The University of Chicago Spanish Dictionary

Diccionario de la Universidad de Chicago Inglés-Español *y* Español-Inglés

Cuarta Edición

Un Diccionario Manual Nuevo y Conciso que Contiene las Voces y Locuciones Básicas de Ambos Idiomas y Además una Lista de 500 Modismos y Refranes Españoles con Variantes y Traducción al Inglés

Recopilación de
Carlos Castillo *y* Otto F. Bond

Con la ayuda de
Barbara M. García

Revisada y Ampliada por
D. Lincoln Canfield

The University of Chicago Press
Chicago & London

The University of Chicago Spanish Dictionary

Fourth Edition

A New Concise Spanish-English and English-Spanish Dictionary of Words and Phrases Basic to the Written and Spoken Languages of Today, plus a List of 500 Spanish Idioms and Sayings, with Variants and English Equivalents

Compiled by
Carlos Castillo & Otto F. Bond

With the Assistance of
Barbara M. García

Revised and Enlarged by
D. Lincoln Canfield

The University of Chicago Press
Chicago & London

The University of Chicago Press, Chicago 60637
The University of Chicago Press, Ltd., London

First Edition published 1948
Fourth Edition 1987
Printed in the United States of America

07 06 05 04 03 02 01 00 99 98 14 15 16 17

Library of Congress Cataloging-in-Publication Data

The University of Chicago Spanish dictionary.

Added t.p. in Spanish: Diccinario de la Universidad de Chicago, inglés-español y español-inglés.
1. Spanish language—Dictionaries—English.
2. English language—Dictionaries—Spanish.
I. Castillo, Carlos, 1890– . II. Bond,
Otto Ferdinand, 1885– . III. García, Barbara M.
IV. Canfield, D. Lincoln (Delos Lincoln), 1903–

V. University of Chicago. IV. Title: Diccionario
inglés-español y español-inglés.
PC4640.US 1987 463′.21 86-24886
ISBN 0-226-10400-1
ISBN 0-226-10402-8 (pbk.)

This book is printed on acid-free paper.

Contents

Foreword to the Fourth Edition

The University of Chicago Spanish Dictionary has been compiled for the general use of the American learner of Spanish and the Spanish-speaking learner of English, with special reference to New World usages as found in the United States and Spanish America.

With this purpose in mind, the editors and the author of the revisions of this new fourth edition have gone far beyond the frequency-based vocabulary of the revised second edition of 1972, with its numerous new entries from such realms as aviation, energy, rocketry, and linguistics, and the augmented third edition of 1977, with its thorough syllabication and phonetic transcriptions and its highly useful section of idiomatic expressions, including many dialectal variants, of the Spanish-speaking world.

This edition incorporates hundreds of current terms from the basic vocabularies of the office worker, the welder, the machinist, the builder, and the automotive mechanic, as well as important entries relating to food preparation and serving, the environment, computer science, and telecommunications.

Indications of regional occurrence, used to show that a term is characteristic of the Spanish of Mexico or Chile, for instance, or that it is common to all of Central America, Colombia, and Venezuela, have been considerably refined.

One of the distinctive features of this dictionary, among the bilingual lexicons, has always been the parenthetical synonym that helps to distinguish meanings or shades of meaning. More than a thousand of these helpful expressions have been added in this fourth edition.

A short history of the Spanish language has been added in the form of descriptions of typical developments in the Vulgar Latin that eventually became Castilian or Spanish.

The much-used section on the Spanish of America in the introductory material for the first half of the dictionary has a short counterpart in the English-Spanish half in the form of a map with brief commentary on the dialectal manifestations of English in the United States.

Part One Spanish-English

List of Abbreviations

adj.	adjective	*math.*	mathematics
adv.	adverb	*neut.*	neuter
arith.	arithmetic	*num.*	numeral
conj.	conjunction	*p.p.*	past participle
contr.	contraction	*pers.*	personal
def.	definite	*pers. pron.*	personal pronoun
def. art.	definite article	*pl.*	plural
dem.	demonstrative	*poss.*	possessive
dem. adj.	demonstrative adjective	*prep.*	preposition
dem. pron.	demonstrative pronoun	*pron.*	pronoun
etc.	et cetera	*refl.*	reflexive
f.	feminine noun	*refl. pron.*	reflexive pronoun
fam.	familiar	*rel.*	relative
indef.	indefinite	*rel. adv.*	relative adverb
indef. art.	indefinite article	*rel. pron.*	relative pronoun
inf.	infinite	*sing.*	singular
interj.	interjection	*subj.*	subjunctive
interr.	interrogative	*v.*	verb
irr.	irregular	*v. irr.*	irregular verb
m.	masculine noun		

Special Words and Abbreviations Used to Indicate Regional Occurrence

Am.[1]	Spanish-American
Andalusia	
Andes	(Ecuador, Peru, Bolivia)
Arg.	Argentina
Bol.	Bolivia
Carib.	(Cuba, Puerto Rico, Dominican Republic)
C.A.	Central America (Guatemala, El Salvador, Honduras, Nicaragua, Costa Rica)
Ch.	Chile
Col.	Colombia
C.R.	Costa Rica
Cuba	
Ec.	Ecuador
Guat.	Guatemala
Hond.	Honduras
Mex.	Mexico
Nic.	Nicaragua
N.Sp.	Northern Spain
Pan.	Panama
Par.	Paraguay
Peru	
P.R.	Puerto Rico
Riopl.	Rio de la Plata region (Eastern Argentina, Uruguay)
S.A.	South America
Sal.	El Salvador
Spain	
Ur.	Uruguay
Ven.	Venezuela

Spanish Pronunciation

The Spanish of central and northern Spain has 24 phonemes, or minimum units of sound-meaning distinction. The Spanish of southwest Spain and most of Spanish America has 22 phonemes. These minimum units of sound are indicated in the

[1]This abbreviation is employed to indicate general Spanish-American usage, usually with the implication of obsolescence in Spain. It is also used to identify words that are currently little used but which may occur in literary works of bygone days.

Phonetic Manifestations of the Consonant Phonemes of Spanish

	Bilabial		Labiodental		Interdental		Dental		Alveolar		Palatal		Velar		Glottal	
Voice	vs	vd	vs	vd	vs	vd	vs	vd	vs	vd	vs	vd	vs	vd	vs	vd
Occlusive	p	b											k	g		
Fricative	ɸ	ƀ	f		θ	đ						y	x	ǥ	h	
Sibilant							s	z	S	Z	Š	Ž				
Affricate											č	ŷ				
Nasal										n		ñ		ŋ		
Lateral										l		l̬				
Vibrant										r rr						
Semiconsonant		w										j				

following charts and descriptions by slashes, /b/, /e/, /č/, and stand for an abstract representation of a group or class of sounds, the individual members of which are variants or allophones. The latter are indicated by brackets: [ƀ], [e], [ȳ]. Some of the phonemes of Spanish have two or three variants, depending on position within the phrase.

The two principal characteristics of Spanish pronunciation as contrasted with English are tenseness of articulation and continuity in transition from word to word within the breath group. Thus all the vowels have a clear nondiphthongal character and sound "clipped" to the English-speaking person. The consonants, especially /p/, /t/, /k/, /l/, /r/, /rr/, have much less vocalic interference than in English, and the first three have no aspiration. The glottal stop, so common in the Germanic languages, including English, is very rare in Spanish. The transition between vowels of contiguous words is smooth. **El hado, helado, el lado** sound very much alike. **Para hacerlo** is [paraasérlo] or in rapid speech [parasérlo]. So marked is the continuity that following sounds influence the preceding ones: **los dos niños** [lozdozníños]; **un peso** [umpéso] **en que** [éŋke].

The Consonantal Phonemes of the Spanish of Northern Spain

/p/ /b/ /t/ /d/ /k/ /g/
/f/ /θ/ /S/ /y/ /x/
/č/
/m/ /n/ /ñ/ 24
/l/ /l̬/
/r/ /rr/

The Vocalic Phonemes of Spanish

i u
e o
a

The Consonantal Phonemes of Andalusian and Latin American Spanish

/p/ /b/ /t/ /d/ /k/ /g/
/f/ /s/ /y /x/
/č/
/m/ /n/ /ñ/ 22 or 23
/l/ (/l̬/) [Bolivia, Paraguay, Peru]
/r/ /rr/

The Spanish Spelling System and the Sounds Represented

I. The Vowels

1. **i** as a single vowel always represents [i], similar to the second vowel of *police*. Examples: **hilo, camino, piso.** As a part of a diphthong, it represents [j], much like English /y/ in *yes, year*. Examples: **bien** [bjen], **diablo** [djaƀlo], **ciudad, baile, reina, boina.** The first syllable of **baile** is much like *by* in English.

2. **e** represents [e], which has no exact equivalent in most English dialects. It is higher than the /e/ of *get* but without the diphthong of *they*. It is much more tense in articulation than either English sound. It varies slightly according to adjacent sounds. The vowel of **perro** is more open than that of **pero.** Generally it is more open in a closed syllable. Examples: **mesa, del, hablé, en, tres.**
3. **a** represents [a], which is similar to the first vowel of *mama,* stressed on the first syllable. Examples: **caso, cano, ¡ah!, América.** Even when not stressed, it has the same clear sound. English *America* has at least two neutral or *schwa* sounds [ə].
4. **o** represents [o], which is more like the first syllable of the American slang expression *gonna* (''going to'') than the British or American *old*. It has no off-glide or diphthongal character such as is heard in the latter. It varies slightly according to adjacent sounds: the first syllable of **corro** is slightly more open than the first of **coro. Sol** is slightly more open than **no.** Examples: **boto, modo, señor, oso, amó.**
5. **u** represents [u], which always has the value of the sound indicated by English *oo* in *boot, fool,* never that of *book,* nor that of the *u* in *union*. Examples: **cura, agudo, uno.**
   a. Note that the spelling combinations **qui, que, gui, gue** represent [ki], [ke], [gi], [ge].
   b. **u** is used to represent the semiconsonant [w] in a diphthong: **cuida, cuento, cuadro, cuota** [kwíđa], [kwénto], [kwáđro], [kwóta].
   c. Likewise **u** is used to represent the semivocalic element of a diphthong: **bou, deuda, causa** [bow], [déwđa], [káwsa].

II. The Consonants

1. **p** represents [p], which never has the aspiration of English /p/ *(pill, papa),* but is like that of *spot*. Examples: **padre, capa, apuro, punto.**
2. **b** and **v** represent /b/, which has two variants, according to position in the phrase: [b], [ƀ]. These do not depend on spelling, which goes back centuries to the Latin. Either letter represents [b] at the beginning of a breath group or when preceded by [m] (spelled either **m** or **n**), and is much like English /b/. Examples: **bomba, burro, en vez de, vine, invierno.** In spite of spelling, the last three examples are [embézđe], [bíne], [imbjérno]. Either letter represents [ƀ] in all other situations. English has no equivalent. It is a /b/ with the lips slightly open. Examples: **haba, uva, Cuba, la vaca, habla, la barba.**
3. **m** represents [m], which is essentially the same as English /m/ *(much).* Examples: **madre, mano, cama.** [m] does not occur syllable final in Spanish. **Álbum** is pronounced [álƀun].
4. **f** represents [f], which is similar to the /f/ of English. In some areas and among certain strata of Hispanic society the articulation is bilabial [ɸ] rather than labiodental.
5. **t** represents [t], which never has the aspiration of English /t/ in prevocalic stressed position *(tea, two, ten)*. It is more similar to the English /t/ of the

cluster [st] *(stop, step)*. Examples in Spanish: **tela, tino, tinta.** The point of articulation is dental.

6. **d** represents /d/, which has three variants according to position in the phrase: [d], [đ], [ø]. At the beginning of the breath group or after /n/ and /l/, **d** represents [d], which is similar to the English /d/ of *dame, did, darn.* Examples: **donde, falda, conde.** In all other situations the letter represents [đ], or even silence. There is a tendency in modern Spanish to move from the fricative [đ] (similar to the sound represented by the *th* in *mother, this, then*) to zero articulation [ø]. Examples: **hado, cuerda, es de, dos dados, cuadro, padre, abad, usted, Madrid.** The last two words are usually pronounced without final consonant, and the consonant tends to be very weak or even to disappear in the ending /-ado/: **hablado, estado, mercado.**

7. **s** in Spain, except the south, represents [S], an apicoalveolar sibilant, similar to the /s/ of southern Scotland and that of older speakers of the Midland dialect of the United States. Examples: **solo, casa, es.** Before a voiced consonant within the phrase it usually represents [Z]. Examples: **desde, mismo, es verde, los labios, las manos.**
   In southern Spain and in all of Spanish America except a small area of Colombia, this letter represents [s], a dental sibilant of high resonance similar to the usual ''feminine'' sibilant of much of the United States. In some areas it is actually lisped. Before a voiced consonant within the phrase it usually represents [z], a voiced sibilant similar to the /z/ of English *razor, ooze,* Examples: **desde, mismo, es verde, los labios, las manos.** In the Caribbean and in coastal Spanish generally, there is a strong tendency to aspirate or eliminate the /s/ syllable final, and the above voicing does not occur.

8. **z,** and **c** before **e** and **i** represent in Spain, except the southwest, [θ], an interdental fricative of tenser and more prolonged articulation than that represented by English *th* in *thin, cloth, ether*. Examples: **zagal, zorro, luz** [θagál], [θórro], [luθ]; or **luces, ciento, cerro** [lúθes], [θjento], [θerro].
   In southern Spain and in Spanish America, these letters represent [s] (see paragraph 7). Examples: **zagal, zorro, luz, luces, ciento, cerro** [sagál], [sórro], [lus], [lúses], [sjénto], [sérro]. Before a voiced consonant in the phrase, the **z** represents [z] (see paragraph 7). Examples: **en vez de, mayorazgo, la luz de.**

9. **l** always represents [l], a clear alveolar lateral that is rarely heard in English, except in Irish and Scottish dialects. It is never velar as in English *bell, full.* Examples: **lado, ala, el, al, sol.**

10. **n** represents /n/, which has variants according to the following consonants. It stands for [n] in all cases except before /b/, /p/, /m/, where it represents [m], and before /k/, /g/, /x/, where it represents [ŋ] (similar to the final consonant of *sing*). Examples of [n]: **no, nada, mano, aman;** of [m]: **en vez de, en Barcelona, un peso;** of [ŋ]: **anca, banco, en que, tengo, naranja.**

11. **ll** represents [ľ] (a palatal lateral) in northern Spain and in Bolivia, parts of Ecuador, Paraguay, and most of Peru, as well as in the eastern cordillera of Colombia. This sound is similar to that heard in English *million*. In other parts of the Spanish-speaking world, *ll* represents [y]. Examples: **calle, llano, olla.**

12. **ñ** represents [ñ] among all speakers of Spanish. It is similar to the sound heard in English *canyon,* but is more one articulation than the English. Examples: **cañón, año, ñato.**

13. **ch** represents [č], which is similar to English /č/ *(church, cheek, reach).* Examples: **chato, chaleco, mucho.**

14. **y** represents [y], which varies regionally from [y] to [ž] (as in *azure*), and in most regions it represents [ŷ] (similar to *just* of English) in initial position in the phrase and after /l/ and /n/. Examples: **ayer, mayo** [ayér], [máyo]; **¡yo! un yugo, el yerno** [ŷo], [unŷúǥo], [elŷérno]. In nearly all areas, Spanish /y/ has more palatal friction than English /y/.

15. a. **x** represents between vowels [ǥs] or simply [S] in Spain (see paragraph 7) and [ks] in Spanish America. Examples: **examen, próximo.**
    b. Before a consonant **x** represents [S] in Spain and [s] in Spanish America, except in affected speech, when one hears [ks]. Examples: **extranjero, experiencia.** Before *c* [s] it is [k]: [eksépto].
    c. In several Indian words of Mexico and Central America **x** represents [x] (see paragraph 20). **México** is one of these and is spelled **Méjico** in Spain.

16. a. **c** represents [k] before **a, o, u, l,** or **r.** The [k] of Spanish does not have the aspiration of English /k/ in the word-initial position *(can, quill, coal)* but is more like the sound in *scan.* Examples: **casa, cosa, cuna, quinto, queso, crudo, aclamar.** Note that **quinto** and **queso** are [kinto] and [késo]. The syllable final [k] in Spanish occurs only in "learned" terms and is dealt with in various ways by the people. In Spain generally it tends to voice to [ǥ]: **técnico, acto, doctor** [téǥnico], [áǥto], doǥtór], but today in Madrid and farther north, the latter becomes [doθtór]. In Central America, Cuba, Venezuela, and Colombia [kt] often becomes [pt] and vice versa; [ps] is [ks]: **Pepsi Cola** [péksi kóla].
    b. **c** before **e** and **i** represents [θ] in Spain, except the southwest, and [s] in Spanish America (see paragraph 8).

17. **k** represents [k] in certain words of foreign origin, mainly Greek, German, and English: **kilo, kilómetro, kermesse, kiosko.**

18. **q** combined with **u** represents [k]. Examples: **queso, aquí, quien** [késo], [akí], [kjen]. **qu** occurs only before **e** and **i.**

19. a. **g** represents [g] before **a, o, u** when initial in the breath group or after /n/. Examples: **ganga, goma, guarda, tengo. gue, gui** represents [ge], [gi], **güe, güi** represent [gwe], [gwi].
    Before **a, o, u** under other circumstances, **g** represents [ǥ], a voiced velar fricative. Examples: **la guerra** [laǥérra], **lago** [láǥo], **la goma** [laǥóma], **agrado** [aǥráđo].
    b. **g** before **e, i,** represents [x], a palatal or velar fricative, which is also represented by **j.** Examples: **gente, giro** [xénte], [xíro]. In the Caribbean and Central America, as well as in southern Spain, the /x/ is simply [h].

20. **j** always represents /x/. The usual manifestation of this phoneme is [x], but in some areas (see paragraph 19) it is [h]. Examples: **jamás, jugo, jota** [xamás], [xúǥo], [xóta].

21. **h** represents a former aspiration that is no longer present except in some rural areas of southern Spain and Spanish America. Examples: **hoja** [óxa], **humo** [úmo], **harto** [árto].
22. **r** represents [r], a single alveolar flap, similar to the sound represented by *tt* in American English *kitty* in rapid speech. However, at the beginning of a word or after **n, l, s,** it represents [rr], a multiple vibrant (trill). Examples of [r]: **caro, farol, mero, tren, comer.** Examples of [rr] written **r: rosa, rana, Enrique, Israel, alrededor.**
rr represents [rr] under all circumstances. Examples: **carro, correr, guerrero.**

The Noun

I. Gender[2]

A. *Masculine Gender*

1. Names of male beings are naturally masculine: **el hombre** the man; **el muchacho** the boy; **el tío** the uncle; **el rey** the king; **el buey** the ox.
2. Nouns ending in **-o** are masculine: **el libro** the book; **el banco** the bank. *Exception:* **la mano** the hand, **la radio** the radio.
3. Days of the week, months, rivers, oceans, and mountains are masculine: **el martes** Tuesday; **enero** January; **el Pacífico** the Pacific; **el Rin** the Rhine; **los Andes** the Andes.
4. Most nouns in **-l** or **-r,** and nouns of Greek origin ending in **-ma** are masculine: **el papel** the paper; **el azúcar** the sugar; **el favor** the favor; **el drama** the drama. *Common exceptions:* **la miel** the honey; **la sal** the salt; **la catedral** the cathedral; **la flor** the flower. Note that **mar** is both masculine and feminine.

B. *Feminine Gender*

1. Names of female beings are naturally feminine: **la mujer** the woman; **la muchacha** the girl; **la tía** the aunt; **la vaca** the cow.
2. Nouns ending in **-a** are feminine: **la pluma** the pen; **la carta** the letter; **la casa** the house. *Common exceptions:* **el día** the day; **el mapa** the map; nouns of Greek origin ending in **-ma: el dogma** the dogma; **el programa** the program.
3. Letters of the alphabet are feminine: **la** *e,* **la** *s,* **la** *t.*
4. Nouns ending in **-ión, -tad, -dad, -tud, -umbre** are feminine: **la canción** the song; **la facultad** the faculty; **la ciudad** the city; **la virtud** the virtue; **la muchedumbre** the crowd. *Exceptions:* **el gorrión** the sparrow; **el sarampión** the measles; **el camión** the truck; **el avión** the airplane.

Note that *(a)* some nouns have different genders according to their meanings: **el corte** the cut or the cutting edge; **la corte** the court; **el guía** the guide; **la guía** the guidebook; **el capital** the capital (money); **la capital** the capital (city); *(b)* some nouns have invariable endings which are used for both the masculine and the feminine: **arista** (and all nouns ending in **-ista**), **amante, mártir, testigo, reo, demócrata, aristócrata, intérprete, consorte, comensal, homicida, suicida, indígena, cómplice, cliente.**

2. There is no general gender rule for the type of nouns not treated in this section.

C. *Formation of the Feminine*

1. Nouns ending in **-o** change **-o** to **-a: tío** uncle, **tía** aunt; **niño** boy, **niña** girl.
2. Nouns ending in **-ón, -or,** and **-án** add **-a: patrón** patron, **patrona** patroness; **pastor** shepherd, **pastora** shepherdess; **holgazán** lazy man, **holgazana** lazy woman.
3. Certain nouns have a special form for the feminine: **el poeta, la poetisa; el cantante, la cantatriz; el sacerdote, la sacerdotisa; el emperador, la emperatriz; el abad, la abadesa; el conde, la condesa; el duque, la duquesa.**

II. Plural of Nouns[3]

1. Nouns ending in an unaccented vowel add **-s** to form the plural: **el libro, los libros; la casa, las casas.**
2. Nouns ending in a consonant, in **-y,** or in an accented vowel add **-es: el papel, los papeles; la canción, las canciones: la ley, las leyes; el rubí, los rubíes.** The accepted plural, however, of **papá** is **papás,** and of **mamá** is **mamás,** and of **café** is **cafés.**
3. Nouns ending in unaccented **-es** and **-is** do not change in the plural: **el lunes** Monday, **los lunes** Mondays; **la tesis** the thesis, **las tesis** the theses.

The Adjective and the Adverb

I. The Adjective

A. *Agreement.* The adjective in Spanish agrees in gender and number with the noun it modifies: **el lápiz rojo** the red pencil; **la casa blanca** the white house; **los libros interesantes** the interesting books; **las muchachas hermosas** the beautiful girls.

B. *Formation of the plural.* Adjectives follow the same rules as nouns for the formation of the plural: **pálido, pálidos** pale; **fácil, fáciles** easy; **cortés, corteses** courteous; **capaz, capaces** capable.

C. *Formation of the feminine.*

1. Adjectives ending in **-o** change **-o** to **-a: blanco, blanca.**
2. Adjectives ending in other vowels are invariable: **verde** green; **fuerte** strong; **indígena** indigenous, native; **pesimista** pessimistic; **baladí** trivial.
3. Adjectives ending in a consonant are invariable: **fácil** easy; **cortés** courteous. *Exceptions: (a)* adjectives ending in **-ón, -án, -or** (except comparatives) add **-a** to form the feminine: **holgazán, holgazana** lazy; **preguntón, preguntona** inquisitive; **hablador, habladora** talkative (Note that **mayor, mejor, menor, peor, superior, inferior, exterior, interior, anterior,** and **posterior** are invariable). **Superior** adds an **-a** when it is used as a noun meaning (''mother

3. The plurals of certain masculine nouns may include the masculine and feminine genders: **los padres** the father(s) and mother(s), the parents; **los tíos** the uncle(s) and aunt(s); **los reyes** the king(s) and queen(s).
Note that *(a)* nouns ending in **-z** change **z** to **c** before **-es: lápiz, lápices;** *(b)* nouns ending in **-ión** lose the written accent in the plural: **canción, canciones.**

superior''). *(b)* adjectives of nationality ending in a consonant add **-a** to form the feminine: **francés, francesa** French; **español, española** Spanish; **alemán, alemana** German; **inglés, inglesa** English.

II. The Adverb

Many adverbs are formed by adding **-mente** to the feminine form of the adjective: **claro, claramente; lento, lentamente; fácil, fácilmente.**

III. Comparison of Adjectives and Adverbs

A. *Comparative of inequality*. The comparative of inequality is formed by placing **más** or **menos** before the positive form of the adjective or adverb: **más rico que** richer than; **menos rico que** less rich than; **más tarde** later; **menos tarde** less late. The superlative is formed by placing the definite article **el** before the comparative: **el más rico** the richest; **el menos rico** the least rich. Note the position of the article in the following examples: **la niña más linda** or **la más linda niña** the prettiest girl.

The following adjectives and adverbs have in addition irregular forms of comparison:

Positive	*Comparative*	*Superlative*
bueno	**mejor**	**el (la) mejor**
malo	**peor**	**el (la) peor**
grande	**mayor**	**el (la) mayor**
pequeño	**menor**	**el (la) menor**
alto	**superior**	**supremo**
bajo	**inferior**	**ínfimo**
mucho	**más**	
poco	**menos**	

B. *Comparative of equality*. With adjectives and adverbs the comparative of equality is formed with **tan . . . como: tan fácil como** as easy as; **tan bien como** as well as; with nouns the comparative of equality is formed with **tanto (tanta, tantos, tantas) . . . como: tanto dinero como** as much money as; **tantas personas como** as many people as.

C. *Absolute superlative of adjectives*. The absolute superlative of adjectives is formed by placing **muy** (very) before the adjective or by adding the suffix **-ísimo:**

Positive	*Absolute Superlative*
feliz	**muy feliz, felicísimo**
fácil	**muy fácil, facilísimo**
importante	**muy importante, importantísimo**
limpio	**muy limpio, limpísimo**
feo	**muy feo, feísimo**
rico	**muy rico, riquísimo**
largo	**muy largo, larguísimo**
notable	**muy notable, notabilísimo**

A few adjectives have, in addition, other forms derived from the Latin superlatives:

bueno **muy bueno, bonísimo**[4]**, óptimo**
malo **muy malo, malísimo, pésimo**
grande **muy grande, grandísimo, máximo**
pequeño **muy pequeño, pequeñísimo, mínimo**

Some adjectives ending in **-ro** or **-re** revert to the corresponding Latin superlative:

acre **muy acre, acrérrimo**
célebre **muy célebre, celebérrimo**
mísero **muy mísero, misérrimo**
salubre **muy salubre, salubérrimo**

D. *Absolute superlative of adverbs*. The absolute superlative of adverbs not ending in **-mente** is formed in the same manner as that of adjectives:

tarde **muy tarde, tardísimo**
pronto **muy pronto, prontísimo**
mucho **muchísimo**
poco **muy poco, poquísmo**
cerca **muy cerca, cerquísima**
lejos **muy lejos, lejísimos**

Superlative adverbs ending in **-mente** are formed by adding the suffix **-ísima** to the corresponding feminine adjective:

claramente **muy claramente, clarísimamente**
noblemente **muy noblemente, nobilísimamente**

Common Spanish Suffixes

I. Diminutives

The most common diminutive endings in Spanish are:

-ito, -ita **(-cito, -cita, -ecito, -ecita).** Examples: **librito** (from **libro**), **casita** (from **casa**), **corazoncito** (from **corazón**), **mujercita** (from **mujer**), **cochecito** (from **coche**), **florecita** (from **flor**).

-illo, -illa **(-cillo, -cilla, -ecillo, -ecilla).** Examples: **corderillo** (from **cordero**), **dolorcillo** (from **dolor**), **viejecillo** (from **viejo**), **piedrecilla** (from **piedra**).

-ico, -ica **(-cico, -cica, -ecico, -ecica).** Examples: **niñico** (from **niño**), **hermanica** (from **hermana**), **corazoncico** (from **corazón**), **mujercica** (from **mujer**), **pobrecico** (from **pobre**).

-uelo, -uela **(-zuelo, -zuela, -ezuelo, -ezuela).** Examples: **arroyuelo** (from **arroyo**), **mozuela** (from **moza**), **mujerzuela** (from **mujer**), **reyezuelo** (from **rey**), **piedrezuela** (from **piedra**).

-ete, -eta Examples: **vejete** (from **viejo**), **vejeta** (from **vieja**).
-uco, -uca Example: **casuca** (from **casa**).
-ucho, -ucha Examples: **serrucho** (from **sierra**), **casucha** (from **casa**).

4. Also **buenísimo.**

II. Augmentatives

The most common augmentative endings in Spanish are:

-acho, -acha Example: **ricacho** (from **rico**).

-azo, -aza Examples: **gigantazo** (from **gigante**), **bribonazo** (from **bribón**), **manaza** (from **mano**), **bocaza** (from **boca**).

-on, -ona Examples: **hombrón** (from **hombre**), **mujerona** (from **mujer**), **almohadón** (from **almohada**), **borrachón** (from **borracho**).

-ote, -ota Examples: **grandote** (from **grande**), **muchachote** (from **muchacho**), **muchachota** (from **muchacha**).

III. Depreciatives

The most common depreciative endings in Spanish are:

-aco, -aca Example: **pajarraco** ugly bird.

-ejo, -eja Example: **librejo** old, worthless book.

Note that a depreciative or ironic connotation is often conveyed by many of the augmentatives and by the diminutive endings **-uelo, -ete, -uco, -ucho, -illo.**

IV. Other Suffixes

-ada *a*. is sometimes equal to the English suffix *-ful:* **cucharada** spoonful; **palada** shovelful;
b. often indicates a blow: **puñada** blow with the fist; **puñalada** stab or blow with a dagger; **topetada** butt, blow with the head;
c. indicates a group or a crowd of: **peonada** a group or crowd of peons; **indiada** a group or crowd of Indians.

-al, -ar denote a grove, field, plantation or orchard: **naranjal** orange grove; **cauchal** rubber plantation; **pinar** pine grove.

-azo indicates a blow or explosion: **puñetazo** blow with the fist; **topetazo** butt, blow with the head; **escobazo** blow with a broom; **cañonazo** cannon shot; **cabezazo** header (soccer)

-dad, -tad are suffixes forming many abstract nouns and are usually equivalent to the English suffix *-ty:* **fraternidad** fraternity; **facultad** faculty; **cantidad** quantity; **calidad** quality.

-dizo is an adjective-forming suffix which means sometimes *tending to,* or *in the habit of:* **resbaladizo** slippery; **olvidadizo** forgetful; **enojadizo** irritable, easily angered; **asustadizo** easily frightened, scary, timid; **movedizo** movable, loose, changeable.

-ería *a*. denotes a place where something is made or sold: **panadería** bakery; **librería** bookstore; **zapatería** shoestore; **pastelería** pastry shop;

	b. indicates a profession, business or occupation: **carpintería** carpentry; **ingeniería** engineering. *c.* means sometimes a collection: **pastelería** pastry, pastries; *d.* is sometimes equivalent to English suffix *-ness;* it also suggests a single act or action: **tontería** foolishness; foolish act; **niñería** childishness; childish act.
-ero	*a.* indicates a person who makes, sells, or is in charge of: **panadero** baker; **librero** bookseller; **zapatero** shoemaker, **carcelero** jailer; **cajero** cashier; *b.* is an adjective-forming suffix; **parlero** talkative; **guerrero** warlike; **extranjero** foreign.
-ez, -eza	are used to make abstract nouns: **vejez** old age; **niñez** childhood; **viudez** widowhood; **grandeza** greatness.
ía	*a.* is the ending of the names of many arts and sciences: **geología** geology; **geometría** geometry; **biología** biology; *b.* see **-ería.**
-iento	indicates a *resemblance,* or a *tendency to:* **ceniciento** ashlike; **soñoliento** sleepy, drowsy; **amarillento** yellowish.
ísimo	is the ending of the absolute superlative: **hermosísimo** very beautiful.
-izo	is a suffix meaning *tending to* or *somewhat:* **rojizo** reddish. See **-dizo.**
-mente	is the adverbal ending attached to the feminine form of the adjective: **generosamente** generously; **claramente** clearly.
-ón	*a.* is an augmentative suffix; *b.* is also a suffix without an augmentative force, meaning *in the habit of,* or *full of:* **juguetón** playful; **preguntón** full of questions, inquisitive; **llorón** tearful; crybaby; *c.* indicates suddenness or violence of an action: **estirón** pull, tug, jerk; **apretón** squeeze.
-or, -dor	*a.* are equivalent to the English suffixes *-or, -er,* and indicate the agent or doer: **hablador** talker; **regulador** regulator; *b.* may also be used as adjectives: **hablador** talkative; **regulador** regulating.
-oso	is an adjective-forming suffix which usually means *having, full of,* or *characterized by:* **rocoso** rocky; **tormentoso** stormy; **fangoso** muddy; **herboso** grassy; **lluvioso** rainy; **maravilloso** marvelous; **famoso** famous.
-udo	is an adjective-forming suffix meaning *having* or *characterized by:* **zancudo** long-legged; **peludo** hairy; **panzudo** big-bellied; **caprichudo** stubborn.
-ura	is a suffix forming many abstract nouns: **negrura** blackness; **blancura** whiteness; **altura** height; **lisura** smoothness.

-uzco indicates *resemblance* or *a tendency to;* it is akin to the English suffix *-ish:* **blancuzco** whitish; **negruzco** blackish.

Spanish Regular Verbs

First Conjugation

Infinitive hablar
Pres. Indic. hablo, hablas, habla, hablamos, habláis, hablan
Pres. Subj. hable, hables, hable, hablemos, habléis, hablen
Pret. Indic. hablé, hablaste, habló, hablamos, hablasteis, hablaron
Imp. Indic. hablaba, hablabas, hablaba, hablábamos, hablabais, hablaban
Imp. Subj. hablara or hablase, hablaras or hablases, hablara or hablase, habláramos or hablásemos, hablarais or hablaseis, hablaran or hablasen
Fut. Indic. hablaré, hablarás, hablará, hablaremos, hablaréis, hablarán
Cond. hablaría, hablarías, hablaría, hablaríamos, hablaríais, hablarían
Imper. habla tú, hable Vd., hablad vosotros, hablen Vds.
Pres. Part. hablando
Past Part. hablado

Second Conjugation

Infinitive comer
Pres. Indic. como, comes, come, comemos, coméis, comen
Pres. Subj. coma, comas, coma, comamos, comáis, coman
Pret. Indic. comí, comiste, comió, comimos, comisteis, comieron
Imp. Indic. comía, comías, comía, comíamos, comíais, comían
Imp. Subj. comiera or comiese, comieras or comieses, comiera or comiese, comiéramos or comiésemos, comierais or comieseis, comieran or comiesen
Fut. Indic. comeré, comerás, comerá, comeremos, comeréis, comerán
Cond. comería, comerías, comería, comeríamos, comeríais, comerían
Imper. come tú, coma Vd., comed vosotros, coman Vds.
Pres. Part. comiendo
Past Part. comido

Third Conjugation

Infinitive vivir
Pres. Indic. vivo, vives, vive, vivimos, vivís, viven
Pres. Subj. viva, vivas, viva, vivamos, viváis, vivan
Pret. Indic. viví, viviste, vivió, vivimos, vivisteis, vivieron
Imp. Indic. vivía, vivías, vivía, vivíamos, vivíais, vivían
Imp. Subj. viviera or viviese, vivieras or vivieses, viviera or viviese, viviéramos or viviésemos, vivierais or vivieseis, vivieran or viviesen
Fut. Indic. viviré, vivirás, vivirá, viviremos, viviréis, vivirán
Cond. viviría, vivirías, viviría, viviríamos, viviríais, vivirían
Imper. vive tú, viva Vd., vivid vosotros, vivan Vds.
Pres. Part. viviendo
Past Part. vivido

Spanish Irregular and Orthographic Changing Verbs

The superior number, or numbers, after a verb entry indicate that it is conjugated like the model verb in this section which has the corresponding number. Only the tenses which have irregular forms or spelling changes are given. The irregular forms and spelling changes are shown in bold-face type.

1. pensar (if stressed, the stem vowel **e** becomes **ie**)
   Pres. Indic. **pienso, piensas, piensa,** pensamos, pensáis, **piensan.**
   Pres. Subj. **piense, pienses, piense,** pensemos, penséis, **piensen.**
   Imper. **piensa** tú, **piense** Vd., pensad vosotros, **piensen** Vds.

2. contar (if stressed, the stem vowel **o** becomes **ue**)
   Pres. Indic. **cuento, cuentas, cuenta,** contamos, contáis, **cuentan.**
   Pres. Subj. **cuente, cuentes, cuente,** contemos, contéis, **cuenten.**
   Imper. **cuenta** tú, **cuente** Vd. contad vosotros, **cuenten** Vds.

3.*a*. sentir (if stressed, the stem vowel **e** becomes **ie;** if unstressed, the stem vowel **e** becomes **i** when the following syllable contains stressed **a, ie,** or **ió**)
   Pres. Indic. **siento, sientes, siente,** sentimos, sentís, **sienten.**
   Pres. Subj. **sienta, sientas, sienta, sintamos, sintáis, sientan.**
   Pret. Indic. **sentí, sentiste, sintió,** sentimos, sentisteis, **sintieron.**
   Imp. Subj. **sintiera** or **sintiese, sintieras** or **sintieses, sintiera** or **sintiese, sintiéramos** or **sintiésemos, sintierais** or **sintieseis, sintieran** or **sintiesen.**
   Imper. **siente** tú, **sienta** Vd., sentid vosotros, **sientan** Vds.
   Pres. Part. **sintiendo.**

   b. erguir (this verb has same vowel changes as *sentir,* but the initial **i** of the diphthong **ie** is changed to **y.** For regular spelling changes see No. 12,*a*)
   Pres. Indic. **yergo, yergues, yergue,** erguimos, erguís, **yerguen.**
   Pres. Subj. **yerga, yergas, yerga, irgamos, irgáis, yergan.**
   Pret. Indic. erguí, erguiste, **irguió,** erguimos, erguisteis, **irguieron.**
   Imp. Subj. **irguiera** or **irguiese, irguieras** or **irguieses, irguiera** or **irguieses, irguiéramos** or **irguiésemos, irguierais** or **irguieseis, irguieran** or **irguiesen.**
   Imper. **yergue** tú, **yerga** Vd., erguid vosotros, **yergan** Vds.
   Pres. Part. **irguiendo.**

4. dormir (if stressed, the stem vowel **o** becomes **ue;** if unstressed, the stem vowel **o** becomes **u** when the following syllable contains stressed **a, ie,** or **ió**)
   Pres. Indic. **duermo, duermes, duerme,** dormimos, dormís, **duermen.**
   Pres. Subj. **duerma, duermas, duerma, durmamos, durmáis, duerman.**
   Pret. Indic. dormí, dormiste, **durmió,** dormimos, dormisteis, **durmieron.**
   Imp. Subj. **durmiera** or **durmiese, durmieras** or **durmieses, durmiera** or **durmiese, durmiéramos** or **durmiésemos, durmierais** or **durmieseis, durmieran** or **durmiesen.**
   Imper. **duerme** tú, **duerma** Vd., dormid vosotros, **duerman** Vds.
   Pres. Part. **durmiendo.**

5. pedir (if stressed, the stem vowel **e** becomes **i;** if unstressed, the stem vowel **e** becomes **i** when the following syllable contains stressed **a, ie,** or **ió**)
   Pres. Indic. **pido, pides, pide,** pedimos, pedís, **piden.**
   Pres. Subj. **pida, pidas, pida, pidamos, pidáis, pidan.**

Pret. Indic. **pedí,** pediste, **pidió,** pedimos, pedisteis, **pidieron.**
Imp. Subj. **pidiera** or **pidiese, pidieras** or **pidieses, pidiera** or **pidiese, pidiéramos** or **pidiésemos, pidierais** or **pidieseis, pidieran** or **pidiesen.**
Imper. **pide** tú, **pida** Vd., pedid vosotros, **pidan** Vds.
Pres. Part. **pidiendo.**

6. buscar (verbs ending in **car** change **c** to **qu** before **e**)
Pres. Subj. **busque, busques, busque, busquemos, busquéis, busquen.**
Pret. Indic. **busqué,** buscaste, buscó, buscamos, buscasteis, buscaron.
Imper. busca tú, **busque** Vd., buscad vosotros, **busquen** Vds.

7. llegar (verbs ending in **gar** change the **g** to **gu** before **e**)
Pres. Subj. **llegue, llegues, llegue, lleguemos, lleguéis, lleguen.**
Pret. Indic. **llegué,** llegaste, llegó, llegamos, llegasteis, llegaron.
Imper. llega tú, **llegue** Vd., llegad vosotros, **lleguen** Vds.

8. averiguar (verbs ending in **guar** change the **gu** to **gü** before **e**)
Pres. Subj. **averigüe, averigües, averigüe, averigüemos, averigüéis, averigüen.**
Pret. Indic. **averigüé,** averiguaste, averiguó, averiguamos, averiguasteis, averiguaron.
Imper. averigua tú, **averigüe** Vd., averiguad vosotros, **averigüen** Vds.

9. abrazar (verbs ending in **zar** change **z** to **c** before **e**)
Pres. Subj. **abrace, abraces, abrace, abracemos, abracéis, abracen.**
Pret. Indic. **abracé,** abrazaste, abrazó, abrazamos, abrazasteis, abrazaron.
Imper. abraza tú, **abrace** Vd., abrazad vosotros, **abracen** Vds.

10.*a*. convencer (verbs ending in **cer** preceded by a consonant change **c** to **z** before **a** and **o**)
Pres. Indic. **convenzo,** convences, convence, convencemos, convencéis, convencen.
Pres. Subj. **convenza, convenzas, convenza, convenzamos, convenzáis, convenzan.**
Imper. convence tú, **convenza** Vd., convenced vosotros, **convenzan** Vds.

b. esparcir (verbs ending in **cir** preceded by a consonant change **c** to **z** before **a** and **o**)
Pres. Indic. **esparzo,** esparces, esparce, esparcimos, esparcís, esparcen.
Pres. Subj. **esparza, esparzas, esparza, esparzamos, esparzáis, esparzan.**
Imper. esparce tú, **esparza** Vd., esparcid vosotros, **esparzan** Vds.

c. mecer (two verbs ending in **cer** preceded by a vowel change **c** to **z** before **a** and **o**; see No. 13.*a*): **mecer** and **cocer.**
Pres. Indic. **mezo,** meces, mece, mecemos, mecéis, mecen.
Pres. Subj. **meza, mezas, meza, mezamos, mezáis, mezan.**
Imper. mece tú, **meza** Vd., meced vosotros, **mezan** Vds.

11.*a*. dirigir (verbs ending in **gir** change **g** to **j** before **a** and **o**)
Pres. Indic. **dirijo,** diriges, dirige, dirigimos, dirigís, dirigen.
Pres. Subj. **diríja, dirijas, dirija, dirijamos, dirijáis, dirijan.**
Imper. dirige tú, **dirija** Vd., dirigid vosotros, **dirijan** Vds.

b. coger (verbs ending in **ger** change **g** to **j** before **o** and **a**)
Pres. Indic. **cojo,** coges, coge, cogemos, cogéis, cogen.
Pres. Subj. **coja, cojas, coja, cojamos, cojáis, cojan.**
Imper. coge tú, **coja** Vd., coged vosotros, **cojan** Vds.

12.*a*. distinguir (verbs ending in **guir** drop the **u** before **o** and **a**)
Pres. Indic. **distingo,** distingues, distingue, distinguimos, distinguís, distinguen.
Pres. Subj. **distinga, distingas, distinga, distingamos, distingáis, distingan.**
Imper. distingue tú, **distinga** Vd., distinguid vosotros, **distingan** Vds.

b. delinquir (verbs ending in **quir** change **qu** to **c** before **o** and **a**)
Pres. Indic. **delinco,** delinques, delinque, delinquimos, delinquís, delinquen.
Pres. Subj. **delinca, delincas, delinca, delincamos, delincáis, delincan.**

13.*a*. conocer (verbs ending in **cer** when preceded by a vowel insert **z** before **c** when **c** is followed by **o** or **a;** see No. 10.*c*)
Pres. Indic. **conozco,** conoces, conoce, conocemos, conocéis, conocen.
Pres. Subj. **conozca, conozcas, conozca, conozcamos, conozcáis, conozcan.**
Imper. conoce tú, **conozca** Vd., conoced vosotros, **conozcan** Vds.

b. lucir (verbs ending in **cir** when preceded by a vowel insert **z** before **c** when **c** is followed by **o** or **a;** see No. 25)
Pres. Indic. **luzco,** luces, luce, lucimos, lucís, lucen.
Pres. Subj. **luzca, luzcas, luzca, luzcamos, luzcáis, luzcan.**
Imper. luce tú, **luzca** Vd., lucid vosotros, **luzcan** Vds.

14. creer (unstressed **i** between vowels is changed to **y**)
Pret. Indic. creí, creíste, **creyó,** creímos, creísteis, **creyeron.**
Imp. Subj. **creyera** or **creyese, creyeras** or **creyeses, creyera** or **creyese, creyéramos** or **creyésemos, creyerais** or **creyeseis, creyeran** or **creyesen.**
Pret. Part. **creyendo.**

15. reír (like No. 5, except that when the **i** of the stem would be followed by **ie** or **ió** the two **i**'s are reduced to one)
Pres. Indic. **río, ríes, ríe,** reimos, reís, **ríen.**
Pres. Subj. **ría, rías, ría, riamos, riáis, rían.**
Pret. Indic. rei, reíste, **rió,** reímos, reísteis, **rieron.**
Imp. Subj. **riera** or **riese, rieras** or **rieses, riera** or **riese, riéramos** or **riésemos, rierais** or **rieseis, rieran** or **riesen.**
Imper. **ríe** tú, **ría** Vd., reíd vosotros, **rían** Vds.
Pres. Part. **riendo.**

16. podrir or pudrir
Pres. Indic. **pudro, pudres, pudre,** podrimos or pudrimos, podris or pudrís, **pudren.**
Pres. Subj. **pudra, pudras, pudra, pudramos pudráis, pudran.**
Imp. Indic. pudría or podría, etc. (Seldom *podría* because of confusion with *poder*)
Pret. Indic. podrí or pudrí, podriste or pudriste, **pudrió,** podrimos or pudrimos, podristeis or pudristeis, **pudrieron.**
Imp. Subj. **pudriera** or **pudriese, pudrieras** or **pudrieses, pudriera** or

pudriese, pudriéramos or **pudriésemos, pudrierais** or **pudrieseis, pudrieran** or **pudriesen.**

Fut. Indic. pudriré or podriré, etc.
Cond. pudriría or podriría, etc.
Pres. Part. **pudriendo.**
Past Part. podrido or pudrido.

17. enviar
Pres. Indic. envío, envías, envía, enviamos, enviáis, envían.
Pres. Subj. envíe, envíes, enviemos, enviéis, envíen.
Imper. envía tú, envíe Vd., enviad vosotros, envíen Vds.

18. continuar
Pres. Indic. continúo, continúas, continúa, continuamos, continuáis, continúan.
Pres. Subj. continúe, continúes, continúe, continuemos, continuéis, continúen.
Imper. continúa tú, continúe Vd., continuad vosotros, continúen Vds.

19. gruñir (**i** of the diphthong **ie** or **ió** is lost after **ñ**)
Pret. Indic. gruñí, gruñiste, **gruñó,** gruñisteis, **gruñeron.**
Imp. Subj. **gruñera** or **gruñese, gruñeras** or **gruñeses, gruñera** or **gruñese, gruñéramos** or **gruñésemos, gruñerais** or **gruñeseis, gruñeran** or **gruñesen.**
Pres. Part. **gruñendo.**

20. bullir (**i** of the diphthong **ie** or **ió** is lost after **ll**)
Pret. Indic. bullí, bulliste, **bulló,** bullimos, bullisteis, **bulleron.**
Imp. Subj. **bullera** or **bullese, bulleras** or **bulleses, bullera** or **bullese, bulléramos** or **bullésemos, bullerais** or **bulleseis, bulleran** or **bullesen.**
Pres. Part. **bullendo.**

21. andar
Pret. Indic. **anduve, anduviste, anduvo, anduvimos, anduvisteis, anduvieron.**
Imp. Subj. **anduviera** or **anduviese, anduvieras** or **anduvieses, anduviera** or **anduviese, anduviéramos** or **anduviésemos, anduvierais** or **anduvieseis, anduvieran** or **anduviesen.**

22. asir
Pres. Indic. **asgo,** ases, ase, asimos, asis, asen.
Pres. Subj. **asga, asgas, asga, asgamos, asgáis, asgan.**
Imper. ase tú, **asga** Vd., asid vosotros, **asgan** Vds.

23. caber
Pres. Indic. **quepo,** cabes, cabe, cabemos, cabéis, caben.
Pres. Subj. **quepa, quepas, quepa, quepamos, quepáis, quepan.**
Pret. Indic. **cupe, cupiste, cupo, cupimos, cupisteis, cupieron.**
Imp. Subj. **cupiera** or **cupiese, cupieras** or **cupieses, cupiera** or **cupiese, cupiéramos** or **cupiésemos, cupierais** or **cupieseis, cupieran** or **cupiesen.**
Fut. Indic. **cabré, cabrás, cabrá, cabremos, cabréis, cabrán.**

Cond. **cabría, cabrías, cabría, cabríamos, cabríais, cabrían.**
Imper. cabe tú, **quepa** Vd., cabed vosotros, **quepan** Vds.

24. caer
Pres. Indic. **caigo,** caes, cae, caemos, caéis, caen.
Pres. Subj. **caiga, caigas, caiga, caigamos, caigáis, caigan.**
Pret. Indic. caí, caiste, **cayó,** caímos, caísteis, **cayeron.**
Imp. Subj. **cayera** or **cayese, cayeras** or **cayases, cayera** or **cayese, cayéramos** or **cayésemos, cayerais** or **cayeseis, cayeran** or **cayesen.**
Imper. cae tú, **caiga** Vd., caed vosotros, **caigan** Vds.
Pres. Part. **cayendo.**

25. conducir (all verbs ending in **ducir** have the irregularities of conducir)
Pres. Indic. **conduzco,** conduces, conduce, conducimos, conducís, conducen.
Pres. Subj. **conduzca, conduzcas, conduzca, conduzcamos, conduzcáis, conduzcan.**
Pret. Indic. **conduje, condujiste, condujo, condujimos, condujisteis, condujeron.**
Imp. Subj. **condujera** or **condujese, condujeras** or **condujeses, condujera** or **condujese, condujéramos** or **condujésemos, condujerais** or **condujeseis, condujeran** or **condujesen.**
Imp. conduce tú, **conduzca** Vd., conducid vosotros, **conduzcan** Vds.

26. dar
Pres. Indic. **doy,** das, da, damos, dais, dan.
Pres. Subj. dé, des, dé, demos, deis, den.
Pret. Indic. **di, diste, dio, dimos, disteis, dieron.**
Imp. Subj. **diera** or **diese, dieras** or **dieses, diera** or **diese, diéramos** or **diésemos, dierais** or **dieseis, dieran** or **diesen.**

27. decir[5]
Pres. Indic. **digo, dices, dice,** decimos, decís, **dicen.**
Pres. Subj. **diga, digas, diga, digamos, digáis, digan.**
Pret. Indic. **dije, dijiste, dijo, dijimos, dijisteis, dijeron.**
Imp. Subj. **dijera** or **dijese, dijeras** or **dijeses, dijera** or **dijese, dijéramos** or **dijésemos, dijerais** or **dijeseis, dijeran** or **dijesen.**
Fut. Indic. **diré, dirás, dirá, diremos, diréis, dirán.**
Cond. **diría, dirías, diría, diríamos, diríais, dirían.**
Imper. **di** tú, **diga** Vd., decid vosotros, **digan** Vds.
Pres. Part. **diciendo.**
Past Part. **dicho.**

28. errar (like No. 1, except that the initial **ie** is spelled **ye**)
Pres. Indic. **yerro, yerras, yerra,** erramos, erráis, **yerran.**

5. The compound verbs of *decir* have the same irregularities with the exception of the following:
a. The future and conditional of the compound verbs *bendecir* and *maldecir* are regular: *bendeciré, maldeciré,* etc.; *bendeciría, maldeciría,* etc.
b. The familiar imperative is regular: *bendice tu, maldice tu, contradice tu,* etc.
c. The past participles of *bendecir* and *maldecir* are regular when used with *haber* or in the passive with *ser: bendecido, maldecido;* when used as an adjective with *estar* or with *ser* as a noun, the forms are: *bendito, maldito.*

Pres. Subj. **yerre, yerres, yerre,** erremos, erréis, **yerren.**
Imper. **yerra** tú, **yerre** Vd., errad vosotros, **yerren** Vds.

29. estar
Pres. Indic. **estoy, estás, está,** estamos, estáis, **están.**
Pres. Subj. **esté, estés, esté,** estemos, estéis, **estén.**
Pret. Indic. **estuve, estuviste, estuvo, estuvimos, estuvisteis, estuvieron.**
Imp. Subj. **estuviera** or **estuviese, estuvieras** or **estuvieses, estuviera** or **estuviese, estuviéramos** or **estuviésemos, estuvierais** or **estuvieseis, estuvieran** or **estuviesen.**
Imper. **está** tú, **esté** Vd., estad vosotros, **estén** Vds.

30. haber
Pres. Indic. **he, has, ha, hemos,** habéis, **han.**
Pres. Subj. **haya, hayas, haya, hayamos, hayáis, hayan.**
Pret. Indic. **hube, hubiste, hubo, hubimos, hubisteis, hubieron.**
Imp. Subj. **hubiera** or **hubiese, hubieras** or **hubieses, hubiera** or **hubiese, hubiéramos** or **hubiésemos, hubierais** or **hubieseis, hubieran** or **hubiesen.**
Fut. Indic. **habré, habrás, habrá, habremos, habréis, habrán.**
Cond. **habría, habrías, habría, habríamos, habríais, habrían.**

31. hacer
Pres. Indic. **hago,** haces, hace, hacemos, hacéis, hacen.
Pres. Subj. **haga, hagas, haga, hagamos, hagáis, hagan.**
Pret. Indic. **hice, hiciste, hizo, hicimos, hicisteis, hicieron.**
Imp. Subj. **hiciera** or **hiciese, hicieras** or **hicieses, hiciera** or **hiciese, hiciéramos** or **hiciésemos, hicierais** or **hicieseis, hicieran** or **hiciesen.**
Fut. Indic. **haré, harás, hará, haremos, haréis, harán.**
Cond. **haría, harías, haría, haríamos, haríais, harían.**
Imper. **haz** tú, **haga** Vd., haced vosotros, **hagan** Vds.
Past Part. **hecho.**

32.*a.* huir
Pres. Indic. **huyo, huyes, huye,** huimos, huís, **huyen.**
Pres. Subj. **huya, huyas, huya, huyamos, huyáis, huyan.**
Pret. Indic. huí, huiste, **huyó,** huimos, huisteis, **huyeron.**
Imp. Subj. **huyera** or **huyese, huyeras** or **huyeses, huyera** or **huyese, huyéramos** or **huyésemos, huyerais** or **huyeseis, huyeran** or **huyesen.**
Imper. **huye** tú, **huya** Vd., huid vosotros, **huyan** Vds.
Pres. Part. **huyendo.**

b. argüir
Pres. Indic. **arguyo, arguyes, arguye,** argüimos, argüís, **arguyen.**
Pres. Subj. **arguya, arguyas, arguya, arguyamos, arguyáis, arguyan.**
Pret. Indic. argüí, argüiste, **arguyó,** argüimos, argüisteis, **arguyeron.**
Imp. Subj. **arguyera** or **arguyese, arguyeras** or **arguyeses, arguyera** or **arguyese, arguyéramos** or **arguyésemos, arguyerais** or **arguyeseis, arguyeran** or **arguyesen.**

	Imper.	**arguye** tú, **arguya** Vd., argüid vosotros, **arguyan** Vds.
	Pres. Part.	**arguyendo.**
33.	ir	
	Pres. Indic.	**voy, vas, va, vamos, vais, van.**
	Pres. Subj.	**vaya, vayas, vaya, vayamos, vayáis, vayan.**
	Imp. Indic.	**iba, ibas, iba, íbamos, ibais, iban.**
	Pret. Indic.	**fui, fuiste, fue, fuimos, fuisteis, fueron.**
	Imp. Subj.	**fuera** or **fuese, fueras** or **fueses, fuera** or **fuese, fuéramos** or **fuésemos, fuerais** or **fueseis, fueran** or **fuesen.**
	Imper.	**ve** tú, **vaya** Vd., id vosotros, **vayan** Vds.
	Pres. Part.	**yendo.**
34.	jugar (cf. Nos. 2 and 7)	
	Pres. Indic.	**juego, juegas, juega,** jugamos, jugáis, **juegan.**
	Pres. Subj.	**juegue, juegues, juegue,** juguemos, juguéis, **jueguen.**
	Pret. Indic.	**jugué,** jugaste, jugó, jugamos, jugasteis, jugaron.
	Imper.	**juega** tú, **juegue** Vd., jugad vosotros, **jueguen** Vds.
35.	adquirir	
	Pres. Indic.	**adquiero, adquieres, adquiere,** adquirimos, adquirís, **adquieren.**
	Pres. Subj.	**adquiera, adquieras, adquiera,** adquiramos, adquiráis, **adquieran.**
	Imper.	**adquiere** tú, **adquiera** Vd., adquirid vosotros, **adquieran** Vds.
36.	oír	
	Pres. Indic.	**oigo, oyes, oye,** oímos, oís, **oyen.**
	Pres. Subj.	**oiga, oigas, oiga, oigamos, oigáis, oigan.**
	Pret. Indic.	oí, oíste, **oyó,** oímos, oísteis, **oyeron.**
	Imp. Subj.	**oyera** or **oyese, oyeras** or **oyeses, oyera** or **oyese, oyéramos** or **oyésemos, oyerais** or **oyeseis, oyeran** or **oyesen.**
	Imper.	**oye** tú, **oiga** Vd., oíd vosotros, **oigan** Vds.
	Pres. Part.	**oyendo.**
37.	oler (like No. 2, except that initial **ue** is spelled **hue**)	
	Pres. Indic.	**huelo, hueles, huele,** olemos, oléis, **huelen.**
	Pres. Subj.	**huela, huelas, huela,** olamos, oláis, **huelan.**
	Imper.	**huele** tú, **huela** Vd., oled vosotros, **huelan** Vds.
38.	placer	
	Pres. Indic.	**plazco,** places, place, placemos, placéis, placen.
	Pres. Subj.	**plazca, plazcas, plazca, plazcamos, plazcáis, plazcan.** (There are also the antiquated forms, **plegue** and **plega,** used now only in the third person in poetic language.)
	Pret. Indic.	In addition to the regular forms, there is the antiquated form **plugo,** used now only in poetic language.
	Imp. Subj.	In addition to the regular forms, there are the antiquated forms, **pluguiera** and **pluguiese,** used now only in poetic language.
39.	poder	
	Pres. Indic.	**puedo, puedes, puede,** podemos, podéis, **pueden.**
	Pres. Subj.	**pueda, puedas, pueda,** podamos, podáis, **puedan.**

Pret. Indic. **pude, pudiste, pudo, pudimos, pudisteis, pudieron.**
Imp. Subj. **pudiera** or **pudiese, pudieras** or **pudieses, pudiera** or **pudiese, pudiéramos** or **pudiésemos, pudierais** or **pudieseis, pudieran** or **pudiesen.**
Fut. Indic. **podré, podrás, podrá, podremos, podréis, podrán.**
Cond. **podría, podrías, podría, podríamos, podríais, podrían.**
Pres. Part. **pudiendo.**

40. poner
Pres. Indic. **pongo,** pones, pone, ponemos, ponéis, ponen.
Pres. Subj. **ponga, pongas, ponga, pongamos, pongáis, pongan.**
Pret. Indic. **puse, pusiste, puso, pusimos, pusisteis, pusieron.**
Imp. Subj. **pusiera** or **pusiese, pusieras** or **pusieses, pusiera** or **pusiese, pusiéramos** or **pusiésemos, pusierais** or **pusieseis, pusieran** or **pusiesen.**
Fut. Indic. **pondré, pondrás, pondrá, pondremos, pondréis, pondrán.**
Cond. **pondría, pondrías, pondría, pondríamos, pondríais, pondrían.**
Imper. **pon** tú, **ponga** Vd., poned vosotros, **pongan** Vds.
Past Part. **puesto.**

41. querer
Pres. Indic. **quiero, quieres, quiere,** queremos, queréis, **quieren.**
Pres. Subj. **quiera, quieras, quiera,** queramos, queráis, **quieran.**
Pret. Indic. **quise, quisiste, quiso, quisimos, quisisteis, quisieron.**
Imp. Subj. **quisiera** or **quisiese, quisieras** or **quisieses, quisiera** or **quisiese, quisiéramos** or **quisiémos, quisierais** or **quisieseis, quisieran** or **quisiesen.**
Fut. Indic. **querré, querrás, querrá, querremos, querréis, querrán.**
Cond. **querría, querrías, querría, querríamos, querríais, querrían.**
Imper. **quiere** tú, **quiera** Vd., quered vosotros, **quieran** Vds.

42. saber
Pres. Indic. **sé,** sabes, sabe, sabemos, sabéis, saben.
Pres. Subj. **sepa, sepas, sepa, sepamos, sepáis, sepan.**
Pret. Indic. **supe, supiste, supo, supimos, supisteis, supieron.**
Imp. Subj. **supiera** or **supiese, supieras** or **supieses, supiera** or **supiese, supiéramos** or **supiésemos, supierais** or **supieseis, supieran** or **supiesen.**
Fut. Indic. **sabré, sabrás, sabrá, sabremos, sabréis, sabrán.**
Cond. **sabría, sabrías, sabría, sabríamos, sabríais, sabrían.**
Imper. sabe tú, **sepa** Vd., sabed vosotros, **sepan** Vds.

43. salir
Pres. Indic. **salgo,** sales, sale, salimos, salís, salen.
Pres. Subj. **salga, salgas, salga, salgamos, salgáis, salgan.**
Fut. Indic. **saldré, saldrás, saldrá, saldremos, saldréis, saldrán.**
Cond. **saldría, saldrías, saldría, saldríamos, saldríais, saldrían.**
Imper.[6] **sal** tú, **salga** Vd., salid vosotros, **salgan** Vds.

6. The compound *sobresalir* is regular in the familiar imperative: **sobresale tú.**

44. ser

Pres. Indic. **soy, eres, es, somos, sois, son.**
Pres. Subj. **sea, seas, sea, seamos, seáis, sean.**
Imp. Indic. **era, eras, era, éramos, erais, eran.**
Pret. Indic. **fui, fuiste, fue, fuimos, fuisteis, fueron.**
Imp. Subj. **fuera** or **fuese, fueras** or **fueses, fuera** or **fuese, fuéramos** or **fuésemos, fuerais** or **fueseis, fueran** or **fuesen.**
Imper. **sé** tú, **sea** Vd., sed vosotros, **sean** Vds.

45. tener

Pres. Indic. **tengo, tienes, tiene,** tenemos, tenéis, **tienen.**
Pres. Subj. **tenga, tengas, tenga, tengamos, tengáis, tengan.**
Pret. Indic. **tuve, tuviste, tuvo, tuvimos, tuvisteis, tuvieron.**
Imp. Subj. **tuviera** or **tuviese, tuvieras** or **tuvieses, tuviera** or **tuviese, tuviéramos** or **tuviésemos, tuvierais** or **tuvieseis, tuvieran** or **tuviesen.**
Fut. Indic. **tendré, tendrás, tendrá, tendremos, tendréis, tendrán.**
Cond. **tendría, tendrías, tendría, tendríamos, tendríais, tendrían.**
Imper. **ten** tú, **tenga** Vd., tened vosotros, **tengan** Vds.

46. traer

Pres. Indic. **traigo,** traes, trae, traemos, traéis, traen.
Pres. Subj. **traiga, traigas, traiga, traigamos, traigáis, traigan.**
Pret. Indic. **traje, trajiste, trajo, trajimos, trajisteis, trajeron.**
Imp. Subj. **trajera** or **trajese, trajeras** or **trajeses, trajera** or **trajese, trajéramos** or **trajésemos, trajerais** or **trajeseis, trajeran** or **trajesen.**
Imper. trae tú, **traiga** Vd., traed vosotros, **traigan** Vds.
Pres. Part. **trayendo.**

47. valer

Pres. Indic. **valgo,** vales, vale, valemos, valéis, valen.
Pres. Subj. **valga, valgas, valga, valgamos, valgáis, valgan.**
Fut. Indic. **valdré, valdrás, valdrá, valdremos, valdréis, valdrán.**
Cond. **valdría, valdrías, valdría, valdríamos, valdríais, valdrían.**
Imper. **val** or vale tú, **valga** Vd., valed vosotros, **valgan** Vds.

48. venir

Pres. Indic. **vengo, vienes, viene,** venimos, venís, **vienen.**
Pres. Subj. **venga, vengas, venga, vengamos, vangáis, vengan.**
Pret. Indic. **vine, viniste, vino, vinimos, vinisteis, vinieron.**
Imp. Subj. **viniera** or **viniese, vinieras** or **vinieses, viniera** or **viniese, viniéramos** or **viniésemos, vinierais** or **vinieseis, vinieran** or **viniesen.**
Fut. Indic. **vendré, vendrás, vendrá, vendremos, vendréis, vendrán.**
Cond. **vendría, vendrías, vendría, vendríamos, vendríais, vendrían.**
Imper. **ven** tú, **venga** Vd., venid vostros, **vengan** Vds.
Pres. Part. **viniendo.**

49. ver

Pres. Indic. **veo,** ves, ve, vemos, veis, ven.
Pres. Subj. **vea, veas, vea, veamos, veáis, vean.**

Imp. Indic. **veía, veías, veía, veíamos, veíais, veían.**
Imper. ve tú, **vea** Vd., ved vosotros, **vean** Vds.
Past Part. **visto.**

50. yacer
Pres. Indic. **yazco** or **yazgo,** yaces, yace, yacemos, yacéis, yacen.
Pres. Subj. **yazca** or **yazga, yazcas** or **yazgas, yazca** or **yazga, yazcamos** or **yazgamos, yazcáis** or **yazgáis, yazcan** or **yazgan.**
Imper. yace tú, **yazca** or **yazga** Vd., yaced vosotros, **yazcan** or **yazgan** Vds.

51. Defective Verbs

a. The following verbs are used only in the forms that have an **i** in the ending: abolir, agredir, aterirse, empedernir, transgredir.

b. atañer
This verb is used only in the third person. It is most frequently used in the present indicative: atañe, atañen.

c. concernir
This verb is used only in the third person of the following tenses:
Pres. Indic. **concierne, conciernen.**
Pres. Subj. **concierna, conciernan.**
Imp. Indic. concernía, concernían.
Imp. Subj. concerniera or concerniese, concernieran or concerniesen.
Pres. Part. concerniendo.

d. soler
This verb is used most frequently in the present and imperfect indicative. It is less frequently used in the present subjunctive.
Pres. Indic. **suelo, sueles, suele,** solemos, soléis, **suelen.**
Pres. Subj. **suela, suelas, suela,** solamos, soláis, **suelan.**
Imp. Indic. solía, solías, solía, solíamos, solíais, solían.
The preterit is seldom used. Of the compound tenses, only the present perfect is commonly used: he solido, etc. The other tenses are very rare.

e. roer
This verb has three forms in the first person of the present indicative: **roo, royo, roigo,** all of which are infrequently used. In the present subjunctive the preferable form is **roa, roas, roa,** etc., although the forms **roya** and **roiga** are found.

52. Irregular Past Participles

abrir—**abierto**
absorber—absorbido, **absorto**
bendecir—bendecido, **bendito**
componer—**compuesto**
cubrir—**cubierto**
decir—**dicho**
deponer—**depuesto**
descomponer—**descompuesto**
describir—**descrito**
descubrir—**descubierto**
desenvolver—**desenvuelto**
deshacer—**deshecho**
devolver—**devuelto**
disolver—**disuelto**
encubrir—**encubierto**
entreabrir—**entreabierto**
entrever—**entrevisto**
envolver—**envuelto**
escribir—**escrito**
freir—**frito,** freído
hacer—**hecho**
imprimir—**impreso**

inscribir—**inscrito**
maldecir—maldecido, **maldito**
morir—**muerto**
poner—**puesto**
prescribir—**prescrito**
proscribir—**proscrito**
proveer—proveído, **provisto**
resolver—**resuelto**
revolver—**revuelto**
romper—rompido, **roto**
satisfacer—**satisfecho**
subscribir—**subscrito**
ver—**visto**
volver—**vuelto**

A Short History of the Spanish Language

Introduction

In a sense, Latin is not dead. The speech of Roman soldiers, merchants, and colonists, the spoken Latin of another day, was taken bodily to Iberia, Gaul, Dacia, and many other regions that became parts of the Roman Empire. As this spoken Latin developed under the influence of the languages native to the areas, it became known eventually by several other names, according to the vast political entities that gradually took shape: Spanish, Portuguese, French, Italian, Romanian, and so forth.

The Latin of north central Spain (Iberia) came to be called Castilian, since its speakers were from the province of Castilla (Latin *Castella,* "castles"), and although later it was referred to as Spanish **(español),** to this day the people of many regions call it **castellano,** and the children of Argentina and Chile, for instance, study **composición castellana.**

Castilian became prominent among the other Latin dialects in the Iberian Peninsula during the late Middle Ages because of the hegemony of Christian north-central Iberia in the reconquest of the peninsula from the Arabs, Moors, and other Muslims who had conquered most of it between 711 and 718 and who had coexisted with their Christian enemy in most of the area for several centuries, even as these Christians gradually drove them southward toward Africa. After finally taking over the last stronghold, Granada, in early 1492, these same Christians, who were culturally Castilians, left by the thousands from the ports of southern Spain to take an active part in the discovery and settlement of America. Thus it is that the predominence of Castilian over the other manifestations of Latin *(gallego, leonés, aragonés)* is due not to its own nature but rather to nonlinguistic factors: political and military power and organization, church-state relations, and literary ascendance.

Today Spanish **(castellano** or **español)** is the most extensive manifestation of the former spoken Latin. Those who think and express themselves in this language number many more than 300,000,000 and live in some twenty countries, most of which have rapidly growing populations. It is estimated that by A.D. 2000, Spanish will be the language of nearly 500,000,000 people, most of whom will be **hispanoamericanos.** Spanish is one of the principal languages of the world and is to be found in such widely separated parts of the globe as Morocco, Equatorial Guinea, the Philippines (among older people), and in several parts of the United States where there are about twenty million Spanish speakers. Moreover, hundreds of thousands of Jews who were exiled from Spain in 1492 spoke only Spanish, and their descendants now live in Holland, Greece, Bulgaria, Yugoslavia, Turkey, Israel, Egypt, Libya, Syria, the United States, and many countries of Latin America. They are known as Sephardic Jews and are sometimes referred to as **ladinos.**

As the great essayist Ortega y Gasset reminds us, man has history, not nature, and the history of Spanish is a part of the continuum of those who spoke Latin. It is remarkable that Spanish is still so recognizably Latin after nearly two thousand years. About 85 percent of its present forms were brought to Iberia before the time of Christ!

Since Spain has suffered many invasions and has also engaged in many conquests, vocabulary from other than Latin sources became a part of what was to be called Castilian or Spanish. Lexical adoptions, so to speak, were to be made from the language of the Visigothic invaders who overran the Iberian Peninsula in the fifth century; from Arabic over some seven centuries; and from several Indian languages of America after 1492, notably Caribbean dialects, Náhuatl (Aztec) of Mexico, and Quechua of the Andean cordillera. In modern times, first French and then English have provided important contributions to the vocabulary.

Of major importance in the evolution of Latin to Spanish over the centuries are changes in physical articulation, in function indicators, in order and arrangement of the various elements, and in lexical items (vocabulary), along with changes in the actual meaning of a given form. The pronunciation of syllables and hence words gradually changed through the principle of least effort and through the influence of such substratum languages as Basque, still spoken by the descendents of those who learned the Romance language that was to be Spanish.

Latin usually indicated grammatical function and situation by affixes (*ad-*, *pre-*, *-or*, *-i*, etc.), while the developing Castilian language tended in some cases to signal these circumstances by prepositions: *Catullus fīlĭō Caesarĭs lĭbrum dat* becomes **Catullus da al hijo el libro de César.** Of the six grammatical cases of Latin—nominative, genitive, dative, accusative, ablative, and vocative—Spanish generally kept only the accusative. The functions signaled by *ō* in *fīlĭō* and by *ĭs* in *Caesarĭs* are taken over by **al** and **de** respectively. Although word order in Latin was quite flexible, Spanish order became more fixed because of, among other things, the use of prepositions in the place of suffixes.

During the evolution of the language, some terms gradually took on new shades of meaning, while others were lost or replaced by vocabulary foreign to the Latin continuum. Latin *ĕquus* (''horse'') was replaced by *căballus* (Spanish **caballo**), the original meaning of which was ''nag.'' The Latin *cănis* (''dog'') was replaced by **perro,** probably of Iberian origin. In many cases Castilian developed pairs from one Latin term, one learned and the other popular: *căthedra* (''chair'') gave both **cátedra** (''class,'' ''audience,'' ''professorship''), and **cadera** (''hip''); *causam* (''cause'') became both **causa** (''cause'') and **cosa** (''thing''); for ''cold,'' both **frígido** and **frío** exist, one poetic and one of everyday use.

Sound Changes in the Evolution of Latin to Spanish

All languages tend to change gradually through the centuries, some faster than others, and some more consistently than others. Since the Middle Ages, Spanish appears to have changed much more slowly than English and more consistently than French. In all languages, one can cite and describe certain trends in these changes, and on the basis of frequency of occurrence, one can establish ''rules'' of transformation: this particular sound or syllable tends to become that under these circumstances; e.g. the *ŏ* of Latin tends to change to *ue* when it is stressed. The Latin *pŏrta* becomes **puerta** in Spanish. The forces behind the changes can't always be identified, but one of them is analogy, whereby two distinctive features are leveled to one. One such change in

American English has been the leveling of *wh* and *w* to *w,* so that *which* and *witch* sound alike in the speech of millions, especially in the large cities of the Eastern United States.

One interesting case of leveling is that of the Spanish sibilants or ''whistling sounds.'' Old Spanish (during the Middle Ages and up to 1492, let's say) had six sibilants (dental, alveolar, palatal):

/s/ spelled *ç* or *z* (syllable final): **çapato, luz, haces**
/z/ spelled *z:* **dezir, hazes, zero**
/S/ spelled *s* (*ss* between vowels): **seis, classe, osso**
/Z/ spelled *s* (between vowels or final): **cosa, casas, oso**
/š/ spelled *x:* **dixe, exe, relox**
/ž/ spelled *j* (*g* before *i* and *e*): **jardín, ojo, gente**

These basic sounds (phonemes) first began to ''level'' by losing the distinction between voiced and voiceless qualities (the /z/, /Z/, and /ž/ were voiced). Thus both **haces** and **hazes** leveled to **haces** [háseS] (the *h* represented an aspirate then). Likewise **osso** and **oso** leveled to [óSo] phonetically. To the listener, there was no longer any difference between **osso** (bear) and **oso** (I dare), nor between **haces** (bundles) and **hazes** (you do). The spelling wasn't changed until centuries later. Besides analogy, there is an element of less effort in all this.

In the late sixteenth century another loss of distinction began to be evident. The sibilant spelled *s* or *ss,* and today pronounced in all of northern and central Spain with an alveolar articulation (the point of the tongue turned up toward the upper gum ridge), gradually leveled to the same articulation as the [s] of **çapato,** first in the area of Sevilla and finally in nearly all of Andalucía and much of Extremadura, perhaps reinforced by the speech habits of those who had lived longer under Arabic domination. This change became especially important with the conquest and settlement of the Americas, because about 70 percent of those who settled the American colonies of Spain during the first two centuries of colonization were from southwestern Andalucía and Extremadura.

The final stage of this sibilant leveling has been going on since the seventeenth century in southwestern Spain and in regions of America accessible to influences from the mother country during the colonial period, that is, coastal areas on the trade routes, especially the Caribbean and coastal South America: the aspiration or complete elimination of the sound (**hasta dos o tres** [áhta doh o treh] or [áta do o tre]).

A process that is quite consistent in the evolution of Spanish is the tendency to voice the unvoiced consonants between vowels and to eliminate those that are already voiced. Good examples of the two developments in a single word are **dĭgĭtu** to **dedo** (''finger'') and **cŭbĭtu** to **codo** (''elbow''). A case of three voiceless consonants changing to voiced is to be seen in **apothēca** to **bodega** (''wine cellar,'' ''storeroom''). As in the case of **căthedra** some Latin terms were retained as learned forms but also evolved along popular lines.

Since both Spain and Portugal were exploring and colonizing distant lands after 1485, the spellings of these two languages were applied to the representation of languages spoken in the newly discovered territories and are still in evidence today. The letter *x,* for example, came to represent [š] (the *sh* of English) in the Indian languages of America and in several languages of Asia, because it represented this sound in Spanish and Portuguese at that time. The sound has since changed in Spanish but still prevails in Portuguese. The map of Mexico is filled with words that have an *x*, and **Mexico** itself was pronounced as if the *x* were English *sh*. An Englishman who was there in the sixteenth century wrote *Washaca* for what is today **Oaxaca.** Sephardic Jews pronounce **dixe** [díše].

Since Castilla is adjacent to the Basque Provinces, it is to be expected that Basque might have had some influence on those who learned the Latin that eventually became **castellano.** Basque had no labio-dentals (/f/ and /v/), and Spanish developed /h/ for the /f/ and /b/ for the /v/ of Latin. Although the /h/ has disappeared (**hierro** is actually [yérro]), Spanish /b/ today may be spelled either *v* or *b: va* and *bah* are [ba]. We now believe that the five vowels of Basque may account for the leveling of seven in popular Latin, and that the strong /rr/ of Spanish is that of Basque in contrast to a weaker general Romance /rr/.

While Basque must have contributed considerably to the phonology of Spanish, Arabic contributed a great deal to the vocabulary during the more than seven centuries that it was spoken in at least part of the peninsula. Hundreds of words from Arabic form part of the Castilian lexicon today, among them **ojalá** (''would that, I hope that''), in which we see the Arabic **Allah;** *alcalde* (''mayor''), and incidentally the English *mayor,* is from Spanish! **Alcohol, algebra, alfalfa, algodón** (''cotton'') are all from Arabic, as are *arroz* (''rice''), **azúcar** (''sugar''), *naranja* (''orange''), **Gibraltar, Guadalquivir, Guadalupe, Guadalajara,** and even **cero** (''zero''), an Arabic concept.

The Spanish Language in America

The Spanish of Latin America, like most ''colonial'' speech, tends to be conservative in its structural changes compared with that of the mother country. In addition, it reflects regional traits of the southwestern part of Spain, notably Andalusia and adjacent areas, from where a large part of the sailors, conquistadores, and colonists came. In other words, the Spanish of America would seem to be Andalusian Castilian of the sixteenth and seventeenth centuries, as far as pronunciation and grammar are concerned. But in vocabulary hundreds of Indian words have entered the language, especially in Mexico, Guatemala, the Andes (Ecuador, Peru, and Bolivia), and in the Río de la Plata region. The Indian words of the Caribbean islands were taken to other parts of Latin America by the original Spanish settlers and often form a part of the general Spanish lexicon. It should be noted that these Indian languages belong to distinct, unrelated families, so that an **ahuacate** (avocado) in Mexico and Central America becomes a **palta** in the Andes. Although Spanish Americans generally have little difficulty understanding each other, the following variants represent rather extreme divergences:

	Little boy	*bus*	*blond*
Mexico	**chamaco**	**camión**	**güero**
Guatemala	**patojo**	**camioneta**	**canche**
El Salvador	**cipote**	**camioneta**	**chele**
Panama	**chico**	**chiva**	**fulo**
Colombia	**pelado**	**autobús**	**mono**
Argentina	**pibe**	**colectivo**	**rubio**
Chile	**cabro**	**micro**	**rubio**
Cuba	**chico**	**guagua**	**rubio**

Although most of these words are actually Spanish (of Latin origin), several are from the Indian languages of the respective areas. The fact that there are differences of this sort is to be expected in a general culture that contains so many national boundaries.

The Pronunciation of Latin-American Spanish

The fundamental phonological traits of American Spanish are to be found in Castilla, but only changes that have taken place in the Andalusian dialect of Castilian have become established in America. Furthermore, these changes apparently took place between the fifteenth and the eighteenth centuries, during the settlement of Latin America. Evidence indicates that inaccessible areas of Spanish America (the mountainous regions of Mexico, Guatemala, Colombia, Ecuador, Peru, Bolivia, as well as Paraguay, inland Venezuela, and northern Argentina) received only the early changes of Andalusian Castilian, while the accessible coastal areas and port cities tend to reflect both early changes and those of the late colonial period. Thus it is that Cuban and Panamanian Spanish resemble that of present-day Sevilla more than does Mexican Spanish or that of Bogotá. In the meantime Madrid Spanish (called Castilian by many North Americans) developed one or two features that never reached America.

The outstanding common feature of American-Spanish pronunciation that goes back to the early colonial period is the so-called **seseo.** About the time of Columbus the people of southwestern Spain began to confuse the two sibilant sounds of **casa** [káSa] (''house'') and **caza** [kása] (''hunt'') (the capital [S] representing a ''thick'' alveolar sound and the [s] representing a ''normal'' dental sound), with the result that only the dental sound survived. Since most settlers of America were from the south, this became the general Spanish-American tendency. **Coser** and **cocer** are alike in southern Spain and in Latin America. The sibilant is a delicate dental one. In northern and central Spain a distinction between these two sounds is still maintained, and the second or dental one has become interdental [θ], similar to the voiceless *th* of English. The former [S] is still apicoaveolar, and to the foreigner approaches the sound represented by English *sh*.

In the seventeenth and eighteenth centuries other changes occurred in the pronunciation of southern Spanish. As has been indicated, these became part of the Spanish of the accessible areas of America, but most did not reach the high mountains and plateaus. The first of these was the aspiration or even the loss of /s/ syllable final. **Estos** becomes [ehtoh] or even [éto], the result of what might be termed a ''relaxed'' articulation. About the same time the /l̆/ (written *ll*) tended to be ''relaxed'' to the extent that it coincided with the /y/ (written *y*), so that **valla** and **vaya** were levelled to [báya] in Andalusia and parts of America. Today Bolivia, Paraguay, and much of Peru and Ecuador still maintain a distinction. One of the latest levelings of Andalusia was the confusion of /l/ and /r/ syllable final. This is heard today in Puerto Rico, Panama, and Venezuela, and to a certain extent in Cuba, the Dominican Republic, and central Chile. **Puerta** sounds like [pwelta], **mar** like [mal] and the infinitives seem to end in /l/. A final Andalusian trait is the velar /n/ [ŋ] as a sign of word boundaries. **Enamora** is [enamóra], but **en amor** is [eŋamór]. English-speakers think of *ng* when they hear **son** and **pan** pronounced [soŋ] and [paŋ].

Perhaps the only outstanding feature of American Spanish that is not traceable to Andalusia is the assibilation of /rr/ [ř̌] and /r/ [ř] final and postconsonantal. This occurs in vast areas of America: Guatemala, Costa Rica, in the eastern cordillera of Colombia, highland Ecuador, Bolivia, Chile, western and northern Argentina, and Paraguay.

The maps show the distribution of the distinguishing features of Spanish-American pronunciation.

Syntactic Features

The familiar form of address in Spanish, **tú,** is a direct descendant of the Latin *tu*. The Latin plural form *vos* also came down to Spanish, but by the late Middle Ages it had assumed the function of polite singular as well as familiar plural. To make the distinction, people began to say **vosotros** (you others) for the plural. In the sixteenth century there came into being a very polite form of address: **vuestra merced** (your mercy), used with the third person of the verb, as one might say, "Does his majesty wish to enter?" It has been shortened to **usted.** With this new polite form, **vos,** the former polite singular, lost prestige and became a familiar form. This was the state of affairs when the colonists came to America. As a result, vast sections of Latin America use **vos** instead of **tú** as the singular familiar form of address. All of Spanish America uses **ustedes** for the familiar plural as well as the polite plural. It will be noted in map 1 that the **vos** areas are generally far from the old Viceroyalties of Mexico and Lima. Only in Chile is there a social distinction.

The verb used with **vos** is the modified plural of Old Spanish: **hablás, comés, vivís;** the imperative is **hablá, comé, viví.** The object pronoun and the possessive are from the singular **te, tu,** the object of the preposition, **vos:** and **llevate tu perro con vos.** Since the imperative of **ir** would be simply **i,** the verb **andar** is used instead: **¡andate!** Another interesting syntactic trait is the general tendency to differentiate gender of nouns of occupation and status of people and to create feminine forms where they may not have existed in so-called standard Spanish. **Presidenta, ministra, dependienta, liberala, abogada,** and **arquitecta** have been heard. Equally general are the tendencies to use adjectives as adverbs **(corre ligero, toca el piano lindo)** and to make certain adverbs "agree" with adjectives they modify **(media muerta; medias locas)** as well as to use the impersonal **haber** in the plural **(habían dos; ¿cuántos habrán?).**

The Vocabulary of Spanish America

There are three main tendencies in the development of Hispanic-American lexical elements: (1) to use words that were popular at the time of the settlement of America, especially maritime terms or rural expressions, often out of popular etymology; (2) to adopt Indian words, especially those related to the domestic scene; and (3) to borrow directly from English and to develop cases of correlative analogy due to English influence.

Of the first category are such terms as **flota** for a bus line, **amarrar** for **atar; botar** for **echar; virar** for **volverse.** In the tropical zone of America (from Guatemala south

Map 1

Vos used instead of tú in informal address.

In Chile the distinction is one of class: vos is used in the lower economic levels.

Map 2

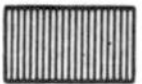

Aspiration or loss of /s/ syllable final

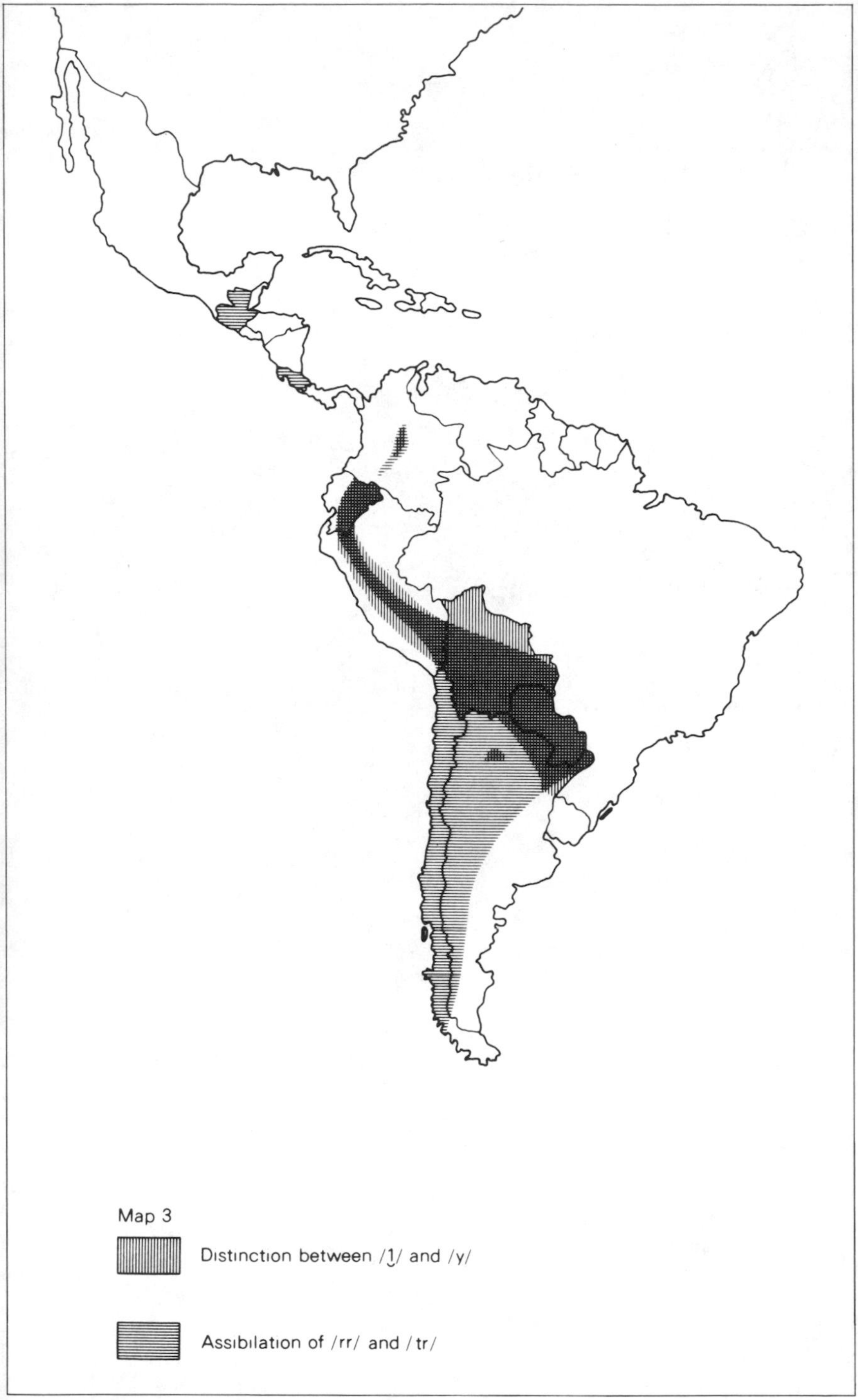

Map 3

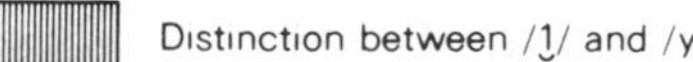

through Peru), where there are no seasons of heat and cold, since these depend on altitude, the Spaniards began to call the wet periods **invierno** (winter) and the dry, **verano** (summer). The custom continues to this day in Guatemala, El Salvador, Honduras, Nicaragua, Costa Rica, Panama, Colombia, Venezuela, Ecuador, and Peru. One may ask, **¿qué tal el invierno?** ("How was the winter?") and receive the answer **¡copioso!** ("copious").

Indian words entered the Spanish of America by the hundreds. In the Caribbean the Spaniards learned **tabaco, canoa, huracán, maíz, ají;** in Mexico, from Náhuatl, **chocolate, tomate, coyote, chicle, cacao;** in the Andes, from Quechua, **pampa, quinina, cóndor, puma, poncho;** and in the Río de la Plata region, from Guaraní, **ananá, ñandú, ombú, yajá, tapioca.**

During the twentieth century the influence of English has been strong in Latin America, and the direct borrowings in some areas could be counted in the hundreds: **control, lonche, lonchería, sándwich, jáibol** ("highball"), **cóctel, ponche, bar, twist, chance, fútbol, béisbol, fildear** ("to field"), **jonrón** ("home run"), **noquear** ("to knock out"), **lobista,** and even such verbs as **taipear** ("to type") and **blofear** ("to bluff"). In the realm of correlative analogy or sense loans, English has tremendous influence, and **educación** ("upbringing") takes the place of **pedagogía, instrucción,** and **enseñanza; argumento** ("plot of a story") moves into the slot of **discusión; atender** ("to wait on") into that of **asistir; audiencia** into that of **concurrencia; acta** ("minutes") takes the place of **ley; complexión** ("physical constitution") takes the place of **tez.**

Regional Features: Mexico

Among speakers of Spanish, a Mexican is recognized by his intonation and by his tendency to lengthen the articulation of his /s/ and by his general preference for the consonant over the vowel. If intonation of Spanish is represented in a pattern of four levels, Mexicans, especially males in a "man-about-town" mood, tend to strike a terminal point between standard statement and emphatic statement, giving the utterance a "minor-key" effect. The tensely-grooved /s/ of Mexican Spanish leads to the virtual elimination of unstressed vowels, especially /e/, in rapid speech: **accidentes de coches** may tend to be [aksiđénts đe kočs].

Typical adjectives of Mexico are **mero** and **puro.** The first of these is so popular that it means not only "mere" but "very," "real," "just," "same," and many other things, and is even used adverbially: **ya merito** ("It won't be long now").

As has been noted, Mexico is the center of Aztec vocabulary that has entered Spanish and eventually many languages of the world; **tomate, chocolate, cacao, coyote, chicle,** and hundreds of less common terms.

Guatemala

The Spanish of Guatemala is characterized by a strong assibilated /rr/ [řř] and by [ř] for /r/ except in intervocalic position. The **jota** tends to be [h] rather than [x], and velar [ŋ] marks open transition. Along with those of other Central-American areas, Guatemalan speakers tend to weaken intervocalic /y/ to the extent that **silla** sounds like [sía] and **bella** like [bea]. Through a process of ultracorrection, **vea** may become [béya]. Guatemalans generally pronounce their /s/ syllable final with clarity and tension.

A fairly universal feature of the Spanish of Guatemala is the **voseo,** or use of **vos** as the subject form of familiar address in the singular. The verb used with this is the plural familiar, but the pronoun objects and possessives are always singular **Cuando te vayas, llévate tu perro contigo,** as one might say in Spain or in Mexico, would be **Cuando te vayás, llevate tu perro con vos** in Guatemala.

Little boys are **patojos** in Guatemala, and blonds are **canches.**

El Salvador, Honduras, Nicaragua

Perhaps more than any other group of independent countries, these three form a linguistic unity in most respects. They represent in phonology a middle point between the highland conservatism (Mexico and the Andes, for instance) and the later trends of the lowlands (Cuba and Panamá, for example). The inhabitants of these countries call each other **guanacos, catrachos,** and **nicas** respectively, and are always talking of Central-American union.

The phonological phenomenon of recent discovery—although it is probably an "archaic" trait—is the occlusive pronunciation of /b/, /d/, /g/ after another consonant, a situation in which they would be fricative in "standard" Spanish.

It is in this region of Central America that one hears a lisped /s/ that approaches [θ] among many residents, and especially among the working classes. As in northern Mexico, the intervocalic /y/ (representing orthographic **y** and **ll**) tends to be a semivowel or even disappears. The **jota** /x/ is [h] in all speakers, and there is a strong tendency to aspirate syllable final /s/.

The Salvador-Honduras-Nicaragua region is rich in forms of combinative analogy, especially noun formation on the basis of other nouns. The suffixes **-ada** and **-ón** are of extensive application: **babosada, pendejada, lambida, atolada, paisanada, perrada, barbón, narizón, pistón, quemazón;** and the longer diminutive form **-ecito** that might be used in Spain and in Mexico is simply **-ito: llavita, lucita, crucita, piedrita.** The place where things grow or are to be found is indicated by the suffix **-al: cañal, guacal, platanal, cafetal, piñal, pinal.**

Along with Guatemala and the other Central-American countries, except Panama, this region uses the **vos** form of familiar address, and in the way described for Guatemala: **Vení y decime, ¿son vos y tu padre carpinteros?**

Many indigenous words are used in everyday conversation, most of them from the Pipil, a sublanguage of the Náhuatl. A blond is a **chele,** a boy is a **cipote, pushco** is dirty, **peche** is slender, and there is the usual stock of Aztec terms that were imported after the conquest of Mexico.

Costa Rica

Like Guatemala, Costa Rica is noted for its assibilated /rr/, along with assibilated /r/ syllable final. It also shares with Guatemala a fairly conservative articulation of /s/ syllable final. As in all Central-American and Caribbean countries, the /n/ is velar when final, as a sign of open juncture: [eŋ amor] but [enamorár], and intervocalic /y/ weakens to the point of elimination through vocalization.

As a part of the syntactic structure of the dialect, **vos** and related forms operate where **tú** would prevail in Spain or Mexico today, and lexically, Costa Rica shows less Aztec influence than Guatemala, El Salvador, or Honduras.

Costa Ricans are known affectionately as **ticos.**

Panama

The Spanish of Panama might be termed "trade route Spanish," in that it has the phonological character of parts of America that were in constant communication with Spain at the grass-roots level and yet were removed from the courtly influences of the viceregal centers (Mexico and Lima). It resembles strongly the Spanish of Cuba, Puerto Rico, and Venezuela and the northern coast of Colombia.

Along with other Caribbean residents, the Panamanians tend to aspirate their /s/ at the end of a syllable, or to eliminate it entirely.

Colombia

The development of the language in Colombia, which has three high mountain ranges and several important ports, might serve as an example of how American Spanish grew in disparate ways from Peninsular models. The relative inaccessibility of the high sierras and valleys makes it possible to find at least five distinct linguistic zones in the former Nueva Granada. The "dialects" therefore represent stages in the historical development of southern Peninsular Spanish, the most inaccessible regions generally representing the earliest and the most accessible in general representing the latest in Andalusian vogues, before independence.

Strange as it may seem, Colombian Spanish has two general traits in common with that of El Salvador, Honduras, and Nicaragua: the /x/ is [h] in all regions, and the /b/, /d/, /g/ are occlusive after any consonant. Thus **pardo, barba, algo, desde, las vacas,** all have occlusives where a Spaniard or a Mexican would use fricatives.

The Spanish of older Bogotá residents has the conservative distinction of /l/ and /y/ and, like that of Costa Rica and Guatemala, tends to assibilate the /rr/, the /tr̆/, and the /r/ final.

Pastuso Spanish (or Nariño) is in many ways Ecuadorean, and like the Spanish of highland Mexico, slights the vowel in favor of the consonant, tends to pronounce the /d/ of **-ado,** and uses an apicodental /s/, strong and well defined.

Antioquia's Spanish is unique in America in one way. The /s/ is apicoalveolar [S], like that of Spain, and although no distinction is made between **casa** and **caza,** one Colombian ambassador to Spain, an **antioqueño,** gave the impression of "talking like a Spaniard." The second distinguishing feature of this region's Spanish is the /y/ of such tenseness that it even becomes affricate intervocalically [maŷo, kaƀaŷo].

Colombia is unusually formal in most sections as far as direct address is concerned. Many speakers use **usted** almost exclusively—even to cats and dogs. Not only is this the case within the family, but some relatives speak to each other as **su merced.** The **voseo** prevails in Antioquia and in Santander and in the **Valle,** while Bogotá and the Coast always employ the **tuteo.**

Typical of Colombia are the idiomatic expressions **¡siga!** and **¡a la orden!** The first is said to invite one to enter, and the other to ask, "What can I do for you?" Black coffee, especially the demitasse, is a **tinto,** and to invite one to partake, one says: **¿Le provoca un tinto?** This same sentence to a Spaniard might mean, "Does red wine make you fight?" Instead of sending regards with **saludos,** Colombians use **saludes** ("healths").

Venezuela

The speech pattern of Venezuela is for the most part that of the Caribbean, and therefore late Andalusian. One "eats" his final /s/; /l/ and /r/ are confused at syllable end; /n/ is velar [ŋ] as a sign of word finality; and as in El Salvador, Honduras, and Nicaragua, many people pronounce the /s/ as [θ].

As far as address is concerned most of Venezuela is **tuteo** country, but sections near the Colombian frontier are **vos** areas.

Ecuador

In a country where thousands speak Quechua (the language of the Incas) in preference to Spanish and where many are bilingual, the Spanish language of the upper inter-Andean region is very conservative in its phonological evolution. Ecuadoreans (except those of the coast) still distinguish /l̮/ and /y/ as [ž] and [y], still pronounce /s/ with deliberate tenseness and, like many Mexicans, slight the vowel in favor of the consonant. Because Quechua is so widely spoken, and because this language has a simple three-vowel system, the Spanish of the highlands tends to heighten /o/ to /u/ and /e/ to /i/. Unique in Latin America is the final /s/ as [z] before a vowel in the following word: [laz aǥwas].

Peru

About 19,000,000 **peruanos,** or as their neighbors may say, **peruleros** or **cholos,** occupy the territory of the central Inca Empire of preconquest days. Their money is counted in **soles** and their babies are **guaguas.** Along with Ecuador and Bolivia, Peru belongs to heavily populated Andean Spanish America, and besides having many Quechua-speaking inhabitants, the region boasts a clear Spanish that gives evidence of sixteenth-century origin and viceregal nurture.

Except in Lima and along the northern coast, Peruvians still distinguish the /l̮/ and /y/, and the general impression of Peruvian Spanish is similar to that of Mexico, Bolivia, and Ecuador.

Nearly all of Peru uses the **tú** form of familiar address, and as one might expect, hundreds of Quechua words have entered the Spanish of everyday life. In fact, several **quechuismos** have become universal terms: **pampa, cóndor, puma, puna, quinina, llama, alpaca, gaucho, china** ("sweetheart"), **poncho,** and many others.

Bolivia

This country, once Alto Peru, was settled by Spanish colonists from two directions, the high altiplano from Peru and the llanos from Paraguay and Argentina. As a result, Bolivia has two principal manifestations of Andalusian Spanish, a very early type in the highlands and a later form in the lowlands. The later includes changes brought from the Iberian Peninsula via the main trade route to Buenos Aires during the late colonial period.

Bolivia is one of two countries of Spanish America that still maintain a universal distinction between the phonemes /l̮/ and /y/: *valla* and *vaya* are different.

The highlands, especially La Paz and Potosí, tend to have the apico-alveolar /S/ of northern and central Spain, and the /rr/ tends to be a fricative [řř]. As in Mexico, vowel reduction in the unstressed syllable is common: *Potsí, ofsina, cochs.*

In the lowlands, /s/ syllable final tends to be aspirated or dropped.

Chile

Linguistically, Chile can be divided into three sections, north, middle, and south. The north and the south resemble each other more than they do the middle. The heavily populated central valley partakes of many of the traits of late Andalusian, through the port of Valparaíso and the city of Santiago. Final /s/ is aspirated, /l/ and /r/ are confused in the syllable final situation, and /l̮/ and /y/ are not distinguished. Chiloé still distinguishes these latter two, and in the north there are vowel-heightening influences of Quechua. Two features that seem to characterize all Chilean Spanish are the /č/ of alveolar articulation rather than palatal and the /x/ with a palatal element of semiconsonantal nature before /e/. One seems to hear **la gente de Chile** as [la xjénte de tSíle].

The **five o'clock** tea of Argentina may be **onces** in Chile.

Argentina, Uruguay, Paraguay

The Spanish of this vast territory is of two main types, according to the direction from which the settlers came. The western and northwestern sections were settled from Peru and Chile from about 1590. Although Buenos Aires and the humid Pampa were first settled about 1535, it was not until 1580 that a permanent settlement was established. The important factor producing the differences of today was the accessibility of Buenos Aires and surrounding country to constant influences from the ports of southern Spain in the colonial period. Thus the interior shows more conservative features: an /s/ of more tense articulation, a distinction between /l̮/ and /y/ in some areas, and the assibilated /rr/ of Costa Rica, Bogotá, and Guatemala.

The **porteño** of the Río de la Plata region is noted for his /y/ with strong [ž] articulation: **bayo, calle** [bážo], [káže] and sometimes even [š], especially among women.

Both Argentina and Uruguay are **voseo** territories, and the style has been recorded extensively in gaucho poetry. As a cattle region, the pampas have a lexicon that is rich in the terminology of the ranch and of horses. English and French are contributors to the vocabulary of the area, and one hears of **five o'clock tea a todas horas,** and the frequency of **chau** for "good-by" attests the influence of Italian, the original language of more than half of the inhabitants of Argentina. **Argentinos** are often called **che,** since they use this term to attract attention.

Paraguay, being more inaccessible, has two conservative features in its phonology: the distinction of /l̮/ and /y/, and the assibilation of /rr/. It is unique in that nearly all its inhabitants are bilingual. They speak the original Indian language, Guaraní, and Spanish. The occasion usually dictates which will be used, and speakers will often shift from one to the other in the same utterance.

Cuba, The Dominican Republic, and Puerto Rico

The Spanish of the Caribbean, like that of Panama, could be termed "trade route" Spanish, since it shows rather typically the American evolution of Andalusian trends of the seventeenth and eighteenth centuries, trends that do not seem to be present in the more inaccessible hinterland. Add to this the Afro-Cuban influences of slave days and the many American English loans of the twentieth century, and we have perhaps the least "conservative" Castilian.

Cubans tend to aspirate their syllable final /s/ or drop it altogether, and the tendency is as marked or more so in Puerto Rico and Santo Domingo. In all three, syllable final /l/ and /r/ are confused, most of all in Puerto Rico, where the /l/ is favored: **puerta, izquierdo** [pwélta], [ihkjéldo]. In contrast to Mexico, Ecuador, Peru, and Bolivia, where the vowel may be slighted, those of the Caribbean tend to slight the consonant in favor of the vowel. In Puerto Rico /rr/ is now velar in about half of the population. It resembles the **jota** of Spain: [x]. Thus **rota** sounds like **jota** to other Spanish speakers.

Cuba, Puerto Rico, and the Dominican Republic are **tuteo** countries.

This brief description of some of the features of the Castilian of America may help to show that distinctive features do not correspond to geographical or political entities to the extent that has been believed, and one might indicate as many as a hundred dialects—and yet it is all Spanish.

Numerals—Números

Cardinal Numbers	*Números Cardinales*	*Ordinal Numbers*	*Números Ordinales*[7]
1 .... one	uno, una	first	primero
2 .... two	dos	second	segundo
3 .... three	tres	third	tercero
4 .... four	cuatro	fourth	cuarto
5 .... five	cinco	fifth	quinto
6 .... six	seis	sixth	sexto
7 .... seven	siete	seventh	séptimo (sétimo)
8 .... eight	ocho	eighth	octavo
9 .... nine	nueve	ninth	noveno, nono
10 .... ten	diez	tenth	décimo
11 .... eleven	once	eleventh	undécimo
12 .... twelve	doce	twelfth	duodécimo
13 .... thirteen	trece	thirteenth	décimotercio
14 .... fourteen	catorce	fourteenth	décimocuarto
15 .... fifteen	quince	fifteenth	décimoquinto
16 .... sixteen	dieciséis, diez y seis	sixteenth	décimosexto
17 .... seventeen	diecisiete, diez y siete	seventeenth	décimoséptimo
18 .... eighteen	dieciocho, diez y ocho	eighteenth	décimoctavo
19 .... nineteen	diecinueve, diez y nueve	nineteenth	décimonono
20 .... twenty	veinte	twentieth	vigésimo
21 .... twenty-one	veintiuno, veinte y uno	twenty-first	vigésimo primero
30 .... thirty	treinta	thirtieth	trigésimo
40 .... forty	cuarenta	fortieth	cuadragésimo
50 .... fifty	cincuenta	fiftieth	quincuagésimo
60 .... sixty	sesenta	sixtieth	sexagésimo
70 .... seventy	setenta	seventieth	septuagésimo

7. The ordinals beyond the "tenth" are less used in Spanish than in English. They are often replaced by the cardinals: *Alfonso the Thirteenth* **Alfonso trece.**

80	eighty	ochenta	eightieth	octogésimo
90	ninety	noventa	ninetieth	nonagésimo
100	one hundred	ciento, cien	(one) hundredth	centésimo
101	one hundred and one	ciento (y) uno	(one) hundred and first	centésimo primo
200	two hundred	doscientos	two-hundredth	ducentésimo
300	three hundred	trescientos	three-hundredth	tricentésimo
400	four hundred	cuatrocientos	four-hundredth	cuadringentésimo
500	five hundred	quinientos	five-hundredth	quingentésimo
600	six hundred	seiscientos	six-hundredth	sexcentésimo
700	seven hundred	setecientos	seven-hundredth	septingentésimo
800	eight hundred	ochocientos	eight-hundredth	octingentésimo
900	nine hundred	novecientos	nine-hundredth	noningentésimo
1000	one thousand	mil	(one) thousandth	milésimo
100,000	one hundred thousand	cien mil	(one) hundred thousandth	cienmilésimo
1,000,000	one million	un millón	(one) millionth	millonésimo

Nations, Cities, and Adjectives of Nationality

Afganistán	afgano
Albania	albanés
Alto Volta	voltaico
Arabia Saudita	árabe saudita
Argelia	argelino
Argentina	argentino
Asunción	asunceño
Basutolandia	basutolandés
Bechuanalandia	bechuanalandés
Bélgica	belga
Birmania	birmano
Bogotá	bogotano
Bolivia	boliviano
Brasil	brasileño
Bruselas	bruselense
Buenos Aires	bonaerense or porteño
Bulgaria	búlgaro
Burundi	burundi
Camboya	camboyano
Camerún	camerunés
Canadá	canadiense
Caracas	caraqueño
Ceilán (Sri Lanka)	ceilanés
Colombia	colombiano
Congo (both)	congoleño
Costa de Marfil	marfileño
Costa Rica	costarricense

Cuba	cubano
Chad	chadiano
Checoslovaquia	checoslovaco
Chile	chileno
China	chino
Chipre	chipriota
Dahomey	dahomeyano
Dinamarca	dinamarqués or danés
Ecuador	ecuatoriano
El Salvador	salvadoreño
Escocia	escocés
España	español
Estados Unidos de América	estadounidense
Etiopía	etíope
Filipinas	filipino
Finlandia	finlandés or finés
Francia	francés
Gabón	gabonés
Gales	galés
Gambia	gambio
Ghana	ghanés
Ginebra	ginebrino
Grecia	griego
Guatemala	guatemalteco
Guayaquil	guayaquileño
Guinea	guineo
Haití	haitiano
Honduras	hondureño
Hungría	húngaro
Ifni	ifneño
India	indio
Indonesia	indonesio
Inglaterra	inglés
Irak	iraqués
Irán	iranio
Irlanda	irlandés
Islandia	islandés
Israel	israelí
Italia	italiano
Jamaica	jamaicano
Japón	japonés
Jordania	jordanio
Jerusalém	jerosolimitano
Kenia	kenio
Kuwait	kuwaiteño

Laos	laosiano
La Paz	paceño
Líbano	libanés
Liberia	liberiano
Libia	libio
Lima	limeño
Lisboa	lisboeta or lisbonense
Londres	londinense
Luxemburgo	luxemburgués
Madagascar	malache
Madrid	madrileño
Malasia	malayo
Malavi	malavio
Malí	maliense
Managua	managüense
Marruecos	marroquí
Mauritania	mauritano
México (Méjico)	mexicano (mejicano in Spain)
Mongolia	mongol
Montevideo	montevideño or montevideano
Nepal	nepalés
Nicaragua	nicaragüense
Níger	nigerino
Nigeria	nigeriano
Noruega	noruego
Nueva York	neoyorquino
Nueva Zelanda	neozelandés
Países Bajos	holandés
Pakistán	pakistano
Panamá	panameño
Paraguay	paraguayo
París	parisiense
Perú	peruano
Polonia	polaco
Portugal	portugués
Puerto Rico	puertorriqueño or portorriqueño
Reino Unido de Gran Brctaña e Irlanda del Norte	británico
República Arabe Unida	egipcio
República Centroafricana	centroafricano
República Dominicana	dominicano
República Socialista Soviética de Bielorrusia	bieloruso
República Socialista Soviética de Ucrania	ucranio
Río de Janeiro	carioca

Río Muni	ríomuniense
Rodesia	rodesio
Rumania	rumano
Rusia	ruso
Rwanda	rwandés
San José	josefino
San Pablo	paulista
Santa Cruz	cruceño
Santiago	santiagueño or santiaguino
Senegal	senegalés
Sierra Leona	leonense
Siria	sirio
Somalia	somalí
Suazilandia	suazilandés
Sudáfrica	sudafricano
Sudán	sudanés
Suecia	sueco
Suiza	suizo
Tailandia	tailandés
Tangañica	tangañicano
Tanzania	tanzanio
Tegucigalpa	tegucigalpense
Tenerife	tinerfeño
Tetuán	tetuaní
Togo	togolés
Trinidad y Tobago	trinitario
Túnez	tunecí
Turquía	turco
Uganda	ugandés
Unión de Repúblicas Socialistas Soviéticas	ruso
Uruguay	uruguayo
Venecia	veneciano or véneto
Venezuela	venezolano
Viena	vienés
Yemen	yemenita
Yugoslavia	yugoslavo
Wáshington	washingtoniano
Zambia	zambio
Zanzíbar	zanzibareño

Monetary Units

Exchange rates vary from day to day. Consult your bank.

Country	*Basic Unit*	*Standard Subdivision*	*Symbol*
Argentina	peso nuevo	100 centavos	$
Bolivia	peso	100 centavos	$b
Brazil	cruzeiro	100 centavos	Cr$
Chile	peso	100 centésimos	$
Colombia	peso	100 centavos	$
Costa Rica	colón	100 céntimos	¢
Cuba	peso	100 centavos	$
Dominican Republic	peso	100 centavos	$
Ecuador	sucre	100 centavos	S/
El Salvador	colón	100 centavos	¢
Guatemala	quetzal	100 centavos	Q
Haiti	gourde	100 centimes	G
Honduras	lempira	100 centavos	L
Mexico	peso	100 centavos	$
Nicaragua	córdoba	100 centavos	C$
Panama	balboa	100 centésimos	B
Paraguay	guaraní	100 céntimos	G
Peru	sol	100 centavos	S/
Spain	peseta	100 céntimos	Pts.
Uruguay	peso	100 centésimos	N$
Venezuela	bolívar	100 céntimos	Bs

A

A:a

a [a] *prep.* to; in, into; on; by.
abacería [a·ƀa·se·rí·a] *f.* grocery; grocery store; **abacero** [a·ƀa·sé·ro] *m.* grocer.
abad [a·ƀáđ] *m.* abbot; **abadía** [a·ƀa·đí·a] *f.* abbey.
abadejo [a·ƀa·đé·xo] *m. N.Sp.* codfish.
abadesa [a·ƀa·đé·sa] *f.* abbess.
abajarse [a·ƀa·xár·se] *v.* to lower oneself, humiliate oneself.
abajeño [a·ƀa·xé·ño] *adj. Mex., C.A.* lowland; *n.* lowlander.
abajo [a·ƀá·xo] *adv.* down, below; downstairs.
abalanzar[9] [a·ƀa·lan·sár] *v.* to balance; to hurl, impel; **-se** to hurl oneself; to rush (upon), swoop down (upon); *Am.* to rear, balk.
abalear [a·ƀa·le·ár] *v.* to "shoot up"; *Am.* to winnow.
abanderado [a·ƀan·de·rá·đo] *adj.* standard-bearing; *n.* standard-bearer.
abandonamiento [a·ƀan·do·na·mjén·to] = **abandono.**
abandonar [a·ƀan·do·nár] *v.* to abandon, desert; to give up.
abandono [a·ƀan·dó·no] *m.* abandon; desertion; neglect.
abanicar[6] [a·ƀa·ni·kár] *v.* to fan.
abanico [a·ƀa·ní·ko] *m.* fan.
abaratar [a·ƀa·ra·tár] *v.* to cheapen, lower the price of.
abarcar[6] [a·ƀar·kár] *v.* to embrace, contain, include; *Carib., Ríopl.* to buy up, monopolize.
abarrancarse[6] [a·ƀa·rran·kár·se] *v.* to fall into an opening; to get into a difficult situation.
abarrotería [a·ƀa·rro·te·rí·a] *f. Mex., C.A., Andes* grocery, grocery store; **abarrotero** [a·ƀa·rro·té·ro] *m. Mex., C.A., Andes* grocer.
abarrotes [a·ƀa·rró·tes] *m. pl.* small packages (*in hold of a ship*); *Mex., C.A., Andes* groceries; **tienda de —** *Mex., C.A., Andes* grocery store.
abastecer[13] [a·ƀas·te·sér] *v. irr.* to supply.
abastecimiento [a·ƀas·te·si·mjén·to] *m.* supply; provisions.
abasto [a·ƀás·to] *m.* supply; **no dar — a** to be unable to cope with.
abatido [a·ƀa·tí·đo] *adj.* dejected, depressed, crestfallen, humbled; fallen; lowered.
abatimiento [a·ƀa·ti·mjén·to] *m.* discouragement, dejection, depression; descent, swoop, drop.
abatir [a·ƀa·tir] *v.* to lower; to knock down; to depress; to humble; **-se** to become discouraged; to swoop down.
abdicar[6] [aƀ·đi·kár] *v.* to abdicate.
abdomen [aƀ·đó·men] *m.* abdomen.
abecedario [a·ƀe·se·đá·rjo] *m.* alphabet; primer.
abedul [a·ƀe·đúl] *m.* birch.
abeja [a·ƀé·xa] *f.* bee; **abejera** [a·ƀe·xé·ra] *f.* beehive; **abejón** [a·ƀe·xón] *m.* drone; bumblebee; **abejorro** [a·ƀe·xó·rro] *m.* bumblebee.
aberración [a·ƀe·rra·sjón] *f.* aberration, mental or moral deviation.
abertura [a·ƀer·tú·ra] *f.* aperture, opening, hole, slit.
abeto [a·ƀé·to] *m.* fir (*tree and wood*).
abierto [a·ƀjér·to] *p.p. of* **abrir** opened; *adj.* open; frank; *Am.* proud, self-satisfied; *Am.* generous.
abigarrado [a·ƀi·ǥa·rrá·đo] *adj.* motley; multicolored; variegated.
abigeato [a·ƀi·xe·á·to] *m.* cattle stealing.
abismado [a·ƀiz·má·đo] *p.p.* absorbed, buried in thought; overwhelmed.
abismal [a·ƀiz·mál] *adj.* abysmal.
abismar [a·ƀiz·már] *v.* to overwhelm; to depress; **-se** to be plunged (into); to bury oneself (*in thought, grief, etc.*).
abismo [a·ƀíz·mo] *m.* abyss, precipice, chasm.
abjurar [aƀ·xu·rár] *v.* to abjure; to renounce solemnly.
ablandar [a·ƀlan·dár] *v.* to soften.
ablativo [a·ƀla·tí·ƀo] *m.* ablative.
abnegación [aƀ·ne·ǥa·sjón] *f.* abnegation, self-denial, self-sacrifice.
abnegado [aƀ·ne·ǥá·đo] *adj.* self-sacrificing.
abnegarse[7] [aƀ·ne·ǥár·se] *v.* to deny oneself, sacrifice oneself.
abobado [a·ƀo·ƀá·đo] *adj.* stupid, silly.
abocar[6] [a·ƀo·kár] *v.* to bite; to bring near; to flow into.
abocinador [a·ƀo·si·na·đór] *m.* flaring tool.
abocinar [a·ƀo·si·nár] *v.* to flare; to fall on one's face.
abochornar [a·ƀo·čor·nár] *v.* to overheat; to embarrass; **-se** to get overheated; to blush; to be embarrassed.
abofetear [a·ƀo·fe·te·ár] *v.* to slap.
abogacía [a·ƀo·ǥa·sí·a] *f.* the legal profession; a law career.
abogado [a·ƀo·ǥá·đo] *m.* lawyer.
abogar[7] [a·ƀo·ǥár] *v.* to advocate, plead in favor of; to intercede.
abolengo [a·ƀo·léŋ·go] *m.* lineage, ancestry; inheritance, patrimony.
abolición [a·ƀo·li·sjón] *f.* abolition.
abolir[51] [a·ƀo·lír] *v.* to abolish; to repeal.
abolsarse [a·ƀol·sár·se] *v.* to bag.
abollado [a·ƀo·yá·đo] *p.p. & adj.* dented; bumped; bruised.
abolladura [a·ƀo·ya·đú·ra] *f.* dent, bump.
abollar [a·ƀo·yár] *v.* to dent; to bump, to crush, crumple; to bruise.
abombar [a·ƀom·bár] *v.* to make bulge; **-se** *Ríopl.* to get drunk.
abominable [a·ƀo·mi·ná·ƀle] *adj.* abominable, detestable.
abominar [a·ƀo·mi·nár] *v.* to abominate, abhor, detest.
abonado [a·ƀo·ná·đo] *m.* subscriber; *p.p. of* **abonar.**
abonar [a·ƀo·nár] *v.* to credit with; to make a payment; to endorse, back (*a person*); to fertilize (*soil*); **-se** to subscribe.
abonaré [a·ƀo·na·ré] *m.* promissory note; I.O.U.
abono [a·ƀó·no] *m.* (*monetario*) payment; installment; endorsement; guarantee; (*del suelo*) fertilizer; (*suscripción*) subscription.
abordar [a·ƀor·đár] *v.* to board (*a ship*); to dock, put into port; to approach; to undertake, take up (*a matter, problem, etc.*).
aborigen [a·ƀo·rí·xen] *adj.* aboriginal, indigenous, native; **aborigenes** [a·ƀo·rí·xe·nes] *m. pl.* aborigines, primitive inhabitants.
aborrascarse[6] [a·ƀo·rras·kár·se] *v.* to become stormy.
aborrecer[13] [a·ƀo·rre·sér] *v. irr.* to abhor, hate, detest.
aborrecible [a·ƀo·rre·sí·ƀle] *adj.* abominable, hateful.
aborrecimiento [a·ƀo·rre·si·mjén·to] *m.* abhorrence; hatred.
abortar [a·ƀor·tár] *v.* to miscarry, have a miscarriage; to give birth prematurely; to fail.
aborto [a·ƀór·to] *m.* abortion, miscarriage; monster.
abotagarse[7] [a·ƀo·ta·ǥár·se] *v.* to bloat; to swell.
abotonador [a·ƀo·to·na·đór] *m.* buttonhook.
abotonar [a·ƀo·to·nár] *v.* to button, button up; to bud; **-se** to button up.
abovedar [a·ƀo·ƀe·đár] *v.* to vault, cover with a vault; to arch.

abozalar [a·ƀo·sa·lár] *v.* to muzzle.
abra [á·ƀra] *f.* cove; mountain gap or pass; dale; *Am.* breach (*in the jungle*); *Am.* leaf (*of a door*).
abrasador [a·ƀra·sa·dór] *adj.* burning, very hot.
abrasar [a·ƀra·sár] *v.* to burn; to parch; **-se** to burn up, be consumed.
abrasivo [a·ƀra·si·ƀo] *adj.* abrasive.
abrazar[9] [a·ƀra·sár] *v.* to hug, embrace; to include.
abrazo [a·ƀrá·so] *m.* hug, embrace.
abrebotellas [a·ƀre·ƀo·té·yas] *m.* bottle opener.
abrelatas [a·ƀre·lá·tas] *m.* can opener.
abrevadero [a·ƀre·ƀa·đé·ro] *m.* drinking trough; watering place for cattle.
abrevar [a·ƀre·ƀár] *v.* to water (*livestock*).
abreviación [a·ƀre·ƀja·sjón] *f.* abbreviation.
abreviar [a·ƀre·ƀjár] *v.* to abbreviate, shorten, condense.
abreviatura [a·ƀre·ƀja·tú·ra] *f.* abbreviation.
abrigar[7] [a·ƀri·ǥár] *v.* to shelter, cover, protect; to wrap up; to harbor (*fear*), cherish (*hope*); **-se** to find shelter; to wrap oneself up.
abrigo [a·ƀri·ǥo] *m.* shelter, cover, protection; wrap; overcoat.
abril [a·ƀríl] *m.* April.
abrillantar [a·ƀri·yan·tár] *v.* to polish, shine; to glaze.
abrir[52] [a·ƀrír] *v.* to open; to unlock.
abrochar [a·ƀro·čár] *v.* to button; to clasp; to fasten.
abrogación [a·ƀro·ǥa·sjón] *f.* repeal.
abrogar[7] [a·ƀro·ǥár] *v.* to abrogate, repeal, annul.
abrojo [a·ƀró·xo] *m.* thistle, thorn; **-s** reef.
abrumador [a·ƀru·ma·đór] *adj.* crushing, overwhelming; oppressive; fatiguing.
abrumar [a·ƀru·már] *v.* to crush, overwhelm; to trouble, annoy; **-se** to become foggy.
abrupto [a·ƀrúp·to] *adj.* abrupt, steep.
absceso [aƀ·sé·so] *m.* abscess.
absolución [aƀ·so·lu·sjón] *f.* absolution; acquittal.
absoluto [aƀ·so·lú·to] *adj.* absolute; unconditional.
absolver[2, 52] [aƀ·sol·ƀér] *v. irr.* to absolve, free from guilt; to pardon, acquit.
absorbente [aƀ·sor·ƀén·te] *adj. & m.* absorbent.
absorber[52] [aƀ·sor·ƀér] *v.* to absorb.
absorción [aƀ·sor·sjón] *f.* absorption.
absorto [aƀ·sór·to] *p.p. irr. of* **absorber** *& adj.* absorbed, engrossed; amazed.
abstenerse[45] [aƀs·te·nér·se] *v. irr.* to abstain, refrain.
abstinencia [aƀs·ti·nén·sja] *f.* abstinence; fasting.
abstracción [aƀs·trak·sjón] *f.* abstraction, reverie.
abstracto [aƀs·trák·to] *adj.* abstract.
abstraer[46] [aƀs·tra·ér] *v. irr.* to abstract; to withdraw, remove; **-se** to be lost in thought.
abstraído [aƀs·tra·í·đo] *adj.* lost in thought, absentminded; aloof.
absuelto [aƀ·swél·to] *p.p. of* **absolver** absolved, acquitted.
absurdo [aƀ·súr·đo] *adj.* absurd, ridiculous, senseless; *m.* absurdity.
abuela [a·ƀwé·la] *f.* grandmother.
abuelo [a·ƀwé·lo] *m.* grandfather; **-s** grandparents; ancestors.
abulia [a·ƀú·lja] *f.* abulia, loss of will power.
abultado [a·ƀul·tá·đo] *adj.* bulky, bulgy.
abultar [a·ƀul·tár] *v.* to bulge; to be bulky; to enlarge.
abundancia [a·ƀun·dán·sja] *f.* abundance, plenty.
abundante [a·ƀun·dán·te] *adj.* abundant, plentiful.
abundar [a·ƀun·dár] *v.* to abound, be plentiful.
aburrido [a·ƀu·rrí·đo] *p.p. & adj.* bored; boring, tiresome; weary.
aburrimiento [a·ƀu·rri·mjén·to] *m.* weariness, dullness, boredom.
aburrir [a·ƀu·rrír] *v.* to bore, vex; **-se** to become bored or vexed.
abusar [a·ƀu·sár] *v.* to abuse, mistreat; to misuse; — **de** to take unfair advantage of; to impose upon.
abuso [a·ƀú·so] *m.* abuse; misuse.
abyecto [aƀ·yék·to] *adj.* abject.
acá [a·ká] *adv.* here, over here; this way, hither.
acabado [a·ka·ƀá·đo] *m.* a finishing material; paint, varnish; **acabado y compostura** *m.* finish and repair.
acabamiento [a·ka·ƀa·mjén·to] *m.* finish, completion, end; death; *Am.* exhaustion, physical decline.
acabar [a·ka·ƀár] *v.* to end, finish, complete; — **de** (+ *inf.*) to have just; — **por** (+ *inf.*) to end by; — **con** to put an end to, make short work of; to destroy; **-se** to be over, finished; to be consumed; *Am.* to wear oneself out; *Ríopl., Mex., C.A.* to age or decline in health.
academia [a·ka·đé·mja] *f.* academy; a special school; a scientific, literary, or artistic society.
académico [a·ka·đé·mi·ko] *adj.* academic; *m.* academician, member of an academy.
acaecer[13] [a·ka·e·sér] *v. irr.* to happen, occur.
acaecimiento [a·ka·e·si·mjén·to] *m.* event, happening.
acalorado [a·ka·lo·rá·đo] *adj.* heated, excited, angry.
acaloramiento [a·ka·lo·ra·mjén·to] *m.* heat, ardor, excitement.
acalorar [a·ka·lo·rár] *v.* (*calentar*) to heat, warm; (*emocionar*) to excite.
acallar [a·ka·yár] *v.* to silence; to calm, quiet.
acampar [a·kam·pár] *v.* to encamp; to camp.
acanalar [a·ka·na·lár] *v.* to groove; to flute (*as a column*); to form a channel in.
acantilado [a·kan·ti·lá·đo] *adj.* sheer, steep (*cliff*); *m.* bluff, cliff.
acantonar [a·kan·to·nár] *v.* to quarter (*troops*).
acaparar [a·ka·pa·rár] *v.* to corner (*the market*); to monopolize; to gather in.
acaramelarse [a·ka·ra·me·lár·se] *v.* to caramelize.
acarear [a·ka·re·ár] *v.* to bring face to face; to confront.
acariciar [a·ka·ri·sjár] *v.* to caress, pet; to cherish (*a hope or illusion*).
acarreador [a·ka·rre·a·đór] *m.* carter; carrier.
acarrear [a·ka·rre·ár] *v.* to cart, transport; to bring about (*harm, disaster*).
acarreo [a·ka·rré·o] *m.* cartage, carriage, transport, haul.
acaso [a·ká·so] *adv.* perhaps; by chance; **por si** — just in case; *m.* chance, accident.
acatamiento [a·ka·ta·mjén·to] *m.* homage, reverence, respect.
acatar [a·ka·tár] *v.* to revere, respect; to pay homage to; *Mex., C.A. Ven.* to realize; *Mex., C.A., Ven.* to notice, pay attention.
acatarrar [a·ka·ta·rrár] *v.* to chill; *Mex. Ven.* to bother, annoy; **-se** to get chilled, catch cold; *Ríopl.* to get tipsy.
acaudalado [a·kaw·đa·lá·đo] *adj.* wealthy.
acaudillar [a·kaw·đi·yár] *v.* to lead, command.
acceder [ak·se·đér] *v.* to accede.
accesible [ak·se·sí·ƀle] *adj.* accessible; approachable.
acceso [ak·sé·so] *m.* access; entrance, admittance; attack; fit (*of madness, anger, etc.*).
accesorio [ak·se·só·rjo] *adj. & m.* accessory.
accidentado [ak·si·đen·tá·đo] *adj.* seized with a fit; in a swoon; rough, uneven (*ground*).
accidental [ak·si·đen·tál] *adj.* accidental, casual.
accidentarse [ak·si·đen·tár·se] *v.* to have a seizure or fit; to swoon, faint.
accidente [ak·si·đen·te] *m.* accident, mishap; chance;

sudden fit, swoon.
acción [ak·sjón] *f.* (*física*) action; act; gesture; (*militar*) battle; (*de bolsa*) share of stock; — **de gracias** thanksgiving.
accionador [ak·sjo·na·đór] *m.* switch; — **de corriente** power switch.
accionar [ak·sjo·nár] *v.* to gesticulate, make gestures; *Am.* to act, be active.
accionista [ak·sjo·nís·ta] *m.* & *f.* shareholder, stockholder.
acecinar [a·se·si·nár] *v.* to dry-cure; to salt down.
acecino [a·se·sí·no] *m.* corned beef.
acechanza [a·se·čán·sa] *f.* snare; ambush.
acechar [a·se·čár] *v.* to lurk; to spy.
acecho [a·sé·čo] *m.* ambush; spying; **al** (*or* **en**) — waiting in ambush, lying in wait.
acedo [a·sé·đo] *adj.* rancid; acid; sour; harsh, disagreeable.
aceitar [a·sej·tár] *v.* to oil, grease.
aceite [a·séj·te] *m.* oil; — **alcanforado** camphorated oil; — **de hígado de bacalao** cod-liver oil; — **de oliva** olive oil; — **de ricino** castor oil.
aceitera [a·sej·té·ra] *f.* oil can; oil cruet (*bottle for the table*).
aceitoso [a·sej·tó·so] *adj.* oily.
aceituna [a·sej·tú·na] *f.* olive; **aceitunado** *adj.* olive green.
aceituno [a·sej·tú·no] *m.* olive tree.
aceleración [a·se·le·ra·sjón] *f.* acceleration.
acelerador [a·se·le·ra·đór] *m.* accelerator.
acelerante [a·se·le·rán·te] *adj.* stimulator.
acelerar [a·se·le·rár] *v.* to accelerate, speed up; to quicken; to hurry, hasten.
acelga [a·sél·ga] *f.* chard.
acémila [a·sé·mi·la] *f.* pack mule.
acendrado [a·sen·drá·đo] *adj.* pure, without blemish; purified.
acendrar [a·sen·drár] *v.* to refine (*metals*); to purify, cleanse.
acento [a·sén·to] *m.* accent; emphasis.
acentuar[18] [a·sen·twár] *v.* to accentuate, emphasize; to accent; **-se** to become worse (*as an illness*).
acepción [a·sep·sjón] *f.* acceptation, usual meaning.
acepillar [a·se·pi·yár] *v.* to brush; to plane.
aceptación [a·sep·ta·sjón] *f.* acceptance; approval.
aceptar [a·sep·tár] *v.* to accept; to approve; to admit.
acequia [a·sé·kja] *f.* irrigation canal or ditch; *Peru, Ch.* small stream; *Ven., Mex., Andes* sewer.
acera [a·sé·ra] *f.* sidewalk.
acerado [a·se·rá·đo] *adj.* steely, made of steel; steel-like; sharp.
acerar [a·se·rár] *v.* to steel.
acerbo [a·sér·bo] *adj.* bitter; harsh, cruel.
acerca de [a·sér·ka·đe] *prep.* about, concerning.
acercamiento [a·ser·ka·mjén·to] *m.* approach; approaching; rapprochement (*coming together*).
acercar[6] [a·ser·kár] *v.* to bring near, draw up; **-se** to get near, approach.
acero [a·sé·ro] *m.* steel; — **parco en carbono** mild steel.
acérrimo [a·sé·rri·mo] *adj.* very sour, very tart; very harsh; very strong, stanch, stalwart, steadfast.
acertado [a·ser·tá·đo] *adj.* accurate; right; sure.
acertar[1] [a·ser·tár] *v. irr.* to hit (*the mark*); to hit upon; find by chance; to guess right; — **a** (+ *inf.*) to happen to.
acertijo [a·ser·tí·xo] *m.* riddle.
acetileno [a·se·ti·lé·no] *m.* acetylene.
acetona [a·se·tó·na] *f.* acetone.
aciago [a·sjá·go] *adj.* ill-fated, unlucky.
acicalado [a·si·ka·lá·đo] *p.p.* & *adj.* polished; dressed up; adorned; trim, neat.
acicalar [a·si·ka·lár] *v.* to polish; to adorn; **-se** to dress up, doll up.
acicate [a·si·ká·te] *m.* spur; incentive.
acidez [a·si·đés] *f.* acidity, sourness.
ácido [á·si·đo] *m.* acid; *adj.* acid, sour.
acierto [a·sjér·to] *m.* right guess; lucky hit; good aim; good judgment; **con** — effectively, successfully.
aclamación [a·kla·ma·sjón] *f.* acclamation, applause.
aclamar [a·kla·már] *v.* to acclaim, cheer, hail, applaud.
aclaración [a·kla·ra·sjón] *f.* explanation.
aclarar [a·kla·rár] *v.* to clarify, explain; to clear up, (*enjuagar*) to rinse; (*amanecer*) to dawn.
aclimatar [a·kli·ma·tár] *v.* to acclimatize, accustom to a climate or new environment.
acné [ak·né] *m.* acne.
acobardar [a·ko·bar·đár] *v.* to frighten, intimidate.
acogedor [a·ko·xe·đór] *adj.* friendly; hospitable.
acoger[11] [a·ko·xér] *v.* to receive; to give shelter; **-se** to take refuge.
acogida [a·ko·xí·đa] *f.* reception, welcome; refuge.
acogimiento [a·ko·xi·mjén·to] *m.* reception, welcome.
acojinar [a·ko·xi·nár] *v.* to cushion; to quilt.
acolchar [a·kol·čár] *v.* to quilt.
acólito [a·kó·li·to] *m.* acolyte, altar boy.
acometer [a·ko·me·tér] *v.* to attack; (*emprender*) to undertake.
acometida [a·ko·me·tí·đa] *f.* **acometimiento** [a·ko·me·ti·mjén·to] *m.* attack, assault.
acomodadizo [a·ko·mo·đa·đí·so] *adj.* obliging; accommodating.
acomodado [a·ko·mo·đá·đo] *adj.* well-off, wealthy; suitable, convenient; *p.p. of* **acomodar.**
acomodador [a·ko·mo·đa·đór] *m.* usher (*in a theater*).
acomodar [a·ko·mo·đár] *v.* (*cosa*) to arrange, adjust; (*a una persona*) to lodge; to give employment to; **-se** to make oneself comfortable; to adapt oneself.
acomodo [a·ko·mó·đo] *m.* occupation, employment; arrangement.
acompañador [a·kom·pa·ña·đór] *m.* companion; accompanist.
acompañamiento [a·kom·pa·ña·mjén·to] *m.* accompaniment; retinue, company.
acompañante [a·kom·pa·ñán·te] *m.* companion; escort; attendant; accompanist.
acompañar [a·kom·pa·ñár] *v.* to accompany; to escort; to be with; (*incluir*) to enclose (*in a letter*).
acompasado [a·kom·pa·sá·đo] *adj.* rhythmical; measured; slow, deliberate.
acondicionado [a·kon·di·sjo·ná·đo] *adj.* conditioned; comfortable; air-conditioned; *Am.* adequate, suitable.
acondicionar [a·kon·di·sjo·nár] *v.* to condition; to prepare; to arrange; **-se** to become conditioned or prepared.
acongojar [a·koŋ·go·xár] *v.* to grieve; **-se** to grieve; to be distressed.
aconsejar [a·kon·se·xár] *v.* to advise, counsel.
acontecer[13] [a·kon·te·sér] *v. irr.* to happen, occur.
acontecimiento [a·kon·te·si·mjén·to] *m.* event, happening.
acopiar [a·ko·pjár] *v.* to gather, accumulate, store up.
acopio [a·kó·pjo] *m.* storing; accumulation; stock, store, supply.
acoplamiento [a·ko·pla·mjén·to] *m.* coupling; joint, connection.
acoplador [a·ko·pla·dór] *m.* coupler; — **acústico** acoustic coupler.
acoplar [a·ko·plár] *v.* to couple, connect; to fit or join together; (*enyugar*) to yoke; to pair, mate.

acorazado [a·ko·ra·sá·ɗo] *m.* armored ship, battleship.
acorazar[9] [a·ko·ra·sár] *v.* to armor.
acordar[2] [a·kor·ɗár] *v. irr* (*estar conforme*) to arrange, to decide; (*instrumento*) to tune, put in harmony (*stringed instrument*); *Peru, Ch., Ríopl., Mex., Cuba* to grant; **-se** to remember.
acorde [a·kór·ɗe] *adj.* in harmony; in tune; *m.* chord.
acordelar [a·kor·ɗe·lár] *v.* to measure with a cord; to rope off, put a cord around.
acordeón [a·kor·ɗe·ón] *m.* accordion.
acordonar [a·kor·ɗo·nár] *v.* to tie with a cord, string, or rope; to rope off, tie a rope around (*a place*); (*acuñar*) to mill (*a coin*).
acornear [a·kor·ne·ár] *v.* to gore, wound with a horn; (*topar*) to butt.
acorralar [a·ko·rra·lár] *v.* to corral; to surround.
acortamiento [a·kor·ta·mjén·to] *m.* shortening.
acortar [a·kor·tár] *v.* to shorten, diminish; **-se** to shrink; to be shy, bashful.
acosar [a·ko·sár] *v.* to pursue, harass.
acostado [a·kos·tá·ɗo] *adj.* reclining, lying down, in bed; tilted.
acostar[2] [a·kos·tár] *v. irr.* to put to bed; to lay down; **-se** to lie down, go to bed; to tilt.
acostumbrado [a·kos·tum·brá·ɗo] *adj.* accustomed, used, usual, habitual.
acostumbrar [a·kos·tum·brár] *v.* (*enseñar*) to accustom, train; (*soler*) to be used to, be accustomed to; **-se** to get accustomed.
acotación [a·ko·ta·sjón] *f.* marginal note; stage directions (*for a play*); (*límites*) boundary mark; mark on a map showing altitude.
acotar [a·ko·tár] *v.* to mark off (*with boundary marks*); to make marginal notes or citations; to put the elevation marks on (*maps*).
acre [á·kre] *adj.* sour, (*sabor*) tart, sharp; (*tosco*) rude, harsh; *m.* acre.
acrecentamiento [a·kre·sen·ta·mjén·to] *m.* growth, increase.
acrecentar[1] [a·kre·sen·tár] *v. irr.* to increase; to advance, promote.
acreditar [a·kre·ɗi·tár] *v.* to credit; to bring fame or credit to; (*autorizar*) to accredit, authorize; **-se** to win credit or fame.
acreedor [a·kre·e·ɗór] *adj.* worthy, deserving; *m.* creditor.
acribillar [a·kri·ƀi·yár] *v.* to riddle; to perforate; to pierce.
acriollar [a·krjo·yár] *v.* to make Spanish American; **-se** to become Spanish American like; to take on Spanish-American customs.
acróbata [a·kró·ƀa·ta] *m. & f.* acrobat.
acta [ák·ta] *f.* minutes (*of a meeting*); document; **levantar** — to write the minutes.
actitud [ak·ti·túɗ] *f.* attitude; posture, pose.
activar [ak·ti·ƀár] *v.* to activate, make active; to speed up, hasten.
actividad [ak·ti·ƀi·ɗaɗ] *f.* activity; energy.
activista [ak·ti·ƀís·ta] *m. & f.* activist.
activo [ak·tí·ƀo] *adj.* active, lively; *m.* assets.
acto [ák·to] *m.* act; action, deed; ceremony; — **continuo** (*or* **seguido**) immediately after; **en el** — immediately.
actor [ak·tór] *m.* actor; ***actriz*** *f.* actress.
actuación [ak·twa·sjón] *f.* action; intervention, participation, performance; **-es** legal proceedings.
actual [ak·twál] *adj* present (*time*); of the present month; **-mente** *adv.* at present, nowadays.
actualidad [ak·twa·li·ɗáɗ] *f.* present time; **-es** latest news, fashions, or events; **de** — current, up-to-date.
actuar[18] [ak·twár] *v.* to act, perform a function or act; to set in motion, cause to act.
acuarela [a·kwa·ré·la] *f.* water color.
acuario [a·kwá·rjo] *m.* aquarium.
acuartelar [a·kwar·te·lár] *v.* to quarter (*troops*).
acuático [a·kwá·ti·ko] *adj.* aquatic; **deportes -s** water sports.
acuchillar [a·ku·či·yár] *v.* to knife; to stab; to slash.
acudir [a·ku·ɗír] *v.* to come up to; to respond to a call; (*asistir*) to attend, be present; to resort or turn to for help.
acueducto [a·kwe·ɗúk·to] *m.* aqueduct, water channel or pipe.
acuerdo [a·kwér·ɗo] *m.* agreement; decision, resolution; opinion; (*recuerdo*) remembrance; **estar de** — to be in agreement; **ponerse de** — to come to an agreement; **tomar un** — to take a decision.
acullá [a·ku·yá] *adv.* yonder, over there.
acumulación [a·ku·mu·la·sjón] *f.* accumulation.
acumulador [a·ku·mu·la·ɗór] *m.* storage battery.
acumular [a·ku·mu·lár] *v.* to accumulate, gather, pile up.
acuñación [a·ku·ña·sjón] *f.* coinage, minting; wedging.
acuñar [a·ku·ñár] *v.* to mint, coin, to wedge.
acuoso [a·kwó·so] *adj.* watery.
acurrucarse[6] [a·ku·rru·kár·se] *v.* to cuddle, nestle; to huddle.
acusación [a·ku·sa·sjón] *f.* accusation, charge.
acusado [a·ku·sá·ɗo] *p.p. & adj.* accused; *m.* defendant.
acusar [a·ku·sár] *v.* to accuse, denounce; to acknowledge (*receipt*).
acusativo [a·ku·sa·tí·ƀo] *adj.* accusative.
acuse [a·kú·se] *m.* acknowledgment (*of receipt*).
acústica [a·kús·ti·ka] *f.* acoustics.
acústico [a·kús·ti·ko] *adj.* acoustic.
achacar[6] [a·ča·kár] *v.* to impute, attribute.
achacoso [a·ča·kó·so] *adj.* sickly.
achaparrado [a·ča·pa·rrá·ɗo] *adj.* shrub, of shrub size; squat, squatty.
achaque [a·čá·ke] *m.* slight chronic illness; excuse; pretext; infirmity.
achicar[6] [a·či·kár] *v.* to shorten, to make small; (*vaciar*) to bail (*water*); (*humillar*) to humiliate; *Col.* to kill; *Ríopl.* to tie, fasten; **-se** to get smaller; to shrink.
achicoria [a·či·kó·rja] *f.* chicory.
adagio [a·ɗá·xjo] *m.* adage, proverb, wise saying.
adaptar [a·ɗap·tár] *v.* to adapt, fit, adjust.
adecuado [a·ɗe·kwá·ɗo] *adj.* adequate, fit, suitable.
adecuar [a·ɗe·kwár] *v.* to fit, adapt.
adefesio [a·ɗe·fé·sjo] *m.* absurdity, nonsense; ridiculous sight, dress, or person.
adelantado [a·ɗe·lan·tá·ɗo] *p.p. & adj.* anticipated; advanced; ahead; forward, bold; **por** — in advance; *m.* governor of a province (*in colonial Spanish America*).
adelantamiento [a·ɗe·lan·ta·mjén·to] *m.* advancement, progress, betterment.
adelantar [a·ɗe·lan·tár] *v.* to advance; to move forward; to progress; (*mejorar*) to better; **-se** to get ahead.
adelante [a·ɗe·lán·te] *adv.* forward, ahead; **en** — from now on.
adelanto [a·ɗe·lán·to] *m.* advance; advancement, progress; (*mejoramiento*) betterment.
adelfa [a·ɗél·fa] *f.* oleander.
adelgazar[9] [a·ɗel·ǥa·sár] *v.* to thin out, taper; **-se** to get thin, slender.
ademán [a·ɗe·mán] *m.* gesture, gesticulation; attitude.

además [a·de·más] *adv.* moreover, besides; — **de** *prep.* in addition to, besides.
adentro [a·dén·tro] *adv.* within, inside; **tierra** — inland; **mar** — out to sea; **hablar para sus -s** to talk to oneself.
aderezamiento [a·de·re·sa·mjén·to] *m.* dressing; (*adorno*) adornment, decoration.
aderezar [a·de·re·sár] *v.* (*embellecer*) to fix up, adorn, beautify, garnish; (*condimentar*) to season, prepare; (*almidonar*) to starch, stiffen.
aderezo [a·de·ré·so] *m.* (*adorno*) adornment, garnish, trappings, finery, set of jewels; (*alimento*) seasoning; (*almidón*) starch, stiffener, filler (*used in cloth*).
adestrado [a·des·trá·do] *adj.* trained, skilled.
adestrar[1] [a·des·trár] *v. irr.* to train; to guide.
adeudado [a·dew·dá·do] *adj.* indebted; in debt; *p.p. of* **adeudar.**
adeudar [a·dew·dár] *v.* to owe; to debit, charge; **-se** to run into debt.
adeudo [a·déw·do] *m.* debt, indebtedness; (*derechos*) duty (*on imports*); debit, charge.
adherencia [a·de·rén·sja] *f.* adherence; attachment.
adherir[3] [a·de·rír] *v. irr.* to adhere, stick.
adhesión [a·de·sjón] *f.* adhesion; attachment.
adicto [a·dík·to] *adj.* addicted; devoted; *m.* addict; follower.
adiestrado [a·djes·trá·do] = **adestrado.**
adiestramiento [a·djes·tra·mjén·to] *m.* training; drill.
adiestrar [a·djes·trár] = **adestrar.**
adinerado [a·di·ne·rá·do] *adj.* wealthy.
¡adiós! [a·djós] *interj.* good-bye!; farewell!; (*hola*) hello!; *Am.* you don't say!
aditamento [a·di·ta·mén·to] *m.* addition; annex.
aditivo [a·di·tí·bo] *m.* additive.
adivinación [a·di·bi·na·sjón] *f.* divination, prediction; guess.
adivinanza [a·di·bi·nán·sa] *f.* conundrum, riddle.
adivinar [a·di·bi·nár] *v.* to guess.
adivino [a·di·bí·no] *m.* fortuneteller; soothsayer.
adjetivo [ad·xe·tí·bo] *m. & adj.* adjective.
adjudicar[6] [ad·xu·di·kár] *v.* to adjudge, award, assign; **-se** to appropriate.
adjuntar [ad·xun·tár] *v.* to put with; to bring together; (*incluir*) to enclose (*in a letter*).
adjunto [ad·xún·to] *adj.* adjoining; attached, enclosed.
adminículo [ad·mi·ní·ku·lo] *m.* accessory; gadget.
administración [ad·mi·nis·tra·sjón] *f.* administration, management; headquarters; *Ven., Mex., Cuba* extreme unction, last sacrament; **administración y gerencia** *f.* public administration and management.
administrador [ad·mi·nis·tra·dór] *m.* administrator, manager.
administrar [ad·mi·nis·trár] *v.* to administer; to manage; **-se** *Ven., Mex., Cuba* to receive the extreme unction or last sacrament.
administrativo [ad·mi·nis·tra·tí·bo] *adj.* administrative.
admirable [ad·mi·rá·ble] *adj.* admirable, wonderful.
admiración [ad·mi·ra·sjón] *f.* admiration, wonder; **punto de** — exclamation point.
admirador [ad·mi·ra·dór] *m.* admirer.
admirar [ad·mi·rár] *v.* to admire; **-se** to be astonished or amazed; to wonder.
admisible [ad·mi·sí·ble] *adj.* admissible, allowable.
admisión [ad·mi·sjón] *f.* admission; acceptance; acknowledgment.
admitir [ad·mi·tír] *v.* (*dejar entrar*) to admit; to let in; (*aceptar*) to accept; (*permitir*) to allow, permit.
adobar [a·do·bár] *v.* to fix, cook, prepare (*food*), to tan (*hides*); to pickle (*meats, fish*).
adobe [a·dó·be] *m.* adobe, sun-dried mud brick.
adobo [a·dó·bo] *m.* repairing; (*salsa*) sauce for seasoning or pickling; mixture for dressing skins or cloth; rouge.
adoctrinamiento [a·dok·tri·na·mjén·to] *m.* indoctrination, teaching, instruction.
adoctrinar [a·dok·tri·nár] *v.* to indoctrinate, teach, instruct.
adolecer[13] [a·do·le·sér] *v. irr.* to suffer (*from an illness, defect, etc.*).
adolescencia [a·do·le·sén·sja] *f.* adolescence.
adolescente [a·do·le·sén·te] *adj.* adolescent.
adonde [a·dón·de] *rel. adv.* where; **¿adónde?** *interr. adv.* where to?; where?
adoptar [a·dop·tár] *v.* to adopt; to accept (*an opinion*).
adoptivo [a·dop·ti·bo] *adj.* adoptive, related by adoption; adopted.
adoración [a·do·ra·sjón] *f.* adoration, worship.
adorar [a·do·rár] *v.* to adore, worship.
adormecer[13] [a·dor·me·sér] *v. irr.* to make sleepy or drowsy; to lull; **-se** to get sleepy; to get numb; to fall asleep.
adormilado [a·dor·mi·lá·do] *adj.* drowsy.
adornar [a·dor·nár] *v.* to adorn, decorate, ornament.
adorno [a·dór·no] *m.* adornment, ornament, decoration.
adquirir[35] [ad·ki·rír] *v. irr.* to acquire, gain, win, obtain.
adquisición [ad·ki·si·sjón] *f.* acquisition, attainment.
adrede [a·dré·de] *adv.* on purpose, intentionally.
aduana [a·dwá·na] *f.* customhouse.
aduanero [a·dwa·né·ro] *m.* customhouse officer; *adj.* customhouse.
aduar [a·dwár] *m.* gypsy camp; *Ríopl.* Indian camp or ranch.
aducir[25] [a·du·sír] *v. irr.* to cite, allege, offer as proof.
adueñarse [a·dwe·ñár·se] *v.* to take possession.
adulación [a·du·la·sjón] *f.* flattery.
adulador [a·du·la·dór] *m.* flatterer.
adular [a·du·lár] *v.* to flatter.
adulterar [a·dul·te·rár] *v.* to adulterate, corrupt, make impure.
adulterio [a·dul·té·rjo] *m.* adultery.
adúltero [a·dúl·te·ro] *m.* adulterer.
adulto [a·dúl·to] *m. & adj.* adult.
adusto [a·dús·to] *adj.* stern, severe, austere.
advenedizo [ad·be·ne·dí·so] *m.* newcomer, stranger; upstart; *Mex., Carib., Andes* novice, beginner; *adj.* newly arrived; upstart; *Mex., Carib., Andes* inexperienced.
advenimiento [ad·be·ni·mién·to] *m.* advent, arrival, coming.
adverbio [ad·bér·bjo] *m.* adverb.
adversario [ad·ber·sá·rjo] *m.* adversary, opponent; foe.
adversidad [ad·ber·si·dád] *f.* adversity; calamity.
adverso [ad·bér·so] *adj.* adverse; contrary; unfavorable.
advertencia [ad·ber·tén·sja] *f.* notice; warning; advice.
advertir[3] [ad·ber·tír] *v. irr.* to notice; to warn; to advise.
adyacente [ad·ya·sén·te] *adj.* adjacent.
aéreo [a·é·re·o] *adj.* aerial; airy; **correo** — air mail.
aerodinámico [a·e·ro·di·ná·mi·ko] *adj.* aerodynamic; *f.* aerodynamics.
aeródromo [a·e·ró·dro·mo] *m.* airport.
aerofluyente [a·e·ro·flu·yén·te] *adj.* streamlined.

AC

aeronautica [a·e·ro·náw·ti·ka] *f.* aeronautics.
aeronave [a·e·ro·ná·ƀe] *f.* airship.
aeropista [a·e·ro·pís·ta] *f.* landing strip; runway.
aeroplano [a·e·ro·plá·no] *m.* airplane.
aeropuerto [a·e·ro·pwér·to] *m.* airport.
aerosol [a·e·ro·sól] *m.* aerosol.
afabilidad [a·fa·ƀi·li·đáđ] *f.* friendliness, pleasantness, courtesy; **afable** [a·fá·ƀle] *adj.* affable, pleasant, courteous.
afamado [a·fa·má·đo] *adj.* famous.
afán [a·fán] *m.* eagerness, anxiety, ardor.
afanar [a·fa·nár] *v.* to urge, press; **-se** to hurry; to worry; to work eagerly; to toil.
afanoso [a·fa·nó·so] *adj.* laborious, hardworking.
afasia [a·fá·sja] *f.* aphasia.
afear [a·fe·ár] *v.* to make ugly; to disfigure; to blame, censure, condemn.
afección [a·fek·sjón] *f.* affection, fondness; disease.
afectado [a·fek·tá·đo] *p.p. & adj.* affected; *Am.* hurt, harmed; *Am.* **estar — del corazón** to have heart trouble.
afectar [a·fek·tár] *v.* (*promover*) to affect, move; (*fingir*) to pretend to have or feel; *Am.* to hurt, to harm, to injure.
afecto [a·fék·to] *m.* affection; *adj.* fond; **— a** fond of; given to; prone to.
afectuoso [a·fek·twó·so] *adj.* affectionate, tender.
afeitada [a·fej·tá·đa] *f. Am.* shave, shaving.
afeitar [a·fej·tár] *v.* to shave; **-se** to shave oneself; to put on make-up.
afeite [a·féj·te] *m.* make-up, cosmetics.
afelpado [a·fel·pá·đo] *adj.* velvety.
afeminado [a·fe·mi·ná·đo] *adj.* effeminate.
aferrado [a·fe·rrá·đo] *adj.* stubborn, obstinate; *p.p. of* **aferrar.**
aferramiento [a·fe·rra·mjén·to] *m.* grasping, seizing; attachment; subbornness; tenacity.
aferrar [a·fe·rrár] *v.* to seize, grasp, grapple; **-se** to take or seize hold of; to cling; **-se a una opinión** to cling to an opinion.
afianzar[9] [a·fjan·sár] *v.* to fasten, secure; to steady; to give bail or bond.
afición [a·fi·sjón] *f.* taste, inclination; fondness, affection.
aficionado [a·fi·sjo·ná·đo] *adj.* fond; *m.* amateur, fan.
aficionar [a·fi·sjo·nár] *v.* to inspire a liking or fondness; **-se a** to become fond of.
afiche [a·fí·če] *m. Ríopl.*, poster.
afijo [a·fí·xo] *m.* affix.
afilador [a·fi·la·đór] *m.* grinder, sharpener.
afilar [a·fi·lár] *v.* to sharpen; to grind; *Am.* to make love to, woo; *Am.* to flatter; *Am.* **— con** to flirt with.
afín [a·fín] *adj.* kindred, related; **ideas afines** related ideas.
afinado [a·fi·ná·đo] *m.* polishing.
afinador [a·fi·na·đór] *m.* piano tuner.
afinar [a·fi·nár] *v.* to refine, polish; (*instrumento*) to tune.
afinidad [a·fi·ni·đáđ] *f.* affinity; similarity, relationship.
afirmación [a·fir·ma·sjón] *f.* affirmation, assertion.
afirmado [a·fir·mã·đo] *m.* tamping.
afirmar [a·fir·már] *v.* to affirm, assert; to make firm; *Am.* **— un golpe** to deal a blow.
afirmativa [a·fir·ma·tí·ƀa] *f.* affirmative.
afirmativo [a·fir·ma·tí·ƀo] *adj.* affirmative.
aflicción [a·flik·sjón] *f.* affliction, trouble, (*dolor*) pain, grief.
afligir[11] [a·fli·xír] *v.* to afflict, trouble, grieve; *Ríopl., Ven.* to mistreat, harm, beat, strike; **-se** to worry, grieve.
aflojar [a·flo·xár] *v.* to slacken; to loosen, unfasten; to let go; *Mex. Ríopl., Carib.* to let go of money, spend easily; *Mex. Ríopl., Carib.* **— un golpe** to hit.
afluente [a·flwén·te] *m.* tributary; *adj.* abundant.
afluir[32] [a·flwír] *v. irr.* to flow (into).
afortunado [a·for·tu·ná·đo] *adj.* fortunate; lucky.
afrenta [a·frén·ta] *f.* affront, offense, insult.
afrentar [a·fren·tár] *v.* to insult, offend, dishonor.
afrentoso [a·fren·tó·so] *adj.* outrageous, shameful, disgraceful.
africado [a·fri·ká·đo] *adj.* affricative; *f.* affricate.
africano [a·fri·ká·no] *adj & m.* African.
afrontar [a·fron·tár] *v.* to face; to confront.
afuera [a·fwé·ra] *adv.* out, outside; **-s** *f. pl.* outskirts.
agachar [a·ǥa·čár] *v.* to lower; to bend down; **-se** to stoop, bend down, duck; to crouch; *Am.* to give in, yield; *Col.* **-se con algo** to make away with or steal something.
agalla [a·ǥá·ya] *f.* gill; tonsil; *Col., Ven.* greed; **tener -s** to have guts, have courage; *Ríopl., Ch., Carib.* to be unscrupulous and bold in business deals; *Ríopl., Ch., Carib.* to be greedy or stingy; *C.A.* to be smart, astute, cunning.
agarrar [a·ǥa·rrár] *v.* to seize, grasp, grab; **-se** to cling, hold on.
agarro [a·ǥá·rro] *m.* clench, clutch, grasp, grip. grab; **agarrón** *m.* tight clench, sudden grasp, grab; *Mex., Col., Ven., C.A.* pull, tug.
agasajar [a·ǥa·sa·xár] *v.* to entertain; to flatter.
agasajo [a·ǥa·sá·xo] *m.* entertainment, kind reception; friendliness; (*adulación*) flattery.
agazapar [a·ǥa·sa·pár] *v.* to nab, seize (*a person*), **-se** to crouch; to squat.
agencia [a·xén·sja] *f.* agency; *Ch.* pawnshop.
agenciar [a·xen·sjár] *v.* to negotiate; to procure by negotiation; to promote.
agente [a·xén·te] *m.* agent; *Am.* police officer, official.
ágil [á·xil] *adj.* agile, nimble, limber.
agilidad [a·xi·li·đáđ] *f.* agility, nimbleness.
agitación [a·xi·ta·sjón] *f.* agitation; excitement.
agitador [a·xi·ta·đór] *m.* agitator; *adj.* agitating; stirring.
agitar [a·xi·tár] *v.* to agitate, excite; (*menear*) to stir; to wave; to shake.
aglomeración [a·ǥlo·me·ra·sjón] *f.* conglomeration, heap, pile, mass.
aglomerar [a·ǥlo·me·rár] *v.* to mass together; to cluster; **-se** to crowd together, pile up.
aglutinante [a·ǥlu·ti·nán·te] *adj.* agglutinative.
agobiar [a·ǥo·ƀjár] *v.* to oppress, weigh down; to overwhelm.
agolparse [a·ǥol·pár·se] *v.* to crowd together, jam.
agonía [a·ǥo·ní·a] *f.* agony.
agonizante [a·ǥo·ni·sán·te] *adj.* dying; *m.* dying person.
agonizar[9] [a·ǥo·ni·sár] *v.* to be dying.
agorero [a·ǥo·ré·ro] *adj.* ominous, of bad omen; prophetic; *m.* augur, prophet, fortune-teller.
agostar [a·ǥos·tár] *v.* to parch, dry up; to pasture; to plow (*in August*).
agosto [a·ǥós·to] *m.* August; harvest; **hacer su —** to make hay while the sun shines.
agotado [a·ǥo·tá·đo] *adj. & p.p.* exhausted; out-of-print.
agotamiento [a·ǥo·ta·mjén·to] *m.* exhaustion; draining.
agotar [a·ǥo·tár] *v.* to exhaust, use up; to drain off; **-se** (*acabarse*) to be exhausted, used up;

(*terminarse la edición*) to go out of print.
agraciado [a·ǥra·sjá·đo] *adj.* graceful; *m.* winner (*of a favor, prize, etc.*).
agraciar [a·ǥra·sjár] *v.* to grace; to adorn.
agradable [a·ǥra·đá·ƀle] *adj.* agreeable, pleasant.
agradar [a·ǥra·đár] *v.* to please, be agreeable (to).
agradecer[13] [a·ǥra·đe·sér] *v. irr.* to thank for; to be grateful for.
agradecido [a·ǥra·đe·si·đo] *adj.* thankful, grateful.
agradecimiento [a·ǥra·đe·si·mjén·to] *m.* gratitude, thankfulness.
agrado [a·ǥrá·đo] *m.* agreeableness; liking, pleasure; **de su** — to his liking.
agrandar [a·ǥran·dár] *v.* to enlarge; to aggrandize, make greater.
agravar [a·ǥra·ƀár] *v.* to aggravate, make worse; to make heavier; (*oprimir*) to oppress; **-se** to get worse.
agraviar [a·ǥra·ƀjár] *v.* to offend, insult, affront.
agravio [a·ǥrá·ƀjo] *m.* offense, insult, affront.
agredir[51] [a·ǥre·đír] *v.* to assail, assault, attack.
agregado [a·ǥre·ǥá·đo] *m.* attaché, person attached to a staff; (*colección*) aggregate, collection.
agregar[7] [a·ǥre·ǥár] *v.* to add; to join; to attach.
agresivo [a·ǥre·sí·ƀo] *adj.* aggressive, offensive.
agresor [a·ǥre·sór] *m.* aggressor; assailant.
agreste [a·ǥrés·te] *adj.* rustic; (*flora*) wild (*fruit, flower, etc.*).
agriar[17] [a·ǥrjár] *v.* to sour, make sour; **-se** to sour, turn sour, become sour.
agrícola [a·ǥrí·ko·la] *adj.* agricultural.
agricultor [a·ǥri·kul·tór] *m.* agriculturist, farmer.
agricultura [a·ǥri·kul·tú·ra] *f.* agriculture.
agridulce [a·ǥri·đúl·se] *adj.* bittersweet, tart.
agrietarse [a·ǥrje·tár·se] *v.* to crack; to chap (*said of the skin*).
agrimensor [a·gri·men·sór] *m.* surveyor.
agrimensura [a·ǥri·men·sú·ra] *f.* survey, surveying (*of land*).
agrio [á·ǥrjo] *adj.* sour; disagreeable.
agropecuario [a·ǥro·pe·kwá·rjo] *adj.* farming (*crops and cattle*).
agrupación [a·ǥru·pa·sjón] *f.* group; bunch; grouping; gathering.
agrupar [a·ǥru·pár] *v.* to group, bunch up.
agrura [a·ǥrú·ra] *f.* sourness.
agua [á·ǥwa] *f.* water; rain; — **abajo** downstream; — **arriba** upstream; **aguas inmundas** *f.* sewage.
aguacate [a·ǥwa·ká·te] *m. Mex., C.A., Carib., Col., Ven.* avocado, alligator pear; *Am.* avocado tree; *Am.* phlegmatic person.
aguacero [a·ǥwa·sé·ro] *m.* shower. *C.A.*, party to honor.
aguada [a·ǥwá·đa] *f.* watering place; supply of drinking water; flood; wall wash; water color.
aguadero [a·ǥwa·đé·ro] *m.* watering place.
aguado [a·ǥwá·đo] *adj.* watery; watered; *Am.* soft, unstarched; *Am.* weak, limp; *Andes* insipid, uninteresting, dull; **sopa aguada** thin soup; *p.p. of* **aguar.**
aguaitar [a·ǥwaj·tár] *v. Col., Ven., Andes, Ch.* to spy; to watch; to wait for.
aguantar [a·ǥwan·tár] *v.* to endure, bear; to resist; **-se** to be silent, restrain oneself.
aguante [a·ǥwán·te] *m.* endurance, fortitude, resistance.
aguar[9] [a·ǥwár] *v.* to water, dilute with water; to spoil (*pleasure*); *Ríopl., Ven., C.A.* to water (*livestock*); **-se** to become diluted; to get watery; to fill up with water; **se aguó la fiesta** the party was spoiled.
aguardar [a·ǥwar·đár] *v.* to wait; to wait for.
aguardentoso [a·ǥwar·đen·tó·so] *adj.* alcoholic; (*ronco*) hoarse, raucous.
aguardiente [a·ǥwar·đjén·te] *m.* brandy, hard liquor; — **de caña** rum.
aguarrás [a·ǥwa·rrás] *m.* turpentine, oil of turpentine.
aguazal [a·ǥwa·sál] *m.* marsh, swamp.
agudeza [a·ǥu·đé·sa] *f.* sharpness; keenness; (*viveza*) wit; witty remark or saying.
agudo [a·ǥú·đo] *adj.* sharp; sharp-pointed; (*listo*) keen, witty; acute; shrill.
agüero [a·ǥwé·ro] *m.* augury, prediction; sign, omen; *Ríopl., Mex., Carib.* fortune-teller.
aguijar [a·ǥi·xár] *v.* (*picar*) to prick, goad, spur; (*animar*) to encourage, excite.
aguijón [a·ǥi·xón] *m.* prick; sting; spur, goad.
aguijonear [a·ǥi·xo·ne·ár] *v.* to goad; to prick.
águila [á·ǥi·la] *f.* eagle; **es un** — he is sharp.
aguileño [a·ǥi·lé·ño] *adj.* aquiline; eaglelike.
aguinaldo [a·ǥi·nál·do] *m.* Christmas or New Year's gift; bonus.
aguja [a·ǥú·xa] *f.* needle; crochet hook; watch hand; church spire; railroad switch.
agujerear [a·ǥu·xe·re·ár] *v.* to pierce, perforate; to riddle.
agujero [a·ǥu·xé·ro] *m.* hole; (*vendedor*) needle peddler; (*caja*) needle box; pincushion; **agujeros de burbuja** *m.* blowholes.
aguzar[9] [a·ǥu·sar] *v.* to sharpen; to goad, stimulate; — **las orejas** to prick up one's ears.
ahí [a·í] *adv.* there; **por** — over there.
ahijado [a·i·xá·đo] *m.* godchild.
ahijar [a·i·xár] *v.* to adopt.
ahínco [a·íŋ·ko] *m.* effort, eagerness, zeal.
ahogar[7] [a·o·ǥár] *v.* to drown; (*estrangular*) to choke, strangle; to smother; (*apagar*) to quench, extinguish.
ahogo [a·ó·ǥo] *m.* suffocation; breathlessness; (*angustia*) anguish, grief.
ahondar [a·on·dár] *v.* to deepen, to dig; to penetrate, go deep into.
ahora [a·ó·ra] *adv.* now; — **mismo** right now; **por** — for the present; — **que** *Am.* as soon as; **ahorita** [a·o·rí·ta] instantly, this very minute; **ahoritica** [a·o·ri·tí·ka], **ahoritita** [a·o·ri·tí·ta] *Am.* this very second, in a jiffy.
ahorcar[6] [a·or·kár] *v.* to hang, kill by hanging.
ahorrar [a·o·rrár] *v.* to save; to spare; to avoid.
ahorro [a·ó·rro] *m.* saving, economy; **caja de -s** savings bank.
ahuecar[6] [a·we·kár] *v.* to make hollow; to hollow out; — **la voz** to speak in a hollow voice; *Am.* **¡ahueca!** get out of here!; **-se** to become puffed up, get conceited.
ahuehuete [a·we·wé·te] *m. Mex., C.A.* a Mexican cypress.
ahumado [a·u·má·đo] *adj.* smoked; smoky.
ahumar [a·u·már] *v.* to smoke; to fume.
ahuyentar [a·u·yen·tár] *v.* to drive away; to scare away; **-se** to go away, flee; *Ven., Carib., Mex.* to stop frequenting a place.
aindiado [ajn·djá·đo] *adj.* Indian-like.
airado [aj·rá·đo] *adj.* irate; angry.
airar [aj·rár] *v.* to annoy, irritate; **-se** to get angry.
aire [áj·re] *m.* air; wind; (*melodía*) tune; (*aspecto*) appearance; conceit; **-cito** *m.* breeze; a little tune; a certain air or appearance.
airear [aj·re·ár] *v.* to air, ventilate.
airoso [aj·ró·so] *adj.* windy; airy; graceful, elegant; lively, spirited.
aislador [ajz·la·đór] *m.* insulator; isolator; *adj.*

insulating; isolating.
aislamiento [ajz·la·mjén·to] *m.* isolation; insulation.
aislar [ajz·lár] *v.* to isolate, place apart; to insulate.
¡ajá! [a·xá] *interj.* great! fine! so!
ajar [a·xár] *v.* to crumple, wither.
ajedrez [a·xe·đrés] *m.* chess.
ajenjo [a·xéŋ·xo] *m.* absynthe.
ajeno [a·xé·no] *adj.* (*de otro*) another's; (*inconciente*) unaware; (*extranjero*) alien; — **a mi voluntad** beyond my control; — **de cuidados** free from cares.
ajetrearse [a·xe·tre·ár·se] *v.* to hustle and bustle, (*cansarse*) to get tired out.
ajetreo [a·xe·tré·o] *m.* bustle, hustle; hubbub; fuss; (*cansancio*) fatigue.
ají [a·xí] *m. S.A., Carib.* chili pepper, chili sauce.
ajo [á·xo] *m.* garlic; garlic clove; garlic sauce; (*maldición*) swear word.
ajuar [a·xwár] *m.* furniture set; trousseau, bride's outfit; bride's portion or dowry.
ajustado [a·xus·tá·đo] *adj.* tight, fitting tight; (*acordado*) agreed upon (*as a price*); — **a la ley** in accordance with the law; *p.p. of* **ajustar.**
ajustamiento [a·xus·ta·mjén·to] *m.* adjustment.
ajustar [a·xus·tár] *v.* to adjust; to fit tight; to regulate; to tighten; to settle (*accounts*); (*nombrar*) to hire (*a person*); *Col.* to stint, scrimp, save; *C.A.* — **una bofetada** to give a good slap; *C.A., Mex.* **hoy ajusta quince años** he is just fifteen years old today; **-se** to come to an agreement.
ajuste [a·xús·te] *m.* adjustment, fit; agreement; settlement (*of accounts*); truing.
adjusticiar [a·xus·ti·sjár] *v.* to execute, put to death.
al [al] = **a** + **el** to the.
ala [á·la] *f.* wing; hat brim.
alabanza [a·la·ƀán·sa] *f.* praise.
alabar [a·la·ƀár] *v.* to praise.
alabastro [a·la·bás·tro] *m.* alabaster.
alacena [a·la·sé·na] *f.* cupboard; closet; *Am.* booth, stall, market stand.
alacrán [a·la·krán] *m.* scorpion.
alado [a·la·đo] *adj.* winged.
alambicado [a·lam·bi·ka·đo] *p.p. & adj.* distilled; over-refined, (*sutil*) over-subtle (*applied to style*).
alambique [a·lam·bí·ke] *m.* still.
alambrada [a·lam·brá·đa] *f.* wire, entanglement.
alambrado [a·lam·brá·đo] *m.* wire fence; wire screening; wiring.
alambre [a·lám·bre] *m.* wire.
alameda [a·la·mé·đa] *f.* poplar grove; park.
álamo [á·la·mo] *m.* poplar.
alancear [a·lan·se·ár] *v.* to lance, spear.
alano [a·lá·no] *m.* mastiff.
alarde [a·lár·đe] *m.* boast, bluff, brag.
alardear [a·lar·đe·ár] *v.* to boast, brag.
alargar[7] [a·lar·ǥár] *v.* to lengthen; to prolong; to stretch out, extend.
alarido [a·la·rí·đo] *m.* shout, scream, howl.
alarma [a·lár·ma] *f.* alarm.
alarmar [a·lar·már] *v.* to alarm.
alazán [a·la·sán] *adj.* chestnut-colored; sorrel.
alba [ál·ƀa] dawn; alb (*white robe worn by priest*).
albacea [al·ƀa·sé·a] *m.* executor.
albañal [al·ƀa·ñál] *m.* sewer.
albañil [al·ƀa·ñíl] *m.* mason, brickmason; **albañilería** [al·ƀa·ñi·le·rí·a] *f.* masonry.
albaricoque [al·ƀa·ri·kó·ke] *m.* apricot; **albaricoquero** [al·ƀa·ri·ko·ke·ro] *m.* apricot tree.
albayalde [al·ƀa·yál·de] *m.* white lead.
albazo [al·ƀá·so] *m. Mex.* early morning serenade; *Mex.* bad surprise, surprise attack at dawn.
albear [al·ƀe·ár] *v.* to show white (*in the distance*); *Am.* to rise at dawn.
albedrío [al·ƀe·đrí·o] *m.* free will.
albéitar [al·ƀéj·tar] *m.* veterinary.
alberca [al·ƀér·ka] *f.* water reservoir, tank; *Mex.* swimming pool.
albergar[7] [al·ƀer·ǥár] *v.* to house, shelter, lodge; **-se** to take shelter; to lodge.
albino [al·ƀí·no] *m. & f.* albino.
albo [ál·ƀo] *adj.* white; *Am.* white-footed (*horse*).
albóndiga [al·ƀón·di·ǥa] *f.* meat ball; fish ball.
albor [al·ƀór] *f.* dawn; whiteness.
alborada [al·ƀo·rá·đa] *f.* dawn; reveille (*morning bugle call*).
alborear [al·ƀo·re·ár] *v.* to dawn.
alborotador [al·ƀo·ro·ta·đór] *m.* agitator, troublemaker.
alborotar [al·ƀo·ro·tár] *v.* to disturb, upset; *Am.* to excite, arouse enthusiasm; **-se** to get upset; to mutiny; to riot; *Am.* to get excited; *Am.* to rear, balk (*said of a horse*).
alboroto [al·ƀo·ró·to] *m.* uproar, disturbance; riot; *Am.* excitement, enthusiasm; *Col., C.A.* popcorn, candied popcorn ball.
alborozado [al·ƀo·ro·sá·đo] *adj.* elated, excited.
alborozar[9] [al·ƀo·ro·sár] *v.* to gladden; **-se** to rejoice.
alborozo [al·ƀo·ró·so] *m.* joy, delight.
albricias [al·ƀrí·sjas] *f. pl.* good news; reward (*for good news*).
alcachofa [al·ka·čó·fa] *f.* artichoke; *Ch.* blow.
alcahuete [al·ka·wé·te] *m.* procurer, panderer; go-between; **alcahueta** *f.* bawd, procuress, go-between.
alcaide [al·káj·đe] *m.* warden (*of a fortress, prison, etc.*).
alcalde [al·kál·de] *m.* mayor; justice of the peace; — **mayor** mayor.
alcance [al·kán·se] *m.* (*extensión*) reach, scope; (*capacidad*) talent, capacity; (*noticas*) last minute news, newspaper extra; **cortos -s** meagre intellect; **dar** — **a** to catch up with.
alcancía [al·kan·sí·a] *f.* money box (*with slit for coin*); savings bank.
alcanfor [al·kan·fór] *m.* camphor.
alcantarilla [al·kan·ta·rí·ya] *f.* conduit; drain.
alcantarillado [al·kan·ta·ri·yá·đo] *m.* sewage system.
alcanzado [al·kan·sá·đo] *adj.* needy; broke, short of funds.
alcanzar[9] [al·kan·sár] *v.* to reach; to overtake; (*obtener*) to obtain; (*suceder*) to befall; (*bastar*) to be enough; *Am.* to hand, pass, put within reach.
alcaravea [al·ka·ra·ƀé·a] *f.* caraway.
alcayata [al·ka·yá·ta] *f.* wall hook; meat hook.
alcázar [al·ká·sar] *m.* castle, fortress.
alcoba [al·kó·ƀa] *f.* alcove, bedroom.
alcohol [al·ko·ól] *m.* alcohol; **alcohólico** [al·ko·ó·li·ko] *adj.* alcoholic.
alcor [al·kór] *m.* hill.
alcornoque [al·kor·nó·ke] *m.* cork tree; cork wood; (*tonto*) blockhead, dunce.
alcuza [al·kú·sa] *f.* oil can; cruet, oil bottle.
aldaba [al·dá·ƀa] *f.* knocker (*of a door*); crossbar, bolt, latch; handle (*of a door, chest, etc.*); **tener buenas -s** to have "pull", influential connections.
aldabón [al·da·ƀón] *m.* large iron knocker; large handle; **aldabonazo** [al·da·ƀo·ná·so] *m.* knock, knocking.
aldea [al·dé·a] *f.* village; **aldehuela** [al·de·wé·la] *f.* little village, hamlet.
aldeano [al·de·á·no] *adj.* rustic, countrified; *m.* villager; peasant.

aleación [a·le·a·sjón] *f.* alloy; alloying.
alear [a·le·ár] *v.* to alloy, mix (*metals*); (*moverse*) to flutter; to flap (*wings, arms, etc.*).
aleccionar [a·lek·sjo·nár] *v.* to coach; to teach, instruct; to train; to drill.
aledaños [a·le·đá·ños] *m. pl.* borders, frontiers.
alegar[7] [a·le·ǥár] *v.* to allege, assert; *Am.* to argue, dispute.
alegato [a·le·ǥá·to] *m.* allegation; assertion.
alegrar [a·le·ǥrár] *v.* to cheer up, gladden; to brighten; **-se** to be glad, rejoice; to get tipsy.
alegre [a·lé·ǥre] *adj.* merry, gay, joyful, cheerful, bright; tipsy.
alegría [a·le·ǥrí·a] *f.* joy, mirth, gaiety, merriment.
alejamiento [a·le·xa·mjén·to] *m.* withdrawal; retirement, aloofness.
alejar [a·le·xár] *v.* to remove, move away from; **-se** to move away; to withdraw, be aloof.
alelado [a·le·lá·đo] *adj.* stupefied, open-mouthed; silly.
alemán [a·le·mán] *adj. & m.* German.
alentar[1] [a·len·tár] *v. irr.* to breathe; (*animar*) to encourage, cheer, cheer up; **-se** to take heart; *Am.* to recover (*from illness*).
alergia [a·lér·xja] *f.* allergy.
alero [a·lé·ro] *m.* eaves; projecting edge.
alerón [a·le·rón] *m.* aileron; flap.
alerto [a·lér·to] *adj.* alert, watchful; **¡alerta!** attention! look out!; **estar alerta** to be on the alert.
aleta [a·lé·ta] *f.* small wing; flap; fin.
aletargado [a·le·tar·ǥá·đo] *adj.* drowsy, sluggish.
aletargarse[7] [a·le·tar·ǥár·se] *v.* to fall into a state of lethargy; to become drowsy.
aletazo [a·le·tá·so] *m.* flap, blow with a wing.
aletear [a·le·te·ár] *v.* to flap, flutter.
aleteo [a·le·té·o] *m.* flapping, flutter (*of wings*).
aleve [a·lé·ƀe] *adj.* treacherous.
alevosía [a·le·ƀo·sí·a] *f.* treachery.
alevoso [a·le·ƀó·so] *adj.* treacherous.
alfabeto [al·fa·ƀé·to] *m.* alphabet.
alfalfa [al·fál·fa] *f.* alfalfa; **alfalfar** [al·fa·fár] *m.* alfalfa field.
alfarería [al·fa·re·rí·a] *f.* pottery; **alfarero** [al·fa·ré·ro] *m.* potter.
alfeñicar[6] [al·fe·ñi·kár] *v.* to frost with sugar (*a cake, cookie, etc.*); **-se** to get frail, delicate; to act affectedly.
alfeñique [al·fe·ñí·ke] *m.* sugar paste; delicate person; gingerbread.
alférez [al·fé·res] *m.* ensign; second lieutenant.
alfil [al·fíl] *m.* bishop (*in chess*).
alfiler [al·fi·lér] *m.* pin; brooch; **-es** pin money; **ponerse de veinticinco -es** to doll up, dress up.
alfombra [al·fóm·bra] *f.* carpet; **alfombrilla** [al·fom·brí·ya] *f.* (*tapete*) carpet, rug; (*enfermedad*) measles; *Mex.* plant of the vervain family; *Carib.* black smallpox; *Carib.* skin eruption.
alforja [al·fór·xa] *f.* saddlebag; knapsack; food provisions for a trip; *Am.* **pasarse a la otra** — to take undue liberties.
alforza [al·fór·sa] *f.* tuck, fold, pleat; (*cicatriz*) scar.
alga [ál·ǥa] *f.* seaweed; alga.
algarabía [al·ǥa·ra·ƀí·a] *f.* jargon; chatter; (*alboroto*) uproar.
algarrobo [al·ǥa·rró·ƀo] *m.* locust tree; carob tree.
algazara [al·ǥa·sá·ra] *f.* clamor; shouting; uproar.
álgebra [ál·xe·ƀra] *f.* algebra.
algo [ál·ǥo] *pron.* something; *adv.* somewhat.
algodón [al·ǥo·đón] *m.* cotton; **algodonal** [al·ǥo·đo·nál] *m.* cotton plantation.
algoritmo [al·go·rít·mo] *m.* algorithm.
alguacil [al·ǥwa·síl] *m.* constable.
alguien [ál·ǥjen] *pron.* somebody, someone.
algún(o) [al·ǥún(o)] *adj.* some; any; *pron.* someone.
alhaja [a·lá·xa] *f.* jewel.
alharaca [a·la·rá·ka] *f.* rumpus, clamor, racket.
aliado [a·ljá·đo] *adj.* allied; *m.* ally.
alianza [a·lján·sa] *f.* alliance, union; *Andes* wedding ring; *Am.* mixture of liquors.
aliar[17] [a·ljár] *v.* to ally; to unite; **-se** to form an alliance; to unite.
alicaído [a·li·ka·í·đo] *adj.* crestfallen, downcast, discouraged; drooping.
alicatado [a·li·ka·ta·đo] *m.* tiling.
alicates [a·li·ká·tes] *m. pl.* pliers, small pincers; tongs.
aliciente [a·li·sjén·te] *m.* inducement, incentive, attraction.
alienista [a·lje·nís·ta] *m.* alienist (*doctor who treats mental diseases*).
aliento [a·ljén·to] *m.* (*de los pulmones*) breath; (*ánimo*) encouragement.
aligerar [a·li·xe·rár] *v.* to lighten; to hasten; **-se** to hurry.
alijar [a·li·xár] *v.* to smooth.
alimentación [a·li·men·ta·sjón] *f.* nourishment, food, nutrition; feeding; — **por fricción** friction-feed; — **por tracción** tractor-feed.
alimentar [a·li·men·tár] *v.* to feed, nourish.
alimenticio [a·li·men·tí·sjo] *adj.* nutritious, nourishing; related to food.
alimento [a·li·mén·to] *m.* food; **-s** meals.
alinear [a·li·ne·ár] *v.* to line up, put into line; to range; **-se** to fall in line; form into a line.
aliño [a·lí·ño] *m.* ornament, decoration; neatness; (*alimento*) condiment, dressing, seasoning.
alisar [a·li·sár] *v.* to smooth; to polish; to plane.
alistamiento [a·lis·ta·mjén·to] *m.* enlistment; enrollment.
alistar [a·lis·tár] *v.* to enlist; to enroll; to make ready; **-se** to enlist; to get ready; *Am.* to dress up.
aliviar [a·li·ƀjár] *v.* to lighten; to alleviate, relieve, remedy, soothe; **-se** to get better, recover.
alivio [a·lí·ƀjo] *m.* relief, remedy; aid, (*ayuda*) help; (*mejora*) improvement.
aljibe [al·xí·ƀe] *m.* cistern, reservoir, tank; water tanker; *Ríopl.* well, artesian well, spring.
alma [ál·ma] *f.* soul, spirit; inhabitant.
almacén [al·ma·sén] *m.* warehouse; (*tienda*) department store; store.
almacenaje [al·ma·se·ná·xe] *m.* storage.
almacenamiento [al·ma·se·na·mjén·to] *m.* storage
almacenar [al·ma·se·nár] *v.* to store, store up; to put in storage.
almacenista [al·ma·se·nís·ta] *m. & f.* department store owner; warehouse owner or manager; wholesale merchant.
almanaque [al·ma·ná·ke] *m.* almanac, calendar.
almeja [al·mé·xa] *f.* clam.
almendra [al·mén·dra] *f.* almond; **almendrado** [al·men·drá·đo] *m.* almond paste; **almendro** [al·mén·dro] *m.* almond tree.
almíbar [al·mí·ƀar] *m.* syrup.
almidón [al·mi·đón] *m.* starch; *Col., Ven.* paste (*for gluing*); **almidón de arrarruz** arrowroot starch; **almidón de maíz** corn starch; *Mex.* **maicena**.
almidonar [al·mi·đo·nár] *v.* to starch.
alminar [al·mi·nár] *m.* turret.
almirante [al·mi·rán·te] *m.* admiral.
almirez [al·mi·rés] *m.* metal mortar.
almohada [al·mo·á·đa] *f.* pillow; **almohadón** *m.* large cushion or pillow.

almohadillar [al·mo·a·di·yár] *m.* padding.
almohaza [al·mo·á·sa] *f.* currycomb (*for grooming horses*).
almoneda [al·mo·né·da] *f.* auction.
almorranas [al·mo·rrá·nas] *f.* hemorrhoids, piles.
almorzar[2, 9] [al·mor·sár] *v. irr.* to lunch, eat lunch.
almuerzo [al·mwér·so] *m.* lunch.
alojamiento [a·lo·xa·mjén·to] *m.* lodging.
alojar [a·lo·xár] *v.* to lodge; to house; to quarter (*troops*); **-se** to lodge, room.
alondra [a·lón·dra] *f.* lark.
alpaca [al·pá·ka] *f.* alpaca (*sheeplike animal of South America*); alpaca wool; alpaca cloth.
alpargata [al·par·gá·ta] *f.* sandal (*usually of canvas and with hemp sole*).
alpinismo [al·pi·níz·mo] *m.* mountain climbing.
alpinista [al·pi·nís·ta] *m. & f.* mountain climber.
alquería [al·ke·rí·a] *f.* farmhouse.
alquilar [al·ki·lár] *v.* to rent; to hire; **-se** to hire out.
alquiler [al·ki·lér] *m.* rent, rental; **de** — for rent, for hire.
alquitrán [al·ki·trán] *m.* tar.
alrededor [al·rre·de·dór] *adv.* about, around; — **de** *prep.* around; **-es** *m. pl.* environs, outskirts.
altanería [al·ta·ne·rí·a] *f.* haughtiness.
altanero [al·ta·né·ro] *adj.* haughty, proud.
altar [al·tár] *m.* altar; — **mayor** high altar.
altavoz [al·ta·bós] *m.* loud-speaker.
alteración [al·te·ra·sjón] *f.* alteration, change; disturbance.
alterar [al·te·rár] *v.* to alter, change; to disturb.
altercar[6] [al·ter·kár] *v.* to argue, dispute; to quarrel.
alternador [al·ter·na·dór] *m.* alternator.
alternar [al·ter·nár] *v.* to alternate; to take turns; — **con** to rub elbows with, be friendly with.
alternativa [al·ter·na·tí·ba] *f.* alternative, choice, option.
alternativo [al·ter·na·tí·bo] *adj.* alternating, alternative.
alterno [al·tér·no] *adj.* alternate.
alteza [al·té·sa] *f.* highness (*title*); lofty height.
altibajo [al·ti·bá·xo] *m.* (*esgrima*) downward thrust (*in fencing*); **-s** ups and downs; uneven ground.
altiplanicie [al·ti·pla·ní·sje] *f.* upland; high plateau.
altiplano [al·ti·plá·no] *m. Am.* high plateau.
altisonante [al·ti·so·nán·te] *adj.* high-sounding.
altitud [al·ti·túd] *f.* altitude.
altivez [al·ti·bés] *f.* haughtiness, arrogance.
altivo [al·tí·bo] *adj.* haughty, proud, arrogant.
alto [ál·to] *adj.* (*tamaño*) high; *m.* height; upper story (*of a building*); *Am.* heap, pile; **-s** *Am.* upper floors; *v.* **hacer** — to halt, stop; **pasar por** — to omit, overlook; **¡—!** halt!
altoparlante [al·to·par·lán·te] *m.* loud-speaker.
altura [al·tú·ra] *f.* height, altitude.
alud [a·lúd] *m.* avalanche.
aludir [a·lu·dír] *v.* to allude, refer indirectly.
alumbrado [a·lum·brá·do] *m.* lighting; *adj.* lit, lighted; (*borracho*) tipsy.
alumbramiento [a·lum·bra·mjén·to] *m.* childbirth; lighting.
alumbrar [a·lum·brár] *v.* to light, give light; to enlighten; to give birth; **-se** to get tipsy.
aluminio [a·lu·mí·njo] *m.* aluminum.
alumnado [a·lum·ná·do] *m.* student body.
alumno [a·lúm·no] *m.* student.
alusión [a·lu·sjón] *f.* allusion.
alveolar [al·be·o·lár] *adj.* alveolar.
alza [ál·sa] *f.* rise; lift (*for shoes*).
alzada [al·sá·da] *f.* height (*of a horse*).
alzamiento [al·sa·mjén·to] *m.* raising, lifting; uprising, insurrection.
alzaprima [al·sa·prí·ma] *f.* crowbar, lever.
alzar[9] [al·sár] *v.* to lift, raise; (*la baraja*) to cut (*cards*); **-se** to rebel, rise up in arms; *Col., Ven., C.A., Mex., Andes* to puff up with pride; **-se con algo** to run off with something, steal something.
allá [a·yá] *adv.* there, over there; **más** — farther.
allanar [a·ya·nár] *v.* to level, even off; (*invadir*) to invade, break into (*a house*); to raid; — **una dificultad** to smooth out a difficulty.
allegado [a·ye·gá·do] *adj.* near; related; allied; *m.* relative; partisan, follower.
allegar[7] [a·ye·gár] *v.* to accumulate, heap up, gather.
allende [a·yén·de] *adv.* on the other side; beyond; — **el mar** across the sea, overseas.
allí [a·yí] *adv.* there; **por** — through that place, around there.
ama [á·ma] *f.* mistress, owner; — **de leche** wet nurse; — **de llaves** housekeeper.
amabilidad [a·ma·bi·li·dád] *f.* kindness, courtesy.
amable [a·má·ble] *adj.* kind, amiable.
amador [a·ma·dór] *m.* lover.
amaestrar [a·ma·es·trár] *v.* to teach, coach, train.
amagar[7] [a·ma·gár] *v.* (*amenazar*) to threaten; (*fingir*) to feint, make a threatening motion; (*golpear*) to strike at.
amago [a·má·go] *m.* threat; indication.
amalgamar [a·mal·ga·már] *v.* to amalgamate, combine, mix, blend.
amamantar [a·ma·man·tár] *v.* to nurse, suckle.
amanecer[13] [a·ma·ne·sér] *v. irr.* to dawn; — **malo** to wake up ill; *Mex.* to get up; *m.* dawn, sunrise.
amanecida [a·ma·ne·sí·da] *f.* dawn, sunrise.
amansar [a·man·sár] *v.* to tame; to subdue; to pacify.
amante [a·mán·te] *m.* lover; — **de** fond of.
amañarse [a·ma·ñár·se] *v. Ec., Col., Ven.* to be accustomed; to acclimate oneself.
amapola [a·ma·pó·la] *f.* poppy.
amar [a·már] *v.* to love.
amargar[7] [a·mar·gár] *v.* to embitter, make bitter.
amargo [a·már·go] *adj.* bitter; *m.* bitters; *Am.* mate (*Paraguayan tea*) without sugar.
amargor [a·mar·gór] *m.* bitterness.
amargura [a·mar·gú·ra] *f.* bitterness; grief.
amarillear [a·ma·ri·ye·ár] *v.* to show or have a yellowish tinge; to turn yellow.
amarillento [a·ma·ri·yén·to] *adj.* yellowish.
amarillo [a·ma·rí·yo] *adj.* yellow.
amarra [a·má·rra] *f.* cable; rope; strap.
amarrar [a·ma·rrár] *v.* to tie, fasten, rope; to moor (*a ship*); *Am.* **amarrárselas** [a·ma·rrár·se·las] to get "tight," drunk.
amasar [a·ma·sár] *v.* to knead, mix; to mash; *Am.* to amass, accumulate (*a fortune*).
amatista [a·ma·tís·ta] *f.* amethyst.
ambages [am·bá·xes] *m. pl.* circumlocutions; **hablar sin** — to go straight to the point, speak plainly, not to beat about the bush.
ámbar [ám·bar] *m.* amber; **ambarino** [am·ba·rí·no] *adj.* amber; like amber.
ambición [am·bi·sjón] *f.* ambition; aspiration.
ambicionar [am·bi·sjo·nár] *v.* to seek, aspire after; to covet.
ambicioso [am·bi·sjó·so] *adj.* ambitious, eager; (*codicioso*) greedy, grasping.
ambiente [am·bjén·te] *m.* atmosphere, environment.
ambigüedad [am·bi·gwe·dád] *f.* ambiguity.
ambiguo [am·bí·gwo] *adj.* ambiguous; uncertain, doubtful.
ámbito [ám·bi·to] *m.* precinct, enclosure.
ambos [ám·bos] *adj. & pron.* both.

ambulancia [am·bu·lán·sja] *f.* ambulance; field hospital.
ambulante [am·bu·lán·te] *adj.* walking; itinerant; (*movedizo*) moving; wandering.
amedrentar [a·me·đren·tár] *v.* to scare, frighten.
amenaza [a·me·ná·sa] *f.* menace, threat.
amenazador [a·me·na·sa·đór], **amenazante** [a·me·na·sán·te] *adj.* threatening.
amenazar[9] [a·me·na·sár] *v.* to menace, threaten.
amenguar[8] [a·meŋ·gwár] *v.* to lessen, diminish; to defame, dishonor.
amenidad [a·me·ni·đáđ] *f.* pleasantness.
amenizar[9] [a·me·ni·sár] *v.* to make pleasant, cheer, brighten.
ameno [a·mé·no] *adj.* pleasant, agreeable.
americana [a·me·ri·ká·na] *f.* suit coat.
americanismo [a·me·ri·ka·níz·mo] *m.* Americanism; characteristic of any part of America.
americano [a·me·ri·ká·no] *adj.* & *m.* American.
ametrallador [a·me·tra·ya·đór] *m.* gunner; **ametralladora** [a·me·tra·ya·đó·ra] *f.* machine gun.
amigable [a·mi·ǥá·ƀle] *adj.* friendly; affable, pleasant.
amígdala [a·míǥ·đa·la] *f.* tonsil; **amigdalitis** [a·miǥ·đa·lí·tis] *f.* tonsilitis.
amigo [a·mí·ǥo] *m.* friend; — **de** fond of.
aminorar [a·mi·no·rár] *v.* to lessen.
amistad [a·mis·táđ] *f.* friendship; friendliness.
amistoso [a·mis·tó·so] *adj.* friendly.
amnistía [am·nis·tí·a] *f.* amnesty.
amo [á·mo] *m.* master, owner, boss.
amodorrado [a·mo·đo·rrá·đo] *adj.* drowsy.
amodorrar [a·mo·đo·rrár] *v.* to make drowsy; **-se** to become drowsy.
amolador [a·mo·la·đór] *m.* grinder, sharpener; *adj.* grinding, sharpening.
amoladora [a·mo·la·đó·ra] *f.* grinding machine.
amolar [a·mo·lár] *v. irr.* to grind, hone, sharpen; (*molestar*) to annoy; *Col., Mex., C.A.* to ruin, harm; **-se** *Mex., C.A., Col.* to go to rack and ruin.
amoldar [a·mol·dár] *v.* to mold; to shape; (*ajustar*) to adjust; to adapt.
amonestación [a·mo·nes·ta·sjón] *f.* admonition, advice, warning; **-es** marriage banns.
amonestar [a·mo·nes·tár] *v.* to admonish, advise, warn.
amoníaco [a·mo·ní·a·ko] *m.* ammonia.
amontonamiento [a·mon·to·na·mjén·to] *m.* accumulation, pile, heap.
amontonar [a·mon·to·nár] *v.* to heap up, pile up, crowd up.
amor [a·mór] *m.* love; — **propio** self-esteem.
amoratado [a·mo·ra·tá·đo] *adj.* livid, bluish, purplish.
amordazar[9] [a·mor·đa·sár] *v.* to gag; to muzzle.
amorío [a·mo·rí·o] *m.* love affair; love-making.
amoroso [a·mo·ró·so] *adj.* loving, tender, affectionate.
amortajar [a·mor·ta·xár] *v.* to shroud.
amortiguador [a·mor·ti·ǥwa·đór] *m.* shock absorber; silencer, muffler.
amortiguar[8] [a·mor·ti·ǥwár] *v.* to muffle; to deafen (*a sound*); to deaden (*a blow or sound*); to soften, tone down (*a color or sound*).
amortizar[9] [a·mor·ti·sár] *v.* to pay on account; to liquidate, pay (*a debt*); to provide a sinking fund.
amoscarse[6] [a·mos·kár·se] *v.* to get peeved, annoyed; *Am.* to blush, be inhibited or embarrassed.
amostazar[9] [a·mos·ta·sár] *v.* to anger, irritate; **-se** to get angry or irritated.
amotinar [a·mo·ti·nár] *v.* to incite to rebellion; **-se** to mutiny; to riot.
amparar [am·pa·rár] *v.* to protect; to defend; *Am.* to grant mining rights; **-se** to seek protection or refuge; to protect oneself.
amparo [am·pá·ro] *m.* protection; habeas corpus (*protection against imprisonment*); *Am.* mining rights.
amperio [am·pé·rjo] *m.* ampere; **amperaje** *m.* amperage.
ampliación [am·plja·sjón] *f.* enlargement, widening.
ampliar[17] [am·pljár] *v.* to enlarge, widen.
amplificador [am·pli·fi·ka·đór] *m.* amplifier.
amplificar[6] [am·pli·fi·kár] *v.* to amplify, expand, extend, enlarge; to magnify.
amplio [ám·pljo] *adj.* ample; wide, large, roomy.
amplitud [am·pli·túđ] *f.* breadth, extent, width.
ampolla [am·pó·ya] *f.* (*condición*) blister, water bubble; (*vasija*) narrow-necked bottle or vase, cruet.
ampollar [am·po·yár] *v.* to blister; **-se** to blister.
ampuloso [am·pu·ló·so] *adj.* inflated, wordy, bombastic, pompous.
amputar [am·pu·tár] *v.* to amputate, cut off.
amueblar [a·mwe·ƀlár] *v.* to furnish (*with furniture*).
ánade [á·na·đe] *m.* & *f.* duck; **anadeja** [a·na·đé·xa] *f.* duckling.
anadear [a·na·đe·ár] *v.* to waddle.
anales [a·ná·les] *m. pl.* annals, historical records.
analfabeto [a·na·fal·ƀé·to] *adj.* & *m.* illiterate; **analfabetismo** [a·nal·fa·ƀe·tíz·mo] *m.* illiteracy.
analgésico [a·nal·xé·si·ko] *adj.* analgesic.
analisis [a·ná·li·sis] *m.* analysis.
analítico [a·na·lí·ti·ko] *adj.* analytical.
analizador [a·na·li·sa·đór] *m.* digital differential.
analizar[9] [a·na·li·sár] *v.* to analyze, examine.
analogía [a·na·lo·xí·a] *f.* analogy, similarity.
análogo [a·ná·lo·ǥo] *adj.* analogous, similar, comparable.
ananá [a·na·ná], **ananás** [a·na·nás] *f.* pineapple. *See* **piña**.
anaquel [a·na·kél] *m.* shelf; bookshelf; **anaquelería** [a·na·ke·le·rí·a] *f.* shelves, bookshelves, library stacks.
anaranjado [a·na·raŋ·xá·đo] *adj.* orange-colored; *m.* orange color.
anarquía [a·nar·ki·a] *f.* anarchy.
anatomía [a·na·to·mí·a] *f.* anatomy.
anatómico [a·na·tó·mi·ko] *adj.* anatomical.
anca [áŋ·ka] *f.* haunch, hind quarter, rump; *Andes* popcorn.
ancianidad [an·sja·ni·đáđ] *f.* old age.
anciano [an·sjá·no] *adj.* old, aged; *m.* old man.
ancla [áŋ·kla] *f.* anchor.
anclar [aŋ·klár] *v.* to anchor.
ancho [án·čo] *adj.* wide, broad; loose; roomy; *Col., Ven.* self-satisfied, conceited; **a sus anchas** at one's ease; comfortable; leisurely; *m.* width.
anchoa [an·čó·a], **anchova** [an·čó·ƀa] *f.* anchovy.
anchura [an·čú·ra] *f.* width, breadth; comfort, ease.
anchuroso [an·ču·ró·so] *adj.* vast, extensive; spacious.
andada [an·dá·đa] *f. Mex., Ven.* walk, stroll; **-s** tracks, footprints; **volver a las -s** to fall back into one's old ways or habits.
andadura [an·da·đú·ra] *f.* gait, pace.
andaluz [an·da·lús] *adj.* Andalusian, of or pertaining to Andalusia, Spain; *m.* Andalusian, native or Andalusia.
andamiada [an·da·mjá·đa] *f.* **andamiaje** [an·da·mjá·xe] *m.* scaffolding; framework.
andamio [an·dá·mjo] *m.* scaffold, scaffolding.
andanada [an·da·ná·đa] *f.* (*localidad*) grandstand; (*descarga*) broadside; **soltar una** — to discharge a

broadside; (*regañar*) to reprimand.
andante [an·dán·te] *adj.* walking; errant, wandering; moderately slow (*music*); **caballero** — knight-errant.
andanzas [an·dán·sas] *f. pl.* rambles, wanderings.
andar[21] [an·dár] *v. irr.* to walk; to go, go about; to run (*as a watch or machinery*); — **con cuidado** to be careful; **anda en quince años** he is about fifteen; **a todo** — at full (walking) speed; **a más** — walking briskly; **¡anda!** move on!; **¿qué andas haciendo?** what are you doing?; *Am.* — **andando** to be walking around; *Am.* **¡ándale!** hurry!; *Mex.* O.K., fine! now you're talking!
andariego [an·da·rjé·ɡo] *adj.* fond of walking; roving; *m.* walker.
andas [án·das] *f. pl.* portable platform; litter.
andén [an·dén] *m.* railway station platform; *C.A., Col., Ven.,* sidewalk.
andino [an·dí·no] *adj.* Andean, of or from the Andes.
andrajo [an·drá·xo] *m.* rag.
andrajoso [an·dra·xó·so] *adj.* ragged, in rags.
anécdota [a·nék·đo·ta] *f.* anecdote, story.
anegar[7] [a·ne·ɡár] *v.* to drown; to flood.
anejo [a·né·xo] *adj.* annexed, attached.
anestesia [a·nes·té·sja] *f.* anesthesia.
anestésico [a·nes·té·si·ko] *m. & adj.* anesthetic.
anexar [a·nek·sár] *v.* to annex.
anexo [a·nék·so] *m.* annex; *adj.* annexed, joined.
anfibio [an·fí·ƀjo] *adj.* amphibian.
anfiteatro [an·fi·te·á·tro] *m.* amphitheater.
anfitrión [an·fi·trjón] *m.* generous host.
ángel [áŋ·xel] *m.* angel.
angélico [aŋ·xé·li·ko] *adj.* angelic.
angina [aŋ·xí·na] *f.* angina, inflammation of the throat; *Mex., Ven.* tonsil; — **del pecho** angina pectoris.
anglosajón [aŋ·glo·sa·xón] *adj & m.* Anglo-Saxon.
angostar [aŋ·gos·tár] *v.* to narrow; **-se** to narrow, become narrow; (*contratar*) to contract.
angosto [aŋ·gós·to] *adj.* narrow.
angostura [aŋ·gos·tú·ra] *f.* narrowness; narrows.
anguila [aŋ·gí·la] *f.* eel.
angular [aŋ·gu·lár] *adj.* angular; **piedra** — cornerstone.
ángulo [áŋ·gu·lo] *m.* angle, corner.
anguloso [aŋ·gu·ló·so] *adj.* angular, sharp-cornered.
angustia [aŋ·gús·tia] *f.* anguish, sorrow, grief, (*preocupación*) worry.
angustiar [aŋ·gus·tjár] *v.* to distress, grieve, (*preocuparse*) worry.
angustioso [aŋ·gus·tjó·so] *adj.* anguished, worried, grievous; distressing.
anhelante [a·ne·lán·te] *adj.* anxious, desirous, longing; panting.
anhelar [a·ne·lár] *v.* to long for; (*desalentado*) to breathe hard; (*respirar*) to pant.
anhelo [a·né·lo] *m.* longing.
anheloso [a·ne·ló·so] *adj.* anxious; eager.
anidar [a·ni·đár] *v.* to nest; to nestle; to dwell; (*amparar*) to shelter.
anillo [a·ní·yo] *m.* ring; **anillos anuales** *m.* annual rings.
ánima [á·ni·ma] *f.* soul, spirit.
animación [a·ni·ma·sjón] *f.* animation, liveliness, life.
animal [a·ni·mál] *m.* animal; *adj.* animal; (*estúpido*) stupid; beastly; **animalejo** *m.* little animal; **animalucho** *m.* insignificant animal; hideous little beast.
animar [a·ni·már] *v.* to animate, give life to; to inspire, encourage.
ánimo [á·ni·mo] *f.* spirit, mind; courage, valor; (*intención*) intention.
animosidad [a·ni·mo·si·đáđ] *f.* animosity, ill will; courage, energy.
animoso [a·ni·mó·so] *adj.* spirited; courageous.
aniñado [a·ni·ñá·đo] *adj.* boyish; childish; **aniñada** girlish.
aniquilar [a·ni·ki·lár] *v.* to annihilate, wipe out, destroy completely.
anís [a·nís] *m.* anise.
aniversario [a·ni·ƀer·sá·rjo] *m.* anniversary.
anoche [a·nó·če] *adv.* last night.
anochecer[3] [a·no·če·sér] *v. irr.* to grow dark; to be or arrive at nightfall; *m.* nightfall.
anochecida [a·no·če·sí·đa] *f.* nightfall.
anonadar [a·no·na·đár] *v.* to annihilate; (*humillar*) to humiliate.
anónimo [a·nó·ni·mo] *adj.* anonymous; nameless; *m.* anonymous letter or note.
anormal [a·nor·mál] *adj.* abnormal.
anotación [a·no·ta·sjón] *f.* annotation; note.
anotar [a·no·tár] *v.* to annotate, provide with notes; to write down.
anquilosado [aŋ·ki·lo·sá·đo] *adj.* stiff-jointed; gnarled.
anquilosarse [aŋ·ki·lo·sár·se] *v.* to become stiff in the joints; (*ponerse*) to become mentally stagnant.
ansia [án·sja] *f.* anxiety, anguish; longing, eagerness; **-s** anguish; *Col., Ven., P.R.* nausea.
ansiar[17] [an·sjár] *v.* to long for, desire eagerly.
ansiedad [an·sje·đáđ] *f.* anxiety; (*preocupación*) worry.
ansioso [an·sjó·so] *adj.* anxious, troubled; eager.
antagonismo [an·ta·ɡo·niz·mo] *m.* antagonism.
antagonista [an·ta·ɡo·nís·ta] *m. & f.* antagonist, adversary, opponent.
antaño [an·tá·ño] *adv.* yesteryear, formerly; **días de** — days of old.
ante [án·te] *prep.* before, in the presence of; — **todo** above all; *m.* elk; buckskin.
anteanoche [an·te·a·nó·če] *adv.* night before last.
anteayer [an·te·a·yér] *adv.* day before yesterday.
antebrazo [an·te·ƀrá·so] *m.* forearm.
antecámara [an·te·ká·ma·ra] *f.* antechamber, waiting room.
antecedente [an·te·se·đén·te] *m.* antecedent; *adj.* antecedent, preceding.
antecesor [an·te·se·sór] *m.* ancestor; predecessor.
antedicho [an·te·đí·čo] *adj.* aforesaid.
antelación [an·te·la·sjón] *f.* precedence, priority (*in time*).
antemano [an·te·má·no]: **de** — beforehand.
antena [an·té·na] *f.* antenna (*of a radio or wireless*); lateen yard (*of a ship*); **-s** antennae, feelers; — **emisora** *f.* broadcasting antenna; — **receptora** *f.* receiving antenna; — **parabólica** *f.* parabolic (*TV*) antenna.
antenoche [an·te·nó·če] = **anteanoche.**
anteojera [an·te·o·xé·ra] *f.* blinder.
anteojo [an·te·ó·xo] *m.* spyglass; small telescope; eyeglass; **-s** spectacles; **-s de larga vista** field glasses; **-s de seguridad** safety glasses.
antepasado [an·te·pa·sá·đo] *adj.* passed; **el año** — year before last; *m.* ancestor.
antepecho [an·te·pé·čo] *m.* sill, railing.
anteponer[40] [an·te·po·nér] *v. irr.* to place before; to prefer.
antepuesto [an·te·pwés·to] *p.p. of* **anteponer**.
anterior [an·te·rjór] *adj.* front, toward the front; earlier, previous; **el día** — the day before.
antes [án·tes] *adv.* before, formerly; — **de** *prep.* before; — **(de) que** *conj.* before.
antesala [an·te·sá·la] *f.* anteroom, waiting room.

antiaéreo [an·tja·é·re·o] *adj.* antiaircraft.
antibiótico [an·ti·bjó·ti·ko] *adj.* & *m.* antibiotic.
anticipación [an·ti·si·pa·sjón] *f.* anticipation, advance consideration; **con** — in advance.
anticipado [an·ti·si·pa·do] *adj.* early, ahead of time; advanced (*payment*); **por** — in advance; *p.p. of* **anticipar** anticipated.
anticipar [an·ti·si·pár] *v.* to anticipate; to advance, pay in advance; **-se** to get ahead (of).
anticipo [an·ti·sí·po] *m.* advance, advance payment.
anticlericalismo [an·ti·kle·ri·ka·líz·mo] *m.* anticlericalism.
anticoncepción [an·ti·kon·sep·sjón] contraconception; birth control.
anticuado [an·ti·kwá·do] *adj.* antiquated, out-of-date.
antídoto [an·tí·do·to] *m.* antidote.
antigualla [an·ti·gwá·ya] *f.* antique; anything old.
antigüedad [an·ti·gwe·dád] *f.* antiquity, ancient times; **-es** antique objects, antiques.
antiguo [an·tí·gwo] *adj.* ancient, old; antique.
antílope [an·tí·lo·pe] *m.* antelope.
antimonio [an·ti·mó·njo] *m.* antimony.
antiparras [an·ti·pá·rras] *f. pl.* goggles; spectacles.
antipatía [an·ti·pa·tí·a] *f.* antipathy, dislike; mutual antagonism.
antipático [an·ti·pá·ti·ko] *adj.* disagreeable; unlikeable, unpleasant.
antipoliomielítico [an·ti·po·lio·mje·lí·ti·ko] *adj.* antipolio
antiséptico [an·ti·sép·ti·ko] *adj.* & *m.* antiseptic.
antisocial [an·ti·so·sjál] *adj.* & *m.* antisocial; criminal.
antojadizo [an·to·xa·dí·so] *adj.* fanciful, whimsical.
antojarse [an·to·xár·se] *v.*: **antojársele a uno** to take a notion or fancy to; to strike one's fancy; to want, desire.
antojo [an·tó·xo] *m.* whim, notion, fancy.
antorcha [an·tór·ča] *f.* torch; **-de propano** propane torch.
antracita [an·tra·sí·ta] *f.* anthracite, hard coal.
antropología [an·tro·po·lo·xí·a] *f.* anthropology.
antropólogo [an·tro·pó·lo·go] *m.* anthropologist.
anual [a·nwál] *adj.* annual, yearly.
anuario [a·nwá·rjo] *m.* annual, yearbook.
anublar [a·nu·blár] *v.* to cloud; to dim, obscure; **-se** to become cloudy.
anudar [a·nu·dár] *v.* to knot; **anudársele a uno la garganta** to choke up with emotion.
anulación [a·nu·la·sjón] *f.* voiding, cancellation.
anular [a·nu·lár] *v.* to annul, void, cancel, abolish.
anunciador [a·nun·sja·dór] *m.* announcer; advertiser; *adj.* announcing; advertising.
anunciante [a·nun·sján·te] *m.* & *f.* announcer, advertiser.
anunciar [a·nun·sjár] *v.* to announce; to advertise.
anuncio [a·nún·sjo] *m.* announcement; advertisement.
anzuelo [an·swé·lo] *m.* fishhook; lure, attraction.
añadidura [a·ña·di·dú·ra] *f.* addition.
añadir [a·ña·dír] *v.* to add.
añejado [a·ñe·xá·do] *adj.* aged (*wine, cheese, etc.*).
añejo [a·ñé·xo] *adj.* old; of old vintage; stale.
añicos [a·ñí·kos] *m. pl.* bits, shatters, fragments; **hacer(se)** — to shatter, break into a thousand pieces.
añil [a·ñíl] *m.* indigo (*plant*); indigo blue.
año [á·ño] *m.* year; — **bisiesto** leap year; **¿cuántos -s tiene Vd?** how old are you?
añoranza [a·ño·rán·sa] *f.* nostalgia, longing.
añorar [a·ño·rár] *v.* to long for, yearn for, be homesick for; to make reminiscences.
añoso [a·ñó·so] *adj.* old, aged.
aojar [a·o·xár] *v.* to bewitch; to cast the evil eye.
apabullar [a·pa·bu·yár] *v.* to crush, crumple.
apacentar[1] [a·pa·sen·tár] *v. irr.* to graze, pasture; to feed (*the spirit, desires, passions, etc.*); **-se** to graze, pasture.
apacibilidad [a·pa·si·bi·li·dád] *f.* gentleness, mildness, pleasantness; **apacible** [a·pa·sí·ble] *adj.* pleasant, quiet, gentle.
apaciguamiento [a·pa·si·gwa·mjén·to] *m.* appeasement.
apaciguar[8] [a·pa·si·gwár] *v.* to pacify, calm, appease; **-se** to calm down.
apachurrar [a·pa·ču·rrár] *v. Mex., C.A., Carib., Andes* to crush. *See* **despachurrar**.
apadrinar [a·pa·dri·nár] *v.* to sponsor; to act as a godfather; to act as a second in a duel.
apagamiento [a·pa·ga·mjén·to] *m.* quenching.
apagar[7] [a·pa·gár] *v.* to put out, extinguish; to deafen (*a sound*).
apagón [a·pa·gón] *m.* blackout.
apalabrar [a·pa·la·brár] *v.* to speak for, engage, reserve; **-se con** to make a verbal agreement with.
apalear [a·pa·le·ár] *v.* to beat up, thrash, to thresh.
aparador [a·pa·ra·dór] *m.* sideboard; cupboard; showcase; show window; workshop.
aparato [a·pa·rá·to] *m.* apparatus; pomp; **-interuterino** *m.* I.U.D (*interuterine device*).
aparatoso [a·pa·ra·tó·so] *adj.* pompous, ostentatious.
aparcero [a·par·sé·ro] *m.* co-owner of land; *Am.* pal, comrade.
aparear [a·pa·re·ár] *v.* to mate; to match; to pair; **-se** to mate; to match; to pair.
aparecer[13] [a·pa·re·sér] *v. irr.* to appear, show up.
aparecido [a·pa·re·sí·do] *m.* ghost, specter, phantom.
aparejar [a·pa·re·xár] *v.* to prepare; to harness; to rig; to equip.
aparejo [a·pa·ré·xo] *m.* harness; packsaddle; rigging (*of a boat*); preparation; fishing tackle; **-s** equipment, tools.
aparentar [a·pa·ren·tár] *v.* to appear, seem; to pretend, feign, affect.
aparente [a·pa·rén·te] *adj.* apparent.
aparición [a·pa·ri·sjón] *f.* apparition, ghost; appearance.
apariencia [a·pa·rjén·sja] *f.* appearance.
apartado [a·par·tá·do] *m.* compartment; — **postal** post office letter box; *p.p. of* **apartar**.
apartamento [a·par·ta·mén·to] *m.* apartment.
apartamiento [a·par·ta·mjén·to] *m.* separation; retirement; aloofness; retreat, refuge; *Am.* apartment, flat.
apartar [a·par·tár] *v.* to set apart, separate; to remove; *Am.* — **las reses** to sort out cattle; **-se** to withdraw; to step aside; to go away.
aparte [a·pár·te] *adv.* apart; aside; *m.* aside (*in a play*); new paragraph; *Am.* sorting out of cattle.
apasionado [a·pa·sjo·ná·do] *adj.* passionate; very fond (of); impassioned, emotional.
apasionar [a·pa·sjo·nár] *v.* to arouse passion; to fill with passion; **-se** to become impassioned; to fall ardently in love.
apatía [a·pa·tí·a] *f.* apathy, indolence, indifference.
apático [a·pá·ti·ko] *adj.* apathetic, indifferent, indolent.
apear [a·pe·ár] *v.* (*de caballo*) dismount; (*bajar*) to lower, take down; to shackle (*a horse*); (*cortar*) to fell (*a tree*); *Ríopl.* to fire, dismiss from a position; — **el tratamiento** to omit the title (*in addressing a person*); **-se** to get off, alight; *Am.* **-se por la cola** (*or* **por las orejas**) to go off at a tangent, make an irrelevant remark.

apechugar[7] [a·pe·ču·ǥár] *v.* to push with the chest; to push ahead; — **con** to accept reluctantly; to go through with (*something*) courageously; *P.R.* to snatch, take possession of.
apedrear [a·pe·đre·ár] *v.* to stone, hit with stones.
apegado [a·pe·ǥá·đo] *adj.* devoted, attached; *p.p. of* **apegarse**.
apegarse[7] [a·pe·ǥár·se] *v.* to become attached (to); to become fond (of).
apego [a·pé·ǥo] *m.* attachment, fondness.
apelación [a·pe·la·sjón] *f.* appeal.
apelar [a·pe·lár] *v.* to appeal.
apelotonar [a·pe·lo·to·nár] *v.* to form or roll into a ball; to pile up, bunch together.
apellidar [a·pe·yi·đár] *v.* to call, name; **-se** to be named; to have the surname of.
apellido [a·pe·yí·đo] *m.* surname.
apenar [a·pe·nár] *v.* to grieve, afflict; **-se** to be grieved; *Col., Ven., C.A., Carib.* to feel embarrassed, feel ashamed.
apenas [a·pé·nas] *adv.* hardly, scarcely; *conj.* as soon as.
apéndice [a·pén·di·se] *m.* appendix.
apercibir [a·per·si·bír] *v.* to prepare beforehand; to supply; to warn, advise; to perceive; **-se a la pelea** to get ready to fight; *Am.* **-se de** to notice.
apergaminado [a·per·ǥa·mi·ná·đo] *adj.* parchmentlike; dried up.
aperitivo [a·pe·ri·tí·ƀo] *m.* aperitif, appetizer; cocktail.
aperlado [a·per·lá·đo] *adj.* pearly, pearl-colored.
apero [a·pé·ro] *m.* farm equipment; **-s** tools, implements; *Ríopl., Ch., Mex., Ven., Andes* saddle and trappings.
apertura [a·per·tú·ra] *f.* (*acto*) opening; (*crédito*) issue.
apestar [a·pes·tár] *v.* to infect; to corrupt; to sicken; to stink; **-se** to turn putrid, become corrupted; *Am.* to catch cold.
apestoso [a·pes·tó·so] *adj.* putrid, foul-smelling.
apetecer[13] [a·pe·te·sér] *v. irr.* to desire, crave.
apetecible [a·pe·te·sí·ƀle] *adj.* desirable, appetizing.
apetencia [a·pe·tén·sja] *f.* hunger, appetite; desire.
apetito [a·pe·tí·to] *m.* appetite; hunger.
apetitoso [a·pe·ti·tó·so] *adj.* appetizing; gluttonous.
apiadarse [a·pja·đár·se] *v.* to pity; — **de** to pity, take pity on.
ápice [á·pi·se] *m.* apex, top, summit.
apiladores [a·pi·la·đó·res] *m.* stackers.
apilar [a·pi·lár] *v.* to pile up, stack, heap.
apiñado [a·pi·ñá·đo] *p.p. of* **apiñar** *& adj.* crowded, jammed, cone-shaped, shaped like a pine cone.
apiñamiento [a·pi·ña·mjén·to] *m.* crowd, jam (*of people or animals*); crowding together.
apiñar [a·pi·ñár] *v.* to cram together; to crowd; **-se** to pile up, crowd together.
apio [á·pjo] *m.* celery.
apisonadora [a·pi·so·na·đó·ra] *f.* road roller.
apisonar [a·pi·so·nár] *v.* to pack down, flatten by pounding.
aplacar[6] [a·pla·kár] *v.* to appease, pacify, soothe.
aplanamiento [a·pla·na·mjén·to] *m.* flattening, leveling; dejection, depression.
aplanar [a·pla·nár] *v.* to level; to flatten; to astonish; *Am.* — **las calles** to tramp the streets; **-se** to be flattened out; to be leveled to the ground; to lose one's strength; *Col.* to give in, yield.
aplastar [a·plas·tár] *v.* to squash, crush, flatten; *Am.* (*cansar*) to tire out, break (*a horse*); **-se** *Am.* to plump oneself down; *Col., Andes* to overstay a call (*remaining seated*).
aplaudir [a·plaw·đír] *v.* to applaud, clap; to approve, praise.
aplauso [a·pláw·so] *m.* applause; praise, approval.
aplazamiento [a·pla·sa·mjén·to] *m.* postponement; adjournment.
aplazar[9] [a·pla·sár] *v.* to postpone; to adjourn.
aplicable [a·pli·ká·ƀle] *adj.* applicable, suitable, fitting.
aplicación [a·pli·ka·sjón] *f.* application; effort, diligence; **-es** applique.
aplicado [a·pli·ká·đo] *adj.* industrious, diligent.
aplicar[6] [a·pli·kár] *v.* to apply; to put on, lay on; **-se** to apply oneself, work hard.
aplomado [a·plo·má·đo] *adj.* gray, lead-colored; *p.p. of* **aplomar**.
aplomar [a·plo·már] *v.* to plumb (*a wall*); to make vertical; to make heavier; **-se** *Am.* to become ashamed or embarrassed; *Am.* to be slow.
aplomo [a·pló·mo] *m.* assurance, confidence, self-possession, serenity; **estar** — to be plumb, vertical.
apocado [a·po·ká·đo] *adj.* cowardly; timid; *p.p. of* **apocar**.
apocamiento [a·po·ka·mjén·to] *m.* timidity; bashfulness; belittling.
apocar[6] [a·po·kár] *v.* to lessen; to belittle, give little importance to; **-se** to humble oneself.
apodar [a·po·đár] *v.* to nickname.
apoderado [a·po·đe·rá·đo] *m.* attorney; proxy, substitute.
apoderar [a·po·đe·rár] *v.* to empower, give power of attorney; **-se de** to take possession of, seize.
apodo [a·pó·đo] *m.* nickname.
apogeo [a·po·xé·o] *m.* apogee; highest point, height (*of glory, fame, etc.*).
apolillado [a·po·li·yá·đo] *adj.* moth-eaten; worm-eaten.
apología [a·po·lo·xí·a] *f.* praise, apologia.
apoplejía [a·po·ple·xí·a] *f.* apoplexy, stroke.
aporrear [a·po·rre·ár] *v.* to beat; to maul; *Am.* to beat (*in a game*), defeat.
aportación [a·por·ta·sjón] *f.* contribution.
aportar [a·por·tár] *v.* to bring; to contribute; to arrive in port; to reach an unexpected place (*having gone astray*); **-se** *Am.* to appear, approach.
aporte [a·pór·te] *m.* contribution.
aposento [a·po·sén·to] *m.* room; lodging.
apostar[2] [a·pos·tár] *v. irr.* to bet; to post, station.
apóstol [a·pós·tol] *m.* apostle; religious leader.
apostólico [a·pos·tó·li·ko] *adj.* apostolic.
apostura [a·pos·tú·ra] *f.* elegant bearing, graceful carriage.
apoyar [a·po·yár] *v.* to lean, rest; to back, support; to aid, favor; to confirm; **-se** to lean (on).
apoyo [a·pó·yo] *m.* support; favor, protection.
apreciable [a·pre·sjá·ƀle] *adj.* estimable, esteemed; valuable; appraisable; noticeable.
apreciación [a·pre·sja·sjón] *f.* appreciation; valuation; estimation.
apreciar [a·pre·sjár] *v.* to appreciate, value, esteem; to price, fix the price of; to appraise.
aprecio [a·pré·sjo] *m.* esteem, high regard; appraisal, valuation, estimate; *Mex., Ven., Cuba* **hacer** — to notice, pay attention.
aprehender [a·pre·en·dér] *v.* to apprehend, seize, arrest.
aprehensión [a·pre·en·sjón], **aprensión** [a·pren·sjón] *f.* apprehension; fear, dread; seizure, arrest; *Am.* prejudice.
aprehensor [a·pre·en·sór], **aprensor** [a·pren·sór] *m.* captor.
apremiante [a·pre·mján·te] *adj.* pressing, urgent.

apremiar [a·pre·mjár] *v.* to press, urge onward, hurry.
apremio [a·pré·mjo] *m.* pressure; urgency.
aprender [a·pren·dér] *v.* to learn.
aprendiz [a·pren·dís] *m.* apprentice.
aprendizaje [a·pren·di·sá·xe] *m.* apprenticeship; learning (*act of learning*).
apresar [a·pre·sár] *v.* to seize, grab; to capture; to imprison.
aprestar [a·pres·tár] *v.* to prepare, make ready; **-se** to get ready.
apresto [a·prés·to] *m.* preparation; readiness.
apresurado [a·pre·su·rá·đo] *adj.* hasty.
apresurar [a·pre·su·rár] *v.* to hurry, hasten; **-se** to hurry, hasten.
apretado [a·pre·tá·đo] *adj.* tight; compact; (*tacaño*) stingy, miserly; (*difícil*) difficult, dangerous; *p.p. of* **apretar**.
apretar[1] [a·pre·tár] *v. irr.* to press, squeeze, tighten; to urge on; *Am.* to increase in strength or intensity (*as rain, wind, etc.*); *Am.* (*reforzarse*) to redouble one's effort; — **a correr** to start to run; **-se** *Col.* to gorge, overeat.
apretón [a·pre·tón] *m.* sudden pressure; squeeze; dash, short run; — **de manos** hand-shake.
apretura [a·pre·tú·ra] *f.* jam, crush; tight squeeze, narrow place; (*dificultad*) difficulty, predicament; (*pobreza*) dire poverty.
aprieto [a·prjé·to] *m.* tight spot, difficulty.
aprisa [a·prí·sa] *adv.* quickly, fast, speedily.
aprisco [a·prís·ko] *m.* sheepfold.
aprisionar [a·pri·sjo·nár] *v.* to imprison; to tie, fasten.
aprobación [a·pro·ƀa·sjón] *f.* approbation, approval; consent; pass, passing grade.
aprobar[2] [a·pro·ƀár] *v. irr.* to approve; to pass (*in an examination*).
aprontar [a·pron·tár] *v.* to make ready; to expedite; (*entregar*) to hand over without delay; *Am.* to pay in advance.
apropiación [a·pro·pja·sjón] *f.* appropriation; confiscation.
apropiado [a·pro·pjá·đo] *adj.* appropriate, proper, fitting, suitable; *p.p. of* **apropiar**.
apropiar [a·pro·pjár] *v.* to fit; to adapt; **-se** to take possession (of); to confiscate.
aprovechable [a·pro·ƀe·čá·ƀle] *adj.* (*disponible*) available; usable, (*útil*) fit to use.
aprovechado [a·pro·ƀe·čá·đo] *adj.* diligent, industrious; *p.p. of* **aprovechar**.
aprovechamiento [a·pro·ƀe·ča·mjén·to] *m.* use, utilization; exploitation; profit, benefit; progress.
aprovechar [a·pro·ƀe·čár] *v.* to profit, be profitable; to progress, get ahead; to utilize; **-se de** to take advantage of; **¡que aproveche!** may you enjoy it!
aproximado [a·prok·si·má·đo] *adj.* approximate; near; nearly correct.
aproximar [a·prok·si·már] *v.* to place or bring near; to approximate; **-se** to get near, approach.
aproximativo [a·prok·si·ma·tí·ƀo] *adj.* approximate.
aptitud [ap·ti·túđ] *f.* aptitude, capacity, ability.
apto [áp·to] *adj.* apt; competent.
apuesta [a·pwés·ta] *f.* bet, wager.
apuesto [a·pwés·to] *adj.* smart, stylish; goodlooking.
apuntación [a·pun·ta·sjón] *f.* note; memorandum; (*música*) musical notation, set of musical symbols or signs.
apuntalar [a·pun·ta·lár] *v.* to prop; to shore up.
apuntar [a·pun·tár] *v.* (*señalar*) to point; (*arma*) to aim; (*escribir*) to write down; (*a un actor*) to prompt; (*remendar*) to mend, to stitch; to sharpen; (*brotar*) to begin to show; — **el día** to begin to dawn; **-se** to sprout.
apunte [a·pún·te] *m.* note, memorandum.
apuñalar [a·pu·ña·lár] *v.* to stab.
apuración [a·pu·ra·sjón] *f.* worry; trouble.
apurado [a·pu·rá·đo] *adj.* worried; needy; difficult; dangerous; in a hurry.
apurar [a·pu·rár] *v.* (*acabar*) to exhaust, to drain to the last drop; (*preocupar*) to worry, annoy; (*acelerar*) to hurry, press; **-se** to be or get worried; to hurry up.
apuro [a·pú·ro] *m.* need; worry; predicament; *Am.* (*prisa*) rush, hurry.
aquejar [a·ke·xár] *v.* to grieve, afflict.
aquel [a·kél], **aquella** [a·ké·ya] *dem. adj.* that (*at a distance*); **aquellos** [a·ké·yos], **aquellas** [a·ké·yas] those; **aquél, aquélla** *m., f. dem. pron.* that one; the former; **aquello** [a·ké·yo] that, that thing; **aquéllos, aquéllas** *m., f. pl.* those; the former.
aquí [a·kí] *adv.* here; **por** — this way; through here; around here.
aquietar [a·kje·tár] *v.* to quiet, calm; to hush; **-se** to calm down, become calm.
aquilón [a·ki·lón] *m.* north wind.
ara [á·ra] *f.* altar.
árabe [á·ra·ƀe] *m.* Arab; *adj.* Arabic.
arado [a·rá·đo] *m.* plow; *Am.* (*tierra*) plowed land, piece of cultivated land.
aragonés [a·ra·ǥo·nés] *adj.* Aragonese, of or from Aragón, Spain, *m.* Aragonese.
arancel [a·ran·sél] *m.* tariff; — **de aduanas** customs, duties.
arancelario [a·ran·ce·lá·rjo] *adj.* pertaining to tariffs.
arándano [a·rán·da·no] *m.* cranberry.
araña [a·rá·ña] *f.* spider; chandelier.
arañar [a·ra·ñár] *v.* to scratch; to claw.
araño [a·rá·ño] *m.* scratch; **arañazo** [a·ra·ñá·so] *m.* big scratch.
arar [a·rár] *v.* to plow.
arbitración [ar·ƀi·tra·sjón] *f.* arbitration.
arbitrador [ar·ƀi·tra·đór] *m.* arbitrator; referee, umpire.
arbitraje [ar·ƀi·trá·xe] *m.* arbitration.
arbitrar [ar·ƀi·trár] *v.* to arbitrate; to umpire.
arbitrario [ar·ƀi·trá·rjo] *adj.* arbitrary.
arbitrio [ar·ƀí·trjo] *m.* free will; (*plan*) scheme, means; compromise, arbitration; (*fallo*) sentence (*of a judge*); judgment.
árbitro [ár·ƀi·tro] *m.* arbitrator, sole judge, umpire.
árbol [ár·ƀol] *m.* tree; mast; **arbolado** [ar·ƀo·lá·đo] *adj.* wooded; *m.* grove of trees.
arboleda [ar·ƀo·lé·đa] *f.* grove.
arbusto [ar·ƀús·to] *m.* shrub.
arca [ár·ka] *f.* ark; chest, coffer; **arcón** [ar·kón] *m.* large coffer or chest; bin.
arcada [ar·ká·đa] *f.* arcade; archway.
arcaico [ar·káj·ko] *adj.* archaic.
arcano [ar·ká·no] *adj.* hidden, secret; *m.* secret, mystery.
arce [ár·se] *m.* maple, maple tree.
arcilla [ar·sí·ya] *f.* clay.
arco [ár·ko] *m.* arc; arch; bow; violin bow; — **iris** rainbow.
archipiélago [ar·či·pjé·la·ǥo] *m.* archipelago.
archisabido [ar·či·sa·ƀí·đo] *adj.* very well-known.
archivo [ar·čí·ƀo] *m.* archives; file; public records; — **de cinta** tape library; *Am.* (*despacho*) office, business office; **archivero** [ar·či·ƀé·ro] *m.* keeper of archives; city clerk.
arder [ar·đér] *v.* to burn; to be consumed (*with fever or passion*); *C.A. Mex., Col., Carib.* (*picar*) to smart, sting.

ardid [ar·đíđ] *m.* trick, scheme.
ardiente [ar·đjén·te] *adj.* ardent, burning, fervent; (*apasionante*) passionate; fiery.
ardilla [ar·đí·ya] *f.* squirrel.
ardite [ar·đí·te] *m.* ancient coin of small value; bit, trifle; **no valer un** — not to be worth a penny.
ardor [ar·đór] *m.* ardor; heat; fervor, eagerness; *Ríopl., C. A., Mex.* smart.
ardoroso [ar·đo·ró·so] *adj.* ardent, fiery.
arduo [ár·đwo] *adj.* arduous, hard, difficult.
área [á·re·a] *f.* area.
arena [a·ré·na] *f.* sand; arena; **-s** kidney stones; **arenal** [a·re·nál] *m.* sand pit.
arenga [a·réŋ·ga] *f.* address, speech.
arenisco [a·re·nís·ko] *adj.* sandy; gritty; **piedra arenisca** sandstone.
arenoso [a·re·nó·so] *adj.* sandy; gritty.
arenque [a·réŋ·ke] *m.* herring.
arepa [a·ré·pa] *f. Col., Ven., Carib.* a fried (*griddle*) cake made of corn meal that corresponds to the Mexican tortilla.
arete [a·ré·te] *m.* earring.
argamasa [ar·ǥa·má·sa] *f.* mortar.
argentar [ar·xen·tár] *v.* to plate (*with silver*); to polish.
argentino [ar·xen·tí·no] *adj.* silvery; Argentine; *m.* Argentine; Argentine gold coin worth 5 pesos.
argolla [ar·ǥó·ya] *f.* large iron ring; *Am.* (*anillo*) plain finger ring, engagement ring; *Am.* **tener** — to be lucky.
argón [ar·ǥón] *m.* argon (gas).
argucia [ar·ǥú·sja] *f.* cunning, astuteness; scheme; subtlety.
argüir[32] [ar·ǥwír] *v. irr.* to argue; to deduce, infer.
argumentación [ar·ǥu·men·ta·sjón] *f.* argumentation, argument, reasoning.
argumento [ar·ǥu·mén·to] *m.* reasoning; substance, subject matter, (*trama*) plot, resumé (*of a play or story*).
aridez [a·ri·đés] *f.* barrenness; dryness; drought.
árido [á·ri·đo] *adj.* arid, dry, barren; **-s** *m. pl.* grains and dry vegetables; **medida para -s** dry measure.
ariete [a·rjé·te] *m.* ram, battering ram; — **hidráulico** hydraulic ram.
arisco [a·rís·ko] *adj.* gruff, harsh, unsociable; *Am.* (*tímido*) shy, distrustful.
arista [a·rís·ta] *f.* sharp edge; ridge.
aristocracia [a·ris·to·krá·sja] *f.* aristocracy.
aristócrata [a·ris·tó·kra·ta] *m. & f.* aristocrat.
aristocrático [a·ris·to·krá·ti·ko] *adj.* aristocratic.
aritmética [a·rit·mé·ti·ka] *f.* arithmetic.
arma [ár·ma] *f.* arm, weapon; (*ramo*) branch (*of the army*); **-s** armed forces; — **arrojadiza** missile weapon; — **blanca** sword or knife; **de -s tomar** ready for any emergency; ready to fight.
armada [ar·má·đa] *f.* armada, fleet.
armador [ar·ma·đór] *m.* shipbuilder; assembler.
armadura [ar·ma·đú·ra] *f.* armor; armature (*of a generator or dynamo*); framework; mounting.
armamento [ar·ma·mén·to] *m.* armament; equipment.
armar [ar·már] *v.* to arm; (*componer*) to set up, assemble, rig up; — **una pendencia** to start a quarrel; *Col.* — **un trique** to lay a snare, set a trap; *Am.* **-se** to balk, to be stubborn; *Ven., Mex.* **-se con alguna cosa** to refuse to return something.
armario [ar·má·rjo] *m.* wardrobe, clothes closet; cabinet.
armatoste [ar·ma·tós·te] *m.* unwieldy object or machine; clumsy thing; heavy, clumsy fellow.
armazón [ar·ma·són] *f.* framework, skeleton; *m.* skeleton (*of an animal*); — **provisional** balloon framing; *Am.* (*estante*) truss, shelf, set of shelves.
armella [ar·mé·ya] *f.* staple; screw eye.
armiño [ar·mí·ño] *m.* ermine.
armisticio [ar·mis·tí·sjo] *m.* armistice.
armonía [ar·mo·ní·a] *f.* harmony.
armónico [ar·mó·ni·ko] *adj.* harmonic; harmonious.
armonioso [ar·mo·njó·so] *adj.* harmonious, musical.
armonizar[9] [ar·mo·ni·sár] *v.* to harmonize.
arnés [ar·nés] *m.* harness; (*malla*) coat of mail; **-es** harness and trappings; equipment, outfit.
aro [á·ro] *m.* hoop; rim (*of a wheel*); *Am.* (*anillo*) finger ring; *Ch., Ríopl.* (*arete*) earring.
aroma [a·ró·ma] *f.* aroma, scent, perfume.
aromático [a·ro·má·ti·ko] *adj.* aromatic, fragrant, spicy; **sales aromáticas** smelling salts.
arpa [ár·pa] *f.* harp.
arpía [ar·pí·a] *f.* shrew.
arpón [ar·pón] *m.* harpoon, spear.
arqueado [ar·ke·á·đo] *adj.* arched.
arquear [ar·ke·ár] *v.* to arch.
arquitecto [ar·ki·ték·to] *m.* architect.
arquitectónico [ar·ki·tek·tó·ni·ko] *adj.* architectural.
arquitectura [ar·ki·tek·tú·ra] *f.* architecture.
arrabal [a·rra·ƀál] *m.* outlying district; **-es** outskirts, suburbs.
arracada [a·rra·ká·đa] *f.* earring.
arraigar[7] [a·rraj·ǥár] *v.* to root, take root; **-se** to become rooted, attached.
arrancado [a·rraŋ·ká·đo] *adj. Mex., Carib., C.A., Andes* without money, broke.
arrancar[6] [a·rraŋ·kár] *v.* to uproot; to pull out; to start, start out; *Ch., Mex.* to flee, run away.
arranque [a·rráŋ·ke] *m.* start; pull; uprooting; automobile starter; — **de ira** fit or outburst of anger: **punto de** — starting point.
arras [á·rras] *f. pl.* earnest money; pledge; (*dote*) dowry.
arrasar [a·rra·sár] *v.* to level; to tear down, raze; to fill to the brim; **-se** to clear up (*said of the sky*); **-se de lágrimas** to fill up with tears.
arrastrado [a·rras·trá·đo] *adj.* poor, destitute; (*vil*) mean, vile; wretched; rascally; **llevar una vida arrastrada** to lead a dog's life.
arrastrar [a·rras·trár] *v.* to drag, haul; *Ven.* (*rastrear*) to harrow (*land*); **-se** to drag along, crawl.
arrayán [a·rra·yán] *m.* myrtle.
¡arre! [á·rre] *interj.* gee! get up there!
arrear [a·rre·ár] *v.* to drive (*mules, cattle*); *Guat.* (*robar*) to rustle, steal cattle; *Am.* **-le a uno una bofetada** to give a person a slap.
arrebatamiento [a·rre·ƀa·ta·mjén·to] *m.* snatch; (*éxtasis*) ecstasy; rage.
arrebatar [a·rre·ƀa·tár] *v.* to snatch away; **-se de cólera** to have a fit of anger.
arrebatiña [a·rre·ƀa·tí·ña] *f.* grab, snatch; scramble; **arrebatón** [a·rre·ƀa·tón] *m.* quick or violent grab.
arrebato [a·rre·ƀá·to] *m.* rage; rapture, ecstasy; (*rabia*) fit; (*éxtasis*) anger.
arrebol [a·rre·ƀól] *m.* red color of the sky; rouge; **-es** red clouds.
arreciar [a·rre·sjár] *v.* to increase in intensity, get stronger.
arrecife [a·rre·sí·fe] *m.* reef.
arredrar [a·rre·đrár] *v.* to frighten, intimidate; **-se** to be or get scared.
arreglar [a·rre·ǥlár] *v.* to arrange, put in order; to regulate; to fix; to adjust, settle; *Am.* (*pagar*) to pay (*a debt*); *Am.* (*castigar*) to correct, punish; **-se** to doll up, fix oneself up, to settle differences, come to an agreement.
arreglo [a·rré·ǥlo] *m.* arrangement; adjustment;

settlement; conformity, agreement; **con — a** according to.
arrellanarse [a·rre·ya·nár·se] *v.* to sprawl, lounge; (*estar satisfecho*) to be self-satisfied.
arremangado [a·rre·maŋ·gá·đo] *adj. & p.p.* turned up; **nariz arremangada** turned up nose.
arremangar[7] [a·rre·maŋ·gár] *v.* to tuck up, turn up, roll up (*the sleeves, trousers, etc.*); **-se** to roll up one's sleeves; **-se los pantalones** to roll up one's trousers.
arremeter [a·rre·me·tér] *v.* to attack, assail, assault.
arremetida [a·rre·me·tí·đa] *f.* thrust, push, attack.
arremolinarse [a·rre·mo·li·nár·se] *v.* to whirl, swirl; to eddy; to mill around.
arrendamiento [a·rren·da·mjén·to] *m.* renting; lease; rental, rent.
arrendar [a·rren·dár] *v. irr.* to rent, lease, let; to hire; (*amarrar*) to tie (*a horse*); to bridle; *Am.* (*dirigirse*) to head for.
arrendatario [a·rren·da·tá·rjo] *m.* renter, tenant.
arreo [a·rré·o] *m.* raiment; ornament; *Am.* (*animales*) driving of horses or mules; *Ríopl., Ch., Mex., Ven.* (*grupo*) drove of horses or mules; **-s** trappings; equipment; finery; *adv.* uninterruptedly, without interruption.
arrepentido [a·rre·pen·tí·đo] *adj.* repentant; *p.p. of* **arrepentirse**.
arrepentimiento [a·rre·pen·ti·mjén·to] *m.* repentance, regret.
arrepentirse[3] [a·rre·pen·tír·se] *v. irr.* to repent, regret.
arrestado [a·rres·tá·đo] *adj.* daring, rash; *p.p. of* **arrestar**.
arrestar [a·rres·tár] *v.* to arrest; *Am.* to return, strike back (*a ball*); *Peru* (*regañar*) to reprimand; **-se** to dare, venture.
arresto [a·rrés·to] *m.* arrest, imprisonment; detention; daring, rashness; rash act.
arriar[17] [a·rrjár] *v.* to haul down, lower (*the flag*); to lower (*the sails*); (*aflojar*) to slacken (*a rope*).
arriba [a·rrí·ƀa] *adv.* above; upstairs; **de — abajo** from top to bottom; up and down; **río —** upstream; **¡ — !** hurrah!
arribada [a·rri·ƀá·đa] *f.* arrival; *Am.* back talk, impudent answer.
arribar [a·rri·ƀár] *v.* to arrive; to put into port; *Am.* (*prosperar*) to prosper, better one's lot.
arribo [a·rrí·ƀo] *m.* arrival.
arriendo [a·rrjén·do] = **arrendamiento**.
arriero [a·rrjé·ro] *m.* muleteer.
arriesgado [a·rrjez·ǵá·đo] *adj.* risky, daring.
arriesgar[7] [a·rrjez·ǵár] *v.* to risk; **-se** to dare, run a risk.
arrimar [a·rri·már] *v.* to bring or place near; (*apartar*) to lay aside; (*golpear*) to strike (*a blow*); **-se** to lean (on); to get near; to seek shelter.
arrinconar [a·rriŋ·ko·nár] *v.* to corner; to put in a corner; to lay aside; to slight, neglect; **-se** to retire; to live a secluded life.
arriscado [a·rris·ká·đo] *adj.* bold; daring; brisk; spirited (*horse*); craggy, rugged; *Col.* **ser —** to have vigor.
arriscar[6] [a·rris·kár] *v.* to risk, venture; *Mex.* (*arrollar*) to roll up, curl up, tuck up, fold back; *Col.* to have vim and vigor; *Am.* **— a** to reach, amount to; **-se** to get angry; *Peru., C.A.* to dress up, doll up.
arroba [a·rró·ƀa] *f.* weight of 25 pounds.
arrobamiento [a·rro·ƀa·mjén·to] *m.* trance, rapture.
arrobarse [a·rro·ƀár·se] *v.* to be entranced; to be in a trance; to be enraptured.
arrodillarse [a·rro·đi·yár·se] *v.* to kneel.
arrogancia [a·rro·ǵán·sja] *f.* arrogance, pride.
arrogante [a·rro·ǵán·te] *adj.* arrogant, haughty, proud.
arrogarse[7] [a·rro·ǵár·se] *v.* to appropriate, usurp, assume (*power or rights*).
arrojadizo [a·rro·xa·đí·so] *adj.* missile; **arma arrojadiza** missile weapon.
arrojado [a·rro·xá·đo] *adj.* daring, rash, fearless; *p.p. of* **arrojar**.
arrojar [a·rro·xár] *v.* to throw, hurl, cast; to expel; *Am.* (*vomitar*) to throw up, vomit; **— un saldo de** to show a balance of; **-se a** to hurl oneself upon or at; (*osar*) to dare to.
arrojo [a·rró·xo] *m.* boldness, daring.
arrollador [a·rro·ya·đór] *adj.* sweeping, overwhelming, violent; (*que arrolla*) winding (*that serves to wind or roll up*).
arrollar [a·rro·yár] *v.* to roll up; to sweep away; (*pisar*) to trample upon; to destroy.
arropar [a·rro·pár] *v.* to wrap, cover; *Col.* (*aceptar*) to snap up, accept on the spot (*a deal*); **-se** to wrap up, cover up.
arrostrar [a·rros·trár] *v.* to face, defy; **-se** to dare, dare to fight face to face.
arroyada [a·rro·yá·đa] *f.* gully, valley of a stream; bed (*formed by a stream*); (*inundación*) river flood.
arroyo [a·rró·yo] *m.* brook, small stream, rivulet; creek; gutter; **arroyuelo** [a·rro·ywé·lo] *m.* rivulet.
arroz [a·rrós] *m.* rice; **arrozal** [a·rro·sál] *m.* rice field.
arruga [a·rrú·ǵa] *f.* wrinkle.
arrugar[7] [a·rru·ǵár] *v.* to wrinkle; *Carib.* (*fastidiar*) to bother, annoy; **-se** to get wrinkled; *Mex., Col.* (*agacharse*) to crouch with fear, be afraid.
arruinar [a·rrwi·nár] *v.* to ruin, destroy; **-se** to become ruined; *Am.* to go "broke", lose all one's fortune.
arrullar [a·rru·yár] *v.* to lull; to coo.
arrullo [a·rrú·yo] *m.* lullaby; cooing.
arrumbar [a·rrum·bár] *v.* to lay aside (*as useless*), put away in a corner, discard; (*despedir*) to dismiss, remove (*from office or a position of trust*); (orientarse) to take bearings, **— a su adversario** to corner one's opponent, overpower him.
arsenal [ar·se·nál] *m.* arsenal; navy yard.
arsénico [ar·sé·ni·ko] *m.* arsenic.
arte [ár·te] *m. & f.* art; skill, ability; cunning; craft; **por — de** by way or means of; **bellas -s** fine arts.
artefacto [ar·te·fák·to] *m.* piece of workmanship, manufactured object; handiwork; contrivance.
arteria [ar·té·rja] *f.* artery.
artero [ar·té·ro] *adj.* crafty, astute.
artesa [ar·té·sa] *f.* trough.
artesano [ar·te·sá·no] *m.* artisan, craftsman; **artesanía** [ar·te·sa·ní·a] *f.* arts and crafts; workmanship, craftsmanship.
artesonado [ar·te·so·ná·đo] *m.* ceiling decorated with carved panels.
ártico [ár·ti·ko] *adj.* arctic.
articulación [ar·ti·ku·la·sjón] *f.* articulation; pronunciation; (*juntura*) joint.
articular [ar·ti·ku·lár] *v.* to articulate; to join, unite.
artículo [ar·tí·ku·lo] *m.* article; **— de fondo** editorial.
artífice [ar·tí·fi·se] *m.* artisan, craftsman.
artificial [ar·ti·fi·sjál] *adj.* artificial.
artificio [ar·ti·fí·sjo] *m.* artifice, clever device; craft, skill; cunning, deceit.
artificioso [ar·ti·fi·sjó·so] *adj.* cunning, astute, deceitful; skilful.
artillería [ar·ti·ye·rí·a] *f.* artillery, gunnery; **— de plaza** (*or* **de sitio**) heavy artillery; **— de montaña**

light mountain artillery.
artillero [ar·ti·yé·ro] *m.* artilleryman, gunner.
artimaña [ar·ti·má·ña] *f.* trick.
artista [ar·tís·ta] *m. & f.* artist; actor.
artistico [ar·tís·ti·ko] *adj.* artistic.
arveja [ar·ƀé·xa] *f. C.A., Col., Ven.* pea. *Also referred to as* **alverja** [al·ƀér·xa].
arzobispo [ar·so·ƀís·po] *m.* archbishop.
arzon [ar·són] *m.* saddletree.
as [as] *m.* ace.
asa [á·sa] *f.* handle.
asado [a·sá·đo] *m.* roast; *p.p. & adj.* roasted.
asador [a·sa·dór] *m.* spit (*for roasting*).
asaltador [a·sal·ta·đór] *m.* assailant; highway robber.
asaltar [a·sal·tár] *v.* to assault, attack; **-le a uno una idea** to be struck by an idea; *Ríopl., Carib.* — **la casa de un amigo** to give a surprise party.
asalto [a·sál·to] *m.* assault, attack; *Ríopl., Carib.* surprise party.
asamblea [a·sam·blé·a] *f.* assembly, legislature; meeting.
asar [a·sár] *v.* to roast; **-se** to roast; to feel hot.
asaz [a·sás] *adv.* enough, very.
ascendencia [a·sen·dén·sja] *f.* ancestry; origin.
ascendente [a·sen·dén·te] *adj.* ascendant, ascending, upward, rising.
ascender[1] [a·sen·dér] *v. irr.* to ascend, climb; (*de puesto*) to promote; (*sumar*) to amount (to).
ascendiente [a·sen·djén·te] *m.* ancestor; influence.
ascensión [a·sen·sjón] *f.* ascension; ascent.
ascenso [a·sén·so] *m.* ascent, rise; (*de puesto*) promotion.
ascensor [a·sen·sór] *m.* elevator.
asco [ás·ko] *m.* disgust, loathing; nausea; **me da** — it makes me sick; it disgusts me; *Mex., Ven.* **poner a uno del** — to call a person all kinds of bad names; to soil.
ascua [ás·kwa] *f.* ember.
aseado [a·se·á·đo] *adj.* clean, neat; well-groomed; *p.p. of* **asear**.
asear [a·se·ár] *v.* to adorn; to make neat and clean; to groom; **-se** to clean oneself up.
asechanza [a·se·čán·sa] = **acechanza**.
asediar [a·se·đjár] *v.* to besiege, attack.
asedio [a·sé·đjo] *m.* siege.
asegurar [a·se·ǥu·rár] *v.* to assure; to secure; to affirm; to insure; **-se** to make sure; to hold on; to get insured.
asemejar [a·se·me·xár] *v.* to liken, compare; **-se a** to resemble.
asentaderas [a·sen·ta·đé·ras] *f. pl.* buttocks.
asentador [a·sen·ta·đór] *m.* razor strop.
asentar [a·sen·tár] *v.* (*poner*) to set; to put down in writing; (*afirmar*) to assert; to iron out; to establish; (*afilar*) to hone; strop; **-se** to settle.
asentimiento [a·sen·ti·mjén·to] *m.* assent, acquiescence, agreement.
asentir[3] [a·sen·tír] *v. irr.* to assent, agree.
aseo [a·sé·o] *m.* neatness, cleanliness.
asequible [a·se·kí·ƀle] *adj.* obtainable, available.
aserción [a·ser·sjón] *f.* assertion, affirmation.
aserradero [a·se·rra·đé·ro] *m.* sawmill.
aserrar[1] [a·se·rrár] *v. irr.* to saw.
aserrín [a·se·rrín] *m.* sawdust.
aserto [a·sér·to] *m.* assertion.
asesinar [a·se·si·nár] *v.* to assassinate, murder.
asesinato [a·se·si·ná·to] *m.* assassination, murder.
asesino [a·se·sí·no] *m.* assassin, murderer; *adj.* murderous.
asestar [a·ses·tár] *v.* to point, aim, direct; — **un golpe** to deal a blow; — **un tiro** to fire a shot.
aseveración [a·se·ƀe·ra·sjón] *f.* assertion, affirmation, contention.
aseverar [a·se·ƀe·rár] *v.* to assert, affirm.
asfalto [as·fál·to] *m.* asphalt.
asfixia [as·fík·sja] *f.* suffocation.
asfixiar [as·fik·sjár] *v.* to suffocate, smother.
así [a·sí] *adv.* so, thus, like this; therefore; — — so-so; — **que** so that; — **que** (*or* **como**) *conj.* as soon as; *Ríopl., Ch., Ven., Mex., Andes* — **no más** so-so; just so.
asiático [a·sjá·ti·ko] *adj. & m.* Asiatic.
asidero [a·si·đé·ro] *m.* handle; hold.
asiduo [a·si·đwo] *adj.* assiduous, diligent, persevering.
asiento [a·sjén·to] *m.* seat; site, location; bottom; entry (*in bookkeeping*); **-de abono** credit entry; **-de cargo** debit entry; **-s** dregs, sediment.
asignación [a·siǥ·na·sjón] *f.* assignment; allowance.
asignar [a·siǥ·nár] *v.* to assign; to allot; to attribute; to appoint.
asilado [a·si·lá·đo] *m.* inmate (*of an asylum*).
asilar [a·si·lár] *v.* to house, shelter; to put in an asylum.
asilo [a·sí·lo] *m.* asylum, refuge, shelter.
asimilar [a·si·mi·lár] *v.* to assimilate, digest, absorb; (*asemejar*) to liken, compare.
asimismo [a·si·míz·mo] *adv.* likewise, also.
asir[22] [a·sír] *v. irr.* to seize, take hold of.
asistencia [a·sis·tén·sja] *f.* presence; attendance; assistance, help; *Mex.* sitting room; **-s** allowance; *Col., Ven., Mex.* **casa de** — boarding house.
asistente [a·sis·tén·te] *m.* assistant; helper; military orderly; *Col., Ven., P.R.* servant; **los -s** those present.
asistir [a·sis·tír] *v.* to attend, be present; (*ayudar*) to help; *Am.* to board, serve meals.
asno [áz·no] *m.* ass, donkey.
asociación [a·so·sja·sjón] *f.* association.
asociado [a·so·sjá·đo] *m.* associate.
asociar [a·so·sjár] *v.* to associate; **-se** to join; to associate.
asolamiento [a·so·la·mjén·to] *m.* devastation, ravage, havoc, destruction.
asolar[2] [a·so·lár] *v. irr.* to raze; to lay waste; to parch; **-se** to dry up, become parched; (*depositar*) to settle (*as liquids*).
asoleado [a·so·le·á·đo] *adj.* sunny; *p.p. of* **asolear**.
asolear [a·so·le·ár] *v.* to sun; **-se** to bask in the sun; to get sunburnt.
asomar [a·so·már] *v.* to show, appear; — **la cabeza** to stick one's head out; **-se** to look out (*of a window*); to peep out (*or* into); *Peru* (*acercarse*) to draw near, approach.
asombrar [a·som·brár] *v.* (*hacer sombra*) to cast a shadow, darken; (*asustar*) to astonish, amaze, frighten; **-se** to be astonished, amazed.
asombro [a·sóm·bro] *m.* astonishment, amazement; fright.
asombroso [a·som·bró·so] *adj.* astonishing, amazing.
asomo [a·só·mo] *m.* sign, indication; conjecture, suspicion; **ni por** — by no means.
aspa [ás·pa] *f.* wing of a windmill; blade (*of a propeller*); reel (*for winding yarn*).
aspecto [as·pék·to] *m.* aspect, look, appearance.
aspereza [as·pe·ré·sa] *f.* roughness, ruggedness; harshness; severity.
áspero [ás·pe·ro] *adj.* rough, uneven, harsh; gruff.
aspiración [as·pi·ra·sjón] *f.* aspiration, ambition, longing; (*inspiración*) inhalation, breathing in.
aspiradora [as·pi·ra·đó·ra] *f.* vacuum cleaner.
aspirante [as·pi·rán·te] *m. & f.* applicant; candidate.

AR

aspirar [as·pi·rár] *v.* (*anhelar*) to aspire, long for seek; (*inspirar*) to breathe in, to inhale; to aspirate (*a sound*).
asquear [as·ke·ár] *v.* to disgust, nauseate, sicken.
asqueroso [as·ke·ró·so] *adj.* loathsome, disgusting, sickening, filthy.
asta [ás·ta] *f.* horn; antler; (*poste*) mast, pole, staff, flagstaff; (*lanza*) lance; **a media** — at half mast.
asterisco [as·te·rís·ko] *m.* asterisk, star (*used in printing*).
astilla [as·tí·ya] *f.* chip; splinter; splint.
astillar [as·ti·yár] *v.* to chip; to splinter; **-se** to splinter, break into splinters.
astillero [as·ti·yé·ro] *m.* dry dock; shipyard; lumber yard; (*colgadero*) rack (*for lances or spears*).
astringente [as·triŋ·xén·te] *adj.* & *m.* astringent.
astro [ás·tro] *m.* star; planet.
astronauta [as·tro·náw·ta] *m.* & *f.* astronaut.
astronomía [as·tro·no·mí·a] *f.* astronomy; **astrónomo** *m.* astronomer.
astucia [as·tú·sja] *f.* shrewdness, cunning; trick
asturiano [as·tu·rjá·no] *adj.* Asturian, of or from Asturias, Spain; *m.* Asturian.
astuto [as·tú·to] *adj.* astute, shrewd, wily, crafty.
asueto [a·swé·to] *m.* recess, vacation; **dia de** — holiday.
asumir [a·su·mír] *v.* to assume.
asunto [a·sún·to] *m.* topic, subject matter; business; affair.
asustadizo [a·sus·ta·đí·so] *adj.* shy, scary, easily frightened, jumpy.
asustar [a·sus·tár] *v.* to frighten, scare.
atacante [a·ta·kán·te] *m.* attacker; *adj.* attacking.
atacar[6] [a·ta·kár] *v.* to attack; (*apretar*) to tighten, fasten; to ram; (*tapar*) to plug, wad (*a gun*).
atadura [a·ta·đú·ra] *f.* tie, knot; fastening.
atajar [a·ta·xár] *v.* to intercept; to interrupt, cut off; to take a short cut; to cross out.
atajo [a·tá·xo] *m.* short cut; interception; *Col., Ven.* (*rebaño*) drove. *See* **hatajo**.
atalaya [a·ta·lá·ya] *f.* lookout, watchtower; *m.* lookout, watchman, guard.
atañer[19, 51] [a·ta·ñér] *v.* to concern.
ataque [a·tá·ke] *m.* attack; fit.
atar [a·tár] *v.* to tie, fasten; **-se** to get tied up; to be puzzled or perplexed.
atardecer [a·tar·đe·sér] *m.* late afternoon.
atareado [a·ta·re·á·đo] *adj.* busy, over-worked.
atarear [a·ta·re·ár] *v.* to overwork, load with work; **-se** to toil, work hard; to be very busy.
atascadero [a·tas·ka·đé·ro] *m.* muddy place; obstruction.
atascar[6] [a·tas·kár] *v.* to stop up; to jam, obstruct; **-se** to get stuck; to stick; to jam, get obstructed; to stall.
ataúd [a·ta·úđ] *m.* coffin.
ataviar[17] [a·ta·bjár] *v.* to attire, deck, adorn; **-se** to dress up, doll up.
atavío [a·ta·bí·o] *m.* attire, costume; ornaments, finery.
atemorizar[9] [a·te·mo·ri·sár] *v.* to frighten, scare.
atención [a·ten·sjón] *f.* attention, care, thought; courtesy; **-es** business, affairs; **en — a** having in mind, considering.
atender[1] [a·ten·dér] *v. irr.* to heed, pay attention; to attend to, take care of; to take into account or consideration.
atendido [a·ten·dí·đo] *adj. Am.* attentive, courteous; paid.
ateneo [a·te·né·o] *m.* literary forum.
atenerse[45] [a·te·nér·se] *v. irr.* to rely (on); (*aceptar*) to accept, abide (by).
atenido [a·te·ní·đo] *adj. Mex., Carib., C.A., Andes* habitually dependent on another; *p.p. of* **atenerse**.
atentado [a·ten·tá·đo] *m.* offense, violation; crime, violence.
atentar[1] [a·ten·tár] *v. irr.* to attempt, try; — **contra la vida de alguien** to attempt the life of someone.
atento [a·tén·to] *adj.* attentive; courteous, polite.
atenuar[18] [a·te·nwár] *v.* to attenuate, lessen; to tone down; to dim; (*adelgazar*) to make thin or slender.
ateo [a·té·o] *m.* atheist; *adj.* atheistic.
aterciopelado [a·ter·sjo·pe·lá·đo] *adj.* velvety.
aterido [a·te·rí·đo] *adj.* stiff, numb from cold.
aterirse[3, 51] [a·te·rír·se] *v. irr.* to become numb with cold.
aterrador [a·te·rra·đór] *adj.* terrifying, appalling.
aterrar [a·te·rrár] *v.* to terrify, frighten.
aterrizaje [a·te·rri·sá·xe] *m.* landing (*of a plane*); **pista de** — landing strip.
aterrizar[9] [a·te·rri·sár] *v.* to land (*said of a plane*).
aterronar [a·te·rro·nár] *v.* to make lumpy, form into lumps; **-se** to lump, form into lumps, become lumpy.
aterrorizar[9] [a·te·rro·ri·sár] *v.* to terrify, frighten, appal.
atesorar [a·te·so·rár] *v.* to treasure; to hoard, lay up, accumulate.
atestado [a·tes·tá·đo] *adj.* crowded, jammed, stuffed; witnessed; *p.p. of* **atestar**.
atestar [a·tes·tár] *v.* (*legal*) to attest, testify, witness; (*llenar*) to fill up, cram, stuff, crowd; **-se de** to stuff oneself with, to get stuffed with.
atestiguar[8] [a·tes·ti·ǥwár] *v.* to testify, witness; to attest.
atiborrar [a·ti·bo·rrár] *v.* to stuff; **-se** to stuff oneself.
atiesar [a·tje·sár] *v.* to stiffen.
atildado [a·til·dá·đo] *adj.* spruce, trim; painstaking in dress or style.
atinar [a·ti·nár] *v.* to hit the mark; to guess right.
atisbar [a·tiz·bár] *v.* to spy, look cautiously; to watch, pry; to catch a glimpse of; to peek.
atisbo [a·tíz·bo] *m.* glimpse; insight; peek; spying.
atizar[9] [a·ti·sár] *v.* to poke, stir (*the fire*); to kindle, rouse; to trim (*a wick*); — **un bofetón** to give a wallop.
atlántico [ađ·lán·ti·ko] *adj.* Atlantic; **el Atlántico** the Atlantic.
atlas [áđ·las] *m.* atlas.
atleta [ađ·lé·ta] *m.* & *f.* athlete.
atlético [ađ·lé·ti·ko] *adj.* athletic.
atletismo [ađ·le·tíz·mo] *m.* athletics.
atmósfera [ađ·mós·fe·ra] *f.* atmosphere, air.
atmosférico [ađ·mos·fé·ri·ko] *adj.* atmospheric.
atole [a·tó·le] *m. Mex.* Mexican drink made of corn meal; **atol** in C.A.
atolondrado [a·to·lon·drá·đo] *p.p.* & *adj.* confused, muddled; stunned; heedless, harebrained, thoughtless.
atolondramiento [a·to·lon·dra·mjén·to] *m.* thoughtlessness, recklessness; confusion, perplexity.
atolondrar [a·to·lon·drár] *v.* to confuse, muddle, perplex; to stun; **-se** to get muddled, confused; to get stunned.
atómico [a·tó·mi·ko] *adj.* atomic.
atomizar [a·to·mi·zár] *v.* to atomize.
átomo [á·to·mo] *m.* atom; small particle, tiny bit.
atónito [a·tó·ni·to] *adj.* astonished, amazed.
átono [á·to·no] *adj.* unstressed.
atontado [a·ton·tá·đo] *adj.* stupefied, stupid, stunned.
atontar [a·ton·tár] *v.* to stupefy, stun; to confuse.

atorar [a·to·rár] *v.* to jam; to stop up, clog; *Am.* to hold up, stop; **-se** to get stuck (*in the mud*); to get clogged; to get jammed; to choke (*with food*).
atormentar [a·tor·men·tár] *v.* to torment; to worry, afflict; to tease, bother, vex.
atornasolado [a·tor·na·so·lá·đo] = **tornasolado**.
atornillar [a·tor·ni·yár] *v.* to screw; *Am.* (*molestar*) to bother, torment.
atorrante [a·to·rrán·te] *m.* & *f. Col., Ch. Ríopl., Bol.* vagabond, tramp.
atrabancar[6] [a·tra·ƀaŋ·kár] *v.* to rush awkwardly; to run over; **-se** *Ríopl.* (*meterse*) to get involved in difficulties; *Ríopl.* to rush into things.
atrabiliario [a·tra·ƀi·ljá·rjo] *adj.* melancholy; bad-tempered.
atracar [a·tra·kár] *v.* (*llenar*) to cram, stuff; (*amarrar*) to moor, to approach land; (*atacar*) to hold up, assault; *Am.* to seize; *Col.* to pursue, harass; *Mex., C.A.* (*aporrear*) to thrash, beat; **— al muelle** to dock, moor to the wharf; **-se** to stuff oneself, overeat; *Ch.* to have a fist fight; *Ríopl.* (*vacilar*) to falter, stutter; **-se a** to come alongside of (*a ship*).
atracción [a·trak·sjón] *f.* attraction.
atraco [a·trá·ko] *m.* holdup, assault; *Am.* **darse un — de comida** to stuff oneself, gorge.
atracón [a·tra·kón] *m.* stuffing, gorging; *C.A.* (*riña*) violent quarrel; **darse un — de comida** to stuff oneself, gorge.
atractivo [a·trak·tí·ƀo] *adj.* attractive; *m.* attractiveness, charm.
atraer[46] [a·tra·ér] *v. irr.* to attract.
atragantarse [a·tra·ǥan·tár·se] *v.* to gobble up; to choke (*with food*).
atrancar[6] [a·traŋ·kár] *v.* to bolt, fasten with a bolt; *Am.* **-le a una cosa** (*encararse con*) to face something, stand up against something; **-se** to get crammed, obstructed; *Am.* to be stubborn, stick to one's opinion; *Col.* to stuff oneself, choke (*with food*).
atrapar [a·tra·pár] *v.* to trap, ensnare; to seize, grab; (*alcanzar*) to overtake.
atrás [a·trás] *adv.* back; behind; backward; *Am.* **echarse —** (*or* **para —**) to back out, go back on one's word.
atrasado [a·tra·sá·đo] *adj.* late; behind time; backward; behind (*in one's work, payments, etc.*); slow (*said of a clock*); *p.p. of* **atrasar**.
atrasar [a·tra·sár] *v.* to delay; to be slow or behind time; **-se** to get behind, lose time; *Am.* to suffer a setback (*in one's health or fortune*).
atraso [a·trá·so] *m.* backwardness; delay; setback; **-s** arrears.
atravesar[1] [a·tra·ƀe·sár] *v. irr.* to cross; to walk across; to go through; to pierce; *Am.* to buy wholesale.
atreverse [a·tre·ƀér·se] *v.* to dare, risk; (*ser respondón*) to be insolent, saucy.
atrevido [a·tre·ƀí·đo] *adj.* bold, daring; insolent.
atrevimiento [a·tre·ƀi·mjén·to] *m.* boldness, daring; insolence.
atribuir[32] [a·tri·ƀwír] *v. irr.* to attribute, ascribe, impute.
atribular [a·tri·ƀu·lár] *v.* to grieve, distress; **-se** to grieve; to be distressed.
atributo [a·tri·ƀú·to] *m.* attribute, quality.
atril [a·tríl] *m.* lectern, reading desk; book stand; music stand.
atrincherar [a·trin·če·rár] *v.* to entrench, fortify with trenches; **-se** to entrench oneself.
atrio [á·trjo] *m.* court, patio in front of a church; entrance hall.
atrocidad [a·tro·si·đáđ] *f.* atrocity.
atronador [a·tro·na·đór] *adj.* thunderous, deafening.
atronar[2] [a·tro·nár] *v. irr.* to deafen; to stun.
atropellar [a·tro·pe·yár] *v.* to run over, run down, knock down; to trample upon; to insult; **— por** to knock down, overcome with violence; **-se** to rush.
atropello [a·tro·pé·yo] *m.* violent act; insult; outrage; trampling.
atroz [a·trós] *adj.* atrocious, awful; inhuman.
atún [a·tún] *m.* tunny fish, tuna fish.
aturdido [a·tur·đí·đo] *adj.* & *p.p.* stupid, awkward; stunned, bewildered.
aturdimiento [a·tur·đi·mjén·to] *m.* daze, bewilderment, confusion.
aturdir [a·tur·đír] *v.* to stun; to deafen; to bewilder.
atusar [a·tu·sár] *v.* to trim.
audacia [aw·đá·sja] *f.* daring, boldness.
audaz [aw·đás] *adj.* daring, bold.
audencia [aw·đjén·sja] *f.* audience, hearing; court of justice.
audífono [aw·dí·fo·no] *m.* hearing aid; earphone.
auditor [aw·đi·tór] *m.* judge advocate.
auditorio [aw·đi·tó·rjo] *m.* audience.
auge [áw·xe] *f.* boom (*in the market*); (*alza*) boost (*in prices*); (*apogeo*) topmost height (*of fortune, fame, dignity, etc.*); **estar** (*or* **ir**) **en —** to be on the increase.
augurar [aw·ǥu·rár] *v.* to fortell, predict.
augusto [aw·ǥús·to] *adj.* venerable; majestic.
aula [áw·la] *f.* schoolroom, classroom; lecture hall.
aullar [aw·yár] *v.* to howl; to shriek; to bawl.
aullido [aw·yí·đo] *m.* howl.
aumentar [aw·men·tár] *v.* to augment, increase.
aumento [aw·mén·to] *m.* increase, advance, rise.
aun [awn] (**aún**) [a·ún] *adv.* even, still, yet.
aunque [áwŋ·ke] *conj.* though, although.
aura [áw·ra] *f.* breeze; favor, applause; *Carib.* bird of prey, buzzard, vulture.
áureo [áw·re·o] *adj.* golden.
aureola [aw·re·ó·la] *f.* aureole, halo.
aureomicina [aw·re·o·mi·sí·na] *f.* Aureomycin (*trademark for chlortetracycline*).
aurora [aw·ró·ra] *f.* dawn; beginning; **— boreal** aurora borealis, northern lights.
auscultar [aws·kul·tár] *v.* to sound, examine by listening to (*the chest, lungs, heart, etc.*).
ausencia [aw·sén·sja] *f.* absence.
ausentarse [aw·sen·tár·se] *v.* to absent oneself; to be absent; to leave.
ausente [aw·sén·te] *adj.* absent.
auspicios [aws·pí·sjos] *m. pl.* auspices, patronage; omens.
austeridad [aws·te·ri·đáđ] *f.* austerity, severity, sternness, harshness.
austero [aws·té·ro] *adj.* austere, stern, strict; harsh.
austral [aws·trál] *adj.* southern.
austríaco [aws·trí·a·ko] *adj.* & *m.* Austrian.
austro [áws·tro] *m.* south wind.
auténtico [aw·tén·ti·ko] *adj.* authentic, true, genuine.
auto [áw·to] *m.* auto, automobile; one-act play; writ, order; **— sacramental** one-act religious play; **-s** proceedings.
autobús [aw·to·ƀús] *m.* bus, autobus.
autocarga [aw·to·kár·ǥa] *f.* (*computadora*) auto-boot.
autóctono [aw·tók·to·no] *adj.* indigenous, native.
autógena [aw·tó·ge·na] *f.* fusion welding.
autogiro [aw·to·xí·ro] *m.* autogiro.
automático [aw·to·má·ti·ko] *adj.* automatic.
automotriz [aw·to·mo·tríz] *adj.* automotive, self-moving.

automóvil [aw·to·mó·ƀil] *m.* automobile, auto.
automovilista [aw·to·mo·ƀi·lís·ta] *m. & f.* motorist, driver.
autonomía [aw·to·no·mí·a] *f.* autonomy.
autopista [aw·to·pís·ta] *f.* expressway, superhighway, freeway, throughway, turnpike.
autor [aw·tór] *m.* author.
autoridad [aw·to·ri·đáđ] *f.* authority.
autoritario [aw·to·ri·tá·rjo] *adj.* authoritative; authoritarian, domineering; bossy.
autorización [aw·to·ri·sa·sjón] *f.* authorization, sanction.
autorizar[9] [aw·to·ri·sár] *v.* to authorize, give power (to).
autoservicio [aw·to·ser·ƀí·sjo] *m.* self-service.
autoverificar [aw·to·ƀe·ri·fi·kár] *v.* to selftest.
auxiliar [awk·si·ljár] *v.* to aid, help; *adj.* auxiliary, helping, assisting; *m.* assistant.
auxilio [awk·sí·ljo] *m.* aid, help.
avalar [a·ƀa·lár] *v.* to endorse; **avalista** *m. & f.* guarantor.
avaluación [a·ƀa·lwa·sjón] *f.* valuation, appraisal, assessment.
avaluar[18] [a·ƀal·wár] *v.* to value, appraise.
avalúo [a·ƀa·lú·o] *m.* valuation, appraisal.
avance [a·ƀán·se] *m.* advance, progress, headway; advanced payment; attack.
avanzada [a·ƀan·sá·đa] *f.* advance guard; outpost; advanced unit, spearhead.
avanzar[9] [a·ƀan·sár] *v.* to advance.
avaricia [a·ƀa·rí·sja] *f.* avarice, greed.
avariento [a·ƀa·rjén·to] *adj.* avaricious, miserly; *m.* miser.
avaro [a·ƀá·ro] *adj.* miserly, greedy; *m.* miser.
avasallar [a·ƀa·sa·yár] *v.* to subject, dominate, subdue.
ave [á·ƀe] *f.* bird; fowl; — **de corral** domestic fowl; — **de rapiña** bird of prey.
avecindarse [a·ƀe·sin·dár·se] *v.* to settle, locate, establish oneself, take up residence (*in a community*).
avellana [a·ƀe·yá·na] *f.* hazelnut; **avellano** [a·ƀe·yá·no] *m.* hazel; hazelnut tree; **avellanado** [a·ƀe·ya·ná·đo] *adj.* hazel, light brown.
avellanar [a·ƀe·ya·nár] *v.* to countersink.
avena [a·ƀé·na] *f.* oats.
avenencia [a·ƀe·nén·sja] *f.* harmony, agreement; conformity.
avenida [a·ƀe·ní·đa] *f.* avenue; flood.
avenir[48] [a·ƀe·nír] *v. irr.* to adjust; to reconcile; **-se a** to adapt oneself to; **-se con alguien** to get along with someone.
aventador [a·ƀen·ta·đór] *m.* fan (*for fanning a fire*); ventilator; winnower (*machine for separating wheat from chaff*).
aventajar [a·ƀen·ta·xár] *v.* to excel; to be ahead (of); **-se a** to get ahead of.
aventar[1] [a·ƀen·tár] *v. irr.* to fan; to winnow, blow chaff from grain; to throw out, expel; *Am.* (*tirar*) to pitch, throw; *Am.* to dry sugar (*in the open*); *Am.* to rouse (*game*); **-se** to be full of wind; to flee, run away; *Am.* (*atacar*) to attack, hurl oneself (*on someone*).
aventón [a·ƀen·tón] *m. Mex.* free ride, a ''lift''.
aventura [a·ƀen·tú·ra] *f.* adventure; risk, danger; chance.
aventurado [a·ƀen·tu·rá·đo] *adj.* adventurous, risky; bold, daring.
aventurar [a·ƀen·tu·rár] *v.* to venture, risk; **-se a** to risk, run the risk of; to dare.
aventurero [a·ƀen·tu·ré·ro] *adj.* adventurous; *m.* adventurer.
avergonzar[2, 9] [a·ƀer·ǥon·sár] *v. irr.* to shame; **-se** to feel ashamed.
avería [a·ƀe·rí·a] *f.* damage; aviary, (*de pájaros*) birdhouse; *Am.* (*desgracia*) misfortune; *Mex., Cuba* (*travesura*) mischief.
averiar[17] [a·ƀe·rjár] *v.* to damage, spoil, hurt; **-se** to become damaged; to spoil.
averiguar[8] [a·ƀe·ri·ǥwár] *v.* to find out; to investigate.
aversión [a·ƀer·sjón] *f.* aversion, dislike; reluctance.
avestruz [a·ƀes·trús] *m.* ostrich.
avezado [a·ƀe·sá·đo] *p.p. & adj.* accustomed; trained, practiced.
aviación [a·ƀja·sjón] *f.* aviation.
aviador [a·ƀja·đór] *m.* aviator, flyer; (*suplidor*) purveyor, provider; *Am.* moneylender (*to miners or laborers*), promoter.
aviar[17] [a·ƀjár] *v.* to equip; to supply; to prepare, make ready; *Am.* (*prestar*) to lend money or equipment; **estar aviado** to be surrounded by difficulties; to be in a fix.
ávido [á·ƀi·đo] *adj.* eager; greedy.
avinagrado [a·ƀi·na·ǥrá·đo] *adj.* sour; acid; cross.
avinagrar [a·ƀi·na·ǥrár] *v.* to sour, make sour or acid; **-se** to sour, become sour.
avío [a·ƀí·o] *m.* provision, supply; preparation; *Cuba, Mex.* (*préstamo*) loan of money or equipment; **-s** equipment; **-s de pescar** fishing tackle.
avión [a·ƀjón] *m.* airplane; martin (*a bird similar to a swallow*).
avisar [a·ƀi·sár] *v.* to inform, give notice, advise; to announce; to warn.
aviso [a·ƀí·so] *m.* notice, advice, announcement; warning.
avispa [a·ƀís·pa] *f.* wasp; **avispero** [a·ƀis·pé·ro] *m.* wasp's nest; **avispón** [a·ƀis·pón] *m.* hornet.
avispado [a·ƀis·pá·đo] *adj.* lively, keen, clever, wide-awake; *Am.* (*asustado*) frightened, scared.
avispar [a·ƀis·pár] *v.* to spur, incite; **-se** to be on the alert; to be uneasy; *Am.* (*asustarse*) to become frightened, scared.
avistar [a·ƀis·tár] *v.* to glimpse, catch sight of; **-se** to see each other, meet.
avivar [a·ƀi·ƀár] *v.* to enliven, give life to; to revive; to brighten; to quicken.
avizor [a·ƀi·sór] *adj.* alert, watchful.
avizorar [a·ƀi·so·rár] *v.* to spy, watch closely.
aya [á·ya] *f.* child's nurse, governess; **ayo** [á·yo] *m.* tutor guardian.
ayer [a·yér] *adv.* yesterday.
ayuda [a·yú·đa] *f.* aid, help.
ayudante [a·yu·đán·te] *m.* assistant.
ayudar [a·yu·đár] *v.* to aid, help.
ayunar [a·yu·nár] *v.* to fast.
ayunas [a·yú·nas]: **en** — fasting; **en** — **de** totally ignorant of.
ayuno [a·yú·no] *m.* fast; — **de** wholly ignorant of.
ayuntamiento [a·yun·ta·mjén·to] *m.* municipal government; town hall.
azabache [a·sa·ƀá·če] *m.* jet; **-s** jet ornaments.
azada [a·sá·đa] *f.* spade; hoe; **azadón** [a·sa·đón] *m.* hoe.
azafata [a·sa·fá·ta] *f.* airline hostess.
azafrán [a·sa·frán] *m.* saffron.
azahar [a·sa·ár] *m.* orange or lemon blossom.
azar [a·sár] *m.* hazard; chance; accident; disaster.
azaroso [a·sa·ró·so] *adj.* risky; coincidental.
azogue [a·só·ǥe] *m.* quicksilver.
azolvar [a·sol·ƀár] *v.* to clog, obstruct; **-se** to clog, get clogged.
azorar [a·so·rár] *v.* to disturb, startle; to bewilder; **-se**

to be startled, astonished; to be bewildered, perplexed; to be uneasy.

azotaina [a·so·táj·na] *f.* flogging, lashing, beating.

azotar [a·so·tár] *v.* to whip, lash, beat; *Am.* (*trillar*) to thresh (*rice*), — **las calles** to "beat the pavement", walk the streets.

azote [a·só·te] *m.* whip; lash with a whip; (*aflicción*) scourge; affliction, calamity.

azotea [a·so·té·a] *f.* flat roof.

azteca [as·té·ka] *adj., m. & f.* Aztec.

azúcar [a·sú·kar] *m. & f.* sugar.

azucarar [a·su·ka·rár] *v.* to sugar; to sweeten; **-se** to become sweet; *Am.* to crystallize, turn to sugar.

azucarera [a·su·ka·ré·ra] *f.* sugar bowl; sugar mill.

azucarero [a·su·ka·ré·ro] *adj.* sugar (*used as adj.*); *m.* sugar manufacturer, producer or dealer; sugar bowl.

azucena [a·su·sé·na] *f.* white lily.

azufre [a·sú·fre] *m.* sulphur.

azul [a·súl] *adj.* blue; — **celeste** sky-blue; — **marino** navy blue; — **turquí** indigo; *Am.* **tiempos -es** hard times.

azulado [a·su·lá·đo] *adj.* bluish.

azular [a·su·lár] *v.* to dye or color blue.

azulejo [a·su·lé·xo] *m.* glazed tile; *Am.* (*pájaro*) bluebird; *adj.* bluish.

azuzar[9] [a·su·sár] *v.* to urge, egg on; to incite.

B:b

baba [bá·ƀa] *f.* drivel, slaver, saliva; slime, slimy secretion; *Am.* small alligator.

babear [ba·ƀe·ár] *v.* to drivel; to slobber.

babero [ba·ƀé·ro] *m.* baby's bib.

babor [ba·ƀór] *m.* port, port side (*of a ship*).

babosear [ba·ƀo·se·ár] *v.* to slaver, drivel; to keep one's mouth open; to act like a fool.

baboso [ba·ƀó·so] *adj.* driveling, slobbering; slimy; foolishly sentimental; *Am.* silly, idiotic, foolish; **babosa** *f.* slug (*creature like a snail, but without a shell*).

babucha [ba·ƀú·ča] *f.* slipper; *Ríopl.* **a** — pickaback, on the back or shoulders.

bacalao [ba·ka·lá·o], **bacallao** *m. Andalusia, Am.* codfish.

bacía [ba·sí·a] *f.* basin.

bacilo [ba·sí·lo] *m.* bacillus.

bacín [ba·sín] *m.* pot, chamber pot; **bacinica** [ba·si·ní·ka] *f.* chamber pot.

bacteria [bak·té·rja] *f.* bacterium; **-s** bacteria.

bacteriología [bak·te·rjo·lo·xí·a] *f.* bacteriology.

bacteriológico [bak·te·rjo·ló·xi·ko] *adj.* bacteriological, pertaining to bacteriology.

báculo [bá·ku·lo] *m.* staff, cane; aid, support.

bache [bá·če] *m.* rut, hole in the road, pothole.

bachiller [ba·či·yér] *m.* bachelor (*one who holds degree*); talkative person; **bachillerato** [ba·či·ye·rá·to] *m.* bachelor's degree; studies for the bachelor's degree.

badajo [ba·đá·xo] *m.* clapper of a bell; foolish talker.

badana [ba·đá·na] *f.* sheepskin.

bagaje [ba·ǥá·xe] *m.* military baggage, army pack mule.

bagatela [ba·ǥa·té·la] *f.* trifle.

bagazo [ba·ǥá·so] *m.* waste pulp (*of sugarcane, olives, grapes, etc.*).

bagual [ba·ǥwál] *adj. Ríopl.* wild, untamed, unruly; *Ríopl.* rude, discourteous; *Ríopl.* (*flaco*) lanky, awkward; *m. Ríopl.* wild horse.

bahía [ba·í·a] *f.* bay, harbor.

bailador [baj·la·đór] *m.* dancer; *adj.* dancing.

bailar [baj·lár] *v.* to dance; to spin around.

bailarín [baj·la·rín] *m.* dancer; **bailarina** [baj·la·rí·na] *f.* dancer.

baile [báj·le] *m.* dance; ball; ballet.

bailotear [baj·lo·te·ár] *v.* to jig, jiggle; to dance poorly; to dance around.

baivel [baj·ƀél] *m.* bevel.

baja [bá·xa] *f.* fall (*of prices*); war casualty; **dar de** — to discharge, muster out.

bajá [ba·xá] *m.* pasha.

bajada [ba·xá·đa] *f.* descent; slope, dip (*on a road*); **de** — on the way down; — **vertical** *f.* waste stack; **subidas y -s** ups and downs.

bajar [ba·xár] *v.* to go down; to drop (*as price or value*); to lower; to take or carry down; to humble; **-se** to get down or off; to alight.

bajel [ba·xél] *m.* boat, ship.

bajeza [ba·xé·sa] *f.* vile act or remark; meanness; baseness; degradation.

bajío [ba·xí·o] *m.* shoal, sand bank; *Mex., Bol.* lowland.

bajo [bá·xo] *adj.* low; short; soft, bass (*tone or voice*); shallow (*water*); subdued (*color*); (*humilde*) humble; (*vil*) base; **piso** — first floor, ground floor; *prep.* under, underneath; *m.* bass.

bala [bá·la] *f.* bullet, shot, ball; (*bulto*) bale (*of cotton*).

balada [ba·lá·đa] *f.* ballad.

baladí [ba·la·đí] *adj.* trivial; flimsy.

balance [ba·lán·se] *m.* balance; equilibrium; balance sheet; (*vaivén*) rocking, rolling.

balancear [ba·lan·se·ár] *v.* to balance; to rock, roll; to swing, sway; to waver.

balanceo [ba·lan·séo] *m.* rocking, rolling; swinging; balancing; wavering; wobbling.

balanza [ba·lán·sa] *f.* balance, scale.

balar [ba·lár] *v.* to bleat.

balaustrada [ba·laws·trá·đa] *f.* balustrade, banister, railing.

balaustre [ba·láws·tre] *m.* banister.

balazo [ba·lá·so] *m.* shot; (*herida*) bullet wound; *adj. Ch.* (*listo*) clever, cunning.

balbucear [bal·ƀu·se·ár] *v.* to stammer, stutter; to babble.

balbuceo [bal·ƀu·sé·o] *m.* babble.

balcón [bal·kón] *m.* balcony.

baldado [bal·dá·đo] *m.* cripple; *adj. & p.p.* crippled.

baldar [bal·dár] *v.* to cripple; to trump (*a card*).

balde [bál·de] *m.* pail; bucket; **de** — free of charge; **en** — in vain.

baldío [bal·dí·o] *adj.* barren; fallow, uncultivated; *m.* fallow land; wasteland.

baldón [bal·dón] *m.* infamy, insult.

baldosa [bal·dó·sa] *f.* floor tile; paving stone.

balido [ba·lí·đo] *m.* bleat, bleating.

balneario [bal·ne·á·rjo] *m.* bathing resort; *adj.* pertaining to bathing resorts or medicinal springs.

balompié [ba·lom·pjé] *m.* soccer.

balota [ba·ló·ta] *f.* ballot.

balotar [ba·lo·tár] *v.* to ballot, vote.

balsa [bál·sa] *f.* (*de agua*) pond, pool; (*embarcación*) raft; *Mex.* marsh; *Am.* (*árbol*) a species of ceiba (*a tropical tree*).

bálsamo [bál·sa·mo] *m.* balsam, balm.

baluarte [bal·wár·te] *m.* bulwark.

ballena [ba·yé·na] *f.* whale; (*hueso*) whalebone.

bambolear [bam·bo·le·ár] *v.* to sway, swing, rock; **-se** to stagger; to sway.

bambú [bam·bú] *m.* bamboo.
banana [ba·ná·na] *f.* banana; **banano** [ba·ná·no] *m.* banana tree.
banasta [ba·nás·ta] *f.* large basket.
banca [báŋ·ka] *f.* bench; (*naipes*) card game; (*negocio*) banking; banking house.
bancada [baŋ·ká·đa] *f.* work table.
bancario [baŋ·ká·rjo] *adj.* bank, pertaining to a bank.
bancarrota [baŋ·ka·rró·ta] *f.* bankruptcy; failure, collapse.
banco [báŋ·ko] *m.* bank; (*asiento*) bench, stool; (*de peces*) school (*of fish*); *Mex.* pile of grain; *Ven.* (*meseta*) small hill on a plain.
banda [bán·da] *f.* (*musical*) band; (*cinta*) ribbon, sash; (*grupo*) gang, group, party; flock; (*lindero*) side, edge, border.
bandada [ban·dá·đa] *f.* flock of birds; *Am.* (*porra*) gang.
bandeja [ban·dé·xa] *f.* tray; *Mex., Ven., Col.* bowl.
bandera [ban·dé·ra] *f.* banner, flag; *Ríopl., Cuba, Mex.* **parar uno** — to take the lead, be a gangleader.
banderilla [ban·de·rí·ya] *f.* dart with a small flag or streamers (*used in bullfights*); **clavar a uno una** — to goad or taunt someone; **tercio de** — the **banderilla** phase of the bullfight; *Am.* **pegar una** — to touch for a loan.
banderillero [ban·de·ri·yé·ro] *m.* bullfighter who sticks the **banderillas** into the bull.
banderín [ban·de·rín] *m.* small flag; signal flag; pennant; (*oficina*) recruiting office.
banderola [ban·de·ró·la] *f.* streamer, small banner or flag; pennant.
bandidaje [ban·di·đá·xe] *m.* banditry, highway robbery; bandits.
bandido [ban·dí·đo] *m.* bandit, gangster.
bando [bán·do] *m.* (*decreto*) decree, proclamation; (*partido*) party, faction.
bandolero [ban·do·lé·ro] *m.* bandit.
bandurria [ban·dú·rrja] *f.* bandore (*stringed instrument*); *Ríopl.* a species of wading bird.
banquero[baŋ·ké·ro] *m.* banker.
banqueta [baŋ·ké·ta] *f.* bench (*without a back*); stool; footstool; *Mex.* sidewalk.
banquete [baŋ·ké·te] *m* banquet.
banquetear [baŋ·ke·te·ár] *v.* to banquet, feast.
banquillo[baŋ·kí·yo] *m.* bench, stool.
bañada [ba·ñá·đa] *f.* shower, spray; (*inmersión*) dip, bath.
bañar [ba·ñár] *v.* to bathe, wash; to dip; **-se** to take a bath.
bañera [ba·ñé·ra] *f.* bathtub.
bañista [ba·ñís·ta] *m. & f.* bather.
baño [bá·ño] *m.* (*aseo*) bath; bathtub; (*acabado*) cover, coating; — **de María** double boiler; *Am.* — **ruso** steam bath.
baqueta [ba·ké·ta] *f.* rod; whip; **-s** (*muslo*) drumsticks; **tratar a la** — to treat scornfully, despotically.
baquiano [ba·kjá·no], **baqueano** [ba·ke·á·no] *m. Ríopl., Ven., Andes* native guide; *adj. Ríopl., Andes* having an instinctive sense of direction.
bar [bar] *m.* bar, taproom, tavern.
baraja [ba·rá·xa] *f.* pack of cards.
barajar [ba·ra·xár] *v.* to shuffle; to mix, jumble together; to scuffle, wrangle; *Am.* (*impedir*) to hinder, obstruct.
baranda [ba·rán·da] *f.* railing; **barandal** [ba·ran·dál] *m.* banister, railing.
barandilla [ba·ran·dí·ya] *f.* balustrade, rail, railing.
barata [ba·rá·ta] *f.* barter, exchange; *Mex., C.A., Andes, Ven.* bargain sale; *Peru, Ch.* cockroach.
baratear [ba·ra·te·ár] *v.* to sell cheap; to cheapen; to cut the price of.
baratija [ba·ra·tí·xa] *f.* trinket, trifle.
barato [ba·rá·to] *adj.* cheap; *m.* bargain sale; (*premio*) money given by the winning gambler.
baratura [ba·ra·tú·ra] *f.* cheapness.
baraúnda [ba·ra·ún·da] *f.* clamor, uproar, clatter.
barba [bár·ƀa] *f.* chin; beard; **-s** whiskers.
barbacoa [bar·ƀa·kó·a] *f. Mex., C.A., Col., Ríopl.* barbecue; barbecued meat.
barbado [bar·ƀá·đo] *adj.* bearded.
barbaridad [bar·ƀa·ri·đáđ] *f.* cruelty, brutality; rudeness; **una** — **de** a lot of; **¡que** — **!** what nonsense!; what an atrocity!
barbarie [bar·ƀá·rje] *f.* barbarousness; savagery; lack of culture, ignorance; cruelty, brutality.
bárbaro [bár·ƀa·ro] *adj.* barbarous, cruel, savage; crude, coarse; *m.* barbarian.
barbechar [bar·ƀe·čár] *v.* to plow; to fallow.
barbecho [bar·ƀé·čo] *m.* first plowing; plowed land; fallow, fallow land.
barbería [bar·ƀe·rí·a] *f.* barbershop.
barbero [bar·ƀé·ro] *m.* barber; *Mex.* flatterer.
barbilla [bar·ƀí·ya] *f.* point of the chin.
barbón [bar·ƀón], **barbudo** [bar·ƀú·đo] *adj.* bearded.
barca [bár·ka] *f.* boat, launch, barge.
barco [bár·ko] *m.* boat, ship.
bardo [bár·đo] *m.* bard, minstrel, poet.
bario [bá·rjo] *m.* barium.
barítono [ba·rí·to·no] *m.* baritone.
barlovento [bar·lo·ƀén·to] *m.* windward.
barniz [bar·nís] *m.* varnish; glaze; (*de prensa*) printer's ink.
barnizar[9] [bar·ni·sár] *v.* to varnish; to glaze.
barómetro [ba·ró·me·tro] *m.* barometer.
barquero [bar·ké·ro] *m.* boatman; bargeman.
barquillo [bar·kí·yo] *m.* rolled wafer; ice-cream cone.
barquinazo [bar·ki·ná·so] *m.* tumble, bad fall, hard bump, somersault; *Am.* lurch (*of a vehicle or boat*).
barra [bá·rra] *f.* bar; rod; railing; (*de arena*) sand bar; claque, audience; — **de jabón** bar of soap; — **de tabulación** tabulator; — **espaciadora** space bar.
barrabasada [ba·rra·ƀa·sá·đa] *f.* mischief, mean prank; rash, hasty act.
barraca [ba·rrá·ka] *f.* hut, cabin; *Andes* large shed, warehouse.
barranca [ba·rráŋ·ka] *f.*, **barranco** [ba·rráŋ·ko] *m.* ravine, gorge; *Am.* (*peña*) cliff.
barreminas [ba·rre·mí·nas] *m.* mine-sweeper.
barrena [ba·rré·na] *f.* auger, drill; gimlet (*small tool for boring holes*); (*avión*) spinning dive (*of a plane*).
barrenar [ba·rre·nár] *v.* to drill, bore; to scuttle (*a ship*); (*volar*) to blast (*a rock*).
barrendero [ba·rren·dé·ro] *m.* sweeper.
barrer [ba·rrér] *v.* to sweep; to sweep away; *Am.* to defeat; *Am.* **al** — altogether, as a whole.
barrera [ba·rré·ra] *f.* barrier; obstacle; — **arancelarias** tariff barriers.
barreta [ba·rré·ta] *f.* small iron bar; *Mex., Cuba, Col.* pick, pickaxe.
barrica [ba·rrí·ka] *f.* cask, keg.
barrida [ba·rrí·đa] *f. Am.* sweep, sweeping.
barrido [ba·rrí·đo] *m.* sweep, sweeping; sweepings; *p.p. of* **barrer**.
barriga [ba·rrí·ǥa] *f.* belly; (*bombeo*) bulge.
barrigón [ba·rri·ǥón], **barrigudo** [ba·rri·ǥú·đo] *adj.* big-bellied.

barril [ba·rríl] *m.* barrel, keg.
barrilete [ba·rri·lé·te] *m.* clamp; *Arg.* kite.
barrio [bá·rrjo] *m.* district, neighborhood, quarter; **-s bajos** slums.
barro [bá·rro] *m.* (*tierra*) mud, clay; (*granillo*) pimple; *Am.* **hacer** (*or* **cometer**) **un** — to commit a blunder.
barroso [ba·rró·so] *adj.* muddy; pimply; reddish.
barrote [ba·rró·te] *m.* short, thick bar; brace; (*de silla*) rung (*of a ladder or chair*).
barruntar [ba·rrun·tár] *v.* to foresee; to have a presentiment; to conjecture.
barrunto [ba·rrún·to] *m.* foreboding, presentiment; guess; hint, indication, sign.
bártulos [bár·tu·los] *m. pl.* household goods; implements, tools.
barullo [ba·rú·yo] *m.* hubbub, racket, disorder.
basa [bá·sa] *f.* base, pedestal; basis, foundation.
basar [ba·sár] *v.* to base; to put on a base.
basca [bás·ka] *f.* nausea, sickness to one's stomach; **tener -s** to be nauseated, sick to one's stomach.
báscula [bás·ku·la] *f.* scale (*for weighing*), platform scale.
base [bá·se] *f.* base, basis, foundation; — **de datos** data base.
basic [bá·sik] *m.* (*computadora*) basic.
básico [bá·si·ko] *adj.* basic.
basquear [bas·ke·ár] *v.* to heave, try to vomit; to be nauseated, sick to one's stomach.
basquetbol [bas·ke·ƀól] *m.* basketball.
bastante [bas·tán·te] *adj.* enough, sufficient; *adv.* enough.
bastar [bas·tár] *v.* to be enough; to suffice.
bastardilla [bas·tar·đí·ya] *f.* italic type, italics.
bastardo [bas·tár·đo] *adj.* bastard.
bastidor [bas·ti·đór] *m.* (*teatro*) wing (*of a stage*); (*marco*) frame; embroidery frame; (*ventana*) window sash; easel (*support for a picture, blackboard, etc.*); **entre -es** behind the scenes, off stage.
bastilla [bas·tí·ya] *f.* hem.
bastimento [bas·ti·mén·to] *m.* supply, provisions; vessel, ship.
basto [bás·to] *adj.* coarse; *m.* (*naipes*) club (*in cards*); *Am.* saddle pad.
bastón [bas·tón] *m.* cane, walking stick.
basura [ba·sú·ra] *f.* rubbish, scraps; garbage; refuse.
basurero [ba·su·ré·ro] *m.* garbage or rubbish dump; manure pile; garbage man, rubbish man; street cleaner.
bata [bá·ta] *f.* lounging robe; housecoat, wrapper, dressing gown; smock; **batín** [ba·tín] *m.* smock.
batahola [ba·ta·ó·la] *f.* hubbub, racket, uproar.
batalla [ba·tá·ya] *f.* battle; struggle.
batallar [ba·ta·yár] *v.* to battle, fight, struggle.
batallón [ba·ta·yón] *m.* battalion.
batata [ba·tá·ta] *f. Caribe, Sp.* sweet potato.
bate [bá·te] *m.* baseball bat.
batea [ba·té·a] *f.* tray; trough; bowl; *Mex., Ven., Col. C.A.* barge; *Am.* washtub.
bateador [ba·te·a·đór] *m.* batter (*in baseball*).
batear [ba·te·ár] *v. Mex., Carib., C.A., Ven.* to bat.
batería [ba·te·rí·a] *f.* battery (*military, naval, or electric*); — **de cocina** set of kitchen utensils; — **de jazz** a jazz combo; *Mex.* **dar** — to raise a rumpus; (*trabajar*) to plod, work hard.
batidor [ba·ti·đór] *m.* beater; scout; — **de alambre** wire beater.
batintín [ba·tin·tín] *m.* gong.
batir [ba·tír] *v.* (*combatir*) to beat, whip, defeat; (*reconocer*) reconnoiter, explore; (*mover*) to flap; *Ch.* to rinse (*clothes*); *Ríopl.* to denounce; **-se** to fight; — **palmas** to clap, applaud.
batisfera [ba·tis·fé·ra] *f.* bathysphere.
baturrillo [ba·tu·rrí·yo] *m.* medley, mixture; hodgepodge.
batuta [ba·tú·ta] *f.* orchestra conductor's baton or wand; **llevar la** — to lead; to be the leader.
baudio [báw·đjo] *m.* (*computadora*) baud.
baúl [ba·úl] *m.* trunk, chest; — **mundo** large trunk.
bautismo [baw·tíz·mo] *m.* baptism, christening; **nombre de** — Christian name.
bautista [baw·tís·ta] *m. & f.* Baptist; baptizer.
bautizar[9] [baw·ti·sár] *v.* to baptize, christen.
bautizo [baw·tí·so] *m.* christening, baptism.
bauxítica [baw·ksí·ti·ka] *f.* bauxite.
baya [bá·ya] *f.* berry.
bayeta [ba·yé·ta] *f.* flannel; flannelette; **bayetón** *m.* thick wool cloth; *Col.* long poncho lined with flannel.
bayo [bá·yo] *adj.* bay, reddish-brown.
baza [bá·sa] *f.* trick (*cards played in one round*); **meter** — to meddle; to butt into a conversation; **no dejar meter** — not to let a person put a word in edgewise.
bazar [ba·sár] *m.* bazaar; department store.
bazo [bá·so] *m.* spleen.
bazofia [ba·só·fja] *f.* scraps, refuse, garbage; dregs.
beatitud [be·a·ti·túd] *f.* bliss, blessedness.
beato [be·á·to] *adj.* blessed; beatified; devout; overpious; (*hipócrita*) hypocritical.
bebé [be·ƀé] *m.* baby.
bebedero [be·ƀe·đé·ro] *m.* drinking trough; watering place; spout.
bebedor [be·ƀe·đór] *m.* drinker; drunkard.
beber [be·ƀér] *v.* to drink; to drink in, (*absorber*) absorb.
bebida [be·ƀí·đa] *f.* drink, beverage; **dado a la** — given to drink.
beca [bé·ka] *f.* scholarship, fellowship; (*faja*) sash worn over the academic gown.
becario [be·ká·rjo] *m.* scholar, fellow, holder of a scholarship.
becerro [be·sé·rro] *m.* young bull (*less than a year old*); calf; calfskin.
becuadro [be·kwá·đro] *m.* natural sign (*in music*).
bedel [be·đél] *m.* beadle.
befa [bé·fa] *f.* scoff, jeer.
befar [be·fár] *v.* to scoff, jeer at, mock.
bejuco [be·xú·ko] *m.* reed; **silla de** — cane chair.
beldad [bel·dáđ] *f.* beauty.
belga [bél·ǥa] *adj., m. & f.* Belgian.
bélico [bé·li·ko] *adj.* warlike.
beligerante [be·li·xe·rán·te] *adj., m. & f.* belligerent.
bellaco [be·yá·ko] *adj.* sly, deceitful; *m.* villain; rascal.
bellaquear [be·ya·ke·ár] *v.* to cheat; to play tricks; *Ríopl.* to rear, stand up on the hind legs; *Ríopl.* to balk; *Am.* to be touchy, oversensitive.
bellaquería [be·ya·ke·rí·a] *f.* cunning, trickery; sly act or remark.
belleza [be·yé·sa] *f.* beauty.
bello [bé·yo] *adj.* beautiful.
bellota [be·yó·ta] *f.* acorn.
bemol [be·mól] *adj.* flat (*in music*); **tener -es** to have difficulties.
bendecir[27, 52] [ben·de·sír] *v. irr.* to bless.
bendición [ben·di·sjón] *f.* benediction, blessing; *Mex., C.A., Col., Ven.* **echarle la** — **a una cosa** to give something up for lost.
bendito [ben·dí·to] *adj.* blessed; saintly; **es un** — he is a saint, he is a simple soul; *p.p. of* **bendecir**.

benefactor [be·ne·fak·tór] *m.* benefactor; patron.
beneficencia [be·ne·fi·sén·sja] *f.* beneficence, kindness, charity; — **pública** welfare.
beneficiar [be·ne·fi·sjár] *v.* to benefit, do good; to cultivate (*land*); to exploit (*a mine*); to treat (*metals*); *Col., Ven.* (*matar*) to slaughter (*cattle*) for marketing.
beneficio [be·ne·fí·sjo] *m.* (*provecho*) benefit, profit; exploitation of a mine; (*cultivo*) cultivation of land; *Ch.* fertilizer; *Am.* slaughtering (*of cattle*).
benéfico [be·né·fi·ko] *adj.* beneficent, good, kind.
benemérito [be·ne·mé·ri·to] *m.* worthy, notable; *adj.* worthy.
benevolencia [be·ne·ƀo·lén·sja] *f.* benevolence, kindness.
benévolo [be·né·ƀo·lo] *adj.* benevolent, good, kindly.
benigno [be·níǥ·no] *adj.* benign, gentle, mild, kind.
beodo [be·ó·đo] *adj.* drunk; *m.* drunkard.
berbiquí [ber·ƀi·kí] *m.* carpenter's brace.
berenjena [be·reŋ·xé·na] *f.* eggplant; *Mex., C.A.* kind of squash; **berenjenal** *m.* egg-plant patch; **meterse uno en un** — to get into a mess.
bergantín [ber·ǥan·tín] *m.* brigantine, brig (*square-rigged ship with two masts*).
beriberi [be·ri·ƀé·ri] *m.* beriberi.
berilio [be·rí·ljo] *m.* beryllium.
bermejo [ber·mé·xo] *adj.* crimson, bright red.
bermellón [ber·me·yón] *adj.* vermilion (*bright red*).
berrear [be·rre·ár] *v.* to bellow; to scream; to sing off key.
berrido [be·rrí·đo] *m.* bellow, bellowing; scream.
berrinche [be·rrín·če] *m.* fit of anger; tantrum.
berro [bé·rro] *m.* water cress.
berza [bér·sa] *f.* cabbage.
besar [be·sár] *v.* to kiss.
beso [bé·so] *m.* kiss.
bestia [bés·tja] *f.* beast.
bestialidad [bes·tja·li·đáđ] *f.* bestiality, brutality.
besugo [be·sú·ǥo] *m.* sea bream (*a fish*).
besuquear [be·su·ke·ár] *v.* to kiss repeatedly.
betabel [be·ta·ƀél] *f. Mex.* beet.
betún [be·tún] *m.* bitumen (*combustible mineral*); black pitch; (*de zapatos*) shoeblacking.
Biblia [bí·ƀlja] *f.* Bible.
bíblico [bí·ƀli·ko] *adj.* Biblical.
biblioteca [bi·ƀljo·té·ka] *f.* library; set of volumes; bookcase.
bibliotecario [bi·bljo·te·ká·rjo] *m.* librarian.
bicarbonato [bi·kar·ƀo·ná·to] *m.* bicarbonate; — **de sosa** bicarbonate of soda.
bicicleta [bi·si·klé·ta] *f.* bicycle; **biciclista** [bi·si·klís·ta], **bicicletista** [bi·si·kle·tís·ta] *m. & f.* bicyclist, bicycle rider.
bicho [bí·čo] *m.* insect, bug; any small animal; an insignificant person; *C.A.* baby at creeping stage.
biela [bjé·la] *f.* connecting rod (*of an engine*).
bien [bjen] *adv.* well; — **que** although; **ahora** — now then; **más** — rather; **si** — although; *m.* good, benefit; **-es** property; **-es muebles** goods and chattels; **-es inmuebles** real estate; **-es raíces** real estate.
bienaventurado [bje·na·ƀen·tu·rá·đo] *adj.* blessed, happy.
bienaventuranza [bje·na·ƀen·tu·rán·sa] *f.* blessedness; beatitude; bliss.
bienestar [bje·nes·tár] *m.* well-being, comfort, welfare.
bienhechor [bje·ne·čór] *m.* benefactor.
bienvenida [bjem·be·ní·đa] *f.* welcome.
bienvenido [bjem·be·ní·đo] *adj.* welcome.
biftec [bif·ték], **bistec** [bis·ték], **bisté** [bis·té] *m.* beefsteak.
bifurcación [bi·fur·ka·sjón] *f.* fork, forking, branching out; (*empalme*) railway junction; branch, railroad.
bifurcarse[6] [bi·fur·kár·se] *v.* to fork, branch off, divide into two branches.
bigamía [bi·ǥa·mí·a] *f.* bigamy.
bigote [bi·ǥó·te] *m.* mustache.
bikini [bi·kí·ni] *m.* bikini.
bilabial [bi·la·ƀjál] *adj.* bilabial.
bilingüe [bi·líŋ·gwe] *adj.* bilingual.
bilingüismo [bi·liŋ·gwíz·mo] *m.* bilingualism.
bilis [bí·lis] *f.* bile.
billar [bi·yár] *m.* billiards; billiard room.
billete [bi·yé·te] *m.* ticket; note; bill, banknote.
billón [bi·yón] *m.* billion.
bimestre [bi·més·tre] *m.* two-month period; bi-monthly salary, rent, etc.; *adj.* bi-monthly; **bimestral** [bi·mes·trál] *adj.* bimonthly.
binario [bi·ná·rjo] *adj. & n.* (*computadora*) binary system.
biografía [bjo·ǥra·fí·a] *f.* biography.
biología [bjo·lo·xí·a] *f.* biology.
biombo [bjóm·bo] *m.* folding screen.
biopsia [bjóp·sja] *f.* biopsy.
birlar [bir·lár] *v.* to snatch away; to steal; (*matar*) to kill or knock down with one blow.
birrete [bi·rré·te] *m.* academic cap; mortarboard.
bisabuelo [bi·sa·ƀwé·lo] *m.* great-grandfather; **bisabuela** *f.* great-grandmother.
bisagra [bi·sá·ǥra] *f.* hinge.
bisel [bi·sél] *m.* bevel.
bisiesto [bi·sjés·to] *adj.* leap (*year*).
bismuto [biz·mú·to] *m.* bismuth.
bisnieto [biz·njé·to] *m.* great-grandson; **bisnieta** [biz·njé·ta] *f.* great-granddaughter.
bisojo [bi·só·xo] *adj.* squint-eyed.
bisonte [bi·són·te] *m.* bison; the American buffalo.
bisturí [bis·tu·rí] *m.* bistoury, surgical knife.
bitoque [bi·tó·ke] *m.* barrel plug, stopper; *Mex.,* faucet; *Col., Cuba, Mex.* injection point (*of a syringe*).
bizarría [bi·sa·rrí·a] *f.* gallantry, bravery; generosity.
bizarro [bi·sá·rro] *adj.* gallant, brave; generous.
bizco [bís·ko] *adj.* cross-eyed.
bizcocho [bis·kó·čo] *m.* hardtack, hard biscuit; cake; cookie; — **borracho** cake dipped in wine.
biznieto [biz·njé·to] *m.* great-grandson; **biznieta** *f.* great-granddaughter.
blanco [bláŋ·ko] *adj.* (*color*) white; *m.* white man; (*nada escrito*) blank, blank sheet; (*objeto de tiro*) target, goal.
blancura [blaŋ·kú·ra] *f.* whiteness.
blancuzco [blaŋ·kús·ko], **blanquecino** [blaŋ·ke·sí·no], **blanquizco** [blaŋ·kís·ko] *adj.* whitish.
blandir [blan·dír] *v.* to brandish, flourish, swing.
blando [blán·do] *adj.* bland, smooth; soft; **blanducho** *adj.* flabby; soft.
blandura [blan·dú·ra] *f.* softness; mildness, gentleness.
blanquear [blaŋ·ke·ár] *v.* to whiten, bleach; to whitewash; to show white; to begin to turn white; to blanch.
blanqueo [blaŋ·ké·o] *m.* whitening, bleach, bleaching.
blanquillo [blaŋ·kí·yo] *adj.* whitish; white (*flour*); *m. Mex., C.A.* egg; *Peru, Ch., Andes* white peach.
blasfemar [blas·fe·már] *v.* to blaspheme, curse, swear.
blasfemia [blas·fé·mja] *f.* blasphemy.
blasón [bla·són] *m.* coat of arms; honor, glory.
blasonar [bla·so·nár] *v.* to boast.

blindaje [blin·dá·xe] *m.* armor, armor plating.
blindar [blin·dár] *v.* armor.
bloc [blok] *m. Am.* tablet, pad of paper.
blocaje [blo·ká·xe] *m.* action of blocking.
blondo [blón·do] *adj.* blond.
bloque [bló·ke] *m.* block (*of stone, wood, etc.*); *Am.* tablet, pad of paper; *Cuba, Mex., Ríopl.* political bloc; **-s calibradores** gauge blocks.
bloquear [blo·ke·ár] *v.* to blockade.
bloqueo [blo·ké·o] *m.* blockade.
blusa [blú·sa] *f.* blouse.
boato [bo·á·to] *m.* pomp, ostentation.
bobada [bo·bá·da] *f.* foolishness, folly.
bobalicón [bo·ba·li·kón] *adj.* foolish, silly; *m.* simpleton, blockhead, dunce.
bobear [bo·be·ár] *v.* to act like a fool; to fool around; (*mirar*) to gawk, stare foolishly.
bobería [bo·be·rí·a] *f.* foolishness, folly; nonsense; foolish remark.
bobina [bo·bí·na] *f.* bobbin, reel; electric coil; — **distribuidora** feeding reel; — **receptora** rewind reel (*on a tape recorder*).
bobo [bó·bo] *adj.* simple, foolish, stupid; *m.* booby, fool, dunce.
boca [bó·ka] *f.* mouth; opening; — **abajo** face downward; — **arriba** face upward; **a — de jarro** at close range; **bocaza** *f.* large mouth.
bocacalle [bo·ka·ká·ye] *f.* street intersection.
bocado [bo·ká·do] *m.* mouthful, morsel, bite; bit (*of a bridle*); **bocadillo** [bo·ka·dí·yo], **bocadito** [bo·ka·dí·to] *m.* snack; sandwich; tidbit; *Mex.* piece of candy.
bocanada [bo·ka·ná·da] *f.* mouthful; puff (*of smoke*).
boceto [bo·sé·to] *m.* sketch; outline; skit.
bocina [bo·sí·na] *f.* horn; trumpet; automobile horn; speaking tube; megaphone; **bocinazo** *m.* honk.
bochorno [ba·čór·no] *m.* sultry weather; suffocating heat; (*vergüenza*) blush, flush; embarrassment.
bochornoso [bo·čor·nó·so] *adj.* sultry; embarrassing.
boda [bó·da] *f.* marriage, wedding; — **de negros** a noisy party; **-s de Camacho** lavish feast, banquet.
bodega [bo·dé·ga] *f.* cellar; wine cellar; storeroom; (*almacén*) warehouse; *Cuba, Ven., Col.* grocery store; **bodeguero** *m.* keeper of a wine cellar; liquor dealer; *Cuba, Ven., Col.* grocer.
bodoque [bo·dó·ke] *m.* wad; lump; dunce; *Mex.* bump, swelling.
bofe [bó·fe] *m.* lung; *P.R.* snap, easy job; **echar uno los -s** to throw oneself into a job; to work hard; *Am.* **ser un** — to be a bore; to be repulsive.
bofetada [bo·fe·tá·da] *f.* slap; **bofetón** *m.* big slap, blow, hard sock, wallop.
boga [bó·ga] *f.* vogue, fashion; rowing; *m.* rower.
bogar[7] [bo·gár] *v.* to row.
bohemio [bo·é·mjo] *adj. & m.* Bohemian.
bohío [bo·í·o] *m. Carib., Ven.* cabin, shack, hut.
boina [bój·na] *f.* beret.
bola [bó·la] *f.* (*esfera*) ball, bowling; (*mentira*) fib, lie; (*betún*) shoe polish; *C.A.* disturbance, riot, false rumor; **no dar pie con** — not to do things right; not to hit the mark; to make mistakes; *Am.* **darle a la** — to hit the mark.
boleada [bo·le·áda] *f. Ríopl.* lassoing with **boleadoras**; *Ríopl.* hunting expedition (*with* **boleadoras**); *Mex.* shoeshine; *Col.* affront, insult.
boleadoras [bo·le·a·dó·ras] *f. pl. Ríopl.* throwing weapon made of three united thongs with balls at the ends.
bolear [bo·le·ár] *v.* to play billiards; to bowl; to lie, fib; *Ríopl.*, to lasso with **boleadoras**; *Mex.* to entangle; *Am.* to polish (*shoes*); *Am.* to dismiss: *Am.* to blackball, vote against; *Am.* to flunk; **-se** *Am.* to rear, balk (*said of a horse*); *Andes, Ríopl., Mex., Ch.* to blush, be ashamed.
boleta [bo·lé·ta] *f.* certificate; pass; pay order; *Mex., C.A.* ballot; *Ch.* first draft of a deed.
boletín [bo·le·tín] *m.* bulletin.
boleto [bo·lé·to] *m. Am.* ticket; **boletería** *f. Am.* ticket office.
boliche [bo·lí·če] *m.* bowling; bowling alley; *Ríopl.* cheap tavern; *Ch.* gambling joint; *Ríopl.* cheap store or shop, notions store, variety store.
bolígrafo [bo·lí·gra·fo] *m.* ball point pen.
bolillo [bo·lí·yo] *m. Mex., C.A.* hard roll.
bolita [bo·lí·ta] *f.* small ball; *Am.* ballot (*small ball used in voting*); *Col., Ven.* marble; *S.A.* armadillo.
bolo [bó·lo] *m.* one of the pins (*used in bowling*); dunce, stupid fellow; **-s** bowls, bowling; **jugar a los -s** to bowl.
bolsa [ból·sa] *f.* bag, purse; (*de acciones*) stock exchange; *Ríopl.* pocket.
bolsillo [bol·sí·yo] *m.* pocket; pocketbook.
bolsista [bol·sís·ta] *m.* stockbroker, market operator.
bollo [bó·yo] *m.* bun, muffin; (*chichón*) bump, lump; puff (*in a dress*); tuft (*on upholstery*); *Andes* loaf of bread; *Am.* a kind of tamale; **-s** *Am.* difficulties, troubles.
bomba [bóm·ba] *f.* pump; (*bombilla*) lamp bulb; bomb; — **atómica** atomic bomb; — **de hidrógeno** hydrogen bomb; *Carib.* false news; *Carib.* stanza improvised by a dancer; *Ríopl.* firecracker, skyrocket; *Mex., Col.* satirical remark; *P.R.* large drum; — **de líquido refrigerante** coolant pump; — **para incendios** fire engine; *Am.* **estar con una** — to be drunk; **bombita** *f.* soap bubble; *Col.* shame, embarrassment.
bombachas [bom·bá·čas] *f. pl. Ríopl.* loose-fitting breeches.
bombacho [bom·bá·čo] *adj.* loose-fitting (*trousers or breeches*).
bombardear [bom·bar·de·ár] *v.* to bomb.
bombardeo [bom·bar·dé·o] *m.* bombardment, bombing; **avión de** — bomber, bombing plane.
bombardero [bom·bar·dé·ro] *m.* bombardier; bomber.
bombear [bom·be·ár] *v.* (*echar bombas*) to bomb; (*alabar*) to praise, extol *Am.* to pump; *Col.* to fire, dismiss; *Mex.* to puff hard on a cigar or cigarette.
bombero [bom·bé·ro] *m.* fireman; pumper.
bombilla [bom·bí·ya] *f.* electric-light bulb; *Am.* kerosene lamp tube; *Ríopl.* small tube for drinking **mate**.
bombo [bóm·bo] *m.* large drum; bass drum; player on a bass drum; *Mex., Col., Ch.* pomp, ostentation; *Ríopl.* buttocks, rump; **dar** — to praise, extol (*in the press or newspapers*); *Col., Ríopl.* **darse** — to put on airs; *Am.* **irse uno al** — to fail; *adj.* stunned; *Am.* lukewarm; *Am.* slightly rotten; *Cuba* stupid, silly, simple; *Cuba* **fruta bomba** papaya (*tropical fruit*).
bombón [bom·bón] *m.* bonbon, candy; — **de altea** marshmallow.
bonachón [bo·na·čón] *adj.* good-natured; naïve, simple.
bonanza [bo·nán·sa] *f.* fair weather; (*riqueza*) prosperity; rich vein of ore.
bondad [bon·dád] *f.* goodness.
bondadoso [bon·da·dó·so] *adj.* good, kind.
boniato [bo·njá·to] *m. Carib., Ríopl.* sweet potato.
bonito [bo·ní·to] *adj.* pretty, *m.* striped tunny (*a fish*).
bono [bó·no] *m.* certificate; bond.
boñiga [bo·ñí·ga] *f.* dung, manure.
boqueada [bo·ke·á·da] *f.* gape, gasp.

boquear [bo·ke·ár] *v.* to open one's mouth; to gape, gasp; to be dying; *C.R.* break a horse.
boquete [bo·ké·te] *m.* breach, gap, hole, opening.
boquiabierto [bo·kja·ƀjér·to] *adj.* openmouthed.
boquilla [bo·kí·ya] *f.* (*abertura*) little mouth; small opening; (*de cigarro*) holder; tip; (*de instrumento*) mouthpiece; pastry tube.
borbollón [bor·ƀo·yón], **borbotón** [bor·ƀo·tón] *m.* spurt; spurting; big bubble; bubbling up; **a -es** in spurts; **boquillo cortador** *m.* cutting head.
borbotar [bor·ƀo·tár] *v.* to bubble up; to spurt, gush forth; to boil over.
bordado [bor·đá·đo] *m.* embroidery.
bordadura [bor·đa·đú·ra] *f.* embroidery.
bordar [bor·đár] *v.* to embroider.
borde [bór·đe] *m.* border, edge.
bordear [bor·đe·ár] *v.* to skirt, go along the edge of; *Am.* to trim with a border; *Am.* to make a **bordo** (*small, temporary dam*); **-se** *Ch., Mex., Ven.* to approach, get near.
bordo [bór·đo] *m.* board, side of a ship; tack (*of a ship*); *Mex., Ven.* ridge (*of a furrow*); *Mex.,* small dam; **a** — on board.
borla [bór·la] *f.* (*indumentaria*) tassel; doctor's cap; (*título*) doctor's degree; (*cosmético*) powder puff; tuft; **tomar uno la** — to get a doctor's degree.
borlarse [bor·lár·se] *v. Am.* to get a doctor's degree.
boro [bó·ro] *m.* boron.
borrachera [bo·rra·čé·ra] *f.* drunkenness; drunken spree.
borrachín [bo·rra·čin] *m.* toper, drunk.
borracho [bo·rrá·čo] *adj.* drunk; *m.* drunkard; **borrachón** [bo·rra·čón] *m.* drunkard, heavy drinker.
borrador [bo·rra·đór] *m.* rough draft; *Am.* rubber eraser.
borrar [bo·rrár] *v.* to blot out; to erase.
borrasca [bo·rrás·ka] *f.* storm, tempest.
borrascoso [bo·rras·kó·so] *adj.* stormy.
borrego [bo·rré·ğo] *m.* lamb; (*tonto*) fool, simpleton; *Mex., C.A.* false news.
borrico [bo·rrí·ko] *m.* donkey, ass; fool; sawhorse.
borrón [bo·rrón] *m.* blotch (*of ink*), blot.
borronear [bo·rro·ne·ár] *v.* to blot, blotch; (*garrapatear*) to scribble; to blur; to make a rough sketch.
borroso [bo·rró·so] *adj.* blurry.
boruca [bo·rú·ka] *f.* racket, noise.
boscaje [bos·ká·xe] *m.* grove, thicket, woods; (*paisaje*) landscape.
bosque [bós·ke] *m.* forest, woods; **bosquecillo** *m.* small forest, grove.
bosquejar [bos·ke·xár] *v.* to sketch; to outline.
bosquejo [bos·ké·xo] *m.* sketch, plan, outline, rough draft.
bostezar[9] [bos·te·sár] *v.* to yawn.
bostezo [bos·té·so] *m.* yawn.
bota [bó·ta] *f.* (*calzado*) boot; (*bolsa*) leather wine bag; *adj. Am.* stupid, clumsy; *Mex.* drunk.
botar [bo·tár] *v.* (*echar*) to launch; to fling; to throw away; (*rebotar*) to bounce; *Ven.* to waste, squander; *Am.* to fire, dismiss; **-se** *Am.* to lie down.
botarate [bo·ta·rá·te] *m.* fool; braggart; *Mex., Carib.* spendthrift.
bote [bó·te] *m.* (*jarro*) small jar; (*embarcación*) boat; (*rebote*) bounce; (*golpe*) blow; jump; *Ríopl.* liquor bottle; *Mex., C.A.* jail; **estar de — en —** to be crowded, completely filled up.
botella [bo·té·ya] *f.* bottle.
botica [bo·tí·ka] *f.* drugstore.
boticario [bo·ti·ká·rjo] *m.* druggist.
botija [bo·tí·xa] *f.* earthen jug; fat person; *Am.* buried treasure; *Am.* belly; *Col.* **poner a uno como — verde** to dress down, scold, insult a person.
botijo [bo·tí·xo] *m.* earthen jar with spout and handle.
botín [bo·tín] *m.* booty, plunder; (*zapato*) high shoe; *Ch.* sock.
botiquín [bo·ti·kín] *m.* medicine cabinet; medicine kit; *Ven.* liquor store, wine shop.
botón [bo·tón] *m.* bud; button; knob; handle; **-es** bellboy.
bóveda [bó·ƀe·đa] *f.* arched roof; vault, underground cellar; burial place.
boxeador [bok·se·a·đór] *m.* boxer.
boxear [bok·se·ár] *v.* to box, fight with the fists.
boxeo [bok·sé·o] *m.* boxing.
boya [bó·ya] *f.* buoy; float net; *Am.* crease, dent; *Bol.* rich mineral vein; *Am.* **estar en la buena** — to be in a good humor.
bozal [bo·sál] *m.* (*de animal*) nuzzle; (*cascabel*) bells on a harness; (*novicio*) novice; (*negro*) Negro native of Africa; *Am.* headstall (*of a halter*); *Spain* person (*especially a Negro*) who speaks broken Spanish; *Am.* coarse, crude individual; *adj.* green, inexperienced; wild, untamed; stupid.
bozo [bó·so] *m.* down (*on the upper lip*); mustache; outside part of the mouth; headstall (*of a halter*).
bracear [bra·se·ár] *v.* to swing one's arms; to struggle; (*nadar*) to crawl, swim with a crawl.
bracero [bra·sé·ro] *m.* day laborer; **de** — arm in arm; **servir de — a una señora** to serve as an escort, give a lady one's arm.
bracete [bra·sé·te]: **de** — arm in arm.
bragueta [bra·ğé·ta] *f.* fly (*pants*).
bramante [bra·mán·te] *m.* hemp cord, hemp string; Brabant linen; *adj.* roaring, bellowing.
bramar [bra·már] *v.* to bellow, roar, howl; to rage.
bramido [bra·mí·đo] *m.* roar; howl; bellow.
brasa [brá·sa] *f.* red-hot coal.
brasero [bra·sé·ro] *m.* brazier (*pan for burning coal*), grate; hearth, *Ríopl.* brick cooking stove.
bravata [bra·ƀá·ta] *f.* bravado, boastfulness, defiance.
bravear [bra·ƀe·ár] *v.* to bluster; to bully.
bravío [bra·ƀí·o] *adj.* savage, wild; rustic.
bravo [brá·ƀo] *adj.* (*agresivo*) wild, ferocious, harsh; ill-tempered; (*valiente*) brave; *Carib., C.A., Andes* angry; *Ch.* hot, highly seasoned.
bravura [bra·ƀú·ra] *f.* fierceness; courage; bravado, show of boldness.
braza [brá·sa] *f.* fathom; (*natación*) stroke.
brazada [bra·sá·đa] *f.* armful; movement of the arms (*swimming stroke*); **a una** — at arm's length.
brazalete [bra·sa·lé·te] *m.* bracelet.
brazo [brá·so] *m.* arm; branch; **-s** day laborers; *Ríopl., Cuba* **de** — arm in arm; **luchar a — partido** to wrestle; to fight hand to hand.
brea [bré·a] *f.* pitch; tar; (*lona*) canvas.
brecha [bré·ča] *f.* breach, gap.
brega [bré·ğa] *f.* fight, scrap.
bregar[7] [bre·ğár] *v.* to struggle; to fight.
breña [bré·ña] *f.* rough, craggy ground covered with brambles; bramble; **breñal** *m.* brambles; bush country.
breve [bré·ƀe] *adj.* brief, short; **en** — shortly.
brevedad [bre·ƀe·đáđ] *f.* brevity, shortness.
bribón [bri·ƀón] *adj.* idle, indolent; *m.* rascal, rogue; **bribonazo** *m.* scoundrel, cheat.
brida [brí·đa] *f.* bridle; rein.
brigada [bri·ğá·đa] *f.* brigade.
brillante [bri·yán·te] *adj.* brilliant, bright; *m.* diamond.

brillantez [bri·yan·tés] *f.* brilliance, dazzle.
brillar [bri·yár] *v.* to shine.
brillo [brí·yo] *m.* luster, sparkle, shine.
brincar[6] [briŋ·kár] *v.* to hop, skip, jump, bounce.
brinco [bríŋ·ko] *m.* hop, skip, bounce, leap.
brindar [brin·dár] *v.* to toast, drink to the health of; (*ofrecer*) give, to offer.
brindis [brín·dis] *m.* toast (*to a person's health*).
brío [brí·o] *m.* vigor, liveliness; (*valor*) valor, courage.
brioso [brjó·so] *adj.* lively; brave.
brisa [brí·sa] *f.* breeze.
británico [bri·tá·ni·ko] *adj.* British.
brizna [bríz·na] *f.* particle, chip, fragment; blade of grass.
broca [bró·ka] *f.* drill.
brocal [bro·kál] *m.* curb, curbstone (*of a well*).
brocha [bró·ča] *f.* house painter's brush; (*dados*) loaded dice; **cuadro de — gorda** badly done painting; **pintor de — gorda** house painter **brochada** *f.* stroke of the brush, brush stroke; **brochazo** *m.* blow with a brush; brush stroke; **— de pastelero** pastry brush.
broche [bró·če] *m.* brooch; clasp, clip, fastener; hook and eye.
brocheta [bro·čé·ta] *f.* skewer.
broma [bró·ma] *f.* jest, joke; fun, merriment; *Am.* disappointment, irritation; **de —** in jest; **fuera de —** all joking aside.
bromear [bro·me·ár] *v.* to joke, jest.
bronca [bróŋ·ka] *f.* quarrel, dispute, wrangle; **armar una —** to cause a disturbance, raise a rumpus.
bronce [brón·se] *m.* bronze.
bronceado [bron·se·áđo] *adj.* bronzed; bronze-colored; *m.* bronze finish.
bronco [bróŋ·ko] *adj.* hoarse; raspy, harsh; (*burdo*) coarse, rough; uncouth; wild, untamed (*horse*).
bronquio [bróŋ·kjo] *m.* bronchus, bronchial tube.
broquel [bro·kél] *m.* buckler, shield (*worn on the arm*).
brotar [bro·tár] *v.* to shoot forth; to bud; to break out (*on the skin*); to gush, flow; to spring forth.
broza [bró·sa] *f.* brushwood, underbush; (*basura*) rubbish, refuse, trash; coarse, hard brush.
bruces [brú·ses]: **de —** face downward.
bruja [brú·xa] *f.* witch; hag; owl; *adj. Mex.* broke, poor; **brujo** *m.* sorcerer, magician, wizard.
brújula [brú·xu·la] *f.* (*compás*) compass; magnetic needle; (*mira*) peephole; gunsight.
bruma [brú·ma] *f.* mist, fog; **brumoso** *adj.* foggy, misty, hazy.
bruñido interior [bru·ñí·đo in·te·rjór] *m.* honing.
bruñir[19] [bru·ñír] *v. irr.* to burnish, polish; to put on make-up.
brusco [brús·ko] *adj.* blunt, rude, abrupt.
brutal [bru·tál] *adj.* brutal, beastly, savage.
brutalidad [bru·ta·li·đáđ] *f.* brutality.
bruto [brú·to] *adj.* (*tonto*) stupid, brutal; (*burdo*) coarse, rough; **peso —** gross weight; **diamante en —** diamond in the rough, unpolished diamond; *m.* brute, beast.
bucal [bu·kál] *adj.* oral, pertaining to the mouth.
bucear [bu·se·ár] *v.* to dive; to dive into, plunge into; to explore thoroughly a subject.
bucle [bú·kle] *m.* curl, ringlet; (*computadora*) loop.
buche [bú·če] *m.* crop (*of a bird*); (*bocada*) mouthful (*of water*); wrinkle, bag (*in clothes*); *Ríopl., Mex., Ven.* goiter.
budín [bu·đín] *m.* pudding.
buen(o) [bwé·n(o)] *adj.* good; kind; useful; well, in good health; **de buenas a primeras** all of a sudden, unexpectedly, on the spur of the moment; **por la(s) buena(s) o por la(s) mala(s)** willingly or unwillingly, by hook or crook.
buey [bwej] *m.* ox.
búfalo [bú·fa·lo] *m.* buffalo.
bufanda [bu·fán·da] *f.* muffler, scarf.
bufar [bu·fár] *v.* to snort; to puff with anger; **-se** *Mex.* to swell, bulge (*as a wall*).
bufete [bu·fé·te] *m.* desk, writing table; lawyer's office.
bufido [bu·fí·đo] *m.* snort.
bufón [bu·fón] *m.* buffoon, jester, clown; *adj.* comical, funny; **bufonada** [bu·fo·ná·đa] *f.* wisecrack; jest.
bufonear [bu·fo·ne·ár] *v.* to clown; to jest.
buhardilla [bu·ar·đí·ya], [bwar·đí·ya] *f.* garret, attic; skylight; dormer.
búho [bú·o] *m.* owl.
buhonero [bu·o·né·ro] *m.* peddler.
buitre [bwí·tre] *m.* vulture.
buje [bú·xe] *m.* bushing; axle box.
bujía [bu·xí·a] *f.* candle; candle power; candlestick; spark plug.
bula [bú·la] *f.* bull (*papal document*); papal seal.
buldózer [bul·dó·ser] *m.* bulldozer.
bulevar [bu·le·ƀár] *m.* boulevard.
bulto [búl·to] *m.* (*cuerpo*) body, bundle, shadow, lump, swelling; (*tamaño*) bulk, volume; **a —** haphazardly, by guess; **escurrir el —** to dodge; **imagen de —** statue, sculpture; **una verdad de —** an evident truth.
bulla [bú·ya] *f.* shouting, uproar; noisy crowd.
bullicio [bu·yí·sjo] *m.* noise, uproar.
bullicioso [bu·yi·sjó·so] *adj.* boisterous, noisy; (*alegre*) lively; turbulent, stormy.
bullir[20] [bu·yír] *v. irr.* to boil; to buzz about; to bustle; to stir, move; *Mex.* to deride.
buñuelo [bu·ñwé·lo] *m.* fritter; *P.R.* botch, poor piece of work.
buque [bú·ke] *m.* ship, boat.
burbuja [bur·ƀú·xa] *f.* bubble.
burdo [búr·đo] *adj.* coarse.
burgués [bur·ǵés] *adj.* bourgeois, middle-class.
burla [búr·la] *f.* jest, mockery; **de —** in jest.
burlador [bur·la·đór] *m.* practical joker; jester; scoffer; seducer.
burlar [bur·lár] *v.* to mock, ridicule, deceive; **-se de** to scoff at; to make fun of.
burlón [bur·lón] *m.* jester, teaser.
burocracia [bu·ro·krá·sja] *f.* bureaucracy.
burócrata [bu·ró·kra·ta] *m.* bureaucrat.
burro [bú·rro] *m.* ass, donkey; *Mex., Cuba, Ríopl.* stepladder; *adj.* stupid; **burrito** *m.* small donkey; *Am.* saddle rack.
busca [bús·ka] *f.* search; hunting party; *Mex.* **-s** profit on the side; graft.
buscar[6] [bus·kár] *v.* to seek, search, look for; *Mex., Andes* to provoke.
búsqueda [bús·ke·đa] *f.* search.
busto [bús·to] *m.* bust (*upper part of body*).
butaca [bu·tá·ka] *f.* armchair; orchestra seat; **butacón** [bu·ta·kón] *m.* large armchair.
buzo [bú·so] *m.* diver; deep-sea or "skin" diver.
buzón [bu·són] *m.* mailbox; letter drop.

C:c

cabal [ka·ƀál] *adj.* complete, entire; exact; **estar uno en sus -es** to be in one's right mind.
cabalgar[7] [ka·ƀal·ǥár] *v.* to ride, mount (*a horse*); to ride horseback.
caballa [ka·ƀá·ya] *f.* horse mackeral.
caballada [ka·ƀa·yá·đa] *f.* herd of horses; *Am.* nonsense, stupidity, blunder.
caballejo [ka·ƀa·yé·xo] *m.* nag; poor horse.
caballeresco [ka·ƀa·ye·rés·ko] *adj.* gentlemanly; knightly; chivalrous, gallant.
caballería [ka·ƀa·ye·rí·a] *f.* calvary; horsemanship; mount, horse; knighthood; chivalry.
caballeriza [ka·ƀa·ye·rí·sa] *f.* stable; horses of a stable.
caballerizo [ka·ƀa·ye·rí·so] *m.* groom, stableman.
caballero [ka·ƀa·yé·ro] *m.* gentleman; knight, horseman; *adj.* gentlemanly.
caballerosidad [ka·ƀa·ye·ro·si·đáđ] *f.* chivalry, gentlemanly conduct.
caballeroso [ka·ƀa·ye·ró·so] *adj.* chivalrous, gentlemanly.
caballete [ka·ƀa·yé·te] *m.* (*de casa*) ridge of a roof, hip; (*madero*) sawhorse; (*de la cara*) bridge of the nose.
caballo [ka·ƀá·yo] *m.* horse; (*ajedrez*) knight (*in chess*); *Am.* stupid or brutal person; **a —** on horseback; **caballuco** [ka·ƀa·yú·ko] *m.* nag.
cabaña [ka·ƀá·ña] *f* hut, cabin; *Ríopl.* cattle ranch.
cabecear [ka·ƀe·se·ár] *v.* to nod; to shake the head; to pitch (*as a boat*); *Ven.* to begin to rise or fall (*said of a river*).
cabeceo [ka·ƀe·sé·o] *m.* nodding; pitching (*of a boat*).
cabecera [ka·ƀe·sé·ra] *f.* head (*of bed or table*); seat, chief city (*of a district*).
cabecilla [ka·ƀe·sí·ya] *f.* small head; *m.* ringleader.
cabellera [ka·ƀe·yé·ra] *f.* head of hair, long hair; wig; tail of a comet.
cabello [ka·ƀé·yo] *m.* hair; **traer algo por los -s** to bring in a far-fetched fact or quotation; **-s de ángel** cotton candy.
cabelludo [ka·ƀe·yú·đo] *adj.* hairy; **cuero —** scalp.
caber[23] [ka·ƀér] *v. irr.* to fit into, go into; to have enough room for; to befall; **no cabe duda** there is no doubt; **no cabe más** there is no room for more; **no — uno en sí** to be puffed up with pride; **no cabe en lo posible** it is absolutely impossible.
cabestro [ka·ƀés·tro] *m.* halter; leading ox; *Carib., Mex.* rope, cord; *S.A.* advance payment; **cabestrillo** [ka·ƀes·trí·yo] *m.* sling (*for an arm*).
cabeza [ka·ƀé·sa] *f.* (*parte superior*) head; upper part; (*director*) chief, leader; capital (*of a district*); *Carib.* source (*of a river*); **— de playa** beachhead; **— de puente** bridgehead; **— sonora** recording head.
cabezada [ka·ƀe·sá·đa] *f.* butt (*with the head*); bump on the head; (*cabeceo*) nod; shake of the head; pitching (*of a ship*); headgear (*of a harness*).
cabezal [ka·ƀe·sál] *m.* headstock (*lathe*).
cabezazo [ka·ƀe·sá·so] *m.* butt (*with the head*), bump on the head.
cabezudo [ka·ƀe·súđo] *adj.* big-headed; hard-headed, pig-headed, stubborn, headstrong.
cabezón [ka·ƀe·són] *adj.* big-headed; pig-headed, stubborn; *Ch.* strong (*liquor*); *m.* large head; cavesson (*iron noseband used in breaking a horse*); *Col.* rapids or whirlpool in a river.
cabida [ka·ƀí·đa] *f.* space, room, capacity; **tener — con alguien** to have influence with someone.
cabildo [ka·ƀíl·do] *m.* cathedral chapter; municipal council; council room; town hall.
cabina [ka·ƀí·na] *f.* cabin (*of an airplane*).
cabio [ká·ƀjo] *m.* joist; **cabio de cresta** hip rafter.
cabizbajo [ka·ƀiz·ƀá·xo] *adj.* crestfallen, downcast; pensive.
cable [ká·ƀle] *m.* cable.
cablegrafiar[17] [ka·ƀle·ǥra·fjár] *v.* to cable.
cablegrama [ka·ƀle·ǥrá·ma] *m.* cablegram.
cabo [ká·ƀo] *m.* (*cosa*) end, tip, handle; piece of rope; (*geográfico*) cape, headland; (*persona*) foreman, corporal; **al —** finally; **al fin y al —** anyway, in the long run; **de — a rabo** from beginning to end; **estar al — de** to be well informed about; **llevar a —** to carry out, finish.
cabotaje [ka·ƀo·tá·xe] *m.* coastal trade or traffic.
cabra [ká·ƀra] *f.* goat; *Col.* fraud, trick; *Col., Cuba, Ven.* loaded dice; *Am.* light two-wheeled carriage; **cabrillas** [ka·ƀrí·yas] *f. pl.* whitecaps (*small waves with white crests*); Pleiades (*constellation*); game of skipping stones on the water.
cabrero [ka·ƀré·ro] *m.* goatherd.
cabrio [ká·ƀrjo] *m.* rafter.
cabrío [ka·ƀrí·o] *adj.* goatish; **macho —** he-goat; *m.* herd of goats.
cabriola [ka·ƀrjó·la] *f.* caper, leap, hop, skip; somersault; **hacer -s** to cut capers; to prance.
cabriolar [ka·ƀrjo·lár] *v.* to prance; to caper; to romp, frolic, frisk.
cabrito [ka·ƀrí·to] *m.* kid; **cabritilla** [ka·ƀri·tí·ya] *f.* kid, kidskin.
cabrón [ka·ƀrón] *m.* he-goat; cuckold (*man whose wife is unfaithful*).
caca [ká·ka] *f.* excrement (popular children's expression).
cacahuate [ka·ka·wá·te] *m. Mex., C.A.* peanut; *Spain* **cacahuete** [ka·ka·wé·te], **cacahuey** [ka·ka·wéj].
cacao [ka·ká·o] *m.* cocoa.
cacarear [ka·ka·re·ár] *v.* to cackle; to boast; *Am.* to run away from a fight.
cacareo [ka·ka·ré·o] *m.* cackle.
cacería [ka·se·rí·a] *f.* hunt, hunting.
cacerola [ka·se·ró·la] *f.* saucepan.
cacique [ka·sí·ke] *m.* chief; political boss; *Mex.* tyrant; *Ch., Ven.* one who leads an easy life.
caciquismo [ka·si·kíz·mo] *m.* political bossism (*rule by political bosses*).
cacofonía [ka·ko·fo·ní·a] *f.* cacophony.
cacto [kák·to] *m.* cactus.
cacumen [ka·kú·men] *m.* acumen, keen insight.
cacha [ká·ča] *f.* handle (*of a knife or pistol*); *Am.* the horns of a bull; *C.A.* **hacer la —** to complete a task, to get.
cacharro [ka·čá·rro] *m.* earthen pot or vase; broken piece of a pot; crude utensil; *Am.* cheap trinket; "jalopy".
cachaza [ka·čá·sa] *f.* slowness; calm; rum.
cachazudo [ka·ča·sú·đo] *adj.* slow, easy going.
cachetada [ka·če·tá·đa] *f. Am.* slap on the face.
cachete [ka·čé·te] *m.* cheek; slap on the cheek.
cachimbo [ka·čím·bo] *m. Am.* pipe (*for smoking*); *Cuba* small sugar mill; also **cachimba** [ka·čím·ba].
cachivache [ka·či·ƀá·če] *m.* piece of junk; (*persona*) worthless fellow; *Mex., Carib., Ven.* trinket.
cacho [ká·čo] *m. Am.* horn (of an animal); *adj.* bent, crooked.
cachorro [ka·čó·rro] *m.* (*oso*) cub; (*perro*) puppy; small pistol; *Carib.* rude, ill-bred person.
cachucha [ka·čú·ča] *f.* cap; rowboat; popular Andalusian dance, song and music; *Am.* slap.
cada [ká·đa] *adj.* each, every; **— uno** each one; **— y cuando que** whenever; *Am.* **a — nada** every second.

cadalso [ka·đal·so] *m.* gallows; scaffold, platform.
cadáver [ka·đá·ƀer] *m.* corpse; **cadavérico** [ka·đa·ƀé·ri·ko] *adj.* deadly, ghastly, pale, like a corpse.
cadena [ka·đé·na] *f.* chain.
cadencia [ka·đén·sja] *f.* cadence.
cadencioso [ka·đen·sjó·so] *adj.* rhythmical.
cadera [ka·đé·ra] *f.* hip.
cadete [ka·đé·te] *m.* cadet.
cadmio [kađ·mjo] *m.* cadmium.
caducar[6] [ka·đu·kár] *v.* to dote, be in one's dotage; (*vencer*) to lapse, expire; to become extinct, fall into disuse.
caduco [ka·đú·ko] *adj.* decrepit, very old, feeble; perishable.
caer[24] [ka·ér] *v. irr.* to fall; to fall down; to fall off; **-se** to fall down, tumble; — **a** to face, overlook; — **bien** to fit, be becoming; — **en cama** to fall ill; — **en la cuenta** to catch on, get the point; — **en gracia** to please; **al — de la noche** at nightfall; **dejar** — to drop.
café [ka·fé] *m.* coffee, café; *Mex.* annoyance, bad time.
cafeína [ka·fe·í·na] *f.* caffein.
cafetal [ka·fe·tál] *m.* coffee plantation.
cafetera [ka·fe·té·ra] *f.* coffeepot; woman café owner, coffee vendor or merchant; coffee-bean picker.
cafetería [ka·fe·te·rí·a] *f.* café, bar, lunchroom.
cafetero [ka·fe·té·ro] *adj.* pertaining to coffee; *m.* coffee grower; coffee merchant; owner of a café or coffee-house; *Am.* coffee drinker.
cafeto [ka·fé·to] *m.* coffee bush.
cagar[7] [ka·ǥár] *v. irr.* to defecate (*popular term*).
caída [ka·í·đa] *f.* fall, drop; descent; **a la — del sol** (*or* **de la tarde**) at sunset.
caimán [kaj·mán] *m.* cayman, alligator.
caja [ká·xa] *f.* case, box; — **de ahorros** savings bank; — **de cambios** transmission (*automobile*); — **de fusibles** fuse box; **-s de ingletes** mitre boxes; — **de píldora** pillbox; — **fuerte** safe; **echar a uno con -s destempladas** to give someone the gate.
cajero [ka·xé·ro] *m.* cashier; box maker.
cajetilla [ka·xe·tí·ya] *f.* small box; package of cigarettes.
cajón [ka·xón] *m.* large box, chest; drawer; vendor's booth or stand; *Ch., Mex.* narrow canyon; — **de muerto** coffin; *Mex.* — **de ropa** dry-goods and clothing store.
cal [kal] *f.* lime (*mineral*).
calabaza [ka·la·ƀá·sa] *f.* pumpkin, squash; gourd; an ignorant person; **dar -s** to jilt, turn down (*a suitor*); to flunk; fail.
calabozo [ka·la·ƀó·so] *m.* dungeon; prison cell.
calado [ka·lá·đo] *m.* drawn work; openwork (*in wood, metal linen, etc.*), fretwork; draft (*of a ship*).
calafatear [ka·la·fa·te·ar] *v.* to caulk.
calamar [ka·la·már] *m.* squid, cuttlefish.
calambre [ka·lám·bre] *m.* body cramp.
calamidad [ka·la·mi·đáđ] *f.* calamity, misfortune.
calandria [ka·lán·drja] *f.* lark, skylark.
calar [ka·lár] *v.* (*penetrar*) to pierce, penetrate; to soak through; to make openwork (*in cloth, metal*); (*probar*) to probe, search into; **-se el sombrero** to put on one's hat; to pull down one's hat.
calavera [ka·la·ƀé·ra] *f.* skull; *m.* libertine, rounder, reckless fellow; *Mex.* taillight.
calcar[6] [kal·kár] *v.* to trace; to copy, imitate.
calceta [kal·sé·ta] *f.* hose, stocking; **hacer** — to knit; **calcetería** [kal·se·te·rí·a] *f.* hosiery shop; hosiery.
calcetín [kal·se·tín] *m.* sock.
calcinar [kal·si·nár] *v.* to burn, char, heat.
calcio [kál·sjo] *m.* calcium.
calco [kál·ko] *m.* tracing, traced copy; exact copy; imitation.
calculadora [kal·ku·la·đó·ra] *f.* calculator — **electrónica** computer; — **e integradora electrónica numérica** UNIVAC.
calcular [kal·ku·lár] *v.* to calculate, figure, estimate.
cálculo [kál·ku·lo] *m.* calculation, estimate; calculus; gravel (*in the gall bladder, kidney, etc.*).
caldear [kal·de·ár] *v.* to heat; to weld; **-se** *Mex.* to become overheated, excited; *Mex., Ríopl.* to get "lit up", get drunk.
caldera [kal·dé·ra] *f.* boiler; caldron, kettle; **calderilla** [kal·de·rí·ya] *f.* copper coin.
caldo [kál·do] *m.* broth; gravy.
calefacción [ka·le·fak·sjón] *f.* heat, heating.
calendario [ka·len·dá·rjo] *m.* calendar; almanac.
caléndula [ka·lén·du·la] *f.* marigold.
calentador [ka·len·ta·đór] *m.* heater.
calentar[1] [ka·len·tár] *v. irr.* to warm, heat; to spank; *Am.* to annoy, bother; **-se** to warm oneself; to become heated, excited; to be in heat; *Am.* to become angry.
calentura [ka·len·tú·ra] *f.* fever; *Col.* fit of temper; — **de pollo** feigned illness; **calenturón** [ka·len·tu·rón] *m.* high fever.
calenturiento [ka·len·tu·rjén·to] *adj.* feverish; *Ch.* tubercular.
caletre [ka·lé·tre] *m.* judgment, acumen, keen insight.
calibrar [ka·li·ƀrár] *v.* to gauge, measure; to measure the caliber of.
calibre [ka·lí·ƀre] *m.* caliber; bore, gauge (*of a gun*); diameter (*of a pipe, tube, wire*).
calicanto [ka·li·kán·to] *m.* stone masonry.
calicó [ka·li·kó] *m.* calico, cotton cloth.
calidad [ka·li·đáđ] *f.* quality.
cálido [ká·li·đo] *adj.* warm, hot.
caliente [ka·ljén·te] *adj.* warm, hot; heated; fiery; *Am.* angry; *Col.* bold brave; *m. Col.* brandy in hot water; **calientito** *adj.* nice and warm.
calificación [ka·li·fi·ka·sjón] *f.* qualification; (*nota*) grade, mark; (*juicio*) judgment.
calificar[6] [ka·li·fi·kár] *v.* to qualify; to rate, consider, judge; to grade; *Mex.* to compute (*election returns*); **-se** *Ch.* to qualify or register (*as a voter*).
caligrafía [ka·li·gra·fí·a] *f.* penmanship.
calina [ka·lí·na] *f.* haze, mist.
cáliz [ká·lis] *m.* chalice, communion cup; cup, goblet; calyx (*of a flower*).
calma [kál·ma] *f.* calm, quiet.
calmante [kal·mán·te] *adj.* soothing; *m.* sedative; tranquilizer.
calmar [kal·már] *v.* to calm, quiet, soothe.
calmo [kál·mo] *adj.* calm, quiet.
calmoso [kal·mó·so] *adj.* calm; soothing; (*torpe*) phlegmatic, slow.
caló [ka·ló] *m.* underworld jargon.
calor [ka·lór] *m.* heat, warmth; ardor; — **exotérmico** exothermic heat.
caloria [ka·lo·rí·a] *f.* calorie.
calorífero [ka·lo·rí·fe·ro] *m.* heater, radiator; furnace.
calosfrío [ka·los·frí·o], **calofrío** [ka·lo·frí·o] *m.* chill.
calumnia [ka·lúm·nja] *f.* slander.
calumniar [ka·lum·njár] *v.* to slander.
caluroso [ka·lu·ró·so] *adj.* (*literal*) hot, warm; (*figurado*) heated, excited; cordial, enthusiastic.
calva [kál·ƀa] *f.* bald head; bald spot; barren spot.
calvario [kal·ƀá·rjo] *m.* Calvary, place of the Cross; suffering, tribulation.
calvo [kál·ƀo] *adj.* bald; barren.

calza [kál·sa] *f.* wedge; shoehorn; *Col., Ven.* gold inlay, tooth filling; **-s** breeches.
calzada [kal·sá·đa] *f.* paved road; highway; *Mex., Carib.* wide avenue.
calzado [kal·sá·đo] *m.* footwear.
calzador [kal·sa·đór] *m.* shoehorn.
calzar[9] [kal·sár] *v.* to put on (*shoes, gloves, spurs*); to put a wedge under a wheel; *Am.* to fill (*a tooth*).
calzón [kal·són] *m.* (*or* **calzones** [kal·só·nes]) breeches, short trousers; *Mex., Ven.* drawers; *Mex.* white cotton trousers; **calzoncillos** [kal·son·sí·yos] *m. pl.* drawers, men's shorts; **calzoneras** [kal·so·né·ras] *f. p. Mex.* trousers open down the sides.
callado [ka·yá·đo] *adj.* silent, quiet.
callar [ka·yár] *v.* to be silent; to hush; **-se** to be or keep silent.
calle [ká·ye] *f.* street.
calleja [ka·yé·xa] *f.* small street, alley, lane; **callejuela** [ka·ye·xwé·la] *f.* small, narrow street; lane.
callejear [ka·ye·xe·ár] *v.* to walk the streets, ramble.
callejero [ka·ye·xé·ro] *m.* street-rambler, street-stroller; street-loiterer; *adj.* fond of walking the streets; rambling.
callejón [ka·ye·xón] *m.* alley; lane; narrow pass; **— sin salida** blind alley.
callo [ká·yo] *m.* callus, corn; *Spain* **-s** tripe (*food*).
calloso [ka·yó·so] *adj.* callous, hard.
cama [ká·ma] *f.* bed, couch, cot; litter **caer en —** to fall ill; **guardar —** to be confined to bed; *Am.* **tenderle uno la — a otro** to help one in his love affairs; to set a trap for someone; **camastro** [ka·más·tro] *m.* poor, uncomfortable bed.
camada [ka·má·đa] *f.* litter; brood.
camaleón [ka·ma·le·ón] *m.* chameleon.
cámara [ká·ma·ra] *f.* chamber, hall, parlor; house (*of a legislative body*); cabin, stateroom; chamber (*of a gun*); **— de aire** inner tube; **— fotográfica** camera.
camarada [ka·ma·rá·đa] *m.* comrade; **camaradería** [ka·ma·ra·đe·rí·a] *f.* comradeship, companionship.
camarera [ka·ma·ré·ra] *f.* waitress; chambermaid; stewardess.
camarero [ka·ma·ré·ro] *m.* waiter; chamberlain; steward; valet.
camarilla [ka·ma·rí·ya] *f.* political lobby; small group of politicians, "kitchen cabinet", group of unofficial advisers; (*cuarto*) small room.
camarón [ka·ma·rón] *m.* shrimp.
camarote [ka·ma·ró·te] *m.* cabin, stateroom.
cambalache [kam·ba·lá·če] *m.* swap, barter, exchange.
cambalachear [kam·ba·la·če·ár] *v.* to swap, barter, exchange.
cambiador [kam·bja·đór] *m.* barterer; money changer; *Mex., Ch.* switchman.
cambiante [kam·bján·te] *adj.* changing; exchanging; *-s m. pl.* iridescent colors.
cambiar [kam·bjár] *v.* to change; to exchange; to shift; **— de marcha** to shift gears.
cambiavía [kam·bja·ƀí·a] *m. Carib., Mex., Andes* railway switchman. *See* **guardagujas** *and* **cambiador.**
cambio [kám·bjo] *m.* change; exchange; (*ferrocarril*) railway switch; **libre —** free trade; **en —** on the other hand; in exchange; **caja de —** *f.* transmission.
cambista [kam·bís·ta] *m.* exchange broker, banker; *Am.* railway switchman.
camello [ka·mé·yo] *m.* camel.
camilla [ka·mí·ya] *f.* stretcher; cot; **camillero** [ka·mi·yé·ro] *m.* stretcher bearer.
caminante [ka·mi·nán·te] *m. & f.* walker, traveler.
caminar [ka·mi·nár] *v.* to travel; to walk; *Am.* to progress, prosper.
caminata [ka·mi·ná·ta] *f.* long walk; hike; jaunt.
camino [ka·mí·no] *m.* road; course; *Ríopl.* table runner; *Am.* hall runner; **— de hierro** railroad; **— real** highway; **de —** on the way.
camión [ka·mjón] *m.* truck; wagon; *Mex.* bus; **camionero** [ka·mjo·né·ro] *m.* truck driver; **camioneta** [ka·mjo·né·ta] *f.* small truck; station wagon; *C.A.* bus.
camisa [ka·mí·sa] *f.* shirt; **— de fuerza** straitjacket; **meterse en — de once varas** to attempt more than one can manage, bite off more than one can chew; **camiseta** [ka·mi·sé·ta] *f.* undershirt.
camisón [ka·mi·són] *m.* long shirt; *Mex.* nightgown, *Am.* gown, dress.
camote [ka·mó·te] *m. Mex., C.A.* sweet potato.
campamento [kam·pa·mén·to] *m.* encampment; camp.
campana [kam·pá·na] *f.* bell; *Ríopl., Andes* spy, lookout (*for thieves*); **campanada** [kam·pa·ná·đa] *f.* stroke of a bell; *Mex.* **por — de vacante** once in a blue moon, very seldom.
campanario [kam·pa·ná·rjo] *m.* bell tower.
campanilla [kam·pa·ní·ya] *f.* small bell; (*burbuja*) bubble; uvula; tassel, bell-flower.
campanillazo [kam·pa·ni·yá·so] *m.* loud ring of a bell.
campanilleo [kam·pa·ni·yé·o] *m.* ringing; tinkling.
campaña [kam·pá·ña] *f.* (*paisaje*) level, open country; (*política*) campaign; period of active service.
campear [kam·pe·ár] *v.* to pasture; (*enverdecer*) to grow green (*said of the fields*); to excel; (*destacarse*) to be prominent, stand out; to be in the field; *Ríopl.* to search the plains for lost cattle; *Col., Ven.* (*hacer el guapo*) to act the bully.
campechano [kam·pe·čá·no] *adj.* frank, open.
campéon [kam·pe·ón] *m.* champion; defender.
campeonato [kam·pe·o·ná·to] *m.* championship.
campero [kam·pé·ro] *adj.* out in the open; related to the country; *m.* (*auto*) camper.
campesino [kam·pe·sí·no] *adj.* rural, rustic; *m.* peasant, countryman; farmer.
campestre [kam·pés·tre] *adj.* rural, rustic.
campiña [kam·pí·ña] *f.* large field; open country.
campo [kám·po] *m.* country; field; camp; **a — raso** in the open; **a — traviesa** (*or* **travieso**) cross-country.
camposanto [kam·po·sán·to] *m.* churchyard, cemetery.
camuesa [ka·mwé·sa] *f.* pippin (*a variety of apple*).
camuflaje [ka·mu·flá·xe] *m.* camouflage.
can [kan] *m.* dog; (*de arma*) trigger (*of a gun*).
cana [ká·na] *f.* white hair, grey hair; *Carib.* a kind of palm; **echar una — al aire** to go out for a good time; to go out on a fling.
canadiense [ka·na·đjén·se] *adj., m. & f.* Canadian.
canal [ka·nál] *m.* canal, channel; (*telecomunicaciones*) channel; *f.* eaves trough.
canalla [ka·ná·ya] *f.* rabble, mob; *m.* mean fellow.
canana [ka·ná·na] *f.* cartridge belt; **-s** *Col., Ven.* (*esposas*) handcuffs.
canapé [ka·na·pé] *m.* couch, lounge, sofa; settee.
canario [ka·ná·rjo] *m.* canary; native of the Canary Islands; *interj.* gosh!
canasta [ka·nás·ta] *f.* basket; crate.
cancelación [kan·se·la·sjón] *f.* cancellation.
cancelar [kan·se·lár] *v.* to cancel.
canciller [kan·si·yér] *m.* chancellor.
canción [kan·sjón] *f.* song; a kind of lyric poem;

volver a la misma — to repeat, harp on the same thing.
cancha [kán·ča] *f.* court (*for tennis, etc.*); sports ground or field; cockpit, enclosure for cockfights; *Peru* roasted corn or beans; *Am.* **¡abran — !** gangway!; make room!; **¡cancha!** down in front!
candado [kan·dá·do] *m.* padlock; *Col.* goatee.
candela [kan·dé·la] *f. Carib.* fire, forest fire; light.
candelabro [kan·de·lá·bro] *m.* candelabrum.
candelero [kan·de·lé·ro] *m.* candlestick.
candente [kan·dén·te] *adj.* incandescent, white-hot, red-hot.
candidato [kan·di·dá·to] *m.* candidate.
candidatura [kan·di·da·tú·ra] *f.* candidacy.
candidez [kan·di·dés] *f.* candor, simplicity.
cándido [kán·di·do] *adj.* candid, simple, innocent; white.
candil [kan·díl] *m.* lamp; *Ríopl., Mex.* chandelier; **candileja** [kan·di·lé·xa] *f.* small oil lamp; oil receptacle (*of a lamp*); **-s** footlights (*of a stage*).
candor [kan·dór] *m.* candor, simplicity, innocence; frankness, sincerity.
canela [ka·né·la] *f.* cinnamon; (*cosa*) an exquisite thing.
caney [ka·néj] *m. Caribe* hut; crude structure (*often without walls*).
cangrejo [kan·gré·xo] *m.* crab.
canguro [kan·gú·ro] *m.* kangaroo.
caníbal [ka·ní·bal] *m.* cannibal.
canica [ka·ní·ka] *f.* (game) marble (*small glass or marble ball*).
canilla [ka·ní·ya] *f.* long bone (*of the arm or leg*); cock (*of a barrel*), faucet; (*carrete*) spool (*for a sewing machine*); *C.A.* slender leg; *Ch., Col., Ríopl.* calf (*of the leg*); *Mex., Ven.* **tener —** to have physical strength; **canillita** [ka·ni·yí·ta] *m. Ríopl., Ch., C.A., Andes* newspaper boy.
canino [ka·ní·no] *adj.* canine; **tener un hambre canina** to be ravenous; to be hungry as a dog.
canje [káŋ·xe] *m.* interchange, exchange.
canjear [kaŋ·xe·ár] *v.* to exchange, interchange.
cano [ká·no] *adj.* grey-headed, grey-haired.
canoa [ka·nó·a] *f.* canoe.
canon [ká·non] *m.* canon; precept, rule, principle.
canónigo [ka·nó·ni·go] *m.* canon (*churchman*).
canonizar[9] [ka·no·ni·sár] *v.* to canonize, saint.
canoso [ka·nó·so] *adj.* grey, grey-haired.
cansado [kan·sá·do] *adj.* tired; tiresome, boring.
cansancio [kan·sán·sjo] *m.* fatigue, weariness.
cansar [kan·sár] *v.* to tire, fatigue; **-se** to get tired.
cantar [kan·tár] *v.* to sing; (*confesar*) to squeal, confess; *Am.* **— alto** to ask a high price; **— claro** (*or* **-las claras**) to speak with brutal frankness; *m.* song, epic poem.
cántaro [kán·ta·ro] *m.* pitcher, jug.
cantatriz [kan·ta·trís] *f.* singer.
cantera [kan·té·ra] *f.* quarry; *Ríopl., Mex., Carib.* stone block.
cántico [kán·ti·ko] *m.* canticle, religious song.
cantidad [kan·ti·dád] *f.* quantity.
cantilena [kan·ti·lé·na] *f.* song, ballad; monotonous repetition.
cantimplora [kan·tim·pló·ra] *f.* canteen; metal vessel for cooling water; *Col.* flask for carrying gunpowder.
cantina [kan·tí·na] *f.* mess hall; wine cellar; wine shop; canteen; *Carib., Mex., Ríopl.* barroom, tavern; *Col.* saddlebag.
cantinela [kan·ti·né·la] = **cantilena.**
cantinero [kan·ti·né·ro] *m.* bartender; tavern keeper.
canto [kán·to] *m.* song; singing; canto (*division of a long poem*); (*piedra*) stone; edge; *Col.* lap; *P.R.* piece.
cantón [kan·tón] *m.* canton, region; corner; *Mex.* cotton cloth.
cantor [kan·tór] *m.* singer; song bird.
canturrear [kan·tu·rre·ár], **canturriar** [kan·tu·rrjár] *v.* to hum, sing softly.
canturreo [kan·tu·rré·o] *m.* hum, humming.
caña [ká·ña] *f.* cane, reed; tall, thin glass; stem; *Ríopl., Col., Ven.* sugar-cane brandy; *Col.* a kind of dance; *Am.* bluff, boast.
cañada [ka·ñá·da] *f.* narrow canyon, dale, dell, gully, ravine; *Carib.* brook.
cáñamo [ká·ña·mo] *m.* hemp; hemp cloth; *Am.* hemp cord, rope; **cañamazo** [ka·ña·má·so] *m.* (*lona*) canvas.
cañaveral [ka·ña·be·rál] *m.* cane field; reed patch; sugar-cane plantation.
cañería [ka·ñe·rí·a] *f.* conduit, pipe line; tubing, piping; gas or water main.
caño [ká·ño] *m.* pipe, tube; spout; sewer; narrow channel; *Ven.* branch of a river, stream.
cañón [ka·ñón] *m.* (*arma*) cannon, gun; barrel (*of a gun*); (*topográfico*) ravine, gorge, canyon; (*tubo*) pipe, tube; (*figurado*) beard stubble; pinfeather; quill (*of a feather*); chimney shaft; **cañonazo** [ka·ño·ná·so] *m.* cannon shot.
cañonear [ka·ño·ne·ár] *v.* to cannonade, bombard.
cañoneo [ka·ño·né·o] *m.* cannonade; bombardment.
cañonero [ka·ño·né·ro] *m.* gunboat; gunner; **lancha cañonera** gunboat.
caoba [ka·ó·ba] *f.* mahogany.
caos [ká·os] *m.* chaos, confusion.
capa [ká·pa] *f.* (*ropa*) cape, cloak; (*cubierta*) covering, coating; layer; scum; **so — de** under the guise of, under pretense of.
capacidad [ka·pa·si·dád] *f.* capacity; ability.
capacitador [ka·pa·si·ta·dór] *m.* capacitor (condenser).
capacitar [ka·pa·si·tár] *v.* to enable, prepare, fit, qualify; *Col.* to empower, authorize.
capataz [ka·pa·tás] *m.* boss, foreman, overseer.
capaz [ka·pás] *adj.* capable, able, competent; (*extenso*) spacious, roomy.
capellán [ka·pe·yán] *m.* chaplain, priest, clergyman.
caperuza [ka·pe·rú·sa] *f.* pointed hood.
capicúa [ka·pi·kú·a] *f.* a number which reads the same from right to left as from left to right.
capilla [ka·pí·ya] *f.* chapel; hood.
capirote [ka·pi·ró·te] *m.* hood; **tonto de —** dunce, plain fool.
capital [ka·pi·tál] *m.* capital, funds; *f.* capital, capital city; *adj.* capital; **capitalismo** [ka·pi·ta·líz·mo] *m.* capitalism; **capitalista** [ka·pi·ta·lís·ta] *m. & f.* capitalist; *adj.* capitalistic.
capitalino [ka·pi·ta·lí·no] *adj.* relative to the capital city; *m.* a resident of the capital.
capitalizar[9] [ka·pi·ta·li·sár] *v.* to capitalize.
capitán [ka·pi·tán] *m.* captain.
capitanear [ka·pi·ta·ne·ár] *v.* to command, lead.
capitolio [ka·pi·tó·ljo] *m.* capitol.
capitular [ka·pi·tu·lár] *v.* to surrender; to come to an agreement.
capítulo [ka·pí·tu·lo] *m.* chapter.
capó [ka·pó] *m.* hood (of a car).
caporal [ka·po·rál] *m.* boss, leader; *Am.* foreman in a cattle ranch.
capote [ka·pó·te] *m.* cloak (*with sleeves*); bullfighter's cloak; *Ch.* thrashing, beating; **decir para su —** to say to oneself; *Mex.* **de —** in an underhanded way; *Ven., Carib.* **dar —** to get ahead; to deceive.
capricho [ka·prí·čo] *m.* caprice, whim, notion.

caprichoso [ka·pri·čó·so] *adj.* capricious, whimsical; changeable, fickle.
caprichudo [ka·pri·čú·đo] *adj.* whimsical; (*terco*) stubborn, willful.
cápsula [káp·su·la] *f.* capsule; percussion cap, cartridge shell; metal cap (*on bottles*).
captar [kap·tár] *v.* to win, attract; to captivate; *Am.* to tune in.
captura [kap·tú·ra] *f.* capture.
capturar [kap·tu·rár] *v.* to capture, arrest.
capucha [ka·pú·ča] *f.* hood.
capullo [ka·pú·yo] *m.* cocoon; bud; acorn cup.
cara [ká·ra] *f.* face; (*gesto*) expression, countenance; front; **de** — opposite; **de dos -s** two-sided; **echar** (*or* **dar**) **en** — to reproach, blame; **sacar la** — **por alguien** to take someone's part, defend him.
carabina [ka·ra·ƀí·na] *f.* carbine, rifle.
caracol [ka·ra·kól] *m.* snail; (*escalera*) winding stairs; *Mex.* embroidered blouse; *Am.* curl; **¡caracoles!** gosh!
caracolear [ka·ra·ko·le·ár] *v.* to caper, prance around (*said of horses*); *Col., Ven.* to muddle, entangle; *Col.* to sidestep an obligation.
caracoleo [ka·ra·ko·lé·o] *m.* prancing around; (*vuelta*) winding, turn.
carácter [ka·rák·ter] *m.* character; temper; **de** — **alfanumérico** (*computadora*) alphanumeric character.
característico [ka·rak·te·rís·ti·ko] *adj.* characteristic; **característica** [ka·rak·te·rís·ti·ka] *f.* characteristic, trait.
caracterizar[9] [ka·rak·te·ri·sár] *v.* to characterize.
¡caramba! [ka·rám·ba] *interj.* great guns! my goodness!
carámbano [ka·rám·ba·no] *m.* icicle.
caramelo [ka·ra·mé·lo] *m.* caramel; piece of candy.
caramillo [ka·ra·mí·yo] *m.* reed pipe, small flute; **armar un** — to raise a rumpus, create a disturbance.
carancho [ka·rán·čo] *m. Ríopl.* buzzard.
carátula [ka·rá·tu·la] *f.* mask; *Col., Ven., Ríopl., Carib., Andes* title page of a book; *C.A., Mex., Andes* dial, face of a watch.
caravana [ka·ra·ƀá·na] *f.* caravan.
caray [ka·ráj] *m.* tortoise shell; *interj.* gosh!
carbólico [kar·ƀó·li·ko] *adj.* carbolic.
carbón [kar·ƀón] *m.* carbon; coal; — **de leña** charcoal; **carbono** [kar·ƀó·no] *m.* carbon.
carbonera [kar·ƀo·né·ra] *f.* coal bin; coal cellar; woman coal or charcoal vendor; *Am.* coal mine; **carbonero** [kar·ƀo·né·ro] *m.* coal dealer; charcoal vendor; *adj.* coal, relating to coal or charcoal.
carburador [kar·ƀu·ra·đór] *m.* carburetor.
carburo de boro [kar·ƀú·ro·đe·ƀó·ro] *m.* boron carbide; — **de silicio** silicon carbide.
carcajada [kar·ka·xá·đa] *f.* loud laughter, peal of laughter.
cárcel [kár·sel] *f.* jail, prison.
carcelero [kar·se·lé·ro] *m.* jailer; *adj.* relating to a jail.
carcomido [kar·ko·mí·đo] *adj.* worm-eaten; decayed.
cardán [kar·đán] *m.* universal joint.
cardar [kar·đár] *v.* to card, comb (*wool*).
cardenal [kar·đe·nál] *m.* cardinal; cardinal bird; bruise.
cárdeno [kár·đe·no] *adj.* dark-purple.
cardíaco [kar·đí·a·ko] *adj.* cardiac; *m, f.* cardiac.
cardiólogo [kar·đjó·lo·ǥo] *m.* cardiologist.
cardo [kár·đo] *m.* thistle; a kind of cactus.
carear [ka·re·ár] *v.* to confront, bring face to face; to compare; **-se** to meet face to face.
carecer[13] [ka·re·sér] *v. irr.* to lack, be in need of.
carencia [ka·rén·sja] *f.* lack, want.
carente [ka·rén·te] *adj.* lacking.
carero [ka·ré·ro] *adj.* overcharging; profiteering; *m.* profiteer.
carestía [ka·res·tí·a] *f.* dearth, scarcity; high price.
careta [ka·ré·ta] *f.* mask.
carga [kár·ǥa] *f.* load, burden; freight; cargo; charge or gunpowder; **volver a la** — to insist again and again.
cargado [kar·ǥá·đo] *p.p. & adj.* loaded; (*fuerte*) strong (*as tea or coffee*); (*nublado*) cloudy, sultry; — **de espaldas** round-shouldered, stoop-shouldered.
cargador [kar·ǥa·đór] *m.* loader; stevedore; *Mex.* baggage handler.
cargamento [kar·ǥa·mén·to] *m.* cargo.
cargar[6] [kar·ǥár] *v.* (*poner carga*) to load; to charge; (*atacar*) to charge; (*molestar*) to bother, annoy; *Am.* to carry, lug; *Cuba* to punish; — **con** to carry away; to assume (*responsibility*); — **con el muerto** to get the blame (*unjustly*).
cargas [kár·ǥas] *f.* fillers.
cargo [kár·ǥo] *m.* charge, position, duty, burden; loading; accusation; **hacerse** — **de** to take charge of; to realize.
carguero [kar·ǥé·ro] *adj.* load-carrying; freight-carrying; *m. Col., Ríopl.* beast of burden; *Col., Ríopl.* skilled loader of pack animals; *Am.* patient, long suffering person.
cari [ká·ri] *m.* curry.
caribe [ka·rí·ƀe] *adj.* Caribbean; *m.* Carib, Caribbean Indian; (*salvaje*) cannibal; savage.
caricatura [ka·ri·ka·tú·ra] *f.* caricature; cartoon.
caricia [ka·rí·sja] *f.* caress.
caridad [ka·ri·đáđ] *f.* charity; alms.
caries [ká·rjes] *f.* decay (*of a bone*); tooth cavity.
cariño [ka·rí·ño] *m.* affection, love; *Am.* gift.
cariñoso [ka·ri·ñó·so] *adj.* affectionate, loving.
carioca [ka·rjó·ka] *adj. & m.f.* native of Rio de Janeiro.
caritativo [ka·ri·ta·tí·ƀo] *adj.* charitable.
cariz [ka·rís] *m.* aspect, appearance.
carmesí [kar·me·sí] *adj. & m.* crimson.
carmín [kar·mín] *m.* crimson.
carnal [kar·nál] *adj.* carnal, sensual; blood relative; *Mex.* buddy, pal.
carnaval [kar·na·ƀál] *m.* carnival.
carne [kár·ne] *f.* meat; flesh; — **de gallina** ''goose flesh'', ''goose pimples''; **echar -s** to put on weight, get fat; *Am.* — **de res** beef.
carneada [kar·ne·á·đa] *f. Ríopl.* butchering, slaughtering.
carnear [kar·ne·ár] *v. Ríopl.* to butcher; *Ríopl.* to kill.
carnero [kar·né·ro] *m.* (*animal*) ram, male sheep; (*carne*) mutton; *Am.* a weak-willed person; *Ch.* waste basket; *Am.* — **de la tierra** llama (*or any fleece-bearing animal*); *Am.* **cantar uno el** — to die.
carnet [kar·né] *m.* identification card; notebook.
carnicería [kar·ni·se·rí·a] *f.* (*tienda*) meat market; (*matanza*) butchery, slaughter; *C.A., Ec.* slaughterhouse.
carnicero [kar·ni·sé·ro] *m.* butcher; *adj.* carnivorous, flesh-eating; cruel.
carnívoro [kar·ní·ƀo·ro] *adj.* carnivorous.
carnosidad [kar·no·si·đáđ] *f.* fleshiness, fatness; abnormal growth (*on animal or plant tissues*).
carnoso [kar·nó·so] *adj.* fleshy; meaty; pulpy.
caro [ká·ro] *adj.* expensive; dear; *adv.* at a high

price.
carona [ka·ró·na] *f.* saddle pad.
carozo [ka·ró·so] *m.* cob, corncob; fruit pit, seed.
carpa [kár·pa] *f.* carp (*fresh-water fish*); *Mex.* canvas tent, circus tent; — **dorada** goldfish.
carpeta [kar·pé·ta] *f.* (*cubierta*) table cover; desk pad; (*cartera*) portfolio, letter case or file; *Andes* office desk; *Carib.* bookkeeping department; **carpetazo** [kar·pe·tá·so]: **dar** — to table (*a motion*); to set aside, pigeonhole or dismiss.
carpintería [kar·pin·te·rí·a] *f.* carpentry; carpenter's workshop.
carpintero [kar·pin·té·ro] *m.* carpenter; **pájaro** — woodpecker.
carraspear [ka·rras·pe·ár] *v.* to cough up; to clear one's throat; to be hoarse.
carraspera [ka·rras·pé·ra] *f.* hoarseness.
carrera [ka·rré·ra] *f.* career; race, run; course; (*de media*) stocking run.
carreta [ka·rré·ta] *f.* long narrow wagon; cart; *Col., Ven.* wheelbarrow.
carretaje [ka·rre·tá·xe] *m.* cartage (*transporting by cart, truck, etc.*); price paid for cartage.
carrete [ka·rré·te] *m.* spool; reel — **distribuidor** feeding reel; — **receptor** take-up reel (*tape recorder*).
carretel [ka·rre·tél] *m.* reel, spool, bobbin; fishing reel; log reel (*of a boat*).
carretera [ka·rre·té·ra] *f.* highway.
carretero [ka·rre·té·ro] *m.* carter, teamster; cart maker; **camino** — highway.
carretilla [ka·rre·tí·ya] *f.* wheelbarrow; small cart; baggage truck; *Ríopl.* wagon; *Ch.* jaw; *Col.* string, series; *Am.* firecracker; **repetir de** — to rattle off, repeat mechanically.
carretón [ka·rre·tón] *m.* truck; wagon, cart.
carril [ka·rríl] *m.* highway lane; — **prensatelas** work holder; rut; furrow.
carrillo [ka·rrí·yo] *m.* (*de la cara*) cheek; (*mecánico*) pulley; cart.
carrizo [ka·rrí·so] *m.* reed; reed grass.
carro [ká·rro] *m.* cart; cartload; *Am.* car, auto, streetcar, coach; *Am.* **pararle a uno el** — to restrain someone; *Am.* **pasarle a uno el** — to suffer an injury or misfortune; **carroza** [ka·rró·sa] *f.* large and luxurious carriage; chariot; *Am.* hearse; **carrito-guía** track torch; — **portaherramientas** apron (machine).
carrocería [ka·rro·se·rí·a] *f.* chassis; frame for a parade float.
carroña [ka·rró·ña] *f.* dead and decaying flesh; putrid, decaying carcass.
carruaje [ka·rrwá·xe] *m.* carriage, vehicle.
carta [kár·ta] *f.* (*misiva*) letter; (*naipe*) card; (*documento*) charter; map; — **blanca** full authority, freedom to act; — **de naturaleza** naturalization papers; — **de venta** bill of sale; *Ch.* **retirar** — to repent, back down; *Am.* **ser la última** — **de la baraja** to be the worst or most insignificant person or thing.
cartearse [kar·te·ár·se] *v.* to correspond, write to each other.
cartel [kar·tél] *m.* poster, handbill; cartel, written agreement; **cartela** [kar·té·la] *f.* tag, slip of paper, small card, piece of cardboard; **cartelera** [kar·te·lé·ra] *f.* billboard; **cartelón** [kar·te·lón] *m.* large poster.
cartera [kar·té·ra] *f.* (*objeto*) wallet; briefcase; desk pad; (*puesto*) portfolio, cabinet post; **carterista** [kar·te·rís·ta] *m. & f.* pickpocket.
cartero [kar·té·ro] *m.* mailman, letter carrier, postman.
cartilla [kar·tí·ya] *f.* primer; note, short letter; **leerle a uno la** — to scold, lecture someone concerning his duties.
cartografiar[17] [kar·to·ǵra·fjár] *v.* to chart; to make charts.
cartón [kar·tón] *m.* cardboard; pasteboard; **cartulina** [kar·tu·lí·na] *f.* fine cardboard.
cartuchera [kar·tu·čé·ra] *f.* cartridge belt.
cartucho [kar·tú·čo] *m.* cartridge; roll of coins; paper cone or bag.
casa [ká·sa] *f.* (*doméstica*) house, home; household; (*negocio*) business firm; square (*of a chessboard*); *Col.* bet, wager; — **de empeños** pawnshop; — **de huéspedes** boardinghouse; **echar la** — **por la ventana** to spend recklessly, squander everything; **poner** — to set up housekeeping; — **rodante** mobile home.
casabe [ka·sá·ƀe], **cazabe** *m. Am.* cassava; *Am.* cassava bread.
casaca [ka·sá·ka] *f.* long military coat; **volver** — to be a turncoat, change sides or parties.
casamiento [ka·sa·mjén·to] *m.* wedding; marriage.
casar [ka·sár] *v.* to marry; to match; *Ven.* to graft (*trees*); **-se** to get married.
cascabel [kas·ka·ƀél] *m.* jingle bell, tinkle bell; snake's rattle; *Am.* rattlesnake; **cascabela** [kas·ka·ƀé·la] *f. C.R.* rattlesnake.
cascada [kas·ká·đa] *f.* cascade, waterfall.
cascajo [kas·ká·xo] *m.* coarse gravel; crushed stone; pebble; fragment; (*basura*) rubbish.
cascanueces [kas·ka·nwé·ses] *m.* nutcracker.
cascar[6] [kas·kár] *v.* to crack, break; **-se** to crack or break open.
cáscara [kás·ka·ra] *f.* shell, husk, hull, rind; bark of a tree; *Ríopl.* **dar a uno** — **de novillo** to give someone a whipping; **cascarudo** [kas·ka·rú·đo] *adj.* having a thick husk; having a thick rind.
cascarrabias [kas·ka·rrá·ƀjas] *m. & f.* crab, grouch, ill-tempered person; *adj.* grouchy, cranky, irritable.
casco [kás·ko] *m.* (*yelmo*) helmet; (*uña*) hoof; (*calavera*) skull; broken piece of earthenware; cask; (*botella*) empty bottle; hull of a ship; *Mex., Ríopl.* compound, main buildings of a farm; **caliente de -s** hot-headed; **ligero de -s** light-headed, frivolous; **romperse los -s** to rack one's brain.
caserío [ka·se·rí·o] *m.* hamlet, small settlement.
casero [ka·sé·ro] *adj.* domestic; homemade; *m.* landlord; (*consierje*) janitor, caretaker; *Ch.* customer; *Col., Peru, Ven.* delivery boy; **casera** [ka·sé·ra] *f.* landlady; housekeeper.
caseta [ka·sé·ta] *f.* small house, cottage; booth, stall.
casi [ká·si] *adv.* almost.
casilla [ka·sí·ya] *f.* (*puesto*) stall, booth; (*apartado*) post office box; pigeonhole; **sacarle a uno de sus -s** to change someone's way of life or habits; to irritate, annoy, try someone's patience; **salirse de sus -s** to lose one's temper; to do something out of the way.
casino [ka·sí·no] *m.* club, society; clubhouse; recreation hall.
caso [ká·so] *m.* case; point; matter; event — **que** (*or* **en** — **de que**) in case that; **dado** — supposing; **hacer** — **de** to pay attention to; **hacer** — **omiso de** to omit; **no viene al** — that is not to the point.
casorio [ka·só·rjo] *m.* wedding, marriage.
caspa [kás·pa] *f.* dandruff.
casquillo [kas·kí·yo] *m.* tail stock (machine).
casta [kás·ta] *f.* race, breed; caste, distinct class; quality, kind.

castaña [kas·tá·ña] *f.* chestnut; jug; knot or roll of hair; *Mex.* small barrel; *Mex.* trunk, large suitcase.
castañetear [kas·ta·ñe·te·ár] *v.* to rattle the castanets; to chatter (*said of the teeth*); to crackle (*said of the knees or joints*); — **con los dedos** to snap one's fingers.
castañeteo [kas·ta·ñe·té·o] *m.* rattle or sound of castanets; chatter, chattering (*of the teeth*).
castaño [kas·tá·ño] *m.* chestnut (*tree and wood*); *adj.* chestnut-colored.
castañuela [kas·ta·ñwé·la] *f.* castanet.
castellano [kas·te·yá·no] *adj.* & *m.* Castilian, Spanish.
castidad [kas·ti·đáđ] *f.* chastity.
castigar[7] [kas·ti·ǥár] *v.* to chastise, punish.
castigo [kas·tí·ǥo] *m.* punishment; correction.
castillo [kas·tí·yo] *m.* castle.
castizo [kas·tí·so] *adj.* pure, correct (*language*); pure-blooded.
casto [kás·to] *adj.* chaste, pure.
castor [kas·tór] *m.* beaver; beaver cloth.
casual [ka·swál] *adj.* casual, accidental.
casualidad [ka·swa·li·đáđ] *f.* chance, accident.
casuca [ka·sú·ka] *f.* little house; hut, shanty.
casucha [ka·sú·ča] *f.* hut, hovel, shack.
catadura [ka·ta·đú·ra] *f.* aspect, appearance.
catalán [ka·ta·lán] *adj.* Catalan, Catalonian, of or from Catalonia, Spain; *m.* Catalan.
catalejo [ka·ta·lé·xo] *m.* telescope.
catalizador [ka·ta·li·sa·đór] *m.* catalyst.
catalogar[7] [ka·ta·lo·ǥár] *v.* to catalogue.
catálogo [ka·tá·lo·ǥo] *m.* catalogue.
catar [ka·tár] *v.* to look at, examine; (*saber*) to taste, sample.
catarata [ka·ta·rá·ta] *f.* cataract; waterfall.
catarro [ka·tá·rro] *m.* catarrh, cold.
catástrofe [ka·tás·tro·fe] *f.* catastrophe, mishap.
catear [ka·te·ár] *v.* to explore, look around; *Ch., C.A., Mex.* to search or raid (*a home*); *Am.* to explore for ore; *Col., Ríopl.* to test, try.
catecismo [ka·te·síz·mo] *m.* catechism.
cátedra [ká·te·đra] *f.* class; subject; chair, professorship.
catedral [ka·te·đrál] *f.* cathedral.
catedrático [ka·te·đrá·ti·ko] *m.* professor.
categoría [ka·te·ǥo·rí·a] *f.* category, rank; kind, class.
categórico [ka·te·ǥó·ri·ko] *adj.* categorical, positive.
catequizar[9] [ka·te·ki·sár] *v.* to catechize, give religious instruction (to); (*inducir*) to induce, persuade.
católico [ka·tó·li·ko] *adj.* Catholic; universal; *m.* Catholic; **catolicismo** [ka·to·li·síz·mo] *m.* Catholicism.
catorce [ka·tór·se] *num.* fourteen.
catre [ká·tre] *m.* cot, small bed; *Ríopl.* raft, float; *C.A.,* camp stool, folding stool; — **de tijera** folding cot.
catrín [ka·trín] *m. Am.* dandy; *adj. Mex., C.A.* over-elegant, dressy.
cauce [káw·se] *m.* river bed.
caución [kaw·sjón] *f.* precaution; security, guarantee; bail.
cauchero [kaw·čé·ro] *m. Am.* rubber gatherer; *Am.* rubber producer; *adj. Am.* rubber, pertaining to rubber.
caucho [káw·čo] *m.* rubber; — **sintético** synthetic rubber; *Am.* rubber tree; *Col.* rubber raincoat or cloak; **cauchal** [kaw·čál] *m.* rubber grove or plantation.
caudal [kaw·đál] *m.* (*monetario*) wealth; (*torrente*) river current; volume of water.
caudaloso [kaw·đa·ló·so] *adj.* wealthy; abundant.
caudillaje [kaw·đi·yá·xe] *m.* military leadership; *Am.* political bossism; *Am.* tyranny.
caudillo [kaw·đí·yo] *m.* leader, chief; *Am.* political boss.
causa [káw·sa] *f.* cause; (*pleito*) case, lawsuit; *Ch., Perú* light lunch, snack; **a causa de** on account of.
causar [kaw·sár] *v.* to cause.
cautela [kaw·té·la] *f.* caution; cunning, craftiness; trick, deception.
cauteloso [kaw·te·ló·so] *adj.* cautious; crafty.
cautivar [kaw·ti·ƀár] *v.* to capture; to charm, fascinate.
cautiverio [kaw·ti·ƀé·rjo] *m.* captivity.
cautivo [kaw·tí·ƀo] *m.* captive, war prisoner.
cauto [káw·to] *adj.* cautious.
cavar [ka·ƀár] *v.* to dig, spade; to excavate.
caverna [ka·ƀér·na] *f.* cavern, cave.
cavernoso [ka·ƀer·nó·so] *adj.* cavernous, like a cavern; hollow; **voz cavernosa** deep, hollow voice.
cavidad [ka·ƀi·đáđ] *f.* cavity.
cayado [ka·yá·đo] *m.* shepherd's crook, staff.
cayo [ká·yo] *m.* key, island reef.
caza [ká·sa] *f.* hunt, hunting; wild game; *m.* attack plane; **dar** — to pursue, track down.
cazador [ka·sa·đór] *adj.* hunting; *m.* hunter.
cazar[9] [ka·sár] *v.* to chase, hunt; to track down.
cazatorpedero [ka·sa·tor·pe·đé·ro] *m.* destroyer, torpedo-boat.
cazo [ká·so] *m.* dipper; (*cazuela*) pot, pan.
cazuela [ka·swé·la] *f.* stewing pan; earthenware cooking pan; — **para perdigar** braiser; — **plana** sheet pan; topmost theatre gallery; *Ven.* stewed hen; *P.R.* candied sweet potatoes with spices.
cebada [se·ƀá·đa] *f.* barley; *Ríopl.* brewing of **mate; cebadal** [se·ƀa·đál] *m.* barley field.
cebar [se·ƀár] *v.* to feed, fatten (*animals*); to encourage, nourish (*a passion*); to prime (*a gun, pump, etc.*); to bait (*a fishhook*); *Ríopl.* to brew and serve **mate** or tea; **-se** to vent one's fury.
cebo [sé·ƀo] *m.* feed (*for animals*); bait; incentive.
cebolla [se·ƀó·ya] *f.* onion.
cebollanas [se·ƀo·yá·nas] *f.* chives; *Mex.* **cebollines.**
cebollar [se·ƀo·yár] *m.* onion patch.
cecear [se·se·ár] *v.* to lisp.
ceceo [se·sé·o] *m.* lisp, lisping; pronunciation of both /s/ and /θ/ as [θ].
cecina [se·sí·na] *f.* dried beef, jerked beef.
cedazo [se·đá·so] *m.* sieve.
ceder [se·đér] *v.* to cede, transfer; to yield, surrender, submit; to diminish, abate.
cedilla [se·đí·ya] *f.* cedilla.
cedro [sé·đro] *m.* cedar.
cédula [sé·đu·la] *f.* slip of paper; certificate; — **de vecindad** (*or* — **personal**) official identification card.
céfiro [sé·fi·ro] *m.* zephyr, soft breeze; *Am.* fine muslin.
cegar[1, 7] [se·ǥár] *v. irr.* to blind; to become blind; to confuse; to fill up, stop up (*a hole*).
ceguedad [se·ǥe·đáđ], **ceguera** [se·ǥé·ra] *f.* blindness.
ceiba [séj·ƀa] *f. Am.* ceiba, silk-cotton tree.
ceja [sé·xa] *f.* eyebrow; brow of a hill.
cejar [se·xár] *v.* to go backward; to back; to back down, give in, yield; to slacken.
cejijunto [se·xi·xún·to] *adj.* frowning; with knitted eyebrows.
celada [se·lá·đa] *f.* ambush, snare, trap.
celador [se·la·đór] *m.* guard.
celaje [se·lá·xe] *m.* colored clouds; skylight; presage, portent; *P.R.* shadow, ghost; *Am.* **como un** — like

lightning.
celar [se·lár] *v.* to guard, watch; to watch over jealously; (*esconder*) to conceal.
celda [sél·da] *f.* cell.
celebración [se·le·ƀra·sjón] *f.* celebration.
celebrar [se·le·ƀrár] *v.* to celebrate; to praise, honor; to be glad.
célebre [sé·le·ƀre] *adj.* famous; funny, witty; *Col.* graceful, pretty (*woman*).
celebridad [se·le·ƀri·đáđ] *f.* fame, renown; celebrity, famous person; celebration.
celeridad [se·le·ri·đáđ] *f.* swiftness, speed.
celeste [se·lés·te] *adj.* celestial, heavenly.
celestial [se·les·tjál] *adj.* celestial, heavenly, divine.
célibe [sé·li·ƀe] *adj.* unmarried; *m. & f.* unmarried person.
celo [sé·lo] *m.* (*humano*) zeal, ardor; envy; (*animal*) heat (*sexual excitement in animals*); **-s** jealousy, suspicion; **tener -s** to be jealous.
celosía [se·lo·sí·a] *f.* window lattice; Venetian blind.
celoso [se·ló·so] *adj.* jealous; zealous, eager; suspicious.
célula [sé·lu·la] *f.* cell.
celuloide [se·lu·lój·đe] *m.* celluloid.
cellisca [se·yís·ka] *f.* sleet; rain and snow.
cementación [se·men·ta·sjón] *f.* case hardening.
cementar [se·men·tár] *v.* to cement.
cementerio [se·men·té·rjo] *m.* cemetery.
cemento [se·mén·to] *m.* cement; — **armado** reinforced concrete.
cena [sé·na] *f.* supper.
cenagal [se·na·ǥál] *m.* quagmire, muddy ground, swamp.
cenagoso [se·na·ǥó·so] *adj.* muddy, miry.
cenar [se·nár] *v.* to eat supper.
cencerrada [sen·se·rrá·đa] *f.* racket, noise (*with cowbells, tin cans, etc.*); tin pan serenade.
cencerrear [sen·se·rre·ár] *v.* to make a racket (*with cowbells, tin cans, etc.*); serenade with cowbells.
cencerro [sen·sé·rro] *m.* cowbell.
cendal [sen·dál] *m.* gauze; thin veil.
cenicero [se·ni·sé·ro] *m.* ash tray; ash pit; ash pan.
cenicienta [se·ni·sjén·ta] *f.* a Cinderella.
ceniciento [se·ni·sjén·to] *adj.* ashen, ash-colored.
cenit [sé·nit] *m.* zenith.
ceniza [se·ní·sa] *f.* ashes, cinders.
cenizo [se·ní·so] *adj.* ash-colored.
censo [sén·so] *m.* census.
censor [sen·sór] *m.* censor.
censura [sen·sú·ra] *f.* censure, criticism, disapproval; censorship.
censurador [sen·su·ra·đór] *m.* censor, critic; critical person; *adj.* critical.
censurar [sen·su·rár] *v.* to censure, criticize, reprove; to censor.
centavo [sen·tá·ƀo] *m.* cent.
centella [sen·té·ya] *f.* lightning, flash; spark.
centelleante [sen·te·ye·án·te] *adj.* sparkling, flashing.
centellear [sen·te·ye·ár] *v.* to twinkle; to sparkle, glitter; to flash.
centelleo [sen·te·yé·o] *m.* glitter, sparkle.
centenar [sen·te·nár] *m.* one hundred; (*campo*) field of rye.
centenario [sen·te·ná·rjo] *m.* centennial, one hundredth anniversary; *adj.* centennial; old, ancient.
centeno [sen·té·no] *m.* rye.
centésimo [sen·té·si·mo] *adj. & m.* hundredth.
centímetro [sen·tí·me·tro] *m.* centimeter.
céntimo [sén·ti·mo] *m. Sp.* one hundredth part of a **peseta.**
centinela [sen·ti·né·la] *m.* sentry, sentinel.
central [sen·trál] *adj.* central; *f.* main office; headquarters; *Carib.* main sugar mill or refinery.
centrar [sen·trár] *v.* to center.
céntrico [sén·tri·ko] *adj.* central.
centrífugo [sen·trí·fu·ǥo] *adj.* centrifugal.
centrípeto [sen·trí·pe·to] *adj.* centripetal.
centro [sén·tro] *m.* center, middle.
ceñidor [se·ñi·đór] *m.* girdle, belt, sash.
ceñir[5, 19] [se·ñír] *v. irr.* (*rodear*) to gird, girdle; to tighten; to encircle; (*abreviar*) to diminish; to limit; **-se a** to limit oneself to.
ceño [sé·ño] *m.* frown; scowl; **fruncir el** — to frown; to scowl.
cepa [sé·pa] *f.* stump, stub (*of a tree or plant*); vinestock; (*ascendencia*) origin, stock (*of a family*); *Am.* mass of plants growing from a common root; *Am.* excavation (*for a building*), hole, pit (*for planting trees*); **de buena** — of good stock.
cepillo [se·pí·yo] *m.* brush; (*limosna*) alms box; carpenter's plane; *Am.* flatterer; — **de dientes** toothbrush.
cepo [sé·po] *m.* branch, stock.
cera [sé·ra] *f.* wax.
cerámica [se·rá·mi·ka] *f.* ceramics, pottery.
cerca [sér·ka] *adv.* near, near by; — **de** *prep.* near, nearly; *f.* fence, low wall.
cercado [ser·ká·đo] *m.* enclosure; fenced-in garden; fence; *Am.* Peruvian political division; *p.p. of* **cercar.**
cercanía [ser·ka·ní·a] *f.* proximity; **-s** surroundings, vicinity.
cercano [ser·ká·no] *adj.* near; neighboring.
cercar[6] [ser·kár] *v.* to fence, enclose; to surround; (*sitiar*) to besiege.
cercenar [ser·se·nár] *v.* to clip off; to curtail, diminish, reduce.
cerciorar [ser·sjo·rár] *v.* to assure, affirm; **-se** to ascertain, find out.
cerco [sér·ko] *m.* fence enclosure; siege; circle; *Ch.* small farm or orchard.
cerda [sér·đa] *f.* bristle; *Col.* **ir en -s** to go halves or share in a deal.
cerdo [sér·đo] *m.* hog; pig; pork.
cerdoso [ser·đó·so] *adj.* bristly.
cereal [se·re·ál] *m.* cereal, grain.
cerebro [se·ré·ƀro] *m.* brain.
ceremonia [se·re·mó·nja] *f.* ceremony.
ceremonial [se·re·mo·njál] *adj. & m.* ceremonial.
ceremonioso [se·re·mo·njó·so] *adj.* ceremonious.
cereza [se·ré·sa] *f.* cherry; **cerezo** [se·ré·so] *m.* cherry tree; cherry wood.
cerilla [se·rí·ya] *f.* wax taper; *Sp.* wax match; earwax.
cerillo [se·rí·yo] *m. Mex., C.A., Ven., Andes* match.
cerner[1] [ser·nér] *v. irr.* to sift; to drizzle; *Am.* to strain through a sieve; **-se** to hover (*as a bird or plane*).
cero [sé·ro] *m.* zero; nothing.
cerquita [ser·kí·ta] *adv.* quite near, nice and near.
cerrado [se·rrá·đo] *adj.* closed; (*nublado*) cloudy; (*espeso*) thick (*beard*); reserved (*person*); dull; *Am.* stubborn.
cerradura [se·rrá·đú·ra] *f.* locking, closing; lock; — **de golpe** spring lock.
cerrajería [se·rra·xe·rí·a] *f.* locksmith's shop; locksmith's trade.
cerrajero [se·rra·xé·ro] *m.* locksmith.
cerrar[1] [se·rrár] *v. irr.* to close, shut, lock; **-se** to close; **-se el cielo** to become overcast or cloudy.
cerrazón [se·rra·són] *f.* cloudiness, darkness.
cerro [sé·rro] *m.* hill.

cerrojo [se·rró·xo] *m.* latch, bolt.
certamen [ser·tá·men] *m.* contest, literary contest; debate; competition.
certero [ser·té·ro] *adj.* accurate, exact; well-aimed; **tirador** — good shot.
certeza [ser·té·sa] *f.* certainty.
certidumbre [ser·ti·đúm·bre] *f.* certainty.
certificado [ser·ti·fi·ká·đo] *adj.* certified, registered; *m.* certificate.
certificar[6] [ser·ti·fi·kár] *v.* to certify; to register (*a letter*).
cervato [ser·ƀá·to] *m.* fawn, young deer.
cerveza [ser·ƀé·sa] *f.* beer; **cervecería** [ser·ƀe·se·rí·a] *f.* beer tavern; brewery.
cervis [ser·ƀís] *f.* cervix.
cesante [se·sán·te] *adj.* unemployed.
cesar [se·sár] *v.* to cease, stop; to quit.
cesáreo [se·sá·re·o] *adj.* & *m.* Caesarean.
cesio [sé·sjo] *m.* cesium.
cesionario [se·sjo·ná·rjo] *m.* grantee, assignee; **cesionista** [se·sjo·nís·ta] *m., f.* grantor.
cesta [sés·ta] *f.* basket; for playing jai alai (*Basque ball game*).
cesto [sés·to] *m.* large basket, hamper.
cetrino [se·trí·no] *adj.* greenish-yellow, lemon-colored; citronlike; melancholy, gloomy.
cetro [sé·tro] *m.* scepter, staff.
cibernética [si·ƀer·né·ti·ka] *f.* cybernetics, computer science.
cicatero [si·ka·té·ro] *adj.* miserly, stingy.
cicatriz [si·ka·trís] *f.* scar.
cicatrizar[9] [si·ka·tri·sár] *v.* to heal, close (*a wound*).
ciclo [sí·klo] *m.* cycle; period of time; school term.
ciclón [si·klón] *m.* cyclone.
ciclotrón [si·klo·trón] *m.* cyclotron.
ciego [sjé·ǥo] *adj.* blind; **a ciegas** blindly; *m.* blindman.
cielo [sjé·lo] *m.* sky; heaven; — **de la boca** palate; **poner en el** — to praise, extol; **poner el grito en el** — to "hit the ceiling", **cielito** *m. Ríopl.* gaucho group dance and tune.
ciempiés [sjem·pjés], **cientopiés** [sjen·to·pjés] *m.* centipede.
cien(to) [sjén·to] *num.* hundred.
ciénaga [sjé·na·ǥa] *f.* swamp, bog, quagmire, marsh.
ciencia [sjén·sja] *f.* science; learning; skill; **a** (*or* **de**) — **cierta** with certainty.
cieno [sjé·no] *m.* mud, mire.
científico [sjen·tí·fi·ko] *adj.* scientific; *m.* scientist.
cierre [sjé·rre] *m.* clasp, fastener; zipper; closing, fastening, locking; method of closing.
cierto [sjér·to] *adj.* certain, true, sure; **por** — certainly; *Col., C.A.* **ciertas hierbas** so-and-so (*person not named*).
ciervo [sjér·ƀo] *m.* deer; **cierva** [sjér·ƀa] *f.* doe, hind, female deer.
cierzo [sjér·so] *m.* north wind.
cifra [sí·fra] *f.* cipher, number; figure; (*resumen*) abridgment, summary; (*código*) code; monogram; (*emblema*) emblem.
cifrar [si·frár] *v.* to write in code; to summarize; — **la esperanza en** to place one's hop in.
cigarra [si·ǥá·rra] *f.* cicada, locust.
cigarrera [si·ǥa·rré·ra] *f.* cigar or cigarette case; woman cigar maker or vendor.
cigarrillo [si·ǥa·rrí·yo] *m. Sp.* cigarette.
cigarro [si·ǥá·rro] *m.* cigarrette.
cigüeña [si·ǥwé·ña] *f.* stork; (*mecánico*) crank, handle (*for turning*).
cigüeñal [si·ǥwe·ñál] *m.* crankshaft.
cilantro [si·lán·tro] *m.* coriander, also **culantro.**
cilíndrico [si·lín·dri·ko] *adj.* cylindrical.
cilindro [si·lín·dro] *m.* cylinder; *Mex.* hand organ.
cima [sí·ma] *f.* peak, summit, top; **dar** — to complete, carry out.
cimarrón [si·ma·rrón] *adj. Ríopl., Mex., Carib., Ven., Andes* wild, untamed; *Ríopl.* **mate** — black, bitter **mate.**
cimarronear [si·ma·rro·ne·ár] *v. Ríopl.* to drink **mate** without sugar.
cimbrar [sim·brár], **cimbrear** [sim·bre·ár] *v.* to brandish, flourish, swing; to shake; to bend; *Am.* to swing around, change suddenly one's direction, — **a uno de un golpe** to knock a person down with a blow; **-se** to swing, sway; to vibrate, shake.
cimiento [si·mjén·to] *m.* foundation, base; source, root; **abrir los -s** to break ground for a building.
cinc [siŋk] *m.* zinc.
cincel [sin·sél] *m.* chisel.
cincelar [sin·se·lár] *v.* to chisel; to engrave.
cinco [síŋ·ko] *num.* five.
cincuenta [siŋ·kwén·ta] *num.* fifty.
cincha [sín·ča] *f.* cinch, girth; *Mex., C.A.* blows with the flat of a sword; *Col., Ríopl.* **a revienta -s** unwillingly; hurriedly; at breakneck speed.
cinchar [sin·čár] *v.* to cinch, tighten the saddle girth; *Mex., C.A.* to hit with the flat of a sword.
cine [sí·ne], **cinema** [si·né·ma] *m.* cinema, motion picture, movie; **cinematógrafo** [si·ne·ma·tó·ǥra·fo] *m.* motion picture.
cinematografía [si·ne·ma·to·ǥra·fí·a] *f.* cinematography, the science of motion picture photography.
cíngulo [síŋ·gu·lo] *m.* girdle, cord, belt.
cínico [sí·ni·ko] *adj.* cynical, sarcastic, sneering; *m.* cynic.
cinta [sín·ta] *f.* ribbon, band; tape; strip; (*película*) movie film; (*red*) coarse fishing net; — **magnetofónica** recording tape; *Ríopl.* tin can.
cintarada [sin·ta·rá·đa] *f.* beating, flogging; **cintarazo** *m.* blow with the flat of a sword.
cintilar [sin·ti·lár] *v.* to sparkle, twinkle; to glimmer.
cinto [sín·to] *m.* belt; girdle.
cintura [sin·tú·ra] *f.* waist; **meter en** — to subdue, subject.
cinturón [sin·tu·rón] *m.* belt; — **de seguridad** safety belt.
ciprés [si·prés] *m.* cypress.
circo [sír·ko] *m.* circus.
circonio [sir·kó·njo] *m.* zirconium.
circuitería física [sir·kwi·te·rí·a fí·si·ka] *f.* (*computadora*) hardware.
circuito [sir·kwí·to] *m.* circuit.
circulación [sir·ku·la·sjón] *f.* circulation; traffic.
circular [sir·ku·lár] *v.* to circulate; to circle; *adj.* circular; *f.* circular letter, notice.
círculo [sír·ku·lo] *m.* circle; group; club; clubhouse.
circundante [sir·kun·dán·te] *adj.* surrounding.
circundar [sir·kun·dár] *v.* to surround.
circunferencia [sir·kun·fe·rén·sja] *f.* circumference.
circunlocución [sir·kun·lo·ku·sjón] *f.* circumlocution, roundabout expression.
circunspección [sir·kun·spek·sjón] *f.* circumspection, decorum, prudence, restraint.
circunspecto [sir·kuns·pék·to] *adj.* circumspect, prudent.
circunstancia [sir·kuns·tán·sja] *f.* circumstance.
circunstante [sir·kuns·tán·te] *adj.* surrounding; present; **-s** *m. pl.* bystanders, onlookers, audience.
circunvecino [sir·kum·be·sí·no] *adj.* neighboring, surrounding.
cirio [sí·rjo] *m.* wax candle; saguaro cactus.

ciruela [si·rwé·la] *f.* plum; prune; — **pasa** prune, dried prune; **ciruelo** *m.* plum tree.
cirugía [si·ru·xí·a] *f.* surgery.
cirujano [si·ru·xá·no] *m.* surgeon.
cisne [síz·ne] *m.* swan; *Ríopl., Ch.* powder puff.
cisterna [sis·tér·na] *f.* cistern.
cita [sí·ta] *f.* date, appointment; (*citación*) citation, summons; quotation.
citación [si·ta·sjón] *f.* (*de texto*) quotation; citation, summons.
citar [si·tár] *v.* (*convocar*) to make a date or appointment with; (*referir*) to cite, quote; (*incitar*) incite, provoke; to summon.
cítrico [sí·tri·ko] *adj.* citric.
ciudad [sju·đáđ] *f.* city.
ciudadano [sju·đa·đá·no] *m.* citizen; resident of a city; *adj.* of or pertaining to a city; **ciudadanía** [sju·đa·đa·ní·a] *f.* citizenship.
ciudadela [sju·đa·đé·la] *f.* citadel.
cívico [sí·ƀi·ko] *adj.* civic.
civil [si·ƀíl] *adj.* civil; polite, courteous.
civilidad [si·ƀi·li·đáđ] *f.* civility, courtesy.
civilización [si·ƀi·li·sa·sjón] *f.* civilization.
civilizador [si·ƀi·li·sa·đór] *adj.* civilizing; *m.* civilizer.
civilizar[9] [si·ƀi·li·sár] *v.* to civilize.
cizaña [si·sá·ña] *f.* weed; (*vicio*) vice; discord; **sembrar** — to sow discord.
clamar [kla·már] *v.* to clamor, shout; (*gimotear*) to whine.
clamor [kla·mór] *m.* clamor, shout; whine; knell.
clamoreo [kla·mo·ré·o] *m.* clamoring; shouting.
clamorear [kla·mo·re·ár] *v.* to clamor, shout; to toll, knell.
clandestino [klan·des·tí·no] *adj.* clandestine, underhanded, secret.
clara [klá·ra] *f.* white of egg; bald spot; (*calvicie*) thin spot (*in a fabric*); **a las -s** clearly, openly, frankly.
claraboya [kla·ra·ƀó·ya] *f.* skylight.
clarear [kla·re·ár] *v.* (*poner claro*), to clarify, make clear; (*haber más luz*) to grow light, begin to dawn; to clear up; *Mex.* to pierce through and through; **-se** to become transparent; to reveal oneself.
claridad [kla·ri·đáđ] *f.* clarity, clearness; (*franqueza*) blunt remark, slam; fame.
claridoso [kla·ri·đó·so] *adj. Mex., Ven., C.A.* (*franco*) blunt, outspoken, plainspoken.
clarificar[6] [kla·ri·fi·kár] *v.* to clarify, make clear.
clarín [kla·rín] *m.* bugle; (*persona*) bugler; organ stop; *Am.* song bird.
clarinete [kla·ri·né·te] *m.* clarinet; clarinet player.
clarito [kla·rí·to] *adj. & adv.* quite clear, nice and clear.
clarividencia [kla·ri·ƀi·đén·sja] *f.* clairvoyance; keen insight.
claro [klá·ro] *adj.* clear; light (*color*); illustrious; *adv.* clearly; *m.* skylight; space, gap; clearing (*in a forest*); **pasar la noche de — en —** not to sleep a wink; *Mex., Carib.* **en** — without eating or sleeping; *Am.* **poner en** — to copy (*a rough draft*).
clase [klá·se] *f.* class; classroom; kind, sort.
clásico [klá·si·ko] *adj.* classic, classical.
clasificación [kla·si·fi·ka·sjón] *f.* classification.
clasificar[6] [kla·si·fi·kár] *v.* to classify; (*computadora*) to sort.
claustro [kláws·tro] *m.* cloister; (*reunión*) meeting of a university faculty; — **de profesores** university faculty.
cláusula [kláw·su·la] *f.* clause.
clausura [klaw·sú·ra] *f.* closing; seclusion, (*vida*) monastic life.
clavado [kla·ƀá·đo] *m. Mex.* a dive into water.
clavar [kla·ƀár] *v.* to nail; to fix; to deceive, cheat; **-se** to be deceived; *Mex.* to fall into a trap; *Mex.* to dive.
clave [klá·ƀe] *f.* key, code; (*piedra angular*) keystone; clef; **puesta en** — set in code.
clavel [kla·ƀél] *m.* carnation, pink.
clavetear [kla·ƀe·te·ár] *v.* to nail; to stud with nails.
clavícula [kla·ƀí·ku·la] *f.* collarbone.
clavija [kla·ƀí·xa] *f.* peg; electric plug; peg (*of a stringed instrument*).
clavijero [kla·ƀi·xé·ro] *m.* hat or clothes rack.
clavo [klá·ƀo] *m.* nail; (*clavero*) clove (*spice*); (*dolor*) sharp pain or grief; sick headache; *Mex.* rich mineral vein; *Mex., Ch.* bother, worry; *Col.* surprise, disappointment; *Ríopl.* drug on the market (*unsaleable article*); **dar en el** — to hit the nail on the head; *Mex.* **meter a uno en un** — to put a person in a predicament; *P.R.* **ser un** — to be punctual, exact.
clemencia [kle·mén·sja] *f.* mercy; **clemente** [kle·mén·te] *adj.* merciful.
clerical [kle·ri·kál] *adj.* clerical, of a clergyman or the clergy.
clérigo [klé·ri·ǥo] *m.* clergyman.
clero [klé·ro] *m.* clergy.
cliché [kli·čé] *m.* photographic plate; also **clisé.**
cliente [kljén·te] *m. & f.* client; customer; **clientela** [kljen·té·la] *f.* clientele, clients; customers.
clima [klí·ma] *m.* climate.
climatización [kli·ma·ti·sa·sjón] *f.* air conditioning.
clímax [klí·maks] *m.* climax.
clínica [klí·ni·ka] *f.* clinic.
clíper [klí·per] *m.* clipper.
cloaca [klo·á·ka] *f.* sewer.
cloquear [klo·ke·ár] *v.* to cluck.
cloqueo [klo·ké·o] *m.* cluck, clucking.
cloro [kló·ro] *m.* chlorine.
clorofila [klo·ro·fí·la] *f.* chlorophyll.
cloruro [klo·rú·ro] *m.* chloride.
club [kluƀ] *m.* club, society.
clueca [klwé·ka] *f.* brooding hen.
coacción [ko·ak·sjón] *f.* compulsion, force; enforcement.
coagular [ko·a·ǥu·lár] *v.* to coagulate, thicken, clot; to curd, curdle; **-se** to coagulate, clot; to curd, curdle.
coágulo [ko·á·ǥu·lo] *m.* coagulation, clot.
coartar [ko·ar·tár] *v.* to restrain, limit.
coba [kó·ƀa] *f.* flattery; fib; **dar** — to flatter; to tease.
cobalto [ko·ƀál·to] *m.* cobalt.
cobarde [ko·ƀár·đe] *adj.* cowardly; timid; weak; *m.* coward.
cobardía [ko·ƀar·đí·a] *f.* cowardice.
cobertizo [ko·ƀer·tí·so] *m.* shed; shanty.
cobertor [ko·ƀer·tór] *m.* bedcover, quilt.
cobertura [ko·ƀer·tú·ra] *f.* cover, covering.
cobija [ko·ƀí·xa] *f.* cover; shelter; roof; *Mex., C.A., Col., Ríopl.* blanket; *Am.* shawl, serape, poncho; **-s** *Mex.* bedclothes.
cobijar [ko·ƀi·xár] *v.* to cover; to shelter.
cobrador [ko·ƀra·đór] *m.* collector; ticket collector.
cobranza [ko·ƀrán·sa] *f.* collection (*of a sum of money*); cashing.
cobrar [ko·ƀrár] *v.* to collect (*bills, debts*); (*cargar*) to charge; (*hacer efectivo*) to cash (*a draft, check, etc.*); to recover, regain; to gain, acquire; *Am.* to demand payment; — **cariño a** to take a liking to; — **a la entrega** C.O.D. (collect on delivery).

cobre [kó·ƀre] *m.* copper; copper kitchen utensils; *Am.* copper coin; **-s** brass musical instruments; **batir el** — to hustle, work with energy; *Am.* **mostrar el** — to show one's worse side.
cobrizo [ko·ƀrí·so] *adj.* coppery, copper-colored.
cobro [kó·ƀro] *m.* collection (*of bills*); **poner en** — to put in a safe place; **ponerse en** — to take refuge, get to a safe place.
coca [kó·ka] *f. Andes* coca (*South American shrub and its leaves*); *Am.* cocaine; *Col.* coca tea; *Col.* eggshell; *Col.* fruit skin or rind; *Am.* **de** — free of charge; in vain.
cocaína [ko·ka·í·na] *f.* cocaine.
cocear [ko·se·ár] *v.* to kick.
cocer[2, 10] [ko·sér] *v. irr.* to cook; to boil; to bake.
cocido [ko·sí·đo] *m.* Spanish stew; *p.p. of* **cocer.**
cociente [ko·sjén·te] *m.* quotient.
cocimiento [ko·si·mjén·to] *m.* cooking; baking; liquid concoction (*generally made of medicinal herbs*).
cocina [ko·sí·na] *f.* kitchen; cuisine, cooking; — **económica** stove, range.
cocinar [ko·si·nár] *v.* to cook.
cocinero [ko·si·né·ro] *m.* cook.
coco [kó·ko] *m.* coconut; coconut palm; bogeyman, goblin; *Col.* derby hat; *Mex., Carib., Ríopl.* head; *Am.* blow on the head; **hacer -s a** to make eyes at, flirt with; *Col., Ven., Andes* **pelar a** — to crop the hair; **cocotal** [ko·ko·tál] *m.* grove of coconut palms; coconut plantation; **cocotero** [ko·ko·té·ro] *m.* coconut palm.
cocodrilo [ko·ko·đri·lo] *m.* crocodile.
cocoliche [ko·ko·lí·če] *m. Ríopl.* jargon of Italians who are learning Spanish.
coche [kó·če] *m.* coach; car; taxi.
cochero [ko·čé·ro] *m.* coachman; cabman; taxi driver.
cochinada [ko·či·ná·đa] *f.* filth, filthiness; filthy act or remark; dirty trick; herd of swine.
cochinilla [ko·čí·no] *m.* hog, pig; dirty person; *Ch.* stingy person; *Am.* — **de monte** wild boar; *adj.* filthy, dirty; *Ch.* miserly, stingy.
codazo [ko·đá·so] *m.* nudge; poke (*with the elbow*).
codear [ko·đe·ár] *v.* to elbow; to nudge; **-se con alguien** to rub elbows with someone.
códice [kó·đi·se] *m.* codex.
codicia [ko·đí·sja] *f.* greed; greediness.
codiciar [ko·đi·sjár] *v.* to covet.
codicioso [ko·đi·sjó·so] *adj.* covetous, greedy.
codificación [ko·đi·fi·ka·sjón] *f.* coding.
código [kó·đi·ǥo] *m.* code of laws.
codo [kó·đo] *m.* elbow; bend; — **doble** double elbow (plumbing); **alzar (empinar) el** — to drink too much; **hablar por los -s** to talk too much; **meterse** (*or* **estar metido**) **hasta los -s** to be up to the elbows, be very busy.
codorniz [ko·đor·nís] *f.* partridge.
coetáneo [ko·e·tá·ne·o] *adj.* contemporary.
cofrade [ko·frá·đe] *m. & f.* fellow member (*of a brotherhood, club, society, etc.*).
cofradía [ko·fra·đí·a] *f.* brotherhood; sisterhood; guild; trade union.
cofre [kó·fre] *m.* coffer, jewel box; chest, truck.
coger[11] [ko·xér] *v.* to seize; to catch; to grasp; to gather; *Mex., Ch. Ven. Col. Ríopl.* to copulate; *Am.* **-se una cosa** to steal something.
cogollo [ko·ǥó·yo] *m.* heart (*of lettuce*), head (*of cabbage*).
cogote [ko·ǥó·te] *m.* nape, back of the neck.
cohechar [ko·e·čár] *v.* to bribe.
coheredero [ko·e·re·đé·ro] *m.* joint heir.
coherente [ko·e·rén·te] *adj.* coherent; connected.
cohete [ko·é·te] *m.* skyrocket; rocket; *Ríopl.* **al** — in vain, uselessly.
cohetería [ko·e·te·rí·a] *f.* rocketry; rocket weaponry; shop for making fireworks.
cohibición [koj·ƀi·sjón] *f.* repression, inhibition, restraint.
cohibido [koj·ƀí·đo] *p.p. & adj.* inhibited; embarrassed, uneasy.
cohibir [koj·ƀír] *v.* to restrain, repress; to inhibit.
coincidencia [kojn·si·đén·sja] *f.* coincidence.
coincidir [kojn·si·đír] *v.* to coincide.
cojear [ko·xe·ár] *v.* to limp; **cojeamos del mismo pie** we both have the same weakness.
cojera [ko·xé·ra] *f.* limp, lameness.
cojín [ko·xín] *m.* cushion; pad; **cojincillo** *m.* pad.
cojinete [ko·xi·né·te] *m.* small pillow or cushion, pad; (*balero*) bearing, ball bearing; — **del cabezal** headstock bearing (machine).
cojo [kó·xo] *adj.* lame, crippled; one-legged.
col [kol] *f.* cabbage; — **de Bruselas** Brussels sprouts.
cola [kó·la] *f.* (*rabo*) tail; train of a dress; (*hilera de gente*) line of people; glue; **piano de** — grand piano; **piano de media** — baby grand; **hacer** — to stand in line; *Ríopl.* **comer** — to be the last one in a contest.
colaboración [ko·la·ƀo·ra·sjón] *f.* collaboration, mutual help.
colaborar [ko·la·ƀo·rár] *v.* to collaborate, work together.
coladera [ko·la·đé·ra] *f.* colander, strainer, sieve; *Mex., Ven.* drain.
colador [ko·la·dór] *m.* colander.
colar[2] [ko·lár] *v. irr.* to strain, filter; to bleach with lye; **-se** to slip in or out, sneak in.
colcha [kól·ča] *f.* quilt; bedspread; **-s** *Ríopl.* saddle and trappings; *Ríopl.* gaucho clothing.
colchón [kol·čón] *m.* mattress.
colear [ko·le·ár] *v.* to wag the tail; to grab a bull by the tail and throw him over; *Ch.* to flunk (*a student*); *Am.* to trail, tag behind (*a person*); *Col.* to bother, nag, harass; *Mex.* to smoke one cigarette after another.
colección [ko·lek·sjón] *f.* collection; set; gathering.
coleccionar [ko·lek·sjo·nár] *v.* to collect, make a collection.
coleccionista [ko·lek·sjo·nís·ta] *m. & f.* collector (*of stamps, curios, etc.*).
colecta [ko·lék·ta] *f.* collection of voluntary gifts; assessment; collect (*a short prayer of the mass*).
colectivo [ko·lek·tí·ƀo] *adj.* collective; *m. Ríopl.* small bus.
colector [ko·lek·tór] *m.* collector; water pipe, drain.
colega [ko·lé·ǥa] *m. & f.* colleague, fellow worker.
colegiatura [ko·le·xja·tú·ra] *f.* college fellowship or scholarship; *C.A.* tuition in a college.
colegio [ko·lé·xjo] *m.* boarding school; high school, academy; college, body of professional persons; *Col.* any private school.
colegir[5, 11] [ko·le·xír] *v.* to gather; to conclude, infer.
cólera [kó·le·ra] *f.* anger, rage; *m.* cholera (*disease*).
colérico [ko·lé·ri·ko] *adj.* irritable; angry.
coleto [ko·lé·to] *m.* leather jacket; one's inner self; *Am.* impudence, shamelessness; **decir para su** — to say to oneself; **echarse al** — to drink down; to devour.
colgadero [kol·ǥa·đé·ro] *m.* hanger; hook, peg; (*percha*) hat or clothes rack.
colgadura [kol·ǥa·đú·ra] *f.* drape, hanging; drapery; tapestry.
colgante [kol·ǥán·te] *adj.* hanging; dangling; **puente** — suspension bridge.

colgar[2, 7] [kol·ǥár] *v. irr.* (*suspender*) to hang, suspend; to dangle; to drape (*walls*); (*achacar*) to impute, attribute; *Cuba* to flunk, fail (*a student*); *Col.* **-se** to fall behind.
colibrí [ko·li·ƀrí] *m.* hummingbird.
coliflor [ko·li·flór] *f.* cauliflower.
coligarse[7] [ko·li·ǥár·se] *v.* to league together, band together.
colilla [ko·lí·ya] *f.* small tail; butt (*of a cigarette*), stub (*of a cigar*).
colina [ko·lí·na] *f. N. Sp.* hill.
colindante [ko·lin·dán·te] *adj.* contiguous, neighboring, adjacent.
colindar [ko·lin·dár] *v.* to border (on); to be adjoining.
colisión [ko·li·sjón] *f.* collision, clash.
colmar [kol·már] *v.* to fill to the brim; — **de** to fill with; to shower with (*gifts, favors, etc.*); **-le a uno el plato** to exhaust one's patience.
colmena [kol·mé·na] *f.* beehive; *Mex.* bee.
colmillo [kol·mí·yo] *m.* eyetooth, canine tooth; (*animal*) tusk; fang.
colmo [kól·mo] *m.* overfullness; limit; — **de la locura** height of folly; **¡eso es el — !** that's the limit! *adj.* overfull, filled to the brim.
colocación [ko·lo·ka·sjón] *f.* placing, arrangement; (*puesto*) position, job.
colocar[6] [ko·lo·kár] *v.* to place; to put in place, arrange; (*emplear*) to give employment to.
colocho [ko·ló·čo] *m. C.A.* curly hair; wood shavings.
colombiano [ko·lom·bjá·no] *adj.* Colombian, of or pertaining to Colombia, South America.
colon [kó·lon] *m.* colon (*of the large intestine*).
colonia [ko·ló·nja] *f.* colony; silk ribbon; *Mex., Carib.* city district; *Am.* sugar plantation.
coloniaje [ko·lo·njá·xe] *m. Am.* colonial period.
colonial [ko·lo·njál] *adj.* colonial.
colonización [ko·lo·ni·sa·sjón] *f.* colonization.
colonizador [ko·lo·ni·sa·đór] *m.* colonizer, colonist; *adj.* colonizing.
colonizar[9] [ko·lo·ni·sár] *v.* to colonize.
colono [ko·ló·no] *m.* colonist, settler; tenant farmer; *Carib.* owner of a sugar plantation; *Am.* bootlicker, flatterer.
coloquio [ko·ló·kjo] *m.* conversation, talk; literary dialogue; *Col.* street comedy farce.
color [ko·lór] *m.* color; coloring; paint; rouge; **so — de** under the pretext of.
coloración [ko·lo·ra·sjón] *f.* coloring.
colorado [ko·lo·ra·đo] *adj.* red, reddish; colored; **ponerse** — to blush.
colorante [ko·lo·rán·te] *adj. & m.* coloring.
colorar [ko·lo·rár] *v.* to color; to stain; to dye.
colorear [ko·lo·re·ár] *v.* to color; to redden; to give color to.
colorete [ko·lo·ré·te] *m.* rouge.
colorido [ko·lo·rí·đo] *m.* coloring; color; *adj.* colored; colorful.
colosal [ko·lo·sál] *adj.* colossal, huge.
columbrar [ko·lum·brár] *v.* to see faintly; to glimpse.
columna [ko·lúm·na] *f.* column.
columpiar [ko·lum·pjár] *v.* to swing; **-se** to swing; to sway.
columpio [ko·lúm·pjo] *m.* swing.
collado [ko·yá·đo] *m.* hillock, knoll.
collar [ko·yár] *m.* necklace; dog collar; *Am.* collar (*of a draft horse*); **collera** [ko·yé·ra] *f.* collar (*for draft animals*).
coma [kó·ma] *f.* comma; *m.* (*inconsciente*) coma, stupor, prolonged unconsciousness.
comadre [ko·má·đre] *f.* (*amiga*) woman friend; (*chismosa*) gossip; (*partera*) midwife; (*alcahueta*) go-between; *name used to express kinship between mother and godmother;* **comadrona** [ko·ma·đró·na] *f.* midwife.
comadreja [ko·ma·đré·xa] *f.* weasel.
comandancia [ko·man·dán·sja] *f.* command; position and headquarters of a commander.
comandante [ko·man·dán·te] *m.* major; commander.
comandar [ko·man·dár] *v.* to command (*troops*).
comandita [ko·man·dí·ta] *f.* silent partnership; **sociedad en** — limited company.
comando [ko·mán·do] *m.* military command; (*computadora*) command.
comarca [ko·már·ka] *f.* district, region.
comba [kóm·ba] *f.* bulge, warp.
combar [kom·bár] *v.* to warp, bend, twist; **-se** to warp; to sag; to bulge.
combate [kom·bá·te] *m.* combat, battle, fight.
combatiente [kom·ba·tjén·te] *m.* combatant, fighter.
combatir [kom·ba·tír] *v.* to combat; to fight.
combinación [kom·bi·na·sjón] *f.* combination.
combinar [kom·bi·nár] *v.* to combine, unite.
comburente [kom·bu·rén·te] *m.* the chemical agent that causes combustion, e.g., oxygen; *adj.* causing combustion.
combustible [kom·bus·tí·ƀle] *adj.* combustible; *m.* fuel.
combustión [kom·bus·tjón] *f.* combustion.
comedero [ko·me·đé·ro] *m.* trough (*for feeding animals*); *adj.* edible, eatable.
comedia [ko·mé·đja] *f.* comedy; farce.
comediante [ko·me·đján·te] *m.* actor, comedian.
comedido [ko·me·đí·đo] *adj.* courteous, polite; obliging; *p.p. of* **comedirse.**
comedirse[5] [ko·me·đír·se] *v. irr.* to be civil, polite, obliging; *Ec.* to meddle; *Am.* — **a hacer algo** to volunteer to do something.
comedor [ko·me·đór] *m.* dining room; (*comilón*) great eater.
comején [ko·me·xén] *m.* termite.
comelón [ko·me·lón] *m. Am.* big eater. *See* **comilón.**
comendador [ko·men·da·đór] *m.* commander (*of certain military orders*).
comensal [ko·men·sál] *m. & f.* table companion; dinner guest.
comentador [ko·men·ta·đór] *m.* commentator.
comentar [ko·men·tár] *v.* to comment.
comentario [ko·men·tá·rjo] *m.* commentary, explanation.
comentarista [ko·men·ta·rís·ta] *m. & f.* commentator.
comenzar[1, 9] [ko·men·sár] *v. irr.* to begin.
comer [ko·mér] *v.* to eat; to dine; to take (*in chess or checkers*); **dar de** — to feed; **ganar de** — to earn a living; **-se** to eat; to eat up; to skip (*a letter, syllable, word, etc.*); *Ríopl., Col.* **-se uno a otro** to deceive each other.
comercial [ko·mer·sjál] *adj.* commercial.
comerciante [ko·mer·sján·te] *m.* merchant; storekeeper.
comerciar [ko·mer·sjár] *v.* to trade; to have dealings (with).
comercio [ko·mér·sjo] *m.* commerce, trade.
comestible [ko·mes·tí·ƀle] *adj.* edible, eatable; **-s** *m. pl.* food, groceries.
cometa [ko·mé·ta] *m.* comet; *Mex., Ch., C.A.* person seldom seen; *f.* kite.
cometer [ko·me·tér] *v.* to commit; to entrust; to use (*a figure of speech*).
cometido [ko·me·tí·đo] *m.* commission, assignment, charge; task, duty.
comezón [ko·me·són] *f.* itch.

comicios [ko·mí·sjos] *m. pl.* primaries, elections.
cómico [kó·mi·ko] *adj.* comic, of comedy; comical, funny, amusing; *m.* comedian, actor.
comida [ko·mí·đa] *f.* meal; dinner; good; **comidilla** *f* small meal; gossip; **la comidilla de la vecindad** the talk of the town.
comienzo [ko·mjén·so] *m.* beginning; origin.
comilitona [ko·mi·li·tó·na] *f.* spread, big feast.
comilón [ko·mi·lón] *m.* big eater.
comillas [ko·mí·yas] *f. pl.* quotation marks.
comino [ko·mí·no] *m.* cuminseed.
comisar [ko·mi·sár] *v.* to confiscate.
comisario [ko·mi·sá·rjo] *m.* commissary, deputy, delegate; manager; *Mex., Arg.* police inspector.
comisión [ko·mi·sjón] *f.* commission; committee.
comisionado [ko·mi·sjo·ná·đo] *adj.* commissioned, charged, delegated; *m.* commissioner; *Cuba* constable.
comisionar [ko·mi·sjo·nár] *v.* to commission.
comistrajo [ko·mis·trá·xo] *m.* mess, strange food concoction, mixture.
comité [ko·mi·té] *m.* committee, commission.
comitiva [ko·mi·tí·ƀa] *f.* retinue, group of attendants or followers.
como [kó·mo] *adv. & conj.* as, like, such as; if, provided that, since, when; *Mex., Ven.* about, approximately; **¿cómo?** [kó·mo] *interr. adv.* how?, what (did you say)?; *Am.* **¡cómo no!** yes, of course!
cómoda [kó·mo·đa] *f.* bureau, chest of drawers.
comodidad [ko·mo·đi·đáđ] *f.* comfort; convenience.
comodín [ko·mo·đín] *m.* joker, wild card.
cómodo [kó·mo·đo] *adj.* comfortable; convenient; *m. Am.* bedpan.
compactar [kom·pak·tár] *v.* roll out (fiber glass).
compacto [kom·pák·to] *adj.* compact.
compadecer[13] [kom·pa·đe·sér] *v. irr.* to pity, sympathize with; **-se con** to be in harmony with; **-se de** to take pity on.
compadrazgo [kom·pa·đráz·go] *m.* compaternity (*spiritual affinity between the godfather and the parents of a child*); friendship; relationship; clique, group of friends; cronyism.
compadre [kom·pá·đre] *m.* (*amigo*) pal, crony, comrade; (*padrino*) cosponsor; *name used to express kinship between father and godfather.*
compañero [kom·pa·ñé·ro] *m.* companion; partner; mate; **compañerismo** [kom·pa·ñe·ríz·mo] *m.* companionship.
compañía [kom·pa·ñí·a] *f.* company; *Mex.* — **del ahorcado** silent companion, poor company.
comparación [kom·pa·ra·sjón] *f.* comparison.
comparar [kom·pa·rár] *v.* to compare.
comparativo [kom·pa·ra·tí·ƀo] *adj.* comparative.
comparecer[13] [kom·pa·re·sér] *v. irr.* to appear (*before a judge or tribunal*).
compartimiento [kom·par·ti·mjén·to] *m.* compartment.
compartir [kom·par·tír] *v.* to share; to divide into shares.
compás [kom·pás] *m.* compass; measure; beat; **llevar el** — to beat time; — **de gruesas** calipers.
compasión [kom·pa·sjón] *f.* compassion, pity.
compasivo [kom·pa·sí·ƀo] *adj.* compassionate, sympathetic.
compatible [kom·pa·tí·ƀle] *adj.* compatible, in harmony.
compatriota [kom·pa·trjó·ta] *m. & f.* compatriot, fellow countryman.
compeler [kom·pe·lér] *v.* to compel, force.
compendiar [kom·pen·djár] *v.* to abstract, summarize, condense.
compendio [kom·pén·djo] *m.* summary, condensation.
compensación [kom·pen·sa·sjón] *f.* compensation; recompense.
compensar [kom·pen·sár] *v.* to balance; to make equal; to compensate, recompense.
competencia [kom·pe·tén·sja] *f.* competition, rivalry; competence, ability.
competente [kom·pe·tén·te] *adj.* competent; capable; adequate.
competidor [kom·pe·ti·đór] *m.* competitor; rival; *adj.* competing.
competir[5] [kom·pe·tír] *v. irr.* to compete, vie.
compilador [kom·pi·la·đór] *m.* (*computadora*) compiler.
compilar [kom·pi·lár] *v.* to compile.
compinche [kom·pín·če] *m.* chum, pal, comrade.
complacencia [kom·pla·sén·sja] *f.* complacency, satisfaction, contentment.
complacer[38] [kom·pla·sér] *v. irr.* to please, humor; to comply; **-se** to take pleasure or satisfaction (in).
coplaciente [kom·pla·sjén·te] *adj.* obliging, agreeable, willing to please.
complejidad [kom·ple·xi·đáđ] *f.* complexity.
complejo [kom·plé·xo] *adj. & m.* complex.
complemento [kom·ple·mén·to] *m.* complement; (*gramática*) object (*of a verb*).
completamiento [kom·ple·ta·mjén·to] *m.* completion.
completar [kom·ple·tár] *v.* to complete; to finish.
completo [kom·plé·to] *adj.* complete, full, perfect.
complexión [kom·plek·sjón] *f.* constitution, make-up.
complicar[6] [kom·pli·kár] *v.* to complicate.
cómplice [kóm·pli·se] *m. & f.* accomplice, companion in crime.
complot [kom·plót], [kom·pló] *m.* plot, conspiracy; intrigue.
componenda [kom·po·nén·da] *f.* adjustment; compromise.
componente [kom·po·nén·te] *adj.* component, constituent; *m.* component, essential part.
componer[40] [kom·po·nér] *v. irr.* to fix, repair; to fix up; to adorn, trim; to compose; (*imprenta*) to set up (*type*); (*arreglar*) to settle (*a dispute*); *Col.* to set (*bones*).
comportamiento [kom·por·ta·mjén·to] *m.* conduct, behavior.
composición [kom·po·si·sjón] *f.* composition; settlement.
compositor [kom·po·si·tór] *m.* composer.
compostura [kom·pos·tú·ra] *f.* (*arreglo*) repair; settlement, adjustment; (*aseo*) neatness, composition; (*dignidad*) composure, dignity.
compota [kom·pó·ta] *f.* fruit preserves; — **de manzana** applesauce.
compra [kóm·pra] *f.* purchase; buying; **ir de -s** to go shopping.
comprador [kom·pra·đór] *m.* buyer, purchaser.
comprar [kom·prár] *v.* to buy, purchase.
comprender [kom·pren·dér] *v.* to understand, grasp, comprehend; to comprise, embrace.
comprensible [kom·pren·sí·ƀle] *adj.* comprehensible, understandable.
comprensión [kom·pren·sjón] *f.* understanding; comprehension; keenness.
comprensivo [kom·pren·sí·ƀo] *adj.* comprehensive; understanding.
compresión [kom·pre·sjón] *f.* compression.
compresor [kom·pre·sór] *m.* compressor.
comprimido [kom·pri·mí·đo] *adj.* compressed; *m.* medicinal tablet.
comprimir [kom·pri·mír] *v.* to compress; to repress.

comprobación [kom·pro·ƀa·sjón] *f.* confirmation, check, proof, test.
comprobante [kom·pro·ƀán·te] *adj.* proving, verifying; *m.* proof; evidence; certificate; voucher; warrant.
comprobar[2] [kom·pro·ƀár] *v. irr.* to verify; to check; to prove.
comprometer [kom·pro·me·tér] *v.* (*exponer*) to compromise; to endanger; to bind; to force; (*concordar*) to come to an agreement; **-se** to promise, bind oneself; to become engaged; to compromise oneself.
compromiso [kom·pro·mí·so] *m.* (*convenio*) compromise; (*obligación*) engagement; appointment; (*dificultad*) predicament, trouble.
compuerta [kom·pwér·ta] *f.* sluice, floodgate.
compuesto [kom·pwés·to] *p.p. of* **componer** *& adj.* repaired; fixed, adorned; composed; *m.* composite; compound.
compungirse[11] [kom·puŋ·xír·se] *v.* to feel regret or remorse.
computación [kom·pu·ta·sjón] *f.* (*computadora*) computing.
computadora electrónica [kom·pu·ta·đó·ra e·lek·tró·ni·ka] *f.* electronic computer; — **analógica** analogical computer; — **digital** digital computer; — **casera** home computer; — **personal** personal computer.
computar [kom·pu·tár] *v.* to compute, calculate.
cómputo [kóm·pu·to] *m.* computation, calculation.
comulgar[7] [ko·mul·ǵár] *v.* to commune, take communion.
común [ko·mún] *adj.* common; **por lo** — generally; *m.* toilet; **el** — **de las gentes** the majority of the people; the average person.
comunero [ko·mu·né·ro] *adj.* common, popular; *Am.* pertaining to a community; *m.* commoner (*one of the common people*); *Col., Ven., Andes* member of an Indian community.
comunicación [ko·mu·ni·ka·sjón] *f.* communication.
comunicar[6] [ko·mu·ni·kár] *v.* to communicate; to notify; **-se** to communicate; to correspond; to be in touch (with); to connect.
comunicativo [ko·mu·ni·ka·tí·ƀo] *adj.* communicative, talkative.
comunidad [ko·mu·ni·đáđ] *f.* community; commonwealth; the common people; commonness; guild.
comunión [ko·mu·njón] *f.* communion; political party.
comunismo [ko·mu·níz·mo] *m.* communism; **comunista** [ko·mu·nís·ta] *m. & f.* communist; *adj.* communistic, communist.
con [kon] *prep.* with; — **ser** in spite of being; — **tal que** provided that; — **todo** however.
conato [ko·ná·to] *m.* attempt, effort; (*asalto*) assault (*law*).
concavidad [koŋ·ka·ƀi·đáđ] *f.* hollow, cavity; hollowness.
cóncavo [kóŋ·ka·ƀo] *adj.* concave, hollow.
concebible [kon·se·ƀí·ƀle] *adj.* conceivable.
concebir[5] [kon·se·ƀír] *v. irr.* to conceive; to imagine; to understand, grasp.
conceder [kon·se·đér] *v.* to concede, grant; (confesar) to admit.
concejal [kon·se·xál] *m.* councilman, alderman.
concejo [kon·sé·xo] *m.* town council.
concentración [kon·sen·tra·sjón] *f.* concentration.
concentrar [kon·sen·trár] *v.* to concentrate.
concepción [kon·sep·sjón] *f.* conception.
concepto [kon·sép·to] *m.* concept, idea, thought.
concernir[51] [kon·ser·nír] *v. irr.* to concern.
concertar[1] [kon·ser·tár] *v. irr.* (*arreglar*) to arrange, plan, settle; (*llevar a cabo*) to conclude (*a treaty or business deal*); (*concordar*) to harmonize; to agree.
concesión [kon·se·sjón] *f.* concession, grant; granting; acknowledgment.
conciencia [kon·sjén·sja] *f.* conscience.
concienzudo [kon·sjen·sú·đo] *adj.* conscientious.
concierto [kon·sjér·to] *m.* concert; harmony; agreement; **de** — by common agreement.
conciliar [kon·si·ljár] *v.* to conciliate, win over; to reconcile, bring into harmony; — **el sueño** to get to sleep.
concilio [kon·sí·ljo] *m.* council.
concision [kon·si·sjón] *f.* conciseness, brevity.
conciso [kon·sí·so] *adj.* concise, brief.
conciudadano [kon·sju·đa·đá·no] *m.* fellow citizen, fellow countryman.
concluir[32] [koŋ·klwír] *v. irr.* to conclude, finish; to infer.
conclusión [koŋ·klu·sjón] *f.* conclusion.
concordancia [koŋ·kor·đán·sja] *f.* concord, agreement, harmony.
concordar[2] [koŋ·kor·đár] *v. irr.* to agree; to be in harmony; to put in harmony.
concordia [koŋ·kór·đja] *f.* concord, harmony, agreement.
concretar [koŋ·kre·tár] *v.* to summarize, condense; to limit; **-se a** to limit oneself to.
concreto [koŋ·kré·to] *adj.* concrete, real, specific; **en**— concretely; to sum up; *m. Mex.* concrete.
concupiscente [koŋ·ku·pi·sen·te] *adj.* sensual.
concurrencia [koŋ·ku·rrén·sja] *f.* gathering, audience; concurrence, simultaneous meeting or happening; competition.
concurrido [koŋ·ku·rrí·đo] *adj.* well-patronized, well-attended, much frequented.
concurrir [koŋ·ku·rrír] *v.* to concur, (*reunirse*) meet together; to happen at the same time or place; (*asistir*) to attend; to agree.
concurso [koŋ·kúr·so] *m.* gathering; (*contienda*) contest; competitive examination; assistance.
concha [kón·ča] *f.* shell; shellfish; (*de teatro*) prompter's box; *Mex.* **tener** — to be indifferent, unruffled, tough.
conchabar [kon·ča·ƀár] *v.* to unite, join; *Mex., S.A.* to hire (*labor*); **-se** to join, gang together; to conspire; *Ríopl.* to hire oneself out, get a job.
conchabo [kon·čá·ƀo] *m. Am.* hiring of a laborer or servant; *Ríopl.* job, menial job.
conde [kón·de] *m.* count; condesa *f.* countess.
condecoración [kon·de·ko·ra·sjón] *f.* decoration; badge, medal.
condecorar [kon·de·ko·rár] *v.* to decorate (*with a badge or medal*).
condena [kon·dé·na] *f.* term in prison, sentence, penalty.
condenación [kon·de·na·sjón] *f.* condemnation; conviction; (*teología*) damnation.
condenar [kon·de·nár] *v.* to condemn; to sentence; *Ven.* to annoy, irritate; **-se** to be damned, go to hell.
condensación [kon·den·sa·sjón] *f.* condensation; "sweating" of containers.
condensar [kon·den·sár] *v.* to condense.
condescendencia [kon·de·sen·dén·sja] *f.* condescension, patronizing attitude.
condescender[1] [kon·de·sen·dér] *v. irr.* to condescend; to comply, yield.
condición [kon·di·sjón] *f.* condition.

condimentar [kon·di·men·tár] *v.* to season.
condimento [kon·di·mén·to] *m.* condiment, seasoning.
condiscípulo [kon·di·sí·pu·lo] *m.* schoolmate, classmate.
condolerse[2] [kon·do·lér·se] *v. irr.* to condole (with), sympathize (with), be sorry (for).
condón [kon·dón] *m.* condom.
cóndor [kón·dor] *m. Am.* condor, vulture; *Am.* gold coin of Ecuador, Chile and Colombia.
conducir[25] [kon·du·sír] *v. irr.* to conduct, lead; (*manejar*) to drive (*an auto*); **-se** to behave, act.
conducta [kon·dúk·ta] *f.* conduct; behavior; convoy, escort; management.
conducto [kon·dúk·to] *m.* conduit, pipe, channel; — **lacrimar** tear duct; **por — de** through.
conductor [kon·duk·tór] *adj.* conducting; *m.* leader; (*motorista*) chauffeur; guide; conductor (*electrical*); *Am.* conductor, ticket collector (*on trains, buses, streetcars*); *Ríopl.* teamster, driver.
conectar [ko·nek·tár] *v.* to connect.
conejera [ko·ne·xé·ra] *f.* burrow; rabbit warren (*piece of land for breeding rabbits*); (*tasca*) den, joint, dive (*of ill repute*).
conejo [ko·né·xo] *m.* rabbit; *Am.* guinea pig; **conejillo de Indias** [ko·ne·xí·yo·đe ín·djas] guinea pig.
conexión [ko·nek·sjón] *f.* connection.
conexo [ko·nék·so] *adj.* connected; coherent.
confección [kon·fek·sjón] *f.* making; confection; manufactured article; workmanship; concoction, compound.
confeccionar [kon·fek·sjo·nár] *v.* to make; to manufacture; to mix, put up (*a prescription*).
confederación [kon·fe·đe·ra·sjón] *f.* confederation, alliance, league.
confederar [kon·fe·đe·rár] *v.* to confederate; **-se** to confederate, form into a confederacy.
conferencia [kon·fe·rén·sja] *f.* lecture; conference, meeting.
conferenciante [kon·fe·ren·sján·te] *m. & f.* lecturer.
conferencista [kon·fe·ren·sís·ta] *m. & f. Am.* lecturer.
conferir[3] [kon·fe·rír] *v. irr.* to confer; to give, bestow.
confesar[1] [kon·fe·sár] *v. irr.* to confess.
confesión [kon·fe·sjón] *f.* confession.
confesionario [kon·fe·sjo·ná·rjo] *m.* confessional, confessional box.
confesor [kon·fe·sór] *m.* confessor.
confiado [kon·fjá·đo] *adj.* confident, trusting, credulous; (*presuntuoso*) presumptuous, self-confident.
confianza [kon·fján·sa] *f.* confidence, trust; familiarity; informality; **reunión de** — informal gathering or party.
confianzudo [kon·fjan·sú·đo] *adj.* over-friendly, over-familiar; *Ven.* meddlesome.
confiar[17] [kon·fjár] *v.* to confide, entrust; to trust, hope firmly.
confidencia [kon·fi·đén·sja] *f.* confidence, trust; secret, confidential remark; **confidencial** [kon·fi·đen·sjál] *adj.* confidential.
confidente [kon·fi·đén·te] *m.* confidant; spy, secret agent; (*sofá*) settee or sofa for two people, love seat; *adj.* faithful, trustworthy.
confín [kon·fín] *m.* limit, border, boundary; *adj.* bordering, limiting.
confinar [kon·fi·nár] *v.* to border (upon); to confine, (*desterrar*) exile to a specific place.
confirmación [kon·fir·ma·sjón] *f.* confirmation.
confirmar [kon·fir·már] *v.* to confirm.
confiscar[6] [kon·fis·kár] *v.* to confiscate.
confitar [kon·fi·tár] *v.* to candy; to make into candy or preserves; to sweeten.
confite [kon·fí·te] *m.* candy, bonbon; **confitería** [kon·fi·te·rí·a] *f.* confectionery; candy shop; **confitura** [kon·fi·tú·ra] *f.* confection.
conflicto [kon·flík·to] *m.* conflict.
confluencia [kon·flwén·sja] *f.* junction (*of two rivers*).
conformar [kon·for·már] *v.* to adapt, adjust; **-se** to conform, comply; to agree; to be resigned (to); to be satisfied.
conforme [kon·fór·me] *adj.* in agreement; resigned, satisfied; alike, similar; — **a** in accordance with.
conformidad [kon·for·mi·đáđ] *f.* conformity; agreement, harmony; compliance; — **con la voluntad de Dios** resignation to the will of God; **en — con** in compliance with; **estar de — con** to be in accordance or agreement with.
confortar [kon·for·tár] *v.* to comfort, console.
confraternidad [kon·fra·ter·ni·đáđ] *f.* brotherhood.
confrontar [kon·fron·tár] *v.* to confront; to face; to compare, check.
confundir [kon·fun·dír] *v.* to confound, confuse, mix up; to bewilder; (*avergonzar*) to shame.
confusión [kon·fu·sjón] *f.* confusion.
confuso [kon·fú·so] *adj.* confused, bewildered; blurred; (*vago*) vague.
congelado [koŋ·xe·lá·đo] *p.p. & adj.* frozen; icy
congelador [koŋ·xe·la·dór] *m.* freezer.
congelar [koŋ·xe·lár] *v.* to congeal, freeze.
congenial [koŋ·xe·njál] *adj.* congenial.
congeniar [koŋ·xe·njár] *v.* to be congenial (with), to harmonize, be in harmony (with).
congoja [koŋ·gó·xa] *f.* anguish, grief, anxiety.
congratular [koŋ·gra·tu·lár] *v.* to congratulate.
congregación [koŋ·gre·ga·sjón] *f.* congregation, assembly; religious fraternity.
congregar[7] [koŋ·gre·gár] *v.* to congregate, call together; to assemble; **-se** to congregate, assemble.
congresista [koŋ·gre·sís·ta] *m.* congressman; conventionite; *f.* congresswoman.
congreso [koŋ·gré·so] *m.* congress, assembly; convention; — **de los Diputados** House of Representatives.
conjetura [koŋ·xe·tú·ra] *f.* conjecture, guess, surmise.
conjeturar [koŋ·xe·tu·rár] *v.* to conjecture, guess, surmise.
conjugación [koŋ·su·ga·sjón] *f.* conjugation; (*juntura*) coupling, joining together.
conjugar[7] [koŋ·xu·gár] *v.* to conjugate.
conjunción [koŋ·xun·sjón] *f.* conjunction; union, combination.
conjunto [koŋ·xún·to] *m.* total, whole, entirety; set aggregate; **en** — as a whole; *adj.* joined; related, allied; — **lógico** *m.* (*computadora*) software.
conjuración [koŋ·xu·ra·sjón] *f.* conspiracy, plot.
conjurado [koŋ·xu·rá·đo] *m.* conspirator.
conjurar [koŋ·su·rár] *v.* to conspire, plot; to join a conspiracy; to entreat; to conjure; to ward off.
conjuro [kon·xú·ro] *m.* conspiracy; exorcism.
conmemorar [kom·me·mo·rár] *v.* to commemorate.
conmemorativo [kom·me·mo·ra·tí·bo] *adj.* memorial, serving to commemorate.
conmigo [kom·mí·go] with me.
conminación [kom·mi·na·sjón] *f.* threat.
conminatorio [kom·mi·na·tó·rjo] *adj.* threatening.
conmoción [kom·mo·sjón] *f.* commotion.
conmovedor [kom·mo·be·đór] *adj.* moving, touching; stirring.
conmover[2] [kom·mo·bér] *v. irr.* to move, touch, affect (*with emotion*); to stir (*emotions*).
conmutador [kom·mu·ta·đór] *m.* electric switch; **cuadro** — switchboard.

connatural [kon·na·tu·rál] *adj.* inborn.
cono [kó·no] *m.* cone; pine cone.
conocedor [ko·no·se·đór] *adj.* knowing, aware, expert; *m.* connoisseur, judge, expert; **ser — de** to be judge of.
conocer[13] [ko·no·sér] *v. irr.* (*tener idea de*) to know, be acquainted with; to recognize; (*llegar a conocer*) to meet; **se conoce que** it is clear or evident that.
conocido [ko·no·sí·đo] *p.p. & adj.* known; well-known; *m.* acquaintance.
conocimiento [ko·no·si·mjén·to] *m.* (*inteligencia*) knowledge, understanding; acquaintance; (*documento*) bill of lading; **-s** knowledge, learning; **poner en —** to inform.
conque [kóŋ·ke] *conj.* so then, well then, and so.
conquista [koŋ·kís·ta] *f.* conquest.
conquistador [koŋ·kis·ta·đór] *m.* conqueror; *adj.* conquering, victorious.
conquistar [koŋ·kis·tár] *v.* to conquer, defeat; to win.
consabido [kon·sa·ƀí·đo] *adj.* aforementioned, aforesaid.
consagración [kon·sa·ǥra·sjón] *f.* consecration.
consagrar [kon·sa·ǥrár] *v.* to consecrate.
consciencia [kon·sjén·sja] *f.* consciousness.
consciente [kon·sjén·te] *adj.* conscious.
consecución [kon·se·ku·sjón] *f.* attainment.
consecuencia [kon·se·kwén·sja] *f.* consequence; result; **a — de** as a result of; **por** (*or* **en**) — therefore; consequently.
consecuente [kon·se·kwén·te] *adj.* consequent, logical; consistent; *m.* consequence, result.
consecutivo [kon·se·ku·tí·ƀo] *adj.* consecutive, successive.
conseguir[5, 12] [kon·se·ǥír] *v. irr.* to get, obtain; to reach, attain.
conseja [kon·sé·xa] *f.* old wives' tale, fable.
consejero [kon·se·xé·ro] *m.* adviser counselor.
consejo [kon·sé·xo] *m.* counsel, advice; council; (*lugar*) council hall.
consentimiento [kon·sen·ti·mjén·to] *m.* consent.
consentir[3] [kon·sen·tír] *v. irr.* to consent, permit; to pamper, spoil.
conserje [kon·sér·xe] *m.* janitor, caretaker.
conserva [kon·sér·ƀa] *f.* preserve; (*en escabeche*) pickled fruit or vegetables; *Ch.* filling (*for tarts or candy*).
conservación [kon·ser·ƀa·sjón] *f.* conservation.
conservador [kon·ser·ƀa·đór] *m.* conservative; preserver; guardian; *adj.* conservative.
conservar [kon·ser·ƀár] *v.* to conserve, keep; to preserve.
considerable [kon·si·đe·rá·ƀle] *adj.* considerable.
consideración [kon·si·đe·ra·sjón] *f.* consideration.
considerado [kon·si·đe·rá·đo] *adj.* considerate, thoughtful; respected; prudent.
considerar [kon·si·đe·rár] *v.* to consider; to treat with consideration.
consigna [kon·síǥ·na] *f.* watchword, password; *Am.* checkroom.
consignar [kon·siǥ·nár] *v.* to consign; to deliver; to deposit; to assign; (*facturar*) to check (*baggage*).
consigo [kon·sí·ǥo] with oneself; with himself (herself, themselves).
consiguiente [kon·si·ǥjén·te] *adj.* consequent; *m.* consequence; **por —** consequently.
consistente [kon·sis·tén·te] *adj.* firm, substantial.
consistir [kon·sis·tír] *v.* to consist; to be based on; **¿en qué consiste?** of what does it consist?
consocio [kon·só·sjo] *m.* associate, partner.
consola [kon·só·la] *f.* console.
consolación [kon·so·la·sjón] *f.* consolation.
consolar[2] [kon·so·lár] *v. irr.* to console, cheer.
consolidar [kon·so·li·đár] *v.* to consolidate, make solid; to unite, combine.
consonante [kon·so·nán·te] *m.* perfect rhyme; *f.* consonant; *adj.* in harmony.
consorte [kon·sór·te] *m. & f.* consort; mate; companion.
conspicuo [kons·pí·kwo] *adj.* conspicuous.
conspiración [kons·pi·ra·sjón] *f.* conspiracy, plot.
conspirador [kons·pi·ra·đór] *m.* conspirator, plotter.
conspirar [kons·pi·rár] *v.* to conspire, plot.
constancia [kons·tán·sja] *f.* (*firmeza*) constancy; perseverance; (*certeza*) evidence, certainty; *Am.* documentary proof, record.
constante [kons·tán·te] *adj.* constant; continual; (*fiel*) firm, faithful.
constar [kons·tár] *v.* to be evident, clear; (*consistir en*) to consist (of), be composed (of); to be on record.
constatación [kons·ta·ta·sjón] *f. Am.* proof, check, evidence.
constelación [kons·te·la·sjón] *f.* constellation.
constipado [kons·ti·pá·đo] *adj.* suffering from a cold; *m.* cold in the head.
constipar [kons·ti·pár] *v.* to stop up (*the nasal passages*); to cause a cold; **-se** to catch cold.
constitución [kons·ti·tu·sjón] *f.* constitution.
constitucional [kons·ti·tu·sjo·nál] *adj.* constitutional.
constituir[32] [kons·ti·twír] *v. irr.* to constitute, form; to set up, establish; **-se en** to set oneself up as.
constitutivo [kons·ti·tu·tí·ƀo] = **constituyente.**
constituyente [kons·ti·tu·yén·te] *adj.* constituent.
constreñir[5, 19] [kons·tre·ñír] *v. irr.* to constrain; to compel, oblige.
construcción [kons·truk·sjón] *f.* construction; structure; building.
construir[32] [kons·trwír] *v. irr.* to construct, build.
consuelo [kon·swé·lo] *m.* consolation, comfort; relief; cheer.
consuetudinario [kon·swe·tu·đi·ná·rjo] *adj.* habitual, customary; **derecho —** common law.
consul [kón·sul] *m.* consul.
consulado [kon·su·lá·đo] *m.* consulate.
consulta [kon·súl·ta] *f.* consultation; opinion.
consultar [kon·sul·tár] *v.* to consult.
consultoría [kon·sul·to·rí·a] *f.* consulting (services).
consultorio [kon·sul·tó·rjo] *m.* office for consultation; doctor's office or clinic.
consumado [kon·su·má·đo] *p.p. of* **consumar;** *adj.* consummate, perfect, complete; accomplished.
consumar [kon·su·már] *v.* to consummate, complete.
consumidor [kon·su·mi·đór] *m.* consumer; *adj.* consuming.
consumir [kon·su·mír] *v.* to consume; to waste; **-se** to be consumed; to burn out; to be exhausted; (*acabarse*) to waste away.
consumo [kon·sú·mo] *m.* consumption (*of food, provisions, etc.*).
consunción [kon·sun·sjón] *f.* consumption (*illness*).
contabilidad [kon·ta·ƀi·li·đáđ] *f.* accounting; bookkeeping.
contacto [kon·ták·to] *m.* contact.
contado [kon·tá·đo]: **al —** in cash; **de —** immediately; **por de —** of course; **contados** *adj.* few, scarce, rare.
contador [kon·ta·đór] *m.* accountant; purser, cashier; counter; (*medidor*) meter (*for water, gas, or electricity*); **— geiger** Geiger counter; Geiger-Müller counter.
contaduría [kon·ta·đu·rí·a] *f.* accounting; accountant's

or auditor's office; box office; cashier's office.
contagiar [kon·ta·xjár] *v.* to infect; to corrupt; to contaminate.
contagio [kon·tá·xjo] *m.* contagion; infection.
contagioso [kon·ta·xjó·so] *adj.* contagious; infectious.
contaminar [kon·ta·mi·nár] *v.* to contaminate, defile; to corrupt.
contar[2] [kon·tár] *v. irr.* to count; to tell, relate; — **con** to count on, rely on; **a — desde** starting from, beginning with.
contemplación [kon·tem·pla·sjón] *f.* contemplation; gazing; meditation.
contemplar [kon·tem·plár] *v.* to contemplate, gaze at; (*examinar*) to examine; to meditate.
contemporáneo [kon·tem·po·rá·ne·o] *adj.* contemporary.
contender[1] [kon·ten·dér] *v. irr.* to contend, fight; to compete.
contener[45] [kon·te·nér] *v. irr.* to contain; to restrain, check; **-se** to refrain; to restrain oneself.
contenido [kon·te·ní·đo] *m.* contents; *adj.* restrained, moderate.
contentamiento [kon·ten·ta·mjén·to] *m.* contentment, joy.
contentar [kon·ten·tár] *v.* to give pleasure, make happy; **-se** to be satisfied, pleased; *Am.* to make up, renew friendship.
contento [kon·tén·to] *adj.* content, contented, satisfied, glad; *m.* gladness, contentment.
conteo [kon·té·o] *m.* (blood) count.
contera [kon·té·ra] *f.* metal tip (*of a cane, umbrella, etc.*); tip, end; (*refrán*) refrain of a song; **por** — as a finishing touch.
contertulio [kon·ter·tú·ljo] *m.* fellow-member.
contestación [kon·tes·ta·sjón] *f.* answer, reply; argument.
contestar [kon·tes·tár] *v.* to answer, reply.
contextura [kon·tes·tú·ra] *f.* texture, composition; structure (*of animal or vegetable tissues*).
contienda [kon·tjén·da] *f.* fight; dispute; contest.
contigo [kon·tí·ǥo] with you (with thee).
contiguo [kon·tí·ǥwo] *adj.* contiguous, next, neighboring.
continental [kon·ti·nen·tál] *adj.* continental.
continente [kon·ti·nén·te] *m.* continent; countenance; *adj.* continent, moderate, sober.
contingencia [kon·tiŋ·xén·sja] *f.* contingency, possibility; risk.
contingente [kon·tiŋ·xén·te] *adj.* contingent.
continuación [kon·ti·nwa·sjón] *f.* continuation; continuance; **a** — below, as follows.
continuar[18] [kon·ti·nwár] *v.* to continue; to last.
continuidad [kon·ti·nwi·đáđ] *f.* continuity.
continuo [kon·tí·nwo] *adj.* continuous, connected; continual; steady, constant.
contonearse [kon·to·ne·ár·se] *v.* to strut, swagger; to waddle.
contoneo [kon·to·né·o] *m.* strut; waddle.
contorno [kon·tór·no] *m.* (*circuito*) environs, surrounding country (*usually used in plural*); (*línea*) contour, outline.
contra [kón·tra] *prep.* against; **el pro y el** — the pro and con; *f.* opposition; *Am.* antidote, remedy; **-s** *Am.* play-off, final game (*to determine the winner*); **llevar a uno la** — to contradict a person, take the opposite view.
contraalmirante [kon·tra·al·mi·rán·te] *m.* rear admiral.
contrabajo [kon·tra·ƀá·xo] *m.* bass fiddle, string bass.
contrabandear [kon·tra·ƀan·de·ár] *v.* to smuggle.
contrabandista [kon·tra·ƀan·dís·ta] *m.* smuggler.
contrabando [kon·tra·ƀán·do] *m.* contraband; smuggled goods; smuggling.
contracción [kon·trak·sjón] *f.* contraction; *Ch., Peru* diligence, application, devotion.
contradecir[27] [kon·tra·đe·sír] *v. irr.* to contradict.
contradicción [kon·tra·đik·sjón] *f.* contradiction.
contradictorio [kon·tra·đik·tó·rjo] *adj.* contradictory, contrary, opposing.
contradicho [kon·tra·đí·čo] *p.p. of* **contradecir.**
contraer[46] [kon·tra·ér] *v. irr.* to contract; — **matrimonio** to get married; **-se** to shrink; to contract.
contraflujo [kon·tra·flú·xo] *m.* counterflow.
contrafuerte [kon·tra·fwér·te] *m.* buttress; spur (*of a mountain*); **-s** secondary chain of mountains.
contrahacer[31] [kon·tra·a·sér] *v. irr.* to counterfeit; (*forjar*) to forge; to copy, imitate; to mimic.
contrahecho [kon·tra·é·čo] *p.p. of* **contrahacer** & *adj.* counterfeit; forged; deformed.
contralor [kon·tra·lór] *m. Ven., Col., C.A., Andes, Ríopl.* controller or comptroller (*of accounts or expenditures*). *See* **controlador.**
contraorden [kon·tra·ór·đen] *f.* countermand; cancellation of an order.
contrapartida [kon·tra·par·tí·đa] *f.* balancing entry.
contrapelo [kon·tra·pé·lo]: **a** — against the grain.
contrapesar [kon·tra·pe·sár] *v.* to counterbalance, balance; to offset.
contrapeso [kon·tra·pé·so] *m.* counterpoise, counterweight, counterbalance; *Ch.* fear, uneasiness.
contrariar[17] [kon·tra·rjár] *v.* to oppose; to contradict; (*molestar*) to irritate, vex.
contrariedad [kon·tra·rje·đáđ] *f.* opposition; contradiction; bother, irritation; disappointment.
contrario [kon·trá·rjo] *adj.* contrary; opposite; *m.* opponent.
contrarrestar [kon·tra·rres·tár] *v.* to counteract; to resist, oppose; to strike back (*a ball*).
contrarrevolución [kon·tra·rre·ƀo·lu·sjón] *f.* counterrevolution.
contraseña [kon·tra·sé·ña] *f.* password, watchword mark; (*talón*) check (*for baggage*); — **de salida** theatre check.
contrastar [kon·tras·tár] *v.* (*contrapesar*) to contrast; to test (*scales, weights, measures, etc.*); to assay (*metals*); (*resistir*) to resist, oppose.
contraste [kon·trás·te] *m.* contrast; (*prueba*) assay, test; assayer, tester; assayer's office.
contrata [kon·trá·ta] *f.* contract, bargain, agreement.
contratar [kon·tra·tár] *v.* to contract for; to trade; to engage, hire (*someone*); **-se** to come to, or make, an agreement.
contratiempo [kon·tra·tjém·po] *m.* accident, mishap.
contratista [kon·tra·tís·ta] *m. & f.* contractor.
contrato [kon·trá·to] *m.* contract.
contraventana [kon·tra·ƀen·tá·na] *f.* shutter.
contribución [kon·tri·ƀu·sjón] *f.* contribution; (*impuesto*) tax.
contribuir[32] [kon·tri·ƀwír] *v. irr.* to contribute.
contribuyente [kon·tri·ƀu·yén·te] *m.* contributor; taxpayer; *adj.* contributing.
contrincante [kon·triŋ·kán·te] *m.* rival.
control [kon·tról] *m. Am.* control; — **de calidad** quality control.
controlador [kon·tro·la·đór] *Mex., Ch.* (*desacato*) controller.
controlar [kon·tro·lár] *v. Am.* to control.
controversia [kon·tro·ƀér·sja] *f.* controversy.
contumacia [kon·tu·má·sja] *f.* stubbornness, obstinacy; contempt of court, failure to appear in court; rebelliousness.

contumaz [kon·tu·más] *adj.* stubborn; rebellious.
contusión [kon·tu·sjón] *f.* bruise.
convalecer[13] [kom·ba·le·sér] *v. irr.* to convalesce, recover from an illness.
convecino [kom·be·sí·no] *adj.* near, neighboring; *m.* neighbor.
convencedor [kom·ben·se·đór] *adj.* convincing.
convencer[10] [kom·ben·sér] *v.* to convince.
convencimiento [kom·ben·si·mjén·to] *m.* conviction, belief; convincing.
convención [kom·ben·sjón] *f.* convention, assembly; pact, agreement; *Ríopl., Col., Ven., Mex., Carib.* political convention; **convencional** [kom·ben·sjo·nál] *adj.* conventional.
convenido [kom·be·ní·đo] *adj.* agreed; O.K., all right; *p.p. of* **convenir.**
conveniencia [kom·be·njén·sja] *f.* convenience; comfort; (*utilidad*) utility, profit.
conveniente [kom·be·njén·te] *adj.* convenient, useful, profitable; (*propio*) fit, proper, suitable; opportune.
convenio [kom·bé·njo] *m.* pact, agreement.
convenir[48] [kom·be·nír] *v. irr.* to agree; to convene, assemble; (*cuadrar*) to be suitable, proper, advisable; to suit, fit; **-se** to agree.
conventillo [kom·ben·tí·yo] *m. Ríopl., Ch.* tenement house.
convento [kom·bén·to] *m.* convent.
convergente [kom·ber·xén·te] *adj.* convergent, coming together.
converger[11] [kom·ber·xér], **convergir**[11] [kom·ber·xír] *v.* to converge.
conversación [kom·ber·sa·sjón] *f.* conversation.
conversar [kom·ber·sár] *v.* to converse.
conversión [kom·ber·sjón] *f.* conversion.
convertidores [kom·ber·ti·đó·res] *m.* transformers.
convertir[3] [kom·ber·tír] *v. irr.* to convert.
convicción [kom·bik·sjón] *f.* conviction.
convicto [kom·bík·to] *p.p. irr. of* **convencer**; convicted, guilty.
convidado [kom·bi·đá·đo] *m.* guest; *Am.* — **y con ollita** guest who abuses hospitality.
convidar [kom·bi·đár] *v.* to invite; **-se** to volunteer one's services; to invite oneself.
convincente [kom·bin·sén·te] *adj.* convincing.
convite [kom·bí·te] *m.* invitation; banquet.
convocación [kom·bo·ka·sjón] *f.* convocation.
convocar[6] [kom·bo·kár] *v.* to convoke, call together.
convoyar [kom·bo·yár] *v.* to convoy, escort.
convulsión [kom·bul·sjón] *f.* convulsion.
convulsivo [kom·bul·sí·ƀo] *adj.* convulsive; **tos convulsiva** whooping cough.
conyugal [kon·ŷu·ǥál] *adj.* conjugal, pertaining to marriage or a married couple; **vida** — married life.
cónyuge [kón·yu·xe] *m.* husband; *f.* wife.
cooperación [ko·o·pe·ra·sjón] *f.* cooperation.
cooperador [ko·o·pe·ra·đór] *adj.* cooperating, cooperative; *m.* cooperator, co-worker.
cooperar [ko·o·pe·rár] *v.* to cooperate.
cooperativo [ko·o·pe·ra·tí·ƀo] *adj.* cooperative; **cooperativa** *f.* cooperative, cooperative society.
coordinación [ko·or·đi·na·sjón] *f.* coordination.
coordinar [ko·or·đi·nár] *v.* to coordinate.
copa [kó·pa] *f.* (*vaso*) goblet; (*de árbol*) treetop; (*de sombrero*) crown; (*palo de la baraja*) card in the suit of copas (*Spanish deck of cards*); *Am.* **empinar la** — to drink, get drunk.
copartícipe [ko·par·tí·si·pe] *adj.* participant; *m. & f.* joint partner.
copete [ko·pé·te] *m.* tuft; crest; top, summit; ornamental top on furniture; **de** — of high rank, important; proud; **estar uno hasta el** — to be stuffed; to be fed up; **tener mucho** — to be arrogant, haughty.
copia [kó·pja] *f.* copy, imitation; (*computadora*) — **de seguridad** backup copy, — **dura** hard copy, printout; (*cantidad*) abundance.
copiar [ko·pjár] *v.* to copy.
copioso [ko·pjó·so] *adj.* copious, abundant.
copita [ko·pí·ta] *f.* little glass; little drink.
copla [kó·pla] *f.* couplet; stanza (*of variable length and meter*); popular song.
copo [kó·po] *m.* (*de nieve*) snowflake; (*mechón*) wad, tuft (*of wool or cotton*).
copularse [ko·pu·lár·se] *v.* to have sexual relations.
coqueta [ko·ké·ta] *f.* coquette, flirt.
coquetería [ko·ke·te·rí·a] *f.* coquetry, flirting.
coraje [ko·rá·xe] *m.* courage, valor; anger.
coral [ko·rál] *m.* coral; *Am.* red poisonous snake; **-es** coral beads; *adj.* choral, pertaining to a choir; **coralino** [ko·ra·lí·no] *adj.* coral, like coral.
coraza [ko·rá·sa] *f.* cuirass, armor; armor plate or plating; (*concha*) shell (*of a turtle*).
corazón [ko·ra·són] *m.* heart; core, center.
corazonada [ko·ra·so·ná·đa] *f.* presentiment, foreboding; hunch.
corbata [kor·ƀá·ta] *f.* necktie; cravat; *Ríopl.* colorful kerchief, scarf.
corcel [kor·sél] *m.* charger, steed.
corcova [kor·kó·ba] *f.* hump, hunch; **corcovado** [kor·ko·ƀá·đo] *adj.* hunchbacked; *m.* hunchback.
corcovear [kor·ko·ƀe·ár] *v.* to prance about, leap; *Ch.* to kick, protest against.
corchete [kor·čé·te] *m.* hook and eye.
corcho [kór·čo] *m.* cork; (*colmena*) beehive; *adj. Am.* cork-like, spongy.
cordel [kor·đél] *m.* cord, rope; — **entizado** chalk line.
cordero [kor·đé·ro] *m.* lamb; lambskin.
cordial [kor·đjál] *adj.* cordial, friendly; **dedo** — middle finger.
cordialidad [kor·đja·li·đáđ] *f.* cordiality, friendliness, warmth.
cordillera [kor·đi·yé·ra] *f.* mountain range.
cordobés [kor·đo·ƀés] *adj.* Cordovan, of or pertaining to Cordova; *m.* native of Cordova.
cordón [kor·đón] *m.* cord; braid; cordon, line of soldiers; *Ríopl.* — **de la acera** curb, curbstone of the sidewalk — **de rizo** ripple beads; **cordonería** [kor·đo·ne·rí·a] *f.* lace or cord maker's shop; collection of cords and laces; cordmaker's work; braiding.
cordoncillo [kor·đon·sí·yo] *m.* small cord, drawstring, lace, lacing; braid; (*de moneda*) mill (*ridged edge of a coin*); ridge, rib (*of certain fabrics*).
cordura [kor·đú·ra] *f.* good judgment, wisdom; sanity.
corindón [ko·rin·dón] *m.* corundum.
cornada [kor·ná·đa] *f.* goring; butt with the horns; **dar -s** to gore, horn, butt with the horns.
corneta [kor·né·ta] *f.* cornet; bugle; horn; *m.* (*persona*) bugler.
cornisa [kor·ní·sa] *f.* cornice.
coro [kó·ro] *m.* choir; chorus.
corona [ko·ró·na] *f.* crown; wreath.
coronar [ko·ro·nár] *v.* to crown; to top.
coronel [ko·ro·nél] *m.* colonel.
coronilla [ko·ro·ní·ya] *f.* small crown; crown of the head; **estar uno hasta la** — to be fed up, be satiated.
corpanchón [kor·pan·čón] *m.* large body; carcass.
corpiño [kor·pí·ño] *m.* bodice.
corporación [kor·po·ra·sjón] *f.* corporation.

corporal [kor·po·rál] *adj.* corporal, of the body; *m.* (*de iglesia*) corporal.
corpóreo [kor·pó·re·o] *adj.* corporeal, bodily; tangible, material.
corpulento [kor·pu·lén·to] *adj.* corpulent, fat, stout.
corral [ko·rrál] *m.* yard; corral, cattle yard; **corralón** [ko·rra·lón] *m.* large corral; *Am.* lumber warehouse.
correa [ko·rré·a] *f.* leather strap; (*resistencia*) resistance; *Ch.* **-s** leather blanket carrier; *Am.* **tener muchas -s** to be phlegmatic, calm.
corrección [ko·rrek·sjón] *f.* correction; correctness.
correcto [ko·rrék·to] *adj.* correct, proper.
corredizo [ko·rre·đí·so] *adj.* sliding, slipping; **nudo** — slip knot.
corredor [ko·rre·đór] *m.* (*que corre*) runner, racer; (*pasillo*) corridor; gallery around a patio; (*revendedor*) broker; *Carib., Andes* covered porch; *Am.* beater of wild game; *adj.* running; speedy.
corregidor [ko·rre·xi·đór] *m.* corrector; Spanish magistrate.
corregir[5, 11] [ko·rre·xír] *v. irr.* to correct; to reprove; to punish; **-se** to mend one's ways.
correligionario [ko·rre·li·xjo·ná·rjo] *adj.* of the same religion; of the same political party or sympathies; *m.* coreligionist.
correntada [ko·rren·tá·đa] *f. Ch., Ríopl., C.A., Carib.* strong river current.
correo [ko·rré·o] *m.* mail; mail service; postman; post office; — **aéreo** air mail.
correón [ko·rre·ón] *m.* large strap.
correoso [ko·rre·ó·so] *adj.* flexible, leathery, tough; **correosidad** [ko·rre·o·si·đáđ] *f.* toughness; flexibility.
correr [ko·rrér] *v.* (*caminar*) to run; to blow (*said of the wind*); (*encarrera*) to race; to chase; (*pasar*) to pass, elapse (*time*); to draw (*a curtain*); *Mex.* to dismiss, throw out; **-se** to slip through; to slide; (*apenarse*) to be embarrassed.
correría [ko·rre·rí·a] *f.* foray, raid for plunder; (*viaje*) excursion, short trip; **-s** wanderings, travels; raids.
correspondencia [ko·rres·pon·dén·sja] *f.* correspondence; letters, mail; agreement; interchange.
corresponder [ko·rres·pon·dér] *v.* to reciprocate, return (*love, favors*); (*pertenecer*) to belong; (*tratarse de*) to concern; to correspond (*one thing with another*).
correspondiente [ko·rres·pon·djén·te] *adj.* corresponding, agreeing; respective; *m.* correspondent.
corresponsal [ko·rres·pon·sál] *m.* correspondent; agent; newspaper reporter.
corretaje [ko·rre·tá·xe] *m.* brokerage.
corretear [ko·rre·te·ár] *v.* to run around; to roam, rove; *Am.* to pursue, chase.
corretelas [ko·rre·té·las] *m.* puller (*drape*).
corrida [ko·rrí·đa] *f.* race; *Ch.* row, file; *P.R.* night spree; *Am.* beating up of game; — **del tiempo** swiftness of time; — **de toros** bullfight; **de** — without stopping; **comida** — **a** the regular meal.
corrido [ko·rrí·đo] *adj.* embarrassed, ashamed; worldly-wise; flowing, fluent; **de** — without stopping; *m. Mex., Col., Ven., Ríopl., Andes* popular ballad.
corriente [ko·rrjén·te] *adj.* (*que corre*) running; flowing, fluent; (*común*) usual, common, ordinary; *Am.* frank, open; **¡ — !** all right! O.K.!; **el ocho del** — the eighth of the current month; **estar al** — to be up-to-date; to be well-informed (*about current news*); **poner a uno al** — to keep someone posted or well informed; *f.* current; flow; course; *Am.* **hay que llevarle la** — one must humor him; — **alternativa** A.C. (alternating current); — **continua** D.C. (direct current).
corrillo [ko·rrí·yo] *m.* circle or group of gossipers.
corro [kó·rro] *m.* group of talkers or spectators.
corroer[51] [ko·rro·ér] *v. irr.* to corrode.
corromper [ko·rrom·pér] *v.* to corrupt; to seduce; to bribe; **-se** to rot; to become corrupted.
corrompido [ko·rrom·pí·đo] *adj.* corrupt; rotten, spoiled; degenerate; *p.p. of* **corromper.**
corrupción [ko·rrup·sjón] *f.* corruption.
corrupto [ko·rrúp·to] *adj.* corrupt, rotten.
corsé [kor·sé] *m.* corset.
corsetería [kor·se·te·rí·a] *f.* maker or seller of inner garments.
cortacircuito [kor·ta·sir·kwí·to] *m.* circuit breaker, cut-out.
cortada [kor·tá·đa] *f. Col., Ven., Carib.* cut, slash.
cortador [kor·ta·đór] *m.* cutter.
cortadura [kor·ta·đú·ra] *m.* cut; gash; slash.
cortafrío [kor·ta·frí·o] *m.* cold chisel.
cortante [kor·tán·te] *adj.* cutting; sharp.
cortaplumas [kor·ta·plú·mas] *m.* penknife.
cortar [kor·tár] *v.* to cut; to cut off; to cut out; to cut down; to interrupt; *Ven.* to harvest, pick (*fruit*); to gossip, speak ill of someone; **-se** to be embarrassed, ashamed; to sour, curdle (*said of milk*); *Mex., Arg.* to become separated, cut off, *Mex., Cuba* to leave in a hurry; *Am.* to die.
corte [kór·te] *m.* cut; cutting; cutting edge; fit, style; *Carib., Mex., Ríopl.* cut (*in cards*); — **por arco y aire** arc-air cutting (*welding*); *Am.* harvest; *Mex., Carib.* weeding; *Arg.* gracefulness in dancing; *f.* royal court; retinue; *P.R., Ven.* court of justice; **-s** Spanish parliament; **hacer la** — to court, woo; *Am.* **darse uno** — to put on airs.
cortedad [kor·te·đáđ] *f.* smallness; timidity; bashfulness, shyness.
cortejar [kor·te·xár] *v.* to court, woo.
cortejo [kor·té·xo] *m.* cortege, procession; retinue; courtship; suitor.
cortés [kor·tés] *adj.* courteous, polite.
cortesana [kor·te·sá·na] *f.* courtesan, prostitute.
cortesano [kor·te·sá·no] *m.* courtier; *adj.* courtlike; courteous.
cortesía [kor·te·sí·a] *f.* courtesy, politeness.
corteza [kor·té·sa] *f.* bark; crust; peel.
cortijo [kor·tí·xo] *m.* farmhouse.
cortina [kor·tí·na] *m.* curtain.
corto [kór·to] *adj.* short; scanty; bashful.
cortocircuito [kor·to·sir·kwí·to] *m.* short circuit.
corveta [kor·ƀé·ta] *f.* buck, leap, bound (*of a horse*); **hacer -s** to prance.
corvo [kór·ƀo] *m. C.A.* machete.
cosa [kó·sa] *f.* thing; — **de** approximately, about; **no es** — it is not worth anything; **otra** — something else; **como si tal** — serene, as if nothing had happened; *Mex.* **ni por una de estas nueve -s** absolutely not, not for anything in the world.
cosecha [ko·sé·ča] *f.* crop; harvest.
cosechar [ko·se·čár] *v.* to reap; to harvest.
coser [ko·sér] *v.* to sew; to stitch.
cosmético [koz·mé·ti·ko] *m. & adj.* cosmetic.
cosquillas [kos·kí·yas] *f. pl.* ticklishness; tickling; **hacer** — to tickle; to excite (*one's desire or curiosity*); **tener** — to be ticklish.
cosquillear [kos·ki·ye·ár] *v.* to tickle; to excite (*one's curiosity or desire*).
cosquilleo [kos·ki·yé·o] *m.* tickle, tickling sensation.
cosquilloso [kos·ki·yó·so] *adj.* ticklish; touchy.
costa [kós·ta] *f.* coast; (*precio*) cost, expense, price; **a**

toda — at all costs, by all means.
costado [kos·tá·đo] *m.* side; (*de animal*) flank.
costal [kos·tál] *m.* sack; **estar hecho un — de huesos** to be nothing but skin and bones; to be very thin.
costanero [kos·ta·né·ro] *adj.* coastal, relating to a coast; (*inclinado*) sloping.
costar[2] [kos·tár] *v. irr.* to cost; — **trabajo** to be difficult.
costarricense [kos·ta·rri·sén·se] *adj., m. & f.* Costa Rican.
coste [kós·te], **costo** [kós·to] *m.* cost; expense.
costear [kos·te·ár] *v.* (*pagar*) to defray or pay costs; to pay, (*valer*) be profitable; (*pasar junto a*) to navigate along the coast; to go along the edge of; **no costea** it does not pay.
costero [kos·té·ro] *adj.* coastal; **navegación costera** coastal navigation.
costilla [kos·tí·ya] *f.* rib; (*carne*) chop, cutlet.
costoso [kos·tó·so] *adj.* costly, expensive.
costra [kós·tra] *f.* crust; scab; — **de óxido** scale.
costroso [kos·tró·so] *adj.* crusty, scabby.
costumbre [kos·túm·bre] *f.* custom, habit.
costura [kos·tú·ra] *f.* sewing; stitching; seam; — **invisible** blind stitching; — **cruzada** cross stitching.
costurera [kos·tu·ré·ra] *f.* seamstress.
costurero [kos·tu·ré·ro] *m.* sewing table or cabinet; sewing box; sewing room.
costurón [kos·tu·rón] *m.* coarse stitching; large seam; (*remiendo*) patch, mend; (*cicatriz*) big scar.
cotejar [ko·te·xár] *v.* to confront, compare; collate.
cotejo [ko·té·xo] *m.* comparison; collation.
contense [ko·tén·se] *m. Ch., Mex.* burlap.
cotidiano [ko·ti·đjá·no] *adj.* daily.
cotizable [ko·ti·sá·ƀle] *adj.* quotable (*price*).
cotización [ko·ti·sa·sjón] *f.* quotation of prices; current price.
cotizar[9] [ko·ti·sár] *v.* to quote (*prices*); *Ch.* to contribute one's share or quota; *Am.* to prorate, distribute proportionally.
coto [kó·to] *m.* enclosure; (*mojón*) landmark; (*límite*) limitation; limit, boundary; **poner — a** to set a limit to; to put an end to.
cotón [ko·tón] *m. Mex., C.A.* shirt of cheap fabric (muslin).
cotorra [ko·tó·rra] *f.* small parrot; magpie; (*persona*) talkative person, chatterbox.
cotorrear [ko·to·rre·ár] *v.* to chatter; to gossip.
covacha [ko·ƀá·ča] *f.* small cave; grotto; *Mex., Cuba, Andes* hut, shanty; *Col.* cubbyhole, small dark room.
coyote [ko·yó·te] *m. Am.* coyote, prairie wolf; *Mex.* (*traficante*) shyster, tricky, lawyer; *Mex., C.A.* agent, broker (*often illegal*).
coyuntura [ko·yun·tú·ra] *f.* joint; articulation; occasion; precise moment.
coz [kos] *f.* kick; recoil of a gun; butt of a firearm; **dar** (*or* **tirar**) **coces** to kick.
cráneo [krá·ne·o] *m.* cranium, skull.
craso [krá·so] *adj.* fat; (*bruto*) thick, coarse, gross; **ignorancia crasa** gross ignorance.
cráter [krá·ter] *m.* crater of a volcano.
creación [kre·a·sjón] *f.* creation.
creador [kre·a·đór] *m.* creator; *adj.* creating, creative.
crear [kre·ár] *v.* to create.
crecer[13] [kre·sér] *v. irr.* to grow; to increase; **-se** to swell (*as a river*); to become or feel important.
crecida [kre·sí·đa] *f.* river flood.
crecido [kre·sí·đo] *adj.* grown, increased; large; swollen.
creciente [kre·sjén·te] *adj.* growing, increasing; crescent (*moon*); *f.* river flood; *m.* crescent.
crecimiento [kre·si·mjén·to] *m.* growth, increase.
credenciales [kre·đen·sjá·les] *f. pl.* credentials.
crédito [kré·đi·to] *m.* credit; (*creencia*) credence, belief; (*fama*) fame, reputation; letter of credit; **dar a** — to loan on credit.
credo [kré·đo] *m.* creed; **en un** — in a jiffy, in a minute.
crédulo [kré·đu·lo] *adj.* credulous, too ready to believe.
creencia [kre·én·sja] *f.* belief, faith.
creer[14] [kre·ér] *v.* to believe; to think, suppose; **¡ya lo creo!** I should say so!; yes, of course!
creíble [kre·í·ƀle] *adj.* credible, believable.
crema [kré·ma] *f.* cream; custard; cold cream.
cremallera [kre·ma·yé·ra] *f.* rack (*rack and pinion*).
crémor tártaro [kre·mor·tár·ta·ro] *m.* cream of tartar.
crepitar [kre·pi·tár] *v.* to crackle, snap; to creak; to rattle.
crepuscular [kre·pús·ku·lár] *adj.* twilight.
crepúsculo [kre·pús·ku·lo] *m.* twilight.
crespo [krés·po] *adj.* curly; artificial (*style*); angry, crisp.
crespón [kres·pón] *m.* crepe.
cresta [krés·ta] *f.* crest; top, summit; tuft, comb (*of a bird*).
cretona [kre·tó·na] *f.* cretonne.
creyente [kre·yén·te] *m. & f.* believer; *adj.* believing.
creyón [kre·yón] *m. Am.* crayon.
cría [krí·a] *f.* brood; suckling; breeding.
criadero [krja·đé·ro] *m.* tree nursery; breeding place; (*semillero*) hotbed; rich mine.
criado [krjá·đo] *m.* servant; *adj.* bred; **mal** — ill-bred; **criada** *f.* maid, servant.
criador [krja·đór] *m.* breeder, raiser, rearer; creator; *adj.* creating, creative; breeding; nourishing.
crianza [krján·sa] *f.* breeding; nursing; (*modales*) manners.
criar[17] [krjar] *v.* to breed; to bring up, rear, educate; to nurse.
criatura [krja·tú·ra] *f.* creature; baby, child.
criba [krí·ƀa] *f.* sieve.
cribar [kri·ƀár] *v.* to sift.
crimen [krí·men] *m.* crime.
criminal [kri·mi·nál] *adj., m. & f.* criminal.
crin [krin] *f.* mane.
crinudo [kri·nú·đo] *adj. Am.* with a long or thick mane.
criollo [krjó·yo] *m. Am.* Creole; native of Spanish America; *adj. Am.* national, domestic (*not foreign to Spanish America*).
criptón [krip·tón] *m.* krypton.
crisantema [kri·san·té·ma] *f.*, **crisantemo** [kri·san·té·mo] *m.* chrysanthemum.
crisis [krí·sis] *f.* crisis.
crisol [kri·sól] *m.* crucible, melting pot; (*hogar*) hearth of a blast furnace.
crispar [kris·pár] *v.* to contract (*muscles*); to clench (*fists*); to put (*nerves*) on edge.
cristal [kris·tál] *m.* crystal; glass; (*espejo*) mirror; (*lente*) lens; — **líquido** liquid glass.
cristalería [kris·ta·le·rí·a] *f.* glassware shop or factory; glassware.
cristalino [kris·ta·lí·no] *adj.* crystalline, transparent, clear; *m.* lens of the eye.
cristalizar[9] [kris·ta·li·sár] *v.* to crystallize.
cristiandad [kris·tjan·đáđ] *f.* Christianity; Christendom.
cristianismo [kris·tja·níz·mo] *m.* Christianity.
cristiano [kris·tjá·no] *m.* Christian; person; **hablar en**

— to speak clearly; *adj.* Christian.
criterio [kri·té·rjo] *m.* criterion, rule, standard; judgment.
crítica [krí·ti·ka] *f.* criticism; censure; (*chisme*) gossip.
criticador [kri·ti·ka·đór] *adj.* critical; *m.* critic, faultfinder.
criticar[6] [kri·ti·kár] *v.* to criticize; to censure; to find fault with.
crítico [krí·ti·ko] *adj.* critical; *m.* critic, judge; *Am.* faultfinder, slanderer; **criticón** [kri·ti·kón] *m.* critic, knocker, faultfinder; *adj.* critical, over-critical, faultfinding.
croar [kro·ár] *v.* to croak.
cromo [kró·mo] *m.* chromium.
cromosoma [kro·mo·só·ma] *m.* chromosome.
crónica [kró·ni·ka] *f.* chronicle, history; **cronista** [kro·nís·ta] *m.* & *f.* chronicler.
crónico [kró·ni·ko] *adj.* chronic.
cronómetro [kro·nó·me·tro] *m.* chronometer, timepiece.
croquis [kró·kis] *m.* rough sketch.
cruce [krú·se] *m.* crossing; crossroads; crossbreeding.
crucero [kru·sé·ro] *m.* (*cruciforme*) crossing; crossbearer; crossroads; transept (*of a church*); crossbeam; cross (*a constellation*); (*buque*) cruiser.
cruceta [kru·sé·ta] *f.* crosspiece; crosstree; universal joint (*automobile*).
crucificar[6] [kru·si·fi·kár] *v.* to crucify.
crucifijo [kru·si·fí·xo] *m.* crucifix.
crucigrama [kru·si·ǥrá·ma] *m.* crossword puzzle.
crudo [krú·đo] *adj.* raw; (*sin cocer*) uncooked; unripe; harsh; **agua cruda** hard water; **petróleo** — crude oil; *Mex.* **estar** — to have a hang-over; **cruda** *f. Mex.* hang-over.
cruel [krwel] *adj.* cruel.
crueldad [krwel·dáđ] *f.* cruelty.
crujido [kru·xí·đo] *m.* creak, crack, creaking; rustle.
crujir [kru·xír] *v.* to creak, crackle; to grate (*one's teeth*); to rustle; to crunch.
cruz [krus] *f.* cross.
cruzada [kru·sá·đa] *f.* crusade; holy war; campaign.
cruzado [kru·sá·đo] *m.* crusader; *adj.* crossed; cross, crosswise, transverse.
cruzamiento [kru·sa·mjén·to] *m.* crossing; crossroads.
cruzar[9] [kru·sár] *v.* to cross; *Ch.* to fight, dispute; **-se con** to meet.
cuaco [kwá·ko] *m. Mex.* horse; *S.A.* cassava flour.
cuaderno [kwa·đér·no] *m.* notebook; memorandum book; booklet; *Mex., Ven.* pamphlet.
cuadra [kwá·đra] *f.* hall, large room; stable; hospital or prison ward; *Am.* city block; *Perú* reception room.
cuadrado [kwa·đrá·đo] *adj.* square; *m.* square; square ruler; die, metal block or plate.
cuadrante [kwa·đrán·te] *m.* dial, face of a clock or watch; sundial; quadrant (*fourth part of circle; instrument used in astronomy*).
cuadrar [kwa·đrár] *v.* (*cuadriforme*) to square; to form into a square; (*agradar*) to please; to conform; to harmonize; to set well; *Am.* to be becoming (*said of clothes*); *Ch.* to be ready; *Am.* to contribute a large sum; *P.R.* to come out well, succeed; **-se** to stand at attention.
cuadricular [kwa·đri·ku·lár] *v.* to square off, divide into squares.
cuadrilla [kwa·đrí·ya] *f.* group, troupe, gang; armed band; quadrille, (*baile*) square dance.
cuadro [kwá·đro] *m.* square; picture; scene; frame; flower bed; *Col.* blackboard; *Ch.* slaughterhouse.
cuajada [kwa·xá·đa] *f.* curd.
cuajado [kwa·xá·đo] *p.p.* & *adj.* coagulated, curdled; filled, covered; — **de** full or covered with (*flowers, dew, etc.*).
cuajar [kwa·xár] *v.* to coagulate, thicken, curd, curdle; to turn out well; to jell; to please; *Am.* to chatter, prattle; **-se** to coagulate, curd; to become crowded, be filled; **la cosa no cuajó** the thing did not work, did not jell.
cuajarón [kwa·xa·rón] *m.* clot.
cual [kwal] *rel. pron.* which; **cada** — each one; — **más** — **menos** some people more, others less; **el** —, **la** —, **los -es, las -es** which; who; **lo** — which; *adv.* as, like; **¿cuál?** *interr. pron.* which one? what?
cualidad [kwa·li·đáđ] *f.* quality; trait.
cualquier(a) [kwal·kjér(a)] *indef. adj.* & *pron.* any, anyone; whichever; **un hombre cualquiera** any man whatever.
cuando [kwán·do] *rel. adv.* & *conj.* when; **aun** — even though; **¿cuándo?** *interr. adv.* when?
cuantía [kwan·tí·a] *f.* quantity; rank, importance.
cuantioso [kwan·tjó·so] *adj.* plentiful, abundant; numerous.
cuanto [kwán·to] *rel. adj.* & *pron.* as much as, as many as; all that; — **antes** as soon as possible, immediately; **en** — *conj.* as soon as; **en** — **a** as for, with regard to; **unos -s** a few; **¿cuánto?** *interr. adj.* & *pron.* how much?; **¿cuántos?** how many?
cuaquerismo [kwa·ke·ríz·mo] *m.* the Quaker sect, or doctrine.
cuáquero [kwá·ke·ro] *m.* Quaker.
cuarenta [kwa·rén·ta] *num.* forty.
cuarentena [kwa·ren·té·na] *f.* quarantine; forty units of anything; period of forty days, months, or years.
cuarentón [kwa·ren·tón] *m.* man in his forties; **cuarentona** [kwa·ren·tó·na] *f.* woman in her forties.
cuaresma [kwa·réz·ma] *f.* Lent.
cuarta [kwár·ta] *f.* fourth, fourth part; span of a hand; *Mex.* horse whip; *P.R.* **echar** — to beat, flog.
cuartear [kwar·te·ár] *v.* to quarter, divide into quarters; *P.R.* to whip; **-se** to crack, split (*said of walls or ceilings*); *Mex.* to back down, go back on one's word.
cuartel [kwar·tél] *m.* quarter, one fourth; quarters, barracks; district; quarter, mercy; **no dar** — to give no quarter.
cuartelada [kwar·te·lá·đa] *f.* military coup d'état, uprising, insurrection.
cuartelazo [kwar·te·lá·so] *m. Am.* military coup d'état, insurrection.
cuarterón [kwar·te·rón] *m.* quarter, fourth part; fourth of a pound; panel (*of a door or window*); *adj.* & *m.* quarter-breed (*one fourth Indian and three fourths Spanish*); quadroon (*person of quarter negro blood*).
cuarteto [kwar·té·to] *m.* quartet; (*verso*) quatrain (*stanza of four lines*).
cuartilla [kwar·tí·ya] *f.* (*hoja*) sheet of paper; (*medida*) about 4 quarts; about 1½ pecks; fourth of an **arroba** (about 6 pounds); *Am.* three cents' worth; *Am.* **no valer uno** — not to be worth a penny.
cuartillo [kwar·tí·yo] *m.* fourth of a peck; about a pint; fourth of a **real.**
cuarto [kwár·to] *m.* room; (*cantidad*) quarter, one fourth; **tener -s** to have money; *adj.* fourth.
cuarzo [kwár·so] *m.* quartz.
cuate [kwá·te] *adj., m.* & *f. Mex.* twin; pal, buddy.

cuatrero [kwa·tré·ro] *m.* horse thief, cattle thief; *Mex.* Indian who speaks "broken" Spanish.
cuatro [kwá·tro] *num.* four.
cuba [kú·ba] *f.* cask, barrel; tub, vat; (*panzón*) big-bellied person; drunkard.
cubano [ku·bá·no] *adj. & m.* Cuban.
cubeta [ku·bé·ta] *f.* small barrel or keg; bucket, pail.
cúbico [kú·bi·ko] *adj.* cubic.
cubierta [ku·bjér·ta] *f.* cover; covering; (*carta*) envelope; deck (*of a ship*); *Mex.* sheath.
cubierto [ku·bjér·to] *p.p. of* **cubrir**; *m.* cover; place setting for one person at a table.
cubismo [ku·bíz·mo] *m.* cubism.
cubo [kú·bo] *m.* cube; bucket, pail; hub of a wheel; mill pond; *Arg.* finger bowl.
cubremesa [ku·bre·mé·sa] *f.* table cover.
cubrir[52] [ku·brír] *v.* to cover; to hide; to coat; to settle, pay (*a bill*); **-se** to cover oneself; to put on one's hat.
cucaracha [ku·ka·rá·ča] *f.* cockroach.
cuclillas [ku·klí·yas] **en** — in a squatting position; **sentarse en** — to squat.
cuclillo [ku·klí·yo] *m.* cuckoo.
cuco [kú·ko] *adj.* dainty, cute; sly, shrewd; *m.* cuckoo; a kind of caterpillar; card game; *Ríopl.* peach, peach tree; *Mex.* **hacer — a** to make fun of; to fool.
cucurucho [ku·ku·rú·čo] *m.* paper cone; *Am.* peak, summit; *Peru, C.A., Mex.* cowl, cloak with a hood (*worn by penitents in Holy Week processions*).
cuchara [ku·čá·ra] *f.* spoon; trowel; *Am.* mason's trowel; **media** — mediocre person; *Am.* mason's helper; *Am.* **hacer** — to pout; *Am.* **meter uno su** — to butt into a conversation; to meddle; **cucharada** [ku·ča·rá·da] *f.* spoonful; scoop; **cucharón** [ku·ča·rón] *m.* large spoon; ladle; dipper; scoop.
cuchichear [ku·či·če·ár] *v.* to whisper.
cuchicheo [ku·či·čé·o] *m.* whispering, whisper.
cuchilla [ku·čí·ya] *f.* large knife, cleaver; *Mex., P.R.* mountain ridge; *Am.* gore (*in a garment*); *Am.* narrow tract of land.
cuchillada [ku·či·yá·da] *f.* thrust with a knife, stab, slash; cut, gash.
cuchillo [ku·čí·yo] *m.* knife; gore (*in a garment*); — **de monte** hunting knife; **cuchillería** [ku·či·ye·rí·a] *f.* cutlery; cutlery shop.
cueca [kwé·ka] *f. Ch., Arg.* a Chilean dance.
cuello [kwé·yo] *m.* neck; collar.
cuenca [kwéŋ·ka] *f.* river basin; narrow valley; wooden bowl; socket of the eye.
cuenco [kwéŋ·ko] *m.* earthen bowl.
cuenta [kwén·ta] *f.* (*cálculo*) count, calculation; bill; account; (*bolita*) bead (*of a rosary or necklace*); **a fin de -s** in the final analysis; **caer en la** — to see, get the point; **darse** — to realize; *Col.* **de toda** — anyway; **eso corre de mi** — that is my responsibility; I'll take charge of that; **eso no me tiene** — that does not pay me; it is of no profit to me; **en resumidas -s** in short; *P.R.* **hacerle — una cosa a uno** to be useful or profitable for one; **tomar en** — to take into account; **tomar una cosa por su** — to take charge of something, take the responsibility for it; **vamos a -s** let's understand or settle this.
cuentagotas [kwen·ta·gó·tas] *m.* dropper (*for counting drops*).
cuento [kwén·to] *m.* story, tale; — **de nunca acabar** never-ending tale; **déjese de -s** come to the point; **no viene a** — it is not opportune or to the point.
cuerda [kwér·da] *f.* cord, string, rope; chord; watch spring; **dar — a** to wind (*a watch*).
cuerdo [kwér·do] *adj.* sane; wise.
cuereada [kwe·re·á·da] *f. Mex., C.A., Col., Ven.* flogging, whipping; *Am.* skinning of an animal.
cuerear [kwe·re·ár] *v. Am.* to flog, whip; *Am.* to harm, dishonor; *Am.* to beat (*in a game*); *Arg.* to skin (*an animal*).
cuerno [kwér·no] *m.* horn; antenna, feeler; **poner -s a** to be unfaithful to, deceive (*a husband*); *Am.* **mandar al** — to send to the devil.
cuero [kwé·ro] *m.* hide, skin; leather; wineskin; *Col., Ven.* whip; **en -s** naked.
cuerpeada [kwer·pe·á·da] *f. Ríopl.* dodge; evasion.
cuerpo [kwér·po] *m.* body; bulk; corps; **en** — without hat or coat; **luchar — a** — to fight in single combat; *Am.* **sacar el** — to dodge; to escape, avoid doing something.
cuervo [kwér·bo] *m.* crow; raven; *Ven.* buzzard; *Ch.* dishonest priest; *Ríopl., Ch.* **hacer uno la del** — to leave abruptly and not return.
cuesta [kwés·ta] *f.* hill, slope; **a -s** on one's shoulders or back; in one's care; — **abajo** downhill; — **arriba** uphill.
cuestión [kwes·tjón] *f.* question; controversy, dispute; problem, matter.
cuestionario [kwes·tjo·ná·rjo] *m.* questionnaire, list of questions.
cueva [kwé·ba] *f.* cave, cavern; cellar.
cuico [kwí·ko] *m. Mex.* cop, policeman; *Am.* gossiper, tattletale, "squealer"; *Ch., Bol., Peru* half-breed; *Ríopl.* short, chubby person.
cuidado [kwi·dá·do] *m.* care, attention; worry, misgiving; **al — de** in care of; **tener** — to be careful; **¡ — !** look out!; be careful! **¡cuidadito!** be very careful!
cuidadoso [kwi·da·dó·so] *adj.* careful; attentive; anxious.
cuidar [kwi·dár] *v.* to take care of, look after, keep; to make or do carefully.
cuita [kwí·ta] *f.* grief, care, anxiety; misfortune; *C.A.* bird dung.
cuitado [kwi·tá·do] *adj.* unfortunate; timid, shy.
culata [ku·lá·ta] *f.* haunch, buttock; rear; butt (*of a firearm*).
culatazo [ku·la·tá·so] *f.* blow with the butt of a rifle; recoil, kick of a firearm.
culebra [ku·le·bra] *f.* snake; coil; *Mex.* money belt.
culebrear [ku·le·bre·ár] *v.* to zigzag; to twist; wriggle.
culminación [kul·mi·na·sjón] *f.* culmination, climax.
culminar [kul·mi·nár] *v.* to culminate; to come to a climax.
culo [kú·lo] *m.* anus, behind.
culpa [kúl·pa] *f.* fault; guilt; blame; **echar la — a** to blame; **tener la** — to be to blame.
culpabilidad [kul·pa·bi·li·dád] *f.* guilt; **culpable** [kul·pá·ble] *adj.* guilty.
culpar [kul·pár] *v.* to blame; to declare guilty.
cultivación [kul·ti·ba·sjón] *f.* cultivation.
cultivador [kul·ti·ba·dór] *m.* cultivator; **máquina cultivadora** cultivator.
cultivar [kul·ti·bár] *v.* to cultivate.
cultivo [kul·tí·bo] *m.* cultivation, culture.
culto [kúl·to] *adj.* cultured; *m.* cult, worship; religious sect; **rendir — a** to pay homage to; to worship.
cultura [kul·tú·ra] *f.* culture; cultivation.
cumbre [kúm·bre] *f.* summit; top.
cumpleaños [kum·ple·á·ños] *m.* birthday.
cumplido [kum·plí·do] *adj.* (*completo*) complete, full; perfect; (*cortés*) courteous; *p.p.* fulfilled; due,

fallen due; **tiene tres años -s** he is just over three years old; *m.* courtesy, attention; compliment.
cumplimentar [kum·pli·men·tár] *v.* to compliment; to congratulate; to pay a courtesy visit.
cumplimiento [kum·pli·mjén·to] *m.* fulfilment; courtesy; completion; compliment; **de** — formal, ceremonious.
cumplir [kum·plír] *v.* to fulfill; to comply; to carry out; to fall due; — **año,** to have a birthday; to be (*so many*) years old.
cúmulo [kú·mu·lo] *m.* pile, heap; accumulation; cumulus (*mass of clouds*).
cuna [kú·na] *f.* cradle; origin; *Mex.* coffin for the poor; *Cuba* dive, den (*for gambling and dancing*).
cundir [kun·dír] *v.* to spread (*as news, disease, liquids*); to propagate, extend, multiply.
cuña [kú·ña] *f.* wedge; splinter; beadpan; *Ch., Ríopl.* influential person; *Arg.* spot commercial.
cuñado [ku·ñá·đo] *m.* brother-in-law; **cuñada** [ku·ñá·đa] *f.* sister-in-law.
cuota [kwó·ta] *f.* quota; dues, fee; — **de entrada** admission fee.
cuotidiano [kwo·ti·đjá·no] *adj.* everyday, daily.
cupé [ku·pé] *m.* coupé.
cupo [kú·po] *m.* quota; *Col.* place, seat (*on a plane or train*).
cupón [ku·pón] *m.* coupon.
cúpula [kú·pu·la] *f.* dome.
cura [kú·ra] *f.* cure; *m.* curate, priest.
curación [ku·ra·sjón] *f.* cure.
curandero [ku·ran·dé·ro] *m.* healer (*not a doctor*); quack; medicine man (*among Indians*).
curar [ku·rár] *v.* to cure, heal; to treat; to cure (*meats, tobacco*); to tan (*skins*); *Arg.* to load (*dice*), fix (*cards*); — **de** to take care of; **-se** to cure oneself; to get well; *Ríopl.* to get drunk.
curiosear [ku·rjo·se·ár] *v.* to snoop, peek, peer, pry; to observe with curiosity.
curiosidad [ku·rjo·si·đáđ] *f.* curiosity; neatness, daintiness.
curioso [ku·rjó·so] *adj.* curious; neat, dainty; **libros raros y -s** rare books.
curita [ku·rí·ta] *f.* bandaid.
curro [kú·rro] *adj.* showy, gaudy, flashy; *m.* dandy.
currutaco [ku·rru·tá·ko] *m.* fop, dandy; *adj.* affected (*in one's dress*).
cursi [kúr·si] *adj.* common, in bad taste; cheap, ridiculous; **cursilería** [kur·si·le·rí·a] *f.* bad taste, cheapness, false elegance; group of cheap, ridiculous people.
curso [kúr·so] *m.* course, direction; scholastic year; course of study.
cursor [kur·sór] *m.* (*computadora*) cursor.
curtidor [kur·ti·đór] *m.* tanner.
curtiduría [kur·ti·đu·rí·a] *f.* tannery.
curtir [kur·tír] *v.* to tan; to harden, accustom to hardships; *Col., Ven.* to dirty, soil; **-se** to get tanned or sunburned; to become accustomed to hardships.
curva [kúr·ƀa] *f.* curve.
curvo [kúr·ƀo] *adj.* curved; bent, crooked; arched.
cúspide [kús·pi·đe] *f.* summit, peak, top; spire, steeple.
custodia [kus·tó·đja] *f.* custody; guard, guardian; monstrance (*vessel in which the consecrated Host is exposed*); **en** — in escrow.
custodiar [kus·to·đjár] *v.* to guard, watch; to keep in custody.
custodio [kus·tó·đjo] *m.* guardian, keeper.
cutícula [ku·tí·ku·la] *f.* cuticle.
cutis [kú·tis] *m.* skin; complexion.
cuyo [kú·yo] *rel. poss. adj.* whose, of whom, of which.
cuz! [kus] *interj.* come here! here! (*to a dog*).

CH:ch

chabacano [ča·ƀa·ká·no] *adj.* crude, unpolished; inartistic; cheap, in bad taste; *m. Mex.* a variety of apricot.
chacota [ča·kó·ta] *f.* fun; jest; **echar a** — to take as a joke; **hacer** — **de** to make fun of.
chacotear [ča·ko·te·ár] *v.* to frolic, joke, make merry; to be boisterous; to show off.
chacra [čá·kra] *f. Ec., Peru, Ch.* small farm; *Col., Ec.* cultivated field.
chaflán [ča·flán] *m.* chamfer (arch.).
chagra [čá·ǥra] *f. Col., Ec.* farm, piece of farm land; *m. & f. Ec.* peasant; *adj.* uncivilized, unrefined.
chal [čal] *m.* shawl.
chalán [ča·lán] *m.* horse trader; *Am.* broncobuster, horse breaker; *Mex.* ferry boat.
chaleco [ča·lé·ko] *m.* waistcoat, vest.
chalote [ča·ló·te] *m.* shallot.
chalupa [ča·lú·pa] *f.* sloop, sailboat; launch; *Mex., Col., Ven., Ríopl.* canoe; *P.R.* raft; *Mex.* Mexican tortilla with sauce.
chamaco [ča·má·ko] *m. Mex., C.A.* boy; **chamaquito** *m. Mex., C.A.* little boy.
chamarra [ča·má·rra] *f.* coarse wool jacket or sweater; *Mex.* sheepskin jacket, leather jacket; *Am.* heavy wool blanket.
chamarreta [ča·ma·rré·ta] *f.* short loose jacket; *Am.* square poncho.
chambergo [čam·bér·ǥo] *m.* gaucho sombrero.
chambón [čam·bón] *adj.* clumsy, awkward, unskillful; *m.* bungler, clumsy performer, awkward workman; clumsy player.
champaña [čam·pá·ña] *f.* champagne.
champiñón [čam·pi·ñón] *m.* mushroom.
champú [čam·pú] *m.* shampoo.
champurrado [čam·pu·rrá·đo] *m. Mex.* a mixed drink of chocolate and **atole**; *Col.* a mixed alcoholic beverage.
champurrar [čam·pu·rrár], *Am.* **champurrear** [čam·pu·rre·ár] *v.* to mix (*drinks*).
chamuescar [ča·mwes·kár] *v.* to frizzle.
chamuscada [ča·mus·ká·đa], **chamuscadura** [ča·mus·ka·đú·ra] *f. Am.* singe, scorch.
chamuscar[6] [ča·mus·kár] *v.* to scorch; to singe; to sear; *Am.* to sell at a low cost; **-se** to get scorched, singed, or seared; *Col.* to get peeved, offended.
chamusquina [ča·mus·kí·na] *f.* singe, scorch.
chancear [čan·se·ár] *v.* to fool, joke, jest.
chancero [čan·sé·ro] *m.* jester, joker; *adj.* jolly.
chancla [čáŋ·kla] *f.* slipper; old shoe; **chancleta** *f.* slipper; *m. Am.* good-for-nothing.
chanclo [čáŋ·klo] *m.* galosh, overshoe; clog; rubber overshoe; **-s** rubbers.
chancho [čán·čo] *m. S.A.* pig, pork.
changador [čaŋ·ga·đór] *m. Ríopl.* carrier, porter; *Am.* handy man, person who does odd jobs.
chango [čáŋ·go] *m. Mex.* monkey; **ponerse** — to be alert, wary.
chantaje [čan·tá·xe] *m.* blackmail, blackmailing.
chanza [čán·sa] *f.* joke, jest.
chapa [čá·pa] *f.* metal plate; veneer (*thin leaf of wood*); rosy spot on the cheeks; *Mex., C.A., Andes* lock; *S.A.* Indian spy; **-s** game of tossing coins;

hombre de — serious, reliable man.
chapado [ča·pá·đo] *adj.* veneered (*covered with a thin layer of wood or other material*); — **a la antigua** old-fashioned.
chapalear [ča·pa·le·ár] = **chapotear.**
chapapote [ča·pa·pó·te] *m. Mex.* tar; asphalt.
chaparro [ča·pá·rro] *m.* scrub oak; short, chubby person; *Am.* a kind of tropical shrub with rough leaves; *Am.* short whip; *adj. Mex., C.A.* short, squatty person.
chaparrón [ča·pa·rrón] *m.* downpour, heavy shower.
chapetón [ča·pe·tón] *m.* red spot on the cheek; *Col.* nickname for a Spaniard.
chapitel [ča·pi·tél] *m.* spire, steeple; capital (*of a column*).
chapotear [ča·po·te·ár] *v.* to splash, paddle in the water.
chapoteo [ča·po·té·o] *m.* splash.
chapucear [ča·pu·se·ár] *v.* to fumble; to botch, bungle, do or make clumsily; *Am.* to deceive, trick.
chapulín [ča·pu·lín] *m. Mex., C.A.* grasshopper.
chapurrar [ča·pu·rrár] *v.* to speak (*a language*) brokenly; to mix (*drinks*).
chapuz [ča·pús] *m.* dive, duck, ducking.
chapuza [ča·pú·sa] *f.* botch, clumsy piece of work; *Am.* foul trick, fraud.
chapuzar[9] [ča·pu·sár] *v.* to duck; to dive.
chaqueta [ča·ké·ta] *f.* jacket; **chaquetón** [ča·ke·tón] *m.* long jacket, coat.
charamusca [ča·ra·mús·ka] *f. Mex.* twisted candy stick or cane; *Col., Ven.* brushwood, firewood; *C.A.* hubbub, uproar.
charamusquero [ča·ra·mus·ké·ro] *m. Am.* candystick maker or vendor.
charca [čár·ka] *f.* pond.
charco [čár·ko] *m.* puddle, pool; **pasar el** — to cross the pond, cross the ocean.
charla [čár·la] *f.* chat, chatter, prattle.
charladuría [čar·la·đu·rí·a] *f.* chatter, gossip.
charlar [čar·lár] *v.* to chat, chatter, prate.
charlatán [čar·la·tán] *m.* chatterer, prater; gossiper; charlatan, quack.
charol [ča·ról] *m.* varnish; patent leather; *Col.* tray; **charola** *f. Mex.* tray.
charolar [ča·ro·lár] *v.* to varnish, polish.
charqui [čár·ki] *m.* jerky, jerked beef.
charro [čá·rro] *m. Spain* a villager of Salamanca province; *Mex.* Mexican horseman of special costume and cultural status.
charrúa [ča·rrú·a] *m. & f. Am.* Charruan Indian (*Indian of Uruguay*).
chascarrillo [čas·ka·rrí·yo] *m.* joke, funny story.
chasco [čás·ko] *m.* joke, prank; surprise; disillusionment, disappointment; **llevarse** — to be disappointed, surprised or fooled; *adj. S.A.* thick, curly (*hair*); *Am.* ruffled (*plumage*).
chasquear [čas·ke·ár] *v.* to play a trick on; to disappoint; to crack (*a whip*); to smack (*the lips*); to click (*the tongue*); to crack, snap; *Col., Ven.* to chatter (*said of the teeth*); *Am.* to munch (*food*); **-se** to be disappointed or disillusioned; to be tricked or fooled.
chasqui [čás·ki] *m. Andes, Ríopl.* courier, messenger.
chasquido [čas·kí·đo] *m.* crack of a whip; crackle; smack (*of the lips*); click (*of the tongue*).
chata [čá·ta] *f.* bedpan; scow, barge, flat-bottomed boat; *Ríopl.* platform wagon, platform car, flatcar, **chatita** [ča·tí·ta] *f. Mex.* "honey", "cutie", "funny face".
chato [čá·to] *adj.* snub-nosed, flat-nosed; flat; flattened; squatty; *Mex.* **quedarse uno** — to be left flat or in the lurch; to be disappointed.
chaval [ča·ƀál] *m.* lad; young man.
chayote [ča·yó·te] *m. Mex.* vegetable pear (*a tropical fruit growing on a vine*); *Mex., Ven., C.A.* dunce, silly fool.
che [če] *interj. Ríopl.* word used to attract attention among intimates; say! listen! hey!; nickname for citizens of Argentina; *Bol.* buddy, pal.
cheque [čé·ke] *m.* check, bank check.
chequera [če·ké·ra] *f.* check book.
chica [čí·ka] *f.* little girl; girl, maid, servant.
chicle [čí·kle] *m. Am.* chicle; *Mex.* chewing gum.
chico [čí·ko] *adj.* small, little; *m.* child, boy; *Col.* each game of billiards; *Mex.* = **chicozapote** [či·ko·sa·pó·te] (*tropical fruit and tree from which chicle is extracted*).
chicote [či·kó·te] *m.* cigar; piece of rope; *Am.* whip; *Col., Ven.* cigar butt.
chicotear [či·ko·te·ár] *v. Ríopl., Col., Peru* to lash, whip, flog; *Ven.* to fight, quarrel, *Col.* to kill.
chicoteo [či·ko·té·o] *m. Ríopl.* whipping; *Am.* shooting, killing; *Am.* crackling, rattling (*as of machine guns*); *Am.* quarreling.
chicha [čí·ča] *f. Peru, Col., Ch., Ríopl., C.A.* chicha (*a popular alcoholic beverage*); *Peru* thick-soled shoe; **no ser ni — ni limonada** to be worth nothing, be neither fish nor fowl.
chícharo [čí·ča·ro] *m. Mex.* pea; *Col.* bad cigar; *Mex.* apprentice.
chicharra [či·čá·rra] *f.* cicada, locust; talkative person; *Mex.* person with a shrill voice; *Am.* rickety, squeaky car; *Ch.* harsh-sounding musical instrument or bell; *C.A., Mex., Cuba* piece of fried pork skin.
chicharrón [či·ča·rrón] *m.* crackling, crisp piece of fried pork skin; burned piece of meat; sunburnt person; *Am.* dried-up, wrinkled person; *Mex.* bootlicker, flatterer.
chiche [čí·če] *m. Mex., C.A.* breast, teat; wet nurse.
chichón [či·čón] *m.* bump, lump; *Am.* joker, jester; **chichona** [či·čó·na] *adj. Mex., C.A.* large-breasted; "stacked".
chiflado [či·flá·đo] *adj.* "cracked", nuts, crazy; *p.p. of* **chiflar.**
chifladura [či·fla·đú·ra] *f.* craziness, mania; mockery, jest.
chiflar [či·flár] *v.* to whistle; to hiss; *Mex.* to sing (*said of birds*); **-se** to lose one's head; to become unbalanced, crazy.
chiflido [či·flí·đo] *m.* whistle; hiss; *Am.* **en un** — in a jiffy, in a second.
chile [čí·le] *m.* chili, red pepper.
chileno [či·lé·no] *adj. & m.* Chilean.
chillante [či·yán·te] *adj.* flashy, bright, showy, loud; shrieking.
chillar [či·yár] *v.* to shriek, scream; to hiss; *Am.* to shout, protest, moan; *Mex.* to "squeal", turn informer; *Ríopl., Ven., C.A., P.R.* **no** — not to say a word; *Mex.* **-se** to be piqued, offended.
chillido [či·yí·đo] *m.* shriek, scream.
chillón [či·yón] *adj.* shrieking, screaming; shrill; loud, gaudy; *Col., Andes* whining, discontented; *Ríopl.* touchy.
chimenea [či·me·né·a] *f.* chimney; fireplace, hearth.
china [čí·na] *f.* (*de la China*) Chinese woman; China silk or cotton; porcelain; (*piedra*) pebble; marble; *Andes, Ch., Ríopl., Col.* girl, young woman (*usually half-breed or Indian*); *S.A.* servant girl; *P.R.* sweet orange; *Col.* spinning top; **chinita** [či·ní·ta] *f. Am.* little Indian girl; darling.

chinche [čin·če] *f.* bedbug; thumbtack; tiresome person, bore; *Col., Ven., Ríopl.* touchy or irritable person; *Am.* plump, squatty person.
chinchilla [čin·čí·ya] *f.* chinchilla.
chinchorro [čin·čó·rro] *m. Ven., Col.* hammock.
chingar [čiŋ·gár] *v. S.A.* to frustrate; to fail; *Mex.* to copulate.
chino [čí·no] *adj.* Chinese; *Mex.* curly; *m. Ríopl.* Chinese; Chinaman; *C.R.* pig; *Ríopl.* half-breed (*Negro and Indian, white and Indian*); *Am.* Indian, *Col.* house servant; *Am.* coarse, rough, ugly person, *Col.* straight, coarse hair.
chiquero [či·ké·ro] *m.* pigsty, pigpen; pen for bulls; goat shelter.
chiquilín [či·ki·lín] *m. Mex., C.A.* tot, little boy; **chiquilina** [či·ki·lí·na] *f. Am.* little girl.
chiquito [či·kí·to] *adj.* tiny, very small; *m.* tiny tot, tiny child; **chiquitico** [či·ki·tí·ko] *adj.* tiny.
chiripa [či·rí·pa] *f.* stroke of good luck.
chiripá [či·ri·pá] *m. Ríopl.* loose riding trousers (*square of cloth draped from the waist and between the legs*).
chirola [či·ró·la] *f. Mex., Ven., Ríopl.* "jug", jail; coin of low value.
chirona [či·ró·na] *f.* "jug", jail.
chirriado [či·rrjá·đo] *adj. Col.* attractive; lively.
chirriar[17] [či·rrjár] *v.* to squeak, creak; to sizzle; to chirp; to sing out of tune; *Col.* to go on a spree.
chirrido [či·rrí·đo] *m.* creak, squeak; chirp; squeaking, creaking; chirping.
chisguete [čiz·ǵé·te] *m.* squirt.
chisme [číz·me] *m.* gossip, piece of gossip; trifle, trinket, knickknack, gadget.
chismear [čiz·me·ár] *v.* to gossip; to tattle.
chismería [čiz·me·rí·a] *f.* gossiping, talebearing.
chismero [čiz·mé·ro] *adj.* gossiping; *m.* gossip.
chismoso [čiz·mó·so] *adj.* gossiping; *m.* gossip, talebearer, tattletale.
chispa [čís·pa] *f.* spark; small diamond; wit; *Col.* false rumor, lie; *Am.* two-wheeled cart; *Mex.* brazen, shameless woman; *Am.* **da** — it clicks, works, functions; *Am.* **ponerse** — to get drunk.
chispeante [čis·pe·án·te] *adj.* sparkling.
chispear [čis·pe·ár] *v.* to spark; to sparkle; to twinkle; to drizzle.
chisporrotear [čis·po·rro·te·ár] *v.* to sputter, throw off sparks.
chiste [čís·te] *m.* joke, jest; **dar en el** — to guess right, hit the nail on the head.
chistera [čis·té·ra] *f.* top hat; fish basket.
chistoso [čis·tó·so] *adj.* funny, amusing, humorous.
¡chito! [čí·to] **¡chitón!** [čí·tón] *interj.* hush!
chiva [čí·ƀa] *f.* female goat; *Am.* goatee; *Pan., Col.* flivver, small bus; **chivo** *m.* he-goat; *Am.* fit of anger; *Am.* insulting remark; *C.R.* **estar hecho un** — to be very angry; *adj. Am.* angry; **chivato** [či·ƀá·to] *m. Cuba* informer, squealer.
chocante [čo·kán·te] *adj.* striking, surprising; shocking; disgusting; *Col., Andes* tiresome, annoying, impertinent.
chocar[6] [čo·kár] *v.* to bump, collide, clash; to fight; to shock, surprise, disgust; **me choca ese hombre** I loathe that man.
chocarrear [čo·ka·rre·ár] *v.* to tell coarse jokes; to clown.
chocarrería [čo·ka·rre·rí·a] *f.* coarse joke; **chocarrero** [čo·ka·rré·ro] *adj.* coarse, vulgar; clownish.
choclo [čó·klo] *m.* overshoe; clog; *Mex.* low shoe or slipper; *Andes, Col., Ch., Ríopl.* ear of corn; *Ven.* corn stew, *Ch.* spike, ear of wheat.
chocolate [čo·ko·lá·te] *m.* chocolate.
chochear [čo·če·ár] *v.* to be in one's dotage, act senile.
chochera [čo·čé·ra], **chochez** [čo·čés] *f.* senility, dotage; **chocheras** [čo·čé·ras], **chocheces** [čo·čé·ses] senile actions or habits.
chocho [čó·čo] *adj.* doting; *m.* childish old man.
chófer [čó·fer], [čo·fér] *m.* chauffeur.
cholo [čó·lo] *m. Andes, Ríopl., Ch.* half-breed; *Am.* half-civilized Indian; *adj. Mex., Perú* coarse, rude; *C.R.* dark-skinned; *Ch.* black (*dog*); member of U.S. Southwest anti-social, counter-prestige culture.
chopo [čó·po] *m.* black poplar; *adj. Am.* stupid.
choque [čó·ke] *m.* collision, bump; shock; clash, conflict; dispute.
chorizo [čo·rí·so] *m.* sausage; *Am.* string of things; *Am.* fool.
chorrazo [čo·rrá·so] *m.* spurt, large stream or jet.
chorrear [čo·rre·ár] *v.* to drip; to spout.
chorro [čó·rro] *m.* spurt, jet; stream, flow; *Arg.* strand of a whip; *Col.* river rapids.
choteador [čo·te·a·đór] *m. Carib.* joker, jester.
chotear [čo·te·ár] *v. Cuba* to make fun of, jeer, jest, mock, kid; *Mex., C.A.* to idle, fool around; *Col.* to pamper.
choteo [čo·té·o] *m. Cuba* joking, jeering, kidding.
choza [čó·sa] *f.* hut, cabin.
chubasco [ču·ƀás·ko] *m.* squall, sudden shower; **aguantar el** — to weather the storm.
chuchería [ču·če·rí·a] *f.* trifle, trinket; knick-knack; tidbit.
chueco [čwé·ko] *adj. Mex.* crooked, bent; *Col.* crook-legged, bow-legged, knock-kneed; *Am.* worn-out, dejected; *Mex.* disgusted, annoyed; *Mex.* **commerciar en** — to trade in stolen goods.
chuleta [ču·lé·ta] *f.* cutlet, chop; blow, slap.
chulo [čú·lo] *m.* elegant person; effeminate man; clownish fellow; bullfighter's assistant; *Col.* buzzard; *Mex.* coarse, thick brush; *adj. C.A., Col., Mex.* goodlooking, pretty.
chumpipe [čum·pí·pe] *m. C.A.* turkey; also **chompipe.**
chupada [ču·pá·đa] *f.* sucking; suction; suck, sip; *Mex., C.A., Ven., Andes* puff from a cigarette; *Ríopl.* big swallow of liquor.
chupador [ču·pa·đór] *m.* sucker; teething ring; *Ríopl.* toper, heavy drinker; *Am.* smoker.
chupaflor [ču·pa·flór], **chuparrosa** [ču·pa·rró·sa] *m. Am.* hummingbird.
chupar [ču·pár] *v.* to suck; to sip; to absorb, take in; *Am.* to smoke; *C.A., Ríopl., Andes* to drink, get drunk; **-se** to shrivel up.
churrasco [ču·rrás·ko] *m. Ríopl., Andes* roasted meat; *Ríopl., Andes* barbecued meat; *Ríopl., Andes* large piece of meat for barbecuing.
churrasquear [ču·rras·ke·ár] *v. Ríopl., Andes* to barbecue, roast over coals; *Ríopl., Andes* to prepare (*meat*) for barbecuing; *Ríopl., Andes* to eat barbecued meat.
churrasquito [ču·rras·kí·to] *m.* small piece of roast.
churrigueresco [ču·rri·ǵe·rés·ko] *adj.* baroque, ornate (*architecture*).
churro [čú·rro] *adj.* coarse; *m. Spain* doughnut-like fritter.
chuscada [čus·ká·đa] *f.* jest, joke.
chusco [čús·ko] *adj.* funny, witty; ridiculous; *Peru* **perro** — mongrel dog.
chusma [čúz·ma] *f.* rabble, mob.
chuzo [čú·so] *m.* pike or cane carried by the watchman (*sereno*).

D:d

dable [dá·ƀle] *adj.* feasible, possible.
daca [dá·ka] = **de acá**
dadiva [dá·đi·ƀa] *f.* gift.
dadivoso [da·đi·ƀó·so] *adj.* liberal, generous.
dado [dá·đo] *m.* die; **-s** dice.
dador [da·đór] *m.* giver.
daga [dá·ǥa] *f.* dagger.
dama [dá·ma] *f.* lady; **jugar a las -s** to play checkers.
damajuana [da·ma·xwá·na] *f.* demijohn.
damasquinado [da·mas·ki·ná·đo] *m.* damascene (*incrustation of gold in steel*).
damisela [da·mi·sé·la] *f.* damsel, girl.
danza [dán·sa] *f.* dance.
danzante [dan·sán·te] *m.* & *f.* dancer.
danzar[9] [dan·sár] *v.* to dance.
danzarina [dan·sa·rí·na] *f.* dancer.
dañar [da·ñár] *v.* to harm, hurt, damage; **-se** to spoil, rot; to get hurt; to get damaged.
dañino [da·ñí·no] *adj.* harmful; destructive.
daño [dá·ño] *m.* damage, harm, loss.
dañoso [da·ñó·so] *adj.* harmful.
dar[26] [dar] *v. irr.* (*hacer don*) to give, confer; (*golpear*) to strike, hit; (*emitir*) give off, emit; — **a luz** to give birth to; to publish; — **con** to encounter, find; — **de alta** to discharge, release from the hospital; — **de comer** to feed; — **de si** to give, stretch; — **en** to hit upon; to persist in; — **largas a un asunto** to prolong or postpone a matter; *C.A., Ven., Col.* — **cuero (guasca, puños)** to beat, thrash, lash; **lo misma da** it makes no difference; **-se** to give up; **dárselas de** to boast of.
dardo [dár·đo] *m.* dart, arrow.
dares y tomares [dá·res·i·to·má·res] *m. pl.* give-and-take, dispute; dealings.
dársena [dár·se·na] *f.* dock, wharf.
datar [da·tár] *v.* to date; — **de** to date from.
dátil [dá·til] *m.* date (*fruit of the date palm*).
dato [dá·to] *m.* datum, fact; **-s** data.
de [de] *prep.* of, from; about, concerning; in (*after a superlative*); if (*before inf.*); — **no llegar** if he does not arrive; **el — la gorra azul** the one with the blue cap; **el mejor — América** the best in America; **más — lo que dice** more than he says.
debajo [de·ƀá·xo] *adv.* under, underneath; — **de** *prep.* under.
debate [de·ƀá·te] *m.* debate; dispute, quarrel.
debatir [de·ƀa·tír] *v.* to debate, argue, discuss; to fight; **-se** to struggle.
debe [dé·ƀe] *m.* debit.
debelar [de·ƀe·lár] *v.* to subdue, defeat.
deber [de·ƀér] *v.* to owe; to have to (must, should, ought); **debe de ser** it must be, probably is; **¡me la debes!** I have an account to settle with you!
deber [de·ƀér] *m.* duty, obligation; debt; debit, debit side (*in bookkeeping*).
debido [de·ƀí·đo] *adj.* due, owing; just, appropriate.
débil [dé·ƀil] *adj.* weak, feeble.
debilidad [de·ƀi·li·đáđ] *f.* debility, weakness.
debilitación [de·ƀi·li·ta·sjón] *f.* **debilitamiento** [de·ƀi·li·ta·mjén·to] *m.* weakening; weakness.
debilitar [de·ƀi·li·tár] *v.* to weaken.
débito [dé·ƀi·to] *m.* debt; debit.
debutar [de·ƀu·tár] *v.* to make a debut, make a first public appearance.
década [dé·ka·đa] *f.* decade, ten years; series of ten.
decadencia [de·ka·đén·sja] *f.* decadence, decline, falling off.
decaer[24] [de·ka·ér] *v. irr.* to decay, decline, wither, fade; to fall to leeward.
dacaimiento [de·kaj·mjén·to] *m.* decline, decay; dejection; weakness.
decano [de·ká·no] *m.* dean; senior member of a group.
decantado [de·kan·tá·đo] *p.p.* & *adj.* much talked about; overrated.
decapitar [de·ka·pi·tár] *v.* to behead.
decencia [de·sén·sja] *f.* decency; **decente** [de·sén·te] *adj.* decent; respectable; fair.
decenio [de·sé·njo] *m.* decade.
decepción [de·sep·sjón] *f.* disillusion, disappointment.
decepcionante [de·sep·sjo·nán·te] *adj.* disappointing.
decepcionar [de·sep·sjo·nár] *v.* to disillusion, disappoint.
decibel [de·si·ƀél] *m.* decibel (*unit for the measurement of the intensity of sound*).
decidir [de·si·đír] *v.* to decide, resolve; **-se a** to make up one's mind to; to decide to.
décima [dé·si·ma] *f.* tenth; tithe; stanza of ten octosyllabic lines.
décimo [dé·si·mo] *adj.* tenth.
decir[27] [de·sír] *v. irr.* to say; to tell; to speak; **es** — that is; **querer** — to mean, signify.
decisión [de·si·sjón] *f.* decision.
decisivo [de·si·sí·ƀo] *adj.* decisive, final.
declamar [de·kla·már] *v.* to declaim, recite.
declaración [de·kla·ra·sjón] *f.* declaration; statement; deposition, testimony.
declarar [de·kla·rár] *v.* to declare, state, affirm; to testify; **-se** to propose, declare one's love; to give one's views or opinion.
declinar [de·kli·nár] *v.* to decline; to go down; to lose vigor, decay; to bend down.
declive [de·klí·ƀe] *m.* declivity, slope.
decoración [de·ko·ra·sjón] *f.* decoration, ornament; stage setting.
decorar [de·ko·rár] *v.* to decorate, adorn.
decorativo [de·ko·ra·tí·ƀo] *adj.* decorative, ornamental.
decoro [de·kó·ro] *m.* decorum, propriety, dignity; honor.
decoroso [de·ko·ró·so] *adj.* decorous, becoming, proper, decent.
decrépito [de·kré·pi·to] *adj.* decrepit, old, feeble.
decretar [de·kre·tár] *v.* to decree.
decreto [de·kré·to] *m.* decree; decision, order.
dechado [de·čá·đo] *m.* model, pattern, example.
dedal [de·đál] *m.* thimble.
dedicar[6] [de·đi·kár] *v.* to dedicate; to devote; **-se** to apply oneself.
dedicatoria [de·đi·ka·tó·rja] *f.* dedication, inscription.
dedo [dé·đo] *m.* (*de la mano*) finger; (*del pie*) toe; — **del corazón** middle finger; — **meñique** little finger; — **pulgar** thumb; **no mamarse el** — not to be easily fooled; **dedillo** *m.* small finger; **saber al dedillo** to know perfectly, know by heart.
deducción [de·đuk·sjón] *f.* deduction; inference.
deducir[25] [de·đu·sír] *v. irr.* to deduce, conclude; to deduct.
defecar[6] [de·fe·kár] *v. irr.* to defecate.
defecto [de·fék·to] *m.* defect, fault.
defectuoso [de·fek·twó·so] *adj.* defective, faulty.
defender[1] [de·fen·dér] *v. irr.* to defend.
defensa [de·fén·sa] *f.* defense; *Mex.* automobile bumper.
defensivo [de·fen·sí·ƀo] *adj.* defensive; *m.* defense, safeguard; **defensiva** [de·fen·si·ƀa] *f.* defensive.
defensor [de·fen·sór] *m.* defender.
deficiencia [de·fi·sjén·sja] *f.* deficiency; **deficiente** [de·fi·sjén·te] *adj.* deficient.

déficit [dé·fi·sit] *m.* deficit, shortage.
definición [de·fi·ni·sjón] *f.* definition.
definido [de·fi·ní·đo] *adj.* definite; *p.p. of* **definir.**
definir [de·fi·nír] *v.* to define, explain; to determine.
definitivo [de·fi·ni·tí·ƀo] *adj.* definitive, conclusive, final; **en definitiva** in short, in conclusion; definitely.
deformación [de·for·ma·sjón] *f.* deformation, deformity.
deformar [de·for·már] *v.* to deform; **-se** to become deformed; to lose its shape or form.
deforme [de·fór·me] *adj.* deformed; ugly.
deformidad [de·for·mi·đáđ] *f.* deformity.
defraudar [de·fraw·đár] *v.* to defraud, cheat, rob of.
defunción [de·fun·sjón] *f.* death, decease.
degenerado [de·xe·ne·rá·đo] *adj. & m.* degenerate.
degenerar [de·xe·ne·rár] *v.* to degenerate.
deglución [de·ǥlu·sjón] *f.* swallowing.
deglutir [de·ǥlu·tír] *v.* to swallow.
degollar[2] [de·ǥo·yár] *v. irr* to behead; to slash the throat; to cut (*a dress*) low in the neck.
degradar [de·ǥra·dár] *v.* to degrade; to debase.
degüello [de·ǥwé·yo] *m.* beheading; throat-slashing.
dehesa [de·é·sa] *f.* pasture, grazing ground.
deidad [dej·đáđ] *f.* deity.
dejadez [de·xa·đés] *f.* lassitude, languor, listlessness; self-neglect, slovenliness.
dejado [de·xá·đo] *adj.* indolent, listless; slovenly.
dejar [de·xár] *v.* (*abandonar*) to leave; to quit; to abandon; to omit; (*permitir*) to permit, let; (*soltar*) to let go; — **de** to stop, cease; — **caer** to drop; *Am.* **no -se** not to be an easy mark, not to let others pick on one.
dejo [dé·xo] *m.* (*sabor*) aftertaste; slight taste; (*acento*) slight accent, peculiar inflection.
del [del] = **de** + **el** of the.
delaminación [de·la·mi·na·sjón] *f.* delamination.
delantal [de·lan·tál] *m.* apron.
delante [de·lán·te] *adv.* before, in front; — **de** *prep.* in front of.
delantera [de·lan·té·ra] *f.* lead, forepart, front.
delantero [de·lan·té·ro] *adj.* front, foremost, first.
delatar [de·la·tár] *v.* to denounce, accuse, inform against.
delator [de·la·tór] *m.* accuser, informer.
delegación [de·le·ǥa·sjón] *f.* delegation.
delegado [de·le·ǥá·đo] *m.* delegate.
delegar[7] [de·le·ǥár] *v.* to delegate.
deleitable [de·lej·tá·ƀle] *adj.* delightful, enjoyable.
deleitar [de·lej·tár] *v.* to delight, please.
deleite [de·léj·te] *m.* delight, joy, pleasure.
deleitoso [de·lej·tó·so] *adj.* delightful.
deletrear [de·le·tre·ár] *v.* to spell.
deleznable [de·lez·ná·ƀle] *adj.* perishable; brittle.
delfín [del·fín] *m.* dolphin; dauphin.
delgadez [del·ǥa·dés] *f.* thinness; slimness; fineness.
delgado [del·ǥá·đo] *adj.* thin, slender, slim.
deliberado [de·li·ƀe·rá·đo] *adj.* deliberate; *p.p. of* **deliberar.**
deliberar [de·li·ƀe·rár] *v.* to deliberate, consider, ponder.
delicadeza [de·li·ka·đé·sa] *f.* fineness; delicacy; softness, exquisiteness.
delicado [de·li·ká·đo] *adj.* delicate; weak, frail; exquisite, dainty; tender.
delicia [de·lí·sja] *f.* delight.
delicioso [de·li·sjó·so] *adj.* delicious, delightful.
delincuente [de·liŋ·kwén·te] *adj., m. & f.* deliquent.
delineación [de·li·ne·a·sjón] *f.,* **delineamiento** [de·li·ne·a·mjén·to] *m.* delineation, design, outline, drawing; portrayal.
delinear [de·li·ne·ár] *v.* to delineate, sketch, outline.
delirante [de·li·rán·te] *adj.* delirious, raving.
delirar [de·li·rár] *v.* to be delirious; to rave, talk wildly or foolishly.
delirio [de·lí·rjo] *m.* delirium, temporary madness; wild excitement; foolishness.
delito [de·lí·to] *m.* crime; misdemeanor.
demacrado [de·ma·krá·đo] *adj.* scrawny, emaciated, thin.
demanda [de·mán·da] *f.* demand; petition; question; claim; complaint; lawsuit.
demandado [de·man·dá·đo] *m.* defendant; *p.p. of* **demandar.**
demandante [de·man·dán·te] *m. & f.* plaintiff.
demandar [de·man·dár] *v.* to demand; to petition; to sue, file a suit; to indict.
demás [de·más] *indef. adj. & pron.:* **los** — the rest; the others; **las** — **personas** the other people; **lo** — the rest; **por** — useless; uselessly; **por lo** — as to the rest; moreover.
demasía [de·ma·sí·a] *f.* excess; boldness, insolence; offense, outrage; **en** — excessively.
demasiado [de·ma·sjá·đo] *adv.* too much, excessively; too; *adj.* too much, excessive.
demente [de·mén·te] *adj.* demented, insane, crazy.
democracia [de·mo·krá·sja] *f.* democracy; **demócrata** [de·mó·kra·ta] *m. & f.* democrat; **democrático** [de·mo·krá·ti·ko] *adj.* democratic.
demográfico [de·mo·grá·fi·ko] *adj.* demographic.
demoler[2] [de·mo·lér] *v. irr.* to demolish, tear down.
demonio [de·mó·njo] *m.* demon, devil; evil spirit.
demontre [de·món·tre] *m.* devil; **¡ — !** the deuce!
demora [de·mó·ra] *f.* delay.
demorar [de·mo·rár] *v.* to delay; to retard; **-se** to linger; to be delayed.
demostración [de·mos·tra·sjón] *f.* demonstration; proof, explanation.
demostrar[2] [de·mos·trár] *v. irr.* to demonstrate, show, prove, explain.
demostrativo [de·mos·tra·tí·ƀo] *adj.* demonstrative.
demovilizar[9] [de·mo·ƀi·li·sár] *v.* to demobilize.
demudar [de·mu·đár] *v.* to change, alter; to disguise; **-se** to change color or one's facial expression; to turn pale.
dengoso [deŋ·gó·so], **denguero** [deŋ·gé·ro] *adj.* affected; finicky.
dengue [déŋ·ge] *m.* primness; coyness, affectation; dengue, breakbone fever; *Arg.* marigold; *Ch.* zigzag; *Am.* swagger **hacer -s** to act coy, make grimaces.
denigrar [de·ni·ǥrár] *v.* to blacken, defame, revile, insult.
denodado [de·no·đá·đo] *adj.* dauntless, daring.
denominación [de·no·mi·na·sjón] *f.* denomination; name, title, designation.
denominar [de·no·mi·nár] *v.* to name, call, entitle.
denostar[2] *v. irr.* to insult, outrage, revile.
denotar [de·no·tár] *v.* to denote, indicate, mean.
densidad [den·si·đáđ] *f.* density; (*computadora*) — **doble** double density; — **simple** single density.
denso [dén·so] *adj.* dense, compact; thick.
dentado [den·tá·đo] *adj.* toothed, notched; pinking (sewing).
dentadura [den·ta·đú·ra] *f.* set of teeth.
dentar[1] [den·tár] *v. irr.* to tooth, furnish (*a saw*) with teeth; to indent; to cut teeth, grow teeth (*referring to a child*).
dentellada [den·te·yá·đa] *f.* bite; tooth mark; **a -s** with big bites.
dentición [den·ti·sjón] *f.* teething.
dentífrico [den·tí·fri·ko] *m.* dentrifice, tooth cleanser;

pasta dentífrica toothpaste; **polvos dentífricos** toothpowder.
dentista [den·tís·ta] *m.* dentist.
dentro [dén·tro] *adv.* inside, within; — **de** *prep.* inside of; **por** — on the inside.
denuedo [de·nwé·đo] *m.* spirit, courage, daring.
denuesto [de·nwés·to] *m.* affront, insult.
denuncia [de·nún·sja] *f.* denunciation, condemnation, accusation; miner's claim.
denunciar [de·nun·sjár] *v.* to denounce, accuse; to proclaim, advise, give notice; to claim (*a mine*).
deparar [de·pa·rár] *v.* to furnish, offer, supply.
departamento [de·par·ta·mén·to] *m.* department; compartment; apartment.
departir [de·par·tír] *v.* to talk, converse.
dependencia [de·pen·dén·sja] *f.* dependence; dependency; branch office.
depender [de·pen·dér] *v.* to depend, rely (on).
dependiente [de·pen·djén·te] *m.* clerk; dependent, subordinate; *adj.* dependent.
depilar [de·pi·lár] *v.* to depilate.
depilatorio [de·pi·la·tó·rjo] *adj.* & *m.* depilatory.
deplorar [de·plo·rár] *v.* to deplore, lament, regret.
deponer[40] [de·po·nér] *v. irr.* to set aside; to depose, remove (*an official*); to testify, declare; to have a bowel movement; *Mex., C.A.* to vomit.
deportar [de·por·tár] *v.* to deport, banish.
deporte [de·pór·te] *m.* sport; pastime, recreation.
deportista [de·por·tís·ta] *m.* sportsman; *f.* sportswoman.
deportivo [de·por·ti·ƀo] *adj.* sport, sports (*used as an adj.*); **copa deportiva** loving cup.
deposición [de·po·si·sjón] *f.* declaration, assertion; testimony; dismissal, removal (*from office or power*); bowel movement.
depositar [de·po·si·tár] *v.* to deposit; to deliver, intrust.
depositario [de·po·si·tá·rjo] *m.* receiver, trustee.
depósito [de·pó·si·to] *m.* deposit; storage; warehouse; — **de agua** reservoir.
depravado [de·pra·ƀá·đo] *adj.* depraved, corrupt, degenerate.
depravar [de·pra·ƀár] *v.* to corrupt, pervert, contaminate.
depreciar [de·pre·sjár] *v.* to depreciate, lessen the value of.
depresión [de·pre·sjón] *f.* depression; dip, sag.
deprimente [de·pri·mén·te] *adj.* depressing.
deprimir [de·pri·mír] *v.* to depress; to press down; to humiliate, belittle.
depuesto [de·pwés·to] *p.p. of* **deponer.**
depuración [de·pu·ra·sjón] *f.* (*computadora*) debugging.
depurar [de·pu·rár] *v.* to purify.
derecha [de·ré·ča] *f.* right hand; right side; right wing (*in politics*); **a la** — to the right; **derechazo** [de·re·čá·so] *m.* a blow with the right hand, a right (*boxing*).
derechista [de·re·čís·ta] *adj.* & *m. f.* rightist.
derecho [de·ré·čo] *adj.* right; straight; *m.* law; duty, tax; fee; — **mercantil** business law.
derechura [de·re·čú·ra] *f.* straightness.
deriva [de·rí·ƀa] *f.* drift (*of a boat or plane*); **irse** (*or* **andar**) **a la** — to drift, be drifting.
derivar [de·ri·ƀár] *v.* to derive; to come (from).
dermatólogo [der·ma·tó·lo·go] *m.* dermatologist.
derogar[7] [de·ro·gár] *v.* to revoke, repeal, abolish.
derramamiento [de·rra·ma·mjén·to] *m.* spill, spilling, shedding; overflow; scattering; — **de sangre** bloodshed.
derramar [de·rra·már] *v.* to spill; to spread, scatter; to shed.
derrame [de·rrá·me] *m.* spill, spilling, shedding; overflow; discharge (*of secretion, blood, etc.*); slope; — **cerebral** stroke.
derredor [de·rre·đór] *m.* circuit; contour; **al** — around; **en** — around.
derrengado [de·rreŋ·gá·đo] *p.p.* & *adj.* lame, crippled; dislocated (*said of hip or spine*).
derrengar[1, 7] [de·rreŋ·gár] *v. irr.* to dislocate or sprain (*hip or spine*); to cripple; to bend.
derretimiento [de·rre·ti·mjén·to] *m.* thaw, thawing, melting.
derretir[5] [de·rre·tír] *v. irr.* to melt, dissolve; **-se** to be consumed; to melt.
derribar [de·rri·ƀár] *v.* to demolish, knock down, fell; to overthrow; **-se** to lie down, throw oneself down.
derrocamiento [de·rro·ka·mjén·to] *m.* overthrow.
derrocar[6] [de·rro·kár] *v.* to fling down; to fell; to overthrow.
derrochador [de·rro·ča·đór] *m.* squanderer, spendthrift; *adj.* wasteful, extravagant.
derrochar [de·rro·čár] *v.* to waste; to squander.
derroche [de·rró·če] *m.* waste; dissipation, lavish spending.
derrota [de·rró·ta] *f.* rout, defeat; ship's route or course.
derrotar [de·rro·tár] *v.* to defeat; to squander; to destroy, ruin; to lose or shift its course (*said of a ship*).
derrotero [de·rro·té·ro] *m.* course, direction; ship's course; book of marine charts.
derrumbadero [de·rrum·ba·đé·ro] *m.* precipice.
derrumbamiento [de·rrum·ba·mjén·to] *m.* landslide; collapse.
derrumbar [de·rrum·bár] *v.* to fling down, *Mex.* to knock down; *Mex.* to go down in a hurry; **-se** to crumble away; to topple over; *Col., Ven.* to dwindle (*as a business*).
derrumbe [de·rrúm·be] *m.* landslide; collapse.
desabotonar [de·sa·ƀo·to·nár] *v.* to unbutton.
desabrido [de·sa·ƀrí·đo] *adj.* tasteless, insipid; harsh; sour.
desabrigar[7] [de·sa·ƀri·ǥár] *v.* to uncover; **-se** to uncover oneself.
desabrimiento [de·sa·ƀri·mjén·to] *m.* tastelessness; harshness; sourness.
desabrochar [de·sa·ƀro·čár] *v.* to unfasten, unbutton, unclasp; **-se** to unbutton oneself, unfasten one's clothes.
desacato [de·sa·ká·to] *m.* irreverence, disrespect; profanation.
desacierto [de·sa·sjér·to] *m.* mistake, error.
desacoplar [de·sa·ko·plár] *v.* to uncouple, disconnect.
desacostumbrado [de·sa·kos·tum·brá·đo] *adj.* unaccustomed; unusual; *p.p. of* **desacostumbrar.**
desacostumbrar [de·sa·kos·tum·brár] *v.* to disaccustom, rid of a habit; **-se** to become unaccustomed; to lose a custom.
desacreditar [de·sa·kre·đi·tár] *v.* to discredit; to disgrace.
desacuerdo [de·sa·kwér·đo] *m.* disagreement; discord; blunder; forgetfulness.
desafiar[17] [de·sa·fjár] *v.* to challenge; to compete; to defy.
desafinado [de·sa·fi·ná·đo] *adj.* out of tune.
desafinar [de·sa·fi·nár] *v.* to be discordant; to be out of tune; **-se** to get out of tune.
desafío [de·sa·fí·o] *m.* challenge, defiance; duel; contest.
desafortunado [de·sa·for·tu·ná·đo] *adj.* unfortunate,

unlucky.

desafuero [de·sa·fwé·ro] *m.* violation; outrage, abuse.

desagradable [de·sa·ǥra·đá·ƀle] *adj.* disagreeable, unpleasant.

desagradar [de·sa·ǥra·đár] *v.* to displease.

desagradecido [de·sa·ǥra·đe·sí·đo] *adj.* ungrateful.

desagrado [de·sa·ǥrá·đo] *m.* displeasure; discontent.

desagraviar [de·sa·ǥra·ƀjár] *v.* to make amends; to compensate for a damage or injury; to right a wrong; to apologize; to vindicate.

desagravio [de·sa·ǥrá·ƀjo] *m.* reparation; compensation for a wrong or injury; vindication; apology.

desaguadero [de·sa·ǥwa·đé·ro] *m.* drain, drain pipe, water outlet.

desaguar[8] [de·sa·ǥwár] *v.* to drain, draw off; to flow (into); *Ch.* to wash (*something*) two or more times; *Ch.* to extract the juice from; *Col., Ven., Mex.* to urinate; **-se** to drain.

desagüe [de·sá·ǥwe] *m.* drainage; drain.

desaguisado [de·sa·ǥi·sá·đo] *m.* outrage, violence, wrong.

desahogado [de·sa·o·ǥá·đo] *p.p. & adj.* (*aliviado*) relieved; (*espacioso*) roomy, spacious; **estar —** to be in easy or comfortable circumstances; to be well-off.

desahogar[7] [de·sa·o·ǥár] *v.* to relieve from pain or trouble; **-se** to find relief or release; to unbosom oneself, disclose one's feelings.

desahogo [de·sa·ó·ǥo] *m.* relief from pain or trouble; release; ease, comfort, relaxation; freedom, unrestraint.

desairar [de·saj·rár] *v.* to slight, snub, disdain; to rebuff; to disappoint; to neglect.

desaire [de·sáj·re] *m.* rebuff, snub, slight, disdain.

desajustar [de·sa·xus·tár] *v.* to put out of order.

desalentar[1] [de·sa·len·tár] *v. irr.* to put out of breath; to discourage; **-se** to get discouraged.

desaliento [de·sa·ljén·to] *m.* discouragement, dejection.

desaliñado [de·sa·li·ñá·đo] *adj.* disheveled, slovenly, unkempt, untidy; disorderly.

desaliño [de·sa·lí·ño] *m.* slovenliness, untidiness; neglect, carelessness; disorder.

desalmado [de·sal·má·đo] *adj.* soulless, cruel, inhuman.

desalojar [de·sa·lo·xár] *v.* to dislodge; to evict, expel from a lodging; to vacate.

desamarrar [de·sa·ma·rrár] *v.* to untie, unfasten; to unmoor (*a ship*).

desamparar [de·sam·pa·rár] *v.* to abandon, forsake.

desamparo [de·sam·pá·ro] *m.* desertion, abandonment.

desamueblado [de·sa·mwe·ƀlá·đo] *adj.* unfurnished.

desangrar [de·saŋ·grár] *v.* to bleed, draw blood from; to drain; **-se** to bleed, lose blood.

desanimado [de·sa·ni·má·đo] *adj.* discouraged; lifeless; dull.

desanimar [de·sa·ni·már] *v.* to dishearten, discourage.

desaparecer[13] [de·sa·pa·re·sér] *v. irr.* to disappear; to hide; **-se** to disappear, vanish.

desaparición [de·sa·pa·ri·sjón] *f.* disappearance.

desapasionado [de·sa·pa·sjo·ná·đo] *adj.* dispassionate; free from passion; calm; impartial.

desapego [de·sa·pé·ǥo] *m.* aloofness, indifference, detachment.

desapercibido [de·sa·per·si·ƀí·đo] *adj.* unprepared; unprovided; unnoticed.

desaprobación [de·sa·pro·ƀa·sjón] *f.* disapproval.

desaprobar[2] [de·sa·pro·ƀár] *v. irr.* to disapprove.

desarmar [de·sar·már] *v.* to disarm; to dismount, take apart.

desarme [de·sár·me] *m.* disarmament.

desarraigar[7] [de·sa·rraj·ǥár] *v.* to root out, uproot.

desarreglado [de·sa·rre·ǥlá·đo] *p.p. & adj.* disordered; disorderly; slovenly.

desarreglar [de·sa·rre·ǥlár] *v.* to disarrange, disorder, disturb, upset.

desarreglo [de·sa·rré·ǥlo] *m.* disorder, confusion.

desarrollar [de·sa·rro·yár] *v.* to unroll, unfold; to develop, explain; **-se** to develop; to unfold.

desarrollo [de·sa·rró·yo] *m.* development.

desaseado [de·sa·se·á·đo] *adj.* unkempt, untidy.

desaseo [de·sa·sé·o] *m.* slovenliness, untidiness.

desasir[22] [de·sa·sír] *v. irr.* to loosen, unfasten; **-se** to get loose (from); to let go (of).

desasosiego [de·sa·so·sjé·ǥo] *m.* unrest, uneasiness, restlessness.

desastrado [de·sas·trá·đo] *adj.* unfortunate, unhappy; ragged, dirty, untidy.

desastre [de·sás·tre] *m.* disaster.

desastroso [de·sas·tró·so] *adj.* disastrous, unfortunate.

desatar [de·sa·tár] *v.* to untie, loosen; to dissolve; to unravel, clear up; **-se** to let loose, let go; to break loose; **-se en improperios** to let out a string of insults.

desatascar[6] [de·sa·tas·kár] *v. irr.* to extricate, dislodge; to pull out of the mud.

desatención [de·sa·ten·sjón] *f.* inattention, lack of attention; discourtesy.

desatender[1] [de·sa·ten·dér] *v. irr.* to disregard, pay no attention (to); to slight, neglect.

desatento [de·sa·tén·to] *adj.* inattentive; discourteous.

desatinado [de·sa·ti·ná·đo] *adj.* senseless; reckless.

desatinar [de·sa·ti·nár] *v.* to act foolishly; to talk nonsense; to blunder; to rave; to lose one's bearings.

desatino [de·sa·tí·no] *m.* blunder, error; folly, nonsense.

desatracar[6] [de·sa·tra·kár] *v.* to push off (*from shore or from another ship*); to cast off, unmoor.

desavenencia [de·sa·ƀe·nén·sja] *f.* disagreement, discord; dispute, misunderstanding.

desayunarse [de·sa·yu·nár·se] *v.* to eat breakfast; **— con la noticia** to hear a piece of news for the first time.

desayuno [de·sa·yú·no] *m.* breakfast.

desazón [de·sa·són] *f.* uneasiness, anxiety; insipidity, flatness, tastelessness; displeasure.

desbandarse [dez·ƀan·dár·se] *v.* to disband, scatter, disperse; to desert the army or a party.

desbaratar [dez·ƀa·ra·tár] *v.* to destroy, ruin; to upset, disturb; to disperse, put to flight; to talk nonsense; **-se** to be upset, be in disorder; to fall to pieces.

desbocado [dez·ƀo·ká·đo] *adj.* runaway (*horse*), dashing headlong; foul-mouthed, abusive; broken-mouthed (*jar, pitcher, etc.*).

desbordamiento [dez·ƀor·đa·mjén·to] *m.* overflow, flood.

desbordante [dez·ƀor·đán·te] *adj.* overflowing; *Am.* frantic.

desbordar [dez·ƀor·đár] *v.* to overflow, flood; **-se** to spill over; to get overexcited.

desbravar [dez·ƀra·ƀár] *v.* to tame; **-se** to calm down.

descabalar [des·ka·ƀa·lár] *v.* to break (*a given amount, making it thereby incomplete*).

descabello [des·ka·ƀé·yo] *m.* the act of killing the bull by piercing the brain with the sword.

descabezado [des·ka·ƀe·sá·đo] *p.p.* beheaded; *adj.* headless; harebrained, thoughtless.

descabezar[9] [des·ka·ƀe·sár] *v.* to behead; to chop off

the head or tip of; — **el sueño** to take a nap; **-se** to break one's head; to rack one's brain.
descaecido [des·ka·e·sí·đo] *adj.* feeble, weak; — **de ánimo** depressed, dejected, despondent.
descaecimiento [des·ka·e·si·mjén·to] *m.* languor, weakness; depression, dejection.
descalabradura [des·ka·la·bra·đú·ra] *f.* blow or wound on the head; scar on the head.
descalabrar [des·ka·la·brár] *v.* to wound on the head; to hurt, injure; to damage; **-se** to suffer a head wound or skull fracture.
descalabro [des·ka·lá·bro] *m.* loss, misfortune.
descalzar[9] [des·kal·sár] *v.* to take off (*someone's*) shoes or (and) stockings; **-se** to take off one's shoes or (and) stockings; to lose a shoe (*said of horses*).
descalzo [des·kál·so] *adj.* barefoot; shoeless.
descaminar [des·ka·mi·nár] *v.* to mislead, lead astray; **-se** to go astray.
descamisado [des·ka·mi·sá·đo] *adj.* shirtless; in rags; *m.* ragamuffin, ragged fellow.
descansar [des·kan·sár] *v.* to rest.
descanso [des·kán·so] *m.* rest; staircase landing.
descarado [des·ka·rá·đo] *adj.* shameless, impudent, brazen.
descarga [des·kár·ga] *f.* discharge; unloading.
descargar[7] [des·kar·gár] *v.* to discharge; to unload.
descargo [des·kár·go] *m.* discharge (*of a duty or obligation*); unloading; relief.
descargue [des·kár·ge] *m.* unloading; discharge.
descarnado [des·kar·ná·đo] *adj.* fleshless, scrawny.
descarnar [des·kar·nár] *v.* to pull the flesh from the bone; to corrode, eat away; **-se** to become thin, emaciated.
descaro [des·ká·ro] *m.* effrontery, shamelessness, impudence, audacity.
descarriar[17] [des·ka·rrjár] *v.* to mislead, lead astray; to separate (*cattle*) from the herd; **-se** to stray; to go astray.
descarrilar [des·ka·rri·lár] *v.* to derail (*cause a train to run off the track*); to wreck (*a train*); **-se** to get or run off the track; to go astray.
descartar [des·kar·tár] *v.* to discard; to put aside.
descascarado [des·kas·ka·rá·đo] *p.p. & adj.* peeled off; chipped off.
descascarar [des·kas·ka·rár] *v.* to shell, hull, husk; to peel; to chip off (*plaster*); *Am.* to defame, discredit; *Col.* to flay; **-se** to chip off, peel off.
descendencia [de·sen·dén·sja] *f.* descent, lineage; descendants, offspring.
descendente [de·sen·dén·te] *adj.* descending, downward.
descender[1] [de·sen·dér] *v. irr.* to descend, go down; to get down; to come (from), originate.
descendiente [de·sen·djén·te] *m. & f.* descendant; *adj.* descending.
descendimiento [de·sen·di·mjén·to] *m.* descent.
descenso [de·sén·so] *m.* descent; fall.
descifrar [de·si·frár] *v.* to decipher, puzzle out, figure out.
descolgar[2, 7] [des·kol·gár] *v. irr.* to unhang, take down; to let down; **-se** to climb down (*a rope, tree, etc.*); to drop in, appear unexpectedly.
descolorar [des·ko·lo·rár] *v.* to discolor; to fade; **-se** to fade, lose its color; to discolor.
descolorido [des·ko·lo·rí·đo] *adj.* pale.
descollar[2] [des·ko·yár] *v. irr.* to excel; to stand out; tower (above).
descomedido [des·ko·me·đí·đo] *adj.* rude, discourteous, impolite; unobliging.
descompletar [des·kom·ple·tár] *v.* to make incomplete, break (*a unit, sum, set, etc.*)
descomponer[40] [des·kom·po·nér] *v. irr.* (*estorbar*) to upset, disturb; (*echar a perder*) to put out of order; to decompose; **-se** to decompose, rot; to become upset, ill; to get out of order; *Col., Ven., C.A., Carib., Mex.* **se me descompuso el brazo** I dislocated my arm, my arm got out of joint.
descomposición [des·kom·po·si·sjón] *f.* decomposition; decay, corruption; disorder, confusion.
decompuesto [des·kom·pwés·to] *p.p. of* **descomponer**; *adj.* out of order; insolent; brazen; immodest.
descomunal [des·ko·mu·nál] *adj.* colossal, enormous, monstrous.
desconcertante [des·kon·ser·tán·te] *adj.* disconcerting, disturbing, confusing, baffling, embarrassing.
desconcertar[1] [des·kon·ser·tár] *v. irr.* to disconcert, bewilder, confuse; to disturb; **-se** to be confused, perplexed.
desconcierto [des·kon·sjér·to] *m.* disorder; confusion; disagreement; feeling of discomfort.
desconchadura [des·kon·ča·đú·ra] *f.* chip (*chipped off place*); chipping off, peeling off (*of plaster, varnish, etc.*).
desconchar [des·kon·čár] *v.* to scrape off (*plaster or stucco*); **-se** to peel off, chip off (*as plaster*).
desconectar [des·ko·nek·tár] *v.* to disconnect.
desconfiado [des·kon·fjá·đo] *adj.* distrustful, suspicious.
desconfianza [des·kon·fján·sa] *f.* mistrust, distrust.
desconfiar[17] [des·kon·fjár] *v.* to distrust; to lose confidence.
desconocer[13] [des·ko·no·sér] *v. irr.* to fail to recognize or remember; to disown; to disregard, slight; not to know.
desconocido [des·ko·no·sí·đo] *adj.* unknown; unrecognizable; *m.* stranger.
desconocimiento [des·ko·no·si·mjén·to] *m.* disregard; ignorance.
desconsolado [des·kon·so·lá·đo] *p.p. & adj.* disconsolate, forlorn; disheartened, grieved.
desconsolador [des·kon·so·la·đór] *adj.* disheartening, saddening.
desconsolar[2] [des·kon·so·lár] *v. irr.* to sadden, grieve; to discourage; **-se** to become disheartened, grieved.
desconsuelo [des·kon·swé·lo] *m.* dejection, sadness, distress.
descontar[2] [des·kon·tár] *v. irr.* to discount, deduct; to allow for.
descontentadizo [des·kon·ten·ta·đí·so] *adj.* discontented, fretful, hard to please.
descontentar [des·kon·ten·tár] *v.* to displease.
descontento [des·kon·tén·to] *adj.* discontent, displeased; *m.* discontent, displeasure.
descorazonado [des·ko·ra·so·ná·đo] *adj.* disheartened, discouraged, depressed.
descorchar [des·kor·čár] *v.* to uncork; to remove the bark from (*a cork tree*); to force or break open.
descortés [des·kor·tés] *adj.* discourteous, rude, impolite.
descortesía [des·kor·te·sí·a] *f.* discourtesy, rudeness, impoliteness.
descortezar[9] [des·kor·te·sár] *v.* to bark, strip the bark from (*trees*); to remove the crust or shell from; to peel; to civilize, remove the rough manners from.
descoser [des·ko·sér] *v.* to rip, unsew, unstitch; **-se** to rip, come unstitched; to talk too much or indiscreetly.
descosido [des·ko·sí·đo] *m.* rip; *adj.* too talkative, indiscreet; disorderly; *p.p. of* **descoser.**

descostrar [des·kos·trár] *v.* to flake; to scale off; to remove the crust from; **-se** to flake, scale off.
descoyuntado [des·ko·yun·tá·đo] *p.p. & adj.* dislocated, out of joint.
descoyuntar [des·ko·yun·tár] *v.* to dislocate, put out of joint; **-se** to get out of joint.
descrédito [des·kré·đi·to] *m.* discredit.
descreído [des·kre·í·đo] *adj.* incredulous, unbelieving; *m.* unbeliever.
descreimiento [des·krej·mjén·to] *m.* unbelief, lack of faith.
describir[52] [des·kri·ƀír] *v.* to describe.
descripción [des·krip·sjón] *f.* description.
descriptivo [des·krip·ti·ƀo] *adj.* descriptive.
descrito [des·krí·to] *p.p. irr. of* **describir.**
descuartizar[9] [des·kwar·ti·sár] *v.* to quarter (*an animal*); to tear or cut into parts.
descubierto [des·ku·ƀjér·to] *p.p. of* **descubrir** *& adj.* (*sin cubierta*) uncovered; hatless, bareheaded; (*hallado*) discovered; *m.* deficit, shortage; **al** — openly, in the open; **en** — uncovered, unpaid; no funds.
descubridor [des·ku·ƀri·đór] *m.* discoverer.
descubrimiento [des·ku·ƀri·mjén·to] *m.* discovery; find; invention.
descubrir[52] [des·ku·ƀrír] *v.* to discover; to uncover; **-se** to uncover; to take off one's hat.
descuento [des·kwén·to] *m.* discount; deduction.
descuidado [des·kwi·đá·đo] *adj.* careless, negligent; untidy, slovenly; unaware; thoughtless.
descuidar [des·kwi·đár] *v.* to neglect; to overlook; to be careless or negligent; **-se** to be careless or negligent.
descuido [des·kwí·đo] *m.* carelessness; neglect; oversight; disregard; inattention; slip, error.
desde [déz·đe] *prep.* from; since; — **luego** of course; — **que** *conj.* since, ever since.
desdecir[27] [dez·đe·sir] *v. irr.* to be out of harmony (with); to detract (from); **-se** to retract; to contradict oneself.
desdén [dez·đén] *m.* disdain, scorn.
desdentado [dez·đen·tá·đo] *adj.* toothless.
desdeñar [dez·đe·ñár] *v.* to disdain, scorn.
desdeñoso [dez·đe·ñó·so] *adj.* disdainful, scornful.
desdicha [dez·đí·ča] *f.* misfortune; misery; poverty.
desdichado [dez·đi·čá·đo] *adj.* unfortunate; unhappy, wretched; miserable; *m.* wretch.
desdoblamiento [dez·đo·ƀla·mjén·to] *m.* unfolding.
desdoblar [dez·đo·ƀlár] *v.* to unfold; to spread out.
desdorar [dez·đo·rár] *v.* to remove the gilt from; to tarnish; to dishonor.
desdoro [dez·đó·ro] *m.* tarnish, blemish; dishonor.
deseable [de·se·á·ƀle] *adj.* desirable.
desear [de·se·ár] *v.* to desire, want.
desecación [de·se·ka·sjón] *f.*, **desecamiento** [de·se·ka·mjén·to] *m.* drying; drainage.
desecar[6] [de·se·kár] *v.* to dry; to dry up; to drain (*land*).
desechar [de·se·čár] *v.* to discard; to reject; to refuse, decline; *Col.* to cut across, take a short cut.
desecho [de·sé·čo] *m.* remainder, residue; waste material; piece of junk; discard; **-s** refuse, scraps, junk; **hierro de** — scrap iron; **papel de** — wastepaper, scraps of paper.
desembalar [de·sem·ba·lár] *v.* to unpack.
desembarazar[9] [de·sem·ba·ra·sár] *v.* to rid, free, clear; *Ch.* to give birth; **-se** to get rid of.
desembarazo [de·sem·ba·rá·so] *m.* freedom, ease, naturalness; *Ch.* childbirth.
desembarcadero [de·sem·bar·ka·đé·ro] *m.* dock, wharf, pier.
desembarcar[6] [de·sem·bar·kár] *v.* to disembark, land; to unload; to go ashore.
desembarco [de·sem·bár·ko], **desembarque** [de·sem·bár·ke] *m.* landing; unloading.
desembocadura [de·sem·bo·ka·đú·ra] *f.* mouth (*of a river, canal, etc.*); outlet.
desembocar[6] [de·sem·bo·kár] *v.* to flow (into); to lead (to).
desembolsar [de·sem·bol·sár] *v.* to disburse, pay out.
desembolso [de·sem·ból·so] *m.* disbursement, outlay, expenditure.

DE

desembragar[7] [de·sem·bra·ǥár] *v.* to throw out the clutch; to disconnect.
desemejante [de·se·me·xán·te] *adj.* unlike.
desempacar[6] [de·sem·pa·kár] *v.* to unpack.
desempañar [de·sem·pa·ñár] *v.* to wipe clean; to remove steam or smudge (*from glass*).
desempeñar [de·sem·pe·ñár] *v.* to recover, redeem, take out of pawn; — **un cargo** to perform the duties of a position; — **un papel** to play a part; **-se** to get out of debt.
desempeño [de·sem·pé·ño] *m.* fulfillment, carrying out, discharge; performance (*of a duty*); (*teatro*) acting (*of a role*); redeeming (*of a thing pawned*).
desempleado [de·sem·ple·á·đo] *adj.* unemployed.
desempleo [de·sem·plé·o] *m.* unemployment.
desempolvar [de·sem·pol·ƀár] *v.* to dust, remove the dust from.
desencadenar [de·seŋ·ka·đe·nár] *v.* to unchain, free from chains; to loosen, set free; **-se** to free oneself; to break loose.
desencajado [de·seŋ·ka·xá·đo] *p.p. & adj.* disjointed; disfigured; sunken (*eyes*); emaciated.
desencajar [de·seŋ·ka·xár] *v.* to dislocate; **-se** to become dislocated.
desencantar [de·seŋ·kan·tár] *v.* to disillusion, disappoint.
desencanto [de·seŋ·kán·to] *m.* disillusion, disappointment.
desenfadar [de·sen·fa·đár] *v.* to free of anger; **-se** to calm down.
desenfado [de·sen·fá·đo] *m.* ease, freedom; calmness.
desenfrenado [de·sen·fre·ná·đo] *p.p. & adj.* unbridled; wanton, reckless; loose, immoral.
desenganchar [de·seŋ·gan·čár] *v.* to unhitch; to unhook; to unfasten.
desengañador [de·seŋ·ga·ña·đór] *adj.* disappointing, disillusioning.
desengañar [de·seŋ·ga·ñár] *v.* to undeceive, disillusion, disappoint.
desengaño [de·seŋ·gá·ño] *m.* disillusion, disappointment, blighted hope.
desengranar [de·seŋ·gra·nár] *v.* to throw out of gear.
desenmarañar [de·sem·ma·ra·ñár] *v.* to untangle; to unravel.
desenmascarar [de·sem·mas·ka·rár] *v.* to unmask.
desenredar [de·sen·rre·đár] *v.* to disentangle, unravel.
desenrollar [de·sen·rro·yár] *v.* to unroll.
desensartar [de·sen·sar·tár] *v.* to unstring; to unthread; to unfasten from a ring.
desensillar [de·sen·si·yár] *v.* to unsaddle.
desentenderse[1] [de·sen·ten·dér·se] *v. irr.* to neglect, ignore, pay no attention to; to pretend not to see, hear or understand.
desentendido [de·sen·ten·dí·đo] *adj.* unmindful, heedless; *p.p. of* **desentenderse; hacerse el** — to pretend not to notice.
desenterrar[1] [de·sen·te·rrár] *v. irr.* to unearth, dig up.
desentonado [de·sen·to·ná·đo] *adj.* inharmonious, out of tune.
desentonar [de·sen·to·nár] *v.* to be out of tune; to be

out of harmony; to sing off key, play out of tune.
desenvoltura [de·sem·bol·tú·ra] *f.* freedom, ease, abandon; boldness, impudence.
desenvolver[2, 52] [de·sem·bol·bér] *v. irr.* to unroll, unfold; to unwrap; to develop.
desenvolvimiento [de·sem·bol·bi·mjén·to] *m.* development, unfolding.
desenvuelto [de·sem·bwél·to] *adj.* free, easy; forward, bold; shameless, brazen; *p.p. of* **desenvolver.**
deseo [de·sé·o] *m.* desire, wish.
deseoso [de·se·ó·so] *adj.* desirous, eager.
desequilibrado [de·se·ki·li·brá·do] *adj.* unbalanced; *p.p. of* **desequilibrar.**
desequilibrar [de·se·ki·li·brár] *v.* to unbalance; to derange.
desequilibrio [de·se·ki·lí·brjo] *m.* lack of balance; derangement, mental disorder.
deserción [de·ser·sjón] *f.* desertion.
desertar [de·ser·tár] *v.* to desert; to abandon; **-se de** to desert.
desertor [de·ser·tór] *m.* deserter; quitter.
desesperación [de·ses·pe·ra·sjón] *f.* despair; desperation; fury.
desesperado [de·ses·pe·rá·do] *adj.* desperate; despairing; hopeless; *p.p. of* **desesperar.**
desesperanzado [de·ses·pe·ran·sá·do] *p.p. & adj.* discouraged; hopeless; desperate, in despair.
desesperanzar[9] [de·ses·pe·ran·sár] *v.* to discourage, deprive of hope; **-se** to be discouraged; to despair, lose one's hope.
desesperar [de·ses·pe·rár] *v.* to despair, lose hope; to make (*someone*) despair; **-se** to despair, be desperate; to be furious.
desfachatez [des·fa·ča·tés] *f.* shamelessness, effrontery, impudence.
desfalcar[6] [des·fal·kár] *v.* to embezzle; to remove a part of.
desfalco [des·fál·ko] *m.* embezzlement; diminution, decrease.
desfallecer[13] [des·fa·ye·sér] *v. irr.* to grow weak; to faint.
desfallecimiento [des·fa·ye·si·mjén·to] *m.* faintness; weakness; languor; swoon, faint.
desfavorable [des·fa·bo·rá·ble] *adj.* unfavorable.
desfigurar [des·fi·gu·rár] *v.* to disfigure; to deface; to distort.
desfiladero [des·fi·la·dé·ro] *m.* narrow passage, narrow gorge; road on the edge of a precipice.
desfilar [des·fi·lár] *v.* to march, parade, pass by.
desfile [des·fí·le] *m.* parade.
desgana [dez·gá·na] *f.* lack of appetite; reluctance.
desgarrado [dez·ga·rrá·do] *p.p.* torn; *adj.* shameless; impudent.
desgarradura [dez·ga·rra·dú·ra] *f.* tear.
desgarrar [dez·ga·rrár] *v.* to tear, rend; to expectorate, cough up; **-se** to tear; to separate oneself (from).
desgastar [dez·gas·tár] *v.* to waste, consume, wear away; **-se** to waste away, lose one's strength or vigor; to wear off.
desgaste [dez·gás·te] *m.* waste; wear and tear.
desgracia [dez·grá·sja] *f.* misfortune, mishap; disgrace.
desgraciado [dez·gra·sjá·do] *adj.* unfortunate, wretched.
desgranar [dez·gra·nár] *v.* to thrash, thresh (*grain*); to remove the grain from; to shell (*peas, beans, etc.*).
desgreñado [dez·gre·ñá·do] *adj.* disheveled.
desgreñar [dez·gre·ñár] *v.* to dishevel; **-se** to muss up one's own hair.
deshabitado [de·sa·bi·tá·do] *adj.* uninhabited, deserted; empty, vacant.
deshacer[31] [de·sa·sér] *v. irr.* to undo; to dissolve; to destroy; to untie; **-se** to dissolve; to melt; to waste away; **-se de** to get rid of.
desharrapado, desarrapado [de·sa·rra·pá·do] *adj.* ragged, shabby, tattered.
deshecha [de·sé·ča] *f.* simulation, pretense; **hacer la** — to feign, pretend.
deshecho [de·sé·čo] *p.p. of* **deshacer** *& adj.* undone; ruined, destroyed, in pieces; violent (*said of rainstorms*); worn-out, fatigued; *Arg.* disorderly, untidy.
desheladora automática [de·se·la·dó·ra aw·to·má·ti·ka] *f.* automatic defroster.
deshelar[1] [de·se·lár] *v. irr.* to melt; to thaw; **-se** to melt; to thaw.
desherbar[1] [de·ser·bár] *v. irr.* to weed.
deshielo [dez·yé·lo] *m.* thaw.
deshierbe [dez·yér·be] *m.* weeding.
deshilachar [de·si·la·čár] *v.* to ravel, fray.
deshilar [de·si·lár] *v.* to unravel; **-se** to unravel; to fray.
deshojar [de·so·xár] *v.* to strip off the leaves, petals, or pages; **-se** to lose its leaves (*said of a plant or book*); to lose petals.
deshollejar [de·so·ye·xár] *v.* to husk, hull; to peel, pare, skin; to shell (*beans*).
deshonesto [de·so·nés·to] *adj.* immodest; unchaste, lewd.
deshonra [de·són·rra] *f.* dishonor; disgrace.
deshonrar [de·son·rrár] *v.* to dishonor, disgrace; to insult, offend; to seduce.
deshonroso [de·son·rró·so] *adj.* dishonorable; shameful.
deshora [de·só·ra] *f.* inopportune time; **a** — (*or* **a -s**) unexpectedly; **comer a** — to piece, eat between meals.
deshuesar [dez·we·sár] *v.* to stone, remove the pits or stones from (*fruits*); to bone, remove the bones from (*an animal*).
deshumanizar[9] [de·su·ma·ni·sár] *v. irr.* to dehumanize.
desidia [de·sí·dja] *f.* indolence, laziness.
desidioso [de·si·djó·so] *adj.* indolent, negligent, lazy; listless.
desierto [de·sjér·to] *adj.* deserted, uninhabited; alone; lonely; *m.* desert, wilderness.
designación [de·sig·na·sjón] *f.* designation; appointment.
designar [de·sig·nár] *v.* to designate, appoint, select; to design, plan, intend.
designio [de·síg·njo] *m.* design, plan, purpose.
desigual [de·si·gwál] *adj.* unequal; uneven; variable, changeable.
desigualdad [de·si·gwal·dád] *f.* inequality; unevenness; roughness (*of the ground*).
desilusión [de·si·lu·sjón] *f.* disillusion, disappointment.
desilusionar [de·si·lu·sjo·nár] *v.* to disillusion, disappoint; **-se** to become disillusioned; to lose one's illusions.
desinencia [de·si·nén·sja] *f.* termination, ending (*of a word*).
desinfectante [de·sin·fek·tán·te] *adj.* disinfecting; *m.* disinfectant.
desinfectar [de·sin·fek·tár] *v.* to disinfect.
desinflado [de·sin·flá·do] *adj.* deflated, not inflated, flat.
desinflar [de·sin·flár] *v.* to deflate.
desinterés [de·sin·te·rés] *m.* disinterestedness,

unselfishness, impartiality.
desinteresado [de·sin·te·re·sá·đo] *adj.* disinterested, unselfish, fair, impartial.
desistir [de·sis·tír] *v.* to desist, stop, cease.
deslavado [dez·la·ƀá·đo] *p.p. & adj.* half-washed; weakened; faded; pale; saucy.
deslavar [dez·la·ƀár] *v.* to wash away; to fade; to wash superficially.
desleal [dez·le·ál] *adj.* disloyal, faithless.
desleír[15] [dez·le·ír] *v. irr.* to dissolve; to dilute, make thin or weak; **-se** to become diluted.
deslindar [dez·lin·dár] *v.* to mark off, mark the boundaries of.
desliz [dez·lís] *m.* slip, slide; error.
deslizador [dez·li·sa·đór] *m.* glider.
deslizamiento [dez·li·sa·mjén·to] *m.* slip, slipping; glide; sliding, skidding.
deslizar[9] [dez·li·sár] *v.* to slip, slide; **-se** to slip; to skid; to glide; to slip out.
deslucido [dez·lu·sí·đo] *p.p. & adj.* tarnished; dull; discredited; dingy, shabby; awkward, ungraceful; inelegant.
deslucir[13] [dez·lu·sír] *v. irr.* to tarnish, dull the luster of; to discredit.
deslumbrador [dez·lum·bra·đór] *adj.* dazzling, glaring.
deslumbramiento [dez·lum·bra·mjén·to] *m.* dazzle, glare; daze, confusion.
deslumbrar [dez·lum·brár] *v.* to dazzle.
deslustrado [dez·lus·trá·đo] *adj. & p.p.* tarnished; dim, dull; opaque.
deslustrar [dez·lus·trár] *v.* to tarnish; to soil, stain (*one's honor or reputation*).
deslustre [dez·lús·tre] *m.* tarnish; disgrace.
desmadejado [dez·ma·đe·xá·đo] *p.p. & adj.* enervated, exhausted; depressed.
desmadejar [dez·ma·đe·xár] *v.* to enervate, weaken.
desmán [dez·mán] *m.* misconduct, abuse, insult; calamity, disaster.
desmantelar [dez·man·te·lár] *v.* to dismantle, strip of furniture, equipment, etc.
desmañado [dez·ma·ñá·đo] *adj.* unskillful, awkward, clumsy.
desmayar [dez·ma·yár] *v.* to dismay; to lose strength, courage; **-se** to faint.
desmayo [dez·má·yo] *m.* faint, swoon; dismay, discouragement.
desmazalado [dez·ma·sa·lá·đo] *adj.* dejected, depressed.
desmedido [dez·me·đí·đo] *adj.* limitless; excessive.
desmejorar [dez·me·xo·rár] *v.* to impair; to make worse; **-se** to grow worse; to waste away, lose one's health.
desmentir[3] [dez·men·tír] *v. irr.* to contradict; to give the lie; **-se** to contradict oneself; to retract, take back one's word.
desmenuzar[9] [dez·me·nu·sár] *v.* to crumble, break into bits; to mince; to shred; **-se** to crumble, fall to pieces.
desmerecer[13] [dez·me·re·sér] *v. irr.* to become unworthy of; to deteriorate, lose merit or value; to be inferior to.
desmigajar [dez·mi·ǥa·xár] *v.* to crumb (*bread*); to crumble; **-se** to crumble.
desmochar [dez·mo·čár] *v.* to cut off, chop off (*the top or tip*).
desmolado [dez·mo·lá·đo] *adj.* toothless, without molars.
desmontar [dez·mon·tár] *v.* to dismount; to cut down (*a forest*); to clear or level off (*ground*); to dismantle, take apart; to tear down; **-se** to dismount, alight, get off.
desmoronar [dez·mo·ro·nár] *v.* to crumble, **-se** to crumble down, fall gradually to pieces.
desnatar [dez·na·tár] *v.* to skim, take the cream from (*milk*).
desnaturalizado [dez·na·tu·ra·li·sá·đo] *adj.* unnatural, cruel; **alcohol** — denatured alcohol (*made unfit for drinking*); **madre desnaturalizada** unnatural mother (*one without motherly instincts*).
desnudar [dez·nu·đár] *v.* to undress, uncover; **-se** to undress.
desnudez [dez·nu·dés] *f.* nudity, nakedness.
desnudo [dez·nú·đo] *adj.* nude, naked, bare.
desobedecer[13] [de·so·ƀe·đe·sér] *v. irr.* to disobey.
desobediencia [de·so·ƀe·đjén·sja] *f.* disobedience;
desobediente [de·so·ƀe·đjén·te] *adj.* disobedient.
desocupación [de·so·ku·pa·sjón] *f.* unemployment; idleness; vacationing.
desocupado [de·so·ku·pá·đo] *adj.* unoccupied; unemployed, idle; empty, vacant.
desocupar [de·so·ku·pár] *v.* to empty, vacate; **-se de un negocio** to get rid of, or not pay attention to, a business.
desoír[36] [de·so·ír] *v. irr.* to turn a deaf ear to, not to heed; to refuse (*a petition*).
desolación [de·so·la·sjón] *f.* desolation; ruin; loneliness; anguish, affliction, grief.
desolado [de·so·lá·đo] *adj.* desolate; *p.p. of* **desolar.**
desolar[2] [de·so·lár] *v. irr.* to lay waste, ruin; **-se** to be in anguish; to grieve.
desollar[2] [de·so·yár] *v. irr.* to skin, flay; to fleece, extort money from.
desorbitado [de·sor·ƀi·tá·đo] *adj.* out of its orbit; out of place or proportion; decentered; *Ch. Andes* popeyed, with bulging eyes; *Am.* crazy, eccentric.
desorden [de·sór·đen] *m.* disorder, confusion.
desordenado [de·sor·đe·ná·đo] *adj.* disorderly; lawless; unsettled; *p.p. of* **desordenar.**
desordenar [de·sor·đe·nár] *v.* to disturb, confuse, upset.
desorientar [de·so·rjen·tár] *v.* to throw off one's bearings; to lead astray; to misdirect, mislead; to confuse; **-se** to lose one's bearings; to go astray, get lost.
desoxidar [de·sok·si·đár] *v.* to deoxidize.
despabilado [des·pa·ƀi·lá·đo] *adj.* wakeful; wide-awake; bright, lively.
despabilar [des·pa·ƀi·lár] *v.* to snuff, trim the wick of (*a candle*); to enliven, awaken (*the mind*), sharpen (*the wits*); **-se** to wake up, rouse oneself, shake off drowsiness.
despacio [des·pá·sjo] *adv.* slowly.
despacioso [des·pa·sjó·so] *adj.* slow.
despachar [des·pa·čár] *v.* to dispatch; to send; to facilitate; to ship.
despacho [des·pá·čo] *m.* (*oficina*) office, bureau; salesroom; (*communicación*) dispatch; (*envío*) sending; shipment; (*sin demora*) promptness; *Ch.* country store, farm store.
despachurrar [des·pa·ču·rrár] *v.* to crush, squash.
desparejo [des·pa·ré·xo] *adj.* unequal, uneven.
desparpajar [des·par·pa·xár] *v.* to upset, disarrange; to rant, talk too much; *Mex.* to disperse, scatter.
desparpajo [des·par·pá·xo] *m.* ease, freedom of manner; freshness, pertness; *Col.* dispersion, scattering; *Am.* disorder, jumble.
desparramar [des·pa·rra·már] *v.* to scatter, spread; to spill; to squander; **-se** to "spread" oneself, spend lavishly; to scatter; to spill.
desparramo [des·pa·rrá·mo] *m. Ch., C.A.* scattering, spreading, spilling; *Ríopl., Carib.* disorder,

commotion.
despatarrarse [des·pa·ta·rrár·se] *v.* to sprawl; to fall sprawling to the ground.
despecho [des·pé·čo] *m.* spite; grudge; despair; weaning; **a — de** in spite of.
despedazar[9] [des·pe·đa·sár] *v.* to break, cut, tear into pieces.
despedida [des·pe·đí·đa] *f.* farewell; departure; dismissal.
despedir[5] [des·pe·đír] *v. irr.* (*cesar*) to discharge, dismiss, (*emitir*) emit, throw off, give off; to see (*a person*) off (*at a station, airport, etc.*); **-se** to take leave, say good-bye.
despegar[7] [des·pe·ǵár] *v.* to detach; to unfasten; to take off (*said of a plane*); *Am.* to unhitch; **no — los labios** not to say a word, not to open one's mouth; **-se** to grow apart; to come loose or become detached.
despego [des·pé·ǵo] = **desapego.**
despegue [des·pé·ǵe] *m.* takeoff (*of an airplane*).
despejado [des·pe·xá·đo] *adj.* clear, cloudless; smart, bright; *p.p. of* **despejar.**
despejar [des·pe·xár] *v.* to clear; to remove obstacles from; **-se** to clear up (*as the sky*); to clear one's mind.
despellejar [des·pe·ye·xár] *v.* to skin, flay.
despensa [des·pén·sa] *f.* pantry; storeroom (*for food*); food provisions.
despensero [des·pen·sé·ro] *m.* butler; steward.
despeñadero [des·pe·ña·đé·ro] *m.* steep cliff, precipice.
despeñar [des·pe·ñár] *v.* to fling down a precipice; **-se** to fall down a precipice; to throw oneself down a cliff.
despepitar [des·pe·pi·tár] *v.* to seed, remove the seeds from; **-se** to talk or shout vehemently; to rave, talk wildly; **-se por una cosa** to long for something; to be crazy about something.
desperdiciado [des·per·đi·sjá·đo] *adj.* wasteful; *p.p. of* **desperdiciar.**
desperdiciar [des·per·đi·sjár] *v.* to squander; to waste.
desperdicio [des·per·đí·sjo] *m.* waste; extravagance; **-s** leftovers, garbage; residue.
desperdigar[7] [des·per·đi·ǵár] *v.* to disperse; to scatter; to strew.
desperezarse[9] [des·pe·re·sár·se] *v.* to stretch oneself.
desperfecto [des·per·fék·to] *m.* damage; flaw, defect.
despertador [des·per·ta·đór] *m.* alarm clock.
despertar[1] [des·per·tár] *v. irr.* to awaken; to wake up; **-se** to wake up.
despiadado [des·pja·đá·đo] *adj.* pitiless, heartless, cruel.
despido [des·pí·đo] *m.* dismissal.
despierto [des·pjér·to] *adj.* awake; wide-awake.
despilfarrado [des·pil·fa·rrá·đo] *adj.* wasteful, extravagant; ragged; *p.p. of* **despilfarrar.**
despilfarrar [des·pil·fa·rrár] *v.* to squander; to waste.
despilfarro [des·pil·fá·rro] *m.* extravagance, squandering; waste.
despistar [des·pis·tár] *v.* to throw off the track.
desplantador [des·plan·ta·đór] *m.* garden trowel.
desplante [des·plán·te] *m.* arrogance; impudent remark or act.
desplazar[9] [des·pla·sár] *v.* to displace.
desplegar[1, 7] [des·ple·ǵár] *v. irr.* to unfold; to unfurl; to show, manifest.
desplomar [des·plo·már] *v.* to cause (*a wall*) to lean; **-se** to slump; to topple over, tumble down, collapse.
desplome [des·pló·me] *m.* collapse; toppling over; landslide.
desplumar [des·plu·már] *v.* to pick, pluck (*a fowl*); to fleece, skin, rob, strip; **-se** to molt, shed the feathers.
despoblado [des·po·ƀlá·đo] *adj.* uninhabited, desolate; **— de árboles** treeless; *m.* open country; uninhabited place; wilderness.
despojar [des·po·xár] *v.* to despoil, rob; to strip (of), deprive (of); **-se** to undress; to deprive oneself.
despojo [des·pó·xo] *m.* plundering, robbery; spoil, booty; leftover, scrap; **-s** remains.
desportilladura [des·por·ti·ya·đú·ra] *f.* chip; nick.
desportillar [des·por·ti·yár] *v.* to chip; to nick.
desposar [des·po·sár] *v.* to marry; **-se** to become formally engaged; to get married.
déspota [dés·po·ta] *m. & f.* despot, tyrant.
despótico [des·pó·ti·ko] *adj.* despotic, tyrannical.
despotismo [des·po·tíz·mo] *m.* despotism, tyranny.
despreciable [des·pre·sjá·ƀle] *adj.* contemptible; worthless; insignificant, negligible.
despreciar [des·pre·sjár] *v.* to despise, scorn.
desprecio [des·pré·sjo] *m.* scorn, contempt.
desprender [des·pren·dér] *v.* to unfasten, loosen; to detach; **-se** to get loose, come unfastened; to climb down; to get rid (of); to be inferred, be deduced.
desprendimiento [des·pren·di·mjén·to] *m.* detachment; generosity; unfastening; landslide.
despreocupado [des·pre·o·ku·pá·đo] *p.p. & adj.* unbiased; liberal, broadminded; unconventional, carefree; *Am.* careless, slovenly; *Am.* indifferent to criticism.
desprestigiar [des·pres·ti·xjár] *v.* to discredit, harm the reputation of; **-se** to lose one's prestige.
desprestigio [des·pres·tí·xjo] *m.* discredit, loss of prestige.
desprevenido [des·pre·ƀe·ní·đo] *adj.* unprepared; unaware.
despropósito [des·pro·pó·si·to] *m.* absurdity, nonsense.
desprovisto [des·pro·ƀís·to] *adj.* destitute; lacking; devoid.
después [des·pwés] *adv.* after, afterward; then, later; **— de** *prep.* after; **— (de) que** *conj.* after.
despuntado [des·pun·tá·đo] *adj.* blunt, dull; *p.p. of* **despuntar.**
despuntar [des·pun·tár] *v.* (*quitar la punta*) to blunt; to cut off (*a point*); nip; (*brotar*) to bud or sprout; (*sobresalir*) to excel; to be clever, witty; **— el alba** to begin to dawn.
desquiciar [des·ki·sjár] *v.* to unhinge; to perturb.
desquitar [des·ki·tár] *v.* to retrieve, restore (*a loss*); **-se** to get even, take revenge; to win back one's money; to make up (for).
desquite [des·kí·te] *m.* retaliation, revenge; getting even; recovery of a loss; return game or match.
desrazonable [des·rra·so·ná·ƀle] *adj.* unreasonable.
destacado [des·ta·ká·đo] *adj.* outstanding; *p.p. of* **destacar.**
destacamento [des·ta·ka·mjén·to] *m.* military detachment.
destacar[6] [des·ta·kár] *v.* to detach (*troops*); to make stand out; to stand out; **hacer —** to emphasize; to make stand out; **-se** to stand out.
destapar [des·ta·pár] *v.* to uncover; to uncork; *Mex.* to start running; **-se** to uncover, get uncovered; to get uncorked; *Am.* to burst out talking.
destartalado [des·tar·ta·la·đo] *adj.* in disorder; in rack and ruin; dismantled, stripped of furniture.
destechado [des·te·čá·đo] *adj.* roofless.
destellar [des·te·yár] *v.* to flash; to sparkle, twinkle; to gleam.
destello [des·té·yo] *m.* flash, sparkle, gleam.

destemplado [des·tem·plá·đo] *adj.* out of tune, out of harmony; immoderate; **sentirse** — not to feel well, to feel feverish.
desteñir[5, 19] [des·te·ñír] *v. irr.* to discolor; to fade; to bleach; **-se** to become discolored; to fade.
desternillarse [des·ter·ni·yár·se] *v.* — **de risa** to split one's sides with laughter.
desterrado [des·te·rrá·đo] *m.* exile; outcast; *p.p. & adj.* exiled, banished.
desterrar[1] [des·te·rrár] *v. irr.* to exile, banish; to remove earth (from).
destetar [des·te·tár] *v.* to wean.
destierro [des·tjé·rro] *m.* exile.
destilación [des·ti·la·sjón] *f.* distillation.
destiladera [des·ti·la·đé·ra] *f.* still; *Am.* filter.
destilar [des·ti·lár] *v.* to distill; to drip, trickle; to filter.
destilería [des·ti·le·rí·a] *f.* distillery.
destinación [des·ti·na·sjón] *f.* destination.
destinar [des·ti·nár] *v.* to destine; to employ.
destinatario [des·ti·na·tá·rjo] *m.* addressee.
destino [des·tí·no] *m.* destiny, fate; destination; employment, job.
destituido [des·ti·twí·đo] *adj.* destitute; *p.p. of* **destituir.**
destituir[32] [des·ti·twír] *v. irr.* to deprive.
destorcer[10] [des·tor·sér] *v. irr.* to untwist.
destornillador [des·tor·ni·ya·đór] *m.* screwdriver.
destornillar [des·tor·ni·yár] *v.* to unscrew.
destrabar [des·tra·ƀár] *v.* to unlock, unfasten; to untie; to separate; to unfetter.
destreza [des·tré·sa] *f.* dexterity, skill, ability.
destronar [des·tro·nár] *v.* to dethrone, depose, overthrow.
destrozar[9] [des·tro·sár] *v.* to shatter, cut to pieces; to destroy; to squander.
destrozo [des·tró·so] *m.* destruction; ruin.
destrucción [des·truk·sjón] *f.* destruction.
destructivo [des·truk·tí·ƀo] *adj.* destructive.
destructor [des·truk·tór] *adj.* destructive; *m.* destroyer.
destruir[32] [des·trwír] *v. irr.* to destroy; to ruin.
desunir [de·su·nír] *v.* to divide, separate.
desusado [de·su·sá·đo] *adj.* unusual, unaccustomed; obsolete, out of use.
desuso [de·sú·so] *m.* disuse; obsoleteness.
desvaído [dez·ƀa·í·đo] *adj.* lanky, tall and awkward; gaunt; dull, faded.
desvainar [dez·ƀaj·nár] *v.* to shell (*peas, beans, etc.*).
desvalido [dez·ƀa·lí·đo] *adj.* abandoned; destitute; helpless.
desvalijar [dez·ƀa·li·xár] *v.* to ransack the contents of a valise; to rob.
desván [dez·ƀán] *m.* garret, attic.
desvanecer[13] [dez·ƀa·ne·sér] *v. irr.* to fade, dissolve; to make vain; to make dizzy; **-se** to evaporate; to vanish; to fade out, disappear; to get dizzy.
desvanecido [dez·ƀa·ne·sí·đo] *adj.* (*desmayado*) dizzy, faint; (*orgulloso*) proud, haughty; *p.p. of* **desvanecer.**
desvanecimiento [dez·ƀa·ne·si·mjén·to] *m.* dizziness, faintness; vanity.
desvariar[17] [dez·ƀa·rjár] *v.* to rave, be delirious; to rant, talk excitedly; to talk nonsense.
desvarío [dez·ƀa·rí·o] *m.* raving; delirium; madness; inconstancy.
desvelado [dez·ƀe·lá·đo] *adj.* sleepless, awake; watchful; *p.p. of* **desvelar.**
desvelar [dez·ƀe·lár] *v.* to keep (*another*) awake; **-se** to keep awake; to have insomnia, lose sleep; to be worried, anxious.
desvelo [dez·ƀé·lo] *m.* lack of sleep; restlessness; vigilance, watchfulness; worry, anxiety.
desvencijado [dez·ƀen·si·xá·đo] *adj.* tottering, rickety, shaky, falling apart.
desventaja [dez·ƀen·tá·xa] *f.* disadvantage.
desventura [dez·ƀen·tú·ra] *f.* misfortune, unhappiness.
desventurado [dez·ƀen·tu·rá·đo] *adj.* unfortunate, unhappy, miserable, wretched.
desvergonzado [dez·ƀer·ǥon·sá·đo] *adj.* shameless, brazen.
desvergüenza [dez·ƀer·ǥwén·sa] *f.* shamelessness; disgrace; shame; insolence; impudent word.
desvestir[5] [dez·ƀes·tír] *v. irr.* to undress; **-se** to undress.
desviación [dez·ƀja·sjón] *f.* deviation, turning aside, shift; detour.
desviar[17] [dez·ƀjár] *v.* to deviate, turn aside; to swerve; **-se** to shift direction; to branch off, turn off the main road; to swerve.
desvío [dez·ƀí·o] *m.* deviation, turning aside; indifference, coldness; side track, railroad siding; detour.
desvirtuar[18] [dez·ƀir·twár] *v.* to impair, diminish the value or quality of.
desvivirse [dez·ƀi·ƀír·se] *v.* — **por** to long for; to be excessively fond of, be crazy about, make a fuss over; to do one's best for; **ella se desvive por complacerme** she does her utmost to please me.
desyerbar [dez·yer·ƀár] = **desherbar.**
detallar [de·ta·yár] *v.* to detail, report in detail; to retail.
detalle [de·tá·ye] *m.* detail; retail; **¡ahí está el — !** that's the point.
detallista [de·ta·yís·ta] *m. & f.* retailer; detailer, person fond of detail.
detective [de·tek·tí·ƀe], **detectivo** [de·tek·tí·ƀo] *m.* detective.
detención [de·ten·sjón] *f.* detention, arrest; stop, halt; delay.
detener[45] [de·te·nér] *v. irr.* to detain, stop; to arrest; **-se** to halt; to delay oneself, stay.
detenimiento [de·te·ni·mjén·to] *m.* detention; delay; care, deliberation.
deteriorar [de·te·rjo·rár] *v.* to deteriorate, damage; **-se** to deteriorate, become impaired or damaged; to wear out.
deterioro [de·te·rjó·ro] *m.* deterioration, impairment.
determinación [de·ter·mi·na·sjón] *f.* determination; firmness.
determinar [de·ter·mi·nár] *v.* to determine; to decide; **-se** to resolve, decide.
detestable [de·tes·tá·ƀle] *adj.* detestable; hateful.
detestar [de·tes·tár] *v.* to detest.
detonación [de·to·na·sjón] *f.* detonation, report (*of a gun*), loud explosion; pop.
detonar [de·to·nár] *v.* to detonate, explode with a loud noise; to pop.
detrás [de·trás] *adv.* behind; — **de** *prep.* behind; **por** — from the rear, by the rear, from behind.
deuda [déw·đa] *f.* debt; indebtedness.
deudo [déw·đo] *m.* relative, kinsman.
deudor [dew·đór] *m.* debtor; *adj.* indebted, obligated.
devanar [de·ƀa·nár] *v.* to spool, wind on a spool; **-se los sesos** to rack one's brain.
devaneo [de·ƀa·né·o] *m.* frenzy; dissipation; wandering; idle pursuit; giddiness.
devastar [de·ƀas·tár] *v.* to devastate, lay waste, destroy.
devenir[48] [de·ƀe·nír] *v. irr.* to befall; to become, be transformed into.
devoción [de·ƀo·sjón] *f.* devotion; piety; attachment.

devocionario [de·ƀo·sjo·ná·rjo] *m.* prayer book.
devolución [de·ƀo·lu·sjón] *f.* return, giving back; replacement.
devolver[2, 52] [de·ƀol·ƀér] *v. irr.* to return, give back, pay back.
devorador [de·ƀo·ra·đór] *adj.* devouring; absorbing; ravenous; *m.* devourer.
devorar [de·ƀo·rár] *v.* to devour, gobble up.
devoto [de·ƀó·to] *adj.* devout, religious, pious; very fond (of).
devuelto [de·ƀwél·to] *p.p. of* **devolver.**
día [dí·a] *m.* day; **al otro** — on the next day; **hoy** — nowadays; **un — sí y otro no** every other day.
diablo [djá·ƀlo] *m.* devil, demon.
diablura [dja·ƀlú·ra] *f.* deviltry, mischief, devilish prank.
diabólico [dja·ƀó·li·ko] *adj.* diabolic, devilish, fiendish.
diácono [djá·ko·no] *m.* deacon.
diadema [dja·đé·ma] *f.* diadem, crown.
diáfano [djá·fa·no] *adj.* transparent, clear; sheer.
diagnosticar[6] [djaǥ·nos·ti·kár] *v.* to diagnose.
diagrama [dja·ǥrá·ma] *m.* diagram; graph; — **de flujo** (*computadora*) flow chart.
dialecto [dja·lék·to] *m.* dialect.
dialectología [dja·lek·to·lo·xí·a] *f.* dialectology.
dialogar[7] [dja·lo·ǥár] *v.* to dialogue.
diálogo [djá·lo·ǥo] *m.* dialogue.
diamante [dja·mán·te] *m.* diamond.
diámetro [djá·me·tro] *m.* diameter.
diantre [dján·tre] *m.* devil.
diapasón [dja·pa·són] *m.* pitch (*of a sound*); tuning fork.
diapositiva [dja·po·si·tí·ƀa] *f. Spain* slide, lantern slide.
diario [djá·rjo] *adj.* daily; *m.* newspaper; daily expense; journal, diary.
diarrea [dja·rré·a] *f.* diarrhea.
dibujante [di·ƀu·xán·te] *m. & f.* draftsman; designer.
dibujar [di·ƀu·xár] *v.* (*diseñar*) to draw, make a drawing of; (*describir*) depict, portray; describe; **-se** to appear, show.
dibujo [di·ƀú·xo] *m.* drawing; delineation, protrayal, picture; — **natural** drawing of the human figure, drawing from life.
dicción [dik·sjón] *f.* diction; word; choice of words, style.
diciembre [di·sjém·bre] *m.* December.
dictado [dik·tá·đo] *m.* dictation; title; dictate; **escribir al** — to take dictation.
dictador [dik·ta·đór] *m.* dictator.
dictadura [dik·ta·đú·ra] *f.* dictatorship.
dictamen [dik·tá·men] *m.* opinion, judgment.
dictaminar [dik·ta·mi·nár] *v.* to give an opinion or judgment.
dictar [dik·tár] *v.* to dictate.
dicha [dí·ča] *f.* happiness; good luck.
dicharachero [di·ča·ra·čé·ro] *adj.* fond of making wisecracks; witty.
dicharacho [di·ča·rá·čo] *m.* wisecrack, smart remark; malicious remark.
dicho [dí·čo] *p.p. of* **decir** said; — **y hecho** no sooner said than done; *m.* saying, popular proverb.
dichoso [di·čó·so] *adj.* happy, lucky.
diecinueve [dje·si·nwé·ƀe] *num.* nineteen.
dieciocho [dje·sjó·čo] *num.* eighteen.
dieciséis [dje·si·séjs] *num.* sixteen.
diecisiete [dje·si·sjé·te] *num.* seventeen.
diente [djén·te] *m.* tooth; tusk; — **de león** dandelion, — **de leche** baby tooth; **de -s afuera** insincerely; *Am.* **pelar el** — to smile affectedly.
diéresis [djé·re·sis] *f.* diaeresis (*as in* **vergüenza**).
diesel [dí·sel] *m.* diesel; diesel motor.
diestra [djés·tra] *f.* right hand.
diestro [djés·tro] *adj.* skillful; right; *m.* matador; skillful swordsman; halter.
dieta [djé·ta] *f.* diet; assembly; salary, fee.
dietista [dje·tís·ta] *m. & f.* dietician.
diez [djes] *num.* ten.
diezmo [djéz·mo] *m.* tithe.
difamación [di·fa·ma·sjón] *f.* libel, slander.
difamador [di·fa·ma·đór] *m.* slanderer.
difamar [di·fa·már] *v.* to defame, libel, malign, slander.
difamatorio [di·fa·ma·tó·rjo] *adj.* scandalous, slandering.
diferencia [di·fe·rén·sja] *f.* difference.
diferencial [di·fe·ren·sjál] *m.* differential.
diferenciar [di·fe·ren·sjár] *v.* to differentiate, distinguish; to differ, disagree; **-se** to distinguish oneself; to become different.
diferente [di·fe·rén·te] *adj.* different.
diferir[3] [di·fe·rír] *v. irr.* to defer, put off, delay; to differ, disagree; to be different.
difícil [di·fí·sil] *adj.* difficult.
dificultad [di·fi·kul·tád] *f.* difficulty.
dificultar [di·fi·kul·tár] *v.* to make difficult; — **el paso** to impede or obstruct the passage; **-se** to become difficult.
dificultoso [di·fi·kul·tó·so] *adj.* difficult, hard.
difteria [dif·té·rja] *f.* diphtheria.
difundir [di·fun·dír] *v.* to diffuse, spread out, scatter; to broadcast by radio.
difunto [di·fún·to] *adj.* deceased, dead; *m.* corpse.
difusión [di·fu·sjón] *f.* diffusion, spreading, scattering; wordiness; broadcasting.
difuso [di·fú·so] *adj.* diffuse; diffused, widespread.
digerible [di·xe·rí·ƀle] *adj.* digestible.
digerir[3] [di·xe·rír] *v. irr.* to digest.
dígito [dí·xi·to] *m.* digit; (*computadora*) — **binario** binary (bit).
dignarse [diǥ·nár·se] *v.* to deign, condescend.
dignatario [diǥ·na·tá·rjo] *m.* dignitary (*person in a high office*).
dignidad [diǥ·ni·đáđ] *f.* dignity.
digno [díǥ·no] *adj.* worthy; dignified.
digresión [di·ǥre·sjón] *f.* digression.
dije [dí·xe] *m.* trinket, small piece of jewelry; locket; woman of fine qualities a ''jewel''; *Am.* locket or charm.
dilación [di·la·sjón] *f.* delay.
dilatado [di·la·tá·đo] *adj.* vast, spacious; extensive; *p.p. of* **dilatar.**
dilatar [di·la·tár] *v.* to dilate, widen, enlarge; to expand; to lengthen, extend; to spread out; to defer, put off, retard; **-se** to expand; to be diffuse, wordy; *Mex.* to delay oneself, take long.
diligencia [di·li·xén·sja] *f.* diligence, care, industry; speed; stagecoach; business, errand.
diligente [di·li·xén·te] *adj.* diligent; quick, speedy.
diluir[32] [di·lwír] *v. irr.* to dilute.
diluvio [di·lú·ƀjo] *m.* flood.
dimensión [di·men·sjón] *f.* dimension.
dimes: — **y diretes** [dí·mes·i·đi·ré·tes] quibbling, arguing; **andar en — y diretes** to quibble, argue.
diminución [di·mi·nu·sjón] *f.* diminution, decrease; — **progresiva** tapering off.
diminutivo [di·mi·nu·tí·ƀo] *adj.* diminutive, tiny; diminishing; *m.* diminutive.
diminuto [di·mi·nú·to] *adj.* tiny, little.
dimisión [di·mi·sjón] *f.* resignation (*from an office*).
dimitir [di·mi·tír] *v.* to resign, give up (*a position,*

office, etc.).
dinámica [di·ná·mi·ka] *f.* dynamics; **dinámico** *adj.* dynamic.
dinamismo [di·na·míz·mo] *m.* vigor, forcefulness; dynamic force or energy.
dinamita [di·na·mí·ta] *f.* dynamite.
dínamo [dí·na·mo] *m.* dynamo.
dinastía [di·nas·tí·a] *f.* dynasty.
dineral [di·ne·rál] *m.* a lot of money.
dinero [di·né·ro] *m.* money; currency; *Peru* Peruvian silver coin equivalent to about ten cents; — **contante y sonante** ready cash, hard cash.
diodo electroluminiscente [djó·đo e·lek·tro·lu·mi·ni·sén·te] *m.* (*computadora*) light emitting diode (LED).
dios [djos] *m.* god; **Dios** God; **a la buena de** — without malice; without plan, haphazard, at random.
diosa [djó·sa] *f.* goddess.
diplomacia [di·plo·má·sja] *f.* diplomacy; tact.
diplomático [di·plo·má·ti·ko] *adj.* diplomatic; tactful; *m.* diplomat.
diputación [di·pu·ta·sjón] *f.* deputation; committee.
diputado [di·pu·tá·đo] *m.* deputy, representative.
diputar [di·pu·tár] *v.* to depute, delegate, commission.
dique [dí·ke] *m.* dike; barrier; — **de carena** dry dock.
dirección [di·rek·sjón] *f.* direction, course; advice, guidance; management; board of directors; office of the board of directors; address.
directivo [di·rek·tí·bo] *adj.* directive, directing, guiding; **mesa directiva** board of directors.
directo [di·rék·to] *adj.* direct, straight.
director [di·rek·tór] *m.* director, manager; *adj.* directing.
directorio [di·rek·tó·rjo] *adj.* directory, directive, directing; *m.* directory, book of instructions; directorate, board of directors.
directrices [di·rek·trí·ses] *f. pl.* directives.
dirigente [di·ri·xén·te] *adj.* directing, leading; *m.* leader, director.
dirigible [di·ri·xí·ble] *adj.* & *m.* dirigible.
dirigir[11] [di·ri·xír] *v.* to direct, manage, govern; to guide; to address (*letters, packages*); to dedicate; **-se a** to address (*a person*); to go to or toward.
discernimiento [di·ser·ni·mjén·to] *m.* discernment, keen judgment, insight, discrimination.
discernir[3] [di·ser·nír] *v. irr.* to discern; to distinguish; to discriminate.
disciplina [di·si·plí·na] *f.* discipline, training; rule of conduct; order; any art or science; scourge, whip.
disciplinar [di·si·pli·nár] *v.* to discipline; train; to drill; **-se** to discipline oneself; to scourge oneself.
discípulo [di·sí·pu·lo] *m.* pupil; disciple.
disco [dís·ko] *m.* disk; discus; phonograph record; — **flexible** (*computadora*) floppy disk, — **rígido** hard disk.
díscolo [dís·ko·lo] *adj.* unruly, disobedient; unfriendly.
discordancia [dis·kor·đán·sja] *f.* discord, disagreement.
discordia [dis·kór·đja] *f.* discord.
discreción [dis·kre·sjón] *f.* discretion; keenness; wit; **darse** (*or* **rendirse**) **a** — to surrender unconditionally; **discrecional** [dis·kre·sjo·nál] *adj.* optional.
discrepancia [dis·kre·pán·sja] *f.* discrepancy.
discreto [dis·kré·to] *adj.* discreet, prudent; clever.
disculpa [dis·kúl·pa] *f.* excuse; apology.
disculpable [dis·kul·pá·ble] *adj.* excusable.
disculpar [dis·kul·pár] *v.* to excuse, free from blame; **-se** to excuse oneself, apologize.
discurrir [dis·ku·rrír] *v.* (*charlar*) to discuss, (*recorrer*) to ramble about; (*imaginar*) to invent, think out.
discursear [dis·kur·se·ár] *v.* to make speeches.
discurso [dis·kúr·so] *m.* discourse; speech; reasoning; lapse of time.
discusión [dis·ku·sjón] *f.* discussion.
discutible [dis·ku·tí·ble] *adj.* debatable, questionable.
discutir [dis·ku·tír] *v.* to discuss.
disecar[6] [di·se·kár] *v.* to dissect; to stuff and mount (*the skins of animals*).
diseminación [di·se·mi·na·sjón] *f.* dissemination, spread, scattering.
diseminar [di·se·mi·nár] *v.* to disseminate, scatter, spread.
disensión [di·sen·sjón] *f.* dissension, dissent, disagreement.
disentería [di·sen·te·rí·a] *f.* dysentery.
disentir[3] [di·sen·tír] *v. irr.* to dissent, differ, disagree.
diseñador [di·se·ña·đór] *m.* designer.
diseñar [di·se·ñár] *v.* to design; to sketch, outline; — **la política** to outline policy.
diseño [di·sé·ño] *m.* design; sketch, outline; — **gráfico** graphic design.
disertar [di·ser·tár] *v.* to discourse, discuss.
disforme [dis·fór·me] *adj.* deformed; ugly, hideous; out of proportion.
disfraz [dis·frás] *m.* disguise, mask; masquerade costume.
disfrazar[9] [dis·fra·sár] *v.* to disguise, conceal; **-se** to disguise oneself; to masquerade.
disfrutar [dis·fru·tár] *v.* to enjoy; to reap benefit or advantage; to make use of.
disfrute [dis·frú·te] *m.* enjoyment, benefit, use.
disgustar [diz·gus·tár] *v.* to disgust, displease; **-se** to get angry; to get bored.
disgusto [diz·gús·to] *m.* displeasure; unpleasantness; annoyance; quarrel; grief; disgust.
disidente [di·si·đén·te] *m.* & *f.* dissident; protester.
disimulado [di·si·mu·lá·đo] *adj.* underhanded, sly, cunning; *p.p. of* **disimular.**
disimular [di·si·mu·lár] *v.* to feign, hide, mask; to overlook, excuse.
disimulo [di·si·mú·lo] *m.* dissimulation, feigning, pretense; slyness; reserve.
disipación [di·si·pa·sjón] *f.* dissipation; waste, extravagance.
disipar [di·si·pár] *v.* to dissipate, scatter; to squander; **-se** to vanish.
dislocar[6] [diz·lo·kár] *v.* to dislocate, put out of joint; **-se** to become dislocated, get out of joint.
disminución [diz·mi·nu·sjón] = **diminución.**
disminuir[32] [di·mi·nwír] *v. irr.* to diminish, decrease, lessen.
disociación [di·so·sja·sjón] *f.* dissociation, separation.
disociar [di·so·sjár] *v.* to dissociate, separate.
disolución [di·so·lu·sjón] *f.* dissolution, breaking up; dissoluteness, lewdness.
disoluto [di·so·lú·to] *adj.* dissolute, loose, immoral, dissipated.
disolver[2, 52] [di·sol·bér] *v. irr.* to dissolve; to melt.
disonancia [di·so·nán·sja] *f.* discord.
disparada [dis·pa·rá·đa] *f. C.A., Mex., Carib., Riopl.* rush, run.
disparar [dis·pa·rár] *v.* to shoot, fire, discharge; to throw; **-se** to run away, dart out.
disparatado [dis·pa·ra·tá·đo] *adj.* absurd, foolish, senseless.
disparatar [dis·pa·ra·tár] *v.* to talk nonsense; to

blunder; to act foolishly.
disparate [dis·pa·rá·te] *m.* nonsense, blunder.
disparidad [dis·pa·ri·đáđ] *f.* inequality.
disparo [dis·pá·ro] *m.* shooting, discharge, explosion; shot; sudden dash, run.
dispensa [dis·pén·sa] *f.* dispensation; exemption.
dispensar [dis·pen·sár] *v.* to excuse, absolve, pardon; to grant, give.
dispensario [dis·pen·sá·rjo] *m.* dispensary; pharmaceutical laboratory; pharmacopoeia (*book containing list and description of drugs*).
dispersar [dis·per·sár] *v.* to disperse, scatter.
dispersión [dis·per·sjón] *f.* dispersion, dispersal.
displicencia [dis·pli·sén·sja] *f.* displeasure, discontent, dislike.
displicente [dis·pli·sén·te] *adj.* unpleasant, disagreeable, cross.
disponer[40] [dis·po·nér] *v. irr.* (*arreglar*) to dispose; to arrange, put in order; to prepare; (*mandar*) to order, command; **-se** to get ready; to make one's will and testament.
disponible [dis·po·ní·ƀle] *adj.* spare, available; on hand.
disposición [dis·po·si·sjón] *f.* disposition; arrangement; order, command; aptitude; disposal; — **legales** ordinances.
dispositivos [dis·po·si·tí·ƀos] *m. pl.* devices.
dispuesto [dis·pwés·to] *p.p. of* **disponer** & *adj.* disposed; ready; fit; smart, clever.
disputa [dis·pú·ta] *f.* dispute.
disputar [dis·pu·tár] *v.* to dispute.
distancia [dis·tán·sja] *f.* distance.
distante [dis·tán·te] *adj.* distant.
distar [dis·tár] *v.* to be distant, far (from).
distender[1] [dis·ten·dér] *v. irr.* to distend, stretch; to inflate; **-se** to distend, expand.
distinción [dis·tin·sjón] *f.* distinction.
distinguido [dis·tiŋ·gí·đo] *adj.* & *p.p.* distinguished.
distinguir[12] [dis·tiŋ·gír] *v.* to distinguish; **-se** to distinguish oneself, excel; to differ, be different.
distintivo [dis·tin·tí·ƀo] *adj.* distinctive, distinguishing; *m.* distinguishing characteristic; mark, sign; badge.
distinto [dis·tín·to] *adj.* distinct, plain, clear; different.
distracción [dis·trak·sjón] *f.* distraction; diversion, amusement; lack of attention.
distraer[46] [dis·tra·ér] *v. irr.* to distract; to divert, amuse; to lead astray; to divert (*funds*); **-se** to have a good time; to be absentminded; to be inattentive.
distraído [dis·tra·í·đo] *adj.* distracted; inattentive; absentminded; *Am.* slovenly, untidy.
distribución [dis·tri·ƀu·sjón] *f.* distribution, apportionment.
distribuidor [dis·tri·ƀwi·đór] *m.* distributor; *adj.* distributing.
distribuir[32] [dis·tri·ƀwír] *v. irr.* to distribute; to sort; classify.
distrito [dis·trí·to] *m.* district; region.
disturbio [dis·túr·ƀjo] *m.* disturbance.
disuadir [di·swa·đír] *v.* to dissuade.
disuelto [di·swél·to] *p.p. of* **disolver.**
diurno [djúr·no] *adj.* day, of the day.
divagación [di·ƀa·ǥa·sjón] *f.* rambling, digression.
divagar[7] [di·ƀa·ǥár] *v.* to ramble; to digress.
diván [di·ƀán] *m.* divan, sofa.
divergencia [di·ƀer·xén·sja] *f.* divergence; difference (*of opinion*).
divergir[11] [di·ƀer·xír] *v.* to diverge; to differ.
diversidad [di·ƀer·si·đáđ] *f.* diversity; variety.
diversión [di·ƀer·sjón] *f.* amusement.
diverso [di·ƀér·so] *adj.* diverse; different; **-s** several, various.
divertido [di·ƀer·tí·đo] *adj.* amusing, funny.
divertir[3] [di·ƀer·tír] *v. irr.* to amuse, entertain; to divert, turn aside; **-se** to have a good time, amuse oneself.
dividendo [di·ƀi·đén·do] *m.* dividend.
dividir [di·ƀi·đír] *v.* to divide, split.
divinidad [di·ƀi·ni·đáđ] *f.* divinity, deity; **¡qué—!** what a beauty!
divino [di·ƀí·no] *adj.* divine.
divisa [di·ƀí·sa] *f.* device, emblem; foreign exchange.
divisar [di·ƀi·sár] *v.* to sight; to make out, distinguish.
división [di·ƀi·sjón] *f.* division.
divisorio [di·ƀi·só·rjo] *adj.* dividing.
divorciar [di·ƀor·sjár] *v.* to divorce; to separate.
divorcio [di·ƀór·sjo] *m.* divorce.
divulgar[7] [di·ƀul·ǥár] *v.* to divulge, spread, make public, give out.
diz [dis] = **dice; dizque** [dís·ke] *they say that* ...
do [do] *m.* the first note of the diatonic scale in solfeggio.
dobladillar [do·ƀla·đi·yár] *v.* to hem.
dobladillo [do·ƀla·đí·yo] *m.* hem; — **de ojo** hemstitch.
doblar [do·ƀlár] *v.* to bend, fold; to double; to toll, knell; *Ríopl.* to knock down; — **la esquina** to turn the corner; **-se** to stoop; to bend down; to give in.
doble [dó·ƀle] *adj.* double, twofold; double-faced, hypocritical; *Ch., Perú, P.R.* broke, poor; *m.* fold, toll, tolling of bells, knell.
doblegar[7] [do·ƀle·ǥár] *v.* to bend; to fold; **-se** to bend over; to stoop; to submit, yield.
doblete [do·ƀlé·te] *m.* doublet; a two-base hit.
doblez [do·ƀlés] *m.* fold, crease; duplicity, hypocrisy.
doce [dó·se] *num.* twelve.
docena [do·sé·na] *f.* dozen.
docente [do·sén·te] *adj.* teaching; educational; **cuerpo** — faculty (*of a school*).
dócil [dó·sil] *adj.* docile, obedient, manageable, meek; flexible; **docilidad** [do·si·li·đáđ] *f.* obedience, meekness, gentleness; flexibility.
docto [dók·to] *adj.* learned; expert.
doctor [dok·tór] *m.* doctor.
doctorar [dok·to·rár] *v.* to grant a doctor's degree to; **-se** to get a doctor's degree.
doctrina [dok·trí·na] *f.* doctrine.
documentar [do·ku·men·tár] *v.* to document.
documento [do·ku·mén·to] *m.* document.
dogal [do·ǥál] *m.* halter; noose.
dogma [dóǥ·ma] *m.* dogma; **dogmático** [doǥ·má·ti·ko] *adj.* dogmatic, pertaining to dogma; positive.
dolencia [do·lén·sja] *f.* ailment; ache, aching.
doler[2] [do·lér] *v. irr.* to ache, hurt, cause pain; to cause grief; **-se de** to feel pity for, feel sorry for; to repent from.
doliente [do·ljén·te] *adj.* sorrowful; suffering; aching; *m.* sick person, patient; mourner.
dolor [do·lór] *m.* pain, ache; sorrow, grief.
dolorido [do·lo·rí·đo] *adj.* aching, sore; afflicted; repentant; doleful.
doloroso [do·lo·ró·so] *adj.* painful; sorrowful.
doma [dó·ma] *f.* breaking of horses.
domador [do·ma·đór] *m.* horsebreaker, broncobuster.
domar [do·már] *v.* to tame, subdue.
domeñar [do·me·ñár] *v.* to tame; to subdue; to dominate.
domesticar[6] [do·mes·ti·kár] *v.* to domesticate, tame.
doméstico [do·més·ti·ko] *adj.* domestic; *m.* house servant.

domiciliar [do·mi·si·ljár] *v.* to house, lodge; *Ríopl.* to address (*a letter*); **-se** to take up residence; to settle down; to dwell, reside.
domicilio [do·mi·sí·ljo] *m.* home, dwelling.
dominación [do·mi·na·sjón] *f.* domination, rule, authority.
dominador [do·mi·na·dór] *adj.* dominant, dominating; domineering, bossy; *m.* ruler, boss.
dominante [do·mi·nán·te] *adj.* dominant; domineering; tyrannical; prevailing, predominant.
dominar [do·mi·nár] *v.* to dominate, rule, lead; to stand out, tower above; to master.
dómine [dó·mi·ne] *m.* teacher; pedagogue; pedant.
domingo [do·míŋ·go] *m.* Sunday; — **de ramos** Palm Sunday.
dominio [do·mí·njo] *m.* domain; dominion; authority; mastery (*of a science, art, language, etc.*).
dominó [do·mi·nó] *m.* domino.
don [don] *m.* gift; ability, knack; Don (*title used only before Christian names of men*).
donación [do·na·sjón] *f.* donation; grant.
donador [do·na·dór] *m.* donor, giver.
donaire [do·náj·re] *m.* grace, elegance; wit; humor; witty remark.
donairoso [do·naj·ró·so] *adj.* elegant, graceful; witty.
donar [do·nár] *v.* to donate.
doncella [don·sé·ya] *f.* virgin, maiden; maidservant; *Col.* felon (*sore or inflammation near a finger or toenail*).
donde [dón·de] *rel. adv.* where, in which; **a — (adonde)** where, to which; *C.A., Ríopl.* to the house of; **de** — from where, from which; **en** — where, in which; **por** — where, through which; wherefore; — **no** otherwise; if not; **¿donde?** *interr. adv.* where?; **¿por —?** which way?
dondequiera [don·de·kjé·ra] *adv.* wherever; anywhere.
donjuanismo [doŋ·xwa·níz·mo] *m.* Don Juanism, conduct reminiscent of Don Juan Tenorio.
donoso [do·nó·so] *adj.* witty, gay; graceful.
doña [dó·ña] *f.* Doña (*title used only before Christian names of women*).
dorada [do·rá·da] *f.* gilthead (fish).
dorado [do·rá·do] *p.p. & adj.* gilded, gilt; golden; *m.* gilding; *Am.* a kind of hummingbird; **doradillo** [do·ra·dí·yo] *adj. C.R., Ríopl.* honey-colored, golden (*applied to horses*).
dorar [do·rár] *v.* to gild.
dormir[4] [dor·mír] *v. irr.* to sleep; **-se** to go to sleep, fall asleep; to become numb.
dormitar [dor·mi·tár] *v.* to doze.
dormitorio [dor·mi·tó·rjo] *m.* dormitory; bedroom.
dorso [dór·so] *m.* back, reverse.
dos [dos] *num.* two.
DOS [dos] *m.* (*computadora*) disk operating system.
dosel [do·sél] *m.* canopy.
dosis [dó·sis] *f.* dose.
dotación [do·ta·sjón] *f.* endowment, endowing; donation, foundation; dowry; complement (*personnel of a warship*); office force.
dotar [do·tár] *v.* to endow; to provide with a dowry.
dote [dó·te] *m. & f.* dowry; *f.* natural gift, talent, or quality.
draga [drá·ga] *f.* dredge, dredging machine.
dragado [dra·gá·do] *m.* dredging.
dragaminas [dra·ga·mí·nas] *m.* mine sweeper.
dragar[7] [dra·gár] *v.* to dredge.
dragón [dra·gón] *m.* dragon.
drama [drá·ma] *m.* drama.
dramático [dra·má·ti·ko] *adj.* dramatic; *m.* dramatic actor; playwright, dramatist.
dramatizar[9] [dra·ma·ti·sár] *v.* to dramatize.
dramaturgo [dra·ma·túr·go] *m.* playwright, dramatist.
drenaje [dre·ná·xe] *m. Am.* drainage.
drenar [dre·nár] *v. Am.* to drain.
dril [dril] *m.* drill (*strong cotton or linen cloth*).
droga [dró·ga] *f.* (*medicina*) drug, medicine; (*mentira*) lie, fib; trick; (*molestia*) bother, nuisance; *Peru, Carib.* bad debt; *Ríopl.* drug on the market unsalable article.
drogadicto [dro·ga·dik·to] *m.* drug addict.
droguería [dro·ge·rí·a] *f.* drugstore; drug business.
droguero [dro·gé·ro] *m.* druggist; *Mex.* cheat, debt evader.
droguista [dro·gís·ta] *m. & f.* druggist; (*tramposo*) cheat, crook.
dúctil [dúk·til] *adj.* ductile.
ductilidad [duk·ti·li·dád] *f.* ductility.
ducha [dú·ča] *f.* shower bath; douche.
ducho [dú·čo] *adj.* expert, skillful.
duda [dú·da] *f.* doubt.
dudable [du·dá·ble] *adj.* doubtful.
dudar [du·dár] *v.* to doubt; to hesitate.
dudoso [du·dó·so] *adj.* doubtful; uncertain.
duela [dwé·la] *f.* stave (*of a barrel*); *Mex., Andes* long, narrow floor board.
duelo [dwé·lo] *m.* (*luto*) grief, sorrow; mourning; mourners (*pleito*) duel; **estar de** — to be in mourning; to mourn.
duende [dwén·de] *m.* goblin.
dueña [dwé·ña] *f.* owner, landlady; duenna, chaperon or governess.
dueño [dwé·ño] *m.* owner; master.
dueto [dwé·to], **dúo** [dú·o] *m.* duet.
dulce [dúl·se] *adj.* sweet; pleasant, agreeable; fresh (*water*); soft (*metal*); *m.* sweetmeat; candy; preserves; *Am.* sugar, honey; **dulcería** [dul·se·rí·a] *f.* candy shop.
dulcificar[6] [dul·si·fi·kár] *v.* to sweeten; to soften.
dulzón [dul·són] *adj.* over-sweet, sickeningly sweet.
dulzura [dul·sú·ra] *f.* sweetness; meekness.
duna [dú·na] *f.* dune, sand dune.
dúplex [dú·ples] *m.* (*computadora*) full duplex.
duplicado [du·pli·ká·do] *adj. & m.* duplicate; **por** — in duplicate; *p.p. of* **duplicar.**
duplicadora [du·pli·ka·dó·ra] *f.* duplicator (machine).
duplicar[6] [du·pli·kár] *v.* to duplicate, double; to repeat.
duplicidad [du·pli·si·dád] *f.* duplicity, deceit, deceitfulness, treachery.
duque [dú·ke] *m.* duke.
duquesa [du·ké·sa] *f.* duchess.
durabilidad [du·ra·bi·li·dád] *f.* durability, durable quality, wear.
durable [du·rá·ble] *adj.* durable.
duración [du·ra·sjón] *f.* duration.
duradero [du·ra·dé·ro] *adj.* durable, lasting.
durante [du·rán·te] *prep.* during, for.
durar [du·rár] *v.* to last, endure; to wear well.
durazno [du·ráz·no] *m.* peach; peach tree; **duraznero** [du·raz·né·ro] *m.* peach tree.
dureza [du·ré·sa] *f.* hardness; harshness.
durmiente [dur·mjén·te] *adj.* sleeping; *m.* sleeper; crossbeam; *Col., Ven., Mex., Ch.* railroad tie.
duro [dú·ro] *adj.* (*sólido*) hard; firm, solid; untiring; (*cruel*) cruel; harsh; rigid; (tacaño) stubborn; stingy; **a duras penas** with difficulty; *Mex., Ch., Arg.* — **y parejo** eagerly, tenaciously; *Am.* **hacer** — to resist stubbornly; *m.* **duro** (*Spanish dollar*).

E:e

e[e] *conj.* and (*before words beginning with* **i** *or* **hi**).
ebanista [e·ƀa·nís·ta] *m.* cabinetmaker.
ébano [é·ƀa·no] *m.* ebony.
ebrio [é·brjo] *adj.* drunk
ebullición [e·ƀu·yi·sjón] *f.* boiling, bubbling up.
eclesiástico [e·kle·sjás·ti·ko] *adj.* ecclesiastic, belonging to the church; *m.* clergyman.
eclipsar [e·klip·sár] *v.* to eclipse; to outshine, surpass.
eclipse [e·klíp·se] *m.* eclipse.
écloga [é·klo·ǥa] *f.* eclogue, pastoral poem, idyll.
eco [é·ko] *m.* echo.
economía [e·ko·no·mí·a] *f.* economy; —**política** economics, political economy.
económico [e·ko·nó·mi·ko] *adj.* economic; economical, saving; **economista** [e·ko·no·mís·ta] *m.* economist.
economizar[9] [e·ko·no·mi·sár] *v.* to economize, save.
ecuación [e·kwa·sjón] *f.* equation.
ecuador [e·kwa·đór] *m.* equator.
echar [e·čár] *v.* (*tirar*) to throw, cast; to expel; to throw out; (*emitir*) to give off; to sprout; — **a correr** to run away; **-(se) a perder** to spoil; — **a pique** to sink; **-(se) a reír** to burst out laughing; — **carnes** to get fat; — **de menos** to miss; — **de ver** to notice; to make out; — **mano** to seize; — **papas** to fib; — **raíces** to take root; — **suertes** to draw lots; **-se** to lie down; *Am.* **echársela** [e·čár·se·la] to boast.
edad [e-đáđ] *f.* age.
edecán [e·đe·kán] *m.* aide-de-camp.
edén [e·đén] *m.* Eden; paradise.
edición [e·đi·sjón] *f.* edition; publication; — **en pantalla** (*computadora*) screen editing.
edificación [e·đi·fi·ka·sjón] *f.* edification (*moral or spiritual uplift*); construction.
edificar[6] [e·đi·fi·kár] *v.* to construct, build; to edify, uplift.
edificio [e·đi·fí·sjo] *m.* edifice, building.
editar [e·đi·tár] *v.* to publish.
editor [e·đi·tór] *m.* publisher; *adj.* publishing.
editorial [e·đi·to·rjál] *adj.* publishing, editorial; *m.* editorial; *f.* publishing house.
edredón [e·đre·đón] *m.* down quilt, comforter, quilted blanket.
educación [e·đu·ka·sjón] *f.* education, training; breeding, manners.
educador [e·đu·ka·đór] *m.* educator; *adj.* educating.
educando [e·đu·kán·do] *m.* pupil; inmate (*of an orphanage, boarding school, etc.*).
educar[6] [e·đu·kár] *v.* to educate, teach, train, raise, bring up.
educativo [e·đu·ka·tí·ƀo] *adj.* — educational.
efectivo [e·fek·tí·ƀo] *adj.* effective; real; in operation, active; *m.* cash; **-s por cobrar** accounts receivable.
efecto [e·fék·to] *m.* (*resultado*) effect, result; (*fin*) end, purpose, **-s** goods, personal property; **en** — in fact, actually; **llevar a** — to carry out; **surtir** — to come out as expected; to give good results.
efectuar[18] [e·fek·twár] *v.* to effect, bring about.
eficacia [e·fi·ká·sja] *f.* efficacy; efficiency; effectiveness.
eficaz [e·fi·kás] *adj.* effective; active; efficient.
eficiencia [e·fi·sjén·sja] *f.* efficiency; **eficiente** [e·fi·sjén·te] *adj.* efficient.
efímero [e·fí·me·ro] *adj.* ephemeral, short-lived, brief.
efluvio [e·flú·ƀjo] *m.* emanation, exhalation, vapors.
efusión [e·fu·sjón] *f.* effusion, unrestrained expression of feeling, gushy manner; — **de sangre** bloodshed.
efusivo [e·fu·sí·ƀo] *adj.* effusive, too demonstrative, over-emotional.
egipcio [e·xíp·sjo] *adj.* & *m.* Egyptian.
egocéntrico [e·ǥo·sén·tri·ko] *adj.* egocentric, self-centered.
egoísmo [e·ǥo·íz·mo] *m.* selfishness.
egoísta [e·ǥo·ís·ta] *adj.* selfish; *m.* & *f.* selfish person.
egolatría [e·ǥo·la·trí·a] *f.* self-worship.
egreso [e·ǥré·so] *m.* outlay, expenses; graduation.
eje [é·xe] *m.* axis; axle; arbor (*machine*).
ejecución [e·xe·ku·sjón] *f.* execution; carrying out; (*computadora*) execution, running.
ejecutar [e·xe·ku·tár] *v.* to execute; to carry out; to perform, do.
ejecutivo [e·xe·ku·tí·ƀo] *adj.* executive; active; *m.* executive.
ejecutor [e·xe·ku·tór] *m.* executor; — **de la justicia** executioner.
ejemplar [e·xem·plár] *adj.* exemplary, model; *m.* copy; specimen.
ejemplo [e·xém·plo] *m.* example; model, pattern.
ejercer[10] [e·xer·sér] *v.* to practice (*a profession*); to exert.
ejercicio [e·xer·sí·sjo] *m.* exercise; practice; tenure; military drill; exercise (*of authority*); **hacer** — to take exercise; — **contable** accounting period.
ejercitar [e·xer·si·tár] *v.* to practice, exercise; to drill, train; **-se** to train oneself; to practice.
ejército [e·xér·si·to] *m.* army.
ejido [e·xí·đo] *m.* public land, common.
ejote [e·jó·te] *m. Mex., Guat.* string bean.
el [el] *def. art. m.* the; — **de** the one with, that one with; — **que** *rel. pron.* he who, the one that; **él** *pers. pron.* he; him, it (*after a prep.*).
elaboración [e·la·ƀo·ra·sjón] *f.* manufacture, making; development.
elaborar [e·la·ƀo·rár] *v.* to elaborate.
elasticidad [e·las·ti·si·đáđ] *f.* elasticity.
elástico [e·lás·ti·ko] *adj.* elastic; flexible; *m.* elastic; elastic tape; wire spring; **-s** *Am.* suspenders.
elección [e·lek·sjón] *f.* election; choice.
electo [e·lék·to] *adj.* elect, chosen; *m.* elect, person chosen.
elector [e·lek·tór] *m.* elector, voter; *adj.* electoral, electing.
electoral [e·lek·to·rál] *adj.* electoral.
electricidad [e·lek·tri·si·đáđ] *f.* electricity.
electricista [e·lek·tri·sís·ta] *m.* electrician; electrical engineer.
eléctrico [e·lék·tri·ko] *adj.* electric, electrical.
electrizar[9] [e·lek·tri·sár] *v.* to electrify; to thrill, excite; *Am.* to anger, irritate.
electrocardiógrafo [e·lek·tro·kar·đjó·gra·fo] *m.* electrocardiograph.
electroimán [e·lek·troj·mán] *m.* electromagnet.
electrólisis [e·lek·tró·li·sis] *f.* electrolysis.
electromagnético [e·lek·tro·maǥ·né·ti·ko] *adj.* electromagnetic.
electrón [e·lek·trón] *m.* electron.
electrónico [e·lek·tró·ni·ko] *adj.* electronic; **electrónica** [e·lek·tró·ni·ka] *f.* electronics.
elefante [e·le·fán·te] *m.* elephant.
elegancia [e·le·ǥán·sja] *f.* elegance, grace, distinguished manner.
elegante [e·le·ǥán·te] *adj.* elegant, graceful, polished; stylish.
elegir[5, 11] [e·le·xír] *v. irr.* to elect, choose.
elemental [e·le·men·tál] *adj.* elementary; elemental, fundamental.
elemento [e·le·mén·to] *m.* element; **-s** elements, fundamentals; personnel; — **químicos** chemical

elements, simple substances; — **físico** (*computadora*) hardware; *Am.* **ser** (*or* **estar**) **hecho un** — to be an idiot, a fool.
elevación [e·le·ƀa·sjón] *f.* elevation; height; rise; rapture.
elevador [e·le·ƀa·đór] *m. Am.* elevator, hoist.
elevar [e·le·ƀár] *v.* to elevate, raise, lift; **-se** to go up; to soar.
eliminación [e·li·mi·na·sjón] *f.* elimination, removal.
eliminar [e·li·mi·nár] *v.* to eliminate.
elocuencia [e·lo·kwén·sja] *f.* eloquence.
elocuente [e·lo·kwén·te] *adj.* eloquent.
elogiar [e·lo·xjár] *v.* to praise.
elogio [e·ló·xjo] *m.* praise.
elote [e·ló·te] *m. Mex., C.A.* ear of corn, corn on the cob.
elucidación [e·lu·si·đa·sjón] *f.* elucidation, explanation.
elucidar [e·lu·si·đár] *v.* to elucidate, illustrate, explain.
eludir [e·lu·đír] *v.* to elude, avoid, dodge.
ella [é·ya] *pers. pron.* she; her, it (*after a prep.*).
ello [é·yo] *pron.* it; — **es que** the fact is that.
emanación [e·ma·na·sjón] *f.* emanation, flow; fumes, vapor, odor; manifestation.
emanar [e·ma·nár] *v.* to emanate, spring, issue.
emancipación [e·man·si·pa·sjón] *f.* emancipation.
emancipar [e·man·si·pár] *v.* to emancipate, set free; **-se** to become free.
embajada [em·ba·xá·da] *f.* embassy; errand, mission.
embajador [em·ba·xa·dór] *m.* ambassador.
embalador [em·ba·la·dór] *m.* packer.
embalaje [em·ba·lá·xe] *m.* packing.
embalar [em·ba·lár] *v.* to pack; to bale, crate.
embaldosar [em·bal·do·sár] *v.* to pave with flagstones or tiles.
embalsamar [em·bal·sa·már] *v.* to embalm; to scent, perfume.
embarazar[9] [em·ba·ra·sár] *v.* (*impedir*) to hinder, to obstruct; (*preñar*) to make pregnant; **-se** to become pregnant; to become embarrassed.
embarazo [em·ba·rá·so] *m.* (*obstáculo*) impediment, obstacle; (*preñez*) pregnancy; (*timidez*) bashfulness, awkwardness.
embarazoso [em·ba·ra·só·so] *adj.* embarrassing; cumbersome, unwieldly.
embarcación [em·bar·ka·sjón] *f.* ship, boat; embarkation.
embarcadero [em·bar·ka·đé·ro] *m.* wharf pier.
embarcador [em·bar·ka·đór] *m.* shipper.
embarcar[6] [em·bar·kár] *v.* to embark; to ship; *Am.* to ship by train or any vehicle; **-se** to embark, sail; to engage (in); *Am.* to board, get on a train.
embarco [em·bár·ko] *m.* embarkation.
embargar[7] [em·bar·ǥár] *v.* to impede; to restrain; to attach, confiscate; to lay an embargo on; **estar embargado de emoción** to be overcome with emotion.
embargo [em·bár·ǥo] *m.* embargo, restriction on commerce; attachment, confiscation; **sin** — nevertheless.
embarque [em·bár·ke] *m.* shipment.
embarrado [em·ba·rrá·đo] *p.p. & adj.* smeared; plastered; muddy.
embarrar [em·ba·rrár] *v.* to smear, daub.
embaucador [em·baw·ka·đór] *m.* cheat, impostor.
embaucar[6] [em·baw·kár] *v.* to fool, trick, swindle, deceive.
embebecido [em·be·ƀe·sí·đo] *p.p. & adj.* absorbed; amazed.
embebecimiento [em·be·ƀe·si·mjén·to] *m.* absorption; rapture.
embeber [em·be·ƀér] *v.* to imbibe, absorb; to soak; take up; to shrink; **-se** to be fascinated; to be absorbed.
embelesar [em·be·le·sár] *v.* to enrapture, delight, charm.
embeleso [em·be·lé·so] *m.* delight, ectasy.
embellecer[13] [em·be·ye·sér] *v. irr.* to embellish, beautify, adorn.
embestida [em·bes·tí·đa] *f.* sudden attack, onset, assault.
embestir[5] [em·bes·tír] *v. irr.* to attack, assail.
embetunar [em·be·tu·nár] *v.* to cover with pitch; to black.
emblanquecer[13] [em·blaŋ·ke·sér] *v. irr.* to whiten; to bleach; to become white; **-se** to whiten, become white.
emblema [em·blé·ma] *m.* emblem.
embobar [em·bo·ƀár] *v.* to fool; to amuse; to fascinate; to amaze; **-se** to be amazed; to be fascinated.
embobinado [em·bo·ƀi·ná·đo] *m.* reel assembly (*of a tape recorder or computer*).
embocadura [em·bo·ka·đú·ra] *f.* mouth (*of a river*); entrance (*through a narrow passage*); mouthpiece (*of a wind instrument*); bit (*of a bridle*); taste, flavor (*said of wines*).
embolado [em·bo·lá·đo] *m.* bull whose horns have been tipped with balls; impotent, ineffectual person; *p.p. of* **embolar**.
embolar [em·bo·lár] *v.* (*al toro*) to tip a bull's horns with balls; (*dar lustre*) to polish, to black; **-se** *C.A.* to get drunk.
embolia [em·bó·lja] *f.* clot.
émbolo [ém·bo·lo] *m.* piston; plunger (*of a pump*); embolus (*clot in a blood vessel*).
embolsar [em·bol·sár] *v.* to put into a pocket or purse; **-se** to pocket, put into one's pocket.
emborrachar [em·bo·rra·čár] *v.* to intoxicate; **-se** to get drunk.
emborronar [em·bo·rro·nár] *v.* to blot; to scribble.
emboscada [em·bos·ká·đa] *f.* ambush.
emboscar[6] [em·bos·kár] *v.* to ambush; **-se** to lie in ambush; to go into a forest.
embotado [em·bo·tá·đo] *adj.* dull, blunt; *p.p. of* **embotar**.
embotamiento [em·bo·ta·mjén·to] *m.* dullness, bluntness; dulling, blunting; glazing.
embotar [em·bo·tár] *v.* to dull, blunt; to enervate, weaken.
embotellador [em·bo·te·ya·đór] *m.* bottling machine; **embotelladora** [em·bo·te·ya·đó·ra] bottling works.
embotellar [em·bo·te·yár] *v.* to bottle; to bottle up; *Mex.* to jail; *Cuba* to learn by heart.
embozado [em·bo·sá·đo] *adj.* cloaked; muffled, covered up to the face.
embozar[7] [em·bo·sár] *v.* to muffle; to cloak, conceal, disguise; to muzzle; **-se** to muffle oneself, wrap oneself.
embragar[7] [em·bra·ǥár] *v.* to engage or throw in the clutch.
embrague [em·brá·ǥe] *m.* clutch (*of a machine*); coupling.
embriagar[7] [em·brja·ǥár] *v.* to intoxicate; **-se** to get drunk, intoxicated.
embriaguez [em·brja·ǥés] *f.* intoxication; drunkenness.
embrión [em·brjón] *m.* embryo.
embrollar [em·bro·yár] *v.* to involve, ensnare, entangle; to confuse.
embrollo [em·bró·yo] *m.* confusion, tangle; trickery,

lie, deception.

embromar [em·bro·már] *v.* to chaff, make fun of, "kid"; *Am.* to bother, molest; *Mex., Ch.* to delay unnecessarily; *Col., Ven.* to ruin, harm; **-se** *Am.* to be bothered, disgusted; *Mex.* to get delayed.

embrujar [em·bru·xár] *v.* to bewitch, enchant.

embrujo [em·brú·xo] *m.* charm, enchantment; glamour.

embrutecer[13] [em·bru·te·sér] *v. irr.* to stupefy, render brutish; to dull the mind, make insensible.

embudo [em·bú·đo] *m.* funnel; trick.

embuste [em·bús·te] *m.* lie, fraud; trinket.

embustero [em·bus·té·ro] *m.* liar; *adj.* deceitful, tricky.

embutido [em·bu·tí·đo] *m.* sausage; inlaid work; *Am.* insertion of embroidery or lace; *p.p. of* **embutir.**

embutir [em·bu·tír] *v.* to insert, inlay; to stuff.

emerger[11] [e·mer·xér] *v.* to emerge, come out.

emigración [e·mi·ǥra·sjón] *f.* emigration.

emigrante [e·mi·ǥrán·te] *m. & f.* emigrant.

emigrar [e·mi·ǥrár] *v.* to emigrate; to migrate.

eminencia [e·mi·nén·sja] *f.* eminence; height.

eminente [e·mi·nén·te] *adj.* eminent, high, lofty.

emisión [e·mi·sjón] *f.* issue (*of bonds, money, etc.*); radio broadcast.

emisor [e·mi·sór] *adj.* emitting; broadcasting; *m.* radio transmitter; **emisora** [e·mi·só·ra] *f.* broadcasting station.

emitir [e·mi·tír] *v.* to emit, give off; to utter; to send forth; to issue; to broadcast.

emoción [e·mo·sjón] *f.* emotion.

emocional [e·mo·sjo·nál] *adj.* emotional.

emocionante [e·mo·sjo·nán·te] *adj.* moving, touching, thrilling.

emocionar [e·mo·sjo·nár] *v.* to cause emotion, touch, move; **-se** to be touched, moved, stirred.

emotivo [e·mo·tí·ƀo] *adj.* emotional.

empacador [em·pa·ka·đór] *m.* packer.

empacar[6] [em·pa·kár] *v.* to pack up, wrap up, bale, crate; *Ríopl.* to goad, irritate (*an animal*); **-se** to be stubborn; to get angry; *Ríopl.* to balk; *Ríopl.* to put on airs.

empachado [em·pa·čá·đo] *p.p. & adj.* (*relleno*) clogged; stuffed; upset from indigestion; (*tímido*) embarrassed; bashful.

empachar [em·pa·čár] *v.* to stuff, cram; to cause indigestion; **-se** to get upset; to get clogged; to be stuffed; to suffer indigestion; to get embarrassed.

empacho [em·pá·čo] *m.* indigestion; bashfulness; **no tener — en** to have no objection to; to feel free to.

empalagar[7] [em·pa·la·ǥár] *v.* to cloy; to pall on, become distasteful; to disgust.

empalagoso [em·pa·la·ǥó·so] *adj.* cloying; sickeningly sweet; boring, wearisome.

empalizada [em·pa·li·sá·đa] *f.* stockade, palisade.

empalmar [em·pal·már] *v.* to splice; to join; — **con** to join (*as railroads or highways*).

empalme [em·pál·me] *m.* junction; joint, connection; splice.

empanada [em·pa·ná·đa] *f.* pie, meat pie; swindle, fraud.

empanar [em·pa·nár] *v.* to bread.

empanizar[9] [em·pa·ni·sár] *v. Carib., C.A., Mex.* to bread.

empañado [em·pa·ñá·đo] *adj. & p.p.* tarnished; dim, blurred.

empañar [em·pa·ñár] *v.* to blur, dim, tarnish.

empapada [em·pa·pá·đa] *f. Am.* drenching, soaking.

empapar [em·pa·pár] *v.* to soak, drench, saturate.

empapelador [em·pa·pe·la·đór] *m.* paper hanger.

empapelar [em·pa·pe·lár] *v.* to paper; to wrap in paper.

empaque [em·pá·ke] *m.* (*bulto*) packing; (*parecer*) looks, appearance, air; airs, importance; *Am., Peru* impudence.

empaquetadura [em·pa·ke·ta·đú·ra] *f.* gasket.

empaquetar [em·pa·ke·tár] *v.* to pack; to pack in; to make a package; **-se** to dress up, doll up.

emparedado [em·pa·re·đá·đo] *adj.* shut up, confined between walls; *m.* sandwich; prisoner confined in a narrow cell.

emparejar [em·pa·re·xár] *v.* to even up, level off; to match; to pair off; to overtake, catch up with.

emparentado [em·pa·ren·tá·đo] *adj. & p.p.* related by marriage.

emparentar [em·pa·ren·tár] *v.* to become related by marriage.

emparrado [em·pa·rrá·đo] *m.* vine, arbor.

empastar [em·pas·tár] *v.* to paste; to fill (*a tooth*) to bind (*books*); **-se** *Ch.* to get lost in the pasture; *Mex.* to become overgrown with grass.

empaste [em·pás·te] *m.* tooth filling; binding (*of a book*).

empatar [em·pa·tár] *v.* (*igualar*) to tie (*in a game*), have an equal score; to have an equal number of votes; (*impedir*) to hinder, obstruct; *Col., Ven., Carib.* to tie, join.

empate [em·pá·te] *m.* tie, draw, equal score, equal number of votes; hindrance, obstruction; *Am.* joint, junction.

empecinado [em·pe·si·ná·đo] *adj. Am.* stubborn.

empedernido [em·pe·đer·ní·đo] *adj.* hardened, hardhearted.

empedernir[51] [em·pe·đer·nír] *v.* to harden, toughen; **-se** to become hardened.

empedrado [em·pe·đrá·đo] *m.* cobblestone pavement; *p.p. & adj.* paved with stones.

empedrar[1] [em·pe·đrár] *v. irr.* to pave with stones.

empeine [em·péj·ne] *m.* instep; groin (*hollow between lower part of abdomen and thigh*).

empellón [em·pe·yón] *m.* push, shove; **a -es** by pushing.

empeñar [em·pe·ñár] *v.* (*dar en prenda*) to pawn; (*obligar*) to oblige, compel; **-se** to persist, insist; to apply oneself; to go into debt; **-se por** to plead for, intercede for; **se empeñaron en una lucha** they engaged in a fight.

empeño [em·pé·ño] *m.* (*fianza*) pledge, pawn; (*deseo*) persistence, insistence; eagerness; perseverance; *Mex.* pawnshop; **tener — en** to be eager to.

empeorar [em·pe·o·rár] *v.* to impair; to make worse; to grow worse; **-se** to grow worse.

empequeñecer[13] [em·pe·ke·ñe·sér] *v. irr.* to diminish, make smaller; to belittle.

emperador [em·pe·ra·đór] *m.* emperor; **emperatriz** [em·pe·ra·trís] *f.* empress.

emperifollar [em·pe·ri·fo·yár] *v.* to decorate, adorn; **-se** to dress up, deck out, doll up.

empero [em·pé·ro] *conj.* however, nevertheless.

empezar[1, 9] [em·pe·sár] *v. irr.* to begin.

empiezo [em·pjé·so] *m. Carib., Mex., C.A.* beginning.

empinado [em·pi·ná·đo] *adj.* steep; lofty.

empinar [em·pi·nár] *v.* to raise, lift; to incline, bend; — **el codo** to drink; **-se** to stand on tiptoes; to rear (*said of horses*); to rise high; *Am.* to overeat.

empiojado [em·pjo·xá·đo] *adj.* lousy, full of lice.

emplasto [em·plás·to] *m.* plaster, poultice.

empleado [em·ple·á·đo] *m.* employee; *p.p. of* emplear.

emplear [em·ple·ár] *v.* to employ; to invest, spend;

-se en to be employed in.
empleo [em·plé·o] *m.* employment, position, job; employ; occupation; aim; investment.
emplumar [em·plu·már] *v.* to feather; to adorn with feathers; to tar and feather; *C.A.* to deceive; *Ec.* to send away to a house of correction or prison; *Am.* — **con algo** to run away with something, steal it; *Ch., Col., Ven.* **-las** (*or* **emplumárselas** [em·plu·már·se·las]) to take to one's heels, flee, escape.
empobrecer[13] [em·po·ƀre·sér] *v. irr.* to impoverish; **-se** to become poor.
empobrecimiento [em·po·ƀre·si·mjén·to] *m.* impoverishment.
empolvado [em·pol·ƀá·đo] *adj.* dusty, covered with dust or powder.
empolvar [em·pol·ƀár] *v.* to sprinkle powder; to cover with dust; **-se** to get dusty; to powder one's face.
empollar [em·po·yár] *v.* to hatch, brood.
emponzoñar [em·pon·so·ñár] *v.* to poison.
empotrado [em·po·trá·đo] *adj.* built-in, set in.
emprendedor [em·pren·de·đór] *adj.* enterprising.
emprender [em·pren·dér] *v.* to undertake.
empreñar [em·pre·ñár] *v.* to impregnate, make pregnant.
empresa [em·pré·sa] *f.* enterprise, undertaking; symbol; company, management; **empresarial** managerial.
empresario [em·pre·sá·rjo] *m.* manager; impresario, promoter.
empréstito [em·prés·ti·to] *m.* loan.
empujar [em·pu·xár] *v.* to push, shove.
empuje [em·pú·xe] *m.* push; shove; impulse; energy.
empujón [em·pu·xón] *m.* shove, push.
empuñar [em·pu·ñár] *v.* to grasp, grab, clutch, seize.
émulo [é·mu·lo] *m.* rival, competitor.
en [en] *prep.* in, on, upon.
enaguas [e·ná·ǥwas] *f. pl.* underskirt, petticoat; short skirt.
enajenamiento [e·na·xe·na·mjén·to] *m.* trance; abstraction, absence of mind; transfer (*of property*); — **mental** mental disorder; — **de los sentidos** loss of consciousness.
enajenar [e·na·xe·nár] *v.* (*distraer*) to enrapture, charm; to deprive (*of one's sense*); (*trasladar*) to transfer property; to dispossess; — **el afecto de** to alienate the affection of; **-se** to be enraptured, be in a trance.
enaltecer[13] [e·nal·te·sér] *v.* to extol, exalt.
enamorado [e·na·mo·rá·đo] *adj.* in love; *m.* lover.
enamorar [e·na·mo·rár] *v.* to make love, woo, court; to enamor; **-se** to fall in love.
enano [e·ná·no] *m.* dwarf; *adj.* dwarfish, tiny, little.
enarbolar [e·nar·ƀo·lár] *v.* to hoist, lift, raise on high; to brandish (*a sword, cane, etc.*); **-se** to rear, balk.
enarcado [e·nar·ká·đo] *p.p.* arched.
enarcar[6] [e·nar·kár] *v.* to arch; to hoop (*barrels, kegs, etc.*); — **las cejas** to arch one's eyebrows.
enardecer[13] [e·nar·đe·sér] *v. irr.* to excite, kindle, fire with passion; **-se** to become excited; to become passionate; to get angry.
enardecimiento [e·nar·đe·si·mjén·to] *m.* ardor, passion, unbridled enthusiasm; inflaming.
encabezado [eŋ·ka·ƀe·sá·đo] *m.* headline; heading.
encabezamiento [eŋ·ka·ƀe·sa·mjén·to] *m.* heading; headline; list or roll of taxpayers; registration of taxpayers.
encabezar[9] [eŋ·ka·ƀe·sár] *v.* to give a heading or title to; to head; to lead; to make up (*a list or tax roll*); to strengthen (*wine*).
encabritarse [eŋ·ka·ƀri·tár·se] *v.* to rear, rise up on the hind legs.
encadenar [eŋ·ka·đe·nár] *v.* to chain; to link together.
encajar [eŋ·ka·xár] *v.* to thrust in, fit into, insert; **-se** to squeeze into; to intrude, meddle.
encaje [eŋ·ká·xe] *m.* lace; adjustment; fitting together; (*enchufe*) socket, groove, hole; inlaid work; — **de electrodo** electrode holder (stinger).
encajonar [eŋ·ka·xo·nár] *v.* to box (*put or pack in a box*).
encallar [eŋ·ka·yár] *v.* to strand, run aground; to get stuck.
encamado [eŋ·ka·má·đo] *p.p.* confined in bed.
encaminar [eŋ·ka·mi·nár] *v.* to direct, guide; **-se** to betake oneself, go (toward); to start out on a road.
encanecer[13] [eŋ·ka·ne·sér] *v. irr.* to get grey, get grey-haired.
encanijado [eŋ·ka·ni·xá·đo] *adj.* emaciated, thin, sickly.
encanijarse [eŋ·ka·ni·xár·se] *v.* to get thin, emaciated.
encantado [eŋ·kan·tá·đo] *p.p. & adj.* delighted, charmed; enchanted.
encantador [eŋ·kan·ta·đór] *adj.* charming; *m.* charmer, enchanter.
encantamiento [eŋ·kan·ta·mjén·to] *m.* enchantment.
encantar [eŋ·kan·tár] *v.* to charm, enchant.
encanto [eŋ·kán·to] *m.* charm, enchantment, delight.
encapillar [eŋ·ka·pi·yár] *v. P.R.* to confine in the death cell.
encapotado [eŋ·ka·po·tá·đo] *p.p. & adj.* cloaked; overcast, cloudy; in a bad humor.
encapotarse [eŋ·ka·po·tár·se] *v.* to become overcast, cloudy; to cover up, put on a cloak or raincoat; to frown.
encapricharse [eŋ·ka·pri·čár·se] *v.* to persist in one's whims; to get stubborn.
encaramar [eŋ·ka·ra·már] *v.* to raise; to elevate; to extol; **-se** to climb; to climb upon, get upon, perch upon; *Ch.* to be ashamed; *Carib.* to go to one's head (*said of liquor*).
encarar [eŋ·ka·rár] *v.* to face; to aim; **-se con** to face; to confront.
encarcelación [eŋ·kar·se·la·sjón] *f.* imprisonment.
encarcelamiento [eŋ·kar·se·la·mjén·to] = **encarcelación.**
encarcelar [eŋ·kar·se·lár] *v.* to imprison, jail.
encarecer[13] [eŋ·ka·re·sér] *v. irr.* (*alzar precio*) to go up in value; to make dear, raise the price of; (*ponderar*) to exaggerate; to extol; to recommend highly, to enhance.
encarecidamente [eŋ·ka·re·si·đa·mén·te] *adv.* earnestly.
encargar[7] [eŋ·kar·ǥár] *v.* (*dar cargo*) to put in charge; to entrust; to commission; (*aconsejar*) to recommend, advise; (*pedir*), to order; to beg; **-se de** to take charge of.
encargo [eŋ·kár·ǥo] *m.* recommendation, advice; charge; order; commission; errand.
encariñado [eŋ·ka·ri·ñá·đo] *adj. & p.p* attached, fond, enamored.
encariñamiento [eŋ·ka·ri·ña·mjén·to] *m.* affection, fondness, attachment.
encariñar [eŋ·ka·ri·ñár] *v.* to awaken love or affection; **-se** to become fond (of), attached (to).
encarnado [eŋ·kar·ná·đo] *adj.* flesh-colored; red; *p.p. of* **encarnar.**
encarnar [eŋ·kar·nár] *v.* to incarnate, embody; to bait (*a fishhook*).
encarnizado [eŋ·kar·ni·sá·đo] *adj.* bloody; hard-fought, fierce.
encarnizar[9] [eŋ·kar·ni·sár] *v.* to infuriate, enrage; **-se** to get furious, enraged; to fight with fury.

encasillar [eŋ·ka·si·yár] *v.* to pigeonhole, put in a pigeonhole or compartment; to put in a stall; to classify, sort out.
encauzamiento [eŋ·kaw·sa·mjén·to] *m.* channeling.
encender[1] [en·sen·dér] *v. irr.* to light, kindle; to set on fire; **-se** to take fire, be on fire; to get red.
encendido [en·sen·dí·đo] *adj.* red; *p.p. of* **encender;** *m.* ignition (*of a motor*).
encerado [en·se·rá·đo] *m.* blackboard; oilcloth; wax coating; *p.p. & adj.* waxed; wax-colored; **papel** — wax paper.
encerar [en·se·rár] *v.* to wax; to thicken (*lime*).
encerramiento [en·se·rra·mjén·to] *m.* enclosure, confinement; locking up; retreat; prison.
encerrar[1] [en·se·rrár] *v. irr.* to enclose; to lock up; to contain; **-se** to lock oneself up, go into seclusion.
encía [en·sí·a] *f.* gum (*of the teeth*).
enciclopedia [en·si·klo·pé·đja] *f.* encyclopedia.
encierro [en·sjé·rro] *m.* confinement; retreat; prison.
encima [en·sí·ma] *adv.* above, overhead, over, on top; besides, in addition; — **de** on top of; **por** — **de** over; *Col., Perú* **de** — besides, in addition; *Col., C.A., Ríopl., Carib.* **echárselo todo** — to spend everything on clothes.
encina [en·sí·na] *f.* live oak.
encinta [en·sín·ta] *adj.* pregnant.
encintado [en·sin·tá·đo] *m.* curb (*of a sidewalk*).
enclaustrar [eŋ·klaws·trár] *v.* to cloister.
enclavar [eŋ·kla·ƀár] *v.* to nail, fix, fasten.
enclenque [eŋ·klén·ke] *adj.* sickly, wan; weak, feeble.
enclítico [eŋ·klí·ti·ko] *adj.* enclitic.
encobar [eŋ·ko·ƀár] *v.* to brood.
encoger[11] [eŋ·ko·xér] *v.* to shrink, shrivel, shorten, contract; **-se** to shrink; to shrivel; **-se de hombros** to shrug one's shoulders.
encogido [eŋ·ko·xí·đo] *p.p. & adj.* shrunk, shrivelled; timid, shy.
encogimiento [eŋ·ko·xi·mjén·to] *m.* shrinking; timidity; — **de hombros** shrug.
encolerizar[9] [eŋ·ko·le·ri·sár] *v.* to anger; **-se** to get angry.
encomendar[1] [eŋ·ko·men·dár] *v. irr.* (*encargar*) to charge, advise; to entrust; (*recomendar*) to recommend, commend; **-se** to put oneself in the hands (of); to send regards; to pray (to).
encomiar [eŋ·ko·mjár] *v.* to extol, praise.
encomienda [eŋ·ko·mjén·da] *f.* charge, commission; recommendation; royal land grant (*including Indian inhabitants*); *Mex.* warehouse (*for agricultural products*); *Col.* parcel-post package.
encomio [eŋ·kó·mjo] *m.* encomium, high praise.
enconado [eŋ·ko·ná·đo] *p.p. & adj.* inflamed; infected; sore; angry.
enconar [eŋ·ko·nár] *v.* to inflame; to infect; to irritate; **-se** to become inflamed, infected; to get irritated.
encono [eŋ·kó·no] *m.* rancor, animosity, ill will; *Cuba, Mex.* inflammation, swelling.
encontrado [eŋ·kon·trá·đo] *adj.* opposite; opposing; contrary; *p.p. of* **encontrar.**
encontrar[2] [eŋ·kon·trár] *v. irr.* to encounter, meet; to find; **-se** to meet; to coincide; to be; to be found, be situated; to collide; to conflict; **-se con** to come across, meet up with.
encontrón [eŋ·kon·trón], **encontronazo** [eŋ·kon·tro·ná·so] *m.* bump, collision; **darse un** — to collide (with) bump (into); to bump into each other.
encordelar [eŋ·kor·đe·lár] *v.* to string; to tie with strings.
encorvar [eŋ·kor·ƀár] *v.* to curve, bend; **-se** to bend down; to stoop.
encrespar [eŋ·kres·pár] *v.* (*rizar*) to curl; to ruffle; (*agitar*) to irritate; **-se** to curl; to get ruffled; to become involved or entangled (*a matter or affair*); to become rough (*said of the sea*).
encrucijada [eŋ·kru·si·xá·đa] *f.* crossroads, street intersection; ambush.
encuadernación [eŋ·kwa·đer·na·sjón] *f.* binding (*of books*).
encuadernar [eŋ·kwa·đer·nár] *v.* to bind (*books*).
encuadrar [eŋ·kwa·đrár] *v.* to enclose in a frame; to encompass; to fit (into); *Arg.* to suit; *Ven.* to summarize briefly, give a synthesis of.
encubierto [eŋ·ku·ƀjér·to] *p.p. of* **encubrir.**
encubrir[52] [eŋ·ku·ƀrír] *v.* to cover, hide.
encuentro [eŋ·kwén·tro] *m.* (*hallazgo*) encounter, meeting; find, finding; (*conflicto*) conflict, clash; collision; **salir al** — **de** to go out to meet; to make a stand against, oppose; *Am.* **llevarse de** — to run over, knock down; to drag along.
encuerado [eŋ·kwe·rá·đo] *adj. Am.* naked.
encuerar [eŋ·kwe·rár] *v. Am.* to strip off clothes; *Am.* to skin, fleece, strip of money; **-se** *Am.* to strip, get undressed.
encuesta [eŋ·kwés·ta] *f.* search, inquiry, investigation; survey.
encumbrado [eŋ·kum·brá·đo] *p.p. & adj.* elevated; exalted; high, lofty.
encumbramiento [eŋ·kum·bra·mjén·to] *m.* elevation; exaltation; height; eminence.
encumbrar [eŋ·kum·brár] *v.* to elevate; to exalt, extol; **-se** to climb to the top; to rise up; to hold oneself high; to soar.
encurtido [eŋ·kur·tí·đo] *m.* pickle; *p.p. of* **encurtir.**
encurtir [eŋ·kur·tír] *v.* to pickle.
enchapar [en·ča·pár] *v.* to plate, to overlay.
enchilada [en·či·lá·đa] *f. Mex., C.A.* rolled **tortilla** served with chili.
enchuecar[6] [en·čwe·kár] *v.* to bend, twist; **-se** *Col., Ven., Mex., Ríopl.* to get bent or twisted.
enchufar [en·ču·fár] *v.* to plug in; to telescope; to fit (*a tube or pipe*) into another.
enchufe [en·čú·fe] *m.* socket; plug; electric outlet; *Spain* influence; position obtained through influence.
ende [én·de]: **por** — hence, therefore.
endeble [en·dé·ƀle] *adj.* weak, feeble; flimsy.
endemoniado [en·de·mo·njá·đo] *adj.* possessed by the devil; devilish, fiendish; mischievous.
endentar[1] [en·den·tár] *v. irr.* to indent, form notches in; to furnish (*a saw, wheel, etc.*) with teeth; to mesh.
enderezar[9] [en·de·re·sár] *v.* to straighten; to set upright; to right, correct; to direct; to address; **-se** to go straight (to); to straighten up.
endeudado [en·dew·đá·đo] *p.p. & adj.* indebted; in debt.
endeudarse [en·dew·đár·se] *v.* to get into debt, become indebted.
endiablado [en·dja·ƀlá·đo] *adj.* devilish; possessed by the devil; ugly; mean, wicked; *Col., Ven., Mex., Ríopl.* dangerous, risky.
endibia [en·dí·ƀja] *f.* endive.
endomingado [en·do·miŋ·gá·đo] *p.p. & adj.* dressed up in one's Sunday, or best, clothes.
endosante [en·do·sán·te] *m.* endorser.
endosar [en·do·sár] *v.* to endorse (*a check, draft, etc.*).
endose [en·dó·se], **endoso** [en·dó·so] *m.* endorsement.
endulzar[9] [en·dul·sár] *v.* to sweeten; to soften.

endurecer[13] [en·du·re·sér] *v. irr.* to harden; **-se** to get hardened; to get cruel.
enebro [e·né·ƀro] *m.* juniper.
enemigo [e·ne·mí·ǥo] *m.* enemy; devil; *adj.* hostile; unfriendly; **ser — de una cosa** to dislike a thing.
enemistad [e·ne·mis·táđ] *f.* enmity, hatred.
enemistar [e·ne·mis·tár] *v.* to cause enmity between; **-se con** to become an enemy of.
energía [e·ner·xí·a] *f.* energy; **— nuclear** nuclear energy.
enérgico [e·nér·xi·ko] *adj.* energetic.
enero [e·né·ro] *m.* January.
enervar [e·ner·ƀár] *v.* to enervate, weaken.
enfadar [en·fa·đár] *v.* to anger; **-se** to get angry.
enfado [en·fá·đo] *m.* anger, disgust.
enfadoso [en·fa·đó·so] *adj.* annoying.
enfardar [en·far·đár] *v.* to bale, pack.
énfasis [én·fa·sis] *m.* emphasis; **enfático** [en·fá·ti·ko] *adj.* emphatic.
enfermar [en·fer·már] *v.* to become ill; to make ill; to weaken; **-se** to become ill.
enfermedad [en·fer·me·đáđ] *f.* sickness, illness.
enfermería [en·fer·me·rí·a] *f.* infirmary.
enfermero [en·fer·mé·ro] *m.* male nurse; **enfermera** [en·fer·mé·ra] *f.* nurse (*for the sick*).
enfermizo [en·fer·mí·so] *adj.* sickly; unhealthy.
enfermo [en·fer·mo] *adj.* sick, ill; feeble; *m.* patient.
enflaquecer [en·fla·ke·sér] *v. irr.* to become thin; to make thin; to weaken.
enfocar[6] [en·fo·kár] *v.* to focus.
enfoque [en·fó·ke] approach.
enfrenar [en·fre·nár] *v.* to bridle; to brake, put the brake on; to check, curb.
enfrentar [en·fren·tár] *v.* to put face to face; **-se con** to confront, face, meet face to face.
enfrente [en·frén·te] *adv.* in front, opposite; **— de** in front of, opposite.
enfriamiento [en·frja·mjén·to] *m.* cooling; chill; refrigeration.
enfriar[17] [en·frjár] *v.* to cool, chill; *Carib.* to kill; **-se** to cool, cool off; to get chilled.
enfurecer[13] [en·fu·re·sér] *v. irr.* to infuriate, enrage; **-se** to rage; to get furious; to get rough, stormy (*said of the sea*).
enfurruñarse [en·fu·rru·ñár·se] *v.* to get angry; to grumble.
engalanar [eŋ·ga·la·nár] *v.* to adorn, decorate; **-se** to dress up, primp.
enganchamiento [eŋ·gan·ča·mjén·to] = **enganche.**
enganchar [eŋ·gan·čár] *v.* to hitch; to hook; to ensnare; to draft; to attract into the army; *Col., Ven., Mex., Ríopl.* to hire (*labor with false promises*); **-se** to engage, interlock; to get hooked; to enlist in the army.
enganche [eŋ·gán·če] *m.* hooking; coupling; draft (*into the army*); *Col., Ven., Mex., Ríopl.* enrolling of laborers (*for a rubber plantation or other risky business under false promises*); *Mex.* down payment.
engañador [eŋ·ga·ña·đór] *adj.* deceitful, deceiving; *m.* deceiver.
engañar [eŋ·ga·ñár] *v.* to deceive; to while away (*time*); to ward off (*hunger or sleep*); **-se** to deceive oneself; to be mistaken.
engaño [eŋ·gá·ño] *m.* deceit, trick, fraud; mistake, misunderstanding; *Ch., C.A.* bribe.
engañoso [eŋ·ga·ñó·so] *adj.* deceitful; tricky; misleading.
engastar [eŋ·gas·tár] *v.* to mount, set (*jewels*).
engaste [eŋ·gás·te] *m.* setting (*for a gem or stone*).
engatusar [eŋ·ga·tu·sár] *v.* to coax, entice; to fool.
engendrar [eŋ·xen·drár] *v.* to engender, beget; produce; to cause.
engolfarse [eŋ·gol·fár·se] *v.* to get deep (into); to go deeply (into); to become absorbed, lost in thought.
engomar [eŋ·go·már] *v.* to gum; to glue.
engordar [eŋ·gor·đár] *v.* to fatten; to get fat; to get rich.
engorroso [eŋ·go·rró·so] *adj.* cumbersome; bothersome.
engranaje [eŋ·gra·ná·xe] *m.* gear, gears, gearing.
engranar [eŋ·gra·nár] *v.* to gear, throw in gear; to mesh gears.
engrandecer[13] [eŋ·gran·de·sér] *v. irr.* to aggrandize, make greater; to magnify; to exalt.
engrane [eŋ·grá·ne] *m.* engagement (*of gears*); gear.
engrasar [eŋ·gra·sár] *v.* to lubricate, grease; to stain with grease; to fertilize, manure; to dress (*cloth*).
engrase [eŋ·grá·se] *m.* grease job.
engreído [eŋ·gre·í·đo] *adj. & p.p.* conceited, vain; *Col.* attached, fond.
engreír[15] [eŋ·gre·ír] *v. irr.* to make vain, conceited; **-se** to puff up, get conceited; *Col.* to become fond (of), become attached (to).
engrosar[2] [eŋ·gro·sár] *v. irr.* to enlarge; to thicken; to fatten; to get fat.
engrudo [eŋ·grú·đo] *m.* paste (*for gluing*).
engullir[20] [eŋ·gu·yír] *v.* to gobble, devour; to gorge.
enhebrar [en·e·ƀrár] *v.* to thread (*a needle*); to string (*beads*).
enhiesto [en·jés·to] *adj.* straight, upright, erect.
enhorabuena [en·o·ra·ƀwé·na] *f.* congratulation; *adv.* safely; well and good; all right; with much pleasure.
enigma [e·níǥ·ma] *m.* enigma, riddle, puzzle.
enjabonar [en·xa·ƀo·nár] *v.* to soap; to soft-soap, flatter.
enjaezar[9] [eŋ·xa·e·sár] *v.* to harness.
enjalbegar[7] [eŋ·xal·ƀe·ǥar] *v.* to whitewash; **-se** to paint (*one's face*).
enjambre [eŋ·xám·bre] *m.* swarm of bees; crowd.
enjaular [eŋ·xaw·lár] *v.* to cage; to confine; to jail.
enjuagar[7] [eŋ·xwa·ǥár] *v.* to rinse, rinse out.
enjuague [eŋ·xwá·ǥe] *m.* mouth wash; rinse; rinsing; scheme, plot.
enjugar[7] [eŋ·xu·ǥár] *v.* to dry; to wipe; **-se** to dry oneself.
enjuiciar [eŋ·xwi·sjár] *v.* to indict; to prosecute, bring suit against; to try (*a case*); to judge.
enjundia [eŋ·xún·dja] *f.* substance, essence; fat; force, strength.
enjuto [en·xú·to] *adj.* dried; thin, skinny; **-s** *m. pl.* dry kindling.
enlace [en·lá·se] *m.* link; tie, bond; marriage.
enladrillado [en·la·đri·yá·đo] *m.* brick pavement or floor.
enladrillar [en·la·đri·yár] *v.* to pave with bricks.
enlatar [en·la·tár] *v.* to can; *Col.* to roof with tin.
enlazar[9] [en·la·sár] *v.* to join, bind, tie; to rope; *Ven., Mex.* to lasso; **-se** to join; to marry; to become related through marriage.
enlodar [en·lo·đár] *v.* to cover with mud; to smear, sully, soil, dirty; **-se** to get in the mud; to get muddy.
enloquecer[13] [en·lo·ke·sér] *v. irr.* to make crazy; to drive mad; to lose one's mind; **-se** to go crazy.
enlosado [en·lo·sá·đo] *m.* flagstone pavement; *p.p. of* **enlosar.**
enlosar [en·lo·sár] *v.* to pave with flagstones.
enmantecado [em·man·te·ká·đo] *m. Am.* ice cream. *See* **mantecado.**
enmantecar[6] [em·man·te·kár] *v.* to butter; to grease

(*with lard or butter*).
enmarañar [emma·ra·ñár] *v.* to entangle; to snarl; to confuse, mix up.
enmascarar [em·mas·ka·rár] *v.* to mask; **-se** to put on a mask; to masquerade.
enmendar[1] [em·men·dár] *v. irr.* to amend, correct; to indemnify, compensate; **-se** to reform, mend one's ways.
enmienda [em·mjén·da] *f.* correction; amendment; reform; indemnity, compensation.
enmohecer[13] [em·mo·e·sér] *v.* to rust; to mold; **-se** to rust, become rusty; to mold.
enmudecer[13] [em·mu·đe·sér] *v. irr.* to silence; to remain silent; to lose one's voice; to become dumb.
ennegrecer[13] [en·ne·ǥre·sér] *v. irr.* to blacken; to darken; **-se** to become dark; to get cloudy.
ennoblecer[13] [en·no·ƀle·sér] *v. irr.* to ennoble, dignify.
enojadizo [e·no·xa·đí·so] *adj.* irritable, ill-tempered.
enojado [e·no·xá·đo] *adj.* angry.
enojar [e·no·xár] *v.* to make angry, vex, annoy; **-se** to get angry.
enojo [e·nó·xo] *m.* anger; annoyance.
enojoso [e·no·xó·so] *adj.* annoying, bothersome.
enorgullecer[13] [e·nor·ǥu·ye·sér] *v. irr.* to fill with pride; **-se** to swell up with pride; to be proud.
enorme [e·nór·me] *adj.* enormous.
enramada [en·rra·má·đa] *f.* arbor, bower; shady grove.
enrarecer[13] [en·rra·re·sér] *v. irr.* to rarefy, thin, make less dense (*as air*); **-se** to become rarefied; to become scarce.
enrarecimiento [en·rra·re·si·mjén·to] *m.* rarity, thinness (*of the air*); rarefaction (*act of making thin, rare or less dense*).
enredadera [en·rre·đa·đé·ra] *f.* climbing vine.
enredar [en·rre·đár] *v.* (*enmarañar*) to entangle, snare; to snarl; to mix up; to wind (*on a spool*); (*enemistar*) to raise a rumpus; **-se** to get tangled up, mixed up; to get trapped; **-se con** to have an affair with.
enredista [en·rre·đís·ta] *m. Am.* liar; gossip; *Am.* talebearer.
enredo [en·rré·đo] *m.* tangle; confusion; lie; plot.
enredoso [en·rre·đó·so] *adj.* tangled up; *Am.* tattler.
enrejado [en·rre·xá·đo] *m.* trellis; grating.
enrevesado [en·rre·ƀe·sá·đo] *adj.* turned around; intricate, complicated; unruly.
enriquecer[13] [en·rri·ke·sér] *v. irr.* to enrich; to become rich; **-se** to become rich.
enrojecer[13] [en·rro·xe·sér] *v. irr.* to redden; **-se** to get red, blush.
enrollar [en·rro·yár] *v.* to roll, roll up; to coil.
enronquecer[13] [en·rroŋ·ke·sér] *v. irr.* to make hoarse; to become hoarse; **-se** to become hoarse.
enroscar[6] [en·rros·kár] *v.* to coil; to twist, twine; **-se** to coil; to curl up.
ensacar[6] [en·sa·kár] *v.* to sack, bag, put in a bag or sack.
ensalada [en·sa·lá·đa] *f.* salad; hodgepodge, mixture.
ensalmo [en·sál·mo] *m.* incantation.
ensalzar[9] [en·sal·sár] *v.* to exalt, praise.
ensanchar [en·san·čár] *v.* to widen, enlarge; **-se** to expand; to puff up.
ensanche [en·sán·če] *m.* widening, expansion, extension.
ensangrentado [en·saŋ·gren·tá·đo] *adj.* gory, bloody; *p.p. of* **ensangrentar.**
ensangrentar [en·saŋ·gren·tár] *v.* to stain with blood; **-se** to be covered with blood; to get red with anger.
ensartar [en·sar·tár] *v.* to string; to thread; to link; to rattle off (*tales, stories, etc.*); *Ch.* to tie to a ring; *Mex.* to swindle, trick; **-se** *Andes* to fall into a trap.
ensayar [en·sa·yár] *v.* to try; to attempt; to test; to rehearse; **-se** to practice, train oneself.
ensayo [en·sá·yo] *m.* trial, attempt; rehearsal; test; experiment; essay.
ensenada [en·se·ná·đa] *f.* small bay, cove.
enseñanza [en·se·ñán·sa] *f.* teaching; education, training.
enseñar [en·se·ñár] *v.* to show; to teach; to train; to point out.
enseres [en·sé·res] *m. pl.* household goods; utensils; implements; equipment.
ensillar [en·si·yár] *v.* to saddle; *Ch.* to abuse, mistreat, domineer; *Ríopl.* — **el picazo** to get angry.
ensimismarse [en·si·miz·már·se] *v.* to become absorbed in thought; *Col., Ven., Ch.* to become conceited or vain.
ensoberbecer[13] [en·so·ƀer·ƀe·sér] *v. irr.* to make proud or haughty; **-se** to puff up with pride; to become haughty; to get rough, choppy (*said of the sea*).
ensordecer[13] [en·sor·đe·sér] *v. irr.* to deafen; to become deaf.
ensortijar [en·sor·ti·xár] *v.* to curl; to ring the nose of (*an animal*); **-se** to curl.
ensuciar [en·su·sjár] *v.* to dirty, soil; to stain; **-se** to get dirty; to soil oneself.
ensueño [en·swé·ño] *m.* illusion, dream.
entablar [en·ta·ƀlár] *v.* to board up; to plank; to splint; — **una conversación** to start a conversation; — **un pleito** to bring a lawsuit.
entablillar [en·ta·ƀli·yár] *v.* to splint; *Mex.* to cut (*chocolate*) into tablets or squares.
entallar [en·ta·yár] *v.* to fit closely (*a dress*); to carve.
entapizar[9] [en·ta·pi·sár] *v.* to cover with tapestry; to drape with tapestries; to upholster.
entarimar [en·ta·ri·már] *v.* to floor (*with boards*).
ente [én·te] *m.* entity, being; queer fellow.
enteco [en·té·ko] *adj.* sickly, skinny.
entender[1] [en·ten·dér] *v. irr.* to understand; — **de** to know, be an expert in; — **en** to take care of; to deal with; **-se con** to have dealings or relations with; to have an understanding with.
entendido [en·ten·dí·đo] *p.p.* understood; *adj.* wise, prudent; well-informed; able, skillful; **no darse por** — to pretend not to hear or understand; not to take the hint.
entendimiento [en·ten·di·mjén·to] *m.* understanding; intellect; mind.
enterado [en·te·rá·đo] *p.p. & adj.* informed; aware.
enterar [en·te·rár] *v.* to inform, acquaint; **-se** to know, learn, find out; to understand, get the idea.
entereza [en·te·ré·sa] *f.* entirety; integrity; fortitude; serenity; firmness; perfection.
enternecedor [en·ter·ne·se·đór] *adj.* touching, moving, pitiful.
enternecer[13] [en·ter·ne·sér] *v. irr.* to soften, touch, stir, move; **-se** to become tender; to be touched, stirred.
entero [en·té·ro] *adj.* (*completo*) entire, whole; (*justo*) just, right; firm; *m.* integer, whole number; *Col.* payment, reimbursement; *Ch.* balance of an account; **caballo** — stallion.
enterramiento [en·te·rra·mjén·to] *m.* burial.
enterrar[1] [en·te·rrár] *v. irr.* to bury; *Am.* to sink,

stick into.
entibiar [en·ti·ƀjár] *v.* to make lukewarm; **-se** to become lukewarm.
entidad [en·ti·đáđ] *f.* entity; unit, group, organization; **de —** of value or importance.
entierro [en·tjé·rro] *m.* burial; funeral; grave; *Am.* hidden treasure.
entintar [en·tin·tár] *v.* to ink; to stain with ink; to dye.
entoldar [en·tol·dár] *v.* to cover with an awning; **-se** to puff up with pride; to become overcast, cloudy.
entonación [en·to·na·sjón] *f.* intonation.
entonar [en·to·nár] *v.* to sing in tune; to start a song (*for others to follow*); to be in tune; to harmonize; **-se** to put on airs.
entonces [en·tón·ses] *adv.* then, at that time; **pues —** well then.
entornado [en·tor·ná·đo] *adj.* half-open; half-closed, ajar.
entornar [en·tor·nár] *v.* to half-open.
entorpecer[13] [en·tor·pe·sér] *v. irr.* to stupefy; to be numb, make numb; to delay, obstruct; to thwart, frustrate.
entorpecimiento [en·tor·pe·si·mjén·to] *m.* numbness; dullness; delay, obstruction.
entrada [en·trá·đa] *f.* (*apertura*) entrance; entry; gate; opening; (*acción o privilegio*) entering, admission; entrée (*dish or dinner course*); ticket; (*computadora*) entry; *Mex., Cuba* attack, assault, goring; *Mex.* beating; **-s** cash receipts; **mecanismos de —** input.
entrambos [en·trám·bos] *adj. & pron.* both.
entrampar [en·tram·pár] *v.* to trap, ensnare; to trick; to burden with debts; **-se** to get trapped or entangled; to run into debt.
entrante [en·trán·te] *adj.* entering; incoming; **el año —** next year.
entraña [en·trá·ña] *f.* entrail; innermost recess; heart; disposition, temper; **-s** entrails, "innards", insides; **hijo de mis -s** child of my heart; **no tener -s** to be cruel.
entrar [en·trár] *v.* to enter, go in, come in; to attack; **me entró miedo** I became afraid; **-se** to slip in, get in, sneak in; to enter.
entre [én·tre] *prep.* between; among; **dijo — sí** he said to himself; **— tanto** meanwhile; *Am.* **— más habla menos dice** the more he talks the less he says.
entreabierto [en·tre·a·ƀjér·to] *p.p. of* **entreabrir;** *adj.* ajar, half-open, partly open.
entreabrir[52] [en·tre·a·ƀrír] *v.* to half-open.
entreacto [en·tre·ák·to] *m.* intermission; intermezzo (*entertainment between the acts*); small cigar.
entrecano [en·tre·ká·no] *adj.* greyish.
entrecejo [en·tre·sé·xo] *m.* space between the eyebrows; **fruncir el —** to wrinkle one's brow.
entrecortado [en·tre·kor·tá·đo] *adj.* hesitating, faltering (*speech*); breathless, choking; *p.p.* interrupted.
entrecortar [en·tre·kor·tár] *v.* to cut halfway through or in between; to interrupt at intervals.
entrecruzar[9] [en·tre·kru·sár] *v.* to intercross, cross; to interlace; **-se** to cross.
entredicho [en·tre·đí·čo] *m.* prohibition, injunction.
entrega [en·tré·ğa] *f.* (*acto de ceder*) delivery; surrender; (*parte suelta*) installment (*of a book*); **novela por -s** serial novel.
entregar[7] [en·tre·ğár] *v.* to deliver, hand over; **-se** to surrender, submit, give up; to devote oneself (to); to abandon oneself (to).
entrelace [en·tre·lá·se] *m.* bridging.
entrelazar[9] [en·tre·la·sár] *v.* to interlace; to weave together.
entremés [en·tre·més] *m.* relish, side dish (*of olives, pickles, etc.*); one-act farce (*formerly presented between the acts of a play*).
entremeter [en·tre·me·tér] *v.* to insert; to place between; **-se** to meddle; to intrude.
entremetido [en·tre·me·tí·đo] *adj.* meddlesome; *m.* meddler; intruder.
entremetimiento [en·tre·me·ti·mjén·to] *m.* intrusion, meddling.
entremezclar [en·tre·mes·klár] *v.* to intermix, intermingle.
entrenador [en·tre·na·đór] *m. Am.* trainer.
entrenamiento [en·tre·na·mjén·to] *m. Am.* training, drill.
entrenar [en·tre·nár] *v. Am.* to train, drill; **-se** *Am.* to train.
entresacar[6] [en·tre·sa·kár] *v.* to pick out, select.
entresuelo [en·tre·swé·lo] *m.* mezzanine; second floor.
entretanto [en·tre·tán·to] *adv.* meanwhile.
entretejer [en·tre·te·xér] *v.* to weave together; to intertwine.
entretener[45] [en·tre·te·nér] *v. irr.* to delay, detain; to amuse, entertain; **-se** to amuse oneself; to delay oneself; **— el tiempo** to while away the time.
entretenido [en·tre·te·ní·đo] *adj.* entertaining, amusing; *p.p. of* **entretener.**
entretenimiento [en·tre·te·ni·mjén·to] *m.* entertainment; pastime; delay.
entrever[49] [entre·ƀér] *v.* to glimpse, catch a glimpse of; to half-see, see vaguely.
entreverar [en·tre·ƀe·rár] *v.* to intermingle, intermix.
entrevista [en·tre·ƀís·ta] *f.* interview; date, appointment.
entrevistar [en·tre·ƀis·tár] *v.* to interview; **-se con** to have an interview with.
entrevisto [en·tre·ƀís·to] *p.p. of* **entrever.**
entristecer[13] [en·tris·te·sér] *v. irr.* to sadden, make sad; **-se** to become sad.
entrometer [en·tro·me·tér] = **entremeter.**
entrometido [en·tro·me·tí·đo] = **entremetido.**
entumecer[13] [en·tu·me·sér] *v. irr.* to make numb; **-se** to get numb; to surge; to swell.
entumido [en·tu·mí·đo] *adj.* numb, stiff; *Am.* timid, shy, awkward.
entumirse [en·tu·mír·se] *v.* to get numb.
enturbiar [en·tur·ƀjár] *v.* to make muddy; to muddle; to disturb; to obscure; **-se** to get muddy; to get muddled.
entusiasmar [en·tu·sjaz·már] *v.* to excite, fill with enthusiasm; **-se** to get enthusiastic, excited.
entusiasmo [en·tu·sjáz·mo] *m.* enthusiasm.
entusiasta [en·tu·sjás·ta] *m. & f.* enthusiast; **entusiástico** *adj.* enthusiastic.
enumeración [e·nu·me·ra·sjón] *f.* enumeration, counting.
enumerar [e·nu·me·rár] *v.* to enumerate.
enunciar [e·nun·sjár] *v.* to express, state, declare.
envainar [em·baj·nár] *v.* to sheathe.
envalentonar [em·ba·len·to·nár] *v.* to make bold or haughty; **-se** to get bold; to brag, swagger.
envanecer[13] [em·ba·ne·sér] *v. irr.* to make vain; **-se** to become vain.
envasar [em·ba·sár] *v.* to pack, put up in any container; to bottle; to can.
envase [em·bá·se] *m.* packing; container, jar, bottle, can (*for packing*).
envejecer[13] [em·be·xe·sér] *v. irr.* to make old; to grow old, get old; **-se** to grow old, get old.
envenenamiento [em·be·ne·na·mjén·to] *m.* poisoning.

envenenar [em·be·ne·nár] *v.* to poison; to infect.
envergadura [em·ber·ǥa·đú·ra] *f.* span (*of an airplane*); spread (*of a bird's wings*); breadth (*of sails*).
envés [em·bés] *m.* back or wrong side.
enviado [em·bjá·đo] *m.* envoy.
enviar[17] [em·bjár] *v.* to send; — **a uno a paseo** to give someone his walking papers.
enviciar [em·bi·sjár] *v.* to vitiate, corrupt; **-se** to become addicted (to), overly fond (of).
envidar [em·bi·đjár] *v.* to bid (*in cards*); to bet.
envidia [em·bi·đja] *f.* envy.
envidiable [em·bi·đjá·ƀle] *adj.* enviable, desirable.
envidiar [em·bi·đjár] *v.* to envy.
envidiso [em·bi·đjó·so] *adj.* envious.
envilecer[13] [em·bi·le·sér] *v. irr.* to revile, malign, degrade; **-se** to degrade or lower oneself.
envilecimiento [em·bi·le·si·mjén·to] *m.* degradation, humiliation, shame.
envío [em·bí·o] *m.* remittance, sending; shipment.
envite [em·bí·te] *m.* bid; stake (*in cards*); offer; push.
envoltorio [em·bol·tó·rjo] *m.* bundle, package.
envoltura [em·bol·tú·ra] *f.* wrapping, cover; wrapper.
envolver[2, 52] [em·bol·ƀér] *v. irr.* to involve, entangle; to wrap; to wind (*a thread, rope, etc.*); to surround; **-se** to become involved, entangled; to cover up, wrap up.
envuelto [em·bwél·to] *p.p. of* **envolver.**
enyesar [en·ŷe·sár] *v.* to plaster; to chalk; to put a cast on.
enzolvar [en·sol·ƀár] *v. Mex.* to clog, obstruct; *Am.* **-se** to clog, get clogged. *See* **azolvar.**
¡epa! [é·pa] *interj. Ríopl., Ven., Col., Mex.* hey! listen! stop! look out!
épico [é·pi·ko] *adj.* epic.
epidemia [e·pi·đe·mja] *f.* epidemic.
episodio [e·pi·só·đjo] *m.* episode.
epístola [e·pís·to·la] *f.* epistle; letter.
epitafio [e·pi·tá·fjo] *m.* epitaph.
época [é·po·ka] *f.* epoch.
epopeya [e·po·pé·ya] *f.* epic poem.
equidad [e·ki·đáđ] *f.* equity, justice, fairness.
equidistante [e·ki·đis·tán·te] *adj.* equidistant, equally distant, halfway, midway.
equilibrar [e·ki·li·ƀrár] *v.* to balance, poise.
equilibrio [e·ki·lí·ƀrjo] *m.* equilibrium, balance; poise.
equilibrista [e·ki·li·ƀrís·ta] *m. & f.* acrobat.
equipaje [e·ki·pá·xe] *m.* baggage, luggage; equipment, outfit; crew.
equipar [e·ki·pár] *v.* to equip, fit out; to man, cquip and provision (*a ship*).
equipo [e·kí·po] *m.* (*materiales*) equipment, equipping; outfit; (*grupo*) work crew; sport team; — **de novia** trousseau.
equitación [e·ki·ta·sjón] *f.* horsemanship; horseback riding.
equitativo [e·ki·ta·tí·ƀo] *adj.* fair, just.
equivalente [e·ki·ƀa·lén·te] *adj.* equivalent.
equivaler[47] [e·ki·ƀa·lér] *v. irr.* to be equivalent.
equivocación [e·ki·ƀo·ka·sjón] *f.* error, mistake.
equivocado [e·ki·ƀo·ká·đo] *p.p. & adj.* mistaken.
equivocar[6] [e·ki·ƀo·kár] *v.* to mistake; **-se** to be mistaken; to make a mistake.
equívoco [e·kí·ƀo·ko] *adj.* equivocal, ambiguous, vague; *Am.* mistaken; *m.* pun, play on words; *Am.* mistake, error.
era [é·ra] *f.* era, age; threshing floor.
erario [e·rá·rjo] *m.* public treasury.
erguido [er·ǥí·đo] *adj.* erect; *p.p. of* **erguir.**
erguir[3] [er·ǥír] *v. irr.* to erect, set upright; to lift (*the head*) **-se** to sit up or stand erect; to become proud and haughty.
erial [e·rjál] *m.* uncultivated land; *adj.* unplowed, untilled.
erigir[11] [e·ri·xír] *v.* to erect, build; to found.
erizado [e·ri·sá·đo] *adj.* bristly, prickly; — **de** bristling with.
erizar[9] [e·ri·sár] *v.* to set on end, make bristle; **-se** to bristle; to stand on end (*hair*).
erizo [e·rí·so] *m.* hedgehog, porcupine; thistle; — **de mar** sea urchin; **ser un** — to be irritable, harsh.
ermitaño [er·mi·tá·ño] *m.* hermit.
erosion [e·ro·sjón] *f.* erosion.
errabundo [e·rra·ƀún·do] *adj.* wandering.
errado [e·rrá·đo] *adj.* mistaken, wrong, in error; *p.p. of* **errar.**
errante [e·rrán·te] *adj.* errant, roving, wandering.
errar[28] [e·rrár] *v. irr.* to err, make mistakes; to miss (*target, road*); to rove, wander.
errata [e·rrá·ta] *f.* misprint, printer's error.
erróneo [e·rró·ne·o] *adj.* erroneous, mistaken, wrong, incorrect.
error [e·rrór] *m.* error, fault, mistake.
eructar [e·ruk·tár] *v.* to belch, to burp.
eructo [e·rúk·to] *m.* belch.
erudición [e·ru·đi·sjón] *f.* erudition, learning.
erudito [e·ru·đí·to] *adj.* erudite, scholarly, learned; *m.* scholar.
erupción [e·rup·sjón] *f.* eruption; outburst; rash.
esbelto [ez·ƀel·to] *adj.* slender.
esbozar[9] [ez·ƀo·sár] *v.* to sketch, outline.
esbozo [ez·ƀó·so] *m.* sketch, outline.
escabechar [es·ka·ƀe·čár] *v.* to pickle.
escabeche [es·ka·ƀé·če] *m.* pickled fish; pickle (*solution for pickling*).
escabel [es·ka·ƀél] *m.* stool; footstool.
escabrosidad [es·ka·ƀro·si·đáđ] *f.* roughness, unevenness; harshness; improper word or phrase.
escabroso [es·ka·ƀró·so] *adj.* rough; rugged; scabrous, rather indecent.
escabullirse[20] [es·ka·ƀu·yír·se] *v. irr.* to slip away; to slip through; to scoot, scamper, scurry.
escala [es·ká·la] *f.* ladder; scale; port of call; stopover; **hacer — en** to stop over at; **escalafón** [es·ka·la·fón] *m.* army register.
escalar [es·ka·lár] *v.* to scale; to climb.
escaldar [es·kal·dár] *v.* to scald; to make red-hot; **-se** to get scalded.
escalera [es·ka·lé·ra] *f.* stairs, staircase; ladder; — **mecánica** escalator.
escalfar [es·kal·fár] *v.* to poach (*eggs*).
escalinata [es·ka·li·ná·ta] *f.* flight of stairs (*usually on the outside*).
escalofriarse[17] [es·ka·lo·frjár·se] *v.* to become chilled.
escalofrío [es·ka·lo·frí·o] *m.* chill; **-s** chills and fever.
escalón [es·ka·lón] *m.* step (*of a ladder or staircase*); stepping stone; *Arg.* **-es** tribe of **quichua** Indians.
escalonar [es·ka·lo·nár] *v.* to echelon (*arrange in step-like formation*); to terrace; **-se** to rise in terraces.
escaloñas [es·ka·ló·ñas] *f. pl.* scallions.
escama [es·ká·ma] *f.* scale, fish scale; flake.
escamoso [es·ka·mó·so] *adj.* scaly.
escamotear [es·ka·mo·te·ár] *v.* to whisk out of sight; to steal or snatch away with cunning; to conceal by a trick of sleight of hand.
escampar [es·kam·pár] *v.* to clear (*weather*).
escandalizar[9] [es·kan·da·li·sár] *v.* scandalize, shock; **-se** to be shocked.
escándalo [es·kán·da·lo] *m.* scandal; bad example.
escandaloso [es·kan·da·ló·so] *adj.* scandalous,

shocking; *Mex., C.A., Col., Andes* showy, loud (*color*).
escandio [es·kán·djo] *m.* scandium.
escapada [es·ka·pá·đa] *f.* escape, flight.
escapar [es·ka·pár] *v.* to escape, flee, avoid; **-se** to run away, escape.
escaparate [es·ka·pa·rá·te] *m.* show window; glass case, glass cabinet or cupboard.
escapatoria [es·ka·pa·tó·rja] *f.* escape, loophole, excuse.
escape [es·ká·pe] *m.* escape; vent, outlet; exhaust; **a** — rapidly, at full speed.
escarabajo [es·ka·ra·ƀá·xo] *m.* black beetle.
escaramuza [es·ka·ra·mú·sa] *f.* skirmish; quarrel.
escarbar [es·kar·ƀár] *v.* to scrape, scratch; to dig out; to pry into, investigate.
escarcear [es·kar·se·ár] *v. Ch., Ríopl.* to prance.
escarcha [es·kár·ča] *f.* frost; frosting.
escarchar [es·kar·čár] *v.* to frost; to freeze.
escardar [es·kar·đár] *v.* to weed; to weed out.
escarlata [es·kar·lá·ta] *f.* scarlet; scarlet fever; scarlet cloth; **escarlatina** [es·kar·la·tí·na] *f.* scarlet fever.
escarmentar[1] [es·kar·men·tár] *v. irr.* to punish (*as an example or warning*); to profit by one's misfortunes, punishment, etc.; — **en cabeza ajena** to profit by another's mistake or misfortune.
escarmiento [es·kar·mjén·to] *m.* lesson, example, warning; punishment.
escarnecer[13] [es·kar·ne·sér] *v. irr.* to jeer, insult, mock.
escarnio [es·kár·njo] *m.* scoff, jeer.
escarpa [es·kár·pa] *f.* steep slope, bluff, cliff; scarp (*of a fortification*).
escarpado [es·kar·pá·đo] *adj.* steep; rugged.
escarpia [es·kár·pja] *f.* hook (*for hanging something*).
escasear [es·ka·se·ár] *v.* to be scarce; to grow less, become scarce; to stint.
escasez [es·ka·sés] *f.* scarcity, lack, scantiness.
escaso [es·ká·so] *adj.* scarce, limited; scant; scanty; stingy.
escatimar [es·ka·ti·már] *v.* to stint, skimp; to curtail.
escena [e·sé·na] *f.* scene; scenery, theatre, stage.
escenario [e·se·ná·rjo] *m.* stage.
escenificación [e·se·ni·fi·ka·sjón] *f.* dramatization, stage adaptation.
escepticismo [e·sep·ti·síz·mo] *m.* scepticism; doubt, unbelief.
escéptico [e·sép·ti·ko] *m. & adj.* sceptic.
esclarecer[13] [es·kla·re·sér] *v. irr.* to lighten, illuminate; to elucidate, make clear, explain.
esclarecimiento [es·kla·re·si·mjén·to] *m.* clarification, illumination, illustration; worth, nobility.
esclavitud [es·kla·ƀi·túđ] *f.* slavery.
esclavizar[9] [es·kla·ƀi·sár] *v.* to enslave.
esclavo [es·klá·ƀo] *m.* slave.
esclusa [es·klú·sa] *f.* lock (*of a canal*); sluice, floodgate.
escoba [es·kó·ƀa] *f.* broom.
escobazo [es·ko·ƀá·so] *m.* blow with a broom.
escobilla [es·ko·ƀí·ya] *f.* whisk broom; small broom.
escobillón [es·ko·ƀi·yón] *m.* swab; push broom.
escocer[2, 10] [es·ko·sér] *v. irr.* to sting, smart.
escocés [es·ko·sés] *adj.* Scottish; Scotch; *m.* Scot; Scotchman.
escoger[11] [es·ko·xér] *v.* to choose, select, pick out.
escolar [es·ko·lár] *adj.* scholastic, academic; *m.* scholar, student.
escolástico [es·ko·lás·ti·ko] *adj. & m.* scholastic.
escolta [es·kól·ta] *f.* escort; convoy.
escollo [es·kó·yo] *m.* reef; danger; obstacle.
escombro [es·kóm·bro] *m.* debris, rubbish; mackerel.
esconder [es·kon·dér] *v.* to hide, conceal; **-se** to hide, go into hiding.
escondidas [es·kon·dí·đas]: **a** — on the sly, under cover; *Am.* **jugar a las** — to play hide-and-seek.
escondite [es·kon·dí·te] *m.* hiding place; *Spain* **jugar al** — to play hide-and-seek.
escondrijo [es·kon·drí·xo] *m.* hiding place.
escopeta [es·ko·pé·ta] *f.* shotgun.
escopetazo [es·ko·pe·tá·so] *m.* gunshot; gunshot wound; (*malas noticias*) sudden bad news; *Am.* offensive or ironic remark.
escoplo [es·kó·plo] *m.* chisel.
escoria [es·kó·rja] *f.* slag; scum; **escorial** [es·ko·rjál] *m.* dump, dumping place; pile of slag.
escorpión [es·kor·pjón] *m.* scorpion.
escote [es·kó·te] *m.* low neck; **convite a** — Dutch treat (*where everyone pays his share*).
escotilla [es·ko·tí·ya] *f.* hatchway; **escotillón** *m.* hatch, hatchway; trap door.
escozor [es·ko·zór] *m.* smarting sensation, sting.
escribano [es·kri·ƀá·no] *m.* court clerk; lawyer's clerk; notary.
escribiente [es·kri·ƀjén·te] *m.* clerk, office clerk.
escribir[52] [es·kri·ƀír] *v.* to write.
escrito [es·krí·to] *p.p. of* **escribir** written; *m* — writing; manuscript.
escritor [es·kri·tór] *m.* writer.
escritorio [es·kri·tó·rjo] *m.* desk; office.
escritura [es·kri·tú·ra] *f.* writing, handwriting; deed, document; **Sagrada Escritura** Holy Scripture.
escrúpulo [es·krú·pu·lo] *m.* scruple, doubt.
escrupuloso [es·kru·pu·ló·so] *adj.* scrupulous; particular, exact.
escrutador [es·kru·ta·đór] *adj.* scrutinizing, examining; peering; penetrating; *m.* scrutinizer, examiner; inspector of election returns.
escrutar [es·kru·tár] *v.* to scrutinize.
escrutinio [es·kru·tí·njo] *m.* scrutiny, careful inspection.
escuadra [es·kwá·đra] *f.* squadron; fleet; square (*instrument for drawing or testing right angles*); — **de ángulo** angle plate; — **de hierro** steel square.
escuadrón [es·kwa·đrón] *m.* squadron.
escualidez [es·kwa·li·đés] *f.* squalor.
escuálido [es·kwá·li·đo] *adj.* squalid, filthy; thin, emaciated.
escuchar [es·ku·čár] *v.* to listen; to heed.
escudar [es·ku·đár] *v.* to shield.
escudero [es·ku·đé·ro] *m.* squire.
escudo [es·kú·đo] *m.* shield; escutcheon, coat of arms; gold crown (*ancient coin*); *Am.* Chilean gold coin; — **protector** hood (*machine*).
escudriñar [es·ku·đri·ñár] *v.* to scrutinize, search, pry into.
escuela [es·kwé·la] *f.* school.
escuelante [es·kwe·lán·te] *m. & f. Col.* schoolboy; schoolgirl.
escueto [es·kwé·to] *adj.* plain, unadorned, bare.
esculcar[6] [es·kul·kár] *v. Am.* to search; *Carib., Col., Ven.* to frisk (*a person's pockets*).
esculpir [es·kul·pír] *v.* to sculpture; to engrave.
escultor [es·kul·tór] *m.* sculptor.
escultura [es·kul·tú·ra] *f.* sculpture.
escupidera [es·ku·pi·đé·ra] *f.* cuspidor.
escupir [es·ku·pír] *v.* to spit.
escurridero [es·ku·rri·đé·ro] *m.* drain pipe; drainboard.
escurrir [es·ku·rrír] *v.* to drip; to drain; to trickle; **-se** to ooze out, trickle; to slip out, sneak out.
ese [é·se], **esa** [é·sa] *dem. adj.* that; **esos** [é·sos], **esas** [é·sas] those; **ése, ésa** *m., f. dem. pron.* that one;

ésos, ésas *m., f. pl.* those.
esencia [e·sén·sja] *f.* essence.
esencial [e·sen·sjál] *adj.* essential.
esfera [es·fé·ra] *f.* sphere; clock dial.
esférico [es·fé·ri·ko] *adj.* spherical.
esforzado [es·for·sá·do] *adj.* strong; valiant; courageous.
esforzar[2, 9] [es·for·sár] *v. irr.* to give or inspire strength; to encourage; **-se** to make an effort; to strive, try hard.
esfuerzo [es·fwér·so] *m.* effort; spirit, courage, vigor; stress.
esfumar [es·fu·már] *v.* to shade, tone down; **-se** to vanish, disappear.
esgrima [ez·grí·ma] *f.* fencing.
esgrimir [ez·gri·mír] *v.* to fence; to brandish; to wield (*the sword or pen*).
eslabón [ez·la·bón] *m.* link of a chain; steel knife sharpener; black scorpion.
eslabonar [ez·la·bo·nár] *v.* to link; to join; to connect.
esmaltar [ez·mal·tár] *v.* to enamel; to beautify; adorn.
esmalte [ez·mál·te] *m.* enamel; enamel work; smalt (*a blue pigment*).
esmerado [ez·me·rá·do] *adj.* painstaking, careful, conscientious; *p.p. of* **esmerar.**
esmeralda [ez·me·rál·da] *f.* emerald; *Am.* an eel-like fish; *Col.* hummingbird; *Mex.* variety of pineapple.
esmerar [ez·me·rár] *v.* to polish, clean; **-se** to strive, take special pains, use great care.
esmeril [ez·me·ríl] *m.* emery.
esmeriladora [ez·me·ri·la·dó·ra] *f.* emery wheel.
esmero [ez·mé·ro] *m.* care, precision.
esmoquin [ez·mó·kin] *m.* tuxedo, dinner coat.
eso [é·so] *dem. pron.* that, that thing, that fact; — **es** that is it; **a — de** at about (*referring to time*); *Am.* **¡eso!** that's right!
espaciado [es·pa·sjá·do] *m.* pitch.
espaciar[17] [es·pa·sjár] *v.* to space; to spread; to expand; **-se** to enlarge (*upon a subject*); to relax, amuse oneself.
espacio [es·pá·sjo] *m.* space; interval; slowness, delay; (*imprenta*) pitch; *adv. Mex.* slowly.
espacioso [es·pa·sjó·so] *adj.* spacious; slow.
espada [es·pá·da] *f.* sword; skilled swordsman; matador (*bull-fighter who kills the bull*); **-s** swords (*Spanish card suit*).
espalda [es·pál·da] *f.* back, shoulders; **-s** back, back part; **a -s** behind one's back; **de -s** on one's back; **dar la — a** to turn one's back on; **espaldilla** [es·pal·dí·ya] *f.* shoulder blade.
espaldar [es·pal·dár] *m.* back (*of a chair*); trellis (*for plants*); backplate of a cuirass (*armor*).
espantadizo [es·pan·ta·dí·so] *adj.* scary, shy, timid.
espantajo [es·pan·tá·xo] *m.* scarecrow.
espantapájaros [es·pan·ta·pá·xa·ros] *m.* scarecrow.
espantar [es·pan·tár] *v.* to frighten, scare; to scare away; *Col.* to haunt; **-se** to be scared; to be astonished; *Mex.* **espantárselas** [es·pan·tár·se·las] to be wide-awake, catch on quickly.
espanto [es·pán·to] *m.* fright, terror; astonishment; *Col., Ven., Mex.* ghost.
espantoso [es·pan·tó·so] *adj.* frightful, terrifying; wonderful.
español [es·pa·ñól] *adj.* Spanish; *m.* Spaniard; Spanish language.
esparadrapo [es·pa·ra·drá·po] *m.* court plaster, adhesive tape. *See* **tela adhesiva.**
esparcir[10] [es·par·sír] *v.* to scatter, spread; **-se** to relax, amuse oneself.
espárrago [es·pá·rra·go] *m.* asparagus.
esparto [es·pár·to] *m.* esparto grass (*used for making ropes, mats, etc.*).
espasmo [es·páz·mo] *m.* spasm; horror.
espátula [es·pá·tu·la] *f.* spatula.
especia [es·pé·sja] *f.* spice.
especial [es·pe·sjál] *adj.* special; **en** — in particular, specially.
especialidad [es·pe·sja·li·dád] *f.* specialty.
especialista [es·pe·sja·lís·ta] *m. & f.* specialist.
especializar[9] [es·pe·sja·li·sár] *v.* to specialize; **-se en** to specialize in.
especie [es·pé·sje] *f.* species; kind, sort; pretext; idea.
especificar[6] [es·pe·si·fi·kár] *v.* to specify; to name.
específico [es·pe·sí·fi·ko] *adj.* specific; *m.* specific (*medicine*).
espécimen [es·pé·si·men] *m.* specimen, sample.
espectacular [es·pek·ta·ku·lár] *adj.* spectacular.
espectáculo [es·pek·tá·ku·lo] *m.* spectacle.
espectador [es·pek·ta·dór] *m.* spectator.
espectro [es·pék·tro] *m.* spectre, ghost; spectrum.
espectrógrafo [es·pek·tró·gra·fo] *m.* spectrograph.
especulación [es·pe·ku·la·sjón] *f.* speculation.
especulador [es·pe·ku·la·dór] *m.* speculator.
especular [es·pe·ku·lár] *v.* to speculate.
especulativo [es·pe·ku·la·tí·bo] *adj.* speculative.
espejismo [es·pe·xíz·mo] *m.* mirage; illusion.
espejo [es·pé·xo] *m.* mirror; model; — **de cuerpo entero** full-length mirror.
espejuelos [es·pe·xwé·los] *m. pl.* glasses, goggles.
espeluznante [es·pe·luz·nán·te] *adj.* hair-raising, terrifying.
espeluznarse [es·pe·luz·nár·se] *v.* to be terrified; to bristle with fear.
espera [es·pé·ra] *f.* wait; stay (*granted by judge*), delay; extension of time (*for payment*); **sala de** — waiting room; **estar en — de** to be waiting for; to be expecting.
esperanza [es·pe·rán·sa] *f.* hope; expectation.
esperanzado [es·pe·ran·sá·do] *adj.* hopeful.
esperanzar[9] [es·pe·ran·sár] to give hope to.
esperar [es·pe·rár] *v.* (*tener esperanza*) to hope; to expect; to trust; (*permanecer*) to wait, wait for; — **en alguien** to place hope or confidence in someone.
esperezarse [es·pe·re·sár·se] = **desperezarse.**
esperma [es·pér·ma] *f.* sperm.
esperpento [es·per·pén·to] *m.* ugly thing; nonsense.
espesar [es·pe·sár] *v.* to thicken; to make dense; **-se** to thicken; to become thick or dense.
espeso [es·pé·so] *adj.* thick, dense; compact; slovenly; *Ríopl.* bothersome, boring.
espesor [es·pe·sór] *m.* thickness.
espesura [es·pe·sú·ra] *f.* density, thickness; thicket; thickest part (*of a forest*).
espetar [es·pe·tár] *v.* to spring (*a joke, story, etc.*) on (*a person*), surprise with (*a joke, speech, story, etc.*); to pop (*a question*); to run a spit through (*meat, fish, etc. for roasting*); to pierce; **-se** to be stiff, pompous.
espía [es·pí·a] *m. & f.* spy.
espiar[17] [es·pjár] *v.* to spy; *Col., Mex.* **-se** to bruise the hoofs, get lame (*said of horses*).
espiga [es·pí·ga] *f.* ear of wheat; peg; spike.
espigar[7] [es·pi·gár] *v.* to glean; to grow spikes (*said of corn or grain*); **-se** to grow tall and slender.
espina [es·pí·na] *f.* thorn; sharp splinter; fish bone; spine; fear, suspicion; **darle a uno mala** — to arouse one's suspicion.
espinaca [es·pi·ná·ka] *f.* spinach.
espinazo [es·pi·ná·so] *m.* spine, backbone.
espinilla [es·pi·ní·ya] *f.* shin (*front part of leg*); blackhead (*on the skin*).

espino [es·pí·no] *m.* hawthorn; thorny shrub; thorny branch.

espinoso [es·pi·nó·so] *adj.* thorny; difficult, dangerous.

espionaje [es·pjo·ná·xe] *m.* espionage, spying.

espiral [es·pi·rál] *adj.* & *f.* spiral.

espirar [es·pi·rár] *v.* to exhale; to emit, give off; to die. *See* **expirar.**

espíritu [es·pí·ri·tu] *m.* spirit; soul; courage; vigor; essence; ghost.

espiritual [es·pi·ri·tuál] *adj.* spiritual.

espita [es·pí·ta] *f.* spigot, faucet, tap; toper, drunkard.

esplendidez [es·plen·di·đés] *f.* splendor.

espléndido [es·plén·di·đo] *adj.* splendid.

esplendor [es·plen·dór] *m.* splendor.

esplendoroso [es·plen·do·ró·so] *adj.* resplendent, shining.

espliego [es·pljé·ǥo] *m.* lavender (*plant*).

espolear [es·po·le·ár] *v.* to spur; to incite.

espoleta [es·po·lé·ta] *f.* bomb fuse.

espolón [es·po·lón] *m.* spur (*on a cock's leg*); ram (*of a boat*); spur; buttress.

espolvorear [es·pol·ƀo·re·ár] *v.* to powder, sprinkle with powder.

esponja [es·póŋ·xa] *f.* sponge; sponger, parasite; *Col., Peru, Ch., Ríopl.* souse, habitual drunkard.

esponjado [es·poŋ·xá·đo] *adj.* fluffy; spongy; puffed up; *p.p. of* **esponjar.**

esponjar [es·poŋ·jár] *v.* to fluff; to make spongy or porous; **-se** to fluff up; to become spongy or porous; to swell, puff up; to puff up with pride.

esponjoso [es·poŋ·xó·so] *adj.* spongy.

esponsales [es·pon·sá·les] *m. pl.* betrothal.

espontaneidad [es·pon·ta·nej·đáđ] *f.* spontaneity, ease, naturalness.

espontáneo [es·pon·tá·ne·o] *adj.* spontaneous.

esposa [es·pó·sa] *f.* wife; **-s** handcuffs.

esposo [es·pó·so] *m.* husband.

espuela [es·pwé·la] *f.* spur.

espulgar[7] [es·pul·ǥár] *v.* to delouse, remove lice or fleas from; to scrutinize.

espuma [es·pú·ma] *f.* foam, froth; scum; — **de jabón** suds.

espumar [es·pu·már] *v.* to skim; to froth, foam.

espumarajo [es·pu·ma·rá·xo] *m.* froth, foam (*from the mouth*); **echar -s** to froth at the mouth; to be very angry.

espumoso [es·pu·mó·so] *adj.* foamy.

esputo [es·pú·to] *m.* sputum, spit, saliva.

esquela [es·ké·la] *f.* note, letter; announcement.

esqueleto [es·ke·lé·to] *m.* skeleton; carcass; framework; *Mex., C.A., Col., Ven.* blank (*to fill out*); *Am.* outline.

esquema [es·ké·ma] *f.* scheme, outline.

esquí [es·kí] *m.* ski, skiing; — **náutico,** — **acuático** water ski.

esquiar[17] [es·kjár] *v.* to ski.

esquila [es·kí·la] *f.* small bell; cow bell; sheep-shearing.

esquilar [es·ki·lár] *v.* to shear; to clip; to crop.

esquina [es·kí·na] *f.* corner, angle; **esquinazo** [es·ki·ná·so] *m.* corner; *Am.* serenade; **dar esquinazo** to avoid meeting someone; to "ditch" someone.

esquivar [es·ki·ƀár] *v.* to avoid, dodge; to shun; **-se** to withdraw, shy away.

esquivez [es·ki·ƀés] *f.* shyness; aloofness; disdain.

esquivo [es·kí·ƀo] *adv.* reserved, unsociable; shy; disdainful, aloof.

estabilidad [es·ta·ƀi·li·đáđ] *f.* stability.

estable [es·tá·ƀle] *adj.* stable, firm, steady.

establecer[13] [es·ta·ƀle·sér] *v. irr.* to establish; to found; to decree, ordain.

establecimiento [es·ta·ƀle·si·mjén·to] *m.* establishment; foundation; statute, law.

establo [es·tá·ƀlo] *m.* stable; **establero** [es·ta·ƀlé·ro] *m.* groom.

estaca [es·tá·ka] *f.* stake, club; stick; picket.

estacada [es·ta·ká·đa] *f.* stockade; picket fence; *Am.* predicament.

estacar[6] [es·ta·kár] *v.* to stake; to tie on a stake; to stake off, mark with stakes; *Am.* to fasten down with stakes; **-se** to remain stiff or rigid.

estación [es·ta·sjón] *f.* station; season; railway station.

estacionar [es·ta·sjo·nár] *v.* to station; to place; to park (*a car*); **-se** to remain stationary; to park.

estacionario [es·ta·sjo·ná·rjo] *adj.* stationary; motionless.

estada [es·tá·đa] *f.* sojourn, stay.

estadía [es·ta·đí·a] *f.* detention, stay; stay in port (*beyond time allowed for loading and unloading*); *C.A., Carib.* sojourn, stay (*in any sense*).

estadio [es·tá·đjo] *m.* stadium.

estadista [es·ta·đís·ta] *m.* statesman.

estadística [es·ta·đís·ti·ka] *f.* statistics.

estado [es·tá·đo] *m.* state, condition; station, rank; estate; — **mayor** army staff; **hombre de** — statesman; *Am.* **en** — **interesante** pregnant.

estadounidense [es·ta·đow·ni·đén·se] *adj.* from the United States, American.

estafa [es·tá·fa] *f.* swindle, fraud, trick.

estafador [es·ta·fa·đór] *m.* swindler, crook.

estafar [es·ta·fár] *v.* to swindle, defraud, cheat.

estalactita [es·ta·lak·tí·ta] *f.* stalactite.

estalagmita [es·ta·laǥ·mí·ta] *f.* stalagmite.

estallar [es·ta·yár] *v.* to explode, burst; to creak, crackle.

estallido [es·ta·yí·đo] *m.* explosion, outburst; crash; creaking; crack (*of a gun*), report (*of a gun or cannon*).

estambre [es·tám·bre] *m.* woolen yarn; stamen (*of a flower*).

estampa [es·tám·pa] *f.* image; print; stamp; cut, picture; footprint; figure, appearance.

estampado [es·tam·pá·đo] *m.* print, printed fabric; printing.

estampar [es·tam·pár] *v.* to stamp, print.

estampida [es·tam·pí·đa] *f.* crack, sharp sound; *Col., Ven., C.A.* stampede (*sudden scattering of a herd of cattle or horses*).

estampido [es·tam·pí·đo] *m.* crack, sharp sound; report of a gun.

estampilla [es·tam·pí·ya] *f.* stamp, seal; *Mex., C.A., Andes* postage stamp.

estancar[6] [es·taŋ·kár] *v.* to stem; to stanch; to stop the flow of; to corner (*a market*); **-se** to stagnate, become stagnant.

estancia [es·tán·sja] *f.* (*permanencia*) stay; (*lugar*) hall, room; mansion; *Ríopl.* farm, cattle ranch; *Carib.* main building of a farm or ranch.

estanciero [es·tan·sjé·ro] *m. Ríopl.* rancher, ranch-owner, cattle raiser; *adj.* pertaining to an **estancia.**

estanco [es·táŋ·ko] *m.* monopoly; government store (*for sale of monopolized goods such as tobacco, stamps and matches*); tank, reservoir; *Ec., C.A.* liquor store.

estandar [es·tán·dar] *m. Am.* standard, norm.

estandardizar [es·tan·dar·đi·sár], **estandarizar**[9] [es·tan·da·ri·sár] *v. Am.* standardize.

estandarte [es·tan·dár·te] *m.* standard, flag, banner.

estanque [es·táŋ·ke] *m.* pond, pool, reservoir.

estanquillo [es·táŋ·kí·yo] *m.* tobacco store; *Am.* small

store; *C.A., Mex.* small liquor store, tavern.
estante [es·tán·te] *m.* shelf; bookshelf; *Am.* prop, support; **estantería** [es·tan·te·rí·a] *f.* shelves; bookcases.
estaño [es·tá·ño] *m.* tin.
estaquilla [es·ta·kí·ya] *f.* peg; spike.
estar[29] [es·tár] *v. irr.* to be; **-le bien a uno** to be becoming to one; — **de prisa** to be in a hurry; **¿a cuántos estamos?** what day of the month is it today?; **-se** to keep, remain.
estático [es·tá·ti·ko] *adj.* static; **estática** [es·tá·ti·ka] *f.* statics; radio static.
estatua [es·tá·twa] *f.* statue.
estatura [es·ta·tú·ra] *f.* stature, height.
estatuto [es·ta·tú·to] *m.* statute.
este [és·te], **esta** [és·ta] *dem. adj.* this; **estos** [és·tos], **estas** [és·tas] these; **éste, ésta** *m., f. dem. pron.* this one, this thing; the latter; **esto** [és·to] this, this thing; **éstos, éstas** *m., f. pl.* these; the latter.
este [és·te] *m.* east; east wind.
estela [es·té·la] *f.* wake of a ship.
estenógrafo [es·te·nó·ǥra·fo] *m.* stenographer.
estentóreo [es·ten·tó·re·o] *adj.* loud, thundering (*voice*).
estepa [es·té·pa] *f.* steppe, treeless plain.
estera [es·té·ra] *f.* matting; mat; conveyor belt.
estercolar [es·ter·ko·lár] *v.* to manure, fertilize with manure.
estercolero [es·ter·ko·lé·ro] *m.* manure pile, manure dump; manure collector.
estereoscopio [es·te·re·os·kó·pjo] *m.* stereoscope.
estereotipo [es·te·re·o·tí·po] *m.* stereotype.
estéril [es·té·ril] *adj.* sterile, barren.
esterilidad [es·te·ri·li·đáđ] *f.* sterility, barrenness.
esterilizar[9] [es·te·ri·li·sár] *v.* to sterilize.
esterlina [es·te·ri·lí·na] *adj.* sterling; **libra** — pound sterling.
esternón [es·ter·nón] *m.* sternum.
estero [es·té·ro] *m.* estuary.
estertor [es·ter·tór] *m.* death-rattle; snort.
estético [es·té·ti·ko] *adj.* aesthetic; **estética** [es·té·ti·ka] *f.* aesthetics.
estetoscopio [es·te·tos·kó·pjo] *m.* stethoscope.
estibador [es·ti·ƀa·đór] *m.* stevedore, longshoreman.
estibar [es·ti·ƀár] *v.* to stow (*in a boat*); to pack down, compress.
estiércol [es·tjér·kol] *m.* manure; fertilizer.
estigma [es·tíǥ·ma] *m.* stigma; brand, mark of disgrace; birthmark.
estilar [es·ti·lár] *v.* to use, be accustomed to using; **-se** to be in style (*said of clothes*).
estilete [es·ti·lé·te] *m.* stiletto, narrow-bladed dagger; stylet (*instrument for probing wounds*); long, narrow sword.
estilo [es·tí·lo] *m.* style; fashion.
estima [es·tí·ma] *f.* esteem.
estimación [es·ti·ma·sjón] *f.* esteem, regard; valuation.
estimado al azar *n* a "guesstimate."
estimar [es·ti·már] *v.* to esteem, regard highly; to estimate, appraise; to judge, think.
estimulante [es·ti·mu·lán·te] *adj.* stimulant, stimulating; *m.* stimulant.
estimular [es·ti·mu·lár] *v.* to stimulate, excite, goad.
estímulo [es·tí·mu·lo] *m.* stimulation, incitement; stimulus.
estío [es·tí·o] *m.* summer.
estipulación [es·ti·pu·la·sjón] *f.* stipulation, specification, provision, proviso.
estipular [es·ti·pu·lár] *v.* to stipulate, specify.
estirado [es·ti·rá·đo] *p.p. & adj.* stretched; extended, drawn out; stuck-up, conceited.
estirar [es·ti·rár] *v.* to stretch, extend; — **la pata** to die; **-se** to stretch out; *Mex.* to die.
estirón [es·ti·rón] *m.* hard pull, tug; stretch; **dar un** — to grow suddenly (*said of a child*).
estirpe [es·tír·pe] *f.* lineage, family, race.
estival [es·ti·ƀál] *adj.* summer, relating to the summer.
estocada [es·to·ká·đa] *f.* thrust, stab; stab wound.
estofa [es·tó·fa] *f.* stuff, cloth; class, quality; **gente de baja** — low class people, rabble.
estofado [es·to·fá·đo] *m.* stew, stewed meat; *p.p. of* **estofar.**
estofar [es·to·fár] *v.* to quilt; to stew.
estoico [es·tój·ko] *adj. & m.* stoic.
estola [es·tó·la] *f.* stole; — **de visón** mink wrap.
estómago [es·tó·ma·ǥo] *m.* stomach.
estopa [es·tó·pa] *f.* burlap; oakum (*loose fiber of old ropes*).
estoque [es·tó·ke] *m.* long, narrow sword.
estorbar [es·tor·ƀár] *v.* to hinder; to obstruct.
estorbo [es·tór·ƀo] *m.* hindrance; nuisance, bother.
estornudar [es·tor·nu·đár] *v.* to sneeze.
estornudo [es·tor·nú·đo] *m.* sneeze.
estrado [es·trá·đo] *m.* dais (*platform for a throne, seats of honor, etc.*); main part of a parlor or drawing room.
estragado [es·tra·ǥá·đo] *p.p. & adj.* corrupted; spoiled; ruined; tired, worn out.
estragar[7] [es·tra·ǥár] *v.* to corrupt, contaminate; to spoil; to ruin.
estrago [es·trá·ǥo] *m.* havoc, ruin; massacre.
estragón [es·tra·gón] *m.* tarragon.
estrangulador [es·traŋ·gu·la·đór] *m.* strangler, choke (*of an automobile*); *adj.* strangling.
estrangular [es·traŋ·gu·lár] *v.* to strangle; to choke, throttle.
estratagema [es·tra·ta·xé·ma] *f.* stratagem, scheme.
estrategia [es·tra·té·xja] *f.* strategy.
estratégico [es·tra·té·xi·ko] *adj.* strategic; *m.* strategist, person trained or skilled in strategy.
estrato [es·trá·to] *m.* stratum, layer (*of mineral*).
estratorreactor [es·tra·to·rre·ak·tór] *m.* supersonic jet plane.
estratosfera [es·tra·tos·fé·ra] *f.* stratosphere.
estrechar [es·tre·čár] *v.* to tighten; to narrow down; to embrace, hug; — **la mano** to squeeze, grasp another's hand; to shake hands.
estrechez [es·tre·čés], **estrechura** [es·tre·čú·ra] *f.* narrowness; tightness; austerity; dire straits; poverty; closeness.
estrecho [es·tré·čo] *adj.* narrow; tight; *m.* strait, narrow passage.
estrella [es·tré·ya] *f.* star; — **de mar** starfish.
estrellado [es·tre·yá·đo] *adj.* starry; spangled with stars; **huevos -s** fried eggs.
estrellar [es·tre·yár] *v.* to shatter; to dash to pieces; to star, spangle with stars; **-se** to shatter, break into pieces; to fail.
estremecer[13] [es·tre·me·sér] *v. irr.* to shake; **-se** to shiver, shudder; to vibrate.
estremecimiento [es·tre·me·si·mjén·to] *m.* shiver, shudder; vibration; shaking.
estrenar [es·tre·nár] *v.* to wear for the first time; to perform (*a play*) for the first time; to inaugurate; to begin.
estreno [es·tré·no] *m.* début, first appearance or performance.
estreñimiento [es·tre·ñi·mjén·to] *m.* constipation.
estreñir[5, 19] [es·tre·ñír] *v. irr.* to constipate; **-se** to become constipated.

estrépito [es·tré·pi·to] *m.* racket, noise, crash.
estrepitoso [es·tre·pi·tó·so] *adj.* noisy; boisterous.
estriaciones [es·trja·sjó·nes] *f.* scratches, streaks.
estriado [es·trjá·đo] *p.p.* & *adj.* fluted, grooved; streaked.
estriar[17] [es·trjár] *v.* to groove; to flute (*as a column*).
estribación [es·tri·ƀa·sjón] *f.* spur (*of a mountain or mountain range*).
estribar [es·tri·ƀár] *v.* to rest (upon); **eso estriba en que . . .** the basis or reason for it is that . . .
estribillo [es·tri·ƀí·yo] *m.* refrain.
estribo [es·trí·ƀo] *m.* (*de caballo o vehículo*) stirrup; footboard, running board; (*apoyo*) support; brace; spur (*of a mountain*); **perder los -s** to lose one's balance; to lose control of oneself.
estribor [es·tri·ƀór] *m.* starboard.
estricto [es·trík·to] *adj.* strict.
estrofa [es·tró·fa] *f.* strophe, stanza.
estroncio [es·trón·sjo] *m.* strontium.
estropajo [es·tro·pá·xo] *m.* fibrous mass (*for scrubbing*); **tratar a uno como un —** to treat someone scornfully.
estropear [es·tro·pe·ár] *v.* to spoil, ruin, damage; to cripple.
estructura [es·truk·tú·ra] *f.* structure.
estructural [es·truk·tu·rál] *adj.* structural.
estruendo [es·trwén·do] *m.* clatter; clamor, din, racket.
estruendoso [es·trwen·dó·so] *adj.* thunderous, uproarious, deafening.
estrujamiento [es·tru·xa·mjén·to] *m.* crushing, squeezing.
estrujar [es·tru·xár] *v.* to squeeze, press, crush.
estrujón [es·tru·xón] *m.* squeeze, crush; smashing.
estuario [es·twá·rjo] *m.* estuary.
estuco [es·tú·ko] *m.* stucco.
estuche [es·tú·če] *m.* jewel box; instrument case, kit; small casket; sheath; **— de primer auxilio** first aid kit.
estudiantado [es·tu·đjan·tá·đo] *m.* the student body (*of a school or college*).
estudiante [es·tu·đján·te] *m.* & *f.* student.
estudiantil [es·tu·đjan·tíl] *adj.* pertaining to students.
estudiar [es·tu·đjár] *v.* to study.
estudio [es·tú·đjo] *m.* study; studio.
estudioso [es·tu·đjó·so] *adj.* studious; *m.* learner.
estufa [es·tú·fa] *f.* heater; stove; hothouse; steam room; steam cabinet.
estupefacto [es·tu·pe·fák·to] *adj.* stunned; speechless.
estupendo [es·tu·pén·do] *adj.* stupendous, marvelous.
estupidez [es·tu·pi·đés] *f.* stupidity.
estúpido [es·tú·pi·đo] *adj.* stupid.
esturión [es·tu·rjón] *m.* sturgeon.
etapa [e·tá·pa] *f.* stage, lap (*of a journey or race*); army food rations; epoch, period.
éter [é·ter] *m.* ether.
etéreo [e·té·re·o] *adj.* ethereal; heavenly.
eternidad [e·ter·ni·đáđ] *f.* eternity.
eternizar[9] [e·ter·ni·sár] *v.* to prolong excessively; to perpetuate, make eternal.
eterno [e·tér·no] *adj.* eternal, everlasting.
ética [é·ti·ka] *f.* ethics; **ético** *adj.* ethical, moral.
etimología [e·ti·mo·lo·xí·a] *f.* etymology.
etiqueta [e·ti·ké·ta] *f.* etiquette; formality; tag; **de —** formal (*dress, function, etc.*).
étnico [ét·ni·ko] *adj.* ethnic.
eucalipto [ew·ka·líp·to] *m.* eucalyptus.
Eucaristía [ew·ka·ris·tí·a] *f.* Eucharist.
euforia [ew·fó·rja] *f.* euphoria.
europeo [ew·ro·pé·o] *adj.* & *m.* European.
evacuación [e·ƀa·kwa·sjón] *f.* evacuation; bowel movement.
evacuar[18] [e·ƀa·kwár] *v.* to evacuate, empty; to vacate.
evadir [e·ƀa·đír] *v.* to evade, elude; **-se** to slip away, escape.
evaluar[18] [e·ƀa·lwár] *v.* to evaluate, appraise.
evangelio [e·ƀaŋ·xé·ljo] *m.* gospel.
evaporar [e·ƀa·po·rár] *v.* to evaporate; **-se** to evaporate; to vanish, disappear.
evasión [e·ƀa·sjón] *f.* evasion, dodge, escape.
evasiva [e·ƀa·sí·ƀa] *f.* evasion, dodge, escape.
evasivo [e·ƀa·sí·ƀo] *adj.* evasive.
evasor [e·ƀa·sór] *m.* evader, dodger.
evento [e·ƀén·to] *m.* event.
evidencia [e·ƀi·đén·sja] *f.* evidence.
evidenciar [e·ƀi·đen·sjár] *v.* to prove, show, make evident.
evidente [e·ƀi·đén·te] *adj.* evident.
evitable [e·ƀi·tá·ƀle] *adj.* avoidable.
evitar [e·ƀi·tár] *v.* to avoid, shun.
evocar[6] [e·ƀo·kár] *v.* to evoke, call forth.
evolución [e·ƀo·lu·sjón] *f.* evolution.
evolucionar [e·ƀo·lu·sjo·nár] *v.* to evolve; to perform maneuvers; to go through changes.
exacerbar [ek·sa·ser·ƀár] *v.* to exasperate, irritate; to aggravate, make worse.
exactitud [ek·sak·ti·túđ] *f.* exactness, precision; punctuality.
exacto [ek·sák·to] *adj.* exact, precise; punctual.
exagerar [ek·sa·xe·rár] *v.* to exaggerate.
exaltación [ek·sal·ta·sjón] *f.* exaltation; excitement.
exaltado [ek·sal·tá·đo] *adj.* elated; excited; hotheaded.
exaltar [ek·sal·tár] *v.* to exalt, elevate, glorify; to praise; **-se** to get excited; to become upset emotionally.
examen [ek·sá·men] *m.* examination; inspection.
examinar [ek·sa·mi·nár] *v.* to examine; to inspect.
exangüe [ek·sáŋ·gwe] *adj.* lacking blood; anemic; exhausted.
exánime [ek·sá·ni·me] *adj.* lifeless, motionless; weak, faint.
exasperar [ek·sas·pe·rár] *v.* to exasperate, irritate, annoy.
excavar [es·ka·ƀár] *v.* to excavate, dig, dig out.
excedente [ek·se·đén·te] *m.* surplus; *adj.* exceeding, extra.
exceder [ek·se·đér] *v.* to exceed, surpass; to overdo; **-se** to go beyond the proper limit; to misbehave.
excelencia [ek·se·lén·sja] *f.* excellence, superiority; excellency (*title*).
excelente [ek·se·lén·te] *adj.* excellent.
excelso [ek·sél·so] *adj.* lofty, elevated; sublime; **El Excelso** the Most High.
excéntrico [ek·sén·tri·ko] *adj.* eccentric; queer, odd.
excepción [ek·sep·sjón] *f.* exception.
excepcional [ek·sep·sjo·nál] *adj.* exceptional, unusual.
excepto [ek·sép·to] *adv.* except, with the exception of.
exceptuar[18] [ek·sep·twár] *v.* to except.
excesivo [ek·se·sí·ƀo] *adj.* excessive.
exceso [ek·sé·so] *m.* excess; crime; **— de equipaje** excess baggage; **en —** in excess, excessively.
excitación [ek·si·ta·sjón] *f.* excitement.
excitante [ek·si·tán·te] *adj.* exciting; stimulating.
excitar [ek·si·tár] *v.* to excite, stir; **-se** to get excited.
exclamación [es·kla·ma·sjón] *f.* exclamation.
exclamar [es·kla·már] *v.* to exclaim.
excluir[32] [es·klwír] *v. irr.* to exclude.
exclusivo [es·klu·sí·ƀo] *adj.* exclusive.
excomunicar[6] [es·ko·mu·ni·kár] *v.* to excommunicate.
excomunión [es·ko·mu·njón] *f.* excommunication.

excrecencia [es·kre·sén·sja], **excrescencia** [es·kre·sén·sja] *f.* excrescence (*abnormal growth or tumor*).
excremento [es·kre·mén·to] *m.* excrement.
excursión [es·kur·sjón] *f.* excursion, tour, outing.
excusa [es·kú·sa] *f.* excuse.
excusado [es·ku·sá·đo] *p.p. & adj.* excused; exempt; superfluous; unnecessary; reserved, private; *m.* toilet.
excusar [es·ku·sár] *v.* (*disculpar*) to excuse; to exempt; (*evitar*) to avoid, shun; **-se** to excuse oneself, apologize; to decline.
exención [ek·sen·sjón] *f.* exemption.
exentar [ek·sen·tár] *v.* to exempt. *See* **eximir.**
exento [ek·sén·to] *adj.* exempt, freed; free, unobstructed.
exequias [ek·sé·kjas] *f. pl.* obsequies, funeral rites.
exhalar [ek·sa·lár] *v.* to exhale; to emit, give off; to breathe forth; **-se** to evaporate; to run away.
exhibición [ek·si·ƀi·sjón] *f.* exhibition; exposition; *Mex.* payment of an installment.
exhibir [ek·si·ƀír] *v.* to exhibit; *Mex.* to pay for in installments (*stocks, policies, etc.*); **-se** to exhibit oneself, show off.
exhortar [ek·sor·tár] *v.* to exhort, admonish.
exigencia [ek·si·xén·sja] *f.* demand; urgent want; emergency.
exigente [ek·si·xén·te] *adj.* demanding, exacting; urgent.
exigir[11] [ek·si·xír] *v.* to require; to demand; to exact.
exiguo [ek·sí·ǥwo] *adj.* scanty, meager.
eximio [ek·sí·mjo] *adj.* very distinguished.
eximir [ek·si·mír] *v.* to exempt, except, excuse; **-se dé** to avoid, shun.
existencia [ek·sis·tén·sja] *f.* existence; **-s** stock on hand, goods; **en** — in stock, on hand.
existente [ek·sis·tén·te] *adj.* existent, existing; in stock.
existir [ek·sis·tír] *v.* to exist.
éxito [ék·si·to] *m.* outcome, result; success; **tener buen (mal)** — to be successful (unsuccessful).
éxodo [ék·so·đo] *m.* exodus, emigration.
exonerar [ek·so·ne·rár] *v.* to exonerate, free from blame; to relieve of a burden or position; to dismiss.
exorbitante [ek·sor·ƀi·tán·te] *adj.* exorbitant, excessive, extravagant.
exótico [ek·só·ti·ko] *adj.* exotic, foreign, strange; quaint.
expansión [es·pan·sjón] *f.* expansion; relaxation; recreation.
expansivo [es·pan·sí·ƀo] *adj.* expansive; demonstrative, effusive.
expatriar [es·pa·trjár] *v.* to expatriate, exile; **-se** to expatriate oneself, renounce one's citizenship; to emigrate.
expectación [es·pek·ta·sjón] *f.* expectation.
expectativa [es·pek·ta·tí·ƀa] *f.* expectation; hope, prospect; **estar en — de algo** to be expecting, or on the lookout for, something.
expectorar [es·pek·to·rár] *v.* to expectorate, cough up.
expedición [es·pe·đi·sjón] *f.* expedition; dispatch, promptness; papal dispatch or bull.
expedicionario [es·pe·đi·sjo·ná·rjo] *adj.* expeditionary; *m.* member of an expedition; explorer.
expediente [es·pe·đjén·te] *m.* certificate; papers pertaining to a business matter; expedient, means; dispatch, promptness; — **personal** curriculum vitae.
expedir[5] [es·pe·đír] *v. irr.* to dispatch; to issue officially; to remit, send.
expeler [es·pe·lér] *v.* to expel, eject.
experiencia [es·pe·rjén·sja] *f.* experience; experiment.
experimentado [es·pe·ri·men·tá·đo] *adj. & p.p.* experienced.
experimental [es·pe·ri·men·tál] *adj.* experimental.
experimentar [es·pe·ri·men·tár] *v.* to experiment, try, test; to experience, feel.
experimento [es·pe·ri·mén·to] *m.* experiment, trial.
experto [es·pér·to] *adj.* expert, skillful; *m.* expert.
expiación [es·pja·sjón] *f.* expiation, atonement.
expiar[17] [es·pjár] *v.* to atone for; to make amends for; to purify.
expirar [es·pi·rár] *v.* to die; to expire, come to an end.
explayar [es·pla·yár] *v.* to extend; **-se** to become extended; to relax in the open air; to enlarge upon a subject; **-se con un amigo** to unbosom oneself, speak with utmost frankness with a friend.
explicable [es·pli·ká·ƀle] *adj.* explainable.
explicación [es·pli·ka·sjón] *f.* explanation.
explicar[6] [es·pli·kár] *v.* to explain; — **una cátedra** to teach a course; **-se** to explain oneself; to account for one's conduct.
explicativo [es·pli·ka·tí·ƀo] *adj.* explanatory, explaining.
explícito [es·plí·si·to] *adj.* explicit, express, clear, definite.
exploración [es·plo·ra·sjón] *f.* exploration.
explorador [es·plo·ra·đór] *m.* explorer, scout; *adj.* exploring.
explorar [es·plo·rár] *v.* to explore.
explosión [es·plo·sjón] *f.* explosion.
explosivo [es·plo·sí·ƀo] *adj. & m.* explosive.
explotación [es·plo·ta·sjón] *f.* exploitation; operation of a mine; development of a business; plant.
explotar [es·plo·tár] *v.* to exploit, operate, develop; to utilize, profit by; to make unfair use of; *Am.* to explode.
exponer[40] [es·po·nér] *v. irr.* (*dejar ver*) to expose, reveal; to show, exhibit; to display; (*sin protección*) to leave unprotected, to expose (*film*); (*explicar*) to expound; to explain; **-se a** to expose oneself to; to run the risk of.
exportación [es·por·ta·sjón] *f.* exportation; export.
exportar [es·por·tár] *v.* to export.
exposición [es·po·si·sjón] *f.* exposition; exhibition; explanation; exposure.
exprés [es·prés] *m. Am.* express; *Am.* express company.
expresar [es·pre·sár] *v.* to express; **-se** to express oneself, speak.
expresión [es·pre·sjón] *f.* expression; utterance; **-es** regards.
expresivo [es·pre·sí·ƀo] *adj.* expressive; affectionate.
expreso [es·pré·so] *adj.* expressed; express, clear, exact; fast; *m.* express train.
exprimir [es·pri·mír] *v.* to squeeze, extract (*juice*); to wring out; to express, utter.
expuesto [es·pwés·to] *p.p. of* **exponer** *& adj.* exposed; expressed; displayed; risky, dangerous; **lo** — what has been said.
expulsar [es·pul·sár] *v.* to expel, eject.
expulsión [es·pul·sjón] *f.* expulsion, expelling.
exquisitez [es·ki·si·tés] *f.* exquisiteness.
exquisito [es·ki·sí·to] *adj.* exquisite.
extasiado [es·ta·sjá·đo] *adj.* rapt, in ecstasy; *p.p. of* **extasiar.**
extasiar[17] [es·ta·sjár] *v.* to delight; **-se** to be in ecstasy; to be entranced.
éxtasis [és·ta·sis] *m.* ecstasy.

extender[1] [es·ten·dér] *v. irr.* to extend; to spread; to unfold; to draw up (*a document*); **-se** to extend, spread; to expatiate, be too wordy.
extensión [es·ten·sjón] *f.* extension; extent; expanse; expansion.
extensivo [es·ten·sí·ƀo] *adj.* extensive.
extenso [es·tén·so] *p.p. irr of* **extender** extended; *adj.* extensive, vast, spacious; **por** — extensively, in detail.
extenuado [es·te·nwá·đo] *adj.* wasted, weak, emaciated.
exterior [es·te·rjór] *adj.* exterior, outer; *m.* exterior; outside; outward appearance.
exterminar [es·ter·mi·nár] *v.* to exterminate.
exterminio [es·ter·mí·njo] *m.* extermination, destruction.
externo [es·tér·no] *adj.* external, outward.
extinción [es·tin·sjón] *f.* extinction; — **de derecho** foreclosure.
extinguir[12] [es·tiŋ·gír] *v.* to extinguish, put out; to destroy.
extinto [es·tín·to] *adj.* extinct.
extintor [es·tin·tór] *m.* extinguisher; — **de espuma** fire extinguisher.
extirpar [es·tir·pár] *v.* to eradicate, pull out by the roots, root out, remove completely; to destroy completely.
extorsión [es·tor·sjón] *f.* extortion.
extorsionar [es·tor·sjo·nár] *v. Am.* to extort, extract money, blackmail.
extorsionista [es·tor·sjo·nís·ta] *m. Am.* extortioner, profiteer, racketeer.
extracto [es·trák·to] *m.* extract; abstract, summary.
extraer[46] [es·tra·ér] *v. irr.* to extract.
extranjero [es·traŋ·xé·ro] *adj.* foreign; *m.* foreigner.
extrañamiento [es·tra·ña·mjén·to] *m.* wonder, surprise, amazement.
extrañar [es·tra·ñár] *v.* to wonder at; to banish; *Am.* to miss (*a person or thing*); **-se** to marvel, be astonished.
extrañeza [es·tra·ñé·sa] *f.* strangeness; surprise, astonishment; oddity, odd thing.
extraño [es·trá·ño] *adj.* strange; rare; odd; *m.* stranger.
extraordinario [es·tra·or·đi·ná·rjo] *adj.* extraordinary.
extravagancia [es·tra·ƀa·ǵán·sja] *f.* extravagance; folly.
extravagante [es·tra·ƀa·ǵán·te] *adj.* extravagant, fantastic; queer, odd.
extraviar[17] [es·tra·ƀjár] *v.* to lead astray; to strand; to misplace; **-se** to lose one's way; to get stranded; to get lost; to miss the road.
extravío [es·tra·ƀí·o] *m.* deviation, straying; error; misconduct; damage.
extremado [es·tre·má·đo] *adj.* extreme; extremely good or extremely bad; *p.p. of* **extremar.**
extremar [es·tre·már] *v.* to carry to an extreme; **-se** to take great pains, exert great effort.
extremidad [es·tre·mi·đáđ] *f.* extremity; extreme degree; remotest part; **-es** extremities, hands and feet.
extremo [es·tré·mo] *adj.* extreme, last; farthest; excessive; utmost; *m.* extreme, highest degree or point; end, extremity; extreme care; **con (en** *or* **por)** — very much, extremely.
exuberante [ek·su·ƀe·rán·te] *adj.* exuberant; luxuriant.

F:f

fa [fa] *m.* fourth note of the musical scale.
fabada [fa·ƀá·đa] *f.* a bean and bacon soup popular in Spain.
fábrica [fá·ƀri·ka] *f.* manufacture; factory, mill; structure.
fabricación [fa·ƀri·ka·sjón] *f.* manufacture.
fabricante [fa·ƀri·kán·te] *m.* manufacturer, maker.
fabricar[6] [fa·ƀri·kár] *v.* to manufacture, make; to construct, build; to fabricate, make up, invent.
fabril [fa·ƀríl] *adj.* manufacturing.
fábula [fá·ƀu·la] *f.* fable, tale; falsehood.
fabuloso [fa·ƀu·ló·so] *adj.* fabulous; false, imaginary.
facción [fak·sjón] *f.* faction, band, party; battle; **-es** features; **estar de** — to be on duty.
faceta [fa·sé·ta] *f.* facet.
faceto [fa·sé·to] *adj. Mex.* cute, funny; *Am.* affected.
fácil [fá·sil] *adj.* easy; docile, yielding, manageable; likely; probable.
facilidad [fa·si·li·đáđ] *f.* facility, ease; opportunity.
facilitar [fa·si·li·tár] *v.* to facilitate, make easy; to furnish; give; — **todos los datos** to furnish all the data.
facón [fa·kón] *m. Ríopl., Bol.* dagger, large knife;
faconazo [fa·ko·ná·so] *m. Ríopl., Bol.* stab.
factible [fak·tí·ƀle] *adj.* feasible.
factor [fak·tór] *m.* factor; element, joint cause; commercial agent; baggage man.
factoría [fak·to·rí·a] *f.* trading post; *Mex.* factory.
factura [fak·tú·ra] *f.* (*cuenta*) invoice, itemized bill; (*hechura*) make; workmanship, form; *Am.* roll, biscuit, muffin; — **simulada** temporary invoice, memorandum.
facturar [fak·tu·rár] *v.* to invoice, bill; to check (*baggage*).
facultad [fa·kul·táđ] *f.* faculty; ability, aptitude; power, right; permission; branch of learning; school or college of a university.
facultativo [fa·kul·ta·tí·ƀo] *m.* doctor, physician.
facundia [fa·kún·dja] *f.* eloquence, fluency, facility in speaking, gift of expression.
facha [fá·ča] *f.* appearance, figure, aspect, looks.
fachada [fa·čá·đa] *f.* façade, front (*of a building*); title page.
fachenda [fa·čén·da] *f.* ostentation, vanity.
fachendoso [fa·čen·dó·so] *adj.* vain, boastful, ostentatious.
faena [fa·é·na] *f.* task, job, duty; *Carib., Mex., C.A.* extra job; *Ch.* work crew, labor gang.
faja [fá·xa] *f.* sash; girdle; band; *Am.* belt, waist band.
fajar [fa·xár] *v.* to girdle; to bind, wrap, or bandage with a strip of cloth; *Am.* to beat, strike, thrash; *Am.* — **un latigazo a uno** to whip, thrash someone; **-se** to put on a sash or belt; to tighten one's sash or belt; *Am.* **-se con** to have a fight with, come to blows with.
fajo [fá·xo] *m.* bundle; sheaf.
falaz [fa·lás] *adj.* illusive, illustory; deceitful, deceiving.
falda [fál·da] *f.* skirt; lap; hat brim; foothill, slope;
faldón [fal·dón] *m.* coattail; shirttail.
faldear [fal·de·ár] *v.* to skirt (*a hill*).
falsario [fal·sá·rjo] *m.* crook, forger; liar.
falsear [fal·se·ár] *v.* to falsify, misrepresent; to counterfeit; to forge; to pick (*a lock*); to flag, grow weak; to hit a wrong note.
falsedad [fal·se·đáđ] *f.* falsehood, lie; deceit.
falsificación [fal·si·fi·ka·sjón] *f.* falsification, forgery; counterfeit.
falsificar[6] [fal·si·fi·kár] *v.* to falsify, make false; to

EX

counterfeit; to forge.
falso [fál·so] *adj.* false; untrue, unreal; deceitful; counterfeit; sham; *C.A.* cowardly; *m.* inside facing of a dress; lining; *Mex.* false testimony, slander; **en** — upon a false foundation; without proper security; *Am.* **coger a uno en** — to catch one lying.
falta [fál·ta] *f.* (*defecto*) lack, want; fault, mistake; defect; absence; (*infracción*) misdemeanor, offense; **a — de** for want of; **hacer** — to be necessary; to be missing; **me hace** — I need it; **sin** — without fail.
faltar [fal·tár] *v.* to be lacking, wanting; to be absent or missing; to fail, be of no use or help; to fail to fulfill (*a promise or duty*); to die; *Mex., C.A.* to insult; — **poco para las cinco** to be almost five o'clock; **¡no fáltaba más!** that's the last straw!; why, the very idea!
falto [fál·to] *adj.* lacking; deficient, short; *Am.* foolish, stupid.
faltriquera [fal·tri·ké·ra] *f.* pocket.
falla [fá·ya] *f.* fault, defect; failure; fault (*fracture in the earth's crust*); *Ríopl.* baby's bonnet; **-s** popular *fiestas* of Valencia, Spain.
fallar [fa·yár] *v.* (*juzgar*) to render a verdict; (*fracasar*) to fail, be deficient; to default; to miss; to fail to hit; to give way, break; to trump.
fallecer[13] [fa·ye·sér] *v. irr.* to die.
fallecimiento [fa·ye·si·mjén·to] *m.* decease, death.
fallido [fa·yí·đo] *adj.* frustrated; bankrupt.
fallo [fá·yo] *m.* verdict, judgment; decision; *adj.* lacking (*a card, or suit, in card games*); *Ch.* silly, foolish.
fama [fá·ma] *f.* fame, reputation; rumor, report; *Ch.* bull's-eye, center of a target.
famélico [fa·mé·li·ko] *adj.* ravenous, hungry, starved.
familia [fa·mí·lja] *f.* family.
familiar [fa·mi·ljár] *adj.* domestic, homelike; familiar, well-known; friendly, informal; colloquial (*phrase or expression*); *m.* intimate friend; member of a household; domestic servant; familiar spirit, demon; *Am.* relative.
familiaridad [fa·mi·lja·ri·đáđ] *f.* familiarity, informality.
familiarizar[9] [fa·mi·lja·ri·sár] *v.* to familiarize, acquaint; **-se** to acquaint oneself, become familiar (with).
famoso [fa·mó·so] *adj.* famous; excellent.
fanal [fa·nál] *m.* beacon, lighthouse; lantern; headlight; bell jar, glass cover.
fanático [fa·ná·ti·ko] *adj. & m.* fanatic.
fanatismo [fa·na·tíz·mo] *m.* fanaticism.
fanega [fa·né·ǥa] *f.* Spanish bushel (1.58 bushels); — **de tierra** land measure (1.59 acres).
fanfarrón [fan·fa·rrón] *m.* braggart, boaster; bluffer.
fanfarronada [fan·fa·rro·ná·đa] *f.* boast, brag, swagger, bluff.
fanfarronear [fan·fa·rro·ne·ár] *v.* to bluff, brag; to swagger.
fango [fáŋ·go] *m.* mud, mire.
fangoso [faŋ·gó·so] *adj.* muddy, miry.
fantasear [fan·ta·se·ár] *v.* to fancy; to imagine.
fantasía [fan·ta·sí·a] *f.* fantasy, imagination, fancy, whim; **-s** string of pearls; *Ven.* **tocar por** — to play by ear.
fantasma [fan·táz·ma] *m.* phantom, image; vision, ghost; *f.* scarecrow.
fantasmagórico [fan·taz·ma·ǥó·ri·ko] *adj.* fantastic, unreal, illusory.
fantástico [fan·tás·ti·ko] *adj.* fantastic.
fardel [far·đél] *m.* knapsack, bag; bundle.
fardo [fár·đo] *m.* bundle; bale, *Ríopl., Andes* **pasar el** — to "pass the buck", shift the responsibility to someone else.
faringe [fa·ríŋ·xe] *f.* pharynx.
faríngeo [fa·ríŋ·xe·o] *adj.* pharyngeal.
farmacéutico [far·ma·séw·ti·ko] *m.* pharmacist, druggist; *adj.* pharmaceutical.
farmacia [far·má·sja] *f.* pharmacy; drugstore.
faro [fá·ro] *m.* lighthouse; beacon; *Am.* headlight.
farol [fa·ról] *m.* (*linterna*) lantern; street lamp; (*fachendoso*) conceit, self-importance; *Ríopl.* balcony; *Am.* presumptuous man; *Am.* bluff; **darse** — to show off; to put on airs.
farola [fa·ró·la] *f.* street light; lamppost.
farolero [fa·ro·lé·ro] *adj.* vain, ostentatious; *m.* lamp maker or vendor; lamplighter (*person*).
farra [fá·rra] *f. Ríopl., Ch., Col., Ven., Andes* spree, revelry, wild party, noisy merrymaking; *Ríopl., Ch., Col., Ven., Andes* **ir de** — to go on a spree.
farsa [fár·sa] *f.* farce; company of actors; sham, fraud.
farsante [far·sán·te] *m.* charlatan, bluffer; quack; comedian; wag.
fascinación [fa·si·na·sjón] *f.* fascination; glamour.
fascinador [fa·si·na·đór] *adj.* fascinating, glamorous; charming.
fascinar [fa·si·nár] *v.* to fascinate, bewitch, charm; to allure.
fascismo [fa·síz·mo] *m.* fascism.
fascista [fa·sís·ta] *m. & f.* fascist.
fase [fá·se] *f.* phase, aspect.
fastidiar [fas·ti·đjár] *v.* to annoy, bother; to bore; *Col., P.R.* to hurt, harm, ruin.
fastidio [fas·tí·đjo] *m.* boredom; disgust; nuisance, annoyance.
fastidioso [fas·ti·đjó·so] *adj.* annoying, bothersome; boring, tiresome.
fatal [fa·tál] *adj.* fatal; mortal, deadly; unfortunate.
fatalidad [fa·ta·li·đáđ] *f.* fatality, destiny; calamity, misfortune.
fatalismo [fa·ta·líz·mo] *m.* fatalism.
fatiga [fa·tí·ǥa] *f.* fatigue, weariness; toil; **-s** hardships.
fatigar[7] [fa·ti·ǥár] *v.* to fatigue, weary; to bother.
fatigoso [fa·ti·ǥó·so] *adj.* fatiguing, tiring.
fatuo [fá·two] *adj.* foolish, stupid; vain; **fuego** — will-o'-the-wisp.
favor [fa·ƀór] *m.* favor; kindness; help, aid; protection; *Col.* ribbon bow; **a — de** in favor of; **hágame el** — please.
favorable [fa·ƀo·rá·ƀle] *adj.* favorable.
favorecer[13] [fa·ƀo·re·sér] *v. irr.* to favor, help; protect.
favoritismo [fa·ƀo·ri·tíz·mo] *m.* favoritism.
favorito [fa·ƀo·rí·to] *adj. & m.* favorite.
faz [fas] *f.* face.
fe [fe] *f.* faith; — **de bautismo** baptismal certificate.
fealdad [fe·al·dáđ] *f.* ugliness, homeliness; foulness, foul or immoral action.
febrero [fe·ƀré·ro] *m.* February.
febril [fe·ƀríl] *adj.* feverish.
fécula [fé·ku·la] *f.* starch.
fecundar [fe·kun·dár] *v.* to fertilize.
fecundo [fe·kún·do] *adj.* fruitful, fertile, productive.
fecha [fé·ča] *f.* date.
fechar [fe·čár] *v.* to date.
fechoría [fe·čo·rí·a] *f.* misdeed, misdemeanor.
federación [fe·đe·ra·sjón] *f.* federation, union.
federal [fe·đe·rál] *adj.* federal.
felicidad [fe·li·si·đáđ] *f.* happiness; **¡-es!** congratulations.

felicitación [fe·li·si·ta·sjón] *f.* congratulation.
felicitar [fe·li·si·tár] *v.* to congratulate.
feligrés [fe·li·grés] *m.* parishioner.
feliz [fe·lís] *adj.* happy; lucky.
felpa [fél·pa] *f.* plush.
felpudo [fel·pú·do] *adj.* plushy, like plush; *m.* small plushlike mat; door mat.
femenil [fe·me·níl] *adj.* womanly, feminine.
femenino [fe·me·ní·no] *adj.* feminine.
fementido [fe·men·tí·do] *adj.* false; treacherous.
fenecer[13] [fe·ne·sér] *v. irr.* to die; to finish, end.
fénico [fé·ni·ko] *adj.* carbolic; **acido** — carbolic acid.
fénix [fé·nis] *m.* phoenix (*mythical bird*).
fenómeno [fe·nó·me·no] *m.* phenomenon.
feo [fé·o] *adj.* ugly, homely; *Am., Col.* (*referring to taste or odor*); **feote** [fe·ó·te] *adj.* hideous, very ugly.
féretro [fé·re·tro] *m.* bier; coffin.
feria [fé·rja] *f.* fair; market; *Mex.* change (*money*); *C.A.* tip; **-s** *Am.* present given to servants or the poor during holidays.
feriante [fe·rján·te] *m. & f.* trader at fairs; trader; peddler.
feriar [fe·rjár] *v.* to trade.
fermentar [fer·men·tár] *v.* to ferment.
fermento [fer·mén·to] *m.* ferment; yeast, leaven.
ferocidad [fe·ro·si·dád] *f.* ferocity, fierceness.
feroz [fe·rós] *adj.* ferocious, wild, fierce.
férreo [fé·rre·o] *adj.* ferrous (*pertaining to or derived from iron*); ironlike; harsh; **vía férrea** railroad.
ferretería [fe·rre·te·rí·a] *f.* hardware shop; hardware.
ferrocarril [fe·rro·ka·rríl] *m.* railroad.
ferroso [fe·rró·so] *adj.* iron-like.
ferroviario [fe·rro·bjá·rjo] *adj.* railway, railroad (*used as adj.*); *m.* railroad man; railroad employee.
fértil [fér·til] *adj.* fertile, productive; **fertilidad** [fer·ti·li·dad] *f.* fertility.
fertilizar[9] [fer·ti·li·sár] *v.* to fertilize.
ferviente [fer·bjén·te] *adj.* fervent, ardent.
fervor [fer·bór] *m.* fervor, zeal, devotion.
fervoroso [fer·bo·ró·so] *adj.* fervent, ardent; pious, devout; zealous.
festejar [fes·te·xár] *v.* to feast, entertain; to celebrate; to woo; *Mex.* to thrash, beat.
festejo [fes·té·xo] *m.* entertainment, festival, celebration; courtship; *Ch.* revelry.
festín [fes·tín] *m.* feast; banquet.
festividad [fes·ti·bi·dád] *f.* festival; holiday; holy day; festivity, gaiety, rejoicing.
festivo [fes·tí·bo] *adj.* festive, gay; **día** — holiday.
fétido [fé·ti·do] *adj.* foul, foul-smelling.
fiado [fjá·do] *p.p. of* **fiar; al** — on credit.
fiador [fja·dór] *m.* guarantor, backer, bondsman; *Ec., Ch.* chin strap, hat guard.
fiambre [fjám·bre] *m.* cold meat; cold or late news; *Ríopl., Mex., Col., Ven.* cold meat salad; *Am.* flop, failure (*referring to a party*).
fianza [fján·sa] *f.* bond, security, surety, guarantee; bail.
fiar[17] [fjar] to trust; to guarantee, back; *Am.* to borrow on credit; **-se de** to place confidence in.
fibra [fí·bra] *f.* fiber; wood grain; — **de vidrio** fiber glass; **-s de vidrio trituradas** milled fibers; **fibroso** *adj.* fibrous.
ficción [fik·sjón] *f.* fiction.
ficticio [fik·tí·sjo] *adj.* fictitious.
ficha [fí·ča] *f.* (*pieza*) chip; token; domino; (*tarjeta*) file card; *Am.* check (*used in barbershops and stores*); *Am.* rascal, scamp; **fichero** [fi·čé·ro] *m.* file, card index, filing cabinet.
fidedigno [fi·de·díg·no] *adj.* trustworthy, reliable.
fidelidad [fi·de·li·dád] *f.* fidelity, faithfulness.
fideo [fi·dé·o] *m.* vermicelli, thin noodle; thin person.
fiebre [fjé·bre] *f.* fever; excitement, agitation; *Ch.* astute person.
fiel [fjel] *adj.* faithful; true, accurate; *m.* public inspector; pointer of a balance or scale; pin of the scissors; **los -es** the worshipers, the congregation.
fieltro [fjél·tro] *m.* felt; felt hat; felt rug.
fiera [fjé·ra] *f.* wild beast; *Cuba, Mex.* go-getter, hustler; **ser una — para el trabajo** to be a demon for work.
fiereza [fje·ré·sa] *f.* ferocity, fierceness; cruelty; ugliness.
fiero [fjé·ro] *adj.* fierce, ferocious, wild; cruel; ugly, horrible; huge; *m.* threat; **echar** (*or* **hacer**) **-s** to threaten; to boast.
fierro [fjé·rro] *m. Am.* iron; *Am.* iron bar; *Am.* cattle brand; — **fundido** cast iron; **-s** *Mex.* tools, implements. *See* **hierro.**
fiesta [fjés·ta] *f.* festivity, celebration, entertainment; holiday; **estar de** — to be in a holiday mood; **hacer -s a uno** to fawn on a person.
fiestero [fjes·té·ro] *adj.* fond of parties, fond of entertaining; gay, festive; playful; *m.* merrymaker.
figón [fi·gón] *m.* cheap eating house; "joint."
figura [fi·gú·ra] *f.* figure; shape, form; countenance; face card.
figurado [fi·gu·rá·do] *adj.* figurative.
figurar [fi·gu·rár] *v.* to figure; to form; to represent, symbolize; **-se** to imagine; **se me figura** I think, guess, or imagine.
figurín [fi·gu·rín] *m.* fashion plate; dandy.
fijar [fi·xár] *v.* to fix, fasten; to establish; **-se** to settle; **-se en** to notice, pay attention to.
fijeza [fi·xé·sa] *f.* firmness, solidity, steadiness.
fijo [fí·xo] *adj.* fixed; firm; secure.
fila [fí·la] *f.* row, tier; rank.
filamento [fi·la·mén·to] *m.* filament.
filatelia [fi·la·té·lja] *f.* philately.
filete [fi·lé·te] *m.* (*moldura*) edge, rim; (*carne*) fillet, tenderloin; (*freno*) snaffle bit (*for horses*); hem; screw thread; **en** — fillet welding.
filial [fi·ljál] *adj.* filial.
filigrana [fi·li·grá·na] *f.* filigree.
filmar [fil·már] *v.* to film, screen (*a play or novel*).
filo [fí·lo] *m.* cutting edge; *Andes* hunger; **por** — exactly; *Am.* **de** — resolutely.
filología [fi·lo·lo·xí·a] *f.* philology.
filólogo [fi·ló·lo·go] *m.* philologist.
filón [fi·lón] *m.* seam, layer (*of metallic ore*).
filoso [fi·ló·so] *adj. Am.* sharp, sharp-edged.
filosofía [fi·lo·so·fí·a] *f.* philosophy.
filosófico [fi·lo·só·fi·ko] *adj.* philosophic, philosophical.
filósofo [fi·ló·so·fo] *m.* philosopher.
filtrar [fil·trár] *v.* to filter; **-se** to leak through, leak out; to filter.
filtro [fíl·tro] *m.* filter; — **de aire** air filter.
filudo [fi·lú·do] *adj. Am.* sharp, sharp-edged.
fin [fin] *m.* end, ending; purpose; **al** — at last; **al — y al cabo** at last; anyway; in the end; **a — de que** so that; **a -es del mes** toward the end of the month; **en** — in conclusion; well; in short.
finado [fi·ná·do] *m.* the deceased.
final [fi·nál] *adj.* final.
finalizar[9] [fi·na·li·sár] *v.* to finish; to end.
financiamiento [fi·nan·sja·mjén·to] *m. Am.* financing.
financiar [fi·nan·sjár] *v. Am.* to finance.
financiero [fi·nan·sjé·ro] *adj.* financial; *m.* financier.
financista [fi·nan·sís·ta] *m. Am.* financier.
finanza [fi·nán·sa] *f. Am.* finance; **-s** *Col.* public

FA

treasury, government funds.
finca [fíŋ·ka] *f.* real estate; property; country house; *Mex., C.A., Col., Ven.* ranch, farm.
fincar [fiŋ·kár] *v.* to buy real estate; *Am.* to rest (on), be based (on); *Am.* to build a farmhouse or country house.
fineza [fi·né·sa] *f.* fineness; nicety; courtesy; favor, kindness; present.
fingimiento [fiŋ·xi·mjén·to] *m.* pretense, sham.
fingir[11] [fiŋ·xír] *v.* to feign, pretend, fake; to imagine.
finiquito [fi·ni·kí·to] *m.* settlement (*of an account*); quittance, final receipt; **dar** — to finish up.
fino [fí·no] *adj.* fine; nice; delicate; sharp; subtle; refined.
finura [fi·nú·ra] *f.* fineness; nicety; subtlety; courtesy, good manners.
fiordo [fjór·đo] *m.* fjord.
firma [fír·ma] *f.* signature; firm, firm name.
firmamento [fir·ma·mén·to] *m.* firmament, sky.
firmante [fir·mán·te] *m. & f.* signer.
firmar [fir·már] *v.* to sign.
firme [fír·me] *adj.* firm; solid, hard; **de** — without stopping, hard, steadily.
firmeza [fir·mé·sa] *f.* firmness.
fiscal [fis·kál] *m.* public prosecutor, district attorney; *adj.* fiscal.
fisgar[7] [fiz·ǥár] *v.* to pry; to snoop; to spy on.
fisgón [fiz·ǥón] *m.* snoop, snooper; *adj.* snooping; curious.
fisgonear [fiz·ǥo·ne·ár] *v.* to pry about; to snoop.
física [fí·si·ka] *f.* physics.
físico [fí·si·ko] *adj.* physical; *Ven., Cuba* vain, prudish, affected; *Arg.* real; *m.* physicist.
fisiología [fi·sjo·lo·xía] *f.* physiology.
fisiológico [fi·sjo·ló·xi·ko] *adj.* physiological.
fisionomía [fi·sjo·no·mí·a] *f.* face, features.
flaco [flá·ko] *adj.* lean, skinny; frail, weak; **su lado** — his weak side, his weakness.
flacura [fla·kú·ra] *f.* thinness.
flama [flá·ma] *f.* flame.
flamante [fla·mán·te] *adj.* bright, shiny; brand-new.
flameante [fla·me·án·te] *adj.* flaming, flashing.
flamear [fla·me·ár] *v.* to flame; to flap, flutter (*in the wind*).
flamenco [fla·méŋ·ko] *adj.* Flemish; *C.A., P.R.* skinny; *m.* Flemish, Flemish language; flamingo; Andalusian dance.
flan [flan] *m.* custard.
flanco [fláŋ·ko] *m.* flank, side.
flanquear [flaŋ·ke·ár] *v.* to flank.
flaps [flaps] *m. pl.* flaps (*of an airplane*).
flaquear [fla·ke·ár] *v.* to weaken, flag.
flaqueza [fla·ké·sa] *f.* thinness, leanness; weakness, frailty.
flauta [fláw·ta] *f.* flute; **flautista** [flaw·tís·ta] *m. & f.* flute player; flutist.
fleco [flé·ko] *m.* fringe; bangs, fringe of hair.
flecha [flé·ča] *f.* arrow, dart.
flechar [fle·čár] *v.* to dart, shoot (*an arrow*); to strike, wound or kill with an arrow; to cast an amorous or ardent glance; *Ven.* to prick, sting; *Am.* to burn (*said of the sun*).
flechazo [fle·čá·so] *m.* arrow shot; wound from an arrow.
flema [flé·ma] *f.* phlegm.
flequillos [fle·kí·yos] *m. pl.* bangs.
fletamento [fle·ta·mén·to] *m.* charter, charter party (*of a ship*).
fletar [fle·tár] *v.* to charter (*a ship*); to freight; *Ch.* to hire (*pack animals*); *Peru* to let loose (*strong words*); *Am.* to scatter (*false rumors*); **-se** *Col., Mex., Carib., Ch.* to run away, slip away; *Am.* to slip in uninvited; *Am.* **salir fletado** to leave on the run.
flete [flé·te] *m.* freight, freightage; cargo; load; *Col., Ríopl.* fine horse, race horse; *Arg.* bother, nuisance; *Col., Ven.* **salir sin -s** to leave in a hurry.
flexibilidad [flek·si·ƀi·li·đáđ] *f.* flexibility; **flexible** [flek·sí·ƀle] *adj.* flexible.
flexión [flek·sjón] *f.* bending, bend; sag.
flojear [flo·xe·ár] *v.* to slacken; to weaken; to idle, to be lazy.
flojedad [flo·xe·đáđ] *f.* laxity, looseness; slackness; laziness; slack.
flojera [flo·xé·ra] = **flojedad.**
flojo [fló·xo] *adj.* (*mal atado*) lax; loose, slack; (*sin fuerza*) lazy; weak.
flor [flor] *f.* flower, blossom; compliment; — **de la edad** prime; — **de lis** iris (*flower*); — **y nata** the best, the cream, the chosen few; **a** — **de** flush with; **echar -es** to throw a bouquet; to compliment, flatter.
floreado [flo·re·á·đo] *p.p. & adj.* flowered; made of the finest wheat.
florear [flo·re·ár] *v.* to decorate with flowers; to brandish, flourish; to make a flourish on the guitar; to flatter, compliment; to bolt, sift out (*the finest flour*); *Am.* to flower, bloom; *Ch.* to choose the best; **-se** *C.A.* to shine, excel; *Am.* to burst open like a flower.
florecer[13] [flo·re·sér] *v. irr.* to flower, bloom; to flourish, thrive.
floreciente [flo·re·sjén·te] *adj.* flourishing, thriving; prosperous.
florecimiento [flo·re·si·mjén·to] *m.* flourishing, flowering, bloom.
floreo [flo·ré·o] *m.* flourish; idle talk; flattery, compliment.
florería [flo·re·rí·a] *f.* florist's shop.
florero [flo·ré·ro] *m.* florist; flower vase; flatterer; *adj.* flattering.
floresta [flo·rés·ta] *f.* wooded place, grove; arbor.
florete [flo·ré·te] *m.* fencing foil.
florido [flo·rí·đo] *adj.* flowery.
flota [fló·ta] *f.* fleet; *Col.,* **echar -s** to brag, boast.
flotador [flo·ta·đór] *m.* floater; float; pontoon (*of a hydroplane*); *adj.* floating.
flotante [flo·tán·te] *adj.* floating; *m. Col., Ven.* bluffer, braggart.
flotar [flo·tár] *v.* to float.
flote [fló·te]: **a** — afloat.
fluctuación [fluk·twa·sjón] *f.* fluctuation; wavering, hesitation.
fluctuar[18] [fluk·twár] *v.* to fluctuate; to waver; to hesitate.
fluente [flwén·te] *adj.* fluent, flowing.
fluidez [flwi·đés] *f.* fluidity, easy flow, fluency; **temperatura crítica de** — pour point.
flúido [flú·i·đo] *adj.* fluid, flowing, fluent; *m.* fluid.
fluir[32] [flwir] *v. irr.* to flow.
flujo [flú·xo] *m.* flux; flow; flood tide.
flúor [flú·or] *m.* fluorin.
fluorescente [flwo·re·sén·te] *adj.* fluorescent.
fluoroscopio [flwo·ros·kó·pjo] *m.* fluoroscope.
flux [flus] *f.* flush (*in cards*); *P.R., Col., Ven.* suit of clothes; **hacer** — to use up one's funds, lose everything; *Am.* tener uno — to be lucky.
foca [fó·ka] *f.* seal, sea lion.
foco [fó·ko] *m.* focus, center; *Mex., C.A., Andes* electric-light bulb.

fofo [fó·fo] *adj.* spongy, porous; light (*in weight*); soft.
fogata [fo·ǥá·ta] *f.* fire, blaze, bonfire.
fogón [fo·ǥón] *m.* hearth, fireplace; grill (*for cooking*); vent of a gun; *C.A., Mex.* fire, bonfire; **fogonazo** [fo·ǥo·ná·so] *m.* flash (*of gunpowder*).
fogoso [fo·ǥó·so] *adj.* fiery, ardent; lively, spirited.
follaje [fo·yá·xe] *m.* foliage.
folletín [fo·ye·tín] *m.* small pamphlet; serial story.
folleto [fo·yé·to] *m.* pamphlet.
fomentar [fo·men·tár] *v.* to foment, encourage, promote, foster.
fomento [fo·mén·to] *m.* promotion, encouragement; development; aid.
fonda [fón·da] *f.* inn; restaurant.
fondear [fon·de·ár] *v.* to cast anchor; to sound, make soundings; to search (*a ship*); to sound out; **-se** *Cuba* to save up for the future.
fondero [fon·dé·ro] *m. Am.* innkeeper.
fondillos [fon·dí·yos] *m. pl.* seat of trousers.
fondista [fon·dís·ta] *m. & f.* innkeeper.
fondo [fón·do] *m.* (*hondura*) bottom; depth; background; back, rear end; (*esencia*) nature, heart, inner self; fund; *Cuba, Ven.* underskirt; **-s** funds; **a —** thoroughly; **echar a —** to sink.
fonducho [fon·dú·čo] *m.* cheap eating place.
fonema [fo·né·ma] *m.* phoneme.
fonética [fo·né·ti·ka] *f.* phonetics, study of pronunciation.
fonógrafo [fo·nó·ǥra·fo] *m.* phonograph.
fonología [fo·no·lo·xí·a] *f.* phonology.
foque [fó·ke] *m.* jib (sail).
forajido [fo·ra·xí·đo] *m.* outlaw, fugitive; highwayman, bandit.
foráneo [fo·rá·ne·o] *adj.* foreign; *m.* outsider, stranger.
forastero [fo·ras·té·ro] *m.* stranger; foreigner; outsider; *adj.* foreign.
forcejear [for·se·xe·ár], **forcejar** [for·se·xar] *v.* to struggle; to strive; to oppose, resist.
fórceps [fór·seps] *m.* forceps.
forja [fór·xa] *f.* forge; forging; blacksmith's shop.
forjador [for·xa·đór] *m.* forger (*of metals*); smith, blacksmith; inventor (*of lies, stories, tricks, etc.*).
forjar [for·xár] *v.* to forge; to form, shape; to invent, feign, fake.
forma [fór·ma] *f.* form, shape, figure; manner; format (*size and shape of a book*); (*hostia*) host (*unleavened bread for communion*).
formación [for·ma·sjón] *f.* formation.
formal [for·mál] *adj.* formal; serious, trustworthy, punctual; reliable.
formalidad [for·ma·li·đáđ] *f.* formality; seriousness, reliability; gravity, dignity; punctuality; red tape.
formalismo [for·ma·líz·mo] *m.* formality, red tape (*excess of formalities*); **formalista** [for·ma·lís·ta] *adj.* fond of excessive formalities, fond of red tape.
formalizar[9] [for·ma·li·sár] *v.* to give proper form to; to legalize; to make official; **-se** to settle down, become serious.
formar [for·már] *v.* to form; to shape, mold; **-se** to get into line; to be molded, educated; to take form.
formatear [for·ma·te·ár] *v.* (*computadora*) to format; **formato** *m.* format; **formateo** *m.* formatting.
fórmico [fór·mi·ko] *adj.* formic.
formidable [for·mi·đá·ƀle] *adj.* formidable; fearful.
formón [for·món] *m.* wide chisel; wood chisel.
fórmula [fór·mu·la] *f.* formula.
formular [for·mu·lár] *v.* to formulate, word.
fornido [for·ní·đo] *adj.* stout, strong, sturdy.
foro [fó·ro] *m.* stage; back, rear (*of a stage*); forum, court; bar (*profession of law*).
forraje [fo·rrá·xe] *m.* forage, green grass, fodder, feed.
forrajear [fo·rra·xe·ár] *v.* to forage, gather forage.
forrar [fo·rrár] *v.* to line; to cover, put a sheath, case, or covering on; **-se** *Ríopl., C.A.* to eat well; *Am.* to supply oneself with provisions; *Ríopl., Mex., Cuba* to save money.
forro [fó·rro] *m.* lining; sheathing, casing; covering; book cover.
fortalecer[13] [for·ta·le·sér] *v. irr.* to fortify; to strengthen.
fortaleza [for·ta·lé·sa] *f.* fortress; fortitude; strength, vigor; *Ch.* stench, stink.
fortificación [for·ti·fi·ka·sjón] *f.* fortification; fort.
fortificar[6] [for·ti·fi·kár] *v.* to fortify.
fortuito [for·twí·to] *adj.* fortuitous, accidental, unexpected.
fortuna [for·tú·na] *f.* fortune; fate, chance; wealth; **por —** fortunately.
forzar[9] [for·sár] *v. irr.* to force; to compel; to take (*a fort*); to rape; **— la entrada en** to break into.
forzoso [for·só·so] *adj.* compulsory; necessary.
fosa [fó·sa] *f.* grave; cavity.
fosco [fós·ko] *adj.* dark; cross, irritable, frowning; *see* **hosco.**
fosfato [fos·fá·to] *m.* phosphate.
fosforecer[13] [fos·fo·re·sér], **fosforescer** [fos·fo·re·sér] *v.* to glow.
fósforo [fós·fo·ro] *m.* phosphorus; match.
fósil [fó·sil] *adj. & m.* fossil.
foso [fó·so] *m.* hole, pit; stage pit; ditch.
fotingo [fo·tíŋ·go] *m.* "jalopy".
foto [fó·to] *f.* snapshot.
fotocopia [fo·to·có·pja] *f.* photocopy.
fotoeléctrico [fo·to·e·lék·tri·ko] *adj.* photoelectric.
fotograbado [fo·to·ǥra·ƀá·đo] *m.* photoengraving.
fotografía [fo·to·ǥra·fí·a] *f.* photograph; photography.
fotografiar[17] [fo·to·ǥra·fjár] *v.* to photograph.
fotógrafo [fo·tó·ǥra·fo] *m.* photographer.
fotosíntesis [fo·to·sín·te·sis] *f.* photosynthesis.
fracasado [fra·ka·sá·đo] *adj.* failed; *m.* failure.
fracasar [fra·ka·sár] *v.* to fail; to come to ruin; to crumble to pieces.
fracaso [fra·ká·so] *m.* failure, ruin; calamity; crash.
fracción [frak·sjón] *f.* fraction.
fractura [frak·tú·ra] *f.* fracture; break, crack.
fracturar [frak·tu·rár] *v.* to fracture, break.
fragancia [fra·ǥán·sja] *f.* fragrance, scent, perfume.
fragante [fra·ǥán·te] *adj.* fragrant; **en —** in the act.
fragata [fra·ǥá·ta] *f.* frigate.
frágil [frá·xil] *adj.* fragile, breakable; frail, weak.
fragilidad [fra·xi·li·đáđ] *f.* brittleness.
fragmento [fraǥ·mén·to] *m.* fragment.
fragor [fra·ǥór] *m.* clang, din; crash.
fragoroso [fra·ǥo·ró·so] *adj.* deafening, thunderous.
fragoso [fra·ǥó·so] *adj.* rugged, craggy, rough, uneven; noisy.
fragua [frá·ǥwa] *f.* forge; blacksmith's shop.
fraguar [fra·ǥwár] *v.* to forge; to scheme, hatch (*a plot*).
fraile [fráj·le] *m.* friar; priest; **frailuco** [fraj·lú·ko] *m.* little old friar.
frambuesa [fram·bwé·sa] *f.* raspberry; **frambueso** [fram·bwé·so] *m.* raspberry bush.
francés [fran·sés] *adj.* French; *m.* Frenchman; French language.
franco [fráŋ·ko] *adj.* (*sincero*) frank, open, candid, sincere; (*exento*) free; *m.* franc; **francote** [fraŋ·kó·te] *adj.* very frank, blunt, outspoken.

franela [fra·né·la] *f.* flannel.
franja [fráŋ·xa] *f.* fringe, border; stripe; braid.
franquear [fraŋ·ke·ár] *v.* to exempt; to free; to frank (*a letter*); to dispatch, send; to make grants; — **el paso** to permit the passage (of); **-se** to unbosom oneself, disclose one's innermost thoughts and feelings.
franqueo [fraŋ·ké·o] *m.* postage; franking (*of a letter*); freeing (*of slaves or prisoners*).
franqueza [fraŋ·ké·sa] *f.* frankness; freedom.
franquicia [fraŋ·kí·sja] *f.* franchise, grant, privilege; freedom or exemption (*from fees*).
frasco [frás·ko] *m.* flask, vial, small bottle.
frase [frá·se] *f.* phrase; sentence.
fraternal [fra·ter·nál] *adj.* fraternal, brotherly.
fraternidad [fra·ter·ni·đáđ] *f.* fraternity; brotherhood.
fraude [fráw·đe] *m.* fraud.
fraudulento [fraw·đu·lén·to] *adj.* fraudulent, tricky, deceitful, dishonest.
fray [fraj] *m.* (*contr. of* **fraile** [fráj·le], *used before Christian name*) friar.
frazada [fra·sá·đa] *f.* blanket.
frecuencia [fre·kwén·sja] *f.* frequency; **con** — frequently.
frecuentar [fre·kwen·tár] *v.* to frequent.
frecuente [fre·kwén·te] *adj.* frequent.
fregadero [fre·ǥa·đé·ro] *m.* sink.
fregado [fre·ǥá·đo] *m.* scrub, scrubbing; *p.p. of* **fregar**; *adj. Ch., Andes, Mex.* bothersome, annoying; *Col.* stubborn; *Mex., C.A.* brazen.
fregar[7] [fre·ǥár] *v. irr.* to scour; to scrub; to rub; to wash (*dishes*); *Am.* to molest, annoy.
fregona [fre·ǥó·na] *f.* scrub woman; dishwasher, kitchen maid.
freír[15] [fre·ír] *v. irr.* to fry; to tease, bother.
frenar [fre·nár] *v.* to apply the brakes; to restrain.
frenesí [fre·ne·sí] *m.* frenzy, madness.
frenético [fre·né·ti·ko] *adj.* frantic; furious; in a frenzy.
freno [fré·no] *m.* bridle; brake; control; bit (*for horses*).
frente [frén·te] *f.* forehead; countenance; *m.* front; **en — de** in front of; — **a** in front of, facing; **hacer** — to face.
freón [fre·ón] *m.* freon.
fresa [fré·sa] *f.* strawberry.
fresado [fre·sá·đo] *m.* milling; — **de refrentar** face milling; — **en superficie plana** slab milling.
fresca [frés·ka] *f.* fresh air; fresh remark.
fresco [frés·ko] *adj.* (*bastante frío*) fresh; cool, (*sereno*) calm, serene; (*descarado*) forward, bold; *m.* coolness; cool air; fresco (*painting*); *C.A., Col.* refreshment; **al** — in the open air; **pintura al** — painting in fresco.
frescor [fres·kór] *m.* freshness, coolness.
frescura [fres·kú·ra] *f.* (*temperatura baja*) freshness; coolness; (*serenidad*) calm; freedom; ease; (*insolencia*) boldness, impudence; impudent remark.
fresno [fréz·no] *m.* ash, ash tree.
fresquecillo [fres·ke·sí·yo] *adj.* nice and cool; *m.* cool air, fresh breeze; **fresquecito** [fres·ke·sí·to], **fresquito** [fres·kí·to] *adj.* nice and cool.
frialdad [frjal·dáđ] *f.* coldness; coolness, indifference.
fricativo [fri·ka·tí·ƀo] *adj.* fricative.
fricción [frik·sjón] *f.* friction, rub, rubbing.
friccionar [frik·sjo·nár] *v.* to rub; to massage.
friega [frjé·ǥa] *f.* rub, rubbing; *Am.* bother, nuisance, irritation; *Am.* flogging, beating.
frigorífico [fri·ǥo·rí·fi·ko] *adj.* freezing; *m. Spain* refrigerator, icebox; *Ríopl.* meatpacking house.
frijol [fri·xól] *m.* bean; kidney bean, navy bean.
frío [frí·o] *adj.* cold; frigid; cool, indifferent; *m.* cold; **-s** *Mex.* chills and fever; *Col., C.A., Ven.* malaria.
friolento [frjo·lén·to] *adj.* cold-blooded, sensitive to cold; chilly.
friolera [frjo·lé·ra] *f.* trifle.
fritada [fri·tá·đa] *f.* dish of fried food.
frito [frí·to] *p.p. irr. of* **freír** fried; *m.* fry, dish of fried food.
fritura [fri·tú·ra] *f.* fry, dish of fried food; fritter.
frivolidad [fri·ƀo·li·đáđ] *f.* frivolity; **frívolo** [frí·ƀo·lo] *adj.* frivolous.
fronda [frón·da] *f.* leaf; fern leaf; foliage.
frondoso [fron·dó·so] *adj.* leafy.
frontera [fron·té·ra] *f.* frontier, border; **fronterizo** [fron·te·rí·so] *adj.* frontier (*used as an adj.*); opposite, facing.
frontero [fron·té·ro] *adj.* facing, opposite.
frontis [frón·tis] *m.* façade, front (*of a building*).
frontispicio [fron·tis·pí·sjo] *m.* front, façade (*front of a building*); title page.
frontón [fron·tón] *m.* main wall of a handball court; handball court; jai alai court; game of *pelota*.
frotación [fro·ta·sjón] *f.* friction, rubbing.
frotar [fro·tár] *v.* to rub; to scour.
frote [fró·te] *m.* rubbing; friction.
fructificar[6] [fruk·ti·fi·kár] *v.* to fruit, bear or produce fruit; to yield profit.
fructuoso [fruk·twó·so] *adj.* fruitful.
frugal [fru·ǥál] *adj.* frugal, economical, saving, thrifty; **frugalidad** [fru·ǥa·li·đáđ] *f.* frugality, thrift.
fruncir[10] [frun·sír] *v.* to wrinkle; to gather in pleats; to contract, shrivel; to shir; — **las cejas** to frown; to knit the eyebrows; — **los labios** to purse or curl the lips.
fruslería [fruz·le·rí·a] *f.* trifle, trinket.
frustración [frus·tra·sjón] *f.* frustration; failure.
frustrar [frus·trár] *v.* to frustrate, thwart, foil; **-se** to fail, be thwarted.
fruta [frú·ta] *f.* fruit; **frutería** [fru·te·rí·a] *f.* fruit store.
frutero [fru·té·ro] *m.* fruit vendor; fruit dish; *adj.* fruit (*used as adj.*); **buque** — fruit boat; **plato** — fruit dish.
fruto [frú·to] *m.* fruit (*any organic product of the earth*); result; benefit, profit.
¡fuche! [fú·če] *interj. Mex.* phew! ugh! pew! phooey!
fuego [fwé·ǥo] *m.* (*incendio*) fire; (*pasión*) passion; (*erupción*) skin eruption; *Am.* cold sore; **-s artificiales** fireworks; **hacer** — to fire, shoot; **estar hecho un** — to be very angry; **romper** — to begin to fire, start shooting.
fuelle [fwé·ye] *m.* (*instrumento*) bellows; (*arruga*) pucker, wrinkle, fold; (*hablador*) tattletale, windbag, gossiper.
fuente [fwén·te] *f.* fountain; source, origin; spring; platter, serving dish; — **de alimentación** (*computadora*) power supply (source).
fuera [fwé·ra] *adv.* outside, out; — **de** *prep.* outside of; in addition to.
fuereño [fwe·ré·ño] *m. Mex., Ven., Andes* outsider, stranger.
fuero [fwé·ro] *m.* law, statute; power, jurisdiction; code of laws; exemption, privilege.
fuerte [fwér·te] *adj.* (*robusto*) strong; loud; secure, fortified; (*grave*) grave, serious; (*áspero*) excessive; *Ch.* stinking; *m.* fort; forte, strong point; forte (*music*); *Mex.* alcohol, liquor; *adv.* strongly; excessively; loud; hard.
fuerza [fwér·sa] *f.* force; power, strength; violence;

compulsion; **a — de** by dint of; **a la — (por —, por la —, de por —,** *Am.* **de —)** by force, forcibly; necessarily; **ser —** to be necessary.
fuete [fwé·te] *m. Col., Cuba, Ríopl., Mex., Ven., Andes* whip; **fuetazo** [fwe·tá·so] *m. Am.* lash.
fuga [fú·ga] *f.* flight, escape; leak, leakage; fugue (*musical composition*).
fugarse[7] [fu·gár·se] *v.* to flee, escape.
fugaz [fu·gás] *adj.* fleeing; fleeting, brief, passing.
fugitivo [fu·xi·tí·bo] *adj.* fugitive; fleeting, passing; perishable; *m.* fugitive.
fulano [fu·lá·no] *m.* so-and-so (*referring to person*).
fulgor [ful·gór] *m.* radiance, brilliance.
fulgurar [ful·gu·rár] *v.* to gleam, flash, shine.
fulminar [ful·mi·nár] *v.* to thunder, thunder forth; to utter (*threats*).
fulo [fú·lo] *m. Pan.* blond.
fullero [fu·yé·ro] *m.* cardsharp; crooked gambler; cheat.
fumada [fu·má·da] *f.* puff, whiff (*of smoke*).
fumadero [fu·ma·dé·ro] *m.* smoking room.
fumador [fu·ma·dór] *m.* smoker, habitual smoker.
fumar [fu·már] *v.* to smoke (*tobacco*); *Am.* **-se a uno** to swindle or cheat someone.
fumigar[7] [fu·mi·gár] *v.* to fumigate.
función [fun·sjón] *f.* (*actividad*) function; functioning; (*empleo*) office; occupation; (*espectáculo*) show, performance; religious festival.
funcionamiento [fun·sjo·na·mjén·to] *m.* functioning, action, working, operation.
funcionar [fun·sjo·nár] *v.* to function, to work, run (*said of machines*).
funcionario [fun·sjo·ná·rjo] *m.* public employee, officer or official.
funda [fún·da] *f.* cover, case; *Col.* skirt; **— de almohada** pillowcase.
fundación [fun·da·sjón] *f.* foundation.
fundador [fun·da·dór] *m.* founder.
fundamental [fun·da·men·tál] *adj.* fundamental.
fundamento [fun·da·mén·to] *m.* foundation, groundwork; basis; *Col.* skirt.
fundar [fun·dár] *v.* to found, establish; to erect; to base, ground.
fundición [fun·di·sjón] *f.* foundry; smelting.
fundido [fun·dí·do] *adj.* molten.
fundir [fun·dír] *v.* to smelt, fuse, melt; to cast, mold; *Am.* to ruin; **-se** to fuse, melt together; to unite; *Ríopl., Mex.* to be ruined.
fundo [fún·do] *m. Ch.* farm, country estate; property, land.
fúnebre [fú·ne·bre] *adj.* funeral; funereal, gloomy, dismal.
funeral [fu·ne·rál] *adj. & m.* funeral.
funeraria [fu·ne·rá·rja] *f.* undertaking establishment, funeral parlor.
funesto [fu·nés·to] *adj.* ill-fated, unlucky; sad, unfortunate.
fungosidad [fuŋ·go·si·dád] *f.* fungus, fungous growth.
funicular [fu·ni·ku·lár] *adj. & m.* funicular.
furgón [fur·gón] *m.* freight car, boxcar; baggage car; **furgonada** [fur·go·ná·da] *f.* carload.
furia [fú·rja] *f.* fury, rage; speed.
furibundo [fu·ri·bún·do] *adj.* furious.
furioso [fu·rjó·so] *adj.* furious.
furor [fu·rór] *m.* fury, rage, anger; frenzy.
furtivo [fur·tí·bo] *adj.* furtive, sly, secret.
fuselaje [fu·se·lá·xe] *m.* fuselage (*of an airplane*).
fusible [fu·sí·ble] *adj.* fusible; *m.* electric fuse.
fusil [fu·síl] *m.* gun, rifle.
fusilar [fu·si·lár] *v.* to shoot, execute.
fusión [fu·sjón] *f.* fusion; melting; **— nuclear** nuclear fusion; **punto de —** melting point.
fustigar[7] [fus·ti·gár] *v.* to lash, whip; to censure severely, scold sharply.
fútbol [fú·bol] *m.* soccer.
fútil [fú·til] *adj.* futile, useless; trivial; **futilidad** [fu·ti·li·dád] *f.* futility, uselessness.
futuro [fu·tú·ro] *adj.* future; *m.* fiancé, future husband; future.

G:g

gabacho [ga·bá·čo] *adj.* from or of the Pyrenees; Frenchlike; foreigner; *m.* Frenchman (*used depreciatively*); *Am.* **me salió —** it turned out wrong.
gabán [ga·bán] *m.* overcoat.
gabeta [ga·bé·ta] = **gaveta.**
gabinete [ga·bi·né·te] *m.* cabinet (*of a government*); studio; study, library room; dressing room; sitting room; private room; dentist's office; laboratory; *Am.* glassed-in **mirador.**
gablete [ga·blé·te] *m.* (*techo de dos aguas*) gable.
gaceta [ga·sé·ta] *f.* gazette, official newspaper; professional periodical; *Col.* any newspaper.
gacetilla [ga·se·tí·ya] *f.* short newspaper article; column of short news items; gossip column; *m. & f.* newsmonger, tattletale; **gacetillero** [ga·se·ti·yé·ro] *m.* newspaper reporter; newsmonger.
gacha [gá·ča] *f.* watery mass or mush; *Col.* china or earthenware bowl; **-s** porridge, mush; caresses; **-s de avena** oatmeal.
gacho [gá·čo] *adj.* drooping; bent downward; turned down; stooping; slouching; with horns curved downward; **sombrero —** slouch hat; **a gachas** on all fours; **con las orejas gachas** with drooping ears; crestfallen, discouraged.
gachupín [ga·ču·pín] *m. Mex.* Spaniard (generally derogatory).
gafas [gá·fas] *f. pl.* spectacles; grappling hooks.
gaita [gáj·ta] *f.* flageolet, a kind of flute; *Mex.* good-for-nothing, lazy bum; **— gallega** bagpipe; **sacar la —** to stick out one's neck; **gaitero** [gaj·té·ro] *m.* piper, bagpipe player.
gaje [gá·xe] *m.* fee; **-s** wages, salary; fees.
gajo [gá·xo] *m.* broken branch; bunch.
gala [gá·la] *f.* elegance; full dress or uniform; ostentation; *Am.* award, prize, tip; **-s** finery, regalia, best clothes; **-s de novia** trousseau; **hacer — de** to boast of.
galán [ga·lán] *m.* gallant, lover; leading man (*in a play*).
galante [ga·lán·te] *adj.* gallant, attentive to ladies; polite.
galanteador [ga·lan·te·a·dór] *m.* gallant, lady's man; flatterer.
galantear [ga·lan·te·ár] *v.* to court, woo; to make love.
galanteo [ga·lan·té·o] *m.* wooing, courtship.
galantería [ga·lan·te·rí·a] *f.* gallantry, compliment, attention to ladies; courtesy; gracefulness; generosity.
galardón [ga·lar·dón] *m.* recompense, reward.
galeote [ga·le·ó·te] *m.* galley slave.
galera [ga·lé·ra] *f.* galley; large wagon; women's jail; printer's galley; *Mex.* jail; *Ch., Ríopl.* tall hat.
galerada [ga·le·rá·da] *f.* galley, galley proof; wagon load, van load.
galería [ga·le·rí·a] *f.* gallery; corridor.
galgo [gál·go] *m.* greyhound; *adj. Col.* gluttonous,

always hungry.
galicismo [ga·li·síz·mo] *m.* gallicism.
galillo [ga·lí·yo] *m.* uvula.
galio [gá·ljo] *m.* gallium.
galón [ga·lón] *m.* galloon, braid, trimming; gallon.
galoneado [ga·lo·ne·á·đo] *adj.* gallooned, trimmed with braid.
galopada [ga·lo·pá·đa] *f.* gallop; **pegar una —** to break into a gallop.
galopar [ga·lo·pár] *v.* to gallop.
galope [ga·ló·pe] *m.* gallop; **a (al** *or* **de) —** at a gallop; speedily.
galopear [ga·lo·pe·ár] = **galopar.**
galpón [gal·pón] *m. Ríopl., Andes* large open shed.
galvanómetro [gal·ƀa·nó·me·tro] *m.* galvanometer.
gallardete [ga·yar·đé·te] *m.* streamer.
gallardía [ga·yar·đí·a] *f.* elegance; gracefulness; bravery.
gallardo [ga·yár·đo] *adj.* elegant, graceful; brave.
gallego [ga·yé·ǥo] *adj.* Galician, from or of Galicia, Spain; *m.* Galician; *Carib., Ríopl.* Spaniard (*used as a nickname*).
galleta [ga·yé·ta] *f.* cracker; hardtack, hard biscuit; hard cookie; blow, slap; small pot; *Ríopl.* bread of coarse meal or bran; *Ch.* reproof; *Mex., Arg.* **colgarle la — a uno** to fire, dismiss someone; *Am.* **tener —** to have strength, muscle.
gallina [ga·yí·na] *f.* hen; *m. & f.* chickenhearted person.
gallinero [ga·yi·né·ro] *m.* chicken coop, house, or yard; flock of chickens; basket for carrying chickens; poultryman; noisy gathering; top gallery of a theater.
gallo [gá·yo] *m.* cock, rooster; (*agresivo*) aggressive, bossy, person; cork float; false note (*in singing*); frog (*in one's throat*); *Am.* secondhand clothing; *Am.* fire wagon; *Mex., Ríopl.* serenade.
gama [gá·ma] *f.* gamut.
gamba [gám·ba] *f. Spain* large shrimp.
gamo [gá·mo] *m.* buck, male deer.
gamonal [ga·mo·nál] *m. Am.* boss; overseer.
gamuza [ga·mú·sa] *f.* chamois, chamois skin.
gana [gá·na] *f.* desire, appetite; **de buena (mala) —** willingly (unwillingly); **tener —** (*or* **-s**) to feel like, want to; **no me da la —** I don't want to.
ganadero [ga·na·đé·ro] *m.* cattleman; cattle dealer; *adj.* cattle, pertaining to cattle.
ganado [ga·ná·đo] *m.* cattle; herd; livestock; **— mayor** cattle; horses; mules; **— menor** sheep; **— de cerda** swine.
ganador [ga·na·đór] *m.* winner; *adj.* winning.
ganancia [ga·nán·sja] *f.* profit, gain; *Am.* something to boot, something extra.
ganancioso [ga·nan·sjó·so] *adj.* winning; profitable; *m.* winner.
ganar [ga·nár] *v.* to win; to profit, gain; to earn; to get ahead of.
gancho [gán·čo] *m.* hook; hooked staff; *Mex., Cuba, Ríopl., Col., C.A.* hairpin; *Am.* bait, lure, trick; *Arg.* bonus; **aguja de —** crochet hook; **echar a uno el —** to hook someone; **tener —** to be attractive, alluring.
gandul [gan·dúl] *m.* bum, loafer.
ganga [gáŋ·ga] *f.* bargain; snap, easy job; kind of prairie hen.
gangoso [gaŋ·gó·so] *adj.* twangy, nasal (*voice*).
gangrena [gaŋ·gré·na] *f.* gangrene.
gangrenar [gaŋ·gre·nár] *v.* to gangrene, cause gangrene; **-se** to gangrene.
ganguear [gaŋ·ge·ár] *v.* to talk "through the nose."
ganoso [ga·nó·so] *adj.* desirous; *Am.* lively, spirited (*horse*).
ganso [gán·so] *m.* goose, gander; lazy, slovenly person; dunce.
ganzúa [gan·sú·a] *f.* hook; picklock (*tool for picking locks*); *m. & f.* burglar.
garabato [ga·ra·ƀá·to] *m.* hook; scrawl, scribble; **hacer -s** to scribble, write poorly.
garaje [ga·rá·xe] *m.* garage.
garantía [ga·ran·tí·a] *f.* guarantee; security; bail, bond.
garantizar[9] [ga·ran·ti·sár] *v.* to guarantee, vouch for.
garañón [*ga·ra·ñón*] *m.* jackass, male ass; male camel (*for breeding*); *Ríopl., Mex., C.A.* stallion.
garapiñar [*ga·ra·pi·ñár*] *v.* to candy (*almonds, fruits, etc.*); to decorate (cake).
garbanzo [gar·ƀán·so] *m.* chickpea.
garbo [gár·ƀo] *m.* elegance, graceful air, good carriage.
garboso [gar·ƀó·so] *adj.* graceful; elegant; sprightly.
garduña [gar·đú·ña] *f.* marten.
garfio [gár·fjo] *m.* hook.
garganta [gar·ǥán·ta] *f.* throat, neck; gorge, ravine; **gargantilla** [gar·ǥan·tí·ya] *f.* necklace.
gárgara [gár·ǥa·ra] *f.* gargling; **-s** *Am.* gargle, gargling solution; **hacer -s** to gargle.
gargarear [gar·ǥa·re·ár] *v. Am.* to gargle.
gargarismo [gar·ǥa·ríz·mo] *m.* gargling; gargle, gargling solution.
gargarizar[9] [gar·ǥa·ri·sár] *v.* to gargle.
garita [ga·rí·ta] *f.* sentry box; watchman's booth; *Col.* vendor's booth.
garito [ga·rí·to] *m.* gambling house, gambling joint; gambler's winnings.
garra [gá·rra] *f.* claw, paw; hook; *Mex.* strength; *Col.* leather or cloth remnant; *Col.* skinny person or animal; *Am.* margin of profit in a business deal; **echar la —** to arrest; to grab; *Mex., C.A., Ven., Andes* **hacer -s** to tear to pieces.
garrafa [ga·rrá·fa] *f.* decanter; **garrafón** [ga·rra·fón] *m.* large decanter; demijohn.
garrapata [ga·rra·pá·ta] *f.* tick (*an insect*).
garrapatear [ga·rra·pa·te·ár] *v.* to scribble, scrawl, write poorly.
garrocha [ga·rró·ča] *f.* pole; iron-pointed staff; **salto de —** pole vault; *Mex.* goad (*for goading oxen*).
garrote [ga·rró·te] *m.* club, cudgel, heavy stick; *Mex., Ríopl., C.A.* brake; **dar —** to strangle; *Mex.* to brake, set the brakes; **garrotazo** [ga·rro·tá·so] *m.* blow with a club; huge stick.
garrotero [ga·rro·té·ro] *m. Mex., Ven.* brakeman; *Am.* beater (*one who beats with a club*); *adj. Am.* stingy.
garrucha [ga·rrú·ča] *f.* pulley.
garúa [ga·rú·a] *f. C.A., Ríopl., Ven., Andes* drizzle.
garza [gár·sa] *f.* heron; egret.
garzo [gár·so] *adj.* blue, bluish; blue-eyed.
gas [gas] *m.* gas, vapor; *Col., Ríopl., Ven.* gasoline; **— lacrimógeno** tear gas.
gasa [gá·sa] *f.* gauze.
gaseosa [ga·se·ó·sa] *f.* soda water; soda pop.
gaseoso [ga·se·ó·so] *adj.* gaseous.
gasolina [ga·so·lí·na] *f.* gasoline.
gastador [gas·ta·đór] *adj.* lavish, extravagant, wasteful; *m.* spendthrift, lavish spender.
gastar [gas·tár] *v.* to spend; to wear; to use; to waste; **-se** to wear out; to get old.
gasto [gás·to] *m.* expense, expenditure; wear.
gatas [gá·tas] **a —** on all fours; **andar a —** to creep, crawl; **salir a —** to crawl out of a difficulty.
gateado [ga·te·á·đo] *adj.* catlike; veined, streaked; *m. Am.* light-colored horse with black streaks.

gatear [ga·te·ár] *v.* to creep, crawl; to walk on all fours; to claw, scratch; to steal.
gatillo [ga·tí·yo] *m.* kitten; trigger; forceps (*for extracting teeth*); petty thief.
gato [gá·to] *m.* cat; moneybag; jack (*for lifting weights*); sneak thief; sly fellow; *Am.* trigger; *Perú* outdoor market; *Ch.* hot-water bottle; *Ríopl.* a gaucho song and tap dance (*by extension,* the dancer); *Arg.* blunder.
gatuperio [ga·tu·pé·rjo] *m.* fraud, intrigue.
gauchada [gaw·čá·đa] *f. Ríopl.* gaucho deed or exploit.
gauchaje [gaw·čá·xe] *m. Ríopl.* band of Gauchos, Gaucho folk.
gauchesco [gaw·čés·ko] *adj. Am.* relating to Gauchos.
gaucho [gáw·čo] *m. Am.* Gaucho, Argentine and Uruguayan cowboy; *Ríopl., Ven.* good horseman; *adj. Am.* relating to Gauchos, Gaucho-like; *Ríopl.* sly, crafty.
gaveta [ga·ƀé·ta] *f.* drawer.
gavilla [ga·ƀí·ya] *f.* sheaf; gang, band (*of rogues, thieves, etc.*).
gaviota [ga·ƀjó·ta] *f.* sea gull.
gaza [gá·sa] *f.* loop; *Carib.* noose of a lasso.
gazmoñería [gaz·mo·ñe·rí·a] *f.* prudery, affected modesty; **gazmoño** [gaz·mó·ño] *adj.* prudish, affected, coy.
gaznate [gaz·ná·te] *m.* windpipe; a kind of fritter; *Andes* a sweetmeat made a pineapple or coconut.
gazpacho [gas·pá·čo] *m. Spain* cold vegetable soup.
gela (*resina coloide coagulada*) [xé·la] *f.* gel (*fiber glass*); **gela-capa** gel-coat.
gelatina [xe·la·tí·na] *f.* gelatin; jelly; — **de caldo de tomate** aspic.
gema [xé·ma] *f.* gem, jewel; bud.
gemelo [xe·mé·lo] *m.* twin; **-s** twins; binoculars, opera glasses, field glasses; cuff links.
gemido [xe·mí·đo] *m.* moan; wail, cry.
gemir[5] [xe·mír] *v. irr.* to moan; to wail, cry.
gendarme [xen·dár·me] *m. Mex., Ven., Ríopl., C.A.* policeman; (now less used than *policía, agente*).
genealogía [xe·ne·a·lo·xí·a] *f.* genealogy.
generación [xe·ne·ra·sjón] *f.* generation.
generador [xe·ne·ra·đór] *m.* generator; — **molecular** atom smasher.
general [xe·ne·rál] *adj. & m.* general; **por lo** — generally.
generalidad [xe·ne·ra·li·đáđ] *f.* generality; majority.
generalizar[9] [xe·ne·ra·li·sár] *v.* to generalize; **-se** to spread, become general.
genérico [xe·né·ri·ko] *adj.* generic.
género [xé·ne·ro] *m.* (*clase*) kind, sort, class; gender; (*tela*) goods, material, cloth; — **humano** human race.
generosidad [xe·ne·ro·si·đáđ] *f.* generosity.
generoso [xe·ne·ró·so] *adj.* generous; best (*wine*).
genial [xe·njál] *adj.* genial, jovial, pleasant.
genio [xé·njo] *m.* genius; temperament, disposition; spirit.
gente [xén·te] *f.* (*personas*) people; crowd; (*pueblo*) race, nation; clan; *Am.* — **bien** upper-class or important person; *Am.* **ser** — to be a somebody; to be cultured; to be socially important.
gentil [xen·tíl] *adj.* graceful; genteel; courteous; gentile; *m.* pagan; gentile.
gentileza [xen·ti·lé·sa] *f.* grace, courtesy; nobility; gavor.
gentilicio [xen·ti·lí·sjo] *adj.* national; *m.* name used to identify national or local origin.
gentío [xen·tí·o] *m.* crowd, throng.
gentuza [xen·tú·sa] *f.* rabble.
genuino [xe·nwí·no] *adj.* genuine.
geofísica [xe·o·fí·si·ka] *f.* geophysics.
geografía [xe·o·ǥra·fí·a] *f.* geography; **geográfico** [xe·o·ǥrá·fi·ko] *adj.* geographical.
geología [xe·o·lo·xí·a] *f.* geology; **geológico** [xe·o·ló·xi·ko] *adj.* geological.
geometría [xe·o·me·trí·a] *f.* geometry; **geométrico** [xe·o·mé·tri·ko] *adj.* geometric.
geranio [xe·rá·njo] *m.* geranium.
gerencia [xe·rén·sja] *f.* management, administration.
gerente [xe·rén·te] *m.* manager.
germen [xér·men] *m.* germ; origin, source.
germinar [xer·mi·nár] *v.* to germinate.
gerundio [xe·rún·djo] *m.* gerund; present participle.
gesticular [xes·ti·ku·lár] *v.* to gesticulate.
gestión [xes·tjón] *f.* action, step, maneuver; intervention; **-es** negotiations.
gestionar [xes·tjo·nár] *v.* to manage; to take steps; to negotiate or carry out (*a deal, transaction, etc.*); (*computadora*) to control.
gesto [xés·to] *m.* face, expression; grimace; gesture; **estar de buen** (*or* **mal**) — to be in a good (*or* bad) humor; **hacer -s a** to make faces at.
giba [xí·ƀa] *f.* hump, hunch.
gigante [xi·ǥán·te] *adj.* gigantic; *m.* giant.
gigantesco [xi·ǥan·tés·ko] *adj.* gigantic.
gimnasia [xim·ná·sja] *f.* gymnastics; **gimnasio** [xim·ná·sjo] *m.* gymnasium; German institute (*for secondary instruction*).
gimotear [xi·mo·te·ár] *v.* to whimper, whine.
gimoteo [xi·mo·té·o] *m.* whimper, whining.
ginebra [xi·né·ƀra] *f.* gin (*liquor*).
ginecología [xi·ne·ko·lo·xí·a] *f.* gynecology.
gira [xí·ra] *f.* excursion, tour; outing, picnic.
girador [xi·ra·đór] *m.* drawer (*of a check or draft*).
girar [xi·rár] *v.* to revolve, rotate, whirl; to send, issue, or draw (*checks, drafts, etc.*); to manage (*a business*).
girasol [xi·ra·sól] *m.* sunflower.
giratorio [xi·ra·tó·rjo] *adj.* rotary, revolving.
giro [xí·ro] *m.* (*movimiento circular*) rotation; bend, turn; (*dirección*) direction, trend; (*estructura*) turn of phrase; (*monetario*) draft; — **postal** money order; *adj.* yellowish (*rooster*); *Am.* black and white (*rooster*); *Am.* cocky.
gitano [xi·tá·no] *adj.* gypsy; gypsylike; sly, clever; *m.* gypsy.
gitomate [xi·to·má·te] *Mex.* = **jitomate.**
glacial [gla·sjál] *adj.* glacial, icy, very cold.
glaciar [gla·sjár] *m.* glacier.
glándula [glán·du·la] *f.* gland.
glasear [gla·se·ár] *v.* to glaze (*paper, fruits, etc.*), make glossy.
glaucoma [glaw·kó·ma] *m.* glaucoma.
globo [gló·ƀo] *m.* globe, sphere; world; balloon.
glóbulo [gló·ƀu·lo] *m.* globule; corpuscle.
gloria [gló·rja] *f.* glory; gloria (*song of praise to God*).
gloriarse[17] [glo·rjár·se] *v.* to glory (in), delight (in), be proud (of); to boast (of).
glorieta [glo·rjé·ta] *f.* arbor, bower; secluded nook in a park (*with benches*); traffic circle.
glorificar[6] [glo·ri·fi·kár] *v.* to glorify; **-se** to glory (in), take great pride (in).
glorioso [glo·rjó·so] *m.* glorious.
glosa [gló·sa] *f.* gloss.
glosar [glo·sár] *v.* to gloss, comment upon, explain (*a text*).
glosario [glo·sá·rjo] *m.* glossary.
glotal [glo·tál] *adj.* glottal.
glotis [gló·tis] *f.* glottis.

glotón [glo·tón] *adj.* gluttonous; *m.* glutton.
glotonería [glo·to·ne·rí·a] *f.* gluttony.
gobernador [go·ƀer·na·đór] *adj.* governing; *m.* governor, ruler.
gobernante [go·ƀer·nán·te] *adj.* governing, ruling; *m.* governor, ruler.
gobernar[1] [go·ƀer·nár] *v. irr.* to govern, rule; to lead, direct; to steer (*a boat*).
gobierno [go·ƀjér·no] *m.* government; management; control; helm, rudder.
goce [gó·se] *m.* enjoyment; joy.
goleta [go·lé·ta] *f.* schooner, sailing vessel.
golfo [gól·fo] *m.* gulf; open sea; faro (*gambling game*); vagabond, bum, ragamuffin.
golondrina [go·lon·drí·na] *f.* swallow; swallow fish.
golosina [go·lo·sí·na] *f.* sweet, dainty, tidbit; trifle; appetite, desire.
goloso [go·ló·so] *adj.* sweet-toothed, fond of sweets; gluttonous.
golpazo [gol·pá·so] *m.* bang, whack, heavy blow, hard knock.
golpe [gól·pe] *m.* blow, hit, stroke; knock; beat; *Col.* facing (*of a garment*); *Mex.* sledge hammer; — **de fortuna** stroke of good luck; — **de gente** crowd, throng; — **de gracia** death blow; finishing stroke; **de** — suddenly; **de un** — all at once; **pestillo de** — spring latch; *Am.* **al** — instantly, at once; *Am.* **al** — **de vista** at one glance.
golpear [gol·pe·ár] *v.* to strike, hit; to knock; to beat; *Mex.* to knock at a door.
golpetear [gol·pe·te·ár] *v.* to tap, knock or pound continuously; to flap; to rattle.
golpeteo [gol·pe·té·o] *m.* tapping, pounding, knocking; flapping; rattling.
gollería [go·ye·rí·a] *f.* dainty, delicacy; superfluous thing.
goma [gó·ma] *f.* gum; rubber; elastic; eraser; tire; — **de repuesto** spare tire; *Am.* **estar de** — to have a hang-over (*after excessive drinking*).
gomero [go·mé·ro] *adj.* rubber, pertaining to rubber; *m. Ríopl.* gum or rubber tree; *S.A.* rubber producer; *S.A.* rubber-plantation worker; *Mex., Ch., Ven.* glue container or bottle.
gomífero [go·mí·fe·ro] *adj.* rubber-bearing, rubber-producing.
gomoso [go·mó·so] *adj.* gummy, sticky; *m.* dandy.
gordiflón [gor·đi·flón] *adj.* fat; chubby.
gordo [gór·đo] *adj.* fat; plump; *m.* suet, fat; **gorda** [gór·đa] *f. Mex.* thick tortilla or cornmeal cake; **se armo la gorda** all hell broke loose; there was a big rumpus.
gordura [gor·đú·ra] *f.* fatness; stoutness; fat.
gorgojo [gor·ǥó·xo] *m.* weevil; (*persona*) puny person; *Am.* wood borer, wood louse; **gorgojoso** *adj.* infested with weevils.
gorila [go·rí·la] *m.* gorilla.
gorjeador [gor·xe·a·đór] *m.* warbler; *adj.* warbling; **pájaro** — warbler.
gorjear [gor·xe·ár] *v.* to warble; to chirp.
gorjeo [gor·xé·o] *m.* warble; warbling.
gorra [gó·rra] *f.* cap; bonnet; **de** — at another's expense; **vivir de** — to sponge, live at another's expense.
gorrino [go·rrí·no] *m.* sucking pig.
gorrión [go·rrjón] *m.* sparrow.
gorro [gó·rro] *m.* cap; bonnet.
gorrón [go·rrón] *m.* sponge, parasite; bum; rake (*dissolute fellow*).
gota [gó·ta] *f.* (*líquido*) drop; (*enfermedad*) gout; **sudar la** — **gorda** to sweat profusely, toil, work hard.
gotear [go·te·ár] *v.* to drip; to leak; to dribble, trickle; to sprinkle, begin to rain; **-se** to leak.
goteo [go·té·o] *m.* trickle, drip.
gotera [go·té·ra] *f.* leak, hole (*in the roof*); eaves, trough; **-s** *Mex.* surroundings, outskirts.
gotero [go·té·ro] *m. Carib., Mex.* dropper (*for counting drops*).
gótico [gó·ti·ko] *adj.* Gothic; *m.* Goth; Gothic language.
gozar[9] [go·sár] *v.* to enjoy; to possess, have; **-se** to rejoice.
gozne [góz·ne] *m.* hinge.
gozo [gó·so] *m.* pleasure, joy.
gozoso [go·só·so] *adj.* joyful, glad, merry.
gozque, [gós·ke] **gozquejo,** [gos·ké·xo] **gozquecillo** [gos·ke·sí·yo] *m.* a small dog.
grabación [gra·ƀa·sjón] *f.* recording (*tape*).
grabado [gra·ƀá·đo] *adj.* engraved; recorded; *m.* engraving; woodcut, print; — **al agua fuerte** etching.
grabadora [gra·ƀa·đó·ra] *f.* tape recorder; *Spain* **grabadora magnetofónica.**
grabar [gra·ƀár] *v.* to engrave; to carve; to fix, impress; to record on tape; — **al agua fuerte** to etch.
gracejada [gra·se·xá·đa] *f. C.A.* clownish act or expression.
gracejo [gra·sé·xo] *m.* grace; cuteness; humor, wit.
gracia [grá·sja] *f.* (*humorismo*) witty remark; joke; humor; (*garbo*) grace; gracious act; (*favor*) favor; pardon; **caer en** — to please; **hacer** — to amuse, make (*someone*) laugh; **¡-s!** thanks!; **dar -s** to thank.
gracioso [gra·sjó·so] *adj.* (*chistoso*) amusing; funny; witty; (*con garbo*) graceful, attractive; *m.* comedian, clown.
grada [grá·đa] *f.* step of a staircase; harrow; **-s** steps; seats of an amphitheater; bleachers.
gradación [gra·đa·sjón] *f.* gradation.
gradería [gra·đe·rí·a] *f.* series of steps; rows of seats (*in an amphitheater or stadium*); — **cubierta** grandstand; **-s** bleachers.
grado [grá·đo] *m.* (*medida*) degree; step; (*título*) degree; **de (buen)** — willingly, with pleasure; **de mal** — unwillingly; **de** — **en** — by degrees, gradually.
graduación [gra·đwa·sjón] *f.* graduation; military rank.
gradual [gra·đwál] *adj.* gradual; *m.* response sung at mass.
graduar[18] [gra·đwár] *v.* to graduate, give a diploma, rank or degree to; to gauge; to classify, grade; **-se** to graduate, take a degree.
gráfico [grá·fi·ko] *adj.* graphic; vivid, lifelike; **gráfica** *f.* graph, diagram, chart.
grafito [gra·fí·to] *m.* graphite.
grajo [grá·xo] *m.* rook; crow.
grama [grá·ma] *f.* grama grass.
gramática [gra·má·ti·ka] *f.* grammar; **gramatical** [gra·ma·ti·kál] *adj.* grammatical; **gramático** [gra·má·ti·ko] *adj.* grammatical; *m.* grammarian.
gramo [grá·mo] *m.* gram.
gran [gran] *contr. of* **grande.**
grana [grá·na] *f.* cochineal, kermes (*insects used for producing a red dye*); scarlet color; scarlet cloth; any small seed.
granada [gra·ná·đa] *f.* pomegranate; grenade, shell, small bomb; — **de mano** hand grenade.
granado [gra·ná·đo] *m.* pomegranate tree; *adj.* notable; illustrious; select.
grande [grán·de] *adj.* large, big; great, grand; *Mex.,*

C.A., Ven., Andes **mamá (papá)** — grandmother (grandfather); *m.* grandee (*Spanish or Portuguese nobleman*); **en** — on a large scale.
grandeza [gran·dé·sa] *f.* greatness; grandeur, splendor; bigness; size; grandeeship; body of grandees.
grandiosidad [gran·djo·si·đáđ] *f.* grandeur, grandness; greatness; **grandioso** [gran·djó·so] *adj.* grandiose, great, grand, magnificent.
granero [gra·né·ro] *m.* granary; grain bin; country or region rich in grain.
granito [gra·ní·to] *m.* granite; small grain; small pimple.
granizada [gra·ni·sá·đa] *f.* hailstorm; shower, volley.
granizar[9] [gra·ni·sár] *v.* to hail.
granizo [gra·ní·so] *m.* hail; hailstorm; web or film in the eye; *adj. Mex.* spotted (*horse*).
granja [gráŋ·xa] *f.* grange, farm; country house.
granjear [graŋ·xe·ár] *v.* to earn, gain; to acquire, obtain; *Ch., C.A.* to steal; **-se** to win for oneself (*favor, goodwill, esteem, etc.*).
granjería [graŋ·xe·rí·a] *f.* farming; business profit.
granjero [graŋ·xé·ro] *m.* farmer.
grano [grá·no] *m.* (*cereal*) grain; seed; grain (*unit of measure*); **ir al** — to come to the point.
granuja [gra·nú·xa] *m.* ragamuffin, urchin; scamp.
granular [gra·nu·lár] *v.* to granulate; **-se** to become granulated; to break out with pimples.
grapa [grá·pa] *f.* clamp; staple; (*carbunclo*) pimple.
grasa [grá·sa] *f.* grease; fat; tallow; *Mex., Ríopl., Ven.* shoe polish; *Am.* **dar** — to polish (*shoes*).
grasiento [gra·sjén·to] *adj.* greasy, oily.
grasoso [gra·só·so] *adj.* greasy, oily.
gratificación [gra·ti·fi·ka·sjón] *f.* gratuity, bonus, tip; recompense, reward.
gratis [grá·tis] *adv.* gratis, for nothing, free of charge.
gratitud [gra·ti·túđ] *f.* gratitude.
grato [grá·to] *adj.* pleasing, pleasant; gratuitous; **su grata** your favor, your letter.
gratuito [gra·twí·to] *adj.* gratuitous, free, free of charge.
grava [grá·ƀa] *f.* gravel.
gravamen [gra·ƀá·men] *m.* burden; mortgage; assessment, levy.
grave [grá·ƀe] *adj.* grave; serious; weighty, heavy; grievous; deep, low (*in pitch*).
gravedad [gra·ƀe·đáđ] *f.* (*fuerza*) gravity; (*seriedad*) seriousness, gravity; (*tono*) depth (*of a sound*); — **específica** specific gravity.
gravoso [gra·ƀó·so] *adj.* burdensome; **serle a uno** — to be burdensome; to weigh on one's conscience.
graznar [graz·nár] *v.* to caw, croak, squawk, cackle, quack.
graznido [graz·ní·đo] *m.* caw, croak, squawk, cackle, quack.
greca [gré·ka] *f.* fret; ornamental design.
greda [gré·đa] *f.* clay, chalk; chalk cleaner.
gremial [gre·mjál] *adj.* pertaining to a labor union; *m.* member of a union.
gremio [gré·mjo] *m.* guild, society, brotherhood, trade union; fold (*referring to the Church*).
greña [gré·ña] *f.* shock of hair, tangled mop of hair (*usually* **greñas**): **greñudo** [gre·ñú·đo] *adj.* shaggy, with long, unkempt hair.
grey [grej] *f.* flock; congregation (*of a church*).
griego [grjé·ǥo] *adj.* Greek, Grecian; *m.* Greek.
grieta [grjé·ta] *f.* crevice; crack; fissure.
grifo [grí·fo] *m.* faucet; *Andes* cheap tavern (*where* **chicha** *is sold*); *Peru* gas station; *Cuba, P.R.* colored person; *Col.* drug addict; *Mex.* drunkard; *adj.* curly, kinky, woolly (*hair*); *Col.* vain, conceited; **letra grifa** script; **ponerse** — to bristle, stand on end (*said of hair*); **grifería** faucets.
grillo [grí·yo] *m.* cricket; sprout, shoot; **-s** fetters; obstacle, hindrance.
grima [grí·ma] *f.* uneasiness; displeasure, disgust; *Ríopl., Carib.* sadness, compassion, pity; *Ch.* bit, small particle; **dar** — to disgust; to make uneasy; *Am.* to make sad, inspire pity.
gringo [gríŋ·go] *adj. Ch., Ríopl.* (*Italian*) foreign (*not Spanish*); *m. Ch., Ríopl.* (*Italian*) foreigner (*not Spanish*); *Mex., C.A., Andes, Col., Ven.* Yankee or English-speaking person.
griñones [gri·ñó·nes] *m. pl.* nectarines.
gripe [grí·pe] *f.* grippe, flu, influenza.
gris [gris] *adj.* grey; **grisáceo** *adj.* greyish.
grita [grí·ta] *f.* shouting, hooting; clamor, uproar.
gritar [gri·tár] *v.* to shout, cry.
gritería [gri·te·rí·a] *f.* shouting, clamor, uproar.
grito [grí·to] *m.* shout, cry; **poner el** — **en el cielo** to complain loudly, "hit the ceiling".
grosella [gro·sé·ya] *f.* currant; — **blanca** gooseberry; **grosellero** [gro·se·yé·ro] *m.* currant bush.
grosería [gro·se·rí·a] *f.* rudeness; coarseness; crudeness; insult.
grosero [gro·sé·ro] *adj.* rough, coarse; rude, impolite.
grosor [gro·sór] *m.* thickness.
grotesco [gro·tés·ko] *adj.* grotesque, fantastic; absurd.
grúa [grú·a] *f.* crane, derrick.
gruesa [grwé·sa] *f.* gross, twelve dozen.
grueso [grwé·so] *adj.* (*voluminoso*) fat, stout; thick; bulky, big, heavy; (*burdo*) dense; coarse; *m.* thickness; bulk; density; main part; **en** — in gross, in bulk, by wholesale.
grulla [grú·ya] *f.* crane (*bird*).
gruñido [gru·ñí·đo] *m.* growl, grumble; grunt.
gruñir[19] [gru·ñír] *v. irr.* to grunt; to growl; to snarl; to grumble.
gruñón [gru·ñón] *adj.* growling; grunting; grumbly; *m.* growler; grumbler.
grupa [grú·pa] *f.* rump; **volver -s** to turn around (*usually on horseback*).
grupo [grú·po] *m.* group; set.
gruta [grú·ta] *f.* grotto, cavern.
guacal [gwa·kál] *m. Col., Mex., C.A.* crate (*for transporting fruit, vegetables, etc., carried on the back*). *Also* **huacal.**
guacamayo [gwa·ka·má·yo] *m. Am.* macaw (*large parrot*); *Am.* flashily dressed person.
guacamole [gwa·ka·mó·le] *m. Mex., C.A., Cuba* avocado salad; also **guacamol.**
guacho [gwá·čo] *m.* birdling, chick; young animal; *Andes, Ríopl.* orphan; *Andes, Ríopl.* foundling, abandoned child; *adj. Am.* odd, not paired; *Andes, Ríopl.* forlorn, alone, abandoned.
guadal [gwa·đál] *m. Am.* small dune, sand hill; *Ven.* quagmire, bog, swamp; *Am.* growth of bamboo grass.
guadaña [gwa·đá·ña] *f.* scythe.
guagua [gwá·ǥwa] *f. Carib., Ven.* bus; trifle, insignificant thing; *m. & f. Andes, Ch., Ríopl.* baby; **de** — for nothing, gratis, free.
guaje [gwá·xe] *m. Am.* a species of gourd; *Mex.* vessel or bowl made of a gourd; *Mex.* simpleton, fool; *Am.* trifle, trinket, piece of junk; *adj. Mex.* foolish; *Am.* **hacerse uno** — to play the fool; *Am.* **hacer a uno** — to fool, deceive someone.
guajiro [gwa·xí·ro] *m.* Indian of the Guajira peninsula (*in Venezuela and Colombia*); *Cuba* rustic, peasant.
guajolote [gwa·xo·ló·te] *m. Mex.* turkey; *Mex.* fool.

guanaco [gwa·ná·ko] *m. Andes, Ch., Ríopl.* guanaco (*a kind of llama*); *Ch., Arg.* tall, lanky, gawky person; *Mex., C.A.* fool, simpleton; nickname for Salvadoreans.
guanajo [gwa·ná·xo] *m. Carib.* turkey, dunce.
guano [gwá·no] *m. Carib.* palm tree; *Carib.* palm leaves (*used for thatching*); *Am.* guano, bird dung, fertilizer.
guantada [gwan·tá·ɗa] *f.* wallop, blow, slap.
guante [gwán·te] *m.* glove; *Andes* whip, scourge; **echar el — a uno** to seize or grab a person; **guantelete** [gwan·te·lé·te] *m.* gauntlet.
guapo [gwá·po] *adj.* handsome, good-looking; ostentatious, showy; daring, brave; *Ch., Andes* harsh, severe; *Carib., Mex.* angry; *m.* brawler, quarreler, bully.
guarache [gwa·rá·če] *m. Mex.* Mexican leather sandal; *Mex.* tire patch. *Also* **huarache** [wa·rá·če].
guaraní [gwa·ra·ní] *adj.* pertaining to the Guarani Indians of Paraguay; *m. & f.* Guarani Indian.
guarapo [gwa·rá·po] *m. Col., C.A., Andes* juice of the sugar cane; *Col., C.A., Andes* sugar-cane liquor; *Col., C.A., Andes* low-grade brandy.
guarda [gwár·ɗa] *m. & f.* guard; keeper; *Ríopl.* ticket collector on a streetcar; *f.* custody, care, keeping; observance of a law; **-s** outside ribs of a fan; flyleaves.
guardabarros [gwar·ɗa·ƀá·rros], **guardafango** [gwar·ɗa·fáŋ·go] *m.* fender.
guardabosques [gwar·ɗa·ƀós·kes] *m.* forest ranger, forester, forest keeper.
guardabrisa [gwar·ɗa·ƀrí·sa] *f.* windshield.
guardacostas [gwar·ɗa·kós·tas] *m.* coast guard.
guardafrenos [gwar·ɗa·fré·nos] *m.* brakeman.
guardagujas [gwar·ɗa·ǵú·xas] *m.* switchman.
guardalmacén [gwar·ɗal·ma·sén] *m.* warehouse keeper, storekeeper.
guardamonte [gwar·ɗa·món·te] *m.* trigger guard; forest keeper.
guardapapeles [gwar·ɗa·pa·pé·les] *m.* file, filing cabinet or box.
guardapelo [gwar·ɗa·pé·lo] *m.* locket.
guardar [gwar·ɗár] *v.* to guard, watch over; to keep; to store; to observe (*laws, customs*); **-se de** to guard against, keep from, avoid.
guardarropa [gwar·ɗa·rró·pa] *m.* wardrobe; cloakroom; keeper of a cloakroom.
guardia [gwár·ɗja] *f.* guard, body of guards; defense, protection; *m.* guard, guardsman.
guardiamarina [gwar·ɗja·ma·rí·na] *f.* midshipman.
guardián [gwar·ɗján] *m.* guardian, keeper; superior of a Franciscan monastery.
guarecer[13] [gwa·re·sér] *v. irr.* to protect, shelter; **-se** to take shelter.
guarida [gwa·rí·da] *f.* den, cave, lair.
guarismo [gwa·ríz·mo] *m.* number.
guarnecer[13] [gwar·ne·sér] *v. irr.* to garnish, decorate; to adorn; to trim; to harness; to garrison; to set (*jewels*).
guarnición [gwar·ni·sjón] *f.* adornment; trimming; setting of a jewel; guard of a sword; garrison; **-es** trappings, harness.
guaro [gwá·ro] *m. C.A.* rum.
guasa [gwá·sa] *f.* joking; foolishness.
guasca [gwás·ka] *f. Andes, Ch., Ríopl.* leather thong; *Andes, Ch., Ríopl.* rope, cord; *Andes, Ch.* whip; *Andes, Ch., Ríopl.* **dar —** to whip, beat, thrash.
guaso [gwá·so] *m. Am.* stag, male deer; *Ch., Andes, Ríopl.* peasant; *Cuba* half-breed; *Am.* lasso; *adj.* rustic, peasant-like.
guasón [gwa·són] *adj.* funny, comical; *m.* joker, jester.
guata [gwá·ta] *f. Am.* padding; *Ven.* fib; *Col.* a species of potato; *Ch., Andes* paunch, belly; *Am.* **echar —** to get fat.
guatemalteco [gwa·te·mal·té·ko] *m. & adj.* Guatemalan.
guayaba [gwa·yá·ƀa] *f.* guava (*pear-shaped tropical fruit*); **guayabo** *m.* guava tree; *Am.* lie, fraud, trick.
guayabera [gwa·ya·ƀé·ra] *f.* tropical pleated jacket.
gubernativo [gu·ƀer·na·tí·ƀo] *adj.* governmental, administrative.
gubia [gú·ƀja] *f.* gouge (chisel).
guedeja [ge·ɗé·xa] *f.* forelock; lock of hair; lion's mane.
güero [gwé·ro] *adj. Mex.* blond; *m. Ven.* cassava liquor. *See* **huero.**
guerra [gé·rra] *f.* war; **— a muerte** war to the finish; **dar —** to bother, trouble.
guerrear [ge·rre·ár] *v.* to war; *Am.* to do mischief or to bother (*said of children*).
guerrero [ge·rré·ro] *adj.* warlike, martial; *m.* warrior, soldier.
guerrilla [ge·rrí·ya] *f.* small war; skirmish; body of soldiers; band of fighters.
guerrillero [ge·rri·yé·ro] *m.* guerrilla fighter.
guía [gí·a] *m. & f.* guide, leader; *f.* guidebook, directory; signpost; shoot, sprout; *Ríopl.* garland of flowers.
guiar[17] [gjar] *v.* to guide; to drive (*a car*).
guija [gí·xa] *f.* pebble; **guijarro** [gi·xá·rro] *m.* cobblestone.
guijo [gí·xo] *m.* gravel.
guinda [gín·da] *f.* sour cherry.
guindilla [gin·dí·ya] *f. Spain* small hot pepper.
guineo [gi·né·o] *m. C.A.* banana.
guiñada [gi·ñá·ɗa] *f.* wink.
guiñapo [gi·ñá·po] *m.* tag, tatter, rag; ragamuffin, ragged person.
guiñar [gi·ñár] *v.* to wink.
guiño [gí·ño] *m.* wink.
guión [gjón] *m.* hyphen; repeat sign (*in music*); cross (*carried before a prelate in a procession*); guide, leader (*among birds and animals*); leader in a dance.
guirnalda [gir·nál·da] *f.* garland, wreath.
guisa [gí·sa] *f.* way, manner; **a — de** like, in the manner of.
guisado [gi·sá·ɗo] *m.* stew.
guisante [gi·sán·te] *m. Sp.* pea; **— de olor** sweet pea.
guisar [gi·sár] *v.* to cook; to prepare, arrange.
guiso [gí·so] *m.* dish, dish of food.
güisquil [gwis·kíl] *m. C.A.* chayote (*a pear-shaped fruit*).
guitarra [gi·tá·rra] *f.* guitar.
gula [gú·la] *f.* gluttony.
gusano [gu·sá·no] *m.* worm; caterpillar; **— de la conciencia** remorse; **— de luz** glowworm; *Col., Mex.* **matar el —** to satisfy a need or desire (*particularly hunger or thirst*).
gustar [gus·tár] *v.* (*agradar*) to please, be pleasing; (*saborear*) to taste; to experience; **-le a uno una cosa** to like something; **— de** to have a liking for, be fond of.
gusto [gús·to] *m.* (*agrado*) pleasure; whim, fancy; (*sabor*) taste; flavor; **dar —** to please; **estar a —** to be comfortable, contented; **tener — en** to be glad to; **tomar el — a una cosa** to become fond of something.
gustoso [gus·tó·so] *adj.* (*con agrado*) glad; pleasant; willing; merry; (*sabroso*) tasty; *adv.* willingly.

H:h

haba [á·ƀa] *f.* large bean; Lima bean.
habano [a·ƀá·no] *m.* Havana cigar.
haber[30] [a·ƀér] *v. irr.* to have (*auxiliary verb*); **habérselas con** to have it out with; **ha de llegar mañana** he is to arrive tomorrow; **ha de ser verdad** it must be true; **hay (había, hubo,** *etc.*) there is, there are (there was, there were, *etc.*); **hay que** (+ *inf.*) it is necessary; **no hay de qué** you are welcome? **¿qué hay?** what's the matter?
haber [a·ƀér] *m.* credit, credit side (*in book-keeping*); **-es** property, goods, cash, assets.
habichuela [a·ƀi·čwé·la] *f.* bean; — **verde** string bean.
hábil [á·ƀil] *adj.* skilful, capable, able.
habilidad [a·ƀi·li·đáđ] *f.* ability, skill.
habilitar [a·ƀi·li·tár] *v.* to enable; to equip; to qualify.
habitación [a·ƀi·ta·sjón] *f.* apartment; room; lodging.
habitante [a·ƀi·tán·te] *m.* inhabitant; resident.
habitar [a·ƀi·tár] *v.* to inhabit; to live, reside.
hábito [á·ƀi·to] *m.* habit; custom.
habitual [a·ƀi·twál] *adj.* habitual, customary.
habituar[18] [a·ƀi·twár] *v.* to accustom; **-se** to get used, accustomed.
habla [á·ƀla] *f.* speech; language, dialect; **al** — within speaking distance; in communication (with).
hablador [a·ƀla·đór] *m.* talker; gossip; *adj.* talkative.
habladuría [a·ƀla·đu·rí·a] *f.* gossip, rumor; empty talk; impertinent remark.
hablar [a·ƀlár] *v.* to speak; to talk; — **alto** (*or* **en voz alta**) to speak loudly; — **bajo (quedo** *or* **en voz baja)** to speak softly; — **por los codos** to chatter constantly.
hablilla [a·ƀlí·ya] *f.* gossip, rumor, malicious tale.
hacedero [a·se·đé·ro] *adj.* feasible.
hacedor [a·se·đór] *m.* maker; **el Supremo Hacedor** the Maker.
hacendado [a·sen·dá·đo] *m.* landholder; *Ríopl., Ch., Ven.* owner of a farm, plantation, or ranch.
hacendoso [a·sen·dó·so] *adj.* industrious, diligent.
hacer[31] [a·sér] *v. irr.* (*crear*) to do; to make; (*formar*) to form; to accustom; (*causar*) to cause, order (*followed by inf.*); — **caso** to mind, pay attention; — **frío (calor)** to be cold (warm); — **la maleta** to pack one's suitcase; — **la mortecina** play possum; — **un papel** to play a part; *Am.* — **aprecio** to pay attention; *Ríopl., Mex.* — **caras** (*or* **caritas**) to flirt; **no le hace** it makes no difference; **-se** to become, grow, get to be; **-se a** to get used to; **-se de rogar** to want to be coaxed.
hacia [á·sja] *prep.* toward; about; — **adelante** forward; — **atrás** backward.
hacienda [a·sjén·da] *f.* estate; property; finance; large farm; *Ríopl.* cattle, livestock.
hacina [a·sí·na] *f.* shock (*of grain*), stack, pile.
hacinar [a·si·nár] *v.* to shock (*grain*); to stack, pile up; to accumulate.
hacha [á·ča] *f.* ax; hatchet; torch.
hachero [a·čé·ro] *m.* axman, woodcutter.
hachuela de uña [a·čwé·la de ú·ña] claw (tool).
hada [á·đa] *f.* fairy.
hado [á·đo] *m.* fate, fortune, destiny.
halagar[7] [a·la·ǥár] *v.* to coax; to flatter; to allure, attract.
halago [a·lá·ǥo] *m.* flattery; caress; allurement.
halagüeño [a·la·ǥwé·ño] *adj.* alluring, attractive; flattering; promising.
halar [a·lár] = **jalar.**
halcón [al·kón] *m.* falcon.
hálito [á·li·to] *m.* breath; vapor.
hallar [a·yár] *v.* to find; to discover, find out; **-se** to be; to fare, get along.
hallazgo [a·yáz·ǥo] *m.* find; discovery; reward (*for finding something*).
hamaca [a·má·ka] *f.* hammock.
hambre [ám·bre] *f.* hunger; famine; appetite; **tener** — to be hungry; **hambruna** [am·brú·na] *f. Am.* great hunger, starvation.
hambrear [am·bre·ár] *v.* to starve; to be hungry.
hambriento [am·brjén·to] *adj.* hungry; greedy; *C.A., Mex., Andes* stingy.
hampa [ám·pa] *f. Spain* underworld.
hangar [aŋ·gár] *m.* hangar.
haragán [a·ra·ǥán] *adj.* lazy, indolent; *m.* loafer, idler.
haraganear [a·ra·ǥa·ne·ár] *v.* to lounge, loaf, be lazy.
haraganería [a·ra·ǥa·ne·rí·a] *f.* laziness.
harapiento [a·ra·pjén·to] *adj.* tattered, ragged.
harapo [a·rá·po] *m.* rag, tatter; **andar hecho un** — to be in tatters.
haraposo [a·ra·pó·so] *adj.* tattered, ragged.
harina [a·rí·na] *f.* flour; — **de utilidad general** all-purpose flour; **eso es — de otro costal** that is something entirely different; **harinoso** [a·ri·nó·so] *adj.* floury; flourlike.
harmonía [ar·mo·ní·a] *f.* harmony.
hartar [ar·tár] *v.* to fill up, gorge; to sate, satiate; **-se** to have one's fill; to overeat, eat too much.
harto [ár·to] *adj.* full; sated, satiated; fed up; too much; *adv.* too much; *Mex., C.A., Col., Ven., Ríopl., Andes* much, very much.
hasta [ás·ta] *prep.* till, until; up to; — **luego** good-bye, see you later; *conj.* even; — **que** until.
hastiar[17] [as·tjár] *v.* to surfeit; to cloy; to disgust.
hastío [as·tí·o] *m.* surfeit, excess; boredom; loathing, disgust.
hato [á·to] *m.* herd; flock; sheepfold; shepherd's hut; gang, crowd; pile; *Col., Ven.* cattle ranch.
haya [á·ya] *f.* beech; **hayuco** *m.* beechnut.
haz [as] *f.* face; surface; *m.* fagot, bundle, bunch.
hazaña [a·sá·ña] *f.* deed, exploit, feat.
hazmerreír [az·me·rre·ír] *m.* laughing stock.
he [e] (*used with* **aquí** *or* **allí**) behold, here is, here you have; **heme aquí** here I am; **helo aquí** here it is.
hebilla [e·ƀí·ya] *f.* buckle.
hebra [é·ƀra] *f.* thread; fiber; fine string; *Am.* **de una** — all at once, at one stroke, *Col.* **ni** — absolutely nothing; — **de vidrio troceadas** chopped strand (fiber glass); **hebroso** adj. fibrous, stringy.
hecatombe [e·ka·tóm·be] *m.* massacre, great slaughter; hecatomb (*sacrifice of 100 oxen*).
hectárea [ek·tá·re·a] *m.* hectare.
hechicera [e·či·sé·ra] *f.* witch, enchantress; hag.
hechicería [e·či·se·rí·a] *f.* witchcraft; magic; charm; enchantment.
hechicero [e·či·sé·ro] *adj.* bewitching, charming; *m.* magician; charmer; sorcerer.
hechizar[9] [e·či·sár] *v.* to bewitch; to charm.
hechizo [e·čí·so] *m.* charm; enchantment.
hecho [é·čo] *m.* fact; act, deed; **de** — in fact; *p.p. of* **hacer** done, made.
hechura [e·čú·ra] *f.* make; shape, cut; workmanship.
heder[1] [e·đér] *v. irr.* to stink; to reek.
hediondez [e·đjon·dés] *f.* stink, stench.
hediondo [e·đjón·do] *adj.* foul-smelling, stinking; filthy; *m. Ríopl.* skunk.
hedor [e·đór] *m.* stink, stench.
helada [e·lá·đa] *f.* frost.
helado [e·lá·đo] *adj.* frozen; freezing; frosty; icy; *m.* ice cream; ice, sherbet; **heladería** [e·la·đe·rí·a] *f.*

Am. ice-cream parlor.
heladora [e·la·đó·ra] *f.* freezer.
helar[1] [e·lár] *v. irr.* to freeze.
helecho [e·lé·čo] *m.* fern.
hélice [é·li·se] *f.* screw propeller; helix, spiral.
helicóptero [e·li·kóp·te·ro] *m.* helicopter.
helio [e·ljo] *m.* helium.
heliógrafo [e·ljó·gra·fo] *m.* blueprint.
helipuerto [e·li·pwér·to] *m.* heliport.
hembra [ém·bra] *f.* female; staple; nut (*of a screw*), **macho y** — hook and eye.
hemisferio [e·mis·fé·rjo] *m.* hemisphere.
hemofilia [e·mo·fí·lja] *f.* hemophilia.
hemoglobina [e·mo·ǥlo·ƀí·na] *f.* hemoglobin.
hemorragia [e·mo·rrá·xja] *f.* hemorrhage.
henchir[5] [en·čír] *v. irr.* to swell, stuff, fill.
hendedura [en·de·đú·ra], **hendidura** [en·di·đú·ra] *f.* crack, crevice, fissure.
hender[1] [en·dér] *v. irr.* to split, crack, cleave.
henequén [e·ne·kén] *m. Mex., Ven., C.A., Col.* sisal, sisal hemp.
heno [é·no] *m.* hay.
henil [e·níl] *m.* hayloft.
hepatitis [e·pa·tí·tis] *f.* hepatitis.
heráldico [e·rál·di·ko] *adj.* heraldic; **heráldica** heraldry.
heraldo [e·rál·do] *m.* herald.
herbazal [er·ƀa·sál] *m.* field of grass.
herboso [er·ƀó·so] *adj.* grassy; weedy.
heredad [e·re·đáđ] *f.* parcel of land; rural property; estate.
heredar [e·re·đár] *v.* to inherit; to bequeath, leave in a will.
heredero [e·re·đé·ro] *m.* heir; successor; **heredera** [e·re·đé·ra] *f.* heiress.
hereditario [e·re·đi·tá·rjo] *adj.* hereditary.
hereje [e·ré·xe] *m.* heretic; **cara de** — hideous face.
herejía [e·re·xí·a] *f.* heresy; offensive remark.
herencia [e·rén·sja] *f.* inheritance; heritage; heredity.
herida [e·rí·đa] *f.* wound; injury.
herido [e·rí·đo] *adj.* wounded; *m.* wounded man; *Am.* small drainage channel.
herir[3] [e·rír] *v. irr.* to wound; to hurt; to strike; to offend.
hermana [er·má·na] *f.* sister.
hermanastro [er·ma·nás·tro] *m.* stepbrother, half brother; **hermanastra** [er·ma·nás·tra] *f.* stepsister, half sister.
hermandad [er·man·dáđ] *f.* brotherhood, fraternity.
hermano [er·má·no] *m.* brother.
hermético [er·mé·ti·ko] *adj.* hermetic; airtight; tight-lipped; close-mouthed; **hermetismo** [er·me·tíz·mo] *m.* complete silence.
hermosear [er·mo·se·ár] *v.* to beautify, adorn.
hermoso [er·mó·so] *adj.* beautiful, handsome.
hermosura [er·mo·sú·ra] *f.* beauty.
hernia [ér·nja] *f.* hernia.
héroe [é·ro·e] *m.* hero; **heroína** [e·ro·í·na] *f.* heroine; heroin (*drug*).
heroico [e·rój·ko] *adj.* heroic.
heroísmo [e·ro·íz·mo] *adj.* heroism.
herradura [e·rra·đú·ra] *f.* horseshoe.
herraje [e·rrá·xe] *m.* ironwork; iron trimmings; horseshoes and nails; *Am.* silver saddle trimmings; *Arg.* horseshoe.
herramienta [e·rra·mjén·ta] *f.* tool; — **con punta de diamante** diamond tool; *pl.* set of tools.
herrar[1] [e·rrár] *v. irr.* to shoe (*a horse*); to brand; to trim with iron.
herrería [e·rre·rí·a] *f.* blacksmith's shop or trade; forge; ironworks.
herrero [e·rré·ro] *m.* blacksmith.
herrete [e·rré·te] *m.* metal tip (*for a shoelace, for instance*); *Am.* branding iron.
herrumbre [e·rrúm·bre] *f.* rust; plant rot.
hervidero [er·ƀi·đé·ro] *m.* bubbling sound (*of boiling water*); bubbling spring; swarm, crowd; **un — de gente** a swarm of people.
hervir[3] [er·ƀír] *v. irr.* to boil; — **de gente** to swarm with people.
hervor [er·ƀór] *m.* boiling; boiling point; **soltar el** — to come to a boil.
heterodoxia [e·te·ro·đók·sja] *f.* heterodoxy.
heterogéneo [e·te·ro·xé·ne·o] *adj.* heterogeneous.
hez [es] *f.* scum; **la — del pueblo** the scum of society; **heces** [é·ses] dregs, sediment.
hiato [já·to] *m.* hiatus.
híbrido [í·ƀri·đo] *adj. & m.* hybrid.
hidalgo [i·đál·ǥo] *m.* hidalgo (*Spanish nobleman*); *adj.* noble, courteous.
hidalguía [i·đal·ǥí·a] *f.* nobility; generosity; courtesy.
hidrato [i·đrá·to] *m.* hydrate.
hidráulico [i·đráw·li·ko] *adj.* hydraulic; **fuerza hidráulica** water power; **ingeniero** — hydraulic engineer.
hidroavión [i·đro·a·ƀjón] *m.* hydroplane, seaplane.
hidroeléctrico [i·đro·e·lék·tri·ko] *adj.* hydroelectric.
hidrógeno [i·đró·xe·no] *m.* hydrogen.
hidropesía [i·đro·pe·sí·a] *f.* dropsy.
hidroplano [i·đro·plá·no] *m.* hydroplane.
hiedra [jé·đra] *f.* ivy.
hiel [jel] *f.* gall, bile; bitterness.
hielo [jé·lo] m. ice; frost.
hierba [jér·ƀa] *f.* grass; herb; weed; *Ríopl., Andes* mate (*Paraguayan tea*); *Mex., Ven., Cuba* marihuana (*a narcotic*); *C.A.* **ciertas -s** so-and-so (*person not named*).
hierbabuena [jer·ƀa·ƀwé·na] *f.* mint. *Also* **yerbabuena** [ŷer·ƀa·ƀwé·na].
hierro [jé·rro] *m.* iron; brand; iron tool, instrument, or weapon; **-s** irons, chains, handcuffs; **-s para soldar** soldering iron.
hígado [í·ǥa·đo] *m.* (*órgano*) liver; (*valentía*) courage; valor; **malos -s** ill will.
higiene [i·xjé·ne] *f.* hygiene; **higiénico** [i·xjé·ni·ko] *adj.* hygienic, sanitary.
higo [í·ǥo] *m.* fig; **higuera** [i·ǥé·ra] *f.* fig tree; **higuerilla** [i·ǥe·rí·ya] *f. Am.* castor-oil plant.
higrómetro [i·ǥró·me·tro] *m.* hygrometer.
hija [í·xa] *f.* daughter; native daughter.
hijo [í·xo] *m.* son; native son; offspring, fruit, result.
hilachas [i·lá·čas] *f. pl.* lint; **mostrar uno la hilacha** to show one's worst side or nature; **hilachos** [i·lá·čos] *m. pl. Am.* rags, tatters.
hilado [i·lá·đo] *m.* yarn; *p.p. of* **hilar.**
hilandera [i·lan·dé·ra] *f.* spinner.
hilandería [i·lan·de·rí·a] *f.* spinning mill; art of spinning; spinning.
hilandero [i·lan·dé·ro] *m.* spinner; spinning room.
hilar [i·lár] *v.* to spin, make into thread; — **muy delgado** to be very subtle.
hilas [í·las] *f. pl.* lint, fine ravelings (*for dressing wounds*).
hilaza [i·lá·sa] *f.* coarse thread; yarn.
hilera [i·lé·ra] *f.* file, row, line; — **de perlas** strand or string of pearls.
hilo [í·lo] *m.* (*hebra*) thread; fine yarn; string; (*alambre*) filament; thin wire; (*tela*) linen; **a** — without interruption; **al** — along the thread; *Am.* very well, all right; **de** — straight, without stopping; *Am.* **de un** — constantly, without stopping; **tener el alma en un** — to be frightened

to death; to be in great anxiety or suspense.
hilván [il·ƀán] *m.* basting stitch; basting; *Am.* hem.
hilvanar [il·ƀa·nár] *v.* to baste; to put together, connect; to do hastily; *Ven.* to hem.
himno [ím·no] *m.* hymn.
hincapié [iŋ·ka·pjé]: **hacer** — to emphasize, stress; to insist (upon).
hincar[6] [iŋ·kár] *v.* to drive, thrust (into); **-se** (*or* **-se de rodillas**) to kneel down.
hinchado [in·čá·đo] *adj.* & *p.p.* swollen; inflated; presumptuous.
hinchar [in·čár] *v.* to swell; **-se** to swell; to swell up, puff up.
hinchazón [in·ča·són] *f.* swelling; inflation; conceit; bombast, inflated style.
hinojo [i·nó·xo] *m.* fennel.
hinojos [i·nó·xos]: **de** — on one's knees.
hipérbole [i·pér·ƀo·le] *f.* hyperbole.
hiperbólico [i·per·ƀó·li·ko] *adj.* hyperbolic.
hipo [í·po] *m.* hiccough; sob; longing; grudge, ill will.
hipocresía [i·po·kre·sía] *f.* hypocrisy.
hipócrita [i·pó·kri·ta] *adj.* hypocritical, insincere; *m.* & *f.* hypocrite.
hipódromo [i·pó·đro·mo] *m.* race track.
hipoteca [i·po·té·ka] *f.* mortgage.
hipotecar[6] [i·po·te·kár] *v.* to mortgage.
hipótesis [i·pó·te·sis] *f.* hypothesis, theory.
hipotético [i·po·té·ti·ko] *adj.* hypothetic(al).
hirviente [ir·ƀjén·te] *adj.* boiling.
hispanidad [is·pa·ni·đáđ] *f.* Hispanic solidarity.
hispanista [is·pa·nís·ta] *m.* & *f.* Hispanist; one who is interested in Hispanic studies.
hispano [is·pá·no] *adj.* Hispanic, Spanish; *m.* Spanish-speaking person.
hispanoamericano [is·pa·no·a·me·ri·ká·no] *adj.* Spanish-American.
histamina [is·ta·mí·na] *f.* histamine.
histerectomía [is·te·rek·to·mí·a] *f.* hysterectomy.
histérico [is·té·ri·ko] *adj.* hysterical.
historia [is·tó·rja] *f.* history; story; tale, fable; **dejarse de -s** to stop fooling and come to the point; **historieta** [is·to·rjé·ta] *f.* story, anecdote.
historiador [is·to·rja·đór] *m.* historian.
historial [is·to·rjál] *m.* record, data (*concerning a person or firm*); *adj.* historic.
histórico [is·tó·ri·ko] *adj.* historic, historical.
hito [í·to] *adj.* firm, fixed; **de hito en hito** fixedly.
hocico [o·sí·ko] *m.* snout; **caer de -s** to fall on one's face; **meter el — en todo** to meddle, stick one's nose in everything.
hogaño [o·ǥá·ño] *adv.* nowadays.
hogar [o·ǥár] *m.* hearth, fireplace; home.
hogareño [o·ǥa·ré·ño] *adj.* home-loving, domestic; homelike.
hogaza [o·ǥá·sa] *f.* loaf of bread.
hoguera [o·ǥé·ra] *f.* bonfire.
hoja [ó·xa] *f.* leaf; petal; sheet of paper or metal; blade; — **de lata** tin plate; — **electrónica** (*computadora*) spread sheet.
hojalata [o·xa·lá·ta] *f.* tin plate.
hojaldre [o·xál·dre] *m.* & *f.* puff pastry.
hojarasca [o·xa·rás·ka] *f.* fallen leaves; dry foliage; superfluous ornament; trash; useless words.
hojear [o·xe·ár] *v.* to leaf, turn the pages of; to browse.
hojuela [o·xwé·la] *f.* leaflet, small leaf; thin leaf (*of metal*); flake; thin pancake; — **de estaño** tin foil.
¡hola! [ó·la] *interj.* hello!; ho!; ah!
holandés [o·lan·dés] *adj.* Dutch; *m.* Dutchman; Dutch language.
holgado [ol·ǥá·đo] *adj.* (*libre*) free, at leisure; comfortable; (*ancho*) wide, loose; roomy, spacious; *p.p. of* **holgar.**
holganza [ol·ǥán·sa] *f.* idleness.
holgar[2] [ol·ǥár] *v. irr.* to rest; to loaf; **-se** to be glad; to relax, have a good time; **huelga decir** needless to say.
holgazán [ol·ǥa·sán] *m.* idler, loafer; *adj.* lazy, idle.
holgazanear [ol·ǥa·sa·ne·ár] *v.* to loiter, lounge, idle, bum around.
holgazanería [ol·ǥa·sa·ne·rí·a] *f.* idleness, laziness.
holgorio [ol·ǥó·rjo] *m.* spree.
holgura [ol·ǥú·ra] *f.* (*descanso*) ease; rest, comfort; (*lugar*) roominess, plenty of room.
holocausto [o·lo·káws·to] *m.* holocaust, burnt offering, sacrifice.
hollar [o·yár] *v.* to tread, trample upon.
hollejo [o·yé·xo] *m.* skin, peel; husk.
hollín [o·yín] *m.* soot.
hombrada [om·brá·đa] *f.* manly act; show of bravery.
hombre [óm·bre] *m.* man; **hombría** [om·brí·a] *f.* manliness, manly strength; — **de bien** honesty.
hombro [óm·bro] *m.* shoulder; **arrimar** (*or* **meter**) **el** — to help.
hombruno [om·brú·no] *adj.* mannish, masculine.
homenaje [o·me·ná·xe] *m.* homage, honor.
homeópata [o·me·ó·pa·ta] *adj.* homeopathic.
homicida [o·mi·sí·đa] *m.* murderer; *f.* murderess; *adj.* homicidal, murderous.
homicidio [o·mi·sí·đjo] *m.* homicide, murder.
homófono [o·mó·fo·no] *adj.* homophonous.
homogeneidad [o·mo·xe·nej·đáđ] *f.* homogeneity.
homogéneo [o·mo·xé·ne·o] *adj.* homogeneous, of the same kind or nature.
honda [ón·da] *f.* sling, slingshot.
hondo [ón·do] *adj.* deep; low; *m.* bottom, depth.
hondonada [on·do·ná·đa] *f.* hollow, dip, gully, ravine.
hondura [on·dú·ra] *f.* depth; **meterse en -s** to go beyond one's depth; to get into trouble.
honestidad [o·nes·ti·đáđ] *f.* chastity, modesty, decency; decorum, propriety.
honesto [o·nés·to] *adj.* chaste, modest, decent; just; honest.
hongo [óŋ·go] *m.* mushroom; fungus; derby hat.
honor [o·nór] *m.* honor; glory; dignity.
honorario [o·no·rá·rjo] *m.* fee (*for professional services*); *adj.* honorary.
honorífico [o·no·rí·fi·ko] *adj.* honorary; **mención honorífica** honorable mention.
honra [ón·rra] *f.* honor; reputation; **-s** obsequies, funeral rites.
honradez [on·rra·đés] *f.* honesty, honor, integrity.
honrado [on·rrá·đo] *adj.* honest, honorable; honored.
honrar [on·rrár] *v.* to honor; **-se** to be honored; to consider it an honor.
honroso [on·rró·so] *adj.* honorable; honoring.
hora [ó·ra] *f.* hour; time; **-s** canonical hours, office (*required daily prayers for priests and nuns*); **es — de** it is time to; **no ver la — de** (+ *inf.*) to be anxious to; **¿qué — es?** what time is it?
horadar [o·ra·đár] *v.* to pierce, bore, perforate.
horario [o·rá·rjo] *m.* schedule, timetable; hour hand.
horca [ór·ka] *f.* (*cadalso*) gallows; (*horcón*) pitchfork; *P.R.* birthday present; — **de ajos** string of garlic.
horcajadas [or·ka·xá·đas]: **a** — astride (*with one leg on each side*); **ponerse a** — to straddle.
horcón [or·kón] *m.* forked pole, forked prop; *Mex., Cuba, Ven.* post, roof support; *Am.* roof.
horda [ór·đa] *f.* horde.

horizontal [o·ri·son·tál] *adj.* horizontal.
horizonte [o·ri·són·te] *m.* horizon.
horma [ór·ma] *f.* form, mold; block (*for shaping a hat*); shoe last; shoe tree.
hormiga [or·mí·ǥa] *f.* ant.
hormigón [or·mi·ǥón] *m.* concrete.
hormigonera [or·mi·ǥo·né·ra] *f.* concrete mixer.
hormiguear [or·mi·ǥe·ár] *v.* to swarm; to be crawling with ants; **me hormiguea el cuerpo** I itch all over.
hormigueo [or·mi·ǥé·o] *m.* itching, creeping sensation; tingle, tingling sensation.
hormiguero [or·mi·ǥé·ro] *m.* ant hill; ant nest; swarm; **oso** — anteater.
hormona [or·mó·na] *f.* hormone.
hornada [or·ná·đa] *f.* batch of bread, baking.
hornear [or·ne·ár] *v.* to bake (*in an oven*).
hornilla [or·ní·ya] *f.* burner; grate (*of a stove*).
hornillo [or·ní·yo] *m.* kitchen stove; hot plate.
horno [ór·no] *m.* furnace; oven; kiln (*for baking bricks*); **alto** — blast furnace; — **de convección** convection oven; — **microhonda** microwave oven.
horquilla [or·kí·ya] *f.* hairpin; forked pole; small pitchfork.
horrendo [o·rrén·do] *adj.* horrible, hideous.
horrible [o·rrí·ƀle] *adj.* horrible.
horripilante [o·rri·pi·lán·te] *adj.* horrifying.
horror [o·rrór] *m.* horror; atrocity; **dar** — to cause fright; to horrify; **tenerle** — **a uno** to feel a strong dislike for one.
horrorizar[9] [o·rro·ri·sár] *v.* to horrify, shock, terrify.
horroroso [o·rro·ró·so] *adj.* horrid; frightful, hideous.
hortaliza [or·ta·lí·sa] *f.* vegetables; vegetable garden.
hortelano [or·te·lá·no] *m.* gardener.
hosco [ós·ko] *adj.* sullen; frowning; dark.
hospedaje [os·pe·đá·xe] *m.* board and lodging; lodging.
hospedar [os·pe·đár] *v.* to lodge, give lodging; **-se** to take lodging; to room, to stop (*at a hotel*).
hospedero [os·pe·đé·ro] *m.* innkeeper.
hospicio [os·pí·sjo] *m.* asylum; orphanage, orphan asylum; poorhouse; **hospiciano** [os·pi·sjá·no] *m.* inmate of a poorhouse or asylum.
hospital [os·pi·tál] *m.* hospital; — **de primera sangre** first-aid station.
hospitalidad [os·pi·ta·li·đáđ] *f.* hospitality.
hostería [os·te·rí·a] *f.* hostelry, inn.
hostia [ós·tja] *f.* host (*consecrated wafer*).
hostigar[7] [os·ti·ǥár] *v.* to harass, vex; to beat, lash; *C.A., Col.* to cloy.
hostil [os·tíl] *adj.* hostile; **hostilidad** [os·ti·li·đáđ] *f.* hostility.
hotel [o·tél] *m.* hotel; villa; **hotelero** [o·te·lé·ro] *m.* hotel-keeper; *adj.* pertaining to hotels.
hoy [oj] *adv.* today; — **día** nowadays; **de** — **en adelante** from now on; — **por** — at present; **de** — **más** henceforth.
hoya [ó·ya] *f.* pit, hole; grave; valley; *Col., Ch.* river basin.
hoyo [ó·yo] *m.* hole; pit; grave; *Ríopl., Carib* dimple.
hoyuelo [o·ywé·lo] *m.* dimple; tiny hole.
hoz [os] *f.* sickle; narrow ravine.
hozar[9] [o·sár] *v.* to root, turn up the earth with the snout (*as hogs*).
huacal [wa·kál] = **guacal.**
huarache [wa·rá·če] = **guarache.**
huaso [wá·so] = **guaso.**
hueco [wé·ko] *adj.* (*vacío*) hollow, empty; (*vano*) vain, affected; puffed up; high-sounding; *m.* gap, space, hole.
huelga [wél·ǥa] *f.* labor strike; rest; leisure; **declararse en** — to strike.
huelguista [wel·ǥís·ta] *m.* striker.
huella [wé·ya] *f.* trace; footprint.
huérfano [wér·fa·no] *adj.* & *m.* orphan.
huero [wé·ro] *adj.* empty; rotten, spoiled (*egg*). *See* **güero.**
huerta [wér·ta] *f.* orchard and vegetable garden; irrigated land.
huerto [wér·to] *m.* small orchard and vegetable garden; garden patch.
hueso [wé·so] *m.* bone; stone, pit; big seed; **la sin** — the tongue; **soltar la sin** — to talk too much; **no dejarle un** — **sano** to pick him to pieces.
huésped [wés·peđ] *m.* (*convidado*) guest; (*anfitrión*) host; **ser** — **en su casa** to be seldom at home.
hueste [wés·te] *f.* host, army, multitude.
huesudo [we·sú·đo] *adj.* bony.
huevo [wé·ƀo] *m.* egg; — **duro** hard-boiled egg; — **estrellado** fried egg; — **pasado por agua** soft-boiled egg; **-s revueltos** scrambled eggs; *Mex., C.A., Col., Ven.* **-s tibios** soft-boiled eggs; *Col., Ven.* **-s pericos** scrambled eggs; *Ven., Andes* **costar un** — to be very expensive.
huída [wí·đa] *f.* flight; escape.
huir[32] [wir] *v. irr.* to flee, excape; to avoid, shun.
huizache [wi·sá·če] *m. Mex., C.A.* huisache (*a species of acacia*).
hule [ú·le] *m.* rubber; oilcloth; *Col., Ven.* rubber tree.
hulla [ú·ya] *f.* soft coal.
humanidad [u·ma·ni·đáđ] *f.* humanity, mankind; humaneness; **-es** humanities, letters.
humanitario [u·ma·ni·tá·rjo] *adj.* humanitarian, humane, kind, charitable.
humano [u·má·no] *adj.* human; humane; *m.* man, human being.
humareda [u·ma·ré·đa] *f.* cloud of smoke.
humeante [u·me·án·te] *adj.* smoking, smoky; steaming.
humear [u·me·ár] *v.* to smoke, give off smoke; to steam; *Am.* to fumigate.
humedad [u·me·đáđ] *f.* humidity, moisture, dampness.
humedecer[13] [u·me·đe·sér] *v. irr.* to moisten, wet, dampen.
húmedo [ú·me·đo] *adj.* humid, moist, wet, damp.
humero [u·mé·ro] *m.* flue.
humildad [u·mil·dáđ] *f.* humility; humbleness; meekness.
humilde [u·míl·de] *adj.* humble, lowly, meek.
humillación [u·mi·ya·sjón] *f.* humiliation; submission.
humillar [u·mi·yár] *v.* to humiliate, humble, lower, crush; **-se** to humiliate oneself; to bow humbly.
humillos [u·mí·yos] *m. pl.* airs, conceit, vanity.
humo [ú·mo] *m.* smoke, fume, vapor; **-s** conceit, vanity.
humor [u·mór] *m.* substance; mood, disposition.
humorada [u·mo·rá·đa] *f.* pleasantry, witty remark; caprice, notion.
humorismo [u·mo·ríz·mo] *m.* humor, humorous style.
humorístico [u·mo·rís·ti·ko] *adj.* humorous.
humoso [u·mó·so] *adj.* smoky.
hundimiento [un·di·mjén·to] *m.* sinking, collapse, cave-in.
hundir [un·dír] *v.* (*sumir*) to sink, submerge; (*batir*) to crush, oppress; to destroy; **-se** to sink; to collapse, cave in.
huracán [u·ra·kán] *m.* hurricane.
huraño [u·rá·ño] *adj.* diffident, shy, bashful; unsociable.
¡hurra! [ú·rra] *interj.* hurrah!
hurtadillas [ur·ta·đí·yas]·; **a** — on the sly, secretly,

stealthily.
hurtar [ur·tár] *v*. to steal, rob; **-se** to withdraw, slip away; to hide; — **el cuerpo** to dodge; to flee.
hurto [úr·to] *m*. robbery, theft; stolen article; **a** — stealthily, on the sly.
husillo [u·sí·yo] *m*. lead screw, spindle.
husmear [uz·me·ár] *v*. to scent, smell, follow the track of; to nose, pry (into).
husmeo [uz·mé·o] *m*. sniff, sniffing, smelling; prying.
huso [ú·so] *m*. spindle.

I:i

ibérico [i·ƀé·ri·ko], **ibero** [i·ƀé·ro] *adj*. Iberian; **iberoamericano** [i·ƀe·ro·a·me·ri·ká·no] *adj*. Ibero-American (*Spanish or Portuguese American*).
iconoclasta [i·ko·no·klás·ta] *m*. & *f*. iconoclast.
ida [í·đa] *f*. departure; sally; **billete de — y vuelta** round-trip ticket; **-s y venidas** goings and comings.
idea [i·dé·a] *f*. idea; notion.
ideal [i·đe·ál] *m*. & *adj*. ideal.
idealismo [i·đe·a·líz·mo] *m*. idealism.
idealista [i·đe·a·lís·ta] *adj*. idealistic; *m*. & *f*. idealist; dreamer.
idear [i·đe·ár] *v*. to form an idea of; to devise, think out, plan.
ídem [í·đen] idem (*abbreviation*, id.), ditto, the same.
idéntico [i·đén·ti·ko] *adj*. identical.
identidad [i·đen·ti·đáđ] *f*. identity.
identificar[6] [i·đen·ti·fi·kár] *v*. to identify.
idilio [i·đí·ljo] *m*. idyl.
idioma [i·đjó·ma] *m*. language, tongue.
idiosincrasia [i·đjo·siŋ·krá·sja] *f*. idiosyncrasy.
idiota [i·đjó·ta] *m*. & *f*. idiot; *adj*. idiotic, foolish.
idiotez [i·đjo·tés] *f*. idiocy.
idiotismo [i·đjo·tíz·mo] *m*. idiom; idiocy.
idolatrar [i·đo·la·trár] *v*. to idolize, worship.
ídolo [í·đo·lo] *m*. idol.
idóneo [i·đó·ne·o] *adj*. fit, suitable; qualified.
iglesia [i·ǥlé·sja] *f*. church.
ignición [iǥ·ni·sjón] *f*. ignition.
ignominia [iǥ·no·mí·nja] *f*. infamy, shame, disgrace.
ignominioso [iǥ·no·mi·njó·so] *adj*. ignominious; infamous, shameful, disgraceful.
ignorancia [iǥ·no·rán·sja] *f*. ignorance.
ignorante [iǥ·no·rán·te] *adj*. ignorant.
ignorar [iǥ·no·rár] *v*. to be ignorant of, not to know.
ignoto [iǥ·nó·to] *adj*. unknown, undiscovered.
igual [i·ǥwál] *adj*. (*semejante*) equal; (*liso*) even, smooth; uniform; (*siempre*) constant; **serle — a uno** to be all the same to one, make no difference to one; *m*. equal; **al** — equally.
igualar [i·ǥwa·lár] *v*. to equal; to equalize; to match; to level, smooth; to adjust; to be equal.
igualdad [i·ǥwal·dáđ] *f*. equality.
igualitario [i·ǥwa·li·tá·rjo] *adj*. equalitarian (*promoting the doctrine of equality*).
iguana [i·ǥwá·na] *f*. iguana.
ijada [i·xá·đa] *f*. loin; flank (*of an animal*); pain in the side; **ijar** *m*. flank (*of an animal*).
ilegal [i·le·ǥál] *adj*. illegal, unlawful.
ilegítimo [i·le·xí·ti·mo] *adj*. illegitimate; illegal.
ileso [i·lé·so] *adj*. unharmed, uninjured, unhurt, safe and sound.
ilícito [i·lí·si·to] *adj*. illicit, unlawful.
ilimitado [i·li·mi·tá·đo] *adj*. unlimited.
iluminación [i·lu·mi·na·sjón] *f*. illumination.
iluminar [i·lu·mi·nár] *v*. to illuminate; to light; to enlighten.
ilusión [i·lu·sjón] *f*. illusion.
ilusivo [i·lu·sí·ƀo] *adj*. illusive.
iluso [i·lú·so] *adj*. deluded; *m*. visionary, dreamer.
ilusorio [i·lu·só·rjo] *adj*. illusive; deceptive; worthless.
ilustración [i·lus·tra·sjón] *f*. illustration; elucidation, explanation.
ilustrado [i·lus·trá·đo] *adj*. learned; enlightened.
ilustrador [i·lus·tra·đór] *m*. illustrator.
ilustrar [i·lus·trár] *v*. to illustrate.
ilustre [i·lús·tre] *adj*. illustrious, distinguished.
imagen [i·má·xen] *f*. image.
imaginable [i·ma·xi·ná·ƀle] *adj*. imaginable, conceivable.
imaginación [i·ma·xi·na·sjón] *f*. imagination.
imaginar [i·ma·xi·nár] *v*. to imagine.
imaginario [i·ma·xi·ná·rjo] *adj*. imaginary.
imaginativo [i·ma·xi·na·tí·ƀo] *adj*. imaginative; **imaginativa** [i·ma·xi·na·tí·ƀa] *f*. imagination.
imán [i·mán] *m*. magnet; attraction.
imantar [i·man·tár] *v*. to magnetize.
imbécil [im·bé·sil] *adj*. imbecile, stupid.
imborrable [im·bo·rrá·ƀle] *adj*. indelible, not erasable; unforgettable.
imbuir[32] [im·bwír] *v*. *irr*. to imbue; to instill, infuse, inspire (with).
imitación [i·mi·ta·sjón] *f*. imitation.
imitador [i·mi·ta·đor] *m*. imitator; follower; *adj*. imitative, imitating.
imitar [i·mi·tár] *v*. to imitate.
impaciencia [im·pa·sjén·sja] *f*. impatience.
impaciente [im·pa·sjén·te] *adj*. impatient.
impar [im·pár] *adj*. odd; **número** — odd number.
imparcial [im·par·sjál] *adj*. impartial; **imparcialidad** [im·par·sja·li·đáđ] *f*. impartiality, fairness, justice.
impasible [im·pa·sí·ƀle] *adj*. impassive, insensitive, insensible, unfeeling, unmoved.
impávido [im·pá·ƀi·đo] *adj*. fearless; calm; *Am*. impudent, brazen.
impedimento [im·pe·đi·mén·to] *m*. impediment, hindrance, obstacle.
impedir[5] [im·pe·đír] *v*. *irr*. to impede, prevent, hinder.
impeler [im·pe·lér] *v*. to impel, push; to incite, spur.
impenetrable [im·pe·ne·trá·ƀle] *adj*. impenetrable; impervious; incomprehensible.
impensado [im·pen·sá·đo] *adj*. unforeseen, unexpected; offhand, done without thinking; **impensadamente** [im·pen·sa·đa·mén·te] *adv*. offhand, without thinking; unexpectedly.
imperar [im·pe·rár] *v*. to rule, command, dominate; prevail.
imperativo [im·pe·ra·tí·ƀo] *adj*. imperative; urgent, compelling; *m*. imperative mood.
imperceptible [im·per·sep·tí·ƀle] *adj*. imperceptible.
imperdible [im·per·đí·ƀle] *m*. safety pin; *adj*. safe, that cannot be lost.
imperecedero [im·pe·re·se·đé·ro] *adj*. imperishable, enduring, everlasting.
imperfecto [im·per·fék·to] *adj*. imperfect; *m*. imperfect tense.
imperial [im·pe·rjál] *adj*. imperial; *f*. coach top; top seats on a coach or bus.
impericia [im·pe·rí·sja] *f*. inexperience.
imperio [im·pé·rjo] *m*. empire; command, rule; sway, influence.
imperioso [im·pe·rjó·so] *adj*. imperious, arrogant, domineering; urgent.
impermeable [im·per·me·á·ƀle] *adj*. waterproof,

impervious, rainproof; *m.* raincoat.
impersonal [im·per·so·nál] *adj.* impersonal.
impertinencia [im·per·ti·nén·sja] *f.* impertinence; impudence; insolent remark or act; **decir -s** to talk nonsense; to make insolent remarks.
impertinente [im·per·ti·nén·te] *adj.* impertinent, impudent; meddlesome; irrelevant, not to the point; **-s** *m. pl.* lorgnette (*eyeglasses mounted on a handle*).
ímpetu [ím·pe·tu] *m.* impetus; violent force; impulse; *C.A., Ríopl.* vehement desire; — **de ira** fit of anger.
impetuoso [im·pe·twó·so] *adj.* impetuous, violent.
impío [im·pí·o] *adj.* impious, irreligious; profane.
implacable [im·pla·ká·ƀle] *adj.* implacable, relentless.
implantación [im·plan·ta·sjón] *f.* implantation, establishment, introduction (*of a system*).
implantar [im·plan·tár] *v.* to implant, establish, introduce.
implicar[6] [im·pli·kár] *v.* to imply; to implicate, involve.
implorar [im·plo·rár] *v.* to implore, entreat, beg.
imponente [im·po·nén·te] *adj.* imposing.
imponer[40] [im·po·nér] *v. irr.* to impose; to invest (*money*); — **miedo** to inspire fear; — **respeto** to inspire or command respect; **-se** to inspire fear or respect; to dominate; *Mex.* **-se a** to become accustomed to.
importancia [im·por·tán·sja] *f.* importance.
importante [im·por·tán·te] *adj.* important.
importar [im·por·tár] *v.* to be important; to matter; to amount to; to be necessary; to concern; to import.
importe [im·pór·te] *m.* amount, price, value; — **global** over-all costs.
importunar [im·por·tu·nár] *v.* to importune, nag, tease, pester.
importuno [im·por·tú·no] *adj.* annoying, persistent.
imposibilidad [im·po·si·ƀi·li·đáđ] *f.* impossibility.
imposibilitado [im·po·si·ƀi·li·tá·đo] *p.p. & adj.* disabled, unfit; helpless.
imposibilitar [im·po·si·ƀi·li·tár] *v.* to make impossible; to disable.
imposible [im·po·sí·ƀle] *adj.* impossible; intolerable, unbearable; *Col., Ven.* disabled (*because of illness*); *Am.* slovenly, untidy.
imposición [im·po·si·sjón] *f.* imposition; burden; tax.
impostor [im·pos·tór] *m.* impostor, cheat; **impostura** [im·pos·tú·ra] *f.* imposture, fraud, deceit.
impotencia [im·po·tén·sja] *f.* impotence.
impotente [im·po·tén·te] *adj.* impotent, powerless.
impreciso [im·pre·sí·so] *adj.* vague, indefinite; inaccurate.
impregnar [im·preg̶·nár] *v.* to impregnate, saturate.
imprenta [im·prén·ta] *f.* press; printing shop; printing.
imprescindible [im·pre·sin·dí·ƀle] *adj.* essential, indispensable.
impresión [im·pre·sjón] *f.* impression; printing; mark; footprint.
impresionante [im·pre·sjo·nán·te] *adj.* impressive.
impresionar [im·pre·sjo·nár] *v.* to impress; to move, affect, stir; **-se** to be stirred, moved.
impreso [im·pré·so] *p.p. irr. of* **imprimir** printed; impressed, imprinted; *m.* printed matter.
impresor [im·pre·sór] *m.* printer (*person*).
impresora [im·pre·só·ra] *f.* printer (*device*); — **de margarita** daisy wheel printer; — **de matriz de puntos** dot-matrix printer; — **de cilindro** barrel printer; — **de bola** ball printer; — **gráfica** plotter.
imprevisión [im·pre·ƀi·sjón] *f.* carelessness, lack of foresight.
imprevisto [im·pre·ƀís·to] *adj.* unforeseen, unexpected.
imprimir [im·pri·mír] *v.* to print; to imprint, impress.
improbable [im·pro·ƀá·ƀle] *adj.* improbable, unlikely.
improperio [im·pro·pé·rjo] *m.* affront, insult.
impropio [im·pró·pjo] *adj.* improper; unsuitable.
improvisar [im·pro·ƀi·sár] *v.* to improvise.
improviso [im·pro·ƀí·so] *adj.* unforeseen; **de** — suddenly; *Col., Ven., Mex.* **en un** — in a moment, in the twinkling of an eye.
imprudencia [im·pru·đén·sja] *f.* imprudence, indiscretion, rash act.
imprudente [im·pru·đén·te] *adj.* imprudent; unwise; indiscreet.
impuesto [im·pwés·to] *p.p. of* **imponer** imposed; informed; *Am.* **estar** — **a** to be used or accustomed to; *m.* tax, duty.
impulsar [im·pul·sár] *v.* to impel, push, move; to force.
impulso [im·púl·so] *m.* impulse; push.
impulsor [im·pul·sór] *m.* (*computadora*) driving mechanism; — **de discos** disk drive.
impureza [im·pu·ré·sa] *f.* impurity.
impuro [im·pú·ro] *adj.* impure.
imputar [im·pu·tár] *v.* to impute, attribute.
inacabable [i·na·ka·ƀá·ƀle] *adj.* unending, endless.
inacabado [i·na·ka·ƀá·đo] *adj.* unfinished.
inaccesible [i·nak·se·sí·ƀle] *adj.* inaccessible, unobtainable.
inacción [i·nak·sjón] *f.* inaction, inactivity, idleness.
inaceptable [i·na·sep·tá·ƀle] *adj.* unacceptable, unsatisfactory.
inactividad [i·nak·ti·ƀi·đáđ] *f.* inactivity.
inactivo [i·nak·tí·ƀo] *adj.* inactive.
inadecuado [i·na·đe·kwá·đo] *adj.* inadequate.
inadvertencia [i·nađ·ƀer·tén·sja] *f.* oversight; inattention, heedlessness.
inadvertido [i·nađ·ƀer·tí·đo] *adj.* careless, heedless; unnoticed.
inafectado [i·na·fek·tá·đo] *adj.* unaffected.
inagotable [i·na·g̶o·tá·ƀle] *adj.* inexhaustible.
inaguantable [i·na·g̶wan·tá·ƀle] *adj.* insufferable, unbearable.
inalámbrico [i·na·lám·bri·ko] *adj.* wireless.
inalterable [i·nal·te·rá·ƀle] *adj.* unalterable, unchangeable.
inalterado [i·nal·te·rá·đo] *adj.* unchanged.
inamovible [i·na·mo·ƀí·ƀle] = **inmovible.**
inanición [i·na·ni·sjón] *f.* starvation.
inanimado [i·na·ni·má·đo] *adj.* inanimate, lifeless.
inapelable [i·na·pe·lá·ƀle] *adj.* unappealable; unavoidable.
inapetencia [i·na·pe·tén·sja] *f.* lack of appetite.
inaplicable [i·na·pli·ká·ƀle] *adj.* inapplicable, unsuitable; — **al caso** irrelevant.
inapreciable [i·na·pre·sjá·ƀle] *adj.* invaluable; inappreciable, too small to be perceived, very slight.
inasequible [i·na·se·kí·ƀle] *adj.* inaccessible, not obtainable; hard to attain or obtain.
inaudito [i·naw·đí·to] *adj.* unheard-of; unprecedented.
inauguración [i·naw·g̶u·ra·sjón] *f.* inauguration.
inaugurar [i·naw·g̶u·rár] *v.* to inaugurate, begin, open.
incaico [iŋ·káj·ko], **incásico** [in·ká·si·ko] *adj.* Incan (*of or pertaining to the Incas*).
incalculable [iŋ·kal·ku·lá·ƀle] *adj.* incalculable; innumerable, untold.
incandescente [iŋ·kan·de·sén·te] *adj.* incandescent.
incansable [iŋ·kan·sá·ƀle] *adj.* untiring, tireless.
incapacidad [iŋ·ka·pa·si·đáđ] *f.* incompetence,

inability, unfitness.
incapacitar [iŋ·ka·pa·si·tár] *v.* to cripple, disable, handicap, unfit, make unfit.
incapaz [iŋ·ka·pás] *adj.* incapable, unable.
incauto [iŋ·káw·to] *adj.* unwary, heedless, reckless.
incendiar [iŋ·sen·djár] *v.* to set fire to; **-se** to catch fire.
incendio [iŋ·sén·djo] *m.* conflagration, fire.
incentivo [in·sén·ti·ƀo] *m.* incentive, inducement.
incertidumbre [in·ser·ti·đúm·bre] *f.* uncertainty, doubt.
incesante [in·se·sán·te] *adj.* incessant.
incidental [in·si·đen·tál] *adj.* incidental.
incidente [in·si·đén·te] *adj.* incidental; *m.* incident.
incienso [in·sjén·so] *m.* incense.
incierto [in·sjér·to] *adj.* uncertain, doubtful; unstable; unknown; untrue.
incisión [in·si·sjón] *f.* incision, cut, slit, gash.
incisivo [in·si·sí·ƀo] *adj.* incisive; *m.* incisor.
incitamiento [in·si·ta·mjén·to] *m.* incitement, inducement, incentive.
incitar [in·si·tár] *v.* to incite, rouse, stir up.
incivil [in·si·ƀíl] *adj.* uncivil, rude, impolite.
inclemencia [iŋ·kle·mén·sja] *f.* inclemency, severity, harshness; **inclemente** [iŋ·kle·mén·te] *adj.* unmerciful, merciless.
inclinación [iŋ·kli·na·sjón] *f.* inclination, affection; tendency, bent; bow; incline, slope.
inclinar [iŋ·kli·nár] *v.* (*bajar*) to incline; (*persuadir*) to persuade; **-se** to bow; to stoop; to incline, slope, slant; to lean, bend.
incluir[32] [iŋ·klwír] *v. irr.* to include; to inclose.
inclusive [iŋ·klu·sí·ƀe] *adv.* inclusive, including; even; **inclusivo** [in·klu·sí·ƀo] *adj.* inclusive; comprehensive.
incluso [iŋ·klú·so] *adj.* inclosed; included; including; even.
incógnito [iŋ·kóǥ·ni·to] *adj.* unknown; **de —** incognito (*with one's name or rank unknown*); **incógnita** *f.* unknown quantity (*in mathematics*).
incoherente [iŋ·ko·e·rén·te] *adj.* incoherent, disconnected, rambling.
incoloro [iŋ·ko·ló·ro] *adj.* colorless.
incombustible [iŋ·kom·bus·tí·ƀle] *adj.* incombustible; fireproof.
incomestible [iŋ·ko·mes·tí·ƀle] *adj.* inedible.
incomodar [iŋ·ko·mo·đár] *v.* to inconvenience, disturb, trouble, annoy.
incomodidad [iŋ·ko·mo·đi·đáđ] *f.* inconvenience, discomfort; bother, annoyance.
incómodo [iŋ·kó·mo·đo] *adj.* inconvenient, bothersome; uncomfortable.
incomparable [iŋ·kom·pa·rá·ƀle] *adj.* incomparable.
incompasivo [iŋ·kom·pa·sí·ƀo] *adj.* merciless, pitiless.
incompatible [iŋ·kom·pa·tí·ƀle] *adj.* incompatible; unsuitable, uncongenial.
incompetencia [iŋ·kom·pe·tén·sja] *f.* incompetence, inability, unfitness; **incompentente** [in·kom·pe·tén·te] *adj.* incompetent, unfit.
incompleto [iŋ·kom·plé·to] *adj.* incomplete.
incomprensible [iŋ·kom·pren·sí·ƀle] *adj.* incomprehensible.
inconcebible [iŋ·kon·se·ƀí·ƀle] *adj.* inconceivable.
inconcluso [iŋ·koŋ·klú·so] *adj.* unfinished.
incondicional [iŋ·kon·di·sjo·nál] *adj.* unconditional.
inconexo [iŋ·ko·nék·so] *adj.* unconnected; incoherent, disconnected.
inconfundible [iŋ·kon·fun·dí·ƀle] *adj.* unmistakable.
incongruente [iŋ·koŋ·grwén·te] *adj.* unsuitable, not appropriate; not harmonious.
inconquistable [iŋ·koŋ·kis·tá·ƀle] *adj.* unconquerable.
inconsciencia [iŋ·kon·sjén·sja] *f.* unconsciousness; unawareness.
inconsciente [iŋ·kon·sjén·te] *adj.* unconscious; unaware.
inconsecuente [iŋ·kon·se·kwén·te] *adj.* inconsistent; illogical.
inconsiderado [iŋ·kon·si·đe·rá·đo] *adj.* inconsiderate, thoughtless.
inconstancia [iŋ·kons·tán·sja] *f.* inconstancy, changeableness, fickleness.
inconstante [iŋ·kons·tán·te] *adj.* inconstant, fickle, changeable, variable.
incontable [iŋ·kon·tá·ƀle] *adj.* countless, innumerable.
inconveniencia [iŋ·kom·be·njén·sja] *f.* inconvenience; trouble.
inconveniente [iŋ·kom·be·njén·te] *adj.* inconvenient; improper; *m.* obstacle; objection.
incorporar [iŋ·kor·po·rár] *v.* to incorporate, unite; to embody; to include; **-se** to sit up; **-se a** to join.
incorrecto [iŋ·ko·rrék·to] *adj.* incorrect.
incredulidad [iŋ·kre·đu·li·đáđ] *f.* incredulity, unbelief.
incrédulo [iŋ·kré·đu·lo] *adj.* incredulous, unbelieving; *m.* unbeliever.
increíble [iŋ·kre·í·ƀle] *adj.* incredible, unbelievable.
incremento [iŋ·kre·mén·to] *m.* increment, increase.
incrustar [iŋ·krus·tár] *v.* to inlay; to encrust (*cover with a crust or hard coating*); **-se en** to penetrate impress itself deeply into.
incubadora [iŋ·ku·ƀa·đó·ra] *f.* incubator.
inculcar[6] [iŋ·kul·kár] *v.* to inculcate, instill, impress.
inculto [iŋ·kúl·to] *adj.* uncultured; uncultivated; unrefined.
incumbencia [iŋ·kum·bén·sja] *f.* concern, duty, obligation; **no es de mi —** it does not concern me, it is not within my province.
incurable [iŋ·ku·rá·ƀle] *adj.* incurable.
incurrir [iŋ·ku·rrír] *v.* to incur, fall (into); **— en un error** to fall into or commit an error; **— en el odio de** to incur the hatred of.
incursión [iŋ·kur·sjón] *f.* raid, invasion.
indagación [in·da·ǥa·sjón] *f.* investigation, inquiry.
indagador [in·da·ǥa·dór] *m.* investigator; inquirer; *adj.* investigating; inquiring.
indagar[7] [in·da·ǥár] *v.* to find out, investigate; to inquire.
indebido [in·de·ƀí·đo] *adj.* undue, improper; illegal; **indebidamente** [in·de·ƀi·đa·mén·te] *adv.* unduly; illegally.
indecencia [in·de·sén·sja] *f.* indecency, obscenity, indecent act or remark.
indecente [in·de·sén·te] *adj.* indecent, improper.
indecible [in·de·sí·ƀle] *adj.* inexpressible, untold.
indeciso [in·de·sí·so] *adj.* undecided; doubtful, uncertain.
indefectible [in·de·fek·tí·ƀle] *adj.* unfailing; **-mente** unfailingly.
indefenso [in·de·fén·so] *adj.* defenseless, unprotected.
indefinible [in·de·fi·ní·ƀle] *adj.* indefinable.
indefinido [in·de·fi·ní·đo] *adj.* indefinite.
indeleble [in·de·lé·ƀle] *adj.* indelible.
indemnización [in·dem·ni·sa·sjón] *f.* indemnity, compensation.
indemnizar[9] [in·dem·ni·sár] *v.* to indemnify, compensate.
independencia [in·de·pen·dén·sja] *f.* independence.
independiente [in·de·pen·djén·te] *adj.* independent.
indescriptible [in·des·krip·tí·ƀle] *adj.* indescribable.
indeseable [in·de·se·á·ƀle] *adj.* undesirable, unwelcome.
indiada [in·djá·đa] *f. Ríopl., C.A., Col.* community,

group, or crowd of Indians; *Col., Ven., Carib., Andes* an Indian-like remark or act; *Am.* an uncontrollable fit of anger.

indianista [in·dja·nís·ta] *m. & f.* student of Indian culture; *adj.* pertaining to Indian culture.

indiano [in·djá·no] *adj.* of or pertaining to the West or East Indies; *m.* Spaniard who goes back to settle in his country after having lived for some time in Spanish America.

indicación [in·di·ka·sjón] *f.* indication.

indicar[6] [in·di·kár] *v.* to indicate, show, point out.

indicativo [in·di·ka·tí·ƀo] *adj.* indicative; *m.* indicative, indicative mood.

índice [ín·di·se] *m.* index; catalogue; sign; pointer; forefinger.

indicio [in·dí·sjo] *m.* indication, sign.

indiferencia [in·di·fe·rén·sja] *f.* indifference.

indiferente [in·di·fe·rén·te] *adj.* indifferent.

indígena [in·dí·xe·na] *adj.* indigenous, native; *m. & f.* native inhabitant; *Am.* Indian.

indigestión [in·di·xes·tjón] *f.* indigestion.

indignación [in·diǥ·na·sjón] *f.* indignation.

indignado [in·diǥ·ná·đo] *p.p. & adj.* indignant, irritated, angry.

indignar [in·diǥ·nár] *v.* to irritate, anger; **-se** to become indignant, angry.

indignidad [in·diǥ·ni·đáđ] *f.* indignity, affront, insult; unworthy or disgraceful act.

indigno [in·díǥ·no] *adj.* unworthy; low, contemptible.

indio [ín·djo] *adj. & m.* Indian; Hindu; indium (*element*).

indirecta [in·di·rék·ta] *f.* hint, indirect remark, innuendo, insinuation.

indirecto [in·di·rék·to] *adj.* indirect.

indisciplinado [in·di·si·pli·ná·đo] *adj.* undisciplined, untrained.

indiscreto [in·dis·kré·to] *adj.* indiscreet, imprudent, unwise, rash.

indiscutible [in·dis·ku·tí·ƀle] *adj.* indisputable, unquestionable.

indispensable [in·dis·pen·sá·ƀle] *adj.* indispensable.

indisponer[40] [in·dis·po·nér] *v. irr.* to indispose; to make ill; — **a uno con otro** to prejudice someone against another; **-se** to become ill; **-se con** to fall out with, quarrel with.

indisposición [in·dis·po·si·sjón] *f.* indisposition, upset, slight illness; reluctance, unwillingness.

indispuesto [in·dis·pwés·to] *p.p. of* **indisponer** *& adj.* indisposed, unwilling; ill.

indisputable [in·dis·pu·tá·ƀle] *adj.* unquestionable.

indistinto [in·dis·tín·to] *adj.* indistinct, dim, vague, not clear.

individual [in·di·ƀi·đwál] *adj.* individual.

individualidad [in·di·ƀi·đwa·li·đáđ] *f.* individuality.

individualismo [in·di·ƀi·đwa·líz·mo] *m.* individualism.

individuo [in·di·ƀí·đwo] *adj.* individual; indivisible; *m.* individual; person; member.

indócil [in·dó·sil] *adj.* unruly, disobedient, headstrong.

indocto [in·dók·to] *adj.* uneducated, ignorant.

índole [ín·do·le] *f.* disposition, temper; kind, class.

indolencia [in·do·lén·sja] *f.* indolence, laziness; insensitiveness, indifference.

indolente [in·do·lén·te] *adj.* indolent, lazy; insensitive, indifferent.

indomable [in·do·má·ƀle] *adj.* indomitable, unconquerable; unmanageable; untamable.

indómito [in·dó·mi·to] *adj.* untamed; uncontrollable, unruly.

inducir[25] [in·du·sír] *v. irr.* to induce; to persuade.

indudable [in·du·đá·ƀle] *adj.* unquestionable, certain.

indulgencia [in·dul·xén·sja] *f.* indulgence, tolerance, forgiveness; remission of sins.

indulgente [in·dul·xén·te] *adj.* indulgent, lenient.

indultar [in·dul·tár] *v.* to pardon, set free; to exempt.

indulto [in·dúl·to] *m.* pardon, forgiveness; exemption; privilege.

indumentaria [in·du·men·tá·rja] *f.* costume, dress; manner of dressing.

industria [in·dús·trja] *f.* industry; cleverness, skill; **de** — intentionally, on purpose.

industrial [in·dus·trjál] *adj.* industrial; *m.* industrialist; manufacturer.

industrioso [in·dus·trjó·so] *adj.* industrious.

inédito [i·né·đi·to] *adj.* unpublished.

inefable [i·ne·fá·ƀle] *adj.* ineffable, inexpressible.

ineficaz [i·ne·fi·kás] *adj.* ineffective; inefficient.

inepto [i·nép·to] *adj.* incompetent; unsuitable.

inequívoco [i·ne·kí·ƀo·ko] *adj.* unmistakable.

inercia [i·nér·sja] *f.* inertia, lifelessness; inactivity.

inerme [i·nér·me] *adj.* unarmed, defenseless.

inerte [i·nér·te] *adj.* inert; inactive, sluggish, slow.

inesperado [i·nes·pe·rá·đo] *adj.* unexpected.

inestable [i·nes·tá·ƀle] *adj.* unstable; unsettled; unsteady.

inestimable [i·nes·ti·má·ƀle] *adj.* inestimable, invaluable.

inevitable [i·ne·ƀi·tá·ƀle] *adj.* inevitable, unavoidable.

inexacto [i·nek·sák·to] *adj.* inexact, inaccurate.

inexorable [i·nek·so·rá·ƀle] *adj.* inexorable.

inexperiencia [i·nes·pe·rjén·sja] *f.* inexperience.

inexperto [i·nes·pér·to] *adj.* unskillful, unskilled, inexperienced.

inexplicable [i·nes·pli·ká·ƀle] *adj.* inexplicable.

inextinguible [i·nes·tiŋ·gí·ƀle] *adj.* inextinguishable, unquenchable.

infalible [in·fa·lí·ƀle] *adj.* infallible.

infame [in·fá·me] *adj.* infamous; *m.* scoundrel.

infamia [in·fá·mja] *f.* infamy, dishonor; wickedness.

infancia [in·fán·sja] *f.* infancy.

infante [in·fán·te] *m.* infant; infante (*royal prince of Spain, except the heir to the throne*); infantryman.

infantería [in·fan·te·rí·a] *f.* infantry.

infantil [in·fan·tíl] *adj.* infantile, childlike, childish.

infatigable [in·fa·ti·ǥá·ƀle] *adj.* tireless, untiring.

infausto [in·fáws·to] *adj.* unfortunate; unhappy.

infección [in·fek·sjón] *f.* infection; **infeccioso** *adj.* infectious.

infectar [in·fek·tár] *v.* to infect; to corrupt; **-se** to become infected.

infeliz [in·fe·lís] *adj.* unhappy, unfortunate; *m.* poor wretch.

inferior [in·fe·rjór] *adj.* inferior; lower; *m.* inferior.

inferioridad [in·fe·rjo·ri·đáđ] *f.* inferiority.

inferir[3] [in·fe·rír] *v. irr.* (*concluir*) to infer; to imply; (*causar*) to inflict.

infernal [in·fer·nál] *adj.* infernal.

infestar [in·fes·tár] *v.* to infest, invade, overrun, plague; to corrupt, infect.

inficionar [in·fi·sjo·nár] *v.* to infect; to contaminate.

infiel [in·fjél] *adj.* unfaithful, faithless; infidel; inaccurate.

infiernillo [in·fjer·ní·yo] *m.* chafing dish.

infierno [in·fjér·no] *m.* hell; **en el quinto** — very far away, at the end of nowhere.

infiltrar [in·fil·trár] *v.* to filter through; **-se** to leak (into), filter (through), infiltrate.

infinidad [in·fi·ni·đáđ] *f.* infinity; **una** — **de** a large number of.

infinito [in·fi·ní·to] *adj.* infinite; *adv.* infinitely; *m.* infinity.

inflamación [in·fla·ma·sjón] *f.* inflammation.

inflamado [in·fla·má·đo] *p.p. & adj.* inflamed; sore.
inflamar [in·fla·már] *v.* to inflame, excite; to kindle, set on fire; **-se** to become inflamed.
inflar [in·flár] *v.* to inflate; to exaggerate; **-se** to become inflated; to swell up with pride.
inflexible [in·flek·sí·ƀle] *adj.* inflexible, stiff, rigid; unbending.
inflexión [in·flek·sjón] *f.* inflection.
infligir[11] [in·fli·xír] *v.* to inflict.
influencia [in·flwén·sja] *f.* influence.
influenza [in·flwén·sa] *f.* influenza, grippe, flu.
influir[32] [in·flwír] *v. irr.* to influence.
influjo [in·flú·xo] *m.* influence; influx, inward flow.
influyente [in·flu·yén·te] *adj.* influential.
información [in·for·ma·sjón] *f.* information.
informal [in·for·mál] *adj.* informal; unconventional; unreliable, not dependable, not punctual.
informar [in·for·már] *v.* to inform; to give form to; to give a report; to present a case; **-se** to find out.
informática [in·for·má·ti·ka] *f.* (*computadora*) computer science.
informatizar [in·for·ma·ti·sár] *v.* to computerize.
informe [in·fór·me] *m.* report, account; information; brief; *adj.* formless, shapeless.
infortunio [in·for·tú·njo] *m.* misfortune, mishap; misery.
infracción [in·frak·sjón] *f.* infraction, breach, violation (*of a law, treaty, etc.*).
infractor [in·frak·tór] *m.* transgressor, lawbreaker, violator (*of a law*).
infrascrito [in·fras·krí·to] *m.* undersigned, subscriber, signer (*of a letter, document, etc.*); **el — secretario** the secretary whose signature appears below.
infringir[11] [in·friŋ·xír] *v.* to infringe, break, violate.
infructuoso [in·fruk·twó·so] *adj.* fruitless.
ínfulas [ín·fu·las] *f. pl.* airs, false importance; **darse —** to put on airs.
infundado [in·fun·dá·đo] *adj.* groundless, without foundation.
infundir [in·fun·dír] *v.* to infuse, inspire; to instill.
infusión [in·fu·sjón] *f.* infusion (*liquid extract obtained by steeping*); infusion, inspiration; **poner en —** to steep (*as tea leaves*).
ingeniería [iŋ·xe·nje·rí·a] *f.* engineering.
ingeniero [iŋ·xe·njé·ro] *m.* engineer.
ingenio [iŋ·xé·njo] *m.* genius; talent; ingenuity; mentality, mental power, mind; wit; **— de azúcar** sugar refinery; sugar plantation.
ingeniosidad [iŋ·xe·njo·si·đáđ] *f.* ingenuity, cleverness.
ingenioso [iŋ·xe·njó·so] *adj.* ingenious, clever.
ingenuidad [iŋ·xe·nwi·đáđ] *f.* candor, frankness; unaffected simplicity.
ingenuo [iŋ·xé·nwo] *adj.* frank, sincere; simple, unaffected; naive.
ingerir [iŋ·xe·rír] = **injerir.**
ingestion [iŋ·xes·tjón] *f.* ingestion.
ingle [íŋ·gle] *f.* groin.
inglés [iŋ·glés] *adj.* English; **a la inglesa** in the English fashion; *Am.* **ir a la inglesa** to go Dutch treat; *m.* Englishman; the English language.
inglete [iŋ·glé·te] *m.* miter.
ingobernable [iŋ·go·ƀer·ná·ƀle] *adj.* ungovernable, unruly, uncontrollable.
ingratitud [iŋ·gra·ti·túđ] *f.* ingratitude.
ingrato [iŋ·grá·to] *adj.* ungrateful, thankless; harsh; cruel; disdainful.
ingrediente [iŋ·gre·đjén·te] *m.* ingredient.
ingresar [iŋ·gre·sár] *v.* to enter; (*computadora*) to input; **— en** to join (*a society, club, etc.*).
ingreso [iŋ·gré·so] *m.* entrance; entry; **-s** receipts., profits; revenue.
inhábil [i·ná·ƀil] *adj.* unskilled; unskilful; unfit.
inhabilidad [i·na·ƀi·li·đáđ] *f.* inability; unfitness.
inhabilitar [i·na·ƀi·li·tár] *v.* to disqualify; to unfit, disable.
inherente [i·ne·rén·te] *adj.* inherent.
inhibir [i·ni·ƀír] *v.* to inhibit.
inhospitalario [i·nos·pi·ta·lá·rjo] *adj.* inhospitable.
inhumano [i·nu·má·no] *adj.* inhuman, cruel.
iniciador [i·ni·sja·đór] *m.* initiator; pioneer; *adj.* initiating.
inicial [i·ni·sjál] *adj. & f.* initial.
iniciar [i·ni·sjár] *v.* to initiate; to begin.
iniciativa [i·ni·sja·tí·ƀa] *f.* initiative.
inicuo [i·ní·kwo] *adj.* wicked.
iniquidad [i·ni·ki·đáđ] *f.* iniquity, wickedness; sin.
injerir[3] [iŋ·xe·rír] *v. irr.* to inject, insert; **-se** to interfere, meddle.
injertar [iŋ·xer·tár] *v.* to graft.
injerto [iŋ·xér·to] *m.* graft.
injuria [iŋ·xú·rja] *f.* affront, insult; harm, damage.
injuriar [iŋ·xu·rjár] *v.* to insult, offend; to harm, damage.
injurioso [iŋ·xu·rjó·so] *adj.* insulting, offensive; harmful.
injusticia [iŋ·xus·tí·sja] *f.* injustice.
injustificado [iŋ·xus·ti·fi·ká·đo] *adj.* unjustified; unjustifiable.
injusto [iŋ·xús·to] *adj.* unjust, unfair.
inmaculado [im·ma·ku·lá·đo] *adj.* immaculate, clean; pure.
inmediación [im·me·đja·sjón] *f.* vicinity; nearness; **-es** environs, outskirts.
inmediato [im·me·đjá·to] *adj.* near, close; *Am.* **de —** immediately; suddenly; **inmediatamente** *adv.* immediately, at once.
inmejorable [im·me·xo·rá·ƀle] *adj.* unsurpassable.
inmensidad [im·men·si·đáđ] *f.* immensity, vastness; vast number.
inmenso [im·mén·so] *adj.* immense, vast, huge; boundless.
inmersión [im·mer·sjón] *f.* immersion, dip.
inmigración [im·mi·gra·sjón] *f.* immigration.
inmigrante [im·mi·grán·te] *adj., m. & f.* immigrant.
inmigrar [im·mi·grár] *v.* to immigrate.
inminente [im·mi·nén·te] *adj.* imminent.
inmiscuir[32] [im·mis·kwír] *v. irr.* to mix; **-se** to meddle, interfere.
inmoble [im·mó·ƀle] *adj.* motionless; unshaken.
inmoral [im·mo·rál] *adj.* immoral; **inmoralidad** [im·mo·ra·li·đáđ] *f.* immorality.
inmortal [im·mor·tál] *adj.* immortal; **inmortalidad** *f.* immortality.
inmovible [im·mo·ƀí·ƀle] *adj.* immovable, fixed; steadfast.
inmóvil [im·mó·ƀil] *adj.* motionless, still; immovable.
inmuebles [im·mwé·ƀles] *m. pl.* real estate.
inmundicia [im·mun·dí·sja] *f.* filth, dirt; nastiness.
inmundo [im·mún·do] *adj.* filthy, dirty; impure; nasty.
inmune [im·mú·ne] *adj.* immune; exempt.
inmunidad [im·mu·ni·đáđ] *f.* immunity.
inmutable [im·mu·tá·ƀle] *adj.* unchangeable, invariable.
inmutar [im·mu·tár] *v.* to alter, change; **-se** to show emotion (*either by turning pale or blushing*).
innato [in·ná·to] *adj.* innate, natural inborn.
innecesario [in·ne·se·sá·rjo] *adj.* unnecessary.
innegable [in·ne·gá·ƀle] *adj.* undeniable, not to be denied.

innocuo [in·nó·kwo] *adj.* innocuous, harmless; **innocuidad** *f.* harmlessness.
innovación [in·no·ƀa·sjón] *f.* innovation; novelty.
innumerable [in·nu·me·rá·ƀle] *adj.* innumerable.
inobservancia [i·noƀ·ser·ƀán·sja] *f.* nonobservance, violation (*of a law*), lack of observance (*of a law, rule, or custom*).
inocencia [i·no·sén·sja] *f.* innocence.
inocente [i·no·sén·te] *adj.* innocent; *m.* innocent person; **inocentón** *adj.* quite foolish or simple; easily fooled; *m.* dupe, unsuspecting victim.
inocular [i·no·ku·lár] *v.* to inoculate.
inodoro [i·no·đó·ro] *adj.* odorless; *m. C.A., Ven., Col.* toilet, water closet.
inofensivo [i·no·fen·sí·ƀo] *adj.* inoffensive; harmless.
inolvidable [i·nol·ƀi·đá·ƀle] *adj.* unforgettable.
inopinado [i·no·pi·ná·đo] *adj.* unexpected.
inoportuno [i·no·por·tú·no] *adj.* inopportune, untimely, unsuitable.
inoxidable [i·nok·si·đá·ƀle] *adj.* rust proof.
inquietar [iŋ·kje·tár] *v.* to worry, disturb, make uneasy; **-se** to become disturbed, uneasy.
inquieto [iŋ·kjé·to] *adj.* restless; uneasy, anxious.
inquietud [iŋ·kje·túđ] *f.* restlessness; anxiety, uneasiness; fear.
inquilino [iŋ·ki·lí·no] *m.* tenant, renter; lodger.
inquina [iŋ·kí·na] *f.* aversion, grudge, dislike.
inquirir[35] [iŋ·ki·rír] *v. irr.* to inquire, investigate; to find out.
inquisición [iŋ·ki·si·sjón] *f.* inquisition; inquiry, investigation.
insaciable [in·sa·sjá·ƀle] *adj.* insatiable, never satisfied, greedy.
insalubre [in·sa·lú·ƀre] *adj.* unhealthy, unhealthful, unwholesome.
insano [in·sá·no] *adj.* insane, crazy; unhealthy.
inscribir[52] [ins·kri·ƀír] *v.* to inscribe; to register, enroll; to record; **-se** to register.
inscripción [ins·krip·sjón] *f.* inscription; registration.
inscripto [ins·kríp·to], **inscrito** [ins·krí·to] *p.p. of* inscribir.
insecto [in·sék·to] *m.* insect.
inseguro [in·se·ǥú·ro] *adj.* insecure; unsafe; doubtful, uncertain.
insensato [in·sen·sá·to] *adj.* senseless; foolish.
insensibilidad [in·sen·si·ƀi·li·đáđ] *f.* insensibility, unconsciousness; lack of feeling.
insensible [in·sen·sí·ƀle] *adj.* insensible; unfeeling; imperceptible.
inseparable [in·se·pa·rá·ƀle] *adj.* inseparable.
inserción [in·ser·sjón] *f.* insertion; insert.
insertar [in·ser·tár] *v.* to insert.
inserto *adj.* inserted.
inservible [in·ser·ƀi·ƀle] *adj.* useless.
insidioso [in·si·đjó·so] *adj.* insidious; sly, crafty.
insigne [in·síǥ·ne] *adj.* famous.
insignia [in·síǥ·nja] *f.* badge, medal, decoration; flag, pennant; **-s** insignia.
insignificante [in·siǥ·ni·fi·kán·te] *adj.* insignificant.
insinuación [in·si·nwa·sjón] *f.* insinuation; intimation, hint.
insinuar[18] [in·si·nwár] *v.* to insinuate, hint; **-se** to insinuate oneself (*into another's friendship*); to creep (into) gradually.
insipidez [in·si·pi·đés] *f.* flatness, tastelessness, dullness; **insípido** *adj.* insipid; tasteless.
insistencia [in·sis·tén·sja] *f.* insistence, persistence, obstinacy; **insistente** [in·sis·tén·te] *adj.* insistent, persistent.
insistir [in·sis·tír] *v.* to insist; to persist.
insociable [in·so·sjá·ƀle] *adj.* unsociable.
insolación [in·so·la·sjón] *f.* sunstroke.
insolencia [in·so·lén·sja] *f.* insolence.
insolentarse [in·so·len·tár·se] *v.* to sauce, become insolent, act with insolence.
insolente [in·so·lén·te] *adj.* insolent.
insólito [in·só·li·to] *adj.* unusual; uncommon.
insolvente [in·sol·ƀén·te] *adj.* insolvent, bankrupt.
insomne [in·sóm·ne] *adj.* sleepless.
insondable [in·son·dá·ƀle] *adj.* fathomless, deep; impenetrable.
insoportable [in·so·por·tá·ƀle] *adj.* unbearable.
insospechado [in·sos·pe·čá·đo] *adj.* unsuspected.
inspección [ins·pek·sjón] *f.* inspection.
inspeccionar [ins·pek·sjo·nár] *v.* to inspect.
inspector [ins·pek·tór] *m.* inspector; overseer.
inspiración [ins·pi·ra·sjón] *f.* inspiration; inhalation, breathing in.
inspirar [ins·pi·rár] *v.* to inspire; to inhale.
instalación [ins·ta·la·sjón] *f.* installation.
instalar [ins·ta·lar] *v.* to install.
instancia [ins·tán·sja] *f.* instance, urgent request; petition; **a -s de** at the request of.
instantánea [ins·tan·tá·ne·a] *f.* snapshot.
instantáneo [ins·tan·tá·ne·o] *adj.* instantaneous; sudden.
instante [ins·tán·te] *m.* instant, moment; **al** — at once, immediately; **por -s** continually; from one moment to another; *adj.* instant, urgent.
instar [ins·tár] *v.* to urge, press; to be urgent.
instigar[7] [ins·ti·ǥár] *v.* to instigate, urge on, incite.
instintivo [ins·tin·tí·ƀo] *adj.* instinctive.
instinto [ins·tín·to] *m.* instinct.
institución [ins·ti·tu·sjón] *f.* institution; establishment, foundation; **-se** institutes, collection of precepts and principles.
instituir[32] [ins·ti·twír] *v. irr.* to institute; — **por heredero** to appoint as heir.
instituto [ins·ti·tú·to] *m.* institute; established principle, law, or custom; — **de segunda enseñanza** high school.
institutriz [ins·ti·tu·trís] *f.* governess.
instrucción [ins·truk·sjón] *f.* instruction; education.
instructivo [ins·truk·tí·ƀo] *adj.* instructive.
instruir[32] [ins·trwír] *v. irr.* to instruct, teach; to inform.
instrumento [ins·tru·mén·to] *m.* instrument.
insuficiencia [in·su·fi·sjén·sja] *f.* insufficiency, deficiency; incompetence; dearth, scarcity, lack.
insuficiente [in·su·fi·sjén·te] *adj.* insufficient.
insufrible [in·su·frí·ƀle] *adj.* insufferable, unbearable.
insula [ín·su·la] *f.* island.
insulina [in·su·lí·na] *f.* insulin.
insultante [in·sul·tán·te] *adj.* insulting, abusive.
insultar [in·sul·tár] *v.* to insult; **-se** to be seized with a fit.
insulto [in·súl·to] *m.* insult; sudden fit or attack.
insuperable [in·su·pe·rá·ƀle] *adj.* insuperable; insurmountable.
insurgente [in·sur·xén·te] *adj., m. & f.* insurgent.
insurrección [in·su·rrek·sjón] *f.* insurrection, uprising, revolt.
insurrecto [in·su·rrék·to] *m.* insurgent, rebel; *adj.* rebellious.
intacto [in·ták·to] *adj.* intact.
intachable [in·ta·čá·ƀle] *adj.* faultless, irreproachable.
integrador [in·te·ǥra·dór] *m.* integrator; *m.* **-s** members.
integral [in·te·ǥrál] *adj.* integral; *f.* integral (*math*).
integrante [in·te·ǥrán·te] *adj.* integral; integrating.
integrar [in·te·ǥrár] *v.* to form; to integrate.
integridad [in·te·ǥri·đáđ] *f.* integrity; wholeness;

honesty; purity.
íntegro [ín·te·ǥro] *adj.* whole, complete, honest, upright.
intelecto [in·te·lék·to] *m.* intellect.
intelectual [in·te·lek·twál] *adj.* intellectual.
inteligencia [in·te·li·xén·sja] *f.* intelligence.
inteligente [in·te·li·xén·te] *adj.* intelligent.
intemperancia [in·tem·pe·rán·sja] *f.* intemperance, excess.
intemperie [in·tem·pé·rje] *f.* open air; bad weather; **a la** — unsheltered, outdoors, in the open air; exposed to the weather.
intención [in·ten·sjón] *f.* intention; **intencional** [in·ten·sjo·nál] *adj.* intentional.
intendente [in·ten·dén·te] *m.* manager, superintendent, supervisor; *Ríopl.* governor of a province; *Am.* police commissioner.
intensidad [in·ten·si·đáđ] *f.* intensity; stress.
intenso [in·tén·so] *adj.* intense; intensive; ardent, vehement.
intentar [in·ten·tár] *v.* to attempt, try; to intend.
intento [in·tén·to] *m.* intent, purpose, intention; **de** — on purpose.
intercalar [in·ter·ka·lár] *v.* to insert, place between.
intercambio [in·ter·kám·bjo] *m.* interchange; exchange.
interceder [in·ter·se·đér] *v.* to intercede.
interceptar [in·ter·sep·tár] *v.* to intercept.
intercesión [in·ter·se·sjón] *f.* intercession, mediation.
interdental [in·ter·đen·tál] *adj.* interdental.
interdicción [in·ter·đik·sjón] *f.* interdiction; prevention.
interés [in·te·rés] *m.* interest; — **compuesto** compound interest.
interesante [in·te·re·sán·te] *adj.* interesting.
interesar [in·te·re·sár] *v.* to interest; to give an interest or share; **-se** to be or become interested.
interfaz [in·ter·fás] *f.* (*computadora*) interface.
interferencia [in·ter·fe·rén·sja] *f.* interference.
ínterin [ín·te·rin] *m.* interim, meantime; **en al** — in the meantime.
interino [in·te·rí·no] *adj.* acting, temporary.
interior [in·te·rjór] *adj.* interior; inner; internal; *m.* interior, inside.
interjección [in·ter·xek·sjón] *f.* interjection, exclamation.
interlineal [in·ter·li·ne·ál] *adj.* interlinear.
interlocutor [in·ter·lo·ku·tór] *m.* participant in a dialogue.
intermedio [in·ter·mé·đjo] *adj.* intermediate; intervening; *m.* intermission; interval; **por** — **de** by means of, through the intervention of.
interminable [in·ter·mi·ná·ƀle] *adj.* interminable, unending, endless.
intermisión [in·ter·mi·sjón] *f.* intermission, interruption, pause, interval.
intermitente [in·ter·mi·tén·te] *adj.* intermittent, occurring at intervals; **calentura** (*or* **fiebre**) — intermittent fever.
internacional [in·ter·na·sjo·nál] *adj.* international.
internado [in·ter·ná·đo] *m.* a boarding student.
internar [in·ter·nár] *v.* to intern, confine; **-se** to penetrate, go into the interior.
interno [in·tér·no] *adj.* internal; interior; *m.* boarding-school student.
interoceánico [in·te·ro·se·á·ni·ko] *adj.* interoceanic; transcontinental.
interpelar [in·ter·pe·lár] *v.* to interrogate, question, demand explanations; to ask the aid of.
interponer[40] [in·ter·po·nér] *v. irr.* to interpose, put between, insert; to place as a mediator; **-se** to intervene, mediate.
interpretación [in·ter·pre·ta·sjón] *f.* interpretation.
interpretar [in·ter·pre·tár] *v.* to interpret.
intérprete [in·tér·pre·te] *m.* & *f.* interpreter.
interpuesto [in·ter·pwés·to] *p.p. of* **interponer.**
interrogación [in·te·rro·ǥa·sjón] *f.* interrogation, question; **signo de** — question mark.
interrogador [in·te·rro·ǥa·đór] *m.* questioner; *adj.* questioning.
interrogar[7] [in·te·rro·ǥár] *v.* to interrogate, question.
interrogativo [in·te·rro·ǥa·tí·ƀo] *adj.* interrogative.
interrogatorio [in·te·rro·ǥa·tó·rjo] *m.* interrogation, questioning.
interrumpir [in·te·rrum·pír] *v.* to interrupt.
interrupción [in·te·rrup·sjón] *f.* interruption.
interruptor [in·te·rrup·tór] *m.* interrupter; (*rilai fusible*) electric switch; — **de circuitos** circuit breaker.
intersección [in·ter·sek·sjón] *f.* intersection.
intersticio [in·ters·tí·sjo] *m.* interval.
intervalo [in·ter·ƀá·lo] *m.* interval.
intervención [in·ter·ƀen·sjón] *f.* intervention; mediation; participation; auditing of accounts.
intervenir[48] [in·ter·ƀe·nír] *v. irr.* to intervene; to mediate; to audit (*accounts*).
interventor [in·ter·ƀen·tór] *m.* inspector; controller, comptroller; auditor.
intestino [in·tes·tí·no] *m.* intestine; *adj.* intestine, internal.
intimación [in·ti·ma·sjón] *f.* intimation; hint, insinuation, suggestion.
intimar [in·ti·már] *v.* to announce, notify; to intimate, hint; to become intimate, become friendly.
intimidad [in·ti·mi·đáđ] *f.* intimacy.
intimidar [in·ti·mi·đár] *v.* to intimidate.
íntimo [ín·ti·mo] *adj.* intimate.
intitular [in·ti·tu·lár] *v.* to entitle; to give a title to (*a person or a thing*); **-se** to be entitled, be called; to call oneself (*by a certain name*).
intolerable [in·to·le·rá·ƀle] *adj.* intolerable.
intolerancia [in·to·le·rán·sja] *f.* intolerance; **intolerante** [in·to·le·rán·te] *adj.* intolerant, narrow-minded.
intoxicante [in·tok·si·kán·te] *m.* poison.
intoxicar[6] [in·tok·si·kár] *v.* to poison.
intranquilo [in·traŋ·kí·lo] *adj.* disturbed, uneasy.
intranquilidad [in·traŋ·ki·li·đáđ] *f.* uneasiness, restlessness.
intransigencia [in·tran·si·xén·sja] *f.* uncompromising act or attitude; intolerance.
intransigente [in·tran·si·xén·te] *adj.* uncompromising, unwilling to compromise or yield; intolerant.
intratable [in·tra·tá·ƀle] *adj.* unsociable; rude; unruly.
intravenoso [in·tra·ƀe·nó·so] *adj.* intravenous (*within a vein or the veins; into a vein*).
intrepidez [in·tre·pi·đés] *f.* fearlessness, courage.
intrépido [in·tré·pi·đo] *adj.* intrepid, fearless.
intriga [in·trí·ǥa] *f.* intrigue; scheme; plot.
intrigante [in·tri·ǥán·te] *m.* & *f.* intriguer, plotter; *adj.* intriguing.
intrigar[7] [in·tri·ǥár] *v.* to intrigue.
intrincado [in·triŋ·ká·đo] *adj.* intricate, complicated, entangled.
introducción [in·tro·đuk·sjón] *f.* introduction.
introducir[25] [in·tro·đu·sír] *v. irr.* to introduce; (*computadora*) to input; **-se** to introduce oneself; to get in; to penetrate.
intromisión [in·tro·mi·sjón] *f.* meddling; insertion.
introvertido [in·tro·ƀer·tí·đo] *m.* & *f.* introvert.
intruso [in·trú·so] *adj.* intrusive, intruding; *m.* intruder.

intuición [in·twi·sjón] *f.* intuition.
intuir[32] [in·twír] *v. irr.* to sense, feel by intuition.
inundación [i·nun·da·sjón] *f.* inundation, flood.
inundar [i·nun·dár] *v.* to inundate, flood.
inusitado [i·nu·si·tá·đo] *adj.* unusual, rare.
inútil [i·nú·til] *adj.* useless.
inutilidad [i·nu·ti·li·đáđ] *f.* uselessness.
inutilizar[9] [i·nu·ti·li·sár] *v.* to make useless, put out of commission; to disable; to ruin, spoil.
invadir [im·ba·đír] *v.* to invade.
invalidar [im·ba·li·dár] *v.* to render invalid; to void, annul.
inválido [im·bá·li·đo] *adj.* invalid; void, null; sickly, weak; *m.* invalid.
invariable [im·ba·rjá·ƀle] *adj.* invariable.
invasión [im·ba·sjón] *f.* invasion.
invasor [im·ba·sór] *m.* invader; *adj.* invading; **ejército** — invading army.
invencible [im·ben·sí·ƀle] *adj.* invincible, unconquerable.
invención [im·ben·sjón] *f.* invention.
invendible [im·ben·dí·ƀle] *adj.* unsaleable.
inventar [im·ben·tár] *v.* to invent.
inventariar[17] [im·ben·ta·rjár] *v.* to inventory, take an inventory of.
inventario [im·ben·tá·rjo] *m.* inventory.
inventiva [im·ben·tí·ƀa] *f.* inventiveness, power of inventing, ingenuity.
inventivo [im·ben·tí·ƀo] *adj.* inventive.
invento [im·ben·to] *m.* invention.
inventor [im·ben·tór] *m.* inventor; storyteller, fibber.
invernáculo [im·ber·ná·ku·lo] *m.* greenhouse, hothouse.
invernada [im·ber·ná·đa] *f.* wintering; *Am.* pasturing.
invernadero [im·ber·na·đé·ro] *m.* winter quarters; winter resort; winter pasture; greenhouse, hothouse.
invernal [im·ber·nál] *adj.* wintry, winter.
invernar[1] [im·ber·nár] *v. irr.* to winter, spend the winter.
inverosímil [im·be·ro·sí·mil] **inverisímil** [im·be·ri·sí·mil] *adj.* unlikely, improbable.
inversión [im·bér·sjón] *f.* inversion; investment.
inverso [im·bér·so] *adj.* inverse, inverted; reverse; **a** (*or* **por**) **la inversa** on the contrary.
invertir[3] [im·ber·tír] *v. irr.* to invert; to reverse; to invest; to employ, spend (*time*).
investigación [im·bes·ti·ǥa·sjón] *f.* investigation.
investigador [im·bes·ti·ǥa·đór] *m.* investigator; *adj.* investigating.
investigar[7] [im·bes·ti·ǥár] *v.* to investigate.
invicto [im·bík·to] *adj.* unconquered; always victorious.
invierno [im·bjér·no] *m.* winter; *C.A., Col., Ven., Ec., Peru* the rainy season.
invisible [im·bi·sí·ƀle] *adj.* invisible.
invitación [im·bi·ta·sjón] *f.* invitation.
invitar [im·bi·tár] *v.* to invite.
invocación [im·bo·ka·sjón] *f.* invocation.
invocar[6] [im·bo·kár] *v.* to invoke.
involuntario [im·bo·lun·tá·rjo] *adj.* involuntary.
inyección [in·ŷek·sjón] *f.* injection.
inyectado [in·ŷek·tá·đo] *p.p.* injected; *adj.* bloodshot, inflamed.
inyectar [in·ŷek·tár] *v.* to inject.
ion [jon] *m.* ion.
ionizar[9] [jo·ni·sár] *v. irr.* to ionize.
ir[33] [ír] *v. irr.* to go; to walk; — **corriendo** to be running; — **entendiendo** to understand gradually; to begin to understand; — **a caballo** to ride horseback; — **a pie** to walk; — **en automóvil** to drive, ride in an automobile; **no irle ni venirle a uno** to make no difference to one; **¿cómo le va?** how are you? **no me va nada en eso** that doesn't concern me; **¡vamos!** let's go! come on! **¡vaya!** well now!, **¡vaya un hómbre!** what a man!; **-se** to go, go away; to escape; **-se abajo** to fall down, topple over; to collapse; **-se a pique** to founder, sink.
ira [í·ra] *f.* ire, anger.
iracundo [i·ra·kún·do] *adj.* irritable; angry.
iridio [i·rí·đjo] *m.* iridium.
iris [í·ris] *m.* iris (*of the eye*); **arco** — rainbow.
irisado [i·ri·sá·đo] *adj.* iridescent, rainbow-hued.
ironía [i·ro·ní·a] *f.* irony.
irónico [i·ró·ni·ko] *adj.* ironic, ironical.
irracional [i·rra·sjo·nál] *adj.* irrational, unreasonable.
irradiar [i·rra·djár] *v.* to radiate.
irreal [i·rre·ál] *adj.* unreal.
irreflexión [i·rre·flek·sjón] *f.* thoughtlessness.
irreflexivo [i·rre·flek·sí·ƀo] *adj.* thoughtless.
irrefrenable [i·rre·fre·ná·ƀle] *adj.* uncontrollable.
irrefutable [i·rre·fu·tá·ƀle] *adj.* irrefutable.
irregular [i·rre·ǥu·lár] *adj.* irregular.
irreligioso [i·rre·li·xjó·so] *adj.* irreligious.
irremediable [i·rre·me·đjá·ƀle] *adj.* irremediable; hopeless, incurable.
irreprochable [i·rre·pro·čá·ƀle] *adj.* irreproachable, flawless.
irresistible [i·rre·sis·tí·ƀle] *adj.* irresistible.
irresoluto [i·rre·so·lú·to] *adj.* irresolute, undecided, hesitating.
irrespetuoso [i·rres·pe·twó·so] *adj.* disrespectful.
irreverencia [i·rre·ƀe·rén·sja] *f.* irreverence.
irreverente [i·rre·ƀe·rén·te] *adj.* irreverent.
irrigación [i·rri·ǥa·sjón] *f.* irrigation.
irrigar[7] [i·rri·ǥár] *v.* to irrigate.
irrisión [i·rri·sjón] *f.* mockery, ridicule, derision.
irritación [i·rri·ta·sjón] *f.* irritation.
irritante [i·rri·tán·te] *adj.* irritating.
irritar [i·rri·tár] *v.* to irritate.
irrumpir [i·rrum·pír] *v.* to enter violently; to invade.
irrupción [i·rrup·sjón] *f.* sudden attack, raid, invasion.
isla [iz·la] *f.* island.
islamismo [iz·la·míz·mo] *m.* islamism.
islandés [iz·lan·dés] *adj.* Icelandic.
isleño [iz·lé·ño] *m.* islander.
isobara [i·so·ƀá·ra] *f.* isobar.
islote [iz·ló·te] *m.* islet, small rocky island.
istmo [iz·mo] *m.* isthmus.
italiano [i·ta·ljá·no] *adj.* & *m.* Italian.
itinerario [i·ti·ne·rá·rjo] *m.* itinerary; timetable, schedule; railroad guide.
itrio [í·trjo] *m.* yttrium.
izar[9] [i·sár] *v.* to hoist; to heave.
izquierda [is·kjér·đa] *f.* left hand; left side; left wing (*in politics*); **a la** — to the left; **izquierdista** [is·kjer·đís·ta] *m.* & *f.* leftist, radical.
izquierdo [is·kjér·đo] *adj.* left; left-handed.

J:j

jabalí [xa·ƀa·lí] *m.* wild boar.
jabalina [xa·ƀa·lí·na] *f.* javelin; wild sow.
jabón [xa·ƀón] *m.* soap; *Ríopl.* fright, fear; **dar** — to soft-soap, flatter; **dar un** — to give a good scolding; to beat, thrash.
jabonadura [xa·ƀo·na·đú·ra] *f.* washing, soaping; **-s** suds, lather; **dar a uno una** — to reprimand or

scold someone.
jabonar [xa·ƀo·nár] *v.* (*lavar*) to lather, soap; (*reprender*) to scold; reprimand.
jabonera [xa·ƀo·né·ra] *f.* soap dish; woman soap vendor or maker.
jaca [xá·ka] *f.* pony, small horse; **jaco** [xa·ko] *m.* small nag; poor horse.
jacal [xa·kál] *m. Mex.* shack, adobe hut; **jacalucho** [xa·ka·lú·čo] *m. Am.* poor, ugly shack.
jacinto [xa·sín·to] *m.* hyacinth.
jactancia [xak·tán·sja] *f.* boast, brag; boasting.
jactancioso [xak·tan·sjó·so] *adj.* braggart, boastful.
jactarse [xak·tár·se] *v.* to brag, boast.
jaculatoria [xa·ku·la·tó·rja] *f.* short, fervent prayer.
jadeante [xa·đe·án·te] *adj.* breathless, panting, out of breath.
jadear [xa·đe·ár] *v.* to pant.
jadeo [xa·đé·o] *m.* pant, panting.
jaez [xa·és] *m.* harness; kind, sort; **jaeces** [xa·é·ses] trappings.
jaguar [xa·ǥwár] *m.* jaguar.
jagüey [xa·ǥwéj] *m.* puddle, pool.
jai alai [xaj·a·láj] *m.* Basque game played with basket and *pelota*.
jalar [xa·lár] *v. Am.* to pull; to haul; to jerk; *C.A.* to court, make love; *Ven., Andes* to flunk (*a student*); *Mex.* **¡jala!** [xá·la] (*or* **¡jálale!** [xá·la·le]) get going! get a move on there!; **-se** *Mex.* to get drunk; *Mex.* to go away, move away.
jalea [xa·lé·a] *f.* jelly.
jalear [xa·le·ár] *v.* to shout (*to hunting dogs*); to rouse, beat up (*game*); to shout and clap (*to encourage dancers*).
jaleo [xa·lé·o] *m.* shouting and clapping (*to encourage dancers*); an Andalusian dance; revelry, merrymaking; jesting; gracefulness.
jaletina [xa·le·tí·na] *f.* gelatin.
jalón [xa·lón] *m.* marker (*for boundaries*); *Am.* pull, jerk, tug; *Mex., C.A.* swallow of liquor; *Bol., C.A.* stretch, distance.
jalonear [xa·lo·ne·ár] *v. C.A., Mex.* to pull, jerk.
jamás [xa·más] *adv.* never.
jamón [xa·món] *m.* ham; *P.R.* fix, difficulty.
jamona [xa·mó·na] *f.* popular term for a fat middle-aged woman.
japonés [xa·po·nés] *adj. & m.* Japanese.
jaque [xá·ke] *m.* check (*in chess*); braggart, bully; — **mate** checkmate (*in chess*); **tener a uno en** — to hold someone under a threat.
jaqueca [xa·ké·ka] *f.* headache; sick headache.
jara [xá·ra] *f.* rockrose (*shrub*); *Ven., Col.* reed; **jaral** [xa·rál] *m.* bramble of rockroses; *Am.* reeds, clump of reeds.
jarabe [xa·rá·ƀe] *m.* syrup; sweet beverage; *Mex., C.A.* a kind of tap dance; *Mex.* song and musical accompaniment of the **jarabe.**
jarana [xa·rá·na] *f.* merrymaking, revelry; trick; fib; jest; *Col., Ec., Carib.* a dance; *Mex.* small guitar; **ir de** — to go on a spree.
jarcia [xár·sja] *f.* rigging (*ropes, chains, etc. for the masts, yards and sails of a ship*); fishing tackle; pile, heap; jumble of things.
jardín [xar·đín] *m.* flower garden.
jardinero [xar·đi·né·ro] *m.* gardener.
jarra [xá·rra] *f.* jar, vase, pitcher; **de** (*or* **en**) **-s** akimbo (*with hands on the hips*).
jarro [xá·rro] *m.* jar, jug, pitcher.
jarrón *m.* large vase or jar.
jaspe [xás·pe] *m.* jasper; veined marble; **jaspeado** *adj.* veined, streaked, mottled.
jaula [xáw·la] *f.* cage; cagelike cell or prison; *Am.* roofless cattle car or freight car.
jauría [xaw·rí·a] *f.* pack of hounds.
jazmín [xaz·mín] *m.* jasmine.
jefatura [xe·fa·tú·ra] *f.* position of chief; headquarters of a chief.
jefe [xé·fe] *m.* chief, leader, head.
jengibre [xeŋ·xí·ƀre] *m.* ginger.
jerez [xe·rés] *m.* sherry wine.
jerga [xér·ǥa] *f.* (*tela*) thick coarse cloth; straw mattress; (*dialecto*) jargon; slang; *Am.* saddle pad; *Col.* poncho made of coarse cloth.
jergón [xer·ǥón] *m.* (*material*) straw mattress; ill-fitting suit or dress; (*persona*) big clumsy fellow; *Ríopl., Mex., Ven.* cheap coarse rug.
jerigonza [xe·ri·ǥón·sa] *f.* jargon; slang.
jeringa [xe·ríŋ·ga] *f.* syringe; **jeringazo** [xe·riŋ·gá·so] *m.* injection; squirt.
jeringar[7] [xe·riŋ·gár] *v.* to inject; to squirt; to bother, molest, vex, annoy.
jeroglífico [xe·ro·ǥlí·fi·ko] *m.* hieroglyphic.
jesuita [xe·swi·ta] *m.* Jesuit.
jeta [xé·ta] *f.* snout; thick lips.
jiba [xí·ƀa] = **giba.**
jíbaro [xí·ƀa·ro] *adj. P.R.* rustic, rural, rude, uncultured; *m. P.R.* bumpkin, peasant.
jibia [xí·ƀja] *f.* cuttlefish.
jícara [xí·ka·ra] *f.* chocolate cup; *Am.* small bowl made out of a gourd; *Mex.* any small bowl; *Mex.* bald head.
jilguero [xil·ǥé·ro] *m.* linnet.
jinete [xi·né·te] *m.* horseman, rider.
jineteada [xi·ne·te·á·đa] *f. Ríopl., C.A.* roughriding, horse-breaking.
jinetear [xi·ne·te·ár] *v.* to ride horseback; to perform on horseback; *Mex., C.A.* to break in (*a horse*); *Mex.* to ride a bronco or bull.
jira [xí·ra] *f.* excursion, tour; outing, picnic; strip of cloth.
jirafa [xi·rá·fa] *f.* giraffe; boom mike (*broadcasting*).
jitomate [xi·to·má·te] *m. Mex.* tomato. *Also* gitomate.
jocoso [xo·kó·so] *adj.* jocular.
jofaina [xo·fáj·na] *f.* basin, washbowl.
jolgorio [xol·ǥó·rjo] = **holgorio.**
jornada [xor·ná·đa] *f.* day's journey; military expedition; working day; act (*of a Spanish play*).
jornal [xor·nál] *m.* day's wages; bookkeeping journal; **a** — by the day.
jornalero [xor·na·lé·ro] *m.* day laborer.
joroba [xo·ró·ƀa] *f.* hump; nuisance, annoyance.
jorobado [xo·ro·ƀá·đo] *adj.* hunchbacked; annoyed, bothered, in a bad fix; *m.* hunchback.
jorobar [xo·ro·ƀár] *v.* to bother, pester, annoy.
jorongo [xo·róŋ·go] *m. Mex.* Mexican poncho.
jota [xó·ta] *f.* name of the letter *j*; iota (*anything insignificant*); Aragonese and Valencian dance and music; *Andes* (= **ojota**) leather sandal; **no saber una** — not to know anything.
joven [xó·ƀen] *adj.* young; *m. & f.* youth; young man; young woman.
jovial [xo·ƀjál] *adj.* jovial, jolly, merry; **jovialided** [xo·ƀja·li·đáđ] *f.* gaiety, merriment, fun.
joya [xó·ya] *f.* jewel; piece of jewelry; **-s** jewels; trousseau.
joyería [xo·ye·rí·a] *f.* jeweler's shop.
joyero [xo·yé·ro] *m.* jeweler; jewel box.
juanete [xwa·né·te] *m.* bunion.
jubilación [xu·ƀi·la·sjón] *f.* retirement (*from a position or office*); pension.
jubilar [xu·ƀi·lár] *v.* to pension; to retire; **-se** to be pensioned or retired; to rejoice; *Col.* to decline, fall into decline; *Ven., Guat.* to play hooky or

IN

truant.
jubileo [xu·ƀi·lé·o] *m.* jubilee; time of rejoicing; concession by the Pope of plenary (*complete*) indulgence.
júbilo [xú·ƀi·lo] *m.* joy, glee.
jubiloso [xu·ƀi·ló·so] *adj.* jubilant, joyful.
jubón [xu·ƀón] *m.* jacket; bodice.
judía [xu·đí·a] *f. Spain* bean; string bean; Jewess; **-s tiernas** (*or* **verdes**) string beans.
judicial [xu·đi·sjál] *adj.* judicial; **-mente** *adv.* judicially.
judío [xu·đí·o] *adj.* Jewish; *m.* Jew.
judo [xú·đo] *m.* judo.
juego [xwé·ǥo] *m.* game; play; sport; gambling; pack of cards; set; — **de palabras** pun, play on words; — **de te** tea set; **hacer** — to match; **poner en** — to coordinate; to set in motion.
juerga [xwér·ǥa] *f.* spree, revelry, wild festivity; **irse de** — to go out on a spree; **juerguista** *m. & f.* merrymaker.
jueves [xwé·ƀes] *m.* Thursday.
juez [xwes] *m.* judge; juror, member of a jury; — **arbitrador** (*or* **árbitro**) arbitrator, umpire.
jugada [xu·ǥá·đa] *f.* play, move; stroke; trick.
jugador [xu·ǥa·đór] *m.* player; gambler; — **de manos** juggler.
jugar[34] [xu·ǥár] *v. irr.* to play; to gamble; to toy; — **a la pelota** to play ball; *Mex.* — **a dos cartas** to be double-faced.
jugarreta [xu·ǥa·rré·ta] *f.* bad play, wrong play; mean trick; tricky deal; *Am.* noisy game.
jugo [xú·ǥo] *m.* juice; sap.
jugosidad [xu·ǥo·si·đáđ] *f.* juiciness; **jugoso** *adj.* juicy.
juguete [xu·ǥé·te] *m.* plaything, toy; jest, joke; — **cómico** skit; **por** (*or* **de**) — jokingly.
juguetear [xu·ǥe·te·ár] *v.* to play around, romp, frolic; to toy; to tamper (with), fool (with).
juguetón [xu·ǥe·tón] *adj.* playful.
juicio [xwí·sjo] *m.* judgment; sense, wisdom; opinion; trial; **perder el** — to lose one's mind, go crazy.
juicioso [xwi·sjó·so] *adj.* judicious, wise; sensible.
julio [xú·ljo] *m.* July.
jumento [xu·mén·to] *m.* ass, donkey.
juncal [xun·kál] *m.* growth of rushes.
junco [xúŋ·ko] *m.* rush, reed; junk (*Chinese sailboat*).
jungla [xúŋ·gla] *f. Am.* jungle.
junio [xú·njo] *m.* June.
junquillo [xuŋ·kí·yo] *m.* reed; jonquil (*yellow flower similar to the daffodil*), species of narcissus.
junta [xún·ta] *f.* (*reunión*) meeting, conference; (*funcionarios*) board, council; **-s** joints (plumbing); — **a inglete** miter joint; — **a traslapo** lap joint; **-s en tope** butt joints; — **en V** vee-butt; — **por puntas** tack weld; (*cepillo mecánico*) **juntera** jointer.
juntar [xun·tár] *v.* to join, unite; to connect; to assemble; to collect; **-se** to assemble, gather; to be closely united; to associate (with).
junto [xún·to] *adj.* joined, united; **-s** together; *adv.* near; — **a** neat to, close to; **en** — all together, in all; **por** — all together, in a lump; wholesale.
juntura [xun·tú·ra] *f.* juncture; junction; joint, seam.
jurado [xu·rá·đo] *m.* jury; juror, juryman; *adj. & p.p.* sworn.
juramentar [xu·ra·men·tár] *v.* to swear in; **-se** to take an oath, be sworn in.
juramento [xu·ra·mén·to] *m.* oath; vow; curse.
jurar [xu·rár] *v.* to swear, vow; to take oath; to curse.
jurisconsulto [xu·ris·kon·súl·to] *m.* jurist, expert in law; lawyer.
jurisdicción [xu·riz·đik·sjón] *f.* jurisdiction.
jurisprudencia [xu·ris·pru·đén·sja] *f.* jurisprudence, law.
juro; de — [xú·ro] *adv.* certainly, of course.
justa [xús·ta] *f.* joust, tournament, combat (*between horsemen with lances*); contest.
justicia [xus·tí·sja] *f.* justice; court of justice; judge; police.
justiciero [xus·ti·sjé·ro] *adj.* strictly just, austere (*in matters of justice*).
justificación [xus·ti·fi·ka·sjón] *f.* justification.
justificante [xus·ti·fi·kán·te] *adj.* justifying; *m.* voucher; written excuse; proof.
justificar[6] [xus·ti·fi·kár] *v.* to justify; to vindicate, clear of blame.
justo [xús·to] *adj.* just; pious; exact, correct; tight; *adv.* duly; exactly; tightly; *m.* just man; **los -s** the just.
juvenil [xu·ƀe·níl] *adj.* juvenile, young, youthful.
juventud [xu·ƀen·túđ] *f.* youth; young people.
juzgado [xuz·ǥá·đo] *m.* court, tribunal.
juzgar[7] [xuz·ǥár] *v.* to judge.

K:k

kermesse [ker·mé·se] *f.* country fair; bazaar for charity.
keroseno [ke·ro·sé·no] *f.* kerosene, coal oil.
kilo [kí·lo] *m.* kilo, kilogram.
kilo-byte (KB) [ki·lo·bájt] *m.* (*computadora*) kilobyte (KBYTE).
kilociclo [ki·lo·sí·klo] *m.* kilocycle.
kilogramo [ki·lo·ǥrá·mo] *m.* kilogram.
kilometraje [ki·lo·me·trá·xe] *m.* number of kilometers.
kilómetro [ki·ló·me·tro] *m.* kilometer.
kilovatio [ki·lo·ƀá·tjo] *m.* kilowatt.

L:l

la [la] *def. art. f.* the; — **de** the one with, that one with; *obj. pron.* her; it; — **que** *rel. pron.* she who, the one that; which.
la [la] *m.* sixth note on the musical scale.
laberinto [la·ƀe·rín·to] *m.* labyrinth, maze; labyrinth, internal ear.
labia [la·ƀja] *f.* fluency, talkativeness, gift of gab; **tener mucha** — to be a good talker.
labial [la·ƀjál] *adj.* labial.
labio [lá·ƀjo] *m.* lip.
labiodental [la·ƀjo·đen·tál] *adj.* labiodental.
labor [la·ƀór] *f.* (*trabajo*) labor, work; (*cosido*) embroidery; needlework; (*agrícola*) tillage; — **de punto** knitting; **laborable** [la·ƀo·rá·ƀle] *adj.* workable; tillable; **día laborable** work day; **laboral** [la·ƀo·rál] *adj.* pertaining to labor.
laboratorio [la·ƀo·ra·tó·rjo] *m.* laboratory.
laboriosidad [la·ƀo·rjo·si·đáđ] *f.* laboriousness, industry.
laborioso [la·ƀo·rjó·so] *adj.* laborious; industrious.
laborista [la·ƀo·rís·ta] *m. & f.* laborite.
labrado [la·ƀrá·đo] *p.p. & adj.* (*agrícola*) tilled, cultivated; (*hecho*) wrought; manufactured; carved; *m.* carving; — **en madera** woodwork, carving; **-s**

cultivated lands.
labrador [la·ƀra·đór] *m.* farmer; peasant.
labranza [la·ƀrán·sa] *f.* farming, tillage, plowing; cultivated land, farm.
labrar [la·ƀrár] *v.* (*la tierra*) to till, cultivate, farm; to plow; (*crear*) to carve; to embroider; to work (*metals*); to build (*a monument*).
labriego [la·ƀrjé·ĝo] *m.* peasant.
laca [lá·ka] *f.* lacquer; shellac.
lacayo [la·ká·yo] *m.* lackey, footman, flunky.
lacio [lá·sjo] *adj.* withered; languid; limp; straight (*hair*).
lacra [lá·kra] *f.* trace of an illness; blemish, defect; *Mex., Ven., C.A.* sore, ulcer, scab, scar.
lacre [lá·kre] *m.* red sealing wax; *adj. Am.* red.
lacrimógeno [la·kri·mó·xe·no] *adj.* tear-producing.
lactar [lak·tár] *v.* to nurse, suckle; to feed with milk.
lácteo [lák·te·o] *adj.* milky; **fiebre láctea** milk fever; **régimen** — milk diet; **Vía láctea** milk Way; **productor -s** milk products.
ladear [la·đe·ár] *v.* to tilt, tip; to go along the slope or side of; to turn aside (*from a way or course*); **-se** to tilt; to sway; to incline or lean (towards); to move to one side; *Ch.* to fall in love.
ladeo [la·đé·o] *m.* inclination, tilt.
ladera [la·đé·ra] *f.* slope.
ladino [la·đí·no] *adj.* crafty, sly, shrewd; conversant with two or three languages; *m.* Sephardic Jew (*Spanish-speaking*); Romansch (*a Romance language of Switzerland*); *Guat.* Spanish-speaking person (*as opposed to one who speaks an Indian language*); *C.A.*, mestizo, half-breed; *Mex., Col., Ven.* talker, talkative person.
lado [lá·đo] *m.* side; **al** — near, at hand, at one's side; **de** — tilted, obliquely; sideways; — **a** — side by side; **¡a un — !** gangway! **hacerse a un** — to move over, step aside, move to one side; *Mex., Ven.* **echársela de** — to boast.
ladrar [la·đrár] *v.* to bark.
ladrido [la·đrí·đo] *m.* bark, barking.
ladrillo [la·đrí·yo] *m.* brick.
ladrón [la·đrón] *m.* thief, robber; **ladronzuelo** [la·đron·swé·lo] *m.* petty thief.
lagartija [la·ĝar·tí·xa] *f.* small lizard.
lagarto [la·ĝár·to] *m.* lizard; rascal, sly fellow.
lago [lá·ĝo] *m.* lake.
lágrima [lá·ĝri·ma] *f.* tear; **llorar a — viva** to weep abundantly.
lagrimear [la·ĝri·me·ár] *v.* to weep, shed tears.
laguna [la·ĝú·na] *f.* lagoon; gap, blank space.
laico [láj·ko] *adj.* lay; *m.* layman.
laísta [la·ís·ta] *m. & f.* one who uses *la* for indirect object.
laja [lá·xa] *f.* slab; flat stone.
lamedero [la·me·đé·ro] *m.* salt lick (*for cattle*).
lamentable [la·men·tá·ƀle] *adj.* lamentable, pitiful.
lamentación [la·men·ta·sjón] *f.* lamentation.
lamentar [la·men·tár] *v.* to lament, deplore; **-se** to moan, complain, wail.
lamento [la·mén·to] *m.* lament, moan, cry.
lamer [la·mér] *v.* to lick; to lap.
lamida [la·mí·đa] *f. Mex., C.A.* lick; also **lambida.**
lámina [lá·mi·na] *f.* metal plate; sheet of metal; engraving; book illustration.
laminar [la·mi·nár] *v.* to laminate; **laminación a mano** hand lay-up; **con pistola de aire** spray-up.
lámpara [lám·pa·ra] *f.* lamp.
lampiño [lam·pí·ño] *adj.* hairless; beardless.
lana [lá·na] *f.* wool; *C.A.* tramp, vagabond.
lanar [la·nár] *adj.* wool-bearing; of wool.
lance [lán·se] *m.* occurrence, event; cast, throw, move, turn; accident; quarrel; predicament.
lancear [lan·se·ár] *v.* to lance, spear.
lancha [lán·ča] *f.* launch; boat; slab; **lanchón** [lan·čón] *m.* barge.
langosta [laŋ·gós·ta] *f.* lobster; locust.
languidecer[13] [laŋ·gi·đe·sér] *v. irr.* to languish.
languidez [laŋ·gi·đés] *f.* languor, faintness, weakness.
lánguido [láŋ·gi·đo] *adj.* languid.
lanilla [la·ní·ya] *f.* nap (*of cloth*).
lanudo [la·nú·đo] *adj.* woolly; *Ven.* coarse, crude, ill-bred; *Am.* dull, slow, weak-willed; *Ch., C.A., Col.* wealthy.
lanza [lán·sa] *f.* lance, spear; *Col.* swindler, cheat; *m.* **lanzabombas** [lan·sa·ƀóm·bas] bomb launcher; *m.* **lanzacohetes** [lan·sa·ko·é·tes] rocket launcher; *m.* **lanzallamas** [lan·sa·yá·mas] flame thrower.
lanzada [lan·sá·đa] *f.* thrust (*with a spear*).
lanzadera [lan·sa·đé·ra] *f.* shuttle.
lanzamiento [lan·sa·mjén·to] *m.* launching (*boat or rocket*).
lanzar[9] [lan·sár] *v.* to fling, throw; to eject; to launch; **-se** to rush, fling oneself; to dart out.
lanzazo [lan·sá·so] *m.* thrust with a lance.
lapicero [la·pi·sé·ro] *m.* pencil (*a mechanical pencil, one with an adjustable lead*).
lápida [lá·pi·đa] *f.* slab, tombstone; stone tablet.
lapidar [la·pi·đár] *v.* to stone; *Col., Ch.* to cut precious stones; **lapidado** lapping.
lapidario [la·pi·đá·rjo] *m.* lapidary.
lápiz [lá·pis] *m.* pencil; crayon; — **para los labios** lipstick; — **óptico** (*computadora*) light pen.
lapso [láp·so] *m.* lapse.
lardo [lár·đo] *m.* lard; **lardear** to baste.
lares [lá·res] *m. pl.* home.
largar[7] [lar·ĝár] *v.* to loosen; to let go; to set free; to unfold (*a flag or sails*); *Am.* to hurl, throw; *Col.* to strike (*a blow*); *Ríopl.* to give, hand over; **-se** to go away, slip away; to leave.
largo [lár·ĝo] *adj.* long; generous; *m.* length; largo (*music*); — **de arco** arc length; — **del encaje** length of engagement (machine) **a la larga** in the long run; slowly; **a lo** — along; lengthwise; **¡ — de aquí!** get out of here!
largor [lar·ĝór] *m.* length.
largucho [lar·ĝú·čo] *adj.* lanky.
larguero [lar·ĝé·ro] *m.* stud (machine).
largueza [lar·ĝé·sa] *f.* generosity, liberality; length.
larguísimo [lar·gí·si·mo] *adj.* very long.
largura [lar·ĝú·ra] *f.* length.
laringe [la·ríŋ·xe] *f.* larynx.
laríngeo [la·ríŋ·xe·o] *adj.* laryngeal.
laringitis [la·riŋ·xí·tis] *f.* laryngitis.
larva [lár·ƀa] *f.* larva.
las [las] *def. art. f. pl.* the; *obj. pron.* them; — **que** *rel. pron.* those which; which.
lascivia [la·sí·ƀja] *f.* lewdness.
lascivo [la·sí·ƀo] *adj.* lascivious, lewd.
lástima [lás·ti·ma] *f.* pity; compassion, grief.
lastimadura [las·ti·ma·đú·ra] *f.* sore, hurt.
lastimar [las·ti·már] *v.* to hurt; to offend; **-se** to get hurt; **-se de** to feel pity for.
lastimero [las·ti·mé·ro] *adj.* pitiful; mournful.
lastimoso [las·ti·mó·so] *adj.* pitiful.
lastre [lás·tre] *m.* ballast, weight.
lata [lá·ta] *f.* (*metal*) tin plate, tin can, can; (*madero*) small log; thin board; (*pesadez*) annoyance; embarrassment; boring speech; *Arg.* gaucho saber; *Arg.* prop.
latente [la·tén·te] *adj.* latent.
lateral [la·te·rál] *adj.* lateral, side; [l] (*phonetically*).
latido [la·tí·đo] *m.* palpitation, throb, beat; bark,

JU

howl.

latifundio [la·ti·fún·djo] *m.* large landed estate.

latigazo [la·ti·ǥá·so] *m.* lash, stroke with a whip; crack of a whip; harsh reprimand; unexpected blow or offense.

látigo [lá·ti·ǥo] *m.* whip; *Am.* whipping, beating; *Ch.* end or goal of a horse race; (*encaje de electrodo y su cable*) whip.

latín [la·tín] *m.* Latin language.

latinismo [la·ti·níz·mo] *m.* Latinism; imitating Latin.

latino [la·tí·no] *adj.* Latin; *m.* Latinist, Latin scholar; Latin.

latir [la·tír] *v.* to throb, beat, palpitate; to bark.

latitud [la·ti·túđ] *f.* latitude; extent, breadth.

latón [la·tón] *m.* brass.

latrocinio [la·tro·sí·njo] *m.* larceny, theft, robbery.

laúd [la·úđ] *m.* lute; catboat (*long, narrow boat with a lateen sail*).

laudable [law·đá·ƀle] *adj.* laudable, praiseworthy.

laurel [law·rél] *m.* laurel; laurel wreath.

lauro [láw·ro] *m.* laurel; glory, fame.

lava [lá·ƀa] *f.* lava; washing of minerals.

lavable [la·ƀá·ƀle] *adj.* washable.

lavabo [la·ƀá·ƀo] *m.* lavatory, washroom; washstand; washbowl.

lavadero [la·ƀa·đé·ro] *m.* washing place.

lavado [la·ƀá·đo] *m.* wash, washing; laundry, laundry work; — **de cerebro** brain washing.

lavador [la·ƀa·đór] *m.* washer; cleaner; *adj.* washing; cleaning; **lavadora** [la·ƀa·đó·ra] *f.* washer, washing machine.

lavadura [la·ƀa·đú·ra] *f.* washing; slops, dirty water.

lavamanos [la·ƀa·má·nos] *m.* lavatory, washbowl, washstand.

lavendera [la·ƀan·dé·ra] *f.* laundress, washerwoman.

lavandería [la·ƀan·de·rí·a] *f.* laundry.

lavar [la·ƀár] *v.* to wash; to launder; to whitewash.

lavativa [la·ƀa·tí·ƀa] *f.* enema; syringe; bother, nuisance.

lavatorio [la·ƀa·tó·rjo] *m.* washing (*act of washing*); wash (*liquid or solution for washing*); lavatory (*ceremonial act of washing*); washbowl, washstand; *Am.* washroom.

lavazas [la·ƀá·sas] *f. pl.* slops, dirty water.

laxante [lak·sán·te] *m.* laxative.

lazada [la·sá·đa] *f.* bow, bowknot; *Am.* throwing of the lasso, lassoing.

lazar[9] [la·sár] *v.* to rope, lasso; to noose.

lazarillo [la·sa·rí·yo] *m.* blindman's guide.

lazo [lá·so] *m.* (*nudo*) bow, knot; slipknot; lasso, lariat; (*vínculo*) tie, bond; (*trampa*) snare, trap; trick.

le [le] *obj. pron.* him; you (*formal*); to him; to her; to you (*formal*).

leal [le·ál] *adj.* loyal.

lealtad [le·al·táđ] *f.* loyalty.

lebrel [le·ƀrél] *m.* greyhound.

lebrillo [le·ƀrí·yo] *m.* earthenware basin or tub.

lección [lek·sjón] *f.* lesson; reading; **dar la** — to recite the lesson; **dar** — to teach; **tomarle a uno la** — to have someone recite his lesson.

lector [lek·tór] *m.* reader; lecturer.

lectura [lek·tú·ra] *f.* reading; **libro de** — reader.

lechada [le·čá·đa] *f.* whitewash; *Am.* milking.

leche [lé·če] *f.* milk; *Col., Ven., C.A., Andes, Ríopl.* luck (*in games*); — **homogeneizada** homogenized milk; — **desnatada** skim milk; — **en polvo** powdered milk.

lechería [le·če·rí·a] *f.* dairy, creamery; **lechero** [le·čé·ro] *adj.* milk; milch, giving milk (*applied to animals*); *Am.* lucky (*in games of chance*); *m.* milkman; **lechera** [le·čé·ra] *f.* milkmaid; milk can; milk pitcher.

lecho [lé·čo] *m.* bed; river bed.

lechón [le·čón] *m.* suckling pig; pig.

lechoso [le·čó·so] *adj.* milky; *m.* papaya tree; **lechosa** [le·čó·sa] *f. P.R.* papaya (*tropical fruit*).

lechuga [le·čú·ǥa] *f.* lettuce; — **romana** romaine lettuce.

lechuza [le·čú·sa] *f.* screech owl, barn owl.

leer[14] [le·ér] *v.* to read.

legación [le·ǥa·sjón] *f.* legation.

legado [le·ǥá·đo] *m.* (*donación*) legacy; legato; (*representante*) representative, ambassador.

legajo [le·ǥá·xo] *m.* bundle of papers; dossier.

legal [le·ǥál] *adj.* legal, lawful; truthful; reliable; *Col., Ven., Andes* excellent, best; *Mex.* just, honest.

legalizar[9] [le·ǥa·li·sár] *v.* to legalize.

legar[7] [le·ǥár] *v.* to will, bequeath; to send as a delegate.

legendario [le·xen·dá·rjo] *adj.* legendary.

legión [le·xjón] *f.* legion.

legislación [le·xiz·la·sjón] *f.* legislation.

legislador [le·xiz·la·đór] *m.* legislator; *adj.* legislating, legislative.

legislar [le·xiz·lár] *v.* to legislate.

legislativo [le·xiz·la·tí·ƀo] *adj.* legislative.

legislatura [le·xiz·la·tú·ra] *f.* legislature, legislative assembly.

legítimo [le·xí·ti·mo] *adj.* legitimate; real, genuine.

lego [lé·ǥo] *adj.* lay; ignorant; *m.* layman.

legua [lé·ǥwa] *f.* league (*about 3 miles*).

leguleyo [le·ǥu·lé·yo] *m.* shyster.

legumbre [le·ǥúm·bre] *f.* vegetable.

leída [le·í·đa] *f. Am.* reading. *See* **lectura.**

leísta [le·ís·ta] *m. & f.* one who uses the pronoun *le* for masculine direct object (*le conozco*).

lejanía [le·xa·ní·a] *f.* distance; distant place.

lejano [le·xá·no] *adj.* distant; remote.

lejía [le·xí·a] *f.* lye; harsh reprimand; *Am.* bleach.

lejos [lé·xos] *adv.* far, far away; **a lo** — in the distance; *Am.* **a un** — in the distance; **de** (*or* **desde**) — from afar; *m.* view, perspective; background.

lelo [lé·lo] *adj.* silly, stupid, foolish.

lema [lé·ma] *m.* motto; theme; slogan.

lencería [len·se·rí·a] *f.* dry goods, dry-goods store; linen room or closet.

lengua [léŋ·gwa] *f.* tongue; language; interpreter; — **de tierra** point, neck of land.

lenguado [leŋ·gwá·đo] *m.* sole (*a fish*).

lenguaje [leŋ·gwá·xe] *m.* language (*manner of expression*); — **de alto nivel** (*computadora*) high level language; — **de ensamble** assembly language; — **de máquina** machine language.

lenguaraz [leŋ·gwa·rás] *adj.* talkative, loose-tongued.

lengüeta [leŋ·gwé·ta] *f.* small tongue; **lengüetada** [leŋ·gwe·ta·đa] *f.* lick.

leninismo [le·ni·níz·mo] *m.* Leninism.

lente [lén·te] *m. & f.* lens; — **filtrador** filter lens; **-s** *m. pl.* eyeglasses.

lenteja [len·té·xa] *f.* lentil; lentil seed; **lentejuela** [len·te·xwé·la] *f.* spangle.

lentitud [len·ti·túđ] *f.* slowness.

lento [lén·to] *adj.* slow; dull.

leña [lé·ña] *f.* firewood, kindling; beating; **leñera** [le·ñé·ra] *f.* woodshed, woodbox.

leñador [le·ña·đór] *m.* woodcutter, woodman.

leño [lé·ño] *m.* log, timber, piece of firewood.

león [le·ón] *m.* lion; **leona** [le·ó·na] *f.* lioness; **leonera** [le·o·né·ra] *f.* lion's den or cage; dive, gambling

joint; disorderly room.
leontina [le·on·tí·na] *f. Mex., Carib., Col.* watch chain.
leopardo [le·o·pár·đo] *m.* leopard.
leopoldina [le·o·pol·dí·na] *f. Mex., Ven.* watch chain.
lerdo [lér·đo] *adj.* dull, heavy, stupid, slow.
les [les] *obj. pron.* to them; to you (*formal*).
lesión [le·sjón] *f.* wound, injury.
lesionar [le·sjo·nár] *v.* to injure, to wound, to hurt, to damage.
lesna [léz·na] = **lezna.**
letargo [le·tár·ǥo] *m.* lethargy, stupor, drowsiness.
letra [lé·tra] *f.* letter (*of the alphabet*); printing type; hand; handwriting; letter (*exact wording or meaning*); words of a song; — **abierta** letter of credit; — **de cambio** draft, bill of exchange; — **mayúscula** capital letter; — **minúscula** small letter; **al pie de la** — literally; **-s** letters, learning.
letrado [le·trá·đo] *adj.* learned; *m.* lawyer.
letrero [le·tré·ro] *m.* notice, poster, sign; legend (*under an illustration*).
leva [lé·ƀa] *f.* levy, draft; weighing anchor, setting sail; **echar** — to draft, conscript; *Col.* **echar -s** to boast.
levadizo [le·ƀa·dí·so] *adj.* lift (*bridge*).
levadura [le·ƀa·đú·ra] *f.* leaven, yeast; — **en polvo** baking powder. — **instante** instant yeast.
levantamiento [le·ƀan·ta·mjén·to] *m.* (*revuelta*) uprising, revolt, insurrection; (*altura*) elevation; (*alzar*) lifting, raising; (*reunión*) adjournment (*of a meeting*); — **de un plano** surveying.
levantar [le·ƀan·tár] *v.* to raise, lift; to set up; to erect; to rouse, stir up; to recruit; *Ch.* to break land, plow; — **el campo** to break camp; — **la mesa** to clear the table; — **la sesión** to adjourn the meeting; — **un plano** to survey, map out; — **falso testimonio** to bear false witness; **-se** to stand up, get up, rise; to rebel.
levante [le·ƀán·te] *m.* east; east wind.
levantisco [le·ƀan·tís·ko] *adj.* turbulent; rebellious.
levar [le·ƀár] *v.* to weigh (*anchor*); — **el ancla** to weigh anchor; **-se** to weigh anchor, set sail.
leve [lé·ƀe] *adj.* light; slight; unimportant.
levita [le·ƀí·ta] *f.* frock coat; *m.* Levite, member of the tribe of Levi.
léxico [lék·si·ko] *m.* lexicon, dictionary; vocabulary; glossary.
lexicografía [lek·si·ko·ǥra·fí·a] *f.* lexicography.
lexicología [lek·si·ko·lo·xí·a] *f.* lexicology.
ley [lej] *f.* law; rule; loyalty; standard quality; **de buena** — of good quality; **plata de** — sterling silver; **-es** jurisprudence, law; system of laws.
leyenda [le·yén·da] *f.* legend; reading; inscription.
lezna [léz·na] *f.* awl.
liar[17] [ljar] *v.* to tie, bind; to roll up; to deceive; — **el petate** *Mex.* to kick the bucket; **-se** to bind oneself; to get tangled up.
libelo [li·ƀé·lo] *m.* libel.
libélula [li·ƀé·lu·la] *f.* dragon fly.
liberación [li·ƀe·ra·sjón] *f.* liberation; deliverance.
liberal [li·ƀe·rál] *adj.* liberal; generous; **liberalidad** [li·ƀe·ra·li·đáđ] *f.* liberality; generosity.
liberalismo [li·ƀe·ra·líz·mo] *m.* liberalism.
libertad [li·ƀer·táđ] *f.* liberty.
libertador [li·ƀer·ta·đór] *m.* liberator, deliverer.
libertar [li·ƀer·tár] *v.* to liberate, free, set free; **-se** to get free; to escape.
libertinaje [li·ƀer·ti·ná·xe] *m.* license, licentiousness, lack of moral restraint.
libertino [li·ƀer·tí·no] *m.* libertine.
libido [li·ƀí·đo] *m.* libido.
libra [lí·ƀra] *f.* pound; Libra (*sign of the Zodiac*).
librado [li·ƀrá·do] *m.* drawee.
librador [li·ƀra·đór] *m.* drawer (*of a bill, draft, etc.*); deliverer, liberator; measuring scoop.
libranza [li·ƀrán·sa] *f.* bill of exchange, draft.
librar [li·ƀrár] *v.* to free, set free; to issue; to draw (*a draft*); — **guerra** to wage war; **-se** to save oneself; to escape; **-se de** to get rid of, escape from.
libre [lí·ƀre] *adj.* free; unmarried; loose; vacant.
librea [li·ƀré·a] *f.* livery (*uniform*).
librecambista [li·ƀre·kam·bís·ta] *m., f.* free trader.
librería [li·ƀre·rí·a] *f.* bookstore.
librero [li·ƀré·ro] *m.* bookseller; *Am.* bookcase, bookshelves.
libreta [li·ƀré·ta] *f.* notebook, memorandum book; bankbook; — **de ahorros** savings book.
libreto [li·ƀré·to] *m.* libretto.
libro [lí·ƀro] *m.* book; — **de caja** cashbook; — **mayor** ledger.
licencia [li·sén·sja] *f.* license; permission; furlough, leave; looseness; license to practice.
licenciado [li·sen·sjá·đo] *m.* licenciate (*person having a degree approximately equivalent to a master's degree*); *Ríopl., Mex., C.A.* lawyer.
licenciar [li·sen·sjár] *v.* to license; to give a license or permit; to dismiss, discharge (*from the army*); to confer the degree of **licenciado; -se** to get the degree of **licenciado.**
licenciatura [li·sen·sja·tú·ra] *f.* degree of **licenciado.**
licencioso [li·sen·sjó·so] *adj.* licentious, lewd.
liceo [li·sé·o] *m.* lyceum; high school; *Col.* private primary school or high school.
lícito [lí·si·to] *adj.* lawful; permissible, allowable.
licor [li·kór] *m.* liquid; liquor.
licuadora [li·kwa·đó·ra] *f.* blender.
lid [liđ] *f.* fight; contest.
líder [lí·đer] *m. Am.* (labor or political) leader.
lidiar [li·đjár] *v.* to fight; to combat; to contend.
liebre [ljé·ƀre] *f.* hare; coward.
lienzo [ljén·so] *m.* cotton or linen cloth; canvas; painting.
liga [lí·ǥa] *f.* (*alianza*) league; alliance; (*cinta*) garter; allow; birdlime.
ligador [li·ǥa·đór] *m.* binder.
ligadura [li·ǥa·đú·ra] *f.* binding; tie, bond; — **de laca** shellac bond.
ligar[7] [li·ǥár] *v.* to bind, tie, unite; to alloy (*combine metals*); **-se** to unite, combine, form an alliance.
legereza [li·xe·ré·sa] *f.* lightness; swiftness; flippancy; frivolity.
ligero [li·xé·ro] *adj.* (*leve*) light; (*rápido*) swift; nimble; flippant; *adv. C.A., Col., Ven.* quickly; **a la ligera** quickly, superficially.
lija [lí·xa] *f.* sandpaper.
lijar [li·xár] *v.* to sandpaper; **lijadora** sander.
lila [lí·la] *f.* lilac; pinkish-purple.
lima [lí·ma] *f.* file; lime (*fruit*); finishing, polishing.
limar [li·már] *v.* to file; to file down; to smooth, polish.
limeño [li·mé·ño] *adj.* of or from Lima, Peru.
limero [li·mé·ro] *m.* lime tree.
limitación [li·mi·ta·sjón] *f.* limitation; district.
limitar [li·mi·tár] *v.* to limit; to restrict; to bound.
límite [lí·mi·te] *m.* limit; boundary.
limítrofe [li·mí·tro·fe] *adj.* limiting; bordering.
limo [lí·mo] *m.* slime.
limón [li·món] *m.* lemon; lemon tree; *Am.* lime; — **italiano** lemon; **limonada** *f.* lemonade; **limonero** *m.* lemon tree lemon dealer or vendor.
limosna [li·móz·na] *f.* alms, charity.
limosnero [li·moz·né·ro] *m.* beggar.

limpiabotas [lim·pja·ƀó·tas] *m.* bootblack; *Ch.* bootlicker, flatterer.
limpiadientes [lim·pja·đjén·tes] *m.* toothpick.
limpiaparabrisas [lim·pja·pa·ra·ƀrí·sas] *m.* windshield wiper.
limpiar [lim·pjár] *v.* to clean; to wipe; to cleanse, purify; *Am.* to beat up, whip, lash.
limpias [lím·pjas] *f.* cleanouts.
límpido [lím·pi·đo] *adj.* limpid, clear.
limpieza [lim·pjé·sa] *f.* cleanliness, neatness; purity; honesty.
limpio [lím·pjo] *adj.* clean; neat; pure; **poner en —** to make a clean copy; *Col.* **— y soplado** absolutely broke, wiped out.
linaje [li·ná·xe] *m.* lineage, family, race.
linajudo [li·na·xú·đo] *adj.* highborn.
linaza [li·ná·sa] *f.* linseed.
lince [lín·se] *m.* lynx; sharp-sighted person.
linchar [lin·čár] *v.* to lynch.
lindar [lin·dár] *v.* to border, adjoin.
linde [lín·de] *m. & f.* limit, border, boundary; landmark.
lindero [lin·dé·ro] *adj.* bordering upon; *m. Carib., C.A.* landmark; boundary.
lindeza [lin·dé·sa] *f.* prettiness; exquisiteness; neatness; witty act or remark.
lindo [lín·do] *adj.* pretty; **de lo —** wonderfully; very much; to the utmost.
línea [lí·ne·a] *f.* line; limit.
lineal [li·ne·ál] *adj.* lineal, linear.
lingüista [liŋ·gwís·ta] *m. & f.* linguist.
lingüística [liŋ·gwís·ti·ka] *f.* linguistics.
lingüístico [liŋ·gwís·ti·ko] *adj.* linguistic.
lino [lí·no] *m.* linen; flax; **linón** *m.* lawn, thin linen or cotton.
linotipia [li·no·tí·pja] *f.* linotype.
linterna [lin·tér·na] *f.* lantern.
lío [lí·o] *m.* (*bulto*) bundle; (*enredo*) fib; mess, confusion; **armar un —** to raise a rumpus; to cause confusion; **hacerse un —** to be confused, get tangled up; **meterse en un —** to get oneself into a mess.
liquidación [li·ki·đa·sjón] *f.* liquidation; settlement (*of an account*).
liquidar [li·ki·đár] *v.* to liquidate; to settle (*an account*).
líquido [lí·ki·đo] *m.* liquid; **— refrigerador** coolant.
lira [lí·ra] *f.* lyre, small harp; a type of metrical composition; lira (*Italian coin*).
lírico [lí·ri·ko] *adj.* lyric, lyrical; *Am.* fantastic; *m. Ríopl.* visionary, dreamer.
lirio [lí·rjo] *m.* lily.
lirismo [li·ríz·mo] *m.* lyricism (*lyric quality*); *Am.* idle dream, fantasy.
lisiado [li·sjá·đo] *adj.* lame, hurt, injured.
liso [lí·so] *adj.* smooth, even; flat; evident, clear; *Am.* crafty, sly; *Col., Ven., C.A., Andes* fresh, impudent.
lisonja [li·sóŋ·xa] *f.* flattery.
lisonjear [li·soŋ·xe·ár] *v.* to flatter; to fawn on; to please.
lisonjero [li·soŋ·xé·ro] *adj.* flattering, pleasing; *m.* flatterer.
lista [lís·ta] *f.* list; strip; stripe; **pasar —** to call the roll; **— de correos** general delivery.
listado [lis·tá·đo] *adj.* striped.
listar [lis·tár] *v.* to register, enter in a list; *Ríopl., Mex., Ven.* to stripe, streak.
listo [lís·to] *adj.* ready, prompt; clever; *Ríopl., Ch.* mischievous.
listón [lis·tón] *m.* ribbon, tape; strip; **-s de enrasar** furring (carpentry).
lisura [li·sú·ra] *f.* smoothness; sincerity, frankness; *Am.* freshness, impudence; *Andes* insulting or filthy remark.
litera [li·té·ra] *f.* berth (*on a boat or train*); litter (*for carrying a person*).
literario [li·te·rá·rjo] *adj.* literary.
literato [li·te·rá·to] *adj.* literary, learned; *m.* literary man, writer.
literatura [li·te·ra·tú·ra] *f.* literature.
litigio [li·tí·xjo] *m.* litigation, lawsuit.
litio [lí·tjo] *m.* lithium.
litoral [li·to·rál] *adj.* seaboard, coastal; *m.* coast, shore.
litro [lí·tro] *m.* liter (*about 1.05 quarts*).
liviandad [li·ƀja·ni·đáđ] *f.* lightness; frivolity; lewdness.
liviano [li·ƀjá·no] *adj.* (*leve*) light; slight, unimportant; (*lascivo*) frivolous, fickle; lewd; unchaste.
lívido [lí·ƀi·đo] *adj.* livid, having a dull-bluish color; pale.
lo [lo] *obj. pron.* him; you (*formal*); it; so; *dem. pron.* **— de** that of, that affair of, that matter of; **— bueno** the good, what is good; **sé — bueno que Vd. es** I know how good you are; **— que** that which, what.
loable [lo·á·ƀle] *adj.* laudable, worthy of praise.
loar [lo·ár] *v.* to praise.
lobanillo [lo·ƀa·ní·yo] *m.* growth, tumor.
lobo [ló·ƀo] *m.* wolf.
lóbrego [ló·ƀre·go] *adj.* dark, gloomy.
lobreguez [lo·ƀre·ǥés] *f.* darkness, gloominess.
lóbulo [ló·ƀu·lo] *m.* lobe.
lobuno [lo·ƀú·no] *adj.* related to the wolf.
local [lo·kál] *adj.* local; *m.* place, quarters; site; premises.
localidad [lo·ka·li·đáđ] *f.* location; locality, town; place; seat (*in a theater*).
localización [lo·ka·li·sa·sjón] *f.* localization, localizing.
localizar[9] [lo·ka·li·sár] *v.* to localize.
loco [lo·ko] *adj.* insane, mad, crazy; **— de remate** stark mad; *m.* lunatic, insane person.
locomotor [lo·ko·mo·tór] *adj.* locomotive.
locomotora [lo·ko·mo·tó·ra] *f.* locomotive; **— diesel** diesel locomotive.
locuaz [lo·kwás] *adj.* loquacious, talkative.
locución [lo·ku·sjón] *f.* phrase; diction.
locura [lo·kú·ra] *f.* madness, insanity.
locutor [lo·ku·tór] *m.* radio announcer.
lodazal [lo·đa·sál] *m.* muddy place; mire.
lodo [ló·đo] *m.* mud; **lodoso** [lo·đó·so] *adj.* muddy, miry.
logaritmo [lo·ǥa·rím·mo] *m.* logarithm.
logia [ló·xja] *f.* lodge (*secret society*).
lógica [ló·xi·ka] *f.* logic; reasoning.
logical [lo·xi·kál] *m.*, (*computadora*) software.
lógico [ló·xi·ko] *adj.* logical.
lograr [lo·ǥrár] *v.* to gain, obtain, accomplish; — (+ *inf.*) to succeed in; **-se** to succeed; to turn out well.
logrero [lo·ǥré·ro] *m.* usurer; profiteer.
logro [ló·ǥro] *m.* profit, gain; usury; attainment; realization.
loísta [lo·ís·ta] *m. & f.* one who uses the pronoun *lo* for the masculine direct object (*lo conozco*).
loma [ló·ma] *f.* small hill; **lomerío** [lo·me·rí·o] *m. Am.* group of hills.
lombriz [lom·brís] *f.* earthworm.
lomillo [lo·mí·yo] *m.* cross-stitch.

lomo [ló·mo] *m.* back (*of an animal, book, knife, etc.*); loin; ridge between two furrows; *Mex., Ven.* **hacer** — to bear with patience, resign oneself.
lona [ló·na] *f.* canvas.
lonche [lón·če] *m. Col., Ven., Mex.* lunch; **lonchería** [lon·če·rí·a] *f. Col., Ven., Mex.* lunchroom.
londinense [lon·di·nén·se] *m. & f.* of or from London.
longaniza [loŋ·ga·ní·sa] *f.* pork sausage.
longevidad [loŋ·xe·ƀi·đáđ] *f.* longevity, long life; span of life, length of life.
longitud [loŋ·xi·túđ] *f.* longitude; length.
longitudinal [loŋ·xi·tu·đi·nál] *adj.* longitudinal, lengthwise; **-mente** *adv.* longitudinally, lengthwise.
lonja [lóŋ·xa] *f.* (*mercado*) exchange; market; (*carne*) slice of meat; (*correa*) leather strap; *Ríopl.* rawhide.
lontananza [lon·ta·nán·sa] *f.* background; **en** — in the distance, in the background.
loro [ló·ro] *m.* parrot.
los [los] *def. art. m. pl.* the; *obj. pron.* them; — **que** *rel. pron.* those which; which.
losa [ló·sa] *f.* flagstone; slab; gravestone.
lote [ló·te] *m.* lot, share, part; *Am.* remnant lot; *Col.* swallow of liquor; *Am.* blockhead, dunce.
lotear [lo·te·ár] *v. Am.* to subdivide into lots; *Am.* to divide into portions.
lotería [lo·te·rí·a] *f.* lottery; raffle.
loza [ló·sa] *f.* fine earthenware; crockery; — **fina** chinaware.
lozanía [lo·sa·ní·a] *f.* luxuriance (*rich foliage or growth*); vigor.
lozano [lo·sá·no] *adj.* luxuriant; exuberant, vigorous, lusty.
lubricar[6] [lu·ƀri·kár] *v.* to lubricate, or grease; **lubricante** lubricant.
lucero [lu·sé·ro] *m.* morning star; any bright star; star on the forehead of certain animals; splendor, brightness.
lúcido [lú·si·đo] *adj.* lucid, clear; shining, bright.
luciente [lu·sjén·te] *adj.* shining, bright.
luciérnaga [lu·sjér·na·ǥa] *f.* firefly; glowworm.
lucimiento [lu·si·mjén·to] *m.* splendor; brilliance; success.
lucir[13] [lu·sír] *v. irr.* (*brillar*) to shine, to illuminate, to brighten; (*superar*) to excel; (*alardear*) to show off; **-se** to shine, be brilliant; show off; to be successful.
lucrativo [lu·kra·tí·ƀo] *adj.* lucrative, profitable.
lucro [lú·kro] *m.* profit, gain.
luctuoso [luk·twó·so] *adj.* sad, mournful, dismal.
lucha [lú·ča] *f.* fight, struggle; dispute; wrestling match.
luchador [lu·ča·đór] *m.* fighter; wrestler.
luchar [lu·čár] *v.* to fight, to wrestle, to struggle, to dispute.
luego [lwé·ǥo] *adv.* soon, presently; afterwards, then, next; **desde** — immediately, at once; naturally; of course; — **de** after; — **que** as soon as; **hasta** — good-bye, so long; — — right away.
luengo [lwéŋ·go] *adj.* long; **-s años** many years.
lugar [lu·ǥár] *m.* (*sitio*) place; site; town; space; (*empleo*) position, employment; (*ocasión*) time, occasion, opportunity; **dar** — **a** to give cause or occasion for; **hacer** (*or* **dar**) — to make room; **en** — **de** instead of.
lugareño [lu·ǥa·ré·ño] *m.* villager.
lúgubre [lú·ǥu·ƀre] *adj.* mournful, gloomy.
lujo [lú·xo] *m.* luxury, extravagance.
lujoso [lu·xó·so] *adj.* luxurious; elegant; showy.
lujuria [lu·xú·rja] *f.* lust, lewdness, sensuality.
lujurioso [lu·xu·rjó·so] *adj.* lustful, lewd, sensual.
lumbre [lúm·bre] *f.* fire; brightness.
luminoso [lu·mi·nó·so] *adj.* luminous, bright, shining.
luna [lú·na] *f.* moon; mirror, glass for mirrors.
lunar [lu·nár] *adj.* lunar; *m.* mole; blemish, spot.
lunático [lu·ná·ti·ko] *adj. & m.* lunatic.
lunes [lú·nes] *m.* Monday; *Ch.* **hacer San Lunes** to lay off on Monday.
lunfardo [lun·fár·đo] *m.* social dialect of the Buenos Aires underworld.
lustre [lús·tre] *m.* luster, shine; glory.
lustroso [lus·tró·so] *adj.* lustrous, glossy, shining.
luto [lú·to] *m.* mourning; sorrow, grief.
luz [lus] *f.* light; clarity; hint, guidance; **dar a** — to give birth; to publish; **entre dos luces** at twilight.

LL:ll

llaga [ŷá·ǥa] *f.* wound; ulcer, sore.
llama [ŷá·ma] *f.* flame; (*animal*) llama.
llamada [ŷa·má·đa] *f.* call; beckon, sign; knock; reference mark (*as an asterisk*).
llamador [ŷa·ma·đór] *m.* knocker (*of a door*); caller.
llamamiento [ŷa·ma·mjén·to] *m.* call, calling; calling together; appeal.
llamar [ŷa·már] *v.* to call; to summon; to name; to invoke; — **a la puerta** to knock at the door; **-se** to be called, named; *Mex.* to break one's word or promise.
llamarada [ŷa·ma·rá·đa] *f.* flash; sudden flame or blaze; sudden flush, blush.
llamativo [ŷa·ma·tí·ƀo] *adj.* showy, loud, gaudy, flashy; thirst-exciting.
llameante [ŷa·me·án·te] *adj.* flaming.
llana [ŷá·na] *f.* mason's trowel.
llanero [ŷa·né·ro] *m. Ven., Col.* plainsman.
llaneza [ŷa·né·sa] *f.* simplicity, frankness, sincerity, plainness.
llano [ŷá·no] *adj.* plain, simple; even, smooth, level; frank; *m.* plain, flat ground.
llanta [ŷán·ta] *f. Spain* rim of a wheel; *Am.* tire; tire casing; *Peru* large sunshade (*used in Peruvian markets*).
llanto [ŷán·to] *m.* crying, weeping; tears.
llanura [ŷa·nú·ra] *f.* extensive plain; prairie; evenness, flatness.
llapa [ŷá·pa] *f. Andes, Ríopl.* a small gift from the vendor to the purchaser; also **yapa, ñapa.**
llave [ŷá·ƀe] *f.* key; faucet; clef; — **de tuercas** wrench; — **inglesa** monkey wrench; — **maestra** master key.
llavera [ŷa·ƀé·ra] *f. Ch.* housekeeper.
llavero [ŷa·ƀé·ro] *m.* key ring; key maker; keeper of the keys.
llavín [ŷa·ƀín] *m.* small key.
llegada [ŷe·ǥá·đa] *f.* arrival.
llegar[7] [ŷe·ǥár] *v.* to arrive; to reach; to amount; — **a ser** to get or come to be; — **a las manos** to come to blows; **-se** to approach, get near.
llenar [ŷe·nár] *v.* to fill; to stuff; **-se** to fill up; to overeat; **-se de** to get filled with; to get covered with, spattered with.
lleno [ŷé·no] *adj.* full; *m.* fullness, completeness; **de** — totally, completely; **un** — **completo** a full house (*said of a theater*).
llenura [ŷe·nú·ra] *f.* fullness; abundance.
llevadero [ŷe·ƀa·đé·ro] *adj.* bearable, tolerable.
llevar [ŷe·ƀár] *v.* (*transportar*) to carry; to bear; to

transport; to wear; (*conducir*) to take; to lead; (*cobrar*) to charge; to ask a certain price; to keep (*accounts*); — **ventaja** to be ahead, have the advantage; — **un año a** to be one year older than; — **un mes aquí** to have been here one month; — **un castigo** to suffer punishment; **-se** to carry away; **-se bien con** to get along with.
llorar [ŷo·rár] *v.* to cry, weep.
lloriquear [ŷo·ri·ke·ár] *v.* to whimper, whine, weep.
lloriqueo [ŷo·ri·ké·o] *m.* whimper, whining.
lloro [ŷó·ro] *m.* weeping.
llorón [ŷo·rón] *adj.* weeping; **sauce** — weeping willow; *m.* weeper, crybaby, whiner.
llorona [ŷo·ró·na] *f.* weeping woman; **-s** *Arg., Bol.* large spurs.
lloroso [ŷo·ró·so] *adj.* tearful; weeping.
llovedizo [ŷo·ƀe·đí·so] *adj.* rain (*used as adj.*); **agua llovediza** rain water.
llover[2] [ŷo·ƀér] *v. irr.* to rain, shower.
llovizna [ŷo·ƀíz·na] *f.* drizzle.
lloviznar [ŷo·ƀiz·nár] *v.* to drizzle, sprinkle.
lluvia [ŷú·ƀja] *f.* rain; shower.
lluvioso [ŷu·ƀjó·so] *adj.* rainy.

M:m

macana [ma·ká·na] *f. Am.* club, cudgel, stick; *Ríopl., Ch., Bol.* lie, absurdity, nonsense.
macanudo [ma·ka·nú·đo] *adj. Ríopl.* tremendous! great!
macarrón [ma·ka·rrón] *m.* macaroon; **-es** macaroni.
maceta [ma·sé·ta] *f.* (*tiesto*) flowerpot; (*martillo*) small mallet; stonecutter's hammer; handle of tools; *Am.* head; *adj. Am.* slow.
macilento [ma·si·lén·to] *adj.* thin, emaciated; pale.
macizo [ma·sí·so] *adj.* solid, firm; massive; *m.* massiveness; firmness; thicket; clump.
machacar[6] [ma·ča·kár] *v.* to pound, crush; to insist, harp on.
machacón [ma·ča·kón] *adj.* persistent; tenacious.
machete [ma·čé·te] *m.* machete, large heavy knife; **machetazo** *m.* large machete; blow with a machete.
machismo [ma·číz·mo] *m.* the quality of being a male; proven daring; male chauvinism.
macho [má·čo] *m.* male; he-mule; hook (*of a hook and eye*); abutment; pillar; stupid fellow; sledgehammer; *C.R.* a blond; North American; *Am.* **pararle a uno el** — to halt or repress a person; *adj.* masculine, male; strong.
machucar[6] [ma·ču·kár] *v.* to pound, beat, bruise; *Am.* to crush; *Am.* to break (*a horse*).
machucón [ma·ču·kón] *m.* smash; bruise.
madeja [ma·đé·xa] *f.* skein; mass of hair; limp, listless person.
madera [ma·đé·ra] *f.* wood; timber; lumber; — **contrachapada** (*triplay*) plywood; **maderero** *m.* lumberman, lumber dealer.
maderaje [ma·đe·rá·xe] *m.* timber, lumber; timber work; woodwork.
maderamen [ma·đe·rá·men] *m.* timber; timber work; woodwork.
madero [ma·đé·ro] *m.* beam; plank; timber, piece of lumber; blockhead, dunce.
madrastra [ma·đrás·tra] *f.* stepmother.
madre [má·đre] *f.* mother; womb; root, origin; river bed; **salirse de** — to overflow (*said of rivers*).
madrepeña [ma·đre·pé·ña] *f. Am.* moss.
madreperla [ma·đre·pér·la] *f.* mother-of-pearl.
madreselva [ma·đre·sél·ƀa] *f.* honeysuckle.
madriguera [ma·đri·ǥé·ra] *f.* burrow; den, lair.
madrileño [ma·đri·lé·ño] *adj.* Madrilenian, from or pertaining to Madrid; *m.* Madrilenian.
madrina [ma·đrí·na] *f.* (*patrocinadora*) godmother; bridesmaid; sponsor; (*correa*) strap for yoking two horses; (*ganado*) leading mare; prop; *Am.* small herd of tame cattle (*used for leading wild cattle*).
madrugada [ma·đru·ǥá·đa] *f.* dawn; early morning; **de** — at daybreak.
madrugador [ma·đru·ǥa·đór] *m.* early riser.
madrugar[7] [ma·đru·ǥár] *v.* to rise early; to be ahead of others; to "get the jump" on someone.
madurar [ma·đu·rár] *v.* to mature; to ripen.
madurez [ma·đu·rés] *f.* maturity; ripeness.
maduro [ma·đú·ro] *adj.* ripe; mature; prudent, wise; *Am.* bruised, sore.
maestría [ma·es·trí·a] *f.* mastery; great skill; advanced teaching degree.
maestro [ma·és·tro] *m.* master, teacher; chief craftsman; *adj.* master; masterly, skillful; **llave maestra** master key; **obra maestra** masterpiece.
MAGI (soldura) *s.* **en atmósfera de gas inerte** MIG welding.
magia [má·xja] *f.* magic; charm.
mágico [má·xi·ko] *adj.* magic; *m.* magician.
magín [ma·xín] *m.* imagination, fancy.
magisterio [ma·xis·té·rjo] *m.* teaching profession.
magistrado [ma·xis·trá·đo] *m.* magistrate, judge.
magistral [ma·xis·trál] *adj.* masterly; masterful; authoritative.
magnánimo [maǥ·ná·ni·mo] *adj.* magnanimous, noble, generous.
magnesia [maǥ·né·sja] *f.* magnesia.
magnesio [maǥ·né·sjo] *m.* magnesium.
magnético [maǥ·né·ti·ko] *adj.* magnetic; attractive.
magnetofónico [maǥ·ne·to·fó·ni·ko] *adj.* recording (*tape or wire*).
magnetófono [maǥ·ne·tó·fo·no] *m.* tape recorder.
magnificencia [maǥ·ni·fi·sén·sja] *f.* magnificence, splendor.
magnífico [maǥ·ní·fi·ko] *adj.* magnificent, splendid.
magnitud [maǥ·ni·túđ] *f.* magnitude, greatness.
magno [máǥ·no] *adj.* great.
magnolia [maǥ·nó·lja] *f.* magnolia.
mago [má·ǥo] *m.* magician, wizard; **los tres Reyes Magos** the Three Wise Men.
magra [máǥ·ra] *f.* slice of ham.
magro [máǥ·ro] *adj.* lean.
maguey [ma·ǥéj] *m.* maguey, century plant.
magullar [ma·ǥu·yár] *v.* to bruise; to maul; to mangle; *Ríopl., Ch., Col., Andes, P.R.* to crumple.
magullón [ma·ǥu·yón] *m.* a bruise.
mahometano [ma·o·me·tá·no] *adj. & m.* Mohammedan.
maicillo [maj·sí·yo] *m. Am.* gravel.
maíz [ma·ís] *m.* corn; **maizal** [maj·sál] *m.* cornfield.
majada [ma·xá·đa] *f.* sheepfold; dung, manure; *Ríopl., Ch.* flock of sheep or goats.
majadería [ma·xa·đe·rí·a] *f.* foolishness, nonsense.
majadero [ma·xa·đé·ro] *adj.* foolish; bothersome.
majar [ma·xár] *v.* to pound; to crush; to bruise; to crumple; to mash; to annoy, bother.
majestad [ma·xes·táđ] *f.* majesty; dignity.
majestuoso [ma·xes·twó·so] *adj.* majestic, stately.
majo [má·xo] *adj.* gaudy, showy; gaily attired; pretty; *m.* dandy; **maja** [má·xa] *f.* belle.
mal [mal] *m.* evil; illness; harm; wrong. *See* **malo.**
malabarista [ma·la·ƀrís·ta] *m. & f.* juggler; *Ch.* sly

thief.
malacate [ma·la·ká·te] *m.* hoist, hoisting machine, winch; *Am.* spindle (*for cotton*); *Am.* **parecer uno un** — to be constantly on the go, be in constant motion.
malagueña [ma·la·gé·ña] *f.* song and dance of Málaga; native (*f.*) of Málaga.
malandanza [ma·lan·dán·sa] *f.* misfortune.
malaquita [ma·la·kí·ta] *f.* malachite.
malaventura [ma·la·ben·tú·ra] *f.* misfortune, disaster.
malazo [ma·lá·so] *adj.* perverse, evil, wicked; vicious.
malbaratar [mal·ba·ra·tár] *v.* to undersell, sell at a loss; to squander.
malcontento [mal·kon·tén·to] *adj.* discontented; *m.* malcontent, troublemaker.
malcriado [mal·krjá·do] *adj.* ill-bred, rude.
maldad [mal·dád] *f.* badness, evil, wickedness.
maldecir[27, 52] [mal·de·sír] *v. irr.* to curse; to damn.
maldiciente [mal·di·sjén·te] *adj.* cursing.
maldición [mal·di·sjón] *f.* curse.
maldispuesto [mal·dis·pwés·to] *adj.* unwilling, not inclined.
maldito [mal·dí·to] *p.p. of* **maldecir** & *adj.* cursed; wicked; damned; *Ch.* tricky; *Mex.* bold, boastful.
maleable [ma·le·á·ble] *adj.* malleable, easily spoiled.
maleante [ma·le·án·te] *m.* crook, rogue, rascal, villain.
malecón [ma·le·kón] *m.* mole; dike.
maledicencia [ma·le·di·sén·sja] *f.* slander.
maleficio [ma·le·fí·sjo] *m.* spell, charm, witchery.
maléfico [ma·lé·fi·ko] *adj.* evil, harmful.
malestar [ma·les·tár] *m.* indisposition; slight illness; discomfort.
maleta [ma·lé·ta] *f.* travelling bag; suitcase; *Col., Ven., C.A.* bundle of clothes; *Col.* hump (*on the back*); *Ch.* saddlebag; *C.A.* rogue, rascal; *Ch.* lazy fellow.
maletín [ma·le·tín] *m.* small valise, satchel.
malevo [ma·lé·bo] *adj. Bol., Ríopl.* bad, wicked.
malévolo [ma·lé·bo·lo] *adj.* bad, evil, wicked.
maleza [ma·lé·sa] *f.* underbrush; thicket; weeds.
malgastar [mal·gas·tár] *v.* to squander, waste.
¡malhaya! [ma·lá·ya] *interj.* cursed; *Ríopl.* were it so!
malhechor [ma·le·čór] *m.* malefactor, evildoer, criminal.
malhora [ma·ló·ra] *f. Ríopl., C.A., Ven.* trouble, misfortune.
malhumorado [ma·lu·mo·rá·do] *adj.* ill-humored.
malicia [ma·lí·sja] *f.* malice; wickedness; shrewdness; suspicion; *Ch.* bit of brandy or cognac added to another drink.
maliciar [ma·li·sjár] *v.* to suspect.
malicioso [ma·li·sjó·so] *adj.* malicious; wicked; shrewd; suspicious.
maligno [ma·líg·no] *adj.* malign, malignant; pernicious, harmful.
malmandado [mal·man·dá·do] *adj.* disobedient; stubborn.
mal(o) [mál(o)] *adj.* bad, evil; wicked; ill; difficult; *Am.* **a la mala** treacherously; *Ríopl.* **de malas** by force; **estar de malas** to be out of luck; **por la mala** unwillingly, by force; **venir de malas** to come with evil intentions; **mal** *adv.* badly; poorly; wrongly.
malograr [ma·lo·grár] *v.* to waste, lose; **-se** to turn out badly; to fail.
malón [ma·lón] *m.* mean trick; *Ríopl.* surprise Indian raid; *Ven.* tin-pan serenade, boisterous surprise party.
malpagar[7] [mal·pa·gár] *v.* to underpay, pay poorly.
malparto [mal·pár·to] *m.* miscarriage, abortion.
malquerencia [mal·ke·rén·sja] *f.* aversion, dislike, ill will.
malsano [mal·sá·no] *adj.* unhealthy; sickly.
malta [mál·ta] *f.* malt.
maltratar [mal·tra·tár] *v.* to treat badly; to misuse, abuse.
maltrato [mal·trá·to] *m.* mistreatment, abuse.
maltrecho [mal·tré·čo] *adj.* battered, bruised, injured.
malvado [mal·bá·do] *adj.* wicked; malicious.
malversación [mal·ber·sa·sjón] *f.* graft, corruption, misuse of public funds.
malversar [mal·ber·sár] *v.* to misuse (*funds in one's trust*); to embezzle.
malla [má·ya] *f.* mesh; coat of mail; *Ch.* species of potato; **hacer** — to knit.
mamá [ma·má] *f.* mamma.
mamada [ma·má·da] *f.* suck, sucking.
mamado [ma·má·do] *adj. Am.* drunk.
mamar [ma·már] *v.* to suckle; to suck; to gorge; **-se** *Ríopl., C.A.* to get drunk; *Col.* to go back on one's promise; *Col.* to fold up, crack up; **-se a uno** to get the best of someone, deceive someone; *Col., C.A.* to kill someone.
mamarracho [ma·ma·rrá·čo] *m.* a mess; a worthless guy.
mamífero [ma·mí·fe·ro] *m.* mammal; *adj.* mammalian, of mammals.
mamón [ma·món] *adj.* suckling; *m.* suckling (*very young animal or child*); shoot, sucker (*of a tree*); a tropical tree and its fruit; *Mex.* a kind of cake; *C.A.* public employee.
mampara [mam·pá·ra] *f.* screen.
mampostería [mam·pos·te·rí·a] *f.* masonry, stone masonry.
manada [ma·ná·da] *f.* herd, drove, pack, flock.
manantial [ma·nan·tjál] *m.* spring; source, origin.
manar [ma·nár] *v.* to spring, flow (from); to abound.
manaza [ma·ná·sa] *f.* large hand.
manazo [ma·ná·so] *m. Ríopl.* slap. *See* **manotazo.**
mancarrón [maŋ·ka·rrón] *m.* one-armed or one-handed man; cripple; old nag; *Ríopl., Andes* crude, clumsy fellow; *S.A.* disabled workman; *S.A.* dike, small dam.
mancebo [man·sé·bo] *m.* youth, young man; bachelor.
mancera [man·sé·ra] *f.* handle of a plough.
mancilla [man·sí·ya] *f.* stain, spot; dishonor.
manco [máŋ·ko] *adj.* one-armed; one-handed; maimed; lame (*referring to an arm* or *the front leg of an animal*); faulty, defective; *m. Ch.* nag.
mancuerna [maŋ·kwér·na] *f.* pair of animals tied together; *Mex., C.A. f. pl.* cuff links.
mancha [mán·ča] *f.* spot, stain, blemish; *Am.* cloud, swarm; *Ven., Cuba, Col.* roving herd of cattle.
manchar [man·čár] *v.* to stain, soil, spot; to tarnish.
manchego [man·čé·go] *adj.* of or belonging to La Mancha (*region of Spain*); *m.* inhabitant of La Mancha.
manchón [man·čón] *m.* large stain; large patch.
mandadero [man·da·dé·ro] *m.* messenger, errand boy.
mandado [man·dá·do] *m.* (*orden*) command, order; (*recado*) errand; *p.p. of* **mandar; bien** — well-behaved; **mal** — ill-behaved.
mandamiento [man·da·mjén·to] *m.* command, order; writ; commandment.
mandar [man·dár] *v.* (*pedir*) to command, order; rule; (*enviar*) to send; to bequeath; will; *Col., Ven.* to throw, hurl; — **hacer** to have made, order; *Col., Ven., Mex., Carib., Andes* — **una bofetada** to give a slap; *Col., Ven., Mex., Carib., Andes* —

una pedrada to throw a stone; **-se** *Am.* to be impudent; **-se mudar** *Ríopl., Carib.* to go away.

mandatario [man·da·tá·rjo] *m.* attorney, representative; *Am.* magistrate, chief.

mandato [man·dá·to] *m.* mandate; order, command; term of office; (*computadora*) command.

mandíbula [man·dí·ƀu·la] *f.* jaw, jawbone.

mandioca [man·djó·ka] *f.* manioc.

mando [mán·do] *m.* command, authority, power; (*computadora*) joystick.

mandolina [man·do·lí·na] *f.* mandolin.

mandón [man·dón] *adj.* bossy, domineering; *m.* bossy person; *Arg.* boss or foreman of a mine; *Ch.* race starter.

mandril [man·dríl] *m.* chuck, reamer; — **de la barra taladradora** boring bar holder.

maneador [ma·ne·a·đór] *m. Ríopl., Ven., Col.* hobble, leather lasso (*for the legs of an animal*); *Arg.* whip; *Ven., Andes* halter.

manear [ma·ne·ár] *v.* to hobble, lasso, tie the legs of (*an animal*); **-se** *Col., Ven.* to get tangled up.

manecilla [ma·ne·sí·ya] *f.* small hand; hand of a watch or clock.

manejable [ma·ne·xá·ƀle] *adj.* manageable.

manejar [ma·ne·xár] *v.* to manage, handle; to drive (*a car*); (*computadora*) to control; **-se** to move about, get around (*after an illness or accident*); *Carib., Ven.* to behave oneself.

manejo [ma·né·xo] *m.* handling; management; trick, intrigue.

manera [ma·né·ra] *f.* manner, way, mode; side opening in a shirt; front opening in breeches; **-s** customs; manners, behavior; **a — de** (*or* **a la — de**) like, in the style of; **de — que** so that; **sobre —** exceedingly; extremely.

manga [mán·ga] *f.* sleeve; bag; hose (*for watering*); body of troops; *Am.* multitude, herd, swarm; *Am.* cattle chute (*narrow passageway*); *Col., Ec.* corral; **— de agua** waterspout, whirlwind over the ocean; *Mex.* **— de hule** raincape; **por angas o por -s** by hook or crook, in one way or another.

mangana [man·gá·na] *f.* lariat, lasso.

manganeso [man·ga·né·so] *m.* manganese.

mangle [mán·gle] *m.* mangrove.

mango [mán·go] *m.* handle; *Am.* mango (*tropical tree and its fruit*).

manguera [man·gé·ra] *f.* hose (*for water*); waterspout; *Ríopl.* large corral (*for livestock*).

manguito [man·gí·to] *m.* muff; knitted half-sleeve (*worn on the forearm*); oversleeve; bushing.

maní [ma·ní] *m. Carib., C.A., Ch., Andes, Ven., Col.* peanut; **manicero** [ma·ni·sé·ro] *m. Carib., C.A., Ch., Andes, Ven., Col.* peanut vendor.

manía [ma·ní·a] *f.* mania, frenzy; craze, whim.

maniatar [ma·nja·tár] *v.* to tie the hands; to handcuff; to hobble (*an animal*).

maniático [ma·njá·ti·ko] *m.* crank, queer fellow; *adj.* cranky, queer, odd.

manicomio [ma·ni·kó·mjo] *m.* insane asylum.

manicura [ma·ni·kú·ra] *f.* manicure; manicurist.

manicurar [ma·ni·ku·rár] *v.* to manicure.

manido [ma·ní·đo] *adj.* rotting; *Ríopl., Carib., Col., Andes* trite, commonplace.

manifestación [ma·ni·fes·ta·sjón] *f.* manifestation; demonstration.

manifestar[1] [ma·ni·fes·tár] *v. irr.* to manifest; to show.

manifiesto [ma·ni·fjés·to] *adj.* manifest, clear, plain; *m.* manifesto, public declaration; customhouse manifest.

manigua [ma·ní·ǥwa] *f. Col., Ríopl., Cuba, P.R.* Cuban jungle or thicket; *Carib.* **coger —** to get feverish; *Ríopl., Carib.* **irse a la —** to rise up in rebellion.

manija [ma·ni·xa] *f.* handle; crank; fetter.

manilla [ma·ní·ya] *f.* small hand; bracelet; **-s de hierro** handcuffs.

maniobra [ma·njó·ƀra] *f.* maneuver; operation.

maniobrar [ma·njo·ƀrár] *v.* to maneuver.

manipulación [ma·ni·pu·la·sjón] *f.* manipulation.

manipular [ma·ni·pu·lár] *v.* to manipulate, handle.

maniquí [ma·ni·kí] *m.* manikin, model, dummy, figure of a person; puppet.

manivela [ma·ni·ƀé·la] *f.* crank.

manjar [maŋ·xár] *m.* dish, food; choice bit of food.

mano [má·no] *f.* (*del cuerpo*) hand; forefoot; (*reloj*) clock hand; (*acabado*) coat of paint or varnish; quire (*25 sheets*) of paper; *Am.* adventure, mishap; *Am.* handful; **— de obra** workmanship; labor; **a —** at hand; by hand; *Am.* **estamos a —** we are even, we are quits; *Am.* **doblar las -s** to give up; **ser —** to be first (*in a game*); to lead (*in a game*); **venir a las -s** to come to blows.

manojo [ma·nó·xo] *m.* handful; bunch.

manopla [ma·nó·pla] *f.* gauntlet; heavy glove; huge hand.

manosear [ma·no·se·ár] *v.* to handle, touch, feel with the hand; *Am.* to fondle, pet, caress.

manotada [ma·no·tá·đa] *f.* slap, blow; sweep of the hand; *Col.* handful, fistful; **manotazo** [ma·no·tá·so] *m.* slap.

manotear [ma·no·te·ár] *v.* to gesticulate; to strike with the hands; *Ríopl.* to embezzle, steal; *Arg.* to snatch away.

mansalva [man·sál·ƀa]: **a —** without danger or risk; treacherously; **matar a —** to kill without warning or without giving a person a chance to defend himself.

mansedumbre [man·se·đúm·bre] *f.* meekness; gentleness.

mansión [man·sjón] *f.* sojourn, stay; abode, dwelling.

manso [mán·so] *adj.* meek; mild, gentle; tame; *Ríopl., Ch.* cultivated (*plant*), civilized (*Indian*); *m.* leading sheep, goat, or ox.

manta [mán·ta] *f.* blanket; large shawl; tossing in a blanket; *Mex., C.A., Ven., Ríopl.* coarse cotton cloth; *Arg.* poncho; *Am.* **— mojada** dull person, dunce; **darle a uno una —** to toss someone in a blanket.

mantear [man·te·ár] *v.* to toss (*someone*) in a blanket.

manteca [man·té·ka] *f.* fat; lard; butter; **— de hojaldre** pastry lard; *Am.* **— de cacao** cocoa butter; *Am.* **— de coco** coconut oil; **mantequera** [man·te·ké·ra] *f.* churn; butter dish; woman who makes or sells butter.

mantecado [man·te·ká·đo] *m.* ice cream.

mantel [man·tél] *m.* tablecloth; altar cloth; *C.A., Mex.* **estar de -es largos** to dine in style.

mantener[45] [man·te·nér] *v. irr.* to maintain; to support; to sustain; to defend; **-se** to continue, remain; to support oneself; **-se firme** to remain firm; **-se quieto** to stay or keep quiet.

mantenimiento [man·te·ni·mjén·to] *m.* maintenance, support; sustenance; livelihood.

mantequilla [man·te·kí·ya] *f.* butter; **mantequillería** [man·te·ki·ye·rí·a] *f. Am.* creamery, dairy (*for making butter*).

mantilla [man·tí·ya] *f.* mantilla (*Spanish veil or scarf for the head*); saddlecloth.

manto [mán·to] *m.* mantle, cloak; cape: large mantilla; mantel, mantelpiece.

mantón [man·tón] *m.* large shawl; — **de Manila** embroidered silk shawl.
manuable [ma·nwá·ƀle] *adj.* handy, easy to handle.
manual [ma·nwál] *adj.* manual; handy; *m.* manual, handbook.
manubrio [ma·nú·ƀrjo] *m.* crank; handle.
manufacturar [ma·nu·fak·tu·rár] *v.* to manufacture.
manufacturero [ma·nu·fak·tu·ré·ro] *adj.* manufacturing; *m.* manufacturer.
manuscrito [ma·nus·krí·to] *adj.* written by hand; *m.* manuscript.
manutención [ma·nu·ten·sjón] *f.* maintenance; support; conservation.
manzana [man·sá·na] *f.* apple; block of houses; *Ríopl., Ch., Col., Ven., C.A.* Adam's apple; **manzano** [man·sá·no] *m.* apple tree.
manzanar [man·sa·nár] *m.* apple orchard.
maña [má·ña] *f.* skill, knack; cunning; **malas -s** bad tricks or habits.
mañana [ma·ñá·na] *f.* morning; *Ríopl.* **media** — mid-morning snack; *adv.* tomorrow, in the near future; **pasado** — day after tomorrow; **muy de** — very early in the morning; *m.* morrow; **mañanitas** [ma·ña·ní·tas] *f. pl. Mex., C.A.* popular song sung early in the morning to celebrate a birthday, saint's day, etc.
mañanero [ma·ña·né·ro] *m.* early riser; *adj.* early rising; **mañanista** [ma·ña·nís·ta] *m. & f. Am.* procrastinator, one who puts things off until tomorrow.
mañero [ma·ñe·ro] *adj.* astute, artful, clever; *Arg., P.R., C.A.* tricky; *Ch.* shy (*animal*); *Ríopl.* indolent, lazy (*child*).
mañoso [ma·ñó·so] *adj.* skillful; clever; (*tramposo*) sly; tricky; deceitful; *Am.* slow, lazy; *Am.* greedy; gluttonous (*child*).
mapa [má·pa] *m.* map, chart.
mapache [ma·pá·če] *m. Ch.* raccoon.
mapurite [ma·pu·rí·te], **mapurito** [ma·pu·rí·to] *m. Col., Ven.* skunk. *See* **zorrino, zorrillo.**
maqueta [ma·ké·ta] *f.* mock-up.
máquina [má·ki·na] *f.* machine; engine; — **de coser** sewing machine; — **de escribir** typewriter; — **amoladora** grinder; — **de rebanar** slicer.
maquinación [ma·ki·na·sjón] *f.* machination, scheming, plotting; plot, scheme.
maquinador [ma·ki·na·đór] *m.* schemer, plotter.
maquinal [ma·ki·nál] *adj.* mechanical, automatic; **-mente** *adv.* mechanically, automatically, in a mechanical manner.
maquinar [ma·ki·nár] *v.* to plot, scheme.
maquinaria [ma·ki·ná·rja] *f.* machinery; mechanism; mechanics.
maquinista [ma·ki·nís·ta] *m.* engineer, locomotive engineer; machinist; mechanic.
mar [mar] *m. & f.* sea; — **alta** rough sea; — **llena** high tide (*see* **pleamar**); — **de fondo** swell; **a -es** abundantly; **baja** — low tide; **en alta** — on the high seas; **la** — **de cosas** a lot of things.
maraca [ma·rá·ka] *f. Carib., Col., Ven.* maraca (*rhythm instrument made of a dried gourd filled with seeds or pebbles*).
maraña [ma·rá·ña] *f.* tangle; snarl; thicket; maze; plot, intrigue.
marañón [ma·ra·ñón] *m.* cashew.
maravedí [ma·ra·ƀe·đí] *m.* maravedi (*an old Spanish coin*).
maravilla [ma·ra·ƀí·ya] *f.* wonder, marvel; marigold; **a las mil -s** wonderfully, perfectly.
maravillar [ma·ra·ƀi·yár] *v.* to astonish, dazzle; **-se** to wonder, marvel.
maravilloso [ma·ra·ƀi·yó·so] *adj.* marvellous, wonderful.
marbete [mar·ƀé·te] *m.* label, stamp; baggage tag or check.
marca [már·ka] *f.* mark, stamp; sign; brand, make; gauge, rule; march, frontier, province; — **de fábrica** trademark; **de** — of excellent quality.
marcapasos [mar·ka·pá·sos] *m.* pacemaker.
marcar[6] [mar·kár] *v.* to mark, stamp, brand; to note, observe.
marcial [mar·sjál] *adj.* martial, warlike; frank, abrupt.
marco [már·ko] *m.* frame; mark (*German coin*); mark (*unit of weight, equal to 8 ounces*).
marcha [már·ča] *f.* march; course, progress; speed; gait; running, functioning; movement of a watch.
marchamo [mar·čá·mo] *m.* customhouse mark; *Am.* tax on each slaughtered animal.
marchante [mar·čán·te] *m.* (*vendedor*) merchant, dealer; (*cliente*) customer, regular client.
marchar [mar·čár] *v.* to march, mark step; to walk; to parade; to run (*said of machinery*); **-se** to go away.
marchitar [mar·či·tár] *v.* to wither; **-se** to wither; to fade; to shrivel up.
marchito [mar·čí·to] *adj.* withered; faded; shriveled up.
marea [ma·ré·a] *f.* tide; *Ríopl., Ch.* sea fog.
mareado [ma·re·á·đo] *adj.* seasick; dizzy.
marear [ma·re·ár] *v.* (*navegar*) to navigate, sail; (*fastidiar*) to annoy, upset (*a person*); to make dizzy; **-se** to get seasick, nauseated; dizzy.
mareo [ma·ré·o] *m.* seasickness; nausea; vexation, annoyance.
marfil [mar·fíl] *m.* ivory; *Ven.* fine-toothed comb.
margarita [mar·ga·rí·ta] *f.* marguerite, daisy; pearl.
margen [már·xen] *m.& f.* margin, border; river bank; **dar** — **a** to give an occasion to.
mariachi [ma·rjá·či] *m. Mex.* band and music typical of Guadalajara; *pl.* members of the band.
maricón [ma·ri·kón] *adj.* sissy, effeminate; *m.* sissy.
marido [ma·rí·đo] *m.* husband.
marimacho [ma·ri·má·čo] *m.* mannish woman.
marimba [ma·rím·ba] *f.* marimba.
marina [ma·rí·na] *f.* (*costa*) seacoast, shore; (*fuerza naval*) fleet; navy; (*arte u oficio*) seascape; seamanship; — **de guerra** navy; — **mercante** merchant marine.
marinar [ma·ri·nár] *v.* to marinate.
marinero [ma·ri·né·ro] *m.* mariner, seaman, sailor.
marino [ma·rí·no] *adj.* marine; *m.* mariner, seaman, sailor.
mariposa [ma·ri·pó·sa] *f.* butterfly; moth, *Col.* blindman's bluff (*a game*).
mariquita [ma·ri·kí·ta] *f.* sissy; (*cap.*) Molly.
mariscal [ma·ris·kál] *m.* marshal; blacksmith; — **de campo** field marshal.
marisco [ma·rís·ko] *m.* shellfish.
marítimo [ma·rí·ti·mo] *adj.* maritime, marine.
marmita [mar·mí·ta] *f.* kettle, boiler, teakettle; — **doble** double boiler.
mármol [már·mol] *m.* marble.
marmóreo [mar·mó·re·o] *adj.* marble, of marble, like marble.
maroma [ma·ró·ma] *f.* rope; *Am.* somersault; *Am.* acrobatic performance; *Col.* sudden change of political views; **andar en la** — to walk the tightrope; **maromero** [ma·ro·mé·ro] *m. Carib.* acrobat.
marqués [mar·kés] *m.* marquis.
marquesa [mar·ké·sa] *f.* marquise; *Ch.* couch.

marrano [ma·rrá·no] *m.* pig, hog; filthy person.
marrazo [ma·rrá·so] *m. Am.* bayonet, dagger.
marrón [ma·rrón] *adj.* reddish brown; *Spain* brown.
marroquí [ma·rro·kí] *adj.* from Morocco; *pl.* **marroquíes** [ma·rro·kí·es].
marrullero [ma·rru·yé·ro] *adj.* sly, wily.
martes [már·tes] *m.* Tuesday; — **de carnestolendas** Shove Tuesday (*Tuesday before Lent*).
martillar [mar·ti·yár] *v.* to hammer, pound.
martillo [mar·tí·yo] *m.* hammer; — **de orejas** claw hammer; — **de desbastar** chipping hammer.
martinete [mar·ti·né·te] *m.* pile driver; drop hammer; hammer of a piano.
mártir [már·tir] *m.& f.* martyr.
martirio [mar·tí·rjo] *m.* martyrdom; torture, torment.
martirizar[9] [mar·ti·ri·sár] *v.* to martyr; to torture, torment.
marxismo [mark·síz·mo] *m.* Marxism.
marzo [már·so] *m.* March.
mas [mas] *conj.* but.
más [mas] *adj.* more; most; *adv.* more; most; plus; — **bien** rather; — **de** more than, over; — **que** more than, **no . . .** — **que** only; **a** — **de** in addition to; **a lo** — at the most; **está de** — it is superfluous, unnecessary; *am.* **no** — only; *Am.* **no quiero** — **nada** (*instead of* **no quiero nada** —) I don't want anything more.
masa [má·sa] *f.* (*volumen*) mass; volume; (*pueblo*) crowd, the masses; (*pasta*) dough, paste; mortar; — **coral** glee club, choral society; **agarrarle a uno con las manos en la** — to catch someone in the act; **masilla** *f.* putty.
masaje [ma·sá·xe] *m.* massage.
mascada [mas·ká·đa] *f.* chewing; *Am.* mouthful; *Ríopl.* chew or quid of tobacco; *Am.* reprimand, scolding; *Mex.* silk handkerchief, scarf.
mascar[6] [mas·kár] *v.* to chew.
máscara [más·ka·ra] *f.* mask; **-s** masquerade; *m. & f.* masquerader; **mascarada** [mas·ka·rá·đa] *f.* masquerade.
masculino [mas·ku·lí·no] *adj.* masculine.
mascullar [mas·ku·yár] *v.* to mumble; to munch.
masón [ma·són] *m.* mason, freemason; **masonería** [ma·so·ne·rí·a] *f.* masonry, freemasonry.
masticar[6] [mas·ti·kár] *v.* to chew.
mástico [más·ti·ko] *m.* mastic; — **para tubos** pipe "dope".
mástil [más·til] *m.* mast; post.
mastín [mas·tín] *m.* mastiff.
mastuerzo [mas·twér·so] *m.* (*flor*) nasturtium; (*tonto*) simpleton, fool.
mata [má·ta] *f.* shrub, plant, bush; grove; clump of trees; *Ven., Col.* thicket, jungle; — **de pelo** head of hair.
matadero [ma·ta·đé·ro] *m.* slaughterhouse; hard work.
matador [ma·ta·đór] *m.* killer, murderer; bullfighter who kills the bull.
matamoros [ma·ta·mó·ros] *m.* bully; boastful person.
matamoscas [ma·ta·mós·kas] *m.* fly swatter.
matanza [ma·tán·sa] *f.* massacre, butchery; slaughter of livestock; *Mex.* slaughterhouse.
matar [ma·tár] *v.* to kill; to murder; **-se** to commit suicide; to overwork; **-se con alguien** to fight with somebody.
matasanos [ma·ta·sá·nos] *m.* quack, quack doctor.
matasellos [ma·ta·sé·yos] *m.* canceller (*of stamps*).
mate [má·te] *m.* checkmate (*winning move in chess*); *Ríopl., Ch.* Paraguayan tea (*used also in Argentina and Uruguay*); *Andes, Col.* teapot (*for* **mate**), any small pot; *Am.* bald head; *adj.* unpolished, dull (*surface*).
matear [ma·te·ár] *v.* to plant seeds or shoots; to hunt among the bushes; *Ríopl., Ch.* to drink **mate;** *Am.* to checkmate (*make the winning move in chess*).
matemática [ma·te·má·ti·ka] *f. pl.* mathematics.
matemático [ma·te·má·ti·ko] *adj.* mathematical; *m.* mathematician.
materia [ma·té·rja] *f.* matter; material; school subject; pus; — **prima** (*or* **primera** —) raw material.
material [ma·te·rjál] *adj.* material; rude, coarse; *m.* ingredient; material; equipment; *Ven.* **de** — made of adobe; — **que se trabaja** work at hand.
maternal [ma·ter·nál] *adj.* maternal.
maternidad [ma·ter·ni·đáđ] *f.* maternity, motherhood.
materno [ma·tér·no] *adj.* maternal.
matinal [ma·ti·nál] *adj.* morning, of the morning.
matiné [ma·ti·né] *m. Am.* matinée.
matiz [ma·tís] *m.* tint, shade, color, hue; shading.
matizar[9] [ma·ti·sár] *v.* to blend (*colors*); to tint; to shade, tone down.
matón [ma·tón] *m.* bully.
matorral [ma·to·rrál] *m.* thicket.
matoso [ma·tó·so] *adj.* bushy; weedy, full of weeds.
matrero [ma·tré·ro] *adj.* astute, shrewd; cunning, sly; *m. Col.* trickster, swindler; *Ríopl.* bandit, outlaw, cattle thief.
matrícula [ma·trí·ku·la] *f.* register, list; matriculation, registration; certificate of registration.
matricular [ma·tri·ku·lár] *v.* to matriculate, enroll, register.
matrimonio [ma·tri·mó·njo] *m.* matrimony, marriage; married couple.
matriz [ma·trís] *f.* matrix, mold, form; womb; screw nut; *adj.* main, principal, first; **casa** — main office (*of a company*); — **estencil** stencil master.
matungo [ma·tún·go] *m. Ríopl.* nag, old worn-out horse.
matutino [ma·tu·tí·no] *adj.* morning, of the morning.
maula [máw·la] *m.* a good-for-nothing.
maullar [maw·yár] *v.* to mew.
maullido, [maw·yí·đo] **maúllo** [ma·ú·yo] *m.* mew.
máxima [mák·si·ma] *f.* maxim, rule; proverb.
máxime [mák·si·me] *adj.* principally, especially.
máximo [mák·si·mo] *adj. & m.* maximum.
maya [má·ya] *f.* daisy; May queen; *m. & f.* Maya, Mayan Indian; *m.* Mayan language.
mayo [má·yo] *m.* May; Maypole; *Am.* Mayo Indian (*from Sonora, Mexico*); *Am.* language of the Mayo Indian.
mayonesa [ma·yo·né·sa] *f.* mayonnaise; dish served with mayonnaise.
mayor [ma·yór] *adj.* greater; larger; older; greatest; largest; oldest; main; major; high (*altar, mass*); *m.* major; chief; **-es** elders; ancestors; — **de edad** of age; **por** — (*or* **al por** —) wholesale; *f.* major premise (*of a syllogism*).
mayoral [ma·yo·rál] *m.* head shepherd; stagecoach driver; foreman; overseer, boss.
mayorazgo [ma·yo·ráz·go] *m.* primogeniture (*right of inheritance by the first-born*); first-born son and heir; family estate left to the eldest son.
mayordomo [ma·yor·đó·mo] *m.* majordomo, steward, butler; manager of an estate.
mayorear [ma·yo·re·ár] *v. Mex., Arg., Ch.* to wholesale, sell at wholesale.
mayoreo [ma·yo·ré·o] *m. Mex., Arg., Ch.* wholesale.
mayoría [ma·yo·rí·a] *f.* majority.
mayorista [ma·yo·rís·ta] *m. Am.* wholesale dealer.
maza [má·sa] *f.* mace (*weapon, staff*); — **química** chemical mace.
mazmorra [maz·mó·rra] *f.* dungeon.
mazo [má·so] *m.* mallet; sledgehammer; bunch,

handful.
mazorca [ma·sór·ka] *f.* ear of corn; *Ríopl.* tyrannical government; *Ch., Arg.* cruel torture (*imposed by tyrants*).
me [me] *obj. pron.* me; to me; for me; myself.
mear [me·ár] *v.* to urinate.
mecánico [me·ká·ni·ko] *adj.* mechanical; *m.* mechanic, machinist, repairman; driver, chauffeur.
mecanismo [me·ka·níz·mo] *m.* mechanism.
mecanografía [me·ka·no·ǥra·fí·a] *f.* stenography, typewriting.
mecanógrafo [me·ka·nó·ǥra·fo] *m.* stenographer, typist.
mecate [me·ká·te] *m. Mex., C.A., Col., Ven.* rope, cord.
mecedor [me·se·đór] *m.* swing; *adj.* swinging, rocking.
mecedora [me·se·đó·ra] *f.* rocking chair.
mecer[10] [me·sér] *v.* to swing, rock, sway; to shake.
mecha [mé·ča] *f.* wick; lock of hair; fuse; strip of salt pork or bacon (*for larding meat*); *Ven.* tip of a whip; *Am.* scare, fright; *Andes, Col.* fib; *Andes, Col.* jest, joke; *Col.* trifle, worthless thing.
mechar [me·čár] *v.* to lard (*meat or fowl*).
mechero [me·čé·ro] *m.* (*canutillo*) lamp burner; gas jet; candlestick socket; (*encendedor*) pocket lighter; large wick; *Col.* disheveled hair; *Am.* joker, jester.
mechón [me·čón] *m.* large wick; large lock of hair.
medalla [me·đa·ya] *f.* medal.
médano [mé·đa·no] *m.* dune, sand hill, sand bank; *Ríopl., Carib.* sandy marshland.
media [mé·đja] *f.* stocking; *Col., Ríopl., Ven.* — **corta** (*or* — —) sock.
mediación [me·đja·sjón] *f.* mediation.
mediador [me·đja·đór] *m.* mediator.
mediados: [me·đjá·đos] **a — de** about the middle of.
medianero [me·đja·né·ro] *m.* mediator; go-between; *adj.* mediating; intermediate; **pared medianera** partition wall.
medianía [me·đja·ní·a] *f.* mediocrity; average; middle ground; moderate circumstances; moderation; *Col.* partition wall.
mediano [me·đjá·no] *adj.* medium; moderate; middle-sized; average; mediocre.
medianoche [me·đja·nó·če] *f.* midnight.
mediante [me·đján·te] *adj.* intervening; **Dios** — God willing; *prep.* by means of, through, with the help of.
mediar [me·đjár] *v.* to mediate, intervene; to intercede; to arrive at, or be in, the middle.
medible [me·đí·ƀle] *adj.* measurable.
medicamento [me·đi·ka·mén·to] *m.* medicament, medicine.
medicastro [me·đi·kás·tro] *m.* quack, quack doctor.
medicina [me·đi·sí·na] *f.* medicine.
medicinar [me·đi·si·nár] *v.* to doctor, treat, prescribe medicine for; **-se** to take medicine.
medición [me·đi·sjón] *f.* measurement; measuring.
médico [mé·đi·ko] *m.* doctor, physician; *adj.* medical.
medida [me·đí·đa] *f.* measure; measurement; gauge, rule; — **para áridos** dry measure; **a — del deseo** according to one's desire; **a — que** as, in proportion as; at the same time as.
medidor [me·đi·đór] *m. Am.* meter gauge; — **de la humedad** wet tube.
medio [mé·đjo] *adj.* half; middle; intermediate; medium, average; **media noche** midnight; **hacer una cosa a medias** to do something halfway; **ir a medias** to go halves; *adv.* half, not completely; *m.* middle; means, way; medium; environment; **-s** means, resources; **meterse de por** — to intervene, meddle in a dispute.
mediocre [me·đjó·kre] *adj.* mediocre, **mediocridad** [me·đjo·kri·đáđ] *f.* mediocrity.
mediodía [me·đjo·đí·a] *m.* midday, noon; south.
medioeval [me·djo·e·ƀál], **medieval** [me·đje·ƀál] *adj.* medieval.
medir[5] [me·đír] *v. irr.* to measure; to scan (*verses*); *Col., Ven., Mex.* — **las calles** to walk the streets, be out of a job; **-se** to measure one's words or actions; *Mex., C.A., Ven., Col., Ríopl.* **-se con otro** to try one's strength or ability against another; to fight with another.
meditación [me·đi·ta·sjón] *f.* meditation.
meditar [me·đi·tár] *v.* to meditate; to muse.
medrar [me·đrár] *v.* to flourish, thrive; to prosper.
medroso [me·đró·so] *adj.* timid, faint-hearted; fearful, dreadful.
médula [mé·đu·la] *f.* marrow; pith; — **oblongada** medulla oblongata (*the posterior part of the brain tapering off into the spinal cord*).
megáfono [me·ǥá·fo·no] *m.* megaphone.
megatón [me·ǥa·tón] *m.* megaton.
mejicano [me·xi·ká·no] *adj.* Mexican; *m.* Mexican; the Aztec language; inhabitant of Mexico City. *Also* **mexicano.**
mejilla [me·xí·ya] *f.* cheek.
mejor [me·xór] *adj.* better; **el** — the best; *adv.* better; **a lo** — suddenly, unexpectedly; **tanto** — so much the better.
mejora [me·xó·ra] *f.* betterment; improvement.
mejoramiento [me·xo·ra·mjén·to] *m.* improvement.
mejorana [me·xo·rá·na] *f.* sweet marjoram.
mejorar [me·xo·rár] *v.* to better, improve; to get better, recover; **-se** to get better, recover.
mejoría [me·xo·rí·a] *f.* betterment, improvement; superiority.
melado [me·lá·đo] *adj.* honey-colored; *m.* sugar-cane syrup; honey cake.
melancolía [me·laŋ·ko·lí·a] *f.* melancholy, gloom.
melancólico [me·laŋ·kó·li·ko] *adj.* melancholy, gloomy.
melaza [me·lá·sa] *f.* molasses.
melena [me·lé·na] *f.* mane.
melindre [me·lín·dre] *m.* (*acto*) affectation; affected act or gesture; whim; (*comestible*) fritter, marzipan (*sweetmeat made of almond paste*).
melindroso [me·lin·dró·so] *adj.* affected; too particular, finicky, fussy.
melocotón [me·lo·ko·tón] *m.* peach; **melocotonero** [me·lo·ko·to·ne·ro] *m.* peach tree.
melodía [me·lo·dí·a] *f.* melody; **melodioso** [me·lo·djó·so] *adj.* melodious.
melón [me·lón] *m.* melon; cantaloupe; musk-melon; melon vine.
melosidad [me·lo·si·đáđ] *f.* sweetness; softness, gentleness.
meloso [me·ló·so] *adj.* honeyed; soft, sweet; *m. Am.* honey-voiced person; *Ch.* over-affectionate person.
mella [mé·ya] *f.* nick; dent; **hacer** — to make a dent or impression; to cause pain, worry, or suffering.
mellar [me·yár] *v.* to notch, to nick, to dent; to impair, damage.
mellizo [me·yí·so] *adj. & m.* twin.
membrete [mem·bré·te] *m.* heading; letterhead; memorandum.
membrillo [mem·brí·yo] *m.* quince (*tree and its fruit*).
membrudo [mem·brú·đo] *adj.* sinewy, robust, strong, muscular.
memorable [me·mo·rá·ƀle] *adj.* memorable, notable.
memorándum [me·mo·rán·dun] *m.* memorandum,

note; memorandum book, notebook.
memoria [me·mó·rja] *f.* memory; remembrance; reminiscence; memoir, note, account; memorandum; (*computadora*) memory; — **residente** internal memory; — **de acceso aleatorio** random access memory (RAM); — **de sólo lectura** read only memory (ROM); **de** — by heart; **hacer** — to remember, recollect; — **de gallo** poor memory; **-s** regards; memoirs.
memorial [me·mo·rjál] *m.* memorandum book; memorial, brief, petition.
mención [men·sjón] *f.* mention.
mencionar [men·sjo·nár] *v.* to mention.
mendigar[7] [men·di·gár] *v.* to beg; to ask alms.
mendigo [men·dí·go] *m.* beggar.
mendrugo [men·drú·go] *m.* crumb of bread.
menear [me·ne·ár] *v.* to move, shake, stir; to wiggle, to wag; **-se** to hustle about; to wag; to wiggle.
meneo [me·né·o] *m.* shaking, swaying, wagging, wiggle, wiggling.
menester [me·nes·tér] *m.* need; job, occupation; **-es** bodily needs; implements, tools; tasks, chores; **ser** — to be necessary.
menesteroso [me·nes·te·ró·so] *adj.* needy, in want.
mengua [méŋ·gwa] *f.* diminution, decrease; waning; poverty, want; discredit.
menguante [meŋ·gwán·te] *adj.* waning, diminishing, declining.
menguar[8] [meŋ·gwár] *v.* to diminish, decrease; to wane.
menjurje [meŋ·xúr·xe] *m.* stuff, mixture.
menor [me·nór] *adj.* smaller, lesser, younger; smallest, least, youngest; minor; *m. & f.* — **de edad** minor; *m.* minor (*music*); Minorite, Franciscan; *f.* minor premise (*of a syllogism*); **por** — (**al por** —) at retail; in small quantities.
menoría [me·no·rí·a] = **minoría.**
menos [mé·nos] *adv.* less; least; except; *adj. & pron.* less, least; *m.* minus; — **de** (*or* — **que**) less than; **a lo** — (**al** —, *or* **por lo** —) at least; **a** — **que** unless; **echar de** — to miss, feel or notice the absence of; **no puede** — **de hacerlo** he cannot help doing it; **venir a** — to decline; to become weak or poor.
menoscabar [me·nos·ka·bár] *v.* to diminish, lessen; to impair, damage; — **la honra de** to undermine the reputation of.
menoscabo [me·nos·ká·bo] *m.* impairment; damage; diminution, lessening.
menospreciar [me·nos·pre·sjár] *v.* to despise, scorn; to underestimate.
menosprecio [me·nos·pré·sjo] *m.* scorn, contempt; underestimation.
mensaje [men·sá·xe] *m.* message.
mensajero [men·sa·xé·ro] *m.* messenger.
menstruo [méns·trwo] *m.* menstruation.
mensual [men·swál] *adj.* monthly.
mensualidad [men·swa·li·dád] *f.* monthly allowance; monthly payment.
mensurable [men·su·rá·ble] *adj.* measurable.
menta [mén·ta] *f.* mint; peppermint; *Ríopl.* rumor, hearsay; *Ríopl., Andes* **por -s** by hearsay; *Ríopl.* **persona de** — famous person.
mentado [men·tá·do] *adj.* famous; *p.p.* mentioned.
mental [men·tál] *adj.* mental.
mentalidad [men·ta·li·dád] *f.* mentality.
mentar[1] [men·tár] *v. irr.* to mention; to call, name.
mente [mén·te] *f.* mind; intellect.
mentecato [men·te·ká·to] *adj.* foolish, simple; *m.* fool.
mentir[3] [men·tír] *v. irr.* to lie, tell lies.
mentira [men·tí·ra] *f.* lie, falsehood, fib; white spot on the fingernails.
mentiroso [men·ti·ró·so] *adj.* lying; deceptive, false; *m.* liar, fibber; **mentirosillo** *m.* little fibber.
mentís [men·tís]: **dar un** — to give the lie (to).
mentón [men·tón] *m.* chin.
menú [me·nú] *m.* menu; (*computadora*) menu.
menudear [me·nu·de·ár] *v.* to occur frequently; to repeat over and over; to fall incessantly (*as rain, stones, projectiles, etc.*); to tell in detail; *Mex., C.A., Col., Ven.* to retail, sell at retail; *Arg.* to meet together often.
menudeo [me·nu·dé·o] *m.* retail; **vender al** — to retail, sell at retail.
menudo [me·nú·do] *adj.* minute, small; insignificant; exact, detailed; **dinero** — change; **a** — often; **por** — in detail; retail; *m.* entrails, "innards"; (*cambio*) change, small coins.
meñique [me·ñí·ke] *adj.* tiny, wee; **dedo** — little finger.
meollo [me·ó·yo] *m.* marrow; pith; kernel; substance; brain; brains.
meple [mé·ple] *m. Ríopl.* maple.
merca [mér·ka] *f.* purchase.
mercachifle [mer·ka·čí·fle] *m.* peddler, vendor; cheap merchant; cheap fellow.
mercadear [mer·ka·de·ár] *v.* to trade.
mercader [mer·ka·dér] *m.* trader, merchant.
mercadería [mer·ka·de·rí·a] *f.* merchandise; trade.
mercado [mer·ká·do] *m.* market; mart.
mercadotecnia [mer·ka·do·ték·nja] *f.* marketing management.
mercancía [mer·kan·sí·a] *f.* merchandise; goods.
mercantil [mer·kan·tíl] *adj.* mercantile, commercial.
mercar[6] [mer·kár] *v.* to purchase, buy.
merced [mer·séd] *f.* favor; present, gift; mercy; **Vuestra Merced** Your Honor; **a** — **de** at the mercy of; at the expense of.
mercería [mer·se·rí·a] *f.* notions (*pins, buttons, etc.*); notions store; *Ríopl., P.R.* drygoods store.
mercurio [mer·kú·rjo] *m.* mercury; quicksilver.
merecedor [me·re·se·dór] *adj.* worthy, deserving.
merecer[13] [me·re·sér] *v. irr.* to deserve.
merecido [me·re·sí·do] *adj. & p.p.* deserved; *m.* deserved punishment.
merecimiento [me·re·si·mjén·to] *m.* merit.
merendar[1] [me·ren·dár] *v. irr.* to have an afternoon snack or refreshment; *Carib., Ven.* **-se uno a alguien** to fleece or skin someone (*in a game or business deal*); to kill someone.
merendero [me·ren·dé·ro] *m.* lunchroom.
meridiano [me·ri·djá·no] *adj. & m.* meridian.
meridional [me·ri·djo·nál] *adj.* southern; *m.* southerner.
merienda [me·rjén·da] *f.* light afternoon meal; afternoon refreshments.
mérito [mé·ri·to] *m.* merit; **de** — notable.
merito [me·rí·to] *dim. of* **mero.**
meritorio [me·ri·tó·rjo] *adj.* meritorious, worthy, deserving; *m.* employee without salary (*learning trade or profession*).
merluza [mer·lú·sa] *f.* hake (*species of codfish*); drunken state.
merma [mér·ma] *f.* reduction, decrease.
mermar [mer·már] *v.* to dwindle; to decrease, reduce.
mermelada [mer·me·lá·da] *f.* marmalade.
mero [mé·ro] *adj.* mere, pure; *Mex., C.A.* exact, real; **la mera verdad** the real truth; *adv. Mex., C.A.* very, very same, exactly; *Mex., C.A.* soon; *Col.* only; *Mex., C.A.* **una mera de las tres** only

one of the three; *Mex., C.A.* **ya** — (*or* **merito**) very soon; *Mex., C.A.* **allí** — (*or* **merito**) right there; *m.* species of perch; *Ch.* species of thrush.
merodear [me·ro·đe·ár] *v.* to rove in search of plunder.
mes [mes] *m.* month.
mesa [mé·sa] *f.* table; executive board; staircase landing; mesa, plateau; **levantar la** — to clear the table; **poner la** — to set the table; *Col., Carib., C.A., Mex.* **quitar la** — to clear the table.
mesada [me·sá·đa] *f.* monthly salary or allowance.
mesarse [me·sár·se] *v.* to tear (*one's hair or beard*).
mesero [me·sé·ro] *m. Mex., C.A., Ven., Col.* waiter.
meseta [me·sé·ta] *f.* plateau; staircase landing.
mesón [me·són] *m.* inn.
mesonero [me·so·né·ro] *m.* innkeeper.
mestizo [mes·tí·so] *adj.* half-breed; hybrid; **perro** — mongrel dog; *m.* mestizo, half-breed.
mesura [me·sú·ra] *f.* moderation; composure; dignity; politeness.
mesurado [me·su·rá·đo] *adj.* moderate, temperate; dignified.
meta [mé·ta] *f.* goal; objective.
metabolismo [me·ta·ƀo·líz·mo] *m.* metabolism.
metafísica [me·ta·fí·si·ka] *f.* metaphysics.
metáfora [me·tá·fo·ra] *f.* metaphor.
metafórico [me·ta·fó·ri·ko] *adj.* metaphorical.
metal [me·tál] *m.* metal; — **base** base metal; — **no ferroso** non-ferrous metal.
metálico [me·tá·li·ko] *adj.* metallic, metal; *m.* specie, coined money; cash in coin.
metalurgia [me·ta·lúr·xja] *f.* metallurgy.
metamorfosis [me·ta·mor·fó·sis] *f.* metamorphosis.
metate [me·tá·te] *m. Mex.* flat stone (*used for grinding corn, etc.*).
metátesis [me·tá·te·sis] *f.* metathesis.
meteorito [me·te·o·rí·to] *m.* meteorite.
meteoro [me·te·ó·ro] *m.* meteor.
meteorología [me·te·o·ro·lo·xí·a] *f.* meteorology; **meteorológico** [me·te·o·ro·ló·xi·ko] *adj.* meteorological; **oficina meteorológica** weather bureau.
meter [me·tér] *v.* to put (in); to get (in); to insert; to smuggle; to make (*noise, trouble, etc.*); to cause (*fear*); *Carib.* to strike (*a blow*); *Ríopl., Carib.* **-le** to hurry up; **-se** to meddle, interfere; to plunge (into); **-se monja** (*Am.* **-se de monja**) to become a nun; also **-se a monja; -se con** to pick a quarrel with.
metódico [me·tó·đi·ko] *adj.* methodical.
método [mé·to·đo] *m.* method.
metralleta [me·tra·yé·ta] *f.* hand machine gun.
métrico [mé·tri·ko] *adj.* metric.
metro [mé·tro] *m.* meter; subway; — **plegadizo** folding rule.
metrópoli [me·tró·po·li] *f.* metropolis.
metropolitano [me·tro·po·li·tá·no] *adj.* metropolitan; *m.* (*metro*) the subway.
mexicano [me·xi·ká·no] = **mejicano** (*pronounced identically*).
mezcal [mes·kál] *m. Mex.* mescal (*a species of* **maguey** *and an alcoholic beverage made from it*).
mezcla [més·kla] *f.* mixture; mortar; mixed cloth; **mezclilla** [mes·klí·ya] *f.* mixed cloth (*generally black and white*); tweed.
mezclar [mes·klár] *v.* to mix, blend; **-se** to mix, mingle; to meddle.
mezcolanza [mes·ko·lán·sa] *f.* jumble, mess, mixture.
mezquindad [mes·ki·ni·đáđ] *f.* meanness; stinginess; dire poverty.
mezquino [mes·kí·no] *adj.* poor, needy; mean, stingy; meager; small, tiny; *m. Col., Mex.* wart (*usually on a finger*).
mezquita [mes·kí·ta] *f.* mosque.
mi [mi] *adj.* my.
mí [mi] *pers. pron* (*used after prep.*) me, myself.
miaja [mjá·xa] = **migaja.**
miau [mjáw] *m.* mew.
mico [mí·ko] *m.* long-tailed monkey; *C.A.* jack (*for lifting heavy objects*).
micro [mí·kro] *m. Peru, Ch.* bus.
microbio [mi·kró·ƀjo] *m.* microbe.
microbús [mi·kro·ƀús] *m.* microbus.
microfilm [mi·kro·fíln] *m.* microfilm.
micrófono [mi·kró·fo·no] *m.* microphone.
microprocesador [mi·kro·pro·se·sa·dór] *m.* (*computadora*) microprocessor.
microscopio [mi·kros·kó·pjo] *m.* microscope; — **electrónico** electron microscope; **microscópico** [mi·kro·skó·pi·ko] *adj.* microscopic.
miedo [mjé·đo] *m.* fear; dread; **tener** — to be afraid.
miedoso [mje·đó·so] *adj.* afraid, fearful, timid.
miel [mjel] *f.* honey; molasses.
mielga [mjél·ǥa] *f.* plot of ground for planting.
miembro [mjém·bro] *m.* member; limb.
mientes [mjén·tes] *f. pl.* thought, mind; **parar** — **en** to consider, reflect on; **traer a las** — to recall; **venírsele a uno a las** — to occur to one, come to one's mind.
mientras [mjén·tras] *conj.* while; — **que** while; — **tanto** in the meantime, meanwhile; — **más . . .** — **menos . . .** the more . . . the less . . .
miércoles [mjér·ko·les] *m.* Wednesday.
mies [mjes] *f.* ripe grain; harvest; **-es** fields of grain.
miga [mí·ǥa] *f.* crumb; soft part of bread; substance; **-s** crumbs; fried crumbs of bread; **hacer buenas -s** (*or* **malas -s**) **con** to get along well (*or* badly) with.
migaja [mi·ǥá·xa] *f.* crumb; bit, fragment, small particle.
migración [mi·ǥra·sjón] *f.* migration.
mil [mil] *num.* thousand.
milagro [mi·lá·ǥro] *m.* miracle; wonder.
milagroso [mi·la·ǥró·so] *adj.* miraculous.
milicia [mi·lí·sja] *f.* militia; military science; military profession.
miligramo [mi·li·ǥrá·mo] *m.* milligram.
milímetro [mi·lí·me·tro] *m.* millimeter.
militar [mi·li·tár] *adj.* military; *m.* soldier, military man; *v.* to serve in the army; to militate, fight (against).
milpa [míl·pa] *f. Mex., C.A.* cornfield.
milla [mí·ya] *f.* mile.
millar [mi·yár] *m.* thousand; **-es** thousands, a great number.
millón [mi·yón] *m.* million; **millonario** [mi·yo·ná·rjo] *adj. & m.* millionaire; **millonésimo** [mi·yo·né·si·mo] *adj. & m.* millionth.
mimar [mi·már] *v.* to pamper, spoil, humor; to pet.
mimbre [mím·bre] *m.* wicker; **mimbrera** [mim·bré·ra] *f.* willow.
mímico [mí·mi·ko] *adj.* mimic.
mimo [mí·mo] *m.* pampering; caress; coaxing.
mimoso [mi·mó·so] *adj.* tender, sensitive; delicate; finicky, fussy.
mina [mí·na] *f.* mine; source; fortune.
minar [mi·nár] *v.* to mine; to undermine; to sow with explosive mines.
mineral [mi·ne·rál] *m.* mineral; mine; ore; wealth, fortune; *adj.* mineral.
minería [mi·ne·rí·a] *f.* mining; miners.
minero [mi·né·ro] *m.* miner; wealth, fortune; source;

adj. mining; **compañía minera** mining company.
miniatura [mi·nja·tú·ra] *f.* miniature.
minifalda [mi·ni·fál·da] *f.* miniskirt.
minifundio [mi·ni·fún·djo] *m.* small farm (*privately owned*).
mínimo [mí·ni·mo] *adj.* least, smallest; *m.* minimum.
minino [mi·ní·no] *m.* kitten, kitty, pussy.
ministerio [mi·nis·té·rjo] *m.* ministry; administration, ministering; portfolio (*office of a cabinet member*); minister's office.
ministrar [mi·nis·trár] *v.* to minister; to give (*money, aid, etc.*).
ministro [mi·nís·tro] *m.* minister; cabinet member; office of justice.
minoría [mi·no·rí·a] *f.* minority.
minoridad [mi·no·ri·đáđ] *f.* minority (*in age*).
minucioso [mi·nu·sjó·so] *adj.* minute, detailed; scrupulous.
minúsculo [mi·nús·ku·lo] *adj.* small; **letra minúscula** small letter.
minuta [mi·nú·ta] *f.* minutes; memorandum; first draft (*of a contract, deed, etc.*); memorandum list; lawyer's bill; *Carib.* **a la** — breaded and fried (*said of meat or fish*).
minuto [mi·nú·to] *m.* minute; **minutero** [mi·nu·té·ro] *m.* minute hand.
mío [mí·o] *poss. adj.* my, of mine; *poss. pron.* mine; *Ríopl., Ch.* **detrás** — behind me.
miope [mjó·pe] *adj.* shortsighted, nearsighted; *m. & f.* nearsighted person.
miopía [mjo·pí·a] *f.* near-sightedness.
mira [mí·ra] *f.* (*de puntería*) gun sight; guiding point; (*intención*) intention, design; outlook; **estar a la — de** to be on the lookout for; to be on the alert for; **poner la — en** to fix one's eyes on; to aim at.
mirada [mi·rá·đa] *f.* glance, gaze, look.
mirador [mi·ra·đór] *m.* mirador, enclosed balcony (*commanding an extensive view*); watchtower; lookout site; onlooker, spectator; *Ríopl.* penthouse.
miramiento [mi·ra·mjén·to] *m.* consideration, respect, regard; reverence; circumspection, prudence.
mirar [mi·rár] *v.* to look; to glance; to behold; to see; — **por alguien** to take care of someone; **¡mira (tú)!** look!
miríada [mi·rjá·đa] *f.* myriad, multitude, great number.
miriñaque [mi·ri·ñá·ke] *m.* crinoline.
mirlo [mír·lo] *m.* blackbird.
mirón [mi·rón] *m.* bystander, onlooker, spectator; *adj.* curious.
mirra [mí·rra] *f.* myrrh.
mirto [mír·to] *m.* myrtle.
misa [mí·sa] *f.* mass; — **del gallo** midnight mass.
misántropo [mi·sán·tro·po] *m.* misanthrope.
misceláneo [mi·se·lá·ne·o] *adj.* miscellaneous.
miserable [mi·se·rá·ƀle] *adj.* miserable, unhappy; forlorn; miserly, stingy; mean.
miseria [mi·sé·rja] *f.* misery; poverty; stinginess; bit, trifle.
misericordia [mi·se·ri·kór·đja] *f.* mercy, compassion, pity.
misericordioso [mi·se·ri·kor·đjó·so] *adj.* merciful, compassionate.
mísero [mí·se·ro] *adj.* miserable, unhappy; forlorn; stingy.
misi [mí·si] *interj.* word used to call cats.
misión [mi·sjón] *f.* mission.
misionero [mi·sjo·né·ro] *m.* missionary.
mismo [míz·mo] *adj.* same; self, very; **ahora** — right away.
misterio [mis·té·rjo] *m.* mystery; secret.
misterioso [mis·te·rjó·so] *adj.* mysterious.
místico [mís·ti·ko] *adj.* mystical, mystic; *m.* mystic.
mitad [mi·táđ] *f.* half; middle.
mitigar[7] [mi·ti·ǥár] *v.* to mitigate, soften, soothe.
mitin [mí·tin] *m.* meeting.
mito [mí·to] *m.* myth; **mitología** [mi·to·lo·xí·a] *f.* mythology.
mitra [mí·tra] *f.* bishop's miter.
mixto [mís·to] *adj.* mixed; half-breed; *m.* composite; match; explosive compound.
mobiliario [mo·ƀi·ljá·rjo] *m.* furniture.
moblaje [mo·ƀlá·xe] = **mueblaje.**
mocasín [mo·ka·sín] *m.* (*zapatilla y culebra*) moccasin.
mocedad [mo·se·đáđ] *f.* youth; youthfulness; youthful prank.
mocetón [mo·se·tón] *m.* tall, robust lad.
moción [mo·sjón] *f.* motion.
moco [mó·ko] *m.* mucus; snot.
mocoso [mo·kó·so] *adj.* sniffling; *m.* brat, scamp; sniffling boy.
mochar [mo·čár] *v. Am.* to cut off, chop off, cut, trim (*see* **desmochar**); *Arg.* to snitch, pilfer; *Col.* to depose, dismiss, put out of a job.
mochila [mo·čí·la] *f.* knapsack; soldier's kit.
mocho [mó·čo] *adj.* cut off; cropped, shorn; *Am.* maimed, mutilated; *Mex.* reactionary, conservative; *m.* butt of a firearm; *Col., Ven.* nag; *Carib.* cigar butt.
moda [mó·đa] *f.* mode, custom, style, fashion; **de** — fashionable.
modelar [mo·đe·lár] *v.* to model.
modelo [mo·đé·lo] *m.* model, copy, pattern; *m. & f.* life model.
modem m. (*computadora*) modem.
moderación [mo·đe·ra·sjón] *f.* moderation.
moderado [mo·đe·rá·đo] *adj.* moderate; conservative.
moderar [mo·đe·rár] *v.* to moderate, temper; to regulate; to restrain.
moderno [mo·dér·no] *adj.* modern.
modestia [mo·đés·tja] *f.* modesty.
modesto [mo·đés·to] *adj.* modest.
módico [mó·đi·ko] *adj.* moderate, reasonable (*price*).
modificación [mo·đi·fi·ka·sjón] *f.* modification.
modificar[6] [mo·đi·fi·kár] *v.* to modify.
modismo [mo·đíz·mo] *m.* idiom.
modista [mo·đís·ta] *f.* dressmaker; milliner.
modo [mó·đo] *m.* mode, manner, way; mood (*grammar*); (*computadora*) mode; — **directo** direct mode; — **indirecto** indirect mode; **a** (*or* **al**) — **de** like, in the manner of; **de — que** so that; and so; **de todos -s** at any rate, anyway.
modorra [mo·đó·rra] *f.* drowsiness; gid (*a disease of sheep*).
modular [mo·đu·lár] *v.* to modulate, tone down.
mofa [mó·fa] *f.* scoff, jeer, taunt; mockery.
mofar [mo·fár] *v.* to mock, scoff, jeer; **-se de** to make fun of, scoff at.
mofeta [mo·fé·ta] *f. S.A.* skunk.
moflete [mo·flé·te] *m.* fat cheek; **mofletudo** [mo·fle·tú·đo] *adj.* fat-cheeked.
mohín [mo·ín] *m.* grimace; wry face.
mohíno [mo·í·no] *adj.* moody, discontented, sad, melancholy; black (*referring to a horse, cow, or bull*).
moho [mó·o] *m.* rust; mold.
mohoso [mo·ó·so] *adj.* musty, moldy; rusty.
mojada [mo·xá·đa] *f.* drench, drenching, wetting.
mojado [mo·xá·đo] *adj.* wet, damp, moist; *p.p. of* **mojar.**
mojadura [mo·xa·đú·ra] *f.* wetting, dampening,

drenching.
mojar [mo·xár] *v.* to dampen, wet, moisten; *Ríopl., Ch.* to accompany (*a song*); *P.R.* to bribe; *Ríopl., Carib., Mex.* to celebrate by drinking; *Am.* **mojársele a uno los papeles** to get things mixed up.
mojicón [mo·xi·kón] *m.* punch, blow; muffin, bun.
mojigatería [mo·xi·ga·te·rí·a] *f.* prudery; false humility; affected piety.
mojigato [mo·xi·gá·to] *adj.* prudish; affectedly pious, overzealous (*in matters of religion*); hypocritical; *m.* prude; hypocrite.
mojón [mo·xón] *m.* landmark; milestone; heap, pile.
molde [mól·de] *m.* mold, cast; form; pattern, model; **venir de** — to come pat, be to the point; **letras de** — printed letters; print.
moldear [mol·de·ár] *v.* to mold; to cast; to decorate with moldings.
moldura [mol·dú·ra] *f.* molding.
mole [mó·le] *f.* mass, bulk; *adj.* soft, mild; *m. Mex.* — **de guajolote** a Mexican dish of turkey served with a chili gravy.
molécula [mo·lé·ku·la] *f.* molecule.
moler[2] [mo·lér] *v. irr.* to mill; to grind; to tire, fatigue; to wear out, destroy; to bother; — **a palos** to give a thorough beating.
molestar [mo·les·tár] *v.* to molest, disturb; to bother, annoy.
molestia [mo·lés·tja] *f.* bother, annoyance; discomfort.
molesto [mo·lés·to] *adj.* bothersome, annoying; uncomfortable.
molibdeno [mo·lib·dé·no] *m.* molybdenum.
molicie [mo·lí·sje] *f.* softness; fondness for luxury.
molienda [mo·ljén·da] *f.* grind, grinding, milling; portion to be, or that has been, ground; grinding season (*for sugar cane or olives*); fatigue, weariness; bother.
molinero [mo·li·né·ro] *m.* miller.
molinete [mo·li·né·te] *m.* small mill; ventilating fan; pin wheel; twirl, whirl, flourish.
molinillo [mo·li·ní·yo] *m.* small mill or grinder; chocolate beater; restless person.
molino [mo·lí·no] *m.* mill; restless person; — **de viento** windmill.
molusco [mo·lús·ko] *m.* mollusk.
mollejas [mo·yé·xas] *f. pl.* sweetbreads.
mollera [mo·yé·ra] *f.* crown of the head; judgment, good sense; **ser duro de** — to be stubborn; **no tener sal en la** — to be dull, stupid.
momentáneo [mo·men·tá·ne·o] *adj.* momentary; sudden, quick.
momento [mo·mén·to] *m.* moment; importance; momentum; **al** — immediately, without delay; **a cada** — continually; frequently.
momia [mó·mja] *f.* mummy.
mona [mó·na] *f.* female monkey; mimic; drunkenness; **dormir la** — to sleep it off; **pillar una** — to get drunk.
monada [mo·ná·da] *f.* (*típico de mono*) monkeyshine; monkey face; (*cosa graciosa*) cute little thing; cute gesture; nonsense; flattery.
monarca [mo·nár·ka] *m.* monarch.
monarquía [mo·nar·kí·a] *f.* monarchy.
monasterio [mo·nas·té·rjo] *m.* monastery.
mondadientes [mon·da·djen·tes] *m.* toothpick.
mondadura [mon·da·dú·ra] *f.* trimming; peeling.
mondar [mon·dár] *v.* to pare; to peel; to prune; to clean out; *Am.* to beat, thrash; *Am.* to beat, defeat; **-se los dientes** to pick one's teeth.
moneda [mo·né·da] *f.* coin; money; — **corriente** currency; — **menuda** (*or* **suelta**) change, small coins; **casa de** — mint.
monería [mo·ne·rí·a] *f.* monkeyshine, antic; trifle, trinket; cute little thing.
monetario [mo·ne·tá·rjo] *adj.* monetary, pertaining to money; financial.
monigote [mo·ni·gó·te] *m.* puppet, ridiculous figure; dunce.
monitor [mo·ni·tór] *m.* (*computadora*) monitor.
monitorear [mo·ni·to·re·ár] *v.* to monitor (*a radio or TV program*).
monja [móŋ·xa] *f.* nun.
monje [móŋ·xe] *m.* monk.
mono [mó·no] *m.* monkey; silly fool; mimic; coveralls; *Ch.* pile of fruit or vegetables (*in a market*); **-s** *Ch.* worthless household utensils and furniture; *Am.* **meterle a uno los -s en el cuerpo** to frighten, terrify someone; *adj.* pretty, neat, cute; *Am.* sorrel, reddish-brown; *Col.* blond.
monóculo [mo·nó·ku·lo] m. monocle.
monologar[7] [mo·no·lo·gár] *v.* to soliloquize, talk to oneself; to recite monologues; to monopolize the conversation.
monólogo [mo·nó·lo·go] *m.* monologue.
monopolio [mo·no·pó·ljo] *m.* monopoly.
monopolizar[9] [mo·no·po·li·sár] *v.* to monopolize; to corner (*a market*).
monosílabo [mo·no·sí·la·bo] *adj.* monosyllabic, of one syllable; *m.* monosyllable.
monotonía [mo·no·to·ní·a] *f.* monotony; **monótono** [mo·nó·to·no] *adj.* monotonous.
monousuario [mo·now·swá·rjo] *adj.* used by a single person.
monserga [mon·sér·ga] *f.* gabble.
monstruo [móns·trwo] *m.* monster.
monstruosidad [mons·trwo·si·dád] *f.* monstrosity; monster, freak.
monstruoso [mons·trwó·so] *adj.* monstrous.
monta [món·ta] *f.* amount, sum; value, importance; **de poca** — of little value or importance.
montaje [mon·tá·xe] *m.* assembly, assembling (*of machinery*); mount, support for a cannon.
montante [mon·tán·te] *m.* broadsword; transom; upright; post; *Carib., Ven.* sum, amount, cost; *f.* high tide.
montaña [mon·tá·ña] *f.* mountain; — **rusa** roller coaster.
montañés [mon·ta·ñés] *adj.* mountain (*used as adj.*) of, from or pertaining to the mountains; *m.* mountaineer; native of the province of Santander, Spain.
montañismo [mon·ta·ñíz·mo] *m.* mountaineering.
montañoso [mon·ta·ñó·so] *adj.* mountainous.
montar [mon·tár] *v.* to mount; to ride horseback; to amount (to); to set (*jewels*); to cock (*a gun*); to assemble, set up (*machinery*); *Carib., C.A.* to organize, establish.
montaraz [mon·ta·rás] *adj.* wild, primitive, uncivilized; *m.* forester.
monte [món·te] *m.* mount, mountain; forest; thicket; monte (*a card game*); *C.A., Mex.* grass, pasture; *Am.* country, outskirts; **montecillo** [mon·te·sí·yo] *m.* mound, small hill; **montepío** [mon·te·pí·o] *m.* pawnshop.
montera [mon·té·ra] *f.* cap; *Andes* Bolivian cone-shaped hat (*worn by Indians*).
montés [mon·tés] *adj.* wild, mountain (*used as adj.*); *f.* **cabra** — mountain goat; *m.* **gato** — wildcat.
montículo [mon·tí·ku·lo] *m.* mound.
montón [mon·tón] *m.* pile, heap; mass, great number; **a -es** in abundance, in heaps, by heaps.

montonera [mon·to·né·ra] *f. Col., Ven., Ríopl.* band of mounted rebels or guerrilla fighters; *Col.* pile of wheat, hay, straw, etc.; *P.R.* pile, heap (*of anything*).
montuoso [mon·twó·so] *adj.* hilly; mountainous.
montura [mon·tú·ra] *f.* mount, horse; saddle and trappings.
monumento [mo·nu·mén·to] *m.* monument; **monumental** [mo·nu·men·tál] *adj.* monumental.
moña [mó·ña] *f.* doll; hair ribbon.
moño [mó·ño] *m.* knot or roll of hair; bow of ribbon; crest, tuft of feathers; *Mex.* forelock (*lock of hair on the fore part of the head*); *Am.* crest, peak (*of anything*); *Col.* whim; *Col.* a Colombian popular dance; **-s** frippery, gaudy ornaments; *Col.* **estar con el — torcido** to be in an ugly humor.
mora [mó·ra] *f.* blackberry; mulberry; brambleberry; *Ch.* blood pudding, sausage.
morada [mo·rá·đa] *f.* dwelling, residence; stay.
morado [mo·rá·đo] *adj.* purple; *m.* (*moretón*) bruise.
morador [mo·ra·đór] *m.* dweller, resident.
moral [mo·rál] *adj.* moral; *f.* ethics, moral philosophy; morale; *m.* mulberry tree; blackberry bush.
moraleja [mo·ra·lé·xa] *f.* moral, lesson, maxim.
moralidad [mo·ra·li·đáđ] *f.* morality.
moralista [mo·ra·lís·ta] *m. & f.* moralist.
morar [mo·rár] *v.* to live, dwell, reside.
morbidez [mor·bi·đés] *f.* softness; mellowness.
mórbido [mór·bi·đo] *adj.* morbid; soft.
morboso [mor·bó·so] *adj.* morbid, unhealthy, diseased.
morcilla [mor·sí·ya] *f.* blood pudding, blood sausage; gag (*an amusing remark by a comedian*).
mordacidad [mor·đa·si·đáđ] *f.* sharpness (*of tongue*).
mordaz [mor·đás] *adj.* biting, cutting, sarcastic.
mordaza [mor·đá·sa] *f.* gag (*for the mouth*); clamp; **— de tierra** ground clamp.
mordedor [mor·đe·đór] *adj.* biting; snappy; *m.* biter; slanderer.
mordedura [mor·đe·đú·ra] *f.* bite; sting.
mordelón [mor·đe·lón] *adj. Col., Ven.* biting, snappy; *m. Am.* biter; *Mex.* public official who accepts a bribe.
morder[2] [mor·đér] *v. irr.* to bite; to nip; to gnaw; to corrode; to backbite, slander; *Ven.* to swindle; *Mex., C.A.* to "shake down", exact a bribe.
mordida [mor·đí·đa] *f. Am.* bite; *Mex., C.A., Carib., Ven.* graft, money obtained by graft; bribe.
mordiscar[6] [mor·đis·kár], **mordisquear** [mor·đis·ke·ár] *v.* to nibble; to gnaw.
mordisco [mor·đís·ko] *m.* bite; nibble.
moreno [mo·ré·no] *adj.* brown; dark, brunette; *m. Ríopl., Carib., Mex., Ven., Andes* colored person.
moretón [mo·re·tón] *m.* bruise, black-and-blue mark.
morfema [mor·fé·ma] *m.* morpheme.
morfina [mor·fí·na] *f.* morphine; **morfinómano** [mor·fi·nó·ma·no] *m.* morphine addict, drug fiend.
morfología [mor·fo·lo·xí·a] *f.* morphology.
moribundo [mo·ri·bún·do] *adj.* dying.
morir[4, 52] [mo·rír] *v. irr.* to die; **-se** to die; to die out, be extinguished.
morisco [mo·rís·ko] *adj.* Moorish; Moresque, in the Moorish style; *m.* Morisco (*Christianized Moor*); language of the Moriscos.
mormonismo [mor·mo·níz·mo] *m.* Mormonism.
moro [mó·ro] *adj.* Moorish; *Mex., Ven., Ríopl., Cuba* dappled, spotted (*horse*); *Col., Ch., Andes* unbaptized; *m.* Moor; *Col.* frosted cookie.
morocho [mo·ró·čo] *adj. Am.* robust, strong; *Ríopl.* of dark complexion; *Ch.* rough, tough; *Andes* of low social condition.
moroso [mo·ró·so] *adj.* delinquent.
morral [mo·rrál] *m.* nose bag; knapsack; hunter's bag.
morrillo [mo·rrí·yo] *m.* fat of the neck (*especially the bull*).
morriña [mo·rrí·ña] *f.* melancholy, blues, sadness.
morro [mó·rro] *m.* knoll.
morsa [mór·sa] *f.* walrus.
mortaja [mor·tá·xa] *f.* shroud; *Am.* cigarette paper; mortise (carpentry).
mortal [mor·tál] *adj.* mortal, fatal, deadly; *m.* mortal; **mortalidad** [mor·ta·li·đáđ] *f.* mortality; death rate.
mortandad [mo·tan·dáđ] *f.* mortality, death rate; massacre, slaughter.
mortecino [mor·te·sí·no] *adj.* deathly pale; dying; **hacer la mortecina** to pretend to be dead.
morterete [mor·te·ré·te] *m.* small mortar, small canon.
mortero [mor·té·ro] *m.* mortar (*for grinding*).
mortífero [mor·tí·fe·ro] *adj.* deadly, fatal.
mortificar[6] [mor·ti·fi·kár] *v.* to mortify; to torment; to vex, annoy; **-se** to do penance; to be grieved; *Mex., C.A., Ven.* to be embarrassed.
mortuorio [mor·twó·rjo] *adj.* funeral; funereal, mournful; *m.* funeral, burial.
mosaico [mo·sáj·ko] *adj. & m.* mosaic.
mosca [mós·ka] *f.* fly; bore; bother; *Am.* sponger, parasite; *Mex., C.A., Ven.* bull's-eye, center of a target; **moscón** *m.* large fly; *Am.* **ir de moscón** to go along as a chaperone.
mosquear [mos·ke·ár] *v.* to brush off or drive away flies; to whip, beat; *Ríopl.* to rage, be furious; **-se** to show pique or resentment; *Ch.* to go away.
mosquito [mos·kí·to] *m.* mosquito; gnat; *Am.* Mosquito Indian of Nicaragua; **mosquitero** *m.* mosquito net.
mostacho [mos·tá·čo] *m.* mustache.
mostaza [mos·tá·sa] *f.* mustard; mustard seed; bird shot.
mostrador [mos·tra·đór] *m.* demonstrator; store counter; clock dial.
mostrar[2] [mos·trár] *v. irr.* to show; to demonstrate; to exhibit.
mostrenco [mos·tréŋ·ko] *adj.* (*sin dueño*) ownerless; homeless; stray (*animal*); (*torpe*) slow, dull; fat, heavy; *m.* dunce; *C.A.* worthless animal.
mota [mó·ta] *f.* mote, speck; knot in cloth; slight defect; mound, knoll; *Col., Ven., Carib.* powder puff; *Am.* tuft.
mote [mó·te] *m.* motto; slogan; nickname; *Andes, Ch., Col.* stewed corn; *Andes* grammatical error; *Ch.* **— pelado** hominy.
motear [mo·te·ár] *v.* to speck, speckle; to spot; *Am.* to mispronounce, enunciate badly.
motejar [mo·te·xár] *v.* to jeer at; to call bad names; to insult; to censure; **— de** to brand as.
motín [mo·tín] *m.* mutiny; riot.
motivar [mo·ti·bár] *v.* to cause; to give a cause for.
motivo [mo·tí·bo] *m.* motive, reason; motif, theme; *m.* **con — de** because of; on the occasion of; *adj.* motive.
motocicleta [mo·to·si·klé·ta] *f.* motorcycle; **motociclista** [mo·to·si·kle·tís·ta] *m. & f.* motorcyclist, motorcycle rider.
motociclismo [mo·to·si·klíz·mo] *m.* motorcycling.
motor [mo·tór] *m.* motor; **— de reacción** jet engine; **— de avance** feed motor; *adj.* motor, causing motion.
motorista [mo·to·rís·ta] *m. & f.* motorist; motorman, motorwoman.

motorreactor [mo·to·rre·ak·tór] *m.* jet engine.
motriz [mo·trís] *adj.* motive, impelling, driving; **fuerza** — power, driving force.
movedizo [mo·ƀe·đi·so] *adj.* movable; shaky; shifting; **arena movediza** quicksand.
mover[7] [mo·ƀér] *v. irr.* (*físicamente*) to move; (*persuadir*) to persuade; to stir, excite; to touch, affect; **-se** to move.
movible [mo·ƀí·ƀle] *adj.* movable; mobile; fickle.
móvil [mó·ƀil] *m.* motive, inducement, incentive; *adj.* mobile, movable; unstable.
movilización [mo·ƀi·li·sa·sjón] *f.* mobilization.
movilizar[9] [mo·ƀi·li·sár] *v.* to mobilize.
movimiento [mo·ƀi·mjén·to] *m.* movement; motion; commotion, disturbance; (*computadora*) — **vertical** scrolling.
moza [mó·sa] *f.* maid; girl; last hand of a game; *Ch.* last song or dance of a fiesta.
mozalbete [mo·sal·ƀé·te] *m.* youth, lad.
mozárabe [mo·sá·ra·ƀe] *adj.* Mozarabic (*Christian in Moslem Spain*).
mozo [mó·so] *adj.* young; unmarried; *m.* youth; manservant; waiter; porter; errand boy; **buen** — handsome man.
mozuela [mo·swé·la] *f.* lass, young girl.
mozuelo [mo·swé·lo] *m.* lad, young boy.
mucama [mu·ká·ma] *f. Andes, Ríopl.* servant girl; **mucamo** [mu·ká·mo] *m. Andes, Ríopl.* servant.
mucoso [mu·kó·so] *adj.* mucous; slimy; **membrana mucosa** mucous membrane.
muchacha [mu·čá·ča] *f.* child; girl; servant, maid.
muchacho [mu·čá·čo] *m.* child; boy, lad.
muchedumbre [mu·če·đúm·bre] *f.* multitude; crowd.
mucho [mú·čo] *adj.* much, a lot of; long (*referring to time*); **-s** many; *adv.* much; a great deal; **ni con** — not by far, not by a long shot; **ni** — **menos** not by any means, nor anything like it; **por** — **que** no matter how much; **no es** — **que** it is no wonder that.
muda [mú·đa] *f.* change; change of clothes; molt (*act or time of shedding feathers*); *Ríopl.* relay of draft animals.
mudable [mu·đá·ƀle] *adj.* changeable; fickle.
mudanza [mu·đán·sa] *f.* change; removal; inconstancy.
mudar [mu·đár] *v.* to change; to remove; to molt; — **de casa** to move; — **de traje** to change one's suit or costume; **-se** to change one's clothes; to change one's habits; to move, change one's abode.
mudez [mu·đés] *f.* muteness, dumbness.
mudo [mú·đo] *adj.* mute, dumb; silent; *m.* dumb person.
mueblaje [mwe·ƀlá·xe] *m.* furniture.
mueble [mwé·ƀle] *m.* piece of furniture; **-s** furniture, household goods; *adj.* movable; **bienes -s** chattels, movable possessions.
mueblería [mwe·ƀle·rí·a] *f.* furniture store.
mueca [mwé·ka] *f.* grimace; wry face.
muela [mwé·la] *f.* (*diente*) molar tooth; (*piedra*) millstone; grindstone; — **ahuecada** recessed wheel; — **cordal** (*or* — **del juicio**) wisdom tooth.
muelle [mwé·ye] *adj.* soft; voluptuous; *m.* spring; wharf; loading platform; — **real** main spring of a watch.
muerte [mwér·te] *f.* death.
muerto [mwér·to] *p.p. of* **morir** & *adj.* dead; withered; faded; **naturaleza muerta** still life; *m.* corpse.
muesca [mwés·ka] *f.* notch; groove.
muestra [mwés·tra] *f.* sample; pattern, model; shop sign; sign, indication; presence, bearing; face, dial (*of a clock or watch*); **muestrario** [mwes·trá·rjo] *m.* book or collection of samples.
mugido [mu·xí·đo] *m.* moo; mooing, lowing of cattle.
mugir[11] [mu·xír] *v.* to moo, low.
mugre [mú·ǥre] *f.* dirt, grime.
mugriento [mu·ǥrjén·to] *adj.* grimy, dirty.
mujer [mu·xér] *f.* woman; wife.
mujeriego [mu·xe·rjé·ǥo] *adj.* fond of women; womanly.
mujeril [mu·xe·ríl] *adj.* womanly, feminine; womanish, like a woman.
mula [mú·la] *f.* mule; *Mex.* cushion for carrying loads; *Am.* worthless merchandise; *Ríopl.* cruel, treacherous person; *Mex.* **echar a uno la** — to give someone the dickens, scold someone.
muladar [mu·la·đár] *m.* rubbish pile or dump; dunghill, pile of manure.
mulato [mu·lá·to] *adj.* & *m.* mulatto.
muleta [mu·lé·ta] *f.* crutch; red cloth draped over a rod (*used by bullfighters*).
muletilla [mu·le·tí·ya] *f.* cane with a crutchlike handle; red cloth draped over a rod (*used by bullfighters*); cliché (*hackneyed or trite phrase*); refrain; repetitious word or phrase; braid frog (*fastener for a coat*).
mulo [mú·lo] *m.* mule.
multa [múl·ta] *f.* fine.
multicolor [mul·ti·ko·lór] *adj.* many-colored, motley.
múltiple [múl·ti·ple] *adj.* multiple.
multiplicación [mul·ti·pli·ka·sjón] *f.* multiplication.
multiplicar[6] [mul·ti·pli·kár] *v.* to multiply.
multiplicidad [mul·ti·pli·si·đáđ] *f.* multiplicity, manifold variety.
múltiplo [múl·ti·plo] *m.* multiple number.
multitud [mul·ti·túđ] *f.* multitude; crowd.
mullido [mu·yí·đo] *adj.* soft; fluffy; *m.* stuffing for mattresses or pillows; soft cushion or mattress.
mullir[20] [mu·yír] *v.* to fluff; to soften.
mundanal [mun·da·nál] *adj.* worldly.
mundano [mun·dá·no] *adj.* mundane, worldly.
mundial [mun·djál] *adj.* universal; **la guerra** — the World War.
mundo [mún·do] *m.* world; trunk; **todo el** — everybody.
munición [mu·ni·sjón] *f.* ammunition; buckshot; — **de guerra** war supplies.
municipal [mu·ni·si·pál] *adj.* municipal; **municipalidad** [mu·ni·si·pa·li·đáđ] *f.* municipality; town hall; city government.
municipio [mu·ni·sí·pjo] *m.* municipality; *Arg.* city hall.
muñeca [mu·ñé·ka] *f.* doll; wrist; manikin (*figure for displaying clothes*); **muñeco** *m.* boy doll; dummy, puppet.
muñón [mu·ñón] *m.* stump (*of an arm or leg*).
muralla [mu·rá·ya] *f.* surrounding wall; rampart.
murciano [mur·sjá·no] *adj.* of or from Murcia, Spain; *m.* native of Murcia.
murciélago [mur·sjé·la·ǥo] *m.* bat.
murga [múr·ǥa] *f.* brass band.
murmullo [mur·mú·yo] *m.* murmur, rumor; whisper; muttering.
murmuración [mur·mu·ra·sjón] *f.* slander, gossip; grumbling.
murmurar [mur·mu·rár] *v.* to murmur; to slander, gossip; to whisper; to grumble.
muro [mú·ro] *m.* wall.
murria [mú·rrja] *f.* sulkiness, sullenness, melancholy, blues; **tener** — to be sulky; to have the blues.
musa [mú·sa] *f.* Muse; muse, poetic inspiration;

poetry; **-s** fine arts.
muscular [mus·ku·lár] *adj.* muscular.
musculatura [mus·ku·la·tú·ra] *f.* muscles; muscular system.
músculo [mús·ku·lo] *m.* muscle.
musculoso [mus·ku·ló·so] *adj.* muscular; sinewy.
muselina [mu·se·lí·na] *f.* muslin.
museo [mu·sé·o] *m.* museum.
musgo [múz·ǥo] *m.* moss.
musgoso [muz·ǥó·so] *adj.* mossy.
música [mú·si·ka] *f.* music.
musical [mu·si·kál] *adj.* musical.
músico [mú·si·ko] *adj.* musical; *m.* musician.
musitar [mu·si·tár] *v.* to mutter, mumble; to whisper.
muslo [múz·lo] *m.* thigh.
mustio [mús·tjo] *adj.* sad; withered; humble.
mutación [mu·ta·sjón] *f.* mutation; unsettled weather.
mutilar [mu·ti·lár] *v.* to mutilate; to butcher; to mar.
mutismo [mu·tíz·mo] *m.* muteness, silence.
mutuo [mú·two] *adj.* mutual; reciprocal.
muy [mwi(múj)] *adv.* very; greatly; most.

N:n

nabo [ná·ƀo] *m.* turnip.
nácar [ná·kar] *m.* mother-of-pearl; pearl color.
nacarado [na·ka·rá·đo] *adj.* pearly.
nacer[13] [na·sér] *v. irr.* (*salir del vientre*) to be born; (*brotar*) to spring, originate; to bud; to sprout, grow (*said of plants*) — **de pie** (*or* — **de pies**) to be born lucky.
naciente [na·sjén·te] *adj.* rising (*sun*); *m.* orient, east.
nacimiento [na·si·mjén·to] *m.* birth; origin; beginning; descent; source; crèche (*representation of the Nativity*).
nación [na·sjón] *f.* nation.
nacional [na·sjo·nál] *adj.* national; *m.* national, citizen.
nacionalidad [na·sjo·na·li·đáđ] *f.* nationality.
nada [ná·đa] *f.* nothingness; *indef. pron.* nothing, not . . . anything; *adv.* not at all; **de** — you are welcome, don't mention it (*as a reply to* **«gracias»**); *Am.* **a cada** — constantly; **una nadita** [na·đí·ta] a trifle, just a little.
nadada [na·đá·đa] *f.* swim.
nadador [na·đa·đór] *m.* swimmer; *Ven.* fish-net float.
nadar [na·đár] *v.* to swim; to float.
nadería [na·đe·rí·a] *f.* a mere nothing, trifle, worthless thing.
nadie [ná·đje] *indef. pron.* nobody, no one, not . . . anyone.
nafta [náf·ta] *f.* naphtha.
naguas [ná·ǥwas] = **enaguas.**
náhuatl [ná·watl] *adj.* the language of the Aztec Indians.
naipe [náj·pe] *m.* playing card.
nalgas [nál·ǥas] *f. pl.* buttocks; rump; **nalgada** [nal·ǥá·đa] *f.* spank; **-s** spanking.
nana [ná·na] *f.* grandma; (*canción*) lullaby; *Mex., Ríopl., Ven.* child's nurse; *Spain* nice old lady.
naranja [na·ráŋ·xa] *f.* orange; — **tangerina** [taŋ·xe·rí·na] tangerine; **naranjada** [na·raŋ·xá·đa] *f.* orangeade; orange juice; orange marmalade; **naranjal** [na·raŋ·xál] *m.* orange grove; **naranjo** [na·ráŋ·xo] *m.* orange tree.
narciso [nar·sí·so] *m.* narcissus; daffodil; fop, dandy.
narcótico [nar·kó·ti·ko] *adj. & m.* narcotic.
narcotizar[9] [nar·ko·ti·sár] *v.* to dope, drug with narcotics.
nariz [na·rís] *f.* nose; nostril; **narices** [na·rí·ses] nostrils.
narración [na·rra·sjón] *f.* narration, account, story.
narrar [na·rrár] *v.* to narrate, tell, relate.
narrativo [na·rra·ti·ƀo] *adj.* narrative; **narrativa** [na·rra·tí·ƀa] *f.* narrative.
nata [ná·ta] *f.* cream; best part; scum; **-s** whipped cream with sugar; custard; **natoso** [na·tó·so] *adj.* creamy.
natación [na·ta·sjón] *f.* swimming.
natal [na·tál] *adj.* natal; native; **natalicio** [na·ta·lí·sjo] *m.* birthday; **natalidad** [na·ta·li·đáđ] *f.* birth rate.
natillas [na·tí·yas] *f. pl.* custard.
nativo [na·tí·ƀo] *adj.* native.
natural [na·tu·rál] *adj.* natural; native; simple, unaffected; *m. & f.* native; *m.* nature, disposition; **al** — without affectation; **del** — from nature, from life.
naturaleza [na·tu·ra·lé·sa] *f.* nature; disposition; nationality; naturalization; — **muerta** still life.
naturalidad [na·tu·ra·li·đáđ] *f.* naturalness; simplicity; birthright.
naturalista [na·tu·ra·lís·ta] *adj.* naturalistic; *m. & f.* naturalist.
naturalización [na·tu·ra·li·sa·sjón] *f.* naturalization.
naturalizar[9] [na·tu·ra·li·sár] *v.* to naturalize; to acclimatize, accustom to a new climate; **-se** to become naturalized.
naufragar[7] [naw·fra·ǥár] *v.* to be shipwrecked; to fail.
naufragio [naw·frá·xjo] *m.* shipwreck; failure, ruin.
náufrago [náw·fra·ǥo] *m.* shipwrecked person.
náusea [náw·se·a] *f.* nausea; **dar -s** to nauseate, sicken; to disgust; **tener -s** to be nauseated, be sick to one's stomach.
nauseabundo [naw·se·a·ƀún·do] *adj.* nauseating, sickening.
nauseado [naw·se·á·đo] *adj.* nauseated, sick to one's stomach.
náutica [náw·ti·ka] *f.* navigation (*science of navigation*).
navaja [na·ƀá·xa] *f.* jackknife, pocketknife; penknife; razor.
navajazo [na·ƀa·xá·so] *m.* stab with a jackknife or razor; stab wound.
naval [na·ƀál] *adj.* naval.
navarro [na·ƀá·rro] *adj.* Navarrese, of or pertaining to Navarre, Spain; *m.* Navarrese.
nave [ná·ƀe] *f.* ship, boat; nave; — **cósmica** spaceship; — **cósmica pilotada** manned space vehicle.
navegable [na·ƀe·ǥá·ƀle] *adj.* navigable.
navegación [na·ƀe·ǥa·sjón] *f.* navigation; sea voyage; — **aérea** aviation.
navegador [na·ƀe·ǥa·đór] **navegante** [na·ƀe·ǥán·te] *m.* navigator; *adj.* navigating.
navegar[7] [na·ƀe·ǥár] *v.* to navigate; to sail.
navidad [na·ƀi·đáđ] *f.* Nativity; Christmas; **-es** Christmas season.
navideño [na·ƀi·đé·ño] *adj.* pertaining to Christmas.
navío [na·ƀí·o] *m.* vessel, ship — **de guerra** warship.
neblina [ne·ƀlí·na] *f.* fog, mist.
nebulosidad [ne·ƀu·lo·si·đáđ] *f.* cloudiness; nebulousness.
necedad [ne·se·đáđ] *f.* foolishness, nonsense.
necesario [ne·se·sá·rjo] *adj.* necessary.
neceser [ne·se·sér] *m.* toilet case; sewing kit.
necesidad [ne·se·si·đáđ] *f.* necessity, need, want.
necesitado [ne·se·si·tá·đo] *adj.* needy; in need, destitute, poor; *p.p. of* **necesitar;** *m.* needy person.

necesitar [ne·se·si·tár] *v.* to need; to necessitate.
necio [né·sjo] *adj.* stupid, ignorant; foolish; stubborn, *Col.* touchy.
necrología [ne·kro·lo·xí·a] *f.* necrology.
nefando [ne·fán·do] *adj.* abominable; wicked.
nefasto [ne·fás·to] *adj.* ominous; tragic.
nefritis [ne·frí·tis] *f.* nephritis.
negación [ne·ǥa·sjón] *f.* negation, denial; negative (*negative particle*).
negar[1, 7] [ne·ǥár] *v. irr.* to deny; to refuse; to prohibit; to disown; **-se** to refuse, decline.
negativa [ne·ǥa·tí·ƀa] *f.* negative; denial, refusal.
negativo [ne·ǥa·tí·ƀo] *adj.* negative.
negligencia [ne·ǥli·xén·sja] *f.* negligence, neglect, carelessness.
negligente [ne·ǥli·xén·te] *adj.* negligent, neglectful, careless.
negociación [ne·ǥo·sja·sjón] *f.* negotiation; business; business house; management; transaction, deal.
negociante [ne·ǥo·sján·te] *m.* merchant, trader, dealer; businessman; *adj.* negotiating.
negociar [ne·ǥo·sjár] *v.* to negotiate; to trade; to transact.
negocio [ne·ǥó·sjo] *m.* business; business deal; negotiation, transaction; *Ríopl., Carib., C.A., Ven., Andes* store; **hombre de -s** businessman.
negrear [ne·ǥre·ár] *v.* to become black; to appear black, look black (*in the distance*).
negrero [ne·ǥré·ro] *m.* slave trader.
negro [né·ǥro] *adj.* black; dark; sad, gloomy; unfortunate; *m.* black color; negro; *Ríopl., C.A., Ven., Col.* dear, darling; **negra** [né·ǥra] *f.* negress; *Ríopl., C.A., Ven., Col.* dear, darling.
negrura [ne·ǥrú·ra] *f.* blackness.
negruzco [ne·ǥrús·ko] *adj.* blackish.
nena [né·na] *f.* baby girl; **nene** [né·ne] *m.* baby boy.
neón [ne·ón] *m.* neon.
neófito [ne·ó·fi·to] *m.* & *f.* neophyte.
neologismo [ne·o·lo·xíz·mo] *m.* neologism.
neoplasma [ne·o·pláz·ma] *m.* neoplasm.
nepotismo [ne·po·tíz·mo] *m.* nepotism.
nervio [ner·ƀio] *m.* nerve.
nervioso [ner·ƀjó·so], **nervoso** [ner·ƀó·so] *adj.* nervous, sinewy, strong.
nerviosidad [ner·ƀjo·si·đáđ], **nervosidad** [ner·ƀo·si·đáđ] *f.* nervousness; flexibility; vigor.
nervudo [ner·ƀú·đo] *adj.* sinewy, tough, powerful.
neto [né·to] *adj.* clear, pure; net (*profit, price, etc.*); **netamente** [ne·ta·mén·te] *adv.* clearly, distinctly.
neumático [new·má·ti·ko] *m.* tire; *adj.* pneumatic.
neuralgia [new·rál·xja] *f.* neuralgia.
neurastenia [new·ras·té·nja] *f.* neurasthenia.
neutralidad [new·tra·li·đáđ] *f.* neutrality.
neutralizar[9] [new·tra·li·sár] *v.* to neutralize, counteract.
neutro [néw·tro] *adj.* neutral; neuter; sexless.
neutrón [new·trón] *m.* neutron.
nevada [ne·ƀá·đa] *f.* snowfall.
nevado [ne·ƀá·đo] *adj.* snowy, white as snow; covered with snow.
nevar[1] [ne·ƀár] *v. irr.* to snow.
nevasca [ne·ƀás·ka] *f.* snowstorm.
nevera [ne·ƀe·ra] *f.* icebox; refrigerator; ice storehouse; ice or ice-cream vendor (*woman*).
nevería [ne·ƀe·rí·a] *f.* ice cream parlor.
ni [ni] *conj.* & *adv.* not; not even; neither; — **siquiera** not even.
nicotina [ni·ko·tí·na] *f.* nicotine.
nicho [ní·čo] *m.* niche; recess, hollow in a wall.
nidada [ni·đá·đa] *f.* nestful of eggs; brood of chicks; hatch, brood.
nido [ní·đo] *m.* nest; abode; *Am.* **patearle el — a alguien** to "upset the applecart", upset someone's plans.
niebla [njé·ƀla] *f.* fog, mist; confusion.
nieto [njé·to] *m.* grandson, grandchild; **nieta** [njé·ta] *f.* granddaughter.
nieve [njé·ƀe] *f.* snow; *Mex., Ríopl., Ven.* sherbet, ice cream; **tiempo de -s** snowy season.
nigua [ní·ǥwa] *f.* chigger, chigoe, "sand flea," "red bug."
nihilismo [ni·i·líz·mo] *m.* nihilism.
nilon [náj·lon] *m.* nylon.
nimio [ní·mjo] *adj.* miserly, stingy; *Am.* very small, insignificant.
ninfa [nín·fa] *f.* nymph.
ningun(o) [niŋ·gún(o)] *indef. adj.* & *pron.* no one, none, not . . . any; nobody.
niña [ní·ña] *f.* girl; baby girl; *Andes, Ríopl., Mex., Carib.* lady, mistress (*title of respect and endearment given to adults*); — **del ojo** pupil of the eye.
niñada [ni·ñá·đa] *f.* childishness, childish act or remark.
niñera [ni·ñé·ra] *f.* child's nurse.
niñería [ni·ne·rí·a] *f.* childish act; child's play; trifle; foolishness.
niñez [ni·ñés] *f.* infancy; childhood.
niño [ní·ño] *m.* child, boy; infant; *C.A.* master (*title of respect given to a young man by his servants*); *adj.* childlike, childish; very young, immature.
niple [ní·ple] *m.* nipple (machine).
níquel [ní·kel] *m.* nickel.
niquelado [ni·ke·lá·đo] *adj.* nickel-plated; *m.* nickel plating; nickel plate.
níspero [nís·pe·ro] *m.* loquat; medlar tree.
nitidez [ni·ti·đés] *f.* clarity, clearness.
nítido [ní·ti·đo] *adj.* clear.
nitrato [ni·trá·to] *m.* nitrate; saltpeter.
nítrico [ní·tri·ko] *adj.*
nitro [ní·tro] *m.* niter, saltpeter.
nitrógeno [ni·tró·xe·no] *m.* nitrogen.
nitroglicerina [ni·tro·ǥli·se·rí·na] *f.* nitroglycerine.
nivel [ni·ƀél] *m.* level.
nivelar [ni·ƀe·lár] *v.* to level; to grade; to equalize.
no [no] *adv.* no; not; nay; — **bien** as soon as; **un — sé qué** something indefinable; **por sí o por —** just in case, anyway.
noble [nó·ƀle] *adj.* noble; *m.* nobleman.
nobleza [no·ƀlé·sa] *f.* nobility; nobleness.
noción [no·sjón] *f.* notion, idea.
nocivo [no·sí·ƀo] *adj.* noxious, harmful, injurious.
nocturno [nok·túr·no] *adj.* nocturnal, night, nightly; *m.* nocturne (*musical or lyrical composition*).
noche [nó·če] *f.* night; darkness; **a la —** tonight; **de —** by (at) night; **por (en) la —** at night, in the evening; **dejar a uno a buenas -s** to leave a person in the lurch.
Nochebuena [no·če·ƀwé·na] *f.* Christmas Eve.
nocherniego [no·čer·nje·ǥo] *m.* night owl (*person*).
nodriza [no·đrí·sa] *f.* child's nurse; wet nurse.
nogal [no·ǥál] *m.* walnut (*tree and wood*).
nomás [no·más] *Am.* = **no más** just; only.
nombradía [nom·bra·đí·a] *f.* renown, fame.
nombramiento [nom·bra·mjén·to] *m.* nomination; appointment; naming.
nombrar [nom·brár] *v.* to nominate; to name; to appoint.
nombre [nóm·bre] *m.* name; fame; noun; watchword; **— de pila** (*or* **— de bautismo**) Christian name.
nomenclatura [no·meŋ·kla·tú·ra] *f.* nomenclature.
nomeolvides [no·me·ol·ƀí·đes] *f.* forget-me-not

MU

(flower).

nómina [nó·mi·na] *f.* list (*of names*); pay roll.

nominación [no·mi·na·sjón] *f.* nomination; appointment.

nominal [no·mi·nál] *adj.* nominal; **valor** — small, insignificant value.

nominar [no·mi·nár] *v.* to nominate.

non [non] *adj.* odd, uneven; *m.* odd number, uneven number; **estar** (*or* **quedar**) **de** — to be left alone, be left without a partner or companion.

nonada [no·ná·đa] *f.* trifle, mere nothing.

nopal [no·pál] *m.* nopal, prickly pear tree (*species of cactus*).

nordeste [nor·đés·te] *adj.* & *m.* northeast.

nórdico [nór·đi·ko] *adj.* Nordic.

noria [nó·rja] *f.* draw well; chain pump.

norma [nór·ma] *f.* norm, standard, model.

normal [nor·mál] *adj.* normal, standard; *f.* perpendicular line; normal school.

normalizar[9] [nor·ma·li·sár] *v.* to normalize, make normal; to standardize.

noroeste [nor·o·és·te] *adj.* & *m.* northwest.

nortada [nor·tá·đa] *f.* strong north wind.

nortazo [nor·tá·so] *m. Mex., Ven.* sudden gust of wind, strong north wind.

norte [nór·te] *m.* north; north wind; guide; North Star; direction; *C.A.* wind.

norteamericano [nor·te·a·me·ri·ká·no] *adj.* North American; American (*from or of the United States*).

nortear [nor·te·ár] *v.* to blow from the north; *Sal.* to blow from any direction.

norteño [nor·té·ño] *adj.* northern; *m.* northerner.

noruego [no·rwé·ǥo] *adj.* & *m.* Norwegian.

nostalgia [nos·tál·xja] *f.* nostalgia, longing, homesickness.

nostálgico [nos·tál·xi·ko] *adj.* homesick; lonesome; longing.

nota [nó·ta] *f.* note; mark; fame.

notable [no·tá·ƀle] *adj.* notable; noticeable.

notar [no·tár] *v.* to note, observe; to mark; to write down.

notario [no·tá·rjo] *m.* notary.

noticia [no·tí·sja] *f.* notice, information; news; **recibir -s** to receive word, hear (from).

noticiario [no·ti·sjá·rjo] *m.* news sheet, news column, news bulletin or film; **noticiero** [no·ti·sjé·ro] *m.* = **noticiario;** *adj.* news (*used as adj.*); newsy, full of news.

noticioso [no·ti·sjó·so] *adj.* newsy, full of news; well-informed.

notificación [no·ti·fi·ka·sjón] *f.* notification, notifying; notice; summons.

notificar[6] [no·ti·fi·kár] *v.* to notify.

notorio [no·tó·rjo] *adj.* well-known; obvious, evident.

novato [no·ƀá·to] *m.* novice, beginner.

novedad [no·ƀe·đáđ] *f.* novelty; latest news, event, or fashion; change; newness; **hacerle a uno** — to seem strange or new to one; to excite one's curiosity or interest; **sin** — as usual; well.

novel [no·ƀél] *adj.* new, inexperienced.

novela [no·ƀé·la] *f.* novel; fiction.

novelesco [no·ƀe·lés·ko] *adj.* novelistic, fictional; fantastic.

novelista [no·ƀe·lís·ta] *m.* & *f.* novelist.

novena [no·ƀé·na] *f.* novena of the Church.

noventa [no·ƀén·ta] *num.* ninety.

novia [nó·ƀja] *f.* fiancée; sweetheart; bride.

noviazgo [no·ƀjáz·ǥo] *m.* betrothal, engagement; courtship.

novicio [no·ƀí·sjo] *m.* novice; beginner; apprentice; *adj.* inexperienced.

noviembre [no·ƀjém·bre] *m.* November.

novilla [no·ƀí·ya] *f.* heifer, young cow.

novillada [no·ƀi·yá·đa] *f.* herd of young bulls; bullfight (*using young bulls*).

novillero [no·ƀi·yé·ro] *m.* a novice bullfighter; a fighter of 3-year-old bulls.

novillo [no·ƀí·yo] *m.* young bull; steer; **-s** bullfight (*using young bulls*); **hacer -s** to play hooky, cut classes; to play truant.

novio [nó·ƀjo] *m.* fiancé; sweetheart; bridegroom.

novocaína [no·ƀo·ka·í·na] *f.* novocaine.

nubarrón [nu·ƀa·rrón] *m.* large storm cloud.

nube [nú·ƀe] *f.* cloud; film on the eyeball; **poner por las -s** to praise to the skies.

nublado [nu·ƀlá·đo] *m.* storm cloud; imminent danger; *adj.* cloudy.

nublar [nu·ƀlar] *v.* to cloud; to darken, obscure; **-se** to grow cloudy.

nubloso [nu·ƀló·so] *adj.* cloudy; gloomy.

nuboso [nu·ƀó·so] *adj. Spain* cloudy.

nuca [nú·ka] *f.* nape.

nuclear [nu·kle·ár] *adj.* nuclear.

núcleo [nú·kle·o] *m.* nucleus; kernel.

nudillo [nu·đí·yo] *m.* small knot; knuckle; loop, knitted stitch.

nudo [nú·đo] *m.* (*vinculo*) knot; joint; union, bond, tie; (*crisis*) crisis, turning point (*of a play*); knot, nautical mile; — **ciego** hard knot; — **corredizo** slip knot.

nudoso [nu·đó·so] *adj.* knotty, gnarled, knotted.

nuera [nwé·ra] *f.* daughter-in-law.

nueva [nwé·ƀa] *f.* news.

nueve [nwe·ƀe] *num.* nine.

nuevecito [nwe·ƀe·sí·to] *adj.* nice and new, brandnew.

nuevo [nwé·ƀo] *adj.* new; newly arrived; **de** — again; **¿qué hay de — ?** what's new? what's the news?

nuez [nwes] *f.* walnut; nut; — (*or* — **de Adán**) Adam's apple; — **moscada** (*or* — **de especia**) nutmeg.

nulidad [nu·li·đáđ] *f.* nullity (*state or quality of being null*); incompetence; nonentity, a nobody.

nulo [nú·lo] *adj.* null, void; useless.

numeral [nu·me·rál] *adj.* & *m.* numeral.

numerar [nu·me·rár] *v.* to number; to calculate; to enumerate.

numérico [nu·mé·ri·ko] *adj.* numerical.

número [nú·me·ro] *m.* number; numeral.

numeroso [nu·me·ró·so] *adj.* numerous.

numismática [nu·miz·má·ti·ka] *f.* numismatics.

nunca [núŋ·ka] *adv.* never; **no . . .** — not . . . ever; **más que** — more than ever.

nuncio [nún·sjo] *m.* herald, messenger; nuncio, Papal envoy.

nupcial [nup·sjál] *adj.* nuptial, relating to marriage or weddings.

nupcias [núp·sjas] *f. pl.* nuptials, wedding.

nutria [nú·trja] *f.* otter.

nutrición [nu·tri·sjón] *f.* nutrition; nourishment.

nutrido [nu·trí·đo] *adj.* full, abundant; substantial; *p.p. of* **nutrir.**

nutrimento [nu·tri·mén·to], **nutrimiento** [nu·tri·mjén·to] *m.* nutrition; nourishment, food.

nutrir [nu·trír] *v.* nourish, feed.

nutritivo [nu·tri·tí·ƀo] *adj.* nutritious, nourishing.

Ñ:ñ

ñandú [ñan·dú] *m.* nandu; American ostrich.
ñapa [ñá·pa] *f. Andes, Ríopl., Cuba, Ven., Col.* additional amount, something extra; *Am.* **de** — to boot, in addition, besides.
ñato [ñá·to] *adj. C.A., Col., Ven., Andes* flat-nosed, pug-nosed, snub-nosed; *Am.* ugly, deformed; *Am.* insignificant.
ñoñería [ño·ñe·rí·a] *f.* silly remark or action; *Am.* dotage.
ñoño [ñó·ño] *adj.* feeble-minded; silly; *Am.* old, decrepit, feeble; *Col., Ec.* old-fashioned, out of style.
ñu [ñu] *m.* gnu.

O:o

o [o] *conj.* or, either.
oasis [o·á·sis] *m.* oasis.
obedecer[13] [o·ƀe·đe·sér] *v. irr.* to obey; — **a cierta causa** to arise from, be due to, a certain cause; **esto obedece a que . . .** this is due to the fact that . . .
obediencia [o·ƀe·đjén·sja] *f.* obedience.
obediente [o·ƀe·đjén·te] *adj.* obedient.
obelisco [o·ƀe·lís·ko] *m.* obelisk.
obertura [o·ƀer·tú·ra] *f.* musical overture.
obispado [o·ƀis·pá·đo] *m.* bishopric.
obispo [o·ƀís·po] *m.* bishop; *Cuba, Andes* **a cada muerte de** (*or* **por la muerte de un**) — once in a blue moon.
objeción [oƀ·xe·sjón] *f.* objection.
objetar [oƀ·xe·tár] *v.* to object.
objetivo [oƀ·xe·tí·ƀo] *adj.* objective; *m.* objective (*lens of any optical instrument*); objective.
objeto [oƀ·xé·to] *m.* object, purpose, aim; thing.
oblea [o·ƀlé·a] *f.* wafer.
oblicuo [o·ƀlí·kwo] *adj.* oblique, slanting, bias.
obligación [o·ƀli·ǥa·sjón] *f.* obligation; duty; bond, security; engagement.
obligar[7] [o·ƀli·ǥár] *v.* to oblige; to obligate, bind, compel, put under obligation; **-se** to bind oneself, obligate oneself.
obligatorio [o·ƀli·ǥa·tó·rjo] *adj.* obligatory; compulsory; binding.
oboe [o·ƀó·e] *m.* oboe.
óbolo [ó·ƀo·lo] *m.* mite, small contribution.
obra [ó·ƀra] *f.* (*resultado de acción*) work; act; labor, toil; (*creación artística*) book; building (*under construction*); masterpiece of art; repair; — **de** approximately; **por** — **de** through, by virtue of power of; **hacer mala** — to interfere, hinder; **poner por** — to undertake, begin; to put into practice.
obrar [o·ƀrár] *v.* to work; to act; to operate; to function; to perform; to make; to do; to have a bowel movement; **obra en nuestro poder** we are in receipt of; **la carta que obra en su poder** the letter that is in his possession.
obrero [o·ƀré·ro] *m.* workman, laborer.
obscenidad [oƀ·se·ni·đáđ] *f.* obscenity.
obsceno [oƀ·sé·no] *adj.* obscene.
obscurecer[13] [oƀs·ku·re·sèr] *v. irr.* to obscure, darken; to tarnish; to grow dark; **-se** to get dark or cloudy.
obscuridad [oƀs·ku·ri·đáđ] *f.* obscurity; darkness; dimness.
obscuro [oƀs·kú·ro] *adj.* obscure; dark; dim; **a obscuras** (= **a oscuras**) in the dark; *m.* shade (*in painting*).
obsequiar [oƀ·se·kjár] *v.* to regale, entertain; to court; *Am.* to give, make a present of.
obsequio [oƀ·sé·kjo] *m.* attention, courtesy; gift; **en** — **de** for the sake of, in honor of.
obsequioso [oƀ·se·kjó·so] *adj.* attentive, courteous, obliging; obsequious, servile.
observación [oƀ·ser·ƀa·sjón] *f.* observation; remark.
observador [oƀ·ser·ƀa·đór] *m.* observer; *adj.* observing.
observancia [oƀ·ser·ƀán·sja] *f.* observance (*of a law, rule, custom, etc.*).
observante [oƀ·ser·ƀán·te] *adj.* observant (*of a law, custom, or rule*).
observar [oƀ·ser·ƀár] *v.* to observe; to watch; to remark.
observatorio [oƀ·ser·ƀa·tó·rjo] *m.* observatory.
obsesión [oƀ·se·sjón] *f.* obsession.
obsesionar [oƀ·se·sjo·nár] *v.* to obsess.
obstáculo [oƀs·tá·ku·lo] *m.* obstacle.
obstante: [oƀs·tán·te] **no** — notwithstanding; nevertheless.
obstar [oƀs·tár] *v.* to hinder, impede, obstruct.
obstétrica [oƀs·té·tri·ka] *f.* obstetrics.
obstinación [oƀs·ti·na·sjón] *f.* obstinacy, stubbornness.
obstinado [oƀs·ti·ná·đo] *adj.* obstinate, stubborn.
obstinarse [oƀs·ti·nár·se] *v.* to persist (in); to be obstinate, stubborn (about).
obstrucción [oƀs·truk·sjón] *f.* obstruction.
obstruir[32] [oƀs·trwír] *v. irr.* to obstruct, block.
obtener[45] [oƀ·te·nér] *v. irr.* to obtain, get; to attain.
obtenible [oƀ·te·ní·ƀle] *adj.* obtainable, available.
obturador [oƀ·tu·ra·đór] *m.* choke (*of an automobile*); throttle; plug, stopper; shutter (*of a camera*).
obviar [oƀ·ƀjár] *v.* to obviate, clear away, remove.
obvio [óƀ·ƀjo] *adj.* obvious.
ocasión [o·ka·sjón] *f.* occasion, opportunity; cause; danger, risk; **de** — reduced, bargain; **avisos de** — want ''ads'' (*advertisements*); *Am.* **esta** — this time.
ocasional [o·ka·sjo·nál] *adj.* occasional.
ocasionar [o·ka·sjo·nár] *v.* to occasion, cause.
ocaso [o·ká·so] *m.* sunset; setting (*of any star or planet*); west; decadence, decline, end.
occidental [ok·si·đen·tál] *adj.* occidental, western.
occidente [ok·si·đén·te] *m.* occident, west.
océano [o·sé·a·no] *m.* ocean.
oceanografía [o·se·a·no·ǥra·fí·a] *f.* oceanography.
ocelote [o·se·ló·te] *m.* ocelot.
ocio [ó·sjo] *m.* leisure, idleness; recreation, pastime.
ociosidad [o·sjo·si·đáđ] *f.* idleness, leisure.
ocioso [o·sjó·so] *adj.* idle; useless.
ocre [ó·kre] *m.* ocher.
octava [ok·tá·ƀa] *f.* octave.
octubre [ok·tú·ƀre] *m.* October.
ocular [o·ku·lár] *adj.* ocular; **testigo** — eye witness; *m.* eyepiece, lens (*for the eye in a microscope or telescope*).
oculista [o·ku·lís·ta] *m. & f.* oculist; *Am.* flatterer.
ocultar [o·kul·tár] *v.* to hide, conceal.
oculto [o·kúl·to] *adj.* hidden, concealed; *m. Am.* species of mole (*small animal*).
ocupación [o·ku·pa·sjón] *f.* occupation; employment.
ocupante [o·ku·pán·te] *m. & f.* occupant.
ocupar [o·ku·pár] *v.* to occupy; to employ; **-se en** (*Am.* **-se de**) to be engaged in; to pay attention to, be interested in.
ocurrencia [o·ku·rrén·sja] *f.* occurrence, event; witticism, joke; bright or funny idea.
ocurrente [o·ku·rrén·te] *adj.* witty, funny, humorous;

occurring.
ocurrir [o·ku·rrír] *v.* to occur.
ocurso [o·kúr·so] *m. Ríopl.* petition, application.
ochavo [o·čá·ƀo] *m.* an ancient coin; **no tener** — not to have a red cent.
ochenta [o·čén·ta] *num.* eighty.
ochentón [o·čen·tón] *m.* octogenarian.
ocho [ó·čo] *num.* eight.
oda [ó·đa] *f.* ode.
odiar [o·đjár] *v.* to hate.
odio [ó·đjo] *m.* hatred.
odioso [o·đjó·so] *adj.* odious, hateful.
odontología [o·đon·to·lo·xí·a] *f.* odontology.
odre [ó·đre] *m.* wine bag; drunk.
oeste [o·és·te] *m.* west; west wind.
ofender [o·fen·dér] *v.* to offend; to displease; **-se** to get offended; to become angry, take offense.
ofensa [o·fén·sa] *f.* offense.
ofensivo [o·fen·sí·ƀo] *adj.* offensive; obnoxious; attacking; **ofensiva** [o·fen·sí·ƀa] *f.* offensive.
ofensor [o·fen·sór] *m.* offender; *adj.* offending.
oferta [o·fér·ta] *f.* offer; promise.
oficial [o·fi·sjál] *m.* official, officer, skilled workman; *adj.* official.
oficiar [o·fi·sjár] *v.* to officiate, serve, minister; perform the duties of a priest or minister; to communicate officially; — **de** to serve as, act as.
oficina [o·fi·sí·na] *f.* office; shop; **oficinesco** *adj.* clerical, pertaining to an office.
oficio [o·fí·sjo] *m.* trade; function; official communication; religious office (*prayers*).
oficioso [o·fi·sjó·so] *adj.* officious, meddlesome.
ofrecer[13] [o·fre·sér] *v. irr.* to offer; to promise; **-se** to offer, occur, present itself; to offer oneself, volunteer; **¿qué se le ofrece a Vd.?** what do you wish?
ofrecimiento [o·fre·si·mjén·to] *m.* offer; offering.
ofrenda [o·frén·da] *f.* offering, gift.
ofuscamiento [o·fus·ka·mjén·to] *m.* clouded vision, blindness; cloudiness of the mind, bewilderment, mental confusion.
ofuscar[6] [o·fus·kár] *v.* to darken, cast a shadow on; to blind; to cloud; to bewilder, confuse.
ogro [ó·ǥro] *m.* ogre.
ohm, ohmio [on, ó·mjo] *m.* ohm; **ohmiómetro** ohmmeter.
oído [o·í·đo] *m.* hearing; ear; **al** — confidentially; **de** (*or* **al**) — by ear; **de -s** (*or* **de oídas**) by hearsay or rumor.
oidor [oj·đór] *m.* hearer, listener; judge.
oír[36] [o·ír] *v. irr.* to hear; to listen; to understand; — **misa** to attend mass; — **decir que** to hear that; — **hablar de** to hear about.
ojal [o·xál] *m.* buttonhole; hole.
¡ojalá! [o·xa·lá] *interj.* God grant!; I hope so!; — **que** would that, I hope that.
ojazo [o·xá·so] *m.* large eye.
ojeada [o·xe·á·đa] *f.* glimpse, quick glance.
ojear [o·xe·ár] *v.* to eye, stare; to bewitch; to beat up, rouse (*wild game*).
ojera [o·xé·ra] *f.* dark circle under the eye; eyecup.
ojeriza [o·xe·rí·sa] *f.* grudge, spite.
ojeroso [o·xe·ró·so] *adj.* with dark circles under the eyes.
ojete [o·xé·te] *m.* eyelet.
ojiva [o·xí·ƀa] *f.* pointed arch; **ojival** [o·xi·ƀál] *adj.* pointed (*arch*); **ventana ojival** window with a pointed arch.
ojo [ó·xo] *m.* (*órgano*) eye; (*agujero*) keyhole; hole; **¡—!** careful! look out!; **a** — by sight, by guess; **a -s vistas** visibly, clearly; — **de agua** spring (*of water*); — **de buey** porthole; **mal** (*or* **mal de**) — evil eye; *Am.* **hacer** — to cast the evil eye; *Am.* **pelar el** — to be alert, keep one's eye peeled; *Mex., Ven.* **poner a uno los -s verdes** to deceive someone; **tener entre -s a** to have ill will toward, have a grudge against.
ojoso [o·xó·so] *adj.* full of holes.
ojota [o·xó·ta] *f. Andes, Ch., Ríopl.* leather sandal.
ola [ó·la] *f.* wave.
¡ole! [ó·le] *interj.* bravo! good!
oleada [o·le·á·đa] *f.* big wave; swell; surge; abundant yield of oil.
oleaje [o·le·á·xe], **olaje** [o·lá·xe] *m.* swell, surge, succession of waves.
óleo [ó·le·o] *m.* oil, holy oil; **pintura al** — oil painting.
oleoducto [o·le·o·đúk·to] *m.* pipe line.
oleoso [o·le·ó·so] *adj.* oily.
oler[37] [o·lér] *v. irr.* to smell; to scent; — **a** to smack of; to smell like; *Am.* **olérselas** to suspect it, "smell a rat".
olfatear [ol·fa·te·ár] *v.* to scent, sniff, smell.
olfateo [ol·fa·té·o] *m.* sniff, sniffing.
olfato [ol·fá·to] *m.* sense of smell.
olfatorio [ol·fa·tó·rjo] *adj.* olfactory.
oligarquía [o·li·ǥar·kí·a] *f.* oligarchy.
olimpiada [o·lim·pjá·đa] *f.* Olympiad; Olympic games.
olímpico [o·lím·pi·ko] *adj.* Olympian.
oliva [o·lí·ƀa] *f.* olive; olive tree; **olivar** *m.* olive grove; **olivo** *m.* olive tree.
olmo [ól·mo] *m.* elm.
olor [o·lór] *m.* (*en el olfato*) smell, odor, fragrance; (*fama*) smack, trace, suspicion; *Ch.* spice; **olorcillo** [o·lor·sí·yo] *m.* faint odor.
oloroso [o·lo·ró·so] *adj.* fragrant.
olote [o·ló·te] *m. Mex., C.A.* cob, corncob.
olvidadizo [ol·ƀi·đa·đí·so] *adj.* forgetful.
olvidar [ol·ƀi·đár] *v.* to forget; to neglect; **-se de** to forget; **olvidársele a uno algo** to forget something.
olvido [ol·ƀí·đo] *m.* forgetfulness; oblivion; neglect; **echar al** — to cast into oblivion; to forget on purpose.
olla [ó·ya] *f.* pot, kettle; — **profunda para freír** deep fat fryer; olla (*vegetable and meat stew*); — **podrida** Spanish stew of mixed vegetables and meat.
ombligo [om·blí·ǥo] *m.* navel; middle center.
ombú [om·bú] *m.* umbra tree.
omisión [o·mi·sjón] *f.* omission; oversight, neglect.
omiso [o·mí·so] *adj.* careless, neglectful; *N. Arg.* guilty; **hacer caso** — to omit.
omitir [o·mi·tír] *v.* to omit; to overlook.
ómnibus [óm·ni·ƀus] *m.* omnibus, bus.
omnipotente [om·ni·po·tén·te] *adj.* omnipotent, almighty.
once [ón·se] *num.* eleven.
onda [ón·da] *f.* wave; ripple; sound wave; scallop.
ondear [on·de·ár] *v.* to wave; to waver; to ripple; to sway, swing.
ondulación [on·du·la·sjón] *f.* undulation, waving motion; wave; — **permanente** permanent wave.
ondulado [on·du·lá·đo] *p.p. & adj.* wavy; scalloped (*edge*); — **permanente** permanent wave.
ondulante [on·du·lán·te] *adj.* wavy, waving.
ondular [on·du·lár] *v.* to undulate, wave.
oneroso [o·ne·ró·so] *adj.* onerous.
onomástico [o·no·más·ti·ko] *adj.* onomastic; *m.* saint's day.
onomatopeya [o·no·ma·to·pé·ya] *f.* onomatopoeia.
ontología [on·to·lo·xí·a] *f.* ontology.

onza [ón·sa] *f.* ounce; ounce, wildcat; *Ríopl., Bol.* small tiger.
opacidad [o·pa·si·đáđ] *f.* opacity; sadness.
opaco [o·pá·ko] *adj.* opaque, dim, dull.
ópalo [ó·pa·lo] *m.* opal.
ópera [ó·pe·ra] *f.* opera.
operación [o·pe·ra·sjón] *f.* operation; business transaction.
operador [o·pe·ra·đór] *m.* operator, surgeon.
operante [o·pe·rán·te] *adj.* operant (*behavior*).
operar [o·pe·rár] *v.* to operate; to take effect, work; to speculate (*in business*); to manipulate, handle.
operario [o·pe·rá·rjo] *m.* operator, workman, worker.
opereta [o·pe·ré·ta] *f.* operetta.
opinar [o·pi·nár] *v.* to express an opinion; to think; to judge; to argue.
opinión [o·pi·njón] *f.* opinion; reputation.
opio [ó·pjo] *m.* opium.
oponer[40] [o·po·nér] *v. irr.* to oppose; **-se** to disapprove; **-se a** to oppose, be against.
oporto [o·pór·to] *m.* port wine.
oportunidad [o·por·tu·ni·đáđ] *f.* opportunity.
oportuno [o·por·tú·no] *adj.* opportune; convenient, timely.
oposición [o·po·si·sjón] *f.* opposition; competition; **-es** competitive examinations.
opositor [o·po·si·tór] *m.* opponent; competitor.
opresión [o·pre·sjón] *f.* oppression.
opresivo [o·pre·sí·bo] *adj.* oppressive.
opresor [o·pre·sór] *m.* oppressor.
oprimir [o·pri·mír] *v.* to oppress; to crush; to press down; to press a button.
oprobio [o·pró·bjo] *m.* infamy; insult; shame; dishonor.
optar [op·tár] *v.* to choose, select; — **por** to decide upon; to choose.
óptica [óp·ti·ka] *f.* optics.
óptico [óp·ti·ko] *adj.* optical, optic; *m.* optician.
optimismo [op·ti·míz·mo] *m.* optimism; **optimista** *m. & f.* optimist; *adj.* optimistic.
óptimo [óp·ti·mo] *adj.* very good, very best.
opuesto [o·pwés·to] *p.p. of* **oponer** opposed; *adj.* opposite; contrary.
opulencia [o·pu·lén·sja] *f.* opulence, abundance, wealth.
opulento [o·pu·lén·to] *adj.* opulant, wealthy.
oquedad [o·ke·đáđ] *f.* cavity, hollow; chasm.
ora [ó·ra] *conj.* now, then; whether; either.
oración [o·ra·sjón] *f.* oration; prayer; sentence.
oráculo [o·rá·ku·lo] *m.* oracle.
orador [o·ra·đór] *m.* orator, speaker.
oral [o·rál] *adj.* oral.
orar [o·rár] *v.* to pray.
oratoria [o·ra·tó·rja] *f.* oratory, eloquence.
oratorio [o·ra·tó·rjo] *m.* oratory, private chapel; oratorio (*a religious musical composition*); *adj.* oratorical, pertaining to oratory.
orbe [ór·be] *m.* orb, sphere, globe; the earth; world, universe.
órbita [ór·bi·ta] *f.* orbit; eye socket.
orden [ór·đen] *m.* (*colocación*) order; succession, series; class, group; relation; proportion; *f.* (*mando*) order, command; (*sociedad*) honorary or religious order; *m. & f.* sacrament of ordination; **a sus órdenes** at your service.
ordenado [or·đe·ná·đo] *p.p. & adj.* ordered; ordained; orderly; neat.
ordenanza [or·đe·nán·sa] *f.* ordinance, decree, law; command, order; *m.* orderly (*military*).
ordenar [or·đe·nár] *v.* to arrange, put in order; to order, command; to ordain; **-se** to become ordained.
ordeño [or·đé·ña] *m.* milking.
ordeñar [or·đe·ñár] *v.* to milk.
ordinariez [or·đi·na·rjés] *f.* commonness, lack of manners.
ordinario [or·đi·ná·rjo] *adj.* ordinary; usual; common, coarse; *m.* ordinary (*a bishop or judge*); ordinary mail; daily household expense; **de** — usually, ordinarily.
orear [o·re·ár] *v.* to air; **-se** to be exposed to the air; to dry in the air.
orégano [o·ré·ga·no] *m.* wild marjoram, oregano.
oreja [o·ré·xa] *f.* ear; hearing; loop; small flap; *Am.* handle (*shaped like an ear*); **orejano** [o·re·xá·no] *adj.* unbranded (*cattle*); *Ven., Col.* cautious; *m. Cuba* aloof, unsociable person; **orejera** [o·re·xé·ra] *f.* ear muff, ear flap; **orejón** [o·re·xón] *m.* a pull by the ear; *Col.* rancher or inhabitant of the *sabana; adj. Col.* long-eared, long-horned; *Col.* unbranded (*cattle*); *Col.* coarse, crude, uncouth.
orfandad [or·fan·dáđ] *f.* orphanage (*state of being an orphan*).
orfanato [or·fa·ná·to] *m.* orphanage, orphan asylum.
orfanatorio [or·fa·na·tó·rjo] *Mex., C.A., Andes* = **orfanato.**
orfebre [or·fé·bre] *m.* goldsmith; silversmith.
orfebrería [or·fe·bre·rí·a] *f.* silver or gold work.
orfeón [or·fe·ón] *m.* glee club, choir.
orgánico [or·gá·ni·ko] *adj.* organic.
organigrama [or·ga·ni·grá·ma] *m.* organization chart.
organillo [or·ga·ní·yo] *m.* hand organ, hurdy-gurdy.
organismo [or·ga·níz·mo] *m.* organism.
organización [or·ga·ni·sa·sjón] *f.* organization.
organizador [or·ga·ni·sa·đór] *m.* organizer.
organizar[9] [or·ga·ni·sár] *v.* to organize; to arrange.
órgano [ór·ga·no] *m.* organ; **organillo** [or·ga·ní·yo] *m.* hand organ.
orgía [or·xí·a] *f.* orgy, wild revel.
orgullo [or·gú·yo] *m.* pride; haughtiness, arrogance.
orgulloso [or·gu·yó·so] *adj.* proud; haughty, arrogant.
oriental [o·rjen·tál] *adj.* oriental, eastern.
orientar [o·rjen·tár] *v.* to orientate, orient; **-se** to orient oneself, find one's bearings.
oriente [o·rjén·te] *m.* orient, east; east wind; source, origin.
orificación [o·ri·fi·ka·sjón] *f.* gold filling.
orificio [o·ri·fí·sjo] *m.* orifice, small hole, aperture, outlet.
origen [o·rí·xen] *m.* origin; source.
original [o·ri·xi·nál] *adj.* original; strange, quaint; *m.* original; manuscript, copy; queer person; **originalidad** [o·ri·xi·na·li·đáđ] *f.* originality.
originar [o·ri·xi·nár] *v.* to originate, cause to be; **-se** originate, arise.
orilla [o·rí·ya] *f.* shore, bank; beach; edge, border; **-s** *Am.* outskirts, environs.
orillar [o·ri·yár] *v.* border, trim the edge of; to skirt, go along the edge of; to reach the edge or shore.
orín [o·rín] *m.* rust; **orines** *m. pl.* urine.
orina [o·rí·na] *f.* urine.
orinar [o·ri·nár] *v.* to urinate.
oriol [o·rjól] *m.* oriole.
oriundo [o·rjún·do] *adj.* native; **ser** — **de** to hail from, come from.
orla [ór·la] *f.* border; trimming, fringe.
orlar [or·lár] *v.* to border, edge, trim with a border or fringe.
orlón [or·lón] *m.* orlon.
ornado [or·ná·đo] *adj.* ornate; *p.p.* adorned, ornamented.
ornamentar [or·na·men·tár] *v.* to ornament, adorn.

ornamento [or·na·mén·to] *m.* ornament; decoration; **-s** sacred vestments.
ornar [or·nár] *v.* to adorn.
oro [ó·ro] *m.* gold; gold ornament; **-s** "gold coins" (*Spanish card suit*).
orondo [o·rón·do] *adj.* self-satisfied, puffed up, vain; *Am.* serene, calm.
oropel [o·ro·pél] *m.* tinsel.
orquesta [or·kés·ta] *f.* orchestra.
orquestar [or·kés·tár] *v.* to orchestrate.
orquídea [or·kí·đe·a] *f.* orchid.
ortiga [or·tí·ǥa] *f.* nettle.
ortodoxo [or·to·đók·so] *adj.* orthodox.
ortografía [or·to·ǥra·fí·a] *f.* orthography, spelling.
ortográfico [or·to·ǥrá·fi·ko] *adj.* orthographic (*pertaining to orthography or spelling*).
oruga [o·rú·ǥa] *f.* caterpillar.
orzuelo [or·swé·lo] *m.* sty (*on the eyelid*).
osadía [o·sa·đí·a] *f.* boldness, daring.
osado [o·sá·đo] *adj.* bold, daring.
osamenta [o·sa·mén·ta] *f.* bones; skeleton.
osar [o·sár] *v.* to dare, venture.
oscilación [o·si·la·sjón] *f.* oscillation, sway; fluctuation, wavering.
oscilar [o·si·lár] *v.* to oscillate, swing, sway; to waver.
oscilatorio [o·si·la·tó·rjo] *adj.* oscillatory.
oscurecer [os·ku·re·sér] = **obscurecer.**
oscuridad [os·ku·ri·đáđ] = **obscuridad.**
oscuro [os·kú·ro] = **obscuro.**
oso [ó·so] *m.* bear; — **blanco** polar bear; — **hormiguero** anteater; — **marino** seal.
ostentación [os·ten·ta·sjón] *f.* ostentation, show, display.
ostentar [os·ten·tár] *v.* to display, show; (*jactarse*) to show off; to boast.
ostentoso [os·ten·tó·so] *adj.* ostentatious, showy.
ostión [os·tjón] *m.* large oyster.
ostra [ós·tra] *f.* oyster.
otate [o·tá·te] *m. Mex., C.A.* species of bamboo; *Mex., C.A.* bamboo stick or cane.
otero [o·té·ro] *m.* hillock, small hill, knoll.
otoñal [o·to·ñál] *adj.* autumnal, of autumn.
otoño [o·tó·ño] *m.* autumn, fall.
otorgante [o·tor·ǥan·te] *m.* grantor; maker of a deed.
otorgar[7] [o·tor·ǥár] *v.* to grant; to promise; to consent to.
otro [ó·tro] *adj.* another; **otra vez** again; *Am.* **como dijo el** — as someone said.
otrora [o·tró·ra] *adv.* formerly, in other times.
ovación [o·ƀa·sjón] *f.* ovation, enthusiastic applause.
oval [o·ƀál], **ovalado** [o·ƀa·lá·đo] *adj.* oval; **óvalo** [ó·ƀa·lo] *m.* oval.
oveja [o·ƀé·xa] *f.* sheep.
ovejero [o·ƀe·xé·ro] *m.* shepherd; sheep dog.
ovejuno [o·ƀe·xú·no] *adj.* sheep, pertaining or relating to sheep.
overo [o·ƀé·ro] *adj.* peach-colored (*applied to horses and cattle*); *Ríopl.* mottled, spotted; *Ríopl.* multicolored; *Ríopl.* **ponerle a uno** — to insult someone.
overol [o·ƀe·ról], **overoles** [o·ƀe·ró·les] *m. Ch., Col.* overalls.
ovillar [o·ƀi·yár] *v.* to ball, wind or form into a ball; **-se** to curl up into a ball.
ovillo [o·ƀí·yo] *m.* ball of yarn or thread; tangle; prewinder; **hacerse uno un** — to curl up into a ball; to become entangled, confused.
oxidado [ok·si·đá·đo] *p.p.* rusted; *adj.* rusty.
oxidar [ok·si·đár] *v.* to oxidize; to rust; **-se** to become oxidized; to rust.
óxido [ók·si·đo] *m.* oxide.
oxígeno [ok·sí·xeno] *m.* oxygen.
oyente [o·yén·te] *m. & f.* listener, auditor, hearer; *adj.* listening.
ozono [o·só·no] *m.* ozone.

P:p

pabellón [pa·ƀe·yón] *m.* pavilion; canopy; banner, flag; shelter, covering; external ear.
pabilo [pa·ƀí·lo] *m.* wick; snuff (*of a candle*).
pacer[13] [pa·sér] *v. irr.* to pasture; to graze.
paciencia [pa·sjén·sja] *f.* patience.
paciente [pa·sjén·te] *adj.* patient; *m. & f.* patient.
pacienzudo [pa·sjen·sú·đo] *adj.* patient, long-suffering.
pacificar[6] [pa·si·fi·kár] *v.* to pacify; to appease.
pacífico [pa·sí·fi·ko] *adj.* pacific, peaceful, calm.
pacifismo [pa·si·fíz·mo] *m.* pacifism.
pacto [pák·to] *m.* pact, agreement.
padecer[13] [pa·đe·sér] *v. irr.* to suffer.
padecimiento [pa·đe·si·mjén·to] *m.* suffering.
padrastro [pa·đrás·tro] *m.* stepfather; hangnail.
padre [pá·đre] *m.* father; **-s** parents; ancestors; *adj. Am.* very great, stupendous.
padrenuestro [pa·đre·nwés·tro] *m.* paternoster, the Lord's Prayer.
padrino [pa·đrí·no] *m.* godfather; sponsor, patron; second in a duel; best man (*at a wedding*).
paella [pa·é·ya] *f.* a popular rice dish with chicken, vegetables, etc.
paga [pá·ǥa] *f.* payment; pay, salary.
pagadero [pa·ǥa·đé·ro] *adj.* payable.
pagado [pa·ǥá·đo] *p.p. & adj.* paid; self-satisfied, conceited; — **de sí mismo** pleased with oneself.
pagador [pa·ǥa·đór] *m.* payer; paymaster; paying teller (*in a bank*).
paganismo [pa·ǥa·níz·mo] *m.* paganism, heathenism.
pagano [pa·ǥá·no] *adj.* pagan; *m.* pagan; payer; dupe, sucker.
pagar[7] [pa·ǥár] *v.* to pay; to pay for; to requite, return (*love*); **-se de** to be proud of; to boast of; to be pleased with; *Ríopl.* **-se de palabras** to let oneself be tricked; *Ch.* — **a nueve** to pay in excess.
pagaré [pa·ǥa·ré] *m.* promissory note; I.O.U.
página [pá·xi·na] *f.* page.
paginar [pa·xi·nár] *v.* to page.
pago [pá·ǥo] *m.* (*premio*) payment; prize, reward; (*distrito*) country district; *Ríopl.* one's native farm land or district; *adj.* paid; *Am.* **estar -s** to be quits; to be even.
paila [páj·la] *f.* large pan; *C.A.* saucer.
país [pa·ís] *m.* nation, country; region.
paisaje [paj·sá·xe] *m.* landscape.
paisanaje [paj·sa·ná·xe] *m.* peasantry, country people; civilians; *Andes* gang of farm laborers.
paisano [paj·sá·no] *m.* countryman; peasant; fellow countryman; civilian.
paja [pá·xa] *f.* straw; chaff; rubbish; *Andes* grass for pasture; **echar -s** to draw lots; **por quítame allá esas -s** for an insignificant reason or pretext; **en un quítame allá esas -s** in a jiffy, in a second; **a humo de -s** thoughtlessly; lightly; **no lo hizo a humo de -s** he did not do it without a special reason or intention.
pajar [pa·xár] *m.* straw loft, barn.
pájaro [pá·xa·ro] *m.* bird; shrewd, cautious person;

Ch. absent-minded person; *Ch., Ríopl.* person of suspicious conduct; — **carpintero** woodpecker; — **mosca** hummingbird.

paje [pá·xe] *m.* page, valet, attendant.

pajizo [pa·xí·so] *adj.* made of straw; covered with straw; straw colored.

pajonal [pa·xo·nál] *m.* plain or field of tall coarse grass.

pala [pá·la] *f.* shovel; trowel; scoop; paddle; blade of an oar; racket; upper (*of a shoe*); cunning, craftiness; **meter la** — to deceive with cunning; *Am.* **hacer la** — to deceive with cunning; to stall, pretend to work; to flatter; **palada** [pa·lá·đa] *f.* scoop, shovelful; stroke of an oar.

palabra [pa·lá·ƀra] *f.* word; promise; — **clave** (*computadora*) reserved word, key word; **de** — by word of mouth; **cuatro -s** a few words; **empeñar la** — to promise, pledge; **tener la** — to have the floor; *Am.* **¡—!** I mean it, it is true!

palabrero [pa·la·ƀré·ro] *adj.* wordy, talkative.

palabrita [pa·la·ƀrí·ta] *f.* a little word, a few words, a word of advice.

palacio [pa·lá·sjo] *m.* palace; **palaciego** [pa·la·sjé·ǥo] *m.* courtier; *adj.* relating to a palace or court; court (*used as an adj.*).

paladar [pa·la·đár] *m.* palate; taste, relish.

paladear [pa·la·đe·ár] *v.* to relish, taste with relish.

paladín [pa·la·đín] *m.* knight; champion, defender.

paladio [pa·lá·đjo] *m.* palladium.

palanca [pa·láŋ·ka] *f.* lever; crowbar; bar used for carrying a load; joystick; — **de arranque y detención** start-stop lever; — **del engranaje** gear lever; — **del embrague** clutch lever; influence, a "pipe line".

palangana [pa·laŋ·gá·na] *f.* washbowl, basin; *S.A.* platter; *Ch.* large wooden bowl; *m. Andes* bluffer, charlatan.

palatal [pa·la·tál] *adj.* palatal.

palco [pál·ko] *m.* theater box; — **escénico** stage.

palenque [pa·léŋ·ke] *m.* palisade, fence; enclosure; *Ríopl.* hitching post or plank.

paleta [pa·lé·ta] *f.* small flat shovel; mason's trowel; shoulder blade; blade (*of a rudder, of a ventilating fan*); paddle (*of a paddle wheel*); painter's palette; *Am.* candy, sweetmeat or ice cream attached to a stick; *Am.* a wooden paddle to stir with, or for beating clothes; **en dos -s** in a jiffy, in a second; **paletilla** [pa·le·tí·ya] *f.* shoulder blade.

palidecer[13] [pa·li·đe·sér] *v. irr.* to turn pale.

palidez [pa·li·đés] *f.* pallor, paleness.

pálido [pá·li·đo] *adj.* pallid, pale.

palillo [pa·lí·yo] *m.* small stick; toothpick; **tocar todos los -s** (*Ch.* **menear uno los -s**) to try every possible means.

paliza [pa·lí·sa] *f.* beating (*with a stick*), thrashing.

palizada [pa·li·sá·đa] *f.* palisade; stockade.

palma [pál·ma] *f.* palm tree; palm leaf; palm of the hand; **batir -s** to clap, applaud; **llevarse la** — to triumph, win, carry off the honors; to be the best.

palmada [pal·má·đa] *f.* slap; clap.

palmario [pal·má·rjo] *adj.* clear, evident.

palmatoria [pal·ma·tó·rja] *f.* small candlestick with handle.

palmear [pal·me·ár] *v.* to clap, applaud; *Am.* to pat, slap on the back; *Ríopl.* to flatter.

palmera [pal·mé·ra] *f.* palm tree.

palmo [pál·mo] *m.* span (*about 9 inches*); — **a** — slowly, foot by foot.

palmotear [pal·mo·te·ár] *v.* to clap, applaud.

palo [pá·lo] *m.* stick; pole; log; mast; wood; blow with a stick; suit (*in a deck of cards*); *Am.* tree; *Ríopl.* reprimand, reproof; *P.R., Ven.* large swallow of liquor; — **del Brasil** Brazil wood; *Ven.* — **a pique** rail fence, barbed wire fence; *Mex., C.A.* **a medio** — half-done; half-drunk; *Am.* **a** — **entero** drunk.

paloma [pa·ló·ma] *f.* dove, pigeon; pleasant, mild person; **-s** whitecaps.

palomar [pa·lo·már] *m.* dovecot (*shelter for doves or pigeons*).

palomilla [pa·lo·mí·ya] *f.* little dove; moth; small butterfly; **-s** small whitecaps.

palomita [pa·lo·mí·ta] *f.* little dove; **-s** *Am.* popcorn.

palpable [pal·pá·ƀle] *adj.* palpable (*that can be felt or touched*); clear, obvious, evident.

palpar [pal·pár] *v.* to feel; to touch; to grope.

palpitación [pal·pi·ta·sjón] *f.* palpitation; beat, throb.

palpitante [pal·pi·tán·te] *adj.* palpitating, throbbing, trembling; exciting; **la cuestión** — the burning question.

palpitar [pal·pi·tár] *v.* to palpitate; to throb, beat.

palta [pál·ta] *f. Col., Ven., Andes, Ríopl., Ch.* avocado, alligator pear; **palto** [pál·to] *m. Col., Ven., Andes, Ríopl., Ch.* avocado tree. *See* **aguacate.**

palúdico [pa·lú·đi·ko] *adj.* marshy; **fiebre palúdica** malarial, or marsh fever; malaria; **paludismo** *m.* malaria.

pampa [pám·pa] *f. Am.* (*vast treeless plain of South America*); *Am.* prairie; *Ch.* drill field (*military*); *m.* & *f.* pampa Indian of Argentina; *m. Ríopl.* language of the pampa Indian; *adj. Ríopl.* pertaining to the pampa Indian; *Ríopl.* **caballo** — horse with head and body of different colors; *Ríopl.* **trato** — dubious or dishonest deal; *Col., Arg.* **estar a la** — to be in the open; *Ríopl.* **tener todo a la** — to be ragged or to be indecently exposed; *Ch.* **quedar en** — to be left without clothes; to be left in the lurch.

pampeano [pam·pe·á·no] *adj. Ríopl.* of, or pertaining to the pampa.

pampero [pam·pé·ro] *adj. Ríopl.* of, or pertaining to, the pampas; *m. Ríopl.* inhabitant of the pampas; *Ríopl.* violent wind of the pampa.

pan [pan] *m.* bread; loaf of bread; wheat; — **rallado** crumbs; **-es** fields of grain; breadstuffs; *Arg.* **echar -es** to brag, boast.

pana [pá·na] *f.* corduroy.

panadería [pa·na·đe·rí·a] *f.* bakery.

panadero [pa·na·đé·ro] *m.* baker; *Ch.* flatterer.

panal [pa·nál] *m.* honeycomb; sweetmeat (*made of sugar, egg white, and lemon*).

panamericano [pa·na·me·ri·ká·no] *adj.* Pan-American.

pandearse [pan·de·ár·se] *v.* to bulge, warp; to sag.

pandeo [pan·dé·o] *m.* sag; bulge.

pandilla [pan·dí·ya] *f.* gang, band.

panela [pa·né·la] *f. Col., C.A.* unrefined sugar.

panfleto [pan·flé·to] *m. Am.* pamphlet.

pánico [pá·ni·ko] *m.* panic; *adj.* panic, panicky.

panne [pán·ne] *f.* accident, car trouble.

panocha [pa·nó·ča] *f.* ear of corn; *Mex.* Mexican raw sugar; *Col., C.R.* a kind of tamale.

panqué [paŋ·ké] *m. Col., C.A., Mex.* small cake, cup cake; *Am.* pancake.

pantalón [pan·ta·lón] *m.* trousers; pants; **un par de -es** a pair of trousers.

pantalla [pan·tá·ya] *f.* light shade; screen; fireplace screen; motion-picture screen; — **de cabeza** helmet (welding); *C.R.* fan, palm leaf fan; *P.R.* earring.

pantano [pan·tá·no] *m.* swamp; dam; difficulty.

pantanoso [pan·ta·nó·so] *adj.* swampy, marshy; muddy.

panteón [pan·te·ón] *m.* cemetery.

pantera [pan·té·ra] *f.* panther.

pantorrilla [pan·to·rrí·ya] *f.* calf (*of the leg*).

pantufla [pan·tú·fla] *f.* bedroom slipper.

panza [pán·sa] *f.* paunch, belly.

panzón [pan·són], **panzudo** [pan·sú·đo] *adj.* big-bellied.

pañal [pa·ñál] *m.* diaper; **estar en -es** to be in one's infancy; to have little or no knowledge of a thing.

paño [pá·ño] *m.* cloth (*any cloth, especially woolen*); blotch or spot on the skin; film on the eyeball; *Mex., Cuba* parcel of tillable land; *Mex.* kerchief; shawl; — **de manos** towel; — **de mesa** tablecloth; **al** — off-stage; **-s** clothes, garments; **-s menores** underwear; **pañero** *m.* clothier.

pañolón [pa·ño·lón] *m.* scarf, large kerchief; shawl.

pañuelo [pa·ñwé·lo] *m.* handkerchief.

papa [pá·pa] *m.* pope; *f.* potato; fib, lie; *Am.* snap, easy job; **-s** pap (*soft food for babies*); **-s horneadas** baked potatoes; soup; *Ríopl., Ch.* **cosa** — something good to eat; excellent thing; **echar -s** to fib, lie; *Am.* **importarle a uno una** — not to matter to one a bit; *Am.* **no saber ni** — not to know a thing; to be completely ignorant.

papá [pa·pá] *m.* papa; *Mex., C.A., Andes* — **grande** grandfather.

papagayo [pa·pa·ǥá·yo] *m.* parrot; talker, chatterer.

papal [pa·pál] *adj.* papal.

papalote [pa·pa·ló·te], **papelote** [pa·pe·ló·te] *m.* *Carib., Mex.* kite.

papamoscas [pa·pa·mós·kas] *m.* flycatcher (*a bird*); simpleton, half-wit, dunce.

papanatas [pa·pa·ná·tas] *m.* simpleton, fool, dunce.

paparrucha [pa·pa·rrú·ča] *f.* fib, lie; **paparruchero** [pa·pa·rru·čé·ro] *m.* fibber.

papaya [pa·pá·ya] *f.* papaya.

papel [pa·pél] *m.* (*hoja*) paper; sheet of paper; document; (*parte dramática*) role; — **de estraza** brown wrapping paper; — **de lija** sandpaper; — **de seda** tissue paper; — **continuo** (*computadora*) fan-fold paper; — **moneda** paper money; — **secante** blotting paper; **hacer el** — **de** to play the role of; **hacer buen** (*or* **mal**) — to cut a good (*or* bad) figure.

papelera [pa·pe·lé·ra] *f.* folder, file, case or device for keeping papers; *Am.* wastepaper basket; **papelero** [pa·pe·lé·ro] *m.* paper manufacturer; *adj.* pertaining to paper; vain, ostentatious.

papelería [pa·pe·le·rí·a] *f.* stationery store; stationery; lot of papers.

papeleta [pa·pe·lé·ta] *f.* card, file card, slip of paper.

papelucho [pa·pe·lú·čo] *m.* worthless piece of paper.

papera [pa·pé·ra] *f.* goiter; **-s** mumps.

paquete [pa·ké·te] *m.* package; bundle; (*buque*) packet boat (*mail boat*); *adj. S.A.* dolled up, dressed up; *Ríopl., Col.* important, pompous; *Ríopl., Col.* insincere.

par [par] *adj.* even; *m.* pair, couple; peer; **a la** — at par; jointly; at the same time; **al** — **de** on a par with; **bajo** — below par; **sin** — peerless, without an equal, having no equal; **sobre** — above par; **de** — **en** — wide-open.

para [pá·ra] *prep.* for; to; toward; in order to; **¿— qué?** what for?; — **que** so that; — **siempre** forever; — **mis adentros** to myself; **sin qué ni** — **qué** without rhyme or reason; *m. Ríopl.* Paraguayan tobacco; *Ríopl.* Paraguayan (*used as nickname*).

parabién [pa·ra·ƀjén] *m.* congratulations; **dar el** — to congratulate.

parabrisas [pa·ra·ƀrí·sas] *m.* windshield.

paracaídas [pa·ra·ka·í·đas] *m.* parachute; **paracaidista** [pa·ra·kaj·đís·ta] *m. & f.* parachutist.

parachoques [pa·ra·čó·kes] *m.* bumper.

parada [pa·rá·đa] *f.* stop; stopping place; bet, stake; military review; *P.R.* parade; *Ríopl.* boastfulness; *Ríopl.* **tener mucha** — to dress very well.

paradero [pa·ra·đé·ro] *m.* stopping place; whereabouts; end.

parado [pa·rá·đo] *p.p. & adj.* stopped; unoccupied, unemployed; fixed, motionless; *Am.* standing, erect, straight up; *Ch., P.R.* stiff, proud; *Ríopl.* cold, unenthusiastic; *P.R., Ch., Andes* **caer uno** — to land on one's feet; to be lucky; *Mex.* **estar bien** — to be well-fixed, well-established; to be lucky; *m. Mex.* air, appearance.

paradoja [pa·ra·đó·xa] *f.* paradox.

paradójico [pa·ra·đó·xi·ko] *adj.* paradoxical.

parafina [pa·ra·fí·na] *f.* paraffin.

paráfrasis [pa·rá·fra·sis] *f.* paraphrase.

paraguas [pa·rá·ǥwas] *m.* umbrella; **paragüero** [pa·ra·gwé·ro] *m.* umbrella stand; umbrella maker or seller.

paraguayo [pa·ra·ǥwá·yo] *adj. & m.* Paraguayan.

paraíso [pa·ra·í·so] *m.* paradise, heaven; upper gallery (*in a theater*).

paraje [pa·rá·xe] *m.* place; spot; situation.

paralelo [pa·ra·lé·lo] *adj.* parallel; similar; *m.* parallel; similarity; **paralela** [pa·ra·lé·la] *f.* parallel line; **paralelismo** [pa·ra·le·líz·mo] *m.* parallelism.

parálisis [pa·rá·li·sis] *f.* paralysis.

paralítico [pa·ra·lí·ti·ko] *adj.* paralytic.

paralizar[9] [pa·ra·li·sár] *v.* to paralyze; to stop.

parámetro [pa·rá·me·tro] *m.* parameter.

páramo [pá·ra·mo] *m.* high, bleak plain; cold region; *Andes* blizzard or a cold drizzle.

parangón [pa·raŋ·gón] *m.* comparison.

parangonar [pa·raŋ·go·nár] *v.* to compare.

paraninfo [pa·ra·nín·fo] *m.* assembly hall, lecture hall, auditorium.

parapeto [pa·ra·pé·to] *m.* parapet.

parar [pa·rár] *v.* to stop; to end, end up, come to an end; to parry (*in fencing*); to set up (*type*); *Am.* to stand, place in upright position; — **atención** to notice; — **mientes en** to observe; notice; *Ríopl.* — **las orejas** to prick up one's ears; to pay close attention; **-se** to stop; *Am.* to stand up, get up.

pararrayos [pa·ra·rrá·yos] *m.* lightning rod.

parásito [pa·rá·si·to] *m.* parasite; *adj.* parasitic.

parasol [pa·ra·sól] *m.* parasol.

parcela [par·sé·la] *f.* parcel of land; particle, small piece.

parcial [par·sjál] *adj.* partial; *m.* follower, partisan; **parcialidad** [par·sja·li·đáđ] *f.* partiality; faction, party.

parche [pár·če] *m.* mending patch; sticking plaster; medicated plaster; drum.

pardal [par·đál] *m.* sparrow; linnet; sly fellow.

pardear [par·đe·ár] *v.* to grow dusky; to appear brownish-grey.

pardo [pár·đo] *adj.* dark-grey; brown; dark; cloudy; *m.* leopard; *Carib., Ríopl.* mulatto; **pardusco** [par·đús·ko] *adj.* greyish; brownish.

parear [pa·re·ár] *v.* to pair, couple, match, mate.

parecer[13] [pa·re·sér] *v. irr.* to seem; to appear, show up; **-se** to resemble each other, look alike; *m.* opinion; appearance, looks; **al** — apparently, seemingly.

parecido [pa·re·sí·đo] *adj.* alike, similar; **bien** — good-looking; *p.p. of* **parecer;** *m.* similarity, likeness, resemblance.

pared [pa·réđ] *f.* wall; — **maestra** main wall; —

medianera partition wall.
paredón [pa·re·đón] *m.* execution wall; thick wall.
pareja [pa·ré·xa] *f.* pair, couple; match; partner; *Am.* team of two horses; *Ríopl.* horse race.
parejero [pa·re·xé·ro] *m. Ríopl.* race horse; *Ríopl.* over-familar person, backslapper, hail fellow-well-met.
parejo [pa·ré·xo] *adj.* even; smooth; equal; *adv. Ríopl.* hard.
parentela [pa·ren·té·la] *f.* relatives, kin.
parentesco [pa·ren·tés·ko] *m.* kinship, relationship.
paréntesis [pa·rén·te·sis] *m.* parenthesis; digression; **entre** — by the way.
pargo [pár·go] *m.* red snapper.
paria [pá·rja] *m. & f.* outcast.
paridad [pa·ri·đáđ] *f.* par, equality, parity.
pariente [pa·rjén·te] *m. & f.* relative, relation.
parir [pa·rír] *v.* to give birth; to bear (*children*).
parlamentar [par·la·men·tár] *v.* to converse; to parley, discuss terms with an enemy.
parlamentario [par·la·men·tá·rjo] *adj.* parliamentary; *m.* member of parliament; envoy to a parley.
parlamento [par·la·mén·to] *m.* speech (*of a character in a play*); parley; parliament, legislative assembly.
parlanchín [par·lan·čín] *adj.* talkative; *m.* talker, chatterer.
parlero [par·lé·ro] *adj.* talkative; gossipy; chattering, chirping.
parlotear [par·lo·te·ár] *v.* to prate, prattle, chatter, chat.
parloteo [par·lo·té·o] *m.* chatter, prattle, idle talk.
paro [pá·ro] *m.* work, stoppage; lockout; *Am.* throw (*in the game of dice*); *Am.* — **y pinta** game of dice.
parodia [pa·ró·đja] *f.* parody, take-off, humorous imitation.
parodiar [pa·ro·đjár] *v.* to parody, take off, imitate.
parótidas [pa·ró·ti·đas] *f. pl.* mumps.
parpadear [par·pa·đe·ár] *v.* to wink; to blink; to flutter the eyelids; to twinkle.
parpadeo [par·pa·đé·o] *m.* winking; blinking; fluttering of the eyelids; twinkling.
párpado [pár·pa·đo] *m.* eyelid.
parque [pár·ke] *m.* park; *Am.* ammunition.
parra [pá·rra] *f.* grapevine; earthenware jug.
parrafada [pa·rra·fá·đa] *f.* chat.
párrafo [pá·rra·fo] *m.* paragraph; **echar un** — **con** to have a chat with.
parral [pa·rrál] *m.* grape arbor.
parranda [pa·rrán·da] *f.* revel, orgy, spree; *Col.* gang, band; **andar** (*or* **ir**) **de** — to go on a spree.
parrandear [pa·rran·de·ár] *v.* to revel, make merry, go on a spree.
parrilla [pa·rrí·ya] *f.* grill, gridiron, broiler; grate.
párroco [pá·rro·ko] *m.* parish priest.
parroquia [pa·rró·kja] *f.* parish; parish church; clientele, customers.
parroquiano [pa·rro·kjá·no] *m.* client, customer; parishioner; *adj.* parochial, of a parish.
parsimonia [par·si·mó·nja] *f.* thrift, economy; moderation; prudence.
parsimonioso [par·si·mo·njó·so] *adj.* thrifty; stingy; cautious; slow.
parte [pár·te] *f.* part; share; place; party (*legal term*); **-s** qualities; **parte** *m.* notice, announcement; *Am.* unnecessary excuses or explanations; **de algún tiempo a esta** — for some time past; **de** — **de** on behalf of; in favor of; **de** — **a** — through, from one side to the other; **dar** — to inform; **echar a mala** — to take amiss; **en** — partly; **por todas -s** everywhere; *m.* telegram; message.
partera [par·té·ra] *f.* midwife.
partición [par·ti·sjón] *f.* partition, division.
participación [par·ti·si·pa·sjón] *f.* participation, share; notice.
participante [par·ti·si·pán·te] *m. & f.* participant; *adj.* participating, sharing.
participar [par·ti·si·pár] *v.* to participate, share; to inform, notify.
partícipe [par·tí·si·pe] *m. & f.* participant; *adj.* participating.
participio [par·ti·sí·pjo] *m.* participle.
partícula [par·tí·ku·la] *f.* particle.
particular [par·ti·ku·lár] *adj.* particular, special; peculiar; private; personal; odd, strange; **en** — specially; **lecciones -es** private lessons; *m.* private citizen; individual; point, detail; matter.
partida [par·tí·đa] *f.* (*salida*) departure, leave; (*entidad*) item, entry; record; band, group; squad; shipment; game; set (*in tennis*); *Am.* part in the hair; — **de bautismo (de matrimonio** *or* **de defunción)** birth (marriage, *or* death) certificate; — **de campo** picnic; — **de caza** hunting party; — **doble** double-entry bookkeeping; *Mex., Ríopl.* **confesar la** — to tell the truth, speak plainly; **jugar una mala** — to play a mean trick.
partidario [par·ti·đá·rjo] *m.* partisan, follower, supporter.
partido [par·tí·đo] *m.* party, faction, group; contest, game; profit; district; *Bol.* **a** (*or* **al**) — in equal shares; *Am.* **dar** — to give a handicap or advantage (*in certain games*); **darse a** — to yield, give up; **sacar** — **de** to derive advantage from, make the best of; **tomar un** — to decide, make a decision.
partir [par·tír] *v.* (*dividir*) to split, divide; to crack, break; (*salir*) to depart, leave; **a** — **de hoy** starting today; from this day on; *Am.* **a** (*or* **al**) — in equal parts; *Am.* — **a uno por el eje** to ruin someone.
partitura [par·ti·tú·ra] *f.* musical score.
parto [pár·to] *m.* childbirth, delivery; product, offspring; **estar de** — to be in labor.
parvada [par·ƀá·đa] *f.* pile of unthreshed grain; brood; *Andes* flock (*of birds or children*).
parvedad [par·ƀe·đáđ] *f.* smallness; trifle; snack, bit of food.
párvulo [pár·ƀu·lo] *m.* child; *adj.* small; innocent.
pasa [pá·sa] *f.* raisin; woolly hair of negros.
pasada [pa·sá·đa] *f.* passing, passage; *Am.* stay; *Col.* embarrassment, shame; **una mala** — a mean trick; **de** — on the way; incidentally, by the way; **dar una** — **por** to pass by, walk by.
pasadizo [pa·sa·dí·so] *m.* aisle; narrow hall; narrow passageway.
pasado [pa·sá·đo] *m.* past; *p.p.* past, gone; *adj.* overripe, spoiled; *Mex.* dried (*fruits*); *Col.* thin, bony (*animal*); — **mañana** day after tomorrow; **el año** — last year; **en días -s** in days gone by.
pasaje [pa·sá·xe] *m.* passage; fare, ticket; total number of passengers; *Carib., Mex., Col.* private alley; *Col., Ven.* anecdote.
pasajero [pa·sa·xé·ro] *adj.* passing, temporary, fleeting, transitory; *m.* passenger; guest (*of a hotel*).
pasamano [pa·sa·má·no] *m.* railing, hand rail; gangplank; gangway (*of a ship*).
pasaporte [pa·sa·pór·te] *m.* passport.
pasar [pa·sár] *v.* to pass; to cross; to surpass, exceed; to pierce; to go forward; to go over (in, by, to); to enter; to carry over, take across; to happen; to get along; to swallow; to overlook; to tolerate; to suffer; — **a la computadora** to feed to the

computer; — **las de Caín** to have a hard time; — **por alto** to omit, overlook; — **por las armas** to execute; **-se** to transfer, change over; to get overripe, spoiled; to exceed, go beyond; **se me pasó decirte** I forgot to tell you; *Ch.* **pasársela a uno** to deceive someone, break someone's confidence; **un buen** — enough to live on.

pasarela [pa·sa·ré·la] *f.* gangplank.

pasatiempo [pa·sa·tjém·po] *m.* pastime; *Am.* cookie.

pascua [pás·kwa] *f.* Easter; Jewish Passover; — **florida** (*or* **de resurrección**) Easter Sunday; — **de Navidad** Christmas.

pase [pá·se] *m.* pass, permit; thrust (*in fencing*); pass (*with the cape in bullfighting*).

pasear [pa·se·ár] *v.* to walk; to take a walk; to ride; **-se** to take a walk; to parade; **-se en automóvil** to take an automobile ride; **-se a caballo** to go horseback riding.

paseo [pa·sé·o] *m.* walk, ride; parade; public park; boulevard; — **en automóvil** automobile ride; **dar un** — to take a walk.

pasillo [pa·sí·yo] *m.* aisle; hallway, corridor; short step; short skit; *Col., Ec.* a type of dance music; *Mex.* runner, hall carpet.

pasión [pa·sjón] *f.* passion; suffering.

pasivo [pa·sí·bo] *adj.* passive; inactive; *m.* liabilities, debts; debit, debit side (*in bookkeeping*).

pasmar [paz·már] *v.* to astound, stun; **-se** to be amazed, stunned; to marvel; to get a sudden chill; to get frostbitten; *P.R.* to become dried up, shriveled up; *P.R., Mex.* to get bruised by the saddle or pack (*said of horses and mules*).

pasmo [páz·mo] *m.* amazement, astonishment; wonder, awe.

pasmoso [paz·mó·so] *adj.* astonishing, astounding; marvellous.

paso [pá·so] *m.* pass; step; pace; gait; passage; passing; skit; incident; *P.R., Ch., Andes* ford; *Mex.* ferry, ferryboat wharf; *adv.* slowly; **de** — by the way, in passing; **al** — **que** while; **salir del** — to get out of a difficulty; *Am.* **marcar el** — to mark step, obey humbly; *adj.* dried (*figs, grapes, prunes, etc.*); **paso a nivel** grade crossing.

pasta [pás·ta] *f.* paste; dough; noodles; book cover, binding; *Am.* cookie, cracker; **de buena** — of good temper or disposition.

pastal [pas·tál] *m. Am.* range, grazing land, large pasture.

pastar [pas·tár] *v.* to pasture, graze.

pastear [pas·te·ár] *v. Mex., Ríopl.* to graze, pasture.

pastel [pas·tél] *m.* pie; pastry roll; filled pastry; trick, fraud; secret pact, plot; pastel crayon; **pintura al** — pastel painting.

pastelería [pas·te·le·rí·a] *f.* pastry shop, bakery; pastry.

pastelero [pas·te·lé·ro] *m.* pastry cook; *Cuba* turncoat (*person who changes easily from one political party to another*); *Ríopl.* political intriguer.

pasterizar[9] [pas·te·ri·sár], **pasteurizar**[9] [pas·tew·ri·sár] *v.* to pasteurize.

pastilla [pas·tí·ya] *f.* tablet (*of medicine, candy, etc.*); bar (*of chocolate*); cake (*of soap*); (*computadora*) chip.

pastinaca [pas·ti·ná·ka] *f.* parsnip.

pastizal [pas·ti·sál] *m.* pasture, grassland.

pasto [pás·to] *m.* pasture; grassland; grazing, nourishment; *Am.* grass; *Ch.* **a todo** — without restraint.

pastor [pas·tór] *m.* shepherd; pastor.

pastoral [pas·to·rál] *adj.* pastoral; *f.* pastoral play; idyll; pastoral letter; **pastorela** [pas·to·ré·la] *f.* pastoral, pastoral play; **pastoril** [pas·tó·ríl] *adj.* pastoral.

pastoso [pas·tó·so] *adj.* pasty, soft; mellow (*said of the voice*); *Am.* grassy.

pastura [pas·tú·ra] *f.* pasture; fodder, feed.

pata [pá·ta] *f.* foot, leg (*of an animal, table, chair, etc.*); female duck; (*computadora*) pin; — **de gallo** crow's-foot (*wrinkle at the corner of the eye*); *Ch., Andes* — **de perro** wanderer; *Ríopl.* **hacer** — **ancha** to stand firm, face a danger; **meter la** — to put one's foot in it, make an embarrassing blunder; **-s arriba** upside down, head over heels.

patacón [pa·ta·kón] *m. Ríopl.* silver coin worth about one peso.

patada [pa·tá·da] *f.* kick; stamp (*with the foot*); footprint; "kick", intoxicating effect; **a -s** with kicks; in great abundance; *Andes* **en dos -s** in a jiffy, in a second.

patalear [pa·ta·le·ár] *v.* to kick around; to stamp.

pataleo [pa·ta·lé·o] *m.* kicking; stamping.

pataleta [pa·ta·lé·ta] *f.* convulsion; fainting fit.

patán [pa·tán] *m.* boor, ill-mannered person; rustic; *adj.* rude, boorish, ill-mannered.

patata [pa·tá·ta] *f.* potato.

patear [pa·te·ár] *v.* to kick; to stamp the foot; to tramp about; to trample on; to humiliate; *Am.* to kick, spring back (*as a gun*); *Ch.* to have a kick or intoxicating effect.

patentar [pa·ten·tár] *v.* to patent.

patente [pa·tén·te] *adj.* patent, evident, clear; *f.* patent; grant; privilege; *Carib.* **de** — excellent, of best quality.

patentizar[9] [pa·ten·ti·sár] *v.* to evidence, reveal, show.

paternal [pa·ter·nál] *adj.* paternal; fatherly.

paternidad [pa·ter·ni·dád] *f.* paternity, fatherhood; authorship.

paterno [pa·tér·no] *adj.* paternal, fatherly.

patético [pa·té·ti·ko] *adj.* pathetic.

patibulario [pa·ti·bu·lá·rjo] *adj.* harrowing, frightful, hair-raising; criminal.

patíbulo [pa·tí·bu·lo] *m.* scaffold, gallows.

patilla [pa·tí·ya] *f.* small foot or paw; *Col., Ven.* watermelon; *Ríopl.* stone or brick bench (*near a wall*); *Ríopl.* railing of a balcony; *Ch.* slip from a plant; **-s** side whiskers; sideburns; **Patillas** [pa·tí·yas] the Devil.

patín [pa·tín] *m.* skate; a small patio; goosander (*a kind of duck*); — **de ruedas** roller skate; **patinadero** [pa·ti·na·dé·ro] *m.* skating rink.

patinar [pa·ti·nár] *v.* to skate; to skid.

patio [pá·tjo] *m.* patio, open court, courtyard; *Am.* railway switchyard; *Am.* **pasarse uno al** — to take undue liberties.

patitieso [pa·ti·tjé·so] *adj.* dumbfounded.

patituerto [pa·ti·twér·to] *adj.* crook-legged; knock-kneed; bow-legged.

patizambo [pa·ti·sám·bo] *adj.* knock-kneed.

pato [pá·to] *m.* duck; **pagar el** — to be the goat; to get the blame; *Ríopl.* **andar** — to be flat broke, penniless; *Am.* hacerse — to play the fool; *Mex., Ríopl.* **pasarse de** — **a ganso** to take undue liberties; *Am.* **ser el** — **de la boda** to be the life of the party; **patito** *m.* duckling.

patochada [pa·to·čá·da] *f.* stupidity, blunder, nonsense.

patojo [pa·tó·xo] *adj.* crooked-legged; bowlegged; *m. & f. Guat.* child; young person.

patología [pa·to·lo·xí·a] *f.* pathology.

patológico [pa·to·ló·xi·ko] *adj.* pathological.

patraña [pa·trá·ña] *f.* fabulous tale; lie, falsehood.

patria [pá·trja] *f.* fatherland, native country.

patriarca [pa·trjár·ka] *m.* patriarch; **patriarcal** [pa·trjar·kál] *adj.* patriarchal.
patrimonio [pa·tri·mó·njo] *m.* patrimony; inheritance.
patrio [pá·trjo] *adj.* native, of one's native country; paternal, belonging to the father.
patriota [pa·trjó·ta] *m. & f.* patriot.
patriótico [pa·trjó·ti·ko] *adj.* patriotic.
patriotismo [pa·trjo·tíz·mo] *m.* patriotism.
patrocinar [pa·tro·si·nár] *v.* to patronize, favor, sponsor.
patrocinio [pa·tro·sí·njo] *m.* patronage, protection.
patrón [pa·trón] *m.* (*protector*) patron; patron saint; sponsor; (*amo*) master, boss; proprietor, landlord; host; skipper; (*dechado*) pattern, standard, model; **patrona** [pa·tró·na] *f.* landlady; patroness; hostess.
patronato [pa·tro·ná·to] *m.* board of trustees; foundation (*for educational, cultural, or charitable purposes*).
patrono [pa·tró·no] *m.* patron, protector; trustee; patron saint.
patrulla [pa·trú·ya] *f.* patrol; squad, gang.
patrullar [pa·tru·yár] *v.* to patrol.
pausa [páw·sa] *f.* pause, stop, rest.
pausar [paw·sár] *v.* to pause.
pauta [páw·ta] *f.* norm, rule, standard; guide lines (*for writing*).
pava [pá·ƀa] *f.* turkey hen; *Ríopl.* kettle, teapot, teakettle; *Andes, Ch.* jest, coarse joke; **pelar la** — to talk by night at the window (*said of lovers*).
pavear [pa·ƀe·ár] *v.* to talk nonsense.
pavesa [pa·ƀé·sa] *f.* cinder; small firebrand; burnt wick or snuff of a candle; **-s** cinders.
pavimentar [pa·ƀi·men·tár] *v.* to pave.
pavimento [pa·ƀi·mén·to] *m.* pavement.
pavo [pá·ƀo] *m.* turkey; *Ch.* sponger, parasite; — **real** peacock; **comer** — to be a wallflower at a dance; *adj.* silly, foolish; vain.
pavón [pa·ƀón] *m.* peacock.
pavonearse [pa·ƀo·ne·ár·se] *v.* to strut, swagger.
pavoneo [pa·ƀo·né·o] *m.* strut, swagger.
pavor [pa·ƀór] *m.* awe, dread, terror.
pavoroso [pa·ƀo·ró·so] *adj.* frightful, dreadful.
payador [pa·ya·đór] *m. Ríopl.* one who sings an improvised song accompanied on the guitar.
payasada [pa·ya·sá·đa] *f.* clownish act or remark.
payasear [pa·ya·se·ár] *v.* to clown, play the fool.
payaso [pa·yá·so] *m.* clown.
paz [pas] *f.* peace.
pazguato [paz·ǥwá·to] *adj.* simple, dumb, stupid; *m.* simpleton.
peaje [pe·á·xe] *m.* toll (*for crossing a bridge or ferry*).
peal [pe·ál] = **pial.**
pealar [pe·a·lár] = **pialar.**
peatón [pe·a·tón] *m.* pedestrian.
peca [pé·ka] *f.* freckle.
pecado [pe·ká·đo] *m.* sin.
pecador [pe·ka·đór] *m.* sinner; *adj.* sinful.
pecaminoso [pe·ka·mi·nó·so] *adj.* sinful.
pecar[6] [pe·kár] *v.* to sin; — **de bueno** to be too good; — **de oscuro** to be exceedingly unclear, too complicated.
pecera [pe·sé·ra] *f.* fish bowl.
pécora [pé·ko·ra] *f.* head of sheep.
pecoso [pe·kó·so] *adj.* freckly, freckled.
peculado [pe·ku·lá·đo] *m.* embezzlement.
peculiar [pe·ku·ljár] *adj.* peculiar; **peculiaridad** [pe·ku·lja·ri·đáđ] *f.* peculiarity.
pechada [pe·čá·đa] *f. Ríopl.* bump, push, shove with the chest; *Arg.* bumping contest between two riders; *Ríopl., Ch.* overthrowing an animal (*by bumping it with the chest of a horse*).
pechar [pe·čár] *v. Ríopl., Ch., Bol.* to bump, push, shove with the chest; *Ríopl., Ch., Bol.* to drive one's horse against; *Ch., Ríopl.* to borrow, strike (*someone*) for a loan.
pechera [pe·čé·ra] *f.* shirtfront; chest protector; bib (*of an apron*).
pecho [pé·čo] *m.* chest; breast; bosom; heart; courage; **dar el** — to nurse; **tomar a -s** to take to heart; *P.R., Col.* **a todo** — shouting; *Am.* **en -s de camisa** in shirt sleeves.
pechuga [pe·čú·ǥa] *f.* breast, breast meat of a fowl; bosom; *C.A., Col., Ch., Andes* courage, nerve, audacity, impudence.
pedagogía [pe·đa·ǥo·xí·a] *f.* pedagogy, science of education.
pedagógico [pe·đa·ǥó·xi·ko] *adj.* pedagogic, relating to education or teaching.
pedagogo [pe·đa·ǥó·ǥo] *m.* pedagogue, teacher, educator.
pedal [pe·đál] *m.* pedal.
pedalear [pe·đa·le·ár] *v.* to pedal.
pedante [pe·đán·te] *adj.* pedantic, affected, vain, superficial; *m.* pedant; **pedantesco** [pe·đan·tés·ko] *adj.* pedantic.
pedazo [pe·đá·so] *m.* piece, portion, bit; **hacer -s** to tear or break into pieces; **caerse a -s** fall into pieces.
pedernal [pe·đer·nál] *m.* flint.
pedestal [pe·đes·tál] *m.* pedestal, base.
pedestre [pe·đés·tre] *adj.* pedestrian, walking, going on foot; commonplace, vulgar, low.
pediatra [pe·đjá·tra] *m., f.* pediatrician; **pediatría** pediatrics.
pedido [pe·đí·đo] *m.* commercial order; request petition; *p.p. of* **pedir.**
pedigüeño [pe·đi·ǥwé·ño] *adj.* begging, demanding.
pedir[5] [pe·đír] *v. irr.* to ask, beg, petition; to ask for; to demand; to require; to order (*merchandise*); **a — de boca** exactly as desired.
pedo [pé·đo] *m.* wind, flatulence; *Mex.* **andar** — to be drunk.
pedrada [pe·đrá·đa] *f.* hit or blow with a stone; throw with a stone; mark or bruise made by a stone (*thrown*); **a -s** by stoning; with stones; **dar una** — to hit with a stone; **echar a alguien a -s** to stone someone out; **matar a -s** to stone to death.
pedregal [pe·đre·ǥál] *m.* rocky ground, ground strewn with rocks.
pedregoso [pe·đre·ǥó·so] *adj.* rocky, stony, pebbly.
pedrería [pe·đre·rí·a] *f.* precious stones; precious stone ornament; jewelry.
pedrusco [pe·đrús·ko] *m.* boulder.
pedúnculo [pe·đúŋ·ku·lo] *m.* stem (*of a leaf, flower or fruit*), stalk.
pegajoso [pe·ǥa·xó·so] *adj.* sticky; contagious.
pegar[7] [pe·ǥár] *v.* (*golpear*) to hit, strike, slap, beat; (*adherir*) to stick, paste, glue; to sew on (*a button*); to infect; to be becoming; to be fitting, opportune, to the point; *Am.* to tie, fasten; *Am.* to yoke; — **fuego** to set on fire; — **un chasco** to play a trick; to surprise; disappoint; — **un susto** to give a scare; — **un salto (una carrera)** to take a jump (a run); **-se** to stick, cling; **pegársela a uno** to fool somebody.
pegote [pe·ǥó·te] *m.* sticky thing; sticking plaster; clumsy patch; sponger; thick, sticky concoction; clumsy addition or insertion (*in a literary or artistic work*).
peinado [pej·ná·đo] *m.* coiffure, hairdo; hairdressing; *p.p.* combed; groomed; *adj.* effeminate; **bien** —

spruce, trim.
peinador [pej·na·đór] *m.* hairdresser; short wrapper or dressing gown; **peinadora** [pej·na·đó·ra] *f.* woman hairdresser.
peinar [pej·nár] *v.* to comb; *Ríopl.* to flatter.
peine [péj·ne] *m.* comb.
peineta [pej·né·ta] *f.* large ornamental comb.
peje [pé·xe] *m. C.A.* fish.
peladilla [pe·la·đí·ya] *f.* small pebble; sugar-coated almond.
pelado [pe·lá·đo] *p.p. & adj.* peeled; plucked; skinned; hairless; featherless; barren, treeless, bare; penniless, broke; *m. Mex.* ragged fellow (*generally a peon*); *Mex.* ill-bred person; *Col.* child.
pelafustán [pe·la·fus·tán] *m.* tramp, vagabond.
pelagatos [pe·la·ǥá·tos] *m.* ragged fellow, tramp.
pelaje [pe·lá·xe] *m.* animal's coat, fur; external appearance.
pelar [pe·lár] *v.* to cut the hair of; to pluck the feathers or hair from; to peel, shell, skin, husk; to fleece, rob; *Am.* to beat, thrash; *Am.* to slander; *C.R.* — **los dientes** to show one's teeth; to smile affectedly; *C.A., Mex., Carib., Col., Andes* — **los ojos** to keep one's eyes peeled; to open one's eyes wide; **-se** to peel off; to lose one's hair; *Col., Ven.* to be confused; *Col., Ven.* to be careless, unaware; *Col., Ven.* to slip away; *Col., Ven.* to die; **pelárselas por algo** to be dying for something, want something very much; **peladora** peeler.
peldaño [pel·dá·ño] *m.* step (*of a staircase*).
pelea [pe·lé·a] *f.* fight, quarrel.
pelear [pe·le·ár] *v.* to fight; to quarrel.
peletería [pe·le·te·rí·a] *f.* fur store; fur trade; furs; *Am.* leather goods, leather shop; *Cuba* shoe store.
pelicano [pe·li·ká·no] *adj.* gray-haired.
pelícano [pe·lí·ka·no] *m.* pelican.
película [pe·lí·ku·la] *f.* thin skin; membrane; film; motion-picture film.
peligrar [pe·li·ǥrár] *v.* to be in danger.
peligro [pe·lí·ǥro] *m.* danger.
peligroso [pe·li·ǥró·so] *adj.* dangerous.
pelillo [pe·lí·yo] *m.* short, fine hair; **-s** trouble, nuisance; **echar -s a la mar** to "bury the hatchet", become reconciled; **no pararse en -s** not to stop at small details, not to bother about trifles; **no tener -s en la lengua** to speak frankly.
pelirrojo [pe·li·rró·xo] *adj.* redheaded, red-haired.
pelo [pé·lo] *m.* (*cabello*) hair; (*haz*) nap (*of cloth*); (*fibra*) grain (*in wood*); **al** — perfectly; agreed; apropos, to the point; along the grain; **eso me viene al** — that suits me perfectly; **con todos sus -s y señales** with every possible detail; *Am.* **por** (*or* **en**) **un** — on the point of, almost, by a hair's breadth; **montar en** — to ride bareback; **tomar el — a** to kid, make fun of; *Ríopl., Carib., Mex., Andes* **no aflojar un** — not to yield an inch.
pelón [pe·lón] *adj.* bald.
pelota [pe·ló·ta] *f.* ball; ball game; *Ríopl.* boat made of cowhide; **en** — (*or* **en -s**) naked; *Am.* **darle a la** — to hit upon by chance; **pelotilla** [pe·lo·tí·ya] *f.* pellet, little ball.
pelotari [pe·lo·tá·ri] *m.* pelota (*jai-alai*) player.
pelotera [pe·lo·té·ra] *f.* brawl, row, riot; *C.A., Ven.* crowd.
pelotón [pe·lo·tón] *m.* large ball; crowd, gang; heap, pile; platoon of soldiers; firing squad.
peluca [pe·lú·ka] *f.* wig.
pelucón [pe·lu·kón] *adj.* wig-wearing; *Ch.* conservative.
peludo [pe·lú·đo] *adj.* hairy; shaggy; *m.* plush carpet with shaggy pile; *Am.* a species of armadillo; *Ríopl.* **agarrar un** — to get drunk.
peluquería [pe·lu·ke·rí·a] *f.* barbershop, hairdresser's shop.
peluquero [pe·lu·ké·ro] *m.* hairdresser, barber.
pelusa [pe·lú·sa] *f.* down; fuzz; nap (*of cloth*).
pellejo [pe·yé·xo] *m.* hide; skin; peel; **salvar el** — to save one's skin, escape punishment; *Am.* **jugarse el** — to gamble one's life.
pellizcar[6] [pe·yis·kár] *v.* to pinch, nip.
pellizco [pe·yís·ko] *m.* pinching, nipping; pinch, nip.
pena [pé·na] *f.* penalty; grief, worry; hardship; toil; *Mex., Carib., C.A., Col., Ven.* embarrassment; **a duras -s** with great difficulty; hardly; **me da** — it grieves me; *C.A., Ven., Col., Carib.* it embarrasses me; **valer la** — to be worthwhile; **tener** (*or* **estar con**) **mucha** — to be terribly sorry; *Am.* to be greatly embarrassed.
penacho [pe·ná·čo] *m.* tuft, crest; plume.
penado [pe·ná·đo] *adj.* afflicted.
penal [pe·nál] *adj.* penal; **código** — penal code.
penalidad [pe·na·li·đáđ] *f.* hardship; trouble; penalty.
penar [pe·nár] *v.* to suffer; to worry, fret; to impose a penalty; — **por** to long for; to suffer because of.
penca [péŋ·ka] *f.* leaf of a cactus plant; *Arg.* sweetheart; *Ven.* **coger una** — to get drunk.
penco [péŋ·ko] *m.* nag, horse; *Am.* boor.
pendencia [pen·dén·sja] *f.* quarrel; scuffle, fight.
pendenciero [pen·den·sjé·ro] *adj.* quarrelsome.
pender [pen·dér] *v.* to hang; to dangle; to depend.
pendiente [pen·djén·te] *f.* slope; *m.* earring; pendant; *Am.* watch chain; *adj.* hanging, dangling; pending.
pendón [pen·dón] *m.* banner.
péndulo [pén·du·lo] *m.* pendulum.
pene [pé·ne] *m.* penis.
penetración [pe·ne·tra·sjón] *f.* penetration; acuteness; keen judgment.
penetrante [pe·ne·trán·te] *adj.* penetrating; acute; keen.
penetrar [pe·ne·trár] *v.* to penetrate; to pierce; to fathom, comprehend.
penicilina [pe·ni·si·lí·na] *f.* penicillin.
península [pe·nín·su·la] *f.* peninsula.
peninsular [pe·nin·su·lár] *adj.* peninsular.
penitencia [pe·ni·tén·sja] *f.* penance.
penitenciaría [pe·ni·ten·sja·rí·a] *f.* penitentiary.
penitente [pe·ni·tén·te] *adj.* repentant, penitent; *m. & f.* penitent.
penoso [pe·nó·so] *adj.* painful; hard, difficult; embarrassing; fatiguing; *Mex., Carib., C.A., Ven., Col.* timid, shy.
pensador [pen·sa·đór] *m.* thinker; *adj.* thinking.
pensamiento [pen·sa·mjén·to] *m.* thought; mind; pansy.
pensar[1] [pen·sár] *v. irr.* to think; to think over; to intend.
pensativo [pen·sa·tí·ƀo] *adj.* pensive.
pensión [pen·sjón] *f.* pension; board; scholarship for study; boardinghouse; *Col.* apprehension, anxiety; — **completa** room and board.
pensionado [pen·sjo·ná·đo] *m.* pensioner (*person receiving a pension*); *adj. & p.p.* pensioned.
pensionar [pen·sjo·nár] *v.* to pension.
pensionista [pen·sjo·nís·ta] *m. & f.* boarder; pensioner (*person receiving a pension*).
pentagrama [pen·ta·ǥrá·ma] *m.* musical staff.
penúltimo [pe·núl·ti·mo] *adj.* next to the last.
penumbra [pe·núm·bra] *f.* partial shadow, dimness.
penumbroso [pe·num·bró·so] *adj.* dim.
peña [pé·ña] *f.* rock, large stone.
peñasco [pe·ñás·ko] *m.* large rock; crag.
peñascoso [pe·ñas·kó·so] *adj.* rocky.

peón [pe·ón] *m.* unskilled laborer; foot soldier; spinning top; pawn (*in chess*); *Ch., Ríopl., C.A., Carib., Mex.* farm hand; *Am.* apprentice; *Mex.* — **de albañil** mason's helper.
peonada [peo·ná·đa] *f.* gang of laborers or peons.
peonaje [pe·o·ná·xe] *m.* gang of laborers.
peonza [pe·on·sa] *f.* top (*toy*).
peor [pe·ór] *adj. & adv.* worse; worst; — **que** worse than; — **que** — that is even worse; **tanto** — so much the worse.
pepa [pé·pa] *f. Andes, Col., Ven., Ch., Mex., Ríopl.* seed (*of an apple, melon, etc.*); *Am.* marble (*to play with*); **Pepa** *nickname for* **Josefa.**
pepenar [pe·pe·nár] *v. Mex.* to pick up; *Am.* to seize, grab.
pepino [pe·pí·no] *m.* cucumber.
pepita [pe·pí·ta] *f.* seed (*of an apple, melon, etc.*); pip (*a disease of birds*); nugget (*lump of gold or other minerals*); *Am.* fruit stone, pit; **Pepita** = **Josefita** *dim. of* **Josefa.**
pequeñez [pe·ke·ñés] *f.* smallness; childhood; trifle; meanness.
pequeño [pe·ké·ño] *adj.* small, little; young; low, humble; *m.* child.
pera [pé·ra] *f.* pear; goatee; sinecure, easy job; *Am.* Peruvian alligator pear (*see* **aguacate**); *Am.* **hacerle a uno la** — to play a trick on someone; **peral** *m.* pear tree; pear orchard.
perca [pér·ka] *f.* perch (*fish*)
percal [per·kál] *m.* percale (*fine cotton cloth*).
percance [per·kán·se] *m.* misfortune, accident; occurrence.
percepción [per·sep·sjón] *f.* perception; idea.
perceptible [per·sep·tí·ƀle] *adj.* perceptible, noticeable.
percibir [per·si·ƀír] *v.* to perceive; to collect, receive.
percudido [per·ku·đí·đo] *adj.* dirty, grimy.
percudir [per·ku·đir] *v.* to soil, make dirty or grimy; **-se** to get grimy.
percusión [per·ku·sjón] *f.* percussion.
percusor [per·ku·sór] *m.* firing pin.
percha [pér·ča] *f.* clothes or hat rack; pole; perch, roost; perch (*a fish*); **perchero** [per·čé·ro] *m.* clothes or hat rack.
perder[1] [per·đér] *v. irr.* to lose; to squander; to ruin, harm; to miss (*a train*); — **de vista** to lose sight of; **-se** to lose one's way; to get lost; to go astray; to get spoiled; to become ruined.
perdición [per·đi·sjón] *f.* perdition, damnation, hell, ruin.
pérdida [pér·đi·đa] *f.* loss; damage.
perdidamente [per·đi·đa·mén·te] *adv.* excessively.
perdido [per·đí·đo] *p.p. & adj.* lost; strayed; mislaid; ruined; **estar** — **por alguien** to be crazy about, or very fond of, someone; *m.* rake, dissolute fellow; bum, vagabond.
perdigar [per·đi·ǥár] *v.* to braise.
perdigón [per·đi·ǥón] *m.* young partridge; bird shot, buckshot; losing gambler.
perdiz [per·đís] *f.* partridge.
perdón [per·đón] *m.* pardon; forgiveness; remission.
perdonar [per·đo·nár] *v.* to pardon; to forgive.
perdulario [per·đu·lá·rjo] *m.* rake, dissolute person; reckless fellow; good-for-nothing; tramp.
perdurable [per·đu·rá·ƀle] *adj.* lasting, everlasting.
perdurar [per·đu·rár] *v.* to last, endure.
perecedero [pe·re·se·đé·ro] *adj.* perishable.
perecer[13] [pe·re·sér] *v. irr.* to perish; to die; **-se** to long (for), pine (for).
peregrinación [pe·re·ǥri·na·sjón] *f.* pilgrimage; long journey.
peregrinar [pe·re·ǥri·nár] *v.* to journey; to go through life.
peregrino [pe·re·ǥrí·no] *m.* pilgrim; *adj.* foreign, strange; rare; beautiful, perfect; travelling, wandering; **ave peregrina** migratory bird, bird of passage.
perejil [pe·re·xíl] *m.* parsley; **-es** frippery, showy clothes or ornaments.
perenne [pe·rén·ne] *adj.* perennial, enduring, perpetual.
pereza [pe·ré·sa] *f.* laziness; idleness.
perezoso [pe·re·só·so] *adj.* lazy; *m. Am.* sloth (*an animal*); *Am.* safety pin; *Ch.* bed cushion.
perfección [per·fek·sjón] *f.* perfection; **a la** — to perfection, perfectly.
perfeccionamiento [per·fek·sjo·na·mjén·to] *m.* perfecting, perfection; completion.
perfeccionar [per·fek·sjo·nár] *v.* to perfect, finish, complete.
perfecto [per·fék·to] *adj.* perfect.
perfidia [per·fí·đja] *f.* perfidy, treachery.
pérfido [pér·fi·đo] *adj.* perfidious, treacherous, faithless.
perfil [per·fíl] *m.* profile; outline; *Col., Ec.* pen or pen point.
perfilar [per·fi·lár] *v.* to silhouette; to outline; **-se** to show one's profile; to be silhouetted.
perforación [per·fo·ra·sjón] *f.* perforation, hole; puncture; perforating, boring, drilling; — **aumentadora** counter bore.
perforar [per·fo·rár] *v.* to perforate, pierce; to drill, bore.
perfumar [per·fu·már] *v.* to perfume, scent.
perfume [per·fú·me] *m.* perfume; fragrance.
perfumería [per·fu·me·rí·a] *f.* perfumery; perfume shop.
pergamino [per·ǥa·mí·no] *m.* parchment.
pericia [pe·rí·sja] *f.* expertness, skill.
perico [pe·rí·ko] *m.* parakeet, small parrot; *Col.* **huevos -s** scrambled eggs.
periferia [pe·ri·fé·rja] *f.* periphery; **periférico** belt-line highway; *adj.* peripheral.
perifollos [pe·ri·fó·yos] *m. pl.* frippery, finery, showy ornaments.
perifrasear [pe·ri·fra·se·ár] *v.* to periphrase.
perífrasis [pe·rí·fra·sis] *f.* periphrase.
perigeo [pe·ri·xé·o] *m.* perigee.
perilla [pe·rí·ya] *f.* small pear; pear-shaped ornament; knob; pommel of a saddle; goatee; **de** — apropos, to the point.
perímetro [pe·rí·me·tro] *m.* perimeter.
periódico [pe·rjó·đi·ko] *m.* newspaper; periodical; *adj.* periodic, periodical.
periodismo [pe·rjo·đíz·mo] *m.* journalism; **periodista** [pe·rjo·đís·ta] *m. & f.* journalist; newspaper editor or publisher; **periodístico** [pe·rjo·đís·ti·ko] *adj.* journalistic.
período [pe·rí·o·đo] [pe·rjó·đo] *m.* period; cycle; sentence.
peripecia [pe·ri·pé·sja] *f.* vicissitude, change in fortune; unforeseen incident.
peripuesto [pe·ri·pwés·to] *adj.* dressed up, dolled up, decked out.
perito [pe·rí·to] *adj.* learned; experienced; skillful; skilled; *m.* expert.
peritoneo [pe·ri·to·né·o] *m.* peritoneum.
peritonitis [pe·ri·to·ní·tis] *f.* peritonitis.
perjudicar[6] [per·xu·đi·kár] *v.* to damage, impair, harm.
perjudicial [per·xu·đi·sjál] *adj.* harmful, injurious.
perjuicio [per·xwí·sjo] *m.* damage, ruin, mischief;

harm.
perjurar [per·xu·rár] *v.* to perjure oneself; to commit perjury; to curse, swear.
perjurio [per·xú·rjo] *m.* perjury.
perla [pér·la] *f.* pearl; **de -s** perfectly, just right, to the point.
perlino [per·lí·no] *adj.* pearly, pearl-colored.
permanecer[13] [per·ma·ne·sér] *v. irr.* to remain, stay.
permanencia [per·ma·nén·sja] *f.* permanence, duration; stability; stay, sojourn.
permanente [per·ma·nén·te] *adj.* permanent.
permiso [per·mí·so] *m.* permission; permit; **con —** with your permission; excuse me.
permitir [per·mi·tír] *v.* to permit, let; to grant.
permuta [per·mú·ta] *f.* exchange, barter.
permutar [per·mu·tár] *v.* to exchange; to barter; to change around.
pernetas [per·né·tas] **en —** barelegged, with bare legs.
pernicioso [per·ni·sjó·so] *adj.* pernicious, harmful.
perno [pér·no] *m.* bolt; spike; **-s** *Ch.* (*trampa*) tricks, frauds.
pero [pé·ro] *conj* but, except, yet; *m.* objection, exception; defect; a variety of apple tree; a variety of apple; **perón** [pe·rón] *m. Am.* a variety of apple.
perogrullada [pe·ro·ǥru·yá·đa] *f.* platitude, trite or commonplace remark.
peroración [pe·ro·ra·sjón] *f.* peroration, speech, harangue.
perorar [pe·ro·rár] *v.* to make an impassioned speech; to declaim, harangue; to plea, make a plea.
perorata [pe·ro·rá·ta] *f.* harangue, speech.
peróxido [pe·rók·si·đo] *m.* peroxide; **— benzoico** benzoyl peroxide.
perpendicular [per·pen·di·ku·lár] *adj., m. & f.* perpendicular.
perpetuar[18] [per·pe·twár] *v.* to perpetuate.
perpetuo [per·pé·two] *adj.* perpetual; **perpetua** [per·pé·twa] *f.* everlasting (*plant*).
perplejidad [per·ple·xi·đáđ] *f.* perplexity.
perplejo [per·plé·xo] *adj.* perplexed, bewildered.
perra [pé·rra] *f.* bitch, female dog; drunkenness; **— chica** five-centime copper coin; **— grande** (*or* **gorda**) ten-centime copper coin.
perrada [pe·rrá·đa] *f.* pack of dogs; **hacer una —** to play a mean trick.
perrera [pe·rré·ra] *f.* kennel; toil, hard work, hard job; tantrum; *Carib., Mex., Ven.* brawl, dispute.
perrilla [pe·rrí·ya] *f. Am.* sty (*on the eyelid*). *See* **orzuelo.**
perro [pé·rro] *m.* dog; **— de arrastre** dog, pawl (machine); **— de busca** hunting dog; **— dogo** bulldog; **— de lanas** poodle; *adj.* dogged, tenacious; *Mex., C.A.* hard, selfish, mean, stingy; *Ven.* vagabond.
perruno [pe·rrú·no] *adj.* canine, doglike.
persecución [per·se·ku·sjón] *f.* persecution; pursuit.
perseguidor [per·se·ǥi·đór] *m.* pursuer; persecutor.
perseguimiento [per·se·ǥi·mjén·to] *m.* pursuit; persecution.
perseguir[5, 12] [per·se·ǥír] *v. irr.* to pursue; to persecute; to harass, annoy.
perseverancia [per·se·ƀe·ran·sja] *f.* perseverance.
perseverar [per·se·ƀe·rár] *v.* to persevere.
persiana [per·sjá·na] *f.* Venetian blind; window shade.
persistencia [per·sis·tén·sja] *f.* persistence; **persistente** [per·sis·tén·te] *adj.* persistent.
persistir [per·sis·tír] *v.* to persist.
persona [per·só·na] *f.* person; personage.
personaje [per·so·ná·xe] *m.* personage; character (*in a book or play*).
personal [per·so·nál] *adj.* personal; *m.* personnel.
personalidad [per·so·na·li·đáđ] *f.* personality; individuality; person, personage.
personalismo [per·so·na·líz·mo] *m.* personalism; individualism.
perspectiva [per·spek·tí·ƀa] *f.* perspective; view; appearance; outlook; prospect.
perspicacia [pers·pi·ká·sja] *f.* keenness of mind, penetration, keen insight.
perspicaz [pers·pi·kás] *adj.* keen, shrewd.
persuadir [per·swa·đír] *v.* to persuade.
persuasión [per·swa·sjón] *f.* persuasion.
persuasivo [per·swa·sí·ƀo] *adj.* persuasive.
pertenecer[13] [per·te·ne·sér] *v. irr.* to belong; to pertain; to concern.
perteneciente [per·te·ne·sjén·te] *adj.* pertaining, belonging, concerning.
pértiga [pér·ti·ǥa] *f.* pole, bar, rod; **salto con —** pole vault.
pertinente [per·ti·nén·te] *adj.* pertinent, to the point, apt, fitting.
pertrechos [per·tré·čos] *m. pl.* military supplies; tools, implements.
perturbación [per·tur·ƀa·sjón] *f.* uneasiness, agitation, disturbance.
perturbar [per·tur·ƀár] *v.* to perturb, disturb.
peruano [pe·rwá·no] *adj. & m.* Peruvian.
perulero [pe·ru·lé·ro] *adj., m & f.* Peruvian (*slang expression*).
perversidad [per·ƀer·si·đáđ] *f.* perversity, wickedness.
perverso [per·ƀér·so] *adj.* perverse, wicked; *m.* pervert.
pervertir[3] [per·ƀer·tír] *v. irr.* to pervert; to corrupt; to distort; **-se** to become perverted; to go wrong.
pesa [pé·sa] *f.* weight (*for scales*); **— de reloj** clock weight; **-s y medidas** weights and measures.
pesadez [pe·sa·dés] *f.* heaviness; dullness, drowsiness; slowness; bother; stubbornness.
pesadilla [pe·sa·đí·ya] *f.* nightmare.
pesado [pe·sá·đo] *adj.* heavy; sound (*sleep*); tiresome, boring; annoying; slow; dull.
pesadumbre [pe·sa·đúm·bre] *f.* grief, sorrow; weight, heaviness.
pésame [pé·sa·me] *m.* condolence, expression of sympathy.
pesantez [pe·san·tés] *f.* gravity; heaviness.
pesar [pe·sár] *v.* (*penar*) to cause grief, sorrow, or regret; (*tener gravedad*) to weigh; to consider, to have weight, value, or importance; *m.* grief, sorrow; **a — de** in spite of.
pesaroso [pe·sa·ró·so] *adj.* grieved, sad; repentant.
pesca [pés·ka] *f.* fishing; catch, fish caught.
pescadería [pes·ka·đe·rí·a] *f.* fish market; **pescadero** [pes·ka·đé·ro] *m.* fishmonger, dealer in fish.
pescado [pes·ká·đo] *m.* fish (*especially after being caught*); salted codfish.
pescador [pes·ka·đór] *m.* fisherman.
pescar[6] [pes·kár] *v.* to fish; to catch; to catch unaware, catch in the act.
pescozón [pes·ko·són] *m.* blow on the back of the head or neck.
pescuezo [pes·kwé·so] *m.* neck.
pesebre [pe·sé·ƀre] *m.* manger.
peseta [pe·sé·ta] *f.* peseta (*monetary unit of Spain*).
pesimismo [pe·si·míz·mo] *m.* pessimism; **pesimista** [pe·si·mís·ta] *m. & f.* pessimist; *adj.* pessimistic.
pésimo [pé·si·mo] *adj.* very bad.
peso [pé·so] *m.* weight; weighing; burden; importance; *Am.* peso (*monetary unit of several Spanish American countries*).

pespunte [pes·pún·te] *m.* backstitching.
pesquera [pes·ké·ra] *f.* fishery (*place for catching fish*); **pesquería** [pes·ke·rí·a] *f.* fishery; fishing.
pesquero [pes·ké·ro] *adj.* fishing; **buque** — fishing boat; **industria pesquera** fishing industry.
pesquisa [pes·kí·sa] *f.* investigation, inquiry; *m. Am.* police investigator.
pestaña [pes·tá·ña] *f.* eyelash; edging, fringe; **quemarse las -s** to burn the midnight oil, study hard at night.
pestañear [pes·ta·ñe·ár] *v.* to blink; to wink; to flicker.
peste [pés·te] *f.* pest, pestilence, plague; epidemic; stench, stink, foul odor; overabundance, excess; *Arg., Ch.* smallpox; *Col.* head cold; **echar -s** to utter insults.
pestillo [pes·tí·yo] *m.* bolt; latch; lock.
pesuña [pe·sú·ña] *f.* hoof (*cloven*).
pesuño [pe·sú·ño] *m.* half of the cloven hoof.
petaca [pe·tá·ka] *f.* tobacco pouch; cigar case; leather covered hamper (*used as a pack*); *Mex.,* trunk; *adj. Andes* heavy, clumsy.
pétalo [pé·ta·lo] *m.* petal.
petate [pe·tá·te] *m.* bundle; impostor; *Mex., C.A., Ven., Col.* mat (*of straw or palm leaves*); *Am.* dunce; *Andes* coward; **llar el** — to pack up and go; *Mex.* to die; *Col., Ven.* **dejar a uno en un** — to ruin a person, leave him penniless.
petición [pe·ti·sjón] *f.* petition, request.
petirrojo [pe·ti·rró·xo] *m.* robin, robin redbreast.
petiso [pe·tí·so] *adj. Ríopl., Ch., Andes* small, short, dwarfish; *m. Am.* small horse, pony.
pétreo [pé·tre·o] *adj.* stone, stony.
petróleo [pe·tró·le·o] *m.* petroleum.
petrolero [pe·tro·lé·ro] *m.* oil man; dealer in petroleum; **compañía petrolera** oil company.
petulancia [pe·tu·lán·sja] *f.* flippancy; insolence; **petulante** [pe·tu·lán·te] *adj.* impertinent, flippant.
petunia [pe·tú·nja] *f.* petunia.
pez [pes] *m.* fish; *f.* pitch, tar.
pezón [pe·són] *m.* nipple; stem, stalk (*of a fruit, leaf or flower*); small point of land.
pezuña [pe·sú·ña] *f.* hoof.
piadoso [pja·đó·so] *adj.* pious; kind, merciful.
pial [pjal] *m. Mex.* lasso, lariat (*thrown in order to trip an animal*); *Ríopl.* snare, trap.
pialar [pja·lár] *v.* to lasso by tripping with a **pial.**
piano [pjá·no] *m.* piano; — **de cola** grand piano; — **vertical** upright piano.
piar[17] [pjar] *v.* to peep, chirp; to cry, whine.
pibe [pí·be] *m. Ríopl.* urchin, boy.
pica [pí·ka] *f.* pike, spear; picador's goad or lance; stonecutter's hammer; *Ven.* tapping of rubber trees; *Col.* trail; *Col., Ch.* pique, resentment; *Am.* cockfight.
picada [pi·ká·đa] *f.* prick; bite (*as of an insect or fish*); puncture; sharp pain; dive (*of a plane*); *Cuba, Ríopl.* path, trail (*cut through a forest*); *Am.* narrow ford; *Col., Ven., Mex.* peck.
picadillo [pi·ka·đí·yo] *m.* meat and vegetable hash; minced meat, mincemeat.
picador [pi·ka·đór] *m.* picador (*mounted bullfighter armed with a goad*); horse-breaker; chopping block; *Ven.* tree tapper.
picadura [pi·ka·đú·ra] *f.* biting; pricking; bite; prick; sting; puncture; cut tobacco.
picante [pi·kán·te] *adj.* (*acerbo*) pricking, biting stinging; (*con chile o ají*) spicy; highly seasoned; *m.* strong seasoning; *Am.* highly seasoned sauce (*usually containing chili pepper*).
picapleitos [pi·ka·pléj·tos] *m.* quarrelsome person (*one who likes to pick a fight*); shyster.
picaporte [pi·ka·pór·te] *m.* latch; latchkey; door knocker.
picar[6] [pi·kár] *v.* to prick; to pierce; to bite (*said of fish or insects*); to sting; to peck; to nibble; to mince, chop up; to goad; to stick, poke; to hew, chisel; to pique, vex; to itch, smart, burn; *Am.* to chop (*wood*); *Mex., Carib.* to open a trail; *Am.* to tap (*a tree*); *Am.* to slaughter (*cattle*); — **muy alto** to aim very high; — **en** to border on, be somewhat of; *Mex., Ven.* **¡pícale!** [pí·ka·le] hurry! **-se** to be piqued, angry; to be motheaten; to begin to sour; to begin to rot; *C.A., Ven.* to get tipsy; **-se de** to boast of.
picardía [pi·kar·đí·a] *f.* roguishness; offensive act or remark; roguish trick; mischief.
picaresco [pi·ka·rés·ko] *adj.* picaresque, roguish.
pícaro [pí·ka·ro] *m.* rogue, rascal; *adj.* roguish; mischievous; crafty, sly; low, vile; **picarón** [pa·ka·rón] *m.* big rascal.
picazo [pi·ká·so] *adj.* piebald; *m.* piebald horse.
picazón [pi·ka·són] *f.* itch, itching.
pico [pí·ko] *m.* beak, bill; sharp point; peak, pickaxe, pick, spout; mouth; additional amount, a little over; *C.A., Carib., Ríopl., Ven.* a small balance; *Mex.* a goodly sum; **tener el** — **de oro** to be very eloquent; **tener mucho** — to be very talkative.
picotada [pi·ko·tá·đa] *f.*, **picotazo** [pi·ko·tá·so] *m.* peck.
picotear [pi·ko·te·ár] *v.* to peck; to chatter; *Am.* to mince, cut into small pieces.
pichel [pi·čél] *m.* pitcher; mug.
pichón [pi·čón] *m.* young pigeon; *C.A.* any male bird (*except a rooster*); *Mex.* dupe, easy mark; *Am.* novice, inexperienced person, apprentice, *adj. Am.* timid, shy.
pie [pje] *m.* foot; leg; stand; stem; base; *Am.* down payment; *Mex.* strophe, stanza; *Am.* — **de amigo** wedge; prop; — **de banco** silly remark; **a** — **juntillas** steadfastly, firmly; **al** — **de la letra** to the letter, literally, exactly; **de** — (*or* **en** —) standing; **a cuatro -s** on all fours; **dar** — to give an opportunity or occasion; *Am.* **estar a** — **en** to be ignorant of; **ir a** — to walk.
piececito [pje·se·sí·to], **piecito** [pje·sí·to] *m.* little foot.
piedad [pje·đáđ] *f.* piety; pity; mercy; **monte de** — pawnshop.
piedra [pjé·đra] *f.* stone; gravel; hailstone; *Ven.* piece of a domino set; — **angular** (*or* **fundamental**) cornerstone; — **caliza** limestone; — **de aceite;** oil stone; — **de amolar** hone; — **pómez** pumice, pumice stone; **a** — **y lodo** shut tight; **ser** — **de escándalo** to be an object of scandal.
piel [pjel] *f.* skin; hide; leather; fur.
piélago [pjé·la·go] *m.* high sea; sea; great abundance, great plenty.
pienso [pjén·so] *m.* feed; thought; **ni por** — not even in thought.
pierna [pjér·na] *f.* leg; **dormir a** — **suelta** to sleep like a log, sleep soundly; *Am.* **ser una buena** — to be a good fellow, be always in a good mood.
pieza [pjé·sa] *f.* (*pedazo*) piece; part; (*cuarto*) room; (*comedia*) play; **de una** — solid, in one piece; *Am.* **ser de una** — to be an honest, upright man.
pífano [pí·fa·no] *m.* fife.
pifia [pí·fja] *f.* a miss, miscue.
pigmento [pig·men·to] *m.* pigment.
pijama [pi·yá·ma] [pi·xá·ma] *m.* pajamas.
pila [pí·la] *f.* (*pieza cóncava*) basin; baptismal font, trough; (*cúmulo*) pile; heap; electric battery; — **atómica** atomic pile; *Am.* fountain; *Andes* hairless

dog; *N. Arg.* bald head; **nombre de** — Christian name; *Andes* **andar** — to go naked; *Mex.* **tener las -s** (*or* **tener por -s**) to have a lot, have heaps.
pilar [pi·lár] *m.* pillar, column; basin of a fountain.
pilcha [píl·ča] *f. Ríopl.* any article of clothing; *Ríopl., Ch.* mistress; **-s** *Ríopl.* belongings.
píldora [píl·do·ra] *f.* pill.
pilmama [pil·má·ma] *f. Mex.* child's nurse, wet nurse.
pilón [pi·lón] *m.* basin (*of a fountain*); watering trough; sugar loaf; large wooden or metal mortar (*for grinding grain*); counterpoise; *Mex.* an additional amount, premium (*given to a buyer*); *Mex.* **de** — to boot, in addition, besides; **piloncillo** [pi·lon·sí·yo] *m. Mex.* unrefined sugar loaf.
pilotar [pi·lo·tár], **pilotear** [pi·lo·te·ár] *v.* to pilot.
pilote [pi·ló·te] *m.* pile (*for building*).
piloto [pi·ló·to] *m.* pilot; *Mex.* generous entertainer or host.
pillaje [pi·yá·xe] *m.* pillage, plunder.
pillar [pi·yár] *v.* to pillage, plunder; to pilfer; to seize, snatch, grasp; to catch; *Mex., P.R., Arg.* to surprise, catch in the act.
pillo [pí·yo] *adj.* roguish; sly, crafty; *m.* rogue, rascal; *Ch.* a species of heron; *Ch.* long-legged person; **pilluelo** [pi·ywé·lo] *m.* little rascal, scamp.
pimentero [pi·men·té·ro] *m.* pepper plant; pepperbox, pepper shaker.
pimentón [pi·men·tón] *m.* large pepper; cayenne, red pepper; paprika.
pimienta [pi·mjén·ta] *f.* black pepper.
pimiento [pi·mjén·to] *m.* green pepper; red pepper.
pimpollo [pim·pó·yo] *m.* rosebud; bud; shoot, sprout; attractive youth.
pináculo [pi·ná·ku·lo] *m.* pinnacle, top, summit.
pinar [pi·nár] *m.* pine grove.
pincel [pin·sél] *m.* artist's brush; **pincelada** [pin·se·lá·đa] *f.* stroke of the brush.
pinchar [pin·čár] *v.* to prick; to puncture.
pinchazo [pin·čá·so] *m.* prick; puncture; stab.
pingajo [piŋ·gá·xo] *m.* tag, tatter, rag.
pingo [píŋ·go] *m. Ríopl., Andes* saddle horse; *Mex.* devil.
pingüe [píŋ·gwe] *adj.* abundant, copious; fat, greasy.
pingüino [piŋ·gwí·no] *m.* penguin.
pino [pí·no] *m.* pine; *Ch.* filling for a meat pie; **hacer -s** (*or* **hacer pinitos**) to begin to walk (*said of a baby*); to begin to do things (*said of a novice*).
pinta [pín·ta] *f.* spot, mark; outward sign, aspect; pint; *Mex.* **hacer** — to play hooky, cut class.
pintar [pin·tár] *v.* to paint; to describe, depict; to feign; to begin to turn red, begin to ripen (*said of fruit*); to fancy, imagine; *Mex.* to play hooky, play truant; *S.A.* to fawn, flatter; **no — nada** to be worth nothing, count for nothing; **las cosas no pintaban bien** things did not look well; *Mex.* — **venados** to play hooky; **-se** to put on make-up; *Arg.* to excel (in); to praise oneself; *Ven.* to go away.
pintarrajear [pin·ta·rra·xe·ár] *v.* to daub; to smear with paint or rouge.
pinto [pín·to] *adj. Am.* spotted, speckled.
pintor [pin·tór] *m.* painter, artist; — **de brocha gorda** house painter; poor artist; *adj. Am.* boastful, conceited.
pintoresco [pin·to·rés·ko] *adj.* picturesque.
pintura [pin·tú·ra] *f.* painting; picture; paint, color; description.
pinzas [pín·sas] *f. pl.* pincers; tweezers; claws (*of lobsters, crabs, etc.*); *Ríopl., Mex., Carib.* pliers, tongs.
piña [pí·ña] pineapple; pine cone; piña cloth; cluster; *Cuba* pool (*a billiard game*).
piñata [pi·ñá·ta] *f.* pot; hanging pot or other container (*filled with candies, fruit, etc.*).
piñón [pi·ñón] *m.* pine nut; nut pine; pinion.
pío [pí·o] *adj.* pious, devout; kind; merciful; dappled, spotted (*horse*); **obras pías** pious works, charitable deeds.
piocha [pjó·ča] *adj. Mex.* great! excellent.
piojo [pjó·xo] *m.* louse.
piojoso [pjo·xó·so] *adj.* lousy; mean, stingy.
pionero [pjo·né·ro] *m.* pioneer; boy scout.
pip (piip) [pip, piíp] *m.* beep.
pipa [pí·pa] *f.* tobacco pipe; (*barril*) keg, barrel; reed pipe (*musical instrument*); fruit seed (*of a lemon, orange, melon*); *Col.* green coconut; *Am.* potato; *Ven.* **estar** — to be drunk; *m. Ch.* species of green frog.
pipiar[17] [pi·pjár] *v.* to peep, chirp.
pipiolo [pi·pjó·lo] *m.* novice, beginner; *Am.* child, youngster.
pique [pí·ke] *m.* pique, resentment; chigger (*insect*); flea; *Am.* small chili pepper; *Arg.* trail; **a — de** in danger of, on the point of; **echar a** — to sink (*a ship*); to destroy; **irse a** — to capsize; to sink.
piquete [pi·ké·te] *m.* prick; bite, sting (*of insects*); small hole; picket, stake; picket (*military*); *Cuba* small band of musicians; *Arg., Col.* small corral; *Am.* cutting edge of scissors.
piragua [pi·rá·gwa] *f. Ríopl., Carib., Ven., Col., Andes* Indian canoe; dugout.
pirámide [pi·rá·mi·đe] *f.* pyramid.
pirata [pi·rá·ta] *m.* pirate.
piratear [pi·ra·te·ár] *v.* to pirate.
piropo [pi·ró·po] *m.* flattery, compliment; a variety of garnet (*a semiprecious stone*); **echar un** — to "throw a bouquet"; to compliment.
pirotecnia [pi·ro·ték·nja] *f.* pyrotechnics; fireworks.
pirueta [pi·rwé·ta] *f.* whirl; somersault; caper; **hacer -s** to cut capers; to turn somersaults; to do stunts.
pisada [pi·sá·đa] *f.* footstep; footprint; **dar una** — to step on, stamp on; **seguir las -s de** to follow in the footsteps of; to imitate.
pisapapeles [pi·sa·pa·pé·les] *m.* paperweight.
pisar [pi·sár] *v.* to step on, tread upon; to trample under foot; to pound; to cover (*said of a male bird*).
piscina [pi·sí·na] *f.* swimming pool, swimming tank; fish pond.
pisco [pís·ko] *m. Peru, Col.* fine anisette made in Pisco, Peru.
pise [pí·se] *m. Ven.* rut; *Ch.* tread (*of a wheel*). *See* **rodadura.**
piso [pí·so] *m.* floor; story; pavement; apartment, flat; tread; *Ríopl., Mex., Carib., Ven.* fee for pasturage rights; *Mex., Ch.* table scarf; *Am.* stool, footstool; *Am.* small rug.
pisón [pi·són] *m.* heavy mallet (*for pounding, flattening, crushing*).
pisotear [pi·so·te·ár] *v.* to tramp, tramp on, trample; to tread.
pisotón [pi·so·tón] *m.* hard step, stamp (*of the foot*); **dar un** — to step hard, stamp (upon).
pista [pís·ta] *f.* track, trace, trail; clew; race track; — **de aterrizaje** landing field.
pistola [pis·tó·la] *f.* pistol; **pistolera** [pis·to·lé·ra] *f.* holster.
pistolero [pis·to·lé·ro] *m.* gangster; body guard.
pistón [pis·tón] *m.* piston; *Col.* cornet.
pita [pí·ta] *f. Am.* agave or century plant; *Am.* fiber, or thread made from the fiber, of the agave or

maguey.

pitar [pi·tár] *v.* to toot; to whistle; *Ríopl., Andes* to smoke; *Ven.* to hiss; *Carib., Mex.* to slip away, escape; *Am.* **-se una cosa** to steal something; *Ch., Col., Ven., C.A.* (*pitado*) **salir pitando** to leave on the run.

pitazo [pi·tá·so] *m.* toot, whistle, blast.

pitillo [pi·tí·yo] *m. Spain* cigarette; **pitillera** [pi·ti·yé·ra] *f.* cigarette case.

pito [pí·to] *m.* whistle; cigarette; *Am.* tick (*an insect*); **no vale un** — it is not worth a straw; *Am.* **no saber ni — de una cosa** not to know anything about a subject.

pitón [pi·tón] *m.* lump; horn of an animal.

pizarra [pi·sá·rra] *f.* slate; blackboard; **pizarrín** [pi·sa·rrín] *m.* slate pencil; **pizarrón** [pi·sa·rrón] *m.* blackboard.

pizca [pís·ka] *f.* pinch, small bit; *Mex.* harvest.

placa [plá·ka] *f.* badge, insignia; plaque, tablet; metal plate; photographic plate; license plate; (*computadora*) board, card; *Ven.* scab or skin blemish.

placentero [pla·sen·té·ro] *adj.* pleasant, agreeable.

placer[38] [pla·sér] *v. irr.* to please, content; *m.* pleasure; sand bank, shoal; placer (*place where gold is obtained by washing*); *Am.* pearl fishing.

placero [pla·sé·ro] *m.*, **placera** *f.* market vendor.

plácido [plá·si·đo] *adj.* placid, calm.

plaga [plá·ǥa] *f.* plague; calamity.

plagar[7] [pla·ǥár] *v.* to plague, infest; **-se de** to become plagued or infested with.

plagiar [pla·xjár] *v.* to plagiarize, steal and use as one's own (*the writings, ideas, etc. of another*); to kidnap, abduct.

plan [plan] *m.* plan; design; project; drawing; mine floor; *C.A., Cuba, Ch.* clearing; *Am.* building grounds of a ranch.

plana [plá·na] *f.* page (*of a newspaper*); plain, flat country; mason's trowel; tally sheet; **enmendar la — a uno** to correct a person's mistakes.

plancton [pláŋk·ton] *m.* plankton.

plancha [plán·ča] *f.* flatiron; metal plate; gangplank; blunder; *Cuba* railway flatcar; *Ven., Col.* dental plate; — **de blindaje** armor plate; **hacer una** — to make a ridiculous blunder; **tirarse una** — to place oneself in a ridiculous situation.

planchado [plan·čá·đo] *m.* ironing; clothes ironed or to be ironed; *adj. Am.* smart, clever; *Mex.* brave; *Ven.* dolled up, dressed up; *Peru, Ch.* broke, penniless.

planchar [plan·čár] *v.* to iron; to smooth out; *Mex.* to leave (*someone*) waiting; *Ven., Arg.* to strike with the flat of a blade; *P.R.* to flatter; *Mex., Ven.* — **el asiento** to be a wallflower at a dance.

planeador [pla·ne·a·đór] *m.* glider airplane.

planear [pla·ne·ár] *v.* to plan; to glide (*said of an airplane or bird*).

planeo [pla·né·o] *m.* planning; glide, gliding (*of an airplane*).

planeta [pla·né·ta] *m.* planet.

planetario [pla·ne·tá·rjo] *m.* planetary.

plano [plá·no] *adj.* plane, flat, level; *m.* plane; plan; map; **de** — flatly, clearly, openly; **dar de** — to hit with the flat of anything.

planta [plán·ta] *f.* (*ser orgánico*) plant; plantation; (*proyecto*) plan; ground plan, ground floor; (*del pie*) sole of the foot; — **baja** ground floor; **buena** — good looks; **echar -s** to brag.

plantación [plan·ta·sjón] *f.* plantation; planting.

plantar [plan·tár] *v.* plant; to strike (*a blow*); **-se** to stand firm; to balk; *C.A.* to doll up, dress up; **dejar a uno plantado** to "stand someone up", keep someone waiting indefinitely.

plantear [plan·te·ár] *v.* to plan; to establish; to carry out; to state, present (*a problem*); to try.

plantel [plan·tél] *m.* establishment; firm; plant; nursery.

plantío [plan·tí·o] *m.* planting; plantation; recently planted garden; tree nursery.

plañidero [pla·ñi·đé·ro] *m.* professional mourner.

plasma [pláz·ma] *m.* plasma.

plástico [plás·ti·ko] *adj.* plastic; **-s reforzados con fibra de vidrio** fiber glass.

plata [plá·ta] *f.* silver; silver money; **hablar en** — to speak in plain language; *Carib., C.A., Ven., Col.* money.

plataforma [pla·ta·fór·ma] *f.* platform; — **de lanzamiento** launching pad.

platanal [pla·ta·nál], **platanar** [pla·ta·nár] *m.* grove of banana trees; banana plantation.

plátano [plá·ta·no] *m.* banana; banana tree; plane tree.

platea [pla·té·a] *f.* main floor of a theatre; a lower box seat.

plateado [pla·te·á·đo] *adj.* silver-plated; silvery.

platear [pla·te·ár] *v.* to silver, plate, cover with silver.

platel [pla·tél] *m.* platter; tray.

platero [pla·té·ro] *m.* silversmith; jeweler.

plática [plá·ti·ka] *f.* conversation, talk, chat; informal lecture.

platicador [pla·ti·ka·đór] *m.* talker; *adj.* talkative.

platicar[6] [pla·ti·kár] *v.* to converse, talk, chat.

platillo [pla·tí·yo] *m.* saucer; pan (*of a pair of scales*); cymbal; stew.

platino [pla·tí·no] *m.* platinum.

plato [plá·to] *m.* plate; dish; dinner course; — **de tocadiscos** turntable; — **de sujeción** chuck (machine).

platón [pla·tón] *m.* large plate; platter.

platudo [pla·tú·đo] *adj. Am.* wealthy, rich.

playa [plá·ya] *f.* beach, shore; *Ven.* wide, open space in front of a ranch house; *Ríopl., Andes* — **de estacionamiento** parking lot.

plaza [plá·sa] *f.* (*pública*) plaza, public square; public market; (*empleo*) job; employment; *Ríopl., Ch., Cuba, Ven.* park, promenade; — **de armas** parade ground; public square; fortress; — **fuerte** fortress; — **de gallos** cockpit (*for cockfights*); — **de toros** bull ring; **sacar a** — to bring out into the open, make public; **sentar** — to enlist; **plazoleta** [pla·so·lé·ta], **plazuela** [pla·swé·la] *f.* small square, court.

plazo [plá·so] *m.* term, time; **a** — on credit; in installments.

pleamar [ple·a·már] *m.* flood tide, high tide.

plebe [plé·ƀe] *f.* rabble; masses.

plebeyo [ple·ƀé·yo] *adj.* plebeian.

plebiscito [ple·ƀi·sí·to] *m.* plebiscite, direct vote.

plegadizo [ple·ǥa·đí·so] *adj.* folding; pliable, easily bent.

plegar[1, 7] [ple·ǥár] *v.* to fold; to pleat; to crease; **-se** to bend, yield, submit.

plegaria [ple·ǥá·rja] *f.* supplication, prayer, prayer hour.

pleito [pléj·to] *m.* litigation, lawsuit; dispute; debate; duel; — **de acreedores** bankruptcy proceedings; **pleitista** *m. & f.* quarrelsome person.

plenario [ple·ná·rjo] *adj.* plenary (*session*).

plenipotenciario [ple·ni·po·ten·sjá·rjo] *m.* plenipotentiary (*diplomatic agent having full power or authority*); *adj.* plenipotentiary, having full

PI

power.
plenitud [ple·ni·túđ] *f.* plenitude, fullness, completeness; abundance.
pleno [plé·no] *adj.* full, complete; **sesión plena** joint session; **en — día** in broad daylight, openly; **en — rostro** (*or* **en plena cara**) right on the face; *m.* joint session (*of a legislative body*).
pleuresía [plew·re·sí·a] *f.* pleurisy.
pliego [pljé·ǥo] *m.* sheet of paper; sealed letter or document.
pliegue [pljé·ǥe] *m.* fold, crease, pleat.
plomada [plo·má·đa] *f.* plumb, lead weight, plumb bob.
plomazo [plo·má·so] *m. Col., Ven., Mex.* shot, bullet.
plomería [plo·me·rí·a] *f.* plumbing; plumber's shop; lead roof.
plomero [plo·mé·ro] *m.* plumber.
plomizo [plo·mí·so] *adj.* leaden, lead-colored.
plomo [pló·mo] *m.* lead; plumb, lead weight; bullet; boring person; **a —** vertical; vertically; *adj. Carib., Mex.* lead-colored.
pluma [plú·ma] *f.* (*de ave*) feather; plume; (*instrumento*) pen; quill; **— estilográfica** (*or* **— fuente**) fountain pen; **plumada** [plu·má·đa] *f.* dash, stroke of the pen, flourish; **plumaje** [plu·má·xe] *m.* plumage; plume, **plumero** [plu·mé·ro] *m.* feather duster; box for feathers; feather ornament (*on hats, helmets, etc.*); **plumón** [plu·món] *m.* down; feather mattress; **plumoso** [plu·mó·so] *adj.* downy, feathery.
plural [plu·rál] *adj.* plural.
plutonio [plu·tó·njo] *m.* plutonium.
pluralidad [plu·ra·li·đáđ] *f.* plurality.
pluvial [plu·ƀjál] *adj.* rain (*used as adj.*); **capa —** cope (*long cape used by priests during certain religious ceremonies*).
pluviómetro [plu·ƀjó·me·tro] *m.* rain gauge.
población [po·ƀla·sjón] *f.* (*acto*) populating; settlement; (*número*) population; (*lugar*) town, city.
poblado [po·ƀlá·đo] *m.* inhabited place; village; *p.p.* populated; covered with growth.
poblador [po·ƀla·đór] *m.* settler (*of a colony*).
poblar[2] [po·ƀlár] *v. irr.* to populate, people; to colonize, settle; to stock (*a farm*); to breed; **-se** to become covered (*with leaves or buds*).
pobre [pó·ƀre] *adj.* poor; *m.* poor man; beggar; **pobrete** [po·ƀré·te] *m.* poor devil, poor wretch; **pobretón** [po·ƀre·tón] *m.* poor old fellow, poor wretch.
pobreza [po·ƀré·sa] *f.* poverty; need; lack, scarcity; barrenness.
pocilga [po·síl·ǥa] *f.* pigsty, pigpen.
pocillo [po·sí·yo] *m.* cup.
poco [pó·ko] *adj.* little, scanty; small; short (*time*); **-s** few, some; *m.* a little, a bit; *adv.* little; **a —** presently, after a short time; **a — rato** (*or* **al — rato**) after a short while; **— a —** slowly, little by little; **a los -s meses** after a few months; **por — me caigo** I almost fell; **tener en — a** to hold in low esteem.
podadera [po·đa·đé·ra] *f.* pruning hook or knife.
podar [po·đár] *v.* to prune, trim, cut off.
podenco [po·đéŋ·ko] *m.* hound.
poder[39] [po·đér] *v. irr.* to be able; can; may; **él puede mucho** (*or* **poco**) he has much (*or* little) power; **puede que** it is possible that, it may be that, perhaps; **hasta más no —** to the utmost, to the limit; **no — más** not to be able to do more; to be exhausted; **no puede menos de hacerlo** he cannot help doing it; **no — con la carga** not to be equal to the burden, not to be able to lift the load; *Col., Ven.* **-le a uno algo** to be worried or affected by something, *m.* power, authority.
poderío [po·đe·rí·o] *m.* power, dominion; might; wealth.
poderoso [po·đe·ró·so] *adj.* powerful; wealthy.
podre [pó·đre] *f.* pus; decayed matter; **podredumbre** [po·đre·đúm·bre] *f.* corruption, decay; pus; rotten matter.
podrido [po·đrí·đo] *adj.* rotten; *p.p. of* **podrir.**
podrir[16] [po·đrír] = **pudrir**[16]
poema [po·é·ma] *m.* poem.
poesía [po·e·sí·a] *f.* poetry; poem.
poeta [po·é·ta] *m.* poet; **poetastro** [po·e·tás·tro] *m.* bad poet.
poético [po·é·ti·ko] *adj.* poetic; **poética** [po·é·ti·ka] *f.* poetics.
poetisa [po·e·tí·sa] *f.* poetess.
polaco [po·lá·ko] *adj.* Polish; *m.* Polish, Polish language; Pole.
polaina [po·láj·na] *f.* legging.
polar [po·lár] *adj.* polar.
polea [po·lé·a] *f.* pulley; **— cono** cone pulley.
polémica [po·lé·mi·ka] *f.* controversy; polemics.
polen [pó·len] *m.* pollen.
policía [po·li·sí·a] *f.* police; *m.* policeman.
policial [po·li·sjál] *m. Col., Ven.* policeman.
policíaco [po·li·sjá·ko] [po·li·sí·a·ko] *adj.* police, detective (*story*).
poligamia [po·li·ǥá·mja] *f.* polygamy.
políglota [po·lí·ǥlo·ta] *m. & f.* polyglot; one who speaks several languages.
polilla [po·lí·ya] *f.* moth; larva of the moth.
poliomielitis [po·ljo·mje·lí·tis] *f.* poliomyelitis, polio.
política [po·lí·ti·ka] *f.* politics; policy; *Am.* **— de campanario** politics of a clique.
politicastro [po·lí·ti·kás·tro] *m.* bad or incapable politician.
político [po·lí·ti·ko] *adj.* political; politic; polite; **madre política** mother-in-law; *m.* politician.
polivalente [po·li·ƀa·lén·te] *adj.* multiple.
póliza [pó·li·sa] *f.* policy, written contract; draft; customhouse certificate; **— de seguros** insurance policy.
polizonte [po·li·són·te] *m.* policeman.
polo [pó·lo] *m.* pole (*of a magnet or of an axis*); polo (*a game*); **— acuático** water polo.
polonio [po·ló·njo] *m.* polonium.
poltrón [pol·trón] *adj.* lazy, idel; **silla poltrona** easy chair.
polvareda [pol·ƀa·ré·đa] *f.* cloud of dust; **armar** (*or* **levantar**) **una —** to kick up the dust; to raise a rumpus.
polvera [pol·ƀé·ra] *f.* powder box; compact; powder puff.
polvo [pól·ƀo] *m.* dust; powder; pinch of snuff or powder; **— férrico** iron oxide filings (*coating for recording tape*); **-s** toilet powder; **-s para dientes** tooth powder; **limpio de — y paja** entirely free; net; *Am.* cleaned out, without a penny; *Am.* innocent, ignorant, unaware; *Mex., Col., Ven.* **tomar el —** to escape, "beat it".
pólvora [pól·ƀo·ra] *f.* gunpowder; fireworks.
polvorear [pol·ƀo·re·ár] *v.* to powder, sprinkle with powder.
polvoriento [pol·ƀo·rjén·to] *adj.* dusty.
polvorín [pol·ƀo·rín] *m.* powder magazine; priming powder; powder flask; *Am.* tick (*parasitic insect*); *Ríopl.* spitfire, quick-tempered person.
polla [pó·ya] *f.* pullet (*young hen*); young lass; pool

(*in cards*).
pollada [po·yá·đa] *f.* hatch, brood; flock of chicks.
pollera [po·yé·ra] *f.* woman who raises and sells chickens; chicken coop; a bell-shaped basket for chickens; petticoat; *Ríopl., Ch., Col., Andes* skirt.
pollino [po·yí·no] *m.* young donkey, ass.
pollo [pó·yo] *m.* young chicken; nestling, young bird; *Spain* young man; **polluelo** [po·ywé·lo] *m.* chick.
pomelo [po·mé·lo] *m. Spain* grapefruit.
pómez [pó·mes] *m.* pumice.
pompa [póm·pa] *f.* pomp; pageant, procession; bubble; pump.
pomposo [pom·pó·so] *adj.* pompous.
pómulo [pó·mu·lo] *m.* cheek bone.
ponche [pón·če] *m.* punch (*a beverage*); **ponchera** [pon·čé·ra] *f.* punch bowl.
poncho [pón·čo] *m. Andes, Ch., Ríopl.* poncho; cape.
ponderación [pon·de·ra·sjón] *f.* pondering, careful consideration, weighing; exaggeration.
ponderar [pon·de·rár] *v.* (*pensar*) to ponder, consider, weigh; (*exagerar*) to exaggerate; to extol.
ponderativo [pon·de·ra·tí·ƀo] *adj.* exaggerating.
ponderoso [pon·de·ró·so] *adj.* ponderous, heavy.
poner[40] [po·nér] *v. irr.* to put; to place; to set; to lay; to suppose; — **como nuevo a alguien** to cover someone with insults; — **en claro** to clarify; — **en limpio** to recopy, make a clean copy; — **en tela de juicio** to doubt; — **todo de su parte** to do one's best; **pongamos que** . . . let us suppose that . . .; **-se** to place oneself; to become; **-se a** to begin to; **-se al corriente** to become informed; **-se de pie** to stand up; *Carib., Mex., Ch., Andes* **-se bien con alguien** to ingratiate oneself with someone, get on his good side; **-se en la sábana** strike it rich; *Am.* **ponérsela** to get drunk.
poniente [po·njén·te] *m.* west; west wind; **el sol** — the setting sun.
pontón [pon·tón] *m.* pontoon; scow, flat-bottomed boat; log bridge; pontoon bridge.
ponzoña [pon·só·ña] *f.* venom, poison.
ponzoñoso [pon·so·ñó·so] *adj.* venomous, poisonous.
popa [pó·pa] *f.* poop, stern; **viento en** — speedily; going well.
popote [po·pó·te] *m. Mex.* straw for brooms; *Mex.* drinking straw or tube.
populacho [po·pu·lá·čo] *m.* populace, rabble.
popular [po·pu·lár] *adj.* popular.
popularidad [po·pu·la·ri·đáđ] *f.* popularity.
populoso [po·pu·ló·so] *adj.* populous, densely populated.
popurrí [po·pu·rrí] *m.* potpourri.
poquito [po·kí·to] *adj.* very little; *Cuba, Ven., Col.* timid, shy; *m.* a small bit; **a -s** in small quantities.
por [por] *prep.* by; for; for the sake of, on account of, on behalf of; because of; through; along; on exchange for; in the place of; during; about, around; to, with the idea of; — **ciento** percent; — **consiguiente** consequently; — **entre** among, between; — **escrito** in writing; — **poco se muere** he almost died; **está** — **hacer** it is yet to be done; **él está** — **hacerlo** he is in favor of doing it; **recibir** — **esposa** to receive as a wife; **tener** — to consider, think of as; **¿— qué?** *interr. adv.* why? for what reason?
porcelana [por·se·lá·na] *f.* porcelain, china; enamel.
porcentaje [por·sen·tá·xe] *m.* percentage.
porcino [por·sí·no] *adj.* porcine; related to the pig.
porción [por·sjón] *f.* portion; part, share; **una** — **de gente** a lot of people.
porche [pór·če] *m.* porch.
pordiosear [por·đjo·se·ár] *v.* to beg.
pordiosero [por·đjo·sé·ro] *m.* beggar.
porfía [por·fí·a] *f.* stubbornness, obstinacy; persistence, insistence; **a** — in competition; with great insistence.
porfiado [por·fjá·đo] *adj.* stubborn, obstinate, persistent.
porfiar[17] [por·fjár] *v.* to persist, to insist; to dispute obstinately; to argue.
pormenor [por·me·nór] *m.* detail.
pormenorizar[9] [por·me·no·ri·sár] *v.* to detail, tell in detail; to itemize.
pornografía [por·no·ǵra·fí·a] *f.* pornography.
pornográfico [por·no·ǵrá·fi·ko] *adj.* pornographic.
poro [pó·ro] *m.* pore.
porosidad [po·ro·si·đáđ] *f.* porosity.
poroso [po·ró·so] *adj.* porous.
poroto [po·ró·to] *m. Ch., Ríopl., Andes* bean; *Ch., Ríopl., Andes* runt; urchin.
porque [pór·ke] *conj.* because; so that.
porqué [por·ké] *m.* cause, reason, motive.
porquería [por·ke·rí·a] *f.* filth; filthy act or word; nasty piece of food; trifle, worthless object.
porra [pó·rra] *f.* club, stick; mob; *Am.* **mandar a uno a la** — to send someone to the devil; **porrazo** *m.* blow; knock; bump; **porrón** *m.* wine vessel with long snout.
porta [pór·ta] *f.* porthole; cover for a porthole; goal (*in football*).
portaaviones [por·ta·a·ƀjó·nes] *m.* airplane carrier.
portabroca [por·ta·ƀró·ka] *m.* chuck.
portada [por·tá·đa] *f.* façade, front (*of a building*); title page.
portador [por·ta·đór] *m.* carrier; bearer; tray.
portaherramientas [por·ta·e·rra·mjén·tas] *m.* tool post.
portal [por·tál] *m.* portal; entrance, vestibule; portico, porch; *C.A.* Christmas crèche; **-es** arcades, galleries; **portalón** [por·ta·lón] *m.* large portal; gangway (*of a ship*).
portamonedas [por·ta·mo·né·đas] *m.* pocketbook, coin purse.
portapapeles [por·ta·pa·pé·les] *m.* briefcase.
portaplumas [por·ta·plú·mas] *m.* penholder.
portar [por·tár] *v. Am.* to carry; **-se** to behave.
portátil [por·tár] *adj.* portable.
portaviones [por·ta·ƀjó·nes] *m.* aircraft carrier; also **portaaviones.**
portavoz [por·ta·ƀós] *m.* megaphone; mouthpiece; spokesman.
portazgo [por·táz·ǵo] *m.* toll.
portazo [por·tá·so] *m.* bang or slam of a door; **dar un** — to bang or slam the door.
porte [pór·te] *m.* portage, cost of carriage; freight; postage; manner, bearing; size, capacity; *Ch.* birthday present; *C.A.* size.
portear [por·te·ár] *v.* to carry on one's back; *Am.* to get out in a hurry; **porteador** carrier.
portento [por·tén·to] *m.* portent; wonder, marvel.
portentoso [por·ten·tó·so] *adj.* marvelous, extraordinary, amazing, terrifying.
porteño [por·té·ño] *adj.* from a port; *Ríopl.* from Buenos Aires.
portería [por·te·ría] *f.* porter's quarters; main door of a building.
portero [por·té·ro] *m.* doorkeeper, doorman; janitor.
pórtico [pór·ti·ko] *m.* portico, porch.
portilla [por·tí·ya] *f.* porthole; small gate or passageway.
portón [por·tón] *m.* gate.
portugués [por·tu·ǵés] *adj.* Portuguese; *m.*

Portuguese; Portuguese language.
porvenir [por·ƀe·nír] *m.* future.
pos [pos]: **en — de** after; in pursuit of.
posada [po·sá·đa] *f.* lodging; inn; boardinghouse; dwelling, home; *Mex.* **las -s** a Christmas festivity lasting nine days; **posadero** [po·sa·đé·ro] *m.* innkeeper.
posaderas [po·sa·đé·ras] *f. pl.* posterior, buttocks, rump.
posar [po·sár] *v.* to lodge; to rest; to sit down; to pose (*as a model*); to perch (*said of birds*); **-se** to settle (*said of sediment*).
posdata [poz·đá·ta] *f.* postscript.
poseedor [po·se·e·đór] *m.* possessor, owner.
poseer[14] [po·se·ér] *v.* to possess, own; to master, know well; **-se** to have control of oneself.
posesión [po·se·sjón] *f.* possession.
posesivo [po·se·sí·ƀo] *adj. & m.* possessive.
posesor [po·se·sór] *m.* possessor, owner.
posibilidad [po·si·ƀi·li·đáđ] *p.* possibility.
posible [po·sí·ƀle] *adj.* possible; **hacer lo —** to do one's best; **-s** *m. pl.* goods, property, means.
posición [po·si·sjón] *f.* position; posture; status, rank, standing; placing.
positivo [po·si·tí·ƀo] *adj.* positive; effective; true; practical.
posponer[40] [pos·po·nér] *v. irr.* to postpone, put off; to put after; to subordinate.
pospuesto [pos·pwés·to] *p.p. of* **posponer.**
posta [pós·ta] *f.* (*bala*) small bullet; (*apuesta*) bet, wager; (*relevo*) relay (*of post horses*); post station; **-s** buckshot; **por la —** posthaste; fast, speedily; *m.* postboy, courier, messenger.
postal [pos·tál] *adj.* postal; **tarjeta —** postcard.
postdata [poz·đá·ta] = **posdata.**
poste [pós·te] *m.* post, pillar; **— de soporte** bearing post.
postergar[7] [pos·ter·ǥár] *v.* to delay; to postpone; to disregard someone's right.
posteridad [pos·te·ri·đáđ] *f.* posterity.
posterior [pos·te·rjór] *adj.* posterior, back, rear; later.
postigo [pos·tí·ǥo] *m.* wicket, small door or gate; shutter; peep window.
postizo [pos·tí·so] *adj.* false, artificial; *m.* switch, false hair.
postración [pos·tra·sjón] *f.* prostration, collapse, exhaustion; dejection, lowness of spirits.
postrar [pos·trár] *v.* to prostrate; to humiliate; to throw down; to weaken, exhaust; **-se** to kneel to the ground; to be weakened, exhausted; to collapse.
postre [pós·tre] *m.* dessert; **a la —** at last.
postrer(o) [pos·tré·r(o)] *adj.* last; hindmost, nearest the rear.
postulante [pos·tu·lán·te] *m. & f.* petitioner; applicant, candidate.
póstumo [pós·tu·mo] *adj.* posthumous, after one's death.
postura [pos·tú·ra] *f.* posture, position; bid; wager; pact, agreement; egg-laying.
potable [po·tá·ƀle] *adj.* drinkable; **agua —** drinking water.
potaje [po·tá·xe] *m.* pottage, thick soup; porridge; mixed drink.
potasio [po·tá·sjo] *m.* potassium.
pote [pó·te] *m.* pot; jar; jug; *Carib., Ven., Mex., Ríopl.* flask; *Ch.* buzzard.
potencia [po·tén·sja] *f.* potency; power; faculty, ability; powerful nation.
potenciómetro [po·ten·sjó·me·tro] *m.* (*computadora*) paddle.
potentado [po·ten·tá·đo] *m.* potentate.
potente [po·tén·te] *adj.* potent, powerful, strong.
potestad [po·tes·táđ] *f.* power; dominion, authority.
potranca [po·tráŋ·ka] *f.* filly, young mare.
potrero [po·tré·ro] *m.* herdsman of colts; fenced-in pasture land; *Carib., Mex., C.A., Ven., Col., Ch.* cattle ranch, stock farm.
potro [pó·tro] *m.* colt; rack, torture; *Col., Ven., Mex., Ch., Ríopl.* wild horse.
poyo [pó·yo] *m.* stone or brick bench (*usually built against a wall*).
pozo [pó·so] *m.* well; hole, pit; mine shaft; hold of a ship; *Hond.* pool, puddle; *Ríopl., Ch., Ven., Col., Mex.* spring, fountain.
pozole [po·só·le] *m. Mex.* stew made of hominy and pig's head.
práctica [prák·ti·ka] *f.* practice; exercise; custom, habit; method.
practicante [prak·ti·kán·te] *m. & f.* doctor's assistant; hospital intern.
practicar[6] [prak·ti·kár] *v.* to practice; to put into practice.
práctico [prák·ti·ko] *adj.* practical; experienced, skilful; *m.* **— de puerto** harbor pilot.
pradera [pra·đé·ra] *f.* prairie; meadow.
prado [prá·đo] *m.* meadow, field; lawn.
preámbulo [pre·ám·bu·lo] *m.* preamble, introduction, prologue.
precario [pre·ká·rjo] *adj.* precarious.
precaución [pre·kaw·sjón] *f.* precaution.
precaver [pre·ka·ƀér] *v.* to guard (against), keep (from); to warn, caution; **-se** to guard oneself (against); to take precautions.
precavido [pre·ka·ƀí·đo] *adj.* cautious, on guard.
precedencia [pre·se·dén·sja] *f.* precedence; priority.
precedente [pre·se·dén·te] *adj.* preceding; *m.* precedent.
preceder [pre·se·dér] *v.* to precede; to have precedence.
precepto [pre·sép·to] *m.* precept; rule; order.
preceptor [pre·sep·tór] *m.* teacher, tutor.
preciado [pre·sjá·đo] *adj.* prized, esteemed; precious, valuable.
preciar [pre·sjár] *v.* to appraise; to value; **-se de** to boast of, be proud of.
precio [pré·sjo] *m.* price; value, worth; esteem.
precioso [pre·sjó·so] *adj.* precious, valuable; fine, exquisite; beautiful.
precipicio [pre·si·pí·sjo] *m.* precipice; ruin.
precipitación [pre·si·pi·ta·sjón] *f.* precipitation; rush, haste, hurry.
precipitado [pre·si·pi·tá·đo] *adj.* precipitate, hasty, rash; *m.* precipitate (*chemical term*).
precipitar [pre·si·pi·tár] *v.* to precipitate; to hasten, rush; to hurl, throw headlong; **-se** to throw oneself headlong; to rush (into).
precipitoso [pre·si·pi·tó·so] *adj.* precipitous, steep; rash.
precisar [pre·si·sár] *v.* to determine precisely; to force, compel, make necessary; *Ríopl., Col., Ven., Mex., Andes;* to be necessary or urgent; *Am.* to need.
precisión [pre·si·sjón] *f.* precision, exactness; accuracy; compulsion, force, necessity; *Am.* haste.
preciso [pre·sí·so] *adj.* necessary; precise, exact; clear; *m. Am.* small travelling bag.
precoz [pre·kós] *adj.* precocious.
precursor [pre·kur·sór] *m.* precursor, forerunner.
predecir[27] [pre·đe·sír] *v. irr.* to predict, prophesy, forecast, foretell.
predestinar [pre·đes·ti·nár] *v.* to predestine.

predicación [pre·ði·ka·sjón] *f.* preaching.
predicado [pre·ði·ká·ðo] *adj.* & *m.* predicate; *p.p. of* **predicar.**
predicador [pre·ði·ka·ðór] *m.* preacher.
predicar[6] [pre·ði·kár] *v.* to preach.
predicción [pre·ðik·sjón] *f.* prediction.
predilección [pre·ði·lek·sjón] *f.* predilection, preference, liking.
predilecto [pre·ði·lek·to] *adj.* favorite, preferred.
predisponer[40] [pre·ðis·po·nér] *v. irr.* to predispose, bias, prejudice.
predispuesto [pre·ðis·pwés·to] *p.p. of* **predisponer** & *adj.* predisposed, prejudiced, biased.
predominante [pre·ðo·mi·nán·te] *adj.* predominant; prevailing, ruling.
predominar [pre·ðo·mi·nár] *v.* to predominate, prevail.
predominio [pre·ðo·mí·njo] *m.* predominance; sway, influence.
prefacio [pre·fá·sjo] *m.* preface.
prefecto [pre·fék·to] *m.* prefect (*military or civil chief; sometimes a mayor, sometimes governor of a province, as in Peru*).
preferencia [pre·fe·rén·sja] *f.* preference; **de** — with preference; preferably.
preferente [pre·fe·rén·te] *adj.* preferable; preferred; preferential; **acciones -s** preferred shares.
preferible [pre·fe·rí·ƀle] *adj.* preferable.
preferir[3] [pre·fe·rír] *v. irr.* to prefer.
prefijar [pre·fi·xár] *v.* to prefix; to set beforehand (*as a date*).
prefijo [pre·fí·xo] *m.* prefix.
pregonar [pre·ǥo·nár] *v.* to proclaim, cry out; to make known.
pregunta [pre·ǥún·ta] *f.* question; **hacer una** — to ask a question.
preguntar [pre·ǥun·tár] *v.* to ask, inquire.
preguntón [pre·ǥun·tón] *adj.* inquisitive.
prejuicio [pre·xwí·sjo] *m.* prejudice.
prejuzgar[7] [pre·xuz·ǥár] *v. irr.* to prejudge.
prelado [pre·lá·ðo] *m.* prelate.
preliminar [pre·li·mi·nár] *adj.* & *m.* preliminary.
preludiar [pre·lu·ðjár] *v.* to be the prelude or beginning of; to initiate, introduce; to try out (*a musical instrument*).
preludio [pre·lú·ðjo] *m.* prelude; introduction.
prematuro [pre·ma·tú·ro] *adj.* premature, untimely.
premeditado [pre·me·ði·tá·ðo] *adj.* premeditated, deliberate.
premiar [pre·mjár] *v.* to reward.
premio [pré·mjo] *m.* prize; reward; recompense; premium; **a** — with interest, at interest.
premisa [pre·mí·sa] *f.* premise (*either of the first two propositions of a syllogism*).
premura [pre·mú·ra] *f.* pressure, urgency, haste.
prenda [prén·da] *f.* (*fianza*) pawn, pledge, security; token; (*partes del vestido*) article of clothing; anything valuable; loved person; jewel; **-s** good qualities, gifts, talents; — **de vestir** garment; **juego de -s** game of forfeits; **en** — **de** as a proof of, as a pledge of.
prendar [pren·dár] *v.* to pawn, pledge; to charm, please; **-se de** to get attached to; to fall in love with.
prendedor [pren·de·ðór] *m.* clasp; stickpin; tie pin; brooch; *Am.* light.
prender [pren·dér] *v.* (*asir*) to seize, catch, grab; to bite (*said of an insect*); to fasten, clasp; to arrest, imprison; (*empezar*) to take root; to begin to burn; catch fire; *Ríopl., Carib., C.A., Mex.* to light (*a lamp*); *Am.* to start, begin, undertake; — **el fuego** to start the fire; *Col.* **-las** to take to one's heels; **-se** to dress up.
prendero [pren·dé·ro] *m.* pawnbroker; second-hand dealer.
prensa [prén·sa] *f.* press; printing press; — **de tornillo** vise.
prensar [pren·sár] *v.* to press.
prensil [pren·síl] *adj.* prehensile.
preñado [pre·ñá·ðo] *adj.* pregnant; full.
preñez [pre·ñés] *f.* pregnancy.
preocupación [pre·o·ku·pa·sjón] *f.* preoccupation; worry; bias, prejudice.
preocupar [pre·o·ku·pár] *v.* to preoccupy; to worry; to prejudice; **-se** to be preoccupied; to worry; to be prejudiced.
preparación [pre·pa·ra·sjón] *f.* preparation.
preparar [pre·pa·rár] *v.* to prepare; **-se** to get ready; to be prepared.
preparativo [pre·pa·ra·tí·ƀo] *adj.* preparatory; *m.* preparation.
preparatorio [pre·pa·ra·tó·rjo] *adj.* preparatory.
preponderancia [pre·pon·de·rán·sja] *f.* preponderance.
preposición [pre·po·si·sjón] *f.* preposition.
prerrogativa [pre·rro·ǥa·tí·ƀa] *f.* prerogative, right, privilege.
presa [pré·sa] *f.* prey; dam; fang, tusk; claw; **hacer** — to seize.
presagiar [pre·sa·xjár] *v.* to foretell.
presagio [pre·sá·xjo] *m.* presage, omen, sign.
presbítero [prez·ƀí·te·ro] *m.* priest.
prescindir [pre·sin·dír] *v.* to disregard, set aside, leave aside; to omit; to dispense (with).
prescribir[52] [pres·kri·ƀír] *v.* to prescribe.
prescrito [pres·krí·to] *p.p. of* **prescribir.**
presencia [pre·sén·sja] *f.* presence; figure, bearing; — **de ánimo** presence of mind, serenity.
presenciar [pre·sen·sjár] *v.* to see, witness; to be present at.
presentación [pre·sen·ta·sjón] *f.* presentation; personal introduction; *Ven.* petition.
presentar [pre·sen·tár] *v.* to present; to introduce; **-se** to appear, present oneself; to introduce oneself; to offer one's services; *Ch., Arg.* to have recourse to justice, file suit.
presente [pre·sén·te] *adj.* present; *m.* present, gift; **al** — now, at the present time; **por el (la,** *or* **lo)** — for the present; **mejorando lo** — present company excepted; **tener** — to bear in mind.
presentimiento [pre·sen·ti·mjén·to] *m.* presentiment, foreboding.
presentir[3] [pre·sen·tír] *v. irr.* to have a presentiment, foreboding or hunch.
preservación [pre·ser·ƀa·sjón] *f.* preservation.
preservar [pre·ser·ƀár] *v.* to preserve, guard, protect, keep.
presidencia [pre·si·ðén·sja] *f.* presidency; office of president; presidential term; chairmanship.
presidencial [pre·si·ðen·sjál] *adj.* presidential.
presidente [pre·si·ðén·te] *m.* president; chairman; presiding judge.
presidiario [pre·si·ðjá·rjo] *m.* prisoner, convict.
presidio [pre·sí·ðjo] *m.* garrison; fortress; penitentiary, prison; **diez años de** — ten years at hard labor (*in a prison*).
presidir [pre·si·ðír] *v.* to preside; to direct.
presilla [pre·sí·ya] *f.* loop, fastener; clip.
presión [pre·sjón] *f.* pressure.
preso [pré·so] *m.* prisoner; *p.p. irr. of* **prender** imprisoned.
prestado [pres·tá·ðo] *adj.* & *p.p.* loaned, lent; **dar** — to lend; **pedir** — to borrow.

prestamista [pres·ta·mís·ta] *m. & f.* moneylender.
préstamo [prés·ta·mo] *m.* loan.
prestar [pres·tár] *v.* to loan, lend; *Col., Ven., C.A., Andes* to borrow; — **ayuda** to give help; — **atención** to pay attention; *Andes* **presta acá** give it here, give it to me; **-se** to lend oneself or itself.
presteza [pres·té·sa] *f.* promptness, speed.
prestidigitación [pres·ti·đi·xi·ta·sjón] *f.* juggling, sleight of hand.
prestidigitador [pres·ti·đi·xi·ta·đór] *m.* juggler.
prestigio [pres·tí·xjo] *m.* prestige; influence, authority; good reputation.
presto [prés·to] *adj.* quick; nimble; prompt; ready; *adv.* soon, at once; **de** — quickly, promptly.
presumido [pre·su·mí·đo] *adj.* conceited, presumptuous; *p.p. of* **presumir.**
presumir [pre·su·mír] *v.* to presume; to boast; to show off; *Am.* to court, woo; — **de valiente** to boast of one's valor.
presunción [pre·sun·sjón] *f.* presumption, assumption; conceit, arrogance.
presunto [pre·sún·to] *adj.* presumed; supposed; prospective; **heredero** — heir apparent.
presuntuoso [pre·sun·twó·so] *adj.* presumptuous, conceited.
presuponer[40] [pre·su·po·nér] *v. irr.* to presuppose, take for granted, imply; to estimate.
presupuesto [pre·su·pwés·to] *p.p. of* **presuponer** presupposed; estimated; *m.* budget, estimate.
presuroso [pre·su·ró·so] *adj.* quick, prompt; hasty.
pretencioso [pre·ten·sjó·so] *adj.* presumptuous; conceited.
pretender [pre·ten·dér] *v.* to pretend; to solicit; seek; to claim; to try; to court.
pretendiente [pre·ten·djén·te] *m.* pretender, claimant; suitor; office seeker.
pretensión [pre·ten·sjón] *f.* pretension; claim; presumption; pretense.
pretérito [pre·té·ri·to] *adj.* preterite, past; *m.* preterite, the past tense.
pretexto [pre·tés·to] *m.* pretext, pretense, excuse.
pretil [pre·tíl] *m.* stone or brick railing; *Am.* ledge; *Mex., Ven.* stone or brick bench (*built against a wall*).
pretina [pre·tí·na] *f.* belt, girdle; waistband.
prevalecer[13] [pre·ƀa·le·sér] *v. irr.* to prevail.
prevaleciente [pre·ƀa·le·sjén·te] *adj.* prevalent, current.
prevención [pre·ƀen·sjón] *f.* prevention; foresight, preparedness; bias, prejudice; provision, supply; admonition, warning; police station; guardhouse.
prevenido [pre·ƀe·ní·đo] *adj. & p.p.* prepared, ready; forewarned; cautious; supplied.
prevenir[48] [pre·ƀe·nír] *v. irr.* to prevent, avoid; to prepare beforehand; to foresee; to warn; to predispose; **-se** to get prepared, get ready.
prever[49] [pre·ƀér] *v. irr.* to foresee.
previo [pré·ƀjo] *adj.* previous; *m. Am.* preliminary examination.
previsión [pre·ƀi·sjón] *f.* foresight.
previsto [pre·ƀís·to] *p.p. of* **prever.**
prieto [prjé·to] *adj.* dark, black; tight; compact; *Ríopl., Ven., Col., Mex., C.A., Andes* dark-complexioned, swarthy.
prima [prí·ma] *f.* female cousin; premium; prime (*first of the canonical hours*).
primacía [pri·má·sja] *f.* priority, precedence; superiority.
primario [pri·má·rjo] *adj.* primary, principal.
primavera [pri·ma·ƀé·ra] *f.* spring; primrose; print, flowered silk cloth.
primaveral [pri·ma·ƀe·rál] *adj.* spring, pertaining to spring.
primer(o) [pri·mér(o)] *adj.* first; former; leading, principal; **primera enseñanza** primary education; **primera materia** raw material; **de buenas a primeras** all of a sudden, unexpectedly; **a primera luz** at dawn; *adv.* first; rather.
primicia [pri·mí·sja] *f.* first fruit; first profit; **-s** first fruits.
primitivo [pri·mi·tí·ƀo] *adj.* primitive; primary; original.
primo [prí·mo] *m.* cousin; simpleton, sucker, dupe; — **hermano** (*or* — **carnal**) first cousin; *Carib.* **coger a uno de** — to deceive someone easily; *adj.* first; **número** — prime number.
primogénito [pri·mo·xé·ni·to] *adj. & m.* first-born; **primogenitura** [pri·mo·xe·ni·tú·ra] *f.* birthright; rights of the first-born.
primor [pri·mór] *m.* beauty; excellence; exquisiteness; skill, ability.
primordial [pri·mor·đjál] *adj.* primordial.
primoroso [pri·mo·ró·so] *adj.* excellent, fine, exquisite; skillful.
prímula [prí·mu·la] *f.* primrose.
princesa [prin·sé·sa] *f.* princess.
principal [prin·si·pál] *adj.* principal; renowned, famous; **piso** — main floor (*usually, the second floor*); *m.* principal, capital sum; chief, head.
príncipe [prín·si·pe] *m.* prince; *adj.* princeps, first (*edition*).
principiante [prin·si·pján·te] *m.* beginner.
principiar [prin·si·pjár] *v.* to begin.
principio [prin·sí·pjo] *m.* principle; beginning; origin, source; entrée (*main dinner course*); **a -s de** towards the beginning of.
pringar[7] [priŋ·gár] *v. irr.* to dip (*in grease*).
pringoso [priŋ·gó·so] *adj.* greasy.
pringue [príŋ·ge] *m. & f.* grease drippings (*from bacon, ham, etc.*).
prioridad [prjó·ri·đáđ] *f.* priority; precedence.
prisa [prí·sa] *f.* speed, haste; **de** (*or* **a**) — quickly, speedily; **a toda** — with the greatest speed; **eso corre** — that is urgent; **dar** — **a** to hurry; **darse** — to hurry; **tener** (*or* **estar de**) — to be in a hurry.
prisión [pri·sjón] *f.* prison; imprisonment; seizure; shackle; **-es** shackles, fetters, chains.
prisionero [pri·sjo·né·ro] *m.* prisoner.
prisma [príz·ma] *f.* prism.
pristino [pris·tí·no] *adj.* first, early, former, primitive.
privación [pri·ƀa·sjón] *f.* privation; want, lack; loss.
privado [pri·ƀá·đo] *adj.* private; personal; unconscious; *p.p.* deprived; *m.* favorite.
privar [pri·ƀár] *v.* (*destituir*) to deprive; to prohibit; (*tener aceptación*) to enjoy the favor of someone; to be in vogue; **-le a uno del sentido** to stun, daze; **ya no privan esas costumbres** those customs are no longer in vogue or in existence; **-se** to lose consciousness; **-se de** to deprive oneself of.
privativo [pri·ƀa·tí·ƀo] *adj.* exclusive; particular, distinctive.
privilegiado [pri·ƀi·le·xjá·đo] *adj.* privileged.
privilegiar [pri·ƀi·le·xjár] *v.* to favor; to give a privilege to.
privilegio [pri·ƀi·lé·xjo] *m.* privilege; exemption; patent; copyright; — **de invención** patent on an invention.
pro [pro] *m. & f.* profit, advantage; **en** — **de** on behalf of; **en** — **y en contra** pro and con, for and against; **hombre de** — man of worth.

proa [pró·a] *f.* prow.
probabilidad [pro·ƀa·ƀi·li·đáđ] *f.* probability.
probable [pro·ƀá·ƀle] *adj.* probable.
probar[2] [pro·ƀár] *v. irr.* (*examinar*) to test; to taste; to prove; to try; to try on; (*gustar*) to suit, agree with; **no me prueba el clima** the climate does not agree with me.
probeta [pro·ƀé·ta] *f.* test tube; pressure gauge.
probidad [pro·ƀi·đáđ] *f.* integrity, uprightness, honesty.
problema [pro·ƀlé·ma] *m.* problem.
problemático [pro·ƀle·má·ti·ko] *adj.* problematic.
procedente [pro·se·đén·te] *adj.* proceeding (from), originating; according to law.
proceder [pro·se·đér] *v.* to proceed; to originate; to behave; to take action (against); *m.* behavior, conduct.
procedimiento [pro·se·đi·mjén·to] *m.* procedure; method; process; conduct.
prócer [pró·ser] *m.* distinguished person; hero; great statesman.
procesado [pro·se·sá·đo] *p.p. & adj.* relating to, or included in, a lawsuit; accused, prosecuted; *m.* defendant.
procesar [pro·se·sár] *v.* to prosecute; to accuse; to indict; to sue; **procesamiento de datos** data processing.
procesión [pro·se·sjón] *f.* procession; parade.
proceso [pro·sé·so] *m.* process; lawsuit, legal proceedings; lapse of time; — **fundacional** chartering; — **verbal** minutes, record.
proclama [pro·klá·ma] *f.* proclamation, ban; marriage banns.
proclamación [pro·kla·ma·sjón] *f.* proclamation.
proclamar [pro·kla·már] *v.* to proclaim.
proclítico [pro·klí·ti·ko] *adj.* proclitic.
procurador [por·ku·ra·đór] *m.* attorney.
procurar [pro·ku·rár] *v.* (*pretender*) to try, endeavor; (*obtener*) to procure, obtain, get.
prodigar[7] [pro·đi·ǥár] *v.* to lavish; to bestow upon; to squander, waste.
prodigio [pro·đí·xjo] *m.* prodigy, wonder, marvel; miracle.
prodigioso [pro·đi·xjóso] *adj.* prodigious, marvelous; fine, exquisite.
pródigo [pró·đi·ǥo] *adj.* prodigal, wasteful; lavish; generous; *m.* spendthrift.
producción [pro·đuk·sjón] *f.* production; produce; — **masiva** mass production.
producir[25] [pro·đu·sír] *v. irr.* to produce; to bring about; to yield; **-se** to express oneself, explain oneself; *Col., Ven.* to occur, happen.
productivo [pro·đuk·tí·ƀo] *adj.* productive; fruitful; profitable.
producto [pro·đúk·to] *m.* product; yield; result.
productor [pro·đuk·tór] *m.* producer; *adj.* producing, productive.
proeza [pro·é·sa] *f.* prowess; *Col.* boast, exaggeration.
profanación [pro·fa·na·sjón] *f.* profanation.
profanar [pro·fa·nár] *v.* to profane; to defile.
profano [pro·fá·no] *adj.* profane, not sacred; irreverent; lay, uninformed (*about a branch of learning*).
profecía [pro·fe·sí·a] *f.* prophecy; prediction.
proferir[3] [pro·fe·rír] *v. irr.* to utter, express, speak.
profesar [pro·fe·sár] *v.* to profess; to avow, confess.
profesión [pro·fe·sjón] *f.* profession; avowal, declaration.
profesional [pro·fe·sjo·nál] *adj., m. & f.* professional.
profesionista [pro·fe·sjo·nís·ta] *m. & f. Am.* professional.
profesor [pro·fe·sór] *m.* professor, teacher;
profesorado [pro·fe·so·rá·đo] *m.* faculty; body of teachers; teaching profession; professorship.
profeta [pro·fé·ta] *m.* prophet.
profético [pro·fé·ti·ko] *adj.* prophetic.
profetizar[9] [pro·fe·ti·sár] *v.* to prophesy.
proficiente [pro·fi·sjén·te] *adj.* proficient, skilled.
profilaxis [pro·fi·lák·sis] *f.* prophylaxis (*disease prevention*).
prófugo [pró·fu·ǥo] *adj. & m.* fugitive.
profundidad [pro·fun·di·đáđ] *f.* profundity, depth.
profundizar[9] [pro·fun·di·sár] *v.* to deepen; to go deep into.
profundo [pro·fún·do] *adj.* profound; deep; low.
profuso [pro·fú·so] *adj.* profuse; lavish.
progenitor [pro·xe·ni·tór] *m.* progenitor.
programa [pro·ǥrá·ma] *m.* program; plan.
programación [pro·ǥra·ma·sjón] *f.* programming.
programador [pro·ǥra·ma·đór] *m.* programmer.
programar [pro·ǥra·már] *v.* to plan; to program.
progresar [pro·ǥre·sár] *v.* to progress.
progresista [pro·ǥre·sís·ta] *m., f. & adj.* progressive.
progresivo [pro·ǥre·sí·ƀo] *adj.* progressive.
progreso [pro·ǥré·so] *m.* progress.
prohibición [proj·ƀi·sjón] *f.* prohibition; ban.
prohibir [proj·ƀír] *v.* to prohibit, forbid.
prohijar [pro·i·xár] *v.* to adopt.
prójimo [pró·xi·mo] *m.* neighbor, fellow being; *Ríopl., Carib., C.A.* **ese** — that fellow.
prole [pró·le] *f.* progeny, offspring.
proletariado [pro·le·ta·rjá·đo] *m.* proletariat, working class.
proletario [pro·le·tá·rjo] *adj.* proletarian, belonging to the working class; plebeian; *m.* proletarian.
prolijo [pro·lí·xo] *adj.* prolix, too long, drawn out, too detailed; boring, tedious.
prologar[7] [pro·lo·ǥár] *v.* to preface, write a preface for.
prólogo [pró·lo·ǥo] *m.* prologue.
prolongación [pro·loŋ·ga·sjón] *f.* prolongation; extension; lengthening.
prolongar[7] [pro·loŋ·gár] *v.* to prolong, lengthen, extend.
promediar [pro·me·đjár] *v.* to average; to divide or distribute into two equal parts; to mediate; **antes de — el mes** before the middle of the month.
promedio [pro·mé·đjo] *m.* middle; average.
promesa [pro·mé·sa] *f.* promise.
prometedor [pro·me·te·đór] *adj.* promising, hopeful.
prometer [pro·me·tér] *v.* to promise; to show promise; *Ríopl., C.A.* to affirm, assure; **-se** to become engaged, betrothed.
prometido [pro·me·tí·đo] *adj. & p.p.* betrothed; *m.* fiancé, betrothed; promise.
prominente [pro·mi·nén·te] *adj.* prominent.
promiscuo [pro·mís·kwo] *adj.* promiscuous.
promisorio [pro·mi·só·rjo] *adj.* promissory.
promoción [pro·mo·sjón] *f.* promotion, advancement.
promontorio [pro·mon·tó·rjo] *m.* promontory, headland, cape; anything bulky; bulge.
promotor [pro·mo·tór] *m.* promoter.
promovedor [pro·mo·ƀe·đór] *m.* promoter.
promover[2] [pro·mo·ƀér] *v. irr.* to promote; to advance.
promulgación [pro·mul·ǥa·sjón] *f.* promulgation, publication, proclamation (*of a law*).
promulgar[7] [pro·mul·ǥár] *v.* to promulgate, proclaim, announce publicly.
pronombre [pro·nóm·bre] *m.* pronoun.
pronominal [pro·no·mi·nál] *adj.* pronominal.

pronosticar[6] [pro·nos·ti·kár] *v.* to prophesy, predict.
pronóstico [pro·nós·ti·ko] *m.* forecast; prediction; omen.
prontitud [pron·ti·túđ] *f.* promptness; quickness.
pronto [prón·to] *adj.* quick, speedy; ready; prompt; *adv.* soon; quickly; **de** — suddenly; **al** — at first; **por de** (*or* **por lo**) — for the present; *m.* sudden impulse.
pronunciación [pro·nun·sja·sjón] *f.* pronunciation.
pronunciar [pro·nun·sjár] *v.* to pronounce; to utter; **-se** to rise up in rebellion.
propagación [pro·pa·ǥa·sjón] *f.* propagation, spread, spreading.
propaganda [pro·pa·ǥán·da] *f.* propaganda; advertising.
propagar[7] [pro·pa·ǥár] *v.* to propagate, reproduce; to spread.
propalar [pro·pa·lár] *v.* to spread (*news*).
propasarse [pro·pa·sár·se] *v.* to overstep one's bounds; to exceed one's authority, go too far.
propensión [pro·pen·sjón] *f.* tendency, inclination; bent, natural tendency or ability.
propenso [pro·pén·so] *adj.* prone, susceptible, inclined.
propiciar [pro·pi·sjár] *v.* to calm one's anger; *Am.* to propose.
propicio [pro·pí·sjo] *adj.* propitious, favorable.
propiedad [pro·pje·đáđ] *f.* property; ownership; attribute, quality; propriety, appropriateness.
propietario [pro·pje·tá·rjo] *m.* proprietor, owner.
propina [pro·pí·na] *f.* tip (*voluntary gift of money for service*).
propinar [pro·pi·nár] *v.* to give (*something to drink*); to give (*a beating, kick, slap*); *Am.* to tip, give a tip to; — **una paliza** to give a beating.
propio [pró·pjo] *adj.* proper; suitable; own; same; **amor** — vanity, pride, self-esteem; *m.* messenger.
proponer[40] [pro·po·nér] *v. irr.* to propose; to resolve; to present; **-se** to resolve, make a resolution.
proporción [pro·por·sjón] *f.* proportion; dimension; ratio; opportunity, chance.
proporcionar [pro·por·sjo·nár] *v.* to proportion; to adapt, adjust; to furnish, supply, give.
proposición [pro·po·si·sjón] *f.* proposition; proposal; assertion.
propósito [pro·pó·si·to] *m.* purpose, aim, design; **a** — apropos, suitable, fitting; by the way; **de** — on purpose; **fuera de** — irrelevant, beside the point.
propuesta [pro·pwés·to] *f.* proposal, offer; proposition.
propuesto [pro·pwés·to] *p.p. of* **proponer.**
propulsar [pro·pul·sár] *v.* to propel.
propulsión [pro·pul·sjón] *f.* propulsion; — **a chorro** (*por reacción*) jet propulsion; — **a cohete** rocket propulsion.
propulsor [pro·pul·sór] *m.* propeller; *adj.* propelling; *m.* propelling force.
prorratear [pro·rra·te·ár] *v.* to prorate, distribute or assess proportionally; to average.
prorrateo [pro·rra·té·o] *m.* apportionment, proportional distribution.
prórroga [pró·rro·ǥa] *f.* renewal, extension of time.
prorrogar[7] [pro·rro·ǥar] *v.* to put off, postpone; to adjourn; to extend (*time limit*).
prorrumpir [pro·rrum·pír] *v.* to break forth; — **en llanto** to burst into tears; — **en una carcajada** to let out a big laugh.
prosa [pró·sa] *f.* prose.
prosaico [pro·sáj·ko] *adj.* prosaic; dull; tedious.
proscribir[52] [pros·kri·ƀír] *v.* to proscribe, banish; to outlaw.
proscripción [pros·krip·sjón] *f.* banishment.
proscripto [pros·kríp·to], **proscrito** [pros·krí·to] *p.p. of* **proscribir;** *m.* exile, outlaw.
proseguir[5, 12] [pro·se·ǥír] *v. irr.* to continue; to follow.
prosélito [pro·sé·li·to] *m.* proselyte.
prosódico [pro·só·đi·ko] *adj.* prosodic.
prosperar [pros·pe·rár] *v.* to prosper.
prosperidad [pros·pe·ri·đáđ] *f.* prosperity; success.
próspero [prós·pe·ro] *adj.* prosperous; successful.
próstata [prós·ta·ta] *f.* prostate.
prostituir[32] [pros·ti·twír] *v.* to prostitute, corrupt.
prostituta [pros·ti·tú·ta] prostitute.
protagonista [pro·ta·ǥo·nís·ta] *m. & f.* protagonist (*main character or actor*).
protección [pro·tek·sjón] *f.* protection; support.
proteccionista [pro·tek·sjo·nís·ta] *adj.* protective; **tarifa** — protective tariff; *m. & f.* protectionist (*follower of the economic principles of protection*).
protector [pro·tek·tór] *m.* protector, guardian; *adj.* protecting, protective.
protectorado [pro·tek·to·rá·đo] *m.* protectorate.
proteger[11] [pro·te·xér] *v.* to protect; to shelter; to defend.
protegido [pro·te·xí·đo] *m.* protege.
proteína [pro·te·í·na] *f.* protein.
proteínico [pro·te·í·ni·ko] *adj.* related to the proteins.
protesta [pro·tés·ta] *f.* protest; protestation.
protestación [pro·tes·ta·sjón] *f.* protestation, solemn declaration; protest.
protestante [pro·tes·tán·te] *m.* Protestant; one who protests.
protestar [pro·tes·tár] *v.* (*confesar*) to assert, assure; to avow publicly; (*negar*) to protest; — **una letra** to protest a draft.
protocolo [pro·to·kó·lo] *m.* protocol.
protón [pro·tón] *m.* proton.
protoplasma [pro·to·pláz·ma] *m.* protoplasm.
protuberancia [pro·tu·ƀe·rán·sja] *f.* protuberance, bulge.
protuberante [pro·tu·ƀe·rán·te] *adj.* protuberant, prominent, bulging.
provecho [pro·ƀé·čo] *m.* profit; benefit; utility; advantage; **hombre de** — worthy, useful man.
provechoso [pro·ƀe·čó·so] *adj.* profitable; useful; beneficial; advantageous.
proveedor [pro·ƀe·e·đór] *m.* provisioner, provider; supply man.
proveer[14, 52] [pro·ƀe·ér] *v. irr.* to provide; to supply; to confer, bestow; to decide; **-se de** to supply oneself with.
provenir[48] [pro·ƀe·nír] *v. irr.* to originate, arise, come (from).
proverbio [pro·ƀer·ƀjo] *m.* proverb.
providencia [pro·ƀi·đén·sja] *f.* providence; foresight; Providence, God; legal decision, sentence; provision, measure; **tomar una** — to take a step or measure.
providencial [pro·ƀi·đen·sjál] *adj.* providential.
provincia [pro·ƀín·sja] *f.* province.
provincial [pro·ƀin·sjál] *adj.* provincial.
provinciano [pro·ƀin·sjá·no] *adj.* & *m.* provincial.
provisión [pro·ƀi·sjón] *f.* provision; supply, stock.
provisional [pro·ƀi·sjo·nál] *adj.* temporary; provisional.
provisorio [pro·ƀi·só·rjo] *adj.* provisional, temporary.
provisto [pro·ƀís·to] *p.p. of* **proveer.**
provocación [pro·ƀo·ka·sjón] *f.* provocation; dare, defiance.
provocador [pro·ƀo·ka·đór] *adj.* provoking; *m.* provoker.

provocar[6] [pro·ƀo·kár] *v.* to provoke; to excite, rouse; to stimulate.
provocativo [pro·ƀo·ka·tí·ƀo] *adj.* provocative.
proximidad [prok·si·mi·đáđ] *f.* proximity, nearness.
próximo [prók·si·mo] *adj.* next; neighboring; near; **del — pasado** of last month.
proyección [pro·yek·sjón] *f.* projection; jut.
proyectar [pro·yek·tár] *v.* to project; to plan; to throw; to cast; **-se** to be cast (*as a shadow*).
proyectil [pro·yek·tíl] *m.* projectile.
proyectista [pro·yek·tís·ta] *m. & f.* designer; schemer, planner.
proyecto [pro·yék·to] *m.* project; plan; **— de ley** bill (*in a legislature*).
prudencia [pru·đén·sja] *f.* prudence, practical wisdom, discretion.
prudente [pru·đén·te] *adj.* prudent, wise, discreet.
prueba [prwé·ƀa] *f.* proof; trial; test; fitting; sample; evidence; *Andes, Ríopl., Col., C.A.* acrobatic performance, stunt, trick, sleight of hand; **a — de incendio** fireproof; **— de doblaje** bend test.
prurito [pru·rí·to] *m.* itch; keen desire.
psicología [si·ko·lo·xí·a] *f. see* **sicología.**
psicosis [si·kó·sis] *f. see* **sicosis.**
psiqiatría [si·kja·trí·a] *f. see* **siqiatría.**
psitacosis [si·ta·kó·sis] *f. see* **sitacosis.**
ptomaína [toma·í·na] *f.* ptomaine.
púa [pú·a] *f.* prick; barb; prong; thorn; quill (*of a porcupine, etc.*); sharp, cunning person; *Ríopl.* cock's spur; **alambre de -s** barbed wire.
publicación [pu·ƀli·ka·sjón] *f.* publication.
publicar[6] [pu·ƀli·kár] *v.* to publish; to reveal; to announce.
publicidad [pu·ƀli·si·đáđ] *f.* publicity.
público [pú·ƀli·ko] *adj. & m.* public.
puchero [pu·čé·ro] *m.* pot, kettle; meat and vegetable stew; pout; **hacer -s** to pout.
pucho [pú·čo] *m.* cigar or cigarette butt; *C.A.* something of little value.
pudiente [pu·đjén·te] *adj.* powerful; rich, wealthy; *m.* man of means.
pudín [pu·đín] *m.* pudding.
pudor [pu·đór] *m.* modesty; shyness.
pudrir[16] [pu·đrír] *v.* to rot; to vex, annoy; **-se** to rot.
pueblero [pwe·ƀlé·ro] *m. Ríopl.* townsman (*as opposed to countryman*).
pueblo [pwé·ƀlo] *m.* town, village; people, race, nation; populace; common people.
puente [pwén·te] *m.* bridge; *Carib., Mex., Ríopl.* dental bridge; *Am.* knife and fork rest; **— colgante** suspension bridge; **— levadizo** drawbridge.
puerca [pwér·ka] *f.* sow.
puerco [pwér·ko] *m.* pig, hog; **— espín** porcupine; *adj.* filthy, dirty; coarse, ill-bred.
pueril [pwe·ríl] *adj.* puerile, childish.
puerro [pwé·rro] *m.* scallion.
puerta [pwér·ta] *f.* door; gate; entrance; **— accessoria (excusada,** *or* **falsa)** side door; **— de golpe** spring door; trap door; **— franca** open door; free entrance or entry; **— trasera** back door; **a — cerrada** secretly, behind closed doors; *Am.* **en —** in view, in sight, very near.
puerto [pwér·to] *m.* port; harbor; refuge; mountain pass; **— franco** free port.
puertorriqueño [pwer·to·rri·ké·ño] *adj. & m.* Puerto Rican.
pues [pwes] *conj.* since, because, for, inasmuch as; then; *adv.* then; well; **— bien** well then, well; **— que** since.
puesta [pwés·ta] *f.* set, setting (*of a star or planet*); stake at cards; **— de sol** sunset.
puestero [pwes·té·ro] *m. Carib., Mex., Ríopl.* vendor, seller (*at a stand or stall*); *Ríopl.* man in charge of livestock on Argentine ranches.
puesto [pwés·to] *p.p. of* **poner** placed, put, set; **mal** (*or* **bien**) **—** badly (*or* well) dressed; *m.* place; vendor's booth or stand; post, position, office; military post; *Andes, Ríopl.* station for watching and taking care of cattle on a ranch; **— de socorros** first-aid station; **— que** *conj.* since.
pugilato [pu·xi·lá·to] *m.* boxing.
pugilista [pu·xi·lís·ta] *m.* boxer, prize fighter.
pugna [púǥ·na] *f.* struggle; conflict; **estar en — con** to be in conflict with; to be opposed to.
pugnar [puǥ·nár] *v.* to fight; to struggle; to strive; to persist.
pujanza [pu·xán·sa] *f.* push, force, power.
pujar [pu·xár] *v.* to make a strenuous effort; to grope for words; to falter; to outbid (*offer a higher bid than*); *C.A.* to grunt; *Peru* to reject; *Ven.* to dismiss; *Mex.* **— para adentro** to forbear, keep silent; *Peru* **andar pujado** to go around crestfallen; to be in disgrace.
pujido [pu·xí·đo] *m. Am.* grunt.
pulcritud [pul·kri·túđ] *f.* neatness, trimness; excellence, perfection.
pulcro [púl·kro] *adj.* neat, trim; beautiful.
pulga [púl·ǥa] *f.* flea; *Ríopl.* small and insignificant person; **tener malas -s** to be illtempered; *Col., Andes* **ser de pocas -s** to be touchy, oversensitive; **pulgón** *m.* blight, plant louse.
pulgada [pul·ǥá·đa] *f.* inch.
pulgar [pul·ǥár] *m.* thumb.
pulguero [pul·ǥé·ro] *m.* jail (*slang*).
pulido [pu·lí·đo] *adj.* polished, refined; polite; neat; exquisite.
pulidor [pu·li·đór] *adj.* polishing; *m.* polisher.
pulimentar [pu·li·men·tár] *v.* to polish.
pulimento [pu·li·mén·to] *m.* polish; gloss.
pulir [pu·lír] *v.* to polish.
pulmón [pul·món] *m.* lung.
pulmonar [pul·mo·nár] *adj.* pulmonary, pertaining to the lungs.
pulmonía [pul·mo·ní·a] *f.* pneumonia.
pulpa [púl·pa] *f.* pulp; boneless meat.
pulpería [pul·pe·rí·a] *f. Ríopl., C.A., Ch., Ven., Andes* country general store; *Am.* tavern.
pulpero [pul·pé·ro] *m. Ríopl., C.A., Ch., Ven., Andes* owner of a country store or tavern.
púlpito [púl·pi·to] *m.* pulpit.
pulpo [púl·po] *m.* octopus.
pulque [púl·ke] *m. Mex.* pulque (*fermented juice of the maguey*).
pulquería [pul·ke·rí·a] *f. Mex.* pulque bar or *cantina.*
pulsación [pul·sa·sjón] *f.* pulsation, beat, throb; pulse, beating.
pulsar [pul·sár] *v.* to pulsate, throb, beat; to feel the pulse of; to sound out; examine; to play (*the harp*); *Mex., C.A.* to judge or try the weight of (*by lifting*).
pulsera [pul·sé·ra] *f.* bracelet; wrist bandage; **reloj de —** wrist watch.
pulso [púl·so] *m.* pulse; steadiness; tract; *Ríopl., Carib., Col.* bracelet, wrist watch; **un hombre de —** a prudent, steady man; *Cuba, Mex.* **beber a —** to drink straight down, gulp down; **levantar a —** to lift with the strength of the wrist or hand; **sacar a — un negocio** to carry out a deal by sheer perseverance.
pulsorreactor [pul·so·rre·ak·tór] *m.* jet engine of movable intake valves.
pulular [pu·lu·lár] *v.* to swarm; to multiply rapidly; to

sprout, bud.
pulverizar[9] [pul·ƀe·ri·sár] *v.* to pulverize.
pulla [pú·ya] *f.* taunt; mean dig, quip, cutting remark; filthy word or remark.
puma [pú·ma] *f.* puma, mountain lion.
puna [pú·na] *f. Andes* cold, arid tableland of the Andes; *Ríopl.* desert; *Andes* sickness caused by high altitude.
pundonor [pun·do·nór] *m.* point of honor.
púnico [pú·ni·ko] *adj.* Punic.
punta [pún·ta] *f.* point, tip; bull's horn; cigar or cigarette butt; *Ven.* gang, band, herd, a lot (*of things, people, etc.*); *Am.* small leaf of fine tobacco; *Am.* jeer, cutting remark; **-s** point lace; scallops; **de —** on end; **de -s** (*or* **de puntillas**) on tiptoe; *Am.* **a — de** by dint of, by means of; **estar de — con** to be on bad terms with; **sacar — a un lápiz** to sharpen a pencil; **tener sus -s de poeta** to be something of a poet.
puntada [pun·ta·đa] *f.* stitch; hint; *Andes* prick, pricking, sting, sharp pain; **no he dado — en este asunto** I have left this matter completely untouched.
puntal [pun·tál] *m.* prop; support, basis; bull's horn; *Col.* snack (*between meals*).
puntapié [pun·ta·pjé] *m.* kick (*with the toe of the shoe*).
puntazo [pun·tá·so] *m. Col., Ven., Mex., Cuba* stab, jab.
puntear [pun·te·ár] *v.* to pluck (*the strings of a guitar*); to play (*a guitar*); to make dots; to engrave, draw or paint by means of dots; to stitch; to tack (*said of a boat*).
puntería [pun·te·rí·a] *f.* aim.
puntero [pun·té·ro] *m.* pointer; chisel; blacksmith's punch; *C.A., Col., Ch.* clock or watch hand; *Col., Ch.* leader of a parade; *Cuba, Mex., Ven., Col.* leading ox (*or other animal*); *Arg.* guide.
puntiagudo [pun·tja·ǥú·đo] *adj.* sharp, sharp-pointed.
puntilla [pun·tí·ya] *f.* small point; tip; small dagger; tracing point; point lace; *Ven.* penknife; *Mex., Ch.* toe rubber; *Ch.* ridge (*of a hill*); **de -s** on tiptoe; **puntillazo** *m.* stab (*with a dagger*).
punto [pún·to] *m.* (*parada*) period; stop; point; dot; (*puntada*) stitch; mesh; (*sitio*) place; moment; (*mira*) gun sight; (*computadora*) pixel; **— de admiración** exclamation mark; **— de interrogación** question mark; **— y coma** semicolon; **dos -s** colon; **al —** at once, immediately; **a — de** on the point of; **de —** knitted, porous knit, stockinet or jersey weave; **en —** exactly, on the dot; **a — fijo** with certainty; **subir de —** to increase or get worse.
puntuación [pun·twa·sjón] *f.* punctuation.
puntual [pun·twál] *adj.* punctual, prompt; exact.
puntualidad [pun·twa·li·đáđ] *f.* punctuality, promptness; certainty.
puntualizar [pun·twa·li·sár] *v.* to point out.
puntuar[18] [pun·twár] *v.* to punctuate.
punzada [pun·sá·đa] *f.* puncture; prick; sharp pain.
punzante [pun·sán·te] *adj.* sharp; pricking; piercing, penetrating.
punzar[9] [pun·sár] *v.* to puncture; to sting; to prick; to punch, perforate.
punzón [pun·són] *m.* punch, puncher; pick; awl; **— de marcar** center punches (machine).
puñada [pu·ñá·đa] *f.* punch, box, blow with the fist.
puñado [pu·ñá·đo] *m.* fistful, handful; **a -s** abundantly; by handfuls.
puñal [pu·ñál] *m.* dagger.
puñalada [pu·ña·la·đa] *f.* stab; sharp pain; **coser a -s** to stab to death.
puñetazo [pu·ñe·tá·so] *m.* punch, blow with the fist.
puño [pú·ño] *m.* fist; fistful, handful; cuff; hilt, handle; *Ven., Col.* blow with the fist; **a — cerrado** firmly; **ser como un —** to be stingy; **tener -s** to be strong, courageous.
pupila [pu·pí·la] *f.* pupil (*of the eye*).
pupilo [pu·pí·lo] *m.* ward; boarding-school pupil; boarder.
pupitre [pu·pí·tre] *m.* desk, school desk.
puré [pu·ré] *m.* purée; thick soup.
pureza [pu·ré·sa] *f.* purity; chastity.
purga [púr·ǥa] *f.* purge, laxative, physic.
purgante [pur·ǥán·te] *adj.* purgative, laxative; *m.* purgative, physic, laxative.
purgar[7] [pur·ǥár] *v.* to purge; to purify; to atone for; **-se** to purge oneself; to take a laxative.
purgatorio [pur·ǥa·tó·rjo] *m.* purgatory.
purificar[6] [pu·ri·fi·kár] *v.* to purify.
purista [pu·rís·ta] *m. & f.* purist.
puro [pú·ro] *adj.* (*limpio*) pure; clean; chaste; (*sólo*) mere, only, sheer; **a pura fuerza** by sheer force; **a puros gritos** by just shouting; *m.* cigar.
púrpura [púr·pu·ra] *f.* purple; purple cloth.
purpúreo [pur·pú·re·o] *adj.* purple.
pus [pus] *m.* pus.
pusilánime [pu·si·lá·ni·me] *adj.* pusillanimous.
puta [pú·ta] *f.* whore, prostitute.
putativo [pu·ta·tí·ƀo] *adj.* reputed, supposed; **padre —** foster father.
putrefacción [pu·tre·fak·sjón] *f.* putrefaction, decay, rotting.
putrefacto [pu·tre·fák·to] *adj.* putrid, rotten, decayed.
puya [pú·ya] *f.* goad; lance head.

Q:q

que [ke] *rel. pron.* that; which; who; whom; **el —** who; which; the one who; the one which; *conj* that; for, because; **más (menos) —** more (less) than; **el mismo —** the same as; **—** (= *subj.*) let, may you, I hope that; **por mucho —** no matter how much; **quieras — no** whether you wish or not.
qué [ke] *interr. adj. & pron.* what?; what a!; *interr. adv.* how; **¡— bonito!** how beautiful!; **¿a —?** what for?; **¿para —?** what for?; **¿por —?** why?; **¿— tal?** how?; hello!; **¡— más da!** what's the difference!; **¡a mí —!** so what! and what's that to me!
quebracho [ke·ƀrá·čo] *m.* quebracho, breakax wood.
quebrada [ke·ƀrá·đa] *f.* ravine; gorge; failure, bankruptcy; *Ríopl., Col., Ven., C.A., Mex.* brook.
quebradizo [ke·ƀra·đí·so] *adj.* breakable; brittle; fragile; delicate.
quebrado [ke·ƀrá·đo] *adj.* broken; weakened; ruptured; bankrupt; rough or rugged (*ground*); *m.* common fraction; *Ven.* navigable waters between reefs.
quebrantar [ke·ƀran·tár] *v.* to break; to break open; to pound, crush; to violate (*a law*); to weaken; to vex; *Mex., Col.* to tame, break in (*a colt*); **— el agua** to take the chill off the water.
quebranto [ke·ƀrán·to] *m.* breaking; grief, affliction; discouragement; damage, loss.
quebrar[1] [ke·ƀrár] *v. irr.* to break; to crush; to interrupt; to wither (*said of the complexion*); to become bankrupt; **-se** to break; to get broken; to be ruptured; **-se uno la cabeza** to rack one's brain.

quebrazón [ke·ƀra·són] *m. Ven., Col.* breakage, breaking.
quechua [ké·čwa] *adj. Am.* Quechua; *m. & f.* Quechua, Quechua Indian; *m.* Quechua language.
queda [ké·đa] *f.* curfew.
quedar [ke·đár] to stay; to remain; to be left over; to be left (*in a state or condition*); — **en** to agree to; *Am.* — **de** to agree to; — **bien** to acquit oneself well; to come out well; *Am.* to suit, become (*said of a dress, hat, etc.*); *Am.* — **bien con alguien** to please someone; **-se** to remain; **-se con una cosa** to keep something; to take something (*buy it*); *Am.* **-se como si tal cosa** to act as if nothing had happened.
quedo [ké·đo] *adj.* quiet, still; gentle; *adv.* softly; in a low voice; **quedito** [ke·đí·to] *adj.* nice and quiet; *adv.* very softly.
quehacer [ke·a·sér] *m.* work, occupation; task, duty, chore.
queja [ké·xa] *f.* complaint; groan, moan; grudge.
quejarse [ke·xár·se] *v.* to complain; to grumble; to moan; to lament.
quejido [ke·xí·đo] *m.* moan; groan.
quejoso [ke·xó·so] *adj.* complaining, whining.
quejumbre [ke·xúm·bre] *f.* whine, moan; murmur, complaint; **-s** *m. Cuba, Ven.* grumbler, whiner; **quejumbroso** [ke·xum·bró·so] *adj.* whining, complaining.
quemada [ke·má·đa] *f.* burned forest; *Am.* burn.
quemado [ke·má·đo] *m.* burned portion of a forest; *Col.* burned field; *Ec.* hot alcoholic drink; *adj* dark, tan; *Am.* peeved, piqued; *Col., Ven., Cuba, Mex.* ruined; *p.p. of* **quemar.**
quemadura [ke·ma·đú·ra] *f.* burn; burning; scald; smut (*plant disease*).
quemar [ke·már] *v.* to burn; to scald; to scorch; to sell at a loss; to annoy; *Am.* to deceive, swindle; **-se** to burn; to be hot.
quemazón [ke·ma·són] *f.* (*calor*) burn, burning; great heat; fire, conflagration; (*desazón*) pique, anger; bargain sale; *Am.* mirage on the pampas.
quena [ké·na] *f. Andes* flute of the Quechua Indians.
querella [ke·ré·ya] *f.* quarrel; complaint; controversy.
querellante [ke·re·yán·te] *m.* plaintiff.
querellarse [ke·re·yár·se] *v.* to complain.
querencia [ke·rén·sja] *f.* affection; longing; favorite spot; haunt; stable.
querer[41] [ke·rér] *v. irr.* to want, wish, desire; to will; to be willing; to love; — **decir** to mean; **sin** — unwillingly; **no quiso hacerlo** he refused to do it; **quiere llover** it is trying to rain, it is about to rain; **como quiera** in any way; **como quiera que** since; no matter how; **cuando quiera** whenever; **donde quiera** wherever; anywhere; **-se** to love each other; *Ríopl., Ven., Col.* to be on the point of, be about to; **se quiere caer esa pared** that wall is about to fall.
querido [ke·rí·đo] *p.p.* wanted, desired; *adj.* beloved, dear; *m.* lover; **querida** *f.* darling; mistress.
queroseno [ke·ro·sé·no] *m. variant of* **keroseno.**
querubín [ke·ru·ƀín] *m.* cherub.
quesería [ke·se·rí·a] *f.* dairy, creamery, cheese factory; **quesera** [ke·sé·ra] *f.* dairy, cheese factory; cheese dish; dairymaid, woman cheese vendor or cheesemaker; **quesero** [ke·sé·ro] *adj.* pertaining to cheese; *m.* cheesemaker.
queso [ké·so] *m.* cheese; *Ven.* — **de higos** fig paste; — **crema (de natas)** cream cheese.
quetzal [ket·sál] *m.* bird of paradise; quetzal (*monetary unit of Guatemala*).
quicio [kí·sjo] *m.* hinge of a door; **sacar a uno de** — to exasperate someone.
quichua [kí·čwa] = **quechua.**
quiebra [kjé·ƀra] *f.* (*rotura*) break; crack; fissure; fracture; (*pérdida*) loss, damage; bankruptcy.
quien [kjen] *rel. pron.* who, whom; he who, she who; **¿quién?** *interr. pron.* who? whom?
quienquiera [kjen·kjé·ra] *pron.* whoever, whosoever, whomsoever.
quieto [kjé·to] *adj.* quiet, still; calm.
quietud [kje·túđ] *f.* quiet, stillness, calmness.
quijada [ki·xá·đa] *f.* jaw; jawbone.
quijotada [ki·xo·tá·đa] *f.* quixotic deed.
quilate [ki·lá·te] *m.* carat (*twenty-fourth part in weight and value of gold*); unit of weight for precious stones and pearls; **-s** qualities; degree of perfection or purity.
quilla [kí·ya] *f.* keel.
quimbombó [kim·bom·bó] *m.* okra.
quimera [ki·mé·ra] *f.* absurd idea, wild fancy.
química [kí·mi·ka] *f.* chemistry.
químico [kí·mi·ko] *adj.* chemical; *m.* chemist.
quina [kí·na], **quinina** [ki·ní·na] *f.* quinine.
quincalla [kin·ká·ya] *f.* hardware.
quincallería [kin·ka·ye·rí·a] *f.* hardware; hardware store; hardware trade.
quince [kín·se] *num.* fifteen.
quincena [kin·sé·na] *f.* fortnight; semimonthly pay.
quinqué [kin·ké] *m.* oil lamp.
quinta [kín·ta] *f.* (*casa*) villa, country house; (*militar*) draft, military conscription; (*cartas*) sequence of five cards.
quintaesencia [kin·ta·e·sén·sja] *f.* quintessence, pure essence, purest form.
quiosco [kjós·ko] *m.* kiosk, small pavilion.
quiropráctico [ki·ro·prák·ti·ko] m. chiropractor.
quirúrgico [ki·rúr·xi·ko] *adj.* surgical.
quisquilloso [kis·ki·yó·so] *adj.* touchy, oversensitive.
quisto [kís·to]: **bien** — well-liked, well received, welcome; **mal** — disliked; unwelcome.
quitamanchas [ki·ta·mán·čas] *m.* cleaner, stain remover.
quitar [ki·tár] *v.* to remove; to take away (off, *or* from); to rob of; to deprive of; to subtract; to parry (*in fencing*); **-se** to take off (*clothing*); to remove oneself, withdraw; **-se de una cosa** to give up something, get rid of something; **-se a alguien de encima** to get rid of someone; **¡quita allá!** don't tell me that!; **¡quítese de aquí!** get out of here!
quitasol [ki·ta·sól] *m.* large sunshade, parasol.
quite [kí·te] *m.* parry (*in fencing*); revenge; dodge, dodging; *Ven., Col., Mex.* **andar a los -s** to be on the defensive; to take offense easily; to be afraid of one's own shadow; **eso no tiene** — that can't be helped.
quizá [ki·sá], **quizás** [ki·sás] *adv.* perhaps, maybe.

R:r

rabadilla [rra·ƀa·đí·ya] *f.* end of the spinal column; coccyx; tail of a fowl; rump.
rábano [rrá·ƀa·no] *m.* radish; **tomar el — por las hojas** to take one thing for another; to misinterpret something.
rabia [rrá·ƀja] *f.* rabies; rage; **tener — a alguien** to hate someone; *Ríopl., Carib., Mex.* **volarse de** — to get furious, angry.
rabiar [rra·ƀjár] *v.* to have rabies; to rage; to rave; to suffer a severe pain; — **por** to be dying to or for, be very eager to; **quema que rabia** it burns

terribly.
rabieta [rra·ƀjé·ta] *f.* tantrum, fit of temper.
rabino [rra·ƀí·no] *m.* rabbi.
rabioso [rra·ƀjó·so] *adj.* rabid (*having rabies*), mad; furious, angry, violent.
rabo [rrá·ƀo] *m.* tail; **de cabo a** — from beginning to end; **mirar con el** — **del ojo** to look out of the corner of one's eye.
rabón [rra·ƀón] *m.* bobtail.
racimo [rra·sí·mo] *m.* bunch; cluster.
raciocinio [rra·sjo·sí·njo] *m.* reasoning.
ración [rra·sjón] *f.* ration; allowance; supply.
racional [rra·sjo·nál] *adj.* rational; reasonable.
racionamiento [rra·sjo·na·mjén·to] *m.* rationing.
racionar [rra·sjo·nár] *v.* to ration.
racismo [rra·síz·mo] *m.* racism.
racista [rra·sís·ta] *m. & f.* racist.
radar [rra·đár] *m.* radar.
radaroscopio [rra·đa·ros·kó·pjo] *m.* radarscope.
radiación [rra·đja·sjón] *f.* radiation; — **cósmica** cosmic radiation.
radiatividad [rra·đjak·ti·ƀi·đáđ] *f.* radioactivity.
radiactivo [rra·đjak·tí·ƀo] *adj.* radioactive.
radiador [rra·đja·đór] *m.* radiator.
radiante [rra·đján·te] *adj.* radiant; shining; beaming.
radiar [rra·đjár] *v.* to radiate; to radio; to broadcast.
radical [rra·đi·kál] *adj.* (*básico*) fundamental, basic; radical; (*extremista*) extreme; *m.* radical; root of a word.
radicalismo [rra·đi·ka·líz·mo] *m.* radicalism.
radicar[6] [rra·đi·kár] *v.* to take root; to be, be found (*in a certain place*); **-se** to take root; to locate, settle.
radio [rrá·đjo] *m.* radius; radium; *m. & f.* radio.
radiodifundir [rra·đjo·đi·fun·dír] *v.* to broadcast by radio. *See* **difundir.**
radiodifusión [rra·đjo·đi·fu·sjón] *f.* broadcasting. *See* **difusión.**
radiodifusora [rra·đjo·đi·fu·só·ra], **radioemisora** [rra·đjo·e·mi·só·ra] *f.* broadcasting station.
radioeléctrico [rra·djo·e·lék·tri·ko] *adj.* radioelectric.
radioescucha [rra·đjo·es·kú·ča] *m. & f.* radio listener.
radiofónico [rra·đjo·fó·ni·ko] *adj.* radio (*used as adj.*); **estación radiofónica** radio station.
radiografía [rra·đjo·ǥra·fí·a] *f.* radiography, X-ray photography; X-ray picture.
radiografiar[17] [rra·đjo·ǥra·fjár] *v.* to take X-ray pictures.
radiolocutor [rra·đjo·lo·ku·tór] *m.* radio announcer. *See* **locutor.**
radiotelefonía [rra·đjo·te·le·fo·ní·a] *f.* radiotelephony, radio, wireless.
radiotelegrafía [rra·đjo·te·le·ǥra·fí·a] *f.* radiotelegraphy, radio, wireless telegraphy.
radiotransmisor [rra·djo·trans·mi·sór] *m.* radio transmitter.
radón [rra·đón] *m.* radon.
radioyente [rra·đjo·yén·te] = **radioescucha.**
raer[24] [rra·ér] *v. irr.* to scrape off; to rub off; to scratch off; to fray; to erase.
ráfaga [rrá·fa·ǥa] *f.* gust of wind; flash of light.
raído [rra·í·đo] *p.p. & adj.* scraped off; rubbed off; frayed; worn, threadbare.
raigón [rraj·ǥón] *m.* large root; root of a tooth.
raíz [rra·ís] *f.* root; origin; foundation; — **cuadrada** square root; **a** — **de** close to, right after; **de** — by the roots, completely; **echar raíces** to take root, become firmly fixed.
raja [rrá·xa] *f.* slice; splinter; crack; split, crevice; **hacer -s** to slice; to tear into strips; to cut into splinters; **hacerse uno -s** to wear oneself out (*by dancing, jumping or any violent exercise*).
rajá [rra·xá] *m.* rajah.
rajadura [rra·xa·đú·ra] *f.* crack, crevice.
rajar [rra·xár] *v.* to split; to crack; to cleave; to slice; to chatter; to brag; *Col., Cuba, Mex., Andes* to defame, insult; *Col.* to flunk, fail (*a student*); **-se** to split open; to crack; *Mex.* to get afraid, back down.
rajatablas [rra·xa·tá·ƀlas] *m. Col.* reprimand, scolding; **a** — in great haste.
ralea [rra·lé·a] *f.* breed, race, stock; species, kind.
ralear [rra·le·ár] *v.* to thin out, make less dense; to become less dense.
ralo [rrá·lo] *adj.* sparse, thin, thinly scattered.
rallador [rra·ya·đór] *m.* grater.
rallar [rra·yár] *v.* to grate; to grate on, annoy; *Am.* to goad, spur.
rama [rrá·ma] *f.* branch, limb; **en** — crude, raw; **andarse por las -s** to beat about the bush, not to stick to the point.
ramada [rra·má·đa] *f.* branches, foliage; arbor; *Am.* shed, tent.
ramaje [rra·má·xe] *m.* foliage; branches.
ramal [rra·mál] *m.* strand (*of a rope, etc.*); branch; branch railway line; halter.
rambla [rrám·bla] *f.* avenue (*especially in Barcelona*).
ramera [rra·mé·ra] *f.* harlot, prostitute.
ramificación [rra·mi·fi·ka·sjón] *f.* (*computadora*) branching.
ramificarse[6] [rra·mi·fi·kár·se] *v.* to branch off, divide into branches.
ramillete [rra·mi·yé·te] *m.* bouquet; flower cluster.
ramo [rrá·mo] *m.* bunch (*of flowers*), bouquet; line, branch (*of art, science, industry, etc.*); branch, bough; **domingo de -s** Palm Sunday.
ramonear [rra·mo·ne·ár] *v.* to cut off twigs or tips of branches; to nibble grass, twigs, or leaves; *Am.* to eat scraps or leftovers.
rampa [rrám·pa] *f.* ramp; apron (*airport*); — **de cohetes,** — **de lanzamiento** launching ramp.
ramplón [rram·plón] *adj.* coarse; crude, uncouth; slovenly.
ramplonería [rram·plo·ne·rí·a] *f.* coarse act or remark; crudeness, coarseness; slovenliness.
rana [rrá·na] *f.* frog.
rancio [rrán·sjo] *adj.* rancid, stale; old (*wine*); **linaje** — old, noble lineage.
ranchero [rran·čé·ro] *m. Mex.* rancher, farmer; **ranchería** [rran·če·rí·a] *f.* group of huts; *Col.* inn (*for* **arrieros**).
rancho [rrán·čo] *m.* camp; hamlet; mess (*meal for a group and the group itself*); *Carib., Ven., Col., Andes, Ríopl.* hut; *Carib., Ven., Col., Andes, Ríopl.* country house; *Mex.* ranch, small farm (*usually for cattle raising*).
rango [rráŋ·go] *m.* rank, position.
ranura [rra·nú·ra] *f.* groove; slot; — **de acceso** (*computadora*) head slot, — **de protección** protect tab.
rapar [rra·pár] *v.* to shave off; to crop (*hair*); to strip bare, rob of everything.
rapaz [rra·pás] *adj.* rapacious, grasping, greedy; *m.* lad; **rapaza** *f.* lass, young girl.
rape [rrá·pe] *m.* quick or close haircut.
rapé [rra·pé] *m.* snuff (*pulverized tobacco*).
rapidez [rra·pi·đés] *f.* rapidity, speed.
rápido [rrá·pi·đo] *adj.* rapid, swift; *m.* rapids.
rapiña [rra·pí·ña] *f.* plunder; **ave de** — bird of prey.
rapiñar [rra·pi·ñár] *v.* to plunder; to steal.
raposa [rra·pó·sa] *f.* fox.

raptar [rrap·tár] *v.* to kidnap, abduct.
rapto [rráp·to] *m.* (*delito*) abduction, kidnapping; (*sentimiento*) ecstasy, rapture; outburst.
raqueta [rra·ké·ta] *f.* racket (*used in games*); tennis.
raquítico [rra·kí·ti·ko] *adj.* rickety, feeble, weak, skinny, sickly.
rareza [rra·ré·sa] *f.* rarity; oddity; strangeness; freak; curiosity; queer act or remark; peculiarity; **por** — seldom.
raro [rrá·ro] *adj.* rare; thin, not dense; scarce; strange, odd; ridiculous; **rara vez** (*or* **raras veces**) rarely, seldom.
ras [rras]: **a — de** flush with, even with; **al — con** flush with; **estar — con —** to be flush, perfectly even.
rascacielos [rras·ka·sjé·los] *m.* skyscraper.
rascar[6] [rras·kár] *v.* to scratch; to scrape; *Andes, Mex.* to dig up potatoes; *Am.* **— uno para adentro** to seek one's own advantage, look out for oneself.
rasete [rra·sé·te] *m.* sateen.
rasgado [rraz·gá·do] *adj.* torn; open; *Col.* generous; *Carib.* outspoken; **ojos -s** large, wideopen eyes.
rasgadura [rraz·ga·dú·ra] *f.* tear, rip, rent.
rasgar[7] [rraz·gár] *v.* to tear; to rip.
rasgo [rráz·go] *m.* (*propiedad*) trait, characteristic; (*rúbrica*) stroke of the pen, flourish; (*hazaña*) feat; *Am.* irrigation ditch; *Ven.* **un — de terreno** a parcel of land; **-s** features; traits.
rasgón [rraz·gón] *m.* large tear, rent, rip.
rasguñar [rraz·gu·ñár] *v.* to scratch; to claw.
rasguño [rraz·gú·ño] *m.* scratch.
raso [rrá·so] *adj.* (*llano*) plain; flat, smooth; (*despejado*) clear, cloudless; *Ríopl., Mex.* even, level (*when measuring wheat, corn, etc.*); *Am.* scarce, scanty; **soldado —** private; **al —** in the open air; *m.* satin.
raspadura [rras·pa·dú·ra] *f.* scrape; scraping; erasure; shaving (*of wood or metal*).
raspar [rras·pár] *v.* to scrape, scrape off; to steal; *Andes* to scold, upbraid; *Col.* to leave.
rastra [rrás·tra] *f.* drag; sled; large rake; harrow; **a -s** dragging; unwillingly.
rastreador [rras·tre·a·dór] *m.* trailer, tracker, tracer.
rastrear [rras·tre·ár] *v.* to trail, track, trace; to rake, harrow; to drag (*a dragnet*); to skim, scrape the ground.
rastrero [rras·tré·ro] *adj.* low, vile.
rastrillar [rras·tri·yár] *v.* to rake; to comb (*flax or hemp*); *Ven.* to scrape; *Col.* to shoot; *Am.* to barter, exchange; *Ch.* to pilfer, steal (*in stores*).
rastrillo [rras·trí·yo] *m.* rake; *Col.* barter, exchange; *Am.* business deal.
rastro [rrás·tro] *m.* track, trail, scent; trace, sign; rake, harrow; slaughterhouse.
rastrojo [rras·tró·xo] *m.* stubble.
rasura [rra·sú·ra] *f.* shave, shaving.
rasurar [rra·su·rár] *v.* to shave.
rata [rrá·ta] *f.* rat; *m.* pickpocket.
ratear [rra·te·ár] *v.* to pilfer; to pick pockets; to creep, crawl.
ratería [rra·te·rí·a] *f.* petty larceny; meanness.
ratero [rra·té·ro] *m.* pickpocket; *adj.* comtemptible, mean.
ratificar[6] [rra·ti·fi·kár] *v.* to ratify.
rato [rrá·to] *m.* short time, little while; **buen —** pleasant time; long time; **-s perdidos** leisure hours; **a -s** at intervals, from time to time; **pasar el —** to while away the time, kill time; *Am.* **¡hasta cada — !** so long!; see you later!
ratón [rra·tón] *m.* mouse; *Am.* **tener un —** to have a hangover; **ratonera** [rra·to·né·ra] *f.* mousetrap.
raudal [rraw·dál] *m.* torrent, downpour, flood; *Ríopl., Ch., Col., Ven., Andes* rapids.
raudo [rraw·do] *adj.* rapid, swift.
raya [rrá·ya] *f.* line; dash; stripe; boundary line; part in the hair; *Mex.* pay, wage; *Mex.* **día de —** payday; **tener a —** to keep within bounds; to hold in check; **pasar de la —** to overstep one's bounds, take undue liberties; *m.* sting ray (*a species of fish*).
rayador [rra·ya·dór] *m. Mex.* paymaster; *Ch.* umpire in a game.
rayar [rra·yár] *v.* to line, make lines on; to streak; to scratch, mark; to cross out; score; *Mex.* to pay or collect wages; *Am.* to stop a horse all of a sudden; *S.A.* to spur a horse to run at top speed; **— el alba** to dawn; **— en** to border on; *Am.* **-se uno** to help oneself; to get rich.
rayo [rrá·yo] *m.* ray, beam; lightning, thunderbolt; spoke; **-s X** X-rays; **-s infrarrojos** infrared rays.
rayón [rra·yón] *m.* rayon.
raza [rrá·sa] *f.* race; clan; breed; fissure, crevice; **caballo de —** thoroughbred horse.
razón [rra·són] *f.* (*facultad*) reason; (*justicia*) right, justice; (*cuenta*) ratio; account, information, word, message; **— social** firm, firm name; **a — de** at the rate of; **¡con — !** no wonder!; **dar —** to inform; **dar la — a una persona** to admit that a person is right; **perder la —** to lose one's mind; **poner en —** to pacify; **tener —** to be right.
razonable [rra·so·ná·ble] *adj.* reasonable.
razonamiento [rra·so·na·mjén·to] *m.* reasoning.
razonar [rra·so·nár] *v.* to reason; to discourse, talk; to argue.
re [rre] *m.* second note of the musical scale (*solfeggio*).
reabierto [rre·a·bjér·to] *p.p. of* **reabrir.**
reabrir[52] [rre·a·brír] *v.* to reopen.
reacción [rre·ak·sjón] *f.* reaction; **— nuclear** nuclear reaction; **— en cadena** chain reaction.
reaccionar [rre·ak·sjo·nár] *v.* to react.
reaccionario [rre·ak·sjo·ná·rjo] *adj. & m.* reactionary.
reacio [rre·á·sjo] *adj.* stubborn, obstinate.
reactor [rre·ak·tór] *m.* reactor; **— atómico** atomic reactor; **— nuclear** nuclear reactor.
reajustar [rre·a·xus·tár] *v.* to readjust.
reajuste [rre·a·xús·te] *m.* readjustment.
real [rre·ál] *adj.* real; royal; *m.* army camp; fairground; real (*Spanish coin worth one fourth of a peseta*); **-es** *Andes* money (*in general*); **levantar el —** (*or* **los -es**) to break camp.
realce [rre·ál·se] *m.* (*adorno*) embossment, raised work, relief; (*lustre*) prestige; lustre, splendor; **dar —** to enhance; to emphasize.
realeza [rre·a·lé·sa] *f.* royalty (*royal dignity*).
realidad [rre·a·li·dád] *f.* reality; truth; fact; **en —** really, truly, in fact.
realismo [rre·a·líz·mo] *m.* realism; royalism.
realista [rre·a·lís·ta] *adj.* realistic; royalist; *m.* realist; royalist.
realización [rre·a·li·sa·sjón] *f.* realization, fulfillment; conversion into money, sale.
realizar[9] [rre·a·li·sár] *v.* to realize, fulfill, make real; to convert into money; to sell out.
realzar[9] [rre·al·sár] *v.* to emboss; to raise; to enhance; to make stand out; to emphasize.
reanimar [rre·a·ni·már] *v.* to revive; to comfort; to cheer; to encourage.
reanudación [rre·a·nu·da·sjón] *f.* renewal.
reanudar [rre·a·nu·dár] *v.* to renew, resume, begin again.

reaparecer[13] [rre·a·pa·re·sér] *v. irr.* to reappear.
reasumir [rre·a·su·mír] *v.* to resume.
reata [rre·á·ta] *f.* lariat, rope, lasso.
reavivar [rre·a·ƀi·ƀár] *v.* to revive.
rebaba [rre·ƀá·ƀa] *f.* fin, flange.
rebaja [rre·ƀá·xa] *f.* deduction; reduction; discount.
rebajar [rre·ƀa·xár] *v.* to diminish; to lower, reduce; to tone down (*a painting*); to humiliate; — **una superficie** to grind; **-se** to lower or humble oneself.
rebajo [rre·ƀá·xo] *m.* rabbet; groove, offset.
rebanada [rre·ƀa·ná·đa] *f.* slice.
rebanar [rre·ƀa·nár] *v.* to slice.
rebaño [rre·ƀá·ño] *m.* flock; herd.
rebatir [rre·ƀa·tír] *v.* to beat over and over; to repel, resist; to refute; to rebut (*come back with an argument*); to argue; to parry (*in fencing*).
rebato [rre·ƀá·to] *m.* alarm, call to arms; surprise attack.
rebelarse [rre·ƀe·lár·se] *v.* to rebel.
rebelde [rre·ƀél·de] *adj.* rebellious; *m.* rebel; defaulter (*one who fails to appear in court*).
rebeldía [rre·ƀel·dí·a] *f.* rebelliousness; defiance; default, failure to appear in court; **en** — in revolt.
rebelión [rre·ƀe·ljón] *f.* rebellion, revolt.
rebencazo [rre·ƀeŋ·ká·so] *m. Ríopl., Ch., Andes* crack of a whip; *Am.* lash, stroke with a whip.
rebenque [rre·ƀéŋ·ke] *m.* rawhide whip.
reborde [rre·ƀór·đe] *m.* edge, border.
rebosante [rre·ƀo·sán·te] *adj.* brimming, overflowing.
rebosar [rre·ƀo·sár] *v.* to overflow, brim over; to abound.
rebotar [rre·ƀo·tár] *v.* to rebound, bounce back or again; to make rebound; to repel, reject; to annoy, vex; **-se** to become vexed, upset; *Col., Mex.* to become cloudy or muddy (*said of water*); *Am.* **rebotársele a uno la bilis** to get angry, become upset.
rebote [rre·ƀó·te] *m.* rebound, bounce; **de** — on the rebound; indirectly.
rebozar[9] [rre·ƀo·sár] *v.* to muffle up; **-se** to muffle oneself up; to wrap oneself up.
rebozo [rre·ƀó·so] *m.* shawl; **sin** — frankly, openly.
rebullir[20] [rre·ƀu·yír] *v. irr.* to stir, move; to boil up.
rebusca [rre·ƀús·ka] *f.* research; search; searching; gleaning; residue.
rebuscar[6] [rre·ƀus·kár] *v.* to search thoroughly; to pry into; to glean.
rebuznar [rre·ƀuz·nár] *v.* to bray.
rebuzno [rre·ƀúz·no] *m.* bray.
recabar [rre·ka·ƀár] *v.* to obtain, gain by entreaty.
recado [rre·ká·đo] *m.* message; errand; gift; daily food supply, daily marketing; precaution; equipment; *Ríopl., Andes* saddle and trappings; — **de escribir** writing materials; **-s a** regards to.
recaer[24] [rre·ka·ér] *v. irr.* to fall (upon); to fall again; to relapse; to have a relapse.
recaída [rre·ka·í·đa] *f.* relapse; falling again.
recalar [rre·ka·lár] *v.* to saturate, soak through; to reach port; to come within sight of land; to land, end up, stop at; *Am.* — **con alguien** to "land" on somebody, take it out on somebody.
recalcar[6] [rre·kal·kár] *v.* to emphasize; to harp on; to press down.
recalcitrante [rre·kal·si·trán·te] *adj.* obstinate, disobedient, stubborn.
recalentar[1] [rre·ka·len·tár] *v. irr.* to reheat, warm over; to overheat, heat too much.
recamar [rre·ka·már] *v.* to embroider (*usually with gold or silver*).
recámara [rre·ká·ma·ra] *f.* dressing room; *Mex., C.A., Col.* bedroom; *Ríopl., Col.* chamber for an explosive charge.
recapitular [rre·ka·pi·tu·lár] *v.* to recapitulate, sum up, tell briefly.
recargar[7] [rre·kar·ǥár] *v.* to overload; to emphasize.
recargo [rre·kár·ǥo] *m.* overload; extra load; extra charge; increase (*of fever*); new charge, new accusation.
recatado [rre·ka·tá·đo] *adj.* cautious, prudent; modest; *p.p.* concealed.
recatar [rre·ka·tár] *v.* to cover, conceal; **-se** to show timidity; to be cautious; to hide (from), shun.
recato [rre·ká·to] *m.* caution, prudence; reserve, restraint, secrecy; modesty.
recaudación [rre·kaw·đa·sjón] *f.* collection, collecting; office of tax collector.
recaudador [rre·kaw·đa·đór] *m.* tax collector.
recaudar [rre·kaw·đár] *v.* to collect (*money, taxes, rents, etc.*).
recaudo [rre·kaw·đo] *m.* collection, collecting; precaution; bond, security; *Mex.* spices, seasonings; *Ch., Guate.* daily supply of vegetables; **estar a buen** — to be safe; **poner a buen** — to place in safety.
recelar [rre·se·lár] *v.* to suspect, fear; **-se de** to be suspicious or afraid of.
recelo [rre·sé·lo] *m.* suspicion, fear.
receloso [rre·se·ló·so] *adj.* suspicious, distrustful, fearful.
recepción [rre·sep·sjón] *f.* reception; admission.
receptáculo [rre·sep·tá·ku·lo] *m.* receptacle.
receptivo [rre·sep·tí·ƀo] *adj.* receptive, capable of receiving, quick to receive.
receptor [rre·sep·tór] *m.* receiver; *adj.* receiving.
receta [rre·sé·ta] *f.* recipe; prescription.
recetar [rre·se·tár] *v.* to prescribe (*a medicine*).
recibidor [rre·si·ƀi·đór] *m.* receiver; reception room.
recibimiento [rre·si·ƀi·mjén·to] *m.* reception; welcome; reception room; parlor.
recibir [rre·si·ƀír] *v.* to receive; to admit, accept; to go out to meet; — **noticias de** to hear from; **-se de** to receive a title or degree of.
recibo [rre·sí·ƀo] *m.* (*monetario*) receipt; (*acción*) reception; (*sala*) reception room; parlor; **sala de** — reception room; **estar de** — to be at home for receiving callers; **ser de** — to be acceptable, be fit for use.
reciedumbre [rre·sje·đúm·bre] *f.* strength, force, vigor.
recién [rre·sjén] *adv.* recently, lately, newly (*used before a past participle*); *Ríopl., Ch., Andes* just now; *Ríopl., Ch., Andes* a short time ago; *Ríopl., Ch., Andes* — **entonces** just then.
reciente [rre·sjén·te] *adj.* recent, new.
recinto [rre·sín·to] *m.* enclosure; precinct; campus.
recio [rré·sjo] *adj.* strong, robust; harsh; hard, severe; fast; *adv.* strongly; harshly; rapidly; hard; loud.
recipiente [rre·si·pjén·te] *m.* receptacle, container; recipient, receiver (*he who receives*).
recíproco [rre·sí·pro·ko] *adj.* reciprocal, mutual.
recitación [rre·si·ta·sjón] *f.* recitation, recital.
recital [rre·si·tál] *m.* musical recital.
recitar [rre·si·tár] *v.* to recite.
reclamación [rre·kla·ma·sjón] *f.* protest, complaint; claim, demand.
reclamador [rre·kla·ma·đór] *m.* claimant; complainer.
reclamante [rre·kla·mán·te] *m. & f.* claimant; complainer; *adj.* complaining; claiming.
reclamar [rre·kla·már] *v.* (*protestar*) to complain, protest (*against*); (*exigir*) to claim, demand; to lure, call back (*a bird*).
reclamo [rre·klá·mo] *m.* (*protesta*) protest; claim;

advertisement; (*llamada*) call; bird call; decoy bird; lure.
reclinar [rre·kli·nár] *v.* to recline, lean; **-se** to recline, lean back.
recluir[32] [rre·klwír] *v. irr.* to seclude, shut up; **-se** to isolate oneself.
recluso [rre·klú·so] *m.* recluse, hermit; *adj.* shut in, shut up.
recluta [rre·klú·ta] *f.* recruiting; *Am.* roundup of cattle; *m.* recruit.
reclutamiento [rre·klu·ta·mjén·to] *m.* recruiting; levy, draft.
reclutar [rre·klu·tár] *v.* to recruit, enlist; *Am.* to round up (*cattle*).
recobrar [rre·ko·brár] *v.* to recover, regain; **-se** to recover; to recuperate.
recobro [rre·kó·bro] *m.* recovery.
recocido [rre·ko·sí·do] *m.* annealing.
recodo [rre·kó·do] *m.* bend, turn; elbow (*of a road*).
recoger[11] [rre·ko·xér] *v.* (*juntar*) to gather; to collect; to pick up; (*ceñir*) to take in, tighten; (*abrigar*) to shelter; **-se** to retire, go home; to withdraw; to seclude oneself; to take shelter.
recogida [rre·ko·xí·da] *f.* harvest.
recogimiento [rre·ko·xi·mjén·to] *m.* seclusion; concentration of thought, composure; retreat; collecting, gathering.
recolección [rre·ko·lek·sjón] *f.* collecting, gathering; harvest, crop; summary.
recolectar [rre·ko·lek·tár] *v.* to harvest; to gather.
recomendable [rre·ko·men·dá·ble] *adj.* praiseworthy, laudable; advisable.
recomendación [rre·ko·men·da·sjón] *f.* recommendation; request.
recomendar[1] [rre·ko·men·dár] *v. irr.* to recommend; to commend, praise; to enjoin, urge; to advise.
recompensa [rre·kom·pén·sa] *f.* recompense; compensation.
recompensar [rre·kom·pen·sár] *v.* to recompense, reward; to compensate.
reconcentrar [rre·kon·sen·trár] *v.* to concentrate, bring together; to hide in the depth of one's heart; **-se** to concentrate, become absorbed in thought, collect one's thoughts.
reconciliación [rre·kon·si·lja·sjón] *f.* reconciliation.
reconciliar [rre·kon·si·ljár] *v.* to reconcile; **-se** to become reconciled.
recóndito [rre·kón·di·to] *adj.* hidden, concealed; profound.
reconocer[13] [rre·ko·no·sér] *v. irr.* to recognize; to admit, acknowledge; to examine carefully; to reconnoiter, scout, explore.
reconocimiento [rre·ko·no·si·mjén·to] *m.* recognition; acknowledgment; gratitude; examination; scouting, exploring.
reconstruir[32] [rre·kons·trwír] *v. irr.* to reconstruct, rebuild.
recontar[2] [rre·kon·tár] *v. irr.* to recount; to tell, relate.
recopilar [rre·ko·pi·lár] *v.* to compile; to digest, make a digest of.
record [rré·kor] *m.* record.
recordación [rre·kor·da·sjón] *f.* recollection; remembrance.
recordar[2] [rre·kor·dár] *v. irr.* to remember; to recall; to remind; *Ríopl., C.A., Ven.* to rouse, awaken; **-se** to remember; to wake up.
recordativo [rre·kor·da·tí·bo] *m.* reminder; *adj.* reminding.
recordatorio [rre·kor·da·tó·rjo] *m.* reminder.
recorrer [rre·ko·rrér] *v.* to go over; to travel over; to read over; to look over; to overhaul.
recorrido [rre·ko·rrí·do] *m.* trip, run; mileage, distance traveled.
recortar [rre·kor·tár] *v.* to trim, clip; to shorten; to cut out (*figures*); to pare off; **-se** to project itself (*as a shadow*); to outline itself.
recorte [rre·kór·te] *m.* clipping; cutting; outline; *Mex.* gossip, slander.
recostar [rre·kos·tár] *v.* to recline, lean; **-se** to recline, lean back.
recoveco [rre·ko·bé·ko] *m.* turn, bend; nook; sly or underhanded manner.
recreación [rre·kre·a·sjón] *f.* recreation.
recrear [rre·kre·ár] *v.* to entertain, amuse; to gratify, please; **-se** to amuse oneself; to take delight (in).
recreo [rre·kré·o] *m.* recreation, entertainment; place of amusement.
recrudecer[13] [rre·kru·de·sér] *v.* to recur, break out again, flare up, become worse (*said of an illness or evil*).
rectángulo [rrek·táŋ·gu·lo] *m.* rectangle; *adj.* rectangular, right-angled.
rectificar[6] [rrek·ti·fi·kár] *v.* to rectify, correct, amend; to refine (*liquors*); **rectificado cilíndrico** cylindrical grinding.
rectitud [rrek·ti·túd] *f.* rectitude, uprightness, righteousness; straightness; accuracy.
recto [rrék·to] *adj.* straight; right; just, honest; **ángulo** — right angle; *m.* rectum; *adv. C.A.* straight ahead.
rector [rrek·tór] *m.* college or university president; principal; rector, curate, priest.
recua [rré·kwa] *f.* drove of pack animals; drove, crowd.
recuento [rre·kwén·to] *m.* recount.
recuerdo [rre·kwér·do] *m.* remembrance; recollection; souvenir, keepsake; memory; **-s** regards; *adj. Ríopl., Col., Ven.* awake.
reculada [rre·ku·lá·da] *f.* recoil.
recular [rre·ku·lár] *v.* to recoil, spring back; to fall back, go back, retreat; to yield, back down.
recuperación [rre·ku·pe·ra·sjón] *f.* recovery.
recuperar [rre·ku·pe·rár] *v.* to recuperate, recover, regain; **-se** to recuperate, recover one's health.
recurrir [rre·ku·rrír] *v.* to resort (to); to have recourse (to).
recurso [rre·kúr·so] *m.* recourse, resort; petition, appeal; **-s** means, resources; **sin** — without remedy; without appeal.
recusar [rre·ku·sár] *v.* to reject; decline.
rechazar[9] [rre·ča·sár] *v.* to reject; to repel, drive back; to rebuff.
rechifla [rre·čí·fla] *f.* hooting; hissing; ridicule.
rechiflar [rre·či·flár] *v.* to hoot; to hiss; to ridicule.
rechinamiento [rre·či·na·mjén·to] *m.* creak; squeak; squeaking; gnashing.
rechinar [rre·či·nár] *v.* to squeak; to creak; *Mex.* to be furious, angry; *Ven.* to grumble, growl; — **los dientes** to gnash one's teeth.
rechino [rre·čí·no] = **rechinamiento.**
rechoncho [rre·čón·čo] *adj.* plump; chubby; squat.
rechuparse [rre·ču·pár·se] *v.* to smack one's lips.
red [rred] *f.* net; netting; network; snare; **redecilla** [rre·de·sí·ya] *f.* small net; mesh; hair net.
redacción [rre·dak·sjón] *f.* (*acto*) wording; editing; (*lugar*) newspaper offices; editorial department; (*cuerpo*) editorial staff.
redactar [rre·dak·tár] *v.* to word, compose; to edit.
redactor [rre·dak·tór] *m.* editor.
redada [rre·dá·da] *f.* catch; haul (*of criminals*).
redargüir[32] [rre·dar·gwír] *v. irr.* to retort, answer

back; to contradict, call in question; to reargue.
rededor [rre·đe·đór] *m.* surroundings; **al** (*or* **en**) — around, about.
redención [rre·đen·sjón] *f.* redemption.
redentor [rre·đen·tór] *m.* redeemer, savior; **el Redentor** the Savior.
redil [rre·đíl] *m.* sheepfold.
redimir [rre·đi·mír] *v.* to redeem; to ransom; to set free.
rédito [rré·đi·to] *m.* interest, revenue, yield.
redituar[18] [rre·đi·twár] *v.* to produce, yield (*interest*).
redoblar [rre·đo·ƀlár] *v.* to double; to clinch (*a nail*); to reiterate, repeat; to roll (*a drum*).
redoble [rre·đó·ƀle] *m.* roll (*of a drum*).
redoma [rre·đó·ma] *f.* flask, vial.
redomón [rre·đo·món] *m. Ríopl.* half-tame horse or bull; *adj. Ríopl.* half-civilized, rustic.
redonda [rre·đón·da] *f.* surrounding district, neighborhood; whole note (*music*); **a la** — all around, round-about.
redondear [rre·đon·de·ár] *v.* to round, make round; to round off; to round out.
redondel [rre·đon·dél] *m.*arena, bull ring; circle.
redondez [rre·đon·dés] *f.* roundness.
redondo [rre·đón·do] *adj.* round; whole, entire; clear, evident; *Andes* stupid; *Mex.* honest; **en** — all around.
redopelo [rre·đo·pé·lo]: **a** — against the grain.
redor [rre·đór] *m.* round mat; **en** — around.
reducción [rre·đuk·sjón] *f.* reduction; cut, discount; decrease.
reducido [rre·đu·sí·đo] *p.p. & adj.* reduced; compact, small.
reducir[25] [rre·đu·sír] *v. irr.* to reduce; to diminish; to convert (into); to reset (*a bone*); **-se** to adapt oneself, adjust oneself; to be constrained, forced.
redundante [rre·đun·dán·te] *adj.* redundant.
reedificar[6] [rre·e·đi·fi·kár] *v.* to rebuild, reconstruct.
reelección [rre·e·lek·sjón] *f.* re-election.
reelegir[11] [rre·e·le·xír] *v.* to re-elect.
reembolsar [rre·em·bol·sár] *v.* to reimburse, refund, repay, pay back.
reembolso [rre·em·ból·so] *m.* reimbursement, refund.
reemitir [rre·mi·tír] *v.* to emit again; to issue again; to rebroadcast; to relay (*a broadcast*).
reemplazable [rre·em·pla·sá·ƀle] *adj.* replaceable.
reemplazar[9] [rre·em·pla·sár] *v.* to replace; to substitute.
reemplazo [rre·em·plá·so] *m.* replacement; substitute, substitution.
reexpedir[5] [rre·es·pe·đír] *v. irr.* to forward (*mail*).
refacción [rre·fak·sjón] *f.* (*alimento*) light lunch, refreshment; (*compostura*) repair, reparation; *Mex., Col.* spare part; *Carib.* help, aid, loan.
refajo [rre·fá·xo] *m.* underskirt; short skirt.
referencia [rre·fe·rén·sja] *f.* reference; narration, account.
referente [rre·fe·rén·te] *adj.* referring.
referir[3] [rre·fe·rír] *v. irr.* to refer; to narrate; to relate; **-se** to refer (to), relate (to).
refinamiento [rre·fi·na·mjén·to] *m.* refinement.
refinar [rre·fi·nár] *v.* to refine; to purify.
refinería [rre·fi·ne·rí·a] *f.* refinery.
reflector [rre·flek·tór] *m.* reflector; floodlight.
reflejar [rre·fle·xár] *v.* to reflect; to think over; **-se** to be reflected.
reflejo [rre·flé·xo] *m.* reflection, image; reflex; *adj.* reflected; reflex.
reflexión [rre·flek·sjón] *f.* reflection; meditation, consideration.
reflexionar [rre·flek·sjo·nár] *v.* to reflect, meditate, think over.
reflexivo [rre·flek·sí·ƀo] *adj.* reflexive; reflective, thoughtful.
reflujo [rre·flú·xo] *m.* ebb; ebb tide.
refocilar [rre·fo·si·lár] *v.* to cheer.
reforma [rre·fór·ma] *f.* reform; reformation; improvement.
reformador [rre·for·ma·đór] *m.* reformer.
reformar [rre·for·már] *v.* to reform; to correct, amend; to improve; **-se** to reform.
reformista [rre·for·mís·ta] *m. & f.* reformer.
reforzar[2,9] [rre·for·sár] *v. irr.* to reinforce; to strengthen.
refracción [rre·frak·sjón] *f.* refraction.
refractario [rre·frak·tó·rjo] *adj.* refractory; impervious; rebellious, unruly; stubborn.
refrán [rre·frán] *m.* popular proverb or saying.
refrenar [rre·fre·nár] *v.* to restrain, keep in check; to curb; to rein.
refrendar [rre·fren·dár] *v.* to legalize by signing; to countersign (*confirm by another signature*); — **un pasaporte** to visé a passport.
refrescante [rre·fres·kán·te] *adj.* refreshing.
refrescar[6] [rre·fres·kár] *v.* to refresh, renew; to cool; to get cool (*said of the weather*); **-se** to cool off; to take the fresh air; to take a cooling drink or refreshment; *Cuba, C.A.* to take an afternoon refreshment.
refresco [rre·frés·ko] *m.* refreshment.
refresquería [rre·fres·ke·rí·a] *f. Mex., C.A., Ven.* refreshment shop, outdoor refreshment stand.
refriega [rre·frjé·ǥa] *f.* strife, fray, scuffle.
refrigeración [rre·fri·xe·ra·sjón] *f.* refrigeration; light meal or refreshment.
refrigerador [rre·fri·xe·ra·đór] *m. Am.* refrigerator, freezer; *adj.* refrigerating, freezing; refreshing.
refrigerar [rre·fri·xe·rár] *v.* to cool.
refrigerio [rre·fri·xé·rjo] *m.* refreshment; relief, comfort; coolness.
refrito [rre·frí·to] *adj.* refried; frijoles refritos (*Mexican fried beans*).
refuerzo [rre·fwér·so] *m.* reinforcement.
refugiado [rre·fu·xjá·đo] *m.* refugee; *p.p. of* **refugiar.**
refugiar [rre·fu·xjár] *v.* to shelter; **-se** to take shelter or refuge.
refugio [rre·fú·xjo] *m.* refuge, shelter.
refulgente [rre·ful·xén·te] *adj.* refulgent, radiant, shining.
refundir [rre·fun·dír] *v.* to remelt, refound, recast (*metals*); to recast, rewrite, reconstruct.
refunfuñar [rre·fun·fu·ñár] *v.* to grumble, mumble, growl, mutter.
refunfuño [rre·fun·fú·ño] *m.* grumble, growl; **refunfuñón** [rre·fun·fu·ñón] *adj.* grouchy; grumbly, grumbling.
refutar [rre·fu·tár] *v.* to refute.
regadera [rre·ǥa·đé·ra] *f.* sprinkler; *Mex.* shower bath.
regadío [rre·ǥa·đí·o] *adj.* irrigable, that can be irrigated; irrigated; *m.* irrigated land; **tierras de** — irrigable lands.
regalar [rre·ǥa·lár] *v.* (*dar*) to give, present as a gift; to regale; (*recrear*) to entertain; to delight, please; **-se** to treat oneself well, live a life of ease.
regalo [rre·ǥá·lo] *m.* present, gift; pleasure, delight; dainty, delicacy; luxury, comfort.
regañadientes [rre·ǥa·ña·đjén·tes]: **a** — much against one's wishes; unwillingly.
regañar [rre·ǥa·ñár] *v.* to growl; to grumble; to quarrel; to scold.
regaño [rre·ǥá·ño] *m.* scolding, reprimand.

regañón [rre·ga·ñón] *adj.* grumbling; scolding; quarrelsome; *m.* growler, grumbler, scolder.
regar[1, 7] [rre·gár] *v. irr.* to irrigate; to water; to sprinkle, scatter; *Col.* to spill, throw off (*said of a horse*); **-se** *Am.* to scatter, disperse (*said of a group, herd, etc.*).
regatear [rre·ga·te·ár] *v.* to haggle, bargain; to dispute; to sell at retail; to race (*in a regatta or boat race*).
regateo [rre·ga·té·o] *m.* bargaining.
regazo [rre·gá·so] *m.* lap.
regencia [rre·xén·sja] *f.* regency.
regentar [rre·xen·tár] *v.* to direct, conduct, manage; — **una cátedra** to teach a course (*at a university*).
regente [rre·xén·te] *m.* regent; manager; *adj.* ruling.
regidor [rre·xi·dór] *m.* councilman, alderman; *adj.* governing, ruling.
régimen [rré·xi·men] *m.* regime; government, rule, management; — **lácteo** milk diet.
regimiento [rre·xi·mjén·to] *m.* regiment; (*administrativo*) administration; municipal council; position of alderman.
regio [rré·xjo] *adj.* regal, royal; splendid, magnificient.
región [rre·xjón] *f.* region.
regir[5, 11] [rre·xír] *v. irr.* to rule, govern; to direct, manage; to be in force (*said of a law*); to move (*said of the bowels*).
registrador [rre·xis·tra·dór] *m.* registrar, recorder; city clerk, official in charge of records; inspector (*in a customhouse*); searcher; *adj.* registering; **caja registradora** cash register.
registrar [rre·xis·trár] *v.* to examine, inspect, scrutinize; to register, record; **-se** to register, enroll.
registro [rre·xís·tro] *m.* search, inspection; registration; census; registration office; register; record; registration certificate; watch regulator; bookmark; organ stop; (*computadora*) record; *Ven.* wholesale textile store.
regla [rré·gla] *f.* (*precepto*) rule; ruler; order; precept, principle; (*medida*) measure, moderation; menstruation; **en** — in order, in due form; **por — general** as a general rule; usually.
reglamento [rre·gla·mén·to] *m.* regulations, rules; rule, bylaw.
regocijado [rre·go·si·xá·do] *adj.* joyful, merry, gay; *p.p. of* **regocijar.**
regocijar [rre·go·si·xár] *v.* to gladden, delight; **-se** to be glad; to rejoice.
regocijo [rre·go·sí·xo] *m.* joy; rejoicing.
regordete [rre·gor·dé·te] *adj.* plump.
regresar [rre·gre·sár] *v.* to return.
regreso [rre·gré·so] *m.* return; **estar de** — to be back.
reguero [rre·gé·ro] *m.* stream, rivulet; trickle; irrigation ditch.
regulación [rre·gu·la·sjón] *f.* regulation; adjustment.
regulador [rre·gu·la·dór] *m.* regulator; controller, governor (*of a machine*) — **de tiro** damper; *adj.* regulating.
regular [rre·gu·lár] *v.* to regulate; to adjust; *adj.* regular; ordinary; moderate; fair, medium; **por lo** — as a rule, usually; *adv.* fairly well.
regularidad [rre·gu·la·ri·dád] *f.* regularity.
regularizar[9] [rre·gu·la·ri·sár] *v.* to regulate, make regular.
rehacer[31] [rre·a·sér] *v. irr.* to remake; to make over; to repair; **-se** to recover one's strength; to rally.
rehen [rre·én] *m.* hostage; **en rehenes** as a hostage.
rehuir[32] [rre·wír] *v. irr.* to shun, avoid; to shrink (from).
rehusar [rre·u·sár] *v.* to refuse; **-se a** to refuse to.
reina [réj·na] *f.* queen.
reinado [rrej·ná·do] *m.* reign.
reinante [rrej·nán·te] *adj.* reigning; prevailing.
reinar [rrej·nár] *v.* to reign; to rule; to prevail.
reincidir [rrej·si·dír] *v.* to relapse, slide back (into).
reino [rréj·no] *m.* kingdom.
reintegro [rrejn·té·gro] *m.* reimbursement, refund.
reir[15] [rre·ír] *v. irr.* to laugh; **-se de** to laugh at; *Ríopl., Andes, Col., Ven., Carib.* — **de dientes para afuera** to laugh outwardly, laugh hypocritically.
reiterar [rrej·te·rár] *v.* to reiterate, repeat.
reivindicación [rrej·bin·di·ka·sjón] *f.* recovery.
reja [rré·xa] *f.* grate, grating; plowshare (*blade of the plow*); plowing; *Carib., C.A.* jail.
rejilla [rre·xí·ya] *f.* small grating, lattice; small latticed window; fireplace grate; cane upholstery; *Ch.* wire dish-cover.
rejo [rré·xo] *m.* point; plow share.
rejonear [rre·xo·ne·ár] *v.* to fight a bull from horseback (*Portuguese style*).
rejuvenecer[13] [rre·xu·be·ne·sér] *v. irr.* to rejuvenate, make young; **-se** to become rejuvenated.
relación [rre·la·sjón] *f.* relation; story, account; long speech in a play; *Ríopl.* verse recited alternately by a couple in a folk dance; **-es** personal relations, connections; acquaintances.
relacionar [rre·la·sjo·nár] *v.* to relate, connect; **-se** to be related, connected; to become acquainted, establish friendly connections.
relajación [rre·la·xa·sjón] *f.*, **relajamiento** [rre·la·xa·mjén·to] *m.* relaxation; laxity; slackening; hernia.
relajar [rre·la·xár] *v.* to relax; to slacken; to release from a vow or oath; **-se** to get a hernia or rupture; to become weakened; to become lax (*said of laws, customs, etc.*).
relajo [rre·lá·xo] *m. Carib., Mex.* disorderly conduct; lewdness; scandal.
relamerse [rre·la·mér·se] *v.* to lick one's lips; to gloat; to boast; to slick oneself up.
relámpago [rre·lám·pa·go] *m.* lightning; flash.
relampaguear [rre·lam·pa·ge·ár] *v.* to lighten; to flash; to sparkle, blink.
relampagueo [rre·lam·pa·gé·o] *m.* flashing; sheet lightning.
relatar [rre·la·tár] *v.* to relate, narrate.
relativo [rre·la·tí·bo] *adj.* relative; — **a** relative to, regarding.
relato [rre·lá·to] *m.* narration, account, story.
relé [rre·lé] *m.* relay; — **de televisión** television relay system.
relegar[7] [rre·le·gár] *v.* to relegate, banish; to postpone; to set aside, put away.
relente [rre·lén·te] *m.* night dampness; *Am.* fresh night breeze.
relevar [rre·le·bár] *v.* to relieve; to release; to absolve; to replace, substitute; to emboss; to make stand out in relief.
relevo [rre·lé·bo] *m.* relief (*from a post or military duty; person who relieves another from the performance of a duty*).
relicario [rre·li·ká·rjo] *m.* reliquary (*small box or casket for keeping relics*); *Col., Ven., Cuba, Mex., Andes* locket.
relieve [rre·ljé·be] *m.* relief, embossment, raised work; **-s** scraps, leftovers; **de** — in relief; prominent, outstanding; **poner de** — to make stand out; to emphasize.

religión [rre·li·xjón] *f.* religion.
religiosidad [rre·li·xjo·si·đáđ] *f.* religiousness, piety; faithfulness.
religioso [rre·li·xjó·so] *adj.* religious; faithful; punctual; *m.* friar, monk.
relinchar [rre·lin·čár] *v.* to neigh.
relincho [rre·lín·čo] *m.* neigh.
reliquia [rre·lí·kja] *f.* relic; vestige; **-s** relics, remains.
reloj [rre·ló] *m.* clock; watch; — **de pulsera** wristwatch; — **de sol** (*or* — **solar**) sundial; — **despertador** alarm clock.
relojería [rre·lo·xe·rí·a] *f.* watch shop; jewelry store.
reluciente [rre·lu·sjén·te] *adj.* shining; sparkling.
relucir[13] [rre·lu·sír] *v. irr.* to glitter, sparkle; to shine.
relumbrante [rre·lum·brán·te] *adj.* brilliant, flashing, resplendent.
relumbrar [rre·lum·brár] *v.* to glare; to glitter.
relumbre [rre·lúm·bre] *m.* glare, glitter.
rellenar [rre·ye·nár] *v.* to refill; to fill up; to pad; to stuff.
relleno [rre·yé·no] *adj.* stuffed; *m.* meat stuffing; filling.
remachar [rre·ma·čár] *v.* to clinch; to hammer down; to flatten; to rivet; to fix firmly; **-se** *Am.* to be tight-lipped, stubbornly silent.
remache [rre·má·če] *m.* clinching; fastening, securing; riveting; rivet.
remanente [rre·ma·nén·te] *m.* remainder, balance; remnant; residue.
remar [rre·már] *v.* to row; to struggle.
rematado [rre·ma·tá·đo] *adj.* & *p.p.* (*acabado*) finished; (*vendido en subasta*) sold at auction; **loco** — completely crazy.
rematar [rre·ma·tár] *v.* (*acabar*) to finish; to end; to give the final or finishing stroke; (*vender*) to auction; (*afianzar*) to fasten (*a stitch*); *Ch.* to stop (*a horse*) suddenly; *Am.* to buy or sell at auction; **-se** to be finished, be completely destroyed or ruined.
remate [rre·má·te] *m.* (*fin*) finish, end; (*postura*) highest bid at an auction; sale at auction; (*punta*) pinnacle, spire; *Mex.* selvage, edge of a fabric; **de** — absolutely, without remedy; **loco de** — completely crazy, stark mad.
remedar [rre·me·đár] *v.* to imitate; to mimic.
remediar [rre·me·đjár] *v.* to remedy; to help; to avoid.
remedio [rre·mé·đjo] *m.* remedy; help; amendment; recourse, resort; **sin** — without help, unavoidable; **no tiene** — it can't be helped.
remedo [rre·mé·đo] *m.* imitation; mockery.
remembranza [rre·mem·brán·sa] *f.* remembrance, memory.
rememorar [rre·me·mo·rár] *v.* to remember, call to mind.
remendar[1] [rre·men·dár] *v. irr.* to mend, patch; to darn; to repair.
remendón [rre·men·dón] *m.* cobbler, shoe repairman; mender, patcher.
remero [rre·mé·ro] *m.* rower.
remesa [rre·mé·sa] *f.* shipment; remittance, payment.
remesar [rre·me·sár] *v.* to remit; to ship.
remiendo [rre·mjén·do] *m.* mend; mending; patch; darn; repair; **a -s** piecemeal, piece by piece.
remilgado [rre·mil·ǵá·đo] *adj.* prudish, prim, affected.
remilgo [rre·míl·ǵo] *m.* prudery, primness, affection.
reminiscencia [rre·mi·ni·sén·sja] *f.* reminiscence.
remisión [rre·mi·sjón] *f.* (*disculpa*) remission; forgiveness; (*remesa*) remittance, remitting; (*disminución*) abatement, slackening; *Mex., Ven.* anything shipped or sent.
remitente [rre·mi·tén·te] *m.* & *f.* sender; shipper.
remitir [rre·mi·tír] *v.* (*enviar*) to remit; to send; (*diferir*) to defer; to pardon; to refer; to abate; **-se** to defer, yield (*to another's judgment*).
remo [rré·mo] *m.* oar; hard and long work; leg of a horse; **al** — at the oar; at hard labor.
remojar [rre·mo·xár] *v.* to soak; to steep; *Am.* to tip, bribe.
remojo [rre·mó·xo] *m.* soaking; steeping; *Am.* tip, bribe.
remolacha [rre·mo·lá·ča] *f.* beet.
remolcador [rre·mol·ka·đór] *m.* towboat, tug, tugboat; **lancha remolcadora** tugboat.
remolcar[6] [rre·mol·kár] *v.* to tow, tug; to take (*a person*) in tow.
remolino [rre·mo·lí·no] *m.* swirl, whirl; whirlwind; whirlpool; commotion; *Ríopl.* pin wheel; *Am.* ventilating wheel (*fan*); — **de gente** throng, crowd.
remolón [rre·mo·lón] *adj.* indolent, lazy.
remolque [rre·mól·ke] *m.* tow; towrope; **llevar a** — to tow; to take in tow.
remontar [rre·mon·tár] *v.* (*alzar*) to elevate, raise; (*reparar*) to repair, patch up; to resole; to revamp; *Am.* to go up; *Ríopl., Carib., C.A., Ven., Col.* to go upstream; **-se** to rise; to soar, fly upward; to date (from), go back (to); *Ríopl.* to take to the woods or hills.
rémora [rré·mo·ra] *f.* impediment, obstacle, hindrance.
remorder[4] [rre·mor·đér] *v. irr.* to sting.
remordimiento [rre·mor·đi·mjén·to] *m.* remorse.
remoto [rre·mó·to] *adj.* remote, distant; improbable.
remover[2] [rre·mo·ƀér] *v. irr.* to remove; to dismiss; to stir.
rempujar [rrem·pu·xár] *v.* to jostle, push.
rempujón [rrem·pu·xón] *m.* jostle, push.
remuda [rre·mú·đa] *f.* change; substitution; replacement; change of clothes; spare tire; relay of horses; *Am.* spare horse, spare pack animal.
remudar [rre·mu·đár] *v.* to change; to replace.
remuneración [rre·mu·ne·ra·sjón] *f.* remuneration, compensation, pay, reward.
remunerar [rre·mu·ne·rár] *v.* to remunerate, compensate, pay, reward (*for services*).
renacer[13] [rre·na·sér] *v. irr.* to be reborn; to spring up, grow up again.
renacimiento [rre·na·si·mjén·to] *m.* renascence, renaissance; revival; rebirth.
rencilla [rren·sí·ya] *f.* quarrel.
renco [rréŋ·ko] *adj.* lame.
rencor [rreŋ·kór] *m.* rancor, resentment, hatred, grudge.
rencoroso [rreŋ·ko·ró·so] *adj.* resentful, spiteful.
rendición [rren·di·sjón] *f.* (*comportamiento*) surrender; submission; yield, profit.
rendido [rren·dí·đo] *p.p.* & *adj.* tired out, fatigued; devoted; obsequious, servile.
rendija [rren·dí·xa] *f.* crack, crevice.
rendimiento [rren·di·mjén·to] *m.* yield, output, profit; surrender, submission; (*cansancio*) fatigue; performance.
rendir[5] [rren·dír] *v. irr.* to subdue; to surrender, hand over; to yield, produce; to fatigue; to render, do (*homage*); *Cuba, Ven.* — **la jornada** to end or suspend the day's work; **-se** to surrender, give up; to become fatigued, worn out.
renegado [rre·ne·ǵá·đo] *m.* renegade, traitor; *adj.* renegade, disloyal; wicked.
renegar[1, 7] [rre·ne·ǵárd] *v. irr.* to deny insistently; to

detest; to blaspheme, curse; — **de** to deny, renounce (*one's faith*); *Am.* to hate, protest against.
renglón [rreŋ·glón] *m.* line (*written or printed*); item; *Ríopl., Col., Ven., Mex., Carib., Andes* line of business, specialty.
renio [rré·njo] *m.* rhenium.
reno [rré·no] *m.* reindeer.
renombrado [rre·nom·brá·đo] *adj.* renowned, famous.
renombre [rre·nóm·bre] *m.* renown, fame.
renovación [rre·no·ƀa·sjón] *f.* renovation, restoration; renewal.
renovar[2] [rre·no·ƀár] *v. irr.* to renovate; to renew; to replace.
renquear [rreŋ·ke·ár] *v.* to limp.
renta [rrén·ta] *f.* rent, rental; income; revenue.
renuencia [rre·nwén·sja] *f.* reluctance, unwillingness.
renuente [rre·nwén·te] *adj.* reluctant, unwilling.
renuevo [rre·nwé·ƀo] *m.* (*vástago*) sprout, shoot; (*acto*) renovation, restoration.
renunciar [rre·nun·sjár] *v.* to renounce; to resign; to refuse; to renege (*fail to follow suit in cards*).
reñidor [rre·ñi·đór] *adj.* quarrelsome.
reñir[5, 19] [rre·ñír] *v. irr.* to quarrel; to fight; to scold.
reo [rré·o] *adj.* guilty; *m.* culprit, criminal; defendant.
reojo [rre·ó·xo] **mirar de** — to look out of the corner of one's eye; to look scornfully.
repantigarse[7] [rre·pan·ti·ǥár·se] *v.* to lounge, stretch out (*in a chair*).
reparación [rre·pa·ra·sjón] *f.* reparation; repair; indemnity.
reparar [rre·pa·rár] *v.* (*renovar*) to repair; to regain; to recover; (*corregir*) to make amends for, atone for; to remedy; to ward off (*a blow*); *Am.* to rear, buck (*said of horses*); — **en** to observe, notice.
reparo [rre·pá·ro] *m.* (*arreglo*) repair; restoration; (*observación*) notice; observation; (*duda*) doubt, objection; (*abrigo*) shelter; parry (*fencing*); *Mex.* sudden bound or leap of a horse.
repartimiento [rre·par·ti·mjén·to] *m.* distribution, division; assessment.
repartir [rre·par·tír] *v.* to distribute; to allot.
reparto [rre·pár·to] *m.* distribution; mail delivery; cast of characters.
repasar [rre·pa·sár] *v.* to review, look over, go over again; to mend (*clothes*); to pass by again.
repaso [rre·pá·so] *m.* review; revision.
repelente [rre·pe·lén·te] *adj.* repellent, repulsive, repugnant.
repeler [rre·pe·lér] *v.* to repel; to reject.
repelón [rre·pe·lón] *m.* pull; kink.
repente [rre·pén·te] *m.* sudden movement; *Am.* attack, fit; **de** — suddenly.
repentino [rre·pen·tí·no] *adj.* sudden.
repercutir [rre·per·ku·tír] *v.* to resound, echo back; to rebound; to reflect back (*as light*).
repetición [rre·pe·ti·sjón] *f. repetition.*
repetido [rre·pe·tí·đo] *p.p.* repeated; **repetidas veces** repeatedly, often.
repetir[5] [rre·pe·tír] *v. irr.* to repeat; to belch.
repicar[6] [rre·pi·kár] *v.* (*tañer*) to chime, ring; (*hacer menudo*) to mince, chop fine; *Carib., Ven.* to drum, tap (*with the fingers or heels*); **-se** to boast; to be conceited.
repique [rre·pí·ke] *m.* (*tañido*) chime, ringing, peal; (*acción de picar*) mincing, chopping.
repiquetear [rre·pi·ke·te·ár] *v.* to chime, ring; to jingle; *Am.* to tap (*with fingers or heels*).
repiqueteo [rre·pi·ke·té·o] *m.* chiming, ringing; jingling, tinkling; *Ríopl., Carib., Ven.* clicking sound of heels.
repisa [rre·pí·sa] *f.* shelf, ledge; sill; wall bracket; — **de ventana** window sill.
replegar[1, 7] [rre·ple·ǥár] *v. irr.* to fold, pleat; **-se** to retreat, fall back.
réplica [rré·pli·ka] *f.* reply, answer, retort; replica, copy; *Am. m.* examiner.
replicar[6] [rre·pli·kár] *v.* to reply, answer back; to retort.
repliegue [rre·pljé·ǥe] *m.* fold, crease; retreat (*of troops*).
repollo [rre·pó·yo] *m.* cabbage.
reponer[40] [rre·po·nér] *v. irr* (*devolver*) to replace, put back; to restore; (*contestar*) to reply, retort; **-se** to recover one's health or fortune; to collect oneself, become calm.
reportaje [rre·por·tá·xe] *m.* newspaper report; reporting.
reportar [rre·por·tár] *v.* to check, control, restrain; to attain, obtain; to bring; to carry; *Am.* to report; **-se** to control oneself.
reporte [rre·pór·te] *m.* report, news.
repórter [rre·pór·ter], **reportero** *m.* reporter.
reposado [rre·po·sá·đo] *p.p. & adj.* reposed; quiet, calm; restful.
reposar [rre·po·sár] *v.* to repose; to rest, to lie buried; **-se** to settle (*said of sediment*).
reposición [rre·po·si·sjón] *f.* replacement; recovery (*of one's health*).
reposo [rre·pó·so] *m.* repose, rest; calm.
repostada [rre·pos·tá·đa] *f.* sharp answer, back talk.
repostería [rre·pos·te·rí·a] *f.* pastry shop.
reprender [rre·pren·dér] *v.* to reprimand, scold.
reprensible [rre·pren·sí·ƀle] *adj.* reprehensible, deserving reproof.
reprensión [rre·pren·sjón] *f.* reproof, rebuke.
represa [rre·pré·sa] *f.* dam; damming, stopping; *Col., Ven.* reservoir.
represalia [rre·pre·sá·lja] *f.* reprisal.
represar [rre·pre·sár] *v.* to bank, dam; to recapture (*a ship*) from the enemy; to repress, check.
representación [rre·pre·sen·ta·sjón] *f.* representation; play, performance; authority, dignity; petition, plea.
representante [rre·pre·sen·tán·te] *adj.* representing; *m. & f.* representative; actor.
representar [rre·pre·sen·tár] *v.* (*declarar*) to represent; to declare, state; to express, show; (*actuar*) to act, play, perform; **-se** to imagine, picture to oneself.
representativo [rre·pre·sen·ta·tí·ƀo] *adj.* representative.
represión [rre·pre·sjón] *f.* repression, control, restraint.
reprimenda [rre·pri·mén·da] *f.* reprimand, rebuke.
reprimir [rre·pri·mír] *v.* to repress, check, curb; **-se** to repress oneself; to refrain.
reprobar[2] [rre·pro·ƀár] *v. irr.* to reprove, blame; to condemn; to flunk, fail.
reprochar [rre·pro·čár] *v.* to reproach.
reproche [rre·pró·če] *m.* reproach.
reproducción [rre·pro·đuk·sjón] *f.* reproduction.
reproducir[25] [rre·pro·đu·sír] *v. irr.* to reproduce.
reptil [rrep·tíl] *m.* reptile.
república [rre·pú·ƀli·ka] *f.* republic.
republicano [rre·pu·ƀli·ká·no] *adj. & m.* republican.
repudiar [rre·pu·đjár] *v.* to repudiate; to disown.
repuesto [rre·pwés·to] *m.* stock, supply, provisions; sideboard; **de** — spare, extra; *p.p. of* **reponer** & *adj.* recovered (*from an illness, loss, fright, etc.*); replaced; restored.
repugnancia [rre·puǥ·nán·sja] *f.* repugnance, disgust;

aversion; dislike, reluctance.

repugnante [rre·puǥ·nán·te] *adj.* repugnant, disgusting, loathsome.

repugnar [rre·puǥ·nár] *v.* to be repugnant; to disgust; to oppose, contradict.

repulido [rre·pu·lí·đo] *adj.* polished up, slick; shiny; spruce.

repulsa [rre·púl·sa] *f.* repulse; rebuff; rebuke.

repulsar [rre·pil·sár] *v.* to repulse, repel, reject.

repulsivo [rre·pul·sí·ƀo] *adj.* repulsive, repugnant.

repuntar [rre·pun·tár] *v. Am.* to round up (*cattle*).

reputación [rre·pu·ta·sjón] *f.* reputation.

reputar [rre·pu·tár] *v.* to repute.

requebrar[1] [rre·ke·ƀrár] *v. irr.* to compliment; to flatter; to flirt with; to court, woo; to break again.

requemado [rre·ke·má·đo] *p.p. & adj.* burned; parched; tanned, sunburned.

requemar [rre·ke·már] *v.* to parch, dry up; to burn; to overcook; **-se** to become overheated; to burn inwardly; to get tanned, sunburned.

requerimiento [rre·ke·ri·mjén·to] *m.* requisition; requirement; summons; **-s** amorous advances, insinuations.

requerir[3] [rre·ke·rír] *v. irr.* (*exigir*) to require; to need; to summon; (*indagar*) to examine, investigate; (*avisar*) to notify; — **de amores** to court, woo.

requesón [rre·ke·són] *m.* cottage cheese.

requiebro [rre·kjé·ƀro] *m.* flattery; compliment.

requisito [rre·ki·sí·to] *m.* requirement, requisite; — **previo** prerequisite.

res [rres] *f.* head of cattle; any large animal.

resabio [rre·sá·ƀjo] *m.* disagreeable aftertaste; bad habit.

resaca [rre·sá·ka] *f.* undertow; surge, surf; redraft (*of a bill of exchange*); *Carib.* beating, thrashing; *Mex., Ríopl.* mud and slime (*left by a flood*).

resaltar [rre·sal·tár] *v.* to stand out; to project, jut out; to rebound, bounce or spring back; to be evident, obvious.

resarcir[10] [rre·sar·sír] *v.* to indemnify, compensate, repay; to make amends for; **-se de** to make up for.

resbaladero [rrez·ƀa·la·đé·ro] *m.* slide, slippery place.

resbaladizo [rrez·ƀa·la·đí·so] *adj.* slippery.

resbalar [rrez·ƀa·lár] *v.* to slide; **-se** to slip; to slide; to skid; **resbalársele a uno una cosa** to let a thing slide off one's back, be impervious to a thing.

resbalón [rre·ƀa·lón] *m.* sudden or violent slip; slide; error; **darse un** — to slip.

resbaloso [rrez·ƀa·ló·so] *adj.* slippery.

rescatar [rres·ka·tár] *v.* to ransom; to redeem; to barter, exchange, trade; *Mex.* to resell.

rescate [rres·ká·te] *m.* ransom; redemption; barter, exchange.

rescoldo [rres·kól·do] *m.* embers, hot cinders, hot ashes; doubt, scruple.

resecar[6] [rre·sé·kár] *v.* to dry up; to parch.

reseco [rre·sé·ko] *adj.* very dry; dried up, parched; thin, skinny.

resentimiento [rre·sen·ti·mjén·to] *m.* resentment; impairment, damage (*to one's health*).

resentirse[3] [rre·sen·tír·se] *v. irr* (*tener pesar*) to show resentment, hurt, or grief; to resent; (*empoerar*) to weaken; to become worse.

reseña [rre·sé·ña] *f.* military review; book review; brief account; sign, signal.

reseñar [rre·se·ñár] *v.* to review (*a book*); to review (*troops*); to outline briefly, give a short account of.

resero [rre·sé·ro] *m. Ríopl.* cowboy, herdsman; *Ríopl.* dealer in livestock.

reserva [rre·ser·ƀa] *f.* reserve; reservation; exception; caution; **a — de** reserving the right to, intending to; **sin** — without reserve, frankly.

reservación [rre·ser·ƀa·sjón] *f.* reservation.

reservar [rre·ser·ƀár] *v.* to reserve; to put aside; to postpone; to exempt; to keep secret; **-se** to conserve one's strength, spare oneself (*for another time*).

resfriado [rres·frjá·đo] *m.* cold (*illness*); *p.p. of* **resfriar;** *adj. Ríopl.* indiscreet.

resfriar[17] [rres·frjár] *v.* to cool; to chill; **-se** to catch cold; to cool.

resfrío [rres·frí·o] *m.* chill; cold.

resguardar [rrez·ǥwar·đár] *v.* to guard, defend; to shield; **-se de** to guard oneself against; to seek shelter from.

resguardo [rrez·ǥwár·đo] *m.* defense; security; guarantee; guard.

residencia [rre·si·đén·sja] *f.* residence; office or post of a resident foreign minister; *Am.* luxurious dwelling.

residente [rre·si·đén·te] *adj.* resident, residing; *m. & f.* resident, dweller; resident foreign minister; *Col., C.A., Ríopl.* alien resident.

residir [rre·si·đír] *v.* to reside; to live, dwell; to be inherent, belong (to).

residuo [rre·sí·đwo] *m.* residue; remainder.

resignación [rre·siǥ·na·sjón] *f.* resignation; strength.

resignar [rre·siǥ·nár] *v.* to resign; to hand over; **-se** to resign oneself.

resiliencia [rre·si·ljén·sja] *f.* resilience; — **al choque o al desgaste** toughness (machine).

resina [rre·sí·na] *f.* resin.

resistencia [rre·sis·tén·sja] *f.* resistance.

resistente [rre·sis·tén·te] *adj.* resistant; resisting.

resistir [rre·sis·tír] *v.* to resist; to tolerate, endure; **-se** to resist, struggle.

resolución [rre·so·lu·sjón] *f.* (*ánimo*) resolution; courage, determination; (*resultado*) solution; **en** — in brief.

resolver[2, 52] [rre·sol·ƀér] *v. irr.* to resolve, decide; to solve; to dissolve; **-se** to resolve, decide; to be reduced (to), dissolve (into).

resollar[2] [rre·so·yár] *v. irr.* to breathe hard; to pant.

resonar[2] [rre·so·nár] *v. irr.* to resound.

resoplar [rre·so·plár] *v.* to puff, breathe hard; to snort.

resoplido [rre·so·plí·đo] *m.* puff, pant; snort.

resorte [rre·sór·te] *m.* spring; elasticity; means (*to attain an object*); *Col.* elastic, rubber band; *Ven.* **no es de mi** — it doesn't concern me.

respaldar [rres·pal·dár] *v.* to endorse; to guarantee; *Am.* to back, support; **-se** to lean back; *Ch.* to protect one's rear.

respaldo [rres·pál·do] *m.* back (*of a chair or sheet of paper*); protecting wall; endorsement; *Am.* protection, security, guarantee.

respectivo [rres·pek·tí·ƀo] *adj.* respective.

respecto [rres·pék·to] *m.* respect, relation, reference; point, matter; (**con**) — **a** (*or* — **de**) with respect to, with regard to.

respetable [rres·pe·tá·ƀle] *adj.* respectable.

respetar [rres·pe·tár] *v.* to respect.

respeto [rres·pé·to] *m.* respect; reverence, regard; consideration.

respetuoso [rres·pe·twó·so] *adj.* respectful; respectable.

respingar[7] [rres·piŋ·gár] *v.* to buck; to balk (*said of a horse*); to grumble; to curl up (*said of the edge of a garment*).

respingo [rres·píŋ·go] *m.* buck, balking; muttering, grumbling.

respiración [rres·pi·ra·sjón] *f.* respiration, breathing.
respirar [rres·pi·rár] *v.* to breathe.
respiro [rres·pí·ro] *m.* breathing; breath; respite, pause, moment of rest; extension of time (*for payment*).
resplandecer[13] [rres·plan·de·sér] *v. irr.* to shine; to glitter.
resplandeciente [rres·plan·de·sjén·te] *adj.* resplendent, shining.
resplandor [rres·plan·dór] *m.* splendor, brilliance, brightness; *Am.* sun's glare.
responder [rres·pon·dér] *v.* to respond; to answer; to correspond, harmonize; to answer (for), be responsible (for).
respondón [rres·pon·dón] *adj.* saucy, pert, insolent (*in answering*).
responsabilidad [rres·pon·sa·bi·li·dád] *f.* responsibility.
responsable [rres·pon·sá·ble] *adj.* responsible.
respuesta [rres·pwés·ta] *f.* response; answer, reply.
resquebradura [rres·ke·bra·dú·ra], **resquebrajadura** [rres·ke·bra·xa·dú·ra] *f.* fissure, crevice, crack.
resquebrajar [rres·ke·brá·xár] = **resquebrar.**
resquebrar[1] [rres·ke·brár] *v. irr.* to crack; to split.
resquicio [rres·kí·sjo] *m.* crack, slit, crevice; opening; *Col., Ven., Mex.* vestige, sign, trace.
resta [rrés·ta] *f.* subtraction (*as an arithmetical operation*); remainder.
restablecer[13] [rres·ta·ble·sér] *v. irr.* to re-establish; to restore; **-se** to recover.
restante [rres·tán·te] *adj.* remaining; *m.* residue, remainder.
restañar [rres·ta·ñár] *v.* to staunch (*a wound*); to check the flow of.
restar [rres·tár] *v.* to deduct; to subtract; to remain, be left over; to strike back (*a ball*).
restauración [rres·taw·ra·sjón] *f.* restoration.
restaurante [rres·taw·rán·te] *m.* restaurant.
restaurantismo [rres·taw·ran·tíz·mo] *m.* food service; restaurant business.
restaurar [rres·taw·rár] *v.* to restore; to recover; to re-establish; to repair.
restitución [rres·ti·tu·sjón] *f.* restitution, restoration, return.
restituir[32] [rres·ti·twír] *v. irr.* to return, give back; to restore.
resto [rrés·to] *m.* rest, remainder; stakes at cards; return (*of a tennis ball*); player who returns the ball; **-s** remains.
restorán [rres·to·rán] *m. Am.* restaurant.
restregar[1, 7] [rres·tre·gár] *v. irr.* to rub hard; to scrub.
restricción [rres·trik·sjón] *f.* restriction; restraint; curb; limitation.
restringir[11] [rres·triŋ·xír] *v.* to restrict; to restrain; to limit.
resucitar [rre·su·si·tár] *v.* to resuscitate, bring to life; to come to life; to revive.
resuelto [rre·swél·to] *p.p. of* **resolver** resolved, determined; *adj.* resolute, bold; quick.
resuello [rre·swé·yo] *m.* breath; breathing, panting.
resulta [rre·súl·ta] *f.* result; effect, consequence; **de -s** as a result, in consequence.
resultado [rre·sul·tá·do] *m.* result, effect, consequence.
resultante [rre·sul·tán·te] *adj.* resulting; *f.* resultant (*force*).
resultar [rre·sul·tár] *v.* to result; to spring, arise as a consequence; to turn out ot be; **resulta que** it turns out that.
resumen [rre·sú·men] *m.* résumé, summary; **en —** summing up, in brief.
resumidero [rre·su·mi·dé·ro] *m. Am.* = **sumidero.**
resumir [rre·su·mír] *v.* to summarize, sum up; **-se** to be reduced or condensed.
resurgir[11] [rre·sur·xír] *v.* to arise again; to reappear.
retablo [rre·tá·blo] *m.* altarpiece; religious picture hung as a votive offering; series of pictures that tell a story.
retaguardia [rre·ta·gwár·dja] *f.* rear guard.
retal [rre·tál] *m.* remnant.
retar [rre·tár] *v.* to challenge, defy; to reprimand, scold; *Ch., Andes* to insult; **retable** challenging; **poco —** unprofitable.
retardar [rre·tar·dár] *v.* to retard, delay.
retazo [rre·tá·so] *m.* remnant; piece; fragment.
retener[45] [rre·te·nér] *v. irr.* to retain; to keep; to withhold; to detain.
retintín [rre·tin·tín] *m.* jingle, tinkle; sarcastic tone of ring.
retirada [rre·ti·rá·da] *f.* retreat; withdrawal.
retirado [rre·ti·rá·do] *p.p. & adj.* retired; distant, remote; isolated; pensioned.
retirar [rre·ti·rár] *v.* to withdraw; to take away; **-se** to retire, withdraw; to retreat.
retiro [rre·tí·ro] *m.* retreat; retirement; withdrawal; place of refuge; pension of a retired officer.
reto [rré·to] *m.* challenge; defiance; *Ríopl.* scolding; *Andes* insult.
retobado [rre·to·bá·do] *adj. Col., Ríopl.* saucy; *Andes* stubborn, unruly; *Andes* peevish; *Am.* sly, astute.
retobar [rre·to·bár] *v. Col., Andes* to cover with leather; *Ch., Peru* to wrap with leather, oilcloth, or burlap; *Am.* to tan (*leather*); **-se** *Ríopl.* to revel, talk back, act saucy; *Andes, Col.* to become disagreeable and aloof.
retocar[6] [rre·to·kár] *v.* to retouch, touch up; to finish, perfect.
retoñar [rre·to·ñár] *v.* to sprout; to bud; to sprout again; to reappear.
retoño [rre·tó·ño] *m.* sprout, shoot; bud.
retoque [rre·tó·ke] *m.* retouching; finishing touch.
retorcer[2, 10] [rre·tor·sér] *v. irr.* to twist; to retort; to distort; **-se** to wriggle; to squirm.
retorcimiento [rre·tor·si·mjén·to] *m.* twisting; squirming.
retórica [rre·tó·ri·ka] *f.* rhetoric.
retornar [rre·tor·nár] *v.* to return; to give back.
retorno [rre·tór·no] *m.* return; repayment; barter.
retozar[9] [rre·to·sár] *v.* to gambol, frisk about, frolic, romp; to stir within (*said of passions*).
retozo [rre·tó·so] *m.* frolic; **retozón** [rre·to·són] *adj.* frisky, playful.
retractarse [rre·trak·tár·se] *v.* to retract, take back one's word.
retraer[46] [rre·tra·ér] *v. irr.* to withdraw, draw back, take back; **-se de** to withdraw from; to keep aloof or away from; to shun.
retraído [rre·tra·í·do] *adj.* shy, reserved.
retraimiento [rre·traj·mjén·to] *m.* retirement; reserve, aloofness, shyness.
retranca [rre·tráŋ·ka] *f. Cuba* brake; **retranquero** [rre·traŋ·ké·ro] *m. Am.* brakeman.
retrancar[6] [rre·traŋ·kár] *v. Cuba* to brake, put the brake on; *Cuba* **se ha retrancado el asunto** the affair has come to a standstill.
retrasado [rre·tra·sá·do] *p.p. & adj.* behind, behind time; backward; postponed, delayed.
retrasar [rre·tra·sár] *v.* to delay, retard; to set back; to go backward; **-se** to fall behind; to be late, behind time.
retraso [rre·trá·so] *m.* delay.

retratar [rre·tra·tár] *v.* to portray; to photograph; to copy, imitate; **-se** to be portrayed; to be photographed; to be reflected.
retrato [rre·trá·to] *m.* portrait; photograph; copy, imitation; reflection.
retrete [rre·tré·te] *m.* toilet, water closet; place of retreat.
retroactivo [rre·tro·ak·tí·ƀo] *adj.* retroactive.
retroceder [rre·tro·se·đér] *v.* to turn back; to fall back, draw back; to recede.
retroceso [rre·tro·sé·so] *m.* retrogression, backward step; retreat; setback, relapse.
retrocohete [rre·tro·ko·é·te] *m.* retrorocket.
retropropulsión [rre·tro·pro·pul·sjon] *f.* retropropulsion.
retruécano [rre·trwé·ka·no] *m.* pun.
retumbar [rre·tum·bár] *v.* to resound; to rumble.
retumbo [rre·túm·bo] *m.* loud echo or sound; rumble (*of thunder, cannon, etc.*).
reubicar [rre·u·ƀi·kár] *v.* relocate.
reuma [rréw·ma] *m.* rheumatism.
reumatismo [rrew·ma·tíz·mo] *m.* rheumatism.
reunión [rrew·njón] *f.* reunion; meeting.
reunir [rrew·nír] *v.* to reunite; to unite; to group; to gather; to assemble; to collect; **-se** to meet, assemble; to reunite.
revancha [rre·ƀán·ča] *f.* revenge; return game or match.
revelación [rre·ƀe·la·sjón] *f.* revelation.
revelador [rre·ƀe·la·đór] *adj.* revealing; *m.* developer (*in photography*).
revelar [rre·ƀe·lár] *v.* reveal; to develop (*a film*).
revendedor [rre·ƀen·de·đór] *m.* retailer; reseller; ticket scalper.
reventa [rre·ƀén·ta] *f.* resale.
reventar[1] [rre·ƀen·tár] *v. irr.* (*estallar*) to burst; to burst forth; to explode; to smash; (*fatigar*) to fatigue, exhaust; to bother; **-se** to burst; to blow out, explode.
reventón [rre·ƀen·tón] *m.* burst, bursting; blowout; steep hill; hard work, toil; *adj.* bursting.
reverdecer[13] [rre·ƀer·đe·sér] *v. irr.* to grow fresh and green again; to gain new strength and vigor.
reverencia [rre·ƀe·rén·sja] *f.* reverence; bow.
reverenciar [rre·ƀe·ren·sjár] *v.* to revere, venerate.
reverendo [rre·ƀe·rén·do] *adj.* reverend; *Cuba, Ríopl., Mex., Andes* large, big (*ironically*).
reverente [rre·ƀe·rén·te] *adj.* reverent.
reverso [rre·ƀér·so] *m.* reverse; back side.
revertir[3] [rre·ƀer·tír] *v. irr.* to revert.
revés [rre·ƀés] *m.* reverse; back, wrong side; setback; backstroke or slap; backhanded thrust (*in fencing*); (*desgracia*) misfortune; **al** — backwards; wrong side out; in the opposite way; from left to right.
revestir[5] [rre·ƀes·tír] *v. irr.* to dress, clothe; to coat, cover with a coating; **-se** to dress, put on an outer garment or vestment; to be invested (*with power, authority, etc.*); **-se de paciencia** to arm oneself with patience; **revestimiento duro** hard surfacing.
revisar [rre·ƀi·sár] *v.* to revise; to review; to examine, inspect.
revisión [rre·ƀi·sjón] *m.* revision; review (*of a case*), new trial; inspection (*of baggage*).
revisor [rre·ƀi·sór] *m.* corrector; inspector, overseer.
revista [rre·ƀís·ta] *f.* (*inspección*) review; inspection; (*publicación*) magazine, journal; (*proceso*) second trial or hearing; **pasar** — to pass in review; to examine carefully; to review (*troops*).
revistar [rre·ƀis·tár] *v.* to review, inspect (*troops*).
revivir [rre·ƀi·ƀír] *v.* to revive.
revocación [rre·ƀo·ka·sjón] *f.* repeal, cancellation.
revocar[6] [rre·ƀo·kár] *v.* to revoke, repeal.
revolcar[6] [rre·ƀol·kár] *v.* (*derribar*) to knock down; to turn over and over; to floor, defeat; (*suspender*) to fail, flunk; **-se** to wallow; to roll over and over; to flounder.
revolotear [rre·ƀo·lo·te·ár] *v.* to fly about, flutter around; to hover; to circle around.
revoltijo [rre·ƀol·tí·xo], **revoltillo** [rre·ƀol·tí·yo] *m.* jumble, mixture, mess; tangle, muddle; **revoltillo de huevos** scrambled eggs.
revoltoso [rre·ƀol·tó·so] *adj.* turbulent, unruly, rebellious; mischievous; intricate; *m.* agitator, troublemaker; rebel.
revolución [rre·ƀo·lu·sjón] *f.* revolution; **-es por minuto** RPM.
revolucionario [rre·ƀo·lu·sjo·ná·rjo] *adj.* revolutionary; *m.* revolutionist, revolutionary.
revolver[2] [rre·ƀol·ƀér] *v. irr.* to revolve; to turn over; to stir up; to mix up; to turn around swiftly (*a horse*); **-se** to move back and forth; to roll over and over; to change (*said of the weather*).
revólver [rre·ƀól·ƀer] *m.* revolver, pistol.
revuelo [rre·ƀwé·lo] *m.* whirl; stir, commotion; flying around.
revuelta [rre·ƀwél·ta] *f.* revolt, revolution; second turn; turn, bend; quarrel, fight; *Ch.* sudden turning of a horse.
revuelto [rre·ƀwél·to] *p.p. of* **revolver** *& adj.* confused; mixed up; intricate, complicated; choppy (*sea*); changeable (*weather*); **huevos -s** scrambled eggs.
rey [rrej] *m.* king.
reyerta [rre·yér·ta] *f.* quarrel, dispute.
rezagado [rre·sa·ǥá·đo] *adj.* back, behind; *m.* straggler, slowpoke, latecomer.
rezagar[7] [rre·sa·ǥár] *v.* to leave behind; to separate (*the weak cattle*) from the herd; *Am.* to reserve, set aside; **-se** to lag behind.
rezar[9] [rre·sár] *v.* to pray; to say or recite (*a prayer*); to mutter, grumble; **así lo reza el libro** so the book says; **eso no reza conmigo** that has nothing to do with me.
rezo [rré·so] *m.* prayer.
rezongar[7] [rre·son·gár] *v.* to grumble, growl, mutter.
rezongón [rre·son·gón] *adj.* growling, grumbling; *m.* grumbler, growler; scolder.
rezumar [rre·su·már] *v.* to ooze; to leak; **se rezuma** it oozes, it seeps through.
ría [rrí·a] *f.* mouth of a river, estuary.
riachuelo [rrja·čwé·lo] *m.* rivulet, brook.
ribazo [rri·ƀá·so] *m.* bank, ridge.
ribera [rri·ƀé·ra] *f.* shore, bank, beach.
ribereño [rri·ƀe·ré·ño] *adj.* of, pertaining to, or living on, a river bank.
ribete [rri·ƀé·te] *m.* trimming, border, edge, binding; addition; **tiene sus -s de poeta** he is something of a poet.
ribetear [rri·ƀe·te·ár] *v.* to bind, put a binding on; to border, trim the edge or border of.
ricacho [rri·ká·čo] *adj.* quite rich (*often said sarcastically*); **ricachón** [rri·ka·čón] *adj.* extremely rich, disgustingly rich.
rico [rrí·ko] *adj.* rich, wealthy; delicious; exquisite; **ricote** [rri·kó·te] = **ricacho.**
ridiculizar[9] [rri·đi·ku·li·sár] *v.* to ridicule, deride.
ridículo [rri·đí·ku·lo] *adj.* ridiculous; queer, strange; *m.* ridicule; ridiculous situation; **hacer el** — to be ridiculous; to act the fool.
riego [rrjé·ǥo] *m.* irrigation; watering.
riel [rrjel] *m.* rail; **-es** track, railroad track.
rienda [rrjén·da] *f.* rein, bridle; moderation, restraint;

a — **suelta** with free rein, without restraint; violently, swiftly; **soltar la** — to let loose, act without restraint; **tirar las -s** to draw rein, tighten the reins; to restrain.
riente [rrjén·te] *adj.* laughing, smiling.
riesgo [rrjez·go] *m.* risk.
rifa [rrí·fa] *f.* raffle; scuffle, quarrel.
rifar [rrí·fár] *v.* to raffle; to scuffle, quarrel.
rifeño [rri·fé·ño] *m.* riff.
rifle [rrí·fle] *m.* rifle.
rigidez [rri·xi·dés] *f.* rigidity, stiffness; severity, strictness.
rígido [rrí·xi·do] *adj.* rigid, stiff; severe, strict.
rigor [rri·gór] *m.* rigor; severity; harshness; rigidity, stiffness; **en** — in reality; strictly; **ser de** — to be absolutely indispensable, be required by custom.
rigoroso [rri·go·ró·so], **riguroso** [rri·gu·ró·so] *adj.* rigorous; harsh; severe; strict.
rima [rrí·ma] *f.* rhyme; **-s** poems.
rimar [rri·már] *v.* to rhyme.
rimbombante [rrim·bom·bán·te] *adj.* high-sounding; resounding.
rimero [rri·mé·ro] *m.* pile, heap.
rincón [rriŋ·kón] *m.* corner; nook; *Am.* narrow valley.
rinconada [rriŋ·ko·ná·da] *f.* corner; nook.
rinconera [rriŋ·ko·né·ra] *f.* corner cupboard, corner table, corner bracket.
ringlera [rriŋ·glé·ra] *f.* tier, row, line.
rinoceronte [rri·no·se·rón·te] *m.* rhinoceros.
riña [rri·ña] *f.* quarrel, dispute, fight.
riñón [rri·ñón] *m.* kidney; center, interior.
río [rrí·o] *m.* river.
ripio [rrí·pjo] *m.* rubble, stone or brick fragments; padding (*in a verse, speech, etc.*), useless word.
riqueza [rri·ké·sa] *f.* riches; wealth.
risa [rrí·sa] *f.* laugh; laughter; **reventar de** — to burst with laughter; **tomar a** — to take lightly; to laugh off.
risada [rri·sá·da] *f.* gale of laughter, loud laugh.
risco [rrís·ko] *m.* rocky cliff, crag; honey fritter.
risible [rri·sí·ble] *adj.* laughable, ridiculous.
risotada [rri·so·tá·da] *f.* guffaw, big laugh.
ristra [rrís·tra] *f.* string (*of onions, garlic, etc.*); series, row.
risueño [rri·swé·ño] *adj.* smiling; pleasant; delightful.
rítmico [rríd·mi·ko] *adj.* rhythmical.
ritmo [rríd·mo] *m.* rhythm.
rito [rrí·to] *m.* rite, ceremony.
rival [rri·bál] *m.* & *f.* rival, competitor; enemy.
rivalidad [rri·ba·li·dád] *f.* rivalry, competition; enmity.
rivalizar[9] [rri·ba·li·sár] *v.* to rival, compete.
rizado [rri·sá·do] *p.p.* curled; *adj.* wavy, curly; *m.* curling; curls.
rizar[9] [rri·sár] *v.* to curl; to ripple; to ruffle, gather into ruffles; **-se** to curl one's hair; to curl.
rizo [rrí·so] *m.* curl; ripple; *adj.* curly; **rizoso** [rri·só·so] *adj.* curly.
roano [rro·á·no] *adj.* roan (*red, bay, or chestnut-colored, mixed with white; applied to a horse*).
robalo [rro·bá·lo] *m.* bass.
robar [rro·bár] *v.* to rob, steal; to abduct, kidnap.
roble [rró·ble] *m.* oak tree; oak wood; **robledal** [rro·ble·dál], **robledo** [rro·blé·do] *m.* oak grove.
robo [rró·bo] *m.* robbery, theft; loot, plunder.
robusto [rró·bús·to] *adj.* robust, vigorous.
roca [rró·ka] *f.* rock, boulder; rocky cliff, crag.
rocalloso [rro·ka·yó·so] *adj.* rocky.
roce [rró·se] *m.* graze; friction; contact; **no tener — con** to have no contact with (*a person*).
rociada [rro·sjá·da] *f.* sprinkling; spray; dew; sprinkle, shower; volley of harsh words.
rociar[17] [rro·sjár] *v.* to sprinkle; to spray; to fall (*said of dew*).
rocín [rro·sín] *m.* nag, hack; draft horse; coarse, ill-bred man; *Ríopl., Mex., Andes* riding horse.
rocío [rro·sí·o] *m.* dew; sprinkle; shower; spray; *adj. Am.* reddish, roan (*horse*).
rocoso [rro·kó·so] *adj.* rocky.
rodada [rro·dá·da] *f.* rut, wheel track; *Ríopl.* tumble, fall.
rodado [rro·dá·do] *adj.* dapple (*horse*); *p.p. of* **rodar.**
rodadura [rro·da·dú·ra] *f.* rolling; rut; — **del neumático** tire tread.
rodaja [rro·dá·xa] *f.* disk; small wheel; round slice.
rodaje [rro·dá·xe] *m.* works (*of a watch*); — **de película** the filming of a movie.
rodar[2] [rro·dár] *v. irr.* to roll; to revolve; to roam, wander about; to fall down (*rolling*) *Mex.* — **a patadas** to kick down.
rodear [rro·de·ár] *v.* to go around; to go by a roundabout way; to surround, encircle; *Ríopl., Cuba, Ven.* to round up (*cattle*).
rodela [rro·dé·la] *f.* round shield; *Mex., Ch.* padded ring for carrying loads on the head; *Am.* round slice; *Ch.* kettle lid; *Ch.* hoop; *Ch.* game of rolling a hoop.
rodeo [rro·dé·o] *m.* detour, roundabout way; circumlocution, roundabout expression; dodge, evasion; corral, stockyard; rodeo, roundup.
rodilla [rro·dí·ya] *f.* knee; **de -s** on one's knees; **hincarse de -s** to kneel down.
rodillo [rro·dí·yo] *m.* roller; rolling pin; road roller; (*computadora*) platen.
rodio [rró·djo] *m.* rhodium.
rododendro [rro·do·dén·dro] *m.* rhododendron.
roedor [rro·e·dór] *m.* rodent.
roer[51] [rro·ér] *v. irr.* to gnaw; to corrode, eat away; to torment, harass.
rogar[2, 7] [rro·gár] *v. irr.* to pray, beg, beseech; **hacerse** — to let oneself be coaxed.
rojez [rro·xés] *f.* redness.
rojizo [rro·xí·so] *adj.* reddish.
rojo [rró·xo] *adj.* red; red, radical.
rojura [rro·xú·ra] *f.* redness.
rollizo [rro·yí·so] *adj.* plump; *m.* log.
rollo [rró·yo] *m.* roll; bundle; rolling pin; log.
romadizo [rro·ma·dí·so] *m.* nasal catarrh, head cold.
romance [rro·mán·se] *adj.* Romance, Romanic (*language*); *m.* Romance language; Spanish language; romance, chivalric novel; ballad; eight-syllable meter with even verses rhyming in assonance; **en buen** — in plain language.
románico [rro·má·ni·ko] *adj.* Romanesque (*architecture*); Romance (*language*).
romano [rro·má·no] *adj.* & *m.* Roman.
romanticismo [rro·man·ti·síz·mo] *m.* romanticism.
romántico [rro·mán·ti·ko] *adj.* romantic; sentimental; *m.* romantic; sentimentalist.
rombo [rróm·bo] *m.* rhombus.
romería [rro·me·rí·a] *f.* pilgrimage.
romero [rro·mé·ro] *m.* pilgrim; rosemary (*shrub*).
romo [rró·mo] *adj.* blunt; snub-nosed.
rompe [rróm·pe]: **de — y rasga** resolute, bold; **al** — *Am.* suddenly.
rompecabezas [rrom·pe·ka·bé·sas] *m.* puzzle, riddle.
rompenueces [rrom·pe·nwé·ses] *m.* nutcracker.
rompeolas [rrom·pe·ó·las] *m.* breakwater, mole.
romper[52] [rrom·pér] *v.* to break; to shatter; to tear; to wear through; *Ven.* to leave suddenly or on the run; — **el alba** to dawn; — **a** to start to; **-se** to

break.
rompiente [rrom·pjén·te] *m.* shoal, sand bank, reef; **-s** breakers, surf.
rompimiento [rrom·pi·mjén·to] *m.* rupture, break; crack; breach; quarrel.
rompopo [rrom·pó·po] *m.* eggnog.
ron [rron] *m.* rum.
roncar[6] [rroŋ·kár] *v.* to snore; to roar; to brag.
ronco [rróŋ·ko] *adj.* hoarse; harsh-sounding.
roncha [rrón·ča] *f.* hive; welt.
ronda [rrón·da] *f.* patrol; night serenaders; round (*of a game, of drinks, etc.*); *Ríopl., C.A., Andes* ring-around-a-rosy (*a children's* game); **hacer la — a** to court; *Ch.* to surround, trap (*an animal*).
rondar [rron·dár] *v.* to go around, hover around; to patrol; to make the rounds; to serenade.
ronquera [rron·ké·ra] *f.* hoarseness.
ronquido [rron·kí·đo] *m.* snore; snort.
ronronear [rron·rro·ne·ár] *v.* to purr.
ronroneo [rron·rro·né·o] *m.* purr.
ronzal [rron·sál] *m.* halter.
roña [rró·ña] *f.* scab, mange; (*suciedad*) filth; (*infección*) infection; (*avaricia*) stinginess; trickery; *Ríopl., Col., Ven., Cuba* ill will, grudge, *Am., Col.* **hacer** — to fake an illness.
roñoso [rro·ñó·so] *adj.* scabby, mangy; dirty; stingy; *Carib., Mex.* spiteful; *Arg.* fainthearted, cowardly.
ropa [rró·pa] *f.* clothing, clothes; — **blanca** linen; — **vieja** old clothes; stew made from leftover meat; **a quema** — at close range (*when shooting*); suddenly, without warning.
ropaje [rro·pá·xe] *m.* clothes, clothing apparel; robe.
ropería [rro·pe·rí·a] *f.* clothing store.
ropero [rro·pé·ro] *m.* clothier; wardrobe, clothespress; wardrobe keeper; *Ven.* clothes rack.
roqueño [rro·ké·ño] *adj.* rocky; hard, like rock.
rorro [rró·rro] *m.* popular term for a baby.
rosa [rró·sa] *f.* rose; red spot on the skin; rose color; *Ch., Mex.* rosebush; — **de los vientos** (*or* — **náutica**) mariner's compass.
rosado [rro·sá·đo] *adj.* rosy, rose-colored; frosted (*drink*); *Am.* roan, reddish-brown (*horse*).
rosal [rro·sál] *m.* rosebush.
rosario [rro·sá·rjo] *m.* rosary; — **de desdichas** chain of misfortunes.
rosbif [rroz·ƀíf] *m.* roast beef.
rosca [rrós·ka] *f.* screw and nut; screw thread; spiral, twist; ring-shaped roll; *Mex., Ven., Col.* ring-shaped cushion (*for carrying loads on the head*); *Am.* circle of card players; **roscada de tornillo** screw thread.
roseta [rro·sé·ta] *f.* rosette; small rose; **-s** popcorn; **rosetón** [rro·se·tón] *m.* large rosette; rose window.
rosillo [rro·sí·yo] *adj.* light red; roan (*horse*).
rostro [rrós·tro] *m.* face; **hacer** — to face.
rota [rró·ta] *f.* rout, defeat; ship's course; Rota (*ecclesiastical court*); rattan palm tree.
rotación [rro·ta·sjón] *f.* rotation.
rotario [rro·tá·rjo] *m.* member of the Rotary Club.
rotativo [rro·ta·tí·ƀo] *adj.* rotary; *f.* printing press.
rotatorio [rro·ta·tó·rjo] *adj.* rotary.
roto [rró·to] *p.p. irr.* of **romper** *& adj.* broken; shattered; torn; worn out, ragged; *m. Ch.* person of the poorer class.
rotular [rro·tu·lár] *v.* to label; to letter.
rótulo [rró·tu·lo] *m.* title, inscription; label.
rotundo [rro·tún·do] *adj.* round; sonorous; **una negativa rotunda** a flat denial.
rotura [rro·tú·ra] *f.* breach, opening; break; tear, rip; rupture; fracture.
roturar [rro·tu·rár] *v.* to break ground; to plow (*new ground*).
rozadura [rro·sa·đú·ra] *f.* friction; chafe; chafing.
rozamiento [rro·sa·mjén·to] *m.* friction; rubbing.
rozar[9] [rro·sár] *v.* to graze; to scrape; to chafe; to clear of underbush; **-se con alguien** to have connections, contact, or dealings with someone.
rozón [rro·són] *m.* graze, sudden or violent scrape; short, broad scythe.
ruana [rrwá·na] *f. Col., Ven.* a woolen poncho.
ruano [rrwá·no] = **roano.**
rubí [rru·ƀí] *m.* ruby.
rubicundo [rru·ƀi·kún·do] *adj.* reddish; ruddy, healthy red; reddish-blond.
rubidio [rru·ƀí·đjo] *m.* rubidium.
rubio [rrú·ƀjo] *adj.* blond, blonde.
rubor [rru·ƀór] *m.* blush; bashfulness, shyness.
ruborizarse[9] [rru·ƀo·ri·sár·se] *v.* to blush; to feel ashamed.
rúbrica [rrú·ƀri·ka] *f.* scroll, flourish (*added to a signature*); title, heading; **de** — according to ritual, rule, or custom.
rucio [rrú·sjo] *adj.* grey (*horse or donkey*); — **rodado** dapple-grey.
rudeza [rru·đé·sa] *f.* rudeness; coarseness; roughness.
rudo [rrú·đo] *adj.* rude; coarse; rough; stupid.
rueca [rrwé·ka] *f.* distaff (*used for spinning*).
rueda [rrwé·đa] *f.* (*máquina*) wheel; circle; spread of a peacock's tail; round object; (*grupo*) circle; group; **en** — in turn; in a circle; **hacer la — a** to court; to flatter; — **manivela** handwheel.
ruedo [rrwé·đo] *m.* circuit, tour; border, rim; circumference.
ruego [rrwé·ǥo] *m.* prayer, supplication, request.
rufián [rru·fján] *m.* ruffian; bully.
rugido [rru·xí·đo] *m.* roar; rumbling.
rugir[11] [rru·xír] *v.* to roar; to bellow.
rugoso [rru·ǥó·so] *adj.* wrinkled; furrowed.
ruibarbo [rrwi·ƀár·ƀo] *m.* rhubarb.
ruidazo [rrwi·đá·so] *m.* big noise.
ruido [rrwí·đo] *m.* noise; din; dispute; talk, rumor; **hacer** (*or* **meter**) — to make a noise; to create a sensation; to cause a disturbance.
ruidoso [rrwi·đó·so] *adj.* noisy; loud; sensational.
ruin [rrwin] *adj.* (*vicioso*) vile, base, mean; vicious (*animal*); (*mezquino*) small; petty; puny; stingy.
ruina [rrwí·na] *f.* ruin; destruction; downfall.
ruindad [rrwin·dáđ] *f.* baseness; meanness; stinginess; mean or vile act.
ruinoso [rrwi·nó·so] *adj.* ruinous; in a state of ruin or decay.
ruiseñor [rrwi·se·ñór] *m.* nightingale.
rumba [rrúm·ba] *f. Ven., Col., Carib., Mex., Ríopl.* rumba (*dance and music*); *Carib., Ven., Andes* spree; *Carib., Ven., Andes* **irse de** — to go on a spree.
rumbear [rrum·be·ár] *v. Ríopl., Andes* to head (towards), take a certain direction; *Am.* to cut a path through a forest; *S.A., Cuba* to go on a spree.
rumbo [rrúm·bo] *m.* (*ruta*) direction, course; route; (*pompa*) pomp; ostentation; *Arg.* cut on the head; *C.A.* revel, noisy spree; **hacer — a** to head or sail towards; *Am.* **ir al** — to be going in the right direction, be on the right track.
rumboso [rrum·bó·so] *adj.* pompous, ostentatious; generous.
rumiante [rru·mján·te] *m.* ruminant.
rumiar [rru·mjár] *v.* to ruminate; to chew the cud; to ponder, meditate.
rumor [rru·mór] *m.* rumor, report; murmur; rumble.
runfla [rrún·fla] *f.* series (*of things of the same kind*); sequence (*in cards*).

runrún [rrun·rrún] *m.* rumor; murmur.
ruptura [rrup·tú·ra] *f.* rupture; break; fracture.
rural [rru·rál] *adj.* rural.
ruso [rrú·so] *adj.* Russian; *m.* Russian; Russian language.
rústico [rrús·ti·ko] *adj.* rustic, rural; crude, coarse; *m.* peasant; **en** (*or* **a la**) **rústica** unbound, paperbound.
ruta [rrú·ta] *f.* route, course, way.
rutenio [rru·té·njo] *m.* ruthenium.
rutina [rru·tí·na] *f.* routine.

S:s

sábado [sá·ƀa·đo] *m.* Saturday.
sábalo [sá·ƀa·lo] *m.* shad; *Am.* tarpon.
sábana [sá·ƀa·na] *f.* bed sheet; altar cloth.
sabana [sa·ƀá·na] *f. Col.* savanna, treeless plain; *Col.* **ponerse en la** — to become suddenly rich.
sabandija [sa·ƀan·dí·xa] *f.* small reptile; small lizard.
sabañón [sa·ƀa·ñón] *m.* chilblain.
sabedor [sa·ƀe·đór] *adj.* knowing; aware, informed.
saber[42] [sa·ƀér] *v. irr.* to know; to know how to, be able to; to learn, find out; *Ríopl., Ven., Col.* to be in the habit of; — **a** to taste of, taste like; **sabe bien** it tastes good; **a** — namely; that is; *Am.* **¡a — si venga!** who knows whether he will come!; **un no sé qué** an indefinable something; **¿sabe Vd. a la plaza?** do you know the way to the square?; *m.* knowledge, learning.
sabiduría [sa·ƀi·đu·rí·a] *f.* wisdom; knowledge.
sabiendas [sa·ƀjén·das]: **a** — consciously, knowingly.
sabino [sa·ƀí·no] *adj.* roan.
sabio [sá·ƀjo] *adj.* wise; judicious; learned; *m.* savant, scholar; sage, wise man.
sable [sá·ƀle] *m.* saber; **sablazo** [sa·ƀlá·so] *m.* blow with a saber; saber wound; **dar un sablazo** to strike for a loan.
sabor [sa·ƀór] *m.* savor, taste, flavor.
saborear [sa·ƀo·re·ár] *v.* to savor, flavor, season; to relish, taste with pleasure; to enjoy; **-se** to eat or drink with relish; to smack one's lips.
sabotaje [sa·ƀo·tá·xe] *m.* sabotage.
sabotear [sa·ƀo·te·ár] *v.* to sabotage.
sabroso [sa·ƀró·so] *adj.* savory, tasty; delicious; delightful.
sabueso [sa·ƀwé·so] *m.* hound.
sacabocados [sa·ka·ƀo·ká·đos] *m.* punch (*tool*).
sacacorchos [sa·ka·cór·čos] *m.* corkscrew.
sacamuelas [sa·ka·mwé·las] *m. & f.* tooth puller; quack dentist.
sacapuntas [sa·ka·pún·tas] *m.* pencil sharpener.
sacar[6] [sa·kár] *v.* to draw, draw out, pull out, get out, or take out; to get, obtain; to infer; to make (*a copy*); to take (*a snapshot or picture*); to stick out (*one's tongue*); to serve (*a ball*); — **a bailar** to ask to dance, lead on to the dance floor; — **a luz** to publish; — **el cuerpo** to dodge; — **en claro** (*or* — **en limpio**) to deduce, conclude; *Am.* — **el sombrero** to take off one's hat; *Am.* **¡sáquese de allí!** get out of there!
sacarina [sa·ka·rí·na] *f.* saccharine.
sacerdocio [sa·ser·đó·sjo] *m.* priesthood.
sacerdote [sa·ser·đó·te] *m.* priest.
saciar [sa·sjár] *v.* to satiate, satisfy; **-se** to be satiated, satisfied completely.
saco [sá·ko] *m.* sack, bag; sackful, bagful; loose-fitting coat; sack, plundering; *Am.* suit coat; — **de noche** overnight bag, satchel.
sacramento [sa·kra·mén·to] *m.* sacrament.
sacrificar[6] [sa·kri·fi·kár] *v.* to sacrifice.
sacrificio [sa·kri·fí·sjo] *m.* sacrifice.
sacrilegio [sa·kri·lé·xjo] *m.* sacrilege.
sacrílego [sa·krí·le·ǥo] *adj.* sacrilegious.
sacristán [sa·kris·tán] *m.* sacristan, sexton; *Am.* busybody, meddler.
sacro [sá·kro] *adj.* sacred.
sacrosanto [sa·kro·sán·to] *adj.* sacrosanct, holy and sacred.
sacudida [sa·ku·đí·đa] *f.* shake, jolt, jerk.
sacudimiento [sa·ku·đi·mjén·to] *m.* shaking; shake, jerk; shock, jolt.
sacudir [sa·ku·đír] *v.* to shake; to jerk; to beat; to beat the dust from; to shake off; **-se** to shake oneself; to brush oneself off; **-se de alguien** to shake someone off, get rid of someone.
sádico [sá·đi·ko] *adj.* sadistic, cruel.
sadismo [sa·đíz·mo] *m.* sadism.
saeta [sa·é·ta] *f.* arrow, dart.
sagacidad [sa·ǥa·si·đáđ] *f.* sagacity.
sagaz [sa·ǥás] *adj.* sagacious, shrewd.
sagrado [sa·ǥrá·đo] *adj.* sacred; consecrated; *m.* asylum, refuge.
sahumar [sa·u·már] *v.* to perfume with incense; to fumigate.
sahumerio [sa·u·mé·rjo] *m.* vapor, fume; incense; burning of incense; fumigation.
sainete [saj·né·te] *m.* one-act comedy or farce; delicacy, tasty tidbit; flavor, relish; sauce.
sajón [sa·xón] *adj. & m.* Saxon.
sal [sal] *f.* salt; wit, humor; grace; *Mex., Cuba, C.A., Col., Andes* misfortune, bad luck.
sala [sá·la] *f.* parlor; hall, large room; — **de justicia** courtroom.
salado [sa·lá·đo] *adj.* salty; salted; witty; (*gracioso*) charming; *Ch., Arg.* costly; *Mex., Cuba, C.A., Col., Andes* **estar** — to be unlucky; *m. Col.* salt pit, salt mine.
salar [sa·lár] *v.* to salt; to cure or preserve with salt; *Mex., Cuba, C.A., Col., Andes* to bring bad luck (to); *Am.* to dishonor; *Am.* to ruin, spoil; *Am.* to bribe; *Am.* to feed salt to cattle; *m. Am.* salt pit.
salario [sa·lá·rjo] *m.* salary, wages.
salchicha [sal·čí·ča] *f.* sausage; **salchichón** [sal·či·čón] *m.* large sausage.
saldar [sal·dár] *v.* to balance, settle (*an account*).
saldo [sál·do] *m.* balance, settlement (*of an account*); bargain sale.
saledizo [sa·le·dí·so] = **salidizo.**
salero [sa·lé·ro] *m.* (*vaso*) saltcellar, saltshaker; place for storing salts; salt lick; (*gracia*) wit, grace, charm; *Col.* salt dealer.
saleroso [sa·le·ró·so] *adj.* charming; witty; attractive (*more common in feminine*).
salida [sa·lí·đa] *f.* departure; exit; sally; outlet; way out; loophole; outskirts; outcome; jut, projection; outlay, expenditure; witty remark; (*computadora*) output; — **de pie de banco** silly remark, nonsense; **de fácil** — best-seller; — **doble** loop vent; — **del sol** sunrise; *Cuba* — **de teatro** evening wrap.
salidizo [sa·li·đí·so] *m.* jut, ledge, projection; *adj.* salient, jutting, projecting.
saliente [sa·ljén·te] *adj.* salient, standing out; projecting; *m.* salient, salient angle; jut, projection; — **de la rosca** depth of thread (screw).
salina [sa·lí·na] *f.* salt mine or pit; salt works.
salir[43] [sa·lír] *v. irr.* (*partir*) to go out; to leave, depart; to get out (*of*); to come out; to sprout; to come (*from*); (*resultar*) to turn out to be; — **bien**

RO

to turn out well; to come out well; — **a su padre** to turn out to be or look like his father; *Am.* — **a mano** to come out even; **-se** to get out, slip out; to leak out; **-se con la suya** to get one's own way.
salitral [sa·li·trál] *m.* saltpeter bed or mine.
salitre [sa·lí·tre] *m.* saltpeter; **salitrera** [sa·li·tré·ra] *f.* saltpeter mine or bed; **salitroso** [sa·li·tró·so] *adj.* nitrous, abounding in saltpeter.
saliva [sa·lí·ƀa] *f.* saliva.
salmo [sál·mo] *m.* psalm.
salmodiar [sal·mo·đjár] *v.* to chant; to talk in a monotone or singsong.
salmón [sal·món] *m.* salmon.
salmuera [sal·mwé·ra] *f.* brine.
salobre [sa·ló·ƀre] *adj.* briny, salty.
salón [sa·lón] *m.* salon, hall, large room; salted meat or fish.
salpicadero [sal·pi·ka·đé·ro] *m.* dashboard.
salpicadura [sal·pi·ka·đú·ra] *f.* spatter, splash.
salpicar[6] [sal·pi·kár] *v.* to sprinkle, spray, spatter.
salpicón [sal·pi·kón] *m.* hash; hodgepodge; *Ec.* fruit drink.
salpimentar[1] [sal·pi·men·tár] *v. irr.* to salt and pepper.
salpimienta [sal·pi·mjén·ta] *f.* salt and pepper.
salpullido [sal·pu·yí·đo] *m.* rash, skin eruption.
salsa [sál·sa] *f.* sauce; gravy; *Ch.* sound whipping or beating; **salsera** [sal·sé·ra] *f.* sauce dish.
saltamontes [sal·ta·món·tes] *m.* grasshopper.
saltar [sal·tár] *v.* (*brincar*) to jump; to jump over; to leap; to bounce; to skip; (*estallar*) to burst, break into pieces; to come off; — **a la vista** to be obvious, evident; — **a tierra** to disembark, land; *Mex.* — **las trancas** to lose one's patience; to lose one's head.
salteador [sal·te·a·đór] *m.* bandit, highway robber.
saltear [sal·te·ár] *v.* to assault, attack; to hold up, rob; to take by surprise; to jump or skip around; to sautee.
salto [sál·to] *m.* jump; leap; precipice; gap; — **de agua** waterfall; **a -s** by jumps; **en un** (*or* **de un**) — in a jiffy; quickly; **dar un** — to jump, leap.
saltón [sal·tón] *adj.* jumping, skipping, hopping; jumpy; protruding; *Col.* half-cooked; **ojos -es** popeyes, bulging eyes; *m.* grasshopper.
salubre [sa·lú·ƀre] *adj.* healthy, healthful.
salubridad [sa·lu·ƀri·đáđ] *f.* healthfulness, health; sanitation.
salud [sa·lúđ] *f.* health; welfare; salvation; **¡ — !** greetings!; your health!
saludable [sa·lu·đá·ƀle] *adj.* wholesome, healthful beneficial.
saludador [sa·lu·đa·đór] *m.* greeter; healer, quack.
saludar [sa·lu·đár] *v.* to salute, greet; to fire a salute.
saludo [sa·lú·đo] *m.* salute, nod, greeting.
salutación [sa·lu·ta·sjón] *f.* salutation; greeting.
salva [sál·ƀa] *f.* salvo, salute with guns; greeting, welcome.
salvación [sal·ƀa·sjón] *f.* salvation.
salvado [sal·ƀá·đo] *m.* bran.
salvador [sal·ƀa·đór] *m.* savior, rescuer; Savior (Saviour); *adj.* saving.
salvaguardar [sal·ƀa·ǥwar·đár] *v.* to safeguard, defend, protect.
salvaguardia [sal·ƀa·ǥwár·đja] *m.* safeguard, protection; guard; *f.* safe-conduct paper, passport; password.
salvajada [sal·ƀa·xá·đa] *f.* savage act or remark.
salvaje [sal·ƀá·xe] *adj.* savage, wild; *m.* savage.
salvajez [sal·ƀa·xés] *f.* wildness, savagery.
salvajismo [sal·ƀa·xíz·mo] *m.* savagery; *Am.* savage act or remark. *See* **salvajada.**
salvamento [sal·ƀa·mén·to] *m.* salvation, rescue; place of safety; salvage (*rescur of property*); **bote de** — lifeboat.
salvar [sal·ƀár] *v.* (*librar*) to save; to except; to exclude; (*vencer*) to clear, jump over; **-se** to be saved; to save oneself, escape.
salvavidas [sal·ƀa·ƀí·đas] *m.* life preserver; **lancha** — lifeboat.
¡salve! [sál·ƀe] *interj.* hail!; **Salve** [sál·ƀe] *f.* Salve Regina, prayer to the Virgin Mary.
salvia [sal·ƀja] *f.* sage (*a plant*).
salvo [sál·ƀo] *adj.* saved; safe; *prep.* save, except but; **a** — safe, without injury; **en** — in safety; out of danger.
salvoconducto [sal·ƀo·kon·dúk·to] *m.* safe-conduct, pass.
san [san] *adj.* (*contr. of* **santo**) saint.
sanalotodo [sa·na·lo·tó·đo] *m.* cure-all.
sanar [sa·nár] *v.* to heal, cure; to recover, get well.
sanatorio [sa·na·tó·rjo] *m.* sanitarium.
sanción [san·sjón] *f.* sanction.
sancionar [san·sjo·nár] *v.* to sanction; to authorize, ratify.
sancochar [saŋ·ko·čár] *v.* to parboil.
sancocho [saŋ·kó·čo] *m.* parboiled meat.
sandalia [san·dá·lja] *f.* sandal.
sandez [san·dés] *f.* stupidity; folly; foolish remark.
sandía [san·dí·a] *f.* watermelon.
sandio [san·dí·o] *adj.* silly, foolish.
saneamiento [sa·ne·a·mjén·to] *m.* sanitation; drainage of land.
sanear [sa·ne·ár] *v.* to make sanitary (*land, property, etc.*); to drain, dry up (*land*).
sangrar [saŋ·gár] *v.* to bleed; to drain; to tap (*a tree*); to pilfer; to exploit (*someone*); to indent (*a line*).
sangre [sáŋ·gre] *f.* blood; — **fría** calmness, coolness of mind; **a** — **fría** in cold blood.
sangría [saŋ·grí·a] *f.* a refreshing Spanish drink made of red wine, fruit juice, and sugar.
sangriento [saŋ·grjén·to] *adj.* bleeding; bloody; bloodstained; bloodthirsty, cruel.
sanguijuela [saŋ·gi·xwé·la] *f.* leech.
sanguinario [saŋ·gi·ná·rjo] *adj.* bloody, cruel; bloodthirsty, murderous.
sanidad [sa·ni·đáđ] *f.* health; soundness; healthfulness; sanitation; — **pública** health department.
sanitario [sa·ni·tá·rjo] *adj.* sanitary.
sano [sá·no] *adj.* (*de salud*) sound, healthy; healthful; sane, sensible; (*íntegro*) whole; unbroken; undamaged; — **y salvo** safe and sound.
sanseacabó [san·se·a·ka·ƀó] that's all; that's the end.
santiamén [san·tja·mén]: **en un** — in a jiffy.
santidad [san·ti·đáđ] *f.* sanctity, holiness, saintliness; **su Santidad** his Holiness.
santificar[6] [san·ti·fi·kár] *v.* to sanctify; to consecrate.
santiguar[8] [san·ti·ǥwár] *v.* to bless; to make the sign of the cross; to beat, hit, punish; **-se** to cross oneself; to show astonishment (*by crossing oneself*).
santísimo [san·tí·si·mo] *adj.* most holy; *m.* the Holy Sacrament.
santo [sán·to] *adj.* saintly, holy; sacred; **esperar todo el** — **día** to wait the whole blessed day; — **y bueno** well and good; *Ríopl., Col., Ven., Mex., Carib., Andes* **¡santa palabra!** that's my final and last word! *m.* saint; saint's day; *Mex., Ven.* **tener el** — **de espaldas** to have a streak of bad luck; **santurrón** *m.* religious hypocrite, affectedly pious

person.
santuario [san·twá·rjo] *m.* sanctuary; *Col.* buried treasure; *Am.* Indian idol.
saña [sá·ña] *f.* fury, rage.
sañudo [sa·ñú·đo] *adj.* furious, enraged.
sapo [sá·po] *m.* toad; *Col.* despicable little man; *Col.* chubby person; *Mex., Ch.* sly person; **echar -s y culebras** to swear, curse.
saque [sá·ke] *m.* serve, service (*in tennis*); server.
saquear [sa·ke·ár] *v.* to sack, plunder, pillage, loot.
saqueo [sa·ké·o] *m.* sacking, pillaging, plunder; loot, booty.
saquillo [sa·kí·yo] *m.* small bag, handbag, satchel.
sarampión [sa·ram·pjón] *m.* measles.
sarao [sa·rá·o] *m.* soirée, evening party.
sarape [sa·rá·pe] *m. Mex.* serape, blanket.
sarcasmo [sar·káz·mo] *m.* sarcasm.
sarcástico [sar·kás·ti·ko] *adj.* sarcastic.
sarcófago [sar·kó·fa·go] *m.* sarcophagus.
sardina [sar·đí·na] *f.* sardine.
sardo [sár·đo] *adj.* Sardinian.
sargento [sar·xén·to] *m.* sergeant.
sarmentoso [sar·men·tó·so] *adj.* vinelike; full of vine shoots; gnarled, knotty.
sarmiento [sar·mjén·to] *m.* shoot or branch of a vine.
sarna [sár·na] *f.* itch; mange.
sarnoso [sar·nó·so] *adj.* itchy, scabby, mangy.
sarpullido [sar·pu·yí·đo] = **salpullido.**
sarro [sá·rro] *m.* tartar (*on teeth*); crust, sediment (*in utensils*).
sarta [sár·ta] *f.* string (*of beads*); series.
sartén [sar·tén] *f.* frying pan; **sartencillo** skillet.
sastre [sás·tre] *m.* tailor.
sastrería [sas·tre·rí·a] *f.* tailor shop.
satánico [sa·tá·ni·ko] *adj.* satanic, devilish.
satélite [sa·té·li·te] *m.* satellite; suburban development; — **artificial** artificial satellite.
satén [sa·tén] *m.* sateen.
sátira [sá·ti·ra] *f.* satire.
satírico [sa·tí·ri·ko] *adj.* satirical.
satirizar[9] [sa·ti·ri·sár] *v.* to satirize.
satisfacción [sa·tis·fak·sjón] *f.* satisfaction; apology, excuse; **tomar** — to vindicate oneself; to take revenge; **dar una** — to offer an apology; to apologize.
satisfacer[31] [sa·tis·fa·sér] *v. irr.* to satisfy; to pay (*a debt*); — **una letra** to honor a draft; **-se** to be satisfied; to take satisfaction.
satisfactorio [sa·tis·fak·tó·rjo] *adj.* satisfactory.
satisfecho [sa·tis·fé·čo] *p.p. of* **satisfacer** satisfied, gratified; *adj.* content, contented.
saturar [sa·tu·rár] *v.* to saturate; to satiate.
sauce [sáw·se] *m.* willow.
savia [sá·bja] *f.* sap.
saxófono [sak·só·fo·no] *m.* saxophone; also **saxofón** [sak·so·fón], **sazón** [sa·són] *f.* (*época*) season, opportune time; (*sabor*) taste, flavor; ripeness; **a la** — then, at that time; **en** — in season; ripe; opportunely; *adj. Ríopl., Mex., Cuba* ripe.
sazonado [sa·so·ná·đo] *adj. & p.p.* seasoned; mellow, ripe; expressive (*said of a phrase*).
sazonar [sa·so·nár] *v.* to season; to flavor; **-se** to become seasoned; to ripen, mature.
se [se] *obj. pron.* (*before* **le, la, lo, las,** *and* **los**) to him, to her; to you (*formal*); to them; *refl. pron.* himself, herself, yourself (*formal*), yourselves (*formal*) themselves; *reciprocal pron.* each other, one another.
sebo [sé·bo] *m.* tallow, fat; suet.
seboso [se·bó·so] *adj.* fatty; tallowy.
secador [se·ka·đór] *m. Am.* dryer (*clothes, hair*); *Arg.* towel.
secante [se·kán·te] *adj.* drying, blotting; **papel** — blotter; *f.* secant (*math.*).
secar[6] [se·kár] *v.* to dry; to wipe dry; **-se** to dry or wipe oneself; to dry up; to wither; to get thin.
sección [sek·sjón] *f.* section; division; cutting.
seccionar [sek·sjo·nár] *v.* to section.
seco [sé·ko] *adj.* (*sin humedad*) dry; dried; withered; (*áspero*) harsh; abrupt; plain, unadorned; **en** — on dry land, out of the water; **parar en** — to stop short, stop suddenly; **a secas** plain; alone, without anything else; *Mex., Carib., Ríopl., Andes* simply, straight to the point; **comer pan a secas** to eat just bread; *Mex., Ven.* **bailar a secas** to dance without musical accompaniment.
secreción [se·kre·sjón] *f.* secretion.
secretar [se·kre·tár] *v.* to secrete.
secretaría [se·kre·ta·rí·a] *f.* secretary's office; position of secretary.
secretariado [se·kre·ta·rjá·đo] *m.* secretariat.
secretario [se·kre·tá·rjo] *m.* secretary; confidant; **secretaria** [se·kre·ta·rja] *f.* woman secretary; secretary's wife.
secretear [se·kre·te·ár] *v.* to whisper; **-se** to whisper to each other.
secreto [se·kré·to] *adj.* secret, hidden; secretive; *m.* secret; secrecy; secret place; — **a voces** open secret; **en** — secretly; **hablar en** — to whisper.
secta [sék·ta] *f.* sect.
sector [sek·tór] *m.* sector.
secuaz [se·kwás] *m.* partisan, follower.
secuela [se·kwé·la] *f.* sequel, outcome, consequence.
secuencia [se·kwén·sja] *f.* sequence.
secuestrador [se·kwes·tra·đór] *m.* kidnapper; confiscator.
secuestrar [se·kwes·trár] *v.* to seize; to kidnap; to confiscate.
secuestro [se·kwés·tro] *m.* kidnapping; seizure.
secular [se·ku·lár] *adj.* secular; lay, worldly; centennial; *m.* secular, secular priest.
secundar [se·kun·dár] *v.* to second, favor, back up.
secundario [se·kun·dá·rjo] *adj.* secondary.
sed [sed] *f.* thirst; craving, desire; **tener** — to be thirsty.
seda [sé·đa] *f.* silk; **como una** — soft as silk; sweet-tempered; smoothly, easily.
sedal [se·đál] *m.* fishing line.
sedán [se·đán] *m.* sedan.
sedativo [se·đa·tí·bo] *adj. & m.* sedative.
sede [sé·đe] *f.* seat, see; **Santa Sede** Holy See.
sedentario [se·đen·tá·rjo] *adj.* sedentary.
sedeño [se·đé·ño] *adj.* silky, silken.
sedería [se·đe·rí·a] *f.* silk goods; silk shop.
sedero [se·đé·ro] *m.* silk dealer or weaver; *adj.* silk, pertaining to silk; **industria sedera** silk industry.
sedición [se·đi·sjón] *f.* sedition.
sedicioso [se·đi·sjó·so] *adj.* seditious, turbulent.
sediento [se·đjén·to] *adj.* thirsty; dry, parched; anxious, desirous.
sedimento [se·đi·mén·to] *m.* sediment; dregs, grounds.
sedoso [se·đó·so] *adj.* silken, silky.
seducción [se·đuk·sjón] *f.* seduction.
seducir[25] [se·đu·sír] *v. irr.* to seduce; to entice; to charm.
seductivo [se·đuk·tí·bo] *adj.* seductive, alluring; inviting, enticing.
seductor [se·đuk·tór] *adj.* tempting, fascinating; *m.* seducer; tempter; charming person.
sefardí [se·far·đí] *adj.* Sephardic; *m.* Spanish-speaking Jew.

segador [se·ǥa·đór] *m.* harvester, reaper; **segadora** [se·ǥa·đó·ra] *f.* harvester, mowing machine; woman reaper.
segar[1, 7] [se·ǥár] *v. irr.* to mow, reap; to cut off.
seglar [se·ǥlár] *adj.* secular, lay; *m.* layman.
segmento [seǥ·mén·to] *m.* segment.
segregar[7] [se·ǥre·ǥár] *v. irr.* to segregate.
seguida [se·ǥí·đa] *f.* succession; series, continuation; **de** — without interruption, continuously; **en** — at once, immediately.
seguido [se·ǥí·đo] *p.p.* followed; continued; *adj.* continuous; straight, direct; *adv.* without interruption; *Am.* often; *Col., Ven.* **de** — at once, immediately.
seguidor [se·ǥi·đór] *m.* follower.
seguimiento [se·ǥi·mjén·to] *m.* pursuit.
seguir[5, 12] [se·ǥír] *v. irr.* to follow; to continue; to pursue; **-se** to follow as a consequence.
según [se·ǥún] *prep.* according to; *conj.* as; according to; — **y conforme** (*or* — **y como**) exactly as, just as; that depends.
segundar [se·ǥun·dár] *v.* to repeat a second time; to second.
segundero [se·ǥun·dé·ro] *m.* second hand (*of a watch or clock*).
segundo [se·ǥún·do] *adj. & m.* second.
segundón [se·ǥun·dón] *m.* second child.
seguridad [se·ǥu·ri·đáđ] *f.* security; safety; certainty; **alfiler de** — safety pin.
seguro [se·ǥú·ro] *adj.* secure; sure, certain; safe; *Ríopl., Mex., Carib., Andes* honest, trustworthy; *m.* assurance; insurance; safety device; **a buen** — (**al** —, *or* **de** —) truly, certainly; **en** — in safety; **sobre** — without risk; without taking a chance; *Am.* **irse uno del** — to lose one's temper; *Ch., Mex., Cuba, Andes* **a la segura** without risk.
seibó [sej·ƀó] *m. Cuba, Ven.* sideboard, hutch.
seis [sejs] *num.* six.
selección [se·lek·sjón] *f.* selection choice.
seleccionar [se·lek·sjo·nár] *v.* to select, choose.
selecto [se·lék·to] *adj.* select, choice.
selenio [se·lé·njo] *m.* selenium.
selectivo [se·lek·tí·ƀo] *adj.* selective.
selva [sél·ƀa] *f.* forest; jungle.
sellar [se·yár] *v.* (*imprimir*) to stamp; to seal; (*cerrar*) to close tightly, seal; (*concluir*) to conclude.
sello [sé·yo] *m.* seal; stamp; *Arg.* official stamped paper.
semáforo [se·má·fo·ro] *m.* traffic light.
semana [se·má·na] *f.* week; week's wages; **días de** — week days; **entre** — during the week.
semanal [se·ma·nál] *adj.* weekly; **-mente** *adv.* weekly, every week.
semanario [se·ma·ná·rjo] *m.* weekly publication; *adj.* weekly.
semblante [sem·blán·te] *m.* countenance; facial expression; appearance.
semblanza [sem·blán·sa] *f.* portrait, literary sketch.
sembrado [sem·brá·đo] *m.* sown ground; cultivated field.
sembradora [sem·bra·đó·ra] *f.* seeder, sowing machine.
sembrar[1] [sem·brár] *v. irr.* to sow; to scatter.
semejante [se·me·xán·te] *adj.* similar, like; such a; *m.* fellow man; **nuestros -s** our fellow men.
semejanza [se·me·xán·sa] *f.* resemblance, similarity; simile; **a** — **de** in the manner of.
semejar [se·me·xár] *v.* to resemble; **-se** to resemble.
semental [se·men·tál] *adj.* sowing (*crops*); breeding (*animals*); used as stud.
semestre [se·més·tre] *m.* semester.
semiconsonante [se·mi·kon·so·nán·te] *f.* semiconsonant.
semiduplex [se·mi·du·plés] *m.* (*computadora*) half duplex.
semilla [se·mí·ya] *f.* seed.
semillero [se·mi·yé·ro] *m.* seed bed; plant nursery; — **de vicios** hotbed of vice.
seminario [se·mi·ná·rjo] *m.* seminary; plant nursery, seed plot.
semítico [se·mí·ti·ko] *adj.* Semitic.
semivocal [se·mi·ƀo·kál] *f.* semivowel.
sempiterno [sem·pi·tér·no] *adj.* everlasting; evergreen.
senado [se·ná·đo] *m.* senate.
senador [se·na·đór] *m.* senator.
sencillez [sen·si·yés] *f.* simplicity; plainness.
sencillo [sen·sí·yo] *adj.* simple; easy; plain; unadorned; unaffected; *m.* loose change, small coins.
senda [sén·da] *f.* path; way, course.
sendero [sen·dé·ro] *m.* path.
sendos [sén·dos] *adj. pl.* one for each of two or more persons or things.
senectud [se·nek·túđ] *f.* senility, old age.
senil [se·níl] *adj.* senile.
seno [sé·no] *m.* (*pecho*) breast, bosom; (*hueco*) cavity, hollow; womb; lap; cove, bay; innermost recess; sinus (*cavity in a bone*); sine (*math.*); *C.A.* armpit.
sensación [sen·sa·sjón] *f.* sensation.
sensacional [sen·sa·sjo·nál] *adj.* sensational.
sensatez [sen·sa·tés] *f.* prudence, common sense.
sensato [sen·sá·to] *adj.* sensible, wise, prudent.
sensibilidad [sen·si·ƀi·li·đáđ] *f.* sensibility; sensitiveness.
sensible [sen·sí·ƀle] *adj.* sensitive; perceptible; regrettable.
sensitivo [sen·si·tí·ƀo] *adj.* sensitive.
sensual [sen·swál] *adj.* sensual; sensuous.
sensualidad [sen·swa·li·đáđ] *f.* sensuality; lewdness.
sentada [sen·tá·đa] *f.* sitting; **de una** — at one sitting.
sentado [sen·tá·đo] *adj.* seated, sitting; **dar por** — to take for granted.
sentar[1] [sen·tár] *v. irr.* to seat; to set; to establish; to become, suit, fit; to agree with one (*as food or climate*); **-se** to sit down; to settle down; *Col.* **-se en la palabra** to do all the talking, monopolize the conversation.
sentencia [sen·tén·sja] *f.* sentence; verdict; judgment, maxim, proverb; statement.
sentenciar [sen·ten·sjár] *v.* to sentence; to pass judgment on; to decide.
sentido [sen·tí·đo] *p.p.* felt; experienced; *adj.* heartfelt, filled with feeling; sensitive; touchy; **darse por** — to take offense; to have one's feelings hurt; **estar** — **con alguien** to be offended or peeved at someone; *m.* sense; meaning; judgment; **aguzar el** — to prick up one's ears; **perder el** — to faint.
sentimental [sen·ti·men·tál] *adj.* sentimental.
sentimentalismo [sen·ti·men·ta·líz·mo] *m.* sentimentalism, sentimentality.
sentimiento [sen·ti·mjén·to] *m.* sentiment; sensation, feeling; grief, regret.
sentir[3] [sen·tír] *v. irr.* to feel; to sense; to hear; to regret; **-se** to feel (*well, strong, sad, etc.*); to feel oneself, consider oneself; to feel resentment; to feel a pain; **sin** — without being realized or felt; inadvertently; unnoticed; *m.* feeling; judgment, opinion.

señá [se·ñá] *C.A., Ven., Col. familiar contraction of* **señora.**
seña [sé·ña] *f.* sign, mark; signal; password; **-s** address (*name and place of residence*); **por mas -s** as an additional proof.
señal [se·ñál] *f.* (*marca*) sign, mark; signal; trace, vestige; scar; (*indicio*) reminder; indication; token, pledge; *Ríopl., Andes* earmark, brand (*on the ear of livestock*); **en — de** in proof of, in token of.
señalar [se·ña·lár] *v.* to mark; to point out; to indicate; to determine, fix; to appoint; to signal; to assign; *Am.* to earmark, brand (*cattle*); **-se** to distinguish oneself.
señero [se·ñé·ro] *adj.* unique.
señor [se·ñór] *m.* mister; sir; owner; master, lord; gentleman; **el Señor** the Lord.
señora [se·ñó·ra] *f.* lady; madam; mistress; Mrs.
señorear [se·ño·re·ár] *v.* to lord it over, domineer; to dominate; to master, control.
señoría [se·ño·rí·a] *f.* lordship.
señoril [se·no·ríl] *adj.* lordly.
señorío [se·ño·rí·o] *m.* dominion, rule; domain of a lord; lordship; dignity; mastery, control; body of noblemen.
señorita [se·ño·rí·ta] *f.* miss; young lady.
señorito [se·ño·rí·to] *m.* master, young gentleman.
señuelo [se·ñwé·lo] *m.* decoy; lure, bait; *Ven.* leading or guiding oxen.
separación [se·pa·ra·sjón] *f.* separation.
separado [se·pa·rá·đo] *p.p. & adj.* separate; separated; **por —** separately.
separar [se·pa·rár] *v.* to separate; to set aside, to remove (*from*); to dismiss (*from*); **-se** to separate; to retire, resign; to withdraw, leave.
separata [se·pa·rá·ta] *f.* reprint; offprint.
septentrional [sep·ten·trjo·nál] *adj.* northern.
septiembre [sep·tjém·bre] *m.* September.
sepulcral [se·pul·král] *adj.* sepulchral (*pertaining to sepulchers or tombs*); **lápida —** tombstone.
sepulcro [se·púl·kro] *m.* sepulcher, tomb, grave.
sepultar [se·pul·tár] *v.* to bury; to hide.
sepultura [se·pul·tú·ra] *f.* burial; grave; **dar —** to bury.
sepulturero [se·pul·tu·ré·ro] *m.* gravedigger.
sequedad [se·ke·đáđ] *f.* dryness; gruffness.
sequía [se·kí·a] *f.* drought.
séquito [sé·ki·to] *m.* retinue, following.
ser[44] [ser] *v. irr.* to be; to exist; to happen, occur; **— de** (*or* **para**) **ver** to be worth seeing; *m.* being; essence, nature; existence; *Am.* **estar en un —** to be always in the same condition.
serafín [se·ra·fín] *m.* seraph.
serenar [se·re·nár] *v.* to pacify; to calm down; *Col.* to drizzle, rain gently; **-se** to become serene, calm down; to clear up (*said of the weather*).
serenata [se·re·ná·ta] *f.* serenade.
serenidad [se·re·ni·đáđ] *f.* serenity, calm.
sereno [se·ré·no] *adj.* serene, calm; clear, cloudless; *m.* night humidity, dew; night watchman; **al —** in the night air.
serie [sé·rje] *f.* series.
seriedad [se·rje·đáđ] *f.* seriousness; gravity; earnestness; dignity.
serio [sé·rjo] *adj.* serious; grave; earnest; dignified; formal; **en —** seriously.
sermón [ser·món] *m.* sermon; reproof.
sermonear [ser·mo·ne·ár] *v.* to preach; to admonish, reprimand.
serpentear [ser·pen·te·ár] *v.* to wind, twist, turn, zigzag.
serpentín [ser·pen·tín] *m.* coil.
serpentino [ser·pen·tí·no] *adj.* serpentine.
serpiente [ser·pjén·te] *f.* serpent, snake.
serrado [se·rrá·đo] *adj.* toothed, notched (*like a saw*); jagged.
serrana [se·rrá·na] *f.* mountain girl; **serranilla** [se·rra·ní·ya] *f.* lyric poem with a rustic theme.
serranía [se·rra·ní·a] *f.* mountainous region; chain of mountains.
serrano [se·rrá·no] *m.* mountaineer; *adj.* of, pertaining to, or from the mountains.
serrar [se·rrár] = **aserrar.**
serrín [se·rrín] *m.* sawdust.
serrucho [se·rrú·čo] *m.* handsaw.
servible [ser·ƀí·ƀle] *adj.* serviceable, useful.
servicial [ser·ƀi·sjál] *adj.* helpful, obliging.
servicio [ser·ƀí·sjo] *m.* service; table service; tea or coffee set; chamber pot; *Am.* toilet, water closet.
servidor [ser·ƀi·đór] *m.* servant; waiter; **— de Vd.** at your service; **su seguro —** yours truly.
servidumbre [ser·ƀi·đúm·bre] *f.* domestic help, servants; servitude, slavery; service.
servil [ser·ƀíl] *adj.* servile; **servilón** [ser·ƀi·lón] *adj.* very servile; *m.* bootlicker, great flatterer.
servilismo [ser·ƀi·líz·mo] *m.* servility, servile behavior or attitude, servile submission.
servilleta [ser·ƀi·yé·ta] *f.* napkin.
servir[5] [ser·ƀír] *v. irr.* to serve; to be of use; **— de** to serve as, act as; to be used as; **— para** to be good for; to be used for; **-se** to serve or help oneself; to be pleased to; **-se de** to make use of; **sírvase Vd. hacerlo** please do it.
sésamo [sé·sa·mo] *m.* sesame.
sesenta [se·sén·ta] *num.* sixty.
seseo [se·sé·o] *m.* pronunciation of all sibilants as /s/.
sesgado [sez·ǥá·đo] *adj.* slanting, oblique, bias.
sesgar[7] [sez·ǥár] *v.* to slant; to cut on the bias; to follow an oblique line.
sesgo [séz·ǥo] *m.* bias; slant; diagonal cut; turn; **al —** on the bias; diagonally, obliquely.
sesión [se·sjón] *f.* session; meeting, conference.
seso [sé·so] *m.* brain; wisdom, intelligence; **devanarse los -s** to rack one's brain.
sestear [ses·te·ár] *v.* to snooze, take a nap.
sesudo [se·sú·đo] *adj.* sensible, wise, prudent; *Mex., C.A.* stubborn.
seta [sé·ta] *f.* mushroom.
setenta [se·tén·ta] *num.* seventy.
setiembre [se·tjém·bre] *m. Spain* preferred form for **septiembre.**
sétimo [sé·ti·mo] *adj. Spain* preferred form for **séptimo.**
seto [sé·to] *m.* fence; hedge.
seudónimo [sew·đó·ni·mo] *m.* pseudonym, pen name.
severidad [se·ƀe·ri·đáđ] *f.* severity; strictness; seriousness.
severo [se·ƀé·ro] *adj.* severe; strict; stern.
sevillano [se·ƀi·yá·no] *adj.* of, from, or pertaining to Seville, Spain.
sexo [sék·so] *m.* sex.
sexual [sek·swál] *adj.* sexual.
si [si] *conj.* if; whether; **¡— ya te lo dije!** but I already told you!; **— bien** although; **por — acaso** just in case.
sí [si] *adv.* yes; **— que** certainly, really; **un — es no es** a trifle, somewhat; **¡sí, fuí!** I *did* go!; *m.* assent, consent; *refl. pron.* (*used after a prep.*) himself, herself, yourself (*formal*), themselves; **de por —** separately, by itself; **estar sobre —** to be on the alert.
sibilante [si·ƀi·lán·te] *adj.* sibilant, whistling.
sicología [si·ko·lo·xí·a] *f.* psychology.
sicológico [si·ko·ló·xi·ko] *adj.* psychological.

sicólogo [si·kó·lo·ǥo] *m.* psychologist.

sicosis [si·kó·sis] *f.* psychosis.

siderurgia [si·đe·rúr·xja] *f.* iron and steel industry.

sidra [sí·đra] *f.* cider.

siega [sjé·ǥa] *f.* reaping, mowing; harvesting; harvest, harvest season.

siembra [sjém·bra] *f.* sowing; seedtime, sowing time; sown field.

siempre [sjém·pre] *adv.* always; *Mex., C.A., Col., Andes* in any case, anyway; **para** (*or* **por**) — forever, for always; **por — jamás** forever and ever; — **que** whenever; provided that; *Am.* — **sí me voy** I've decided to go anyway.

siempreviva [sjem·pre·ƀí·ƀa] *f.* evergreen; everlasting.

sien [sjen] *f.* temple (*of the forehead*).

sierpe [sjér·pe] *f.* serpent, snake.

sierra [sjé·rra] *f.* saw; — **caladora** jigsaw; — **para metales** hacksaw; — **sin fin** bandsaw; (*cordillera*) mountain range.

siervo [sjér·ƀo] *m.* serf; slave; servant.

siesta [sjés·ta] *f.* siesta, afternoon nap; early afternoon; **dormir la** — to take an afternoon nap.

siete [sjé·te] *num.* seven.

sifón [si·fón] *m.* siphon; siphon bottle; trap (*in plumbing fixtures*).

sigilo [si·xí·lo] *m.* secret; secrecy.

sigla [sí·ǥla] *f.* initial abbreviation.

siglo [sí·ǥlo] *m.* century; period, epoch; the world; worldly matters.

significación [siǥ·ni·fi·ka·sjón] *f.* meaning; significance.

significado [siǥ·ni·fi·ká·đo] *m.* significance, meaning.

significar[6] [siǥ·ni·fi·kár] *v.* to signify; to mean; to make known, show; to matter, have importance.

significativo [siǥ·ni·fi·ka·tí·ƀo] *adj.* significant.

signo [síǥ·no] *m.* sign; mark; symbol.

siguiente [si·ǥjén·te] *adj.* following.

sílaba [sí·la·ƀa] *f.* syllable.

silabario [si·la·ƀá·rjo] *m.* speller, spelling book.

silabear [si·la·ƀe·ár] *v.* to syllabicate.

silbar [sil·ƀár] *v.* to whistle; to hiss.

silbato [sil·ƀá·to] *m.* whistle.

silbido [sil·ƀí·đo] *m.* whistle; hiss.

silenciador [si·len·sja·đór] *m.* silencer; muffler (*of an automobile*).

silencio [si·lén·sjo] *m.* silence; pause; *adj. Am.* silent, quiet, motionless.

silencioso [si·len·sjó·so] *adj.* silent, quiet.

silicio [si·lí·sjo] *m.* silicon.

silo [sí·lo] *m.* silo; cave.

silogismo [si·lo·xíz·mo] *m.* syllogism.

silueta [si·lwé·ta] *f.* silhouette.

silvestre [sil·ƀés·tre] *adj.* wild, uncultivated.

silvicultor [sil·ƀi·kul·tór] *m.* forester; **silvicultura** [sil·ƀi·kul·tú·ra] *f.* forestry.

silla [sí·ya] *f.* chair; saddle; — **de montar** saddle; *Ven.* — **de balanza** rocking chair. *See* **mecedora.**

sillón [si·yón] *m.* large chair; easy chair; *Am.* — **de hamaca** rocking chair.

sima [sí·ma] *f.* chasm, abyss.

simbólico [sim·bó·li·ko] *adj.* symbolic.

simbolismo [sim·bo·líz·mo] *m.* symbolism.

símbolo [sím·bo·lo] *m.* symbol; — **de la fe** (*or* **de los Apóstoles**) the Apostle's creed; — **de status** status symbol.

simetría [si·me·trí·a] *f.* symmetry.

simétrico [si·mé·tri·ko] *adj.* symmetrical.

simiente [si·mjén·te] *f.* seed.

símil [sí·mil] *m.* simile; similarity; *adj.* similar.

similar [si·mi·lár] *adj.* similar.

simpatía [sim·pa·tí·a] *f.* attraction, attractiveness; accord, harmony; liking.

simpático [sim·pá·ti·ko] *adj.* sympathetic, congenial; pleasant, agreeable, nice.

simpatizar[9] [sim·pa·ti·sár] *v.* to be attractive to; to get on well with; to be congenial; **no me simpatiza** I don't like him or her.

simple [sím·ple] *adj.* simple; mere; plain; pure, unmixed; naïve, innocent; silly, foolish; *m.* simpleton.

simpleza [sim·plé·sa] *f.* simplicity; simpleness, stupidity, foolishness.

simplicidad [sim·pli·si·đáđ] *f.* simplicity; candor.

simplificar[6] [sim·pli·fi·kár] *v.* to simplify.

simplista [sim·plís·ta] *adj.* simplistic; *m. & f.* a person who is inclined to oversimplify.

simplón [sim·plón] *m.* simpleton.

simposio [sim·pó·sjo] *m.* symposium.

simulacro [si·mu·lá·kro] *m.* mimic battle, sham or mock battle; image, vision.

simular [si·mu·lár] *v.* to simulate, feign.

simultáneo [si·mul·tá·ne·o] *adj.* simultaneous.

sin [sin] *prep.* without; besides, not counting; — **que** *conj.* without; — **embargo** nevertheless, still, yet; — **qué ni para qué** without rhyme or reason.

sinagoga [si·na·ǥó·ǥa] *f.* synagogue.

sinapismo [si·na·píz·mo] *m.* mustard plaster; irritating person, nuisance, pest, bore.

sincerar [sin·se·rár] *v.* to square, justify, excuse; **-se** to square oneself (with), justify oneself (with).

sinceridad [sin·se·ri·đáđ] *f.* sincerity.

sincero [sin·sé·ro] *adj.* sincere.

síncopa [sín·ko·pa] *f.* syncopation; syncope.

sincronizar[9] [sin·kro·ni·sár] *v. irr.* to synchronize.

sindicar[6] [sin·di·kár] *v.* to syndicate; **-se** to syndicate, form a syndicate.

sindicato [sin·di·ká·to] *m.* syndicate; labor union.

síndico [sín·di·ko] *m.* receiver (*person appointed to take charge of property under litigation or to liquidate a bankrupt business*); trustee.

sinecura [si·ne·kú·ra] *f.* sinecure (*easy and well paid position*).

sinfonía [sin·fo·ní·a] *f.* symphony.

singular [sin·gu·lár] *adj.* singular; unique; striking; odd, strange.

singularizar[9] [sin·gu·la·ri·sár] *v.* to single out, choose; to distinguish; **-se** to distinguish oneself; to be singled out.

siniestro [si·njés·tro] *adj.* sinister; left (*side*); *m.* unforeseen loss, damage; **siniestra** [si·njés·tra] *f.* left hand; left-hand side.

sinnúmero [sin·nú·me·ro] *m.* great number, endless number.

sino [sí·no] *conj.* but; *prep.* except; **no hace — lo que le mandan** he only does what he is told; — **que** *conj.* but; *m.* fate, destiny.

sinónimo [si·nó·ni·mo] *m.* synonym; *adj.* synonymous.

sinrazón [sin·rra·són] *f.* injustice, wrong.

sinsabor [sin·sa·ƀór] *m.* displeasure; trouble, grief, distress.

sintaxis [sin·ták·sis] *f.* syntax.

síntesis [sín·te·sis] *f.* synthesis; summary.

sintético [sin·té·ti·ko] *adj.* synthetic.

sintetizar[9] [sin·te·ti·sár] *v.* to synthesize.

síntoma [sín·to·ma] *m.* sympton; indication, sign.

sintonizar[9] [sin·to·ni·sár] *v.* to tune in (on).

sinuoso [si·nwó·so] *adj.* sinuous, winding; wavy.

sinvergüenza [sim·ber·ǥwén·sa] *m. & f.* shameless person; scoundrel.

siquiatra [si·kjá·tra] *m. & f.* psychiatrist, alienist.

siquiatría [si·kja·trí·a] *f.* psychiatry.

siquiera [si·kjé·ra] *adv.* at least; even; **ni** — not even; *conj.* even though.
sirena [si·ré·na] *f.* siren; whistle, foghorn.
sirviente [sir·ƀjén·te] *m.* servant; waiter; **sirvienta** [sir·ƀjén·ta] *f.* housemaid; waitress.
sisa [sí·sa] *f.* petty theft; dart (*made in a garment*).
sisal [si·sál] *m. Am.* sisal or sisal hemp.
sisar [si·sár] *v.* to take in (*a garment*); to pilfer; to cheat out of, defraud.
sisear [si·se·ár] *v.* to hiss.
siseo [si·sé·o] *m.* hiss, hissing.
sistema [sis·té·ma] *m.* system; — **operativo** (*computadora*) operating sustem; — **binario** (*computadora*) binary system.
sistemático [sis·te·má·ti·ko] *adj.* systematic.
sitial [si·tjál] *m.* chair of a presiding officer; place of honor.
sitiar [si·tjár] *v.* to besiege; to surround.
sitio [sí·tjo] *m.* site, location; place, spot, space; siege; *Am.* cattle ranch; *Mex.* taxicab station; **poner — a** to lay siege to.
sito [sí·to] *adj.* situated, located.
situación [si·twa·sjón] *f.* situation; position; location; state, condition; *Mex., Carib., Ven., Col.* **hombre de la** — man of the hour, man of influence.
situado [si·twá·đo] *p.p.* situated; placed.
situar[18] [si·twár] *v.* to locate; to place; **-se** to station oneself, place oneself; to be located, placed, situated.
snobismo [ez·no·ƀíz·mo] *m.* snobism (*in the European sense*); the tendency to try to do whatever seems to be in style.
so [so] *prep.* — **capa de** under the guise of; — **pena de** under penalty of; — **pretexto de** under the pretext of.
sobaco [so·ƀá·ko] *m.* armpit.
sobar [so·ƀár] *v.* (*ablandar*) to rub; to knead; to massage; to touch, handle; to fondle, pet; (*fastidiar*) to bother; to beat, slap; *Col., Ven., Mex.* to set bones; *Col.* to flay, skin; *Am.* to win (*in a fight*); *Am.* to tire out (*a horse*).
soberanía [so·ƀe·ra·ní·a] *f.* sovereignty.
soberano [so·ƀe·rá·no] *adj. & m.* sovereign.
soberbia [so·ƀér·ƀja] *f.* pride, arrogance; ostentation, pomp.
soberbio [so·ƀer·ƀjo] *adj.* proud, haughty, arrogant; pompous; (*excelente*) superb, magnificent; spirited (*horse*).
sobornar [so·ƀor·nár] *v.* to bribe.
soborno [so·ƀór·no] *m.* bribery; bribe; *Andes* overload (*on a pack animal*), extra load.
sobra [só·ƀra] *f.* surplus, excess; **-s** leftovers, leavings; **de** — more than enough; superfluous, unnecessary.
sobrado [so·ƀrá·đo] *m.* attic; loft; *Am.* pantry shelf; **-s** *Col., Ven.* leftovers, leavings; *adj.* leftover; excessive; superfluous; forward, brazen; **sobradas veces** many times, repeatedly.
sobrante [so·ƀrán·te] *adj.* leftover, surplus, excess, spare; *m.* surplus, excess, remainder.
sobrar [so·ƀrár] *v.* to exceed; to remain, be left over; to be more than enough.
sobre [só·ƀre] *prep.* (*encima de*) over; above; on, upon; (*acerca de*) about; approximately; besides; — **manera** excessively; **estar — sí** to be cautious, on the alert; — **que** besides, in addition to the fact that; *m.* envelope; address (*on an envelope*).
sobrecama [so·ƀre·ká·ma] *f.* bedspread.
sobrecarga [so·ƀre·kár·ǥa] *f.* overload; overburden.
sobrecargar[7] [so·ƀre·kar·ǥár] *v.* to overload; to overburden.
sobrecargo [so·ƀre·kár·ǥo] *m.* purser (*on a ship*); *f.* airline hostess.
sobrecoger[11] [so·ƀre·ko·xér] *v.* to surprise, catch unaware; to startle; **-se** to be startled; **-se de miedo** to be seized with fear.
sobreentender[1] [so·ƀre·en·ten·dér] *v. irr.* to assume, understand; **-se** to be assumed, be obvious, be understood.
sobreescrito [so·ƀre·es·krí·to] *m.* address (*on an envelope*).
sobreesdrújulo [so·ƀre·ez·đrú·xu·lo] *adj.* accented on syllable before antepenult.
sobreexcitación [so·ƀre·ek·si·ta·sjón] *f.* overexcitement; thrill.
sobreexcitar [so·ƀre·ek·si·tár] *v.* to overexcite.
sobregirar [so·ƀre·xi·rár] *v.* to overdraw.
sobrehumano [so·ƀre·u·má·no] *adj.* superhuman.
sobrellevar [so·ƀre·ye·ƀár] *v.* to endure, bear; to tolerate; to lighten (*another's burden*).
sobremesa [so·ƀre·mé·sa] *f.* table runner; after dinner conversation at the table; **de** — during the after dinner conversation.
sobrenadar [so·ƀre·na·đár] *v.* to float.
sobrenatural [so·ƀre·na·tu·rál] *adj.* supernatural.
sobrenombre [so·ƀre·nóm·bre] *m.* surname; nickname.
sobrepasar [soƀ·re·pa·sár] *v.* to exceed; to excel; **-se** to overstep, go too far.
sobreponer[40] [so·ƀre·po·nér] *v. irr.* to lay on top; **-se** to dominate oneself; **-se a** to overcome; to dominate.
sobrepuesto [so·ƀre·pwés·to] *p.p. of* **sobreponer;** *m.* appliqué (*trimming laid on a dress*); *C.A.* mend, patch.
sobrepujar [so·ƀre·pu·xár] *v.* to exceed, excel, surpass; to outweigh.
sobresaliente [so·ƀre·sa·ljén·te] *adj.* outstanding; projecting; excellent; *m. & f.* substitute (*a person*); understudy.
sobresalir[43] [so·ƀre·sa·lír] *v. irr.* to stand out; to project, jut out; to excel.
sobresaltar [so·ƀre·sal·tár] *v.* to startle, frighten; to assail; to stand out clearly **-se** to be startled, frightened.
sobresalto [so·ƀre·sál·to] *m.* start, scare, fright, shock; **de** — suddenly.
sobrestante [so·ƀres·tán·te] *m.* overseer; boss, foreman.
sobresueldo [so·ƀre·swél·do] *m.* overtime pay, extra pay or wages.
sobretodo [so·ƀre·tó·đo] *m.* overcoat.
sobrevencer [so·ƀre·ƀen·sér] *v.* to be overdue.
sobrevenir[48] [so·ƀre·ƀe·nír] *v. irr.* to happen, occur, come unexpectedly; to follow, happen after.
sobreviviente [so·ƀre·ƀi·ƀjén·te] *m. & f.* survivor; *adj.* surviving.
sobrevivir [so·ƀre·ƀi·ƀír] *v.* to survive.
sobriedad [so·ƀrje·đáđ] *f.* sobriety, soberness, temperance, moderation.
sobrina [so·ƀrí·na] *f.* niece.
sobrino [so·ƀrí·no] *m.* nephew.
sobrio [só·ƀrjo] *adj.* sober, temperate, moderate.
socarrar [so·ka·rrár] *v.* to sear, singe.
socarrón [so·ka·rrón] *adj.* cunning, sly, crafty.
socarronería [so·ka·rro·ne·rí·a] *f.* craftiness, slyness, cunning.
socavar [so·ka·ƀár] *v.* to dig under; to undermine.
socavón [so·ka·ƀón] *m.* tunnel; cave, cavern; underground passageway.
social [so·sjál] *adj.* social; sociable, friendly.
socialismo [so·sja·líz·mo] *m.* socialism.

socialista [so·sja·lís·ta] *adj.* socialist, socialistic; *m. & f.* socialist.
sociedad [so·sje·đáđ] *f.* society; partnership; company, firm, corporation; — **anónima** (*or* — **por acciones**) stock company.
socio [só·sjo] *m.* associate, partner; member.
sociología [so·sjo·lo·xí·a] *f.* sociology.
socorrer [so·ko·rrér] *v.* to help, aid, assist.
socorro [so·kó·rro] *m.* help, aid, assistance, relief; *Am.* partial advance payment on a workman's wages.
sodio [só·đjo] *m.* sodium.
sodomía [so·đo·mí·a] *f.* sodomy.
soez [so·és] *adj.* low, vile, vulgar; coarse, ill-mannered.
sofá [so·fá] *m.* sofa, davenport.
sofocante [so·fo·kán·te] *adj.* suffocating, stifling.
sofocar[6] [so·fo·kár] *v.* to suffocate, choke; to smother; to bother; to embarrass.
sofoco [so·fó·ko] *m.* suffocation, choking; upset, annoyance; embarrassment.
sofrenar [so·fre·nár] *v.* to check; to control; to reprimand.
sofrito [so·frí·to] *m.* a preparation of lightly fried ingredients.
soga [só·ǥa] *f.* rope; *Ven., Col., Andes, Ch.* leather lasso or rope.
soja [só·xa] *f.* soy.
sojuzgamiento [so·xuz·ǥa·mjén·to] *m.* subjugation, subjection.
sojuzgar[7] [so·xuz·ǥár] *v.* to subjugate, subdue, subject.
sol [sol] *m.* sun; sunshine; sol (*fifth note of the scale*); sol (*monetary unit of Peru*); **de — a —** from sunrise to sunset; **hace —** it is sunny; **tomar el —** to bask in the sun; to enjoy the sunshine.
solana [so·lá·na] *f.* sunny place; sunroom; sun porch; intense sunlight; **solanera** [so·la·né·ra] *f.* sunburn; sunny place.
solapa [so·lá·pa] *f.* lapel.
solapado [so·la·pá·đo] *adj.* sly, crafty, cunning, deceitful, underhanded.
solapo [so·lá·po] *m.* overlap.
solar [so·lár] *m.* lot, plot of ground; ancestral mansion, manor; *Carib., Mex.* tenement house; *Mex., Ven.* back yard; *Col.* town lot, field (*for growing alfalfa, corn, etc.*); *adj.* solar, of the sun.
solar[2] [so·lár] *v. irr.* to sole (*shoes*); to pave, floor.
solariego [so·la·rjé·ǥo] *adj.* manorial, pertaining to a manor; **casa solariega** ancestral manor or mansion.
solaz [so·lás] *m.* solace, comfort; relaxation, recreation.
solazar[9] [so·la·sár] *v.* to console, cheer, comfort; **-se** to seek relaxation or pleasure; to enjoy oneself.
soldado [sol·dá·đo] *m.* soldier; — **raso** private; — **de línea** regular soldier.
soldadura [sol·da·đú·ra] *f.* soldering; welding; — **autógena** arc welding; — **oxiacetilénica** oxyacetylene welding; solder.
soldar[2] [sol·dár] *v. irr.* to solder; to weld.
soleado [so·le·á·đo] *adj.* sunny; *p.p.* sunned.
solear [so·le·ár] = **asolear.**
soledad [so·le·đáđ] *f.* solitude; loneliness; homesickness; lonely retreat.
solemne [so·lém·ne] *adj.* solemn; imposing; — **disparate** downright foolishness, huge blunder.
solemnidad [so·lem·ni·đáđ] *f.* solemnity; solemn ceremony.
soler[2, 51] [so·lér] *v. irr.* to have the custom of, be in the habit of.
solera [so·lé·ra] *f.* sill.
solfeo [sol·fé·o] *m.* sol-faing, solfeggio style.
solferino [sol·fe·rí·no] *adj.* reddish-purple.
solicitante [so·li·si·tán·te] *m. & f.* solicitor; applicant.
solicitar [so·li·si·tár] *v.* to solicit; to apply for; to beg, ask for; to court, woo.
solícito [so·lí·si·to] *adj.* solicitous, careful; anxious, concerned, diligent.
solicitud [so·li·si·túđ] *f.* solicitude; care, concern, anxiety.
solidaridad [so·li·đa·ri·đáđ] *f.* solidarity; union; bond, community of interests.
solidez [so·li·đés] *f.* solidity; compactness.
solidificar[6] [so·li·đi·fi·kár] *v.* to solidify.
sólido [só·li·đo] *adj.* solid; firm; strong; *m.* solid.
soliloquio [so·li·ló·kjo] *m.* soliloquy, monologue.
solista [so·lís·ta] *m. & f.* soloist.
solitario [so·li·tá·rjo] *adj.* solitary; lonely; *m.* recluse, hermit; solitaire (*card game*); solitaire (*gem set by itself*).
sólito [só·li·to] *adj.* customary.
sólito [só·li·to] *adj.* customary.
solo [só·lo] *adj.* sole, only; single; alone; lonely **a solas** alone; *m.* solo; **sólo** [só·lo] *adv.* only.
solomillo [so·lo·mí·yo], **solomo** [so·ló·mo] *m.* sirloin; loin; loin of pork (**lomo**).
solsticio [sols·tí·sjo] *m.* solstice.
soltar[2] [sol·tár] *v. irr.* to loosen, untie, unfasten; to let loose; to set free; to let go; to let out; to utter; **-se** to set oneself free; to come loose; to lose restraint; to loosen up; **-se a** to begin to, start to.
soltero [sol·té·ro] *adj.* single, unmarried; *m.* bachelor; **soltera** [sol·té·ra] *f.* spinster; **solterón** [sol·te·rón] *m.* old bachelor; **solterona** [sol·te·ró·na] *f.* old maid.
soltura [sol·tú·ra] *f.* looseness; freedom; facility, ease; agility, nimbleness; release (*of a prisoner*).
solución [so·lu·sjón] *f.* solution; loosening, untying.
solucionar [so·lu·sjo·nár] *v.* to solve, to resolve.
solventar [sol·ƀen·tár] *v.* to pay (*a bill*), settle (*an account*); to solve (*a problem or difficulty*).
sollozar[9] [so·yo·sár] *v.* to sob.
sollozo [so·yó·so] *m.* sob.
sombra [sóm·bra] *f.* (*oscuridad*) shadow; shade; darkness; (*abrigo*) shelter, protection; (*imagen*) image, reflection (*in the water*); *Am.* guide lines (*under writing paper*); *Ven.* awning, sunshade; **hacer** — to shade; to cast a shadow (on).
sombreado [som·bre·á·đo] *adj.* shady; shaded.
sombrear [som·bre·ár] *v.* to shade; **-se** *Mex., Ven., Col.* to seek the shade, stand in the shade.
sombrerería [som·bre·re·rí·a] *f.* hat shop.
sombrero [som·bré·ro] *m.* hat; — **de copa** top hat, high hat; — **hongo** derby; — **de jipijapa** Panama hat; *C.A., Col., Ven.* — **de pelo** top hat.
sombrilla [som·brí·ya] *f.* parasol, sunshade.
sombrío [som·brí·o] *adj.* somber, gloomy; shady.
somero [so·mé·ro] *adj.* superficial, shallow; summary, concise.
someter [so·me·tér] *v.* to submit; to subject; **-se** to submit.
sometimiento [so·me·ti·mjén·to] *m.* submission; subjection.
somnolencia [som·no·lén·sja] *f.* drowsiness, sleepiness; **con** — sleepily.
son [son] *m.* sound; tune; rumor; **en — de guerra** in a warlike manner; **sin ton ni —** without rhyme or reason.
sonaja [so·ná·xa] *f.* jingles, tambourine (*to accompany certain dances*); rattle; **sonajero** [so·na·xé·ro] *m.* child's rattle.
sonámbulo [so·nám·bu·lo] *m.* sleepwalker.

sonante [so·nán·te] *adj.* sounding; ringing; sonorous; **en dinero — y contante** in hard cash.
sonar[2] [so·nár] *v. irr.* to sound; to ring; to sound familiar; **— a** to sound like; seem like; **-se** to blow one's nose; **suena que** it is rumored that.
sonda [són·da] *f.* plumb, string with lead weight (*for sounding the depth of water*); sounding; surgeon's probe.
sondar [son·dár] = **sondear.**
sondear [son·de·ár] *v.* to sound, fathom; to sound out; to probe; to examine into.
sondeo [son·dé·o] *m.* sounding, fathoming.
soneto [so·né·to] *m.* sonnet.
sonido [so·ní·ɗo] *m.* sound.
sonoro [so·nó·ro] *adj.* sonorous; **consonante sonora** voiced consonant.
sonreír[15] [son·rre·ír] *v. irr.* to smile; **-se** to smile.
sonriente [son·rrjén·te] *adj.* smiling, beaming, radiant.
sonrisa [son·rrí·sa] *f.* smile.
sonrojarse [son·rro·xár·se] *v.* to blush.
sonrojo [son·rró·xo] *m.* blush.
sonrosado [son·rro·sá·ɗo] *adj.* rosy.
sonsacar[6] [son·sa·kár] *v.* to lure away; to draw (*someone*) out; to extract (*a secret*); to take on the sly.
sonsonete [son·so·né·te] *m.* singsong, rhythmical tapping sound.
soñador [so·ña·ɗór] *m.* dreamer.
soñar[2] [so·ñár] *v. irr.* to dream; **— con** (*or* **— en**) to dream of; **— despierto** to daydream.
soñoliento [so·ño·ljén·to] *adj.* sleepy, drowsy.
sopa [só·pa] *f.* soup; **— juliana** julienne soup; sop; **estar hecho una —** to be sopping wet; *Am.* **es un -s** he is a fool.
sopapo [so·pá·po] *m.* chuck, tap, pat (*under the chin*); slap.
sopera [so·pé·ra] *f.* soup tureen.
sopero [so·pé·ro] *m.* soup dish.
sopesar [so·pe·sár] *v.* to weigh, consider.
sopetón [so·pe·tón] *m.* box, slap; **de —** all of a sudden, unexpectedly.
soplar [sop·lár] *v.* (*despedir aire*) to blow; to blow away; to blow up, inflate; (*robar*) to swipe, steal; (*informar*) to prompt; to ''squeal'' on, inform against; *Col., Ven., Mex., Cuba, Andes* **— una bofetada** to strike a blow; **-se** to swell up, puff up; to eat up, gobble up; to gulp down; **se sopló el pastel** he gobbled up the pie; *Am.* **-se a uno** to deceive someone, get the best of someone.
soplete [so·plé·te] *m.* blow torch; blowpipe.
soplo [só·plo] *m.* (*de aire*) blowing; puff, gust of wind; breath; (*aviso*) whispered warning or advice; ''squealing'', informing; **en un —** in a jiffy, in a second.
soplón [so·plón] *m.* informer, ''squealer'' (*one who tells on someone*), tattletale.
sopor [so·pór] *m.* stupor; lethargy.
soportal [so·por·tál] *m.* arcade.
soportar [so·por·tár] *v.* to support, hold up, bear; to stand, endure, tolerate.
soporte [so·pór·te] *m.* support; (*computadora*) storage medium; **-s para el cabezal** arm braces (*machine*).
sorber [sor·ƀér] *v.* to sip; to suck; to swallow; to absorb; to snuff up one's nose.
sorbete [sor·ƀé·te] *m.* sherbet; fruit ice; *C.A., Mex., Ven.* cone, ice-cream cone; *Mex.* silk top hat.
sorbo [sór·ƀo] *m.* sip, swallow, gulp; sniff.
sordera [sor·ɗé·ra], **sordez** [sor·ɗés] *f.* deafness.
sórdido [sór·ɗi·ɗo] *adj.* sordid.
sordina [sor·ɗí·na] *f.* mute (*of a musical instrument*).
sordo [sór·ɗo] *adj.* deaf; silent, noiseless; dull; muffled; **consonante sorda** voiceless consonant; *m.* deaf person; **hacerse el —** to pretend not to hear; to turn a deaf ear.
sordomudo [sor·ɗo·mú·ɗo] *adj.* deaf and dumb; *m.* deaf-mute.
sorna [sór·na] *f.* slyness, cunning; sneer.
soroche [so·ró·če] *m. Andes* shortness of breath, sickness caused by high altitude; *Am.* blush, flush.
sorprendente [sor·pren·dén·te] *adj.* surprising.
sorprender [sor·pren·dér] *v.* to surprise; **-se** to be surprised.
sorpresa [sor·pré·sa] *f.* surprise.
sortear [sor·te·ár] *v.* to draw lots; to raffle; to dodge; to shun; to fight (*bulls*) skillfully.
sorteo [sor·té·o] *m.* drawing or casting of lots; raffle.
sortija [sor·tí·xa] *f.* ring; finger ring; ringlet, curl.
sosa [só·sa] *f.* soda.
sosegado [so·se·ǵá·ɗo] *adj.* calm, quiet, peaceful.
sosegar[1, 7] [so·se·ǵár] *v.* to calm, quiet; to be quiet; **-se** to quiet down.
sosiego [so·sjé·ǵo] *m.* calm, peace, quiet.
soslayo [soz·lá·yo]: **al —** obliquely; slanting; on the bias; **de —** oblique, slanting; at a slant; sideways; **mirada de —** side glance; **pegar de —** to glance, hit at a slant.
soso [só·so] *adj.* flat, tasteless, insipid; dull, silly; awkward.
sospecha [sos·pé·ča] *f.* suspicion; mistrust.
sospechar [sos·pe·čár] *v.* to suspect; to mistrust.
sospechoso [sos·pe·čó·so] *adj.* suspicious; *m.* suspect.
sostén [sos·tén] *m.* support; prop; supporter; brassière.
sostener[45] [sos·te·nér] *v. irr.* to sustain; to hold; to support, maintain; to defend, uphold; to endure.
sostenido [sos·te·ní·ɗo] *p.p. & adj.* sustained; supported, held up; *m.* sharp (*in music*).
sota [só·ta] *f.* jack (*at cards*); *m. Am.* foreman, boss, overseer.
sotana [so·tá·na] *f.* cassock (*black outer robe of a priest*).
sótano [só·ta·no] *m.* cellar, basement.
sotavento [so·ta·ƀén·to] *m.* leeward.
soterrar [so·te·rrár] *v.* to bury.
soto [só·to] *m.* grove; thicket.
sotreta [so·tré·ta] *m. Andes, Ríopl.* nag, old horse.
soviet [so·ƀjét] *m.* soviet; **soviético** [so·ƀjé·ti·ko] *adj.* soviet, of, or pertaining to, soviets.
esténcil [es·tén·sil] *m.* stencil.
suave [swá·ƀe] *adj.* soft; smooth; mild; bland; gentle.
suavidad [swa·ƀi·ɗáɗ] *f.* softness; smoothness; mildness; gentleness.
suavizar[9] [swa·ƀi·sár] *v.* to smooth; to soften.
subalterno [su·ƀal·tér·no] *adj. & m.* subordinate.
subarrendar [su·ƀa·rren·dár] *v.* to sublet.
subasta [su·ƀás·ta] *f.* public auction.
subastar [su·ƀás·tar] *v.* to sell at auction.
subconsciente [suƀ·kon·sjén·te] *adj.* subconscious.
subdesarrollado [suƀ·ɗe·sa·rro·yá·ɗo] *adj.* underdeveloped.
súbdito [súƀ·ɗi·to] *m.* subject.
subida [su·ƀí·ɗa] *f.* rise; ascent; carrying up; **de —** on the way up; **muchas -s y bajadas** many ups and downs; much going up and down.
subir [su·ƀír] *v.* to ascend, go up, climb; to raise, lift; to carry up; to mount; **— al tren** to board the train, get on the train.
súbito [sú·ƀi·to] *adj.* sudden; **de —** suddenly.
sublevación [su·ƀle·ƀa·sjón] *f.* revolt, uprising, insurrection.
sublevar [suƀ·le·ƀár] *v.* to excite to rebellion; **-se** to

revolt.
sublimado [suƀ·li·má·đo] *adj.* sublimated.
sublime [su·ƀlí·me] *adj.* sublime.
submarino [suƀ·ma·rí·no] *m.* & *adj.* submarine; *m.* — **atómico** atomic submarine.
subordinado [su·ƀor·đi·ná·đo] *adj.* & *m.* subordinate.
subordinar [su·ƀor·đi·nár] *v.* to subordinate; to subdue.
subrayar [suƀ·rra·yár] *v.* to underline; to emphasize.
subrutina [suƀ·rru·tí·na] *f.* (*computadora*) subroutine.
subsanar [suƀ·sa·nár] *v.* to mend, remedy, repair (*a damage, error, defect, etc.*); to make up for (*an error, fault, etc.*); to excuse (*a fault or error*).
subscribir [suƀs·kri·ƀír] = **suscribir.**
subscripción [suƀs·krip·sjón] = **suscripción.**
subscriptor [suƀs·krip·tór] = **suscritor.**
subsecretario [suƀ·se·kre·tá·rjo] *m.* undersecretary.
subsecuente [suƀ·se·kwén·te] *adj.* subsequent.
subsiguiente [suƀ·si·ǥjén·te] *adj.* subsequent.
subsistencia [suƀ·sis·tén·sja] *f.* living, livelihood; sustenance; permanence.
subsistir [suƀ·sis·tír] *v.* to subsist; to exist; to last.
substancia [suƀs·tán·sja] = **sustancia.**
substancial [suƀs·tan·sjál] = **sustancial.**
substancioso [suƀs·tan·sjó·so] = **sustancioso.**
substituíble [suƀs·ti·twí·ƀle] = **sustituíble.**
substantivo [suƀs·tan·tí·ƀo] = **sustantivo.**
substitución [suƀs·ti·tu·sjón] = **sustitución.**
substituir [suƀs·ti·twír] = **sustituir.**
substituto [suƀs·ti·tú·to] = **sustituto.**
substracción [suƀs·trak·sjón] = **sustracción.**
substraer [suƀs·tra·ér] = **sustraer.**
subsuelo [suƀ·swé·lo] *m.* subsoil.
subteniente [suƀ·te·njén·te] *m.* second lieutenant.
subterfugio [suƀ·ter·fú·xjo] *m.* subterfuge.
subterráneo [suƀ·te·rrá·ne·o] *adj.* subterranean, underground; *m.* underground; cave, tunnel, vault.
suburbano [su·ƀur·ƀá·no] *adj.* suburban; *m.* suburban resident.
suburbio [su·ƀur·ƀjo] *m.* suburb.
subvención [suƀ·ƀen·sjón] *f.* subsidy.
subvencionar [suƀ·ƀen·sjo·nár] *v.* to subsidize.
subyugar [suƀ·yu·ǥár] *v.* to subdue.
succión [suk·sjón] *f.* suction.
suceder [su·se·đér] *v.* to happen, occur; to succeed, follow.
sucesión [su·se·sjón] *f.* succession; heirs, offspring.
sucesivo [su·se·sí·ƀo] *adj.* successive; **en lo** — hereafter, in the future.
suceso [su·sé·so] *m.* event; outcome, result.
sucesor [su·se·sór] *m.* successor.
suciedad [su·sje·đáđ] *f.* dirt, filth; filthiness; filthy act or remark.
sucinto [su·sín·to] *adj.* compact, concise, brief.
sucio [sú·sjo] *adj.* dirty; foul, filthy.
suculento [su·ku·lén·to] *adj.* juicy.
sucumbir [su·kum·bír] *v.* to succumb; to yield.
sucursal [su·kur·sál] *f.* branch, branch office (*of a post office, bank, etc.*); *adj.* branch.
suche [sú·če] *adj. Ven.* sour, unripe; *m. Andes* pimple; *Ch.* office boy, insignificant employee; *Andes* suche (*a tree*).
sud [suđ] *m.* south; south wind; **sudeste** [su·đés·te] *m.* & *adj.* southeast; **sudoeste** [su·đo·és·te] *m.* & *adj.* southwest.
sudamericano [su·đa·me·ri·ká·no] *adj.* & *m.* South American.
sudar [su·đár] *v.* to sweat, perspire; to ooze, to toil.
sudario [su·đá·rjo] *m.* shroud.
sudor [su·đór] *m.* sweat, perspiration; toil.
sudoroso [su·đo·ró·so] *adj.* sweaty, sweating, perspiring.
sueco [swé·ko] *adj.* Swedish; *m.* Swede; Swedish language; **hacerse el** — to pretend not to see or understand.
suegra [swé·ǥra] *f.* mother-in-law.
suegro [swé·ǥro] *m.* father-in-law.
suela [swé·la] *f.* sole of a shoe; shoe leather.
sueldo [swél·do] *m.* salary.
suelo [swé·lo] *m.* soil, ground; floor; pavement; bottom.
suelto [swél·to] *adj.* (*no atado*) loose; free, easy; (*ágil*) agile, nimble; blank (*verse*); *m.* small change; short newspaper article, news item.
sueño [swé·ño] *m.* sleep; dream; sleepiness, drowsiness; **en -s** in one's sleep; **conciliar el** — to get to sleep; **tener** — to be sleepy.
suero [swé·ro] *m.* serum.
suerte [swér·te] *f.* (*fortuna*) fate; fortune; chance; luck; (*clase*) sort, kind; way, manner; (*truco*) trick; **de** — **que** so that, in such a way that; and so; **echar -s** to cast lots; **tener** — to be lucky; **tocarle a uno la** — to fall to one's lot; to be lucky.
suéter [swé·ter] *m. Am.* sweater.
suficiente [su·fi·sjén·te] *adj.* sufficient; competent, able.
sufijo [su·fí·xo] *m.* suffix; *adj.* suffixed.
sufragar[7] [su·fra·ǥár] *v.* to defray, pay; to help, aid; *Am.* — **por** to vote for.
sufragio [su·frá·xjo] *m.* suffrage; vote; help, aid.
sufrido [su·frí·đo] *adj.* suffering, long-suffering, patient; **mal** — impatient.
sufridor [su·fri·đór] *m.* sufferer; *adj.* suffering.
sufrimiento [su·fri·mjén·to] *m.* suffering; patience, endurance.
sufrir [su·frír] *v.* to suffer; to endure; to allow, permit; to sustain; to undergo; — **un examen** to take an examination.
sugerencia [su·xe·rén·sja] *f. Am.* suggestion, hint.
sugerir[3] [su·xe·rír] *v. irr.* to suggest; to hint.
sugestión [su·xes·tjón] *f.* suggestion; hint.
sugestivo [su·xes·tí·ƀo] *adj.* suggestive.
suicida [swi·sí·đa] *m.* & *f.* suicide (*person who commits suicide*).
suicidarse [swi·si·đár·se] *v.* to commit suicide.
suicidio [swi·sí·đjo] *m.* suicide (*act of suicide*).
suizo [swí·so] *adj.* & *m.* Swiss.
sujeción [su·xe·sjón] *f.* subjection; control; submission.
sujetapapeles [su·xe·ta·pa·pé·les] *m.* paper clip.
sujetar [su·xe·tár] *v.* to subject; to control; to subdue; to fasten; to grasp, hold; **-se** to subject oneself; to submit; to adhere (to).
sujeto [su·xé·to] *adj.* subject; liable; fastened; under control; *m.* subject matter; subject; fellow, individual.
sulfamida [sul·fa·mí·đa] *f.* common name for the sulfa drugs.
sulfato [sul·fá·to] *m.* sulphate.
sulfurarse [sul·fu·rár·se] *v.* to get angry.
sulfúrico [sul·fú·ri·ko] *adj.* sulphuric.
sulfuro [sul·fú·ro] *m.* sulphide.
sultán [sul·tán] *m.* sultan.
suma [sú·ma] *f.* sum; addition; substance; summary; **en** — in short.
sumador [su·ma·đór] *adj.* adding; **máquina sumadora** adding machine.
sumar [su·már] *v.* to add; to add up (to), amount (to); to sum up; **-se a** to join.
sumario [su·má·rjo] *m.* summary; indictment; *adj.* summary, brief, concise; swift (*punishment*).
sumergible [su·mer·xí·ƀle] *adj.* submergible; *m.*

submarine.
sumergir[11] [su·mer·xír] *v.* to submerge, plunge, sink, to immerse; **-se** to submerge; to sink.
sumidero [su·mi·đé·ro] *m.* sink; sewer, drain.
suministrar [su·mi·nis·trár] *v.* to give, supply with, provide with.
sumir [su·mír] *v.* to sink; to submerge; to immerse; *Ríopl., Mex., Carib.* to dent; **-se** to sink; *Andes* to shrink, shrivel; *Andes* to cower, crouch in fear; *Am.* **-se el sombrero hasta las cejas** to pull one's hat over one's eyes.
sumisión [su·mi·sjón] *f.* submission; obedience.
sumiso [su·mí·so] *adj.* submissive; obedient; meek.
sumo [sú·mo] *adj.* supreme, highest, high; greatest; — **pontífice** Sovereign Pontiff (*the Pope*); **a lo** — at the most.
suntuoso [sun·twó·so] *adj.* sumptuous, magnificent, luxurious.
superable [su·pe·rá·ƀle] *adj.* superable.
superabundancia [su·pe·ra·ƀun·dán·sja] *f.* superabundance, great abundance, overflow.
superar [su·pe·rár] *v.* to surpass; to exceed; to overcome.
superávit [su·pe·rá·ƀit] *m.* surplus.
superficial [su·per·fi·sjál] *adj.* superficial; shallow; frivolous; **superficialidad** [su·per·fi·sja·li·đáđ] *f.* superficiality, shallowness, frivolity.
superficie [su·per·fí·sje] *f.* surface; area.
superfluo [su·pér·flwo] *adj.* superfluous.
superintendente [su·pe·rin·ten·dén·te] *m.* superintendent; supervisor; overseer.
superior [su·pe·rjór] *adj.* superior; higher; better; upper; *m.* superior; father superior; **superiora** [su·pe·rjó·ra] *f.* superior, mother superior.
superioridad [su·pe·rjo·ri·đáđ] *f.* superiority; excellence.
superlativo [su·per·la·tí·ƀo] *adj. & m.* superlative.
supersónico [su·per·só·ni·ko] *adj.* supersonic.
superstición [su·pers·ti·sjón] *f.* superstition.
supersticioso [su·pers·ti·sjó·so] *adj.* superstitious.
supervivencia [su·per·ƀi·ƀén·sja] *f.* survival.
superviviente [su·per·ƀi·ƀjén·te] = **sobreviviente.**
suplantar [su·plan·tár] *v.* to supplant; to forge (*a document or check*).
suplementar [su·ple·men·tár] *v.* supplement.
suplementario [su·ple·men·tá·rjo] *adj.* supplementary, extra.
suplemento [su·ple·mén·to] *m.* supplement; supply, supplying.
suplente [su·plén·te] *adj., m. & f.* substitute.
súplica [sú·pli·ka] *f.* entreaty; request; petition; prayer.
suplicante [su·pli·kán·te] *adj.* suppliant, beseeching; *m. & f.* suppliant; petitioner.
suplicar[6] [su·pli·kár] *v.* to beg, entreat, implore; to pray humbly; to appeal, petition.
suplicio [su·plí·sjo] *m.* torture; torment; anguish; execution; instrument of torture; scaffold, gallows.
suplir [su·plír] *v.* to supply; to make up for; to substitute, take the place of (*temporarily*).
suponer[40] [su·po·nér] *v. irr.* to suppose; to assume; to be important.
suposición [su·po·si·sjón] *f.* supposition; assumption.
supremacía [su·pre·ma·sía] *f.* supremacy.
supremo [su·pré·mo] *adj.* supreme; final, last.
supresión [su·pre·sjón] *f.* suppression; omission; elimination.
suprimir [su·pri·mír] *v.* to suppress; to abolish; to omit.
supuesto [su·pwés·to] *p.p. of* **suponer** supposed, assumed; — **que** supposing that; since; **por** — of course; naturally; *m.* supposition; assumption.
supuración [su·pu·ra·sjón] *f.* formation or discharge of pus.
supurar [su·pu·rár] *v.* to fester, form or discharge pus.
sur [sur] *m.* south; south wind; **sureste** [su·rés·te] *m.* southeast; **suroeste** [su·ro·és·te] *m.* southwest.
suramericano [su·ra·me·ri·ká·no] = **sudamericano.**
surcar[6] [sur·kár] *v.* to furrow; to plow; to plow through; to cut through.
surco [súr·ko] *m.* furrow; rut; groove; wrinkle.
sureño [su·ré·ño] *adj.* southern, from the south; *m.* a southerner.
surgir[11] [sur·xír] *v.* to surge, rise; to spurt; spout; to appear.
surrealismo [su·rre·a·líz·mo] *m.* surrealism.
surtido [sur·tí·đo] *m.* stock, supply, assortment; *adj.* assorted.
surtidor [sur·ti·đór] *m.* supplier; spout, jet.
surtir [sur·tír] *v.* to provide, supply, stock (with); to spout, spurt; — **efecto** to produce the desired result; — **un pedido** to fill an order.
susceptible [su·sep·tí·ƀle] *adj.* susceptible; sensitive; touchy.
suscitar [su·si·tár] *v.* to raise, stir up, provoke.
suscribir[52] [sus·kri·ƀír] *v.* to subscribe; to endorse; to agree (to); **-se** to subscribe.
suscripción [sus·krip·sjón] *f.* subscription.
suscrito [sus·krí·to] *p.p. of* **suscribir.**
suscritor [sus·kri·tór] *m.* subscriber.
susodicho [su·so·dí·čo] *adj.* aforesaid, above-mentioned.
suspender [sus·pen·dér] *v.* (*colgar*) to suspend; to hang; (*detener*) to stop; to defer; (*no aprobar*) to fail, flunk; to dismiss temporarily; to astonish.
suspensión [sus·pen·sjón] *f.* suspension; postponement, delay; uncertainty; cessation; a system of supporting devices (*automobile*).
suspenso [sus·pén·so] *adj.* suspended; hanging; pending; perplexed, astonished; **en** — in suspense; *m.* failure (*in an examination*).
suspicaz [sus·pi·kás] *adj.* suspicious.
suspirar [sus·pi·rár] *v.* to sigh; to sigh (for), long (for).
suspiro [sus·pí·ro] *m.* sigh; brief pause (*in music*).
sustancia [sus·tán·sja] *f.* substance; essence; *Andes* broth.
sustancial [sus·tan·sjál] *adj.* substantial; nourishing.
sustancioso [sus·tan·sjó·so] *adj.* substantial; nourishing.
sustantivo [sus·tan·tí·ƀo] *m.* noun; *adj.* substantive; real; independent.
sustentar [sus·ten·tár] *v.* to sustain; to support; to feed, nourish; to maintain; uphold.
sustento [sus·tén·to] *m.* sustenance; food; support.
sustitución [sus·ti·tu·sjón] *f.* substitution.
sustituíble [sus·ti·twí·ƀle] *adj.* replaceable.
sustituir[32] [sus·ti·twír] *v. irr.* to substitute.
sustituto [sus·ti·tú·to] *m.* substitute.
susto [sús·to] *m.* scare, fright.
sustracción [sus·trak·sjón] *f.* subtraction.
sustraer[46] [sus·tra·ér] *v. irr.* to subtract; to remove, withdraw; **-se a** to evade, avoid, slip away from.
susurrar [su·su·rrár] *v.* to whisper; to murmur; to rustle; **-se** to be whispered or rumored about.
susurro [su·sú·rro] *m.* whisper; murmur; rustle.
sutil [su·tíl] *adj.* subtle; keen; clever; crafty; thin, fine, delicate.
sutileza [su·ti·lé·sa] , **sutilidad** [su·ti·li·đáđ] *f.* subtlety; keenness, cleverness; cunning; thinness, fineness.
suyo [sú·yo] *adj.* his, of his; her, of hers; your, of

yours (*formal*); their, of theirs; *pron.* his, hers, yours (*formal*), theirs; **de** — naturally, by nature; **salirse con la suya** to get one's own way; **hacer de las suyas** to be up to one's tricks; **los -s** his (hers, theirs); his (her, their) own people.

T:t

tabaco [ta·ƀá·ko] *m.* tobacco; *Carib., Ven., Col.* cigar; snuff; *Col.* blow with the fist; **tabaquería** [ta·ƀa·ke·rí·a] *f.* tobacco store, cigar store.
tábano [tá·ƀa·no] *m.* horsefly, gadfly.
taberna [ta·ƀér·na] *f.* tavern, bar, liquor store.
tabernáculo [ta·ƀer·ná·ku·lo] *m.* tabernacle.
tabique [ta·ƀí·ke] *m.* partition, partition wall.
tabla [tá·ƀla] *f.* board, plank; plate of metal; slab; table, list; strip of ground; *Col.* chocolate tablet; **-s** draw, tie (*in games*); stage boards, the stage; **a raja** — cost what it may; *Am.* in great haste; **hacer — rasa de algo** to disregard, omit, or ignore something; *Am.* to clear away all obstacles in the way of something.
tablado [ta·ƀlá·đo] *m.* platform, stage; scaffold; floor boards.
tablero [ta·ƀlé·ro] *m.* board; panel; timber, piece of lumber; chessboard, checkerboard; store counter; large work table; gambling table; dashboard; instrument panel; (*computadora*) keyboard; *Col., Ven., Mex.* blackboard; **poner al** — to risk, endanger; — **de mando** control panel.
tableta [ta·ƀlé·ta] *f.* tablet; small thin board; memorandum pad.
tabletear [ta·ƀle·te·ár] *v.* to rattle; to make a continuous rattling or tapping sound.
tableteo [ta·ƀle·té·o] *m.* rattling sound; tapping.
tablilla [ta·ƀlí·ya] *f.* tablet; slat, small thin board; splint; small bulletin board; **-s** wooden clappers.
tablón [ta·ƀlón] *m.* plank; large, thick board.
taburete [ta·ƀu·ré·te] *m.* stool; footstool; *Sal.* chair.
tacañería [ta·ka·ñe·rí·a] *f.* stinginess, tightness, miserliness.
tacaño [ta·ka·ño] *adj.* stingy, tight, miserly; sly.
tácito [tá·si·to] *adj.* tacit, implied; silent.
taciturno [ta·si·túr·no] *adj.* taciturn, silent, sullen; sad.
taco [tá·ko] *m.* wad; roll; plug, stopper; billiard cue; bite, snack; swear word; *Mex., C.A.* Mexican folded tortilla sandwich; *Am.* leather legging; *Ch., Andes* short, fat person; *Mex.* heel of a shoe; *Am.* pile, heap; **echar -s** to curse, swear; *Mex.* **darse uno** — to strut, put on airs.
tacón [ta·kón] *m.* heel of a shoe.
taconear [ta·ko·ne·ár] *v.* to click the heels, walk hard on one's heels.
taconeo [ta·ko·né·o] *m.* click, clicking (*of the heels*).
táctica [ták·ti·ka] *f.* tactics.
tacto [ták·to] *m.* tact; touch, sense of touch.
tacha [tá·ča] *f.* flaw, defect, blemish.
tachar [ta·čár] *v.* (*borrar*) to cross out; to scratch out; to blot out; (*culpar*) to blame; to find fault with; to censure.
tachón [ta·čón] *m.* stud; trimming, braid; blot.
tachonar [ta·čo·nár] *v.* to stud, ornament with studs; to adorn with trimming.
tachuela [ta·čwé·la] *f.* tack, small nail; *Am.* metal dipper; *Am.* runt, "shorty".
tafetán [ta·fe·tán] *m.* taffeta; — **inglés** court plaster; — **adhesivo** "Band-Aid".
tahúr [ta·úr] *m.* gambler; cardsharp.
taimado [taj·má·đo] *adj.* sly, crafty; *Am.* sullen, gloomy, gruff.
taita [táj·ta] = **tatita.** *See* **tata.**
tajada [ta·xá·đa] *f.* slice; cut.
tajalápiz [ta·xa·lá·pis] *m.* pencil sharpener.
tajante [ta·xán·te] *adj.* cutting, sharp.
tajar [ta·xár] *v.* to slice; to cut; to sharpen (*a pencil*).
tajo [tá·xo] *m.* cut; gash; cutting edge; sheer cliff; chopping block.
tal [tal] *adj.* such; such a; — **cual** such as; so-so, fair; — **vez** perhaps; **el — Pedro** that fellow Peter; **un — García** a certain García; — **para cual** two of a kind; **un — por cual** a nobody; *adv.* just as, in such a way; **estaba — como le dejé** he was just as I left him; **con — (de) que** provided that; **¿qué —?** how are you?; hello!
talabarte [ta·la·ƀár·te] *m.* sword belt.
taladrar [ta·la·đrár] *v.* to bore, drill; to pierce; to penetrate.
taladro [ta·lá·đro] *m.* auger, drill; bore, drill hole; *Am.* mine tunnel.
tálamo [tá·la·mo] *m.* bridal bed or chamber.
talante [ta·lán·te] *m.* disposition; mood; appearance, manner.
talar [ta·lár] *v.* to cut down; *Am.* to prune.
talco [tál·ko] *m.* talc (*a soft mineral*); — **en polvo** talcum powder.
talega [ta·lé·ǥa] *f.* money bag, sack.
talento [ta·lén·to] *m.* talent; ability, natural gift.
talentoso [ta·len·tó·so] *adj.* talented, gifted.
talio [tá·ljo] *m.* thallium.
talismán [ta·liz·mán] *m.* talisman, charm.
talón [ta·lón] *m.* heel; stub, check, coupon.
talonario [ta·lo·ná·rjo] *m.* stub book; **libro** — stub book.
talonear [ta·lo·ne·ár] *v.* to tap with one's heel; to walk briskly.
taloneo [ta·lo·né·o] *m.* tapping with the heel; loud footsteps.
talla [tá·ya] *f.* (*altura*) stature, height; size; (*labrado*) carving; (*lance entero*) round of a card game; (*rescate*) ransom; *Col.* chat; *Arg.* thrashing, beating.
tallar [ta·yár] *v.* to carve; to cut (*stone*); to appraise; to deal (*cards*); *Ch.* to court, make love; *Andes, Col.* to bother, disturb.
tallarín [ta·ya·rín] *m.* noodle.
talle [tá·ye] *m.* figure, form; waist; fit (*of a dress*); looks, appearance; *Ven.* bodice.
taller [ta·yér] *m.* workshop; laboratory; studio; factory.
tallo [tá·yo] *m.* stalk; stem; shoot, sprout.
tamal [ta·mál] *m. Mex., C.A.* tamale; *Cuba, Mex.* vile trick, intrigue; *Am.* clumsy bundle.
tamaño [ta·má·ño] *m.* size; *adj.* such a; of the size of; — **disparate** such a (big) mistake; — **como un elefante** big as an elephant; **tamañito** [ta·ma·ñí·to] *adj.* very small; **tamañito así** about this little; **se quedó tamañito** he was (left) astonished, amazed.
tamarindo [ta·ma·rín·do] *m.* tamarind; *Mex.* traffic cop (*because of color of uniform*).
tambalearse [tam·ba·le·ár·se] *v.* to totter, stagger, sway, reel.
también [tam·bjén] *adv.* also, too; likewise.
tambor [tam·bór] *m.* drum; drum-like object; drummer; pair of embroidery hoops; *Mex.* bedspring, spring mattress; — **de freno** brake drum; **tambora** [tam·bó·ra] *f.* bass drum; **tamboril** [tam·bo·ríl] *m.* small drum; **tamborilero** [tam·bo·ri·lé·ro] *m.* drummer.

tamborilear [tam·bo·ri·le·ár] *v.* to drum; to extol.
tamiz [ta·mís] *m.* fine sieve.
tamizar [ta·mi·sár] *v.* to sift; to blend.
tampoco [tam·pó·ko] *conj.* either (*after a negative*); **no lo hizo** — he did not do it either; **ni yo** — nor I either.
tan [tan] *adv.* (*contr. of* **tanto**) so, as; such a.
tanda [tán·da] *f.* turn; round, bout; task; gang, group; shift, relay; *Col., Ven., Mex., Carib.* section of a theatrical performance.
tangente [taŋ·xén·te] *adj. & f.* tangent; **salirse por la** — to go off at a tangent; to avoid the issue.
tangible [taŋ·xí·ƀle] *adj.* tangible.
tango [táŋ·go] *m.* tango.
tanque [táŋ·ke] *m.* tank; reservoir; *Col., Ven.* pond; *Mex.* swimming pool.
tantán [tan·tán] *m.* clang; knock! knock!; sound of a bell, drum, etc.
tantear [tan·te·ár] *v.* to probe, test; to sound out, feel out; to estimate, calculate approximately; *Cuba, Ven., Ríopl.* to grope, feel one's way; *Am.* to lie in wait; *Mex.* to fool, make a fool of; *Ven., Mex., C.A.* **¡tantee Vd.!** just imagine!
tanteo [tan·té·o] *m.* trial, test; calculation, estimate; score; **al** — by guess; hit or miss.
tanto [tán·to] *adj., pron. & adv.* so much, as much; so; **-s** so many, as many; *m.* certain amount; counter, chip (*to keep score*); **cuarenta y -s** forty odd; **el — por ciento** percentage, rate; **un** — (*or* **algún** —) somewhat; — **como** as well as; as much as; — . . . **como** both . . . and; — **en la ciudad como en el campo** both in the city and in the country; **entre** (*or* **mientras**) — meanwhile; **por lo** — therefore.
tañer [ta·ñér] *v.* to play (*an instrument*); to ring.
tañido [ta·ñí·đo] *m.* sound, tune; ring; twang (*of a guitar*).
tapa [tá·pa] *f.* cover; cap; lid; book cover; heel lift.
tapacubos [ta·pa·kú·ƀos] *m.* hubcap.
tapadera [ta·pa·đé·ra] *f.* cover, lid; one who shields another.
tapar [ta·pár] *v.* to cover; to plug, stop up; to veil; to hide; *Am.* to fill (*a tooth*); *Col.* to crush, crumple; *Ch.* to cover with insults; **-se** to cover up; to wrap oneself up.
taparrabo [ta·pa·rrá·ƀo] *m.* loincloth; trunks.
tapera [ta·pé·ra] *f. Ríopl.* ruins; *Ríopl., Andes* abandoned room or house.
tapete [ta·pé·te] *m.* rug; table scarf.
tapia [tá·pja] *f.* abode wall; wall fence.
tapiar [ta·pjár] *v.* to wall up; to block up (*a door or window*).
tapicería [ta·pi·se·rí·a] *f.* tapestry; upholstery; tapestry shop; tapestry making.
tapioca [ta·pjó·ka] *f.* tapioca.
tapiz [ta·pís] *m.* tapestry.
tapizar[9] [ta·pi·sár] *v. irr.* to carpet; to cover.
tapón [ta·pón] *m.* plug, stopper, cork; bottle cap.
taquigrafía [ta·ki·ǥra·fí·a] *f.* shorthand.
taquígrafo [ta·kí·ǥra·fo] *m.* stenographer.
taquilla [ta·kí·ya] *f.* ticket office; box office; file (*for letters, papers, etc.*); *C.R.* tavern, liquor store.
tarántula [ta·rán·tu·la] *f.* tarantula.
tararear [ta·ra·re·ár] *v.* to hum.
tarareo [ta·ra·ré·o] *m.* hum, humming.
tarascada [ta·ras·ká·đa] *f.* snap, bite; snappy or harsh answer.
tardanza [tar·đán·sa] *f.* delay; slowness.
tardar [tar·đár] *v.* to delay; to be late; to be long (in); to take long (in); **-se** to delay oneself; to be delayed; **a más** — at the very latest.
tarde [tár·đe] *f.* afternoon; *adv.* late; **de — en** — from time to time, now and then.
tardío [tar·đí·o] *adj.* late; slow.
tardo [tár·đo] *adj.* slow, lazy; tardy, late; stupid, dull; **tardón** [tar·đón] *adj.* very slow; *m.* slowpoke, slow person.
tarea [ta·ré·a] *f.* task, job; anxiety, care.
tarifa [ta·rí·fa] *f.* tariff; list of duties, taxes, or prices; fare.
tarima [ta·rí·ma] *f.* wooden platform; low bench.
tarjeta [tar·xé·ta] *f.* card; (*computadora*) board, card; — **postal** postcard; — **de perforadora** key punchcard; — **registradora** time card.
tarro [tá·rro] *m.* earthen jar; glass jar; *Mex.* horn (*of an animal*); *Ch., Cuba, Andes* can; *Andes* top hat.
tarta [tár·ta] *f.* tart.
tartamudear [tar·ta·mu·đe·ár] *v.* to stutter, stammer.
tartamudeo [tar·ta·mu·đé·o] *m.* stammer, stammering.
tartamudo [tar·ta·mú·đo] *m.* stutterer, stammerer; *adj.* stuttering, stammering.
tártaro [tár·ta·ro] *m.* tartar.
tartera [tar·té·ra] *f.* griddle; baking pan.
tarugo [ta·rú·ǥo] *m.* wooden block; wooden peg; blockhead, dunce; *adj. Andes* mischievous, devilish.
tasa [tá·sa] *f.* measure; standard; rate; appraisal; valuation.
tasación [ta·sa·sjón] *f.* assessment, valuation, appraisal.
tasajo [ta·sá·xo] *m.* piece of jerked beef.
tasar [ta·sár] *m.* to measure; to appraise; to rate.
tata [tá·ta] *f.* daddy, dad; *Mex., Andes* chief (*said by Indians to a superior*); **tatita** [ta·tí·ta] *m.* daddy; *Mex., Andes* dear chief or daddy (*said by Indians*).
tataranieto [ta·ta·ra·njé·to] *m.* great-great-grandson.
tatuar[18] [ta·twár] *v.* to tattoo.
taurino [taw·rí·no] *adj.* related to bullfighting.
tauromaquia [taw·ro·má·kja] *f.* bullfighting.
taxear [tak·se·ár] *v.* to taxi (*said of a plane*).
taxi [ták·si], **taxímetro** [tak·sí·me·tro] *m.* taxi, taxicab.
taxista [tak·sís·ta] *m. & f.* taxi driver.
taxonomía [tak·so·no·mí·a] *f.* taxonomy.
taza [tá·sa] *f.* cup; bowl; basin of a fountain.
tazón [ta·són] *m.* large cup; bowl; basin of a fountain.
té [te] *m.* tea; *f.* T-square, T-shaped ruler.
te [te] *obj. pron.* you (*fam. sing.*); to you; for you; yourself.
teatral [te·a·trál] *adj.* theatrical.
teatro [te·á·tro] *m.* theater; stage; scene, setting; **hacer** — to put on airs, show off.
tecla [té·kla] *f.* key (*of a piano, typewriter, computer, etc.*); — **para mayúsculas** capital letter key; — **de cambio** shift key; — **funcional** (*computadora*) function key; — **de retroceso** backspace key; **dar uno en la** — to hit the nail on the head, find the right way to do something.
teclado [te·klá·đo] *m.* keyboard; — **numérico** (*computadora*) keypad.
teclear [te·kle·ár] *v.* to finger the keys; to play the piano; to type.
tecleo [te·klé·o] *m.* fingering; movement of the keys (*typewriter, piano*).
técnica [ték·ni·ka] *f.* technique.
técnico [ték·ni·ko] *adj.* technical; *m.* technical expert, technician.
tecnología [tek·no·lo·xí·a] *f.* technology.
tecolote [te·ko·ló·te] *m. Mex.* owl.
techado [te·čá·đo] *m.* roof; shed; *p.p. of* **techar.**
techar [te·čár] *v.* to roof.

techo [té·čo] *m.* roof; ceiling; — **a cuatro vertientes** hip roof; — **a la holandesa** gabled roof.
techumbre [te·čúm·bre] *f.* roof; ceiling.
tedio [te·đjo] *m.* tediousness; boredom; bother.
tedioso [te·đjó·so] *adj.* tedious, boring, tiresome.
teja [té·xa] *f.* tile; linden tree; *Am.* rear part of a saddle; **de -s abajo** here below, in this world.
tejado [te·xá·đo] *m.* roof; shed; roofing.
tejamanil [te·xa·ma·níl] *m.* shingle; small thin board; shake.
tejar [te·xár] *m.* tile factory; *v.* to cover with tiles.
tejedor [te·xe·đór] *m.* weaver.
tejer [te·xér] *v.* to weave; to interlace; to braid; to knit.
tejido [te·xí·đo] *m.* textile, fabric; texture; weave; weaving; tissue.
tejo [té·xo] *m.* disk; quoit; weight.
tejón [te·xón] *m.* badger; bar of gold.
tela [té·la] *f.* cloth; membrane; web; film (*on the surface of liquids*); — **adhesiva** adhesive tape; — **de cebolla** onion skin; flimsy fabric; *Am.* — **emplástica** court plaster; — **metálica** wire screen; **poner en — de juicio** to call in question.
telar [te·lár] *m.* loom.
telaraña [te·la·rá·ña] *f.* cobweb, spider's web.
telecomunicación [te·le·co·mu·ni·ka·sjón] *f.* telecommunication
teleférico [te·le·fé·ri·ko] *m.* telpher; car suspended on aerial cables.
telefonear [te·le·fo·ne·ár] *v.* to telephone.
telefónico [te·le·fó·ni·ko] *adj.* telephonic, telephone (*used as adj.*); **receptor** — telephone receiver.
teléfono [te·lé·fo·no] *m.* telephone; **telefonista** [te·le·fo·nísta] *m.* & *f.* telephone operator.
telegrafía [te·le·ǥra·fí·a] *f.* telegraphy.
telegrafiar[17] [te·le·ǥra·fjár] *v.* to telegraph.
telegráfico [te·le·ǥrá·fi·ko] *adj.* telegraphic.
telégrafo [te·lé·gra·fo] *m.* telegraph; — **sin hilos** (*or* — **inalámbrico**) wireless telegraph; **telegrafista** [te·le·ǥra·fís·ta] *m.* & *f.* telegraph operator.
telegrama [te·le·ǥra·ma] *m.* telegram.
telémetro [te·lé·me·tro] *m.* telemeter; range finder.
telepatía [te·le·pa·tí·a] *f.* telepathy.
telescopio [te·les·kó·pjo] *m.* telescope.
telesquí [te·les·kí] *m.* ski lift.
teletipo [te·le·tí·po] *m.* teletype.
televidente [te·le·ƀi·đén·te] *m.* & *f.* televiewer; one who watches television.
televisión [te·le·ƀi·sjón] *f.* television.
televisor [te·le·ƀi·sór] *m.* TV set.
telón [te·lón] *m.* theater curtain; — **de boca** drop curtain; — **de foro** drop scene.
telurio [te·lú·rjo] *m.* tellurium.
tema [té·ma] *m.* theme; subject; *f.* fixed idea, mania; **temario** agenda.
temático [te·má·ti·ko] *adj.* thematic; persistent.
temblar[1] [tem·blár] *v. irr.* to tremble; to shake; to quiver.
temblón [tem·blón] *adj.* tremulous, trembling, shaking, quivering.
temblor [tem·blór] *m.* tremor, trembling; shiver; quake; — **de tierra** earthquake.
tembloroso [tem·blo·ró·so] *adj.* trembling, shaking.
temer [te·mér] *v.* to fear; to dread; to suspect.
temerario [te·me·rá·rjo] *adj.* rash, reckless.
temeridad [te·me·ri·đáđ] *f.* temerity, recklessness; folly.
temeroso [te·me·ró·so] *adj.* fearful; suspicious; timid.
temible [te·mí·ƀle] *adj.* terrible, dreadful.
temor [te·mór] *m.* fear; dread, suspicion.
témpano [tém·pa·no] *m.* thick slice or chunk (*of anything*); kettledrum; drumhead (*parchment stretched over the end of a drum*); — **de hielo** block of ice; iceberg.
temperamento [tem·pe·ra·mén·to] *m.* temperament; climate.
temperatura [tem·pe·ra·tú·ra] *f.* temperature.
tempestad [tem·pes·táđ] *f.* tempest, storm.
tempestuoso [tem·pes·twó·so] *adj.* tempestuous, stormy.
templado [tem·plá·đo] *p.p.* & *adj.* (*moderado*) tempered; tuned; moderate; temperate; lukewarm; (*valiente*) brave; *Andes* in love; *Col., P.R.* half-drunk; *Col., Ven.* hard, severe; **estar mal** — to be in a bad humor.
templanza [tem·plán·sa] *f.* temperance; moderation; mildness.
templar [tem·plár] *v.* to temper; to moderate; to calm; to soften; to tune; **-se** to be tempered, moderate; to control oneself; *Andes* to fall in love; *Col.* to take to one's heels; *Mex., Ch.* to stuff oneself.
temple [tém·ple] *m.* temper; temperament; valor, courage; harmony (*of musical instruments*); *Arg.* sweetheart; **de mal** — in a bad humor.
templo [tém·plo] *m.* temple; church.
temporada [tem·po·rá·đa] *f.* period of time, season; — **de ópera** opera season.
temporal [tem·po·rál] *adj.* temporal; secular, worldly; temporary; *m.* weather; storm; spell of rainy weather.
tempranero [tem·pra·né·ro] *adj.* habitually early or ahead of time; **ser** — to be an early riser.
temprano [tem·prá·no] *adj.* early; premature; *adv.* early.
tenacidad [te·na·si·đáđ] *f.* tenacity; tenaciousness; perseverance.
tenacillas [te·na·sí·yas] *f. pl.* small tongs; pincers, tweezers; sugar tongs; curling iron.
tenaz [te·nás] *adj.* tenacious; firm; strong, resistant; stubborn.
tenazas [te·ná·sas] *f. pl.* pincers; pliers; tongs; — **de agarre de tornillo** vise grip pliers; forceps (*for pulling teeth*); **tenazuelas** [te·na·swé·las] *f. pl.* tweezers, small pincers.
tendedero [ten·de·đé·ro] *m.* place to hang or spread clothes; clothesline.
tendencia [ten·dén·sja] *f.* tendency, inclination.
tender[1] [ten·dér] *v. irr.* (*extender*) to spread out; to hang to dry; to stretch out; to lay out; (*propender*) to tend, have a tendency, move (*toward*); *Carib., Mex., C.A., Ríopl., Andes* to make (*a bed*); **-se** to stretch oneself out; to lay all one's cards on the table; to run at full gallop; **tendedor** spreader.
ténder [tén·der] *m.* tender (*of a train*).
tendero [ten·dé·ro] *m.* storekeeper; tentmaker.
tendido [ten·dí·đo] *m.* laying; a wash hung up to dry.
tendón [ten·dón] *m.* tendon, sinew.
tenducho [ten·dú·čo] *m.* wretched little shop.
tenebroso [te·ne·ƀró·so] *adj.* dark, shadowy; gloomy.
tenedor [te·ne·đór] *m.* table fork; holder, possessor, keeper; — **de libros** bookkeeper.
teneduría [te·ne·đu·rí·a] *f.* office and position of bookkeeper; — **de libros** bookkeeping.
tener[45] [te·nér] *v. irr.* to have; to possess; to hold; — **en mucho** to esteem highly; — **por** to consider, judge; — **que** (+ *inf.*) to have to; — **gana** (*or* — **ganas**) **de** to desire, feel like; — **miedo (sueño, frío, hambre,** *etc.*) to be afraid (sleepy, cold, hungry, *etc.*); — . . . **años** to be . . . years old; **-se** to stand firm; to hold on.
tenería [te·ne·rí·a] *f.* tannery.

tenia [té·nja] *f.* tapeworm.
teniente [te·njén·te] *m.* first lieutenant; substitute, deputy.
tenis [té·nis] *m.* tennis.
tenista [te·nís·ta] *m.* & *f.* tennis player.
tenor [te·nór] *m.* tenor; text, literal meaning; kind, sort, nature.
tensión [ten·sjón] *f.* tension; strain.
tenso [tén·so] *adj.* tense; tight, taut.
tentación [ten·ta·sjón] *f.* temptation.
tentáculo [ten·tá·ku·lo] *m.* tentacle, feeler.
tentador [ten·ta·đór] *adj.* tempting; *m.* tempter; the devil.
tentalear [ten·ta·le·ár] *v.* to grope, feel around; to finger, touch; to fumble (*for something*).
tentar[1] [ten·tár] *v. irr.* to tempt; to touch, feel with the fingers; to grope; to attempt, try; to test; to probe, examine with a probe.
tentativa [ten·ta·tí·ƀa] *f.* attempt, trial.
tentativo [ten·ta·tí·ƀo] *adj.* tentative.
tenue [té·nwe] *adj.* delicate, thin; flimsy; worthless.
teñir[5, 19] [te·ñír] *v. irr.* to dye; to tinge; to darken (*the color of a painting*).
teologal [te·o·lo·gál], **teológico** *adj.* theological.
teología [te·o·lo·xí·a] *f.* theology.
teólogo [te·ó·lo·go] *m.* theologian.
teoría [te·o·rí·a] *f.* theory.
teórico [te·ó·ri·ko] *adj.* theoretical.
tequila [te·kí·la] *m. Mex.* tequila (*liquor made from the maguey plant*).
terapéutico [te·ra·péw·ti·ko] *adj.* therapeutic.
tercería [ter·se·rí·a] *f.* arbitration.
tercero [ter·sé·ro] *adj.* third; *m.* third person; mediator; go-between; tertiary (*member of the third order of St. Francis*).
terciar [ter·sjár] *v.* (*atravesar*) to sling across one's shoulders; (*dividir*) to divide into three parts; (*intervenir*) to intervene, mediate; to meddle, join (*in*); (*equilibrar*) to balance the load on a pack animal; *Mex., Col.* to load or carry on the back; *Am.* to adulterate, add water to; *Am.* to mix.
tercio [tér·sjo] *adj.* third; *m.* one third; half of a mule load; military regiment or division; *Col., Carib., Mex.* bale, bundle; **hacer uno mal** — to hinder, interfere; — **de varas** the banderilla part of the bullfight.
terciopelo [ter·sjo·pé·lo] *m.* velvet.
terco [tér·ko] *adj.* obstinate, stubborn; hard; *Ch., Ec.* harsh, severe.
tergiversar [ter·xi·ƀer·sár] *v.* to distort, twist.
terminación [ter·mi·na·sjón] *f.* termination, end; ending.
terminal [ter·mi·nál] *adj.* terminal, final.
terminante [ter·mi·nán·te] *adj.* closing, ending; decisive, final.
terminar [ter·mi·nár] *v.* to terminate, end; to finish; **-se** to end.
término [tér·mi·no] *m.* end; completion; goal, object; boundary, limit; terminal; term; word, phrase; **en otros -s** in other words; **por — medio** on an average; as a rule; **primer** — foreground.
termo [tér·mo] *m.* thermos bottle.
termómetro [ter·mó·me·tro] *m.* thermometer.
termonuclear [ter·mo·nu·kle·ár] *adj.* thermonuclear.
termoplástico [ter·mo·plás·ti·co] *adj.* thermoplastic.
Termos [tér·mos] *f.* Thermos bottle (*trademark*).
termóstato [ter·mós·ta·to] *m.* thermostat.
ternera [ter·né·ra] *f.* calf; veal.
terneza [ter·né·sa] *f.* tenderness; softness; affection; affectionate word; caress.
terno [tér·no] *m.* group or combination of three; suit of clothes; *Carib., Mex.* set of jewels (*earrings, necklace, and brooch*); *Col., Mex.* cup and saucer; **echar** (*or* **soltar**) **un** — to utter a bad word; to curse, swear.
ternura [ter·nú·ra] *f.* tenderness.
terquedad [ter·ke·đáđ] *f.* obstinacy, stubbornness.
terrado [te·rrá·đo] *m.* terrace; flat roof.
terraja [te·rrá·xa] diestock; **-s para tubos** pipe laps.
terramicina [te·rra·mi·sí·na] *f.* Terramycin.
terraplén [te·rra·plén] *m.* railroad embankment.
terrateniente [te·rra·te·njén·te] *m.* & *f.* landholder.
terraza [te·rrá·sa] *f.* terrace, veranda; flat roof.
terremoto [te·rre·mó·to] *m.* earthquake.
terrenal [te·rre·nál] *adj.* earthly, worldly.
terreno [te·rré·no] *m.* land; ground; field; *adj.* earthly, worldly.
terrestre [te·rrés·tre] *adj.* terrestrial; earthly.
terrible [te·rrí·ƀle] *adj.* terrible.
terrífico [te·rrí·fi·ko] *adj.* terrific.
territorial [te·rri·to·rjál] *adj.* territorial.
territorio [te·rri·tó·rjo] *m.* territory.
terrón [te·rrón] *m.* clod; lump (*of sugar*).
terror [te·rrór] *m.* terror.
terrorista [te·rro·rís·ta] *m.* & *f.* terrorist.
terruño [te·rrú·ño] *m.* native soil.
terso [tér·so] *adj.* polished, smooth.
tertulia [ter·tú·lja] *f.* evening party; social gathering; club; conversation; *Ríopl., Cuba, Ven.* theater gallery.
tertuliano [ter·tu·ljá·no], **tertulio** [ter·tú·ljo] *m.* member of a **tertulia.**
tesis [té·sis] *f.* thesis.
tesón [te·són] *m.* grit, endurance, pluck, persistence.
tesonero [te·so·né·ro] *adj. Mex., Cuba, Andes* tenacious, stubborn, persevering, persistent.
tesorería [te·so·re·rí·a] *f.* treasury; **tesorero** [te·so·ré·ro] *m.* treasurer.
tesoro [te·só·ro] *m.* treasure; treasury.
testa [tés·ta] *f.* head; crown of the head; front.
testamento [tes·ta·mén·to] *m.* testament; will.
testarudez [tes·ta·ru·đés] *f.* stubbornness, obstinacy.
testarudo [tes·ta·rú·đo] *adj.* stubborn.
testigo [tes·tí·go] *m.* & *f.* witness; *m.* testimony, proof, evidence; — **de cargo** witness for the prosecution; — **de vista** eyewitness.
testimoniar [tes·ti·mo·njár] *v.* to give testimony of; to serve as a witness.
testimonio [tes·ti·mó·njo] *m.* testimony; proof, evidence; **levantar falso** — to bear false witness.
testuz [tes·tús] *m.* nape; crown of the head (*of certain animals*).
teta [té·ta] *f.* teat, nipple; breast; udder.
tétano [té·ta·no] *m.* tetanus.
tetera [te·té·ra] *f.* teapot; teakettle; *Mex., Cuba, Col.* **tetero** [te·té·ro] nursing bottle.
tétrico [té·tri·ko] *adj.* sad, melancholy, gloomy.
teutónico [tew·tó·ni·ko] *adj.* teutonic.
textil [tes·tíl] *adj.* textile.
texto [tés·to] *m.* text; quotation; textbook; **textual** textual; **textualmente** literally.
tez [tes] *f.* complexion, skin.
ti [ti] *pers. pron.* (*used after prep.*) you; yourself (*fam. sing.*).
tía [tí·a] *f.* aunt, older woman; *Ven.* — **rica** pawnshop; **no hay tu** — there is no use or hope; there is no way out of it; **quedarse una para** — to remain an old maid.
tibio [tí·ƀjo] *adj.* tepid, lukewarm; indifferent; *Col.* annoyed, angry.
tiburón [ti·ƀu·rón] *m.* shark.
tico [tí·ko] *adj.* & *m. Am.* Costa Rican (*humorous*

nickname).

tictac [tik·ták] *m.* tick-tock.

tiempo [tjém·po] *m.* time; weather; tense; **a** — in time, on time; **a su** — in due time, at the proper time; **a un** — at one and the same time; **andando el** — in time, as time goes on; — **extra** overtime; — **y medio** time and a half.

tienda [tjén·da] *f.* store; tent; — **de campaña** camping tent, army tent.

tienta [tjén·ta] *f.* probe (*surgical instrument*); **a -s** gropingly, feeling one's way; **andar a -s** to grope, feel one's way.

tiento [tjén·to] *m.* touch; tact; blind man's stick; steady hand; blow; tentacle, feeler (*of an insect*); *Andes, Ríopl.* saddle strap, leather strap, thong; *Am.* snack; *Arg.* swallow of liquor; **dar un** — to make a trial or attempt; **hacer algo con mucho** — to do something with great care or caution; **perder el** — to lose one's skill; *Andes* **tener a uno a los -s** to keep someone within sight; *Ven.* **tener la vida en un** — to be in great danger.

tierno [tjér·no] *adj.* tender; soft; young; recent, new; sensitive; affectionate; *Am.* green, unripe.

tierra [tjé·rra] *f.* earth; land; ground; soil; native land; — **adentro** inland; — **firme** mainland; solid ground; **dar en** — **con alguien** to overthrow someone; **echar por** — to knock down; to demolish; **tomar** — to land.

tieso [tjé·so] *adj.* stiff, rigid; stuck-up; firm; stubborn.

tiesto [tjés·to] *m. Spain* flowerpot; broken piece of earthenware; *Ch.* pot.

tiesura [tje·sú·ra] *f.* stiffness.

tifo [tí·fo] *m.* typhus; **tifoidea** [ti·foj·đe·a] *f.* typhoid fever.

tifón [ti·fón] *m.* typhoon; waterspout.

tifus [tí·fus] *m.* typhus.

tigre [tí·ǥre] *m.* tiger.

tijera [ti·xé·ra] *f.* (*usually* **tijeras**) scissors; sawhorse; **silla de** — folding chair; **tener buena** — (*or* **tener buenas -s**) to have a sharp tongue; to be a gossip.

tijeretada [ti·xe·re·tá·đa] *f.*, **tijeretazo** [ti·xe·re·tá·so] *m.* snip, cut, clip (*with the scissors*).

tijeretear [ti·xe·re·te·ár] *v.* to snip, cut, clip (*with scissors*); to criticize others, gossip.

tila [tí·la] *f.* linden; linden blossom tea.

tildar [til·dár] *v.* to accent (*a word*); to put a tilde over the **n**; to stigmatize.

tilde [tíl·de] *f.* tilde (*mark over an* **n**); blemish; jot, bit, speck; *Col.* accent mark.

timbrar [tim·brár] *v.* to stamp, mark with a seal.

timbrazo [tim·brá·so] *m.* ring of an electric bell.

timbre [tim·bre] *m.* revenue stamp; seal; crest (*on a coat of arms*); call bell; timbre (*quality of tone, tone color*); merit, fame; glorious deed; *Am.* postage stamp.

timidez [ti·mi·đés] *f.* timidity, shyness.

tímido [tí·mi·đo] *adj.* timid; shy.

timón [ti·món] *m.* helm; rudder; beam of a plow; *Col.* steering wheel.

timonear [ti·mo·ne·ár] *v.* to steer (*a ship*).

timorato [ti·mo·rá·to] *adj.* timorous, timid.

tímpano [tím·pa·no] *m.* eardrum; kettledrum.

tina [tí·na] *f.* large earthen jar; vat, tank, tub; bathtub.

tinaco [ti·ná·ko] *m.* tank, vat, tub.

tinaja [ti·ná·xa] *f.* large earthen jar.

tinglado [tiŋ·glá·đo] *m.* shed.

tinieblas [ti·njé·ƀlas] *f. pl.* darkness; obscurity; ignorance, confusion; Tenebrae (*Holy Week religious service*).

tino [tí·no] *m.* acumen, keen insight, good judgment; tact; accurate aim; good sense of touch; tank, vat.

tinta [tín·ta] *f.* ink; dye; tint, hue; **-s** paints; — **simpática** invisible ink; **saber de buena** — to know on good authority.

tinte [tín·te] *m.* tint, hue; tinge; color; dye; dyeing.

tinterillo [tin·te·rí·yo] *m.* shyster. *See* **picapleitos.**

tintero [tin·té·ro] *m.* inkwell, inkstand; ink roller (*printing*); *Am.* writing materials, desk set.

tintinear [tin·ti·ne·ár] *v.* to tinkle.

tintineo [tin·ti·né·o] *m.* tinkle, tinkling.

tinto [tín·to] *adj.* tinged; red (*wine*); *m. Col.* black coffee; *Am.* dark-red; *p.p. irr. of* **teñir.**

tintorería [tin·to·re·rí·a] *f.* cleaner's and dyer's shop.

tintorero [tin·to·ré·ro] *m.* dyer.

tintura [tin·tú·ra] *f.* tincture; tint; color; dye.

tinturar [tin·tu·rár] *v.* to tincture; to tinge; to dye.

tiñoso [ti·ñó·so] *adj.* scabby, mangy; stingy.

tío [tí·o] *m.* uncle; old man; good old man; fellow, guy; *Ríopl., Mex., Ven., Andes* **el cuento del** — deceitful story (*told to extract money*).

tíovivo [tí·o·ƀí·ƀo] *m.* merry-go-round.

típico [tí·pi·ko] *adj.* typical; *Am.* corrected (*edition*).

tiple [tí·ple] *m. & f.* high soprano singer; *m.* treble; soprano voice; treble guitar.

tipo [tí·po] *m.* type; class; model, standard; fellow, guy; *Am.* rate of interest; *Am.* — **de cambio** rate of exchange; **buen** — good-looking fellow.

tipografía [ti·po·ǥra·fí·a] *f.* typography, printing; press, printing shop.

tira [tí·ra] *f.* strip; stripe; *Mex.* **estar hecho -s** to be in rags; *Ven.* **sacar a uno las -s** to tan one's hide, beat one to pieces; — **bimetálica** bimetallic strip.

tirabuzón [ti·ra·ƀu·són] *m.* corkscrew.

tirada [ti·rá·đa] *f.* throw; issue, edition, printing; *Am.* tirade, long speech; *P.R.* sly trick; *Ch.* dash (*on horseback*); **de una** — all at once, at one fell swoop.

tirador [ti·ra·đór] *m.* shooter; thrower; slingshot; bell cord; handle; printer; *Am.* leather belt with pockets; — **de goma** slingshot.

tiranía [ti·ra·ní·a] *f.* tyranny.

tiránico [ti·rá·ni·ko] *adj.* tyrannical.

tirano [ti·rá·no] *adj.* tyrannical; *m.* tyrant.

tirante [ti·rán·te] *adj.* pulling; stretched, taut; strained; *m.* trace (*of a harness*); brace; **-s** suspenders; supporters (*for stockings*).

tirantez [ti·ran·tés] *f.* tension, tightness; strain; pull.

tirar [ti·rár] *v.* (*lanzar*) to throw; to throw away; to shoot, fire; (*imprimir*) to draw; to print; (*atraer*) to pull; to attract; *Cuba, Col., Ch.* to cart; — **a** to tend toward; to resemble; to aim at; — **de** to pull, tug; — **bien a la espada** to handle a sword well; **ir tirando** to get along; **a todo** (*or* **a más**) — at the most; *Ch.* **al** — haphazardly; **-se** to throw oneself; to lie down; *Mex., C.A., Col., Ven., Ríopl., Andes* **tirársela de** to boast of.

tiritar [ti·ri·tár] *v.* to shiver.

tiro [tí·ro] *m.* (*disparo*) throw; shot; (*pieza*) piece of artillery; (*alcance*) range of a gun; shooting range; (*carga*) charge of a gun; team (*of horses*); chimney draft; mine shaft; *Am.* issue, printing; *Am.* cartage, transport; — **al blanco** target practice; *Ch., Andes* **al** — at once; *Ven.* **de a** (*or* **de al**) — all at once; completely; **caballo de** — draft horse; **ni a -s** absolutely not (*not even if you shoot me*).

tirón [ti·rón] *m.* jerk, sudden pull; **de un** — all at once, with one big pull.

tironear [ti·ro·ne·ár] *v. C.A., Mex., Ríopl.* to pull, jerk; *Col.* to attract.

tirotear [ti·ro·te·ár] *v.* to shoot around; to shoot at random; **-se** to exchange shots.

tiroteo [ti·ro·té·o] *m.* shooting; exchange of shots; skirmish.

tirria [tí·rrja] *f.* aversion, grudge; **tenerle — a una persona** to have a strong dislike for someone; to hold a grudge against someone.

tísico [tí·si·ko] *adj.* tubercular, consumptive.

tisis [tí·sis] *f.* tuberculosis, consumption.

titanio [ti·tá·njo] *m.* titanium.

títere [tí·te·re] *m.* puppet; ridiculous little fellow; **-s** puppet show.

titilación [ti·ti·la·sjón] *f.* flicker; twinkle; **titileo** *m.* flickering; twinkling; glimmer.

titilar [ti·ti·lár] *v.* to flicker; to twinkle; (*computadora*) to blink.

titubear [ti·tu·be·ár] *v* to hesitate; to totter, stagger; to grope; to stutter, stammer.

titubeo [ti·tu·bé·o] *m.* hesitation, wavering.

titular [ti·tu·lár] *v.* to entitle; to name; **-se** to be called or named; to call oneself; to receive a title; *adj.* titular, in name only; *m.* officer; holder of a title.

título [tí·tu·lo] *m.* (*letrero*) title; heading; sign; inscription; (*derecho*) claim, legal right; (*grado*) degree, diploma; credential; titled person; merit; bond, certificate; **a — de** under the pretext of; in the capacity of.

tiza [tí·sa] *f.* chalk.

tiznado [tiz·ná·do] *adj.* sooty, covered with soot; smutty; dirty; *Ven.* drunk; *p.p. of* **tiznar.**

tiznar [tiz·nár] *v.* to smudge, smut; to smear with soot.

tizne [tíz·ne] *m.* soot; smut; **tiznón** [tiz·nón] *m.* smudge.

tizón [ti·són] *m.* firebrand (*piece of burning wood*); rust, blight (*on plants*); stain (*on one's honor*).

toalla [to·á·ya] *f.* towel.

tobillo [to·bí·yo] *m.* ankle.

tocadiscos [to·ka·dís·kos] *m.* record player; phonograph.

tocado [to·ká·do] *m.* headdress; hairdo, coiffure; *adj.* "touched", half-crazy; *p.p. of* **tocar.**

tocador [to·ka·dór] *m.* dressing table; boudoir, dressing room; dressing case; player (*of a musical instrument*).

tocar[6] [to·kár] *v.* to touch; to play (*an instrument*); to toll, ring; to knock, rap; **— en** to stop over in; **-le a uno** to fall to one's lot; to be one's share; to be one's turn; to concern one; **-se** to fix one's hair; to become "touched," go slightly crazy.

tocayo [to·ká·yo] *m.* namesake; one who has the same name.

tocino [to·sí·no] *m.* bacon; salt pork; lard.

tocón [to·kón] *m.* stub, stump (*of a tree, arm or leg*).

todavía [to·da·bí·a] *adv.* still; yet; even.

todo [tó·do] *adj.* all, whole; every, each; **— hombre** every man; **-s los días** every day; **a — correr** at full or top speed; *m.* whole; all; everything; **-s** everybody; **ante —** first of all; **así y —** in spite of that; **con —** in spite of that; **del —** wholly.

todopoderoso [to·do·po·de·ró·so] *adj.* almighty.

toga [tó·ga] *f.* gown, robe (*worn by a judge, professor, etc.*); Roman toga.

toldería [tol·de·rí·a] *f. Ríopl.* Indian camp, Indian village.

toldo [tól·do] *m.* awning; pomp, vanity; *Ríopl.* Indian hut.

tolerancia [to·le·rán·sja] *f.* tolerance, toleration; **tolerante** [to·le·rán·te] *adj.* tolerant.

tolerar [to·le·rár] *v.* to tolerate; to allow; to overlook, let pass.

tolete [to·lé·te] *m. Col., Mex., Cuba* stick, club, cudgel; *Col.* raft.

toma [tó·ma] *f.* taking; seizure, capture; dose; tap (*of a water main*); *Col.* irrigation ditch; **— de corriente** plug, electric outlet; *m.* **tomacorrientes** socket.

tomar [to·már] *v.* (*asir*) to take; to grasp, catch; to capture; (*beber*) to drink; **— a pechos** to take to heart, take seriously; **-lo a mal** to take it amiss; **— el pelo a** to make fun of, make a fool of; **— por la derecha** to turn to the right; **-se con** to quarrel with.

tomate [to·má·te] *m.* tomato.

tómbola [tóm·bo·la] *f.* raffle for charity.

tomillo [to·mí·yo] *m.* thyme.

tomo [tó·mo] *m.* tome, volume; *Am.* heavy person; *Ch.* dull, silent person; *Ch.* **buen —** a heavy drinker; **de — y lomo** bulky; important.

ton [ton]: **sin — ni son** without rhyme or reason.

tonada [to·ná·da] *f.* tune, song; *Andes* singsong; *Andes, Mex., Carib., Ríopl.* local accent; **tonadilla** [to·na·dí·ya] *f.* little tune; short popular song.

tonel [to·nél] *m.* keg, cask, barrel.

tonelada [to·ne·lá·da] *f.* ton.

tonelaje [to·ne·lá·xe] *m.* tonnage.

tónico [tó·ni·ko] *adj. & m.* tonic.

tono [tó·no] *m.* tone; tune; key, pitch; accent; manner; vigor, strength; **de buen —** of good taste, stylish; **subirse de —** to put on airs.

tonsura [ton·sú·ra] *f.* shearing.

tontera [ton·té·ra] = **tontería.**

tontería [ton·te·rí·a] *f.* foolishness; stupidity.

tonto [tón·to] *adj.* foolish; stupid; **a tontas y a locas** recklessly, without thought; *m.* fool; dunce; *Col., Ch.* a game of cards.

topar [to·pár] *v.* to collide with, run into, bump into; to encounter; to find; to run across; to butt; *Am.* to gamble; *Col.* to fight with the fists; *Carib., Mex., Ríopl., Andes, Col.* to meet, greet.

tope [tó·pe] *m.* butt, bump, collision; encounter; bumper; dead-end; **hasta el —** up to the top; **estar hasta los -s** to be filled up; *Mex.* speed checks (on road); **-s marginales** margin regulators (stops) (typewriter).

topetada [to·pe·tá·da] *f.*, **topetazo** [to·pe·tá·so] *m.* butt; bump, bump on the head; **topetón** [to·pe·tón] *m.* hard bump, collision; butt.

topetear [to·pe·te·ár] *v.* to butt; to bump.

tópico [tó·pi·ko] *m.* topic, subject.

topo [tó·po] *m.* mole (*small animal*); dunce; awkward person.

topografía [to·po·gra·fí·a] *f.* topography.

toque [tó·ke] *m.* touch; ringing; beat (*of a drum*); tap, sound (*of a trumpet, clarinet, etc.*); assay; **piedra de —** touchstone; **¡allí está el —!** there is the difficulty!; there is the real test!

toquilla [to·kí·ya] *f.* triangular handkerchief; ribbon; hatband.

tórax [tó·raks] *m.* thorax.

torbellino [tor·be·yí·no] *m.* whirlwind; rush, bustle, confusion.

torcedura [tor·se·dú·ra] *f.* twist; sprain, strain.

torcer[2, 10] [tor·sér] *v. irr.* to twist; to turn; to bend; to sprain; to distort; **-se** to become twisted, bent, or sprained; to get crooked; to go astray; to turn sour (*said of wine*); *Am.* to get offended, angry.

torcido [tor·sí·do] *p.p. & adj.* twisted, turned, bent; crooked; angry, resentful; *Am.* unfortunate, unlucky; **estar — con** to be on unfriendly terms with; *m.* twisted roll of candied fruit; coarse silk twist; *Mex., Carib.* gesture or look of disdain; *Andes* lasso made of twisted leather.

tordillo [tor·đí·yo] *adj.* greyish, dapple-grey.
tordo [tór·đo] *adj.* dapple-grey; *m.* thrush; dapple-grey horse.
torear [to·re·ár] *v.* to perform in a bullfight; to incite, provoke (*a bull*); to tease.
torero [to·ré·ro] *m.* bullfighter; *adj.* relating to bullfighting.
tormenta [tor·mén·ta] *f.* storm, tempest; misfortune.
tormento [tor·mén·to] *m.* torment; torture; rack (*instrument of torture*); anguish; pain.
tornar [tor·nár] *v.* to return; to turn; to change, alter; — **a hacerlo** to do it again.
tornasol [tor·na·sól] *m.* sunflower.
tornadizo [tor·na·đí·so] *adj.* changeable; fickle.
tornasolado [tor·na·so·lá·đo] *adj.* iridescent, rainbow-colored; changeable (*silk*).
tornear [tor·ne·ár] *v.* to turn in a lathe; to do lathe work; to fight in a tournament.
torneo [tor·né·o] *m.* tournament.
tornillo [tor·ní·yo] *m.* screw; clamp, vise; **faltarle a uno un** — to have little sense, "have a screw loose"; — **sin fin** worm gear; — **de banco para tubos** pipe vise; — **de cabeza ranurada** slotted screw; — **de cabeza phillips (en cruz)** Phillips head.
torniquete [tor·ni·ké·te] *m.* turnbuckle; tourniquet.
torno [tór·no] *m.* turn; lathe; turnstile; revolving server; winch or windlass (*machine for lifting or pulling, turned by a crank*); — **de hilar** spinning wheel; **en** — around.
toro [tó·ro] *m.* bull; *Mex., Col.* difficult question; **-s** bullfight; *Am.* **estar en las astas del** — to be in a predicament.
toronja [to·róŋ·xa] *f. Am.* grapefruit.
torpe [tór·pe] *adj.* stupid, dull; clumsy; slow; lewd.
torpedo [tor·pé·đo] *m.* torpedo; **torpedero** [tor·pe·đé·ro] *m.* torpedo boat.
torpeza [tor·pé·sa] *f.* stupidity, dullness; clumsiness; slowness; moral turpitude, lewdness.
torrar [to·rrár] *v.* to parch.
torre [tó·rre] *f.* tower; turret; castle (*in chess*).
torrencial [to·rren·sjál] *adj.* torrential.
torrente [to·rrén·te] *m.* torrent; flood; — **de voz** powerful voice.
torreón [to·rre·ón] *m.* large tower (*of a fortress, castle, etc.*).
tórrido [tó·rri·đo] *adj.* torrid.
torsión [tor·sjón] *f.* twist; sprain.
torta [tór·ta] *f.* torte, round cake; round loaf.
tortilla [tor·tí·ya] *f.* omelet; *Mex., C.A.* tortilla (*flat, thin cornmeal cake*).
tórtola [tór·to·la] *f.* turtledove.
tortuga [tor·tú·ǥa] *f.* tortoise; turtle.
tortuoso [tor·twó·so] *adj.* tortuous, twisting, winding; sly.
tortura [tor·tú·ra] *f.* torture; grief, affliction.
torturar [tor·tu·rár] *v.* to torture.
torvo [tór·ƀo] *adj.* grim, stern, severe.
tos [tos] *f.* cough; — **ferina** whooping cough.
tosco [tós·ko] *adj.* coarse, harsh, rough.
toser [to·sér] *v.* to cough; *Am.* to brag, boast.
tosquedad [tos·ke·đáđ] *f.* coarseness, crudeness, roughness; rudeness.
tostada [tos·tá·đa] *f.* toast, toasted bread; *Am.* boring visit or conversation; *Ven.* toasted **tortilla; dar** (*or* **pegar) una — a uno** to play a mean trick on someone; *Mex.* to make someone very angry.
tostado [tos·tá·đo] *p.p. & adj.* toasted; roasted; tanned; *Am.* worn out, tired out; *m.* toasting; *Am.* roasted corn.
tostador [tos·ta·đór] *m.* toaster.
tostar[2] [tos·tár] *v. irr.* to toast; to tan; to overheat; to roast (*coffee*).
tostón [tos·tón] *m.* toast dipped in oil; small roasted pig; *Mex., C.A.* coin worth half a Mexican peso.
total [to·tál] *adj. & m.* total.
totalidad [to·ta·li·đáđ] *f.* entirety, whole.
totalitario [to·ta·li·tá·rjo] *adj.* totalitarian.
totuma [to·tú·ma] *f.* calabash.
tóxico [tók·si·ko] *adj.* toxic.
toxina [tok·sí·na] *f.* toxin (*poison produced within animals and plants*).
toza [tó·sa] *f.* wooden block; stump; log; piece of bark.
traba [trá·ƀa] *f.* bond, tie; binding or locking device; fastener, fetter, shackle; hindrance, obstacle.
trabado [tra·ƀá·đo] *adj. Col., Ríopl., Mex.* tongue-tied; *p.p. of* **trabar.**
trabajador [tra·ƀa·xa·đor] *adj.* industrious; *m.* worker, laborer.
trabajar [tra·ƀa·xár] *v.* to work; to labor; to strive.
trabajo [tra·ƀá·xo] *m.* work; labor; difficulty, obstacle; trouble; hardship.
trabajoso [tra·ƀa·xó·so] *adj.* laborious, difficult; troublesome; *Am.* unobliging; *Am.* demanding.
trabalenguas [tra·ƀa·lén·gwas] *m.* tongue twister.
trabar [tra·ƀár] *v.* to join, fasten; to clasp; to shackle; to brace; to impede; — **amistad con alguien** to become friends with someone; — **batalla** to join in battle; — **conversación** to be engaged in conversation; to engage in conversation; **-se** *Ríopl., Mex., Ven.* to stammer; **-se de palabras** to get into an argument.
tracción [trak·sjón] *f.* traction; **resistencia a la** — tensile strength.
tractor [trak·tór] *m.* tractor.
tradición [tra·đi·sjón] *f.* tradition.
tradicional [tra·đi·sjo·nál] *adj.* traditional.
traducción [tra·đuk·sjón] *f.* translation.
traducir[25] [tra·đu·sír] *v. irr.* to translate; to interpret.
traductor [tra·đuk·tór] *m.* translator.
traer[46] [tra·ér] *v. irr.* to bring; to carry; to lead, conduct; to have; to bring about; to wear; — **a uno inquieto** to keep one disturbed; — **a uno a mal** — to mistreat someone; to bother someone; **-se bien** to dress well; to carry oneself well.
trafagar[7] [tra·fa·ǥár] *v.* to traffic, trade; to roam about; to bustle, hustle; to toil.
tráfago [trá·fa·ǥo] *m.* trade, commerce; bustle, hustle; toil.
traficante [tra·fi·kán·te] *m.* trader; dealer; tradesman.
traficar[6] [tra·fi·kár] *v.* to traffic, trade; *Ven.* to pass or move back and forth (*as traffic*). *See* **transitar.**
tráfico [trá·fi·ko] *m.* traffic; trade, commerce.
tragaluz [tra·ǥa·lús] *f.* skylight.
tragar[7] [tra·ǥár] *v.* to swallow; to gulp; to engulf, swallow up.
tragedia [tra·xé·đja] *f.* tragedy.
trágico [trá·xi·ko] *adj.* tragic.
trago [trá·ǥo] *m.* swallow, gulp; misfortune; *Am.* brandy, hard liquor; **a -s** slowly, by degrees; **echar un** — to take a drink; **tragón** *m.* glutton; *adj.* gluttonous.
traición [traj·sjón] *f.* treason; treachery; **a** — treacherously; deceitfully.
traicionar [traj·sjo·nár] *v.* to betray.
traicionero [traj·sjo·né·ro] *adj.* treacherous; deceitful; *m.* traitor.
traído [tra·í·đo] *adj.* used, old, worn out; **muy — y llevado** very worn out; *p.p. of* **traer.**
traidor [traj·đór] *adj.* treacherous; *m.* traitor; betrayer.

traje [trá·xe] *m.* dress; suit; gown; — **de etiqueta** (— **de ceremonia,** *or Am.* — **de parada)** formal gown; formal suit; dress uniform; — **de luces** bullfighter's costume; *Col., C.A., Mex., Ríopl.* — **sastre** woman's tailor-made suit.
trajeado [tra·xe·á·đo] *p.p. & adj.* dressed, clothed.
trajín [tra·xín] *m.* traffic, going and coming; hustle, bustle, commotion.
trajinar [tra·xi·nár] *v.* to carry, cart back and forth; to go back and forth; to bustle, hustle.
trama [trá·ma] *f.* plot; scheme; conspiracy; woof (*horizontal threads of a fabric*).
tramar [tra·már] *v.* to weave; to plot; to scheme.
tramitar [tra·mi·tár] *v.* to transact; to take legal steps; to negotiate.
trámite [trá·mi·te] *m.* transaction, procedure, step, formality.
tramo [trá·mo] *m.* stretch, lap, span; short distance; regular interval; flight of stairs.
tramoya [tra·mó·ya] *f.* stage devices and machinery.
trampa [trám·pa] *f.* trap; snare; hatch, trap door; hinged section of a counter; spring door; fraud; trick.
trampear [tram·pe·ár] *v.* to trick, cheat, swindle.
trampista [tram·pís·ta] *m. & f.* cheat, crook, swindler.
trampolín [tram·po·lín] *m.* springboard.
tramposo [tram·pó·so] *adj.* deceitful, tricky; *m.* swindler, cheat.
tranca [tráŋ·ka] *f.* crossbar, bolt; pole, prop; club, stick; *Ven., Ríopl.* rustic gate, *Ríopl.* fence with gates; *Mex., Ven.* **saltar las -s** to jump over the fence; to lose one's patience, rebel, get angry; *Ch., Ríopl., Andes, Mex.* **tener una** — to be drunk.
trance [trán·se] *m.* critical moment; dangerous situation; **el último** — the last moment of life; **a todo** — at any cost, cost what it may.
tranco [tráŋ·ko] *m.* stride, long step; threshold; **a -s** hurriedly; **en dos -s** in a jiffy; *Ríopl.* **al** — striding, with long steps.
tranquear [traŋ·ke·ár] *v.* to stride along.
tranquera [traŋ·ké·ra] *f.* stockade, wooden fence; *Ríopl., Cuba, Ven.* large gate (*made with* **trancas**).
tranquilidad [traŋ·ki·li·đáđ] *f.* tranquility, peacefulness.
tranquilizar[9] [traŋ·ki·li·sár] *v.* to quiet, calm down; to pacify; **-se** to become tranquil, calm down.
tranquilo [traŋ·kí·lo] *adj.* tranquil, peaceful.
transacción [tran·sak·sjón] *f.* transaction, negotiation; compromise.
transar [tran·sár] *v. Am.* to compromise, yield, give in.
transatlántico [tran·sa·tlán·ti·ko] *adj.* transatlantic; *m.* transatlantic steamer.
transbordar [trans·bor·đár] = **trasbordar.**
transbordo [trans·bór·đo] = **trasbordo.**
transcendencia [trans·sen·dén·sja] *f.* consequence, importance; penetration.
transcendental [tran·sen·den·tál] *adj.* consequential, important, far-reaching.
transcribir [trans·kri·bír] *v.* to transcribe.
transcurrir [trans·ku·rrír] *v.* to pass, elapse.
transcurso [trans·kúr·so] *m.* passing, lapse (*of time*).
transeúnte [tran·se·ún·te] *m.* passer-by; pedestrian; transient; *adj.* transient.
transferencia [trans·fe·rén·sja] *f.* transference, transfer.
transferible [trans·fe·rí·ble] *f.* transference, transfer.
transferible [trans·fe·rí·ble] *adj.* transferable.
transferir[3] [trans·fe·rír] *v. irr.* to transfer.
transformación [trans·for·ma·sjón] *f.* transformation.
transformador [trans·for·ma·đór] *m.* transformer.
transformar [trans·for·már] *v.* to transform.
transfusión [trans·fu·sjón] *f.* transfusion.
transgredir[51] [trans·gre·đír] *v.* to transgress.
transgresión [trans·gre·sjón] *f.* transgression.
transgresor [trans·gre·sór] *m.* transgressor, offender.
transición [tran·si·sjón] *f.* transition.
transigente [tran·si·xén·te] *adj.* compromising, yielding, pliable.
transigir[11] [tran·si·xír] *v.* to compromise, yield, make concessions; to settle by compromise.
transistor [tran·sis·tór] *m.* transistor.
transitable [tran·si·tá·ble] *adj.* passable (*road*).
transitar [tran·si·tár] *v.* to pass or move back and forth (*as traffic*).
tránsito [trán·si·to] *m.* transit; traffic; passing; passage; transition; **de** — on the way, in transit, passing through.
transitorio [tran·si·tó·rjo] *adj.* transitory.
transmisión [trans·mi·sjón] *f.* transmission; — **automática** automatic transmission.
transmisor [trans·mi·sór] *m.* transmitter; *adj.* transmitting.
transmitir [trans·mi·tír] *v.* to transmit.
transparencia [trans·pa·rén·sja] *f.* transparency.
transparente [trans·pa·rén·te] *adj.* transparent; lucid, clear; *m.* window shade; stained-glass window.
transpirar [trans·pi·rár] *v.* to transpire; to leak out.
transponer[40] [trans·po·nér] *v. irr.* to transpose; to transfer; to transplant; to go beyond, go over to the other side; **-se** to hide from view, go behind; to set, go below the horizon.
transportación [trans·por·ta·sjón] *f.* transportation, transport.
transportar [trans·por·tár] *v.* to transport; to transpose (*music*); **-se** to be transported, carried away by strong feeling; to be in ecstasy.
transporte [trans·pór·te] *m.* transport; transportation; transport vessel; ecstasy; — **de locura** fit of madness.
transpuesto [trans·pwés·to] *p.p. of* **transponer.**
transversal [trans·ber·sál] *adj.* transversal, transverse; **sección** — cross section.
transverso [trans·bér·so] *adj.* transverse, cross.
tranvía [tram·bí·a] *m.* streetcar; streetcar track.
trapacear [tra·pa·se·ár] *v.* to swindle, cheat; to racketeer.
trapacería [tra·pa·se·rí·a] *f.* racket, fraud, swindle.
trapacero [tra·pa·sé·ro] *m.* racketeer; cheat, swindler; *adj.* cheating, deceiving.
trapacista [tra·pa·sís·ta] *m. & f.* racketeer; swindler, cheat.
trapeador [tra·pe·a·đór] *m. Am.* mopper; *Andes, Ven., Col., C.A., Mex., Cuba* mop.
trapear [tra·pe·ár] *v. Am.* to mop; *C.A.* to beat up, give (*someone*) a licking.
trapecio [tra·pé·sjo] *m.* trapeze.
trapiche [tra·pí·če] *m.* sugar mill; press (*for extracting juices*); *Andes* grinding machine (*for pulverizing minerals*).
trapisonda [tra·pi·són·da] *f.* escapade, prank; brawl; noisy spree.
trapo [trá·po] *m.* rag; *C.A., Ven., Ur.* cloth; **-s** clothes; **a todo** — at full sail; speedily; **poner a uno como un** — to make one feel like a rag; **sacarle a uno los -s al sol** to exhibit somebody's dirty linen; **soltar el** — to burst out laughing or crying.
traposo [tra·pó·so] *adj. Ch., P.R.* ragged, tattered, in rags.
tráquea [trá·ke·a] *f.* trachea, windpipe.

traquetear [tra·ke·te·ár] *v.* to rattle; to shake; to jolt; to crack, crackle.
traqueteo [tra·ke·té·o] *m.* rattling; shaking; jolting; cracking, crackling; *Ríopl., Col., Ven., C.A., Mex., Carib., Andes* uproar, din; *Am.* noisy, disorderly traffic.
tras [tras] *prep.* after; in search of; behind, in back of; — **de** behind, after; besides, in addition to; *interj.* **¡—!** bang!
trasbordar [traz·ƀor·đár] *v.* to transfer.
trasbordo [traz·ƀór·đo] *m.* transfer.
trascendencia [tra·sen·dén·sja] = **transcendencia.**
trascendental [tra·sen·den·tál] = **transcendental.**
trasegar[1, 7] [tra·se·ǥár] *v. irr.* to upset, overturn; to change from one place to another; to pour from one container to another.
trasero [tra·sé·ro] *adj.* rear, hind, back; *m.* rump.
trasladar [traz·la·đár] *v.* to move, remove; to transfer; to postpone; to translate; to transcribe, copy.
traslado [traz·lá·đo] *m.* transfer; transcript, written copy.
traslapo [traz·lá·po] *m.* overlap.
traslucirse[13] [traz·lu·sír·se] *v. irr.* to be translucent; to be transparent, clear, evident.
trasnochar [traz·no·čár] *v.* to sit up all night; to stay awake all night; to spend the night out.
traspalar [tras·pa·lár] *v.* to shovel.
traspapelar [tras·pa·pe·lár] *v.* to mislay, misplace (*a paper, letter, document, etc.*); **-se** to become mislaid among other papers.
traspasar [tras·pa·sár] *v.* to pass over, cross over; to go beyond; to pass through; to pierce; to transfer (*property*); to trespass.
traspaso [tras·pá·so] *m.* transfer; transgression, trespass.
traspié [tras·pjé] *m.* stumble, slip; **dar un** — to stumble or trip.
trasplantar [tras·plan·tár] *v.* to transplant.
trasponer[40] [tras·po·nér] = **transponer.**
trasquila [tras·kí·la], **trasquiladura** [tras·ki·la·đú·ra] *f.* shearing, clip, clipping; bad haircut.
trasquilar [tras·ki·lár] *v.* to shear; to clip; to crop; to cut badly (*hair*).
trastazo [tras·tá·so] *m.* thump, blow.
traste [trás·te] *m.* fret, stop (*of a guitar*); buttocks; *C.A.* utensil, implement; **dar al** — **con** to destroy, ruin.
trasto [trás·to] *m.* household utensil; piece of junk; rubbish, trash; **-s** utensils; implements; **-s de pescar** fishing tackle.
trastornar [tras·tor·nár] *v.* to overturn; to upset; to disturb.
trastorno [tras·tór·no] *m.* upset; disorder; disturbance.
trastrocar[2, 6] [tras·tro·kár] *v. irr.* to invert, change; to upset.
trasudar [tra·su·đár] *v.* to perspire, sweat slightly.
trasudor [tra·su·đór] *m.* slight perspiration or sweat.
tratable [tra·tá·ƀle] *adj.* friendly, sociable; manageable.
tratado [tra·tá·đo] *m.* treaty; treatise.
tratamiento [tra·ta·mjén·to] *m.* treatment; title of courtesy; form of address; — **de texto** word processing.
tratante [tra·tán·te] *m. & f.* dealer, tradesman, trader.
tratar [tra·tár] *v.* to treat; to handle; to discuss; to have social relations with; — **con** to have dealings with; — **de** to try to; to treat of, deal with; **-le a uno de** to address someone as; to treat someone as; — **en** to deal in; **-se bien** to treat oneself well; to behave well; **-se de** to be a question of; **no se trata de eso** that isn't the question, that isn't the point.
trato [trá·to] *m.* (*acuerdo*) treatment; deal, pact; trade; (*manera*) manner, behavior; social relations; dealings; *Am.* — **pampa** unfair deal; **¡** — **hecho!** it's a deal!; **tener buen** — to be affable, sociable.
traumático [traw·má·ti·ko] *adj.* traumatic.
través [tra·ƀés] *m.* crossbeam; reverse, misfortune; **a** (*or* **al**) — **de** through, across; **de** — across; **dar al** — **con** to ruin, destroy; to squander; **mirar de** — to squint in a sinister manner.
travesaño [tra·ƀe·sá·ño] *m.* crosspiece, crossbar; bolster, long bedpillow; *Ven., Andes* railway tie.
travesear [tra·ƀe·se·ár] *v.* to romp, frisk, frolic; to fool around; to misbehave.
travesía [tra·ƀe·sí·a] *f.* crossing; sea voyage; wind blowing towards a coast; *Col.* wasteland, desert land; *Arg.* partition wall or fence.
travesura [tra·ƀe·sú·ra] *f.* mischief; prank; lively wit.
traviesa [tra·ƀjé·sa] *f.* railway tie; rafter, crossbeam; *Col.* midyear crop.
travieso [tra·ƀjé·so] *adv.* mischievous; lively; restless; **a campo** (*or* **a campo traviesa**) cross-country.
trayecto [tra·yék·to] *m.* run, stretch, lap, distance (*traveled over*).
trayectoria [tra·yek·tó·rja] *f.* path (*of a bullet, missile, etc.*).
traza [trá·sa] *f.* (*plan*) plan; design; plot; invention; (*apariencia*) appearance; semblance; aspect; indication, sign; **darse -s** to use one's wits or ingenuity; **tener -s de** to have the appearance or signs of; **tiene** (*or* **lleva**) **-s de no acabar nunca** it looks as if he would never end.
trazado [tra·sá·đo] *m.* draft, plan, sketch, outline; drawing; *p.p. & adj.* traced, sketched, outlined.
trazador [tra·sa·đór] m. tracer; — **gráfico** (*computadora*) touch tablet.
trazar[9] [tra·sár] *v.* to trace, sketch; to draw, mark out; to plan.
trébol [tré·ƀol] *m.* clover.
trece [tré·se] *num.* thirteen.
trecho [tré·čo] *m.* space, distance; lap (*in a race*); **a -s** by or at intervals; **de** — **en** — at certain points or intervals; from time to time.
tregua [tré·ǥwa] *f.* truce; rest, respite.
treinta [trejn·ta] *num.* thirty.
tremedal [tre·me·đál] *m.* quagmire, bog.
tremendo [tre·mén·do] *adj.* tremendous, huge; terrible.
trementina [tre·men·tí·na] *f.* turpentine.
tremolar [tre·mo·lár] *v.* to flutter, wave (*as a flag*).
trémolo [tré·mo·lo] *m.* tremolo (*of the voice*), quaver.
trémulo [tré·mu·lo] *adj.* tremulous, trembling, quivering; flickering.
tren [tren] *m.* train; *Mex., Guate.* traffic; — **correo** mail train; — **de aterrizaje** landing gear; *Ven., Carib.* — **de lavado** laundry; *Cuba, Ven.* — **de mudadas** moving company; — **de recreo** excursion train; — **mixto** freight and passenger train.
trenza [trén·sa] *f.* tress; braid; *Mex., Cuba, Ven.* string (*of garlic, onions, etc.*); **trencilla** *f.* braid.
trenzar[9] [tren·sár] *v.* to braid; **-se** to braid one's hair; *Ríopl., Andes, Col.* to fight hand to hand.
trepador [tre·pa·đór] *adj.* climbing.
trepar [tre·pár] *v.* to climb; to clamber; **-se** to climb; to clamber; to perch.
trepidación [tre·pi·đa·sjón] *f.* jar, vibration; trembling, shaking.
trepidar [tre·pi·đár] *v.* to shape, vibrate, tremble, jar.
tres [tres] *num.* three.

treta [tré·ta] *f.* trick, wile; **malas -s** bad tricks, bad habits.
triaca [trjá·ka] *f.* treacle.
triangular [trjaŋ·gu·lár] *adj.* triangular.
triángulo [trjáŋ·gu·lo] *m.* triangle; — **de refuerzo** gusset.
tribu [trí·bu] *f.* tribe.
tribulación [tri·bu·la·sjón] *f.* tribulation, trouble.
tribuna [tri·bú·na] *f.* rostrum (*speaker's platform*).
tribunal [tri·bu·nál] *m.* tribunal; court of justice; body of judges.
tributar [tri·bu·tár] *v.* to pay tribute, pay homage.
tributario [tri·bu·tá·rjo] *adj.* & *m.* tributary.
tributo [tri·bú·to] *m.* tribute; contribution, tax.
triciclo [tri·sí·klo] *m.* tricycle.
trifulca [tri·fúl·ka] *f.* fight, quarrel, wrangle, row.
trigo [trí·go] *m.* wheat.
trigueño [tri·gé·ño] *adj.* swarthy; brunet; dark.
trilogía [tri·lo·xí·a] *f.* trilogy.
trillado [tri·yá·do] *p.p.* beaten; *adj.* trite, hackneyed, commonplace; **camino** — beaten path.
trilladora [tri·ya·dó·ra] *f.* threshing machine.
trillar [tri·yár] *v.* to thresh; to beat, mistreat; *Cuba* to cut a path.
trimestre [tri·més·tre] *m.* quarter, period of three months; quarterly payment, income, or salary; **trimestral** [tri·mes·trál] *adj.* quarterly.
trinar [tri·nár] *v.* to trill (*in singing*); to warble; to quaver (*said of the voice*); to get furious.
trinchante [trin·čán·te] *m.* carving fork; carving knife; carver.
trinchar [trin·čár] *v.* to carve (*meat*).
trinche [trín·če] *m. Col., Ven., C.A., Mex.* fork; *Ch., Ec.* carving table; *Am.* **plato** — carving platter.
trinchera [trin·čé·ra] *f.* trench; ditch; *C.A., Ven., Andes* stockade, fence; *Mex.* curved knife.
trinchero [trin·čé·ro] *m.* carving table; **plato** — carving platter.
trineo [tri·né·o] *m.* sleigh; sled.
trino [trí·no] *m.* trill (*in singing*).
tripa [trí·pa] *f.* intestine, bowel; paunch, belly; **-s** entrails, insides.
triple [trí·ple] *adj.* & *m.* triple.
triplicar[6] [tri·pli·kár] *v.* to triplicate, triple, treble.
trípode [trí·po·de] *m.* tripod.
tripulación [tri·pu·la·sjón] *f.* crew, ship's company.
tripular [tri·pu·lár] *v.* to man (*a ship*).
trique [trí·ke] *m.* crack, snap; *Mex.* utensil, trinket; *Col.* clever trick in a game; *Am.* drink made from barley; **-s** *Mex.* poor household utensils, goods, etc.
triquinosis [tri·ki·nó·sis] *f.* trichinosis.
triscar[6] [tris·kár] *v.* to romp, frisk, frolic; to stamp or shuffle the feet; *Col., Cuba* to tease, make fun of.
triste [trís·te] *adj.* sad; sorrowful; *Mex.* bashful, backward; *m. Ríopl.* melancholy love song.
tristeza [tris·té·sa] *f.* sadness; sorrow; *Arg.* tick fever.
tristón [tris·tón] *adj.* wistful, quite sad, melancholy.
triunfal [trjun·fál] *adj.* triumphal.
triunfante [trjun·fán·te] *adj.* triumphant.
triunfar [trjun·fár] *v.* to triumph; to trump (*at cards*).
triunfo [trjún·fo] *m.* triumph; trump card; trophy.
trivial [tri·bjál] *adj.* trivial, commonplace, trite.
triza [trí·sa] *f.* shred, fragment, small piece; cord, rope (*for sails*); **hacer -s** to tear into shreds; to tear to pieces.
trocar[2, 6] [tro·kár] *v. irr.* to change; to barter, exchange; to do one thing instead of another; **-se** to change; to be transformed; to exchange.
trocear [tro·se·ár] *v.* to divide into pieces.
troceadores [tro·se·a·dó·res] *m. pl.* choppers.
trocha [tró·ča] *f.* path, trail; *Ríopl.* gauge (*of a railway*); *Col.* trot; *Am.* slice or serving of meat.
trofeo [tro·fé·o] *m.* trophy; booty, spoils.
troj [tro], **troje** [tró·xe] *m.* barn, granary.
trole [tró·le] *m.* trolley.
trolebús [tro·le·bús] *m.* trolleybus.
tromba [tróm·ba] *f.* waterspout.
trombón [trom·bón] *m.* trombone.
trompa [tróm·pa] *f.* trumpet; trunk of an elephant; large spinning top; *Am.* snout; *Col.* cowcatcher (*of a locomotive*).
trompada [trom·pá·da] *f.* blow with the fist; bump.
trompeta [trom·pé·ta] *f.* trumpet; *m.* trumpeter; useless individual; *Andes* drunk, drunkard; *Andes* bold, shameless fellow.
trompetear [trom·pe·te·ár] *v.* to trumpet, blow the trumpet.
trompo [tróm·po] *m.* spinning top; stupid fellow, dunce.
tronada [tro·ná·da] *f.* thunderstorm.
tronar[2] [tro·nár] *v. irr.* to thunder; to explode, burst; *Mex., C.A.* to execute by shooting; — **los dedos** to snap one's fingers; **por lo que pueda** — just in case.
tronco [tróŋ·ko] *m.* tree trunk; log; stem; trunk (*of the human body*); team (*of horses*).
tronchar [tron·čár] *v.* to bend or break (*a stalk or trunk*); to chop off; to break off; **-se** to break off or get bent (*said of a stalk or trunk*); *Col.* to get twisted or bent.
tronera [tro·né·ra] *f.* opening; porthole (*through which to shoot*); small, narrow window; pocket of a billiard table; *m.* madcap, reckless fellow.
tronido [tro·ní·do] *m.* thunder; detonation; sharp, sudden sound.
trono [tró·no] *m.* throne.
tropa [tró·pa] *f.* troop; crowd; *Ríopl.* herd of cattle, drove of horses (*often* **tropilla**).
tropel [tro·pél] *m.* throng; bustle, rush; jumble, confusion.
tropezar[1, 9] [tro·pe·sár] *v. irr.* to stumble; to blunder; — **con** to meet, come across, encounter.
tropezón [tro·pe·són] *m.* stumbling; stumble; slip; **a -es** falteringly, stumbling along clumsily; **darse un** — to stumble, trip.
tropical [tro·pi·kál] *adj.* tropical.
trópico [tró·pi·ko] *m.* tropic.
tropiezo [tro·pjé·so] *m.* stumble; stumbling block; slip, fault; dispute.
tropilla [tro·pí·ya] *f.* small troop; *Ríopl.* drove of horses guided by the **madrina;** *Mex.* pack of dogs; *Am.* group of spare saddle horses.
tropillero [tro·pi·yé·ro] *m. Am.* horse wrangler, herdsman.
troquel [tro·kél] *m.* die (machine); **troqueladora** clicker; **troqueles roscados** pipe-threading dies.
trotar [tro·tár] *v.* to trot; to hurry.
trote [tró·te] *m.* trot; **al** — quickly.
trovador [tro·ba·dór] *m.* troubadour, minstrel.
troza [tró·sa] *f.* log.
trozar[9] [tro·sár] *v.* to cut off, break off (*a piece*); to break or cut into pieces.
trozo [tró·so] *m.* piece, bit, fragment; passage, selection.
truco [trú·ko] *m.* clever trick; pocketing of a ball (*in the game of pool*); *Am.* blow with the fist; *Andes, Ríopl.* a card game; **-s** game of pool (*game similar to billiards*); **-s devices.**
truculencia [tru·ku·lén·sja] *f.* cruelty, ferocity, ruthlessness.

truculento [tru·ku·lén·to] *adj.* cruel, fierce, ruthless.
trucha [trú·ča] *f.* trout; *C.A.* vendor's portable stand.
trueno [trwé·no] *m.* thunder; explosion, report of a gun; wild youth, troublemaker; *Col., Ven.* firecracker, rocket.
trueque [trwé·ke], **trueco** [trwé·ko] *m.* exchange; barter; *Col., Ven., Andes* change, small money; **a** (*or* **en**) — **de** in exchange for.
truhán [tru·án] *m.* scoundrel; swindler; cheat; buffoon, jester.
truncar[6] [truŋ·kár] *v. irr.* to truncate.
tu [tu] *adj.* thy; your (*fam. sing.*).
tú [tu] *pers. pron.* thou; you (*fam. sing.*).
tuba [tú·ƀa] *f.* tuba (*instrument*).
tubérculo [tu·ƀér·ku·lo] *m.* tuber.
tuberculosis [tu·ƀer·ku·ló·sis] *f.* tuberculosis; **tuberculoso** [tu·ƀer·ku·ló·so] *adj.* tuberculous, tubercular.
tubería [tu·ƀe·rí·a] *f.* tubing, piping; pipe line; — **principal** (water) main; — **vertical** riser; — **de fundición** cast iron pipe.
tubo [tú·ƀo] *m.* tube; pipe; lamp chimney; — **de ensayo** test tube; — **de escape** tail pipe; **-s de paso** yoke vents; — **en T** tee.
tuerca [twér·ka] *f.* nut (*of a screw*); **llave de -s** wrench.
tuerto [twér·to] *adj.* one-eyed; blind in one eye; *m.* wrong, injustice; **a — o a derecho** (*or* **a tuertas o a derechas**) rightly or wrongly; thoughtlessly.
tuétano [twé·ta·no] *m.* marrow; pith; innermost part; **mojado hasta los -s** soaked through and through.
tufo [tú·fo] *m.* vapor, fume; disagreeable odor; airs, conceit; **tufillo** [tu·fí·yo] *m.* whiff, pungent odor.
tul [tul] *m.* tulle (*a thin, fine net for veils*); **tul** [tul], **tule** [tú·le] *m. Mex.* a kind of reed or bulrush (*used in the manufacture of seats and backs of chairs*).
tulipán [tu·li·pán] *m.* tulip; *Mex.* hibiscus.
tullido [tu·yí·đo] *p.p.* crippled; paralyzed; numb.
tullirse[20] [tu·yír·se] *v. irr.* to become crippled; to become numb or paralyzed.
tumba [túm·ba] *f.* tomb; grave; *Col., Cuba, Mex.* felling of timber; *Ven.* forest clearing.
tumbar [tum·bár] *v.* to knock down; *Col., Mex., Cuba* to fell timber; **-se** to lie down.
tumbo [túm·bo] *m.* tumble; somersault; **dar -s** to jump, bump along.
tumor [tu·mór] *m.* tumor; **tumorcillo** [tu·mor·sí·yo] *m.* boil; small tumor.
tumulto [tu·múl·to] *m.* tumult, uproar; mob, throng.
tumultuoso [tu·mul·twó·so] *adj.* tumultuous.
tuna [tú·na] *f.* prickly pear; *Spain* singing group.
tunante [tu·nán·te] *m. & f.* rascal, rogue, scamp; loafer; *Andes, Ch., C.A.* libertine, licentious or lewd person.
tunco [túŋ·ko] *m. C.A.* pig.
tunda [tún·da] *f.* whipping, thrashing; shearing (*the nap of cloth*).
tundir [tun·dír] *v.* to lash, beat, whip; to shear (*the nap of cloth*).
túnel [tú·nel] *m.* tunnel.
túnica [tú·ni·ka] *f.* tunic; gown, robe.
tungsteno [tuns·té·no] *m.* tungsten; — **en atmósfera de gas inerte** tungsten in inert gas.
tupido [tu·pí·đo] *adj.* dense; compact, thick; blocked, obstructed; constipated.
tupir [tu·pír] *v.* to press, pack, squeeze together; to stop up, clog; **-se** to get stopped up; to stuff oneself; to become dense (*as a forest*); *Am.* to get astonished or confused.
turba [túr·ƀa] *f.* mob, throng.
turbación [tur·ƀa·sjón] *f.* disturbance, confusion; embarrassment.
turbamulta [tur·ƀa·múl·ta] *f.* throng, mob, crowd.
turbar [tur·ƀár] *v.* to perturb; to disturb; to trouble; **-se** to get disturbed, confused, embarrassed.
turbina [tur·ƀí·na] *f.* turbine.
turbio [túr·ƀjo] *adj.* muddy; muddled, confused.
turbión [tur·ƀjón] *m.* thunderstorm; heavy shower.
turbogenerador [tur·ƀo·xe·ne·ra·dór] *m.* turbogenerator.
turbopropulsor [tur·ƀo·pro·pul·sór] *m.* turboprop.
turborreactor [tur·ƀo·rre·ak·tór] *m.* turbojet.
turbulento [tur·ƀu·lén·to] *adj.* turbulent; restless; disorderly.
turco [túr·ko] *adj.* Turkish; *m.* Turk; Turkish, Turkish language; *Am.* peddler.
turismo [tu·ríz·mo] *m.* tourist travel; touring, sightseeing; **oficina de** — travel bureau; **turista** [tu·rís·ta] *m. & f.* tourist; **turístico** [tu·rís·ti·ko] *adj.* tourist; related to tourism.
turnar [tur·nár] *v.* to alternate; **-se** to alternate; to take turns.
turno [túr·no] *m.* turn, alternate order.
turquesa [tur·ké·sa] *f.* turquoise.
turrón [tu·rrón] *m.* nougat, nut confection; almond cake; *Mex.* **romper el** — to decide to use the **tú** form of address (*as a mark of close friendship*).
tusa [tú·sa] *f. Am.* corn, corncob; *Cuba, Mex.* corn husk; *Am.* corn silk, tassel of an ear of corn.
tusar [tu·sár] *v. Cuba, Mex., Ríopl., Andes* to shear; *Ríopl.* to crop, cut badly (*hair*).
tutear [tu·te·ár] *v.* to address familiarly (*using the* **tú** *form*).
tutela [tu·té·la] *f.* guardianship; guidance, protection.
tutelar [tu·te·lár] *v.* to guide, coach, direct; *adj.* guiding, guardian (*used as adj.*).
tutor [tu·tór] *m.* tutor; guardian.
tuyo [tú·yo] *poss. adj.* your, of yours (*fam. sing.*); *poss. pron.* yours.

U:u

u [u] *conj.* (*before words beginning with* **o** *or* **ho**) or.
ubicar[6] [u·ƀi·kár] *v.* to be located; **-se** *am.* to situate.
ubre [ú·ƀre] *f.* udder.
ufanarse [u·fa·nár·se] *v.* to glory (in); to be proud (of).
ufano [u·fá·no] *adj.* proud; gay; self-satisfied.
ujier [u·xjér] *m.* usher, doorman.
úlcera [úl·se·ra] *f.* ulcer; sore.
ulterior [ul·te·rjór] *adj.* ulterior; further; later.
ultimar [ul·ti·már] *v.* to put an end to; *Am.* to give the finishing blow, kill.
último [úl·ti·mo] *adj.* last, final; ultimate; latest; **estar en las últimas** to be on one's last legs; to be at the end of one's rope, be at the end of one's resources.
ultrajar [ul·tra·xár] *v.* to outrage, insult; to scorn.
ultraje [ul·trá·xe] *m.* outrage, insult.
ultramar [ul·tra·már] *m.* country or place across the sea; **de** — overseas, from across the sea; **en** (*or* **a**) — overseas.
ultramarinos [ul·tra·ma·rí·nos] *m. pl.* delicatessen; imported foods.
ultratumba [ul·tra·túm·ba] *adv.* beyond the grave.
ultravioleta [ul·tra·ƀjo·lé·ta] *adj.* ultraviolet.
ulular [u·lu·lár] *v.* to howl, shriek, hoot.
umbral [um·brál] *m.* threshold.
umbrío [um·brí·o] *adj.* shady.

un(o) [ú·no] *indef. art.* a, an; **-s** some, a few; **-s cuantos** a few; **uno** *pron. & num.* one.
unánime [u·ná·ni·me] *adj.* unanimous.
unanimidad [u·na·ni·mi·đáđ] *f.* unanimity, complete accord.
unción [un·sjón] *f.* unction (*anointing with oil*); religious fervor; spiritual grace; **Extremaunción** [es·tre·mawn·sjón] Extreme Unction (*the Last Sacrament of the Church*).
uncir[10] [un·sír] *v.* to yoke.
ungir[11] [uŋ·xír] *v.* to anoint; to consecrate.
ungüento [uŋ·gwén·to] *m.* ointment; salve.
único [ú·ni·ko] *adj.* only, sole; unique, singular, rare.
unicornio [u·ni·kór·njo] *m.* unicorn.
unidad [u·ni·đáđ] *f.* unity; unit; (*computadora*) unit, housing; — **de discos** disk drive; — **central de proceso** (UCP) control processing unit (CPU).
unificar[6] [u·ni·fi·kár] *v.* to unify; to unite.
uniformar [u·ni·for·már] *v.* to standardize; to make uniform; to furnish with uniforms.
uniforme [u·ni·fór·me] *adj. & m.* uniform.
uniformidad [u·ni·for·mi·đáđ] *f.* uniformity.
unilateral [u·ni·la·te·rál] *adj.* unilateral, one-sided.
unión [u·njón] *f.* union.
unir [u·nír] *v.* to unite; to join; to bring together; **-se** to unite, join together; to wed.
unísono [u·ní·so·no] *adj.* unison.
universal [u·ni·ƀer·sál] *adj.* universal.
universidad [u·ni·ƀer·si·đáđ] *f.* university.
universitario [u·ni·ƀer·si·tá·rjo] *adj.* pertaining to the university; *m. Am.* a university student.
universo [u·ni·ƀér·so] *m.* universe.
uno(a) [ú·no] *num.* one.
untar [un·tár] *v.* to anoint; to smear; to oil, grease; to bribe; to corrupt; **-se** to smear oneself; to get smeared.
unto [ún·to] *m.* grease, fat; ointment.
untuosidad [un·two·si·đáđ] *f.* greasiness; **untuoso** *adj.* unctuous; oily, greasy.
uña [ú·ña] *f.* fingernail; toenail; claw; hoof; hook (*on a tool*); **a — de caballo** at full gallop, at full speed; **largo de -s** prone to stealing; *Mex., C.A. Ven., Col., Andes* **largas -s** thief; **vivir de sus -s** to live by stealing; *Mex., C.A., Ven., Col., Andes* **echar la —** to steal; **ser — y carne** to be inseparable friends.
uñir [u·ñír] *v.* to yoke.
uranio [u·rá·njo] *m.* uranium.
urbanidad [ur·ƀa·ni·đáđ] *f.* courtesy, politeness; refinement.
urbanizar[9] [ur·ƀa·ni·sár] *v. irr.* to urbanize.
urbano [ur·ƀá·no] *adj.* urban; courteous, polite.
urbe [úr·ƀe] *f.* metropolis, large city.
urdimbre [ur·đím·bre] *f.* warp (*of a fabric*); scheme.
urdir [ur·đír] *v.* to warp (*in weaving*); to plot, scheme; to invent (*a lie, story, etc.*).
uremia [u·ré·mja] *f.* uremia.
uretra [u·ré·tra] *f.* urethra.
urgencia [ur·xén·sja] *f.* urgency; pressing need.
urgente [ur·xén·te] *adj.* urgent, pressing.
urgir[11] [ur·xír] *v.* to urge; to be urgent.
úrico [ú·ri·ko] *adj.* uric.
urna [úr·na] *f.* urn; — **electoral** ballot box.
urólogo [u·ró·lo·ǥo] *m.* urologist.
urraca [u·rrá·ka] *f.* magpie.
usado [u·sá·đo] *p.p. & adj.* used; accustomed; worn; threadbare.
usanza [u·sán·sa] *f.* usage, custom, habit.
usar [u·sár] *v.* to use; to wear; to wear out; to be accustomed; **-se** to be in use, be in vogue.
uso [ú·so] *m.* (*empleo*) use; usage; wear; (*costumbre*) usage; practice; habit; custom; **al — de la época** according to the custom or usage of the period; **estar en buen —** to be in good condition (*said of a thing*).
usted [us·té(đ)] *pers. pron.* (*abbreviated as* **Vd., V.,** *or* **Ud.**) you.
usual [u·swál] *adj.* usual; ordinary, customary.
usuario [u·swá·rjo] *m.* user.
usufructo [u·su·frúk·to] *m.* use, enjoyment; profit.
usufructuar[18] [u·su·fruk·twár] *v.* to enjoy the use of; to make use of.
usura [u·sú·ra] *f.* usury.
usurero [u·su·ré·ro] *m.* usurer, loan shark.
usurpar [u·sur·pár] *v.* to usurp.
utensilio [u·ten·sí·ljo] *m.* utensil; implement, tool.
útero [ú·te·ro] *m.* uterus, womb.
útil [ú·til] *adj.* useful; profitable; **-es** *m. pl.* tools, instruments.
utilidad [u·ti·li·đáđ] *f.* utility; profit; usefulness.
utilitario [u·ti·li·tá·rjo] *adj.* utilitarian.
utilizar[9] [u·ti·li·zár] *v.* to utilize; to use.
utopía [u·to·pí·a] *f.* utopia.
uva [ú·ƀa] *f.* grape; — **espina** gooseberry; — **pasa** raisin; **estar hecho una —** to be tipsy, drunk.
úvula [ú·ƀu·la] *f.* uvula.
uvular [u·ƀu·lár] *adj.* uvular.
¡uy! [uj] *interj.* ouch! oh!

V:v

vaca [bá·ka] *f.* cow; **carne de —** beef; **cuero de —** cowhide; *Am.* **hacer —** to play hooky, play truant, cut class; to join in a quick business deal.
vacación [ba·ka·sjón] *f.* vacation (*usually* **vacaciones**).
vacada [ba·ká·đa] *f.* herd of cows.
vacancia [ba·kán·sja] *f.* vacancy.
vacante [ba·kán·te] *adj.* vacant, unfilled, unoccupied; *f.* vacancy.
vaciar[17] [ba·sjár] (*dejar vacío*) to empty; to drain; to flow; (*amoldar*) to cast into a mold; (*ahuecar*) to hollow out; **-se** to spill; to empty; to become empty; to flow (into).
vaciedad [ba·sje·đáđ] *f.* emptiness; nonsense, silliness.
vacilación [ba·si·la·sjón] *f.* hesitation; wavering; doubt.
vacilante [ba·si·lán·te] *adj.* vacillating, hesitating, wavering; unsteady.
vacilar [ba·si·lár] *v.* to vacillate, waver, hesitate; to sway.
vacío [ba·sí·o] *adj.* empty; vacant; unoccupied; hollow; *m.* void; hollow; vacuum; vacancy; gap, blank.
vacuna [ba·kú·na] *f.* vaccine; vaccination; cowpox (*eruptive disease of the cow*); **vacunación** [ba·ku·na·sjón] *f.* vaccination; — **antipoliomelítica** antipolio inoculation.
vacunar [ba·ku·nár] *v.* to vaccinate.
vadear [ba·đe·ár] *v.* to ford; to wade; to avoid (*a difficulty*).
vado [bá·đo] *m.* ford; **no hallar —** to find no way out.
vagabundear [ba·ǥa·ƀun·de·ár] *v.* to tramp around, wander, rove; to loiter.
vagabundo [ba·ǥa·ƀún·do] *adj.* vagabond, wandering; *m.* vagabond, tramp; vagrant; wanderer.
vagar[7] [ba·ǥár] *v.* to wander, roam; to loiter; to loaf;

TR

m. leisure; loitering.
vagina [ba·xí·na] *f.* vagina.
vago [bá·go] *adj.* vague; roaming; idle; vagrant; *m.* vagrant, tramp.
vagón [ba·gón] *m.* railway car or coach; **vagoneta** [ba·go·né·ta] *f.* small railway car or tram (*used in mines*); **vagonada** [ba·go·ná·da] *f.* carload.
vaguear [ba·ge·ár] = **vagar.**
vahido [ba·í·do] *m.* dizziness, dizzy spell.
vaho [bá·o] *m.* vapor, steam, fume, mist; odor.
vaina [báj·na] *f.* sheath, scabbard; case; pod, husk; *Ven., Col., C.A., Mex.* bother, nuisance; *Ven., Col.* luck.
vainilla [baj·ní·ya] *f.* vanilla.
vaivén [baj·bén] *m.* sway; fluctuation, wavering; traffic, coming and going; **-es** comings and goings; ups and downs; inconstancy.
vajilla [ba·xí·ya] *f.* tableware; set of dishes; — **de plata** silverware; — **de porcelana** chinaware.
vale [bá·le] *m.* bond, promissory note; voucher; adieu, farewell; *m. & f. Col., Ven., Mex.* comrade, pal, chum.
valedero [ba·le·dé·ro] *adj.* valid, binding, effective.
valedor [ba·le·dór] *m.* defender, protector; *Am.* pal, comrade.
valenciano [ba·len·sjá·no] *adj.* Valencian, of or from Valencia, Spain; *m.* Valencian.
valentía [ba·len·tí·a] *f.* courage, valor; exploit; boast.
valentón [ba·len·tón] *adj.* blustering, boastful; *m.* bully, braggart.
valer[47] [ba·lér] *v. irr.* to favor, protect; to cost; to be worth; to be worthy; to be equivalent to; to be valid; to prevail; to be useful; *Spain* **¡vale!** O.K.; now you're talking; — **la pena** to be worth while; — **por** to be worth; **-se de** to avail oneself of, make use of; **más vale** it is better; **¡válgame Dios!** heaven help me! good heavens!
valeroso [ba·le·ró·so] *adj.* valiant, brave; valuable.
valía [ba·lí·a] *f.* worth, value; influence.
validez [ba·li·dés] *f.* validity; stability, soundness.
válido [bá·li·do] *adj.* valid.
valiente [ba·ljén·te] *adj.* valiant, brave; powerful; *m.* brave man; bully.
valija [ba·lí·xa] *f.* valise, satchel; mailbag.
valimiento [ba·li·mjén·to] *m.* favor, protection; **gozar de** — to enjoy protection or favor.
valioso [ba·ljó·so] *adj.* valuable; worthy; wealthy.
valor [ba·lór] *m.* value; worth; price; significance; valor, courage; boldness; efficacy, power; **-es** stocks, bonds.
valoración [ba·lo·ra·sjón] *f.* valuation, appraisal.
valorar [ba·lo·rár] *v.* to evaluate, value, appraise.
valorizar[9] [ba·lo·ri·sár] *v. Cuba, Ven., Ríopl., Andes* to value, appraise; *Am.* to realize, convert into money.
vals [bals] *m.* waltz.
valsar [bal·sár] *v.* to waltz.
valuación [ba·lwa·sjón] *f.* valuation, appraisal.
valuar[18] [ba·lwár] *v.* to value, price, appraise; to rate.
válvula [bál·bu·la] *f.* valve; — **de retención** check valve.
valla [bá·ya] *f.* stockade, fence; barrier; obstacle; *Cuba, Col.* cockpit (*for cockfights*).
vallado [ba·yá·do] *m.* stockade, fenced-in place; fence.
valle [bá·ye] *m.* valley; vale.
vampiro [bam·pí·ro] *m.* vampire.
vanadio [ba·ná·djo] *m.* vanadium.
vanagloria [ba·na·gló·rja] *f.* vainglory, boastful vanity.
vanagloriarse[17] [ba·na·glo·rjár·se] *v.* to glory, take great pride (in), boast (of).
vanaglorioso [ba·na·glo·rjó·so] *adj.* vain, boastful, conceited.
vándalo [bán·da·lo] *m.* vandal.
vanguardia [baŋ·gwár·dja] *f.* vanguard.
vanidad [ba·ni·dád] *f.* vanity; conceit; emptiness.
vanidoso [ba·ni·dó·so] *adj.* vain, conceited.
vano [bá·no] *adj.* vain; empty; hollow; *m.* opening in a wall (*for a door or window*).
vapor [ba·pór] *m.* vapor, steam, mist; steamer, steamship.
vaporoso [ba·po·ró·so] *adj.* vaporous, steamy, misty; vaporlike.
vapulear [ba·pu·le·ár] *v.* to beat, whip, thrash.
vapuleo [ba·pu·lé·o] *m.* beating, whipping, thrashing.
vaquería [ba·ke·rí·a] *f.* herd of cows; stable for cows; dairy.
vaquerizo [ba·ke·rí·so] *m.* herdsman; *adj.* pertaining to cows; **vaqueriza** [ba·ke·rí·sa] *f.* stable for cows.
vaquero [ba·ké·ro] *m.* cowherd, herdsman; cowboy; *Cuba* milkman; *adj.* relating to cowherds, cowboys, or cattle.
vaqueta [ba·ké·ta] *f.* sole leather; cowhide; *Mex.* **zurrar a uno la** — to tan someone's hide, beat someone up.
vara [bá·ra] *f.* twig; stick; rod; wand; staff; yard, yardstick; thrust with a picador's lance.
varadero [ba·ra·dé·ro] *m.* shipyard.
varar [ba·rár] *v.* to beach (*a boat*), run aground; to stop, come to a standstill (*said of business*).
varear [ba·re·ár] *v.* to beat; to whip; to sell by the yard; to measure with a **vara;** *Ríopl.* to exercise (*a horse before a race*).
variable [ba·rjá·ble] *adj.* variable, unstable, changeable; *f.* variable.
variación [ba·rja·sjón] *f.* variation.
variado [ba·rjá·do] *p.p. & adj.* varied; variegated.
variar[17] [ba·rjár] *v.* to vary; to change; to shift; to differ.
várices [bá·ri·ses] *f. pl.* varicose veins.
variedad [ba·rje·dád] *f.* variety; variation, change.
varilla [ba·rí·ya] *f.* small rod; wand; long, flexible twig; rib (*of an umbrella or fan*); corset stay; — **de aporte** filler rod. *Mex.* peddler's wares.
varillero [ba·ri·yé·ro] *m. Mex.* peddler.
vario [bá·rjo] *adj.* various; different; changeable; varied; **-s** various, several.
varón [ba·rón] *m.* male, man; *Am.* long beam, timber.
varonil [ba·ro·níl] *adj.* manly; strong; brave.
vasallo [ba·sá·yo] *adj. & m.* vassal, subject.
vasco [bás·ko], **vascongado** [bas·koŋ·gá·do] *adj. & m.* Basque.
vascuence [bas·kwén·se] *m.* the Basque language.
vasectomía [ba·sek·to·mí·a] *f.* vasectomy.
vaselina [ba·se·lí·na] *f.* vaseline.
vasija [ba·sí·xa] *f.* vessel, container, receptacle.
vaso [bá·so] *m.* drinking glass; glassful; vase; vessel; hull of a ship; horse's hoof; — **de elección** person chosen by God.
vástago [bás·ta·go] *m.* (*de planta*) shoot, sprout; stem; (*persona*) scion, offspring; *Mex., Col., Ven.* stem, trunk of a banana tree.
vasto [bás·to] *adj.* vast, extensive, large.
vate [bá·te] *m.* bard, poet.
vaticinar [ba·ti·si·nár] *v.* to prophesy, predict, foretell.
vaticinio [ba·ti·sí·njo] *m.* prophecy, prediction.
vecindad [be·sin·dád] *f.* vicinity; neighborhood; neighborliness; **casa de** — tenement.
vecindario [be·sin·dá·rjo] *m.* neighborhood;

neighbors; vicinity.
vecino [be·sí·no] *m.* neighbor; resident; citizen; *adj.* neighboring; next, near.
vedar [be·đár] *v.* to prohibit; to impede.
vega [bé·ga] *f.* fertile lowland or plain; *Cuba, Ven.* tobacco plantation.
vegetación [be·xe·ta·sjón] *f.* vegetation.
vegetal [be·xe·tál] *adj.* vegetable; *m.* vegetable, plant.
vegetar [be·xe·tár] *v.* to vegetate.
vegetariano [be·xe·ta·rjá·no] *m.* vegetarian.
vehemente [be·e·mén·te] *adj.* vehement, passionate, impetuous; violet.
vehículo [be·í·ku·lo] *m.* vehicle.
veinte [béjn·te] *num.* twenty.
veintena [bejn·té·na] *f.* score, twenty.
veintiuno [bejn·tjú·no] *num.* twenty-one.
vejamen [be·xá·men] annoyance, vexation.
vejar [be·xár] *v.* to annoy; to criticize.
vejestorio [be·xes·tó·rjo] *m.* wrinkled old person.
vejete [be·xé·te] *m.* little old man.
vejez [be·xés] *f.* old age.
vejiga [be·xí·ga] *f.* bladder; blister; smallpox sore; — **de la bilis** (*or* — **de la hiel**) gall bladder.
vela [bé·la] *f.* vigil, watch; night watch; candle; sail; **a toda** — under full sail; at full speed; **en** — on watch, without sleep; **hacerse a la** — to set sail.
velada [be·lá·đa] *f.* watch, vigil; evening party; evening function or meeting.
velador [be·la·đór] *m.* night watchman; keeper, guard; lamp table; bedside table; candlestick; *Ríopl., Mex., Cuba, Col.* lamp shade.
velar [be·lár] *v.* to keep vigil; to stay up at night; to be vigilant; to watch over; to veil; to cover, hide.
velatorio [be·la·tó·rjo] *m.* wake (*vigil over a corpse*). *See* **velorio.**
veleidoso [be·lej·đó·so] *adj.* inconstant, fickle, changeable.
velero [be·lé·ro] *m.* sailboat; sailmaker; candlemaker; *adj.* swift-sailing; **buque** — sailboat.
veleta [be·lé·ta] *f.* weathervane, weathercock; *m. & f.* fickle person.
velís [be·lís] *m. Mex.* valise.
velo [bé·lo] *m.* veil; curtain, covering; — **del paladar** velum, soft palate.
velocidad [be·lo·si·đáđ] *f.* velocity.
velocímetro [be·lo·sí·me·tro] *m.* speedometer.
velorio [be·ló·rjo] *m. Am.* wake (*vigil over a corpse*); *Mex., C.A., Ven., Col., Ch., Andes* dull party.
veloz [be·lós] *adj.* swift, quick, fast.
vello [bé·yo] *m.* hair (*on the body*); down, fuzz; nap (*of cloth*).
vellón [be·yón] *m.* fleece; tuft of wool; sheepskin with fleece; silver and copper alloy; an ancient copper coin.
velloso [be·yó·so] *adj.* hairy; downy, fuzzy.
velludo [be·yú·đo] *adj.* hairy; downy; fuzzy; *m.* plush, velvet.
vena [bé·na] *f.* vein; lode, vein of metal ore; mood, disposition; **estar en** — to be in the mood; to be inspired.
venado [be·ná·đo] *m.* deer; venison, deer meat; *Mex.* **pintar** — to play hooky.
vencedor [ben·se·đór] *adj.* conquering, winning, victorious; *m.* conqueror, winner, victor.
vencer[10] [ben·sér] *v.* to conquer; vanquish; to defeat; to overcome; to surpass; to win; **-se** to control oneself; to mature, fall due; **se venció el plazo** the time limit expired.
vencido [ben·sí·đo] *p.p. & adj.* conquered; defeated; due, fallen due.
vencimiento [ben·si·mjén·to] *m.* conquering, defeat; maturity (*of a debt*), falling due; expiration (*of a period of time*).
venda [bén·da] *f.* bandage.
vendaje [ben·dá·xe] *m.* bandage.
vendar [ben·dár] *v.* to bandage; to blindfold.
vendaval [ben·da·bál] *m.* strong wind, gale.
vendedor [ben·de·đór] *m.* vendor, seller, peddler.
vender [ben·dér] *v.* to sell; to betray; **-se** to be sold; **se vende** for sale; to sell oneself; accept a bribe.
vendimia [ben·dí·mja] *f.* vintage; profit.
venduta [ben·dú·ta] *f. Col.* auction; *Cuba* small fruit and vegetable store.
veneno [be·né·no] *m.* venom, poison.
venenoso [be·ne·nó·so] *adj.* poisonous.
venerable [be·ne·rá·ble] *adj.* venerable.
veneración [be·ne·ra·sjón] *f.* veneration, reverence.
venerando [be·ne·rán·do] *adj.* venerable, worthy of respect.
venerar [be·ne·rár] *v.* to venerate, revere; to worship.
venéreo [be·né·re·o] *adj.* venereal.
venero [be·né·ro] *m.* water spring; source, origin; lode, layer, seam (*of mineral*).
venezolano [be·ne·so·lá·no] *adj.* Venezuelan; *m.* Venezuelan; *Ven.* Venezuelan silver coin.
vengador [beŋ·ga·đór] *adj.* avenging, revenging; *m.* avenger.
venganza [beŋ·gán·sa] *f.* vengeance, revenge.
vengar[7] [beŋ·gár] to avenge, revenge; **-se de** to take revenge on.
vengativo [beŋ·ga·tí·bo] *adj.* vindictive, revengeful.
venia [bé·nja] *f.* pardon; permission, leave; bow, nod; *C.A., Ven., Ríopl.* military salute.
venida [be·ní·đa] *f.* arrival; return; river flood, onrush of water; attack (*in fencing*).
venidero [be·ni·đé·ro] *adj.* coming, future; **en lo** — in the future; **-s** *m. pl.* successors.
venir[48] [be·nír] *v. irr.* to come; to arrive; to fit; **-le a uno bien** (*or* **mal**) to be becoming (*or* unbecoming); — **a menos** to decline, decay; — **a pelo** to come just at the right moment; to suit perfectly; to be pat, opportune, to the point; — **en** to agree to; — **sobre** to fall upon; **¿a qué viene eso?** what is the point of that? **-se abajo** to fall down; to collapse; to fail.
venoso [be·nó·so] *adj.* veined; venous (*of or pertaining to the veins; with veins*).
venta [bén·ta] *f.* sale; roadside inn; *Ur.* store, vendor's stand; — **pública** auction.
ventaja [ben·tá·xa] *f.* advantage; gain, profit; bonus; odds.
ventajoso [ben·ta·xó·so] *adj.* advantageous, beneficial, profitable; *Mex.* self-seeking, profiteering.
ventana [ben·tá·na] *f.* window; window shutter; *Col.* clearing (*in a forest*); — (*or* **ventanilla** [ben·ta·ní·ya]) **de la nariz** nostril.
ventarrón [ben·ta·rrón] *m.* gale, strong wind.
ventear [ben·te·ár] *v.* (*oler*) to scent, sniff; (*soplar*) to blow, be windy; (*poner al aire*) to air; (*indagar*) to nose around; *Ven.* to toss in the wind; *Arg.* to flee; *Am.* to outrun; **-se** to expel air, break wind; *Col.* to stay outdoors.
ventero [ben·té·ro] *m.* innkeeper.
ventilación [ben·ti·la·sjón] *f.* ventilation.
ventilador [ben·ti·la·đór] *m.* ventilator; fan (*for ventilation*); — **de taller** blower.
ventilar [ben·ti·lár] *v.* to ventilate; to air.
ventisca [ben·tís·ka] *f.* blizzard, snowstorm; snowdrift.
ventiscar[6] [ben·tis·kár] *v.* to snow hard and blow (*as in a blizzard*); to drift (*as snow in a blizzard*).

ventisquero [ben·tis·ké·ro] *m.* blizzard, snowstorm; glacier; snowdrift; snow-capped mountain peak.
ventolera [ben·to·lé·ra] *f.* gust of wind; pride, vanity; whim; pin wheel; **darle a uno la — de** to take the notion to.
ventoso [ben·tó·so] *adj.* windy.
ventura [ben·tú·ra] *f.* happiness; fortune, chance; risk, danger; **a la —** at random; **buena —** fortune; **por —** perchance.
venturoso [ben·tu·ró·so] *adj.* fortunate, lucky; happy.
ver[49] [ver] *v. irr.* to see; to look; to look at; to look into, examine; **— de** to try to, see to it that; **a más** (*or* **hasta más —** good-bye; **no — la hora de** to be anxious to; **no tener nada que — con** not to have anything to do with; **-se** to be seen; to be; **-se obligado a** to be obliged to, be forced to; **a mi modo de —** in my opinion; **de buen —** good-looking; **ser de —** to be worth seeing.
vera [bé·ra] *f.* edge; **a la — del camino** at the edge of the road.
veracidad [ve·ra·si·đáđ] *f.* truthfulness.
veraneante [be·ra·ne·án·te] *m. & f.* summer resorter, vacationist, or tourist.
veranear [be·ra·ne·ár] *v.* to spend the summer.
veraneo [be·ra·né·o] *m.* summering, summer vacation.
veraniego [be·ra·njé·ǥo] *adj.* summer, of summer.
verano [be·rá·no] *m.* summer.
veras [bé·ras] *f. pl.* reality, truth; **de —** in truth; truly; in earnest.
veraz [be·rás] *adj.* truthful.
verbal [ber·ƀál] *adj.* verbal; oral.
verbena [ber·ƀé·na] *f.* verbena (*a plant*); festival or carnival (*on eve of a religious holiday*).
verbigracia [ber·ƀi·ǥrá·sja] *adv.* for instance, for example.
verbo [bér·ƀo] *m.* verb; **el Verbo** the Word (*second person of the Trinity*).
verboso [ber·ƀó·so] *adj.* verbose, wordy.
verdad [ber·đáđ] *f.* truth; **¿—?** really?; is that so?; isn't that so?; **— de Perogrullo** truism, evident truth; **de —** (*or* **a la —**) in truth, in earnest; **en —** really, truly.
verdadero [ber·đa·đé·ro] *adj.* real; true; truthful; sincere; **verdadero/falso** true/false.
verde [bér·đe] *adj.* green; unripe; young; offcolor, indecent; *m.* green; verdure; *Ur., Ven.* country, countryside.
verdear [ber·đe·ár] *v.* to grow green; to look green.
verdinegro [ber·đi·né·ǥro] *adj.* dark-green.
verdor [ber·đór] *m.* verdure, greenness.
verdoso [ber·đó·so] *adj.* greenish.
verdugo [ber·đú·ǥo] *m.* executioner; cruel person; torment; rapier (*light sword*); lash, whip; welt; shoot of a tree; **verdugón** [ber·đu·ǥón] *m.* large welt.
verdulera [ber·đu·lé·ra] *f.* woman vendor of green vegetables; **verdulería** [ber·đu·le·rí·a] *f.* green vegetable store or stand.
verdura [ber·đú·ra] *f.* verdure; greenness; green vegetables.
vereda [be·ré·đa] *f.* path; *Ch., Ríopl., Andes* sidewalk; *Col.* small village; *C.R.* bank of a stream.
veredicto [be·re·đík·to] *m.* verdict.
vergonzoso [ber·ǥon·só·so] *adj.* shameful, disgraceful; shy, bashful; *m.* species of armadillo.
vergüenza [ber·ǥwén·sa] *f.* shame; disgrace; shyness, bashfulness; **tener —** to have shame; to be ashamed.
vericueto [be·ri·kwé·to] *m.* rugged, wild place (*often rocky*).
verídico [be·rí·đi·ko] *adj.* truthful; true.
verificar[6] [be·ri·fi·kár] *v.* to verify; to confirm; to test, check; to carry out, fulfill; **-se** to be verified; to take place; **verificador** checking device.
verijas [be·rí·xas] *f. pl. Ríopl., Mex.* groin (*hollow between lower part of abdomen and thigh*); *Am.* flanks of a horse.
verja [bér·xa] *f.* grate, grating.
verónica [be·ró·ni·ka] *f.* veronica; a bullfighting pass executed with the cape held behind the body with both hands.
verruga [be·rrú·ǥa] *f.* wart; nuisance.
versado [ber·sá·đo] *adj.* versed, skilled, expert.
versar [ber·sár] *v.* to deal (with), treat (of); **-se en** to become versed in.
versátil [ber·sá·til] *adj.* versatile.
versificar[6] [ber·si·fi·kár] *v. irr.* to versify.
versión [ber·sjón] *f.* version; translation.
verso [bér·so] *m.* verse; meter; **— suelto** (*or* **— libre**) free or blank verse.
vertebrado [ber·te·ƀrá·đo] *adj. & m.* vertebrate.
verter[1] [ber·tér] *v. irr.* to pour; to empty; to spill; to translate; to flow down.
vertical [ber·ti·kál] *adj.* vertical.
vértice [bér·ti·se] *m.* top, apex, summit.
vertiente [ber·tjén·te] *f.* slope; watershed; *adj.* flowing.
vertiginoso [ber·ti·xi·nó·so] *adj.* whirling, dizzy, giddy.
vértigo [bér·ti·ǥo] *m.* dizziness, giddiness; fit of madness.
vesícula [be·sí·ku·la] *f.* gall bladder.
vestíbulo [bes·tí·ƀu·lo] *m.* vestibule; lobby.
vestido [bes·tí·đo] *m.* clothing, apparel; dress; garment; suit.
vestidura [bes·ti·đú·ra] *f.* vestment; attire, apparel; raiment.
vestigio [bes·tí·xjo] *m.* vestige, sign, trace.
vestir[5] [bes·tír] *v. irr.* (*cubrir*) to dress; to clothe; to put on; to adorn; to cover; (*llevar*) to wear; **-se** to dress, get dressed; to be clothed; to be covered.
vestuario [bes·twá·rjo] *m.* wardrobe, apparel; theatrical costumes; cloakroom; dressing room; vestry (*room for church vestments*).
veta [bé·ta] *f.* vein, seam (*of mineral*); streak, grain (*in wood*); stripe; *Cuba* rope.
vetar [be·tár] *v.* to veto.
veteado [be·te·á·đo] *adj.* veined; striped; streaked.
veterano [be·te·rá·no] *adj. & m.* veteran.
veterinario [be·te·ri·ná·rjo] *m.* veterinary.
veto [bé·to] *m.* veto.
vetusto [be·tús·to] *adj.* old, ancient.
vez [bes] *f.* time, occasion; turn; **a la —** at the same time; **cada — más** more and more; **cada — que** whenever; **de — en cuando** from time to time; **de una —** all at once; **en — de** instead of; **otra —** again; **una que otra —** rarely, once in a while; **tal —** perhaps; **a veces** sometimes; **raras veces** seldom; **hacer las veces de** to take the place of.
vía [bí·a] *f.* way; road; track; railroad track; conduit; **Vía Crucis** the Way of the Cross; **Vía Láctea** the Milky Way.
viaducto [bja·đúk·to] *m.* viaduct.
viajante [bja·xán·te] *m.* traveler; **— de comercio** traveling salesman.
viajar [bja·xár] *v.* to travel.
viaje [bjá·xe] *m.* voyage; trip; travel; **— de ida y vuelta** (*or* **— redondo**) round trip.
viajero [bja·xé·ro] *m.* traveler; *adj.* traveling.
vianda [bján·da] *f.* viands, food; meal.

viandante [bjan·dán·te] *m. & f.* wayfarer, walker, pedestrian; passer by; vagabond.
viático [bjá·ti·ko] *m.* provisions for a journey; viaticum (*communion given to dying persons*).
víbora [bí·ƀo·ra] *f.* viper.
vibración [bi·ƀra·sjón] *f.* vibration.
vibrante [bi·ƀrán·te] *adj.* vibrant, vibrating.
vibrar [bi·ƀrár] *v.* to vibrate.
vicecónsul [bi·se·kón·sul] *m.* vice consul.
vicepresidente [bi·se·pre·si·đén·te] *m.* vice-president.
viceversa [bi·se·ƀér·sa] *adv.* vice versa, conversely.
viciado [bi·sjá·đo] *adj.* contaminated, foul; corrupt; *p.p. of* **viciar.**
viciar [bi·sjár] *v.* to vitiate, corrupt; to adulterate; to falsify; **-se** to become corrupt.
vicio [bí·sjo] *m.* vice; bad habit; fault; craving; **de** — as a habit; **hablar de** — to talk too much; **-s** *Am.* articles and ingredients used for serving **mate.**
vicioso [bi·sjó·so] *adj.* vicious, evil, wicked; having bad habits; licentious; faulty, incorrect (*grammatical construction, reasoning, etc.*).
vicisitud [bi·si·si·túđ] *f.* vicissitude; **-es** vicissitudes, ups and downs, changes of fortune or condition.
víctima [bík·ti·ma] *f.* victim.
victoria [bik·tó·rja] *f.* victory, triumph; victoria (*carriage*).
victorioso [bik·to·rjó·so] *adj.* victorious.
vicuña [bi·kú·ña] *f.* vicuña (*an Andean animal allied to the alpaca and llama*); vicuña wool; vicuña cloth.
vid [biđ] *f.* vine, grapevine.
vida [bí·đa] *f.* life; living; livelihood; — **mía** dearest; **hacer** — to live together; **pasar a mejor** — to die; **tener la** — **en un hilo** to be in great danger.
vidalita [bi·đa·lí·ta] *f. Ríopl., Ch.* melancholy song of Argentina and Chile.
vidente [bi·đén·te] *m.* seer, prophet; *adj.* seeing.
video [bi·đé·o] *m.* video; **video inverso** inverse video.
vidriado [bi·đrjá·đo] *m.* glaze; glazed earthenware; *p.p. & adj.* glazed.
vidriar[17] [bi·đrjár] *v.* to glaze (*earthenware*).
vidriera [bi·đrjé·ra] *f.* glass window; glass door; *Am.* show case, show window; — **de colores** stained-glass window.
vidriero [bi·đrjé·ro] *m.* glazier (*one who installs windowpanes*); glass blower; glass maker; glass dealer.
vidrio [bí·đrjo] *m.* glass; any glass article.
vidrioso [bi·đrjó·so] *adj.* glassy; brittle; slippery, icy; touchy; irritable.
viejo [bjé·xo] *adj.* old; ancient; worn-out; *m.* old man; — **verde** old man who boasts of his youth and vigor; "dirty" old man; *Am.* **los -s** the old folks (*applied to one's parents*); **viejota** *f.* old hag.
viento [bjén·to] *m.* wind; scent; **hace** — it is windy; **a los cuatro -s** in all directions; **vientecito** *m.* gentle breeze.
vientre [bjén·tre] *m.* abdomen; belly; bowels; entrails; womb.
viernes [bjér·nes] *m.* Friday.
vierteaguas [bjer·te·a·ǥwas] *m.* flashing (roof).
viga [bí·ǥa] *f.* beam, rafter; — **central** collar beam.
vigencia [bi·xén·sja] *f.* operation (*of a law*); **entrar en** — to take effect (*said of a law*); **estar en** — to be in force (*said of a law*).
vigente [bi·xén·te] *adj.* effective, in force (*as a law*).
vigía [bi·xí·a] *f.* lookout, watchtower; watch (*act of watching*); reef; *m.* lookout, watchman.
vigilancia [bi·xi·lán·sja] *f.* vigilance.
vigilante [bi·xi·lán·te] *adj.* vigilant, watchful; *m.* watchman.
vigilar [bi·xi·lár] *v.* to keep guard; to watch over.
vigilia [bi·xí·lja] *f.* vigil, watch; wakefulness, sleeplessness; night hours (*spent in study*); eve before certain church festivals; vesper service; **día de** — day of abstinence; **comer de** — to abstain from meat.
vigor [bi·ǥór] *m.* vigor; **en** — in force (*said of a law*); **entrar en** — to become effective (*as a law, statute, etc.*).
vigorizar[9] [bi·ǥo·ri·sár] *v.* to invigorate, tone up, give vigor to, strengthen.
vigoroso [bi·ǥo·ró·so] *adj.* vigorous.
viguería [bi·ǥe·rí·a] *f.* beams.
vihuela [bi·wé·la] *f.* guitar.
vil [bil] *adj.* vile, base, low, mean.
vileza [bi·lé·sa] *f.* villainy; baseness; vile act.
vilipendiar [bi·li·pen·djár] *v.* to revile.
vilo [bí·lo]: **en** — in the air; suspended; undecided; in suspense; **llevar en** — to waft.
villa [bí·ya] *f.* village; villa, country house.
villancico [bi·yan·sí·ko] *n.* carol; Christmas carol.
villanía [bi·ya·ní·a] *f.* villainy; lowliness.
villano [bi·yá·no] *adj.* rustic; uncouth; villainous, mean, base; *m.* villain; rustic, peasant.
villorrio [bi·yó·rrjo] *m.* small village, hamlet.
vinagre [bi·ná·ǥre] *m.* vinegar; **vinagrera** [bi·na·ǥré·ra] *f.* vinegar cruet.
vincular [biŋ·ku·lár] *v.* to tie, bond, unite; to entail (*limit the inheritance of property*); to found, base (on).
vínculo [bíŋ·ku·lo] *m.* bond, tie, chain; entailed inheritance.
vindicar[6] [bin·di·kár] *v.* to vindicate; to avenge; to defend, assert (*one's rights*); **-se** to avenge oneself; to defend oneself.
vino [bí·no] *m.* wine; — **amontillado** good grade of pale sherry (*originally from Montilla*); — **tinto** dark-red wine; **vinería** [bi·ne·rí·a] *f. Ríopl., Andes* wineshop; **vinero** [bi·né·ro] *adj. Am.* pertaining to wine; **vinoso** [bi·nó·so] *adj.* winy.
viña [bí·ña] *f.* vineyard.
viñedo [bi·ñé·đo] *m.* vineyard.
viola [bjó·la] *f.* viola.
violación [bjo·la·sjón] *f.* violation.
violado [bjo·lá·đo] *adj.* violet; *m.* violet, violet color; *p.p.* violated.
violar [bjo·lár] *v.* to violate; to rape.
violencia [bjo·lén·sja] *f.* violence.
violentar [bjo·len·tár] *v.* to force; to break into (*a house*); **-se** to force oneself; to get angry.
violento [bjo·lén·to] *adj.* violent; impetuous; forced; strained; unnatural.
violeta [bjo·lé·ta] *f.* violet.
violín [bjo·lín] *m.* violin; *m. & f.* violinist; *Ven.* **estar hecho un** — to be very thin.
violinista [bjo·li·nís·ta] *m. & f.* violinist.
violonchelo [bjo·lon·čé·lo] *m.* violincello, cello.
virada [bi·rá·đa] *f.* tack, change of direction, turn.
viraje [bi·rá·xe] *m.* change of direction; turn.
virar [bi·rár] *v.* to turn, turn around, change direction; to tack (*said of a ship*).
virgen [bír·xen] *adj. & f.* virgin.
virginal [bir·xi·nál] *adj.* virginal, virgin, pure.
viril [bi·ríl] *adj.* virile, manly.
virilidad [bi·ri·li·đáđ] *f.* virility, manhood, manly strength, vigor.
virreinal [bi·rrej·nál] *adj.* viceregal.
virreinato [bi·rrej·ná·to] *m.* viceroyalty (*office or jurisdiction of a viceroy*).
virrey [bi·rréj] *m.* viceroy.
virtud [bir·túđ] *f.* virtue.

virtuoso [bir·twó·so] *adj.* virtuous; *m.* virtuoso (*person skilled in an art*).
viruela [bir·wé·la] *f.* smallpox; pock (*mark left by smallpox*); **-s locas** (*or* **-s bastardas**) chicken pox.
viruta [bi·rú·ta] *f.* wood shaving.
visado [bi·sá·đo] *m.* visa.
visaje [bi·sá·xe] *m.* grimace; wry face; **hacer -s** to make faces.
visar [bi·sár] *v.* to visé; to approve; to O.K.
viscoso [bis·kó·so] *adj.* slimy, sticky; **viscosidad** viscosity; **viscosímetro** viscometer.
visera [bi·sé·ra] *f.* visor; eye shade; *Cuba, Mex.* blinder (*on a horse's bridle*).
visible [bi·sí·ƀle] *adj.* visible; evident; conspicuous, notable.
visigodo [bi·si·ǥó·đo] *adj.* visigothic; *m.* visigoth.
visillo [bi·sí·yo] *m.* window curtain.
visión [bi·sjón] *f.* vision; sight; fantasy; apparition; sight (*ridiculous-looking person or thing*).
visionario [bi·sjo·ná·rjo] *adj. & m.* visionary.
visita [bi·sí·ta] *f.* visit, call; visitor; callers, company; — **de confianza** informal call; — **de cumplimiento** (*or* — **de cumplido**) formal courtesy call; — **domiciliaria** police inspection of a house; home call (*of a social worker, doctor, etc.*).
visitación [bi·si·ta·sjón] *f.* visitation, visit.
visitador [bi·si·ta·đór] *m.* visitor, caller; inspector.
visitante [bi·si·tán·te] *m. & f.* caller, visitor; *adj.* visiting.
visitar [bi·si·tár] *v.* to visit; in inspect.
vislumbrar [biz·lum·brár] *v.* to catch a glimpse of; to guess, surmise; **-se** to be faintly visible.
vislumbre [biz·lúm·bre] *f.* glimmer; glimpse; vague idea; faint appearance.
viso [bí·so] *m.* appearance; semblance; pretense, pretext; luster, brilliance, glitter; glass curtain; **a dos -s** with a double view; with a double purpose.
visón [bi·són] *m.* mink.
víspera [bís·pe·ra] *f.* eve, evening or day before; time just before; **-s** vespers; **en -s de** on the eve of; about to.
vista [bís·ta] *f.* (*panorama*) view; landscape; sight; (*sentido*) sight; vision; (*acción*) look, glance; **a — de** in the presence of; in front of, within view of; **pagadero a la** — payable at sight or upon presentation; **¡hasta la —!** good-bye!; **bajar la** — to lower one's eyes; **conocer de** — to know by sight; **hacer la — gorda** to pretend not to see; **pasar la — por** to glance over; **perder de** — to lose sight of; **tener a la** — to have before one; to have received (*a letter*).
vistazo [bis·tá·so] *m.* glance; **dar un — a** to glance over.
visto [bís·to] *p.p. of* **ver** seen; *adj.* evident, clear; **bien** — well thought of, proper; **mal** — looked down upon, improper; — **bueno** (V°.B°.) approved (O.K.); **dar el — bueno** to approve, O.K.; — **que** whereas, considering that.
vistoso [bis·tó·so] *adj.* showy; colorful.
visualizar [bi·swa·li·sár] *v.* (*computadora*) to display; **visualización** *f.* display.
vital [bi·tál] *adj.* vital; important. necessary.
vitalicio [bi·ta·lí·sjo] *adj.* for life; *m.* life-insurance policy; lifetime pension.
vitalidad [bi·ta·li·đáđ] *f.* vitality.
vitamina [bi·ta·mí·na] *f.* vitamin.
vitaminado [bi·ta·mi·ná·đo] *adj.* containing vitamins.
vítor [bí·tor] *m.* cheer, applause; **¡ — !** hurrah!
vitorear [bi·to·re·ár] *v.* to cheer, applaud.
vitrina [bi·trí·na] *f.* glass case; show case; show window.
vituallas [bi·twá·yas] *f. pl.* victuals, food, provisions.
vituperar [bi·tu·pe·rár] *v.* to revile, insult, call bad names.
vituperio [bi·tu·pé·rjo] *m.* affront, insult; reproach; censure.
viuda [bjú·đa] *f.* widow.
viudez [bju·đés] *f.* widowhood.
viudo [bjú·đo] *m.* widower.
¡viva! [bí·ƀa] *interj.* hurrah for; long live!
vivac [bi·ƀák], **vivaque** [bi·ƀá·ke] *m.* bivouac, military encampment; *Am.* police headquarters.
vivacidad [bi·ƀa·si·đáđ] *f.* vivacity; brightness; liveliness.
vivaracho [bi·ƀa·rá·čo] *adj.* lively; vivacious, gay.
vivaz [bi·ƀás] *adj.* vivacious, lively; bright, keen, witty.
víveres [bí·ƀe·res] *m. pl.* food supplies, provisions.
vivero [bi·ƀé·ro] *m.* fish pond, fish hatchery, tree nursery.
viveza [bi·ƀé·sa] *f.* vivacity; animation, liveliness; quickness; brilliance, cleverness.
vívido [bí·ƀi·đo] *adj.* vivid; colorful.
vivienda [bi·ƀjén·da] *f.* dwelling; apartment.
viviente [bi·ƀjén·te] *adj.* living.
vivir [bi·ƀír] *v.* to live; to endure, last; **¡viva!** hurrah! long live!; **¿quién vive?** who goes there?; *m.* existence, living.
vivisección [bi·ƀi·sek·sjón] *f.* vivisection.
vivo [bí·ƀo] *adj.* (*no muerto*) alive; living; (*ágil*) lively; quick; (*vistoso*) vivid; bright; (*listo*) clever, wide-awake; **tío** — merry-go-round; **al** — vividly; **de viva voz** by word of mouth; **tocar en lo** — to hurt to the quick, touch the most sensitive spot.
vizcacha [bis·ká·ča] *f. Andes, Ríopl.* viscacha (*South American rodent about the size of a hare*).
vizcachera [bis·ka·čé·ra] *f. Andes, Ríopl.* viscacha burrow or hole; *Arg.* room filled with junk; **vizcacheral** [bis·ka·če·rál] *m. Andes, Ríopl.* ground full of viscacha burrows.
vizcaíno [bis·ka·í·no] *adj.* Biscayan, of or from Biscay, Spain.
vocablo [bo·ká·ƀlo] *m.* word, term.
vocabulario [bo·ka·ƀu·lá·rjo] *m.* vocabulary.
vocación [bo·ka·sjón] *f.* vocation; aptness, talent.
vocal [bo·kál] *adj.* vocal; oral; vowel; *f.* vowel; *m.* voter (*in an assembly or council*).
vocear [bo·se·ár] *v.* to shout; to cry out; to hail.
vocecita [bo·se·sí·ta] *f.* sweet little voice.
vocería [bo·se·rí·a] *f.* clamor, shouting.
vocerío [bo·se·rí·o] *m. Am.* clamor, shouting.
vocero *m.* spokesman.
vociferar [bo·si·fe·rár] *v.* to shout, clamor; to yell; to boast loudly of.
vodevil [bo·đe·ƀíl] *m.* vaudeville.
volado [bo·lá·đo] *m.* superior letter in printing; *Col.* angry person.
volante [bo·lán·te] *adj.* flying; floating; **papel** (*or* **hoja**) — handbill, circular; *m.* ruffle, frill; steering wheel; balance wheel; flywheel.
volar[2] [bo·lár] *v. irr.* to fly; to fly away; to explode; to irritate, pique; to rouse (*bird game*); **-se** *Carib., Col.* to fly off the handle, lose one's temper.
volátil [bo·lá·til] *adj.* volatile; fickle, changeable; flying.
volcán [bol·kán] *m.* volcano; *Col.* precipice; *S.A.* swift torrent; *C.A.* **un — de** many; lots of; a pile of.
volcánico [bol·ká·ni·ko] *adj.* volcanic.
volcar[2, 6] [bol·kár] *v. irr.* to overturn; to capsize; to upset; to make dizzy; **-se** to upset, get upset.

volear [bo·le·ár] *v.* to volley, hit (*a ball*) in the air.
volición [bo·li·sjón] *f.* volition.
voltaje [bol·tá·xe] *m.* voltage.
voltear [bol·te·ár] *v.* to turn, turn around; to revolve; to turn inside out; to overturn; to tumble or roll over; to turn a somersault; *Am.* to go prying around; *Col., Ven., C.A., Mex., Andes* — **la espalda** to turn one's back; **-se** to turn over; to change sides.
voltereta [bol·te·ré·ta] *f.* somersault, tumble.
voltio [ból·tjo], **volt** *m.* volt; **voltímetro** voltmeter.
voluble [bo·lú·ƀle] *adj.* fickle; moody; changeable; twining (*as a climbing vine*).
volumen [bo·lú·men] *m.* volume.
voluminoso [bo·lu·mi·nó·so] *adj.* voluminous, bulky, very large.
voluntad [bo·lun·tád] *f.* will; desire; determination; benevolence, good will; consent; **última** — last will, testament; **de** (*or* **de buena**) — willingly, with pleasure.
voluntario [bo·lun·tá·rjo] *adj.* voluntary; willful; *m.* volunteer.
voluntarioso [bo·lun·ta·rjó·so] *adj.* willful.
voluptuoso [bo·lup·twó·so] *adj.* voluptuous; sensual.
voluta [bo·lú·ta] *f.* scroll, spiral-like ornament; **-s de humo** spirals of smoke.
volver[2, 52] [bol·ƀér] *v. irr.* (*regresar*) to return; (*dar vuelta*) to turn; to turn up, over, or inside out; to restore; — **loco** to drive crazy; — **a** (+ *inf.*) to do again; — **en sí** to come to, recover one's senses; — **por** to return for; to defend; **-se** to become; to turn; to turn around; to change one's ideas; **-se atrás** to go back; to back out, go back on one's word; **-se loco** to go crazy.
vomitar [bo·mi·tár] *v.* to vomit.
vómito [bó·mi·to] *m.* vomit; vomiting.
voracidad [bo·ra·si·đáđ] *f.* voraciousness, greediness.
vorágine [bo·rá·xi·ne] *f.* vortex, whirlpool.
voraz [bo·rás] *adj.* voracious, ravenous, greedy.
vórtice [bór·ti·se] *m.* vortex, whirlpool; whirlwind, tornado; center of a cyclone.
votación [bo·ta·sjón] *f.* voting; vote, total number of votes.
votante [bo·tán·te] *m. & f.* voter.
votar [bo·tár] *v.* to vote; to vow; to curse; **¡voto a tal!** by Jove!
voto [bó·to] *m.* vote; vow; prayer; votive offering; oath; wish; — **de confianza** vote of confidence.
voz [bos] *f.* (*capacidad*) voice; (*sonido*) shout, outcry; (*palabra*) word; rumor; — **común** common rumor or gossip; **a — en cuello** (*or* **a — en grito**) shouting; at the top of one's lungs; **en — alta** aloud; **a voces** shouting, with shouts; **secreto a voces** open secret; **dar voces** to shout, yell.
vozarrón [bo·sa·rrón] *m.* loud, strong voice.
vuelco [bwél·ko] *m.* upset; overturning; capsizing; tumble.
vuelo [bwé·lo] *m.* flight; width, fullness (*of a dress or cloak*); frill, ruffle; jut, projection (*of a building*); **al** (*or* **a**) — on the fly; quickly; **levantar** (*or* **alzar**) **el** — to fly away; to soar.
vuelta [bwél·ta] *f.* (*giro*) turn; return; repetition; (*parte opuesta*) reverse side; cuff, facing of a sleeve; cloak lining; (*cambio*) change (*money returned*); **a la** — around the corner; on returning; **a la — de los años** within a few years; *Am.* **otra** — again; **dar -s** to turn over and over; to wander about; **dar una** — to take a walk; **estar de** — to be back; **no tiene — de hoja** there are no two ways about it.
vuelto [bwél·to] *p.p. of* **volver;** *m. Am.* change (*money returned*).
vuestro [bwés·tro] *poss. adj.* your, of yours (*fam. pl.*); *poss. pron.* yours.
vulgar [bul·ǥár] *adj.* common, ordinary; in common use; low, vile, base.
vulgaridad [bul·ǥa·ri·đáđ] *f.* vulgarity, coarseness, commonness.
vulgarismo [bul·ǥa·ríz·mo] *m.* slang, slang expression, vulgar or ungrammatical expression.
vulgo [búl·ǥo] *m.* populace, the common people; *adv.* commonly, popularly.
vulva [búl·ƀa] *f.* external female genitalia.

water [gwá·ter] *m. Spain* toilet.

xilófono [si·ló·fo·no] *m.* xylophone.

Y:y

y [i] *conj.* and.
ya [ŷa] *adv.* already; now; finally; soon, presently; in time; **¡—!** now I see!; I understand; enough!; **¡ — lo creo!** I should say so!; yes, of course!; — **no** no longer; — **que** since; although; — **se ve** of course; it is clear; — **voy** I am coming.
yacer[50] [ŷa·sér] *v. irr.* to lie (*in the grave*); to be lying down; to lie, be situated.
yacimiento [ŷa·si·mjén·to] *m.* bed, layer (*of ore*); — **de petróleo** oil field.
yanqui [ŷáŋ·ki] *m. & f.* North American, native of the United States; Yankee.
yantar [ŷan·tár] *v.* to eat; *m.* food, meal.
yapa [ŷá·pa] *f. Ríopl., Andes* a small gift from the vendor to the purchaser; also **llapa, ñapa; pilón** in Mexico.
yarará [ŷa·ra·rá] *f. Ríopl.* Argentine poisonous snake.
yarda [ŷár·đa] *f.* yard (*unit of measure*).
yate [ŷá·te] *m.* yacht.
yedra [ŷé·đra] = **hiedra.**
yegua [ŷé·ǥwa] *f.* mare; *C.A., Bol.* cigar butt; *adj. Am.* big, large; **yeguada** [ŷe·ǥwá·đa] *f.* herd of mares.
yelmo [ŷél·mo] *m.* helmet.
yema [ŷé·ma] *f.* egg yolk; bud, shoot; candied egg yolk; — **del dedo** finger tip.
yerba [ŷér·ƀa] = **hierba.**
yerbabuena [ŷer·ƀa·ƀwé·na] *f.* mint; peppermint.
yerbero [ŷer·ƀé·ro] *m. Mex., Cuba, Ven., Col., Andes* herb vendor.
yermo [ŷér·mo] *m.* desert, wilderness; *adj.* desert uninhabited; uncultivated; sterile.
yerno [ŷér·no] *m.* son-in-law.
yerro [ŷé·rro] *m.* error, fault, mistake.
yerto [ŷér·to] *adj.* stiff, motionless, rigid.
yesca [ŷés·ka] *f.* tinder; anything highly inflammable; incentive (*to passion*); *Ríopl., Mex.* **estar hecho una** — to be in great anger.

VI

yeso [ŷé·so] *m.* gypsum, chalk; plaster; chalk (*for blackboard*); — **blanco** whitewash; — **mate** plaster of Paris; **yesoso** [ŷe·só·so] *adj.* chalky.
yo [ŷo] *pers. pron.* I.
yod [ŷod] *f.* yod (linguistic symbol).
yodo [ŷó·do] *m.* iodine.
yoduro [ŷo·dú·ro] *m.* iodide.
yogi [ŷó·xi] *m.* yogi.
yuca [ŷú·ka] *f.* yucca; cassava.
yugo [ŷú·go] *m.* yoke; marriage tie; burden.
yogur [ŷo·gúr] *m.* yogurt.
yoyo [ŷó·yo] *m.* yo-yo.
yunga [ŷuŋ·ga] *f.* valley of Peru and Bolivia.
yunque [ŷúŋ·ke] *f.* anvil.
yunta [ŷún·ta] *f.* yoke of oxen; pair of draft animals.
yuyo [ŷú·yo] *m. Cuba, Mex., Ríopl., Andes* wild grass, weeds; *C.A., Col.* an herb sauce; *Ec., Peru* garden stuff; *Andes, Ch.* **estar** — to be lifeless insipid; *Col.* **volverse uno** — to faint.

Z:z

zacate [sa·ká·te] *m. Mex., C.A.* grass, forage; hay.
zafado [sa·fá·do] *adj.* impudent, brazen, shameless; *Ven.* smart, wide-awake, keen; *Col., Mex., Andes* "touched", half-crazy; *p.p.* of **zafar.**
zafar [sa·fár] *v.* to release, set free; to dislodge; *Am.* to exclude; **-se** to slip away; to dodge; to get rid (of); to get loose; *Col., Ven., Andes* to get dislocated (*said of a bone*); *Col., Mex., Andes* to go crazy; *Col.* to use foul language.
zafio [sá·fjo] *adj.* coarse, uncouth, rude.
zafir [sa·fír], **zafiro** [sa·fí·ro] *m.* sapphire.
zafra [sá·fra] *f.* sugar-making season; sugar making; sugar crop.
zaga [sá·ga] *f.* rear; **a la** — (**a** *or* **en** —) behind.
zagal [sa·gál] *m.* young shepherd; lad; **zagala** [sa·gá·la] *f.* young shepherdess; lass, maiden; **zagalejo** [sa·ga·lé·xo] *m.* young shepherd; short skirt; petticoat.
zaguán [sa·gwán] *m.* vestibule.
zaherir[3] [sa·e·rír] *v. irr.* to hurt (*feelings*); to censure, reprove; to reproach.
zaino [sáj·no] *adj.* treacherous; vicious; chestnut-colored (*horse*).
zalamero [sa·la·mé·ro] *m.* fawner, flatterer, servile person; **zalamería** [sa·la·me·rí·a] *f.* flattery, scraping and bowing.
zalea [sa·lé·a] *f.* pelt, undressed sheepskin.
zamacueca [sa·ma·kwé·ka] *f.* popular dance of Peru and Chile.
zambo [sám·bo] *adj.* knock-kneed; *m. Col.* a species of South American monkey.
zambra [sám·bra] *f. Spain* uproar; lively *fiesta.*
zambullida [sam·bu·yí·da] *f.* dive, dip, plunge.
zambullir[20] [sam·bu·yír] *v.* to plunge, dip, duck; **-se** to dive; to plunge.
zambullón [sam·bu·yón] *m.* quick, sudden dip or dive.
zanahoria [sa·na·ó·rja] *f.* carrot.
zanca [sáŋ·ka] *f.* long leg of any fowl; long leg; long prop; **zancada** [saŋ·ká·da] *f.* stride, long step.
zanco [sáŋ·ko] *m.* stilt; **andar en -s** to walk on stilts.
zancón [saŋ·kón] *adj.* lanky, long-legged; *Col., Guat., Mex.* too short (*skirt or dress*).
zancudo [saŋ·kú·do] *adj.* long-legged; *m. Mex., C.A., Ven., Col., Andes* mosquito.
zángano [sáŋ·ga·no] *m.* drone; loafer, sponger; *Am.* rogue, rascal.
zangolotear [saŋ·go·lo·te·ár] *v.* to shake, jiggle; **-se** to shake; to waddle; to sway from side to side.
zangoloteo [saŋ·go·lo·té·o] *m.* jiggle, jiggling; shaking; waddling.
zanguanga [saŋ·gwáŋ·ga] *f.* feigned illness; **hacer la** — to pretend to be ill; **zanguango** [saŋ·gwáŋ·go] *adj.* lazy; silly; *m.* fool.
zanja [sáŋ·xa] *f.* ditch; trench; *Am.* irrigation ditch.
zanjar [sa·xár] *v.* to excavate; to dig ditches in; to settle (*disputes*).
zapallo [sa·pá·yo] *m. Pan., Col., Ven., Andes* pumpkin; squash.
zapapico [sa·pa·pí·ko] *m.* pickaxe.
zapata [sa·pá·ta] *f.* half-boot; — **de freno** brake shoe.
zapateado [sa·pa·te·á·do] *m.* a Spanish tap dance.
zapatear [sa·pa·te·ár] *v.* to tap with the feet; to tap-dance.
zapateo [sa·pa·té·o] *m.* tapping with the feet; *Am.* a popular tap dance.
zapatería [sa·pa·te·rí·a] *f.* shoe store; shoemaker's shop.
zapatero [sa·pa·té·ro] *m.* shoemaker; shoe dealer.
zapatilla [sa·pa·tí·ya] *f.* slipper, pump.
zapato [sa·pá·to] *m.* shoe.
zapote [sa·pó·te] *m.* sapodilla.
zaragüeya [sa·ra·gwe·ya] *f.* opossum.
zarandajas [sa·ran·dá·xas] *f. pl.* trifles, trinkets, worthless things.
zarandear [sa·ran·de·ár] *v.* to winnow (*separate the chaff from grain*); to sift; to sift out; to move (*something*) quickly, wiggle, jiggle; *C.A., Ríopl.* to whip, lash, mistreat, abuse; **-se** to wiggle, jiggle; to bump along; to waddle; to strut, swagger.
zarandeo [sa·ran·dé·o] *m.* jiggle, jiggling; sifting; waddling; strutting.
zarcillo [sar·sí·yo] *m.* earring; tendril (*coil of a climbing vine*); *Andes, Mex.* earmark (*on the ear of an animal*).
zarco [sár·ko] *adj.* light-blue (*eyes*).
zarpa [sár·pa] *f.* paw, claw; weighting anchor; **echar la** — to grasp, seize; **zarpada** [sar·pá·da] *f.* pounce; blow with a paw; **zarpazo** [sar·pá·so] *m.* blow with the paw; big blow, thud; hard fall.
zarpar [sar·pár] *v.* to weigh anchor; to set sail.
zarpazo [sar·pá·so] *m.* blow with a claw or paw.
zarza [sár·sa] *f.* bramble; blackberry bush.
zarzamora [sar·sa·mó·ra] *f.* blackberry.
zarzuela [sar·swé·la] *f.* Spanish musical comedy.
¡zas! *interj.* [sas] *interj.* bang!
zigzag [sig·ság] *m.* zigzag.
zigzaguear [sig·sa·ge·ár] *v.* to zigzag, weave.
zinc [siŋk] = **cinc.**
zócalo [só·ka·lo] *m.* base (*of a pedestal*); *Mex.* public square.
zodíaco [so·dí·a·ko] *m.* zodiac.
zona [só·na] *f.* zone; band, girdle; shingles (*a disease*); **zonificación** zoning.
zonzo [són·so] *adj.* dull, stupid, silly, foolish.
zoología [so·o·lo·xí·a] *f.* zoology.
zoológico [so·o·ló·xi·ko] *adj.* zoological; **jardín** — zoo.
zopenco [so·péŋ·ko] *adj.* stupid, dull, thick-headed *m.* blockhead, dunce.
zopilote [so·pi·ló·te] *m. Mex., C.A.* buzzard.
zoquete [so·ké·te] *m.* (*cosa*) block, chunk of wood; hunk of bread; (*persona*) blockhead, dunce, fool; ugly fat person; *Am.* grease, dirt, filth; *Am.* slap.
zorra [só·rra] *f.* fox; foxy person; drunkenness;

prostitute; **pillar una** — to get drunk.
zorro [só·rro] *m.* fox; foxy person; **-s** fox skins; duster made of cloth or leather strips; **estar hecho un** — to be drowsy; **hacerse uno el** — to pretend to be stupid or not to hear; *adj.* foxy; zorrillo [so·rrí·yo], **zorrino** [so·rrí·no] *m. Ríopl.* **skunk; zorruno** [so·rrú·no] *adj.* foxy.
zorzal [sor·sál] *m.* thrush; (*persona*) crafty fellow; *Am.* fool, scapegoat, dupe.
zozobra [so·só·bra] *f.* foundering; sinking; anxiety, worry.
zozobrar [so·so·brár] *v.* to founder; to capsize; to sink; to be in great danger; to fret, to worry.
zumbar [sum·bár] *v.* to buzz; to hum; to ring (*said of the ears*); to scoff at; to strike, hit; *Ven., Col.* to throw out or away; *Andes* to punish; — **una bofetada** to give a slap; **-se** *Am.* to slip away, disappear.
zumbido [sum·bí·do] *m.* buzzing, humming; ringing (*in one's ears*); hit, blow, whack.
zumbón [sum·bón] *adj.* funny, playful; sarcastic; *m.* jester.
zumo [sú·mo] *f. Spain* juice; (*ganancias*) profit; **zumoso** [su·mó·so] *adj.* juicy.
zurcido [sur·sí·do] *m.* darn; darning; *p.p. of* **zurcir.**
zurcir[10] [sur·sír] *v.* to darn; to invent, make up (*lies*).
zurdo [súr·do] *adj.* left-handed; left; **a zurdas** with the left hand; clumsily.
zuro [sú·ro] *m.* cob, corncob.
zurra [sú·rra] *f.* beating, flogging; tanning (*of leather*).
zurrar [su·rrár] *v.* to flog, thrash; to tan (*leather*).
zurrón [su·rrón] *m.* pouch; bag; leather bag; *Ven., Col.* coward.
Zutano [su·tá·no] *m.* so-and-so; a certain person. (*Used often with* **Fulano** *and* **Mengano**).

A Spanish–English List of Five Hundred Common Idioms and Proverbs, with Dialectal Variants

The Spanish idioms, proverbs, and sayings are listed alphabetically, followed by American Spanish variants, then English equivalents, some of which are also idiomatic. American Spanish locutions that seem to be fairly common to most of Latin America are listed without regional designation, while local variations are indicated by country or region with the abbreviations employed in the text of the Dictionary. An English index follows the chart of idioms to facilitate the use of the compilation. It is to be noted that the basic element is the Spanish expression and also that the Spanish variants are intentionally more numerous than the English. This is because of the many political entities represented in the Spanish-speaking world, in contrast to American English idiomatic expression which tends to level to a general American form.

Quinientos Modismos, Refranes, y Dichos Españoles con Variantes Dialectales y Tradducción al Inglés

El cuadro de modismos, refranes, y dichos españoles tiene orden alfabético según la letra inicial de la primera palabra. Siguen variantes hispanoamericanas y luego equivalentes o semejantes del inglés, con ciertas variantes. Los modismos hispanoamericanos que son bastante generales no llevan indicación regional, y se señalan con abreviaturas del texto del Diccionario los que son típicos de ciertos países o regiones. Sigue al cuadro un índice inglés con los números de las locuciones castellanas correspondientes. Se nota que lo básico es la locución española y también que se dan más variantes dialectales en español, con motivo de las numerosas entidades políticas de América. El inglés, por lo visto, ha sufrido más nivelación en este siglo.

	Academy Spanish	*American Spanish Variants*	*English Equivalents*
1.	A aquél loar debemos cuyo pan comemos	No hay que darle patadas al pesebre	Don't bite the hand that feeds you
2.	¡A buenas horas!	¡Qué horitas! (*Mex.*)	Better late than never. It's about time!
3.	A buen hambre no hay pan duro	A buen hambre no hay gordas duras (*Mex.*)	Hunger is the best sauce
4.	A caballo regalado no hay que mirarle el diente	A caballo dado no se le mira el colmillo	Don't look a gift horse in the mouth
5.	A carta cabal		Through and through
6.	A continuación	Como sigue	Following; as follows
7.	¿A cuántos estamos?	¿Cuál es la fecha?	What is the date?
8.	A duras penas	Con gran dificultad	With great difficulty
9.	A empujones (empellones)	A codazos	By pushing; by shoving; by elbowing
10.	A fines de		Toward (around) the end of (month, week)
11.	A fondo		Thoroughly
12.	A grandes rasgos		Briefly; in outline form; in a sketchy way
13.	A la americana; a escote	Al aleluya, cada quien paga la suya; Americanamente (*Col.*)	Dutch treat; go Dutch

	Academy Spanish	American Spanish Variants	English Equivalents
14.	A la buena de Dios		Casually; as luck would have it
15.	A la carrera	Fletado (*Ven., Col.*)	On the run
16.	A la corta o a la larga	Tarde o temprano	Sooner or later
17.	A la larga	Al fin	In the long run; when all is said and done
18.	A la vez		At the same time
19.	A lo largo de		Along; bordering
20.	A lo más	Cuando más	At (the) most
21.	A lo mejor	Puede que; a la mejor (*Mex.*)	Like as not; it could be that
22.	A mano		By hand; at hand; tied (even)
23.	A más no poder	Hasta sacarse los zapatos (*Ch.*)	To the utmost
24.	A mediados de		About (around) the middle of (month)
25.	A menos que	A no ser que	Unless
26.	A menudo		Often
27.	A mi ver	En mi opinión	In my opinion; to my way of thinking
28.	A palabras necias, oídos sordos	A boca de borracho, oídos de cantinero	For foolish talk, deaf ears
29.	A pedir de boca		Exactly as desired; just as you want it
30.	A pesar de		In spite of
31.	A principios de		The early part of; around the first of (month)
32.	A propósito		By the way; on purpose
33.	A prueba de		Proof against (fire, etc.)
34.	A quemarropa	A boca de jarro	Point blank; at very close range
35.	A quien corresponda		To whom it may concern
36.	A quien madruga, Dios le ayuda		The early bird catches the worm
37.	A razón de		At the rate of
38.	A rienda suelta		Without restraint
39.	A saber	Es decir; o sea	Namely; that is
40.	A ver si como repican doblan	A ver si como roncan duermen	His bark is worse than his bite; all talk and no cider
41.	Abierto de par en par		Wide open
42.	Abundar como la mala hierba	Ser ajonjolí de todos los moles (*Mex.*)	To be as common as dirt; to be a dime a dozen
43.	Acabar de	Venir de (*Col.*); recién (*plus verb*) (*Riopl., Ch.*)	To have just
44.	Acusar recibo de		To acknowledge receipt of
45.	Aguzar los oídos	Parar la oreja	To prick up one's ears
46.	Al fin y al cabo	Al fin y al fallo (*Ch.*)	In the very end; when all is said and done
47.	Al fin se canta la gloria	Nadie diga ¡zape! hasta que no escape; el que quiera huevos, que aguante los cacareos (*Riopl.*)	Don't count your chickens before they're hatched
48.	Al mejor cazador se le escapa la liebre	Al mejor mono se le cae el zapote (*C.A.*); A la mejor cocinera se le queman los frijoles	Everyone makes mistakes; it's a good horse that never stumbles
49.	Al pie de la letra		To the letter; thoroughly
50.	Al por mayor	Al mayoreo	Wholesale
51.	Al por menor		Retail; in detail
52.	Algo por el estilo		Something like that; something on that order
53.	Amigo del buen tiempo, múdase con el viento	Al nopal lo van a ver sólo cuando tiene tunas (*Mex.*)	Fair-weather friend
54.	Andarse por las ramas	Andarse con medias tazas; emborrachar la perdiz (*Ch.*)	To beat around the bush
55.	Antes doblar que quebrar	Más vale rodear que rodar	Better bend than break; if you can't lick 'em, join 'em
56.	Aprovecha gaviota, que no hay otra	Atáscate ahora que hay lodo	Gather ye rosebuds while ye may; here's your chance

	Academy Spanish	American Spanish Variants	English Equivalents
57.	Armar un San Quintin	Armar una bronca; revolver el gallinero (*Ch.*)	To start a fight; to raise Cain
58.	¡Arriba los corazones!	¡No le afloje!	Courage! Cheer up! Chin up!
59.	A sus órdenes	Para servirle	At your service
60.	Aunque la mona se vista de seda, mona se queda		Clothes don't make the man
61.	Bajo cuerda	Por debajo del agua	In an underhanded manner; under the table
62.	Barrer para adentro	Rascarse para adentro es gran contento; antes mis dientes que mis parientes	To look after oneself first; to take care of number one
63.	Borracho como una cuba	Borracho perdido	Dead drunk; plastered; tight
64.	¡Buen provecho!	¡Que aproveche!	Good appetite!
65.	Buscarle tres pies al gato	Buscarle mangas al chaleco; buscarle cuatro pies al gato (*Ec.*)	To look for knots in a bulrush; to complicate things
66.	Buscar pelos en la sopa		To be given to fault finding; to look for an excuse to gripe
67.	Cada muerte de obispo	Como visita de obispo	In a month of Sundays; once in a blue moon
68.	Caer atravesado	Caer gordo; caer mal; caer gacho (*Col.*)	To rub (one) the wrong way; to be a pain in the neck
69.	Caer de bruces	Dar el azotón; caer de ancho; echarse de boca (*Andes*)	To fall flat; to bite the dust
70.	Caer en la cuenta		To realize; to take note of
71.	Caerse de su propio peso		To be self-evident (obvious)
72.	Calentarse los cascos		To rack one's brains
73.	Cara o cruz	Aguila o sol (*Mex.*); cara o sello	Heads or tails
74.	Carne de gallina		Goose flesh; goose pimples; burr(brrr) bumps (South)
75.	Colgarle a uno el milagro	Colgarle a uno el muerto	To shift responsibility; to pass the buck
76.	Como perros y gatos	Como dos gatos en un costal	Like cats and dogs
77.	¿Cómo te (le) va?	¿Qué tal?	How are you? How's it going? What gives?
78.	Comprar a ciegas	Comprar potrillo en panza de yegua	To buy blindly; to buy a pig in a poke
79.	Con el ojo y con la fe jamás me burlaré	Aunque te digan que sí, espérate a que lo veas	Seeing is believing; (to say one is) from Missouri
80.	Con guante blanco	Con mucha mano izquierda	With kid gloves
81.	Con la cuchara que elijas, con ésa comerás	Cada quien se pone la corona que se labra	As you make your bed, so you must lie in it
82.	Con las bocas cosidas	¡Chitón!	To keep to oneself; mum's the word; button the lip
83.	Con las manos en la masa		To be caught in the act; to be caught red-handed
84.	Estar con los pelos de la dehesa	Estar con el pelo del potrero	To be a country bumpkin; (hayseed, hick)
85.	Con razón		No wonder! Small wonder!
86.	Con tal que	A condición de que	Provided that; if
87.	Contigo pan y cebolla	Más vale atole con risas que chocolate con lágrimas	Whither thou goest . . .; love in a cottage
88.	Con todas las de ley	Como Dios manda	According to Cocker (Hoyle)
89.	Consultar con la almohada		To think something over; to sleep on something
90.	Contra viento y marea		Come what may; come hell or high water
91.	Correr la voz	Correr la bola (*C.A.*); dizque (*Col. Andes*)	To be rumored; to be noised about; they say; people say
92.	Cortar el hilo	Cortar la hebra	To interrupt; to cut off
93.	Cosa de		About; more or less; a matter of
94.	Cosido a faldas de		To be tied to the apron strings of
95.	Costar un ojo de la cara	Costar un huevo (*Ven., Col., Andes*)	To cost a mint; to cost plenty; to bring a stiff price

	Academy Spanish	American Spanish Variants	English Equivalents
96.	Cruzarse de brazos		To remain indifferent; to be not interested
97.	Cuanto antes	Tan pronto como posible	As soon as possible; the sooner the better
98.	Cuanto más . . . más	Mientras más . . . más; entre más . . . más (*C.A., Col., Andes*)	The more . . . the more
99.	Cuatro letras		
100.	Dar a luz		To give birth
101.	Dar al borracho las llaves de la bodega		To set the fox to keep the geese; to put the cat among the pigeons
102.	Dar calabazas	Cortar: dar ayotes (*C.A.*)*;* dar opio (*Andes*)	To break off relations; to give (one) the brush-off; to give (one) the mitten (N.E.)
103.	Dar cuerda a		To wind (clock, etc.)
104.	Dar de baja		To discharge; to drop (from a team, list, etc.)
105.	Dar el pésame por		To present one's condolences for; to extend one's sympathy for
106.	Dar en		To hit; to take a notion to
107.	Dar gato por liebre	Hacerle guaje a uno (*Mex.*)*;* pasársela a uno (*Ch.*)	To deceive; to cheat
108.	Dar guerra		To make trouble
109.	Dar (la) lata	Poner gorro (*Mex.*)*;* poner pereque (*Col.*)	To bother; to annoy; to be a nuisance; to bug
110.	Dar la razón a alguien		To acknowledge (a person) to be right; give credit for being right
111.	Dar la vuelta a algo		To go around something; to rotate something
112.	Dar parte	Avisar	To inform; to report
113.	Dar por hecho	Suponer	To assume; to take for granted
114.	Dar rienda suelta a	Dar curso libre	To give free rein to; to let go
115.	Dar salida a	Disponer de	To dispose of; to clear out; to get rid of
116.	Dar un paso en falso	Dar una metida de pata	To make a false move; to pull a boner
117.	Dar una mano		To apply (a coat of paint, etc.)
118.	Darle a uno coraje	Darle rabia a uno (*Carib.*)*;*	To make one angry (mad)
119.	Darle a uno en la matadura	Darle a uno en la mera matada (*Mex.*)	To touch to the quick; to strike home
120.	Darle a uno la gana; apetecer	Provocarle a uno (*Col.*)	To feel like; to want to
121.	Darle a uno lo mismo	Serle a uno igual	To be all the same to one; to make no difference to one
122.	Darle a uno una soberana paliza	Darle a uno hasta por debajo de la lengua; aplanchar a uno (*Col.*)	To give one a trouncing; to knock the spots off one
123.	Darse aires; darse tono; ¡cuántos humos!	Darse mucho taco (*Mex.*)*;* Botarse el pucho (*Ch.*)*;* Darse corte; darse paquete (*Ec.*)	To put on airs; to put on the dog; to be stuck up
124.	Darse cuenta de		To realize; to be aware of
125.	De bote en bote	Hasta el tope (*Mex.*)	Full to the brim; full up
126.	De buena gana		Willingly
127.	De buenas a primeras	En un improviso (*Ven., Col.*)	Without warning; suddenly
128.	De cabo a rabo	De punta a punta	From beginning to end; from head to tail
129.	De categoria	De número (*Ríopl.*)*;* de oro (*Col.*)*;* de mentas (*Arg.*)	Of importance; of class
130.	De cuando en cuando	De vez en cuando; de pronto (*C.A.; Ríopl.*)	From time to time
131.	De golpe	En un improviso (*Ven., Col.*)	Suddenly; all of a sudden

	Academy Spanish	*American Spanish Variants*	*English Equivalents*
132.	De gran subida, gran caida	De la subida más alta es la caida más lastimosa	The bigger they are, the harder they fall
133.	De la noche a la mañana		Overnight; all at once
134.	De lado		Sideways
135.	De lleno		Fully; adequately
136.	De lo contrario		Otherwise
137.	De mala gana		Unwillingly
138.	De mala muerte	Chafa (*Mex.*)	Worthless; crumby
139.	De nuevo	Otra vez	Again; anew; once more
140.	De paso		In passing; on the way
141.	De pura casualidad		Purely by chance
142.	De repente	De golpe; en un improviso (*Ven., Col.*)	All of a sudden
143.	De tal palo, tal astilla	Cual el cuervo, tal su huevo; de tal jarro, tal tepalcate (*Mex.*)	Like father, like son; a chip off the old block
144.	Descubrir el pastel	Hacer aparecer el peine	To let the cat out of the bag; to spill the beans
145.	De una vez y para siempre	De una vez	Once and for all
146.	De un solo sentido		One-way
147.	De vuelta a las andadas	Otra vez la burra en el trigo	Back to the old tricks
148.	Decidirse a		To make up one's mind to; to decide to
149.	Decir a todo amén		To be a yes man
150.	Decir entre dientes		To mumble; to mutter
151.	Decir para sí	Decir para sus adentros	To say to oneself
152.	Dejar de		To cease; to stop
153.	Dejar a uno en la calle	Dejar a uno en la tendida; dejar a uno en un petate (*Col.; Ven.*)	To bleed (one) white; to take (one) to the cleaners
154.	Dejar a uno plantado	Dejar a uno en la ecstacada; dejar a uno embarcado (*Mex.*)	To stand someone up
155.	Dejarse de cuentos	Dejarse de historias; dejarse de rodeos	To come to the point; to stop beating around the bush
156.	Del dicho al hecho hay gran trecho		Saying and doing are two different things; there's many a slip twixt the cup and the lip
157.	Desde luego		Of course; naturally
158.	Despedirse a la francesa	Irse como burro sin mecate; Pintarse (*Ven.*); emplumárselas (*Col., Ven.*)	To take French leave
159.	Dia hábil		Workday
160.	Dicho y hecho		No sooner said than done
161.	Dijo la sartén a la caldera, quítate de allá, que me tiznas	El comal le dijo a la olla, qué tiznada estás (*Mex.*)	The pot called the kettle black
162.	Dime con quien andas y te diré quién eres	Dime quien es tu junta y te diré si haces yunta	A man is known by the company he keeps; birds of a feather flock together
163.	Dios mediante	Si Dios nos da vida; primero Dios (*C.A.*)	God willing; I hope so
164.	Dirigir la palabra		To address; to speak to; to talk to
165.	Doblar la hoja	Cambiar el disco	To change the subject
166.	Don de gentes		Winning manners; a way with people
167.	Donde hubo fuego hay cenizas	Donde camotes quemaron, cenizas quedaron (*Andes*)	Where there's smoke, there's fire
168.	Donde menos se piensa salta la liebre	De cualquier maya salta un ratón (*Ríopl.*)	The unexpected always happens; it happens when least expected
169.	Echar de ver	Catar de ver (*Col., Ven.*)	To notice; to observe
170.	Echar indirectas		To make insinuations
171.	Echar la casa por la ventana		To go all out; to kill the fatted calf; to blow the works

	Academy Spanish	American Spanish Variants	English Equivalents
172.	Echar la llave		To lock the door
173.	Echar sapos y culebras	Echar tacos (*Mex.*) Echar ajos y cebollas; subir la prima (*Arg.*)	To swear a blue streak; to turn the air blue
174.	Echar todo a rodar	Patearle el nido a alguien	To spoil things; to upset everything; to make a mess of everything
175.	Echar un sueño (una siesta)	Tomar una siestita; tomar una pestañita (*Mex.*)	To take a nap; to catch a little shut-eye
176.	Echar una mano		To lend a hand; to help out
177.	Echar un párrafo	Echar guáguara (*Mex.*)	To pass the time of day; to chew the rag (fat)
178.	Echarse un trago	Echarse un fogonazo (*Mex.*); empinar el codo; empinar el cacho (*Ch.*); pegarse un palo (*Carib., Col.*)	To take a drink (swig); to wet the whistle
179.	El gallito del lugar	El mero mero (*Mex.*)	The cock of the walk; the top banana; the top dog
180.	El hombre propone y Dios dispone	El hombre propone, Dios dispone y la mujer descompone	Man proposes, God disposes
181.	El que no se arriesga no pasa la mar	El que no arriesga no gana	Nothing ventured, nothing gained
182.	Empleo de cuello y levita	Empleo de camisa blanca y corbata	White-collar job
183.	En calidad de		In the capacity of
184.	En cuanto	Tan pronto como	As soon as
185.	En cuanto a		Regarding; as for
186.	En cueros	En traje de Adán; en pelota; pila (*Andes*)	Naked; in one's birthday suit; naked as a jay bird
187.	En efectivo	En dinero contante y sonante; al chaz-chaz (*Mex.*)	In hard cash; in cold cash; cash on the barrel-head
188.	En el extranjero		Abroad
189.	En el peligro se conoce al amigo	En la cárcel se conocen los amigos	A friend in need is a friend indeed
190.	En firme	A la segura (*Ch., Andes*); a la fija (*Col.*)	Definite; binding
191.	En gustos no hay disputa	Sobre gustos se rompen géneros	Every man to his taste; some like it hot; some like it cold
192.	En hora buena		Safely; luckily; o.k.
193.	En la actualidad	Hoy; estos dias	At the present time; nowadays
194.	En mi perra vida	En mi cochina vida	Never in all my life; never in all my born days
195.	En principio		In principle; basically
196.	En rueda	Entre pura raza (*Mex.*)	A friendly gathering; among friends
197.	En un abrir y cerrar de ojos		In the twinkling of an eye
198.	En un dos por tres	En menos que canta un gallo	When least expected; quick as a wink; in the shake of a lamb's tail
199.	En vez de		Instead of
200.	En voz alta		Out loud
201.	En voz baja	Despacio	In a soft (low) voice
202.	Entrado en años	Ya veterano	Well along in years; to be no spring chicken
203.	Entrar en materia	Llegar al caso	To come to the point; get down to business
204.	Entre azul y buenas noches	Entre dos aguas; ni un sí ni un no	To be undecided; to be on the fence
205.	Entre bastidores		To be behind the scenes
206.	Entre la espada y la pared	Entre dos fuegos	To be between the devil and the deep blue sea
207.	Es decir	O sea	That is to say; in other words
208.	Es fama que	Dizque (*Col.*); corre la bola que (*C.A.*)	It is rumored that; they say that

	Academy Spanish	*American Spanish Variants*	*English Equivalents*
209.	Es harina de otro costal	Es otro cantar; no viene al cuento	That's a horse of a different color
210.	Es más bravo que un león	Es un perro; es una fiera	He is a tiger (wildcat)
211.	¡Esto es Jauja!	¡Esta es la tierra de Dios y María Santísima!	This is Seventh Heaven! This is Never-Never Land!
212.	Escurrir el bulto	Emplumárselas (*Col., Ven.*); pelarse	To sneak away; to slip away
213.	Está hasta en la sopa	Le dicen el diosito	There's no getting away from him; I'm sick of the sight of him
214.	Está que pela	Está como para desplumar pollos	It's piping hot; It's as hot as blue blazes
215.	Estar a disgusto		To be ill at ease; to feel awkward
216.	Estar a gusto		To be contented; to be comfortable
217.	Estar a la expectativa	Catiar la laucha (*Ch.*)	To be on the lookout for
218.	Estar con ánimo de		To have a notion to
219.	Estar chiflado	Le patina el embrague a uno; tener los alambres pelados (*Ch.*)	To have a screw loose; not to have all one's marbles
220.	Estar de malas	Tener la de malas; tener el santo a espaldas (*Ven., Mex.*); estar salado *(Col., Andes)*	To be out of luck
221.	Estar de moda	Estar en boga	To be fashionable; to be popular; to be the "in" thing
222.	Estar de sobra		To be superfluous; to be too much
223.	Estar de turno		To be on duty; to be on one's shift
224.	Estar de viaje		To be traveling; to be on the road
225.	Estar en buen uso	Estar en buenas condiciones	To be in good condition; to be in good shape
226.	Estar en la luna		To be up in the clouds
227.	Estar en las nubes		To daydream; to be high (prices)
228.	Estar en los huesos	Estar hecho un violín (*Ven.*); no quedarle a uno más que hueso y cuero	To be nothing but skin and bone
229.	Estar en plan de		To be in the mood for; to be out for
230.	Estar en vigor		To be in effect; to be in force
231.	Estar en vísperas de		To be on the eve of; to be about to
232.	Estar hecho una furia	Estar como agua para chocolate; estar hecho un chivo; estar hecho un quique (*Ch.*)	To be beside oneself; to be hot under the collar
233.	Estar muy metido en		To be deeply involved in
234.	Estar para	Estar por	To be about to
235.	Estar por	Estar a favor de	To be in favor of; to be for
236.	Estar quebrado	Estar arrancado; estar bruja (*Mex.*); estar pato (*Ch.*)	To be broke (flat broke)
237.	Estar rendido	Estar reventado	To be exhausted; to be all tired out; to be pooped
238.	Estar sentido	Estar resentido	To be offended; to be hurt
239.	Estar todo patas arriba	Ser todo un verdadero relajo	To be topsy-turvy; to be helter-skelter
240.	Fuera de sí		Unconscious; beside oneself
241.	Función corrida	Permanencia voluntaria	All-day program; come-and-go function
242.	Fulano	Ciertas hierbas (*Col., C.A.*)	Mr. So-and-so; what's-his-name
243.	Ganar a uno la mano	Coger a uno la delantera; madrugarle a uno	To get up too early for one; to beat one to it
244.	Genio y figura hasta la sepultura	Al que nace barrigón, es al ñudo que lo fajen (*Ríopl.*)	You can't make a silk purse out of a sow's ear; the leopard doesn't change its spots

	Academy Spanish	*American Spanish Variants*	*English Equivalents*
245.	Gente menuda	La chiquilleria	Small fry
246.	Guiñar un ojo	Hacer ojos (*Col.*)*;* hacer ojitos (*Mex.*)*;* hacer caras (*Ríopl.*)	To make eyes at; to flirt; to give the glad eye to
247.	Haber de		To be expected to; to be scheduled to
248.	Haber de todo como en botica		There's a little of everything
249.	Haber moros en la costa		The coast is not clear; something's up
250.	Hablar como una cotorra	No pararle la boca a uno (*Mex.*)	To be a chatterbox; to be a windbag
251.	Hablar entre dientes		To mumble; to mutter
252.	Hablar hasta por los codos	Ser lengualarga	To chatter; to talk idly; to talk too much
253.	Hacer buenas migas		To get along well together
254.	Hacer caso a uno	Dar boleto a uno	To pay attention to one
255.	Hacer cola		To queue up; to stand in line; to line up
256.	Hacer comedia	Hacer tango	To put on a show; to make a scene
257.	Hacer la vista gorda		To pretend not to see; to wink at
258.	Hacer escala		To make a scheduled stop; to stopover
259.	Hacer falta		To be necessary; to have need of
260.	Hacer frente a		To confront; to face up to
261.	Hacer gracia	Parecer chistoso	To strike one as funny
262.	Hacer hincapié	Poner énfasis; porfiar	To emphasize; to insist upon
263.	Hacer juego		To match; to go well with
264.	Hacer novillos	Pintar venado (*Mex.*)	To cut classes; to play hooky
265.	Hacer presente		To notify; to remind
266.	Hacer puente		To take the intervening day off
267.	Hacer su agosto		To feather one's nest; to make a killing
268.	Hacer un mandado	Hacer un recado	To run an errand
269.	Hacerle a uno un flaco servicio	Hacerle a uno la pera; jugar sucio (*Ch.*)	To do someone a bad turn; to play a dirty trick on someone
270.	Hacerse tarde		To become (get) late
271.	Hallarse en el pellejo de otro		To be in somebody else's shoes
272.	Harto da quien da lo que tiene	El que da lo suyo, harto hace	You can't get blood from a turnip (stone)
273.	Hasta el tuétano	Hasta las cachas *(Mex.)*	To the core; to the very center
274.	Hay que	Es necesario	It is necessary; you have to
275.	Hecho a la medida		Custom-made; made to order
276.	Hecho y derecho		Mature; grown-up
277.	Historias de cuartel	Cuentos colorados; chistes verdes *(Mex.)*	Off-color jokes; pool-room talk
278.	Ida y vuelta		Round-trip
279.	Ir a medias	Ir mitad mitad	To go fifty-fifty
280.	Ir al grano	Ir a lo que truje	To get down to brass tacks; to get to the point
281.	Irle a úno bien (mal)		To be becoming (unbecoming); to be well
282.	Irse de juerga	Irse de parranda; irse de tuna *(Col.);* irse de farras *(Ríopl.);* irse de jarana *(Ven.);* irse de rumba *(Carib.)*	To go on a spree; to paint the town red
283.	Irsele a uno el santo al cielo	Irsele a uno la onda	One's mind goes blank; one clean forgets; to be spacy
284.	Jugar con dos barajas	Mamar a dos tetas	To double-cross; to play both ends against the middle
285.	Jugarle una mala pasada a uno	Hacerle a uno la cama *(Ch.)*	To play foul with one; to play a dirty trick on one
286.	La mar de	Cantidad de; un montón de; un volcán de *(C.A.);* a patadas *(Ec.);* a ponchadas *(Andes)*	Lots of; loads of; oodles of; right smart of

	Academy Spanish	American Spanish Variants	English Equivalents
287.	La madeja se enreda	Se enreda la pita	The plot thickens
288.	La letra con sangre entra		There's no royal road to learning
289.	La niña de mis (tus, etc.) ojos		The apple of one's eye
290.	La piedra quieta cría malva	Piedra que rueda no cría moho	A rolling stone gathers no moss
291.	Levantar la mesa	Quitar la mesa	To clear the table
292.	Levantarse del pie izquierdo	Levantarse de malas	To get up on the wrong side of the bed
293.	Lo de menos		The least of it
294.	Los estadistas de café		Arm-chair strategists; sidewalk superintendents
295.	Los niños y los locos dicen las verdades	Los niños y los borrachos siempre dicen la verdad	Out of the mouths of babes and sucklings
296.	Llegar a las manos	Irse a los moquetes; irse al moño (entre mujeres) *(Ch.)*	To come to blows; to get into a fight
297.	Llevar a cabo		To accomplish; to carry out
298.	Llevar la contra		To oppose; to contradict
299.	Llevar la delantera		To be ahead
300.	Llevar uno su merecido		To get what's coming (to one)
301.	Llevarse un chasco	Pegarse palo	To be disappointed; to have a setback
302.	Llorar a lágrima viva	Llorar como becerro en llano; soltar puchero *(Ch.)*	To cry like a baby
303.	Llover a cántaros	Llover con rabia *(Carib.);* caer burros aparejados *(Carib.)*	To rain bucketfuls; to pour; to rain cats and dogs
304.	Mal que le pese a uno		Whether one likes it or not
305.	Más allá (de)		Farther on; beyond
306.	Más bien		Rather
307.	Más falso que Judas		As false as a counterfeit penny; worthless as a plugged nickel
308.	Más vale pájaro en mano que buitre volando	Más vale pájaro en mano que cien(to) volando; más vale guajito tengo que acocote tendré *(Mex.)*	A bird in the hand is worth two in the bush
309.	Más vale prevenir que lamentar	Un gramo de previsión vale más que una tonelada de curación	An ounce of prevention is worth a pound of cure
310.	Matar dos pájaros de un tiro	Matar dos pájaros de una pedrada	To kill two birds with one stone
311.	Media naranja		Better half; spouse
312.	Mejor dicho		Or rather; better yet
313.	Menos mal	Date de santos que no fue peor	So much the better; it could have been worse
314.	Meter en un puño a uno	Tener a uno agarrado de las greñas	To have someone by the neck; to have someone over a barrel
315.	Meterlo en el bolsillo	Echarse a uno a la bolsa	To wrap someone around one's little finger
316.	Meterse con		To pick a fight with
317.	Mientras más . . . más	Entre más . . . más *(C.A., Col.)*	The more . . . the more
318.	Mientras menos . . . menos	Entre menos . . . menos *(C.A., Col.)*	The less . . . the less
319.	Mirar de hito en hito	Mirar fijamente	To stare at; to eye up and down
320.	¡Mucho ojo!	Un ojo al gato y otro al garabato	Look out! Watch your step!
321.	Mucho ruido, pocas nueces	Tanto cacarear para no poner huevo; más la bulla que la cabuya *(Ven.);* es más la bulla que las mazorcas *(Col.)*	Much ado about nothing; his bark is worse than his bite
322.	Muy campante	Como si nada; da muchas correas	Cool as a cucumber
323.	Nacer con estrella	Nacer de pie	To be born lucky; to be born with a silver spoon in one's mouth
324.	Nadar en la abundancia	Estar muy pesudo; estar bien parado	To be rolling in money (dough)

	Academy Spanish	American Spanish Variants	English Equivalents
325.	Negocio redondo		Good sound bargain
326.	¡Ni a tiros!	¡En absoluto! ¡ni de vainas! *(Col.);* ¡ni bamba! *(Col.)*	Not for anything; not for love or money
327.	¡Ni en sueños!	¡Qué esperanza! *(Ríopl.; Andes);* ¡cuando! *(Ec.);* ¡frijoles! *(Carib.)*	By no means! Not on your life!
328.	¡Ni mucho menos!		Far from it! Not by a long shot!
329.	No cabe duda		There is no doubt; beyond a shadow of a doubt; have (has) got to be *(Jones has got to be the best pitcher)*
330.	No caber en si de gozo	No caber en el pellejo de gozo	To be beside oneself with joy; to be overcome with joy
331.	No caer en la cuenta	No encontrarle el chiste	Not to see the point; not to get it
332.	No dar el brazo a torcer	No aflojar un pelo (*Ríopl.*) *Andes;* hacer pata ancha (*Ríopl.*)	To be stubborn; to be not easily deceived; to be unyielding; to stick to one's guns
333.	No darse por entendido		To pretend not to understand
334.	No dejarle a uno ni a sol ni a sombra	Seguirlo hasta que se eche	To breathe down someone's neck; to dog someone's footsteps; to bug someone
335.	No hay de qué	De nada; por nada (*Mex.*)	Don't mention it; you're welcome
336.	No hay mal que por bien no venga	Una afortunada desgracia	It's an ill wind that blows no good; it's a blessing in disguise
337.	No hay que darle vueltas		There's no getting around it
338.	No me importa un comino	No me importa un pito; no me importa un cacahuate (*Mex.*); no me importa un cacao (*C.A.*)	I don't care a bit
339.	No le suena a uno		It doesn't mean a thing; It doesn't ring a bell
340.	No morderse la lengua	Cantar claro; ser claridoso (*Ven., C.A.*)	Not to mince words; to speak straight from the shoulder
341.	No poder con	No ser un hueso fácil de roer	Not to be able to stand something (someone); to be too much for one
342.	No saber ni jota	No saber ni papa	Not to know a blessed thing; not to know enough to come in out of the rain
343.	No se ganó Zamora en una hora	No se ganó Toledo en un credo	Rome wasn't built in a day
344.	No tener ni en qué caerse muerto	No tener ni segunda camisa; estar arrancado; andar pato (*Ch., Ríopl.*)	Not to have a penny to call one's own; not to have a red cent
345.	No tener pelos en la lengua	Ser claridoso (*Ven., C.A.*); hablar a calzón quitado (*Ch., Col.*)	To be outspoken; to speak one's mind
346.	No tener remedio		To be beyond repair (help, recourse); (to say something) can't be helped
347.	No valer un comino	No valer un cacahuate (*Mex.*); no valer un cacao; *(C.A.);* no valer un palo de tabaco (*Col.*); no valer un taco (*Col.*); estar para el gato (*Ch.*)	Not to be worth a brass farthing (cent)
348.	Obras son amores, que no buenas razones	Acciones son amores, no besos ni apachurrones	Actions speak louder than words
349.	Oír hablar de	Oír mentar	To hear about
350.	Ojos que no ven, corazón que no siente	Ojos que no ven tienen menos que sentir	Ignorance is bliss; out of sight, out of mind
351.	Padre mercader, hijo caballero, nieto limosnero	Padre pulpero, hijo caballero, nieto limosnero (*Perú*)	Three generations from shirt sleeve to shirt sleeve

	Academy Spanish	*American Spanish Variants*	*English Equivalents*
352.	¡Palabra!	¡Palabra de honor! ¡En serio!	Word of honor! On the level! No fooling! Sure enough!
353.	¡Pamplinas!	¡Pura guasa! ¡Frijoles! (*Carib.*)	Nonsense! Horsefeathers! Baloncy!
354.	Para colmo de males	¡No faltaba más!	That's the last straw! That does it! That's the straw that broke the camel's back
355.	Parar (la) oreja		To prick up one's ears; to sit up and take notice
356.	Pararle los pies a uno	Pararle el carro a uno; pararle el macho a uno	To put an end to something; to put one's foot down
357.	Parece mentira		It hardly seems possible; it seems impossible
358.	Pasar estrecheces	Pasar hambres; andar torcido	To feel the pinch
359.	Pasar la mano por el lomo	Darle la suave a uno; ser barbero (*Mex.*)	To butter someone up; to soft-soap someone; to polish the apple; to brown-nose
360.	Pasársele a uno		To get over; to forget
361.	Pasársele a uno la mano		To overdo; to go too far
362.	Pedir prestado	Prestar (*C.A., Col.*)	To ask (someone) to lend (one something); to borrow
363.	Pedirle peras al olmo	Andar buscando guayabas en los magueyes	To try to get blood from a turnip (stone)
364.	Perder el hilo de	Perder la hebra de	To lose the thread of
365.	Perder los estribos		To lose one's mind; to flip one's lid
366.	Perro ladrador nunca buen mordedor	Perro que ladra no muerde	Barking dogs seldom bite
367.	Poner a uno al corriente	Ponerle al tanto a uno	To inform one; to bring one up to date
368.	Poner el grito en el cielo		To make a great fuss; to hit the ceiling
369.	Poner en marcha		To start; to put in motion
370.	Poner la mesa		To set the table
371.	Poner mucho ojo		To pay close attention
372.	Poner pies en polvorosa	Tomar el polvo (*Mex., Col.*); Emplumárselas (*Col.*); salir fletado (*Ven.*)	To run away; to beat it; to take a powder; to hightail it
373.	Poner reparo(s)		To raise objections
374.	Ponerse a la obra		To get to work
375.	Ponerse disgustado	Ponerse bravo; picarse (*Col.*)	To get angry
376.	Ponérsele a uno carne de gallina		To get gooseflesh; to get goose pimples; to get burr (brrr) bumps
377.	Por adelantado	Con anticipación	In advance; beforehand
378.	Por casualidad		By chance; by the way
379.	Por consiguiente	Por lo tanto	Therefore; so
380.	Por extenso		At length; in detail
381.	Por el hilo se saca el olvillo	Por la hebra se saca el olvillo; En el modo de cortar el queso se conoce al tendero	By their fruits shall ye know them; a fool is known by his laughing
382.	Por las buenas o por las malas	De mangas o de faldas (*Ec.*)	Whether one likes it or not; by hook or by crook
383.	Por las nubes		Sky-high; up in the clouds
384.	Por lo demás		As for the rest; moreover
385.	Por lo menos	Cuando menos; al menos	At least
386.	Por lo pronto	Por el momento	For the time being
387.	Por lo visto		Apparently; evidently
388.	Por más quc		However much
389.	Por poco	Por un pelito de rana; casi, casi	Almost; like(d) to
390.	Por sabido se calla	¡Clarinete!	It goes without saying
391.	Por si acaso		Just in case; if by chance
392.	Por supuesto	Claro que sí; ¿cómo no?	Of course; certainly
393.	Por sus puños		On one's own
394.	Por término medio		On the average

	Academy Spanish	American Spanish Variants	English Equivalents
395.	Preguntarse si, cuándo, cómo, etc.		To wonder (if, when, how, etc.)
396.	Prender fuego a	Prender candela (*Col., Andes*)	To set fire to; to set on fire
397.	Presumir de		To consider oneself to be
398.	Prometer el oro y el moro	Prometer las perlas de la Virgen	To promise wonders (the moon)
399.	Puesto que	Ya que	Because of the fact that; since
400.	Puro jarabe de pico	Pura guasa; pura parada (*Mex.*)	Just talk; lip service; eyewash
401.	Que Dios le tenga en la gloria	Que en paz descanse	God rest his soul; may he rest in peace
402.	¿Qué más da?		What's the difference? So what?
403.	¿Qué mosca te picó?		What's the matter with you? What's bugging you?
404.	¿Qué hay de nuevo?	¿Quiubo? (qué hubo) (*Mex., Col.*)	What's up? What's the good word? How goes it?
405.	Quedar en		To agree (on)
406.	Quedar en (de)		To promise to
407.	Quedar en los huesos	No quedar más que hueso y cuero	To be a mere skeleton; to be nothing but skin and bones
408.	Quedar en paz	Quedar a mano	To be even; to be square
409.	Quedar mal con		Not to be on good terms with; not to make a hit with
410.	Quedarse a la luna de Valencia	Dejarle a uno de a pie; quedarse a la luna de Paita (*Andes*)	To be left holding the bag
411.	Quedarse con		To agree to buy (take)
412.	Quedarse para vestir santos	Quedarse para vender estampas y milagros	To be left on the shelf
413.	Quemarse las cejas	Quemarse las pestañas; ponerse barbero (*Col.*); machetear (*Mex.*)	To burn the midnight oil; to cram for an exam
414.	Querer decir		To mean
415.	Quien bien te quiere, te hará llorar	Porque te quiero, te aporreo	Spare the rod and spoil the child
416.	Quien fue a Sevilla perdió su silla	El que se fue para la villa perdió su silla	Finders keepers, losers weepers
417.	Quien porfía mata venado	Quien mucho porfía logra algún día; hay que hacer collera (*Ch.*)	If at first you don't succeed, try, try again; never say die
418.	Quitarse de en medio	Hacerse a un lado; borrarse	To get out of the way
419.	Rezar con	Tener que ver con	To have to do with
420.	Risa de conejo	Reir de dientes afuera (*Col., Mex.*); reir a diente pelado (*Ven.*)	Half-hearted laugh
421.	Ropa blanca	Ropa interior; ropa intima (feminine)	Underclothes; underwear
422.	Saber a (la) gloria		To be delicious
423.	Saber al dedillo		To know perfectly; to know in detail
424.	Saber de sobra		To be fully aware; to know only too well
425.	Saber llevar el compás		To be able to beat time
426.	Sacar en limpio		To deduce; to understand
427.	Sacar jugo de		To get a lot out of
428.	Sacar partido de		To profit (gain) by
429.	Salir a pedir de boca	Salir al pelo	To be all one could wish for; to suit to a T
430.	Salir de Málaga y entrar en Malagón	Salir de Guatemala y entrar en Guatepeor	Out of the frying pan and into the fire
431.	Salir del paso		To manage; to get by
432.	Saltar a la vista		To be obvious; not to be able to miss
433.	Según el caso		According to the situation; it all depends
434.	Sentir en el alma		To be terribly sorry
435.	Sentir crecer la hierba	Tener oídos de tísico	To have ears like a fox; to have a sharp ear

	Academy Spanish	*American Spanish Variants*	*English Equivalents*
436.	Ser cabeza de turco		To be the scapegoat; to be the whipping boy; to be a patsy
437.	Ser correcto		To be well-mannered
438.	Ser de fiar		To be trustworthy; to be dependable
439.	Ser de rigor		To be proper; to be indispensable
440.	Ser mala pieza	Ser una mala ficha (*Col.*)	To be a misfit (bad penny)
441.	Ser mano	Llevar la punta	To lead; to be first
442.	Ser un éxito de taquilla		To be a box-office success (hit)
443.	Sin embargo		Nevertheless
444.	Sin faltar una jota		In minutest detail
445.	Sin fin de		Numberless; endless amount
446.	Sin ton ni son		Without rhyme or reason
447.	Sudar la gota gorda	Sudar petróleo	To have a hard time; to sweat blood; to be in a sweat
448.	Tal vez	A saber (*C.A.*)*;* ¡quién quita! (*Col.*)	Perhaps; maybe
449.	Tanto peor		So much the worse
450.	Tener al corriente		To keep someone posted; to keep someone up to date
451.	Tener buenas aldabas	Tener buenas agarraderas; tener palanca; tener enchufe (*Spain*)	To know the right people; to know influential people; to have a pipeline; to have pull
452.	Tener el riñón bien cubierto	Estar bien parado; tener la canasta baja y el riñón bien cubierto (*Mex.*)	To be well-off; to be well-heeled
453.	Tener en cuenta		To consider; to keep in mind
454.	Tener en poco		To hold in low esteem; not to think much of
455.	Tener ganas de	Apetecer (*Spain*)*;* provocarle a uno (*Col.*)	To feel like; to desire
456.	Tener gracia	Ser chistoso	To be funny
457.	Tener la palabra		To have permission to speak; to have the floor
458.	Tener lugar		To take place; to be held
459.	Tener mucho mundo		To be sophisticated
460.	Tener pesar por	Darle a uno pena	To be sorry about
461.	Tener presente		To realize; to bear in mind
462.	Tener sin cuidado		Not to be concerned; to care less
463.	Tener trazas		To show signs
464.	Tocar de oído		To play by ear
465.	Tocar en lo vivo		To hurt deeply; to cut to the quick
466.	Tocarle a uno		To concern one; to be one's turn
467.	Todo bicho viviente		Every living soul
468.	Todo lo contrario		Just the opposite
469.	Toma y daca	Dando y dando, pajarito volando	Cash and carry; put your money where your mouth is
470.	Tomar a pecho		To take to heart
471.	Tomar cuerpo		To take shape
472.	Tomar el rábano por las hojas		To put the cart before the horse
473.	Tomarla con		To pick on; to have a grudge against
474.	Tomarle el pelo a uno	Hacerle guaje a uno (*Mex.*)	To pull someone's leg; to kid someone
475.	Trabajar como una fiera	Trabajar como burro; trabajar como negro	To work like a dog
476.	Trabar amistad		To strike up a friendship
477.	Traer retraso		To be behind schedule; to be late
478.	¡Trato hecho!	¡Chóquela! ¡Echeme esos cinco!	It's a deal! Shake on it! Put 'er there!

	Academy Spanish	*American Spanish Variants*	*English Equivalents*
479.	¡Tres hurras por fulano!	¡Una porra!	Three cheers for
480.	Un bribón de siete suelas	Uno capaz de empeñar la sábana sagrada	An errant rogue; a dirty rat
481.	Un no sé qué		A certain something
482.	Una comilona	Un banquetazo	A feast fit for a king; quite a spread
483.	Uno que otro		An occasional one; some; a few
484.	Unos cuantos		Some; a few
485.	Valerse de		To avail oneself of; to make use of
486.	Variar de opinión		To hold a different opinion; to change one's mind
487.	Venir a parar		To turn out; to end up
488.	Venirse a tierra		To collapse; to fail
489.	¡Vete a freír espárragos!	¡Vete a freír chongos! (*Mex.*); ¡vete a freír monos! (*Col.*); ¡vete a freír mocos! (*Andes*)	Go peddle your papers! Get lost!
490.	Vísteme despacio que tengo prisa	Más vale paso que dure y no que apresure	Haste makes waste; easy does it
491.	Volver el estómago	Huacarear (*Mex.*); echar las migas; dársele vuelta la vianda a uno (*Ch.*)	To vomit; to have the heaves; to upchuck; to toss one's cookies
492.	Voy y vengo	No me tardo un minuto; oritita vengo (*Mex.*)	I'll be right back; it won't be a minute
493.	Y así sucesivamente		And so on
494.	Y pico		And some odd; and something
495.	Y sanseacabó	Ahí muere	That's final. It's all over with
496.	Ya cayó el chivo en el lazo	Este arroz ya se coció	It's in the bag
497.	Ya lo creo	A la fija (*Ríopl.*) ¿Cómo no?	Of course; certainly
498.	Ya ni llorar es bueno	Nada logras con llorar delante del bien perdido	Don't cry over spilt milk
499.	Zapatero a tus zapatos		Mind your own business
500.	¡Zas!		Bang!

English Index to Spanish Idioms and Proverbs

Parte Segunda Inglés-Español

Al Lector

El auge que desde el principio de la Segunda Guerra Mundial viene cobrando en la América española el aprendizaje del inglés, nos ha movido a recopilar en este breve Diccionario las voces y locuciones más indispensables de esta lengua tal como se habla y escribe en los Estados Unidos de América.

Al igual que en la Sección española-inglesa hemos antepuesto la abreviatura *Am.* y otras de señalados países o regiones a aquellos vocablos o modismos que son de uso exclusivo en alguna región de la América española, o bien de uso frecuentísimo en ésta, aunque ya hayan caído en desuso en la Península. Todo lo cual no excluye la posibilidad de que alguna acepción así designada se oiga en labios de un español o sea de uso esporádico en España.

Lo que sí hemos procurado con gran ahinco y anhelamos lograr, presentando al estudioso este caudal indispensable de palabras, es el acercamiento lingüístico de las Américas, como base para nuestra mutua comprensión y como instrumento poderosísimo para nuestra solidaridad.

LOS EDITORES

Lista de Abreviaturas

adj.	adjetivo
adv.	adverbio
art.	articulo
art. indef.	artículo indefinido
aux.	auxiliar
comp.	comparativo
conj.	conjunción
contr.	contracción
defect.	defectivo
etc.	etcétera
ger.	gerundio
gram.	gramatical, gramática
imperf.	imperfecto
indic.	indicativo
interj.	interjección
interr.	interrogativo
irr.	irregular
p.p.	participio pasado o pasivo
pers.	personal
pl.	plural
pos.	posesivo
prep.	preposición
pron.	pronombre
pron. pers.	pronombre personal
pron. pos.	pronombre posesivo
s.	sustantivo
sing.	singular
subj.	subjuntivo
v.	verbo
v. defect.	verbo defectivo
v. irr.	verbo irregular

Abreviaturas Especiales de Indicación Regional

Am.[1]	Americanismo
Andalucía	
Andes	(Ecuador, Perú, Bolivia)
Arg.	Argentina
Bol.	Bolivia
Carib.	(Cuba, Puerto Rico, República Dominicana)

1. Esta abreviatura se emplea para indicar uso general hispanoamericano; se implica a la vez carácter arcaizante en cuanto a España. Se usa también para señalar los vocablos ya poco usados que puedan encontrarse en obras literarias del siglo pasado.

C.A.	Centroamérica (Guatemala, El Salvador, Honduras, Nicaragua, Costa Rica)
Ch.	Chile
Col.	Colombia
C.R.	Costa Rica
Cuba	
Ec.	El Ecuador
Esp.	España
Guat.	Guatemala
Hond.	Honduras
Méx.	México
N. Esp.	Norte de España
Nic.	Nicaragua
Pan.	Panamá
Par.	Paraguay
Perú	
P.R.	Puerto Rico
Ríopl.	Río de la Plata (La Argentina oriental, el Uruguay)
S.A.	Sudamérica
Sal.	El Salvador
Ur.	El Uruguay
Ven.	Venezuela

Pronunciación Inglesa[2]

I. Vocales

Símbolo fonético	*Ortografía inglesa*	*Ortografía fonética*	*Explicación de los sonidos*
i	see pea	si pi	Equivale a la *i* en *hilo.*
ɪ	bit	bɪt	El sonido más aproximado es la *i* en *virtud,* pero la [ɪ] inglesa es una *i* más abierta tirando a *e* cerrada
e	late they	let ðe	Equivale aproximadamente a *ei;* la *i* de este diptongo es muy relajada y más abierta que en español.
ɛ	bet	bɛt	El sonido más aproximado en español es la *e* abierta de *perro.*
æ	sat	sæt	Es una vocal intermedia entre la *a* y la *e.*
ɑ	car	kɑr	Equivale aproximadamente a la *a* en *cargo.*
ɔ	forge	fɔrdʒ	Equivale aproximadamente a la *o* en *corto, corre.*
o	mode	mod	Equivale aproximadamente a *ou;* la *u* de este diptongo es muy relajada y más abierta que en español.
ʊ	pull	pʊl	El sonido más aproximado en español es la *u* en *turrón,* pero la [ʊ] inglesa es todavía más abierta.
u	June moon	dʒun mun	Equivale aproximadamente a la *u* en *uno.*
ə	cudgel apply	kʌ́dʒəl əpláɪ	Es una *e* muy relajada. No tiene equivalente en español.
ɚ	teacher	títʃɚ	Es una *e* muy relajada, articulada simultáneamente con la *r.* No tiene equivalente en español.

2. El estudioso puede consultar el importante diccionario de pronunciación norteamericana: Kenyon and Knott, *A Pronouncing Dictionary of American English* (Springfield, Massachusetts: G & C. Merriam Company, Publishers, 1944).

Símbolo fonético	*Ortografía inglesa*	*Ortografía fonética*	*Explicación de los sonidos*
ɝ	earth fur	ɝθ fɝ	Es un sonido intermedio entre la *e* y la *o* articulado simultáneamente con la *r*. Se acerca más a la *e* que a la *o*. No tiene equivalente en español.
ʌ	duck	dʌk	Es una vocal intermedia entre la *e* muy abierta y la *o*. Se acerca más a la *o* que a la *e*. No tiene equivalente en español.

II. Diptongos

aɪ	aisle nice	aɪl naɪs	Equivale aproximadamente a *ai* en *aire*.
aʊ	now	naʊ	Equivale aproximadamente a *au* en *causa*.
ɔɪ	coy	kɔɪ	Equivale aproximadamente a *oy* en *hoy*. El segundo elemento del diptongo es más abierto y débil, tirando a *e*.
ju	used	juzd	Equivale aproximadamente a *iu* en *ciudad*.
jʊ	cure	kjʊr	Equivale aproximadamente al diptongo *iu*, pero la *u* es más abierta.

III. Consonantes

p	paper	pépɚ	Equivale aproximadamente a la *p* española, pero es aspirada.
b	bat	bæt	La *b* inglesa es semejante a la *b* inicial española, pero se pronuncia más explosivamente.
t	tea	ti	Es bastante diferente de la *t* española. Se articula colocando flojamente la lengua arriba de los dientes incisivos superiores y es aspirada.
d	day	de	Equivale a la *d* inicial española pronunciada con mayor énfasis y se articula arriba de los dientes.
k	cat kill	kæt kɪl	Equivale aproximadamente a la *c* española delante de *a, o, u* pronunciada con aspiracion.
g	go gum ago	go gʌm əgó	Equivale aproximadamente, a la *g* inicial delante de *a, o, u: goma, guerra, gana;* sólo que la *g* inglesa se pronuncia con mayor explosión.
f	fun affair	fʌn əfǽr	Equivale aproximadamente a la *f* española.
v	very	vɛ́rɪ	De vez en cuando se oye en español como ultracorrección. Es una labiodental que se articula con el labio inferior y los dientes incisivos superiores.
θ	thin	θɪn	Equivale aproximadamente a la *z* en el castellano *cazar*.
ð	then other	ðɛn ʌ́ðɚ	Equivale aproximadamente a la *d* española en *nada*.
s	send case cent	sɛnd kes sɛnt	Equivale aproximadamente a la *s* inicial española de Hispanoamérica; *santo*.
z	rose these zero	roz ðiz zíro	Equivale aproximadamente a la *s* sonora en *mismo*, pero se pronuncia con más sonoridad en inglés.
ʃ	sheet machine nation	ʃit maʃín néʃən	Es una *s* palatal que no tiene equivalente en español. Suena como la *ch* francesa; *chapeau*.
ʒ	vision	viʒən	Es una palatal fricativa sonora, semejante a la y argentina y uruguaya o la *j* de *jouer* en francés.
tʃ	chase	tʃes	Equivale aproximadamente a la *ch* en *charla*.
dʒ	judge gentle	dʒʌdʒ dʒɛ́ntl	No tiene equivalente exacto en español. Se parece a la *y* de *inyectar* en la pronunciación de muchos hispanoamericanos.

Símbolo fonético	*Ortografía inglesa*	*Ortografía fonética*	*Explicación de los sonidos*
m	much	mʌtʃ	Equivale aproximadamente a la *m* española.
n	none any	nʌn ɛ́nɪ	Equivale aproximadamente a la *n* española en *nada*.
n̩	eaten button lesson	itn̩ bʌ́tn̩ lɛ́sn̩	No tiene equivalente en español. Representa la *n* sin la articulación de la vocal anterior.
ŋ	ankle angle ring	ǽŋkl̩ ǽŋgl̩ rɪŋ	Equivale a la *n* española en *mango, banco*.
l	late altar fall folly	let ɔ́ltɚ fɔl fálɪ	La *l* inicial equivale aproximadamente a la *l* española en *lado*. La *l* final de sílaba es más débil que la inicial y semejante a la portuguesa o a la catalana.
l̩	able ankle	ébl̩ ǽŋkl̩	No tiene equivalente en español. Se pronuncia como la *l* final de sílaba, omitiendo la vocal precedente.
w	weed well wall	wid wɛl wɔl	Equivale a la *u* de los diptongos; *ui, ue, ua, uo*.
h	hat whole	hæt hol	No tiene equivalente exacto en español. Equivale aproximadamente a una *j* suave que se reduce a una simple aspiración.
hw	where	hwɛr	Equivale a una *j* suave seguida de una *w* arriba explicada, y se usa en la mayoría de los dialectos norteamericanos.
j	year yawn yet	jɪr jɔn jɛt	Equivale a la *i* española en los diptongos *ie, ia, io, iu: hiena*.
r	rose bear	roz bɛr	No tiene equivalente en español. La punta de la lengua se arrolla hacia atrás sin tocar el paladar. A veces se pierde al grado de vocalizarse.

Pronunciación de la *S* del Plural[3]

I. La **-s** del plural es sorda cuando la palabra termina en las consonantes sordas representadas por los símbolos fonéticos [p], [t], [k], [f], [θ]. Pronúnciase como la *s* de *santo:* **caps** [kæps], **gates** [gets], **cats** [kæts], **books** [bʊks], **cliffs** [klɪfs], **lengths** [leŋkθs].
Las excepciones más comunes son: **oath** [oθ], **oaths** [oðz]; **leaf** [lif], **leaves** [livz], **wife** [waɪf], **wives** [waɪvz]; **knife** [naɪf], **knives** [naɪvz]; **calf** [kæf], **calves** [kævz]; **half** [hæf], **halves** [hævz].

II. La **-s** del plural es sonora cuando la palabra termina en vocal (incluyendo la **-y** que se cambia en **-ies**), o en las consonantes sonoras representadas por los símbolos fonéticos [b], [d], [g], [v], [ð], [m], [n], [ŋ], [l]: **cries** [kraɪz], **robes** [robz], **beds** [bɛdz], **logs** [lɔgz], **stoves** [stovz], **lathes** [leðz], **farms** [farmz], **bins** [bɪnz], **kings** [kɪŋz], **falls** [fɔlz], **furs** [fɝz], **papers** [pépɝz], **plows** [plaʊz].

III. Cuando la palabra termina **-en** las consonantes representadas por los símbolos [s], [ʃ], [tʃ], [z], [ʒ], [dʒ], se añade **-es** [ɪz], o **s** [ɪz], si la palabra termina en **-ce, -se, -dge, -ge: face** [fes], **faces** [fésɪz]; **kiss** [kɪs], **kisses** [kɪ́sɪz]; **ash** [æʃ], **ashes** [æʃɪz]; **lunch** [lʌntʃ], **lunches** [lʌntʃɪz]; **rose** [roz], **roses** [rózɪz]; **judge** [dʒʌdʒ], **judges** [dʒʌdʒɪz].

3. Las mismas reglas se aplican a la pronunciación del genitivo y de la tercera persona del presente de indicativo, singular: **keeps** [kips]; **Kate's** [kets]; **saves** [sevz]; **John's** [dʒanz]; **judges** [dʒʌ́dʒɪz]; **Alice's** [ǽlɪsɪz].

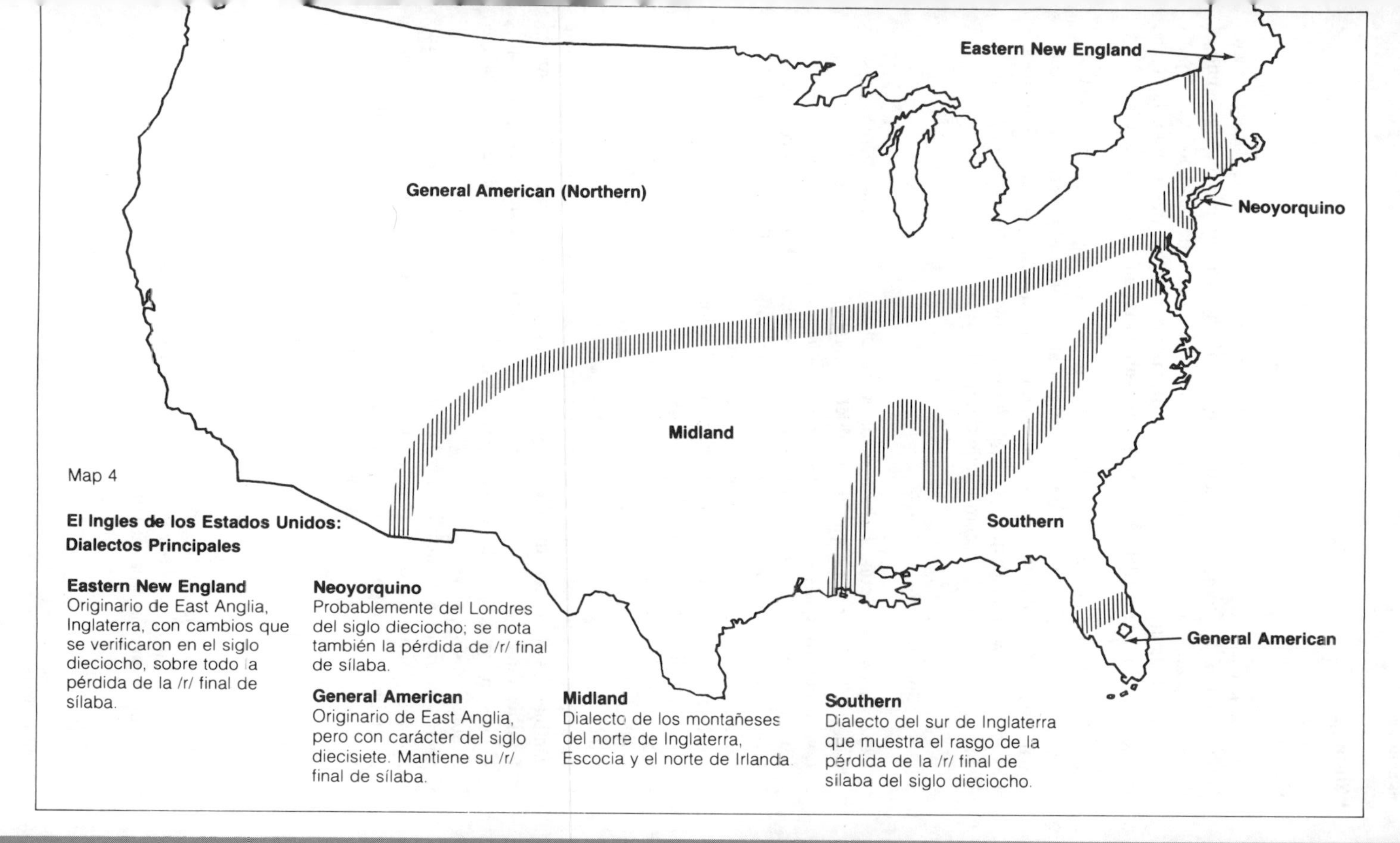
Eastern New England
General American (Northern)
Neoyorquino
Midland
Southern
General American
Map 4
El Ingles de los Estados Unidos:
Dialectos Principales
Eastern New England
Originario de East Anglia, Inglaterra, con cambios que se verificaron en el siglo dieciocho, sobre todo la pérdida de la /r/ final de sílaba.
Neoyorquino
Probablemente del Londres del siglo dieciocho; se nota también la pérdida de /r/ final de sílaba.
General American
Originario de East Anglia, pero con carácter del siglo diecisiete. Mantiene su /r/ final de sílaba.
Midland
Dialecto de los montañeses del norte de Inglaterra, Escocia y el norte de Irlanda.
Southern
Dialecto del sur de Inglaterra que muestra el rasgo de la pérdida de la /r/ final de sílaba del siglo dieciocho.

El Sustantivo

I. Género

En la gramática inglesa el género tiene papel mínimo y resulta ser fenómeno léxico. Son masculinos los nombres de varón o animal macho, y son femeninos los nombres de mujer o animal hembra. Los demás son neutros. El artículo definido **the** se aplica a todos los sustantivos, singular y plural: **the man** el hombre; **the men** los hombres; **the book** el libro; **the books** los libros; **the woman** la mujer; **the women** las mujeres.

En ciertos sustantivos se distingue el género femenino por medio del sufijo **-ess: actor** actor; **actress** actriz. A veces es indispensable indicar el género por medio de las palabras **male** o **female, boy** o **girl, man** o **woman, she** o **he: baby boy** niño; **baby girl** niña; **woman writer** escritora; **she-bear** osa. En otros casos hay una palabra distinta para cada género; **uncle** tío; **aunt** tía.

II. Plural de los Sustantivos[4]

1. Generalmente se forma el plural añadiendo **-s** al singular: **paper, papers** papel, papeles; **book, books** libro, libros; **chief, chiefs** jefe, jefes.
2. Los sustantivos que terminan en **-ch** (pronunciada como la *ch* española), **-ss, -x, -sh, -z,** y **-o** añaden **-es** para formar el plural: **arch, arches** arco, arcos; **kiss, kisses** beso, besos; **box, boxes** caja, cajas; **dish, dishes** plato, platos; **buzz, buzzes** zumbido, zumbidos; **hero, heroes** héroe, héroes. Nótese que los sustantivos terminados en **-ch** (pronunciada [**k**]) forman el plural añadiendo **-s: monarch, monarchs** monarca, monarcas.
3. Los sustantivos que terminan en **-fe,** y ciertos sustantivos que terminan en **-f,** cambian estas letras en **v** y añaden **-es: leaf, leaves** hoja, hojas; **life, lives** vida, vidas; **wife, wives** esposa, esposas; **knife, knives** cuchillo, cuchillos.
4. Para formar el plural de los sustantivos terminados en **-y** precedida de consonante cámbiase la **-y** en **-ies: fly, flies** mosca, moscas; **cry, cries** grito, gritos; **family, families** familia, familias; **quantity, quantities** cantidad, cantidades. Nótese que los sustantivos terminados en **-y** precedida de vocal forman el plural añadiendo **-s** al singular: **day, days** día, días.
5. Ciertos sustantivos forman el plural de una manera irregular: **man, men** hombre, hombres; **woman, women** mujer, mujeres; **mouse, mice** ratón, ratones; **louse, lice** piojo, piojos; **goose, geese** ganso, gansos; **tooth, teeth** diente, dientes; **foot, feet** pie, pies; **ox, oxen** buey, bueyes.
6. Ciertos sustantivos que terminan en **-is** forman el plural cambiando la **i** de la terminación en **e: axis, axes** eje, ejes; **the crisis, the crises** la crisis, las crisis.

El Adjetivo

El adjetivo inglés es invariable en cuanto a género y número. Normalmente se coloca delante del sustantivo: **an interesting book** un libro interesante; **a large table** una mesa grande; **beautiful women** mujeres hermosas.

4. Véase las reglas para la pronunciación del plural.

Los comparativos y superlativos. Aunque no hay una regla general, por lo común los adjetivos monosílabos, los adjetivos acentuados en la última sílaba y algunos bisílabos fácilmente pronunciados forman *el comparativo de aumento y el superlativo* añadiendo **-er** y **-est.** Los demás adjetivos van precedidos de **more** y **most.** Nótese que (1) sólo se añaden **-r** y **-st** a los que terminan en **-e** muda; (2) los adjetivos terminados en **-y** cambian esta letra en **i;** (3) los adjetivos terminados en consonante precedida de vocal doblan la consonante:

Positivo	*Comparativo*	*Superlativo*
tall alto	**taller** más alto	**the tallest** el más alto
wise sabio	**wiser** más sabio	**the wisest** el más sabio
polite cortés	**politer** más cortés	**the politest** el más cortés
happy feliz	**happier** más feliz	**the happiest** el más feliz
fat gordo	**fatter** más gordo	**the fattest** el más gordo
careful cuidadoso	**more careful** maś cuidadoso	**the most careful** el más cuidadoso

El superlativo absoluto se forma anteponiendo **very** y a veces **most: very intelligent** muy inteligente; **she is a most beautiful woman** es una mujer hermosísima.

El comparativo y el superlativo de inferioridad se forman con los adverbios **less** y **least: less important** menos importante; **the least important** el menos importante.

El comparativo de igualdad se forma con el adverbio **as: as poor as** tan pobre como; **as much as** tanto como; **as much money as** tanto dinero como.

Los adjetivos siguientes forman el comparativo y el superlativo de una manera irregular:

good, well	**better**	**best**
bad, ill	**worse**	**worst**
little	**less, lesser**	**least**
far	**farther, further**	**farthest, furthest**
much, many	**more**	**most**
old	**older, elder**	**oldest, eldest**

El Adverbio

Fórmanse muchos adverbios, añadiendo **-ly** al adjetivo: **courteous** cortés, **courteously** cortésmente; **bold** atrevido, **boldly** atrevidamente. Existen las irregularidades siguientes en la formación de los adverbios que terminan en **-ly:** (1) los adjetivos terminados en **-ble** cambian la **-e** en **-y: possible, possibly;** (2) los terminados en **ic** añaden **-ally: poetic, poetically;** (3) los terminados en **-ll** añaden sólo la **-y: full, fully;** (4) los terminados en **-ue** pierden la **-e** final: **true, truly;** (5) los terminados en **-y** cambian la **-y** en **i: happy, happily.**

Como los adjetivos, la mayor parte de los adverbios forman el *comparativo* y el *superlativo* con los adverbios **more** (más), **most** (más), y **very** (muy). Asimismo los adverbios monosílabos añaden **-er** y **-est:**

Positivo	*Comparative*	*Superlativo*	*Superlativo Absoluto*
boldly	**more boldly**	**most boldly**	**very boldly**
generously	**more generously**	**most generously**	**very generously**
soon	**sooner**	**soonest**	**very soon**
early	**earlier**	**earliest**	**very early**

late	**later**	**latest**	**very late**
near	**nearer**	**nearest**	**very near**
fast	**faster**	**fastest**	**very fast**

Los adverbios siguientes forman el comparativo y el superlativo de una manera irregular:

well	**better**	**best**	**very well**
badly, ill	**worse**	**worst**	**very badly**
little	**less**	**least**	**very little**
much	**more**	**most**	**very much**
far	**farther, further**	**farthest, furthest**	**very far**

Sufijos Comunes en Inglés

-dom denota dominio, jurisdicción, estado, condición, etc.: **kingdom** reino; **martyrdom** martirio; **boredom** aburrimiento; **freedom** libertad.

-ed, -d es la terminación del pretérito y del participio pasivo o pasado de los verbos regulares: **I called** llamé; **called** llamado.

-ee indica la persona que recibe la acción: **addressee** destinatario; **employee** empleado.

-eer denota oficio u ocupación: **engineer** ingeniero; **auctioneer** subastador.

-en *a)* terminación del participio de muchos verbos irregulares: **fallen, broken, shaken;**
b) sufijo que significa *hecho de:* **golden** dorado, de oro; **wooden** de madera; **leaden** de plomo;
c) terminación verbal equivalente a *hacer:* **whiten** hacer blanco, emblanquecer; **darken** hacer obscuro, obscurecer.

-er *a)* indica la persona que hace o el agente de la acción del verbo: **player** jugador; **speaker** orador;
b) indica el residente de un lugar: **New Yorker** habitante o residente de Nueva York; **islander** isleño;
c) denota ocupación: **carpenter** carpintero; **baker** panadero.
d) es la terminación del comparativo de adjetivos y adverbios; **taller** más alto; **faster** más aprisa.

-ess úsase para formar el género femenino de ciertos sustantivos: **actress** actriz; **princess** princesa; **countess** condesa.

-est terminación del superlativo: **tallest** el más alto.

-fold sufijo que significa *veces:* **twofold** dos veces; **hundredfold** cien veces.

-ful *a)* equivale a *lleno,* y tratándose de adjectivos es igual a *-oso:* **hopeful** lleno de esperanzas; **careful** cuidadoso; **willful** voluntarioso; **merciful** misericordioso; **glassful** un vaso *(lleno);*
b) indica a veces hábito o inclinación: **forgetful** olvidadizo;
c) es a veces equivalente a los sufijos españoles *-ado, -ada:* **handful** puñado; **spoonful** cucharada.

-hood indica estado, condición, carácter, grupo: a menudo equivale a -*dad:* **motherhood** maternidad; **brotherhood** fraternidad; **childhood** niñez; **likelihood** probabilidad.

-ician denota especialidad en cierto ramo: **musician** músico; **technician** técnico; **electrician** electricista.

-ie sufijo diminutivo: **birdie** pajarito; **Annie** Anita.

-ing *a)* sufijo del gerundio: **speaking** hablando;
b) sufijo del participio activo: **threatening** amenazante; **surprising** sorprendente;
c) úsase a menudo para formar adjetivos: **running water** agua corriente; **drinking water** agua potable; **waiting room** sala de espera; **washing machine** máquina lavadora;
d) úsase para formar sustantivos: **understanding** entendimiento; **supplying** abastecimiento; **clothing** ropa; **covering** cobertura; equivale al infinitivo castellano: **swimming is good exercise** el nadar es buen ejercicio.

-ish *a)* úsase para formar ciertos adjetivos de nacionalidad: **Spanish** español; **English** inglés; **Turkish** turco;
b) indica semejanza: **boyish** como niño, aniñado; **womanish** como mujer, mujeril, afeminado; **whitish** blancuzco, medio blanco, que tira a blanco.

-less equivale a *sin, falto de:* **childless** sin hijos; **penniless** sin dinero; en ciertos casos el sufijo inglés se traduce por medio de un prefijo: **countless** innumerable, sin número; **endless** interminable, sin fin.

-like significa *semejanza,* y equivale a *como, a manera de:* **lifelike** que parece vivo; **childlike** como niño, infantil; **tigerlike** como tigre.

-ly *a)* sufijo adverbial: **slowly** lentamente; **happily** felizmente; **possibly** posiblemente;
b) añadido a ciertos sustantivos equivale a *como, a la manera de:* **motherly** como madre, materno; **gentlemanly** como caballero, caballeroso; **friendly** amigable; **manly** varonil;
c) equivale a *cada* en estos ejemplos: **daily** cada día; diario; **weekly** cada semana, semanal; **monthly** cada mes, mensual; **yearly** cada año, anual.

-ness úsase para formar sustantivos abstractos: **goodness** bondad; **darkness** obscuridad; **foolishness** tontería; **shamelessness** desvergüenza.

-ship *a)* úsase para formar sustantivos abstractos: **friendship** amistad; **relationship** relación, parentesco;
b) denota arte o destreza: **horsemanship** equitación;
c) expresa dignidad, oficio, cargo, o título: **professorship** profesorado o cátedra; **chairmanship** presidencia (*de un comité, asamblea, etc.*); **lordship** señoría;
d) a veces expresa tan sólo un estado y su duración: **courtship** galanteo, cortejo, noviazgo.

-some expresa en alto grado la cualidad representada por el vocablo al cual se añade: **tiresome** que cansa, cansado; **quarrelsome** dado a riñas, pendenciero; **loathsome** que repugna, asqueroso; **burdensome** gravoso.

-th úsase para formar números ordinales: **fifth** quinto; **tenth** décimo.

-ty *a)* terminación de los múltiples de diez: **twenty** veinte; **thirty** treinta; **forty** cuarenta;

	b) terminación de muchos sustantivos abstractos; equivale frecuentemente al sufijo español *-tad* o *-dad:* **beauty** beldad; **paternity** paternidad; **falsity** falsedad.
-ward, -wards	denotan *hacia:* **homeward** hacia casa; **downward** hacia abajo.
-ways, -wise	expresan manera, dirección, posición, etc.: **edgewise** de lado; **sideways** de lado; **lengthwise** a lo largo.
-y	*a)* terminación equivalente a los sufijos españoles *-ia, -ía:* **victory** victoria; **glory** gloria; **courtesy** cortesía; **biology** biología; **astronomy** astronomía; *b)* sufijo diminutivo: **doggy** perrito; **Johnny** Juanito; *c)* denota abundancia, y es a menudo equivalente a *-udo, -oso, -ado:* **rocky** lleno de rocas, rocoso, pedregoso; **rainy** lluvioso; **hairy** lleno de pelo, peludo; **bulky** abultado; **wavy** ondulado; **angry** enojado; *d)* expresa semejanza: **rosy** rosado, como una rosa, color de rosa.

Números

Consúltese la tabla de la página 38 de la Sección Española-Inglesa para el aprendizaje de los números cardinales y ordinales desde uno hasta un millón.

Verbos Irregulares de la Lengua Inglesa

Se denominan verbos irregulares los que no forman el pretérito o el participio pasivo con la adición de **-d** o **-ed** al presente. Obsérvese que en ciertos verbos coexiste la forma regular al lado de la irregular. En otros coexisten dos formas irregulares juntamente con la regular.

Presente	*Pretérito*	*Participio pasivo o pasado*
abide	abode	abode
am, is, are	was, were	been
arise	arose	arisen
awake	awoke, awaked	awaked, awoke
bear	bore	born, borne
beat	beat	beat, beaten
become	became	become
befall	befell	befallen
beget	begat	begotten
begin	began	begun
behold	beheld	beheld
bend	bent	bent
bereave	bereft, bereaved	bereft, bereaved
beseech	besought, beseeched	besought, beseeched
beset	beset	beset
bet	bet	bet
bid	bid, bade	bidden, bid
bind	bound	bound
bite	bit	bitten, bit
bleed	bled	bled
blow	blew	blown
break	broke	broken
breed	bred	bred
bring	brought	brought
build	built	built
burn	burnt, burned	burnt, burned
burst	burst	burst
buy	bought	bought
can *(verbo defectivo)*	could	—

Presente	*Pretérito*	*Participio pasivo o pasado*
cast	cast	cast
catch	caught	caught
chide	chided, chid	chided, chidden
choose	chose	chosen
cleave	cleft, clove, cleaved	cleft, cleaved, cloven
cling	clung	clung
clothe	clad, clothed	clad, clothed
come	came	come
cost	cost	cost
creep	crept	crept
crow	crew, crowed	crowed
cut	cut	cut
deal	dealt	dealt
dig	dug, digged	dug, digged
dive	dived, dove	dived, dove
do	did	done
draw	drew	drawn
dream	dreamt, dreamed	dreamt, dreamed
drink	drank	drunk
drive	drove	driven
dwell	dwelled	dwelt, dwelled
eat	ate	eaten
fall	fell	fallen
feed	fed	fed
feel	felt	felt
fight	fought	fought
find	found	found
flee	fled	fled
fling	flung	flung
fly	flew	flown
forbear	forbore	forborne
forbid	forbade	forbidden
foresee	foresaw	foreseen
foretell	foretold	foretold
forget	forgot	forgotten, forgot
forgive	forgave	forgiven
forsake	forsook	forsaken
freeze	froze	frozen
get	got	got, gotten
gild	gilded	gilt, gilded
gird	girded	girt, girded
give	gave	given
go	went	gone
grind	ground	ground
grow	grew	grown
hang[5]	hung	hung
have, has	had	had
hear	heard	heard
heave	hove, heaved	hove, heaved
hew	hewed	hewn, hewed
hide	hid	hidden, hid
hit	hit	hit
hold	held	held
hurt	hurt	hurt
inlay	inlaid	inlaid
keep	kept	kept
kneel	knelt	knelt
knit	knit, knitted	knit, knitted
know	knew	known
lay	laid	laid
lead	led	led
lean	leaned	leaned, leant
leap	leapt, leaped	leapt, leaped
learn	learned	learned, learnt

5. Es regular cuando significa «ahorcar.»

Presente	*Pretérito*	*Participio pasivo o pasado*
leave	left	left
lend	lent	lent
let	let	let
lie[6] **(yacer; echarse)**	lay	lain
light	lit, lighted	lit, lighted
load	loaded	loaded, laden
lose	lost	lost
make	made	made
may *(verbo defectivo)*	might	—
mean	meant	meant
meet	met	met
melt	melted	melted, molten
mistake	mistook	mistaken
mow	mowed	mown, mowed
must *(verbo defectivo)*	—	—
ought *(verbo defectivo)*	ought	—
pay	paid	paid
plead	pled, pleaded	pled, pleaded
put	put	put
quit	quit, quitted	quit, quitted
read [rid]	read [rɛd]	read [rɛd]
rend	rent	rent
rid	rid, ridded	rid, ridded
ride	rode	ridden
ring	rang, rung	rung
rise	rose	risen
run	ran	run
saw	sawed	sawn, sawed
say	said	said
see	saw	seen
seek	sought	sought
sell	sold	sold
send	sent	sent
set	set	set
sew	sewed	sewn, sewed
shake	shook	shaken
shall	should	—
shave	shaved	shaved, shaven
shear	sheared	shorn, sheared
shed	shed	shed
shine[7]	shone	shone
shoe	shod	shod
shoot	shot	shot
show	showed	shown, showed
shred	shred, shredded	shred, shredded
shrink	shrank, shrunk	shrunk, shrunken
shut	shut	shut
sing	sang, sung	sung
sink	sank	sunk
sit	sat	sat
slay	slew	slain
sleep	slept	slept
slide	slid	slid, slidden
sling	slung	slung
slink	slunk	slunk
slit	slit	slit
smell	smelled	smelt, smelled
smite	smote	smitten
sow	sowed	sown, sowed
speak	spoke	spoken
speed	sped, speeded	sped, speeded
spell	spelled, spelt	spelled, spelt
spend	spent	spent

6. Es regular cuando significa «mentir.»
7. Es por lo común regular cuando significa «pulir, dar brillo.»

Presente	*Pretérito*	*Participio pasivo o pasado*
spill	spilled, spilt	spilled, spilt
spin	spun	spun
spit	spit, spat	spit, spat
split	split	split
spread	spread	spread
spring	sprang, sprung	sprung
stand	stood	stood
stave	staved, stove	staved, stove
steal	stole	stolen
stick	stuck	stuck
sting	stung	stung
stink	stank, stunk	stunk
strew	strewed	strewn, strewed
stride	strode	stridden
strike	struck	struck, striken
string	strung	strung
strive	strove, strived	striven, strived
swear	swore	sworn
sweep	swept	swept
swell	swelled	swollen, swelled
swim	swam	swum
swing	swung	swung
take	took	taken
teach	taught	taught
tear	tore	torn
tell	told	told
think	thought	thought
thrive	throve, thrived	thriven, thrived
throw	threw	thrown
thrust	thrust	thrust
tread	trod	trod, trodden
understand	understood	understood
undertake	undertook	undertaken
undo	undid	undone
uphold	upheld	upheld
upset	upset	upset
wake	woke, waked	waked
wear	wore	worn
weave	wove	woven
wed	wedded	wedded, wed
weep	wept	wept
wet	wet, wetted	wet, wetted
will *(verbo auxiliar)*	would	—
win	won	won
wind	wound	wound
withdraw	withdrew	withdrawn
withhold	withheld	withheld
withstand	withstood	withstood
work	worked, wrought	worked, wrought
wring	wrung	wrung
write	wrote	written

A:a

a [ə, e] *art. indef.* un, una; **what — ...!** ¡qué ...!; **such** — tal; tan.

a·ban·don [əbǽndən] *v.* abandonar; dejar; *s.* abandono, desahogo, desenvoltura; entrega.

a·ban·doned [əbǽndənd] *adj.* abandonado; dejado; perverso; inmoral.

a·ban·don·ment [əbǽndənmənt] *s.* abandono, abandonamiento; desamparo; desenvoltura, desembarazo.

a·bashed [əbǽʃt] *adj.* humillado, avergonzado.

a·bate [əbét] *v.* bajar, rebajar; disminuir; acabar con; mitigar(se); calmarse.

a·bate·ment [əbétmənt] *s.* diminución, merma; rebaja, descuento; mitigación.

ab·bess [ǽbəs] *s.* abadesa.

ab·bey [ǽbɪ] *s.* abadía, monasterio.

ab·bot [ǽbət] *s.* abad.

ab·bre·vi·ate [əbríviet] *v.* abreviar, acortar, reducir.

ab·bre·vi·a·tion [əbriviéʃən] *s.* abreviación, abreviatura; **initial** — sigla.

ab·di·cate [ǽbdəket] *v.* abdicar, renunciar.

ab·do·men [ǽbdəmən] *s.* abdomen; vientre.

ab·duct [ǽbdʌ́kt] *v.* secuestrar, raptar, *Am.* plagiar (*a alguien*).

ab·duc·tion [ǽbdʌ́kʃən] *s.* rapto, robo, secuestro (*de una persona*).

ab·er·ra·tion [ǽbəréʃən] *s.* aberración, extravío (*de la mente*).

a·bet [əbɛ́t] *v.* incitar; fomentar.

a·bey·ance [əbéəns] *s.* suspensión; **in** — pendiente.

ab·hor [əbhór] *v.* aborrecer, odiar, abominar.

ab·hor·rence [əbhɔ́rəns] *s.* aborrecimiento, aversión.

a·bide [əbáɪd] *v.* quedar, permanecer; morar, habitar; aguardar; soportar, tolerar; **to — by** conformarse a; atenerse a.

a·bil·i·ty [əbíləti] *s.* habilidad, capacidad.

ab·ject [æbdʒɛ́kt] *adj.* abatido; vil.

ab·jure [æbdʒúr] *v.* abjurar.

ab·la·tive [ǽblətɪv] *adj.* ablativo.

a·ble [ébl̩] *adj.* hábil, capaz; competente; **a·ble-bod·ied** de cuerpo sano; **to be — to** poder; saber.

a·bly [éblɪ] *adv.* hábilmente.

ab·nor·mal [æbnɔ́rml̩] *adj.* anormal.

a·board [əbórd] *adv.* a bordo; en el tren; **to go** — embarcarse; **all — !** *Sp.* ¡viajeros al tren!; *Méx., C.A.* ¡vámonos!

a·bode [əbód] *s.* morada, domicilio, casa; *pret. & p.p. de* **to abide**.

a·bol·ish [əbálɪʃ] *v.* abolir; anular.

ab·o·li·tion [æbəlíʃən] *s.* abolición.

a·bom·i·na·ble [əbámnəbl̩] *adj.* abominable, aborrecible.

a·bort [əbɔ́rt] *v.* abortar.

a·bor·tion [əbɔ́rʃən] *s.* aborto.

a·bound [əbáʊnd] *v.* abundar; **to — with** abundar en.

a·bout [əbáʊt] *prep.* (*concerning*) acerca de, tocante a, respecto de; (*near, surrounding*) alrededor de, por; *adv.* (*almost*) casi, poco más o menos; **at — ten o'clock** a eso de las diez; **to be — one's business** atender a su negocio; **to be — to** estar para, estar a punto de; **to face** — dar media vuelta; **to have no money — one's person** no llevar dinero consigo.

a·bove [əbʌ́v] *prep.* por encima de; sobre; *adv.* arriba; — **all** sobre todo; **a·bove-men·tioned** susodicho, ya mencionado; **from** — de arriba; del cielo, de Dios; *adj.* — **-the -line** presupuesto corriente.

ab·ra·sive [əbrésɪv] *adj.* abrasivo; tosco.

a·breast [əbrɛ́st] *adj. adv.* al lado; **to keep abreast** ponerse al corriente.

a·bridge [əbrídʒ] *v.* abreviar; compendiar, condensar; privar (*a uno de sus derechos*).

a·broad [əbrɔ́d] *adv.* en el extranjero; fuera de casa; **to go** — ir al extranjero; **to spread** — divulgar o publicar por todas partes.

a·brupt [əbrʌ́pt] *adj.* repentino; precipitado; (*steep*) áspero, brusco; escarpado; **-ly** *adv.* de repente; bruscamente.

ab·scess [ǽbsɛs] *s.* absceso.

ab·sence [ǽbsn̩s] *s.* ausencia; falta; — **of mind** distracción; **leave of** — licencia (*para ausentarse*).

ab·sent [ǽbsn̩t] *adj.* ausente; abstraído, distraído; **ab·sent-mind·ed** absorto, abstraído; [æbsɛ́nt] *v.* **to — oneself** ausentarse.

ab·sinthe [ǽbsɪnθ] *s.* ajenjo.

ab·so·lute [ǽbsəlut] *adj.* absoluto; **the** — lo absoluto; **-ly** *adv.* absolutamente; en absoluto.

ab·so·lu·tion [æbsəlúʃən] *s.* absolución.

ab·solve [æbsálv] *v.* absolver, remitir; perdonar, alzar la pena o el castigo.

ab·sorb [əbsɔ́rb] *v.* absorber.

ab·sorb·ent [əbsɔ́rbənt] *adj. & s.* absorbente.

ab·sorp·tion [əbsɔ́rpʃən] *s.* absorción; abstracción, embebecimiento.

ab·stain [əbstén] *v.* abstenerse, privarse.

ab·sti·nence [ǽbstənəns] *s.* abstinencia.

ab·stract [ǽbstrækt] *adj.* abstracto; *s.* sumario; resúmen; **in the** — en abstracto; — **of account current** resúmen de cuenta corriente; — **of title** certificado de tradición [æbstrǽkt] *v.* abstraer; considerar aisladamente; separar, retirar; resumir, compendiar.

ab·strac·tion [æbstrǽkʃən] *s.* abstracción; idea abstracta.

ab·surd [əbsɛ́d] *adj.* absurdo; insensato; ridículo, disparatado.

ab·sur·di·ty [əbsɛ́dətɪ] *s.* absurdo, disparate.

a·bun·dance [əbʌ́ndəns] *s.* abundancia, copia.

a·bun·dant [əbʌ́ndənt] *adj.* abundante, copioso.

a·buse [əbjús] *s.* abuso; maltrato; ultraje; [əbjúz] *v.* abusar de; maltratar; injuriar; ultrajar.

a·bu·sive [əbjúsɪv] *adj.* abusivo; insultante, injurioso.

a·byss [əbís] *s.* abismo; sima.

ac·a·dem·ic [ækədɛ́mɪk] *adj.* académico; escolar.

a·cad·e·my [əkǽdəmɪ] *s.* academia; colegio, instituto; escuela preparatoria.

ac·cede [æksíd] *v.* acceder, consentir.

ac·cel·er·ate [æksɛ́ləret] *v.* acelerar(se).

ac·cel·er·a·tion [æksɛləréʃən] *s.* aceleración.

ac·cel·er·a·tor [æksɛ́lərətɚ] *s.* acelerador.

ac·cent [ǽksɛnt] *s.* acento; [æksɛ́nt] *v.* acentuar; recalcar.

ac·cen·tu·ate [æksɛ́ntʃuet] *v.* acentuar; recalcar; realzar.

ac·cept [əksɛ́pt] *v.* aceptar; admitir; acoger; aprobar.

ac·cept·a·ble [əksɛ́ptəbl̩] *adj.* aceptable; grato; acepto.

ac·cep·tance [əksɛ́ptəns] *s.* aceptación; aprobación, buena acogida, recibimiento.

ac·cess [ǽksɛs] *s.* acceso; (*attack*) ataque (*de una enfermedad*); arrebato (*de furia*).

ac·ces·si·ble [æksɛ́səbl̩] *adj.* accesible; asequible, obtenible.

ac·ces·so·ry [ǽksɛ́sərɪ] *adj.* accesorio; adjunto; *s.* accesorio; cómplice; **ac·ces·so·ries** cosas accesorias, adornos, adminículos.

ac·ci·dent [ǽksədənt] *s.* accidente; percance, contratiempo; **by** — por casualidad.

ac·ci·den·tal [æksədέntl] *adj.* accidental; casual; **-ly** *adv.* accidentalmente; por casualidad.
ac·claim [əklém] *v.* aclamar, aplaudir; *s.* aclamación, aplauso.
ac·cla·ma·tion [ækləméʃən] *s.* aclamación, aplauso.
ac·cli·mate [əkláɪmət], [ǽkləmet] *v.* aclimatar(se); acostumbrar(se).
ac·cli·ma·tize [əkláɪmətaɪz] *v.* aclimatar(se).
ac·com·mo·date [əkamədét] *v.* (*adjust*) acomodar, ajustar, ayudar, hacer un favor; (*lodge*) hospedar, alojar, tener cabida para; **to — oneself** conformarse, adaptarse.
ac·com·mo·da·tion [əkamədéʃən] *s.* (*help*) favor, (*help*) ayuda; conveniencia; (*lodging*) alojamiento (*en un* hotel, casa, *etc.*); cabida; (*adjustment*) adaptación; ajuste.
ac·com·pa·ni·ment [əkʌ́mpənɪmənt] *s.* acompañamiento.
ac·com·pa·nist [əkʌ́mpənɪst] *s.* acompañador, acompañante.
ac·com·pa·ny [əkʌ́mpənɪ] *v.* acompañar.
ac·com·plice [əkámplɪs] *s.* cómplice.
ac·com·plish [əkámplɪʃ] *v.* cumplir; completar; lograr, conseguir; realizar, efectuar.
ac·com·plished [əkámplɪʃt] *adj.* cumplido; realizado; consumado; establecido; diestro; perfecto.
ac·com·plish·ment [əkámpɪʃmənt] *s.* cumplimiento; logro, realización; (*skill*) habilidad; perfección; mérito, proeza.
ac·cord [əkɔ́rd] *s.* acuerdo, convenio; armonía, concierto; **of one's own —** voluntariamente; espontáneamente; **in — with** de acuerdo con; **with one —** unánimemente; *v.* otorgar, conceder, dar; concordar.
ac·cord·ance [əkɔ́rdn̩s] *s.* conformidad, acuerdo; **in — with** de acuerdo con, de conformidad con.
ac·cord·ing [əkɔ́rdɪŋ]: **— to** según; conforme a; de acuerdo con; **— as** según (que), a medida que.
ac·cord·ing·ly [əkɔ́rdɪŋlɪ] *adv.* en conformidad; así; como tal; por lo tanto; pro consiguiente.
ac·cor·di·on [əkɔ́rdɪən] *s.* acordeón.
ac·cost [əkɔ́st] *v.* abordar (*a alguien*) en la calle, acosar; molestar, perseguir.
ac·count [əkáʊnt] *s.* (*bill*) cuenta, computación; **-s payable (receivable)** cuentas por pagar, (*story*) relato; **on — of** a causa de; con motivo de; por; **on my —** por mí; **on my own —** por mi propia cuenta; **on no —** de ninguna manera; **of no —** de ningún valor o importancia; **to turn to —** aprovechar, hacer útil o provechoso; *v.* dar cuenta (a); considerar, tener por; **to — for** dar cuenta o razón de; explicar; **how do you — for that?** ¿cómo se explica eso?
ac·count·a·ble [əkáʊntəbl̩] *adj.* responsable; explicable.
ac·count·ant [əkáʊntənt] *s.* contador, tenedor de libros; **certified public — (CPA)** contador público nacional; Ch. registrado.
ac·count·ing [əkáʊntɪŋ] *s.* contabilidad, contaduría; **-firm** empresa de contadores públicos; **— period** ejercicio contable; *Col.* período fiscal; **— system** sistema de contabilidad.
ac·cred·it [əkrέdɪt] *v.* acreditar.
ac·crue [əkrú] *v.* acumular(se); **-d assets** activo acumulado; **-d interest** interés acumulado.
ac·cul·tur·ate [əkʌ́ltʃɝet] *v.* aculturar(se).
ac·cu·mu·late [əkjúmjəlet] *v.* acumular(se), juntar(se), amontonar(se).
ac·cu·mu·la·tion [əkjumjəléʃən] *s.* acumulación, amontonamiento.
ac·cu·ra·cy [ǽkjərəsɪ] *s.* precisión, exactitud, esmero.
ac·cu·rate [ǽkjərɪt] *adj.* preciso, exacto; correcto; esmerado; cierto; certero; acertado; **-ly** *adv.* con exactitud; correctamente; con esmero.
ac·cursed [əkɝst] *adj.* maldito; infame.
ac·cu·sa·tion [ǽkjəzéʃən] *s.* acusación.
ac·cu·sa·tive [əkjúzətɪv] *adj.* acusativo.
ac·cuse [əkjúz] *v.* acusar; denunciar.
ac·cus·er [əkjúzɚ] *s.* acusador; delator, denunciador.
ac·cus·tom [əkʌ́stəm] *v.* acostumbrar; **to — oneself** acostumbrarse; **to be -ed to** tener la costumbre de, acostumbrar, soler; estar acostumbrado a, estar hecho a.
ace [es] *s.* as; as, el mejor de su clase (*como un aviador excelente*); **within an — of** a punto de; muy cerca de.
ac·e·tate [ǽsətet] *s.* acetato.
a·cet·y·lene [əsέtəlin] *s.* acetileno.
ache [ek] *s.* dolor; **tooth —** dolor de muelas; *v.* doler.
a·chieve [ətʃív] *v.* acabar, llevar a cabo; realizar; conseguir, lograr; alcanzar.
a·chieve·ment [ətʃívmənt] *s.* logro, realización; proeza, hazaña.
ac·id [ǽsɪd] *adj.* ácido; agrio; *s.* ácido; **— test** prueba de ácido.
ac·id·i·ty [əsídətɪ] *s.* acidez.
ac·knowl·edge [əknálɪdʒ] *v.* reconocer, admitir; confesar; **to — receipt** acusar recibo.
ac·knowl·edg·ment [əknálɪdʒmənt] *s.* reconocimiento, expresión de gratitud; confesión, admisión; **— of receipt** acuse de recibo.
a·corn [ékɔrn] *s.* bellota.
a·cous·tics [əkústɪks] *s.* acústica; **a·cous·tic coup·ler** [kʌplɚ] acoplador acustico.
ac·quaint [əkwént] *v.* enterar, informar; dar a conocer; familiarizar; **to — oneself with** ponerse al corriente de; enterarse de; **to be -ed with** conocer a (*una persona*); estar enterado de (*algo*); conocer (*una ciudad, un pais, etc.*).
ac·quain·tance [əkwéntəns] *s.* conocimiento; conocido; **-s** amistades.
ac·qui·esce [ækwɪέs] *v.* asentir; consentir, quedar conforme.
ac·qui·es·cence [ækwɪέsns] *s.* asentimiento, consentimiento; conformidad.
ac·quire [əkwáɪr] *v.* adquirir; obtener, conseguir; contraer (*costumbres, vicios*).
ac·qui·si·tion [ækwəzíʃən] *s.* adquisición.
ac·quit [əkwít] *v.* absolver, exonerar; pagar, redimir, librar de (*una obligación*); **to — oneself well** quedar bien; portarse bien; **acquitance** descarga de una deuda.
ac·quit·tal [əkwítl] *s.* absolución.
a·cre [ékɚ] *s.* acre (*medida de superficie*).
ac·ro·bat [ǽkrəbæt] *s.* acróbata.
ac·ro·nym [ǽkrənɪm] *s.* acrónimo.
a·cross [əkrɔ́s] *prep.* a través de; al otro lado de; por; por medio de; *adv.* a través, de través; **to go —** atravesar; **to come —**, **run —** encontrarse con; tropezar con.
a·cryl·ic [əkrílɪk] *adj.* acrílico.
act [ækt] *s.* acto; acción, hecho; (*law*) ley, decreto *v.* (*play the part*) hacer, desempeñar (*un papel*); representar (*en el teatro*); (*function*) obrar; actuar; portarse; funcionar; **to — as** servir de, estar de.
act·ing [ǽktɪŋ] *s.* representación, desempeño (*de un papel dramático*); acción, actuación; *adj.* interino, suplente.
ac·tion [ǽkʃən] *s.* acción; acto; actuación: funcionamiento.
ac·ti·vate [ǽktɪvet] *v.* activar.

ac·tive [ǽktɪv] *adj.* activo; — **capital** capital disponible; — **trade balance** balanza comercial favorable.
ac·tiv·ism [ǽktəvɪzm] *s.* activismo.
ac·tiv·ist [ǽktəvɪst] *s.* activista.
ac·tiv·i·ty [ætkívətɪ] *s.* actividad.
ac·tor [ǽktɚ] *s.* actor.
ac·tress [ǽktrɪs] *s.* actriz.
ac·tu·al [ǽktʃuəl] *adj.* (*legitimate*) verdadero, real; (*current*) actual, existente; — **cost** costo efectivo; — **output** rendimiento efectivo; — **sales** ventas efectivas; **-ly** *adv.* realmente, en realidad; de hecho, electivamente.
ac·tu·ar·ial [æktuérɪal] *adj.* actuarial.
a·cu·men [əkjúmɪn] *s.* caletre, tino, perspicacia.
a·cute [əkjút] *adj.* agudo; perspicaz; penetrante.
ad·a·mant [ǽdəmænt] *adj.* duro; firme, inflexible.
a·dapt [ədǽpt] *v.* adaptar; **to — oneself** adaptarse, acomodarse.
ad·ap·ta·tion [ædæptéʃən] *s.* adaptación.
add [æd] *v.* sumar; añadir, agregar; **adding machine** máquina sumadora; — **sign** signo de suma.
ad·dict [ǽdɪkt] *s.* adicto (*persona adicta al uso de narcóticos*); **drug** — morfinómano, drogadicto.
ad·dic·ted [ədíktɪd] *adj.* adicto, dado, (*keen*) entregado, habituado.
ad·di·tion [ədíʃən] *s.* adición; suma; añadidura, aditamento; **in — to** además de.
ad·di·tion·al [ədíʃənḷ] *adj.* adicional.
ad·di·tive [ǽdətɪv] *s.* & *adj.* aditivo.
ad·dress [ədrɛ́s] *s.* (*street*) dirección, domicilio, señas; sobrescrito; (*speech*) discurso, arenga, conferencia; **form of** — tratamiento; *v.* dirigir, poner la dirección, señas o sobrescrito a; hablar, dirgir la palabra a; dirigirse a; **to — oneself to a task** aplicarse a una tarea; **addressing machine** máquina rotuladora.
ad·dress·ee [ədrɛsí] *s.* destinatario.
ad·duce [ədús] *v.* aducir.
a·dept [ədɛ́pt] *adj.* hábil; perito.
ad·e·quate [ǽdəkwɪt] *adj.* adecuado; proporcionado; suficiente.
ad·here [ədhír] *v.* adherirse; pegarse.
ad·her·ence [ədhírəns] *s.* adherencia.
ad·he·sion [ədhíʒən] *s.* adhesión.
ad·he·sive [ədhísɪv] *adj.* adhesivo; pegajoso; — **tape** tela adhesiva, esparadrapo.
ad·ja·cent [ədʒésṇt] *adj.* adyacente, contiguo.
ad·jec·tive [ǽdʒɪktɪv] *s.* adjetivo.
ad·join [ədʒɔ́ɪn] *v.* estar contiguo o adyacente a, lindar con.
ad·journ [ədʒɝ́n] *v.* aplazar, diferir; **to — the meeting** suspender o levantar la sesión; **meeting -ed** se levanta la sesión.
ad·journ·ment [ədʒɝ́nmənt] *s.* aplazamiento, levantamiento (*de una sesión*).
ad·junct [ǽdʒʌŋkt] *s.* adjunto, aditamento, añadidura; asociado, acompañante; *adj.* adjunto, unido, subordinado.
ad·just [ədʒʌ́st] *v.* (*fix*) ajustar; (*adapt*) acomodar; arreglar; graduar; **to — oneself** adaptarse, conformarse; **adjuster** asesor.
ad·just·ment [ədʒʌ́stmənt] *s.* ajuste; ajustamiento; arreglo; regulación.
ad·lib [ædlíb] *v.* improvisar; expresarse espontáneamente.
ad·min·is·ter [ədmínəstɚ] *v.* (*control*) administrar; dirigir, regir, gobernar; (*apply*) aplicar (*remedio, castigo, etc.*); **to — an oath** tomar juramento.
ad·min·is·tra·tion [ədmɪnəstréʃən] *s.* administración; dirección, gobierno; gerencia; manejo.
ad·min·is·tra·tive [ədmínəstretɪv] *adj.* administrativo; ejecutivo; gubernativo; — **agencies** órganos (agencias) administrativas.
ad·min·is·tra·tor [ədmínəstretɚ] *s.* administrador.
ad·mi·ra·ble [ǽdmərəbl] *adj.* admirable.
ad·mi·ra·bly [ǽdmərəblɪ] *adv.* admirablemente.
ad·mi·ral [ǽdmərəl] *s.* almirante.
ad·mi·ra·tion [ædməréʃən] *s.* admiración.
ad·mire [ədmáɪr] *v.* admirar; estimar.
ad·mir·er [ədmáɪrɚ] *s.* admirador; pretendiente.
ad·mis·si·ble [ædmísəbl] *adj.* admisible.
ad·mis·sion [ədmíʃən] *s.* (*entrance*) entrada, precio de entrada o de ingreso; (*confession*) confesión, admisión.
ad·mit [ədmít] *v.* admitir; aceptar; confesar, reconocer; conceder; dar entrada.
ad·mit·tance [ədmítṇs] *s.* entrada; derecho de entrar; admisión.
ad·mon·ish [ədmánɪʃ] *v.* amonestar.
ad·mo·ni·tion [ædmənɪ́ʃən] *s.* amonestación, consejo.
a·do [ədú] *s.* actividad; bulla; disturbio.
a·do·be [ədóbɪ] *s.* adobe; casa de adobe.
ad·o·les·cence [ædəlɛ́sṇs] *s.* adolescencia.
ad·o·les·cent [ædəlɛ́sṇt] *adj.* & *s.* adolescente.
a·dopt [ədápt] *v.* adoptar; ahijar, prohijar.
a·dop·tion [ədápʃən] *s.* adopción.
a·dor·a·ble [ədórəbl] *adj.* adorable; encantador.
ad·o·ra·tion [ædəréʃən] *s.* adoración.
a·dore [ədór] *v.* adorar.
a·dorn [ədɔ́rn] *v.* adornar; ornar; embellecer.
a·dorn·ment [ədɔ́rnmənt] *s.* adorno.
ad·re·nal [ədrínl] *adj.* suprarrenal.
ad·ren·a·lin [ædrɛ́nəlɪn] *s.* adrenalina.
a·drift [ədríft] *adj.* & *adv.* a la deriva, flotando, flotante.
a·droit [ədrɔ́ɪt] *adj.* hábil, diestro.
a·dult [ədʌ́lt] *adj.* & *s.* adulto.
a·dul·ter·ate [ədʌ́ltəret] *v.* adulterar.
a·dul·ter·er [ədʌ́ltərɚ] *s.* adúltero.
a·dul·ter·y [ədʌ́ltərɪ] *s.* adulterio.
ad·vance [ədvǽns] *v.* (*progress*) avanzar, adelantar; progresar; acelerar; (*promote*) promover; proponer; (*pay beforehand*) pagar por adelantado (anticipado); *s.* avance; progreso; adelanto, anticipo; alza aumento de precio; **-s** requerimientos, pretensiones, insinuaciones; **in** — por adelantado, con anticipación.
ad·vanced [ədvǽnst] *adj.* avanzado; adelantado; — **in years** entrado en años, viejo, anciano.
ad·vance·ment [ədvǽnsmənt] *s.* adelantamiento, mejora, progreso; promoción.
ad·van·tage [ədvǽntɪdʒ] *s.* ventaja; beneficio; provecho; **to have the — over** llevar ventaja a; **to take — of** aprovecharse de; **to take — of a person** abusar de la confianza o paciencia de alguien.
ad·van·ta·geous [ædvəntédʒəs] *adj.* ventajoso; provechoso.
ad·vent [ǽdvɛnt] *s.* advenimiento; venida.
ad·ven·ture [ədvɛ́ntʃɚ] *s.* aventura; riesgo.
ad·ven·tur·er [ədvɛ́ntʃərɚ] *s.* aventurero.
ad·ven·tur·ous [ədvɛ́ntʃərəs] *adj.* aventurero; atrevido; aventurado; arriesgado.
ad·verb [ǽdvɝb] *m.* adverbio.
ad·ver·sar·y [ǽdvɚsɛrɪ] *s.* adversario, antagonista, contrario.
ad·verse [ədvɝ́s] *adj.* adverso; opuesto, contrario; hostil; desfavorable.
ad·ver·si·ty [ədvɝ́sətɪ] *s.* adversidad; infortunio.
ad·ver·tise [ǽdvɚtaɪz] *v.* anunciar; avisar, dar aviso; hacer propaganda (publicidad) *Arg.* reclame.

ad·ver·tise·ment [ædvɚtáɪzmənt] *s.* anuncio, aviso.
ad·ver·tis·er [ǽdvɚtaɪzɚ] *s.* anunciador, anunciante.
ad·ver·tis·ing [ǽdvɚtaɪzɪŋ] *s.* anuncios; arte o negocio de anunciar.
ad·vice [ədváɪs] *s.* aviso, advertencia; consejo; noticia.
ad·vis·a·ble [ədváɪzəbḷ] *adj.* conveniente; prudente; recomendable.
ad·vise [ədváɪz] *v.* (*counsel*) aconsejar; (*inform*) avisar, informar, advertir; **to — with** consultar con; aconsejarse con.
ad·vis·er, ad·vi·sor [ədváɪzɚ] *s.* consejero, aconsejador.
ad·vo·cate [ǽdvəkɪt] *s.* abogado; defensor, intercesor; partidario; [ǽdvəket] *v.* abogar por; defender.
aer·i·al [ɛ́rɪəl] *adj.* aéreo; *s.* antena.
aer·o·dy·nam·ic [ɛrodaɪnǽmɪk] *adj.* aerodinámico
aer·o·dy·nam·ics [ɛrodaɪnǽmɪks] *s.* aerodinámica.
aer·o·plane [ɛ́rəplen] = **airplane.**
aer·o·sol [ɛ́rosol] *s.* aerosol.
aes·thet·ic [ɛsθɛ́tɪk] *adj.* estético; **-s** *s.* estética.
a·far [əfár] *adv.* lejos; **from —** desde lejos.
af·fa·ble [ǽfəbḷ] *adj.* afable, amable.
af·fair [əfɛ́r] *s.* (*social*) función, tertulia, fiesta, convite; (*venture*) asunto; negocio; lance; cosa; **love —** amorío.
af·fect [əfɛ́kt] *v.* afectar; conmover; fingir; hacer ostentación de.
af·fec·ta·tion [æfɛktéʃən] *s.* afectación.
af·fect·ed [əfɛ́ktɪd] *adj.* (*emotion*) afectado, conmovido, enternecido; (*feigned*) fingido, artificioso.
af·fec·tion [əfɛ́kʃən] *s.* afecto, cariño; inclinación; afección, dolencia.
af·fec·tion·ate [əfɛ́kʃənɪt] *adj.* afectuoso, cariñoso.
af·fi·da·vit [æfədévɪt] *s.* declaración jurada.
af·fil·i·ate [əfílɪet] *v.* afiliar; afiliarse, unirse, asociarse.
af·fin·i·ty [əfínətɪ] *s.* afinidad.
af·firm [əfɝ́m] *v.* afirmar, asegurar, aseverar.
af·firm·a·tive [əfɝ́mətɪv] *adj.* afirmativo; *s.* afirmativa.
af·fix [əfíks] *v.* fijar, pegar; **to — one's signature** poner su firma, firmar.
af·flict [əflíkt] *v.* afligir; **to be -ed with** padecer de sufrir de, adolecer de.
af·flic·tion [əflíkʃən] *s.* aflicción; pena, dolor; achaque; angustia; infortunio.
af·flu·ent [ǽflʊənt] *adj.* acaudalado; abundante.
af·ford [əfórd] *v.* proveer, proporcionar; **I cannot — that expense** no puedo hacer ese gasto; **he cannot — to waste time** no le conviene perder el tiempo; no tiene tiempo que perder; **I cannot — that risk** no puedo (*o* no quiero) exponerme a ese riesgo.
af·fri·cate [ǽfrɪkət] *adj. & s.* africado.
af·front [əfrʌ́nt] *s.* afrenta, agravio, ultraje; *v.* afrentar, agraviar, ultrajar.
a·fire [əfáɪr] *adj.* ardiendo, quemándose.
a·float [əflót] *adj. & adv.* flotante; flotando; a flote; a flor de agua; a bordo; inundado; (*flooded*) a la deriva, sin rumbo; **the rumor is —** corre la voz.
a·foot [əfʊ́t] *adv.* a pie; en marcha, en movimiento.
a·fore·said [əfórsɛd] *adj.* susodicho, ya dicho.
a·fraid [əfréd] *adj.* miedoso, medroso; atemorizado, amedrentado; **to be —** temer, tener miedo.
a·fresh [əfrɛ́ʃ] *adv.* de nuevo, desde el principio.
Af·ri·can [ǽfrɪkən] *adj. & s.* africano; negro.
af·ter [ǽftɚ] *prep.* (*temporal*) después de, tras, tras de; (*position*) detrás de; (*following*) en busca de; *adv.* después; detrás; *conj.* después (de) que; *adj.* subsiguiente; siguiente; **— all** después de todo; de todos modos; **day — tomorrow** pasado mañana; **after-dinner** de sobremesa; **— effect** consecuencia, resultado; **— math** consecuencias, resultados (*usualmente desastrosos*); **— thought** idea tardía.
af·ter·noon [æftɚnún] *s.* tarde.
af·ter·taste [ǽftɚtest] *s.* dejo, dejillo (*sabor que queda en la boca*).
af·ter·wards [ǽftɚwɚdz] *adv.* después.
a·gain [əgɛ́n] *adv.* otra vez, de nuevo; además; por otra parte; **— and —** repetidas veces; **never —** nunca jamás; **to come —** volver; **to do it —** volver a hacerlo.
a·gainst [əgɛ́nst] *prep.* contra; frente a; en contraste con; **— the grain** a contrapelo, a redopelo; **— a rainy day** para cuando llueva.
age [edʒ] *s.* edad; época; siglo; generación; **of —** mayor de edad; **old —** vejez, ancianidad; **to become of —** llegar a mayor edad; **under —** menor de edad; *v.* envejecer(se).
a·ged [édʒɪd, édʒd] *adj.* viejo, anciano, añejo; envejecido; **— forty years** de cuarenta años; **— in wood** añejado en toneles o barriles (*dícese del vino*).
a·gen·cy [édʒənsɪ] *s.* agencia; (*means*) medio, intermedio.
a·gen·da [ədʒɛ́ndə] *s.* temario; asuntos que han de tratarse en una reunión.
a·gent [édʒənt] *s.* agente; intermediario, representante; apoderado.
ag·glu·ti·na·tive [əglútɪnətɪv] *adj.* aglutinante.
ag·gran·dize [əgrǽndaɪz] *v.* engrandecer; agrandar.
ag·gra·vate [ǽgrəvet] *v.* agravar, empeorar; irritar, exasperar.
ag·gre·gate [ǽgrɪgɪt] *s.* agregado, conjunto, colección; suma global; *adj.* agregado, unido; **in the —** en conjunto.
ag·gres·sion [əgrɛ́ʃən] *s.* agresión.
ag·gres·sive [əgrɛ́sɪv] *adj.* agresivo; emprendedor.
ag·gres·sor [əgrɛ́sɚ] *s.* agresor.
a·ghast [əgǽst] *adj.* espantado, pasmado.
ag·ile [ǽdʒəl] *adj.* ágil.
a·gil·i·ty [ədʒílətɪ] *s.* agilidad.
ag·i·tate [ǽdʒətet] *v.* agitar; turbar, perturbar; alborotar; discutir acaloradamente; maquinar, tramar.
ag·i·ta·tion [ædʒətéʃən] *s.* agitación; alboroto.
ag·i·ta·tor [ǽdʒətetɚ] *s.* agitador, alborotador, revoltoso.
ag·nos·tic [ægnástɪk] *adj. s.* agnóstico.
a·go [əgó] *adj. & adv.* pasado; en el pasado; **many years —** hace muchos años; muchos años ha, mucho tiempo ha; **long —** hace mucho tiempo; ha mucho.
ag·o·nize [ǽgənaɪz] *v.* agonizar; sufrir angustiosamente; retorcerse de dolor; (*fight*) luchar.
ag·o·ny [ǽgənɪ] *s.* agonía; angustia; tormento; dolor; lucha.
a·gree [əgrí] *v.* (*accede*) acordar, concordar, consentir, estar de acuerdo, ponerse de acuerdo; (*suit*) sentarle bien a uno (*dícese del clima, del alimento, etc.*).
a·gree·a·ble [əgríəbḷ] *adj.* agradable, afable; complaciente; conveniente; satisfactorio.
a·gree·ment [əgrímənt] *s.* (*concord*) acuerdo, convenio, conformidad; (*grammatical*) concordancia; **to be in —** estar de acuerdo; **to come to an —** ponerse de acuerdo.
ag·ri·cul·tur·al [ægrɪkʌ́ltʃɚḷ] *adj.* agrícola.
ag·ri·cul·ture [ǽgrɪkʌltʃɚ] *s.* agricultura.
ag·ri·cul·tur·ist [ægrɪkʌ́ltʃərɪst] *s.* agricultor.

a·ground [əgráUnd] *adj. & adv.* encallado.
a·head [əhέd] *adv.* delante, al frente; adelante; — **of time** adelantado; antes de tiempo; **to go** — ir adelante; **to get** — adelantar(se).
aid [ed] *s.* ayuda, auxilio, socorro; (*assistant*) ayudante, auxiliar; *v.* ayudar, auxiliar, socorrer.
aide-de-camp [édəkæmp] *s.* edecán.
ail [el] *v.* adolecer, padecer; **what -s you?** ¿qué tienes? ¿qué te aflige?
ai·le·ron [éləran] *s.* alerón.
ail·ment [élmənt] *s.* achaque, dolencia.
aim [em] *s.* (*pointing*) puntería; tino; (*objective*) fin, objeto; proposición; *v.* apuntar (*un arma*); dirigir, asestar; dirigir la puntería; aspirar (a); **to** — **to please** proponerse (*o* tratar de agradar).
aim·less [émlɪs] *adj.* sin propósito, sin objeto.
air [ɛr] *s.* (*atmosphere*) aire, brisa; (*music*) tonada; **in the** — en el aire; indeciso; incierto; **in the open** — al raso, al aire libre; **to be on the** — emitir, radiodifundir; **to put on -s** darse tono; *adj.* de aire; aéreo; — **brake** freno neumático; — **line** línea aérea; ruta aérea; **air traffic control** control de tránsito aéreo; — **pocket** bache aéreo; bolsa de aire; **by** — **mail** por correo aéreo, por avión; **air-conditioned** de aire acondicionado; *v.* airear; orear; ventilar; publicar, pregonar; ostentar.
air·borne [έrborn] aéreo; aerotransportado.
air·craft [έrkræft] *s.* avión, aeroplano; aeronave; aviones; — **carrier** portaaviones.
air·foil [έrfɔɪl] *s.* superficie de control en los aviones.
air·line [έrlaɪn] *s.* aerovía; línea aérea; compañía de transporte aéreo.
air·plane [έrplen] *s.* aeroplano, avión; — **carrier** portaaviones.
air·port [έrport] *s.* aeropuerto, aerodromo.
air·ship [έrʃɪp] *s.* aeronave.
air·tight [έrtaɪt] *adj.* hermético.
air·y [έrɪ] *adj.* airoso; aireado, ventilado; ligero; tenue.
aisle [aɪl] *s.* pasillo, pasadizo; nave (*de una iglesia*).
a·jar [ədʒár] *adj.* entreabierto, entornado.
al·a·bas·ter [ǽləbæstɚ] *s.* alabastro.
a·larm [əlárm] *s.* alarma; arrebato; inquietud; — **clock** despertador; *v.* alarmar; inquietar.
al·bi·no [ælbáɪno] *s.* albino.
al·bum [ǽlbəm] *s.* álbum.
al·che·my [ǽlkəmɪ] *s.* alquimia.
al·co·hol [ǽlkəhɔl] *s.* alcohol.
al·co·hol·ic [ælkəhɔ́lɪk] *adj.* alcohólico.
al·cove [ǽlkov] *s.* alcoba.
al·der·man [ɔ́ldɚmən] *s.* concejal, regidor.
ale [el] *s.* cerveza de tipo espeso y amargo.
a·lert [əlɝ́t] *adj.* alerto, vigilante; despierto; vivo; listo; *s.* alarma, rebato; **to be on the** — estar alerta.
al·fal·fa [ælfǽlfə] *s.* alfalfa.
algae [ǽldʒɪ] *s. pl.* algas.
al·ge·bra [ǽldʒəbrə] *s.* álgebra.
al·go·rithm [ǽlgərɪəm] *s.* algoritmo.
al·i·bi [ǽləbaɪ] *s.* coartado; excusa.
a·li·en [éljən] *s.* extranjero; residente extranjero; *adj.* extraño, ajeno.
al·ien·ate [éljənet] *v.* enajenar; apartar, alejar (*a una persona de otra*).
al·ien·ist [éljənɪst] *s.* alienista, psiquiatra.
a·light [əláɪt] *v.* apearse, desmontarse, bajar(de); posarse (*dícese de pájaros, mariposas, etc.*).
a·lign [əláɪn] *v.* alinear(se).
a·like [əláɪk] *adj.* semejante; parecido; **to be** — parecerse, asemejarse; ser iguales; *adv.* del mismo modo.
al·i·mo·ny [ǽləmonɪ] *s.* asistencia de divorcio; alimento.
a·live [əláɪv] *adj.* vivo; con vida; viviente; activo; — **with** lleno de.
al·ka·li [ǽlkəlaɪ] *s.* álcali.
all [ɔl] *adj.* todo (el); todos (los); *s.* todo; todo el mundo, todos; *adv.* enteramente; — **at once** de una vez; de un tirón; de repente; — **right** bueno; bien; — **the worse** tanto peor; — **around** en (por) todas partes; — **-round** global; **not at** — de ninguna manera; no hay de qué; **nothing at** — nada en absoluto; — **told** (*o* **in** —) en conjunto; **once (and) for** — por última vez; una vez por todas; **to be** — **in** estar agotado, estar rendido de fatiga; **it is** — **over** se acabó, ha terminado todo.
al·lay [əlé] *v.* aliviar; calmar.
al·le·ga·tion [æləgéʃən] *s.* alegación, alegato; aseveración.
al·lege [əlέdʒ] *v.* alegar; declarar; sostener, asegurar.
al·le·giance [əlídʒəns] *s.* lealtad, fidelidad; homenaje.
al·le·go·ry [ǽləgorɪ] *s.* alegoría.
al·ler·gy [ǽlɚdʒɪ] *s.* alergia (*sensibilidad anormal a ciertos alimentos o sustancias*).
al·le·vi·ate [əlívɪet] *v.* aliviar.
al·ley [ǽlɪ] *c.* callejón; callejuela; **blind** — callejón sin salida; **bowling** — boliche, *Am.* bolera.
al·li·ance [əláɪəns] *s.* alianza.
al·lied [əláɪd] *adj.* aliado; relacionado.
al·li·ga·tor [ǽləgetɚ] *s.* lagarto; caimán; — **pear** aguacate.
al·lot [əlát] *v.* asignar; repartir; **allotment** asignación, cuota
al·low [əláU] *v.* permitir, dejar; conceder; admitir; asignar; abonar; **to** — **for certain errors** tener en cuenta ciertos errores.
al·low·a·ble [əláUəbl] *adj.* permisible, admisible, lícito.
al·low·ance [əláUəns] *s.* asignación; abono, pensión; ración; (*discount*) rebaja, descuento; (*permission*) permiso; concesión; **monthly** — mesada, mensualidad; **to make** — **for** tener en cuenta.
al·loy [ǽlɔɪ] *s.* aleación, liga, mezcla (*de dos o más metales*); [əlɔ́ɪ] *v.* alear, ligar, mezclar (*metales*).
al·lude [əlúd] *v.* aludir.
al·lure [əlÚr] *v.* seducir, cautivar; atraer, halagar.
al·lure·ment [əlÚrmənt] *s.* seducción, tentación; atractivo, halago.
al·lur·ing [əlÚrɪŋ] *adj.* seductivo, halagüeño, encantador.
al·lu·sion [əlúʒən] *s.* alusión; indirecta, insinuación.
al·lu·vi·um [əlúvɪəm] *s.* aluvión.
al·ly [əláɪ *v.* unir; aliarse; **to** — **oneself (itself) with** aliarse con, unirse con; [ǽlaɪ] *s.* aliado.
al·ma·nac [ɔ́lmənæk] *s.* almanaque, calendario.
al·might·y [ɔlmáɪtɪ] *adj.* todopoderoso, omnipotente.
al·mond [ámənd] *s.* almendra; — **tree** almendro.
al·most [ɔ́lmost] *adv.* casi; **I** — **fell down** por poco me caigo.
alms [amz] *s.* limosna; — **box** cepo o cepillo, alcancía (*para limosnas*).
a·lone [əlón] *adj.* solo; solitario; único; *adv.* sólo, solamente; **all** — a solas; completamente solo; solito; **to let** — no tocar; no molestar; dejar en paz; no hacer caso de.
a·long [əlɔ́ŋ] *prep.* a lo largo de; por; al lado de; — **with** junto con; en compañía de; **all** — todo el tiempo; de un extremo a otro; **all** — **the coast** por toda la costa; **to carry** — **with one** llevar consigo; **to go** — **with** acompañar; to get — ir bien; **to get** — **with** llevarse bien con; **get** — ! ¡vete! ¡váyase!

¡largo de aquí!
a·long·side [əlɔ́ŋsaɪd] *prep. & adv.* al lado (de); al costado (de); lado a lado.
a·loof [əlúf] *adj.* aislado, apartado, retirado; huraño; reservado; *adv.* aparte; lejos.
a·loof·ness [əlúfnɪs] *s.* alejamiento, desapego, aislamiento.
a·loud [əláʊd] *adv.* alto, recio, fuerte, en voz alta.
al·pha·bet [ǽlfəbɛt] *s.* alfabeto.
al·pha·num·er·ic [æfənumɛ́rɪk] *adj. (computer)* alfanumérico.
al·read·y [ɔlrɛ́dɪ] *adv.* ya.
al·so [ɔ́lso] *adv.* también, además, igualmente.
al·tar [ɔ́ltɚ] *s.* altar; **high** — altar mayor; — **piece** retablo.
al·ter [ɔ́ltɚ] *v.* alterar; cambiar; variar.
al·ter·a·tion [ɔltəréʃən] *s.* alteración, cambio; mudanza; modificación.
al·ter·nate [ɔ́ltɚnɪt] *adj.* alternativo; alterno; alternado; *s.* suplente; **-ly** *adv.* alternativamente, por turno; [ɔ́ltɚnet] *v.* alternar; variar; turnar.
al·ter·na·tive [ɔltɝ́nətiv] *adj.* alternativo; *s.* alternativa.
al·ter·na·tor [ɔltɝ́nétɚ] *s.* alternador.
al·though [ɔlðó] *conj.* aunque, si bien, bien que.
al·tim·e·ter [æltímətɚ] *s.* altímetro.
al·ti·tude [ǽltətjud] *s.* altitud, altura, elevación; — **sickness** *Am.* soroche.
al·to [ǽlto] *s. & adj.* contralto.
al·to·geth·er [ɔltəgɛ́ðɚ] *adv.* del todo, completamente; en conjunto.
a·lu·mi·num [əlúmɪnəm] *s.* aluminio.
a·lum·nus [əlʌ́mnəs] *s.* graduado, exalumno.
al·ways [ɔ́lwɪz] *adv.* siempre.
am [æm] *1ª persona del presente de indic. del verbo* **to be**: soy, estoy.
a·mal·ga·mate [əmǽlgəmet] *v.* amalgamar; combinar; unir.
a·mass [əmǽs] *v.* amontonar, acumular, apilar, *Am.* amasar.
am·a·teur [ǽmətʃʊr] *s.* aficionado; novicio, principiante.
a·maze [əméz] *v.* pasmar, maravillar, asombrar.
a·maze·ment [əmézmənt] *s.* pasmo, admiración, asombro.
a·maz·ing [əmézɪŋ] *adj.* pasmoso, asombroso, maravilloso.
am·bas·sa·dor [æmbǽsədɚ] *s.* embajador.
am·ber [ǽmbɚ] *s.* ámbar; color de ámbar; *adj.* ambarino; de ámbar.
am·bi·ance [ǽmbiəns] *s.* ambiente.
am·bi·gu·i·ty [æmbɪgjúətɪ] *s.* ambigüedad.
am·big·u·ous [æmbígjʊəs] *adj.* ambiguo.
am·bi·tion [æmbíʃən] *s.* ambición, aspiración.
am·bi·tious [æmbíʃəs] *adj.* ambicioso.
am·biv·a·lent [æmbívələnt] *adj.* ambivalente.
am·ble [ǽmbl̩] *v.* andar, vagar.
am·bu·lance [ǽmbjələns] *s.* ambulancia.
am·bush [ǽmbʊʃ] *s.* emboscada; celada; acecho; *Ven.* aguaite **to lie in** — estar emboscado, estar al acecho; *Ven.* estar al aguaite; *v.* emboscar; poner celada a.
a·me·na·ble [əmínəbl̩] *adj.* dócil; tratable.
a·mend [əmɛ́nd] *v.* enmendar; rectificar; **-s** *s. pl.* satisfacción, compensación; **to make** — **for** resarcir, dar satisfacción por, compensar por.
a·mend·ment [əmɛ́ndmənt] *s.* enmienda.
A·mer·i·can [əmɛ́rəkən] *adj. & s.* (*continental*) americano; (*U.S.A.*) norteamericano.
A·mer·i·can·ism [əmɛ́rɪkənɪzəm] *s.* americanismo.
am·e·thyst [ǽməθɪst] *s.* amatista.
a·mi·a·ble [émɪəbl̩] *adj.* amable, afable, amistoso.
am·i·ca·ble [ǽmɪkəbl̩] *adj.* amigable, amistoso.
a·mid [əmíd] *prep.* en medio de; entre; **amidst** [əmídst] = **amid.**
a·miss [əmís] *adj.* errado, equivocado; (*improper*) impropio; *adv.* mal, fuera de lugar, impropiamente; **to take** — llevar a mal.
am·mo·nia [əmónjə] *s.* amoníaco.
am·mu·ni·tion [æmjəníʃən] *s.* munición.
am·ne·sia [æmníʒjə] *s.* amnesia.
am·nes·ty [ǽmnɛstɪ] *s.* amnestía.
a·mong [əmʌ́ŋ] *prep.* entre, en medio de; **amongst** [əmʌ́ŋst] = **among.**
am·o·rous [ǽmərəs] *adj.* amoroso.
a·mor·phous [əmɔ́rfəs] *adj.* amorfo.
am·or·tize [ǽmɝtaɪz] *v.* amortizar.
a·mount [əmáʊnt] *s.* suma; cantidad; total; importe; valor; *v.* montar, subir, importar, ascender (a); valer; **that -s to stealing** eso equivale a robar.
am·pere [ǽmpɪr] *s.* amperio; **amperage** amperaje.
am·per·sand [ǽmpɚsænd] *s.* signo &.
am·phib·i·ous [æmfíbɪəs] *adj.* anfibio.
am·phi·the·a·ter [ǽmfəθiətɚ] *s.* anfiteatro.
am·ple [ǽmpl̩] *adj.* amplio; abundante; bastante; suficiente.
am·pli·fy [ǽmpləfaɪ] *v.* ampliar; amplificar.
am·pu·tate [ǽmpjətet] *v.* amputar.
a·muck [əmʌ́k] *adv.* con frenesí; **to run** — atacar a ciegas.
a·muse [əmjúz] *v.* divertir, entretener, distraer; **to** — **oneself** divertirse.
a·muse·ment [əmjúzmənt] *s.* diversión, entretenimiento, pasatiempo, recreo, distracción.
a·mus·ing [əmjúzɪŋ] *adj.* divertido, entretenido; gracioso, chistoso.
an [ən, æn] *art. indef.* un, una.
a·nach·ro·nism [ənǽkrənɪzm] *s.* anacronismo.
an·al·ge·sic [ænəldʒízɪk] *s.* analgésico.
a·nal·o·gous [ənǽləgəs] *adj.* análogo.
a·nal·o·gy [ənǽlədʒɪ] *s.* analogía, semejanza.
a·nal·y·sis [ənǽləsɪs] *s.* análisis.
an·a·lyt·ic [ænəlítɪk] *adj.* analítico.
an·a·lyze [ǽnəlaɪz] *v.* analizar.
an·ar·chist [ǽnɚkɪst] *s.* anarquista.
an·ar·chy [ǽnɚkɪ] *s.* anarquía.
a·nath·e·ma [ənǽθəmə] *s.* anatema.
an·a·tom·i·cal [ænətámɪkl] *adj.* anatómico.
a·nat·o·my [ənǽtəmɪ] *s.* anatomía.
an·ces·tor [ǽnsɛstɚ] *s.* antepasado; **-s** abuelos, antepasados.
an·ces·tral [ænsɛ́strəl] *adj.* solariego, de los antepasados; hereditario.
an·ces·try [ǽnsɛstrɪ] *s.* linaje, abolengo, ascendencia.
an·chor [ǽŋkɚ] *s.* ancla; **anchorage** anclaje; — **man** ancla; **to drop** — anclar, echar anclas, dar fondo, fondear; **to weigh** — levar el ancla; *v.* anclar; echar anclas; fijar, asegurar.
an·cho·vy [ǽntʃovɪ] *s.* anchoa, anchova.
an·cient [énʃənt] *adj.* antiguo; vetusto; **the -s** los antiguos; la antigüedad.
and [ənd, ænd] *conj.* y; e (*delante de* i *o* hi); — **so forth** etcétera; y así sucesivamente; **let us try** — **do it** tratemos de hacerlo; **let us go** — **see him** vamos a verle.
An·da·lu·sian [ændəlúʒən] *adj.* andaluz.
an·ec·dote [ǽnɪkdot] *s.* anécdota.
a·ne·mi·a [ənímɪə] *s.* anemia.
an·es·the·sia [ænɪsθíʒə] *s.* anestesia.
an·es·thet·ic [ænəsθɛ́tɪk] *adj. & s.* anestésico.
a·new [ənjú] *adv.* otra vez, de nuevo; nuevamente.
an·gel [éndʒəl] *s.* ángel.

an·gel·ic [ændʒɛ́lɪk] *adj.* angélico.
an·ger [ǽŋgɚ] *s.* enojo, enfado, ira, cólera; *v.* enojar, enfadar, encolerizar.
an·gi·na [ændʒáɪnə] *s.* angina; — **pectoris** angina de pecho.
an·gle [ǽŋgl] *s.* ángulo; (*interior*) rincón; (*exterior*) esquina; punto de vista, aspecto; *v.* pescar.
An·glo-Sax·on [ǽnglosǽksn̩] *adj.* & *s.* anglosajón.
an·gry [ǽŋgrɪ] *adj.* enojado; colérico; airado.
an·guish [ǽŋgwɪʃ] *s.* angustia, ansia, pena, dolor.
an·gu·lar [ǽŋgjəlɚ] *adj.* angular; anguloso.
an·i·mal [ǽnəml̩] *s.* & *adj.* animal.
an·i·mate [ǽnəmɪt] *adj.* animado, viviente; **animated cartoon** dibujo animado; [ǽnəmet] *v.* animar; alentar.
an·i·ma·tion [ænəméʃən] *s.* animación; viveza.
an·i·mos·i·ty [ænəmásətɪ] *s.* animosidad, ojeriza, inquina, rencor.
an·ise [ǽnɪs] *s.* anís.
an·kle [ǽŋkl̩] *s.* tobillo.
an·nals [ǽnl̩z] *s.* *pl.* anales.
an·nex [ǽnɛks] *s.* (*building*) pabellón, ala; (*dependent addition*) anexo; añadidura; [ənɛ́ks] *v.* anexar.
an·nex·a·tion [ænɛkséʃən] *s.* anexión.
an·ni·hi·late [ənáɪəlet] *v.* aniquilar; anonadar.
an·ni·ver·sa·ry [ænəvɝ́sərɪ] *s.* & *adj.* aniversario.
an·no·tate [ǽnotet] *v.* anotar.
an·no·ta·tion [ænotéʃən] *s.* anotación, acotación, nota.
an·nounce [ənáʊns] *v.* anunciar; proclamar.
an·nounce·ment [ənáʊnsmənt] *s.* anuncio; aviso; noticia.
an·nounc·er [ənáʊnsɚ] *s.* anunciador; **radio** — locutor.
an·noy [ənɔ́ɪ] *v.* molestar; fastidiar; incomodar; enfadar.
an·noy·ance [ənɔ́ɪəns] *s.* molestia; fastidio; enfado; vejamen.
an·nu·al [ǽnjʊəl] *adj.* anual; *s.* anuario; planta anual; **-ly** *adv.* anualmente, cada año, todos los años.
an·nu·i·ty [ənúətɪ] *s.* anualidad, renta anual; **annuitant** beneficiario de anualidad.
an·nul [ənʌ́l] *v.* anular; abolir.
an·nul·ment [ənʌ́lmənt] *s.* revocación; anulación.
a·noint [ənɔ́ɪnt] *v.* ungir; untar; administrar la Extremaunción.
a·non [ənán] *adv.* pronto, luego; otra vez.
a·non·y·mous [ənánəməs] *adj.* anónimo.
an·oth·er [ənʌ́ðɚ] *adj.* & *pron.* otro; **one** — uno a otro, unos a otros.
an·swer [ǽnsɚ] *s.* respuesta, contestación; réplica; (*solution*) solución; *v.* responder; contestar; replicar; **to** — **for** ser responsable de (*o* por); responder de; ser (salir) fiador de; **to** — **the purpose** ser adecuado, servir para el objeto; **answering service** servicio telefónico contratado.
ant [ænt] *s.* hormiga; — **eater** oso hormiguero; — **hill** hormiguero.
ant·ac·id [æntǽsɪd] *s.* & *adj.* antiácido.
an·tag·o·nism [æntǽgənɪzəm] *s.* antagonismo, oposición, antipatía.
an·tag·o·nist [æntǽgənɪst] *s.* antagonista, adversario.
an·tag·o·nize [æntǽgənaɪz] *v.* contrariar, oponerse a, hostilizar.
an·te·ce·dent [æntəsídn̩t] *adj.* & *s.* antecedente.
an·te·lope [ǽntl̩op] *s.* antílope.
an·ten·na [æntɛ́nə] (*pl.* **antennae** [æntɛ́ni]) *s.* antena.
an·te·ri·or [æntírɪɚ] *adj.* anterior; delantero.
an·te·room [ǽntɪrum] *s.* antecámara; sala de espera.
an·them [ǽnθəm] *s.* himno.
an·thol·o·gy [ænθálədʒɪ] *s.* antología.
an·thra·cite [ǽnθrəsaɪt] *s.* antracita.
an·thro·pol·o·gist [ænθrəpálədʒɪst] *s.* antropólogo.
an·thro·pol·o·gy [ænθrəpálədʒɪ] *s.* antropología.
an·ti·air·craft [æntɪɛ́rkræft] *adj.* antiaéreo.
an·ti·bi·ot·ic [æntɪbaɪátɪk] *s.* & *adj.* antibiótico.
an·ti·bod·y [ǽntɪbadɪ] *s.* anticuerpo.
an·tic·i·pate [æntísəpet] *v.* anticipar(se); prever; esperar.
an·tic·i·pa·tion [æntɪsəpéʃən] *s.* anticipación; expectación; previsión.
an·tics [ǽntɪks] *s.* *pl.* travesuras, cabriolas.
an·ti·dote [ǽntɪdot] *s.* antídoto.
an·ti·freeze [ǽntɪfriz] *s.* anticongelante.
an·ti·mo·ny [æntəmónɪ] *s.* antimonio.
an·tip·a·thy [æntípəθɪ] *s.* antipatía, repugnancia.
an·ti·quat·ed [ǽntəkwetɪd] *adj.* anticuado; desusado.
an·tique [æntík] *adj.* antiguo; anticuado; *s.* antigualla.
an·tiq·ui·ty [æntíkwətɪ] *s.* antigüedad; vejez, ancianidad.
an·ti·sep·tic [æntəsɛ́ptɪk] *adj.* & *s.* antiséptico.
an·ti·so·cial [æntɪsóʃel] *adj.* antisocial; *s.* *Am.* criminal.
an·tith·e·sis [æntíθəsɪs] *s.* antítesis.
an·ti·trust [æntɪtrʌ́st] *adj.* antimonopolio.
ant·ler [ǽntlɚ] *s.* asta, cuerno (*del venado, ciervo, etc.*).
an·vil [ǽnvɪl] *s.* yunque.
anx·i·e·ty [æŋzáɪətɪ] *s.* ansiedad, zozobra; ansia, anhelo, afán.
anx·ious [ǽŋkʃəs] *adj.* ansioso; inquieto, preocupado; (*desirous*) anheloso, deseoso; **-ly** *adv.* con ansiedad, con ansia, ansiosamente.
an·y [ɛ́nɪ] *adj.* & *pron.* cualquier(a), cualesquier (a); alguno, algunos; **in** — **case** de todos modos, en todo caso; **I have not** — **bread** no tengo pan; **she does not sing** — **more** ya no canta; **he does not want to work** — **more** no quiere trabajar más.
an·y·bod·y [ɛ́nɪbadɪ] *pron.* alguien, alguno; cualquiera; **not** . . . — no . . . nadie, no . . . ninguno; **he does not know** — no conoce a nadie.
an·y·how [ɛ́nɪhaʊ] *adv.* de todos modos; de cualquier modo.
an·y·one [ɛ́nɪwʌn] *pron.* = **anybody.**
an·y·thing [ɛ́nɪθɪŋ] *pron.* alguna cosa; cualquier cosa; algo; **not** . . . — no . . . nada; **not to know** — no saber nada; — **you wish** todo lo que quiera Vd.
an·y·way [ɛ́nɪwe] *adv.* de todos modos; en cualquier caso.
an·y·where [ɛ́nɪhwɛr] *adv.* dondequiera; en cualquier parte o lugar; en todas partes; **not** . . . — no . . . en (*o* a) ninguna parte; **not to go** — no ir a ninguna parte.
a·part [əpárt] *adj.* aparte; *adv.* separadamente; (*aside*) a un lado; *adj.* aislado, separado; **to take** — desarmar, desmontar; **to tear** — despedazar, hacer pedazos.
a·part·ment [əpártmənt] *s.* departamento, piso, apartamento; vivienda, habitación.
ap·a·thet·ic [æpəθɛ́tɪk] *adj.* apático.
ap·a·thy [ǽpəθɪ] *s.* apatía, indiferencia, indolencia.
ape [ep] *s.* mono; **ape-like** símico; *v.* remedar, imitar.
ap·er·ture [ǽpɚtʃɚ] *s.* abertura.
a·pex [épɛks] *s.* ápice, cumbre.
a·pha·sia [əfézɪə] *s.* afasia.
a·piece [əpís] *adv.* cada uno, a cada uno, por persona.
a·poc·o·pe [əpákəpɪ] *s.* apócope.

ap·o·gee [ǽpədʒɪ] *s.* apogeo.
a·pol·o·get·ic [əpalədʒέtɪk] *adj.* que se excusa o disculpa.
a·pol·o·gize [əpálədʒaɪz] *v.* disculparse, excusarse.
a·pol·o·gy [əpálədʒɪ] *s.* apología; excusa, disculpa, (*reason*) justificación, satisfacción.
ap·o·plex·y [ǽpəplεksɪ] *s.* apoplejía.
a·pos·tle [əpásl] *s.* apóstol.
ap·os·tol·ic [æpəstálɪk] *adj.* apostólico.
a·pos·tro·phe [əpástrəfɪ] *s.* apóstrofe; (*punctuation*) apóstrofo.
ap·pall [əpɔ́l] *v.* aterrorizar, aterrar; asombrar, espantar.
ap·pall·ing [əpɔ́lɪŋ] *adj.* aterrador; espantoso, asombroso.
ap·pa·ra·tus [æpərétəs] *s.* aparato; aparejo.
ap·par·el [əpǽrəl] *s.* ropa; ropaje; vestidos; indumentaria.
ap·par·ent [əpǽrənt] *adj.* aparente; visible; claro, evidente; patente; **heir** — heredero presunto; **-ly** *adv.* aparentemente, al parecer, por lo visto.
ap·pa·ri·tion [æpəríʃən] *s.* aparición; aparecido, espectro, fantasma.
ap·peal [əpíl] *s.* (*legal*) apelación, recurso; (*request*) súplica; (*attraction*) atracción, atractivo, llamamiento; *v.* apelar; recurrir, acudir; atraer, despertar interés o simpatía; llamar la atención.
ap·pear [əpír] *v.* aparecer(se); parecer; comparecer.
ap·pear·ance [əpírəns] *s.* apariencia, semblante; facha; aparición; cariz.
ap·pease [əpíz] *v.* apaciguar, aplacar; pacificar; conciliar; sosegar.
ap·pease·ment [əpízmənt] *s.* apaciguamiento; conciliación.
ap·pel·late court [əpέlətkort] *s.* tribunal de apelaciones.
ap·pen·dix [əpέndɪks] *s.* apéndice.
ap·per·tain [æpɚtén] *v.* pertenecer.
ap·pe·tite [ǽpətaɪt] *s.* apetito; gana, deseo.
ap·pe·tiz·er [ǽpətaɪzɚ] *s.* aperitivo.
ap·pe·tiz·ing [ǽpətaɪzɪŋ] *adj.* apetecible; apetitoso.
ap·plaud [əplɔ́d] *v.* aplaudir.
ap·plause [əplɔ́z] *s.* aplauso.
ap·ple [ǽpl̩] *s.* manzana; — **tree** manzano; — **grove** manzanar; **Adam's** — nuez (*del cuello*); *Ven., C.A., Col* manzana; — **of my eye** niña de mis ojos; **apple-pie order** orden (estado) perfecto.
ap·ple·sauce [ǽplsɔs] *s.* compota de manzana.
ap·pli·ance [əpláɪəns] *s.* utensilio, instrumento; herramienta; mueble utilitario.
ap·pli·ca·ble [æplɪkəbl] *adj.* aplicable.
ap·pli·cant [ǽpləkənt] *s.* solicitante, aspirante, candidato.
ap·pli·ca·tion [æpləkéʃən] *s.* (*dedication*) aplicación; (*petition*) solicitud, petición; *Méx., Carib., Ven.* aplicación; — **blank** formulario de solicitud.
ap·plied [əpláɪd] *adj. & p.p.* aplicado; — **for** pedido, solicitado.
ap·ply [əplái] *v.* aplicar(se); **to** — **to** dirigirse a, acudir a, recurrir a; **to** — **for** solicitar, pedir; **to** — **oneself** aplicarse, dedicarse; **to** — **on account** acreditar en cuenta.
ap·point [əpɔ́ɪnt] *v.* (*designate*) nombrar, designar, señalar; (*furnish*) amueblar, equipar; **a well -ed house** una casa bien amueblada.
ap·point·ee [əpɔɪntí] *s.* electo.
ap·point·ment [əpɔ́ɪntmənt] *s.* (*designation*) nombramiento, designación; (*engagement*) cita, compromiso; **-s** mobiliario, mueblaje; accesorios.
ap·por·tion [əpórʃən] *v.* repartir proporcionadamente, prorratear.
ap·por·tion·ment [əpórʃənmənt] *s.* prorrateo, distribución, repartimiento.
ap·prais·al [əprézl̩] *s.* tasa, valuación.
ap·praise [əpréz] *v.* avaluar, valuar, tasar.
ap·pre·cia·ble [əpríʃəbl̩] *adj.* (*prized*) apreciable; (*perceived*) perceptible; (*quantity*) bastante.
ap·pre·ci·ate [əpríʃɪet] *v.* apreciar; estimar; agradecer; **to** — **in value** subir de valor.
ap·pre·ci·a·tion [əpriʃɪéʃən] *s.* apreciación; aprecio; valuación; agradecimiento; aumento, alza, subida (*de precio*).
ap·pre·hend [æprɪhέnd] *v.* aprehender, asir, prender; comprender; percibir.
ap·pre·hen·sion [æprɪhέnʃən] *s.* aprehensión, aprensión, recelo, desconfianza, presentimiento; captura.
ap·pre·hen·sive [æprɪhέnsɪv] *adj.* aprensivo.
ap·pren·tice [əprέntɪs] *s.* aprendiz; novicio, principiante; *v.* poner de aprendiz.
ap·pren·tice·ship [əprέntɪsʃɪp] *s.* aprendizaje.
ap·prise [əpráɪz] *v.* enterar, informar; apreciar; dar parte.
ap·proach [əprótʃ] *s.* acercamiento; aproximación; acceso, entrada; **method of** — técnica o modo de plantear (*un problema*); enfoque; *v.* acercarse, aproximarse; abordar (*a alguien*).
ap·pro·ba·tion [æprəbéʃən] *s.* aprobación.
ap·pro·pri·ate [əprópriɪt] *adj.* apropiado, propio, apto, conveniente, a propósito; [əprópriet] *v.* apropiarse, apoderarse de; asignar (*una suma de dinero*).
ap·pro·pri·a·tion [əproprɪéʃən] *s.* apropiación; asignación, suma asignada.
ap·prov·al [əprúvl̩] *s.* aprobación, asentimiento.
ap·prove [əprúv] *v.* aprobar; asentir a; **approved** visto bueno (V. B.).
ap·prox·i·mate [əpráksəmɪt] *adj.* aproximado; aproximativo; **-ly** *adv.* aproximadamente, casi, poco más o menos; [əpráksəmet] *v.* aproximar; aproximarse, acercarse.
a·pri·cot [éprɪkat] *s.* albaricoque; *Am.* chabacano.
A·pril [éprəl] *s.* abril.
a·pron [éprən] *s.* delantal.
ap·ro·pos [æprəpó] *adv.* a propósito; *adj.* oportuno; pertinente; — **of** a propósito de.
apt [æpt] *adj.* apto, capaz; pertinente, a propósito; — **to** propenso a.
ap·ti·tude [ǽptətjud] *s.* aptitud, capacidad; habilidad.
aq·ua·ma·rine [akwəmərín] *s.* aguamarina.
a·quar·i·um [əkwέrɪəm] *s.* acuario; pecera.
a·quat·ic [əkwǽtɪk] *adj.* acuático.
aq·ue·duct [ǽkwidʌkt] *s.* acueducto.
Ar·ab [ǽrəb] *adj. & s.* árabe.
Ar·a·go·nese [ǽrəgəniz] *adj. & s.* aragonés.
ar·bi·ter [árbɪtɚ] *s.* árbitro, arbitrador, juez árbitro.
ar·bi·trar·y [árbətrεrɪ] *adj.* arbitrario; despótico.
ar·bi·trate [árbətret] *v.* arbitrar; decidir; someter al arbitraje; terciar.
ar·bi·tra·tion [arbətréʃən] *s.* arbitraje, arbitración.
ar·bi·tra·tor [árbətretɚ] *s.* arbitrador, árbitro; medianero.
ar·bor [árbɚ] *s.* emparrado, enramada, glorieta.
arc [ark] *s.* arco; — **lamp** lámpara de arco.
ar·cade [arkéd] *s.* arcada; galería; soportal.
arch [artʃ] *s.* arco; bóveda; **semicircular** — arco de medio punto; — **enemy** enemigo acérrimo; *v.* arquear(se); enarcar(se).
ar·chae·ol·o·gy [arkɪálədʒɪ] *s.* arqueología.
ar·cha·ic [arkéɪk] *adj.* arcaico, desusado, anticuado.
arch·bish·op [ártʃbíʃəp] *s.* arzobispo.
arch·bish·op·ric [artʃbíʃəprɪk] *s.* arzobispado.

arch·er·y [ártʃərɪ] *s.* tiro de flechas.
ar·chi·pel·a·go [arkəpéləgo] *s.* archipiélago.
ar·chi·tect [arkətɛkt] *s.* arquitecto.
ar·chi·tec·tur·al [arkətéktʃərəl] *adj.* arquitectónico.
ar·chi·tec·ture [árkətɛktʃɚ] *s.* arquitectura.
ar·chives [árkaɪvz] *s.* archivo.
arch·way [ártʃwe] *s.* pasadiz (*bajo un arco*); arcada, galería abovedada.
arc·tic [árktɪk] *adj.* ártico.
ar·dent [árdn̩t] *adj.* ardiente, apasionado.
ar·dor [árdɚ] *s.* ardor; enardecimiento; fervor.
ar·du·ous [árdʒuəs] *adj.* arduo, trabajoso.
are [ar] *2ª persona y pl. del presente de indic. del verbo* **to be:** eres, estás; somos, estamos; sois, estáis; son, están.
ar·e·a [ɛ́rɪə] *s.* área, superficie; espacio; región.
a·re·na [ərínə] *s.* arena, redondel, plaza.
Ar·gen·ti·ne [árdʒəntin] *adj. & s.* argentino.
ar·gon [árgan] *s.* argón.
ar·gue [árgju] *v.* argüir; debatir; altercar; **to — into** persuadir a.
ar·gu·ment [árgjəmənt] *s.* disputa; polémica; razonamiento; sumario, resumen.
ar·id [ǽrɪd] *adj.* árido.
a·rise [əráɪz] *v.* levantarse; elevarse; surgir; provenir.
a·ris·en [ərízn̩] *p.p. de* **to arise.**
ar·is·toc·ra·cy [ærəstákrəsɪ] *s.* aristocracia.
a·ris·to·crat [ərístəkræt] *s.* aristócrata.
a·ris·to·crat·ic [ərɪstəkrǽtɪk] *adj.* aristocrático.
a·rith·me·tic [əríθmətɪk] *s.* aritmética; *adj.* aritmético — **data processing** sistematizacion de datos aritméticos.
ark [ark] *s.* arca; — **of the covenant** arca del testamento; **Noah's** — arca de Noé.
arm [arm] *s.* (*anatomy*) brazo; (*weapon*) arma; — **in** — de bracete, de bracero; *Ríopl., Cuba* de brazo, de brazos; **at -'s length** a una brazada; **with open -s** con los brazos abiertos; *v.* armar(se).
ar·ma·da [armádə] *s.* armada, flota.
ar·ma·ment [ármәmənt] *s.* armamento.
ar·ma·ture [ármətʃɚ] *s.* armadura.
arm·chair [ármtʃɛr] *s.* silla de brazos, sillón, butaca.
armed for·ces [ármd fórsəz] *s.* fuerzas armadas.
arm·ful [ármful] *s.* brazada.
ar·mi·stice [árməstɪs] *s.* armisticio.
ar·mor [ármɚ] *s.* armadura; blindaje, coraza; arnés; *v.* blindar, acorazar.
ar·mor·ed [ármɚd] *p.p.* blindado, acorazado.
ar·mor·y [ármərɪ] *s.* armería; arsenal.
arm·pit [ármpɪt] *s.* sobaco.
ar·my [ármɪ] *s.* ejército; muchedumbre; — **doctor** médico militar; **regular** — tropa de línea.
a·ro·ma [əróma] *s.* aroma; fragancia.
ar·o·mat·ic [ærəmǽtɪk] *adj.* aromático.
a·rose [əróz] *pret. de* **to arise.**
a·round [əráund] *adv.* alrededor; en redor; a la redonda; en torno; en derredor; cerca; **all** — por todos lados; *prep.* alrededor de; cerca de; — **here** por aquí; **to go — in circles** dar vueltas; **to go — the world** dar la vuelta al mundo.
a·rouse [əráuz] *v.* despertar, *Ríopl., C.A., Ven.* recordar (*al dormido*); excitar; promover, animar.
ar·raign [ərén] *v.* acusar; procesar (*a un criminal*).
ar·range [ərénd ʒ] *v.* arreglar; disponer, colocar; acomodar; hacer arreglos (para), hacer planes (para).
ar·range·ment [əréndʒmənt] *s.* arreglo; disposición; colocación, orden; convenio.
ar·ray [əré] *s.* (*order*) arreglo, formación, orden; orden (*de batalla*); (*pomp*) pompa; gala, atavío; *v.* formar (*tropas*); poner en orden; ataviar, adornar.
ar·rears [ərírz] *s. pl.* atrasos, pagos o rentas vencidos y no cobrados; **in** — atrasado (*en el pago de una cuenta*).
ar·rest [ərɛ́st] *s.* arresto, captura, aprehensión, detención; *v.* aprehender o prender, arrestar; detener; llamar, atraer (*la atención*).
ar·ri·val [əráɪvl̩] *s.* llegada; arribo; venida; **the new -s** los recién llegados.
ar·rive [əráɪv] *v.* llegar; arribar; **to — at a result** lograr (*o* conseguir) un resultado.
ar·ro·gance [ǽrəgəns] *s.* arrogancia.
ar·ro·gant [ǽrəgənt] *adj.* arrogante.
ar·row [ǽro] *s.* saeta, flecha.
ar·se·nal [ársn̩əl] *s.* arsenal.
ar·se·nic [ársn̩ɪk] *s.* arsénico.
ar·son [ársən] *s.* delito de incendio.
art [art] *s.* arte; destreza; astucia; **fine -s** bellas artes; **master of -s** licenciado en letras, maestro en artes.
ar·ter·y [ártərɪ] *s.* arteria; **arterial** arterial; — **highway** carretera troncal.
art·ful [ártful] *adj.* artero, mañero, ladino.
ar·ti·choke [ártɪtʃok] *s.* alcachofa.
ar·ti·cle [ártɪkl̩] *s.* artículo; — **of clothing** prenda de vestir; — **of merchandise** mercancía, mercadería; — **of agreement** convenio, contrato.
ar·tic·u·late [artíkjəlɪt] *adj.* articulado; claro, inteligible; capaz de hablar; [artíkjəlet] *v.* articular; enunciar; enlazar.
ar·tic·u·la·tion [artɪkjəléʃən] *s.* articulación; coyuntura.
ar·ti·fact [ártəfækt] *s.* artefacto.
ar·ti·fice [ártəfɪs] *s.* artificio; ardid.
ar·ti·fi·cial [artəfɪʃəl] *adj.* artificial; postizo; afectado, artificioso.
ar·til·ler·y [artílərɪ] *s.* artillería; — **man** artillero.
ar·ti·san [ártəzn̩] *s.* artesano; artífice.
art·ist [ártɪst] *s.* artista.
ar·tis·tic [artístɪk] *adj.* artístico; **-ally** *adv.* artísticamente.
as [æz] *adv., conj., prep.* como; mientras; a medida que, según; en el momento en que; — **far** — hasta, hasta donde; — **for** (— **to**) en cuanto a; — **if** como si; — **it were** por decirlo así; — **large** — tan grande como; — **much** — tanto como; — **well** tan bien; también; — **yet** hasta ahora, todavía; — **long** — **you wish** todo el tiempo que Vd. quiera; **strong** — **he is** aunque es tan fuerte; **the same** — lo mismo que; — **of** con fecha de; — **per** según.
as·bes·tos [æsbɛ́stəs] *s.* asbesto.
as·cend [əsɛ́nd] *v.* ascender; subir, elevarse.
as·cen·sion [əsɛ́nʃən] *s.* ascensión; subida.
as·cent [əsɛ́nt] *s.* ascenso; subida; ascensión.
as·cer·tain [æsɚtén] *v.* averiguar, indagar.
as·cet·ic [əsɛ́tɪk] *adj.* ascético; *s.* asceta.
as·cribe [əskráɪb] *v.* atribuir, imputar, achacar.
ash [æʃ] *s.* ceniza; — **tray** cenicero; — **tree** fresno; **Ash Wednesday** miércoles de ceniza; **ash-colored** *adj.* ceniciento, cenizo.
a·shamed [əʃémd] *adj.* avergonzado, corrido; **to be** — tener vergüenza; avergonzarse.
a·shore [əʃór] *adv.* a tierra; en tierra; **to go** — desembarcar.
A·si·at·ic [əʒɪǽtɪk] *adj. & s.* asiático.
a·side [əsáɪd] *adv.* aparte; a un lado; al lado; *s.* aparte (*en un drama*).
ask [æsk] *v.* (*request*) pedir, rogar, solicitar; (*inquire*) preguntar; (*invite*) invitar; **to — for** pedir; **to — for** (about, after) preguntar por; **to — a question** hacer una pregunta; **asking price** precio de oferta.
a·skance [əskǽns] *adv.* de soslayo; con recelo,

recelosamente; **to look** — mirar con recelo; no aprobar.

a·sleep [əslíp] *adj.* dormido; **to fall** — dormirse; **my arm is** — se me ha dormido (entumecido *o* entumido) el brazo.

as·par·a·gus [əspǽrəgəs] *s.* espárrago.

as·pect [ǽspɛkt] *s.* aspecto; cariz.

as·phalt [ǽsfɔlt] *s.* asfalto; chapapote.

as·pi·ra·tion [æspəréʃən] *s.* aspiración; anhelo.

as·pire [əspáɪr] *v.* aspirar; anhelar, ambicionar.

as·pi·rin [ǽspɝɪn] *s.* aspirina.

ass [æs] *s.* asno, burro; pollino.

as·sail [əsél] *v.* asaltar, acometer, agredir.

as·sail·ant [əsélənt] *s.* asaltador, agresor.

as·sas·sin [əsǽsɪn] *s.* asesino.

as·sas·si·nate [əsǽsn̩et] *v.* asesinar.

as·sas·si·na·tion [əsæsn̩éʃən] *s.* asesinato.

as·sault [əsɔ́lt] *s.* asalto, acometida; conato; ataque; *v.* asaltar, acometer, atacar; violar.

as·say [əsé] *v.* ensayar (*metales*); analizar, examinar; contrastar (*pesas, moneda*); *s.* ensaye (*de metales*); contraste (*de pesas, moneda*).

as·sem·ble [əsɛ́mbl̩] *v.* reunir(se), congregar(se), juntar(se); convocar; armar, montar (*maquinaria*).

as·sem·bly [əsɛ́mblɪ] *s.* asamblea; reunión; montaje (*de maquinaria*); — **hall** salón de sesiones; paraninfo; — **line** cadena de producción, tren de ensamblaje, línea de montaje; — **language** *s.* (*computer*) lenguaje de ensamble.

as·sent [əsɛ́nt] *s.* asentimiento; consentimiento; *v.* asentir; consentir.

as·sert [əsɝ́t] *v.* aseverar, asegurar, afirmar; **to** — **oneself** hacerse valer; obrar con firmeza; vindicarse.

as·ser·tion [əsɝ́ʃən] *s.* aserción, aserto, afirmación.

as·sess [əsɛ́s] *v.* avaluar; tasar; asignar, imponer (*impuestos, multas, contribuciones, etc.*).

as·sess·ment [əsɛ́smənt] *s.* avaluación, tasación; imposición (*de contribuciones, multas, etc.*); contribución, (*tax*) impuesto.

as·set [ǽsɛt] *s.* cualidad, ventaja; **-s** capital, fondos, caudal; haber, activo; **personal -s** bienes muebles; **-s in hand** bienes disponibles; **capital -s** activo fijo; *Arg.* valores patrimoniales.

as·sid·u·ous [əsídʒuəs] *adj.* asiduo, diligente.

as·sign [əsáɪn] *v.* asignar; señalar, designar; traspasar, ceder a favor de.

as·sign·ment [əsáɪnmənt] *s.* asignación; encargo; traspaso de bienes, designación; cesión (*de bienes*); tarea (*asignada*); lección (*señalada*).

as·sim·i·late [əsímlet] *v.* asimilar(se), absorber(se).

as·sist [əsíst] *v.* asistir, ayudar.

as·sis·tance [əsístəns] *s.* asistencia, ayuda.

as·sis·tant [əsístənt] *s.* asistente; ayudante; auxiliar; *adj.* subordinado, auxiliar.

as·so·ci·ate [əsóʃɪɪt] *adj.* asociado; *s.* asociado; socio; compañero; colega; [əsóʃɪet] *v.* asociar(se); relacionar.

as·so·ci·a·tion [əsosɪéʃən] *s.* asociación; sociedad; conexión, relación.

as·sort [əsɔ́rt] *v.* ordenar, clasificar.

as·sort·ed [əsɔ́rtɪd] *adj.* surtido, mezclado, variado, de todas clases.

as·sort·ment [əsɔ́rtmənt] *s.* variedad; clasificación; surtido; colección, grupo.

as·sume [əsúm] *v.* asumir; tomar; dar por sentado, dar por supuesto; arrogarse, apropiarse.

as·sump·tion [əsʌ́mpʃən] *d.* suposición; toma, apropiación; presunción; asunción (*de la Virgen*).

as·sur·ance [əʃúrəns] *s.* seguridad, certeza; convicción; confianza; **life** — seguro de vida. *Véase* **insurance.**

as·sure [əʃúr] *v.* asegurar; afirmar; infundir confianza; **assured** asegurado.

as·sur·ed·ly [əʃúrɪdlɪ] *adv.* seguramente; sin duda, con seguridad.

as·ta·tine [ǽstətin] *s.* astato.

as·ter·isk [ǽstərɪsk] *s.* asterisco.

a·stig·ma·tism [əstígmətɪzəm] *s.* astigmatismo.

as·ton·ish [əstɑ́nɪʃ] *v.* asombrar, pasmar, espantar.

as·ton·ish·ing [əstɑ́nɪʃɪŋ] *adj.* asombroso, pasmoso, maravilloso.

as·ton·ish·ment [əstɑ́nɪʃmənt] *s.* asombro, pasmo, sorpresa.

as·tound [əstáund] *v.* pasmar; aterrar, aturdir.

a·stray [əstré] *adv.* fuera de camino; *adj.* desviado, extraviado, descaminado; **to go** — perderse; errar el camino; extraviarse; **to lead** — desviar, extraviar; llevar por mal camino; seducir.

a·stride [əstráɪd] *adv.* a horcajadas.

as·trin·gent [æstríndʒənt] *adj.*, *s.* astringente.

as·tro·dome [ǽstrədom] *s.* astródomo.

as·trol·o·gy [əstrɑ́lədʒɪ] *s.* astrología.

as·tro·naut [ǽstrənɔt] *s.* astronauta.

as·tron·o·mer [əstrɑ́nəmɚ] *s.* astrónomo.

as·tron·o·my [estrɑ́nəmɪ] *s.* astronomía.

as·tro·phys·ics [ǽstrofízɪks] *s.* astrofísica.

As·tu·ri·an [æstjúrɪən] *adj.* & *s.* asturiano.

as·tute [əstjút] *adj.* astuto, sagaz.

a·sun·der [əsʌ́ndɚ] *adj.* separado; **to cut** — separar, apartar; dividir en dos.

a·sy·lum [əsáɪləm] *s.* asilo; hospicio; **orphan** — orfanato, casa de huérfanos, *Méx., C.A., Andes* orfanatorio.

at [æt] *prep.* a; en; en (la) casa de; — **last** por fin, al fin; — **once** al punto; **to be** — **work** estar trabajando; **to enter** — **that door** entrar por aquella puerta.

at·a·vism [ǽtəvɪzəm] *s.* atavismo.

ate [et] *pret. de* **to eat.**

a·the·ist [éθɪɪst] *s.* ateo.

ath·lete [ǽθlit] *s.* atleta.

ath·let·ic [æθlɛ́tɪk] *adj.* atlético.

ath·let·ics [æθlɛ́tɪks] *s.* gimnasia; atletismo; deportes.

At·lan·tic [ətlǽntɪk] *adj.* atlántico; *s.* el Atlántico.

at·las [ǽtləs] *s.* atlas.

at·mos·phere [ǽtməsfɪr] *s.* atmósfera; ambiente.

at·mos·pher·ic [ætməsférɪk] *adj.* atmosférico.

at·om [ǽtəm] *s.* átomo; — **bomb** bomba atómica.

a·tom·ic [ətɑ́mɪk] *adj.* atómico; — **age** edad atómica; — **energy** fuerza atómica; — **pile** pila atómica; — **weight** peso atómico.

a·tone [ətón] *v.* expiar, purgar; reparar.

a·tone·ment [ətónmənt] *s.* expiación; reparación.

a·tro·cious [ətróʃəs] *adj.* atroz.

a·troc·i·ty [ətrɑ́sətɪ] *s.* atrocidad; maldad.

at·ro·phy [ǽtrəfɪ] *s.* atrofia.

at·tach [ətǽtʃ] *v.* unir, juntar; sujetar, pegar, adherir; poner (*sello o firma*); embargar (*bienes*); asignar; atribuir.

at·ta·ché [ǽtəʃe] *s.* agregado.

at·tach·ment [ətǽtʃmənt] *s.* adhesión; apego; vinculación; afición, cariño; embargo (*de bienes*); (*accessory*) accesorio.

at·tack [ətǽk] *s.* ataque, asalto; acceso; *v.* atacar; acometer, embestir.

at·tain [ətén] *v.* lograr, conseguir, alcanzar; llegar a.

at·tain·ment [əténmənt] *s.* logro, consecución; adquisición; dote; habilidad.

at·tempt [ətɛ́mpt] *s.* tentativa; prueba, ensayo; esfuerzo; atentado; *v.* tentar, intentar; procurar, tratar (de), probar; **to** — **the life of** atentar contra

la vida de.
at·tend [ətɛ́nd] *v.* atender, cuidar, mirar por; asistir a; acompañar.
at·ten·dance [ətɛ́ndəns] *s.* asistencia; presencia; concurrencia.
at·ten·dant [ətɛ́ndənt] *s.* acompañante; sirviente, servidor; asistente; *adj.* acompañante.
at·ten·tion [ətɛ́nʃən] *s.* (*care*) cuidado; (*courtesy*) fineza, urbanidad, atención; **to pay** — hacer caso; prestar atención.
at·ten·tive [ətɛ́ntɪv] *adj.* atento; cortés.
at·test [ətɛ́st] *v.* atestiguar, atestar; certificar; dar fe.
at·tic [ǽtɪk] *s.* desván.
at·tire [ətáɪr] *s.* atavío; vestidura; vestido, traje; *v.* ataviar, adornar.
at·ti·tude [ǽtətjud] *s.* actitud; postura.
at·tor·ney [ətɝ́nɪ] *s.* abogado; procurador; apoderado; — **general** fiscal (*de una nación o estado*); **district** — fiscal de distrito; **power of** — procuración, poder.
at·tract [ətrǽkt] *v.* atraer; cautivar; **to — attention** llamar la atención.
at·trac·tion [ətrǽkʃən] *s.* atracción; atractivo; **-s** diversiones; lugares o sitios de interés.
at·trac·tive [ətrǽktɪv] *adj.* atractivo; seductor; simpático.
at·trac·tive·ness [ətrǽktɪvnɪs] *s.* atracción; atractivo.
at·trib·ute [ǽtrəbjut] *s.* atributo; propiedad; [ətríbjʊt] *v.* atribuir, achacar.
at·tri·tion [ətríʃən] *s.* agotamiento; atrición.
auc·tion [ɔ́kʃən] *s.* subasta, almoneda, remate, *Am.* venduta; *v.* subastar; rematar; **auctioneer** subastador, *Arg.* martillo.
au·da·cious [ɔdéʃəs] *adj.* audaz, atrevido, osado.
au·dac·i·ty [ɔdǽsətɪ] *s.* audacia, osadía; descaro.
au·di·ble [ɔ́dəbl̩] *adj.* audible.
au·di·ence [ɔ́dɪəns] *s.* auditorio, concurrencia, público; audiencia.
au·di·o fre·quen·cy [ɔdɪofríkwɛnsɪ] *s.* audiofrecuencia.
au·di·o-vis·u·al [ɔdɪovíʒuəl] *adj.* audiovisual.
au·dit [ɔ́dɪt] *v.* intervenir (*cuentas*); glosar, revisar; asistir a (*una clase*) de oyente; *s.* intervención, comprobación de cuentas.
au·di·tion [ɔdíʃən] *s.* audición.
au·di·tor [ɔ́dɪtɚ] *s.* interventor; censor de cuentas; oyente.
au·di·to·ri·um [ɔdətórɪəm] *s.* salón de conferencias o conciertos; paraninfo.
au·di·to·ry [ɔ́dətorɪ] *adj.* auditivo.
au·ger [ɔ́gɚ] *s.* taladro, barrena.
aught [ɔt] *s.* algo.
aug·ment [ɔgmɛ́nt] *v.* aumentar.
au·gur [ɔ́gɚ] *s.* agorero; *v.* augurar, pronosticar; **to — well** (*o* **ill**) ser de buen (*o* mal) agüero.
Au·gust [ɔ́gəst] *s.* agosto.
aunt [ænt] *s.* tia.
aus·pic·es [ɔ́spɪsɪz] *s. pl.* auspicios; protección.
aus·pi·cious [ɔspíʃəs] *adj.* propicio; favorable.
aus·tere [ɔstír] *adj.* austero, adustro, severo.
aus·ter·i·ty [ɔstérətɪ] *s.* austeridad, severidad.
Aus·tri·an [ɔ́strɪən] *adj.* & *s.* austríaco.
au·then·tic [ɔθɛ́ntɪk] *adj.* auténtico.
au·thor [ɔ́θɚ] *s.* autor; escritor.
au·thor·i·ta·tive [əθɔ́rətetɪv] *adj.* autorizado, que tiene autoridad; autoritario.
au·thor·i·ty [əθɔ́rətɪ] *s.* autoridad; facultad; **to have on good** — saber de buena tinta.
au·thor·ize [ɔ́θəraɪz] *v.* autorizar.
au·to [ɔ́to] *s.* auto, automóvil.
au·to-boot [ɔ́tobut] *s.* (*computer*) autocarga.
au·to·crat [ɔ́təkræt] *s.* autócrata.
au·to·graph [ɔ́təgræf] *s.* autógrafo.
au·to·mat·ic [ɔtəmǽtɪk] *adj.* automático; **-ally** *adv.* automáticamente; **automation** automatización.
au·to·mo·bile [ɔ́təməbil] *s.* automóvil; **automotive** automovilístico.
au·ton·o·my [ɔtɑ́nəmɪ] *s.* autonomía.
au·top·sy [ɔ́tɑpsɪ] *s.* autopsia.
au·tumn [ɔ́təm] *s.* otoño.
au·tum·nal [ɔtʌ́mnl] *adj.* otoñal.
aux·il·ia·ry [ɔgzíljərɪ] *adj.* & *s.* auxiliar.
a·vail [əvél] *v.* aprovechar; beneficiar; **to — oneself of** aprovecharse de; *s.* provecho; ventaja; **of no** — de ninguna utilidad o ventaja.
a·vail·a·ble [əvéləbl̩] *adj.* disponible; aprovechable; obtenible.
av·a·lanche [ǽvl̩æntʃ] *s.* alud; torrente.
av·a·rice [ǽvərɪs] *s.* avaricia.
av·a·ri·cious [ævəríʃəs] *adj.* avaro, avariento.
a·venge [əvɛ́ndʒ] *v.* vengar; vindicar.
a·veng·er [əvɛ́ndʒɚ] *s.* vengador.
av·e·nue [ǽvənu] *s.* avenida.
a·ver [əvɝ́] *v.* afirmar, asegurar.
av·er·age [ǽvrɪdʒ] *s.* promedio, término medio; **on an** — por término medio; *adj.* medio, mediano; ordinario; *v.* promediar, calcular o sacar el promedio; **to — a loss** prorratear una pérdida; **he -s 20 miles an hour** avanza o recorre un promedio de 20 millas por hora.
a·verse [əvɝ́s] *adj.* adverso, renuente.
a·ver·sion [əvɝ́ʒən] *s.* aversión; malquerencia, inquina.
a·vert [əvɝ́t] *v.* apartar, desviar; evitar; impedir.
a·vi·a·tion [evɪéʃən] *s.* aviación.
a·vi·a·tor [évɪetɚ] *s.* aviador.
av·o·ca·do [ɑvəkɑ́do] *s.* aguacate, *Andes* palta.
av·o·ca·tion [ævəkéʃən] *s.* distracción; ocupación de distracción o diversión.
a·void [əvɔ́ɪd] *v.* evitar; eludir.
a·vow [əváʊ] *v.* confesar, reconocer, admitir.
a·vow·al [əváʊəl] *s.* confesión, admisión.
a·wait [əwét] *v.* esperar, aguardar.
a·wake [əwék] *adj.* despierto; alerto; **wide-awake** muy despierto; avispado; *v.* despertar(se).
a·wak·en [əwékən] *v.* despertar(se).
a·ward [əwɔ́rd] *s.* premio; decisión, sentencia; *v.* asignar; otorgar; conferir; adjudicar (*un premio, medalla, etc.*).
a·ware [əwɛ́r] *adj.* consciente; enterado, sabedor; cauto; sobre aviso.
a·way [əwé] *adv.* lejos; fuera; *adj.* ausente; **right** — ahora mismo, ahorita; **ten miles** — a diez millas de aquí; **to give** — regalar; **to go** — irse; **to take** — quitar.
awe [ɔ] *s.* pavor; pasmo; **to stand in** — quedarse, o estar, pasmado; pasmarse; *v.* atemorizar; infundir avor; maravillar.
aw·ful [ɔ́fʊl] *adj.* terrible; horroroso; tremendo; impresionante; **-ly** *adv.* terriblemente; horrorosamente; muy.
a·while [əhwáɪl] *adv.* (por) un rato; (por) algún tiempo.
awk·ward [ɔ́kwɚd] *adj.* torpe, desmañado; molesto, embarazoso; incómodo; inconveniente.
awl [ɔl] *s.* lezna, punzón.
aw·ning [ɔ́nɪŋ] *s.* toldo.
a·woke [əwók] *pret.* & *p.p. de* **to awake.**
ax, axe [æks] *s.* hacha.
ax·is [ǽksɪs] *pl.* **ax·es** (ǽksiz) *s.* eje.
ax·le [ǽksl] *s.* eje (*de una rueda*); **front** — eje delantero; **rear** — eje trasero.

aye [aɪ] *adv.* si; *s.* voto afirmativo.
Az·tec [ǽztɛk] *adj.* & *s.* azteca.
az·ure [ǽʒɚ] *adj.* azul; *s.* azur, azul celeste.

B:b

bab·ble [bǽbl] *s.* balbuceo; parloteo, charla; *v.* balbucear; parlotear, charlar.
babe [beb] = **baby.**
ba·boon [bæbún] *s.* mandril (*especie de mono*).
ba·by [bébɪ] *s.* nene, bebé, criatura; *Andes, Ch.* guagua; *C.A.* tierno; *adj.* infantil; de niño; — **girl** nena; — **sitter** [bébɪsɪtɚ] *s.* cuidaniños, niñera por horas; *v.* mimar.
bach·e·lor [bǽtʃəlɚ] *s.* bachiller; soltero.
ba·cil·lus [bəsíləs] *s.* bacilo.
back [bæk] *s.* (*anatomy*) espalda; lomo (de animal); (*opposite side*) revés; respaldo (*de silla*), espaldar; **behind one's** — a espaldas de uno, a espaldas vueltas; **in — of** detrás de, tras; **to fall on one's** — caer de espaldas, caer boca arriba; **to turn one's** — volver las espaldas; *adj.* posterior; trasero; retrasado, atrasado, rezagado; — **pay** sueldo atrasado; — **talk** respuesta insolente;— **yard** patio interior; corral; *adv.* atrás, detrás; — **and forth** de aquí para allá; **to come** — volver, regresar; **to give** — devolver; *v.* respaldar, endosar; sostener, apoyar, retroceder; hacer retroceder; **to — down** hacerse (para) atrás; retractarse.
back·bone [bǽkbón] *s.* espinazo, espina dorsal; firmeza; apoyo, sostén.
back·er [bǽkɚ] *s.* fiador; sostenedor, defensor; (*politics*) partidario.
back·fire [bǽkfaɪr] *s.* petardeo; *v.* fracasar, ser contraproducente.
back·ground [bǽkgraʊnd] *s.* fondo; educación; experiencia; **to keep in the** — dejar en último término; quedarse en último término; mantenerse retirado.
back·hand [bǽkhænd] *s.* revés; escritura inclinada a la izquierda; **-ed stroke** revés; **a -ed remark** una ironía; una indirecta.
back·ing [bǽkɪŋ] *s.* apoyo, garantía; endose, endoso; respaldo.
back·lash [bǽklæʃ] *s.* contragolpe; culateo.
back·log [bǽklɔg] *s.* reserva pendiente.
back·space [bǽkspes] *v.* espaciar hacia atrás.
back·stage [bækstédʒ] *adv.* detrás del telón.
back·up [bǽkəp] *adj.* de reserva.
back·ward [bǽkwɚd] *adj.* atrasado; retrasado; retrógrado; lerdo, tardo; huraño, tímido, esquivo; *adv.* = **backwards.**
back·ward·ness [bǽkwɚdnɪs] *s.* torpeza; atraso; timidez.
back·wards [bǽkwɚdz] *adv.* hacia (*o* para) atrás; de espaldas; **to go** — retroceder, andar hacia (*o* para) atrás.
ba·con [békən] *s.* tocino.
bac·te·ri·a [bæktírɪə] *s. pl.* bacterias.
bac·te·ri·ol·o·gy [bæktɪrɪálədʒɪ] *s.* bacteriología.
bad [bæd] *adj.* malo; perverso; dañoso; podrido; **to go from — to worse** ir de mal en peor; **to look** — tener mal cariz, tener mala cara o mal aspecto; **-ly** *adv.* mal, malamente.
bade [bæd] *pret. de* **to bid.**
badge [bædʒ] *s.* insignia, divisa; distintivo; *Méx.* chapa.
bad·ger [bǽdʒɚ] *s.* tejón; *v.* atormentar, acosar, molestar.
bad·ness [bǽdnɪs] *s.* maldad.
baf·fle [bǽfl] *v.* desconcertar, confundir; frustrar, impedir.
bag [bæg] *s.* (*sack*) saco, bolsa, talega; costal; (*baggage*) maleta; zurrón, morral; *v.* ensacar; cazar; agarrar; adueñarse de; inflarse; abolsarse.
bag·gage [bǽgɪdʒ] *s.* equipaje; bagaje; — **car** furgón, vagón de equipajes; — **check** talón, contraseña de equipajes; — **tag** marbete, etiqueta; — **inspection** revisión de equipaje.
bag·pipe [bǽgpaɪp] *s.* gaita.
bail [bel] *s.* fianza, caución; **to let out on** — poner en libertad bajo fianza; *v.* dar fianza; salir fiador; (*empty*) achicar (*agua*), vaciar; **to — out of a plane** tirarse (*con paracaídas*) de un aeroplano; **bailee** depositario.
bait [bet] *s.* cebo; atractivo, aliciente; *v.* tentar, atraer; cebar; acosar, perseguir.
bake [bek] *v.* hornear, cocer al horno; calcinar.
bak·er [békɚ] *s.* panadero, pastelero, hornero; — **'s dozen** la docena del fraile.
bak·ery [békərɪ] *s.* panadería, pastelería, tahona.
bak·ing [békɪŋ] *s.* hornado; cocimiento; — **powder** polvo de hornear.
bal·ance [bǽləns] *s.* (*instrument*) balanza; (*equilibrium*) contrapeso, equilibrio, balance; (*debit, credit*) saldo; — **of payments** balanza de pagos; — **wheel** volante del reloj; — **of trade** balanza comercial; — **due** saldo pagadero; — **sheet** estado de contabilidad, *Arg.* hoja de balance; — **of power** equilibrio político; **to lose one's** — perder el equilibrio; *v.* contrapesar; pesar; balancear(se); equilibrar; saldar (*una cuenta*).
bal·co·ny [bǽlkənɪ] *s.* balcón; galería (*de teatro*).
bald [bɔld] *adj.* calvo; pelado; pelón; sin vegetación; escueto, sin adornos; — **spot** calva.
bale [bel] *s.* bala, fardo (*de mercancías*); *v.* embalar, enfardar, empacar.
balk [bɔk] *v.* oponerse, rebelarse, resistirse; pararse de repente; negarse a seguir; encabritarse; **to — someone's plans** frustrar los planes de alguien.
ball [bɔl] *s.* (*plaything*) pelota, bola; (*string, thread*) ovillo; (*weapon*) bala; (*dance*) baile; — **bearing** cojinete de bolas; — **game** juego de pelota; béisbol; — **printer** *(computer)* impresora de bola; *v.* ovillar; **to — up** enredar, confundir.
bal·lad [bǽləd] *s.* romance; copla, canción; balada.
bal·last [bǽləst] *s.* lastre; grava (*usada en terraplenes, caminos, etc.*); *v.* lastrar, poner el lastre a (*una embarcación*).
bal·let [bælé] *s.* ballet.
bal·lis·tics [balístɪks] *s.* balística.
bal·loon [bəlún] *s.* globo (*aerostático*); **ballooning of prices** alza artificial de precios.
bal·lot [bǽlət] *s.* balota, *Méx., C.A.* boleta, cédula para votar; voto; — **box** urna electoral; *v.* balotar, votar.
ball point [bɔ́lpɔɪnt] *s.* bolígrafo.
balm [bɑm] *s.* bálsamo.
bal·my [bɑ́mɪ] *adj.* balsámico; fragante; refrescante, suave; algo loco, chiflado.
bal·sam [bɔ́lsəm] *s.* bálsamo; especie de abeto.
bam·boo [bæmbú] *s.* bambú.
ban [bæn] *s.* bando, proclama; excomunión; prohibición; **marriage -s** (*o* **banns**) amonestaciones; *v.* proscribir, prohibir; condenar.
ba·nan·a [bənǽnə] *s.* plátano; banana; *C.A.* guineo; — **tree** banano; plátano.
band [bænd] *s.* (*group*) banda, partida, pandilla, cuadrilla; (*musicians*) banda; (*strip*) faja, lista,

AY

cinta, tira; partida, pandilla, cuadrilla; **rubber —** liga de goma; *v.* unir, juntar; atar, ligar; **to — together** confederarse, juntarse.
ban·dage [bǽndɪdʒ] *s.* venda, vendaje; *v.* vendar.
bandanna [bændǽnə] *s.* pañuelo de hierbas.
ban·dit [bǽndɪt] *s.* bandido, bandolero.
bang [bæŋ] *s.* golpe, golpazo; estallido; fleco (*de pelo*); **with a —** de golpe, de golpazo; de repente; con estrépito; **—!** ¡pum!; *v.* golpear; hacer estrépito; cortar (*el pelo*) en fleco; **to — the door** dar un portazo.
ban·ish [bǽnɪʃ] *v.* proscribir, desterrar; **to — fear** desechar el temor.
ban·ish·ment [bǽnɪʃmənt] *s.* proscripción; destierro.
ban·is·ter [bǽnɪstɚ] *s.* balaustre; barandilla, barandal, pasamano.
ban·jo [bǽndʒo] *s.* banjo.
bank [bæŋk] *s.* (*institution*) banco; (*in card game*) banca; (*of a river*) orilla, ribera, banda; escarpa; (*pile*) montón; **savings —** caja de ahorros; **— statement** estado de cuenta; **— vault** bóveda, deposito de seguridad; *adj.* bancario; de banco; *v.* depositar en un banco; amontonar (*tierra o arena*); cubrir con cenizas, tapar (*el* fuego); ladear (*un aeroplano*); **to — upon** (*o* **on**) contar con.
bank·book [bǽŋkbʊk] *s.* libreta de banco.
bank·er [bǽŋkɚ] *s.* banquero.
bank·ing [bǽŋkɪŋ] *s.* transacciones bancarias banca; *adj.* bancario, de banca; **— house** banca, casa de banca.
bank·note [bǽŋknot] *s.* billete de banco.
bank·rupt [bǽŋkrʌpt] *adj.* en quiebra, arruinado, insolvente; *v.* quebrar; arruinar.
bank·rupt·cy [bǽŋkrʌptsɪ] *s.* bancarrota, quiebra; *Arg., Ch., Perú, Bol.* falencia; **to go into —** declararse insolvente; quebrar, hacer bancarrota.
ban·ner [bǽnɚ] *s.* bandera, estandarte, pendón; *adj.* primero, principal, sobresaliente.
ban·quet [bǽŋkwɪt] *s.* banquete; *v.* banquetear.
bap·tism [bǽptɪzəm] *s.* bautismo; bautizo.
Bap·tist [bǽptɪst] *s.* bautista.
bap·tize [bæptáɪz] *v.* bautizar.
bar [bɑr] *s.* (*of iron*) barra; barrote; tranca; (*obstacle*) barrera, obstáculo; (*of justice*) tribunal; foro; (*saloon*) cantina, taberna; (*counter*) mostrador; (*piece*) barra (*de jabón*); pastilla (*de chocolate*); **sand —** banco de arena; **-s** reja; **to be admitted to the —** recibirse de abogado; *v.* atrancar (*la puerta*); estorbar; prohibir; excluir; **barring error or omission** salvo error u omisión.
barb [bɑrb] *s.* púa.
bar·bar·i·an [bɑrbέrɪən] *s.* & *adj.* bárbaro; salvaje.
bar·ba·rous [bɑ́rbərəs] *adj.* bárbaro; salvaje; inculto.
bar·be·cue [bɑ́rbɪkju] *s. Méx., C.A., Col.* barbacoa; *Ríopl.* churrasco; *v.* hacer barbacoa; *Ríopl.* churrasquear.
barbed [bɑrbd] *adj.* con púas; **— wire** alambre de púas.
bar·ber [bɑ́rbɚ] *s.* barbero; peluquero.
bar·ber·shop [bɑ́rbɚʃɑp] *s.* barbería; peluquería.
bard [bɑrd] *s.* bardo, vate, poeta.
bare [bɛr] *adj.* (*naked*) desnudo; descubierto; pelado; (*evident*) manifiesto, patente; (*unfurnished*) desamueblado, vacío; **— majority** mayoría escasa; **to lay —** poner de manifiesto, hacer patente, revelar; **to ride — back** montar en pelo.
bare·foot [bέrfʊt] *adj.* descalzo, con los pies desnudos; **-ed** [bέrfʊtɪd] = **barefoot.**
bare·head·ed [bέrhέdɪd] *adj.* descubierto, sin sombrero.
bare·leg·ged [bέrlέgɪd] *adj.* con las piernas desnudas; sin medias.
bare·ly [bέrlɪ] *adv.* apenas; escasamente; **— three pounds** tres libras escasas.
bare·ness [bέrnɪs] *s.* desnudez.
bar·gain [bɑ́rgɪn] *s.* (*agreement*) convenio, pacto; negocio, trato; (*cheap*) ganga; **— sale** ganga, *Méx., C.A., Ven., Andes* barata; **into the —** por añadidura; de ganancia; **to make a —** cerrar un convenio; *v.* regatear; negociar; **to — for** regatear; contar con, esperar.
barge [bɑrdʒ] *s.* lanchón; barca.
bar·i·tone [bǽrəton] *s.* & *adj.* barítono.
bar·i·um [bǽrɪəm] *s.* bario.
bark [bɑrk] *s.* ladrido; corteza (*de árbol*); barco velero; *v.* ladrar; descortezar, quitar la corteza.
bar·ley [bɑ́rlɪ] *s.* cebada.
barn [bɑrn] *s.* establo, cuadra; granero, troje; pajar; **streetcar —** cobertizo para tranvías.
bar·na·cle [bɑ́rnəkəl] *s.* cirrópodo.
barn·yard [bɑ́rnjard] *s.* corral; **— fowl** aves de corral.
ba·rom·e·ter [bərɑ́mətɚ] *s.* barómetro.
bar·on [bǽrən] *s.* barón.
ba·roque [bərók] *adj.* & *s.* barroco.
bar·rage [bərɑ́ʒ] *s.* fuego de barrera; presa.
bar·rel [bǽrəl] *s.* barril, barrica, tonel, cuba; (*gun*) cañón (*de fusil, pistola, etc.*); *v.* embarrilar (*meter en barril*).
bar·ren [bǽrən] *adj.* árido; estéril.
bar·ren·ness [bǽrənnɪs] *s.* aridez; esterilidad.
bar·rette [bərέt] *s.* broche, prendedor (*para sujetar el pelo*).
bar·ri·cade [bærəkéd] *s.* barricada, barrera; *v.* poner barricadas; obstruir el paso con barricadas.
bar·ri·er [bǽrɪɚ] *s.* barrera, valla; obstáculo.
bar·room [bárum] *s.* cantina; bar.
bar·ter [bɑ́rtɚ] *v.* permutar, trocar, cambiar; *s.* permuta, trueque, cambio.
base [bes] *s.* base; basa; fundamento; *adj.* bajo, vil, ruin; inferior; *v.* basar, fundar; establecer.
base·ball [bésbɔ́l] *s.* baseball o béisbol.
base·ment [bésmənt] *s.* sótano.
base·ness [bésnɪs] *s.* bajeza, ruindad, vileza.
bash·ful [bǽʃfəl] *adj.* tímido, encogido, vergonzoso.
bash·ful·ness [bǽʃfəlnɪs] *s.* timidez, vergüenza, cortedad, apocamiento.
ba·sic [bésɪk] *adj.* básico; fundamental.
ba·sin [bésn̩] *s.* palangana, jofaina; lebrillo; tazón (*de fuente*); (*pond*) estanque, depósito de agua; **river —** cuenca de río.
ba·sis [bésɪs] (*pl.* **bases** [bésiz]) *s.* base, fundamento.
bask [bæsk] *v.* calentarse (*al sol*); asolearse, tomar el sol.
bas·ket [bǽskɪt] *s.* cesta, cesto, canasta.
bas·ket·ball [bǽskɪtbɔl] *s.* basquetbol.
Basque [bæsk] *adj.* & *s.* (*person*) vasco; (*language*) vascuence, vasco; (*territory*) vascongado, vasco.
bass [bes] *s.* bajo (*en música*); *adj.* bajo, grave; **— drum** tambora, bombo; **— horn** tuba.
bas·tard [bǽstɚd] *s.* & *adj.* bastardo.
baste [best] *v.* hilvanar; pringar (*empapar la carne con grasa*); apalear.
bat [bæt] *s.* palo, *Méx., Carib., Ven., C.A.* bate (*de béisbol*); garrote; golpe, garrotazo; (*animal*) murciélago; *v.* apalear; dar palos; *Méx., Carib., Ven., C.A.* batear; **not to — an eye** no pestañear.
batch [bætʃ] *s.* hornada; colección, grupo; partida; conjunto.
bath [bæθ] *s.* baño.
bathe [beð] *v.* bañar(se).
bath·er [béðɚ] *s.* bañista.

bath·house [bǽθhaʊs] *s.* casa de baños; bañadero.
bath·robe [bǽθrob] *s.* bata de baño.
bath·room [bǽθrum] *s.* baño, cuarto de baño.
bath·tub [bǽθtʌb] *s.* bañera, tina.
bath·y·sphere [bǽθɪsfɪr] *s.* batisfera.
bat·tal·ion [bətǽljən] *s.* batallón.
bat·ter [bǽtɚ] *s.* batido, masa; *Am.* bateador (*de béisbol*); *v.* golpear; **to — down** demoler.
bat·ter·y [bǽtərɪ] *s.* batería; acumulador; pila; (*assault*) asalto.
bat·tle [bǽtl̩] *s.* batalla, lucha, combate; *v.* batallar, luchar, combatir.
bat·tle·field [bǽtlfild] *s.* campo de batalla
bat·tle·ship [bǽtl̩ʃɪp] *s.* buque de guerra, acorazado.
baud [bɔd] *s.* (*computer*) baudio.
bawl [bɔl] *s.* aullido; grito; *v.* aullar; gritar; pregonar; **to — out** regañar, reprender.
bay [be] *s.* bahía; ladrido, balido, aullido; **— rum** ron de laurel; **— tree** laurel; **— window** ventana saliente, mirador; **to hold at —** tener a raya; *adj.* bayo; *v.* dar aullidos, ladridos o balidos.
bay·o·net [béənɪt] *s.* bayoneta; *v.* traspasar; herir con bayoneta.
ba·zaar [bəzɑ́r] *s.* bazar; feria.
ba·zoo·ka [bəzúka] *s.* bazuca.
be [bi] *v.* (*innately*) ser; (*state or condition*) estar, verse, hallarse, encontrarse; **— that as it may** sea como sea; **to — cold (warm, hungry, right,** *etc.*) tener frío (calor, hambre, razón, *etc.*); **to — in a hurry** tener prisa; **he is to —** ha de ser; va a ser; **it is cold (hot, windy,** *etc.*) hace frío (calor, viento, *etc.*).
beach [bitʃ] *s.* playa, ribera; *v.* varar, poner en seco (*una embarcación*), encallar.
beach·head [bítʃhed] *s.* cabeza de playa.
bea·con [bíkən] *s.* faro, fanal; boya luminosa; señal; **aviation —** radiofaro.
bead [bid] *s.* cuenta (*de rosario, collar, etc.*); abalorio, glóbulo; gota (*de sudor*); **-s** rosario; collar de cuentas; *v.* adornar con abalorios o cuentecitas.
beak [bik] *s.* (*bird*) pico (*de ave*); (*ship*) espolón (*de nave*).
beak·er [bíkɚ] *s.* tazón.
beam [bim] *s.* rayo (*de luz o de calor*); (*smile*) sonrisa; viga; vigueta; (*scale*) brazo (*de balanza*); **radio —** línea de radiación, radiofaro; *v.* (*light*) emitir (*luz, rayos*); brillar; sonreír, estar radiante de alegría; radiar, transmitir por radio.
beam·ing [bímɪŋ] *adj.* radiante, resplandeciente; sonriente.
bean [bin] *s.* judía, habichuela; *Méx., C.A., Ven., Col.* frijol; *Ch., Ríopl.* poroto; **coffee —** grano de café; **Lima —** haba; **string —** judía o habichuela verde; *Méx., C.A.* ejote; *Ch., Ríopl.* chaucha.
bear [bɛr] *s.* oso, osa; (*market*) bajista; *v.* (*stand*) soportar; llevar; sobrellevar; tolerar, aguantar; (*give birth*) parir, dar a luz; producir; **to — down** deprimir; apretar; **to — a grudge** guardar rencor; **to — in mind** tener en cuenta; **to — on a subject** tener relación con un asunto; **to — oneself with dignity** portarse con dignidad; **to — out** confirmar; **to — testimony** dar testimonio; **to — interest** devengar interés.
beard [bɪrd] *s.* barba, barbas; aristas (*de trigo o maíz*); **-ed** *adj.* barbado, barbudo.
bearer [bɛ́rɚ] *s.* portador; mensajero; **bearing** [bɛ́rɪŋ] *s.* (*posture*) porte, presencia; (*relation*) relación, conexión; (*direction*) rumbo, orientación; (*mechanical*) cojinete; **ball —** cojinete de bolas; **beyond —** inaguantable, insufrible; **to lose one's -s** perder el rumbo, desorientarse; **fruit-bearing** *adj.* fructífero.
beast [bist] *s.* bestia, animal.
beat [bit] *s.* golpe; toque (*de tambor*); latido, palpitación; compás; ronda (*que hace el policía*); *v.* batir; golpear; azotar; vencer, ganar; marcar (*el compás*); pulsar, latir; sonar (*tambores*); **to — around the bush** andarse por las ramas; valerse de rodeos; *pret. & p.p. de* **to beat.**
beat·en [bítn̩] *p.p. de* **to beat** *& adj.* batido; vencido; fatigado; **— path** camino trillado.
beat·er [bítɚ] *s.* batidor; molinillo; golpeador; **egg —** batidor de huevos.
be·a·t·if·ic [beətífɪk] *adj.* beatífico.
beat·ing [bítɪŋ] *s.* paliza, tunda, zurra; latido, pulsación.
be·at·i·tude [bɪǽtətjud] *s.* beatitud, bienaventuranza; **the Beatitudes** las bienaventuranzas.
beau [bo] *s.* galán, pretendiente.
beau·te·ous [bjútɪəs] *adj.* bello, hermoso.
beau·ti·ful [bjútəfəl] *adj.* bello, hermoso.
beau·ti·fy [bjútəfaɪ] *v.* hermosear, embellecer.
beau·ty [bjútɪ] *s.* belleza, hermosura; beldad; **— parlor** salón de belleza.
bea·ver [bívɚ] *s.* castor; **— board** cartón para tabiques.
be·came [bɪkém] *pret. de* **to become.**
be·cause [bɪkɔ́z] *conj.* porque; **— of** *prep.* por, a causa de.
beck·on [bɛ́kən] *s.* seña, llamada; *v.* llamar a señas.
be·come [bɪkʌ́m] *v.* (*suit*) sentar bien a, quedar bien a; convenir a; (*turn out to be*) hacerse; ponerse; llegar a ser; convertirse en; **to — crazy** volverse loco; enloquecer; **to — angry** enojarse; **to — frightened** asustarse; **to — old** envejecer(se); **what has — of him?** ¿qué ha sido de él?; ¿qué se ha hecho él?; *p.p. de* **to become.**
be·com·ing [bɪkʌ́mɪŋ] *adj.* propio, conveniente; decente, decoroso; **that dress is — to you** le sienta bien ese traje.
bed [bɛd] *s.* cama, lecho; cauce (*de un río*); fondo (*de lago o mar*); cuadro (*de jardín*); yacimiento (*mineral*); **to go to —** acostarse; **to put to —** acostar.
bed·bug [bɛ́dbʌg] *s.* chinche.
bed·clothes [bɛ́dkloðz] *s. pl.* ropa de cama.
bed·ding [bɛ́dɪŋ] = **bedclothes.**
bed·pan [bɛ́dpæn] *s.* silleta; cómoda.
bed·rid·den [bɛ́drɪdən] *adj.* en cama; postrado.
bed·rock [bɛ́drák] *s.* roca sólida; lecho de roca.
bed·room [bɛ́drum] *s.* cuarto de dormir, alcoba, dormitorio, *Méx., C.A.* recámara.
bed·side [bɛ́dsaɪd]: **at the —** al lado de la cama; **— table** velador, mesilla de noche.
bed·spread [bɛ́dsprɛd] *s.* colcha, sobrecama.
bed·time [bɛ́dtaɪm] *s.* hora de acostarse, hora de dormir.
bee [bi] *s.* abeja; reunión (*para trabajar o competir*); **to have a — in one's bonnet** tener una idea metida en la cabeza.
beech [bitʃ] *s.* haya; **— nut** nuez de haya, hayuco.
beef [bif] *s.* carne de vaca o toro; vaca, toro (*engordados para matar*); **roast —** rosbif.
beef·steak [bífstek] *s.* bistec, biftec o bisté.
bee·hive [bíhaɪv] *s.* colmena; abejera.
been [bɪn, bɛn] *p.p. de* **to be.**
beep [bip] *s.* pip, piip, piiip.
beer [bɪr] *s.* cerveza; **— tavern** cervecería.
beet [bit] *s.* remolacha, *Mex.* betabel.
bee·tle [bítl̩] *s.* escarabajo.
be·fall [bɪfɔ́l] *v.* sobrevenir, acaecer, suceder.
be·fall·en [bɪfɔ́lən] *p.p. de* **to befall.**

be·fell [bɪfɛ́l] *pret. de* **to befall.**
be·fit [bɪfɪ́t] *v.* convenir.
be·fore [bɪfór] *adv.* (*temporal*) antes; (*spatial*) delante; al frente; *prep.* antes de; delante de; enfrente de; ante; *conj.* antes (de) que.
be·fore·hand [bɪfórhænd] *adv.* de antemano, por adelantado, con antelación, con anticipación.
be·friend [bɪfrɛ́nd] *v.* ofrecer o brindar amistad a; favorecer; amparar.
beg [bɛg] *v.* rogar, suplicar, pedir; mendigar, pordiosear; **to — the question** dar por sentado lo mismo que se arguye.
be·gan [bɪgǽn] *pret. de* **to begin.**
be·get [bɪgɛ́t] *v.* engendrar; causar, producir.
beg·gar [bɛ́gɚ] *s.* mendigo, pordiosero; pobre; infeliz, miserable.
be·gin [bigɪ́n] *v.* comenzar, empezar, principiar.
be·gin·ner [bigɪ́nɚ] *s.* principiante; novicio.
be·gin·ning [bigɪ́nɪŋ] *s.* principio; comienzo, empiezo; origen; **— with** comenzando con (*o* por); a partir de; **at the —** al principio.
be·got [bɪgát] *pret. & p.p. de* **to beget.**
be·got·ten [bɪgátn̩] *p.p. de* **to beget.**
be·grudge [bigrʌ́dʒ] *v.* envidiar; ceder de mala gana.
be·guile [bɪgáɪl] *v.* engañar; defraudar; seducir.
be·gun [bɪgʌ́n] *p.p. de* **to begin.**
be·half [bɪhǽf]: **in (on) — of** por; en nombre de; a favor de; en defensa de; **in my —** en mi nombre; a mi favor; por mí.
be·have [bɪhév] *v.* portarse, conducirse, obrar, proceder (*bien o mal*); **— yourself!** ¡pórtate bien!
be·hav·ior [bɪhévjɚ] *s.* comportamiento, proceder, conducta; funcionamiento; reacción.
be·head [bɪhɛ́d] *v.* decapitar, degollar, descabezar.
be·held [bɪhɛ́ld] *pret. & p.p de* **to behold.**
be·hind [bɪháɪnd] *adv.* detrás; atrás; a la zaga, en zaga; *prep.* detrás de, tras; **— one's back** a espaldas de uno; **— time** atrasado, retrasado **from —** por detrás; **to arrive ten minutes — time** llegar con diez minutos de retraso; **to fall —** atrasarse; retrasarse.
be·hold [bɪhóld] *v.* contemplar, mirar; **—!** ¡he aquí!
be·hoove [bɪhúv] *v.* serle necesario a uno; corresponderle a uno; atañerle a uno.
be·ing [bíɪŋ] *s.* ser; ente; esencia; existencia; *ger. de* **to be** siendo; **for the time —** por ahora; por el momento.
be·lat·ed [bɪlétɪd] *adj.* tardío; atrasado.
belch[bɛltʃ] *v.* eructar; **to — forth** echar, arrojar, vomitar; *s.* eructo.
bel·fry [bɛ́lfrɪ] *s.* campanario.
Bel·gian [bɛ́ldʒən] *adj. & s.* belga.
be·lief [bəlíf] *s.* creencia; fe; convicción; opinión.
be·liev·a·ble [bəlívəbl̩] *adj.* creíble.
be·lieve [bəlív] *v.* creer; pensar; **to — in** creer en, tener fe en; confiar en.
be·liev·er [bəlívɚ] *s.* creyente, fiel.
be·lit·tle [bilɪ́tl̩] *v.* menospreciar, apocar, empequeñecer; dar poca importancia a.
bell [bɛl] *s.* campana; campanilla; **cow —** cencerro, esquila; **call —** timbre; **jingle —** cascabel; **— flower** campanilla, campánula; **— jar** campana de cristal.
bell·boy [bɛ́lbɔɪ] *s.* mozo de hotel, botones.
belle [bɛl] *s.* beldad, mujer bella.
bel·lig·er·ent [bəlídʒərənt] *adj. & s.* beligerante.
bel·low [bɛ́lo] *s.* bramido, rugido; *v.* rugir, bramar, berrear; gritar.
bel·lows [bɛ́loz] *s.* (*sing. & pl.*) fuelle.
bel·ly [bɛ́lɪ] *s.* barriga; panza, vientre; estómago.
bel·ly·ache [bɛ́liek] *s.* dolor de barriga (*estómago*).
be·long [bəlɔ́ŋ] *v.* pertenecer, corresponder; **it does not — here** está fuera de su sitio; está mal colocado.
be·long·ings [bəlɔ́ŋɪŋz] *s. pl.* posesiones, bienes, efectos, cosas.
be·lov·ed [bɪlʌ́vɪd] *adj.* querido, amado.
be·low [bəló] *adv.* abajo; bajo; debajo; **here —** aquí abajo; en este mundo, de tejas abajo; *prep.* bajo, debajo de.
belt [bɛlt] *s.* cinturón, cinto; correa; zona; **sword —** talabarte; **— conveyor** cinta (banda) transportadora; *v.* ceñir, fajar.
belt line [bɛ́ltlaɪn] *s.* vía de circunvalación.
be·moan [bɪmón] *v.* lamentarse de, quejarse de.
bench [bɛntʃ] *s.* banco, banca; tribunal.
bend [bɛnd] *s.* curva; vuelta, recodo; *v.* encorvar(se), doblar(se), *Col., Ven., Ríopl., Méx.* enchuecar(se); inclinar(se); someter(se), ceder; **to — one's efforts** esforzarse (por), dirigir sus esfuerzos.
be·neath [bɪníθ] *prep.* debajo de, bajo; indigno de; inferior a.
ben·e·dic·tion [bɛnədɪ́kʃən] *s.* bendición.
ben·e·fac·tor [bɛ́nəfæktɚ] *s.* benefactor, bienhechor; patrón.
be·nef·i·cent [bənɛ́fəsn̩t] *adj.* benéfico.
ben·e·fi·cial [bɛnəfɪ́ʃəl] *adj.* benéfico; ventajoso, provechoso.
ben·e·fi·ci·ar·y [bɛnɪfɪ́ʃiɛrɪ] *s.* beneficiario.
ben·e·fit [bɛ́nəfɪt] *s.* beneficio; provecho, ventaja; **— performance** función de beneficio; **— payments** beneficios; *v.* beneficiar; hacer bien; **to — by the advice** aprovecharse del consejo; **he -ed by the medicine** le hizo bien la medicina.
be·nev·o·lence [bənɛ́vələns] *s.* benevolencia.
be·nev·o·lent [bənɛ́vələnt] *adj.* benévolo.
be·nign [bɪnáɪn] *adj.* benigno; afable.
bent [bɛnt] *s.* inclinación; tendencia; propensión; *pret. & p.p. de* **to bend;** *adj.* encorvado; inclinado, doblado; corvo; (*stooped*) gacho; **to be — on** estar resuelto a.
ben·zene [bɛ́nzin] *s.* benceno.
be·queath [bɪkwíð] *v.* heredar, legar, dejar en testamento.
be·quest [bɪkwɛ́st] *s.* legado, donación.
be·rate [bɪrét] *v.* regañar, reñir, reprender.
be·ret [bəré] *s.* boina.
ber·ry [bɛ́rɪ] *s.* baya (*como mora, fresa, etc.*); grano (*de café*).
berth [bɝθ] *s.* litera (*de un camarote*); **to give a wide — de** sacarle el cuerpo a, hacerse a un lado para dejar pasar.
be·ryl·li·um [bərɪ́liəm] *s.* berilio.
be·seech [bɪsítʃ] *v.* suplicar, rogar.
be·set [bɪsɛ́t] *v.* atacar; rodear; acosar; *pret. & p.p. de* **to beset.**
be·side [bɪsáɪd] *prep.* (*spatial*) al lado de; cerca de; (*in addition*) además de; fuera de; **to be — oneself** estar fuera de sí, estar loco; **that is — the question** eso no hace al caso; no se trata de eso; no viene al caso; *adv.* además.
be·sides [bɪsáɪdz] *adv.* además; *prep.* además de.
be·siege [bɪsídʒ] *v.* sitiar, cercar; acosar, importunar.
be·sought [bɪsɔ́t] *pret. & p.p. de* **to beseech.**
best [bɛst] *adj.* mejor; *adv.* mejor; más; **the —** el mejor; lo mejor; **— girl** novia; querida; **— man** padrino de boda; **— seller** éxito de venta; de mayor venta; **at —** a lo más, cuando más; **to do one's —** hacer todo lo posible; **to get the — of a person** vencer o ganarle a una persona; **to make the — of** sacar el major partido de.
be·stow [bɪstó] *v.* otorgar, conferir; **to — gifts upon**

hacer regalos (*o* dádivas) a; **time well -ed** tiempo bien empleado.

bet [bɛt] *s.* apuesta; *v.* apostar; *pret. & p.p. de* **to bet.**

be·take [bɪték] *v.* **to — oneself** encaminarse, dirigirse.

be·tak·en [bɪtékən] *p.p. de* **to betake.**

be·took [bɪtúk] *pret. de* **to betake.**

be·tray [bɪtré] *v.* traicionar, vender, hacer traición; revelar, no guardar (*un secreto*); **to one's ignorance** hacer patente su ignorancia.

be·tray·er [bɪtréɚ] *s.* traidor, traicionera.

be·troth·al [bɪtrɔ́θəl] *s.* esponsales, compromiso, mutua promesa de matrimonio.

be·trothed [bɪtrɔ́θt] *s.* prometido, desposado; novio, novia.

bet·ter [bɛ́tɚ] *adj.* mejor; *adv.* mejor; más; **— half** cara mitad; **so much the** — tanto mejor; **to be — off** estar mejor así; estar en mejores condiciones; **to change for the** — mejorar(se); **to get** — (mejorar(se), restablecerse, aliviarse; *v.* mejorar; **to — oneself** mejorarse, mejorar de situación.

bet·ter·ment [bɛ́tɚmənt] *s.* mejoramiento, mejora, mejoría.

be·tween [bətwín] *prep.* entre, en medio de; *adv.* en medio.

bev·el [bɛ́vəl] *s.* bisel; *adj.* biselado; *v.* biselar.

bev·er·age [bɛ́vrɪdʒ] *s.* bebida.

bev·y [bɛ́vɪ] *s.* bandada, manada.

be·wail [bɪwél] *v.* lamentar; quejarse de.

be·ware [bɪwɛ́r] *v.* guardarse (de), cuidarse (de); **— !** ¡cuidado! ¡guárdese!

be·wil·der [bɪ́wɪ́ldɚ] *v.* confundir, turbar, perturbar, dejar perplejo; **to be -ed** estar turbado o perplejo; estar desorientado.

be·wil·der·ment [bɪwɪ́ldɚmənt] *s.* perplejidad, aturdimiento.

be·witch [bɪwɪ́tʃ] *v.* hechizar; encantar, cautivar.

be·yond [bɪjɑ́nd] *adv.* más allá, más lejos; *prep.* allende; más allá de; fuera de; **— my reach** fuera de mi alcance; **— the grave** ultratumba.

bi·as [báɪəs] *s.* (*tendency*) prejuicio; inclinación, tendencia; (*diagonal*) sesgo, oblicuidad; **on the —** sesgado, al sesgo, de lado; *adj.* sesgado, oblicuo; *v.* predisponer, inclinar, influir en.

bib [bɪb] *s.* babero; pechera (*de delantal*).

Bi·ble [báɪbl] *s.* Biblia.

bib·li·cal [bɪ́blɪkl] *adj.* bíblico.

bib·li·og·ra·pher [bɪblɪɑ́grəfɚ] *s.* bibliógrafo.

bib·li·og·ra·phy [bɪblɪɑ́grəfɪ] *s.* bibliografía.

bi·car·bon·ate [baɪkárbənet] *s.* bicarbonato.

bick·er [bɪ́kɚ] *v.* disputar, reñir.

bi·cy·cle [báɪsɪkl] *s.* bicicleta; *v.* andar en bicicleta.

bid [bɪd *s.* postura, oferta; licitación, puja; envite (*en naipes*); turno (*para envidar*); invitación; *v.* ofrecer (*precio*); mandar; invitar, convidar; rogar; envidar (*en naipes*); **to — fair** parecer muy probable; **to — good-bye** decir adiós; despedirse; **to — up** alzar, pujar (*la oferta en una subasta*); *pret. & p.p. de* **to bid.**

bid·den [bɪ́dn̩] *p.p. de* **to bid & to bide.**

bide [baɪd] *v.* aguardar; **to — one's time** esperar una buena oportunidad.

bi·en·ni·um [baɪɛ́nɪəm] *s.* bienio.

bier [bɪr] *s.* féretro.

big [bɪg] *adj.* grande; importante; imponente; **— Dipper** Osa Mayor; **— game** caza mayor; **— sister** hermana mayor; **— with child** encinta; **to talk** — darse bombo, *Am.* darse corte; **big-bellied** panzudo, panzón, barrigón; **big-hearted** magnánimo.

big·a·my [bɪ́gəmɪ] *s.* bigamía.

big·ot [bɪ́gət] *s.* fanático.

big·ot·ry [bɪ́gətrɪ] *s.* fanatismo; intolerancia.

bi·ki·ni [bɪkínɪ] *s.* traje bikini.

bi·la·bi·al [baɪlébɪəl] *adj.* bilabial.

bile [baɪl] *s.* bilís, hiel, cólera, mal humor.

bi·lin·gual [baɪlɪ́ŋgwəl] *adj. & s.* bilingüe.

bill [bɪl] *s.* (*statement*) cuenta; factura; (*poster*) cartel, anuncio; (*bank note*) billete de banco; programa de teatro; (*bird*) pico; (*legislative*) proyecto de ley; **— of exchange** libranza, letra de cambio; **— of fare** menú; **— of lading** conocimiento de embarque; **— of rights** declaración de derechos; **— of sale** escritura o acta de venta; **-s payable** efectos a pagar; **— of credit** carta de crédito; *v.* cargar en cuenta; enviar una cuenta a; **to — and coo** acariciarse y arrullar (*como las palomas*).

bill·board [bɪ́lbord] *s.* cartelera.

bill·fold [bɪ́lfold] *s.* cartera; billetera.

bil·liards [bɪ́ljɚdz] *s.* billar.

bill·ing [bɪ́lɪŋ] *s.* importancia relativa de los anuncios de artistas de teatro.

bil·lion [bɪ́ljən] *s.* billón, millón de millones; mil millones (*en los Estados Unidos y Francia*).

bil·low [bɪ́lo] *s.* oleada; ola grande; *v.* alzarse en olas.

bin [bɪn] *s.* arcón, depósito; **coal** — carbonera; **grain** — granero.

bi·nar·y [báɪnərɪ] *adj.* (*computer*) binario.

bind [baɪnd] *v.* (*unite*) unir, juntar; (*tie*) ligar; amarrar; vendar; ceñir; (*compel*) restringir; obligar, compeler; (*enclose*) encuadernar, empastar; rivetear; **binder** garantía.

bind·ing [báɪndɪŋ] *s.* encuadernación; ribete, cinta; **cloth** — encuadernación en tela; **paper** — encuadernación en rústica; *adj.* obligatorio.

binge [bɪndʒ] *s.* jarana; parranda; borrachera.

bi·og·ra·phy [baɪɑ́grəfɪ] *s.* biografía.

bi·ol·o·gy [baɪɑ́lədʒɪ] *s.* biología.

bi·par·ti·san [baɪpártəzən] *adj.* de dos partidos; bipartito.

birch [bɝtʃ] *s.* abedul.

bird [bɝd] *s.* ave; pájaro; persona extraña o mal vista; **— of prey** ave de rapiña; **— seed** alpiste; **— shot** perdigones.

birth [bɝθ] *s.* nacimiento; parto; linaje; origen, principio; **— certificate** certificado (*o* fe) de nacimiento; **— control** control de la natalidad; anticoncepcionismo; limitación de partos; **— rate** natalidad; **to give** — dar a luz, parir.

birth·day [bɝ́θde] *s.* cumpleaños, natalicio.

birth·place [bɝ́θples] *s.* lugar de nacimiento, suelo natal.

birth·right [bɝ́θraɪt] *s.* derechos naturales o de nacimiento; naturalidad; primogenitura.

bis·cuit [bɪ́skɪt] *s.* bizcocho; galleta; panecillo.

bish·op [bɪ́ʃəp] *s.* obispo; alfil (*en ajedrez*).

bish·op·ric [bɪ́ʃəprɪk] *s.* obispado.

bis·muth [bɪ́zməθ] *s.* bismuto.

bi·son [báɪsn̩] *s.* bisonte, búfalo.

bit [bɪt] *s.* pedacito, trocito; pizca, miaja, migaja; poquito; bocado (*del freno*); taladro; (*computer*) dígito binario; bit; **I don't care a** — no me importa un ardite; *pret. & p.p. de* **to bite.**

bitch [bɪtʃ] *s.* perra; ramera, prostituta.

bite [baɪt] *s.* (*act*) mordedura, mordisco; (*morsel*) bocado, bocadito; picadura (*de insecto*); *v.* morder; mordiscar; picar.

bit·ten [bɪtn̩] *p.p. de* **to bite.**

bit·ter [bɪ́tɚ] *adj.* amargo; agrio, acre; (*harsh*)

áspero; mordaz; **to fight to the — end** luchar hasta morir; **-s** *s. pl.* amargo; **-ly** *adv.* amargamente; con amargura.
bit·ter·ness [bítənɪs] *s.* amargura, amargor; (*anger*) rencor; aspereza.
black [blæk] *adj.* negro; obscuro; (*somber*) sombrío; **black-and-blue** amoratado, lleno de moretones; **— mark** mancha, estigma, marca de deshonra; *s.* negro; luto; **— out** obscurecimiento; **to put down in — and white** poner por escrito *v.* teñir de negro; embetunar, dar bola o betún a (*los zapatos*).
black·ber·ry [blǽkbɛrɪ] *s.* zarzamora; mora.
black·bird [blǽkbɝd] *s.* mirlo.
black·board [blǽkbord] *s.* encerado; pizarrón; pizarra.
black·en [blǽkən] *v.* ennegrecer; (*weather*) obscurecer; teñir de negro; (*lower*) denigrar.
black·head [blǽkhɛd] *s.* espinilla.
black·ish [blǽkɪʃ] *adj.* negruzco.
black·jack [blǽkdʒæk] *s.* (*weapon*) cachiporra flexible; (*card game*) veintiuna.
black·mail [blǽkmel] *s.* chantaje, extorsión; *v.* ejercer el chantaje, extorsionar.
black·ness [blǽknɪs] *s.* negrura; obscuridad.
black·smith [blǽksmɪθ] *s.* herrero; **-'s shop** herrería.
black·top [blǽktap] *s.* camino de superficie bituminosa.
blad·der [blǽdə] *s.* vejiga.
blade [bled] *s.* hoja (*de navaja, cuchillo, etc.*); hoja (*de hierba*); espada; pala (*de remo*); aspa (*de hélice*); **shoulder —** espaldilla o paletilla.
blame [blem] *s.* culpa; *v.* culpar, echar la culpa a; **to be to —** tener la culpa.
blame·less [blémlɪs] *adj.* inculpable.
blanch [blæntʃ] *v.* blanquear; palidecer; escaldar (*almendras*).
bland [blænd] *adj.* blando, suave.
blank [blæŋk] *adj.* (*no writing*) en blanco; (*void*) vacío; (*confused*) aturdido; **— cartridge** cartucho vacío; **— face** cara sin expresión; **— form** blanco, forma en blanco, *Méx., C.A., Ven.* esqueleto; **— verse** verso suelto o libre; *s.* blanco; vacío; hueco, intermedio; papel en blanco; forma en blanco; **application —** forma (*o* blanco) para memorial o solicitud.
blan·ket [blǽŋkɪt] *s.* manta, frazada, cobertor; *Ríopl., C.A., Méx., Ven., Col.* cobija; *Méx.* sarape, poncho; *adj.* general, inclusivo, que abarca un grupo o clase.
blare [blɛr] *s.* fragor, son de trompetas, clarinada; *v.* trompetear, proclamar; sonar (*las trompetas*); hacer estruendo.
blas·pheme [blæsfím] *v.* blasfemar.
blas·phe·my [blǽsfɪmɪ] *s.* blasfemia.
blast [blæst] *s.* (*wind*) ráfaga de viento, golpe de viento; soplo repentino; (*trumpet*) trompetazo; (*whistle*) silbido; (*explosion*) explosión; estallido; carga de dinamita; **— furnace** alto horno; *v.* volar (*con dinamita, etc.*); destruir.
blaze [blez] *s.* llama, llamarada, incendio; resplandor; **— of anger** arranque de ira; *v.* arder; resplandecer; **to — a trail** abrir (*o* marcar) una senda.
bleach [blitʃ] *s.* blanqueador; blanqueo; *v.* blanquear(se); desteñir(se).
bleach·ers [blítʃəz] *s. pl.* graderías.
bleak [blik] *adj.* yermo, desierto; helado.
blear [blɪr] *v.* nublar (*los ojos*).
blear·y [blírɪ] *adj.* nublado, inflamado, lagrimoso, lagañoso.
bleat [blit] *s.* balido; *v.* balar.
bled [blɛd] *pret. & p.p. de* **to bleed.**
bleed [blid] *v.* sangrar; desangrar; extorsionar.
blem·ish [blɛ́mɪʃ] *s.* mancha, tacha, defecto; *v.* manchar; empañar.
blend [blɛnd] *s.* mezcla, entremezcla; gradación (*de colores, sonidos, etc.*); *v.* mezclar, entremezclar; graduar (*colores o sonidos*); entremezclarse, fundirse; armonizar.
bless [blɛs] *v.* bendecir; **God — you!** ¡que Dios te bendiga!
bless·ed [blɛ́sɪd] *adj.* bendito; santo, beato; bienaventurado; **the whole — day** todo el santo día; [blɛst] *pret. & p.p. de* **to bless.**
bless·ing [blɛ́sɪŋ] *s.* bendición; gracia, don, beneficio.
blest [blɛst] *adj.* = **blessed.**
blew [blu] *pret. de* **to blow.**
blight [blaɪt] *s.* pulgón (*parásito*); tizón (*honguillo parásito*); quemadura (*enfermedad de las plantas*); roña (*de las plantas*); (*failure*) malogro, ruina; *v.* destruir, arruinar; frustrar (*esperanzas*).
blimp [blɪmp] *s.* dirigible pequeño.
blind [blaɪnd] *adj.* ciego; tapado, oculto; hecho a ciegas; **— alley** callejón sin salida; **— choice** selección hecha a ciegas; **— flying** vuelo ciego, vuelo a ciegas; **— man** ciego; **— man's buff** juego de la gallina ciega; **— date** [blaɪnddet] *s.* cita a ciegas; persiana, cortinilla, biombo; venda (*para los ojos*); anteojera (*para resguardar los ojos del caballo*); **to be a — for someone** ser tapadera de alguien; *v.* cegar; ofuscar; encubrir, tapar.
blind·er [bláɪndə] *s.* anteojera, *Méx., Cuba* visera (*para caballos de tiro*).
blind·fold [bláɪndfold] *v.* vendar (*los ojos*); *adj.* vendado (*de ojos*); *s.* venda (*para los ojos*).
blind·ly [bláɪndlɪ] adv. ciegamente; a ciegas.
blind·ness [bláɪndnɪs] *s.* ceguera, ceguedad.
blink [blɪŋk] *s.* pestaño; parpadeo; guiño; guiñada; *v.* pestañear; parpadear; guiñar; (*computer*) parpadear, titilar.
blip [blɪp] *s.* bache de radar.
bliss [blɪs] *s.* beatitud, bienaventuranza, gloria; felicidad.
blis·ter [blístə] *s.* ampolla, vejiga (*en la piel o en cualquier superficie*); *v.* ampollar, levantar ampollas; ampollarse.
blitz [blɪts] *s.* ataque relámpago.
bliz·zard [blízəd] *s.* ventisca; *v.* ventiscar.
bloat [blot] *v.* inflar(se); abotagarse.
blob [blɑb] *s.* burbuja.
block [blɑk] *s.* (*piece*) bloque, trozo de piedra; zoquete; (*city section*) manzana (*de casas*); *Am.* cuadra; (*obstacle*) estorbo, obstáculo; (*group*) grupo, sección (*hat*) horma; **— pulley** polea; **chopping —** tajo; *v.* estorbar; tapar; bloquear; planchar (*sobre horma*); parar (*una pelota, una jugada*); **to — out** esbozar, bosquejar; **to — the door** impedir el paso; **to — up a door** tapiar una puerta.
block·ade [blɑkéd] *s.* bloqueo, obstrucción; *v.* bloquear.
block·head [blɑ́khɛd] *s.* zoquete, tonto, zopenco.
blond(e) [blɑnd] *adj. & s.* rubio, blondo; *Méx.* huero güero; *Guat.* canche; *Sal., Hond.,* chele; *C.R.* macho; *Col.* mono; *Ven.* catire.
blood [blʌd] *s.* sangre; **— count** análisis cuantitativo de la sangre; **— pudding** (*o* **— sausage**) morcilla; **— relative** pariente consanguíneo; **— vessel** vena; arteria; **in cold —** en sangre fría; **— bank** banco de sangre; **— poisoning** septicemia.

blood·shed [blʌ́dʃɛd] *s.* matanza; derrame, derramiento o efusión de sangre.
blood·shot [blʌ́dʃat] *adj.* inyectado de sangre.
blood·thirst·y [blʌ́dθɝstɪ] *adj.* sanguinario.
blood·y [blʌ́dɪ] *adj.* sangriento; ensangrentado; sanguinario, feroz.
bloom [blum] *s.* flor; florecimiento, floración; lozanía; color rosado (*en las mejillas*) *v.* florecer, *Am,* florear.
bloom·ing [blúmɪŋ] *adj.* floreciente; fresco, lozano, vigoroso.
blos·som [blɑ́səm] *s.* flor; floración, florecimiento; *v.* florecer.
blot [blɑt] *s.* mancha, borrón; tacha; *v.* manchar; borrar; secar (*con papel secante*); emborronar, echar manchas o borrones; **to — out** borrar, tachar; destruir; **this pen -s** esta pluma echa borrones; **blotting paper** papel secante.
blotch [blɑtʃ] *v.* emborronar o borronear, manchar, cubrir con manchas; *s.* mancha, borrón.
blot·ter [blɑ́tɚ] *s.* papel secante; libro borrador.
blouse [blaʊs] *s.* blusa.
blow [blo] *s.* (*stroke*) golpe; porrazo; (*shock*) choque, sorpresa, desastre; (*wind*) soplo, soplido; **to come to -s** venir a las manos; *v.* soplar; (*wind*) ventear; *C.A.* nortear; resoplar; sonar (*una trompeta*); fanfarronear; **to — a fuse** quemar un fusible; **to — one's nose** sonarse; **to — one's brains out** levantarse la tapa de los sesos; **to — open** abrirse; **to — out** apagar(se); estallar, reventar(se) (*un neumático*); **to — over** pasar; disiparse; **to — up** inflar, hinchar; volar (*con dinamita*); estallar, reventar.
blow·er [blóɚ] *s.* soplador; fuelle; ventilador, aventador.
blown [blon] *p.p. de* **to blow** *& adj.* soplado; inflado; **full-blown rose** rosa abierta.
blow·out [blóaʊt] *s.* reventón (*de neumático*); escape violento de gas, aire, etc.
blow·pipe [blópaɪp] *s.* soplete.
blow·torch [blótɔrtʃ] *s.* soplete.
blow·up [blóəp] *s.* ampliación.
blue[blu] *adj.* azul; (*sad*) triste, melancólico; **— chip** de primera línea; *s.* azul; **light** — (*ojos*) zarco; **the -s** melancolía, morriña, murria; *v.* azular, teñir de azul; **blue-pencil** tachar, vedar.
blue·bell [blúbɛl] *s.* campanilla azul (*flor*).
blue·bird [blúbɝd] *s.* pájaro azul, *Am.* azulejo.
blue·jay [blúdʒe] *s.* gayo, especie de azulejo (*pájaro*).
blue·print [blúprɪnt] *s.* heliografía.
bluff [blʌf] *s.* acantilado, escarpa, risco; fanfarronada; fanfarrón, farsante; *v.* fanfarronear; alardear, hacer alarde; echar bravatas; embaucar.
bluff·er [blʌ́fɚ] *s.* farsante, fanfarrón.
blu·ing [blúɪŋ] *s.* añil (*para ropa blanca*).
blu·ish [blúɪʃ] *adj.* azulado, azulejo.
blun·der [blʌ́ndɚ] *s.* disparate, desatino; despropósito; *v.* disparatar, desatinar; equivocarse.
blunt [blʌnt] *adj.* despuntado, embotado; brusco, grosero, *Méx.* claridoso; *v.* despuntar, embotar.
blur [blɝ] *s.* mancha; tacha; nube, cosa obscura o confusa; *v.* empañar, borronear, manchar; nublar, ofuscar; empañarse, nublarse.
blush[blʌʃ] *s.* sonrojo; rubor; *v.* sonrojarse, ruborizarse, ponerse colorado.
blus·ter [blʌ́stɚ] *v.* ventear o soplar recio (*el viento*); fanfarronear; *s.* ventolera, ventarrón, fuerte golpe de viento; jactancia, fanfarronada.
blus·ter·ing [blʌ́stərɪŋ] *adj.* fanfarrón, jactancioso; **— wind** ventarrón.
boar [bor] *s.* jabalí.
board [bord] *s.* (*wood*) tabla, tablero; mesa; (*meals*) comidas; (*directors*) junta, consejo; (*pasteboard*) en pasta; cartón; (*computer*) tarjeta, placa; **the -s** las tablas, el teatro; **room and** — cuarto y comida, pensión completa; asistencia; **— of directors** junta directiva; **bulletin** — tabilla para anuncios; **free on — (f.o.b.)** franco a bordo; **on** — a bordo; en el tren; **to go by the** — caer en el mar; perderse; ser descartado; *v.* ir a bordo; subir (*al tren*); entablar, cubrir con tablas; tomar a pupilaje, dar asistencia, pensión o pupilaje; residir o comer (*en casa de huéspedes*).
board·er [bórdɚ] *s.* huésped, pupilo, pensionista.
board·ing·house [bórdɪŋhaʊs] *s.* casa de huéspedes, pensión.
boast [bost] *s.* jactancia; alarde; bravata; gloria, orgullo; *v.* jactarse, alardear; hacer alarde de; ostentar.
boast·ful [bóstfəl] *adj.* jactancioso.
boast·ful·ness [bóstfəlnɪs] *s.* jactancia; ostentación.
boat [bot] *s.* bote; barco, buque; lancha, chalupa.
boat·house [bóthaʊs] *s.* casilla o cobertizo para botes.
boat·ing [bótɪŋ] *s.* paseo en lancha o bote; **to go** — pasear en bote.
boat·man [bótmən] (*pl.* **boatmen** [bótmɛn]) *s.* barquero.
bob [bɑb] *s.* meneo, sacudida; pesa (*de metal*); **to wear a** — llevar el pelo corto (*o* en melena); *v.* menearse; **to — one's hair** cortarse el pelo en melena; **to — up** aparecer de repente; **to — up and down** saltar, brincar; cabecear (*dícese de una embarcación*).
bob·bin [bɑ́bɪn] *s.* carrete; bobina.
bob·tail [bɑ́btel] *s.* rabón.
bob·white [bɑ́bhwait] *s.* codorniz.
bode [bod] *pret. & p.p. de* **to bide.**
bod·ice [bɑ́dɪs] *s.* corpiño, jubón.
bod·i·ly [bɑ́dli] *adj.* corpóreo; corporal; *adv.* todos juntos, colectivamente; **they rose** — se levantaron todos a una, se levantaron-todos juntos.
bod·y [bɑ́dɪ] *s.* cuerpo; agregado, conjunto; gremio; carrocería (*de automóvil*); fuselaje (*de aeroplano*); **— of water** extensión de agua; — **politic** grupo político; estado.
bod·y·guard [bɑ́dɪgɑrd] *s.* guardaespaldas; *Am.* pistolero.
bog [bɑg] *s.* pantano; tremedal; *v.* hundir(se); atascarse.
Bo·he·mi·an [bohímɪən] *adj. & s.* bohemio.
boil [bɔɪl] *s.* hervor; (*skin*) tumorcillo; **to come to a** — soltar el hervor, hervir; *v.* hervir; cocer; bullir; **to — down** hervir hasta evaporar; abreviar.
boil·er [bɔ́ɪlɚ] *s.* caldera, marmita; caldera de vapor; calorífero central.
boil·ing point [bɔɪlɪŋpɔɪnt] *s.* punto de ebullición.
bois·ter·ous [bɔ́ɪstərəs] *adj.* bullicioso; estrepitoso, ruidoso; tumultuoso.
bold [bold] *adj.* atrevido, osado; arriesgado; audaz; insolente; (*clear*) claro, bien delineado; **— cliff** risco escarpado; **bold-faced** descarado; **bold-faced type** negritas.
bold·ness [bóldnɪs] *s.* atrevimiento; osadía; audacia; descaro, insolencia.
bo·lo·gna [bəlónɪ] *s.* especie de embutido.
Bol·she·vik [bólʃəvik] *adj. & s.* bolchevique.
bol·ster [bólstɚ] *s.* travesaño, almohada larga (*para la cabecera de la cama*); refuerzo, sostén, soporte; *v.* sostener, apoyar; apuntalar; **to — someone's courage** infundirle ámino a alguien.

bolt [bolt] *s.* (*door lock*) pestillo, cerrojo; (*pin*) perno, tornillo grande; (*movement*) salida de repente; (*cloth*) rollo; **thunder** — rayo; *v.* cerrar con cerrojo; tragar, engullir; romper con (*un partido político*); echarse a correr, lanzarse de repente; caer como rayo; **to — out** salir de golpe.
bomb [bɑm] *s.* bomba; *v.* bombardear; — **shelter** [bɑ́mʃɛlɚ] *s.* refugio antiaéreo.
bom·bard [bɑmbɑ́rd] *v.* bombardear, cañonear.
bom·bar·dier [bɑmbɚdír] *s.* bombardero.
bom·bard·ment [bɑmbɑ́rdmənt] *s.* bombardeo, cañoneo.
bom·bas·tic [bɑmbǽstɪk] *adj.* ampuloso, altisonante.
bom·ber [bɑ́mɚ] *s.* bombardero, avión de bombardeo.
bo·na fide [bónəfaɪd] *adj.* de buena fe.
bon·bon [bɑ́nbɑn] *s.* bombón, confite.
bond [bɑnd] *s.* (*tie*) lazo, vínculo; ligadura; (*obligation*) fianza, vale; obligación, bono; — **issue** emisión de bonos; **bonded debt** deuda consolidada.
bond·age [bɑ́ndɪdʒ] *s.* servidumbre, esclavitud.
bonds·man [bɑ́ndzmən] *s.* fiador.
bone [bon] *s.* hueso; espina (*de pez*); **-s** restos; osamenta; — **of contention** materia de discordia; **to make no -s about it** no pararse en pelillos; obrar francamente; *v.* deshuesar, quitar los huesos o espinas.
bon·fire [bɑ́nfaɪr] *s.* hoguera, fogata.
bon·net [bɑ́nɪt] *s.* gorra; sombrero (*de mujer*).
bo·nus [bónəs] *s.* prima, premio, gratificación; sobresueldo.
bon·y [bónɪ] *adj.* huesudo.
boo [bu] *v.* mofarse, burlarse (*a gritos*); — ! *interj.* ¡bu!; **-s** *s. pl.* rechifla, gritos de mofa.
boo·by [búbɪ] *s.* bobo, bobalicón.
book [bʊk] *s.* libro; **The book** la Biblia; **cash** — libro de caja; **memorandum** — libreta; **on the -s** cargado en cuenta; **to keep -s** llevar los libros o la contabilidad *v.* inscribir, asentar (*en un libro*); **to — passage** reservar pasaje.
book·case [bʊ́kkes] *s.* estante, estantería, armario para libros.
book·end [bʊ́kɛnd] *s.* apoyalibros, sujetalibros.
book·keep·er [bʊ́kkipɚ] *s.* tenedor de libros, contador.
book·keep·ing [bʊ́kkipɪŋ] *s.* teneduría de libros, contabilidad; **double entry** — partida doble.
book·let [bʊ́klɛt] *s.* librillo, librito, cuaderno, folleto.
book·sel·ler [bʊ́ksɛlɚ] *s.* librero.
book·shelf [bʊ́kʃɛlf] *s.* estante, repisa para libros.
book·shop [bʊ́kʃɑp] *s.* librería.
book·store [bʊ́kstor] *s.* librería.
boom [bum] *s.* (*noise*) estampido; (*increase*) alza, auge (*en el mercado o bolsa*); bonanza, prosperidad momentánea; *v.* rugir, resonar, hacer estampido; prosperar, medrar, florecer, estar en bonanza; fomentar.
boon [bun] *s.* don; bendición, gracia, favor; *adj.* jovial, congenial.
boon·dog·gle [búndagl] *s.* proyecto inútil y costoso.
boor [bʊr] *s.* patán, hombre zafio o grosero.
boor·ish [bʊ́rɪʃ] *adj.* grosero, zafio.
boost [bust] *s.* empuje, empujón (*de abajo* arriba); — **in prices** alza o auge de precios; *v.* empujar, alzar, levantar; hacer subir; (*advocate*) fomentar, promover.
boost·er [bústɚ] *s.* aumentador; (*rocket*) cohete de lanzamiento; (*electronics*) amplificador.
boot [but] *s.* bota, calzado; **to** — por añadidura, de ganancia, *Méx.* de pilón, *Ven.* de ñapa; *Ríopl.*, *Andes* de yapa (*llapa*); *v.* dar un puntapié; **to — out** echar a puntapiés, echar a patadas.
boot·black [bútblæk] *s.* limpiabotas.
booth [buθ] *s.* casilla, puesto.
boot·leg·ger [bútlɛgɚ] *s.* contrabandista (*de licores*).
boot·lick·er [bútlɪkɚ] *s.* servilón, zalamero.
boo·ty [bútɪ] *s.* botín, saqueo.
bo·rax [bóræks] *s.* bórax.
bor·der [bɔ́rdɚ] *s.* borde, margen, orilla; orla, franja; ribete; frontera; *v.* ribetear, guarnecer (*el borde*); orlar; **to — on** (*o* **upon**) lindar con, confinar con; rayar en; **it -s on madness** raya en locura.
bor·der·ing [bɔ́rdɚɪŋ] *adj.* limítrofe.
bor·der·line [bɔ́rdɚlaɪn] *adj.* fronterizo; indefinido.
bore [bor] *s.* taladro, barreno; agujero (*hecho con taladro*); calibre (*de un cañón, cilindro, etc.*); persona o cosa aburrida; *v.* taladrar, horadar, barrenar; aburrir, fastidiar; *pert. de* **to bear.**
bored [bord] *adj.* cansado, aburrido; *p.p. de* **to bore.**
bore·dom [bórdəm] *s.* aburrimiento, tedio, hastío fastidio.
bo·ric ac·id [bórɪk ǽsəd] *a.* ácido bórico.
bor·ing [bórɪŋ] *adj.* aburrido, fastidioso, tedioso.
born [bɔrn] *p.p. de* **to bear** & *adj.* nacido; innato; **to be** — nacer.
borne [born] *p.p.* **to bear.**
bo·ron [bóran] *s.* boro.
bor·ough [bɝo] *s.* villa, distrito de municipio.
bor·row [bɔ́ro] *v.* pedir prestado; tomar prestado; tomar fiado.
bor·row·er [bɔ́rowɚ] *s.* el que pide prestado; prestatario.
bos·om [búzəm] *s.* seno, pecho, corazón; (*shirt*) pechera (*de camisa*); **in the — of the family** en el seno de la familia; *adj.* querido; — **friend** amigo intimo.
boss [bɔs] *s.* jefe; patrón; mayoral, capataz; *Am.* gamonal; **political** — cacique político; *v.* mandar, dominar, dirigir.
boss·y [bɔ́sɪ] *adj.* mandón, autoritario.
bo·tan·i·cal [bətǽnɪkl] *adj.* botánico.
bot·a·ny [bɑ́tn̩ɪ] *s.* botánica.
botch [bɑ́tʃ] *s.* chapucería.
both [boθ] *adj. & pron.* ambos, entrambos, los dos; — **this and that** tanto esto como aquello; — **of them** ambos, ellos dos, los dos; — **(of) his friends** sus dos amigos, ambos amigos; — **-to-blame-clause** cláusula de responsabilidad mútua.
both·er [bɑ́ðɚ] *s.* molestia; fastidio; incomodidad, enfado; *v.* molestar(se); fastidiar, enfadar; incomodar; estorbar.
both·er·some [bɑ́ðɚsəm] *adj.* molesto.
bot·tle [bɑ́tl] *s.* botella; *v.* embotellar.
bot·tle·neck [bɑ́tlnɛk] *s.* embotellamiento; gollete; cuello de botella; factor que impide.
bot·tom [bɑ́təm] *s.* fondo; base; fundamento; (*naval*) casco, barco; asiento (*de silla*); **to be at the — of the class** ser el último de la clase; **what is at the — of all this?** ¿qué hay en el fondo de todo esto?
bou·doir [budwɑ́r] *s.* tocador.
bough [baʊ] *s.* rama.
bought [bɔt] *pret. & p.p. de* **to buy.**
bouil·lon [bʊ́ljɑ́n] *s.* caldo.
boul·der [bóldɚ] *s.* peña, roca, guijarro grande, pedrusco.
boul·e·vard [búləvɑrd] *s.* bulevar.
bounce [baʊns] *s.* bote, rebote (*de una pelota*); salto, brinco; *v.* hacer saltar; saltar, brincar; botar; echar, arrojar (*a alguien*); echar, despedir de un empleo.
bounc·er [baʊnsɚ] *s.* apagabroncas.
bound [baʊnd] *s.* (*jump*) salto, brinco; (*bounce*)

BL

bote, rebote; (*limit*) límite, confín; *adj.* ligado; confinado; obligado; ceñido; encuadernado; **to be — for** ir para, ir con rumbo a; **to be — up in one's work** estar absorto en su trabajo; **it is — to happen** es seguro que sucederá; **I am — to do it** estoy resuelto a hacerlo; *v.* botar, resaltar; saltar, brincar; (*limit*) limitar; ceñir, cercar; *pret. & p.p. de* **to bind.**

bound·a·ry [báUndərɪ] *s.* límite, linde; confín; frontera.

bound·less [báUndlɪs] *adj.* ilimitado, sin límite, sin término.

boun·ti·ful [báUntəfəl] *adj.* generoso, liberal; abundante.

boun·ty [báUntɪ] *s.* largueza, generosidad; don, favor, gracia; premio, recompensa; subvención, prima.

bou·quet [buké] *s.* ramillete, ramo de flores; aroma, fragancia.

bour·geois [bUrʒwá.] *adj. & s.* burgués.

bout [baUt] *s.* combate, lucha, contienda, asalto; **a — of pneumonia** un ataque de pulmonía.

bow [baU] *s.* (*inclination*) reverencia; inclinación, saludo; (*of a ship*) proa; *v.* hacer una reverencia, inclinarse (*para saludar*); someterse; **to — one's head** inclinar la cabeza **-ed down** agobiado.

bow [bo] *s.* arco (*para tirar flechas*); arco (*de violín*); curva; lazo, moño (*de cintas*); **bow-legged** *adj.* patizambo, patituerto; *v.* arquear; tocar (*un instrumento*) con arco.

bow·els [báUəlz] *s. pl.* intestinos; entrañas; tripas.

bow·er [báUɚ] *s.* enramada, ramada, glorieta.

bowl [bol] *s.* cuenco; tazón; jícara; (*game*) boliche, bola; **wash** — palangana, lavamanos; **-s** juego de bolos; *v.* bolear, jugar a los bolos, jugar al boliche.

box [bɑks] *s.* caja; estuche; palco de teatro; casilla; compartimiento; bofetada; — **car** furgón; — **office** taquilla; — **seat** asiento de palco; *v.* encajonar; meter en una caja; abofetear; boxear.

box·er [bɑ́ksɚ] *s.* boxeador, pugilista.

box·ing [bɑ́ksɪŋ] *s.* boxeo, pugilato.

boy [bɔi] *s.* niño; muchacho; mozo.

boy·cott [bɔ́ɪka.t] *v.* boicotear; *s.* boicoteo.

boy·hood [bɔ́ɪhUd] *s.* niñez; mocedad, juventud.

boy·ish [bɔ́ɪɪʃ] *adj.* pueril; juvenil; aniñado.

brace [bres] *s.* traba; tirante; apoyo, refuerzo; corchete ({}); **carpenter's** — berbiquí; *v.* trabar; apoyar, reforzar; (*support*) asegurar; estimular, fortalecer; **to — up** animarse, cobrar ánimo.

brace·let [bréslɪt] *s.* brazalete, pulsera.

brack·et [brǽkɪt] *s.* ménsula, soporte, sostén; categoría; repisa; **-s** paréntesis cuadrados; *v.* colocar entre paréntesis; unir; agrupar.

brag [bræg] *s.* jactancia; *v.* jactarse (de); hacer alarde de.

brag·gart [brǽgɚt] *ajd. & s.* jactancioso, fanfarrón; matamoros, matamoscas.

braid [bred] *s.* trenza; galón, trencilla; *v.* trenzar; galonear, guarnecer con galones.

brain [bren] *s.* cerebro; seso; **to rack one's -s** devanarse los sesos, romperse la cabeza; *v.* saltar la tapa de los sesos; — **trust** [bréntrʌst] *s.* grupo de consejeros expertos; — **washing** [brénwɔʃɪŋ] *s.* lavado cerebral.

brake [brek] *s.* freno; *Ven., Col., Cuba* retranca; *Méx., Ríopl., C.A., Carib.* garrote; — **lining** forro de freno; — **shoe** zapata de freno; — **drum** tambor de freno; — **fluid** flúido de freno; **to apply the -s** frenar; *v.* frenar, enfrenar; *Ven., Col.* retrancar; *Méx., Ríopl., C.A., Carib.* dar garrote.

brake·man [brékmən] *s.* guardafrenos, *Ven., Col.* retranquero, *Méx., Ríopl., C.A., Carib.* garrotero.

bram·ble [brǽmbl] *s.* zarza, breña.

bran [bræn] *s.* salvado.

branch [bræntʃ] *s.* rama (*de árbol*); gajo; ramo (*de la ciencia*); sucursal; bifurcación; sección; dependencia; tributario (*de un río*); ramificación; — **railway** ramal; *v.* ramificarse; bifurcarse.

brand [brænd] *s.* (*make*) marca; marca de fábrica; marca registrada; hechura; (*cattle mark*) hierro; *Ríopl., Méx.* fierro (*de marcar*); estigma; **brand-new** nuevecito, flamante, acabado de hacer o comprar; *v.* marcar; herrar, marcar (*con hierro candente*); difamar; **to — as** motejar de.

bran·dish [brǽndɪʃ] *v.* blandir; *s.* floreo, molinete.

bran·dy [brǽndɪ] *s.* aguardiente; coñac.

brash [bræʃ] *adj.* insolente; impetuoso; temerario.

brass [bræs] *s.* (*metal*) latón, bronce; (*actitud*) desfachatez, descaro; **-es** utensilios de latón; instrumentos músicos de metal; — **band** murga.

bras·siere [brəzír] *s.* corpiño, sostén (*para ceñir los pechos*).

brat [bræt] *s.* mocoso.

bra·va·do [brəvɑ́do] *s.* bravata; jactancia.

brave [brev] *adj.* bravo, valiente, valeroso; *v.* arrostrar; desafiar, hacer frente a.

brav·ery [brévərɪ] *s.* valor, valentía.

brawl [brɔl] *v.* reyerta, pendencia, riña; alboroto; *v.* armar una pendencia, alborotar, reñir.

bray [bre] *s.* rebuzno; *v.* rebuznar.

bra·zen [brézn̩] *adj.* bronceado; de bronce; de latón; descarado, desvergonzado.

bra·zier [brezjɚ] *s.* brasero; cazuela para perdigar.

breach [britʃ] *s.* (*opening*) brecha, abertura; (*infraction*) infracción; rompimiento; — **of contract** incumplimiento de contrato; — **of faith** abuso de confianza; — **of promise** violación de un compromiso; — **of peace** perturbación del orden público; *v.* abrir brecha.

bread [brɛd] *s.* pan; — **box** caja para pan; — **line** cola del pan; *v. Méx., C.A., Carib.* empanizar; *Ríopl., Ch.* empanar.

breadth [brɛdθ] *s.* anchura, ancho; extensión; amplitud.

break [brek] *s.* rompimiento; rotura; (*pause*) interrupción, pausa; bajón (*en la bolsa o mercado*); **to have a bad (good)** — tener mala (buena) suerte; **to make a bad** — cometer un disparate; *v.* romper(se), quebrantar(se), quebrar(se); amansar, domar; arruinar; **to — away** fugarse, escaparse; — **even** salir a mano; **to — into** forzar la entrada en, allanar (*una morada*); **to — loose** escaparse, desprenderse, soltarse; **to — out** estallar (*una guerra*); **to — out of prison** escaparse de la cárcel; **to — a promise** faltar a la palabra; **to — up** desmenuzar, despedazar; disolver; perturbar.

break·a·ble [brékəbl̩] *adj.* quebradizo.

break·down [brékdaUn] *s.* parado imprevista; análisis, (*automobile*) avería, pane; *v.* descomponerse.

break·er [brékɚ] *s.* rompiente (*ola*); **law** — infractor.

break·fast [brɛ́kfəst] *s.* desayuno; **to eat** — tomar el desayuno; *v.* desayunarse.

break·through [brékθru] *s.* adelanto repentino; brecha.

break·wa·ter [brékwɔtɚ] *s.* rompeolas, malecón.

breast [brɛst] *s.* pecho; seno; teta; pechuga (*de ave*); **to make a clean — of it** confesarlo todo.

breath [brɛθ] *s.* aliento; resuello; respiro; soplo, hálito; **in the same** — al mismo instante, con el mismo aliento; **out of** — sin aliento, jadeante;

under one's — en voz baja, entre dientes.

breathe [brið] *v.* respirar; resollar; tomar aliento; exhalar; **to — into** infundir; **he -ed his last** exhaló el último suspiro; **he did not — a word** no dijo palabra.

breath·less [bréθlɪs] *adj.* jadeante; sin aliento.

breath·tak·ing [bréθtekɪŋ] *adj.* conmovedor; emocionante.

bred [brɛd] *pret. & p.p. de* **to breed.**

breech·es [brítʃɪz] *s. pl.* bragas, calzones; **riding —** pantalones de montar.

breed [brid] *s.* casta, raza; ralea, especie; *v.* criar; procrear, engendrar; educar; producirse; multiplicarse.

breed·er [brídɚ] *s.* criador; animal de cría.

breed·ing [brídɪŋ] *s.* cría, crianza; educación, modales.

breeze [briz] *s.* brisa, vientecillo.

breez·y [brízɪ] *adj.* airoso, ventilado; refrescado (*por la brisa*); animado, vivaz; **it is —** hace brisa.

breth·ren [bréðrɪn] *s. pl.* hermanos (*los fieles de una iglesia o los miembros de una sociedad*).

brev·i·ty [brévətɪ] *s.* brevedad.

brew [bru] *s.* cerveza; mezcla; *v.* fermentar, hacer (*licores*); preparar (*té*); fomentar, tramar; fabricar cerveza; amenazar (*una tormenta, calamidad etc.*).

brew·er·y [brúərɪ] *s.* cervecería, fábrica de cerveza.

bri·ar, bri·er [bráɪɚ] *s.* zarza; rosal silvestre.

bribe [braɪb] *s.* soborno, cohecho; *Méx.* mordida; *v.* sobornar, cohechar.

brib·er·y [bráɪbərɪ] *s.* soborno, choecho.

brick [brɪk] *s.* ladrillo; ladrillos; *v.* enladrillar.

brick·bat [bríkbæt] *s.* pedazo de ladrillo; insulto.

bri·dal [bráɪdl̩] *adj.* nupcial; de bodas; de novia; **— dress** vestido de novia.

bride [braɪd] *s.* novia, desposada.

bride·groom [bráɪdgrum] *s.* novio, desposado.

brides·maid [bráɪdzmed] *s.* madrina de boda.

bridge [brɪdʒ] *a.* puente; caballete de la nariz; **draw —** puente levadizo; **suspension —** puente colgante; *v.* tender un puente; **to — a gap** llenar un vacío; salvar un obstáculo.

bri·dle [bráɪdl] *s.* brida, freno de caballo; freno, restricción; **— path** camino de harradura; *v.* embridar, enfrenar; reprimir, subyugar; erguirse, erguir la cabeza.

brief [brif] *adj.* breve, corto, conciso; *s.* sumario, resumen; (*report*) informe, memorial; breve apostólico; **to hold a — for** abogar por; **-ly** *adv.* brevemente; en resumen, en breve; *v.* dar instrucciones, aleccionar.

brief·case [brífkes] *s.* portapapeles, cartera grande.

brief·ing [brifɪŋ] *s.* reunión preparatoria.

bri·gade [brɪgéd] *s.* brigada.

bright [braɪt] *adj.* (*light*) brillante, claro, luciente; radiante; (*smart*) inteligente; (*cheerful*) alegre; listo, vivo; **— color** color subido.

bright·en [bráɪtn̩] *v.* abrillantar, pulir, dar lustre; avivar(se); alegrar(se); animar(se); aclararse, despejarse (*el cielo*).

bright·ness [bráɪtnɪs] *s.* brillo, lustre, esplendor; claridad; viveza, agudeza, inteligencia.

bril·liance [brílјəns] *s.* brillantez, brillo; lustre; resplandor.

bril·liant [brílјənt] *adj.* brillante; resplandeciente; espléndido; (*smart*) talentoso; *s.* brillante; diamante.

brim [brɪm] *s.* borde, margen, orilla; (*hat*) ala; **to fill to the —** llenar o arrasar hasta el borde; **to be filled to the —** estar hasta los topes; estar de bote en bote; *v.* **to — over** rebosar.

brine [braɪn] *s.* salmuera.

bring [brɪŋ] *v.* traer; llevar; ocasionar, causar; **to — about** producir, efectuar, ocasionar; **to — down** bajar; **to — forth** dar a luz; producir; **— back** devolver; **to — to** resucitar; **to — up** criar, educar; **to — up a subject** traer a discusión un asunto.

brink [brɪŋk] *s.* borde, orilla, margen; **on the — of** al borde de.

brisk [brɪsk] *adj.* vivo, animado; fuerte; rápido; **-ly** *adv.* aprisa; fuerte.

bris·tle [brɪsl] *s.* creda; *v.* erizar(se); **to — with** estar erizado (*o* lleno) de.

bris·tly [brɪstɪ] *adj.* serdoso; erizado.

Brit·ish [brítɪʃ] *adj.* británico; **the —** los ingleses.

brit·tle [brítl] *adj.* quebradizo; frágil.

broach [brotʃ] *v.* tracer a colación, comenzar a hablar de (*un asunto*).

broad [brɔd] *adj.* ancho; amplio, vasto, extenso; tolerante; **— hint** insinuación clara; **in — daylight** en pleno día; **broad-minded** tolerante; de amplias miras.

broad·cast [brɔ́dkæst] *s.* radiodifusión, difusión, emisión; transmisión; **broadcasting** radiodifusión; **— station** emisora, radiodifusora; *v.* difundir; radiodifundir, radiar, emitir; propalar, perifonear.

broad·cloth [brɔdklɔθ] *s.* paño fino de algodón o de lana.

broad jump [brɔ́ddʒəmp] *s.* salto de longitud.

broad·side [brɔ́dsaɪd] *s.* (*guns*) andanada; (*announcement*) hoja suelta de propaganda.

bro·cade [brokéd] *s.* brocado.

brochure [brosúr] *s.* folleto.

broil [brɔil] *v.* asar(se).

broke [brok] *pret. de* **to break**; *adj.* quebrado, arruinado; pelado, sin dinero; **to go —** quebrar, arruinarse.

bro·ken [brókən] *p.p. de* **to break** & *adj.* roto; rompido; quebrado; quebrantado; arruinado; abatido; **— English** inglés champurrado o champurreado; inglés mal pronunciado.

bro·ker [brókɚ] *s.* corredor, agente; bolsista; comisionista; **money —** cambista, corredor de cambio; **brokerage** corretaje.

bro·mide [brómaɪd] *s.* bromuro.

bro·mine [brómin] *s.* bromo.

bron·chi·tis [brɑnkáɪtɪs] *s.* bronquitis.

bron·co, bron·cho [brɑ́ŋko] *s.* potro o caballo bronco, *Ríopl.* redomón; **— buster** domador.

bronze [brɑnz] *s.* bronce; color de bronce; *v.* broncear.

brooch [brutʃ] *s.* broche (*alfiler de pecho*).

brood [brud] *s.* pollada; nidada; cría; casta; *v.* empollar; encobar; **to — over** cavilar.

brook [brʊk] *s.* arroyuelo, riachuelo, *C.A., Col., Ven.* quebrada; caño; *Méx., Ríopl.* arroyo, *Col., Cuba* cañada; *v.* tolerar, aguantar.

broom [brum] *s.* escoba; retama (*arbusto*); **— stick** palo o mango de escoba.

broth [brɔθ] *s.* caldo.

broth·er [brʌ́ðɚ] *s.* hermano; cofrade.

broth·er·hood [brʌ́ðɚhʊd] *s.* hermandad; fraternidad; cofradía.

broth·er-in-law [brʌ́ðərɪnlɔ] *s.* cuñado.

broth·er·ly [brʌ́ðɚlɪ] *adj.* fraternal.

brought [brɔt] *pret. & p.p. de* **to bring.**

brow [braʊ] *s.* ceja; frente.

brown [braʊn] *adj.* moreno; café; castaño; pardo oscuro; tostado; *v.* tostar(se).

browse [braʊz] *v.* hojear; ramonear, pacer, pastar (*el ganado*).

bruise [bruz] *s.* magulladura, cardenal, magullón, contusión; *v.* magullar(se); estropear(se).
bru·net, bru·nette [brunét] *adj.* moreno, trigueño.
brunt [brʌnt] *s.* fuerza (*de un golpe o ataque*); **the — of the battle** lo más reñido del combate.
brush [brʌʃ] *s.* (*tooth, clothes*) cepillo; (*paint, shaving*) brocha; (*artist's*) pincel; (*vegetation*) matorral; (*contact*) roce; encuentro; *v.* cepillar, acepillar; rozar; **to — aside** desechar, echar a un lado; **to — up** cepillarse; repasar (*una materia, una técnica, etc.*).
brush·wood [brʌ́ʃwʊd] *s.* broza; maleza, matorral, zarzal.
brusque [brʌsk] *adj.* brusco.
Brus·sels sprouts [brʌ́sls spraʊts] *s.* coles de Bruselas.
bru·tal [brútl] *adj.* brutal, bruto.
bru·tal·i·ty [brutǽlətɪ] *s.* brutalidad.
brute [brut] *s.* bruto, bestia; *adj.* bruto, brutal; bestial.
bub·ble [bʌ́bl] *s.* burbuja; borbollón; ampolla; *v.* borbotar; hacer espuma; bullir; **to — over with joy** rebosar de gozo.
bub·ble gum [bʌ́bl̩ gʌm] *s.* chicle hinchable; chicle de globo.
buck [bʌk] *s.* (*goat*) macho cabrío, cabrón; (*deer*) gamo; macho (*del ciervo, antílope, etc.*); (*act*) corveta, respingo (*de un caballo*); embestida; — **private** soldado raso; **to pass the** — *Ríopl., Andes* pasar el fardo; *v.* cabriolear, respingar; embestir; encabritarse; bregar con (*el viento*); **to — up** cobrar ánimo; **the horse -ed the rider** el caballo tiró al jinete.
buck·et [bʌ́kɪt] *s.* cubo, cubeta, balde.
buck·le [bʌ́kl̩] *s.* hebilla; *v.* abrochar con hebilla; doblarse; abollarse; **to — down to** aplicarse con empeño a; **to — with** luchar con.
buck·shot [bʌ́kʃɑt] *s.* posta, perdigón.
buck·skin [bʌ́kskɪn] *s.* badana; ante.
buck·wheat [bʌ́khwit] *s.* trigo sarraceno.
bud [bʌd] *s.* botón, yema; capullo, pimpollo; retoño; *v.* echar botones o retoños; florecer.
bud·dy [bʌ́dɪ] *s.* camarada, compañero.
budge [bʌdʒ] *v.* mover(se), menear(se), bullir.
bud·get [bʌ́dʒɪt] *s.* presupuesto.
buff [bʌf] *s.* piel de ante o búfalo; color de ante; pulidor; **blindman's** — juego de la gallina ciega; *v.* pulir, pulimentar.
buf·fa·lo [bʌ́flo] *s.* búfalo.
buff·er [bʌ́fɚ] *s.* (*computer*) buffer, amortiguador, almacén temporal.
buf·fet [bʌfé] *s.* aparador; repostería; mostrador para refrescos; fonda de estación.
buf·fet·ing [bʌ́fətɪŋ] *s.* golpeteo, bataneo.
buf·foon [bʌfún] *s.* bufón; payaso.
bug [bʌg] *s.* insecto; bicho; microbio.
bug·gy [bʌ́gɪ] *s.* cochecillo.
bu·gle [bjúgl̩] *s.* clarín; corneta; trompeta.
build [bɪld] *s.* estructura; talle, forma, hechura; *v.* edificar, construir; fabricar; **to — up one's health** reconstituir su salud.
build·er [bíldɚ] *s.* constructor.
build·ing [bíldɪŋ] *s.* edificio; construcción; — **and loan association** sociedad de préstamos.
build-up [bíldʌp] *s.* refuerzo paulatino.
built [bɪlt] *pret. & p.p. de* **to build.**
bulb [bʌlb] *s.* (*plant*) bulbo; planta bulbosa; **electric light** — bombilla, bujía eléctrica, ampolla, *Méx., C.A., Andes* foco; *Ríopl.* bombita.
bulge [bʌldʒ] *s.* bulto; protuberancia; panza; *v.* abultar; combarse.
bulg·y [bʌ́ldʒɪ] *adj.* abultado.
bulk [bʌlk] *s.* bulto, volumen; masa; **the — of the army** el grueso del ejército; **in** — suelto, en grueso.
bulk·y [bʌ́lkɪ] *adj.* abultado, voluminoso, grueso.
bull [bʊl] *s.* toro; — **market** mercado alcista; **Papal** — bula; — **fight** corrida de toros; *adj.* taurino; — **fighter** torero; **bull's-eye** centro del blanco; tiro perfecto; **bullish** en alza.
bull·dog [bʊ́ldɔg] *s.* perro dogo, perro de presa.
bull·doz·er [bʊ́ldozɚ] *s.* topadora; buldózer.
bul·let [bʊ́lɪt] *s.* bala.
bul·le·tin [bʊ́lətn̩] *s.* boletin; — **board** tablilla para fijar anuncios o avisos.
bull·frog [bʊ́lfrɑg] *s.* rana grande.
bull·head·ed [bʊlhédɪd] *adj.* terco, obstinado.
bul·lion [bʊ́ljən] *s.* oro (*o* plata) en barras; metálico; lingotes de oro o plata.
bul·ly [bʊ́lɪ] *s.* pendenciero, valentón, fanfarrón, matón; *adj.* excelente, magnífico; *v.* intimidar; echar bravatas.
bul·wark [bʊ́lwɚk] *s.* baluarte; defensa.
bum [bʌm] *s.* holgazán, vagabundo; gorrón; borracho; **to go on a** — irse de juerga; *adj.* malo, mal hecho, de infima calidad; inútil, inservible; **to feel** — estar indispuesto; *v.* holgazanear; vivir de gorra.
bum·ble·bee [bʌ́mblbi] *s.* abejorro, abejón.
bump [bʌmp] *s.* (*blow*) tope, choque; golpe; (*lump*) chichón; abolladura; hinchazón, protuberancia; *v.* topar, topetear; chocar; abollar; **to — along** zarandearse, ir zarandeándose; **to — off** derribar; matar.
bump·er [bʌ́mpɚ] *s.* parachoques, defensa; tope; *adj.* grande, excelente; — **crop** cosecha abundante.
bun [bʌn] *s.* bollo (*de pan*).
bunch [bʌntʃ] *s.* manojo, puñado; racimo (*de uvas, plátanos, etc.*); grupo; — **of flowers** ramillete de flores; *v.* juntar(se), agrupar(se).
bun·dle [bʌ́ndl] *s.* lío, bulto, fardo, hato; haz; paquete; *v.* liar, atar; envolver; **to — up** abrigarse, taparse bien.
bun·ga·low [bʌ́ŋgəlo] *s.* casita de un piso.
bun·gle [bʌ́ŋgl̩] *v.* chapucear; estropear; echar a perder.
bun·ion [bʌ́njən] *s.* juanete.
bunk [bʌŋk] *s.* litera, camilla (*fija en la pared*); embuste, tontería, paparrucha, papa.
bun·ny [bʌ́nɪ] *s.* conejito.
buoy [bɔɪ] *s.* boya; *v.* boyar, mantener a flote; **to — up** sostener, apoyar.
buoy·ant [bɔ́ɪənt] *adj.* boyante, flotante; vivaz, animado, alegre.
bur·den [bɝ́dn̩] *s.* carga, peso; cuidado; gravamen; *v.* cargar; agobiar.
bur·den·some [bɝ́dn̩səm] *adj.* gravoso; pesado.
bu·reau [bjʊ́ro] *s.* oficina; despacho; división, ramo; cómoda; **travel** — oficina de turismo; **weather** — oficina de meteorología, observatorio meteorológico.
bu·reauc·ra·cy [bjurákrəsɪ] *s.* burocracia.
bu·reau·crat [bjúrəkræt] *s.* burócrata.
bur·glar [bɝ́glɚ] *s.* ladrón; — **alarm** alarma contra ladrones; — **proof** a prueba de ladrones; — **deterrent** disuadeladrones.
bur·gla·ry [bɝ́glərɪ] *s.* robo.
bur·i·al [bérɪəl] *s.* entierro; — **place** cementerio.
bur·lap [bɝ́læp] *s.* arpillera, tela burda de cáñamo.
bur·ly [bɝ́lɪ] *adj.* corpulento, voluminoso, grandote.
burn [bɝn] *s.* quemadura; *v.* quemar(se); incendiar;

arder; abrasar(se).
burn·er [bɝ́nɚ] *s.* (*heat*) quemador; (*lamp*) mechero, (*stove*) hornilla.
bur·nish [bɝ́nɪʃ] *v.* bruñir; pulir; *s.* bruñido, pulimento.
burn·out [bɝ́naʊt] *s.* fundición, apagón.
burnt [bɝ́nt] *pret. & p.p. de* **to burn.**
bur·row [bɝ́o] *s.* madriguera, conejera; *v.* hacer madrigueras en; escarbar; socavar, minar; esconderse.
burst [bɝst] *s.* reventón, explosión; estallido; — **of laughter** carcajada; *v.* reventar(se); abrirse; estallar; **to — into** entrar de repente; **to — into tears** prorrumpir en lágrimas; **to — with laughter** estallar o reventar de risa; *pret. & p.p. de* **to burst.**
bur·y [bɛ́rɪ] *v.* enterrar; sepultar; soterrar; **to be buried in thought** estar absorto, meditabundo o pensativo.
bus [bʌs] *s.* autobús, ómnibus, *Méx.* camión; *C.A.* camioneta; *Ríopl.* colectivo; *Ch.* micro; *Carib.* guagua; (*computer*) bus, conjunto de líneas.
bus·boy [bʌ́sbɔi] *s.* ayudante de camarero.
bush [bʊʃ] *s.* arbusto; mata; matorral, breñal; **rose** — rosal; **to beat around the** — andarse por las ramas.
bush·el [bʊ́ʃəl] *s.* fanega (*medida de áridos*).
bush·ing [bʊʃɪŋ] *s.* buje.
bush·y [bʊ́ʃɪ] *adj.* matoso, espeso; lleno de arbustos.
bus·i·ly [bɪ́zlɪ] *adv.* diligentemente.
busi·ness [bɪ́znɪs] *s.* negocio; ocupación; comercio; asunto; — **house** casa de comercio, establecimiento mercantil; — **transaction** negocio, transacción comercial; — **cycles** ciclos económicos; — **day** día hábil; — **hours** horas habiles; **to do — with** negociar con, comerciar con; **he has no — doing it** no tiene derecho a hacerlo; **not to be one's** — no concernirle a uno, no importarle a uno; **to make a — deal** hacer un trato.
busi·ness·like [bɪ́znɪslaɪk] *adj.* eficaz, eficiente, práctico; formal.
busi·ness·man [bɪ́znɪsmæn] *s.* hombre de negocios, comerciante.
bust [bʌst] *s.* busto; pecho (*de mujer*); **to go out on a** — salir o ir de parranda; *v.* reventar; quebrar; domar (*un potro*).
bus·tle [bʌ́sl̩] *s.* bulla, bullicio, trajín, alboroto; polisón (*para abultar las caderas*); *v.* bullir(se); menearse; trajinar.
bus·y [bɪ́zɪ] *adj.* ocupado; activo; — **body** entremetido; — **street** calle de mucho tráfico; *v.* **to — oneself** ocuparse.
but [bʌt] *conj., prep. & adv.* pero, mas; sino; menos, excepto; sólo, no . . . más que; — **for you** a no ser por Vd.; **not only . . . — also** no sólo . . . sino (que) también; **I cannot help** — no puedo menos de; **she is — a child** no es más que una niña.
bu·tane [bjutén] *s.* butano.
butch·er [bʊ́tʃɚ] *s.* carnicero; **-'s shop** carnicería; *v.* matar (*reses*); hacer una matanza o carnicería; destrozar.
butch·er·y [bʊ́tʃərɪ] *s.* carnicería, matanza.
but·ler [bʌ́tlɚ] *s.* despensero, mayordomo; **-'s pantry** despensa.
butt [bʌt] *s.* culata (*de rifle*); colilla (*de cigarro*); tope; topetazo; (*animal*) cabezada; **the — of ridicule** el blanco de las burlas; *v.* topetear, embestir; **to — in** entremeterse; **to — into a conversation** meter baza, *Am.* meter su cuchara.
but·ter [bʌ́tɚ] *s.* manteca, mantequilla; *v.* enmantecar, untar con manteca o mantequilla.
but·ter·cup [bʌ́tɚkʌp] *s.* botón de oro (*flor*).
but·ter·fly [bʌ́tɚflaɪ] *s.* mariposa; — **stroke** brazada mariposa.
but·ter·milk [bʌ́tɚmɪlk] *s.* suero de mantequilla.
but·ter·scotch [bʌ́tɚskɑ́tʃ] *s.* confite o jarabe de azúcar y mantequilla.
but·tocks [bʌ́təks] *s. pl.* nalgas, asentaderas.
but·ton [bʌ́tn̩] *s.* botón; — **hook** abotonador; *v.* abotonar(se).
but·ton·hole [bʌ́tn̩hol] *s.* ojal; *v.* hacer ojales; **to — someone** detener, demorar a uno (*charlando*).
but·tress [bʌ́trɪs] *s.* contrafuerte; refuerzo, sostén; *v.* sostener, reforzar, poner contrafuerte.
buy [baɪ] *v.* comprar; **to — off** sobornar; **to — up** acaparar; **to — a pig in a poke** cerrar un trato a ciegas; **to — on credit** comprar al fiado; **to — on time** comprar a plazos; **buying power** poder adquisitivo.
buy·er [báɪɚ] *s.* comprador.
buzz [bʌz] *s.* zumbido; murmullo; *v.* zumbar; murmurar; **to — the bell** tocar el timbre.
buz·zard [bʌ́zɚd] *s.* buitre, *Carib.* aura, *Méx., C.A.* zopilote, *Ríopl.* carancho; *Col., Andes* gallinazo.
by [baɪ] *prep.* por; cerca de; al lado de; junto a; según; — **and** — luego, pronto; — **dint of** a fuerza de; — **far** con mucho; — **night** de noche; — **the way** de paso; a propósito; entre paréntesis; — **this time** ya; a la hora de ésta; — **two o'clock** para las dos; **days gone** — días pasados.
by·gone [báɪgɔn] *adj.* pasado; **let -s be -s** lo pasado pasado, lo pasado pisado.
by·law [báɪlɔ] *s.* estatuto; reglamento.
by-line [báɪlaɪn] *s.* nombre del autor con título.
by·pass [báɪpæs] *s.* desviación.
by·path [báɪpæθ] *s.* atajo, vereda.
by-prod·uct [báɪprɑdəkt] *s.* producto secundario o accessorio; derivado, subproducto.
by·stand·ers [báɪstændɚz] *s.* circunstantes, presentes; mirones.
byte [baɪt] (*computer*) *s.* octeto, byte.

C:c

cab [kæb] *s.* coche de alquiler; taxímetro, taxi; casilla (*de una locomotra*); — **driver** cochero; chófer.
cab·bage [kǽbɪdʒ] *s.* col, repollo, berza.
cab·in [kǽbɪn] *s.* cabaña, choza; bohío, *Méx.* jacal; *Carib.* barraca; camarote (*de buque*); **airplane** — cabina de aeroplano.
cab·i·net [kǽbənɪt] *s.* gabinete; armario; escaparate, vitrina; (*dept. heads*) gabinete.
cab·i·net·ma·ker [kǽbənɪtmékɚ] *s.* ebanista.
cab·le [kébl̩] *s.* cable, amarra; cablegrama; — **address** dirección cablegráfica; — **code** clave para cablegramas; *v.* cablegrafiar.
ca·ble·gram [kébl̩græm] *s.* cablegrama.
cab·man [kǽbmən] *s.* cochero; chófer.
ca·boose [kəbús] *s.* vagón de cola.
cack·le [kǽkl̩] *s.* cacareo; (*talk*) charla; (*laughter*) risotada; *v.* cacarear; parlotear, charlar.
cac·tus [kǽktəs] (*pl.* **cacti** [kǽktaɪ]) *s.* cacto, cactos.
cad [kæd] *s.* canalla (*m.*); malcriado.
cad·die [kǽdɪ] *s.* muchacho que lleva los palos de golf; caddy.
ca·dence [kédn̩s] *s.* cadencia.
ca·det [kədɛ́t] *s.* cadete.

cad·mi·um [kǽdmɪəm] *s.* cadmio.
ca·fé [kəfé] *s.* café, restaurante.
caf·e·te·ri·a [kæfətírɪə] *s.* restaurante (*en donde se sirve uno mismo*).
caf·fein [kǽfɪn] *s.* cafeína.
cage [kedʒ] *s.* jaula; *v.* enjaular.
ca·jole [kədʒol] *v.* halagar para consequir algo.
cake [kek] *s.* pastel; bizcocho; bollo; torta; *Ven., C.A., Col.* panqué; (*soap*) pastilla (*de jabón*); — **of ice** témpano de hielo; *v.* apelmazarse, formar masa compacta.
cal·a·bash [kǽləbæʃ] *s.* calabaza.
ca·lam·i·ty [kəlǽmətɪ] *s.* calamidad.
cal·ci·um [kǽlsɪəm] *s.* calcio.
cal·cu·late [kǽlkjəlet] *v.* calcular; **to — on** contar con.
cal·cu·la·tion [kælkjəléʃən] *s.* cálculo; cómputo, cuenta.
cal·cu·lus [kǽlkjələs] *s.* cálculo.
cal·en·dar [kǽləndɚ] *s.* calendario, almanaque; — **year** año corriente, año civil.
calf [kæf] (*pl.* **calves** [kævz]) *s.* ternero, ternera, becerro, becerra; pantorrilla (*de la pierna*); — **skin** piel de becerro o becerrillo.
cal·i·ber [kǽləbɚ] *s.* calibre.
cal·i·co [kǽləko] *s.* calico (*tela de algodón*).
call [kɔl] *s.* (*summons*) llamada; llamamiento; (*visit*) visita; (*demand*) demanda, pedido; **within** — al alcance de la voz; *v.* llamar; gritar; hacer una visita; pasar (*lista*); **to — at a port** hacer escala en un purerto; **to — for** ir por; demandar, exigir, pedir; **to — on** visitar a; acudir a (*en busca de auxilio*); **to — to order a meeting** abrir la sesión; **to — together** convocar; **to — up on the phone** llamar por teléfono.
cal·ler [kɔ́lɚ] *s.* visita, visitante; llamador (*el que llama*).
cal·lous [kǽləs] *adj.* calloso; duro.
cal·lus [kǽləs] *s.* callo.
calm [kɑm] *s.* calma; sosiego; *adj.* calmo, tranquilo, quieto, sosegado; *v.* calmar, tranquilizar, sosegar; desenfadar; **to — down** calmarse; **-ly** *adv.* tranquilamente, con calma.
calm·ness [kɑ́mnɪs] *s.* calma, sosiego, tranquilidad.
cal·o·rie [kǽlərɪ] *s.* caloría.
cal·um·ny [kǽləmnɪ] *s.* calumnia.
cam [kæm] *s.* leva.
cam·bist [kǽmbɪst] *s.* cambista.
came [kem] *pret. de* **to come.**
cam·el [kǽml̩] *s.* camello.
cam·e·o [kǽmɪo] *s.* camafeo.
cam·er·a [kǽmərə] *s.* cámara fotográfica.
cam·ou·flage [kǽməflɑʒ] *s.* camuflaje; disfraz; *v.* encubrir, disfrazar.
camp [kæmp] *s.* campo, campamento; — **chair** silla de tijera; **political** — partido político; *v.* acampar.
cam·paign [kæmpén] *s.* campaña; *v.* hacer campaña; hacer propaganda.
cam·phor [kǽmfɚ] *s.* alcanfor.
cam·pus [kǽmpəs] *s.* campo (*de una universidad*).
can [kæn] *s.* lata, bote, envase; — **opener** abrelatas; *v.* envasar, enlatar; *v. defect. y aux.* (*usado sólo en las formas* **can** *y* **could**) poder, saber.
Ca·na·di·an [kənédɪən] *adj. & s.* canadiense.
ca·nal [kənǽl] *s.* canal; **irrigation** — acequia.
ca·nar·y [kənérɪ] *s.* canario.
can·cel [kǽnsl̩] *v.* cancelar; anular; revocar; techar.
can·cel·er [kǽnsəlɚ] *s.* matasellos.
can·cel·la·tion [kænsl̩éʃən] *s.* cancelación; anulación; revocación.
can·cer [kǽnsɚ] *s.* cáncer.
can·de·la·brum [kændəlǽbrəm] *s.* candelabro.
can·did [kǽndɪd] *adj.* cándido, franco, sincero.
can·di·da·cy [kǽndədəsɪ] *s.* candidatura.
can·di·date [kǽndədet] *s.* candidato; aspirante.
can·dle [kǽndl̩] *s.* candela, vela; bujía; cirio; — **power** potencia lumínica (*en bujías*).
can·dle·stick [kǽndl̩stɪk] *s.* candelero; palmatoria.
can·dor [kǽndɚ] *s.* candor, sinceridad.
can·dy [kǽndɪ] *s.* dulce, confite, bombón; — **shop** confitería, dulcería; *v.* confitar, azucarar; almibarar, garapiñar; cristalizarse (*el almíbar*); **candied almonds** almendras garapiñadas.
cane [ken] *s.* caña; — **plantation** (*o* — **field**) cañaveral; *C.A.* cañal; — **chair** silla de bejuco; **sugar** — caña de azúcar; **walking** — bastón; chuzo (*de sereno*); **to beat with a** — bastonear, apalear.
ca·nine [kénaɪn] *adj.* canino, perruno.
can·ker [kænkɚ] *s.* úlcera, llaga (*de la boca*).
canned [kænd] *adj.* enlatado, envasado, conservado (*en lato o en vidrio*); — **goods** conservas alímenticias.
can·ner·y [kǽnərɪ] *s.* fábrica de conservas alimenticias.
can·ni·bal [kǽnəbl̩] *s.* caníbal.
can·non [kǽnən] *s.* cañón.
can·non·ade [kænənéd] *s.* cañoneo; *v.* cañonear.
can·not [kǽnɑt] = **can not** no puedo, no puede, no podemos, etc.
can·ny [kǽnɪ] *adj.* sagaz; astuto.
ca·noe [kənú] *s.* canoa, *Ríopl.* piragua, *Méx.* chalupa.
can·on [kǽnən] *s.* canon; ley, regla; criterio, norma; canónigo.
can·o·py [kǽnəpɪ] *s.* dosel, pabellón; (*airplane*) capota, cúpula.
can·ta·loupe [kǽntl̩op] *s.* melón.
can·teen [kæntín] *s.* cantina; cantimplora.
can·ton [kǽntən] *s.* cantón, región, distrito.
can·vas [kǽnvəs] *s.* lona; lienzo; toldo; cañamazo.
can·vass [kǽnvəs] *s.* inspección; escrutinio; indagación, encuesta, pesquisa; solicitación (*de votos*); *v.* examinar, escudriñar; recorrer (*un distrito solicitando algo*); hacer una encuesta; solicitar votos o pedidos comerciales.
can·yon [kǽnjən] *s.* cañón, garganta.
cap [kæp] *s.* (*head covering*) gorro, gorra, boina; *Méx.* cachucha; (*academic*) birrete; (*bottle, wheel*) tapa, tapón; (*mountain*) cima, cumbre; **percussion** — cápsula fulminante; *v.* tapar, poner tapón a; **that -s the climax** eso es el colmo.
ca·pa·bil·i·ty [kepəbíləti] *s.* capacidad, aptitud.
ca·pa·ble [képəbl̩] *adj.* capaz; hábil; competente.
ca·pa·cious [kəpéʃəs] *adj.* capaz, amplio, espacioso.
ca·pac·i·ty [kəpǽsətɪ] *s.* capacidad; cabida; habilidad; aptitud; **in the — of a teacher** en calidad de maestro.
cape [kep] *s.* capa; capote; cabo, promontorio.
ca·per [képɚ] *s.* cabriola; voltereta, brinco; (*food*) alcaparra; **to cut -s** cabriolar, retozar, hacer travesuras; *v.* cabriolar, retozar, juguetear, brincar.
cap·il·lar·y [kǽpɪlɛrɪ] *s. & adj.* capilar.
cap·i·tal [kǽpətl̩] *s.* capital (*f.*), ciudad principal; capital (*m.*), caudal; capitel (*de una columna*); letra mayúscula; **to make — of** sacar partido de, aprovecharse de; *adj.* capital; principal; — **investment** inversion de capital; — **gains** ganancias en bienes de capital; excelente; — **punishment** pena capital, pena de muerte.
cap·i·tal·ism [kǽpətl̩ɪzəm] *s.* capitalismo.
cap·i·tal·ist [kǽpətl̩ɪst] *s.* capitalista; **-ic** *adj.*

capitalista.
cap·i·tal·i·za·tion [kæpətlәzéʃən] *s.* capitalización.
cap·i·tal·ize [kǽpətlaɪz] *v.* capitalizar; sacar provecho (de); escribir con mayúscula.
cap·i·tol [kǽpətl] *s.* capitolio.
ca·pit·u·late [kəpítʃəlet] *v.* capitular.
ca·price [kəprís] *s.* capricho.
ca·pri·cious [kəpríʃəs] *adj.* caprichoso.
cap·size [kæpsáɪz] *v.* zozobrar, volcar(se).
cap·sule [kǽpsl] *s.* cápsula.
cap·tain [kǽptɪn] *s.* capitán; *v.* capitanear, mandar; servir de capitán.
cap·ti·vate [kǽptəvet] *v.* cautivar.
cap·tive [kǽptɪv] *s. & adj.* cautivo, prisionero.
cap·tiv·i·ty [kæptívətɪ] *s.* cautiverio, prisión.
cap·tor [kǽptɚ] *s.* aprehensor o aprensor.
cap·ture [kǽptʃɚ] *s.* captura; aprensión; presa; toma; *v.* capturar; prender; tomar (*una ciudad*).
car [kɑr] *s.* coche, automóvil, auto, *Am.* carro; (*de ferrocarril*); camarín (*de ascensor*), ascensor, *Am.* elevador; **dining** — coche comedor; **freight** — furgón, vagón de carga.
car·a·mel [kǽrəml] *s.* caramelo.
car·at [kǽrət] *s.* quilate.
car·a·van [kǽrəvæn] *s.* caravana.
car·bol·ic [kɑrbálɪk] *adj.* carbólico.
car·bon [kárbən] *s.* carbono; — **copy** copia en papel carbón; — **paper** papel carbón; — **monoxide** monóxido de carbono; — **dioxide** dióxido de carbono.
car·bu·re·tor [kárbəretɚ] *s.* carburador.
car·cass [kárkəs] *s.* esqueleto; cuerpo descarnado, despojo; res (*muerta*); casco (*de un buque*).
card [kɑrd] *s.* (*missive*) tarjeta; (*playing*) naipe, carta; carda (*para cardar lana*); — **index** índice de fichas; fichero; — **sharp** fullero; **file** — ficha, papeleta; **post** — tarjeta postal; (*computer*) tarjeta, placa; **pack of -s** baraja, naipes; **to play -s** jugar a la baraja, jugar a los naipes; *v.* cardar (*lana*).
card·board [kárdbord] *s.* cartón; **fine** — cartulina.
car·di·ac [kárdɪæk] *adj.* cardiaco, cardíaco.
car·di·nal [kárdṇəl] *adj.* cardinal; principal, fundamental; rojo, bermellón; — number número cardinal; *s.* cardenal (*dignatario eclesiástico*); — **bird** cardenal.
care [kɛr] *s.* (*worry*) cuidado; aflicción; ansiedad; (*caution*) cuidado, cautela, esmero; (*responsibility*) cargo, custodia; **to take** — **of** cuidar de; *v.* tener interés (por); **to** — **about** tener interés en (*o* por); preocuparse de; importarle a uno; **to** — **for** cuidar de; estimar, tenerle cariño a; gustarle a uno; simpatizarle a uno (*una persona*); **to** — **to** querer, desear, tener ganas de; **what does he** —? ¿a él qué le importa?
ca·reen [kərín] *v.* moverse con rapidez y sin control; volcar (*un buque*).
ca·reer [kərír] *s.* carrera, profesión.
care·free [kérfri] *adj.* libre de cuidado, sin cuidados, despreocupado.
care·ful [kérfəl] *adj.* cuidadoso; esmerado; cauteloso; **to be** — tener cuidado; **-ly** *adv.* cuidadosamente, con cuidado; con esmero.
care·ful·ness [kérfəlnɪs] *s.* cuidado; esmero; cautela.
care·less [kérlɪs] *adj.* descuido; falta de esmero; desaliño; negligencia.
ca·ress [kərés] *s.* caricia; *v.* acariciar.
care·tak·er [kértekɚ] *s.* cuidador, guardián, vigilante, celador.
car·fare [kárfɛr] *s.* pasaje de tranvía.
car·go [kárgo] *s.* carga, cargamento; flete.
car·i·ca·ture [kǽrɪkətʃɚ] *s.* caricatura; *v.* caricaturar o caricaturizar.
car·load [kárlod] *s.* furgonada, vagonada, carga de un furgón o vagón.
car·nal [kárnl] *adj.* carnal.
car·na·tion [kɑrnéʃən] *s.* clavel; color encarnado o rosado.
car·ni·val [kárnəvl] *s.* carnaval; fiesta, holgorio; feria, verbena
car·niv·o·rous [kɑrnívərəs] *adj.* carnívoro, carnicero.

CA

car·ol [kǽrəl] *s.* villancico; **Christmas** — villancico de Navidad; *v.* cantar villancicos; celebrar con villancicos.
car·om [kǽrəm] *s.* carambola; rebote.
ca·rouse [kəráuz] *v.* andar de parranda, *Ríopl., Ch.* andar de farra; embriagarse.
car·pen·ter [kárpəntɚ] *s.* carpintero.
car·pen·try [kárpəntrɪ] *s.* carpintería.
car·pet [kárpɪt] *s.* alfombra; **small** — tapete; *v.* tapizar.
car·pet·bag·ger [kárpətbægɚ] explotador oportunista.
car·port [kárport] *s.* cobertizo.
car·riage [kǽrɪdʒ] *s.* carruaje, coche; acarreo, transporte; porte; — **paid** porte pagado; **good** — buen porte, garbo, manera airosa.
car·ri·er [kǽrɪɚ] *s.* portador; mensajero; carretero, trajinante; transportador; *Méx.* cargador; **airplane** — portaaviones; **disease** — transmisor de gérmenes contagiosos; **mail** — cartero.
car·rot [kǽrət] *s.* zanahoria.
car·ry [kǽrɪ] *v.* llevar; (*cart*) acarrear, transportar; *Am.* cargar; sostener (*una carga*); traer consigo; ganar, lograr (*una elección, un premio, etc.*); **to** — **away** llevarse; cargar con; entusiasmar, encantar; **to** — **on** continuar; no parar; **to** — **oneself well** andar derecho, airoso, garboso; **to** — **out** llevar a cabo, realizar; sacar; **carried forward** suma y sigue; **carry-over** sobrante, saldo anterior; **carrying charges** cargo mensual, gastos afines.
cart [kɑrt] *s.* carro, carreta, vagoncillo; *v.* acarrear.
cart·age [kártɪdʒ] *s.* carretaje, acarreo.
cart·er [kártɚ] *s.* carretero; acarreador.
car·ton [kártṇ] *s.* caja de cartón.
car·toon [kɑrtún] *s.* caricatura.
car·toon·ist [kɑrtúnɪst] *s.* caricaturista.
car·tridge [kártrɪdʒ] *s.* cartucho; — **belt** cartuchera, canana; — **box** cartuchera; — **shell** cápsula.
carve [kɑrv] *v.* tallar; labrar; cincelar; esculpir; trinchar, tajar (*carne*).
carv·er [kárvɚ] *s.* trinchador; trinchante (*cuchillo*); entallador, escultor.
carv·ing [kárvɪŋ] *s.* talla, obra de escultura, entalladura; — **knife** trinchante.
cas·cade [kæskéd] *s.* cascada, salto de agua.
case [kes] *s.* (*instance*) caso; (*box*) caja; (*pillow*) funda, cubierta; (*scabbard*) vaina; **window** — marco de ventana; **in** — **that** caso que, en caso que, dado que; **in any** — en todo caso; **just in** — por si acaso; — **work** trabajo con casos.
case·ment [késmənt] *s.* puerta ventana.
cash [kæʃ] *s.* dinero contante; en efectivo; — **advance** anticipo en efectivo; — **and carry** al contado y transporte cuenta del comprador; — **box** cofre; — **payment** pago al contado; — **on delivery (c.o.d.)** contra reembolso, cóbrese al entregar; — **register** caja registradora (*de dinero*); **to pay** — pagar al contado; — **assets** activo en efectivo, *Arg.* activos disponibles; — **voucher** comprobante; *v.* cambiar, cobrar (*un cheque*).
ca·shew [kǽʃju] *s.* anacardo, marañón.
cash·ier [kæʃír] *s.* cajero; — **'s check** cheque de caja, de gerencia.

cask [kæsk] *s.* tonel, barril, cuba.
cas·ket [kǽskɪt] *s.* ataúd; **jewel** — joyero, cofrecillo.
cas·se·role [kǽsərol] *s.* cacerola.
cas·sette [kəsɛ́t] *s.* carrete pequeña de cinta magnetofónica; pequeña grabadora.
cas·sock [kǽsək] *s.* sotana.
cast [kæst] *s.* (*throw*) tirada (*al pescar*); (*form*) molde; matiz; apariencia; defecto (*del ojo*); (*theater*) reparto (*de papeles dramáticos*); actores; — **iron** hierro fundido o colado; *v.* echar; tirar; arrojar; lanzar; moldear; repartir (*papeles dramáticos*); escoger (*para un papel dramático*); **to** — **a ballot** votar; **to** — **a statue in bronze** vaciar una estatua en bronce; **to** — **about** buscar; hacer planes; **to** — **aside** desechar; **to** — **lots** echar suertes; **to be** — **down** estar abatido; *pret. & p.p. de* **to cast.**
cas·ta·nets [kǽstənɛts] *s. pl.* castañuelas.
caste [kæst] *s.* casta; **to lose** — perder el prestigio social.
Cas·til·ian [kæstíljən] *s. & adj.* castellano.
cas·tle [kǽsl̩] *s.* castillo; alcázar; fortaleza; torre, roque (*en ajedrez*).
cas·tor oil [kǽstɚɔɪl] *s.* aceite de ricino.
cas·trate [kǽstret] *v.* capar, castrar.
cas·u·al [kǽʒuəl] *adj.* casual; accidental.
cas·u·al·ty [kǽʒuəltɪ] *s.* baja o pérdida (*en el ejército*); accidente.
cat [kæt] *s.* gato; gata.
cat·a·log [kǽtlɔg] *s.* catálogo; *v.* catalogar.
cat·a·lyst [kǽtəlist] *s.* catalizador.
cat·a·ract [kǽtərækt] *s.* catarata.
ca·tarrh [kətάr] *s.* catarro.
ca·tas·tro·phe [kətǽstrəfɪ] *s.* catástrofe.
catch [kætʃ] *s.* presa, botin; presa; pestillo (*de la puerta*); trampa; cogida (*de la pelota*); — **phrase** frase llamativa; — **question** pregunta tramposa; **he is a good** — es un buen partido; **to play** — jugar a la pelota; *v.* coger; prender; asir; alcanzar; enganchar; comprender; ser contagioso, pegarse; **to** — **a glimpse of** vislumbrar; **to** — **cold** coger un resfriado, resfriarse; **to** — **on** comprender, caer en la cuenta; **to** — **one's eye** llamarle a uno la atención; **to** — **sight of** avistar; **to** — **unaware** sorprender, coger desprevenido; **to** — **up with** alcanzar a, emparejarse con.
catch·er [kǽtʃɚ] *s.* cogedor, agarrador; parador, (*baseball*) cácher o receptor (*en béisbol*).
catch·ing [kǽtʃɪŋ] *adj.* pegajoso, contagioso; (*attractive*) atractivo.
cat·e·chism [kǽtəkɪzəm] *s.* catecismo.
cat·e·go·ry [kǽtəgorɪ] *s.* categoría.
ca·ter [kétɚ] *v*— surtir, abastecer, proveer los alimentos (*para banquetes, fiestas, etc.*) **to** — **to** proveer a las necesidades o al gusto de; **to** — **to the taste of** halagar el gusto de.
cat·er·pil·lar [kǽtəpɪlɚ] *s.* oruga; — **tractor** tractor.
ca·the·dral [kəθídrəl] *s.* catedral.
cath·ode [kǽθod] *s.* cátodo; — **rays** rayos catódicos.
Cath·o·lic [kǽθəlɪk] *s. & adj.* católico.
Ca·thol·i·cism [kəθάləsɪzəm] *s.* catolicismo.
cat·sup [kǽtsəp] *s.* salsa de tomate.
cat·tle [kǽtl̩] *s.* ganado, ganado vacuno; — **range** potrero; — **raiser** ganadero, *Ríopl.* estanciero; — **raising** ganaderia; — **ranch** hacienda de ganado, *Méx., C.A.* rancho, *Ríopl.* estancia; *Ven., Col.* hato.
caught [kɔt] *pret. & p.p. de* **to catch.**
cau·li·flow·er [kɔ́ləflaʊɚ] *s.* coliflor.
cause [kɔz] *s.* causa; *v.* causar; originar; **to** — **to** hacer; inducir a.
caus·tic [kɔ́stɪk] *adj.* cáustico.
cau·ter·ize [kɔ́tɝraɪz] *v.* cauterizar.
cau·tion [kɔ́ʃən] *s.* precaución, cautela; aviso, advertencia; — **!** ¡cuidado! ¡atención!, *v.* prevenir, avisar, advertir.
cau·tious [kɔ́ʃəs] *adj.* cauto; cauteloso, cuidadoso; precavido.
cav·a·lier [kævəlír] *s.* caballero; galán; *adj.* orgulloso, altivo, desdeñoso.
cav·al·ry [kǽvlrɪ] *s.* caballería.
cave [kev] *s.* cueva; caverna; *v.* **to** — **in** hundirse; desplomarse.
cav·ern [kǽvɚn] *s.* caverna.
cav·ity [kǽvətɪ] *s.* cavidad, hueco; (*tooth*) carie.
ca·vort [kəvɔ́rt] *v.* cabriolar.
caw [kɔ] *s.* graznido; *v.* graznar.
cease [sis] *v.* cesar; parar, desistir; dejar de.
cease·less [síslɪs] *adj.* incesante.
ce·dar [sídɚ] *s.* cedro.
cede [sid] *v.* ceder.
ce·dil·la [sɪdɪlə] *s.* cedilla.
ceil·ing [sílɪŋ] *s.* techo (*interior*); cielo máximo (*en aviación*); altura máxima (*en aviación*); — **price** precio máximo.
cel·e·brate [sɛ́ləbret] *v.* celebrar.
cel·e·brat·ed [sɛ́ləbretɪd] *adj.* célebre, renombrado.
cel·e·bra·tion [sɛləbréʃən] *s.* celebración; fiesta.
ce·leb·ri·ty [səlɛ́brətɪ] *s.* celebridad; renombre.
cel·er·y [sɛ́lərɪ] *s.* apio.
ce·les·tial [səlɛ́stʃəl] *adj.* celestial, celeste.
cell [sɛl] *s.* (*enclosure*) celda; (*structural*) célula; (*battery*) pila eléctrica.
cel·lar [sɛ́lɚ] *s.* bodega, sótano.
cel·lu·loid [sɛ́ljəlɔɪd] *s.* celuloide.
cel·o·tex [séloteks] *s.* cartón de bagazo.
ce·ment [səmɛ́nt] *s.* cemento; hormigón; **reinforced** —cemento armado; — **mixer** hormigonera; *v.* unir, cementar, pegar con cemento; cubrir con cemento.
cem·e·ter·y [sɛ́mətɛrɪ] *s.* cementerio.
cen·sor [sɛ́nsɚ] *s.* censor; censurador, crítico; *v.* censurar (*cartas, periódicos, etc.*).
cen·sor·ship [sɛ́nsɚʃɪp] *s.* censura
cen·sure [sɛ́nʃɚ] *s.* censura, crítica, reprobación; *v.* censurar, criticar, reprobar.
cen·sus [sɛ́nsəs] *s.* censo; — **taker** empadronador.
cent [sɛnt] *s.* centavo (*de peso o dólar*); **per** — por ciento.
cen·ten·ni·al [sɛntɛ́nɪəl] *adj. & s.* centenario.
cen·ter [sɛ́ntɚ] *s.* centro; — **spread** doble página central; *v.* centrar; colocar en el centro; concentrar(se).
cen·ti·grade [sɛ́ntəgred] *adj.* centígrado.
cen·ti·pede [sɛ́ntəpid] *s.* ciempiés, cientopiés.
cen·tral [sɛ́ntrəl] *adj.* central; céntrico; *s.* (la) central de teléfonos.
cen·tral·ize [sɛ́ntrəlaɪz] *v.* centralizar.
cen·trif·u·gal [sɛntrífjʊgl] *adj.* centrífugo.
cen·trip·e·tal [sɛntrípətl̩] *adj.* centrípeto.
cen·tu·ry [sɛ́ntʃərɪ] *s.* siglo.
ce·ram·ic [sərǽmɪk] *adj.* cerámico; **ceramics** *s.* cerámica.
ce·re·al [sírɪəl] *adj.* cereal; *s.* cereal; grano.
cer·e·mo·ni·al [sɛrəmónɪəl] *adj.* ceremonial; *s.* ceremonial; rito.
cer·e·mo·ni·ous [sɛrəmónɪəs] *adj.* ceremonioso.
cer·e·mo·ny [sɛ́rəmonɪ] *s.* ceremonia; ceremonial.
cer·tain [sɝ́tn̩] *adj.* cierto, seguro; **ly** *adv.* ciertamente; por cierto; de cierto; seguramente; de seguro.
cer·tain·ty [sɝ́tn̩tɪ] *s.* certeza; certidumbre; seguridad.

cer·tif·i·cate [sɝtífəkɪt] *s.* certificado; documento; testimonio; — **of baptism** fe de bautismo; — **of stock** bono, obligación; **birth** — partida de nacimiento; **death** — partida (*o* certificado) de defunción.
cer·ti·fi·ca·tion [sɝtɪfɪkéʃən] *s.* certificación.
cer·ti·fy [sɝ́təfaɪ] *v.* certificar; dar fe, atestiguar; **Certified Public Accountant (CPA)** contador público nacional (registrado, juramentado, titulado).
cer·vix [sɝ́vɪks] *s.* cerviz.
ces·sa·tion [sɛséʃən] *s.* suspensión, paro.
cess·pool [séspul] *s.* cloaca, rezumadero.
chafe [tʃef] *s.* rozadura; irritación, molestia; *v.* rozar(se); frotar; irritar(se).
chaff [tʃæf] *s.* hollejo, cáscara; *v.* embromar, bromear.
cha·grin [ʃəgrín] *s.* mortificación, desazón, pesar; **-ed** *p.p.* mortificado, afligido.
chain [ʃen] *s.* cadena; — **of mountains** cordillera; — **store** tiendas en serie (cadena); — **reaction** reacción en cadena; reacción eslabonada; — **saw** aserradora de cadena; — **smoker** el que fuma cigarro tras cigarro; *v.* encadenar.
chair [tʃɛr] *s.* silla; cátedra; presidencia; **arm** — sillón (de brazos); **easy** — butaca, poltrona; **folding** — silla de tijera; **rocking** — mecedora
chair·man [tʃérmən] *s.* presidente, director (*de una junta o de departamento*).
chair·man·ship [tʃérmənʃɪp] *s.* presidencia (*de una junta*).
chal·ice [tʃǽlɪs] *s.* cáliz (*vaso sagrado*).
chalk [tʃɔk] *s.* tiza, yeso; greda; *Méx.* gis; *v.* enyesar; marcar con tiza o yeso; **to** — **down** apuntar con tiza o yeso (*en el pizarrón*); **to** — **out** bosquejar, esbozar con tiza.
chalk·y [tʃɔ́kɪ] *adj.* yesoso; blanco.
chal·lenge [tʃǽlɪndʒ] *s.* desafío; reto; demanda; *v.* desafiar, retar; disputar, poner a prueba; dar el quienvive.
cham·ber [tʃémbɚ] *s.* cámara; aposento; — **of commerce** cámara de comercio.
cham·ber·maid [tʃémbɚmed] *s.* camarera, sirvienta.
cham·ois [ʃǽmɪ] *s.* gamuza.
cham·pi·on [tʃǽmpɪən] *s.* campeón; defensor; *v.* defender.
cham·pi·on·ship [tʃǽmpɪənʃɪp] *s.* campeonato.
chance [tʃæns] *s.* (*opportunity*) oportunidad ocasión; (*possibility*) posibilidad, probabilidad; (*fortune*) suerte, fortuna; casualidad, azar; (*risk*) riesgo; billete de rifa o lotería; **by** — por casualidad; **game of** — juego de azar; **to run a** — correr riesgo; *adj.* casual, accidental; *v.* arriesgar; **to** — **to** acertar a, hacer (*algo*) por casualidad.
chan·cel·lor [tʃǽnsələ] *s.* canciller; primer ministro; magistrado; rector de universidad.
chan·de·lier [ʃændlír] *s.* araña de luces, *Ríopl.*, *Méx.* candil.
change [tʃendʒ] *s.* (*money*) cambio; vuelta, *Am.* vuelto; suelto; *Méx.* feria; (*fresh clothes*) muda de ropa; (*switch*) mudanza; **the** — **of life** la menopausia; *v.* cambiar; mudar; alterar; **to** — **clothes** mudar de ropa; **to** — **trains** transbordar(se), cambiar de tren.
change·a·ble [tʃéndʒəbl] *adj.* mudable, variable; inconstante; tornadizo; — **silk** seda tornasolada.
chan·nel [tʃǽnl] *s.* canal; cauce; canal (*de televisión*).
chant [tʃænt] *s.* canto llano o gregoriano; sonsonete; *v.* cantar (*salmos, himnos, etc.*).
cha·os [kéɑs] *s.* caos; desorden.
cha·ot·ic [keɑ́tɪk] *adj.* caótico.
chap [tʃæp] *s.* grieta, raja, rajadura (*en la piel*); chico; **what a fine** — **he is!** ¡qué buen tipo (*o* sujeto) es!; *v.* agrietarse, rajarse (*la piel*).
chap·el [tʃǽpl] *s.* capilla.
chap·er·on(e) [ʃǽpəron] *s.* acompañante, persona de respeto; **to go along as a** — *Am.* ir de moscón; *v.* acompañar, servir de acompañante.
chap·lain [tʃǽplɪn] *s.* capellán; **army** — capellán castrense.
chap·ter [tʃǽptɚ] *s.* capítulo; cabildo (*de una catedral*).
char [tʃɑr] *v.* requemar, carbonizar.
char·ac·ter [kǽrɪktɚ] *s.* carácter; personaje.
char·ac·ter·is·tic [kærɪktərístɪk] *adj.* característico; típico; *s.* característica, rasgo característico; distintivo; peculiaridad.
char·ac·ter·ize [kǽrɪktəraɪz] *adj.* caracterizar.
cha·rade [ʃəréd] *s.* charada.
char·coal [tʃɑ́rkol] *s.* carbón; carboncillo (*para dibujar*); — **drawing** dibujo al carbón.
charge [tʃɑrdʒ] *s.* (*custody*) cargo; custodia; cuidado; (*order*) mandato, encargo; (*accusation*) cargo, acusación; (*load*) carga; peso; (*cost*) precio, coste; (*attack*) embestida, asalto, ataque; **chargé d'affaires** agregado; — **account** cuenta abierta; — **prepaid** porte pagado; **under my** — a mi cargo; **to be in** — **of** estar encargado de; *v.* cargar; cargar en cuenta; cobrar (*precio*); mandar; exhortar; atacar, embestir, asaltar; **to** — **with murder** acusar de homicidio; **to** — **off a loss** restar una pérdida.
charg·er [tʃɑ́rdʒɚ] *s.* cargador (*de batería*); caballo de guerra, corcel.
char·i·ot [tʃǽrɪət] *s.* carroza; carruaje.
cha·ris·ma [kərízmə] *s.* carisma.
char·i·ta·ble [tʃǽrətəbl] *adj.* caritativo.
char·i·ty [tʃǽrətɪ] *s.* caridad; limosna; beneficencia.
char·la·tan [ʃɑ́rlətn] *s.* charlatán; farsante.
charm [tʃɑrm] *s.* encanto; atractivo; hechizo; talismán; **watch** — dije; *v.* encantar; cautivar; hechizar.
charm·ing [tʃɑ́mɪŋ] *adj.* encantador, atractivo.
chart [tʃɑrt] *s.* carta (*hidrográfica o de navegar*); mapa; gráfica, representación gráfica; **flow—** (*computer*) diagrama de flujo; *v.* cartografiar, delinear mapas o cartas; **to — a course** trazar o planear una ruta o derrotero.
char·ter [tʃɑ́rtɚ] *s.* carta constitucional, constitución, código; título; carta de privilegio; — **member** socio fundador; *v.* fletar (*un barco*); alquilar (*un ómnibus*).
chase [tʃes] *s.* caza, persecución; *v.* cazar; perseguir; **to** — **away** ahuyentar.
chasm [kǽzəm] *s.* abismo; vacío.
chaste [tʃest] *adj.* casto; honesto; puro.
chas·tise [tʃæstáɪz] *v.* castigar.
chas·tise·ment [tʃæstáɪzmənt] *s.* castigo, escarmiento.
chas·ti·ty [tʃǽstətɪ] *s.* castidad; honestidad; pureza.
chat [tʃæt] *s.* charla, *Méx.* plática; *v.* charlar, *Méx.* platicar.
chat·tels [tʃǽtlz] *s. pl.* enseres, bienes muebles.
chat·ter [tʃǽtɚ] *s.* charla, parloteo; (*teeth*) castañeteo (*birds*) chirrido (*de aves*); *v.* charlar, parlotear, cotorrear; castañetear (*los dientes*).
chauf·feur [ʃófɚ] *s.* chófer, cochero de automóvil.
cheap [tʃip] *adj.* barato; cursi, de mal gusto; **to feel** — sentir vergüenza; **-ly** *adv.* barato, a poco precio.
cheap·en [tʃípən] *v.* abaratar.
cheap·ness [tʃípnɪs] *s.* baratura; cursilería.

cheat [tʃit] *s.* fraude, engaño; (*trick*) trampa; (*person*) trampista, tramposo; estafador; embaucador; *v.* engañar; trampear; embaucar; estafar.
check [tʃɛk] *s.* cheque (*de banco*); talón, marbete, contraseña (*de equipajes, etc.*); marca, señal; cuenta (*de restaurante*); restricción, represión; cuadro (*de un tejido o tela*); comprobación; jaque (*en ajedrez*); — **room** vestuario; — **stub** talón; — **tally** recuento; — **test** contraprueba; guardarropa; consigna (equipajes); — **point** punto de inspección; — **list** lista comprobante; *v.* refrenar, reprimir, restringir; facturar, depositar (*equipajes*); (verify) inspeccionar; confrontar, **to** — *Cuba, Col., P.R.* chequear, *Méx.* checar, comprobar; marcar (*con una señal*); dar jaque (*en ajedrez*); **to** — **out of a hotel** desocupar el cuarto o alojamiento de un hotel.
check·book [tʃɛ́kbʊk] *s.* libreta de cheques; talonario.
check·er [tʃɛ́kɚ] *s.* cuadro; casilla (*de un tablero de ajedrez, etc.*); pieza (*del juego de damas*); comprobador; inspector; **-s** juego de damas; — **board** tablero; *v.* cuadricular, marcar con cuadritos; **-ed career** vida azarosa, vida llena de variedad; **-ed cloth** paño o tela a cuadros.
check·mate [tʃɛ́kmet] *s.* jaque mate.
cheek [tʃik] *s.* mejilla, carrillo; cachete; descaro, desfachatez; **fat** — mejilla gorda, moflete; — **bone** pómulo; **red** — chapetón.
cheer [tʃɪr] *s.* alegría; buen ánimo, jovialidad; (*consolation*) consuelo; **-s** aplausos, vivas; *v.* alegrar, alentar, animar; refocilar; aplaudir, vitorear; **to** — **up** alentar, dar ánimo; cobrar ánimo, animarse.
cheer·ful [tʃɪ́rfəl] *adj.* animado, alegre, jovial; **-ly** *adv.* alegremente, con alegría, con júbilo; de buena gana, de buen grado.
cheer·ful·ness [tʃɪ́rfəlnɪs] *s.* jovialidad, alegría; buen humor.
cheer·i·ly [tʃɪ́rəlɪ] = **cheerfully.**
cheer·less [tʃɪ́rlɪs] *adj.* abatido, desalentado, desanimado; triste, sombrío.
cheer·y [tʃɪ́rɪ] = **cheerful.**
cheese [tʃiz] *s.* queso; **cottage** — requesón.
chef [ʃɛf] *s.* cocinero.
chem·i·cal [kɛ́mɪkl] *adj.* químico; *s.* producto químico.
chem·ist [kɛ́mɪst] *s.* químico.
chem·is·try [kɛ́mɪstrɪ] *s.* química.
cher·ish [tʃɛ́rɪʃ] *v.* acariciar, abrigar (*una esperanza, un ideal, etc.*); apreciar.
cher·ry [tʃɛ́rɪ] *s.* cereza; — **tree** cerezo.
cher·ub [tʃɛ́rəb] *s.* querubín.
chess [tʃɛs] *s.* ajedrez; — **board** tablero de ajedrez.
chest [tʃɛst] *s.* cofre, arca; caja; pecho; — **of drawers** cómoda.
chest·nut [tʃɛ́snət] *s.* castaña; — **tree** castaño; *adj.* castaño; — **horse** caballo zaino.
chev·ron [ʃɛ́vrən] *s.* galón.
chew [tʃu] *s.* mascada, mordisco, bocado; *v.* mascar, masticar.
chew·ing gum [tʃúɪŋ gʌm] *s.* goma de mascar; *Am.* chicle.
chick [tʃɪk] *s.* polluelo, pollito; pajarito; **chick-pea** garbanzo.
chick·en [tʃɪ́kɪn] *s.* pollo; polluelo; — **pox** viruelas locas; **chicken-hearted** cobarde, gallina.
chic·o·ry [tʃɪ́kərɪ] *s.* achicoria.
chide [tʃaɪd] *v.* regañar, reprender, reprobar.
chief [tʃif] *s.* jefe, caudillo; cacique (*de una tribu*); **commander in** — comandante en jefe; *adj.* principal; — **clerk** oficial mayor; — **justice** presidente de la corte suprema; **-ly** *adv.* principalmente, mayormente; sobre todo.
chief·tain [tʃíftan] *s.* cacique.
chif·fon [ʃɪfɑ́n] *s.* gasa.
chig·ger [tʃɪ́gɚ] *s.* nigua.
chil·blain [tʃɪ́blen] *s.* sabañón.
child [tʃaɪld] *s.* niño, niña; hijo, hija; **-'s play** cosa de niños; **to be with** — estar encinta.
child·birth [tʃáɪldbɝθ] *s.* parto, alumbramiento.
child·hood [tʃáɪdhʊd] *s.* niñez, infancia.
child·ish [tʃáɪdɪʃ] *adj.* pueril; infantil; — **action** niñería, niñada.
child·less [tʃáɪdlɪs] *adj.* sin hijos.
child·like [tʃáɪldaɪk] *adj.* como niño, aniñado, pueril.
chil·dren [tʃɪ́ldrən] *pl. de* **child.**
Chil·e·an [tʃɪ́lɪən] *adj. & s.* chileno.
chil·i [tʃɪ́lɪ] *s. Méx., C.A.* chile, *Carib., S.A.* ají.
chill [tʃɪl] *s.* frío, (*illness*) resfrío; enfriamiento; (*sensation*) escalofrío; calofrio; **-s and fever** escalofríos; *adj.* frío; *v.* resfriar(se); enfriar(se); **to become -ed** resfriarse, escalofriarse.
chill·y [tʃɪ́lɪ] *adj.* frío; friolento.
chime [tʃaɪm] *s.* repique, campaneo; **-s** órgano de campanas, juego de campanas; *v.* repicar, campanear; tocar, sonar, tañer (*las companas*); **to** — **with** estar en armonía con.
chim·ney [tʃɪ́mnɪ] *s.* chimenea; **lamp** — tubo de lámpara, *Am.* bombilla.
chin [tʃɪn] *s.* barba, mentón.
chi·na [tʃáɪnə] *s.* loza de china, procelana, loza fina; vajilla de porcelana; — **closet** chinero.
chi·na·ware [tʃáɪnəwɛr] = **china.**
Chi·nese [tʃaɪníz] *adj.* chino; *s.* chino; idioma chino.
chink [tʃɪŋk] *s.* grieta, hendidura.
chip [tʃɪp] *s.* astilla, brizna; fragmento; desconchadura; desportilladura; (*poker*) ficha (*de pócar*); (computer) ficha de silicón; *v.* astillar; desconchar(se); descascarar(se); desportillar(se); picar, tajar (*con cincel o hacha*); **to** — **in** contribuir con su cuota.
chip·munk [tʃɪ́pmʌŋk] *s.* especie de ardilla.
chi·ro·prac·tic [kaɪrəprǽktɪk] *adj.* quiropráctico.
chirp [tʃɝp] *s.* chirrido; pío; gorjeo; *v.* chirriar; piar; pipiar; gorjear.
chis·el [tʃɪ́zl] *s.* cincel, *v.* cincelar; sisar, estafar.
chiseler [tʃɪ́zlɚ] *s.* tramposo.
chiv·al·rous [ʃɪ́vl̩rəs] *adj.* caballeresco, caballeroso, galante, cortés.
chiv·al·ry [ʃɪ́vl̩rɪ] *s.* caballería; caballerosidad.
chlo·ride [klóraɪd] *s.* cloruro.
chlo·rine [klórin] *s.* cloro.
chlo·ro·form [klórəfɔrm] *s.* cloroformo.
chlo·ro·phyll [klórəfɪl] *s.* clorofila.
choc·o·late [tʃɔ́klɪt] *s.* chocolate; — **pot** chocolatera.
choice [tʃɔɪs] *s.* selección; preferencia; escogimiento; cosa elegida; favorito, preferido; alternativa; **to have no other** — no tener otra alternativa; *adj.* selecto; bien escogido; excelente.
choir [kwaɪr] *s.* coro.
choke [tʃok] *s.* sofoco, ahogo; (*cough*) tos ahogada; estrangulación; estrangulator, (*auto*) obturador (*de automóvil*); *v.* sofocar(se), ahogar(se); estrangular(se); obstruir, tapar; regularizar (*el motor*).
chol·er·a [kɑ́lərə] *s.* cólera (*m.*).
cho·les·ter·ol [kəlɛ́stɚol] *s.* colesterol.
choose [tʃuz] *v.* escoger; elegir; seleccionar; **to** — **to** optar por; preferir; **I do not** — **to do it** no se me antoja (*o* no es mi gusto) hacerlo.
chop [tʃɑp] *s.* chuleta, costilla, (*slice*) tajada (*de

carne); **-s** quijadas; *v.* tajar, cortar; picar, desmenuzar (*carne*).
chop·py [tʃápɪ] *adj.* picado, agitado.
cho·ral [kórəl] *adj.* coral.
chord [kɔrd] *s.* cuerda; acorde.
chore [tʃor] *s.* tarea; quehacer.
cho·re·og·ra·phy [korɪágrəfɪ] *s.* coreografía.
cho·rus [kórəs] *s.* coro; *v.* cantar o hablar en coro; contestar a una vos.
chose [tʃoz] *pret. de* **to choose.**
cho·sen [tʃózn̩] *p.p. de* **to choose.**
chris·ten [krísn̩] *v.* bautizar.
chris·ten·ing [krínɪŋ] *s.* bautizo, bautismo.
Chris·tian [krístʃən] *s. & adj.* cristiano; — **name** nombre de pila o bautismo.
Chris·ti·an·i·ty [krɪstʃɪǽnətɪ] *s.* cristiandad, cristianismo.
Christ·mas [krísməs] *s.* Navidad, Pascua de Navidad; *adj.* navideño; — **Eve** Nochebuena; — **gift** regalo de Navidad; aguinaldo; **Merry —!** ¡Felices Navidades! ¡Felices Pascuas!
chrome [krom] *s.* cromo; *adj.* cromado.
chro·mi·um [krómɪəm] *s.* cromo.
chro·mo·some [króməsom] *s.* cromosoma.
chron·ic [kránɪk] *adj.* crónico.
chron·i·cle [kránɪkl̩] *s.* crónica; *v.* relatar; escribir la crónica de.
chron·i·cler [kránɪklɚ] *s.* cronista.
chron·o·log·i·cal [kranəládʒɪkl] *adj.* cronológico.
chro·nom·e·ter [krənámətɚ] *s.* cronómetro.
chry·san·the·mum [krɪsǽθəməm] *s.* crisantema, crisantemo.
chub·by [tʃʌ́bɪ] *adj.* rechoncho; gordiflón.
chuck [tʃʌk] *s.* mamola, golpecito, (*caress*) caricia (*debajo de la barba*); *v.* echar, tirar (*lo que no sirve*); **to — under the chin** hacer la mamola.
chuck·le [tʃʌ́kl̩] *s.* risita; *v.* reír entre dientes.
chum [tʃʌm] *s.* compañero, camarada, compinche.
chunk [tʃʌŋk] *s.* trozo; zoquete.
church [tʃɝt] *s.* iglesia.
church·man [tʃɝ́tʃmən] *s.* clérigo, eclesiástico, sacerdote; (*parishoner*) feligrés.
church·yard [tʃɝ́tʃjard] *s.* patio de iglesia; camposanto, cementerio.
churn [tʃɝn] *s.* mantequera (*para hacer manteca*); *v.* batir (*en una mantequera*); agitar, revolver.
ci·der [sáɪdɚ] *s.* sidra.
ci·gar [sɪgár] *s.* puro; *Carib., Col., Ven.* tabaco; — **store** tabaquería, estanquillo.
cig·a·rette [sɪgərét] *s.* cigarrillo, pitillo, *Méx., C.A., Ven., Col.* cigarro; — **case** cigarrera, pitillera; — **holder** boquilla; — **lighter** encendedor.
cinch [sɪntʃ] *s.* cincha; ganga, cosa fácil; *v.* cinchar; apretar.
cin·der [síndɚ] *s.* ceniza; carbón, brasa, ascua; cisco; **-s** cenizas; rescoldo.
cin·na·mon [sínəmən] *s.* canela; — **tree** canelo.
ci·pher [sáɪfɚ] *s.* cifra; número; cero.
cir·cle [sɝ́kl̩] *s.* círculo; cerco, rueda; *v.* cercar, circundar; circular, dar vueltas.
cir·cuit [sɝ́kɪt] *s.* circuito; rode o, vuelta.
cir·cu·lar [sɝ́kjəlɚ] *adj.* circular; redondo; *s.* circular; hoja volante.
cir·cu·late [sɝ́kjəlet] *v.* circular; poner en circulación.
cir·cu·la·tion [sɝkjəléʃən] *s.* circulación.
cir·cum·fer·ence [sɚkʌ́mfərəns] *s.* circunferencia.
cir·cum·flex [sɝ́kəmflɛks] *adj.* circunflejo.
cir·cum·lo·cu·tion [sɝkəmlokjúʃən] *s.* circunlocución, redeo.
cir·cum·scribe [sɝkəmskráɪb] *v.* circunscribir, limitar.
cir·cum·spect [sɝ́kəmspɛkt] *adj.* circunspecto; prudente.
cir·cum·spec·tion [sɝkəmspɛ́kʃən] *s.* circunspección, miramiento, prudencia.
cir·cum·stance [sɝ́kəmstæns] *s.* circunstancia; incidente; ceremonia, pompa.
cir·cum·vent [sɝkəmvɛ́nt] *v.* evitar, embaucar.
cir·cus [sɝ́kəs] *s.* circo.
cir·rho·sis [sɪrósɪs] *s.* cirrosis.
cis·tern [sístɚn] *s.* cisterna.
cit·a·del [sítədl̩] *s.* ciudadela.
ci·ta·tion [saɪtéʃən] *s.* citación; cita; mención.
cite [saɪt] *v.* citar; citar a juicio; mencionar.
cit·i·zen [sítəzn̩] *s.* ciudadano, paisano.
cit·i·zen·ship [sítəzn̩ʃɪp] *s.* ciudadanía.
cit·ron [sítrən] *s.* acitrón.
cit·rus [sítrəs] *s.* cidro.
cit·y [sítɪ] *s.* ciudad, población; municipio; *adj.* municipal, urbano; — **council** ayuntamiento; — **hall** ayuntamiento, casa municipal; — **planning** urbanismo, urbanización.
civ·ic [sívɪk] *adj.* cívico.
civ·ics [sívɪks] *s.* derecho político.
civ·il [sívl̩] *adj.* civil; cortés; — **engineer** ingeniero civil; — **rights** derechos civiles; — **disobedience** desobediencia civil.
ci·vil·ian [səvíljən] *s.* civil; paisano (*persona no militar*).
ci·vil·i·ty [səvílətɪ] *s.* civilidad, cortesía, urbanidad.
civ·i·li·za·tion [sɪvl̩əzéʃən] *s.* civilización.
civ·i·lize [sívl̩aɪz] *v.* civilizar.
civ·i·lized [sívl̩aɪzd] *adj.* civilizado.
clad [klæd] *pret. & p.p. de* **to clothe.**
claim [klem] *s.* demanda; reclamación, reclamo; derecho, título; pretensión; **miner's —** denuncia; *v.* reclamar; demandar; pedir, exigir; afirmar, sostener; **to — a mine** denunciar una mina; **to — to be** pretender ser.
claim·ant [klémənt] *s.* reclamante o reclamador; pretendiente (*a un trono*).
clair·voy·ant [klɛrvɔ́ɪənt] *adj.* clarividente.
clam [klæm] *s.* almeja.
clam·ber [klǽmbɚ] *v.* trepar, encaramarse, subir a gatas, subir gateando.
clam·my [klǽmɪ] *adj.* frío y húmedo.
clam·or [klǽmɚ] *s.* clamor; clamoreo; gritería, vocería; *v.* clamar; vociferar, gritar.
clam·or·ous [klǽmərəs] *adj.* clamoroso.
clamp [klæmp] *s.* grapa; tornillo de banco; *v.* afianzar, sujetar; pisar recio.
clan [klæn] *s.* clan; tribu.
clan·des·tine [klændɛ́stɪn] *adj.* clandestino.
clang [klæŋ] *s.* tantán, retintín; campanada, campanillazo; —! —! ¡tan! ¡tan!; *v.* sonar, repicar (*una campana o timbre*); hacer sonar, tocar fuerte.
clap [klæp] *s.* palmada; golpe seco; — **of thunder** trueno; *v.* palmear, palmotear, aplaudir, dar palmadas; cerrar de golpe (*un libro*); dar una palmada, *Am.* palmear (*sobre la espalda*); **to — in jail** meter (*o* encajar) en la cárcel.
clap·per [klǽpɚ] *s.* badajo.
clar·i·fy [klǽrəfaɪ] *v.* aclarar.
clar·i·net [klærənɛ́t] *s.* clarinete.
clar·i·ty [klǽrətɪ] *s.* claridad, luz.
clash [klæʃ] *s.* choque, encontrón, colisión; (*fight*) riña, conflicto; estruendo; *v.* chocar; darse un encontrón; hacer crujir; oponerse, estar en conflicto.
clasp [klæsp] *s.* (*fastener*) broche; hebilla; cierre; traba; (*grip*) apretón, apretón de manos; *v.* abrochar; asir; agarrar; sujetar, asegurar; abrazar;

apretar (*la mano*).
class [klæs] *s.* clase; *v.* clasificar.
clas·sic [klǽsɪk] *adj.* & *s.* clásico; — **scholar** humanista, erudito clásico.
clas·si·cal [klǽsɪkḷ] *adj.* clásico.
clas·si·cism [klǽsɪsɪzm] *s.* clasicismo.
clas·si·fi·ca·tion [klæsəfəkéʃən] *s.* clasificación.
clas·si·fy [klǽsəfaɪ] *v.* clasificar.
class·mate [klǽsmet] *s.* compañero de clase, condiscípulo.
class·room [klǽsrum] *s.* clase, aula.
clat·ter [klǽrɚ] *s.* estrépito, boruca; traqueteo; bullicio; alboroto; *v.* hacer estrépito o boruca; traquetear; meter bulla o alboroto.
clause [klɔz] *s.* cláusula.
claw [klɔ] *s.* garra; zarpa; uña; (*crab*) pinza (*de langosta, cangrejo, etc.*); (*hammer*) orejas (*de un martillo*); (*scratch*) arañazo; *v.* desgarrar; aranar; rasgar.
claw·ing [klɔ́ɪŋ] *s.* zarpazo.
clay [kle] *s.* barro; arcilla, greda.
clean [klin] *adj.* limpio; puro; *adv.* limpiamente; **clean-cut** bien tallado, de buen talle, de buen parecer; *v.* limpiar; asear; desempañar; **to — up** limpiar(se), asear(se).
clean·er [klínɚ] *s.* limpiador; quitamanchas.
clean·li·ness [klɛ́nlɪnɪs] *s.* limpieza; aseo.
clean·ly [klɛ́nlɪ] *adj.* limpio; aseado; [klínlɪ] *adv.* limpiamente.
clean·ness [klínnɪs] *s.* limpieza; aseo.
cleanse [klɛnz] *v.* limpiar; asear; purificar, depurar.
cleans·er [klɛ́nzɚ] *s.* limpiador.
clear [klɪr] *adj.* (*evident*) claro; patente, manifiesto; (*clean*) límpido; despejado; (*free*) libre (*de culpa, estorbos, deudas, etc.*); — **profit** ganancia neta; **clear-cut** *adj.* bien delineado; clarividente; **to pass — through** atravesar, traspasar de lado a lado; **to be in the** — estar sin deudas; estar libre de culpa; *v.* aclarar(se); despejar(se); escampar; clarificar; quitar (*estorbos*); desmontar (*un terreno*); salvar, saltar por encima de; librar (*de culpa, deudas, etc.*); sacar (*una ganancia neta*); pasar (*un cheque*) por un banco de liquidación; liquidar (*una cuenta*); **to — the table** levantar la mesa; **to — up** aclarar(se).
clear·ance [klírəns] *s.* espacio (*libre entre dos objetos*); despacho de aduana; — **sale** saldo, venta (*de liquidación*), *Méx., C.A., Andes* barata.
clear·ing [klírɪŋ] *s.* aclaramiento; claro, terreno desmontado o desarbolado; liquidación de balances; — **house** banco de liquidación.
clear·ness [klírnɪs] *s.* claridad.
cleav·age [klívɪdʒ] *s.* hendedura.
cleave [kliv] *v.* hender(se); tajar; rajar, partir.
cleav·er [klívɚ] *s.* cuchilla o hacha (*de carnicero*).
clef [klɛf] *s.* clave (*en música*).
cleft [klɛft] *s.* grieta, hendedura; *adj.* hendido, partido, rajado; *pret.* & *p.p. de* **to cleave.**
clem·en·cy [klɛ́mənsɪ] *s.* clemencia.
clem·ent [klɛ́mənt] *adj.* clemente.
clench [klɛntʃ] *s.* agarro, agarrada, agarrón; apretón; *v.* agarrar, asir; apretar (*los dientes, el puño*).
cler·gy [klɝ́dʒɪ] *s.* clero.
cler·gy·man [klɝ́dʒɪmən] *s.* clérigo, eclesiástico, pastor, sacerdote.
cler·i·cal [klɛ́rɪkḷ] *adj.* (*clergy*) clerical, eclesiástico; (office) oficinesco, de oficina; de dependientes; — **error** error de pluma (de copista); — **work** trabajo de escritorio.
clerk [klɝk] *s.* dependiente; empleado (*de oficina*); escribiente; archivero (*de municipio*); **law** — escribano; *v.* estar de dependiente.
clev·er [klɛ́vɚ] *adj.* diestro, hábil; listo; talentoso; mañoso; **-ly** *adv.* hábilmente; con destreza; con maña.
clev·er·ness [klɛ́vɚnɪs] *s.* destreza, habilidad, maña; talento.
clew [klu] *s.* indicio (*que indica el camino para resolver un misterio o problema*).
cli·ché [kliʃé] *s.* (*plate*) clisé; *Am.* cliché; (*phrase*) cliché.
click [klɪk] *s.* golpecito; (*tongue*) chasquido (*de la lengua*); gatillazo (*sonido del gatillo de una pistola*); taconeo (*sonido de tacones*); *v.* sonar (*un pestillo, un broche, un gatillo, etc.*); chasquear (*la lengua*); **to — the heels** cuadrarse (*militarmente*); taconear.
cli·ent [kláɪənt] *s.* cliente.
cli·en·tele [klaɪəntɛ́l] *s.* clientela.
cliff [klɪf] *s.* risco, precipicio, peñasco, escarpa.
cli·mate [kláɪmɪt] *s.* clima.
cli·max [kláɪmæks] *s.* clímax, culminación; *v.* culminar; llegar al clímax.
climb [klaɪm] *s.* subida, ascenso; *v.* subir; trepar; encaramarse; **to — down** bajar a gatas; desprenderse (*de un árbol*).
climb·er [kláɪmɚ] *s.* trepador; enredadera, planta trepadora.
clime [klaɪm] *s.* clima.
clinch [klɪntʃ] *v.* remachar, redoblar (*un clavo*); (*assure*) afianzar, sujetar, asegurar bien; cerrar (*un trato*); abrazarse fuertemente; *s.* remache; abrazo; agarrón; **to be in a** — estar agarrados o abrazados.
cling [klɪŋ] *v.* pegarse, adherirse.
clin·ic [klínɪk] *s.* clínica.
clink [klɪŋk] *s.* tintín.
clip [klɪp] *s.* (*fastener*) broche, presilla; (*cutting*) tijeretada (*corte con tijeras*); trasquila, trasquiladura; **paper** — sujetapapeles; **to go at a good** — ir a paso rápido; andar de prisa; *v.* recortar; cortar; trasquilar (*el pelo o lana de los animales*); **to — together** sujetar.
clip·per [klípɚ] *s.* clíper (*velero o avión de gran velocidad*); trasquilador; recortador; **-s** tijeras; maquinilla (*para recortar el pelo*).
clip·ping [klípɪŋ] *s.* recorte.
cloak [klok] *s.* capa; manto; *v.* tapar, embozar, encubrir.
cloak·room [klókrum] *s.* guardarropa, vestuario.
clock [klɑk] *s.* reloj; **alarm** — despertador; *v.* marcar; cronometrar.
clock·wise [klɑ́kwaɪz] *adv.* en el sentido de las manecillas de reloj.
clock·work [klɑ́kwɝk] *s.* maquinaria de reloj; **like** — con precisión, puntualmente; sin dificultad.
clod [klɑd] *s.* terrón; tonto, necio.
clog [klɑg] *s.* estorbo, obstáculo; (*shoe*) zueco (*zapato de suela gruesa o de madera*); — **dance** zapateado; *v.* estorbar, embarazar; obstruir, atorar, tapar; obstruirse, atascarse, azolvarse (*Am.* enzolvarse), atorarse (*un caño, acequia, etc.*).
clois·ter [klɔ́ɪstɚ] *s.* claustro; monasterio; convento; *v.* enclaustrar.
close [kloz] *s.* fin, terminación, conclusión; cierre; *v.* cerrar(se); concluir; **to — an account** saldar una cuenta; **to — a meeting** levantar una sesión; **to — in upon** cercar, rodear; **to — out** liquidar, vender en liquidación.
close [klos] *adj.* (*near*) cercano, próximo; aproximado; íntimo; (*tight*) estrecho, ajustado; (*stingy*) cerrado; tacaño, mezquino; (*suffocating*) opresivo; sofocante; (*fought*) reñido; — **attention**

suma atención; — **questioning** interrogatorio detallado o minucioso; — **translation** traducción fiel; **at — range** de cerca; *adv.* cerca; **-ly** *adv.* aproximadamente; estrechamente; apretadamente; con sumo cuidado a atención; **closed shop** con sólo obreros sindicados.
closed cir·cuit [klozd sɝ́kət] *s. & adj.* circuito cerrado.
close·ness [klósnɪs] *s.* cercanía, proximidad; aproximación; (*confinement*) estrechez; (*friendship*) intimidad; (*stingyness*) tacañería, avaricia; mala ventilación, falta de aire; fidelidad (*de una traducción*).
clos·et [klɑ́zɪt] *s.* ropero; alacena, armario; (*toilet*) gabinete, retrete, excusado; *v.* encerrar en un cuarto (*para una entrevista secreta*); **to — oneself (themselves)** encerrarse.
clot [klɑt] *v.* coagular(se), cuajar(se); *s.* coágulo, cuajarón.
cloth [klɔθ] *s.* tela, paño, género; (*rag*) trapo; *adj.* de paño; — **binding** encuadernación en tela.
clothe [kloð] *v.* vestir; cubrir; revestir; investir.
clothes [kloz] *s. pl.* ropa; ropaje, vestidos; **suit of —** terno, traje, *Carib., Ven.* flux; — **line** tendedero; — **pin** pinzas, gancho (*para tender la ropa*).
cloth·ier [klóðjɚ] *s.* comerciante en ropa o paño; ropero, pañero.
cloth·ing [klóðɪŋ] *s.* ropa; ropaje, vestidos.
cloud [klaʊd] *s.* nube; **storm —** nubarrón; *v.* nublar(se), anublar(se); obscurecer; manchar.
cloud·burst [kláʊdbɚst] *s.* chaparrón, aguacero; chubasco.
cloud·less [kláʊdlɪs] *adj.* claro, despejado; sin nubes.
cloud·y [kláʊdɪ] *adj.* nublado; *Esp.* nuboso; sombrío.
clove [klov] *s.* clavo (*especia*); — **of garlic** diente de ajo.
clo·ven [klóvən] *adj.* hendido; *S. & adj.* — **hoof** patihendido, pie hendido.
clo·ver [klóvɚ] *s.* trébol; **to be in —** estar o vivir en la abundancia; sentirse próspero.
clo·ver·leaf [klóvɚlɪf] *s.* (*highway*) cruce en trébol.
clown [klɑʊn] *s.* payaso, bufón; *v.* payasear, bufonear, hacer el payaso.
cloy [klɔɪ] *v.* empalagar; hastiar.
club [klʌb] *s.* club, círculo; casino; (*stick*) garrote, porra; palo; (*cards*) basto (*de la baraja*); *v.* golpear, aporrear, apalear; **to — together** formar club; escotar, pagar la cuota que le toca a cada uno, *Am.* cotizar.
club·house [klʌ́bhaʊs] *s.* club, casino.
cluck [klʌk] *s.* cloqueo; *v.* cloquear.
clue = **clew.**
clump [klʌmp] *s.* terrón; pisada fuerte; — **of bushes** matorral; — **of trees** grupo de árboles, arboleda; *v.* apiñar, amontonar; **to — along** andar pesadamente.
clum·sy [klʌ́mzɪ] *adj.* torpe, desmañado; incómodo; difícil de manejar; mal hecho.
clung [klʌŋ] *pret. & p.p. de* **to cling.**
clus·ter [klʌ́stɚ] *s.* racimo; grupo; *v.* agrupar(se); arracimarse (*formar racimo*).
clutch [klʌtʃ] *s.* apretón fuerte; agarro, agarrón; (*auto*) embrague (*de automóvil*); **-es** garras; uñas; — **pedal** pedal del embrague; **to step on the —** pisar el embrague; desembragar, soltar el embrague; **to throw in the —** embragar; *v.* agarrar, asir; apretar.
clut·ter [klʌ́tɚ] *v.* obstruir; atestar (*de cosas*); poner en desorden; *s.* desorden, confusión.
coach [kotʃ] *s.* coche; (*sports*) entrenador (*en deportes*); maestro particular; *v.* aleccionar; guiar, adiestrar, *Am.* entrenar; **to — with** ser instruído o entrenado por.
coach·man [kótʃmən] *s.* cochero.
co·ag·u·late [koǽgjəlet] *v.* coagular(se), cuajar(se).
coal [kol] *s.* carbón; ascua, brasa; **hard—** carbón de piedra, antracita; **soft —** hulla; — **barge** lanchón carbonero; — **bin** carbonera; — **dealer** carbonero; — **oil** kerosina; — **tar** alquitrán de carbón; *v.* cargar de carbón, echar carbón; proveer(se) de carbón.
co·a·li·tion [koəlɪ́ʃən] *s.* coalición.
coarse [kors] *adj.* (*crude*) burdo, basto; tosco; áspero; (*rude*) rudo; grosero; vulgar; tosco; — **sand** arena gruesa.
coarse·ness [kórsnɪs] *s.* tosquedad; vulgaridad, grosería, rudeza.
coast [kost] *s.* costa, litoral; — **guard** guardacostas, guarda de costas; *v.* costear, navegar por la costa; deslizar(se), resbalar(se) cuesta abajo.
coast·al [kóstl̩] *adj.* costero, costanero, de la costa; — **traffic** cabotaje.
coast·line [kóstlaɪn] *s.* costa, litoral.
coat [kot] *s.* chaqueta, americana; *Am.* saco; (*animals*) lana, pelo (*de un animal*); **lady's —** abrigo de senora; — **hanger** colgador; — **of arms** escudo de armas; — **of paint** capa de pintura; *v.* cubrir; revestir, dar una mano (*de pintura*); **to — with sugar** azucarar, bañar en azúcar.
coat·ing [kótɪŋ] *s.* capa.
coat·tail [kóttel] *s.* faldón.
coax [koks] *v.* rogar o persuadir con halagos, halagar, tentar.
cob [kɑb] *s.* (*corn*) carozo, zuro (*de la mazorca del maíz*), *Ven., Col., Carib.* tusa, *Méx., C.A.* elote; *Andes* marlo.
co·balt [kóbɔlt] *s.* cobalto.
cob·bler [kɑ́blɚ] *s.* remendón (*zapatero*); budin de bizcocho y fruta.
cob·ble·stone [kɑ́bl̩ston] *s.* guijarro; *adj.* empedrado.
cob·web [kɑ́bwɛb] *s.* telaraña.
co·caine [kokén] *s.* cocaína.
cock [kɑk] *s.* gallo; macho de ave; (*faucet*) espita, grifo; *Méx.* bidoque; martillo (*de armas de fuego*); — **sure** muy seguro de sí mismo; *v.* amartillar (*un arma de fuego*); ladear (*la cabeza*), ladearse (*el sombrero*).
cock·fight [kɑ́kfaɪt] *s.* pelea de gallos, riña de gallos.
cock·pit [kɑ́kpɪt] *s.* galera; (*airplane*) cabina.
cock·roach [kɑ́krotʃ] *s.* cucaracha.
cock·tail [kɑ́ktel] *s.* coctel; aperitivo (*de ostras, almejas, frutas, etc.*),
cock·y [kɑ́kɪ] *adj.* arrogante, *Ríopl.* retobado.
co·coa [kóko] *s.* cacao; bebida de cacao, chocolate.
co·co·nut [kókənət] *s.* coco (*fruta*).
co·coon [kəkún] *s.* capullo (*del gusano de seda, etc.*).
cod [kɑd] *s. N. Esp.* abadejo; *Andalucía, Am.* bacalao; **cod-liver oil** aceite de hígado de bacalao.
cod·dle [kɑ́dl̩] *v.* mimar, consentir.
code [kod] *s.* código; clave; — **message** comunicación en clave; **signal —** código de señales.
co·dex [kódɛks] *s.* codice.
cod·fish [kɑ́dfɪʃ] = **cod.**
co·erce [koɝ́s] *v.* forzar, obligar.
co·er·cion [koɝ́ʃən] *s.* coacción.
co·ex·is·tence [koɛgzɪ́stəns] *s.* coexistencia.
cof·fee [kɔ́fɪ] *s.* café; — **shop** café; — **tree** cafeto — **bean** grano de café; **black —** café solo; *Col.* tinto.
cof·fee·pot [kɔ́fɪpɑt] *s.* cafetera.
cof·fer [kɔ́fɚ] *s.* cofre, arca.

cof·fin [kɔ́fɪn] *s.* ataúd, féretro.
cog [kɑg] *s.* diente; — **wheel** rueda dentada.
cog·nate [kɑ́gnet] *s.* cognato.
co·her·ent [kohírənt] *adj.* coherente; conexo.
co·he·sion [kohíʒən] *s.* cohesión.
coif·fure [kwɑfjúr] *s.* tocado, peinado.
coil [kɔɪl] *s.* rollo; rosca; espiral de alambre; **electric** — bobina; *v.* arrollar(se), enrollar(se); enroscar(se).
coin [kɔɪn] *s.* moneda; *v.* acuñar; (*make up*) inventar, forjar (*una frase o palabra*).
coin·age [kɔ́ɪnɪdʒ] *s.* acuñación; sistema monetario; moneda, monedas; invención (*de una palabra o frase*).
co·in·cide [koɪnsáɪd] *v.* coincidir.
co·in·ci·dence [koínsədəns] *s.* coincidencia; casualidad.
coke [kok] *s.* cok, coque (*combustible*).
cold [kold] *adj.* frío; — **cream** crema cosmética; — **meat** fiambre; — **storage almacenaje refrigerado, frigorífico;** — **wave** ola de frío; — **war** guerra fría; **to be** — tener frío; **it is** — **today** hace frío hoy; *s.* frío; catarro, resfriado; **to catch a** — resfriarse, acatarrarse.
cold·ness [kóldnɪs] *s.* frialdad; indiferencia, despego.
col·ic [kɑ́lɪk] *s.* cólico.
col·lab·o·rate [kəlǽbəret] *v.* colaborar.
col·lab·o·ra·tion [kəlæbəréʃən] *s.* colaboración.
col·lapse [kəlǽps] *s.* desplome, derrumbe, derrumbamiento; hundimiento; (*person*) postración; *v.* doblar(se), plegar(se); contraer (*el volumen*); hundirse, derrumbarse, desplomarse; sufrir una postración.
col·lar [kɑ́lɚ] *s.* collar; cuello (*de vestido, camisa, etc.*); collera (*para mulas o caballos de tiro*); *v.* acollarar, poner collar a; coger o agarrar por el cuello; prender.
col·late [kəlét, kólet] *v.* cotejar; colacionar.
col·lat·er·al [kəlǽtərəl] *adj.* colateral; auxiliar, subsidiario, accesorio; *s.* garantía (*para un préstamo bancario*).
col·league [kɑ́lig] *s.* colega.
col·lect [kəlékt] *v.* recoger; coleccionar; (*money*) cobrar; (*taxes*) recaudar (*impuestos*); reunir(se); congregarse; **to** — **oneself** calmarse; sosegarse, reportarse; — **on delivery** (C.O.D.) contra reembolso; **collectable** cobradero.
col·lec·tion [kəlɛkjən] *s.* colección; agrupación (*de gente*); recolección, cobranza, cobro, recaudación, colecta.
col·lec·tive [kəléktɪv] *adj.* colectivo; — **bargaining** contrato (convenio) colectivo.
col·lec·tiv·ism [kəléktəvɪzm] *s.* colectivismo.
col·lec·tor [kəlɛktɚ] *s.* colector; coleccionista (*de sellos, objetos artísticos, etc.*); cobrador (*de billetes, deudas, etc.*) recaudador (*de impuestos*).
col·lege [kɑ́lɪdʒ] *s.* universidad; — **of engineering** facultad de ingeniería; — **of medicine** escuela (*facultad*) de medicina.
col·lide [kəláɪd] *v.* chocar; estar en conflicto, oponerse.
col·lie [kɑ́lɪ] *s.* perro de pastor.
col·li·sion [kəlíʒən] *s.* choque, colisión; oposición, pugna (*de intereses, ideas, etc.*).
col·lo·qui·al [kəlókwɪəl] *adj.* familiar; — **expression** locución o frase familiar.
col·lu·sion [kəlúʒɪən] *s.* confabulación.
co·lon [kólən] *s.* colon (*del intestino*); dos puntos (*signo de puntuación*).
colo·nel [ɝ́nl] *s.* coronel.
co·lo·ni·al [kəlónɪəl] *adj.* colonial.
col·o·nist [kɑ́lənɪst] *s.* colono, colonizador.
col·o·ni·za·tion [kɑlənəzéʃən] *s.* colonización.
col·o·nize [kɑ́lənaɪz] *v.* colonizar; establecerse en colonia.
col·o·ny [kɑ́lənɪ] *s.* colonia.
col·or [kʌ́ɚ] *s.* color; colorido; **the -s** la bandera; *v.* colorar; colorear; dar colorido; pintar; teñir; iluminar (*una fotografía, grabado, etc.*); ruborizarse.
col·ored [kʌ́lɚd] *adj.* colorado, teñido, colorido, pintado; de color; coloreado; — **person** persona de color.
col·or·ful [kʌ́lɚfəl] *adj.* lleno de color; colorido; vistoso; vívido; pintoresco.
col·or·ing [kʌ́lərɪŋ] *s.* colorido; coloración; colorante.
col·or·less [kʌ́lɚlɪs] *adj.* incoloro; descolorido.
co·los·sal [kəlɑ́sl̩] *adj.* colosal.
colt [kolt] *s.* potro.
Co·lum·bi·an [kəlʌ́mbɪən] *adj.* colombiano, de Colombia; colombino, referente a Cristóbal Colón.
col·umn [kɑ́lən] *s.* columna; — **inch** pulgada de columna.
co·ma [kómə] *s.* coma.
comb [kom] *s.* peine; peineta (*de mujer*); cresta (*de gallo*); rastrillo, carda (*para lana*); almohaza (*para caballos*); panal (*de miel*); *v.* peinar; rastrillar, cardar (*lana*); escudriñar; **to** — **one's hair** peinarse.
com·bat [kɑ́mbæt] *s.* combate, pelea; *v.* combatir.
com·bat·ant [kɑ́mbətənt] *adj. & s.* combatiente.
com·bi·na·tion [kɑmbənéʃən] *s.* combinación.
com·bine [kəmbáɪn] *v.* combinar(se), unir(se).
com·bo [kɑ́mbo] *s.* batería de jazz.
com·bus·ti·ble [kəmbʌ́stəbl̩] *adj. & s.* combustible.
com·bus·tion [kəmbʌ́stʃən] *s.* combustión.
come [kʌm] *v.* venir; llegar; provenir; **to** — **about** suceder; efectuarse, verificarse; **to** — **again** volver, volver a venir; **to** — **back** volver, regresar; **to** — **downstairs** bajar; **to** — **in** entrar; **to** — **out** salir; **to** — **of age** llegar a mayor edad; **to** — **off** soltarse, zafarse; **to** — **to** volver en sí; **to** — **to terms** ponerse de acuerdo, ajustarse; **to** — **up** subir; surgir (*una cuestión*); *p.p. de* **to come.**
co·me·di·an [kəmídɪən] *s.* cómico, comediante.
com·e·dy [kɑ́mədɪ] *s.* comedia.
come·ly [kʌ́mlɪ] *adj.* agradable a la vista, gentil, bien parecido.
com·et [kɑ́mɪt] *s.* cometa
com·fort [kʌ́mfɚt] *s.* comodidad; bienestar; alivio, consuelo; *v.* consolar, confortar, aliviar.
com·fort·a·ble [kʌ́mfɚtəbl̩] *adj.* cómodo; confortable; — **life** vida holgada; — **income** un buen pasar, renta suficiente; **comfortably** *adv.* cómodamente; con comodidad; holgadamente.
com·fort·er [kʌ́mfɚtɚ] *s.* consolador; edredón, cobertor acolchado.
com·fort·less [kʌ́mfɚtlɪs] *adj.* incómodo; desconsolado.
com·ic [kɑ́mɪk] *adj.* cómico; chistoso, gracioso; **-s** *s. pl.* caricaturas, historietas cómicas.
com·i·cal [kɑ́mɪkl̩] *adj.* cómico, gracioso.
com·ing [kʌ́mɪŋ] *adj.* que viene, que llega; próximo; venidero; *s.* venida, llegada; — **of Christ** advenimiento de Cristo.
com·ma [kɑ́mə] *s.* coma.
com·mand [kəmǽnd] *s.* (*order*) mando; mandato, orden; mandamiento; (*post*) comandancia; (*dominance*) dominio; (*computer*) comando, mandato; **at your** — a la orden de Vd., a la disposición de Vd.; **he has a good** — **of English** domina bien el inglés; *v.* mandar; ordenar;

dominar; comandar; **to — respect** inspirar respeto, imponerse.
com·mand·er [kəmǽndɚ] *s.* jefe; comandante; teniente de navío; comendador (*de ciertas órdenes*); **— in chief** comandante en jefe; general en jefe.
com·mand·ment [kəmǽndmənt] *s.* mandamiento; mandato, orden.
com·man·do [kəmǽndo] *s.* comando.
com·mem·o·rate [kəmɛ́məret] *v.* conmemorar.
com·mence [kəmɛ́ns] *v.* comenzar.
com·mence·ment [kəmɛ́nsmənt] *s.* comienzo, principio; acto de distribución de diplomas.
com·mend [kəmɛ́nd] *v.* alabar, elogiar; encomendar, encargar; recomendar.
com·men·da·tion [kɑməndéʃən] *s.* encomio, alabanza.
com·ment [kɑ́mɛnt] *s.* comentario, observación, nota; *v.* comentar; hacer observaciones; hacer comentarios.
com·men·tar·y [kɑ́məntɛrɪ] *s.* comentario.
com·men·ta·tor [kɑ́məntetɚ] *s.* comentador; comentarista; **radio —** comentarista radial.
com·merce [kɑ́mɚs] *s.* comercio.
com·mer·cial [kəmɝ́ʃəl] *adj.* comercial; (*advertising*) anuncio en radio o televisión; **commercialize** comercializar ocasiones no comerciales.
com·mis·er·a·tion [kəmɪzəréʃən] *s.* compasión.
com·mis·sar [kɑ́mɪsar] *s.* comisario.
com·mis·sar·y [kɑ́məsɛrɪ] *s.* comisario.
com·mis·sion [kəmɪ́ʃən] *s.* comisión; (*charge*) encargo; junta; (*title*) nombramiento; **to put out of —** inutilizar; descomponer, quebrar; retirar del servicio (*un navío*); *v.* comisionar; encargar; nombrar; poner en servicio (*un navío*); **-ed officer** oficial comisionado (*alférez u oficial superior a éste*).
com·mis·sion·er [kəmɪ́ʃənɚ] *s.* comisionado; comisario; **police —** comisario de policía.
com·mit [kəmɪ́t] *v.* (*perpetrate*) cometer; (*entrust*) encargar; **to — to memory** aprender de memoria; **to — to prison** encarcelar; **to — oneself** dar o expresar su opinión, expresarse abiertamente, comprometerse.
com·mit·tee [kəmɪ́tɪ] *s.* comité; comisión, junta; **— of one** comisionado o delegado único.
com·mod·i·ty [kəmɑ́dətɪ] *s.* mercancía; género, mercadería, artículo de consumo, producto.
com·mon [kɑ́mən] *adj.* común; general; corriente; vulgar, ordinario; público; **— law** derecho consuetudinario; **— sense** sentido común; **— soldier** soldado raso; **— market** mercado común; **-s** *s. pl.* refectorio (*de un colegio o universidad*); ejido, campo común; **-ly** *adv.* comúnmente, por lo común.
com·mon·ness [kɑ́mənnɪs] *s.* vulgaridad, ordinariez; frecuencia.
com·mon·place [kɑ́mənples] *adj.* común, trivial; *s.* lugar común.
com·mon·wealth [kɑ́mənwɛlθ] *s.* estado; república; pueblo, colectividad.
com·mo·tion [kəmóʃən] *s.* conmoción; tumulto; bullicio; levantamiento.
com·mune [kəmjún] *v.* comunicarse (con); comulgar.
com·mu·ni·cate [kəmjúnəket] *v.* comunicar(se); transmitir.
com·mu·ni·ca·tion [kəmjunəkéʃən] *s.* comunicación.
com·mu·ni·ca·tive [kəmjúnəketɪv] *adj.* comunicativo.
com·mun·ion [kəmjúnjən] *s.* comunión.
com·mu·nism [kɑ́mjʊnɪzəm] *s.* comunismo.
com·mu·nist [kɑ́mjʊnɪst] *s. & adj.* comunista.
com·mu·ni·ty [kəmjúnətɪ] *s.* comunidad; sociedad; vecindario, barrio; **— chest** caja de beneficencia, fondos de beneficencia.
com·mute [kəmjút] *v.* conmutar; viajar diario de una población a otra.
com·pact [kəmpǽkt] *adj.* compacto; denso; apretado; conciso; sucinto; [kɑ́mpækt] *s.* pacto, trato, convenio; polvera.
com·pact·ness [kəmpǽktnɪs] *s.* solidez; densidad; concisión.
com·pan·ion [kəmpǽnjən] *s.* compañero; acompañante.
com·pan·ion·ship [kəmpǽnjənʃɪp] *s.* compañerismo, camaradería; compañía.
com·pa·ny [kʌ́mpənɪ] *s.* compañía; sociedad; visita; **ship's —** tripulación; **to keep — with** acompañar a; cortejar a; tener relaciones con, frecuentar la compañía de.
com·pa·ra·ble [kɑ́mpərəbl] *adj.* comparable.
com·par·a·tive [kəmpǽrətɪv] *adj.* comparativo.
com·pare [kəmpɛ́r] *v.* comparar; cotejar; confrontar; contrastar; **beyond —** incomparable, sin par, sin igual, sin comparación.
com·par·i·son [kəmpǽrəsn̩] *s.* comparación; símil; **beyond —** incomparable, sin comparación; **in — with** comparado con.
com·part·ment [kəmpɑ́rtmənt] *s.* compartimiento, sección, división; departamento.
com·pass [kʌ́mpəs] *s.* compás (*para dibujar*); brújula; área, ámbito; alcance.
com·pas·sion [kəmpǽʃən] *s.* compasión, lástima.
com·pas·sion·ate [kəmpǽʃənɪt] *adj.* compasivo, misericordioso.
com·pa·tri·ot [kəmpétrɪət] *s.* compatriota.
com·pel [kəmpɛ́l] *v.* compeler, obligar; exigir.
com·pen·sate [kɑ́mpənset] *v.* compensar; recompensar; remunerar.
com·pen·sa·tion [kɑmpənséʃən] *s.* compensación; recompensa; remuneración.
com·pete [kəmpít] *v.* competir.
com·pe·tence [kɑ́mpətəns] *s.* competencia, aptitud, capacidad.
com·pe·tent [kɑ́mpətənt] *adj.* competente; calificado; capaz.
com·pe·ti·tion [kɑmpətɪ́ʃən] *s.* competencia; concurso, certamen; contienda; **cutthroat —** competencia asesina (implacable).
com·pet·i·tive [kəmpɛ́tətɪv] *adj.* en competencia, **— examination** oposición, concurso.
com·pet·i·tor [kəmpɛ́tətɚ] *s.* competidor; rival; opositor.
com·pile [kəmpáɪl] *v.* compilar, recopilar.
com·pil·er [kəmpáɪlɚ] *s.* (*computer*) compilador.
com·pla·cen·cy [kəmplésn̩sɪ] *s.* complacencia, contentamiento.
com·pla·cent [kəmplésn̩t] *adj.* complaciente, satisfecho.
com·plain [kəmplén] *v.* quejarse; querellarse.
com·plain·ant [kəmplénənt] *s.* querellante.
com·plaint [kəmplént] *s.* queja; quejido, lamento; dolencia, enfermedad; **to lodge a —** hacer una reclamación.
com·ple·ment [kɑ́mpləmənt] *s.* complemento; [kɑ́mpləmɛnt] *v.* complementar, completar.
com·plete [kəmplít] *adj.* completo; *v.* completar; terminar; **-ly** *adv.* completamente, por completo.
com·plete·ness [kəmplítnɪs] *s.* perfección; minuciosidad; lo completo; lo cabal; lo acabado.
com·ple·tion [kəmplíʃən] *s.* completamiento; terminación, conclusión; cumplimiento.
com·plex [kɑ́mplɛks] *s.* complejo; [kəmplɛ́ks] *adj.*

complejo; compuesto; complicado.
com·plex·ion [kəmplɛ́kʃən] *s.* (*skin*) cutis, tez; (*make-up*) aspecto.
com·plex·i·ty [kəmplɛ́ksətɪ] *s.* complejidad.
com·pli·ance [kəmpláɪəns] *s.* complacencia; condescendencia; conformidad; cumplimiento; **in — with** en conformidad con; de acuerdo con, conforme a.
com·pli·cate [kámpləket] *v.* complicar.
com·pli·cat·ed [kámpləketɪd] *adj.* complicado.
com·pli·ca·tion [kampləkéʃən] *s.* complicación.
com·plic·i·ty [kəmplísətɪ] *s.* complicidad.
com·pli·ment [kámpləmənt] *s.* cumplido, cumplimiento; (*flattery*) requiebro, lisonja, galantería; **to send one's -s** enviar saludos; [kámpləmɛnt] *v.* cumplimentar; requebrar; lisonjear; alabar.
com·ply [kəmpláɪ] *v.* consentir, conformarse (con), obrar de acuerdo (con); cumplir (con).
com·po·nent [kəmpónənt] *adj.* & *s.* componente.
com·pose [kəmpóz] *v.* componer; **to — oneself** sosegarse, serenarse, calmarse.
com·posed [kəmpózd] *adj.* compuesto; tranquilo, sereno, sosegado; **to be — of** estar compuesto de, componerse de, constar de.
com·pos·er [kəmpózɚ] *s.* compositor; autor.
com·pos·ite [kəmpázɪt] *adj.* compuesto; *s.* compuesto; mezcla.
com·po·si·tion [kampəzíʃən] *s.* composición; arreglo; compuesto.
com·po·sure [kəmpóʒɚ] *s.* compostura, calma, serenidad.
com·pound [kámpaʊnd] *adj.* & *s.* compuesto; [kampáʊnd] *v.* componer; mezclar, combinar; **to — interest** calcular el interés compuesto.
com·pre·hend [kamprɪhɛ́nd] *v.* comprender; abarcar, abrazar, incluir.
com·pre·hen·si·ble [kamprɪhɛ́nsəbl̩] *adj.* comprensible, inteligible.
com·pre·hen·sion [kamprɪhɛ́nʃən] *s.* comprensión.
com·pre·hen·sive [kamprɪhɛ́nsɪv] *adj.* comprensivo; inclusivo.
com·press [kámprɛs] *s.* compresa; [kəmprɛ́s] *v.* comprimir, apretar, condensar.
com·pres·sion [kəmprɛ́ʃən] *s.* compresión.
com·prise [kəmpráɪz] *v.* comprender, abarcar, incluir, abrazar; constar de.
com·pro·mise [kámprəmaɪz] *s.* compromiso; arreglo; avenencia; término medio; *v.* comprometer; avenirse, transigir; *Am.* transar.
comp·trol·ler [kəntrólɚ] *s.* interventor, *Am.* contralor.
com·pul·sion [kəmpʌ́læən] *s.* compulsión, coacción.
com·pul·so·ry [kəmpʌ́lsərɪ] *adj.* obligatorio.
com·pu·ta·tion [kampjətéʃən] *s.* cómputo, cálculo.
com·pute [kəmpjút] *v.* computar.
com·put·er [kəmpjútɚ] *s.* computadora; *Esp.* ordenador; — **science** informática.
com·put·er·ize [kəmpjútɚaɪz] *v.* informatizar, computarizar; suplir con sistema computador.
com·rade [kámræd] *s.* camarada, compañero.
con·cave [kankév] *adj.* cóncavo.
con·ceal [kənsíl] *v.* encubrir, ocultar, esconder.
con·ceal·ment [kənsílmənt] *s.* encubrimiento.
con·cede [kənsíd] *v.* conceder; otorgar; admitir, reconocer.
con·ceit [kənsít] *s.* presunción, amor propio, vanagloria; concepto, agudeza.
con·ceit·ed [kənsitɪd] *adj.* presuntuoso, presumido, vanidoso, engreído.
con·ceiv·a·ble [kənsívəbl̩] *adj.* concebible, imaginable, comprensible.
con·ceive [kənsív] *v.* concebir; imaginar.
con·cen·trate [kánsn̩tret] *v.* concentrar(se), reconcentrar(se).
con·cen·tra·tion [kansn̩tréʃən] *s.* concentración; reconcentración; — **camp** reconcentración de presos.
con·cept [kánsɛpt] *s.* concepto, idea; opinión.
con·cep·tion [kənsɛ́pʃən] *s.* concepción; concepto, idea
con·cern [kənsɝ́n] *s.* (*business*) compañia, negociación; negocio; establecimiento mercantil; (*interest*) cuidado; interés; preocupación; **to be of no —** no ser de consecuencia; *v.* concernir, importar, interesar; preocupar; **in all that -s him** en cuanto le atañe, en cuanto le concierne; **to whom it may —** a quien corresponda.
con·cerned [kənsɝ́nd] *adj.* interesado; preocupado, (*restless*) intranquilo, inquieto, ansioso; **to be — about** interesarse por, preocuparse por; **as far as I am —** por lo que me concierne, por lo que me toca, en cuanto a mí me atañe.
con·cern·ing [kənsɝ́nɪŋ] *prep.* tocante a, respecto a, acerca de.
con·cert [kánsɝt] *s.* concierto; [kənsɝ́t] *v.* concertar, arreglar (*un plan*).
con·ces·sion [kənsɝ́ʃən] *s.* concesión.
con·cil·i·ate [kənsílɪet] *v.* conciliar, poner en armonía; ganar la voluntad de.
con·cise [kənsáɪs] *adj.* conciso, sucinto.
con·cise·ness [kənsáɪsnɪs] *s.* concisión, brevedad.
con·clude [kənklúd] *v.* concluir; acabar, terminar; deducir; decidir.
con·clu·sion [kənklúʒən] *s.* conclusión.
con·clu·sive [kənklúsɪv] *adj.* conclusivo, concluyente.
con·coct [kankákt] *v.* confeccionar; preparar (*combinando diversos ingredientes*); inventar, urdir.
con·coc·tion [kankákʃən] *s.* cocimiento, menjurje; mezcla.
con·cord [kánkɔrd] *s.* concordia, conformidad, acuerdo; convenio, pacto.
con·crete [kankrít] *adj.* concreto; de hormigón, de cemento; *s.* hormigón, cemento, *Am.* concreto.
con·cu·bine [káŋkjubaɪn] *s.* concubina.
con·cur [kənkɝ́] *v.* estar de acuerdo, ser del mismo parecer; unirse.
con·cus·sion [kənkʌ́ʃən] *s.* concusión.
con·demn [kəndɛ́m] *v.* condenar; **to — a building** condenar un edificio.
con·dem·na·tion [kandɛmnéʃən] *s.* condenación.
con·den·sa·tion [kandɛnséʃən] *s.* condensación; resumen, compendio.
con·dense [kəndɛ́ns] *v.* condensar(se).
con·de·scend [kandɪsɛ́nd] *v.* condescender.
con·de·scen·sion [kandɪsɛ́nʃən] *s.* condescendencia.
con·di·ment [kándəmənt] *s.* condimento.
con·di·tion [kəndíʃən] *s.* condición; estado; nota o calificación provisional; **on — that** a condición de que, con tal que; *v.* acondicionar; poner en buena condición; estipular; reprobar provisionalmente (*a un estudiante*).
con·di·tion·al [kəndíʃənl̩] *adj.* condicional.
con·dole [kəndól] *v.* condolerse; **to — with** dar el pésame a; consolar a.
con·do·lence [kəndóləns] *s.* pésame.
con·do·min·i·um [kandəmínɪəm] *s.* condominio.
con·done [kəndón] *v.* dispensar; perdonar; condonar.
con·duce [kəndjús] *v.* conducir.
con·du·cive [kəndjúsɪv] *adj.* conducente.
con·duct [kándʌkt] *s.* (*behavior*) conducta;

comportamiento, proceder; (*handling*) dirección, manejo; [kəndʌ́kt] *v*. conducir; dirigir; manejar; **to — oneself well** portarse bien.
con·duc·tor [kəndʌktə] *s*. conductor; guía; **orchestra —** director de orquesta; **train —** revisor; cobrador, *Am*. conductor.
con·duit [kɑ́nduɪt] *s*. conducto; caño; cañeria, tubería.
cone [kon] *s*. cono; **paper —** cucurucho; **pine —** piña.
con·fec·tion [kənfɛ́kʃən] *s*. confección; confitura; confite, dulce.
con·fec·tion·er·y [kənfɛ́kʃənɛrɪ] *s*. confitería; dulcería; confites, dulces.
con·fed·er·a·cy [kənfɛ́dərəsɪ] *s*. confederación.
con·fed·er·ate [kənfɛ́dərɪt] *adj*. & *s*. confederado; [kənfɛ́dəret] *v*. confederar(se).
con·fed·er·a·tion [kənfɛdəréʃən] *s*. confederación.
con·fer [kənfɝ́] *v*. conferir, conceder; conferenciar, consultar.
con·fer·ence [kɑ́nfərəns] *s*. convención; congreso; (*meeting*) consulta, junta, sesión.
con·fess [kənfɛ́s] *v*. confesar(se); reconocer, admitir.
con·fes·sion [kənfɛ́ʃən] *s*. confesión.
con·fes·sion·al [kənfɛ́ʃənl̩] *s*. confesionario.
con·fes·sor [kənfɛ́sə] *s*. confesor.
con·fi·dant [kɑnfədǽnt] *s*. confidente.
con·fide [kənfáɪd] *v*. confiar; fiar.
con·fi·dence [kɑ́nfədəns] *s*. confianza; confidencia; **— game** estafa; **— man** estafador.
con·fi·dent [kɑ́nfədənt] *adj*. confiado; seguro, cierto; **-ly** *adv*. confiadamente, con toda seguridad.
con·fi·den·tial [kɑnfədɛ́nʃəl] *adj*. confidencial; íntimo; secreto; **-ly** *adv*. en confianza.
con·fine [kɑ́nfaɪn] *s*. confín; [kənfáɪn] *v*. confinar; encerrar; **to — oneself to** limitarse a; **to be -ed in bed** estar encamado, guardar cama.
con·fine·ment [kənfáɪnmənt] *s*. encerramiento; encierro; prisión, encarcelación.
con·firm [kənfɝ́m] *v*. confirmar.
con·fir·ma·tion [kɑnfəméʃən] *s*. confirmación.
con·fis·cate [kɑ́nfɪsket] *v*. confiscar.
con·fla·gra·tion [kɑnfləgréʃən] *s*. conflagración, incendio.
con·flict [kɑ́nflɪkt] *s*. conflicto, oposición, choque; (*fight*) lucha, combate; [kənflɪ́kt] *v*. chocar, oponerse, estar en conflicto.
con·form [kənfɔ́rm] *v*. conformar(se).
con·form·i·ty [kənfɔ́rmətɪ] *s*. conformidad.
con·found [kɑnfáʊnd] *v*. confundir, perturbar, desconcertar, aturdir; **— it!** ¡caramba!
con·front [kənfrʌ́nt] *v*. confrontar; carear, poner cara a cara (*a dos reos*); encararse con, afrontar, hacer frente a, arrostrar.
con·fuse [kənfjúz] *v*. confundir; trastornar; embrollar; desconcertar.
con·fused [kənfjúzd] *adj*. confuso; revuelto; desconcertado, perplejo; **to become —** confundirse; desconcertarse.
con·fus·ing [kənfjúzɪŋ] *adj*. confuso, revuelto; desconcertante.
con·fu·sion [kənfjúʒən] *s*. confusión; desorden; tumulto; perplejidad.
con·geal [kəndʒíl] *v*. congelar(se), helar(se), cuajar(se).
con·gen·ial [kəndʒínjəl] *adj*. congenial; simpático; **to be — with** congeniar con, simpatizar con.
con·ges·tion [kəndʒɛ́stʃən] *s*. congestión; aglomeración.
con·glom·er·a·tion [kənglɑməréʃən] *s*. aglomeración.
con·grat·u·late [kəngrǽtʃəlet] *v*. congratular, felicitar, dar el parabién
con·grat·u·la·tion [kəngrætʃəléʃən] *s*. congratulación, felicitación, parabién, enhorabuena.
con·gre·gate [kɑ́ŋgrɪget] *v*. congregar(se), juntar(se), reunir(se).
con·gre·ga·tion [kɑŋgrɪgéʃən] *s*. congregación; asamblea, reunión; colección, agregado; fieles, feligreses (*de una iglesia*).
con·gress [kɑ́ŋgrəs] *s*. congreso; asamblea.
con·gres·sion·al [kəngrɛ́ʃənl̩] *adj*. perteneciente al congreso.
con·gress·man [kɑ́ŋgrəsmən] *s*. congresista, diputado, representante.
con·ic [kɑ́nɪk] *adj*. cónico.
con·jec·ture [kəndʒɛ́ktʃə] *s*. conjetura, suposición; *v*. conjeturar, suponer.
con·ju·gate [kɑ́ndʒəget] *v*. conjugar.
con·ju·ga·tion [kɑndʒəgéʃən] *s*. conjugación.
con·junc·tion [kəndʒʌ́ŋkʃən] *s*. conjunción.
con·jure [kɑ́ndʒə] *v*. conjurar; **to — up** evocar; [kəndʒʊ́r] rogar, implorar.
con·nect [kənɛ́kt] *v*. conectar; unir(se), juntar(se); enlazar(se); relacionar(se); acoplar.
con·nec·ting rod [kənɛ́ktɪŋ rad] *s*. biela.
con·nec·tion [kənɛ́kʃən] *s*. conexión; enlace; vínculo; unión; relación; **-s** parientes; amigos, amistades.
con·nip·tion [kənɪ́pʃən] *s*. pataleta; **to have a —** darle a uno una pataleta.
con·nive [kənáɪv] *v*. conspirar; disimular; hacerse cómplice.
con·nois·seur [kɑnəsɝ́] *s*. conocedor, perito.
con·quer [kɑ́ŋkə] *v*. conquistar; vencer.
con·quer·or [kɑ́ŋkərə] *s*. conquistador; vencedor.
con·quest [kɑ́ŋkwɛst] *s*. conquista.
con·science [kɑ́nʃəns] *s*. conciencia.
con·sci·en·tious [kɑnʃɪɛ́nʃəs] *adj*. concienzudo.
con·scious [kɑ́nʃəs] *adj*. consciente; sabedor; **-ly** *adv*. conscientemente; a sabiendas.
con·scious·ness [kɑ́nʃəsnɪs] *s*. conciencia, estado conciente; **to lose —** perder el sentido o conocimiento.
con·script [kənskrɪ́pt] *v*. reclutar; [kɑ́nskrɪpt] *s*. recluta
con·se·crate [kɑ́nsɪkret] *v*. consagrar; dedicar.
con·se·cra·tion [kɑnsɪkréʃən] *s*. consagración; dedicación.
con·sec·u·tive [kənsɛ́kjətɪv] *adj*. consecutivo.
con·sen·sus [kənsɛ́nsəs] *s*. consenso.
con·sent [kənsɛ́nt] *s*. consentimiento; permiso, asentimiento; autorización; *v*. consentir; permitir, asentir.
con·se·quence [kɑ́nsəkwɛns] *s*. consecuencia.
con·se·quent [kɑ́nsəkwɛnt] *adj*. consecuente; consiguiente; *s*. consecuente, consiguiente, consecuencia; **-ly** *adv*. por consiguiente, por consecuencia.
con·se·quen·tial [kɑnsəkwɛ́ntʃl̩] *adj*. de consecuencia.
con·ser·va·tion [kɑnsəvéʃən] *s*. conservación; preservación.
con·ser·va·tive [kənsɝ́vətɪv] *adj*. conservador; conservativo; *s*. conservador.
con·ser·va·to·ry [kənsɝ́vətorɪ] *s*. conservatorio; invernadero.
con·serve [kɑ́nsɝv] *s*. conserva, dulce; *v*. [kənsɝ́v] conservar; preservar.
con·sid·er [kənsɪ́də] *v*. considerar.
con·sid·er·a·ble [kənsɪ́dərəbl̩] *adj*. considerable; cuantioso; **considerably** *adv*. considerablemente; **considerable older** bastante más viejo.
con·sid·er·ate [kənsɪ́dərɪt] *adj*. considerado.

con·sid·er·a·tion [kənsɪdəréʃən] *s.* (*respect*) respeto; consideración; importancia; (*pay*) remuneración; **in — of** en atención a, teniendo en cuenta, en razón de, en vista de.
con·sid·er·ing [kənsídərɪŋ] *prep.* en razón de, en vista de; en atención a, en consideración de.
con·sign [kənsáɪn] *v.* consignar; enviar; entregar.
con·sign·ee [kənsaɪní] *s.* consignatario.
con·sign·ment [kənsáɪnmənt] *s.* consignación.
con·sist [kənsíst] *v.* consistir (en); constar (de).
con·sis·ten·cy [kənsístənsɪ] *s.* consecuencia; consistencia, firmeza, solidez.
con·sis·tent [kənsístənt] *adj.* consecuente, lógico; compatible; consistente, coherente.
con·so·la·tion [kɑnsəléʃən] *s.* consolación; consuelo.
con·sole [kənsól] *v.* consolar.
con·sol·i·date [kənsɑ́lədet] *v.* consolidar(se); unir(se), combinar(se).
con·so·nant [kɑ́nsənənt] *adj.* consonante; conforme; *s.* consonante.
con·sort [kɑ́nsɔrt] *s.* consorte; [kənsɔ́rt] *v.* **to — with** asociarse con.
con·spic·u·ous [kənspíkjʊəs] *adj.* conspicuo, notorio; manifiesto, sobresaliente.
con·spir·a·cy [kənspírəsɪ] *s.* conspiración, conjuración.
con·spir·a·tor [kənspírətə˞] *s.* conspirador, conjurado.
con·spire [kənspáɪr] *v.* conspirar; tramar, maquinar.
con·sta·ble [kɑ́nstəbl̩] *s.* alguacil, policía; condestable (*título*).
con·stan·cy [kɑ́nstənsɪ] *s.* constancia.
con·stant [kɑ́nstənt] *adj.* constante; *s.* constante, cantidad constante; **-ly** *adv.* constantemente, contínuamente, siempre; a menudo.
con·stel·la·tion [kɑnstəleʃən] *s.* constelación.
con·ster·na·tion [kɑnstə˞néʃən] *s.* consternación.
con·sti·pate [kɑ́nstəpet] *v.* estreñir
con·sti·pa·tion [kɑnstəpéʃən] *s.* estreñimiento.
con·stit·u·ent [kənstítʃʊənt] *adj.* constituyente; constitutivo; componente; *s.* componente, elemento; elector, votante.
con·sti·tute [kɑ́nstətjut] *v.* constituir; componer; establecer.
con·sti·tu·tion [kɑnstətjúʃən] *s.* constitución.
con·sti·tu·tion·al [kɑstətjúʃənl̩] *adj.* constitucional; *s.* paseo a pie, caminata (*para hacer ejercicio*).
con·strain [kənstrén] *v.* constreñir; obligar, forzar; apretar, comprimir.
con·strict [kənstríkt] *v.* apretar; estrechar.
con·struct [kənstrʌ́kt] *v.* construir, fabricar.
con·struc·tion [kənstrʌ́ktʃən] *s.* construcción; estructura; interpretación.
con·struc·tive [kənstrʌ́ktɪv] *adj.* constructivo; de utilidad positiva; provechoso.
con·strue [kənstrú] *v.* interpretar, explicar.
con·sul [kɑ́nsl̩] *s.* cónsul.
con·su·late [kɑ́nslɪt] *s.* consulado.
con·sult [kənsʌ́lt] *v.* consultar.
con·sult·ant [kənsʌ́ltənt] *s.* consultante.
con·sul·ta·tion [kɑnsl̩téʃən] *s.* consulta.
con·sume [kənsúm] *v.* consumir; gastar; perder (*el tiempo*).
con·sum·er [kənsúmə˞] *s.* consumidor; **— market** mercado de consumo.
con·sum·mate [kɑ́nsəmet] *v.* consumar, completar; llevar a cabo; [kənsʌ́mɪt] *adj.* consumado, perfecto, completo.
con·sump·tion [kənsʌ́mpʃən] *s.* consumo, gasto; consunción; tisis, tuberculosis.
con·sump·tive [kənsʌ́mptɪv] *adj.* tísico.
con·tact [kɑ́ntækt] *s.* contacto; *v.* tocar; poner(se) en contacto con; estar en contacto con.
con·ta·gion [kəntédʒən] *s.* contagio.
con·ta·gious [kəntédʒəs] *adj.* contagioso.
con·tain [kəntén] *v.* contener; encerrar; tener cabida para; reprimir, refrenar; **to — oneself** contenerse, refrenarse.
con·tain·er [kənténə˞] *s.* envase, caja, recipiente.
con·tam·i·nate [kəntǽmənet] *v.* contaminar, viciar, inficionar, infectar.
con·tam·i·na·tion [kəntæmənéʃən] *s.* contaminación; cruce.
con·tem·plate [kɑ́ntəmplet] *v.* contemplar; meditar; tener la intención de; proyectar.
con·tem·pla·tion [kɑntəmpléʃən] *s.* contemplación; meditación; intención, propósito.
con·tem·po·rar·y [kəntέmpərɛrɪ] *adj.* contemporáneo; coetáneo.
con·tempt [kəntέmpt] *s.* desdén, menosprecio; desprecio; **— of court** contumacia.
con·tempt·i·ble [kəntέmptəbl̩] *adj.* despreciable, vil.
con·temp·tu·ous [kəntέmptʃʊəs] *adj.* desdeñoso.
con·tend [kəntέnd] *v.* contender; competir; argüir; altercar; sostener, afirmar.
con·tent [kɑ́ntɛnt] *s.* contenido; sustancia; capacidad, volumen; **-s** contenido; **table of -s** tabla de materias, índice general.
con·tent [kəntέnt] *adj.* contento; satisfecho; *s.* contento; satisfacción; **to one's heart's —** a pedir de boca; hasta saciarse; a su entera satisfacción; *v.* contentar; satisfacer.
con·tent·ed [kəntέntɪd] *adj.* contento, satisfecho.
con·ten·tion [kəntέnʃən] *s.* contención, contienda, disputa, controversia; tema, argumento; aseveración.
con·tent·ment [kəntέntmənt] *s.* contentamiento, contento.
con·test [kɑ́ntɛst] *s.* concurso, certamen; debate; contienda; torneo; [kəntέst] *v.* contender; disputar; luchar por; **to — with** competir con.
con·text [kɑ́ntɛkst] *s.* contexto.
con·tig·u·ous [kəntígjʊəs] *adj.* contiguo; adyacente.
con·ti·nent [kɑ́ntənənt] *s.* continente; *adj.* continente, casto, moderado.
con·ti·nen·tal [kɑntənέntl̩] *adj. & s.* continental.
con·tin·gen·cy [kəntíndʒənsɪ] *s.* contingencia, eventualidad.
con·tin·gent [kəntíndʒənt] *adj. & s.* contingente.
con·tin·u·al [kəntínjʊəl] *adj.* contínuo; frecuente; **-ly** *adv.* de continuo, continuamente, frecuentemente.
con·tin·u·ance [kəntínjʊəns] *s.* continuación; aplazamiento.
con·tin·u·a·tion [kəntɪnjʊéʃən] *s.* continuación.
con·tin·ue [kəntínju] *v.* continuar.
con·ti·nu·i·ty [kɑntənúətɪ] *s.* continuidad.
con·tin·u·ous [kəntínjʊəs] *adj.* continuo, sin parar, sin cesar.
con·tor·tion [kəntɔ́rʃən] *s.* contorsión.
con·tour [kɑ́ntʊr] *s.* contorno; perímetro.
con·tra·band [kɑ́ntrəbænd] *s.* contrabando.
con·tract [kɑ́ntrækt] *s.* contrato, pacto, convenio; contrata; **marriage —** esponsales; [kəntrǽkt] *v.* contratar; contraer(se), encoger(se); **to — an illness** contraer una enfermedad; **to — the brows** fruncir las cejas.
con·trac·tion [kəntrǽkʃən] *s.* contracción.
con·trac·tor [kəntrǽktə˞] *s.* contratista.
con·tra·dict [kɑtrədíkt] *v.* contradecir; contrariar.
con·tra·dic·tion [kɑntrədíkʃən] *s.* contradicción; contrariedad.
con·tra·dic·to·ry [kɑntrədíktərɪ] *adj.* contradictorio; opuesto, contrario.

con·tra·ry [kántrɛrɪ] *adj.* contrario; opuesto; testarudo, obstinado; *s.* contrario; **on the** — al contrario.
con·trast [kántræst] *s.* contraste; [kəntrǽst] *v.* contrastar.
con·tra·vene [kɑntrəvín] *v.* contravenir a; oponerse a.
con·trib·ute [kəntríbjUt] *v.* contribuir.
con·tri·bu·tion [kɑntrəbjúʃən] *s.* contribución; aportación; cuota; dádiva.
con·trib·u·tor [kəntríbjətə˞] *s.* contribuidor; colaborador.
con·trib·u·to·ry [kəntríbjutorɪ] *adj.* contribuidor.
con·trite [kántraɪt] *adj.* contrito.
con·tri·vance [kəntráɪvəns] *s.* (*plan*) traza, maquinación; artificio, invención; designio; artefacto, aparato, máquina.
con·trive [kəntráɪv] *v.* tramar, maquinar; inventar, idear; proyectar; **to** — **to** buscar el medio de, tratar de, procurar.
con·trol [kəntról] *s.* (*authority*) mando, manejo; dirección; (*instrument*) freno, regulador; restricción; *Am.* control; **-s** mandos, controles; — **stick** palanca (*de un aeroplano*); — **tower** torre de mando; — **experiment** experimento controlado; — **key** tecla de control; **to lose** — **of one's temper** perder la paciencia; *v.* gobernar, manejar; (*computer*) gestionar; *Am.* controlar; regular, regularizar; restringir; contener, reprimir; tener a raya; **to** — **oneself** contenerse dominarse.
con·trol·ler [kəntrólə˞] *s.* interventor, registrador, *Ríopl., C.A., Andes, Ven., Col.* contralor, *Ch., Méx.* controlador; regulador; aparato de manejo y control.
con·tro·ver·sy [kántrəvɝsɪ] *s.* controversia, debate, disputa; polémica.
co·nun·drum [kənʌ́ndrəm] *s.* adivinanza, acertijo.
con·va·lesce [kɑnvəlɛ́s] *v.* convalescer.
con·vene [kənvín] *v.* juntar, convocar; reunirse.
con·ven·ience [kənvínjəns] *s.* conveniencia, comodidad; **at one's** — cuando le convenga a uno, cuando tenga oportunidad, cuando buenamente pueda.
con·ven·ient [kənvínjənt] *adj.* conveniente; oportuno; cómodo; a propósito; **-ly** *adv.* convenientemente, cómodamente.
con·vent [kánvɛnt] *s.* convento.
con·ven·tion [kənvɛ́nʃən] *s.* convención; congreso, asamblea; convenio; costumbre, regla.
con·ven·tion·al [kənvɛ́nʃənl̩] *adj.* convencional; tradicional.
con·ven·tion·eer [kənvɛnʃənír] *s.* congresista.
con·verge [kənvɝ́dʒ] *v.* converger o convergir.
con·ver·sant [kánvə˞sn̩t] *adj.*: — **with** versado en.
con·ver·sa·tion [kɑnvə˞séʃən] *s.* conversación.
con·verse [kənvɝ́s] *v.* conversar, hablar, platicar.
con·ver·sion [kənvɝ́ʒən] *s.* conversión.
con·vert [kánvɝt] *s.* converso, persona convertida; catecúmeno (*converso reciente*); [kənvɝ́t] *v.* convertir(se).
con·vex [kɑnvɛ́ks] *adj.* convexo.
con·vey [kənvé] *v.* llevar; transportar; transferir, traspasar; transmitir; comunicar; **to** — **thanks** expresar agradecimiento, dar las gracias.
con·vey·ance [kənvéəns] *s.* vehículo; transporte; (*transfer*) transmisión; entrega; comunicación; traspaso; escritura de propiedad o traspaso.
con·vey·er [kənvéə˞] *s.* correa de transmisión.
con·vict [kánvɪkt] *s.* presidiario; reo; [kənvíkt] *v.* convencer (*de un delito*), declarar culpable; probar la culpabilidad de.
con·vic·tion [kənvíkʃən] *s.* convicción; convencimiento; prueba de culpabilidad.
con·vince [kənvíns] *v.* convencer.
con·vinc·ing [kənvínsɪŋ] *adj.* convincente.
con·vo·ca·tion [kɑnvəkéʃən] *s.* convocación; asamblea
con·voke [kənvók] *v.* convocar.
con·voy [kánvɔɪ] *s.* convoy, escolta, guardia; [kənvɔ́ɪ] *v.* convoyar.
con·vulse [kənvʌ́ls] *v.* crispar; agitar; convulsionar.
con·vul·sion [kənvʌ́lʃən] *s.* convulsión, agitación.
coo [ku] *s.* arrullo; *v.* arrullar.
cook [kUk] *s.* cocinero, cocinera; *v.* cocinar, guisar; cocer; **to** — **up a plan** urdir un plan.
cook·er·y [kÚkərɪ] *s.* cocina, arte de cocinar.
cook·ie, cook·y [kÚkɪ] *s.* bizcochito, bollito.
cook·ing [kÚkɪŋ] *s.* cocina, arte culinaria; — **stove** cocina de gas, cocina eléctrica, estufa; — **utensils** batería de cocina, trastos de cocina.
cool [kul] *adj.* (*weather*) fresco; (*indifferent*) frío, indiferente; (*calm*) calmo, sereno; *s.* fresco, frescura; *v.* refrescar; enfriar; templar, calmar; **to** — **off** enfriarse; calmarse; **cooling-off period** tregua para evitar huelga.
cool·ant [kúlənt] *s.* líquido refrigerador.
cool·ness [kúlnɪs] *s.* fresco, frescura; frialdad, indiferencia.
coon [kun] s. coatí (*cuadrúpedo carnívoro*); **a -'s age** una eternidad, mucho tiempo.
coop [kup] *s.* jaula; **chicken** — gallinero; *v.* enjaular; **to** — **up** encerrar.
co·op·er·ate [koápəret] *v.* cooperar.
co·op·er·a·tion [koɑpəréʃən] *s.* cooperación.
co·op·er·a·tive [koápəretɪv] *adj.* cooperativo; *s.* cooperativa, sociedad cooperativa.
co·or·di·nate [koɔ́rdn̩et] *v.* coordinar; [koɔ́rdn̩ɪt] *adj.* coordinado.
co·or·di·na·tion [koɔrdn̩éʃən] *s.* coordinación.
cop [kɑp] *s.* polizonte, policía.
cope [kop] *v.* **to** — **with** tener suficiente fuerza para; **I cannot** — **with this** no puedo con esto, no puedo dar abasto a esto.
co·pi·ous [kópɪəs] *adj.* copioso, abundante.
cop·per [kápə˞] *s.* cobre; (*cop*) polizonte, policía; — **coin** moneda de cobre, centavo; — **kettle** marmita o caldera de cobre; *adj.* cobrizo.
cop·y [kápɪ] *s.* copia; ejemplar (*de un libro*); manuscrito (*para el impresor*); *v.* copiar; imitar; remedar; **make fair copy** poner en limpio.
cop·y·right [kápɪraɪt] *s.* derecho de propiedad literaria; derechos de autor; *v.* registrar, obtener patente de propiedad literaria.
co·quette [kokɛ́t] *s.* coqueta.
cor·al [kɔ́rəl] *s.* coral; *adj.* coralino, de coral; — **reef** arrecife de coral.
cord [kɔrd] *s.* cuerda; cordón, cordel; cuerda (*medida de leña*); tendón; **-s** pantalones de pana; **spinal** — espinazo, espina dorsal.
cor·dial [kɔ́rdʒəl] *adj. & s.* cordial.
cor·du·roy [kɔrdərɔ́ɪ] *s.* pana; **-s** pantalones de pana; — **road** camino de troncos o maderos.
core [kor] *s.* corazón, centro; núcleo; esencia; *v.* cortar el centro o corazón de; despepitar (*una manzana*).
cork [kɔrk] *s.* corcho; tapón; — **tree** alcornoque; *v.* tapar con corcho.
cork·screw [kɔ́rkskru] *s.* tirabuzón, sacacorchos; *adj.* espiral, de forma espiral.
corn [kɔrn] *s.* maíz; grano, cereal; callo (*de los pies o manos*); — **bread** pan de maiz; — **meal** harina de maíz; — **cob** *Esp.* zuro; *Ven., Col. C.A. Méx.* elote; tusa; *v.* salar, curar, acecinar.
corned beef [kɔ́rnd bif] *s.* carne de vaca curada;

acecino.
cor·ner [kɔ́rnɚ] *s.* (*interior*) rincón; rinconada; ángulo; (*exterior*) esquina; ángulo; (*monopoly*) monopolio; — **stone** piedra angular; — **table** (— **shelf,** — **bracket**) rinconera; *v.* arrinconar; acorralar; acaparar, monopolizar.
cor·net [kɔrnɛ́t] *s.* corneta.
corn·field [kɔ́rnfild] *s.* maizal, *Méx., C.A.* milpa.
cor·nice [kɔ́rnɪs] *s.* cornisa.
cor·ol·lar·y [kɔ́rəlɛrɪ] *s.* corolario; consecuencia natural.
cor·o·na·tion [kɔrənéʃən] *s.* coronación.
cor·o·ner [kɔ́rənɚ] *s.* juez de guardia.
cor·o·net [kɔ́rənɪt] *s.* coronilla, guirnalda.
cor·po·ral [kɔ́rpərəl] *adj.* corporal; corpóreo; *s.* cabo (*militar*).
cor·po·ra·tion [kɔrpəréʃən] *s.* corporación; sociedad mercantil.
corps [kor] *s.* cuerpo (*grupo organizado*); **air** — cuerpo de aviación; **army** — cuerpo de ejército.
corpse [kɔrps] *s.* cadáver.
cor·pu·lent [kɔ́rpjələnt] *adj.* corpulento.
cor·pus·cle [kɔ́rpəsl̩] *s.* corpúsculo; glóbulo.
cor·ral [kərǽl] *s.* corral; *v.* acorralar.
cor·rect [kɔrɛ́kt] *v.* corregir; *adj.* correcto; **it is** — está bien; **-ly** *adv.* correctamente; **-ly done** bien hecho.
cor·rec·tion [kərɛ́kʃən] *s.* corrección.
cor·rect·ness [kərɛ́ktnɪs] *s.* corrección.
cor·rec·tor [kərɛ́ktɚ] *s.* corregidor, corrector.
cor·re·late [kɔ́rəlet] *v.* correlacionar.
cor·re·spond [kɔrəspɑ́nd] *v.* corresponder; corresponderse, cartearse, escribirse.
cor·re·spon·dence [kɔrəspɑ́ndəns] *s.* correspondencia.
cor·re·spon·dent [kɔrəspɑ́ndənt] *adj.* correspondiente; *s.* correspondiente; corresponsal.
cor·re·spond·ing [kɔrəspɑ́ndɪŋ] *adj.* correspondiente; conforme.
cor·ri·dor [kɔ́rədɚ] *s.* corredor, pasillo, pasadizo.
cor·rob·o·rate [kərɑ́bəret] *v.* corroborar.
cor·rode [kəród] *v.* corroer(se).
cor·ru·gat·ed i·ron [kɔ́rəgetəd aɪɚn] *s.* hierro acanalado.
cor·rupt [kərʌ́pt] *adj.* corrupto; perverso, depravado; **to become** — corromperse; *v.* corromper; pervertir; sobornar.
cor·rup·tion [kərʌ́pʃən] *s.* corrupción; soborno; descomposición.
cor·set [kɔ́rsɪt] *s.* corsé.
cor·ti·sone [kɔ́rtəzon] *s.* cortisona.
cos·met·ic [kɑzmɛ́tɪk] *adj. & s.* cosmético.
cos·mic [kɑ́zmɪk] *adj.* cósmico.
cos·mo·naut [kɑ́zmənɔt] *s.* cosmonauta.
cos·mo·pol·i·tan [kɑzməpɑ́lətn̩] *adj.* cosmopolita.
cost [kɔst] *s.* coste, costa o costo; **at all -s** a toda costa; **to sell at** — vender al costo; *v.* costar; *pret. & p.p. de* **to cost.**
cost·ly [kɔ́stlɪ] *adj.* costoso.
cos·tume [kɑ́stjum] *s.* vestuario, traje, vestido; atavío; indumentaria.
cot [kɑt] *s.* catre; **folding** — catre de tijera.
cot·tage [kɑ́tɪdʒ] *s.* casita, caseta; casa de campo; — **cheese** requesón.
cot·ter pin [kɑ́tɚ pɪn] *s.* chaveta.
cot·ton [kɑtn̩] *s.* algodón; — **seed** semilla de algodón; — **wool** algodón en rama; — **yarn** hilaza.
couch [kaʊtʃ] *s.* canapé, diván; *v.* expresar; estar escondido o en acecho; **-ed in difficult language** expresado en lenguaje difícil.
cough [kɔf] *s.* tos; — **drop** pastilla para la tos; **whooping** — tos ferina; *v.* toser; **to** — **up** expectorar.
could [kʊd] *pret. del. v. defect.* **can.**
coun·cil [káʊnsl̩] *s.* concilio; concejo; **city** — concejo muncipal.
coun·cil·man [káʊnsl̩mən] *s.* concejal.
coun·cil·or [káʊnsl̩ɚ] *s.* concejal.
coun·sel [káʊnsl̩] *s.* (*advice*) consejo; parecer, dictamen; (*lawyer*) abogado consultor; *v.* aconsejar; recomendar.
coun·sel·or [káʊnsl̩ɚ] *s.* consejero; abogado consultor.
count [kaʊnt] *s.* (*reckoning*) cuenta, cálculo; cómputo; (*charge*) cargo, acusación; (*noble*) conde; *v.* contar; valer, tener importancia; **to** — **on** contar con, confiar en.
count·down [káʊntdaʊn] *s.* recuento descendiente hasta cero.
coun·te·nance [káʊntənəns] *s.* semblante, aspecto; **to give** — **to** favorecer, apoyar; aprobar; *v.* aprobar; favorecer, apoyar; tolerar.
count·er [káʊntɚ] *s.* contador; mostrador; tablero; (*chip*) ficha; *adj.* contrario, opuesto; *adv.* al contrario; **to run** — **to** ser contrario a, oponerse a; *v.* oponerse; contradecir; **to** — **a blow** devolver un golpe.
coun·ter·act [kaʊntɚǽkt] *v.* contrarrestar, neutralizar.
coun·ter·at·tack [kaʊntɚətæk] *s.* contraataque.
coun·ter·bal·ance [kaʊntɚbǽləns] *v.* contrapesar; equilibrar; [káʊntɚbæləns] *s.* contrapeso.
coun·ter·feit [káʊntɚfɪt] *s.* falsificación; *adj.* falso; falsificado, falseado; contrahecho; — **money** moneda falsa; *v.* contrahacer, falsificar, falsear.
coun·ter·mand [káʊntɚmænd] *s.* contraorden, contramando, revocación, canceleción; [káʊntɚmǽnd] *v.* contramandar, revocar, cancelar.
coun·ter·part [káʊntɚpɑrt] *s.* contraparte.
coun·ter·poise [káʊntɚpɔɪz] *s.* contrapeso; *v.* contrapesar.
coun·ter·rev·o·lu·tion [kaʊntɚrɛvəlúʃən] *s.* contrarrevolución.
coun·ter·sign [káʊntɚsaɪn] *s.* contraseña; *v.* visar, refrendar.
count·ess [káʊntɪs] *s.* condesa.
count·less [káʊntlɪs] *adj.* incontable, innumerable.
coun·try [kʌ́ntrɪ] *s.* (*nation*) país; (*land*) tierra; (*homeland*) patria; (*field*) campo; *adj.* campestre; rural; rústico; campesino.
coun·try·man [kʌ́ntrɪmən] *s.* compatriota, paisano; (*rural type*) campesino, *Méx., C.A.* ranchero, *P.R.* jíbaro; *Cuba* guajiro; *Ch.* huaso; *Arg.* gaucho; *Ec., Col.* paisa.
coun·try·side [kʌ́ntrɪsaɪd] *s.* campiña, campo.
coun·ty [káʊntɪ] *s.* condado (*división de un estado*).
coup d'é·tat [ku detɑ́] *s.* golpe de estado; cuartelazo.
cou·pé [kupé, kup] *s.* cupé.
cou·ple [kʌ́pl̩] *s.* par; pareja; *v.* parear; unir; acoplar.
cou·plet [kʌ́plɪt] *s.* copla, versos pareados.
coup·ling [kʌ́plɪŋ] *s.* unión, conexión; acoplamiento; enganche.
cou·pon [kúpɑn] *s.* cupón; talón.
cour·age [kɝ́ɪdʒ] *s.* coraje, ánimo, valor.
cou·ra·geous [kərédʒəs] *adj.* valeroso, valiente, animoso.
cou·ri·er [kʊ́rɪɚ] *s.* mensajero.
course [kors] *s.* (*way*) curso; rumbo, trayecto; (*advance*) marcha, progreso; (*mode*) método; (*study*) asignatura; (*dish*) plato (*de una comida*); — **of conduct** conducta, proceder; **golf** — campo o cancha de golf; **race** — hipódromo, pista; **in the** — **of a year** en el transcurso de un año; **of** —

claro, por supuesto; **to follow a straight** — seguir una línea recta.
court [kort] *s*. (*house*) patio; (*city*) plazuela, plazoleta; (*justice*) juzgado, tribunal de justicia; corte; **tennis** — cancha para tenis; — **plaster** tela adhesiva, tafetán inglés, esparadrapo; **to pay** — **to** hacer la corte a, cortejar, galantear; *v*. cortejar; galantear; buscar; **to** — **danger** exponerse al peligro.
cour·te·ous [kɝ́tɪəs] *adj*. cortés.
cour·te·sy [kɝ́təsɪ] *s*. cortesía; fineza, atención; reverencia.
court·i·er [kórtɪɚ] *s*. cortesano, palaciego.
court·mar·tial [kórtmɑrʃəl] *s*. consejo de guerra; *v*. someter a consejo de guerra.
court·ship [kórtʃɪp] *s*. cortejo, galanteo.
court·yard [kórtjɑrd] *s*. patio.
cous·in [kʌ́zn̩] *s*. primo; prima; **first** — primo hermano, primo carnal.
cove [kov] *s*. cala, ensenada
cov·e·nant [kʌ́ənənt] *s*. convenio, pacto; contrato.
cov·er [kʌ́vɚ] *s*. (*lid*) cubierta, tapa, tapadera; (*blanket*) cobija; cobertor; (*binding*) encuadernación; envoltura; (*pillow*) funda; (*shelter*) albergue, abrido; **table** — tapete; — **charge** precio fijo que se agrega a la cuenta por servicios; **to send under separate** — enviar por separado; *v*. cubrir; tapar; encubrir; abrigar, proteger; abarcar; **to** — **a distance** recorrer una distancia.
cov·er·age [kʌ́vərɪdʒ] *s*. alcance; amplitud; (*journalism*) reportaje.
cov·er·ing [kʌ́vrɪŋ] *s*. cubierta; cobertura; envoltura; cobija, abrigo.
cov·et [kʌ́vɪt] *v*. codiciar; ambicionar.
cov·et·ous [kʌ́ɪtəs] *adj*. codicioso.
cow [kaʊ] *s*. vaca; hembra (*de elefante y otros cuadrúpedos*); *v*. atemorizar, acobardar.
cow·ard [káʊɚd] *adj*. & *s*. cobarde.
cow·ard·ice [káʊɚdɪs] *s*. cobardía.
cow·ard·li·ness [káʊɚdlɪnɪs] *s*. cobardía.
cow·ard·ly [káʊɚdlɪ] *adj*. cobarde; *adv*. cobardemente.
cow·boy [káʊbɔɪ] *s*. vaquero, *Ríopl*. resero, gaucho; *Ven*., *Col*. llanero.
cow·er [káʊɚ] *v*. agacharse (*de miedo o vergüenza*), achicarse, encogerse (*de miedo*), acobardarse.
cow·hide [káʊhaɪd] *s*. cuero de vaca, vaqueta.
cowl [kaʊl] *s*. capucha.
cox·swain [kɑ́ksən] *s*. timonel.
coy [kɔɪ] *adj*. recatado, esquivo, modesto; tímido; gazmoño.
coy·o·te [káɪot, kaɪótɪ] *s*. coyote.
co·zy [kózɪ] *adj*. cómodo y abrigado; cómodo y agradable.
CPU (Central Processing Unit) *s*. (*computer*) UCP (unidad central de proceso).
crab [kræb] *s*. cangrejo; (*person*) cascarrabias; — **apple** manzana silvestre.
crack [kræk] *s*. (*space*) raja, grieta, rendija; (*sound*) crujido; estallido; trueno, estampido; (*blow*) golpe; (*joke*) pulla, chanza; **at the** — **of dawn** al romper el alba; *adj*. excelente; *v*. rajar(se), hender(se), agrietarse; crujir; estallar; **to** — **a joke** soltar un chiste; **to** — **nuts** cascar nueces.
crack·down [krǽkdaʊn] *s*. reprensión severa.
cracked [krækt] *adj*. agrietado, rajado; quebrado; chiflado, loco.
crack·er [krǽkɚ] *s*. galleta.
crack·le [krǽkl̩] *s*. crujido; crepitación; chasquido; *v*. crujir, crepitar.
crack·pot [krǽkpat] *s*. eccéntrico.
cra·dle [krédl̩] *s*. cuna.
craft [kræft] *s*. (*skill*) maña, destreza; astucia, artificio, cautela; (*occupation*) arte, oficio; (*boat*) embarcación; embarcaciones.
crafts·man [krǽftsmən] *s*. artesano, artífice.
craft·y [krǽftɪ] *adj*. mañoso, astuto, cauteloso, taimado.
crag [kræg] *s*. risco, peñasco.
cram [kræm] *v*. rellenar; atestar; atracar(se), hartar(se); engullir.
cramp [kræmp] *s*. calambre; grapa; *v*. comprimir, apretar, estrechar; afianzar, sujetar (*con grapa*).
cran·ber·ry [krǽnbɛrɪ] *s*. arándano.
crane [kren] *s*. grulla (*ave*); grúa (*máquina para levantar pesos*); *v*. **to** — **one's neck** estirar el cuella.
cra·ni·um [krénɪəm] *s*. cráneo.
crank [kræŋk] *s*. cigüeña, manubrio, manija, manivela; **he is a** — es un maniático; *v*. voltear el manubrio o la cigüeña.
crank·case [krǽŋkes] *s*. cárter del motor.
crank·shaft [krǽŋkʃæft] *s*. cigüeñal.
crank·y [krǽŋkɪ] *adj*. cascarrabias; maniático; enojadizo.
cran·ny [krǽnɪ] *s*. grieta, rendija.
crape [krep] *s*. crespón; crespón negro.
crash [kræʃ] *s*. (*noise*) estallido, golpazo, estruendo; (*collision*) choque; (*failure*) fracaso; quiebra; bancarrota; — **landing** aterrizaje violento; aterrizaje de barriga; — **program** programa de urgencia; *v*. estrellar(se); estallar; chocar; **to** — **an airplane** aterrizar de golpe un aeroplano; **to** — **into** chocar con, estrellarse contra.
crate [kret] *s*. canasto, cesta, jaula (*para el transporte de mercancías, etc*.); *Am*. huacal; *v*. embalar en jaula.
cra·ter [krétɚ] *s*. cráter.
cra·vat [krəvǽt] *s*. corbata.
crave [krev] *v*. ansiar, anhelar, apetecer; **to** — **mercy (pardon)** pedir misericordia (perdón).
crawl [krɔl] *s*. marcha lenta; natación a la marinera; *v*. arrastrarse; gatear, andar a gatas; marchar lentamente; **to be -ing with ants** hormiguear, estar lleno de hormigas.
cray·on [kréən] *s*. lápiz de color, *Am*. creyón; pastel; tiza, yeso.
craze [krez] *s*. manía, locura; (*vogue*) moda; antojo; *v*. enloquecer.
cra·zy [krézɪ] *adj*. loco; trastornado; **to go** — volverse loco, perder el juicio.
creak [krik] *s*. crujido, rechino, rechinamiento; *v*. crujir, rechinar.
cream [krim] *s*. crema; nata; — **of tomato soup** sopa de tomate; **cold** — crema cosmética; **ice** — helado; *v*. desnatar; batir, mezclar (*azúcar y mantequilla*); preparar (*legumbres*) con salsa blanca.
cream·er·y [krímərɪ] *s*. lechería, quesería, *Am*. mantequillería.
cream·y [krímɪ] *adj*. natoso; cremoso.
crease [kris] *s*. pliegue; arruga; *v*. plegar, hacer pliegues; arrugar.
cre·ate [krɪét] *v*. crear.
cre·a·tion [krɪéʃ;ən] *s*. creación; obra.
cre·a·tive [krɪétɪv] *adj*. creativo, creador.
cre·a·tor [krɪétɚ] *s*. creador.
crea·ture [krítʃɚ] *s*. criatura; ser viviente; animalejo.
cre·dence [krídn̩s] *s*. creencia, crédito.
cre·den·tials [krɪdénʃ;əlz] *s*. *pl*. credenciales.
cred·i·ble [kréd;əbl̩] *adj*. creíble.
cred·it [krédɪt] *s*. crédito; buena fama; — **and debit**

haber y deber; activo y pasivo; — **card** tarjeta de crédito; **on** — a crédito, al fiado, a plazo; **to give** — dar crédito, creer; acreditar, abonar; **that does him** — eso le acredita; — **line** línea de crédito; — **underwriters** aseguradores de crédito; *v.*, acreditar; abonar en cuenta; creer, dar credito atribuir.

cred·it·a·ble [krɛ́dɪtəbl̩] *adj.* loable.

cred·i·tor [krɛ́dɪtɚ] *s.* acreedor.

cred·u·lous [krɛ́dʒələs] *adj.* crédulo.

creed [krid] *s.* credo; creencia.

creek [krik, krɪk] *s.* riachuelo, arroyo; *Col.* quebrada; *Ven.* caño; *Cuba* cañada.

creep [krip] *v.* arrastrarse; gatear, andar a gatas; trepar (*las plantas*); andar lentamente; deslizarse; sentir hormigueo (*en el cuerpo*); *s. pl.* hormigueo; aprensión, horror.

creep·er [krípɚ] *s.* enredadera, planta trepadora.

cre·mate [krímet] *v.* incinerar.

Cre·ole [kríol] *s.* criollo; descendiente de los franceses de Luisiana; persona de sangre mestiza.

cre·o·sote [kriəsot] *s.* creosota.

crepe [krep] = **crape.**

crept [krɛpt] *pret. & p.p. de* **to creep.**

cres·cent [krɛ́sn̩t] *adj.* creciente; *s.* luna creciente; media luna (*emblema de turcos y mahometanos*).

crest [krɛst] *s.* cresta; penacho; copete; cima, cumbre; timbre (*de un escudo de armas*).

crest·fall·en [krɛ́stfɔlən] *adj.* cabizbajo, alicaído, abatido.

cre·tonne [krɪtɑ́n] *s.* cretona.

crev·ice [krɛ́vɪs] *s.* grieta, hendedura.

crew [kru] *s.* tripulación; cuadrilla (*de obreros*); *pret. de* **to crow.**

crib [krɪb] *s.* camita de niño; pesebre; (*grain*) granero, arcón; (*construction*) armazón (*usado en la construcción de edificios*); traducción o clave fraudulenta (*en un examen*); *v.* enjaular; usar traducción o clave fraudulenta (*en un examen*).

crick·et [kríkɪt] *s.* grillo; vilorta (*juego*).

crime [kraɪm] *s.* crímen.

crim·i·nal [krímənl̩] *adj. & s.* criminal.

crimp [krɪmp] *v.* rizar; *s.* rizo.

crim·son [krímzn̩] *adj. & s.* carmesí.

cringe [krɪndʒ] *v.* encogerse; arrastrarse.

crip·ple [krípl̩] *s.* cojo, manco; tullido, baldado, inválido; *v.* estropear; mutilar, derrengar; baldar; incapacitar.

cri·sis [kráɪsɪs] *s.* crisis.

crisp [krɪsp] *adj.* (*brittle*) quebradizo; tieso; bien tostado; (*curly*) crespo, encrespado; — **answer** contestación aguda; — **wind** brisa refrescante; *v.* encrespar.

cri·te·ri·on [kraɪtírɪən] *s.* criterio.

crit·ic [krítɪk] *s.* crítico; criticón.

crit·i·cal [krítɪkl̩] *adj.* crítico; criticador, criticón.

crit·i·cism [krítəsɪzəm] *s.* crítica; criticismo.

crit·i·cize [krítəsaɪz] *v.* criticar; censurar.

croak [krok] *v.* croar; graznar; *s.* canto de ranas; graznido.

cro·chet [kroʃé] *s.* labor de gancho; — **hook** aguja de gancho; *v.* hacer labor de gancho.

crock [krɑk] *s.* vasija de loza, jarra.

crock·er·y [krɑ́kərɪ] *s.* loza.

croc·o·dile [krɑ́kədaɪl] *s.* cocodrilo, *Am.* caimán.

cro·ny [krónɪ] *s.* compadre, compinche, camarada, compañero.

crook [krʊk] *s.* (*thief*) falsario; estafador, maleante, pícaro; (*curve*) curva, vuelta; recodo; gancho; **shepherd's** — cayado; *v.* torcer(se); **to** — **one's arm** doblar el brazo o codo.

crook·ed [krʊ́kɪd] *adj.* torcido; curvo, encorvado, *Méx.* chueco; *Ríopl.* chingado; falso, fraudulento.

croon [krun] *v.* cantar «tristes» (*con exagerado patetismo y exagerando los sonidos nasales*).

crop [krɑp] *s.* cosecha; (*bird*) buche (*de ave*); (*whip*) látigo, *Méx.* cuarta; — **of hair** cabellera; *v.* segar; recortar; rapar; **to** — **out** aparecer, asomar; **to** — **up** brotar, manifestarse inesperadamente.

cross [krɔs] *s.* cruz; (*roads*) cruce; cruzamiento (*de razas*); mezcla; *v.* cruzar(se); atravesar(se); santiguar(se); encontrarse; contrariar; *adj.* en cruz, cruzado, transversal; malhumorado; **cross-country** a campo traviesa; **cross-examine** *v.* interrogar, repreguntar; **cross-eyed** bizco; — **word puzzle** crucigrama; — **walk** cruce para transeúntes.

cross·bar [krɔ́sbɑr] *s.* travesaño.

cross·ing [krɔ́siŋ] *s.* cruce; cruzamiento; encrucijada, crucero, travesía; **railroad** — cruce; **river** — vado.

cross·road [krɔ́srod] *s.* vía transversal, encrucijada, crucero.

cross sec·tion [krɛ́s sɛ́kʃən] *s.* corte transversal; sección transversal.

crouch [kraʊtʃ] *v.* agacharse, agazaparse.

crow [kro] *s.* cuervo; canto del gallo; **crow's-foot** pata de gallo (*arrugas en el rabo del ojo*); *v.* cantar (*el gallo*); cacarear; jactarse, hacer alarde.

crow·bar [króbɑr] *s.* barra, palanca de hierro.

crowd [kraʊd] *s.* muchedumbre; gentío, gente; cuadrilla, pandilla; grupo; *v.* agolparse, apiñar(se); estrujar, empujar.

crowd·ed [kráʊ́dɪd] *adj.* atestado, lleno, apiñado.

crown [kraʊn] *s.* corona; copa (*de sombrero*); cima; *v.* coronar.

cru·ci·ble [krúsəbl̩] *s.* crisol.

cru·ci·fix [krúsəfɪks] *s.* crucifijo.

cru·ci·fy [krúsəfaɪ] *v.* crucificar.

crude [krud] *adj.* basto, tosco, rudo; inculto; — **oil** petróleo crudo; — **sugar** azúcar bruto, asúcar crudo.

cru·el [krúəl] *adj.* cruel.

cru·el·ty [krúəltɪ] *s.* crueldad.

cru·et [krúɪt] *s.* ampolla (*pequeña vasija de cristal*); vinajera (*para servir vino en la misa*); **oil** — aceitera; **vinegar** — vinagrera.

cruise [kruz] *s.* travesía, viaje por mar; excursión; *v.* navegar.

cruis·er [krúzɚ] *s.* crucero (*buque*).

crumb [krʌm] *s.* migaja; miga; mendrugo; *v.* desmenuzar, desmigajar.

crum·ble [krʌ́mbl̩] *v.* desmenuzar(se); desmoronarse.

crum·ple [krʌ́mpl̩] *v.* arrugar(se); ajar, apabullar.

crunch [krʌntʃ] *v.* crujir; mascullar.

cru·sade [kruséd] *s.* cruzada; *v.* hacer una campaña; hacer una cruzada.

cru·sad·er [kruséd ɚ] *s.* cruzado.

crush [krʌʃ] *s.* compresión, presión; estrujamiento, apiñamiento de gente; *v.* estrujar; aplastar; majar; subyugar; **to** — **stone** moler piedra.

crust [krʌst] *s.* corteza (*de pan, queso, etc.*); costra; mendrugo; *v.* encostrarse, cubrir(se) de costra.

crust·y [krʌ́stɪ] *adj.* costroso.

crutch [krʌtʃ] *s.* muleta.

cry [kraɪ] *s.* grito; lloro, lamento; **a far** — **from** muy distante de, muy lejos de; *v.* gritar; llorar; clamar; exclamar; vocear; **to** — **for help** pedir socorro.

crys·tal [krístl̩] *s.* cristal; — **clear** cristalino.

crys·tal·line [krístlɪn] *adj.* cristalino. **crys·tal·lize** [krístlaɪz] *v.* cristalizar(se).

cub [kʌb] *s.* cachorro (*de oso, tigre, lobo, león*);

—**reporter** reportero novato.
Cu·ban [kjúbən] *adj.* & *s.* cubano.
cub·by·hole [kʌ́bihol] *s.* chiribitil.
cube [kjúb] *s.* cubo; — **root** raíz cúbica.
cu·bic [kjúbɪk] *adj.* cúbico.
cu·bism [kúbɪzm] *s.* cubismo.
cuck·old [kʌ́kold] *s.* cornudo.
cuck·oo [kúku] *s.* cuco, cuclillo; *adj.* tocado, chiflado, medio loco.
cu·cum·ber [kjúkʌmbɚ] *s.* pepino.
cud [kʌd] *s.* rumia; **to chew the** — rumiar.
cud·dle [kʌ́dl̩] *v.* abrazar, tener en brazos; estar abrazados.
cudg·el [kʌ́dʒəl] *s.* garrote; porra; *v.* aporrear, apalear.
cue [kju] *s.* señal, indicación; (theater) pie. **billiard** — taco de billar.
cuff [kʌf] *s.* puño (*de camisa o de vestido*); doblez (*del pantalón*); bofetada; *v.* bofetear, dar de bofetadas.
cull [kʌl] *v.* entresacar; extraer.
cul·mi·nate [kʌ́lmənet] *v.* culminar.
cul·prit [kʌ́lprɪt] *s.* reo, delincuente, culpable.
cult [kʌlt] *s.* culto; secta religiosa.
cul·ti·vate [kʌ́ltəvet] *v.* cultivar; labrar, barbechar.
cul·ti·vat·ed [kʌ́ltəvetɪd] *adj.* cultivado; culto.
cul·ti·va·tion [kʌltəvéʃən] *s.* cultivación, cultivo; cultura.
cul·ti·va·tor [kʌ́ltəvetɚ] *s.* cultivador; máquina cultivadora.
cul·ture [kʌ́ltʃɚ] *s.* (*societal*) cultura; (*tillage*) cultivo.
cul·tured [kʌ́ltʃɚd] *adj.* culto; cultivado.
cum·ber·some [kʌ́mbɚsəm] *adj.* engorroso, embarazoso, incómodo.
cu·mu·la·tive [kjúmjələtɪv] *adj.* acumulativo.
cun·ning [kʌ́nɪŋ] *adj.* astuto, socarrón, sagaz, taimado; diestro; cuco, mono, gracioso; *s.* astucia, maña, sagacidad.
cup [kʌp] *s.* taza, pocillo; copa (*trofeo*).
cup·board [kʌ́bɚd] *s.* armario, aparador; alacena.
cur [kɝ] *s.* perro mestizo, *Perú* perro chusco; villano, vil, cobarde.
cu·rate [kjúrɪt] *s.* cura.
cu·ra·tor [kjúretɚ] *s.* conservador.
curb [kɝb] *s.* reborde, encintado (*de la acera*); *Ríopl.* cordón de la acera; freno, restricción; barbada (*del freno de un caballo*); brocal de pozo; — **market** bolsa fuera de rueda; *v.* refrenar, reprimir.
curd [kɝd] *s.* cuajada; *v.* cuajar(se), coagular(se).
cur·dle [kɝ́dl̩] *v.* cuajar(se), coagular(se).
cure [kjur] *s.* cura, curación; remedio; *v.* curar(se); sanar.
cur·few [kɚfju] *s.* queda.
cu·ri·o [kjúrɪo] *s.* curiosidad, objeto raro y curioso.
cu·ri·os·i·ty [kjurɪásətɪ] *s.* curiosidad; rareza.
cu·ri·ous [kjúrɪəs] *adj.* curioso; extraño, raro.
curl [kɝl] *s.* rizo, bucle; espiral (*de humo*); *v.* rizar(se); ensortijar(se); enroscar(se); retorcerse, alzarse en espirales (*el humo*).
curl·y [kɝ́lɪ] *adj.* rizo, rizoso, rizado, crespo, *Méx.* chino.
cur·rant [kɝ́ənt] *s.* grosella; — **bush** grosellero.
cur·ren·cy [kɝ́ənsɪ] *s.* moneda corriente; circulación; **paper** — papel moneda.
cur·rent [kɝ́ənt] *adj.* corriente; común, prevaleciente, en boga; *s.* corriente.
cur·ric·u·lum [kəríkjələm] *s.* programa de estudios.
curse [kɝs] *s.* maldicón; calamidad; *v.* maldecir.
cursed [kɝ́st] *adj.* maldito.
curs·ing [kɝ́sɪŋ] *adj.* maldiciente.
cur·sive [kɝ́sɪv] *adj.* cursivo.
cur·sor [kɝ́sɚ] *s.* (*computer*) cursor.
curt [kɝt] *adj.* corto; brusco.
cur·tail [kɝtél] *v.* cercenar; acortar; restringir, reducir.
cur·tain [kɝ́tn̩] *s.* cortina; telón (*de teatro*); *v.* poner cortinas.
cur·va·ture [kɝ́vətʃɚ] *s.* curvatura.
curve [kɝv] *s.* curva; *v.* encorvar(se); torcer(se); doblar(se).
curved [kɝvd] *adj.* encorvado; torcido; curvo, corvo, *Méx., C.A.* chueco.
cush·ion [kúʃən] *s.* cojín; almohadilla; almohadón; amortiguador (*para amortiguar un sonido o golpe*); *v.* acojinar; amortiguar (*un choque*).
cus·tard [kʌ́stɚd] *s.* flan, natillas.
cus·to·dy [kʌ́stədɪ] *s.* custodia, cargo, cuidado; **to hold in** — custodiar.
cus·tom [kʌ́stəm] *s.* costumbre, hábito, uso, usanza; **-s** derechos de aduana; — **made** hecho a la medida; — **tailor** maestro sastre; — **built** construido según pedido; — **quota** cupo arancelario.
cus·tom·ar·y [kʌ́stəmɛrɪ] *adj.* acostumbrado, habitual, usual, de costumbre.
cus·tom·er [kʌ́stəmɚ] *s.* parroquiano, cliente, marchante.
cus·tom·house [kʌ́stəmhaus] *s.* aduana; — **official** aduanero; — **mark** marchamo.
cut [kʌt] *s.* corte (*m.*); cortadura, *Am.* cortada; rebanada, tajada; (*reduction*) rebaja, reducción (*de precios, sueldos*); hechura (*de un traje*); ausencia (*de la clase*); grabado; **short** — atajo, camino corto; *v.* cortar; tajar; truncar; talar (*árboles*) labrar, tallar; segar; rebajar, reducir (*precios, sueldos*); negar el saludo a; alzar (*los naipes*); **to** — **across** cruzar, atravesar; **to** — **capers** hacer cabriolas, cabriolar; **to** — **class** faltar a la clase; **to** — **out** recortar; excluir; **to be** — **out for** estar hecho para, tener vocación para; *pret. & p.p. de* **to cut.**
cut-and-dried [kʌ́tænddráɪd] *adj.* ya determinado; ordinario.
cut·back [kʌ́tbæk] *s.* reducción.
cute [kjut] *adj.* mono, cuco; astuto.
cu·ti·cle [kjútɪkl] *s.* cutícula.
cut·ler·y [kʌ́tlərɪ] *s.* cuchillería, cuchillos.
cut·let [kʌ́tlɪt] *s.* chuleta.
cut·off [kʌ́tɔf] *s.* límite ya indicado.
cut·ter [kʌ́tɚ] *s.* cortador; máquina para cortar; trineo; **wood** — leñador; **coast guard** — barco guardacostas.
cut·ting [kʌ́tɪŋ] *adj.* cortante; penetrante; mordaz, sarcástico.
cy·ber·net·ics [saɪbɚnétɪks] *s.* cibernética.
cy·cle [sáɪkl] *s.* ciclo.
cy·clone [sáɪklon] *s.* ciclón; huracán.
cy·clo·tron [sáɪklətran] *s.* ciclotrón.
cyl·in·der [sílɪndɚ] *s.* cilindro; — **head** émbolo.
cy·lin·dri·cal [sɪlíndrɪkl] *adj.* cilíndrico.
cym·bal [símbl̩] *s.* címbalo, platillo; **to play the -s** tocar los platillos.
cyn·ic [sínɪk] *s.* cínico.
cyn·i·cal [sínɪkl̩] *adj.* cínico.
cyn·i·cism [sínəsɪzəm] *s.* cinismo.
cy·press [sáɪprəs] *s.* ciprés.
cyst [sɪst] *s.* quiste.

D:d

dab·ble [dǽbḷ] *v.* chapotear; trabajar superficialmente.
dad [dæd] *s.* papá, tata; **daddy** *s.* papaíto o papacito, tata, tatita, *Am.* taita.
daf·fo·dil [dǽfədɪl] *s.* narciso.
dag·ger [dǽgɚ] *s.* daga; puñal; **to look -s at** traspasar con la mirada.
dahl·ia [dǽljə] *s.* dalia.
dai·ly [délɪ] *adj.* diario; — **wage** jornal; *adv.* diariamente; *s.* diario, periódico.
dain·ty [déntɪ] *adj.* delicado, fino, primoroso, exquisito; *s.* golosina, manjar exquisito.
dair·y [dέrɪ] *s.* lechería, vaquería; quesería, quesera; *Arg.* tambo.
dai·sy [dézɪ] *s.* margarita, maya; (*computer*) — **wheel** margarita, disco impresor; — **wheel printer** impresora de margarita.
dale [del] *s.* cañada.
dal·ly [dǽlɪ] *v.* juguetear; holgazanear; entretenerse, tardar; malgastar el tiempo.
dam [dæm] *s.* presa, represa; *v.* represar, estancar.
dam·age [dǽmɪdʒ] *s.* daño; perjuicio; avería; **to pay for -s** indemnizar, pagar los daños y perjuicios; *v.* dañar(se); averiar(se).
Dam·a·scene [dǽməsin] *adj. s.* damasquinado.
dame [dem] *s.* dama, señora; **old** — vieja.
damn [dæm] *v.* maldecir; condenar; blasfemar; — **it** ¡maldito sea!
dam·na·tion [dæmnéʃən] *s.* condenación, perdición.
damp [dæmp] *adj.* húmedo; mojado; *s.* humedad; *v.* humedecer, mojar.
damp·en [dǽmpən] *v.* mojar, humedecer; desalentar; amortiguar.
damp·ness [dǽmpnɪs] *s.* humedad.
dam·sel [dǽmzḷ] *s.* damisela.
dance [dæns] *s.* baile; danza; — **music** música de baile; *v.* bailar; danzar.
danc·er [dǽnsɚ] *s.* bailador; bailarín, bailarina; danzante.
dan·de·li·on [dǽndlaɪən] *s.* diente de león.
dan·druff [dǽndrəf] *s.* caspa.
dan·dy [dǽndɪ] *s.* currutaco, majo, afectado; chulo; *adj.* elegante, excelente.
dan·ger [déndʒɚ] *s.* peligro, riesgo.
dan·ger·ous [déndʒərəs] *adj.* peligroso; arriesgado; **-ly** *adv.* peligrosamente; **-ly ill** gravemente enfermo.
dan·gle [dǽŋgl] *v.* pender, colgar, bambolear(se) (*en el aire*).
dap·ple(d) [dǽpl(d)] *adj.* rodado, con manchas (*dícese de los caballos*); **dapple-grey** rucio, moteado, rodado, tordo, tordillo.
dare [dεr] *s.* desafío, reto, provocación; — **devil** atrevido, osado; *v.* atreverse, osar; desafiar.
dar·ing [dέrɪŋ] *s.* atrevimiento, osadía; *adj.* osado, atrevido, arrojado.
dark [dɑrk] *adj.* obscuro; sombrío; — **horse** caballo desconocido (*que gana inesperadamente la carrera*); (*politics*) candidato nombrado inesperadamente; — **secret** secreto profundo; enigma; **darkskinned** moreno, trigueño; *s.* obscuridad; sombra.
dark·en [dɑ́rkən] *v.* obscurecer(se); nublarse.
dark·ness [dɑ́rknɪs] *s.* obscuridad; tinieblas; sombra.
dar·ling [dɑ́rlɪŋ] *adj. & s.* amado, querido; **my** — vida mía (*o* mi vida), amor mío.
darn [dɑrn] *s.* zurcido; **it is not worth a** — no vale un comino, no vale un pito; *v.* zurcir; — **!** ¡caramba! ¡canastos!; **-ing needle** aguja de zurcir.
dart [dɑrt] *s.* dardo, flecha; (*tuck*) sisa (*en un vestido*); movimiento rápido; *v.* lanzar(se); flechar; **to — out** salir como una flecha; **to — in and out** entrar y salir precipitadamente.
dash [dæʃ] *s.* (*line*) raya; (*run*) carrera corta; (*vigor*) ímpetu; (*grace*) garbo; pizca (*de sal, azúcar, etc.*); rociada (*de agua*); — **board** tablero de instrumentos; **with a — of the pen** de una plumada; *v.* lanzar(se); echar(se); estrellar(se); salpicar; frustrar (*esperanzas*); **to — by** pasar corriendo; **to — out** salir a la carrera; **to — off a letter** escribir de prisa una carta.
da·ta [détə] *s. pl.* datos; — **collection** recopilación de datos; — **display** despliegue (presentación) de datos; — **processing** procesamiento de datos; — **base** base de datos.
date [det] *s.* (*time*) fecha; (*statement*) data; (*appointment*) cita, compromiso; (*fruit*) dátil; **out of** — anticuado, desusado; fuera de moda; **up to** — al día, moderno; **up to this** — hasta ahora, hasta la fecha; *v.* fechar; **to — from** datar de; remontarse a.
daub [dɔb] *v.* embarrar, untar; pintarrajear.
daugh·ter [dɔ́tɚ] *s.* hija; **daughter-in-law** nuera.
daunt [dɔnt] *v.* intimidar, asustar, espantar; desanimar.
daunt·less [dɔ́ntlɪs] *adj.* denodado, intrépido.
dav·en·port [dǽvənport] *s.* sofá.
dawn [dɔn] *s.* alba; amanecer, madrugada; *v.* amanecer; alborear, rayar (*el día*); **it just -ed upon me** acabo de darme cuenta.
day [de] *s.* día; — **after tomorrow** pasado mañana; — **before yesterday** anteayer o antier; — **laborer** jornalero; **by** — de día; **by the** — por día; **eight-hour** — jornada de ocho horas; **to win the** — ganar la jornada, triunfar; *adj.* diurno.
day·break [débrek] *s.* amanecer, alba; **at** — al amanecer, al romper el día, al rayar el día.
day·light [délaɪt] *s.* luz del día.
day·time [détaɪm] *s.* día (*tiempo de luz natural*); **in the** — durante el día; de día.
daze [dez] *s.* aturdimiento; deslumbramiento; **to be in a** — estar aturdido; *v.* aturdir; ofuscar; deslumbrar.
daz·zle [dǽzḷ] *s.* brillantez; *v.* deslumbrar; ofuscar.
dea·con [dikən] *s.* diácono.
dead [dεd] *adj.* muerto; — **air** aire viciado o estancado; — **bolt** cerrojo dormido; — **letter** carta no reclamada; — **loss** pérdida absoluta; *adv.* completamente, absolutamente; sumamente, muy; — **sure** completamente seguro; — **tired** muerto de cansancio; *s.* **the** — los muertos; **in the — of the night** en el sigilo de la noche; **in the — of winter** en lo más crudo del invierno.
dead·en [dέdṇ] *v.* amortiguar.
dead·head [dέdhεd] *s.* persona que no paga la entrada; colado.
dead·line [dέdlaɪn] *s.* fin de plazo, vencimiento.
dead·lock [dέdlak] desacuerdo insuperable.
dead·ly [dέdlɪ] *adj.* mortal; fatal; como la muerte, cadavérico; *adv.* mortalmente; — **dull** sumamente aburrido.
deaf [dεf] *adj.* sordo; **deaf-mute** *s. & adj.* sordomudo.
deaf·en [dέfən] *v.* ensordecer; amortiguar, apagar, (*un sonido*).
deaf·en·ing [dέfənɪŋ] *adj.* ensordecedor, estruendoso.
deaf·ness [dέfnɪs] *s.* sordera.
deal [dil] *s.* trato, negocio; (*cards*) mano; distribución, reparto (*de los naipes*); **a great — of** una gran cantidad de, mucho; **to give a square** —

tratar con equidad; *v.* tallar (*en juegos de naipes*); distribuir, repartir; dar (*un golpe*); **to — in** comerciar en; **to — with** tratar de (*un asunto*); tratar con; negociar con.
deal·er [dílɚ] *s.* negociante, comerciante, tratante; tallador (*en el juego de naipes*).
deal·ings [dílɪŋz] *s. pl.* relaciones (*comerciales o amistosas*); comercio, tratos; negocios.
dealt [dɛlt] *pret. & p.p. de* **to deal.**
dean [din] *s.* deán (*dignidad eclesiástica*); decano (*de universidad*).
dear [dɪr] *adj.* (*beloved*) querido, amado; (*expensive*) caro; costoso; *adv.* caro; **— me!** ¡Dios mío!; **oh — !** ¡ay!; **my —** querido mío; **Dear Sir** Muy señor mío; **-ly** *adv.* cariñosamente; a precio alto; **my -ly beloved** muy amado mío; muy amados míos.
dearth [dɝθ] *s.* escasez, carestía, insuficiencia.
death [dɛθ] *s.* muerte; mortandad; **— rate** mortalidad; **— certificate** fe de óbito, partida de difunción.
death·bed [dɛ́θbɛd] *s.* lecho de muerte.
de·base [dɪbés] *v.* rebajar el valor de; degradar, humillar, envilecer.
de·bat·a·ble [dɪbétəbl̩] *adj.* discutible, disputable.
de·bate [dɪbét] *s.* debate, discusión; *v.* debatir, discutir; considerar; deliberar.
de·ben·ture [dɪbɛ́ntʃɚ] *s.* certificado de reintegro.
de·bil·i·tate [dəbɪlətet] *v.* debilitar.
deb·it [dɛ́bɪt] *s.* débito, adeudo, cargo; debe (*de una cuenta*); pasivo (*en contabilidad*); *v.* adeudar, cargar en cuenta.
de·brief·ing [dibrifɪŋ] *s.* informe de vuelo bajo, interrogación; informe.
de·bris [dəbrí] *s.* escombros; ruinas.
debt [dɛt] *s.* deuda; adeudo; débito; **bad —** cuenta incobrable; **to run into —** adeudarse, entramparse, cargarse de deudas.
debt·or [dɛ́tɚ] *s.* deudor.
de·bug·ging [dibʌ́gɪŋ] *s.* depuración.
de·bunk [dibʌ́ŋk] *s.* desbaratar; desenmascarar.
de·but [dɪbjú] *s.* estreno; **to make a —** debutar, estrenarse.
de·cade [dɛ́ked] *s.* década, decenio.
de·ca·dence [dɪkédn̩s] *s.* decadencia.
de·cant·er [dɪkǽntɚ] *s.* garrafa; **large —** garrafón.
de·cay [dɪké] *s.* decaímiento; decadencia, ruina; podredumbre; caries (*de la dentadura*); *v.* decaer; venir a menos; pudrir(se) o podrir(se).
de·cease [dɪsís] *s.* muerte, fallecimiento; *v.* morir, fallecer.
de·ceased [dɪsíst] *adj.* & *s.* muerto, difunto.
de·ceit [dɪsít] *s.* engaño; fraude; trampa.
de·ceit·ful [dɪsítfəl] *adj.* engañador; tramposo; engañoso.
de·ceive [dɪsív] *v.* engañar.
De·cem·ber [dɪsɛmbɚ] *s.* diciembre.
de·cen·cy [dísn̩sɪ] *s.* decencia.
de·cent [dísn̩t] *adj.* decente; decoroso.
de·ci·bel [dɛ́sɪbɛl] *s.* decibelio; decibel.
de·cide [dɪsáɪd] *v.* decidir, resolver, determinar; **to — to** resolverse a, decidirse a.
de·cid·ed [dɪsáɪdɪd] *adj.* decidido, resuelto.
dec·i·mal [dɛ́səml̩] *adj.* decimal; *s.* decimal, fracción decimal.
dec·i·mate [dɛ́sɪmet] *v.* diezmar.
de·ci·pher [dɪsáɪfɚ] *v.* decifrar.
de·ci·sion [dɪsíʒən] *s.* decisión, resolución.
de·ci·sive [dɪsáɪsɪv] *adj.* decisivo; terminante.
deck [dɛk] *s.* cubierta (*de un buque*); baraja; *v.* cubrir; ataviar; **to — oneself out** emperifollarse.
dec·la·ra·tion [dɛkləréʃən] *s.* declaración.
de·clare [dɪklǽr] *v.* declarar; afirmar.
de·cline [dɪkláɪn] *s.* declinación; decadencia; mengua; baja (*de precios*); *v.* declinar; decaer; rehusar; **to — to do something** negarse a hacer algo.
de·cliv·i·ty [dɪklívətɪ] *s.* declive.
de·col·le·te [dekɑlté] *adj.* escotado.
de·com·pose [dikəmpóz] *v.* descomponer(se); corromper(se), pudrir(se).
dec·o·rate [dɛ́kəret] *v.* decorar, adornar; condecorar.
dec·o·ra·tion [dɛkəréʃən] *s.* decoración; adorno; insignia, condecoración.
dec·o·ra·tive [dɛ́kəretɪv] *adj.* decorativo; ornamental.
de·co·rum [dɪkórəm] *s.* decoro; circunspección.
de·coy [dɪkɔ́ɪ] *s.* reclamo, señuelo, figura de ave (*que sirve para atraer aves*); cebo (*artificio para atraer con engaño*); (*trap*) trampa, lazo; *v.* atraer con señuelo o engaño.
de·crease [díkris] *s.* disminución o diminución; merma; mengua; [dɪkrís] *v.* disminuir(se); mermar; menguar.
de·cree [dɪkrí] *s.* decreto; *v.* decretar; mandar.
de·crep·it [dɪkrɛ́pɪt] *adj.* decrépito.
ded·i·cate [dɛ́dəket] *v.* dedicar.
ded·i·ca·tion [dɛdəkéʃən] *s.* dedicación; dedicatoria.
de·duce [dɪdjús] *v.* deducir, inferir.
de·duct [dɪdʌ́kt] *v.* deducir, descontar, rebajar.
de·duc·tion [dɪdʌ́kʃən] *s.* deducción; rebaja, descuento.
deed [did] *s.* hecho, acción, acto; hazaña; título de propiedad, escritura de traspaso.
deem [dim] *v.* juzgar, creer, considerar.
deep [dip] *adj.* (*down*) hondo, profundo; (*obscure*) oscuro; (*tone*) grave, bajo; **— in debt** cargado de deudas; **— in thought** absorto; **— mourning** luto riguroso; **to go off the — end** echarse a pique; caer en el abismo; **— into the night** en las tinieblas de la noche; *s.* **the —** el mar; **-ly** *adv.* profundamente, hondamente; intensamente.
deep·en [dípən] *v.* ahondar, profundizar.
deer [dɪr] *s.* ciervo, venado; **— skin** piel o cuero de venado.
de·face [dɪfés] *v.* desfigurar, estropear, mutilar.
de·fame [dɪfém] *v.* difamar, calumniar, denigrar.
de·fault [dɪfɔ́lt] *s.* falla, falta, negligencia (*de un deber, pago, obligación*); deficiencia; **in —** en mora, moroso; *v.* fallar, faltar (*en el cumplimiento de un deber, pago, obligación*); no comparecer a la cita de un tribunal.
de·feat [dɪfít] *s.* derrota, vencimiento; frustración (*de un plan*); *v.* vencer, derrotar; frustrar.
def·e·cate [dɛ́fəket] *v.* defecar.
de·fect [dɪfɛ́kt] *s.* defecto.
de·fec·tive [dɪfɛ́ktɪv] *adj.* defectuoso; incompleto; subnormal, falto de inteligencia; **— verb** verbo defectivo.
de·fend [dɪfɛ́nd] *v.* defender.
de·fen·dant [dɪfɛ́ndənt] *s.* acusado, demandado, procesado.
de·fend·er [dɪfɛ́ndɚ] *s.* defensor; abogado defensor.
de·fense [dɪfɛ́ns] *s.* defensa.
de·fense·less [dɪfɛ́nslɪs] *adj.* indefenso, inerme.
de·fen·sive [dɪfɛ́nsɪv] *adj.* defensivo; . defensiva.
de·fer [dɪfɝ́] *v.* diferir, posponer, aplazar; **to — to another's opinion** remitirse o ceder al dictamen de otro; **deferred assets** activo diferido; **— payment** pago aplazado.
de·fi·ance [dɪfáɪəns] *s.* reto, desafío, provocación; oposición; **in — of** en abierta oposición con, a despecho de.
de·fi·cien·cy [dɪfíʃənsɪ] *s.* deficiencia; defecto; déficit.
de·fi·cient [dɪfíʃənt] *adj.* deficiente; defectuoso.

def·i·cit [défəsɪt] *s.* déficit; — **spending** gastos deficitarios.
de·file [dɪfáɪl] *v.* viciar, corromper; profanar; (*dirty*) manchar, ensuciar.
de·fine [dɪfáɪn] *v.* definir.
def·i·nite [défənɪt] *adj.* definido; claro, preciso; fijo; — **article** artículo determinado o definido; **-ly** *adv.* definidamente; claramente; **-ly not** terminantemente no.
def·i·ni·tion [dɛfəníʃən] *s.* definición.
de·fin·i·tive [dɪfínətɪv] *adj.* definitivo.
de·flate [dɪflét] *v.* desinflar.
de·flect [dɪflékt] *v.* desviar(se).
de·form [dɪfɔ́rm] *v.* deformar; desfigurar, afear.
de·formed [dɪfɔ́rmd] *adj.* deforme, disforme; deformado; desfigurado.
de·form·i·ty [dɪfɔ́rmətɪ] *s.* deformidad; deformación.
de·fraud [dɪfrɔ́d] *v.* defraudar.
de·fray [dɪfré] *v.* sufragar, costear, pagar (*gastos*).
deft [dɛft] *adj.* diestro, ágil.
de·funct [dɪfʌ́ŋkt] *adj.* difunto.
de·fy [dɪfáɪ] *v.* desafiar; retar; oponerse a, resistirse a.
de·gen·er·ate [dɪdʒénərɪt] *adj. & s.* degenerado; [dɪdʒénərɪt] *v.* degenerar.
deg·ra·da·tion [dɛgrədéʃən] *s.* degradación; envilecimiento.
de·grade [dɪgréd] *v.* degradar; envilecer, rebajar.
de·gree [dɪgrí] *s.* grado; rango; **by -s** gradualmente; **to get a** — graduarse.
de·hu·man·ize [dihjúmənaɪz] *v.* deshumanizar.
de·hy·drate [dɪháɪdret] *v.* deshidratar(se).
deign [den] *v.* dignarse, condescender.
de·i·ty [díətɪ] *s.* deidad.
de·ject·ed [dɪdʒéktɪd] *adj.* abatido.
de·jec·tion [dɪdʒékʃən] *s.* abatimiento, melancolía, depresión.
de·lay [dɪlé] *s.* demora, tardanza, dilación, retraso; *v.* demorar; retardar, dilatar; deferir; tardarse.
de·layed ac·tion [dɪléd ǽkʃən] *adj.* atrasado; retardado.
del·e·gate [déləget] *s.* delegado, representante; *v.* delegar, diputar.
del·e·ga·tion [dɛləgéʃən] *s.* delegación, diputación.
de·le·tion [dɪlíʃən] *s.* suspensión.
de·lib·er·ate [dɪlíbərɪt] *adj.* deliberado, premeditado; cauto, prudente; lento; **-ly** *adv.* deliberadamente; con premeditación; [dɪlíbəret] *v.* deliberar.
de·lib·er·a·tion [dɪlɪbəréʃən] *s.* deliberación.
del·i·ca·cy [déləkəsɪ] *s.* delicadeza; sensibilidad; finura; golosina.
del·i·cate [déləkət] *adj.* delicado; frágil; exquisito.
del·i·ca·tes·sen [dɛləkətésn̩] *s.* tienda de fiambres, queso, ensaladas, ultramarinos, etc.
de·li·cious [dɪlíʃəs] *adj.* delicioso.
de·light [dɪláɪt] *s.* deleite; delicia; *v.* deleitar(se); encantar; agradar; **to** — **in** gozarse en, deleitarse en.
de·light·ed [dɪláɪtɪd] *adj.* encantado; **to be** — **to** alegrarse de, tener mucho gusto en (de).
de·light·ful [dɪláɪtfəl] *adj.* deleitoso; delicioso; ameno, agradable.
de·lin·e·ate [dɪlínɪet] *v.* delinear, trazar.
de·lin·quent [dɪlíŋkwənt] *adj. & s.* delincuente.
de·lir·i·ous [dɪlírɪəs] *adj.* delirante; **to be** — delirar, desvariar.
de·lir·i·um [dɪlírɪəm] *s.* delirio, desvarío.
de·liv·er [dɪlívɚ] *v.* entregar; librar, libertar; pronunciar (*un discurso*); dar (*un golpe*); — **the goods** cumplir.
de·liv·er·ance [dɪlívərəns] *s.* liberación, rescate.
de·liv·er·er [dɪlívərɚ] *s.* libertador; portador, mansajero.
de·liv·er·y [dɪlívərɪ] *s.* (*giving*) entrega; (*saving*) liberación; (*birth*) parto; (*speaking*) elocuencia, manera de hacer una conferencia; — **service** servicio de entrega; — **truck** camión (camioneta) de reparto; **mail** — reparto de correo.
dell [dɛl] *s.* cañada, hondonada.
del·ta wing [déltə wɪŋ] *s.* ala en delta.
de·lude [dɪlúd] *v.* engañar.
del·uge [déljudʒ] *s.* diluvio; *v.* inundar; abrumar.
de·lu·sion [dɪlúʒən] *s.* ilusión; engaño, error.
de·mand [dɪmǽnd] *s.* demanda; exigencia; solicitud; **on** — a solicitud; — **and supply** demanda y oferta; — **note** pagaré a la vista; *v.* demandar, reclamar; exigir.
de·mand·ing [dɪmǽndɪŋ] *adj.* exigente.
de·mean·or [dɪmínɚ] *s.* conducta, comportamiento, proceder.
de·ment·ed [dɪméntɪd] *adj.* demente.
dem·i·john [démidʒan] *s.* damajuana.
de·mise [dɪmáɪz] *s.* fallecimiento.
de·mo·bil·ize [dimóblaɪz] *v.* demovilizar.
de·moc·ra·cy [dəmákrəsɪ] *s.* democracia.
dem·o·crat [déməkræt] *s.* demócrata.
dem·o·crat·ic [dɛməkrǽtɪk] *adj.* democrático.
de·mol·ish [dɪmálɪʃ] *v.* demoler.
de·mon [dímən] *s.* demonio.
dem·on·strate [démənstret] *v.* demostrar.
dem·on·stra·tion [dɛmənstréʃən] *s.* demostración; prueba; (*protest*) manifestación.
de·mon·stra·tive [dɪmánstrətɪv] *adj.* demostrativo; efusivo.
den [dɛn] *s.* guarida; escondrijo; cueva, lugar de retiro.
de·ni·al [dɪnáɪəl] *s.* negación; negativa; **self-denial** abnegación.
den·i·grate [dénɪgret] *v.* calumniar; ennegrecer.
de·nom·i·na·tion [dɪnɑmənéʃən] *s.* (*name*) denominación; nombre; título, designación; (*sect*) secta religiosa.
de·note [dɪnót] *v.* denotar.
de·nounce [dɪnáʊns] *v.* denunciar; delatar, acusar.
dense [dɛns] *adj.* denso; espeso, apretado; estúpido.
den·si·ty [dénsətɪ] *s.* densidad; estupidez.
dent [dɛnt] *s.* abolladura; mella; *v.* abollar; mellar.
den·tal [déntl] *adj.* dental; *s.* dental, consonante dental.
den·ti·frice [déntɪfrɪs] *s.* pasta dentífrica; dentífrico.
den·tist [déntɪst] *s.* dentista.
de·nun·ci·a·tion [dɪnʌnsɪéʃən] *s.* denuncia, acusación.
de·ny [dɪnáɪ] *v.* negar; rehusar; **to** — **oneself** sacrificarse, abnegarse; **to** — **oneself to callers** negarse a recibir visitas.
de·o·dor·ant [diódərənt] *s.* desodorante.
de·ox·i·dize [diáksədaɪz] *v.* desoxidar.
de·part [dɪpárt] *v.* partir, salir, irse; desviarse, apartarse.
de·part·ed [dɪpártɪd] *adj.* ido; ausente; difunto.
de·part·ment [dɪpártmənt] *s.* departamento; distrito; ramo, división; — **store** almacén.
de·par·ture [dɪpártʃɚ] *s.* salida, partida; desviación.
de·pend [dɪpénd] *v.* depender; **to** — **on** depender de; contar con, confiar en.
de·pend·a·ble [dɪpéndəbl̩] *adj.* seguro, fidedigno, digno de confianza; serio, formal.
de·pen·dence [dɪpéndəns] *s.* dependencia; confianza.
de·pen·den·cy [dɪpéndənsɪ] *s.* dependencia; sucursal.
de·pen·dent [dɪpéndənt] *adj.* dependiente; subordinado; *s.* dependiente, familiar.
de·pict [dɪpíkt] *v.* pintar, describir; representar.

dep·i·late [dέpəlet] *v.* depilar.
de·pil·a·to·ry [dɪpflətorɪ] *s.* depilatorio.
de·plete [dɪplít] *v.* agotar; vaciar; **depletion** agotamiento.
de·plor·a·ble [dɪplórəbl̩] *adj.* deplorable, lamentable.
de·plore [dɪplór] *v.* deplorar.
de·port [dɪpórt] *v.* deportar; **to — oneself well** portarse bien.
de·port·ment [dɪpórtmənt] *s.* comportamiento, conducta.
de·pose [dɪpóz] *v.* deponer; declarar, (*testify*) atestiguar.
de·pos·it [dɪpάzɪt] *s.* depósito; (*mineral*) yacimiento; (*ernest money*) prenda, anticipo; *v.* depositar.
dep·o·si·tion [dɛpəzíʃən] *s.* deposición; declaración.
de·pos·i·tor [dɪpάzɪtɚ] *s.* depositador.
de·pot [dípo] *s.* depósito; almacén; estación de ferrocarril.
dep·re·cate [dέprɪket] *v.* desaprobar.
de·pre·ci·ate [dɪpríʃɪet] *v.* depreciar; bajar de precio; abaratar(se); menospreciar.
de·press [dɪprέs] *v.* deprimir; abatir; desanimar; depreciar, rebajar el valor de.
de·pressed [dɪprέst] *adj.* abatido, decaído.
de·press·ing [dɪprέsɪŋ] *adj.* deprimente.
de·pres·sion [dɪprέʃən] *s.* depresión; decaimiento, abatimiento; rebaja (*de precios*).
de·prive [dɪpráɪv] *v.* privar.
depth [dɛpθ] *s.* profundidad; hondura; fondo; (*length*) longitud (*de un solar*); gravedad (*de los sonidos*); viveza (*de los colores*); **in the — of the night** en las tinieblas de la noche; **in the — of winter** en lo más crudo del invierno.
dep·u·ta·tion [dɛpjətéʃən] *s.* diputación, delegación; comisión.
de·pute [dɪpjút] *v.* diputar, delegar.
dep·u·ty [dέpjətɪ] *s.* diputado; agente; delegado.
de·range [dɪréndʒ] *v.* trastornar, desordenar.
der·by [dɝ́bɪ] *s.* sombrero hongo, *Méx., Ven., Col.* sombrero de bola.
der·e·lict [dέrɪlɪkt] *adj.* abandonado; negligente.
de·ride [dɪráɪd] *v.* escarnecer, ridiculizar, mofarse de, burlarse de.
de·ri·sion [dɪríʒən] *s.* mofa, escarnio.
de·rive [dəráɪv] *v.* derivar(se); provenir; sacar (*provecho*); recibir (*placer*).
der·ma·tol·o·gy [dɚmətάlədʒɪ] *s.* dermatología.
der·rick [dέrɪk] *s.* grúa; armazón (*para la explotación del petróleo*).
de·scend [dɪsέnd] *v.* descender; bajar; **to — upon** caer sobre, acometer.
de·scen·dant [dɪsέndənt] *adj. & s.* descendiente.
de·scent [dɪsέnt] *s.* descenso; bajada; (*lineage*) descendencia, linaje; descendimiento; declive.
de·scribe [dɪskráɪb] *v.* describir; trazar.
de·scrip·tion [dɪskrípʃən] *s.* descripción; **of all -s** de todas clases.
de·scrip·tive [dɪskríptɪv] *adj.* descriptivo; — **linguistics** lingüística descriptiva.
des·ert [dέzɚt] *adj.* desierto, despoblado, estéril; *s.* desierto, yermo; páramo; [dɪzɝ́t] *v.* abandonar, desamparar; desertar.
de·sert·er [dɪzɝ́tɚ] *s.* desertor.
de·ser·tion [dɪzɝ́ʃən] *s.* deserción, abandono, desamparo.
de·serve [dɪzɝ́v] *v.* merecer.
de·serv·ing [dɪzɝvɪŋ] *adj.* meritorio; merecedor.
de·sign [dɪzáɪn] *s.* (*sketch*) dibujo, diseño; (*plan*) designio, propósito, intención; plan, proyecto; *v.* diseñar, trazar; proyectar; idear.
des·ig·nate [dέzɪgnet] *v.* designar; señalar, indicar, nombrar.
de·sign·er [dɪzáɪnɚ] *s.* diseñador; dibujante; proyectista; intrigante.
de·sir·a·bil·i·ty [dɪzaɪrəbflətɪ] *s.* conveniencia, utilidad.
de·sir·a·ble [dɪzáɪrəbl̩] *adj.* deseable; agradable; conveniente.
de·sire [dɪzáɪr] *s.* deseo; anhelo, ansia; *v.* desear; anhelar, ansiar.
de·sir·ous [dɪzáɪrəs] *adj.* deseoso.
de·sist [dɪzíst] *v.* desistir.
desk [dɛsk] *s.* escritorio, bufete, (*school*) pupitre, mesa de escribir.
des·o·late [dέslɪt] *adj.* desolado; despoblado, desierto; solitario [dέslet] *v.* desolar; asolar, arrasar; despoblar.
des·o·la·tion [dɛsléʃən] *s.* desolación; soledad.
de·spair [dɪspέr] *s.* desesperación; desesperanza; *v.* desesperarse, perder la esperanza.
de·spair·ing [dɪspέrɪŋ] *adj.* desesperado, sin esperanza.
des·patch [dɪspǽtʃ] = **dispatch.**
des·per·ate [dέsprɪt] *adj.* desesperado; arriesgado, temerario; — **illness** enfermedad gravísima; **-ly** *adv.* desesperadamente; **-ly ill** gravísimamente enfermo.
des·per·a·tion [dɛspəréʃən] *s.* desesperación; temeridad.
des·pi·ca·ble [dέspɪkəbl̩] *adj.* despreciable; desdeñable.
de·spise [dɪspáɪz] *v.* despreciar; desdeñar; menospreciar.
de·spite [dɪspáɪt] *s.* despecho; *prep.* a despecho de, a pesar de.
de·spoil [dɪspɔ́ɪl] *v.* despojar.
de·spon·den·cy [dɪspάndənsɪ] *s.* abatimiento desaliento, descaecimiento o decaimiento del ánimo.
de·spon·dent [dɪspάndənt] *adj.* abatido, descaecido o decaído de ánimo, desalentado, desesperanzado.
des·pot [dέspət] *s.* déspota.
des·pot·ic [dɪspάtɪk] *adj.* despótico.
des·pot·ism [dέspətɪzəm] *s.* despotismo.
des·sert [dɪzɚt] *s.* postre.
des·ti·na·tion [dɛstənéʃən] *s.* destinación, destino; paradero.
des·tine [dέstɪn] *v.* destinar; **-ed for** con rumbo a, con destinación a; destinado a.
des·ti·ny [dέstənɪ] *s.* destino, sino, hado.
des·ti·tute [dέstətjut] *adj.* destituido, necesitado; falto, desprovisto.
de·stroy [dɪstrɔ́ɪ] *v.* destruir.
de·stroy·er [dɪstrɔ́ɪɚ] *s.* destruidor; destructor, cazatorpedero, destroyer.
de·struc·ti·ble [dɪstrʌ́ktəbl] *adj.* destructible.
de·struc·tion [dɪstrʌ́kʃən] *s.* destrucción; ruina.
de·struc·tive [dɪstrʌ́ktɪv] *adj.* destructivo.
de·tach [dɪtǽtʃ] *v.* separar, despegar, desprender; destacar (*una porción de tropa*).
de·tach·ment [dɪtǽtʃmənt] *s.* separación; desprendimiento; desapego, despego, alejamiento; destacamento (*militar*).
de·tail [dítel] *s.* detalle; pormenor; destacamento (*militar*); **to go into —** detallar, pormenorizar; [dɪtél] *v.* detallar; pormenorizar; destacar, asignar.
de·tain [dɪtén] *v.* detener; entretener, demorar, retardar.
de·tect [dɪtέkt] *v.* descubrir.
de·tec·tive [dɪtέktɪv] *s.* detective, detectivo, policía secreto.
de·ten·tion [dɪtέnʃən] *s.* detención.

de·ter [dɪtɝ́] *v.* disuadir.
de·ter·gent [dɪtɝ́dʒənt] *s.* detergente.
de·te·ri·o·rate [dɪtírɪəret] *v.* deteriorar(se).
de·te·ri·o·ra·tion [dɪtɪrɪəréʃən] *s.* deterioro.
de·ter·mi·na·tion [dɪtɝmənéʃən] *s.* determinación; decisión; resolución, firmeza.
de·ter·mine [dɪtɝ́mɪn] *v.* determinar; decidir; **to —** determinarse a, decidirse a, resolverse a.
de·ter·mined [dɪtɝ́mɪnd] *adj.* determinado, decidido, resuelto.
de·test [dɪtést] *v.* detestar, aborrecer.
de·tour [dítʊr] *s.* rodeo, desvío, desviación, vuelta; *v.* dar o hacer un rodeo.
devaluation [divæljuéʃən] *s.* devaluación.
dev·as·tate [dévəstet] *v.* devastar, arruinar, asolar.
de·vel·op [dɪvéləp] *v.* desarrollar(se); desenvolver(se); revelar (*una película o placa fotográfica*); explotar (*una mina*); **developing countries** países en desarrollo.
de·vel·op·ment [dɪvéləpmənt] *s.* (*evolution*) desarrollo; desenvolvimiento; evolución; crecimiento; (*generation*) fomento; explotación, (*photo*) revelado.
de·vi·ate [dívɪet] *v.* desviar(se).
de·vi·a·tion [divɪéʃən] *s.* desviación; desvío, extravío.
de·vice [dɪváɪs] *s.* artificio; mecanismo, aparato; ardid, recurso; divisa; dispositivo, plan; **left to one's own -s** abandonado a sus propios recursos.
dev·il [dévl] *s.* diablo; demonio.
dev·il·ish [dévlɪʃ] *adj.* diabólico; endiablado; travieso.
devilry [dévlrɪ] *s.* diablura.
de·vi·ous [dívɪ;əs] *adj.* desviado; tortuoso; indirecto.
de·vise [dɪváɪz] *v.* idear, trazar, urdir.
de·void [dɪvɔ́ɪd] *adj.* exento, libre, falto, privado, desprovisto.
de·vote [dɪvót] *v.* dedicar; consagrar; **to — oneself to** dedicarse a, consagrarse a, aplicarse a.
de·vot·ed [dɪvótɪd] *adj.* dedicado, consagrado; apegado; **— friend** amigo fiel o leal.
de·vo·tion [dɪvóʃən] *s.* devoción; piedad; afecto; lealtad.
de·vour [dɪváʊr] *v.* devorar.
de·vout [dɪváʊt] *adj.* devoto, piadoso; sincero.
dew [dju] *s.* rocío, sereno; *v.* rociar; caer (*el rocío*).
dew·drop [djúdrɑp] *s.* gota de rocío.
dew·y [djúɪ] *adj.* rociado, húmedo de rocío.
dex·ter·i·ty [dɛkstérətɪ] *s.* destreza.
dex·ter·ous [dékstrəs] *adj.* diestro.
dex·trose [dékstros] *s.* dextrosa.
di·a·dem [dáɪədɛm] *s.* diadema.
di·ag·nose [daɪəgnós] *v.* diagnosticar.
di·ag·o·nal [daɪǽgənl] *adj.* diagonal, oblicuo; *s.* diagonal.
di·a·gram [dáɪəgræm] *s.* diagrama.
di·al [dáɪəl] *s.* esfera; muestra (*del reloj*), *Méx., C.A.* carátula; **— telephone** teléfono automático; (*clock*) cuadrante **— tone** señal para marcar (*girar*); *v.* sintonizar o captar (*una estación radiotelefónica*); (*telephone*) marcar, girar.
di·a·lect [dáɪəlɛkt] *s.* dialecto.
di·a·lec·tol·o·gy [daɪ;əlɛktálədʒɪ] dialectología.
di·a·logue [dáɪəlɔg] *s.* diálogo; *v.* dialogar.
di·am·e·ter [daɪǽmətɚ] *s.* diámetro.
dia·mond [dáɪmənd] *s.* diamante; rombo (*figura geométrica*).
di·a·per [dáɪəpɚ] *s.* pañal.
di·ar·rhe·a [daɪəríə] *s.* diarrea.
di·a·ry [dáɪərɪ] *s.* diario.
dice [daɪs] *s. pl. de* **die** dados; *v.* cuadricular, cortar en cuarterones o cubos.
di·chot·o·my [daɪkɑ́təmɪ] *s.* dicotomía.
dick·er [díkɚ] *v.* regatear.
dic·tate [díktet] *s.* dictado, precepto; *v.* dictar.
dic·ta·tion [dɪktéʃən] *s.* dictado; mando absoluto; **to take —** escribir al dictado.
dic·ta·tor [díktetɚ] *s.* dictador.
dic·ta·tor·ship [dɪktétɚʃɪp] *s.* dictadura.
dic·tion [díkʃən] *s.* dicción.
dic·tion·ary [díkʃənɛrɪ] *s.* diccionario.
did [dɪd] *pret. de* **to do.**
die [daɪ] *s.* (*pl.* **dice**) dado (*para jugar*); (*pl.* **dies**) matriz, molde; cuño (*sello para acuñar moneda*).
die [daɪ] *v.* morir(se); marchitarse; secarse (*las flores, plantas, etc.*); **to — out** morirse, extinguirse, apagarse.
di·er·e·sis [daɪérəsɪs] *s.* diéresis.
di·et [dáɪət] *s.* dieta; régimen; **to be on a —** estar a dieta; **to put on a —** adietar, poner a dieta; *v.* ponerse a dieta; estar a dieta.
dif·fer [dífɚ] *v.* diferir, diferenciarse, distinguirse; disentir; **to — with** no convenir con, no estar de acuerdo con.
dif·fer·ence [dífrəns] *s.* diferencía; distinción; discordia, controversia; **it makes no —** no importa, es igual, da lo mismo.
dif·fer·ent [dífrənt] *adj.* diferente; distinto.
dif·fer·en·tial [dɪfɝénʃəl] *s.* diferencial.
dif·fer·en·ti·ate [dɪfərénʃɪet] *v.* diferenciar(se); distinguir(se).
dif·fi·cult [dífəkʌlt] *adj.* difícil; dificultoso, trabajoso, penoso.
dif·fi·cul·ty [dífəkʌltɪ] *s.* dificultad; apuro, aprieto.
dif·fi·dence [dífədəns] *s.* timidez; desconfianza de sí propio.
dif·fi·dent [dífədənt] *adj.* huraño; tímido.
dif·fuse [dɪfjús] *adj.* difuso; prolijo; [dɪfjúz] *v.* difundir.
dif·fu·sion [dɪfjúʒən] *s.* difusión; diseminación.
dig [dɪg] *v.* cavar; excavar; ahondar; escarbar; trabajar duro; **to — under** socavar; **to — up** desenterrar; *s.* piquete; pulla, sarcasmo.
di·gest [dáɪdʒɛst] *s.* sumario, compendio; recopilación; código; [dədʒést] *v.* digerir; recopilar.
di·gest·i·ble [dədʒéstəbl] *adj.* digestible, digerible.
di·ges·tion [dədʒéstʃən] *s.* digestión.
di·ges·tive [dədʒéstɪv] *adj.* digestivo.
dig·ni·fied [dígnəfaɪd] *adj.* digno, mesurado; serio, grave.
dig·ni·tar·y [dígnətɛrɪ] *s.* dignatario.
dig·ni·ty [dígnətɪ] *s.* dignidad.
di·graph [dáɪgræf] *s.* digrafo.
di·gress [dəgrés] *v.* divagar.
di·gres·sion [dəgréʃən] *s.* digresión, divagación.
dike [daɪk] *s.* dique, represa; zanja.
di·late [daɪlét] *v.* dilatar(se), extender(se), ensanchar(se).
dil·i·gence [dílədʒəns] *s.* diligencia; aplicación, esmero.
dil·i·gent [dílədʒənt] *adj.* diligente, activo, aplicado.
di·lute [dɪlút] *v.* diluir, desleír; aguar; *adj.* diluido.
dim [dɪm] *adj.* penumbroso, obscuro; nublado; confuso; indistinto; deslustrado, sin brillo; *v.* obscurecer; anublar, ofuscar; atenuar.
dime [daɪm] *s.* moneda de diez centavos; **a — a dozen** una baratura.
di·men·sion [dəménʃən] *s.* dimensión.
di·min·ish [dəmínɪʃ] *v.* disminuir; rebajar; **diminishing return** rendimiento decreciente.
dim·i·nu·tion [dɪmənjúʃən] *s.* diminución, mengua.
di·min·u·tive [dəmínjətɪv] *adj.* diminutivo; diminuto;

s. diminutivo.
dim·ness [dímnɪs] *s.* semi-obscuridad, penumbra; ofuscamiento.
dim·ple [dímpl̩] *s.* hoyuelo.
din [dɪn] *s.* estruendo, fragor, estrépito.
dine [daɪn] *v.* comer; festejar u obsequiar con una comida.
din·er [dáɪnɚ] *s.* coche-comedor; comensal (*persona que come a la mesa*).
din·gy [díndʒɪ] *adj.* negruzco; manchado, sucio.
din·ing [dáɪnɪŋ] *ger. de* **to dine**; — **car** coche-comedor; — **room** comedor.
din·ner [dínɚ] *s.* comida; — **coat** smoking o esmoquin.
dint [dɪnt]: **by** — **of** a fuerza de.
di·o·ram·a [daɪərǽmə] *s.* diorama.
dip [dɪp] *s.* zambullida; inmersión; (lower level) bajada; declive, depresión; *v.* meter(se); zambullirse; (*wet*) mojar (*la pluma en el tintero*); teñir; agachar (*la cabeza*); saludar (*con la bandera*); inclinarse (*un camino*); dar un bajón (*un avión*); hundirse (*el sol en el horizonte*); **to** — **out** vaciar (*con cucharón o cazo*).
diph·the·ri·a [dɪθírɪə] *s.* difteria.
diph·thong [dífθɔŋ] *s.* diptongo.
di·plo·ma [dɪplómə] *s.* diploma.
di·plo·ma·cy [dɪplóməsɪ] *s.* diplomacia.
dip·lo·mat [dípləmæt] *s.* diplomático.
dip·lo·mat·ic [dɪpləmǽtɪk] *adj.* diplomático.
dip·per [dípɚ] *s.* cucharón, cazo; **the Big Dipper** la Osa Mayor.
dire [daɪr] *adj.* extremo; horrendo; fatal, de mal agüero.
di·rect [dərέkt] *adj.* (*straight*) directo; derecho, en línea recta; *C.A.* recto; (*immediate*) inmediato; — **current** corriente continua; — **examination** primer interrogatorio; — **object** acusativo; — **mode** (*computer*) modo directo *adv.* directamente; **-ly** *adv.* directamente; inmediatamente; en seguida; *v.* dirigir; guiar; encaminar; dar direcciones u órdenes.
di·rec·tion [dərέkʃən] *s.* dirección; administración; gerencia; rumbo.
di·rec·tion·al an·ten·na [dərέkʃənl̩ æntέnə] *s.* antena direccional.
di·rec·tion·al sig·nal [dərέkʃənl̩ sígnl̩] *s.* señal direccional.
di·rec·tive [dərέktɪv] *adj.* directivo; *s.* orden, mandato.
di·rect·ness [dərέktnɪs] *s.* derechura; franqueza; lo directo; **with** — sin rodeos.
di·rec·tor [dərέktɚ] *s.* director; gerente.
di·rec·to·ry [dərέktərɪ] *s.* directorio; junta directiva; (*computer*) directorio; **telephone** — guía telefónica.
dir·i·gi·ble [dírədʒəbl̩] *adj.* & *s.* dirigible.
dirt [dɝt] *s.* suciedad; mugre; tierra, polvo, lodo; — **cheap** baratísimo.
dirt·y [dɝ́tɪ] *adj.* sucio; mugriento; cochino; enlodado; manchado; *v.* ensuciar; manchar; enlodar.
dis·a·bil·i·ty [dɪsəbílətɪ] incapacidad; — **clause** cláusula de incapacidad; — **claim** reclamación por incapacidad.
dis·a·ble [dɪsébl̩] *v.* incapacitar.
dis·ad·van·tage [dɪsədvǽntɪdʒ] *s.* desventaja; **to be at a** — estar en una situación desventajosa.
dis·a·gree [dɪsəgrí] *v.* (*dissent*) diferir, disentir; no convenir, no estar de acuerdo; (*bad effect*) no sentarle bien a uno (*el clima, la comida, etc.*).
dis·a·gree·a·ble [dɪsəgríəbl̩] *adj.* desagradable; áspero, de mal genio.
dis·a·gree·ment [dɪsəgrímənt] *s.* desavenencia, desacuerdo; disensión; discordia; discordancia.
dis·al·low [dísəlaʊ] *v.* desaprobar; rechazar.
dis·ap·pear [dɪsəpír] *v.* desaparecer.
dis·ap·pear·ance [dɪsəpírəns] *s.* desaparición.
dis·ap·point [dɪsəpɔ́ɪnt] *v.* chasquear; contrariar; decepcionar; faltar a lo prometido; desilusionar **to be -ed** estar desilusionado o decepcionado; estar desengañado; quedar contrariado.
dis·ap·point·ing [dɪsəpɔ́ɪntɪŋ] *adj.* desilusionante, desengañador, decepcionante.
dis·ap·point·ment [dɪsəpɔ́ɪntmənt] *s.* desilusión, desengaño, decepción; chasco; contrariedad.
dis·ap·prov·al [dɪsəprúvl̩] *s.* desaprobación.
dis·ap·prove [dɪsəprúv] *v.* desaprobar.
dis·arm [dɪsárm] *v.* desarmar(se).
dis·ar·ma·ment [dɪsárməmənt] *s.* desarme.
dis·ar·ray [dɪsəré] *s.* desarreglo, confusión, desorden; *v.* desarreglar, desordenar.
dis·as·ter [dizǽstɚ] *s.* desastre.
dis·as·trous [dɪzǽstrəs] *adj.* desastroso.
dis·band [dɪsbǽnd] *v.* dispersar; licenciar (*las tropas*); desbandarse.
dis·be·lieve [dɪsbəlív] *v.* descreer, no creer.
dis·burse [dɪsbɝ́s] *v.* desembolsar.
dis·burse·ment [dɪsbɝ́smənt] *s.* desembolso; gasto.
disc [dɪsk] = **disk.**
dis·card [dískɑrd] *s.* descarte; desecho, cosa desechada; [dɪskɑ́rd] *v.* descartar; desechar.
dis·cern [dɪsɝ́n] *v.* discernir, distinguir; percibir.
dis·cern·ment [dɪsɝ́nmənt] *s.* discernimiento.
dis·charge [dɪstʃɑ́rdʒ] *s.* descarga (*de artillería*); (*obligation*) descargo; (*duty*) desempeño (*de un deber*); (*freedom*) exoneración; despedida; licencia (*militar*); pago (*de una deuda*); derrame, desagüe; supuración; *v.* descargar; exonerar; poner en libertad; despedir; echar, deponer; dar de baja (*a un soldado*); (*hospital*) dar de alta; pagar (*una deuda*); arrojar, supurar; desaguar.
dis·ci·ple [dɪsáɪpl̩] *s.* discípulo.
dis·ci·pline [dísəplɪn] *s.* disciplina; *v.* disciplinar.
dis·close [dɪsklóz] *v.* descubrir; revelar.
dis·col·or [dɪskʌ́lɚ] *v.* descolorar(se), desteñir(se).
dis·com·fort [dɪskʌ́mfɚt] *s.* incomodidad; malestar.
dis·con·cert [dɪskənsɝ́t] *v.* desconcertar.
dis·con·nect [dɪskənέkt] *v.* desconectar; desacoplar; desunir, separar.
dis·con·nect·ed [dɪskənέktɪd] *p.p.* & *adj.* desconectado; desunido; inconexo, incoherente.
dis·con·so·late [dɪskɑ́nsl̩ɪt] *adj.* desconsolado.
dis·con·tent [dɪskəntέnt] *s.* descontento; *v.* descontentar.
dis·con·tent·ed [dɪskəntέntɪd] *adj.* descontento; descontentadizo.
dis·con·tin·ue [dɪskəntínju] *v.* descontinuar; parar; suspender, interrumpir; abandonar.
dis·cord [dískɔrd] *s.* discordia; disonancia, discordancia; desavenencia.
dis·count [dískaʊnt] *s.* descuento; rebaja; — **rate** tipo de descuento (tasa); *v.* descontar; rebajar.
dis·cour·age [dɪskɝ́ɪdʒ] *v.* desanimar, desalentar, abatir; **to** — **from** disuadir de.
dis·cour·age·ment [dɪskɝ́ɪdʒmənt] *s.* desaliento, abatimiento.
dis·course [dískors] *s.* discurso; conversación; [dɪskórs] *v.* disertar, discurrir, hablar.
dis·cour·te·ous [dɪskɝ́tɪəs] *adj.* descortés, desatento.
dis·cour·te·sy [dɪskɝ́təsɪ] *s.* descortesía, desatención.
dis·cov·er [dɪskʌ́vɚ] *v.* descubrir.
dis·cov·er·er [dɪskʌ́vərɚ] *s.* descubridor.

DE

dis·cov·er·y [dɪskʌ́vrɪ] *s.* descubrimiento.
dis·cred·it [dɪskrέdɪt] *s.* descrédito; deshonra; *v.* desacreditar; deshonrar; no creer.
dis·creet [dɪskrít] *adj.* discreto, prudente.
dis·crep·an·cy [dɪskrέpənsɪ] *s.* discrepancia, diferencia, variación.
dis·cre·tion [dɪskrέʃən] *s.* discreción; prudencia; **at one's own** — a discreción.
dis·crim·i·nate [dɪskrímənet] *v.* discernir; distinguir; hacer distinciones, hacer favoritismos; dar trato de inferioridad con motivos de perjuicio; **to — against** hacer favoritismos en perjuicio de.
dis·cuss [dɪskʌ́s] *v.* discutir.
dis·cus·sion [dɪskʌ́ʃən] *s.* discusión.
dis·dain [dɪsdén] *s.* desdén, menosprecio; *v.* desdeñar, menospreciar; desdeñarse de.
dis·dain·ful [dɪsdénfəl] *adj.* desdeñoso.
dis·ease [dɪzíz] *s.* enfermedad.
dis·eased [dɪzízd] *adj.* enfermo.
dis·em·bark [dɪsɪmbɑ́rk] *v.* desembarcar.
dis·en·tan·gle [dɪsɪntǽŋgl̩] *v.* desenredar, desenmarañar, deshacer (*una maraña o enredo*).
dis·fig·ure [dɪsfígjɚ] *v.* desfigurar; afear; desencajar.
dis·fran·chise [dɪsfrǽntʃaɪz] *v.* privar de derecho de voto o de ciudadanía.
dis·grace [dɪsgrés] *s.* ignominia, deshonra; vergüenza; **to be in** — estar desacreditado, haber perdido la gracia o el favor; *v.* deshonrar; degradar; desacreditar; avergonzar.
dis·grace·ful [dɪsgrésfəl] *adj.* vergonzoso.
dis·guise [dɪsgáɪz] *s.* disfraz; *v.* disfrazar.
dis·gust [dɪsgʌ́st] *s.* asco; repugnancia; disgusto; *v.* disgustar, dar asco; repugnar.
dis·gust·ed [dɪsgʌ́stɪd] *adj.* disgustado; descontento; asqueado.
dis·gust·ing [dɪsgʌ́stɪŋ] *adj.* asqueroso, repugnante.
dish [dɪʃ] *s.* plato; manjar, vianda; **-es** vajilla; *v.* servir.
dis·heart·en [dɪshɑ́rtn̩] *v.* desalentar, desanimar, descorazonar.
di·shev·el [dɪʃέvl] *v.* desgreñar.
di·shev·eled [dɪʃέvl̩d] *adj.* desgreñado; desaliñado, desaseado; revuelto.
dis·hon·est [dɪsɑ́nɪst] *adj.* engañoso, falso, tramposo, falto de honradez, fraudulento.
dis·hon·es·ty [dɪsɑ́nɪstɪ] *s.* fraude, falta de honradez.
dis·hon·or [dɪsɑ́nɚ] *s.* deshonra; afrenta; *v.* deshonrar; recusar (*un giro o cheque*).
dis·hon·or·a·ble [dɪsɑ́nərəbl̩] *adj.* deshonroso; infame.
dish·wash·er [dɪ́ʃwɔʃɚ] *s.* (*person*) lavaplatos; (*machine*) máquina de lavar platos.
dis·il·lu·sion [dɪsɪlúʒən] *s.* desilusión, decepción, desengaño; *v.* desilusionar, decepcionar, desengañar.
dis·in·fect [dɪsɪnfέkt] *v.* desinfectar.
dis·in·fec·tant [dɪsɪnfέktənt] *s.* desinfectante.
dis·in·ter·est·ed [dɪsɪ́ntərəstɪd] *adj.* desinteresado.
disk [dɪsk] *s.* disco; (*computer*) disco, disquette; — **drive** impulsor de discos, unidad de discos; **floppy** — disco flexible; **hard** — disco rígido (duro); — **brake** freno de disco.
dis·like [dɪsláɪk] *s.* antipatía, aversión; *v.* sentir o tener aversión por; **I — it** me repugna, no me gusta, me desagrada.
dis·lo·cate [dɪ́sloket] *v.* dislocar, descoyuntar; desencajar.
dis·lodge [dɪslɑ́dʒ] *v.* desalojar.
dis·loy·al [dɪslɔ́ɪəl] *adj.* desleal.
dis·mal [dɪ́zml̩] *adj.* lúgubre, sombrío, tétrico.
dis·man·tle [dɪsmǽntl̩] *v.* desmantelar; desmontar, desarmar.
dis·may [dɪsmé] *s.* desmayo, desaliento, pavor; *v.* desalentar, desanimar; atemorizar.
dis·miss [dɪsmɪ́s] *v.* (*discharge*) despedir, expulsar, destituir; (*dispel*) desechar; (*allow to leave*) licenciar, dar de baja; (*close*) dar por terminado (*un pleito o caso jurídico*); **to — the meeting** disolver la junta, levantar la sesión.
dis·miss·al [dɪsmɪ́sl̩] *s.* despedida, expulsión, destitución (*de un cargo*).
dis·mount [dɪsmáʊnt] *v.* desmontar; apear(se); desarmar (*un cañón, una máquina*); desengastar (*joyas*).
dis·o·be·di·ence [dɪsəbídɪəns] *s.* desobediencia.
dis·o·be·di·ent [dɪsəbídɪənt] *adj.* desobediente.
dis·o·bey [dɪsəbé] *v.* desobedecer.
dis·or·der [dɪsɔ́rdɚ] *s.* (*confusion*) desorden; trastorno; confusión; (*illness*) enfermedad; *v.* desordenar; trastornar; desarreglar.
dis·or·der·ly [dɪsɔ́rdɚlɪ] *adj.* desordenado; desarreglado; revoltoso; escandaloso; *adv.* desordenadamente.
dis·own [dɪsón] *v.* repudiar; desconocer, negar.
dis·par·age [dɪspǽrɪdʒ] *v.* desacreditar; desdorar.
dis·pas·sion·ate [dɪspǽʃənɪt] *adj.* desapasionado.
dis·patch [dɪspǽtʃ] *s.* despacho; envío; parte (*m.*), comunicación, mensaje; prontitud, expedición; *v.* despachar; enviar, expedir; matar.
dis·pel [dɪspέl] *v.* disipar; dispersar.
dis·pen·sa·ry [dɪspέnsərɪ] *s.* dispensario.
dis·pen·sa·tion [dɪspənséʃən] *s.* dispensa, exención; dispensación; distribución.
dis·pense [dɪspέns] *v.* (*give*) dispensar, dar; repartir, distribuir; administrar (*la justicia*); despachar (*recetas, medicamentos*); **to — from** eximir de, dispensar de; **to — with** omitir; pasarse sin, prescindir de.
dis·per·sal [dɪspɝ́sl̩] *s.* dispersión; desbandada.
dis·perse [dɪspɝ́s] *v.* dispersar(se), disipar(se), esparcir(se).
dis·place [dɪsplés] *v.* desalojar; desplazar; poner fuera de su lugar; suplantar.
dis·placed per·son [dɪsplést pɝsən] *s.* persona desplazada.
dis·play [dɪsplé] *s.* manifestación, exhibición; — **poster** cartel de publicidad; ostentación; (*computer*) visualización; *v.* exhibir; mostrar, manifestar; desplegar; (*computer*) visualizar.
dis·please [dɪsplíz] *v.* desagradar; disgustar, fastidiar.
dis·pleas·ure [dɪsplέʒɚ] *s.* desagrado, disgusto, descontento.
dis·pos·al [dɪspózl̩] *s.* disposición; arreglo; venta (*de bienes*).
dis·pose [dɪspóz] *v.* disponer; arreglar; influir; **to — of** deshacerse de.
dis·po·si·tion [dɪspəzɪ́ʃən] *s.* disposición; arreglo; aptitud, inclinación; venta; **good (bad)** — buen (mal) genio.
dis·pos·ses [dɪspozέs] *v.* desposeer; despojar.
dis·prove [dɪsprúv] *v.* refutar.
dis·pute [dɪspjút] *s.* disputa; *v.* disputar.
dis·qual·i·fy [dɪskwɑ́ləfaɪ] *v.* inhabilitar, incapacitar, descalificar.
dis·re·gard [dɪsrɪgɑ́rd] *s.* desatención, falta de atención, negligencia, descuido; falta de respeto o consideración; *v.* desatender, no hacer caso de, desentenderse de.
dis·re·spect [dɪsrɪspέkt] *s.* desacato, falta de respeto.
dis·re·spect·ful [dɪsrɪspέktfəl] *adj.* irrespetuoso.
dis·rupt [dɪsrʌ́pt] *v.* desbaratar; romper.
dis·sat·is·fied [dɪssǽtɪsfaɪd] *adj.* descontento, malcontento, mal satisfecho.

dis·sat·is·fy [dɪssǽtɪsfaɪ] *v.* descontentar, no satisfacer.
dis·sect [dɪsέkt] *v.* disecar, hacer una disección; analizar.
dis·sem·ble [dɪsέmbl̩] *v.* disimular, fingir.
dis·sen·sion [dɪsέnʃən] *s.* disensión, discordia.
dis·sent [dɪsέnt] *v.* disentir; *s.* desacuerdo; disensión, desavenencia.
dis·ser·ta·tion [dɪsɝtéʃən] *s.* disertación; tratado; tesis.
dis·sim·u·la·tion [dɪsɪmjəléʃən] *s.* disimulo.
dis·si·pate [dísəpet] *v.* disipar(se).
dis·si·pa·tion [dɪsəpéʃən] *s.* disipación.
dis·so·lute [dísəlut] *adj.* disoluto.
dis·so·lu·tion [dɪsəlúʃən] *s.* disolución.
dis·solve [dɪzɑ́lv] *v.* disolver(se); anular; derogar, liquidar.
dis·suade [dɪswéd] *v.* disuadir.
dis·taff [dístæf] *s.* rueca.
dis·tance [dístəns] *s.* distancia; lejanía; alejamiento; **in the** — a lo lejos, en lontananza.
dis·tant [dístənt] *adj.* (*far*) distante; apartado, lejano, remoto; (*aloof*) esquivo; **to be** — **from** distar de; **-ly** *adv.* de lejos; remotamente; a distancia; en lontananza.
dis·taste [dɪstést] *s.* disgusto, aversión, repugnancia.
dis·taste·ful [dɪstéstfəl] *adj.* desagradable, repugnante.
dis·tem·per [dɪstέmpɚ] *s.* moquillo; pepita (*de las gallinas*).
dis·tend [dɪstέnd] *v.* dilatar; ensanchar.
dis·til [dɪstíl] *v.* destilar.
dis·til·la·tion [dɪstl̩éʃən] *s.* destilación.
dis·till·er·y [dɪstílərɪ] *s.* destilería.
dis·tinct [dɪstíŋkt] *adj.* distinto, claro; diferente; **-ly** *adv.* distintamente, claramente, con claridad.
dis·tinc·tion [dɪstíŋkʃən] *s.* distinción.
dis·tinc·tive [dɪstíŋktɪv] *adj.* distintivo.
dis·tin·guish [dɪstíŋgwɪʃ] *v.* distinguir; discernir.
dis·tin·guished [dɪstíŋgwɪʃt] *adj.* distinguido.
dis·tin·guish·ing [dɪstíŋgwɪʃɪŋ] *adj.* distintivo, característico.
dis·tort [dɪstɔ́rt] *v.* desfigurar, deformar, torcer, falsear; tergivesar.
dis·tract [dɪstrǽkt] *v.* distraer; perturbar.
dis·trac·tion [dɪstrǽkʃən] *s.* distracción, diversión; perturbación; **to drive to** — volver loco.
dis·tress [dɪstrέs] *s.* angustia, aflicción, congoja; dolor; **to be in** — tener una aflicción; estar apurado; estar en zozobra (*un navío*); *v.* angustiar, acongojar, afligir; **to be -ed** estar afligido o apurado.
dis·trib·ute [dɪstríbjʊt] *v.* distribuir, repartir.
dis·tri·bu·tion [dɪstrəbjúʃən] *s.* distribución; repartimiento.
dis·trib·u·tor [dɪstríbjətɚ] *s.* distribuidor.
dis·trict [dístrɪkt] *s.* distrito; — **attorney** fiscal de distrito.
dis·trust [dɪstrʌ́st] *s.* deconfianza; recelo; *v.* desconfiar; recelar.
dis·trust·ful [dɪstrʌ́stfəl] *adj.* desconfiado, sospechoso, receloso.
dis·turb [dɪstɝ́b] *v.* turbar, perturbar, inquietar; desarreglar; incomodar, molestar; **don't** — **yourself!** ¡no se moleste Vd.!
dis·tur·bance [dɪstɝ́bəns] *s.* disturbio; perturbación; desorden; alboroto; molestia.
dis·use [dɪsjús] *s.* desuso; **to fall into** — caer en desuso; caducar.
ditch [dɪtʃ] *s.* zanja; foso; **irrigation** — acequia; *v.* zanjar, abrir zanjas; meter en la zanja; **to** — **someone** deshacerse de alguien.
dit·to [díto] *s.* idem, lo mismo.
di·u·ret·ic [daɪjʊrέtɪk] *adj.* & *s.* diurético.
di·van [dáɪvæn] *s.* diván.
dive [daɪv] *s.* zambullida (*echándose de cabeza*), buceada, chapuz; picada (*descenso rápido de un avión*); *Méx.* clavado; (*place*) garito, leonera; *v.* echarse de cabeza; zambullirse (*de cabeza*); bucear; sumergirse (*un submarino*); **to** — **into someone** abalanzarse sobre alguien.
div·er [dáɪvɚ] *s.* buzo; zambullidor.
di·verge [dəvɝ́dʒ] *v.* divergir, irse apartando, separarse; diferir.
di·ver·gence [dəvɝ́dʒəns] *s.* divergencia; diferencia (*de opiniones*).
di·vers [dáɪvɚz] *adj.* diversos, varios.
di·verse [dəvɝ́s] *adj.* diverso; diferente.
di·ver·sion [dəvɝ́ʒən] *s.* diversión, recreo; desviación.
di·ver·si·ty [dəvɝ́sətɪ] *s.* diversidad, diferencia, variedad.
di·vert [dəvɝ́t] *v.* divertir, entretener; distraer; desviar, apartar.
di·vide [dəváɪd] *v.* dividir(se); partir.
div·i·dend [dívədεnd] *s.* dividendo.
di·vid·ing [dɪváɪdɪŋ] *adj.* divisorio.
di·vine [dəváɪn] *adj.* divino; *v.* adivinar.
di·vin·i·ty [dəvínətɪ] *s.* divinidad; deidad; teología.
di·vi·sion [dəvíʒən] *s.* división.
di·vorce [dəvórs] *s.* divorcio; *v.* divorciar(se).
di·vulge [dəvʌ́ldʒ] *v.* divulgar.
diz·zi·ness [dízɪnɪs] *s.* vahido o vaguido, desvanecimiento, mareo, vértigo.
diz·zy [dízɪ] *adj.* desvanecido, mareado; (*confused*) confuse; aturdido; — **speed** velocidad vertiginosa.
do [du] *v.* hacer; **to** — **away with** deshacerse de; prescindir de; **to** — **a lesson** estudiar una lección; **to** — **one's hair** peinarse, arreglarse el pelo; **to** — **the dishes** lavar los platos; **to** — **up** envolver; limpiar, arreglar; lavar o planchar; **to** — **well in business** prosperar en los negocios; **to** — **without** pasarse sin; **to have nothing to** — **with** no tener nada que ver con; **that will** — basta, bastará; **that won't** — eso no sirve; eso no resultará bien; **this will have to** — habrá que conformarse con esto; **how** — **you** —? ¿cómo está Vd.?; — **you hear me?** ¿me oye Vd.?; **yes, I** — sí, le oigo; **I** — **say it** sí lo digo.
doc·ile [dɑ́sl̩] *adj.* dócil.
dock [dɑk] *s.* muelle, desembarcadero; dársena; dique; **dry** — carenero, dique de carena; *v.* entrar en el muelle; atracar, meter (*una embarcación*) en el muelle o dique; **to** — **the wages** rebajar la paga.
doc·tor [dɑ́ktɚ] *s.* doctor; médico, facultativo; *v.* medicinar, curar; **to** — **oneself** medicinarse, tomar medicinas.
doc·trine [dɑ́ktrɪn] *s.* doctrina.
doc·u·ment [dɑ́kjəmənt] *s.* documento; [dɑ́kjəmεnt] *v.* documentar.
dod·der [dɑ́dɚ] *v.* tambalear; temblar.
dodge [dɑdʒ] *s.* evasión, evasiva; *v.* evadir(se); escabullirse; hurtar el cuerpo; **to** — **around a corner** dar un esquinazo.
doe [do] *s.* cierva; hembra (*del antílope, del gamo, de la liebre*).
dog [dɔg] *s.* perro, perra; can; **hot** — salchicha caliente, *Ch., C.A.* perro caliente; *Ríopl.* pancho; **to put on a lot of** — emperifollarse; darse mucho tono, *Am.* darse mucho corte; *v.* seguir la pista de, perseguir, acosar; *adv.* sumamente, completamente; **dog-tired** cansadísimo.

dog·ma [dɔ́gmə] *s.* dogma.
dog·mat·ic [dɔgmǽtɪk] *adj.* dogmático.
doi·ly [dɔ́ɪlɪ] *s.* mantelito (*para platos, vasos, lámparas, etc.*).
do·ings [dúɪŋz] *s. pl.* hechos, acciones, acontecimientos; **great** — mucha actividad, fiesta, función.
do-it-your·self [duɪtjʊrsɛ́lf] *adj.* proyectado para que uno pueda hacer sus propios trabajos manuales en casa; autodidáctico.
dole [dol] *s.* reparto gratuito (*de dinero o alimento*); ración, limosna; *v.* repartir gratuitamente.
dole·ful [dólfəl] *adj.* lúgubre, triste, lastimoso.
doll [dɑl] *s.* muñeca, muñeco; *v.* **to — up** emperifollarse, ataviarse; **dolly** *s.* muñequita.
dol·lar [dɑ́lɚ] *s.* dólar; — **diplomacy** diplomacia mercantilista; — **exchange** divisa en dólares.
dol·phin [dɔ́lfɪn] *s.* delfín.
do·main [domén] *s.* dominio; heredad.
dome [dom] *s.* cúpula; media naranja (*de iglesia*).
do·mes·tic [dəmɛ́stɪk] *adj.* doméstico; hogareño; nacional, del país, *Am.* criollo; *s.* criado, sirviente.
do·mi·cile [dɑ́məsaɪl] *s.* domicilio.
dom·i·nant [dɑ́mənənt] *adj.* dominante.
dom·i·nate [dɑ́mənet] *v.* dominar.
dom·i·na·tion [dɑmənéʃən] *s.* dominación, dominio.
dom·i·neer [dɑmənír] *v.* dominar, señorear.
dom·i·neer·ing [dɑmənírɪŋ] *adj.* dominador, mandón, imperioso, tiránico.
do·min·ion [dəmínjən] *s.* dominio.
dom·i·no [dɑ́məno] *s.* dominó, traje de máscara; disfraz; (*game*) ficha (*de dominó*); **dominoes** dominó (*juego*).
don [dɑn] *s.* don (*título*); caballero; *v.* ponerse, vestirse.
do·nate [dónet] *v.* donar, regalar, hacer donación.
do·na·tion [donéʃən] *s.* donación; regalo, dádiva.
done [dʌn] *p.p. de* **to do** hecho; terminado, acabado; **to be — in** estar rendido de cansancio; **the meat is well** — está bien asada la carne.
don·key [dɑ́ŋkɪ] *s.* burro, asno.
doo·dad [dúdæd] *s.* chuchería, chisme.
doom [dum] *s.* hado, sino, destino; mala suerte, perdición, ruina; **the day of** — el día del juicio final; *v.* condenar, sentenciar; predestinar; **to be -ed to failure** estar predestinado al fracaso.
door [dor] *s.* puerta; entrada.
door·bell [dórbɛl] *s.* campanilla o timbre (*de llamada*).
door·knob [dórnɑb] *s.* tirador de puerta, perilla, manija.
door·man [dórmæn] *s.* portero.
door·step [dórstɛp] *s.* escalón de la puerta; umbral.
door·way [dórwe] *s.* puerta, entrada; vano (*de la puerta*).
dope [dop] *s.* (*narcotic*) narcótico; opio; droga; menjurje, medicamento; — **addict** drogadicto; — **racket** tráfico ilícito de narcóticos; (*information*) información; — **fiend** morfinómano; **he is a** — es un zoquete; *v.* narcotizar; **to — out** adivinar, conjeturar; **to — oneself up** medicinarse demasiado.
dor·mi·to·ry [dɔ́rmətorɪ] *s.* dormitorio.
DOS (Disk Operating System) *s.* (*computer*) SOD (Sistema operativo de disquettes)
dose [dos] *s.* dosis; *v.* medicinar; **to — oneself** medicinarse.
dos·si·er [dásie] *s.* expediente; legajo.
dot [dɑt] *s.* punto; **on the** — en punto; **dot-matrix printer** *s.* (*computer*) impresora de matriz de puntos; *v.* marcar con puntos; poner el punto (*sobre la* i).
do·tage [dótɪdʒ] *s.* chochez; **to be in one's** — chochear.
dote [dot] *v.* chochear; **to — on** estar loco por.
dou·ble [dʌ́bl̩] *adj.* doble; doblado; — **boiler** baño de María; — **check** verificar, revisar; — **deal** trato doble; — **entry** partida doble; — **standard** norma de conducta sexual más restringida para la mujer; — **shift** turno doble; *s.* doble; **-s** juego de dobles (*en tenis*); *adv.* doblemente; **double-breasted** cruzado; **double-faced** de dos caras; — **density** (*computer*) doble densidad; — **sided** (de dos) caras; *v.* doblar(se); duplicar(se); **to — up** doblarse; **doubly** *adv.* doblemente; por duplicado.
doubt [daʊt] *s.* duda; *v.* dudar.
doubt·ful [dáʊtfəl] *adj.* dudoso; dudable.
doubt·less [dáʊtlɪs] *adj.* indudable, cierto, seguro; *adv.* sin duda; indudablemente; probablemente.
douche [duʃ] *s.* ducha vaginal.
dough [do] *s.* pasta, masa; dinero.
dough·nut [dónət] *s.* bollito o buñuelo en rosca.
dove [dʌv] *s.* paloma.
dove [dov] *pret. de* **to dive.**
down [daʊn] *adv.* abajo, hacia abajo; — **to** hasta; — **East** en el este; — **the street** calle abajo; **to cut — prices** reducir o rebajar precios; **to get — to work** aplicarse; **to go (come)** — bajar; **to pay** — pagar al contado; **to put** — poner; anotar, apuntar, poner por escrito; *adj.* abatido, descorazonado; — **grade** declive, pendiente; — **payment** pago inicial; *Col.* cuota inicial; *Méx.* enganche; **prices are** — han bajado los precios; **to be — on someone** tenerle ojeriza a alguien; *s.* plumón; vello; pelusa; *v.* echar por tierra, derribar; rebajar (*precios*).
down·cast [dáʊnkæst] *adj.* cabizbajo, abatido; **with — eyes** con los ojos bajos.
down·fall [dáʊnfɔl] *s.* caída; ruina.
down·pour [dáʊnpor] *s.* aguacero, chaparrón.
down·right [dáʊnraɪt] *adj.* claro, positivo, categórico, absoluto; — **foolishness** solemne disparate; *adv.* enteramente; absolutamente.
down·stairs [dáʊnstɛ́rz] *adv.* abajo; en el piso bajo; *adj.* del piso bajo; *s.* piso bajo, piso inferior.
down·stream [dáʊnstrím] *adv.* río abajo, aguas abajo; con la corriente.
down-to-earth [daʊntəɝ́θ] *adj.* sensato; práctico.
down·town [dáʊntáʊn] *adv.* al centro, en el centro (*de una población*); *adj.* del centro; *s.* centro.
down·turn [dáʊntɚn] *s.* tendencia a la baja.
down·ward [dáʊnwɚd] *adj.* descendente; inclinado, *adv.* (= **downwards**) hacia abajo.
dow·ny [dáʊnɪ] *adj.* suave, blando; velloso; plumoso.
dow·ry [dáʊrɪ] *s.* dote.
doze [doz] *s.* siestecita, sueño ligero; *v.* dormitar.
doz·en [dʌ́zn̩] *s.* docena.
drab [dræb] *adj.* pardo, pardusco; monótono.
draft [dræft] *s.* corriente de aire; (*drink*) trago; (*bank*) libranza, letra de cambio, giro bancario; (*tracing*) trazado; plan; leva (*militar*), conscripción; (*stove*) tiro (*de estufa, hogar, etc.*); calado (*de un barco*); — **beer** cerveza de barril; — **horse** caballo de tiro; **rough** — croquis, borrador; *v.* trazar, dibujar, delinear, reclutar, echar leva; redactar (*un documento*).
drafts·man [drǽftsmən] *s.* dibujante.
drag [dræg] *s.* rastra; traba, obstáculo; **to have a — with someone** tener buenas aldabas con alguien; *v.* arrastrar(se); rastrear; moverse despacio; **to — on and on** prolongarse demasiado, prolongarse hasta el fastidio.

drag·on [drǽgən] *s.* dragón.
drain [dren] *s.* (*channel*) desagüe; desaguadero, conducto; (*exhaust*) agotamiento; consumo; *v.* desaguar(se); apurar (*un vaso*); agotar, consumir; escurrir(se), secar(se); desecar (*un terreno*), *Am.* drenar.
drain·age [drénɪdʒ] *s.* desagüe, *Am.* drenaje; desaguadero; sistema de desaguaderos; desecamiento, desecación (*de un terreno, laguna, etc.*).
drake [drek] *s.* pato.
dra·ma [drámə] *s.* drama.
dra·mat·ic [drəmǽtɪk] *adj.* dramático.
dra·ma·tist [drámətɪst] *s.* dramaturgo, dramático.
dra·ma·tize [drǽmətaɪz] *v.* dramatizar.
drank [dræŋk] *pret. de* **to drink.**
drape [drep] *s.* colgadura, cortina, tapiz; *v.* colgar, entapizar, adornar con tapices; cubrir, revestir.
drap·er·y [drépərɪ] *s.* tapicería, colgaduras, cortinas; pañería, paños, géneros.
dras·tic [drǽstɪk] *adj.* extremo, fuerte, violento; **to take — steps** tomar medidas enérgicas.
draught [drǽft] *véase* **draft.**
draw [drɔ] *v.* (*pull*) tirar; estirar; jalar; (*attract*) atraer, sacar; (*design*) dibujar, trazar; (*withdraw*) girar, librar (*una libranza*); hacer (*una comparación*); correr (*la cortina*); **to — aside** apartar(se); **to — a breath** aspirar, tomar aliento; **to — a blank** fracasar; **to — lots** echar suertes, sortear; **to — near** acercarse; **to — out** sacar; sonsacar (*a una persona*); alargar, prolongar; **to — up** acercar(se); redactar (*un documento*); *s.* empate (*en deportes o juegos*); número sacado (*en una rifa*); atracción; — **bridge** puente levadizo.
draw·back [drɔ́bæk] *s.* desventaja; obstáculo, inconveniente.
draw·ee [drɔí] *s.* girado, librado.
drawer [drɔr] *s.* cajón, gaveta; **-s** calzoncillos.
draw·er [drɔ́ɚ] *s.* librador, girador; dibujante.
draw·ing [drɔ́ɪŋ] *s.* (*design*) dibujo; delineación, trazado; (*raffle*) sorteo; — **paper** papel de dibujo; — **room** sala de recibo, recibidor, recibimiento.
drawn [drɔn] *p.p. de* **to draw.**
dread [drɛd] *s.* pavor, temor, aprensión; *adj.* terrible; temido; *v.* temer; sentir aprensión de.
dread·ful [drɛ́dfəl] *adj.* horrendo; espantoso.
dream [drim] *s.* sueño; ensueño; *v.* soñar; **to — of** soñar con, soñar en.
dream·er [drímɚ] *s.* soñador.
dream·land [drímlænd] *s.* tierra del ensueño; región de los sueños.
dreamt [drɛmpt] = **dreamed.**
drea·my [drímɪ] *adj.* soñoliento; soñador; melancólico; como un sueño; **a — recollection** un vago recuerdo.
drea·ry [drírɪ] *adj.* sombrío; melancólico.
dredge [drɛdʒ] *s.* draga; *v.* dragar.
dregs [drɛgz] *s. pl.* heces, sedimento.
drench [drɛnʃ] *s.* mojada, mojadura, empapada; *v.* empapar; mojar; remojar.
dress [drɛs] *s.* vestido, traje; (*apparel*) vestidura, ropaje, atavío; — **rehearsal** ensayo general y último (*antes de una función*); — **suit** traje de etiqueta; *v.* vestir(se); arreglarse, componerse; aderezar; adobar (*carne o pieles*); curar (*heridas*), alinear, formar (*las tropas*); **to — down** reprender, regañar; **to — up** emperifollarse, acicalarse, ataviarse.
dress·er [drɛ́sɚ] *s.* tocador, cómoda (*con espejo*); **she is a good —** viste con elegancia o buen gusto.
dress·ing [drɛ́sɪŋ] *s.* aderezo; salsa (*para ensaladas*); relleno (*para carne, pollo, etc.*); medicamento, vendajes (*para heridas*); **a — down** regaño; — **gown** bata; — **room** tocador; — **table** tocador.
dress·mak·er [drɛ́smekɚ] *s.* modista.
drew [dru] *pret. de* **to draw.**
drib·ble [drɪ́bl̩] *v.* gotear; dejar caer en gotas; babear; *s.* goteo; chorrito.
drib·let [drɪ́blɪt] *s.* gota, gotita; **in -s** gota a gota; en pequeñas cantidades.
dried [draɪd] *pret. & p.p. de* **to dry;** *adj.* seco; paso; — **fig** higo paso.
drift [drɪft] *s.* (*direction*) rumbo dirección, tendencia, deriva; (*pile*) montón, amontonamiento (*de arena, nieve, etc.*); (*off course*) desvío (*de un barco o avión*); **to get the — of a conversation** enterarse a medias de una conversación; *v.* flotar; ir(se) a la deriva; dejarse llevar por la corriente; amontonarse (*la nieve, la arena*); esparcirse (*la arena, la nieve, las nubes*).
drift·wood [drɪ́ftwʊd] *s.* madera o leña flotante; madera de playa.
drill [drɪl] *s.* (*tool*) taladro; barrena; (*training*) ejercicio; adiestramiento; *Am.* entrenamiento; (*cloth*) dril (*tela*); *v.* taladrar, barrenar, perforar; hacer ejercicio; aleccionar; disciplinar (*un ejército*); adiestrar(se), *Am.* entrenar(se).
dri·ly [dráɪlɪ] *adv.* secamente.
drink [drɪŋk] *s.* bebida; trago; *v.* beber; **to — a toast to** beber a la salud de, brindar por; — **it down!** ¡bébaselo! ¡tráguesclo!
drink·a·ble [drɪ́ŋkəbl̩] *adj.* potable.
drip [drɪp] *s.* goteo; *v.* gotear, caer gota a gota; dejar caer gota a gota.
drive [draɪv] *s.* (*ride*) paseo en coche; (*road*) calzada, carretera, paseo; (*campaign*) campaña; (*impulse*) empuje; tiro, tirada (*de una pelota*); *v.* impulsar, impeler, empujar; arrear (*animales*); conducir, guiar o manejar (*un auto*); forzar; encajar, clavar (*una estaca, cuña, o clavo*); tirar, lanzar (*una pelota*); dar un paseo en auto; llevar (*a alguien*) en auto; cavar (*un pozo, túnel, etc.*); **to — away** ahuyentar; **to — a good bargain** hacer un buen trato; **to — a hard bargain** regatear mucho; **to — mad** volver loco; **what are you driving at?** ¿qué quieres decir con eso?
drive-in [dráɪvɪn] *s. adj.* establecimiento como tienda, banco, teatro que tiene pista automovilística que permite al cliente permanecer en su coche; automovilístico.
driv·el [drɪ́vl̩] *s.* baba; ñoñería, tontería; *v.* babear; chochear, decir ñoñerías.
driv·el·ing [drɪvlɪŋ] *adj.* baboso.
driv·en [drɪ́vən] *p.p. de* **to drive.**
driv·er [dráɪvɚ] *s.* cochero, chófer, mecánico, conductor (*de automóvil*); *C.A.* motorista; arriero (*de animales*); uno de los palos de golf; **pile —** martinete (*para clavar pilotes*); **slave —** mandón, tirano; **truck —** carretero, camionero.
drive·way [dráɪvwe] *s.* calzada de entrada, carretera de entrada.
driz·zle [drɪ́zl̩] *v.* lloviznar; *s.* llovizna.
drone [dron] *s.* zángano; holgazán; (*sound*) zumbido; *v.* zumbar; hablar con monotonía; (*be lazy*) holgazanear, perder el tiempo.
droop [drup] *v.* doblarse, andar o estar alicaído, estar abatido; languidecer; marchitarse; bajar (*los hombros, los párpados*); **his shoulders —** tiene los hombros caídos; **-ing eyelids** párpados caídos.
drop [drɑp] *s.* (*liquid*) gota; (*descent*) baja; caída; (*incline*) declive; **cough —** pastilla para la tos; **letter —** buzón; — **curtain** telón (*de teatro*); —

hammer martinete; — **out** dimitente; *v.* dejar caer, soltar; gotear; caer; dejar (*un asunto, una amistad*); **to — a line** poner unos renglones; **to — asleep** quedarse dormido, dormirse; **to — behind** dejar atrás; quedarse atrás; **to — in** hacer una visita inesperada, *Am.* descolgarse; **to — in a mailbox** echar al buzón; **to — out** retirarse; desaparecer; **to — the curtain** bajar el telón.
drought [draʊt] *s.* sequía.
drove [drov] *s.* manada, recua, rebaño; tropel; *pret. de* **to drive.**
drown [draʊn] *v.* ahogar(se), anegar(se); apagar, ahogar (*un sonido*).
drowse [draʊz] *v.* dormitar; estar amodorrado.
drows·i·ness [dráʊzɪnɪs] *s.* modorra, somnolencia.
drow·sy [dráʊzɪ] *adj.* soñoliento; adormilado, amodorrado; **to become** — amodorrarse.
drudge [drʌdʒ] *v.* afanarse, atarearse; *s.* trabajador, esclavo del trabajo.
drug [drʌg] *s.* droga; narcótico; **to be a — on the market** ser invendible (*una mercancía*); — **addict** drogadicto; *v.* jaropar (*administrar drogas en demasía*); narcotizar.
drug·gist [drʌ́gɪst] *s.* boticario, droguista, droguero, farmacéutico.
drug·store [drʌ́gstor] *s.* botica, droguería, farmacia.
drum [drʌm] *s.* tambor; tímpano (*del oído*); barril, tonel; **bass** — tambora, bombo; — **stick** bolillo de tambor; — **major** tambor mayor; *v.* tocar el tambor; tamborilear; **to — a lesson into someone** meterle a uno la lección en la cabeza; **to — up trade** solicitar o fomentar ventas.
drum·mer [drʌ́mɚ] *s.* tambor, tamborilero; viajante de comercio, agente.
drunk [drʌŋk] *p.p. de* **to drink;** *adj.* borracho, ebrio, emborrachado, bebido; *Ríopl.* mamado; *C.A.* bolo; *Ch.* cufifo; *Méx.* pedo; **to get** — emborracharse, embriagarse.
drunk·ard [drʌ́ŋkɚd] *s.* borracho, borrachón, beodo, bebedor.
drunk·en [drʌ́ŋjən] *adj.* borracho, ebrio.
drunk·en·ness [drʌ́ŋkənnɪs] *s.* borrachera, embriaguez.
dry [draɪ] *adj.* seco; árido; **a — book** un libro aburrido; — **cleaner** quitamanchas; tintorero; — **cleaning** lavado o limpieza al seco; — **goods** lencería, géneros, tejidos, telas; — **measure** medida para áridos, — **run** ejercicio de ensayo; ensayo; — **wash** ropa lavada pero no planchada; — **dock** dique seco, carenero; *v.* secar(se); enjugar; **to — up** secarse, resecarse.
dry·ness [dráɪnɪs] *s.* sequedad; aridez.
dub [dʌb] *v.* doblar (*una película*).
du·bi·ous [djúbɪəs] *adj.* dudoso.
duch·ess [dʌ́tjɪs] *s.* duquesa.
duck [dʌk] *s.* pato, pata; ánade; dril (*género*); zambullida, chapuz; agachada rápida (*para evitar un golpe*); *v.* zambullir(se), chapuzar(se); agachar(se); agachar (*la cabeza*).
duck·ling [dʌ́klɪŋ] *s.* patito, anadeja.
duc·tile [dʌ́ktɪl] *adj.* dúctil.
dud [dʌd] *s.* bomba que no estalla.
dude [dud] *s.* caballerete; novato.
due [dju] *adj.* debido; vencido, pagadero; **in — time** a su debido tiempo; **the bill is** — se ha vencido la cuenta; **the train is — at two o'clock** el tren debe llegar a las dos; *adv.* directamente; — **east** hacia el este, rumbo al oriente; *s.* derecho, privilegio; **-s** cuota.
du·el [djúəl] *s.* duelo, desafío, combate; *v.* batirse en duelo.
du·et [djuɛ́t] *s.* duo, dueto.
dug [dʌg] *pret. & p.p. de* **to dig.**
dug·out [dʌ́gaʊt] *s.* piragua.
duke [djuk] *s.* duque.
duke·dom [djúkdəm] *s.* ducado.
dull [dʌl] *adj.* (*dim*) opaco, empañado, mate; sin brillo; (*boring*) aburrido; (*blunt*) embotado, sin punta, sin filo; (*stupid*) torpe; tardo; — **pain** dolor sordo; — **sound** sonido sordo o apagado; — **spell** período de poco movimiento; *v.* embotar(se); empañar(se); ofuscar; amortiguar (*un dolor o sonido*).
dull·ness [dʌ́lnɪs] *s.* (*dimness*) falta de brillo; (*sluggishness*) estupidez, torpeza; (*bluntness*) falta de punta o filo; (*monotony*) aburrimiento; (*heaviness*) pesadez.
du·ly [djúlɪ] *adv.* debidamente.
dumb [dʌm] *adj.* (*silent*) mudo; silencioso, callado; (*dull*) estúpido, torpe; — **creature** animal.
dumb·found·ed [dʌmfáʊndəd] *adj.* patitieso.
dumb·ness [dʌ́mnɪs] *s.* mudez; mutismo; estupidez.
dum·my [dʌ́mɪ] *s.* (*figure*) maniquí, figurón, muñeco; (*fool*) *zoquete,* tonto; *adj.* falso, fingido.
dump [dʌmp] *s.* montón (*de tierra, carbón, etc.*); terrero, vaciadero, escorial; **garbage** — muladar; basurero; **to be in the -s** estar abatido; *v.* echar, vaciar, descargar; echar a la basura; **dumping** inundación del mercado con artículos baratos.
dunce [dʌns] *s.* zopenco, zoquete, tonto.
dune [djun] *s.* duna o médano.
dung [dʌŋ] *s.* boñiga, estiércol.
dun·geon [dʌ́ndʒən] *s.* mazmorra, calabozo.
dung·hill [dʌ́ŋhɪl] *s.* muladar, estercolero.
dupe [djup] *s.* inocentón, incauto, víctima (*de un engaño*); *v.* embaucar.
du·pli·cate [djúpləkɪt] *adj. & s.* doble, duplicado; [djúpləket] *v.* duplicar, copiar.
du·plic·i·ty [djuplísətɪ] *s.* duplicidad, doblez.
du·ra·ble [djʊ́rəbl] *adj.* durable, duradero.
du·ra·tion [djʊréʃən] *s.* duración.
dur·ing [dʊ́rɪŋ] *prep.* durante.
dusk [dʌsk] *s.* crepúsculo (*vespertino*), anochecida; caída de la tarde; sombra, oscuridad; **at** — al atardecer.
dusk·y [dʌ́skɪ] *adj.* obscuro, negruzco; sombrío.
dust [dʌst] *s.* polvo; tierra; **cloud of** — polvareda; *v.* sacudir el polvo, desempolvar, quitar el polvo; empolvar, llenar de polvo; espolvorear.
dust·er [dʌ́stɚ] *s.* limpiador; quitapolvo; **feather** — plumero.
dust·y [dʌ́stɪ] *adj.* polvoriento; empolvado, lleno de polvo.
Dutch [dʌtʃ] *adj. & s.* holandés; — **treat** convite a escote.
Dutch·man [dʌ́tʃmən] *s.* holandés.
du·ty [djútɪ] *s.* deber, obligación; derechos aduanales; impuesto; — **free** libre de derechos aduanales.
dwarf [dwɔrf] *s. & adj.* enano; *v.* achicar, empequeñecer; impedir el desarrollo o crecimiento de.
dwell [dwɛl] *v.* residir, morar, habitar, vivir; **to — on a subject** espaciarse o dilatarse en un asunto.
dwell·er [dwɛ́lɚ] *s.* habitante, morador.
dwell·ing [dwɛ́lɪŋ] *s.* morada, habitación, domicilio.
dwelt [dwɛlt] *pret. & p.p. de* **to dwell.**
dwin·dle [dwɪndl] *v.* menguar, mermar; disminuir(se); gastarse.
dye [daɪ] *s.* tinte, tintura; *v.* teñir, tinturar.
dy·er [dáɪɚ] *s.* tintorero; **-'s shop** tintorería.
dy·ing [dáɪɪŋ] *adj.* moribundo; agonizante.
dy·nam·ic [daɪnǽmɪk] *adj.* dinámico; enérgico; **-s** *s.*

dinámica.
dy·na·mite [dáɪnəmaɪt] *s.* dinamita; *v.* dinamitar, volar con dinamita.
dy·na·mo [dáɪnəmo] *s.* dínamo.
dy·nas·ty [dáɪnəstɪ] *s.* dinastía.
dys·en·ter·y [dísn̩tɛrɪ] *s.* disentería.

E:e

each [itʃ] *adj.* cada; *pron.* cada uno; — **other** el uno al otro, uno(s) a otro(s).
ea·ger [ígɚ] *adj.* anhelante, ansioso, deseoso; **-ly** *adv.* con anhelo; con ahinco; ansiosamente.
ea·ger·ness [ígɚnɪs] *s.* anhelo, ansia, deseo vehemente; ahinco; ardor.
ea·gle [ígl̩] *s.* águila.
ear [ɪr] *s.* (*outer*) oreja; (*hearing*) oído; — **drum** tímpano; — **muff** orejera; — **of corn** mazorca; — **of wheat** espiga; **by** — de oído; **within** — **shot** al alcance del oído.
earl [ɝl] *s.* conde.
ear·ly [ɝ́lɪ] *adv.* temprano; *adj.* temprano; primitivo, remoto; — **riser** madrugador, tempranero, mañanero; **at an** — **date** en fecha a próxima.
earn [ɝn] *v.* ganar; merecer; *s.* **earned income** ingreso devengado.
ear·nest [ɝ́nɪst] *adj.* serio, formal; ardiente; **in** — en serio, con toda formalidad; de buena fe; — **money** dinero en prenda; **-ly** *adv.* seriamente; con ahinco; encarecidamente, ansiosamente.
ear·nest·ness [ɝ́nɪstnɪs] *s.* seriedad; celo; solicitud; sinceridad; **in all** — con todo ahinco; con toda formalidad; con toda sinceridad.
earn·ings [ɝ́nɪŋz] *s.* ganancias; sueldo, salario, paga.
ear·ring [írrɪŋ] *s.* arete, zarcillo, pendiente, arracada; *C.A.* arito; *P.R.* pantalla.
earth [ɝθ] *s.* tierra; suelo.
earth·en [ɝ́θən] *adj.* de tierra; de barro.
earth·en·ware [ɝ́θənwɛr] *s.* loza de barro; trastos, cacharros.
earth·ly [ɝ́θlɪ] *adj.* terrenal, terrestre, mundano; terreno; **to be of no** — **use** no servir para nada.
earth·quake [ɝ́θkwek] *s.* terremoto, temblor de tierra.
earth·shak·ing [ɝ́θʃekɪŋ] *adj.* desmedido.
earth·worm [ɝ́θwɝm] *s.* lombriz.
ease [iz] *s.* (*facility*) facilidad; naturalidad; soltura; (*comfort*) comodidad; tranquilidad; **at** — tranquilo; cómodo; (*military*) a discreción; *v.* facilitar; aliviar; mitigar; tranquilizar; aligerar (*el peso*); aflojar.
ea·sel [ízl̩] *s.* caballete (*de pintor*).
eas·i·ly [ízəlɪ] *adv.* fácilmente; sin dificultad; cómodamente.
east [ist] *s.* este; oriente, levante; *adj.* del este, oriental; *adv.* (*eastbound*) al este, hacia el este; en el este.
East·er [ístɚ] *s.* Pascuas, Pascua Florida; — **Sunday** Domingo de Resurrección o de Pascuas.
east·ern [ístɚn] *adj.* oriental; del este.
east·ward [ístwɚd] *adv.* & *adj.* hacia el este u oriente.
eas·y [ízɪ] *adj.* (*simple*) fácil; (*comfortable*) cómodo; tranquilo; — **chair** silla cómoda, poltrona, butaca; **easy-going man** hombre cachazudo o calmo; **at an** — **pace** a paso moderado; **within** — **reach** al alcance; a la mano.
eat [it] *v.* comer; **to** — **away** corroer, destruir; **to** — **breakfast** desayunarse, tomar el desayuno; **to** — **dinner** tomar la comida, comer; **to** — **supper** tomar la cena, cenar; **to** — **one's heart out** sufrir en silencio; **to** — **one's words** retractarse.
eat·en [ítn̩] *p.p. de* **to eat.**
eaves [ivz] *s. pl.* alero (*de un tejado*).
ebb [ɛb] *s.* reflujo, decadencia; — **tide** marea menguante; **to be at a low** — estar decaído; *v.* menguar, decaer.
eb·on·y [ɛ́bənɪ] *s.* ébano.
ec·cen·tric [ɪksɛ́ntrɪk] *adj.* & *s.* excéntrico.
ec·cle·si·as·tic [ɪklizɪǽstɪk] *adj.* & *s.* eclesiástico.
ech·e·lon [ɛ́ʃəlɑn] *s.* escalón.
ech·o [ɛ́ko] *s.* eco; *v.* hacer eco, repetir; resonar, repercutir.
ec·lec·tic [ɪklɛ́ktɪk] *adj.* ecléctico.
e·clipse [ɪklíps] *s.* eclipse; *v.* eclipsar.
ec·o·nom·ic [ɪkənɑ́mɪk] *adj.* económico.
ec·o·nom·i·cal [ɪkənɑ́mɪkl] *adj.* económico.
ec·o·nom·ics [ɪkənɑ́mɪks] *s.* economía política.
e·con·o·mist [ɪkɑ́nəmɪst] *s.* economista.
e·con·o·mize [ɪkɑ́nəmaɪz] *v.* economizar.
e·con·o·my [ɪkɑ́nəmɪ] *s.* economía; parsimonia; **planned** — economía dirigida.
e·con·o·my class [ɪkánəmi klæs] *s.* segunda clase en las líneas aéreas.
ec·sta·sy [ɛ́kstəsɪ] *s.* éxtasis.
ec·u·men·i·cal [ɛkjumɛ́nəkl] *adj.* ecuménico.
ed·dy [ɛ́dɪ] *s.* remolino; *v.* arremolinarse.
E·den [ídn̩] *s.* Edén; paraíso.
edge [ɛdʒ] *s.* orilla, borde; filo; **to be on** — estar nervioso.
edge·wise [ɛ́dʒwaɪz] *adv.* de lado; de filo.
ed·i·ble [ɛ́dəbl̩] *adj.* & *s.* comestible.
ed·i·fice [ɛ́dəfɪs] *s.* edificio.
ed·i·fy [ɛ́dəfaɪ] *v.* edificar (*moral, espiritualmente*).
ed·it [ɛ́dɪt] *v.* redactar; preparar o corregir (*un manuscrito*) para la imprenta; cuidar (*una edición*).
e·di·tion [ɪdɪ́ʃən] *s.* edición.
ed·i·tor [ɛ́dɪtɚ] *s.* redactor; director de un periódico; revisor (*de manuscritos*).
ed·i·to·ri·al [ɛdətórɪəl] *adj.* editorial; *s.* editorial (*m.*), artículo de fondo.
ed·i·to·ri·al·ize [ɛdɪtórɪəlaɪz] *v.* expresar opiniones como en artículo de fondo; editorializar.
ed·u·cate [ɛ́dʒəket] *v.* educar; instruir.
ed·u·ca·tion [ɛdʒəkéʃən] *s.* (*up-bringing*) educación; crianza; (*instruction*) instrucción, enseñanza; pedagogía.
ed·u·ca·tion·al [ɛdʒəkéʃənl̩] *adj.* educativo, docente; pedagógico.
ed·u·ca·tor [ɛ́dʒəketɚ] *s.* educador.
eel [il] *s.* anguila.
ef·fect [əfɛ́kt] *s.* efecto; **-s** bienes, efectos; **to go into** — hacerse vigente, ponerse en operación (*una ley*); *v.* efectuar; ejecutar; realizar.
ef·fec·tive [əfɛ́ktɪv] *adj.* efectivo, eficaz; vigente (*una ley*); — **date** fecha de vigencia; **-ly** *adv.* eficazmente.
ef·fec·tu·al [əfɛ́ktʃuəl] *adj.* eficaz.
ef·fem·i·nate [əfɛ́mənɪt] *adj.* afeminado.
ef·fete [ɪfít] *adj.* gastado; estéril; decadente.
ef·fi·ca·cy [ɛ́fəkəsɪ] *s.* eficacia.
ef·fi·cien·cy [əfíʃəsɪ] *s.* eficiencia; eficacia.
ef·fi·cient [əfíʃənt] *adj.* eficiente; eficaz.
ef·fi·gy [ɛ́fɪdʒɪ] *s.* efigie; **to burn in** — quemar en efigie.
ef·fort [ɛ́fɚt] *s.* esfuerzo; empeño; conato.
ef·front·er·y [əfrʌ́ntərɪ] *s.* descaro, desvergüenza, desfachatez.
ef·fu·sive [ɛfúsɪv] *adj.* efusivo, demostrativo, expansivo.

egg [ɛg] *s.* huevo; **fried** — huevo frito o estrellado; **hard-boiled** — huevo cocido, huevo duro; **scrambled -s** huevos revueltos; **soft-boiled** — huevo pasado por agua; *Méx.* huevo tibio; *v.* **to — on** incitar.
egg·nog [ɛ́gnag] *s.* rompope.
egg·plant [ɛ́gplænt] *s.* berenjena.
e·go·cen·tric [igosɛ́ntrɪk] *adj.* egocéntrico.
e·go·tism [ígətɪzəm] *s.* egotismo; egoísmo.
E·gyp·tian [ɪdʒípʃən] *adj.* & *s.* egipcio.
eight [et] *num.* ocho.
eight·een [etín] *num.* dieciocho.
eight·y [étɪ] *num.* ochenta.
ei·ther [íðɚ] *adj.* & *pron.* uno u otro; — **of the two** cualquiera de los dos; **in — case** en ambos casos; *adv.* tampoco; **nor I** — ni yo tampoco; *conj.* o.
ejac·u·late [ɪdʒǽkjulet] *v.* eyacular.
e·ject [ɪdʒɛ́kt] *v.* echar, arrojar, expulsar.
e·jec·tion [ɪdʒɛ́kʃən] *s.* expulsión; — **seat** asiento lanzable.
e·lab·o·rate [ɪlǽbərɪt] *adj.* elaborado, primoroso; esmerado; [ɪlǽbəret] *v.* elaborar.
e·lapse [ɪlǽps] *v.* transcurrir, pasar.
e·las·tic [ɪlǽstɪk] *adj.* elástico; *s.* elástico; goma elástica; cordón elástico; liga elástica.
e·las·tic·i·ty [ɪlæstísətɪ] *s.* elasticidad.
e·lat·ed [ɪlétɪd] *adj.* exaltado, gozoso, alborozado.
el·bow [ɛ́lbo] *s.* codo; recodo, ángulo; **to be within — reach** estar a la mano; *v.* codear, dar codazos; **to — one's way through** abrirse paso a codazos.
eld·er [ɛ́ldɚ] *adj.* mayor, más grande, más viejo, de más edad; *s.* mayor; anciano; dignatario (*en ciertas iglesias*); **our -s** nuestros mayores; nuestros antepasados.
el·der·ly [ɛ́ldɚlɪ] *adj.* viejo, anciano.
el·dest [ɛ́ldɪst] *adj.* mayor.
e·lect [ɪlɛ́kt] *adj.* & *s.* electo; elegido; *v.* elegir.
e·lec·tion [ɪlɛ́kʃən] *s.* elección.
e·lec·tor [ɪlɛ́ktɚ] *s.* elector.
e·lec·tor·al [ɪlɛ́ktərəl] *adj.* electoral.
e·lec·tric [ɪlɛ́ktrɪk] *adj.* eléctrico; — **meter** electrómetro, contador eléctrico; — **storm** tronada, tempestad; — **eye** ojo eléctrico; — **sign** anuncio luminoso; — **power plant** central generadora; *s.* tranvía o ferrocarril eléctrico.
e·lec·tri·cal [ɪlɛ́ktrɪkl̩] *adj.* eléctrico; — **engineering** electrotecnia, ingeniería eléctrica; — **engineer** ingeniero electricista; electrotécnico.
e·lec·tri·cian [ɪlɛktríʃən] *s.* electricista.
e·lec·tric·i·ty [ɪlɛktrísətɪ] *s.* electricidad.
e·lec·tri·fy [ɪlɛ́ktrəfaɪ] *v.* electrizar; electrificar.
e·lec·tro·car·di·o·graph [ɪlɛktrokárdɪəgræf] *s.* electrocardiógrafo.
e·lec·tro·cute [ɪlɛ́ktrəkjut] *v.* electrocutar.
e·lec·trol·y·sis [ilɛktrálɪsɪs] *s.* electrólisis.
e·lec·tro·mag·net [ɪlɛktromǽgnət] *s.* electroimán.
e·lec·tron [ɪlɛ́ktrɑn] *s.* electrón; — **microscope** microscopio electrónico.
e·lec·tron·ics [ɪlɛktrɑ́nɪks] *s.* electrónica.
el·e·gance [ɛ́ləgəns] *s.* elegancia.
el·e·gant [ɛ́ləgənt] *adj.* elegante.
el·e·ment [ɛ́ləmənt] *s.* elemento.
el·e·men·tal [ɛləmɛ́ntl̩] *adj.* elemental.
el·e·men·ta·ry [ɛləmɛ́ntərɪ] *adj.* elemental.
el·e·phant [ɛ́ləfənt] *s.* elefante.
el·e·vate [ɛ́ləvet] *v.* elevar; alzar, levantar.
el·e·va·tion [ɛləvéʃən] *s.* elevación; altura; exaltación.
el·e·va·tor [ɛ́ləvetɚ] *s.* ascensor, *Am.* elevador; **grain** — almacén de granos.
e·lev·en [əlɛ́vən] *num.* once.
e·lic·it [ɪlísɪt] *v.* extraer, sonsacar; **to — admiration** despertar admiración; **to — applause** suscitar el aplauso o los aplausos.
el·i·gi·ble [ɛ́lɪdʒəbl̩] *adj.* elegible.
e·lim·i·nate [ɪlímənet] *v.* eliminar.
e·lim·i·na·tion [ɪlɪmənéʃən] *s.* eliminación.
e·lite [ɛlít] *s.* lo selecto; los selectos; los escogidos.
elk [ɛlk] *s.* ante.
el·lip·tic [ɪlíptɪk] *adj.* elíptico.
elm [ɛlm] *s.* olmo.
e·lope [ɪlóp] *v.* fugarse (*con su novio*).
el·o·quence [ɛ́ləkwəns] *s.* elocuencia.
el·o·quent [ɛ́ləkwənt] *adj.* elocuente.
else [ɛls] *adj.* & *adv.* otro (*úsase sólo en ciertas combinaciones*); más, además; **or** — de otro modo; si no; **nobody** — ningún otro; **nothing** — nada más; **somebody** — algún otro, otra persona; **what** —? ¿qué más?
else·where [ɛ́lshwɛr] *adv.* en otra parte, a otra parte.
e·lu·ci·date [ɪlúsədet] *v.* elucidar, esclarecer, aclarar, clarificar.
e·lu·ci·da·tion [ɪlusədéʃən] *s.* elucidación, esclarecimiento, explicación.
e·lude [ɪlúd] *v.* eludir, evadir.
e·lu·sive [ɪlúsɪv] *adj.* evasivo; que elude.
e·ma·ci·at·ed [ɪméʃɪetɪd] *adj.* demacrado, escuálido, macilento.
em·a·nate [ɛ́mənet] *v.* emanar, brotar.
em·a·na·tion [ɛmənéʃən] *s.* emanación; efluvio.
e·man·ci·pate [ɪmǽnsəpet] *v.* emancipar.
e·man·ci·pa·tion [ɪmænsəpéʃən] *s.* emancipación.
em·balm [ɪmbɑ́m] *v.* embalsamar.
em·bank·ment [ɪmbǽŋkmənt] *s.* terraplén; dique.
em·bar·go [ɪmbɑrgo] *s.* embargo; prohibición; **to put an — on** embargar.
em·bark [ɪmbɑ́rk] *v.* embarcar(se).
em·bar·rass [ɪmbǽrəs] *v.* turbar, desconcertar; apenar; avergonzar; embarazar; **to be financially -ed** encontrarse escaso de fondos.
em·bar·rass·ing [ɪmbǽrəsɪŋ] *adj.* embarazoso, penoso; desconcertante; angustioso.
em·bar·rass·ment [ɪmbǽrəsmənt] *s.* turbación, vergüenza, desconcierto; aprieto, apuro, dificultad; estorbo, embarazo.
em·bas·sy [ɛ́mbəsɪ] *s.* embajada.
em·bel·lish [ɪmbɛ́lɪʃ] *v.* embellecer, hermosear.
em·ber [ɛ́mbɚ] *s.* ascua; **-s** ascuas, rescoldo.
em·bez·zle [ɪmbɛ́zl̩] *v.* desfalcar.
em·bez·zle·ment [ɪmbɛ́zl̩mənt] *s.* desfalco, peculado.
em·bit·ter [ɪmbítɚ] *v.* amargar.
em·blem [ɛ́mbləm] *s.* emblema.
em·bod·y [ɪmbɑ́dɪ] *v.* encarnar, dar cuerpo a; incorporar, abarcar.
em·boss [ɪmbɔ́s] *v.* realzar, grabar en relieve.
em·brace [ɪmbrés] *s.* abrazo; *v.* abrazar(se); abarcar.
em·broi·der [ɪmbrɔ́ɪdɚ] *v.* bordar; recamar; ornar, embellecer.
em·broi·der·y [ɪmbrɔ́ɪdərɪ] *s.* bordado; bordadura; recamo.
em·bry·o [ɛ́mbrɪo] *s.* embrión.
em·er·ald [ɛ́mərəld] *s.* esmeralda.
e·merge [ɪmɝ́dʒ] *v.* emerger; surtir.
e·mer·gen·cy [ɪmɝ́dʒənsɪ] *s.* caso fortuito; aprieto, urgencia; emergencia.
em·i·grant [ɛ́məgrənt] *adj.* & *s.* emigrante.
em·i·grate [ɛ́məgret] *v.* emigrar.
em·i·gra·tion [ɛməgréʃən] *s.* emigración.
em·i·nence [ɛ́mənəns] *s.* eminencia.
em·i·nent [ɛ́mənənt] *adj.* eminente.
e·mit [ɪmít] *v.* emitir; exhalar, arrojar; despedir (*olor, humo, etc.*).
e·mo·tion [ɪmóʃən] *s.* emoción.

e·mo·tion·al [ɪmóʃənḷ] *adj*. emocional; emotivo; sentimental; sensible.
em·pa·thy [ɛ́mpəθɪ] *s*. empatía.
em·per·or [ɛ́mpərɚ] *s*. emperador.
em·pha·sis [ɛ́mfəsɪs] *s*. énfasis.
em·pha·size [ɛ́mfəsaɪz] *v*. dar énfasis; hacer hincapié en; subrayar, recalcar; acentuar.
em·phat·ic [ɪmfǽtɪk] *adj*. enfático; recalcado; **-ally** *adv*. enfáticamente.
em·phy·se·ma [ɛmfəsímə] *s*. enfisema.
em·pire [ɛ́mpaɪr] *s*. imperio.
em·pir·i·cal [ɛmpírəkḷ] *adj*. empírico.
em·ploy [ɪmplɔ́ɪ] *v*. emplear; dar empleo a; ocupar; **to be in his** — ser su empleado; trabajar a sus órdenes.
em·ploy·ee [ɪmplɔɪí] *s*. empleado.
em·ploy·er [ɪmplɔ́ɪɚ] *s*. patrón, amo, principal.
em·ploy·ment [ɪmplɔ́ɪmənt] *s*. empleo; ocupación; — **legislation** legislación laboral.
em·pow·er [ɪmpáUɚ] *v*. autorizar; apoderar (*dar poder a un abogado*).
em·press [ɛ́mprɪs] *s*. emperatriz.
emp·ti·ness [ɛ́mptɪnɪs] *s*. vaciedad, futilidad, vanidad.
emp·ty [ɛ́mptɪ] *adj*. vacío; vacante, desocupado; vano; *v*. vaciar; desaguar, desembocar.
emp·ty-hand·ed [ɛmptɪhǽndɪd] *adj*. sin posesión.
em·u·late [ɛ́mjUlet] *v*. emular.
en·a·ble [ɪnébḷ] *v*. capacitar, hacer capaz; habilitar; dar poder; facilitar; hacer posible.
en·act [ɪnǽkt] *v*. decretar, promulgar; hacer el papel de.
en·am·el [ɪnǽmḷ] *s*. esmalte; *v*. esmaltar.
en·am·or [ɪnǽmɚ] *v*. enamorar, mover a amar; encantar; **to be -ed of** estar enamorado de.
en·camp [ɪnkǽmp] *v*. acampar.
en·chant [ɪntʃǽnt] *v*. encantar, embelesar, hechizar.
en·chant·er [ɪntʃǽntɚ] *s*. encantador, hechicero, mago, brujo.
en·chant·ment [ɪntʃǽntmənt] *s*. encanto, encantamiento, hechicería.
en·chant·ress [ɪntʃǽntrɪs] *s*. encantadora, hechicera, bruja.
en·cir·cle [ɪnsɝ́kḷ] *v*. cercar, rodear, ceñir.
en·clit·ic [enklítɪk] *adj*. enclítico.
en·close [ɪnklóz] *v*. encerrar; cercar, rodear, circundar; incluir.
en·clo·sure [ɪnklóʒɚ] *s*. recinto, cercado, vallado; remesa, lo remitido (*dentro de una carta*), lo adjunto; encerramiento.
en·com·pass [ɪnkʌ́mpəs] *v*. abarcar; encuadrar; rodear, ceñir, circundar.
en·coun·ter [ɪnkáUntɚ] *s*. encuentro; combate; *v*. encontrar(se); encontrarse con; tropezar con.
en·cour·age [ɪnkɝ́ɪdʒ] *v*. alentar, animar; fomentar.
en·cour·age·ment [ɪnkɝ́ɪdʒmənt] *s*. aliento, ánimo; estímulo; fomento.
en·croach [ɪnkrótʃ] *v*. **to — upon** usurpar, invadir, meterse en; quitar (*el tiempo*).
en·cum·ber [ɛnkʌ́mbɚ] *v*. impedir; estorbar.
en·cy·clo·pe·di·a [ɪnsaɪkləpídɪə] *s*. enciclopedia.
end [ɛnd] *s*. (*temporal*) fin; cabo; término; (*spatial*) término; extremo; **no — of things** un sin fin de cosas; **odds and -s** retazos; **on** — de punta; **to put an — to** acabar con, poner fin a; *v*. acabar; terminar; concluir, dar fin.
en·dan·ger [ɪndéndʒɚ] *v*. poner en peligro, arriesgar.
en·dear [ɪndír] *v*. hacer amar, hacer querer; **to — oneself** hacerse querer.
en·deav·or [ɪndɛ́vɚ] *s*. esfuerzo, empeño; tentativa; tarea; *v*. procurar, tratar de, intentar; esforzarse por o en.
en·dem·ic [ɛndɛ́mɪk] *adj*. endémico.
end·ing [ɛ́ndɪŋ] *s*. final; terminación; conclusión.
end·less [ɛ́ndlɪs] *adj*. sin fin, interminable, inacabable; eterno.
en·dorse [ɛndɔ́rs] *v*. endosar; respaldar; apoyar, garantizar.
en·dorse·ment [ɛndɔ́rsmənt] *s*. (*signature*) endose, endoso; (*backing*) respaldo; garantía, apoyo.
en·dors·er [ɛndɔ́rsɚ] *s*. endosante.
en·dow [ɪndáU] *v*. dotar.
en·dow·ment [ɪndáUmənt] *s*. dotación; dote, don; — **annuity** anualidad dotal; — **fund** fondo dotal; — **policy** póliza dotal.
en·dur·ance [ɪndjÚrəns] *s*. resistencia, aguante; paciencia; duración.
en·dure [ɪndjÚr] *v*. aguantar, soportar, sufrir; durar, perdurar.
en·e·ma [ɛ́nəmə] *s*. lavativa.
en·e·my [ɛ́nəmɪ] *s*. enemigo.
en·er·get·ic [enɚdʒɔ́tɪk] *adj*. enérgico.
en·er·gy [ɛ́nɚdʒɪ] *s*. energía.
en·er·vate [ɛ́nɚvet] *v*. enervar, debilitar.
en·fold = **infold.**
en·force [ɪnfórs] *v*. dar fuerza a; hacer cumplir (*una ley*); **to — obedience** hacer obedecer, imponer obediencia.
en·force·ment [ɪnfórsmənt] *s*. coacción; cumplimiento forzoso (*de una ley*).
en·gage [ɪngédʒ] *v*. (*employ*) ocupar; emplear, contratar; (*reserve*) alquilar; (*attract*) atraer; (*mesh*) engranar, acoplar; **to — in battle** trabar batalla; **to — (oneself) to do it** comprometerse a hacerlo; **to be -ed in something** estar ocupado en algo; **to be -ed to be married** estar comprometido para casarse.
en·gage·ment [ɪngédʒmənt] *s*. compromiso; cita; noviazgo; convenio, contrato; pelea; traba, engrane, acoplamiento (*de maquinaria*).
en·gen·der [ɪndʒɛ́ndɚ] *v*. engendrar, producir.
en·gine [ɛ́ndʒən] *s*. máquina; motor; (*locomotive*) locomotora.
en·gi·neer [ɛndʒənír] *s*. ingeniero; (*of locomotive*) maquinista; *v*. dirigir, planear.
en·gi·neer·ing [ɛndʒənírɪŋ] *s*. ingeniería; manejo, planeo.
Eng·lish [íŋglɪʃ] *adj*. inglés; *s*. inglés, idioma inglés; **the** — los ingleses.
Eng·lish·man [íŋglɪʃmən] *s*. inglés.
en·grave [ɪngrév] *v*. grabar, esculpir.
en·grav·ing [ɪngrévɪŋ] *s*. grabado; estampa, lámina; **wood** — grabado en madera.
en·gross [ɛngrós] *v*. absorber; (*edit*) redactar en limpio.
en·grossed [ɪngróst] *adj*. absorto, ensimismado.
en·gulf [ɪngʌ́lf] *v*. engolfar, absorber, tragar.
en·hance [ɪnhǽns] *v*. realzar; engrandecer.
e·nig·ma [ɪnígmə] *s*. enigma.
en·join [ɪndʒɔ́ɪn] *v*. mandar, ordenar; **to — from** prohibir, vedar.
en·joy [ɪndʒɔ́ɪ] *v*. gozar de; disfrutar de; **to — oneself** divertirse, gozar, deleitarse; **to — the use of** usufructuar.
en·joy·a·ble [ɪndʒɔ́ɪəbḷ] *adj*. agradable, deleitable.
en·joy·ment [ɪndʒɔ́ɪmənt] *s*. placer, goce; disfrute; usufructo.
en·large [ɪnlárdʒ] *v*. agrandar(se); ensanchar; ampliar; **to — upon** explayarse en, extenderse en; comentar.
en·large·ment [ɪnlárdʒmənt] *s*. (*photo*) ampliación; ensachamiento.

en·light·en [ɪnláɪtn̩] *v.* alumbrar; iluminar; ilustrar, instruir.
en·list [ɪnlíst] *v.* alistar(se); sentar plaza (*de soldado*); reclutar.
en·list·ment [ɪnlístmənt] *s.* reclutamiento; alistamiento.
en·li·ven [ɪnláɪvən] *v.* avivar, animar, alegrar.
en·mi·ty [ɛ́nmətɪ] *s.* enemistad.
en·no·ble [ɪnóbl̩] *v.* ennoblecer.
e·nor·mous [ɪnɔ́rməs] *adj.* enorme.
e·nough [ənʌ́f] *adj.* & *adv.* bastante; *s.* lo bastante, lo suficiente; **that is** — eso basta, con eso basta; — **!** ¡basta!
en·quire = **inquire.**
en·rage [ɪnréd ʒ] *v.* enrabiar, hacer rabiar; enfurecer.
en·rap·ture [ɪnrǽptʃɚ] *v.* extasiar, embelesar, enajenar.
en·rich [ɪnrítʃ] *v.* enriquecer.
en·roll [ɪnról] *v.* alistar(se); matricular(se); inscribir(se); hacerse miembro.
en·roll·ment [ɪnrólmənt] *s.* alistamiento; registro, matrícula.
en·sem·ble [ɑnsɑ́mbl̩] *s.* (*music*) conjunto musical; (*dress*) traje armonioso.
en·sign [ɛ́nsn] *s.* alférez (*de la marina*); [ɛ́nsaɪn] bandera; insignia.
en·slave [ɪnslév] *v.* esclavizar.
en·snare [ɛnsnɛ́r] *v.* enredar, entrampar, embaucar.
en·sue [ɛnsú] *v.* sobrevenir, seguir(se), resultar.
en·tail [ɪntél] *v.* envolver, ocasionar; vincular (*una herencia*).
en·tan·gle [ɪntǽŋgl̩] *v.* enredar, enmarañar, embrollar.
en·tente [ɑntɑ́nt] *s.* pacto no formal.
en·ter [ɛ́ntɚ] *v.* entrar en; ingresar en; asentar (*una partida, cantidad, etc.*); registrar; salir (*al escenario*).
en·ter·prise [ɛ́ntɚpraɪz] *s.* empresa.
en·ter·pris·ing [ɛ́ntɚpraɪzɪŋ] *adj.* emprendedor.
en·ter·tain [ɛntɚtén] *v.* divertir; agasajar; obsequiar; banquetear; acariciar (*una idea*); abrigar (*una esperanza, un rencor*); **she -s a great deal** es muy fiestera u obsequiosa.
en·ter·tain·ing [ɛntɚténɪŋ] *adj.* entretenido, divertido, chistoso.
en·ter·tain·ment [ɛntɚténmənt] *s.* entretenimiento; pasatiempo; diversión; fiesta; convite.
en·thu·si·asm [ɪnθjúzɪæzəm] *s.* entusiasmo.
en·thu·si·ast [inθjúzɪæstɪk] *adj.* entusiasta, entusiástico; **to be** — estar entusiasmado.
en·tice [ɪntáɪs] *v.* atraer, tentar, seducir, halagar.
en·tire [ɪntáɪr] *adj.* entero, cabal; **the** — **world** todo el mundo; **-ly** *adv.* enteramente, por entero.
en·tire·ty [ɪntáɪrtɪ] *s.* totalidad, entereza; conjunto; todo.
en·ti·tle [ɪntáɪtl̩] *v.* titular, intitular; autorizar, dar derecho.
en·ti·ty [ɛ́ntətɪ] *s.* entidad; ente, ser.
en·trails [ɛ́ntrəlz] *s. pl.* entrañas; tripas.
en·trance [ɛ́ntrəns] *s.* entrada; ingreso.
en·treat [ɪntrít] *v.* suplicar, rogar; instar.
en·treat·y [ɪntrítɪ] *s.* súplica, ruego; instancia.
en·trench = **intrench.**
en·trust [ɪntrʌ́st] *v.* confiar; depositar, (*deliver*) entregar.
en·try [ɛ́ntrɪ] *s.* entrada; ingreso; partida, registro, anotación; *(computer)* entrada; **make an** — asentar una partida; **double** — partida doble (*en teneduría*).
e·nu·mer·ate [ɪnjúməret] *v.* enumerar.
e·nun·ci·ate [ɪnʌ́snɪet] *v.* articular; enunciar, declarar.
en·vel·op [ɪnvɛ́ləp] *v.* envolver.
en·ve·lope [ɛ́nvəlop] *s.* sobre, cubierta (*de una carta*).
en·vi·a·ble [ɛ́nvɪəbl̩] *adj.* envidiable.
en·vi·ous [ɛ́nvɪəs] *adj.* envidioso.
en·vi·ron·ment [ɪnváɪrənmənt] *s.* ambiente, medio ambiente; *adj.* **environmental** ambiental.
en·vi·rons [ɛnváɪrənz] *s. pl.* cercanías, contornos, alrededores.
en·vis·age [ɛnvízɪdʒ] *v.* prever; encararse con.
en·voy [ɛ́nvɔɪ] *s.* enviado.
en·vy [ɛ́nvɪ] *s.* envidia; *v.* envidiar.
e·phem·er·al [ɪfɛ́mɚl̩] *adj.* efímero.
ep·ic [ɛ́pɪk] *s.* epopeya, poema, épico; *adj.* épico.
ep·i·dem·ic [ɛpədɛ́mɪk] *s.* epidemia; peste; *adj.* epidémico.
ep·i·logue [ɛ́pəlɔg] *s.* epílogo.
E·piph·a·ny [ɪpífənɪ] *s.* Epifanía.
ep·i·sode [ɛ́pəsod] *s.* episodio.
e·pis·tle [ɪpísl̩] *s.* epístola, carta.
ep·i·taph [ɛ́pətæf] *s.* epitafio.
e·pit·o·me [ɪpítəmɪ] *s.* epítome.
ep·och [ɛ́pək] *s.* época; — **making** transcendental.
EPROM (*computer*) erasable, programmable, read only memory *adj.* borrable, capaz de programarse, léase sólo memoria.
e·qual [íkwəl] *adj.* igual; **to be** — **to a task** ser competente (*o* tener suficientes fuerzas) para una tarea; — **rights** igualdad de derechos; *s.* igual; cantidad igual; *v.* igualar; ser igual a; **-ly** *adv.* igualmente; por igual.
e·qual·i·ty [íkwɑ́lətɪ] *s.* igualdad.
e·qual·ize [íkwəlaɪz] *v.* igualar; emparejar; equilibrar; nivelar.
e·qua·tion [ɪkwéʒən] *s.* ecuación.
e·qua·tor [ɪkwétɚ] *s.* ecuador.
e·qui·lib·ri·um [ikwəlíbrɪəm] *s.* equilibrio.
e·quip [ɪkwíp] *v.* equipar; proveer; habilitar.
e·quip·ment [ɪkwípmənt] *s.* equipo; aparatos; avíos; havilitación; **railroad** — material rodante.
eq·ui·ta·ble [ɛ́kwɪtəbl̩] *adj.* equitativo.
eq·ui·ty [ɛ́kwətɪ] *s.* equidad; justicia; **-s** derechos sobre el activo, valor libre de la hipoteca.
e·quiv·a·lent [ɪkwívələnt] *adj.* & *s.* equivalente.
e·quiv·o·cal [ɪkwívəkl̩] *adj.* equívoco, ambiguo.
e·ra [írə] *s.* era, época.
e·rad·i·cate [ɪrǽdɪket] *v.* desarraigar, extirpar.
e·rase [ɪrés] *v.* borrar; tachar.
e·ras·er [ɪrésɚ] *s.* goma, *Am.* borrador; **blackboard** — cepillo.
e·ra·sure [ɪréʃɚ] *s.* borradura, raspadura.
ere [ɛr] *prep.* antes de; *conj.* antes (de) que.
e·rect [ɪrɛ́kt] *adj.* erguido; derecho; levantado; *Am.* parado; *v.* erigir; levantar, alzar.
er·mine [ɝ́mɪn] *s.* armiño.
e·rode [ɪród] *v.* erosionar.
e·ro·sion [ɪróʒən] *s.* erosión; desgaste.
e·rot·ic [ɪrɑ́tɪk] *adj.* erótico.
err [ɝ] *v.* errar; equivocarse; descarriarse.
er·rand [ɛ́rənd] *s.* mandado, recado, encargo; — **boy** mandadero.
er·rant [ɛ́rənt] *adj.* errante; **knight-errant** caballero andante.
er·rat·ic [ɛrǽtɪk] *adj.* inconstante, errático; vagabundo.
er·ro·ne·ous [ərónɪəs] *adj.* erróneo, errado.
er·ror [ɛ́rɚ] *s.* error; (printing) errata; **-s and omissions excepted** salvo error u omisión.
er·u·di·tion [ɛrʊdíʃən] *s.* erudición.
e·rupt [ɪrʌ́pt] *v.* arrojar.
e·rup·tion [ɪrʌ́pʃən] *s.* erupción.

es·ca·late [éskəlet] *v.* aumentar; intensificar.
es·ca·pade [éskəped] *s.* trapisonda, travesura.
es·cape [əskép] *s.* escape; fuga, huída; escapada; escapatoria; — **clause** cláusula que permite ajuste a las condiciones; *v.* escapar(se); fugarse; huir(se); eludir, evadir; **it -s me** se me escapa.
es·cort [éskɔrt] *s.* escolta; acompañante; convoy; [ɪskɔ́rt] *v.* escoltar; convoyar; acompañar.
es·crow [éskro] *s.* plica; **in** — en custodia.
es·cutch·eon [ɪskʌ́tʃən] *s.* escudo de armas, blasón.
Es·ki·mo [éskəmo] *s.* esquimal.
es·pe·cial [əspéʃəl] *adj.* especial; **-ly** *adv.* especialmente.
es·pi·o·nage [éspɪənɪdʒ] *s.* espionaje.
es·pouse [ɛspáʊs] *v.* patrocinar; casarse.
es·say [ése] *s.* ensayo; [ɛsé] *v.* ensayar.
es·sence [ésṇs] *s.* esencia.
es·sen·tial [əsénʃəl] *adj.* esencial.
es·tab·lish [əstǽblɪʃ] *v.* establecer.
es·tab·lish·ment [əstǽblɪʃmənt] *s.* establecimiento.
es·tate [əstét] *s.* hacienda, heredad; bienes, propiedades; — **tax** impuesto de sucesión; estado, condición; **country** — finca rural.
es·teem [əstím] *s.* estima, estimación, aprecio; *v.* estimar, apreciar; considerar, juzgar.
es·ti·ma·ble [éstəməbl] *adj.* estimable.
es·ti·mate [éstəmɪt] *s.* (*calculation*) tasa, cálculo aproximado; presupuesto; (*judgment*) opinión; [éstəmet] *v.* estimar, tasar, calcular aproximadamente; hacer un presupuesto; juzgar, opinar.
es·ti·ma·tion [ɛstəméʃən] *s.* juicio, opinión; estima; estimación.
es·trange [ɛstréndʒ] *v.* enajenar; apartar.
es·tu·ar·y [éstʃʊɛrɪ] *s.* estuario o estero, desembocadura de un río.
etch [ɛtʃ] *v.* grabar al agua fuerte.
etch·ing [étʃɪŋ] *s.* agua fuerte, grabado al agua fuerte.
e·ter·nal [ɪtɝ́nl] *adj.* eterno.
e·ter·ni·ty [ɪtɝ́nətɪ] *s.* eternidad.
e·ther [íθɚ] *s.* éter.
e·the·re·al [ɪθírɪəl] *adj.* etéreo.
eth·i·cal [éθɪkl] *adj.* ético, moral.
eth·ics [éθɪks] *s.* ética, moral.
eth·nic [éθnɪk] *adj.* étnico.
eth·nol·o·gy [ɛθnálədʒɪ] *s.* etnología.
et·i·quette [étɪkɛt] *s.* etiqueta (*regla de conducta social*).
et·y·mol·o·gy [ɛtəmálədʒɪ] *s.* etimología.
eu·ca·lyp·tus [jukəlíptəs] *s.* eucalipto.
Eu·cha·rist [júkərɪst] *s.* Eucaristía.
eu·phe·mism [júfəmɪzm] *s.* eufemismo.
eu·pho·ri·a [jufórɪə] *s.* euforia.
Eu·ro·pe·an [jʊrəpíən] *adj. & s.* europeo.
e·vac·u·ate [ɪvǽkjʊet] *v.* evacuar; desocupar.
e·vade [ɪvéd] *v.* evadir.
e·val·u·ate [ɪvǽljʊet] *v.* valorar, avaluar.
e·vap·o·rate [ɪvǽpəret] *v.* evaporar(se).
e·vap·o·ra·tion [ɪvæpəréʃən] *s.* evaporación.
e·va·sion [ɪvéʒən] *s.* evasión, evasiva.
e·va·sive [ɪvésɪv] *adj.* evasivo.
eve [iv] *s.* víspera, vigilia; **Christmas Eve** Nochebuena; **New Year's Eve** víspera del Año Nuevo; **on the** — **of** en vísperas de.
e·ven [ívən] *adj.* (*level*) liso, plano, llano, a nivel; (*same*) parejo; uniforme; igual; — **dozen** docena cabal; — **number** número par; — **temper** genio apacible; **to be** — **with someone** estar mano a mano (*o* estar a mano) con alguien; **to get** — **with someone** desquitarse de alguien; *adv.* aun, hasta; — **if** (*o* — **though**) aun cuando; — **so** aun así, **not** — ni siquiera, ni aun; *v.* allanar; nivelar(se); igualar(se); emparejar; **-ly** *adv.* igualmente; de un modo igual; con uniformidad; con suavidad.
eve·ning [ívnɪŋ] *s.* tarde; atardecer; noche (*las primeras horas*); — **gown** vestido de etiqueta; — **star** estrella vespertina, lucero de la tarde.
e·ven·ness [ívənnɪs] *s.* lisura; igualdad; — **of temper** apacibilidad o suavidad de genio.
e·vent [ɪvént] *s.* suceso, acontecimiento; incidente, evento; resultado, coneecuencia; **in any** — en todo caso; **in the** — **of** en caso de.
e·vent·ful [ɪvéntfəl] *adj.* lleno de sucesos; importante, memorable.
e·ven·tu·al [ɪvéntʃʊəl] *adj.* eventual; último, final, terminal; **-ly** *adv.* finalmente, por fin, con el tiempo; eventualmente.
ev·er [évɚ] *adv.* siempre; jamás; alguna vez; — **so much** muchísimo; **for** — **and** — por (*o* para) siempre jamás; **hardly** — casi nunca, apenas; **if** — si alguna vez; **more than** — más que nunca; **the best friend I** — **had** el mejor amigo que en mi vida he tenido.
ev·er·green [évɚgrin] *s.* siempreviva, sempiterna; *adj.* siempre verde.
ev·er·last·ing [ɛvɚlǽstɪŋ] *adj.* sempiterno, eterno, perpetuo; duradero; *s.* eternidad; sempiterna (*planta*); siempreviva; perpetua, flor perpetua.
ev·er·more [ɛvɚmór] *adv.* para siempre; **for** — para siempre jamás.
eve·ry [évrɪ] *adj.* cada; todo; todos los, todas las; — **bit of it** todo, todito; — **day** todos los días; — **once in a while** de vez en cuando; — **one of them** todos ellos; — **other day** cada dos días, un día sí y otro no.
eve·ry·bod·y [évrɪbadɪ] *pron.* todos, todo el mundo.
eve·ry·day [évrɪdé] *adj.* diario, cuotidiano, de todos los días; ordinario.
eve·ry·one [évrɪwʌn] *pron.* todos; todo el mundo; cada uno.
eve·ry·thing [évrɪθɪŋ] *pron.* todo.
eve·ry·where [évrɪhwɛr] *adv.* por (*o* en) todas partes; a todas partes.
e·vict [ɪvíkt] *v.* desalojar; expulsar.
ev·i·dence [évədəns] *s.* evidencia; prueba; demostración, señal; testimonio; **to be in** — mostrarse; *v.* hacer evidente, evidenciar; patentizar, revelar, mostrar.
ev·i·dent [évədənt] *adj.* evidente, patente.
e·vil [ívl] *adj.* malo, malvado, maligno; aciago, de mal agüero; **to cast the** — **eye** aojar; **the Evil One** el Diablo; *s.* mal, maldad; *adv.* mal.
e·vil·do·er [ívldúɚ] *s.* malhechor.
e·voke [ɪvók] *v.* evocar; **to** — **laughter** provocar a risa.
ev·o·lu·tion [ɛvəlúʃən] *s.* evolución.
e·volve [ɪválv] *v.* desarrollar(se), desenvolver(se); urdir; evolucionar.
ewe [ju] *s.* oveja.
ex·act [ɪgzǽkt] *adj.* exacto; *v.* exigir; **-ly** *adv.* exactamente; en punto.
ex·act·ing [ɪgzǽktɪŋ] *adj.* exigente.
ex·ag·ger·ate [ɪgzǽdʒəret] *v.* exagerar.
ex·alt [ɪgzɔ́lt] *v.* exaltar, ensalzar.
ex·al·ta·tion [ɛgzɔltéʃən] *s.* exaltación.
ex·am·i·na·tion [ɪgzæmənéʃən] *s.* examen; reconocimiento (*médico*); (*trial*) interrogatorio.
ex·am·ine [ɪgzǽmɪn] *v.* examinar; reconocer (*dícese del médico*).
ex·am·ple [ɪgzǽmpl] *s.* ejemplo.
ex·as·per·ate [ɪgzǽspəret] *v.* exasperar, irritar.

EN

ex·ca·vate [ékskəvet] *v.* excavar.
ex·ca·va·tor [ékskəvetə˞] *s.* excavadora.
ex·ceed [ɪksíd] *v.* exceder; sobrepasar; propasarse.
ex·ceed·ing·ly [ɪksídɪŋlɪ] *adv.* sumamente, extremamente; — **well** extremamente bien.
ex·cel [ɪksél] *v.* sobresalir en (entre); sobrepujar (a).
ex·cel·lence [ékslṇs] *s.* excelencia.
ex·cel·len·cy [ékslənsɪ] *s.* excelencia.
ex·cel·lent [ékslənt] *adj.* excelente.
ex·cept [ɪksépt] *prep.* excepto, menos; *v.* exceptuar.
ex·cept·ing [ɪkséptɪŋ] *prep.* excepto, salvo, menos, exceptuando.
ex·cep·tion [ɪksépʃən] *s.* (*exclusion*) excepción; (*opposition*) objeción; **with the — of** a excepción de, con excepción de; **to take** — objetar; ofenderse.
ex·cep·tion·al [ɪksépʃənḷ] *adj.* excepcional.
ex·cess [ɪksés] *s.* exceso; sobrante; — **baggage** exceso de equipaje; — **weight** exceso de peso; **to drink to** — beber en exceso; — **profits tax** impuesto sobre ganancias excesivas.
ex·ces·sive [ɪksésɪv] *adj.* excesivo; desmedido; **-ly** *adv.* excesivamente, en exceso, demasiado.
ex·change [ɪkstʃéndʒ] *s.* (*money*) cambio; (*interchange*) trueque; intercambio, canje (*de publicaciones, prisioneros*); (*stock*) lonja, bolsa; **rate of** — cambio, *Am.* tipo de cambio; **telephone** — central de teléfonos; **foreign** — divisa, *v.* cambiar; trocar; canjear (*publicaciones, prisioneros*); **to — greetings** saludarse; mandarse felicitaciones.
ex·cise tax [éksaɪz tæks] *s.* alcabala, sisa.
ex·cite [ɪksáɪt] *v.* excitar; acalorar; agitar.
ex·cit·ed [ɪksáɪtɪd] *adj.* excitado, acalorado; animado; **to get** — entusiasmarse; sobreexcitarse; acalorarse; **-ly** *adv.* acaloradamente, agitadamente.
ex·cite·ment [ɪksáɪtmənt] *s.* excitación; acaloramiento; agitación, alboroto; animación.
ex·cit·ing [ɪksáɪtɪŋ] *adj.* excitante, excitador; estimulante.
ex·claim [ɪksklém] *v.* exclamar.
ex·cla·ma·tion [ɛkskləméʃən] *s.* exclamación; — **point** punto de admiración.
ex·clude [ɪksklúd] *v.* excluir.
ex·clu·sion [ɪksklúʒən] *s.* exclusión.
ex·clu·sive [ɪksklúsɪv] *adj.* exclusivo; privativo; — **of** sin contar.
ex·com·mu·ni·cate [ɛkskəmjúnəket] *v.* excomunicar.
ex·com·mu·ni·ca·tion [ɛkskəmjunəkéʃən] *s.* excomunión.
ex·cre·ment [ékskrɪmənt] *s.* excremento; caca.
ex·cur·sion [ɪkskɝ́ʒən] *s.* excursión; correría; expedición.
ex·cus·a·ble [ɪkskjúzebḷ] *adj.* excusable, disculpable.
ex·cuse [ɪkskjús] *s.* excusa; disculpa; [ɪkskjúz] *v.* excusar; disculpar; perdonar, dispensar; eximir; — **me!** ¡dispense Vd.! ¡perdone Vd.!
ex·e·cute [éksɪkjut] *v.* ejecutar; fusilar; ajusticiar; llevar a cabo; *(computer)* ejecutar.
ex·e·cu·tion [ɛksɪkjúʃən] *s.* ejecución; desempeño; *(computer)* ejecución; — **wall** paredón.
ex·e·cu·tion·er [ɛksɪkjúʃənə˞] *s.* verdugo.
ex·ec·u·tive [ɪgzékjʊtɪv] *adj.* ejecutivo; *s.* ejecutivo, poder ejecutivo; gerente, administrador.
ex·ec·u·tor [ɪgzékjətə˞] *s.* albacea, ejecutor testamentario; [éksɪkjutə˞] ejecutor.
ex·em·pla·ry [ɪgzémplərɪ] *adj.* ejemplar.
ex·empt [ɪgzémpt] *adj.* exento, libre; *v.* eximir, exentar.
ex·emp·tion [ɪgzémpʃən] *s.* exención.
ex·er·cise [éksə˞saɪz] *s.* ejercicio; *v.* ejercitar(se); ejercer (*poder o autoridad*); hacer ejercicio, hacer gimnasia; **to be -d about something** estar preocupado o sobreexcitado por algo.
ex·ert [ɪgzɝ́t] *v.* ejercer; **to — oneself** esforzarse, hacer esfuerzos, empeñarse.
ex·er·tion [ɪgzɝ́ʃən] *s.* ejercicio; esfuerzo, empeño.
ex·hale [ɛkshél] *v.* exhalar, emitir; espirar, soplar.
ex·haust [ɪgzɔ́st] *s.* escape (*de gas o vapor*); *v.* agotar; consumir; debilitar, fatigar; **I am -ed** no puedo más; estoy agotado.
ex·haus·tion [ɪgzɔ́stʃən] *s.* agotamiento; fatiga, postración.
ex·haus·tive [ɛgzɔ́stɪv] *adj.* comprensivo; detallado.
ex·hib·it [ɪgzíbɪt] *v.* exhibir; mostrar, exponer.
ex·hi·bi·tion [ɛksəbíʃən] *s.* exhibición; exposición, manifestación.
ex·hil·a·rate [ɪgzíləret] *v.* alborozar, excitar, animar, entusiasmar; refocilar.
ex·hort [ɪgzɔ́rt] *v.* exhortar.
ex·ile [égzaɪl] *s.* destierro, exilio; desterrado; *v.* desterrar; expatriar.
ex·ist [ɪgzíst] *v.* existir.
ex·is·tence [ɪgzístəns] *s.* existencia.
ex·is·tent [ɪgzístənt] *adj.* existente.
ex·it [égzɪt] *s.* salida; salida (*del foro*); *v.* vase o vanse (*un personaje o personajes al fin de una escena*).
ex·o·dus [éksədəs] *s.* éxodo.
ex·on·er·ate [ɪgzánəret] *v.* exonerar.
ex·or·bi·tant [ɪgzɔ́rbətənt] *adj.* exorbitante.
ex·or·cism [éksɔrsɪzəm] *s.* exorcismo; conjuro.
ex·ot·ic [ɪgzátɪk] *adj.* exótico; raro, extraño.
ex·pand [ɪkspǽnd] *v.* ensanchar(se); dilatar(se); extender(se); agrandar(se); desarrollar (*una ecuación*).
ex·panse [ɪkspǽns] *s.* espacio, extensión.
ex·pan·sion [ɪkspǽnʃən] *s.* expansión; ensanche; desarrollo (*de una ecuación*).
ex·pan·sive [ɪkspǽnsɪv] *adj.* expansivo; efusivo.
ex·pect [ɪkspékt] *v.* esperar; contar con; **I — so** supongo que sí.
ex·pec·ta·tion [ɛkspɛktéʃən] *s.* expectación; expectativa; esperanza.
ex·pec·to·rate [ɪkspéktəret] *v.* expectorar, desgarrar.
ex·pe·di·ent [ɪkspídɪənt] *adj.* conveniente, oportuno; ventajoso; prudente; *s.* expediente, medio.
ex·pe·dite [ékspədaɪt] *v.* facilitar; despachar.
ex·pe·di·tion [ɛkspɪdíʃən] *s.* expedición.
ex·pe·di·tion·ary [ɛkspɪdíʃənɛrɪ] *adj.* expedicionario.
ex·pel [ɪkspél] *v.* expeler; expulsar.
ex·pend [ɪkspénd] *v.* gastar; consumir.
ex·pen·di·ture [ɪkspéndɪtʃə˞] *s.* gasto; desembolso.
ex·pense [ɪkspéns] *s.* gasto; coste, costa o costo.
ex·pen·sive [ɪkspénsɪv] *adj.* costoso.
ex·pen·sive·ness [ɪkspénsɪvnɪs] *s.* precio subido, coste elevado.
ex·pe·ri·ence [ɪkspírɪəns] *s.* experiencia; aventura, lance; *v.* experimentar; pasar (*penas, sufrimientos*); sentir.
ex·pe·ri·enced [ɪkspírɪənst] *adj.* experimentado; ducho, perito, experto.
ex·per·i·ment [ɪkspérəmənt] *s.* experimento, prueba; *v.* experimentar, hacer un experimento.
ex·per·i·men·tal [ɪkspɛrəméntḷ] *adj.* experimental.
ex·pert [ékspɝt] *s.* experto, perito; [ɪkspɝ́t] *adj.* experto, perito, experimentado.
ex·pi·ra·tion [ɛkspəréʃən] *s.* terminación; vencimiento (*de un plazo*); espiración (*del aire*).
ex·pire [ɪkspáɪr] *v.* expirar, morir; acabar; vencerse (*un plazo*); expeler (*el aire aspirado*).
ex·plain [ɪksplén] *v.* explicar.

ex·plain·a·ble [ɪksplénəbl] *adj*. explicable.
ex·pla·na·tion [ɛksplənéʃən] *s*. explicación.
ex·plan·a·to·ry [ɪksplǽnətorɪ] *adj*. explicativo.
ex·plic·it [ɛksplísɪt] *adj*. explícito.
ex·plode [ɪksplód] *v*. estallar, hacer explosión, *Am*. explotar; reventar; volar (*con dinamita*); desacreditar (*una teoría*).
ex·ploit [éksplɔɪt] *s*. hazaña, proeza; [ɪksplɔ́ɪt] *v*. explotar; sacar partido de, abusar de.
ex·ploi·ta·tion [ɛksplɔɪtéʃən] *s*. explotación.
ex·plo·ra·tion [ɛkspləréʃən] *s*. exploración.
ex·plore [ɪksplór] *v*. explorar.
ex·plor·er [ɪksplórɚ] *s*. explorador.
ex·plo·sion [ɪksplóʒən] *s*. explosión, estallido.
ex·plo·sive [ɪksplósɪv] *adj*. & *s*. explosivo.
ex·port [éksport] *s*. exportación; artículo exportado, mercancía exportada; [ɪkspórt] *v*. exportar.
ex·por·ta·tion [ɛksportéʃən] *s*. exportación.
ex·pose [ɪkspóz] *v*. exponer; exhibir, mostrar, poner a la vista; revelar; desenmascarar.
ex·po·si·tion [ɛkspəzíʃn] *s*. exposición; exhibición.
ex·po·sure [ɪkspóʒɚ] *s*. exposición; revelación; **to die of** — morir a efecto de la intemperie.
ex·pound [ɪkspáʊnd] *v*. exponer, explicar.
ex·press [ɪksprés] *adj*. (*rapid*) expreso; (*explicit*) explícito, claro; — **company** compañía de expreso; expreso, *Am*. exprés; — **train** tren expreso; *adv*. por expreso, por exprés; *s*. expreso; tren expreso, *Am*. exprés; *v*. expresar; enviar por expreso (*o* por exprés).
ex·pres·sion [ɪkspréʃən] *s*. expresión.
ex·pres·sive [ɪksprésɪv] *adj*. expresivo.
ex·pul·sion [ɪkspʌ́lʃən] *s*. expulsión.
ex·qui·site [ɛkskwízɪt] *adj*. exquisito.
ex·qui·site·ness [ɪkskwízɪtnɪs] *s*. exquisitez; primor.
ex·tant [ɪkstǽnt] *adj*. existente.
ex·tem·po·ra·ne·ous [ɛkstɛmpərénɪəs] *adj*. improvisado.
ex·tend [ɪksténd] *v*. extender(se); tender; prolongar(se); alargar(se); agrandar; dilatar, prorrogar (*un plazo*); dar (*el pésame, el parabién, ayuda, etc.*).
ex·tend·ed [ɪksténdɪd] *adj*. extenso; prolongado; extendido.
ex·ten·sion [ɪksténʃən] *s*. extensión; prolongación; prórroga (*de un plazo*); añadidura, anexo.
ex·ten·sive [ɪksténsɪv] *adj*. extenso, ancho, dilatado; extensivo; **-ly** *adv*. extensamente, por extenso; extensivamente; **-ly used** de uso general o común.
ex·tent [ɪkstént] *s*. extensión; grado; **to a great** — en gran parte, generalmente; **to such an** — **that** a tal grado que; **to the** — **of one's ability** en proporción a su habilidad; **up to a certain** — hasta cierto punto.
ex·ten·u·ate [ɪksténjʊet] *v*. atenuar, mitigar.
ex·te·ri·or [ɪkstírɪɚ] *adj*. exterior; externo; *s*. exterioridad; exterior, porte, aspecto.
ex·ter·mi·nate [ɪkstɝ́mənet] *v*. exterminar, destruir por completo, extirpar.
ex·ter·mi·na·tion [ɪkstɝmənéʃən] *s*. exterminio.
ex·ter·nal [ɪkstɝ́nl] *adj*. externo; exterior; *s*. exterioridad; lo externo.
ex·tinct [ɪkstíŋkt] *adj*. extinto; extinguido, apagado.
ex·tin·guish [ɪkstíŋgwɪʃ] *v*. extinguir; apagar.
ex·tol [ɪkstól] *v*. enaltecer; ensalzar.
ex·tort [ɪkstɔ́rt] *v*. obtener por fuerza o amenaza, exigir (*dinero, promesa, etc.*), *Am*. extorsionar.
ex·tor·tion [ɪkstɔ́rʃən] *s*. extorsión.
ex·tra [ékstrə] *adj*. extraordinario; de sobra, de más, adicional; suplementario; — **tire** neumático de repuesto o de recambio; — **workman** obrero supernumerario; *adv*. extraordinariamente; *s*. extra, extraordinario (*de un periódico*); suplemento; gasto extraordinario; recargo (*cargo adicional*); actor suplente o supernumerario.
ex·tract [ékstrækt] *s*. extracto; cita, trozo (*entresacado de un libro*); resumen; [ɪkstrǽkt] *v*. extraer; seleccionar; citar.
ex·traor·di·nar·y [ɪkstrɔ́rdnɛrɪ] *adj*. extraordinario; **extraordinarily** *adv*. extraordinariamente; de manera extraordinaria.
ex·trav·a·gance [ɪkstrǽvəgəns] *s*. despilfarro, derroche, gasto excesivo; lujo excesivo; extravagancia, capricho.
ex·trav·a·gant [ɪkstrǽvəgənt] *adj*. gastador, despilfarrado; extravagante, disparatado; — **praise** elogios excesivos; — **prices** precios exorbitantes.
ex·treme [ɪkstrím] *adj*. (*last*) último; extremo; más remoto; (*excessive*) excesivo; riguroso; radical; — **opinions** opiniones extremadas; *s*. extremo; cabo; **to go to -s** extremar, exagerar; hacer extremos; tomar las medidas más extremas; **-ly** *adv*. extremamente, en extremo.
ex·trem·ity [ɪkstréməti] *s*. extremidad, extremo; medida extrema; **in** — en gran peligro; en un apuro.
ex·u·ber·ant [ɪgzjúbərənt] *adj*. exuberante.
ex·ult [ɪgzʌ́lt] *v*. alborozarse, regocijarse.
eye [aɪ] *s*. ojo; — **shade** visera; **in a twinkling of an** — en un abrir y cerrar de ojos; **hook and** — macho y hembra; **to catch one's** — llamar la atención; **to have good -s** tener buena vista; **to have before one's -s** tener a (*o* tener ante) la vista; **to keep an** — **on** cuidar, vigilar; **to see** — **to** — estar completamente de acuerdo; *v*. mirar, observar.
eye·ball [áɪbɔl] *s*. globo del ojo.
eye·bolt [áɪbolt] *s*. perno de argolla.
eye·brow [áɪbraʊ] *s*. ceja.
eye·glass [áɪglæs] *s*. lente, cristal (*de anteojo*); ocular (*de microscopio o telescopio*); **-es** lentes, anteojos.
eye·lash [áɪlæʃ] *s*. pestaña.
eye·lid [áɪlɪd] *s*. párpado.
eye·sight [áɪsaɪt] *s*. vista; **poor** — mala vista.

F:f

fa·ble [fébl] *s*. fábula.
fab·ric [fǽbrɪk] *s*. género, tela; tejido; textura; estructura.
fab·u·lous [fǽbjələs] *adj*. fabuloso.
fa·çade [fəsɑ́d] *s*. fachada.
face [fes] *s*. (*human*) cara, rostro; (*building*) fachada, frente; (*surface*) haz, superficie; (*watch*) muestra; *Ríopl*. esfera; *Méx., C.A., Ven., Col*. carátula; — **value** valor nominal; **in the** — **of** en presencia de, ante, frente a; **to lose** — perder prestigio; **to make -s** hacer muecas o gestos; **to save one's** — salvar el amor propio; *v*. encararse con; enfrentarse con; hacer frente a; mirar hacia; forrar; **to** — **about** volverse, *Méx., C.A., Ven., Col., Andes* voltearse; **to** — **danger** afrontar o arrostrar el peligro; **to** — **with marble** revestir de mármol; **it -s the street** da a la calle.
fac·et [fǽsɪt] *s*. faceta.
fa·cil·i·tate [fəsílətet] *v*. facilitar.
fa·cil·i·ty [fəsílətɪ] *s*. facilidad.
fact [fækt] *s*. hecho; dato; verdad, realidad; **in** — de hecho; en realidad.
fac·tion [fǽkʃən] *s*. facción, bando, partido, pandilla.

fac·tor [fǽktɚ] *s.* factor; elemento; agente; *v.* descomponer en factores.
fac·to·ry [fǽktrɪ] *s.* fábrica; — **automation** automatización fabril.
fac·ul·ty [fǽkltɪ] *s.* facultad; (*college*) profesorado; cuerpo docente.
fad [fæd] *s.* novedad; manía; moda.
fade [fed] *v.* descolorar(se), desteñir(se); marchitar(se); apagarse (*un sonido*); desvanecerse.
fagged [fægd] *adj.* agotado, rendido de cansancio.
fail [fel] *v.* (*not effect*) faltar; fallar; fracasar; no tener éxito; (*wane*) decaer; debilitarse; (*go broke*) quebrar, hacer bancarrota; **to — in an examination** fallar en un examen, salir mal en un examen; **to — a student** reprobar o suspender a un estudiante; **to — to do it** dejar de hacerlo, no hacerlo; **don't — to come** no deje Vd. de venir; **without —** sin falta.
fail·ure [féljɚ] *s.* fracaso; malogro; falta; descuido, negligencia; quiebra, bancarrota; debilitamiento.
faint [fent] *adj.* (*weak*) débil, lánguido; (*indistinct*) imperceptible, tenue, vago, indistinto; **to feel —** sentirse desvanecido; — **hearted** tímido, cobarde; *s.* desmayo; *v.* desmayarse; languidecer; **-ly** *adv.* débilmente; lánguidamente; indistintamente, vagamente, tenuemente; apenas.
faint·ness [féntnɪs] *s.* languidez, debilidad, desfallecimiento; falta de claridad; vaguedad.
fair [fɛr] *adj.* (*just*) justo, recto, honrado; imparcial; equitativo; — **market value** valor justo; — **trade** comercio legítimo; (*mediocre*) regular, mediano; (*complexion*) rubio, blondo; *Méx.* huero; *Guat.* canche; *C.R.* macho; *Pan.* fulo; *Col.* mono; *Ven.* catire; *Sal.* chele; (*weather*) claro, despejado; — **chance of success** buena probabilidad de éxito; — **complexion** tez blanca; — **hair** pelo rubio; — **name** reputación sin mancilla; — **play** juego limpio; — **sex** sexo bello; — **weather** buen tiempo, tiempo bonancible; **to act —** obrar con imparcialidad (*o* con equidad); **to play —** jugar limpio; *s.* feria; mercado; exposición; *Valencia* falla; **-ly** *adv.* justamente; imparcialmente; medianamente; **-ly difficult** medianamente difícil; **-ly well** regular, bastante bien.
fair·ness [fɛ́rnɪs] *s.* justicia, equidad, imparcialidad; blancura (*de la tez*); belleza.
fair·y [fɛ́rɪ] *s.* hada; — **godmother** hada madrina; — **tale** cuento de hadas.
fair·y·land [fɛ́rɪlænd] *s.* tierra de las hadas.
faith [feθ] *s.* fe; fidelidad; **in good —** de buena fe; **to have — in** tener fe o confianza en; **to keep —** cumplir con la palabra.
faith·ful [féθfəl] *adj.* fiel; leal; **-ly** *adv.* fielmente; con fidelidad; puntualmente; **-ly yours** suyo afectísimo; siempre suyo.
faith·ful·ness [féθfəlnɪs] *s.* fidelidad; lealtad; exactitud.
faith·less [féθlɪs] *adj.* infiel; sin fe; desleal; falso.
fake [fek] *s.* fraude, trampa; falsedad; embustero; *adj.* falso, fingido; *v.* falsear; fingir; simular.
fal·con [fɔ́lkən] *s.* halcón.
fall [fɔl] *s.* (*drop*) caída; bajada; (*collapse*) ruina; baja (*de precios*); (*season*) otoño; **-s** cascada, catarata, salto de agua; *v.* caer(se); decaer; bajar; **to — asleep** dormirse, quedarse dormido; **to — back** retroceder; **to — behind** atrasarse, rezagarse, quedarse atrás; **to — in love** enamorarse; **to — out with** reñir con, enemistarse con; **to — to one** tocarle a uno, corresponderle a uno; **his plans fell through** fracasaron (*o* se malograron) sus planes; — **guy** cabeza de turco.
fal·la·cy [fǽləsɪ] *s.* falsedad; error.
fall·en [fɔ́lən] *p.p. de* **to fall.**
fall·out [fɔ́laʊt] *s.* precipitación radiactiva.
fal·low [fǽlo] *adj.* baldío; *s.* barbecho; *v.* barbechar.
false [fɔls] *adj.* falso; postizo (*dientes, barba, etc.*); fingido, simulado; — **pretense** dolo, estafa.
false·hood [fɔ́lshʊd] *s.* falsedad, mentira.
false·ness [fɔ́lsnɪs] *s.* falsedad.
fal·si·fy [fɔ́lsəfaɪ] *v.* falsificar, falsear; mentir.
fal·si·ty [fɔlsətɪ] *s.* falsedad; mentira.
fal·ter [fɔ́ltɚ] *v.* vacilar; titubear; tambalearse; bambolearse; **to — an excuse** balbucear una excusa; *s.* temblor, vacilación.
fame [fem] *s.* fama.
famed [femd] *adj.* afamado, famoso, renombrado.
fa·mil·iar [fəmɪ́ljɚ] *adj.* familiar, íntimo; confianzudo; **to be — with a subject** conocer bien, estar versado en o ser conocedor de una materia; *s.* familiar.
fa·mil·i·ar·i·ty [fəmɪlɪǽrətɪ] *s.* familiaridad; confianza, franqueza.
fam·i·ly [fǽmlɪ] *s.* familia; — **name** apellido; — **tree** árbol genealógico; **to be in the — way** estar encinta.
fam·ine [fǽmɪn] *s.* hambre; escasez, carestía.
fam·ished [fǽmɪʃt] *adj.* hambriento, muerto de hambre; **to be —** morirse de hambre.
fa·mous [féməs] *adj.* famoso.
fan [fæn] *s.* abanico; aventador; ventilador; aficionado (*a deportes*); admirador; *v.* abanicar; ventilar.
fa·nat·ic [fənǽtɪk] *adj. & s.* fanático.
fa·nat·i·cism [fənǽtəsɪzəm] *s.* fanatismo.
fan·ci·ful [fǽnsɪfəl] *adj.* fantástico; caprichoso; imaginario.
fan·cy [fǽnsɪ] *s.* fantasía, antojo, capricho; imaginación; afición, gusto; **to have a — for** tener afición a; **to strike one's —** antojársele a uno; **to take a — to a person** caerle a uno bien (*o* simpatizarle a uno) una persona; *adj.* fantástico, de fantasía; de adorno; elegante; — **ball** baile de fantasía o disfraces; — **free** libre de cuidados; — **work** labor; bordado fino; *v.* imaginar(se); fantasear; forjar, concebir (*una idea*); **to — oneself** imaginarse; **just — the idea!** ¡figúrate qué idea! **I don't — the idea of** no me gusta la idea de.
fan·fare [fǽnfɛr] *s.* toque de trompeta.
Fan-fold pa·per [fǽnfold pepɚ] *s.* papel continuo.
fang [fæŋ] *s.* colmillo (*de ciertos animales*).
fan·tas·tic [fæntǽstɪk] *adj.* fantástico; extravagante.
fan·ta·sy [fǽntəsɪ] *s.* fantasía.
far [fɑr] *adv.* lejos; — **away** muy lejos; — **and wide** por todas partes; — **better** mucho mejor; — **off** muy lejos; a lo lejos; **by —** con mucho; **as — as** hasta; en cuanto a; **as — as I know** según parece; a lo que parece; que yo sepa; **so —** hasta ahora; hasta aquí; hasta entonces; **how —?** ¿hasta dónde?; *adj.* lejano, distante, remoto; — **journey** largo viaje; **it is a — cry from** dista mucho de.
far·a·way [fɑ́rəwé] *adj.* muy lejano, distante, remoto; abstraído.
farce [fɑrs] *s.* farsa.
fare [fɛr] *s.* pasaje, tarifa de pasajes; pasajero; comida, alimento; *v.* pasarla (*vien o mal*); irle a uno (*bien o mal*); **to — forth** salir.
fare·well [fɛrwɛ́l] *s.* despedida, adiós; **to bid — to** despedirse de; **—!** ¡adiós!
far·fetched [fɑ́rfɛ́tʃt] *adj.* traído de muy lejos; forzado; traído por los cabellos; que no hace al caso; improbable, poco creíble.
far·flung [fɑ́rflʌ́ŋ] *adj.* extenso, de gran alcance.

farm [fɑrm] *s.* hacienda, granja, finca; *Ríopl.* estancia, *Méx.* rancho; — **hand** peón; — **produce** productos agrícolas; — **loan bank** caja de crédito agrario campesino; *v.* cultivar, labrar (*la tierra*); **to — out** dar en arriendo; repartir.
farm·er [fɑ́rmɚ] *s.* labrador; granjero; agricultor, *Méx.* ranchero, *Ríopl.* estanciero, *Am.* hacendado.
farm·house [fɑ́rmhaʊs] *s.* alquería, finca.
farm·ing [fɑ́rmɪŋ] *s.* labranza, agricultura, cultivo de los campos; *adj.* agrícola.
farm·yard [fɑ́rmjɑrd] *s.* corral (*de una alquería*).
far·off [fɑ́rɔ́f] *adj.* distance, remoto.
far-sighted [fɑrsáɪtəd] *adj.* (*sight*) présbite.
far·ther [fɑ́rðɚ] *adv.* más lejos; más; — **on** más adelante; *adj.* más remoto, más lejano.
far·thest [fɑ́rðɪst] *adj.* más lejano; más remoto; *adv.* más lejos.
fas·ci·nate [fǽsn̩et] *v.* fascinar.
fas·ci·na·tion [fæsn̩éʃən] *s.* fascinación.
fas·cism [fǽʃɪzm] *s.* fascismo.
fas·cist [fǽʃɪst] *s.* fascista.
fash·ion [fǽʃən] *s.* (*style*) moda, boga, estilo; (*way*) manera, modo; — **plate** figurín; **the latest** — la última moda (*o* novedad); **after a** — medianamente, no muy bien; **to be in** — estar de moda; estilarse; *v.* forjar, hacer, formar; idear.
fash·ion·a·ble [fǽʃnəbl̩] *adj.* de moda; de buen tono; elegante.
fast [fæst] *adj.* rápido, veloz; (*watch*) adelantado (*dícese del reloj*); (*firm*) firme; fiel (*amigo*); fijo; (*dissolute*) disipado, disoluto; *adv.* aprisa, de prisa; firmemente, fijamente; — **asleep** profundamente dormido; *s.* ayuno; *v.* ayunar.
fas·ten [fǽsn̩] *v.* fijar(se); sujetar(se), asegurar(se); atar, unir, abrochar(se).
fas·ten·er [fǽsn̩ɚ] *s.* broche; abrochador.
fas·tid·i·ous [fæstídɪəs] *adj.* melindroso.
fat [fæt] *adj.* (*large*) gordo; (*greasy*) grasiento; mantecoso; — **profits** ganancias pingües; *s.* grasa, manteca; gordura; **the — of the land** lo mejor y más rico de la tierra.
fa·tal [fétl] *adj.* fatal.
fa·tal·i·ty [fətǽlətɪ] *s.* fatalidad; muerte.
fate [fet] *s.* hado, sino, destino; fortuna, suerte.
fa·ther [fɑ́ðɚ] *s.* padre.
fa·ther·hood [fɑ́ðɚhʊd] *s.* paternidad.
fa·ther-in-law [fɑ́ðərɪnlɔ] *s.* suegro.
fa·ther·land [fɑ́ðɚlænd] *s.* patria.
fa·ther·ly [fɑ́ðɚlɪ] *adv.* paternal.
fath·om [fǽðəm] *v.* sondar, sondear; penetrar; *s.* braza (*medida de profundidad*).
fath·om·less [fǽðəmlɪs] *adj.* insondable.
fa·tigue [fətíg] *s.* fatiga, cansancio; *v.* fatigar(se), cansar(se).
fat·ness [fǽtnɪs] *s.* gordura.
fat·ten [fǽtn̩] *v.* engordar.
fat·ty [fǽtɪ] *adj.* grasiento; seboso.
fau·cet [fɔ́sɪt] *s.* grifo, llave, espita, canilla, *Méx.* bitoque.
fault [fɔlt] *s.* (*defect*) falta; defecto; tacha; (*blame*) culpa; (*geological*) falla; **to a** — excesivamente; **to be at** — ser, culpable; **to find — with** criticar a.
fault·find·er [fɔ́ltfaɪndɚ] *s.* criticón, criticador.
fault·less [fɔ́ltlɪs] *adj.* intachable, sin tacha, perfecto.
fault·y [fɔ́ltɪ] *adj.* defectuoso, imperfecto.
fa·vor [févɚ] *s.* favor; **your — of the …** su grata (carta) del …; *v.* favorecer.
fa·vor·able [févrəbl] *adj.* favorable; **favorably** *adv.* favorablemente.
fa·vor·ite [févrɪt] *adj.* & *s.* favorito.
fa·vor·it·ism [févrɪtɪzəm] *s.* favoritismo.
fawn [fɔn] *s.* cervato; color de cervato; *v.* adular; halagar.
fear [fɪr] *s.* temor, miedo; pavor; *v.* temer.
fear·ful [fírfəl] *adj.* terrible, espantoso; temible, temeroso; miedoso.
fear·less [fírlɪs] *adj.* sin temor, intrépido, atrevido, arrojado.
fear·less·ness [fírlɪsnɪs] *s.* intrepidez, arrojo, osadía, atrevimiento.
fea·si·ble [fízəbl̩] *adj.* factible, hacedero, dable.
feast [fist] *s.* fiesta; festín, banquete; *v.* festejar, obsequiar; banquetear; **to — one's eyes on** deleitar la vista en.
feat [fit] *s.* (heroics) proeza, hazaña; (*trick*) acto de destreza; suerte (*en el circo*).
feath·er [féðɚ] *s.* pluma; **-s** plumaje; **a — in one's cap** un triunfo para uno; — **weight** de peso mínimo; — **bedding** empleo de trabajadores innecesarios; *v.* emplumar.
feath·er·y [féðərɪ] *adj.* plumoso; ligero, como una pluma.
fea·ture [fítʃɚ] *s.* facción, rasgo distintivo; película principal (*en el cine*); **-s** facciones (*de la cara*); — **article** artículo sobresaliente o principal; *v.* destacar, hacer sobresalir; dar realce a; mostrar, exhibir (*como cosa principal*), hacer resaltar.
Feb·ru·ar·y [fébrʊɛrɪ] *s.* febrero.
fed [fɛd] *pret.* & *p.p. de* **to feed; to be — up** estar harto, estar hasta la coronilla, estar hasta el copete.
fed·er·al [fédərəl] *adj.* federal.
fed·er·a·tion [fɛdəréʃən] *s.* federación, confederación, liga.
fee [fi] *s.* honorario (honorarios); derechos; cuota; **admission** — derechos de entrada; precio de entrada.
fee·ble [fibl̩] *adj.* débil, endeble; **feebly** *adv.* débilmente.
feed [fid] *s.* forraje, pasto, pienso (*para los caballos*); comida; *v.* alimentar(se); dar de comer; pacer, pastar; **to — coal** echar carbón.
feed·back [fídbæk] *s.* regeneración; reacciones informativas.
feel [fil] *v.* sentir; tocar, tentar; palpar; **to — better** (sad, happy, *etc.*) sentirse mejor (triste, feliz, *etc.*); **to — one's way** tantear el camino; **to — for someone** compadecer a alguien; **it -s soft** está suave; **it -s hot in here** se siente calor aquí; *s.* tacto, sentido del tacto; **this cloth has a nice** — esta tela es suave al tacto.
feel·er [filɚ] *s.* tentáculo, antena (*de los insectos*); tiento; propuesta (*para averiguar la inclinación o pensamiento de alguien*).
feel·ing [filɪŋ] *s.* (*touch*) tacto; sensación (*emotion*) sentimiento; emoción; pasión; (*pity*) compasión; ternura; **to hurt someone's -s** ofender la sensibilidad de alguien; *adj.* sensible, compasivo.
feet [fit] *pl. de* **foot.**
feign [fen] *v.* fingir.
fell [fɛl] *v.* derribar, echar abajo; talar (*un árbol*); *pret. de* **to fall.**
fel·low [félo] *s.* socio, miembro (*de una sociedad, colegio, etc.*); (*scholar*) becario (*estudiante que disfruta una beca*); (*companion*) camarada; compañero; individuo, tipo, sujeto, hombre; — **citizen** conciudadano; — **man** prójimo; — **member** consocio; colega; — **student** condiscípulo.
fel·low·ship [féloʃɪp] *s.* compañerismo; unión; confraternidad; sociedad; beca; **to get a** — obtener una beca.
fel·o·ny [félənɪ] *s.* crimen.

felt [fɛlt] *s.* fieltro; *adj.* de fieltro; *pret. & p.p. de* **to feel.**
fe·male [fímel] *s.* hembra; *adj.* hembra; femenino, mujeril, de la mujer; — **cat (dog,** *etc.*) gata (perra, *etc.*); — **screw** tuerca, hembra de tornillo.
fem·i·nine [fɛ́mənɪn] *adj.* femenino, femenil.
fem·i·nin·i·ty [fɛmɪnínɪtɪ] *s.* feminidad.
fe·mur [fímɚ] *s.* fémur.
fence [fɛns] *s.* cerca, valla, vallado; receptor de cosas robadas; **to be on the** — estar indeciso; *v.* esgrimir; **to — in** cercar, rodear con cerca.
fenc·ing [fɛ́nsɪŋ] *s.* esgrima; cercado.
fend·er [fɛ́ndɚ] *s.* guardabarros, guardafango; *Col.* trompa (*de locomotora*); *Ríopl.* parrilla.
fer·ment [fɝ́mɛnt] *s.* fermento; fermentación; [fɚmɛ́nt] *v.* fermentar; hacer fermentar.
fer·men·ta·tion [fɝməntéʃən] *s.* fermentación.
fern [fɝn] *s.* helecho.
fe·ro·cious [fəróʃəs] *adj.* feroz, fiero.
fe·roc·i·ty [fərɑ́sətɪ] *s.* ferocidad, fiereza.
fer·ret [fɛ́rɪt] *v.* **to — out** buscar, cazar; (*investigate*) escudriñar, indagar.
fer·ry [fɛ́rɪ] *s.* barca de pasaje (*a través de un río o bahía*); embarcadero; *Méx.* chalán, pango; *v.* transportar de una orilla a otra; atravesar (*un río*) en barca de pasaje.
fer·tile [fɝ́tl̩] *adj.* fértil; fecundo.
fer·til·i·ty [fɝtílətɪ] *s.* fertilidad.
fer·til·ize [fɝ́tlaɪz] *v.* fertilizar; abonar; fecundar.
fer·til·iz·er [fɝ́tlaɪzɚ] *s.* abono (*para la tierra*).
fer·vent [fɝ́vənt] *adj.* ferviente; fervoroso.
fer·vor [fɝ́vɚ] *s.* fervor; ardor.
fes·ter [fɛ́stɚ] *v.* supurar; enconarse (*una llaga*); *s.* llaga, úlcera.
fes·ti·val [fɛ́stəvl̩] *s.* fiesta.
fes·tive [fɛ́stɪv] *adj.* festivo; alegre.
fes·tiv·i·ty [fɛstívətɪ] *s.* júbilo, regocijo; festividad.
fetch [fɛtʃ] *v.* ir a buscar; coger; traer.
fete [fet] *s.* fiesta; *v.* festejar; agasajar.
fet·ish [fɛ́tɪʃ] *s.* fetiche.
fet·ter [fɛ́tɚ] *v.* engrillar, meter en grillos encadenar; **-s'** *s. pl.* grillos, cadenas, trabas.
fe·tus [fítəs] *s.* feto.
feud [fjud] *s.* riña, pelea, contienda; **old** — enemistad antigua (*entre dos personas o familias*).
feu·dal [fjúdl] *adj.* feudal.
fe·ver [fívɚ] *s.* fiebre, calentura.
fe·ver·ish [fívərɪʃ] *adj.* calenturiento, febril.
fe·ver·ish·ness [fívərɪʃnɪs] *s.* calentura; agitación febril.
few [fju] *adj. & pron.* pocos; **a** — unos pocos, unos cuantos.
fi·an·cé [fiɑnsé] *s.* novio; **fiancée** *f.* novia.
fi·as·co [fɪǽsko] *s.* fiasco.
fib [fɪb] *s.* bola, mentirilla, paparrucha, papa; *v.* echar papas, decir o contar paparruchas.
fib·ber [fíbɚ] *s.* paparruchero, cuentero, mentirosillo.
fi·ber [fáɪbɚ] *s.* fibra.
fi·brous [fáɪbrəs] *adj.* fibroso.
fick·le [fíkl̩] *adj.* inconstante, voluble, veleidoso, mudable; tornadizo.
fic·tion [fíkʃən] *s.* ficción.
fic·tion·al [fíkʃənl] *adj.* novelesco; ficticio.
fic·ti·tious [fɪktíʃəs] *adj.* ficticio.
fid·dle [fídl̩] *s.* violín; *v.* tocar el violín; **to — around** malgastar el tiempo; juguetear.
fi·del·i·ty [faɪdɛ́lətɪ] *s.* fidelidad.
fid·get [fídʒɪt] *v.* estar inquieto; agitarse, menearse nerviosamente.
fi·du·ci·ar·y [fɪdúʃɛrɪ] *adj.* fiduciario, fideicomisario.
field [fild] *s.* campo; campo o cancha (*de deportes*); (*computer*) campo; — **artillery** artillería de campaña; — **glasses** anteojos de larga vista; — **work** trabajo de investigación en el campo.
fiend [find] *s.* demonio, diablo; **dope** — morfinómano.
fiend·ish [fíndɪʃ] *adj.* diabólico.
fierce [fɪrs] *adj.* feroz, fiero; furioso, espantoso.
fierce·ness [fɪ́rsnɪs] *s.* ferocidad; fiereza; vehemencia.
fier·y [fáɪrɪ] *adj.* fogoso; ardiente; vehemente.
fife [faɪf] *s.* pífano.
fif·teen [fɪftín] *num.* quince.
fif·ty [fíftɪ] *num.* cincuenta.
fig [fɪg] *s.* higo; — **tree** higuera.
fight [faɪt] *s.* lucha; pelea; riña, pleito; **he has a lot of — left** le sobra fuerza para luchar; *v.* luchar (con) pelear; combatir; reñir; batirse; **to — it out** decidirlo a golpes o con argumentos; **to — one's way through** abrirse camino a la fuerza.
fight·er [fáɪtɚ] *s.* luchador; combatiente; guerrero; — **airplane** avión de caza.
fight·ing [fáɪtɪŋ] *s.* lucha, combate pelea; *adj.* combatiente; luchador.
fig·ure [fígjɚ] *s.* (*form*) figura; forma; talle (*de una persona*); (*numerical*) cifra, número; valor; precio; **-s** cuentas, cálculos; — **of speech** figura de dicción; **to be good at -s** sabe hacer bien las cuentas; ser listo en aritmética; **to cut a poor** — tener mala facha, hacer el ridículo; *v.* figurar; imaginarse, figurarse; adornar con dibujos; calcular; **to — on** contar con, confiar en; tener la intención de; proponerse; tomar en cuenta; **to — out** descifrar, resolver.
fil·a·ment [fílәmənt] *s.* filamento.
file [faɪl] *s.* (*records*) fichero; archivo; registro, lista; (*computer*) archivo, fichero; legajo; (*cabinet*) guardapapeles; (*line*) fila; (*tool*) lima; — **card** ficha, papeleta; *v.* archivar; guardar en el fichero; registrar, asentar en el registro; limar; desfilar, marchar en fila; — **a claim** establecer reclamación; — **a suit** entablar un pleito.
fil·i·al [fílɪəl] *adj.* filial.
fil·i·bus·ter [fɪləbʌstɚ] *v.* emplear táctica parlamentaria dilatoria.
fil·i·gree [fílɪgri] *s.* filigrana.
fill [fɪl] *v.* llenar(se); ocupar (*un puesto*); empastar (*un diente*); servir, atender, despachar (*un pedido*); inflar (*un neumático*); tapar (*un agujero*); **to — out a blank** llenar un formulario (*forma o esqueleto*); **to — in** suministrar informes específicos; **her eyes -ed with tears** se le arrasaron los ojos de lágrimas.
fil·let [fɪlé] *s.* filete; [fílɪt] *cinta, lista de adorno.*
fill·ing [fílɪŋ] *s.* relleno; empaste (*dental*); **gold** — orificación.
fil·ly [fílɪ] *s.* potranca.
film [fɪlm] *s.* (*photographic*) película; (*membrane*) membrana; (*on liquid*) tela; (*in eye*) nube (*en el ojo*); *v.* filmar, cinematografiar.
fil·ter [fíltɚ] *s.* filtro; *v.* filtrar(se).
filth [fɪlθ] *s.* suciedad; porquería; mugre.
filth·i·ness [fílθɪnɪs] *s.* suciedad, porquería.
filth·y [fílθɪ] *adj.* sucio; puerco, cochino; mugriento.
fin [fɪn] *s.* aleta (*de pez*).
fi·nal [fáɪnl] *adj.* final; terminante; definitivo; **-ly** *adv.* finalmente; en fin, por fin.
fi·nance [fənǽns] *s.* teoría bancaria, *Am.* finanza; **-s** fondos, recursos monetarios; negocios bancarios, *Am.* finanzas; *v.* hacer operaciones bancarias; fomentar (*un negocio o empresa*), *Am.* financiar.
fi·nan·cial [fənǽnʃəl] *adj.* financiero; monetario; — **backing** respaldo económico, apoyo financiero.
fin·an·cier [fɪnənsɪ́r] *s.* financiero, *Am.* financista.

fi·nanc·ing [fənǽnsɪŋ] *s. Am.* financiamiento.
find [faɪnd] *v.* hallar; encontrar; declarar; **to — fault with** criticar a, censurar a; **to — guilty** declarar o encontrar culpable; **to — out** descubrir; averiguar; *s.* hallazgo.
find·ing [fáɪndɪŋ] *s.* descubrimiento; hallazgo; fallo, decisión; **-s** resultados, datos (*de una investigación*).
fine [faɪn] *adj.* (*delicate*) fino; (*good*) perfecto, excelente; superior; primoroso; **— arts** bellas artes; **— sand** arena fina o menuda; **— weather** tiempo claro o despejado; **to feel —** sentirse muy bien de salud; **to have a — time** pasar un rato muy divertido; **fine-looking** bien parecido, guapo; *s.* multa; **in —** en fin, en resumen; *v.* multar; **-ly** *adv.* finamente; con primor; excelentemente; muy bien, perfectamente.
fine·ness [fáɪnnɪs] *s.* finura; fineza; primor; excelencia, perfección.
fin·er·y [fáɪnərɪ] *s.* galas; atavíos, adornos.
fi·nesse [fɪnέs] *s.* sutileza; artificio; soltura.
fin·ger [fíŋgɚ] *s.* dedo (*de la mano*); **—print** impresión digital; **the little —** el dedo meñique; **middle —** dedo del corazón, dedo de enmedio; **ring —** dedo anular; *v.* tocar; manosear.
fin·ger·nail [fíŋgɚnel] *s.* uña.
fin·ick·y [fínɪkɪ] *adj.* melindroso.
fin·ish [fínɪʃ] *s.* fin, término, conclusión; (*varnish*) acabado; pulimiento; **to have a rough —** estar sin pulir, sin pulimento o al natural; *v.* acabar, acabar con, terminar, finalizar; pulir, pulimentar.
fin·ished [fínɪʃt] *adj.* acabado; pulido, pulimentado; (*good*) excelente.
fir [fɝ] *s.* abeto.
fire [faɪr] *s.* (*flame*) fuego; lumbre; (*destructive*) quemazón; incendio; **— alarm** alarma de incendios; **— department** cuerpo o servicio de bomberos; servicio de incendios; **— engine** bomba (*para incendios*); **— escape** escalera de salvamento; **— insurance** seguro contra incendios; **— trap** edificio sin medios de escape en caso de incendio; **to be on —** estar ardiendo, estar quemándose; **to catch —** incendiarse, quemarse; **to set on —** pegar fuego, incendiar; **to be under enemy —** estar expuesto al fuego del enemigo; *v.* incendiar; pegar fuego; inflamar; disparar; **to — an employee** despedir (*o* expulsar) a un empleado.
fire·arm [fáɪrɑrm] *s.* arma de fuego.
fire·brand [fáɪrbrænd] *s.* tizón; pavesa.
fire·crack·er [fáɪrkrǽkɚ] *s.* triquitraque.
fire·fly [fáɪrflaɪ] *s.* luciérnaga.
fire·man [fáɪrmən] *s.* (*who extinguishes*) bombero; (*who makes*) fogonero.
fire·place [fáɪrples] *s.* chimenea, hogar.
fire·proof [fáɪrpruf] *adj.* incombustible; a prueba de incendio; *v.* hacer incombustible.
fire·side [fáɪrsaɪd] *s.* hogar.
fire·wood [fáɪrwʊd] *s.* leña.
fire·works [fáɪrwɝks] *s.* fuegos artificiales; pirotecnia.
fir·ing pin [fáɪrɪŋ pɪn] *s.* percusor.
firm [fɝm] *adj.* firme; fijo; estable; *s.* firma, razón social (*nombre de una casa comercial*); compañía (*comercial o industrial*); **-ly** *adv.* firmemente, con firmeza.
fir·ma·ment [fɝ́məmənt] *s.* firmamento.
firm·ness [fɝ́mnɪs] *s.* firmeza; estabilidad.
first [fɝst] *adj.* primero; *adv.* primero, en primer lugar, al principio, **from the —** desde el principio; **first-born** primogénito; **first-class** de primera clase; **first-cousin** primo hermano; **first-rate** de primera clase; muy bien; **— hand** de primera mano; **— of exchange** primera de cambio.
first aid [fɝst éd] *s.* primeros auxilios.
fis·cal [fískl] *adj.* monetario, económico; **— period** período económico, *Méx.* año natural.
fish [fɪʃ] *s.* pez; *C.A.* peje; (*for market*) pescado; **— market** pescadería; **— story** patraña, cuento extravagante o increíble; **neither — nor fowl** ni chicha ni limonada; *v.* pescar.
fish·er [fíʃɚ] *s.* pescador.
fish·er·man [fíʃɚmən] *s.* pescador.
fish·er·y [fíʃərɪ] *s.* pesquera; pesquería, pesca.
fish·hook [fíʃhʊk] *s.* anzuelo.
fish·ing [fíʃɪŋ] *s.* pesca, pesquería; **— rod** caña de pescar; **— tackle** avíos o enseres de pescar; **to go —** ir de pesca.
fis·sure [fíʃɚ] *s.* grieta, hendedura, *Am.* rajadura.
fist [fɪst] *s.* puño; **to shake one's — at** amenazar con el puño.
fit [fɪt] *adj.* (*proper*) apto; a propósito, propio, conveniente; (*healthy*) sano, de buena salud, en buen estado; capaz; **— to be tied** frenético; **not to see — to do it** no tener a bien hacerlo; *s.* talle (*de un traje*); ajuste; encaje (*de una pieza en otra*); ataque, convulsión; **— of anger** acceso, arrebato o arranque de cólera; **by -s and starts** espasmódicamente; **that suit is a good —** ese traje le entalla (*o* le viene) bien; *v.* ajustar(se); adaptar; encajar(se), caber (en); acomodar; entallar (*un vestido*); venir bien (*un vestido, zapatos, sombrero, etc.*); ser a propósito para, ser propio para; capacitar, preparar; **to — in with** armonizar con; llevarse bien con; **to — out** equipar, proveer; **it does not — the facts** no está de acuerdo con los hechos; no hace al caso.
fit·ness [fítnɪs] *s.* aptitud; capacidad; conveniencia; propiedad (*de una idea, de una palabra, etc.*); **physical —** buena salud.
fit·ting [fítɪŋ] *adj.* propio, apropiado; a propósito, conveniente; *s.* ajuste; **dress —** prueba de un traje o vestido; **-s** avíos, guarniciones, accesorios.
five [faɪv] *num.* cinco.
fix [fɪks] *v.* (*repair*) remendar; componer; reparar; ajustar; arreglar; (*prearrange*) fijar; asegurar; **to — up** arreglar(se); componer(se); *s.* apuro, aprieto.
fixed [fɪkst] *adj.* fijo, firme.
fix·ed·ly [fíksɪdlɪ] *adv.* de hito en hito; fijamente.
fix·ture [fíksʃɚ] *s.* (*thing*) accesorio fijo; (*person*) persona firmemente establecida (*en un sitio o empleo*); muebles y enseres; **electric light -s** instalaciones eléctricas (*como brazos de lámparas, arañas*).
fiz·zle out [fízl aʊt] *v.* hacer fiasco, fracasar.
flab·by [flǽbɪ] *adj.* blanducho.
flag [flæg] *s.* bandera; banderola; **— lily** flor de lis; *v.* hacer señas con banderola; adornar con banderas; decaer, debilitarse, menguar, flaquear.
fla·grant [flǽgrənt] *adv.* flagrante, notorio, escandaloso.
flag·staff [flǽgstæf] *s.* asta de bandera.
flag·stone [flǽgston] *s.* losa.
flair [flɛr] *s.* instinto, penetración, cacumen; disposición o aptitud natural.
flak [flæk] *s.* fuego antiaéreo; crítica abusiva.
flake [flek] *s.* copo (*de nieve*); escama; hojuela; **corn -s** hojuelas de maíz; *v.* descostrarse, descascararse.
flam·boy·ant [flæmbɔ́jənt] *adj.* rimbombante; flameante.
flame [flem] *s.* llama; flama; **— thrower** lanzallamas; *v.* llamear, flamear, echar llamas; inflamar(se); enardecer(se).

flam·ing [flémɪŋ] *adj.* llameante; flameante; encendido; ardiente, apasionado; — **red** rojo encendido.
flank [flæŋk] *s.* flanco; costado; lado; (*animal*) ijar (*de un animal*); *v.* flanquear; rodear.
flan·nel [flǽnl̩] *s.* franela.
flap [flæp] *s.* (*thing*) aleta; cubierta (*del bolsillo*); (*action*) golpeteo; aleteo; *v.* golpetear; aletear, batir (*las alas*); hojear con violencia (*las páginas*).
flare [flɛr] *s.* llamarada; llama; arranque (*de ira*); vuelo (*de una falda*); *v.* llamear, echar llamaradas; tener vuelo (*una falda*); **to — up** enfurecerse; encenderse; **the illness -ed up** recrudeció la enfermedad.
flash [flæʃ] *s.* rayo; destello, llamarada; fogonazo; — **of hope** rayo de esperanza; — **of lightning** relámpago; — **of wit** agudeza; — **bulb** bombilla de destello; bombilla flash; **in a** — en un instante; **news** — última noticia (*enviada por radio o telégrafo*); *v.* relampaguear; destellar; brillar; centellear; radiar o telegrafiar (*noticias*); **to — by** pasar como un relámpago.
flash·ing [flǽʃɪŋ[*s.* relampagueo, centello; *adj.* relumbrante; flameante.
flash·light [flǽʃlaɪt] *s.* linterna eléctrica.
flash·y [flǽʃɪ] *adj.* relumbrante; llamativo, de relumbrón, ostentoso; chillante, chillón (*dícese de los colores*).
flask [flæsk] *s.* frasco.
flat [flæt] *adj.* (*no curves*) plano, llano, chato; (*smashed*) aplastado; (*tasteless*) insípido; monótono; (*without air*) desinflado; — **denial** negativa terminante; — **note** nota desentonada; — **rate** precio o número redondo; **D** — re bemol (*nota musical*); — **car** vagón de plataforma; **to be — broke** estar completamente pelado, estar sin dinero; **to fall** — caer de plano; caer mal (*un discurso, chiste, etc.*); **to sing** — desafinarse, cantar desentonadamente; **to refuse -ly** negarse absolutamente; *s.* plano; palma (*de la mano*); apartamento, departamento, piso; bemol (*en música*).
flat·iron [flǽtaɪɚn] *s.* plancha.
flat·ness [flǽtnɪs] *s.* llanura; lisura; insipidez; desafinamiento (*en música*).
flat·ten [flǽtn̩] *v.* aplastar(se); aplanar(se); allanar(se).
flat·ter [flǽtɚ] *v.* lisonjear; adular.
flat·ter·er [flǽtərɚ] *s.* lisonjero, adulador.
flat·ter·ing [flǽtərɪŋ] *adj.* lisonjero, halagüeño, adulador.
flat·ter·y [flǽtərɪ] *s.* lisonja, halago; adulación.
flat·u·lence [flǽtjʊləns] *s.* hinchazón, flatulencia.
flaunt [flɔnt] *v.* ostentar; hacer gala de.
fla·vor [flévɚ] *s.* sabor; gusto; (*seasoning*) condimento; *v.* sazonar; dar sabor a; condimentar.
fla·vor·less [flévɚlɪs] *adj.* insípido, sin sabor.
flaw [flɔ] *s.* defecto; falta; tacha; imperfección.
flaw·less [flɔ́lɪs] *adj.* sin tacha, intachable, irreprochable; perfecto.
flax [flæks] *s.* lino.
flay [fle] *s.* desollar.
flea [fli] *s.* pulga.
fled [flɛd] *pret. & p.p. de* **to flee.**
flee [fli] *v.* huir; huir de.
fleece [flis] *s.* vellón, lana; *v.* trasquilar, esquilar; despojar, estafar, defraudar.
fleet [flit] *s.* flota; (*navy*) armada; *adj.* veloz.
fleet·ing [flítiŋ] *adj.* fugaz, transitorio, pasajero, efímero.
Flem·ish [flɛ́mɪʃ] *adj.* flamenco; *s.* flamenco, idioma flamenco; **the** — los flamencos.
flesh [flɛʃ] *s.* carne; — **and blood** carne y hueso; — **color** color encarnado; **in the** — en persona.
flesh·y [flɛ́ʃɪ] *adj.* carnoso; gordo, gordiflón.
flew [flu] *pret. de* **to fly.**
flex·i·bil·i·ty [flɛksəbflətɪ] *s.* flexibilidad.
flex·i·ble [flɛ́ksəbl̩] *adj.* flexible.
flick·er [flɪ́kɚ] *s.* titilación, parpadeo, luz trémula; temblor momentáneo (*de emoción*); aleteo; especie de pájaro carpintero; *v.* titilar; temblar; parpadear; vacilar; aletear; **to — one's eyelash** pestañear.
fli·er [fláɪɚ] *s.* volador; aviador; (*train*) tren rápido.
flight [flaɪt] *s.* vuelo; bandada (*de pájaros*); escuadrilla (*de aviones*); fuga, huída; — **of stairs** tramo de escalera; **to put to** — poner en fuga.
flim·sy [flɪ́mzɪ] *adj.* endeble, débil; tenue; quebradizo; frágil; baladí; **a — excuse** una excusa baladí.
fling [flɪŋ] *v.* arrojar(se), lanzar(se); tirar; echar; **to — open (shut)** abrir (cerrar) de golpe; *s.* tiro; tirada, lanzamiento; tentativa; **to go out on a** — irse a echar una cana al aire.
flint [flɪnt] *s.* pedernal.
flip [flɪp] *v.* arrojar, lanzar al aire; sacudir; dar un dedazo.
flip·pan·cy [flɪ́pənsɪ] *s.* ligereza; frivolidad; impertinencia; petulancia.
flip·pant [flɪ́pənt] *adj.* ligero (*en sus acciones y modales*), ligero de cascos; frívolo; impertinente; petulante.
flirt [flɝt] *s.* coqueta; coquetón, coquetona; *v.* coquetear, flirtear.
flir·ta·tion [flɝtéʃən] *s.* coquetería; **to carry on a** — coquetear.
flit [flɪt] *v.* pasar velozmente; volar; revolotear.
float [flot] *s.* boya; cosa flotante, flotador; (*fishing*) corcho (*de una caña de pescar*); balsa; (*parade*) carro o carroza (*de procesiones, fiestas, etc.*); *v.* flotar; sobrenadar; boyar; poner a flote; lanzar al mercado (*una nueva emisión de valores, bonos, etc.*).
flock [flɑk] *s.* bandada (*de pájaros, niños, etc.*); rebaño, grey; manada (*de animales*); grupo; — **of people** gentío, muchedumbre; *v.* agruparse; congregarse; **to — to** acudir juntos (*o* en bandadas) a; **to — together** andar juntos, volar en bandadas, ir en grupo.
flog [flɑg] *v.* azotar.
flood [flʌd] *s.* inundación; diluvio; avenida (*de agua*), crecida; creciente; torrente; — **gate** compuerta (*de una presa*); esclusa (*de un canal*); — **light** reflector; proyector de luz; — **tide** flujo (*o* marea ascendiente); *v.* inundar.
floor [flor] *s.* (*surface*) suelo; piso; (*story*) piso; (*bottom*) fondo; **to have the** — tener la palabra; *v.* solar; entarimar, enladrillar, enlosar; echar al suelo, derribar; asombrar.
flop [flɑp] *v.* (*flap*) caer o colgar flojamente; aletear; menearse; (*throw*) lanzar; dejar caer; (*fail*) fracasar; fallar; **to — down** dejarse caer; desplomarse, tumbarse; **to — over** voltear(se); dar vueltas; *s.* fracaso.
flop·py disk [flɑ́pɪ dɪsk] *s.* (*computer*) disco flexible.
flo·rist [flórɪst] *s.* florero, florera; **-'s shop** florería.
floss [flɔs] *s.* seda floja; pelusa; fibra sedosa; **dental** — seda dental.
flound·er [fláʊndɚ] *v.* patalear (*en el lodo, nieve, etc.*); forcejear (*por salir del lodo, nieve, o cualquier aprieto*); revolcarse; tropezar, cometer errores; *s.* lenguado (*pez*).
flour [flaʊr] *s.* harina.

flour·ish [flɝ́ɪʃ] *v.* (*prosper*) florecer, prosperar, medrar; (*blandish*) blandir; agitar en el aire; *s.* floreo; adorno o rasgo caprichoso; ostentación; (*with the signature*) rúbrica.
flour·y [fláUrɪ] *adj.* harinoso.
flow [flo] *s.* flujo; corriente;—**chart** (*computer*) diagrama de flujo; — **of words** torrente de palabras; *v.* fluir; correr; flotar, ondear; **to — into** desembocar en; **to be -ing with riches** nadar en la abundancia.
flow·er [fláUɚ] *s.* flor; — **bed** cuadro de jardín; — **vase** florero; *v.* florecer, *Am.* florear.
flow·er·pot [fláUrpɑt] *s. N. Esp.* tiesto, *And. Am.* maceta.
flow·er·y [fláUrɪ] *adj.* florido.
flow·ing [flóɪŋ] *adj.* (*liquid*) fluído, corriente, fluente; (*clothing*) suelto, ondeante.
flown [flon] *p.p. de* **to fly.**
flu [flu] *s.* influenza, gripe.
fluc·tu·ate [flʌ́ktʃUet] *s.* fluctuar.
fluc·tu·a·tion [flʌktʃUéʃən] *s.* fluctuación.
flue [flu] *s.* cañón (*de chimenea*); tubo de escape.
flu·en·cy [flúənsɪ] *s.* fluidez; labia.
flu·ent [flúənt] *adj.* fluente, flúido; **to speak -ly** hablar con facilidad.
fluff [flʌf] *v.* mullir; esponjar.
fluff·y [flʌ́fɪ] *adj.* mullido, suave, blando; cubierto de vello o plumón; — **hair** pelo esponjado o esponjoso.
flu·id [flúɪd] *adj. & s.* flúido.
flung [flʌŋ] *pret. & p.p. de* **to fling.**
flunk [flʌŋk] *s.* reprobación (*en un examen o asignatura*); *v.* reprobar, suspender (*en un examen*); salir mal, fracasar o fallar (*en un examen*).
flun·ky [flʌ́ŋkɪ] *s.* lacayo; ayudante servil; zalamero, persona servil.
flu·o·rine [flúərin] *s.* fluor.
flur·ry [flɝ́ɪ] *s.* (*weather*) ráfaga; nevisca; (*action*) agitación.
flush [flʌʃ] *s.* (*face*) sonrojo, rubor, bochorno; (*liquid*) flujo rápido; (*cards*) flux (*de naipes*); *adj.* lleno; rico; parejo, al mismo nivel; — **with** a flor de, a ras de; *v.* sonrojar(se), ruborizar(se), poner(se) colorado; hacer rebosar (*de agua*); **to — out** vaciar (*un depósito*), enjuagar.
flute [flut] *s.* flauta; (*column*) estría (*de una columna*); *v.* acanalar, estriar (*una columna*).
flut·ter [flʌ́tɚ] *s.* aleteo; agitación; alboroto; (*heart*) vuelco (*del corazón*); *v.* aletear; revolotear; agitar(se); palpitar; menear(se); tremolar (*una bandera*).
flux [flʌks] *s.* flujo.
fly [flaɪ] *s.* mosca; (*pants*) pliegue (*para cubrir botones*); bragueta (*abertura de los pantalones*); **on the** — al vuelo; **to hit a** — pegar una planchita o elevar una palomita (*en béisbol*); — **swatter** matamoscas; *v.* volar; pasar velozmente; huir; ondear; enarbolar (*una bandera*); **to — at** lanzarse sobre; **to — away** volar, irse, escaparse; **to — off the handle** perder los estribos (*o* la paciencia); **to — open (shut)** abrirse (cerrarse) de repente; **to — up in anger** montar en cólera.
fly·er = **flier.**
fly·leaf [fláɪlif] *s.* guarda (*hoja en blanco al principio y al fin de un libro*).
foam [fom] *s.* espuma; *v.* espumar, hacer espuma.
fo·cus [fókəs] *s.* foco; distancia focal; *v.* enfocar(se).
fod·der [fɑ́dɚ] *s.* forraje.
foe [fo] *s.* enemigo.
fog [fɑg] *s.* niebla, neblina, bruma; velo, nube (*en una película o fotografía*); — **horn** sirena; *v.* anublar, ofuscar, obscurecer; ponerse brumoso; velar(se) (*una película*).
fog·gy [fɑ́gɪ] *adj.* brumoso, nublado; obscuro, confuso.
foil [fɔɪl] *s.* oropel, hojuela, laminita de metal; (*sword*) florete (*de esgrima*); realce, contraste; **tin** — hojuela de estaño; *v.* frustrar.
fold [fold] *s.* (*double over*) pliegue, doblez; (*enclosure*) redil; grey; **three** — tres veces; **hundred** — cien veces; *v.* doblar(se); plegar(se); envolver; **to — one's arms** cruzarse de brazos.
fold·er [fóldɚ] *s.* (*pamphlet*) folleto, circular; (*holder*) papelera; pliego, carpeta; plegadera (*máquina para plegar*).
fold·ing [fóldɪŋ] *adj.* plegadizo; — **chair** silla plegadiza, silla de tijera; — **machine** plegadora, máquina plegadora; — **screen** biombo.
fo·li·age [fólɪɪdʒ] *s.* follaje, fronda.
fo·li·o [fólɪo] *s.* folio; infolio, libro en folio; pliego; — **edition** edición en folio.
folk [fok] *s.* gente; pueblo; **-s** parientes, allegados; familia; personas; amigos (*vocativo familiar*); *adj.* popular, del pueblo; — **dance** danza o baile tradicional; (*regional*) — **lore** folklore; cuentos, leyendas y tradiciones populares; — **song** canción popular, canción típica o tradicional; — **music** música del pueblo; música tradicional.
fol·low [fɑ́lo] *v.* seguir; ejercer (*un oficio o profesión*); seguir el hilo de (*un argumento*); seguirse (*como consecuencia*); **to — suit** jugar el mismo palo (*en naipes*); seguir el ejemplo, imitar.
fol·low·er [fɑ́ləwɚ] *s.* seguidor; imitador; partidario.
fol·low·ing [fɑ́ləwɪŋ] *s.* séquito, comitiva, partidarios; *adj.* siguiente; subsiguiente.
fol·ly [fɑ́lɪ] *s.* locura; necedad, tontería; desatino.
fo·ment [fomɛ́nt] *v.* fomentar.
fond [fɑnd] *adj.* aficionado (a); amigo (de); amante (de), encariñado (con); cariñoso, afectuoso; tierno; **to be — of** querer a (*una persona*); estar encariñado con, ser aficionado a; gustar de (*algo*); **-ly** *adv.* cariñosamente, afectuosamente.
fon·dle [fɑ́ndl̩] *v.* acariciar.
fond·ness [fɑ́ndnɪs] *s.* cariño, afecto; afición.
font [fɑnt] *s.* pila bautismal; fuente.
food [fud] *s.* alimento, sustento; comida.
food·stuff [fúdstʌf] *s.* alimento; producto alimenticio; comestibles.
fool [ful] *s.* tonto, necio, zonzo; (*clown*) payaso; **to play the** — payasear, hacer el payaso; *v.* chasquear, chancear(se); bromear, embromar; engañar; **to — away the time** malgastar el tiempo.
fool·ish [fúlɪʃ] *adj.* tonto; necio, bobo, zonzo.
fool·ish·ness [fúlɪʃnɪs] *s.* tontería, necedad, bobería.
foot [fUt] *s.* pie; pata (*de animal*); **on** — a pie; — **soldier** soldado de infantería; **to put one's — in it** meter la pata; *v.* andar a pie; **to — it** andar a pie; **to — the bill** pagar la cuenta; sufragar los gastos.
foot·ball [fÚtbɔl] *s.* fútbol, football.
foot·hold [fÚthold] *s.* arraigo; puesto establecido.
foot·ing [fÚtɪŋ] *s.* base; posición firme; **to be on a friendly — with** tener relaciones amistosas con; **to lose one's** — perder pie.
foot·lights [fÚlaɪts] *s. pl.* candilejas (*del teatro*); tablas, teatro.
foot·man [fÚtmən] *s.* lacayo.
foot·note [fÚtnot] *s.* nota al pie de una página.
foot·path [fÚtpæθ] *s.* vereda, senda, trocha (*para gente de a pie*).
foot·print [fÚtprɪnt] *s.* huella, pisada.
foot·step [fÚtstɛp] *s.* (*action*) pisada, paso; (*trace*)

FL

huella; **to follow in the -s of** seguir las pisadas o huellas de.
foot·stool [fútstul] *s.* banquillo, taburete, escabel.
fop [fap] *s.* currutaco.
for [fɔr] *prep.* por; para; — **all of her intelligence** a pesar de su inteligencia; — **feat that** por miedo (de) que; — **the present** por el presente, por ahora; **as** — **him** en cuanto a él; **to know** — **a fact** saber de cierto, saber de hecho; **to pay him** — **it** pagárselo; **to thank him** — **it** agradecérselo; *conj.* porque, pues.
for·age [fɔ́rɪdʒ] *s.* forraje; *v.* forrajear; dar forraje a.
for·ay [fɔ́re] *s.* correría, incursión; saqueo; *v.* pillar, saquear.
for·bade [fɚbǽd] *pret. de* **to forbid.**
for·bear [fɔ́rbɛr] *s.* antepasado; [fɔrbɛ́r] *v.* abstenerse de; tener paciencia.
for·bid [fɚbíd] *v.* prohibir; vedar.
for·bid·den [fɚbídn̩] *adj.* prohibido; vedado; *p.p. de* **to forbid.**
for·bid·ding [fɚbídɪŋ] *adj.* austero, reservado; pavoroso; impenetrable.
for·bore [fɔrbór] *pret. de* **to forbear.**
for·borne [fɔrbórn] *p.p. de* **to forbear.**
force [fors] *s.* fuerza; (group) cuerpo (*de policía, de empleados, etc.*); **in** — en vigor, vigente; **armed -s** fuerzas armadas; *v.* forzar, obligar; **to** — **one's way** abrirse paso por fuerza; **to** — **out** echar por fuerza, echar a la fuerza.
forced [forst] *adj.* forzado.
force·ful [fórsfəl] *adj.* vigoroso; enérgico.
for·ceps [fɔ́rsəps] *s.* gatillo (*tenazas para sacar muelas*); pinzas.
for·ci·ble [fórsəbl] *adj.* (*strong*) fuerte, enérgico; potente; eficaz; (*by force*) violento; hecho a la fuerza; **forcibly** *adv.* fuertemente; con energía; forzosamente; por fuerza.
ford [ford] *s.* vado; *v.* vadear.
fore [for] *adj.* anterior, delantero; (*ship*) de proa; *s.* frente; puesto delantero; *adv.* delante, hacia adelante; *interj.* ¡cuidado! (*dícese en el campo de golf*).
fore·arm [fórarm] *s.* antebrazo.
fore·bode [forbód] *v.* presagiar; presentir.
fore·bod·ing [forbódɪŋ] *s.* presentimiento; presagio.
fore·cast [fórkæst] *s.* pronóstico; [forkǽst] *v.* pronosticar; predecir; *pret. & p.p. de* **to forecast.**
fore·clo·sure [forklóʒjʊr] *s.* juicio hipotecario.
fore·fa·ther [fórfaðɚ] *s.* antepasado.
fore·fin·ger [fórfɪŋgɚ] *s.* (dedo) índice.
fore·foot [fórfʊt] *s.* pata delantera, mano (*de cuadrúpedo*).
fore·go [forgó] *v.* abstenerse de.
fore·gone [forgɔ́n] *p.p. de* **to forego; a** — **conclusion** una conclusión inevitable.
fore·ground [fórgraʊnd] *s.* frente, primer plano, primer término.
fore·head [fɔ́rɪd] *s.* frente (*f.*).
for·eign [fɔ́rɪn] *adj.* extranjero; (*not local*) foráneo; (*strange*) extraño; — **to his nature** ajeno a su índole; — **office** ministerio de relaciones exteriores; departamento de negocios extranjeros; — **trade** comercio exterior; **foreign-born** extranjero de nacimiento; — **exchange** divisas, cambio extrajero.
for·eign·er [fɔ́rɪnɚ] *s.* extranjero; forastero.
fore·lock [fórlak] *s.* guedeja.
fore·man [fórmən] *s.* capataz; (*jury*) presidente (*de un jurado*); *Méx., C.A., Ven., Col.* caporal (*de un rancho o hacienda*); *Ríopl.* capataz.
fore·most [fórmost] *adj.* (*first*) primero; delantero; (*most important*) principal, más notable, más distinguido.
fore·noon [fornún] *s.* (la) mañana.
fore·run·ner [forrʌ́nɚ] *s.* precursor; presagio.
fore·saw [forsɔ́] *pret. de* **to foresee.**
fore·see [forsí] *s.* prever.
fore·seen [forsín] *p.p. de* **to foresee** previsto.
fore·sight [fórsaɪt] *s.* previsión; **-ed** precavido.
for·est [fɔ́rɪst] *s.* bosque, selva; — **ranger** guardabosques; *v.* arbolar, plantar de árboles.
for·stall [forstɔ́l] *v.* prevenir; madrugar.
for·est·er [fɔ́rɪstɚ] *s.* guardabosques; silvicultor; habitante de un bosque.
for·est·ry [fɔ́rɪstrɪ] *s.* silvicultura.
fore·tell [fortɛ́l] *v.* predecir, pronosticar, presagiar.
fore·told [fortóld] *pret. & p.p. de* **to foretell.**
for·ev·er [fɚɛ́vɚ] *adv.* por (*o* para) siempre.
for·feit [fɔ́rfɪt] *s.* multa; pena; prenda perdida; **game of -s** juego de prendas; *v.* perder, perder el derecho a.
for·gave [fɚgév] *pret. de* **to forgive.**
forge [fɔrdʒ] *s.* fragua; forja; *v.* fraguar; forjar; falsear, falsificar; **to** — **ahead** abrirse paso; avanzar.
for·ger·y [fɔ́rdʒərɪ] *s.* falsificación.
for·get [fɚgɛ́t] *v.* olvidar; olvidarse de; to — **oneself** cometer un desmán impensadamente; perder el tino o la paciencia.
for·get·ful [fɚgɛ́tfəl] *adj.* olvidadizo; negligente.
for·get·ful·ness [fɚgɛ́tfəlnɪs] *s.* olvido; negligencia.
for·get-me-not [fɚgɛ́tminat] *s.* nomeolvides.
for·give [fɚgív] *v.* perdonar.
for·giv·en [fɚgívən] *p.p. de* **to forgive.**
for·give·ness [fɚgívnɪs] *s.* perdón.
for·giv·ing [fɚgívɪŋ] *adj.* perdonador, misericordioso, de buen corazón.
for·got [fɚgát] *pret. & p.p. de* **to forget.**
for·got·ten [fɚgátn̩] *p.p. de* **to forget.**
fork [fɔrk] *s.* tenedor, *Méx., Col., Ven., Andes* trinche; (*hay*) horquilla (*para heno*); horcón; bifurcación; *v.* bifurcarse; levantar o arrojar (*heno*) con horquilla.
for·lorn [fɚlɔ́rn] *adj.* desamparado, desdichado.
form [fɔrm] *s.* forma; (*state*) condición, estado; **blank** — blanco, forma en blanco, *Méx., Ven., Col., S.A.* esqueleto; *v.* formar(se).
for·mal [fɔ́rml̩] *adj.* formal, perteneciente a la forma; convencional, ceremonioso; — **party** reunión de etiqueta; **-ly** *adv.* formalmente, con ceremonia, solemnemente.
for·mal·i·ty [fɔrmǽlətɪ] *s.* formalidad, ceremonia; formalismo.
for·mat [fɔ́rmæt] *s.* (*computer*) formato; **formatting** formateo; *v.* formatear.
for·ma·tion [fɔrméʃən] *s.* formación.
for·ma·tive [fɔ́rmətɪv] *formativo.*
for·mer [fɔ́rmɚ] *adj.* primero, precedente, anterior; antiguo; **in** — **times** en otro tiempo, en días de antaño, antiguamente, anteriormente; **the** — aquél (aquélla, aquéllos, aquéllas); **-ly** *adv.* anterioremente; antes, en tiempos pasados.
for·mi·da·ble [fɔ́rmɪdəbl̩] *adj.* formidable.
for·mu·la [fɔ́rmjələ] *s.* fórmula.
for·mu·late [fɔ́mjəlet] *v.* formular.
for·sake [fɚsék] *v.* desamparar; abandonar.
for·sak·en [fɚsékən] *p.p. de* **to forsake** *& adj.* desamparado, abandonado.
for·sook [fɔrsʊ́k] *pret. de* **to forsake.**
for·swear [fɔrswɛ́r] *v.* abjurar.
fort [fort] *s.* fuerte, fortín, fortaleza.
forth [forθ] *adv.* adelante; hacia adelante; **to go** —

salir; **and so** — etcétera, y así succesivamente.
forth·com·ing [fórθkʌmɪŋ] *adj.* venidero, próximo; **funds will not be — until** no habrá fondos disponibles hasta.
forth·with [forθwíθ] *adv.* en seguida, pronto, al punto.
for·ti·fi·ca·tion [fɔrtəfəkéʃən] *s.* fortificación.
for·ti·fy [fɔ́rtəfaɪ] *v.* fortificar; fortalecer.
for·ti·tude [fɔ́rtətjud] *s.* fortaleza.
fort·night [fɔ́rtnaɪt] quincena, quince días, dos semanas.
for·tress [fɔ́rtrɪs] *s.* fortaleza, fuerte.
for·tu·i·tous [fɔrtjúətəs] *adj.* fortuito; inopinado, inesperado.
for·tu·nate [fɔ́rtʃənɪt] *adj.* afortunado; **-ly** *adv.* afortunadamente, por fortuna.
for·tune [fɔ́rtʃən] *s.* fortuna; — **teller** agorero, adivino.
for·ty [fórtɪ] *num.* cuarenta.
fo·rum [fórəm] *s.* foro; tribunal; ateneo.
for·ward [fɔ́rwɚd] *adj.* (*leading*) delantero; (*progressive*) precoz; progresista; (*daring*) atrevido; descarado; *adv.* adelante, hacia adelante; *v.* transmitir; despachar; reenviar; reexpedir, **to — a plan** fomentar un plan.
fos·sil [fɑ́sl̩] *adj.* fósil; anticuado; *s.* fósil.
fos·ter [fɔ́stɚ] *v.* criar, nutrir; fomentar; promover; *adj.* putativo; adoptivo.
fought [fɔt] *pret. & p.p. de* **to fight.**
foul [faʊl] *adj.* sucio; asqueroso; puerco, cochino; fétido; vil; injusto; — **air** aire viciado; — **ball** pelota foul (*en béisbol*); — **mouthed** mal hablado, obsceno; — **play** juego sucio; fraude; violencia; — **weather** mal tiempo; *s.* mala jugada (*contraria a las reglas del juego*), trampa, *Méx.* chapuza, foul; *v.* ensuciar; violar (*las reglas de un juego*); *Am.* pegar un foul (*en béisbol*).
found [faʊnd] *v.* fundar, establecer; *pret. & p.p de* **to find.**
foun·da·tion [faʊndéʃən] *s.* fundación; base, fundamento; dotación.
foun·der [fáʊndɚ] *s.* fundador; fundidor (*de metales*); *v.* zozobrar, irse a pique; fracasar; tropezar; hacer zozobrar.
foun·dry [fáʊndrɪ] *s.* fundición.
foun·tain [fáʊntn̩] *s.* fuente; manatial; — **pen** pluma (de) fuente, pluma estilográfica.
four [for] *num.* cuatro.
four·score [fórskór] *adj.* cuatro veintenas, ochenta.
four·teen [fortín] *num.* catorce.
fourth [forθ] *adj.* cuarto; *s.* cuarto, cuarta parte; **the Fourth of July** el cuarto de julio.
fowl [faʊl] *s.* ave; gallo, gallina; pollo.
fox [fɑks] *s.* zorra; zorro; persona astuta.
fox·y [fɑ́ksɪ] *adj.* zorro, zorruno, astuto.
frac·tion [frǽkʃən] *s.* fracción; quebrado.
frac·ture [frǽktʃɚ] *s.* fractura; quiebra; rotura; *v.* fracturar; quebrar, romper.
frag·ile [frǽdʒəl] *adj.* frágil.
frag·ment [frǽgmənt] *s.* fragmento.
fra·grance [frégrəns] *s.* fragancia.
fra·grant [frégrənt] *adj.* fragante, oloroso.
frail [frel] *adj.* frágil; endeble, débil.
frail·ty [fréltɪ] *s.* debilidad, flaqueza.
frame [frem] *s.* armazón, armadura, esqueleto; estructura; (*picture*) marco; (*of mind*) disposición (*de ánimo*); **embroidery** — bastidor para bordar; — **house** casa con armazón de madera; *v.* formar, forjar; fabricar; enmarcar (*poner en marco*); inventar; **to — someone** conspirar contra una persona; **to — up a charge** forjar un cargo o acusación.
frame·work [frémwɚk] *s.* armazón, esqueleto; estructura.
franc [fræŋk] *s.* franco (*moneda francesa*).
fran·chise [frǽntʃaɪz] *s.* (*privilege*) franquicia; derecho o privilegio político; (*vote*) sufragio, voto.
fran·ci·um [frǽnsiəm] *s.* francio.
frank [fræŋk] *adj.* franco, sincero; **very** — francote; *s.* sello de franqueo; franquicia de correos; *v.* franquear, despachar, enviar (*carta*) exenta de franqueo; **franking machine** máquina franqueadora.
frank·furt·er [frǽŋkfɚtɚ] *s.* salchicha.
frank·ness [frǽŋknɪs] *s.* franqueza, sinceridad.
fran·tic [frǽntɪk] *adj.* frenético; **-ally** *adv.* frenéticamente.
fra·ter·nal [frətɝ́nl] *adj.* fraternal.
fra·ter·ni·ty [frətɝ́nətɪ] *s.* fraternidad; confraternidad.
frat·er·nize [frǽtɚnaɪz] *v.* fraternizar.
fraud [frɔd] *s.* fraude, engaño; trampa, *Méx.* chapuza; (*person*) trampista, tramposo.
fraud·u·lent [frɔ́dʒələnt] *adj.* fraudulento.
fray [fre] *s.* reyerta, riña, pelea, alboroto; raedura; *v.* raer(se); deshilacharse.
frayed [fred] *adj.* raído, deshilachado.
freak [frik] *s.* (*whim*) capricho; (*rarity*) rareza, hombre o cosa rara; (*monstrosity*) monstruosidad, fenómeno.
freck·le [frékl] *s.* peca; *v.* ponerse pecoso.
freck·led [frékld] *adj.* pecoso.
freck·ly [fréklɪ] *adj.* pecoso.
free [fri] *adj.* (*not bound*) libre; suelto; (*gratis*) gratuito; exento; (*generous*) liberal, generoso; — **of charge** gratis; — **on board (f.o.b.)** libre a bordo; — **port** puerto franco; **postage** — franco de porte; **to give someone a — hand** dar rienda suelta o libertad de acción a una persona; — **hand drawing** dibujo a pulso, dibujo a mano; — **thinker** libre pensador; — **lance** a destajo; *adv.* libremente; gratis, de balde; *v.* librar; libertar; soltar; eximir; **-ly** *adv.* libremente; con soltura.
free·dom [frídəm] *s.* libertad; libre uso; exención.
freeze [friz] *v.* helar(se); congelar(se); (*stop*) bloquear *s.* bloqueo.
freez·ing [frizɪŋ] *adj.* helado, glacial; — **point** punto de congelación.
freight [fret] *s.* flete; carga; — **train** tren de carga, tren de mercancías; — **yard** patio de carga; **by** — por carga; *v.* fletar, cargar; enviar por carga.
French [frɛntʃ] *adj.* francés; **to take — leave** marcharse a la francesa, irse sin despedirse; *s.* francés, idioma francés; **the** — los franceses.
French·man [fréntʃmən] *s.* francés.
fren·zy [frénzɪ] *s.* frenesí.
fre·quen·cy [fríkwənsɪ] *s.* frecuencia.
fre·quent [fríkwənt] *adj.* frecuente; *v.* frecuentar; **-ly** *adv.* frecuentemente, a menudo.
fresh [frɛʃ] *adj.* (*not stale*) fresco; (*new*) reciente; nuevo; (*bold*) impertinente, entremetido; — **water** agua dulce; **-ly** *adv.* frescamente; con frescura; nuevamente, recientemente; **-ly painted** recién pintado, acabado de pintar.
fresh·en [fréʃən] *v.* refrescar(se).
fresh·man [fréʃmən] *s.* novato, novicio, estudiante del primer año.
fresh·ness [fréʃnɪs] *s.* frescura; frescor, fresco; descaro.
fret [frɛt] *v.* irritar(se); apurarse; estar nervioso; agitarse; *s.* agitación, apuro, preocupación; traste (*de guitarra, mandolina, etc.*); — **work** calado.
fret·ful [frétfəl] *adj.* descontentadizo; malhumorado,

enojadizo; nervioso.
fri·ar [fráɪɚ] *s.* fraile.
fric·tion [fríkʃən] *s.* fricción; rozamiento; frotación; desavenencia; — **feed** (*computer*) alimentación por fricción.
Fri·day [fráɪdɪ] *s.* viernes.
fried [fraɪd] *adj.* frito; freído; *p.p. de* **to fry.**
friend [frɛnd] *s.* amigo, amiga.
friend·less [fréndlɪs] *adj.* sin amigos, solo.
friend·li·ness [fréndlɪnɪs] *s.* afabilidad; amistad.
friend·ly [fréndlɪ] *adj.* amistoso, afable, amigable; propicio, favorable; *adv.* amistosamente.
friend·ship [frénʃɪp] *s.* amistad.
frig·ate [frígət] *s.* fragata.
fright [fraɪt] *s.* espanto, susto; terror; espantajo, **she is a** — es un adefesio.
fright·en [fráɪtn] *v.* espantar, asustar, atemorizar; **to — away** espantar, ahuyentar; **to get -ed** espantarse, asustarse.
fright·ened [fráɪtnd] *adj.* espantado, asustado.
fright·ful [fráɪtfəl] *adj.* espantoso, terrible, horroroso.
frig·id [frídʒɪd] *adj.* frígido, frío.
fringe [frɪndʒ] *s.* fleco; flequillo; orla; — **benefits** beneficios laborales; *Col.* prestaciones sociales; *v.* adornar con fleco; orlar.
frip·per·y [frípərɪ] *s.* perifollos, moños, perejiles; cursilería.
frisk [frɪsk] *v.* retozar, cabriolar, saltar, brincar; (*search*) registrar (*los bolsillos*), *Ven., Méx.* exculcar.
frisk·y [frískɪ] *adj.* retozón, juguetón.
frit·ter [frítɚ] *s.* fritura, fruta de sartén; *v.* **to — away** malgastar, desperdiciar poco a poco.
fri·vol·i·ty [frɪválətɪ] *s.* frivolidad.
friv·o·lous [frívələs] *adj.* frívolo.
fro [fro]: **to and** — de una parte a otra; de aquí para allá.
frock [frak] *s.* vestido (*de mujer*); — **coat** levita.
frog [frag] *s.* rana; broche (*de cordoncillos o galones*); — **in the throat** gallo en la garganta.
frol·ic [frálɪk] *s.* retozo, juego; holgorio, diversión; *v.* retozar, travesear, juguetear.
from [fram, frʌm] *prep.* de; desde; **to take something away — a person** quitarle algo a una persona.
front [frʌnt] *s.* frente (*m.*); (*building*) fachada; frontispicio; **in — of** enfrente de; delante de; **shirt** — pechera; *adj.* delantero; frontal; frontero; **front-wheel drive** tracción delantera; *v.* hacer frente a; **to — towards** mirar hacia; dar a, caer a.
fron·tier [frʌntír] *s.* frontera; *adj.* fronterizo.
frost [frɔst] *s.* escarcha; helada; *v.* escarchar; helar; cubrir de escarcha.
frost·ing [frɔ́stɪŋ] *s.* escarcha, (*cooking*) confitura (*para cubrir un pastel*).
frost·y [frɔ́stɪ] *adj.* escarchado, cubierto de escarcha; helado.
froth [frɔθ] *s.* espuma; *v.* espumar, hacer espuma; echar espuma o espumarajos; **to — at the mouth** echar espumarajos por la boca; enfurecerse.
frown [fraUn] *s.* ceño; entrecejo; *v.* fruncir el ceño o las cejas; **to — at** mirar con ceño; desaprobar (*algo*).
froze [froz] *pret. de* **to freeze.**
fro·zen [frózn̩] *p.p. de* **to freeze;** — **assets** recursos inactivos, *Méx.* activo congelado.
fru·gal [frúgl̩] *adj.* frugal.
fruit [frut] *s.* fruto (*en general*); fruta (*comestible*); **to eat** — comer fruta; — **tree** árbol frutal; *v.* fructificar, producir frutas.
fruit·ful [frútfəl] *adj.* fructuoso; productivo; provechoso.
fruit·less [frútlɪs] *adj.* infructuoso, improductivo, estéril.
frus·trate [frʌ́stret] *v.* frustrar.
frus·tra·tion [frʌstréʃən] *s.* frustración.
fry [fraɪ] *v.* freír(se); *s.* fritada; **small** — pececillos; gente menuda; **French fries** patatas fritas a la francesa; **-ing pan** sartén.
fudge [fʌdʒ] *s.* dulce.
fu·el [fjúəl] *s.* combustible; incentivo.
fu·gi·tive [fjúdʒətɪv] *adj.* fugitivo; transitorio; *s.* fugitivo, prófugo.
ful·fill [fUlfíl] *v.* cumplir; cumplir con; (*bring about*) realizar; llevar a cabo; llenar (*un requisito*).
ful·fill·ment [fUlfílmənt] *s.* cumplimiento.
full [fUl] *adj.* lleno; completo; harto; pleno; — **dress** traje de etiqueta; — **moon** plenilunio, luna llena; — **skirt** falda de vuelo entero; — **of fun** muy divertido, muy chistoso; **at — speed** a toda velocidad; **in** — completamente; por completo; **to the** — por completo, por entero, totalmente; — **time** tiempo completo, jornada completa; *adv.* completamente, enteramente; **to know — well** saber perfectamente, saber a ciencia cierta; **full-blooded** de raza pura; **full-fledged** hecho y derecho; maduro; completo; **-y** *adv.* completamente, enteramente, por completo.
full·ness [fÚlnɪs] *s.* plenitud; llenura.
fum·ble [fʌ́mbl̩] *v.* tentalear, buscar a tientas; chapucear, no coger la pelota o soltarla al correr.
fume [fjum] *v.* exhalar vapor o gas; (*rage*) rabiar; **-s** *s. pl.* vapores, emanaciones, gases.
fu·mi·gate [fjúməget] *v.* fumigar, sahumar, *Ríopl.* humear.
fun [fʌn] *s.* diversión; (*joke*) burla, broma, chanza, *Carib., Méx., C.A.* choteo; **for** — en (*o* de) broma; de chanza; de chiste; **full of** — muy divertido; **to have** — divertirse; **to make — of** burlarse de, chancearse con, *Carib., Méx., C.A.* chotear, chotearse con; *Ríopl.* jorobar.
func·tion [fʌ́ŋkʃən] *s.* función; — **key** (*computer*) tecla funcional; *v.* funcionar.
fund [fʌnd] *s.* fondo, caudal; **-s** fondos, recursos; **funded debt** deuda consolidada; *v.* consolidar (*una deuda*); prorrogar el plazo de (*una deuda*).
fun·da·men·tal [fʌndəméntl̩] *adj.* fundamental; *s.* fundamento, principio.
fu·ner·al [fjúnərəl] *adj.* funeral, fúnebre; *s.* funeral, exequias, funerales.
fun·gus [fʌ́ŋgəs] *s.* hongo; fungosidad.
fun·nel [fʌ́nl̩] *s.* embudo; humero (*cañón de chimenea*).
fun·ny [fʌ́nɪ] *adj.* (*comical*) chistoso, cómico, gracioso, divertido; (*odd*) extraño, raro; **the funnies** la sección cómica (*de un periódico*).
fur [fɝ] *s.* piel (*de animales peludos o lanudos*); sarro (*en la lengua*); — **coat** abrigo de pieles; *v.* forrar, cubrir o adornar con pieles.
fur·bish [fɚbɪʃ] *v.* acicalar, pulir.
fu·ri·ous [fjúrɪəs] *adj.* furioso.
furl [fɝl] *v.* arrollar, enrollar; plegar.
fur·lough [fɝ́lo] *s.* licencia militar; *s.* dar licencia militar.
fur·nace [fɝ́nɪs] *s.* calorífero; **blast** — alto horno.
fur·nish [fɝ́nɪʃ] *v.* (*equip*) equipar; amueblar; (*provide*) proveer, suministrar, surtir; **to — a room** amueblar un cuarto.
fur·ni·ture [fɝ́nɪtʃɚ] *s.* muebles, mobiliario, moblaje, mueblaje.
fur·row [fɝ́o] *s.* surco; arruga; *v.* surcar; arar.

fur·ther [fɛ́ðɚ] *adj.* adicional; más lejano, más remoto; *adv.* además; más; más lejos, *v.* promover, fomentar, adelantar.
fur·ther·more [fɝ́ðɚmor] *adv.* además.
fur·thest [fɝ́ðɪst] *adj.* (el) más lejano, (el) más remoto; *adv.* más lejos.
fur·tive [fɝ́tɪv] *adj.* furtivo.
fu·ry [fjúrɪ] *s.* furia; frenesí.
fuse [fjuz] *s.* fusible; mecha; *v.* fundir(se).
fu·se·lage [fjúzlɪdʒ] *s.* fuselaje.
fu·sion [fjúʒən] *s.* fusión; **nuclear** — fusión nuclear.
fuss [fʌs] *s.* melindre, preocupación inútil; bulla innecesaria; **to make a — over someone** darle a alguien demasiada importancia, desvivirse por alguien; *v.* hacer melindres, inquietarse (*por bagatelas*).
fuss·y [fʌ́sɪ] *adj.* melindroso; minucioso (*en demasía*); inquieto, nervioso; — **dress** vestido con demasiados adornos.
fu·tile [fjútl̩] *adj.* fútil; vano; **futility** *s.* futilidad.
fu·ture [fjútʃɚ] *adj.* futuro; **-s market** mercado de futuros; *s.* futuro; porvenir.
fuzz [fʌz] *s.* vello; pelusa.
fuzz·y [fʌ́zɪ] *adj.* velloso; cubierto de plumón fino; cubierto de pelusa.

G:g

gab [gæb] *v.* charlar, parlotear; *s.* charla; **gift of** — labia, facundia.
gab·ar·dine [gǽbɚdin] *s.* gabardina (*paño*).
gab·ble [gǽbl̩] *s.* charla, cotorreo; *v.* charlar, cotorrear.
ga·ble [gébl̩] *s.* gablete (*de un tejado*); — **roof** tejado de caballete o de dos aguas; — **window** ventana con gablete.
gad [gæd] *v.* vagar, callejear; andar de aquí para allá.
gadg·et [gǽdʒɪt] *s.* adminículo, artefacto, chisme, dispositivo.
gag [gæg] *s.* (*obstacle*) mordaza; — **law** ley de la mordaza; (*joke*) broma, burla; morcilla, chiste (*improvisado por un actor*); *v.* amordazar; dar náuseas, hacer vomitar, basquear; interpolar chistes (*en la escena*).
gage *véase* **gauge.**
gai·e·ty [géətɪ] *s.* alegría, viveza, alborozo.
gai·ly [gélɪ] *adv.* alegremente; vistosamente.
gain [gen] *s.* ganancia, provecho; *v.* ganar.
gain·ful [génfl̩] *adj.* ganancioso.
gait [get] *s.* paso, andadura, marcha.
gale [gel] *s.* ventarrón; — **of laughter** risotada, carcajada, risada.
gall [gɔl] *s.* (*bile*) bilis, hiel; (*bitterness*) amargura; odio; descaro; — **bladder** vesícula; *v.* irritar.
gal·lant [gǽlənt] *adj.* valiente; noble; vistoso; [gəlǽnt] *adj.* galante, atento, cortés; galanteador; *s.* galán.
gal·lant·ry [gǽləntrɪ] *s.* galantería; gallardía, valor.
gal·ler·y [gǽlərɪ] *s.* galería; paraíso, gallinero *del* (*teatro*).
gal·ley [gǽlɪ] *s.* galera; cocina (*de un buque*); — **proof** galerada; — **slave** galeote.
gal·lium [gǽliəm] *s.* galio.
gal·lon [gǽlən] *s.* galón (*aproximadamente cuatro litros*).
gal·lop [gǽləp] *s.* galope; *v.* galopar, galopear; ir a galope.
gal·lows [gǽloz] *s.* horca.
gal·osh·es [gəlɑ́ʃɪz] *s. pl.* chanclos, zapatos fuertes, zapatones.
gal·va·nom·e·ter [gælvənámətɚ] *s.* galvanómetro.
gam·ble [gǽmbl̩] *v.* jugar, apostar, aventurar (*algo*) en el juego; **to — away** perder en el juego; **to — everything** jugar el todo por el todo; arriesgarlo todo; *s.* jugada (*en juegos de azar*), apuesta; riesgo.
gam·bol [gǽmbəl] *v.* retozar; cabriolar; juguetear; *s.* retozo, cabriola.
game [gem] *s.* juego; deporte; caza (*animales de caza y su carne*); **to make — of** mofarse de, burlarse de; *adj.* valiente, atrevido; resuelto; — **bird** ave de caza.
gam·ut [gǽmət] *s.* gama.
gan·der [gǽndɚ] *s.* ánsar, ganso.
gang [gǽŋ] *s.* cuadrilla; pandilla; juego (*de herramientas o máquinas*); *v.* agrupar(se); **to — up against** conspirar contra.
gang·plank [gǽŋplæŋk] *s.* plancha, pasamano (*de un buque*), pasarela.
gan·grene [gǽŋgrin] *s.* gangrena; *v.* gangrenar(se).
gang·ster [gǽŋstɚ] *s.* bandolero, bandido, maleante, atracador.
gang·way [gǽŋwe] *s.* paso, pasadizo; plancha; pasamano; portalón (*de un barco*); — **!** ¡a un lado! ¡ábranse!
gant·let = **gauntlet.**
gap [gæp] *s.* brecha, abertura; boquete; hueco; intervalo.
gape [gep] *s.* (*breach*) brecha, abertura; (*open jaws*) bostezo; boqueada; *v.* boquear, abrir la boca; estar boquiabierto (*mirando*); estar embobado; bostezar.
ga·rage [gərɑ́ʒ] *s.* garaje.
garb [gɑrb] *s.* vestido; vestidura; aspecto, apariencia; *v.* vestir, ataviar.
gar·bage [gɑ́rbɪdʒ] *s.* desperdicios, basura.
gar·den [gɑ́rdn̩] *s.* jardín; huerta; huerto; *v.* cultivar un jardín.
gar·den·er [gɑ́rdnɚ] *s.* jardinero, hortelano, horticultor.
gar·gle [gɑ́rgl̩] *s.* gargarismo, *Am.* gárgaras; *v.* gargarizar, hacer gárgaras, *Am.* gargarear.
gar·land [gɑ́rlənd] *s.* guirnalda.
gar·lic [gɑ́rlɪk] *s.* ajo.
gar·ment [gɑ́rmənt] *s.* prenda (*de vestir*).
gar·net [gɑ́rnɪt] *s.* granate.
gar·nish [gɑ́rnɪʃ] *s.* aderezo; adorno; *v.* aderezar; adornar; guarnecer; (*attach*) embargar; **garnishment** embargo.
gar·ret [gǽrɪt] *s.* desván, buhardilla.
gar·ri·son [gǽrəsn̩] *s.* guarnición; *v.* guarnecer o guarnicionar (*una fortaleza*).
gar·ru·lous [gǽrjələs] *adj.* locuaz, lenguaz, gárrulo.
gar·ter [gɑ́rtɚ] *s.* liga (*para sujetar las medias*); *v.* sujetar con liga.
gas [gæs] *s.* (*gaseous*) gas; (*petroleum*) gasolina; — **burner** mechero; — **stove** estufa o cocina de gas; **tear** — gas lacrimante o lacrimógeno; *v.* asfixiar con gas; envenenar con gas.
gas·e·ous [gǽsɪəs] *adj.* gaseoso.
gash [gæʃ] *s.* cuchillada, herida, incisión; *v.* dar una cuchillada, acuchillar.
gas·o·line [gǽslin] *s.* gasolina.
gasp [gæsp] *s.* boqueada; grito sofocado; *v.* boquear; jadear; sofocarse; abrir la boca (*de asombro*).
gas·tric [gǽstrɪk] *adj.* gástrico.
gas·tro·in·tes·ti·nal [gæstroɪntɛ́stɪnl̩] *adj.* gastrointestinal.
gate [get] *s.* portón, entrada; puerta; *Ven., Col.*

tranquera (*puerta de trancas*).
gate·way [gétwe] *s*. paso, entrada.
gath·er [gǽðɚ] *v*. recoger; coger; (*unite*) reunir(se), juntar(se); (*deduce*) deducir, colegir; fruncir (*en pliegues*); cobrar (fuerzas); **to — dust** llenarse de polvo, empolvarse; *s*. pliegue.
gath·er·ing [gǽðrɪŋ] *s*. asamblea, reunión; muchedumbre; pliegue.
gaud·y [gɔ́dɪ] *adj*. vistoso, llamativo, chillón, chillante.
gauge [gedʒ] *s*. calibrador; indicador; medidor; instrumento para medir; medida; **manifold —** manómetro; **vacuum —** vacuómetro; calibre (*de un cañón, pistola, etc.*); (*track*) ancho (*del ferrocarril*), *Ven*. trocha; *v*. medir; calibrar; estimar, calcular.
gaunt [gɔnt] *adj*. macilento, demacrado, flaco.
gaunt·let [gɔ́ntlɪt] *s*. guantelete; manopla; **to throw down the —** retar, desafiar.
gauze [gɔz] *s*. gasa; cendal.
gave [gev] *pret. de* **to give.**
gav·el [gævḷ] *s*. mazo del que preside.
gawk [gɔk] *v*. bobear, mirar embobado; *s*. simplón, bobo.
gawk·y [gɔ́kɪ] *adj*. torpe, desmañado; bobo.
gay [ge] *adj*. alegre; vivo; vistoso; festivo; (*homosexual*) homosexual.
gay·e·ty *véase* **gaiety.**
gaze [gez] *s*.mirada (fija); *v*. contemplar, mirar con fijeza, clavar la mirada.
ga·zette [gəzɛ́t] *s*. gaceta.
gear [gɪr] *s*. (*equipment*) aperos; herramientas; aparejo; equipo; (*wheel*) rueda dentada; (*assembly*) engranaje (*de ruedas dentadas*); **foot —** calzado; **low —** primera velocidad; **steering —** mecanismo de dirección; **to be in —** estar engranado; **to shift —** cambiar de engrane o velocidad; **to throw in —** engranar; **to throw out of —** desengranar; **— shift lever** palanca de engrane, palanca de cambios; *v*. engranar.
geese [gis] *pl. de* **goose.**
Gei·ger count·er [gáɪgɚkáʊntɚ] *s*. contador (de) Geiger.
gel·a·tin [dʒɛ́lətṇ] *s*. gelatina, jaletina.
gem [dʒɛm] *s*. gema, piedra preciosa; joya, alhaja, panecillo, bollo.
gem·i·nate [dʒɛ́mənet] *v*. geminar(se).
gen·der [dʒɛ́ndɚ] *s*. género.
gene [dʒin] *s*. gen.
ge·ne·al·o·gy [dʒiniǽlədʒɪ] *s*. genealogía.
gen·er·al [dʒɛ́nərəl] *adj*. & *s*. general; **in —** en general, por lo común, por lo general; **— delivery** lista de correo.
gen·er·al·i·ty [dʒɛnərǽlətɪ] *s*. generalidad.
gen·er·al·ize [dʒɛ́nərəlaɪz] *v*. generalizar.
gen·er·ate [dʒɛ́nəret] *v*. engendrar; producir; originar.
gen·er·a·tion [dʒɛnəréʃən] *s*. generación; producción.
gen·er·a·tor [dʒɛ́nɚetɚ] *s*. generador.
ge·ner·ic [dʒənɛ́rɪk] *adj*. genérico.
gen·er·os·i·ty [dʒɛnərɑ́sətɪ] *s*. generosidad.
gen·er·ous [dʒɛ́nərəs] *adj*. generoso; magnánimo, liberal; amplio; abundante.
ge·net·ics [dʒənɛ́tɪks] *s*. genética.
gen·ial [dʒínjəl] *adj*. genial, afable.
gen·i·tive [dʒɛ́nətɪv] *adj*. & *s*. genitivo.
gen·ius [dʒínjəs] *s*. genio, ingenio, talento.
gen·teel [dʒɛntíl] *adj*. gentil, cortés; elegante; gallardo.
gen·tile [dʒɛ́ntaɪ] *adj*. & *s*. gentil.
gen·tle [dʒɛ́ntḷ] *adj*. suave; afable; apacible; manso, gentil.
gen·tle·man [dʒɛ́ntḷmən] *s*. caballero; **gentlemen** *pl*. caballeros; señores.
gen·tle·man·ly [dʒɛ́ntḷmənlɪ] *adj*. caballeroso, caballero, cortés.
gen·tle·ness [dʒɛ́ntḷnɪs] *s*. suavidad, dulzura, apacibilidad; mansedumbre.
gen·tly [dʒɛ́ntlɪ] *adv*. suavemente; despacio; dulcemente; con ternura; mansamente.
gen·u·ine [dʒɛ́njʊɪn] *adj*. genuino; sincero.
ge·o·graph·i·cal [dʒiəgrǽfɪkḷ] *adj*. geográfico.
ge·og·ra·phy [dʒiɑ́grəfɪ] *s*. geografía.
ge·o·log·i·cal [dʒiəlɑ́dʒɪkḷ] *adj*. geológico.
ge·ol·o·gy [dʒiɑ́lədʒɪ] *s*. geología.
ge·o·met·ric [dʒiəmɛ́trɪk] *adj*. geométrico.
ge·om·e·try [dʒiɑ́mətrɪ] *s*. geometría.
ge·o·phys·ics [dʒiofízɪks] *s*. geofísica.
ge·ra·ni·um [dʒəréniəm] *s*. geranio.
germ [dʒɝm] *s*. germen; microbio.
Ger·man [dʒɝmən] *adj*. & *s*. alemán.
ger·mane [dʒɚmén] *adj*. pertinente, relacionado.
ger·ma·ni·um [dʒɝméniəm] *s*. germanio.
ger·mi·nate [dʒɝ́mənet] *v*. germinar.
ger·und [dʒɛ́rənd] *s*. gerundio.
ges·ta·tion [dʒɛstéʃən] *s*. gestación.
ges·tic·u·late [dʒɛstíkjəlet] *v*. gesticular, hacer gestos o ademanes, accionar, manotear.
ges·ture [dʒɛ́stʃɚ] *s*. gesto; ademán; **a mere —** una pura formalidad; *v*. gesticular, hacer gestos.
get [gɛt] *v*. (*obtain*) obtener, adquirir, lograr, conseguir; (*earn*) recibir, ganar; (*reach*) llegar (a); traer; (*catch*) coger, atrapar; preparar (*la lección, la comida, etc.*); **to — long** llevarse bien (*con alguien*); ir pasándolo (*o* ir pasándola); **to — angry** ponerse enojado, enojarse; **to — away** escaparse; irse; **to — down** bajar; **to — ill** ponerse enfermo, enfermar(se); **to — in** entrar; meter(se); llegar; **to — married** casarse; **to — off the train** bajar del tren; apearse del tren; **to — old** envejecer(se); **to — on** subir a; montar; **to — out** salir; irse; sacar; divulgarse (*un secreto*); **to — over** pasar por encima de; recuperarse de (*una enfermedad*); olvidar (*una ofensa*); pasársele a uno (*el susto*); **to — ready** preparar(se); alistar(se); **to — rich** enriquecerse, hacerse rico; **to — rid of** deshacerse de, desprenderse de; **to — through** pasar; terminar; **to — together** juntar(se), reunir(se); ponerse de acuerdo; **to — up** levantarse; **I got him to do it** le persuadí a que lo hiciese; **I (have) got to do it** tengo que hacerlo; **I don't — it** no lo comprendo; **that's what -s me** (*or* **-s my goat**) eso es lo que me irrita.
ghast·ly [gǽstlɪ] *adj*. horrible; pálido, lívido, cadavérico.
ghost [gost] *s*. espectro, fantasma; **the Holy Ghost** el Espíritu Santo; **not to have the — of a notion of** no tener la más remota idea de; **— writer** colaborador anónimo.
ghost·ly [góstlɪ] *adj*. como un espectro; de espectros, de aparecidos.
gi·ant [dʒáɪənt] *s*. gigante; *adj*. gigantesco; enorme.
gid·dy [gídɪ] *adj*. ligero de cascos, frívolo; voluble, inconstante; desvanecido; **— speed** velocidad vertiginosa.
gift [gɪft] *s*. regalo, dádiva; don; dote, talento, prenda; donación.
gift·ed [gíftɪd] *adj*. talentoso, de talento.
gi·gan·tic [dʒaɪgǽntɪk] *adj*. gigantesco.
gig·gle [gígḷ] *s*. risita, risilla; risa falsa; *v*. reírse falsamente; reírse sofocando la voz; reír con una risilla afectada.
gild [gɪld] *v*. dorar.

gill [gɪl] *s.* agalla (*de pez*).
gilt [gɪlt] *adj.* & *s.* dorado; *pret.* & *p.p. de* **to gild.**
gim·mick [gímɪk] *s.* adminículo.
gin [dʒɪn] *s.* ginebra (*licor*).
gin·ger [dʒíndʒɚ] *s.* jengibre; — **ale** cerveza de jengibre.
gin·ger·bread [dʒíndʒɚbrɛd] *s.* pan de jengibre; ornato de mal gusto.
ging·ham [gíŋəm] *s.* guinga (*tela de algodón*).
gip·sy *véase* **gypsy.**
gi·raffe [dʒərǽf] *s.* jirafa.
gird [gɝd] *v.* ceñir; rodear; **to — oneself for** prepararse para.
gir·dle [gɝ́dl̩] *s.* ceñidor; cinto; faja; *v.* ceñir; fajar; cercar.
girl [gɝl] *s.* niña; muchacha; joven; chica, moza; criada.
girl·hood [gɝ́lhʊd] *s.* niñez; mocedad, juventud.
girl·ish [gɝ́lɪʃ] *adj.* pueril; de niña, de muchacha; juvenil.
girt [gɝt] *pret.* & *p.p. de* **to gird;** *v. véase* **gird.**
girth [gɝθ] *s.* circunferencia; cincha (*para caballos*); faja; *v.* cinchar; ceñir.
gist [dʒɪst] *s.* substancia, esencia.
give [gɪv] *v.* dar; regalar; (*give in*) ceder; dar de sí; **to — away** regalar; entregar; revelar (*un secreto*); **to — back** devolver; **to — birth** dar a luz, parir; **to — in** ceder; darse por vencido; **to — off** emitir; **to — out** divulgar; repartir; agotarse; **to — up** abandonar; desistir; renunciar a; perder la esperanza; rendir(se); ceder, darse por vencido; **— and take** toma y daca; *s.* elasticidad.
giv·en [gívən] *p.p. de* **to give;** *adj.* (*presented*) (dado); regalado; (*inclined*) adicto, entregado; dispuesto, inclinado; — **name** nombre de pila, nombre de bautismo; — **time** hora determinada; — **that** dada que, supuesto que.
giv·er [gívɚ] *s.* dador, donador.
gla·cial [gléʃəl] *adj.* glacial.
gla·cier [gléʃɚ] *s.* glaciar, helero.
glad [glæd] *adj.* contento; alegre; **to be — to** alegrarse de, tener mucho gusto en (*o* de); **-ly** *adv.* alegremente; con mucho gusto; de buena gana.
glad·den [glǽdn̩] *v.* regocijar, alegrar.
glade [gled] *s.* claro herboso (*en un bosque*).
glad·ness [glǽdnɪs] *s.* alegría, gozo.
glam·our [glǽmɚ] *s.* encanto, hechizo; fascinación, embrujo; — **girl** niña hechicera.
glam·or·ous [glǽmərəs] *adj.* fascinador, hechicero.
glance [glæns] *s.* mirada, vistazo, ojeada; vislumbre; *v.* echar (*o* dar) un vistazo; vislumbrar; pegar de soslayo; **to — off** rebotar de soslayo (*o* de lado).
gland [glænd] *s.* glándula.
glare [glɛr] *s.* (*light*) resplandor, relumbre; (*stare*) mirada furiosa; *v.* resplandecer, relumbrar; **to — at** mirar enfurecido a.
glass [glæs] *s.* (*substance*) vidrio; cristal; (*receptacle*) vaso; copa (*de cristal*); (*eye*) lente; **looking —** espejo; **-es** anteojos, lentes, gafas; *adj.* de vidrio; — **blower** vidriero, soplador de vidrio; — **case** escaparate; vitrina.
glass·ware [glǽswɛr] *s.* vajilla de cristal, cristalería; — **shop** cristalería.
glass·y [glǽsɪ] *adj.* vidrioso.
glau·co·ma [glɔkómə] *s.* glaucoma.
glaze [glez] *s.* vidriado; lustre; superficie lustrosa o glaseada; *v.* vidriar; glasear; lustrar; poner vidrios a.
gla·zier [gléʒɚ] *s.* vidriero.
gleam [glim] *s.* destello, rayo, fulgor, viso; *v.* destellar, fulgurar, centellear.
glean [glin] *v.* recoger; espigar.
glee [gli] *s.* regocijo; júbilo; — **club** orfeón, masa coral.
glib [glɪb] *adj.* locuaz; de mucha labia; — **excuse** excusa fácil.
glide [glaɪd] *s.* deslizamiento; ligadura (*en música*); planeo (*de un aeroplano*); *v.* deslizarse; resbalarse; planear (*un aeroplano*).
glid·er [gláɪdɚ] *s.* deslizador, planeador (*aeroplano*).
glim·mer [glímɚ] *s.* vislumbre; viso; titileo; — **of hope** rayo de esperanza; *v.* titilar, centellear.
glimpse [glɪmps] *s.* vislumbre; vistazo, ojeada; **to catch a — of** vislumbrar; *v.* vislumbrar.
glint [glɪnt] *s.* fulgor, rayo, destello.
glis·ten [glísn̩] *v.* relucir, brillar.
glit·ter [glítɚ] *s.* lustre, brillo, resplandor; *v.* relumbrar, relucir, brillar.
gloat [glot] *v.* gozarse (en), deleitarse (en); relamerse (*de gusto*).
globe [glob] *s.* globo; esfera.
glob·ule [glábjul] *s.* glóbulo.
gloom [glum] *s.* lobreguez, sombra; abatimiento, tristeza, melancolía.
gloom·y [glúmɪ] *adj.* lóbrego, sombrío; triste, melancólico; abatido.
glo·ri·fy [glórəfaɪ] *v.* glorificar.
glo·ri·ous [glórɪəs] *adj.* glorioso; espléndido.
glo·ry [glórɪ] *s.* gloria; *v.* gloriarse; vanagloriarse.
gloss [glɔs] *s.* (*shine*) lustre, brillo; pulimento; (*note*) glosa, comentario; *v.* lustrar, dar brillo a; pulir; glosar, comentar; **to — over** encubrir, dar colorido de bueno (*a algo que no lo es*).
glos·sa·ry [glásərɪ] *s.* glosario.
gloss·y [glásɪ] *adj.* lustroso; pulido.
glove [glʌv] *s.* guante; *v.* enguantar, poner guantes.
glow [glo] *s.* incandescencia; brillo (*de un ascua*); calor vivo; fosforescencia; *v.* lucir, brillar (*como un ascua*); fosforescer; estar encendido o enardecido.
glow·ing [glóɪŋ] *adj.* encendido, ardiente.
glow·worm [glówɝm] *s.* luciérnaga.
glue [glu] *s.* cola (*para pegar*); *v.* encolar, pegar (*con cola*).
glum [glʌm] *adj.* hosco.
glut [glʌt] *s.* exceso, saturación; *v.* saturar.
glut·ton [glʌ́tn̩] *s.* glotón.
glut·ton·ous [glʌ́tn̩əs] *adj.* glotón; goloso.
glut·ton·y [glʌ́tn̩ɪ] *s.* gula, glotonería.
glyc·er·in [glísɚɪn] *s.* glicerina.
gnarled [nɑrld] *adj.* nudoso, torcido.
gnash [næʃ] *v.* crujir, rechinar (*los dientes*).
gnat [næt] *s.* jején (*insecto*).
gnaw [nɔ] *v.* roer.
gnu [ñu] *s.* nu.
go [go] *v.* (*move*) ir(se); andar; (*function*) marchar, funcionar, servir; **to — around** andar alrededor de; dar vueltas; **to — away** irse; **to — back on one's word** faltar a la palabra; **to — by** pasar por; guiarse por (*una regla*); **to — down** bajar; **to — insane** volverse loco; **to — into** entrar en; investigar; caber en; **to — off** hacer explosión; dispararse; irse, salir disparado; **to — on** proseguir, continuar; **to — out** salir; apagarse; **to — over** pasar por encima de; examinar con cuidado; releer; repasar; recorrer; **to — to pot** arruinarse; **to — to sleep** dormirse; **to — under** ir o pasar por debajo de; hundirse; **to — up** subir; **to let —** soltar; **there is not enough to — around** no hay (bastante) para todos; *s.* empuje, energía; **it is a —** trato hecho; **to be on the —** estar en continuo movimiento.

goad [god] *s.* aguijón; puya; *v.* aguijonear; aguijar, incitar.
goal [gol] *s.* meta; fin, objetivo.
goat [got] *s.* cabra; **male** — macho cabrío; **to be the** — ser la víctima, pagar el pato.
goat·ee [gotí] *s.* perilla.
goat·herd [góthɚd] *s.* cabrero.
gob·ble [gabl] *v.* tragar, engullir; **to** — **up** engullirse.
gob·bler [gáblɚ] *s.* pavo.
go-be·tween [góbətwin] *s.* medianero.
gob·let [gáblɪt] *s.* copa grande.
gob·lin [gáblɪn] *s.* duende.
god [gad] *s.* dios; **God** Dios.
god·child [gádtʃaɪld] *s.* ahijado, ahijada.
god·dess [gádɪs] *s.* diosa.
god·fa·ther [gádfaðɚ] *s.* padrino.
god·less [gádlɪs] *adj.* impío, ateo.
god·like [gádlaɪk] *adj.* como Dios; divino.
god·ly [gádlɪ] *adj.* pío, devoto; divino.
god·moth·er [gádmʌðɚ] *s.* madrina.
gog·gles [gáglz] *s. pl.* antiparras, gafas.
go·ing [góɪŋ] *ger. & adj.* que anda, marcha o funciona bien; **to be** — ir, irse; *s.* ida, partida; **comings and -s** idas y venidas.
goi·ter [gɔ́ɪtɚ] *s.* papera; bocio; *Ríopl., Méx., C.A.* buche; *C.A.* güecho.
gold [gold] *s.* oro; — **standard** patrón de oro.
gold·en [góldn̩] *adj.* de oro; áureo; dorado.
gold·finch [góldfɪntʃ] *s.* jilguero amarillo.
gold·fish [góldfɪʃ] *s.* carpa dorada.
gold·smith [góldsmɪθ] *s.* orfebre; — **shop** orfebrería.
golf [galf] *s.* golf.
gon·do·la [gándələ] *s.* góndola; cabina (*de una aeronave*); — **car** vagón de mercancías (*sin techo*), *Am.* jaula.
gone [gɔn] *p.p. de* **to go** *& adj.* ido; perdido; **he is** — se fué; **it is all** — se acabó; ya no hay más.
gong [gɔŋ] *s.* gong, batintín.
good [gʊd] *adj.* bueno; (*valid*) válido; valedero; — **afternoon** buenas tardes; — **day** buenos días; adiós; — **evening** buenas noches; — **morning** buenos días; — **night** buenas noches; **Good Friday** Viernes Santo; **for** — para siempre, permanentemente; **to have a** — **time** pasar un buen rato; divertirse; **to make** — pagar, compensar; cumplir (*una promesa*); salir bien, tener buen éxito; *s.* bien; beneficio, provecho, ventaja; **-s** bienes, efectos; mercancías; — **and services** bienes y servicios.
good-bye [gʊdbáɪ] *s. & interj.* adiós.
good-looking [gúdlúkɪŋ] *adj.* bien parecido, guapo.
good·ly [gʊ́dlɪ] *adj.* grande, considerable; de buena apariencia.
good-na·tured [gʊ́dnétʃɚd] *adj.* de buen genio, bonachón, afable.
good·ness [gʊ́dnɪs] *s.* bondad; — ! ¡Dios mío! ¡cielos!
good·y [gʊdɪ] *s.* golosina, bombón, dulce; *interj.* ¡qué gusto!; **goody-goody** beatuco (*el que afecta virtud*), papanatas.
goof [guf] *v.* chapucear.
goose [gus] *s.* ganso; bobo, tonto; — **flesh** carne de gallina.
goose·ber·ry [glúsbɛrɪ] *s.* grosella; grosellero (*arbusto*).
go·pher [gófɚ] *s.* roedor semejante a la ardilla.
gore [gor] *s.* (*blood*) cuajarón de sangre; sangre; (*cloth*) cuchillo (*Am.* cuchilla), sesga (*tira de lienzo en figura de cuchilla*); *v.* acornear, herir con los cuernos; hacer una sesga en (*un traje*).
gorge [gɔrdʒ] *s.* cañada, barranco, barranca; *v.* engullir(se), atracarse.
gor·geous [gɔ́rdʒəs] *adj.* primoroso, vistoso, hermosísimo.
go·ril·la [gərílə] *s.* gorila.
go·ry [górɪ] *adj.* sangriento, ensangrentado.
gos·pel [gáspl̩] *s.* evangelio; **it is the** — **truth** es la pura verdad.
gos·sip [gásɪp] *s.* (*rumors*) chisme, chismería; murmuración, hablilla; (*person*) murmurador, chismero, chismoso; *v.* chismear, murmurar.
gos·sip·y [gásəpɪ] *adj.* chismero, chismoso.
got [gat] *pret. & p.p. de* **to get.**
Goth·ic [gáθɪk] *adj.* gótico; *s.* gótico (*idioma de los godos*); estilo gótico.
got·ten [gátn̩] *p.p. de* **to get.**
gouge [gaʊdʒ] *s.* gubia (*especie de formón o escoplo curvo*); *v.* excavar con gubia, formón o escoplo; **to** — **someone's eyes out** sacarle los ojos a alguien.
gourd [gord] *s.* calabaza.
gour·met [gʊrmé] *s.* gastrónomo.
gout [gaʊt] *s.* gota (*enfermedad*).
gov·ern [gʌ́vɚn] *v.* gobernar; regir.
gov·ern·ess [gʌ́vɚnɪs] *s.* institutriz.
gov·ern·ment [gʌ́vɚmənt] *s.* gobierno.
gov·ern·ment·al [gʌvɚméntl̩] *adj.* gubernativo.
gov·er·nor [gʌ́vɚnɚ] *s.* gobernador; regulador (*de una máquina*).
gown [gaʊn] *s.* vestido (*de mujer*); toga (*de un juez, profesor, etc.*); **dressing** — bata.
grab [græb] *v.* agarrar, asir; arrebatar; *s.* arrebatiña; agarro, agarrón; presa.
grace [gres] *s.* gracia; favor; donaire, garbo; **to say** — bendecir la mesa, dar gracias; **to be in the good -s of someone** gozar del favor de uno; *v.* agraciar, adornar.
grace·ful [grésfəl] *adj.* gracioso, agraciado, garboso; **-ly** *adv.* graciosamente, con gracia, con garbo.
grace·ful·ness [grésfəlnɪs] *s.* gracia, donaire, gallardía, garbo.
gra·cious [gréʃəs] *adj.* afable; cortés; — ! ¡válgame Dios!
gra·da·tion [gredéʃən] *s.* graduación; gradación; grado.
grade [gred] *s.* (*degree*) grado; (*mark*) nota, calificación; (*slope*) cuesta, declive, pendiente; *Am.* gradiente; — **crossing** cruce a nivel (*de un ferrocarril con una carretera*); **the -s** la escuela primaria; *v.* graduar, clasificar; calificar, dar una calificación; (*level*) nivelar, explanar.
grad·u·al [grǽdʒʊəl] *adj.* gradual; **-ly** *adv.* gradualmente, poco a poco.
grad·u·ate [grǽdʒʊɪt] *adj.* graduado, que ha recibido un grado académico; **to do** — **work** cursar asignaturas superiores (*al bachillerato*); *s.* estudiante graduado (*que estudia para licenciado o doctor*); [grǽdʒʊet] *v.* graduar(se).
grad·u·a·tion [grædʒʊéʃən] *s.* graduación.
graft [græft] *s.* (*insertion*) injerto; tejido injertado; (*extortion*) sisa, malversación (*de caudales públicos*); peculado, chanchullo; ganancia ilegal, *Méx.* mordida; *v.* injertar; malversar fondos ajenos; sisar, exigir gago ilegal, *Méx.* morder.
graft·er [grǽftɚ] *s.* malversador (*de fondos públicos*), estafador, *C.A.* coyote, *Méx.* mordelón.
grain [gren] *s.* (*cereal*) grano; (*markings*) fibra (*de la madera*), veta (*del mármol o madera*); **against the** — a (*o* al) redopelo, a contrapelo.
gram [græm] *s.* gramo.
gram·mar [grǽmɚ] *s.* gramática; — **school** escuela primaria.
gram·mat·i·cal [grəmǽtɪkl̩] *adj.* gramatical,

gramático.
gran·a·ry [grǽnərɪ] *s.* granero.
grand [grænd] *adj.* grande; grandioso, admirable; magnífico.
grand·child [grǽntʃaɪld] *s.* nieto.
grand·chil·dren [grǽntʃɪdrən] *s. pl.* nietos.
grand·daugh·ter [grǽndɔtɚ] *s.* nieta.
gran·deur [grǽndʒɚ] *s.* grandeza, grandiosidad; majestad.
grand·father [grǽnfɑðɚ] *s.* abuelo.
gran·di·ose [grǽndɪos] *adj.* grandioso, magnífico.
grand·ma [grǽnmɑ] *s.* abuela, abuelita, *Am.* mamá grande.
grand·moth·er [grǽnmʌðɚ] *s.* abuela.
grand·ness [grǽndnɪs] *s.* grandeza; grandiosidad; magnificencia.
grand·pa [grǽnpɑ] *s.* abuelo, abuelito, *Am.* papá grande.
grand·par·ent [grǽnpɛrənt] *s.* abuelo, abuela; **-s** abuelos.
grand·son [grǽnsʌn] *s.* nieto.
grand·stand [grǽnstænd] *s.* andanada, gradería cubierta.
grange [grendʒ] *s.* granja; asociación de agricultores.
gran·ite [grǽnɪt] *s.* granito (*roca*).
gran·ny [grǽnɪ] *s.* abuelita; viejecita, viejita.
grant [grænt] *s.* concesión; subvención; donación; dádiva; transferencia de propiedad (*mediante escritura*); *v.* conceder; otorgar; ceder, transferir (*derechos, propiedad, etc.*); **to take for -ed** dar por supuesto, dar por sentado.
gran·u·late [grǽnjələt] *v.* granular(se).
grape [grep] *s.* uva.
grape·fruit [grépfrut] *s.* toronja; *Esp.* pomelo.
grape·vine [grépvaɪn] *s.* vid; parra.
graph [græf] *s.* diagrama, gráfica; *v.* hacer una gráfica o diagrama; *paper* papel cuadriculado.
graph·ic [grǽfɪk] *adj.* gráfico; — **design** (*computer*) diseño gráfico.
graph·ite [grǽfaɪt] *s.* grafito.
grap·ple [grǽpl] *v.* luchar, pelear cuerpo a cuerpo; aferrar, agarrar.
grasp [græsp] *v.* (*seize*) agarrar; asir; apretar; (*understand*) comprender; abarcar; *s.* agarro, asimiento; apretón de manos; **to be within one's** — estar al alcance de uno; **to have a good — of a subject** estar fuerte en una materia, saber a fondo una materia.
grass [græs] *s.* hierba; césped; pasto; *Méx.* zacate; *Méx., Ven., Col.* grama.
grass·hop·per [grǽshɑpɚ] *s.* saltamontes, saltón, *Méx, C.C.* chapulín.
grass·roots [grǽsruts] *adj.* del pueblo; de la gente.
grass·y [grǽsɪ] *adj.* herboso, *Am.* pastoso.
grate [gret] *s.* (*window*) reja, verja, enrejado; (*grill*) parrilla, brasero; *v.* enrejar, poner enrejado; crujir, rechinar (*los dientes*); rallar (*queso*); **to — on** molestar, irritar.
grate·ful [grétfəl] *adj.* agradecido; grato, agradable.
grat·er [grétɚ] *s.* rallador.
grat·i·fy [grǽtəfaɪ] *v.* complacer, dar gusto, agradar; satisfacer.
grat·ing [grétɪŋ] *s.* reja, enrejado, verja; *adj.* rechinante; molesto, áspero.
gra·tis [grétɪs] *adv.* gratis, de balde.
grat·i·tude [grǽtətjud] *s.* gratitud.
gra·tu·i·tous [grətjúətəs] *adj.* gratuito; sin fundamento; — **statement** afirmación arbitraria.
grave [grev] *adj.* grave; serio; *s.* tumba, sepulcro, sepultura; acento grave; —**stone** losa o lápida sepulcral.
grave·dig·ger [grévdɪgɚ] *s.* sepulturero.
grav·el [grǽvl] *s.* grava, guijo, cascajo, *Am.* maicillo; cálculos (*en los riñones, la vejiga, etc.*); mal de piedra; *v.* cubrir con grava.
grave·yard [grévjɑrd] *s.* cementerio.
grav·i·ta·tion [grævɪtéʃən] *s.* atracción; gravitación.
grav·i·ty [grǽvətɪ] *s.* gravedad; seriedad.
gra·vy [grévɪ] *s.* salsa; jugo (*de carne*).
gray [gre] *adj.* gris; (*hair*) cano; pelicano; entrecano (*que empieza a encanecer*); — **horse** rucio, tordo, tordillo; — **matter** seso; **gray-headed** canoso; *s.* gris. color gris; *v.* encanecer; poner(se) gris.
gray·ish [gréɪʃ] *adj.* grisáceo, pardusco; — **hair** pelo entrecano.
gray·ness [grénɪs] *s.* grisura, gris, calidad de gris; encanecimiento.
graze [grez] *v.* (*feed*) pacer; apacentar, *Am.* pastear, pastar; (*brush*) rozar; raspar; *s.* roce, rozón, raspadura.
grease [gris] *s.* grasa; *v.* engrasar; (*anoint*) untar; lubricar; **to — the palm** untar la mano, sobornar.
greas·y [grísɪ] *adj.* grasiento, grasoso; pringoso.
great [gret] *adj.* gran(de); eminente; magnífico, excelente; **a — deal** una gran cantidad; muchos; mucho; **a — many** muchos; **a — while** un largo rato o tiempo; **-ly** *adv.* grandemente; mucho; muy; en gran parte; sobremanera.
great-grand·child [grétgrǽntʃaɪld] *s.* bisnieto.
great-grand·fa·ther [grétgrǽnfɑðɚ] *s.* bisabuelo.
great-grand·moth·er [grétgrǽnmʌðɚ] *s.* bisabuela.
great·ness [grétnɪs] *s.* grandeza.
Gre·cian [gríʃən] *adj. & s.* griego.
greed [grid] *s.* codicia; avaricia; gula.
greed·i·ly [grídlɪ] *adv.* vorazmente; con avaricia; con gula.
greed·i·ness [grídɪnɪs] *s.* codicia; avaricia; gula; voracidad.
greed·y [grídɪ] *adj.* codicioso; avaro; goloso; voraz.
Greek [grik] *adj. & s.* griego.
green [grin] *adj.* (*color*) verde; (*novice*) novato, inexperto; **to grow** — verdear; **the fields look** — verdean los campos; *s.* verde, verdor; césped, prado; campo de golf; **-s** verduras, hortalizas.
green·horn [grínhɔrn] *s.* novato, pipiolo.
green·house [grínhaʊs] *s.* invernáculo, invernadero.
green·ish [grínɪʃ] *adj.* verdoso.
green·ness [grínnɪs] *s.* (*color*) verdor, verdura; (*experience*) inmadurez; impericia.
greet [grit] *v.* saludar; **to — each other** saludarse.
greet·ing [grítɪŋ] *s.* saludo; salutación; **-s!** ¡salud! ¡saludos!
gre·nade [grɪnéd] *s.* granada, bomba pequeña.
grew [gru] *pret. de* **to grow.**
grey = **gray.**
grey·ish = **gray.**
grey·ness = **grayness.**
grey·hound [gréhaʊnd] *s.* lebrel, galgo.
grid·dle [grídl] *s.* tartera; plancha (*para tapar el hornillo*).
grief [grif] *s.* dolor, pesar; **to come to** — sobrevenirle a uno una desgracia; fracasar.
griev·ance [grívəns] *s.* queja; resentimiento; (*injustice*) motivo de queja, injusticia, ofensa.
grieve [griv] *v.* afligir(se); lamentar(se), acongojar(se).
grieved [grivd] *adj.* penado.
griev·ous [grívəs] *adj.* doloroso, penoso; grave, atroz.
grill [grɪl] *s.* parrilla; **men's** — restaurante para hombres; *v.* asar en parrillas; interrogar (*a un sospechoso*).

grim [grɪm] *adj.* austero, áspero; fiero; torvo, siniestro.
gri·mace [grɪmés] *s.* mueca, gesto; *v.* hacer muecas o gestos.
grime [graɪm] *s.* mugre; *v.* ensuciar.
grim·y [gráɪmɪ] *adj.* mugriento.
grin [grɪn] *s.* sonrisa abierta; sonrisa maliciosa; sonrisa canina; *v.* sonreír (*mostrando mucho los dientes*).
grind [graɪnd] *v.* (*crush*) moler; machacar; (*sharpen*) afilar, amolar; (*study hard*) afanarse demasiado; estudiar con empeño; **to — a hand organ** tocar el organillo; **to — one's teeth** rechinar los dientes; *s.* molienda; faena, trabajo penoso; estudiante tesonero; **the daily** — la rutina diaria.
grind·er [gráɪndɚ] *s.* moledor; molinillo (*para moler café*); amolador, afilador; muela (*piedra para afilar*); muela (*diente molar*).
grind·stone [gráɪndston] *s.* piedra de amolar.
grip [grɪp] *v.* (*seize*) agarrar; asir; apretar; empuñar; (*impress*) impresionar; conmover; *s.* agarro; asimiento; apretón; asidero, asa; (*suitcase*) valija, maletín; *Méx.*, velís; **to have a — on someone** tener agarrado a alguien.
grippe [grɪp] *s.* gripe, influenza.
grit [grɪt] *s.* (*gravel*) arenilla, arena; piedra arenisca; (*pluck*) firmeza, tesón; **-s** maíz, avena, o trigo a medio moler; *v.* rechinar, crujir.
grit·ty [grítɪ] *adj.* arenoso; valeroso, firme.
griz·zly [grízlɪ] *adj.* grisáceo, pardusco; — **bear** oso pardo.
groan [gron] *s.* gemido, quejido; *v.* gemir; quejarse; crujir (*por exceso de peso*).
gro·cer [grósɚ] *s.* abacero, *Méx.* abarrotero, *Carib.*, *C.A.* bodeguero; *Ríopl.* almacenero.
gro·cer·y [grósərɪ] *s.* abacería, tienda de comestibles, *Méx.*, abarrotería, *Méx.* tienda de abarrotes; *Ríopl.* almacén; *Carib.*, *C.A.* bodega; **groceries** comestibles, *Méx.* abarrotes.
groom [grum] *s.* (*bridegroom*) novio; (*stable groom*) caballerizo, mozo de caballeriza; establero; *v.* almohazar, limpiar con la almohaza (*a los caballos*), cuidar (*a los caballos*); **to — oneself** asearse, peinarse, componerse; **well-groomed** bien vestido, aseado, limpio.
groove [gruv] *s.* estría, ranura, acanaladura; surco (*en un camino*); muesca, encaje; *v.* acanalar, estriar.
grope [grop] *v.* tentalear, tentar, andar a tientas; **to — for** buscar tentando, buscar a tientas.
gross [gros] *adj.* grueso; burdo; tosco; grosero; *s.* — **earnings** ganancias totales; renta bruta, ingreso bruto; — **ignorance** ignorancia crasa; — **weight** peso bruto; *s.* grueso, totalidad; gruesa (*doce docenas*).
gro·tesque [grotésk] *adj.* & *s.* grotesco.
grot·to [gráto] *s.* gruta.
grouch [graʊtʃ] *s.* mal humor; gruñón, refunfuñón, cascarrabias; **to have a — against someone** tenerle ojeriza (*o* mala voluntad) a una persona; guardarle rencor a alguien; *v.* gruñir, refunfuñar; estar de mal humor.
grouch·y [gráʊtʃɪ] *adj.* gruñón, refunfuñón, malhumorado, cascarrabias.
ground [graʊnd] *s.* (*earth*) suelo, tierra; terreno; (*motive*) motivo, razón; base, fundamento; — **crew** personal de tierra; **-s** heces, desperdicios, sedimento; — **floor** piso bajo, planta baja, **to break** — roturar, arar; cavar; **to give** — retroceder, ceder; **to hold one's** — mantenerse firme; *v.* conectar (*un alambre*) con la tierra; encallar (*una embarcación*); aterrizar (*un aeroplano*); **to be well -ed** poseer las bases o principios fundamentales; *pret.* & *p.p. de* **to grind.**
ground·less [gráʊndlɪs] *adj.* infundado.
group [grup] *s.* grupo; — **insurance** seguros sociales; *v.* agrupar.
grove [grov] *s.* arboleda, bosquecillo.
grow [gro] *v.* crecer; brotar; cultivar; criar; producir; **to — angry** ponerse enojado o enfadado, enfadarse, enojarse; **to — better** ponerse mejor, mejorar; **to — difficult** dificultarse, hacerse difícil; **to — late** hacerse tarde; **to — old** ponerse viejo, envejecer; **to — out of a habit** perder la costumbre; **to — pale** ponerse pálido, palidecer; **to — tired** cansarse.
growl [graʊl] *s.* gruñido; *v.* gruñir.
growl·er [gráʊlɚ] *s.* gruñón; regañón.
grown [gron] *p.p. de* **to grow** & *adj.* crecido; desarrollado; — **man** hombre maduro, hombre hecho; — **with trees** poblado de árboles.
grown-up [grónʌp] *adj.* crecido, adulto; *s.* adulto.
growth [groθ] *s.* (*increase*) crecimiento, acrecentamiento; aumento; (*development*) desarrollo; (*vegetation*) vegetación; (*tissue*) tumor, lobanillo, excrecencia.
grub·by [grʌ́bɪ] *adj.* roñoso; sucio.
grudge [grʌdʒ] *s.* inquina, rencor, resentimiento, mala voluntad; *v.* tener inquina, envidia o mala voluntad; dar de mala gana.
gruff [grʌf] *adj.* áspero, rudo; grosero.
grum·ble [grʌ́mbl̩] *s.* refunfuño, gruñido, queja; *v.* refunfuñar, gruñir, quejarse.
grum·bler [grʌ́mblɚ] *s.* gruñón; regañón.
grump·y [grʌ́mpɪ] *adj.* malhumorado; gruñón.
grunt [grʌnt] *s.* gruñido, *Méx.*, *C.A.*, *Col.*, *Ven.* pujido; *v.* gruñir, *Ríopl.*, *Méx.*, *C.A.*, *Ven.*, *Andes* pujar.
guar·an·tee [gærəntí] *s.* garantía; fianza; fiador; *v.* garantizar; dar fianza; salir fiador de.
guar·an·tor [gǽrəntɚ] *s.* fiador.
guar·an·ty [gǽrəntɪ] *s.* garantía; fianza; fiador; *v.* *véase* **guarantee.**
guard [gɑrd] *s.* guarda; guardia; resguardo; **to be on** — estar alerta; estar en guardia; **to keep** — vigilar; *v.* guardar; resguardar; vigilar; **to — (oneself) against** guardarse de.
guard·i·an [gɑ́rdɪən] *s.* guardián, custodio; tutor; — **angel** ángel custodio, ángel de la guarda.
guard·i·an·ship [gɑ́rdɪənʃɪp] *s.* tutela; guarda, custodia.
guard·rail [gɑ́rdrel] *s.* baranda.
Gua·te·ma·lan [gwɑtəmɑ́lən] *adj.* & *s.* guatemalteco.
guess [gɛs] *s.* conjetura, suposición; adivinación; *v.* adivinar; suponer, creer.
guest [gɛst] *s.* convidado; visita; huésped, pensionista, inquilino.
guf·faw [gʌfɔ́] *s.* risotada, carcajada.
gui·dance [gáɪdn̩s] *s.* guía, dirección.
guide [gaɪd] *s.* guía.
guide·book [gáɪdbʊk] *s.* guía del viajero; **railway** — guía de ferrocarriles.
guide·line [gáɪdlaɪn] *s.* norma; precepto.
guild [gɪld] *s.* gremio; cofradía; asociación.
guile [gaɪl] *s.* engaño, astucia.
guilt [gɪlt] *s.* culpa, delito; culpabilidad.
guilt·less [gíltlɪs] *adj.* libre de culpa; inocente.
guilt·y [gíltɪ] *adj.* culpable; reo, delincuente.
guise [gaɪz] *s.* aspecto, apariencia; modo; **under the — of** so capa de; disfrazado de.
gui·tar [gɪtɑ́r] *s.* guitarra.
gulf [gʌlf] *s.* golfo; abismo.

gull [gʌl] *s.* gaviota.
gul·let [gʌ́lɪt] *s.* gaznate.
gul·ly [gʌ́lɪ] *s.* barranco, barranca; hondonada.
gulp [gʌlp] *s.* trago; *v.* tragar; engullir; **to — it down** tragárselo.
gum [gʌm] *s.* (*product*) goma; (*of mouth*) encía; **chewing —** goma de mascar, *Am.* chicle; **— tree** arbol gomífero, *Col.* gomero; *v.* engomar, pegar con goma.
gun [gʌn] *s.* (*cannon*) cañón; (*rifle*) fusil, rifle; (*shotgun*) escopeta; pistola, revólver; **a 21 — salute** una salva de 21 cañonazos.
gun·boat [gʌ́nbot] *s.* cañonero, lancha cañonera.
gun·ner [gʌ́nɚ] *s.* artillero, cañonero; ametrallador.
gun·pow·der [gʌ́npaʊdɚ] *s.* pólvora.
gur·gle [gɝ́gl] *v.* borbotar, hacer borbollones; *s.* borbollón, borbotón.
gush [gʌʃ] *s.* chorro; borbollón, borbotón; efusión (*de cariño o entusiasmo*); *v.* chorrear, borbotar, borbollar, borbollonear; brotar; ser demasiado efusivo.
gust [gʌst] *s.* ráfaga, ventolera.
gut [gʌt] *s.* tripa, intestino; cuerda de tripa; **to have -s** tener agallas (*ánimo*).
gut·ter [gʌ́tɚ] *s.* arroyo (*de la calle o de un camino*); gotera (*del techo*); zanja.
guy [gaɪ] *s.* (*person*) sujeto, tipo, individuo; (*wire*) tirante, alambre, cadena (*para sostener algo*); *v.* sostener (*algo*) con tirantes; burlarse de, mofarse de.
gym·na·si·um [dʒɪmnézɪəm] *s.* gimnasio.
gym·nas·tics [dʒɪmnǽtɪks] *s.* gimnasia.
gy·ne·col·o·gy [gaɪnəkálədʒɪ] *s.* ginecología.
gyp·sy [dʒípsɪ] *s.* & *adj.* gitano.
gy·rate [dʒaíret] *v.* girar.
gy·ro·scope [dʒaɪrəskop] *s.* giroscopio.

H:h

hab·it [hǽbɪt] *s.* hábito; costumbre; **drinking —** vicio de la bebida; **riding —** traje de montar.
ha·bit·u·al [həbítʃʊəl] *adj.* habitual; acostumbrado.
hack [hæk] *s.* (*cut*) tajo; (*cough*) tos seca; (*horse*) caballo de alquiler; rocín; (*writer*) escritor mercenario; *v.* tajar, picar; toser con tos seca.
hack·neyed [hǽknɪd] *adj.* trillado, muy común.
had [hæd] *pret.* & *p.p. de* **to have; you — better do it** es bueno que Vd. lo haga; sería bueno que Vd. lo hiciese; **I — rather go than stay** preferiría irme a quedarme.
haf·ni·um [hǽfniəm] *s.* hafnio.
hag [hæg] *s.* hechicera, bruja; viejota.
hag·gard [hǽgɚd] *adj.* macilento, flaco.
hag·gle [hǽgl] *v.* regatear.
hail [hel] *s.* (*storm*) granizo; (*greeting*) saludo; llamada, grito; **Hail Mary** Ave María; *interj.* ¡salud!; ¡salve!; *v.* granizar; saludar; llamar; aclamar; **to — from** proceder de, ser oriundo de.
hail·storm [hélstɔrm] *s.* granizada.
hair [hɛr] *s.* pelo; cabello; vello; filamento (*de las plantas*); **— net** red para el cabello.
hair·brush [hɛ́rbrʌʃ] *s.* cepillo para el cabello.
hair·cut [hɛ́rkʌt] *s.* corte de pelo; **close —** rape; **to have a —** hacerse cortar el pelo.
hair·do [hɛ́rdu] *s.* peinado.
hair·dress·er [hɛ́rdrɛsɚ] *s.* peluquero; peinadora.
hair·less [hɛ́rlɪs] *adj.* sin pelo, pelado; lampiño.
hair·pin [hɛ́rpɪn] *s.* horquilla, *Am.* gancho (*para el pelo*).
hair·y [hɛ́rɪ] *adj.* peludo, cabelludo; hirsuto, velloso, velludo.
hale [hel] *adj.* sano, fuerte, robusto; *v.* llevar (*a una persona*) por fuerza.
half [hæf] *s.* mitad; **— an apple** media manzana; *adj.* medio; **— brother** hermanastro; **— cooked** a medio cocer, medio cocido; **— duplex** (*computer*) semiduplex; **half-past one** la una y media; **half-baked** a medio cocer; a medio planear.
half-breed [hǽfbrid] *adj.* & *s.* mestizo.
half-hour [hǽfáʊr] *s.* media hora; *adj.* de media hora.
half-mast [hǽfmǽst] *s.* media asta; *v.* poner a media asta (*la bandera*).
half-o·pen [hǽfópən] *adj.* entreabierto; medio abierto, entornado.
half·way [hǽfwe] *adj.* & *adv.* a medio camino; parcial, incompleto; **— between** equidistante de; **— finished** a medio acabar; **to do something —** hacer algo a medias.
half-wit·ted [hǽfwítɪd] *adj.* imbécil, zonzo.
hal·i·but [hǽləbət] *s.* mero, hipogloso (*pez*).
hall [hɔl] *s.* salón (*para asambleas, funciones, etc.*); edificio (*de un colegio o universidad*); vestíbulo; corredor, pasillo; **town —** ayuntamiento.
hall·mark [hɔ́lmɑrk] *s.* distintivo.
hal·lo = **hello.**
hal·low [hǽlo] *v.* santificar; consagrar.
Hal·low·een [hæloín] *s.* víspera de Todos los Santos.
hall·way [hɔ́lwe] *s.* corredor, pasillo; zaguán.
ha·lo [hélo] *s.* halo; aureola.
halt [hɔlt] *s.* alto, parada; *v.* parar(se), detener(se); hacer alto; vacilar.
hal·ter [hɔ́ltɚ] *s.* ronzal, cabestro.
halt·ing [hɔ́ltɪŋ] *adj.* vacilante; **-ly** *adv.* con vacilación.
halve [hæv] *v.* partir por la mitad; partir en dos.
halves [hævz] *pl. de* **half; to go —** ir a medias.
ham [hæm] *s.* jamón.
ham·burg·er [hǽmbɝgɚ] *s.* carne picada de vaca; bocadillo o emparedado de carne picada, *Am.* hamburguesa.
ham·let [hǽmlɪt] *s.* caserío, aldehuela.
ham·mer [hǽmɚ] *s.* martillo; martinete (*de piano*); **sledge —** macho; *v.* martillar; machacar; clavar.
ham·mock [hǽmək] *s.* hamaca, *Ven., Col.* chinchorro; *Ríopl.* mangangá; coy.
ham·per [hǽmpɚ] *s.* canasto, cesto grande, cuévano; *v.* estorbar, impedir, embarazar.
hand [hænd] *s.* mano; manecilla; (*clock*) aguja (*de reloj*); obrero; letra (*modo de escribir*); **— and glove** uña y carne; **— in —** (cogidos) de la mano; **at —** a la mano, cerca; **made by —** hecho a mano; **on —** disponible; en existencia; listo; a la mano, presente; **on the other —** en cambio, por otra parte; **to have one's -s full** estar ocupadísimo; *v.* entregar, dar; **to — down** bajar (*una cosa para dársela a alguien*); transmitir (*de una a otra generación*); pronunciar (*un fallo*); **to — in** entregar; **to — over** entreger.
hand·bag [hǽndbæg] *s.* bolsa o bolso; saco de noche, maletín.
hand·ball [hǽndbɔl] *s.* pelota; juego de pelota.
hand·bill [hǽndbɪl] *s.* hoja volante (*anuncio*).
hand·cuff [hǽndkʌf] *v.* maniatar; **-s** *s. pl.* esposas, manillas de hierro.
hand·ful [hǽndfəl] *s.* manojo, puñado.
hand·i·cap [hǽndɪkæp] *s.* desventaja, estorbo, impedimento, obstáculo; ventaja o desventaja (*impuesta en ciertas contiendas*); **— race** carrera

de handicap; *v.* estorbar, poner trabas a.
hand·i·work [hǽndɪwɜk] *s.* labor, trabajo hecho a mano; artefacto.
hand·ker·chief [hǽŋkɚtʃɪf] *s.* pañuelo.
han·dle [hǽndl] *s.* mango, asa; (*furniture*) tirador (*de puerta o cajón*); puño (*de espada*); (*crank*) manubrio (*de bicicleta, organillo, etc.*); *v.* manejar; manipular; manosear, tocar; comerciar en; **-s easily** se maneja con facilidad, es muy manuable.
hand·made [hǽndméd] *adj.* hecho a mano.
hand·out [hǽndoʊt] *s.* comunicado, circular informativo; (gift) remuneración sin servicios correspondientes.
hand·saw [hǽndsɔ] *s.* serrucho.
hand·shake [hǽndʃek] *s.* apretón de manos.
hand·some [hǽnsəm] *adj.* (*good-looking*) hermoso, guapo, bien parecido; (*generous*) generoso; **a — sum** una suma considerable.
hand·work [hǽndwɛk] *s.* obra hecha a mano.
hand·writ·ing [hǽndraɪtɪŋ] *s.* letra (*modo de escribir*), escritura.
hand·y [hǽndɪ] *adj.* (near) a la mano, próximo; (*clever*) hábil, diestro; manuable, fácil de manejar.
hang [hæŋ] *v.* colgar; suspender; ahorcar; inclinar (*la cabeza*); **sentenced to —** condenado a la horca; **to — around** andar holgazaneando por un sitio; rondar; esperar sin hacer nada; **to — on** colgarse de; depender de; estar pendiente de; persistir; **to — paper on a wall** empapelar una pared; **to — with tapestries** entapizar; *s.* modo de caerle la ropa a una persona; modo de manejar (*un mecanismo*); modo de resolver (*un problema*); significado (*de un argumento*); **I don't care a —** no me importa un ardite.
han·gar [hǽŋɚ] *s.* hangar, cobertizo.
hang·er [hǽŋɚ] *s.* colgadero; percha, clavijero; **paper —** empapelador.
hang·ing [hǽŋɪŋ] *s.* muerte en la horca; **-s** colgaduras; *adj.* colgante; colgado.
hang·man [hǽŋmən] *s.* verdugo.
hang·nail [hǽŋnel] *s.* padrastro (*pedacito de pellejo que se levanta junto a las uñas*).
hang-o·ver [hǽŋovɚ] *s.* sobrante, remanente, resto; **to have a —** *Ven., Col., Andes* tener un ratón o estar enratonado (*tras una borrachera*), *Méx.* estar crudo o tener una cruda; *Ch.* la mona; *C.A.* de goma; *Ríopl.* resaca.
hap·haz·ard [hæphǽzɚd] *adv.* al azar, al acaso, a la ventura, a la buena de Dios; *adj.* casual; impensado.
hap·haz·ard·ly [hæphǽzɚdlɪ] *adv.* = **haphazard.**
hap·less [hǽplɪs] *adj.* desventurado, desgraciado.
hap·pen [hǽpən] *v.* suceder, pasar, acontecer, sobrevenir, acaecer; **to — to hear (do, be,** *etc.*) oír (hacer, estar, *etc.*) por casualidad; **to — to pass by** acertar a pasar; **to — on (upon)** encontrarse con, tropezar con.
hap·pen·ing [hǽpənɪŋ] *s.* acontecimiento, suceso.
hap·pi·ly [hǽplɪ] *adv.* felizmente; afortunadamente.
hap·pi·ness [hǽpɪnɪs] *s.* felicidad, dicha, contento.
hap·py [hǽpɪ] *adj.* feliz; dichoso, alegre; afortunado; **to be — to** alegrarse de.
ha·rangue [hərǽŋ] *s.* arenga, perorata; *v.* arengar, perorar.
har·ass [hǽrəs] *v.* acosar, hostigar, molestar.
har·bor [hárbɚ] *s.* puerto; (*refuge*) asilo, refugio, abrigo; *v.* abrigar; hospedar; albergar.
hard [hɑrd] *adj.* (*firm*) duro; (*stiff*) tieso; (*difficult*) arduo, difícil; **— cash** dinero contante y sonante, metálico; **— coal** antracita; **— liquor** licor espiritoso (*aguardiente, ron, etc.*); **— luck** mala suerte; **— of hearing** medio sordo; **— sell** técnica de venta agresiva; **— water** agua cruda; **— copy** (*computer*) listado en papel; **— disk** (*computer*) disco rígido; *adv.* fuerte, recio, con fuerza; con empeño, con ahinco; **— by** muy cerca; **— core** núcleo resistente (*de un grupo*); **—hearted** de corazón duro; **hard-working** muy trabajador, industrioso, aplicado.
hard·en [hárdn̩] *v.* endurecer(se).
hard·en·ing [hárdn̩ɪŋ] *s.* endurecimiento.
hard·ly [hárdlɪ] *adv.* apenas; a duras penas; difícilmente; duramente, con aspereza; probablemente no.
hard·ness [hárdnɪs] *s.* dureza; aspereza; dificultad.
hard·ship [hárdʃɪp] *s.* apuro, aflicción; trabajo, penalidad.
hard·ware [hárdwɛr] *s.* **— shop** quincallería, ferretería; *Méx.* tlapalería; (*computer*) circuitería física, elemento físico.
har·dy [hárdɪ[*adj.* robusto, fuerte, recio, atrevido.
hare [hɛr] *s.* liebre.
hare·brained [hɛ́rbrénd] *adj.* atolondrado, ligero de cascos.
hare·lip [hɛ́rlɪp] *s.* labio leporino.
har·em [hɛ́rəm] *s.* harén.
har·lot [hɑrlət] *s.* ramera, prostituta.
harm [hɑrm] *s.* daño, mal; perjuicio; *v.* dañar; hacer mal, hacer daño; perjudicar.
harm·ful [hármfəl] *adj.* dañoso; dañino, nocivo, perjudicial.
harm·less [hármlɪs] *adj.* innocuo; inofensivo; no dañoso, inocente.
harm·less·ness [hármlɪsnɪs] *s.* innocuidad; inocencia, falta de malicia.
har·mon·ic [hɑrmánɪk] *adj.* armónico.
har·mo·ni·ous [hɑrmónɪəs] *adj.* armonioso.
har·mo·nize [hármənaɪz] *v.* armonizar; concordar; congeniar.
har·mo·ny [hármənɪ] *s.* armonía.
har·ness [hárnɪs] *s.* guarniciones (*de caballerías*); jaez, aparejo; **to get back in —** volver al servicio activo, volver a trabajar; volver a la rutina; *v.* enjaezar, poner guarniciones a (*un caballo, mula, etc.*).
harp [hɑrp] *s.* arpa; *v.* tocar el arpa; **to — on** repetir constantemente (*una nota, palabra, tema, etc.*); porfiar en.
har·poon [hɑrpún] *s.* arpón; *v.* arponear, pescar con arpón.
har·row [hǽro] *s.* rastro, rastrillo, grada; *v.* rastrear, rastrillar; atormentar; horrorizar.
har·row·ing [hǽrəwɪŋ] *adj.* horrendo, horripilante, que pone los cabellos de punta; espeluznante.
har·ry [hǽrɪ] *v.* acosar, molestar; asolar.
harsh [hɑrʃ] *adj.* tosco, áspero; severo, austero.
harsh·ness [hárʃnɪs] *s.* aspereza; tosquedad; severidad.
har·vest [hárvɪst] *s.* cosecha; siega, agosto; recolección; recogida; *v.* cosechar; segar.
hash [hæʃ] *s.* picadillo.
haste [hest] *s.* prisa; apresuramiento; **in —** de prisa; **to make —** darse prisa, apresurarse; *Am.* apurarse.
has·ten [hésn̩] *v.* apresurar(se), precipitar(se); darse prisa.
hast·i·ly [héstlɪ] *adv.* aprisa, de prisa, apresuradamente, precipitadamente.
hast·y [héstɪ] *adj.* apresurado; precipitado.
hat [hæt] *s.* sombrero.
hatch [hætʃ] *v.* empollar; criar pollos; idear, maquinar; *s.* cría, nidada, pollada; escotillón,

trampa (*puerta en el suelo*); — **way** escotilla.
hatch·et [hǽtʃɪt] *s.* hacha; **to bury the** — echar pelillos a la mar, olvidar rencores o enemistades.
hate [het] *s.* odio; aborrecimiento; *v.* odiar; aborrecer; detestar.
hate·ful [hétfəl] *adj.* odioso, aborrecible.
ha·tred [hétrɪd] *s.* odio, aversión.
haugh·ti·ly [hɔ́tlɪ] *adv.* con altivez, altaneramente, arrogantemente.
haugh·ti·ness [hɔ́tɪnɪs] *s.* altanería, altivez.
haugh·ty [hɔ́tɪ] *adj.* altivo, altanero, arrogante.
haul [hɔl] *v.* (*transport*) acarrear, transportar; (*pull*) jalar (*halar*); tirar de; (*drag*) arrastrar; **to — down the flag** arriar (*o* bajar) la bandera; *s.* acarreo; transporte; tirón, estirón; buena pesca; ganancia, botín; (*round-up*) redada.
haunch [hɔntʃ] *s.* anca.
haunt [hɔnt] *v.* frecuentar a menudo; andar por, vagar por (*como fantasma o espectro*); **that idea -s me** me persigue esa idea; **-ed house** casa de espantos, fantasmas o aparecidos; *s.* guarida.
have [hæv] *v.* tener; poseer; haber (*v. aux.*); **to — a suit made** mandar hacer un traje; **to — a look at** dar un vistazo a, echar una mirada a; **to — to** tener que; **I'll not — it so** no lo toleraré, no lo permitiré; **what did she — on?** ¿qué vestido llevaba (puesto)?
ha·ven [hévən] *s.* asilo, abrigo, refugio; puerto.
hav·oc [hǽvək] *s.* estrago, estropicio, ruina; **to cause** — hacer estragos.
hawk [hɔk] *s.* halcón; *v.* pregonar (*mercancías*).
haw·thorn [hɔ́θɔrn] *s.* espino.
hay [he] *s.* heno, paja, hierba seca; — **fever** catarro asmático.
hay·loft [hélɔft] *s.* henil, pajar.
hay·stack [héstæk] *s.* montón de heno o paja.
haz·ard [hǽzɚd] *s.* azar; riesgo, peligro; estorbo, obstáculo (*en el campo de golf*); *v.* arriesgar, aventurar.
haz·ard·ous [hǽzɚdəs] *adj.* peligroso.
haze [hez] *s.* bruma, neblina, niebla; *v.* atormentar, hostigar (*con bromas estudiantiles*).
ha·zel [hézl] *s.* avellano; —**nut** avellana; *adj.* de avellano; avellanado, color de avellana.
haz·y [hézɪ] *adj.* (*weather*) nublado, brumoso; (*mind*) confuso.
he [hi] *pron. pers.* él; — **who** el que, quien; **he-goat** macho cabrío.
head [hɛd] *s.* cabeza; cabecera (*de cama*); jefe; — **slot** (*computer*) ranura de acceso; — **of hair** cabellera; **game of -s or tails** juego de cara y cruz, juego de las chapas, *Ven., Col., Andes, Ch.* juego de cara y sello; *Méx.* juego de águila y sol; **to be out of one's** — delirar, estar delirante; **to come to a** — madurar; supurar (*un absceso*); **to keep one's** — conservar la calma, no perder la cabeza; **it goes to his** — le desvanece; se le sube a la cabeza; *adj.* principal, primero; de proa, de frente; **head-on** de frente; *v.* encabezar; ir a la cabeza de; acaudillar; mandar, dirigir; **to — off** atajar; detener, refrenar; **to — towards** dirigirse a, encaminarse a.
head·ache [hɛ́dek] *s.* dolor de cabeza.
head·dress [hɛ́ddrɛs] *s.* tocado, adorno para la cabeza.
head·gear [hɛ́dgɪr] *s.* sombrero, gorro, gorra; tocado, toca (*de mujer*); cabezada (*de guarnición para caballo*).
head·ing [hɛ́dɪŋ] *s.* encabezamiento, título.
head·land [hɛ́dlənd] *s.* cabo, promontorio.
head·light [hɛ́dlaɪt] *s.* linterna delantera, faro delantero.
head·line [hɛ́dlaɪn] *s.* título, encabezado.
head·long [hɛ́dlɔ́ŋ] *adv.* de cabeza; precipitadamente.
head·quar·ters [hɛ́dkwɔ́rtɚz] *s.* cuartel general; jefatura; oficina principal; *Arg.* sede central.
head·set [hɛ́dsɛt] *s.* receptor de cabeza.
head·strong [hɛ́dstrɔŋ] *adj.* testarudo, porfiado, obstinado.
head·way [hɛ́dwe] *s.* progreso, avance; **to make** — avanzar, adelantar, progresar.
heal [hil] *v.* curar; sanar; cicatrizar.
health [hɛlθ] *s.* salud; sanidad; salubridad.
health·ful [hɛ́lθfəl] *adj.* sano; salubre; saludable.
health·ful·ness [hɛ́lθfəlnɪs] *s.* salubridad; sanidad.
health·y [hɛ́lθɪ] *adj.* sano; saludable.
heap [hip] *s.* montón; pila; *v.* amontonar; apilar.
hear [hɪr] *v.* (*listen*) oír; escuchar; (*get news*) tener noticias; **to — about someone** oír hablar de alguien; **to — from someone** tener noticias de alguien; **to — of** saber de, tener noticias de, oír hablar de; **I -d that . . .** oí decir que . . .
heard [hɝd] *pret. & p.p. de* **to hear.**
hear·er [hírɚ] *s.* oyente.
hear·ing [hírɪŋ] *s.* (*sense*) oído; (*trial*) audiencia; examen de testigos; **hard of** — medio sordo, algo sordo; **within** — al alcance del oído; — **aid** aparato auditivo.
hear·say [hírse] *s.* hablilla, rumor; **by** — de oídas.
hearse [hɝs] *s.* carroza fúnebre.
heart [hɑrt] *s.* (*organ*) corazón; (*spirit*) ánimo; **at** — en realidad, en el fondo; **from the bottom of one's** — de corazón, con toda el alma; con toda sinceridad; **to learn by** — aprender de memoria; **to take** — cobrar ánimo; **to take to** — tomar en serio; tomar a pecho; — **attack** ataque cardíaco; — **of lettuce, cabbage** cogollo.
heart·ache [hɑ́rtek] *s.* dolor del corazón; angustia, pesar, congoja.
heart·bro·ken [hɑ́rtbrokən] *adj.* traspasado de dolor, acongojado, angustiado; desengañado.
heart·en [hɑ́rtn̩] *v.* animar.
heart·felt [hɑ́rtfɛlt] *adj.* sentido, cordial, sincero; **my — sympathy** mi más sentido pésame.
hearth [hɑrθ] *s.* hogar; fogón.
heart·i·ly [hɑ́rtlɪ] *adv.* de corazón; cordialmente; de buena gana; **to eat** — comer con apetito; comer bien (*o* mucho).
heart·less [hɑ́rtlɪs] *adj.* de mal corazón; cruel; insensible.
heart·rend·ing [hɑ́rtrɛndɪŋ] *adj.* angustioso; agudo.
heart·y [hɑ́rtɪ] *adj.* sincero, cordial; sano, fuerte; — **food** alimento nutritivo; **a — laugh** una buena carcajada; — **meal** comida abundante.
heat [hit] *s.* (*hot*) calor; ardor (*emotion*) vehemencia; celo (*ardor sexual de la hembra*); calefacción (*para las habitaciones*); corrida, carrera (*de prueba*); *v.* calentar(se); acalorar(se).
heat·er [hítɚ] *s.* calentador; calorífero.
hea·then [híðən] *s.* pagano, gentil, idólatra; pagano; *adj.* pagano; irreligioso.
heat·ing [hítɪŋ] *s.* calefacción.
heave [hiv] *v.* levantar, alzar (*con esfuerzo*); arrojar, lanzar; exhalar (*un suspiro*); jalar (*un cable*); jadear; basquear, hacer esfuerzos por vomitar.
heav·en [hɛ́vən] *s.* cielo.
heav·en·ly [hɛ́vənlɪ] *adj.* celeste; celestial; divino.
heav·i·ly [hɛ́vlɪ] *adv.* pesadamente, lentamente; copiosamente, excesivamente.
heav·i·ness [hɛ́vɪnɪs] *s.* pesadez, pesantez; opresión, abatimiento.
heav·y [hɛvɪ] *adj.* (*weight*) pesado; (*thick*) grueso; (*coarse*) burdo; (*oppressive*) opresivo; — **rain**

aguacero recio o fuerte; — **duty** de servicio pesado; **with a — heart** abatido, acongojado.
heav·y·weight [hévɪwet] *s. & adj.* peso pesado (*fuerte*).
Hebrew [híbru] *adj.* hebreo.
hectare [héktɛr] *s.* hectárea.
hec·tic [héktɪk] *adj.* febril; inquieto.
hedge [hɛdʒ] *s.* seto; vallado, barrera; *v.* cercar; poner valla o seto a; evitar o evadir contestaciones.
hedge·hog [hédʒhɑg] *s.* erizo.
he·don·ism [hídənɪzm] *s.* hedonismo.
heed [hid] *v.* atender; hacer caso; prestar atención; *s.* atención, cuidado; **to pay — to** prestar atención a; hacer caso de.
heed·less [hídlɪs] *adj.* descuidado; desatento.
heel [hil] *s.* talón (*del pie o de una media*); tacón (*del zapato*); **head over -s** patas arriba; *v.* poner tacón a; poner talón a.
he·gem·o·ny [hɪdʒémənɪ] *s.* hegemonía.
heif·er [héfɚ] *s.* novilla, vaquilla.
height [haɪt] *s.* altura; elevación; — **of folly** colmo de la locura.
height·en [háɪtn̩] *v.* avivar; aumentar(se); realzar.
hei·nous [hénəs] *adj.* aborrecible, odioso; malvado.
heir [ɛr] *s.* heredero.
heir·ess [érɪs] *s.* heredera.
held [hɛld] *pret. & p.p. de* **to hold.**
hel·i·cop·ter [héləkɑptɚ] *s.* helicóptero.
he·li·um [hílɪəm] *s.* helio.
hell [hɛl] *s.* infierno.
hel·lo [hɛló] *interj.* ¡hola!; ¡halo!
helm [hɛlm] *s.* timón.
hel·met [hélmɪt] *s.* yelmo.
help [hɛlp] *s.* (*aid*) ayuda; auxilio; remedio; alivio; (*employee*) criado o criados, empleado o empleados; *v.* ayudar, asistir; auxiliar; remediar; servir (*algo de comer*); **to — down** ayudar a bajar; **— yourself** sírvase Vd. (*de comer o beber*); tómelo Vd., está a la disposición de Vd.; **he cannot — it** no puede evitarlo; **he cannot — doing it** no puede menos de hacerlo; **he cannot — but come** no puede menos de venir.
help·er [hélpɚ] *s.* ayudante, asistente.
help·ful [hélpfəl] *adj.* útil, servicial; provechoso.
help·ing [hélpɪŋ] *s.* ayuda; porción (*que se sirve en la mesa*).
help·less [hélplɪs] *adj.* (*defenseless*) desamparado; (*handicapped*) desvalido; imposibilitado; incapaz; (*confused*) perplejo, indeciso (*sin saber qué hacer*); **a — situation** una situación irremediable.
help·less·ness [hélplɪsnɪs] *s.* incapacidad; incompetencia; impotencia, debilidad; abandono, desamparo.
hem [hɛm] *s.* dobladillo, bastilla; *v.* dobladillar, bastillar, hacer dobladillos en (*la ropa*); **to — in** rodear, cercar; **to — and haw** toser y retoser (*fingidamente*); tartamudear, vacilar.
hem·i·sphere [héməsfɪr] *s.* hemisferio.
hem·lock [hémlɑk] *s.* cicuta (*hierba venenosa*); abeto americano.
he·mo·glo·bin [hímoglobɪn] *s.* hemoglobina.
hem·or·rhage [hémərɪdʒ] *s.* hemorragia.
hem·or·rhoids [hémərɔɪdz] *s.* hemorroides.
hemp [hɛmp] *s.* cáñamo, *Am.* sisal.
hem·stitch [hémstɪtʃ] *s.* dobladillo de ojo; *v.* hacer (*o* echar) dobladillo de ojo.
hen [hɛn] *s.* gallina; ave hembra.
hence [hɛns] *adv.* de (*o* desde) aquí; desde ahora; por lo tanto, por consiguiente; **a week** — de hoy en ocho días; de aquí a una semana.
hence·forth [hɛnsfórθ] *adv.* de aquí en adelante; de hoy en adelante; desde ahora.
hep·a·ti·tis [hɛpətáɪtɪs] *s.* hepatitis.
her [hɝ] *pron.* la; le, a ella; ella (*con preposición*); *adj.* su (sus), de ella.
her·ald [hérəld] *s.* heraldo; anunciador, proclamador; precursor; *v.* anunciar, proclamar, publicar.
her·ald·ry [hérəldrɪ] *s.* heráldica.
herb [ɝb] *s.* hierba (yerba).
herd [hɝd] *s.* (*animals*) hato; rebaño; manada; tropel; tropilla; (*cattle*) ganado; (*people*) muchedumbre; **the common** — el populacho, la chusma; *v.* reunir, juntar (*el ganado*); ir en manadas, ir juntos.
herds·man [hɝdzmən] *s.* vaquero, vaquerizo; pastor.
here [hɪr] *adv.* aquí; acá; — **it is** aquí está, helo aquí, aquí lo tiene Vd., — **is to you!** ¡a la salud de Vd.!; **that is neither — nor there** eso no viene al caso; (*to call a dog*) ¡cuz! ¡toma! (*a cat*) ¡mis! ¡mis!
here·af·ter [hɪrǽftɚ] *adv.* de aquí (*o* de hoy) en adelante; desde ahora en adelante; en lo futuro; *s.* **the** — la otra vida.
here·by [hɪrbáɪ] *adv.* por este medio; mediante la presente, por la presente; con estas palabras.
he·red·i·tar·y [hərédətɛrɪ] *adj.* hereditario.
he·red·i·ty [hərédətɪ] *s.* herencia.
here·in [hɪrín] *adv.* aquí dentro; en esto.
her·e·sy [hérəsɪ] *s.* herejía.
her·e·tic [hérətɪk] *s.* hereje.
here·to·fore [hɪrtəfór] *adv.* hasta ahora, hasta el presente.
here·with [hɪrwíθ] *adv.* aquí dentro, con esto, adjunto, incluso.
her·i·tage [hérətɪdʒ] *s.* herencia.
her·met·ic [hɚmétɪk] *adj.* hermético.
her·mit [hɝmɪt] *s.* ermitaño.
her·ni·a [hɝnɪə] *s.* hernia, ruptura, relajamiento.
he·ro [híro] *s.* héroe; protagonista.
he·ro·ic [hɪróɪk] *adj.* heroico.
her·o·ine [hérоɪn] *s.* heroína.
her·o·ism [héroɪzəm] *s.* heroísmo.
he·ron [hérən] *s.* garza.
her·ring [hérɪŋ] *s.* arenque.
hers [hɝz] *pron. pos.* suyo (suya, suyos, suyas), de ella; el suyo (la suya, los suyos, las suyas); el (la los, las) de ella; **a friend of** — un amigo suyo.
her·self [hɚsélf] *pron.* ella misma; se (*como reflexivo*); **by** — sola; por sí (sola); **she — did it** ella misma lo hizo; **she talks to** — ella habla para sí, habla consigo misma, habla para sus adentros, habla sola.
hes·i·tant [hézətənt] = **hesitating.**
hes·i·tate [hézətet] *v.* vacilar; (*stutter*) titubear; (*doubt*) dudar.
hes·i·tat·ing [hésətetɪŋ] *adj.* vacilante; indeciso; irresoluto; **-ly** *adv.* con vacilación.
hes·i·ta·tion [hɛzətéʃən] *s.* vacilación; titubeo, duda.
het·er·o·ge·ne·ous [hɛtɚədʒíniəs] *adj.* heterogéneo.
hew [hju] *v.* tajar, cortar; picar (*piedra*); labrar (*madera, piedra*).
hewn [hjun] *p.p. de* **to hew.**
hey [he] *interj.* ¡he!; ¡oiga!; ¡oye!
hi·a·tus [haɪétəs] *s.* hiato.
hi·ber·nate [háɪbɚnet] *v.* invernar.
hic·cup, hic·cough [híkʌp] *s.* hipo; *v.* hipar, tener hipo.
hick·o·ry [híkərɪ] *s.* nogal americano; — **nut** nuez (*del nogal americano*).
hid [hɪd] *pret. & p.p. de* **to hide.**
hid·den [hídn̩] *p.p. de* **to hide;** *adj.* oculto, escondido.
hide [haɪd] *v.* ocultar(se); esconder(se); **to — from**

esconderse de, recatarse de; *s.* cuero, piel; **to play — and seek** jugar al escondite.
hid·e·ous [hídɪəs] *adj.* horrendo, horripilante, feote.
hi·er·ar·chy [háɪərɑrkɪ] *s.* jerarquía.
hi·er·o·glyph·ic [haɪərəglífɪk] *adj.* & *s.* jeroglífico.
high [haɪ] *adj.* alto; **— altar** altar mayor; **— and dry** enjuto; en seco; solo, abandonado; **— antiquity** antigüedad remota; **— explosive** explosivo de gran potencia; **— tide** plenamar; **— wind** ventarrón, viento fuerte; **— -level language** lenguaje de alto nivel; **in — gear** en directa, en tercera velocidad; **two feet —** dos pies de alto; **it is — time that** ya es hora de que; **to be in — spirits** estar muy animado; *adv.* alto; a precio subido; en alto; **to look — and low** buscar por todas partes; **high-grade** de calidad superior; **high-handed** arbitrario, despótico; **high-minded** magnánimo; orgulloso; **high-sounding** altisonante, rimbombante; **high-strung** muy tenso; **— school** escuela secundaria; **high-powered** de alta potencia; **— seas** alta mar.
high·jack [háɪdʒæk] *v.* asaltar a mano armada.
high·land [háɪlənd] *s.* tierra montañosa; **the Highlands** las montañas de Escocia.
high·light [háɪlaɪt] *s.* lo más notable.
high·ly [háɪlɪ] *adv.* altamente; sumamente, muy; **— paid** muy bien pagado.
high·ness [háɪnɪs] *s.* altura; elevación; Alteza (*título*).
high·way [háɪwe] *s.* camino real; carretera, calzada.
high·way·man [háɪwemən] *s.* forajido, salteador de caminos, bandido.
hike [haɪk] *s.* caminata, paseo largo, *Am.* andada; *v.* dar (*o* echar) una caminata.
hill [hɪl] *s.* colina, collado, cerro; (*pile*) montoncillo de tierra; *Andes, Am.* loma; **ant —** hormiguero; **down—** cuesta abajo; **up—** cuesta arriba.
hill·ock [hílək] *s.* collado, otero, montecillo.
hill·side [hílsaɪd] *s.* ladera.
hill·top [híltɑp] *s.* cumbre, cima (*de una colina*).
hill·y [hílɪ] *adj.* montuoso; accidentado.
hilt [hɪlt] *s.* empuñadura, puño (*de una espada o daga*).
him [hɪm] *pron.* le; lo; él (*con preposición*).
him·self [hɪmsélf] *pron.* él mismo; se (*como reflexivo*); a sí mismo; *véase* **herself.**
hind [haɪnd] *adj.* trasero; posterior; *s.* cierva; **—most** *adj.* último, postrero.
hin·der [híndə] *v.* estorbar, impedir, obstruir.
hin·drance [híndrəns] *s.* estorbo, obstáculo, impedimento.
hinge [hɪndʒ] *s.* gozne; bisagra; *v.* engoznar, poner goznes; **to — on** girar sobre; depender de.
hint [hɪnt] *s.* indirecta, insinuación; sugestión; **not to take the —** no darse por entendido; *v.* insinuar, intimar, sugerir indirectamente.
hip [hɪp] *s.* cadera.
hip·po·pot·a·mus [hɪpəpɑ́təməs] *s.* hipopótamo.
hire [haɪr] *s.* (*rent*) alquiler; (*pay*) paga, sueldo; *v.* alquilar; emplear, dar empleo, *C.A., Ven., Col* enganchar, *S.A.* conchabar; **to — out** alquilarse, ponerse a servir a otro.
his [hɪz] *pron. pos.* suyo (suya, suyos, suyas), de él; el suyo (la suya, los suyos, las suyas); el (la, los, las) de él; **a friend of —** un amigo suyo; *adj.* su (sus), de él.
hiss [hɪs] *s.* silbido, chiflido; siseo; *v.* sisear, silbar, chiflar.
his·ta·mine [hístəmin] *s.* histamina.
his·to·ri·an [hɪstórɪən] *s.* historiador.
his·tor·ic [hɪstɔ́rɪk] *adj.* histórico.
his·tor·i·cal [hɪstɔ́rɪkl] *adj.* histórico.
his·to·ry [hístrɪ] *s.* historia.
his·tri·on·ics [hɪstrɪɑ́nɪks] *s.* histrionismo.
hit [hɪt] *v.* pegar, golpear; dar (*un golpe*); dar en (*o* con); chocar; (*press, type*) presionar, pulsar, tocar, oprimir; **they — it off well** se llevan bien, congenian; **to — the mark** acertar, atinar, dar en el blanco; **to — upon** dar con; encontrarse con, encontrar por casualidad; *pret. & p.p. de* **to hit;** *s.* golpe; choque; golpe de fortuna; pulla, dicharacho; **to be a great —** ser un gran éxito; **to make a — with someone** caerle en gracia a una persona; **hit-and-run** *adj.* que abandona a su víctima atropellada.
hitch [hɪtʃ] *v.* atar, amarrar; enganchar; (*yoke*) uncir (*bueyes*), (*pull*) dar un tirón; **to — one's chair nearer to** acercar su silla a; *s.* tirón; obstáculo, impedimento, tropiezo; enganche, enganchamiento.
hitch·hike [hítʃhaɪk] *v.* viajar de gorra (*en automóvil*), *Méx.* irse o viajar de mosca; *Ch., Ríopl.* hacer dedo, ir a dedo; *Esp.* viajar por autostop.
hith·er [híðə] *adv.* acá; **— and thither** acá y allá.
hith·er·to [híðətú] *adv.* hasta aquí, hasta ahora, hasta hoy.
hive [haɪv] *s.* colmena; enjambre; **-s** ronchas (*de la piel*).
hoard [hord] *s.* tesoro escondido; acumulamiento secreto de provisiones; *v.* atesorar, guardar (*con avaricia*); acumular secretamente.
hoarse [hors] *adj.* bronco, áspero, ronco.
hoarse·ness [hórsnɪs] *s.* ronquera; carraspera.
hoar·y [hórɪ] *adj.* cano, encanecido, canoso.
hoax [hoks] *s.* engaño, estafa.
hob·ble [hɑ́bl] *v.* (*limp*) cojear, renquear; (*tie*) maniatar o manear (*un animal*); (*impede*) impedir, estorbar; *s.* cojera; traba, maniota o manea (*cuerda con que se atan las manos de una bestia*).
hob·by [hɑ́bɪ] *s.* afición; trabajo hecho por afición (*no por obligación*).
ho·bo [hóbo] *s.* vagabundo.
hodge·podge [hɑ́dʒpɑdʒ] *s.* mezcolanza, baturrillo.
hoe [ho] *s.* azada, azadón; *v.* cavar, escardar, limpiar con azadón.
hog [hɑg] *s.* puerco, cerdo, cochino; *S.A.* chancho; *C.A.* tunco, cochi; *adj.* porcino; *v.* apropiárselo todo.
hoist [hɔɪst] *v.* alzar, levantar; (*flag*) izar (*la bandera, las velas*); *s.* elevador, *Am.* malacate; grúa, montacargas.
hold [hold] *v.* tener(se); retener; detener; tener cabida para; sostener; mantener(se); opinar; celebrar (*una reunión, etc.*); ocupar (*un puesto*); ser válido (*un argumento o regla*); **to — back someone** detener (*o* refrenar) a alguien; **to — forth** perorar, hablar largamente; **to — in place** sujetar; **to — off** mantener(se) a distancia; mantenerse alejado; **to — on** agarrar(se); asir(se); persistir; **— on!** ¡agárrese bien!; ¡deténgase! ¡pare!; **to — someone responsible** hacerle a uno responsable; **to — someone to his word** obligar a uno a cumplir su palabra; **to — oneself erect** tenerse o andar derecho; **to — one's own** mantenerse firme; **to — one's tongue** callarse; **to — out** continuar, durar; mantenerse firme; **to — over** aplazar; durar; continuar en un cargo; **to — still** estarse quieto o callado; **to — tight** apretar; **to — to one's promise** cumplir con la promesa; **to — up** levantar, alzar; detener; asaltar, atracar (*para robar*); **how much does it — ?** ¿cuánto le cabe? *s.* agarro; dominio; influencia; autoridad; bodega (*de un barco*); cabina de carga (*de un aeroplano*); **to**

get — of asir, agarrar; atrapar; to take — of coger, agarrar, asir.
hold·er [hóldɚ] *s.* (*person*) tenedor, posesor; (*device*) receptáculo; cojinillo (*para coger un trasto caliente*); **cigarette** — boquilla; **pen**— portaplumas.
hold·up [hóldʌp] *s.* asalto, atraco.
hole [hol] *s.* agujero; abertura; hoyo, (*hollow*) hueco, cavidad; (*pothole*) bache (*de un camino*); **swimming** — charco, remanso; **to be in a** — hallarse en un apuro o aprieto.
hol·i·day [hɑ́lədе] *s.* día de fiesta, día festivo, festividad; **-s** días de fiesta; vacaciones.
ho·li·ness [hólɪnɪs] *s.* santidad.
ho·lis·tic [holístɪk] *adj.* global.
hol·low [hɑ́lo] *adj.* (*empty*) hueco; vacío, (*concave*) cóncavo; hundido; (*insincere*) falso; *s.* hueco; hoyo; cavidad; concavidad; depresión; cañada, hondonada; *v.* ahuecar; excavar; ahondar.
hol·ly [hɑ́lɪ] *s.* agrifolio, acebo.
hol·ster [hólstɚ] *s.* pistolera, funda (*de pistola*).
ho·ly [hólɪ] *adj.* santo; sagrado, sacro; — **water** agua bendita.
hom·age [hɑ́mɪdʒ] *s.* homenaje; reverencia, acatamiento; **to do** — acatar, rendir homenaje, honrar.
home [hom] *s.* casa, hogar; habitación, domicilio; **at** — en casa; *adj.* doméstico; casero; — **office** oficina matriz o central; — **rule** autonomía; — **run** *Méx., C.A., Ven., Col, Carib.* jonrón (*en béisbol*); — **stretch** último trecho (*de una carrera*); — **computer** computadora casera; *adv.* a casa; en casa; **to strike** — herir en lo vivo; dar en el clavo o en el blanco.
home·land [hómlænd] *s.* tierra natal, suelo patrio.
home·less [hómlɪs] *adj.* sin casa; destituido.
home·like [hómlaɪk] *adj.* hogareño, cómodo.
home·ly [hómlɪ] *adj.* feo; llano; (*simple*) sencillo; (*domestic*) casero, doméstico.
home·made [hómméd] *adj.* hecho en casa; doméstico, nacional, del país.
home·sick [hómsɪk] *adj.* nostálgico.
home·sick·ness [hómsɪknɪs] *s.* nostalgia.
home·stead [hómstɛd] *s.* heredad; casa y terrenos adyacentes.
home·ward [hómwɚd] *adv.* a casa; hacia la patria; — **voyage** retorno, viaje de vuelta.
home·work [hómwɝk] *s.* trabajo de casa; trabajo hecho en casa.
hom·i·cide [hɑ́məsaɪd] *s.* homicidio; homicida, asesino.
ho·mo·ge·ne·ous [homədʒínɪəs] *adj.* homogéneo.
ho·mog·e·nize [homɑ́dʒənaɪz] *v.* homogenizar.
ho·mo·sex·u·al [homəsɛ́kʃjʊl] *adj. & s.* homosexual.
hone [hon] *v.* amolar, asentar, afilar; *s.* piedra de afilar.
hon·est [ɑ́nɪst] *adj.* honrado, recto; genuino; — **goods** mercancías genuinas; **-ly** *adv.* honradamente; de veras.
hon·es·ty [ɑ́nɪstɪ] *s.* honradez, rectitud.
hon·ey [hʌ́nɪ] *s.* miel; dulzura; querido, querida.
hon·ey·comb [hʌ́nɪkom] *s.* panal.
hon·eyed [hʌ́nɪd] *adj.* meloso; dulce; melífluo.
hon·ey·moon [hʌ́nɪmun] *s.* luna de miel; viaje de novios, viaje de bodas; *v.* pasar la luna de miel.
hon·ey·suck·le [hʌ́nɪsʌkl] *s.* madreselva.
honk [hɔŋk] *s.* bocinazo, pitazo (*de automóvil*); (*goose*) graznido (*voz del ganso*); *v.* sonar la bocina; graznar.
hon·or [ɑ́nɚ] *s.* honor; honra; señoría (*título*); **upon my** — sobre mi palabra; *v.* honrar; dar honra.
hon·or·a·ble [ɑ́nərəbl] *adj.* honorable; honroso; honrado.
hon·or·ar·y [ɑ́nərɛrɪ] *adj.* honorario, honorífico.
hood [hʊd] *s.* capucha, caperuza; capirote, cubierta (*del motor*); *v.* encapuchar, encapirotar.
hood·lum [húdləm] *s.* maleante; antisocial.
hoof [hʊf] *s.* casco, pezuña; pata (*de caballo, toro, etc.*); (*half of cloven hoof*) pesuño.
hook [hʊk] *s.* gancho, garfio; (*fish*) anzuelo (*para pescar*); — **and eye** corchete; macho y hembra, **by** — **or crook** por la buena o por la mala, por angas o por mangas; **on his own** — por su propia cuenta; *v.* enganchar(se); abrochar(se); pescar, coger con anzuelo; robar, hurtar.
hook·y [hʊ́kɪ]: **to play** — hacer novillos, *Carib.* capear la escuela, *Méx.* pintar venado, *C.A., Ven., Col.* jubilarse; *Ríopl.* hacerse la rata (*la rabona*).
hoop [hup] *s.* aro; argolla; *v.* poner aro a; ceñir, cercar.
hoot [hut] *v.* (*owl*) ulular; (*make fun of*) rechiflar, ridiculizar; *s.* alarido, chillido.
hoot·ing [hútɪŋ] *s.* grita, rechifla.
hop [hɑp] *s.* salto, brinco; (*dance*) baile; *v.* saltar; brincar.
hope [hop] *s.* esperanza; *v.* esperar; **to** — **for** esperar; **to** — **against** — esperar desesperando; esperar lo que no puede ser, esperar lo imposible.
hope·ful [hópfəl] *adj.* esperanzado, lleno de esperanza; **a young** — un joven prometedor; **-ly** *adv.* con esperanza; con ansia; lleno de esperanza.
hope·less [hóplɪs] *adj.* sin esperanza, falto de esperanza, desesperanzado; desesperado; irremediable; — **cause** causa perdida; — **illness** enfermedad incurable; **it is** — no tiene remedio; **-ly** *adv.* sin esperanza, sin remedio.
hope·less·ness [hóplɪsnɪs] *s.* falta de esperanza; falta de remedio; desesperanza, desaliento.
horde [hord] *s.* horda; muchedumbre, gentío; enjambre.
ho·ri·zon [həráɪzn̩] *s.* horizonte.
hor·i·zon·tal [hɔrəzɑ́ntl] *adj.* horizontal.
hor·mone [hɔ́rmon] *s.* hormona.
horn [hɔrn] *s.* (*animal*) cuerno; asta; cacho; (*automobile*) bocina, klaxon, trompa; (*musical*) corneta; trompeta; — **of plenty** cuerno de la abundancia; *v.* acornear, dar cornadas; **to** — **in** extremeterse; — **tip** piton.
hor·net [hɔ́rnɪt] *s.* avispón; **-'s nest** avispero.
hor·o·scope [hɔ́rəskop] *s.* horóscopo.
hor·ri·ble [hɔ́rəbl] *adj.* horrible; **horribly** *adv.* horriblemente.
hor·rid [hɔ́rɪd] *adj.* horrendo, horrible.
hor·ri·fy [hɔ́rəfaɪ] *v.* horrorizar, aterrorizar, espantar.
hor·ror [hɔ́rɚ] *s.* horror.
hors d'oeuvre [ɔrdɝ́vrə] *s.* entremés; bocadillos.
horse [hɔrs] *s.* caballo; caballete (*de madera*), borriquete (*de carpinteros*); **saddle** — caballo de silla; — **dealer** chalán; — **race** carrera de caballos; — **sense** sentido común.
horse·back [hɔ́rsbæk] *s.* lomo de caballo; **to ride** — montar a caballo, cabalgar, jinetear.
horse·fly [hɔ́rsflaɪ] *s.* tábano, mosca de caballo.
horse·laugh [hɔ́rslæf] *s.* carcajada, risotada.
horse·man [hɔ́rsmən] *s.* jinete.
horse·man·ship [hɔ́rsmənʃɪp] *s.* equitación.
horse·pow·er [hɔ́rspaʊɚ] *s.* caballo de fuerza.
horse·rad·ish [hɔ́rsrǽdɪʃ] *s.* rábano picante.
horse·shoe [hɔ́rsʃu] *s.* herradura.
hose [hoz] *s.* medias; manga o manguera (*para regar*); **men's** — calcetines.
ho·sier·y [hóʒrɪ] *s.* medias; calcetines; calcetería

(*negocio*); — **shop** calcetería.
hos·pi·ta·ble [hɑ́spɪtəbl] *adj*. hospitalario.
hos·pi·tal [hɑ́spɪtl] *s*. hospital.
hos·pi·tal·i·ty [hɑ̀spɪtǽlətɪ] *s*. hospitalidad.
host [host] *s*. huésped (*el que hospeda*), anfitrión (*el que convida*); hospedero, mesonero; hueste; ejército, multitud; hostia; **sacred** — hostia consagrada.
hos·tage [hɑ́stɪdʒ] *s*. rehén (*persona que queda como prenda en poder del enemigo*).
hos·tel·ry [hɑ́stəlrɪ] *s*. hostería.
host·ess [hóstɪs] *s*. huéspeda (*la que hospeda o convida*).
hos·tile [hɑ́stl] *adj*. hostil.
hos·til·i·ty [hɑstɪ́lətɪ] *s*. hostilidad.
hot [hɑt] *adj*. caliente; caluroso; cálido; (*spicy*) picante (*como el pimentón, chile, ají, etc.*); (*angry*) furioso; fresco, (*recent*) reciente; — **bed** semillero; **hot-headed** enojadizo, impetuoso; exaltado; — **house** invernáculo, invernadero; **it is** — **today** hace calor hoy.
ho·tel [hotɛ́l] *s*. hotel.
ho·tel-keep·er [hotɛ́lkípə˞] *s*. hotelero.
hot·ly [hɑ́tlɪ] *adv*. calurosamente, con vehemencia.
hound [haʊnd] *s*. perro de busca, lebrel, galgo, sabueso, podenco; *v*. acosar, perseguir; azuzar, incitar.
hour [hʊr] *s*. hora; — **hand** horario.
hour·ly [áʊrlɪ] *adv*. por horas; a cada hora; a menudo; *adj*. frecuente; por horas.
house [haʊs] *s*. (*residence*) casa, domicilio; (*legislature*) cámara, asamblea legislativa; **country** — casa de campo; **a full** — un lleno completo (*en al teatro*); [haʊz] *v*. alojar; hospedar.
house·hold [háʊshold] *s*. casa, familia; *adj*. casero; doméstico.
house·keep·er [háʊskipə˞] *s*. casera; ama de llaves; **to be a good** — ser una mujer hacendosa.
house·keep·ing [háʊskipɪŋ] *s*. gobierno de casa; quehaceres domésticos.
house·top [háʊstɑp] *s*. techumbre, tejado.
house·wife [háʊswaɪf] *s*. mujer de su casa; madre de familia; ama de casa.
house·work [háʊswɝk] *s*. trabajo de casa; quehaceres domésticos.
hous·ing [háʊzɪŋ] *s*. viviendas; programa de construcción de viviendas; (*computer*) unidad, carcasa, mueble.
hove [hov] *pret. & p.p. de* **to heave.**
hov·el [hʌ́vl] *s*. choza, cabaña, *Carib., Ven.* bohío, *Méx*. jacal; cobertizo; *Ríopl*. tapera.
hov·er [hʌ́və˞] *v*. cernerse (*como un pájaro*); vacilar; **to** — **around** revolotear; rondar.
how [haʊ] *adv*. cómo; — **beautiful!** ¡qué hermoso!; — **early (late, soon)?** ¿cuándo? ¿a qué hora?; — **far is it?** ¿a qué distancia está? ¿cuánto dista de aquí?; — **long?** ¿cuánto tiempo?; — **many?** ¿cuántos?; — **much is it?** ¿cuánto es? ¿a cómo se vende? ¿cuál es el precio?; — **old are you?** ¿cuántos años tiene Vd.?; **no matter** — **much** por mucho que; **he knows** — **difficult it is** él sabe lo difícil que es; él sabe cuán difícil es.
how·ev·er [haʊɛ́və˞] *adv. & conj.* sin embargo, no obstante, con todo, empero; — **difficult it may be** por muy difícil que sea; — **much** por mucho que.
howl [haʊl] *s*. aullido, alarido, chillido, grito; *v*. aullar; chillar, dar alaridos; gritar.
hub [hʌb] *s*. cubo (*de una rueda*); eje, centro de actividad.
hub·bub [hʌ́bʌb] *s*. ajetreo; barullo.
huck·ster [hʌ́kstə˞] *s*. vendedor ambulante.
hud·dle [hʌ́dl] *s*. montón, confusión, tropel; **to be in a** — estar agrupados (*en futbol para planear una jugada*); **to get in a** — agruparse (*para aconsejarse o planear algo*); *v*. amontonar(se); acurrucarse.
hue [hju] *s*. tinte, matiz.
huff [hʌf] *s*. enojo, rabieta; **to get into a** — enojarse.
hug [hʌg] *v*. abrazar, estrechar; **to** — **the coast** costear; *s*. abrazo fuerte.
huge [hjudʒ] *adj*. enorme; descomunal.
hull [hʌl] *s*. casco (*de una nave*); armazón (*de una aeronave*); vaina, hollejo (*de ciertas legumbres*); *v*. mondar, pelar desvainar, deshollejar.
hum [hʌm] *v*. canturrear (*o* canturriar), tararear; zumbar (*dícese de insectos, maquinaria, etc.*); **to** — **to sleep** arrullar; *s*. canturreo, tarareo; zumbido; *interj*. ¡hum!; ¡ejém!
hu·man [hjúmən] *adj*. humano; *s*. ser humano.
hu·mane [hjumén] *adj*. humano; humanitario.
hu·man·ism [hjúmənɪzm] *s*. humanismo.
hu·man·i·tar·i·an [hjumænətɛ́rɪən] *adj*. humanitario; *s*. filántropo.
hu·man·i·ty [hjumǽnətɪ] *s*. humanidad; **-ies** humanidades.
hum·ble [hʌ́mbl] *adj*. humilde; *v*. humillar; **humbly** *adv*. humildemente, con humildad.
hum·ble·ness [hʌ́mblnɪs] *s*. humildad.
hu·mid [hjúmɪd] *adj*. húmedo.
hu·mid·i·fy [hjumɪ́dəfaɪ] *v*. humedecer.
hu·mid·ity [hjumɪ́dətɪ] *d*. humedad.
hu·mil·i·ate [hjumɪ́lɪet] *v*. humillar.
hu·mil·i·a·tion [hjumɪlɪéʃən] *s*. humillación.
hu·mil·i·ty [hjumɪ́lətɪ] *s*. humildad.
hum·ming·bird [hʌ́mɪŋbɝd] *s*. colibrí, pájaro mosca, *Méx*. chuparrosa, *Méx*. chupaflor, *S.A.* guainumbí; *Ríopl., Ch.* picaflor; *C.A.* gurrión.
hu·mor [hjúmə˞] *s*. humor, humorismo, gracia; capricho; **out of** — de mal humor, malhumorado, disgustado; *v*. seguir el humor (*a una persona*), complacer; mimar.
hu·mor·ous [hjúmərəs] *adj*. humorístico, gracioso, cómico, chistoso.
hump [hʌmp] *s*. joroba, corcova, giba; *v*. encorvarse.
hump·back [hʌ́mpbæk] = **hunchback.**
hunch [hʌntʃ] *s*. joroba, corcova, giba; presentimiento, corazonada; *v*. encorvar (*la espalda*).
hunch·back [hʌ́ntʃbæk] *s*. joroba; jorobado.
hun·dred [hʌ́ndrəd] *adj*. cien(to); *s*. ciento; **-s** centenares, cientos.
hun·dredth [hʌ́ndrədθ] *adj*. centésimo.
hung [hʌŋ] *pret. & p.p. de* **to hang.**
hun·ger [hʌ́ŋgə˞] *s*. hambre; *v*. tener hambre, estar hambriento; **to** — **for** ansiar, anhelar.
hun·gri·ly [hʌ́ŋgrɪlɪ] *adv*. con hambre, hambrientamente.
hun·gry [hʌ́ŋgrɪ] *adj*. hambriento; **to be** — tener hambre.
hunk [hʌŋk] *s*. pedazo grande; mendrugo (*de pan*).
hunt [hʌnt] *v*. cazar; perseguir; buscar; escudriñar; **to** — **down** dar caza a; seguir la pista de; **to** — **for** buscar; *s*. caza, cacería; busca, búsqueda; perseguimiento.
hunt·er [hʌ́ntə˞] *s*. cazador; buscador; perro de caza, perro de busca.
hunts·man [hʌ́ntsmən] *s*. cazador.
hurl [hɝl] *v*. arrojar, lanzar.
hur·ly bur·ly [hɝ́lɪbɝ́lɪ] *s*. alboroto, baraúnda, *C.A.* bullas.

hur·rah [hərɔ́] *interj.* ¡hurra! ¡viva!; ¡ole!; *v.* vitorear.
hur·ri·cane [hɝ́ɪken] *s.* huracán.
hur·ried [hɝɪd] *adj.* apresurado; **-ly** *adv.* de prisa, apresuradamente, a escape.
hur·ry [hɝɪ] *v.* apresurar(se); precipitar(se); dar(se) prisa; apurarse; correr; **to — in (out)** entrar (salir) de prisa; **to — up** apresurar(se); dar(se) prisa; *s.* prisa; precipitación; **to be in a —** tener prisa, ir de prisa, estar de prisa.
hurt [hɝt] *v.* hacer daño; dañar; perjudicar; herir; lastimar; doler; **to — one's feelings** darle a uno que sentir; lastimar a uno; **my tooth -s** me duele la muela; *pret. & p.p. de* **to hurt;** *s.* daño; herida; lesión; dolor.
hus·band [hʌ́zbənd] *s.* marido, esposo.
hush [hʌʃ] *v.* acallar, aquietar; callar(se); **—!** ¡chitón! ¡silencio! ¡cállese! ¡quieto!; **to — up a scandal** encubrir un escándalo; *s.* silencio, quietud.
husk [hʌsk] *s.* cáscara, hollejo, (*pod*) vaina; *v.* mondar, pelar, deshollejar.
husk·y [hʌ́skɪ] *adj.* (*voice*) ronco; (*strong*) forzudo, fuerte; cascarudo.
hus·tle [hʌ́sl] *v.* apresurar(se); apurarse; menear(se); atropellar; *s.* prisa, apresuramiento, meneo; actividad; **— and bustle** vaivén.
hut [hʌt] *s.* choza, cabaña, *Carib.* bohío; *Méx.* jacal; *S.A.* rancho.
hy·a·cinth [háɪəsɪnθ] *s.* jacinto.
hy·brid [háɪbrɪd] *adj.* híbrido.
hy·drate [háɪdret] *s.* hidrato.
hy·drau·lic [haɪdrɔ́lɪk] *adj.* hidráulico.
hy·dro·e·lec·tric [haɪdroiléktrɪk] *adj.* hidroeléctrico.
hy·dro·gen [háɪdrədʒən] *s.* hidrógeno.
hy·dro·pho·bi·a [haɪdrofóbɪə] *s.* hidrofobia.
hy·dro·plane [háɪdrəplen] *s.* hidroplano, hidroavión.
hy·giene [háɪdʒin] *s.* higiene.
hymn [hɪm] *s.* himno.
hy·phen [háɪfən] *s.* guión.
hyp·no·sis [hɪpnósɪs] *s.* hipnosis.
hy·poc·ri·sy [hɪpɑ́krəsɪ] *s.* hipocresía.
hyp·o·crite [hɪ́pəkrɪt] *s.* hipócrita.
hyp·o·crit·i·cal [hɪpəkrɪ́tɪkl] *adj.* hipócrita.
hy·poth·e·sis [haɪpɑ́θəsɪs] *s.* hipótesis.
hys·ter·i·cal [hɪstérɪkl] *adj.* histérico.

I:i

I [aɪ] *pron. pers.* yo.
I-beam [ájbɪm] viga de doble.
I·be·ri·an [aɪbɪ́rɪən] *adj.* ibérico, ibero.
ice [aɪs] *s.* (*solid*) hielo; (*food*) helado; mantecado; sorbete; **— cream** helado; **ice-cream parlor** *Am.* heladería; nevería; **— skates** patines de cuchilla; **— water** agua helada; *v.* helar; escarchar, alfeñicar, cubrir con escarcha (*un pastel*).
ice·berg [áɪsbɝg] *s.* montaña de hielo, témpano.
ice·box [áɪsbɑks] *s.* nevera, *Am.* refrigerador.
ice·man [áɪsmæn] *s.* vendedor de hielo.
i·ci·cle [áɪsɪkl] *s.* carámbano.
i·con·o·clasm [aɪkɑ́nəklæzəm] *s.* iconoclasmo.
i·con·o·clast [aɪkánəklæst] *s.* iconoclasta.
i·cy [áɪsɪ] *adj.* helado, frío; congelado; cubierto de hielo.
i·de·a [aɪdíə] *s.* idea.
i·de·al [aɪdíəl] *adj. & s.* ideal.
i·de·al·ism [aɪdíəlɪzəm] *s.* idealismo.
i·de·al·ist [aɪdíəlɪst] *s.* idealista.
i·de·al·is·tic [aɪdíəlɪ́stɪk] *adj.* idealista.
i·den·ti·cal [aɪdéntɪkl] *adj.* idéntico.
i·den·ti·fi·ca·tion [aɪdɛntəfɪkéʃən] *s.* identificación; **I.D. card** carnet.
i·den·ti·fy [aɪdéntəfaɪ] *v.* identificar.
i·den·ti·ty [aɪdéntətɪ] *s.* identidad.
i·de·ol·ogy [aɪdɪɔ́lədʒɪ] *s.* ideología.
id·i·o·cy [Idiəsɪ] *s.* idiotez.
id·i·om [ɪ́dɪəm] *s.* modismo, idiotismo.
id·i·o·syn·cra·sy [ɪdɪosɪ́nkrəsi] *s.* idiosincrasia.
id·i·ot [ɪ́dɪət] *s.* idiota.
id·i·ot·ic [ɪdɪɑ́tɪk] *adj.* idiota.
i·dle [áɪdl] *adj.* ocioso; (*lazy*) perezoso, holgazán; vano; desocupado; *v.* holgazanear; perder el tiempo; funcionar (*el motor solo, sin engranar*); **idly** *adv.* ociosamente; inútilmente; perezosamente.
i·dle·ness [áɪdlnɪs] *s.* ociosidad; ocio, desocupación; pereza, holgazanería.
i·dler [áɪdlɚ] *s.* holgazán, haragán.
i·dol [áɪdl] *s.* ídolo.
i·dol·a·try [aɪdɑ́lətrɪ] *s.* idolatría.
i·dol·ize [áɪdlaɪz] *v.* idolatrar.
i·dyl [áɪdl] *s.* idilio.
if [ɪf] *conj.* si.
ig·nite [ɪgnáɪt] *v.* encender(se), inflamar(se); prender, pegar fuego a.
ig·ni·tion [ɪgnɪ́ʃən] *s.* ignición, encendido (*de un motor*); **— switch** interruptor de encendido, *Méx., C.A., Ven., Carib.* switch de ignición.
ig·no·ble [ɪgnóbl] *adj.* innoble; bajo, vil.
ig·no·rance [ɪ́gnərəns] *s.* ignorancia
ig·no·rant [ɪ́gnərənt] *adj.* ignorante.
ig·nore [ɪgnór] *v.* no hacer caso de, desatender; desairar.
ill [ɪl] *adj.* enfermo; malo; **— nature** mal genio, mala índole; **— will** *s.* mala voluntad, ojeriza, inquina; *s.* mal; enfermedad; calamidad, infortunio; *adv.* mal, malamente; **— at ease** inquieto, intranquilo; **ill-bred** mal criado; **ill-clad** mal vestido; **ill-humored** malhumorado; **ill-mannered** descortés, grosero; **ill-natured** de mala índole, *Ven., Col., Méx.* mal genioso; **ill-advised** mal aconsejado.
il·le·gal [ɪlígl] *adj.* ilegal; ilícito.
il·le·git·i·mate [ɪlɪdʒɪ́təmɪt] *adj.* ilegítimo; bastardo.
il·lic·it [ɪlɪ́sɪt] *adj.* ilícito.
il·lit·er·a·cy [ɪlɪ́tərəsɪ] *s.* analfabetismo.
il·lit·er·ate [ɪlɪ́tərɪt] *adj. & s.* analfabeto.
ill·ness [ɪ́lnɪs] *s.* mal, enfermedad.
il·lu·mi·nate [ɪlúmənet] *v.* iluminar; alumbrar; esclarecer.
il·lu·mi·na·tion [ɪlumənéʃən] *s.* iluminación; alumbrado.
il·lu·sion [ɪlúʒən] *s.* ilusión.
il·lu·sive [ɪlúsɪv] *adj.* ilusorio, ilusivo, falaz.
il·lu·so·ry [ɪlúsərɪ] *adj.* ilusorio, ilusivo, engañoso.
il·lus·trate [ɪətrét] *v.* ilustrar; esclarecer.
il·lus·tra·tion [ɪləstréʃən] *s.* ilustración; grabado, estampa; aclaración, esclarecimiento.
il·lus·tra·tor [ɪ́ləstretɚ] *s.* ilustrador.
il·lus·tri·ous [ɪlʌ́strɪəs] *adj.* ilustre.
im·age [ɪ́mɪdʒ] *s.* imagen.
im·age·ry [ɪ́mɪdʒrɪ] *s.* conjunto de imágenes, figuras; fantasía.
im·ag·i·nar·y [ɪmǽdʒnɛrɪ] *adj.* imaginario.
im·ag·i·na·tion [ɪmædʒənéʃən] *s.* imaginación; imaginativa.
im·ag·i·na·tive [ɪmǽdʒenetɪv] *adj.* imaginativo.
im·ag·ine [ɪmǽdʒɪn] *v.* imaginar(se); figurarse.
im·be·cile [ɪ́mbəsɪl] *adj. & s.* imbécil.
im·bibe [ɪmbáɪb] *v.* embeber, absorber; beber.
im·bue [ɪmbjú] *v.* imbuir, infundir; impregnar,

empapar.
im·i·tate [ímətet] *v.* imitar; remedar.
im·i·ta·tion [ɪmətéʃən] *s.* imitación; remedo; *adj.* imitado, de imitación.
im·i·ta·tor [ímətetɚ] *s.* imitador; remedador.
im·mac·u·late [ɪmǽkjəlɪt] *adj.* inmaculado, sin mancha.
im·ma·te·ri·al [ɪmətírɪəl] *adj.* inmaterial, espiritual; **it is — to me** me es indiferente.
im·me·di·ate [ɪmídɪɪt] *adj.* inmediato; próximo; **-ly** *adv.* inmediatamente; en seguida; al punto, en el acto, al instante.
im·mense [ɪméns] *adj.* inmenso.
im·men·si·ty [ɪménsətɪ] *s.* inmensidad.
im·merse [ɪmɝ́s] *v.* sumergir, sumir.
im·mi·grant [íməgrənt] *adj.* & *s.* inmigrante.
im·mi·grate [íməgret] *v.* inmigrar.
im·mi·gra·tion [ɪməgréʃən] *s.* inmigración.
im·mi·nent [ímənənt] *adj.* inminente.
im·mo·bile [ɪmóbil] *adj.* inmóbil.
im·mod·est [ɪmádɪst] *adj.* deshonesto, impúdico, indecente.
im·mor·al [ɪmɔ́rəl] *adj.* inmoral, licencioso.
im·mor·al·i·ty [ɪmərǽlətɪ] *s.* inmoralidad.
im·mor·tal [ɪmɔ́rtl] *adj.* & *s.* inmortal.
im·mor·tal·i·ty [ɪmɔrtǽlətɪ] *s.* inmortalidad.
im·mov·a·ble [ɪmúvəbl] *adj.* inmovible (*o* inamovible); inmóvil; inmutable.
im·mune [ɪmjún] *adj.* inmune.
im·mu·ni·ty [ɪmjúnətɪ] *s.* inmunidad.
im·mu·ta·ble [ɪmjútəbl] *adj.* inmutable.
imp [ɪmp] *s.* diablillo.
im·pair [ɪmpér] *v.* dañar, perjudicar, menoscabar, desvirtuar, debilitar.
im·pair·ment [ɪmpérmənt] *s.* menoscabo; perjuicio; deterioro.
im·part [ɪmpárt] *v.* impartir, dar, comunicar.
im·par·tial [ɪmpárʃəl] *adj.* imparcial.
im·par·ti·al·i·ty [ɪmparʃǽlətɪ] *s.* imparcialidad.
im·pas·si·ble [ɪmpǽsəbl] *adj.* impasible.
im·pas·sioned [ɪmpǽʃənd] *adj.* apasionado, vehemente, ardiente.
im·pas·sive [ɪmpǽsɪv] *adj.* impasible.
im·pa·tience [ɪmpéʃəns] *s.* impaciencia.
im·pa·tient [ɪmpéʃənt] *adj.* impaciente.
im·peach [ɪmpítʃ] *v.* demandar o acusar formalmente (*a un alto funcionario de gobierno*); **to — a person's honor** poner en tela de juicio el honor de uno.
im·pede [ɪmpíd] *v.* impedir, estorbar, obstruir.
im·ped·i·ment [ɪmpédəmənt] *s.* impedimento, obstáculo, estorbo; traba.
im·pel [ɪmpél] *v.* impeler, impulsar.
im·pend·ing [ɪmpéndɪŋ] *adj.* inminente, amenazador.
im·per·a·tive [ɪmpérətɪv] *adj.* imperativo; imperioso, urgente; *s.* imperativo.
im·per·cep·ti·ble [ɪmpɚséptəbl] *adj.* imperceptible.
im·per·fect [ɪmpɝ́fɪkt] *adj.* imperfecto; defectuoso; *s.* imperfecto (*tiempo del verbo*).
im·pe·ri·al [ɪmpírɪəl] *adj.* imperial.
im·pe·ri·al·ism [ɪmpírɪəlɪzm] *s.* imperialismo.
im·per·il [ɪmpérəl] *v.* poner en peligro, arriesgar.
im·pe·ri·ous [ɪmpírɪəs] *adj.* imperioso; urgente.
im·per·son·al [ɪmpɝ́sn̩l] *adj.* impersonal.
im·per·son·ate [ɪmpɝ́sn̩et] *v.* representar (*un personaje*); remedar, imitar; fingirse otro, pretender ser otro.
im·per·ti·nence [ɪmpɝ́tn̩əns] *s.* impertinencia; insolencia, descaro.
im·per·ti·nent [ɪmpɝ́tn̩ənt] *adj.* impertinente; insolente, descarado.
im·per·vi·ous [ɪmpɝ́vɪəs] *adj.* impermeable; impenetrable; **— to reason** refractario, testarudo.
im·pet·u·ous [ɪmpétʃuəs] *adj.* impetuoso.
im·pe·tus [ímpətəs] *s.* ímpetu.
im·pi·ous [ímpɪəs] *adj.* impío.
im·pla·ca·ble [ɪplékəbl] *adj.* implacable.
im·plant [ɪmplǽnt] *v.* implantar, plantar; inculcar, infundir.
im·ple·ment [ímpləmənt] *s.* herramienta, instrumento; **-s** utensilios, aperos, enseres.
im·pli·cate [ímplɪket] *v.* implicar, envolver, enredar.
im·plic·it [ɪmplísɪt] *adj.* implícito.
im·plore [ɪmplór] *v.* implorar, rogar; suplicar.
im·ply [ɪmpláɪ] *v.* implicar; querer decir; insinuar.
im·po·lite [ɪmpəláɪt] *adj.* descortés.
im·port [ímport] *s.* significado, significación, sentido; importancia; importación; **-s** artículos importados; [ɪmpórt] *v.* importar; significar, querer decir.
im·por·tance [ɪmpɔ́rtn̩s] *s.* importancia.
im·por·tant [ɪmpɔ́rtn̩t] *adj.* importante.
im·pose [ɪmpóz] *v.* imponer; **to — upon** abusar de (*la amistad, hospitalidad, confianza de alguien*); engañar.
im·pos·ing [ɪmpózɪŋ] *adj.* imponente; impresionante.
im·po·si·tion [ɪmpəzíʃən] *s.* imposición; carga, impuesto; abuso (*de confianza*).
im·pos·si·bil·i·ty [ɪmpasəbílətɪ] *s.* imposibilidad.
im·pos·si·ble [ɪmpásəbl̩] *adj.* imposible.
im·pos·tor [ɪmpástɚ] *s.* impostor, embaucador.
im·pos·ture [ɪmpástʃɚ] *s.* impostura, fraude, engaño.
im·po·tence [ímpətəns] *s.* impotencia.
im·po·tent [ímpətənt] *adj.* impotente.
im·pov·er·ish [ɪmpávərɪʃ] *v.* empobrecer.
im·preg·nate [ɪmprégnet] *v.* impregnar; empapar; empreñar.
im·press [ímpres] *s.* impresión, marca, señal, huella; [ɪmprés] *v.* imprimir, estampar, marcar, grabar; impresionar.
im·pres·sion [ɪmpréʃən] *s.* impresión; marca.
im·pres·sive [ɪmprésɪv] *adj.* impresionante; imponente.
im·print [ímprɪnt] *s.* impresión; pie de imprenta; [ɪmprínt] *v.* imprimir; estampar.
im·pris·on [ɪmprízn̩] *v.* aprisionar, encarcelar.
im·pris·on·ment [ɪmprízn̩mənt] *s.* prisión, encarcelación o encarcelamiento.
im·prob·a·ble [ɪmprábəbl] *adj.* improbable.
im·promp·tu [ɪmprámptu] *adv.* de improviso.
im·prop·er [ɪmprápɚ] *adj.* impropio.
im·prove [ɪmprúv] *v.* mejorar(se); **to — upon** mejorar; **to — one's time** aprovechar el tiempo.
im·prove·ment [ɪmprúvmənt] *s.* mejoramiento; mejora; progreso, adelanto; mejoría (*de una enfermedad*).
im·pro·vise [ímprəvaɪz] *v.* improvisar.
im·pru·dent [ɪmprúdn̩t] *adj.* imprudente.
im·pu·dence [ímpjədəns] *s.* impudencia, descaro, insolencia.
im·pu·dent [ímpjədənt] *adj.* impudente, descarado, insolente.
im·pulse [ímpʌls] *s.* impulso; ímpetu; inclinación; **to act on —** obrar impulsivamente.
im·pul·sive [ɪmpʌ́lsɪv] *adj.* impulsivo.
im·pu·ni·ty [ɪmpjúnətɪ] *s.* impunidad, falta o exención de castigo.
im·pure [ɪmpjúr] *adj.* impuro; (*dirty*) sucio; (*watered*) adulterado.
im·pu·ri·ty [ɪmpjúrətɪ] *s.* impureza.
im·pute [ɪmpjút] *v.* imputar, achacar, atribuir.
in [ɪn] *prep.* en; dentro de; de (*después de un superlativo*); **— haste** de prisa; **— the morning**

por (*o* en) la mañana; — **writing** por escrito; **at two — the morning** a las dos de la mañana; **dressed — white** vestido de blanco; **the tallest — his class** el más alto de su clase; **to come — a week** venir de hoy en ocho días, venir dentro de ocho días; *adv*. dentro; adentro; en casa; **to be — and out** estar entrando y saliendo; **to be all** — no poder más, estar rendido de cansancio; **to be — with someone** estar asociado con alguien; disfrutar el aprecio de una persona; **to come** — entrar; **to have it — for someone** tenerle ojeriza a una persona; **to put** — meter; **is the train — ?** ¿ha llegado el tren?

in·a·bil·i·ty [ɪnəbíləti] *s*. inhabilidad, incapacidad.

in·ac·ces·si·ble [ɪnəksέsəbl] *adj*. inaccesible; inasequible.

in·ac·cu·rate [ɪnǽkjərɪt] *adj*. inexacto, impreciso, incorrecto.

in·ac·tive [ɪnǽktɪv] *adj*. inactivo; inerte.

in·ac·tiv·i·ty [ɪnæktívəti] *s*. inactividad, inacción, inercia.

in·ad·e·quate [ɪnǽdəkwɪt] *adj*. inadecuado; insuficiente.

in·ad·ver·tent [ɪnədvɝ́tn̩t] *adj*. inadvertido; descuidado; **-ly** *adv*. inadvertidamente; descuidadamente.

in·ad·vis·a·ble [ɪnədváɪzəbl] *adj*. imprudente.

in·an·i·mate [ɪnǽnəmɪt] *adj*. inanimado.

in·as·much [ɪnəzmʌ́tʃ]: — **as** visto que, puesto que; en cuanto.

in·at·ten·tive [ɪnətέntɪv] *adj*. desatento.

in·au·gu·rate [ɪnɔ́gjəret] *v*. inaugurar, iniciar; investir de una dignidad o cargo.

in·au·gu·ra·tion [ɪnɔgjəréʃən] *s*. inauguración.

in·board [ínbord] *adj*. interior.

in·born [ɪnbɔ́rn] *adj*. innato, connatural.

in·can·des·cent [ɪnkəndέsn̩t] *adj*. incandescente, candente.

in·can·ta·tion [ɪnkæntéʃən] *s*. conjuro.

in·ca·pa·ble [ɪnképəbl] *adj*. incapaz.

in·ca·pac·i·tate [ɪkəpǽsɪtet] *v*. incapacitar.

in·cen·di·ar·y [ɪsέndɪεri] *adj*. incendiario; — **bomb** bomba incendiaria.

in·cense [ínsεns] *s*. incienso; [ɪnsέns] *v*. inflamar, exasperar.

in·cen·tive [ɪnsέntɪv] *s*. incentivo, estímulo.

in·ces·sant [ɪnsέsn̩t] *adj*. incesante, continuo.

inch [ɪntʃ] *s*. pulgada (*2.54 centímetros*); **by -es** poco a poco, gradualmente; **every — a man** nada menos que todo un hombre; **to be within an — of** estar a dos pulgadas de, estar muy cerca de; *v*. avanzar muy despacio (*por pulgadas*).

in·ci·dence [ínsɪdəns] *s*. incidencia.

in·ci·dent [ínsədənt] *s*. incidente, suceso, acontecimiento.

in·ci·den·tal [ɪnsədέntl] *adj*. incidental; accidental; contingente; **-s** *s*. *pl*. gastos imprevistos; **-ly** *adv*. incidentalmente; de paso.

in·cip·i·ent [ɪnsípɪənt] *adj*. incipiente.

in·ci·sion [ɪnsíʒən] *s*. incisión.

in·ci·sive [ɪnsáɪsɪv] *adj*. incisivo.

in·cite [ɪnsáɪt] *v*. incitar.

in·clem·ent [ɪnklέmənt] *adj*. inclemente.

in·cli·na·tion [ɪnklənéʃən] *s*. inclinación.

in·cline [ínklaɪn] *s*. declive, pendiente, cuesta; [ɪnkláɪn] *v*. inclinar(se).

in·close = **enclose.**

in·clo·sure = **enclosure.**

in·clude [ɪnklúd] *v*. incluir, encerrar; abarcar.

in·clu·sive [ɪnklúsɪv] *adj*. inclusivo; **from Monday to Friday** — del lunes al viernes inclusive.

in·co·her·ent [ɪnkohírənt] *adj*. incoherente, inconexo.

in·come [ínkʌm] *s*. renta, rédito, ingreso, entrada; — **tax** impuesto sobre rentas (ingresos); *Arg*. impuesto a los réditos, *Ch*. impuesto cedular.

in·com·pa·ra·ble [ɪnkámpərəbl] *adj*. incomparable, sin par, sin igual.

in·com·pat·i·ble [ɪnkəmpǽtəbl] *adj*. incompatible.

in·com·pe·tent [ɪnkámpətənt] *adj*. incompetente.

in·com·plete [ɪnkəmplít] *adj*. incompleto.

in·com·pre·hen·si·ble [ɪnkamprɪhέnsəbl] *adj*. incomprensible.

in·con·ceiv·a·ble [ɪnkənsívəbl] *adj*. inconcebible.

in·con·clu·sive [ɪnkənklúsɪv] *adj*. inconcluso.

in·con·sid·er·ate [ɪnkənsídərɪt] *adj*. inconsiderado, falto de miramiento.

in·con·sis·ten·cy [ɪnkənsístənsɪ] *s*. inconsecuencia; falta de uniformidad (*en la aplicación de una regla o principio*).

in·con·sis·tent [ɪnkənsístənt] *adj*. inconsecuente; falto de uniformidad.

in·con·spic·u·ous [ɪnkənspíkjuəs] *adj*. poco llamativo.

in·con·stan·cy [ɪnkánstənsɪ] *s*. inconstancia, mudanza.

in·con·stant [ɪnkánstənt] *adj*. inconstante, mudable, voluble.

in·con·test·a·ble [ɪnkəntέstəbl] *adj*. incontestable.

in·con·ven·ience [ɪnkənvínjəns] *s*. inconveniencia; molestia; *v*. *incomodar; molestar*.

in·con·ven·ient [ɪnkənvínjənt] *adj*. inconveniente; inoportuno.

in·cor·po·rate [ɪnkɔ́rperɪt] *adj*. incorporado; asociado; [ɪnkɔ́rpəret] *v*. incorporar; incorporarse, asociarse (*para formar un cuerpo*).

in·cor·rect [ɪnkərέkt] *adj*. *incorrecto*.

in·cor·ri·gi·ble [ɪnkɔ́rɪdʒəbl] *adj*. incorregible.

in·crease [ínkris] *s*. aumento; acrecentamiento; crecimiento; incremento; [ɪnkrís] *v*. aumentar(se); acrecentar(se), crecer; recargar.

in·creas·ing·ly [ɪnkrísɪŋlɪ] *adv*. más y más; cada vez más.

in·cred·i·ble [ɪnkrέdəbl] *adj*. increíble.

in·cre·du·li·ty [ɪnkrədúətɪ] *s*. incredulidad.

in·cred·u·lous [ɪnkrέdʒələs] *adj*. incrédulo, descreído.

in·cre·ment [ínkrəmənt] *s*. incremento.

in·crim·i·nate [ɪnkrímənet] *v*. acriminar.

in·cu·ba·tor [ínkjubetɚ] *s*. incubadora.

in·cul·cate [ɪnkʌ́lket] *v*. inculcar, infundir.

in·cum·bent [ɪnkʌ́mbənt] *s*. incumbente.

in·cur [ɪnkɝ́] *v*. incurrir en.

in·cur·a·ble [ɪnkjʊ́rəbl] *adj*. incurable, irremediable; *s*. incurable.

in·debt·ed [ɪndέtɪd] *adj*. adeudado, endeudado; obligado, agradecido.

in·debt·ed·ness [ɪndέtɪdnɪs] *s*. deuda; obligación.

in·de·cen·cy [ɪndísn̩sɪ] *s*. indecencia.

in·de·cent [ɪndísn̩t] *adj*. indecente.

in·de·ci·sion [ɪndəsíʒən] *s*. indecisión.

in·deed [ɪndíd] *adv*. en verdad, a la verdad; de veras; realmente.

in·de·fen·si·ble [ɪndɪfέnsəbl] *adj*. indefendible.

in·def·i·nite [ɪndέfənɪt] *adj*. indefinido.

in·del·i·ble [ɪndέləbl] *adj*. indeleble.

in·del·i·cate [ɪndέləkət] *adj*. indelicado, indecoroso.

in·dem·ni·fy [ɪndέmnəfaɪ] *v*. indemnizar.

in·dem·ni·ty [ɪndέmnətɪ] *s*. indemnización.

in·dent [ɪndέnt] *v*. dentar, endentar; sangrar (*comenzar un renglón más adentro que los otros*).

in·de·pend·ence [ɪndɪpέndəns] *s*. independencia.

in·de·pend·ent [ɪndɪpέndənt] *adj*. independiente.

in·de·scrib·a·ble [ɪndɪskráɪbəbl] *adj*. indescriptible.

in·dex [índɛks] *s.* índice; — **card** ficha para índices; *v.* alfabetizar, ordenar alfabéticamente; poner en un índice; — **finger** índice.
In·di·an [índɪən] *adj.* & *s.* indio; — **Ocean** Océano Indico.
in·di·cate [índəket] *v.* indicar.
in·di·ca·tion [ɪdəkéʃən] *s.* indicación.
in·dic·a·tive [ɪdíkətɪv] *adj.* & *s.* indicativo.
in·dict [ɪndáɪt] *v.* procesar, demandar (*ante un juez*); enjuiciar, formar causa a.
in·dict·ment [ɪndáɪtmənt] *s.* acusación (*hecha por el Gran Jurado*), denuncia, proceso judicial.
in·dif·fer·ence [ɪndífrəns] *s.* indiferencia; apatía.
in·dif·fer·ent [ɪndífrənt] *adj.* indiferente; apático.
in·dig·e·nous [ɪndídʒənəs] *adj.* indígena, autóctono, nativo.
in·di·gent [índədʒənt] *adj.* & *s.* indigente.
in·di·ges·tion [ɪndədʒɛ́stʃən] *s.* indigestión.
in·dig·nant [ɪndígnənt] *adj.* indignado; **-ly** *adv.* con indignación.
in·dig·na·tion [ɪndɪgnéʃən] *s.* indignación.
in·dig·ni·ty [ɪndígnətɪ] *s.* indignidad, afrenta.
in·di·go [índɪgo] *s.* índigo, añil; — **blue** azul de añil.
in·di·rect [ɪndərɛ́kt] *adj.* indirecto.
in·dis·creet [ɪndɪskrit] *adj.* indiscreto.
in·dis·cre·tion [ɪndɪskrɛ́ʃən] *s.* indiscreción.
in·dis·pen·sa·ble [ɪndɪspɛ́nsəbl] *adj.* indispensable.
in·dis·pose [ɪndɪspóz] *v.* indisponer.
in·dis·posed [ɪndɪspózd] *adj.* indispuesto.
in·dis·po·si·tion [ɪndɪspəzíʃən] *s.* indisposición; malestar.
in·dis·tinct [ɪndɪstíŋkt] *adj.* indistinto.
in·di·um [índiəm] *s.* indio.
in·di·vi·du·al [ɪndəvídʒuəl] *adj.* individual; *s.* individuo, sujeto, persona.
in·di·vid·u·al·ism [ɪndəvídʒuəlɪzm] *s.* individualismo.
in·di·vid·u·al·ist [ɪndəvídʒuəlɪst] *s.* individualista.
in·di·vid·u·al·i·ty [ɪndəvɪdʒuǽlətɪ] *s.* individualidad; individuo, persona.
in·di·vis·i·ble [ɪndəvízəbl] *adj.* indivisible.
in·doc·tri·nate [ɪndáktrɪnet] *v.* adoctrinar.
in·do·lence [índələns] *v.* indolencia, desidia, apatía.
in·do·lent [índələnt] *adj.* indolente, desidioso, apático.
in·dom·i·ta·ble [ɪndámətəbl] *adj.* indomable.
in·door [índor] *adj.* interior, de casa.
in·doors [índórz] *adv.* dentro, en casa; adentro; **to go** — entrar; ir adentro.
in·dorse = **endorse.**
in·dorse·ment = **endorsement.**
in·dors·er = **endorser.**
in·duce [ɪndjús] *v.* inducir.
in·duce·ment [ɪndjúsmənt] *s.* aliciente, incentivo.
in·duct [ɪndʌ́kt] *v.* introducir; iniciar; instalar (*en un cargo*).
in·duc·tion [ɪndʌ́kʃən] *s.* inducción; instalación (*en un cargo*).
in·dulge [ɪnkʌ́ldʒ] *v.* gratificar, complacer; seguir el humor a (*una persona*); mimar, consentir (*a un niño*); **to** — **in** darse a, entregarse a (*un placer*); darse el lujo de, permitirse el placer de.
in·dul·gence [ɪndʌ́ldʒəns] *s.* indulgencia; complacencia (*en el vicio o placer*).
in·dul·gent [ɪndʌ́ldʒənt] *adj.* indulgente.
in·dus·tri·al [ɪnkʌ́strɪəl] *adj.* industrial.
in·dus·tri·al·ist [ɪndʌ́strɪəlɪst] *s.* industrial; fabricante.
in·dus·tri·ous [ɪndʌ́strɪəs] *adj.* industrioso. aplicado, diligente.
in·dus·try [índəstrɪ] *s.* industria; aplicación, diligencia.
in·ed·i·ble [ɪnɛ́dəbl] *adj.* incomestible.
in·ef·fa·ble [ɪnɛ́fəbl] *adj.* inefable.
in·ef·fec·tive [ɪnəfɛ́ktɪv] *adj.* inefectivo, ineficaz.
in·ef·fi·cient [ɪnifíʃənt] *adj.* ineficaz.
in·el·i·gi·ble [ɪnɛ́lədʒəbl] *adj.* inelegible.
in·e·qual·i·ty [ɪnɪkwálətɪ] *s.* desigualdad; disparidad.
in·ert [ɪnɝ́t] *adj.* inerte.
in·er·tia [ɪnɝ́ʃə] *s.* inercia.
in·es·cap·a·ble [ɪnəsképəbl] *adj.* forzoso, inevitable.
in·es·ti·ma·ble [ɪnɛ́stəməbl] *adj.* inestimable.
in·ev·i·ta·ble [ɪnɛ́vətəbl] *adj.* inevitable.
in·ex·haust·i·ble [ɪnɪgzɔ́stəbl] *adj.* inagotable.
in·ex·o·ra·ble [ɪnɛ́ksərəbl] *adj.* inexorable; severo.
in·ex·pe·di·ent [ɪnɛkspídjənt] *adj.* inoportuno; imprudente.
in·ex·pen·sive [ɪnɪkspɛ́nsɪv] *adj.* económico, barato.
in·ex·pe·ri·ence [ɪnɪkspírɪəns] *s.* inexperiencia, falta de experiencia.
in·ex·pe·ri·enced [ɪnɪkspírɪənst] *adj.* inexperto, falto de experiencia.
in·ex·pli·ca·ble [ɪnɛ́ksplɪkəbl] *adj.* inexplicable.
in·ex·press·i·ble [ɪnɪksprɛ́səbl] *adj.* inexpresable, indecible, inefable.
in·fal·li·ble [ɪnfǽləbl] *adj.* infalible.
in·fa·mous [ínfəməs] *adj.* infame, ignominioso
in·fa·my [ínfəmɪ] *s.* infamia.
in·fan·cy [ínfənsɪ] *s.* infancia.
in·fant [ínfənt] *s.* infante, bebé, criatura, nene
in·fan·tile [ínfəntaɪl] *adj.* infantil.
in·fan·try [ínfəntrɪ] *s.* infantería.
in·fect [ɪnfɛ́kt] *v.* infectar, inficionar; contagiar; contaminar.
in·fec·tion [ɪnfɛ́kʃən] *s* infección; contagio.
in·fec·tious [ɪnfɛ́kʃəs] *adj.* infeccioso; contagioso.
in·fer [ɪnfɝ́] *v.* inferir, deducir, colegir.
in·fer·ence [ínfərəns] *s.* inferencia, deducción.
in·fe·ri·or [ɪnfírɪɚ] *adj.* & *s.* inferior.
in·fe·ri·or·i·ty [ɪnfɪrɪɔ́rətɪ] *s.* inferioridad; — **complex** complejo de inferioridad.
in·fer·nal [ɪnfɝ́nl] *adj.* infernal.
in·fer·no [ɪnfɝ́no] *s.* infierno.
in·fest [ɪnfɛ́st] *v.* infestar, plagar.
in·fi·del [ínfədl] *adj.* & *s.* infiel.
in·fil·trate [ɪnfíltret] *v.* infiltrar(se).
in·fi·nite [ínfənɪt] *adj.* & *s.* infinito.
in·fin·i·tive [ɪnfínətɪv] *adj.* & *s.* infinitivo.
in·fin·i·ty [ɪnfínətɪ] *s.* infinidad; infinito.
in·firm [ɪnfɝ́m] *adj.* enfermizo, achacoso, débil.
in·fir·ma·ry [ɪnfɝ́mərɪ] *s.* enfermería.
in·fir·mi·ty [ɪnfɝ́mətɪ] *s.* enfermedad, achaque; flaqueza.
in·flame [ɪnflém] *v.* inflamar(se); enardecer(se).
in·flam·ma·tion [ɪnfləméʃən] *s.* inflamación.
in·flate [ɪnflét] *v.* inflar; hinchar.
in·fla·tion [ɪnfléʃən] *s.* inflación; hinchazón.
in·fec·tion [ɪnflɛ́kʃən] *s.* inflexión.
in·flict [ɪnflíkt] *v.* infligir, imponer.
in·flu·ence [ínfluəns] *s.* influencia, influjo; — **peddler** traficante de influencias; *v.* influir en; ejercer influencia o influjo sobre.
in·flu·en·tial [ɪnfluɛ́nʃəl] *adj.* influyente.
in·flu·en·za [ɪnfluɛ́nzə] *s.* influenza, gripe.
in·flux [ínflʌks] *s.* entrada, afluencia (*de gente*).
in·fold [ɪnfóld] *v.* envolver; abrazar; abarcar.
in·form [ɪnfɔ́rm] *v.* informar; enterar; avisar; **to** — **against** delatar a, denunciar a.
in·for·mal [ɪnfɔ́rml] *adj.* informal, sin ceremonia; — **visit** visita de confianza; **-ly** *adv.* informalmente, sin ceremonia, de confianza.
in·form·ant [ɪnfɔ́rmənt] *s.* informante.
in·for·ma·tion [ɪnfɚméʃən] *s.* (*service*) información; (*details*) informes; (*news*) noticias; (*knowledge*)

conocimientos, saber.
in·frac·tion]ɪnfrǽkʃən] *s.* infracción.
in·fringe [ɪnfríndʒ] *v.* infringir, violar; **to — upon** violar.
in·fu·ri·ate [ɪnfjʊ́rɪet] *v.* enfurecer.
in·fuse [ɪnfjúz] *v.* infundir; inculcar.
in·gen·ious [ɪndʒínjəs] *adj.* ingenioso.
in·ge·nu·i·ty [ɪndʒənúətɪ] *s.* ingeniosidad.
in·grat·i·tude [ɪngrǽtətjud] *s.* ingratitud.
in·gre·di·ent [ɪngrídɪənt] *s.* ingrediente.
in·hab·it [ɪnhǽbɪt] *v.* habitar, vivir en, residir en.
in·hab·i·tant [ɪnhǽbətənt] *s.* habitante.
in·hale [ɪnhél] *v.* inhalar, aspirar, inspirar.
in·her·ent [ɪnhírənt] *adj.* inherente.
in·her·it [ɪnhérɪt] *v.* heredar.
in·her·i·tance [ɪnhérətəns] *s.* herencia.
in·hib·it [ɪnhíbɪt] *v.* inhibir, cohibir, refrenar, reprimir; impedir.
in·hi·bi·tion [ɪnɪbíʃən] *s.* inhibición, cohibición; prohibición, restricción.
in·hos·pi·ta·ble [ɪnhɑ́spɪtəbl] *adj.* inhospitalario.
in·hu·man [ɪnhjúmən] *adj.* inhumano.
in·im·i·ta·ble [ɪnímətəbl] *adj.* inimitable.
in·iq·ui·ty [ɪníkwətɪ *s.* iniquidad, maldad.
in·i·tial [ɪníʃəl] *adj.* & *s.* inicial; — **abbreviation** sigla; *v.* marcar o firmar con iniciales.
in·i·ti·ate [ɪníʃɪet] *v.* iniciar.
in·i·ti·a·tive [ɪníʃɪetɪv] *s.* iniciativa.
in·ject [ɪndʒékt] *v.* inyectar; injerir, introducir.
in·jec·tion [ɪndʒékʃən] *s.* inyección.
in·junc·tion [ɪndʒʌ́ŋkʃən] *s.* mandato, orden; entredicho.
in·jure [índʒɚ] *v.* dañar; herir, lesionar; lastimar.
in·ju·ri·ous [ɪndʒʊ́rɪəs] *adj.* dañoso, dañino, perjudicial.
in·ju·ry [índʒərɪ] *s.* daño; herida, lesión; perjuicio.
in·jus·tice [ɪndʒʌ́stɪs] *s.* injusticia.
ink [ɪŋk] *s.* tinta; *v.* entintar; teñir o manchar con tinta.
ink·ling [íŋklɪŋ] *s.* indicación, indicio, idea, sospecha, noción vaga.
ink·stand [íŋkstænd] *s.* tintero.
ink·well [íŋkwɛl] *s.* tintero.
in·laid [ɪnléd] *adj.* incrustado, embutido; — **work** embutido, incrustación; *pret.* & *p.p. de* **to inlay.**
in·land [ínlənd] *s.* interior (*de un país*); *adj.* interior, del interior de un país; *adv.* tierra adentro.
in·lay [ɪnlé]*v.* incrustar, embutir; [ínle] *s.* embutido.
in·mate [ínmet] *s.* residente, asilado (*de un hospicio, asilo, casa de corrección, etc.*); presidiario; hospiciano.
in·most [ínmost] *adj.* más interior, más íntimo, más secreto o recóndito; más profundo.
inn [ɪn] *s.* posada, mesón, fonda.
in·nate [ɪnét] *adj.* innato, connatural.
in·ner [ínɚ] *adj.* interior; íntimo, recóndito; — **most** = **inmost.**
in·ning [ínɪŋ *s.* entrada, cuadro (*en béisbol*); turno (*del bateador en béisbol y otros juegos*).
inn·keep·er [ínkipɚ] *s.* ventero, mesonero, posadero.
in·no·cence [ínəsn̩s] *s.* inocencia.
in·no·cent [ínəsn̩t] *adj.* & *s.* inocente.
in·noc·u·ous [ɪnɑ́kjʊəs] *adj.* innocuo, inofensivo.
in·no·va·tion [ɪnəvéʃən] *s.* innovación.
in·nu·en·do [ɪnjʊéndo] *s.* insinuación, indirecta.
in·nu·mer·a·ble [ɪnjúmərəbl] *adj.* innumerable.
in·oc·u·late [ɪnɑ́kjəlet] *v.* inocular; contaminar.
in·of·fen·sive [ɪnəfénsɪv] *adj.* inofensivo.
in·op·por·tune [ɪnɑpɚtjún] *adj.* inoportuno.
in·put [ínpʊt] *s.* potencia consumida; (*electric*) entrada; (*contribution*) sugerencias al caso; (*computer*) entrada; *v.* introducir, ingresar.
in·quire [ɪnkwáɪr] *v.* inquirir, indagar; preguntar; **to — about** preguntar por; **to — into** indagar, investigar.
in·qui·ry [ɪnkwáɪrɪ] *s.* indagación, investigación; pregunta; interrogatorio.
in·qui·si·tion [ɪnkwəzíʃən] *s.* inquisición; indagación.
in·quis·i·tive [ɪnkwízətɪv] *adj.* inquisitivo, investigador; preguntón; curioso.
in·road [ínrod] *s.* incursión, invasión, ataque; **to make -s upon** atacar; mermar.
in·sane [ɪnsén] *adj.* insano, loco; — **asylum** manicomio, casa de locos.
in·san·i·ty [ɪnsǽnətɪ] *s.* locura.
in·sa·tia·ble [ɪnséʃɪəbl] *adj.* insaciable.
in·scribe [ɪnskráɪb] *v.* inscribir.
in·scrip·tion [ɪnskrípʃən] *s.* inscripción; letrero.
in·sect [ínsɛkt] *s.* insecto.
in·se·cure [ɪnsɪkjʊ́r] *adj.* inseguro.
in·sen·si·ble [ɪnsénsəbl] *adj.* insensible.
in·sen·si·tive [ɪnsénsətɪv] *adj.* insensible.
in·sep·a·ra·ble [ɪnsépərəbl] *adj.* inseparable.
in·sert [ínsɝt] *s.* inserción; intercalación; hoja (*insertada en un libro*); circular, folleto (*insertado en un periódico*); [ɪnsɝ́t] *v.* insertar; intercalar; encajar; meter.
in·ser·tion [ɪnsɝ́ʃən] *s.* inserción; introducción.
in·side [ínsáɪd] *s.* interior; **-s** entrañas; *adj.* interior, interno; secreto; — **job** delito cometido por el personal; — **track** con datos privados. *adv.* dentro; adentro; **to turn — out** volver(se) al revés; *prep.* dentro de.
in·sight [ínsaɪt] *s.* penetración, discernimiento; intuición; perspicacia; comprensión.
in·sig·ni·a [ɪnsígnɪə] *s. pl.* insignias.
in·sig·nif·i·cant [ɪnsɪgnífəkənt] *adj.* insignificante.
in·sin·u·ate [ɪnsínjʊet] *v.* insinuar.
in·sin·u·a·tion [ɪnsɪnjʊéʃən] *s.* insinuación; indirecta.
in·sip·id [ɪnsípɪd] *adj.* insípido.
in·sist [ɪnsíst] *v.* insistir en; empeñarse(en); porfiar, persistir.
in·sis·tence [ɪnsístəns] *s.* insistencia, empeño, porfía.
in·sis·tent [ɪnsístənt] *adj.* insistente; porfiado, persistente.
in·so·lence [ínsələns] *s.* insolencia.
in·so·lent [ínsələnt] *adj.* insolente.
in·sol·u·ble [ɪnsɑ́ljəbl] *adj.* insoluble.
in·spect [ɪnspékt] *v.* inspeccionar; examinar, registrar.
in·spec·tion [ɪnspékʃən] *s.* inspección; registro.
in·spec·tor [ɪnspéktɚ] *s.* inspector.
in·spi·ra·tion [ɪnspəréʃən] *s.* inspiración.
in·spire [ɪnspáɪr] *v.* inspirar.
in·stall [ɪnstɔ́l] *v.* instalar.
in·stal·la·tion [ɪstəléʃən] *s.* instalación.
in·stall·ment, in·stal·ment [ɪnstɔ́lmənt] *s.* instalación; abono (*pago*); plazos, *Col.* cuotas; entrega o continuación (*semanal o mensual de una novela*); **to pay in -s** pagar por plazos; pagar en abonos.
in·stance [ínstəns] *s.* ejemplo, caso; vez, ocasión; instancia; **for —** por ejemplo.
in·stant [ínstənt] *s.* instante; *adj.* inmediato; urgente; **the 10th** — el 10 del (mes) corriente; **-ly** *adv.* al instante, inmediatamente.
in·stan·ta·ne·ous [ɪnstənténɪəs] *adj.* instantáneo.
in·stead [ɪnstéd] *adv.* en lugar de ello (eso, él, ella, *etc.*); — **of** en lugar de, en vez de.
in·step [ínstɛp] *s.* empeine (*del pie, del zapato*).
in·sti·gate [ínstəget] *v.* instigar.
in·still [ɪnstíl] *v.* inculcar, infundir.
in·stinct [ínstɪŋkt] *s.* instinto.

in·stinc·tive [ɪnstíŋktɪv] *adj.* instintivo.
in·sti·tute [ínstətjut] *s.* instituto; *v.* instituir.
in·sti·tu·tion [ɪnstətjúʃən] *s.* institución.
in·struct [ɪnstrʌ́kt] *v.* instruir; dar instrucciones.
in·struc·tion [ɪnstrʌ́kʃən] *s.* instrucción; enseñanza; **lack of** — falta de saber o conocimientos; **-s** órdenes, instrucciones.
in·struc·tive [ɪnstrʌ́ktɪv] *adj.* instructivo.
in·struc·tor [ɪnstrʌ́ktɚ] *s.* instructor.
in·stru·ment [ínstrəmənt] *s.* instrumento; — **panel** salpicadero.
in·stru·men·tal [ɪnstrəméntl] *adj.* instrumental; **to be** — **in** ayudar a, servir de instrumento para.
in·sub·or·di·nate [ɪnsəbɔ́rdɪnət] *adj.* insubordinado.
in·suf·fer·a·ble [ɪnsʌ́frəbl] *adj.* insufrible, inaguantable.
in·suf·ficien·cy [ɪnsəfíʃənsɪ] *s.* insuficiencia; incompetencia; falta, escasez.
in·suf·fi·cient [insəfíʃənt] *adj.* insuficiente; inadecuado.
in·su·late [ínsəlet] *v.* aislar.
in·su·la·tion [ɪnsəléʃən] *s.* aislamiento; aislación.
in·su·la·tor [ínsəletɚ] *s.* aislador.
in·su·lin [ínsələn] *s.* insulina.
in·sult [ínsʌlt] *s.* insulto; [ɪnsʌ́lt] *v.* insultar.
in·sur·ance [ɪnʃúrəns] *s.* aseguramiento; seguro; prima, premio (*de una póliza de seguro*); — **agent** agente de seguros; — **company** compañía de seguros; — **policy** póliza de seguro; **accident** — seguro contra accidentes; **fire** — seguro contra incendios; **life** — seguro sobre la vida.
in·sure [ɪnʃúr] *v.* asegurar; asegurarse de.
in·sur·gent [ɪnsɝ́dʒənt] *adj.* & *s.* insurgente, insurrecto.
in·sur·mount·a·ble [ɪnsɚmáuntəbl] *adj.* insuperable.
in·sur·rec·tion [ɪnsərékʃən] *s.* insurrección, rebelión, alzamiento.
in·tact [ɪntǽkt] *adj.* intacto.
in·te·ger programming [intəgɚ prográmɪŋ] *s.* programación por integración.
in·te·gral [íntəgrəl] *adj.* integral; integrante; *s.* integral.
in·te·grate [íntəgret] *v.* integrar.
in·teg·ri·ty [ɪntégrətɪ] *s.* integridad, entereza.
in·tel·lect [íntlɛkt] *s.* intelecto; entendimiento.
in·tel·lec·tu·al [ɪntléktʃuəl] *adj.* & *s.* intelectual.
in·tel·li·gence [ɪntélədʒəns] *s.* inteligencia; — **quotient** (I.Q.) cociente de inteligencia; información, noticias; policía secreta.
in·tel·li·gent [ɪntélədʒənt] *adj.* inteligente.
in·tel·li·gi·ble [ɪntélədʒəbl] *adj.* inteligible.
in·tem·per·ance [ɪntémpərəns] *s.* intemperancia.
in·tend [ɪnténd] *v.* intentar, pensar, tener la intención de; proponerse; destinar; **to** — **to do it** pensar hacerlo.
in·tense [ɪnténs] *adj.* intenso.
in·ten·si·fy [ɪnténsɪfaɪ] *v.* intensificar.
in·ten·si·ty [ɪnténsətɪ] *s.* intensidad.
in·ten·sive [ɪnténsɪv] *adj.* intenso; intensivo.
in·tent [ɪntént] *s.* intento, intención, propósito; significado; **to all -s and purposes** en todo caso, en todos sentidos; en realidad; *adj.* atento; — **on** absorto en, reconcentrado en; resuelto a, decidido a.
in·ten·tion [ɪnténʃən] *s.* intención.
in·ten·tion·al [ɪnténʃənl] *adj.* intencional; **-ly** *adv.* intencionalmente, adrede, a propósito.
in·ter [ɪntɝ́] *v.* enterrar, sepultar.
in·ter·cede [ɪntɚsíd] *v.* interceder.
in·ter·cept [ɪntɚsépt] *v.* interceptar; atajar.
in·ter·cep·tion [ɪntɚsépʃən] *s.* interceptación.
in·ter·ces·sion [ɪntɚséʃən] *s.* intercesión.
in·ter·change [íntɚtʃéndʒ] *s.* intercambio; cambio, trueque; [ɪntɚtʃéndʒ] *v.* cambiar, trocar; permutar; alternar.
in·ter·course [íntɚkors] *s.* comunicación; comercio, trato; intercambio (*de ideas, sentimientos, etc.*).
in·ter·den·tal [ɪntɚdéntl] *adj.* interdental.
in·ter·est [íntərɪst] *s.* interés; rédito; participación (*en un negocio*); *v.* interesar.
in·ter·est·ed [íntərɪstɪd] *adj.* interesado; **to be** (*o* **become**) — **in** interesarse en (*o* por).
in·ter·est·ing [íntərɪstɪŋ] *adj.* interesante.
in·ter·face [íntɚfes] *s.* (*computer*) interfaz, interface.
in·ter·fere [ɪntɚfír] *v.* intervenir; interponerse, entremeterse; estorbar; **to** — **with** estorbar, frustrar, dificultar.
in·ter·fer·ence [ɪntɚfírəns] *s.* intervención; obstáculo; interferencia (*en la radio*).
in·ter·im [íntərɪm] *adj.* interino, intermedio.
in·te·ri·or [ɪntírɪɚ] *adj.* interior; interno; *s.* interior.
in·ter·jec·tion [ɪntɚdʒékʃən] *s.* interjección, exclamación; intercalación.
in·ter·lace [ɪntɚlés] *v.* entrelazar, enlazar, entretejer.
in·ter·lin·e·ar [ɪntərlínɪɚ] *adj.* interlineal.
in·ter·lock [ɪntɚlák] *v.* entrelazar(se); trabar(se); **interlocking** entrelazados.
in·ter·lude [íntɚlud] *s.* intervalo.
in·ter·me·di·ate [ɪntɚmídɪɪt] *adj.* intermedio.
in·ter·mi·na·ble [ɪntɝ́mɪnəbl] *adj.* interminable, inacabable.
in·ter·min·gle [ɪntɚmíŋgl] *v.* entremezclar(se), entreverar(se); mezclar(se).
in·ter·mis·sion [ɪntɚmíʃən] *s.* intermisión; intermedio, entreacto.
in·ter·mit·tent [ɪntɚmítn̩t] *adj.* intermitente.
in·tern [ɪntɝ́n] *v.* internar, confinar, encerrar; [íntɝn] *s.* practicante (*de medicina en un hospital*).
in·ter·nal [ɪntɝ́nl] *adj.* interno; interior; — **revenue** rentas internas; — **memory** (*computer*) memoria residente.
in·ter·na·tion·al [ɪntɚnǽʃənl] *adj.* internacional.
in·ter·o·ce·an·ic [ɪntɚoʃɪǽnɪk] *adj.* interoceánico.
in·ter·pose [ɪntɚpóz] *v.* interponer(se).
in·ter·pret [ɪntɝ́prɪt] *v.* interpretar.
in·ter·pre·ta·tion [ɪntɝprɪtéʃən] *s.* interpretación.
in·ter·pret·er [ɪntɝ́prɪtɚ] *s.* intérprete.
in·ter·ro·gate [ɪntérəget] *v.* interrogar.
in·ter·ro·ga·tion [ɪntɛrəgéʃən] *s.* interrogación.
in·ter·o·ga·tive [ɪntərágətɪv] *adj.* interrogativo; *s.* pronombre o palabra interrogativa.
in·ter·rupt [ɪntərʌ́pt] *v.* interrumpir.
in·ter·rup·tion [ɪntərʌ́pʃən] *s.* interrupción.
in·ter·sect [ɪntɚsékt] *v.* cortar(se); cruzar(se).
in·ter·sec·tion [ɪntɚsékʃən] *s.* intersección; **street** — bocacalle.
in·ter·sperse [ɪntɚspɝ́s] *v.* entremezclar, esparcir.
in·ter·stice [ɪntɝ́rstɪs] *s.* intersticio.
in·ter·twine [ɪntɚtwáɪn] *v.* entrelazar, entretejer, trenzar.
in·ter·val [íntɚvl] *s.* intervalo.
in·ter·vene [ɪntɚvín] *s.* intervenir; interponerse; mediar.
in·ter·ven·tion [ɪntɚvénʃən] *s.* intervención.
in·ter·view [íntɚvju] *s.* entrevista; *v.* entrevistar, entrevistarse con.
in·tes·tine [ɪntéstɪn] *s.* intestino; *adj.* intestino, interno.
in·ti·ma·cy [íntəməsɪ] *s.* intimidad.
in·ti·mate [íntəmɪt] *adj.* íntimo; *s.* amigo íntimo; [íntəmet] *v.* intimar, insinuar; indicar, dar a entender.

in·ti·ma·tion [ɪntəméʃən] *s.* intimación, insinuación.
in·tim·i·date [ɪntímədet] *v.* intimidar, acobardar, infundir miedo.
in·to [íntu, íntə] *prep.* en; dentro de; hacia el interior.
in·tol·er·a·ble [ɪntálərəbl] *adj.* intolerable, inaguantable.
in·tol·er·ance [ɪntálərəns] *s.* intolerancia.
in·tol·er·ant [ɪntálərənt] *adj.* intolerante.
in·to·na·tion [ɪntonéʃən] *s.* entonación.
in·tox·i·cate [ɪntáksəket] *v.* embriagar; emborrachar.
in·tox·i·ca·tion [ɪntaksəkéʃən] *s.* embriaguez; envenenamiento, intoxicación (*estado tóxico o envenenamiento parcial*).
in·tran·si·gent [ɪntrǽnsədʒənt] *adj.* intransigente.
in·tra·ve·nous [ɪntrəvínəs] *adj.* intravenoso.
in·trench [ɪntréntʃ] *v.* atrincherar; **to — oneself** atrincherarse; **to — upon another's rights** infringir los derechos ajenos; **to be -ed** estar atrincherado; estar firmemente establecido.
in·trep·id [ɪntrépɪd] *adj.* intrépido.
in·tri·cate [íntrəkɪt] *adj.* intrincado, enredado.
in·trigue [ɪntríg] *s.* intriga; enredo; trama; lío, embrollo; *v.* intrigar; tramar, maquinar.
in·tri·guer [ɪntrígɚ] *s.* intrigante.
in·tro·duce [ɪntrədjús] *v.* introducir; presentar.
in·tro·duc·tion [ɪntrədʌ́kʃən] *s.* introducción; presentación.
in·tro·spec·tion [ɪntrospékʃən] *s.* introspección.
in·tro·vert [íntrovɚt] *s.* introvertido.
in·trude [ɪntrúd] *v.* entremeterse (*o* entrometerse); introducir, meter.
in·trud·er [ɪntrúdɚ] *s.* intruso, entremetido.
in·tru·sion [ɪntrúʒən] *s.* intrusión, entremetimiento.
in·tru·sive [ɪntrúsɪv] *adj.* intruso.
in·trust = **entrust.**
in·tu·i·tion [ɪntuíʃən] *s.* intuición.
in·un·date [ínəndet] *v.* inundar.
in·ure [ɪnjúr] *v.* habituar, acostumbrar.
in·vade [ɪnvéd] *v.* invadir.
in·vad·er [ɪnvédɚ] *s.* invasor.
in·va·lid [ɪnvǽlɪd] *adj.* inválido (*que no vale*), nulo, de ningún valor.
in·va·lid [ínvəlɪd] *adj.* inválido, enfermizo, achacoso; **— diet** dieta para inválidos; *s.* inválido.
in·val·u·a·ble [ɪnvǽljebl] *adj.* de gran precio o valor, inapreciable, inestimable.
in·var·i·a·ble [ɪnvérɪəbl] *adj.* invariable; **invariably** *adv.* invariablementre; sin falta, sin excepción.
in·va·sion [ɪnvéʒən] *s.* invasión.
in·vent [ɪnvént] *v.* inventar.
in·ven·tion [ɪnvénʃən] *s.* invención; invento; inventiva, facultad para inventar.
in·ven·tive [ɪnvéntɪv] *adj.* inventivo.
in·ven·tive·ness [ɪnvéntɪvnɪs] *s.* inventiva.
in·ven·tor [ɪnvéntɚ] *s.* inventor.
in·ven·to·ry [ínvəntorɪ] *s.* inventario; *v.* inventariar.
in·verse [ɪnvɝ́s] *adj.* inverso; **— video** (*computer*) video inverso.
in·vert [ɪnvɝ́t] *v.* invertir; trastrocar; volver al revés.
in·vest [ɪnvést] *v.* invertir, colocar (*fondos*); (*award*) investir (*de una dignidad o cargo*); (*authorize*) revestir (*de autoridad*); sitiar.
in·ves·ti·gate [ɪnvéstəget] *v.* investigar, indagar.
in·ves·ti·ga·tion [ɪnvɛstəgéʃən] *s.* investigación; indagación.
in·ves·ti·ga·tor [ɪnvéstəgetɚ] *s.* investigador; indagador.
in·vest·ment [ɪnvéstmənt] *s.* inversión (*de fondos*); **— broker** corredor de valores.
in·ves·tor [ɪnvéstɚ] *s.* el que invierte fondos.
in·vig·o·rate [ɪnvígəret] *v.* vigorizar, fortalecer.
in·vin·ci·ble [ɪnvínsəbl] *adj.* invencible.
in·vis·i·ble [ɪnvízəbl] *adj.* invisible.
in·vi·ta·tion [ɪnvətéʃən] *s.* invitación.
in·vite [ɪnváɪt] *v.* invitar; convidar.
in·vit·ing [ɪnváɪtɪŋ] *adj.* atractivo; seductivo, tentador.
in·vo·ca·tion [ɪnvəkéʃən] *s.* invocación.
in·voice [ínvɔɪs] *s.* factura; envío, mercancías enviadas; *v.* facturar.
in·voke [ɪnvók] *v.* invocar.
in·vol·un·tar·y [ɪnválənterɪ] *adj.* involuntario.
in·volve [ɪnválv] *v.* complicar, enredar; envolver; implicar; comprometer; **to get -d in difficulties** embrollarse, meterse en embrollos.
in·ward [ínwɚd] *adj.* interior; interno; (*secret*) secreto; *adv.* hacia el interior; hacia dentro, adentro, para dentro; **-s** *adv.* = **inward.**
i·o·dide [áɪədaɪd] *s.* yoduro.
i·o·dine [áɪədaɪn] *s.* yodo.
i·on [áɪən] *s.* ion.
i·on·ize [áɪənaɪz] *v.* ionizar.
ire [aɪr] *s.* ira.
ir·i·des·cent [ɪrədésn̩t] *adj.* iridiscente, tornasolado, irisado.
i·rid·i·um [ɪrídiəm] *s.* iridio.
i·ris [áɪrɪs] *s.* iris; arco iris; flor de lis.
I·rish [áɪrɪʃ] *adj.* irlandés; *s.* irlandés, idioma irlandés; **the —** los irlandeses.
irk·some [ɝ́ksəm] *adj.* fastidioso, engorroso, molesto, tedioso; **irked** fastidiado.
i·ron [áɪɚn] *s.* (*element*) hierro; (*instrument*) plancha (*de planchar ropa*); *adj.* ferro, de hierro; **— work** herraje, trabajo en hierro, **— works** herrería; fábrica de hierro; *v.* planchar; **to — out a difficulty** allanar una dificultad.
i·ron·ic·al [aɪránɪkl] *adj.* irónico.
i·ron·ing [áɪɚnɪŋ] *s.* planchado.
i·ro·ny [áɪrənɪ] *s.* ironía.
ir·ra·di·ate [ɪrédɪet] *v.* irradiar.
ir·ra·tion·al [ɪrǽʃənl] *adj.* irracional.
ir·re·fut·a·ble [ɪrɛfjútəbl] *adj.* irrefutable.
ir·reg·u·lar [ɪrégjəlɚ] *adj.* irregular.
ir·rel·e·vant [ɪréləvənt] *adj.* fuera de propósito, inaplicable al caso, inoportuno, que no viene (*o* no hace) al caso.
ir·re·li·gious [ɪrɪlídʒəs] *adj.* irreligioso, impío.
ir·re·me·di·a·ble [ɪrɪmídɪəbl] *adj.* irremediable; incurable.
ir·re·proach·a·ble [ɪrɪprótʃəbl] *adj.* irreprochable, intachable.
ir·re·sis·ti·ble [ɪrɪzístəbl] *adj.* irresistible.
ir·res·o·lute [ɪrézəlut] *adj.* irresoluto, indeciso.
ir·re·triev·a·ble [ɪrɪtrívəbl] *adj.* inapelable.
ir·rev·er·ence [ɪrévərəns] *s.* irreverencia, desacato.
ir·rev·er·ent [ɪrévərənt] *adj.* irreverente.
ir·ri·gate [írəget] *v.* regar; irrigar, bañar.
ir·ri·ga·tion [ɪrəgéʃən] *s.* riego; irrigación; **— canal** acequia, canal de irrigación.
ir·ri·ta·ble [írətəbl] *adj.* irritable; colérico.
ir·ri·tate [írətet] *v.* irritar.
ir·ri·tat·ing [írətetɪŋ] *adj.* irritante.
ir·ri·ta·tion [ɪrətéʃən] *s.* irritación.
ir·rupt [ɪrʌ́pt] *v.* irrumpir.
is·land [áɪlənd] *s.* isla.
is·land·er [áɪləndɚ] *s.* isleño.
isle [aɪl] *s.* isla, ínsula.
i·so·bar [áɪsəbar] *s.* isobara.
i·so·late [áɪslet] *v.* aislar.
i·so·la·tion [aɪsléʃən] *s.* aislamiento.
i·so·la·tion·ism [aɪsoléʃənɪzəm] *s.* aislamiento.

i·so·met·ric [aɪsométrɪk] *adj.* isométrico.
Is·ra·el [ízriəl] *s.* Israel.
is·sue [íʃu] *s.* (*printing*) tirada, impresión; (*stock, bonds*) emisión (*de valores*); (*problem*) problema, tema; (*result*) resultado, consecuencia; **without —** sin prole, sin sucesión; **to take — with** disentir o diferir de; *v.* publicar, dar a luz; dar, promulgar (*un decreto*); emitir (*valores, acciones, etc.*); emanar; fluir; salir; brotar; provenir.
isth·mus [ísməs] *s.* istmo.
it [ɪt] *pron. neutro* lo, la (*acusativo*); ello, él, ella (*después de una preposición*); *por lo general no se traduce cuando es sujeto del verbo;* **— is there** está allí; **— is I** soy yo; **— is raining** llueve, está lloviendo; **what time is — ?** ¿qué hora es?; **— is two o'clock** son las dos; **how goes — ?** ¿qué tal?
I·tal·ian [ɪtǽljən] *adj. & s.* italiano.
i·tal·ic [ɪtǽlɪk] *adj.* itálico; **-s** *s.* letra bastardilla.
i·tal·i·cize [ɪtǽləsaɪz] *v.* poner en letra bastardilla.
itch [ɪtʃ] *s.* comezón; picazón; sarna (*enfermedad de la piel*); *v.* picar, darle a uno comezón; sentir comezón; **to be -ing** tener ansias de.
itch·y [ítʃɪ] *adj.* sarnoso, *Méx., Ven.* sarniento; **to feel —** sentir comezón.
i·tem [áɪtəm] *s.* artículo; detalle; noticia, suelto (*de un periódico*); partida (*de una lista*).
i·tem·ize [áɪtəmaɪz] *v.* pormenorizar detallar; hacer una lista de.
i·tin·er·ant [aɪtínərənt] *adj.* ambulante.
i·tin·er·ar·y [aɪtínərɛrɪ] *s.* itinerario; ruta; guía de viajeros.
its [ɪts] *pos. neutro* su (sus), de él, de ella, de ello.
it·self [ɪtsélf] *pron. neutro* mismo, misma; **by —** por sí, de por sí, por sí solo; solo, aislado; **in —** en sí.
i·vo·ry [áɪvrɪ] *s.* marfil; **— tower** torre de marfil.
i·vy [áɪvɪ] *s.* hiedra (yedra).

J:j

jab [dʒæb] *v.* picar; pinchar; *s.* piquete, pinchazo.
jack [dʒæk] *s.* (*tool*) gato (*para alzar cosas pesadas*); (*card*) sota (*en naipes*); (*male*) macho (*del burro y otros animales*); (*flag*) bandera de proa; **— of all trades** aprendiz de todo y oficial de nada; sabelotodo; **— pot** premio gordo, premio mayor; **— rabbit** liebre americana; *v.* **to — up** solevantar, alzar con gato (*un objeto pesado*).
jack·ass [dʒǽkæs] *s.* asno, burro.
jack·et [dʒǽkɪt] *s.* chaqueta; envoltura; forro (*de un libro*); hollejo (*de la patata*).
jack·knife [dʒǽknaɪf] *s.* navaja.
jag·ged [dʒǽgɪd] *adj.* serrado, dentado.
jag·uar [dʒǽgwar] *s.* jaguar.
jail [dʒel] *s.* cárcel; *v.* encarcelar.
jail·er [dʒélə˞] *s.* carcelero.
ja·lop·y [dʒalápɪ *s.* fotingo.
jam [dʒæm] *v.* estrujar, apachurrar; atorar(se); obstruir(se), atascar(se); apiñar(se); agolpar(se); **to — on the brakes** frenar de golpe; **to — one's fingers** machucarse los dedos; **to — through** forzar por, meter a la fuerza; *s.* conserva, compota; apretura; atascamiento; **traffic —** aglomeración de transeúntes o automóviles, *Am.* bola; **to be in a —** estar en un aprieto.
jan·i·tor [dʒǽnətə˞] *s.* conserje; portero; casero (*encargado de un edificio*).
Jan·u·ar·y [dʒǽnjuɛrɪ] *s.* enero.
Jap·a·nese [dʒæpəníz] *adj. & s.* japonés.
jar [dʒɑr] *s.* jarra, jarro; tarro; (*collision*) choque; (*shake*) sacudida; (*vibration*) trepidación, vibración; **large earthen —** tinaja; *v.* trepidar; hacer vibrar; hacer temblar; menear; **to — one's nerves** ponerle a uno los nervios de punta.
jar·gon [dʒɑ́rgən] *s.* jerga, jerigonza.
jas·mine [dʒǽzmɪn] *s.* jazmín.
jas·per [dʒǽspə˞] *s.* jaspe.
jaunt [dʒɔnt] *s.* caminata, excursión; *v.* dar un paseíto, hacer una corta caminata.
jaw [dʒɔ] *s.* quijada, mandíbula, *Ch.* carretilla; **-s** grapa (*de herramienta*).
jaw·bone [dʒɔ́bón] *s.* mandíbula, quijada.
jay [dʒe] *s.* grajo; rústico, bobo; **blue —** azulejo; **— walker** el que cruza las bocacalles descuidadamente.
jazz [dʒæz] *s.* jazz (*cierta clase de música sincopada*); *v.* tocar el jazz; bailar el jazz; **to — up** sincopar; animar, alegrar.
jeal·ous [dʒéləs] *adj.* celoso; envidioso; **to be — of someone** tener celos de una persona, tenerle celos a una persona.
jeal·ou·sy [dʒéləsɪ] *s.* celos; envidia.
jeer [dʒɪr] *s.* mofa, befa, escarnio, *Carib.* choteo; *v.* mofar, befar, *Carib.* chotear; **to — at** mofarse de.

IN

jel·ly [dʒélɪ] *s.* jalea; *v.* convertir(se) en jalea, hacer(se) gelatinoso.
jeop·ard·ize [dʒépə˞daɪz] *v.* arriesgar, comprometer.
jeop·ar·dy [dʒépə˞dɪ] *s.* riesgo.
jerk [dʒə˞k] *s.* tirón; sacudida, *Méx., C.A., Ven. Col.* jalón; espasmo muscular; *v.* sacudir(se); dar un tirón; atasajar (*la carne*); **to — out** sacar de un tirón; **-ed beef** tasajo, *Am.* charqui.
jerk·wa·ter [dʒə˞kwɔlə˞] *adj.* de mala muerte.
jer·ry-build [dʒérɪ bɪʃd] *v.* edificar con cualesquiera materiales.
jer·sey [dʒə́˞zɪ *s.* tejido de punto, tejido elástico, *Am.* jersey; chaqueta, blusa, camisa (*de punto*), *Am.* jersey.
jest [dʒɛst] *s.* broma; chanza; chiste; *v.* bromear; chancearse.
jest·er [dʒéstə˞] *s.* chancero, burlón; bufón.
Jes·u·it [dʒéʒuɪt] *s.* jesuita.
jet [dʒɛt] *s.* chorro; surtidor (*de fuente*); **— airplane** avión de reacción; **— engine** motor de reacción; motorreactor; **gas —** mechero de gas; *adj.* de azabache; **jet-black** negro como el azabache; *v.* chorrear, salir en chorro.
jet·ti·son [dʒétɪsən] *v.* echar mercancías al mar.
Jew [dʒu] *s.* judío.
jew·el [dʒúəl] *s.* joya, alhaja; gema; **— box** estuche, joyero.
jew·el·er [dʒúələ˞] *s.* joyero; **-'s shop** joyería.
jew·el·ry [dʒúəlrɪ] *s.* joyas, alhajas, pedrería; **— store** joyería.
Jew·ish [dʒúɪʃ] *adj.* judío.
jib [dʒɪb] *s.* foque (vela).
jif·fy [dʒífɪ] *s.* instante; **in a —** en un instante, en dos paletas; en un decir Jesús, en un santiamén.
jig [dʒɪg] *s.* jiga (*música y baile*); **— saw** sierra mecánica (*para recortar figuras*); **— saw puzzle** rompecabezas (*de recortes*) *v.* tocar una jiga; bailar una jiga; bailotear; menear(se).
jig·gle [dʒígl] *v.* zangolotear(se), zarandear(se), menear(se); *s.* zarandeo, meneo, zangoloteo.
jilt [dʒɪlt] *v.* desairar, dar calabazas, dejar plantado.
jin·gle [dʒíŋgl] *s.* retintín; verso o rima infantil; (*radio*) propaganda cantada; **— bell** cascabel; *v.* hacer retintín.
job [dʒɑb] *s.* tarea, faena; trabajo; empleo, ocupación; **to be out of a —** estar sin trabajo;

estar desocupado; **by the** — a destajo.
job·ber [dʒábɚ] *s.* negociante medianero.
jock·ey [dʒákɪ] *s.* jockey; *v.* maniobrar (*para sacar ventaja o ganar un puesto*).
join [dʒɔɪn] *v.* juntar(se); enlazar(se); acoplar; unirse a, asociarse a.
joint [dʒɔɪnt] *s.* (*point*) juntura, coyuntura; (*function*) articulación; conexión; bisagra; (*public place*) garito (*casa de juego*); fonducho, restaurante de mala muerte; **out of** — descoyuntado; desunido; *adj.* unido, asociado; copartícipe; colectivo; — **account** cuenta en común; — **action** acción colectiva; — **committee** comisión mixta; — **company** en comandita; — **creditor** acreedor copartícipe; — **heir** coheredero; — **owner** condómino, copropietario; — **session** sesión plena; **-ly** *adv.* juntamente, juntos, unidamente, colectivamente.
joke [dʒok] *s.* broma; chiste, chanza; *v.* bromear; chancear(se), *Carib.* chotear; *Ríopl.* farrear; jorobar.
jok·er [dʒókɚ] *s.* bromista, chancero, guasón, *Carib.* choteador; (*card*) comodín.
jok·ing·ly [dʒókɪŋlɪ] *adv.* en (*o* de) chanza, en (*o* de) broma; de chiste.
jol·ly [dʒálɪ] *adj.* jovial; alegre; festivo; *v.* bromear, chancearse.
jolt [dʒolt] *s.* sacudida; sacudimiento; choque; *v.* sacudir.
jos·tle [dʒásl] *v.* rempujar o empujar, dar empellones; codear; *s.* rempujón, empujón, empellón.
jot [dʒɑt] *v.* **to** — **down** apuntar, tomar apuntes; *s.* jota, pizca.
jour·nal [dʒɝ́nl] *s.* diario; periódico; revista; acta (*de una junta o concilio*).
jour·nal·ism [dʒɝ́nlɪzəm] *s.* periodismo.
jour·nal·ist [dʒɝ́nlɪst] *s.* periodista.
jour·nal·is·tic [dʒɝnlístɪk] *adj.* periodístico.
jour·ney [dʒɝ́nɪ] *s.* viaje; jornada; *v.* viajar; peregrinar.
joy [dʒɔɪ] *s.* júbilo, regocijo; alegría, gusto, deleite; felicidad.
joy·ful [dʒɔ́ɪfəl] *adj.* regocijado, jubiloso; alegre; **-ly** *adv.* con regocijo, regocijadamente, con júbilo, alegremente.
joy·ous [dʒɔ́ɪəs] *adj.* jubiloso, alegre, gozoso.
joy·stick [dʒɔ́ɪstɪk] *s.* (*computer*) mando para juegos, palanca de juegos.
ju·bi·lant [dʒúblənt] *adj.* jubiloso, alegre.
ju·bi·lee [dʒúblɪ] *s.* jubileo; júbilo.
judge [dʒʌdʒ] *s.* juez; — **advocate** auditor de un consejo militar; *v. juzgar.*
judg·ment [dʒʌ́dʒmənt] *s.* juicio; sentencia, fallo; opinión; discernimiento; — **day** día del juicio final.
ju·di·cial [dʒudíʃəl] *adj.* judicial.
ju·di·cious [dʒudíʃəs] *adj.* juicioso, cuerdo.
jug [dʒʌg] *s.* cántaro; jarro; jarra; botija; chirona (*cárcel*) *Am.* chirola.
jug·gle [dʒʌ́gl] *v.* hacer juegos de manos; hacer suertes; **to** — **the accounts** barajar (*o* manipular) las cuentas; *s.* juego de manos, suerte; trampa.
jug·gler [dʒʌ́glɚ] *s.* prestidigitador, malabarista.
juice [dʒus] *s.* jugo; zumo.
juic·i·ness [dʒúsɪnɪs] *s.* jugosidad.
juic·y [dʒúsɪ] *adj.* jugoso, zumoso; suculento; **a** — **story** un cuento picante.
juke box [dʒúkbɑks] *s.* tragamonedas; tragaquintos.
Ju·ly [dʒulái] *s.* julio.
jum·ble [dʒʌ́mbl] *s.* revolver(se), barajar; mezclar(se); *s.* mezcolanza, revoltijo; confusión.
jump [dʒʌmp] *v.* saltar; brincar; salvar (*de un salto*); hacer saltar; comerse una pieza (*en el juego de damas*); **to** — **at the chance** asir o aprovechar la oportunidad; **to** — **bail** perder la fianza por evasión; **to** — **over** saltar por encima de, salvar de un salto; **to** — **the track** descarrilarse; **to** — **to conclusions** hacer deducciones precipitadas; *s.* salto; brinco; subida repentina (*del precio*); **to be always on the** — andar siempre de aquí para allá; trajinar, trafagar, ser muy activo.
jump·er [dʒʌ́mpɚ] *s.* saltador; chaquetón holgado (*de obrero*); vestido sin mangas (*puesto sobre la blusa de mujer*); traje de juego (*para niños*).
jump·y [dʒʌ́mpɪ] *adj.* saltón; asustadizo, nervioso.
junc·tion [dʒʌ́ŋkʃən] *s.* unión, juntura; confluencia (*de dos rios*); empalme (*de ferrocarriles*); entronque.
junc·ture [dʒʌ́ŋktʃɚ] *s.* juntura; coyuntura; **at this** — a esta sazón, en esta coyuntura.
June [dʒun] *s.* junio.
jun·gle [dʒʌ́ŋgl] *s.* selva; matorral; *Am.* jungla; *Carib.* manigua.
ju·nior [dʒúnjɚ] *adj.* menor, más joven; — **college** colegio para los dos primeros anõs del bachillerato; **John Smith, Junior** (**Jr.**) John Smith, hijo; *s.* estudiante del tercer año (*en escuela superior, colegio o universidad*).
ju·ni·per [dʒúnɪpɚ] *s.* junípero; enebro.
junk [dʒʌŋk] *s.* basura, desperdicios; trastos viejos; chatarra; cosa inservible; — **dealer** chatarrero, — **yard** chatarrería; **Chinese** — junco chino (*embarcación pequeña*); *v.* desechar, echar a la basura.
ju·ris·dic·tion [dʒurɪskfkʃən] *s.* jurisdicción.
ju·ris·pru·dence [dʒurɪsprúdṇs] *s.* jurisprudencia, derecho.
ju·ror [dʒúrɚ] *s.* jurado, miembro de un jurado.
ju·ry [dʒúrɪ] *s.* jurado; **grand** — jurado de acusación; — **box** tribunal del jurado.
just [dʒʌst] *adj.* justo; recto; exacto; *adv.* ni más ni menos, exactamente, justamente; precisamente; sólo, no más, nada más; apenas; — **now** ahora mismo; **he** — **left** acaba de salir, *Ríopl.* salió recién; **she is** — **a little girl** no es más que una niña, es una niña no más; **to have** — acabar de.
jus·tice [dʒʌ́stɪs] *s.* justicia; juez; magistrado.
jus·ti·fi·ca·tion [dʒʌstəfəkéʃən] *s.* justificación.
jus·ti·fy [dʒʌ́stəfaɪ] *v.* justificar.
just·ly [dʒʌ́stlɪ] *adv.* justamente; con razón.
jut [dʒʌt] *v.* sobresalir, proyectarse, extenderse; *s.* salidizo, proyección.
ju·ve·nile [dʒúvənl] *adj.* juvenil.

K:k

kan·ga·roo [kæŋgərú] *s.* canguro.
kay·o (**K.O.**) [Kéo] *v.* noquear; **-ed** adj. noqueado.
keel [kil] *s.* quilla; *v.* dar de quilla (*voltear un barco*); **to** — **over** volcar(se); zozobrar; caerse patas arriba, desplomarse.
keen [kin] *adj.* agudo; afilado; perspicaz; ansioso.
keen·ness [kínnɪs] *s.* agudeza; perspicacia; anhelo, ansia.
keep [kip] *v.* guardar; tener guardado; tener; retener; conservar(se); preservar(se); mantener(se); **to** — **accounts** llevar las cuentas; **to** — **at it** persistir, seguir dale que dale; **to** — **away** mantener(se)

alejado; **to — back** tener a raya; detener; reprimir, restringir; **to — from** impedir; guardar(se) de; abstenerse de; **to — going** seguir andando, seguir adelante; seguir viviendo; **to — off** no arrimarse, no acercarse; no entrar; mantener(se) a distancia; **to — one's hands off** no tocar; **to — one's temper** contenerse, refrenarse, reprimirse; **— posted** mantener al corriente; **to — quiet** estarse quieto o callado; **to — something up** seguir o continuar haciendo algo; **to — to the right** seguir a la derecha; mantenerse a la derecha; **to — track of** llevar la cuenta de; no perder de vista; seguir la pista de; *s.* manutención, subsistencia; **for -s** para siempre; para guardar; dado, no prestado.

keep·er [kípɚ] *s.* guardián, custodio; **jail —** carcelero.

keep·ing [kípɪŋ] *s.* custodia; mantenimiento; preservación, conservación; **in — with** en armonía con.

keep·sake [kípsek] *s.* prenda, recuerdo, regalo.

keg [kɛg] *s.* tonel, barril.

ken·nel [kɛnl] *s.* perrera.

kept [kɛpt] *pret. & p.p. de* **to keep.**

ker·chief [kɝ́tʃɪf] *s.* pañuelo, pañolón.

ker·nel [kɝ́nl] *s.* simiente; grano (*de trigo o maíz*); meollo (*de ciertas frutas como la nuez*); núcleo.

ker·o·sene [kɛ́rəsin] *s.* kerosina, petróleo para lámparas.

ket·tle [kɛ́tl] *s.* caldera; **· drum** tímpano; **tea —** marmita, tetera, *Am.* pava (*para el mate*).

key [ki] *s.* (*lock*) llave; (*music*) clave; (*instrument*) tecla; (*land*) cayo; isleta; **— ring** llavero; **— lockout** (*computer*) inhibición de teclas; **to be in —** estar a tono, estar templado; estar en armonía; *adj.* (*important*) **— industries** industrias básicas; *v.* poner a tono, afinar, templar (*con llave*); armonizar; **to — up** elevar el tono de; **to be -ed up** estar sobreexcitado, estar en tensión nerviosa.

key·board [kíbord] *s.* teclado, tablero.

key·hole [kíhol] *s.* ojo de la cerradura.

key·note [kínot] *s.* nota tónica; idea o principio fundamental.

key·pad [kípæd] *s.* (*computer*) teclado numérico.

key·stone [kíston] *s.* clave (*de un arco*); base, fundamento principal.

kha·ki [kάki] *s.* kaki, caqui; *adj.* de kaki.

kick [kɪk] *s.* (*foot*) *Esp.* coz; puntapié; *Am.* patada; (*complaint*) queja; protesta; fuerza (*de una bebida*); estímulo; **to have a —** *Am.* patear (*dícese del licor*); *v.* cocear; dar coces o patadas; dar puntapiés; patear; quejarse, protestar; **to — out** echar a patadas; echar, expulsar; **to — the bucket** estirar la pata, morir, *Am.* patear el balde; **to — up a lot of dust** levantar una polvareda.

kick·back [kíkbæk] *s.* comisión ilegal; *Méx* mordida.

kid [kɪd] *s.* cabrito; cabritilla (*piel curtida de cabrito*); niño, niña; **— gloves** guantes de cabritilla; *v.* bromear, embromar; chancearse con, *Carib., Méx.* chotear.

kid·nap [kídnæp] *v.* secuestrar, raptar.

kid·nap·per [kídnæpɚ] *s.* secuestrador; robachicos, ladrón de niños.

kid·nap·ping [kídnæpɪŋ] *s.* rapto, secuestro.

kid·ney [kídnɪ] *s.* riñon; **— bean** judía, frijol; **— stones** cálculos.

kill [kɪl] *v.* matar; destruir; amortiguar; parar (*el motor*); *s.* animal o animales matados (*en la caza*).

kill·er [kílɚ] *s.* matador; asesino.

kiln [kɪln], [kɪl] *s.* horno.

ki·lo [kílo], **ki·lo·gram** [kíləgræm] *s.* kilo; **— computer chip** ficha de 1,024 *bits;* kilogramo.

ki·lo·byte (KBYTE) [kíləbaɪt] *s.* (*computer*) kilo-byte (KB).

ki·lo·cy·cle [kíləsaɪkl] *s.* kilociclo.

kil·o·me·ter [kíləmitɚ] *s.* kilómetro.

kil·o·watt [kíləwat] *s.* kilovatio.

ki·mo·no [kəmónə] *s.* quimono; bata.

kin [kɪn] *s.* parentela, parientes, familia; **to notify the nearest of —** avisar al pariente o deudo más cercano.

kind [kaɪnd] *adj.* bondadoso; benévolo; amable; **to send one's — regards to** enviar afectuosos saludos a; **kindhearted** de buen corazón; **— of tired** algo cansado; *s.* clase, especie, género; **to pay in —** pagar en especie; pagar en la misma moneda.

kin·der·gar·ten [kíndɚgαrtn̩] *s.* escuela de párvulos.

kin·dle [kíndl] *v.* encender(se); inflamar(se); incitar; prender (*el fuego*).

kind·ling [kíndlɪŋ] *s.* encendimiento; leña ligera, astillas, *Andes* charamuscas.

kind·ly [káɪndlɪ] *adj.* bondadoso; benigno; benévolo; amable, apacible; *adv.* bondadosamente, amablemente; con benevolencia; por favor; **not to take — to criticism** no aceptar de buen grado las correcciones.

kind·ness [káɪndnɪs] *s.* bondad, amabilidad; gentileza; benevolencia; favor.

kin·dred [kíndrɪd] *adj.* emparentado; allegado; semejante; **· facts** hechos relacionados; **— spirits** espíritus afines.

ki·nes·ics [kaɪnízɪks] *s.* kinésica; quinésica.

king [kɪŋ] *s.* rey; rey (*en ajedrez*); dama (*en el juego de damas*).

king·dom [kíŋdəm] *s.* reino.

king·ly [kíŋlɪ] *adj.* regio; real; majestuoso; *adv.* regiamente; majestuosamente.

king·pin [kɪŋpɪn] *s.* pivote central.

kink [kɪŋk] *s.* (*bend*) enroscadura; (*pain*) tortícolis.

kink·y [kɪŋkɪ] *adj.* crespo, ensortijado, *Am.* grifo.

kin·ship [kínʃɪp] *s.* parentesco; afinidad; semejanza.

kins·man [kínzmən] *s.* pariente, deudo.

kiss [kɪs] *s.* beso; *v.* besar.

kit [kɪt] *s.* estuche, caja de herramientas; saco, envoltura (*para guardar instrumentos, herramientas, etc.*); gatito; **medicine —** botiquín; **soldier's —** mochila.

kitch·en [kítʃɪn] *s.* cocina; **— ware** trastos de cocina.

kite [kaɪt] *s.* cometa (*f.*), *Méx.* papalote; *Ch.* volantín; *Arg.* barrilete; milano (*pájaro*).

kit·ten [kítn̩] *s.* gatito.

kit·ty [kítɪ] *s.* gatito, minino.

knack [næk] *s.* destreza, maña, habilidad.

knap·sack [nǽpsæk] *s.* mochila, morral, alforja.

knave [nev] *s.* bribón, bellaco, pícaro; sota (*de naipes*).

knead [nid] *v.* amasar, sobar.

knee [ni] *s.* rodilla; **knee-deep** hasta la rodilla; metido hasta las rodillas.

kneel [nil] *v.* arrodillarse; hincarse.

knell [nɛl] *s.* doble (*toque de campanas por los difuntos*) *v* doblar, tocar a muerto.

knelt [nɛlt] *pret. & p.p. de* **to kneel.**

knew [nju] *pret. de* **to know.**

knick·knack [níknæk] *s.* chuchería, baratija, chisme.

knife [naɪf] *s.* cuchillo; cuchilla; **carving —** trinchante; **pocket —** cortaplumas; navaja; *v.* acuchillar.

knight [naɪt] *s.* caballero; campeón; caballo (*en ajedrez*—0; **— errant** caballero andante; *v.* armar caballero.

knight·hood [náɪthʊd] *s.* caballería, orden de la caballería.
knit [nɪt] *v.* tejer (*a punto de aguja*); hacer calceta o malla; enlazar; soldarse (*un hueso*) **to — one's brow** fruncir las cejas, arrugar la frente; *pret. & p.p. de* **to knit.**
knit·ting [nítɪŋ] *s.* labor de punto; — **needle** aguja de media.
knives [naívz] *pl. de* **knife.**
knob [nɑb] *s.* perilla, botón, tirador (*de puerta, cajón, etc.*); protuberancia.
knock [nɑk] *v.* (*pound*) golpear, golpetear; llamar o tocar a la puerta; (*criticize*) criticar, censurar o hablar mal de; desacreditar; **to — down** derribar; desmontar (*una máquina o aparato*); **to — off** suspender (*el trabajo*); rebajar (*del precio*); derribar, echar abajo; **to — out** aplastar de un golpe, poner fuera de combate; dejar sin sentido; noquear; *s.* golpe; golpeteo, toque, llamada, aldabonazo; crítica, censura; **knock-kneed** zambo, patizambo.
knock·er [nɑ́kɚ] *s.* llamador, aldaba, aldabón; criticón, murmurador.
knoll [nol] *s.* colina, loma; eminencia.
knot [nɑt] *s.* nudo; lazo; milla náutica; *v.* anudar(se).
knot·ty [nɑ́tɪ] *adj.* nudoso; (*difficult*) dificultoso, enredado.
know [no] *v.* (*to be acquainted with*) conocer; (*to have knowledge of; to know how to*) saber; (*to recognize*) reconocer; distinguir; **to — how to swim** saber nadar; **to — of** saber de; tener conocimiento de; tener noticias de; estar enterado de.
know·how [nóhaʊ] *s.* idoneidad.
know·ing·ly [nóɪŋlɪ] *adv.* a sabiendas; adrede.
knowl·edge [nɑ́lɪdʒ] *s.* conocimiento; saber, sabiduría; pericia; **not to my** — mo que yo sepa.
known [non] *p.p. de* **to know.**
knuck·le [nʌ́kl] *s.* nudillo; coyuntura, articulación; artejo; *v.* someterse; **to — down** someterse; aplicarse con empeño al trabajo.
kryp·ton [kríptan] *s.* criptón.

L:l

la·bel [lébl] *s.* marbete, etiqueta, rótulo; *v.* marcar, rotular; apodar, llamar.
la·bor [lébɚ] *s.* trabajo; (*cause*) labor; obrerismo, obra; mano de obra; (*class*) la clase obrera; — **union** sindicato; — **gang** peonaje; — **party** Partido Laborista; **to be in** — estar de parto; *adj.* laboral, obrero; *v.* trabajar; (*try*) afanarse; (*give birth*) estar de parto; (*develop*) elaborar (*un punto*).
lab·o·ra·to·ry [lǽbrətorɪ] *s.* laboratorio.
la·bor·er [lébərɚ] *s.* trabajador, obrero; jornalero, peón.
la·bo·ri·ous [ləbóriəs] *adj.* laborioso, trabajoso, penoso; industrioso.
lab·y·rinth [lǽbərɪnθ] *s.* laberinto.
lace [les] *s.* (*cloth*) encaje; (*cord*) cordón, cordoncillo, cinta (*de corsé, etc.*); **gold** — galón de oro (*para guarnecer uniformes*); *v.* atar con cinta o cordón; guarnecer con encajes; enlazar, entrelazar.
lack [læk] *s.* falta; escasez, carencia; deficiencia; *v.* carecer de, faltarle a uno; necesitar; **he -s courage** le falta ánimo.
lack·ey [lǽkɪ] *s.* lacayo.
lack·ing [lǽkɪŋ] *adj.* falto, carente.
lack·lus·ter [lǽklʌstɚ] *adj.* deslustrado.
lac·quer [lǽkɚ] *s.* laca; *v.* barnizar con laca.
lad [læd] *s.* rapaz, chico.
lad·der [lǽdɚ] *s.* escalera de mano.
lad·en [lédn̩] *adj.* cargado; agobiado, abrumado; *v.* cargar; agobiar.
la·dies [lédɪz] *pl. de* **lady.**
la·dle [lédl] *s.* cucharón; *v.* servir (*sopa*) con cucharón.
la·dy [lédɪ] *s.* señora; dama; — **like** como señora, muy fina, elegante; — **love** amada, querida.
lag [læg] *v.* rezagarse, quedarse atrás, atrasarse; andar lentamente; *s.* retardo o retardación, retraso.
la·goon [ləgún] *s.* laguna.
laid [led] *pret. & p.p. de* **to lay; to be — up** estar incapacitado o estropeado.
lain [len] *p.p. de* **to lie.**
lair [lɛr] *s.* guarida; cueva de fieras.
lake [lek] *s.* lago.
lamb [læm] cordero; — **kin** corderito.
lame [lem] *adj.* cojo; (*injured*) lisiado; estropeado; — **excuse** disculpa falsa; — **duck** empleado público entre elección e inauguración; deudor insolvente. *v.* hacer cojo; estropear, incapacitar.
la·ment [ləmέnt] *s.* lamento; *v.* lamentar(se).
lam·ent·a·ble [lǽməntəbl] *adj.* lamentable; doloroso.
lam·en·ta·tion [læməntéʃən] *s.* lamentación, lamento.
lam·i·nate [lǽmənet] *v.* laminar.
lamp [læmp] *s.* lámpara; linterna; (*street*) farol; — **post** poste (de farol); — **shade** pantalla de lámpara.
lance [læns] *s.* lanza; *v.* alancear, lancear, herir con lanza; picar con bisturí.
land [lænd] *s.* tierra; (*lot*) terreno; (*soil*) suelo; *v.* desembarcar; aterrizar (*un avión*); llegar; coger (*un pez*); — **bank** banco de préstamos hipotecarios; — **poor** con propiedad pero sin fondos; **to — a job** conseguir una colocacion, lograr un empleo.
land-grant [lǽndgrænt] *adj.* mediante donación federal de tierras.
land·hold·er [lǽndholdɚ] *s.* terrateniente, propietario, hacendado.
land·ing [lǽndɪŋ] *s.* (*act*) desembarco, desembarque; aterrizaje (*de un avión*); (*place*) desembarcadero; descanso (*de escalera*); — **field** campo de aterrizaje; aeropuerto; — **gear** tren de aterrizaje; — **wheels** ruedas de aterrizaje; — **strip** pista de aterrizaje.
land·la·dy [lǽndledɪ] *s.* patrona, casera, dueña (*de la casa*).
land·lord [lǽndlɔrd] *s.* amo, patrón, propietario, dueño; casero.
land·mark [lǽndmɑrk] *s.* mojón, señal (*para fijar los confines*); marca; suceso culminante.
land·own·er [lǽndonɚ] *s.* terrateniente, propietario, hacendado.
land·scape [lǽndskep] *s.* paisaje.
land·slide [lǽndslaɪd] *s.* derrumbe; alúd, derrumbamiento, desplome; gran mayoría de votos; victoria aplastante, arrolladora.
lane [len] *s.* senda, vereda; callejuela; ruta, derrotero (*de vapores o aviones*).
lan·guage [lǽŋgwɪdʒ] *s.* lengua; idioma; lenguaje.
lan·guid [lǽŋgwɪd] *adj.* lánguido.
lan·guish [lǽŋgwɪʃ] *v.* languidecer.
lan·guor [lǽŋgɚ] *d.* languidez.
lank [læŋk] *adj.* alto y delgado, largucho.
lank·y [lǽŋkɪ *adj.* largucho, zancón, zancudo.
lan·tern [lǽntɚn] *s.* linterna; farol.
lan·tha·nides [lǽnθənaɪdz] *s.* lantánidos.

lap [læp] *s.* falda, regazo; aleta; etapa, trecho (*de una carrera*); *v.* lamer; **to — over** cruzar(se) sobre, entrecruzar(se).
la·pel [ləpɛ́l] *s.* solapa.
lap·i·da·ry [lǽpɪdɛrɪ] *s.* & *adj.* lapidario.
lapse [læps] *s.* lapso; transcurso; desliz; error; *v.* deslizarse; pasar, transcurrir; caer en un desliz; decaer (*el entusiasmo, el interés, etc.*); caducar (*un plazo, un contrato, etc.*).
lar·board [lɑ́rbɚd] *s.* babor; *adj.* de babor; **— side** banda de babor.
lar·ce·ny [lɑ́rsn̩ɪ] *s.* latrocinio, hurto; ratería.
lard [lɑrd] *s.* lardo, manteca de puerco; *v.* mechar.
large [lɑrdʒ] *adj.* grande; **at —** suelto, libre; sin trabas; en general; **-ly** *adv.* grandemente, en gran parte.
large·scale [lɑ́rdʒskél] *adj.* en grande escala; (*computer*) **— integration** 500 a 20,000 entradas lógicas.
lar·i·at [lǽrɪət] *s.* reata.
lark [lɑrk] *s.* (*bird*) alondra; (*fun*) diversión, holgorio, jarana; **to go on a —** ir o andar de jarana.
lar·va [lɑ́rvə] *s.* larva.
lar·ynx [lǽrɪŋks] *s.* laringe.
las·civ·i·ous [ləsívɪəs] *adj.* lascivo.
la·ser [lézɚ] *s.* laser; **— printer** impresora laser.
lash [læʃ] *s.* látigo; azote, latigazo; (*eye*) pestaña; *v.* fustigar; azotar; (*scold*) censurar, reprender; (*tie*) amarrar.
lass [læs] *s.* moza, muchacha, doncella.
las·si·tude [lǽsətjud] *s.* dejadez, flojedad, decaimiento de fuerzas.
las·so [lǽso] *s.* lazo, reata, mangana; *v.* lazar, *Am.* enlazar.
last [læst] *adj.* (*in a series*) último; final; (*just passed*); pasado; **— night** anoche; **— year** el año pasado; **at —** por fin, finalmente, al fin; **next to the —** penúltimo; **to arrive —** llegar el último; *s.* fin, término; horma (*de zapato*); *v.* durar; perdurar; **-ly** *adv.* finalmente, en conclusión.
last·ing [lǽstɪŋ] *adj.* duradero; perdurable.
latch [lætʃ] *s.* pestillo, picaporte, aldaba, cerrojo; *v.* cerrar con aldaba.
late [let] *adj.* (*tardy*) tardío; tardo; (*recent*) reciente; último; **— comer** recién llegado; rezagado; **a — hour** una hora avanzada; **the — Mr. X** el finado (*o* difunto) Sr. X; **to have a — supper** cenar tarde; *adv.* tarde; **— afternoon** atardecer; **— in the night** a una hora avanzada de la noche; **— into the night** a deshoras de la noche; **— in the week** a fines de la semana; **of —** últimamente, recientemente; hace poco; **to be —** ser tarde; llegar tarde; estar atrasado, venir o llegar con retraso (*el tren*); **the train was ten minutes —** el tren llegó con diez minutos de retraso; **-ly** últimamente, recientemente; hace poco, poco ha
la·tent [létn̩t] *adj.* latente.
lat·er [létɚ] *adj.* & *adj.* (*comp. de* **late**) más tarde; después, luego; más reciente; posterior.
lat·er·al [lǽtərəl] *adj.* lateral.
lat·est [létɪst] *adv.* & *adj.* (*superl. de* **late**) más tarde; más reciente, más nuevo; último; **the — fashion** la última moda, las últimas novedades; **the — news** las últimas novedades, las noticias más recientes; **at the —** a más tardar.
lathe [leð] *s.* torno (*de carpintero o mecánico*).
lath·er [lǽðɚ] *s.* jabonadura, espuma de jabón; *v.* jabonar, enjabonar; espumar, hacer espuma.
Lat·in [lǽtn̩] *adj.* latino; *s.* latín.
lat·i·tude [lǽtətjud] *s.* latitud; libertad; amplitud.
lat·ter [lǽtɚ] *adj.* último; **towards the — part of the week** a (*o* hacia) fines de la semana; **the —** éste (ésta, esto, etc.).
lat·tice [lǽtɪs] *s.* celosía; enrejado, rejilla.
laud [lɔd] *v.* loar, encomiar, alabar.
laud·a·ble [lɔ́dəbl] *adj.* laudable, loable.
laugh [læf] *v.* reír(se); **to — at** reírse de; **to — loudly** reírse a carcajadas; **to — in one's sleeve** reírse para sus adentros; **she -ed in his face** se rió en sus barbas; *s.* risa; **loud —** risotada, carcajada, risada.
laugh·a·ble [lǽfəbl] *adj.* risible; ridículo.
laugh·ing·stock [lǽfɪŋstak] *s.* hazmerreír.
laugh·ter [lǽftɚ] *s.* risa.
launch [lɔntʃ] *v.* (*put into water*) botar o echar (*un barco*) al agua; (*a rocket*) lanzar; (*begin*) empezar, poner en operación; **to — forth** lanzarse; **to — forth on a journey** emprender un viaje; *s.* lancha; (*act*) botadura, lanzamiento.
laun·der [lɔ́ndɚ] *v.* lavar y planchar (*la ropa*).
laun·dress [lɔ́ndrɪs] *s.* lavandera.
laun·dry [lɔ́ndrɪ] *s.* lavandería; lavado; ropa (lavada).
lau·rel [lɔ́rəl] *s.* laurel; gloria, honor.
la·va [lɑ́və] *s.* lava.
lav·a·to·ry [lǽvətorɪ] *s.* lavabo; lavamanos; lavatorio.
lav·en·der [lǽvəndɚ] *s.* espliego, lavándula; *adj.* lila, morado claro.
lav·ish [lǽvɪʃ] *adj.* gastador, pródigo, dadivoso; abundante, copioso; profuso; lujoso; *v.* prodigar; malgastar, despilfarrar; **to — praise upon** colmar de alabanzas a; **-ly** pródigamente; copiosamente; lujosamente.
law [lɔ] *s.* ley; derecho, jurisprudencia; regla; *adj.* **— student** estudiante de leyes, estudiante de derecho; **law-abiding** observante de la ley; *s.* **— of nations** derecho internacional.
law·break·er [lɔ́brekɚ] *s.* infractor, transgresor.
law·ful [lɔ́fəl] *adj.* legal; lícito; válido; permitido.
law·less [lɔ́lɪs] *adj.* sin ley; ilegal; desenfrenado; revoltoso; licencioso.
law·mak·er [lɔ́mekɚ] *s.* legislador.
lawn [lɔn] *s.* césped, prado; *Am.* pasto, grama; linón (*tela de hilo o algodón*); **— mower** cortadora de césped.
law·suit [lɔ́sut] *s.* pleito, litigio.
law·yer [lɔ́jɚ] *s.* abogado, jurisconsulto.
lax [læks] flojo; suelto; relajado.
lax·a·tive [lǽksətɪv] *adj.* & *s.* laxante, purgante.
lax·i·ty [lǽksətɪ] *s.* flojedad, flojera; relajamiento (*de una regla, ley, etc.*).
lay [le] *pret. de* **to lie.**
lay [le] *v.* colocar; poner; tender, extender; poner (*huevos*); echar (*la culpa*); atribuir (*la responsabilidad*); presentar, exponer; asentar (*el polvo*); **to — a wager** apostar; **to — aside** poner a un lado; arrinconar; ahorrar; **to — away** (*o* **by**) guardar; **to — bare** revelar; poner al descubierto; exponer; **to — down** poner, colocar; rendir (*las armas*); **to — down the law** mandar, dictar; **to — hold of** asir, agarrar; **to — off a workman** suspender a un obrero; **to — open** exponer a la vista; **to — out a plan** trazar un plan; **to — up** almacenar; guardar, ahorrar; **to be laid up** estar incapacitado o estropeado; **to — waste** asolar; *s.* lay, balada, canción; situación, orientación (*del terreno*); *adj.* lego, laico; profano (*no iniciado en una ciencia*).
lay·er [léɚ] *s.* capa; estrato; (*hen*) gallina ponedora.
lay·man [lémən] *s.* lego, seglar, laico.
lay·off [léɔf] *s.* despido.
la·zi·ly [lézɪlɪ] *adv.* perezosamente.

la·zi·ness [lézɪnɪs] *s.* pereza.
la·zy [lézɪ] *adj.* perezoso, holgazán.
lead [lɛd] *d.* plomo; plomada, pesa de plomo.
lead [lid] *v.* (*guide*) guiar, dirigir; llevar; conducir; mandar (*un ejército*); (*precede*) ir a la cabeza de; sobresalir entre; ser mano (*en el juego de naipes*); **to — an orchestra** dirigir una orquesta, llevar la batuta; **to — astray** llevar por mal camino, extraviar, descarriar; **to — the way** ir por delante, mostrar el camino; *s.* delantera, primer lugar; mando, dirección; indicio; papel principal; primer actor.
lead·en [lɛ́dn̩] *adj.* plomizo; aplomado, color de plomo; pesado.
lead·er [lídɚ] *s.* jefe, caudillo, *Am.* líder; director; guía; caballo delantero; **-s** puntos suspensivos.
lead·er·ship [lídɚʃɪp] *s.* dirección, mando; iniciativa.
lead·ing [lídɪŋ] *adj.* principal; delantero; **— man** primer actor.
lead·off [lídɔf] *adj.* delantero; puntero.
leaf [lif] *s.* hoja; *v.* echar hojas (*un árbol*), cubrirse de hojas; **to — through a book** hojear un libro.
leaf·less [líflɪs] *adj.* sin hojas, deshojado.
leaf·let [líflɪt] *s.* hojilla; folleto, hoja volante, papel volante, circular.
leaf·y [lífɪ] *adj.* frondoso.
league [lig] *s.* (*alliance*) liga, confederación; sociedad; (*distance*) legua; *v.* asociar(se); ligarse, coligarse.
leak [lik] *s.* gotera (*en un techo*); agujero, grieta (*por donde se escapa el agua o el gas*); escape (*de gas, vapor, electricidad, etc.*); *v.* gotear(se); rezumar(se); hacer agua (*dícese de un barco*); salirse, escaparse (*el gas, el vapor, etc.*).
lean [lin] *v.* (*incline*) inclinar(se); recostar(se), reclinar(se); (*support*) apoyar(se); *adj.* magro; flaco; **— year** año estéril, año improductivo.
leant [lɛnt] = **leaned.**
leap [lip] *v.* saltar; brincar; *s.* salto, brinco; **— year** año bisiesto.
leapt [lɛpt] *pret. & p.p. de* **to leap.**
learn [lɝn] *v.* aprender; saber, averiguar, enterarse de.
learn·ed [lɝ́nɪd] *adj.* erudito; docto.
learn·er [lɝnɚ] *s.* aprendedor; estudiante, estudioso.
learn·ing [lɝ́nɪŋ] *s.* erudición, saber; aprendizaje.
learnt [lɝnt] *pret. & p.p. de* **to learn.**
lease [lis] *v.* arrendar, dar o tomar en arriendo; *s.* arriendo, contrato de arrendamiento; *Arg.* contrato de locación.
leash [liʃ] *s.* traílla; cuerda.
least [list] *adj.* (el mínimo, (el) más pequeño; *adv.* menos; **at —** al menos, a lo menos, por lo menos; **the —** lo (el, la) menos.
leath·er [ɛ́ðɚ] *s.* cuero, piel; *adj.* de cuero, de piel; **— strap** correa.
leave [liv] *v.* dejar; abandonar; (*depart*) salir (de); partir; irse; **to — out** dejar fuera; omitir; *s.* permiso, licencia; **— out absence** licencia; **to take — of** despedirse de.
leav·en [lɛ́vən] *s.* levadura, fermento; *v.* fermentar (*la masa*).
leaves [livz] *pl. de* **leaf.**
leav·ings [lívɪŋz] *s.* sobras, desperdicios.
lec·ture [lɛ́ktʃɚ] *s.* conferencia, discurso; reprensión; *v.* dar una conferencia; explicar; reprender.
lec·tur·er [lɛ́ktʃərɚ] *s.* conferenciante; conferencista; lector (*de universidad*).
LED (Light-e·mit·ting di·ode) [lɛd] *s.* (computer) diodo electroluminiscente (LED).
led [lɛd] *pret. & p.p. de* **to lead.**
ledge [lɛdʒ] *s.* borde; salidizo.
ledg·er [lɛ́dʒɚ] *s.* libro mayor (*en contabilidad*); *Arg.* libro de cuentas. **— account** cuenta del mayor; **— balance** saldo del mayor; **— entry** pase en el mayor.
leech [litʃ] *s.* sanguijuela.
leer [lɪr] *s.* mirada de soslayo, mirada lujuriosa; *v.* mirar de soslayo; mirar con lujuria.
lee·ward [líwɚd] *s. & adv.* sotavento.
left [lɛft] *pret. & p.p. de* **to leave; I have two books —** me quedan dos libros; *adj.* izquierdo; *s.* izquierda; mano izquierda; **at (on, to) the —** a la izquierda.
left-hand·ed [lɛ́fthǽndɪd] *adj.* zurdo; a la izquierda; (*awkward*) torpe; (*bad*) malicioso, insincero; **— compliment** alabanza irónica.
left·ist [lɛ́ftɪst] *s.* izquierdista.
left·o·ver [lɛ́ftovɚ] *adj.* sobrante; **-s** *s. pl.* sobras.
left-wing [lɛ́ftwɪŋ] *adj.* izquierdista.
leg [lɛg] *s.* pierna; pata (*de animal, mesa, etc.*); pie o pata (*de banquillo, silla, etc.*); etapa, trecho (*de una carrera o viaje*); **to be on one's last -s** estar en las últimas.
leg·a·cy [lɛ́gəsɪ] *s.* legado, herencia.
le·gal [lígl̩] *adj.* legal; lícito; **— expenses** gastos jurídicos; **— fees** honorarios legales; **— holiday** día feriado; **— opinion** consulta; **— tender** moneda de curso legal.
le·gal·ize [líglaɪz] *v.* legalizar; sancionar, autorizar.
leg·ate [lɛ́gɪt] *s.* legado; delegado.
leg·a·tee [lɛ́gəti] *s.* legatario; *Cuba, Ch.* asignatario.
le·ga·tion [lɪgéʃən] *s.* legación; embajada.
leg·end [lɛ́dʒənd] *s.* leyenda; letrero, inscripción.
leg·en·dar·y [lɛ́dʒəndɛrɪ] *adj.* legendario.
leg·gings [lɛ́gɪŋz] *s. pl.* polainas.
leg·i·ble [lɛ́dʒəbl] *adj.* legible.
le·gion [lídʒən] *s.* legión.
leg·is·late [lɛ́dʒɪslet] *v.* legislar.
leg·is·la·tion [lɛdʒɪsléʃən] *s.* legislación.
leg·is·la·tive [lɛ́dʒɪsletɪv] *adj.* legislativo.
leg·is·la·tor [lɛ́dʒɪsletɚ] *s.* legislador.
leg·is·la·ture [lɛ́dʒɪsletʃɚ] *s.* legislatura, asamblea legislativa
le·git·i·mate [lɪdʒítəmɪt] *adj.* legítimo.
lei·sure [líʒɚ] *s.* ocio; **— hours** horas de ocio; **to be at —** estar ocioso; estar libre o desocupado; **do it at your —** hágalo Vd. cuando pueda o le convenga; hágalo Vd. en sus ratos de ocio.
lei·sure·ly [líʒɚlɪ] *adj.* lento, deliberado, pausado; *adv.* sin prisa, despacio, a sus (mis, tus, *etc.*) anchas.
lem·on [lɛ́mən] *s.* limón; **— tree** limonero; *adj.* de limón; **— color** cetrino.
lem·on·ade [lɛmənéd] *s.* limonada.
lend [lɛnd] *v.* prestar.
lend·er [lɛ́ndɚ] *s.* prestador; **money —** prestamista.
length [leŋkθ] *s.* largo, largor, largura, longitud; duración; cantidad (*de una sílaba*); **at —** largamente, detenidamente; al fin; **to go to any —** hacer cuanto esté de su parte.
length·en [lɛ́ŋkθən] *v.* alargar(se); prolongar(se).
length·wise [lɛ́ŋkθwaɪz] *adv.* a lo largo; longitudinalmente; *adj.* longitudinal.
length·y [lɛ́ŋkθɪ] *adj.* largo, prolongado.
le·ni·ent [línɪənt] *adj.* indulgente, clemente, poco severo.
lens [lɛnz] *s.* lente; cristalino (*del ojo*).
lent [lɛnt] *pret. & p.p. de* **to lend.**
Lent [lɛnt] *s.* cuaresma.
leop·ard [lɛ́pɚd] *s.* leopardo.
lep·ro·sy [lɛ́prəsɪ] *s.* lepra

less [lɛs] *adj.* menor; *adv. & prep.* menos; — **and** — cada vez menos.
less·en [lɛ́sn̩] *v.* aminorar(se), disminuir(se), reducir(se); mermar.
less·er [lɛ́sɚ] *adj.* menor, más pequeño.
les·son [lɛ́sn̩] *s.* lección.
lest [lɛst] *conj.* no sea que, por miedo de que.
let [lɛt] *v.* (*permit*) dejar, permitir; (*rent*) alquilar, arrendar; — **us** (*o* **let's**) **do it** vamos a hacerlo, hagámoslo; — **him come** que venga; **to** — **be** no molestar, dejar en paz; no tocar; **to** — **down** traicionar; **to** — **go** soltar; **to** — **in** dejar entrar, admitir; **to** — **know** avisar, enterar, hacer saber; **to** — **off** soltar; dejar libre; **to** — **through** dejar pasar; **to** — **up** disminuir; *pret. & p.p. de* **to let.**
let·down [lɛ́tdɑʊn] *s.* aflojamiento; desilusión.
le·thal [líθəl] *adj.* letal.
leth·ar·gy [lɛ́θədʒɪ] *s.* letargo; **to fall into a** — aletargarse.
let·ter [lɛ́tɚ] *s.* (*alphabet*) letra; (*missive*) carta; — **box** buzón; — **carrier** cartero; — **head** membrete; — **quality printer** impresora de alta calidad; *v.* rotular, hacer a mano letras de molde.
let·tuce [lɛ́tɪs] *s.* lechuga.
lev·ee [lɛ́vɪ] *s.* dique.
lev·el [lɛ́vl] *adj.* llano, plano; a nivel; igual; parejo; **level-headed** bien equilibrado, sensato; *adv.* a nivel; a ras; *s.* nivel; **to be on the** — obrar rectamente, obrar sin engaño; ser o decir la pura verdad; *v.* nivelar; igualar; allanar; apuntar, asestar (*un arma*); **to** — **to the ground** arrasar, echar por tierra.
le·ver [lɛ́vɚ] *s.* palanca; **control** — palanca de mando.
lev·i·ty [lɛ́vɪtɪ] *s.* frivolidad; levedad.
lev·y [lɛ́vɪ] *s.* imposición, recaudación (*de tributos, impuestos, etc.*); (*draft*) leva, enganche, reclutamiento; embargo (*de propiedad*); *v.* imponer, exigir, recauder (*tributos o multas*); reclutar; **to** — **on someone's property** embargar la propiedad de alguien.
lewd [lud] *adj.* lujurioso, lascivo, deshonesto.
lewd·ness [lúdnɪs] *s.* lascivia, lujuria.
lex·i·cal [lɛ́ksɪkl] *adj.* léxico.
lex·i·cog·ra·phy [lɛksɪkágrəfɪ] *s.* lexicografía.
lex·i·con [lɛ́ksɪkɑn] *s.* léxico.
li·a·bil·i·ty [laɪəbílətɪ] *s.* responsabilidad, obligación; desventaja; **li·a·bil·i·ties** obligaciones, deudas; pasivo; — **insurance** seguro contra daños a terceros; responsabilidad civil.
li·a·ble [láɪəbl] *adj.* responsable, obligado; sujeto, expuesto; propenso; probable.
li·ai·son [liezɑ́n] *s.* enlace; unión.
li·ar [láɪɚ] *s.* mentiroso, embustero.
li·bel [láɪbl] *s.* libelo; difamación; *v.* difamar.
lib·er·al [líbərəl] *adj. & s.* liberal.
lib·er·al·ism [líbɚəlɪzm] *s.* liberalismo.
lib·er·al·i·ty [lɪbərǽlətɪ] *s.* liberalidad; largueza, generosidad.
lib·er·al·ize [líbɚəlaɪz] *v.* liberalizar(se).
lib·er·ate [líbəret] *v.* libertar, librar; soltar.
lib·er·a·tion [lɪbəréʃən] *s.* liberación.
lib·er·a·tor [líbəretɚ] *s.* libertador.
li·ber·tine [líbɚtin] *adj. & s.* libertino.
li·ber·ty [líbɚtɪ] *s.* libertad; **at** — libre.
li·bi·do [lɪbído] *s.* líbido.
li·brar·i·an [laɪbrɛ́rɪən] *s.* bibliotecario.
li·brar·y [láɪbrɛrɪ] *s.* biblioteca.
li·bret·to [lɪbrɛ́to] *s.* libreto.
lice [laɪs] *pl. de* **louse.**
li·cense, licence [láɪsn̩s] *s.* licencia; permiso; (**title**) título; **driver's** — licencia (pase, certificado *o* patente) de chófer; título de conductor; licencia para manejar; — **plate** placa (*o* chapa) de numeración, chapa de circulación, chapa de matrícula; *v.* licenciar, dar licencia a; permitir, autorizar.
li·cen·tious [laɪsɛ́nʃəs] *adj.* licencioso, disoluto.
lick [lɪk] *v.* (*tongue*) lamer; (*thrash*) dar una tunda o zurra; vencer; **to** — **someone's boots** adular a uno con servilismo; **to** — **the dust** morder el polvo; adular; *s.* lamedura, *Am.* lamida; lengüetada; *C.C.* lambida; **salt** — lamedero (*lugar salino donde lame el ganado*); **not to do a** — **of work** no hacer absolutamente nada.
lick·ing [líkɪŋ] *s.* zurra, tunda.
lid [lɪd] *s.* tapadera, tapa; **eye** — párpado.
lie [laɪ] *s.* mentira; embuste; **to give the** — **to** desmentir, dar un mentís; *v.* mentir (*pret. & p.p.* **lied**); tenderse, acostarse; yacer; estar; estar situado; consistir (en); **to** — **back** recostarse, echarse hacia atrás; **to** — **down** acostarse, echarse, tenderse; **to** — **in wait** acechar, espiar.
lien [lin] *s.* obligación, gravámen.
lieu·ten·ant [lutɛ́nənt] *s.* teniente; **second** — subteniente.
life [laɪf] *s.* vida; **from** — del natural; **still** — naturaleza muerta; — **boat** bote de salvamento, lancha salvavidas; — **imprisonment** prisión perpetua; — **insurance** seguro sobre la vida; — **pension** pensión vitalicia; — **preserver** salvavidas, cinto o chaqueta de salvamento.
life·less [láɪflɪs] *adj.* sin vida; muerto; exánime; inanimado; desanimado.
life·less·ness [láɪflɪsnɪs] *s.* falta de vida; inercia; falta de animación.
life·like [láɪflaɪk] *adj.* como la vida; natural, que parece vivo.
life·long [láɪflaɔ́ŋ] *adj.* perpetuo, de toda la vida
life·size [láɪfsɑɪz] *adj.* de tamaño natural.
life·time [láɪftaɪm] *s.* vida, transcurso de la vida.
lift [lɪft] *v.* levantar; alzar; elevar; (**disperse**) disiparse (*las nubes, la niebla, las tinieblas*); **to** — **one's hat** quitarse el sombrero (*para saludar*); *s.* elevación; exaltación de ánimo; alzamiento, levantamiento; carga; ayuda (*para levantar una carga*); (**hoist**) alza (*de un zapato*); ascensor, *Am.* elevador; **to give someone a** — **in a car** llevar a alguien en el auto; *Méx.* dar aventón.
lig·a·ture [lígətʃʊr] *s.* ligadura.
light [laɪt] *s.* luz; lumbre; **tail** — *Am.* farito trasero, *Am.* farol de cola, *Méx.* calavera; *adj.* claro; con luz, (**skin**) de tez blanca; (**weight**) ligero; leve; frívolo; — **drink** bebida suave; — **headed** frívolo, ligero de cascos; — **hearted** alegre; — **opera** opereta; — **pen** (*computer*) lápiz óptico; **to make** — **of** dar poca importancia a; *v.* encender(se); iluminar, alumbrar; **to** — **upon** caer sobre; posarse en (*dícese de los pájaros, mariposas, etc.*).
light·en [láɪtn̩] *v.* aligerar; iluminar; aclarar; relampaguear; alegrar.
light·er [láɪtɚ] *s.* encendedor; (**boat**) barcaza, chalana.
light·house [láɪthaʊs] *s.* faro.
light·ing [láɪtɪŋ] *s.* iluminación; alumbrado.
light·ly [láɪtlɪ] *adv.* ligeramente; levemente; frívolamente; sin seriedad.
light·ness [láɪtnɪs] *s.* ligereza; frivolidad; claridad.
light·ning [láɪtnɪŋ] *s.* relampagueo; relámpago; — **rod** pararrayos.
light·weight [láɪtwet] *s.* peso liviano; peso ligero.
lik·a·ble [láɪkəbl] *adj.* agradable, simpático.

placentero.
like [laɪk] *adv.* & *prep.* como; del mismo modo que; semejante a; *adj.* semejante, parecido; **in — manner** de manera semejante, del mismo modo; **to feel — going** tener ganas de ir; **to look —** someone parecerse a alguien; **it looks — rain** parece que va a llover, quiere llover; *s.* semejante, igual; **-s** gustos; preferencias; *v.* gustarle a uno; **he -s books** le gustan los libros; **do whatever you —** haz lo que gustes.
like·ly [láɪklɪ] *adj.* probable, creíble; prometedor; **— place** lugar a propósito; **it is — to happen** es probable que suceda; *adv.* probablemente.
lik·en [láɪkən] *v.* asemejar, comparar.
like·ness [láɪknɪs] *s.* semejanza; parecido; retrato.
like·wise [láɪkwaɪz] *adv.* igualmente, asimismo; del mismo modo; también.
lik·ing [láɪkɪŋ] *s.* simpatía; afición; preferencia, gusto.
li·lac [láɪlək] *s.* lila; *adj.* lila, morado claro.
lil·y [lílɪ] *s.* lirio; azucena.
lil·y-white [lɪliwáɪt] *adj.* blanquísimo; puro; racialmente segregado.
limb [lɪm] *s.* rama (*de árbol*); miembro (*del cuerpo*), pierna, brazo.
lim·ber [límbɚ] *adj.* flexible; ágil; *v.* hacer flexible; **to — up** agilitar(se), hacer(se) flexible.
lime [laɪm] *s.* cal; lima (*fruta*); *Am.* limón; **— tree** limonero; liga (*para cazar pájaros*).
lime·light [láɪmlaɪt] *s.* luz de calcio; proscenio; **to be in the —** estar a la vista del público.
lime·stone [láɪmston] *s.* piedra caliza.
lim·it [límɪt] *s.* límite; confín; *v.* limitar.
lim·i·ta·tion [lɪmɪtéʃən] *s.* limitación; restricción.
lim·it·ed [límɪtɪd] *adj.* limitado; restringido.
lim·it·ing [límətɪŋ] *adj.* limítrofe.
lim·it·less [límɪtlɪs] *adj.* ilimitado, sin límites; desmedido.
limp [lɪmp] *s.* cojera; *v.* cojear; renguear; *adj.* flojo; flexible.
lim·pid [límpɪd] *adj.* límpido; claro, transparente.
line [laɪn] *s* (*mark*) línea; renglón; raya; (*cord*) cuerda; (*business*) ramo; giro (*de negocios*); especialidad; **of credit** línea de crédito, *Col.* cupo de crédito; **— printer** (*computer*) impresora de líneas; **— of goods** surtido, línea (*Am.* renglón) de mercancías; **branch railway —** ramal; **pipe —** cañería, tubería; **to bring into —** alinear; obligar a proceder de acuerdo con un plan; poner de acuerdo; **to get in —** meterse en fila, hacer (*o* formar) cola; *v.* linear, rayar; alinear; forrar; **to — up** alinear(se); formarse, formar fila.
lin·e·age [línɪɪdʒ] *s.* linaje.
lin·e·ar [lpaaɪnɪɚ] *adj.* lineal.
lined [laɪnd] *adj.* rayado; forrado.
lin·en [línɪn] *s.* lino; ropa blanca.
lin·er [láɪnɚ] *s.* vapor, buque; **air —** avión, transporte aéreo.
line·up [láɪnəp] *s.* formación.
lin·ger [líŋgɚ] *v.* tardar(se), demorarse, dilatarse; (*saunter*) andar ocioso, vagar; (*last*) perdurar; prolongarse.
lin·ge·rie [lǽnʒəri] *s.* ropa interior de mujer.
lin·guist [líŋgwɪst] *s.* lingüista.
lin·guis·tics [lɪŋgwístɪks] *s.* lingüística.
lin·ing [láɪnɪŋ *s.* forro.
link [lɪŋk] *s.* eslabón; enlace; **cuff -s** gemelos; *v.* eslabonar(se); enlazar(se).
lin·net [línɪt] *s.* jilguero.
li·no·le·um [lɪnólɪəm] *s.* linóleo (*tela impermeable para cubrir el suelo*).
lin·seed [línsid] *s.* linaza; **— oil** aceite de linaza.
lint [lɪnt] *s. hilas; hilachas.*
li·on [láɪən] *s.* león.
li·on·ess [láɪənɪs] *s.* leona.
lip [lɪp] *s.* labio.
lip·stick [l'aaɪpstɪk] *s.* lápiz para los labios.
liq·uid [líkwɪd] *adj.* líquido; **— assets** valores líquidos (*o* realizables); **— measure** medida para liquidos; *s.* líquido.
liq·ui·date [líkwɪdet] *v.* liquidar, saldar (*cuentas*); poner término a.
liq·ui·da·tion [lɪkwɪdéʃən] *s.* liquidación; saldo de cuentas.
liq·uor [líkɚ] *s.* licor; bebida espiritosa (*como aguardiente, ron, etc.*).
lira [lɪrə] unidad monetaria de Italia.
lisp [lɪsp] *s.* ceceo; *v.* cecear; balbucir.
list [lɪst] *s.* lista; registro; (*ship*) escora (*inclinación de un barco*); *v.* alistar, registrar poner o apuntar en una lista; hacer una lista de; escorar, inclinarse a la banda.
lis·ten [lísn] *v.* escuchar; atender, dar oídos, prestar atención; — ¡oye! ¡escucha!; ¡oiga! ¡escuche!; **to — in** escuchar por radio; escuchar a hurtadillas (*una conversación*).
lis·ten·er [lísn̩ɚ] *s.* escuchador, oyente; **radio —** radioescucha, radioyente.
list·ing [lístɪŋ] *s.* (*computer*) listado.
list·less [lístlɪs] *adj.* abstraído; indiferente; indolente; desatento.
list·less·ness [lístlɪsnɪs] *s.* indiferencia, inatención, abstracción.
lit [lɪt] *pret.* & *p.p. de* **to light**; *adj.* alumbrado; algo borracho.
lit·er·al [lítərəl] *adj.* literal; **-ly** *adv.* al pie de la letra, literalmente.
lit·er·ar·y [lítərɛrɪ] *adj.* literario.
lit·er·a·ture [lítərətʃʊr] *s.* literatura; impresos, folletos, circulares.
lith·i·um [líθiəm] *s.* litio.
lit·i·ga·tion [lɪtəgéʃən] *s.* litigio, pleito.
lit·ter [lítɚ] *s.* (*young animals*) camada, cría; (*stretcher*) litera; camilla; cama de paja para animales; (*disorder*) cosas esparcidas; desorden; revoltillo; *v.* desarreglar, revolver, esparcir cosas.
lit·tle [lítl] *adj.* pequeño; poco; **Little Bear** Osa Menor; **a — coffee** un poco de café; **a — while** un ratito (*o* ratico), un poco; *adv.* & *s.* poco; **— by —** poco a poco.
live [lɪv] *v.* vivir; **to — down** hacer olvidar, borrar (*el pasado*); **to — up to** vivir en conformidad con, vivir de acuerdo con.
live [laɪv] *adj.* (*not dead*) vivo; (*lively*) enérgico; vivo, activo; **— coal** ascua encendida; **— oak** encina; siempreverde **— question** cuestión palpitante, cuestión de actualidad; **— wire** alambre cargado; persona muy activa.
live·li·hood [láɪvlɪhʊd] *s.* vida, alimento, subsistencia, manutención.
live·li·ness [láɪvlɪnɪs] *s.* viveza, animación; agilidad.
live·long [lívlɔŋ] *adj.* todo; absolutamente todo.
live·ly [láɪvlɪ] *adj.* vivo; vivaz; animado, alegre; airoso; **— horse** caballo brioso; *adv.* vivamente; de prisa.
liv·er [lívɚ] *s.* (*organ*) hígado; (*with life*) vividor.
liv·er·y [lívərɪ] *s.* librea; caballeriza (*para caballos de alquiler*).
lives [laɪvz] *pl. de* **life**.
live·stock [láɪvstɑk] *s.* ganado.
liv·id [lívɪd] *adj.* lívido; amoratado.
liv·ing [lívɪŋ] *s.* (*state*) vida; (*means*) manutención,

subsistencia; *adj.* vivo; viviente; — **room** sala; — **wage** sueldo suficiente para vivir; **the** — los vivos.
liz·ard [lízɚd] *s.* lagarto; **small** — lagartija.
load [lod] *s.* carga; **ship** — cargamento; **-s of** gran cantidad de; montones de; *v.* cargar; agobiar; colmar.
loaf [lof] *s.* hogaza de pan; **sugar** — azúcar de pilón; *v.* holgazanear, haraganear.
loaf·er [lófɚ] *s.* holgazán, haragán, zángano.
loan [lon] *s.* préstamo; empréstito; — **shark** usurero; — **word** préstamo semántico; *v.* prestar (*dinero*).
loath [loθ] *adj.* maldispuesto, renuente; **to be** — **to** repugnarle a uno.
loathe [loð] *v.* repugnarle a uno; abominar.
loath·some [lóðsəm] *adj.* repugnante, asqueroso; aborrecible.
loaves [lovz] *pl. de* **loaf.**
lob [lɑb] *v.* volear.
lob·by [lɑ́bɪ] *s.* (*place*) vestíbulo; antecámara; salón de entrada; hall; (*influence*) camarilla; **hotel** — vestíbulo o patio del hotel, hall; *v.* cabildear; *Ch., Perú* capitulear; **lobbying** cabildeo; **lobbyist** cabildero.
lobe [lob] *s.* lóbulo.
lob·ster [lɑ́bstɚ] *s.* langosta de mar.
lo·cal [lókl] *adj.* local; **train** tren ordinario.
lo·cal·i·ty [lokǽlətɪ] *s.* localidad; comarca.
lo·cal·ize [lóklaɪz] *v.* localizar.
lo·cate [lóket] *v.* situar, establecer; (*find*) localizar, averiguar la posición de; (*move to*) avecindarse, radicarse, establecerse.
lo·ca·tion [lokéʃən] *s.* situación; sitio, localidad.
lock [lak] *s.* (*door*) cerradura; (*canal*) esclusa (*de un canal*); llave (*de un arma de fuego*); guedeja (*de pelo*); bucle, rizo; *v.* cerrar con llave; trabar(se), juntar(se); entrelazar(se); **to** — **in** encerrar; **to** — **out** cerrar la puerta (*a alguien*), dejar afuera; **to** — **up** encerrar; encarcelar.
lock·er [lɑ́kɚ] *s.* alacena; armario.
lock·et [lɑ́kɪt] *s.* guardapelo.
lock·out [lɑ́kaʊt] *s.* paro (*suspensión del trabajo por parte de los empresarios*); cierre de fábrica.
lock·smith [lɑ́ksmɪθ] *s.* cerrajero.
lo·co·mo·tive [lokəmótɪv] *s.* locomotora; —**engineer** maquinista.
lo·cust [lókəst] *s.* langosta, saltamontes; cigarra; — **tree** algarrobo; acacia falsa.
lodge [lɑdʒ] *s.* logia; casita accesoria; casa de campo; *v.* alojar(se); hospedar(se); colocar; **to** — **a complaint** presentar una queja.
lodg·er [lɑ́dʒɚ] *s.* huésped, inquilino.
lodg·ing [lɑ́dʒɪŋ] *s.* alojamiento, hospedaje; vivienda.
loft [lɔft] *s.* desván; galería, balcón interior (*de un templo*); **choir** — coro; **hay** — pajar.
loft·y [lɔ́ftɪ] *adj.* elevado; sublime; altivo.
log [lɔg] *s.* leño, troza, tronco aserrado; (*ship*) corredera (*aparato para medir las millas que anda la nave*); diario de navegación; — **cabin** cabaña de troncos; *v.* cortar (*árboles*); cortar leños y transportarlos; registrar (*en el diario de navegación*); **logging** corte y transporte de trozos, explotación forestal.
log·ic [lɑ́dʒɪk] *s.* lógica; principios de la combinación de circuitos en las computadoras.
log·i·cal [lɑ́dʒʃɪkl] *adj.* lógico.
log·roll [lɔ́rol] *v.* lograr aprobación de leyes mediante favores.
loin [lɔɪn] *s.* ijada, ijar, lomo.
loi·ter [lɔ́ɪtɚ] *v.* holgazanear, vagar, malgastar el tiempo; **to** — **behind** rezagarse.
loll [lɑl] *v.* arrellanarse o repantigarse, recostarse con toda comodidad.
lone [lon] *adj.* solo, solitario.
lone·li·ness [lónlɪnɪs] *s.* soledad.
lone·ly [lónlɪ] *adj.* solo, solitario; triste, desamparado.
lone·some [lónsəm] *adj.* solo, solitario; triste, nostálgico.
long [lɔŋ] *adj.* largo; **the whole day** — todo el santo día; **three feet** — tres pies de largo; **to be** — **in coming** tardar en venir; *adv.* mucho, mucho tiempo; — **ago** hace mucho tiempo; — **shot** muy improbable, de poca esperanza; — **live!** ¡viva! **as** (*o* **so**) — **as** en tanto que, mientras que; **how** — **is it since . . . ?** ¿cuánto tiempo hace que . . . ?; **so** — **!** ¡hasta luego! ¡adiós!; **long-suffering** sufrido, paciente; **long-winded** prolijo, largo (*en hablar*); **long-distance** de larga distancia; *v.* anhelar; ansiar; **to** — **for** anhelar; suspirar por.
long·er [lɔ́ŋgɚ] *adj.* más largo; *adv.* más, más tiempo; **no** — ya no; **not . . . any** — ya no; no . . . más.
lon·gev·i·ty [lɑndʒévətɪ] *s.* longevidad.
long·hand [lɔ́ŋhænd] *s.* letra manuscrita.
long·ing [lɔ́ŋɪŋ] *s.* anhelo, añoranza, nostalgia; *adj.* anhelante, anheloso, nostálgico; **-ly** *adv.* con anhelo, anhelosamente, con ansia.
lon·gi·tude [lɑ́ndʒətjud] *s.* longitud.
long-range [lɔŋréndʒ] *adj.* de largo alcance.
long·shore·man [lɔ́ŋʃormən] *s.* estibador (*de barco o muelle*), cargador.
long-term [lɔ́ŋtɚm] *adj.* a largo plazo.
look [lʊk] *v.* (*see*) mirar; (*seem*) parecer; **it -s well on you** le cae (*o* le sienta) bien; **to** — **after** atender, cuidar; **to** — **alike** parecerse; asemejarse; **to** — **down on a person** mirar con desprecio (*o* menospreciar) a alguien; **to** — **for** buscar; esperar; **to** — **forward to** anticipar con placer; **to** — **into** examinar, investigar; — **out!** ¡cuidado!; ¡tenga cuidado!; **to** — **out of** asomarse a; **to** — **over** examinar; dar un vistazo a; **to** — **up** levantar la vista; buscar; **to** — **up to** admirar, mirar con respeto; *s.* mirada, vistazo; **-s** apariencia, aspecto; **to have good -s** ser bien parecido.
look·ing glass [lʊ́kɪŋglæs] *s.* espejo.
look·out [lʊ́kaʊt] *s.* vigía; atalaya; (*place*) mirador; (*view*) vista, perspectiva; **that is your** — ¡eso a usted!; **to be on the** — estar alerta.
loom [lum] *s.* telar; *v.* destacarse, descollar; asomar(se), aparecer.
loop [lup] *s.* (*closed*) lazo, gaza, presilla; (*road*) vuelta, curva; (*electric*) circuito; (*computer*) bucle; *v.* hacer una gaza (con *o* en); atar con gaza o presilla; hacer un circuito.
loop·hole [lúphol] *s.* agujero, abertura; (*way out*) salida; escapatoria.
loose [lus] *adj.* (*slack*) suelto; flojo; (*unfettered*) desatado; (*licentious*) disoluto; — **change** suelto, moneda suelta; — **jointed** de articulaciones flojas; — **leaf** de hojas sueltas; **to let** — soltar; *v.* soltar, desatar; aflojar; **-ly** *adv.* sueltamente; flojamente; con poca exactitud, sin fundamento.
loos·en [lúsn̩] *v.* soltar(se); aflojar(se) desatar(se); **to** — **one's hold** desasirse, soltarse.
loose·ness [lúsnɪs] *s.* (*limberness*) soltura; flojedad; (*laxness*) flojera; holgura; relajación; (*of bowel*) flujo.
loot [lut] *s.* botín, pillaje, saqueo; *v.* saquear, pillar, robar.
lop [lɑp] *v.* tronchar, desmochar (*Am.* mochar).
lo·qua·cious [lokwéʃəs] *adj.* locuaz, hablador, lenguaraz.

lo·quat [lókwat] *s.* níspero.
lord [lɔrd] *s.* señor; dueño, amo; lord; **Lord's Prayer** Padre Nuestro; **Our Lord** Nuestro Señor; *v.* señorear, mandar; **to — it over** señorear, dominar.
lord·ly [lɔ́rdlɪ] *adj.* señoril; noble; (*haughty*) altivo; despótico; *adv.* altivamente, imperiosamente.
lord·ship [lɔ́rdʃɪp] *s.* señoría (*título*); señorío, dominio.
lose [luz] *v.* perder; **to — sight of** perder de vista.
loss [lɔs] *s.* pédida; **to be at a —** estar perplejo; no saber qué hacer; **to sell at a —** vender con pérdida.
lost [lɔst] *pret. & p.p. de* **to lose;** *adj.* perdido; extraviado; **— in thought** absorto, abstraído; **to get —** perderse, extraviarse.
lot [lɑt] *s.* (*land*) lote; (*section*) parte, porción; (*luck*) suerte; solar, porción de terreno; **a — of** (*o* **-s of**) una gran cantidad de; mucho; muchos; **to draw -s** echar suertes; **to fall to one's —** tocarle a uno, caerle en suerte; *adv.* mucho; **a — better** mucho mejor.
lo·tion [lóʃən] *s.* loción.
lot·ter·y [lɑ́tərɪ] *s.* lotería.
loud [laʊd] *adj.* ruidoso; (*voice*) recio, fuerte; (*colors*) chillón (*dícese también de los colores*); *adv.* ruidosamente, fuerte, recio; alto, en voz alta.
loud-speak·er [láʊdspíkɚ] *s.* altavoz, altoparlante.
lounge [laʊndʒ] *s.* sala de descanso; sofá, diván, canapé; *v.* arrellanarse, repantigarse, recostarse cómodamente; sestear; holgazanear.
louse [laʊs] *s.* piojo.
lous·y [láʊzɪ] *adj.* piojoso; asqueroso.
lov·a·ble [lʌ́vəbl] *adj.* amable.
love [lʌv] *s.* (*affection*) amor; cariño; (*fondness*) afición **— affair** amorío; **to be in —** estar enamorado; **to fall in — with** enamorarse de; **to make — to** enamorar a; *v.* amar, querer; gustar mucho de, gustarle a uno mucho; encantarle a uno algo.
love·li·ness [lʌ́vlɪnɪs] *s.* belleza, hermosura; amabilidad.
love·ly [lʌ́vlɪ]*adj.* amable; lindo, bello; exquisito; encantador; ameno.
lov·er [lʌ́vɚ] *s.* amante; **music —** aficionado a (*o* amante de) la música.
lov·ing [lʌ́vɪŋ] *adj.* amante, amoroso, cariñoso, afectuoso; **-ly** *adv.* cariñosamente, afectuosamente.
low [lo] *adj.* (*not high*) bajo; (*base*) vil; (*humble*) humilde; (*downcast*) abatido; débil; (*lacking*) deficiente; (*sick*) gravemente enfermo; **— comedy** farsa, sainete; **— gear** primera velocidad; **—Mass** misa rezada; **— key** de intensidad minima; **dress with a — neck** vestido escotado (*o* con escote); **to be — on something** estar escaso de algo; **to be in — spirits** estar abatido o desanimado; *adv.* bajo; en voz baja, quedo, quedito; con bajeza, a precio bajo, vilmente; *s.* mugido; *v.* mugir.
low·er [lóɚ] *adj.* más bajo; inferior; **— case letter** letra minúscula; **— classman** estudiante de los dos primeros años; **— house** cámara de diputados; *v.* bajar; disminuir; rebajar; abatir; humillar.
low·land [lólænd] *s.* tierra baja.
low·li·ness [lólɪnɪs] *s.* bajeza; humildad.
low·ly [lólɪ] *adj.* bajo, humilde; inferior; *adv.* humildemente.
low·ness [lónɪs] *s.* bajeza (*humility*) humildad; (*weakness*) abatimiento; gravedad (*de tono*); debilidad (*de un sonido*); baratura.
loy·al [lɔ́ɪəl] *adj.* leal, fiel.
loy·al·ty [lɔ́ɪəltɪ] *s.* lealtad, fidelidad.
LSI (see **large-scale integration.**)
lu·bri·cant [lʊ́brɪkənt] *adj. & s.* lubricante.
lu·bri·cate [lúbrɪket] *v.* lubricar.
lu·cid [lúsɪd] *adj.* lúcido; claro; luciente.
luck [lʌk] *s.* suerte; fortuna; **in —** de buena suerte; **in bad —** de mala suerte.
luck·i·ly [lʌ́klɪ] *adv.* afortunadamente, por fortuna.
luck·y [lʌ́kɪ] *adj.* afortunado, feliz; **to be —** tener suerte, tocarle a uno la suerte.
lu·cra·tive [lúkrətɪv] *adj.* lucrativo.
lu·di·crous [lúdɪkrəs] *adj.* ridículo.
lug [lʌg] *v.* llevar, traer, *Am.* cargar; **to — away** cargar con, llevarse (*una cosa pesada*).
lug·gage [lʌ́gɪdʒ] *s.* equipaje.
luke·warm [lúkwɔ́rm] *adj.* tibio, templado; indiferente.
lull [lʌl] *v.* arrullar; sosegar; calmar(se); *s.* calma, momento de calma.
lul·la·by [lʌ́ləbaɪ] *s.* arrullo, canción de cuna.
lum·ber [lʌ́mbɚ] *s.* madera, maderaje; **— man** maderero, negociante en madera; **— yard** depósito de maderas; **— jack** leñador; *v.* cortar y aserrar madera; explotar los bosques; moverse pesadamente.
lu·min·ous [lúmənəs] *adj.* luminoso.
lump [lʌmp] *s.* (*mass*) terrón; bulto; (*swelling*) hinchazón, chichón; protuberancia; **— of sugar** terrón de azúcar; **— sum** pago global; *v.* amontonar; consolidar (*gastos*); apelotonarse, aterronarse, formar terrones.
lump·y [lʌ́mpɪ] *adj.* aterronado.
lu·na·tic [lʌ́nətɪk] *adj. & s.* lunático, loco.
lunch [lʌntʃ] *s.* almuerzo; merienda; **· room** merendero, *Méx., Ven., Carib.* lonchería; *Ríopl.* confitería; *Spain* cafetería; *v.* almorzar; merendar; *Am.* tomar el lonche.
lun·cheon [lʌ́ntʃən] *s.* almuerzo; merienda.
lung [lʌŋ] *s.* pulmón.
lurch [lɝtʃ] *s.* sacudida; tambaleo repentino; **to give a —** tambalearse; **to leave someone in the —** dejar a uno plantado, dejar a uno a buenas noches; *v.* tambalearse; dar un tambaleo repentino.
lure [lʊr] *s.* aliciente, atractivo; tentación; (*bait*) cebo o reclamo (*para atraer*); *v.* atraer; seducir; atraer (*con cebo o reclamo*).
lurk [lɝk] *v.* estar oculto; estar en acecho; moverse furtivamente.
lus·cious [lʌ́ʃəs] *adj.* exquisito, delicioso, sabroso.
lust [lʌst] *s.* lujuria; deseo vehemente; codicia; *v.* **to — after** codiciar.
lus·ter [lʌ́stɚ] *s.* lustre, brillo.
lus·trous [lʌ́strəs] *adj.* lustroso.
lust·y [lʌ́stɪ] *adj.* vigoroso, fornido, robusto.
lute [lut] *s.* laúd.
lux·u·ri·ant [lʌgʒʊ́rɪənt] *adj.* lozano, frondoso, exuberante.
lux·u·ri·ous [lʌgʒʊ́rɪəs] *adj.* lujoso; dado al lujo; frondoso.
lux·u·ry [lʌ́kʃərɪ] *s.* lujo; **— tax** impuesto suntuario.
lye [laɪ] *s.* lejía.
ly·ing [láɪɪŋ] *ger. de* **to lie;** *adj.* mentiroso; **lying-in hospital** casa de maternidad.
lymph [lɪmpʃ] *s.* linfa.
lynch [lɪntʃ] *v.* linchar.
lynx [lɪŋks] *s.* lince.
lyre [laɪr] *s.* lira.
ly·ric [lírɪk] *s.* poema lírico; *adj.* lírico.
lyr·i·cal [lírɪkl] *adj.* lírico.
lyr·i·cism [lírəsɪzəm] *s.* lirismo.

M:m

mac·a·ro·ni [mækəróni] *s.* macarrón o macarrones.
mac·a·roon [mækərún] *s.* *macarrón, almendrado, bollito de almendra.*
ma·chine [məʃín] *s.* máquina; automóvil; — **gun** ametralladora; — **made** hecho a máquina; — **language** (*computer*) lenguaje de máquina; — **pistol** metralleta; **political** — camarilla política; **sewing** — máquina para coser.
ma·chin·ery [məʃínərɪ] *s.* maquinaria.
ma·chin·ist [məʃínɪst] *s.* mecánico, maquinista.
mack·er·el [mǽkərəl] *s.* escombro, caballa (*pez*).
mad [mæd] *adj.* (*crazy*) loco; (*angry*) rabioso; furioso, enojado; **to drive** — enloquecer; volver loco; **to get** — encolerizarse; **to go** — volverse loco, enloquecerse; **-ly** *adv.* **locamente.**
mad·am, mad·ame [mǽdəm] *s.* madama, señora.
mad·cap [mǽdkæp] *s.* calavera (*m.*), *adj.* temerario; temerario; atolondrado.
mad·den [mǽdn̩] *v.* enloquecer(se).
made [med] *pret. & p.p. de* **to make; to be — of** estar hecho de; ser de; **to have something** — mandar hacer algo; **made-up** fingido, falso; artificial, pintado (*con afeites*).
made-to-order [medtuórdɚ] *adj.* hecho a la medida.
mad·man [mǽdmæn] *s.* loco.
mad·ness [mǽdnɪs] *s.* locura; (*anger*) rabia.
mag·a·zine [mægəzín] *s.* revista; (*storage*) almacén; **powder** — polvorín.
mag·ic [mǽdʒɪk] *s.* magia; *adj.* mágico.
ma·gi·cian [mədʒíʃən] *s.* mágico; prestidigitador; brujo.
mag·is·trate [mǽdʒɪstret] *s.* magistrado.
mag·nan·i·mous [mægnǽnəməs] *adj.* magnánimo.
mag·ne·sia [mægníʒə] *s.* magnesia.
mag·ne·si·um [mægníziəm] *s.* magnesio.
mag·net [mǽgnɪt] *s.* imán.
mag·net·ic [mægnétɪk] *adj.* magnético; — **pole** polo magnético; — **tape** cinta magnetofónica.
mag·net·ise [mǽgnətaɪz] *v.* magnetizar; imantar; cautivar.
mag·nif·i·cence [mægnífəsn̩s] *s.* magnificencia.
mag·nif·i·cent [mægnífəsn̩t] *adj.* magnífico.
mag·ni·fy [mǽgnəfaɪ] *v.* agrandar, engrandecer; amplificar; exagerar.
mag·ni·tude [mǽgnətjud] *s.* magnitud.
mag·pie [mǽgpaɪ] *s.* urraca; cotorra, hablador, habladora.
ma·hog·a·ny [məhɑ́gənɪ] *s.* caoba
maid [med] *s.* criada, sirvienta, camarera, *Méx.* recamarera, *Ríopl., Andes* mucama; doncella; — **of honor** doncella de honor; **old** — solterona.
maid·en [médn̩] *s.* doncella; virgen; mozuela; (*unmarried*) soltera; — **lady** mujer soltera; — **voyage** primer viaje (*de un vapor*).
mail [mel] *s.* correo; correspondencia; **air** — correo aéreo; **coat of** — malla; — **bag** valija; — **order** ventas por correo; — **train** tren correo; *v.* echar al correo.
mail·box [mélbɑks] *s.* buzón.
mail·man [mélmæn] *s.* cartero.
maim [mem] *v.* mutilar, estropear.
main [men] *adj.* principal, mayor, de mayor importancia; (*pipe*)*s.* (*sea*) tubería, cañería principal (*de agua o gas*); — **office** casa matriz; alta mar, océano; **in the** — en su mayor parte; en general, en conjunto; **-ly** *adv.* principalmente.
main·land [ménlænd] *s.* continente, tierra firme.
main·spring [ménsprɪŋ] *s.* muelle real; origen.
main·tain [mentén] *v.* mantener; sostener, afirmar; guardar.
main·te·nance [méntənəns] *s.* mantenimiento; sustento; manutención; sostén, sostenimiento.
maize [mez] *s.* maíz.
ma·jes·tic [mədʒéstɪk] *adj.* majestuoso.
maj·es·ty [mǽdʒɪstɪ] *s.* majestad.
ma·jor [médʒɚ] *adj.* (*greater*) mayor, más grande; (*principal*) principal; — **key** tono mayor; *s.* comandante; mayor, mayor de edad; curso o asignatura de especialización (*en la universidad*); — **league** liga mayor; *v.* especializarse (*en un curso de estudios*).
ma·jor·i·ty [mədʒɔ́etɪ] *s.* mayoría; mayor edad.
make [mek] *v.* (*do*) hacer; (*create*) fabricar; formar; (*deliver*) pronunciar (*un discurso*); **to — a clean breast of** confesar; **to — a train** alcanzar un tren; **to — a turn** dar vuelta; **to — away with** llevarse, robar; matar; **to — fast** asegurar, afianzar; **to — headway** progresar, adelantar, avanzar; **to — much of** dar mucha importancia a; **to — neither head nor tail of** no comprender nada de; **to — nothing out of** no comprender nada de, no sacar nada en limpio; **to — out in the distance** distinguir a lo lejos; **to — over** rehacer, alterar (*un traje*); **to — sure** asegurarse; **to — toward** dirigirse a, encaminarse a; **to — up a story** inventar un cuento; **to — up after a quarrel** hacer las paces; **to — up for a loss** compensar por una pérdida; **to — up one's face** pintarse la cara; **to — up one's mind** resolverse, decidirse; *s.* hechura, forma; marca (*de fábrica*); manufactura.
mak·er [mékɚ] *s.* hacedor; fabricante; artífice.
make·shift [mékʃɪft] *adj.* provisional.
make-up [mékʌp] *s.* (*composition*) compostura, composición, hechura; (*character*) naturaleza, carácter; **facial** — afeite, cosmético; maquillaje.
mal·a·chite [mǽləkaɪt] *s.* malaquita.
mal·a·dy [mǽlədɪ] *s.* mal, enfermedad.
ma·lar·i·a [məlérɪə] *s.* malaria, fiebre palúdica, paludismo.
mal·con·tent [mǽlkəntɛnt] *adj. & s.* malcontento.
male [mel] *adj.* macho; varón; masculino; varonil; de hombres, de varones; *s.* macho; varón; hombre.
mal·ice [mǽlɪs] *s.* malicia.
ma·li·cious [məlíʃəs] *adj.* malicioso, perverso, malévolo.
ma·lign [məláɪn] *v.* calumniar, difamar; *adj.* maligno; pernicioso.
ma·lig·nant [məlígnənt] *adj.* maligno; malévolo.
mal·le·a·ble [mǽliəbl] *adj.* maleable; manejable.
mal·let [mǽlɪt] *s.* mazo, maceta.
mal·nu·tri·tion [mælnutríʃən] *s.* desnutrición.
malt [mɔt] *s.* malta; **-ed milk** leche malteada.
ma·ma, mam·ma [mɑ́mə] *s.* mamá
mam·mal [mǽml] *s.* mamífero.
mam·moth [mǽməθ] *adj.* gigantesco, enorme.
mam·my [mǽmɪ] *s.* mamita; niñera negra. [Hoy día se puede considerar racista.]
man [mæn] *s.* hombre; varón; pieza (*de ajedrez*); — **and wife** marido y mujer; **to a** — unánimente, todos a una; **officers and men** oficiales y soldados; **man-of-war** buque de guerra; — **cook** cocinero; *v.* armar, proveer de gente armada; guarnecer (*una fortaleza*); tripular (*una embarcación*).
man·age [mǽnɪdʒ] *v.* manejar; gobernar, dirigir; gestionar; **to — to do something** arreglárselas para hacer algo.
man·age·a·ble [mǽnɪdʒəbl] *adj.* manejable; domable, dócil.
man·age·ment [mǽnɪdʒmənt] *s.* manejo; dirección; gobierno, administración; (*office*) gerencia.

man·ag·er [mǽnɪdʒɚ] *s.* gerente; director, administrador; empresario.
man·date [mændet] *s.* mandato; *v.* asignar por mandato.
man·do·lin [mǽndəlɪn] *s.* mandolina.
mane [men] *s.* melena (*del león*), crin (*del caballo*).
ma·neu·ver [mənúvɚ] *s.* maniobra; gestión; *v.* maniobrar; manipular, manejar.
man·ful [mǽnfəl] *adj.* varonil; viril.
man·ga·nese [mǽŋgənis] *s.* manganeso.
mange [mendʒ] *s.* sarna, roña.
man·ger [méndʒɚ] *s.* pesebre.
man·gle [mǽŋgl] *v.* magullar, mutilar, destrozar, estropear; planchar en máquina de planchar; *s.* planchadora (*máquina de planchar*).
man·grove [mǽngrov] *s.* mangle.
man·gy [méndʒɪ] *adj.* sarnoso, *Am.* sarniento.
man·hood [mǽnhʊd] *s.* virilidad; edad viril; hombres.
ma·ni·a [ménɪə] *s.* mania.
man·i·cure [mǽnɪkjʊr] *s.* manicura; manicurist; *v.* manicurar.
man·i·fest [mǽnəfɛst] *adj.* manifiesto; *s.* (*ship*) manifiesto; *v.* manifestar; poner de manifiesto; declarar.
man·i·fes·ta·tion [mænəfɛstéʃən] *s.* manifestación.
man·i·fes·to [mænɪfɛ́sto] *s.* manifiesto, bando, proclama.
man·i·fold [mǽnəfold] *adj.* múltiple; numeroso, diverso.
man·i·kin [mǽnəkɪn] *s.* maniquí; muñeco; hombrecillo.
ma·nil·a [mənɪ́lə] *s.* abacá (*cáñamo de Manila*); · **paper** papel de Manila.
man·i·oc [mǽniak] *s.* mandioca.
ma·nip·u·late [mənɪ́pjəlet] *v.* manipular; manejar.
ma·nip·u·la·tion [mənɪpjəléʃən] *s.* manipulación.
man·kind [mænkáɪnd] *s.* humanidad, género humano; los hombres.
man·like [mǽnlaɪk] *adj.* hombruno; varonil; *Méx.* macho *s.* (*woman*) marimacho.
man·ly [mǽnlɪ] *adj.* varonil; viril; muy hombre; *adv.* varonilmente.
man·ner [mǽnɚ] *s.* (*way*) manera; modo; género; (*air*) aire, ademán; **-s** manejas, modales; costumbres; **after the — of** a la manera de; **by no — of means** de ningún modo.
man·ner·ism [mǽnɚɪzm] *s.* costumbre; amaneramiento.
man·nish [mǽnɪʃ] *adj.* hombruno.
ma·noeu·vre = **maneuver.**
man·or [mǽnɚ] *s.* solar, casa solariega.
man·pow·er [mǽnpɑvɚ] *s.* mano de obra, fuerzas disponibles.
man·sion [mǽnʃən] *s.* mansión; palacio.
man·slaugh·ter [mǽnslɔtɚ] *s.* homicidio impremeditado o casual.
man·tel [mǽntl] *s.* manto (*de una chimenea*); repisa de chimenea·
man·tle [mǽntl] *s.* manto; capa.
man·u·al [mǽnjʊəl] *adj.* manual; — **training school** escuela de artes y oficios; *s.* manual; (*keyboard*) teclado de órgano.
man·u·fac·ture [mænjəfǽktʃɚ] *s.* fabricación; elaboración; manufactura; *v.* fabricar, manufacturar; elaborar.
man·u·fac·tur·er [mænjəfǽktʃərɚ] *s.* fabricante.
man·u·fac·tur·ing [mænjəfǽktʃərɪŋ] *s.* fabricación; *adj.* fabril, manufacturero; — **concern** empresa industrial.
man·ure [mənʊ́r] *s.* estiércol, abono; *v.* estercolar, abonar (*la tierra*).
man·u·script [mǽnjəskrɪpt] *adj.* & *s.* manuscrito.
man·y [mɛ́nɪ] *adj.* muchos; — **a time** muchas veces; **a great** — muchísimos; **as — as** tantos como; cuantos; **as — as five** hasta cinco; **how** — ? ¿cuántos?; **three books too** — tres libros de más; **too** — demasiados.
map [mæp] *s.* mapa; *v.* trazar un mapa de; **to — out** proyectar, planear.
ma·ple [mépl] *s.* arce, *Méx.* meple; *Ríopl.* maple.
mar [mɑr] *v.* desfigurar, estropear.
mar·ble [márbl] *s.* mármol; (*plaything*) canica (*para jugar*); **to play -s** jugar a las canicas; *adj.* de mármol; marmóreo.
march [mɑrtʃ] *s.* marcha; *v.* marchar, caminar; hacer marchar; **to — in** entrar marchando; **to — out** marcharse; salirse marchando.
March [martʃ] *s.* marzo.
mare [mɛr] *s.* yegua.
mar·ga·rine [mάrdʒərɪn] *s.* margarina.
mar·gin [mάrdʒɪn] *s.* margen; orilla; sobrante; excedente; reserva (*fondos*).
mar·gin·al [mάrdʒɪnl] *adj.* marginal; — **note** nota marginal, acotación; de rendimiento mínimo.
mar·i·gold [mǽrəgold] *s.* caléndula, maravilla.
ma·rine [mərín] *adj.* marino; marítimo; — **corps** cuerpo de marinos; *s.* marino; soldado de marina; **merchant** — marina mercante.
mar·i·ner [mǽrənɚ] *s.* marinero.
mar·i·time [mǽrətaɪm] *adj.* marítimo.
mark [mɑrk] *s.* marca; señal, seña; nota, calificación; **question** — punto de interrogación; **to come up to the** — alcanzar la norma requerida; **to hit the** — dar en el blanco; **to make one's** — distinguirse; **to miss one's** — fallar; errar el tiro; (*fail*) fracasar; *v.* marcar; señalar; notar; observar; calificar; — **my words!** ¡advierte lo que te digo!; **to — down** anotar, apuntar; rebajar el precio de.
mark·down [mάrkdɑʊn] *s.* rebaja de precios.
mark·er [mάrkɚ] *s.* marcador; marca, señal; jalón.
mar·ket [mάrkɪt] *s.* mercado, plaza; — **place** mercado, plaza; el mundo del comercio — **price** precio corriente; **meat** — carnicería; **stock** — mercado de valores, bolsa; in the — **for** dispuesto a comprar; — **on the market** de venta; *v.* vender; vender o comprar en el mercado; **to go -ing** ir de compras.
mar·ket·ing [mάrkətɪŋ] *s.* mercadotecnia.
mark·up [mάrkəp] *s.* aumento de precios.
mar·ma·lade [mάrmled] *s.* mermelada.
ma·roon [mərún] *s.* & *adj.* rojo obscuro.
ma·rooned [mərúnd] *adj.* abandonado (*en lugar desierto*); aislado; **to get** — encontrarse aislado, perdido o incomunicado.
mar·quis [mάrkwɪs] *s.* marqués.
mar·quise [mɑrkíz] *s.* marquesa.
mar·riage [mǽrɪdʒ] *s.* matrimonio; casamiento, boda; unión, enlace; — **license** licencia de matrimonio.
mar·riage·a·ble [mǽrɪdʒəbl] *adj.* casadero.
mar·ried [mǽrɪd] *adj.* casado; conyugal; — **couple** matrimonio, cónyuges; pareja de casados; **to get** — casarse.
mar·row [mǽro] *s.* meollo, tuétano, médula (*de los huesos*).
mar·ry [mǽrɪ] *v.* casar; casarse; casarse con.
marsh [mɑrʃ] *s.* pantano; ciénaga.
mar·shal [mάrʃəl] *s.* mariscal; (*local*) alguacil; jefe de policía (*en ciertas regiones*); maestro de ceremonia; **fire** — jefe de bomberos; *v.* ordenar, arreglar; guiar, conducir con ceremonia.

marsh·mal·low [mάrʃmælo] *s.* pastilla o bombón de altea.
marsh·y [mάrʃɪ] *adj.* pantanoso, cenagoso.
mart [mɑrt] *s.* mercado.
mar·tial [mάrʃəl] *adj.* marcial; — **law** estado de sitio.
mar·tin [mάrtɪn] *s.* avión (*pájaro*).
mar·tyr [mάrtɚ] *s.* mártir; *v.* martirizar, torturar, atormentar.
mar·tyr·dom [mάrtɚdəm] *s.* martirio.
mar·vel [mάrvl] *s.* maravilla; *v.* maravillarse.
mar·vel·ous [mάrvləs] *adv.* maravilloso.
Marx·ism [márksɪzəm] *s.* marxismo.
mas·cot [mǽskɑt] *s.* mascota.
mas·cu·line [mǽskjəlɪn] *adj.* masculino; varonil; hombruno.
mash [mæʃ] *v.* majar, amasar; machacar, magullar; **-ed potatoes** puré de papas (*o* patatas); patatas majadas.
mask [mæsk] *s.* máscara; disfraz; careta; *v.* disfrazar, enmascarar; encubrir; **-ed ball** baile de máscaras.
ma·son [mésn̩] *s.* albañil; **Mason** masón, francmasón.
ma·son·ry [mésn̩rɪ] *s.* albañilería; mampostería; **Masonry** masonería, francmasonería.
mas·quer·ade [mæskəréd] *s.* mascarada; disfraz, máscara; *v.* enmascararse, disfrazarse; andar disfrazado.
mass [mæs] *s.* masa; montón; mole; (*most*) mayoría, mayor parte; (*church*) misa; — **meeting** mitín popular; — **production** fabricación en serie (*cadena*); — **communication** communicación extensa; — **media** los medios de comunicarse con el público (*radio, televisión, periódicos, etc.*); **the -es** las masas, el pueblo; *v.* juntar(se) en masa.
mas·sa·cre [mǽsəkɚ] *s.* hecatombe, matanza, carnicería, destrozo; *v.* hacer matanza o hecatombe, destrozar.
mas·sage [məsάʒ] *v.* friccionar, dar masaje; *s.* masaje.
mas·sive [mǽsɪv] *adj.* sólido, macizo; (*big*) voluminoso, imponente.
mast [mæst] *s.* mástil, palo.
mas·ter [mǽstɚ] *s.* (*head*) amo, dueño, señor; maestro; patrón; (*skilled*) experto, perito; **band** — director de la banda; — **of arts** maestro en artes, licenciado; **-'s degree** licenciatura, grado de licenciado; *adj.* maestro; — **builder** maestro de obras; — **key** llave maestra; *v.* dominar; domar; gobernar; **to — a language** dominar un idioma.
mas·ter·ful [mǽstɚfəl] *adj.* magistral; dominante.
mas·ter·ly [mǽstɚlɪ] *adj.* magistral; *adv.* magistralmente.
mas·ter·piece [mǽstɚpis] *s.* obra maestra.
mas·ter·y [mǽstərɪ] *s.* maestría, arte, destreza; dominio.
mas·tiff [mǽstɪf] *s.* mastín, alano.
mat [mæt] *s.* (*covering*) estera; esterilla, felpudo, tapete; (*gymnasium*) colchoncillo (*de gimnasia*); borde de cartón (*para hacer resaltar una pintura*).
match [mætʃ] *s.* (*pair*) pareja; (*game*) partida, contienda, juego; (*light*) fósforo, cerilla; *Méx.* cerillo; **he has no** — no tiene igual; **he is a good** — es un buen partido; **the hat and coat are a good** — el abrigo y el sombrero hacen juego; *v.* igualar; aparear; hacer juego, armonizar; **to — one's strength** medir uno sus fuerzas; **these colors do not — well** estos colores no casan bien.
match·less [mǽtʃlɪs] *adj.* sin par, sin igual, incomparable.
mate [met] *s.* compañero, compañera; consorte; macho o hembra (*entre animales o aves*); (*ship*) piloto (*officer*); oficial subalterno (*en la marina*); *v.* aparear(se).
ma·te·ri·al [mətírɪəl] *adj.* material; esencial; *s.* material; tejido, género; materia; **raw** — materia prima.
ma·ter·nal [mətɝ́nl] *adj.* maternal, materno.
ma·ter·ni·ty [mətɝ́nətɪ] *s.* maternidad.
math·e·mat·i·cal [mæθəmǽtɪkl] *adj.* matemático.
math·e·mati·cian [mæθəmətɪ́ʃən] *s.* matemático.
math·e·mat·ics [mæθəmǽtɪks] *s.* matemáticas.
mat·i·née [mætné] *s.* función de la tarde, *Am.* matiné.
ma·tri·arch [métrɪɑrk] *s.* matriarca.
ma·tric·u·late [mətrɪ́kjəlet] *v.* matricular(se).
ma·tric·u·la·tion [mətrɪkjəléʃən] *s.* matriculación, matrícula.
mat·ri·mony [mǽtrəmonɪ] *s.* matrimonio, casamiento.
ma·trix [métrɪks] *s.* matriz; molde.
ma·tron [métrən] *s.* matrona, madre de familia; ama de llaves; vigilante, cuidadora (*de un asilo, cárcel para mujeres, etc.*).
mat·ter [mǽtɚ] *s.* (*substance*) material, materia; sustancia; (*affair*) asunto, cuestión; cosa; (*discharge*) pus; — **for complaint** motivo de queja; — **of two minutes** cosa de dos minutos; **as a — of fact** de hecho; en verdad, en realidad; **business -s** negocios; **printed** — impresos; **serious** — cosa seria; **it is of no** — no tiene importancia; **to do something as a — of course** hacer algo por rutina; **what is the — ?** ¿qué tiene Vd.?; **matter-of-fact person** persona de poca imaginación; *v.* importar; supurar; **it does not** — no importa, no le hace.
mat·tress [mǽtrɪs] *s.* colchón; **spring** — colchón de muelles.
ma·ture [mətjʊ́r] *adj.* maduro; **a — note** un pagaré vencido; *v.* madurar(se); vencerse, hacerse cobrable o pagadero (*un pagaré, una deuda*).
ma·tur·i·ty [mətjʊ́rətɪ] *s.* madurez; vencimiento (*de una deuda u obligación*).
maul [mɔl] *v.* magullar; maltratar; manejar rudamente; golpear.
mav·er·ick [mǽvɚɪk] *s.* animal sin marca; becerro suelto.
max·im [mǽksɪm] *s.* máxima.
max·i·mum [mǽksəməm] *adj.* & *s.* máximo.
may [me] *v. irr. y. defect.* (*able*) poder; (*permitted*) tener permiso para, serle permitido a uno; (*possible*) ser posible; — **I sit down?** ¿puedo sentarme?; — **you have a good time** que se divierta Vd., **it — be that** puede ser que, tal vez sea que; **it — rain** puede (ser) que llueva, es posible que llueva; **she — be late** puede (ser) que llegue ella tarde.
May [me] *s.* mayo, mes de mayo; — **Day** primero de mayo; — **pole** mayo; — **Queen** maya (*reina de la fiesta del primero de mayo*).
may·be [mébɪ] *adv.* quizás, tal vez, acaso.
may·on·naise [meənéz] *s.* mayonesa.
may·or [méɚ] *s.* alcalde, alcalde mayor.
maze [mez] *s.* laberinto; confusión; **to be in a** — estar confuso o perplejo.
me [mi] *pron. pers.* me; mí (*después de preposición*); **give it to** — démelo (a mí); **for** — para mí; **with** — conmigo.
mead·ow [médo] *s.* pradera, prado; — **lark** alondra de los prados.
mea·ger [mígɚ] *adj.* escaso, insuficiente; magro, flaco.

meal [mil] *s.* comida; (*flour*) harina (*a medio moler*); **corn** — harina de maíz; — **time** hora de comer.
mean [min] *adj.* (*malicious*) ruin, bajo; vil; (*humble*) humilde; (*stingy*) mezquino, tacaño; (*difficult*) de mal genio; (*sick*) malo, indispuesto; (*middle*) mediano; medio; intermedio; — **distance** distancia media; *s.* medio; término medio; **-s** medios; recursos; **a man of -s** un hombre pudiente o rico; **by -s of** por medio de; **by all -s** de todos modos; a toda costa; por supuesto; **by no -s** de ningún modo; **golden** — justo medio; *v.* querer decir, significar; pensar, proponerse, tener la intención de; intentar; destinar; **he -s well** tiene buenas intenciones.
me·an·der [miǽndɚ] *v.* serpentear.
mean·ing [mínɪŋ] *s.* (*sense*) significado, sentido; significación; (*intent*) propósito, intención; *adj.* significativo; **well-meaning** bien intencionado.
mean·ing·less [mínɪŋlɪs] *adj.* sin sentido, vacío de sentido.
mean·ness [mínnɪs] *s.* ruindad, vileza, bajeza; mezquindad.
meant [mɛnt] *pret. & p.p. de* **to mean.**
mean·time [míntaɪm] *adv.* mientras tanto, entretanto; *s.* ínterin, entretanto; **in the** — en el ínterin, mientras tanto.
mean·while [mínhwaɪl = **meantime.**
mea·sles [mízlz] *s.* sarampión.
mea·sur·a·ble [mɛ́ʒrəbl] *adj.* medible, mensurable; **mea·sur·a·bly** *adv.* marcadamente.
mea·sure [mɛ́ʒɚ] *s.* (*dimension*) medida; compás (*de música*); cadencia, ritmo; (*law*) proyecto de ley; ley; **beyond** — sobremanera; con exceso; **dry** — medida para áridos; **in large** — en gran parte, en gran manera; *v.* medir; **measuring tape** cinta de medir.
mea·sured [mɛ́ʒɚd] *adj.* medido; moderado; acompasado.
mea·sure·ment [mɛ́ʒɚmənt] *s.* medida; dimensión; tamaño; medición.
meat [mit] *s.* carne; (*pith*) meollo, sustancia; — **ball** albóndiga; — **market** carnicería; — **packer** empacador de carnes; **cold** — fiambre.
meat·y [mítɪ] *adj.* carnoso; sustancioso.
me·chan·ic [məkǽnɪk] *adj. & s.* mecánico; **-s** *s.* mecánica.
me·chan·i·cal [mekǽnɪkl] *adj.* mecánico; maquinal.
mech·a·nism [mɛ́kənɪzəm] *s.* mecanismo.
med·al [mɛ́dl] *s.* medalla.
med·dle [mɛ́dl] *v.* entrometerse o entremeterse; meterse.
med·dler [mɛ́dlɚ] *s.* entremetido.
med·dle·some [mɛ́dlsəm] *adj.* entremetido.
me·di·an [mídɪən] *adj.* mediano, del medio; *s.* punto, línea o número del medio; mediana.
me·di·ate [mídɪet] *v.* mediar; intervenir; arbitrar.
me·di·a·tion [midɪéʃən] *s.* mediación, intervención, intercesión.
me·di·a·tor [mídɪetɚ] *s.* mediador, medianero, árbitro.
me·di·cal [mɛ́dɪkl] *adj.* médico; — **school** escuela de medicina
med·i·ca·tion [mɛdɪkéʃən] *s.* medicación.
med·i·cine [mɛ́dəsn̩] *s.* medicina; medicamento; — **ball** pelota grande de cuero; —**cabinet** botiquín; — **man** curandero indio.
me·di·e·val [midɪívl] *adj.* medioeval o medieval.
me·di·o·cre [midɪókɚ] *adj.* mediocre, mediano; ordinario.
me·di·oc·ri·ty [midɪákrətɪ] *s.* mediocridad, medianía.
med·i·tate [mɛ́dətet] *v.* meditar.
med·i·ta·tion [mɛdətéʃən] *s.* meditación.
me·di·um [mídɪəm] *s.* medio; medio ambiente; *adj.* mediano; intermedio; a medio cocer, a medio asar; — **of exchange** medio (tipo) de cambío.
med·ley [mɛ́dlɪ] *s.* baturrillo, mezcla, mezcolanza.
meek [mik] *adj.* manso, dócil, paciente, sufrido.
meek·ness [míknɪs] *s.* mansedumbre, docilidad.
meet [mit] *v.* encontrar(se); reunirse; conocer (*personalmente*), ser presentado a; (*receive*) ir a esperar (*un tren, vapor, o a alguien*); satisfacer (*deseos, requisitos, etc.*); pagar (*una deuda*); sufragar (*gastos*); responder a (*una acusación*); **to** — **in battle** trabar batalla; **to** — **with** encontrarse con; tropezar con; topar con; reunirse con; **to** — **the expenses** pagar los gastos; **to** — **halfway** partir la diferencia; *s.* concurso; contienda (*tratándose de deportes*); **track** — competencia de atletas.
meet·ing [mítɪŋ] *s.* reunión; (*political*) mitin; sesión; asamblea; encuentro.
Meg·a·byte (MBYTE) [mɛ́gəbaɪt] *s.* (*computer*) mega-byte (MB).
meg·a·phone [mɛ́gəfon] *s.* megáfono, portavoz, bocina.
meg·a·ton [mɛ́gətʌn] *s.* megatón.
mel·an·chol·y [mɛ́lənkɑlɪ] *s.* melancolía; *adj.* melancólico.
me·lee [méle] *s.* reyerta; zafarrancho.
mel·low [mɛ́lo] *adj.* maduro, sazonado; dulce, blando, suave; *v.* madurar(se), sazonar(se); ablandar(se), suavizar(se).
me·lo·di·ous [məlódíəs] *adj.* melodioso.
mel·o·dra·ma [mɛ́lodrɑmə] *s.* melodrama.
mel·o·dy [mɛ́lədɪ] *s.* melodía.
mel·on [mɛ́lən] *s.* melón.
melt [mɛlt] *v.* derretir(se); disolver(se); fundir(se).
mem·ber [mɛ́mbɚ] *s.* miembro; socio.
mem·bership [mɛ́mbɚʃɪp] *s.* número de miembros o socios; asociación; (*los*) miembros (*de un club o sociedad*).
mem·brane [mɛ́mbren] *s.* membrana.
me·men·to [mɪmɛ́nto] *s.* memento, memoria, recuerdo.
mem·oir [mɛ́mwɑr] *s.* memoria, apuntaciones; **-s** memorias; autobiografía
mem·o·ra·ble [mɛ́mərəbl] *adj.* memorable.
mem·o·ran·dum [mɛmərǽndəm] *s.* memorándum; memoria, apunte; — **book** memorándum, librito de apuntes, memorial.
me·mor·i·al [məmórɪəl] *s.* (*monument*) monumento conmemorativo; (*occasion*) obra o fiesta conmemorativa; memorial, petición; *adj.* conmemorativo.
mem·o·rize [*m*ɛ́məraɪz] *v.* aprender de memoria.
mem·o·ry [mɛ́mərɪ] *s.* memoria; recuerdo; **chip** (*computer*), ficha memoria.
men [mɛn] *pl. de* **man.**
men·ace [mɛ́nɪs] *s.* amenaza; *v.* amenazar.
mend [mɛnd] *v.* remendar; reparar, componer; enmendar; **to** — **one's ways** enmendarse, reformarse; *s.* remiendo; reparación; **to be on the** — ir mejorando.
me·ni·al [mínɪəl] *adj.* servil, bajo.
men·stru·a·tion [mɛnstruéʃən] *s.* menstruo o menstruación.
men·tal [mɛ́ntl] *adj.* mental.
men·tal·i·ty [mɛntǽlətɪ] *s.* mentalidad, ingenio.
men·tion [mɛ́nʃən] *s.* mención; alusión; *v.* mencionar, mentar; **don't** — **it** no hay de qué (*contestación a* ''thank you'').
men·u [mɛ́nju] *s.* menú, lista de platos; (*computer*) menú (de entrada).

me·ow [mjaʊ] = **mew.**
mer·can·tile [mɝ́kəntɪl] *adj.* mercantil.
mer·ce·nar·y [mɝ́sn̩ɛrɪ] *adj.* mercenario.
mer·chan·dise [mɝ́tʃəndaɪz] *s.* mercancías, mercaderías; **piece of** — mercancía; **merchandising** mercadotecnia.
mer·chant [mɝ́tʃənt] *s.* comerciante; negociante; mercader; *adj.* mercante, mercantil; — **marine** marina mercante.
mer·ci·ful [mɝ́sɪfəl] *adj.* misericordíoso, piadoso.
mer·ci·less [mɝ́sɪlɪs] *adj.* sin piedad, despiadado, incompasivo.
mer·cu·ry [mɝ́kjərɪ] *s.* mercurio; azogue.
mer·cy [mɝ́sɪ] *s.* (*favor*) merced; favor, gracia; (*compassion*) misericordia, piedad, compasión; **to be at the** — **of** estar a merced de.
mere [mɪr] *adj.* mero; simple, puro; **a** — **formality** una pura formalidad, no más que una formalidad, una formalidad no más; **a** — **trifle** una nonada; **-ly** *adv.* meramente; sólo, solamente; simplemente.
merge [mɝdʒ] *v.* combinar(se), unir(se); absorber(se); fundírse.
merg·er [mɝ́dʒɚ] *s.* amalgamación comercial; fusión.
me·rid·i·an [mərɪ́dɪən] *adj.* & *s.* meridiano.
mer·it [mɛ́rɪt] *s.* mérito; *v.* merecer; — **rating** valoración de meritos.
mer·i·to·ri·ous [mɛrətórɪəs] meritorio.
mer·maid [mɝ́med] *s.* ninfa marina.
mer·ri·ly [mɛ́rəlɪ] *adv.* alegremente, con regocijo.
mer·ri·ment [mɛ́rɪmənt] *s.* alegría, regocijo, júbilo.
mer·ry [mɛ́rɪ] *adj.* alegre; jovial; divertido; festivo; — **Christmas** Felices Navidades, Felices Pascuas; **to make** — divertirse.
mer·ry-go-round [mɛ́rɪgəraʊnd] *s.* tío vivo, *Méx., C.A.* los caballitos; *Ríopl.* calesita.
mer·ry·mak·er [mɛ́rɪmekɚ] *s.* fiestero; juerguista.
mer·ry·mak·ing [mɛ́rɪmekɪŋ] *s.* regocijo; jaleo, juerga, jolgorio; *adj.* regocijado, alegre, festivo, fiestero.
mesh [mɛʃ] *s.* malla; red; **-es** red, redes; *v.* enredar, coger con red; **to** — **gears** engranar.
mess [mɛs] *s.* (*food*) rancho, comida (*en el ejército o la marina*); (*confusion*) lío, confusión; (*dirt*) suciedad; — **of fish** plato o ración de pescado; **to make a** — **of** *v.* revolver, confundir; ensuciar; echar a perder; *v.* revolver, confundir; ensuciar, echar a perder (*generalmente:* **to** — **up**); **to** — **around** revolver o mezclar las cosas; entrometerse;
mess·y [mɛ́sɪ] *adj.* desordenado, desarreglado; sucio.
mes·sage [mɛ́sɪdʒ] *s.* mensaje; parte (*m*), comunicación; recado.
mes·sen·ger [mɛ́sn̩dʒɚ] *s.* mensajero; mandadero.
met [mɛt] *pret.* & *p.p.* *de* **to meet.**
me·tab·o·lism [məwtǽbəlɪzm] *s.* metabolismo.
met·al [mɛ́tl] *s.* metal; *adj.* de metal, metálico.
me·tal·lic [mətǽlɪk] *adj.* metálico.
met·al·lur·gy [mɛ́tlɝdʒɪ] *s.* metalurgia.
met·a·mor·pho·sis [mɛtəmɔ́rfəsɪs] *s.* metamorfosis.
met·a·phor [mɛ́təfɚ] *s.* metáfora.
me·tath·e·sis [mətǽθəsɪs] *s.* metátesis.
me·te·or [mitɪɚ] *s.* meteoro; estrella fugaz.
me·te·or [mítɪoraɪt] *s.* meteorito.
me·te·or·ite [mítɪoraɪt] *s.* meteorito.
me·te·or·ol·o·gy [mitɪərɑ́lədʒɪ] *s.* meteorología.
me·ter [mítɚ] *s.* metro; contador (*de gas, agua, electricidad,*) *Am.* medidor.
meth·od [mɛ́θəd] *s.* método; técnica.
me·thod·i·cal [məθɑ́dɪkl] *adj.* metódico.
me·tre = **meter.**
met·ric [mɛ́trɪk] *adj.* métrico; — **system** sistema métrico; — **ton** tonelada métrica (1000 kg.).
me·trop·o·lis [mətrɑ́plɪs] *s.* metrópoli.
met·ro·pol·i·tan [mɛtrəpɑ́lətn̩] *adj.* metropolitano.
met·tle [mɛ́tl] *s.* temple, brío, ánimo, valor.
mew [mju] *s.* maullido, maúllo, miau; *v.* maullar.
Mex·i·can [mɛ́ksɪkən] *adj.* & *s.* mejicano o mexicano.
mez·za·nine [mɛ́zənin] *s.* entresuelo.
mice [maɪs] *pl.* *de* **mouse.**
mi·crobe [máɪkrob] *s.* microbio.
mi·cro·bus [máɪkrobʌs] *s.* microbús.
mi·cro·com·put·er [maɪkrokəmpjútɚ] *s.* microcomputadóra, *Esp.* microordenador.
mi·cro·eco·nom·ics [maɪkroikanámiks] *s.* microeconomía.
mi·cro·film [máɪkrəfɪlm] *s.* microfilm.
mi·cro·phone [máɪkrəfon] *s.* micrófono.
mi·cro·pro·ces·sor [maɪkroprásɛsɚ] *s.* el circuito integrado de la computadora; microprocesador.
mi·cro·scope [máɪkrəskop] *s.* microscopio.
mi·cro·scop·ic [maɪkrəskɑ́pɪk] *adj.* microscópico.
mi·cro·wave [máɪkrowev] *s.* microonda.
mid [mɪd] *adj.* medio (*úsase por lo general en composición*); **in** — **air** en el aire; *prep.* en medio de, entre.
mid·day [mɪ́dde] *s.* mediodía; *adj.* del mediodía.
mid·dle [mɪ́dl] *adj.* medio; intermedio; **Middle Ages** Edad Media; — **finger** dedo de en medio, dedo del corazón; — **size** tamaño mediano; *s.* medio, centro, mitad; **in the** — **of** en medio de, a la mitad de **towards the** — **of the month** a mediados del mes; — **class** clase media.
mid·dle-aged [mɪ́dlédʒd] *adj.* de edad mediana, de edad madura.
mid·dle·man [mɪ́dlmæn] *s.* revendedor; medianero, corredor, agente.
mid·dle-sized [mɪ́dlsáɪzd] *adj.* de mediano tamaño, de mediana estatura.
mid·dy [mɪ́dɪ] *s.* guardiamarina (*m*); — **blouse** blusa a la marinera.
midg·et [mɪ́dʒɪt] *s.* enanillo.
mid·night [mɪ́dnaɪt] *s.* medianoche; *adj.* de (la) medianoche; — **blue** azul oscuro; **Midnight Mass** misa de gallo.
mid·riff [mɪ́drɪf] *s.* diafragma.
mid·ship·man [mɪ́dʃɪpmən] *s.* guardiamarina (*m*).
midst [mɪdst] *s.* medio, centro; **in the** — **of** en medio de, entre; **in our** — entre nosotros.
mid·stream [mɪ́dstrim] *s.* el medio (*o* el centro) de la corriente.
mid·sum·mer [mɪ́dsʌ́mɚ] *s.* pleno verano, solsticio estival, la mitad del verano.
mid·term [mɪ́dtɝ́m]; — **examination** examen a mitad del curso.
mid·way [mɪ́dwé] *adj.* situado a medio camino; equidistante; *adv.* a medio camino; en medio del camino.
mid·wife [mɪ́dwaɪf] *s.* partera, comadrona.
mien [min] *s.* facha, aspecto.
might [maɪt] *imperf.* *de* **may** podía; podría; pudiera, pudiese; *s.* poder, poderío, fuerza.
might·y [máɪtɪ] *adj.* poderoso, potente, fuerte; *adv.* muy, sumamente.
mi·grant [máɪgrənt] *adj.* migratorio.
mi·grate [máɪgret] *v.* emigrar.
mi·gra·tion [maɪgréʃən] *s.* migración.
mike [maɪk] = **microphone.**
mild [maɪld] *adj.* (*gentle*) suave; blando; apacible; (*moderate*) templado, moderado.
mil·dew [mɪ́ldu] *s.* moho; enmohecimiento.

ME

mild·ness [máɪldnɪs] *s.* suavidad; mansedumbre; apacibilidad; templanza, dulzura.
mile [maɪl] *s.* milla; — **stone** mojón.
mile·age [máɪlɪdʒ] *s.* millaje, número de millas; recorrido (*en millas*). *Compárese* kilometraje, número de kilómetros.
mil·i·tant [mílɪtənt] *s.* militante; belicoso.
mil·i·tar·y [míləteri] *adj.* militar; de guerra; *s.* **the** — el ejército; los militares.
mi·li·tia [məlíʃə] *s.* milicia.
milk [mɪlk] *s.* leche; — **diet** régimen lácteo; *v.* ordeñar.
milk·maid [mílkmed] *s.* lechera.
milk·man [mílkmən] *s.* lechero, *Am.* vaquero.
milk·y [mílkɪ] *adj.* lácteo; lechoso; **Milky Way** Vía Láctea.
mill [mɪl] *s.* (*grinder*) molino; (*factory*) fábrica; taller; (*money*) la milésima parte de un dólar; **saw** — aserradero; **spinning** — hilandería; **sugar** — ingenio de azúcar; **textile** — fábrica de tejidos; *v.* moler; (*wood*) aserrar (*madera*); fabricar; (*coins*) acordonar (*el canto de la moneda*); fresar, estriar; **to** — **around** arremolinarse (*una muchedumbre*).
mill·er [mílɚ] *s.* molinero; mariposa nocturna.
mil·li·gram [míləgræm] *s.* miligramo.
mil·li·me·ter [míləmitɚ] *s.* milímetro.
mil·li·ner [mílənɚ] *s.* modista (*de sombreros para señoras*).
mil·li·ner·y [mílənerɪ] *s.* sombreros de señora; artículos para sombreros de señora; oficio de sombrerera; — **shop** sombrerería.
mil·lion [míljən] *s.* millón; **a** — **dollars** un millón de dólares.
mil·lion·aire [mɪljənér] *adj.* & *s.* millonario.
mil·lionth [míljənθ] *adj.* & *s.* millonésimo.
mill·stone [mílston] *s.* muela o piedra de molino; carga pesada.
mim·ic [mímɪk] *adj.* mímico, imitativo; — **battle** simulacro; *s.* imitador, remedador; *v.* imitar, remedar.
mince [mɪns] *v.* picar, desmenuzar; **not to** — **words** hablar con toda franqueza.
mince·meat [mínsmit] *s.* picadillo (*especialmente el de carne, pasas, manzanas y especias*).
mind [maɪnd] *s.* (*brain*) mente; (*thought*) pensamiento; inteligencia; (*spirit*) ánimo, espíritu; (*purpose*) propósito, intención; (*opinion*) parecer, opinión; **to be out of one's** — estar loco, haber perdido el juicio; **to change one's** — cambiar de parecer; **to give someone a piece of one's** — cantarle a alguien la verdad; echarle a alguien un buen regaño; **to have a** — **to** estar por; sentir ganas de; **to make up one's** — decidirse, resolverse; **to my** — a mi modo de ver; **to speak one's** — **freely** hablar con toda franqueza; *v.* cuidar; atender a, hacer caso de; obedecer; **I don't** — no tengo inconveniente en ello; **never** — no importa; no se preocupe; no se moleste; no haga Vd. caso; **to** — **one's own business** atender a lo suyo, no meterse en lo ajeno.
mind·ful [máɪndfəl] *adj.* atento (a); cuidadoso (de).
mine [maɪn] *pron. pos.* mío (mía, míos, mías); **el** mío (la mía, los míos, las mías); **a book of** — un libro mío.
mine [maɪn] *s.* mina; — **sweeper** dragaminas; *v.* minar; explotar (*una mina*); extraer (*mineral*).
min·er [máɪnɚ] *s.* minero.
min·er·al [mínərəl] *adj.* & *s.* mineral; — **right** derecho de subsuelo.
min·gle [míŋgl] *v.* mezclar(se); entremezclar(se); confundir(se); juntarse.
min·i·a·ture [mínɪtʃɚ] *s.* miniatura; *adj.* en miniatura; diminuto.
min·i·mal [mínəml] *adj.* mínimo.
min·i·mize [mínəmaɪz] *v.* empequeñecer.
min·i·mum [mínəməm] *adj.* & *s.* mínimo.
min·ing [máɪnɪŋ] *s.* minería, explotación de minas; *adj.* minero; — **engineer** ingeniero de minas.
min·i·skirt [mínɪskɚt] *s.* minifalda.
min·is·ter [mínɪstɚ] *s.* ministro; pastor, clérigo; *v.* ministrar, atender; proveer, socorrer.
min·is·try [mínɪstrɪ] *s.* (*agency*) ministerio; (*help*) socorro, ayuda.
mink [mɪŋk] *s.* visón.
min·now [míno] *s.* pececillo de río.
mi·nor [máɪnɚ] *adj.* (*young*) menor; de menor edad; (*secondary*) secundario; — **key** tono menor; *s.* menor de edad; premisa menor (*de un silogismo*); tono menor; curso o asignatura menor.
mi·nor·i·ty [mənɔ́rətɪ] *s.* minoría; minoridad, menorde edad; menor parte; *adj.* minoritario.
min·strel [mínstrəl] *s.* trovador; bardo, vate; actor cómico que remeda al negro norteamericano.
mint [mɪnt] *s.* (*flavor*) menta, hierbabuena (*yerbabuena*); (*candy*) pastilla o bombón de menta; (*money*) casa de moneda; **a** — **of money** un montón de dinero, la mar de dinero; *v.* acuñar.
mint·age [míntədʒ] *s.* acuñación; moneda acuñada.
min·u·et [mɪnjUét] *s.* minué.
mi·nus [máɪnəs] *adj.* negativo; sin, falto de; **seven** — **four** siete menos cuatro; *s.* menos, signo menos.
min·ute [mínɪt] *s.* minuto; **-s** acta (*de una junta*); — **hand** minutero.
mi·nute [mənjút] *adj.* menudo, diminuto; minucioso, detallado.
mir·a·cle [mírəkl] *s.* milagro.
mi·rac·u·lous [mərǽkjələs] *adj.* milagroso.
mi·rage [mərɑ́ʒ] *s.* espejismo.
mire [maɪr] *s.* cieno, fango, lodo; *v.* atascar(se) en el fango; enlodar(se).
mir·ror [mírɚ] *s.* espejo; *v.* reflejar.
mirth [mɝθ] *s.* júbilo, regocijo, alegría.
mirth·ful [mɝ́θfəl] *adj.* jubiloso, regocijado, gozoso, alegre.
mir·y [máɪrɪ] *adj.* cenagoso, fangoso, lodoso.
mis·ad·ven·ture [mɪsədvéntʃɚ] *s.* desgracia; contratiempo.
mis·be·have [mɪsbihév] *v.* portarse mal, obrar mal.
mis·car·riage [mɪskǽrɪdʒ] *s.* aborto, malparto; mal éxito; extravío (*de una carta, papel, etc.*).
mis·car·ry [mɪskǽrɪ] *v.* (*fail*) malograrse, frustrarse; extraviarse (*una carta*); (*abort*) abortar.
mis·cel·la·ne·ous [mɪsléniəs] *adj.* misceláneo, diverso; — **expenses** gastos varios.
mis·chief [místʃɪf] *s.* travesura; diablura; mal, daño; diablillo, persona traviesa.
mis·chie·vous [místʃɪivəs] *adj.* travieso; malicioso; dañino; revoltoso.
mis·con·cep·tion [mɪskənsépʃən] *s.* concepto erróneo.
mis·con·duct [mɪskɑ́ndʌkt] *s.* mala conducta; mala administración; [mɪskəndʌ́kt] *v.* maladministrar, manejar mal; **to** — **oneself** portarse mal, conducirse mal.
mis·cue [mɪskjú] *s.* pifia.
mis·deed [mɪsdíd] *s.* fechoría, mala acción.
mis·de·mean·or [mɪsdɪmínɚ] *s.* mal comportamiento; fechoría.
mi·ser [máɪzɚ] *s.* avaro, avariento.
mis·er·a·ble [mízrebl] *adj.* miserable; infeliz, desdichado.
mi·ser·ly [máɪzɚlɪ] *adj.* avariento, avaro; tacaño,

mezquino.
mis·er·y [mízrɪ] *s.* miseria, desgracia; (*poverty*) estrechez, pobreza; dolor.
mis·for·tune [mɪsfɔ́rtʃən] *s.* infortunio, desgracia, desastre.
mis·giv·ing [mɪsgívɪŋ *s.* mal presentimiento, aprensión, recelo, temor.
mis·guid·ed [mɪsgáɪdəd] *adj.* mal aconsejado.
mis·hap [míshæp] *s.* desgracia, contratiempo, accidente.
mis·judge [mɪsdʒʌ́dʒ] *v.* juzgar mal.
mis·laid [mɪsléd] *pret. & p.p. de* **to mislay.**
mis·lay [mɪslé] *v.* extraviar, perder; poner fuera de su sitio, colocar mal; traspapelar (*una carta, documento, etc.*).
mis·lead [mɪslíd] *v.* guiar por mal camino; extraviar, descarriar; engañar.
mis·led [mɪslɛ́d] *pret. & p.p. de* **to mislead.**
mis·man·age [mɪsmǽnɪdʒ] *v.* administrar mal.
mis·place [mɪsplés] *v.* extraviar, poner fuera de su sitio, colocar mal; traspapelar (*una carta, documento, etc.*).
mis·print [mɪsprínt] *s.* errata, error tipográfico, error de imprenta.
mis·pro·nounce [mísprənɑʊns] *v.* pronunciar mal.
mis·rep·re·sent [mɪsrɛprɪzɛ́nt] *v.* falsear, falsificar; tergiversar; **misrepresentation** tergiversación.
miss [mɪs] *v.* (*not hit*) errar, no acertar; fallar; (*omit*) equivocar; perder; faltar a; (*feel absence of*) echar de menos; *Am.* extrañar; **he just -ed being killed** por poco lo matan; *s.* error; falla, falta.
miss [mɪs] *s.* señorita; **Miss Smith** la señorita Smith.
mis·sile [mísl] *s.* proyectil; arma arrojadiza; *adj.* arrojadizo, que se puede arrojar o tirar.
miss·ing [mísɪŋ] *adj.* ausente; perdido; **one book is** — falta un libro.
mis·sion [míʃən] *s.* misión.
mis·sion·ar·y [míʃənɛrɪ] *adj. & s.* misionero.
mis·spell [mɪsspɛ́l] *v.* escribir con mala ortografía, deletrear mal.
mist [mɪst] *s.* neblina, niebla; llovizna, *Ven., Col., Andes* garúa; *v.* lloviznar; anublar.
mis·take [məsték] *s.* error, yerro, equivocación; errata (*de imprenta*); **to make a** — equivocarse; *v.* equivocar.
mis·tak·en [məstékən] *p.p. de* **to mistake** *& adj.* equivocado; errado; erróneo, incorrecto; **to be** — estar equivocado, equivocarse, errar.
mis·ter [místə˞] *s.* señor.
mis·took [mɪstʊ́k] *pret. de* **to mistake.**
mis·treat [mɪstrít] *v.* maltratar.
mis·tress [místrɪs] *s.* señora; (*in charge*) ama, dueña; (*lover*) querida, amante; **school** — maestra.
mis·tri·al [mɪstráɪl] *s.* pleito viciado de nulidad.
mis·trust [mɪstrʌ́st] *s.* desconfianza; *v.* desconfiar de.
mis·trust·ful [mɪstrʌ́stfəl] *adj.* desconfiado, sospechoso, receloso.
mist·y [místɪ] *adj.* brumoso; nublado; (*filmed*) empañado; (*vague*) vago, indistinto.
mis·un·der·stand [mɪsʌndə˞stǽnd] *v.* comprender mal; entender mal; interpretar mal; no comprender.
mis·un·der·stand·ing [mɪsʌndə˞stǽndɪŋ] *s.* equivocación; mala interpretación, mala inteligencia; desavenencia.
mis·un·der·stood [mɪsʌndə˞stʊ́d] *pret. & p.p. de* **to misunderstand.**
mis·use [mɪsjús] *s.* abuso; mal uso; malversación (*de fondos*); [mɪsjúʃ] *v.* abusar de; maltratar; usar o emplear mal; malversar (*fondos*).
mite [maɪt] *s.* (*small*) óbolo, friolera, pequeñez; (*creature*) criatura.
mi·ter [máɪtə˞] *s.* mitra, dignidad de obispo
mit·i·gate [mítəget] *v.* mitigar.
mit·ten [mítn̩] *s.* mitón.
mix [mɪks] *v.* mezclar(se); unir(se), juntar(se), asociar(se); **to — someone up** confundir a uno; *s.* mezcla; confusión, lío.
mix·ture [míkstʃə˞] *s.* mezcla; mezcolanza.
mix·up [míksʌp] *s.* equívoco; enredo.
moan [mon] *s.* quejido, gemido; *v.* gemir; quejarse; lamentar(se).
moat [mot] *s.* foso.
mob [mɑb] *s.* (*rabble*) populacho; (*crowd*) muchedumbre, gentío, *Am.* bola (*de gente*); *v.* atropellar; apiñarse o agolparse alrededor de.
mo·bile [móbl] *adj.* móvil; movible; movedizo; — **home** casa rodante.
mo·bi·li·za·tion [mobləzéʃən] *s.* movilización.
mo·bi·lize [móblaɪz] *v.* movilizar.
moc·ca·sin [mɑ́kən̩] *s.* (*shoe*) mocasín (*zapato burdo de cuero*); (*snake*) mocasín (*víbora venenosa*).
mock [mɔk] *v.* (*ridicule*) mofar, mofarse de; (*imitate*) remedar, imitar; **to — at** mofarse de; burlarse de; *s.* mofa, burla, escarnio; mímica; remedo; *adj.* falso, ficticio, imitado; — **battle** simulacro, batalla fingida.
mock·er·y [mɔ́kərɪ] *s.* burla, mofa, escarnio; remedo.
mock-up [mɑ́kʌp] *s.* maqueta; modelo.
mode [mod] *s.* modo, manera; moda.
mod·el [mɑ́dl] *s.* (*guide*) modelo; (*pattern*) patrón; (*figure*) figurín, maniquí; *adj.* ejemplar; modelo; — **school** escuela modelo; *v.* modelar; moldear, formar; posar, servir de modelo.
mod·em [modɛm] *s.* (computer) modem, modulador-demodulador.
mod·er·ate [mɑ́dərɪt] *adj.* moderado; templado; módico; [mɑ́dəret] *v.* moderar(se); templar(se).
mod·er·a·tion [mɑdəréʃən] *s.* moderación; templanza.
mod·ern [mɑ́də˞n] *adj.* moderno.
mod·ern·ize [mɑ́də˞naɪz] *v.* modernizar.
mod·est [mɑ́dɪst] *adj.* modesto.
mod·es·ty [mɑ́dəstɪ] *s.* modestia.
mod·i·fi·ca·tion [mɑdəfəkéʃən] *s.* modificación.
mod·i·fy [mɑ́dəfaɪ] *v.* modificar.
mod·u·late [mɑ́dʒəlet] *v.* modular.
mo·hair [móhɛr] *s.* pelo de cabra.
Mo·ham·med·an [mohǽmədən] *adj. & s.* mahometano.
moist [mɔɪst] *adj.* húmedo; mojado.
mois·ten [mɔ́ɪsn̩] *v.* humedecer, mojar.
mois·ture [mɔ́ɪstʃə˞] *s.* humedad.
mo·lar [mólə˞] *adj.* molar; *s.* muela.
mo·las·ses [məlǽsɪz] *s.* melaza, miel de caña.
mold [mold] *s.* (*form*) molde, matriz; (*substance*) moho; tierra vegetal; *v.* moldear, amoldar; modelar; enmohecer(se), cubrir(se) de moho.
mold·er [móldə˞] *v.* desmoronarse.
mold·ing [móldɪŋ] *s.* moldura; moldeamiento.
mold·y [móldɪ] *adj.* mohoso.
mole [mol] *s.* lunar; topo (*animal*); dique, malecón, rompeolas.
mole [mol] *s.* lunar; topo (*animal*); dique, malecón, rompeolas.
mol·e·cule [mɑ́ləkjul] *s.* molécula.
mo·lest [məlɛ́st] *v.* molestar.
mol·li·fy [mɑ́ləfaɪ] *v.* apaciguar.
mol·ten [móltn̩] *adj.* derretido, fundido, en fusión.
mo·lyb·de·num [məlíbdənəm] *s.* molibdeno.
mo·ment [mómənt] *s.* momento; importancia, consecuencia.
mo·men·tar·y [móməntɛrɪ] *adj.* momentáneo.
mo·men·tous [moméntəs] *adj.* importante.

MI

mo·men·tum [moméntəm] *s.* momento (*de una fuerza*); ímpetu.
mon·arch [mánɚk] *s.* monarca.
mon·ar·chy [mánɚkɪ] *s.* monarquía.
mon·as·ter·y [mánəstɛrɪ] *s.* monasterio.
Mon·day [mʌ́ndɪ] *s.* lunes.
mon·e·tar·y [mánətɛrɪ] *adj.* monetario.
mon·ey [mʌ́nɪ] *s.* dinero; — **changer** cambista; — **order** giro postal; — **'s worth** valor cabal; — **standard** patrón (talón) monetario; — **in hand** dinero contante; **paper** — papel moneda; **silver** — moneda de plata; **money-making** lucrativo, provechoso, ganancioso.
mon·ger [máŋgɚ] *s.* traficante; defensor.
mon·grel [mʌ́ŋgrəl] *adj.* & *s.* mestizo, mixto, cruzado, *Perú* chusco (*perro*).
mon·i·tor [manɪtɚ] *s.* (*telecommunications*) monitor.
monk [mʌŋk] *s.* monje.
mon·key [mʌ́ŋkɪ] *s.* mono; — **shine** monada, monería; — **wrench** llave inglesa; *v.* juguetear; hacer monerías; payasear; entremeterse; **to** — **with** juguetear con; meterse con.
mon·o·gram [mánəgræm] *s.* monograma.
mon·o·graph [mánəgræf] *s.* monografía.
mon·o·logue [mánlɔg] *s.* monólogo, soliloquio.
mo·nop·o·lize [mənápIaɪz] *v.* monopolizar, acaparar.
mo·nop·o·ly [mənáplɪ] *s.* monopolio.
mon·o·syl·la·ble [mánəsɪləbl] *s.* monosílabo.
mon·o·tone [mánəton] *adj.* monótono.
mo·not·o·nous [mənátn̩əs] *adj.* monótono.
mo·not·o·ny [mənátn̩ɪ] *s.* monotonía.
mon·ster [mánstɚ] *s.* monstruo; *adj.* enorme.
mon·stros·i·ty [mɑnstrásətɪ] *s.* monstruosidad; monstruo.
mon·strous [mánstrəs] *adj.* monstruoso.
month [mʌnθ] *s.* mes.
month·ly [mʌ́nθlɪ] *adj.* mensual; — **installment** mensualidad *Col., Méx.* abono mensual; *s.* publicación mensual; *adv.* mensualmente.
mon·u·ment [mánjəmənt] *s.* monumento.
mon·u·men·tal [mɑnjəméntl] *adj.* monumental; colosal, grandioso.
moo [mu] *s.* mugido; *v.* mugir.
mood [mud] *s.* humor, disposición de ánimo; modo (*del verbo*); **to be in a good** — estar de buen humor; **to be in the** — **to** estar dispuesto a, tener gana de.
mood·y [múdɪ] *adj.* (*changing*) caprichoso, voluble, mudable; (*sad*) melancólico, mohino.
moon [mun] *s.* luna; mes lunar; **once in a blue** — de Pascuas a San Juan, muy rara vez, *Am.* por campanada de vacante, *Am.* a cada muerte de (*o* por la muerte de un) obispo.
moon·light [múnlaɪt] *s.* luz de la luna; — **dance** baile a la luz de la luna; — **night** noche de luna.
moon·shine [múnʃaɪn] *s.* licor hecho ilegalmente.
moor [mʊr] *v.* amarrar, atracar (*un buque*); anclar estar anclado; *s.* terreno inculto o baldío.
Moor [mʊr] *s.* moro.
Moor·ish [mʊ́riʃ] *adj.* morisco, moro.
mop [mɑp] *s. Am.* trapeador; **dust** — limpiapolvo; — **of hair** greñas, cabellera abundante; *v.* limpiar (*el suelo*), *Am.* trapear; **to** — **one's brow** limpiarse (*o* secarse) la frente; **to** — **up** limpiar; vencer; acabar con.
mope [mop] *v.* andar quejumbroso o abatido.
mor·al [mɔ́rəl] *adj.* moral; — **philosophy** ética, moral; *s.* moraleja; **-s** moral, ética.
mo·rale [mərǽl] *s.* moral, entereza de ánimo.
mor·al·ist [mɔ́rəlɪst] *s.* moralista.
mo·ral·i·ty [mɔrǽlətɪ] *s.* moralidad.
mor·al·ize [mɔ́rəlaɪz] *v.* moralizar.
mor·bid [mɔ́bɪd] *adj.* mórbido, morboso; malsano.
mor·dant [mɔ́rdənt] *adj.* mordaz.
more [mor] *adj.* & *adv.* más; — **and** — cada vez más, más y más; — **or less** poco más o menos; **there is no** — no hay más, ya no hay; se acabó.
more·o·ver [moróvɚ] *adv.* además.
morgue [mɔg] *s.* necrocomio; depósito de cadáveres; (**of newspaper**) archivo de referencias.
morn·ing [mɔ́rnɪŋ] *s.* mañana; **good** — ! ¡buenos días!; **tomorrow** — mañana por la mañana; *adj.* de la mañana; matutino, matinal; **morning-glory** dondiego de día; — **star** lucero del alba.
mor·phine [mɔ́fin] *s.* morfina.
mor·phol·o·gy [mɔrfálədʒɪ] *s.* morfología.
mor·row [mɔ́ro]: **on the** — el día de mañana; mañana.
mor·sel [mɔ́rsl] *s.* bocada; manjar sabroso.
mor·tal [mɔ́rtl̩] *adj.* & *s.* mortal.
mor·tal·i·ty [mɔrtǽlətɪ] *s.* mortalidad; mortandad.
mor·tar [mɔ́tɚ] *s.* mortero; argamasa, mezcla; **metal** — almirez.
mort·gage [mɔ́gɪdʒ] *s.* hipoteca, gravamen; *v.* hipotecar; *adj.* hipotecario; — **deed** escritura hipotecaria; **mort·ga·gee** acreedor hipotecario; **mort·ga·gor** deudor hipotecario.
mor·ti·fy [mɔ́təfaɪ] *v.* mortificar; avergonzar.
mo·sa·ic [mozéɪk] *adj.* & *s.* mosaico.
Mos·lem [mázləm] *adj.* & *s.* musulmán.
mosque [mɔsk] *s.* mezquita.
mos·qui·to [məskíto] *s.* mosquito; zancudo; — **net** mosquitero.
moss [mɔs] *s.* musgo; **moss-grown** musgoso, cubierto de musgo; anticuado.
moss·y [mɔ́sɪ] *adj.* musgoso.
most [most] *adv. más; sumamente, muy; s.* la mayoría, la mayor parte, el mayor número o cantidad; los más; — **people** la mayoría (*o* la mayor parte) de la gente; **at the** — a lo más, a lo sumo; **for the** — **part** por la mayor parte; generalmente, mayormente; **the** — **that I can do** lo más que puedo hacer; **the** — **votes** el mayor número de votos, los más votos.
most·ly [móstlɪ] *adv.* por la mayor parte; mayormente, principalmente.
moth [mɔθ] *s.* polilla; mariposa nocturna; — **ball** bolita de naftalina; **moth-eaten** apolillado.
moth·er [mʌ́ðɚ] *s.* madre; **mother-of-pearl** madreperla, nácar; *adj.* de madre; materno, maternal; nativo, natal; — **country** madre patria; país natal; — **Superior** superiora; — **tongue** lengua materna; *v.* servir de madre a, cuidar de.
moth·er·hood [mʌ́ðɚhʊd] *s.* maternidad.
moth·er-in-law [mʌ́ðərɪnlɔ] *s.* suegra.
moth·er·ly [mʌ́ðɚlɪ] *adj.* maternal, materno.
mo·tif [motíf] *s.* motivo, tema.
mo·tion [móʃən] *s.* (*movement*) moción; movimiento; (*signal*) ademán; señal, seña; — **sickness** mareo; *v.* hacer una seña o señas; indicar.
mo·tion·less [móʃənlɪs] *adj.* inmóvil, inmoble.
mo·tion pic·ture [móʃənpɪktʃɚ] *s.* cine o cinematógrafo; película; fotografia cinematográfica; **motion-picture** *adj.* cinematográfico.
mo·tive [mótɪv] *s.* motivo; tema; *adj.* motriz.
mot·ley [mátlɪ] *adj.* abigarrado, multicolor, de diversos colores; variado, mezclado; *s.* mezcla, mezcolanza.
mo·tor [mótɚ] *s.* motor; automóvil; *v.* pasear o ir en automóvil.
mo·tor·bike [mótɚbaɪk] *s.* motocicleta pequeña; moto.

mo·tor·boat [mótɚbot] *s.* autobote, lancha de gasolina, bote de motor.
mo·tor·car [mótɚkɑr] *s.* automóvil.
mo·tor·coach [mótɚkotʃ] *s.* autobús, ómnibus, *Méx.* camión, *Carib.* guagua; *Ríopl., Ch.* micro; *C.A.* bus.
mo·tor·cy·cle [mótɚsaɪkl] *s.* motocicleta.
mo·tor·ist [mótərɪst] *s.* motorista, automovilista.
mo·tor·man [mótɚmən] *s.* motorista.
mo·tor scoot·er [mótɚskutɚ] *s.* motoneta.
mot·tled [mɑ́tld] *adj.* moteado; jaspeado, manchado.
mot·to [mɑ́to] *s.* mote, divisa, lema.
mould = **mold.**
mould·er = **molder.**
mould·ing = **molding.**
mould·y = **moldy.**
mound [maʊnd] *s.* montecillo, montículo, montón de tierra.
mount [maʊnt] *s.* (*elevation*) monte; (*horse*) montura, cabalgadura, caballo; *v.* montar; montar a caballo; subir, ascender; (*assemble*) armar (*una máquina*); (*jewels*) engastar (*joyas*).
moun·tain [maʊntn̩] *s.* montaña; *adj.* montañés; de montaña; — **goat** cabra montés; — **lion** puma; — **range** cordillera, cadena de montañas.
moun·tain climb·er [máʊntənklaɪmɚ] *s.* alpinista.
moun·tain·eer [maʊntn̩ír] *s.* montañés.
moun·tain·ous [máʊntn̩əs] *adj.* montañoso.
mourn [morn] *v.* lamentar; deplorar; **to** — **for** llorar a; estar de duelo por; **mourn·er** [mornɚ] *s.* dolientes, penitentes.
mourn·ful [mórnfəl] *adj.* fúnebre; lúgubre; lastimero, triste.
mourn·ing [mórnɪŋ] *s.* luto; duelo; lamentación; **to be in** — estar de luto, estar de duelo; *adj.* de luto.
mouse [maʊs] *s.* ratón; — **trap** ratonera.
mous·tache = **mustache.**
mouth [maʊθ] *s.* boca; abertura; desembocadura, embocadura (*de un río*).
mouth·ful [máʊθfəl] *s.* bocado.
mouth·piece [máʊθpis] *s.* boquilla (*de un instrumento de viento*); portavoz.
mov·a·ble [múvəbl] *adj.* movible, móvil; **-s** *s. pl.* muebles, bienes muebles.
move [muv] *v.* (*motion*) mover(se); (*change*) mudar(se), mudar de casa; (*propose*) proponer, hacer la moción de; (*game*) hacer una jugada (*en ajedrez o damas*); (*emotion*) conmover; inducir; — **away** irse; alejarse; apartarse; **to** — **forward** avanzar; **to** — **on** seguir adelante, caminar; **to** — **out** irse, mudarse, mudar de casa; *s.* movimiento; mudanza (*de una casa a otra*); paso, trámite (*para conseguir algo*); jugada, turno (*en juegos*); **moving van** camión de mudanzas; **get a** — **on there!** ¡ande! ¡dése prisa!; *Méx.* ¡ándele!
move·ment [múvmənt] *s.* (*motion*) movimiento; maniobra; meneo; acción; (*mechanism*) mecanismo, movimiento (*de un reloj*); (*bowel*) evacuación.
mov·ie [múvɪ] *s.* cine, película; **-s** cine.
mow [mo] *v.* segar; cortar (*césped*).
mow·er [móɚ] *s.* segador; segadora, cortadora mecánica; máquina segadora.
mown [mon] *adj. & p.p.* segado.
Mr. [místɚ] Sr., señor; **Mrs.** [mísɪz] Sra, señora.
much [mʌtʃ] *adj., adv. & s.* mucho; — **the same** casi lo mismo; **as** — **as** tanto como; **how** — **?** ¿cuánto?; **not** — **of a book** un libro de poco valor; **not** — **of a poet** un poetastro; **so** — **that** tanto que; **too** — demasiado; **very** — muchísimo; **to make** — **of** dar mucha importancia a.
muck [mʌk] *s.* (*manure*) estiércol húmedo; (*mire*) cieno; (*filth*) porquería, suciedad.
mu·cous [mjúkəs] *adj.* mucoso; — **membrane** membrana mucosa.
mud [mʌd] *s.* lodo, fango, cieno; barro; — **wall** tapia.
mud·dle [mʌdl] *v.* enturbiar; (*confuse*) confundir; embrollar; *s.* confusión, embrollo, lío, desorden.
mud·dy [mʌ́dɪ] *adj.* fangoso, lodoso; turbio; confuso; *v.* enlodar, ensuciar; enturbiar.
muff [mʌf] *s.* manguito (*para las manos*); falla, error (*en ciertos juegos*); *v.* no coger, dejar escapar (*la pelota*).
muf·fin [mʌ́fɪn] *s.* bollo, panecillo.
muf·fle [mʌfl] *v.* embozar; tapar; apagar, amortiguar (*un sonido*).
muf·fler [mʌ́flɚ] *s.* bufanda; silenciador (*para maquinaria*); mofle.
mug [mʌg] *s.* pichel, vaso con asa.
mu·lat·to [məlǽto] *s.* mulato.
mul·ber·ry [mʌ́lbɛrɪ] *s.* mora; — **tree** moral.
mule [mjul] *s.* mulo, mula.
mule·teer [mjulətír] *s.* arriero.
mull [mʌl] *v.* meditar, ponderar, revolver en la mente; calentar (*vino, sidra, etc.*) con azúcar y especias.
mul·ti·ple [mʌ́ltəpl] *s.* múltiplo; *adj.* múltiple.
mul·ti·pli·ca·tion [mʌltəpləkéʃən] *s.* multiplicación; — **table** tabla de multiplicar.
mul·ti·plic·i·ty [mʌltəplísətɪ] *s.* multiplicidad.
mul·ti·ply [mʌ́ltəplaɪ] *v.* multiplicar(se).
mul·ti·tude [mʌ́ltətjud] *s.* multitud.
mul·ti·us·er [mʌltɪjúzɚ] *s.* (*computer*) multiusuario.
mum [mʌm] *adj.* callado, silencioso; **to keep** — estarse (*o quedarse*) callado.
mum·ble [mʌ́mbl] *v.* murmurar, hablar entre dientes; mascullar; *s.* murmullo; **to talk in a** — mascullar las palabras, hablar entre dientes.
mum·my [mʌ́mɪ] *s.* momia.
mumps [mʌmps] *s.* parótidas, paperas.
munch [mʌtʃ] *v.* mascar ruidosamente, mascullar.
mun·dane [məndén] *adj.* mundano.
mu·nic·i·pal [mjunísəpl] *adj.* municipal; — **council** cabildo, concejo, ayuntamiento.
mu·nic·i·pal·i·ty [mjunɪsəpǽlətɪ] *s.* municipio; municipalidad.
mu·ni·tion [mjuníʃən] *s.* munición; — **plant** fábrica de municiones, arsenal; *v.* guarnecer, abastecer de municiones.
mu·ral [mjúrəl] *adj. & s.* mural.
mur·der [mɝ́dɚ] *s.* asesinato, homicidio; *v.* asesinar.
mur·der·er [mɝ́dərɚ] *s.* asesino, homicida.
mur·der·ess [mɝ́dərɪs] *s.* asesina, homicida.
mur·der·ous [mɝ́dərəs] *adj.* asesino, homicida.
mur·mer [mɝ́mɚ] *s.* (*noise*) murmullo; susurro; (*complaint*) queja; *v.* murmurar; susurrar; quejarse.
mus·cle [mʌ́sl] *s.* músculo.
mus·cu·lar [mʌ́skjələɚ] *adj.* muscular; musculoso; nervudo.
muse [mjuz] *v.* meditar; *s.* meditación; **Muse** musa.
mu·se·um [mjuzíəm] *s.* museo.
mush [mʌʃ] *s.* potaje espeso de maíz; masa de maíz; cualquier masa blanda; sentimentalismo.
mush·room [mʌ́ʃrum] *s.* seta, hongo.
mu·sic [mjúzɪk] *s.* música; — **stand** atril.
mu·si·cal [mjúzɪkl] *adj.* musical, músico; melodioso; armonioso; aficionado a la música; — **comedy** zarzuela, comedia musical.
mu·si·cian [mjuzíʃən] *s.* músico.
musk·mel·on [mʌ́skmɛlən] *s.* melón.
musk·rat [mʌ́skræt] *s.* almizclera (*roedor semejante a la rata*).

mus·lin [mʌ́slɪn] *s.* muselina.
muss [mʌs] *v.* desarreglar, desordenar; arrugar.
must [mʌst] *v. defect* (*por lo general se usa sólo en el presente*) deber; deber de, haber de; tener que.
mus·tache [mʌ́stæʃ] *s.* bigote, mostacho.
mus·tard [mʌ́stɚd] *s.* mostaza; — **plaster** sinapismo.
mus·ter [mʌ́stɚ] *v.* pasar lista o revista; juntarse para una formación militar; reunir(se); **to — out** dar de baja; **to — up one's courage** cobrar valor o ánimo; *s.* revista (*de soldados o marinos*); **to pass** — pasar lista o revista; ser aceptable (*en una inspección*).
must·y [mʌ́stɪ] *adj.* mohoso; rancio, añejo.
mu·ta·tion [mjutéʃən] *s.* mutación.
mute [mjut] *adj.* mudo; *s.* mudo. letra muda; sordina (*de violín*).
mu·ti·late [mjútlet] *v.* mutilar.
mu·ti·ny [mjútn̩ɪ] *s.* motín; *v.* amotinarse.
mut·ter [mʌ́tɚ] *v.* murmurar, refunfuñar; hablar entre dientes; *s.* murmullo, refunfuño.
mut·ton [mʌ́tn̩] *s.* carne de carnero; — **chop** chuleta de carnero.
mu·tu·al [mjútʃuel] *adj.* mutuo; **wall** pared medianera; **fund** fondo mutuo.
muz·zle [mʌ́sl] *s.* hocico; (*harness*) bozal (*para el hocico*); (*gun*) boca (*de arma de fuego*); *v.* abozalar, poner bozal a; amordazar; hacer callar.
my [maɪ] *adj.* mi (mis).
myr·i·ad [mɪ́rəd] *s.* miríada, diez mil; millares, gran cantidad.
myrrh [mɝ] *s.* mirra.
myr·tle [mɝ́tl] *s.* mirto, arrayán.
my·self [maɪsɛ́lf] *pron.* yo mismo; me (*como reflexivo*); a mí mismo; **by** — solo; **I — did it** yo mismo lo hice; **I talk to** — hablo conmigo mismo, hablo para mis adentros.
mys·te·ri·ous [mɪstɪ́rɪəs] *adj.* misterioso.
mys·ter·y [mɪ́strɪ] *s.* misterio
mys·tic [mɪ́stɪk] *adj.* & *s.* místico.
mys·ti·cal [mɪ́stɪkl] *adj.* místico.
myth [mɪθ] *s.* mito, fábula.
my·thol·o·gy [mɪθɑ́lədʒɪ] *s.* mitología.

N:n

nab [næb] *v.* agarrar, coger; arrestar.
nag [næg] *s.* rocín, caballejo, jaco; *v.* importunar, irritar (*con repetidos regaños*).
nail [nel] *s.* clavo; uña (*del dedo*); — **file** lima (*para las uñas*); *v.* clavar; clavear; agarrar, atrapar.
na·ive [nɑív] *adj.* simple, ingenuo, cándido.
na·ked [nékɪd] *adj.* desnudo.
na·ked·ness [nékɪdnɪs] *s.* desnudez.
name [nem] *s.* (*designation*) nombre; (*fame*) renombre, fama; — **sake** tocayo; **by the — of** nombrado, llamado; apellidado; **family** — apellido; **to call someone -s** motejar o decirle groserías a uno; ponerle apodos a uno; **to make a — for oneself** ganar fama; **what is your — ?** ¿cómo se llama Vd.?; *v.* nombrar; mentar, mencionar; llamar; *adj.* onomástico.
name·less [némlɪs] *adj.* sin nombre; anónimo.
name·ly [némlɪ] *adv.* a saber, esto es, es decir.
name·plate [némplet] *s.* rótulo, placa; *Col.* chapa.
nap [næp] *s.* siesta; pelo (*de un tejido*); **to take a** — echar un sueño, echar una siesta; *v.* dormitar; echar un sueño; sestear.
nape [nep] *s.* nuca, cogote.
naph·tha [nǽfθə] *s.* nafta.
nap·kin [nǽpkɪn] *s.* servilleta.
nar·cis·sus [nɑrsɪ́səs] *s.* narciso.
nar·cot·ic [nɑrkɑ́tɪk] *adj.* & *s.* narcótico.
nar·rate [nærét] *v.* narrar.
nar·ra·tion [næréʃən] *s.* narración.
nar·ra·tive [nǽrətɪv] *adj.* narrativo; *s.* narración; narrativa; relato.
nar·row [nǽro] *adj.* (*cramped*) estrecho; angosto; limitado (*intolerant*) intolerante; — **escape** trance difícil, escapada difícil; — **gauge** de vía angosta; — **search** búsqueda esmerada; **narrow-minded** fanático, intolerante; **-s** *s. pl.* desfiladero, paso; estrecho o estrechos; *v.* angostar(se), estrechar(se); limitar, restringir, reducir; — **the gap** reducir la diferencia; **-ly** *adv.* estrechamente; **he -ly escaped** por poco no se escapa.
nar·row·ness [nǽrənɪs] *s.* (*cramped*) estrechez, estrechura, angostura; limitación; (*intolerance*) intolerancia.
na·sal [nézl] *adj.* nasal.
nas·ti·ness [nǽstɪnɪs] *s.* suciedad, porquería; (*verbal*) grosería.
na·stur·tium [næstɝ́ʃəm] *s.* mastuerzo.
nas·ty [nǽstɪ] *adj.* (*foul*) sucio, asqueroso; feo (*indecent*) grosero; indecente; **a — fall** una caída terrible; **a — disposition** un genio horrible.
na·tal [nétl] *adj.* natal.
na·tion [néʃən] *s.* nación.
na·tion·al [nǽʃənl] *adj.* nacional; *s.* nacional, ciudadano; *v.* **nationalize** nacionalizar.
na·tion·al·ism [nǽʃənəlɪzm] *s.* nacionalismo.
na·tion·al·i·ty [næʃənǽlətɪ] *s.* nacionalidad; **adjective of** — gentilicio.
na·tive [nétɪv] *adj.* nativo; natal; natural; (*original*) indígena; del país, *Am.* criollo; — **of** oriundo de, natural de; *s.* nativo, natural, indígena; habitante.
na·tiv·i·ty [nətɪ́vətɪ] *s.* nacimiento. natividad (*de la Virgen María*); **the Nativity** la Navidad.
nat·u·ral [nǽtʃərəl] *adj.* natural; sencillo, sin afectación; **resources** recursos naturales; riquezas naturales; *s.* becuadro (*signo musical*); **he is a — for that job** tiene aptitud natural para ese puesto; **-ly** *adv.* naturalmente; con naturalidad.
nat·u·ral·ism [nǽtʃərəlɪzəm] *s.* naturalismo.
nat·u·ral·ist [nǽtʃərəlɪst] *s.* naturalista.
nat·u·ral·i·za·tion [nætʃərələzéʃən] *s.* naturalización.
nat·u·ral·ize [nǽtʃərəlaɪz] *v.* naturalizar.
nat·u·ral·ness [nǽtʃərəlnts] *s.* naturalidad.
na·ture [nétʃɚ] *s.* naturaleza; natural, genio, índole; instinto; especíe; **to copy from** — copiar del natural.
naught [nɔt] *s.* cero; nada.
naugh·ty [nɔ́tɪ] *adj.* malo, desobediente; travieso, pícaro; malicioso.
nau·se·a [nɔ́zɪə] *s.* náusea
nau·se·ate [nɔ́zɪet] *v.* dar náuseas, dar bascas, asquear, dar asco; sentir náusea; **to be -ed** tener náuseas.
nau·se·at·ing [nɔ́zɪetɪŋ] *adj.* nauseabundo, asqueroso.
nau·ti·cal [nɔ́tɪkl] *adj.* náutico, naval.
na·val [névl] *adj.* naval; — **officer** oficial de marina.
nave [nev] *s.* nave (*de una iglesia*).
na·vel [névl] *s.* ombligo; — **orange** naranja california (*sin semillas*).
nav·i·ga·ble [nǽvəgəbl] *adj.* navegable.
nav·i·gate [nǽvəget] *v.* navegar.
nav·i·ga·tion [nævəgéʃən] *s.* navegación; náutica.
nav·i·ga·tor [nǽvəgətɚ] *s.* navegador, navegante.
na·vy [névɪ] *s.* marina de guerra; armada; — **blue**

azul marino; — **yard** astillero, arsenal.
nay [ne] *adv*. no; no sólo . . . sino (*que*) también; *s*. no, voto negativo.
near [nɪr] *adv*. (*space, time*) cerca; (*almost*) casi; — **at hand** cerca, a la mano; **I came — forgetting to do it** por poco se me olvida hacerlo; **to come (go, draw)** — acercarse; — **sighted** miope; *prep*. cerca de; — **the end of the month** hacia fines del mes; *adj*. cercano, próximo; estrecho, íntimo; — **silk** seda imitada; **I had a — accident** por poco me sucede un accidente; *v*. acercarse (a).
near·by [nírbáɪ] *adv*. cerca, a la mano; *adj*. cercano, próximo.
near·ly [nírlɪ] *adv*. casi, cerca de; aproximadamente, próximamente; **I — did it** estuve al punto de hacerlo, estuve por hacerlo.
near·ness [nírnɪs] *s*. cercanía, proximidad.
neat [nit] *adj*. (*clean*) pulcro, aseado, limpio; (*ordered*) ordenado; esmerado; (*clever*) hábil, diestro; **-ly** *adv*. aseadamente; esmeradamente; ordenadamente; hábilmente.
neat·ness [nítnɪs] *s*. pulcritud, aseo; limpieza; esmero; claridad.
neb·u·lous [nɛ́bjʊləs] *adj*. nebuloso.
nec·es·sar·i·ly [nɛsəsɛ́rəlɪ] *adv*. necesariamente; forzosamente.
nec·es·sar·y [nɛ́səsɛrɪ] *adj*. necesario, forzoso; **nec·es·sar·ies** *s. pl*. necesidades, requisitos.
ne·ces·si·tate [nəsɛ́sətet] *v*. necesitar, precisar.
ne·ces·si·ty [nəsɛ́sətɪ] *s*. necesidad.
neck [nɛk] *s*. cuello, (*animal*) pescuezo; cerviz; (*throat*) garganta; — **of land** istmo; **low** — escote; — **and** — parejos (*en una carrera*).
neck·lace [nɛ́klɪs] *s*. collar; gargantilla.
neck·tie [nɛ́ktaɪ] *s*. corbata.
ne·crol·o·gy [nɛkrɑ́lədʒɪ] *s*. necrología.
need [nid] *s*. (*lack*) necesidad; (*poverty*) pobreza; **for — of** por falta de; **if — be** si fuere menester, en caso de necesidad; *v*. necesitar; tener necesidad de; hacerle falta a uno; tener que.
need·ful [nídfəl] *adj*. necesario; necesitado.
nee·dle [nídl] *s*. aguja.
nee·dle·point [nídlpɔɪnt] *s*. encaje de mano.
need·less [nídlɪs] *adj*. innecesario, inútil.
nee·dle·work [nídlwɝk] *s*. labor, bordado; costura.
need·y [nídɪ] *adj*. necesitado, menesteroso.
ne'er [nɛr] *adv*. *contr. de* **never; ne'er-do-well** *s*. persona incompetente; haragán.
ne·ga·tion [nɪgéʃən] *s*. negación; negativa.
neg·a·tive [nɛ́gətɪv] *adj*. negativo; *s*. negativa; negación, partícula o voz negativa; negativa (*de una fotografía*).
ne·glect [nɪglɛ́kt] *s*. negligencia; descuido; abandono; *v*. descuidar; desatender; abandonar; **to — to** dejar de, olvidar, olvidarse de.
ne·glect·ful [nɪglɛ́ktfəl] *adj*. negligente, descuidado.
neg·li·gence [nɛ́glədʒəns] *s*. negligencia.
neg·li·gent [nɛ́glədʒənt] *adj*. negligente, descuidado.
ne·go·ti·ate [nɪgóʃɪet] *v*. negociar; agenciar; vencer (*un obstáculo o dificultad*), dar cima a; gestionar.
ne·go·ti·a·tion [nɪgoʃɪéʃən] *s*. negociación.
Ne·gro [nígro] *s. & adj*. negro.
Ne·groid [nígrɔɪd] *adj*. negroide.
neigh [ne] *s*. relincho; *v*. relinchar.
neigh·bor [nébɚ] *s*. vecino; prójimo; *adj*. vecino; cercano.
neigh·bor·hood [nébɚhʊd] *s*. vecindad; vecindario; inmediatión; **in the — of a hundred dollars** cerca de cien dólares.
neigh·bor·ing [nébərɪŋ] *adj*. vecino; cercano; colindante.
nei·ther [níðɚ] *pron*. ninguno, ni (el) uno ni (el) otro; — **of the two** ninguno de los dos; *adj*. ninguno; — **one of us** ninguno de nosotros; *conj*. ni; — . . . — **nor** ni . . . ni; — **will I** tampoco yo, ni yo tampoco.
ne·ol·o·gism [niɑ́lədʒɪzm] *s*. neologismo.
ne·on [nían] *s*. neón.
ne·o·phyte [níofaɪt]*s*. neófito.
neph·ew [nɛ́fju] *s*. sobrino.
ne·phri·tis [nəfráɪtɪs] *s*. nefritis.
nep·o·tism [nɛ́pətɪzm] *s* nepotismo.
nerve [nɝv] *s*. (*anatomy*) nervio; (*courage*) valor, ánimo; audacia; (*effrontery*) descaro; **-s** nervios; nerviosidad; **to strain every** — esforzarse hasta más no poder, poner el mayor empeño posible.
nerv·ous [nɝvəs] *adj*. nervioso.
nerv·ous·ness [nɝ́vəsnɪs] *s*. nerviosidad; agitación.
nest [nɛst] *s*. nido; nidada; — **egg** nidal; ahorros; — **of baskets (boxes, tables)** juego graduado de cestas (cajas, mesitas); **wasp's** — avispero; *v*. anidar.
nes·tle [nɛ́sl] *v*. acurrucarse; abrigar(se); anidar.
net [nɛt] *v*. red; malla; tejido de mallas; *adj*. de mallas, de punto de malla; *v*. redar, enredar, coger con red; cubrir con una red.
net [nɛt] *adj*. neto; — **price** precio neto; — **profit** ganancia neta o líquida; — **worth** *Ch., Perú* patrimonio; *Méx*. capital contable; — **assets** activo neto; *Arg*. patrimonio neto; *Méx*. capital contable; — **income** ingresos netos; *v*. producir una ganancia neta o liquida; obtener una ganancia liquida.
net·tle [nɛ́tl] *s*. ortiga; *v*. picar, irritar, enfadar.
net·work [nɛ́twɝk] *s*. red; malla; cadena, sistema; **radio** — red de estaciones radiofónicas; — **program** transmisión en cadena.
neu·ral·gia [nurǽldʒə] *s*. neuralgia.
neu·ras·the·ni·a [nurəsθíniə] *s*. neurastenia.
neu·rot·ic [njʊrɑ́tɪk] *adj. & s*. neurótico.
neu·ter [njútɚ] *adj*. neutro.
neu·tral [njútrəl] *adj*. neutral; neutro.
neu·tral·i·ty [njutrǽlətɪ] *s*. neutralidad.
neu·tral·ize [njútrəlaɪz] *v*. neutralizar.
neu·tron [nútran] *s*. neutrón.
nev·er [nɛ́vɚ] *adv*. nunca, jamás; — **mind** no importa; no haga Vd. caso; no se moleste Vd.; **never-ending** perpetuo, eterno; de nunea acabar; **nevermore** nunca jamás.
nev·er·the·less [nɛvɚðəlɛ́s] *adv. & conj*. sin embargo, no obstante, con todo, empero.
new [nju] *adj*. (*not old*) nuevo; moderno; (*fresh*) fresco; reciente; *adv*. recién; — **born baby** criatura recién nacida; — **departure** nuevo derrotero.
new·com·er [njúkʌmɚ] *s*. recién llegado.
new·fan·gled [njufǽŋgld] *adj*. de última moda, recién inventado.
new·ly [njúlɪ] *adv*. nuevamente, recientemente; — **arrived** recién llegado; — **sed** recién casado.
new·ness [njúnɪs] *s*. novedad, calidad de nuevo.
news [njuz] *s*. noticias, nuevas; (*happenings*) novedades; **piece of** — noticia, nueva; — **boy** vendedor de periódicos; — **reel** película noticiera; película de noticias mundiales; — **stand** puesto de periódicos; **broadcast,** — **bulletin** noticiero, noticiario; — **advertising** publicidad de prensa; — **clipping** recorte.
news·mong·er [njúzmʌŋgɚ] *s*. chismoso, chismero, gacetilla.
news·pa·per [njúzpepɚ] *s*. periódico.
next [nɛkst] *adj*. (*future*) próximo; entrante, que viene; (*following*) siguiente; contiguo; **in the — life** en la otra vida; **to be — in turn** tocarle a uno,

MU

ser su turno; *adv.* después, luego; — **best** segundo en cualidad o importancia; *prep.;* — **to** junto a; al lado de; después de.
nib·ble [nɪ́bl] *s.* mordisco; *v.* mordiscar, mordisquear; picar, morder.
nice [naɪs] *adj.* (*attractive*) fino; bueno; amable, simpático; lindo; primoroso; (*refined*) refinado; esmerado; preciso, exacto; **-ly** *adv.* con esmero; con finura o primor; sutilmente, con delicadeza; amablemente; bien; **to get along -ly with** llevarse bien con.
ni·ce·ty [náɪsətɪ] *s.* fineza, finura; delicadeza; exactitud.
niche [nɪtʃ] *s.* nicho.
nick [nɪk] *s.* mella, desportilladura; **in the — of time** en el momento crítico; *v.* mellar, desportillar.
nick·el [nɪ́kl] *s.* níquel; moneda de cinco centavos; **nickel-plated** niquelado.
nick·name [nɪ́knem] *s.* mote, apodo; *v.* apodar, poner apodo a.
nic·o·tine [nɪ́kətin] *s.* nicotina.
niece [nis] *s.* sobrina.
nig·gard·ly [nɪ́gɚdlɪ] *adj.* mezquino, ruin, tacaño; *adv.* mezquinamente, ruinmente.
night [naɪt] *s.* noche; **good — !** ¡buenas noches!; **tomorrow** — mañana por la noche; *adj.* nocturno; de noche; — **owl** buho; trasnochador; — **watchmen** sereno, vigilante nocturno; — **shift** turno de noche.
night·fall [náɪtfɔl] *s.* anochecer, caída de la tarde, anochecida.
night·gown [náɪtgaʊn] *s.* camisa de dormir, camisa de noche, *Am.* camisón.
night·in·gale [náɪtn̩gel] *s.* ruiseñor.
night·ly [náɪtlɪ] *adv.* cada noche, todas las noches; *adj.* nocturno, de noche.
night·mare [náɪtmɛr] *s.* pesadilla
ni·hil·ism [náɪɪlɪzm] *s.* nihilismo.
nim·ble [nɪ́mbl] *adj.* ágil, ligero; listo.
nine [naɪn] *num.* nueve.
nine·teen [naɪntín] *num.* diecinueve.
nine·ty [náɪntɪ] *num.* noventa.
ni·o·bi·um [naɪóbiəm] *s.* niobio.
nip [nɪp] *v.* (*pinch*) pellizcar; (*bite*) mordiscar; (*frostbite*) marchitar, helar (*por la acción del frio*); **to — in the bud** cortar en germen, destruir al nacer; **to — off** despuntar; podar; *s.* pellizco; mordisco; trago.
nip·ple [nɪ́pl] *s.* teta, tetilla, pezón; pezón de goma.
ni·trate [náɪtret] *s.* nitrato.
ni·tric a·cid [náɪtrɪkǽsɪd] *s.* ácido nítrico.
ni·tro·gen [naɪ́trədʒən] *s.* nitrógeno.
ni·tro·glyc·er·in [naɪtroglɪ́sɝɪn] *s.* nitroglicerina.
no [no] *adv.* no; — **longer** ya no; **there is — more** no hay más; *adj.* ningun(o); — **matter how much** por mucho que; — **one** ninguno, nadie; — **smoking** se prohibe fumar; **I have — friend** no tengo ningún amigo; **of — use** inútil, sin provecho; *s.* no, voto negativo.
no·bil·i·ty [nobɪ́lətɪ] *s.* nobleza.
no·ble [nóbl] *s.* & *adj.* noble.
no·ble·man [nóblmən] *s.* noble.
no·ble·ness [nóblnɪs] *s.* nobleza.
no·bly [noblɪ] *adv.* noblemente.
no·bod·y [nóbɑdɪ] *pron.* nadie, ninguno.
noc·tur·nal [nɑktɝnl] *adj.* nocturno.
nod [nɑd] *v.* (*signal*) inclinar la cabeza (*para hacer una seña, saludar, o asentir*); (*doze*) cabecear, dar cabezadas (*dormitando*); *s.* inclinación de cabeza, saludo; señal de asentimiento (*con la cábeza*).
noise [nɔɪz] *s.* (*sound*) ruido; (*disorder*) barullo; sonido; *v.* divulgar; **it is being -d about that** corre el rumor que.
noise·less [nɔ́tzlɪs] *adj.* sin ruido, silencioso, quieto; **-ly** *adv.* sin ruido, silenciosamente.
nois·i·ly [nɔ́ɪzɪlɪ] *adv.* ruidosamente.
nois·y [nɔ́ɪzɪ] *adj.* ruidoso.
no·men·cla·ture [nómənkleʃɚ] *s.* nomenclatura.
nom·i·nal [nɑ́mənl] *adj.* nominal.
nom·i·nate [nɑ́mənet] *v.* nombrar, designar.
nom·i·na·tion [nɑmənéʃən] *s.* nombramiento, nominación.
non·con·form·ist [nɑnkənfɔ́rmɪst] *adj.* & *s.* disidente.
none [nʌn] *pron.* ninguno; ningunos; nada; **I want — of that** no quiero nada de eso; **that is — of his business** no le importa a él eso; *adv.* no, de ningún modo; — **the less** no menos; **to be — the happier for that** no estar por eso más contento.
non·en·ti·ty [nɑnɛ́ntətɪ] *s.* nulidad, persona o cosa inútil.
in·ter·ven·tion [nɑnɪntɚvɛ́nʃən] *s.* no intervención.
non·par·ti·san [nɑnpɑ́rtəzən] *adj.* imparcial; independiente.
non·sense [nɑ́nsɛns] *s.* tontería, necedad; disparate, desatino; **to talk** — pavear.
non·stop [nɑnstɑ́p] *adj.* & *adv.* sin escala, directo.
noo·dle [núdl] *s.* tallarín, fideo, pasta (*para sopa*).
nook [nʊk] *s.* rincón; **breakfast** — desayunador.
noon [nun] *s.* mediodía.
noon·day [núnde] *s.* mediodía; *adj.* meridiano, de mediodía — **meal** comida de mediodía.
noon·tide [núntaɪd] *s.* mediodía.
noon·time [núntaɪm] *s.* mediodía.
noose [nus] *s.* dogal; lazo, nudo corredizo, *Carib.* gaza; *v.* lazar, coger con lazo; hacer un lazo corredizo en.
nor [nɔr] *conj.* ni; **neither . . .** — ni . . . ni.
Nor·dic [nɔ́rdɪk] *adj.* nórdico.
norm [nɔrm] *s.* norma.
nor·mal [nɔ́ml] *adj.* normal; *s.* norma; normal, línea perpendicular.
north [nɔrθ] *s.* norte; *adj.* septentrional; norteño; del norte; — **pole** polo norte, polo ártico; — **wind** cierzo, norte; **North American** norteamericano; *adv.* al norte, hacia el norte.
north·east [nɔrθíst] *adj.* & *s.* nordeste; *adv.* hacia el nordeste, rumbo al nordeste.
north·east·ern [nɔrθístɚn] *adj.* del nordeste, nordeste.
north·ern [nɔrðɚn] *adj.* septentrional; norteño; del norte; hacia el norte; — **lights** aurora boreal.
north·ern·er [nɔ́ðɚnɚ] *s.* norteño, habitante del norte.
north·ward [nɔ́rθwɚd] *adv.* hacia el norte, rumbo al norte.
north·west [nɔrθwɛ́st] *adj.* & *s.* noroeste; *adv.* hacia el noroeste.
north·west·ern [nɔrθwɛ́stɚn] *adj.* noroeste, del noroeste.
Nor·we·gian [nɔrwídʒən] *adj.* & *s.* noruego.
nose [noz] *s.* nariz; proa (*de un barco*); — **dive** picada (*de un avión*); *v.* olfatear; **to — around** husmear, curiosear.
nos·tal·gi·a [nɑstǽldʒɪə] *s.* nostalgia, añoranza.
nos·trils [nɑ́strəlz] *s. pl.* narices, ventanas de la nariz.
not [nɑt] *adv.* no; — **at all** de ningún modo; de nada (*contestación a* "thank you"); — **at all sure** nada seguro; — **even a word** ni siquiera una palabra.
no·ta·ble [notəbl] *adj.* notable.
no·ta·ry [nótərɪ] *s.* notario; notario público; — **public notarize** autorizar ante notario.

no·ta·tion [notéʃən] *s.* notación; apunte; anotación.
notch [nɑtʃ] *s.* muesca, ranura; hendidura; *v.* ranurar, hacer una ranura en.
note [not] *s.* nota; apunte, apuntación; **bank —** billete de banco; **promissory —** pagaré, abonaré; *v.* notar, observar, reparar; **to — down** apuntar.
note·book [nótbʊk] *s.* libreta, cuaderno, libro de apuntes.
not·ed [nótɪd] *adj.* notable, célebre, famoso.
note·worth·y [nótwɝðɪ] *adj.* notable, célebre.
noth·ing [nʌ́θɪŋ] *s.* nada; cero; **for —** por nada; inútilmente; de balde, gratis.
no·tice [nótɪs] *s.* (*news*) noticia; (*warning*) aviso; advertencia, anuncio; mención, **to give a short —** avisar a última hora; **to take — of** hacer caso de, prestar atención a; *v.* notar, observar; prestar atención a; hacer caso a (*o* de); notificar.
no·tice·a·ble [nótɪsəbl] *adj.* notable, conspicuo; perceptible.
no·ti·fy [nótəfaɪ] *v.* notificar, avisar.
no·tion [nóʃən] *s.* noción; idea; capricho; **-s** mercería, artículos menudos (*como alfileres, botones, etc.*), chucherías.
no·to·ri·ous [notórɪəs] *adj.* notorio.
not·with·stand·ing [nɑtwɪθstǽndɪŋ] *prep.* a pesar de; *adv.* & *conj.* no obstante, sin embargo; **— that** a pesar (de) que.
nought = **naught.**
noun [naʊn] *s.* nombre, sustantivo.
nour·ish [nɝ́ɪʃ] *v.* nutrir, alimentar.
nour·ish·ing [nɝ́ɪʃɪŋ] *adj.* nutritivo, alimenticio.
nour·ish·ment [nɝ́ɪʃmənt] *s.* nutrimento, sustento, alimento; nutrición.
nov·el [nɑ́vl] *s.* novela; *adj.* novel, nuevo; (*unique*) raro, original.
nov·el·ist [nɑ́vlɪst] *s.* novelista.
nov·el·ty [nɑ́vltɪ] *s.* novedad; innovación **nov·el·ties** novedades.
No·vem·ber [novɛ́mbɚ] *s.* noviembre.
nov·ice [nɑ́vɪs] *s.* novicio; novato, principiante.
now [naʊ] *adv.* ahora; ya; **— . . . —** ya . . . ya, ora . . . ora; **— and then** de vez en cuando, de cuando en cuando; **— that** ahora que; **— then** ahora bien; **he left just —** salió hace poco, *Ríopl., Ch., Andes* recién salió.
now·a·days [náʊədez] *adv.* hoy día.
no·where [nóhwɛr] *adv.* en ninguna parte, a ninguna parte.
nox·ious [nɑ́kʃəs] *adj.* nocivo.
nu·cle·us [njúklɪəs] núcleo.
nude [njud] *adj.* & *s.* desnudo.
nudge [nʌdʒ] *v.* codear, tocar con el codo; *s.* codzao ligero.
nug·get [nʌ́gɪt] *s.* pepita; pedazo.
nui·sance [njúsn̩s] *s.* molestia; lata, fastidio; **— tax** impuesto menor sobre consumo; persona o cosa fastidiosa.
null [nʌl] *adj.* nulo; **— and void** nulo e inválido.
nul·li·fy [nʌ́lɪfaɪ] *v.* invalidar; anular.
numb [nʌm] *adj.* entumecido o entumido, aterido; **to become —** entumecerse, entumirse, aterirse; *v.* entumecer.
num·ber [nʌ́mbɚ] *s.* número; *v.* numerar; ascender a (*cierto número*); **to — him among one's friends** contarle entre sus amigos.
num·ber·less [nʌ́mbɚlɪs] *adj.* innumerable, sin número.
nu·mer·al [njúmrəl] *s.* número, cifra; guarismo; *adj.* numeral.
nu·mer·i·cal [njumɛ́rɪkəl] *adj.* numérico.
nu·mer·ous [njúmrəs] *adj.* numeroso; numerosos, muchos.
nu·mis·mat·ics [numɪsmǽtɪks] *s.* numismática.
nun [nʌn] *s.* monja.
nuptial [nʌ́pʃəl] *adj.* nupcial; **-s** *s. pl.* nupcias, bodas.
nurse [nɝs] *s.* (*for the sick*) enfermera, enfermero; (*for children*) niñera, aya; *Méx., Ven., Col., Andes* nana, *Cuba* manejadora, *Andes* pilmama; *C.A.* china; **wet —** nodriza, ama de cria; *v.* criar, amamantar, dar de mamar, lactar; mamar; cuidar (*a un enfermo*); abrigar (*rencor*).
nurs·er·y [nɝ́srɪ] *s.* cuarto para niños; (*zoological*) criadero, (*plants*) semillero (*de plantas*); **day —** sala donde se cuida y divierte a los niños.
nur·ture [nɝ́tʃɚ] *s.* crianza; nutrimento; *v.* criar; nutrir; cuidar; fomentar.
nut [nʌt] *s.* nuez (*nombre genérico de varias frutas como la almendra, la castaña, la avellana, etc.*); tuerca; (*person*) loco, tipo raro o extravagante.
nut·crack·er [nʌ́tkrækɚ] *s.* cascanueces.
nut·meg [nʌ́tmɛg] *s.* nuez moscada.
nu·tri·ent [nútrɪənt] *s.* nutritivo.
nu·tri·tion [njutrɪ́ʃən] *s.* nutrición; nutrimento, alimento.
nu·tri·tious [njutrɪ́ʃəs] *adj.* nutritivo, alimenticio.
nu·tri·tive [njútrɪtɪv] *adj.* nutritivo.
nut·shell [nʌ́tʃɛl] *s.* cáscara de nuez (*o de otro fruto semejante*); **in a —** en suma, en breve, en pocas palabras.
nymph [nɪmf] *s.* ninfa.

O:o

oak [ok] *s.* roble; encina; **— grove** robledo o robledal; **live —** encina siempreverde.
oar [or] *s.* remo; *v.* remar, bogar.
o·a·sis [oésɪs] *s.* oasis.
oat [ot] *s.* avena (*planta*); **-s** avena, granos de avena.
oath [oθ] *s.* (*pledge*) juramento; maldición, blasfemia, (*curse*) reniego; **to take an oath** prestar juramento.
oat·meal [otmɪl] *s.* harina de avena; gachas de avena.
o·be·di·ence [əbídɪəns] *s.* obediencia.
o·be·di·ent [əbídɪent] *adj.* obediente.
ob·e·lisk [ablɪsk] *s.* obelisco.
o·be·si·ty [obisətɪ] *s.* obesidad, gordura.
o·bey [əbé] *v.* obedecer.
ob·ject [ɑ́bdʒɪkt] *s.* objeto; cosa; complemento (*del verbo*); [əbdʒɛ́kt] *v.* objetar; oponerse; tener inconveniente.
ob·jec·tion [əbdʒɛ́kʃən] *s.* objeción, reparo; inconveniente.
ob·jec·tive [əbdʒɛ́ktɪv] *adj.* objetivo; **— case** caso complementario; *s.* objetivo; fin, propósito.
ob·li·gate [ɑ́bləget] *v.* obligar, constreñir; comprometer.
ob·li·ga·tion [ɑbləgéʃən] *s.* (*duty*) obligación; deber (*debt*) deuda; **to be under — to** estar obligado a; estar agradecido a, deber favores a.
o·blig·a·to·ry [əblɪ́gətorɪ] *adj.* obligatorio.
o·blige [əbláɪdʒ] *v.* obligar; complacer; **much -ed!** ¡muchas gracias! ¡muy agradecido!; **to be very much -ed to someone** quedar muy agradecido con alguien.
o·blig·ing [əbláɪdʒɪŋ] *adj.* complaciente, obsequioso, comedido, cortés.
o·blique [əblík] *adj.* oblicuo.
o·blit·er·ate [əblɪ́təret] *v.* borrar; arrasar, destruir.

o·bliv·i·on [əblívɪən] *s.* olvido.
o·bliv·i·ous [əblívɪəs] *adj.* olvidado, abstraído.
ob·long [áblɔŋ] *adj.* cuadrilongo; oblongo.
ob·nox·ious [əbnákʃəs] *adj.* ofensivo; molesto; odioso.
o·boe [óbo] *s.* oboe.
ob·scene [əbsín] *adj.* obsceno; grosero.
ob·scen·i·ty [əbsɛ́nətɪ] *s.* obscenidad, indecencia; grosería.
ob·scure [əbskjúr] *adj.* obscuro, *v.* obscurecer; ofuscar.
ob·scu·ri·ty [əbskjúrətɪ] *s.* obscuridad.
ob·se·quies [ábsɪkwiz] *s.* exequias, honras, funerales.
ob·se·qui·ous [əbsikwɪəs] *adj.* obsequioso; servil, zalamero.
ob·serv·a·ble [əbzɝvəbl] *adj.* observable.
ob·ser·vance [əbzɝ́vəns] *s.* observancia; ceremonia, rito.
ob·ser·vant [əbzɝ́vənt] *adj.* observador; observante.
ob·ser·va·tion [ɑbzɝvéʃən] *s.* observación.
ob·ser·va·to·ry [əbzɝ́vətorɪ] *s.* observatorio; mirador.
ob·serve [əbzɝ́v] *v.* observar; guardar (*las fiestas religiosas*); celebrar (*una fiesta*).
ob·serv·er [əbzɝ́vɚ] *s.* observador.
ob·sess [əbsɛ́s] *v.* obsesionar, causar obsesíon.
ob·ses·sion [əbsɛ́ʃən] *s.* obsesión; idea fija.
ob·so·lete [ábsəlit] *adj.* anticuado; desusado; **obsolescence** desuso.
ob·sta·cle [ábstəkl] *s.* obstáculo.
ob·stet·rics [abstɛ́trɪks] *s.* obstetricia.
ob·sti·na·cy [ábstənəsɪ] *s.* obstinación, terquedad, porfía.
ob·sti·nate [ábstənɪt] *adj.* obstinado, terco, porfiado.
ob·strep·er·ous [ɑbstrɛ́pɚəs] *adj.* estrepitoso, turbulento.
ob·struct [əbstrʌ́kt] *v.* obstruir.
ob·struc·tion [əbstrʌ́kʃən] *s.* obstrucción; impedimento, estorbo.
ob·tain [əbtén] *v.* obtener, conseguir, alcanzar, adquirir.
ob·tain·a·ble [əbténəbl] *adj.* obtenible, asequible.
ob·tru·sive [əbtrúsɪv] *adj.* intruso, entremetido.
ob·vi·ate [ábvɪet] *v.* obviar; allanar (*una dificultad*).
ob·vi·ous [ábvɪəs] *adj.* obvio, evidente.
oc·ca·sion [əkéʒən] *s.* (*timely*) ocasión; (*chance*) oportunidad; (*cause*) motivo, causa; (*event*) acontecimiento; *v.* ocasionar, causar.
oc·ca·sion·al [əkéʒənl] *adj.* ocasional; infrecuente, poco fecuente; **-ly** *adv.* de vez en cuando, a veces.
oc·ci·den·tal [ɑksədɛ́ntl] *adj.* & *s.* occidental.
oc·clu·sive [oklúsɪv] *adj.* & *s.* oclusivo.
oc·cult [əkʌ́lt] *adj.* oculto, misterioso.
oc·cu·pant [ákjəpənt] *s.* ocupante; inquilino.
oc·cu·pa·tion [ɑkjəpéʃən] *s.* ocupación; trabajo, empleo, oficio; (*tenancy*) tenencia; **occupational hazard** riesgo profesional.
oc·cu·py [ákjəpaɪ] *v.* ocupar.
oc·cur [əkɝ́] *v.* occurrir, suceder; **to — to one** ocurrírsele a uno, venirle a la mente.
oc·cur·rence [əkɝəns] *s.* ocurrencia, suceso, caso, acontecimiento.
o·cean [óʃən] *s.* océano.
o·cean·og·ra·phy [oʃənágrəfɪ] *s.* oceanografía.
o·cher [okɚ] *s.* ocre.
o'clock [əklák] *contr. de* **of the clock; it is two —** son las dos.
oc·tave [áktɪv] *s.* octava.
Oc·to·ber [ɑktóbɚ] *s.* octubre.
oc·to·pus [áktəpəs] *s.* pulpo.
oc·u·list [ákəlɪst] *s.* oculista.
odd [ɑd] *adj.* (*rare*) extraño, singular, raro; (*not even*) non, impar; — **change** suelto, cambio sobrante; — **job** trabajo occasional; — **moments** momentos libres, momentos de ocio; — **shoe** zapato suelto (*sin compañero*) — **volume** tomo suelto; **thirty** — treinta y tantos, treinta y pico; **-ly** *adv.* extrañamente, de un modo raro.
odd·i·ty [ádətɪ] *s.* rareza.
odds [ɑdz] *s. pl. o sing.* diferencia, disparidad (*en apuestas*); (*advantage*) ventaja, puntos de ventaja (*en apuestas*); — **and ends** retazos, trozos sobrantes, pedacitos varios; **the — are against me** la suerte me es contraria, estoy de mala suerte; **to be at -s with** estar reñido o enemistado con; (*not evens*) nones.
ode [od] *s.* oda.
o·di·ous [ódɪəs] *adj.* odioso.
o·dor [ódɚ] *s.* olor; **bad** — mal olor, hedor.
o·dor·ous [ódərəs] *adj.* oloroso.
o'er [or] *contr. de* **over.**
of [ɑv, ʌv] *prep.* de; — **course** por supuesto, claro, ya se ve; — **late** últimamente; **a quarter — five** las cinco menos cuarto; **to smell** — oler a; **to taste** — sabera.
off [ɔf] *adv.* (*distant*) lejos, fuera, a distancia; (*not attached*) suelto; apagado (*la luz*); (*equivale al reflexivo se en ciertos verbos:* marcharse, irse, *etc.*); — **and on** de vez en cuando; a intervalos; — **the record** extraoficial; — **year** de producción decreciente; **ten cents** — rebaja de diez centavos; **ten miles** — a una distancia de diez millas; **to take a day** — ausentarse por un día; descansar por un día; *adj.* ausente; distante, más remoto; quitado; **the — side** el lado más remoto; **with his hat** — con el sombrero quitado; **the electricity is** — está cortada la electricidad; **to be — in one's accounts** estar errado en sus cuentas; **to be — to war** haberse ido a la guerra; **to be well** — ser persona acomodada, estar en buenas circunstancias; *prep.* lejos de; **offcolor** de mal color; verde (*indecente*); **off-grade** de calidad inferior a la indicada; — **shore** a vista de la costa; — **standard** de calidad inferior; — **the road** deviado, descarriado; a un lado del camino; **to be — duty** no estar de turno; estar libre.
of·fend [əfɛ́nd] *v.* ofender.
of·fend·er [əfɛ́ndɚ] *s.* ofensor; transgresor, delincuente.
of·fense [əfɛ́ns] *s.* ofensa; agravio; delito, culpa; **no — was meant** lo hice (*o* lo dije) sin malicia; **weapon of** — arma ofensiva.
of·fen·sive [əfɛ́nsɪv] *adj.* ofensivo; *s.* ofensiva.
of·fer [ɔ́fɚ] *v.* ofrecer; **to — to do it** ofrecerse a hacerlo; *s.* oferta; ofrecimiento; promesa; propuesta.
of·fer·ing [ɔ́fərɪŋ] *s.* (*gift*) ofrenda; (*bid*) oferta, ofrecimiento.
off·hand [ɔ́fhǽnd] *adv.* de improviso, por el momento, sin pensarlo, impensadamente; *adj.* impensado, hecho de improviso; **in an — manner** con indiferencia; descuidadamente; sin plan.
of·fice [ɔ́fɪs] *s.* (*function*) oficio; cargo; función; (*place*) oficina, despacho; — **boy** mandadero de oficina; — **holder** funcionario; —**building** edificio para oficinas; **post** — correo; **box** — taquilla, *Ch., Ríopl.* boletería; **through the good -s of** por el intermedio de.
of·fi·cer [ɔ́fəsɚ] *s.* (*office holder*) oficial; funcionario; (*police*) policia, gendarme; agente de policía; *v.* comandar, dirigir (*como oficial*); proveer de oficiales.
of·fi·cial [əfíʃəl] *adj.* oficial; *s.* oficial, funcionario;

empleado público.
of·fi·ci·ate [əfíʃɪet] *v.* oficiar.
of·fi·cious [əfíʃəs] *adj.* oficioso, intruso, entremetido.
off·set [ɔfsέt] *v.* compensar por; — **the losses** compensar las pérdidas; contrapesar.
off·shore [ɔfʃor] *adj. & adv.* (*land*) terral; (*at sea*) lejos de la playa.
off·spring [ɔ́fsprɪŋ] *s.* prole, hijos, descendientes; hijo, vástago; resultado, consecuencia.
off·stage [ɔfstédʒ] *adv. & adj.* entre bastidores.
oft [ɔft] = **often.**
of·ten [ɔ́fən] *adv.* muchas veces, con frecuencia, frecuentemente, a menudo; **how — ?** ¿cuántas veces?; ¿cada cuándo?
o·gre [ógɚ] *s.* ogro, gigante, monstruo.
oil [ɔɪl] *s.* (*lubricant*) aceite; (*painting*) óleo; (*crude*) petróleo; — **can** alcuza; —**drum** tambor, bidón; — **field** yacimiento petrolero; — **painting** pintura al óleo; — **well** pozo de petróleo; **motor** — aceite para motores; *v.* aceitar, angrasar, lubricar; untar.
oil·cloth [ɔ́ɪlklɔθ] *s.* hule, tela de hule.
oil·y [ɔ́ɪlɪ] *adj.* aceitoso, oleoso; grasiento.
oint·ment [ɔ́ɪntmənt] *s.* ungüento.
O.K. [óké] *adj.* bueno; corriente, convenido; *Méx.* ándale; *adv.* bien; **it's** — está bien; **to give one's** — dar el V°. B°. (visto bueno); *v.* dar el V°. B°., aprobar.
old [old] *adj.* viejo; antiguo; añejo; — **maid** solterona; — **man** anciano, viejo; — **wine** vino añejo; **days of** — días de antaño; **how — are you?** ¿cuántos años tiene Vd.? ¿qué edad tiene Vd.?; **to be — enough to . . .** tener bastante edad para . . .; **to be an — hand at** ser ducho en, ser muy perito o experto en.
old·en [óldn̩] *adj.* viejo, antiguo, de antaño.
old-fash·ioned [óldfǽʃənd] *adj.* pasado de moda; anticuado; chapado a la antigua.
old·time [óldtáɪm] *adj.* vetusto, de tiempos antiguos; de antaño.
old-tim·er [óldtáɪmɚ] *s.* antiguo residente.
o·le·an·der [óliændɚ] *s.* adelfa.
ol·fac·to·ry [ɔlfǽktərɪ] *adj.* olfatorio.
ol·ive [álɪv] *s.* oliva, aceituna; — **grove** olivar; — **oil** aceite de oliva; — **tree** olivo; — **branch** ramo de olivo; *adj.* aceitunado, verde aceituna.
O·lym·pi·ad [olímpiæd] *s.* olimpiada.
O·lym·pic [olímpɪk] *adj.* olímpico.
om·e·let [ámlɪt] *s.* tortilla de huevos.
o·men [ómən] *s.* agüero, presagio.
om·i·nous [ámənəs] *adj.* siniestro, de mal agüero, amenazador.
o·mis·sion [omíʃən] *s.* omisión.
o·mit [omít] *v.* omitar; dejar de.
om·nip·o·tent [ɑmnípətənt] *adj.* omnipotente, todopoderoso.
on [ɑn] *prep.* en; a; sobre, encima de; — **all sides** por todos lados; — **arriving** al llegar; — **board** a bordo; en el tren; — **condition that** con la condición de que; — **credit** al fiado; — **foot** a pie; — **horseback** a caballo; — **Monday** el lunes; — **purpose** a propósito, adrede; — **sale** de venta; — **time** a tiempo; a plazo; *adv.* adelante; **farther** — más adelante; **later** — después; — **and** — sin parar, sin cesar, continuamente; *adj.* puesto; **his hat is** — lleva puesto el sombrero; **the light is** — está encendida la luz.
once [wʌns] *adv.* una vez; en otro tiempo; — **and for all** una vez por todas, definitivamente; — **in a while** de vez en cuando; **once-over** ojeada, vistazo; — **upon a time** érase que se era; en otro tiempo; **at** — al punto; a un mismo tiempo; **just this** — siquiera esta vez, sólo esta vez; *conj.* una vez que, cuando; luego que.
one [wʌn] *adj.* un, uno; — **hundred** cien, ciento; — **thousand** mil; **his — chance** su única oportunidad; **the — and only** el único; **one-armed** manco; **one-eyed** tuerto; **one-sided** de un solo lado; unilateral; parcial; desigual; **one-way** de un sentido; *s. & pron.* uno; — **another** uno a otro; — **by** — uno a uno; uno por uno; **the — who** el que, la que; **the green** — el verde; **this** — éste, ésta; **one-upmanship** necesidad de mantenerse adelante de la competencia.
one·self [wʌnsέlf] *pron.* se (*reflexivo*); **to speak to** — hablar consigo mismo; **by** — solo; por si, por si solo.
on·go·ing [ángoɪŋ] *adj.* que está haciéndose; corriente, que cursa.
on·ion [ʌ́jən] *s.* cebolla; — **patch** cebollar.
on·look·er [ánlʊkɚ] *s.* espectador, mirón.
on·ly [ónlɪ] *adj.* solo, único; *adv.* sólo, solamente; *conj.* sólo que.
on·set [ánsɛt] *s.* embestida, (*attack*) ataque; (*beginning*) impulso inicial, primer impetu.
on·to [ántu] *prep.* a; sobre.
on·ward [ánwɚd] *adv.* adelante; hacia adelante.
on·yx [ánɪks] *s.* onix, ónice.
ooze [uz] *v.* rezumar(se), escurrir(se).
o·pal [ópl] *s.* ópalo;
o·paque [opék] *adj.* opaco; mate.
OPEC (**Organization of Petroleum Exporting Countries**) OPEP (Organización de países exportadores de petróleo).
o·pen [ópən] *v.* abrir(se); **to — into** comunicarse con, tener paso a; **to — onto** dar a, caer a, mirar a; *adj.* abierto; (*frank*) franco, sincero; (*exposed*) expuesto (a); — **country** campo raso, campo abierto; — **and shut** claro, evidente, sin dificultades; — **door policy** política de acceso libre; — **question** cuestión discutible; — **to temptation** expuesto a caer en la tentación; — **winter** invierno sin nieve; **in the — air** al (*o* en el) aire libre; **open-minded** receptivo; de amplias miras; — **mouthed** boquiabierto, con la boca abierta; **open-end** [ópənέnd] sin límites; sin trabas; *s.* campo raso, aire libre.
o·pen·ing [ópənɪŋ] *s.* (*hole*) abertura; (*beginning*) apertura, comienzo; (*clearing*) claro (*en un bosque*); (*vacancy*) puesto vacante; oportunidad; *adj.* primero; — **night of a play** estreno de una comedia; **the — number** el primer número (*de un programa*).
op·er·a [ápərə] *s.* ópera; — **glasses** gemelos; — **house** ópera, teatro de la ópera; **comic** — ópera cómica, zarzuela.
op·er·ant [ápɝənt] *adj.* operante.
op·er·ate [ápəret] *v.* (*function*) operar; funcionar; obrar; (*manage*) maniobrar; manejar; **to — on a person** operar a una persona; **operating capital** capital de explotación; **operating system** (*computer*) sistema operativo.
op·er·a·tion [ɑpəréʃən] *s.* (*function*) operación; funcionamiento; (*management*) manipulación; manejo; maniobra; **to be in** — funcionar, estar funcionando.
op·er·a·tive [ápɚetɪv] *s.* operario.
op·er·a·tor [ápəretɚ] *s.* operador; (*surgeon*) cirujano; maquinista, mecáncio, operario; (*stock*) especulador (*en la Bolsa*); **mine** — explotador de minas; **telegraph** — telegrafista; **telephone** — telefonista.
op·e·ret·a [ɑpərέtə] *s.* opereta, zarzuela.

o·pin·ion [əpínjən] *s.* opinión, parecer.
o·pi·um [ópiəm] *s.* opio.
o·pos·sum [əpásəm] *s.* zarigüeya.
op·po·nent [əpónənt] *s.* contrario, adversario, antagonista.
op·por·tune [ɑpɚtjún] *adj.* oportuno; a propósito.
op·por·tun·ist [ɑpɚtúnɪst] *s.* oportunista.
op·por·tu·ni·ty [ɑpɚtjúnətɪ] *s.* oportunidad; ocasión.
op·pose [əpóz] *v.* oponer(se); oponerse a.
op·pos·ing [əpózɪŋ] *adj.* opuesto, contrario.
op·po·site [ápəzɪt] *adj.* (*contrary*) opuesto; contrario; (*facing*) frontero, de enfrente; — **to** frente a; *prep.* frente a, en frente de; *s.* contrario; **the** — lo opuesto, lo contrario.
op·po·si·tion [ɑpəzíʃən] *s.* oposición; resistencia.
op·press [əprɛs] *v.* oprimir; agobiar.
op·pres·sion [əprɛ́ʃən] *s.* opresión.
op·pres·sive [əprɛ́sɪv] *adj.* (*harsh*) opresivo; (*distressing*) abrumador; gravoso; bochornoso, sofacante.
op·pres·or [əprɛ́sɚ] *s.* opresor.
op·tic [áptɪk] *adj.* óptico; **-s** *s.* óptica.
op·ti·cal [áptɪkl] *adj.* óptico.
op·ti·cian [aptíʃən] *s.* óptico.
op·ti·mism [áptəmizəm] *s.* optimismo.
op·ti·mist [áptəmɪst] *s.* optimista.
op·ti·mis·tic [ɑptəmístɪk] *adj.* optimista.
op·tion [ápʃən] *s.* opción, derecho de escoger; alternativa.
op·tion·al [ápʃənl] *adj.* discrecional.
op·u·lence [ápjələ̀ns] *s.* opulencia, riqueza, abundancia.
op·u·lent [ápjələnt] *adj.* opulento, rico; abundante;
or [ɔr] *conj.* o; u (*delante de* o, ho).
or·a·cle [ɔ́rəkl] *s.* oráculo.
o·ral [órəl] *adj.* oral; bucal.
or·ange [ɔ́rɪndʒ] *s.* naranja; — **blossom** azahar; — **grove** naranjal; — **tree** naranjo; *adj.* de naranja; anaranjado.
or·ange·ade [ɔrindʒéd] *s.* naranjada.
o·ra·tion [oréʃən] *s.* discurso, peroración, arenga.
or·a·tor [ɔ́rətɚ] *s.* orador.
or·a·to·ry [ɔ́ətorɪ] *s.* oratoria, elocuencia; oratorio, capilla.
orb [ɔrb] *s.* orbe.
or·bit [ɔ́rbɪt] *s.* órbita; *v.* moverse en órbita.
or·bit·al [ɔ́rbɪtl] *adj.* orbital.
or·chard [ɔ́rtʃɚd] *s.* huerto.
or·ches·tra [ɔ́rkɪstrə] *s.* orquesta; — **seat** butaca, luneta, *Am.* platea (*de orquesta*).
or·ches·trate [ɔ́rkɪstret] *v.* orquestar.
or·chid [ɔ́rkɪd] *s.* orquídea.
or·dain [ɔrdén] *v.* ordenar; decretar.
or·deal [ɔrdíl] *s.* prueba penosa.
or·der [ɔ́rdɚ] *s.* (*request*) orden (*s.*); pedido; (*group*) clase; orden; (*arrangement*) orden (*m.*); **holy -s** órdenes sagradas; **in** — en orden; en buen estado; en regla; **in** — **to** para, a fin de; **in** — **that** para que, a fin de que; **made to** — mandado hacer, hecho a la medida; **to the** — **of** a la orden de; **to be out of** — estar descompuesto; estar desordenado; no estar en regla; — **clerk** oficinista encargado de pedidos; *v.* ordenar; mandar; arreglar; pedir (*hacer un pedido*); **to** — **away** echar, despedir, expulsar.
or·der·ly [ɔ́rdɚlɪ] *adj.* ordenado; en orden, bien arreglado; bien disciplinado; *s.* ordenanza (*soldado*); asistente de hospital.
or·di·nal [ɔ́rdɪnl] *adj.* ordinal; — **number** número ordinal.
or·di·nance [ɔ́rdnəns] *s.* ordenanza, ley, reglamento.
or·di·nar·i·ly [ɔrdṇɛ́rəlɪ] *adv.* ordinariamente, por lo común.
or·di·nar·y [ɔ́rdṇɛrɪ] *adj.* ordinario.
ore [or] *s.* mineral.
or·gan [ɔ́rgən] *s.* órgano; **hand** — organillo.
or·gan·ic [ɔrgǽnɪk] *adj.* orgánico; constitutivo, fundamental.
or·gan·ism [ɔ́rgənɪzəm] *s.* organismo.
or·gan·ist [ɔ́gənɪst] *s.* organista.
or·gan·i·za·tion [ɔrgənəzéʃən] *s.* organización; organismo; entidad; sociedad.
or·gan·ize [ɔ́rgənaɪz] *v.* organizar(se).
or·gan·iz·er [ɔ́rgənaɪzɚ] *s.* organizador.
or·gy [ɔ́rdʒɪ] *s.* orgia.
o·ri·ent [ɔ́rɪɛnt] *s.* oriente; *v.* orientar.
o·ri·en·tal [ɔrɪɛ́ntl] *adj.* & *s.* oriental.
o·ri·en·tate [ɔ́rɪɛntet] *v.* orientar.
o·ri·en·ta·tion [ɔrɪɛntéʃən] *s.* orientación.
or·i·fice [ɔ́rəfɪs] *s.* orificio.
or·i·gin [ɔ́rədʒɪn] *s.* origen; procedencia.
or·ig·i·nal [ərídʒənl] *adj.* & *s.* original; **-ly** *adv.* originalmente, originariamente; en el principio, al principio.
or·ig·i·nal·i·ty [ərɪdʒənǽlətɪ] *s.* originalidad.
or·ig·i·nate [əídʒənet] *v.* originar(se).
o·ri·ole [órɪol] *s.* oriol (*pájaro*).
Or·lon [ɔ́rlan] *s.* orlón.
or·na·ment [ɔ́rnəmənt] *s.* ornamento, adorno; [ɔ́rnəmɛnt] *v.* ornamentar, adornar, ornar.
or·na·men·tal [ɔrnəmɛ́ntl] *adj.* ornamental, de adorno, decorativo.
or·nate [ɔrnét] *adj.* ornado, adornado en exceso; — **style** estilo florido.
or·ni·thol·o·gy [ɔrnəθálədʒɪ] *s.* ornitologia.
or·phan [ɔ́rfən] *adj.* & *s.* huérfano; — **asylum** hospicio, orfanato, asilo de huérfanos; *v.* dejar huérfano a.
or·tho·dox [ɔ́rθədɑks] *adj.* ortodoxo.
or·thog·ra·phy [ɔrθágrəfɪ] *s.* ortografía.
os·cil·late [ásəlet] *v.* oscilar.
os·cil·la·to·ry [ásələtɔrɪ] *adj.* oscilatorio.
os·mi·um [ázmiəm] *s.* osmio.
os·ten·ta·tion [ɑstəntéʃən] *s.* ostentación, boato.
os·ten·ta·tious [ɑstəntéʃəs] *adj.* ostentoso.
os·trich [ɔ́strɪtʃ] *s.* avestruz.
oth·er [ʌ́ðɚ] *adj.* & *s.* otro; — **than** otra cosa que; más que; **every** — **day** cada dos días, un día sí y otro no; **some** — **day** otro día.
oth·er·wise [ʌ́ðɚwaɪz] *adv.* de otro modo; en otros respetos; *adj.* otro, diferente.
ot·ter [átɚ] *s.* nutria; (*skin*) piel de nutria.
ought [ɔt] *v. defect.* (*por lo general se traduce por el presente y el condicional de* deber) debo, debes, etc.; debería, deberías, etc.; debiera, debieras, etc.
ounce [aʊns] *s.* onza.
our [aʊr] *adj.* nuestro (nuestra, nuestros, nuestras).
ours [aʊrz] *pron. pos.* nuestro (nuestra, nuestros, nuestras); el nuestro (la nuestra, los nuestros, las nuestras); **a friend of** — un amigo nuestro.
our·selves [aʊrsɛ́lvz] *pron.* nosotros mismos; nos (*reflexivo*); a nosotros mismos; **we** — nosotros mismos; **by** — solos; pos nosotros; *véase* **herself.**
oust [aʊst] *v.* echar, expulsar.
out [aʊt] *adv.* fuera; afuera; hacia fuera; — **of fashion** pasado de moda; — **of commission** (**order**) fuera de servicio; — **of fear** por miedo, de miedo; — **of humor** malhumorado; — **of money** sin dinero; — **of print** agotado; — **of stock** agotado; — **of touch with** aislado de, sin contacto con, — **of tune** desentonado; **made** — **of** hecho de; **to fight it** — decidirlo luchando; **to have it** —

with habérselas con; **to speak** — hablar francamente; *adj.* ausente; apagado; — **and — criminal** criminal empedernido; — **and — refusal** una negativa redonda; — **size** tamaño poco común o extraordinario; **before the week is** — antes de que termine la semana; **the book is just** — acaba de publicarse el libro; **the secret is** — se ha divulgado el secreto.
out·bid [ɑutbíd] *v.* hacer mejor oferta.
out·break [áutbrek] *s.* (*eruption*) erupción; (*revolt*) motín, insurrección, tumulto; (*attack*) ataque, arranque (*de ira*); **at the — of the war** al estallar la guerra.
out·burst [áutbɝst] *s.* explosión; estallido; arranque (*de pasión*); erupción.
out·cast [áutkæst] *adj.* excuido, desechado; desterrado; *s.* paria (*persona excluida de la sociedad*).
out·come [áutkʌm] *s.* resultado, consecuencia.
out·cry [áutkraɪ] *s.* grito; clamor.
out·door [áutdor] *adj.* externo; fuera de la casa; — **games** juegos al aire libre.
out·doors [autdórz] *adv.* puertas afuera, fuera de casa, al aire libre, al raso; *s.* aire libre, campo raso, campiña.
out·er [áutɚ] *adj.* exterior, externo; — **harbor** antepuerto.
out·fit [áutfɪt] *s.* equipo; pertrechos; *v.* equipar, habilitar, aviar; proveer, abastecer.
out·go·ing [áutgoɪŋ] *adj.* (*leaving*) saliente; (*extrovert*) extrovertido.
out·guess [autgés] *v.* anticipar; madrugar.
out·ing [áutɪŋ] *s.* excursión, gira (*jira*), caminata.
out·law [áutlɔ] *s.* forajido, bandido; prófugo, fugitivo; *v.* proscribir, declarar ilegal.
out·lay [áutle] *s.* gasto, desembolso; [áutlé] *v.* gastar, desembolsar.
out·let [áutlɛt] *s.* salida; desaguadero, desagüe; escurridero; (*telecommunications*) toma de corriente.
out·line [áutlaɪn] *s.* (*abstract*) bosquejo, esbozo; (*boundary*) contorno; *v.* bosquejar, esbozar; delinear.
out·live [autlív] *v.* sobrevivir.
out·look [áutlʊk] *s.* vista; perspectiva.
out·ly·ing [áutlaɪɪŋ] *adj.* circundante, exterior, remoto (*del centro*).
out-of-date [áutəvdét] *adj.* fuera de moda, anticuado.
out·post [áutpost] *s.* avanzada.
out·put [áutpʊt] *s.* rendimiento; producción total.
out·rage [áutredʒ] *s.* ultraje; *v.* ultrajar.
out·ra·geous [áutrédʒəs] *adj.* afrentoso; atroz.
out·ran [autrǽn] *pret. de* **to outrun.**
out·right —[autráɪt] *adv. & adj.* sin rodeo; cabal; completo.
out·run [aurʌ́n] *v.* aventajar (*en una carrera*); dejar atrás; *p.p. de* **to outrun.**
out·set [áutsɛt] *s.* comienzo, principio.
out·shine [autʃáɪn] *v.* eclipsar, sobrepasar (*en brillo o lucidez*).
out·shone [autʃón] *pret. & p.p. de* **to outshine.**
out·side [áutsáɪd] *adj.* (*external*) exterior; externo; (*foreign*) foráneo, extranjero; *adv.* fuera, afuera; fuera de casa; *prep.* fuera de; *s.* exterior, parte exterior; superficie; lado de afuera; **in a week, at the** — en una semana, a lo sumo; **to close on the** — cerra por fuera.
out·sid·er [ausáɪdɚ] *s.* foráneo, persona de fuera; forastero; intruso; extraño.
out·skirts [áutskɝts] *s. pl.* alrededores, arrabales, cercanías.
out·spo·ken [áutspókən] *adj.* franco, francote, *Ven., Méx., C.A., Carib.* claridoso.
out·stand·ing [áutstǽndɪŋ] *adj.* sobresaliente; destacado, notable; — **bills** cuentas por cobrar; — **debts** deudas por pagar; (*pending*) pendiente.
out·stretched [autstrétʃt] *adj.* extendido; **with — arms** con los brazos abiertos.
out·strip [autstríp] *v.* dejar atrás, adelantar.
out·ward [áutwɚd] *adj.* (*external*) exterior, externo; (*apparent*) aparente; superficial; *adv.* fuera, hacia fuera; — **bound** que sale, de salida; para fuera, para el extranjero; **-ly** *adv.* exteriormente; por fuera; aparentemente.
out·weigh [autwé] *v.* exceder en poso o valor; sobrepujar.
o·val [óvl] *adj.* oval, ovalado; *s.* óvalo.
o·va·ry [óvərɪ] *s.* ovario.
o·va·tion [ovéʃən] *s.* ovación.
ov·en [ʌ́vən] *s.* horno.
o·ver [óvɚ] *prep.* sobre; por; por encima de; encima de; a través de; al otro lado de; más de; — **night** por la noche, durante la noche; (*véase* **overnight**); — **to** a; **all — the city** por toda la cuidad; *adv.* encima; al otro lado; otra vez, de nuevo; — **again** otra vez, de nuevo; — **against** en contraste con; — **and** — una y otra vez, repetidas veces; — **curious** demasiado curioso; — **generous** demasiado generoso; — **here** acá, aquí; — **there** allá, allí; **two years and** — más de dos años; **to do it** — hacerlo otra vez, volver a hacerlo; *adj.* excesivo; **it is all** — ya se acabó, se ha acabado; ha pasado.
o·ver·age [óvɚadʒ] *s.* exceso, sobrante.
o·ver·all [ovɚɔ́l] *adj.* global, total, general, cabal.
o·ver·alls [óvɚɔ̀lz] *s. pl. Am.* overol, overoles (*pantalones de trabajo*); *Esp.* mono.
o·ver·ate [ovɚét] *pret. de* **to overeat.**
o·ver·bid·ding [ovɚbídɪŋ] *s.* puja.
o·ver·board [óvɚbord] *adv.* al mar, al agua.
o·ver·came [ovɚkém] *pret. de* **to overcome.**
o·ver·cast [óvɚkæst] *adj.* encapotado, nublado; **to become** — encapotarse, nublarse; [ovɚkǽst] *v.* nublar o anublar; sobrehilar (*dar puntadas sobre el borde de una tela*); *pret. & p.p. de* **to overcast.**
o·ver·charge [ovɚtʃárdʒ] *v.* cargar demasiado; cobrar demasiado.
o·ver·coat [óvɚkot] *s.* sobretodo, abrigo.
o·ver·come [ovɚkʌ́m] *v.* vencer; rendir; *p.p. & adj.* vencido; rendido; agobiado; **to be — by weariness** estar rendido de fatiga.
o·ver·draft [óvɚdræft] *s.* sobregiro, giro en descubierto.
o·ver·drawn [ovɚdrɔ́n] *adj.* cuenta en descubierto.
o·ver·due [ovɚdú] *adj.* atrasado; vencido sin pago.
o·ver·eat [ovɚít] *v.* hartarse.
o·ver·eat·en [ovɚítn̩] *p.p. de* **to overeat.**
o·ver·ex·cite [óvərɪksáɪt] *v.* sobreexcitar.
o·ver·flow [óvɚflo] *s.* derrame, desbordamiento; inundación; superabundancia; [ovɚfló] *v.* derramarse, desbordarse; rebosar; (*flood*) inundar.
o·ver·grown [óvɚgrón] *adj.* denso, frondoso, poblado (*de follaje, herbaje, etc.*); — **boy** muchachón, muchacho demasiado crecido para su edad.
o·ver·hang [ovɚhǽŋ] *v.* colgar por encima de; proyectarse o sobresalir por encima de; adornar con colgaduras; amenazar (*dícese de un desastre o calamidad*).
o·ver·haul [ovɚhɔ́l] *v.* reparar (*de cabo a rabo*); remendar; alcanzar (*en una carrera*).
o·ver·head [óvɚhɛd] *s.* gastos generales (*renta,*

seguro, alumbrado, calefacción, etc.); *adj.* de arriba; elevado; — **expenses** gastos generales; [óvɚhɛ́d] *adv.* encima de la cabeza, arriba; en lo alto.
o·ver·hear [ovɚhír] *v.* oír por casualidad, alcanzar a oír, acertar a oír.
o·ver·heard [ovɚhɝ́d] *pret. & p.p. de* **to overhear.**
o·ver·heat [óvɚhít] *v.* recalentar(se); calentar(se) demasiado.
o·ver·hung [ovɚhʌ́ŋ] *pret. & p.p. de* **to overhang.**
o·ver·land [óvɚlænd] *adv. & adj.* por tierra; por ruta terrestre.
o·ver·lap [ovɚlǽp] *v.* solapar.
o·ver·lay [ovɚlé] *v.* cubrir; incrustar.
o·ver·load [ovɚlód] *v.* sobrecargar; [óvɚlod] *s.* sobrecarga.
o·ver·look [ovɚlúk] *v.* (*look*) mirar a (*desde lo alto*); dar a, tener vista a; (*omit*) pasar por alto, omitir; (*pardon*) perdonar (*faltas*); descuidar, no notar; (*supervise*) inspeccionar, examinar.
o·ver·ly [óvɚlɪ] *adv.* excesivamente.
o·ver·night [óvɚnáɪt] *adv.* durante la noche; toda la noche; *adj.* de noche; nocturno; — **bag** saco de noche; — **trip** viaje de una noche.
o·ver·pass [óvɚpǽs] *v.* viaducto.
o·ver·price [pvɚpráɪs] *v.* fijar precio excesivo.
o·ver·pow·er [ovɚpáʊɚ] *v.* subyugar, abrumar, vencer.
o·ver·ran [ovɚfǽn] *pret. de* **to overrun.**
o·ver·rate [ovɚrét] *v.* exagerar el valor de.
o·ver·ride [ovɚráɪd] *v.* anular; invalidar.
o·ver·rule [ovərúl] *v.* anular.
o·ver·run [ovɚrʌ́n] *v.* desbordarse, mundar; sobrepasar; infestar, invadir; *p.p. de* **to overrun.**
o·ver·seas [óvɚsíz] *adv.* en ultramar, allende los mares; *adj.* de ultramar.
o·ver·see [ovɚsí] *v.* dirigir; vigilar.
o·ver·se·er [óvɚsɪr] *s.* sobrestante, capataz; inspector, superintendente.
o·ver·shoe [óvɚʃu] *s.* chanclo; zapato de goma, caucho o hule.
o·ver·sight [óvɚsaɪt] *s.* inadvertencia, negligencia, descuido.
o·ver·step [ovɚstɛ́p] *v.* sobrepasarse, propasarse; traspasar; **to — the bounds** traspasar los limites; proparse.
o·ver·take [ovɚték] *v.* alcanzar.
o·ver·tak·en [ovɚtékən] *p.p. de* **to overtake.**
o·ver·tax [ovɚtǽks] *v.* oprimir con tributos; someter a un esfuerzo excesivo.
o·ver·threw [ovɚθrú] *pret. de* **to overthrow.**
o·ver·throw [óvɚθro] *s.* (*overturn*) derrocamiento; (*defeat*) derrota, destrucción; caída; [ovɚθró] *v.* derrocar; derribar, echar abajo, volcar; destronar.
o·ver·thrown [ovɚθrón] *p.p. de* **to overthrow.**
o·ver·time [óvɚtaɪm] *adv. & adj.* en exceso de las horas estipuladas; — **pay** sobresueldo; *s.* sobretiempo, tiempo suplementario.
o·ver·took [ovɚtúk] *pret. de* **to overtake.**
o·ver·ture [óvɚtʃɚ] *s.* obertura, preludio; propuesta, proposición.
o·ver·turn [ovɚtɝ́n] *v.* volcar(se); trastornar; derribar; echar abajo.
o·ver·view [óvɚvju] *s.* vista global, plan general; resumen.
o·ver·whelm [ovɚhwɛ́lm] *v.* abrumar, agobiar; oprimir; arrollar.
o·ver·whelm·ing [ovɚhwɛ́lmɪŋ] *adj.* abrumador; opresivo; arrollador, irresistible, poderoso.
o·ver·work [óvɚwɝ́k] *v.* atarearse, afanarse más de lo debido, trabajar demasiado; *s.* exceso de trabajo.
owe [o] *v.* deber, adeudar.
ow·ing [óɪŋ] *adj.* debido; — **to** debido a.
owl [aul] *s.* lechuza, buho, *Méx., C.A.* tecolote.
own [on] *adj.* propio; **a house of his** — una casa suya; **his** — **people** los suyos; **to be on one's** — no estar a merced ajena; trabajar por su propia cuenta; **to come into one's** — entrar en posesión de lo suyo; **to hold one's** — mantenerse firme; *v.* poseer, tener; admitir, reconocer; **to** — **to** confesar; **to** — **up** confesar.
own·er [ónɚ] *s.* dueño, amo; propietario; poseedor.
own·er·ship [ónɚʃɪp] *s.* posesión, propiedad; pertenencia.
ox [ɑks] (*pl.* **ox·en** [ɑ́ksn̩]) *s.* buey.
ox·ide [áksaɪd] *s.* óxido.
ox·i·dize [áksɚdaɪz] *v.* oxidar.
ox·y·gen [ɑ́ksədʒən] *s.* oxígeno.
oys·ter [ɔ́ɪstɚ] *s.* ostra, ostión; *Sp.* ostrón.
o·zone [ózon] *s.* ozono.

P:p

P-trap [pítræp] *s.* (*plumbing*) bombillo inodoro.
pace [pes] *s.* paso; *v.* pasear, andar; andar al paso; marchar; medir a pasos.
pace·mak·er [pésmekɚ] *s.* marcapaso.
pa·cif·ic [pəsífɪk] *adj.* pacífico.
pa·ci·fy [pǽsəfaɪ] *v.* pacificar, apaciguar; calmar.
pack [pæk] *s.* fardo, lío, carga; (*animals*) manada; cuadrilla, pandilla (*de ladrones*); (*dogs*) jauría (*de perros*); muchedumbre; (*cards*) baraja (*de naipes*); — **animal** acémila, bestía de carga; *v.* empacar, empaquetar; embalar; enlatar; envasar; apiñar(se); cargar (*una bestia*); hacer (*el baúl, la maleta*); **to — off** despedir de repente; echar a la calle; largarse, irse.
pack·age [pǽkɪdʒ] *s.* paquete; fardo, bulto; cajetilla (*de cigarrillos*).
pack·er [pǽkɚ] *s.* empacador; embalador, envasador.
pack·et [pǽkɪt] *s.* paquetillo; cajetilla.
pack·ing [pǽkɪŋ] *s.* (*covering*) embalaje; envase; (*filling*) relleno; — **box** caja para embalar o empacar; — **house** establecimiento frigorífico, fábrica para envasar o enlatar comestibles; — **slip** boleta de envase.
pact [pækt] *s.* pacto, convenio.
pad [pæd] *s.* almohadilla, cojincillo; tableta, block de papel; *v.* rellenar; forrar; acolchar; (*inflate*) aumentar con material superfluo.
pad·ding [pǽdɪŋ] *s.* relleno (*de pelo, algodón, paja, etc.*), *Andes* guata; ripio, palabras o frases inútiles.
pad·dle [pǽdl] *s.* pala; remo de canoa; (*computer*) potenciómetro; — **wheel** rueda de paleta; *v.* remar con pala; apalear; chapotear (*en el agua*).
pad·dock [pǽdək] *s.* dehesa.
pad·lock [pǽdlɑk] *s.* candado; *v.* cerrar con candado.
pa·gan [pégən] *s. & adj.* pagano.
pa·gan·ism [pégənɪzəm] *s.* paganismo.
page [pedʒ] *s.* (*sheet*) página; (*messenger*) paje; "botones" (*de hotel*), mensajero; *v.* paginar; vocear, llamar a voces.
pag·eant [pǽdʒənt] *s.* (*parade*) manifestación, desfile, procesión, pompa; (*drama*) representación al aire libre.
paid [ped] *pret. & p.p. de* **to pay; paid-up** *adj* saldado.
pail [pel] *s.* balde, cubo, cubeta.
pain [pen] *s.* dolor; sufrimiento; **-s** esmero; **on** (**under**) — **of** so pena de; **to be in** — estar

sufriendo, tener dolores; **to take -s** esmerarse, extremarse; *v.* doler; causar dolor; afligir.
pain·ful [pénfəl] *adj.* doloroso; penoso; arduo.
pain·less [pénlɪs] *adj.* sin dolor; libre de dolor.
pains·tak·ing [pénztekɪŋ] *adj.* esmerado, cuidadoso; aplicado.
paint [pent] *s.* (*mixture*) pintura, color; (*rouge*) colorete; *v.* pintar; pintarse (*la cara*); **to — the town red** irse de juerga o de parranda, *Ríopl.* irse de farra.
paint·brush [péntbrʌʃ] *s.* (*art*) pincel; (*house*) brocha.
paint·er [péntɚ] *s.* pintor.
paint·ing [péntɪŋ] *s.* pintura.
pair [pɛr] *s.* par; pareja; **a — of scissors** unas tijeras; *v.* aparear(se); hacer pareja, hacer pares; **to — off** aparear(se).
pa·jam·as [pədʒǽməz] *s. pl.* pijama.
pal [pæl] *s.* compañero, camarada.
pal·ace [pǽlɪs] *s.* palacio.
pal·ate [pǽlɪt] *s.* paladar.
pa·la·tial [pəléʃl] *adj.* suntuoso.
pale [pel] *adj.* pálido; descolorido; *v.* palidecer, ponerse pálido o descolorido.
pale·ness [pélnɪs] *s.* palidez.
pal·i·sade [pæləséd] *s.* palizada, estacada; **-s** riscos, acantilados.
pall [pɔl] *v.* empalagar; aburrir; **it -s on me** me empalaga; me aburre; *s.* paño de ataúd; (*church*) palia (*lienzo que pone encima del cáliz*).
pal·la·di·um [pəlédiəm] *s.* paladio.
pal·li·a·tive [pǽljətɪv] *adj. & s.* paliativo.
pal·lid [pǽlɪd] *adj.* pálido.
pal·or [pǽlɚ] *s.* palidez.
palm [pɑm] *s.* palma; palmera; **— Sunday** Domingo de Ramos; **— tree** palma; palmera; *v.* **to — something off on someone** pasar o dar algo indeseable a una persona (*sin que se dé cuenta de ello*).
pal·pa·ble [pǽlpəbl] *adj.* palpable, tangible; evidente.
pal·pi·tate [pǽlpətèt] *v.* palpitar, latir.
pal·pi·ta·tion [pælpətéʃən] *s.* palpitación; latido.
pal·try [pɔ́ltrɪ] *adj.* mezquino, miserable, despreciable, insignificante.
pam·per [pǽmpɚ] *v.* mimar, consentir (*a un niño*).
pam·phlet [pǽmflɪt] *s.* folleto, *Am.* panfleto.
pan [pæn] *s.* cazuela, cacerola; (*ladle*) cazo; platillo (*de balanza*); **dish —** cazo para lavar platos; **frying —** sartén; **sheet —** cazuela plana; *v.* **to — out (well)** salir bien, dar buen resultado.
Pan-A·mer·i·can [pǽnəmérəkən] *adj.* panamericano.
pan·cake [pǽnkek] *s.* tortita de harina, *Ven., Col.* panqué; *Ríopl.* panqueque.
pan·der [pǽndɚ] *s.* alcahuete, encubridor *v.* alcahuetear, servir de alcahuete.
pane [pen] vidrio, cristal (*de ventana o puerta*); cuadro (*de vidrio*).
pan·el [pǽnl] *s.* panel, tablero; (*door*) cuarterón (*de puerta, ventana, etc.*); (*dress*) tabla; **jury —** jurado; *v.* proveer de (*o* adornar con) paneles.
pang [pæŋ] *s.* dolor agudo; angustia, tormento.
pan·han·dle [pǽnhændl] *s.* mango de sartén; territorio en forma de mango; *v.* mendigar.
pan·ic [pǽnɪk] *adj. & s.* pánico; **pan·ic-strick·en** sobrecogido de pánico.
pan·o·ram·a [pænərǽmə] *s.* panorama.
pan·sy [pǽnzɪ] *s.* pensamiento (*flor*).
pant [pænt] *v.* jadear; palpitar; **to — for** anhelar, ansiar.
pan·ther [pǽnθɚ] *s.* pantera.
pant·ing [pǽntɪŋ] *s.* jadeo, palpitación; *adj.* jadeante.
pan·to·mime [pǽntəmaɪm] *s.* pantomima.
pan·try [pǽntrɪ] *s.* despensa.
pants [pænts] *s. pl.* pantalones.
pa·pa [pɑ́pə] *s.* papá.
pa·pa·cy [pépəsɪ] *s.* papado.
pa·pal [pépl] *adj.* papal.
pa·per [pépɚ] *s.* (*material*) papel; (*daily*) periódico; (*essay*) tema; ensayos; **-s** papeles, documentos, credenciales; **naturalization -s** carta de naturaleza, certificado de ciudadanía; **scholarly —** ponencia; **— of pins** cartón de alfileres; **on —** escrito; por escrito; *adj.* de papel; para papel; **— doll** muñeca de papel; **— money** papel moneda; **— weight** pisapapeles; *v.* empapelar.
pa·per·back [pépɚbæk] *s. & adj.* libro en rústica.
pa·per·work [pépɚwɚk] *s.* preparación de escritos; papeleo.
pa·pri·ka [pæpríka] *s.* pimentón.
par [pɑr] *s.* (*equality*) paridad, igualdad; (*standard*) valor nominal; **— value** valor a la par; **above —** sobre par, a premio, can prima; **at —** a la par; **below —** bajo par, a descuento; **on a — with** al par de, al nivel de, igual a; **to feel above —** sentirse mejor que de ordinario; **to feel below —** sentirse menos bien que de ordinario.
par·a·ble [pǽrəbl] *s.* parábola (*alegoría bíblica*).
par·a·chute [pǽrəʃut] *s.* paracaídas.
par·a·chut·ist [pǽrəʃutɪst] *s.* paracaidista.
pa·rade [pəréd] *s.* (*procession*) desfile, procesión, manifestación; paseo; (*review*) parada; **— ground** campo de maniobras; **to make a — of** ostentar, hacer ostentación de; *v.* desfilar, pasar en desfile; marchar en parada; hacer ostentación de.
par·a·digm [pǽrədɪm], [pǽrədaɪm] *s.* paradigma.
par·a·dise [pǽrədaɪs] *s.* paraíso.
par·a·dox·i·cal [pærədáksɪkl] *adj.* paradójico.
par·a·dox [pǽrədɑks] *s.* paradoja.
par·af·fin [pǽrəfɪn] *s.* parafina.
par·a·graph [pǽrəgræf] *s.* párrafo; *v.* dividir en párrafos.
Par·a·guay·an [pæregwáɪən] *adj. & s.* paraguayo.
par·al·lel [pǽrəlɛl] *adj. & s.* paralelo; *v.* ser (*o* correr) paralelo a; comparar, cotejar.
pa·ral·y·sis [pərǽləsɪs] *s.* parálisis.
par·a·lyt·ic [pærəlítɪk] *adj.* paralítico.
par·a·lyze [pǽrəlaɪz] *v.* paralizar.
pa·ram·e·ter [pərǽmətɚ] *s.* parámetro.
par·a·mount [pǽrəmaʊnt] *adj.* importantísimo, superior, supremo, máximo.
par·a·noi·a [pærənɔ́ja] *s.* paranoia.
par·a·pet [pǽrəpɪt] *s.* parapeto.
par·a·phrase [pǽrəfrez] *v.* parafrasear.
par·a·site [pǽrəsaɪt] *s.* parásito.
par·a·sol [pǽrəsɔl] *s.* parasol, sombrilla.
par·a·troops [pǽrətrups] *s.* tropas paracaidistas.
par·cel [pɑ́rsl] *s.* (*package*) paquete; (*land*) parcela, porción, lote (*de terreno*); **— post** paquete postal; *Col.* encomienda postal; *v.* parcelar, dividir en porciones o parcelas; hacer paquetes; **to — out** repartir.
parch [pɑrtʃ] *v.* resecar(se); tostar(se).
parch·ment [pɑ́rtʃmənt] *s.* pergamino.
par·don [pɑ́rdn̩] *s.* perdón; indulto; **I beg your —** perdone Vd.; dispense Vd.; *v.* perdonar; dispensar; indultar.
pare [pɛr] *v.* mondar, pelar (*manzanas, patatas, etc.*); cortar, recortar; **to — down expenditures** reducir gastos.
par·ent [pɛ́rənt] *s.* padre, madre; (*origin*) origen; **-s** padres.
par·ent·age [pɛ́rəntɪdʒ] *s.* linaje; padres.

pa·ren·tal [pərέntl] *adj*. parental.
pa·ren·the·sis [pərέnθəsɪs] (*pl*. **pa·ren·the·ses** [pərέnθəsiz]) *s*. paréntesis.
par·ish [pǽrɪʃ] *s*. parroquia.
par·ish [pərɪʃənɚ] *s*. parroquiano, feligrés; **-s** fieles, feligreses.
par·i·ty [pǽrɪtɪ] *s*. paridad.
park [pɑrk] *s*. parque; *v*. estacionar, dejar (*un automóvil*); estacionarse; **-ing lot** *Ch*., *Ríopl*. playa de estacionamiento; *Méx*., *Ven*. estacionamiento; *Col*. parqueadero; **-ing space** sitio o lugar para estacionarse; **free -ing** estacionamiento gratis; **no -ing** se prohibe estacionarse; no estacionarse.
par·lance [pάrləns] *s*. lenguaje.
par·ley [pάrlɪ] *s*. parlamento, discusión, conferencia; *v*. parlamentar, discutir.
par·lia·ment [pάrləmənt] *s*. parlamento.
par·lia·men·ta·ry [pɑrləmέntərɪ] *adj*. parlamentario.
par·lor [pάrlɚ] *s*. sala, salón; sala de recibo; — **car** coche salón; **beauty** — salón de belleza.
pa·ro·chi·al [pərókɪəl] *adj*. parroquial.
par·o·dy [pǽrədɪ] *s*. parodia; *v*. parodiar.
pa·role [pəról] *s*. palabra de honor; **to put on** — dejar libre (*a un prisionero*) bajo palabra de honor; *v*. dejar libre bajo palabra de honor.
par·rot [pǽrət] *s*. cotorra, loro, perico, papagayo; *v*. remedar, repetir como loro.
par·ry [pǽrɪ] *v*. parar, quitar o reparar (*un golpe*); *s*. quite, reparo.
pars·ley [pάrslɪ] *s*. perejil.
pars·nip [pάrsnəp] *s*. chirivía (*legumbre*).
par·son [pάrsn̩] *s*. pastor, clérigo.
part [pɑrt] *s*. parte (*f*.); (*role*) papel (*dramático*); (*hair*) raya (*del cabello*); — **and parcel** parte esencial, inherente; — **owner** condueño, dueño en parte; — **time** parte del tiempo; de tiempo incompleto; **in foreign -s** en el extranjero, en países extranjeros; **spare -s** piezas accesorias, piezas de repuesto (*o* de refacción); **do your** — haga Vd. cuanto esté de su parte; *v*. partir(se); separar(se); **to — company** separarse; **to — from** separarse de, despedirse de; **to — one's hair** hacerse la raya; **to — with** separarse de, despedirse de, deshacerse de.
par·take [pɑrték] *v*. tomar parte, tener parte, participar.
par·tak·en [pɑrtékən] *p.p. de* **to partake.**
par·tial [pάrʃəl] *adj*. parcial; **-ly** *adv*. parcialmente, en parte; con parcialidad.
par·ti·al·i·ty [pɑrʃǽlətɪ] *s*. parcialidad.
par·tic·i·pant [pɚtísəpənt] *adj*. & *s*. participante, partícipe, copartícipe.
par·tic·i·pate [pɚtísəpet] *v*. participar.
par·tic·i·pa·tion [pɚtɪsəpéʃən] *s*. participación.
par·ti·ci·ple [pάrtəsɪpl] *s*. participio; **present** — gerundio.
par·ti·cle [pάrtɪkl] *s*. partícula.
par·tic·u·lar [pɚtíkjəlɚ] *adj*. (*single*) particular; peculiar; (*special*) esmerado, exacto; escrupuloso; (*demanding*) quisquilloso; exigente; *s*. particular, detalle, circunstancia; **in** — en particular, especialmente; **-ly** *adv*. particularmente; en particular.
part·ing [pάrtɪŋ] (*departure*) despedida; (*division*) separación; bifurcación; **the — of the ways** encruijada, bifurcación, cruce de caminos; *adj*. de despedida, último.
par·ti·san [pάrtəzn̩] *adj*. partidario; parcial; *s*. partidario; secuaz, seguidor.
par·ti·tion [pɚtíʃən] *s*. (*division*) partición; división, separación; (*wall*) tabique; *Am*. medianía; *v*. partir, dividir; repartir.
par·ti·tive [pάrtətɪv] *adj*. partitivo.
part·ly [pάrtlɪ] *adv*. en parte.
part·ner [pάrtnɚ] *s*. socio, consocio; compañero; **dancing** — pareja de baile.
part·ner·ship [pάrtnɚʃɪp] *s*. sociedad, compañía; colectiva; *Méx*. sociedad en nombre colectivo.
par·took [pɑrtúk] *pret. de* **to partake.**
par·tridge [pάrtrɪdʒ] *s*. perdiz.
par·ty [pάrtɪ] *s*. (*get-together*) tetulia, reunión, fiesta; (*group*) grupo, partida (*de gente*); (*legal*) parte; **hunting** — partida de caza; **political** — partido político.
pass [pæs] *s*. paso; (*motion*) pase, (*permit*) permiso de entrar; (*exam*) aprobación (*en un examen*); (*event*) trance, situación; — **key** llave maestra; **to come to** — suceder; *v*. pasar; pasar por; pronunciar (*sentencia*), dar (*un juicio o parecer*); aprobar (*a un estudiante*); adoptar (*una ley*); ser aprobado en (*un examen*); **to — away** pasar a mejor vida, morir; desaparecer; pasar (*el tiempo*).
pass·a·ble [pǽsəbl] *adj*. (*penetrable*) transitable; (*acceptable*) pasadero, regular, mediano.
pas·sage [pǽsɪdʒ] *s*. (*fare*) pasaje; paso, tránsito; transcurso (*del tiempo*); pasillo, pasadizo; (*trip*) travesía, viaje por mar; aprobación (*de un proyecto de ley*); adopción (*de una ley*).
pas·sage·way [pǽsədʒwe] *s*. corredor; (*isle*) pasaje.
pass·book [pǽsbuk] *s*. libreta de banco (*depósito*).
pas·sen·ger [pǽsn̩dʒɚ] *s*. pasajero; **the -s** los pasajeros; el pasaje.
pas·ser·by [pǽsɚbáɪ] *s*. transeúnte, viandante.
pas·sion [pǽʃən] *s*. pasión; **Passion play** drama de la Pasión; **to fly into a** — montar en cólera, encolerizarse.
pas·sion·ate [pǽʃənɪt] *adj*. apasionado.
pas·sive [pǽsɪv] *adj*. pasivo; *s*. voz pasiva.
pass·port [pǽsport] *s*. pasaporte.
pass·word [pǽswɝd] *s*. consigna, contraseña, santo y seña.
past [pæst] *adj*. pasado; último; — **master** perito; **the — president** el expresidente, el último presidente; — **tense** tiempo pasado; pretérito; **for some time** — desde hace algún tiempo, de poco tiempo a esta parte; *prep*. — **bearing** insoportable; — **understanding** incomprensible; **half — two** las dos y media; **woman — forty** cuarentona, mujer de más de cuarenta años; **to go — the house** pasar por (*o* por enfrente de) la casa; *s*. pasado; pretérito; pretérito imperfecto; **man with a** — hombre de dudosos antecedentes.
paste [pest] *s*. pasta; engrudo; *v*. pegar (*con engrudo*).
paste·board [péstbord] *s*. cartón; — **box** caja de cartón.
pas·teur·ize [pǽstəraɪz] *v*. pasterizar (*o* pasteurizar).
pas·time [pǽstaɪm] *s*. pasatiempo.
pas·tor [pǽstɚ] *s*. pastor, clérigo, cura.
pas·tor·al [pǽstərəl] *adj*. pastoril; pastoral; *s*. pastoral, carta pastoral; (*story*) écloga; pastorela, idilio.
pas·try [péstrɪ] *s*. pasteleria, pasteles; — **cook** pastelero; — **shop** pastelería; repostería.
pas·ture [pǽstʃɚ] *s*. pastura, pasto; dehesa; *v*. pastar, pacer; apacentar(se).
pat [pæt] *adj*. apto, oportuno; **to have a lesson** — saber al dedillo la lección; **to stand** — mantenerse firme; *adv*. a propósito; oportunamente; de molde; *s*. palmadita, caricia, golpecito; — **of butter** cuadrito de mantequilla; *v*. dar palmaditas a; acariciar; pasar la mano (*para alisar o acariciar*).

patch [pætʃ] *s.* (*repair*) remiendo; parche; mancha; (*plot*) pedazo (*de terreno*); sembrado; *v.* remendar; **to — up a quarrel** hacer las paces.
pate [pet] *s.* coronilla (*de la cabeza*); **bald** — calva.
pat·ent [pǽtn̩t] *adj.* patente, evidente, manifiesto; de patente; — **leather** charol; — **medicine** medicina de patente; — **right** patente; *s.* patente; *v.* patentar.
pa·ter·nal [pətɝ́nl] *adj.* paternal, paterno.
pa·ter·ni·ty [pətɝ́nətɪ] *s.* paternidad.
path [pæθ] *s.* senda, sendero; vereda; ruta; trayectoria (*de una bala*).
pa·thet·ic [pəθɛ́tɪk] *adj.* patético.
path·o·log·i·cal [pæθəlɑ́dʒɪkl] *adj.* patalógico.
pa·thol·o·gy [pæθɑ́lədʒɪ] *s.* patología.
pa·thos [péθɑs] *s.* patetismo, cualidad patética.
path·way [pǽθwe] *s.* senda, vereda, vía.
pa·tience [péʃəns] *s.* paciencia.
pa·tient [péʃənt] *adj.* paciente; pacienzudo; *s.* paciente, enfermo.
pa·tri·arch [pétrɪɑrk] *s.* patriarca.
pa·tri·ar·chal [petrɪɑrkl] *adj.* patriarcal.
pa·tri·cian [pətrɪ́ʃən] *s.* patricio.
pat·ri·mo·ny [pǽtrəmonɪ] *s.* patrimonio.
pa·tri·ot [pétrɪət] *s.* patriota.
pa·tri·ot·ic [petrɪɑ́tɪk] *adj.* patriótico.
pa·tri·ot·ism [pétrɪətɪzəm] *s.* patriotismo.
pa·trol [pətról] *s.* patrulla; ronda; *v.* patrullar, rondar.
pa·tron [pétrən] *s.* patrón, patrono; benefactor; (*customer*) cliente, parroquiano; — **saint** santo patrón.
pa·tron·age [pétrənɪdʒ] *s.* (*support*) patrocinio, amparo; (*clientele*) clientela; (*manner*) condescendencia; **political** — control de nombramientos políticos.
pa·tron·ess [pétrənɪs] *s.* patrona, protectora.
pa·tron·ize [pétrənaɪz] *v.* patrocinar, amparar; tratar con condescendencia; favorecer, ser parroquiano de.
pat·ter [pǽtɚ] *v.* golpetear ligeramente; (*feet*) talonear; (*speech*) charlar, parlotear; *s.* golpeteo; golpecitos; taloneo; charla, parloteo.
pat·tern [pǽtɚn] *s.* (*model*) modelo; dechado; muestra; ejemplo; patrón, molde; (*design*) diseño, dibujo (*en tejidos, telas, etc.*) *v.* **to — oneself after** seguir el ejemplo de; **to — something after (on, upon)** forjar o modelar algo a imitación de.
pau·ci·ty [pɔ́sɪtɪ] *s.* escasez; falta.
paunch [pɔntʃ] *s.* panza, barriga.
pause [pɔz] *s.* pausa; *s.* pausar, hacer pausa; detenerse, parar.
pave [pev] *v.* pavimentar; **to — the way for** preparar o abrir el camino para; **to — with bricks** enladrillar; **to — with flagstones** enlosar.
pave·ment [pévmənt] *s.* pavimento; **brick** — enladrillado.
pa·vil·lion [pəvɪ́ljən] *s.* pabellón.
paw [pɔ] *s.* garra, zarpa; *v.* echar la zarpa; arañar; manosear; **to — the ground** patear la tierra (*dícese del caballo*).
pawn [pɔn] *s.* prenda, empeño; (*chess*) peón (*de ajedrez*); — **broker** prestamista, prendero; — **shop** empeño, casa de empeños, montepío; **in** — en prenda; *v.* empeñar, dejar en prenda.
pay [pe] *v.* (*remit*) pagar; (*pay for*) costear; (*profit*) ser provechoso; (*worthwhile*) valer la pena; **to — attention** prestar atención; **to — back** restituir, devolver; reembolsar; **to — court** hacer la corte; **to — down** pagar al contado; **to — homage** hacer o rendir homenaje; **to — one's respects** presentar sus respetos; **to — a visit** hacer una visita; **to hit — dirt** descubrir algo de valor; *s.* pago; recompensa; **to — through the nose** pagar demasiado; paga; **take-home** — sueldo neto; sueldo; — **load** carga útil o de valor; — **day** día de pagos, *Am.*, día de raya; — **master** pagador, — **phone** teléfono público; *Am.* rayador; — **roll** nómina.
pay·a·ble [péəbl] *adj.* pagadero.
pay·ee [peí] *s.* tenedor, portador.
pay·ment [pémənt] *s.* pago; paga; — **in full** pago total.
pay·off [péɔf] *s.* arreglo; pago; resultados favorables.
pea [pi] *s.* guisante, chícharo; **sweet** — guisante de olor.
peace [pis] *s.* paz.
peace·a·ble [písəbl] *adj.* pacífico, tranquílo.
peace·ful [písfəl] *adj.* pacífico; tranquilo, quieto, sosegado.
peach [pitʃ] *s.* melocotón, durazno; persona bella o admirable; — **tree** durazno, duraznero, melocotoner.
pea·cock [píkɑk] *s.* pavón, pavo real; **to act like a** — pavonearse, hacer ostentación.
peak [pik] *s.* pico, cumbre, cima; cúspide; punto máximo; — **level** producción máxima; — **load** de carga máxima; — **- hour traffic** hora de tránsito máximo.
peal [pil] *s.* repique (*de campanas*); — **of laughter** carcajada, risotada; — **of thunder** trueno; *v.* repicar (*las campanas*).
pea·nut [pínət] *s.* cacahuate, *Carib., Ven., Col., Ch., Ríopl., Andes* maní.
pear [pɛ] *s.* pera; — **tree** peral; **alligator** — aguacate, *Ch., Andes, Ríopl.* palta (*variedad sudamericana*).
pearl [pɝl] *s.* perla; — **necklace** collar de perlas; **mother-of-pearl** nácar, madreperla.
pear·ly [pɝ́lɪ] *adj.* perlino; nacarado; aperlado.
peas·ant [pɝ́zn̩t] *adj. & s.* campesino, rústico, *P.R.* jíbaro, *Cuba* guajiro; *Col.* paisa; *Ch.* guaso; *Ríopl.* gaucho.
peb·ble [pɝ́bl] *s.* guija, china, guijarro, piedrecilla.
pe·can [pikɑ́n] *s.* pacana.
peck [pɛk] *v.* picar, picotear; *s.* picotazo, picotada; medida de áridos (*aproximadamente 9 litros*); **a — of trouble** la mar de disgustos o molestias.
pe·cu·liar [pɪkúljɚ] *adj.* peculiar; raro, singular, extraño.
pe·cu·li·ar·i·ty [pɪkjulɪǽrətɪ] *s.* peculiaridad; particularidad; rareza.
ped·a·gogue [pɛ́dəgɑg] *s.* pedagogo, dómine.
ped·a·go·gy [pɛ́əgodʒɪ] *s.* pedagogía.
ped·al [pɛ́dl] *s.* pedal; *v.* pedalear, mover los pedales.
ped·ant [pɛ́dn̩t] *s.* pedante.
pe·dan·tic [pɪdǽntɪk] *adj.* pedante, pedantesco.
ped·dle [pɛ́dl] *v.* ir vendiendo de puerta en puerta; **to — gossip** chismear.
ped·dler [pɛ́dlɚ] *s.* buhonero; vendedor ambulante.
ped·es·tal [pɛ́dɪstl] *s.* pedestal.
pe·des·tri·an [pədɛ́strɪən] *s.* peatón, transeúnte, viandante; *adj.* pedestre.
pe·di·at·rics [pidɪǽtrɪks] *s.* pediatría.
ped·i·gree [pɛ́dəgri] *s.* linaje, genealogía.
peek [pik] *v.* atisbar, espiar; *s.* atisbo.
peel [pil] *s.* corteza, cáscara (*de algunas frutas*); pellejo (*de patatas*); *v.* pelar(se), descortezar(se), deshollejar(se); **to keep one's eye -ed** tener los ojos muy abiertos, estar alerta.
peep [pip] *v.* atisbar, espiar; asomar(se); pipiar, piar; *s.* atisbo; ojeada; pío (*de pollo o ave*).

peer [pir] *s.* (*equal*) par, igual; (*noble*) noble; *v.* mirar con atención, atisbar; asomar; **to — into other people's business** fisgar, curiosear.
peer group [pɪrgrup] *s.* conjunto de personas de la misma edad y condiciones.
peer·less [pírlɛs] *adj.* incomparable; sin par.
peeve [piv] *v.* irritar, poner de mal humor; **to get -d** amoscarse, ponerse de mal humor.
pee·vish [pívɪʃ] *adj.* enojadizo; malhumorado.
peg [pɛg] *s.* espiga, clavo de madera, estaquilla; clavija (*de violín*); **to take a person down a —** rebajar o humillar a alguien; *v.* clavar, clavetear; poner estaquillas; **to — along** atarearse, trabajar con tesón; **pegged value of exchange** tipo arbitrario de cambio.
pe·jor·a·tive [pədʒɔ́rətɪv] *adj.* peyorativo; despectivo.
pel·i·can [pɛ́lɪkən] *s.* pelícano.
pel·let [pɛ́lɪt] *s.* (*ball*) pelotilla; bola; (*pill*) píldora.
pell·mell [pɛ́lmɛ́l] *adj.* confuso, tumultuoso; *adv.* a trochemoche, atropelladamente, en tumulto.
pelt [pɛlt] *s.* zalea, cuero (*especialmente de oveja*); piel; *v.* golpear; **to — with stones** apedrear, arrojar piedras a.
pel·vis [pɛ́lvɪs] *s.* pelvis.
pen [pɛn] *s.* pluma (*para escribir*); corral; redil; **— holder** mango de pluma, portapluma; **— name** nombre de pluma; **fountain —** pluma fuente, pluma estilográfica; **ballpoint —** bolígrafo; **pig —** pocilga; *v.* escribir (*con pluma*); acorralar, encerrar.
pe·nal [pínl] *adj.* penal.
pe·nal·ize [pínəlaɪz] *v.* penar; aplicar sanción.
pen·al·ty [pɛ́nltɪ] *s.* pena, castigo; multa.
pen·ance [pɛ́nəns] *s.* penitencia.
pen·cil [pɛ́nsl] *s.* lápiz; lapicero; **— sharpener** tajalápiz.
pen·dant [pɛ́ndənt] *s.* pendiente (*ardorno que cuelga*); *adj.* pendiente.
pend·ing [pɛ́ndɪŋ] *adj.* pendiente; colgado; *prep.* durante.
pen·du·lum [pɛ́ndʒələm] *s.* péndula.
pen·e·trate [pɛ́nətret] *v.* penetrar.
pen·e·trat·ing [pɛ́nətretɪŋ] *adj.* penetrante.
pen·e·tra·tion [pɛnətréʃən] *s.* penetración.
pen·guin [pɛ́ngwɪn] *s.* pingüino.
pen·i·cil·lin [pɛnəsílɪn] *s.* penicilina.
pen·in·su·la [pənínsələ] *s.* península.
pe·nis [pínɪs] *s.* pene.
pen·i·tent [pɛ́nətənt] *adj.* arrepentido, penitente; *s.* penitente.
pen·i·ten·tia·ry [pɛnətɛ́ʃərɪ] *s.* penitenciaría, presidio.
pen·knife [pɛ́nnaɪf] *s.* cortaplumas; navaja.
pen·man·ship [pɛ́nmənʃɪp] *s.* escritura, caligrafía.
pen·nant [pɛ́nənt] *s.* banderola, gallardete.
pen·ni·less [pɛ́nɪlɪs] *adj.* pobre, sin dinero.
pen·ny [pɛ́nɪ] *s.* centavo (*de dólar*); **to cost a pretty —** costar un ojo de la cara, costar un dineral.
pen·sion [pɛ́nʃən] *s.* pensión, retiro (*de un militar*); **—fund** fondo de pensión; *v.* pensionar.
pen·sive [pɛ́nsɪv] *adj.* pensativo.
pent [pɛnt] *adj.* encerrado; acorralado; **pent-up emotions** sentimientos reprimidos.
pent·house [pɛ́nthaʊs] *s.* casa de azotea; colgadizo.
peo·ple [pípl] *s.* gente; pueblo *v.* poblar.
pep·per [pɛ́pɚ] *s.* pimienta; **— plant** pimentero; **— shaker** pimentero; **green -s** pimientos verdes; **red —** pimentón, chile, *Carib., Col., Ven., Andes, Ch., Ríopl.* ají; *v.* sazonar con pimienta; **to — with bullets** acribillar a balazos.
pep·per·mint [pɛ́pɚmɪnt] *s.* menta; pastilla o bombón de menta.

per [pɚ] *prep.* por; **— capita** por cabeza; **— capita income** renta por habitante; **— cent** por ciento; **— year** al año; **ten cents — dozen** diez centavos por docena (*o* diez centavos la docena).
per·cale [pɚkél] *s.* percal.
per·ceive [pɚsív] *v.* percibir.
per·cent·age [pɚsɛ́ntɪdʒ] *s.* porcentaje, tanto por ciento.
per·cep·ti·ble [pɚsɛ́ptəbl] *adj.* perceptible.
per·cep·tion [pɚsɛ́pʃən] *s.* percepción.
per·cep·tive [pɚrsɛ́ptɪv] *adj.* perceptivo; sensible.
perch [pɝtʃ] *s.* percha (*para pájaros*); perca (*pez*); *v.* encaramar(se); posarse (*en una percha o rama*).
per·chance [pɚtʃǽns] *adv.* por ventura, acaso, quizás, tal vez.
per·co·late [pɝ́kəlet] *v.* filtrar(se), colar(se); rezumarse; penetrar.
per·cus·sion [pɝkʃən] *s.* percusión.
per·di·tion [pɚdíʃən] *s.* perdición.
per·en·ni·al [pərɛ́nɪəl] *adj.* perenne; continuo; perpetuo.
per·fect [pɝ́fɪkt] *adj.* perfecto; completo; *s.* tiempo perfecto (*del verbo*); [pɚfɛ́kt] *v.* perfeccionar.
per·fec·tion [pɚfɛ́kʃən] *s.* perfección.
per·fid·i·ous [pɚfídɪəs] *adj.* pérfido.
per·fi·dy [pɝ́fədɪ] *s.* perfidia.
per·fo·rate [pɝ́fəret] *v.* perforar.
per·force [pɚfɔ́rs] *adj.* necesariamente; por fuerza.
per·form [pɚfɔ́rm] *v.* ejecutar; llevar a cabo, cumplir, hacer; cuncionar (*una máquina*); desempeñar o representar un papel.
per·form·ance [pɚfɔ́rməns] *s.* ejecución; desempeño, cumplimiento; funcionamiento (*de una máquina o motor*); función, representación; acto, acción; **— standard** norma de rendimiento.
per·fume [pɝ́fjum] *s.* perfume; [pɚfjúm] *v.* perfumar.
per·fum·er·y [pɚfjúmərɪ] *s.* perfumería; perfumes.
per·haps [pɚhǽps] *adv.* acaso, tal vez, quizá (*o* quizás), puede ser.
per·i·gee [pɛ́rədʒi] *s.* perigeo.
per·il [pɛ́rəl] *s.* peligro; riesgo; *v.* poner en peligro.
per·il·ous [pɛ́rələs] *adj.* peligroso.
pe·rim·e·ter [pərímətɚ] *s.* perímetro.
pe·ri·od [pírɪəd] *s.* período; punto final; fin, término.
pe·ri·od·ic [pɪrɪádɪk] *adj.* periódico.
pe·ri·od·i·cal [pɪrɪádɪkl] *adj.* periódico; *s.* revista, publicación periódica.
pe·riph·er·al [pɚífɚl] *adj.* periférico; *(computer) s.* periférico.
pe·riph·er·y [pəríførɪ] *s.* periferia.
per·ish [pɛ́rɪʃ] *v.* perecer.
per·ish·a·ble [pɛ́rɪʃəbl] *adj.* perecedero; deleznable.
per·i·to·ne·um [pɛrətəníəm] *s.* peritoneo.
per·i·to·ni·tis [pɛrətənáɪtɪs] *s.* peritonitis.
per·jure [pɝ́dʒɚ] *v.* **to — oneself** perjurar.
per·ju·ry [pɝ́dʒrɪ] *s.* perjurio, juramento falso.
per·ma·nence [pɝ́mənəns] *s.* permanencia.
per·ma·nent [pɝ́mənənt] *adj.* permanente; duradero.
per·me·ate [pɝ́mɪet] *v.* penetrar, saturar; (*scatter*) difundirse por, filtrarse por.
per·mis·si·ble [pɚmísəbl] *adj.* lícito.
per·mis·sion [pɚmíʃən] *s.* permiso, licencia.
per·mis·sive [pɚmísɪv] *adj.* permisivo.
per·mit [pɝ́mɪt] *s.* permiso, pase; licencia; [pɚmít] *v.* permitir.
per·mu·ta·tion [pɚmjutéʃən] *s.* permutación.
per·ni·cious [pɚníʃəs] *adj.* pernicioso.
per·ox·ide [pəráksaɪd] *s.* peróxido.
per·pen·dic·u·lar [pɝrpəndíkjəlɚ] *adj. & s.* perpendicular.

per·pe·trate [pɝ́pətret] *v.* perpetrar, cometar.
per·pet·u·al [pɚpétʃuəl] *adj.* perpetuo.
per·pet·u·ate [pɚpétʃuet] *v.* perpetuar.
per·plex [pɚpléks] *v.* confundir, turbar, aturdir.
per·plexed [pɚplékst] *adj.* perplejo, confuso.
per·plex·i·ty [pɚpléksətɪ] *s.* perplejidad, confusión.
per·se·cute [pɝ́sɪkjut] *v.* perseguir, acosar.
per·se·cu·tion [pɝsɪkjúʃən] *s.* persecución.
per·se·cu·tor [pɝ́sɪkjutɚ] *s.* perseguidor.
per·se·ver·ance [pɝsəvírəns] *s.* perseverancia.
per·se·vere [pɝsəvír] *v.* perseverar; persistir.
per·sist [pɚzíst] *v.* persistir; porfiar.
per·sist·ence [pɚzístəns] *s.* persistencia; porfía.
per·sist·ent [pɚzístənt] *adj.* persistente; porfiado.
per·son [pɝ́sn̩] *s.* persona.
per·son·a·ble [pɝ́sənəbl] *adj.* presentable; bien parecido.
per·son·age [pɝ́sn̩ɪdʒ] *s.* personaje.
per·son·al [pɝ́sn̩l] *adj.* personal; en persona; — **property** bienes muebles.
per·son·al·ism [pɝ́sənəlɪzm] *s.* personalismo.
per·son·al·i·ty [pɝsn̩ǽlətɪ] *s.* personalidad; persona, personaje; alusión personal.
per·son·nel [pɝsn̩él] *s.* personal.
per·spec·tive [pɚspéktɪv] *s.* perspectiva; — **drawing** dibujo en perspectiva.
per·spi·ca·cious [pɚspɪkéʃəs] *adj.* perspicaz.
per·spi·ra·tion [pɝspəréʃən] *s.* sudor.
per·spire [pɚspáɪr] *v.* sudar.
per·suade [pɚswéd] *v.* persuadir.
per·sua·sion [pɚswéʒən] *s.* persuasión; creencia.
per·sua·sive [pɚswésɪv] *adj.* persuasivo.
pert [pɝt] *adj.* insolente, descarado, atrevido, *Am.* retobado.
per·tain [pɚtén] *v.* pertenecer; atañer.
per·ti·nent [pɝ́tn̩ənt] *adj.* pertinente, a propósito, al caso.
per·turb [pɚtɝ́b] *v.* perturbar.
pe·rus·al [pərúzl] *s.* lectura.
pe·ruse [pərúz] *v.* leer con cuidado.
Pe·ru·vi·an [pərúvɪən] *adj. & s.* peruano.
per·vade [pɚvéd] *v.* llenar, penetrar, difundirse por.
per·verse [pɚvɝ́s] *adj.* perverso; terco, obstinado.
per·vert [pɚvɝ́t] *v.* pervertir; (*twist*) falsear; [pɝ́vɝt] *s.* perverso.
pes·si·mism [pésəmizəm] *s.* pesimismo.
pes·si·mist [pésəmɪst] *s.* pesimista; **-ic** *adj.* pesimista.
pest [pɛst] *s.* peste, plaga; pestilencia.
pes·ter [péstɚ] *v.* importunar, molestar.
pes·ti·cide [péstəsaɪd] *s. & adj.* insecticida.
pes·ti·lence [péstləns] *s.* pestilencia.
pet [pɛt] *s.* animal mimado, animal casero o domestico; (*child*) niño mimado; (*favorite*) favorito; *adj.* favorito; mimado; — **name** nombre de cariño (*por lo general diminutivo*); *v.* mimar, acariciar.
petal [pétl] *s.* pétalo.
pet·cock [pétkɑk] *s.* llave de desagüe (*purga*); *Méx.* bitoque.
pe·ti·tion [pətíʃən] *s.* petición, súplica; instancia, memorial, solicitud, *Ríopl.* ocurso; *v.* solicitar, pedir, dirigir una instancia o memorial a; suplicar, rogar.
pet·ri·fy [pétrɪfaɪ] *v.* petrificar.
pe·tro·le·um [pətrólɪəm] *s.* petróleo; — **products** productos petrolíferos.
pet·ti·coat [pétɪkot] *s.* enaguas.
pet·ty [pétɪ] *adj.* insignificante, pequeño; mezquino, inferior, subordinado; — **cash** fondos para gastos menores; caja menor; — **larceny** ratería; — **officer** oficial subordinado (*en la marina*); — **treason** traición menor.
pe·tu·nia [pətúnjə] *s.* petunia.
pew [pju] *s.* banco de iglesia.
pha·lanx [féléŋks] *s.* falanje.
phan·tom [fǽntəm] *s.* fantasma.
phar·ma·cist [fɑ́rməsɪst] *s.* farmacéutico, boticario.
phar·ma·cy [fɑ́rməsɪ] *s.* farmacia, botica.
phar·ynx [fǽrɪŋks] *s.* faringe.
phase [fez] *s.* fase; *v.* **phase out** retirar por etapas.
pheas·ant [fézənt] *s.* faisán.
phe·nom·e·na [fənɑ́mənə] *pl. de* **phenomenon.**
phe·nom·e·non [fənɑ́mənɑn] *s.* fenómeno.
phi·lan·thro·py [fɪlǽnθrəpɪ] *s.* filantropía.
phi·lat·e·ly [fɪlǽtlɪ] *s.* filatelia.
phil·har·mon·ic [fɪlhɑrmɑ́nɪk] *adj.* filarmónico.
phi·lol·o·gy [fɪlɑ́lədʒɪ] *s.* filología.
phi·los·o·pher [fəlɑ́səfɚ] *s.* filósofo.
phil·o·soph·i·cal [fɪləsɑ́fɪkl] *adj.* filosófico.
phi·los·o·phy [fəlɑ́səfɪ] *s.* filosofía.
phlegm [flɛm] *s.* flema.
phone [fon] *s.* teléfono; *v.* telefonear.
pho·neme [fónim] *s.* fonema.
pho·net·ics [fonétɪks] *s.* fonética.
pho·no·graph [fónəgrǽf] *s.* fonógrafo.
pho·nol·o·gy [fonɑ́lədʒɪ] *s.* fonología.
phos·phate [fɑ́sfet] *s.* fosfato.
phos·pho·rus [fɑ́sfərəs] *s.* fósforo (*elemento quimico*).
pho·to [fóto] *s.* fotografía, retrato; (la) foto.
pho·to·e·lec·tric [fotoɪléktrɪk] fotoeléctrico.
pho·to·graph [fótəgræf] *s.* fotografía, retrato; *v.* fotografiar, retratar.
pho·tog·ra·pher [fətɑ́grəfɚ] *s.* fotógrafo.
pho·tog·ra·phy [fətɑ́grəfɪ] *s.* fotografía.
pho·to·syn·the·sis [fotosínθəsɪs] fotosíntesis.
phrase [frez] *s.* frase; expresión, locución; *v.* frasear; espresar, formular.
phys·ic [fízɪk] *s.* purga, purgante; *v.* purgar.
phys·i·cal [fízɪkl] *adj.* físico.
phy·si·cian [fəzíʃən] *s.* médico.
phys·i·cist [fízəsɪst] *s.* físico.
phys·ics [fízɪks] *s.* física.
phys·i·o·log·i·cal [fɪzɪəlɑ́dʒɪkl] *adj.* fisiológico.
phys·i·ol·o·gy [fɪzɪɑ́lədʒɪ] *s.* fisiología.
phy·sique [fɪzík] *s.* complexión, constitución física, talle, cuerpo.
pi·an·o [pɪǽno] *s.* piano; — **bench** banqueta de piano; — **stool** taburete de piano; **grand** — piano de cola; **upright** — piano vertical.
pic·a·resque [pɪkərésk] *adj.* picaresco.
pick [pɪk] *v.* (*choose*) escoger; coger; (*break*) picar; (*clean*) mondarse, limpiarse (*los dientes*); (*pluck*) desplumar (*un ave*); (*gnaw*) roer (*un hueso*); falsear (*una cerradura*); armar (*una pendencia*); **to — flaws** criticar, censurar; **to — out** escoger; **to — pockets** ratear; **to — up** recoger; **to — up speed** acelerar la marcha; **pick-proof** *adj.* a prueba de forzar; *s.* (*tool*) pico (*herramienta*); (*selection*) selección; lo selecto, lo mejor; (*collection*) recolección, cosecha; **ice** — punzón para romper hielo; **tooth** — mondadientes, palillo de dientes.
pick·ax [píkæks] *s.* pico, zapapico.
pick·et [píkɪt] *s.* piquete (*estaca o palo clavado en la tierra*); piquete (*vigilante huelguista*); piquete de soldados; *v.* estacionar piquetes cerca de (*una fábrica, campamento, etc.*); vigilar (*por medio de piquetes*); estar de guardia.
pick·le [píkl] *s.* encurtido; **to be in a** — hallarse en un aprietó; *v.* encurtir, escabechar; **-d cucumbers** pepinillos encurtidos; **-d fish** excabeche, pescado en escabeche.

pick·pock·et [píkpɑkɪt] *s.* rata (*m.*), ratero; *Méx., Ven., Col.* carterista.
pick·up truck [pɪkəptrʌk] *s.* picó.
pic·nic [píknɪk] *s.* partida de campo, día de campo, comida campestre, *Am.* picnic; *v.* hacer una comida campestre; ir a un picnic.
pic·ture [píktʃɚ] *s.* (*painting*) cuadro, pintura; (*portrait*) retrato; (*photo*) fotografía; (*engraving*) grabado; (*movie*) película; — **frame** marco; — **gallery** museo o galería de pinturas; *v.* pintar, dibujar; describir; imaginar(se).
pic·tur·esque [pɪktʃərέsk] *adj.* pintoresco.
pie [paɪ] *s.* pastel; empanada.
piece [pis] *s.* (*section*) pieza; pedazo; parte; sección (*passage*) trozo; (*song*) canción; — **of advice** consejo; — **of land** parcela; — **of money** moneda; — **of news** noticia; — **of nonsense** tontería; — **meal** en pedazos, a, pedazos, por partes; — **rate** precio (pago) por pieza; *v.* remendar; **to** — **between meals** comer a deshoras; **to** — **on to** juntar a, pegar a; **to** — **together** unir, pegar, juntar.
piece·work [píswɝk] *s.* trabajo por unidades.
pier [pɪr] *s.* muelle, embarcadero; (*breakwater*) rompeolas; pilar (*de puente o arco*).
pierce [pɪrs] *v.* atravesar, traspasar; taladrar, agujerar, perforar.
pi·e·ty [páɪətɪ] *s.* piedad, religiosidad.
pig [pɪg] *s.* puerco, cerdo, cochino; *S.A.* chancho; *C.A.* tunco; cuchi; *adj.* porcino; — **iron** hierro en lingotes; — **headed** cabezón, testarudo; **guinea** — conejillo de Indias; **suckling** — gorrino.
pi·geon [pídʒən] *s.* pichón; paloma.
pi·geon·hole [pídʒənhol] *s.* casilla; *v.* encasillar.
pig·ment [pígmənt] *s.* pigmento, color.
pig·my [pígmɪ] *s.* pigmeo.
pike [paɪk] *s.* pica, lanza; lucio (*pez*).
pile [paɪl] *s.* pila, montón; (*surface*) pelo (*de ciertos tejidos*); pilote; (*ailment*) **-s** almorranas (*enfermedad*); — **driver** martinete (*para clavar pilotes*); *v.* apilar(se), amontonar(se); acumular(se).
pil·fer [pílfɚ] *v.* pillar, retear, hurtar, sisar; **pilferage** hurto.
pil·grim [pílgrɪm] *s.* peregrino, romero.
pil·grim·age [pílgrəmɪdʒ] *s.* peregrinación, romería.
pill [pɪl] *s.* pildora; persona fastidiosa.
pil·lage [pílɪdʒ] *v.* pillar, saquear; *s.* pillaje, saqueo.
pil·lar [pílɚ] *s.* pilar, columna; **to go from** — **to post** ir de Ceca en Meca.
pil·low [pílo] *s.* almohada; cojín.
pil·low·case [pílokes] *s.* funda de almohada.
pi·lot [páɪlət] *s.* piloto; guía; timonel; — **light** (*o* — **burner**) mechero, encendedor (*de una cocina o estufa de gas*); **harbor** — prático de puerto; *v.* pilotar o pilotear; dirigir, guiar; *adj.* de ensayo.
pimp [pɪmp] *s.* alcahuete, puto.
pim·ple [pímpl] *s.* grano, barro.
pin [pɪn] *s.* alfiler; (*ornament*) prendedor; (*spike*) espiga; (*bowling*) bolo (*del juego de bolos*); — **money** dinero para alfileres; — **wheel** molinete, *Am.* remolino; **breast** — broche; **safety** — imperdible; (*computer*) pata; (*printing*) espiga; *v.* prender (*con alfiler*); asegurar, fijar, clavar; **to** — **down** fijar, inmovilizar; hacer dar una contestación definitiva; **to** — **one's hope to** poner toda su esperanza en; **to** — **up** prender con alfileres; colgar (*un dibujo o retrato*), fijar con tachuelas.
pin·cers [pínsɚz] *s. pl.* pinzas; tenazas; **small** — tenacillas.
pinch [pɪntʃ] *v.* (*squeeze*) pellizcar; apretar; (*economize*) economizar; (*arrest*) prender, arrestar; **to** — **one's finger in the door** machucarse el dedo en la puerta; — **hit** batear de emergente; sustituir a otro en un apuro; *s.* pellizco; pizca, proción pequeña; punzada, dolor agudo; aprieto, apuro; — **hitter** suplente, sustituto.
pin·chers [píntʃɚz] = **pincers.**
pine [paɪn] *s.* pino; — **cone** piña; — **grove** pinar; — **nut** piñon; *v.* languidecer; **to** — **away** consumirse; **to** — **for** anhelar, suspirar por.
pine·ap·ple [páɪnæpl] *s.* piña, *S.A.* ananá, ananás.
pin·ion [pínjən] *s.* piñón.
pink [pɪŋk] *s.* clavel; color de rosa; **in the** — **of condition** en la major condición; *adj.* rosado, color de rosa.
pin·na·cle [pínəkl] *s.* pináculo, cumbre.
pint [paɪnt] *s.* pinta (*aproximadamente medio litro*).
pi·o·neer [paɪənír] *s.* explorador, colonizador; fundador, iniciador, precursor; pionero; *v.* explorar, colonizar; fundar, promover.
pi·ous [páɪəs] *adj.* pío, piadoso.
pipe [paɪp] *s.* pipa (*de fumar*); tubo, caño; cañon (*de órgano*); caramillo, flauta; — **line** cañería, tubería; oleoducto (*petróleo*); *v.* conducir por cañerías; desaguar por cañería; proveer de tuberías o cañerías; chillar; **to** — **down** bajar la voz.
pip·er [páɪpɚ] *s.* (*bagpipe*) gaitero, (*flute*) flautista.
pip·ing [páɪpɪŋ] *s.* cañería, tubería; (*clothes*) cordoncillo (*de adorno para costuras*); chillido, silbido; *adj.* agudo, chillón; — **hot** muy caliente; hirviendo.
pip·pin [pípɪn] *s.* camuesa.
pique [pik] *s.* enojo, resentimiento; *v.* picar, excitar; enojar, irritar; **to** — **oneself on** picarse de, preciarse de.
pi·rate [páɪrət] *s.* pirata; *v.* piratear; plagiar.
pis·tol [pístl] *s.* pistola; revólver.
pis·ton [pístn̩] *s.* pistón, émbolo; — **ring** aro de pistón; — **rod** vástago del émbolo.
pit [pɪt] *s.* hoyo; foso; hueso (*de ciertas frutas*); — **of the stomach** boca del estómago.
pitch [pɪtʃ] *s.* (*throw*) tiro, lanzamiento (*de una pelota*); cabezada (*de un barco*); (*music*) diapasón, tono; (*inclination*) grado, declive, grado de inclinación; (*printing*) espacio; pez (*f.*), brea; resina; — **dark** oscurísimo; *v.* tirar, lanzar, arrojar; cabecear (*un barco*); graduar el tono de (*un instrumento o voz*); echarse de cabeza; inclinarse; **to** — **a tent** armar una tienda de campaña; acampar; **to** — **into** arremeter contra; reprender, regañar; — **in!** ¡manos a la obra!
pitch·er [pítʃɚ] *s.* cántaro, jarro *o* jarra; tirador, lanzador (*en béisbol*).
pitch·fork [pítʃfɔrk] *s.* horca, horquilla (*para hacinar las mieses, levantar la paja, etc.*).
pit·e·ous [pítɪəs] *adj.* lastimero, lastimoso.
pit·fall [pítfɔl] *s.* trampa, escollo.
pith [pɪθ] *s.* meollo, médula; (*essence*) esencia, sustancia.
pit·i·ful [pítɪfəl] *adj.* lastimoso, lamentable; miserable.
pit·i·less [pítɪlɪs] *adj.* despiadado, incompasivo, cruel.
pit·y [pítɪ] *s.* piedad; lástima; compasión; **for -'s sake** por piedad, por Dios; **what a** — **!** ¡qué lástima!; *v.* compadecer; tener lástima por; apiadarse de, tener piedad de.
pix·el [píksl̩] *s.* (*computer*) punto, pixel.
plac·ard [plǽkɑrd] *s.* letrero, cartel; *v.* fijar carteles.
place [ples] *s.* (*site*) lugar, sitio; localidad; (*position*) puesto; empleo; posición; *Col.* cupo; — **of business** oficina, despacho; — **of worship** templo,

iglesia; **market** — plaza, mercado; **in** — **of** en lugar de, en vez de; **it is not my** — **to do it** no es mi deber hacerlo, no me toca a mí hacerlo; *v.* colocar; situar; poner; acomodar, dar empleo a.

pla·cid [plǽsɪd] *adj.* plácido, apacible, sosegado.

pla·gia·rism [plédʒərɪzəm] *s.* plagio.

plague [pleg] *s.* plaga; peste, pestilencia; calamidad; *v.* plagar, infestar; importunar.

plaid [plæd] *s.* tartán, tela a cuadros; (*scotch*) manta escocesa a cuadros; diseño a cuadros; *adj.* a cuadros.

plain [plen] *adj.* (*flat*) llano; (*simple*) sencillo; claro; franco; ordinario; — **fool** tonto de capirote; — **woman** mujer sin atractivo; **in** — **sight** en plena vista; **plain-clothes man** detectivo; *adv.* claramente; — **stupid** completamente estúpido; **plain-spoken** franco, francote, sincero; *s.* llano, llanura.

plain·tiff [pléntɪf] *s.* demandante.

plain·tive [pléntɪv] *adj.* lastimero, triste.

plan [plæn] *s.* plan; proyecto; (*map*) plano (*dibujo o mapa*); *v.* planear; proyectar, idear; pensar, proponerse; **planning** planeamiento; planificación.

plane [plen] *s.* (*airplane*) avión; aeroplano; (*surface*) plano, superficie plana; (*tool*) cepillo (*de carpintero*); *adj.* plano, llano; — **tree** plátano falso; *v.* acepillar, alisar con cepillo (*la madera o los metales*).

plan·et [plǽnɪt] *s.* planeta.

plan·e·tar·i·um [plænətériəm] *s.* planetario.

plank [plæŋk] *s.* table, tablón; (*tenet*) principio, base (*del programa de un partido político*); *v.* entablar, entarimar, cubrir con tablas; (*broil*) asar (*carne*) en una tabla.

plank·ton [plǽŋktən] *s.* plancton.

plant [plænt] *s.* (*vegetation*) planta; (*industry*) fábrica; taller; *v.* plantar; sembrar; implantar; establecer.

plan·ta·tion [plæntéʃən] *s.* plantación; hacienda plantío; sembrado; **coffee** — cafetal; **cotton** — algodonal; **rubber** — cauchal; **sugar** — ingenio de azúcar.

plant·er [plǽntɚ] *s.* plantador, cultivador.

plaque [plæk] *s.* placa.

plas·ma [plǽzmə] *s.* plasma.

plas·ter [plǽstɚ] *s.* yeso; emplasto; — **of Paris** yeso, yeso mate; **court** — esparadrapo, tafetán inglés; **mustard** — sinapismo; *v.* enyesar; emplastar, poner emplastos a; pegar (*carteles, anuncios*); embarrar.

plas·tic [plǽstɪk] *adj.* plástico.

plat [plæt] *s.* plano; parcela; *v.* levantar o trazar un plano.

plate [plet] *s.* (*eating*) plato; (*metal*) placa; plancha; lámina; **dental** — dentadura postiza; *v.* platear; dorar; niquelar; blindar, proteger con planchas de metal; laminar.

pla·teau [plætó] *s.* antiplanicie, mesa, meseta.

plat·ed [plétəd] *adj.* chapeado; (*armored*) blindado.

plate·ful [plétfʊl] *s.* plato, plato lleno.

plat·en [plǽtən] *s.* (*computer*) rodillo; — **knob** perilla del rodillo.

plat·form [plǽtfɔrm] *s.* plataforma; tablado; programa de un partido político; **railway** — andén.

plat·i·num [plǽtn̩əm] *s.* platino.

plat·i·tude [plǽtətjud] *s.* lugar común, perogrullada.

plat·ter [plǽtɚ] *s.* platel, platón.

play [ple] *v.* (*game*) jugar; juguetear; (*instrument*) tocar; (*drama*) representar; hacer, desempeñar (*un papel*); manipular (*un instrumento, radio, fonógrafo, etc.*); **to** — **a joke** hacer una broma, dar un chasco; **to** — **cards** jugar a los naipes, jugar a la baraja; **to** — **havoc** hacer estragos, causar daño; **to** — **tennis** jugar al tenis; **to** — **the fool** hacerse el tonto, fingirse tonto; **to be all -ed out** no poder más, estar agotado; *s.* juego; jugada (*acción, movimiento en un juego*); pieza, drama, comedia, representación; recreación, diversión; — **on words** juego de palabras, equívoco; **to give full** — **to** dar rienda suelta a.

play·er [pléɚ] *s.* (*games*) jugador; (*music*) músico; (*plays*) cómico, actor; artista; — **piano** piano mecánico, pianola; **piano** — pianista; **violin** — violinista.

play·ful [pléfəl] *adj.* juguetón, retozón; bromista.

play·ground [plégraʊnd] *s.* campo o patio de recreo.

play·mate [plémet] *s.* compañero de juego.

play·thing [pléθɪŋ] *s.* juguete.

play·wright [pléraɪt] *s.* dramático, dramaturgo.

plea [pli] *s.* suplica; ruego; alegato, defensa; pretexto; **on the** — **that** con el pretexto de que.

plead [plid] *v.* abogar; suplicar; argüir; alegar; defender (*una causa*); **to** — **guilty** declararse o confesarse culpable.

pleas·ant [plɛ́zn̩t] *adj.* grato; agradable; simpático.

pleas·ant·ry [plɛ́zn̩trɪ] *s.* chanza, broma, chiste, humorado.

please [pliz] *v.* agradar, gustar, dar gusto a; complacer; — **do it** haga Vd. el favor de hacerlo, tenga Vd. la bondad de hacerlo, sírvase hacerlo; **as you** — como Vd. quiera, como Vd. guste; **if you** — si me hace Vd. (el) favor; **to be -ed to** complacerse en, tener gusto en; alegrarse de; **to be -ed with** gustarle a uno, estar satisfecho de (*o* con).

pleas·ing [plízɪŋ] *adj.* agradable.

pleas·ure [plɛ́ʒɚ] *s.* placer, gusto; deleite, alegría, gozo; — **trip** viaje de recreo; **what is your** — **?** ¿qué deseaba Vd.? ¿en qué puedo servirle?

pleat [plit] *s.* pliegue, doblez; *v.* plegar, hacer pliegues (en).

ple·be·ian [plɪbíən] *adj. & s.* plebeyo.

pledge [plɛdʒ] *s.* promesa; prenda (*garantía*); arras, compromiso, fianza; **as a** — **of** en prenda de; *v.* prometer; empeñar, dar en prenda; hacer firmar una promesa; **to — one's word** empeñar (*o* dar) su palabra; **to — to secrecy** exigir promesa de sigilo.

ple·na·ry [plɛ́nərɪ] *adj.* plenario.

plen·i·po·ten·ti·ar·y [plɛnəpətɛ́nʃərɪ] *adj. & s.* plenipotenciario.

plen·ti·ful [plɛ́ntɪfəl] *adj.* abundante, copioso.

plen·ty [plɛ́ntɪ] *s.* abundancia, copia; — **of time** bastante tiempo; **that is** — con eso basta; basta.

pleu·ri·sy [plʊ́rəsɪ] *s.* pleuresía.

pli·a·ble [pláɪəbl] *adj.* flexible; manejable, (*docile*) dócil; transigénte.

pli·ant [pláɪənt] *adj.* flexible; dócil, sumiso.

pli·ers [pláɪɚz] *s. pl.* alicates, tenazas.

plight [plaɪt] *s.* apuro, aprieto, situación difícil.

plod [plɑd] *v.* bregar, trafagar, afanarse, trabajar asiduamente.

plo·sive [plósɪv] *adj. & s.* oclusivo.

plot [plɑt] *s.* (*outline*) trama, enredo; argumento; (*conspiracy*) complot, conspiración; conjuración; (*land*) parcela (*de tierra*), solar; (*plan*) plano, diagrama; *v.* tramar, urdir; maquinar, conspirar; dibujar, hacer el plano o diagrama de; **to** — **a curve** hacer una gráfica.

plot·ter [plɑ́tɚ] *s.* conspirador; tramador; conjurado; (*computer*) impresora gráfica, trazador gráfico.

plough = **plow.**

plow [plaʊ] *s.* arado; — **share** reja de arado; *v.* arar;

surcar.
pluck [plʌk] *v.* coger; arrancar; (*pick*) desplumar (*un ave*); puntear (*las cuerdar de una guitarra*); **to — at** tirar de; **to — up** arrancar; cobrar ánimo; *s.* ánimo, valor; tirón.
pluck·y [plʌ́kɪ] *adj.* valeroso, animoso.
plug [plʌg] *s.* (*stopper*) taco, tapón; (*horse*) caballejo, penco; (*boost*) elogio incidental (*de un producto comercial o de una persona*); **— of tobacco** tableta de tabaco; **electric —** clavija de conexión; **— strip** toma de corriente múltiple; **fire —** boca de agua para incendios; **spark —** bujía; *v.* tapar; **to — along** afanarse, atarearse; **to — in** enchufar, conectar; **to — up** tapar, obstruir.
plum [plʌm] *s.* (*fruit*) ciruela; (*prize*) la cosa mejor; la mejor colocación; **— pudding** pudín inglés con pasas; **— tree** circuelo.
plum·age [plúmɪdʒ] *s.* plumaje.
plumb [plʌm] *s.* plomo, pesa de plomo; (*sounding line*) sonda; **out of —** no vertical; *adj.* vertical, a plomo, recto; **— bob** plomo, plomada; *adv.* a plomo, verticalmente; **— crazy** completamente loco; *v.* sondear; aplomar (*una pared*).
plumb·er [plʌ́mɚ] *s.* plomero.
plumb·ing [plʌ́mɪŋ] *s.* plomería; cañerías (*de un edificio*); oficio de plomero.
plume [plum] *s.* pluma; plumaje; penacho; *v.* adornar con plumas; **to — its wing** alisarse o componerse el plumaje del ala.
plump [plʌmp] *adj.* rechoncho, regordete, rollizo; *adv.* de golpe; *v.* **to — down** dejar(se) caer; desplomarse, sentarse de golpe.
plun·der [plʌ́ndɚ] *s.* pillaje, saqueo; botín; *v.* pillar; saquear.
plunge [plʌndʒ] *v.* zambullir(se), sumergir(se); hundir(se); lanzar(se), arrojar(se), precipitar(se); **to — headlong** echarse de cabeza; *s.* zambullida; salto (*de arriba abajo*).
plunk [plʌŋk] *v.* (*instrument*) puntear; (*place*) arrojar.
plu·ral [plʊ́rəl] *adj.* & *s.* plural.
plu·ral·i·ty [plʊrǽlɪtɪ] *s.* pluralidad.
plus [plʌs] *s.* más, signo más; **— quantity** cantidad positiva; **two — three** dos más tres.
plush [plʌʃ] *s.* felpa; velludo.
Plu·to [plúto] *s.* Plutón.
plu·ton·ic [plutɑ́nɪk] *adj.* plutónico.
ply [plaɪ] *v.* (*use*) manejar con tesón (*un instrumento o herramienta*); (*ask*) importunar (*con preguntas*); (*run*) hacer con regularidad un recorrido (*entre dos puntos*); **to — a trade** seguir o ejercer un oficio; **to — oneself with** saturarse de, rellenarse de; *s.* doblez, pliegue; capa (*de tejido, goma, etc.*); **three-ply** *Méx.* triplay.
pneu·mat·ic [njumǽtik] *adj.* neumático.
pneu·mo·nia [njumónjə] *s.* pulmonía.
poach [potʃ] *v.* (*eggs*) escalfar (*huevos*); (*invade*) invadir (*un vedado*); cazar o pescar en vedado; (*rob*) robar caza o pesca (*de un vedado*).
pock·et [pɑ́kɪt] *s.* bolsillo, faltriquera, *C.A.* bolsa; tronera (*de billar*); cavidad; hoyo; *v.* embolsarse; apropiarse; ocultar (*el orgullo o rencor*); aguantar (*un insulto*).
pock·et·book [pɑ́kɪtbʊk] *s.* cartera; portamonedas; **woman's —** bolsa.
pock·et·knife [pɑ́kɪtnaɪf] *s.* navaja; cortaplumas.
pod [pɑd] *s.* vaina (*de guisante, frijol, etc.*).
po·di·um [pódɪəm] *s.* podio.
po·em [póɪm] *s.* poema, poesía.
po·et [póɪt] *s.* poeta; vate.
po·et·ess [póɪtɪs] *s.* poetisa.
po·et·ic [poétɪk] *adj.* poético; **-s** *s.* arte poética, poética.
po·et·i·cal [poétɪkl] *adj.* poético.
po·et·ry [póɪtrɪ] *s.* poesía.
poign·ant [pɔ́ɪnjənt] *adj.* intenso; (*spicy*) picante.
point [pɔɪnt] *s.* (*place*) punto; punta (*de lápiz, espada, tierra, etc.*); **it is not to the —** no viene al caso; **not to see the —** no caer en la cuenta; no ver el chiste, propósito o intención; **on the — of** a punto de; *v.* apuntar; señalar; indicar; **to — out** señalar, mostrar, indicar.
point·blank [pɔɪntblǽŋk] *adj.* a quema ropa.
point·ed [pɔ́ɪntɪd] *adj.* puntiagudo, agudo; satírico; apto; a propósito, al caso; **— arch** arco apuntado, arco ojival.
point·er [pɔ́ɪntɚ] *s.* (*indicator*) puntero; indicador, señalador; (*dog*) perro de punta y vuelta; (*advice*) indicación, consejo.
poise [pɔɪz] *s.* equilibrio; porte, compostura; *v.* equilibrar(se); balancear(se).
poi·son [pɔ́ɪzn̩] *s.* veneno; ponzoña; *v.* envenenar, emponzoñar.
poi·son·ous [pɔ́ɪzn̩əs] *adj.* venenoso, ponzoñoso.
poke [pok] *v.* atizar, remover (*el fuego*); picar (*con el dedo o cualquíer objeto puntiagudo*); **to — along** andar perezosamente; **to — around** husmear, curiosear; **to — fun at** burlarse de; **to — into** meter en; **to — out** sacar; poryectarse; *s.* pinchazo; piquete; codazo; aguijonada; **slow —** tardón.
po·lar [pólɚ] *adj.* polar; **— bear** oso blanco.
po·lar·i·ty [polǽrɪtɪ] *s.* polaridad.
po·lar·i·za·tion [polərɪzéʃən] *s.* polarización.
pole [pol] *s.* (*utility*) poste; (*stick*) pértiga, palo largo; (*flag*) asta (*de bandera*); garrocha; polo; **Pole** polaco; **north —** polo norte; polo ártico; **south —** polo sur, polo antártico; **— vault** salto con garrocha (pértiga).
po·lem·ics [polémɪks] *s.* polémica.
po·lice [pəlís] *s.* policía; *v.* vigilar; guardar el orden; *adj.* policíaco.
po·lice·man [pəlísmən] *s.* policía (*m.*), guardia de policía, polizonte, agente; *Ven., Col.* vigilante, *Méx.* gendarme; *Ch.* carabinero.
pol·i·cy [pɑ́ləsɪ] *s.* política; **insurance —** póliza de seguro.
Po·lish [pólɪʃ] *adj.* polaco; *s.* polaco, idioma polaco.
pol·ish [pɑ́lɪʃ] *s.* pulimento; lustre, brillo; (*cultural*) urbanidad, cultura; **shoe —** betún, bola; *v.* pulir, pulimentar; dar brillo o lustre a; embolar, dar bola o brillo a (*zapatos*); *adj.* pulidor.
po·lite [pəláɪt] *adj.* cortés, fino, urbano, político.
po·lite·ness [pəláɪtnɪs] *s.* cortesía; fineza, urbanidad.
pol·i·tic [pɑ́lətɪk] *adj.* político, prudente; conveniente.
po·lit·i·cal [pəlítɪkl] *adj.* político.
pol·i·ti·cian [pɑlətíʃən] *s.* político; (*bad*) politicastro.
pol·i·tics [pɑ́lətɪks] *s.* política.
poll [pol] *s.* (*voters*) votación; lista electoral; **-s** comicios; (*places*) urnas electorales; casilla (*donde se vota*); **— tax** impuesto (*de tanto por cabeza*); (*survey*) encuesta; *v.* registrar los votos de; votar; recibir (*votos*).
pol·len [pɑ́lən] *s.* polen.
pol·li·nate [pɑ́lənet] *v.* polinizar.
po·lo [pólo] *s.* polo.
po·lo·ni·um [pəlóniəm] *s.* polonio.
pol·y·glot [pɑ́lɪglɑt] *s.* políglota.
pome·gran·ate [pʌ́mgrænɪt] *s.* granada; **— tree** granado.
pomp [pɑmp] *s.* pompa, boato.
pom·pous [pɑ́mpəs] *adj.* pomposa, ostentoso.
pond [pɑnd] *s.* charca; estanque; **fish —** vivero.

pon·der [pándɚ] *v.* ponderar, pesar, examinar; **to — over** reflexionar.
pon·der·ous [pándəres] *adj.* ponderoso; pesado.
pon·toon [pɑntún] *s.* pontón, chata, barco chato; flotador (*de hidroavión*); — **bridge** pontón, puente flotante.
po·ny [pónɪ] *s.* caballito, potrillo; (*key*) clave o traducción (*usada ilícitamente en un examen*).
poo·dle [púdl] *s.* perro de lanas.
pool [pul] *s.* charco; charca; (*game*) trucos (*juego parecido al billar*); (*bets*) polla o puesta (*en ciertos juegos*); fondos en común, combinación de fondos (*para una empresa o para especular*); "trust"; **swimming** — piscina; *v.* formar una polla; combinar fondos.
poor [pʊr] *adj.* pobre; malo; de mala calidad; — **student** estudiante pobre; mal estudiante; — **little thing** pobrecito; **the** — los pobres; **-ly** *adv.* pobremente; mal.
poor·house [pʊ́rhaʊs] *s.* hospicio, casa de pobres.
pop [pɑp] *s.* tronido, trueno, estallido; detonación; — **of a cork** taponazo; **soda** — gaseosa; *v.* reventar, estallar; detonar; saltar (*un tapón*); **to — a question** espetar una pregunta; **to — corn** hacer palomitas de maíz, hacer rosetas de maíz; **to — in and out** entrar y salir de sopetón; **to — one's head out** sacar o asomar de repente la cabeza.
pop·corn [pápkɔrn] *s.* rosetas, palomitas de maíz, *Andes* alborotos; *Ch.* cabritas; *Méx.* esquite.
Pope [pop] *s.* Papa.
pop·eyed [pápaɪd] *adj.* de ojos saltones, *Am.* desorbitado.
pop·lar [páplɚ] *s.* álamo; **black** — chopo; — **grove** alameda.
pop·py [pápɪ] *s.* amapola.
pop·u·lace [pápjəlɪs] *s.* pueblo, populacho.
pop·u·lar [pápjəlɚ] *adj.* popular.
pop·u·lar·i·ty [pɑpjəlǽrətɪ] *s.* popularidad.
pop·u·late [pápjəlet] *v.* poblar.
pop·u·la·tion [pɑpjəléʃən] *s.* población.
pop·u·lous [pápjələs] *adj.* populoso.
por·ce·lain [pɔ́rslɪn] *s.* porcelana.
porch [pɔ́rtʃ] *s.* pórtico, porche; galería.
por·cu·pine [pɔ́rkjəpaɪn] *s.* puerco espin.
pore [pɔr] *s.* poro; *v.* **to — over a book** engolfarse en la lectura.
pork [pɔrk] *s.* puerco, carne de puerco — **chop** chulete de puerco; **salt** — tocino salado.
por·nog·ra·phy [pɔrnágrəfɪ] *s.* pornografía.
po·rous [pɔ́rəs] *adj.* poroso.
por·ridge [pɔ́rɪdʒ] *s.* potaje, gachas.
port [pɔrt] *s.* (*harbor*) puerto; (*wine*) oporto; (*left side*) babor (*de un barco*); (*computer*) canal de acceso, conector; — **hole** porta, portilla;— **of call** escala, puerto de escala; — **of entry** puerto aduanero.
port·a·ble [pɔ́rtəbl] *adj.* portátil.
por·tal [pɔ́rtl] *s.* portal.
por·tent [pɔ́tɛnt] *s.* portento, presagio, agüero.
por·ten·tous [pɔrténtəs] *adj.* portentoso; prodigioso; de mal agüero.
por·ter [pɔ́rtɚ] *s.* moso de cordel, *Méx., C.A.* cargador; *Ríopl.* changador; (*pullman*) camarero (*en un coche-cama*); portero.
port·fo·li·o [pɔrtfólɪo] *s.* portafolio, cartera; carpeta; ministerio.
por·tion [pɔ́rʃən] *s.* porción; *v.* repartir.
port·ly [pɔ́rtlɪ] *adj.* corpulento.
por·trait [pɔ́rtret] *s.* retrato.
por·tray [pɔrtré] *v.* retratar, pintar, dibujar, representar.
por·tray·al [pɔrtréəl] *s.* retrato, delineación, delineamiento, representación.
Por·tu·guese [pɔ́rtʃəgiz] *adj.* & *s.* portugués.
pose [poz] *s.* (*posture*) postura, actitud; (*affected attitude*) afectación; *v.* posar (*como modelo*); colocar(se), en cierta postura; afectar una actitud o postura; proponer, plantear (*una cuestión o problema*); **to — as** fingirse, hacerse pasar por.
po·si·tion [pəzíʃən] *s.* posición; postura; situación, empleo, puesto.
pos·i·tive [pázətɪv] *adj.* positivo; cierto, seguro; categórico; dogmático.
pos·sess [pəzɛ́s] *v.* poseer.
pos·ses·sion [pəzɛ́ʃən] *s.* posesión.
pos·ses·sive [pəzɛ́sɪv] *adj.* & *s.* posesivo.
pos·ses·sor [pəzɛ́sɚ] *s.* poseedor, posesor, dueño.
pos·si·bil·i·ty [pɑsəbílətɪ] *s.* posibilidad.
pos·si·ble [pásəbl] *adj.* posible; **possibly** *adv.* posiblemente; acaso, tal vez.
post [post] *s.* (*pole*) poste, pilar; (*position*) puesto; empleo; **army** — guarnición militar; — **haste** por la posta, rápidamente; — **office** correo, casa de correos; **post-office box** apartado, casilla postal; — **paid** porte pagado, franco de porte; *v.* fijar (*anuncios, carteles*); anunciar; (*list*) poner en lista; (*bet*) apostar, (*place*) situar; (*mail*) echar al correo; **to — an entry** asentar o hacer un asiento (*en teneduría*); **to be well -ed** estar al corriente, estar bien enterado.
post·age [póstɪdʒ] *s.* porte, franqueo; — **stamp** sello de correo, *Am.* estampilla, *Méx., Ríopl;* timbre; — **meter** franqueadora.
post·al [póstl] *adj.* postal; — **card** tarjeta postal; — **money order** giro postal.
post·card [póstkɑrd] *s.* tarjeta postal.
post·er [póstɚ] *s.* cartel, cartelón; *Arg., Col.* afiche; fijador de carteles.
pos·te·ri·or [pɑstírɪɚ] *adj.* posterior; trasero.
pos·ter·i·ty [pɑstɛ́rətɪ] *s.* posteridad.
post·hu·mous [pástʃʊməs] *adj.* póstumo.
post·man [póstmən] *s.* cartero.
post·mas·ter [póstmæstɚ] *s.* administrador de correos.
post·pone [postpón] *v.* posponer; aplazar, diferir; postergar.
post·pone·ment [postpónmənt] *s.* aplazamiento.
post·script [pósskrɪpt] *s.* posdata.
pos·ture [pástʃɚ] *s.* postura, actitud; posición; *v.* adoptar una postura.
po·sy [pózɪ] *s.* flor.
pot [pɑt] *s.* pote; olla, puchero, cacharro (*de cocina*); (*chamber*) bacín, bacinica (*de cámara o recámara*); **flower** — tiesto, maceta; — **bellied** panzudo, barrigón; — **hole** bache.
po·tas·si·um [pətǽsɪəm] *s.* potasio.
po·ta·to [pətéto] *s.* patata, papa; **sweet** — *Carib., Esp.* batata, *Méx., C.A., Ch., Andes* camote, *Carib., Ríopl.* boniato.
po·ten·cy [pótn̩sɪ] *s.* potencia, poder, fuerza.
po·tent [pótn̩t] *adj.* potente, poderoso, fuerte.
po·ten·tate [pótəntet] *s.* potentado.
po·ten·tial [pəténʃəl] *adj.* & *s.* potencial.
pot·pour·ri [popurí] *s.* popurrí.
pot·tage [pátɪdʒ] *s.* potaje.
pot·ter [pátɚ] *s.* alfarero, fabricante de loza o cacharros de barro; **-'s field** cementerio de pobres y desconocidos.
pot·ter·y [pátərɪ] *s.* cerámica, alfarería; loza; vasijas de barro.
pouch [paʊtʃ] *s.* bolsa, saquillo; **mail** — valija; **tobacco** — tabaquera, petaca.

poul·tice [póltɪs] *s.* emplasto.
poul·try [póltrɪ] *s.* aves de corral.
pounce [paʊns] *s.* salto (*para agarrar*); zarpada; *v.* **to — into** entrar de sopetón; **to — upon** abalanzarse sobre, saltar sobre, agarrar.
pound [paʊnd] *s.* libra; golpazo; — **sterling** libra esterlina; *v.* golpear; machacar, martillar.
pour [por] *v.* vaciar, verter; (*serve*) servir (*una taza*); (*flow*) fluir; (*rain*) llover a cántaros, llover recio.
pout [paʊt] *v.* hacer pucheros, lloriquear; poner cara de enfado; *s.* puchero, pucherito.
pov·er·ty [pávɚtɪ] *s.* pobreza.
pow·der [páʊdɚ] *s.* polvo; pólvora (*explosivo*); polvos (*de tocador*); — **compact** polvera; — **magazine** polvorín; — **puff** polvera, borla, *Ríopl., Ch.* cisne, *Méx., Andes, Col., Ven.* mota; *v.* empolvar(se); polvorear, espolvorear; pulverizar(se); **to — one's face** empolvarse la cara, ponerse polvos.
pow·er [páʊɚ] *s.* poder; poderío; potencia; fuerza; **motive** — fuerza motriz; — **of attorney** poder; — **plant** planta de fuerza motriz; planta generadora, central eléctrica, luz y fuerza.
pow·er·ful [páʊɚfəl] *adj.* poderoso.
pow·er·less [páʊɚlɪs] *adj.* impotente.
prac·ti·ca·ble [prǽktɪkəbl] *adj.* practicable; factible, hacedero; práctico; — **road** camino transitable.
prac·ti·cal [prǽktɪkl] *adj.* práctico; — **joke** chasco, burla pesada; **-ly** *adv.* casi, virtualmente; realmente, en realidad; prácticamente.
prac·tice [prǽktɪs] *s.* práctica; (*carry on*) ejercicio (*de una profesión*); método; regla, costumbre; (*clientele*) clientela; *v.* practicar; ejercer (*una profesión*); ejercitarse.
prac·ticed [prǽktɪst] *adj.* práctico, experimentado; experto, perito.
prac·ti·tion·er [præktíʃənɚ] *s.* profesional; práctico.
prai·rie [prɛ́rɪ] *s.* pradera, llanura.
praise [prez] *s.* alabanza; elogio; encomio; *v.* alabar; elogiar; encomiar.
praise·wor·thy [prézwɝðɪ] *adj.* laudable.
prance [præns] *v.* cabriolar, hacer cabriolas.
prank [præŋk] *s.* travesura, burla; **to play -s** hacer travesuras.
prate [pret] *v.* parlotear, charlar; *s.* parloteo, charla.
prat·tle [prǽtl] *v.* parlotear, charlar; *s.* parloteo, charla.
pray [pre] *v.* (*religious*) orar, rezar; (*beg*) rogar, suplicar; — **tell me** dígame por favor, le ruego que me diga.
prayer [prɛr] *s.* oración, rezo; ruego, súplica; — **book** devocionario; **Lord's** — Padre Nuestro.
preach [pritʃ] *v.* predicar; sermonear.
preach·er [prítʃɚ] *s.* predicador.
preach·ing [prítʃɪŋ] *s.* predicación; sermón; sermoneo.
pre·am·ble [príæmbl] *s.* preámbulo.
pre·ar·ranged [priəréndʒd] *adj.* arreglado de antemano.
pre·car·i·ous [prɪkɛ́rɪəs] *adj.* precario; inseguro.
pre·cau·tion [prɪkɔ́ʃən] *s.* precaución.
pre·cede [prisíd] *v.* preceder.
pre·ce·dence [prɪsídn̩s] *s.* precedencia; prioridad.
pre·ce·dent [prɛ́sədənt] *s.* precedente.
pre·ced·ing [prisídɪŋ] *adj.* precendente, anterior.
pre·cept [prísɛpt] *s.* precepto.
pre·cinct [prísɪŋkt] *s.* distrito; recinto; **-s** límites, inmediaciones.
pre·cious [prɛ́ʃəs] *adj.* precioso; querido, amado, caro; — **little** poquísimo, muy poco.
prec·i·pice [prɛ́səpɪs] *s.* precipicio.
pre·cip·i·tate [prɪsípətet] *v.* precipitar(se); *adj.* precipitado, apresurado, atropellado; *s.* precipitado.
pre·cip·i·ta·tion [prɪsɪpətéʃən] *s.* precipitación; lluvia (*o* nieve, rocío, granizo, *etc.*); cantidad de agua pluvial.
pre·cip·i·tous [prɪsípətəs] *adj.* precipitoso, excarpado; precipitado.
pre·cise [prɪsáɪs] *adj.* preciso, exacto.
pre·ci·sion [prɪsíʒən] *s.* precisión, exactitud.
pre·clude [prɪklúd] *v.* excluir; impedir.
pre·co·cious [prɪkóʃəs] *adj.* precoz.
pre·cur·sor [prikɝsɚ] *s.* precursor.
pred·e·ces·sor [prɛdɪsɛ́sɚ] *s.* predecesor.
pre·des·tine [prɪdɛ́stɪn] *v.* predestinar.
pre·dic·a·ment [prɪdíkəmənt] *s.* aprieto, apuro, dificultad.
pred·i·cate [prɛ́dɪkɪt] *adj.* & *s.* predicado.
pre·dict [prɪdíkt] *v.* predicir, vaticinar.
pre·dic·tion [prɪdíkʃən] *s.* predicción, pronóstico, vaticinio.
pre·di·lec·tion [pridlɛ́kʃən] *s.* predilección, preferencia.
pre·dis·pose [pridɪspóz] *v.* predisponer.
pre·dom·i·nance [prɪdámənəns] *s.* predominio; ascendiente.
pre·dom·i·nant [prɪdámənənt] *adj.* predominante.
pre·dom·i·nate [prɪdámənet] *v.* predominar.
pref·ace [prɛ́fɪs] *s.* prefacio; prólogo; *v.* prologar.
pre·fect [prífɛkt] *s.* prefecto.
pre·fer [prɪfɝ́] *v.* preferir; **to — a claim** presentar una demanda.
pref·er·a·ble [prɛ́frəbl] *adj.* preferible; preferente; **pref·er·a·bly** *adv.* preferiblemente; preferentemente, de preferencia.
pre·fer·ence [prɛ́frəns] *s.* preferencia.
pre·ferred [prɪfɝ́d] *p.p.* & *adj.* preferido; — **shares** acciones preferentes.
pre·fix [prífɪks] *s.* prefijo; [prifíks] *v.* prefijar, anteponer.
preg·nan·cy [prɛ́gnənsɪ] *s.* preñez, embarazo.
preg·nant [prɛ́gnənt] *adj.* (*animal*) preñado; (*person*) embarazada; encinta; (*full*) lleno, repleto; en estado delicado.
pre·hen·sile [prihɛ́nsɪl] *adj.* prensil.
pre·judge [pridʒʌ́dʒ] *v.* prejuzgar.
prej·u·dice [prɛ́dʒədɪs] *s.* (*preconception*) prejuicio, prevención; (*harm*) daño; *v.* predisponer, prevenir; perjudicar.
prel·ate [prɛ́lɪt] *s.* prelado.
pre·lim·i·nar·y [prɪlímənɛrɪ] *adj.* & *s.* preliminar.
prel·ude [prɛ́ljud] *s.* preludio; *v.* preludiar.
pre·ma·ture [primətjúr] *adj.* prematuro.
pre·med·i·tat·ed [prɪmɛ́dətetɪd] *adj.* premeditado.
pre·mier [prímɪɚ] *s.* primer ministro; *adj.* primero; principal.
prem·ise [prɛ́mɪs] *s.* premisa; **-s** terrenos; predio; local.
pre·mi·um [prímɪəm] *s.* premio; **at a** — muy escaso, muy caro; **insurance** — prima de seguro.
pre·na·tal [prinétl] *adj.* prenatal.
pre·oc·cu·py [priákjəpaɪ] *v.* preocupar; ocupar de antemano.
pre·or·bit·al [príɔ́rbɪtl] *adj.* preorbital.
pre·paid [prípéd] *adj.* pagado de antemano; **to send** — enviar porte pagado, enviar franco de porte.
prep·a·ra·tion [prɛpəréʃən] *s.* preparación; preparativo.
pre·par·a·to·ry [prɪpǽrətorɪ] *adj.* preparatorio.
pre·pare [prɪpɛ́r] *v.* preparar(se).
pre·par·ed·ness [prɪpɛ́rɪdnɪs] *s.* preparación, prevención.

pre·pon·der·ance [pripándɚrəns] *s.* preponderancia.
pre·pon·der·ant [pripándrənt] *adj.* preponderante.
prep·o·si·tion [prɛpəzíʃən] *s.* preposición.
pre·pos·sess [pripozέs] *v.* preocupar; predisponer.
pre·pos·ter·ous [prɪpástrəs] *adj.* absurdo, insensato.
pre·req·ui·site [prirέkwəzɪt] *s.* requisito previo.
pre·rog·a·tive [prɪrágətɪv] *s.* prerrogativa.
pres·age [prέsɪdʒ] *s.* presagio; [prɪsédʒ] *v.* presagiar.
pre·scribe [prɪskráɪb] *v.* prescribir; recetar.
pre·scrip·tion [prɪskrípʃən] *s.* recata; prescripción, precepto, mandato.
pres·ence [prέzn̩s] *s.* presencia; — **of mind** aplomo, serenidad.
pres·ent [prέzn̩t] *s.* (*time*) presente; (*gift*) regalo; **at** — al presente, ahora; **for the** — por ahora; *adj.* presente; corriente, actual; — **company excepted** mejorando lo presente; — **participle** gerundio; **to be** — asistir, estar presente; [prɪzέnt] *v.* presentar; regalar, obsequiar.
pres·en·ta·tion [prɛzn̩téʃən] *s.* presentación; regalo, obsequio.
pre·sen·ti·ment [prɪzέntəmənt] *s.* presentimiento; corazonada.
pres·ent·ly [prέzn̩tlɪ] *adv.* luego, pronto, dentro de poco.
pres·er·va·tion [prɛzɚvéʃən] *s.* preservación; conservación.
pre·serve [prɪzɝ́v] *v.* preservar, guardar; conservar; mantener; *s.* conserva, compota; **forest** — vedado.
pre·side [prizáɪd] *v.* presidir; **to — at (— over) a meeting** presidir una junta.
pres·i·den·cy [prέzədənsɪ] *s.* presidencia.
pres·i·dent [preέzədənt] *s.* presidente.
pres·i·den·tial [prɛzədέnʃəl] *adj.* presidencial.
press [prɛs] *v.* (*bear down*) prensar; apretar; comprimir; (*iron*) planchar (*ropa*); (*force*) forzar; apremiar; urgir; empujar; **to — forward** empujar hacia adelante; avanzar, ganar terreno; **to — one's point** porfiar; insistir en su argumento; **to — through the crowd** abrirse paso por entre la multitud; **to be hard -ed by work** estar abrumado de trabajo; **to be hard -ed for money** estar esacaso de fondos; *s.* prensa; imprenta.
press·ing [prέsɪŋ] *adj.* apremiante, urgente.
pres·sure [prέʃɚ] *s.* presión; apremio, urgencia; — **cooker** cocinilla de presión; — **gauge** manómetro.
pres·sur·ize [prέʃɚaɪz] *v.* sobrecargar.
pres·tige [prɛstíʒ] *s.* prestigio.
pre·sum·a·ble [prɪsúməbl] *adj.* presumible, probable.
pre·sume [prɪzúm] *v.* prèsumir; suponer; **to — on (upon)** abuser de; **to — to** atreverse a.
pre·sump·tion [prɪzʌ́mpʃən] *s.* presunción; pretensión; suposición.
pre·sump·tu·ous [prɪzʌ́mptʃʊəs] *adj.* presuntuoso, pretencioso, presumido.
pre·sup·pose [prisəpóz] *v.* presuponer.
pre·tend [prɪtέnd] *v.* pretender; fingir.
pre·tense [prɪtέns] *s.* pretensión; presunción; ostentación; apariencia; pretexto; **under — of** so pretexto de.
pre·ten·sion [prɪtέnʃən] *s.* pretensión; pretexto.
pre·ten·tious [pritέnʃəs] *adj.* pretencioso.
pre·text [prítɛkst] *s.* pretexto.
pret·ti·ly [prítlɪ] *adv.* lindamente; agradablemente.
pret·ti·ness [prítɪnɪs] *s.* lindeza, gracia.
pret·ty [prítɪ] *adj.* lindo, bonito, bello, *Esp.* guapo; chulo; *Méx., C.A., Col. adv.* medianamente; bastante; un poco, algo; — **well** regular, así así; bastante bien, medianamente.
pre·vail [prɪvél] *v.* prevalecer; **to — on (upon)** persuadir.
pre·vail·ing [prɪvélɪŋ] *adj.* predominante; en boga.
prev·a·lent [prέvələnt] *adj.* prevalenciante; común, corriente.
pre·vent [prɪvέnt] *v.* prevenir, evitar; impedir; estorbar.
pre·ven·tion [prɪvέnʃən] *s.* prevención; precaución.
pre·ven·tive [privέntɪv] *adj.* impeditivo.
pre·view [prívju] *s.* vista previa (*anticipada*).
pre·vi·ous [prívɪəs] *adj.* previo; **-ly** *adv.* previamente; antes; de antemano.
prey [pre] *s.* presa; victima; **birds of** — aves de rapiña; *v.* **to — on** cazar; rapiñar, pillar; robar; **it -s upon my mind** me tiene preocupado, me tiene en zozobra.
price [praɪs] *s.* precio; valor; costo (coste *o* costa); — **ceiling** máximo de precios; — **control** control de precios; — **fixing** estabilización de precios; **at any** — a toda costa, a todo trance; *v.* apreciar, valuar, fijar el precio de; averiguar el precio de.
price·less [práɪslɪs] *adj.* sin precio, inapreciable.
prick [prɪk] *v.* picar; pinchar; punzar; sentir comezón; sentir picazón; **to — up one's ears** aguzar las orejas; *s.* picadura; punzada; pinchazo; piquete; aguijón; púa.
prick·ly [príklɪ] *adj.* espinoso, lleno de espinas; lleno de púas; — **heat** picazón causada por el calor; — **pear** tuna (*de nopal*).
pride [praɪd] *s.* orgullo; soberbia; *v.* **to — oneself on (upon)** enorgullecerse de, preciarse de.
priest [prist] *s.* sacerdote.
priest·hood [prísthʊd] *s.* sacerdocio.
prim [prɪm] *adj.* remilgado; repulido; peripuesto; estirado.
pri·mar·i·ly [praɪmέrəlɪ] *adv.* primariamente, principalmente; en primer lugar.
pri·ma·ry [práɪmɛrɪ] *adj.* (*first*) primario; primero; (*basic*) fundamental; principal; — **colors** colores elementales; — **election** elección primaria; — **necessities** artículos de primera necesidad; — **school** escuela primaria.
prime [praɪm] *adj.* (*main*) principal; primario, primero; (*select*) selecto, de primera calidad; **minister** primer ministro; — **mover** alma, palanca de una empresa; — **number** número primo; *s.* flor (*de la vida o de la edad*); la flor y nata (*lo mejor*); plenitud; número primo; **to be in one's** — estar en la flor de la edad; *v.* preparar, informar, instruir de atemano; cebar (*un carburador, bomba o arma de fuego*).
prim·er [prímɚ] *s.* abecedario, cartilla de lectura; compendio.
pri·me·val [praɪmívl] *adj.* primitivo.
prim·i·tive [prímətɪv] *adj.* primitivo.
prim·ness [prímnɪs] *s.* remilgo, tiesura, demasiada formalidad, dengue, afectación.
primp [prɪmp] *v.* acicalar(se), adornar(se), arreglar(se).
prim·rose [prímroz] *s.* primula o primavera (*flor*); color amarillo pálido.
prince [prɪns] *s.* principe.
prince·ly [prínslɪ] *adj.* noble, regio, magnífico, propio de un príncipe.
prin·cess [prínsɪs] *s.* princesa.
prin·ci·pal [prínsəpl] *adj.* principal; *s.* principal, capital; principal; jefe, director.
prin·ci·ple [prínsəpl] *s.* principio; regla, ley; funadmento, basé.
print [prɪnt] *s.* (*type*) tipo, letra de molde; (*art*) lámina, grabado; estampado (*tejido estampado*); diseño (*estampado*); impresión; **in** — impreso, publicado; **out of** — agotado; *v.* imprimir;

PO

estampar; escribir en letra de molde; **-ed fabric** estampado.
print·er [príntɚ] *s.* (*person*) impresor; (*computer*) impresora; **ball** — (*computer*) impresora de bola; **barrel** — (*computer*) impresor de cilindro.
print·ing [príntɪŋ] *s.* imprenta; impresión; tipografía; — **office** imprenta; — **press** prensa.
print·out [príntawt] *s.* (*computer*) listado.
pri·or [práɪɚ] *adj.* previo, anterior, precedente; — **to** anterior a, con antelación a; *s.* prior (*de un monasterio*).
pri·or·i·ty [praɪ́ɔ́rətɪ] *s.* prioridad, precedencia, antelación.
prism [prízəm] *s.* prisma.
pris·on [prízn̩] *s.* prisión, cárcel; *v.* encarcelar.
pris·on·er [prízn̩ɚ] *s.* prisionero, preso.
pri·va·cy [práɪvəsɪ] *s.* secreto, reserva; retiro; **to have no** — carecer de sitio privado; estar a la vista del público.
pri·vate [práɪvɪt] *adj.* (*no admittance*) privado; personal; (*not public*) particular; (*confidential*) secreto; confidencial; **a** — **citizen** un particular; — **school** escuela particular; — **enterprise** empresa privada; — **sector** sector privado; *s.* soldado raso; **in** — en secreto; a solas, privadamente.
pri·va·tion [praɪvéʃən] *s.* privación.
priv·i·lege [prívlɪdʒ] *s.* privilegio.
priv·i·leged [prívlɪdʒd] *adj.* privilegiado; **to be** — **to** tener el privilegio de.
priv·y [prívɪ] *adj.* privado; enterado de; *s.* excusado exterior.
prize [praɪz] *s.* (*reward*) premio, galardón; (*booty*) presa, botín de guerra; — **fight** boxeo público, pugilato; — **fighter** boxeador, pugilista; — **medal** medalla de premio; *v.* apreciar, estimar, tener en gran estima.
prob·a·bil·i·ty [prɑbəbílətɪ] *s.* probabilidad.
prob·a·ble [prɑ́bəbl] *adj.* probable; **prob·a·bly** *adv.* probablemente.
pro·ba·tion [probéʃən] *s.* probación; noviciado; prueba; **to put a prisoner on** — poner a un prisionero en libertad bajo la vigilancia de un juez.
probe [prob] *v.* tentar, reconocer, (*go into*) sondear (*una herida*); (*examine*) escudriñar, examinar a fondo; indagar; *s.* tienta (*instrumento de cirujano*); indagación.
prob·lem [prɑ́bləm] *s.* problema.
prob·lem·at·i·cal [prabləmǽtɪkl] *adj.* problemático.
pro·ce·dure [prəsídʒɚ] *s.* procedimiento; proceder.
pro·ceed [prəsíd] *v.* proceder; proseguir; seguir adelante; **to** — **to** proceder a, comenzar a, ponerse a.
pro·ceed·ing [prəsídɪŋ] *s.* procedimiento; transacción; **-s** transacciones; actas; proceso.
pro·ceeds [prósidz] *s. pl.* producto, ganancia.
proc·ess [prɑ́sɛs] *s.* (*series*) proceso; (*method*) procedimiento, método; — **of law** procedimiento legal; **in** — **of time** con el transcurso del tiempo, con el tiempo, andando el tiempo; **in the** — **of being made** en vía de preparación; *v.* preparar mediante un procedimiento especial, someter a un procedimiento; elaborar; procesar (*ante un juez*).
pro·ces·sion [prəsɛʃən] *s.* procesión; desfile; **funeral** — cortejo fúnebre.
pro·claim [proklém] *v.* proclamar; promulgar.
proc·la·ma·tion [prɑkləméʃən] *s.* proclamación; proclama.
pro·cliv·i·ty [proklívɪtɪ] *s.* inclinación.
pro·cure [prokjʊ́] *v.* procurar, conseguir, obtener.
prod [prɑd] *v.* aguijonear; picar.
prod·i·gal [prɑ́dɪgl̩] *adj. & s.* pródigo, gastador.
pro·di·gious [prədídʒəs] *adj.* prodigioso.
prod·i·gy [prɑ́dədʒɪ] *s.* prodigio.
pro·duce [prɑ́djus] *s.* producto; (*vegetables*) productos agríeolas; hortalizas; [prədjús] *v.* producir.
pro·duc·er [prədjúsɚ] *s.* productor; **theatrical** — empresario.
prod·uct [prɑ́dəkt] *s.* producto.
pro·duc·tion [prədʌ́kʃən] *s.* producción; producto; obra, composición; representación teatral.
pro·duc·tive [prədʌ́ktɪv] *adj.* productivo.
pro·fa·na·tion [prɑfənéʃen] *s.* profanación, desacato.
pro·fane [prəfén] *adj.* profano; *v.* profanar.
pro·fess [prəfɛ́s] *v.* profesar; pretender.
pro·fes·sion [prəfɛ́ʃən] *s.* profesión.
pro·fes·sion·al [prəfɛ́ʃənl] *adj.* profesional; *s.* profesional, *Méx.* profesionista.
pro·fes·sor [prəfɛ́sɚ] *s.* profesor, catedrático.
prof·fer [prɑ́fɚ] *s.* oferta, propuesta; *v.* ofrecer, proponer.
pro·fi·cien·cy [prəfíʃənsɪ] *s.* pericia, destreza.
pro·fi·cient [prəfíʃənt] *adj.* proficiente, perito, experto.
pro·file [prófaɪl] *s.* perfil; contorno.
prof·it [prɑ́fɪt] *s.* (*gain*) ganancia; lucro; (*usefulness*) provecho, utilidad, beneficio; — **and loss** pérdidas y ganancias; **net** — ganancia neta o liquida; *v.* aprovechar; ganar, sacar provecho; **to** — **by** aprovecharse de, sacar provecho de.
prof·it·a·ble [prɑ́fɪtəbl] *adj.* provechoso; lucrativo.
prof·i·teer [prɑfətír] *s.* extorsionista, carero, explotador, logrero; *v.* extorsionar, explotar, cobrar más de lo justo.
pro·found [prəfáʊnd] *adj.* profundo.
pro·fuse [prəfjús] *adj.* profuso, abundante; pródigo.
prog·e·ny [prɑ́dʒenɪ] *s.* prole.
prog·no·sis [prɑgnósɪs] *s.* pronóstico.
pro·gram [prógræm] *s.* programa; plan.
pro·gram·mer [progrǽmɚ] *s.* (*computer*) programador.
prog·ress [prɑ́grɛs] *s.* progreso; [prəgrɛ́s] *v.* progresar.
pro·gres·sive [prəgrɛ́sɪv] *adj.* progresivo; progresista; *s.* progresista.
pro·hib·it [prohíbɪt] *v.* prohibir; vedar.
pro·hi·bi·tion [proəbíʃən] *s.* prohibición.
proj·ect [prɑ́dʒɛkt] *s.* proyecto, plan; [prədʒɛ́kt] *v.* proyectar(se); extender(se) sobresalir.
pro·jec·tile [prədʒɛ́ktl] *s.* proyectil; *adj.* arrojadizo; — **weapon** arma arrojadiza.
pro·jec·tion [prədʒɛ́kʃən] *s.* proyección; saliente, salidizo.
pro·jec·tor [prədʒɛ́ktɚ] *s.* proyector.
pro·le·tar·i·an [prolətɛ́rɪən] *adj. & s.* proletario.
pro·le·tar·i·at [prolətɛ́rɪət] *s.* proletariado.
pro·lif·ic [prolífɪk] *adj.* prolífico.
pro·logue [prólɔg] *s.* prólogo.
pro·long [prəlɔ́ŋ] *v.* prolongar.
pro·lon·ga·tion [prolɔŋgéʃən] *s.* prolongación.
prom·e·nade [prɑmənéd] *s.* paseo; baile (*usualmente* **prom**); *v.* pasearse.
prom·i·nent [prɑ́mənənt] *adj.* prominente; notable; saliente; conspicuo.
pro·mis·cu·ous [prəmískjʊəs] *adj.* promiscuo.
prom·ise [prɑ́mɪs] *s.* promesa; *v.* prometer; **Promised Land** Tierra de Promisión.
prom·is·ing [prɑ́mɪsɪŋ] *adj.* prometedor.
prom·is·so·ry [prɑ́məsorɪ] *adj.* promisorio; — **note** pagaré.
prom·on·to·ry [prɑ́məntorɪ] *s.* promontorio.
pro·mote [prəmót] *v.* (*favor*) promover; fomentar;

explotar; adelantar; (*raise*) ascender; elevar.
pro·mot·er [prəmótə˞] *s.* promotor, promovedor.
pro·mo·tion [prəmóʃən] *s.* promoción; ascenso; adelantamiento.
prompt [prɑmpt] *adj.* pronto, puntual; listo, presto; *v.* mover, incitar, inducir; apuntar (*servir de apuntador en el teatro*); soplar (*sugerir a otro lo que debe decir en una clase o junta*).
prompt·ly [prɑ́mptlɪ] *adv.* pronto, prontamente, presto; puntualmente; con prontitud, con presteza.
prompt·ness [prɑ́mptnɪs] *s.* prontitud, presteza; puntualidad.
prom·ul·gate [prəmʌ́lget] *v.* promulgar.
prone [pron] *adj.* inclinado; propenso, dispuesto; boca abajo; postrado.
prong [prɔŋ] *s.* púa, punta.
pro·noun [prónaʊn] *s.* pronombre.
pro·nounce [prənáʊns] *v.* pronunciar; declarar.
pro·nounced [prənáʊnst] *adj.* pronunciado, marcado; — **opinions** opiniones decididas.
pro·nun·ci·a·tion [prənʌnsɪéʃən] *s.* pronunciación.
proof [pruf] *s.* prueba; comprobación; *adj.* impenetrable, resistente; — **against** a prueba de; — **reader** corrector de pruebas de imprenta; — **sheet** prueba, pliego de prueba; **galley** — galerada; **bomb** — a prueba de bomba; **fire** — a prueba de incendios; **water** — impermeable.
prop [prɑp] *s.* puntal; sostén, apoyo; *v.* apuntalar, sostener.
prop·a·gan·da [prɑpəgǽndə˞] *s.* propaganda.
prop·a·gate [prɑ́pəget] *v.* propagar(se).
prop·a·ga·tion [prɑpəgéʃen] *s.* propagación; diseminación.
pro·pel [prəpɛ́l] *v.* populsar, impeler.
pro·pel·ler [prəpɛ́lə˞] *s.* hélice (*de un buque o avión*); propulsor, impulsor.
prop·er [prɑ́pə˞] *adj.* propio; conveniente, a propósito; justo; correcto; — **noun** nombre propio; **-ly** *adv.* propiamente; con propiedad, correctamente.
prop·er·ty [prɑ́pə˞tɪ] *s.* propiedad; posesión; posesiones, bienes.
proph·e·cy [prɑ́fəsɪ] *s.* profecía.
proph·e·sy [prɑ́fəsaɪ] *v.* profetizar, predecir, pronosticar, augurar.
proph·et [prɑ́fɪt] *s.* profeta.
pro·phet·ic [prəfɛ́tɪk] *adj.* profético.
pro·pi·ti·ate [propíʃiet] *v.* propiciar.
pro·pi·tious [prəpíʃəs] *adj.* propicio, favorable.
pro·por·tion [prəpórʃən] *s.* proporción; **out of** — desproporcionado; *v.* proporcionar; **well -ed** bien proporcionado.
pro·pos·al [prəpózl] *s.* propuesta; proposición; (*marriage*) declaración (*de amor*).
pro·pose [prəpóz] *v.* proponer; declararse, hacer propuesta de matrimonio; **to — to do something** proponerse hacer algo.
prop·o·si·tion [prɑpəzíʃən] *s.* proposición; propuesta; asunto.
pro·pri·e·tor [prəpráɪətə˞] *s.* propietario, dueño.
pro·pri·e·ty [prəpráɪətɪ] *s.* propiedad, corrección; decoro.
pro·pul·sion [propʌ́lʃən] *s.* propulsión.
pro·rate [prorét] *v.* prorratear, repartir proporcionalmente.
pro·sa·ic [poszéɪk] *adj.* prosaico.
prose [proz] *s.* prosa; *adj.* prosaico.
pros·e·cute [prɑ́sɪkjut] *v.* procesar, enjuciar, demandar ante un juez; (*pursue*) llevar adelante.
pros·e·cu·tion [prɑsɪkjúʃən] *s.* prosecución, seguimiento; parte acusadora (*en un pleito*).
pros·e·cu·tor [prɑ́sɪkjutə˞] *s.* fiscal; acusador.
pros·e·lyte [prɑ́səlaɪt] *s.* prosélito.
pros·pect [prɑ́spɛkt] *s.* (*hope*) perspectiva, vista; esperanza; espectativa; (*candidate*) cliente; (*chances*) probabilidad de éxito; *v.* explorar, andar en busca de.
pro·spec·tive [prəspɛ́ktɪv] *adj.* probable, posible, esperado; presunto.
pros·pec·tor [prəspɛ́ktə˞] *s.* explorador, buscador (*de minas, petróleo, etc.*).
pros·per [prɑ́spə˞] *v.* prosperar, medrar.
pros·per·i·ty [prɑspɛ́rətɪ] *s.* prosperidad.
pros·per·ous [prɑ́sprəs] *adj.* próspero.
pros·tate [prɑ́stet] *s.* próstata.
pros·ti·tute [prɑ́stətjut] *s.* ramera, prostituta; *v.* prostituir.
pros·trate [prɑ́stret] *adj.* postrado; abatido; *v.* postrar; abatir.
pro·tag·o·nist [protǽgənɪst] *s.* protagonista.
pro·tect [prətɛ́kt] *v.* proteger.
pro·tec·tion [prətɛ́kʃen] *s.* protección; amparo.
pro·tec·tive [prətɛ́ktɪv] *adj.* protector; — **tariff** tarifa proteccionista.
pro·tec·tor [prətɛ́ktə˞] *s.* protector.
pro·tec·tor·ate [prətɛ́ktrɪt] *s.* protectorado.
pro·té·gé [prótəge] *s.* protegido.
pro·tein [prótiɪn] *s.* proteína.
pro·test [prótɛst] *s.* protesta, protestación; [prətɛ́st] *v.* protestar.
prot·es·tant [prɑ́tɪstənt] *adj.* & *s.* protestante.
prot·es·ta·tion [prɑtəstéʃən] *s.* protestación, protesta.
pro·to·col [prótəkɔl] *s.* protocol.
pro·to·plasm [prótəplæzəm] *s.* protoplasma.
pro·to·type [prótotaɪp] *s.* prototipo.
pro·tract [protrǽkt] *v.* alargar, extender, prolongar.
pro·trude [protrúd] *v.* sobresalir; resaltar; proyectar(se).
pro·tu·ber·ance [protjúbərəns] *s.* protuberancia.
proud [praʊd] *adj.* orgulloso; soberbio.
prove [pruv] *v.* probar; demostrar; comprobar; resultar.
prov·erb [prɑ́vɝb] *s.* proverbio; refrán.
pro·vide [prəváɪd] *v.* proveer; abastecer; suplir; estipular; **to — for** hacer provisión para; **to — with** proveer de.
pro·vid·ed [prəváɪdɪd] *conj.* con tal (de) que, a condición (de) que; — **that** con tal (de) que.
prov·i·dence [prɑ́vədəns] *s.* providencia.
prov·i·den·tial [prɑvədɛ́nʃəl] *adv.* providencial.
pro·vid·er [prəváɪdə˞] *s.* proveedor.
prov·ince [prɑ́vɪns] *s.* provincia; jurisdicción; **it isn't within my** — no está dentro de mi jurisdicción; no es de mi incumbencia.
pro·vin·cial [prəvínʃəl] *adj.* provincial; *s.* provinciano.
pro·vi·sion [prəvíʒen] *s.* (*goods*) provision; abastecimiento; (*plan*) estipulación; **-s** provisiones; víveres; **to make the necessary -s** tomar las medidas (*o* precauciones) necesarias.
pro·vi·so [prəváɪzo] *s.* condición, estipulación.
prov·o·ca·tion [prɑvəkéʃən] *s.* provocación.
pro·voke [prəvók] *v.* provocar; irritar; enfadar.
prow [praʊ] *s.* proa.
prow·ess [práʊɪs] *s.* proeza.
prowl [praʊl] *v.* rondar en acecho; fisgonear.
prox·im·i·ty [prɑksímətɪ] *s.* proximidad.
prox·y [prɑ́ksɪ] *s.* apoderado, substituto, delegado; **by** — mediante apoderado.
prude [prud] *s.* mojigato, persona gazmoña.
pru·dence [prúdn̩s] *s.* prudencia.
pru·dent [prúdn̩t] *adj.* prudente.

prud·er·y [prúdərɪ] *s.* mojigatería, gazmoñería, remilgo.
prud·ish [prúdɪʃ] *adj.* gazmoño, remilgado.
prune [prun] *s.* ciruela; ciruela pasa; *v.* podar, recortar.
pry [praɪ] *v.* atisbar, espiar; fisgar, fisgonear; curiosear; **to — a secret out** extraer (*o* arrancar) un secreto; **to — apart** separar por fuerza; **to — into other people's affairs** entremeterse en lo ajeno; **to — open** abrir a la fuerza; **to — up** levantar con una palanca.
psalm [sɑm] *s.* salmo.
pseu·do·nym [sjúdn̩ɪm] *s.* seudónimo.
psit·ta·co·sis [sɪtəkósɪs] *s.* psitacósis.
psy·chi·a·trist [saɪkáɪətrɪst] *s.* psiquiatra, alienista.
psy·chi·a·try [saɪkáɪətrɪ] *s.* psiquiatría.
psy·cho·log·i·cal [saɪkəlɑ́dʒɪk] *adj.* psicológico.
psy·chol·o·gist [saɪkɑ́lədʒɪst] *s.* psicólogo.
psy·chol·o·gy [saɪkɑ́lədʒɪ] *s.* psicología.
psy·cho·sis [saɪkósɪs] *s.* sicosis.
pto·maine [tómen] *s.* ptomaína.
pub·lic [pʌ́blɪk] *adj.* público; **— prosecutor** fiscal; **— domain** dominio público; **— lands** territorios nacionales; **— relations** relaciones públicas; **— utilities** servicios públicos; *s.* público.
pub·li·ca·tion [pʌblɪkéʃən] *s.* publicación.
pub·lic·i·ty [pʌblísətɪ] *s.* publicidad, propaganda.
pub·lish [pʌ́blɪʃ] *v.* publicar; editar; **-ing house** editorial o editora.
pub·lish·er [pʌ́blɪʃɚ] *s.* publicador; editor.
puck·er [pʌ́kɚ] *v.* fruncir.
pud·ding [pʊ́ɪŋ] *s.* budín, pudín.
pud·dle [pʌ́dl] *s.* charco.
puff [pʌf] *s.* (*air*) resoplido; (*smoke*) bocanada (*de numo, vapor, etc.*); bullón (*de vestido*); **— of wind** ráfaga, soplo; **— paste** hojaldre; **cream —** bolo de crema; **powder —** polvera, borla, *Méx., Col., Ven., Andes,* mota; *Ríopl.* cisne; *v.* resoplar, jadear; echar bocanadas; **to — up** inflar(se); ahuecar(se); hinchar(se).
pug [pʌg] *s.* perro dogo; **— nose** nariz chata, ñata o respingada.
pull [pʊl] *v.* (*tug*) tirar de; jalar (halar); (*extract*) sacar; arrancar; (*stretch*) estirar; **to — apart** desgarrar; despedazar; descomponer; desmontar; **to — down the curtain** bajar la cortinilla; **to — oneself together** componerse, serenarse; **to — over to the right** hacarse a la derecha, desviarse hacia la derecha; **to — up** parar (*un caballo, un auto*); parar, hacer alto; **to — through** salir de un apuro; sacar (*a alguien*) de un apuro; **to — strings** buscar palanca; **to — a boner** cometer error; **the train -ed into the station** el tren llegó a la estación; **to — out** desatascar; *s.* tirón; estirón; ascenso difícil; esfuerzo (*para subir*); **to have —** tener buenas aldabas, tener influencia (palanca); enchufe.
pul·let [pʊ́lɪt] *s.* polla.
pul·ley [pʊ́lɪ] *s.* polea; garrucha.
pulp [pʌlp] *s.* pulpa.
pul·pit [pʊ́pɪt] *s.* púlpito.
pul·sate [pʌ́lset] *v.* pulsar, latir.
pulse [pʌls] *s.* pulso; pulsación.
pul·ver·ize [pʌ́lvəraɪz] *v.* pulverizar.
pum·ice [pʌ́mɪs] *s.* piedra pómez.
pump [pʌmp] *s.* bomba (*para sacar agua*); (*shoe*) zapatilla; **gasoline —** bomba de gasolina; **hand —** bomba de mano; **tire —** bomba para neumáticos; *v.* manejar la bomba, *Am.* bombear; inflar (*un neumático*); **to — someone** sacarle (*o* sonsacarle) a una persona la verdad o un secreto; **— priming** cebar la bomba.
pump·kin [pʌ́mpkɪn] *s.* calabaza.
pun [pʌn] *s.* equívoco, retruécano, juego de palabras; *v.* decir retruécanos o equívocos, jugar del vocablo.
punch [pʌntʃ] *s.* (*blow*) puñetazo, puñada; (*drink*) ponche; (*drill*) punzón, sacabocados; (*vitality*) fuerza, empuje; vitalidad; **— bowl** ponchera; *v.* dar un puñetazo, dar una puñada; punzar, horadar, perforar; **to — a hole** hacer un agujero o perforación.
punc·tu·al [pʌ́ŋktʃʊəl] *adj.* puntual.
punc·tu·al·i·ty [pʌŋktʃʊǽlətɪ] *s.* puntualidad.
punc·tu·ate [pʌ́ŋktʃʊet] *v.* puntuar.
punc·tu·a·tion [pʌŋktʃʊéʃən] *s.* puntuación.
punc·ture [pʌ́ŋktʃɚ] *v.* picar, punzar, pinchar; agujerear, perforar; **-d tire** neumático picado; *s.* picadura; pinchazo; perforación; **to have a tire —** tener un neumático picado, tener una llanta o goma picada.
pun·ish [pʌ́nɪʃ] *v.* castigar.
pun·ish·ment [pʌ́nɪʃmənt] *s.* castigo.
punt [pʌnt] *s.* puntapié, patada.
pu·ny [pjúnɪ] *adj.* endeble, débil, flaco, enfermizo; insignificante.
pup [pʌp] *s.* cachorro.
pu·pil [pjúpl] *s.* discípulo; **— of the eye** pupila, niña del ojo.
pup·pet [pʌ́pɪt] *s.* títere, muñeco, monigote; **— show** títeres.
pup·py [pʌ́pɪ] *s.* cachorrito.
pur·chase [pɝ́tʃəs] *v.* comprar; mercar; *s.* compra; merca; **to get a — upon** agarrarse fuerte a.
pur·chas·er [pɝ́tʃəsɚ] *s.* comprador, marchante.
pure [pjʊr] *adj.* puro; **-ly** *adv.* puramente; meramente.
pu·ree [pjʊré] *s.* puré.
pur·ga·tive [pɝ́gətɪv] *adj.* purgante; *s.* purga, purgante.
pur·ga·to·ry [pɝ́gətorɪ] *s.* purgatorio.
purge [pɝdʒ] *v.* purgar(se); limpiar; purificar(se); *s.* purga, purgante.
pu·ri·fy [pjʊ́rəfaɪ] *v.* purificar(se); depurar.
pur·ist [pjʊ́rɪst] *s.* purista.
pu·ri·ty [pjʊ́rətɪ] *s.* pureza.
pur·ple [pɝ́pl] *s.* púrpura; *adj.* purpúreo, morado.
pur·port [pɝ́port] *s.* significado; tenor, sustancia; [pɚpórt] *v.* pretender, aparentar.
pur·pose [pɝ́pəs] *s.* (*intention*) propósito, intención; (*goal*) fin, objeto; **for no —** sin objeto, inútilmente, en vano, para nada; **on —** adrede, de propósito; *v.* proponerse.
purr [pɝ] *s.* (*cat*) ronroneo (*del gato*); (*motor*) zumbido (*del motor*); *v.* ronronear (*el gato*).
purse [pɝs] *s.* bolsillo, portamonedas, bolsa; *v.* **to — one's lips** fruncir los labios.
pur·su·ant [pɚsúənt] *adv.* conforme; de acuerdo con.
pur·sue [pɚsú] *v.* perseguir; seguir; dedicarse a (*una carrera, un estudio*).
pur·su·er [pɚsúɚ] *s.* perseguidor.
pur·suit [pɚsút] *s.* perseguimiento; (*search*) busca; ocupación; (practice) ejercicio (*de una profesión, cargo, etc.*); **in — of** a caza de, en seguimiento de, en busca de.
pus [pʌs] *s.* pus, podre.
push [pʊʃ] *v.* (*shove*) empujar; (*promote*) fomentar, promover; (*hurry*) apresurar; **to — aside** hacer a un lado, rechazar, apartar; **to — forward** empujar, abrirse paso; avanzar; **to — through** encajar (*por un agujero o rendija*); abrirse paso a empujones; **to — a button** oprimir (apretar) un botón; *s.* empuje;

empujón, empellón; — **button** botón eléctrico.
push·cart [pÚʃkɑrt] *s.* carretilla de mano.
puss·y [pÚsɪ] *s.* minino, gatito; — **willow** especie de sauce americano.
put [pʊt] *v.* poner; colocar; **to — a question** hacer una pregunta; **to — across an idea** darse a entender bien; hacer aceptar una idea; **to — away** apartar; guardar; **to — before** poner delante, anteponer; proponer ante; **to — by money** ahorrar o guardar dinero; **to — down** apuntar, anotar; sofocar (*una revolución*); rebajar (*los precios*); **to — in words** expresar; **to — in writing** poner por escrito; **to — off** aplazar, posponer; diferir; **to — on** ponerse (*ropa*); **to — on airs** darse tono o ínfulas; **to — on weight** engordar; **to — out** apagar, extinguir; **to — someone out** echar o expulsar a alguien; molestar o incomodar a alguien; **to — to shame** avergonzar; **to — up** enlatar, envasar (*frutas, legumbres*); apostar (*dinero*); alojar(se); erigir; **to — up for sale** poner de venta; **to — up with** aguantar, tolerar; *pret. & p.p. de* **to put.**
pu·tre·fy [pjútrəfaɪ] *v.* podrir (*o* pudrir), corromper.
pu·trid [pjútrɪd] *adj.* putrefacto, podrido.
put·ter [pʌ́tɚ] *v.* trabajar sin orden ni sistema; ocuparse en cosas de poca monta; malgastar el tiempo.
put·ty [pʌ́tɪ] *s.* masilla; *v.* tapar o rellenar con masilla.
puz·zle [pʌ́zl̩] *s.* rompecabezas, acertijo; (*problem*) enigma; **crossword** — crucigrama; *v.* imbrollar, poner perplejo, confundir; **to — out** desenredar, descifrar; **to — over** ponderar; tratar de resolver o descifrar; **to be -d** estar perplejo.
pyr·a·mid [pírəmɪd] *s.* pirámide; **pyramiding** monopolio financiero piramidal.

Q:q

quack [kwæk] *s.* (*duck*) graznido (*del pato*); (*fake*) curandero, matasanos, medicastro; charlatán; *adj.* falso; *v.* graznar.
quag·mire [kwǽgmaɪr] *s.* tremedal, cenagal.
quail [kwel] *s.* codorniz.
quaint [kwent] *adj.* raro, extraño; pintoresco.
quake [kwek] *s.* temblor; terremoto; *v.* temblar.
qual·i·fi·ca·tion [kwɑləfəkéʃən] *s.* (*condition*) calificación; cualidad, calidad; (*requirement*) requisito; aptitud.
qual·i·fy [kwɑ́ləfaɪ] *v.* calificar; capacitar; **to — for a position** estar capacitado para una posición; **his studies — him for the job** sus estudios le capacitan para el puesto.
qual·i·ty [kwɑ́lətɪ] *s.* (*characteristic*) cualidad; (*importance*) calidad.
qualm [kwɑm] *s.* escrúpulo.
quan·ti·fy [kwɑ́ntɪfaɪ] *v.* cuantificar.
quan·ti·ty [kwɑ́ntətɪ] *s.* cantidad.
quar·an·tine [kwɔ́rəntin] *s.* cuarentena; *v.* poner en cuarentena, aislar.
quar·rel [kwɔ́rəl] *s.* riña, reyerta, pendencia; querella; *v.* reñir; pelear, disputar.
quar·rel·some [kwɔ́rəlsəm] *adj.* reñidor, pendenciero.
quar·ry [kwɔ́rɪ] *s.* (*stone*) cantera; (*game*) presa, caza (*animal perseguido*); *v.* explotar (*una cantera*); trabajar en una cantera.
quart [kwɔrt] *s.* cuarto de galón (*0.9463 de un litro*).
quar·ter [kwɔ́rtɚ] *s.* (*one-fourth*) cuarto, cuarta parte; (*coin*) moneda de 25 centavos; (*district*) barrio, distrito; **-s** morada, vivienda; alojamiento; **from all -s** de todas partes; **to give no — to the enemy** no dar cuartel al enemigo; *adj.* cuarto; *v.* cuartear, dividir en cuartos; descuartizar; acuartelar, acantonar, alojar (*tropas*).
quar·ter·ly [kwɔ́rtɚlɪ] *adv.* trimestralmente, por trimestres; *adj.* trimestral; *s.* publicación trimestral.
quar·tet [kwɔrtét] *s.* cuarteto.
quartz [kwɔrts] *s.* cuarzo.
qua·ver [kwévɚ] *v.* temblar; *s.* temblor; trémolo (*de la voz*).
quay [ki] *s.* muelle, embarcadero.
queen [kwin] *s.* reina.
queer [kwɪr] *adj.* raro, extraño, singular; excéntrico; **to feel** — sentirse raro, no sentirse bien; *v.* poner en ridículo, comprometer; **to — oneself with** quedar mal con, ponerse mal con.
quell [kwel] *v.* reprimir; (*put down*) sofocar (*una revuelta*); calmar.
quench [kwɛntʃ] *v.* apagar (*el fuego, la sed*); reprimir, sofocar, ahogar, templar el ardor de.
que·ry [kwírɪ] *s.* (*interrogation*) pregunta; interrogación, signo de interrogación; (*doubt*) duda; *v.* preguntar, expresar duda; marcar con signo de interrogación.
quest [kwɛst] *s.* busca; pesquisa.
ques·tion [kwɛ́stʃən] *s.* (*interrogation*) pregunta; (*issue*) cuestión; problema; duda; proposición; — **mark** signo de interrogación; **beyond** — fuera de duda; **that is out of the** — ¡imposible!; ¡ni pensar en ello!; *v.* preguntar; interrogar; dudar.
ques·tion·a·ble [kwɛ́stʃənəbl] *adj.* dudoso; discutible.
ques·tion·er [kwɛ́stʃənɚ] *s.* interrogador, preguntador.
ques·tion·ing [kwɛ́stʃənɪŋ *s.* interrogatorio; *adj.* interrogador.
ques·tion·naire [kwɛstʃənɛ́r] *s.* cuestionario, lista de preguntas, interrogatorio; encuesta.
quib·ble [kwíbl] *v.* sutilizar, valerse de argucias o sutilezas; andar en dimes y diretes; *s.* sutileza, argucia.
quick [kwɪk] *adj.* (*soon*) pronto, presto; (*smart*) listo; (*speedy*) rápido, veloz; agudo; — **temper** genio violento; — **wit** mente aguda; *adv.* rápidamente, de prisa, con prisa, pronto; *s.* carne viva; **to cut to the** — herir en lo vivo, herir en el alma.
quick·en [kwíkən] *v.* acelerar(se); avivar(se); aguzar (*la mente, el entendimiento*).
quick·ly [kwíklɪ] *adv.* pronto, presto, de prisa, aprisa, rápidamente.
quick·ness [kwíknɪs] *s.* (*speed*) rapidez; presteza, prontitud; (*alertness*) vivezal; agudeza (*de ingenio*).
quick·sand [kwíksænd] *s.* arena movediza.
quick·sil·ver [kwíksɪlvɚ] *s.* mercurio, azogue.
qui·et [kwáɪət] *adj.* quieto; (*not speaking*) callado; tranquilo; en calma; (*not moving*) reposado; *s.* quietud; sosiego, reposo; calma; silencio; *v.* aquietar; sosegar; calmar, tranquilizar; **to — down** aquietarse; calmarse; **-ly** *adv.* quietamente, con quietud; calladamente; tranquilamente.
qui·et·ness [kwáɪətnɪs] *s.* quietud; sosiego, calma.
quill [kwɪl] *s.* pluma; cañón (*de pluma de ave*); púa (*de puerco espín*).
quilt [kwɪlt] *s.* colcha; *v.* acolchar.
quince [kwɪns] *s.* membrillo.
qui·nine [kwáɪnaɪn] *s.* quinina.
quip [kwɪp] *s.* pulla, dicharacho; agudeza.
quirk [kwɚk] *s.* chifladura, extravagancia, capricho; peculiaridad mental.

quit [kwɪt] *v.* (*abandon*) dejar, abandonar; irse; (*cease*) parar, cesar; **to — doing something** dejar de hacer algo; **-s** *adj.* desquitado; **we are -s** no nos debemos nada, estamos desquitados, *Am.* estamos a mano; *pret. & p.p. de* **to quit.**
quite [kwaɪt] *adv.* bastante; del todo, enteramente; **— a person** una persona admirable; **— so** así es, en efecto; **it's — the fashion** está muy en boga.
quit·ter [kwítɚ] *s.* el que deja fácilmente lo empezado, el que se da fácilmente por vencido; evasor; desertor.
quiv·er [kwívɚ] *v.* temblar; estremecerse; *s.* temblor; estremecimiento.
quix·ot·ic [kwiksátɪk] *adj.* quijotesco.
quiz [kwɪz] *s.* examen; interrogatorio; cuestionario; *v.* examinar, interrogar, hacer preguntas.
quiz·zi·cal [kwízəkl] *adj.* curioso; burlón.
quo·ta [kwótə] *s.* cuota.
quo·ta·tion [kwotéʃen] *s.* citación, cita; (*price*) cotización (*de precios*); **— marks** comillas.
quote [kwot] *v.* citar; cotizar (*precios*); **to — from** citar a, entresacar una cita de; *s.* cita, citación; **-s** comillas; **in -s** entre comillas.
quo·tient [kwóʃənt] *s.* cociente.

R:r

rab·bi [rǽbaɪ] *s.* rabí, rabino.
rab·bit [rǽbɪt] *s.* conejo.
rab·ble [rǽbl] *s.* populacho, plebe; canalla.
rab·id [rǽbəd] *adj.* rabioso.
ra·bies [rébiz] *s.* rabia, hidrofobia.
rac·coon [rækún] *s. Méx., C.A., Andes* mapache.
race [res] *s.* (*lineage*) raza; (*competition*) corrida, carrera; contienda; **—track** (*o* **—course**) pista; **boat —** regata; *v.* correr; competir en una carrera; ir corriendo; regatear (*competir en una regata*); acelerar (*un motor*).
rac·er [résɚ] *s.* corredor; caballo de carrera; auto de carrera.
ra·cial [réʃəl] *adj.* racial.
ra·cism [résɪzm] *s.* racismo.
rack [ræk] *s.* (*framework*) percha, colgadero, clavijero; (*torture*) potro de tormento; **baggage —** red; **towel —** toallero; **to fall into — and ruin** caer en un estado de ruina total; **— and pinion** cremallera; *v.* atormentar; **to — one's brain** devanarse los sesos, quebrarse uno la cabeza.
rack·et [rǽkɪt] *s.* (*instrument*) raqueta (*de tenis*); (*noise*) boruca, estrépito, baraúnda; bullicio; trapacería.
rack·et·eer [rækɪtír] *s.* trapacista, trapacero, extorsionista; *v.* trapacear, extorsionar.
ra·dar [rédɑr] *s.* radar.
ra·di·al [rédɪəl] *adj.* radial.
ra·di·ance [rédɪəns] *s.* resplandor, brillo.
ra·di·ant [rédɪənt] *adj.* radiante; resplandeciente, brillante.
ra·di·ate [rédɪet] *v.* irradiar; radiar.
ra·di·a·tor [rédɪetɚ] *s.* radiador; calorífero.
rad·i·cal [rǽdɪkl] *adj. & s.* radical.
rad·i·cal·ism [rǽdɪkəlɪzm] *s.* extremismo.
ra·di·o [rédɪo] *s.* radio (*m. o f.*); radio-telefonía; radiotelegrafía; **— announcer** locutor; **— commentator** comentarista radial; **— commercial** propaganda comercial, anuncio; **— listener** radioescucha, radioyente; **— program** programa radiofónico; **— transmitter** emisora; **by —** por radio; *v.* radiar, emitir, transmitir, radioifundir o difundir.
ra·di·o·ac·tive [redɪoǽktɪv] *adj.* radiactivo.
ra·di·ol·o·gy [redɪáləd͡ʒɪ] *s.* radiología.
rad·ish [rǽdɪʃ] *s.* rábano.
ra·di·um [rédɪəm] *s.* radio (*elemento químico*).
ra·di·us [rédɪəs] *s.* radio (*de un círculo*).
ra·don [rédan] *s.* radón.
raf·fle [rǽfl] *s.* rifa, sorteo; tómbola; *v.* rifar, sortear.
raft [ræft] *s.* balsa; **a — of things** un montón (*o* la mar) de cosas.
raft·er [rǽftɚ] *s.* viga (*del techo*).
rag [ræg] *s.* trapo; harapo, andrajo, *Am.* hilacho; **— doll** muñeca de trapo; **to be in -s** estar hecho andrajos, *Méx.* estar hecho tiras.
rag·a·muf·fin [rǽgəmʌfɪn] *s.* pelagatos, golfo; granuja, pilluelo.
rage [red͡ʒ] *s.* rabia, furor; ira; **to be all the —** estar en boga, estar de moda; *v.* rabiar; enfurecerse; estar enfurecido; bramar; **to — with anger** bramar de ira.
rag·ged [rǽgɪd] *adj.* andrajoso, haraposo, harapiento, desharrapado, roto; **— edge** borde radio o deshilachado; **to be on the — edge** estar al borde del precipicio; estar muy nervioso.
raid [red] *s.* incursión, invasión repentina; allanamiento (*de un local*); **air —** ataque aéreo, bambardeo aéreo; *v.* hacer una incursión; invadir de repente; caer sobre; allanar (*un local*), entrar a la fuerza.
rail [rel] *s.* (*steel bar*) riel, carril; (*railroad*) ferrocarril; (*railing*) barandal, barandilla; **— fence** empalizada, estacada; **by —** por ferrocarril.
rail·ing [rélɪŋ] *s.* baranda, barandilla; pasamano (*de escalera*), balaustrada, barrera; rieles.
rail·road [rélrod] *s.* ferrocarril; *adj.* ferroviario; de ferrocarril; **— company** empresa ferroviaria; **— crossing** paso a nivel, cruce de ferrocarril; **— siding** apartadero.
rail·way [rélwe] *s.* ferrocarril; *adj.* ferroviario; de ferrocarril; **— crossing** cruce, crucero.
rai·ment [rémənt] *s.* vestidura, ropaje.
rain [ren] *s.* lluvia; **— water** agua llovediza; **— check** garantía de prórroga; *v.* llover; **— or shine** que llueva o no; llueva o truene; a todo trance.
rain·bow [rénbo] *s.* arco iris.
rain·coat [rénkot] *s.* impermeable; *Ch.* capa de agua, *Méx.* manga o capa de hule; *Ríopl.* piloto.
rain·drop [réndrɑp] *s.* gota de agua.
rain·fall [rénfɔl] *s.* lluvia, lluvias; cantidad de agua pluvial; aguacero.
rain·y [rénɪ] *adj.* lluvioso.
raise [rez] *v.* (*lift*) levantar, alzar; subir; eregir; (*cultivate*) criar; cultivar; (*collect*) reunir; reclutar; **to — a question** hacer una observación o suscitar una duda; **to — a racket** armar un alboroto; *s.* aumento de sueldo.
rai·sin [réznฺ] *s.* pasa, uva seca.
ra·jah [rád͡ʒə] *s.* rajá.
rake [rek] *s.* rastro, rastrillo, (*man*) libertino, perdulario; *v.* rastrear, rastrillar (*la tierra*); raspar; barrer (*con rastrillo*); atizar (*el fuego*).
rake-off [rékɔf] *s.* tajada de las ganancias.
ral·ly [rǽlɪ] *v.* (*unite*) reunir(se); juntar(se); (*improve*) recobrar(se); mejorar (*de salud*); fortalecerse; revivir; tomar nueva vida; **to — to the side of** acudir al lado de; *s.* junta popular, junta libre; recuperación.
ram [ræm] *s.* (*animal*) carnero; (*tool*) ariete o martillo hidráulico; espolón de buque; **battering —** ariete; **RAM (ran·dom ac·cess mem·o·ry)** memoria accesible al azar (aleatorio); *v.* apisonar, aplanar a

golpes; aplastar de un choque; rellenar atestar; **to — a boat** chocar con un barco; arremeter contra un barco.
ram·ble [rǽmbl] *v.* vagar; divagar; callejear; *s.* paseo, andanza.
ram·page [rǽmpedʒ] *s.* alboroto.
ram·pant [rǽmpənt] *adj.* extravagante; desenfrenado.
ram·part [rǽmpɑrt] *s.* baluarte, muralla.
ran [ræn] *pret. de* to run.
ranch [ræntʃ] *s.* hacienda, *Méx., C.A.* rancho; **cattle —** hacienda de ganado, *Méx., C.A.* rancho, *Ríopl.* estancia; *Ch.* fundo; *Ven., Col.* hato.
ran·cid [rǽnsɪd] *adj.* rancio, acedo.
ran·cor [rǽŋkɚ] *s.* rencor, encono.
ran·dom [rǽndəm] *adj.* impensado; aleatorio fortuito, al azar; **at —** al azar, a la ventura; **— sample** muestra aleatoria.
rang [ræŋ] *pret. de* **to ring.**
range [rendʒ] *v.* (*align*) alinear; poner en fila; arreglar; (*wander*) vagar por; rondar; fluctuar; **to — ten miles** tener un alcance de diez millas (*un arma de fuego*); *s.* (*line*) fila, hilera; alcance; extensión; (*variation*) fluctuación, variación (*dentro de ciertos* límites); distancia; (*grazing place*) pastizal, *C.A.* pastal; (*stove*) estufa; **gas —** cocina de gas; **— of mountains** cordillera, cadena de montañas; **— of vision** campo de visión; **in — with** en línea con; **shooting —** campo de práctica para tirar.
range find·er [réndʒfaɪndɚ] *s.* telemetro.
rank [ræŋk] *s.* (*position*) rango, categoría; orden; calidad; grado; (*line*) fila; línea, hilera; **the — and file** el pueblo, la gente ordinaria; la tropa; *v.* poner en fila; (*arrange*) ordenar, arreglar; (*rate*) clasificar; colocar por grados; **to — above** sobrepasar a; ser de grado superior a; **to — high** tener un alto rango, categoría o renombre; ser tenido en alta estima; **to — second** tener el segundo lugar; **to — with** estar al nivel de, tener el mismo grado que; **he -s high in athletics** sobresale en los deportes.
ran·sack [rǽnsæk] *v.* escudriñar; saquear.
ran·som [rǽnsəm] *s.* rescate; *v.* rescatar; redimir.
rant [rænt] *v.* desvariar; disparatar, gritar necedades.
rap [ræp] *v.* (*strike*) golpear, dar un golpe; (*censure*) criticar, censurar; **to — on the door** llamar o tocar a la puerta; *s.* golpe; **not to care a —** no importarle a uno un ardite.
ra·pa·cious [rəpéʃəs] *adj.* rapaz.
rape [rep] *s.* estupro, violación (*de una mujer*); *v.* forzar, violar (*a una mujer*).
rap·id [rǽpɪd] *adj.* rápido; **-s** *s. pl.* raudal, rápidos (*de un río*).
ra·pid·i·ty [rəpídətɪ] *s.* rapidez, velocidad.
rap·port [rəpɔ́r] *s.* relación de confianza mutua.
rapt [ræpt] *adj.* extasiado; absorto.
rap·ture [rǽptʃɚ] *s.* éxtasis, rapto.
rare [rɛr] *adj.* (*strange*) extraordinario, extraño; raro; (*precious*) raro; precioso; (*not well-done*) a medio asar, a medio freír, medio crudo; **-ly** *adv.* rara vez, raras veces; raramente; extraordinariamente.
rar·i·ty [rérətɪ] *s.* rareza; enrarecimiento (*de la atmósfera*).
ras·cal [rǽskl] *s.* bribón, bellaco, pícaro.
rash [ræʃ] *adj.* temerario, atrevido; (*thoughtless*) precipitado; imprudente; *s.* salpullido, erupción (*de la peil*).
rash·ness [rǽʃnɪs] *s.* temeridad.
rasp [ræsp] *v.* chirriar; irritar; *s.* chirrido, sonido áspero; ronquera, carraspera.
rasp·ber·ry [rǽzbɛrɪ] *s.* frambuesa; **— bush** frambueso.
rasp·y [rǽspɪ] *adj.* ronco; áspero.
rat [ræt] *s.* rata; postizo (*para el pelo*); (*scab*) esquirol.
rate [ret] *s.* proporción; porcentaje, tanto por ciento, *Am.* tipo (*de interés*); tarifa; precio; **— of exchange** cambio, *Am.* tipo de cambio; **— of taxation** tasa de tributación; **— of increase** incremento proporcional; **at any —** en todo caso, de todos modos; **at that —** a ese paso; en esa proporción; **at the — of** a razón de; **first —** de primera clase o calidad; muy bien; *v.* calificar, clasificar, considerar; tasar, valuar; **he -s as the best** se le considera como el mejor; **he -s high** se le tiene en alta estima; **rated capacity** capacidad nominal; **rated power** potencia nominal.
rath·er [rǽðɚ] *adv.* algo, un poco, un tanto; más bien; mejor; mejor dicho; **— than** más bien que; **I would — die than** prefiero antes la muerte que; **I would — not go** preferiría no ir.
rat·i·fy [rǽtəfaɪ] *s.* ratificar.
rat·ing [rétɪŋ] *s.* clasificación; rango, grado; clase; evaluación.
ra·tio [réʃo] *s.* razón, proporción; relación.
ra·tion [réʃən] *s.* ración; *v.* racionar.
ra·tio·nal [rǽʃənl] *adj.* racional.
ra·tion·ale [ræʃənǽl] *s.* exposición razonada, razón fundamental.
ra·tio·nal·ize [rǽʃənlaɪz] *v.* buscar excusas.
ra·tion·ing [réʃənɪŋ] *s.* racionamiento.
rat·tle [rǽtl] *v.* traquetear; golpetear; sacudir ruidosamente; confundir, desconcertar; **to — off** decir de corrido (*o* decir muy aprisa); *s.* traqueteo; golpeteo; **child's —** sonaja, sonajero; **death —** estertor de la muerte.
rat·tle·snake [rǽtlsnek] *s.* culebra de cascabel, *Ríopl., Ch.* cascabel o cascabela.
rau·cous [rɔ́kəs] *adj.* ronco; estentóreo.
rav·age [rǽvɪdʒ] *s.* estrago, ruina, destrucción, asolamiento; saqueo, pillaje; *v.* asolar, arruinar; pillar, saquear.
rave [rev] *v.* desvariar, delirar, disparatar; bramar; **to — about someone** deshacerse en elogios de alguien.
ra·ven [révən] *s.* cuervo; *adj.* negro lustroso.
rav·en·ous [rǽvənəs] *adj.* voraz; devorador; **to be —** tener un hambre canina.
ra·vine [rəvín] *s.* quebrada, hondonada, barranco (*o* barranca).
rav·ish [rǽvɪʃ] *v.* encantar; arrebatar; violar (*a una mujer*).
raw [rɔ] *adj.* (*crude*) crudo; áspero; pelado, descarnado; (*untrained*) inexperto, nuevo; **— material** materia prima; en bruto; **— recruit** recluta nuevo; **— silk** seda en rama, seda cruda; **— sugar** azúcar bruto, azúcar crudo.
raw·hide [rɔ́haɪd] *s.* cuero crudo; **— whip** rebenque.
ray [re] *s.* rayo; raya (*especie de pez*).
ray·on [réɑn] *s.* rayón, seda artificial.
raze [rez] *v.* arrasar, asolar.
ra·zor [rézɚ] *s.* navaja de afeitar; **— blade** hoja de afeitar; **safety —** navaja de seguridad.
reach [ritʃ] *v.* (*go as far as*) llegar a; alcanzar; (*touch*) tocar; (*extend*) extenderse; **to — for** tratar de coger; echar mano a; **to — into** meter la mano en; penetrar en; **to — out one's hand** alargar o tender la mano; *s.* alcance; extensión; **beyond his —** fuera de su alcance; **within his —** a su alcance.
re·act [rɪǽkt] *v.* reaccionar.
re·ac·tion [rɪǽkʃən] *s.* reacción.
re·ac·tion·ar·y [rɪǽkʃənɛrɪ] *adj. & s.* reaccionario.

read [rid] *v.* leer; indicar (*dícese de un contador, termómetro, etc.*); **to — law** estudiar derecho; **it -s thus** dice así, reza así; **it -s easily** se lee fácilmente o sin esfuerzo.
read [rɛd] *pret. & p.p. de* **to read.**
read·er [rídɚ] *s.* lector; libro de lectura.
read·i·ly [rɛ́dlɪ] *adv.* pronto, con presteza; fácilmente, sin esfuerzo.
read·i·ness [rɛ́dɪnɪs] *s.* prontitud, presteza, facilidad; buena disposición; **to be in —** estar preparado, estar listo.
read·ing [rídɪŋ] *s.* lectura; indicación (*de un barómetro, termómetro, etc.*); **— room** sala o salón de lectura.
re·ad·just [riədʒʌ́st] *v.* reajustar, ajustar de nuevo; arreglar de nuevo; readaptar.
re·ad·just·ment [riədʒʌ́stmənt] *s.* reajuste; readaptación; nuevo arreglo.
read·y [rɛ́dɪ] *adj.* listo; preparado; propenso; (*inclined*) dispuesto; **— cash** fondos disponibles; dinero a la mano.
read·y-made [rɛ́dɪméd] *adj.* hecho, ya hecho.
re·al [ríəl] *adj.* real, verdadero; **— estate** bienes raíces, bienes inmuebles; **-ly** *adv.* realmente, verdaderamente.
re·al·ism [ríəlɪzəm] *s.* realismo.
re·al·ist [ríəlɪst] *s.* realista; **-ic** *adj.* realista, vivo, natural.
re·al·i·ty [riǽlətɪ] *s.* realidad.
re·al·i·za·tion [riəlezéʃən] *s.* realización; comprensión.
re·al·ize [ríəlaɪz] *v.* (*comprehend*) darse cuenta de, hacerse cargo de; (*achieve*) realizar, efectuar; convertir en dinero.
realm [rɛlm] *s.* (*kingdom*) reino; (*domain*) dominio, región.
Re·al·tor [ríəltɚ] *s.* corredor de bienes raíces.
reap [rip] *v.* segar; (*harvest*) cosechar; (*collect*) recoger; obtener; sacar provecho.
reap·er [rípɚ] *s.* segador; segadora, máquina segadora.
re·ap·pear [riəpír] *v.* reaparecer.
rear [rɪr] *adj.* trasero, posterior; de atrás; **— admiral** contraalmirante; **— guard** retaguardia; *s.* espalda, parte de atrás; (*back*) trasero; fondo (*de una sala, salón, etc.*); (*end*) cola (*de una fila*); **in the —** detrás, atrás, a la espalda; *v.* criar, educar; encabritarse, empinarse (*el caballo*).
rea·son [rízn̩] *s.* razón; causa, motivo; **by — of a** causa de; **it stands to —** es razonable; *v.* razonar; **to — out** discurrir, razonar.
rea·son·a·ble [ríznəbl] *adj.* razonable; justo; racional; módico, moderado; **rea·son·a·bly** *adv.* razonablemente; con razón; bastante.
rea·son·ing [ríznɪŋ] *s.* razonamiento, raciocinio.
re·as·sure [riəʃúr] *v.* tranquilizar, restaurar la confianza a; asegurar de nuevo.
re·bate [ríbet] *s.* rebaja (*de precio*); reembolso, reintegro; *v.* rebajar (*precio*).
reb·el [rɛ́bl] *s. & adj.* rebelde; [rɪbɛ́l] *v.* rebelarse.
re·bel·lion [rɪbɛ́ljən] *s.* rebelión.
re·bel·lious [rɪbɛ́ljəs] *adj.* rebelde.
re·birth [ribɝ́θ] *s.* renacimiento.
re·bound [rɪbáʊnd] *v.* rebotar; repercutir; [ríbaʊnd] *s.* rebote; **on the —** de rebote.
re·buff [rɪbʌ́f] *s.* desaire; repulsa; *v.* desairar; rechazar.
re·build [ribíld] *v.* reconstruir, reedificar.
re·built [ribílt] *pret. & p.p. de* **to rebuild.**
re·buke [rɪbjúk] *s.* reprensión, reproche, reprimenda, repulsa; *v.* reprender, reprochar.
re·call [ríkɔl] *s.* llamada, aviso (*para hacer volver*); retirada (*de un diplomático*); revocación; [rɪkɔ́l] *v.* recordar; retirar; revocar.
re·ca·pit·u·late [rikəpítʃəlet] *v.* recapitular.
re·cede [rɪsíd] *v.* retroceder; retirarse.
re·ceipt [rɪsít] *s.* recibo; fórmula, receta; **-s** entradas, ingresos; **— in full** quitanza, finiquito; **on — of** al recibo de; **we are in — of your kind letter . . .** obra en nuestro poder su grata . . .; *v.* sellar (*con el recibí*), dar recibo.
re·ceive [rɪsiv] *v.* recibir.
re·ceiv·er [rɪsívɚ] *s.* receptor; recibidor, depositario, síndico; recipiente, receptáculo; **receivership** sindicatura.
re·cent [rísn̩t] *adj.* reciente; **-ly** *adv.* recientemente, *Ch., Ríopl.* recién (*como en* salió recién); **-ly married** recién casados.
re·cep·ta·cle [rɪsɛ́ptəkl] *s.* receptáculo.
re·cep·tion [rɪsɛ́pʃən] *s.* recepción; recibimiento; acogida, acogimiento.
re·cess [rɪsɛ́s] *s.* (*niche*) nicho, hueco; (*cessation*) tregua, intermisión; (*period*) hora de recreo o asueto; **in the -es of** en lo más recóndito de; *v.* suspender el trabajo; levantar (*por corto tiempo*) una sesión; hacer un hueco o nicho en (*la pared*).
re·ces·sion [risɛ́ʃən] *s.* retroceso; contracción económica.
rec·i·pe [rɛ́səpɪ] *s.* receta, fórmula.
re·cip·i·ent [rɪsípɪənt] *s.* recipiente, recibidor; *adj.* receptivo.
re·cip·ro·cal [rɪsíprəkl] *adj.* recíproco, mutuo.
re·cip·ro·cate [rɪsíprəket] *v.* corresponder.
re·cit·al [rɪsáɪtl] *s.* recitación; relación; narración; recital (*músico*).
rec·i·ta·tion [rɛsətéʃən] *s.* recitación.
re·cite [rɪsáɪt] *v.* recitar; relatar; decir o dar la lección.
reck·less [rɛ́klɪs] *adj.* temerario, atrevido, precipitado; descuidado; **— with one's money** derrochador.
reck·less·ness [rɛ́klɪsnɪs] *s.* temeridad, osadía, descuido.
reck·on [rɛ́kən] *v.* contar, computar, calcular; juzgar; suponer.
reck·on·ing [rɛ́kənɪŋ] *s.* cuenta; ajuste de cuentas; cálculo; **the day of —** el día del juicio.
re·claim [rɪklém] *v.* recobrar, aprovechar (*tierras baldías*); (*re-use*) aprovechar o utilizar (*el hule usado*); (*recall*) pedir la devolución de, tratar de recobrar.
re·cline [rɪkláɪn] *v.* reclinar(se), recostar(se).
re·cluse [rɪklús] *adj.* recluso, solitario; *s.* recluso, solitario, ermitaño.
rec·og·ni·tion [rɛkəgníʃən] *s.* reconocimiento.
rec·og·nize [rɛ́kəgnaɪz] *v.* reconocer.
re·coil [rɪkɔ́ɪl] *v.* (*firearm*) recular, *Am.* patear (*un arma de fuego*); (*move back*) retroceder, retirarse; *s.* reculada; (*rebound*) rebote.
rec·ol·lect [rɛkəlɛ́kt] *v.* recordar; [rikəlɛ́kt] recobrar, volver a cobrar; recoger, reunir.
rec·ol·lec·tion [rɛkəlɛ́kʃən] *s.* recuerdo.
rec·om·mend [rɛkəmɛ́nd] *v.* recomendar.
rec·om·men·da·tion [rɛkəmɛndéʃən] *s.* recomendación.
rec·om·pense [rɛ́kəmpɛns] *v.* recompensar; *s.* recompensa.
rec·on·cile [rɛ́kənsaɪl] *v.* reconciliar; ajustar, conciliar; **to — oneself to** resignarse a, conformarse con.
rec·on·cil·i·a·tion [rɛkənsɪliéʃən] *f.* reconciliación; ajuste, conciliación; conformidad, resignación.

re·con·noi·ter [rikənɔ́ɪtɚ] *v.* reconocer, explorar; hacer un reconocimiento o exploración.
re·con·sid·er [rikənsídɚ] *v.* reconsiderar.
re·con·struct [rikənstrʌ́kt] *v.* reconstruir, reedificar.
re·con·struc·tion [rikənstrʌ́kʃən] *s.* reconstrucción.
rec·ord [rékɚd] *s.* registro; (*copy*) copia oficial de un documento; memoria; (*vita*) historial (*de una persona*), hoja de servicios; disco (*fonográfico*); (*sports*) record (*en deportes*); — **player** tocadiscos; **to break the speed** — batir el record de velocidad; **an off-the-record remark** una observación que no ha de constar en el acta; observación hecha en confianza; *adj.* notable, extraordinario; sobresalienta; [rɪkɔ́rd] *v.* [rɪkɔ́rd] registrar; asentar, apuntar; inscribir; (*cut*) grabar en disco fonográfico.
re·cord·er [rɪkɔ́rdɚ] *s.* (*tape*) grabadora; — **of deeds** registrador de propiedad, archivero.
re·cord·ing [rɪkɔ́rdɪŋ] *s.* grabación.
re·count [ríkaʊnt] *s.* recuento, segunda cuenta; [rɪkáʊnt] *v.* contar, narrar, relatar, referir; [rikáʊnt] recontar, volver a contar.
re·course [ríkors] *s.* recurso, refugio, auxilio; **to have** — **to** recurrir a.
re·cov·er [rɪkʌ́vɚ] *v.* recobrar(se), recuperar(se); recobrar la salud; reponerse; [rikʌ́vɚ] volver a cubrir.
re·cov·er·y [rɪkʌ́vrɪ] *s.* recobro; recuperación; cobranza; reivindicación.
rec·re·a·tion [rɛkrɪéʃən] *s.* recreación, recreo.
re·crim·i·nate [rikrímənet] *v.* recriminar.
re·cruit [rɪkrút] *v.* reclutar; alistar; *s.* recluta; novato, nuevo miembro (*de una organización*).
rec·tan·gle [réktæŋgl] *s.* rectángulo.
rec·ti·fy [réktəfaɪ] *v.* rectificar.
rec·tor [rέktɚ] *s.* rector.
rec·tum [réktəm] *s.* recto.
re·cu·per·ate [rɪkjúpəret] *v.* recuperar, recobrar; recobrar la salud.
re·cur [rɪkɝ́] *v.* volver a ocurrir; repetirse; **to** — **to a matter** volver a un asunto.
red [rɛd] *adj.* rojo; colorado, encarnado; **red-hot** candente; (*angry*) enfurecido, furioso; muy caliente; — **tape** formalismo, trámites enojosos papeleo; — **wine** vino tinto; **in the** — con deficit; **to see** — enfurecerse; *s.* color rojo; rojo.
red·den [rédn̩] *v.* enrojecer(se); ruborizarse, ponerse rojo; teñir de rojo.
red·dish [rédɪʃ] *adj.* rojizo.
re·deem [rɪdím] *v.* redimir; (*rescue*) rescatar; (*buy back*) desempeñar (*una prenda*); (*fulfill*) cumplir (*una promesa*).
re·deem·er [rɪdímɚ] *s.* salvador, redentor; **the Redeemer** el Redentor.
re·demp·tion [rɪdémpʃən] *s.* redención; rescate; — **of a note** pago de una obligación.
red·ness [rédnɪs] *s.* rojez o rojura; inflamación.
re·dou·ble [ridʌ́bl] *v.* redoblar; repetir; repercutir.
re·dound [ridáʊnd] *v.* redundar.
re·dress [rídrɛs] *s.* reparación, enmienda; compensación; desagravio; [rɪdrés] *v.* enmendar, rectificar, remediar, reparar; desagraviar.
red snap·per [rɛdsnæpɚ] *s.* pargo; *Méx.* huachinango.
re·duce [rɪdjús] *v.* reducir; mermar; rebajar; adelgazar(se); subyugar.
re·duc·tion [rɪdʌ́kʃən] *s.* reducción; merma; rebaja.
re·dun·dant [ridʌ́ndənt] *adj.* redundante.
red·wood [rédwʊd] *s. Am.* secoya o secuoya (*árbol gigantesco de California*); madera roja de la secoya.
reed [rid] *s.* caña; junco, junquillo; lengüeta, (*musical instrument*) boquilla (*de ciertos instrumentos de viento*); caramillo.
reef [rif] *s.* arrecife, escollo; banco de arena (*en el mar*).
reek [rik] *v.* (*fume*) exhalar, echar (*vaho o vapor*); (*stink*) heder, oler mal; *s.* hedor, mal olor.
reel [ril] *s.* (*spool*) carrete; carretel; (*film*) cinta cinematográfica; *v.* aspar, enredar (*en carretel*); bambolearse, tambalearse; **to** — **off stories** ensartar cuento tras cuento.
re·e·lect [riəlέkt] *v.* reelegir.
re·e·lec·tion [riəlέkʃən] *s.* reelección.
re·en·ter [riέntɚ] *v.* volver a entrar.
re·es·tab·lish [riəstǽblɪʃ] *v.* restablecer.
re·fer [rɪfɝ́] *v.* referir; (*transmit*) transmitir, remitir; dejar al juicio o decisión de; referirse, aludir; acudir, recurrir (*a un tratado, diccionario, etc.*).
ref·er·ee [rɛfərí] *s.* árbitro; *v.* arbitrar.
ref·er·ence [réfrəns] *s.* (*mention*) referencia; mención, alusión; (*sponsor*) fiador, el que recomienda a otro; — **book** libro de referencia, libro de consulta; **commercial -s** fiadores, referencias comerciales; **letter of** — carta de recomendación; **with** — **to** con respecto a, respecto de, en cuanto a.
re·fill [riffl] *v.* rellenar.
re·fine [rɪfáɪn] *v.* refinar, purificar; (*polish*) pulir; perfeccionar.
re·fined [rɪfáɪnd] *adj.* refinado; pulido, fino, culto.
re·fine·ment [rɪfáɪnmənt] *s.* refinamiento, finura; buena crianza; refinación, purificación; perfeccionamiento.
re·fin·er·y [rɪfáɪnərɪ] *s.* refinería.
re·flect [rɪflékt] *v.* reflejar (*luz, calor*); reflexionar; meditar; **to** — **on one's character** desdecir del carácter de uno.
re·flec·tion [rɪflékʃən] *s.* reflexión; reflejo, imagen; tacha, discrédito; **on** — después de reflexionarlo.
re·flec·tive [rifléktɪv] *adj.* reflexivo.
re·flex [ríflɛks] *adj.* reflejo; *s.* reflejo; acción refleja.
re·flex·ive [rɪfléksɪv] *adj.* reflexivo.
re·form [rɪfɔ́rm] *v.* reformar(se); *s.* reforma.
ref·or·ma·tion [rɛfɚméʃən] *s.* reforma.
re·for·ma·to·ry [rɪfɔ́rmətorɪ] *s.* reformatorio.
re·form·er [rɪfɔ́rmɚ] *s.* reformador; reformista.
re·frac·tion [rɪfrǽkʃən] *s.* refracción.
re·frac·to·ry [rɪfrǽktərɪ] *adj.* refractario; terco, obstinado, rebelde.
re·frain [rɪfrén] *v.* refrenarse, abstenerse; *s.* estribillo.
re·fresh [rɪfréʃ] *v.* refrescar(se); renovar.
re·fresh·ing [rɪfréʃɪŋ] *adj.* refrescante; renovador, que renueva; placentero.
re·fresh·ment [rɪfréʃmənt] *s.* refresco.
re·frig·er·a·tion [rɪfrɪdʒəréʃən] *s.* refrigeración, enfriamiento.
re·frig·er·a·tor [rɪfrídʒəretɚ] *s.* nevera, *Am.* refrigerador; — **plant** frigorífico.
ref·uge [réfjudʒ] *s.* refugio, asilo, amparo.
ref·u·gee [rɛfjʊdʒí] *s.* refugiado.
re·fund [rífʌnd] *s.* reembolso, reintegro; *v.* reembolsar, restituir, reintegrar; consolidar (*una deuda*).
re·fur·bish [rɪfɝ́bɪʃ] *v.* retocar.
re·fus·al [rɪfjúzl] *s.* negativa; (*snub*) desaire; opción (*derecho de recusar un convenio provisional*).
re·fuse [rɪfjúz] *v.* rehusar; negar; desechar; rechazar; **to** — **to** rehusarse a, negarse a.
ref·use [réfjus] *s.* desechos, basura, sobras, desperdicios.
re·fute [rɪfjút] *v.* refutar.

RE

re·gain [rɪgén] *v.* recobrar; ganar de nuevo.
re·gal [rígl] *adj.* regio, real.
re·gale [rɪgél] *v.* regalar, agasajar; recrear.
re·ga·lia [rɪgélɪə] *s. pl.* galas, decoraciones, insignias.
re·gard [rɪgárd] *v.* (*look*) mirar; (*consider*) considerar; juzgar; estimar; **as -s this** tocante a esto, en cuanto a esto; por lo que toca a esto; *s.* miramiento, consideración; respeto; estima; mirada; **-s** recuerdos, memorias; **in** (*o* **with**) — **to** con respecto a, tocante a, respecto de.
re·gard·ing [rɪgárdɪŋ] *prep.* tocante a, con respecto a, respecto de, relativo a.
re·gard·less [rɪgárdlɪs]: — **of** sin hacer caso de, prescindiendo de.
re·gen·cy [rídʒənsɪ] *s.* regencia.
re·gent [rídʒənt] *s.* regente.
re·gime [rɪʒím] *s.* régimen.
reg·i·ment [rɛ́dʒəmənt] *s.* regimiento.
re·gion [rídʒən] *s.* región.
reg·is·ter [rɛ́dʒɪstɚ] *s.* (*recording*) registro; matrícula; (*entry*) archivo; lista; (*machine*) contador; indicador; (*voice*) registro; **cash** — caja registradora; *v.* registrar; matricular(se); inscribir(se); marcar, indicar; mostrar, manifestar; certificar (*una carta*).
reg·is·tered [rɛ́dʒɪstɚd] **mail** *adj.* correo certificado; *Col.* correo recomendado; — **stock** acciones nominativas.
reg·is·trar [rɛ́dʒɪstrɑr] *s.* registrador, archivero.
reg·is·tra·tion [rɛdʒɪstréʃən] *s.* registro; asiento (*en un libro*); matrícula; inscripción.
re·gret [rɪgrɛ́t] *s.* pesadumbre, dolor; sentimiento, remordimiento; **to send -s** enviar sus excusas (*al rehusar una invitación*); *v.* sentir, lamentar; arrenpentirse de.
re·gret·ful [rigrɛ́tfUl] *adj.* deplorable.
re·gret·ta·ble [rɪgrɛ́təbl] *adj.* lamentable.
reg·u·lar [rɛ́gjəlɚ] *adj.* regular; metódico, ordenado; **a** — **fool** un verdadero necio, un tonto de capirote; — **price** precio corriente; — **soldier** soldado de línea.
reg·u·lar·i·ty [rɛgjəlǽrətɪ] *s.* regularidad.
reg·u·late [rɛ́gjəlet] *v.* regular, regularizar.
reg·u·la·tion [rɛgjəléʃən] *s.* regulación; regla, orden; **-s** reglamento; — **uniform** uniforme de regla, uniforme de ordenanza.
reg·u·la·tor [rɛ́gjəletɚ] *s.* regulador; registro (*de reloj*).
re·ha·bil·i·tate [rihæbflətet] *v.* rehabilitar.
re·hears·al [rɪhɝ́sl] *s.* ensayo (*de un drama; concierto, etc.*); enumeración, repetición.
re·hearse [rɪhɝ́s] *v.* ensayar; repetir, repasar.
reign [ren] *s.* reino, reinado; *v.* reinar.
re·im·burse [riɪmbɝ́s] *v.* reembolsar.
re·im·burse·ment [riɪmbɝ́smənt] *s.* reembolso, reintegro.
rein [ren] *s.* rienda; *v.* guiar, gobernar; refrenar (*un caballo*).
re·in·car·nate [riɪnkárnet] *v.* reencarnar.
rein·deer [réndɪr] *s.* reno (*especie de ciervo*).
re·in·force [riɪnfórs] *v.* reforzar.
re·in·force·ment [riɪnfórsmənt] *s.* refuerzo.
re·it·er·ate [riítəret] *v.* reiterar, repetir.
re·ject [ridʒɛ́kt] *v.* rechazar; desechar; descartar; rehusar.
re·joice [rɪdʒɔ́ɪs] *v.* regocijar(se).
re·joic·ing [rɪdʒɔ́ɪsɪŋ] *s.* regocijo, júbilo.
re·join [ridʒɔ́ɪn] *v.* reunirse con; volver(se) a unir; [rɪdʒɔ́ɪn] replicar.
re·ju·ve·nate [rɪdʒúvənet] *v.* rejuvenecer.
re·lapse [rɪlǽps] *s.* recaída; *v.* recaer, reincidir.
re·late [rɪlét] *v.* relatar, narrar; relacionar; **it -s to** se relaciona con, se refiere a.
re·lat·ed [rɪlétɪd] *adj.* relatado, narrado; relacionado; **to become** — **by marriage** emparentar; **we are** — somos parientes; estamos emparentados.
re·la·tion [rɪléʃən] *s.* (*association*) relación; (*story*) narración; (*kinship*) parentesco; pariente; **-s** parientes, parentela; **with** — **to** con relación a, con respecto a, tocante a.
re·la·tion·ship [rɪléʃənʃɪp] *s.* relación; parentesco.
rel·a·tive [rɛ́lətɪv] *adj.* relativo; *s.* relativo, — **pronoun** pronombre relativo; pariente, deudo; — **to** relativo a; tocante a; referente a.
re·lax [rɪlǽks] *v.* relajar; aflojar; mitigar(se); esparcirse, recrearse.
re·lax·a·tion [rilækséʃən] *s.* (*loosening*) expansión, esparcimiento; aflojamento o relajamiento; (*recreation*) solaz, recreo; — **of discipline** relajación de la disciplina; — **of one's mind** esparcimiento del ánimo.
re·lay [ríle] *s.* relevo, remuda; — **race** carrera de relevo; **electric** — relevador; [rɪlé] *v.* transmitir, despachar; hacer cundir (*una noticia*); **to** — **a broadcast** reemitir (*o* redifundir) un programa de radio.
re·lease [rɪlís] *v.* soltar; librar; poner en libertad; (*hospital*) dar de alta; relevar, aliviar; **to** — **a piece of news** hacer pública una nueva; **to** — **from blame** exonerar; *s.* liberación; alivio; exoneración; escape; **press** — comunicado de prensa.
rel·e·gate [rɛ́ləget] *v.* relegar; **to** — **to a corner** arrinconar, arrumbar.
re·lent [rɪlɛ́nt] *v.* mitigar(se); ceder; aplacarse.
re·lent·less [rɪlɛ́ntlɪs] *adj.* implacable.
rel·e·vant [rɛ́ləvənt] *adj.* pertinente; a propósito.
re·li·a·bil·i·ty [rɪlaɪəbflətɪ] *s.* formalidad; puntualidad; integridad.
re·li·a·ble [rɪláɪəbl] *adj.* formal; puntual; digno de confianza.
re·li·ance [rɪláɪəns] *s.* confianza; **self-reliance** confianza en sí, confianza en sus propias fuerzas.
rel·ic [rɛ́lɪk] *s.* reliquia.
re·lief [rɪlíf] *s.* (*ease*) alivio; (*rest*) descanso, (*consolation*) consuelo; (*help*) ayuda, socorro; (*projection*) relieve, realce; **low** — bajo relieve; **to be on** — recibir manutención gratuita; **to put in** — realzar, poner en relieve.
re·lieve [rɪlfv] *v.* relevar; (*free*) librar; (*help*) ayudar; (*alleviate*) aliviar; mitigar.
re·li·gion [rɪlídʒən] *s.* religión.
re·li·gious [rɪlídʒəs] *adj. & s.* religioso.
re·lin·quish [rɪlíŋkwɪʃ] *v.* abandonar, dejar.
rel·ish [rɛ́lɪʃ] *s.* (*zest*) buen sabor; (*taste*) gusto; apetito; (*please*) goce; (*condiment*) condimento; entremés; *v.* saborear, paladear; gustarle a uno, agradarle a uno.
re·lo·cate [rilóket] *v.* restablecer.
re·luc·tance [rɪlʌ́ktəns] *s.* repugnancia, renuencia, aversión, desgana.
re·luc·tant [rɪlʌ́ktənt] *adj.* renuente, refractario, opuesto; **-ly** *adv.* renuentemente, con renuencia, de mala gana; a redopelo.
re·ly [rɪláɪ] *v.* **to** — **on** contar con, confiar en, fiarse de.
re·main [rɪmén] *v.* quedar(se), permanecer, estarse; restar, faltar.
re·main·der [rɪméndɚ] *s.* resto; restante; residuo.
re·mains [rɪménz] *s. pl.* restos; reliquias; sobras.
re·make [rimék] *v.* rehacer, hacer de nuevo.

re·mark [rɪmárk] *s.* observación, nota, reparo; *v.* notar, observar; **to — on** comentar; aludir a.
re·mark·a·ble [rɪmárkəbl] *adj.* notable; extraordinario; **remarkably** *adv.* notablemente; extraordinariamente.
rem·e·dy [rémədɪ] *s.* remedio; cura; *v.* remediar; curar.
re·mem·ber [rɪmémbɚ] *v.* recordar; acordarse; **— me to him** déle Vd. recuerdos (*o* memorias) de mi parte.
re·mem·brance [rɪmémbrəns] *s.* recuerdo; recordación; memoria; **-s** recuerdos, saludos.
re·mind [rɪmáɪnd] *v.* recordar.
re·mind·er [rɪmáɪndɚ] *s.* recordatorio, recordativo, memorándum, memoria; advertencia.
rem·i·nis·cence [rɛmənísn̩s] *s.* reminiscencia, memoria, recuerdo.
re·miss [rɪmís] *adj.* descuidado, negligente.
re·mis·sion [rɪmíʃən] *s.* remisión, perdón.
re·mit [rɪmít] *v.* remitir; remesar, enviar una remesa; (*pardon*) perdonar, absolver.
re·mit·tance [rɪmítns] *s.* remisión, envío, remesa (*de fondos*).
rem·nant [rémnənt] *s.* resto; residuo; retazo (*de tela, paño, etc.*); vestigio.
re·mod·el [rimádl] *v.* rehacer, reconstruir; modelar de nuevo.
re·morse [rɪmɔ́rs] *s.* remordimiento.
re·mote [rɪmót] *adj.* remoto; lejano; *s.* **— control** telecontrol; comando a distancia.
re·mov·al [rɪmúvl] *s.* mudanza, traslado; deposición (*de un empleo*); eliminación; extracción; alejamiento.
re·move [rɪmúv] *v.* remover; mudar(se), trasladar(se); quitar; eliminar; extirpar; sacar, extraer; (*fire*) deponer (*de un empleo*); apartar; alejar.
re·moved [rɪmúvd] *adj.* remoto, distante.
re·nais·sance [rɛnəsáns] *s.* renacimiento.
re·na·scence [rɪnǽsn̩s] *s.* renacimiento.
rend [rɛnd] *v.* desgarrar, rasgar; rajar.
ren·der [réndɚ] *v.* dar; entregar; (*make*) hacer; ejecutar, (*represent*) interpretar (*música o un papel dramático*); (*translate*) traducir; **to — an account of** rendir o dar cuenta de; **to — homage** rendir homenaje; **to — thanks** rendir gracias, dar las gracias; **to — useless** inutilizar, incapacitar.
ren·di·tion [rɛndíʃən] *s.* (*surrender*) rendición; (*version*) traducción, ejecución.
re·new [rɪnjú] *v.* renovar; restaurar; reanudar; prorrogar (*un préstamo*).
re·new·al [rɪnjúəl] *s.* renovación; reanudación; prórroga.
re·nounce [rɪnáʊns] *v.* renunciar.
ren·o·vate [rénəvet] *v.* renovar.
re·nown [rɪnáʊn] *s.* renombre.
re·nowned [rɪnáʊnd] *adj.* renombrado.
rent [rɛnt] *s.* alquiler; renta, arrendamiento; **it is for —** se alquila, se arrienda; *v.* alquilar, arrendar.
rent [rɛnt] *pret. & p.p. de* **to rend**; *s.* grieta, hendidura; rasgadura, rotura.
rent·al [réntl] *s.* renta, alquiler.
rent·er [réntɚ] *s.* inquilino.
re·o·pen [riópən] *v.* reabrir(se), volver a abrir(se).
re·pair [rɪpér] *v.* reparar; remendar; componer; restaurar; **to — to** dirigirse a; *s.* reparo, reparación; remiendo; compostura; **in —** en buen estado; compuesto; **— gang** cuadrilla de reparaciones.
rep·a·ra·tion [rɛpəréʃən] *s.* reparación; desagravio.
rep·ar·tee [rɛpartí] *s.* respuesta viva; agudeza en el diálogo.
re·pay [rɪpé] *v.* resarcir; compensar; reembolsar, pagar.
re·pay·ment [rɪpémənt] *s.* reintegro, pago, devolución, restitución.
re·peal [rɪpíl] *v.* derogar, abrogar, revocar, abolir (*una ley*); *s.* abrogación, derogación, revocación, abolición (*de una ley*).
re·peat [rɪpít] *v.* repetir; *s.* repetición.
re·peat·ed [rɪpítɪd] *adj.* repetido; **-ly** *adv.* repetidamente; repetidas veces, una y otra vez.
re·pel [rɪpél] *v.* repeler; rechazar; repugnar; **that idea -s me** me repugna (*o* me es repugnante) esa idea.
re·pel·lent [ripélənt] *s.* repelente; (*water*) impermeable.
re·pent [rɪpént] *v.* arrepentirse (de).
re·pen·tance [rɪpéntəns] *s.* arrepentimiento.
re·pen·tant [rɪpéntənt] *adj.* arrepentido; penitente.
rep·er·toire [répɚtwar] *s.* repertorio.
rep·e·ti·tion [rɛpɪtíʃən] *s.* repetición.
re·place [rɪplés] *v.* reponer, volver a colocar; reemplazar; restituir; remudar.
re·place·a·ble [rɪplésəbl] *adj.* reemplazable; substituible.
re·place·ment [rɪplésmənt] *s.* reposición; reemplazo; devolución, restitución; substitución.
re·plen·ish [rɪpléniʃ] *v.* reabastecer; rellenar, llenar.
re·plete [rɪplít] *adj.* repleto, atestado.
rep·li·ca [réplɪkə] *s.* reproducción, copia exacta.
re·ply [rɪplái] *v.* replicar, contestar, responder; *s.* réplica, contestación, respuesta.
re·port [rɪpórt] *v.* (*inform*) dar cuenta de; (*make known*) avisar; informar; presentar un informe; rendir informe; hacer un reportaje, *Am.* reportar; denunciar, delatar; presentarse; **to — for duty** presentarse; **it is -ed that** dizque, se dice que, corre la voz que; *s.* noticia, reporte; informe; memorial; relación; rumor; estallido, disparo; **news —** reportaje.
re·port·er [rɪpórtɚ] *s.* reportero, repórter.
re·pose [rɪpóz] *v.* reposar, decansar; **to — one's confidence in** confiar en; depositar su confianza en; *s.* reposo.
re·pos·i·to·ry [rɪpázətorɪ] *s.* depósito; almacén.
rep·re·sent [rɛprɪzént] *v.* representar.
rep·re·sen·ta·tion [rɛprɪzɛntéʃən] *s.* representación.
rep·re·sen·ta·tive [rɛprɪzéntətɪv] *adj.* representativo; representante; típico; *s.* representante; delegado, diputado.
re·press [rɪprés] *v.* reprimir; refrenar, restringir; cohibir.
re·pres·sion [rɪpréʃən] *s.* represión.
re·prieve [rɪpriv] *v.* suspensión temporal de pena; alivio.
rep·ri·mand [réprəmænd] *v.* reprender, regañar; *s.* reprimenda, reprensión, regaño.
re·pri·sal [rɪpráɪzl] *s.* represalia.
re·proach [rɪprótʃ] *v.* reprochar; censurar, criticar; echar en cara; *s.* reproche, reprimenda; censura.
re·pro·duce [riprədjús] *v.* reproducir.
re·pro·duc·tion [riprədʌ́kʃən] *s.* reproducción.
re·proof [rɪprúf] *s.* reprensión, reproche, regaño.
re·prove [rɪprúv] *v.* reprobar, reprender, censurar.
rep·tile [réptl] *s.* reptil.
re·pub·lic [rɪpʌ́blɪk] *s.* república.
re·pub·li·can [rɪpʌ́blɪkən] *adj. & s.* republicano.
re·pu·di·ate [rɪpjúdɪet] *v.* repudiar.
re·pug·nance [rɪpʌ́gnəns] *s.* repugnancia; aversión.
re·pug·nant [rɪpʌ́gnənt] *adj.* repugnante; antipático.
re·pulse [rɪpʌ́ls] *v.* repulsar, repeler; rechazar; *s.* repulsa; desaire.
re·pul·sive [rɪpʌ́lsɪv] *adj.* repulsivo, repugnante.

rep·u·ta·ble [répjətəbl] *adj.* de buena reputación.
rep·u·ta·tion [rɛpjətéʃən] *s.* reputación, renombre.
re·pute [rɪpjút] *v.* reputar; estimar, considerar; *s.* reputación; renombre, fama; **of ill** — de mala fama.
re·quest [rɪkwést] *s.* solicitud, petición, demanda; súplica, ruego; **at the** — **of** a solicitud de, a instancias de; *v.* solicitar, pedir, rogar, suplicar.
re·quire [rɪkwáɪr] *v.* requerir; exigir, demandar.
re·quire·ment [rɪkwáɪrmənt] *s.* requerimiento, requisito; exigencia; necesidad.
req·ui·site [rékwəzɪt] *s.* requisito; *adj.* requerido, necesario.
req·ui·si·tion [rɛkwəzíʃən] *s.* requisición, demanda, orden; *v.* demandar, pedir, ordenar.
re·scind [risínd] *v.* rescindir.
res·cue [réskju] *v.* rescatar; librar; salvar; *s.* rescate, salvamento, salvación, socorro; **to go to the** — **of** acudir al socorro de, ir a salvar a.
re·search [rísɝtʃ] *s.* investigación; rebusca, búsqueda, encuesta, investigación; [rɪsɝ́tʃ] *v.* rebuscar, investigar.
re·sem·blance [rɪzémbləns] *s.* semejanza, parecido.
re·sem·ble [rɪzémbl] *v.* asemejarse a, semejar, parecerse a.
re·sent [rɪzént] *v.* resentirse de, sentirse de, darse por agraviado de.
re·sent·ful [rɪzéntfəl] *adj.* resentido; rencoroso.
re·sent·ment [rɪzéntmənt] *s.* resentimiento.
res·er·va·tion [rɛzɚvéʃən] *s.* reservación; reserva.
re·serve [rɪzɝ́v] *v.* reservar; *s.* reserva.
re·served [rɪzɝ́vd] *adj.* retraido; — **word** (*computer*) palabra clave (reservada).
res·er·voir [rézɚvwɔr] *s.* (*stock*) depósito (*de agua, aceite, gas, provisiones, etc.*); (*receptacle*) receptáculo; **water** — alberca, aljibe, tanque, estanque.
re·side [rɪzáɪd] *v.* residir, vivir.
res·i·dence [rézədəns] *s.* residencia; domicilio.
res·i·dent [rézədənt] *adj.* & *s.* residente.
res·i·den·tial [rɛzɪdénʃəl] *adj.* residencial.
res·i·due [rézədju] *s.* residuo; resto.
re·sign [rɪzáɪn] *v.* renunciar; dimitir; **to** — **oneself to** resignarse a.
res·ig·na·tion [rɛzɪgnéʃən] *s.* renuncia, dimisión; resignación.
re·sil·ience [rizíljəns] *s.* elasticidad.
res·in [rézn̩] *s.* resina.
re·sist [rɪzíst] *v.* resistir; oponerse, resistirse a.
re·sis·tance [rɪzístəns] *s.* resistencia.
re·sis·tant [rɪzístənt] *adj.* resistente.
res·o·lute [rézəlut] *adj.* resuelto.
res·o·lu·tion [rɛzəlúʃən] *s.* resolución; acuerdo.
re·solve [rɪzálv] *v.* resolver(se); **to** — **into** resolverse en, reducirse a, transformarse en; **to** — **to** acordar; proponerse, resolverse a.
res·o·nance [rézənəns] *s.* resonancia.
res·o·nant [rézənənt] *adj.* resonante.
re·sort [rɪzɔ́rt] *v.* recurrir, acudir; **to** — **to force** recurrir a la fuerza; *s.* (*refuge*) refugio; (*dwelling*) morada; **as a last** — como último recurso; **summer** — lugar de veraneo; **vice** — garito; casa de mala fama; **to have** — **to** recurrir a.
re·sort·er [rɪzɔ́rtɚ] *s.* **summer** — veraneante.
re·sound [rɪzáʊnd] *v.* resonar; repercutir; retumbar.
re·source [rɪsórs] *s.* recurso; **natural -s** recursos o riquezas naturales.
re·spect [rɪspékt] *v.* respectar; **as -s** por lo que respecta a, por lo que toca a, tocante a; *s.* respeto; consideración; **with** — **to** (con) respecto a, respecto de; por lo que atañe a.
re·spect·a·ble [rɪspéktəbl] *adj.* respetable.
re·spect·ful [rɪspéktfəl] *adj.* respetuoso.
re·spect·ing [rɪspéktɪŋ] *prep.* con respecto a, tocante a.
re·spec·tive [rɪspéktɪv] *adj.* respectivo.
res·pi·ra·tion [rɛspəréʃən] *s.* respiración, respiro.
re·spite [réspɪt] *s.* tregua, pausa, descanso; intervalo; prórroga.
re·splen·dent [rɪspléndənt] *adj.* resplandeciente.
re·spond [rɪspánd] *v.* responder; corresponder; reaccionar.
re·sponse [rɪspáns] *s.* respuesta, contestación; reacción.
re·spon·si·bil·i·ty [rɪspansəbíləti] *s.* responsabilidad.
re·spon·si·ble [rɪspánsəbl] *adj.* responsable; formal, digno de confianza.
rest [rɛst] *s.* (*repose*) descanso; reposo; quietud; tregua; pausa; (*support*) apoyo; **at** — en paz; en reposo; tranquilo; **the** — el resto; los demás; *v.* descansar; reposar; apoyar; **to** — **on** descansar sobre; apoyar(se) en; basar(se) en; contar con, confiar en, depender de.
res·tau·rant [réstərənt] *s.* restaurante; *Am.* restorán.
rest·ful [réstfəl] *adj.* reposado, sosegado, tranquilo.
res·ti·tu·tion [rɛstətjúʃən] *s.* restitución; (*return*) devolución.
res·tive [réstɪv] *adj.* intranquilo.
rest·less [réstlɪs] *adj.* inquieto, intranquilo.
rest·less·ness [réstlɪsnɪs] *s.* inquietud, desasosiego, intranquilidad.
res·to·ra·tion [rɛstəréʃən] *s.* restauración; restitución; renovación.
re·store [rɪstór] *v.* restaurar; (*renew*) renovar; restituir; restablecer.
re·strain [rɪstrén] *v.* refrenar, contener, cohibir, reprimir, coartar; restringir.
re·straint [rɪstrént] *s.* restricción; reserva, circunspección; moderación; cohibición.
re·strict [rɪstríkt] *v.* restringir, limitar.
re·stric·tion [rɪstríkʃən] *s.* restricción.
re·sult [rɪzʌ́lt] *v.* resultar; **to** — **from** resultar de; **to** — **in** parar en; causar; dar por resultado; *s.* resulta, resultado; **as a** — de resultas, como resultado.
re·sume [rɪzúm] *v.* reasumir, volver a tomar; recomenzar; reanudar, continuar.
ré·su·mé [rɛzʊmé] *s.* resumen, sumario.
re·sur·gent [risɝ́dʒənt] *adj.* resurgente.
res·ur·rec·tion [rɛzərékʃən] *s.* resurrección.
re·sus·ci·tate [rɪsʌ́sətet] *v.* resucitar; revivir.
re·tail [rítel] *s.* venta al por menor; menudeo; **at** — al por menor; — **market** mercado minorista; — **shop** tienda detallista; — **trade** comercio minorista; — **merchant** detallista, comerciante al por menor; — **price** precio al por menor; *v.* detallar; vender al menudeo (vender al por menor), *Méx., C.A., Ven., Col.* menudear.
re·tail·er [rítelɚ] *s.* detallista, revendedor, comerciante al por menor.
re·tain [rɪtén] *v.* retener; emplear.
re·tal·i·ate [rɪtǽlɪet] *v.* desquitarse, vengarse.
re·tal·i·a·tion [rɪtælɪéʃən] *s.* desquite; desagravio, represalia, venganza.
re·tard [rɪtárd] *v.* retardar, retrasar, atrasar.
re·ten·tion [riténʃən] *s.* retención.
ret·i·cence [rétəsəns] *s.* reserva.
ret·i·nue [rétn̩ju] *s.* comitiva, séquito, acompañamiento.
re·tire [rɪtáɪr] *v.* retirar(se); jubilar(se); acostarse; apartarse.
re·tire·ment [rɪtáɪrmənt] *s.* retiro; (*from work*) jubilación.

re·tort [rɪtɔ́rt] *v.* replicar; redargüir; *s.* réplica.
re·touch [ritʌ́tʃ] *v.* retocar; *s.* retoque.
re·trace [rɪtrés] *v.* repasar; (*again*) volver a trazar; **to — one's steps** volver sobre sus pasos, retroceder.
re·tract [rɪtrǽkt] *v.* retractar, retractarse de; desdecirse (de); retraer.
re·treat [rɪtrít] *s.* retiro, refugio, (*place*) asilo; (*action*) retirada; (*call*) retreta (*toque de retirada*); *v.* retirarse; retroceder.
re·trench [rɪtréntʃ] *v.* cercenar, reducir, disminuir; economizar.
re·trieve [rɪtrív] *v.* cobrar (*la caza*); recobrar, recuperar; reparar (*una pérdida*).
ret·ro·ac·tive [rɛtroǽktɪv] *adj.* retroactivo.
ret·ro·flex [rétroflɛks] *adj.* retroflejo.
ret·ro·rock·et [rétrorakɪt] *s.* retrocohete.
ret·ro·spect [rétrospɛkt] *s.* retrospección; **in —** retrospectivamente.
re·turn [rɪtɝ́n] *v.* (*come back*) volver, regresar, retornar; (*give back*) devolver; replicar; redituar; (*produce*) producir; restar (*la pelota en tenis*); **to — a favor** corresponder a un favor; **to — a report** rendir un informe; *s.* vuelta, regreso; retorno; recompensa; restitución, devolución; (*reply*) réplica; **— address** señas del remitente; **— key** (*computer*) tecla de retorno; **— a verdict** fallar, dar un veredicto; resto (*en un juego de pelota*); (*production*) rendimiento; rédito, ganancia; informe; **— game** desquite, juego de desquite; **— ticket** boleto de vuelta; **by — mail** a vuelta de correo; **election -s** reportaje de elecciones; **in —** en cambio; **in — for** a cambio de, a trueque de; **income tax —** declaración de rentas; **many happy -s** muchas felicidades (en su día).
re·un·ion [rijúnjən] *s.* reunión; junta.
re·u·nite [rijunáɪt] *v.* reunir(se), volver a unirse; reconciliar(se).
re·veal [rɪvíl] *v.* revelar.
rev·el [rével] *v.* deleitarse, gozarse; (*to "party"*) parrandear, *Ríopl.* farrear; andar de parranda, andar de farra, *s.* parranda, juerga, jarana.
rev·e·la·tion [rɛvléʃən] *s.* revelación; **Revelation(s)** Apocalipsis.
rev·el·ry [révlrɪ] *s.* jaleo, juerga, jarana, parranda.
re·venge [rɪvéndʒ] *v.* vengar, vindicar; *s.* venganza; desquite.
re·venge·ful [rɪvéndʒfəl] *adj.* vengativo.
rev·e·nue [révənju] *s.* renta; rédito; rentas públicas, ingresos; **— authorities** agentes fiscales; **— stamp** sello fiscal; **— tariff** arancel de renta; *Arg.* derechos fiscales.
re·vere [rɪvír] *v.* venerar.
rev·er·ence [révrəns] *s.* reverencia; veneración; *v.* reverenciar, venerar.
rev·er·end [révrənd] *adj.* reverendo; venerable.
rev·er·ent [révrənt] *adj.* reverente.
rev·er·ie, rev·er·y [révərɪ] *s.* ensueño; arrobamiento.
re·verse [rɪvɝ́s] *adj.* inverso, invertido; (*opposite*) contrario, opuesto; *s.* revés; reverso, dorso; lo contrario; (*mishap*) contratiempo; *v.* invertir; voltear; revocar (*una sentencia*).
re·vert [rɪvɝ́t] *v.* revertir, volver atrás, retroceder.
re·view [rɪvjú] *v.* (*study*) repasar, revisar; revistar; (*inspect*) pasar revista a (*las tropas*); (*criticize*) reseñar, hacer una reseña de (*un libro*); *s.* revista; repaso; reseña, crítica (*de un libro, drama, etc.*); revisión (*de un caso jurídico, sentencia, etc.*).
re·vile [rɪváɪl] *v.* vilipendiar, vituperar, denigrar.
re·vise [rɪváɪz] *v.* revisar, repasar, releer (*para corregir*); corregir, enmendar.
re·vi·sion [rɪvíʒən] *s.* revisión; enmienda; edición enmendada o mejorada.
re·viv·al [rɪváɪvl] *s.* (*renewal*) renovación; revivificación; (*repeating*) renacimiento; (*theater*) nueva presentación (*teatral*); **— meeting** junta para revivir el fervor religioso; **religious —** despertamiento (*o* nuevo fervor) religioso.
re·vive [rɪváɪv] *v.* revivar, resucitar; (*come to*) volver en sí; renacer; reavivar, reanimar(se); (*bring around*) avivar.
re·voke [rɪvók] *v.* revocar, abrogar, anular; renunciar (*en los juegos de naipes*).
re·volt [rɪvólt] *s.* revuelta, rebelión, sublevación; *v.* rebelarse, sublevarse; **it -s me** me da asco, me repugna.
re·volt·ing [rivóltɪŋ] *adj.* repugnante; asqueroso.
rev·o·lu·tion [rɛvəlúʃən] *s.* revolución; vuelta (*que da una rueda*).
rev·o·lu·tion·ar·y [rɛvəlúʃənɛrɪ] *adj. & s.* revolucionario.
rev·o·lu·tion·ist [rɛvəlúʃənɪst] *s.* revolucionario.
re·volve [rɪválv] *v.* girar, dar vueltas; rodar; voltear, dar vueltas a; **to — in one's mind** revolver en la mente, ponderar, reflexionar.
re·volv·er [rɪválvɚ] *s.* revólver.
re·ward [rɪwɔ́rd] *v.* premiar; recompensar; *s.* premio, gratificación, recompensa, galardón; albricias (*por haber hallado algún objeto perdido*).
re·write [riráɪt] *v.* volver a escribir; refundir (*un escrito*).
rhap·so·dy [rǽpsədɪ] *s.* rapsodia.
rhe·ni·um [rinɪəm] *s.* renio.
rhet·o·ric [rétərɪk] *s.* retórica.
rheu·ma·tism [rúmətɪzəm] *s.* reumatismo, reuma.
rhi·noc·er·os [raɪnásərəs] *s.* rinoceronte.
rho·di·um [ródiəm] *s.* rodio.
rho·do·den·dron [rodədéndrən] *s.* rododendro.
rhu·barb [rúbɑrb] *s.* ruibarbo.
rhyme [raɪm] *s.* rima; **without — or reason** sin ton ni son; *v.* rimar.
rhythm [ríðəm] *s.* ritmo.
rhyth·mi·cal [ríðmɪkl] *adj.* rítmico, acompasado, cadencioso.
rib [rɪb] *s.* costilla; varilla (*de paraguas*); cordoncillo (*de ciertos tejidos*).
rib·bon [ríbən] *s.* cinta; listón, banda; moña; tira.
rice [raɪs] *s.* arroz; **— field** arrozal.
rich [rɪtʃ] *adj.* rico; costoso, suntuoso; sabroso; **— color** color vivo; **— food** alimento muy mantecoso o dulce.
rich·es [rítʃɪz] *s. pl.* riqueza, riquezas.
rick·et·y [ríkɪtɪ] *adj.* desvencijado; raquítico.
rid [rɪd] *v.* librar, desembarazar; **to get — of** librarse de, deshacerse de, desembarazarse de; *pret. & p.p. de* **to rid.**
rid·den [rídn̩] *p.p. de* **to ride.**
rid·dle [rídl] acertijo, adivinanza, enigma; *v.* acribillar, perforar; **to — with bullets** acribillar a balazos.
ride [raɪd] *v.* (*horse*) cabalgar, montar; (*vehicle*) pasear; ir en (*tranvía, tren*); **to — a bicycle** andar o montar en bicicleta; **to — a horse** montar un caballo; **to — horseback** montar a caballo; **to — over a country** pasar o viajar por un país (*en auto, a caballo o por tren*); **to — someone** dominar a alguien; burlarse de alguien; *s.* paseo (*a caballo o en automóvil*); viaje (*a caballo, en automóvil, por ferrocarril, etc.*).
rid·er [ráɪdɚ] *s.* (*horse*) jinete; (*car*) pasajero (*de automóvil*); biciclista; motociclista; aditamento, cláusula añadida (*a un proyecto de ley*); anexo.
ridge [rɪdʒ] *s.* espinazo; lomo (*entre dos surcos*);

arista, intersección (*de dos planos*); cordillera; cerro; (*building*) caballete (*de tejado*); (*cloth*) cordoncillo (*de ciertos tejidos*).
rid·i·cule [rídɪkjul] *s.* ridículo; burla, mofa; *v.* ridiculizar, poner en ridículo.
ri·dic·u·lous [rɪdíkjələs] *adj.* ridículo.
ri·fle [ráɪfl] *s.* rifle; *v.* pillar, robar; despojar.
rift [rɪft] *s.* (*opening*) raja; abertura; (*disagreement*) desacuerdo.
rig [rɪg] *v.* aparejar, equipar; enjarciar (*un barco de vela*); manipular; **to — oneself up** emperifollarse, ataviarse; *s.* aparejo, equipo; aparato; atavío, traje.
rig·ging [rigɪŋ] *s* — jarcia, aparejo.
right [raɪt] *adj.* (*not left*) derecho; diestro; (*proper*) recto; justo; propio; adecuado; correcto; **— angle** ángulo recto; **— side** lado derecho; derecho (*de un tejido, traje, etc.*); **it is — that** está bien que, es justo que; **to be —** tener razón; **to be all —** estar bien; estar bien de salud; **to be in one's — mind** estar en sus cabales; *adv.* derecho, directamente; rectamente; justamente; bien; correctamente; a la derecha; **— about-face** media vuelta; **— hungry** muy hambriento; **— now** ahora mismo, inmediatamente; **— there** allí mismo, *Am.* allí mero; **go — home!** ¡vete derechito a casa!; **it is — where you left it** está exactamente (*o* en el mero lugar) donde lo dejaste; **to hit — in the eye** dar de lleno en el ojo, *Méx.* dar en el mero ojo; *s.* derecho; autoridad; privilegio; **— of way** derecho de vía; **by — (by -s)** justamente, con justicia; según la ley; **from — to left** de derecha a izquierda; **to the —** a la derecha; **to be in the —** tener razón; *v.* enderezar; corregir.
righ·teous [ráɪtʃəs] *adj.* recto, justo, virtuoso.
righ·teous·ness [ráɪtʃəsnɪs] *s.* rectitud, virtud.
right·ful [ráɪtfəl] *adj.* justo; legítimo.
right-hand [ráɪthǽnd] *adj.* derecho, de la mano derecha; **— man** brazo derecho.
right·ist [ráɪtɪst] *s.* derechista.
right·ly [ráɪtlɪ] *adv.* con razón; justamente, rectamente; propiamente, aptamente, debidamente.
right·wing [ráɪtwɪŋ] *adj.* derechista.
rig·id [rídʒɪd] *adj.* rígido.
ri·gid·i·ty [rɪdʒídətɪ] *s.* rigidez; tiesura.
rig·or [rígɚ] *s.* rigor; rigidez; severidad.
rig·or·ous [rígɚəs] *adj.* rigoroso (*o* riguroso), severo.
rim [rɪm] *s.* borde, orilla; aro.
rime = **rhyme.**
rind [raɪnd] *s.* corteza, cáscara; mondadura.
ring [rɪŋ] *s.* (*finger*) anillo, sortija; argolla; aro; (*stadium*) arena; pista; (*sound*) toque; tañido; repique; (*telephone*) timbrazo; telefonazo; **— leader** cabecilla; **— of defiance** tono de reto; **— of shouts** gritería; **— of a telephone** llamada de teléfono; **ring-shaped** en forma de anillo, anular; **key —** llavero; **sarcastic —** retintín; *v.* tocar (*un timbre, una campanilla o campana*); sonar; tañer, repicar; resonar; zumbar (*los oidos*); **to — for something** llamar para pedir algo; **to — the nose of an animal** ponerle una argolla en la nariz a un animal; **to — up on the phone** llamar por teléfono.
ring·let [ríŋlɪt] *s.* rizo, bucle; pequeña sortija.
rink [rɪŋk] *s.* patinadero (*cancha para patinar*).
rinse [rɪns] *v.* enjuagar; lavar; aclarar (*la ropa*); *s.* enjuague.
ri·ot [ráɪət] *s.* motín, desorden, alboroto, tumulto; **— of color** riqueza o exceso de colores chillantes; *v.* amotinarse, alborotar, armar un tumulto.
ri·ot·ous [ráɪətəs] *adj.* revoltoso.
rip [rɪp] *v.* rasgar(se), romper(se); descoser(se); **to — off** rasgar, arrancar, cortar; **to — out a seam** descoser una costura; *s.* rasgón, rasgadura, rotura; descosido.
ripe [raɪp] *adj.* maduro, sazonado; en sazón; **— for** maduro para, sazonado para; bien preparado para, listo para.
rip·en [ráɪpən] *v.* madurar(se), sazonar(se).
ripe·ness [ráɪpnɪs] *s.* madurez, sazón.
rip·ple [rípl] *v.* (*curl*) rizar(se), agitar(se), ondear, temblar (*la superficie del agua*); (*sound*) murmurar (*un arroyo*); *s.* onda, temblor, ondulación (*en la superficie del agua*); murmullo (*de un arroyo*).
rise [raɪz] *v.* (*go up*) subir; ascender; (*get up*) alzarse, levantarse; elevarse; (*arise*) surgir; (*sun, moon*) salir; hincharse (*la masa del pan*); **to — up in rebellion** sublevarse, levantarse, alzarse (en rebelión); *s.* subida; ascenso; pendiente; elevación; salida (*del sol, de la luna, etc.*); subida, alza (*de precios*).
ris·en [rízn̩] *p.p. de* **to rise.**
risk [rɪsk] *s.* riesgo; *v.* arriesgar, aventurar, poner en peligro; exponerse a; **to — defeat** correr el riesgo de perder, exponerse a perder.
risk·y [rískɪ] *adj.* arriesgado, peligroso, aventurado.
ris·que [rɪské] *adj.* escabroso.
rite [raɪt] *s.* rito, ceremonia.
rit·u·al [rítʃuəl] *adj.* & *s.* ritual, ceremonial.
ritz·y [rítsɪ] *adj.* elegante.
ri·val [ráɪvl] *s.* rival, competidor, émulo; *adj.* competidor; **the — party** el partido opuesto; *v.* rivalizar con, competir con.
ri·val·ry [ráɪvlrɪ] *s.* rivalidad.
riv·er [rívɚ] *s.* río.
riv·et [rívɪt] *s.* remache; *v.* remachar; fijar.
riv·u·let [rívjəlɪt] *s.* riachuelo, arroyuelo.
road [rod] *s.* camino; carretera; vía; **— system** red vial.
road·side [ródsaɪd] *s.* borde del camino.
road·way [ródwe] *s.* camino, carretera.
roam [rom] *v.* vagar, errar, andar errante.
roar [ror] *v.* rugir, bramar; **to — with laughter** reír a carcajadas; *s.* rugido, bramido; **— of laughter** risotada, carcajada.
roast [rost] *v.* asar(se); tostar (*café, maíz, etc.*); ridiculizar, criticar; *s.* asado, carne asada; *adj.* asado; **— beef** rosbif, rosbí.
rob [rɑb] *v.* robar, hurtar; **to — someone of something** robarle algo a alguien.
rob·ber [rɑ́bɚ] *s.* ladrón; **highway —** salteador.
rob·ber·y [rɑ́brɪ] *s.* robo, hurto.
robe [rob] *s.* manto, traje talar, túnica, (*scholar*) toga (*de un juez, letrado, etc.*); (*house*) bata; **automobile —** manta de automóvil.
rob·in [rɑ́bɪn] *s.* petirrojo.
ro·bust [róbʌst] *adj.* robusto, fuerte.
rock [rɑk] *s.* roca, peña; (*crag*) peñasco; **— crystal** cristal de roca; **— salt** sal de piedra, sal gema o sal mineral; **to go on the -s** tropezar en un escollo, *Am.* escollar; *v.* (*move to and fro*) mecer(se), balancear(se); (*stagger*) bambolear(se); (*tremble*) estremecer; **to — to sleep** adormecer (*meciendo*), arrullar.
rock·er [rɑ́kɚ] *s.* mecedora; arco de una mecedora o cuna.
rock·et [rɑ́kɪt] *s.* cohete.
rock·et·ry [rɑ́kətrɪ] *s.* cohetería.
rock·ing [rɑ́kɪŋ] *s.* balanceo; *adj.* oscilante; **— chair** silla mecedora.
rock·y [rɑ́kɪ] *adj.* roqueño, rocoso, rocalloso, peñascoso; pedregoso; (*unsteady*) movedizo; tembloroso; (*weak*) débil, desvanecido.

rod [rɑd] *s.* vara, varilla; medida de longitud (*aproximadamente 5 metros*); **fishing** — caña de pescar.
rode [rod] *pret. de* **to ride.**
ro·dent [ródənt] *s.* roedor.
rogue [rog] *s.* pícaro, bribón, tunante, pillo; **-s' gallery** colección policíaca de retratos de criminales.
ro·guish [rógɪʃ] *adj.* pícaro, pillo, picaresco; travieso.
role [rol] *s.* papel, parte.
roll [rol] *v.* (*move*) rodar; (*rotate*) girar; (*sway*) balancearse (*un barco*); bambolearse; ondular, (*reverberate*) retumbar (*el trueno, un cañón*); (*level*) aplanar, alisar con rodillo; arrollar, enrollar, hacer un rollo o bola; envolver; redoblar (*un tambor*); pronunciar (*la rr doble*); **to — over in the snow** revolverse o revolcarse en la nieve; **to — up** arrollar, enrollar, envolver; **to — back** reducir, rebajar; *s.* rollo (*de papel, paño, tela, etc.*); balanceo (*de un barco*); retumbo (*del trueno, de cañon*); redoble (*de un tambor*); lista ondulación; oleaje; bollo, rosca, panecillo; **to call the** — pasar lista.
roll·er [rólɚ] *s.* rodillo, cilindro (*para aplanar o alisar*); apisonadora; oleada; — **coaster** montaña rusa; — **skate** patín de ruedas.
rolling pin [rolɪŋ pɪn] *s.* rodillo de pastelero.
ROM (**read only memory**) ficha de la computadora con informes permanentes; memoria de sólo lectura.
Ro·man [rómən] *adj.* & *s.* romano; **nose** nariz aguileña.
ro·mance [romǽns] *s.* (*literature*) romance; novela; cuento; fábula; (*affair*) aventura romántica; amorío, lance amoroso; *v.* contar o fingir fábulas; andar en amoríos o aventuras; **Ro·mance** *adj.* romance, románico, neolatino.
ro·man·tic [romǽntɪk] *adj.* romántico; novelesco.
ro·man·ti·cism [romǽntəsɪzəm] *s.* romanticismo.
ro·man·ti·cist [romǽntəsɪst] *s.* romántico, escritor romántico.
romp [rɑmp] *v.* triscar, juguetear, retozar, travesear.
roof [ruf] *s.* (*ceiling*) techo, techumbre, techado; (*outside*) tejado; — **garden** azotea-jardín; — **of the mouth** paladar; **flat** — azotea; *v.* techar.
room [rum] *s.* (*in building*) cuarto, pieza, sala, habitación; (*space*) espacio; lugar, sitio; **there is no — for more** no cabe(n) más, ho hay lugar o cabida para más; **to make** — hacer lugar; — **mate** compañero de cuarto; *v.* vivir, hospedarse, alojarse.
room·er [rúmɚ] *s.* inquilino.
room·i·ness [rúmɪnɪs] *s.* holgura.
room·y [rúmɪ] *adj.* espacioso, amplio, holgado.
roost [rust] *s.* (*house*) gallinero; (*perch*) percha de gallinero; *v.* acurrucarse (*las aves en la percha*); pasar la noche.
roost·er [rústɚ] *s.* gallo.
root [rut] *s.* raíz; *v.* arraigar(se); echar raíces; (*dig*) hocicar, hozar (*dícese de los cerdos*); **to — for** (acclaim) vitorear, aclamar; **to — out** (*o* — **up**) desarraigar, arrancar de raíz; **to become -ed** arraigarse.
rope [rop] *s.* (*cord*) soga, cuerda; (*lasso*) reata, lazo; **to be at the end of one's** — haber agotado el último recurso; estar (*o* andar) en las últimas; no saber qué hacer; **to know the -s** saber todas las tretas de un asunto o negocio; *v.* amarrar; lazar, enlazar; **to — off** acordelar, poner cuerdas tirantes alrededor de (*un sitio*); **to — someone in** embaucar a alguien.
ro·sa·ry [rózərɪ] *s.* rosario.
rose [roz] *pret. de* **to rise.**
rose [roz] *s.* rosa; color de rosa; —**bush** rosal; — **window** rosetón.
rose·bud [rózbʌd] *s.* capullo o botón de rosa, yema, pimpollo.
ros·ette [rozɛ́t] *s.* roseta; rosetón.
ros·ter [rɑ́stɚ] *s.* registro; lista.
ros·trum [rɑ́strəm] *s.* tribuna.
ros·y [rózɪ] *adj.* (*color*) rosado; color de rosa; (*condition*) alegre, risueño; — **future** porvenir risueño.
rot [rɑt] *v.* pudrir(se); corromperse; *s.* podre, podredumbre, putrefacción.
ro·ta·ry [rótərɪ] *adj.* rotatorio, giratorio, rotativo.
ro·tate [rótet] *v.* girar, dar vueltas; hacer girar; turnarse; (*crops*) cultivar en rotación.
ro·ta·tion [rotéʃən] *s.* rotación, vuelta; — **of crops** rotación de cultivos.
rote [rot] *s.* rutina, repetición maquinal; **by** — maquinalmente.
rot·ten [rɑ́tn̩] *adj.* podrido, putrefacto; (*stinking*) hediondo; (*conduct*) corrompido, corrupto.
rouge [ruʒ] *s.* colorete; *v.* pintar(se), poner(se) colorete.
rough [rʌf] *adj.* (*coarse*) áspero; tosco; fragoso; escabroso; (*rude*) brusco; grosero; (*stormy*) borrascoso, tempestuoso; — **diamond** diamante en bruto; — **draft** borrador; bosquejo; — **estimate** cálculo aproximativo, tanteo; presupuesto aproximado; — **ground** terreno escabroso; — **idea** idea aproximada; — **sea** mar picado; — **weather** tiempo borrascoscо; *adv.* *véase* **roughly;** *v.* **to — it** vivir sin lujos ni comodidades, hacer vida campestre.
rough·en [rʌ́fən] *v.* hacer o poner áspero; (*scratch*) picar, rascar (*una superficie*); (*crack*) rajarse, agrietarse (*la piel*).
rough·ly [rʌ́flɪ] *adv.* ásperamente; groseramente, rudamente; aproximadamente; **to estimate** — tantear.
rough·ness [rʌ́fnɪs] *s.* aspereza: escabrosidad; rudeza; tosquedad; **the — of the sea** lo picado del mar; **the — of the weather** lo borrascoso del tiempo.
round [raʊnd] *adj.* redondo; rotundo; circular; — **trip** viaje redondo, viaje de ida y veulta; **round-trip ticket** boleto (*o* billete) de ida y vuelta; *s.* vuelta, rotación, revolución; ronda; vuelta (*en el juego de naipes*); tanda, turno (*en ciertos deportes*); escalón, travesaño (*de escalera de mano*); danza en rueda; — **of ammunition** carga de municiones; descarga; — **amount** cifra redonda; — **of applause** explosión de aplausos; — **of pleasures** sucesión de placeres; **to make the -s** rondar; *prep.* & *adv.* *véase* **around;** — **about** a la redonda; por todos lados; **round-shouldered** cargado de espaldas; **to come — again** volver otra vez; **to go — a corner** doblar una esquina; *v.* redondear; dar vuelta a; **to — a corner** doblar una esquina; **to — out** redondear; completar; **to — up cattle** juntar el ganado, *Ríopl., Ven.* rodear el ganado.
round·a·bout [ráʊndəbaʊt] *adj.* indirecto.
round·ness [ráʊndnɛs] *s.* redondez.
round·up [ráʊndʌp] *s.* (*cattle*) rodeo (*de ganado*); (*criminals*) redada (*de criminales*); *v.* repuntar.
rouse [raʊz] *v.* despertar(se), *Ríopl., C.A., Ven.* recordar; excitar; incitar, provocar; levantar (*la caza*).
rout [raʊt] *s.* derrota, fuga desordenada; *v.* derrotar;

poner en fuga; **to — out** echar, hacer salir a toda prisa.
route [rut] *s.* ruta, camino, vía; (*planned*) itinerario; *v.* dirigir o enviar por cierta ruta.
roust·a·bout [ráustəbaut] *s.* obrero de muelle.
rou·tine [rutín] *s.* rutina.
rove [rov] *v.* vagar, errar, andar errante.
rov·er [róvɚ] *s.* vagabundo.
row [rau] *s.* riña, pelea, pelotera; *v.* pelearse, reñir, armar una riña o pelotera.
row [ro] *s.* fila, hilera; paseo en lancha; *v.* remar, bogar; llevar en bote de remar.
row·boat [róbot] *s.* bote de remos, lancha.
row·er [róɚ] *s.* remero.
roy·al [rɔ́ɪəl] *adj.* real, regio.
roy·al·ist [rɔ́ɪəlɪst] *s.* realista.
roy·al·ty [rɔ́ɪəltɪ] *s.* realeza, soberanía real; persona o personas reales; (*payment*) derechos; *Arg., Méx., Ven.* regalía, *Cuba* canon de producción.
rub [rʌb] *v.* (*apply friction*) frotar; restregar; fregar; (*scrape*) raspar; irritar; **to — out** borrar; **to — someone the wrong way** irritar, contrariar, llevarle a uno la contraria; *s.* fricción, friega, frotación; roce; (*scoff*) sarcasmo; **there is the —** allí está la dificultad.
rub·ber [rʌ́bɚ] *s.* caucho, goma, *Méx., C.A.* hule; goma elástica; goma de borrar; partida (*en ciertos juegos de naipes*); jugada decisiva (*en ciertos juegos de naipes*); **-s** chanclos, zapatos de goma o hule; *adj.* de caucho, de goma, *Méx., C.A.* de hule; **— band** faja o banda de goma; **— plantation** cauchal; **— tree** *Am.* caucho, *Ríopl.* gomero.
rub·bish [rʌ́bɪʃ] *s.* basura, desechos, desperdicios; tonterías.
rub·ble [rʌ́bl] *s.* escombros; (*stone fragments*) ripio, cascajo, fragmentos de ladrillos o piedras; piedra en bruto, piedra sin labrar.
ru·bid·i·um [rubídiəm] *s.* rubidio.
ru·bric [rúbrɪk] *s.* rúbrica.
ru·by [rúbɪ] *s.* rubí.
rud·der [rʌ́dɚ] *s.* timón.
rud·dy [rʌ́dɪ] *adj.* rojo; rojizo; (*complexion*) rubicundo.
rude [rud] *adj.* rudo; grosero; aspero; brusco; tosco.
rude·ness [rúdnɪs] *s.* rudeza; grosería, descortesía; tosquedad.
rue·ful [rúfəl] *adj.* triste; lastimoso, lamentable.
ruf·fi·an [rʌ́fɪən] *s.* rufián, hombre brutal.
ruf·fle [rʌ́fl] *v.* rizar, fruncir (*tela*); (*wrinkle*) arrugar; desarreglar, rizar (*la superficie del agua*); perturbar; (*bother*) molestar; *s.* volante (*de un traje*); frunce, pliegue; (*ripple*) ondulación (*en al agua*).
rug [rʌg] *s.* alfombra, tapete.
rug·ged [rʌ́gɪd] *adj.* escabroso, fragoso; áspero; recio, robusto; tosco; (*weather*) borrascoso, tempestuoso.
ru·in [rúɪn] *s.* ruina; **to go to —** arruinarse, caer en ruinas, venir a menos; *v.* arruinar; echar a perder; estropear.
ru·in·ous [rúɪnəs] *adj.* ruinoso; desastroso.
rule [rul] *s.* (*regulation*) regla; reglamento; precepto; (*control*) mando, gobierno; **as a —** por regla general; **— of thumb** método empírico; *v.* regir, gobernar; mandar; dirigir, guiar; dominar; (*decide*) fallar, decidir; rayar (*con regla*); **to — out** excluir; **to — over** regir, gobernar.
rul·er [rúlɚ] *s.* gobernante; soberano; regla (*para medir o trazar líneas*).
rul·ing [rúlɪŋ] *s.* fallo, decisión; gobierno; *adj.* predominante, prevaleciente; principal.
rum [rʌm] *s.* ron.
rum·ble [rʌ́mbl] *v.* retumbar, hacer estruendo, rugir; *s.* retumbo, éstruendo, rumor, ruido sordo; **— seat** asiento trasero (*de cupé*).
ru·mi·nant [rúmənənt] *s.* rumiante.
ru·mi·nate [rúmənet] *v.* rumiar; reflexionar, meditar.
rum·mage [rʌ́mɪdʒ] *v.* escudriñar revolviéndolo todo; *s.* búsqueda desordenada; **— sale** venta de prendas usadas (*para beneficencia*).
ru·mor [rúmɚ] *s.* rumor; runrún; *C.A.* corre la bola; *v.* murmurar; **it is -ed that** corre la voz que.
rump [rʌmp] *s.* anca; trasero.
rum·ple [rʌ́mpl] *v.* estrujar, ajar; arrugar; *s.* arruga (*en un traje*).
rum·pus [rʌ́mpəs] *s.* barullo, alharaca, boruca, batahola.
run [rʌn] *v.* (*on foot*) correr; (*function*) andar; marchar; funcionar; (*flow*) fluir; chorrear; (*go over*) recorrer; (*direct*) dirigir, manejar; (*un negocio, empresa, máquina, casa, etc.*); extenderse (*de un punto a otro*); correrse (*los colores*); ser candidato (*a un puesto político*); (*computer*) ejecutar; **to — a fever** tener calentura; **to — away** huir; fugarse, escaparse; **to — across a person** encontrarse o tropezar con una persona; **to — down** dejar de funcionar (*una máquina, reloj, etc.*); aprehender a (*un criminal*); hablar mal de; atropellar; **to get — down in health** quebrantársele a uno la salud; **to — dry** secarse; **to — into** tropezar con, encontrarse con; chocar con; **— around with** asociarse con; tener amores con; **to — into debt** adeudarse; **to — something into** meter algo en, clavar algo en; **to — out** salirse; **to — out of money** acabársele a uno el dinero; **to — over** derramarse (*un líquido*); atropellar, pasar por encima de; repasar, echar un vistazo a (*la lección, un libro, etc.*); **to — through a book** hojear un libro; **the play ran for three months** se dió la comedia durante tres meses; *s.* carrera, corrida; curso, marcha; recorrido; manejo; **— of good luck** serie de repetidos éxitos; **— of performances** serie de representaciones; **— on a bank** corrida, demanda extraordinaria de fondos bancarios; **in the long —** a la larga; **stocking —** carrera; **the common — of mankind** el común de las gentes; **to have the — of** tener el libre uso de; *p.p. de* **to run;** *adj.* **— of the mill** de calidad estándar.
run·a·way [rʌ́nəwe] *adj.* fugitivo; **— horse** caballo desbocado; **— marriage** casamiento de escapatoria; *s.* fugitivo; caballo desbocado; fuga.
rung [rʌŋ] *s.* barrote, travesaño (*de silla, escalera de mano, etc.*); *pret. & p.p. de* **to ring.**
run·ner [rʌ́nɚ] *s.* (*who runs*) corredor; (*cover*) tapete (*para un pasillo o mesa*), *Ríopl.* pasillo; carrera (*en una media*); (*edge*) cuchilla (*de patín o de trineo*); contrabandista.
run·ning [rʌ́nɪŋ] *s.* (*race*) corrida, carrera, (*direction*) manejo, dirección; (*flow*) flujo; **to be out of the —** estar fuera de combate; *adj.* corriente; **— board** estribo; **— expenses** gastos corrientes; **— knot** nudo corredizo; **— water** agua corriente; **in — condition** en buen estado; **for ten days —** por diez días seguidos.
runt [rʌnt] *s.* enano; hombrecillo.
run·way [rʌ́nwe] *s.* senda; vía; (*airport*) pista (*de aterrizaje*).
rup·ture [rʌ́ptʃɚ] *s.* ruptura; rompímiento, rotura; hernia; *v.* romper(se); reventar.
ru·ral [rʊ́rəl] *adj.* rural, campestre.
rush [rʌʃ] *v.* (*hurry*) apresurar(se); *Am.* apurarse;

despachar con prisa; (*attack*) lanzar(se), precipitar(se); abalanzarse; acometer; **to — out** salir a todo correr; **to — past** pasar a toda prisa; **rush!** ¡urgente! *s.* precipitación, prisa; acometida; junco, — **chair** silla de junco; — **of business** gran movimiento comercial; — **of people** tropel de gente; — **order** pedido urgente.
Rus·sian [rʌ́ʃən] *adj. & s.* ruso.
rust [rʌst] *s.* moho, orín; herrumbre; tizón (*enfermedad de las plantas*); — **color** color rojizo; *v.* enmohecer(se), oxidar(se).
rus·tic [rʌ́stɪk] *adj. & s.* rústico, campesino.
rus·tle [rʌ́sl] *v.* susurrar, crujir; menear; **to — cattle** robar ganado; *s.* susurro, crujido.
rust-proof [rʌ́stpruf] *adj.* inoxidable.
rust·y [rʌ́stɪ] *adj.* mohoso, cubierto de orín, oxidado; rojizo; entorpecido, falto de uso; (*lost skill*) falto de práctica.
rut [rʌt] *s.* rodada; rutina, método rutinario; **to be in a** — hacer una cosa por rutina, ser esclavo de la rutina.
ru·the·ni·um [ruθíniəm] *s.* rutenio.
ruth·less [rúθlɪs] *adj.* despiadado, cruel, brutal.
ruth·less·ness [rúθlɪsnɪs] *s.* fiereza, falta de miramiento, truculencia, crueldad.
rye [raɪ] *s.* centeno.

S:s

sa·ber [sébɚ] *s.* sable.
sab·o·tage [sǽbətɑʒ] *s.* sabotaje; *v.* sabotear.
sack [sæk] *s.* (*bag*) saco; costal; (*looting*) saqueo, pillaje; *v.* ensacar, meter en un saco; saquear, pillar.
sac·ra·ment [sǽkrəmənt] *s.* sacramento.
sa·cred [sékrɪd] *adj.* sagrado, sacro.
sa·cred·ness [sékrɪdnɪs] *s.* santidad; lo sagrado.
sac·ri·fice [sǽkrəfaɪs] *s.* sacrificio; **to sell at a** — vender con pérdida; *v.* sacrificar.
sac·ri·lege [sǽkrəlɪdʒ] *s.* sacrilegio.
sac·ri·le·gious [sækrɪlídʒəs] *adj.* sacrílego.
sac·ro·sanct [sǽkrosænkt] *adj.* sacrosanto.
sad [sæd] *adj.* triste.
sad·den [sǽdn̩] *v.* entristecer(se).
sad·dle [sǽdl] *s.* silla de montar; silla de bicicleta o motocicleta; — **bag** alforja; — **horse** caballo de silla — **tree** arzón; *v.* ensillar; **to — someone with responsibilities** cargar a alguien de responsabilidades.
sa·dis·tic [sədístɪk] *adj.* sádico, cruel.
sad·ness [sǽdnɪs] *s.* tristeza.
safe [sef] *adj.* (*secure*) seguro; salvo; sin riesgo, sin peligro; (*trustworthy*) digno de confianza; — **and sound** sano y salvo; **safe-conduct** salvo-conducto; **to be** — no correr peligro, estar a salvo; *s.* caja fuerte; **-ly** *adv.* seguramente; con seguridad; sin peligro; **to arrive -ly** llegar bien llegar sin contratiempo alguno.
safe·guard [séfgɑrd] *s.* salvaguardia; resguardo, defensa; *v.* resguardar, proteger, salvaguardar.
safe·ty [séftɪ] *s.* seguridad; protección; **in** — con seguridad; sin peligro; *adj.* de seguridad; — **device** mecanismo de seguridad; — **pin** imperdible, alfiler de seguridad.
saf·fron [sǽfrən] *s.* azafrán; *adj.* azafranado, color de azafrán.
sag [sæg] *v.* combarse, pandearse; doblegarse; deprimirse, hundirse (*en el centro*); encorvarse; **his shoulders** — tiene las espaldas caídas; *s.* pandeo, flexión, depresión; concavidad.
sa·ga·cious [səgéʃəs] *adj.* sagaz, ladino, astuto.
sa·gac·i·ty [səgǽsətɪ] *s.* sagacidad; astucia.
sage [sedʒ] *adj.* sabio; cuerdo, prudente; *s.* sabio; (*plant*) salvia.
said [sɛd] *pret. & p.p. de* **to say.**
sail [sel] *s.* (*canvas*) vela (*de barco*); (*trip*) viaje o paseo en barco de vela; **under full** — a toda vela; **to set** — hacerse a la vela; *v.* navegar; hacerse a la vela; (*set sail*) zarpar, salir (*un buque*); viajar, ir (*en barco, bote, etc.*); pasear en bote de vela; **to — a kite** volar una cometa o papalote; **to — along** deslizarse; navegar; ir bien; **to — along the coast** costear.
sail·boat [sélbot] *s.* bote o barco de vela.
sail·or [sélɚ] *s.* marinero; marino.
saint [sent] *s.* santo; *adj.* santo; san (*delante de nombres masculinos excepto: Santo Tomás, Santo Domingo, Santo Toribio*); *v.* canonizar.
saint·ly [séntlɪ] *adj.* santo; pío, devoto.
sake [sek]: **for the — of** por; por amor a; por consideración a; **for my** — por mí; **for pity's** — por piedad; ¡caramba!; **for the — of argument** por vía de argumento.
sa·la·cious [səléʃəs] *adj.* salaz.
sal·ad [sǽləd] *s.* ensalada; — **dressing** aderezo (*para ensalada*).
sal·a·ry [sǽlərɪ] *s.* salario, sueldo; *Arg., Col.* asignación; — **brackets** categorías salariales.
sale [sel] *s.* venta; saldo, *Méx., C.A., Andes* barata; *Ríopl., Andes* realización; — **by auction** almoneda, subasta; **-s tax** impuesto sobre ventas; **for** — de venta; **-s approach** política de venta; **-s force** personal de ventas.
sales·man [sélzmən] *s.* vendedor; dependiente (*de tienda*); **traveling** — agente viajero, viajante de comercio.
sales·wom·an [sélzwʊmən] *s.* vendedora; dependiente (*de tienda*).
sa·li·ent [sélɪənt] *adj.* saliente, sobresaliente; prominente.
sa·line [sélin] *adj.* salino.
sa·li·va [səláɪvə] *s.* saliva.
sal·low [sǽlo] *adj.* amarillento, pálido.
sal·ly [sǽlɪ] *s.* (*exit*) salida; (*wise crack*) agudeza, chiste agudo; *v.* salir, hacer una salida; **to — forth** salir.
salm·on [sǽmən] *s.* salmón.
sa·loon [səlún] *s.* salón (*de un vapor*); taberna, *Méx., Carib., Ríopl* cantina; *Ríopl.* bar; **dining — of a ship** salón-comedor de un vapor.
salt [sɔlt] *s.* (*sodium chloride*) sal; (*wit*) chiste, agudeza; **smelling -s** sales aromáticas; **the — of the earth** la flor y nata de la humanidad; *adj.* salado; salobre; —**cellar** salero; — **mine** salina; — **pork** tocino salado; — **shaker** salero; — **water** agua salada, agua de mar; *v.* salar; **to — one's money away** guardar o ahorrar su dinero.
salt·pe·ter [sɔ́ltpítɚ] *s.* salitre, nitro; — **mine** salitral, salitrera.
salt·y [sɔ́ltɪ] *adj.* salado; salobre.
sal·u·tar·y [sǽljʊtɛrɪ] *adj.* saludable.
sal·u·ta·tion [sæljətéʃən] *s.* salutación, saludo.
sa·lute [səlút] *s.* saludo; **gun** — salva; *v.* saludar; cuadrarse (*militarmente*).
sal·vage [sǽlvɪdʒ] *s.* salvamento.
sal·va·tion [sælvéʃən] *s.* salvación.
salve [sæv] *s.* untura, ungüento; alivio; *v.* aliviar, aquietar, calmar; untar.
sal·vo [sǽlvo] *s.* salva.

same [sem] *adj.* mismo; igual; idéntico; **it is all the — to me** me es igual, me da lo mismo; **the —** lo mismo; el mismo (la misma, los mismos, las mismas).
sam·ple [sǽmpl] *s.* muestra, prueba; **book of -s** muestrario; *v.* probar; calar.
sam·pling [sǽmplɪŋ] *s.* muestreo.
san·a·to·ri·um[sænətorɪəm] *s.* sanatorio.
sanc·ti·fy [sǽŋktəfaɪ] *v.* santificar.
sanc·tion [sǽŋkʃən] *s.* sanción; aprobación; autorización; *v.* sancionar; ratificar; aprobar, autorizar.
sanc·ti·ty [sǽŋktətɪ] *s.* santidad.
sanc·tu·ar·y [sǽŋktʃuɛrɪ] *s.* santuario; asilo.
sand [sænd] *s.* arena; **— pit** arenal; *v.* enarenar, cubrir de arena; mezclar con arena; refregar con arena.
san·dal [sǽndl] *s.* sandalia; alpargata; *Méx.* guarache (huarache); *Andes* ojota.
sand·pa·per [sǽndpepɚ] *s.* papel de lija; *v.* lijar, pulir o alisar con papel de lija.
sand·stone [sǽndston] *s.* piedra arenisca.
sand·wich [sǽndwɪtʃ] *s.* bocadillo, emparedado, sandwich; *v.* intercalar, meter (entre).
sand·y [sǽndɪ] *adj.* arenoso; arenisco; **— hair** pelo rojizo; rufo; *Méx.* güero; *Ven.* catire; *Guat.* canche; *Col.* mono.
sane [sen] *adj.* sano, sensato, cuerdo.
sang [sæŋ] *pret. de* **to sing.**
san·i·tar·i·um [sænətɛ́rɪəm] *s.* sanatorio.
san·i·tar·y [sǽnətɛrɪ] *adj.* sanitario.
san·i·ta·tion [sænətéʃən] *s.* saneamiento; salubridad; sanidad.
san·i·ty [sǽnətɪ] *s.* cordura.
sank [sæŋk] *pret. de* **to sink.**
sap [sæp] *s.* savia; tonto, bobo; *v.* agotar, debilitar, minar.
sap·ling [sǽplɪŋ] *s.* vástago, renuevo; arbolillo.
sap·phire [sǽfaɪr] *s.* zafiro; color de zafiro.
sar·casm [sɑ́rkæzəm] *s.* sarcasmo.
sar·cas·tic [sɑrkǽstɪk] *adj.* sarcástico.
sar·coph·a·gus [sarkɔ́fəgəs] *s.* sarcófago.
sar·dine [sɑrdín] *s.* sardina.
sar·don·ic [sɑrdɑ́nɪk] *adj.* burlón; sarcástico.
sash [sæʃ] *s.* faja (*cinturón de lana, seda o algodón*); banda, cinta ancha; **window —** bastidor (*o* marco) de ventana.
sas·sy [sǽsɪ] *adj.* respondón, insolente.
sat [sæt] *pret. & p.p. de* **to sit.**
satch·el [sǽtʃəl] *s.* valija, maletín, maleta, saco.
sate [set] *v.* saciar.
sa·teen [sætín] *s.* satén o rasete (*raso de inferior calidad*).
sat·el·lite [sǽtlaɪt] *s.* satélite.
sa·ti·ate [séʃɪet] *v.* saciar, hartar.
sat·in [sǽtn̩] *s.* raso.
sat·ire [sǽtaɪr] *s.* sátira.
sa·tir·i·cal [sətírɪkl] *adj.* satírico.
sat·i·rize [sǽtəraɪz] *v.* satirizar.
sat·is·fac·tion [sætɪsfǽkʃən] *s.* satisfacción.
sat·is·fac·to·ri·ly [sætɪsfǽktrəlɪ] *adv.* satisfactoriamente.
sat·is·fac·to·ry [sætɪsfǽktrɪ] *adj.* satisfactorio.
sat·is·fied [sǽtɪsfaɪd] *adj.* satisfecho, contento.
sat·is·fy [sǽtɪsfaɪ] *v.* satisfacer.
sat·u·rate [sǽtʃəret] *v.* saturar, empapar.
Sat·ur·day [sǽtɚdɪ] *s.* sábado.
sauce [sɔs] *s.* salsa; **— dish** salsera; *v.* aderezar con salsa; sazonar, condimentar; insolentarse con.
sauce·pan [sɔ́spæn] *s.* cacerola.
sau·cer [sɔ́sɚ] *s.* platillo.
sau·ci·ness [sɔ́sɪnɪs] *s.* descaro, insolencia.
sau·cy [sɔ́sɪ] *adj.* descarado, respondón, insolente, *Am.* retobado.
saun·ter [sɔ́ntɚ] *v.* pasearse, vagar.
sau·sage [sɔ́sɪdʒ] *s.* salchicha, salchichón; longaniza; chorizo.
sav·age [sǽvɪdʒ] *adj.* salvaje; fiero; bárbaro, brutal, feroz; *s.* salvaje.
sav·age·ry [sǽvɪdʒrɪ] *s.* salvajismo; crueldad, fiereza.
sa·vant [səvɑ́nt] *s.* sabio.
save [sev] *v.* (*rescue*) salvar; (*hoard*) ahorrar; economizar; (*keep*) guardar; resguardar; **to — from** librar de; **to — one's eyes** cuidarse la vista; *prep.* salvo, menos, excepto.
sav·er [sévɚ] *s.* salvador; libertador; (*hoarder*) ahorrador; **life —** salvavidas.
sav·ing [sévɪŋ] *adj.* (*rescuer*) salvador; (*economizing*) ahorrativo, económico; frugal; *s.* ahorro, economía; **-s** ahorros; **-s bank** caja o banco de ahorros; *prep.* salvo, excepto, con excepción de.
sav·ior [sévjɚ] *s.* salvador.
sa·vor [sévɚ] *s.* sabor; dejo; *v.* saborear; sazonar; **to — of** saber a, tener el sabor de; **it -s of treason** huele a traición.
sa·vor·y [sévərɪ] *adj.* sabroso.
saw [sɔ] *s.* sierra; **—horse** caballete; *v.* aserrar, serrar; **it -s easily** es fácil de aserrar; *pret. de* **to see.**
saw·dust [sɔ́dʌst] *s.* aserrín, serrín.
saw·mill [sɔ́mɪl] *s.* aserradero.
sawn [sɔn] *p.p. de* **to saw.**
Sax·on [sǽksn̩] *adj. & s.* sajón.
sax·o·phone [sǽksəfon] *s.* saxófono; saxofón.
say [se] *v.* decir; declarar; **— !** ¡diga! ¡oiga usted!; **that is to —** es decir; **to — one's prayers** rezar, decir o recitar sus oraciones; **to — the least** por lo menos; **it is said that** dizque, se dice que, dicen que; *s.* afirmación, aserto; **the final —** la autoridad decisiva; **to have a — in a matter** tener voz y voto en un asunto; **to have one's —** expresarse, dar su opinión.
say·ing [séɪŋ] *s.* dicho, refrán; aserto; **as the — goes** como dice el refrán.
scab [skæb] *s.* costra (*de una herida*); roña; (*strikebreaker*) esquirol (*obrero que sustituye a un huelguista*); obrero que acepta un jornal inferior; *v.* encostrarse (*una herida*), cubrirse de una costra.
scab·bard [skǽbɚd] *s.* vaina, (*holster*) funda (*de espada, puñal, etc.*).
scab·by [skǽbɪ] *adj.* costroso; roñoso, sarnoso, tiñoso.
scab·rous [skébrəs] *adj.* escabroso.
scaf·fold [skǽfld] *s.* andamio, tablado; (*execution*) patíbulo; andamiaje, andamios.
scald [skɔld] *v.* escaldar; **to — milk** calentar la leche hasta que suelte el hervor; *s.* escaldadura, quemadura.
scale [skel] *s.* escala; platillo de balanza; balanza; (*fish*) escama (*de pez o de la piel*); costra; **pair of -s** balanza; **platform —** báscula; *v.* escalar; subir, trepar por; graduar (*a escala*); medir según escala; pesar; escamar, quitar las escamas a; pelarse, despellejarse; descostrar(se); **to — down prices** rebajar proporcionalmente los precios.
scal·lop [skɑ́ləp] *s.* onda, pico (*adorno*); (*seafood*) molusco bivalvo; **-s** festón (*recortes en forma de ondas o picos*); *v.* festonear, recortar en forma de ondas o picos, asar con salsa o migas de pan.
scalp [skælp] *s.* cuero cabelludo; *v.* desollar el cráneo; (*resell*) revender (*boletos, billetes*) a precio subido.

scal·y [skélɪ] *adj.* escamoso, lleno de escamas; — **with rust** mohoso.
scamp [skæmp] *s.* pícaro, bribón, bellaco.
scam·per [skǽmpɚ] *v.* correr, escabullirse, escaparse; *s.* escabullida, carrera, corrida.
scan [skæn] *v.* escudriñar; examinar, mirar detenidamente; echar un vistazo a (*en el habla popular*); (*verse*) medir (*el verso*).
scan·dal [skǽndl] *s.* escándalo; maledicencia, murmuración.
scan·dal·ize [skǽndlaɪz] *v.* escandalizar, dar escándalo.
scan·dal·ous [skǽndləs] *adj.* escandaloso; difamatorio; vergonzoso.
scan·di·um [skǽndiəm] *s.* escandio.
scant [skænt] *adj.* escaso; corto; insuficiente; *v.* escatimar, limitar.
scant·y [skǽntɪ] *adj.* escaso; insuficiente.
scar [skɑr] *s.* (*skin blemish*) cicatriz; costurón; (*mark*) raya, marca (*en una superficie pulida*); *v.* marcar, rayar; hacer o dejar una cicatriz en.
scarce [skɛrs] *adj.* escaso; raro; **-ly** *adv.* escasamente; apenas.
scar·ci·ty [skɛ́rsətɪ] *s.* escasez; carestía; insuficiencía.
scare [skɛr] *v.* espantar, asustar; alarmar; sobresaltar; **he -s easily** se asusta fácilmente; **to — away** ahuyentar, espantar; *s.* susto, sobresalto.
scare·crow [skɛ́rkro] *s.* espantajo; espantapájaros.
scarf [skɑrf] *s.* bufanda; mantilla; pañuelo (*para el cuello o la cabeza*); tapete (*para una mesa, tocador, etc.*).
scar·let [skɑ́rlɪt] *s.* escarlata; *adj.* de color escarlata; — **fever** escarlata, escarlatina.
scar·y [skɛ́rɪ] *adj.* espantadizo, asustadizo, miedoso.
scat [skæt] *interj.* ¡zape!
scat·ter [skǽtɚ] *v.* esparcir(se); desparramar(se); dispersar(se); —**brained** ligero de cascos, aturdido.
scene [sin] *s.* escena; escenario; decoración; (*panorama*) vista; **to make a —** causar un escándalo.
scen·er·y [sínərɪ] *s.* paisaje, vista; **stage —** decoraciones.
scent [sɛnt] *s.* (*odor*) olor; (*substance*) perfume; (*trace*) pista, rastro; **to be on the — of** seguir el rastro de; **to have a keen —** tener buen olfato; *v.* oler, olfatear, ventear, husmear; perfumar.
scep·ter [sɛ́ptɚ] *s.* cetro.
scep·tic [skɛ́ptɪk] *adj.* & *s.* escéptico.
scep·ti·cism [skɛ́ptəsɪzəm] *s.* escepticismo.
sched·ule [skɛ́dʒʊl] *s.* horario; itinerario (*de trenes*); lista, inventario (*adjunto a un documento*); *v.* fijar el día y la hora (*para una clase, conferencia, etc.*); establecer el itinerario para (*un tren o trenes*).
scheme [skim] *s.* (*plan*) esquema, plan, proyecto; empresa; (*plot*) ardid, trama, maquinación; **color —** combinación de colores; **metrical —** sistema de versificación; *v.* proyectar, urdir; maquinar, intrigar, tramar.
schem·er [skímɚ] *s.* maquinador, intrigante; proyectista.
schem·ing [skímɪŋ] *adj.* maquinador, intrigante; *s.* maquinación.
schism [sɪzəm] *s.* cisma.
schiz·o·phre·ni·a [skɪzofrínɪə] *s.* esquizofrenia.
schol·ar [skɑ́lɚ] *s.* (*student*) escolar, estudiante; (*fellow*) becario (*el que disfruta una beca*); erudito, docto; (*researcher*) investigador.
schol·ar·ly [skɑ́lɚlɪ] *adj.* erudito, sabio, docto; *adv.* eruditamente, doctamente.
schol·ar·ship [skɑ́lɚʃɪp] *s.* saber; erudición; (*award*) beca; **to have a —** disfrutar una beca.
scho·las·tic [skolǽstɪk] *adj.* escolástico; escolar.
school [skul] *s.* escuela; colegio; — **of fish** banco de peces; *adj.* de escuela; — **day** día de escuela; — **board** consejo de enseñanza; *v.* enseñar, educar, instruir, aleccionar.
school·boy [skúlbɔɪ] *s.* alumno.
school·girl [skúlgɝl] *s.* alumna.
school·house [skúlhaʊs] *s.* escuela.
school·ing [skúlɪŋ] *s.* instrucción; enseñanza, educación.
school·mas·ter [skúlmæstɚ] *s.* maestro de escuela.
school·mate [skúlmet] *s.* condiscípulo, compañero de escuela.
school·room [skúlrum] *s.* clase, aula; sala de clase.
school·teach·er [skúltitʃɚ] *s.* maestro de escuela.
schoo·ner [skúnɚ] *s.* (*ship*) goleta; (*glass*) vaso grande para cerveza; **prairie —** galera con toldo.
sci·ence [sáɪəns] *s.* ciencia.
sci·en·tif·ic [saɪəntífɪk] *adj.* científico; **-ally** *adv.* científicamente.
sci·en·tist [sáɪəntɪst] *s.* científico, hombre de ciencia.
scin·til·late [síntəlet] *v.* centellear; chispear.
sci·on [sáɪən] *s.* vástago.
scis·sors [sízɚz] *s. pl.* tijeras.
scle·ro·sis [skləósɪs] *s.* esclerosis.
scoff [skɔf] *s.* mofa, burla, befa, escarnio; *v.* escarnecer; mofarse; **to — at** mofarse de, burlarse de, escarnecer a.
scold [skold] *v.* reñir, reprender, regañar; *s.* regañon, persona regañona.
scold·ing [skóldɪŋ] *s.* regaño, represión; *adj.* regañón.
scoop [skup] *s.* (*tool*) cuchara, cucharón; (*shovel*) pala; (*quantity*) palada, cucharada; (*winnings*) buena ganancia; **newspaper —** primera publicación de una noticia; *v.* cavar, excavar; ahuecar; cucharear, sacar con cucharón o pala; achicar (*agua*); **to — in a good profit** sacar buena ganancia.
scoot [skut] *v.* escabullirse, correr, irse a toda prisa; **— !** ¡largo de aquí!
scoot·er [skútɚ] *s.* motoneta (*de motor*); monopatín.
scope [skop] *s.* alcance, extensión; (*sphere*) esfera, campo.
scorch [skɔrtʃ] *v.* chamuscar; resecar, agostar; *s.* chamusquina, *Am.* chamuscada o chamuscadura.
score [skor] *s.* cuenta; escor (*en el juego*); (*line*) raya, línea; calificación (*expresada numéricamente*); veintena; **musical —** partitura; **on that —** a ese respecto; **on the — of** a causa de, con motivo de; **to keep the —** llevar el escor, llevar la cuenta; **to settle old -s** desquitarse; *v.* marcar el escor, señalar los tantos en un juego; calificar (*numéricamente*); instrumentar (*música*); rayar, marcar con rayas; **to — a point** ganar un punto o tanto; **to — a success** lograr éxito, obtener un triunfo.
scorn [skɔrn] *s.* desdén, menosprecio; *v.* desdeñar, menospreciar.
scorn·ful [skɔ́rnfəl] *adj.* desdeñoso.
scor·pi·on [skɔ́rpɪən] *s.* escorpión, alacrán.
Scotch [skatʃ] *adj.* escocés; **the —** los escoceses, el pueblo escocés.
scoun·drel [skáʊndrəl] *s.* bellaco, bribón, pícaro.
scour [skaʊr] *v.* fregar, restregar, limpiar; pulir; **to — the country** recorrer la comarca (*en busca de algo*).
scourge [skɝdʒ] *s.* azote; *v.* azotar; castigar.
scout [skaʊt] *s.* explorador (*usualmente militar*); **a good —** un buen explorador; una buena persona,

un buen compañero; *v.* explorar; reconocer.
scowl [skaʊl] *s.* ceño; *v.* fruncir el ceño, mirar con ceño; poner mala cara.
scram·ble [skræmbl] *v.* (*move*) gatear; (*eggs*) hacer un revoltillo; (*mix up*) revolver, mezclar; **to — for something** forcejear por coger algo; pelearse por coger algo; **to — up** trepar o subir a gatas (*una cuesta*); **-d eggs** revoltillo, huevos revueltos; *s.* revoltillo, confusión; pelea.
scrap [skræp] *s.* (*fragment*) fragmento, pedacito; migaja; (*fight*) riña, reyerta; **-s** sobras; desperdicios; desechos; retales; **—book** albúm de recortes; **— iron** recortes o desechos de hierro; *v.* desechar; tirar a la basura; descartar; pelear, reñir.
scrape [skrep] *v.* (*abrasively*) raspar; rasguñar; rascar; (*rub*) raer; rozar; **to — along** ir tirando, ir pasándola; **to — together** recoger o acumular poco a poco; **to bow and** — ser muy servil; *s.* raspadura; rasguño; aprieto, dificultad, lío.
scrap·er [skrépɚ] *s.* (*tool*) raspador; (*scrimping person*) tacaño.
scratch [skrætʃ] *v.* (*mark*) arañar, rasguñar; (*rub*) rascar; raspar; (*line*) rayar; escarbar; (*write badly*) hacer garabatos; **to — out** borrar, tachar; sacar (*los ojos*) con las uñas; *s.* arañazo, araño, rasguño; raya, marca; **to start from** — empezar sin nada; empezar desde el principio; empezar sin ventaja.
scrawl [skrɔl] *s.* garabato; *v.* hacer garabatos, escribir mal.
scraw·ny [skrɔ́nɪ] *adj.* huesudo, flaco.
scream [skrim] *s.* chillido, alarido, grito; **he's a** — es muy cómico o chistoso; *v.* chillar, gritar.
screech [skritʃ] *s.* chillido; **— owl** lechuza; *v.* chillar.
screen [skrin] *s.* (*projection*) pantalla; (*divider*) biombo; mampara; resguardo; (*sifter*) tamiz, cedazo; **—door** antepuerta de tela metálica; **— editing** (*computer*) edición en pantalla; **motion-picture** — pantalla de cinematógrafo; **wire** — pantalla de tela metálica; *v.* tapar; resguardar, proteger con una pantalla o un biombo; (*sift*) cerner; (*project*) proyectar sobre la pantalla, filmar; **to — windows** proteger las ventanas con tela metálica.
screw [skru] *s.* tornillo; **— eye** armella; **— nut** tuerca; **— propeller** hélice; **— thread** rosca; *v.* atornillar; torcer, retorcer; **to — a lid on** atornillar una tapa; **to — up one's courage** cobrar ánimo.
screw·driv·er [skrúdraɪvɚ] *s.* destornillador.
scrib·ble [skrı́bl] *v.* garrapatear, hacer garabatos, borronear, escribir mal o de prisa; *s.* garabato.
script [skrɪpt] *s.* letra cursiva, escritura; manuscrito (*de un drama, de una película*).
scrip·ture [skrı́ptʃɚ] *s.* escritura sagrada; **the Scriptures** la Sagrada Escritura, la Biblia.
scroll [skrol] *s.* rollo de pergamino o papel; voluta, adorno en espiral; (*flourish*) rúbrica (*de una firma*); **scrolling** (*computer*) movimiento vertical (de la imagen).
scrub [skrʌb] *v.* fregar; restregar; *s.* friega, fregado; *adj.* achaparrado; bajo, inferior; **— oak** chaparro; **— pine** pino achaparrado; **— team** equipo de jugadores suplentes o menos bien entrenados; **— woman** fregona.
scru·ple [skrúpl] *s.* escrúpulo; *v.* escrupulizar, tener escrúpulos.
scru·pu·lous [skrúpjələs] *adj.* escrupuloso.
scru·ti·nize [skrútn̩aɪz] *v.* escudriñar, escrutar.
scru·ti·ny [skrútn̩ɪ] *s.* escrutinio.
scuff [skʌf] *v.* raspar; arrastrar los pies.
scuf·fle [skʌ́fl] *s.* refriega, riña, pelea; *v.* forcejear; luchar, pelear; arrastrar los pies.
sculp·tor [skʌ́lptɚ] *s.* escultor.
sculp·ture [skʌ́lptʃɚ] *s.* escultura; *v.* esculpir, cincelar, tallar.
scum [skʌm] *s.* nata, capa, espuma; (*dregs*) escoria; residuo, desechos; (*low life*) canalla, gente baja; *v.* espumar.
scur·ry [skɝ́ɪ] *v.* escabullirse; echar a correr; apresurarse; *s.* apresuramiento; corrida, carrera.
scut·tle [skʌ́tl] *v.* echar a correr; (*ship*) barrenar (*un buque*); echar a pique; *s.* escotilla, escotillón; balde (*para carbón*).
scythe [saɪð] *s.* guadaña.
sea [si] *s.* mar; **to be at** — estar en el mar; estar perplejo o confuso; **to put to** — hacerse a la mar; *adj.* marino, marítimo, de mar; **— biscuit** galleta; **— green** verdemar; **— gull** gaviota; **— level** nivel del mar; **— lion** léon marino, foca; **— power** potencia naval.
sea·board [síbord] *s.* costa, litoral; *adj.* costanero, litoral.
sea·coast [síkost] *s.* costa, litoral.
seal [sil] *s.* (*stamp*) sello; timbre; (*animal*) foca, león marino; **to set one's — to** sellar; aprobar; **sealed bids** propuestas selladas; *v.* sellar; estampar; cerrar; tapar; **to — in** encerrar, cerrar herméticamente; **to — with sealing wax** lacrar.
seal·ing wax [sílɪŋ wæks] *s.* lacre.
seam [sim] *s.* (*sewing*) costura; juntura; (*scar*) cicatriz; filón, (*ore*) veta; *v.* echar una costura, coser.
sea·man [símən] *v.* marino, marinero.
seam·stress [símstrɪs] *s.* costurera.
sea·plane [síplen] *s.* hidroavión.
sea·port [síport] *s.* puerto de mar.
sear [sɪr] *v.* chamuscar(se), tostar(se); resecar(se); herrar, marcar con hierro candente; *adj.* reseco, marchito.
search [sɝtʃ] *v.* buscar; escudriñar; (*''frisk''*) registrar; examinar; **to — a prisoner** registrar a un prisionero; **to — for something** buscar algo; **to — into** investigar, indagar; *s.* busca, búsqueda; registro, inspección; investigación, pesquisa, indagación; **— warrant** mandato judicial de practicar un registro; **in — of** en busca de.
search·light [sɝtʃlaɪt] *s.* reflector.
sea·shore [síʃor] *s.* costa, playa, orilla o ribera del mar.
sea·sick [sísɪk] *adj.* mareado; **to get** — marearse.
sea·sick·ness [sísɪknɪs] *s.* mareo.
sea·side [sísaɪd] *s.* costa, litoral; playa.
sea·son [sízn̩] *s.* estación (*del año*); temporada; sazón, ocasión, tiempo; **— ticket** billete de abono; **Christmas** — navidades; **harvest** — siega, tiempo de la cosecha; **opera** — temporada de la ópera; **to arrive in good** — llegar en sazón, llegar a tiempo; *v.* sazonar; condimentar; aclimatar.
sea·son·ing [síznɪŋ] *s.* condimento; salsa; desecación (*de la madera*).
seat [sit] *s.* (*furniture*) asiento; silla; (*site*) sitio; (*headquarters*) residencia; sede (*episcopal, del gobierno, etc.*); (*body*) nalgas; (*clothes*) fondillos, parte trasera (*de los pantalones o calzones*); **— of learning** centro de estudios, centro de erudición; *v.* sentar; asentar; dar asiento a; **to — oneself** sentarse; **it -s a thousand people** tiene cabida para mil personas.
sea·weed [síwid] *s.* alga marina.
se·cede [sisíd] *v.* separarse (*de una federación o unión*).
se·clude [sɪklúd] *v.* recluir, apartar, aislar; **to — oneself from** recluirse de, apartarse de.

se·clud·ed [sɪklúdɪd] *adj.* apartado, aislado; solitario.
se·clu·sion [seɪklúʒən] *s.* apartamiento, soledad, aislamiento; retiro.
sec·ond [sɛ́kənd] *adj.* segundo; inferior; — **hand** segundero (*de reloj*); — **lieutenant** subteniente; **second-rate** de segunda clase; mediocre, inferior; **on — thought** después de pensarlo bien; *s.* segundo; (*helper*) padrino (*en un desafío*); ayudante; (*defective*) mercancía de segunda calidad; mercancía defectuosa; — **child** segundón; *v.* secundar (*o* segundar), apoyar; apadrinar.
sec·on·dar·y [sɛ́kəndɛrɪ] *adj.* secundario; — **education** segunda enseñanza; — **school** escuela secundaria, escuela de segunda enseñanza.
sec·ond-hand [sɛ́kəndhǽnd] *adj.* de segunda mano; usado; de ocasión; indirecto, por intermedio de otro.
sec·ond·ly [sɛ́kəndlɪ] *adv.* en segundo lugar.
se·cre·cy [síkrəsɪ] secreto, sigilo, reserva.
se·cret [síkrɪt] *s.* secreto; *adj.* secreto; escondido, oculto; — **service** policía secreta; **-ly** *adv.* secretamente, en secreto.
sec·re·tar·i·at [sɛ́krətǽriət] *s.* secretaría.
sec·re·tary [sɛ́krətɛrɪ] *s.* secretario; escritorio (*con estantes para libros*).
se·crete [sɪkrít] *v.* secretar (*una secreción*); esconder, ocultar.
se·cre·tion [sɪkríʃən] *s.* secreción.
se·cre·tive [sɪkrítɪv] *adj.* reservado, callado; — **gland** glándula secretoria.
sect [sɛkt] *s.* secta.
sec·tion [sɛ́kʃən] *s.* sección; (*passage*) trozo; (*slice*) tajada; (*place*) región; (*ward*) barrio; *v.* seccionar, dividir en secciones.
sec·u·lar [sɛ́kjələ˞] *adj. & s.* secular.
se·cure [sɪkjúr] *adj.* seguro; firme; *v.* asegurar; afianzar; obtener; resguardar; **-ly** *adv.* seguramente, con seguridad; firmamente.
se·cu·ri·ty [sɪkjúrətɪ] *s.* seguridad; (*bond*) fianza, garantía, prenda; resguardo, protección; **securities** bonos, obligaciones, acciones, valores; — **in hand** valores en cartera.
se·dan [sɪdǽn] *s.* sedan.
se·date [sɪdét] *adj.* sosegado; tranquilo, sereno; serio.
se·da·tion [sədéʃən] *d.* sedación.
sed·a·tive [sɛ́dətɪv] *adj. & s.* calmante, sedativo.
sed·en·tar·y [sɛ́dn̩tɛrɪ] *adj.* sedentario; inactivo.
sed·i·ment [sɛ́dəmənt] *s.* sedimento, heces, residuo.
se·di·tion [sɪdíʃən] *s.* sedición.
se·di·tious [sɪdíʃəs] *adj.* sedicioso.
se·duce [sɪdjús] *v.* seducir.
se·duc·tion [sɪdʌ́kʃən] *s.* seducción.
see [si] *v.* ver; — **that you do it** no deje Vd. de hacerlo; tenga Vd. cuidado de hacerlo; **I'll — to it** me encargaré de ello; **let me** — a ver; **to — a person home** acompañar a una persona a casa; **to — a person off** ir a la estación para despedir a una persona; **to — a person through a difficulty** ayudar a una persona a salir de un apuro; **to — through a person** adivinar lo que piensa una persona, darse cuenta de sus intenciones; **to — to one's affairs** atender a sus asuntos; **to have seen military service** haber servido en el ejército; *s.* sede, silla; **Holy See** Santa Sede.
seed [sid] *s.* (*grains*) semilla; (*semen*) simiente; (*fruit*) pepita; hueso; **to go to** — producir semillas; decaer, declinar; descuidar de su persona, andar desaseado; *v.* sembrar; despepitar, quitar las pepitas o semillas de; producir semillas.
seed·er [sídə˞] *s.* sembradora.
seed·ling [sídlɪŋ] *s.* planta de semillero; arbolillo (*de menos de tres pies de altura*).
seed·y [sídɪ] *adj.* semilloso, lleno de semillas; raído; desaseado.
seek [sik] *v.* buscar; pedir, solicitar; **to — after** buscar; **to — to** tratar de, esforzarse por.
seem [sim] *v.* parecer; **it -s to me** me parece.
seem·ing·ly [símɪŋlɪ] *adv.* aparentemente, en apariencia, al parecer.
seem·ly [símlɪ] *adj.* propio, decente, decoroso.
seen [sin] *p.p. de* **to see.**
seep [sip] *v.* escurrirse, rezumarse, colarse, filtrarse.
seer [sɪr] *s.* vidente, adivino, profeta.
seeth [sið] *v.* bullir, hervir; burbujear.
seg·ment [sɛ́gmənt] *s.* segmento.
seg·re·gate [sɛ́grəget] *v.* segregar.
seize [siz] *v.* (*grasp*) asir, coger, agarrar; apoderarse de; (*arrest*) prender o aprehender; (*take advantage of*) aprovecharse de; (*capture*) embargar, secuestrar; encautarse de; **to — upon** asir; **to become -d with fear** sobrecogerse de miedo.
sei·zure [síʒə˞] *s.* cogida; captura; aprehensión (*de un criminal*); secuestro, embargo (*de bienes*); ataque (*de una enfermedad*).
sel·dom [sɛ́ldəm] *adv.* rara vez, raras veces, raramente.
se·lect [səlɛ́kt] *adj.* selecto, escogido; *v.* elegir, escoger; entresacar.
se·lec·tion [səlɛ́kʃən] *s.* selección, elección.
se·le·ni·um [sɪlíniəm] *s.* selenio.
self [sɛlf] *pron.* **by one**— por sí, por sí mismo; **for one**— para sí; **one's other** — su otro yo; **his wife and** — su esposa y él (*véase* **herself, himself, ourselves, themselves,** *etc.*); **self-centered** egoísta, egocéntrico; **self-conscious** consciente de sí, cohibido, tímido; **self-control** dominio de sí mismo (*o* de sí propio); **self-defense** defensa propia; **self-denial** abnegación; **self-evident** patente, manifiesto; **self-esteem** respeto de sí mismo; amor propio; **self-government** gobierno autónomo, autonomía; gobierno democrático; **self-interest** propio interés; egoísmo; **self-love** amor propio; **self-possessed** sereno, dueño de sí, tranquilo; **self-sacrifice** abnegación; **self-service** [sɛlfsɝ́vɪs] *s.* autoservicio; **self-satisfied** pagado de sí, satisfecho de sí; *s.* el yo, el propio yo.
self·ish [sɛ́lfɪʃ] *adj.* egoísta; **-ly** *adv.* con egoísmo, por eogísmo.
self·ish·ness [sɛ́lfɪʃnɪs] *s.* egoísmo.
self·same [sɛ́lfsém] *adj.* mismo, idéntico, mismísimo.
sell [sɛl] *v.* vender; (*for sale*) venderse, estar de venta; **to — at auction** vender en almoneda o subasta, subastar; **to — out** venderlo todo; **to — short** vender en descubierto.
sell·er [sɛ́lə˞] *s.* vendedor.
selves [sɛlvz] *pl. de* **self.**
se·man·tics [səmǽntɪks] *s.* semántica.
sem·blance [sɛ́mbləns] *s.* semejanza; apariencia.
se·mes·ter [səmɛ́stə˞] *s.* semestre.
sem·i·cir·cle [sɛ́məsə˞kl] *s.* semicírculo.
sem·i·co·lon [sɛ́məkolən] *s.* punto y coma.
sem·i·con·duc·tor [sɛmikəndʌ́ktə˞] *s.* semiconductor (menos que cobre y más que cristal).
sem·i·nar·y [sɛ́mənɛrɪ] *s.* seminario.
Se·mit·ic [səmítɪk] *adj.* semítico.
sen·ate [sɛ́nɪt] *s.* senado.
sen·a·tor [sɛ́nɪtə˞] *s.* senador.
send [sɛnd] *v.* enviar; mandar; despachar; remitir, expedir; (*throw*) lanzar (*una flecha, pelota, etc.*); **to — away** despedir; despachar; **to — forth** despachar, enviar; emitir; exhalar; echar; **to —**

someone up for 15 years condenar a un reo a 15 años de prisión; **to — word** avisar, mandar decir, mandar recado.
send·er [séndɚ] *s.* remitente; transmisor.
se·nile [sínaɪl] *adj.* senil, caduco; chocho.
se·nil·i·ty [sənílətɪ] *s.* senectud; chochera o chochez.
sen·ior [sínjɚ] *adj.* (*older*) mayor, de más edad; más antiquo; (*superior*) superior; **— class** clase del cuarto año; *s.* persona o socio más antiguo; estudiante del último año; **to be somebody's — by two years** ser dos años mayor que alguien.
sen·sa·tion [sɛnséʃən] *s.* sensación.
sen·sa·tion·al [sɛnséʃənl] *adj.* sensacional; emocionante.
sense [sɛns] *s.* (*function*) sentido; (*sentiment*) sentimiento; sensación; (*judgment*) juicio, sensatez; (*meaning*) significado; **common —** sentido común; **to make —** tener sentido; **to be out of one's -s** estar fuera de sí, estar loco; *v.* percibir, sentir; darse cuenta de.
sense·less [sénslɪs] *adj.* sin sentido; (*foolish*) insensato, absurdo; insensible, privado de sentido.
sen·si·bil·i·ty [sɛnsəbílətɪ] *s.* sensibilidad.
sen·si·ble [sénsəbl] *adj.* (*aware*) sensato, razonable, cuerdo; (*appreciable*) sensible, perceptible; **sensibly** *adv.* sensatamente, con sensatez, con sentido común; sensiblemente, perceptiblemente.
sen·si·tive [sénsətɪv] *adj.* sensitivo; sensible; quisquilloso, susceptible.
sen·si·tive·ness [sénsətɪvnɪs] *s.* sensibilidad.
sen·si·tize [sénsətaɪz] *v.* sensibilizar.
sen·su·al [sénʃuəl] *adj.* sensual, carnal, lujurioso.
sen·su·al·i·ty [sɛnʃuǽlətɪ] *s.* sensualidad; lujuria.
sent [sɛnt] *pret. & p.p. de* **to send.**
sen·tence [séntəns] *s.* sentencia, fallo, decisión; (*grammar*) oración; **death —** pena capital; *v.* sentenciar.
sen·ti·ment [séntəmənt] *s.* sentimiento; sentido.
sen·ti·men·tal [sɛntəméntl] *adj.* sentimental.
sen·ti·men·tal·i·ty [sɛntəmɛntǽlətɪ] *s.* sentimentalismo, sentimentalidad.
sen·ti·nel [séntənl] *s.* centinela.
sen·try [séntrɪ] *s.* centinela.
sep·a·rate [séprɪt] *adj.* (*apart*) separado; apartado; solitario; (*different*) distinto, diferente; **-ly** *adv.* separadamente, por separado; aparte; [sépəret] *v.* separar(se); apartar(se).
sep·a·ra·tion [sɛpəréʃən] *s.* separación.
Se·phar·di [səfárdi] *s.* sefardí, sefardita; **-c** *adj.* sefardí.
Sep·tem·ber [sɛptémbɚ] *s.* setiembre.
sep·ul·cher [séplkɚ] *s.* sepulcro, sepultura.
se·quel [síkwəl] *s.* secuela; continuación, consecuencia; resultado.
se·quence [síkwəns] *s.* (continuity) secuencia, sucesión; serie, continuación; (*result*) consecuencia, resultado; runfla (*serie de tres o más naipes de un mismo palo*).
ser·e·nade [sɛrənéd] *s.* serenata; *v.* dar serenata a.
se·rene [sərín] *adj.* sereno; tranquilo; claro, despejado.
se·ren·i·ty [sərénətɪ] *s.* serenidad; calma.
ser·geant [sárdʒənt] *s.* sargento; **— at arms** oficial que guarda el orden (*en un cuerpo legislativo*).
se·ri·al [sírɪəl] *s.* cuento o novela por entregas; *adj.* consecutivo, en serie; **— novel** novela por entregas.
se·ries [síriz] *s.* serie; series.
se·ri·ous [sírɪəs] *adj.* serio; grave; **-ly** *adv.* seriamente, con seriedad, en serio; gravemente.
se·ri·ous·ness [sírɪəsnɪs] *s.* seriedad; gravedad.
ser·mon [sɝ́mən] *s.* sermón.
ser·pent [sɝ́pənt] *s.* serpiente; sierpe.
se·rum [sírəm] *s.* suero.
ser·vant [sɝ́vənt] *s.* sirviente; criado; servidor; **— girl** criada, *Ríopl.* mucama; *Andes, Col., Ven., Méx.* muchacha de servicio.
serve [sɝv] *v.* (*wait on*) servir; (*supply*) surtir, abastecer; **to — a term in prison** cumplir una condena; **to — a warrant** entregar una citación; **to — as** servir de; **to — for** servir de, servir para; **to — notice on** notificar, avisar, advertir; **to — one's purpose** servir para el caso o propósito; **it -s me right** bien me lo merezco; *s.* saque (*de la pelota en tenis*).
serv·er [sɝ́vɚ] *s.* servidor; (*game*) saque (*el que saca la pelota en el juego de tenis*); bandeja; mesa de servicio.
ser·vice [sɝ́vɪs] *s.* servicio; saque (*de la pelota en tenis*); entrega (*de una citación judicial*); **at your —** a la disposición de Vd., servidor de Vd.; **funeral —** honras fúnebres, funerales, exequias; **mail —** servicio de correos; **table —** servicio de mesa, vajilla; **tea —** juego o servicio de té; **— entrance** entrada para el servicio; **— man** militar; **— station** estación de servicio; *v.* servir; reparar; surtir (*una tienda*).
ser·vice·a·ble [sɝ́vɪsəbl] *adj.* servible; útil; duradero.
ser·vile [sɝ́vl] *adj.* servil.
ser·vi·tude [sɝ́vətjud] *s.* servidumbre; esclavitud.
ses·sion [séʃən] *s.* sesión.
set [sɛt] *v.* (*place*) poner; colocar, asentar; (*fix*) fijar; establecer; ajustar; engastar (*piedras preciosas*); solidificar(se), endurecer(se) (*el cemento, yeso, etc.*); ponerse (*el sol, la luna*); empollar; **to — a bone** componer un hueso dislocado; **to — a trap** armar una trampa; **to — about** ponerse a; **to — an example** dar ejemplo; **to — aside** poner a un lado, poner aparte; apartar; ahorrar; **to — back** retrasar, atrasar; **to — forth** exponer, expresar; manifestar; **to — forth on a journey** ponerse en camino; **to — off** disparar, hacer estallar (*un explosivo*); hacer resaltar; salir; **to — on fire** pegar o poner fuego a, incendiar; **to — one's jaw** apretar las quijadas; **to — one's heart on** tener la esperanza puesta en; **to — one's mind on** resolverse a, aplicarse a; **to — out for** partir para, salir para; **to — out to** empezar a; **to — right** colocar bien; enderezar; rectificar; **to — sail** hacerse a la vela; **to — the brake** frenar, apretar el freno; **to — up** erigir, levantar; armar, montar (*una máquina*); parar (*tipo de imprenta*); establecer, poner (*una tienda, un negocio*); **to — upon someone** acometer, asaltar a alguien; *pret. & p.p. de* **to set;** *adj.* fijo; firme; sólido; (*resolved*) resuelto; rígido; (*fixed*) puesto; establecido; engastado; **— to go** listo para partir; *s.* juego, colección; serie; grupo, clase; partida (*de tenis*); **— of dishes** servicio de mesa, vajilla; **— of teeth** dentadura; **radio —** radio, radiorreceptor; **tea —** servicio para té.
set·back [sétbæk] *s.* atraso, revés, retroceso inesperado.
set·tee [sɛtí] *s.* canapé.
set·ting [sétɪŋ] *s.* (*jewel*) engaste (*de una joya*); (*theater*) escena, escenario; (*sun, moon*) puesta (*del sol, de un astro*); **— sun** sol poniente.
set·tle [sétl] *v.* (*colonize*) colonizar, poblar; establecer(se); fijar(se); asentar(se); (*solve*) arreglar, poner en orden, ajustar (*cuentas*); zanjar (*una disputa*); pagar, liquidar, saldar; **to — down** formalizarse; asentarse; calmarse; poner casa; **to — on a date** fijar o señalar una fecha; **to — property**

on (upon) asignar bienes o propiedad a; **to — the matter** decidir el asunto, concluir con el asunto.
set·tle·ment [sétlmənt] *s.* (*community*) establecimiento; colonia; poblado; población; colonización; (*arrangement*) asignación o traspaso (*de propiedad*); ajuste, arreglo; pago; saldo, finiquito, liquidación; — **house** casa de beneficencia; **marriage** — dote.
set·tler [sétlɚ] *s.* colono, poblador; — **of disputes** zanjador de disputas.
set·up [sétəp] *s.* arreglo; organización; sistema.
sev·en [sévən] *num.* siete.
sev·en·teen [sɛvəntín] *num.* diecisiete.
sev·en·ty [sévəntɪ] *num.* setenta.
sev·er [sévɚ] *v.* desunir(se), partir(se), dividir(se), separar(se); cortar, romper.
sev·er·al [sévrəl] *adj.* varios, diversos; distintos, diferentes.
se·vere [səvír] *adj.* severo; áspero; austero; rígido; (*rigorous*) riguroso; grave, recio, fuerte.
se·ver·i·ty [səvérətɪ] *s.* severidad; austeridad; rigidez; gravedad; rigor.
sew [so] *v.* coser.
sew·er [sjúɚ] *s.* albañal, cloaca; *Mex., Ven., Andes* acequia.
sew·ing [sóɪŋ] *s.* costura; modo de coser; — **machine** máquina de coser; — **room** cuarto de costura.
sewn [son] *p.p. de* **to sew.**
sex [sɛks] *s.* sexo; — **appeal** atracción sexual.
sex·tant [sékstənt] *s.* sextante.
sex·ton [sékstən] *s.* sacristán.
sex·u·al [sékʃuəl] *adj.* sexual.
shab·by [ʃǽbɪ] *adj.* raído, gastado; andrajoso; mal vestido; vil, injusto; **to treat someone shabbily** tratar a alguien injustamente o con menosprecio.
shack [ʃæk] *s.* cabaña, choza, *Carib.* bohío, *Mex.* jacal.
shack·le [ʃǽkl] *v.* encadenar; trabar, echar trabas a, poner grillos a; estorbar; **-s** *s. pl.* cadenas, trabas, grillos, esposas; (*inconvenience*) estorbo.
shad [ʃæd] *s.* sábalo.
shade [ʃed] *s.* (*shadow*) sombra; (*nuance*) tinte, matiz; (*cover*) visillo, cortinilla; (*lamp*) pantalla (*de lámpara*); (*eye*) visera (*para los ojos*); **a — longer** un poco más largo; — **of meaning** matiz; **in the — of** a la sombra de; *v.* sombrear; dar sombra; resguardar de la luz; matizar.
shad·ow [ʃǽdo] *s.* (*darkness*) sombra; oscuridad; (*phantom*) espectro; **under the — of** al abrigo de, a la sombra de; **without a — of doubt** sin sombra de duda; *v.* sombrear; obscurecer; **to — someone** espiarle a alguien los pasos, seguirle por todas partes.
shad·ow·y [ʃǽdəwɪ] *adj.* lleno de sombras, tenebroso; vago, indistinto.
shad·y [ʃédɪ] *adj.* sombrío, sombreado, umbrío; — **business** negocio sospechoso; — **character** persona de carácter dudoso, persona de mala fama.
shaft [ʃæft] *s.* pozo o tiro (*de mina, de elevador*); cañon de chimenea; (*monument*) columna; (*axle*) eje, árbol (*de maquinaria*); flecha.
shag·gy [ʃǽgɪ] *adj.* peludo, velludo; lanudo; desaseado; áspero.
shake [ʃek] *v.* menear(se); estremecer(se); temblar; sacudir(se); agitar(se); titubear, vacilar; hacer vacilar; dar, estrechar (*la mano*); **to — hands** dar un apretón de manos, darse la mano; **to — one's head** mover o menear la cabeza; cabecear; **to — with cold** tiritar de frío, estremecerse de frío; **to — with fear** temblar de miedo, estremecerse de miedo; *s.* sacudida; sacudimiento; estremecimiento, temblor; **hand**— apretón de manos.
shak·en [ʃékən] *p.p. de* **to shake.**
shake-up [ʃékəp] *s.* reorganización.
shak·y [ʃékɪ] *adj.* tembloroso; vacilante.
shall [ʃæl] *v. aux. del futuro del indicativo en las primeras personas* (**I, we**); *en las demás expresa mayor énfasis, mandato u obligación;* **he — not do it** no lo hará, no ha de hacerlo; **thou shalt not steal** no hurtarás.
shal·low [ʃǽlo] *adj.* bajo, poco profundo; superficial; ligero de cascos.
shal·low·ness [ʃǽlonɪs] *s.* poca hondura, poca profundidad; superficialidad; ligereza de juicio.
sham [ʃæm] *s.* fingimiento, falsedad, farsa; *adj.* fingido, simulado; falso; — **battle** simulacro, batalla fingida; *v.* fingir, simular.
sham·bles [ʃǽmblz] *s.* desorden.
shame [ʃem] *s.* vergüenza; deshonra; — **on you!** ¡qué vergüenza!; **it is a —** es una vergüenza; es una lástima; **to bring — upon** deshonrar; *v.* avergonzar; deshonrar.
shame·ful [ʃémfəl] *adj.* vergonzoso.
shame·less [ʃémlɪs] *adj.* desvergonzado, descarado.
shame·less·ness [ʃémlɪsnɪs] *s.* desvergüenza; descaro, desfachatez.
sham·poo [ʃæmpú] *s.* champú, lavado de la cabeza; *v.* dar un champú, lavar (*la cabeza*).
sham·rock [ʃǽmrɑk] *s.* trébol.
shank [ʃæŋk] *s.* canilla (*parte inferior de la pierna*); zanca.
shan·ty [ʃǽntɪ] *s.* choza, cabaña, casucha.
shape [ʃep] *s.* (*form*) forma; (*figure*) figura; (*condition*) estado, condición; **to be in a bad —** estar mal; **to put into —** arreglar, poner en orden, ordenar; *v.* formar, dar forma a; tomar forma; **to — one's life** dar forma a, ajustar o disponer su vida; **his plan is shaping well** va desarrollándose bien su plan.
shape·less [ʃéplɪs] *adj.* informe, sin forma.
share [ʃɛr] *s.* (*portion*) porción, parte; (*participation*) participación; (*stock*) acción (*participación en el capital de una compañía*); *Col.* cupo. *v.* compartir; repartir; participar; **to — in** participar en, tener parte en; **to — a thing with** compartir una cosa con.
share·hold·er [ʃérholdɚ] *s.* accionista.
share·crop·per [ʃérkrɑpɚ] *s.* aparcero.
shark [ʃɑrk] *s.* (*fish*) tiburón; (*swindler*) estafador; (*expert*) perito, experto; (*usurer*) **loan** — usurero; **to be a — at** ser un águila (*o* ser muy listo) para.
sharp [ʃɑrp] *adj.* (*acute*) agudo, puntiagudo; cortante; punzante; (*biting*) mordaz; picante; (*bright*) astuto; (*clear*) claro, distinto, bien marcado; (*sudden*) repentino; — **curve** curva abrupta, curva pronunciada o muy cerrada; — **ear** oído fino; — **features** facciones bien marcadas; — **struggle** lucha violenta; — **taste** sabor acre; — **temper** genio áspero; — **turn** vuelta repentina; *s.* sostenido (*en música*); **card**— tahur, fullero; *adv.* *véase* **sharply** en punto; **at ten o'clock** — a las diez en punto.
sharp·en [ʃárpən] *v.* afilar(se); sacar punta a; aguzar(se), amolar.
sharp·ly [ʃárplɪ] *adv.* agudamente; mordazmente, ásperamente; repentinamente; claramente; **to arrive** — llegar en punto.
sharp·ness [ʃárpnɪs] *s.* agudeza; sutileza; mordacidad; rigor; aspereza; acidez.
shat·ter [ʃǽtɚ] *v.* estrellar(se), astillar(se), hacer(se)

añicos; quebrar(se), romper(se); **to — one's hopes** frustrar sus esperanzas; **his health was -ed** se le quebrantó la salud; **-s** *s. pl.* pedazos, trozos, añicos, fragmentos; **to break into —** hacer(se) añicos.
shave [ʃev] *v.* afeitar(se), rasurar(se); rapar(se); acepillar (*madera*); *s.* rasura, *Am.* afeitada; **he had a close —** por poco no se escapa; se salvó por milagro.
shav·en [ʃévən] *p.p. de* **to shave; clean-shaven** bien afeitado.
shav·ing [ʃévɪŋ] *s.* rasura, *Am.* afeitada; **wood -s** virutas; **— brush** brocha de afeitar; **— soap** jabón de afeitar.
shawl [ʃɔl] *s.* mantón, chal.
she [ʃi] *pron. pers.* ella; **— who** la que; *s.* hembra; **she-bear** osa; **she-goat** cabra.
sheaf [ʃif] *s.* haz, gavilla, manojo; lío; *v.* hacer gavillas.
shear [ʃɪr] *v.* trasquilar, esquilar (*las ovejas*); cortar (*con tijeras grandes*).
shear·ing [ʃírɪŋ] *s.* tonsura.
shears [ʃɪrz] *s. pl.* tijeras grandes.
sheath [ʃiθ] *s.* vaina; funda, envoltura.
sheathe [ʃið] *v.* envainar.
sheaves [ʃivz] *pl. de* **sheaf.**
shed [ʃɛd] *s.* cobertizo; tejadillo; tinglado; *Ríopl., Andes* galpón (*de una estancia*); *v.* derramar; difundir; esparcir; mudar (*de piel, plumas, etc.*); ser impermeable (*un paño, abrigo, sombrero, etc.*); **to — leaves** deshojarse.
sheen [ʃin] *s.* lustre, viso.
sheep [ʃip] *s.* oveja; carnero; **— dog** perro de pastor; **—fold** redil; **—skin** zalea; badana; pergamino; (*certificate*) diploma (*de pergamino*).
sheep·ish [ʃípɪʃ] *adj.* vergonzoso, encogido, tímido.
sheer [ʃɪr] *adj.* (*pure*) puro; completo; (*thin*) fino, delgado, transparente, diáfano; (*steep*) escarpado; **by — force** a pura fuerza.
sheet [ʃit] *s.* (*bed*) sábana; (*paper*) hoja, pliego (*de papel*); (*metal*) lámina (*de metal*); extensión (*de agua, hielo*); **— lightning** relampagueo.
shelf [ʃɛlf] *s.* estante, anaquel; (*sill*) repisa; (*rock*) saliente de roca.
shell [ʃɛl] *s.* (*sea*) concha; (*egg*) cáscara (*de huevo, nuez, etc.*); (*pod*) vaina (*de guisantes, frijoles, garbanzos, etc.*); casco (*de una embarcación*); (*structure*) armazón (*de un edificio*); granada, bomba; (*case*) cápsula (*para cartuchos*); *v.* cascar (*nueces*); desvainar, quitar la vaina a, pelar; desgranar (*maíz, trigo, etc.*); bombardear.
shel·lac [ʃəlǽk] *s.* laca; *v.* barnizar con laca.
shell·fish [ʃɛ́lfɪʃ] *s.* marisco; mariscos.
shel·ter [ʃɛ́ltɚ] *s.* abrigo, refugio, asilo; (*protection*) resguardo, protección; **to take —** refugiarse, abrigarse; *v.* abrigar, refugiar, guarecer; proteger, amparar.
shelve [ʃɛlv] *v.* poner o guardar en un estante; poner a un lado, arrinconar, arrumbar.
shelves [ʃɛlvz] *s. pl.* estantes, anaqueles; estantería.
shep·herd [ʃɛ́pɚd] *s.* pastor; zagal; **— dog** perro de pastor.
sher·bet [ʃɝ́bɪt] *s.* sorbete.
sher·iff [ʃɛ́rɪf] *s.* alguacil mayor (*de un condado en los Estados Unidos*).
sher·ry [ʃɛ́rɪ] *s.* jerez, vino de Jerez.
shield [ʃild] *s.* escudo, rodela, broquel; resguardo, defensa; *v.* escudar, resguardar, proteger.
shift [ʃɪft] *v.* (*change*) cambiar; mudar(se); alternar(se); variar; desviar(se); (*transfer*) trasladar, transferir; **to — for oneself** valerse o mirar por sí mismo; **to — gears** cambiar de marcha; **to — the blame** echar a otro su propio culpa; *s.* cambio; desvío, desviación; tanda, grupo de obreros; turno; **— key** (*computer*) tecla de cambio; **— lock key** tecla de cambio con cerrojo; **gear —** cambio de marcha.
shift·less [ʃíftlɪs] *adj.* negligente; holgazán.
shil·ling [ʃílɪŋ] *s.* chelín.
shim·my [ʃímɪ] *s.* (*dance*) shimmy; (*vibration*) abaniqueo.
shin [ʃɪn] *s.* espinilla (*de la pierna*); *v.* **to — up** trepar.
shine [ʃaɪn] *v.* (*beam*) brillar, resplandecer, lucir; (*polish*) pulir; dar brillo, lustre o bola, embolar (zapatos); *s.* brillo, lustre, resplandor; **rain or —** llueva o truene; **to give a shoe —** dar bola (brillo *o* lustre) a los zapatos; embolar o embetunar los zapatos; limpiar el calzado.
shin·gle [ʃíŋgl] *s.* ripia, tabla delgada, *Méx.* tejamanil o tejamaní; (*hair*) pelo corto escalonado; (*professional*) letrero de oficina; **-s** zona (*erupción de la piel*); *v.* cubrir con tejamaniles; techar con tejamaniles.
shin·ing [ʃáɪnɪŋ] *adj.* brillante; resplandeciente.
shin·y [ʃáɪnɪ] *adj.* brillante; lustroso.
ship [ʃɪp] *s.* (*naval*) buque, barco, navío, nave; (*air*) aeronave, avión; **— builder** ingeniero naval, constructor de buques; **— mate** camarada de a bordo; **— yard** astillero; **on — board** a bordo; *v.* embarcar(se); despachar, enviar; remesar; transportar; alistarse como marino.
ship·ment [ʃípmənt] *s.* embarque; cargamento; despacho, envío; remesa.
ship·per [ʃípɚ] *s.* embarcador; remitente.
ship·ping [ʃípɪŋ] *s.* embarque; despacho, envío; **— charges** gastos de embarque; **— clerk** dependiente de muelle; dependiente encargado de embarques.
ship·shape [ʃípʃep] *adj.* en buen orden.
ship·wreck [ʃíprɛk] *s.* naufragio; *v.* echar a pique, hacer naufragar; naufragar, irse a pique.
shirk [ʃɝk] *v.* evadir, evitar.
shirt [ʃɝt] *s.* camisa; *C.A.* cotón; **— waist** blusa; **in — sleeves** en camisa, en mangas de camisa.
shiv·er [ʃívɚ] *v.* tiritar; temblar; estremecerse; *s.* escalofrío, temblor, estremecimiento.
shoal [ʃol] *s.* bajío, banco de arena; banco (*de peces*).
shock [ʃɑk] *s.* (*blow*) choque; sacudida; sacudimiento; golpe; (*surprise*) sobresalto; **— absorber** amortiguador; **— of grain** hacina o gavilla de mieses; **— of hair** guedeja, greña; **— troops** tropas de asalto; *v.* chocar, ofender; escandalizar; causar fuerte impresión; horrorizar; sacudir; conmover; hacinar, hacer gavillas de (*mieses*).
shock·ing [ʃɑ́kɪŋ] *adj.* chocante, ofensivo, repugnante; espantoso, escandaloso.
shod [ʃɑd] *pret. & p.p. de* **to shoe.**
shoe [ʃu] *s.* zapato; botín; **brake —** zapata de freno; **horse —** herradura; **— blacking** betún, bola; **— polish** brillo, lustre, bola; **— store** zapatería; *v.* calzar; herrar (*un caballo*).
shoe·black [ʃúblæk] *s.* limpiabotas.
shoe·horn [ʃúhɔrn] *s.* calzador.
shoe·lace [ʃúles] *s.* lazo, cinta, cordón de zapato.
shoe·mak·er [ʃúmekɚ] *s.* zapatero.
shoe·string [ʃústrɪŋ] *s.* lazo, cinta, cordón de zapato.
shone [ʃon] *pret. & p.p. de* **to shine.**
shook [ʃʊk] *pret. de* **to shake.**
shoot [ʃut] *v.* (*firearm*) tirar, disparar, descargar;

hacer fuego; fusilar; dar un balazo; (*throw*) lanzar, disparar (*una instantánea*); (*photograph*) fotografiar, filmar (*una escena*); (*dice*) echar (*los dados*); (*sprout*) brotar (*las plantas*); **to — by** pasar rápidamente; **to — forth** brotar, salir; germinar; lanzarse; **to — it out with someone** pelearse a balazos; **to — up a place** entrarse a balazos por un lugar; *s.* vástago, retoño, renuevo; *s.* caza; **to go out for a —** salir a tirar; ir de caza.

shoot·er [ʃútɚ] *s.* tirador.

shoot·ing [ʃútɪŋ] *s.* tiroteo; **— match** certamen de tiradores (*o* de tiro al blanco); **— pain** punzada, dolor agudo; **— star** estrella fugaz.

shop [ʃɑp] *s.* tienda; taller; **— window** escaparate, vitrina, aparador, *Ríopl.*, *Andes* vidriera; **barber —** barbería; **beauty —** salón de belleza; **to talk —** hablar uno de su oficio o profesión; *v.* ir de tiendas; ir de compras, comprar.

shop·keep·er [ʃɑpkipɚ] *s.* tendero.

shop·per [ʃɑpɚ] *s.* comprador.

shop·ping [ʃɑ́pɪŋ] *s.* compra, compras; **to go —** ir de compras, ir de tiendas.

shore [ʃor] *s.* costa, playa, orilla, ribera; puntal; **ten miles off —** a diez millas de la costa; *v.* **to — up** apuntalar, poner puntales.

shorn [ʃorn] *p.p. de* **to shear.**

short [ʃɔrt] *adj.* (*duration*) corto; breve; (*height*) bajo; *Méx.* chaparro; (*amount*) escaso; (*curt*) brusco; **— cut** atajo; **— circuit** cortocircuito; **— wave** onda corta; método corto; **short-legged** de piernas cortas; **— loan** préstamo a corto plazo; **— run (haul, term)** de corto plazo; **for —** para abreviar; **in —** en resumen, en suma, en conclusión; **in — order** rápidamente, prontamente; **in a — time** en poco tiempo; al poco tiempo; **to be — of** estar falto o escaso de; **to cut —** acortar, abreviar, terminar de repente; **to run — of something** acabársele (írsele acabando) a uno algo; **to stop —** parar de repente, parar en seco.

short·age [ʃɔ́rtɪdʒ] *s.* escasez, carestía; déficit; falta.

short·com·ing [ʃɔ́rtkʌmɪŋ] *s.* falta, defecto.

short·en [ʃɔ́rtn̩] *v.* acortar(se), abreviar(se), disminuir(se).

short·en·ing [ʃɔ́rtnɪŋ] *s.* (*lard*) manteca, grasa (*para hacer pasteles*); (*abbreviation*) acortamiento; abreviación.

short·hand [ʃɔ́rthænd] *s.* taquigrafía.

short·hand·ed [ʃɔrthǽndəd] *adj.* carente de operarios.

short·ly [ʃɔ́rtlɪ] *adj.* brevemente; en breve; al instante, pronto, luego; bruscamente, secamente.

short·ness [ʃɔ́rtnɪs] *s.* cortedad; brevedad; pequeñez; deficiencia.

shorts [ʃɔrts] *s. pl.* calzoncillos, calzones cortos.

short·sight·ed [ʃɔ́rtsáɪtɪd] *adj.* miope; corto de vista.

shot [ʃɑt] *pret. & p.p. de* **to shoot**; *s.* (*discharge*) tiro; disparo; balazo; cañonazo; (*pellet*) bala; balas; (*injection*) inyección; (*throw*) tirada; **— of liquor** trago de aguardiente; **buck —** municiones, postas; **not by a long —** ni con mucho, ni por pienso, nada de eso; **he is a good —** es buen tirador, tiene buen tino; **to take a — at** disparar un tiro a; hacer una tentativa de; **within rifle —** a tiro de rifle.

shot·gun [ʃɑ́tgʌn] *s.* escopeta.

should [ʃʊd] *v. aux. del condicional en las primeras personas* **(I, we): I said that I — go** dije que iría; *equivale al imperfecto de subjuntivo*; **if it — rain** si lloviera; *se usa con la significación de deber*: **you — not do it** no debiera (*o* no debería) hacerlo.

shoul·der [ʃóldɚ] *s.* (*person*) hombro; (*animal*) lomo, pernil (*de puerco, cordero*); borde, saliente (*de un camino*); **-s** espalda, espaldas; **— blade** espaldilla, paletilla; **straight from the —** con toda franqueza; **to turn a cold — to** volver las espaldas a, tratar fríamente; *v.* cargar al hombro, echarse sobre las espaldas; cargar con, asumir; empujar con el hombro.

shout [ʃaʊt] *v.* gritar; vocear; *s.* grito.

shove [ʃʌv] *v.* empujar, dar empellones; **to — aside** echar a un lado, rechazar; **to — off** partir, zarpar (*un buque*); salir, irse; *s.* empujón, empellón; empuje.

shov·el [ʃʌ́vl] *s.* pala; *v.* traspalar.

show [ʃo] *v.:* (*exhibit*) mostrar, enseñar; exhibir; (*prove*) probar, demostrar; indicar; (*appear*) verse; asomarse; **— him in** que pase, hágale entrar; **to — off** alardear, hacer ostentación de; lucirse; **to — up** aparecer, presentarse; **to — someone up** hacer subir a alguien; mostrarle el camino (*para subir*); desenmascarar a alguien, poner a alguien en la evidencia; *s.* exhibición; demostración; ostentación; espectáculo; representación, función; apariencia; **— window** escaparate, vitrina, aparador, *Am.* vidriera; **to go to the —** ir al teatro, ir al cine; **to make a — of oneself** exhibirse, hacer ostentación.

show·case [ʃókes] *s.* vitrina, aparador.

show·down [ʃódaʊn] *s.* arreglo terminante.

show·er [ʃáʊɚ] *s.* (*rain*) aguacero, chubasco, chaparrón, lluvia; (*bath*) ducha, baño de ducha; *Méx.* regadera; **bridal —** tertulia para obsequiar a una novia; *v.* llover; caer un aguacero.

shown [ʃon] *p.p. de* **to show.**

show·y [ʃóɪ] *adj.* ostentoso; vistoso, chillón.

shrank [ʃræŋk] *pret. de* **to shrink.**

shred [ʃrɛd] *s.* tira, triza; andrajo; fragmento; pizca; **to be in -s** estar raído; estar andrajoso; estar hecho trizas; **to tear to -s** hacer trizas; *v.* desmenuzar; hacer trizas, hacer tiras; *pret. & p.p. de* **to shred.**

shrew [ʃru] *s.* arpía, mujer brava, mujer de mal genio.

shrewd [ʃrud] *adj.* astuto, sagaz, agudo.

shriek [ʃrik] *v.* chillar, gritar; *s.* chillido, grito.

shrill [ʃrɪl] *adj.* agudo, penetrante, chillón; *v.* chillar.

shrimp [ʃrɪmp] *s.* camarón; *Sp.* gamba; hombrecillo insignificante.

shrine [ʃraɪn] *s.* santuario; altar; lugar venerado.

shrink [ʃrɪŋk] *v.* encoger(se); contraer(se); disminuir; **to — back** retroceder; **to — from** retroceder ante, apartarse de; huir de, rehuir.

shrink·age [ʃrɪ́nkɪdʒ] *s.* encogimiento; contracción; merma.

shriv·el [ʃrɪ́vl] *v.* encoger(se); fruncir(se), marchitar(se); disminuir(se).

shroud [ʃraʊd] *s.* mortaja; *v.* amortajar; cubrir, ocultar.

shrub [ʃrʌb] *s.* arbusto.

shrub·ber·y [ʃrʌ́bərɪ] *s.* arbustos.

shrug [ʃrʌg] *v.* encogerse de hombros; *s.* encogimiento de hombros.

shrunk [ʃrʌŋk] *pret. & p.p. de* **to shrink.**

shrunk·en [ʃrʌ́ŋkən] *p.p. de* **to shrink.**

shuck [ʃʌk] *s.* hollejo; cáscara.

shud·der [ʃʌ́dɚ] *v.* temblar, estremecerse; *s.* temblor, estremecimiento.

shuf·fle [ʃʌ́fl] *v.* barajar; revolver, mezclar; arrastrar (*los pies*); **to — along** ir arrastrando los pies; *s.* mezcla, confusión; evasiva; **— of feet** arrastramiento de pies; **it is your —** a Vd. le toca barajar.

shun [ʃʌn] *v.* esquivar, evadir, rehuir, evitar.

shut [ʃʌt] *v.* cerrar(se); **to — down** parar el trabajo;

SH

cerrar (*una fábrica*); **to — in** encerrar; **to — off** cortar (*el gas, la electricidad, el agua, etc.*); **to — off from** incomunicar, aislar de, cortar la communicación con; excluir; **to — out** impedir la entrada de; cerrar la puerta a; **to — up** (*close*) cerrar bien; tapar; encerrar; (*be quiet*) tapar la boca, hacer callar; callarse; *pret. & p.p. de* **to shut;** *adj.* cerrado.

shut·down [ʃʌ́tdaʊn] *s.* paro, cesación.

shut·ter [ʃʌ́tɚ] *s.* contraventana; postigo (*de ventana*); cerrador; (*lens*) obturador (*de una cámara fotográfica*).

shut·tle [ʃʌ́tl] *s.* lanzadera; *v.* ir y venir acompasadamente (*como una lanzadera*).

shy [ʃaɪ] *adj.* tímido, apocado, retraído; vergonzoso; asustadizo; esquivo; **to be — on** estar escaso de; **to be — two cents** faltarle a uno dos centavos; *v.* esquivarse, hacerse a un lado; asustarse; **to — at something** retroceder ante algo; respingar (*un caballo*) al ver algo; espantarse con algo; **to — away** esquivarse de repente; respingar (*un caballo*); desviarse, apartarse.

shy·ness [ʃáɪnɪs] *s.* apocamiento, timidez, vergüenza.

shy·ster [ʃáɪstɚ] *s.* leguleyo, abogadillo tramposo, picapleitos.

sib·i·lant [síbələnt] *s.* sibilante.

sick [sɪk] *adj.* enfermo, malo; nauseado; angustiado; **— leave** licencia por enfermedad; **to be — for** languidecer por, suspirar por; **to be — of** estar cansado de; estar harto de; **to be — to** (*o* **at**) **one's stomach** tener náuseas; **to make —** enfermar; dar pena, dar lástima; *s.* **the —** los enfermos; *v.* (*dog*) incitar, azuzar (*a un perro*); **— him!** ¡síguele!

sick·en [síkən] *v.* enfermar(se), poner(se) enfermo; dar asco; tener asco; sentir náuseas.

sick·en·ing [síknɪŋ] *adj.* nauseabundo, repugnante; lastimoso.

sick·le [síkl] *s.* hoz.

sick·ly [síklɪ] *adj.* enfermizo; achacoso, enclenque; malsano.

sick·ness [síknɪs] *s.* enfermedad; malestar; náusea.

side [saɪd] *s.* (*surface*) lado; cara; costado; (*hill*) ladera; falda (*de una colina*); (*faction*) partido, facción; **— by —** lado a lado; **by his —** a su lado; **by the — of** al lado de; **on all -s** por todos lados; **to take -s with** ser partidario de, ponerse al lado de; *adj.* lateral; de lado; oblicuo; incidental; secundario, de menos importancia; **— glance** mirada de soslayo, de través o de reojo; **— issue** cuestión secundaria; **— light** luz lateral; noticia, detalle o ilustración incidental; *v.* **to — with** estar por, ser partidario de, apoyar a, opinar con.

side·board [sáɪdbord] *s.* aparador; *Col., Ven.* seibó.

side·line [sáɪdlaɪn] *s.* negocio secundario.

side·burns [sáɪdbɝnz] *s.* patillas; *Méx.* clavos.

side·slip [sáɪdslɪp] *s.* deslizamiento.

side·track [sáɪdtræk] *v.* desviar; echar a un lado.

side·walk [sáɪdwɔk] *s.* acera, *Méx.* banqueta, *Ríopl., Ch., Andes* vereda; *C.A., Col.*, andén.

side·ways [sáɪdwez] *adv.* de lado, de costado; oblicuamente; hacia un lado; *adj.* lateral, de lado, oblicuo.

siege [sidʒ] *s.* cerco, sitio, asedio; **to lay — to** sitiar, cercar.

sieve [sɪv] *s.* tamiz, cedazo; criba; *v. véase* **sift.**

sift [sɪft] *v.* cerner, tamizar; cribar.

sigh [saɪ] *v.* suspirar; *s.* suspiro.

sight [saɪt] *s.* (*sense*) vista; (*view*) visión; espectáculo, escena; (*gun*) mira (*de un arma de fuego*); **in — of** a vista de; **payable at —** pagadero a la vista; **he is a —** es un adefesio o mamarracho; **this room is a —** este cuarto es un horror; **to catch — of** vislumbrar, avistar; **to know by —** conocer de vista; **to lose — of** perder de vista; **to see the -s** ver o visitar los puntos de interés; *v.* avistar; ver.

sight·see·ing [sáɪtsiɪŋ *s.* turismo; **— tour** paseo en auto para ver puntos de interés.

sign [saɪn] *s.* (*signal*) signo; seña, señal; (*indication*) muestra; (*placard*) letrero; **— board** cartel; (*bulletin*) tablero (*para fijar anuncios*); *v.* firmar; contratar, hacer firmar; **to — over property** ceder una propiedad mediante escritura, hacer cesión legal de propiedad; **to — up for a job** firmar el contrato para un empleo; contratar para un empleo.

sig·nal [sígnl] *s.* señal, seña; *v.* señalar, indicar, hacer seña, dar la señal; *adj.* señalado, notable; extraordinario; **— beacon** faro; **— code** código de señales.

sig·na·ture [sígnətʃɚ] *s.* firma.

sign·er [sáɪnɚ] *s.* firmante.

sig·nif·i·cance [sɪgnífəkəns] *s.* significación; significado.

sig·nif·i·cant [sɪgnífəkənt] *adj.* significativo.

sig·ni·fy [sígnəfaɪ] *v.* significar.

si·lence [sáɪləns] *s.* silencio; *v.* (*hush*) acallar; (*extinguish*) apagar (*un sonido*); aquietar, sosegar.

si·lent [sáɪlənt] *adj.* silencioso; callado; tácito; **— partner** socio comanditario (*que no tiene voz ni voto*).

sil·hou·ette [sɪluét] *s.* silueta; *v.* perfilar; **to be -d against** perfilarse contra.

sil·i·con [siləkan] *s.* silicio.

silk [sɪlk] *s.* seda; *adj.* de seda; **— industry** industria sedera; **— ribbon** cinta de seda.

silk·en [sílkən] *adj.* sedoso; de seda.

silk·worm [sílkwɝm] *s.* gusano de seda.

silk·y [sílkɪ] *adj.* sedoso, sedeño; de seda.

sill [sɪl] *s.* umbral; **window —** antepecho de ventana.

sil·ly [sílɪ] *adj.* necio, tonto, bobo, simple; absurdo, insensato.

si·lo [sáɪlo] *s.* silo.

silt [sɪlt] *s.* cieno.

sil·ver [sílvɚ] *s.* (*metal*) plata; (*tableware*) cubierto; (*dishes*) vajilla de plata; (*color*) color de plata; *adj.* de plata; plateado; argentino; **— wedding** bodas de plata; *v.* platear; argentar; **to — a mirror** azogar un espejo.

sil·ver·smith [sílvɚsmɪθ] *s.* platero.

sil·ver·ware [sílvɚwɛr] *s.* vajilla de plata, vajilla plateada; cuchillos, cucharas y tenedores (*por lo general de plata o plateados*).

sil·ver·y [sílvərɪ] *adj.* plateado; argentino.

sim·i·lar [símələɚ] *adj.* semejante; similar; **-ly** *adv.* semejantemente; de la misma manera.

sim·i·lar·i·ty [sɪməlǽrətɪ] *s.* semejanza, parecido.

sim·i·le [síməli] *s.* símil.

sim·mer [símɚ] *v.* hervir a fuego lento.

sim·ple [símpl] *adj.* simple; sencillo; llano; tonto, mentecato; **simpleminded** ingenuo, simple, simplón; *s.* simple.

sim·ple·ton [símpltən] *s.* simplón, papanatas, papamoscas.

sim·plic·i·ty [sɪmplísətɪ] *s.* sencillez; simplicidad; simpleza; ingenuidad.

sim·pli·fy [símpləfaɪ] *v.* simplificar.

sim·ply [símplɪ] *adv.* simplemente; sencillamente; solamente.

sim·u·late [sɪmjəlet] *v.* simular.

si·mul·ta·ne·ous [saɪmlténiəs] *adj.* simultáneo.

sin [sɪn] *s.* pecado, culpa; *v.* pecar.

since [sɪns] *conj.* desde que; después (de) que; puesto

que, como, visto que; dado que, *prep.* desde, después de; *adv.* desde entonces; **ever** — desde entonces; **he died long** — murió hace mucho tiempo; **we have been here** — **five** estamos aquí desde las cinco.
sin·cere [sɪnsír] *adj.* sincero.
sin·cer·i·ty [sɪnsérətɪ] *s.* sinceridad.
si·ne·cure [sínɪkjur] *s.* sinecura (*trabajo fácil y bien pagado*).
sin·ew [sínju] *s.* tendón; fibra, vigor.
sin·ew·y [sínjəwɪ] *adj.* nervudo, nervioso o nervoso; fuerte, vigoroso.
sin·ful [sínfəl] *adj.* pecaminoso; pecador.
sing [sɪŋ] *v.* cantar; **to** — **out of tune** desentonar(se), desafinar; **to** — **to sleep** arrullar.
singe [sɪndʒ] *v.* chamuscar; *s.* chamusquina, *Am.* chamuscada, *Am.* chamuscadura.
sing·er [síŋɚ] *s.* cantor; cantora, cantatriz.
sin·gle [síŋgl] *adj.* (*unique*) solo; (*distinct*) individual; particular; (*unmarried*) soltero; — **entry bookkeeping** teneduría por partida simple; — **room** cuarto para uno; — **woman** mujer soltera; — **density** (*computer*) densidad simple; **not a** — **word** ni una sola palabra; *s.* billete de un dólar; *v.* **to** — **out** singularizar, distinguir, escoger; entresacar.
sin·gle-hand·ed [síŋglhǽndɪd] *adj.* solo, sin ayuda.
sing·song [síŋsɔŋ] *s.* sonsonete, cadencia monótona.
sin·gu·lar [síŋgjələ˞] *adj.* singular; raro, extraordinario; *s.* singular, número singular.
sin·is·ter [sínɪstɚ] *adj.* siniestro, aciago, funesto.
sink [sɪŋk] *v.* hundir(se); sumir(se), sumergir(se); (*boat*) echar a pique; irse a pique, naufragar; (*dig*) cavar (*un pozo*); enterrar, clavar (*un puntal o poste*); **to** — **into one's mind** grabarse en la memoria; **to** — **one's teeth into** clavar el diente en; **to** — **to sleep** caer en el sueño; *s.* sumidero; fregadero.
sin·ner [sínɚ] *s.* pecador.
sin·u·ous [sínjʊəs] *adj.* sinuoso, tortuoso; con vueltas y rodeos.
si·nus [sáɪnəs] *s.* seno, cavidad (*en un hueso*); **frontal** — seno frontal.
sip [sɪp] *v.* sorber; chupar; *s.* sorbo.
si·phon [sáɪfən] *s.* sifón; *v.* sacar (*agua*) con sifón.
sir [sɝ] *s.* señor.
si·ren [sáɪrən] *s.* sirena.
sir·loin [sɝ́lɔɪn] *s.* solomillo, solomo.
sir·up [sírəp] *s.* jarabe.
sis·sy [sísɪ] *adj.* & *s.* afeminado, maricón.
sis·ter [sístɚ] *s.* hermana; **Sister Mary** Sor María.
sis·ter-in-law [sístərɪnlɔ] *s.* cuñada, hermana política.
sit [sɪt] *v.* sentar(se); colocar, asentar; posarse (*un pájaro*); (*be seated*) estar sentado; estar situado; (*hen*) empollar (*las gallinas*); apoyarse; (*meet*) reunirse, celebrar sesión (*un cuerpo legislativo, un tribunal*); sentar, venir o caer (*bien o mal un traje*); **to** — **down** sentarse; **to** — **out a dance** quedarse sentado durante una pieza de baile; **to** — **still** estarse quieto; **to** — **tight** mantenerse firme en su puesto; **to** — **up** incorporarse; **to** — **up all night** velar toda la noche; **to** — **up and take notice** despabilarse.
site [saɪt] *s.* sitio, local, situación.
sit·ting [sítɪŋ] *s.* sesión (*de un cuerpo legislativo, tribunal, etc.*); sentada; **at one** — de una sentada; *adj.* sentado; — **hen** gallina ponedora; — **room** sala (de descanso); sala de espera; antesala.
sit·u·at·ed [sítʃʊetɪd] *adj.* situado, sito, ubicado, colocado.
sit·u·a·tion [sɪtʃʊéʃən] *s.* (*location*) situación, colocación; (*employment*) empleo; posición; (*status*) situación.
six [sɪks] *num.* seis.
six·teen [sɪkstín] *num.* dieciséis.
six·ty [síkstɪ] *num.* sesenta.
size [saɪz] *s.* tamaño; *C.A.* porte; medida; (*clothing*) talla; *v.* clasificar según el tamaño; **to** — **up** tantear, formarse una idea de, juzgar.
siz·zle [sízl] *v.* chirriar (*aplícase al sonido que hace la carne al freírse*); *s.* chirrido (*de la carne al freírse*).
skate [sket] *s.* patín; **ice** — patín de hielo, patín de cuchilla; **roller** — patín de ruedas; *v.* patinar.
skein [sken] *s.* madeja.
skel·e·ton [skélətn̩] *s.* esqueleto; osamenta; armazón; — **key** llave maestra.
skep·tic = **sceptic.**
sketch [skɛtʃ] *s.* (*drawing*) boceto; diseño; croquis; (*outline*) esbozo; bosquejo; *v.* bosquejar; delinear; esbozar, dibujar.
ski [ski] *s.* esquí; *v.* esquiar, patinar con esquís.
skid [skɪd] *v.* patinar, resbalar(se); patinar (*una rueda*); deslizarse.
skill [skɪl] *s.* destreza, maña, habilidad, pericia.
skilled [skɪld] *adj.* experto, práctico, experimentado, hábil; — **worker** obrero calificado.
skil·let [skílɪt] *s.* sartén; cacerola.
skill·ful, skil·ful [skílfəl] *adj.* experto, diestro, ducho, hábil, perito.
skim [skɪm] *v.* (*remove layer*) desnatar, quitar la nata a; (*foam*) espumar, quitar la espuma a; (*read*) leer superficialmente; **to** — **over the surface** rozar la superficie.
skimp [skɪmp] *v.* escatimar; economizar; ser tacaño; hacer (*las cosas*) con descuido.
skimp·y [skímpɪ] *adj.* escaso; tacaño.
skin [skɪn] *s.* piel; cutis; pellejo; cuero; cáscara, hollejo; **to save one's** — salvar el pellejo; **skin-deep** superficial; *v.* desollar; pelar; **to** — **someone out of his money** desplumar a una persona, quitarle a uno el dinero.
skin·ny [skínɪ] *adj.* flaco; descarnado.
skip [skɪp] *v.* saltar; brincar; saltarse (*unos renglones, un párrafo, etc.*), omitir; saltar por encima de, salvar de un brinco; **to** — **out** salir a escape, escabullirse, escaparse, *s.* salto, brinco; omisión.
skip·per [skípɚ] *s.* patrón (*de barco*); capitán; saltador, brincador.
skir·mish [skɝ́mɪʃ] *s.* escaramuza; *v.* escaramuzar, sostener una escaramuza.
skirt [skɝt] *s.* falda, *Ríopl.* pollera; (*side*) orilla, borde; **under** — enaguas; *v.* bordear, orillar, ir por la orilla de; (*circle*) circundar; **to** — **along a coast** costear.
skit [skɪt] *s.* parodia, juguete o paso cómico; boceto satírico o burlesco.
skull [skʌl] *s.* cráneo; calavera.
skunk —[skʌŋk] *s. C.A.*, *Méx.*, *Ríopl.* zorrillo o zorrino, *Ven.*, *Col.* mapurite.
sky [skaɪ] *s.* cielo; — **blue** azul celeste.
sky·lark [skáɪlɑrk] *s.* alondra, calandria.
sky·light [skáɪlaɪt] *s.* claraboya, tragaluz.
sky·rock·et [skáɪrɑkɪt] *s.* cohete.
sky·scrap·er [skáɪskrepɚ] *s.* rascacielos.
slab [slæb] *s.* tabla, plancha, (*tile*) losa; (*slice*) tajada gruesa; **marble** — losa de mármol.
slack [slæk] *adj.* (*not taut*) flojo; (*sluggish*) tardo, lento; inactivo; — **season** temporada inactiva; *s.* flojedad, flojera; inactividad; **to take up the** —

apretar, estirar; **-s** pantalones anchos con pliegues, *v. véase* **slacken**.
slack·en [slǽkən] *v.* aflojar(se); flojear; retardar(se); disminuir.
slag [slæg] *s.* escoria.
slain [slen] *p.p. de* **to slay.**
slam [slæm] *v.* cerrar(se) de golpe; dejar caer de golpe; **to — someone** decirle a alguien una claridad o grosería; **to — the door** dar un portazo; *s.* golpazo; claridad, grosería; **— of a door** portazo; **to make a grand —** ganar todas las bazas (*en el juego de bridge*).
slan·der [slǽndɚ] *s.* calumnia, maledicencia; *v.* calumniar.
slan·der·ous [slǽndərəs] *adj.* calumnioso; maldiciente.
slang [slæŋ] *s.* (*jargon*) jerga, jerigonza; (*argot*) vulgarismo.
slant [slænt] *s.* sesgo; inclinación; (*viewpoint*) punto de vista; *adj.* sesgado; inclinado; oblicuo; *v.* sesgar; inclinar(se); ladear.
slap [slæp] *s.* palmada, manazo, manotada; insulto, desaire; *v.* dar una palmada a, dar un manazo a.
slap·stick [slǽpstɪk] *adj.* de golpe y porrazo.
slash [slæʃ] *v.* acuchillar; dar cuchilladas o tajos; cortar; truncar; hacer fuerte rebaja de (*precios, sueldos*); *s.* cuchillada; tajo, tajada, cortadura.
slat [slæt] *s.* tabla, tablilla.
slate [slet] *s.* pizarra; color de pizarra; lista de candidatos; **— pencil** pizarrín.
slaugh·ter [slɔ́tɚ] *s.* carnicería, matanza, *Ríopl.* carneada; **— house** matadero, *Méx., C.A.* rastro; *v.* matar; *Ríopl.* carnear; hacer una matanza; destrozar.
slave [slev] *s.* esclavo; **— driver** capataz de esclavos; persona que agobia de trabajo a otra; **— labor** trabajo de esclavos; trabajadores forzados; **— dealer** negrero; *v.* trabajar como esclavo.
slav·er [slǽvɚ] *s.* baba; *v.* babosear, babear.
slav·er·y [slévrɪ] *s.* esclavitud.
slav·ish [slévɪʃ] *adj.* servil.
slay [sle] *v.* matar.
slea·zy [slízɪ] *adj.* débil, tenue, inválido.
sled [slɛd] *s.* trineo, rastra.
sleek [slik] *adj.* liso; pulido, resbaloso; suave; (*tricky*) artero, mañoso; *v.* alisar; pulir.
sleep [slip] *v.* dormir; **to — it off** dormir la mona; **to — off a headache** curarse con sueño un dolor de cabeza; **to — on it** consultarlo con la almohada; *s.* sueño; **— walker** sonámbulo; **to go to —** dormirse, quedarse dormido; **to put to —** adormecer; arrullar (*al nene*).
sleep·er [slípɚ] *s.* durmiente; cochecama, coche-dormitorio.
sleep·i·ly [slípɪlɪ] *adv.* con somnolencia.
sleep·i·ness [slípɪnɪs] *s.* sueño, modorra, somnolencia.
sleep·ing [slípɪŋ] *adj.* durmiente; dormido; **— car** coche-cama, coche-dormitorio; **— pills** píldoras para dormir; **— sickness** encefalitis letárgica.
sleep·less [slíplɪs] *adj.* desvelado, insomne, sin sueño.
sleep·y [slípɪ] *adj.* soñoliento; amodorrado; **to be —** tener sueño.
sleet [slit] *s.* cellisca; *v.* cellisquear.
sleeve [sliv] *s.* manga.
sleigh [sle] *s.* trineo; **— bell** cascabel; *v.* pasearse en trineo.
sleight [slaɪt]: **— of hand** juego de manos; prestidigitación, escamoteo.
slen·der [slɛ́ndɚ] *adj.* delgado; tenue; escaso, insuficiente.
slept [slɛpt] *pret. & p.p. de* **to sleep.**
sleuth [sluθ] *s.* detective (*o* detectivo).
slew [slu] *pret. de* **to slay.**
slice [slaɪs] *s.* rebanada, tajada; lonja; *v.* rebanar, tajar; cortar.
slick [slɪk] *v.* alisar; pulir; **to — up** alisar bien, pulir bien; (*one's self*) pulirse, acicalarse, componerse; *adj.* liso; meloso, suave; aceitoso; astuto, mañoso.
slick·er [slíkɚ] *s.* impermeable de hule (*o* de caucho); (*crook*) embaucador.
slid [slɪd] *pret. & p.p. de* **to slide.**
slid·den [slídn̩] *p.p. de* **to slide.**
slide [slaɪd] *v.* resbalar(se); deslizar(se); hacer resbalar; patinar; **to — into** meter(se) en; **to — out** (*o* **— away**) deslizarse, colarse, escabullirse, escaparse; **to let something —** dejar pasar algo; no hacer caso de algo; *s.* resbalón; resbaladero, lugar resbaladizo; ligado (*en música*); (*véase* **landslide**); **— cover** tapa corrediza; **— rule** regla de cálculo; **microscope —** platina.
slight [slaɪt] *s.* desaire, menosprecio, desdén; desatención; *v.* desairar, menospreciar; descuidar, desatender; *adj.* delgado; delicado; leve, ligero; pequeño; insignificante; escaso; **-ly** *adv.* escasamente; ligeramente; un poco, apenas.
slim [slɪm] *adj.* delgado; esbelto; escaso.
slime [slaɪm] *s.* limo, cieno, fango; (*slobber*) baba, secreción viscosa.
slim·y [sláɪmɪ] *adj.* viscoso, mucoso, fangoso; baboso.
sling [slɪŋ] *s.* (*weapon*) honda (*para tirar piedras*); (*arm*) cabestrillo (*para sostener el brazo*); (*rope*) eslinga (*maroma provista de ganchos para levantar pesos*); **— shot** tirador de goma o hule; *v.* tirar, arrojar; **to — a rifle over one's shoulder** echarse el rifle al hombro.
slink [slɪŋk] *v.* andar furtivamente; **to — away** escurrirse, escabullirse, deslizarse.
slip [slɪp] *v.* (*slide*) deslizar(se); resbalar(se); (*err*) cometer un desliz; equivocarse; **to — away** escaparse, escabullirse, escurrirse; **to — in** meter(se); **to — one's dress on** ponerse de prisa el vestido; **to — out** salirse; sacar a hurtadillas; **to — out of joint** dislocarse, *Am.* zafarse (*un hueso*); **to — something off** quitar(se) algo; **to let an opportunity — by** dejar pasar una oportunidad; **it slipped my mind** se me olvidó, se me pasó, **it slipped off** se zafó; *s.* desliz; resbalón; error, equivocación; funda (*de muebles, de almohada*); combinación, enaguas; pedazo (*de papel*), volante, papeleta; embarcadero; guía, sarmiento (*para transplantar*); **— knot** nudo corredizo.
slip·per [slípɚ] *s.* zapatilla; babucha; pantufla.
slip·per·y [slíprɪ] *adj.* resbaloso, resbaladizo; evasivo.
slit [slɪt] *v.* cortar, hacer una rendija, abertura o incisión; **to — into strips** cortar en tiras; *pret. & p.p. de* **to slit;** *s.* abertura, hendedura, rendija; cortada, incisión.
slob·ber [slɑ́bɚ] *s.* baba; *v.* babosear, babear.
slob·ber·ing [slɑ́bərɪŋ] *adj.* baboso.
slo·gan [slógən] *s.* lema, mote; consigna.
sloop [slup] *s.* balandra.
slop [slɑp] *v.* (*soil*) ensuciar; (*splash*) salpicar; (*spill*) derramar(se); *s.* fango, suciedad; **-s** lavazas, agua sucia; desperdicios.
slope [slop] *v.* inclinar(se); *s.* inclinación; declive; falda, ladera; cuesta, bajada; vertiente.
slop·py [slɑ́pɪ] *adj.* puerco, sucio, cochino; desaseado; mal hecho.
slot [slɑt] *s.* (*opening*) abertura, hendedura; (*groove*

for coins) ranura (*en que se introduce una moneda*); — **machine** máquina automática que funciona por medio de una moneda; «traganíqueles,» «tragamonedas»; *v.* hacer una abertura o hendedura.
sloth [slɔθ] *s.* pereza; perezoso (*cuadrúpedo*).
slouch [slaʊtʃ] *s.* (*posture*) postura muy relajada o floja; (*person*) persona perezosa o desaseada; — **hat** sombrero gacho; **to walk with a** — andar con los hombros caídos y la cabeza inclinada; *v.* andar agachado; andar caído de hombros; andar alicaído; arrellanarse, repantigarse (*en una silla*).
slov·en·li·ness [slʌ́vənlɪnɪs] *s.* desaseo, desaliño; suciedad.
slov·en·ly [slʌ́vənlɪ] *adj.* desaseado, desaliñado; desarreglado.
slow [slo] *adj.* (*low speed*) lento, despacio; (*late*) tardo; atrasado; (*sluggish*) lerdo; torpe; *adv.* lentamente, despacio; *v.* **to** — **down** (*o* — **up**) retardar disminuir (*el paso, la marcha, la velocidad*); aflojar el paso; **-ly** *adv.* despacio, lentamente; **slowdown** disminución de actividades.
slow·ness [slónɪs] *s.* lentitud, torpeza, cachaza.
slug [slʌg] *s.* (*bullet*) bala; porrazo, puñetazo; babosa (*molusco sin concha*); (*lazy*) haragán; (*swallow*) trago (*de aguardiente*); (*printing*) lingote (*de imprenta*); *v.* aporrear, (*fist*) abofetear, dar puñetazos.
slug·gard [slʌ́gɚd] *s.* holgazán, haragán.
slug·gish [slʌ́gɪʃ] *adj.* tardo; inactivo.
sluice [slus] *s.* compuerta; caño, canal; — **gate** compuerta.
slum [slʌm] *s.* barrio bajo; *v.* visitar los barrios bajos.
slum·ber [slʌ́mbɚ] *v.* dormitar; dormir; *s.* sueño, sueño ligero.
slump [slʌmp] *v.* hundirse; desplomarse; bajar repentinamente (*los precios o valores*); *s.* desplome, hundimiento, bajón, baja repentina (*de precios, valores, etc.*).
slung [slʌŋ] *pret. & p.p. de* **to sling.**
slunk [slʌŋk] *pret. & p.p. de* **to slink.**
slush [slʌʃ] *s.* (*snow*) nieve a medio derretir; (*mud*) lodazal, fango; (*refuse*) desperdicios; (*drivel*) sentimentalismo.
sly [slaɪ] *adj.* astuto, socarrón, zorro, taimado; **on the** — a hurtadillas, a escondidas.
sly·ness [sláɪnɪs] *s.* disimulo, astucia.
smack [smæk] *s.* (*taste*) sabor, dejo; (*kiss*) beso ruidoso; (*crack*) chasquido (*de látigo*); (*slap*) palmada, manotada; **a** — **of something** una pizca de algo; *v.* dar un beso ruidoso; chasquear (*un látigo*); dar un manazo; **to** — **of** saber a, tener el sabor de; oler a; **to** — **one's lips** chuparse los labios, saborearse, rechuparse, relamerse.
small [smɔl] *adj.* (*size*) pequeño, chico; bajo; (*insignificant*) insignificante; mezquino; — **change** dinero menudo, suelto; — **hours** primeras horas de la mañana; — **letters** letras minúsculas; — **talk** conversación insubstancial, charladuría; — **voice** vocecita; **to feel** — sentirse pequeño o insignificante.
small·ness [smɔ́lnɪs] *s.* pequeñez; bajeza.
small·pox [smɔ́lpɑks] *s.* viruela.
small·wares [smɔ́lwɛrz] *s.* (*notions*) mercería.
smart [smɑrt] *adj.* (*intelligent*) listo, inteligente; (*astute*) ladino; astuto; agudo; (*stylish*) elegante; — **remark** observación aguda o penetrante; — **set** gente de buen tono; *s.* escozor, *Ríopl.*, *C.A.*, *Méx.* ardor; *v.* picar, escocer, *Ríopl.*, *C.A.*, *Méx.* arder.
smash [smæʃ] *v.* quebrantar, quebrar, romper; destrozar; aplastar; **to** — **into** chocar con; topar con, darse un tope contra; *s.* quebrazón, quiebra; fracaso; choque o tope violento; derrota completa.
smat·ter·ing [smǽtərɪŋ] *s.* conocimiento superficial y rudimental.
smear [smɪr] *v.* embarrar, untar, manchar; **to** — **with paint** pintorrear, pintarrajear; *s.* mancha.
smell [smɛl] *v.* oler; **to** — **of** oler a; *s.* olor; olfato; — **of** olor a; **to take a** — oler.
smell·y [smɛ́lɪ] *adj.* oloroso; hediondo.
smelt [smɛlt] *v.* fundir (*metales*); *pret. & p.p. de* **to smell.**
smile [smaɪl] *v.* sonreír(se); *s.* sonrisa.
smil·ing [smáɪlɪŋ] *adj.* risueño, sonriente; **-ly** *adv.* sonriendo, con cara risueña.
smite [smaɪt] *v.* golpear; herir; castigar; afligir; *véase* **smitten.**
smith [smɪθ] *s.* forjador; *véase* **blacksmith, goldsmith, silversmith.**
smith·y [smíθɪ] *s.* herrería, fragua, forja.
smit·ten [smítn̩] *p.p. de* **to smite** *& adj.* afligido; castigado; (*in love*) enamorado; **to be** — **with a disease** darle a uno una enfermedad.
smock [smɑk] *s.* bata corta, batín.
smoke [smok] *s.* humo; — **screen** cortina de humo; **cloud of** — humareda; **to have a** — dar una fumada, fumar; *v.* fumar, *Am.* chupar (*un cigarro*); humear; ahumar; **to** — **out** ahuyentar o echar fuera con humo.
smok·er [smókɚ] *s.* fumador; (*car*) vagón de fumar; reunión o tertulia de fumadores.
smoke·stack [smókstæk] *s.* chimenea.
smok·ing [smókɪŋ] *adj.* humeante; de fumar; para fumadores; — **car** vagón de fumar; — **room** fumadero, cuarto de fumar.
smok·y [smókɪ] *adj.* humeante; humoso, lleno de humo; ahumado.
smooth [smuð] *adj.* (*even*) liso; terso; igual, parejo; plano, llano; (*serene*) tranquilo; (*pleasant*) suave; (*wise*) sagaz; — **disposition** genio afable; — **manners** maneras o modales afables; — **style** estilo flúido y fácil; — **talker** hablador melífluo y sagaz; *v.* alisar; allanar; pulir; emparejar; **to** — **over** allanar, alisar, arreglar; **-ly** *adv.* suavemente; blandamente; fácilmente, con facilidad.
smooth·ness [smúðnɪs] *s.* (*evenness*) lisura; igualdad, uniformidad; (*pleasantness*) suavidad; afabilidad; tranquilidad; facilidad, fluidez.
smote [smot] *pret. de* **to smite.**
smoth·er [smʌ́ðɚ] *v.* ahogar(se); sofocar(se); asfixiar(se).
smudge [smʌdʒ] *v.* tiznar, manchar o ensuciar con tizne; ahumar; *s.* tiznón, mancha (*hecha con tizne*); humareda, nube espesa de humo.
smug·gle [smʌ́gl] *v.* contrabandear, hacer contrabando; **to** — **in** meter de contrabando; **to** — **out** sacar de contrabando.
smug·gler [smʌ́glɚ] *s.* contrabandista.
smut [smʌt] *s.* (*smudge*) tizne; suciedad, mancha; (*obscenity*) obscenidad, dicho obsceno o indecente; (*plant*) tizón (*enfermedad de ciertas plantas*); *v.* tiznar; ensuciar, manchar.
smut·ty [smʌ́tɪ] *adj.* tiznado, manchado de tizne; sucio.
snack [snæk] *s.* (*food*) bocado, bocadillo, tentempié, bocadito; (*meal*) merienda, comida ligera.
snag [snæg] *s.* (*protuberance*) tocón; raigón; (*obstacle*) tropiezo, obstáculo; **to hit a** — tropezar con un obstáculo; *v.* rasgar; enredar.
snail [snel] *s.* caracol.
snake [snek] *s.* culebra, víbora; *v.* culebrear.

snap [snæp] *v.* (*make sound*) chasquear, dar un chasquido; estallar; (*break*) quebrar(se); (*photograph*) fotografiar instantáneamente; **his eyes** — le chispean los ojos; **to — at** echar una mordida o mordisco a; dar una tarascada a, morder; asir (*una oportunidad*); **to — back at** tirar una mordida a; dar una respuesta grosera a; **to — off** soltarse, saltar; quebrar(se); **to — one's fingers** tronar los dedos, castañetear con los dedos; **to — shut** cerrar(se) de golpe; **to — together** apretar, abrochar; **to — up** agarrar, asir; morder; *s.* chasquido; estallido; mordida, mordisco, dentellada; broche de presión; energía, vigor; galleta; cosa fácil, ganga; **cold** — nortazo; repentino descenso de temperatura; **not to care a** — no importarle a uno un ardite o un comino; *adj.* hecho de prisa, impensado; instantáneo; — **fastener** broche de presión; — **judgment** decisión atolondrada; — **lock** cerradura de golpe.

snap·py [snǽpɪ] *adj.* mordedor, *Ven.*, *C.A.*, *Andes* mordelón; (*angry*) enojadizo, *Méx.* enojón; violento, vivo; (*elegant*) elegante; — **cheese** queso acre o picante; — **eyes** ojos chispeantes.

snap·shot [snǽpʃɑt] *s.* instantánea, fotografía instantánea; *v.* sacar una instantánea.

snare [snɛr] *s.* (*trap*) trampa, lazo; (*ambush*) acechanza; (*net*) red; *v.* (*tangle*) enredar; atrapar, coger con trampa; tender lazos a.

snarl [snɑrl] *v.* (*sound*) gruñir; (*tangle*) enmarañar(se), enredar(se); *s.* gruñido; maraña, enredo; pelo enmarañado.

snatch [snætʃ] *v.* arrebatar; agarrar; **to — at** tratar de asir o agarrar; *s.* arrebatiña, arrebatamiento; trozo, pedacito; **to make a — at** tratar de arrebatar, tratar de agarrarse a.

sneak [snik] *v.* andar furtivamente; obrar solapadamente; **to — in** meter(se) a escondidas; colarse; **to — out** escurrirse, salirse a hurtadillas; sacar, llevarse (*algo*) a escondidas; *s.* persona solapada.

sneer [snɪr] *v.* (*smile*) sonreír con sorna; (*gesture*) hacer un gesto de desdén; (*ridicule*) mofarse; **to — at** mofarse de; *s.* sorna, mofa, rechifla; gesto desdeñoso.

sneeze [sniz] *v.* estornudar; *s.* estornudo.

sniff [snɪf] *v.* husmear, olfatear; sorber (*por las narices*); (*snort*) resollar para adentro; **to — at** husmear; (*ridicule*) menospreciar; *s.* husmeo, olfateo; sorbo (*por las narices*).

snif·fle [snɪ́fl] *v.* sorber por las narices.

snip [snɪp] *v.* tijeretear; **to — off** cortar de un tijeretazo, recortar; *s.* tijeretada, tijeretazo; pedacito, recorte.

snipe [snaɪp] *v.* tirar, disparar desde un escondite.

snip·er [snáɪpɚ] *s.* francotirador; tirador emboscado.

snitch [snɪtʃ] *v.* (*tell on*) ratear; (*rob*) hurtar.

sniv·el [snɪvl] *v.* moquear; gimotear.

snob [snɑb] *s.* esnob.

snoop [snup] *v.* fisgar, fisgonear, curiosear; *s.* curioso, fisgón.

snooze [snuz] *v.* dormitar, sestear; *s.* siestecita, siestita; **to take a** — echar un sueñecito o siestita; descabezar el sueño.

snore [snor] *v.* roncar; *s.* ronquido.

snor·kel [snɔ́rkl] *s.* tubo esnorkel.

snort [snɔrt] *v.* resoplar; bufar; *s.* resoplido, bufido.

snout [snaʊt] *s.* hocico, jeta.

snow [sno] *s.* nieve; *v.* nevar; **to be -ed under** estar totalmente cubierto por la nevada.

snow·ball [snóbɔl] *s.* bola de nieve; *v.* tirar bolas de nieve.

snow·drift [snódrɪft] *s.* ventisca, ventisquero, montón de nieve.

snow·fall [snófɔl] *s.* nevada.

snow·flake [snóflek] *s.* copo de nieve.

snow·storm [snóstɔrm] *s.* fuerte nevada, nevasca.

snow·y [snóɪ] *adj.* nevado; (*white*) níveo, blanco como la nieve.

snub [snʌb] *v.* desairar, menospreciar; *s.* desaire; **snub-nosed** chato, *C.A.*, *Col.*, *Ven.*, *Andes* ñato.

snuff [snʌf] *v.* olfatear, husmear, ventear; (*blow out*) aspirar (*por la nariz*); despabilar (*una candela*); **to — at** olfatear, ventear; **to — out** apagar, extinguir; **to — up** sorber (*por las narices*); *s.* sorbo (*por la nariz*); rapé, tabaco en polvo; pabilo, mecha quemada (*de una vela*).

snuf·fle [snʌ́fl] *v.* ganguear; husmear.

snug [snʌg] *adj.* (*squeezed*) apretado; ajustado; compacto; (*comfortable*) abrigado; cómodo.

so [so] *adv.* así; tan, muy; tanto; **so-so** regular; **so-and-so** Fulano (de tal); — **as to** para; — **far** tan lejos; hasta ahora, hasta aquí; — **many** tantos; — **much** tanto; — **much for that** basta por ese lado; — **much the better** tanto mejor; — **that** de modo que; para que; a fin de que; de suerte que; — **then** conque, pues bien, así pues; — **long!** ¡hasta luego!; **and — forth** etcetera; y así sucesivamente; **I believe** — así lo creo; **is that — ?** ¿de veras? ¿de verdad?; ¡ no diga!; **ten minutes or** — poco más o menos diez minutos, como diez minutos.

soak [sok] *v.* remojar(se); empapar(se); **to — up** absorber, embeber; chupar; — **in grease** pringar; **to be -ed through** estar empapado; estar calado hasta los huesos; *s.* remojo, mojada; borrachín; golpe, puñetazo.

soap [sop] *s.* jabón; — **bubble** pompa de jabón, *Ven.*, *Col.* bombita; *Andes*, *Méx.* burbuja de jabón; — **dish** jabonera; **soft** — jabón blando; lisonja, adulación; *v.* enjabonar.

soap·y [sópɪ] *adj.* lleno de jabón.

soar [sor] *v.* remontarse; encumbrarse; subir muy alto; remontar el vuelo.

sob [sɑb] *v.* sollozar; *s.* sollozo.

so·ber [sóbɚ] *adj.* (*temperate*) sobrio; moderado, templado; (*serious*) serio, grave; (*sane*) cuerdo, sensato; (*calm*) tranquilo, sereno; **to be** — estar en su juicio; no estar borracho; *v.* **to — down** sosegar(se), calmar(se); formalizarse; **to — up** desembriagarse, desemborracharse; bajársele a uno la borrachera.

so·ber·ly [sóbɚlɪ] *adv.* sobriamente; cuerdamente, con sensatez; seriamente.

so·ber·ness [sóbɚnɪs] *s.* sobriedad; seriedad.

so·bri·e·ty [səbráɪətɪ] *s.* sobriedad; cordura.

so·called [sókɔ́ld] *adj.* así llamado, llamado.

soc·cer [sɑ́kɚ] *s.* fútbol.

so·cia·ble [sóʃəbl] *adj.* sociable, social, tratable.

so·cial [sóʃəl] *adj.* social; sociable; tratable, de buen trato; *s.* reunión social; tertulia; — **security** seguridad social; — **welfare** beneficencia publica; — **work** servicio social.

so·cial·ism [sóʃəlɪzəm] *s.* socialismo.

so·cial·ist [sóʃəlɪst] *adj.* & *s.* socialista.

so·cial·ize [sóʃəlaɪz] *v.* socializar.

so·ci·e·ty [səsáɪətɪ] *s.* sociedad; compañía.

so·ci·ol·o·gy [soʃɪɑ́lədʒɪ] *s.* sociología.

sock [sɑk] *s.* (*garment*) calcetín; (*blow*) porrazo, golpe, puñetazo; *v.* pegar, apalear, golpear; *Méx.*, *Carib.* batear (*una pelota*).

sock·et [sɑ́kɪt] *s.* (*eye*) cuenca (*del ojo*); portalámparas, enchufe, *Carib.* sóquet.

sod [sɑd] *s.* (*lawn*) césped; (*piece*) terrón (*de tierra*

sembrada de césped); *v.* cubrir de césped.
so·da [sódə] *s.* soda, sosa; — **fountain** *Am.* fuente de soda; — **water** agua gaseosa; **baking** — bicarbonato de sodio.
so·di·um [sódɪəm] *s.* sodio.
sod·om·y [sádəmɪ] *s.* sodomía.
so·fa [sófə] *s.* sofá.
soft [sɔft] *adj.* (*bland*) blando; muelle; suave; (*gentle*) tierno; dulce; **soft-boiled eggs** huevos pasados por agua; *Méx.*, *C.A.*, *Col.*, *Ven.* huevos tibios; — **coal** carbón bituminoso; — **drink** bebida no alcohólica; — **metal** metal dulce, metal maleable; — **money** moneda débil; — **soap** jabón blando; adulación; — **water** agua dulce; *adv.* *véase* **softly.**
sof·ten [sɔ́fən] *v.* ablandar(se); suavizar(se); enternecer(se); templar(se); **to — one's voice** bajar la voz, hablar quedo (*o* quedito).
soft-heart·ed [sɔfthɑrtəd] *adj.* de buen corazón.
soft·ly [sɔ́ftlɪ] *adv.* blandamente; suavemente; quedo, quedito.
soft·ness [sɔ́ftnɪs] *s.* blandura; molicie; suavidad; ternura; dulzura.
software [sɔ́ftwɛr] *s.* (*computer*) logical, conjunto lógico, software.
sog·gy [sɑ́gɪ] *adj.* remojado; empapado.
soil [sɔɪl] *s.* suelo, terreno, tierra; (*spot*) mancha; **native** — terruño; *v.* ensuciar(se); manchar(se).
so·journ [sódʒɝn] *s.* estada, estancia, permanencia, *Andes*, *Méx.*, *Ríopl.* estadía; *v.* permanecer; estarse, residir por una temporada.
sol·ace [sɑ́lɪs] *s.* solaz; *v.* solazar.
so·lar [sólɚ] *adj.* solar, del sol; — **plexis** plexo solar.
sold [sold] *pret. & p.p. de* **to sell; to be — on an idea** estar bien convencido de una idea.
sol·der [sɑ́dɚ] *v.* soldar; *s.* soldadura.
sol·dier [sóldʒɚ] *s.* soldado.
sole [sol] *adj.* solo, único; exclusivo; *s.* (*shoe*) suela (*del zapato*); (*foot*) planta (*del pie*); (*fish*) lenguado (*pez*); — **right** derecho exclusivo; *v.* solar, echar suelas a; **to half-sole** echar o poner medias suelas a.
sole·ly [sóllɪ] *adv.* sólamente, únicamente.
sol·emn [sɑ́ləm] *adj.* solemne.
so·lem·ni·ty [səlɛ́mnətɪ] *s.* solemnidad.
sol-fa·ing [solfáɪŋ] *s.* solfeo.
so·lic·it [səlísɪt] *v.* solicitar.
so·lic·i·tor [səlísətɚ] *s.* solicitador, agente.
so·lic·i·tous [səlísɪtəs] *adj.* solícito.
so·lic·i·tude [səlísətjud] *s.* solicitud, cuidado.
sol·id [sɑ́lɪd] *s.* sólido; *adj.* sólido; firme; macizo; (*sane*) sensato; (*unanimous*) unánime; — **blue** todo azul; — **gold** oro puro; **for one — hour** por una hora entera, por una hora sin parar; **the country is — for** el país está firmemente unido en favor de.
sol·i·dar·i·ty [sɑlədǽrətɪ] *s.* solidaridad.
so·lid·i·fy [səlídəfaɪ] *v.* solidificar(se).
so·lid·i·ty [səlídətɪ] *s.* solidez.
sol·id-state [sɑlədstét] *adj.* física del estado sólido.
so·lil·o·quy [səlíləkwɪ] *s.* soliloquio.
sol·i·tar·y [sɑlətɛrɪ] *adj.* solitario; solo; *s.* solitario, ermitaño.
sol·i·tude [sɑ́lətjud] *s.* soledad.
so·lo [solo] *s.* solo.
so·lo·ist [sóloɪst] *s.* solista.
sol·stice [sálstəs] *s.* solsticio.
sol·u·ble [sɑ́ljəbl] *adj.* soluble, que se disuelve fácilmente.
so·lu·tion [səlúʃən] *s.* solución.
solve [sɑlv] *v.* resolver; explicar, aclarar, desenredar; solucionar.
som·ber [sɑ́mbɚ] *adj.* sombrío.
some [sʌm] *adj.* algún, alguno; algunos, unos; algo de, un poco de; — **one** alguien, alguno; — **twenty people** unas veinte personas; *pron.* algunos, unos; algo, un poco; una parte.
some·bod·y [sʌ́mbɑdɪ] *pron.* alguien; **a** — un personaje de importancia.
some·how [sʌ́mhaʊ] *adv.* de algún modo, de alguna manera; — **or other** de una manera u otra; por alguna razón.
some·one [sʌ́mwʌn] *pron.* alguno, alguien.
som·er·sault [sʌ́mərsɔlt] *s.* voltereta; *v.* dar una voltereta.
some·thing [sʌ́mθɪŋ] *s.* algo, alguna cosa; un poco; — **else** alguna otra cosa, otra cosa.
some·time [sʌ́mtaɪm] *adv.* algún día; alguna vez; en algún tiempo; **-s** *adv.* a veces, algunas veces, de vez en cuando.
some·what [sʌ́mhwɑt] *s.* algo, alguna cosa, un poco; *adv.* algo, un tanto.
some·where [sʌ́mhwɛr] *adv.* en alguna parte; — **else** en alguna otra parte.
son [sʌn] *s.* hijo.
song [sɔŋ] *s.* canción; canto; **the Song of Songs** el Cantar de los Cantares; — **bird** ave canora, pájaro cantor; **to buy something for a** — comprar algo muy barato.
son·ic bar·ri·er [sɑnɪkbǽrɪɚ] *s.* barrera sónica.
son-in-law [sʌ́nɪnlɔ] *s.* yerno, hijo político.
son·net [sɑ́nɪt] *s.* soneto.
so·no·rous [sənórəs] *adj.* sonoro.
soon [sun] *adv.* pronto, presto; luego; — **after** poco después (de); al poco tiempo; **as — as** tan pronto como; luego que, así que; **how — ?** ¿cuándo?
soot [sʊt] *s.* hollín; tizne.
soothe [suð] *v.* calmar, sosegar; aliviar.
sooth·say·er [súθseɚ] *s.* adivino.
soot·y [sʊ́tɪ] *adj.* tiznado, cubierto de hollín.
sop [sɑp] *v.* empapar; **to — up** absorber; **to be sopping wet** estar hecho una sopa, estar mojado hasta los huesos; *s.* sopa (*pan u otra cosa empapada en leche, caldo, etc.*); (*bribe*) soborno, regalo (*para acallar, conciliar, o sobornar*).
so·phis·ti·cat·ed [səfɪstəketəd] *adj.* mundano; exento de simplicidad.
soph·o·more [sɑ́fəmor] *s.* estudiante de segundo año.
so·pran·o [səprǽno] *s.* soprano; **high** — tiple; — **voice** voz de soprano.
sor·cer·er [sɔ́rsərɚ] *s.* brujo, hechicero.
sor·did [sɔ́rdɪd] *adj.* sórdido; (*mean*) vil, indecente; mezquino.
sore [sor] *adj.* (*painful*) dolorido; inflamado, enconado; (*grievous*) afligido, apenado; (*injured*) lastimado; picado; (*offended*) ofendido; — **eyes** mal de ojos; **to be — at** estar enojado con; **to have a — throat** tener mal de garganta, dolerle a uno la garganta; *s.* úlcera, llaga; inflamación; lastimadura; (*sorrow*) pena, aflicción; **-ly** *adv.* dolorosamente, penosamente; **to be -ly in need of** necesitar con urgencia.
sore·ness [sórnɪs] *s.* dolor, dolencia; inflamación.
sor·rel [sɔ́rəl] *adj.* alazán (*rojo canela*); *s.* color alazán; caballo alazán.
sor·row [sɑ́ro] *s.* (*sadness*) dolor, pena, pesar; (*grieving*) pesadumbre; (*repentance*) arrepentimiento; *v.* apenarse, afligirse, sentir pena.
sor·row·ful [sɑ́rəfəl] *adj.* pesaroso, doloroso, lastimoso, afligido; **-ly** *adv.* tristemente, dolorosamente, con pena, desconsoladamente.
sor·ry [sɔ́ri] *adj.* triste, pesaroso, afligido,

arrepentido; lastimoso; **I am** — lo siento; me pesa; **I am — for her** la compadezco.
sort [sɔrt] *s.* suerte, clase, especie; — **of tired** algo cansado, un tanto cansado; **all -s of** toda suerte de, toda clase de; **out of -s** de mal humor, malhumorado; indispuesto; *v.* clasificar, ordenar, arreglar; (*computer*) clasificar; **to — out** separar, clasificar; entresacar; escoger.
sought [sɔt] *pret. & p.p. de* **to seek.**
soul [sol] *s.* alma; **not a** — nadie, ni un alma.
sound [saʊnd] *adj.* (*healthy*) sano; (*sane*) cuerdo; sensato; (*firm*) firme, sólido; ileso; **a — beating** una buena zurra o tunda; — **business** buen negocio, negocio bien organizado; — **reasoning** raciocinio sólido; — **sleep** sueño profundo; — **title** título válido o legal; **of — mind** en su juicio cabal; **safe and** — sano y salvo; **to sleep** — dormir profundamente; *s.* son, sonido; tono; brazo de mar; — **wave** onda sonora; *v.* sonar, tocar; sondear; tantear; auscultar (*el pecho, los pulmones*); cantar, entonar (*alabanzas*); **to — out** tantear, sondear.
sound·ness [sáʊndnɪs] *s.* (*firmness*) solidez; (*healthiness*) cordura, buen juicio; (*validity*) rectitud; validez; — **of body** buena salud corporal.
sound·track [sáʊndtræk] *s.* banda sonora, huella de sonido.
soup [sup] *s.* sopa; **cold vegetable** — gazpacho; — **tureen** sopera; — **dish** sopero.
sour [saʊr] *adj.* (*acid-like*) agrio; acre; ácido; desabrido; rancio; (*peevish*) malhumorado; — **milk** leche cortada; *v.* agriar(se); cortarse (*la leche*); fermentar; poner(se) de mal humor.
source [sors] *s.* origen; manantial, fuente; — **of supply** fuente de abastecimientos.
sour·ness [sáʊrnɪs] *s.* acidez, agrura, desabrimiento.
souse [saʊs] *v.* zambullir; chapuzar.
south [saʊθ] *s.* sur, sud; *adj.* meridional; del sur; austral; **South American** sudamericano, suramericano; — **pole** polo sur, polo antártico; *adv.* hacia el sur.
south·east [saʊθíst] *s. & adj.* sudeste; *adv.* hacia el sudeste.
south·east·ern [saʊθístɚn] *adj.* del sudeste, sudeste.
south·ern [sʌ́ðɚn] *adj.* meridional, del sur, austral, sureño; **Southern Cross** Cruz del Sur.
south·ern·er [sʌ́ðɚnɚ] *s.* sureño, meridional, habitante del sur.
south·ward [sáʊθwɚd] *adv.* hacia el sur, rumbo al sur.
south·west [saʊθwɛ́st] *s. & adj.* sudoeste (*o* suroeste); *adv.* hacia el sudoeste.
south·west·ern [saʊθwɛ́stɚn] *adj.* sudoeste (*o* suroeste), del sudoeste.
sou·ve·nir [suvənír] *s.* recuerdo, memoria.
sov·er·eign [sɑ́vrɪn] *s. & adj.* soberano.
sov·er·eign·ty [sɑ́vrɪntɪ] *s.* soberanía.
so·vi·et [sóvɪɪt] *s.* sóviet; *adj.* soviético.
sow [saʊ] *s.* puerca.
sow [so] *v.* sembrar.
sown [son] *p.p. de* **to sow.**
soy [sɔj] *s.* soja.
space [spes] *s.* espacio; — **science** ciencia del espacio; ciencia espacial; — **station** estación espacial; — **suit** traje espacial; **spacing** espaciado; *v.* espaciar .
space·bar [spésbar] *s.* barra espaciadora.
space·craft [spéskræft] *s.* nave espacial; astronave.
space·man [spésmæn] *s.* astronauta.
spa·cious [spéʃəs] *adj.* espacioso; dilatado, vasto.
spade [sped] *s.* azada, azadón; (*cards*) espada (*del juego de naipes*); *v.* cavar con la azada.
span [spæn] *s.* palmo; espacio; (*distance*) tramo; (*bridge*) arco u ojo (*de puente*); (*width*) envergadura (*de un aeroplano*); — **of life** longevidad; *v.* medir a palmos; atravesar.
span·gle [spǽŋgl] *s.* lentejuela; *v.* adornar con lentejuelas; brillar, centellear; **-d with stars** estrellado, sembrado (*o* tachonado) de estrellas.
Span·iard [spǽnjɚd] *s.* español.
span·iel [spǽnjəl] *s.* perro de aguas.
Span·ish [spǽnɪʃ] *adj.* español; *s.* español, idioma español.
spank [spæŋk] *v.* zurrar, dar una tunda, dar nalgadas; *s.* palmada, nalgada.
spank·ing [spǽŋkɪŋ] *s.* zurra, tunda, nalgadas.
spar [spɑr] *v.* boxear, pelear.
spare [spɛr] *v.* ahorrar; (*avoid*) evitar (*molestias, trabajo, etc.*); (*excuse*) perdonar; **I cannot — another dollar** no dispongo de otro dólar, no tengo más dinero disponible; **I cannot — the car today** no puedo pasarme hoy sin el automóvil; **to — no expense** no escatimar gastos; **to — the enemy** usar de clemencia con el enemigo; **to have time to** — tener tiempo de sobra; *adj.* flaco, descarnado; escaso, frugal; mezquino; sobrante; de sobra; de repuesto; — **parts** piezas de repuesto; *Méx.* refacciones; — **cash** dinero disponible o de sobra; — **time** tiempo libre, tiempo disponible; — **tire** neumático de repuesto.
spark [spɑrk] *s.* chispa; — **plug** bujía; *v.* chispear, echar chispas, chisporrotear.
spar·kle [spɑ́rkl] *s.* (*flash*) chispa, centella; brillo, centelleo; (*spirit*) viveza, animación; *v.* centellear; chispear; relucir, brillar.
spark·ling [spɑ́rklɪŋ] *adj.* centelleante; reluciente; chispeante; — **wine** vino espumoso.
spar·row [spǽro] *s.* gorrión, pardal.
sparse [spɑrs] *adj.* escaso; esparcido; poco denso, poco poblado; — **hair** pelo ralo.
spasm [spǽzəm] *s.* espasmo.
spas·tic [spǽstɪk] *adj.* espástico.
spat [spæt] *pret. & p.p. de* **to spit;** *v.* reñir, disputar; dar un manazo o sopapo; *s.* sopapo, manotada; riña, desavenencia; **-s** polainas cortas.
spat·ter [spǽtɚ] *v.* salpicar; rociar; manchar; *s.* salpicadura; rociada.
speak [spik] *v.* hablar; decir; recitar; — **to the point!** ¡vamos al grano!; **so to** — por decirlo asi; **to — for** hablar por, hablar en nombre o en favor de; pedir, solicitar; apalabrar, reservar; **to — one's mind** hablar sin rodeos, decir claramente lo que se piensa; **to — out** (*o* — **up**) hablar claro; hablar con toda franqueza; hablar en voz alta.
speak·er [spíkɚ] *s.* orador; conferenciante, conferencista; el que habla; **Speaker of the House** presidente de la cámara de representantes; **loud-speaker** altavoz, altoparlante.
spear [spɪr] *s.* lanza; arpón (*para pescar*); (*sprout*) brote, retoño, hoja (*de hierba*); *v.* alancear, lancear, herir con lanza.
spear·mint [spírmɪnt] *s.* yerbabuena (*hierbabuena*), menta.
spe·cial [spɛ́ʃəl] *adj.* especial; particular; — **delivery** entrega especial de correo; *s.* tren o autobús especial; carta urgente, entrega especial; **-ly** *adv.* especialmente; en especial; sobre todo.
spe·cial·ist [spɛ́ʃəlɪst] *s.* especialista.
spe·cial·i·za·tion [spɛʃəlɪzéʃən] *s.* especialización.
spe·cial·ize [spɛ́ʃəlaɪz] *v.* especializarse.
spe·cial·ty [spɛ́ʃəltɪ] *s.* especialidad.
spe·cies [spíʃɪz] *s.* especie; especies.
spe·cif·ic [spɪsífɪk] *adj.* específico; peculiar,

característico; — **gravity** peso específico; *s.* específico; **-ally** *adv.* específicamente; especificadamente; particularmente, en particular.
spec·i·fy [spésəfaɪ] *v.* especificar; estipular.
spec·i·men [spésəmən] *s.* espécimen, muestra, ejemplar.
speck [spɛk] *s.* mota; manchita; partícula; **not a** — ni pizca; *v. véase* **speckle.**
speck·le [spékl] *s.* manchita; mota; *v.* motear, salpicar de motas o manchas; manchar.
speck·led [spékld] *adj.* moteado; — **with freckles** pecoso.
spec·ta·cle [spéktəkl] *s.* espectáculo; **-s** gafas, anteojos; **to make a — of oneself** ponerse en la evidencia, ponerse en ridículo.
spec·tac·u·lar [spɛktǽkjələ˞] *adj.* espectacular, ostentoso, aparatoso.
spec·ta·tor [spéktetə˞] *s.* espectador.
spec·ter [spéktə˞] *s.* espectro, fantasma, aparecido.
spec·tro·graph [spéktrogræf] *s.* espectrógrafo.
spec·trum [spéktrəm] *s.* espectro.
spec·u·late [spékjəlet] *v.* especular; reflexionar.
spec·u·la·tion [spɛkjəléʃən] *s.* especulación; reflexión.
spec·u·la·tive [spékjəletɪv] *adj.* especulativo; teórico.
spec·u·la·tor [spékjəletə˞] *s.* especulador.
sped [spɛd] *pret. & p.p. de* **to speed.**
speech [spitʃ] *s.* habla; lenguaje, idioma; (*formal*) discurso, arenga; (*lecture*) conferencia; (*theater*) parlamento (*de un actor*); **to make a** — pronunciar un discurso, hacer una perorata.
speech·less [spítʃlɪs] *adj.* sin habla; mudo; estupefacto.
speed [spid] *s.* velocidad; rapidez; presteza, (*promptness*) prontitud; — **limit** velocidad máxima; **at full** — a toda velocidad; **speed-up** aceleración, aumento de producción; *v.* apresurar(se), acelerar(se), dar(se) prisa; correr; ir con exceso de velocidad; despachar.
speed·i·ly [spídɪlɪ] *adv.* velozmente, rápidamente; a todo correr; de prisa, con prontitud.
speed·om·e·ter [spidɑ́mətə˞] *s.* velocímetro.
speed·y [spídɪ] *adj.* veloz, rápido.
spell [spɛl] *s.* (*charm*) hechizo, encanto; (*period*) temporada, corto período; (*sickness*) ataque (*de una enfermedad*); **to put under a** — aojar; hechizar, encantar; *v.* deletrear; significar, indicar; **how is it -ed?** ¿cómo se escribe?
spell·er [spélə˞] *s.* silabario; deletreador.
spell·ing [spélɪŋ] *s.* ortografía; deletreo; — **book** silabario.
spelt [spɛlt] *pret. & p.p. de* **to spell.**
spend [spɛnd] *v.* gastar; usar, agotar, consumir; **to — a day** pasar un día.
spend·thrift [spéndθrɪft] *s.* derrochador, gastador, pródigo.
spent [spɛnt] *pret. & p.p. de* **to spend.**
sperm [spə˞m] *s.* esperma.
sphere [sfɪr] *s.* esfera; globo, orbe.
spher·i·cal [sférɪkl] *adj.* esférico.
sphynx [sfɪŋks] *s.* esfinge.
spice [spaɪs] *s.* especia; picante; aroma; *v.* condimentar, sazonar con especias.
spic·y [spáɪsɪ] *adj.* sazonado con especias; picante; aromático.
spi·der [spáɪdə˞] *s.* araña; sartén; — **web** telaraña.
spig·ot [spígət] *s.* espita, grifo, canilla; *Méx.* bitoque.
spike [spaɪk] *s.* (*sprout*) espiga; (*metal*) perno; clavo largo; alcayata; pico; *v.* clavar; clavetear.
spill [spɪl] *v.* verter; derramar(se); desparramar(se); hacer caer (*de un caballo*); (*tell*) revelar (*una noticia, un secreto*); *s.* derrame, derramamiento; vuelco; caída (*de un caballo*).
spilt [spɪlt] *pret. & p.p. de* **to spill.**
spin [spɪn] *v.* hilar; (*whirl*) girar, dar vueltas, rodar; (*dance*) bailar; **to — out** prolongar, alargar; **to — yarns** contar cuentos; *s.* giro, vuelta; (*trip*) paseo (*en automóvil, bicicleta, etc.*); barrena (*hablando de aeroplanos*); **spin-off** entidad que resulta de la división de producto o proceso.
spin·ach [spínɪtʃ] *s.* espinaca.
spi·nal [spáɪnl] *adj.* espinal; — **column** columna vertebral, espina dorsal.
spin·dle [spíndl] *s.* huso; eje; **spindle motor** motor accionador del husillo.
spine [spaɪn] *s.* espina; espinazo, espina dorsal, columna vertebral.
spin·ner [spínə˞] *s.* hilandero, hilandera; máquina de hilar.
spin·ning [spínɪŋ] *s.* hilandería, arte de hilar; — **machine** aparato para hilar, máquina de hilar; — **mill** hilandería; — **top** trompo; — **wheel** torno de hilar.
spin·ster [spínstə˞] *s.* soltera; solterona.
spi·ral [spáɪrəl] *adj.* espiral; — **staircase** caracol, escalera espiral; *s.* espiral.
spire [spaɪr] *s.* aguja, chapitel de torre; cúspide, ápice; punto más alto; — **of grass** brizna de hierba.
spir·it [spírɪt] *s.* (*essence*) espíritu; temple; (*animation*) viveza, animación; ánimo; **low -s** abatimiento; **to be in good -s** estar de buen humor; **to be out of -s** estar triste o abatido; *v.* **to — away** llevarse misteriosamente.
spir·it·ed [spírɪtɪd] *adj.* vivo, brioso, fogoso.
spir·i·tu·al [spírɪtʃuɛl] *adj.* espiritual; *s.* (*song*) espiritual (*tonada religiosa de los negros del sur de los Estados Unidos*).
spit [spɪt] *v.* escupir; expectorar; *pret. & p.p. de* **to spit;** *s.* esputo, saliva; asador.
spite [spaɪt] *s.* despecho, rencor, inquina, ojeriza; **in — of** a despecho de; a pesar de; **out of** — por despecho; *v.* picar, irritar, hacer rabiar.
spite·ful [spáɪtfəl] *adj.* rencoroso.
splash [splæʃ] *v.* salpicar; rociar; (*soil*) enlodar, manchar; chapotear (*en el agua*); *s.* salpicadura; rociada; chapoteo.
spleen [splin] *s.* bazo; mal humor, rencor.
splen·did [spléndɪd] *adj.* espléndido.
splen·dor [spléndə˞] *s.* esplendor; esplendidez.
splice [splaɪs] *v.* empalmar, unir, juntar; *s.* empalme; junta.
splint [splɪnt] *s.* tablilla; astilla; *v.* entablillar.
splin·ter [splíntə˞] *s.* astilla; (*crack*) raja; *v.* astillar(se), hacer(se) astillas; romper(se) en astillas.
split [splɪt] *v.* hender(se), rajar(se); resquebrajar(se); partir(se), dividir(se); **to — hairs** pararse en pelillos; **to — one's dies with laughter** desternillarse de risa, reventar de risa; **to — the difference** partir la diferencia; *pret. & p.p. de* **to split;** *adj.* partido, hendido, rajado; dividido; resquebrajado; *s.* raja, hendedura, grieta; cisma, rompimiento.
splurge [splə˞dʒ] *s.* ostentación; fachenda.
spoil [spɔɪl] *v.* (*decay*) dañar(se); echar(se) a perder, podrir(se), corromper(se); (*harm*) estropear(se); arruinar; (*overindulge*) consentir, mimar; *s.* botín, presa; **-s of war** botín o despojos de guerra.
spoil·age [spɔ́ɪlədʒ] *s.* desperdicio; *Arg., Col.* desechos; *Méx.* deterioro.
spoke [spok] *s.* rayo (*de rueda*); *pret. de* **to speak.**

spo·ken [spókən] *p.p. de* **to speak.**
spokes·man [spóksmən] *s.* portavoz, vocero.
sponge [spʌndʒ] *s.* (*absorbent*) esponja; (*dependent person*) gorrón, parásito; *v.* lavar o limpiar con esponja; vivir de gorra, vivir a costa ajena; **to — up** chupar, absorber.
sponge·cake [spʌ́ndʒkek] *s.* bizcocho esponjoso.
spong·er [spʌ́ndʒɚ] *s.* esponja, gorrón, pegote, parásito, *Am.* pavo.
spon·gy [spʌ́ndʒɪ] *adj.* esponjoso, esponjado.
spon·sor [spɑ́nsɚ] *s.* padrino, madrina; (*patron*) patrón (*el que patrocina una empresa*); (*protector*) defensor; fiador; fomentador, promovedor; *v.* apadrinar; promover, fomentar; patrocinar; ser fiador de.
spon·ta·ne·i·ty [spɑntəníətɪ] *s.* espontaneidad.
spon·ta·ne·ous [spɑnténɪəs] *adj.* espontáneo.
spook [spuk] *s.* espectro, fantasma, aparecido.
spool [spul] *s.* carrete, carretel; *v.* devanar, enredar (*hilo*) en carrete.
spoon [spun] *s.* cuchara; *v.* cucharear, sacar con cuchara.
spoon·ful [spúnfəl] *s.* cucharada.
sport [sport] *s.* deporte; **in —** en broma, de burla; **to make — of** reírse de, burlarse de; **to be a good —** ser buen perdedor (*en el juego*); ser un buen compañero; *v.* jugar; divertirse; bromear, chancearse; **to — a new dress** lucir un traje nuevo; **-s** *adj.* deportivo; **— clothes** trajes deportivos.
sports car [spórtskar] *s.* coche (*carro*) deportivo, esport.
sports·man [spórtsmən] *s.* deportista; jugador generoso, buen perdedor (*en deportes*).
spot [spɑt] *s.* (*blemish*) mancha, mota; (*place*) sitio, lugar; **in -s** aquí y allí; aquí y allá; **on the —** allí mismo; al punto; **to pay — cash** pagar al contado; **— announcement** anuncio breve, anuncio suelto; *v.* manchar, ensuciar; motear; echar de ver, distinguir; avistar; localizar.
spot·less [spɑ́tlɪs] *adj.* sin mancha, limpio.
spot·light [spɑ́tlaɪt] *s.* faro giratorio.
spot·ted [spɑ́tɪd] *adj.* manchado; moteado.
spouse [spaʊz] *s.* esposo, esposa.
spout [spaʊt] *v.* chorrear; brotar; salir en chorro; (*speak*) emitir; declamar, perorar; hablar mucho; *s.* chorro; surtidor; pico (*de tetera, cafetera, jarra, etc.*); espita.
sprain [spren] *v.* torcer (*una coyuntura o músculo*); **to — one's ankle** torcerse el tobillo; *s.* torsión, torcedura.
sprang [spræŋ] *pret. de* **to spring.**
sprawl [sprɔl] *v.* despatarrarse; estar despatarrado; tenderse; **to — one's legs** abrir las piernas; *s.* postura floja (*abiertos los brazos y piernas*).
spray [spre] *s.* (*liquid*) rocío, rociada; líquido para rociar; (*branch*) ramita; **sea —** espuma del mar; *v.* rociar.
spread [sprɛd] *v.* extender(se); desparramar(se); esparcir(se); difundir(se), diseminar(se), dispersar(se); propalar(se) (*noticias, rumores, etc.*), propagar(se); **to — apart** abrir(se), separar(se); **to — butter on** poner mantequilla en; **to — out the tablecloth** tender el mantel; **to — paint on** dar una mano de pintura a; **to — with** cubrir de; untar con; *s.* extensión; amplitud, anchura; envergadura (*de un aeroplano*); difusión; diseminación; propagación; cubierta, sobrecama; comilitona, festín; mantequilla, queso, etc., que se le unta al pan; *pret. & p.p. de* **to spread; — sheet** (*computer*) hoja electrónica.
spree [spri] *s.* juerga, parranda, holgorio; **to go on a —** andar (*o* ir) de parranda o juerga, *Ríopl.* ir de farra.
sprig [sprɪg] *s.* ramita.
spright·ly [spráɪtlɪ] *adj.* vivo, animado, brioso; alegre.
spring [sprɪŋ] *v.* saltar; brincar; hacer saltar; **to — a leak** hacer agua (*un barco*); comenzar a gotearse (*la cañería, el techo, etc.*); formarse una gotera; **to — a trap** hacer saltar una trampa; **to — at** abalanzarse sobre; **to — from** salir de, nacer de, brotar de; **to — news of a surprise** dar de sopetón una noticia o sorpresa; **to — something open** abrir algo a la fuerza; **to — to one's feet** levantarse de un salto; **to — up** brotar; surgir; crecer; levantarse de un salto; *s.* (*season*) primavera; (*coil*) muelle (*de metal*); resorte; elasticidad; salto, brinco; (*water*) manantial, fuente; origen; *adj.* primaveral; **— board** trampolín; **— mattress** colchón de muelles; **— water** agua de manantial.
spring·bolt [sprɪ́ŋbolt] *s.* pestillo de golpe.
spring·time [sprɪ́ŋtaɪm] *s.* primavera.
sprink·le [sprɪ́ŋkl] *v.* (*scatter*) rociar; regar; espolvorear; salpicar; (*rain*) lloviznar; *s.* rociada, rocío; llovizna; **— of salt** pizca de sal.
sprint [sprɪnt] *v.* echar una carrera; *s.* carrera, carrerilla, corrida corta.
sprout [spraʊt] *v.* brotar; retoñar, germinar; hacer germinar o brotar; *s.* retoño, renuevo; **Brussels -s** bretones, coles de Bruselas.
spruce [sprus] *s.* abeto; *adj.* pulcro, aseado, pulido; elegante; *v.* **to — up** asearse, componerse, emperifollarse.
sprung [sprʌŋ] *pret. & p.p. de* **to spring.**
spun [spʌn] *pret. & p.p. de* **to spin.**
spur [spɝ] *s.* espuela; acicate; (*stimulus*) aguijón, estímulo; (*rooster*) espolón (*del gallo*); estribación (*de una montaña*); **— track** ramal corto (*de ferrocarril*); **on the — of the moment** impensadamente, sin la reflexión debida; por el momento; *v.* espolear, aguijar, picar, incitar; **to — on** animar, incitar a obrar o a seguir adelante.
spu·ri·ous [spúrɪəs] *adj.* espurio.
spurn [spɝn] *v.* rechazar, desdeñar, menospreciar.
spurt [spɝt] *v.* salir a borbotones; chorrear; echar chorros; (*effort*) hacer un repentino esfuerzo (*para ganar una carrera*); *s.* borbotón, chorrazo, chorro repentino; esfuerzo repentino; **— of anger** arranque de ira; **-s of flame** llamaradas.
sput·ter [spʌ́tɚ] *v.* chisporrotear; (*grumble*) refunfuñar; *s.* chisporroteo; refunfuño.
spu·tum [spjútəm] *s.* esputo.
spy [spaɪ] *s.* espía; *v.* espiar; acechar; atisbar; **to — on** espiar, atisbar.
spy·glass [spáɪglæs] *s.* anteojo de larga vista.
squab [skwɑb] *s.* pichón.
squab·ble [skwɑ́bl] *s.* reyerta; *v.* reñir, disputar.
squad [skwɑd] *s.* escuadra, patrulla, partida.
squad·ron [skwɑ́drɑn] *s.* escuadra; escuadrón.
squal·id [skwɑ́lɪd] *adj.* escuálido.
squall [skwɔl] *s.* (*rain*) chubasco; (*sound*) chillido; *v.* chillar.
squan·der [skwɑ́ndɚ] *v.* despilfarrar, derrochar, malgastar, disipar.
square [skwɛr] *s.* (*rectangle*) cuadro; cuadrado; (*central park*) plaza; (*block*) manzana de casas; *Am.* cuadra; escuadra (*de carpintero*); (*chess*) casilla (*de tablero de ajedrez, damas, etc.*); **he is on the —** obra de buena fe; *v.* cuadrar; ajustar, arreglar, (*balance*) saldar (*cuentas*); justificar; cuadricular; **to — one's shoulders** enderezar los

hombros; cuadrarse; **to — oneself with** sincerarse con, justificarse ante; **to — a person with another** poner bien a una persona con otra; *adj.* cuadrado, en cuadro, a escuadra, en ángulo recto; saldado; justo, recto, equitativo; franco; **— corner** esquina en ángulo recto; **— meal** comida completa, comida en regla; **— mile** milla cuadrada; **— root** raíz cuadrada; **— dance** danza de figuras; cuadrilla; **to be — with someone** estar en paz con alguien, no deberle nada, *Am.* estar a mano; *adv.* véase **squarely.**

square·ly [skwɛ́rlɪ] *adv.* equitativamente, honradamente; firmemente; de buena fe; derecho, derechamente; **to hit the target — in the middle** pegar de lleno en el blanco.

squash [skwɑʃ] *s.* calabaza; *v.* aplastar, despachurrar o apachurrar.

squat [skwɑt] *v.* agazaparse, sentarse en cuclillas; agacharse; ocupar tierras baldías para ganar título de propietario; *adj.* agazapado, sentado en cuclillas; (*short*) rechoncho, achaparrado, *Méx., C.A., Andes* chaparro.

squawk [skwɔk] *v.* (*noise*) graznar; chillar; (*complain*) quejarse; *s.* graznido; chillido; queja.

squeak [skwik] *v.* rechinar, chirriar; chillar; *s.* rechinamiento; chirrido, chillico.

squeal [skwil] *v.* chillar; (*complain*) quejarse, protestar; (*"snitch"*) soplar, delatar; *s.* chillido.

squea·mish [skwímɪʃ] escrupuloso; delicado; remilgado.

squeeze [skwiz] *v.* estrujar; despachurrar o apachurrar; exprimir; prensar; apretar; **to — into** meter(se) a estrujones, encajar(se) en; **to — out the juice** exprimir el jugo; **to — through a crowd** abrirse paso a estrujones por entre la muchedumbre; *s.* estrujón; apretón; abrazo fuerte; apretura.

squelch [skwɛltʃ] *v.* (*crush*) aplastar; (*silence*) acallar, imponer silencio; (*scold*) reprender; **to — a revolt** sofocar o apagar una revuelta.

squid [skwɪd] *s.* calamar.

squint [skwɪnt] *v.* mirrar de través; mirar de soslayo; mirar achicando los ojos; mirar furtivamente; bizquear (*mirar bizco*); *s.* mirada de soslayo; mirada bizca; mirada furtiva; **squint-eyed** *adj.* bisojo o bizco.

squire [skwaɪr] *s.* escudero; *v.* acompañar, escoltar.

squirm [skwɝm] *v.* retorcerse; **to — out of a difficulty** forcejear para salir de un aprieto.

squir·rel [skwɝ́əl] *s.* ardilla.

squirt [skwɝt] *v.* jeringar; echar un chisguete; salir a chorritos (*o* a chisguetes); *s.* jeringazo; chisguete.

stab [stæb] *v.* apuñalar, dar una puñalada, dar de puñalada, acuchillar; pinchar; *s.* puñalada, cuchillada, estocada; pinchazo.

sta·bil·i·ty [stəbɪ́lətɪ] *s.* estabilidad.

sta·ble [stébl] *adj.* estable; *s.* establo, cuadra; caballerizà; *v.* poner (*los animales*) en la caballeriza.

stack [stæk] *s.* pila, montón, rimero; (*hay*) hacina (*de paja o heno*); (*chimney*) chimenea, cañón de chimenea; **library -s** estanterías o anaqueles de biblioteca; *v.* amontonar, apilar.

sta·di·um [stédɪəm] *s.* estadio.

staff [stæf] *s.* (*stick*) báculo, cayado, bastón, vara; (*pole*) asta (*de bandera, de lanza*); (*group*) cuerpo, consejo administrativo; funcionarios; **— of life** sostén de la vida; **— officer** oficial de estado mayor; **army —** estado mayor; **editorial —** redacción; **musical —** pentagrama; **teaching —** cuerpo docente; *v.* proveer de funcionarios y empleados (*una organización*).

staff·ing [stǽfɪŋ] *s.* planilla de personal, *Méx.* integración.

stag [stæg] *s.* venado, ciervo; (*male*) macho, hombre; **— dinner** banquete exclusivo para hombres.

stage [stedʒ] *s.* (*platform*) tablado; tablas, escenario; escena; (*theater*) teatro; (*period*) etapa, tramo; período; (*stop*) parada; **— coach** ómnibus, autobús; **— hand** tramoyista; **by easy -s** por grados, gradualmente; *v.* representar, poner en escena; **to — a hold-up** hacer un asalto, atracar; **to — a surprise** dar una sorpresa.

stag·ger [stǽgɚ] *v.* (*totter*) tambalearse, tratabillar, bambolearse; hacer tambalear; (*overwhelm*) azorar, asombrar; **to — working hours** escalonar las horas de trabajo; *s.* tambaleo, bamboleo.

stag·nant [stǽgnənt] *adj.* estancado; **to become —** estancarse.

staid [sted] *adj.* grave, serio.

stain [sten] *v.* manchar; teñir; colorar; **stained-glass window** vidriera de colores; *s.* mancha, mancilla; tinte, tintura; materia colorante.

stain·less [sténlɪs] *adj.* sin mancha, inmaculado, limpio; **— steel** acero inempañablé o inoxidable.

stair [stɛr] *s.* peldaño, escalón; **-s** escalera.

stair·case [stɛ́rkes] *s.* escalera.

stair·way [stɛ́rwe] *s.* escalera.

stake [stek] *s.* (*pole*) estaca; (*investment*) puesta, apuesta; **his future is at —** su porvenir está en peligro o riesgo; **to die at the —** morir en la hoguera; **to have a — in the future of** tener interés en el porvenir de; **to have much at —** irle a uno mucho en una cosa; haber aventurado mucho; *v.* estacar; atar a una estaca; apostar; arriesgar, aventurar; **to — off** señalar con estacas (*un perímetro*).

sta·lac·tite [stəlǽktaɪt] *s.* estalactita.

sta·lag·mite [stəlǽgmaɪt] *s.* estalagmita.

stale [stel] *adj.* viejo; rancio; gastado, improductivo.

stale·mate [stélmet] *s.* punto muerto; estancación.

stalk [stɔk] *s.* tallo; caña.

stall [stɔl] *s.* casilla, puesto (*de un mercado o feria*); (*stable*) casilla o sección de un establo; *v.* encasillar, meter en casilla; (*stick*) atascarse (*un auto*); pararse (*el motor*); **he is -ing** está haciendo la pala; **to be -ed in the mud** estar atascado en el lodo.

stal·lion [stǽljən] *s.* caballo de cría, caballo padre, *Ven., Col., Ríopl.* padrillo; *Méx., C.A.* garañón.

stam·mer [stǽmɚ] *v.* tartamudear, balbucear; *s.* tartamudeo, balbuceo.

stam·mer·er [stǽmərɚ] *s.* tartamudo.

stam·mer·ing [stǽmərɪŋ] *s.* tartamudeo; *adj.* tartamudo.

stamp [stæmp] *v.* (*affix*) sellar; timbrar; poner un sello a; estampar; (*mark*) marcar, imprimir, señalar; (*with foot*) patear, patalear; **to — one's foot** dar patadas en el suelo; **to — out** extirpar, borrar; *s.* sello; timbre, estampilla; estampa; marca, impresión; patada (*en el suelo*); **postage —** sello, *Méx., C.A., Andes* estampilla, *Méx.* timbre; **revenue —** timbre.

stam·pede [stæmpíd] *s.* estampida; huída en desorden; tropel; éxodo repentino; *v.* arrancar, huir en tropel; ir en tropel; ahuyentar, hacer huir en desorden.

stanch [stɑntʃ] *v.* restañar, estancar; *adj.* fuerte, firme; leal, constante, fiel.

stand [stænd] *v.* poner derecho, colocar verticalmente; (*rise*) ponerse de pie, levantarse; *Am.* parar(se); (*be erect*) estar de pie; *Am.* estar

SP

parado; (*withstand*) aguantar, sufrir, tolerar; **to — a chance of** tener probabilidad de; **to — an expense** sufragar un gasto; **to — aside** apartarse; mantenerse apartado; **to — back of** colocarse detrás de; salir fiador de, garantizar a, respaldar a; **to — by** mantenerse a corta distancia; apoyar, defender; estar alerta; **to — for** significar; estar por, apoyar; tolerar; **to — in the way** estorbar; **to — on end** poner(se) de punta; erizarse (*el pelo*); **to — one's ground** mantenerse firme; **to — out** resaltar, destacarse; sobresalir; **to — six feet** tener seis pies de altura; **to — up for** apoyar, defender; **it -s to reason** es razonable, es lógico; *s.* puesto; mesilla; pedestal; posición; actitud; alto, parada (*para resistir*); quiosco; **grand —** andanada, gradería cubierta (*para espectadores*); **music —** atril; **umbrella —** paragüero.

stan·dard [stǽndɚd] *s.* (*norm*) norma; nivel normal; criterio; (*model*) modelo, patrón; *Am.* estándar; (*base*) base, pedestal; (*banner*) estandarte; **gold —** patrón de oro; **to be up to —** satisfacer las normas requeridas; *adj.* normal, que sirve de norma; de uso general; corriente; **standard-bearer** portaestandarte; **— deviation** desviación típica; **— of life** nivel de vida; **— time** hora normal.

stan·dard·i·za·tion [stændɚdəzéʃən] *s.* normalización, uniformación, igualación.

stan·dard·ize [stǽndɚdaɪz] *v.* normalizar, uniformar, *Méx.*, *C.A.*, *Carib.* estandardizar.

stand·by [stǽndbaɪ] *s.* sustituto; de reserva, auxiliar.

stand·ing [stǽndɪŋ] *s.* (*position*) posición; (*fame*) fama, reputación; **of long —** que ha prevalecido largo tiempo; muy antiguo; *adj.* derecho, en pie; de pie; establecido, permanente; **— water** agua estancada; **— order** pedido vigente (*permanente*); **there is — room only** no quedan asientos.

stand·off [stǽndɔf] *s.* empate.

stand·point [stǽndpɔɪnt] *s.* punto de vista.

stand·still [stǽndstɪl] *s.* alto; pausa; **to come to a —** pararse; hacer alto.

stank [stæŋk] *pret. de* **to stink.**

stan·za [stǽnzə] *s.* estrofa.

sta·ple [stépl] *s.* broche de alambre (*para sujetar papeles*); grapa, argolla, armella; artículo principal; **-s** artículos de necesidad prima; *adj.* principal; (*basic*) de uso corriente; indispensable; *v.* asegurar (*papeles*) con broche de alambre; sujetar con armellas.

sta·pler [stéplɚ] *s.* grapadora.

star [stɑr] *s.* estrella; (*asterisk*) asterisco; **star-spangled** estrellado; artista (actor); *adj.* sobresaliente, excelente; *v.* estrellar, adornar o señalar con estrellas; marcar con asterisco; presentar como estrella (*a un actor*); lucir(se) en las tablas o el cine, hacer el papel principal.

star·board [stɑ́rbord] *s.* estribor; *adj.* de estribor; **— side** banda de estribor; *adv.* a estribor.

starch [stɑrtʃ] *s.* almidón; fécula; *v.* almidonar.

stare [stɛr] *v.* mirar, mirar con fijeza o curiosidad; mirar azorado; clavar la mirada, fijar la vista; *s.* mirada fija, mirada persistente.

star·fish [stɑ́rfɪʃ] *s.* estrella de mar.

stark [stɑrk] *adj.* (*utter*) tieso; (*grim*) escueto; **— folly** pura tontería; **— in death** tieso, muerto; **— narrative** narración escueta, sin adornos; *adv.* completamente, totalmente; **— mad** loco de remate; **— naked** enteramente desnudo, en cueros, *Am.* encuerado.

star·light [stɑ́rlaɪt] *s.* luz estelar, luz de las estrellas.

star·ry [stɑ́rɪ] *adj.* estrellado, sembrado de estrellas; como estrellas, brillante.

start [stɑrt] *v.* comenzar, empezar, principiar; poner(se) en marcha; (*depart*) partir, salir; (*jump*) dar un salto, sobresaltarse; **the motor -s** el motor arranca; **to — after someone** salir en busca de alguien; **to — off** salir, partir; dar principio a; **to — out on a trip** empezar una jornada, emprender un viaje; **to — the motor** hacer arrancar el motor; *s.* comienzo, empiezo, principio; sobresalto; respingo (*de un caballo*); (*motor*) arranque; ventaja (*en una carrera*).

start·er [stɑ́rtɚ] *s.* (*automobile*) arranque; (*person*) arrancador; iniciador; (*first*) primero de la serie; **self-starter** arranque automático.

star·tle [stɑ́rtl] *v.* asustar(se), sobresaltar(se), espantar(se).

start·ling [stɑ́rtlɪŋ] *adj.* sobresaltante, pasmoso, asombroso, sorprendente.

star·va·tion [stɑrvéʃən] *s.* inanición, hambre.

starve [stɑrv] *v.* morir(se) de hambre; hambrear; matar de hambre.

starv·ing [stɑ́rvɪŋ] *adj.* hambriento.

state [stet] *s.* estado; condición, situación; **in great —** con gran pompa; *adj.* de estado; del estado; de ceremonia; *v.* declarar, decir; expresar, exponer.

state·ly [stétlɪ] *adj.* majestuoso, imponente.

state·ment [stétmənt] *s.* (*declaration*) declaración; exposición; (*information*) informe, relato; (*bill*) cuenta, estado de cuentas.

state·room [stétrum] *s.* camarote (*de un buque*).

states·man [stétsmən] *s.* estadista, hombre de estado.

stat·ic [stǽtɪk] *adj.* estático; *s.* estática

sta·tion [stéʃən] *s.* (*operations point*) estación; (*post*) paradero; puesto; (*condition*) estado, posición social; **broadcasting —** transmisora o emisora; *v.* estacionar, colocar, apostar; **— wagon** *Esp.* rubia; *Méx.* camioneta, huayin; *C.A.* camionetilla.

sta·tion·ar·y [stéʃənɛrɪ] *adj.* estacionario; fijo.

sta·tion·er·y [stéʃənɛrɪ] *s.* (*shop*) papelería; efectos de escritorio.

sta·tis·tics [stətístɪks] *s.* estadística; datos estadísticos; **statistical sampling** muestreo estadístico.

stat·u·ar·y [stǽtʃuɛrɪ] *s.* estatuaria, arte de hacer estatuas; colección de estatuas.

stat·ue [stǽtʃu] *s.* estatua.

stat·ure [stǽtʃɚ] *s.* estatura.

stat·us [stétəs] *s.* estado, condición; posición social o profesional.

stat·ute [stǽtʃut] *s.* estatuto, ordenanza; **— of limitations** ley de prescripciones.

staunch = **stanch.**

stave [stev] *s.* duela de barril; *v.* poner duelas (*a un barril*); **to — off** mantener a distancia; evitar; rechazar.

stay [ste] *v.* (*remain*) quedarse, permanecer; parar(se); detener(se); (*sojourn*) hospedarse, alojarse; (*check*) resistir; **to — an execution** diferir o aplazar una ejecución; **to — one's hunger** engañar el hambre; **to — up all night** velar toda la noche; *s.* estada, estancia, permanencia; (*postponement*) suspensión; (*supports*) sostén, apoyo; (*corset*) varilla o ballena de corsé; **to grant a —** conceder una prórroga.

stead [stɛd]: **in her (his) —** en su lugar; **to stand one in good —** servirle a uno, ser de provecho para uno.

stead·fast [stɛ́dfæst] *adj.* fijo, firme; constante.

stead·i·ly [stɛ́dɪlɪ] *adv.* constantemente; firmemente; sin parar, de continuo; sin vacilar.

stead·i·ness [stɛ́dɪnɪs] *s.* firmeza; constancia; estabilidad.

stead·y [stɛ́dɪ] *adj.* firme; estable; invariable,

constante; continuo, — **customer** cliente fijo; **market** mercado sostenido; *v.* afianzar, mantener firme, asegurar; calmar (*los nervios*).
steak [stek] *s.* biftec o bisté; tajada (*para asar o freír*).
steal [stil] *v.* (*rob*) robar, hurtar; (*move*) andar furtivamente; **to — away** colarse, escabullirse, escaparse; **to — into a room** meterse a hurtadillas en un cuarto; **to — out of a room** salirse a escondidas de un cuarto, colarse, escabullirse; *s.* robo, hurto.
stealth [stɛlθ]: **by** — a hurtadillas, a escondidas, con cautela.
stealth·y [stɛ́lθɪ] *adj.* cauteloso, furtivo, secreto.
steam [stim] *s.* vapor; vaho; *adj.* de vapor; por vapor; — **engine** máquina de vapor; — **heat** calefacción por vapor; — **roller** apisonadora de vapor; — **shovel** excavadora; *v.* cocer al vapor; dar un baño de vapor; saturar de vapor; echar vapor; **to — into port** llegar a puerto (*un vapor*).
steam·boat [stímbot] *s.* buque de vapor.
steam·er [stímɚ] *s.* vapor, buque de vapor.
steam·ship [stímʃɪp] *s.* vapor, buque de vapor.
steed [stid] *s.* corcel, caballo de combate; caballo brioso.
steel [stil] *s.* acero; — **industry** siderurgia; — **mill** fundición de acero; **mild** — acero parco en carbono; *adj.* acerado, de acero; *v.* acerar, revestir de acero; **to — oneself against** fortalecerse contra.
steep [stip] *adj.* empinado, escarpado, pendiente; muy alto; — **price** precio alto o excesivo; *v.* remojar, empapar; saturar; poner o estar en infusión.
stee·ple [stípl] *s.* aguja, chapitel; cúspide.
steep·ness [stípnɪs] *s.* inclinación abrupta; lo empinado, lo escarpado; (*prices*) altura (*de precios*).
steer [stɪr] *s.* novillo; buey; *v.* guiar, conducir, manejar, gobernar; (*ship*) timonear; **to — a course** seguir un rumbo; **the car -s easily** se maneja fácilmente el auto, es de fácil manejo.
steer·ing wheel [stírɪnhwil] *s.* volante; *Col.* timón.
stel·lar [stɛ́lɚ] *adj.* estelar.
stem [stɛm] *s.* (*plant*) tallo; (*tree*) tronco; (*leaf*) pedúnculo (*de hoja, flor o fruto*); raíz (*de una palabra*); pie (*de copa*); cañón (*de pipa de fumar*); (*ship*) proa; *v.* estancar, represar; resistir, refrenar; contraponerse a; **to — from** provenir de.
stench [stɛnʃ] *s.* hedor, hediondez.
sten·cil [stɛ́nsl] *s.* patrón picado; esténcil.
ste·nog·ra·pher [stənágrəfɚ] *s.* estenógrafo, taquígrafo, mecanógrafo.
step [stɛp] *s.* (*walking*) paso; pisada; (*staircase*) peldaño, escalón, grada; (*degree*) grado; (*effort*) gestión; — **by** — paso a paso; **to be in — with** marchar a compás con; estar de acuerdo con; **to take -s** dar pasos; tomar medidas; gestionar; *v.* andar, caminar; dar un paso; **to — aside** hacerse a un lado, apartarse; **to — back** dar un paso o pasos atrás; retroceder; **to — down** bajar; **to — off a distance** medir a pasos una distancia; **to — on** pisar, pisotear; **to — on the gas** pisar el acelerador; (*hurry*) darse prisa; **to — out** salir; **to — up** subir; acelerar; **step-by-step** *adj.* escalonado; **stepped-up** progresivo.
step·fa·ther [stɛ́pfɑðɚ] *s.* padrastro.
step·mo·ther [stɛ́pmʌðɚ] *s.* madrastra.
steppe [stɛp] *s.* estepa.
ster·e·o·type [stírɪotaɪp] *s.* estereotipo.
ster·ile [stɛ́rəl] *adj.* estéril.
ste·ril·i·ty [stərílətɪ] *s.* esterilidad.
ster·il·ize [stɛ́rəlaɪz] *v.* esterilizar.
ster·ling [stɝ́lɪŋ] *s.* vajilla de plata esterlina; *adj.* genuino; de ley; — **silver** plata de ley, plata esterlina; **pound** — libra esterlina.
stern [stɝn] *adj.* austero, severo; firme; *s.* popa.
stern·ness [stɝ́nnɪs] *s.* austeridad, severidad; firmeza.
steth·o·scope [stɛ́θəskop] *s.* estetoscopio.
ste·ve·dore [stívədor] *s.* estibador, cargador.
stew [stju] *v.* estofar; (*worry*) preocuparse, apurarse; *s.* estofado, guisado; cocido, puchero, sancocho; **to be in a** — estar preocupado o apurado.
stew·ard [stjúwɚd] *s.* mayordomo; camarero (*de buque o avión*).
stew·ard·ess [stjúwɚdɪs] *s.* camarera (*de buque o avión*); *Esp.* azafata.
stick [stɪk] *s.* palo; vara; garrote; (*fire wood*) raja de leña; — **of dynamite** barra de dinamita; **control** — palanca (*de aeroplano*); **walking** — bastón; chuzo (*de sereno*); **stick-up** atraco (*para robar*), asalto; *v.* pegar(se), adherir(se), permanecer; estar pegado; picar, pinchar; herir (*con cuchillo, puñal, etc.*); fijar (*con clavos, alfileres, tachuelas, etc.*); atascarse (*en el fango un carro, auto, etc.*); **to — something in** (*o* **into**) clavar o meter algo en; encajar en; **to — out** salir, sobresalir; proyectarse; **to — out one's head** asomar la cabeza; **to — out one's tongue** sacar la lengua; **to — to a job** perseverar (*o* persistir) en una tarea; **to — up** sobresalir, destacarse; estar de punta (*el pelo*); **to — one's hands up** alzar las manos; **to — someone up** asaltar o atracar a alguien (*para robar*); *véase* **stuck**.
stick·er [stíkɚ] *s.* marbete engomado; etiqueta.
stick·y [stíkɪ] *adj.* pegajoso.
stiff [stɪf] *adj.* tieso; rígido; entumido; duro; (*stubborn*) terco; (*strong*) fuerte; — **climb** subida ardua o difícil; — **price** precio alto o subido; **stiff-necked** terco, obstinado; **sacred** — yerto, muerto de miedo; *s.* cadáver.
stiff·en [stífən] *v.* atiesar(se), poner(se) tieso; entumir(se); endurecer(se); espesar(se); subir de punto, aumentar (*la resistencia*).
stiff·ness [stífnɪs] *s.* tiesura; rigidez; dureza; rigor; terquedad.
sti·fle [stáɪfl] *v.* ahogar(se), asfixiar(se), sofocar(se); apagar, extinguir.
stig·ma [stígmə] *s.* estigma; baldón.
stig·ma·tize [stígmətaɪz] *v.* estigmatizar.
still [stɪl] *adj.* (*quiet*) quieto; callado, silencioso; (*at ease*) tranquilo; inmóvil; — **born** nacido muerto; — **life** naturaleza muerta; *v.* aquietar; calmar; acallar; *adv.* todavía, aún; *conj.* empero, no obstante, sin embargo; *s.* destiladera, alambique; silencio.
still·ness [stílnɪs] *s.* quietud, calma, silencio.
stilt [stɪlt] *s.* (*walking*) zanco; (*support*) pilote, puntal, soporte.
stilt·ed [stíltɪd] *adj.* tieso, afectado, pomposo.
stim·u·lant [stímjələnt] *adj.* & *s.* estimulante.
stim·u·late [stímjəlet] *v.* estimular.
stim·u·la·tion [stɪmjəléʃən] *s.* estimulación, estímulo.
stim·u·lus [stímjələs] *s.* estímulo.
sting [stɪŋ] *v.* (*pierce*) picar; pinchar, aguijonear; (*irritate*) escocer; *Méx., C.A., Col., Carib.* arder; (*cheat*) embaucar; estafar; *s.* picadura, piquete, mordedura, picazón; aguijón; escozor; — **of remorse** remordimiento.
stin·gi·ness [stíndʒɪnɪs] *s.* tacañería, mezquindad.
stin·gy [stíndʒɪ] *adj.* mezquino, ruin, tacaño; escaso; *Ríopl., Méx.* codo.
stink [stɪŋk] *v.* heder, oler mal; apestar; *s.* hedor,

mal olor, hediondez.
stint [stɪnt] *v.* escatimar; ser frugal o económico; **to — oneself** privarse de lo necesario, economizar demasiado; *s.* tarea, faena; **without** — sin límite; sin escatimar; generosamente.
stip·u·late [stípjəlet] *v.* estipular.
stip·u·la·tion [stɪpjəléʃən] *s.* estipulación, condición.
stir [stɝ] *v.* menear(se); mover(se); bullir(se); (*fire*) atizar (*el fuego*); incitar; conmover; perturbar; revolver; **to — up** incitar; conmover; revolver; suscitar (*un argumento, pelea, etc.*); *s.* meneo, agitación, movimiento; alboroto.
stir·ring [stɝ́ɪŋ] *adj.* conmovedor.
stir·rup [stírəp] *s.* estribo.
stitch [stɪtʃ] *v.* coser; dar puntadas; *s.* puntada; punzada; **to be in -es** desternillarse de risa.
stock [stɑk] *s.* (*supply*) surtido; existencias, provisión; (*cattle*) ganado; (*lineage*) cepa, linaje, estirpe; (*shares*) acciones, valores; **in** — en existencia; **live** — ganado; **meat** — caldo de carne; *adj.* en existencia, existente, disponible; común, trivial; — **answer** contestación corriente, común o trivial; — **company** sociedad anónima; compañía teatral; — **exchange** bolsa; *Col.* bolsa de corredores; *Mex.* bolsa de acciones; *Ur.* bolsa de comercio; — **farm** hacienda de ganado, *Am.* rancho, *Am.* estancia; — **market** mercado de valores, bolsa; — **room** almacén; — **size** tamaño ordinario (*regularmente en existencia*); — **yard** matadero; *v.* surtir, abastecer; tener en existencia (*para vender*); **to — a farm** surtir o proveer de ganado un rancho; **to — up with** surtirse de, acumular; **to stockpile** acopiar reservas.
stock·ade [stɑkéd] *s.* estacada, empalizada; vallado; *v.* empalizar, rodear de empalizadas.
stock·bro·ker [stɑ́kbrokɚ] *s.* bolsista, corredor de bolsa.
stock·hold·er [stɑ́kholdɚ] *s.* accionista.
stock·ing [stɑ́kɪŋ] *s.* media.
sto·ic [stóɪk] *adj.* & *s.* estoico.
stoke [stok] *v.* atizar (*el fuego*); (*feed*) cebar, alimentar (*un horno*).
stole [stol] *pret. de* **to steal.**
sto·len [stólən] *p.p. de* **to steal.**
stol·id [stɑ́lɪd] *adj.* estólido, insensible.
stom·ach [stʌ́mək] *s.* estómago; *v.* aguantar, tolerar.
stomp [stɑmp] *v.* pisar violentamente.
stone [ston] *s.* piedra; (*seed*) hueso (*de las frutas*); **within a -'s throw** a tiro de piedra; *adj.* pétreo, de piedra; **Stone Age** Edad de Piedra; **stone-deaf** totalmente sordo, sordo como una tapia; *v.* apedrear; deshuesar (*las frutas*).
ston·y [stónɪ] *adj.* pedregoso; pétreo, de piedra; duro.
stood [stʊd] *pret.* & *p.p. de* **to stand.**
stool [stul] *s.* (*furniture*) taburete; *C.A.* banquillo; (*toilet*) bacín, bacinica; (*excrement*) excremento; — **pigeon** soplón (*el que delata a otro*).
stoop [stup] *v.* agacharse; doblarse, inclinarse; encorvarse; andar encorvado o caído de hombros; rebajarse, humillarse, abajarse; *s.* encorvamiento, inclinación (*de espaldas*); **to walk with a** — andar encorvado o caído de hombros; **stoop-shouldered** cargado de espaldas encorvado.
stop [stɑp] *v.* (*pause*) parar(se), hacer alto, detener(se); (*cease*) acabar(se); cesar; parar de, dejar de; (*block*) atajar; reprimir; suspender; obstruir, tapar; **to — at a hotel** hospedarse o alojarse en un hotel; **to — at nothing** no pararse en escrúpulos; **to — from** impedir; **to — over at** hacer escala en; **to — short** parar(se) de sopetón, parar(se) en seco; **to — up** tapar, obstruir; atascar; *s.* parada; alto, pausa; estada, estancia; detención; suspensión; llave (*de instrumento de viento*); traste (*de guitarra*); registro (*de órgano*); — **consonant** consonante oclusiva.
stop·o·ver [stɑ́povɚ] *s.* parada, escala; **to make a — in** hacer escala en.
stop·page [stɑ́pidʒ] *s.* detención; obstrucción; **work** — paro.
stop·per [stɑ́pɚ] *s.* tapón.
stor·age [stórɪdʒ] *s.* almacenaje; (*computer*) almacenamiento; — **battery** acumulador; — **medium** (*computer*) soporte; **to keep in** — almacenar.
store [stor] *s.* (*shop*) tienda; almacén; (*supply*) depósito; acopio; **-s** provisiones; bastimentos; víveres; **department** — almacén; **dry-goods** — lencería, *Méx.*, *Ríopl.*, *Andes* mercería, *Méx.* cajón de ropa; **fruit** — frutería; **hat** — sombrerería; **grocery** — abacería, tienda de comestibles, *Méx.*, *C.A.* tienda de abarrotes, *Carib.* bodega; **shoe** — zapatería; **to have in** — tener guardado; *v.* almacenar; guardar; abastecer; **to — up** acumular.
store·house [stórhaʊs] *s.* almacén, depósito.
store·keep·er [stórkipɚ] *s.* tendero; almacenista; guardalmacén.
store·room [stórrum] *s.* almacén; bodega; despensa.
stork [stɔrk] *s.* cigüeña.
storm [stɔrm] *s.* (*weather*) tormenta, tempestad, borrasca, temporal; (*disturbance*) tumulto; asalto; — **troops** tropas de asalto; **hail** — granizada; **snow** — nevasca; **wind** — vendaval; *v.* asaltar, atacar; rabiar; **it is -ing** hay tormenta, hay tempestad.
storm·y [stɔ́rmɪ] *adj.* tempestuoso, borrascoso; turbulento.
sto·ry [stórɪ] *s.* (*tale*) cuento, historia, historieta; relato; (*gossip*) chisme; rumor; bola; (*plot*) argumento, trama; (*floor*) piso (*de un edificio*); **newspaper** — artículo de periódico, gacetilla.
stout [staʊt] *adj.* corpulento, robusto, fornido; fuerte; firme; leal; valiente.
stove [stov] *s.* estufa; cocina de gas, cocina eléctrica; *pret.* & *p.p. de* **to stave**.
stow [sto] *v.* meter, guardar; esconder; estibar, acomodar la carga de un barco; rellenar; **to — away on a ship** embarcarse clandestinamente, esconderse en un barco.
strad·dle [strǽdl] *v.* ponerse o estar a horcajadas; ponerse a caballo, cabalgar; favorecer ambos lados (*de un pleito, controversia, etc.*).
strafe [stref] *v.* ametrallar; *Am.* abalear.
strag·gle [strǽgl] *v.* vagar, desviarse; (*get lost*) extraviarse; andar perdido; dispersarse; **to — behind** rezagarse.
straight [stret] *adj.* (*direction*) recto; derecho; directo; (*proper*) honrado; franco; erguido; correcto; en orden; — **face** cara seria; — **hair** pelo lacio; — **hand of five cards** runfla de cinco naipes del mismo palo; — **rum** ron puro, sin mezcla; **for two hours** — por dos horas seguidas, por dos horas sin parar; **to set a person** — dar consejo a una persona; mostrarle el camino, modo o manera de hacer algo; *adv.* directamente, derecho, en línea recta; francamente; honradamente; — **away** (*o* — **off**) en seguida, al punto; **to talk — from the shoulder** hablar con toda franqueza o sinceridad.
straight·en [strétn̩] *v.* enderezar(se); arreglar, poner en orden.
straight·for·ward [stretfɔ́rwɚd] *adj.* derecho, recto; honrado; franco, sincero; *adv.* directamente, en línea recta.

straight·ness [strétnɪs] *s.* derechura; rectitud; honradez.
straight·way [strétwe] *adv.* luego, inmediatamente, en seguida.
strain [stren] *v.* (*force*) estirar demasiado, hacer fuerza; poner tirante; violentar, forzar (*los músculos, los nervios, la vista, etc.*); (*sift*) colar, tamizar; **to — one's wrist** torcerse la muñeca; *s.* tensión excesiva; tirantez; torcedura; esfuerzo excesivo; linaje, rasgo racial; aire, tonada.
strain·er [strénɚ] *s.* coladera; cedazo.
strait [stret] *s.* estrecho; **-s** estrecho; aprieto, apuro; **— jacket** camisa de fuerza.
strait·laced [strétlest] *adj.* estricto.
strand [strænd] *v.* encallar; dejar perdido (*sin medios de salir*), dejar aislado, extraviar; **to be -ed** estar encallado; estar extraviado (*sin medios de salir*), estar aislado, andar perdido; *s.* ribera, playa; ramal (*de cuerda, cable, etc.*); hebra, hilo; **— of hair** guedeja; trenza; **— of pearls** hilera de perlas.
strange [strendʒ] *adj.* extraño; raro, singular; desconocido.
strange·ness [stréndʒnɪs] *s.* extrañeza, rareza.
stran·ger [stréndʒɚ] *s.* extraño, desconocido; forastero.
stran·gle [strǽŋgl] *v.* estrangular(se).
strap [stræp] *s.* correa; tira de cuero o de tela; correón; (*suspender*) tirante; **metal** — banda de metal; *v.* amarrar o atar con correas; azotar (*con correa*); *véase* **strop.**
strat·a·gem [strǽtədʒəm] *s.* estratagema.
stra·te·gic [strətídʒɪk] *adj.* estratégico.
strat·e·gy [strǽtədʒɪ] *s.* estrategia.
strat·o·sphere [strǽtəsfɪr] *s.* estratosfera.
straw [strɔ] *s.* paja; **I don't care a** — no me importa un comino; *adj.* de paja; pajizo; **straw-colored** pajizo, color de paja; **— hat** sombrero de paja; **— vote** voto no oficial (*para averiguar la opinion pública*).
straw·ber·ry [strɔ́bɛrɪ] *s.* fresa.
stray [stre] *v.* extraviarse, descarriarse, desviarse; perderse, errar el camino; vagar; *adj.* extraviado, perdido; **— remark** observación aislada; *s.* animal perdido o extraviado.
streak [strik] *s.* (*line*) raya, línea, lista; (*vein*) vena; (*trace*) rasgo; (*beam*) rayo (*de luz*); **— of lightning** relámpago, rayo; *v.* rayar, *Ríopl., Méx., Ven.* listar, hacer rayas o listas.
stream [strim] *s.* corriente; chorro; río, arroyo, arroyuelo; **— of cars** desfile de autos; **down** — río abajo, agua abajo, con la corriente; **up** — río arriba, agua arriba, contra la corriente; *v.* correr (*el agua*), fluir; brotar, manar; derramarse; flotar (*en el viento*), ondear; **to — out of** salir a torrentes de.
stream·er [strímɚ] *s.* banderola; gallardete; listón, cinta (*que flota en el aire*).
stream·lined [strímlaɪnd] *adj.* aerodinámico.
street [strit] *s.* calle.
street·car [strítkɑr] *s.* tranvía.
strength [strɛŋkθ] *s.* fuerza; poder; potencia; fortaleza; **on the — of his promise** fundado en su promesa.
strength·en [strɛ́ŋkθən] *v.* fortalecer(se); reforzar(se).
stren·u·ous [strɛ́njuəs] *adj.* arduo; enérgico, vigoroso.
strep·to·my·cin [strɛptomáɪsɪn] *s.* estreptomicina.
stress [strɛs] *s.* (*force*) fuerza, esfuerzo; tensión, torsión, compresión; (*importance*) urgencia; énfasis; (*intensity*) acento; *v.* acentuar; recalcar, dar énfasis a, hacer hincapié en.
stretch [strɛtʃ] *v.* estirar(se); alargar(se); tender(se); ensanchar; **to — oneself** estirarse, desperezarse; **to — out one's hand** tender o alargar la mano; *s.* trecho, distancia; extensión, período de tiempo; elasticidad; tensión; esfuerzo (*de la imaginación*); estirón; **home** — último trecho (*de una carrera*).
stretch·er [strɛ́tʃɚ] *s.* estirador, ensanchador, dilatador; camilla (*para los heridos*).
strew [stru] *v.* regar, esparcir.
strewn [strun] *p.p. de* **to strew; — with** regado de, cubierto de.
strick·en [stríkən] *p.p. de* **to strike**; *adj.* herido; afligido; agobiado; atacado.
strict [strɪkt] *adj.* estricto; **in — confidence** en absoluta confianza, con toda reserva.
strid·den [strídn̩] *p.p. de* **to stride.**
stride [straɪd] *v.* tranquear, caminar a paso largo, dar zancadas, andar a trancos; *s.* zancada, tranco, paso largo.
strife [straɪf] *s.* refriega, contienda, pleito.
strike [straɪk] *v.* (*hit*) dar, golpear, pegar; azotar; herir; atacar; (*collide with*) chocar con; (*find*) dar con, encontrar (*oro, petróleo, etc.*); ocurrírsele a uno (*una idea*); (*assume*) asumir, afectar (*una postura, una actitud*); dar (*la hora un reloj*); (*light*) encender (*un fósforo*); acuñar (*moneda*); declararse o estar en huelga; **to — at** amagar; acometer; **to — off** borrar, tachar; cortar; **to — one's attention** atraer o llamar la atención; **to — one's fancy** antojársele a uno; **to — one's head against** darse un cabezazo contra; **to — out in a certain direction** tomar cierto rumbo, encaminarse o irse en cierta dirección; **to — out** ponchar; **to — someone for a loan** darle un sablazo a alguien; **to — up a friendship** trabar amistad; **to — with terror** sobrecoger de terror; **how does she — you?** ¿qué tal le parece?; ¿qué piensa Vd. de ella;? *s.* golpe; huelga; caídos; (*baseball*) estrái; descubrimiento repentino (*de petróleo, de una mina, etc.*); **—breaker** esquirol, rompehuelgas **sit-down** — huelga de brazos.
strik·er [stráɪkɚ] *s.* (*person on strike*) huelguista; (*device*) golpeador.
strik·ing [stráɪkɪŋ] *adj.* (*unusual*) notable; llamativo; conspicuo, manifiesto; sorprendente; extraordinario; (*on strike*) que está de huelga; que está en huelga.
string [strɪŋ] *s.* (*strand*) cuerda; cordel, cinta, cordón; sarta (*de perlas, cuentas, etc.*); (*fiber*) fibra (*de habichuelas, porotos, etc.*); (*line*) fila, hilera; **— bean** habichuela, judía verde, *Méx.* ejote, *Ch., Ríopl.* poroto; **— of lies** sarta de mentiras; *v.* ensartar; tender (*un cable, un alambre*); desfibrar, quitar las fibras a; encordar (*una raqueta, un violín*); encordelar, atar con cordeles, lazos o cuerdas; tomar el pelo, engañar; **to — out** extender(se), prolongar(se); **to — up** colgar.
strip [strɪp] *v.* despojar; robar; desnudar(se); desvestir(se), desmantelar; **to — the gears** estropear el engranaje; **to — the skin from** desollar, pelar; *s.* tira, lista, listón; **— of land** faja de tierra.
stripe [straɪp] *s.* (*band*) franja, raya, lista, tira; banda, galón; (*kind*) tipo, índole; *v.* rayar, *Am.* listar, adornar con listas.
striped [straɪpt, stráɪpɪd] *adj.* listado.
strive [straɪv] *v.* esforzarse; luchar, forcejear; hacer lo posible; **to — to** esforzarse por.
striv·en [strívən] *p.p. de* **to strive.**
strode [strod] *pret. de* **to stride.**
stroke [strok] *s.* golpe; ataque, apoplejía; **— of a bell** campanada; **— of a painter's brush**

pincelada; — **of lightning** rayo; — **of the hand** caricia; — **of the pen** plumada; **at the** — **of ten** al dar las diez; *v.* frotar suavemente, pasar suavemente la mano, acariciar; alisar.

stroll [strol] *v.* dar un paseo, pasearse; vagar; **to** — **the streets** callejear; *s.* paseo, paseíto.

strong [strɔŋ] *adj.* fuerte; forzudo, fornido; vigoroso; recio; enérgico; firme; bien marcado; acérrimo; — **chance** buena probabilidad; — **coffee** café cargado; — **market** mercado firme; **strong-willed** de voluntad fuerte, decidido; **strong-arm** violento; *adv.* fuertemente; firmemente.

strong·hold [strɔ́ŋhold] *s.* fuerte, plaza fuerte.

stron·ti·um [stránt∫iəm] *s.* estroncio.

strop [strɑp] *v.* asentar (*navajas de afeitar*); *s.* asentador de navajas.

strove [strov] *pret. de* **to strive.**

struck [strʌk] *pret. & p.p. de* **to strike**; **to be** — **with a disease** darle a uno una enfermedad; **to be** — **with terror** estar o quedar sobrecogido de terror.

struc·tu·ral [strʌ́kt∫ərəl] *adj.* estructural, relativo a la estructura.

struc·ture [strʌ́kt∫ɚ] *s.* estructura; construcción; edificio.

strug·gle [strʌ́gl] *v.* bregar, luchar, pugnar; forcejear; esforzarse; *s.* esfuerzo; contienda; lucha, pugna.

strung [strʌŋ] *pret. & p.p. de* **to string.**

strut [strʌt] *v.* pavonearse, contonearse; *s.* contoneo; (*support*) tirante, puntal.

stub [stʌb] *s.* trozo, fragmento, pedazo mochado; (*tree*) tocón (*de árbol*); (*ticket*) talón (*de libro talonario, boleto, etc.*); — **book** libro talonario; — **pen** pluma de punta mocha; *v.* **to** — **one's foot** dar(se) un tropezón.

stub·ble [stʌ́bl] *s.* (*crop*) rastrojo; (*beard*) cañones (*de la barba*).

stub·born [stʌ́bɚn] *adj.* terco, testarudo, obstinado, porfiado, cabezón.

stub·born·ness [stʌ́bɚnnɪs] *s.* terquedad, testarudez, porfía, obstinación.

stuc·co [stʌ́ko] *s.* estuco; *v.* estucar, cubrir de estuco.

stuck [stʌk] *pret. & p.p. de* **to stick** pegado; atorado; atascado; — **full of holes** agujereado; **stuck-up** tieso, estirado, orgulloso.

stud [stʌd] *s.* (*knob*) tachón, tachuela de adorno; (*button*) botón postizo para camisa; (*bolt*) perno; — **horse** caballo padre; *v.* tachonar; clavetear.

stu·dent [stjúdn̩t] *s.* estudiante; *adj.* estudiantil.

stud·ied [stʌ́dɪd] *adj.* estudiado.

stu·di·o [stjúdɪo] *s.* estudio, taller.

stu·di·ous [stjúdɪəs] *adj.* estudioso; aplicado; estudiado.

stud·y [stʌ́dɪ] *s.* estudio; cuidado, solicitud; gabinete de estudio; *v.* estudiar.

stuff [stʌf] *s.* (*material*) materia; material; (*cloth*) género, tela; (*thing*) cosa; (*medicine*) menjurje, medicina; (*junk*) cachivaches, baratijas; **of good** — de buena estofa; *v.* rellenar; henchir; hartar(se), atracar(se), atiborrar(se).

stuf·fing [stʌ́fɪŋ] *s.* relleno; material para rellenar.

stum·ble [stʌ́mbl] *v.* tropezar, dar(se) un tropezón; dar un traspié; hablar o recitar equivocándose a cada paso; **to** — **upon** tropezar con; *s.* tropiezo, tropezón, traspié.

stump [stʌmp] *s.* (*tree*) tocón (*tronco que queda de un árbol*); (*tooth*) raigón (*de muela*); (*limb*) muñón (*de brazo o pierna cortada*); **of a tail** rabo; **to be up a** — hallarse en un apuro, estar perplejo; *v.* trozar el tronco de (*un árbol*); renquear, cojear; dejar confuso, confundir; **to** — **the country** recorrer el país pronunciando discursos políticos.

stump·y [stʌ́mpɪ] *adj.* rechoncho, *Am.* chaparro; lleno de tocones.

stun [stʌn] *v.* aturdir, pasmar; atolondrar.

stung [stʌŋ] *pret. & p.p. de* **to sting.**

stunk [stʌŋk] *pret. & p.p. de* **to stink.**

stun·ning [stʌ́niŋ] *adj.* aplastante; elegante, bellísimo.

stunt [stʌnt] *v.* (*make short*) achaparrar, impedir el desarrolo de, no dejar crecer; (*do tricks*) hacer suertes. hacer piruetas; *s.* suerte; pirueta, suerte acrobática, maniobra gimnástica; hazaña sensacional.

stu·pe·fy [stjúpəfaɪ] *v.* atontar; entorpecer; aturdir, atolondrar, pasmar, dejar estupefacto.

stu·pen·dous [stjupɛ́ndəs] *adj.* estupendo.

stu·pid [stjúpɪd] *adj.* estúpido; atontado.

stu·pid·i·ty [stjupɪ́dətɪ] *s.* estupidez.

stu·por [stjúpɚ] *s.* letargo, modorra; sopor; aturdimiento; **in a** — aletargado.

stur·dy [stɝ́dɪ] *adj.* fornido, fuerte, robusto; firme.

stut·ter [stʌ́tɚ] *v.* tartamudear; *s.* tartamudeo; tartamudez.

stut·er·er [stʌ́tərɚ] *s.* tartamudo.

stut·ter·ing [stʌ́tərɪŋ] *adj.* tartamudo; *s.* tartamudeo.

sty [staɪ] *s.* pocilga; orzuelo (*en el párpado*), *Méx.* perilla; *Ríopl.* chiquero.

style [staɪl] *s.* estilo; moda; **to be in** — estar de moda, estilarse; *v.* intitular, nombrar; **to** — **a dress** cortar un vestido a la moda.

styl·ish [stáɪlɪ∫] *adj.* elegante; a la moda.

styl·ize [stáɪlaɪz] *v.* estilizar.

sub·con·scious [sʌbkán∫əs] *adj.* subconsciente.

sub·di·vi·sion [sʌbdəvɪ́ʒən] *s.* subdivisión; parcelación de terrenos.

sub·due [səbdjú] *v.* subyugar, someter; sujetar, dominar; amansar, domar.

sub·dued [səbdjúd] *p.p. de* **to subdue**; *adj.* sumiso; sujeto; manso; suave; tenue; — **light** luz tenue.

sub·ject [sʌ́bdʒɪkt] *s.* súbdito; sujeto; asunto, tema, materia; *adj.* sujeto; sometido; inclinado, propenso; expuesto; [səbdʒɛ́kt] *v.* sujetar; someter; subyugar, sojuzgar.

sub·jec·tion [səbdʒɛ́k∫ən] *s.* sujeción; dominación; sumisión.

sub·jec·tive [səbdʒɛ́ktɪv] *adj.* subjetivo.

sub·ju·gate [sʌ́bdʒəget] *v.* subyugar, sojuzgar.

sub·li·mate [sʌ́bləmet] *v.* sublimar.

sub·lime [səbláɪm] *adj.* sublime.

sub·ma·rine [sʌbmərín] *adj.* submarino; [sʌ́bmərin] *s.* submarino.

sub·merge [səbmɝ́dʒ] *v.* sumergir(se), hundir(se), sumir(se).

sub·mis·sion [səbmɪ́∫ən] *s.* sumisión, sometimiento.

sub·mis·sive [səbmɪ́sɪv] *adj.* sumiso.

sub·mit [səbmɪ́t] *v.* someter; **to** — **a report** someter (presentar *o* rendir) un informe; **to** — **to punishment** someterse a un castigo.

sub·or·di·nate [səbɔ́rdn̩ɪt] *adj. & s.* subordinado; subalterno; dependiente; [səbɔ́rdn̩et] *v.* subordinar.

sub·rou·tine [sʌbrutín] *s.* (*computer*) subrutina.

sub·scribe [səbskráɪb] *v.* subscribir(se); firmar; **to** — **five dollars** prometer una cuota o subscripción de cinco dólares; **to** — **for** subscribirse a, abonarse a; **to** — **to a plan** subscribirse a (*o* aprobar) un plan.

sub·scrib·er [səbskráɪbɚ] *s.* suscritor, abonado; infrascrito (*que firma un documento*), firmante.

sub·scrip·tion [səbskrɪ́p∫ən] *s.* subscripción, abono.

sub·se·quent [sʌ́bsɪkwɛnt] *adj.* subsiguiente, subsecuente, posterior; **-ly** *adv.* después, posteriormente, subsiguientemente.

sub·ser·vi·ent [səbsɝ́vɪənt] *adj.* servil, servilón.
sub·side [səbsáɪd] *v.* menguar, disminuir; bajar (*de nivel*); calmarse, aquietarse.
sub·sid·i·ar·y [səbsídiɛrɪ] *s.* subsidiario; sucursal.
sub·si·dize [sʌ́bsədaɪz] *v.* subvencionar.
sub·si·dy [sʌ́bsədɪ] *s.* subvención.
sub·sist [səbsíst] *v.* subsistir.
sub·stance [sʌ́bstəns] *s.* substancia (sustancia).
sub·stan·tial [səbstǽnʃəl] *adj.* substancial, substancioso; sólido; considerable; importante; **to be in — agreement** estar en substancia de acuerdo.
sub·stan·ti·ate [səbstǽnʃɪet] *v.* comprobar; verificar.
sub·stan·tive [sʌ́bstəntɪv] *adj.* & *s.* sustantivo.
sub·sti·tute [sʌ́bstətjut] *v.* sustituir (substituir); reemplazar; *s.* sustituto, suplente; reemplazo.
sub·sti·tu·tion [sʌbstətjúʃən] *s.* sustitución (substitución); reemplazo.
sub·stra·tum [sʌ́bstrætəm] *s.* sustrato.
sub·ter·fuge [sʌ́btɚfjudʒ] *s.* escapatoria; subterfugio.
sub·ter·ra·ne·an [sʌbtərénɪən] *adj.* subterráneo.
sub·tle [sʌ́tl] *adj.* sutil.
sub·tle·ty [sʌ́tltɪ] *s.* sutileza; agudeza.
sub·tract [səbtrǽkt] *v.* sustraer (substraer); restar.
sub·trac·tion [səbtrǽkʃən] *s.* sustracción (substracción), resta.
sub·urb [sʌ́bɝb] *s.* suburbio, arrabal.
sub·ur·ban [səbɝ́bən] *adj.* & *s.* suburbano.
sub·ver·sive [səbvɝ́sɪv] *adj.* subversivo (*en contra de la autoridad constituida*); trastornador, destructivo.
sub·way [sʌ́bwe] *s.* subterráneo, túnel; metro, ferrocarril subterráneo.
suc·ceed [səksíd] *v.* suceder a; medrar, tener buen éxito, salir bien.
suc·cess [səksɛ́s] *s.* éxito, buen éxito; triunfo.
suc·cess·ful [səksɛ́sfəl] *adj.* afortunado; próspero; **to be** — tener buen éxito; **-ly** *adv.* con buen éxito, prósperamente.
suc·ces·sion [səksɛ́ʃən] *s.* sucesión.
suc·ces·sive [səksɛ́sɪv] *adj.* sucesivo.
suc·ces·sor [səksɛ́sɚ] *s.* sucesor; heredero.
suc·cor [sʌ́kɚ] *s.* socorro; *v.* socorrer.
suc·cumb [səkʌ́m] *v.* sucumbir.
such [sʌtʃ] *adj.* tal; semejante; — **a** tal, semejante; — **a good man** un hombre tan bueno; — **as** tal como, tales como; **at — an hour** a tal hora; **at — and — a place** en tal o cual lugar.
suck [sʌk] *v.* chupar; mamar; **to — up** chupar; sorber; *s.* chupada; mamada.
suck·er [sʌ́kɚ] *s.* chupador; mamón, mamantón; dulce (*que se chupa*); (*gullible*) primo (*persona demasiado crédula*).
suck·le [sʌ́kl] *v.* mamar; amamantar, dar de mamar.
suc·tion [sʌ́kʃən] *s.* succión; chupada, aspiración.
sud·den [sʌ́dn̩] *adj.* súbito, repentino; precipitado; inesperado; **all of a** — de súbito, de repente, de sopetón; **-ly** *adv.* de súbito, de repente, de sopetón.
sud·den·ness [sʌ́dn̩nɪs] *s.* precipitación; rapidez.
suds [sʌdz] *s.* espuma, jabonadura.
sue [su] *v.* demandar; poner pleito; **to — for damages** demandar por daños y perjuicios; **to — for peace** pedir la paz.
su·et [súɪt] *s.* sebo, gordo, grasa.
suf·fer [sʌ́fɚ] *v.* sufrir; padecer.
suf·fer·er [sʌ́fərɚ] *s.* sufridor.
suf·fer·ing [sʌ́fərɪŋ] *s.* sufrimiento, padecimiento; *adj.* doliente; sufrido, paciente.
suf·fice [səfáɪs] *v.* bastar, ser bastante o suficiente.
suf·fi·cient [səfíʃənt] *adj.* suficiente, bastante; **-ly** *adv.* suficientemente, bastante.
suf·fix [sʌ́fɪks] *s.* sufijo.
suf·fo·cate [sʌ́fəket] *v.* sofocar(se), ahogar(se), asfixiar(se).
suf·fo·ca·tion [sʌfəkéʃən] *s.* asfixia, sofoco.
suf·frage [sʌ́frɪdʒ] *s.* sufragio; voto.
sug·ar [ʃúgɚ] *s.* azúcar; — **bowl** azucarera; — **cane** caña de azúcar; **lump of** — terrón de azúcar; *v.* azucarar; cristalizarse (*el almíbar*), *Am.* azucararse.
sug·gest [səgdʒɛ́st] *v.* sugerir, indicar.
sug·ges·tion [səgdʒɛ́stʃən] *s.* sugestión, *Am.* sugerencia; indicación.
sug·ges·tive [səgdʒɛ́stɪv] *adj.* sugestivo.
su·i·cide [súəsaɪd] *s.* (*act*) suicidio; (*person*) suicida; **to commit** — suicidarse.
suit [sut] *s.* traje, terno, *Carib.*, *Ven.* flux (*o* flus); (*cards*) palo (*de la baraja*); (*court*) demanda, pleito; petición; galanteo; *v.* adaptar, acomodar; agradar; satisfacer; sentar bien, venir bien; caer bien; convenir; ser a propósito; — **yourself** haz lo que quieras, haga Vd. lo que guste.
suit·a·ble [sútəbl] *adj.* propio, conveniente, debido, a propósito, apropiado, adecuado.
suit·a·bly [sútəblɪ] *adv.* propiamente, adecuadamente, convenientemente.
suit·case [sútkes] *s.* maleta, valija.
suite [swit] *s.* serie; comitiva, acompañamiento; — **of rooms** vivienda, apartamento, habitación; **bedroom** — juego de muebles para alcoba.
suit·or [sútɚ] *s.* pretendiente, galán; (*court*) demandante (*en un pleito*).
sulk [sʌlk] *v.* tener murria; estar hosco o malhumorado; *s.* murria.
sulk·y [sʌ́lkɪ] *adj.* malcontento, hosco, malhumorado; **to be** — tener murria.
sul·len [sʌ́lɪn] *adj.* hosco, sombrío, tétrico; malhumorado, taciturno.
sul·ly [sʌ́lɪ] *v.* manchar, ensuciar; empañar.
sul·phate [sʌ́lfet] *s.* sulfato.
sul·phide [sʌ́lfaɪd] *s.* sulfuro.
sul·phur [sʌ́lfɚ] *s.* azufre.
sul·phur·ic [sʌlfjʊ́rɪk] *adj.* sulfúrico; — **acid** ácido sulfúrico.
sul·tan [sʌ́ltn̩] *s.* sultán.
sul·try [sʌ́ltrɪ] *adj.* bochornoso, sofocante; — **heat** bochorno, calor sofocante.
sum [sʌm] *s.* suma; monto; cantidad; (*nature*) esencia, substancia; — **total** total; *v.* sumar; **to — up** resumir, recapitular.
sum·ma·rize [sʌ́məraɪz] *v.* resumir, compendiar.
sum·ma·ry [sʌ́mərɪ] *s.* sumario, resumen; compendio; *adj.* sumario; breve.
sum·mer [sʌ́mɚ] *s.* verano; estío; *adj.* veraniego, estival de verano; — **resort** balneario, lugar de veraneo; *v.* veranear.
sum·mit [sʌ́mɪt] *s.* cima, cúspide, cumbre.
sum·mon [sʌ́mən] *v.* citar; convocar, llamar; **-s** *s.* notificación; cita judicial, citación, emplazamiento.
sump·tu·ous [sʌ́mptʃʊəs] *adj.* suntuoso.
sun [sʌn] *s.* sol; — **bath** baño de sol; — **lamp** lámpara de rayos ultravioletas; — **porch** solana; *v.* asolear; **to — oneself** asolearse, tomar el sol.
sun·beam [sʌ́nbim] *s.* rayo de sol.
sun·burn [sʌ́nbɝn] *s.* quemadura de sol; *v.* asolear(se); quemar(se) al sol, tostar(se) al sol.
Sun·day [sʌ́ndɪ] *s.* domingo.
sun·di·al [sʌ́ndaɪəl] *s.* cuadrante solar, reloj de sol.
sun·down [sʌ́ndaʊn] *s.* puesta del sol.
sun·dry [sʌ́ndrɪ] *adj.* varios, diversos.
sun·flow·er [sʌ́nflaʊɚ] *s.* girasol; tornasol.
sung [sʌŋ] *pret.* & *p.p.* de **to sing.**
sun·glass·es [sʌ́nglæsəz] *s.* gafas (*anteojos*) de sol.

sunk [sʌŋk] *pret. & p.p. de* **to sink.**
sunk·en [sʌ́ŋkən] *adj.* hundido, sumido.
sun·light [sʌ́nlaɪt] *s.* luz del sol, luz solar.
sun·ny [sʌ́nɪ] *adj.* asoleado o soleado; alegre, risueño, resplandeciente; — **day** día de sol.
sun·rise [sʌ́nraɪz] *s.* salida del sol, amanecer, amanecida.
sun·set [sʌ́nsɛt] *s.* puesta del sol.
sun·shine [sʌ́nʃaɪn] *s.* luz del sol, solana.
sun·stroke [sʌ́nstrok] *s.* insolación.
sun·tan [sʌ́ntæn] *s.* bronceado.
sup [sʌp] *v.* cenar.
su·perb [sʊpɝ́b] *adj.* soberbio.
su·per·fi·cial [supɚfíʃəl] *adj.* superficial.
su·per·flu·ous [supɝ́flʊəs] *adj.* superfluo.
su·per·hu·man [supɚhjúmən] *adj.* sobrehumano.
su·per·in·tend [suprɪntɛ́nd] *v.* dirigir, inspeccionar, vigilar.
su·per·in·ten·dent [suprɪntɛ́ndənt] *s.* superintendente; inspector; capataz.
su·pe·ri·or [səpírɪɚ] *adj. & s.* superior; — **letter** volado.
su·pe·ri·or·i·ty [səpɪrɪɔ́rətɪ] *s.* superioridad.
su·per·la·tive [səpɝ́lətɪv] *adj. & s.* superlativo.
su·per·mar·ket [súpɚmɑrkət] *s.* supermercado.
su·per·nat·u·ral [supɚnǽtʃrəl] *adj.* sobrenatural; **the** — lo sobrenatural.
su·per·sede [supɚsíd] *v.* reemplazar.
su·per·sti·tion [supɚstíʃən] *s.* superstición.
su·per·sti·tious [supɚstíʃəs] *adj.* supersticioso.
su·per·vise [supɚváɪz] *v.* dirigir, inspeccionar, vigilar.
su·per·vi·sion [supɚvíʒən] *s.* inspección, vigilancia.
su·per·vi·sor [supɚváɪzɚ] *s.* superintendente, inspector; interventor.
sup·per [sʌ́pɚ] *s.* cena.
sup·plant [səplǽnt] *v.* suplantar; reemplazar.
sup·ple [sʌ́pl] *adj.* flexible; dócil.
sup·ple·ment [sʌ́pləmənt] *s.* suplemento; apéndice; [sʌ́pləmɛnt] *v.* suplementar, completar.
sup·pli·ant [sʌ́plɪənt] *adj. & s.* suplicante.
sup·pli·ca·tion [sʌplɪkéʃən] *s.* súplica, plegaria; ruego.
sup·ply [səpláɪ] *v.* (*provide*) proveer; abastecer, surtir; suplir; (*give*) dar, suministrar; *s.* provisión, abastecimiento; bastimento; abasto; surtido; — **and demand** oferta y demanda; **supplies** provisiones; materiales; víveres; pertrechos; — **pipe** cañería o caño de abastecimiento, tubería, tubo de suministro.
sup·port [səpórt] *v.* (*keep from falling*) sostener; apoyar; (*provide for*) mantener; sustentar; (*bear*) soportar, aguantar; *s.* apoyo; sostén, soporte, puntal; sustento, manutención; amparo.
sup·port·er [səpórtɚ] *s.* defensor; partidario; mantenedor; sostén, apoyo; tirante (*para medias*).
sup·pose [səpóz] *v.* suponer.
sup·posed [səpózd] *adj.* supuesto; presunto; **-ly** *adv.* supuestamente.
sup·po·si·tion [sʌpəzíʃən] *s.* suposición.
sup·press [səprɛ́s] *v.* suprimir; reprimir; parar, suspender; **to — a revolt** sofocar una revuelta o motín.
sup·pres·sion [səprɛ́ʃən] *s.* supresión; represión.
su·prem·a·cy [səprɛ́məsɪ] *s.* supremacía.
su·preme [səprím] *adj.* supremo.
sur·charge [sɝ́tʃardʒ] *s.* recargo.
sure [ʃʊr] *adj.* seguro; cierto; (*stable*) estable; *adv.* *véase* **surely, be — to do it** hágalo sin falta, no deje Vd. de hacerlo; **-ly** *adv.* seguramente; ciertamente; con toda seguridad; sin falta.
sure·ty [ʃʊ́rtɪ] *s.* seguridad; garantía, fianza; fiador.
surf [sɝf] *s.* oleaje, rompientes; (*undertow*) resaca.
sur·face [sɝ́fɪs] *s.* superficie; cara; *v.* (*level*) alisar, allanar; (*coat*) poner superficie a.
surf·board [sɝ́fbord] *s.* patín de mar.
sur·feit [sɝ́fɪt] *s.* hastío, exceso; *v.* hastiar; empalagar.
surge [sɝ́dʒ] *s.* oleada, oleaje; *v.* agitarse, hinchar(se) (*el mar*); surgir.
sur·geon [sɝ́dʒən] *s.* cirujano.
sur·ger·y [sɝ́dʒərɪ] *s.* cirujía.
sur·gi·cal [sɝ́dʒɪkl] *adj.* quirúrgico.
sur·ly [sɝ́lɪ *adj.* rùdo, hosco, malhumorado.
sur·mise [sɚmáɪz] *v.* conjeturar, suponer, presumir; *s.* conjetura, suposición.
sur·mount [sɚmáʊnt] *v.* superar, vencer; coronar.
sur·name [sɝ́nem] *s.* sobrenombre, apellido; *v.* apellidar, llamar.
sur·pass [sɚpǽs] *v.* sobrepasar, superar, sobrepujar, exceder, aventajar.
sur·pass·ing [sɚpǽsɪŋ] *adj.* sobresaliente, excelente.
sur·plus [sɝ́plʌs] *s.* sobra, sobrante, exceso, excedente; superávit; *adj.* sobrante, excedente, de sobra.
sur·prise [səpráɪz] *s.* sorpresa; *v.* sorprender.
sur·pris·ing [səpráɪzɪŋ] *adj.* sorprendente.
sur·ren·der [sərɛ́ndɚ] *v.* rendir(se), entregar(se), darse; ceder; *s.* rendición; entrega; cesión; sumisión.
sur·round [səráʊnd] *v.* rodear, cercar, circundar.
sur·round·ing [səráʊndɪŋ] *adj.* circundante, circunvecino, circunstante.
sur·round·ings [səráʊndɪŋz] *s. pl* alrededores, inmediaciones, cercanías; ambiente.
sur·vey [sɝ́ve] *s.* (*inspection*) examen, reconocimiento, inspección, estudio; (*measure*) medición, agrimensura (*de un terreno*); plano (*de un terreno*); bosquejo o esbozo general (*de historia, literatura, etc.*); investigación por encuestas; — **course** curso general o comprensivo; [sɚvé] *v.* examinar, inspeccionar, reconocer, medir (*un terreno*), levantar un plano (*el agrimensor*).
sur·vey·or [sɚvéɚ] *s.* agrimensor.
sur·viv·al [sɚváɪvl] *s.* supervivencia; sobreviviente; resto.
sur·vive [sɚváɪv] *c.* sobrevivir; quedar vivo, salvarse.
sur·vi·vor [sɚváɪvɚ] *s.* sobreviviente.
sus·cep·ti·ble [səsɛ́ptəbl] *adj.* susceptible; — **of proof** capaz de probarse; — **to** propenso a.
sus·pect [sʌ́spɛkt] *s.* sospechoso; [səspɛ́kt] *v.* sospechar.
sus·pend [səspɛ́nd] *v.* suspender.
sus·pend·ers [səspɛ́ndɚz] *s.* tirantes (*de pantalón*).
sus·pense [səspɛ́ns] *s.* (*uncertainty*) suspensión, incertidumbre; (*anxiety*) ansiedad; **to keep in** — tener en suspenso, tener en duda.
sus·pen·sion [səspɛ́nʃən] *s.* suspensión; — **bridge** puente colgante.
sus·pi·cion [səspíʃən] *s.* sospecha.
sus·pi·cious [səspíʃəs] *adj.* sospechoso; suspicaz.
sus·tain [səstén] *v.* (*prolong*) sostener; mantener; (*support*) sustentar; (*bear, endure*) aguantar; (*defend*) apoyar, defender; (*undergo*) sufrir (*un daño o pérdida*).
sus·te·nance [sʌ́stənəns] *s.* sustento; subsistencia; alimentos; mantenimiento.
swab [swab] *s.* escobillón; *v.* fregar.
swag·ger [swǽgɚ] *v.* pavonearse, contonearse; fanfarronear; *s.* pavoneo, contoneo; fanfarronada.
swain [swen] *s.* galán.

swal·low [swálo] *s.* (*bird*) golondrina; (*drink*) trago; *v.* tragar; deglutir.
swam [swæm] *pret. de* **to swim.**
swamp [swɑmp] *s.* pantano; ciénaga; — **land** cenagal, terreno pantanoso; *v.* inundar(se); sumergir(se); **to be -ed with work** estar abrumado de trabajo.
swamp·y [swámpɪ] *adj.* pantanoso, cenagoso, fangoso.
swan [swɑn] *s.* cisne.
swap [swɑp] *v.* cambalachear, cambiar, trocar; *s.* cambalache, cambio, trueque; — **shop** cambalache.
swarm [swɔrm] *s.* enjambre; *v.* pulular; bullir, hervir, hormiguear.
swarth·y [swɔ́rðɪ] *adj.* trigueño, moreno, *Am.* prieto.
swat [swɑt] *v.* pegar, aporrear; aplastar de un golpe (*una mosca*); *s.* golpe.
sway [swe] *v.* mecer(se); cimbrar(se); balancearse; ladear(se); oscilar; tambalear; influir; *s.* oscilación; vaivén; balanceo; influjo, influencia; mando; predominio.
swear [swɛr] *v.* jurar; renegar, (*curse*) blasfemar, echar maldiciones; (*take oath*) juramentar, tomar juramento; **to — by** jurar por; poner toda su confianza en; **to — in** juramentar; **to — off smoking** jurar no fumar más, renunciar al tabaco.
sweat [swɛt] *v.* sudar; trasudar; hacer sudar; *s.* sudor; trasudor.
sweat·er [swɛ́tɚ] *s.* suéter; sudador, el que suda.
sweat·y [swɛ́tɪ] *adj.* sudoroso.
Swede [swid] *s.* sueco.
Swed·ish [swidɪʃ] *adj.* sueco; *s.* sueco, idioma sueco.
sweep [swip] *v.* barrer; (*dredge*) drager (*puertos, ríos, etc.*); extenderse; **to — down upon** caer sobre; asolar; **to — everything away** barrer con todo; **she swept into the room** entró garbosamente en la sala; *s.* barrida; extensión; (*blow*) soplo (*del viento*).
sweep·er [swípɚ] *s.* barrendero; **carpet** — escoba mecánica.
sweep·ing [swípɪŋ] *s.* barrido; **-s** basura; *adj.* abarcador, que lo abarca todo, vasto; asolador; — **victory** victoria completa.
sweet [swit] *adj.* (*flavor*) dulce; oloroso; (*fresh*) fresco; — **butter** mantequilla sin sal; — **corn** maiz tierno; — **milk** leche fresca; — **pea** guisante de olor; — **potato** batata, *Méx., C.A.* camote, *Carib.* boniato; **to have a — tooth** ser goloso, gustarle a uno los dulces; *s.* dulce, golosina; **my** — mi vida, mi alma.
sweet·en [swítn̩] *v.* endulzar(se), dulcificar(se); suavizar.
sweet·heart [swíthɑrt] *s.* querida, novia, prometida; amante, querido, galán, novio.
sweet·meat [swítmit] *s.* confite, confitura dulce, golosina.
sweet·ness [swítnɪs] *s.* dulzura; (*pleasantness*) melosidad; (*gentleness*) suavidad.
swell [swɛl] *v.* hinchar(se), henchir(se), inflar(se); dilatar(se), abultar(se); acrecentar; *s.* hinchazón; protuberancia; oleaje; *adj.* elegante; muy bueno, excelente, magnífico; **to have a — head** creerse gran cosa; ser vanidoso.
swel·ling [swɛ́lɪŋ] *s.* hinchazón; chichón, bulto; protuberancia.
swel·ter [swɛ́ltɚ] *v.* sofocarse de calor.
swept [swɛpt] *pret. & p.p. de* **to sweep.**
swerve [swɝv] *v.* desviar(se); torcer; cambiar repentinamente de rumbo; *s.* desvío brusco, cambio repentino de dirección; **to make a — to the right** torcer a la derecha.
swift [swɪft] *adj.* veloz, rápido.
swift·ness [swíftnɪs] *s.* velocidad, rapidez, presteza, prontitud.
swim [swɪm] *v.* nadar; flotar; **to — across** pasar a nado, atravesar nadando; **my head is swimming** tengo vértigo, se me va la cabeza, estoy desvanecido; *s.* nadada; — **suit** traje de baño o natación.
swim·mer [swímɚ] *s.* nadador.
swin·dle [swíndl] *v.* estafar; *s.* *estafa.*
swine [swaɪn] *s.* marrano, puerco, cerdo, cochino; *S.A.* chancho; *C.A.* cuchi; marranos, puercos, cerdos.
swing [swɪŋ] *v.* columpiar(se), mecer(se), balancear(se); oscilar; hacer oscilar; (*blandish*) blandir (*un bastón, espada, etc.*); (*hang*) colgar; girar; hacer girar; **to — a deal** llevar a cabo un negocio; **to — around** dar vuelta, girar; **to — one's arms** girar o menear los brazos; **to — open** abrirse de pronto (*una puerta*); *s.* columpio; hamaca; balanceo; vaivén; compás; ritmo; golpe, guantada, puñetazo; — **door** puerta giratoria; — **shift** turno de trabajo desde las dieciséis hasta medianoche; **in full** — en su apogeo, en pleno movimiento; **to give someone full** — darle a alguien completa libertad de acción.
swipe [swaɪp] *v.* hurtar, sisar.
swirl [swɝl] *v.* arremolinarse; girar, dar vueltas; *s.* remolino; torbellino; vuelta, movimiento giratorio.
Swiss [swɪs] *adj. & s.* suizo.
switch [swɪtʃ] *s.* (*change*) mudanza; (*whip*) látigo, (*blow*) azote; *Méx., Andes* chicote, *Ríopl.* rebenque; *Méx., Andes* fuste; latigazo; pelo postizo; cambio; **electric** — interruptor, conmutador; **railway** — aguja, cambio; —**man** guardagujas, *Andes, Ríopl.* cambiavía; *Méx.* guardavía; *v.* azotar; desviar(se); cambiar(se); **to — off** cortar (*la communicación o la corriente eléctrica*); apagar (*la luz eléctrica*); **to — on the light** encender la luz; (*computer*) accionar.
switch·board [swítʃbɔrd] *s.* cuadro o tablero de distribución; cuadro conmutador.
swiv·el [swívl] *adj.* giratorio.
swol·len [swólən] *p.p. de* **to swell.**
swoon [swun] *v.* desvanecerse, desmayarse; *s.* desmayo.
swoop [swup] *v.* **to — down upon** caer de súbito sobre; abalanzarse sobre; acometer; **to — off** cortar de un golpe; **to — up** agarrar, arrebatar; *s.* descenso súbito; arremetida; **at one** — de un golpe.
sword [sord] *s.* espada; — **belt** talabarte.
swore [swor] *pret. de* **to swear.**
sworn [sworn] *p.p. de* **to swear.**
swum [swʌm] *p.p. de* **to swim.**
swung [swʌŋ] *pret. & p.p. de* **to swing.**
syl·lab·i·cate [sɪlǽbəket] *v.* silabear.
syl·la·ble [sílәbl] *s.* sílaba.
syl·la·bus [síləbəs] *s.* sílabo.
syl·lo·gism [sílədʒɪzəm] *s.* silogismo.
sym·bol [símbl] *s.* símbolo.
sym·bol·ic [sɪmbálɪk] *adj.* simbólico.
sym·bol·ism [símblɪzəm] *s.* simbolismo.
sym·met·ri·cal [sɪmɛ́trɪkl] *adj.* simétrico.
sym·me·try [símɪtrɪ] *s.* simetría.
sym·pa·thet·ic [sɪmpəθɛ́tɪk] *adj.* compasivo; favorablemente dispuesto; que compadece; — **towards** favorablemente dispuesto a (*o* hacia).
sym·pa·thize [símpəθaɪz] *v.* compadecer(se); condolerse.

SU

sym·pa·thy [sɪ́mpəθɪ] *s.* compasión, lástima; armonía; **to extend one's** — dar el pésame.
sym·pho·ny [sɪ́mfənɪ] *s.* sinfonía; — **orchestra** orquesta sinfónica.
sym·po·si·um [sɪmpósɪəm] *s.* coloquio; simposio.
symp·tom [sɪ́mptəm] *s.* síntoma.
syn·a·gogue [sɪ́nəgag] *s.* sinagoga.
syn·chro·nize [sɪ́nkənaɪz] *v.* sincronizar.
syn·di·cate [sɪ́ndɪkɪt] *s.* sindicato; **newspaper** — sindicato periodístico; [sɪ́ndɪket] *v.* sindicar, formar un sindicato; sindicarse, combinarse para formar un sindicato; vender (*un cuento, caricatura, serie de artículos, etc.*) a un sindicato.
syn·drome [sɪ́ndrom] *s.* síndrome.
syn·o·nym [sɪ́nənɪm] *s.* sinónimo.
syn·on·y·mous [sɪnɑ́nəmes] *adj.* sinónimo.
syn·op·sis [sɪnɑ́psɪs] *s.* sinopsis.
syn·tax [sɪ́ntæks] *s.* sintaxis.
syn·the·sis [sɪ́nθəsɪs] *s.* síntesis.
syn·the·size [sɪ́nθəsaɪz] *v.* sintetizar.
syn·thet·ic [sɪnθétik] *adj.* sintético.
syr·inge [sɪ́rɪndʒ] *s.* jeringa.
syr·up = **sirup.**
sys·tem [sɪ́stəm] *s.* sistema.
sys·tem·at·ic [sɪstəmǽtɪk] *adj.* sistemático.
sys·tem·a·tize [sɪstəmətɑ́ɪz] *v.* sistematizar, metodizar.
sys·tem·ic [sɪstémɪk] *adj.* sistemático.

T:t

tab [tæb] *s.* (*flap*) lengüeta; (*bill*) cuenta; — **key** tecla de tabulación.
tab·er·na·cle [tǽbɚnækl] *s.* tabernáculo.
ta·ble [tébl] *s.* (*furniture*) mesa; tabla (*de materias, de multiplicar, etc.*); — **cover** tapete, cubremesa; —**land** mesa, meseta; *v.* poner sobre la mesa; formar tabla o índice; **to — a motion** dar carpetazo a una moción, aplazar la discusión de una moción.
ta·ble·cloth [téblklɔθ] *s.* mantel.
ta·ble·spoon [téblspun] *s.* cuchara grande.
ta·ble·spoon·ful [téblspunfʊl] *s.* cucharada.
tab·let [tǽblɪt] *s.* tableta; tablilla, (*pill*) pastilla; comprimido; bloc de papel; (*stone*) lápida, placa.
ta·ble·ware [téblwɛr] *s.* vajilla, servicio de mesa.
ta·boo [tæbú] *s.* tabú.
tab·u·late [tǽbjəlet] *v.* formar tablas o listas; tabular.
tac·it [tǽsɪt] *adj.* tácito.
tac·i·turn [tǽsətɝn] *adj.* taciturno, silencioso.
tack [tæk] *s.* (*nail*) tachuela; (*hem*) hilván; (*boat*) virada o cambio de rumbo (*de una embarcación*); amura, jarcia (*para sostener el ángulo de una vela*); **to change** — cambiar de amura, cambiar de rumbo; *v.* clavetear con tachuelas; coser, hilvanar; pegar, clavar; juntar, unir; virar, cambiar de rumbo; zigzaguear (*un barco de vela*).
tack·le [tǽkl] *s.* aparejo, equipo, enseres, avíos; (*football*) agarrada (*en fútbol*); (*person*) atajador (*en fútbol*); **fishing** — avíos de pescar; *v.* agarrar, asir, atajar (*en futbol*); atacar (*un problema*); acometer (*una empresa*).
tact [tækt] *s.* tacto, tino, tiento.
tact·ful [tǽktfəl] *adj.* cauto, prudente, diplomático.
tac·tics [tǽktɪks] *s.* táctica.
tact·less [tǽktlɪs] *adj.* falto de tacto o de tino; imprudente, incauto.
taf·fe·ta [tǽfɪtɚ] *s.* tafetán.
tag [tæg] *s.* (*label*) marbete, etiqueta; cartela; (*loose end*) pingajo, rabito, cabo; **to play** — jugar al tócame tú, jugar a la pega; *v.* pegar un marbete a, marcar; **to — after** seguir de cerca a, pisar los talones a; **to — something on to** juntar, añadir o agregar algo a.
tail [tel] *s.* (*animal*) cola, rabo; (*object*) cabo, extremo, extremidad; — **light** farol trasero, farol de cola; — **spin** barrena.
tai·lor [télɚ] *s.* sastre; — **shop** sastrería.
taint [tent] *s.* tacha, mancha; corrupción; *v.* manchar; corromper(se), inficionar(se).
take [tek] *v.* tomar; coger; (*carry*) llevar; (*conduct*) conducir; dar (*un paseo, vuelta, paso, salto*); hacer (*un viaje*); asumir; (*photo*) sacar o tomar (*una fotografía*); **to — a chance** aventurarse, correr un riesgo; **to — a fancy to** caerle en gracia a uno; aficionarse a; antojársele a uno; **to — a look at** mirar a, echar una mirada a; **to — a notion to** antojársele a uno; **to — after** salir a, parecerse a; seguir el ejemplo de; **to — amiss** interpretar mal, echar a mala parte; **to — an oath** prestar juramento; **to — apart** desarmar, desmontar; **to — away** llevarse; **to — back one's words** desdecirse, retractarse; **to — back to** devolver (*algo*) a; **to — by surprise** coger desprevenido, coger de sorpresa; **to — care of** cuidar de, atender a; **to — charge of** encargarse de; **to — cold** resfriarse, acatarrarse; **to — down in writing** poner por escrito, apuntar; **to — effect** surtir efecto, dar resultado; entrar en vigencia (*una ley*); **to — exercise** hacer ejercicio; hacer gimnasia; **to — from** quitar a; sustraer de, restar de; **to — in** meter en; recibir; abarcar; embaucar; reducir, achicar (*un vestido*); **to — leave** decir adiós, despedirse; **to — off** quitar; descontar, rebajar; despegar (*un aeroplano*); remedar, parodiar (*a alguien*); **to — offense** ofenderse, darse por ofendido; **to — on a responsibility** asumir una responsabilidad; **to — out** sacar; **to — place** tener lugar, suceder, ocurrir; **to — stock** hacer inventario; **to — stock in** creer, tener confianza en; **to — the floor** tomar la palabra; **to — to heart** tomar a pechos, tomar en serio; **to — to one's heels** poner pies en polvorosa; **to — to task** reprender, regañar; **to — up a matter** tratar un asunto; **to — up space** ocupar espacio; **I — it that** supongo que; *s.* toma; **take-off** despegue (*de un aeroplano*); remedo, parodia.
tak·en [tékən] *p.p. de* **to take**; **to be — ill** caer enfermo.
tal·cum [tǽlkəm] *s.* talco; — **powder** talco en polvo.
tale [tel] *s.* (*story*) cuento, relato, fábula; (*gossip*) chisme; **to tell -s** contar cuentos o chismes; chismear, murmurar.
tale·bear·er [télbɛrɚ] *s.* soplón, chismoso.
tal·ent [tǽlənt] *s.* talento.
tal·ent·ed [tǽləntɪd] *adj.* talentoso.
talk [tɔk] *v.* hablar; (*chat*) charlar, platicar, conversar; **to — into** inducir o persuadir a; **to — nonsense** decir tonterías, hablar disparates; **to — out of** disuadir de; **to — over** discutir; **to — up** alabar; hablar claro o recio, hablar en voz alta; *s.* charla, conversación, plática; habla; discurso; conferencia; rumor; — **of the town** comidilla, tema de murmuración.
talk·a·tive [tɔ́kətɪv] *adj.* hablador, locuaz, platicador.
talk·er [tɔ́kɚ] *s.* hablador; conversador; platicador; orador.
tall [tɔl] *adj.* alto; — **tale** cuento exagerado o increíble; **six feet** — seis pies de altura o de alto.

tal·low [tǽlo] *s.* sebo.
tal·low·y [tǽlowɪ] *adj.* seboso.
tal·ly [tǽlɪ] *s.* cuenta; tarja; · **sheet** plana para llevar la cuenta; *v.* llevar la cuenta; **to — up** contar, sumar; **to — with** corresponder con, concordar con.
tam·a·rind [tǽmərɪnd] *s.* tamarindo.
tame [tem] *adj.* manso; dócil; — **amusement** diversión poco animada o desabrida; *v.* amansar, domar, domeñar, domesticar, desbravar.
tam·per [tǽmpɚ] *v.* **to — with** meterse con, juguetear con; falsificar (*un documento*); **to — with a lock** tratar de forzar una cerradura.
tan [tæn] *v.* (*cure*) curtir, adobar (*pieles*); (*punish*) zurrar, azotar; (*sunburn*) tostar(se), requemar(se); *adj.* tostado, requemado; color de canela; bayo, amarillento; *s.* color moreno, de canela o café con leche.
tang [tæŋ] *s.* sabor u olor picante.
tangent [tǽndʒənt] *adj.* & *s.* tangente; **to go off at a —** salirse por la tangente.
tan·ger·ine [tǽndʒərin] *s.* naranja tangerina o mandarina.
tan·gi·ble [tǽndʒəbl] *adj.* tangible, palpable; corpóreo.
tan·gle [tǽŋgl] *v.* enredar(se), enmarañar(se); confundir(se), embrollar(se); *s.* enredo, maraña, embrollo; confusión.
tank [tæŋk] *s.* tanque; depósito; **swimming —** piscina.
tan·ner [tǽnɚ] *s.* curtidor.
tan·ner·y [tǽnərɪ] *s.* curtiduría, tenería.
tan·nic ac·id [tǽnɪkǽsəd] *s.* ácido tánico.
tan·ta·lize [tǽntlaɪz] *v.* molestar; hacer desesperar; exasperar.
tan·ta·lum [tǽntələm] *s.* tantalio.
tan·ta·mount [tæntəmaʊnt] *adj.* equivalente.
tan·trum [tǽntrəm] *s.* berrinche.
tap [tæp] *s.* (*blow*) palmadita; golpecito; (*faucet*) espita, grifo, llave; — **dance** zapateado, *Andes, Ríopl.* zapateo; — **room** bar; **beer on —** cerveza del barril, cerveza de sifón; *v.* tocar, golpear ligeramente; dar una palmadita o golpecito; taladrar; extraer; **to — a tree** sangrar un árbol.
tape [tep] *s.* cinta, cintilla; — **measure** cinta para medir; — **recorder** magnetófono; grabadora; **adhesive —** tela adhesiva, esparadrapo; *v.* atar o vendar con cinta; medir con cinta.
ta·per [tépɚ] *s.* (*candle*) velita, candela; (*diminished size*) adelgazamiento paulatino; *v.* adelgazar, disminuir gradualmente; **to — off** ahusar(se), ir disminuyendo (*hasta rematar en punta*).
tap·es·try [tǽpɪstrɪ] *s.* tapiz, colgadura; tapicería; tela (*para forrar muebles*).
tape·worm [tépwɚm] *s.* tenia, solitaria.
tap·i·o·ca [tæpɪókə] *s.* tapioca.
tar [tɑr] *s.* alquitrán, brea, pez (*f.*); *Méx.* chapapote; *v.* alquitranar, embrear, poner brea o alquitrán.
tar·dy [tɑ́rdɪ] *adj.* tardo, tardío; **to be —** llegar tarde (retrasado).
tar·get [tɑ́rgɪt] *s.* blanco; — **practice** tiro al blanco.
tar·iff [tǽrɪf] *s.* tarifa; arancel, impuesto.
tar·nish [tɑ́rnɪʃ] *v.* empañar(se); manchar; perder el lustre; *s.* deslustre, falta de lustre, empañamiento; mancha.
tar·ry [tǽrɪ] *v.* demorarse, tardar(se).
tart [tɑrt] *adj.* acre, agridulce; agrio; picante; — **reply** respuesta mordaz o agria; *s.* tarta, torta rellena con dulce de frutas.
tar·tar[tártɚ] *s.* tártaro.
task [tæsk] *s.* faena, tarea, quehacer; **to take to —** reprender, regañar.
task force [tǽskfɔrs] *s.* Comisión de investigación para misión especial.
tas·sel [tǽsl] *s.* borla.
taste [test] *v.* gustar; probar; saborear, paladear; **to — of onion** saber a cebolla; **it -s sour** sabe agrio, tiene un sabor o gusto agrio; *s.* gusto; sabor; prueba; afición; **after —** dejo; **in good —** de buen gusto; **to take a — of** probar.
taste·less [téstlɪs] *adj.* insípido; desabrido; de mal gusto.
tast·y [téstɪ] *adj.* sabroso, gustoso; de buen gusto.
tat·ter [tǽtɚ] *s.* harapo, *Carib.* hilacho.
tat·ter·ed [tǽtɚd] *adj.* roto, harapiento, andrajoso.
tat·tle [tǽtl] *v.* chismear, murmurar; *s.* habladuría, murmuración, hablilla; — **tale** chismoso, soplón.
tat·too [tætú] *s.* tatuaje; *v.* tatuar.
taught [tɔt] *pret.* & *p.p. de* **to teach.**
taunt [tɔnt] *v.* mofarse de, echar pullas; reprochar; *s.* mofa, pulla.
tav·ern [tǽvén] *s.* taberna; posada.
tax [tæks] *s.* impuesto, contribución; esfuerzo; *v.* imponer contribuciones a; (*impose*) tasar; (*burden*) abrumar; reprender, reprobar; (*collect*) cobrar; **to — one's patience** abusar de la paciencia; **taxable funds** fondos gravables.
tax·a·tion [tækséʃən] *s.* impuestos, contribuciones; imposición de contribuciones.
tax·i [tǽksɪ] *s.* taxímetro, taxi, automóvil de alquiler; *v.* ir en taxímetro; taxear (*un aeroplano*).
tax·i·cab [tǽksɪkæb] = **taxi.**
tax·i·der·my [tǽksɪdɚmɪ] *s.* taxidermia.
tax·on·o·my [tæksɑ́nəmɪ] *s.* taxonomía.
tax·pay·er [tǽkspeɚ] *s.* contribuyente; *Méx.* causante de impuestos.
tea [ti] *s.* té; **linden —** tila.
teach [titʃ] *v.* enseñar; instruir.
teach·er [títʃɚ] *s.* maestro, maestra.
teach·ing [títʃɪŋ] *s.* enseñanza; instrucción; doctrina.
tea·cup [tíkʌp] *s.* taza para té.
tea·ket·tle [tíkɛtl] *s.* marmita, tetera, *Ríopl.* pava (*para el mate*).
team [tim] *s.* equipo (*de jugadores*); partido, grupo; tronco (*de caballos, mulas, etc.*); (*yoke*) yunta (*de bueyes*): — **work** cooperación; trabajo aunado; *v.* uncir, enganchar; formar pareja; acarrear, transportar; **to — up** unirse, formar un equipo.
team·ster [tímstɚ] *s.* carretero.
tea·pot [típɑt] *s.* tetera.
tear [tɪr] *s.* lágrima; · **gas** gas lacrimógeno o lacrimante; **to burst into -s** romper a llorar; deshacerse en lágrimas.
tear [tɛr] *v.* rasgar(se); desgarrar, romper; **to — along** ir a toda velocidad; andar aprisa, correr; **to — apart** desarmar, desmontar; separar, apartar; **to — away** arrancar; irse; **to — down** demoler, derribar (*un edificio*); desarmar, desmontar (*una máquina*); **to — off in a hurry** salir corriendo, salir a la carrera; **to — one's hair** mesarse los cabellos; *s.* desgarradura, rasgadura; rasgón, rotura; prisa; **wear and —** desgaste.
tear·ful [tírfəl] *adj.* lloroso.
tease [tiz] *v.* embromar; molestar; importunar.
tea·spoon [tíspun] *s.* cucharilla, cucharita.
tea·spoon·ful [tíspunfʊl] *s.* cucharadita.
teat [tit] *s.* teta.
tech·ne·ti·um [tɛkníʃəm] *s.* tecnecio.
tech·ni·cal [tɛ́knɪkl] *adj.* técnico.
tech·ni·cian [tɛkníʃən] *s.* técnico.
tech·nique [tɛkník] *s.* técnica.
tech·nol·o·gy [teknɑ́lədʒɪ] *s.* tecnología.
te·di·ous [tídɪəs] *adj* tedioso, pesado, aburrido,

SY

fastidioso.
te·di·ous·ness [tídɪəsnɪs] *s.* tedio.
teem [tim] *v.* **to — with** abundar en, estar lleno de.
teen·ag·er [tínedʒɚ] *s.* joven de le edad de 13 a 19 años; *Col.* cocacolo.
teens [tinz] *s. pl.* edad de trece a diecinueve años; números de trece a diecinueve; **to be in one's —** tener de trece a diecinueve años.
teeth [tiθ] *s. pl. de* **tooth; he escaped by the skin of his —** por poco no se escapa, se escapó por milagro.
tele·cast [tɛ́ləkæst] *s.* teledifusión.
tele·com·mu·ni·ca·tion [tɛlɪkəmjunɪkéʃən] *s.* telecomunicación.
tele·gram [tɛ́ləgræm] *s.* telegrama.
tele·graph [tɛ́ləgræf] *s.* telégrafo; *v.* telegrafiar.
tele·graph·ic [tɛləgrǽfɪk] *adj.* telegráfico.
te·leg·ra·phy [təlɛ́grəfɪ] *s.* telegrafía.
te·lep·a·thy [təlɛ́pəθɪ] *s.* telepatía.
tele·phone [tɛ́ləfon] *s.* teléfono; **— booth** casilla de teléfono; **— operator** telefonista; **— receiver** receptor telefónico; *v.* telefonear, llamar por teléfono.
tele·scope [tɛ́ləskop] *s.* telescopio; *v.* enchufar(se), encajar(se) un objeto en otro.
Tele·type [tɛ́lətɑɪp] *s.* teletipo.
tele·vi·sion [tɛ́ləvɪʒən] *s.* televisión; **— viewer** televidente.
tell [tɛl] *v.* (*recount*) decir; contar; expresar; explicar; (*identify*) adivinar; **to — on someone** delatar a alguien, contar chismes de alguien; **to — someone off** decirle a alguien cuatro verdades; **his age is beginning to —** ya comienza a notársele la edad.
tell·er [tɛ́lɚ] *s.* narrador, relator; (*bank*) pagador o recibidor (*de un banco*); escrutador de votos.
tel·lu·ri·um [təlúrɪəm] *s.* telurio.
te·mer·i·ty [təmɛ́rətɪ] *s.* temeridad.
tem·per [tempɚ] *v.* templar; *s.* temple (*de un metal*); genio, temple, humor; mal genio; **to keep one's —** contenerse, dominarse; **to lose one's —** perder la calma, encolerizarse.
tem·per·a·ment [tɛ́mprəmənt] *s.* temperamento; disposición; temple.
tem·per·ance [tɛ́mprəns] *s.* templanza, sobriedad.
tem·per·ate [tɛ́mprɪt] *adj.* templado, moderado; sobrio.
tem·per·a·ture [tɛ́mprətʃɚ] *s.* temperatura; **to have a —** tener calentura o fiebre.
tem·pest [tɛ́mpɪst] *s.* tempestad.
tem·pes·tu·ous [tɛmpɛstʃʊəs] *adj.* tempestuoso, borrascoso.
tem·ple [tɛ́mpl] *s.* templo; sien.
tem·po·ral [tɛ́mpərəl] *adj.* temporal.
tem·po·rar·i·ly [tɛ́mpərɛrəlɪ] *adv.* temporalmente.
tem·po·rar·y [tɛ́mpərɛrɪ] *adj.* temporal, transitorio, provisorio; provisional; interino.
tempt [tɛmpt] *v.* tentar; incitar; provocar; atraer.
temp·ta·tion [tɛmptéʃən] *s.* tentación.
tempt·er [tɛ́mptɚ] *s.* tentador.
tempt·ing [tɛ́mptɪŋ] *adj.* tentador, atractivo.
ten [tɛn] *num.* diez.
ten·a·ble [tɛ́nəbl] *adj.* defendible.
te·na·cious [tɪnéʃəs] *adj.* tenaz, aferrado.
te·nac·i·ty [tɪnǽsətɪ] *s.* tenacidad; aferramiento; tesón.
ten·ant [tɛ́nənt] *s.* inquilino, arrendatario.
tend [tɛnd] *v.* (*care for*) cuidar, vigilar, guardar; atender; (*lean toward*) tender, inclinarse.
ten·den·cy [tɛ́ndənsɪ] *s.* tendencia; propensión.
ten·der [tɛ́ndɚ] *adj.* tierno; delicado; (*sensitive*) sensible; **tender-hearted** de corazón tierno; *s.* oferta, ofrecimiento; ténder (*de un tren*); lancha (*de auxilio*); cuidador, vigilante; **legal —** moneda corriente; *v.* ofrecer.
ten·der·loin [tɛ́ndɚlɔɪn] *s.* filete; filet mignon.
ten·der·ness [tɛ́ndɚnɪs] *s.* ternura, terneza; delicadeza.
ten·don [tɛ́ndən] *s.* tendón.
ten·dril [tɛ́ndrɪl] *s.* zarcillo (*tallito de una planta trepadora*).
ten·e·ment [tɛ́nəmənt] *s.* casa de vecindad.
ten·nis [tɛ́nɪs] *s.* tenis; **— court** cancha de tenis.
ten·or [tɛ́nɚ] *s.* (*voice*) tenor; (*meaning*) significado; **— voice** voz de tenor.
tense [tɛns] *adj.* tenso; tirante; *s.* tiempo (*del verbo*).
ten·sion [tɛ́nʃən] *s.* tensión; tirantez.
tent [tɛnt] *s.* tienda de campaña; pabellón; *v.* acampar.
ten·ta·cle [tɛ́ntəkl] *s.* tentáculo.
ten·ta·tive [tɛ́ntətɪv] *adj.* tentativo.
ten·u·ous [tɛ́njʊəs] *adj.* tenue.
ten·ure [tɛ́njʊr] *s.* tenencia.
tep·id [tɛ́pɪd] *adj.* tibio.
term [tɝm] *s.* (*word*) término; (*period*) período; plazo; sesión; **-s** términos, expresiones, palabras; condiciónes; **to be on good -s** estar en buenas relaciones; **not to be on speaking -s** no hablarse, no dirigirse la palabra; **to come to -s** ajustarse, ponerse de acuerdo; *v.* nombrar, llamar, denominar.
ter·mi·na·ble [tɝmɪnəbl] *adj.* terminable.
ter·mi·nal [tɝ́mənl] *adj.* terminal, final, último; *s.* término, fin; estación terminal; **electric —** toma de corriente; borne (*de aparato eléctrico*).
ter·mi·nate [tɝ́mənet] *v.* terminar, acabar.
ter·mi·na·tion [tɝmənéʃən] *s.* terminación, fin; desinencia (*gramatical*).
ter·mite [tɝmaɪt] *s.* termita.
ter·race [tɛ́rɪs] *s.* terraplén; terraza, terrado; *v.* terraplenar.
ter·res·tri·al [tərɛ́strɪəl] *adj.* terrestre, terreno, terrenal.
ter·ri·ble [tɛ́rəbl] *adj.* terrible; **terribly** *adv.* terriblemente.
ter·ri·er [tɛ́rɪɚ] *s.* perro de busca.
ter·ri·fic [tərífɪk] *adj.* terrífico.
ter·ri·fy [tɛ́rəfaɪ] *v.* aterrar, aterrorizar.
ter·ri·to·ry [tɛ́rətorɪ] *s.* territorio.
ter·ror [tɛ́rɚ] *s.* terror, espanto.
ter·ror·ist [tɛ́rərɪst] *s.* terrorista.
test [tɛst] *s.* prueba, ensayo, experimento; comprobación; examen; **— tube** probeta, tubo de ensayo; **to undergo a —** sufrir una prueba; *v.* probar, ensayar, comprobar, experimentar; poner a prueba; examinar.
tes·ta·ment [tɛ́stəmənt] *s.* testamento.
tes·ti·cle [tɛ́stɪkl] *s.* testículo.
tes·ti·fy [tɛ́stəfaɪ] *v.* atestiguar, atestar.
tes·ti·mo·ny [tɛ́stəmonɪ] *s.* testimonio.
tet·a·nus [tɛ́tənəs] *s.* tétanos.
Teu·ton·ic [tutánɪk] *adj.* teutónico.
text [tɛkst] *s.* texto; **— editing** (*computer*) edición de texto.
text·book [tɛ́kstbʊk] *s.* texto, libro de texto.
tex·tile [tɛ́kstl] *adj.* textil; de tejidos; **— mill** fábrica de tejidos; *s.* tejido, materia textil.
tex·ture [tɛ́kstʃɚ] *s.* textura, contextura; tejido.
thal·li·um [θǽliəm] *s.* talio.
than [ðæn] *conj.* que; **more — once** más de una vez; **more — he knows** más de lo que él sabe.
thank [θæŋk] *v.* dar gracias, agradecer; **— heaven!** ¡gracias a Dios!; **— you** gracias; **to have oneself**

to — for tener la culpa de; ser responsable de; -s *s. pl.* gracias.
thank·ful [θǽŋkfəl] *adj.* agradecido; **-ly** *adv.* agradecidamente, con agradecimiento, con gratitud.
thank·ful·ness [θǽŋkfəlnɪs] *s.* gratitud, agradecimiento.
thank·less [θǽŋklɪs] *adj.* ingrato; — **task** tarea ingrata o infructuosa.
thanks·giv·ing [θæŋksgívɪŋ] *s.* acción de gracias; **Thanksgiving Day** día de acción de gracias.
that [ðæt] *adj.* ese, esa, aquel, aquella; — **one** ése, ésa, aquél, aquélla; *pron.* ése, eso, aquél, aquélla, aquello; *pron. rel.* que; — **is** es decir; — **of** el de, la de, lo de; — **which** el que, la que, lo que; *conj.* que; para que, a fin de que; **so** — para que; de modo que, a fin de que, de suerte que, de tal manera que; *adv.* tan; — **far** tan lejos; hasta allí; hasta allí; — **long** así de largo; de este tamaño; tanto tiempo.
thatch [θætʃ] *s.* paja (*para techar*); *v.* techar con paja; **-ed roof** techumbre o techo de paja.
thaw [θɔ] *v.* deshelar(se), derretir(se); volverse más tratable o amistoso; *s.* deshielo, derretimiento.
the [*delante de consonante* ðə; *delante de vocal* ðɪ] *art.* el, la; lo; los, las; *adv.* — **more . . .** — **less** cuanto más . . . tanto menos; mientras más . . . tanto menos.
the·a·ter [θíətɚ] *s.* teatro.
the·at·ri·cal [θɪǽtrɪkl] *adj.* teatral.
thee [ði] *pron.* te.
theft [θɛft] *s.* hurto, robo.
their [ðɛr] *adj.* su (sus), de ellos, de ellas.
theirs [ðɛrz] *pron. pos.* suyo (suya, suyos, suyas), de ellos, de ellas; el suyo (la suya, los suyos, las suyas); el (la, los, las) de ellos; **a friend of** — un amigo suyo, un amigo de ellos.
them [ðɛm] *pron.* los, las; les; ellos, ellas (*con preposición*).
the·mat·ic [θimǽtɪk] *adj.* temático.
theme [θim] *s.* tema; ensayo; — **song** tema central.
them·selves [ðəmsɛ́lvz] *pron.* ellos mismos, ellas mismas; se (*como reflexivo*); **to** — a sí mismos; *véase* **herself.**
then [ðɛn] *adv.* entonces; en aquel tiempo; en aquella ocasión; (*after*) después, luego, en seguida; *conj.* pues, en tal caso; **now** — ahora bien; **now and** — de vez en cuando, de cuando en cuando; **now . . .** — ora . . . ora; ya . . . ya; **well** — conque, pues entonces; ahora bien.
thence [ðɛns] *adv.* desde allí; de allí; desde entonces; desde aquel tiempo; por eso, por esa razón; — **forth** de allí en adelante, desde entonces.
the·o·log·i·cal [θiəlɑ́dʒɪkl] *adj.* teológico; teologal.
the·ol·o·gy [θiɑ́lədʒɪ] *s.* teología.
the·o·ret·i·cal [θiərɛ́tɪll] *adj.* teórico.
the·o·ry [θíərɪ] *s.* teoría.
ther·a·peu·tic [θɛrəpjútɪk] *adj.* terapéutico.
ther·a·py [θɛ́rəpɪ] *s.* terapia.
there [ðɛr] *adv.* allí, allá, ahí; — **is,** — **are** hay; — **followed an argument** siguió una disputa.
there·a·bouts [ðɛrəbáʊts] *adv.* por allí, por ahí; aproximadamente.
there·after [ðɛrǽftɚ] *adv.* después de eso, de allí en adelante.
there·by [ðɛrbáɪ] *adv.* en relación con eso; así, de ese modo; por allí cerca.
there·fore [ðɛ́rfor] *adv.* por eso, por consiguiente, por lo tanto.
there·in [ðɛrín] *adv.* en eso, en ello; allí dentro.
there·of [ðɛrɑ́v] *adv.* de eso, de ello.
there·on [ðɛrɑ́n] *adv.* encima; encima de (*o* sobre) él, ella, ello, etc.
there·up·on [ðɛrəpɑ́n] *adv.* luego, después, en eso, en esto; por consiguiente, por eso, por lo tanto.
there·with [ðɛrwíθ] *adv.* con eso, con ello, con esto; luego, en seguida.
ther·mal [θɚml] *adj.* termal.
ther·mom·e·ter [θɚmɑ́mətɚ] *s.* termómetro.
ther·mo·nu·cle·ar [θɚmonúkljɚ] *adj.* termonuclear.
ther·mos [θɝ́məs] (*marca de fábrica*); — **bottle** termos.
ther·mo·stat [θɝ́məstæt] *s.* termóstato.
these [ðiz] *adj.* estos, estas; *pron.* éstos, éstas.
the·sis [θísɪs] *s.* tesis.
they [ðe] *pron.* ellos, ellas.
thick [θɪk] *adj.* (*not thin*) espeso; grueso; (*dense*) denso; tupido; (*slow*) torpe, estúpido; — **voice** voz ronca; **one inch** — una pulgada de espesor; *adv. véase* **thickly; thick-headed** cabezudo; testarudo; estúpido; **thick-set** grueso, rechoncho; **thick-skinned** insensible; que no se avergüenza fácilmente; *s.* espesor; densidad, lo más denso; **the** — **of the crowd** lo más denso de la muchedumbre; **the** — **of the fight** lo más reñido del combate; **through** — **and thin** por toda suerte de penalidades.
thick·en [θíkən] *v.* espesar(se); engrosar; **the plot -s** se complica el enredo.
thick·et [θíkɪt] *s.* espesura, maleza, matorral, *Carib., Col., Ríopl.* manigua.
thick·ly [θíklɪ] *adv.* espesamente; densamente.
thick·ness [θíknɪs] *s.* espesor; espesura, grueso, grosor; densidad.
thief [θif] *s.* ladrón.
thieve [θiv] *v.* hurtar, robar.
thieves [θivz] *pl. de* **thief.**
thigh [θaɪ] *s.* muslo.
thim·ble [θímbl] *s.* dedal.
thin [θɪn] *adj.* (*slim*) delgado; flaco; (*sparse*) ralo; escaso; (*fine*) tenue, fino; transparente; (*weak*) débil; aguado; — **broth** caldo aguado; — **hair** pelo ralo; *v.* adelgazar(se); enflaquecer; aguar (*el caldo*); **to** — **out** ralear (*el pelo*); ralear o aclarar (*un bosque*).
thine [ðaɪn] *pron. pos.* tuyo (tuya, tuyos, tuyas); el tuyo (la tuya, los tuyos, las tuyas); *adj.* tu, tus.
thing [θɪŋ] *s.* cosa; **no such** — nada de eso; **that is the** — **to do** eso es lo que debe hacerse; eso es lo debido.
think [θɪŋk] *v.* (*cerebrate*) pensar; (*believe*) creer, juzgar; opinar; **to** — **it over** pensarlo; **to** — **of** pensar en; pensar de; **to** — **up an excuse** urdir una excusa; **to** — **well of** tener buena opinión de; — **nothing of it** no haga Vd. caso de ello, no le dé Vd. importancia; **what do you** — **of her?** ¿qué piensa Vd. de ella?; **to my way of -ing** a mi modo de ver.
think·er [θíŋkɚ] *s.* pensador.
thin·ly [θínlɪ] *adv.* delgadamente; escasamente.
thinness [θínnɪs] *s.* delgadez; flacura; (*hair*) raleza (*del cabello*); (*rarity*) enrarecimiento (*del aire*).
third [θɝd] *adj.* tercero; *s.* tercio, tercera parte.
thirst [θɝst] *s.* sed; anhelo, ansia; *v.* tener sed; **to** — **for** tener sed de; anhelar, ansiar.
thirst·y [θɝ́stɪ] *adj.* sediento; **to be** — tener sed.
thir·teen [θɝtín] *num.* trece.
thir·ty [θɝ́tɪ] *num.* treinta.
this [ðɪs] *adj.* este, esta; *pron.* éste, ésto.
this·tle [θísl] *s.* abrojo; cardo.
thith·er [θíðɚ] *adv.* allá, hacia allá, para allá.
tho [ðo] = **though.**
thong [θɔŋ] *s.* correa, tira de cuero, *Am.* guasca.

tho·rax [θóræks] *s.* tórax.
thorn [θɔrn] *s.* espina, púa; espino; abrojo.
thorn·y [θɔ́rnɪ] *adj.* espinosa; arduo, difícil.
thor·ough [θɝ́o] *adj.* (*finished*) completo, entero, cabal, cumplido, acabado; (*careful*) esmerado.
thor·ough·bred [θɝ́obrɛd] *adj.* de casta pura, de raza pura; bien nacido; *s.* animal o persona de casta; caballo de casta.
thor·ough·fare [θɝ́ofɛr] *s.* vía pública, carretera, camino real; pasaje.
thor·ough·ly [θɝ́olɪ] *adj.* completamente, enteramente, cabalmente; a fondo.
those [ðoz] *adj.* esos, esas, aquellos, aquellas; *pron.* ésos, ésas, aquéllos, aquéllas; — **of** los de, las de; — **which** los que, las que; aquellos que; — **who** los que, las que, quienes.
thou [ðaʊ] *pron.* tú.
though [ðo] *conj.* aunque, si bien, bien que; aun cuando; sin embargo; **as** — como si.
thought [θɔt] *s.* (*cogitation*) pensamiento; (*idea*) idea, intención; reflexión, meditación; (*concern*) consideracion; cuidado; **to be lost in** — estar abstraído; **to give it no** — no pensar en ello, no darle importancia, no hacerle caso; *pret. & p.p. de* **to think.**
thought·ful [θɔ́tfəl] *adj.* pensativo; (*attentive*) considerado; atento, solícito, cuidadoso; **to be — of others** pensar en los demás, tener consideración o solicitud por las demás; **-ly** *adv.* con reflexión; consideradamente, con consideración; con solicitud.
thought·ful·ness [θɔ́tfəlnɪs] *s.* consideración, atención, cuidado, solicitud.
thought·less [θɔ́tlɪs] *adj.* inconsiderado; descuidado; irreflexivo, atolondrado; **-ly** *adv.* inconsideradamente, sin consideración; sin reflexión; sin pensar; descuidadamente, irreflexivamente, atolondradamente.
thought·less·ness [θɔ́tlɪsnɪs] *s.* irreflexión, inadvertencia, descuido; atolondramiento.
thou·sand [θáʊzənd] *num.* mil.
thrash [θræʃ] *v.* trillar, desgranar (*las mieses*); zurrar, azotar; **to — around** revolcarse, agitarse, menearse; **to — out a matter** ventilar un asunto.
thread [θrɛd] *s.* hilo; hebra, fibra; **screw** — rosca de tornillo; *v.* ensartar, enhebrar; **to — a screw** roscar un tornillo; **to — one's way through a crowd** colarse por entre la muchedumbre.
thread·bare [θrɛ́dbɛr] *adj.* raído, gastado.
threat [θrɛt] *s.* amenaza; amago.
threat·en [θrɛ́tn̩] *v.* amenazar; amagar.
threat·en·ing [θrɛ́tnɪŋ] *adj.* amenazante, amenazador.
three [θri] *num.* tres.
thresh [θrɛ] *véase* **thrash.**
thresh·old [θrɛ́ʃold] *s.* umbral, entrada.
threw [θru] *pret. de* **to throw.**
thrice [θraɪs] *adv.* tres veces.
thrift [θrɪft] *s.* economía, frugalidad.
thrift·y [θrɪ́ftɪ] *adj.* económico, frugal; próspero.
thrill [θrɪl] *v.* emocionar(se), conmover(se); estremecerse de emoción, sobreexcitarse; *s.* emoción viva, estremecimiento emotivo, sobreexcitación.
thrive [θraɪv] *v.* medrar, prosperar; florecer.
thriv·en [θrɪvən] *p.p. de* **to thrive.**
throat [θrot] *s.* garganta.
throb [θrɑb] *v.* latir, pulsar, palpitar; *s.* latido, palpitación.
throe [θro] *s.* agonía; congoja.
throne [θron] *s.* trono.
throng [θrɔŋ] *s.* muchedumbre, multitud, tropel, gentío; *v.* agolparse, apiñarse; atestar.
throt·tle [θrɑ́tl] *s.* válvula reguladora, obturador, regulador; — **lever** palanca del obturador o regulador; *v.* ahogar; estrangular; **to — down** disminuir o reducir la velocidad.
through [θru] *prep.* por; a través de; (*agent*) por medio de; por conducto de; por entre; *adv.* (*complete*) de un lado a otro; de parte a parte, a través; de cabo a cabo; desde el principio hasta el fin; completamente, enteramente; **loyal — and —** leal a toda prueba; **to be wet** — estar empapado; estar mojado hasta los tuétanos; **to carry a plan** — llevar a cabo un plan; *adj.* directo, continuo; — **ticket** billete (*Am.* boleto) directo; — **train** tren rápido, tren de servicio directo; **to be — with** haber acabado con; no querer ocuparse más de.
through·out [θruáʊt] *prep.* (*all through*) por todo; por todas partes de; (*during*) desde el principio; hasta el fin de; — **the year** durante todo el año; *adv.* por todas partes; en todas partes; en todo, en todos respetos; desde el principio hasta el fin.
throve [θurov] *pret. de* **to thrive.**
throw [θro] *v.* tirar, arrojar, lanzar; echar; **to — away** tirar, arrojar; malgastar; **to — down** arrojar, echar por tierra, derribar; **to — in gear** engranar; **to — in the clutch** embragar; **to — off a burden** librarse o deshacerse de una carga; **to — out** echar fuera; expeler; **to — out of gear** desengranar; **to — out of work** privar de trabajo, quitar el empleo a; **to — out the clutch** desembragar; **to — overboard** echar al agua; **to — up** vomitar; *s.* tiro, tirada.
thrown [θron] *p.p. de* **to throw.**
thrush [θrʌl] *s.* tordo, zorzal.
thrust [θrʌst] *v.* (*push into*) meter; hincar, clavar; encajar; (*shove*) empujar; **to — a task upon someone** imponer una tarea a una persona, obligar a alguien a desempeñar un quehacer; **to — aside** echar o empujar a un lado; rechazar; **to — in** (*o* **into**) meter en, encafar en, intercalar en; **to — out** sacar; echar fuera; **to — someone through with a sword** atravesar a alguien de parte a parte con la espada; *pret. & p.p. de* **to thrust**; *s.* estocada, cuchillada, puñalada, lanzada; empuje, empujón o empellón; arremetida, acometida.
thud [θʌd] *s.* porrazo, golpazo, golpe sordo.
thug [θʌg] *s.* ladrón, salteador.
thumb [θʌm] *s.* pulgar; **under the — of** bajo el poder o influencia de; *v.* hojear (*con el pulgar*).
thumb·tack [θʌ́mtæk] *s.* chinche.
thump [θʌmp] *s.* golpazo, porrazo, trastazo; golpe sordo; *v.* golpear, golpetear, aporrear, dar un porrazo.
thun·der [θʌ́ndɚ] *s.* trueno; tronido; estruendo; *v.* tronar.
thun·der·bolt [θʌ́ndɚbolt] *s.* rayo.
thun·der·ing [θʌ́ndərɪŋ] *adj.* atronador.
thun·der·ous [θʌ́ndərəs] *adj.* atronador, estruendoso.
thun·der·storm [θʌ́ndɚstɔrm] *s.* tronada, tormenta o tempestad de truenos.
Thurs·day [θɝ́zdɪ] *s.* jueves.
thus [θʌs] *adv.* así; — **far** hasta aquí, hasta ahora, hasta hoy.
thwart [θwɔrt] *v.* frustrar; estorbar; impedir.
thy [ðaɪ] *adj.* tu, tus.
thyme [taɪm] *s.* tomillo.
thy·roid [θáɪɔɪd] *s.* tiroides.
thy·self [ðaɪsɛ́lf] *pron.* tú mismo; a tí mismo; te (*como reflexivo*); *véase* **herself.**
tick [tɪk] tic tac; funda (*de colchón o almohada*); garrapata (*insecto parásito*); *v.* hacer tic tac (*como*

un reloj); latir (*el corazón*); **to — off** marcar.
tick·et [tíkɪt] *s.* billete, *Méx., Ch.*, boleto; *C.A., Col.* tiquete; lista de candidatos (*de un partido*); balota (*para votar*); **— office** taquilla; despacho de boletos, *Ec., Peru* boletería.
tick·le [tíkl] *v.* (*touch*) cosquillear, hacer cosquillas; (*feel*) sentir o tener cosquillas; (*please*) halagar, gustarle a uno; **to be -d to death** morirse de gusto, estar muy contento; *s.* cosquilleo, cosquillas.
tick·lish [tíklɪʃ] *adj.* cosquilloso; delicado, arriesgado, difícil.
tid·bit [tídbɪt] *s.* bocado, bocadito, golosina.
tide [taɪd] *s.* marea; corriente; **Christmas —** navidades, temporada de navidad; *v.* **to — someone over a difficulty** ayudar a alguien durante una crisis o dificultad.
tide·wa·ter [táɪdwɔtɚ] *adj.* costanero.
tid·ings [táɪdɪŋz] *s. pl.* noticias, nuevas.
ti·dy [táɪdɪ] *adj.* aseado, limpio, ordenado; **a — sum** una suma considerable; *v.* asear, arreglar, poner en orden; **to — oneself up** asearse.
tie [taɪ] *v.* (*fasten*) atar, liar, ligar; *Am.* amarrar; (*unite*) enlazar, vincular; (*equal*) empatar (*en juegos, etc.*); **to — tight** amarrar bien, apretar fuerte; **to — up the traffic** obstruir el tráfico; *s.* paralización; lazo, ligadura, atadura; enlace, vínculo; corbata; empate (*en carreras, juegos, etc.*); **railway —** traviesa, *Andes, C.A., Méx.* durmiente; *Ríopl., Ch.* travesaño.
tier [tɪr] *s.* fila, hilera, ringlera.
ti·ger [táɪgɚ] *s.* tigre; **— cat** gato montés.
tight [taɪt] *adj.* (*squeezed*) apretado, ajustado, estrecho; (*sealed*) hermético; (*firm*) firme, tieso; (*stingy*) tacaño, mezquino; (*drunk*) borracho; **to be in a — spot** estar en un aprieto; **to close —** apretar, cerrar herméticamente; **to hold on —** agarrarse bien; **it fits —** está muy estrecho o ajustado.
tight·en [táɪtn̩] *v.* apretar; estrechar; estirar, poner tirante.
tight·ness [táɪtnɪs] *s.* estrechez; tirantez, tensión; mezquindad, (*stingyness*) tacañería.
tight·wad [táɪtwɑd] *s.* tacaño; cicatero.
ti·gress [táɪgrɪs] *s.* tigre hembra; *Am.* tigra.
tile [taɪl] *s.* teja; baldosa, azulejo; **— roof** tejado; *v.* tejar, cubrir con tejas; cubrir con azulejos, embaldosar.
till [tɪl] *prep.* hasta; *conj.* hasta que; *v.* cultivar, labrar, arar; *s.* gaveta o cajón para el dinero.
till·age [tílədʒ] *s.* labranza, cultivo, labor.
tilt [tɪlt] *s.* ladeo, inclinación; declive; altercación disputa; **at full —** a toda velocidad; *v.* ladear(se), inclinar(se).
tim·ber [tímbɚ] *s.* madera de construcción; maderaje; madero; viga.
time [taɪm] *s.* tiempo; (*hour*) hora; (*occasion*) vez; (*payments*) plazo; **at -s** a veces; **at one and the same —** a la vez; **at this —** ahora, al presente; **behind —** atrasado, retrasado; **from — to —** de vez en cuando; **in —** a tiempo; andando el tiempo; **on —** puntual; con puntualidad; a tiempo; a la hora debida; **several -s** varias veces; **to beat —** marcar el compás; **to buy on —** comprar a plazo; **to have a good —** divertirse, pasar un buen rato; **what — is it?** ¿qué hora es?; *v.* cronometrar, medir el tiempo de; regular, poner en punto (*el reloj, el motor*); escoger el momento oportuno para; **— zone** zona horaria; huso horario.
time·keep·er [táɪmkipɚ] *s.* listero, apuntador; *Ec.* guardatiempo; *Mex.* rayador.
time·less [táɪmlɛs] *adj.* eterno, infinito.
time·ly [táɪmlɪ] *adj.* oportuno.
time·piece [táɪmpis] *s.* reloj; cronómetro.
time·ta·ble [táɪmtebl] *s.* itinerario, horario.
tim·id [tímɪd] *adj.* tímido.
ti·mid·i·ty [tɪmídətɪ] *s.* timidez.
tim·ing [táɪmɪŋ] *s.* medida del tiempo; cronometraje; (*pace*) selección del momento oportuno; sincronización.
tim·or·ous [tímərəs] *adj.* timorato, tímido, miedoso.
tin [tɪn] *s.* estaño; hojalata, lata; cosa de hojalata; **— can** lata; **— foil** hoja de estaño; *v.* estañar, cubrir con estaño; enlatar.
tinc·ture [tíŋktʃɚ] *s.* tintura; tinte; **— of iodine** tintura de yodo; *v.* tinturar, teñir.
tin·der [tíndɚ] *s.* yesca.
tinge [tɪndʒ] *v.* teñir; matizar; *s.* tinte, matiz; dejo, saborcillo.
tin·gle [tíŋgl] *v.* hormiguear, sentir hormigueo; **to — with excitement** estremecerse de entusiasmo; *s.* hormigueo, picazón, comezón.
tin·ker [tɪŋkɚ] *v.* ocuparse vanamente.
tin·kle [tíŋkl] *v.* tintinear; hacer retintín; *s.* tintineo; retintín.
tin·sel [tísl] *s.* oropel; *adj.* de oropel.
tint [tɪnt] *s.* tinte, matiz; *v.* teñir, matizar.
ti·ny [táɪnɪ] *adj.* diminuto, menudo, chiquitico, chiquitín.
tip [tɪp] *s.* (*point*) punta, extremo, extremidad; (*money*) propina; (*hint*) noticia o aviso secreto; *v.* ladear(se), inclinar(se); dar propina (a); **to — a person off** dar aviso secreto a; **to — one's hat** tocarse el sombrero; **to — over** volcar(se), voltear(se).
tip·sy [típsɪ] *adj.* alumbrado, algo borracho; ladeado.
tip·toe [típto] *s.* punta del pie; **on —** de puntillas; *v.* andar de puntillas.
ti·rade [táɪred] *s.* invectiva.
tire [taɪr] *s.* llanta, neumático, goma; **flat —** llanta o goma reventada; *v.* cansar(se), fatigar(se).
tired [taɪrd] *adj.* cansado, fatigado; **— out** extenuado de fatiga, rendido.
tire·less [táɪrlɪs] *adj.* incansable, infatigable.
tire·some [táɪrsəm] *adj.* cansado, aburrido, pesado.
tis·sue [tíʃu] *s.* tejido; **— paper** papel de seda.
ti·tan·ic [taɪtǽnɪk] *adj.* titánico.
ti·ta·ni·um [taɪténɪəm] *s.* titanio.
tithe [taɪð] *s.* diezmo.
ti·tle [táɪtl] *s.* título **— holder** titulado; **— page** portada; **— deed** título de propiedad.
to [tu] *prep.* a; hasta; hacia; para; **— try —** tratar de; esforzarse por; **a quarter — five** las cinco menos cuarto; **bills — be paid** cuentas por pagar; **frightened — death** muerto de susto; **from house — house** de casa en casa; **he has — go** tiene que ir; **near —** cerca de; **not — my knowledge** no que yo sepa; *adv.* **— and fro** de acá para allá; **to come —** volver en sí.
toad [tod] *s.* sapo o escuerzo.
toast [tost] *v.* tostar(se); brindar por, beber a la salud de; *s.* tostada; brindis.
toast·er [tóstɚ] *s.* tostador.
to·bac·co [təbǽko] *s.* tabaco.
to·day [tədé] *adv.* hoy; hoy día.
toe [to] *s.* dedo del pie; (*shoe*) punta (*de la media, del zapato, etc.*); *v.* **to — in** andar con la punta de los pies para dentro.
toe·nail [tónel] *s.* uña del dedo del pie.
to·geth·er [təgɛ́ðɚ] *adv.* juntamente; a un mismo tiempo, a la vez; juntos; **— with** junto con; **all —** juntos; en junto; **to call —** convocar; juntar; **to come —** juntarse, unirse; ponerse de acuerdo; **to**

walk — andar juntos.
toil [tɔɪl] *v.* afanarse, trafagar, atarearse; *s.* esfuerzo, trabajo, faena, fatiga.
toi·let [tɔ́lɪt] *s.* retrete, excusado, común, *C.A., Col., Ven.* inodoro; — **articles** artículos de tocador; — **case** neceser; — **paper** papel de excusado, papel higiénico.
to·ken [tókən] *s.* señal, símbola; prenda; recuerdo; prueba, muestra; ficha (*de metal*); — **payment** pago nominal.
told [told] *pret. & p.p. de* **to tell.**
tol·er·ance [tάlərəns] *s.* tolerancia.
tol·er·ant [tάlərənt] *adj.* tolerante.
tol·er·ate [άləret] *v.* tolerar.
tol·er·a·tion [taləréʃan] *s.* tolerancia.
toll [tol] *s.* doble, tañido (*de las companas*); peaje; portazgo; — **bridge** puente de peaje; — **gate** barrera de peaje; — **call** llamada por cobrar; — **road** camino de cuota; **to pay** — pagar peaje o portazgo; *v.* tañer, doblar (*las campanas*).
to·ma·to [təméto] *s.* tomate, *Méx.* jitomate.
tomb [tum] *s.* tumba.
tomb·stone [túmston] *s.* lápida sepulcral.
tom·cat [tάmkœt] *s.* gato.
tome [tom] *s.* tomo.
to·mor·row [təmɔ́ro] *adv.* mañana; — **morning** mañana por la mañana; — **noon** mañana al mediodía; **day after** — pasado mañana.
ton [tʌn] *s.* tonelada.
tone [ton] *s.* (*pitch*) tono; timbre; (*sound*) sonido; *v.* dar tono a, modificar el tono de; **to** — **down** bajar de tono; suavizar; **to** — **down one's voice** moderar la voz; **to** — **in well with** armonizar con, entonar bien con; **to** — **up** subir de tono; tonificar, vigorizar.
tongs [tɔŋz] *s. pl.* tenazas.
tongue [tʌn] *s.* lengua; idioma; **to be tongue-tied** tener trabada la lengua.
ton·ic [tάnɪk] *s. & adj.* tónico.
to·night [tənάɪt] *adv.* esta noche, a la noche.
ton·nage [tʌ́nɪdʒ] *s.* tonelaje.
ton·sil [tάnsl] *s.* amígdala.
ton·sil·li·tis [tansláɪtɪs] *s.* amigdalitis.
too [tu] *adv.* también; demasiado; — **many** demasiados; — **much** demasiado; **it is** — **bad!** ¡es una lástima!
took [tuk] *pret. de* **to take.**
tool [tul] *s.* instrumento; herramienta; — **box** caja de herramientas.
toot [tut] *v.* tocar o sonar la bocina; pitar; tocar (*un cuerno, trompa o trompeta*); **to** — **one's own horn** alabarse, cantar sus propias alabanzas; *s.* toque o sonido (*de bocina, trompeta, etc.*); silbido, pitido; pitazo (*de locomotora*).
tooth [tuθ] *s.* diente; muela; — **mark** dentellada; **to fight** — **and nail** luchar a brazo partido; **to have a sweet** — ser amigo de golosinas.
tooth·ache [túθek] *s.* dolor de muelas.
tooth·brush [túθbrʌʃ] *s.* cepillo de dientes.
toothed [tuθt] *adj.* dentado.
tooth·less [túθlɪs] *adj.* desdentado.
tooth·paste [túθpest] *s.* pasta para los dientes, pasta dentífrica.
tooth·pick [túθpɪk] *s.* mondadientes, palillo de dientes.
top [tap] *s.* (*peak*) cumbre, cima; cúspida; tope; pináculo; remate; cabeza; (*surface*) superficie; copa (*de árbol*); (*cover*) tapa, cubierta; (*toy*) trompo; peonza; **at the** — **of his class** a la cabeza de su clase; **at the** — **of one's voice** a voz en cuello; **filled up to the** — lleno hasta el tope; **from** — **to bottom** de arriba abajo; **from** — **to toe** de pies a cabeza; **on** — **of** encima de, sobre; *adj.* superior; más alto; — **coat** abrigo, sobretodo; **at** — **speed** a velocidad máxima; *v.* coronar; exceder; sobresalir, sobrepujar; rematar; **to** — **off** rematar; terminar.
top-flight [tapfláɪt] *adj.* destacado, sobresaliente.
to·paz [tópæz] *s.* topacio.
top·er [tópɚ] *s.* bebedor, borrachín.
top-heav·y [taphέvɪ] *adj.* más pesado arriba que abajo.
top·ic [tάpɪk] *s.* tema, asunto, materia, tópico.
top·most [tάpmost] *adj.* más alto; superior.
to·pog·ra·phy [təpάgreəfɪ] *s.* topografía.
to·pon·y·my [təpánəmɪ] *s.* toponimia.
top·ple [tάpl] *v.* echar abajo, derribar; volcar; **to** — **over** venirse abajo; volcarse.
top·sy-tur·vy [tάpsɪtɝ́vɪ] *adj. & adv.* patas arriba; en confusión; trastornado; enrevesado, al revés.
torch [tɔrtʃ] *s.* antorcha; **blow** — soplete.
tore [tor] *pret. de* **to tear.**
tor·ment [tɔ́rmεnt] *s.* tormento; [tɔrmέnt] *v.* atormentar; afligir.
torn [torn] *p.p. de* **to tear** roto, rompido, rasgado.
tor·na·do [tɔrnédo] *s.* tornado.
tor·pe·do [tɔrpído] *s.* torpedo; — **boat** torpedero; *v.* torpedear.
torque [tɔrk] *s.* fuerza rotatoria.
tor·rent [tɔ́rənt] *s.* torrente.
tor·rid [tɔ́rɪd] *adj.* tórrido.
tor·sion [tɔ́rʃən] *s.* torsión.
tor·toise [tɔ́rtəs] *s.* tortuga.
tor·tu·ous [tɔ́rtʃuəs] *adj.* tortuoso.
tor·ture [tɔ́rtʃɚ] *s.* tortura, tormento; *v.* torturar, atormentar.
toss [tɔs] *v.* tirar, echar, arrojar, lanzar; menear(se); cabecear (*un buque*); **to** — **aside** echar a un lado; desechar; **to** — **up** echar para arriba; aventar; *s.* tiro, tirada; meneo, sacudida.
tot [tat] *s.* chiquitín, chiquitina, chiquitico, chiquitica, niñito, niñita, nene, nena.
to·tal [tótl] *adj. & s.* total.
to·tal·i·tar·i·an [totælətέrɪən] *adj.* totalitario.
tot·ter [tάtɚ] *v.* tambalear(se), bambolear(se); estar para desplomarse.
touch [tʌtʃ] *v.* tocar; palpar, tentar; conmover, enternecer; compararse con, igualar; **to** — **at a port** hacer escala en un puerto; **to** — **off an explosive** prender la mecha de un explosivo; **to** — **up** retocar; *s.* toque; tacto, sentido del tacto; tiento; — **stone** piedra de toque; — **tablet** (*computer*) trazador gráfico; **a** — **of fever** algo de calentura; **to keep in** — **with** mantener(se) en comunicación con.
touch-and-go [tʌ́tʃəndgó] *adj.* arriesgado.
touch·ing [tʌ́tʃɪŋ] *adj.* conmovedor, enternecedor.
touch·y [tʌ́tʃɪ] *adj.* quisquilloso, susceptible, sensible, sensitivo.
tough [tʌf] *adj.* correoso; fuerte; firme; duro; (*difficult*) arduo, difícil; (*stubborn*) terco; (*bad*) empedernido, malvado.
tough·en [tʌ́ʃn̩] *v.* curtir(se); endurecer(se), empedernir(se); hacer(se) correoso.
tough·ness [tʌ́fnɪs] *s.* dureza; correosidad; flexibilidad; tenacidad; resistencia; dificultad.
tou·pee [tupé] *s.* peluca.
tour [tur] *s.* viaje, excursión; vuelta; jira; *v.* viajar por; recorrer; hacer una jira; hacer un viaje de turismo.
tour·ism [túrɪzəm] *s.* turismo.
tour·ist [túrɪst] *s.* turista.
tour·na·ment [tɝ́nəmənt] *s.* torneo; certamen,

concurso.
tow [to] *v.* remolcar; *s.* remolque; — **boat** remolcador; — **truck** remolcador; — **rope** cuerda de remolque; **to take in** — remolcar, llevar a remolque.
to·ward [tord] *prep.* hacia; rumbo a; alrededor de; para, para con; — **four o'clock** a eso de las cuatro.
to·wards [tordz] = **toward.**
tow·el [taUl] *s.* toalla.
tow·er [táUɚ] *s.* torre; torreón; **bell** — campanario; *v.* sobresalir, sobrepujar; destacarse, descollar; elevarse.
tow·er·ing [táUrɪŋ] *adj.* encumbrado; elevado, muy alto; sobresaliente.
town [taUn] *s.* (*center*) población, ciudad, pueblo, aldea; (*administration*) municipio; — **hall** ayuntamiento.
town·ship [táUnʃɪp] *s.* unidad primaria de gobierno local; sección de seis millas cuadradas (*en terrenos públicos*).
tox·in [táksɪn] *s.* toxina.
toy [tɔɪ] *s.* juguete; *adj.* de juego, de juguete; pequeñito; *v.* jugar, juguetear.
trace [tres] *s.* señal, indicio, vestigio; huella, rastro; tirante (*de una guarnición*); *v.* trazar; calcar; rastrear, seguir la huella de; rebuscar, investigar; **to** — **the source of** remontarse al origen de, buscar el origen de.
tra·che·a [trékɪə] *s.* tráquea.
tra·cho·ma [trəkomə] *s.* tracoma
track [træk] *s.* pista, huella, rastro; pisada; (*path*) vereda, senda; vía; — **sports** deportes de pista; — **ball** (*computer*) control por bola; **race** — pista; **railroad** — rieles, vía del tren, vía férrea o ferrovía; **disk** — pista; **to be off the** — estar extraviado, estar descarrilado; **to be on the** — **of** rastrear, ir siguiendo la pista de; **to keep** — **of** llevar la cuenta de; no perder de vista; *v.* rastrear, seguir la huella de; **to** — **down** coger, atrapar; descubrir; **to** — **in mud** traer lodo en los pies, entrar con los pies enlodados.
tract [trækt] *s.* área; terreno; folleto; **digestive** — canal digestivo.
trac·tion [trǽkʃən] *s.* tracción.
trac·tor [trǽktɚ] *s.* tractor; — **feed** (*computer*) alimentación por tracción.
trade [tred] *s.* (*business*) comercio; trato, negocio; (*swap*) trueque, cambio; (*occupation*) oficio; (*customers*) clientela, parroquianos; — **school** escuela de artes y oficios; — **union** gremio obrero o de obreros; *v.* comerciar, negociar, traficar, tratar; trocar, cambiar; feriar, mercar.
trade·mark [trédmɑrk] *s.* marca de fábrica.
trad·er [trédɚ] *s.* mercader, comerciante, negociante, traficante.
trades·man [trédzmən] *s.* mercader, comerciante, traficante; tendero.
tra·di·tion [trədɪ́ʃən] *s.* tradición.
tra·di·tion·al [trədɪ́ʃənl] *adj.* tradicional.
traf·fic [trǽfɪk] *s.* tráfico; tráfago; tránsito; circulación; *v.* traficar, comerciar, negociar.
trag·e·dy [trǽdʒədɪ] *s.* tragedia.
trag·ic [trǽdʒɪk] *adj.* trágico.
trail [trel] *s.* (*trace*) pista, rastro, huella; (*path*) senda, sendero, trocha, vereda; cola (*de vestido*); *v.* arrastrar(se); rastrear, seguir la pista de; andar detrás de; **to** — **behind** ir rezagado, rezagarse.
train [tren] *s.* (*railroad*) tren; (*dress*) cola (*de vestido*); (*retinue*) séquito, comitiva; *v.* amaestrar(se), ejercitar(se); adiestrar(se) o adestrar(se), *Am.* entrenar(se); educar; disciplinar (*tropas*); (*point*) apuntar (*un cañón*).
train·er [trénɚ] *s.* amaestrador; *Méx., C.A., Andes, Ven., Col., Carib.* entrenador.
train·ing [trénɪŋ] *s.* adiestramiento, disciplina, *Méx., C.A., Andes, Ven., Col., Carib.*, entrenamiento; educación; — **camp** campo de entrenamiento o práctica.
trait [tret] *s.* rasgo, característica; cualidad.
trai·tor [trétɚ] *s.* traidor.
tram [træm] *s.* vagoneta (*de una mina de carbón*).
tramp [træmp] *v.* pisotear; andar a pie; vagabundear; *s.* vago, vagabundo; caminata, marcha; pisadas.
tram·ple [trǽmpl] *v.* pisar, hollar, pisotear; **to** — **on** pisotear, hollar; *s.* pisadas.
trance [træns] *s.* rapto, arrobamiento, enajenamiento, éxtasis; **to be in a** — estar arrobado, estar enajenado; estar distraído o ensimismado.
tran·quil [trǽnkwɪl] *adj.* tranquilo.
tran·quil·iz·er [trǽŋkwəlaɪzɚ] *s.* tranquilizador.
tran·quil·li·ty [trænkwɪ́lətɪ] *s.* tranquilidad.
trans·act [trænsǽkt] *v.* tramitar, despachar, llevar a cabo.
trans·ac·tion [trænsǽkʃən] *s.* transacción, trato, negocio; trámite; negociación; **-s** actas; memorias.
trans·at·lan·tic [trænsətlǽntɪk] *adj.* transatlántico.
tran·scend [trænsέnd] *v.* trascender, ir más allá de.
trans·con·ti·nen·tal [trænskɑntənέntl] *adj.* transcontinental.
tran·scribe [trænskráɪb] *v.* transcribir.
tran·script [trǽnskrɪpt] *s.* transcripción, copia.
trans·fer [trǽnsfɝ] *s.* transferencia; traslado; traspaso; trasbordo; — **of ownership** cesión o traspaso de propiedad; **streetcar** — transferencia, contraseña, cupón de trasbordo; [trænsfɝ́] *v.* transferir; trasbordar (*de un tren a otro*), cambiar (*de tren, de tranvía*); traspasar (*propiedad*), trasladar.
trans·fer·a·ble [trænsfɝ́əbl] *adj.* transferible.
trans·fig·ure [trænsfɪ́gjɚ] *v.* transfigurar.
trans·form [trænsfɔ́rm] *v.* transformar(se).
trans·for·ma·tion [trænsfɚméʃən] *s.* transformación.
trans·gress [trænsgrέs] *v.* transgredir, violar, (*break*) quebrantar (*una ley*); pecar; **to** — **the bounds of** traspasar los límites de.
trans·gres·sion [trænsgrέʃən] *s.* transgresión; violación de una ley; pecado.
trans·gres·sor [trænsgrέsɚ] *s.* transgresor.
tran·sient [trǽnʃənt] *s.* transeúnte; *adj.* transeúnte; transitorio, pasajero.
tran·sis·tor [trænzɪ́stɚ] *s.* transistor.
tran·sit [trǽnsɪt] *s.* tránsito; **in** — en tránsito, de paso.
tran·sition [trænzɪ́ʃən] *s.* transición; tránsito, paso.
tran·si·tive [trǽnsətɪv] *adj.* transitivo.
tran·si·to·ry [trǽnsətorɪ] *adj.* transitorio, pasajero.
trans·late [trænslét] *v.* traducir, verter; trasladar.
trans·la·tion [trænsléʃən] *s.* traducción, versión; translación (*de un lugar a otro*).
trans·la·tor [trænslétɚ] *s.* traductor.
trans·lu·cent [trænslúsn̩t] *adj.* translúcido; **to be** — traslucirse.
trans·mis·sion [trænsmɪ́ʃən] *s.* transmisión; caja de velocidades.
trans·mit [trænsmɪ́t] *v.* transmitir; emitir.
trans·mit·ter [trænsmɪ́tɚ] *s.* transmisor; emisor.
tran·som [trǽnsəm] *s.* montante.
trans·par·ent [trænspέrənt] *adj.* transparente.
trans·plant [trænsplǽnt] *v.* trasplantar.
trans·port [trǽnsport] *s.* (*moving*) transporte; acarreo; (*rapture*) éxtasis; — **plane** aeroplano de transporte;

[trænspórt] *v.* transportar; acarrear; **to be -ed with joy** estar enajenado de placer.
trans·por·ta·tion [trænspɚtéʃən] *s.* transportación, transporte; boleto, pasaje.
trans·pose [trænspóz] *v.* transponer.
trans·verse [trænsvɝ́s] *adj.* transverso, transversal, puesto de través.
trap [træp] *s.* trampa, lazo, red; — **door** trampa; **mouse** — ratonera; *v.* entrampar, coger con trampa; atrapar.
tra·peze [træpíz] *s.* trapecio.
trap·e·zoid [trǽpəzɔɪd] *s.* trapezoide.
trap·pings [trǽpɪŋz] *s. pl.* arreos, jaeces, guarniciones.
trash [træʃ] *s.* basura; hojarasca; cachivaches; gentuza, plebe.
trau·ma [trɔ́mə] *s.* traumatismo.
trau·mat·ic [trɔmǽtɪk] *adj.* traumático.
trav·el [trǽvl] *v.* viajar; viajar por; recorrer; *s.* viaje; tráfico.
trav·el·er [trǽvlɚ] *s.* viajero; — **'s check** cheque de viajero.
trav·el·ing [trǽvlɪŋ] *adj.* de viaje, para viaje; — **expenses** gastos de viaje; — **salesman** agente viajero, viajente de comercio.
trav·e·logue [trǽvəlɔg] *s.* conferencia sobre viajes.
trav·erse [trǽvɚs] *v.* atravesar, cruzar; recorrer; *s.* travesaño.
trav·es·ty [trǽvɪstɪ] *s.* parodia; *v.* parodiar, falsear.
tray [tre] *s.* bandeja; batea; *Mex.* charola.
treach·er·ous [trɛ́tʃərəs] *adj.* traicionero, traidor, alevoso.
treach·er·y [trɛ́tʃərɪ] *s.* traición, perfidia, alevosía.
tread [trɛd] *v.* (*trample*) pisar, hollar; pisotear; (*walk*) andar a pie, caminar; *s.* paso; pisada, huella; *Ch.* pise (*de una rueda*); **tire** — rodadura del neumático, *Am.* banda rodante.
tread·mill [trɛ́dmɪl] *s.* noria; rueda de andar.
trea·son [trízn̩] *s.* traición.
trea·son·a·ble [tríznəbl] *adj.* traidor, traicionero.
treas·ure [trɛ́ʒɚ] *s.* tesoro; *v.* atesorar.
treas·ur·er [trɛ́ʒərɚ] *s.* tesorero.
treas·ur·y [trɛ́ʒərɪ] *s.* tesorería; tesoro, erario; **Secretary of the Treasury** ministro de hacienda.
treat [trit] *v.* tratar; curar; convidar, invitar; *s.* obsequio, agasajo, convite; placer, gusto.
trea·tise [trítɪs] *s.* tratado.
treat·ment [trítmənt] *s.* trato; **medical** — tratamiento médico.
trea·ty [trítɪ] *s.* tratado, pacto, convenio.
treb·le [trɛ́bl] *adj.* triple; — **voice** voz atiplada; *s.* tiple; *v.* triplicar.
tree [tri] *s.* árbol; **apple** — manzano; **family** — árbol genealógico; **shoe** — horma de zapato; **to be up a** — estar subido a un árbol; estar en un gran aprieto; estar perplejo.
tree·less [trílɪs] *adj.* pelado, sin árboles, despoblado de árboles.
tree·top [trítɑp] *s.* copa de árbol.
trel·lis [trɛ́lɪs] *s.* emparrado, enrejado.
trem·ble [trɛ́mbl] *v.* temblar; estremecerse; *s.* temblor; estremecimiento.
tre·men·dous [trɪmɛ́ndəs] *adj.* tremendo.
trem·or [trɛ́mɚ] *s.* temblor.
trem·u·lous [trɛ́mjələs] *adj.* trémulo; tembloroso.
trench [trɛntʃ] *s.* trinchera; zanja, foso.
trend [trɛnd] *s.* tendencia; rumbo, dirección.
tres·pass [trɛ́spəs] *v.* invadir, traspasar; violar, infringir; pecar; **to** — **on property** meterse sin derecho en la propiedad ajena; **no -ing** prohibida la entrada; *s.* transgresión; pecado.
tress [trɛs] *s.* trenza; bucle.
tres·tle [trɛsl] *s.* caballete; puente de caballetes.
tri·al [tráɪəl] *s.* ensayo, prueba; tentativa; aflicción; juicio, proceso; — **flight** vuelo de prueba; — **balance** balance de comprobación; — **and error** ensayo y error.
tri·an·gle [tráɪæŋgl] *s.* triángulo.
tri·an·gu·lar [traɪǽŋgjəlɚ] *adj.* triangular.
tribe [traɪb] *s.* tribu.
trib·u·la·tion [trɪbjəléʃən] *s.* tribulación.
tri·bu·nal [trɪbjúnl] *s.* tribunal, juzgado.
trib·u·tar·y [trɪ́bjətɛrɪ] *adj.* & *s.* tributario.
trib·ute [trɪ́bjut] *s.* tributo; homenaje.
trich·i·no·sis [trɪkənósɪs] *s.* triquinosis.
trick [trɪk] *s.* treta; suerte; truco, artificio; maña, ardid, trampa; travesura; (cards) baza (*en el juego de naipes*); **to be up to one's old -s** hacer de las suyas; *v.* embaucar, trampear, hacer trampa; burlar; **to** — **oneself up** componerse, emperifollarse.
trick·er·y [trɪ́kərɪ] *s.* engaños, malas mañas, astucia.
trick·le [trɪ́kl] *v.* gotear; escurrir; *s.* goteo.
trick·y [trɪ́kɪ] *adj.* tramposo, *C.A., Arg., P.R.* mañero; intrincado, complicado.
tri·cy·cle [tráɪsɪkl] *s.* triciclo.
tried [traɪd] *p.p. de* **to try** & *adj.* probado.
tri·fle [tráɪfl] *s.* fruslería, friolera, nadería, nonada; bagatela; *v.* chancear(se), bromear; jugar, juguetear.
trig·ger [trɪ́gɚ] *s.* gatillo (*de pistola, rifle, etc*).
trill [trɪl] *v.* trinar; **to** — **the r** pronunciar la erre doble; *s.* trino.
tril·o·gy [trɪ́lədʒɪ] *s.* trilogía.
trim [trɪm] *v.* guarnecer, adornar; atusar; recortar; (*cut*) podar, mondar; (*clip*) despabilar (*una vela*); (*win*) ganarle a uno (*en el juego*); **to** — **up** adornar, componer; *adj.* aseado, limpio, pulcro, acicalado; *s.* adorno, franja, ribete, guarnición; **to be in** — **for** estar en buena salud para; estar bien entrenado para.
trim·ming [trɪ́mɪŋ] *s.* adorno, aderezo, guarnición; orla, ribete, franja; paliza, zurra; **-s** adornos; accesorios; recortes.
trin·i·ty [trɪ́nətɪ] *s.* trinidad.
trin·ket [trɪ́ŋkɪt] *s.* chuchería, baratija; miriñaque.
trip [trɪp] *s.* viaje; travesía; recorrido, jira; tropezón; *v.* tropezar; dar un traspié; equivocarse; hacer tropezar, hacer caer; saltar, brincar, corretear.
triph·thong [trɪ́fθɔŋ] *s.* triptongo.
trip·le [trɪ́pl] *adj.* & *s.* triple; *v.* triplicar.
trip·li·cate [trɪ́pləkət] *adj.* triplicado.
tri·pod [tráɪpɑd] *s.* trípode.
trite [traɪt] *adj.* trillado, trivial, vulgar.
tri·umph [tráɪəmf] *s.* triunfo; *v.* triunfar.
tri·um·phal [traɪʌ́mfl] *adj.* triunfal.
tri·um·phant [traɪʌ́mfənt] *adj.* triunfante; **-ly** *adv.* triunfantemente, en triunfo.
triv·i·al [trɪ́vjəl] *adj.* trivial, insignificante.
trod [trɑd] *pret.* & *p.p. de* **to tread.**
trod·den [trɑ́dn̩] *p.p. de* **to tread.**
trol·ley [trɑ́lɪ] *s.* trole; tranvía de trole; — **bus** trolebús.
trom·bone [trɑ́mbon] *s.* trombón.
troop [trup] *s.* tropa; cuadrilla.
tro·phy [trófɪ] *s.* trofeo.
trop·ic [trɑ́pɪk] *s.* trópico; — **of Cancer** trópico de Cáncer; — **of Capricorn** trópico de Capricornio; *adj.* tropical.
trop·i·cal [trɑ́pɪkl] *adj.* tropical.
trot [trɑt] *v.* trotar; hacer trotar; *s.* trote.
trou·ba·dour [trúbədor] *s.* trovador.
troub·le [trʌ́bl] *v.* perturbar, turbar; molestar,

incomodar; afligir; preocupar(se); **don't — to come** no se moleste Vd. en venir; *s.* pena, aflicción; inquietud, perturbación; dificultad; molestia; panne, avería, accidente (*a un mecanismo*); **heart —** enfermedad de corazón; **to be in —** estar en un aprieto o apuro; **it is not worth the —** no vale la pena; **— shooter** investigador de fallas o averías.
troub·le·mak·er [trʌ́blmekɚ] *s.* agitador, alborotador, malcontento.
troub·le·some [trʌ́blsəm] *adj.* molesto, fastidioso, enfadoso, dificultoso; penoso.
trough [trɔf] *s.* comedero; artesa; batea; **eaves —** canal, gotera del tejado; **drinking —** abrevadero.
trou·sers [tráuzɚz] *s. pl.* pantalones.
trous·seau [trúso] *s.* ajuar de novia.
trout [traut] *s.* trucha.
trow·el [tráuəl] *s.* llana, *Am.* cuchara (*de albañil*); desplantador (*de jardín*).
tru·ant [trúənt] *s.* novillero, holgazán (*que se ausenta de la escuela*); **to play —** hacer novillos, *Am.* capear la escuela, *Mx.* pintar venado, *Am.* jubilarse; *adj.* vago, perezoso.
truce [trus] *s.* tregua.
truck [trʌk] *s.* camión; carretón; carreta; basura; baratijas; **garden —** hortalizas, legumbres y verduras; **— garden** hortaliza, huerta de legumbres; *v.* acarrear, transportar en camión o carretón.
truck·age [trʌ́kədʒ] *s.* acarreo, camionaje.
trudge [trʌdʒ] *v.* caminar, caminar con esfuerzo; *s.* caminata.
true [tru] *adj.* (*not false*) verdadero; cierto; verídico; fiel; (*exact*) exacto, preciso; legítimo—; **—/false** verdadero/falso, cierto/falso.
tru·ly [trúlɪ] *adv.* (*not falsely*) verdaderamente, en verdad; en realidad; (*exactly*) exactamente, correctamente; fielmente; **very — yours** su seguro servidor.
trump [trʌmp] *s.* triunfo (*en el juego de naipes*); *v.* matar con un triunfo (*en el juego de naipes*); **to — up an excuse** forjar o inventar una excusa.
trum·pet [trʌ́mpɪt] *s.* trompeta; clarín; **ear —** trompetilla acústica; *v.* trompetear; tocar la trompeta; pregonar, divulgar.
trunk [trʌŋk] *s.* (*tree*) tronco; (*receptacle*) baúl; (*animal*) trompa (*de elefante*); **-s** calzones cortos (*para deportes*); **— line** línea principal.
trust [trʌst] *s.* (*reliance*) confianza, fe; (*credit*) crédito; (*charge*) cargo; custodia; depósito; (*firms*) trust, sindicato monopolista; **— account** cuenta fiduciaria; **— fund** fondo en custodia; *v.* confiar; fiar en, tener confianza en, fiarse de; esperar; dar crédito a.
trus·tee [trʌstí] *s.* fideicomisario, depositario; síndico; **university -s** regentes universitarios; **board of -s** patronato; consejo.
trus·tee·ship [trʌstísɪp] *s.* fideicomiso.
trust·ful [trʌ́stfəl] *adj.* confiado.
trust·ing [trʌ́stɪŋ] *adj.* confiado.
trust·wor·thy [trʌ́stwɝðɪ] *adj.* fidedigno, digno de confianza.
trus·ty [trʌ́stɪ] *adj.* fidedigno; honrado, leal; *s.* (*prisoner*) presidiario fidedigno.
truth [truθ] *s.* verdad.
truth·ful [trúθfəl] *adj.* verdadero; verídico; veraz.
truth·ful·ness [trúθfəlnɪs] *s.* veracidad.
try [traɪ] *v.* probar, ensayar; hacer la prueba; poner a prueba; (*attempt*) intentar, procurar; procesar, (*court*) enjuiciar, formar causa (*a un acusado*); ver (*una causa*); **to — on a suit** probarse un traje; **to — one's luck** probar fortuna; **to — someone's patience** poner a prueba la paciencia de alguien; **to — to** tratar de, procurar, intentar; *s.* prueba, tentativa, ensayo.
try·ing [tráɪɪŋ] *adj.* molesto; penoso, irritante.
tub [tʌb] *s.* (*bath*) tina, bañera; baño; (*wash*) batea, cuba; *v.* lavar en tina o cuba.
tu·ba [túbə] *s.* tuba.
tube [tjub] *s.* tubo; **inner —** cámara (*de un neumático*); **radio —** lámpara o tubo de radio.
tu·ber·cu·lar [tjubɝ́kjələɚ] *adj.* tuberculoso, tísico.
tu·ber·cu·lo·sis [tjubɝkjəlósɪs] *s.* tuberculosis.
tuck [tʌk] *v.* alforzar, hacer o echar alforzas; **to — in** meter en; **to — in bed** arropar; **to — under one's arm** meter bajo el brazo; **to — up** arremangar, recoger; **to — up one's sleeves** arremangarse; *s.* alforza.
Tues·day [tjúzdɪ] *s.* martes.
tuft [tʌft] *s.* (*cluster*) penacho, copete; borla; (*clump*) macizo (*de plantas*).
tug [tʌg] *v.* (*tow*) remolcar; (*pull*) jalar (halar); (*drag*) arrastrar; trabajar con esfuerzo; **to — at** tirar de, jalar; *s.* tirón, estirón, *Am.* jalón; remolcador; **— boat** remolcador; **— of war** lucha a tirones de cuerda.
tu·i·tion [tjuɪʃən] *s.* derechos de enseñanza; matrícula; *C.A.* colegiatura.
tu·lip [tjúləp] *s.* tulipán.
tum·ble [tʌ́mbl] *v.* caer(se); voltear; dar volteretas; **to — down** caerse; desplomarse; **to — down** caerse; desplomarse; **to — into someone** tropezar con alguien; **to — over** volcar, tumbar, derribar; venirse abajo; *s.* caída, tumbo, vuelco, voltereta, *Am.* rodada; desorden.
tum·bler [tʌ́mblɚ] *s.* (*glass*) vaso (*de mesa*); (*person*) acróbata.
tu·mor [tjúmɚ] *s.* tumor.
tu·mult [tjúmʌlt] *s.* tumulto.
tu·mul·tu·ous [tjumʌ́ltʃuəs] *adj.* tumultuoso.
tu·na [túnə] *s.* atún (*pez*).
tune [tjun] *s.* (*melody*) tonada; (*pitch*) tono; armonía; **to be in —** estar a tono, estar afinado o templado; estar entonado; **to be out of —** estar desentonado o desafinado; desentonar; *v.* afinar, templar; armonizar; **to — in** sintonizar; **to — up the motor** poner al punto el motor.
tung·sten [tʌ́ŋstən] *s.* tungsteno.
tu·nic [tjúnɪk] *s.* túnica.
tunnel [tʌ́nl] *s.* túnel; socavón; *v.* socavar; abrir un túnel.
tur·ban [tɚbən] *s.* turbante.
tur·bine [tɚbaɪn], [tɚbɪn] *s.* turbina.
tur·bo·prop [tɝ́boprap] *s.* turbopropulsor.
tur·bu·lent [tɝ́bjələnt] *adj.* turbulento; revoltoso.
turf [tɝf] *s.* (*lawn*) césped; (*piece*) terrón de tierra (*con césped*); hipódromo, pista (*para carreras*).
Turk [tɝk] *s.* turco.
tur·key [tɝ́kɪ] *s.* pavo, *Méx.* guajolote (*o* guajalote); *C.A.* jolote, chumpe, chompipe; *Col.* pisco.
Turk·ish [tɝ́kɪʃ] *adj.* turco; *s.* turco, idioma turco.
tur·moil [tɝ́mɔɪl] *s.* alboroto; confusión.
turn [tɝn] *v.* (*rotate*) volver(se); voltear(se); girar, dar vueltas, rodar; virar; (*shape*) tornear, labrar al torno; (*become*) ponerse (*pálido, rojo, etc.*); **to — back** volver atrás; volverse, retroceder; devolver; **to — down an offer** rechazar una oferta; **to — in** entregar; recogerse, acostarse; **to — inside out** voltear o volver al revés; **to — into** convertir(se) en; **to — off** apagar (*la luz*); cortar (*el agua, el gas, etc.*); **to — off the main road** salirse o desviarse de la carretera; **to — on** encender (*la*

TR

luz); abrir la llave (*del gas, del agua*); **to — on someone** volverse contra, acometer o caer sobre alguien; **to — out** apagar (*la luz*); echar, expulsar, arrojar; producir; **to — out well** salir o resultar bien; **to — over** volcar(se), voltear(se); doblar; revolver (*en la mente*); entregar; **to — over and over** dar repetidas vueltas; **to — sour** agriarse, fermentarse; **to — the corner** doblar la esquina; **to — to** acudir a; volverse a; dirigirse a; convertir(se) en; **to — to the left** doblar o torcer a la izquierda; **to — up** aparecer; **to — up one's nose at** desdeñar; hacer ascos a; **to — up one's sleeves** arremangarse; **to — upside down** trastornar; volcar; **it -s my stomach** me da asco o náusea; *s.* vuelta; revolución; giro; recodo (*del camino*); turno; virada, cambio de rumbo; **— of mind** actitud mental; **at every** — a cada paso; **to be one's** — tocarle a uno; **to do one a good** — hacerle a uno un favor; **to take -s** turnarse.

tur·nip [tɝ́nəp] *s.* nabo.

turn·o·ver [tɝ́novɚ] *s.* (*accident*) vuelco (*de un coche*); (*change*) cambio (*de empleados*); **business** — movimiento de mercancías, número de transacciones; rotación de existencias; **labor** — movimiento de obreros, cambio frecuente de trabajadores; **apple** — pastel de manzana; — **collar** cuello doblado.

turn·stile [tɝ́nstaɪl] *s.* torniquete.

turn·ta·ble [tɚ́ntebl] *s.* plato giratorio.

tur·pen·tine [tɝ́pəntaɪn] *s.* trementina; aguarrás.

tur·pi·tude [tɝ́pətjud] *s.* torpeza, vileza.

tur·quoise [tɝ́kwɔɪz] *s.* turquesa.

tur·ret [tɝ́ɪt] *s.* torrecilla; torre blindada; alminar.

tur·tle [tɚ́tl] *s.* tortuga; — **dove** tórtola.

tusk [tʌsk] *s.* colmillo.

tu·tor [tútɚ] *s.* tutor, maestro particular; *v.* enseñar, instruir.

tux·edo [tʌksído] *s.* smoking.

twang [twæŋ] *s.* (*music*) tañido (*de una cuerda de guitarra*); (*speech*) nasalidad, tonillo gangoso; *v.* puntear, tañer (*una cuerda*); hablar con voz nasal, hablar con tonillo gangoso.

twang·y [twǽŋɪ] *adj.* gangoso, nasal.

tweed [twid] *s.* mezclilla de lana; — **suit** traje de mezclilla.

tweez·ers [twízɚz] *s. pl.* pinzas, tenacillas.

twelve [twɛlv] *num.* doce.

twen·ty [twɛ́ntɪ] *num.* veinte.

twice [twaɪs] *adv.* dos veces.

twig [twɪg] *s.* ramita; varita.

twi·light [tsáɪlaɪt] *s.* crepúsculo; **at** — entre dos luces; *adj.* crepuscular.

twin [twɪn] *adj. & s.* gemelo, mellizo, *Méx.* cuate.

twine [twaɪn] *s.* cuerda, cordel; *v.* enroscar(se), torcer(se), retorcer(se); entrelazar.

twinge [twɪndʒ] *s.* punzada (*dolor agudo*); *v.* punzar.

twin·kle [twíŋkl] *v.* titilar, parpadear, pestañear; chispear; *s.* titilación; parpadeo; pestañeo; guiño, guiñada; **in the — of an eye** en un abrir y cerrar de ojos.

twirl [twɝl] *v.* girar; dar vueltas; *s.* giro, vuelta; molinete, floreo.

twist [twɪst] *v.* (*turn*) torcer(se); retorcer(se); (*coil*) enroscar(se); *s.* torsión, torcedura; torzal, cordoncillo (*hecho de varias hebras torcidas*); curva, recodo, vuelta; rosca (*de pan*); **mental** — sesgo de la mente, sesgo mental.

twitch [twɪtʃ] *v.* crisparse, contraerse, torcerse convulsivamente (*un músculo*); (*tremble*) temblar (*los párpados*); (*pull*) dar un tirón; *s.* temblor, ligera, convulsión, contracción nerviosa; tirón.

twit·ter [twítɚ] *v.* (*birds*) gorjear (*los pájaros*); (*tremble*) temblar; agitarse; *s.* gorjeo; agitación, estremecimiento nervioso.

two [tu] *num.* dos.

two-faced [túfest] *adj.* de dos caras.

two-fisted [túfɪstəd] *adj.* vigoroso; de dos puños.

two·fold [túfold] *adj.* doble.

two-way [túwe] *adj.* de dos sentidos.

type [taɪp] *s.* tipo; *v.* escribir a máquina; (*press a key*) presionar, oprimir, tocar.

type·write [táɪpraɪt] *v.* escribir a máquina.

type·writ·er [táɪpraɪtɚ] *s.* máquina de escribir.

type·writ·ing [táɪpraɪtɪŋ] *s.* mecanografía; trabajo de mecanógrafo.

type·writ·ten [táɪprɪtn̩] *adj.* escrito a máquina.

ty·phoid [táɪfɔɪd] *s.* tifoidea, fiebre tifoidea.

ty·phus [táɪfəs] *s.* tifus.

typ·i·cal [típɪkl] *adj.* típico.

typ·ist [táɪpɪst] *s.* mecanógrafo; mecanógrafa.

typ·o·graph·i·cal [taɪpogrǽfɪkl̩] *adj.* tipográfico; — **error** error de máquina; errata.

ty·ran·ni·cal [tɪrǽnɪkl] *adj.* tiránico, tirano.

tyr·an·ny [tírənɪ] *s.* tiranía.

ty·rant [táɪrənt] *s.* tirano.

U:u

u·biq·ui·tous [jubíkwɪtəs] *adj.* ubicuo.

ud·der [ʌ́dɚ] *s.* ubre.

ug·li·ness [ʌ́glɪnɪs] *s.* fealdad; fiereza.

ug·ly [ʌ́glɪ] *adj.* feo; (*cruel*) fiero; repugnante; (*bad temper*) de mal genio; desagradable.

ul·cer [ʌ́lsɚ] *s.* úlcera.

ul·te·ri·or [ʌltírɪɚ] *adj.* ulterior.

ul·ti·mate [ʌ́ltəmɪt] *adj.* último; final; fundamental; **-ly** *adv.* finalmente, a la larga.

ul·tra·mod·ern [ʌltrəmádɚn] *adj.* ultramoderno.

ul·tra·vi·o·let [ʌltrəvaíələt] *adj.* ultravioleta.

um·bil·i·cal cord [ʌmbíləklkɔrd] *s.* cordón umbilical.

um·brel·la [ʌmbrɛ́lə] *s.* paraguas; sombrilla.

um·pire [ʌ́mpaɪr] *s.* árbitro, arbitrador; *v.* arbitrar.

un [ʌn-] *prefijo negativo equivalente a:* sin, no, in-, des-.

un·a·ble [ʌnébl] *adj.* incapaz, inhábil; **to be — to come** no poder venir.

un·ac·cent·ed [ʌnǽksɛntəd] *adj.* inacentuado.

un·ac·cus·tomed [ʌnəkʌ́stəmd] *adj.* desacostumbrado; insólito, inusitado.

un·af·fect·ed [ʌnəfɛ́ktɪd] *adj.* inafectado, sin afectación, natural, sincero.

un·al·ter·a·ble [ʌnɔ́ltərəbl] *adj.* inalterable.

u·na·nim·i·ty [junənímətɪ] *s.* unanimidad.

u·nan·i·mous [jʊnǽnəməs] *adj.* unánime.

un·armed [ʌnármd] *adj.* desarmado.

un·at·tached [ʌnətǽtʃt] *adj.* suelto; libre; (*law*) no embargado.

un·a·void·a·ble [ʌnəvɔ́ɪdəbl] *adj.* inevitable, ineludible; forzoso.

un·a·ware [ʌnəwɛ́r] *adj.* desprevenido; inadvertido; ignorante; incauto; **-s** *adv.* inesperadamente, inopinadamente; impensadamente.

un·bal·anced [ʌnbǽlənst] *adj.* desequilibrado; — **account** cuenta no saldada.

un·bear·a·ble [ʌnbɛ́rəbl] *adj.* inaguantable, insoportable.

un·be·com·ing [ʌnbɪkʌ́mɪŋ] *adj.* impropio; **an — dress** un vestido que no sienta bien o que cae mal.

un·be·lief [ʌnbəlíf] *s.* incredulidad.

un·be·liev·a·ble [ʌnbəlívəbl] *adj*. increíble.
un·be·liev·er [ʌnbəlívɚ] *s*. descreído, incrédulo.
un·be·liev·ing [ʌnbəlívɪŋ] *adj*. descreído, incrédulo.
un·bend·ing [ʌnbɛ́ndɪŋ] *adj*. imflexible.
un·bi·ased [ʌnbáɪəst] *adj*. imparcial, libre de prejuicio.
un·bos·om [ʌnbʊ́zəm] *v*. revelar, confesar, descubrir (*secretos*); **to — oneself** desahogarse con alguien, revelarle sus más íntimos secretos.
un·bound [ʌnbáʊnd] *adj*. desencuadernado, no encuadernado; suelto, desatado.
un·bro·ken [ʌnbrókən] *adj*. intacto, entero; indómito; ininterrumpido, continuo.
un·but·ton [ʌnbʌ́tn̩] *v*. desabotonar, desabrochar.
un·can·ny [ʌnkǽnɪ] *adj*. extraño, raro, misterioso.
un·ceas·ing [ʌnsísɪŋ] *adj*. incesante.
un·cer·tain [ʌnsɝ́tn̩] *adj*. incierto; dudoso; indeciso.
un·cer·tain·ty [ʌnsɝ́tn̩tɪ] *s*. incertidumbre; falta de certeza.
un·change·a·ble [ʌntʃəndʒəbl] *adj*. inmutable, inalterable, invariable.
un·changed [ʌntʃéndʒd] *adj*. inalterado, igual.
un·char·i·ta·ble [ʌntʃǽrətəbl] *adj*. duro; falto de caridad.
un·cle [ʌŋkl] *s*. tío.
un·clean [ʌnklín] *adj*. inmundo, sucio; impuro.
un·com·fort·a·ble [ʌnkʌ́mfɚtəbl *adj*. incómodo; molesto.
un·com·mon [ʌnkɑ́mən] *adj*. poco común, insólito, raro.
un·com·pro·mis·ing [ʌnkɑ́mprəmaɪzɪŋ] *adj*. intransigente; inflexible.
un·con·cern [ʌnkənsɝ́n] *s*. indiferencia.
un·con·di·tion·al [ʌnkəndíʃənl] *adj*. incondicional, absoluto.
un·con·ge·ni·al [ʌnkəndʒínjəl] *adj*. que no congenia, incompatible.
un·con·quer·a·ble [ʌnkɑ́ŋkərəbl] *adj*. invencible, inconquistable.
un·con·quered [ʌnkɑ́ŋkɚd] *adj*. no conquistado, no vencido.
un·con·scious [ʌnkɑ́nʃəs] *adj*. inconsciente; privado.
un·con·scious·ness [ʌnkɑ́nʃəsnɪs] *s*. inconsciencia; insensibilidad.
un·con·sti·tu·tion·al [ʌnkɑ́nstɪtuʃənl *adj*. inconstitucional.
un·con·trol·la·ble [ʌnkəntróləbl] *adj*. irrefrenable, ingobernable.
un·con·ven·tion·al [ʌnkənvɛ́nʃənl] *adj*. despreocupado, libre de trabas o reglas.
un·coup·le [ʌnkʌ́pl] *v*. desacoplar.
un·couth [ʌnkúθ] *adj*. rudo, tosco, inculto, grosero; desmañado.
un·cov·er [ʌnkʌ́vɚ] *v*. descubrir(se); revelar; destapar(se); desabrigar(se).
unc·tion [ʌ́ŋkʃən] *s*. unción; fervor; **Extreme Unction** Extremaunción; *Ven., Méx., Cuba* administración.
unc·tu·ous [ʌ́ŋkʃəs] *adj*. untuoso.
un·cul·ti·vat·ed [ʌnkʌ́ltəvetɪd] *adj*. inculto; baldío.
un·cul·tured [ʌnkʌ́ltʃɚd] *adj*. inculto; grosero.
un·daunt·ed [ʌndɔ́ntəd] *adj*. impávido.
un·de·cid·ed [ʌndɪsáɪdɪd] *adj*. indeciso.
un·de·ni·a·ble [ʌndɪnáɪəbl] *adj*. innegable.
un·der [ʌ́ndɚ] *prep*. (*beneath*) bajo; debajo de; (*less*) menos de; — **age** menor de edad; — **cover** a cubierto; — **the cover of** al abrigo de, al amparo de; — **pretense of** so pretexto de; — **twelve** menos de doce; **to be — obligation to** deber favores a; *adv*. debajo; abajo; menos; *adj*. inferior, de abajo (*en ciertas combinaciones*); — **dose** dosis escasa o corta; — **secretary** subsecretario; — **side** lado de abajo, lado inferior; **the — dogs** los de abajo.
un·der·brush [ʌ́ndɚbrʌʃ] *s*. maleza.
un·der·clothes [ʌ́ndɚkloz] *s. pl*. ropa interior.
und·er·cut [ʌndɚkʌ́t] *v*. vender a menos.
un·der·de·vel·oped [ʌndɚdɪvɛ́ləpt] *adj*. subdesarrollado.
un·der·dog [ʌ́ndɚdɔg] *s*. el (la) de abajo; perdidoso, víctima.
un·der·es·ti·mate [ʌ́ndɚɛ́stəmet] *v*. menospreciar, apreciar en menos de lo justo; salir corto en un cálculo.
un·der·fed [ʌ́ndɚfɛ́d] *adj*. malnutrido.
un·der·go [ʌndɚgó] *v*. sufrir, aguantar, padecer.
un·der·gone [ʌndɚgɔ́n] *p.p. de* **to undergo.**
un·der·grad·u·ate [ʌndɚgrǽdʒʊɪt] *s*. estudiante del bachillerato; — **course** cursos o asignaturas para el bachillerato.
un·der·ground [ʌ́ndɚgraʊnd] *adj*. subterráneo; *s*. subterráneo; *adv*. bajo tierra; (*secretly*) en secreto; ocultamente.
un·der·hand·ed [ʌ́ndɚhǽndɪd] *adj*. socarrón, secreto, disimulado, clandestino.
un·der·line [ʌndɚláɪn] *v*. subrayar.
un·der·ly·ing [ʌndɚláɪɪŋ] *adj*. fundamental.
un·der·mine [ʌndɚmáɪn] *v*. minar, socavar.
un·der·neath [ʌndɚníθ] *prep*. bajo, debajo de; *adv*. debajo.
un·der·pay [ʌ́ndɚpé] *v*. malpagar; escatimar la paga.
un·der·pin·ning [ʌ́ndɚpɪnɪŋ] *s*. apuntalamiento.
un·der·score [ʌ́ndɚskor] *v*. subrayar.
un·der·sell [ʌndɚsɛ́l] *v*. malbaratar; vender a menos precio que.
un·der·shirt [ʌ́ndɚshɝt] *s*. camiseta.
un·der·signed [ʌndɚsáɪnd] *s*. firmante, infrascrito; **the** — el infrascrito, los infrascritos; el que suscribe.
un·der·sized [ʌ́ndɚsáɪzd] *adj*. achaparrado, de tamaño inferior al normal.
un·der·skirt [ʌ́ndɚskɝt] *s*. enaguas, refajo.
un·der·staffed [ʌndɚstǽft] *adj*. de personal insuficiente.
un·der·stand [ʌndɚstǽnd] *v*. extender; comprender; sobrentender.
un·der·stand·a·ble [ʌndɚstǽndəbl] *adj*. comprensible.
un·der·stand·ing [ʌndɚstǽndɪŋ] *s*. comprensión; entendimiento, inteligencia; acuerdo; *adj*. comprensivo.
un·der·stood [ʌndɚstʊ́d] *pret. & p.p. de* **to understand;** *adj*. entendido; convenido; sobrentendido.
un·der·stud·y [ʌ́ndɚstʌdɪ] *s*. sobresaliente, actor suplente; *v*. servir de sobresaliente o actor suplente.
un·der·take [ʌndɚték] *v*. emprender; tratar de, intentar; comprometerse a.
un·der·tak·en [ʌndɚtékən] *p.p. de* **to undertake.**
un·der·tak·er [ʌ́ndɚtekɚ] *s*. director de funeraria; embalsamador.
un·der·tak·ing [ʌndɚtékɪŋ] *s*. empresa.
un·der·took [ʌndɚtʊ́k] *pret. de* **to undertake.**
un·der·tow [ʌ́ndɚto] *s*. resaca.
un·der·wa·ter [ʌ́ndɚwɔtɚ] *adj*. submarino; subacuático.
un·der·wear [ʌ́ndɚwɛr] *s*. ropa interior.
un·der·went [ʌndɚwɛ́nt] *pret. de* **to undergo.**
un·der·world [ʌ́ndɚwɝ́ld] *s*. hampa, bajos fondos de la sociedad; clase criminal; — **jargon** caló.
un·der·write [ʌ́ndɚraɪt] *v*. asegurar; subscribir.

un·de·sir·a·ble [ʌndɪzáɪrəbl] *adj.* indeseable; inconveniente.
un·did [ʌndíd] *pret. de* **to undo.**
un·dis·turbed [ʌndɪstɝ́bd] *adj.* impasible; sereno, tranquilo; intacto.
un·do [ʌndú] *v.* deshacer; desatar; desabrochar; desenredar; anular **to — one's hair** soltarse el cabello.
un·do·ing [ʌndúɪŋ] *s.* destrucción; pérdida.
un·done [ʌndʌ́n] *p.p. de* **to undo**; inacabado, sin hacer; sin terminar; **it is still** — está todavía por hacer, está inacabado; **to come** — desatarse.
un·doubt·ed·ly [ʌndáʊtɪdlɪ] *adv.* indudablemente, sin duda.
un·dress [ʌndrέs] *v.* desnudar(se), desvestir(se).
un·due [ʌndjú] *adj.* indebido; impropio; excesivo.
un·du·late [ʌ́ndjəlet] *v.* ondular, ondear.
un·du·ly [ʌndjúlɪ] *adv.* indebidamente.
un·dy·ing [ʌndáɪɪŋ] *adj.* imperecedero, eterno.
un·earth [ʌnɝ́θ] *v.* desenterrar.
un·eas·i·ly [ʌnízlɪ] *adv.* intranquilamente, inquietamente, con inquietud; incómodamente.
un·eas·i·ness [ʌnízɪnɪs] *s.* malestar, inquietud, intranquilidad, desasosiego.
un·eas·y [ʌnízɪ] *adj.* ansioso, inquieto, intranquilo; (*inhibited*) cohibido; incómodo.
un·ed·u·cat·ed [ʌnέdʒəketɪd] *adj.* inculto, indocto, falto de instrucción, ignorante.
un·em·ployed [ʌnɪmplɔ́ɪd] *adj.* desocupado, desempleado, cesante; (*idle*) ocioso; — **funds** fondos no invertidos, inactivos.
un·em·ploy·ment [ʌnɪmplɔ́ɪmənt] *s.* desempleo; — **compensation** compensación por desempleo; cesantía, falta de empleo, desocupación.
un·end·ing [ʌnέndɪŋ] *adj.* inacabable, interminable.
un·e·qual [ʌníkwəl] *adj.* desigual; (*not enough*) insuficiente, ineficaz.
un·e·quiv·o·cal [ʌnɪkwívəkl] *adj.* inequívoco.
un·err·ing [ʌnέɪŋ] *adj.* infalible.
un·es·sen·tial [ʌnɪsέnʃl] *adj.* no esencial.
un·e·ven [ʌnívən] *adj.* desigual, desparejo; (not level) irregular, accidentado; — **numbers** números impares o nones.
un·e·ven·ness [ʌnívənnɪs] *s.* desigualdad; desnivel; irregularidad, escabrosidad (*del terreno*).
un·e·vent·ful [ʌnɪvέntfl] *adj.* sin novedad.
un·ex·pect·ed [ʌnɪkspέktɪd] *adj.* inesperado; **-ly** *adv.* de improviso, inesperadamente.
un·ex·pres·sive [ʌnɪksprέsɪv] *adj.* sin emoción.
un·fail·ing [ʌnfélɪŋ] *adj.* que nunca falta, constante, indefectible; infalible.
un·fair [ʌnfέr] *adj.* injusto; (*tricky*) tramposo; **to act -ly** obrar de mala fe.
un·faithful [ʌnféθfəl] *adj.* infiel; desleal.
un·fa·mil·iar [ʌnfəmíljɚ] *adj.* poco familiar; desconocido; **to be — with** no tener conocimiento de; no estar al tanto de, ignorar; no conocer bien.
un·fas·ten [ʌnfǽsn̩] *v.* desabrochar; desatar; aflojar.
un·fa·vor·a·ble [ʌnfévrəbl] *adj.* desfavorable, contrario, adverso.
un·feel·ing [ʌnfílɪŋ] *adj.* insensible; incompasivo.
un·fin·ished [ʌnfínɪʃt] *adj.* inacabado, inconcluso; sin terminar, sin acabar; sin barnizar, sin pulir.
un·fit [ʌnfít] *adj.* incompetente, inepto, incapaz; inservible; impropio; *v.* incapacitar.
un·fold [ʌnfóld] *v.* desenvolver(se), desarrollar(se); desdoblar; revelar.
un·fore·seen [ʌnforsín] *adj.* imprevisto.
un·for·get·ta·ble [ʌnfɚgέtəbl] *adj.* inolvidable.
un·for·tu·nate [ʌnfɔ́rtʃənɪt] *adj.* desventurado, infeliz, desgraciado, desdichado; **-ly** *adv.* desgraciadamente, por desgracia.
un·found·ed [ʌnfáʊndəd] *adj.* infundado.
un·fre·quent·ed [ʌnfríkwəntəd] *adj.* poco frecuentado.
un·friend·ly [ʌnfrέndlɪ] *adj.* hostil, enemigo; poco amistoso; *adv.* hostilmente.
un·fruit·ful [ʌnfrútfl] *adj.* infructuoso.
un·fund·ed [ʌnfʌ́ndəd] *adj.* flotante.
un·furl [ʌnfɝ́l] *v.* desplegar.
un·fur·nished [ʌnfɝ́nɪʃt] *adj.* desamueblado.
un·gain·ly [ʌngénlɪ] *adj.* desgarbado, torpe.
un·grate·ful [ʌngrétfəl] *adj.* ingrato, desagradecido.
un·guard·ed [ʌngɑ́rdəd] *adj.* desprevenido; descuidado.
un·hap·py [ʌnhǽpɪ] *adj.* infeliz; desgraciado, desventurado, desdichado.
un·harmed [ʌnhɑ́rmd] *adj.* sin daño, ileso.
un·health·y [ʌnhέlθɪ] *adj.* malsano, insalubre, enfermizo.
un·heard-of [ʌnhɝ́dɑv] *adj.* inaudito; desconocido.
un·hinge [ʌnhíndʒ] *v.* desquiciar.
un·hitch [ʌnhítʃ] *v.* desenganchar; desatar; desacoplar.
un·ho·ly [ʌnhólɪ] *adj.* impío, malo.
un·hook [ʌnhʊ́k] *v.* desenganchar; desabrochar.
un·hurt [ʌnhɝ́t] *adj.* ileso.
u·ni·form [júnəfɔrm] *adj.* & *s.* uniforme.
u·ni·for·mi·ty [junəfɔ́rmətɪ] *s.* uniformidad.
u·ni·fy [júnəfaɪ] *v.* unificar, unir.
u·ni·lat·er·al [junɪlǽtɚl] *adj.* unilateral.
un·im·port·ant [ʌnɪmpɔ́rtn̩t] *adj.* insignificante, poco importante.
un·im·prov·a·ble [ʌnɪmprúvəbl] *adj.* inmejorable.
un·in·hib·i·ted [ʌnɪnhíbətəd] *adj.* sin inhibición.
un·ion [júnjən] *s.* unión; **labor** — sindicato; — **leader** jefe de un gremio obrero; **trade-union** gremio obrero; — **shop** obreros sindicados o agremiados; *adj.* gremial; — **labor** mano de obra sindicalizada.
u·nique [juník] *adj.* único, singular; señero.
u·ni·son [júnəzn̩]: **in** — al unísono (*en el mismo tono*); al compás.
u·nit [júnɪt] *s.* unidad; (*housing*) carcasa, mueble.
u·nite [jʊnáɪt] *v.* unir(se).
u·ni·ty [júnətɪ] *s.* unidad; unión.
u·ni·ver·sal [junəvɝ́sl] *adj.* universal; — **joint** cruceta.
u·ni·verse [júnəvɝs] *s.* universo.
u·ni·ver·si·ty [junəvɝ́sətɪ] *s.* universidad.
un·just [ʌndʒʌ́st] *adj.* injusto.
un·just·i·fi·a·ble [ʌndʒʌ́stəfaɪəbl] *adj.* injustificable, injustificado.
un·kempt [ʌnkɝ́mpt] *adj.* desaseado, desaliñado; desgreñado.
un·kind [ʌnkáɪnd] *adj.* falto de bondad; descortés; cruel.
un·known [ʌnnón] *adj.* desconocido; no sabido; ignoto; — **quality** incógnita; **it is** — se ignora, no se sabe, se desconoce.
un·law·ful [ʌnlɔ́fəl] *adj.* ilegal, ilícito.
un·leash [ʌnlíʃ] *v.* soltar.
un·less [ʌnlέs] *conj.* a menos que, a no ser que.
un·li·censed [ʌnláɪsənzd] *adj.* sin autorización.
un·like [ʌnláɪk] *adj.* desemejante, distinto, diferente; *prep.* a diferencia de.
un·like·ly [ʌnláɪklɪ] *adj.* improbable, inverosímil.
un·lim·it·ed [ʌnlímɪtɪd] *adj.* ilimitado.
un·load [ʌnlód] *v.* descargar; vaciar; deshacerse de (*acciones, mercancías*).
un·lock [ʌnlɑ́k] *v.* abrir (*con llave*); soltar, destrabar; revelar, penetrar (*secretos*).

un·loose [ʌnlús] *v.* soltar.
un·luck·y [ʌnlʌ́kɪ] *adj.* (*unfortunate*) desdichado, desventurado, desgraciado, desafortunado; (*of bad omen*) aciago, de mal agüero, funesto; **an — number** un número de mala suerte.
un·man·age·a·ble [ʌnmǽnɪdʒəbl̩] *adj.* inmanejable, ingobernable, intratable, indomable.
un·manned [ʌnmǽnd] *adj.* desguarnecido; sin tripulación.
un·marked [ʌnmɑ́rkt] *adj.* sin identificación.
un·mar·ried [ʌnmǽrɪd] *adj.* soltero.
un·mask [ʌnmǽsk] *v.* desenmascar(se).
un·mer·ci·ful [ʌnmɝ́sɪfəl] *adj.* despiadado, inclemente.
un·mis·tak·a·ble [ʌnməstékəbl̩] *adj.* inequívoco, claro, inconfundible.
un·moved [ʌnmúvd] *adj.* fijo; inmutable, impasible; indiferente.
un·nat·u·ral [ʌnnǽtʃərəl] *adj.* afectado, artificial; anormal; **an — mother** una madre desnaturalizada.
un·nec·es·sar·y [ʌnnɛ́səsɛrɪ] *adj.* innecesario.
un·not·iced [ʌnnótɪst] *adj.* inadvertido.
un·o·blig·ing [ʌnəbláɪdʒɪŋ] *adj.* poco complaciente, descortés, descomedido.
un·ob·served [ʌnəbzɝ́vd] *adj.* inadvertido; sin ser visto.
un·ob·tain·a·ble [ʌnəbténəbl̩] *adj.* inobtenible, inasequible, inaccesible.
un·ob·tru·sive [ʌnəbtrusɪv] *adj.* discreto; sin ser visto.
un·oc·cu·pied [ʌnɑ́kjəpaɪd] *adj.* desocupado; vacío; desalquilado.
un·of·fi·cial [ʌnəfíʃl̩] *adj.* extraoficial.
un·or·gan·ized [ʌnɔ́rgənaɪzd] *adj.* sin organización; inorganizado.
un·o·rig·i·nal [ʌnərídʒənl̩] *adj.* trivial; ordinario.
un·or·tho·dox [ʌnɔ́rθədɑks] *adj.* heterodoxo.
un·pack [ʌnpǽk] *v.* desempacar; desembalar.
un·paid [ʌnpéd] *adj.* no pagado; sin pagar; **— bills** cuentas por pagar.
un·pleas·ant [ʌnplɛ́zn̩t] *adj.* desagradable.
un·pleas·ant·ness [ʌnplɛ́zn̩tnɪs] *s.* manera desagradable; desazón; desavenencia; **the — of a situation** lo desagradable de una situación; **to have an — with** tener una desavenencia con.
un·prec·e·dent·ed [ʌnprɛ́sədɛntɪd] *adj.* sin precedente; inaudito.
un·pre·med·i·tat·ed [ʌnprimɛ́dətetəd] *adj.* impremeditado.
un·pre·pared [ʌnprɪpɛ́rd] *adj.* desprevenido; no preparado; no listo.
un·pre·ten·tious [ʌnpritɛ́nʃəs] *adj.* modesto; sin pretenciones.
un·print·a·ble [ʌnpríntəbl̩] *adj.* que no puede imprimirse.
un·pro·duc·tive [ʌnprədʌ́ktɪv] *adj.* improductivo.
un·pro·fes·sion·al [ʌnprəfɛ́ʃənl] *adj.* no profesional.
un·prof·it·a·ble [ʌnprɑ́fɪtəbl] *adj.* infructuoso.
un·pub·lished [ʌnpʌ́blɪʃt] *adj.* inédito, no publicado.
un·qual·i·fied [ʌnkwɑ́ləfaɪd] *adj.* incompetente; inepto.
un·quench·a·ble [ʌnkwɛ́ntʃəbl̩] *adj.* inapagable, inextinguible.
un·question·a·ble [ʌnkwɛ́stʃənəbl̩] *adj.* indisputable, indudable; irreprochable.
un·rav·el [ʌnrǽvl] *v.* desenredar; desenmarañar; deshilachar(se); deshilar.
un·real [ʌnríəl] *adj.* irreal; ilusorio; imaginario.
un·rea·son·a·ble [ʌnrízənəbl̩] *adj.* desrazonable, fuera de razón; irracional.
un·rec·og·niz·a·ble [ʌnrɛ́kəgnaɪzəbl̩] *adj.* irreconocible, no conocible, incapaz de reconocerse; desconocido.
un·re·fined [ʌnrɪfáɪnd] *adj.* no refinado; (*uncouth*) inculto, grosero.
un·re·li·a·ble [ʌnrɪlaɪbl] *adj.* informal; indigno de confianza.
un·rest [ʌnrɛ́st] *s.* inquietud, desasosiego.
un·roll [ʌnról] *v.* desenrollar(se), desenvolver(se).
un·ru·ly [ʌnrúlɪ] *adj.* indómito; indócil; desobediente.
un·safe [ʌnséf] *adj.* inseguro, peligroso.
un·sal·a·ble [ʌnséləbl̩] *adj.* invendible.
un·sat·is·fac·to·ry [ʌnsætɪsfǽktrɪ] *adj.* no satisfactorio, inaceptable.
un·scru·pu·lous [ʌnskrúpjʊləs] *adj.* poco escrupuloso.
un·sea·son·a·ble [ʌnsízənəbl̩] *adj.* intempestivo.
un·seat [ʌnsít] *v.* destituir.
un·seen [ʌnsín] *adj.* no visto, oculto; invisible.
un·self·ish [ʌnsɛ́lfɪʃ] *adj.* desinteresado.
un·self·ish·ness [ʌnsɛ́lfɪʃnɪs] *s.* desinterés, abnegación.
un·set·tled [ʌnsɛ́tl̩d] *adj.* (*disturbed*) desordenado, en desorden; turbio; inestable; (*uncertain*) incierto; indeciso; (*unpopulated*) deshabitado; no establecido; **— bills** cuentas no liquidadas, cuentas pendientes; **— weather** tiempo variable; **an — liquid** un líquido revuelto o turbio.
un·shak·en [ʌnʃékən] *adj.* inmóvil, inmovible, firme.
un·sight·ly [ʌnsáɪtlɪ] *adj.* feo, desagradable a la vista.
un·skilled [ʌnskíld] *adj.* inexperto.
un·skill·ful [ʌnskílfəl] *adj.* inhábil, desmañado, inexperto.
un·so·cia·ble [ʌnsóʃəbl̩] *adj.* insociable, huraño, intratable, arisco.
un·so·phis·ti·cat·ed [ʌnsəfístəketəd] *adj.* cándido, sencillo.
un·sound [ʌnsɑ́ʊnd] *adj.* erróneo, falso.
un·speak·a·ble [ʌnspíkəbl̩] *adj.* indecible; inefable; atroz.
un·sta·ble [ʌnstébl̩] *adj.* inestable.
un·stead·y [ʌnstɛ́dɪ] *adj.* inseguro, inestable; movedizo; variable, inconstante.
un·suc·cess·ful [ʌnsəksɛ́sfəl] *adj.* sin éxito; desafortunado; **to be —** no tener éxito.
un·suit·a·ble [ʌnsútəbl̩] *adj.* impropio, inapropiado; (*unskilled*) inepto; inconveniente; incongruente; incompatible.
un·sus·pect·ed [ʌnsəspɛ́ktɪd] *adj.* insospechado.
un·ten·a·ble [ʌntɛ́nəbl] *adj.* insostenible.
un·think·a·ble [ʌnθíŋkəbl̩] *adj.* impensable.
un·ti·dy [ʌntáɪdɪ] *adj.* desaliñado, desaseado; desarreglado, en desorden.
un·tie [ʌntáɪ] *v.* desatar(se); desamarrar; deshacer (*un nudo o lazo*).
un·til [ʌntíl] *prep.* hasta; *conj.* hasta que.
un·time·ly [ʌntáɪmlɪ] *adj.* inoportuno; prematuro; *adv.* inoportunamente; fuera de sazón; demasiado pronto.
un·tir·ing [ʌntáɪrɪŋ] *adj.* incansable.
un·told [ʌntóld] *adj.* indecible, innumerable, incalculable, inestimable.
un·touched [ʌntʌ́ʃt] *adj.* (*unscathed*) intacto, no tocado, íntegro; (*impassive*) impasible, no conmovido; **to leave —** no tocar, dejar intacto; dejar impasible, no conmover.
un·trained [ʌntrénd] *adj.* indisciplinado, falto de disciplina; sin educación; inexperto.
un·tried [ʌntráɪd] *adj.* no probado, no ensayado, no experimentado; **— law case** causa todavía no vista.
un·troub·led [ʌntrʌ́bl̩d] *adj.* sosegado, tranquilo, quieto.

un·true [ʌntrú] *adj.* falso; infiel; desleal; mentiroso.
un·truth [ʌntrúθ] *s.* falsedad; mentira.
un·tu·tored [ʌntútɚd] *adj.* sin instrucción; ingenuo.
un·twist [ʌntwíst] *v.* destorcer.
un·used [ʌnjúzs] *adj.* no usado; (*unaccustomed*) desacostumbrado; — **to** no hecho a, desacostumbrado a.
un·u·su·al [ʌnjúʒuəl] *adj.* inusitado, insólito; desusado; raro, extraño; extraordinario.
un·var·nished [ʌnvárnɪʃt] *adj.* sin barnizar; sin adornos.
un·veil [ʌnvél] *v.* quitar el velo a; revelar, descubrir.
un·war·rant·ed [ʌnwɔ́rəntəd] *adj.* no justificado.
un·war·y [ʌnwɛ́rɪ] *adj.* incauto.
un·washed [ʌnwɔ́ʃt] *adj.* no lavado, sin lavar; sucio.
un·wel·come [ʌnwɛ́lkəm] *adj.* indeseable, no deseado; mal acogido, (*badly received*) mal recibido, mal quisto.
un·whole·some [ʌnhólsəm] *adj.* malsano; (*harmful*) insalubre, dañino.
un·wield·y [ʌnwíldɪ] *adj.* inmanejable, difícil de manejar, embarazoso, engorroso.
un·will·ing [ʌnwílɪŋ] *adj.* renuente, maldispuesto, reacio; **to be — to** no querer, no estar dispuesto a; **-ly** *adv.* de mala gana, sin querer.
un·will·ing·ness [ʌnwílɪŋnɪs] *s.* renuencia, falta de voluntad; mala gana.
un·wise [ʌnwáɪz] *adj.* imprudente, indiscreto; necio.
un·wont·ed [ʌnwʌ́ntəd] *adj.* inusitado, inacostumbrado; inédito.
un·wor·thy [ʌnwɝ́ðɪ] *adj.* indigno.
un·wrap [ʌnrǽp] *v.* desenvolver.
un·writ·ten [ʌnrítən] *adj.* no escrito.
up [ʌp] *adv.* (*above*) arriba, hacia arriba; en lo alto; (*standing*) de pie; *adj.* levantado, derecho, erecto; (*finished*) terminado, concluido; — **and down** de arriba abajo; de acá para allá; **-s and downs** altibajos; fluctuaciones, vaivenes; — **the river** río arriba; — **to now** hasta ahora; **his time is** — ha expirado su tiempo; se ha cumplido su plazo; **prices are** — los precios han subido; **that is — to you** queda a la discreción de Vd.; eso es cosa suya; **to be — against it** estar perplejo, no saber qué hacer; estar en un aprieto; **to be — on the news** estar al corriente (*o* al tanto) de las noticias; **to be — to one's old tricks** hacer de las suyas; **to eat it** — comérselo; **what's — ? ¿qué pasa?**; *v.* levantar, alzar.
up·braid [ʌpbréd] *v.* reprender, regañar.
up·date [ʌ́pdét] *v.* poner al día.
up·grade [ʌ́pgréd] *v.* adelantar; mejorar.
up·heav·al [ʌphívl̩] *s.* trastorno.
up·held [ʌphɛ́ld] *pret. & p.p. de* **to uphold.**
up·hill [ʌphíl] *adv.* cuesta arriba; *adj.* ascendente; trabajoso, arduo.
up·hold [ʌphóld] *v.* sostener; apoyar.
up·hol·ster [ʌphólstɚ] *v.* tapizar y rellenar (*muebles*).
up·hol·ster·y [ʌphólstrɪ] *s.* tapicería.
up·keep [ʌ́pkip] *s.* manutención; conservación.
up·land [ʌ́plənd] *s.* altiplanicie, tierra alta.
up·lift [ʌ́plɪft] *s.* elevación; edificación (*espiritual*); [ʌplíft] *v.* elevar; edificar (*espiritualmente*).
up·on [əpán] *prep.* en, sobre, encima de; — **arriving** al llegar.
up·per [ʌ́pɚ] *adj.* superior; alto; — **berth** litera alta, cama alta (*de un coche dormitorio*); **to have the — hand** ejercer dominio o mando; llevar la ventaja; *s.* litera alta, cama alta; pala (*parte superior del calzado*).
up·right [ʌ́praɪt] *adj.* recto; derecho; vertical; (*just*) justo, honrado; — **piano** piano vertical; *s.* poste; puntal.
up·right·ness [ʌ́praɪtnɪs] *s.* rectitud.
up·ris·ing [ʌpráɪzɪŋ] *s.* alzamiento, levantamiento; revuelta.
up·roar [ʌ́pror] *s.* tumulto, alboroto; bulla, gritería;
up·roar·i·ous [ʌprórɪəs] *adj.* estruendoso, bullicioso, tumultuoso.
up·root [ʌprút] *v.* desarraigar, arrancar de raíz.
up·set [ʌpsɛ́t] *v.* (*capsize*) volcar, tumbar; (*distress*) trastornar; perturbar, turbar; desquiciar; **to become** — volcarse; turbarse; trastornársele a uno el estómago; *pret. & p.p. de* **to upset**; *adj.* indispuesto, descompuesto; desarreglado, trastornado; [ʌ́psɛt] *s.* vuelco; trastorno; desorden; indisposición.
up·shot [ʌ́pʃat] *s.* resultado, fin.
up·side [ʌ́psaɪd] *s.* lado o parte superior; — **down** al revés; patas arriba; en desorden.
up·stage [ʌpstédʒ] *v.* quitarle la escena a uno.
up·stairs [ʌpstɛ́rz] *adv.* arriba, en el piso de arriba; *adj.* de arriba; *s.* piso (*o* pisos) de arriba.
up·start [ʌ́pstart] *s.* advenedizo, principiante presuntuoso.
up-to-date [ʌ́ptədét] *adj.* moderno; al corriente, al tanto.
up·turn [ʌ́ptɝn] *s.* alza, subida (*de precios*); mejora.
up·ward [ʌ́pwɚd] *adv.* arriba, para arriba, hacia arriba; más; — **of** más de; *adj.* ascendente, hacia arriba, para arriba.
up·wards [ʌ́pwɚdz] *adv.* para arriba, hacia arriba.
u·ra·ni·um [jʊréniəm] *s.* uranio.
ur·ban [ɝ́bən] *adj.* urbano; — **renewal** renovación urbana.
ur·chin [ɝ́tʃɪn] *s.* granuja, pilluelo; *Col.* gamín; **sea** — erizo de mar.
u·re·thra [juríθrə] *s.* uretra.
urge [ɝdʒ] *v.* urgir, instar; exhortar; recomendar o solicitar con instancia; apremiar, incitar, estimular; *s.* impulso; gana, ganas; estímulo.
ur·gen·cy [ɝ́dʒənsɪ] *s.* urgencia; apremio.
ur·gent [ɝ́dʒənt] *adj.* urgente, apremiante.
u·ric [júrɪk] *adj.* úrico.
u·ri·nal [júrɪnl̩] *s.* urinario.
u·ri·nate [júrənet] *v.* orinar.
u·rine [júrɪn] *s.* orina, (los) orines.
urn [ɝn] *s.* urna; **coffee** — cafetera.
us [ʌs] *pron.* nos; nosotros (*con preposición*).
us·age [júsɪdʒ] *s.* usanza; uso; **hard** — uso constante.
use [jus] *s.* (*application*) uso; empleo; (*goal*) utilidad; **it is of no** — es inútil; no sirve; **out of** — desusado, ya no usado; pasado de moda; **to have no further — for** ya no necesitar, ya no tener necesidad de; **what is the — of it?** ¿para qué sirve?; ¿qué ventaja tiene?; ¿qué objeto tiene?; [juz] *v.* usar; emplear; servirse de, hacer uso de; acostumbrar, soler, *Am.* saber; — **your judgment** haz lo que te parezca; **to — up** gastar, agotar; consumir; **to be -d to** estar hecho, acostumbrado o habituado a; **he -d to do it** solía hacerlo, lo hacía.
use·ful [júsfəl] *adj.* útil.
use·ful·ness [júsfəlnɪs] *s.* utilidad.
use·less [júslɪs] *adj.* inútil; inservible.
use·less·ness [júslɪsnɪs] *s.* inutilidad.
u·ser [júzɚ] *s.* usuario.
ush·er [ʌ́ʃɚ] *s.* acomodador (*en un teatro o iglesia*); ujier; *v.* conducir, llevar, acompañar; introducir.
u·su·al [júʒuəl] *adj.* usual; corriente, común, general; **-ly** *adv.* usualmente, generalmente, por lo general.
u·su·rer [júʒərɚ] *s.* usurero.
u·surp [juzɝ́p] *v.* usurpar.

u·su·ry [júʒərɪ] *s.* usura.
u·ten·sil [juténsl] *s.* utensilio.
u·ter·us [jútərəs] *s.* útero.
u·til·i·tar·i·an [jutɪlətérɪən] *adj.* utilitario.
u·til·i·ty [jutɪ́lətɪ] *s.* utilidad; servicio.
u·til·ize [jútlaɪz] *v.* utilizar; aprovechar.
ut·most [ʌ́tmost] *adj.* (*extreme*) sumo, extremo; más distante; más grande, mayor; más alto; (*last*) último; **he did his** — hizo cuanto pudo; **to the** — hasta más no poder.
u·to·pi·a [jutópjə] *s.* utopía.
ut·ter [ʌ́tɚ] *v.* proferir; decir, expresar; **to — a cry** dar un grito; *adj.* completo, total; absoluto.
ut·ter·ance [ʌ́tərəns] *s.* declaración; expresión; modo de hablar.
ut·ter·most [ʌ́tɚmost] = **utmost.**
u·vu·la [júvjələ] *s.* campanilla, galillo de la garganta; úvula.
u·vu·lar [júvjʊlɚ] *adj.* uvular.

V:v

va·can·cy [vékənsɪ] *s.* vacante, empleo vacante; (*empty space*) vacío; habitación o apartamento desocupado.
va·cant [vékənt] *adj.* vacante; vacío; desocupado; libre.
va·cate [véket] *v.* desocupar, dejar vacío; dejar vacante.
va·ca·tion [vekéʃən] *s.* vacación; vacaciones.
vac·ci·nate [vǽksn̩et] *v.* vacunar.
vac·ci·na·tion [væksn̩éʃən] *s.* vacunación.
vac·cine [vǽksin] *s.* vacuna.
vac·il·late [vǽsl̩et] *v.* vacilar.
vac·u·um [vǽkjʊəm] *s.* vacío; — **cleaner** escoba eléctrica; aspiradora.
vag·a·bond [vǽgəbɑnd] *adj.* & *s.* vagabundo.
va·gi·na [vədʒáɪnə] *s.* vagina.
va·gran·cy [végrənsɪ] *s.* vagancia.
va·grant [végrənt] *adj.* vago, vagabundo, errante; *s.* vago, vagabundo.
vague [veg] *adj.* vago.
vain [ven] *adj.* vano; vanidoso; **in** — en vano.
vain·glor·y [venglórɪ] *s.* vanagloria.
vale [vel] *s.* valle; cañada.
val·en·tine [vǽləntaɪn] *s.* tarjeta o regalo del día de San Valentín (*el día de los enamorados*); **to my Valentine** a mi querido, a mi querida.
val·et [vǽlɪt] *s.* criado, camarero; (*ironer*) planchador de trajes.
val·iant [vǽljənt] *adj.* valiente, valeroso.
val·id [vǽlɪd] *adj.* válido; valedero.
va·lid·i·ty [vəlɪ́dətɪ] *s.* validez.
va·lise [vəlís] *s.* valija, maleta, *Méx.* velís, *Méx.* petaca.
val·ley [vǽlɪ] *s.* valle.
val·or [vǽlɚ] *s.* valor, ánimo, valentía.
val·or·ous [vǽlərəs] *adj.* valeroso, valiente.
val·u·a·ble [vǽljəbl̩] *adj.* valioso; precioso; preciado; **-s** *s. pl.* objetos de valor, joyas, alhajas.
val·u·a·tion [væljʊéʃən] *s.* valuación, valoración; avalúo; tasa.
val·ue [vǽljʊ] *s.* (*price*) valor; precio; (*merit*) mérito; (*consideration*) estimación, aprecio; *v.* valorar, avaluar, valuar; apreciar, estimar.
val·ue·less [vǽljʊlɪs] *adj.* sin valor.
valve [vælv] *s.* válvula; valva (*de los moluscos*); **safety** — válvula de seguridad.
vam·pire [vǽmpaɪr] *s.* vampiro.
van [væn] *s.* camión (*para transportar muebles*); — **guard** vanguardia.
va·na·di·um [vənédiəm] *s.* vanadio.
van·dal [vǽndl] *s.* vándalo.
vane [ven] *s.* veleta; aspa (*de molino de viento*); paleta (*de hélice*).
van·guard [vǽngɑrd] *s.* vanguardia.
va·nil·la [vənɪ́lə] *s.* vainilla.
van·ish [vǽnɪʃ] *v.* desvanecerse, desaparecer(se).
van·i·ty [vǽnətɪ] *s.* vanidad; — **case** neceser; — **table** tocador.
van·quish [vǽnkwɪʃ] *v.* vencer.
van·tage [vǽntɪdʒ] *s.* ventaja; **point of** — lugar estratégico.
va·por [vépɚ] *s.* vapor; vaho.
va·por·ize [vépɚaɪz] *v.* vaporizar.
var·i·a·ble [vɛ́rɪəbl̩] *adj.* & *s.* variable.
var·i·ance [vɛ́rɪəns] *s.* variación, cambio; desavenencia; **to be at** — estar desavenidos; no estar de acuerdo.
var·i·ant [vǽrɪənt] *s.* variante.
var·i·a·tion [vɛrɪéʃən] *s.* variación; variedad.
var·ied [vɛ́rɪd] *adj.* variado, vario.
var·i·e·gat·ed [vɛ́rɪgetɪd] *adj.* abigarrado.
va·ri·e·ty [vəráɪətɪ] *s.* variedad.
var·i·ous [vɛ́rɪəs] *adj.* varios; diferentes, distintos.
var·nish [vɑ́rnɪʃ] *s.* barniz; *v.* barnizar.
var·y [vɛ́rɪ] *v.* variar; cambiar.
vase [ves] *s.* vaso, jarrón.
Vas·e·line [vǽsəlin] *s.* vaselina.
vas·sal [vǽsl] *adj.* & *s.* vasallo.
vast [væst] *adj.* vasto; inmenso; anchuroso; **-ly** *adv.* vastamente, sumamente, muy.
vast·ness [vǽstnɪs] *s.* inmensidad.
vat [væt] *s.* tina, tanque.
vaude·ville [vódəvɪl] *s.* vodevil, función de variedades.
vault [vɔlt] *s.* bóveda; (*tomb*) tumba; **bank** — caja fuerte, depósito; **pole** — salto con garrocha; *v.* abovedar, edificar una bóveda; dar figura de bóveda; saltar con garrocha; saltar por encima de.
vaunt [vɔnt] *v.* jactarse; ostentar, alardear; *s.* jactancia.
veal [vil] *s.* carne de ternera; — **cutlet** chuleta de ternera.
veer [vɪr] *v.* virar; *s.* virada.
veg·e·ta·ble [vɛ́dʒtəbl̩] *s.* (*plant*) vegetal, planta; (*food*) legumbre; **-s** hortaliza, legumbres; **green -s** verduras; *adj.* vegetal; de legumbres, de hortaliza; — **garden** hortaliza.
veg·e·tar·i·an [vɛdʒətɛ́riən] *s.* vegetariano.
veg·e·tate [vɛ́dʒətet] *v.* vegetar.
veg·e·ta·tion [vɛdʒətéʃən] *s.* vegetación.
ve·he·mence [víəməns] *s.* vehemencia.
ve·he·ment [víəmənt] *adj.* vehemente.
ve·hi·cle [víɪkl] *s.* vehículo.
veil [vel] *s.* velo; *v.* velar; tapar, encubrir.
vein [ven] *s.* (*body*) vena; (*ore*) veta, filón.
veined [vend] *adj.* veteado, jaspeado; (*blood*) venoso.
ve·loc·i·ty [vəlɑ́sətɪ] *s.* velocidad.
vel·vet [vɛ́lvɪt] *s.* terciopelo; velludo; *adj.* de terciopelo; aterciopelado.
vel·vet·y [vɛ́lvɪtɪ] *adj.* aterciopelado.
ven·dor [vɛ́ndɚ] *s.* vendedor; buhonero, vendedor ambulante.
ve·neer [vənír] *s.* chapa; *v.* chapar o chapear, *Am.* enchapar.
ven·er·a·ble [vɛ́nərəbl̩] *adj.* venerable; venerando.
ven·er·ate [vɛ́nəret] *v.* venerar.
ven·er·a·tion [vɛnəréʃən] *s.* veneración.

ve·ne·re·al [vənírɪəl] *adj.* venéreo.
Ven·e·zue·lan [vɛnəzwílən] *adj.* & *s.* venezolano.
ven·geance [véndʒəns] *s.* venganza; **with a** — con furia; con violencia.
ven·i·son [vénəzn̩] *s.* venado, carne de venado.
ven·om [vénəm] *s.* veneno, ponzoña.
ven·om·ous [vénəməs] *adj.* venenoso, ponzoñoso.
vent [vɛnt] *s.* (*opening*) abertura; (*escape*) escape; (*utterance*) desahogo; fogón (*de arma de fuego*); **to give — to anger** desahogar la ira, dar desahogo a la cólera; *v.* dar salida o desahogo; desahogar, descargar.
ven·ti·late [véntl̩et] *v.* ventilar.
ven·ti·la·tion [vɛntl̩éʃən] *s.* ventilación.
ven·ti·la·tor [véntletɚ] *s.* ventilador.
ven·ture [véntʃɚ] *s.* ventura, riesgo; **business —** especulación; empresa o negocio arriesgado; *v.* aventurar, arriesgar; **to — outside** aventurarse a salir; **to — to** aventurarse a, atreverse a, osar.
ven·tur·ous [véntʃərəs] *adj.* aventurado.
ve·ran·da [vərǽndə] *s.* galería; terraza; balcón corrido.
verb [vɝb] *s.* verbo.
ver·bal [vɝ́bl̩] *adj.* verbal; oral.
ver·bal·ize [vɚbəlaɪz] *v.* expresar por medio de palabras.
ver·bose [vɚbós] *adj.* verboso; palabrero.
ver·dict [vɝ́dɪkt] *s.* veredicto; fallo, decisión, sentencia; — **of "not guilty"** veredicto de inculpabilidad.
ver·dure [vɝ́dʒɚ] *s.* verdura, verdor, verde.
verge [vɝdʒ] *s.* borde, margen, orilla; **on the — of** al borde de; a punto de; *v.* **to — on** rayar en, estar al margen de; **to — toward** tender a, inclinarse a.
ver·i·fy [vérəfaɪ] *v.* verificar; comprobar.
ver·i·ly [vérəlɪ] *adv.* en verdad.
ver·i·ta·ble [vérətəbl] *adj.* verdadero.
ver·mil·lion [vɚmíljən] *adj.* bermejo.
ver·nac·u·lar [vɚnǽkjʊlɚ] *adj.* vernáculo; *s.* idioma corriente.
ver·sa·tile [vɚsətl̩] *adj.* hábil para muchas cosas; flexible; versátil.
verse [vɝs] *s.* verso.
versed [ʌɝst] *adj.* versado, experto, perito.
ver·sion [vɝ́ʒən] versión.
ver·te·brate [vɚtəbrɪt] *adj.* vertebrado.
ver·ti·cal [vɝ́tɪkl] *adj.* vertical.
ver·y [vérɪ] *adv.* muy; — **much** muchísimo; — **many** muchísimos; **it is — cold today** hace mucho frío hoy; *adj.* mismo; mismísimo; mero; **the — man** el mismísimo hombre; **the — thought of** la mera idea de.
ves·pers [véspɚz] *s. pl.* vísperas.
ves·sel [vésl̩] *s.* vasija; vaso; barco, embarcación; **blood** — vaso sanguíneo, vena, arteria.
vest [vɛst] *s.* chaleco; *v.* conferir; **to — with power** revestir de autoridad, conferir poder a.
vest·ed in·ter·ests [véstəd íntrɛsts] *s.* intereses creados.
ves·ti·bule [véstəbjul] *s.* vestíbulo; zaguán.
ves·tige [vɛstɪdʒ] *s.* vestigio.
vest·ment [véstmənt] *s.* vestidura.
vet·er·an [vétərən] *adj.* & *s.* veterano.
vet·er·i·nar·y [vétrənɛrɪ] *s.* veterinario o albéitar.
ve·to [víto] *s.* veto; prohibición; *v.* vedar, prohibir; poner el veto a; negarse a aprobar.
vex [vɛks] *v.* molestar, hostigar; incomodar, enfadar; perturbar.
vex·a·tion [vɛkséʃən] *s.* molestia, incomodidad; enojo; vejamen.
vi·a [váɪə] *prep.* por, por la vía de.
vi·a·ble [váɪəbl̩] *adj.* viable.
vi·a·duct [váɪədʌkt] *s.* viaducto.
vi·al [váɪəl] *s.* frasco, redoma; **small** — ampolleta.
vi·ands [váɪəndz] *s. pl.* vianda, alimentos, comida.
vi·brate [váɪbret] *v.* vibrar.
vi·bra·tion [vaɪbréʃən] *v.* vibración.
vi·car·i·ous [vaɪkérɪəs] *adj.* vicario.
vice [vaɪs] *s.* vicio; falta, defecto.
vice-pres·i·dent [váɪsprézədənt] *s.* vice-presidente.
vice·re·gal [vaɪsrígl̩] *adj.* virreinal.
vice·roy [váɪsrɔɪ] *s.* virrey.
vice versa [váɪsɪvɝsə] *adv.* vice versa.
vi·cin·i·ty [vəsínətɪ] *s.* vecindad; cercanía; inmediaciones.
vi·cious [víʃəs] *adj.* vicioso; malo; maligno; malicioso; — **dog** perro mordedor, perro bravo.
vi·cis·si·tude [vəsísətjud] *s.* vicisitud, peripecia.
vic·tim [víktɪm] *s.* víctima.
vic·tim·ize [víktɪmaɪz] *v.* inmolar; engañar.
vic·tor [víktɚ] *s.* vencedor.
vic·to·ri·ous [vɪktórɪəs] *adj.* victorioso.
vic·to·ry [víktrɪ] *s.* victoria.
vic·tuals [vítl̩z] *s. pl.* vituallas, víveres.
vie [vaɪ] v. competir.
view [vju] *s.* (*field of vision*) vista; paisaje; (*opinion*) parecer, opinión; (*inspection*) inspección; (*aim*) mira, propósito; **in — of** en vista de; **to be within** — estar al alcance de la vista; **with a — to** con el propósito de; con la esperanza o expectación de; con la mira puesta en; *v.* mirar; examinar.
view·point [vjúpɔɪnt] *s.* punto de vista.
vig·il [vídʒəl] *s.* vigilia, velada; **to keep** — velar.
vig·i·lance [vídʒələns] *s.* vigilancia, desvelo.
vig·i·lant [vídʒələnt] *adj.* vigilante.
vig·or [vígɚ] *s.* vigor.
vig·or·ous [vígərəs] *adj.* vigoroso.
vile [vaɪl] *adj.* vil, bajo, ruin; pésimo.
vil·la [vílə] *s.* quinta, casa de campo.
vil·lage [vílɪdʒ] *s.* villa, aldea.
vil·lag·er [vílɪdʒɚ] *s.* aldeano.
vil·lain [vílən] *s.* villano, malvado, bellaco.
vil·lain·ous [vílənəs] *adj.* villano, ruin, vil, bellaco.
vil·lain·y [vílənɪ] *s.* villanía, vileza.
vim [vɪm] *s.* vigor, fuerza, energía.
vin·di·cate [víndəket] *v.* vindicar, vengar.
vin·dic·tive [vɪndíktɪv] *adj.* vengativo.
vine [vaɪn] *s.* vid, parra; enredadera.
vin·e·gar [vínɪgɚ] *s.* vinagre.
vine·yard [vínjɚd] *s.* viña, viñedo.
vin·tage [víntɪdʒ] *s.* vendimia; (*age*) edad, época.
vi·o·late [váɪəlet] *v.* violar; infringir.
vi·o·la·tion [vaɪəléʃən] *s.* violación; infracción.
vi·o·lence [váɪələns] *s.* violencia.
vi·o·lent [váɪələnt] *adj.* violento.
vi·o·let [váɪəlɪt] *s.* violeta; violado, color de violeta; *adj.* violado.
vi·o·lin [vaɪəlín] *s.* violín.
vi·o·lin·ist [vaɪəlínɪst] *s.* violinista.
vi·o·lon·cel·lo [viəlontʃélo] *s.* violonchelo.
vi·per [váɪpɚ] *s.* víbora.
vir·gin [vɝ́dʒɪn] *adj.* & *s.* virgen.
vir·gin·al [vɝ́dʒɪnl] *adj.* virginal.
vir·ile [vírl̩] *adj.* viril.
vir·tu·al [vɝ́tʃʊəl] *adj.* virtual; **-ly** *adv.* virtualmente.
vir·tue [vɝ́tʃʊ] *s.* virtud.
vir·tu·ous [vɝ́ʃʊəs] *adj.* virtuoso.
vi·sa [vízə] *s.* visa, visado; *v.* visar, refrendar.
vis·cer·al [vɪsɚl̩] *adj.* visceral.
vi·sé = **visa.**
vise [vaɪs] *s.* tornillo de banco.

vis·i·ble [vízəbl̩] *adj.* visible.
Vis·i·goth [vízəgɔθ] *s.* visigodo.
vi·sion [víʒən] *s.* visión; vista.
vi·sion·ar·y [víʒənɛrɪ] *adj.* visionario; imaginario; *s.* visionario, iluso, soñador.
vis·it [vízɪt] *v.* visitar; **to — punishment upon** mandar un castigo a, castigar a; *s.* visita.
vis·i·ta·tion [vɪzətéʃən] *s.* visitación, visita; castigo, calamidad.
vis·i·tor [vízɪtɚ] *s.* visita; visitador.
vi·sor [váɪzɚ] *s.* visera.
vis·ta [vístə] *s.* vista, paisaje.
vis·u·al [vízjul̩] *adj.* visual; visible.
vis·u·al·ize [vízjʊalaɪz] *v.* representarse en la mente.
vi·tal [váɪtl̩] *adj.* vital.
vi·tal·i·ty [vɑɪtǽlətɪ] *s.* vitalidad.
vi·tal·ize [váɪtəlaɪz] *v.* vitalizar.
vi·ta·min [váɪtəmɪn] *s.* vitamina.
vi·ta·min·ized [váɪtəmənaɪzd] *adj.* vitaminado.
vi·va·cious [vaɪvéʃəs] *adj.* vivaz, vivaracho, vivo, alegre, animado.
vi·vac·i·ty [vaɪvǽsətɪ] *s.* viveza, vivacidad.
viv·id [vívɪd] *adj.* vívido, vivo; animado.
viv·i·fy [vívəfaɪ] *v.* vivificar.
VLSI (*computer*) **(very large scale integration)** *s.* circuitos integrados de 20,000 entradas lógicas.
vo·cab·u·lar·y [vəkǽbjəlɛrɪ] *s.* vocabulario.
vo·cal [vókl̩] *adj.* vocal; oral; **— cords** cuerdas vocales; **to be —** hablar, expresarse.
vo·ca·tion [vokéʃən] *s.* vocación.
vogue [vog] *s.* boga, moda; **in —** en boga, de moda.
voice [vɔɪs] *s.* (*vocalization*) voz; (*speech*) habla; (*opinion*) voto; *v.* expresar, decir; **-d consonant** consonante sonora.
voice·less [vɔ́ɪslɪs] *adj.* mudo; sin voz; **— consonant** consonante sorda.
void [vɔɪd] *adj.* vacío; nulo, inválido; **— of** falto de, desprovisto de; **voided check** cheque anulado; *s.* vacío; *v.* vaciar, evacuar; anular, invalidar.
vol·a·tile [vɑ́lətl̩] *adj.* volátil; inconstante.
vol·can·ic [vɑlkǽnɪk] *adj.* volcánico.
vol·ca·no [vɑlkéno] *s.* volcán.
vo·li·tion [volíʃən] *s.* volición; voluntad.
vol·ley [vɑ́lɪ] *s.* (*discharge*) descarga, lluvia (*de piedras, flechas, balas, etc.*); (*back and forth*) voleo (*de la pelota*); *v.* descargar una lluvia de proyectiles; volear una pelota.
volt [volt] *s.* voltio.
volt·age [vóltɪdʒ)] *s.* voltaje.
vol·u·ble [vɑ́ljəbl̩] *adj.* facundo.
vol·ume [vɑ́ljəm] *s.* (*book*) volumen; tomo; (*capacity*) bulto; suma, cantidad.
vo·lu·mi·nous [vəlúmənəs] *adj.* voluminoso.
vol·un·tar·y [vɑ́ləntɛrɪ] *adj.* voluntario.
vol·un·teer [vɑləntír] *s.* voluntario; *adj.* voluntario; de voluntarios; *v.* ofrecer, dar voluntariamente; ofrecerse.
vo·lup·tu·ous [vəlʌ́ptʃʊəs] *adj.* voluptuoso.
vom·it [vɑ́mɪt] *s.* vómito; *v.* vomitar, *Méx.* deponer.
vo·ra·cious [voréʃəs] *adj.* voraz.
vor·tex [vɔ́rtɛks] *s.* vórtice; vorágine.
vote [vot] *s.* voto; votación; *v.* votar; votar por.
vot·er [vótɚ] *s.* votante, elector.
vouch [vaʊtʃ] *v.* **to — for** dar fe de; garantizar, responder de; salir fiador de.
vouch·er [váʊtʃɚ] *s.* comprobante, justificante; recibo; fiador.
vouch·safe [vaʊtʃséf] *v.* otorgar, conceder.
vow [vaʊ] *s.* voto; juramente; *v.* votar, jurar, hacer voto de.
vow·el [váʊəl] *s.* & *adj.* vocal.
voy·age [vɔɪɪdʒ] *s.* viaje; travesía; *v.* viajar.
vul·gar [vʌ́lgɚ] *adj.* soez, ordinario, grosero; vulgar.
vul·ner·a·ble [vʌ́nɚəbl] *adj.* vulnerable.
vul·ture [vʌ́ltʃɚ] *s.* buitre, *Andes, Ríopl.* cóndor; *Méx., C.A.* zopilote; *Carib.* aura; *Col.* gallinazo.
vul·va [vʌ́lvə] *s.* vulva.

W:w

wab·ble [wɑ́bl̩] *variante de* **wobble** *v.* tambalear(se), bambolear(se); vacilar; temblar; *s.* tambaleo, bambolea; balanceo.
wad [wɑd] *s.* (*filling*) taco; bodoque; (*ball*) pelotilla, bolita, rollo; **— of money** rollo de billetes (*de banco*); dinero; *v.* atacar (*un arma de fuego*); rellenar; hacer una pelotilla de.
wad·dle [wɑ́dl̩] *v.* anadear; contonearse, zarandearse (*al andar*); *s.* anadeo; zarandeo, contoneo.
wade [wed] *v.* vadear; (*splash*) chapotear; andar descalzo por la orilla del agua; **to — through a book** leer con dificultad un libro.
wa·fer [wéfɚ] *s.* oblea; hostia (*consagrada*); (*computer*) ficha de silicón o otro semiconductor.
waft [wæft] *v.* llevar en vilo, llevar por el aire; llevar a flote; *s.* ráfaga de aire; movimiento (*de la mano*).
wag [wæg] *v.* menear; sacudir; **to — the tail** colear, menear la cola; *s.* meneo; (*comic*) bromista, farsante.
wage [wedʒ] *v.* hacer (*guerra*); dar (*batalla*); *s.* (*generalmente*) **wages** paga, jornal; **— earner** jornalero, obrero; trabajador; **wageworker** obrero asalariado; **— scale** escala de salarios (*sueldos*).
wa·ger [wédʒɚ] *s.* apuesta; *v.* apostar.
wag·gle [wǽgl̩] *s.* meneo rápido.
wag·on [wǽgən] *s.* carro, carreta; carretón.
wail [wel] *v.* gemir, lamentar; *s.* gemido, lamento.
waist [west] *s.* cintura; talle; (*garment*) blusa; **— band** pretina.
waist·coat [wéstkot] *s.* chaleco.
waist·line [wéstlaɪn] *s.* talle.
wait [wet] *v.* (*stay*) esperar, aguardar; (*serve*) servir; **to — for** esperar, aguardar; **to — on (upon)** servir a; atender a; **to — table** servir la mesa, servir de mozo o camarero (*en un restaurante*); *s.* espera; **to lie in — for** estar en acecho de.
wait·er[wétɚ] *s.* mozo, camarero, sirviente, *Méx., C.A.* mesero.
wait·ing [wétɪŋ] *s.* espera; **— room** sala de espera.
wait·ress [wétrɪs] *s.* camarera, moza, *Méx.* mesera.
waive [wev] *v.* renunciar a; **to — one's right** renunciar voluntariamente a sus derechos.
waiv·er [wévɚ] *s.* renuncia.
wake [wek] *v.* despertar(se); **to — up** despertar(se); despabilarse; *s.* (*at death*) velatorio (*acto de velar a un muerto*), *Am.* velorio; (*ship*) estela (*huella que deja un barco en el agua*); **in the — of** después de, detrás de.
wake·ful [wékfəl] *adj.* desvelado, despierto; insomne.
wak·en [wékən] *v.* despertar(se); *Ríopl., C.A., Ven.* recordar (*a una persona que está dormida*).
walk [wɔk] *v.* andar, caminar, ir a pie; recorrer a pie; pasear; **to — away** irse, marcharse; **to — back home** volverse a casa (a pie); **to — down** bajar; **to — in** entrar; **to — out** salirse, irse; parar el trabajo, declararse en huelga; **to — the streets** callejear; **to — up** subir; *s.* paseo; (*path*) senda, vereda; (*sidewalk*) acera; (*pace*) paso (*del caballo*);

(*style*) manera de andar; — **of life** vocación; **a ten minutes'** — una caminata de diez minutos.
walk·out [wɔ́kaʊt] *s*. paro, huelga.
wall [wɔl] *s*. (*interior*) pared; (*garden*) muro; (*fort*) muralla; **execution** — paredón; **low mud** — tapia; **to drive to the** — poner entre la espada y la pared, poner en un aprieto.
wal·let [wɑ́lɪt] *s*. cartera.
wall·flow·er [wɔ́lflaʊɚ] *s*. alelí; **to be a — at a dance** comer pavo, *Andes, Méx*. planchar el asiento.
wal·lop [wɑ́ləp] *v*. pegar, zurrar, golpear; *s*. guantada, bofetón, golpazo.
wal·low [wɑ́lo] *v*. revolcarse; chapalear o chapotear (*en el lodo*).
wall·pa·per [wɔ́lpepɚ] *s*. papel (de empapelar).
wal·nut [wɔ́lnət] *s*. nuez de nogal; nogal; — **tree** nogal.
waltz [wɔlts] *s*. vals; *s*. valsar, bailar el vals.
wan [wɑn] *adj*. pálido, enfermizo, enclenque; lánguido.
wand [wɑnd] *s*. vara, varita; **magic** — varita de virtud.
wan·der [wɑ́ndɚ] *v*. vagar, errar; **to — away** extraviarse; **to — away from** apartarse de, desviarse de; **my mind -s easily** me distraigo fácilmente.
wan·der·er [wɑ́ndərɚ] *s*. vago, vagabundo.
wane [wen] *v*. menguar; decaer; *s*. mengua; diminución; **to be on the** — ir menguando; ir desapareciendo.
want [want] *v*. (*desire*) querer, desear; (*lack*) necesitar; *s*. falta; necesidad; escasez, carencia; **to be in** — estar necesitado.
want·ing [wɑ́ntɪŋ] *adj*. falto; deficiente; (*poor*) necesitado.
wan·ton [wɑ́ntən] *adj*. desenfrenado, libre; licencioso; inconsiderado; temerario.
war [wɔ́r] *s*. guerra; *v*. guerrear, hacer guerra; **to — on** guerrear con.
war·ble [wɔ́rbḷ] *v*. gorjear; trinar; *s*. gorjeo; trino.
war·bler [wɔ́rblɚ] *s*. cantor; pájaro gorjeador.
ward [wɔrd] *s*. pupilo, menor o huérfano (*bajo tutela*); (*section*) cuadra (*de hospital, prisión, etc*.); (*district*) distrito (*de una ciudad*); *v*. **to — off** resguardarse de; evitar; parar (*un golpe*).
war·den [wɔ́rdṇ] *s*. guardián; alcaide; **prison** — alcaide de una prisión.
ward·robe [wɔ́rdrob] *s*. (*closet*) guardarropa, ropero, armario; (*garments*) vestuario; ropa.
ware·house [wɛ́rhaʊs] *s*. almacén, depósito.
wares [wɛrz] *s*. *pl*. artículos, mercancías, mercaderías, efectos.
war·fare [wɔ́rfɛr] *s*. guerra.
war·head [wɔ́rhɛd] *s*. punta de combate; (*nuclear*) proyectil.
war·like [wɔ́rlaɪk] *adj*. guerrero, bélico.
warm [wɔrm] *adj*. (*temperature*) caliente, cálido, caluroso; (*enthusiastic*) acalorado; (*fresh*) reciente; — **hearted** de buen corazón; — **blooded** apasionado; ardiente; **he is** — tiene calor; **it is — today** hace calor hoy; *v*. calentar(se); **to — over** recalentar; **to — up** calentar(se); acalorarse; entusiasmarse.
warmth [wɔrmpθ] *s*. (*heat*) calor; (*friendship*) cordialidad.
warn [wɔrn] *v*. avisar, advertir, amonestar; prevenir, precaver.
warn·ing [wɔ́rnɪŋ] *s*. aviso, advertencia, amonestación; escarmiento; **let that be a — to you** que te sirva de escarmiento.
warp [wɔrp] *s*. (*weaving*) urdimbre (*de un tejido*); (*deformation*) torcedura, deformación; comba; *v*. combar(se), deformar(se), torcer(se); urdir (*los hilos de un telar*).
war·rant [wɔ́rənt] *s*. (*sanction*) autorización; (*right*) garantia, justificación; (*writ*) comprobante; orden, mandato, citación (*ante un juez*); *v*. autorizar; garantizar; justificar.
war·ri·or [wɔ́rɪɚ] *s*. guerrero.
war·ship [wɔ́rʃɪp] *s*. buque de guerra, acorazado.
wart [wɔrt] *s*. verruga.
war·y [wɛ́rɪ] *adj*. cauteloso, cauto, precavido, prevenido; **to be — of** desconfiar de.
was [wɑz] *pret. de* **to be** (*primera y tercera persona del singular*).
wash [wɑʃ] *v*. lavar(se); **to — away** deslavar(se); **to be -ed away by the waves** ser arrastrado por las olas; *s*. lavado; lavadura; lavatorio; lavazas, agua sucia; **mouth—** enjuague o enjuagatorio; **—bowl** lavabo, palangana, lavamanos; **—cloth** paño para lavarse; **—dress** vestido lavable; **—room** lavabo, lavatorio.
wash·a·ble [wɑ́ʃəbḷ] *adj*. lavable.
wash-and-wear [wɔ́ʃændwɛ́r] *adj*. de lava y pon.
washed·out [wɑ́ʃtáʊt] *adj*. desteñido; agotado, sin fuerzas.
washed-up [wɔʃtʌ́p] *adj*. fracasado.
wash·er [wɑ́ʃɚ] *s*. lavador; máquina de lavar; arandela (*para una tuerca*); — **woman** lavandera.
wash·ing [wɑ́ʃɪŋ] *s*. (*act*) lavado; (*clothing*) ropa sucia o para lavar; ropa lavada; — **machine** lavadora, máquina de lavar.
wash·out [wɔʃaʊt] *s*. derrubio; fracaso.
wasp [wɑsp] *s*. avispa.
waste [west] *v*. gastar; desgastar; malgastar, despediciar, derrochar; disipar; **to — away** gastarse, consumirse; desgastarse; *s*. desperdicio; gasto inútil; desgaste; desechos, desperdicios; terreno baldío; desierto; *adj*. inútil, desechado; (*desert*) desierto; baldío; — **of time** pérdida de tiempo; — **basket** cesto para papeles; — **land** terreno baldío; — **paper** papeles inútiles, papel de desecho; **to go to** — gastarse, perderse; malgastarse, desperdiciarse; **to lay** — asolar, arruinar.
waste·ful [wéstfəl] *adj*. despilfarrado, gastador; desperdiciado; ineconómico.
watch [wɑtʃ] *v*. (*look*) mirar; observar; (*be alert*) vigilar; velar; cuidar; — **out!** ¡cuidado!; **to — out for** tener cuidado con; cuidar; vigilar; *s*. reloj (de bolsillo); vela, vigilia; guardia; centinela, vigilante; — **chain** cadena de reloj, *Ven., Méx*. leontina; — **charm** dije; **wrist** — reloj de pulsera; **to be on the** — tener cuidado; estar alerta; **to keep — over** vigilar a.
watch·ful [wɑ́tʃfəl] *adj*. alerto, vigilante, despierto, atento, prevenido.
watch·mak·er [wɑ́tʃmekɚ] *s*. relojero.
watch·man [wɑ́tʃmən] *s*. vigilante, guardia, sereno.
watch·tow·er [wɑ́tʃtaʊɚ] *s*. atalaya, mirador.
watch·word [wɑ́tʃwɝd] *s*. contraseña, santo y seña, (*motto*) consigna; lema.
wa·ter [wɔ́tɚ] *s*. agua; — **color** acuarela; color para acuarela — **power** fuerza hidráulica; — **shed** vertiente; — **sports** deportes acuáticos; — **supply** abastecimiento de agua; *v*. (*irrigate*) regar; aguar, (*dilute*) diluir con agua; abrevar, (*give*) dar de beber (*al ganado*); beber agua (*el ganado*); tomar agua (*un barco, locomotora, etc*.); **my eyes** — me lloran los ojos; **my mouth -s** se me hace agua la boca.

wa·ter·cress [wɔ́tɚkrɛs] *s.* berro.
wa·ter·fall [wɔ́tɚfɔl] *s.* cascada, catarata, caída de agua.
wa·ter·front [wɔ́tɚfrʌnt] *s.* terreno ribereño.
wa·ter·mel·on [wɔ́tɚmɛlən] *s.* sandía; *Col.* patilla.
wa·ter·pow·er [wɔ́tɚpaʊɚ] *s.* fuerza hidráulica.
wa·ter·proof [wɔ́tɚpruf] *adj. & s.* impermeable; *v.* hacer impermeable.
wa·ter-ski [wɔ́tɚski] *s.* esquí acuático.
wa·ter·spout [wɔ́tɚspaʊt] *s.* surtidor; tromba, manga de agua.
wa·ter·way [wɔ́tɚwe] *s.* vía de agua, río navegable, canal.
wa·ter·y [wɔ́tərɪ] *adj.* aguado; acuoso; mojado, húmedo.
wave [wev] *v.* ondear; ondular; agitar; (*blandish*) blandir (*una espada, bastón, etc.*); **to — aside** apartar, rechazar; **to — good-bye** hacer una seña o ademán de despedida; **to — hair** ondular el pelo; **to — one's hand** hacer una seña o señas con la mano; mover la mano; *s.* onda; ola; ondulación; **— of the hand** ademán, movimiento de la mano; **permanent** — ondulación permanente.
wave·length [wévlɛŋθ] *s.* longitud de onda.
wa·ver [wévɚ] *v.* oscilar; (*hesitate*) vacilar, (*stutter*) titubear; (*stagger*) tambalear(se); *s.* vacilación, titubeo.
wa·vy [wévɪ] *adj.* rizado, ondulado; ondulante.
wax [wæks] *s.* cera; **— candle** vela de cera; **— paper** papel encerado; *v.* encerar; pulir con cera; hacerse, ponerse; crecer (*la luna*).
way [we] s. (*road*) camino; ruta; senda; (*manner*) modo, manera; **— in** entrada; **out** salida; **— through** paso, pasaje; **a long — off** muy lejos, a una larga distancia; **by — of** por, por vía de; **by — of comparison** a modo de comparación; **by the** — de paso; **in no** — de ningún modo; **on the — to** camino de, rumbo a; **out of the** — fuera del camino; apartado; a un lado; impropio; extraordinario; **to be in a bad** — hallarse en mal estado; **to be well under** — estar (*un trabajo*) ya bastante avanzado; **to give** — ceder; quebrarse; **to have one's** — hacer su capricho, salirse con la suya; **to make — for** abrir paso para
way·far·er [wéfɛrɚ] *s.* caminante.
way·lay [welé] *v.* estar en acecho de (*alguien*); (*attack*) asaltar; (*stop*) detener (*a una persona*).
way·side [wésaɪd] *s.* borde del camino; **— inn** posada al borde del camino.
way·ward [wéwɚd] *adj.* voluntarioso, desobediente.
we [wi] *pron.* nosotros, nosotras.
weak [wik] *adj.* débil; flaco; endeble, **— market** mercado flojo; **weak-minded** de voluntad débil; simple; **— tea** té claro o suave.
weak·en [wíkən] *v.* debilitar(se); desmayar, flaquear, perder ánimo.
weak·ly [wíklɪ] *adv.* débilmente; *adj.* enfermizo, débil, enclenque.
weak·ness [wíknis] *s.* debilidad; flaqueza.
wealth [wɛlθ] *s.* riqueza; copia, abundancia.
wealth·y [wɛ́lθɪ] *adj.* rico; acaudalado.
wean [win] *v.* destetar; (*gradually estrange*) apartar gradualmente (*de un hábito, de una amistad*).
weap·on [wɛ́pən] *s.* arma.
wear [wɛr] *v.* (*have on*) llevar, tener o traer puesto; usar; (*waste away*) gastar, desgastar; **to — away** gastar(se), degastar(se); consumir(se); **to — off** degastar(se), gastar(se); borrarse; **to — out** gastar(se); degastar(se); consumir(se); agotar; cansar; **it -s well** es duradero; dura mucho; **as the day wore on** a medida que pasaba el día; *s.* uso, gasto; durabilidad; **— and tear** desgaste; uso; **men's** — ropa para hombres; **clothes for summer** — ropa de verano.
wea·ri·ly [wírɪlɪ] *adv.* penosamente, con cansancio, con fatiga, fatigadamente.
wea·ri·ness [wírɪnɪs] *s.* cansancio, fatiga.
wear·ing [wɛ́rɪŋ] *adj.* cansado, aburrido, fastidioso.
wea·ri·some [wírɪsəm] *adj.* fatigoso, molesto, fastidioso.
wea·ry [wírɪ] *adj.* cansado, fatigado; aburrido; *v.* cansar(se), fatigar(se).
wea·sel [wízl] *s.* comadreja.
weath·er [wɛ́ðɚ] *s.* tiempo; **weather-beaten** desgastado o curtido por la intemperie; **— bureau** oficina meteorológica; **— conditions** condiciones atmosféricas; **— vane** veleta; **it is fine** — hace buen tiempo; **to be under the** — estar enfermo; estar indispuesto; *v.* exponer a la intemperie; orear, secar al aire; **to — a storm** aguantar un chubasco; salir ileso de una tormenta.
weave [wiv] *v.* (cloth) tejer, entretejer; (*to plan*) urdir; **to — together** entretejer, entrelazar; combinar; *s.* tejido.
weav·er [wívɚ] *s.* tejedor.
web [wɛb] *s.* tela; (*membrane*) membrana; **spider's** — telaraña.
wed [wɛd] *v.* casarse; casarse con; casar; *p.p. de* **to wed.**
wed·ded [wɛ́dɪd] *p.p. & adj.* casado; unido; **— to an idea** aferrado a una idea.
wed·ding [wɛ́dɪŋ] *s.* boda, casamiento, nupcias, enlace; **— day** día de bodas; **— trip** viaje de novios; **silver** — bodas de plata.
wedge [wɛdʒ] *s.* cuña; **entering** — cuña, entrada, medio de entrar, modo de penetrar; *v.* acuñar, meter cuñas; **to be -d between** estar encajado entre.
Wednes·day [wɛ́nzdɪ] *s.* miércoles.
wee [wi] *adj.* diminuto, chiquitico, pequeñito.
weed [wid] *s.* cizaña, mala hierba; *v.* desherbar (*o* desyerbar), quitar o arrancar la mala hierba; **to — a garden** desherbar un huerto; **to — out** escardar; eliminar, arrancar, entresacar.
weed·y [wídɪ] *adj.* herboso, lleno de malas hierbas.
week [wik] *s.* semana; **— day** día de trabajo, día laborable, día hábil; **— end** fin de semana; **a — from today** de hoy en ocho días.
week·ly [wíklɪ] *adj.* semanal, semanario; *adv.* semanalmente, por semana; *s.* semanario, periódico o revista semanal.
weep [wip] *v.* llorar.
weep·ing [wípɪŋ] *adj.* llorón; lloroso; **— willow** sauce llorón; *s.* llanto, lloro, lágrimas.
wee·vil [wívl] *s.* gorgojo.
weigh [we] *v.* pesar; ponderar, considerar; **to — anchor** zarpar, levar el ancla; **to — down** agobiar; abrumar; **to — on one's conscience** serle a uno gravoso, pesarle a uno.
weight [wet] *s.* peso; (*clock*) pesa (*de reloj o medida para pesar*); (*load*) carga; **paper** — pisapapeles; *v.* cargar, sobrecargar; añadir peso a; asignar un peso o valor relativo a.
weight·y [wétɪ] *adj.* grave, ponderoso; de mucho peso; importante.
weird [wɪrd] *adj.* extraño, raro, misterioso, fantástico.
wel·come [wɛ́lkəm] *s.* bienvenida; buena acogida; *adj.* grato, agradable; (*received*) bien acogido, bien quisto; bien-venido; bien recibido; **— home!** ¡bienvenido!; **— rest** grato reposo o descanso; **you are** — no hay de qué; de nada (*para contestar a*

"thank you"); **you are — here** está Vd. en su casa; **you are — to use it** se lo presto con todo gusto; está a su disposición; *v.* dar la bienvenida a; acoger o recibir con gusto.
weld [wɛld] *v.* soldar(se); *s.* soldadura.
wel·fare [wɛ́lfɛr] *s.* bienestar; bien; felicidad; — **work** labor social o de beneficencia; — **society** sociedad benéfica.
well [wɛl] *adv.* bien; **he is — over fifty** tiene mucho más de cincuenta años; — **then** pues bien, ahora bien, conque; **well-being** bienestar; **well-bred** bien criado; bien educado; **well-done** bien cocido; **well-fixed** acomodado, well-groomed acicalado; **well-meaning** bien intencionado; **well-nigh** casi, muy cerca de; *adj.* bueno; bien de salud, sano; conveniente; — **and good** santo y muy bueno; **well-off** acomodado; adinerado; en buenas condiciones; **well-to-do** próspero, adinerado; **all is** — no hay novedad, todo va bien; **it is — to do it** conviene hacerlo, es conveniente hacerlo.
well [wɛl] *s.* (*shaft*) pozo; (*cistern*) cisterna; (*spring*) manantial; **artesian** — pozo artesiano; *v.* manar; **tears -ed up in her eyes** se le arrasaron los ojos de lágrimas.
welsh [wɛlʃ] *v.* no pagar una obligación.
welt [wɛlt] *s.* verdugo, verdugón, roncha.
went [wɛnt] *pret. de* **to go.**
wept [wɛpt] *pret. & p.p. de* **to weep.**
were [wɝ] *pret. de* **to be** (*en el plural y en la segunda persona del singular del indicativo; es además el imperfecto del subjuntivo*); **if I — you** si yo fuera Vd.; **there** — había, hubo.
west [wɛst] *s.* oeste, occidente, ocaso; *adj.* occidental, del oeste; **West Indies** Antillas; *adv.* hacia el oeste, al oeste; en el oeste.
west·ern [wɛ́stɚn] *adj.* occidental, del oeste.
west·ern·er [wɛ́stɚnɚ] *s.* natural del oeste, habitante del oeste, occidental.
west·ward [wɛ́stwɚd] *adv.* hacia el oeste; *adj.* occidental, oeste.
wet [wɛt] *adj.* húmedo; mojado; — **nurse** nodriza, ama de leche; *s.* humedad; (*pro-liquor*) antiprohibicionista; *v.* mojar; humedecer; *pret. & p.p. de* **to wet**.
wet·back [wɛ́tbæk] *s.* panza mojada.
wet·ness [wɛ́tnɪs] *s.* humedad.
whack [hwæk] *v.* golpear, pegar; *s.* golpe; golpazo; tentativa, prueba.
whale [hwel] *s.* ballena; *v.* pescar ballenas.
wharf [hwɔrf] *s.* muelle, embarcadero.
what [hwɑt] *pron. interr.* ¿qué?; ¿qué cosa?; ¿cuál?; *pron. rel.* lo que; — **for?** ¿para qué? *adj. qué;* — **book?** ¿qué libro? — **a man!** ¡qué hombre!; — **happy children!** ¡qué niños más (*o* tan) felices!; **take — books you need** tome Vd. los libros que necesite.
what·ev·er [hwɑtɛ́vɚ] *pron.* cualquiera cosa que, lo que, cuanto, todo lo que; — **do you mean?** ¿qué quiere Vd. decir?; **do it, — happens** hágalo suceda lo que suceda; *adj.* cualquiera; **any person** — una persona cualquiera; **no money** — nada de dinero.
what·so·ev·er [hwɑtsoɛ́vɚ] = **whatever.**
wheat [hwit] *s.* trigo; **cream of** — crema de trigo.
whee·dle [hwídl] *v.* engatusar.
wheel [hwil] *s.* (*disc*) rueda; rodaja; disco; (*bike*) bicicleta; — **chair** silla rodante, silla de ruedas; **steering** — volante (*de automóvil*); (*ship*) rueda del timón; *v.* rodar; hacer rodar; girar; acarrear; andar en bicicleta; **to — around** dar una vuelta; girar sobre los talones; **to — the baby** pasear al bebé en su cochecito.
wheel·bar·row [hwílbæro] *s.* carretilla.
wheeze [hwiz] *s.* resuello ruidoso.
when [hwɛn] *adv. & conj.* cuando; *adv. interr.* ¿cuándo?
whence [hwɛns] *adv.* de donde; de que.
when·ev·er [hwɛnɛ́vɚ] *adj. & conj.* cuando, siempre que, cada vez que.
where [hwɛr] *adv.* donde; adonde; en donde; por donde; — **?** ¿dónde?; ¿adónde?
where·a·bouts [hwɛ́rəbaʊts] *s.* paradero; *adv. interr.* ¿dónde?
where·as [hwɛrǽz] *conj.* mientras que; puesto que, visto que, considerando que.
where·by [hwɛrbáɪ] *adv.* por donde, por lo cual; con lo cual.
where·fore [hwɛ́rfor] *adv.* por lo que; por lo cual; por eso, por lo tanto.
where·in [hwɛrín] *adv.* en que; en donde; en lo cual.
where·of [hwɛrɑ́v] *adv.* de que; de donde; de quien, de quienes.
where·up·on [hwɛrəpɑ́n] *adv.* después de lo cual; entonces.
where·ev·er [hwɛrɛ́vɚ] *adv.* dondequiera que, adondequiera que, por dondequiera que.
where·with·al [hwɛ́rwɪðɔl] *s.* medios, fondos; dinero.
whet [hwɛt] *v.* amolar, afilar; (*stimulate*) aguzar, estimular.
wheth·er [hwɛ́ðɚ] *conj.* si; ya sea que, sea que; — **we escape or not** ya sea que escapemos o no; **I doubt** — dudo (de) que.
which [hwɪtʃ] *pron. interr.* ¿cuál?; ¿cuáles?; *pron. rel.* que; el cual, la cual, los cuales, las cuales; el que, la que, los que, las que; *adj. interr.* ¿qué?; — **boy has it?** ¿cuál de los muchachos lo tiene? ¿qué muchacho lo tiene?; — **way did he go?** ¿por qué camino se fué?; ¿por dónde se fué?; **during — time** tiempo durante el cual.
which·ev·er [hwɪtʃɛ́vɚ] *pron. & adj.* cualquiera (que), cualesquiera (que); el que, la que; — **road you take** cualquier camino que Vd. siga.
whiff [hwɪf] *s.* (*waft*) soplo; fumada, bocanada; (*odor*) repentino olor o hedor; *v.* soplar; echar bocanadas.
while [hwaɪl] *s.* rato; tiempo, temporada; **a short** — un ratito; **a short — ago** hace poco, hace poco rato; **to be worth** — valer la pena; *conj.* mientras, mientras que; *v.* **to — away the time** pasar el tiempo.
whilst [hwaɪlst] *conj.* mientras, mientras que.
whim [hwɪm] *s.* capricho, antojo.
whim·per [hwímpɚ] *v.* lloriquear, gimotear; quejarse; *s.* lloriqueo, gimoteo; quejido.
whim·si·cal [hwímzɪkl] *adj.* caprichoso.
whine [hwaɪn] *v.* lloriquear; quejarse; *s.* gemido, quejido.
whin·er [hwáɪnɚ] *s.* llorón, persona quejosa, *Méx., Carib., Ven.* quejumbres; *Andes* quejumbroso; *Ríopl.* rezongón.
whip [hwɪp] *v.* azotar, fustigar; (*beat*) zurrar, dar una paliza a, dar latigazos a; (*cream*) batir (*crema, huevos*); vencer; **to — up** batir, coger (*o* asir) de repente; hacer de prisa; *s.* azote, látigo, fuete; batido.
whip·ping [hwípɪŋ] *s.* tunda, zurra, paliza; — **cream** crema para batir.
whir [hwɝ] *v.* zumbar; *s.* zumbido.
whirl [hwɝl] *v.* girar, dar vueltas; arremolinarse; **my head -s** siento vértigo, estoy desvanecido; *s.* giro, vuelta; remolino; (*column*) espiral (*de humo*); confusión.

whirl·pool [hwɝ́lpul] *s.* remolino, vorágine, vórtice.
whirl·wind [hwɝ́lwɪnd] *s.* remolino, torbellino.
whisk [hwɪsk] *v.* barrer; (*brush*) desempolvar (*con escobilla*); (*beat*) batir (*huevos*); **to — away** barrer de prisa; llevarse de prisa, arrebatar; irse de prisa, escaparse; **to — something out of sight** escamotear algo, esconder algo de prisa; *s.* — **broom** escobilla; **with a — of the broom** de un escobillazo.
whis·ker [hwɪ́skɚ] *s.* pelo de la barba; **-s** barbas; patillas; bigotes (*del gato*).
whis·key [hwɪ́skɪ] *s.* whisky (*aguardiente de maíz, centeno, etc.*).
whis·per [hwɪ́spɚ] *v.* cuchichear, hablar en secreto; soplar, decir al oído; susurrar; secretearse; **it is -ed that** corre la voz que; dizque, dicen que; *s.* cuchicheo, secreteo; susurro; murmullo; **to talk in a —** hablar en secreto; susurrar.
whis·tle [hwɪ́sḷ] *v.* siblar; chiflar; (*instrument*) pitar; **to — for someone** llamar a uno con un silbido; *s.* silbido, chiflido; silbato, pito.
whit [hwɪt] *s.* jota, pizca.
white [hwaɪt] *adj.* (*color*) blanco; (*pure*) puro; inocente; (*honorable*) honrado, recto; **— caps** cabrillas o palomas (*olas con crestas blancas*); — **lead** albayalde; **— lie** mentirilla, mentira venial; **white-livered** cobarde; **white-collar** de oficina; **to show the — feather** mostrar cobardía, portarse como cobarde; *s.* blanco; clara (*del huevo*).
whit·en [hwáɪtn̩] *v.* blanquear; emblanquecer(se), poner(se) blanco.
white·ness [hwáɪtnɪs] *s.* blancura; palidez; pureza.
white·wash [hwáɪtwɑʃ] *v.* (*paint*) blanquear, enjalbegar; (*gloss over*) encubrir, disimular (*faltas, errores*); (*absolve*) absolver (*sin justicia*); *s.* lechada.
whith·er [hwɪ́ðɚ] *adv.* adonde; **— ?** ¿adónde?
whit·ish [hwáɪtɪʃ] *adj.* blancuzco, blanquecino, blanquizco.
whit·tle [hwɪ́tḷ] *v.* cortar mondar, tallar; (*slice*) tajar, sacar punta a (*un lápiz*); **to — down expenses** cercenar o reducir los gastos.
whiz [hwɪz] *v.* zumbar; *s.* zumbido, silbido; **to be a —** ser un águila, ser muy listo.
who [hu] *pron. rel.* quien, quienes, que, el que, la que, los que, las que; **he —** el que, quien; *pron. interr.* *¿quién?; ¿quiénes?;* **— is it?** ¿quién es?
who·ev·er [huɛ́vɚ] *pron.* quienquiera que, cualquiera que; el que.
whole [hol] *adj.* todo; entero; íntegro; **the — day** todo el día; **— hearted** sincero, cordial; — **heartedly** de todo corazón; con todo ánimo; *s.* todo, total, totalidad; **as a —** en conjunto; **on the —** en general, en conjunto.
whole·sale [hólsel] *s.* venta al por mayor, *Méx., Arg., Ch.* mayoreo; **by —** al por mayor; *adj.* al por mayor; en grandes cantidades; **— dealer** comerciante al por mayor; *Méx., Arg., Ch.* mayorista; **— slaughter** matanza; gran hecatombe; **— trade** comercio al por mayor; *Méx., Arg., Ch.* comercio mayorista; *adv.* al por mayor, por mayor; *v.* vender al por mayor, *Méx., Arg., Ch.* mayorear.
whole·some [hólsəm] *adj.* saludable, sano; salubre; **— man** hombre normalmente bueno o de buena índole.
whol·ly [hólɪ] *adv.* enteramente, completamente, totalmente.
whom [hum] *pron. pers.* a quien, a quienes; que; al que (a la que, a los que, *etc.*); al cual (a la cual, a los cuales, *etc.*); **for —** para quien; **— did you see?** ¿a quién vió Vd.?
whoop [hup] *s.* grito, chillido, alarido; (*cough*) respiro convulsivo (*que acompaña a la tos ferina*); *v.* gritar, vocear, echar gritos; respirar convulsivamente (*al toser*); **to — it up** armar una gritería, gritar; **whooping cough** tos ferina.
whore [hor] *s.* ramera, puta, prostituta.
whose [huz] *pron.* cuyo, cuya, cuyos, cuyas; *pron. interr.* ¿de quién?; ¿de quiénes?; **— book is this?** ¿de quién es este libro?
why [hwaɪ] *adv.* *¿por qué?;* **the reason —** la razón por la que (*o* la cual); **—, of course!** ¡sí, por supuesto!; ¡claro que sí!; **—, that is not true!** ¡si eso no es verdad! *s.* porqué, causa, razón, motivo.
wick [wɪk] *s.* mecha, pabilo.
wick·ed [wɪ́kɪd] *adj.* malvado, malo, inicuo; nefasto.
wick·ed·ness [wɪ́kɪdnɪs] *s.* maldad, iniquidad, perversidad.
wick·er [wɪ́kɚ] *s.* mimbre; **— chair** silla de mimbre.
wick·et [wɪ́kɪt] *s.* postigo; ventanilla.
wide [waɪd] *adj.* ancho; amplio; (*extensive*) vasto; extenso; **— apart** muy apartados; **wide-awake** muy despierto; alerta, vigilante; **— eyed** ojoso; — **of the mark** muy lejos del blanco; **— open** muy abierto; abierto de par en par; **far and —** por todas partes, extensamente; **to open —** abrir mucho; abrir (*la puerta*) de par en par; **two feet —** dos pies de ancho (*o* de anchura).
wide·ly [wáɪdlɪ] *adv.* ampliamente; extensamente; muy; mucho.
wid·en [wáɪdn̩] *v.* ensanchar(se), ampliar(se), dilatar(se).
wide·spread [wáɪdsprɛ́d] *adj.* muy esparcido, muy extensivo; bien difundido; extendido; general, extendido por todas partes.
wid·ow [wɪ́do] *s.* viuda.
wid·ow·er [wɪ́dəwɚ] *s.* viudo.
width [wɪdθ] *s.* ancho, anchura.
wield [wild] *v.* manejar; esgrimir (*la espada o la pluma*); ejercer (*el poder*).
wife [waɪf] *s.* esposa.
wig [wɪg] *s.* peluca.
wig·gle [wɪ́gḷ] *v.* menear(se); *s.* meneo.
wig·wam [wɪ́gwɑm] *s.* choza de los indios norteños.
wild [waɪld] *adj.* salvaje; (*animal*) feroz, fiero; indómito; montaraz; (*plant*) silvestre; *Ven., Méx.* cimarrón; (*uncontrolled*) impetuoso, desenfrenado; bullicoso; violento; loco; enojado; desatinado; ansioso; **to talk —** disparatar, desatinar; *s.* yermo, desierto, monte.
wild·cat [wáɪldkæt] *s.* gato montés; **— scheme** empresa arriesgada; *adj.* de prueba.
wil·der·ness [wɪ́ldɚnɪs] *s.* yermo, desierto, monte; inmensidad.
wild·eyed [wáɪldaɪd] *adj.* de ojos huraños,
wild·ness [wáɪldnɪs] *s.* salvajez; ferocidad, fiereza; locura.
wile [waɪl] *s.* ardid, engaño; (*cleverness*) astucia.
will [wɪl] *v.* (*desire*) querer, decidir; (*order*) ordenar, mandar; (*dispose of legally*) legar; *v. defect. y aux.* querer; *rigurosamente debe usarse para formar el futuro en las segundas y terceras personas*: **she — go** ella irá; *en las primeras personas indica voluntad o determinación*: **I — not do it** no lo haré, no quiero hacerlo.
will [wɪl] *s.* (*wish*) voluntad; albedrío; (*legal disposition*) testamento; **free —** libre albedrío; **ill —** mala voluntad, malquerencia.
will·ful, wil·ful [wɪ́lfəl] *adj.* voluntarioso, testarudo, caprichudo; intencional.
wil·ling [wɪ́lɪŋ] *adj.* bien dispuesto, deseoso, complaciente; voluntario; **-ly** *adv.* con gusto, de

buena gana, de buena voluntad; voluntariamente.
will·ing·ness [wílɪŋnɪs] *s.* buena voluntad, buena gana.
wil·low [wílo] *s.* sauce; mimbrera; **weeping** — sauce llorón.
wilt [wɪlt] *v.* marchitar(se); ajar(se); desmayar; languidecer.
wi·ly [wáɪlɪ] *adj.* astuto, artero.
win [wɪn] (*achieve*) ganar; lograr, obtener; alcanzar; (*persuade*) persuadir; **to — out** ganar, triunfar; salirse con la suya; **to — over** persuadir; atraer; alcanzar o ganar el favor de.
wince [wɪns] *v.* cejar (*ante una dificultad o peligro*); encogerse (*de dolor, susto, etc.*).
winch [wɪntʃ] *s.* malacate.
wind [wɪnd] *s.* viento, aire; resuello; — **instrument** instrumento de viento; **to get — of** barruntar; tener noticia de.
wind [waɪnd] *v.* enredar; devanar, ovillar; (*watch*) dar cuerda a (*un reloj*); (*road*) serpentear (*un camino*); dar vueltas; **to — someone around one's finger** manejar fácilmente a alguien, gobernarle; **to — up one's affairs** terminar o concluir uno sus negocios; *s.* vuelta; recodo.
wind·bag [wíndbœg] *s.* (*instrument*) fuelle; (*person*) parlanchín, hablador.
wind·fall [wíndfɔl] *s.* golpe de fortuna, ganancia repentina, herencia inesperada.
wind·ing [wáɪndɪŋ] *adj.* sinuoso, tortuoso, que da vueltas; — **staircase** escalera de caracol.
wind·mill [wíndmɪl] *s.* molino de viento.
win·dow [wíndo] *s.* ventana; **show** — escaparate, vitrina, aparador, *Am.* vidriera; — **shade** visillo, cortinilla; — **sill** antepecho, repisa de ventana.
win·dow·pane [wíndopen] *s.* cristal de ventana, vidriera.
wind·pipe [wíndpaɪp] *s.* tráquea, gaznate.
wind·shield [wíndʃild] *s.* parabrisa, guardabrisa; — **wiper** limpiaparabrisas.
wind tunnel [wíndtʌnl] *s.* túnel aerodinámico.
wind·ward [wíndwɚd] *s.* barlovento.
wind·y [wíndɪ] *adj.* airoso; ventoso; **it is** — hace aire, ventea, sopla el viento.
wine [waɪn] *s.* vino; *adj.* vinícola; — **cellar** bodega
wing [wɪŋ] *s.* ala; bastidor (*de escenario*); **under the — of** bajo la tutela de; **to take** — levantar el vuelo.
winged, wing·ed [wɪŋd, wíŋɪd] *adj.* alado.
wing·spread [wíŋsprɛd] *s.* envergadura.
wink [wɪŋk] *v.* guiñar; pestañear, parpadear; *s.* guiño, guiñada; **I didn't sleep a** — no pegué los ojos en toda la noche.
win·ner [wínɚ] *s.* ganador; vencedor; — **of a prize** agraciado, premiado.
win·ning [wínɪŋ] *adj.* (*successful*) ganancioso; triunfante, victorioso; (*charming*) atractivo, encantador; **-s** *s. pl.* ganancias.
win·some [wínsəm] *adj.* simpático, atractivo, gracioso.
win·ter [wíntɚ] *s.* invierno; — **clothes** ropa de invierno; *v.* invernar, pasar el invierno.
win·try [wíntrɪ] *adj.* invernal, de invierno; frío, helado.
wipe [waɪp] *v.* secar; enjugar; limpiar; **to — away one's tears** limpiarse las lágrimas; **to — off** borrar; limpiar; **to — out a regiment** destruir o aniquilar un regimiento.
wire [waɪr] *s.* (*strand*) alambre; (*telegram*) telegrama; **by** — por telégrafo; — **entanglement** alambrada; — **fence** alambrado; — **netting** tela metálica, alambrado; **to pull -s** mover los hilos; *v.* poner alambrado, instalar alambrado eléctrico; atar con alambre; telegrafiar.
wire·less [wáɪrlɪs] *adj.* inalámbrico, sin hilos; — **telegraphy** radiotelegrafía; *s.* radio, radiotelegrafía; telegrafía sin hilos; radiotelefonía; radiograma.
wire·tap·ping [wáɪrtæpɪŋ] *s.* conexión secreta interceptora de teléfono.
wir·y [wáɪrɪ] *adj.* de alambre; como alambre; nervudo.
wis·dom [wízdəm] *s.* sabiduría, saber; (*sanity*) cordura; prudencia; — **tooth** muela del juicio.
wise [waɪz] *adj.* (*judicious*) sabio, cuerdo, sensato; (*prudent*) discreto, prudente; **the Three Wise Men** los Tres Reyes Magos; **to get — to** darse cuenta de; modo, manera; **in no** — de ningún modo.
wise·crack [wáɪzkræk] *s.* bufonada, dicho agudo o chocarrero, dicharacho.
wish [wɪʃ] *v.* desear, querer; **to — for** desear; anhelar; **I — it were true!** ¡ojalá (que) fuera verdad!; *s.* deseo.
wish·ful think·ing [wíʃfʊl θíŋkɪŋ] *s.* optimismo ilusorio.
wist·ful [wístfəl] *adj.* anhelante, anheloso, ansioso; tristón, melancólico.
wit [wɪt] *s.* agudeza, sal, chiste; (*person*) ingenio; hombre agudo o de ingenio; **to be at one's wit's end** haber agotado todo su ingenio; **to be out of one's -s** estar fuera de sí, estar loco; **to lose one's -s** perder el juicio; **to use one's -s** valerse de su industria o ingenio.
witch [wɪtʃ] *s.* hechicera; bruja.
witch·craft [wítʃkræft] *s.* hechicería.
with [wɪð, wɪθ] *prep.* con; para con; en compañía de; **filled** — lleno de; **ill** — enfermo de; **the one — the black hat** el del (*o* la del) sombrero negro.
with·draw [wɪðdrɔ́] *v.* retirar(se); apartar(se); separar(se); **to — a statement** retractarse.
with·draw·al [wɪðdrɔ́əl] *s.* retirada, retiro.
with·drawn [wɪðdrɔ́n] *p.p. de* **to withdraw.**
with·drew [wɪðdrú] *pret. de* **to withdraw.**
with·er [wíðɚ] *v.* marchitar(se); ajar(se); secar(se).
with·held [wɪθhέld] *pret. & p.p. de* **to withhold.**
with·hold [wɪθhóld] *v.* retener; detener; **to — one's consent** negarse a dar su consentimiento.
with·hold·ing [wɪθhóldɪŋ] *adj.* de retención.
with·in [wɪðín] *prep.* dentro de; — **call** al alcance de la voz; — **five miles** a poco menos de cinco millas; **it is — my power** está en mi mano; *adv.* dentro, adentro.
with·out [wɪðáʊt] *prep.* sin; — **my seeing him** sin que yo le viera; *adv.* fuera, afuera.
with·stand [wɪθstǽnd] *v.* resistir; aguantar, padecer.
with·stood [wɪθstʊ́d] *pret. & p.p. de* **to withstand.**
wit·ness [wítnɪs] *s.* testigo; testimonio; *v.* ver, presenciar; ser testigo de; atestiguar, dar fe de.
wit·ti·cism [wítəsɪzem] *s.* ocurrencia, agudeza, dicho agudo.
wit·ty [wítɪ] *adj.* agudo, ocurrente, gracioso, divertido, chistoso; — **remark** dicho agudo, agudeza, ocurrencia
wives [waɪvz] *s. pl. de* **wife.**
wiz·ard [wɪzɚd] *s.* genio, hombre de ingenio; mago, mágico.
wob·ble [wɑ́bl̩] *s.* bamboleo, tambaleo; balanceo; *v.* tambalear(se), bombolear(se); vacilar; temblar.
woe [wo] *s.* miseria, aflicción, infortunio; — **is me!** ¡miserable de mi!
woe·ful [wófʊl] *adj.* miserable; abatido.
woke [wok] *pret. de* **to wake.**
wolf [wʊlf] (*pl.* **wolves** [wʊlvz]) *s.* lobo.
wom·an [wʊ́mən] (*pl.* **women** [wímɪn]) *s.* mujer; — **writer** escritora; — **chaser** mujeriego, faldero.

wom·an·hood [wúmənhud] *s.* estado de mujer; la mujer (las mujeres); integridad femenil; feminidad.
wom·an·kind [wúmənkaɪnd] *s.* la mujer, las mujeres, el sexo femenino.
wom·an·ly [wúmənlɪ] *adj.* femenil, mujeril, femenino; *adv.* femenilmente, como mujer.
womb [wum] *s.* (*uterus*) útero, matriz; (*insides*) vientre, entrañas.
won [wʌn] *pret. & p.p. de* **to win.**
won·der [wʌ́ndɚ] *s.* (*marvel*) maravilla; prodigio; (*emotion*) admiración; **in** — maravillado; **no — that** no es mucho que; no es extraño que; *v.* asombrarse, maravillarse, pasmarse, admirarse; **to — at** admirarse de, maravillarse de; **I — what time it is** ¿qué hora será? **I — when he came** ¿cuándo vendría? **I should not — if** no me extrañaría que.
won·der·ful [wʌ́ndɚfəl] *adj.* maravilloso, admirable; **-ly** *adv.* maravillosamente, admirablemente, a las mil maravillas; **-ly well** sumamente bien.
won·drous [wʌ́ndrəs] *adj.* maravilloso, pasmoso, extraño.
wont [wʌnt] *adj.* acostumbrado; **to be — to** soler, acostumbrar, *C.A.* saber; *s.* costumbre, hábito, uso.
woo [wu] *v.* cortejar, enamorar, galantear.
wood [wud] *s.* (*material*) madera; (*stick*) palo; (*firewood*) leña; **-s** bosque; selva; **— engraving** grabado en madera; **— shed** leñera, cobertizo par leña; **fire —** leña; **piece of fire —** leño.
wood·cut [wúdkʌt] *s.* grabado en madera.
wood·cut·ter [wúdkʌtɚ] *s.* leñador.
wood·ed [wúdɪd] *adj.* arbolado, poblado de árboles.
wood·en [wúdn̩] *adj.* de madera, de palo; tieso.
wood·land [wúdlænd] *s.* monte, bosque, selva.
wood·man [wúdmən] *s.* (*vendor*) leñador; (*dweller*) habitante del bosque.
wood·peck·er [wúdpɛkɚ] *s.* pájaro carpintero.
wood·work [wúdwɝk] *s.* maderaje; labrado en madera; obra de carpintería; (*cabinet*) ebanistería.
woof [wuf] *s.* trama (*de un tejido*); tejido.
wool [wul] *s.* lana; *adj.* de lana; lanar; **wool-bearing** lanar; **— dress** vestido de lana.
wool·en [wúlɪn] *adj.* de lana; lanudo; **— mill** fábrica de tejidos de lana; *s.* tejido de lana; género o paño de lana.
wool·ly [wúlɪ] *adj.* lanudo; de lana.
word [wɝd] *s.* (*vocable*) palabra; vocablo, voz; (*news*) noticia, aviso; (*order*) mandato, orden; **— processing** (*computer*) tratamiento de textos; **pass —** contraseña; **by — of mouth** de palabra, verbalmente; *v.* expresar; redactar, formular.
word·y [wɝ́dɪ] *adj.* palabrero, verboso, ampuloso.
wore [wor] *pret. de* **to wear.**
work [wɝk] *s.* (*effort*) trabajo; (*masterpiece*) obra maestra; (*task*) tarea; faena; (*employment*) empleo, ocupación; oficio; (*accomplishment*) labor; **-s** taller, fábrica; maquinaria, mecanismo; **at —** trabajando; ocupado; *v.* trabajar; funcionar; obrar; surtir efecto; manejar, manipular; resolver (*un problema*); explotar (*una mina*); hacer trabajar; **to — havoc** hacer estropicios, causar daño; **to — loose** soltarse, aflojarse; **to — one's way through college** sufragar los gastos universitarios con su trabajo; **to — one's way up** subir por sus propios esfuerzos; **to — out a plan** urdir un plan; **to be all -ed up** estar sobreexcitado; **it didn't — out** no dió resultado; **the plan -ed well** tuvo buen éxito el plan.
work·a·ble [wɝkəbl̩] *adj.* practicable; explotable.
work·er [wɝ́kɚ] *s.* trabajador; obrero; operario.
work·ing [wɝ́kɪŋ] *s.* funcionamiento, operación; cálculo (*de un problema*); explotación (*de una mina*); *adj.* obrero, trabajador; **— class** clase obrera o trabajadora; **— hours** horas de trabajo; horas laborables; **a hard-working man** un hombre muy trabajador.
work·ing·man [wɝ́kɪŋmæn] *s.* trabajador; obrero.
work·man [wɝ́kmən] *s.* trabajador, obrero, operario.
work·man·ship [wɝ́kmənʃɪp] *s.* hechura; trabajo; mano de obra.
work·shop [wɝ́kʃɑp] *s.* taller.
world [wɝld] *s.* mundo; **the World War** la Guerra Mundial; **world-shaking** de gran importancia.
world·ly [wɝ́ldlɪ] *adj.* mundano, mundanal, terreno, terrenal.
worm [wɝm] *s.* gusano; lombriz; **worm-eaten** comido de gusanos; carcomido, apolillado; *v.* **to — a secret out of someone** extraerle o sonsacarle un secreto a una persona; **to — oneself into** insinuarse en, meterse en.
worn [worn] *p.p. de* **to wear**; **worn-out** gastado, roto; rendido de fatiga.
wor·ry [wɝ́ɪ] *s.* inquietud, ansiedad, cuidado, preocupación, apuro, apuración; *v.* inquietar(se), preocupar(se), afligir(se), apurar(se).
worse [wɝs] *adj.* peor; más malo; *adv.* peor; **— and —** cada vez peor; **— than ever** peor que nunca; **from bad to —** de mal en peor; **so much the —** tanto peor; **to be — off** estar peor que antes; **to change for the —** empeorar(se); **to get —** empeorar(se).
wor·ship [wɝ́ʃəp] *s.* adoración, culto; veneración; *v.* adorar; reverenciar.
wor·ship·er [wɝ́ʃəpɚ] *s.* adorador; **the -s** los fieles.
worst [wɝst] *adj.* peor; *adv.* peor; **the —** el peor; la peor; lo peor; *v.* derrotar.
worth [wɝθ] *s.* valor, valía, mérito; (*price*) precio; **ten cent's — of** diez centavos de; **to get one's money's — out of** sacar todo el provecho posible del dinero gastado en; *adj.* digno de; **— hearing** digno de oírse; **to be —** valer; **to be — doing** valer la pena de hacerse; **to be —while** valer la pena.
worth·less [wɝ́θlɪs] *adj.* sin valor; inútil; despreciable.
wor·thy [wɝ́ðɪ] *adj.* (*good*) digno; (*valued*) valioso, apreciable; meritorio, merecedor; *s.* benemérito, hombre ilustre.
would [wud] *imperf. de indic. y de subj. del verbo defect.* **will: she — come every day** solía venir (*o* venía) todos los días; **if you — do it** si lo hiciera Vd.; *expresa a veces deseo:* **— that I knew it!** ¡quién lo supiera!; ¡ojalá que yo lo supiera!; *v. aux. del condicional:* **she said she — go** dijo que iría.
wound [wund] *s.* herida; llaga, lesión; *v.* herir; lastimar; agraviar.
wound [waund] *pret. & p.p. de* **to wind.**
wove [wov] *pret. de* **to weave.**
wo·ven [wóvən] *p.p. de* **to weave.**
wow [wau] *v.* entusiasmar.
wran·gle [rǽŋgl̩] *v.* (*quarrel*) altercar, disputar; reñir. (*herd*) juntar; *Am.* rodear (*el ganado*); *s.* (*quarrel*) riña, pendencia.
wrap [ræp] *v.* envolver; enrollar, arrollar; **to — up** envolver(se); abrigar(se), tapar(se); **to be wrapped up in** estar envuelto en; estar absorto en; *s.* abrigo, manto.
wrap·per [rǽpɚ] *s.* envoltura, cubierta; **woman's —** bata.
wrap·ping [rǽpɪŋ] *s.* envoltura; **— paper** papel de

envolver.
wrath [ræθ] *s.* ira, cólera, rabia.
wrath·ful [rǽθfəl] *adj.* colérico, rabioso, iracundo.
wreath [riθ] *s.* guirnalda, corona; — **of smoke** espiral de humo.
wreathe [rið] *v.* hacer guirnaldas; adornar con guirnaldas; **-d in smiles** sonriente.
wreck [rɛk] *s.* (*destruction*) ruina; destrucción; (*shipwreck*) naufragio; (*accident*) accidente; (*wreckage*) destrozos, despojos (*de un naufragio*); *v.* arruinar; naufragar; echar a pique; destrozar, demoler; **to — a train** descarrilar un tren.
wrench [rɛntʃ] *v.* torcer, retorcer; (*pull away*) arrancar, arrebatar; *s.* torcedura, torsión; tirón, arranque, *Andes, Méx., C.A.* jalón; (*tool*) llave de tuercas; **monkey** — llave inglesa.
wrest [rɛst] *v.* arrebatar, arrancar; usurpar.
wres·tle [rέsl̩] *v.* luchar a brazo partido; luchar; *s.* lucha a brazo partido.
wres·tler [rέslɚ] *s.* luchador (*a brazo partido*).
wres·tling [rέslɪŋ] *s.* lucha libre.
wretch [rɛtʃ] *s.* miserable, infeliz; villano.
wretch·ed [rέtʃɪd] *adj.* (*miserable*) miserable; afligido; (*unfortunate*) desdichado, infeliz; (*bad*) bajo, vil; malísimo; **a — piece of work** un trabajo pésimo o malísimo.
wrig·gle [rígl̩] *v.* menear(se); retorcer(se); **to — out of** salirse de, escaparse de; escabullirse de.
wring [rɪŋ] *v.* torcer, retorcer; exprimir, estrujar; **to — money from someone** arrancar dinero a alquien; **to — out** exprimir (*la ropa*).
wrin·kle [ríŋkl] *s.* arruga; surco; **the latest — in style** la última novedad; *v.* arrugar(se).
wrist [rɪst] *s.* muñeca; — **watch** reloj de pulsera.
writ [rɪt] *s.* auto, orden judicial, mandato jurídico; **the Holy Writ** la Sagrada Escritura.
write [raɪt] *v.* escribir; **to — back** contestar por carta; **to — down** apuntar, poner por escrito; **to — off** cancelar (*una deuda*); **to — out** poner por escrito; escribir por entero; **to — up** relatar, describir; redactar; *s.* **— protect notch** (*computer*) ranura de protección.
writ·er [ráɪtɚ] *s.* escritor; autor.
writhe [raɪð] *v.* retorcerse.
writ·ing [ráɪtɪŋ] *s.* escritura; escrito; composición literaria; forma o estilo literario; **hand** — letra; — **desk** escritorio; — **paper** papel de escribir; **to put in** — poner por escrito.
writ·ten [rítn̩] *p.p. de* **to write.**
wrong [rɔŋ] *adj.* (*incorrect*) falso, incorrecto; equivocado; (*wicked*) malo; injusto; mal hecho; (*improper*) inoportuno; inconveniente; **the — side of a fabric** el envés o el revés de un tejido; **the — side of the road** el lado izquierdo o contrario del camino; **that is the — book** ése no es el libro; **it is in the — place** no está en su sitio, está mal colocado; *adv.* mal; al revés; **to go** — extraviarse, descaminarse; resultar mal; *s.* mal, daño, perjuicio; injusticia; agravio; **to be in the** — no tener razón, estar equivocado; **to do** — hacer mal; *v.* perjudicar; agraviar; hacer mal a.
wrote [rot] *pret. de* **to write.**
wrought [rɔt] *pret. & p.p. irr. de* **to work;** *adj.* labrado; forjado; — **iron** hierro forjado; — **silver** plata labrada; **to be wrought-up** estar sobreexcitado.
wrung [rʌŋ] *pret. & p.p. de* **to wring.**
wry [raɪ] *adj.* torcido; **to make a — face** hacer una mueca.

X:x

xe·non [zinɑn] *s.* xenón.

Y:y

yacht [jɑt] *s.* yate; *v.* navegar en yate.
Yan·kee [jǽŋkɪ] *adj. & s.* yanqui.
yard [jɑrd] *s.* (*measure*) yarda (*medida*); (*enclosure*) patio; cercado; terreno (*adyacente a una casa*); **back** — corral; **barn** — corral; **navy** — arsenal; **ship** — astillero.
yard·stick [jάrdstɪk] *s.* yarda (*de medir*); (*measure*) medida (*metro, vara, etc.*); (*criterion*) patrón, norma.
yarn [jɑrn] *s.* (*material*) estambre; hilado, hilaza; (*story*) cuento enredado y poco probable.
yawn [jɔn] *v.* bostezar; *s.* bostezo.
year [jɪr] *s.* año; — **book** anuario; **-'s income** renta anual; **by the** — por año; **leap** — año bisiesto.
year·ling [jírlɪŋ] *s.* primal; becerro.
year·ly [jírlɪ] *adj.* anual; *adv.* anualmente; una vez al año, cada año.
yearn [jɝn] *v.* anhelar; **to — for** anhelar; suspirar por.
yearn·ing [jέnɪŋ] *s.* anhelo.
yeast [jist] *s.* levadura, fermento.
yell [jɛl] *v.* gritar, dar gritos, vociferar; *s.* grito, alarido.
yel·low [jέlo] *adj.* amarillo; (*coward*) cobarde; — **fever** fiebre amarilla; *s.* amarillo; *v.* poner(se) amarillo.
yel·low·ish [jέloɪʃ] *adj.* amarillento.
yelp [jɛlp] *v.* aullar, ladrar; *s.* aullido, ladrido.
yes [jɛs] *adv.* sí.
yes·ter·day [jέstɚdɪ] *adv. & s.* ayer; **day before** — anteayer o antier.
yet [jɛt] *adv. & conj.* todavía, aún; con todo, sin embargo; no obstante; **as** — todavía, aún; **not** — todavía no.
yield [jild] *v.* (*surrender*) ceder; rendir; someterse; (*produce*) producir; **to — five percent** redituar el cinco por ciento; *s.* (*production*) rendimiento, (*surrender*) rendición; rédito; beneficio.
yo·del [jódl̩] *s.* canto en que la voz fluctúa entre natural y falsete.
yo·ga [jógə] *s.* yoga.
yo·gurt [jógɚt] *s.* yogurt.
yoke [jok] *s.* yugo; yunta (*de bueyes, mulas, etc.*); *v.* uncir; unir.
yolk [jok] *s.* yema (*de huevo*).
yon·der [jάndɚ] *adj.* aquel, aquella, aquellos, aquellas; *adv.* allá, allí, más allá, acullá
yore [jor]: **in days of** — antaño, en días de antaño.
you [ju] *pron. pers.* tú, usted, vosotros, ustedes; te, le, lo, la, os, las, los; **to** — a tí, a usted, a vosotros, a ustedes; te, le, les; *pron. impers.* se, uno.
young [jʌŋ] *adj.* joven; nuevo; — **leaves** hojas tiernas; — **man** joven; **her — ones** sus niños, sus hijitos; **the — people** la gente joven, los jóvenes, la juventud; *s.* jóvenes; cría, hijuelos (*de los animales*).
young·ster [jʌ́ŋstɚ] *s.* muchacho, niño, jovencito, chiquillo.
your [jʊr] *adj.* tu (tus), vuestro (vuestra, vuestros,

vuestras), su (sus), de usted, de ustedes.

yours [jurz] *pron. pos.* tuyo (tuya, tuyos, tuyas); vuestro (vuestra, vuestros, vuestras); suyo (suya, suyos, suyas), de usted, de ustedes; el tuyo (la tuya, los tuyos, las tuyas); el suyo (la suya, los suyos, las suyas); el (la, los, las) de usted; el (la, los, las) de ustedes; **a friend of** — un amigo tuyo, un amigo vuestro; un amigo suyo, un amigo de usted o ustedes.

your·self [jursélf] *pron.* te, se (*como reflexivo*); **to** — a tí mismo; a usted mismo; **you** — tú mismo; usted mismo; *véase* **herself**.

your·selves [jursélvz∫ *pron.* os, se (*como reflexivo*); **to** — a vosotros mismos; a ustedes mismos; **you** — vosotros mismos; ustedes mismos.

youth [juθ] *s.* joven; juventud; jóvenes.

youth·ful [júθfəl] *adj.* joven; juvenil.

yt·tri·um [ítriəm] *s.* itrio.

yuc·ca [jʌ́kə] *s.* yuca.

Yule·tide [júltaɪd] *s.* Pascua de Navidad; Navidades.

Z:z

zeal [zil] *s.* celo, fervor, ardor, entusiasmo.

zeal·ot [zélət] *s.* fanático.

zeal·ous [zéləs] *adj.* celoso, ardiente, fervoroso.

ze·bra [zíbrə] *s.* cebra.

ze·nith [zínɪθ] *s.* cenit, cumbre.

zeph·yr [zéfɚ] *s.* céfiro.

ze·ro [ziro] *s.* cero.

zest [zɛst] *s.* entusiasmo; buen sabor.

zig·zag [zígzæg] *s.* zigzag; *adj. & adv.* en zigzag; *v.* zigzaguear, culebrear, andar en zigzag, serpentear.

zinc [zɪŋk] *s.* cinc (zinc).

zip code [zíp kod] *s.* sistema numérico de zonas postales; código postal.

zip·per [zípɚ] *s.* cierre relámpago, abrochador corredizo o de corredera; zíper; cierre cremallera.

zir·co·ni·um [zɪrkóniəm] *s.* circonio.

zo·di·ac [zódɪæk] *s.* zodíaco.

zone [zon] *s.* zona; *v.* dividir en zonas.

zoo [zu] *s.* jardín zoológico.

zo·o·log·i·cal [zoəlɑ́dʒɪkl̩] *adj.* zoológico.

zo·ol·o·gy [zoɑ́lədʒɪ] *s.* zoología.